EXPOSITORY DICTIONARY OF BIBLE WORDS

EXPOSITORY DICTIONARY OF BIBLE WORDS

Word Studies for Key English Bible Words
Based on the Hebrew and Greek Texts

Coded to the Revised
Strong's Numbering System

STEPHEN D. RENN
EDITOR

HENDRICKSON
PUBLISHERS

P. O. Box 3473
Peabody, Massachusetts 01961-3473

ISBN 1-56563-938-3

Printed in the United States of America

First Printing — March 2005

Library of Congress Cataloging-in-Publication Data

Expository dictionary of Bible words : word studies for key English Bible words /
edited by Stephen D. Renn.
p. cm.
Includes bibliographical references and indexes.
ISBN 1-56563-938-3 (alk. paper)
1. Bible—Dictionaries. I. Renn, Stephen D.
BS440.E97 2005
220.3—dc22
2004031094

TABLE OF CONTENTS

INTRODUCTION

The Nature and Purpose of the Dictionary

This dictionary is designed as a non-technical reference book for pastors, teachers, and lay students of Scripture. It offers a comprehensive (though not exhaustive) analysis and discussion of both Old Testament Hebrew (and Aramaic) and New Testament Greek terms.

While there are a number of excellent Old and New Testament dictionaries on the market, this volume offers unique features that will enhance the reader's understanding of the whole of Scripture—in particular, the relationship between the Testaments. The dictionary is organized into entries by English word, with each main entry divided into Old Testament and New Testament words. However, the "Additional Notes" sections set this dictionary apart from others. These notes explain how the theme, concept, or doctrine shaped by the Hebrew terminology is fulfilled in the Greek vocabulary of the New Testament, especially in relation to the consummation of God's plan of salvation through the person of Christ. In short, the reader has not so much a "word study" as an analysis of a redemptive-historical theme—a "motif study"—that has its origins in the Old Testament and finds its completion in the New Testament.

The question of what constitutes accurate translation is of prime significance for a dictionary of this nature. It is important to note that there is rarely (if ever) a full, or exclusive "one-for-one" semantic equivalent in English for corresponding terms in Hebrew and Greek. Most often, two or more English words are required to accurately convey the meaning of one Hebrew or Greek term. There is thus frequent cross-referencing between the different entries throughout the dictionary. While the expression "dynamic equivalent" refers to an area of meaning common to both Hebrew and Greek terms, such "dynamic equivalence" does not suggest a *precise* identification between the semantic fields of each term. But the concept of dynamic equivalence *does* affirm that Hebrew terminology in the Old Testament may correlate in a significant way to New Testament Greek vocabulary, anticipating a parallel area of meaning in the New Testament. Consequently, one is able to argue that there are many themes, concepts, and motifs that span both Testaments of Holy Scripture. The analyses of these concepts serve to make the reader significantly more aware of the unity of the Old and New Testaments.

Furthermore, the precise meaning of any particular term is never determined just by its lexical definition or its etymology (i.e., by tracing the evolution of meaning throughout the linguistic history of a particular word). Rather, it is literary usage and context that determine the precise sense of any given term—a significant principle that underlies the compilation of this work.

Hebrew and Greek Transliteration

In common with normal practice in "non-technical" works, all Hebrew, Aramaic, and Greek terms have been transliterated, using essentially a simplified phonetic transliteration scheme.

Hebrew

Consonants

א	*alef*	’
בּ, ב	*bet*	***b***
גּ, ג	*gimel*	***g***
דּ, ד	*dalet*	***d***
ה	*he*	***h***
ו	vav	***w***
ז	zayin	***z***
ח	*khet*	***ḥ***
ט	*tet*	***t***
י	*yod*	***y***
כ, כּ, ך	*kaf*	***k***
ל	*lamed*	***l***
מ, ם	*mem*	***m***
נ, ן	*nun*	***n***
ס	*samek*	***s***
ע	*ayin*	’
פּ	*pe* (hard)	***p***
פ, ף	*pe* (soft)	***ph***
צ, ץ	*tsade*	***ṣ***
ק	*qof*	***q***
ר	*resh*	***r***
שׂ	*sin*	***s***
שׁ	*shin*	***sh***
ת, תּ	*tav*	***t***

Vowels

◌ַ	*patakh*	***a***
◌ָ	*qamets*	***ā***
◌ָ	*qamets khatuf* (in a closed and unaccented syllable)	***o***
◌ֶ	*segol*	***e***
◌ֵ	*tsere*	***ē***
◌ֵי	*tsere yod*	***ê***
◌ִ	*hireq*	***i***
◌ִי	*hireq yod*	***î***
◌ֹ	*holem*	***ō***
וֹ	full *holem*	***ô***
◌ֻ	*qibbuts*	***u***
וּ	*shureq*	***û***
◌ֳ	*khatef qamets*	***o***
◌ֲ	*khatef patakh*	***a***
◌ֱ	*khatef segol*	***e***
◌ְ	vocal *shewa*	***e***

The Hebrew script, unlike English, is written from right to left. Although Hebrew makes no distinction between uppercase and lowercase letters, there are five letters which have a different form when they are the last letter of a word: kaf (כ becomes ך), mem (מ becomes ם), nun (נ becomes ן), pe (פ becomes ף), and tsade (צ becomes ץ).

In addition, the letters bet (בּ), gimel (גּ), dalet (דּ), kaf (כּ), pe (פּ), and tav (תּ) each have both a "hard" (voiced) and a "soft" (unvoiced or spirant) form. The hard form is distinguished by a dot, called a *dagesh,* placed in the center of the letter, as shown in the list above. For this work, the same English letter is used to transliterate both forms [with the exception of pe (פּ)]. The dagesh can also appear in these or other letters in the middle of a word to indicate that the letter is doubled. This is indicated in the transliteration (i.e., גַּנָּה becomes ***gannāh***).

The Hebrew consonants alef (א) and ayin (ע) have no counterpart in English or other western alphabets, and so are represented in English by an apostrophe ('). The Hebrew letter khet (ח) is pronounced as a rough "ch" as in the German word "Achtung."

Most Hebrew vowels do not have a letter form. Instead they are indicated by "pointing"—small markings placed underneath or after a consonant. There are, however, a few Hebrew letters, he (ה), vav (ו), and yod (י), which can function as either consonants or as vowels, similar to the English use of the letter y. The shewa (ְ) is not a vowel, and thus is often silent. However, in some cases, it is vocalized (i.e., pronounced). When it is vocalized, it is transliterated as "e", as shown in the list of vowels above.

Aramaic

Aramaic is a Semitic language closely related to Hebrew. (*Strong's Concordance* refers to it as Chaldee.) Parts of the books Daniel and Ezra, as well as a few phrases in Genesis and Jeremiah, were written in Aramaic, and individual Aramaic terms can be found in both the Old and New Testament. Aramaic uses the same alphabet script as Hebrew, and for the purposes of this work can be transliterated the same as Hebrew.

Greek

α	*alpha*	***a***	ρ	*rho*	***r***
β	*bēta*	***b***	ῥ	initial *rho*	***rh***
γ	*gamma*	***g***	σ, ς	*sigma*	***s***
γ	*gamma* nasal (before γ, κ, ξ, χ)	***n***	τ	*tau*	***t***
δ	*delta*	***d***	υ	*upsilon* (not in diphthong)	***y***
ε	*epsilon*	***e***	υ	*upsilon* (in diphthongs: *au, eu, ēu, ou, ui*)	***u***
ζ	*zēta*	***z***			
η	*ēta*	***ē***	φ	*phi*	***ph***
θ	*thēta*	***th***	χ	*chi*	***ch***
ι	*iōta*	***i***	ψ	*psi*	***ps***
κ	*kappa*	***k***	ω	*ōmega*	***ō***
λ	*lambda*	***l***	῾	rough breathing *(precedes initial vowel or diphthong)*	***h***
μ	*mu*	***m***			
ν	*nu*	***n***			
ξ	*xi*	***x***			
ο	*omicron*	***o***			
π	*pi*	***p***			

As far as the Greek alphabet is concerned, little needs to be provided by way of special explanation. Since the reading orientation is the same as English, the similarities to the English alphabet are much closer and, unlike Hebrew, all vowels are indicated by letters. Hence, the reader should be able to correlate the Greek terms and their transliteration with relative ease.

SAMPLE ENTRY

English Entry
A word or words used in English translations of Scripture.

Language Article
A separate entry is given for each Hebrew or Greek word that can be translated with the English word(s) listed in the Main Entry.

Additional Notes
A unique feature of this dictionary, the Additional Notes explain how the theme, concept, or doctrine shaped by the Hebrew terminology is fulfilled in the Greek vocabulary of the New Testament, especially in relation to the consummation of God's plan of salvation through the person of Christ.

See Also
Directs the reader to related entries for further study.

Cross Reference
Directs the reader to the entry which discusses the term.

ANGER, ANGRY

OT Words

'aph **[אַף, 639]**

This noun occurs approximately 270 times and usually means "anger" or "wrath" (both human and divine).

ḥēmāh **[חֵמָה, 2534]**

This noun is synonymous with ***'aph*** (see above); it is derived, however, from the verb ***yāḥam*** (→ CONCEIVE), whose root meaning is "to be hot." Thus the primary meaning for ***ḥēmāh*** is "anger" or "fury" — even though the literal meaning of "heat" (or more accurately "fever") is found only in Hosea 7:5. It can also mean "venom" or "poison." (→ VENOM) . . .

qāṣaph **[קָצַף, 7107];** ***qeṣeph*** **[קֶצֶף, 7110]**

Once again these terms refer to both human and divine anger. ***qāṣaph*** indicates the former on ten . . .

NT Words

orgē [**ὀργή,** *3709*]

The noun ***orgē*** occurs around forty times in a variety of contexts, meaning "anger," "wrath" throughout.

orgizō [**ὀργίζω,** *3710*]

The verb ***orgizō*** is found eight times with the . . .

Additional Notes

Given the number of synonyms for "anger" in the New Testament, it is impossible to precisely identify any one of them as a dynamic equivalent for any of the corresponding Old Testament terms. There is, however, a significant overlap between the two groups of words. For example, the major New Testament terms for "anger" also preserve the distinction between God's anger and human anger. With regard to the latter, see particularly the discussions of ***orgē*** and ***thymos***, as well as their related verbs. The verb from which ***'aph*** is derived (*'ānaph*) means . . .

As in the Old Testament, the New Testament addresses the matter of God's wrath with an emphasis . . .

→ WRATH

. . . .

INDIGNATION → ANGER

Transliteration. *A phonetic spelling of Hebrew or Greek word under discussion. See Introduction for details on transliteration.*

Hebrew or Greek. *See Introduction for details on Hebrew and Greek alphabets.*

Cross Reference (in text). *Indicated by arrow. Directs the reader to related entries.*

Strong's Number. *All entries are coded to Strong's Concordance to simplify finding the word in other reference works.*

The Strong's number for Greek words is italicized.

Boldface, italicized word. *Indicates a word which has a language entry in this dictionary.*

If a Hebrew or Greek word does not appear in a language entry, it is indicated by italics only.

A

ABASE ➞ HUMBLE

ABHOR

OT Words

gā'al [גָּעַל, 1602]

This word carries with it the primary sense of "abhorrence," "despising," or "loathing" in the face of something or someone detestable. In Lev. 26, for example, ***gā'al*** signifies first of all God's solemn declaration not to abhor his people, provided they follow his decrees in terms of the Mosaic covenant (Lev. 26:11). If they despise and disobey his laws (Lev. 26:15, 43), the result will be divine abhorrence (Lev. 26:30). Finally, Lev. 26:44 indicates Yahweh's promise not to so loathe his people as to violate his covenant agreement with them.

gā'al conveys similar meanings in Jer. 14:19 and Ezek. 16:45. Jeremiah asks his God, "Do you abhor Zion?" The context makes plain that he is fully conscious that his countrymen are guilty of violating the sacred articles of the covenant law. In Ezekiel the reference is an allegorical one, indicting Israel and Judah as immoral women who have abhorred or despised their husband (i.e., Yahweh) and family (i.e., fellow Israelites). The fundamental charge against the people of God is one of adultery. In each use of the term, the context is clearly covenantal.

tā'ab [תָּעַב, 8581]

The root meaning here again suggests abhorrence or repulsion; and the term is used in a variety of scriptural contexts. As with ***gā'al***, above, ***tā'ab*** refers to God's abhorrent disdain of both the wickedness of his people (cf. Ps. 106:40; Ezek. 16:25, 52; Mic. 3:9; Amos 5:10) and of corrupt humankind in general (cf. Pss. 5:6; 14:1; 53:1; Isa. 14:19). There are also similar commands for the people of Israel to keep away from any object or practice that will provoke a divine response of abhorrence and loathing (cf. Deut. 7:26). See also Deut. 23:7 for a slightly different perspective.

On another level, there are general expressions of abhorrence towards Job, for example, in Job 9:31; 15:16; 19:19; 30:10; as well as such general usage by the psalmist, as in Ps. 107:18.

There is an intriguing use of ***tā'ab*** in 1 Chr. 21:6, where Joab expresses abhorrence at David's command to take a census of the people in violation of the Mosaic law. Because of his abhorrence, Joab refuses to include Levi and Benjamin in the count. Similarly, Ps. 119:163 expresses the godly person's abhorrence of sin.

Finally, in Isa. 49:7, the redemptive purposes of God negate and overcome the hatred and abhorrence of the godly servant king. For God will cause the once despised ruler to be glorified in the eyes of all people.

shiqqēṣ [שִׁקֵּץ, 8262]

This verb and its derivative noun are not extensively used in the Old Testament, but the meaning is predominantly a ritual one. ***shiqqēṣ*** refers to the ceremonial uncleanness of certain animals and foods which are deemed abhorrent and detestable to both God and Israel (cf. Lev. 11:11, 13, 43; 20:25; Deut. 7:26).

In Ps. 22:24, the psalmist refers to Yahweh's refusal to disdain or abhor his suffering servant. It is clear from the context that the object of God's concern is none other than the Messianic King. Ps. 22 is generally recognized as a messianic psalm.

NT Words

apostygeō [ἀποστυγέω, *655*]

apostygeō is a rare verb, found only in Rom. 12:19, constituting an injunction to "abhor" or "hate" what is evil.

bdelyssō [βδελύσσω, *948*]

bdelyssō is another rare verb referring to the "abhorring" or "despising" of idols in Rom. 2:22. In Rev. 21:8 it is used participially to refer to those who are "abhorrent" (i.e., vile, abominable) to God.

Additional Notes

With ***apostygeō*** in Rom. 12:9, the admonition to hate or abhor what is evil reflects the Levitical and Deuteronomic usage of both ***tā'ab*** and ***shiqqēṣ***.

In regard to ***bdelyssō***, again the idea about abhorring idols carries a ritual association. And it is this preoccupation with the Jews' relationship to the law that forms the context of Romans 2.

Also, in Rev. 21:8, it is significant that those who are designated as "vile" or "abhorrent" constitute part of the apostate company of unbelievers who will suffer the ultimate divine penalty.

Although these terms for "abhor" do not occur frequently in the New Testament, the meaning is consistent throughout the whole Bible. Those who are abhorred by God in either a relative or absolute sense find themselves beyond the sphere of covenant blessing.

See Also: → ABOMINABLE → DESPISE

ABIDE, ABODE

OT Words

yāshab [יָשַׁב, 3427]

The primary meanings of this very common verb are: "sit"; "remain"; "dwell"; "inhabit." ***yāshab*** occurs in its various forms about 1,200 times, a significant number of which refer specifically to Israel living in the land of Canaan (concentrated in the historical and prophetic books of the Old Testament canon). These references do not indicate merely the preexilic occupation of Canaan, but also the postexilic restoration and return to the land. This aspect of the meaning of ***yāshab*** is theologically significant, for dwelling in the land of Canaan is one of the key provisions of the old covenant promises relating to God's plan of salvation for his people.

NT Words

menō [μένω, *3306*]

menō is a common verb found in 120 different places with the primary senses of "abide," "remain," or "stay," both literal and metaphorical.

Literal references to "staying" include "lodging as a guest" in someone's home, cf. Matt. 10:11; Luke 1:56; John 4:40; Acts 9:43; 21:7ff.; "remaining" in someone's company, cf. Matt. 26:38; John 14:25; Luke 24:29; "remaining" in the same geographic location, cf. John 7:9; 10:40; Acts 27:31; 2 Tim. 4:20; "remaining" in the same physical position, in particular with reference to the Spirit of God on the person of Christ in John 1:32ff. (see also John 19:31). In John 1:38ff. ***menō*** means "reside" or "live."

The verb also means to "remain" in the sense of "endure," "continue," or "last" in a number of places. It is used hypothetically, for example, of the city of Sodom in Matt. 11:23 and Mark 14:34. Jesus declares that "heavenly food," figuratively speaking, "lasts forever" in John 6:27. Paul encourages those who are unmarried to "remain" in their single state in 1 Cor. 7:8ff. 1 Cor. 13:13 and Heb. 13:1 speak of the "enduring" qualities of faith, hope, and love. The "veil" of unbelief is said to "remain" over the minds of unbelievers in 2 Cor. 3:14 (see also John 9:41; 12:46 for related nuances). The "lasting" nature of a person's life and ministry will be assessed on the day of judgment, cf. 1 Cor. 3:14. Rom. 9:11 notes the eternal qualities of God's purposes in election. John 8:35 and 12:34 mention Christ, the Son, who "continues" or "lives" forever. Then the priest-king Melchizedek is said to be a priest who "remains" forever in that position in Heb. 7:23; as is Christ who fulfills that role, cf. Heb. 7:24. The word of God is said to "remain" forever in 1 Pet. 1:23ff.; and God himself is described thus in 2 Tim. 2:13 (cf. also Heb. 12:27). For this meaning see also Acts 5:4; 1 Cor. 5:6.

There are a number of places where the meaning "abide" or "remain" expresses a significant theological nuance. When the word of God "remains" in the life of the believer, it has a significant sanctifying effect on that person's life, cf. John 5:38 (cf. also 1 John 2:27). The phenomenon of "abiding (or remaining) in Christ" indicates an intimate spiritual relationship with Christ on the part of the believer, cf. John 6:56; 1 John 2:6ff. The same phenomenon is evident in John 15:4ff., which describes the believer's intimate relationship with Christ via the metaphor of "branches" and "the vine." The love of God is said "to remain" in the life of the believer in 1 John 3:17. John 8:31 refers to the state of continuing to live by the word of God. See also 1 John 2:6ff.

John 3:36 expresses the metaphorical sense of "rest upon," where the anger of God is said to "rest upon" unbelievers.

Other metaphorical uses of ***menō*** are found in connection with the person of God, who "dwells" in Christ, cf. John 14:10; 1 John 4:15, and also in the believer, cf. 1 John 3:24; 4:12ff. The Holy Spirit is also promised to the believer, guaranteeing to "remain" with him or her forever, cf. John 14:16ff. See also John 1:2; 1 John 4:16; 2 John 9.

epimenō [ἐπιμένω, *1961*]

epimenō is a related form of ***menō***, above, occurring nineteen times with the meanings "abide," "stay," "remain," and "continue."

The sense of "remain" or "abide" is found in Acts 10:48; 21:4, 10; 28:12ff.; 1 Cor. 16:7ff.; Gal. 1:18. In each case the intended meaning is that of "staying over" as a guest.

paramenō [παραμένω, *3887*]

paramenō is a rare synonym for ***menō***, found in only three places and meaning "abide" or "stay," in the sense of "spending time" as a guest in 1 Cor. 16:6.

hypomenō [ὑπομένω, *5278*]

hypomenō is another variant of ***menō*** with the primary sense of "endure" evident in the majority of the eighteen occurrences of the term. In Luke 2:43 and Acts 17:14, however, the term expresses the meaning "stay behind" or "remain."

diatribō [διατρίβω, *1304*]

diatribō is a verb found in ten contexts with the consistent meaning "remain," "spend time" in a particular location, cf. John 3:22; 11:54; Acts 12:19; 14:3, 28; 15:35; 16:12; 20:6; 25:6, 14.

aulizomai [αὐλίζομαι, *835*]

aulizomai is a rare verb found only twice, in both places referring to "lodging" or "spending the night," cf. Matt. 21:17; Luke 21:37.

Additional Notes

Of all the New Testament terms for "abide" listed above, ***menō*** is the most theologically significant in relation to its dynamic equivalent ***yāshab*** in the Old Testament. As noted above, ***yāshab*** pointed to the phenomenon of dwelling or living in the promised land. The usage of ***yāshab*** in this respect has a primarily literal or physical sense: that is, under the old covenant the promises of God related fundamentally to his people's occupation of a specific geographic location. In the New Testament, ***menō*** likewise carries a literal sense of "dwell;" but it also indicates the very significant theological and spiritual nuance of "remaining" or "abiding," viz. in intimate relationship with God through the person of Jesus Christ his Son. Just as ***yāshab*** in the Old Testament pointed to the physical reality of God's people dwelling in his chosen land, so ***menō*** indicates the spiritual reality of believers maintaining and being maintained in close spiritual bonds with their Lord and God.

To illustrate this perspective: ***menō*** describes the relationships of God to Christ (cf. John 14:10), of Christians to Christ (cf. John 6:56; 15:4ff.; 1 John 2:6, 24), of Christ to believers (cf. John 15:4, 5), of believers to God (cf. 1 John 2:24ff.; 3:6, 24; 4:12ff.). The physical reality of dwelling in Canaan in the old covenant relationship with Israel, therefore, anticipates the consummation of that union with God in Christ and with his people in the new covenant.

See Also: ➞ CONTINUE ➞ ENDURE ➞ REMAIN ➞ RISE ➞ STAND

ABILITY, ABLE

OT Words

yākōl [יָכֹל, 3201]

This verb is the usual term employed for the concept of ability or inability in the broad sense. The word occurs approximately 140 times throughout the Old Testament.

Secondly, ***yākōl*** carries the idea of both ability and inability in the moral sense, usually translated "may" or "might," "can" or "could," with the negative sense as well. This sense is most commonly found in the Pentateuch: Gen. 43:32, for example, refers to the Egyptian custom of refusing to eat with Hebrews. The remaining uses of ***yākōl*** with this meaning are found in the legislative sections associated with the giving of the covenant law at Mt. Sinai (cf. Exod. 19:23; Deut. 7:22; 12:17; 14:24; 16:5; 17:15; 21:16ff.; 24:4). Other examples of ***yākōl*** expressing moral inability in a non-ritual setting are found in Num. 22:38; 24:13; 1 Kgs. 13:16; 20:9.

yākōl can also mean "prevailing," "overcoming," or "overpowering" in both a literal and metaphorical sense (cf., e.g., Gen. 30:8; Num. 22:6; Judg. 16:5; 1 Sam. 17:9; Esth. 6:13; Hos. 12:5; Jer. 20:7, 9, 10, 11; Isa. 16:12).

Finally, ***yākōl*** can convey an interesting connotation of "endurance." All instances of this are negative, indicating an inability or refusal to tolerate that which is objectionable. This applies to both God and human beings (cf. Job 31:23; Ps. 101:5; Isa. 1:13).

ḥayil [חַיִל, 2428]

In relation to the idea of ability, ***ḥayil*** has two relevant meanings. In the first place it signifies "strength," "valor," or "power," and has this meaning in about ninety different places. It is primarily found in military contexts, concerned with the strength of armies, soldiers, etc. Occasionally, ***ḥayil*** refers to national powers such as Media and Persia (cf. Esth. 1:3; 8:11). The psalmist also frequently uses ***ḥayil*** to refer to the power of God (cf. Pss. 33:17; 59:11; 108:13; 110:3; 118:15, 16), as does the prophet Zechariah (Zech. 4:6).

The second meaning of ***ḥayil*** relates specifically to the idea of general ability, but with special emphasis on moral worth, or virtue. For example, Exod. 18 refers to the elders Moses chose as able men (Exod. 18:15, 21). Ruth (3:11) is described as a virtuous lady, a woman of noble character. There is a similar usage of the word in 1 Kgs. 1:52. The writer of Proverbs also refers to women of virtue in Prov. 12:4; 31:10.

kōaḥ [כֹּחַ, 3581]

Here is another word that links power and strength to the idea of ability, both divine and human. See, for example, Deut. 8:18; 1 Sam. 30:4; 1 Chr. 29:24; Ezra 2:69.

kōaḥ can also simply refer to human strength. Samson, whose legendary physical prowess is recorded in Judg. 16, is a notable example of this.

Finally, this term can also indicate divine power, as in God's creative power (cf. Job 26:12; Jer. 10:12; 27:5; 32:17; 51:15), his power in accomplishing of salvation for his people (cf. Deut. 4:37; 9:29; 2 Chr. 25:8; Ps. 147:5; Isa. 50:2; 63:1; Nah. 1:3; Zech. 4:6), his equipping the prophets through the power of his Spirit (cf. Mic. 3:8), or his divine power in general (cf. Job 36:22; 39:11, 21; Ps. 29:4).

'āzaz [עָזַז, 5810]; *'ōz* [עֹז, 5797]; *'az* [עַז, 5794]

The root ***'āzaz*** and its derivative forms are synonymous with ***kōaḥ*** (see above). It describes both human and divine strength, including Yahweh in his creative and redemptive capacities. The three terms occur approximately 180 times: for ***'āzaz***, cf. Pss. 68:28; 89:13; Eccl. 7:19; for ***'az***, cf. Gen. 49:3; Num. 13:28; 2 Sam. 22:18; Isa. 25:3; for ***'ōz***, cf. Exod. 15:2, 13; Lev. 26:19; 1 Chr. 16:27; Pss. 28:8; 59:16ff.; 68:28ff.

gābar [גָּבַר, 1396]

Like ***yākōl***, above, this verb means indicates prevailing or overcoming, on the part of both God and human beings. ***gābar*** occurs twenty-three times. One of the most theologically significant of these occurrences is found in Dan. 9:27, where the messianic ruler is said to "confirm a covenant with the many for one 'seven.'" The meaning here is that this covenant agreement will ultimately succeed, and it will run no risk of being cast aside. This term would seem to imply, therefore, the absolute effectiveness of God's ability to carry out his plan of salvation on behalf of his people.

NT Words

dynamis [δύναμις, *1411*]

dynamis is a noun with the primary meaning of "power," emphasizing "strength" and "ability" in most of its 120 occurrences (→ STRENGTH). ***dynamis*** can also suggest the sense of "miracle." In addition, ***dynamis*** also signifies "mighty works" or "deeds."

References to "power" or "strength" are varied. The power of God is indicated in a number of general contexts, cf. Matt. 22:29; Mark 12:24; Luke 1:35; Acts 8:10; 1 Cor. 2:5; 2 Cor. 6:7; Rev. 4:11; 19:1. In a related context, ***dynamis*** signifies a "word of power" in Heb. 1:3, denoting a divine catalyst for creation. The term also refers to the "power" of the Son of Man in Matt. 24:30; Mark 13:26; Luke 21:27; and to the person of Christ in Mark 5:30; Luke 4:36; 1 Cor. 5:4; 2 Cor. 12:9. Specifically, Christ's power is manifested in his resurrection as noted in Phil. 3:10 (cf. also Rev. 5:12). There is a general reference to the power of the Spirit in Luke 4:14. 1 Cor. 4:20 and Rev. 12:10 speak of the power of the kingdom of God. In negative contexts, ***dynamis*** denotes the "power" of sin in 1 Cor. 15:56 and refers to the power of the dragon in Rev. 13:2 (cf. also Rev. 17:13). References to the "powers" of natural, cosmic forces include Matt. 24:29; Mark 13:25; Luke 21:26. Other general references to "power" include those in Acts 3:12; 2 Tim. 3:5; Heb. 11:11; Rev. 1:16; 3:8; 15:8.

Elsewhere, ***dynamis*** has particular reference to the "power of God" in significant theological contexts. This power is declared effective for salvation in Rom. 1:16; 1 Cor. 1:18, 24; 1 Pet. 1:5; for the reality of resurrection in 1 Cor. 6:14; 15:43; and for godly living in 2 Cor. 13:4; Eph. 1:19; 2 Pet. 1:13. This divine power is given to the disciples for exorcising demons in Luke 9:1; for gospel ministry in Acts 4:33; 2 Tim. 1:8; and for performing miraculous signs in Acts 6:8.

God equips the disciples for ministry with the "power" of the Spirit in 1 Thess. 1:5; 2 Thess. 1:11. Christ also receives the Spirit's power, as noted in Acts 10:38; Rom. 1:4, as do the believers (Rom. 15:13; 2 Tim. 1:7). Such a power is promised to the disciples in Luke 24:49; Acts 1:8. God also provides the Spirit's power for effective gospel ministry in 1 Cor. 2:4; Eph. 3:7, 20.

dynamis also denotes "powers" with reference to "spiritual forces" of darkness in Rom. 8:38; 1 Cor. 15:24; Eph. 1:21; 2 Thess. 2:9; and to the heavenly "powers" in Heb. 6:5; 1 Pet. 3:22.

dynamis indicates a sense of "ability," with reference to natural talent, in Matt. 25:15. Conversely, ***dynamis*** is also used to describe the "inability" to cope with overwhelming persecution in 2 Cor. 1:8.

Elsewhere, ***dynamis*** refers to "miracles" (i.e., signs of power from God) in Gal. 3:5; Acts 2:4, 22; 8:13; 19:11; 1 Cor. 12:10, 28ff.

ischys [ἰσχύς, *2479*]

ischys is a noun found in eleven different places, meaning "strength," "power," "ability."

The meaning "strength" is indicated in Mark 12:30ff.; Luke 10:27 with reference to the "force of one's entire being" in the context of being devoted to loving and serving God.

The "power" of God is indicated in the use of ***ischys*** in general terms in Eph. 1:19; 6:10; 2 Thess. 1:9. Divine power is given to the people of God for godly living, as noted in 1 Pet. 4:11; and also to "the Lamb" (i.e., the heavenly Christ on the throne of God) in Rev. 5:12. In Rev. 7:12, the heavenly saints ascribe power to God. The power of angels is attested in 2 Pet. 2:11.

ischyō [ἰσχύω, *2480*]

ischyō is a less common synonym for ***dynamai*** (see below) found in approximately thirty places with the meanings "to be able" or "to exercise power (or strength) over."

With regard to human ability, Phil. 4:13 declares that all things "are possible" for the believer through the indwelling strength of Christ. More frequently, ***ischyō*** is used in the negative, to indicate humankind's inability in certain areas, cf. Mark 5:4; 9:18; 14:37; Luke 6:48; 14:29ff.; John 21:6; Acts 15:10. Jas. 5:16, however, affirms that the prayer of a righteous person "is powerful" in its effects. The physical sense of "overpower" is evident in Acts 19:16.

In Acts 19:20, the word of God is said to have a powerful impact on those who hear it.

dynamai [δύναμαι, *1410*]

dynamai is a common verb found over two hundred times with the primary meanings "can" and "be able," used both positively and negatively.

The "ability" of God is indicated in several contexts. For example, God is able to keep believers from falling away in Jude 24; and has a supreme ability to forgive sin, cf. Mark 2:7; Luke 5:21. See also Matt. 3:9; Luke 3:8; Eph. 3:20. Then, 2 Tim. 2:13 affirms that God is "unable" to deny himself.

Where the person of Christ is concerned, several contexts refer to his ability to effect miracle cures, cf. Matt. 8:2; 9:28; Mark 1:40ff.; Luke 5:12. In his role as eternal high priest, he is able to help those of his people who are tempted, cf. Heb. 2:18, and is always able to intercede on their behalf before the throne of God, cf. Heb. 7:25. There is also the false accusation that he is unable to save himself from death by crucifixion (cf. Matt. 27:42). In addition, John 5:19 declares that Christ is incapable of doing anything independently of his Father.

In the human sphere, ***dynamai*** refers positively to humankind's ability (or capacity) to receive spiritual insight, as noted in Matt. 19:12. Elsewhere, God is said to give human beings the ability to overcome temptation and satanic attack, cf. 1 Cor. 10:13; Eph. 6:11ff. Examples of negative contexts include the innate inability of human beings to please God by their own merit (cf. Rom. 8:8); to see the kingdom of God without the new birth (cf. John 3:3ff.; 6:44, 65; Acts 15:1; 1 Cor. 15:56). Elsewhere, specific inability is indicated with respect to speaking (cf. Luke 1:20); to hearing and understanding the word of God (cf. John 8:43; 1 Cor. 2:14); to casting out demons (cf. Mark 9:28; Luke 9:40). See also Matt. 6:24ff.; 16:3; Luke 16:13; John 10:29; Acts 5:39; Heb. 3:19; Rev. 5:3.

dynamai also speaks of ability and inability with reference to inanimate, though highly significant, phenomena. For example, Jesus declares in Mark 3:24ff. that any kingdom divided against itself is unable to stand, and that the word of God is incapable of being broken (John 10:35). Paul affirms in Rom. 8:39 that nothing is able to separate God's people from his love. Positively, the word of God is able to build up one's spiritual vitality (cf. Acts 20:32), and to save one's soul (cf. Jas. 1:21; 2:14).

Additional Notes

As with the corresponding Old Testament terms, ***dynamai*** combines the concept of ability with the meanings of "power" and "strength." Of prime significance is the way in which ***dynamai*** is used to indicate the absolute effectiveness of God's power in accomplishing his purposes through the person of Jesus Christ, his son. This is particularly evident in the gospels (cf. Matt. 3:9; 8:2; 9:28; 12:29; 26:61; John 5:19, 30, plus synoptic parallels), but is also to be found in Acts 5:39; 20:32; Rom. 8:39; 16:25; Heb. 2:18; 4:15; 5:2; 7:25. In other contexts, it is the power of God that enables believers to serve him obediently and faithfully (e.g., Eph. 6:11, 13, 16), and that preserves them for salvation.

dynamis is the principal nominal form derived from ***dynamai***, and likewise reflects the same range of meaning. The power referred to here is that generated by the redemptive plan and purpose of God in the gospel, in the person of Christ, and in the indwelling Holy Spirit. In both Testaments there is a consistency of usage with regard to God-given ability and strength for the accomplishment of his purpose.

See Also: → ARMY → RICH → STRENGTH

ABOLISH

NT Words

katargeō [καταργέω, *2673*]

katargeō is a verb occurring around thirty times with a variety of meanings centered around the idea of depriving a person or thing of influence, force, or existence. Primary meanings include "abolish," "nullify," "destroy," "make void."

The sense of "nullify," "make void" is hypothetically applied to the faithfulness of God in Rom. 3:3. Rom. 7:2 affirms that death "nullifies" the marriage bond. This same metaphorical sense is applied to one's obligation to the law after one's conversion, cf. Rom. 7:16.

The meaning "abolish" or "nullify" occurs with reference to the law of God, which may never be "nullified" or "abolished" by faith, cf. Rom. 3:31. Conversely, the bondage of the law is declared to be "abolished" by the death of Christ, cf. Eph. 2:15. The promises of God are deemed to be "nullified" or "abolished" only if salvation were ever to come via the law, i.e., an impossible scenario. Therefore the promises of God are certain to stand. There is also, in Gal. 3:17, the outright claim that the promises of God may never be abolished. Sin is depicted as "abolished" in Rom. 6:6; Gal. 5:11.

katargeō can also suggest the closely related nuance of "destroy." The abolition or destruction of our human bodies at the hand of God is in view in 1 Cor. 6:13. 1 Cor. 15:24 affirms that all human rule and authority will be destroyed by God; as is death itself in 1 Cor. 15:26; 2 Tim. 1:10. The "veil of unbelief" is abolished (i.e., removed, destroyed) only through Christ (cf. 2 Cor. 3:14). Likewise, the "lawless one" in 2 Thess. 2:8, and the devil in Heb. 2:14, are both destroyed solely through the work of Christ.

katargeō also expresses the sense of "put away," "discard" in 1 Cor. 13:11 with reference to "childish things."

See Also: → WIPE

ABOMINABLE, ABOMINATION

OT Words

tô'ēbāh [תּוֹעֵבָה, **8441**]

tô'ēbāh derives from the verbal root ***tā'ab*** (→ ABHOR), and means "abomination," or "that which is abhorrent or repugnant." It has two distinct senses: one ethical, the other religio-cultural. One example of this is in Gen. 43:32, where reference is made to the Egyptian custom of refusing to associate with Hebrews. Such association was regarded as an abomination to the Egyptians — a social and cultural anathema (cf. also Gen. 46:34).

The ethical meaning is far more common, referring in general to God's response of extreme loathing of Israel's covenant disobedience and also of the abhorrent practices of the Canaanite peoples. Such abominations in the sight of God include: unlawful sexual practices (Lev. 18:22ff.); intermarriage with pagans (Ezra 9:1, 11, 14); shrine prostitution (Deut. 23:18); dishonesty, wickedness, and lying in various contexts (Prov. 6:16; 8:7; 11:1; 12:22; 15:8; 20:23; 29:27, etc.).

By far the most common use of ***tô'ēbāh***, however, is in reference to God's abhorrence of idolatry in all its forms. Idolatry is a mixture of ethical and religious malpractice on the part of both Israel and the Gentile nations. The term is used in this way in about fifty different places.

NT Words

athemitos [ἀθέμιτος, *111*]

athemitos is a rare adjective found only twice. It designates as "unlawful" any association between Jew and Gentile, as noted in Acts 10:28. In 1 Pet. 4:3 the term refers to idolatries as "abominable."

bdelyktos [βδελυκτός, *947*]

bdelyktos is a rare adjective describing the deeds of false teachers as "abominable" or "detestable."

bdelygma [βδέλυγμα, *946*]

bdelygma is a noun found in six different contexts with the consistent meaning "abomination."

The idolatrous altar placed in the Jerusalem temple, known as "the abomination of desolation," is referred to in Matt. 24:15; Mark 13:14. Human wickedness, designated as "abomination(s)" is indicated in Luke 16:15; Rev. 17:4ff.; 21:27.

Additional Notes

There is a consistent pattern of meaning among the Old and New Testament usage of ***tô'ēbāh*** and ***bdelygma***. Both words emphasize idolatry and blasphemy as the fundamental catalysts for the outpouring of divine wrath. With ***bdelygma*** in the New Testament, this is true whether one is speaking of the offensive altar of the antichrist or the metaphorical representation of Babylon the Great. And it is ***tô'ēbāh*** in the Old Testament that anticipates this perspective in the New by making clear that this behavior is offensive to God.

See Also: → ABHOR

ABOUND → ABUNDANCE

ABSENCE, ABSENT

NT Words

apousia [ἀπουσία, *666*]

apousia is a rare noun denoting personal, physical "absence" only in Phil. 2:12.

apeimi [ἄπειμι, *548*]

apeimi is a verb with the consistent meaning "to be absent, away" in each of the seven occurrences of the term. The sense is that of physical, personal absence (cf. 1 Cor. 5:3; 2 Cor. 10:1, 11; 13:2, 10; Phil. 1:27; Col. 2:5).

ekdēmeō [ἐκδημέω, *1553*]

ekdēmeō is a verb found in three places, all expressing the metaphorical sense of "being absent" from the Lord, in that one is still "home" (i.e., alive) in one's body, cf. 1 Cor. 5:6ff.

ABSTAIN, ABSTINENCE

NT Words

apechomai [ἀπέχομαι, *567*]

apechomai is a verb found in six contexts with the consistent sense of "abstain (i.e., refrain) from" idol worship and immorality (cf. Acts 15:20, 29; 1 Thess. 4:3; 5:22; 1 Tim. 4:3; 1 Pet. 2:11).

asitia [ἀσιτία, *776*]

asitia is a rare noun found only in Acts 27:21, referring to "abstinence" from food.

ABUNDANCE, ABUNDANT

OT Words

yātar [**יָתַר, 3498**]

yātar is a verbal root with the primary meaning "remain," "left over." There are, however, several references that indicate the meaning "abundance," "plenty," or "excess." In two instances, the meaning "abundance" is not directly related to the primary idea of "that which remains" (cf. Deut. 28:11; 30:9). The remaining references do, however, indicate a connection with the idea of "remainder." In both cases, what remains is declared to be "abundant" (cf. Exod. 36:7; 2 Chr. 31:10).

rōb [**רֹב, 7230**]; ***rab*** [**רַב, 7227**]; ***me'ōd*** [**מְאֹד, 3966**]

The noun ***rōb*** is a commonly used term for the idea of "abundance." It is also translated "many" or "much." The term occurs approximately 160 times — the majority of which refer to impersonal phenomena such as animals and wealth (approximately one hundred references). The remaining occurrences refer to people (approximately twenty) and quality (approximately forty), both positive and negative. In the latter category, for example, there is reference to the greatness of God's compassion in Ps. 51:1. This mention of the quality of God's attributes is the most theologically significant aspect of the word's usage. The psalmist, for example, frequently refers to the greatness of God's character, in particular to his grace, mercy, and compassion (cf. Pss. 5:7; 51:1; 69:13, 16; 106:7, 45; 150:2). Jeremiah also provides an example of this perspective in Lam. 3:32. Reference is also made to the greatness of God's power and might (cf. Isa. 40:26; 63:1). Greatness is expressed not only in the positive terms of God's essential attributes, but also in negative terms of human wickedness (cf. Jer. 13:22; 30:14, 15; Lam. 1:5; Ezek. 28:18; Hos. 9:7; Nah. 3:4). The adjective ***rab*** is synonymous with ***rōb***, and it is used with essentially the same force (approximately five hundred times). The term ***me'ōd*** also conveys a similar meaning, though it is primarily adverbial. It commonly translates as "very," "much," "exceedingly," or "greatly." ***me'ōd*** occurs about 350 times.

One specific use of ***rōb*** centers on the idea of "multitude" or "greatness," with several nuances. "Numerical greatness" (i.e., large numbers) is indicated with reference to God's people in Gen. 16:10; 30:30; Deut. 1:10; 7:7; 28:62; to armies in Judg. 7:12; Ps. 33:16; and to years in Lev. 25:16.

Elsewhere, ***rōb*** expresses the sense of "abundant quality" with reference to grain in Gen. 27:28; to animals in 1 Kgs. 1:19; to materials for the construction of the temple in 1 Chr. 22:3ff.; to sacrifices in Isa. 1:11; to sin in Ezek. 28:18; Hos. 9:7; Nah. 3:4; and to wealth in 2 Chr. 9:1ff.; 17:5; Ps. 49:6; Prov. 20:15; Ezek. 27:12.

The general meaning "greatness" or "abundance" is also indicated in relation to God's majesty in Exod. 15:17; to divine power in Ps. 66:3; Isa. 40:26; 63:1; to divine mercy in Neh. 13:22; Pss. 5:7; 69:13; 106:45; Lam. 3:32; to wisdom in Eccl. 1:18; Ezek. 28:5; and to strength in Ps. 33:17.

rābāh [רָבָה, 7235]

rābāh is the verbal root from which ***rōb*** and ***rab*** (see above) are derived. ***rābāh*** primarily means "increase," either in numerical strength or in quality. It is most commonly translated with the word "increase" or a synonymous term. ***rābāh*** occurs approximately three hundred times. As with the related words ***rōb*** and ***rab***, this verb denotes people, animals, objects and spiritual qualities, both good and bad. Of considerable importance is the notion that it is the greatness of God's power and authority that lies behind the redemptive process evident in human history, whether it is his power in blessing or in judgment.

To illustrate this observation we note first of all God's promise to Abraham to multiply or increase his progeny to incalculable proportions so that God's own chosen people will flourish. Ultimately, such promises will provide the context for the arrival of the Messiah (cf. Gen. 16:10; 17:2; 22:17). Such promises are also given to the other patriarchs, and to David as well (cf. Jer. 33:22). There is also the declaration to the Egyptians that God will multiply signs and wonders against them so that they will confess him as the one true and living God (cf. Exod. 7:3ff.). Ezekiel 36 also refers to the restoration of Israel, when God promises to replenish the numbers of his people and return them to the land of Israel (cf. Ezek. 36:10, 11). Such promises indicate not only material restoration, but forgiveness as well (cf. e.g., Isa. 55:7).

hāmôn [הָמוֹן, 1995]

hāmôn is a noun found about eighty times, usually with the sense of "multitude," "abundance." It is occasionally used adjectivally.

The adjectival sense of "many" (lit., "a multitude of") refers to nations in Gen. 17:4ff.; and to wives in 2 Chr. 11:13.

The nominal sense of "multitude" indicates a "horde" or "crowd of people." Such general references are found in 1 Sam. 14:16; 1 Kgs. 20:13; Job 31:34; Isa. 17:12; Ezek. 7:12ff.; Dan. 10:6. References to the "multitude" of Israelites are found in 2 Sam. 6:19; 2 Kgs. 7:13; Isa. 5:14. ***hāmôn*** also denotes the size of an army in 2 Chr. 20:12ff.; Isa. 16:14; Dan. 11:10ff.; Joel 3:14. The "hordes" of the nations are indicated in Isa. 29:7ff.; Ezek. 30:15. Specific reference to the "hordes" of Gog and Magog is found in Ezek. 39:11; and to those of Egypt in Ezek. 32:12ff.

hāmôn also expresses the meaning "abundance" in the sense of quantity. It refers to wealth (Ps. 37:16; Eccl. 5:10; Ezek. 30:10); and to property (Ezek. 7:11).

NT Words

perisseuō [περισσεύω, *4052*]

perisseuō is a verb found in approximately forty places with the primary meaning "abound," as well as several related nuances.

"Abound," with the underlying sense of "increase in magnitude," is indicated with respect to God's glory in Rom. 3:7; to God's grace in Rom. 5:15; to thanksgiving to God in 2 Cor. 4:15; Col. 2:7; to the hope of salvation in Rom. 15:13 and love in Phil. 1:9; 1 Thess. 3:12. The meaning "increase in number" is evident in Acts 16:5.

The meaning "exceed" with the sense of "going beyond a fixed measure" is found in relation to Pharisaic righteousness in Matt. 5:20. See also 2 Cor. 3:9.

perisseuō also expresses the meaning "have abundance" (i.e., have a great deal). It occurs in Matt. 13:12; 25:29 in relation to spiritual knowledge, and also in regard to material wealth in Matt. 12:44; Luke 12:15; 21:4.

The meaning "excel," "achieve a high standard" is indicated in relation to the work of the Lord in 1 Cor. 15:58, and to faith and love in 2 Cor. 8:7.

perisseia [περισσεία, *4050*]

perisseia is a noun derived from ***perisseuō*** (see above) found in four places indicating an "abundance" of grace (Rom. 5:17); joy (2 Cor. 8:2); and wickedness (Jas. 1:21). ***perisseia*** is used adverbially in 2 Cor. 10:15 with the sense of "greatly."

perisseuma [περίσσευμα, *4051*]

perisseuma is a synonym for ***perisseia***, above. It is found in five places, indicating the "abundance" of the heart in Matt. 12:34; Luke 6:45. In 2 Cor. 8:14 the term refers to "abundance," denoting material wealth. Mark 8:8 refers to bread that is "left over."

hyperperisseuō [ὑπερπερισσεύω, *5248*]

hyperperisseuō is a rare variant form of ***perisseuō***, above, with the meaning "to abound, exceed beyond all measure." The word expresses this sense in Rom. 5:20 in relation to the grace of God. In 2 Cor. 7:4 the term denotes "being filled (i.e., to overflowing)" with comfort.

perissos [περισσός, *4053*]

perissos is an adjectival form with the underlying adverbial sense of "more abundantly" (i.e., to a high degree, to the greatest extent). It is translated variously throughout the ten contexts in which it is found.

The meaning "more abundantly" is applied to the gaining of life through the person and work of Christ in John 10:10. In Eph. 3:20 ***perissos*** refers to God's infinite capacity to act in ways that far exceed the limits of our imaginations.

Elsewhere ***perissos*** is translated "utterly," with reference to people's astonishment in Mark 6:51; "vehemently," in relation to the expression of anger in Mark 14:31; "very earnestly," in connection with prayer in 1 Thess. 3:10; "very highly," with regard to the expression of esteem in 1 Thess. 5:13. See also Matt. 5:37, 47; Rom. 3:1; 2 Cor. 9:1.

perissoteron [περισσότερον, *4054, 4056*]

perissoteron is an adverbial comparative form with the sense of "more abundantly," "all the more," "far more," which is found in nearly twenty contexts, with related nuances (cf. Mark 7:36; 15:14; 1 Cor. 15:10; 2 Cor. 2:4; 7:13ff.; 11:23; 12:15; Gal. 1:14; 1 Thess. 2:17; Heb. 7:15; 13:19).

perissōs [περισσῶς, *4057*]

perissōs is an adverbial form derived from ***perissos*** (see above) with the meaning "greatly," "exceedingly," "all the more" in all three occurrences of the term (cf. Matt. 27:23; Mark 10:26; Acts 26:11).

hyperperissōs [ὑπερπερισσῶς, *5249*]

hyperperissōs is a rare adverbial variant of ***perissōs***, above, with the meaning "exceedingly" or "beyond measure." It is found only in Mark 7:37, where it refers to people's astonishment at the miracle cures Christ performed.

pleonazō [πλεονάζω, *4121*]

pleonazō is a verb synonymous with ***perisseuō*** (see above) with the meanings "abound," "increase" evident throughout the ten occurrences of the term.

The phenomenon of "increasing" or "abounding" grace is indicated in Rom. 5:20; 6:1; 2 Cor. 4:15; as is the proliferation of sin in Rom. 5:20. Reference to Christian virtues (i.e., "fruit") "increasing" in the life of the believer is made in Phil. 4:17; 2 Pet. 1:8, and to love in particular, in 1 Thess. 3:12; 2 Thess. 1:3. See also 2 Cor. 8:15.

hyperpleonazō [ὑπερπλεονάζω, *5250*]

hyperpleonazō is a rare variant form of ***pleonazō***, above, found only in 1 Tim. 1:14 with the meaning "overflow" (i.e., be exceedingly abundant).

plēthynō [πληθύνω, *4129*]

plēthynō is another synonym for the entries above. It is found in twelve places, with the consistent meanings of "multiply," "abound," or "increase."

The "increase" or "proliferation" of wickedness is indicated in Matt. 24:12.

References to the growth or increase of the early church due to new converts are found in Acts 6:1, 7; 7:17; 9:31. Acts 12:24 refers to the "growth" or "spread" of God's word.

Heb. 6:14 mentions the Abrahamic covenant promise in which God pledges to "multiply" the descendants of the patriarch.

The invoking of God's grace and peace, "multiplied" in the life of the believer, is noted in 1 Pet. 1:2; 2 Pet. 1:2; Jude 2. See also 2 Cor. 9:10.

hyperbolē [ὑπερβολή, *5236*]

hyperbolē is a noun found in eight places variously translated as "abundance" or "exceeding(ly)."

The adverbial meaning "exceedingly" refers to the phenomenon of increased sin in Rom. 7:13; to the experience of persecution in 2 Cor. 1:8; Gal. 1:13; to the anticipation of eternal glory in 2 Cor. 4:17.

hyperbolē is also translated "more excellent" when it describes the way of salvation in 1 Cor. 12:31. See also 2 Cor. 4:7.

2 Cor. 12:7 makes reference to the "abundance" of revelations given to the apostle Paul.

plousiōs [πλουσίως, *4146*]

plousiōs is an adverbial form with the meaning "richly," "abundantly" evident in all four occurrences of the term. Each reference indicates the granting of salvation by God as something rich and abundant (cf. 1 Tim. 6:17; Titus 3:6; 2 Pet. 1:11). In particular, Col. 3:16 makes reference to the word of God dwelling "richly" in the life of the believer.

Additional Notes

Of all the New Testament terms that signify "abundance" and related meanings, the verb ***perisseuō*** is probably the closest dynamic equivalent of the Hebrew term ***yātar***. This Greek verb likewise refers to natural phenomena as well as spiritual qualities. The point of interest to note here, in a theological sense, is the identical emphasis on the abundant, outpouring of God's love and grace to his people in the new covenant (cf. 2 Cor. 9:8; Eph. 1:8; Phil. 1:9). The significant difference is that, in distinction from the old covenant, divine grace is made possible in the new covenant solely through the person and work of Christ.

pleonazō is a dynamic equivalent of the Hebrew verb ***rābāh***. Although ***pleonazō*** does not occur very frequently, there are similarities of emphasis between the two words. All the occurrences of ***pleonazō*** are in theological contexts that refer primarily to the overflowing of divine love and grace for the building up of the new covenant people of God.

See Also: ➡ REMNANT

ACCEPT, ACCEPTABLE

OT Words

qābal [קָבַל, **6901**]

qābal is a verb occurring thirteen times with the primary meaning of "receive," "take." Several places, however, express the allied sense of "accept" that overlaps with "receiving" or "taking." Esth. 4:4 records Mordecai's refusal to "accept" fresh clothing from the queen. Job 2:10 speaks of submission to God by one's preparedness to "accept" both good and bad from him. Prov. 19:20 contains the exhortation to "accept" instruction from God.

NT Words

prosdechomai [προσδέχομαι, *4327*]

prosdechomai is a verb found in fourteen places with the primary meanings "wait for," "receive." A couple of occurrences, however, express the meaning "accept." Heb. 10:34 refers to believers who willingly "accepted" the trauma of persecution; and Heb. 11:35 specifically mentions martyrs who refused to "accept" a release from death so that they could rise again to a better life.

dektos [δεκτός, *1184*]

dektos is an adjective meaning "accepted," "acceptable," and is found in five contexts. Luke 4:19 refers to the "acceptable" year of the Lord (i.e., the divinely ordained time for the coming of the Messiah and the kingdom of God). Acts 10:35 and Phil. 4:18 describe the condition of being "acceptable" to God. See also Luke 4:24; 2 Cor. 6:2.

apodektos [ἀπόδεκτος, *587*]

apodektos is synonymous with ***dektos***, above, and is found twice only, indicating "that which is acceptable" to God in 1 Tim. 2:3; 5:4.

euprosdektos [εὐπρόσδεκτος, *2144*]

euprosdektos is another synonym for ***dektos*** and ***apodektos***, above, and is found in five contexts. Rom. 15:16; 1 Pet. 2:5 refer to the state of being "acceptable" to God. Rom. 15:31 refers to Christian service deemed "acceptable" to the saints in Jerusalem. See also 2 Cor. 6:2; 8:12.

euarestos [εὐάρεστος, *2101*]

euarestos is an adjective used to describe "that which is well-pleasing or acceptable." It occurs nine times.

Devoted service, or commitment, to God is "well pleasing" to him in Rom. 12:1ff.; 14:18; 2 Cor. 5:9; Eph. 5:10; Phil. 4:18; Heb. 13:21. In particular, children's obedience to their parents and a slave's submission to his master are "pleasing" to God, cf. Col. 3:20; Titus 2:9.

apodochē [ἀποδοχή, *594*]

apodochē is a rare noun denoting that which is worthy of full "acceptance" in the eyes of God (cf. 1 Tim. 1:15; 4:9).

See Also: ➡ RECEIVE ➡ TAKE

ACCESS

OT Words

nāgash [נָגַשׁ, **5066**]

This verb conveys the principal idea of "draw near" or "approach." It occurs 125 times in a number of different contexts, including those having to do with drawing near to Yahweh for the purposes of sacrifice and general worship. It was only through the Levitical ritual system that Israelites under the old covenant could gain access to God. References to this phenomenon include the following: priests drawing near to God (cf. Exod. 19:22; Jer. 30:21; Ezek. 44:13); priests approaching the altar (cf. Exod. 28:43; Lev. 21:21ff.); Moses approaching the holy presence of God (Exod. 20:21; 24:2); and Israel drawing near (hypocritically) to God in worship (cf. Isa. 29:13).

qārab [קָרַב, **7126**]

Synonymous with ***nāgash***, this word also emphasizes drawing near to God for worship. ***qārab*** is distinct in that it assumes the status of a virtual technical term in the books of Exodus, Leviticus, and Numbers as it refers to the bringing of sacrifices to Yahweh. It is used in this sense approximately 160 times (e.g., Exod.

29:3ff.; Lev. 1:2ff.; 2:1ff.; 3:1ff.; 9:2ff.; 16:1ff.; 22:18ff.; Num. 7:2ff.; 15:4ff.; 28:3ff).

NT Words

prosagōgē [προσαγωγή, *4318*]

prosagōgē is a noun found three times, denoting "access" to God made possible through the saving work of Christ through faith (cf. Rom. 5:2; Eph. 2:18; 3:12).

Additional Notes

Although there is no direct dynamic equivalent for either ***nāgash*** or ***qārab*** in the New Testament, the use of ***prosagōgē*** indicates a similarity of thought. The New Testament term makes it clear that access to the Father is only made possible through the person and work of Christ. It is that reality to which the old covenant system of worship points.

ACCOMPANY

NT Words

synepomai [συνέπομαι, *4902*]

synepomai is a rare verb, found only in Acts 20:4 and meaning "accompany" in the context of Paul traveling with his companions.

synerchomai [συνέρχομαι, *4905*]

synerchomai is a verb found in approximately thirty places with the primary meanings "come together," "go with." In several places, the meaning "accompany" is also evident in contexts where people are traveling together (cf. John 11:33; Acts 1:21; 9:39; 10:23, 45; 15:38; 21:16). In particular, Acts 11:16 records the Spirit's command to Peter to "accompany" fellow-believers to the home of Cornelius.

propempō [προπέμπω, *4311*]

propempō is a verb found in nine places with the underlying meaning "to send on one's way," in the context of journeying or traveling. In Acts 20:38 the term carries the connotation of "accompany" (i.e., travel together with).

See Also: → COME → GO → ASSEMBLE

ACCOMPLISH, ACCOMPLISHMENT

OT Words

kālāh [**כָּלָה, 3615**]

The root meaning of ***kālāh*** is bound up with the idea of "completion" or "coming to an end." Several shades of meaning are evident, one of which has to do with "accomplishment" in the sense of fulfillment — both positive in terms of God's promises, and negative in terms of divine anger. In 2 Chr. 36:22, for example, reference is made to the fulfillment of God's word in relation to the significance of Cyrus' decree to allow the Israelites to return to their homeland (cf. Ezra 1:1). With regard to divine wrath, Ezek. 5:13; 6:12; 7:8 and 13:15 mention God "spending" his wrath on his people because they have rejected him. The use of ***kālāh*** in these contexts clearly implies that God's response is a measured one, consistent with the terms of the covenant sanctions he had imposed on them. In other words, this anger is the appropriate response to Israel's violation of the terms of the covenant. Thus God's anger is said to run its full course. This same thought is also clearly expressed in Dan. 11:36 with regard to the godless king of the north.

mālē' [**מָלֵא, 4390**]

The verb ***mālē'*** (and its adjectival form) expresses the primary meaning of "fill," and it is generally translated as such. The word occurs overall about 250 times. Like ***kālāh***, above, ***mālē'*** also conveys the idea of accomplishment in several places. 2 Chr. 6:4, 15, for example, expresses Solomon's conviction that God has fulfilled the promise to his father David with the building of the temple in Jerusalem. In 1 Kgs. 2:27, Solomon's removal of Abiathar from the high-priestly office is also declared to be a fulfillment of prophecy (cf. 1 Sam. 3). Then, in Dan. 9:2, ***mālē'*** is used to indicate that the exile in Babylon "would last" (i.e., run its full course) seventy years. This again is implicitly declared to be a fulfillment of prophecy, since Daniel here refers to Jer. 25:11 as the source of his conviction.

Additional Notes

There is a high degree of correlation between the meanings of the three Greek terms, ***teleō***, ***teleioō***, and ***plēroō*** (→ FINISH → FULFILL), and those of the Hebrew ***mālē'*** and ***kālāh***. It is not possible, however, to consider any one of these Greek terms as a precise equivalent of the Hebrew. Rather, the Old and New Testaments consistently affirm the idea of the divine fulfilling or accomplishing of the plan of redemption. While the Old Testament lays the foundation, the New brings it to completion in the person of Christ.

See Also: → FINISH → FULFILL

ACCOUNT

OT Words

ḥāshab **[חָשַׁב, 2803]**

The sense of this term is quite broad. Its basic meanings are "reckon," "consider," "think," and "devise," with other related meanings (such as "account") flowing from these. ***ḥāshab*** occurs about 120 times, with the major emphasis on the idea of evaluating people and objects. Eli in 1 Sam. 1:13, for example, thinks that Hannah is drunk — but in reality she is deep in prayer. In a prophetic indictment against the people of God, Isaiah conveys God's rebuke for Israel's arrogance towards him in reckoning the potter to be like the clay (Isa. 29:16). Num. 18:27, referring to the requirement of the Levites' tithe, declares that this offering will be considered as a grain or juice offering. Finally, in the well-known Servant Song of Isa. 53, the suffering Servant-Messiah is declared to have been of no account to humankind, and reckoned as one stricken (Isa. 53:3, 4).

In another significant theological sense, ***ḥāshab*** conveys the meaning of "impute" in several contexts: Shimei, for example, in 2 Sam. 19:19, implores David not to hold him guilty for his insult against the king on a previous occasion. In Ps. 32:2, the writer declares that person blessed to whom God does not impute sin. Lev. 7:18 decrees that if the offerer eats any remainder of a fellowship offering on the third day (which is prohibited), then any benefit accruing from that offering will not be imputed to the worshiper. In Gen. 15:6, Abraham is credited with righteousness for the expression of his faith in God. An identical tribute is paid to Phinehas in Ps. 106:31 for his role in allaying the plague judgment against Israel at the time of the Baal Peor incident (cf. Num. 25).

NT Words

ellogeō [ἐλλογέω, *1677*]

ellogeō is a rare verb found only twice, meaning "impute," or "charge to one's account." The term is used literally in Phlm. 18 with reference to Paul's own financial "account," and symbolically in Rom. 5:13 in relation to sin "not being imputed" (i.e., charged to one's "spiritual account") where there is no law.

See Also: → COUNT → RECKON → THINK → WORTHY

ACCURATELY

NT Words

akribōs [ἀκριβῶς, *199*]

akribōs is an adverb meaning "accurately" in Acts 18:25 in relation to Apollos' thorough knowledge of the Scriptures.

ACCURSED → CURSE

ACCUSATION, ACCUSE

OT Words

pûaḥ **[פּוּחַ, 6315]**

The root meaning of this word is "breathe" or "blow," and by extension "to speak," with a particular emphasis in the book of Proverbs on uttering lies (cf. Prov. 6:19; 14:5, 25; 19:5, 9). The implied link, then, is between speaking lies or false witness and accusation.

NT Words

aitia [αἰτία, *156*]

The noun ***aitia*** occurs twenty times with the principal meanings "cause," "reason." In several places, however, the meaning "accusation" or "charge" is evident — all in relation to legal indictments applied to Christ at his trial (Matt. 27:37; Mark 15:26); and to Paul (Acts 23:28; 25:18, 27).

aitiōma [αἰτίωμα, *157*]

aitiōma is a rare synonym for ***aitia***, above, referring to the "charges" brought against Paul in Acts 25:7.

enklēma [ἔγκλημα, *1462*]

enklēma is another rare synonym for ***aitia*** and ***aitiōma*** (see above), found only in Acts 23:29; 25:16 with reference to "legal charges" or "accusations."

katēgoria [κατηγορία, *2724*]

The noun ***katēgoria*** is found in four places with the technical sense of a "legal charge" in Luke 6:7; John 18:29. It has a more general sense of "accusation" in 1 Tim. 5:19; Titus 1:6.

katēgoreō [κατηγορέω, *2723*]

The verb ***katēgoreō*** is found in approximately twenty-five different contexts with the consistent meaning "accuse," "bring an accusation against." The usage is primarily one of legal indictment (e.g., Matt. 12:10;

27:12; Mark 3:2; 15:3; Luke 11:54; 23:2, 10, 14; John 5:45; 8:6; Acts 22:30; 24:2ff.; 25:5ff.).

Then, in Rom. 2:15, ***katēgoreō*** refers to people's consciences "accusing" them. In Rev. 12:10, ***katēgoreō*** is used nominally (i.e., participially) to refer to Satan as "the accuser."

katēgoros [κατήγορος, *2725*]

katēgoros is a participial noun derived from ***katēgoreō*** (see above) occurring six times with the meaning "accuser."

There are general references to "those who accuse," "accusers," in Acts 23:30, 35; 24:8; 25:16, 18. In Rev. 12:10, Satan is implicitly referred to as the "accuser" of the saints.

diaballō [διαβάλλω, *1225*]

diaballō is a rare verb found only in Luke 16:1 with the meaning "accuse," "bring an accusation against."

enkaleō [ἐγκαλέω, *1458*]

The verb ***enkaleō*** is synonymous with ***katēgoreō*** and ***diaballō***, above, meaning "bring charge(s), accusation(s) against" in seven places (cf. Acts 19:38ff.; 23:28ff.; 26:2ff.; Rom. 8:33).

sykophanteō [συκοφαντέω, *4811*]

sykophanteō is a rare verb found only in Luke 3:14, with the meaning "falsely accuse," and in Luke 19:8, where it describes the act of "defrauding" (i.e., taking by false accusation).

krisis [κρίσις, *2920*]

The noun ***krisis*** occurs about fifty times with the primary meaning "judgment." In 2 Pet. 2:11; Jude 9, however, the term denotes a "slanderous accusation."

diabolos [διάβολος, *1228*]

diabolos is the standard term in the New Testament for "the devil," occurring nearly forty times. In several places, however, it denotes those who "slander" (i.e., who spread "false accusations," cf. 1 Tim. 3:11; 2 Tim. 3:3; Titus 2:3). (→ SATAN)

See Also: → JUDGE → JUDGMENT → REASON → STRIVE → THINK

ACCUSER → SATAN

ACKNOWLEDGE → KNOW

ACT, ACTIONS

OT Words

'abôdāh [עֲבוֹדָה, **5656**]

The noun ***'abôdāh***, meaning "work," "service," "labor," occurs about 140 times. In Isa. 28:21, ***'abôdāh*** refers to the strange "action" or "deed" of God.

ṣedāqāh [צְדָקָה, **6666**]

ṣedāqāh is a common noun denoting "righteousness," "justice" in almost all of its approximately 160 occurrences. In several texts, the sense of "righteous acts" is evident. Judg. 5:11 refers to the "righteous acts" of both Yahweh and the warriors in Israel. 1 Sam. 12:7 refers solely to the "righteous acts" of the Lord in the context of his saving deeds on behalf of his people.

yārē' [יָרֵא, **3372**]

yārē' is a common verb found over 300 times with the primary meanings "fear," "be afraid," plus related nuances. One of these nuances is found in Ps. 145:6, where ***yārē'*** refers to the "terrible or awesome acts" of Yahweh.

gebûrāh [גְּבוּרָה, **1369**]

The noun ***gebûrāh*** is found approximately sixty times with the primary meanings of "might," "strength," or "power." In four contexts, reference is made to "the mighty acts, or deeds" of Yahweh (cf. Pss. 106:2; 145:4, 12; 150:2).

dābār [דָּבָר, **1697**]

dābār is a very common noun, occurring nearly 1,500 times. While it means "word" in about half of these contexts, it has a wide variety of meanings throughout the rest of its occurrences. One of these meanings is "affairs" or "actions" and refers exclusively to the deeds of kings of Israel and Judah (cf. 1 Kgs. 10:6; 11:41; 15:23ff.; 2 Kgs. 1:18; 10:34; 13:8ff.; 15:6ff.; 2 Chr. 9:5; 20:34; 36:8).

NT Words

dikaiōma [δικαίωμα, *1345*]

The noun ***dikaiōma*** occurs ten times with the senses of "righteousness," "judgment," "justification." In Rom. 5:18 the term denotes precisely "an act of righteousness," viz. the atoning work of Christ.

See Also: → PRACTICE → SERVICE → WORK

ADD

OT Words

yāsaph **[יָסַף, 3254]**

In addition to its root meanings "add" or "increase," ***yāsaph*** is also used as an intensifying verb to indicate either the force of repetition or the cessation of activity. Any verb may be intensified in this way, and translates ". . . (not) again" or ". . . (no) more." For example, Lev. 16:21 reads: "I will multiply your afflictions seven times over." The literal rendering, however, is: "I will add to punish you seven times more." The great majority of the nearly 350 occurrences of ***yāsaph*** use the verb in this way.

The remaining twenty or so occurrences of ***yāsaph*** carry the precise meaning of "add" or "increase." For example, 2 Kgs. 20:6 refers to God's promise to add fifteen years to the life of King Hezekiah (cf. also Isa. 38:5). In Gen. 30:24, Rachel, on the occasion of Joseph's birth, prays that God will add to her another son. Ezra laments in Ezra 10:10 that Israel's intermarriage with foreign women had increased her guilt. Deut. 4:2 contains the divine admonition not to add to or subtract from any of the laws God had communicated to the people. Proverbs contains several promises of blessings that will come to those who fear God and adhere to his principles for godly living (cf. Prov. 11:5; 3:2; 9:9, 11; 10:22, 27; 16:21, 23). In this latter category, there is an emphasis on the fact that it is God alone who determines an increase of blessing or judgment, depending on the behavior and attitude of those to whom he is relating. Such a perspective is also clearly evident in a significant number of references where ***yāsaph*** is used as an "intensifying" verb.

NT Words

epitithēmi [**ἐπιτίθημι,** *2007*]

The verb ***epitithēmi*** is found in about fifty places with the predominant sense of "lay," "put," plus several related nuances. In Rev. 22:18 the term is twice translated "add," referring to the warning "not to add" anything to the prophetic words of the book of Revelation, and also to the inevitable punishments that God would "add" to any who would do such a thing.

prostithēmi [**προστίθημι,** *4369*]

prostithēmi is a verb found in eighteen places, in several different contexts, with the meanings "add," "increase."

The term is predicated of God in Matt. 6:33; Luke 12:31 where Christ declares that God will "add" material blessings to those who make the kingdom of God first priority in their lives. Elsewhere, both implicitly and explicitly, God is declared to be responsible for "adding" new converts to the fledgling Christian church (cf. Acts 2:41, 47; 5:14; 11:24).

In non-personal contexts, Matt. 6:27; Luke 12:25 affirm the impossibility of anyone "adding" to his or her own life span. Paul explains in Gal. 3:19 that the law "was added" by God because of transgressions. Luke 3:20 describes the action of "adding" an extra transgression to one's list of sins. In Luke 17:5, the disciples appeal to Christ to "increase their faith."

prosanatithēmi [**προσανατίθημι,** *4323*]

prosanatithēmi is a rare variant form of ***prostithēmi***, above, found in Gal. 2:6 with reference to the rivals of the apostle Paul of whom he declares "added nothing" to his message.

epidiatassomai [**ἐπιδιατάσσομαι,** *1928*]

epidiatassomai is a rare verb found only in Gal. 3:15, where the declaration is made that no one "adds" to a human covenant.

epichorēgeō [**ἐπιχορηγέω,** *2023*]

epichorēgeō is a verb found in five contexts with the sense of "furnish," "supply" in most of these. 2 Pet. 1:5 contains the exhortation to "add" virtue to one's faith.

Additional Notes

It is evident that ***epitithēmi***, of all the Greek terms cited here, most closely approximates the force of ***yāsaph***, as discussed in the Old Testament entry above. There is, however, no precise equivalent. The significance of ***epitithēmi*** emerges particularly in contexts where its meaning is "add" or "increase." Of the eighteen occurrences of this term, nine relate specifically to God as the source of blessing for the new covenant community of God's people (cf. Matt. 6:33; Mark 4:24; Luke 12:31; Acts 2:41, 47; 5:14; 11:24; Gal. 3:19; Heb. 12:19). Of particular interest are the references in Acts which mention the fact that God's power was the sole factor in the amazing growth of the early church community. It was God alone who added to their numbers.

ADJURE
→ CHARGE → OATH

ADMONISH, ADMONITION

OT Words

yāsar **[יָסַר, 3256]**

This word occurs about forty times and has the threefold root meaning of "instruct," "admonish," and "discipline." The concept of chastisement or punishment is linked with the latter, and there is a certain overlap within this semantic range. Of these meanings, that of instruction or teaching is the least frequent, occurring only four times (cf. Job 4:3; Ps. 16:7; Isa. 28:26; Ps. 2:10). In one of these texts a close connection between instruction and admonishment is clear: Ps. 2:10 exhorts world rulers to "be warned." In this context it is clear that they should take great care to learn what they can about Yahweh and how to serve him, lest they incur his wrath.

yāsar most commonly means discipline. The contexts range from the importance of parental discipline (cf. Deut. 21:18; Prov. 19:18; 29:17), to punishment resulting from civil disobedience (cf. 1 Kgs. 12:11, 14), to the divine chastening of Israel for violation of their covenant responsibilities to God. It is in this latter context that the most significant uses of the term are found. Reference is frequently made, for example, to the necessity of Israel's punishment as a consequence of her disobedience to Yahweh under the covenant (cf. Hos. 10:10; Lev. 26:18, 23, 28; Jer. 30:11; 31:38; 46:28) What is important to note here is that such admonition or chastening is never an end in itself — at least as far as the elect, the faithful in Israel, are concerned. Their chastising is temporary, albeit severe, for in the end the mercy and faithfulness of God to his covenant promises will always guarantee their ultimate preservation and salvation.

NT Words

nouthesia [**νουθεσία,** *3559*]

The noun ***nouthesia*** is found in three contexts with the meanings "admonition," "instruction" in relation to divine teaching in 1 Cor. 10:11; Eph. 6:4; and "warning" in Titus 3:10.

paraineō [**παραινέω,** *3867*]

paraineō is a rare verb found only twice, with the meaning "warn" in the context of physical danger in Acts 27:9, and "urge" or "exhort" in Acts 27:22.

chrēmatizō [**χρηματίζω,** *5537*]

The verb ***chrēmatizō*** has the primary sense of "warned by God" for the majority of the nine occurrences of the term, cf. Matt. 2:12, 22; Acts 10:22; Heb. 8:5; 11:7.

Additional Notes

It is the Greek term ***nouthesia*** that most closely approximates the meaning of ***yāsar*** in the Old Testament. The main difference is that there is little evidence in the New Testament for the explicit meaning of "punishment" or "chastisement" that is found with ***yāsar.*** The concept of discipline or punishment may be implied in 1 Thess. 5:14, although the word is translated "warn" or "admonish" in regard to those who are idle in the Thessalonian congregation.

The main thrust of these terms involves the idea of "admonishment," "warning," or "instruction."

See Also: → CHASTEN → REVEAL → WARN

ADOPTION

NT Words

hyiothesia [**υἱοθεσία,** *5206*]

The noun ***hyiothesia*** is found five times, with the underlying sense of "adoption" in each case, all referring to the status of believers as children, sons adopted by God in and through Christ (cf. Rom. 8:15, 23; 9:4; Gal. 4:5; Eph. 1:5).

Additional Notes

There is no specific Hebrew term for adoption, but the usage of "son" in metaphorical allusion to Israel's relationship with God is to be noted. This motif is touched on in Exod. 4:22ff.; Hos. 11:1. (→ SON)

ADULTERER, ADULTERY

OT Words

nā'aph **[נָאַף, 5003]**

Adultery is mentioned in the Old Testament in two related but distinct contexts. The first refers to the violation of the marriage relationship whereby either husband or wife has an illicit sexual relationship with a third party. It is expressly forbidden in the Decalogue (cf. Exod. 20:14; Deut. 5:18) and constitutes a capital offense (cf. Lev. 20:10).

nā'aph occurs thirty times, mainly in the prophetic literature, where there is also reference to adultery as a moral stain on the fabric of Israelite society (cf. Jer. 7:9; 23:14; 29:23; Hos. 4:2; Mal. 3:5).

A second perspective on adultery in the Old Testament carries a heightened theological significance. This sort of adultery has to do with Israel's persistent idolatry that characterized her as a nation throughout the Old Testament era. This particular sin, more than any other, led to her ultimate demise as an independent nation — resulting first of all in the downfall of the northern kingdom at the hands of the Assyrians and then later in the destruction of Judah and Jerusalem by the Babylonians. An equation of idolatry with spiritual adultery expresses the powerful indictment of Israel's rebellion against God in this respect (cf. Jer. 3:9; 5:7, 8; Hos. 4:13, 14; Isa. 57:3).

This metaphor underlies the intimate nature of Yahweh's relationship with his people Israel as expressed throughout the Old Testament. The consistent image is that of marriage: Yahweh takes Israel as his bride (cf. Jer. 2:33). Thus it is easy to see how naturally the sin of Israel's idolatry is linked with that of adultery against her God and "husband." This is nowhere more poignantly expressed than in the book of Hosea, where that prophet's own bitter life experience exposes the scandal of Israel's unfaithfulness to her God. In taking Gomer as a "wife of prostitution" (see ***moichalis*** below), Hosea dramatically illustrates the reality of Israel's idolatrous (and adulterous) rejection of her covenant Lord (cf. Hosea 2:3). Similarly, in Ezekiel 23 the prophet Ezekiel also illustrates this sin of both Israel and Judah in an allegorical picture of the two nations as the adulterous sisters Oholah and Oholibah, respectively (cf. Ezek. 23:37, 43, 45; cf. also Ezek. 16:32).

NT Words

moichos [μοιχός, *3432*]

The noun ***moichos*** is found in four places, meaning "adulterer" in each case. Three of these contexts make a literal reference to those who are guilty of marital infidelity (cf. Luke 18:11; 1 Cor. 6:9; Heb. 13:4). In Jas. 4:4, the term "adulterer" is metaphorical, referring to the people of God who have "betrayed" their allegiance to Christ by being ensnared by the world.

moichalis [μοιχαλίς, *3428*]

moichalis is the feminine form of ***moichos*** (see above). It is found in seven contexts with the meanings "adulteress," "adultery," and "adulterous."

moichalis is used adjectivally and metaphorically by Christ in Matt. 12:39; 16:4; Mark 8:38 to refer to his unbelieving, hostile, and skeptical hearers as an "adulterous" and evil generation.

The literal meaning "adulteress" is found in Rom. 7:3; and in Jas. 4:4 it refers metaphorically to faithless, backslidden believers.

In 2 Pet. 2:14, ***moichalis*** refers to the sin of "adultery."

moicheia [μοιχεία, *3430*]

The noun ***moicheia*** is found in four places referring to the physical sin of "adultery" (cf. Matt. 15:19; Mark 7:21; John 8:3; Gal. 5:19).

moichaō [μοιχάω, *3429*]

The verb ***moichaō*** refers to the act of "committing adultery" in six contexts (cf. Matt. 5:32 [twice]; 19:9 [twice]; Mark 10:11, 12).

moicheuō [μοιχεύω, *3431*]

moicheuō is a synonym for ***moichaō***, above. It occurs around twenty times, with the consistent literal physical sense of "commit adultery" (cf. Matt. 5:27ff.; 19:18; Mark 10:19; Luke 16:18; 18:20; John 8:4; Rom. 2:22; 13:9; Jas. 2:11). The term is used metaphorically in Rev. 2:22, where it signifies the act of adultery in relation to idol worship.

Additional Notes

With one exception, all occurrences of ***moicheuō*** and its derivatives in the New Testament point to the moral impurity of adultery in the lives of God's people, and the inevitable judgment it will bring if left unconfessed. The exceptional reference is found in Rev. 2:22, where the church in Thyatira is condemned for tolerating a certain false prophetess named Jezebel. This woman clearly led the Thyatiran congregation into immoral practices very similar to the pagan orgies of Canaanite worship.

In the book of Revelation metaphorical allusions to spiritual adultery and idolatry are linked to the vision of Babylon, the "Mother of Prostitutes" (cf. Rev. 17:2; 18:3; 19:2). In these cases, the term ***porneia*** is used, which includes not just adultery, but all kinds of sexual immorality (→ FORNICATION). It is clear in the context of these chapters that the great offense of this visionary woman is her sexual immorality, which clearly symbolizes the sin of idolatry (cf. Rev. 18 and Isa. 47). One key difference, however, between the force of ***porneia*** in Revelation 17ff. and ***nā'aph*** in the Old Testament prophets, is that the New Testament material stresses the sin of the world at large rather than of God's people in particular. Indeed, there is a strong exhortation for the people of

God to avoid all contaminating association with just such a figure (cf. Rev. 18:4).

See Also: → FORNICATION

ADVANTAGE

NT Words

perissos [περισσός, *4053*]

The adjective ***perissos*** occurs ten times and means "more," "abundant." In Rom. 3:1, however, it expresses the sense of "advantage" in Paul's question as to what spiritual "advantage" belongs to the Jews.

ophelos [ὄφελος, *3786*]

The noun ***ophelos*** is found only three times, meaning "profit" or "gain" in the non-material sense of an "advantage" (cf. 1 Cor. 15:32; Jas. 2:14, 16).

ōpheleia [ὠφέλεια, *5622*]

The noun ***ōpheleia*** occurs twice and is synonymous with ***ophelos***, above, with the same sense of non-material "profit" or "advantage" (cf. Rom. 3:1; Jude 16).

ōpheleō [ὠφελέω, *5623*]

ōpheleō is a verb found in nineteen places, usually with the sense of "gain," "profit" in both a material and non-material sense.

In Matt. 15:5; Mark 7:11 ***ōpheleō*** means "to draw a financial gain from."

General references to "gaining an advantage" are found in Matt. 16:26; Luke 9:25; 1 Cor. 13:3; Heb. 13:9. In particular, Heb. 4:2 indicates that the unbelieving generation of Israelites who failed to enter the land of Canaan because of their unbelief had no spiritual gain.

ōpheleō also expresses the sense of "to be of value," used positively in relation to circumcision in Rom. 2:25. The term also occurs in a negative context in Gal. 5:2, where Christ is said to be of no spiritual advantage if one receives circumcision as a perceived means of becoming right with God.

pleonekteō [πλεονεκτέω, *4122*]

pleonekteō is a verb found in five places with the meaning "to gain, take advantage of." The contexts all reflect the underlying sense of "wrong" or "defraud" (cf. 2 Cor. 2:11; 7:2; 12:17, 18; 1 Thess. 4:6).

See Also: → GAIN

ADVERSARY

NT Words

antidikos [ἀντίδικος, *476*]

antidikos is a noun found five times with the underlying senses of "adversary." In Matt. 5:35; Luke 12:58 (twice); Luke 18:3, the term designates a "legal opponent." In 1 Pet. 5:8 the devil is described as an "adversary" prowling around like a roaring lion.

antikeimai [ἀντίκειμαι, *480*]

antikeimai is a verb with the underlying sense of "to oppose," "set over against." It is found in eight contexts.

In the majority of its usage, ***antikeimai*** occurs in a participial noun with the sense of "enemy," "opponent" in general (cf. Luke 13:17; 21:15; 1 Cor. 16:9; Phil. 1:28). In 1 Tim. 5:14 it designates the devil as "the enemy" in particular.

The sense of "be opposed to" is found in the context of the antipathy between the flesh and the Spirit in Gal. 5:17. See also 2 Thess. 2:4 and 1 Tim. 5:10.

hypenantios [ὑπεναντίος, *5227*]

hypenantios is a rare adjectival form found only twice. In Col. 2:14 it refers to the impact of the law standing "against" the people of God, which Christ removed by his death. In Heb. 10:27 the term is used nominally to refer to "the enemies" who will be consumed by the fiery judgment of God.

See Also: → SATAN → ENEMY

ADVICE, ADVISE

OT Words

'ēṣāh [**עֵצָה, 6098**]

The basic meaning of this term revolves around the concept of "counsel" or "advice," with an extended meaning of "plan" or "purpose" in some contexts. ***'ēṣāh*** occurs about eighty times, and in the majority of instances the word is translated "counsel" or "advice," with reference to both God and human beings. The instruction may be positive or negative: that is, the counsel of human beings is either wise and good (e.g., Hushai's advice to Absalom in 2 Sam. 7:14; the elders' wise advice to Rehoboam in 1 Kgs. 12:8, which he soon rejected), or wicked and foolish (cf. Ps. 1:1; Isa. 19:11; Ezek. 11:2). God's counsel is always perfect (cf. Prov. 8:14; Job 12:13; Ps. 33:11), and those who accept it will be greatly blessed (cf. Ps. 73:24). God will advise against those who reject him and his ways, however, and bring about their judgment. It is in this context that the counsel of God assumes the meaning of "plan" or "purpose" (cf. Isa. 19:17; 46:10; Jer. 49:20; 50:45; Mic. 4:12). Such plans may also constitute blessing and salvation for God's people (cf. Isa. 5:19; 25:1; 28:29).

In addition, the counsel of God is spiritually communicated to his chosen Messianic Servant (cf. Isa. 11:2). And, finally, there is a clear inference in Isa. 40:13 that God is independent of any external source of knowledge. He is the source of all wisdom and needs no advice from outside his own being.

NT Words

gnōmē [γνώμη, *1106*]

The noun ***gnōmē*** is found in nine contexts with the meanings "mind," "opinion," "purpose," and "advice." It denotes the human faculty of rational knowledge in general.

The sense of "purpose" or "intention" is indicated in Acts 20:3; 1 Cor. 1:10; Rev. 17:13, 17. Other texts make reference to "advice," "opinion," or "judgment" (cf. 1 Cor. 7:25, 40; 2 Cor. 8:10). Then, in Phlm. 14, ***gnōmē*** denotes "consent" or "permission."

boulē [βουλή, *1012*]

The noun ***boulē*** is found twelve times with the consistent meaning of "counsel" or "will" throughout, except for Acts 27:12, where the term refers to "advice" given regarding the commencement of an ocean journey.

Additional Notes

Though the term ***boulē*** occurs infrequently in the New Testament, its meaning is very close to that of ***'ēṣāh***. Like ***'ēṣāh***, ***boulē*** refers to both human and divine purpose, plan, or will. When referring to people, ***boulē*** suggests the process of decision-making or determination on a particular course of action (e.g., Acts 27:12, 42). When speaking about God, however, ***boulē*** refers to the divine purpose or plan of salvation for his people, especially the raising up of Jesus Christ as the fulfillment of that plan (cf. Acts 2:23; 4:28; Eph. 1:11; Heb. 6:17).

In these respects ***boulē*** may be said to represent a valid dynamic equivalent to the Hebrew noun ***'ēṣāh***, even though the latter term carries a broader range of meaning in the Old Testament.

See Also: ➡ COUNSEL

ADVOCATE ➡ COMFORT

AFAR ➡ FAR

AFFLICT, AFFLICTION

OT Words

'ānāh [**עָנָה, 6031**]

This verb has a wide range of meaning, including "answer," "sing," and "afflict." It is used in both the active and passive voice, and in the passive it usually means "humble" or "afflict" (approximately seventy times).

With regard to affliction, ***'ānāh*** is translated several ways, all meaning to bring about pain, sorrow, or trouble of some kind.

In the first instance, the idea of oppression is evident: ***'ānāh*** is used, for example, to refer to the Egyptians' harsh treatment of Israel in Egypt (cf. Gen. 15:13; Exod. 1:11, 12). Then the Mosaic legislation forbids any oppressive treatment of disadvantaged groups within Hebrew society (e.g., widows, cf. Exod. 22:22, 23). The term is also used to indicate that God will remove the threat of those nations who have oppressed his people, and that he will punish them (cf. Num. 24:24; Isa. 60:14; Zeph. 3:19).

'ānāh can also refer to physical harm. In particular, several references are made to rape and violent abuse (cf. Gen. 34:2; Deut. 22:24, 29; Judg. 19:24; 20:5; 2 Sam. 13:22; Lam. 5:11; Ezek. 22:10, 11). The idea of physical harm is also found in another context with much greater significance. In Isa. 53:4, 7 ***'ānāh*** refers to the affliction of the messianic suffering servant whose terrible pain is the prelude to his exaltation and glorification.

In another significant use of ***'ānāh***, God pours out affliction upon the people of Israel for their disobedience against him, or as a test of their trust in him. In other words, their affliction is an indicator of divine discipline (cf. Deut. 8:16; 1 Kgs. 8:35; 11:39; 2 Kgs. 17:20; Pss. 88:7; 90:15; 102:23; 107:17; 119:75; Nah. 1:12).

Finally, this verb can express that kind of "self-affliction" which is often translated "to humble oneself." The idea is that of self-denial (cf. Lev. 16:31; 23:27, 32; Num. 29:7; Ps. 35:13; Ezra 8:21; Dan. 10:12).

rā'a' [**רָעַע, 7489**]

The fundamental idea associated with this verb is that of "harm" or "evil." Of the nearly one hundred occurrences of ***rā'a'***, a little less than a quarter of them mean to cause harm or inflict hurt and punishment. The majority of these texts speak of affliction, punishment, or disaster in terms of explicit divine punishment (cf. Num. 11:11; Josh. 24:20; Mic. 4:6; Jer. 25:29; 31:28; Zech. 8:14) or testing (cf. Exod. 5:22, 23; Ruth 1:21; 1 Kgs. 17:20).

Other uses of ***rā'a'*** suggest the idea of affliction in a general sense, apart from chastisement or trial (cf. Gen. 31:7; 1 Sam. 25:34; Num. 20:15; Deut. 26:6; 1 Chr. 16:22).

ṣārar [צָרַר, 6887]

The basic meanings of this term include the ideas of showing hostility, disturbing, distressing, or harassing. Most of the contexts in which this verb occurs reflect the notion of affliction in the above sense (approximately sixty occurrences).

There are a number of references in the Psalms that indicate emotional distress, trouble, or affliction in different non-specific circumstances (cf. Pss. 31:9; 69:17; 129:1, 2).

As with ***rā'a'***, above, however, ***ṣārar*** also conveys the idea of divine judgment in affliction, oppression, or distress. For example, in Num. 33:55 God warns the Israelites that if they fail to eradicate the Canaanites living in the land, they will have to endure harassment and oppression from those same people. The idea of divine judgment in affliction is very clear in this context. Similarly, God pronounces divine affliction or chastisement against the people of Israel and Judah for their disobedience and rejection of him. The settings of these texts clearly reflect the covenant curse, which God invokes for his people's violation of the law of Moses (cf. Jer. 10:18; Lam. 1:20; Zeph. 1:17; 2 Chr. 28:22; Neh. 9:27).

Finally, there are texts in which ***ṣārar*** indicates hostility and oppression towards the enemies of Israel (cf. Exod. 23:22; 25:18; Num. 25:17; Ps. 143:12) as part of the divine judgment against them, as well as indicating the deliverance of Israel as a result of the oppression of those enemies (cf. Isa. 11:3).

ṣārāh [צָרָה, 6869]

This noun is synonymous with ***ṣārar*** and means "trouble," "distress," "affliction," and "adversity." ***ṣārāh*** occurs approximately seventy times, and all contexts in which it is found reflect the same theological emphases as for ***ṣārar***.

lāḥaṣ [לָחַץ, 3905]; ***laḥaṣ*** [לַחַץ, 3906]

These two synonymous terms also mean "oppression," "distress." The verb ***lāḥaṣ*** occurs nineteen times, and the derivative noun ***laḥaṣ*** occurs about ten times. The majority of these occurrences refer to the political and military oppression of Israel by a succession of enemies such as Egypt (cf. Exod. 3:9), the Canaanites (cf. Judg. 2:18; 4:3; 6:9), and Syria (cf. 2 Kgs. 13:4). In addition Amos 6:14 refers to the oppression of Israel by Assyria as the direct result of Israel's rebellion against God. And, finally, Jer. 30:20 refers to the deliverance of Israel from domination by all her enemies in the context of her promised deliverance from exile.

'ānî [עָנִי, 6041]

The noun ***'ānî*** occurs in eighty places with the predominant sense of "poor." In a number of contexts, however, the word also means "afflicted," with one or two related nuances.

The people of Israel are said to be "afflicted" in the sense of "humbled," "humiliated," or "cast down" in 2 Sam. 22:8; Ps. 18:27; Zeph. 3:12.

Elsewhere, and more commonly, people are described as "afflicted" in the sense of being "oppressed" or "harassed" (cf. Job 34:28; Pss. 9:12; 10:12; 88:15; 102:1; Prov. 15:15; 22:22). This plight is also predicated of the individual "Suffering Servant" figure of Ps. 22:24 (cf. also Ps. 25:16); and also as a judgment from God on his people (cf. Isa. 51:21; 54:11).

'onî [עֳנִי, 6040]

'onî is a noun found in about forty places with the consistent sense of "affliction," with a variety of nuances.

"Affliction" in the general sense of "suffering," "torment," or "trauma" is indicated with respect to individuals in Gen. 16:11; 31:42; 1 Sam. 1:11; 2 Sam. 16:12; Job 10:15; Pss. 25:18; 119:50; and to people in general in Prov. 31:5.

'onî also denotes "affliction" in the sense of "physical oppression," particularly in relation to Israel's period of enslavement in Egypt from which Yahweh had delivered them (cf. Exod. 3:7, 17, 4:31; Deut. 26:7; Neh. 9:9). Other general references to the "affliction" or "oppression" of God's people include 2 Kgs. 14:26; Pss. 44:24; 107:41. In addition, there are several places where such "affliction" experienced by the people of God is portrayed as an act of divine judgment against them (cf. Isa. 48:10; Lam. 1:3ff.).

There is also a metaphorical use of *'onî* in Deut. 16:3, where Israel's slavery in Egypt is associated with her "bread of affliction."

NT Words

kakoō [κακόω, *2559*]

kakoō is a verb found in seven places with the meaning "to treat harmfully," "mistreat." With this sense, the meaning "afflict" is evident in Acts 7:6; 18:10; 1 Pet. 3:13. (See also Acts 7:19; 12:1; 14:2.)

kakoucheō [κακουχέω, *2558*]

kakoucheō is a rare verb with the meaning "oppress," "afflict" in the sense of "mistreat," "harm" found in Heb. 11:37; 13:3.

kakopatheō [κακοπαθέω, *2553*]

The verb ***kakopatheō*** occurs in five places with the consistent sense of "endure affliction, or suffering." Jas. 5:13 refers to this in general terms; and 2 Tim. 2:3, 9; 4:5 all suggest the context of persecution.

kakopatheia [κακοπάθεια, *2552*]

kakopatheia is a rare noun derived from ***kakopatheō***, above, and found only in Jas. 5:10, meaning "the suffering of affliction, or distress."

kakōsis [κάκωσις, *2561*]

kakōsis is a rare noun found only in Acts 7:34 with reference to the "affliction" the Israelites suffered in Egypt.

thlibō [θλίβω, *2346*]

The verb ***thlibō*** means "to trouble," "afflict," "oppress" in most of its ten occurrences.

The passive sense of "being afflicted, oppressed" in the content of tribulation or persecution is indicated in 2 Cor. 1:6; 4:8; 7:5; 2 Thess. 1:7; Heb. 11:37. The allied sense of "suffering affliction" is evident in 1 Thess. 3:4. The active sense of "to afflict, oppress or trouble" in relation to one's persecutors is found in 2 Thess. 1:6. The participial, nominal sense of "those who are afflicted" is evident in 1 Tim. 5:10.

thlipsis [θλίψις, *2347*]

thlipsis is the noun derived from ***thlibō*** (see above). It occurs around fifty times with the predominant sense of "affliction" or "tribulation," with an underlying sense of deep-seated anguish and suffering.

The general sense of "affliction" or "tribulation" giving rise to anguish is indicated, for example, in Matt. 13:21; 24:9, 21, 29; Mark 13:9ff.; John 16:21, 33; Acts 7:11; Rom. 8:35; 1 Cor. 7:28; 2 Cor. 1:4ff.; 1 Thess. 3:3ff.; Jas. 1:27. Acts 7:10; 20:23 refer to the "affliction" of individuals. Viewed as punishment from God, such "affliction" is evident in Rom. 2:9; Rev. 2:22. This kind of suffering is said to produce endurance in the life of the believer in Rom. 5:3; 12:12; 2 Cor. 6:4. The "afflictions" of Christ are noted in Col. 1:24.

The specific nuance of persecution in "affliction" is evident in Acts 11:19; Heb. 10:33; Rev. 1:9; 2:9ff.; 7:14.

pathēma [πάθημα, *3804*]

The noun ***pathēma***, meaning "suffering," "affliction" is found sixteen times.

General references to "affliction" and "suffering," mostly linked to persecution, are found in Rom. 8:18; 2 Cor. 1:6ff.; Col. 1:24; 2 Tim. 3:11; Heb. 2:10; 10:32; 1 Pet. 5:9. In particular, the "suffering(s)" of Christ are indicated in 2 Cor. 1:5; Phil. 3:10; Heb. 2:9; 1 Pet. 1:11; 4:13; 5:1.

Additional Notes

There is some overlap of meaning among all the Greek and Hebrew terms discussed above. ***kakoō***, for example, and all terms derived from it, emphasize suffering and distress resulting from external factors.

It is with the terms ***pathēma***, ***thlibō***, and ***thlipsis***, however, that we find the closest semantic connections with the set of Hebrew synonyms above. With ***pathēma***, for instance, there is fairly equal emphasis in the New Testament between the value of suffering and persecution as Christians, the redemptive value of Jesus' own sufferings, and the identification of believers' trials with that of our Lord. Secondly, ***thlipsis*** is the most commonly used term for suffering, persecution, and affliction in the New Testament. And, like its dynamic Hebrew equivalents above, ***thlipsis*** has a fairly wide range of meaning within the broad theme of suffering. Both ***thlipsis*** and the corresponding verb ***thlibō*** refer to anguish that largely arises from sources external to the person(s) concerned.

Here we see a similar line of thinking with Old Testament usage. Israel suffered much for her rebellion against God, who determined to have his people undergo very severe chastening so that they might become more like him and live for him wholeheartedly. In the New Testament it is Jesus Christ himself who willingly submits to a divine judgment that is incomprehensible to any and every other human being. It is that affliction, which is incomparably powerful in its saving effect on his people, that testifies to the supreme perfection of our Lord in every aspect of his person and work.

See Also: → ENEMY → OPPRESS → SUFFER

AFFORD

OT Words

***nāsag* [נָשַׂג, 5381]**

The verb ***nāsag*** is found in fifty contexts with the predominant meanings "overtake," "reach," along with a variety of related nuances including "afford," in the sense of "having the means to purchase or supply."

The term is used in the context of the Israelite worship referring to those who "can or cannot afford" to bring certain items for sacrificial offering to the Lord (cf. Lev. 5:11; 14:21ff.; Num. 6:21).

AFRAID → FEAR

AGE

OT Words

***'ôlām* [עוֹלָם, 5769]**

This very common Hebrew noun occurs over four hundred times in the Old Testament. Its main connotation is that of lengthy duration, with both a past and future sense. When referring to the past its meaning is normally "ancient" or "(of) old" (twenty occurrences). However, it is most commonly translated "forever," "always," or "everlasting," with most of these references indicating indefinite future or continuous existence. It is within this future orientation that the word's most significant theological emphasis is to be found. Out of approximately 380 references to the indefinite future, approximately 100 of these have to do either with some aspect of the promised new covenant of redemption or the covenants with Abraham, Moses, and David. In every instance the common emphasis is that such divine plans and purposes will have permanent and lasting effectiveness. This includes both blessing and judgment.

To begin with, ***'ôlām*** refers to the enduring character of God's covenant with his people. He will never break it either in total or in part (cf. Lev. 24:8; Num. 18:19; 25:13; Judg. 2:1; 2 Sam. 23:5; Ps. 105:8, 10). Israel, however, will not maintain her covenant obligations with God, and will have to suffer his punishment as a result (see below). Nevertheless, in spite of Israel's sin, God guarantees never to ultimately abandon his people, but promises to bring them back into intimate relationship with himself. This will be accomplished by a renewed covenant that will never be broken through the weakness and sinfulness of human beings (cf. Isa. 55:13; 61:8; Jer. 32:40; 50:5; Ezek. 16:60; 37:26). The passage in Jer. 31:31–34 describes this phenomenon most succinctly of all. Even though the term ***'ôlām*** is not used in this context, an eternally unbroken covenant is clearly implied.

Secondly, some specific Levitical ordinances are said to be everlasting in their effect. Such references are confined to the Pentateuch, with one exception in the book of Ezekiel (cf. Exod. 27:21; 28:43; 29:9; 30:21; Lev. 3:17; 6:18, 22; 7:34, 36; 10:9, 15; 16:29ff.; 17:7; 23:14ff.; Num. 18:8ff.; Ezek. 46:14).

Finally, there are a number of references to the eternally binding nature of the divine covenant promises. They will last forever and are guaranteed by the person of God himself. This is true whether the promises are applied to the land of Canaan (cf. Deut. 5:29; 12:28; Josh. 4:7; 14:9; Isa. 60:21; Jer. 7:7), or to King David and his future royal posterity (cf. 2 Sam. 7:13ff.; 1 Chr. 20:7; Deut. 5:29; Josh. 4:7). In a negative sense, ***'ôlām*** also refers to the nature of divine punishment for disobedience (the invoking of the covenant curse), whether to Israel (cf. Deut. 28:46; Jer. 23:40; 25:9) or to a nation like Babylon (cf. Jer. 25:12; 51:26, 39, 57, 62).

Although there is no precise equivalent for the concept of "age" in the sense of "era" in the Old Testament, a word like ***'ôlām*** evokes this idea. As a result, this word may be seen to reflect the enduring, unbroken nature of God's promises to Israel and the nations as recorded in Scripture. God is declared to be fully consistent in both word and deed — whether in the past, present, or future age.

***dôr* [דּוֹר, 1755]**

This word is almost uniformly translated "generation" in the English Bible. ***dôr*** refers to clans or generations of people from all time: past, present, and future. The word also refers metaphorically both to the people of God and the nations in terms of an indefinite future with a continuous existence. In this latter sense, it closely approximates ***'ôlām*** (see above). The word is found in both the singular and the plural and occurs some 125 times.

dôr refers first of all to a contemporary generation of people in the biblical era (cf. Exod. 1:6; Deut. 1:35; 32:20; Judg. 2:10; Ps. 14:5; Jer. 2:31). These people are spoken of both positively and negatively (i.e., as those either blessed or condemned by God). Secondly, ***dôr*** refers both positively and negatively to generations of people in the past (cf. Deut. 32:7; Pss. 78:8; 95:10; Isa. 41:4; 51:8; 61:4). Thirdly, ***dôr*** refers to generations in the immediate and not-too-distant future (cf. Gen. 15:16; Exod. 17:16; Pss. 48:13; 102:18).

Finally, the meaning of ***dôr*** is fairly close to that of ***'ôlām*** in the large majority of instances (approximately eighty occurrences), where it refers to an unending succession of generations to come. In this sense it is virtually a technical expression, commonly translated ". . . from generation to generation."

To translate ***dôr*** with the meaning "age" would not be inappropriate in many contexts. It certainly carries a greater nominal sense than does ***'ôlām***, which is most often translated with adjectival or adverbial force.

zequnîm **[זְקֻנִים, 2208]**

zequnîm is the plural form of the noun ***zāqûn***, found only in four contexts in the plural, referring to "old age" (cf. Gen. 21:2, 7; 37:3; 44:20).

zōqen **[זֹקֶן, 2207];** ***sêb*** **[שֵׂיב, 7869]**

Both of these terms occur in only one context, meaning "age" with particular reference to "old age." ***zōqen*** is found in Gen. 48:10, and ***sêb*** in 1 Kgs. 14:4.

NT Words

hēlikia **[ἡλικία,** ***2244*****]**

The noun ***hēlikia*** is found eight times in all, with the meanings "stature," "age." The latter sense is indicated in John 9:21ff. with reference to "being of age" (i.e., adult maturity). In Heb. 11:11, the term refers to "the age" of a woman in relation to her childbearing capacity.

hēmera **[ἡμέρα,** ***2250*****]**

The noun ***hēmera*** means "day(s)" throughout its usage (approximately forty times). In Luke 2:36, the prophetess Anna is described as being of a "great age" (lit., "a woman of many days").

See Also: → DAY → EVER → GENERATION → OLD → WORLD

AGED → ELDER → OLD

AGONY → PAIN

AGREE, AGREEMENT

OT Words

'ôt **[אוֹת, 225]**

This is a rare verb in the Old Testament, occurring only four times (Gen. 34:15ff.; 2 Kgs. 12:8) and meaning "agreement" (i.e., consent given between the parties involved).

shāma' **[שָׁמַע, 8085]**

This very common verb means "hear," "listen(to)," or "obey." On occasion it may also be translated "agree," when the underlying sense is that relevant parties hear what the other has to say and either accept or reject the proposed outcome (e.g., Gen. 16:2; 23:16; 34:24; 1 Sam. 28:23). Context is the sole factor in determining whether "agree" or "listen to" is the most appropriate translation. In either case, the underlying meaning is very similar.

qāshar **[קָשַׁר, 7194]**

The root meaning of this verb is "bind," in a literal sense, and "conspire (together)" in a related, metaphorical sense (i.e., to bind oneself with another party in a conspiracy). Again, these nuances are simply variations on the concept of agreement. The literal and metaphorical meanings of ***qāshar*** are fairly evenly distributed throughout the Old Testament. Of the forty-four occurrences of the term, a little over half of them express the idea of conspiring or plotting. Almost all of these are found in the narratives of Samuel, Kings, and Chronicles, where they illustrate the treachery that surrounded the violent deaths of a number of Israelite and Judean kings — a negative characteristic of certain periods in the royal courts of Israel and Judah.

There is one text, however, that illustrates the metaphorical connotation of ***qāshar*** in a unique way. In 1 Sam. 18:1, David's close friendship with Jonathan is described literally, in terms of Jonathan's soul being bound to the soul of David. This description is a prelude to the solemn covenant they swore to each other a little later on (cf. 1 Sam. 20:16, 17). This rare positive connotation of ***qāshar*** (as opposed to that of "conspiracy") likewise illustrates the underlying meaning of "agreement" inherent in the term.

NT Words

symphōneō **[συμφωνέω,** ***4856*****]**

symphōneō is a verb found in seven contexts, each of which expresses the meaning "to agree," "come to an agreement" (cf. Matt. 18:19; 20:2, 13; Luke 5:36; Acts 5:9; 15:15).

phroneō [φρονέω, *5426*]

The verb ***phroneō*** is found in nearly forty different contexts, with the primary meaning of "think," plus related senses. One of these is "to agree," "be of one mind or like-minded" (cf. Rom. 12:16; 15:5; 2 Cor. 13:11; Phil. 2:2; 4:2).

syntithēmi [συντίθημι, *4934*]

syntithēmi is a verb with the meaning "to agree," "make a formal pledge." It is found in only four places (cf. Luke 22:5; John 9:22; Acts 23:20; 24:9).

synkatathesis [συγκατάθεσις, *4783*]

synkatathesis is a rare noun denoting an "agreement" in the sense of "that which is compatible." It is found only in 2 Cor. 6:16, where Paul asks the rhetorical question: "What agreement is there between the temple of God and idols?" The implicit answer is "None."

asymphōnos [ἀσύμφωνος, *800*]

asymphōnos is a rare adjectival term found only in Acts 28:25 with reference to a "disagreement."

isos [ἴσος, *2470*]

The adjective ***isos*** occurs in eight contexts and expresses the meaning "equal" in most of them. In Mark 14:56, 59, however, the term is used negatively in the sense of "not agreeing" with reference to the false testimony given against Christ at his trial.

Additional Notes

Of all the Greek terms listed here, only ***symphōneō*** and ***syntithēmi*** overlap in meaning with the Hebrew terms above in any significant way. On two of the four occasions ***syntithēmi*** is used in the New Testament, there is a distinct overtone of conspiracy evident in the context. In Luke 22:5, first of all, it is recorded that the chief priests came to an agreement with Judah to pay him money. The betrayal of Jesus is imminent. Then, in Acts 24:9, Paul is falsely accused by his Jewish opponents of being a troublemaker and of having desecrated the temple. Because the Jews here joined in this accusation, the idea of a conspiracy against Paul is clearly evident.

AIR

NT Words

aēr [ἀήρ, *109*]

aēr is a noun denoting "air" in each of the seven contexts in which it is found. Most of these refer to the atmosphere (cf. Acts 22:23; 1 Cor. 9:26; 14:9; 1 Thess. 4:17; Rev. 9:2; 16:17). In Eph. 2:2, the term refers to the satanic "prince of the power of the air." The term "air" denotes the atmospheric region between earth and heaven as the domain of Satan.

ouranos [οὐρανός, *3772*]

ouranos is a common noun denoting "heaven" as the dwelling place of God throughout most of the nearly three hundred occurrences of the term. In several places, however, ***ouranos*** also denotes "air," or the atmosphere above, the earth the domain of birds (cf. Matt. 6:26; 8:20; 13:32; Mark 4:4, 32; Luke 8:5; 9:58; 13:19; Acts 10:12; 11:6).

See Also: → HEAVEN

ALIEN, ALIENATE

OT Words

zûr [זוּר, **2114**]

This Hebrew term occurs seventy-five times and designates that which is strange, foreign, or alien. In its less common verbal sense it indicates "estrangement" or "alienation" (six occurrences), while its participial (nominal) form is more common and generally means "stranger," "foreigner," or "alien." It is also used adjectivally.

The connotation of ***zûr*** in relation to the idea of "stranger" varies according to context. In the Pentateuch, for example, the word refers to all those outside the priestly class (i.e., strangers), who are forbidden to participate in certain civil and ceremonial rituals that are reserved exclusively for the priesthood. It is clear that this word refers to both "lay" Israelites and non-Israelites (cf. Exod. 29:33; 30:33; Lev. 22:10; Num. 1:51; 16:40; 18:4, 7).

zûr refers to a quite different phenomenon in Proverbs. Of the fourteen occurrences in the book, seven focus on morally corrupt women who are "strange" (i.e., prostitutes or adulteresses), and the young men in Israel are warned against consorting with them (cf. Prov. 2:16; 5:3, 10, 17, 20; 7:5; 22:14).

In the prophetic literature, ***zûr*** refers to foreigners who will be used by God to bring judgment upon his rebellious people, Israel (cf. Jer. 51:51; Lam. 5:2; Ezek. 11:9; 28:7, 10; 31:12; Hos. 8:7). The word is also used in two places in a positive sense to promise a divine restoration, when foreigners will no longer harass them (cf. Jer. 30:8; Joel 3:17).

In several places, ***zûr*** refers to the "strangeness" of foreign gods in contexts where Israel is being indicted for her idolatry (cf. Deut. 32:16; Ps. 81:9; Isa. 43:12; Jer. 3:13).

One intriguing use of ***zûr*** occurs in relation to "strange" fire or incense. The most famous of these relates the execution (by God) of Nadab and Abihu, sons of Aaron, for offering such a fire to God (cf. Lev. 10:1; see also Exod. 30:9; Num. 3:4; 16:40). The implication is that any incense offering not presented in the duly prescribed manner under the law is deemed "strange" and liable to very severe sanction.

gēr [גֵּר, 1616]

This term is broadly synonymous with ***zûr*** (see above), although its semantic range is much narrower. ***gēr*** occurs more frequently than ***zûr***, but it refers exclusively to that class of non-Israelites living in the promised land who were temporary residents or newcomers. ***gēr*** is also used to refer to Abraham and Moses (see below) prior to the establishment of Israel as a nation. Although these people had no inherited rights in the land (as did the descendants of Abraham under the provisions of the covenant promise), they were nevertheless granted concessional rights, privileges, and also responsibilities, under the law. The Mosaic legislation required that all such foreigners or "sojourners" (as they are often described) be treated humanely and compassionately.

For example, ***gēr*** describes Abraham at Hebron (cf. Gen. 23:4); Moses in the desert (cf. Exod. 2:22); Yahweh (metaphorically, cf. Jer. 14:8); and Israel in Egypt (cf. Gen. 15:13; Exod. 22:30; 23:9). The sojourner is expected to observe the Sabbath rest (cf. Exod. 20:10; 23:12; Deut. 5:14) and to share obligations with the Israelite population (cf. Exod. 12:19, Lev. 16:29; 17:8ff.; Num. 15:14ff.). He also has rights similar to those of the Israelites (cf. Deut. 16:11, 14; 26:11; 29:11). The Israelites must also treat foreigners kindly (cf. Lev. 19:10; 23:22; 19:33, 34; Deut. 10:18, 19; 14:29; 24:19–21; 26:12, 13), and not oppress them (cf. Lev. 19:33; Deut. 24:14; Exod. 22:20; 23:9; Jer. 7:6; 22:3).

nēkār [נֵכָר, 5236]

Yet another synonym for the two terms above, ***nēkār*** focuses on that which is foreign or alien to Israel — in both a personal and impersonal sense. In the first instance, it refers generally to those who are strangers in Israel (nineteen occurrences). Two of these texts are of particular interest in that they speak of proselytes (i.e., foreign converts to the worship of Yahweh as the one true and living God) who come to share in the blessings of the covenant (Isa. 53:3, 6).

The large majority of the remaining occurrences of ***nēkār*** refer to idols as foreign and once again (like ***zûr***) are found in the context of indictments against or warnings to Israel.

nokrî [נָכְרִי, 5237]

This adjectival form of ***nēkār***, above, carries a nominal sense as well. Again, it designates that which is strange, foreign, or alien. A little less than half of the occurrences of ***nokrî*** refer to women who are foreign. Of these twenty occurrences, eleven refer to both the foreign women that Solomon married (cf. 1 Kgs. 11:1, 8) and those who had married in like manner prior to the return of Ezra in 457 B.C. (cf. Ezra 10:2ff.; Neh. 13:27). The remaining nine passages are in Proverbs and refer to those "strange" women who are in fact adulterous and promiscuous (→ ***zûr*** above, and cf. Prov. 2:16; 5:10, 20; 6:24; 7:5; 20:16; 23:27; 27:2, 13).

NT Words

allotrios [ἀλλότριος, *245*]

The noun ***allotrios*** occurs fourteen times with the senses of "other," "stranger and alien," or "foreigner." The term is also used adjectivally.

The meaning "stranger," merely in the sense of "someone else" or "other people" who may or may not be known, is indicated in Matt. 17:25, 26; Luke 16:12; John 10:5; Rom. 14:4; 15:20; 2 Cor. 10:15, 16; 1 Tim. 5:22. In Heb. 9:25, the specific reference to the blood of the high priest's sacrifice that "does not belong to him" literally designates it as "the blood of others." In Heb. 11:9, ***allotrios*** is used nominally to refer to Abraham, likening him to a "foreigner" in the land of promise. In Heb. 11:34 the usage is adjectival, denoting "foreign" armies; and in Acts 7:6 ***allotrios*** refers to a "foreign" land.

apallotrioō [ἀπαλλοτριόω, *526*]

The verb ***apallotrioō*** is found three times, meaning "to be alienated" or "separated" and referring to estrangement from God or his people (cf. Eph. 2:12; 4:18; Col. 1:21).

Additional Notes

The relatively rare term ***allotrios*** occurs fourteen times in the New Testament, and of these only one text refers to the concept of one who is a stranger or an alien (viz. Heb. 11:9). In the rest of the occurrences ***allotrios*** carries the above meaning.

apallotrioō expresses the idea of alienation in all three of its occurrences (viz. Eph. 2:12; 4:18; Col. 1:21). Each of these refers to the former state of alienation or separation from God in which Gentiles found themselves prior to their conversion to Christ. Although the phenomenon is much more fully developed in the Old Testament, it is nevertheless clear that all distinctions between Jew and Gentile, native and alien, have been obliterated by the coming of Christ and the inauguration of the new covenant kingdom of God.

ALL

OT Words

kōl **[כֹּל, 3605]**

There are over five thousand occurrences of this particle in the Old Testament. There is essentially no distinction in meaning between the Hebrew ***kōl*** and the Greek ***pas*** (see below). The meaning "all" is almost universal, with the accompanying senses of "whole," "each," and "every," encompassing animals, people objects, places, and events. Examples of this usage include Gen. 1:26; Exod. 40:38; Lev. 16:30ff.; Num. 4:9ff.; Deut. 5:1ff.; Josh. 10:15ff.; Judg. 9:34ff.; 1 Sam. 8:4ff.; Ezra 1:1ff.; Neh. 4:6; Job 28:3; Ps. 100:1ff.; Prov. 1:13ff.; 8:8ff.; Eccl. 2:3ff.; Isa. 44:9; Jer. 23:3; Ezek. 8:10; Dan. 2:12; Hos. 7:2ff.; Joel 1:12; Amos 9:1ff.; Mic. 7:12; Nah. 3:1; Hab. 2:8; Hag. 2:4ff.; Zech. 4:2.

The following terms are also worthy of note.

tāmîm **[תָּמִים, 8549]**

The adjective ***tāmîm*** occurs about ninety times, meaning "without blemish," "perfect." In several places the meaning "whole," "entire" is also indicated (cf. Lev. 3:9; Josh. 10:13; Prov. 1:12; Ezek. 15:5).

kālîl **[כָּלִיל, 3632]**

kālîl is an adjectival particle in part synonymous with ***kōl*** (see above), meaning "whole," "wholly," "all" in about half of the fifteen occurrences of the term (cf. Exod. 28:31; 39:22; Lev. 6:22ff.; Num. 4:6; Deut. 13:16; 33:10; 1 Sam. 7:9; Ps. 51:19).

NT Words

pas [πᾶς, *3956*]

pas is an adjectival particle synonymous with ***kōl***, above, its dynamic Hebrew equivalent. It occurs over one thousand times, denoting "all," "each," "every" in relation to people and all sorts of non-personal phenomena (e.g., Matt. 2:3ff.; Mark 4:11ff.; Luke 1:63ff.; John 3:15ff.; Acts 1:18ff.; 2:5; Rom. 1:16; 3:2; 9:5ff.; 1 Cor. 2:15; 2 Cor. 8:7; Gal. 3:8ff.; Eph. 1:3; Phil. 1:3ff.; Col. 1:6ff.; 1 Thess. 5:14ff.; 1 Tim. 2:1ff.; 2 Tim. 3:16; Heb. 1:2ff.; Jas. 3:7; 1 Pet. 1:24; 1 John 1:7ff.; Rev. 6:14; 13:7ff.).

hapas [ἅπας, *537*]

hapas is a variant adjectival form of ***pas***, above, occurring around forty times with the primary meanings "all," "all things."

The word means "all," in a general descriptive sense, in Matt. 24:39; Mark 16:5; Luke 4:6; 7:16; Acts 2:4, 44; 13:29; Jas. 3:2.

The designation "all things" or "everything" is found in Matt. 6:32; 28:11; Luke 2:39; Acts 2:44; 4:32; 10:8.

holos [ὅλος, *3650*]

holos is another synonym for the entries listed above, an adjective denoting "all," "whole" throughout the more than one hundred occurrences of the term (cf. Matt. 1:22; 4:23–24; 20:6; Mark 6:55; 12:30ff.; Luke 8:43; 13:21; Acts 2:2; 13:49; Rom. 16:23; Gal. 5:3; Jas. 3:2ff.; Rev. 13:3).

ALLEGORY

OT Words

ḥîdāh **[חִידָה, 2420]**

The basic meaning of this term is "riddle," "puzzle," or "hard question." It occurs seventeen times in a variety of contexts. First of all, Moses' unique role as the prophet of Yahweh (Num. 12:8) is declared to be that of an intimate divine confidant who enjoys plain speech from his God rather than puzzling or perplexing riddles. Judg. 14 contains the account of Samson's "riddle" which he puts to his Philistine companions on the occasion of his wedding. The solving of the riddle provides a God-given opportunity for Samson to take vengeance on these enemies of Israel. In the book of Kings, the Queen of Sheba plies Solomon with a number of hard questions in order to test the caliber of his reputed wisdom (cf. 1 Kgs. 10:1; 2 Chr. 9:1). Other texts (viz. Pss. 49:4; 78:2; Prov. 1:6; Dan 8:23; Hab. 2:6) all utilize the term ***ḥîdāh*** to convey the idea of puzzling words with hidden meanings.

Of all the Old Testament uses of ***ḥîdāh***, the one in Ezek. 17:2 most closely approximates the meaning of allegory (i.e., a piece of symbolic writing with a veiled spiritual or theological significance). Ezekiel 17 depicts

Israel's deportation at the hands of the Babylonians and her subsequent restoration by God under the symbolic guise of two eagles and a vine. Interestingly enough, Ezek. 23 contains another allegorical depiction of Israel's sinfulness, via the imagery of two adulterous sisters (viz. Israel and Judah). Then, in Judg. 9, Jotham's parable warns his countrymen of the dangers of giving allegiance to Abimelech, Gideon's son. Although there is no specific use of any term for allegory or parable in these two latter passages, this is clearly implied.

Finally, the verbal form of ***ḥîdāh*** (*ḥûd*) occurs only four times: three in the Samson narrative mentioned above (cf. Judg. 14:12, 13, 16), and once in Ezek. 17:2.

māshāl **[מָשָׁל, 4912]**

The noun ***māshāl*** is synonymous with ***ḥîdāh***, above, in certain respects, but it also has a slightly broader range of meaning. In two of the thirty-eight occurrences of ***māshāl***, the connotation of parable or allegory (as defined above) is clearly evident (viz. Ezek. 17:2; 24:3). In both cases, the context is one of indictment against Israel for her sinfulness.

In the remaining passages where ***māshāl*** is used, the primary meaning is that of "proverb" or "wise saying." It is commonly used this way in the wisdom writings (cf. Pss. 49:14, 15; 49:4; 69:11; Prov. 1:1, 6; 10:1; 25:1; 26:7, 9; Eccl. 12:9); and also in the prophets (cf. Ezek. 12:22, 23; 14:8; 18:2, 3; Mic. 2:4) and several times elsewhere (cf. Deut. 28:37; 1 Sam. 10:12; 24:13; 1 Kgs. 4:32; 9:7; 2 Chr. 7:20).

In Num. 23:7, 18 and 24:3ff., ***māshāl*** refers to Balaam's prophetic oracles.

Like ***ḥîdāh***, ***māshāl*** also has a verbal form (*māshal*), which occurs sixteen times with similar usage.

NT Words

allēgoreō [ἀλληγορέω, *238*]

allēgoreō is a rare verb found only in Gal. 4:24 with the meaning "to speak allegorically" or simply "to be an allegory."

ALLOW

OT Words

nātan **[נָתַן, 5414]**

nātan is a very common verb with the predominant meaning "to give," plus a wide variety of related senses throughout the nearly two thousand occurrences of the term. In Exod. 3:19; Num. 22:13, however, it expresses the meaning "to let, allow," in negative contexts of refusing to give permission.

shālaḥ **[שָׁלַח, 7971]**

shālaḥ is a common verb meaning "to send," plus a variety of related nuances throughout the nearly 850 occurrences of the term. In a number of contexts, however, the meaning "let (someone or something) go" in the sense of "allowing" them to go is also indicated (cf. Exod. 4:23; 21:26ff.; Lev. 16:10; Deut. 15:12ff.; 1 Sam. 24:19; Jer. 34:14; 40:1ff.).

yālak **[יָלַךְ, 3212]**

yālak is a very common Hebrew verb expressing the meanings "go," "walk" in most of the 1,000 or so uses of the term. In a few contexts, ***yālak*** means "to let go" (i.e., give permission, allow to leave, cf. Deut. 20:5ff.).

NT Words

epitrepō [ἐπιτρέπω, *2010*]

The verb ***epitrepō*** occurs nineteen times in a variety of contexts with the primary meaning "persist," "allow" throughout.

In a number of places, people ask Jesus to "allow" them a number of things — to bury their loved ones, for example (cf. Matt. 8:21; Luke 9:59), or to say farewell to family (cf. Luke 9:61). Even demons beg permission of him to be sent away into a herd of swine (cf. Matt. 8:31; Mark 5:13; Luke 8:32).

Other contexts where permission is granted include Jesus "allowing" people to get divorced (cf. Matt. 19:8; Mark 10:4). Pilate "allows" the disciples of Christ to take his body down from the cross (cf. John 19:38). Permission to speak is both sought and granted in Acts 21:39ff.; 26:1; 1 Cor. 14:34. Women are refused permission to teach in 1 Tim. 2:12. See also Acts 27:3; 28:16; 1 Cor. 16:7; Heb. 6:3.

apolyō [ἀπολύω, *630*]

The verb ***apolyō*** is found in about ninety contexts, and in about sixty of these it means "release," with the sense of "permitting, allowing to leave."
(→ RELEASE)

aphiēmi [ἀφίημι, *863*]

aphiēmi is a verb found in more than 150 contexts with the predominant sense of "forgive," "leave" in most of these occurrences. (→ FORGIVE → LEAVE)

The general sense of "permit," "let," or "allow" something to happen is evident in Matt. 7:4; 8:22; 13:30; Luke 6:42; 9:60. In particular, Matt. 19:14; Luke 10:14 make reference to Jesus' request to "allow" little children to come to him for blessing. The exhortation "let it be" (i.e., allow to happen) is found in Matt. 3:15. See also Mark 11:6; John 11:44.

The negative use of ***aphiēmi***, indicating a "refusal to allow," is evident in Matt. 23:13, where Jesus indicts the Pharisees for refusing to allow people to enter the kingdom of heaven (cf. also Mark 7:12). In Mark 1:34 Jesus refuses demons permission to speak. See also Mark 5:37; 11:16; Rev. 11:9.

eaō [ἐάω, *1439*]

eaō is a verb expressing the meaning "allow," "permit" in most of its thirteen occurrences.

eaō is predicated of God in Acts 14:16, where he is said to "have granted permission" (or allowed) the nations to go their own way in the past. In 1 Cor. 10:13, the promise is made that God "will not allow" his people to be tempted beyond their strength. There is an indictment in Rev. 2:20 against the church at Thyatira for "tolerating" an ungodly prophetess (i.e., allowing her to minister) within the congregation.

General references to a refusal to allow or permit include Matt. 24:43; Acts 19:30; 28:4. Christ refuses to allow demons to speak in Luke 4:41. In Acts 16:7, the Spirit of Christ refuses to allow Paul and his companions to journey into Bithynia.

proseaō [προσεάω, *4330*]

proseaō is a rare verb found only in Acts 27:7 with reference to the wind "not allowing" a boat to proceed from its anchorage.

See Also: → APPROVE → CONSENT

ALMIGHTY

OT Words

ṣebā'ôt [צְבָאוֹת, **6635**]

This word is the plural form of the noun *ṣābā'*, which is rendered "army," "host," "war(fare)." It is a very common term that occurs around 450 times. Roughly half of these instances have a literal, military connotation referring primarily to the armies of Israel, as well as to those of other nations. The remaining occurrences (approximately 270) are linked to the divine title "Lord of Hosts," or "Lord Almighty." This designation is found from the books of Samuel onward in the canon, and it is most prevalent in the Prophets. Though the usage of this term is widespread, there are several features that may be distinguished. Underlying the meaning of this title is the concept of Yahweh as the omnipotent divine warrior, who guards and guides the fortunes of his people by granting them victory over their enemies (cf. 2 Sam. 5:10; 7:8ff., 26), handing them over to their enemies for punishment (cf. Isa. 9:19; 10:23; Jer. 6:6), effecting their return from captivity (cf. Jer. 31:23), or promising them ultimate salvation and deliverance (cf. Isa. 24:21).

It also needs to be pointed out that while the title "Lord of hosts" is not found prior to 1 Samuel, the concept of Yahweh as the divine warrior watching over his people is still to be found in the earlier material. Several texts refer to the hosts or armies of Yahweh as his agents of redemption (e.g., Exod. 7:4 and 12:41 in relation to the Exodus, and Josh. 5:14, 15 in reference to the occupation of the land of Canaan).

shadday [שַׁדַּי, **7706**]

This term is used exclusively as a divine name. It is commonly, though not exclusively, linked with the word ***'ēl*** (→ GOD) to yield the meaning "God Almighty." Altogether it occurs forty-eight times in all, thirty-one in the book of Job and seventeen elsewhere. ***El-shadday*** (→ GOD) is the name by which God revealed himself to the patriarchs Abraham, Isaac, and Jacob (cf. Exod. 6:3). The name gives general expression to the omnipotence of God. In several contexts, however, there is reference to a significant aspect of God's sovereign power. For example, Ps. 68:14 refers to the Almighty scattering kings in the land of Canaan so as to facilitate the conquest by his people. Then, in Isa. 13:6, the wrath and judgment of the Almighty comes on Israel, punishing her and thereby invoking the curse of the covenant for her rebellion against him.

NT Words

pantokratōr [παντοκράτωρ, *3841*]

The noun ***pantokratōr*** denotes the divine title "Lord (God) Almighty" throughout the ten occurrences of the term (cf. 2 Cor. 6:18; Rev. 1:8; 4:8; 11:17; 15:3; 16:7, 14; 19:6, 15; 21:22).

ALMS → MERCY → RIGHTEOUS

ALONE

OT Words

lebad [לְבַד, **905**]

This term is formed from a root (*bad*) that has both a broad abstract meaning ("separation") and a concrete sense ("part" or "portion"). The former sense concerns us here, for the specific meanings "alone," "only," and "besides" are obtained when the prefix *le* is attached to the word and the particle *min* is linked with it. Several contexts may be noted as follows.

Some texts indicate this sense of separation where ***lebad*** may be translated "only," "alone," or "by itself," "oneself." Exod. 26:9 refers to the arrangement of the tabernacle curtain in sets by themselves. Judg. 7:5 describes the procedure whereby Gideon set apart those who lapped the water from those who knelt down to drink. Zech. 12:12–14 describes the mourning process of the clans of Israel, each by itself. Gen. 2:18 expresses the divine rationale for human marriage — "it is not good for man to be alone . . . ." Deut. 8:3 contains another divine maxim — "man shall not live by bread alone." See also Gen. 43:32; Exod. 18:14; Num. 11:14; 1 Kgs. 19:10; Eccl. 7:29. This word also attests the uniqueness of God (e.g., Isa. 44:24; 63:3; Ps. 71:16).

When ***lebad*** combines with the particle *min* it carries a prepositional force with the meaning "besides" or "apart from" (e.g., Gen. 26:1; Exod. 12:37; Judg. 8:26; Josh. 22:29). Deut. 4:35 likewise affirms God's uniqueness (". . . besides him there is no other"), as does Isa. 45:2 (". . . there is no God apart from me").

NT Words

monos [μόνος, *3441*]

monos is an adjectival form occurring about fifty times with the meaning "alone," as well as the adverbial sense of "alone," "only." There is, however, some degree of overlap between these two meanings.

The meaning "alone" in an adverbial sense is indicated in relation to people in Matt. 18:15; Mark 9:8; Luke 24:18; Gal. 6:4; 1 Thess. 3:1; Heb. 9:7. Jesus is described as being alone in Matt. 14:23; John 6:15; 8:9. Matt. 4:4; Luke 4:4 both contain the affirmation that human beings do not live by bread alone. See also Luke 24:12; John 12:24.

References with the general adverbial sense of "only" are found in Matt. 12:4; 17:8; Luke 6:4; 1 Cor. 9:6. The command to serve God "only" (or "alone") is noted in Matt. 4:10; Luke 4:8. Luke 5:21 affirms that "only" God (or God alone) can forgive sin. God's knowledge of the day of judgment is also unique (i.e., only he knows, cf. Matt. 24:36).

monos is also used with the adjectival sense of "only" or "sole" with reference to the person of God as divine (cf. John 5:44; 17:3; Rom. 16:27; 1 Tim. 1:17; 6:15ff.; Jude 4, 25; Rev. 15:4). See also Col. 4:11.

monon [μόνον, *3440*]

monon is a variant adverbial form of ***monos***, above, found in nearly seventy contexts, with the consistent sense of "only."

Usage of this term in relation to people is evident in Matt. 5:47; Luke 8:50; John 11:52; Acts 8:16 and also concerning Jews in particular (cf. Rom. 3:29; 9:24).

More frequently, ***monon*** is used in the context of non-personal phenomena, including the expression "not only . . . but also." The sense of "only" is found in particular association with commands or instruction in Matt. 8:8; circumcision in Rom. 4:12; Gal. 6:12; the mercy of God in 1 Thess. 1:5; the gospel in 1 Thess. 2:8; the baptism of John in Acts 18:25. Jas. 2:24 makes the significant declaration that people are justified by works with faith, indicating in context that faith without the evidence of accompanying good works is invalid.

Other general references to ***monon*** include Matt. 21:19; Acts 27:10; Rom. 8:23; 1 Cor. 15:19; 2 Tim. 2:20; Heb. 12:26; 1 John 2:2.

See Also: → REST

ALTAR

OT Words

mizbēaḥ **[מִזְבֵּחַ, 4196]**

This term denotes a place of slaughter or sacrifice for ritual purposes. It is universally translated "altar" in the Old Testament and occurs about 360 times. About half of these instances are found in the Pentateuch, with the remainder spread throughout the Former Prophets and Writings (approximately 130 times) and the Prophets (approximately fifty times).

In the period prior to the establishment of the tabernacle, there are several references to the patriarchs building altars for the express purpose of worshiping Yahweh or as a memorial to his deeds on their behalf: Noah (Gen. 8:20); Abraham (Gen. 12:7, 8; 13:18; 22:9); Isaac (Gen. 26:25); Jacob (Gen. 33:20; 35:7)

Once the Mosaic legislation is in the process of transmission, the focus of the pentateuchal material is squarely on the sacred furniture of the tabernacle. The large bronze altar in the forecourt, as well as the smaller altar of incense in the Holy Place, carry special significance for Israelite worship. Every ceremonial requirement and ritual involving these altars is spelled out in meticulous detail in Exodus, Leviticus, and Numbers, where the bulk of the occurrences of

mizbēaḥ are found. This term occurs only ten times in the book of Deuteronomy.

The first references to pagan altars are found in Exod. 34:13, Deut. 7:5, and 12:3. These Canaanite altars must be destroyed under the terms of the divine covenant. Such altars are idolatrous, and the remainder of the Old Testament continues to refer to them (approximately fifty times) alongside the legitimate centers of worship in the tabernacle and temple. The theological significance here is that the presence of these altars exposes the primary flaw in Israel's relationship with her God — namely her persistent failure to acknowledge and worship Yahweh alone as the one true and living God. Testimony to this phenomenon is abundant. An altar to Baal, for example, is mentioned in Judg. 6:24ff. in connection with the idolatrous worship of Gideon's hometown. Then, Jeroboam's construction of an illegitimate altar at Bethel is mentioned in 1 Kgs. 13:1–5. Similarly, pagan altars are mentioned in relation to particular, godless kings of Israel and Judah such as Manasseh (2 Kgs. 21:3ff.) and Ahaz (2 Chr. 28:24). Periodically, rulers initiated reforms in an attempt to rid the land of these idolatrous centers of worship — including Joash (2 Chr. 23:17); Hezekiah (2 Chr. 30:14; 31:1); Josiah (2 Chr. 34:4–7). But all such attempts at reformation ultimately floundered. The prophets also mention Israel's constant failure in this area, and they bring severe indictments against the nation for these practices (e.g., Jer. 11:13; 17:1; Ezek. 6:4ff.; Hosea 8:11; 10:1, 2, 8; Amos 2:8; 3:14).

Besides the emphasis on Israel's idolatry, there is clear confirmation in the Old Testament of the central importance of rightly ordered worship around the altars of the tabernacle and the temple. The evidence from the Pentateuch has already been mentioned. The books of the Chronicler are also suggestive in this regard. Here the postexilic community is again reminded of the centrality of the altar in the temple (thirty references) as the focus of divine attention in dealing with the sin of God's people under the Mosaic covenant. The people's neglect of that worship principle had led to their exile and to the destruction of their land many years before. The prophet Ezekiel frequently alludes to the importance of exclusive worship and reverence for Yahweh in the vision of a renewed temple in Ezekiel 40–48. These chapters disclose the details of this new center of worship, and the altar occupies a central place in its function (cf. Ezek. 40:46, 47; 41:22; 43:13ff.; 45:19; 47:1).

Two clear conclusions emerge. First, throughout the entire Old Testament, devotion to Yahweh through obedience to his laws and right attitudes result in abundant blessing from him. Secondly, and conversely, neglect of those laws results in harsh punishment from the hand of God. The altar is one element in the worship of Israel that carries a great deal of significance for the people of God. Due respect for Yahweh is bound up with due respect for the altar as a focal point of old covenant worship.

NT Words

thysiastērion [θυσιαστήριον, *2379*]

thysiastērion is a dynamic equivalent for the Hebrew term ***mizbēaḥ*** (see above), and it also usually denotes the sacrificial altar of the temple. The term occurs around twenty times (cf. Matt. 5:23ff.; 23:18ff.; Luke 11:51; 1 Cor. 9:13; Heb. 7:13). In Rev. 6:9; 8:5; 11:1; 14:18; 16:7, ***thysiastērion*** denotes the visionary altar in the heavenly temple as seen by the apostle John.

Elsewhere, the term refers to the golden altar of incense that stood in front of the veil enclosing the Holy of Holies (cf. Luke 1:11; Rev. 8:3; 9:13). Heb. 13:10 makes mention of the "heavenly altar" at which the people of God now "serve" in anticipation of the coming consummation of the Lord in his glory. Jas. 2:21 refers to the primitive altar Abraham built when he prepared to offer up his son Isaac to Yahweh.

bōmos [βωμός, *1041*]

bōmos is a rare noun found only in Acts 17:23 with reference to an elevated high place, a pagan altar.

Additional Notes

There are fewer references to "altars" in the New Testament than in the Old. One distinctive difference in usage may be noted, however, even though there is only one text involved: ***bōmos*** is distinguished from ***thysiastērion*** in that the former term (found in Acts 17:23 alone, see above) is the only New Testament reference to a pagan altar. ***thysiastērion*** refers to both the divinely ordained altar of burnt offering and the altar of incense.

There is, however, another perspective on ***thysiastērion*** that is significant for a full understanding of the term in the New Testament. On eight occasions, this term refers to the heavenly altar, of which the altar(s) in the earthly temple are but a foreshadowing (cf. Heb. 9:1–14). All but one of these references come from the book of Revelation (i.e., Heb. 13:10; Rev. 6:9; 8:3 (twice), 5; 9:13; 14:18; 16:7). In the Revelation texts, it seems clear from the context of these visions that the golden altar of incense is intended because of its close association with the majestic presence and voice of God, which in turn indicates an intimate connection with the Holy of Holies. The Hebrews text is more problematic, yet the book of Hebrews makes it very clear that access to the very presence of God is only made possible through the finished work of Christ. Thus, the reference to this (presumably) heavenly altar in Heb. 13:10 symbolizes the unique privilege of new covenant believers that was not available to believers under the old covenant. Whether or not the symbolism indicates the altar of burnt offering or incense is not clear. Yet the reality of an unhindered audience with God remains, arguably, the clear focus of the text.

AMAZE, AMAZEMENT

OT Words

ḥarādāh [חֲרָדָה, 2731]; *ḥārēd* [חָרֵד, 2730]

ḥarādāh occurs nine times with the predominant meaning "trembling" or "fear." At least three of these occurrences may be linked with the reaction of amazement in the face of divine intervention, which evokes a response of awesome terror in the observer. This is seen first in 1 Sam. 14:15, where God afflicts the Philistine army with panic and then paves the way for their defeat at the hands of the Israelite army under Saul. Secondly, Ezek. 26:16 depicts the reaction of awe and fear in the rulers of the neighboring nations in the vicinity of Tyre, whose dramatic fall they had just witnessed. The context suggests that they were aware of the hand of God in this destruction. Dan. 10:7 records the terror of those who stood by Daniel on the bank of the Tigris River when God gave him a vision of the angel of the Lord. Although Daniel's companions saw nothing, they sensed the divine presence and were struck with terror.

The verbal form ***ḥārēd*** occurs in eight places and simply reinforces the general sense of the noun.

pāḥad [פָּחַד, 6342]; *paḥad* [פַּחַד, 6343]

This verb and noun, respectively, mean "fear" or "dread." They occur a total of approximately seventy times. There are, however, several instances where the expression "fear of the Lord" occurs — contexts which may suggest the accompanying response of amazement on the part of those experiencing the awareness of God's presence. Mic. 7:17, for example, predicts that the fear of the Lord will fall upon the nations who will repent and respond to God's offer of salvation. 2 Chr. 14:14 records the fear of the Lord falling on the army of the Cushites, leading to their destruction at the hands of Asa's army (cf. also 2 Chr. 17:10). Job 13:11 carries a similar connotation, along with Pss. 14:5; 53:5, 6; Isa. 2:10, 19, 21. The psalmist reflects positively on his reverential awe in response to God's presence as well as in response to his laws.

shāmēm [שָׁמֵם, 8074]

This term occurs ninety times and means "made desolate," or "destroy," "be appalled or overwhelmed" (i.e., with dismay or terror). (→ DESOLATE)

On the twenty or so occasions when ***shāmēm*** means "appalled" or "overwhelmed," there is the strong probability that astonishment or amazement is linked with these reactions. In the main, these references describe the dismay and astonishment surrounding the catastrophe of divine judgment against both Israel and the nations. In most cases the term is translated "appalled" (e.g., the dismay of Israel's own reaction to God's anger towards them, cf. Jer. 4:9; Ezek. 4:17; Ezra 9:3; 4:1). Ezekiel and Daniel's response to divine revelation concerning Israel's fate is significant in this regard (cf. Ezek. 3:15; Dan. 8:27). The nations are depicted as being horrified and amazed not only at Israel's punishment (cf. Lev. 26:32; Jer. 2:12; 18:16; 19:8; 1 Kgs. 9:8), but also at the fate of countries such as Edom (cf. Jer. 49:17), Babylon (cf. Jer. 50:13), and Tyre (cf. Ezek. 26:16; 27:35; 28:19). The word also refers to God's dismay at Israel's sin (cf. Isa. 59:16) and Israel's horror at the fate of the Suffering Servant (cf. Isa. 52:14).

tāmah [תָּמַהּ, 8539]; *timmāhôn* [תִּמָּהוֹן, 8541]

Unlike the terms discussed above, ***tāmah*** and its derivative noun mean "astound," "astonishment." Though these are not common words (***tāmah*** occurs nine times, ***timmāhôn*** twice), the contexts in which they are found are similar to those of ***ḥarādāh*** and ***shāmēm*** (see above). In Isa. 29:9; Hab. 1:5; Jer. 4:9 the people of Jerusalem and Judah are astounded (***tāmah***) at the nature and magnitude of God's judgment against them The emphasis is on their amazement rather than on their fear, though they must have felt fear as well. Similarly, the kings of the earth are astounded at God's power as they confront their imminent destruction by him (cf. Ps. 48:5). Then Isa. 13:8 records the astonishment of the nations as they witness the demise of Babylon at the hand of God.

timmāhôn, the derivative noun from ***tāmah***, only occurs twice in the Old Testament, but on each occasion it refers to the reaction of people in the face of divine wrath and judgment. Deut. 28:28 predicts the invasion of Israel by foreign armies as a result of Israel's disobedience. This is followed by a promise of inevitable panic, to be sent by God as part of the judgment. Then in Zech. 12:4 it is the hostile nations who are at war with Judah and Jerusalem, who will be stricken with panic and bewilderment and will finally be overthrown by God through Judah.

NT Words

ekstasis [ἔκστασις, *1611*]

The noun ***ekstasis*** is found in seven different places. In four of these it denotes the "astonishment," "amazement" of people in response to miraculous signs from God (cf. Mark 5:42; 16:8; Luke 5:26; Acts 3:10).

thambos [θάμβος, *2285*]

thambos is synonymous with ***ekstasis***, above, also denoting "wonder," "amazement" as a response to miraculous signs. It is found only three times (cf. Luke 4:36; 5:9; Acts 3:10).

thambeō [θαμβέω, *2284*]

The verb ***thambeō*** occurs four times, meaning "to be amazed, astonished" in reaction to the teaching ability of Jesus Christ (cf. Mark 1:27; 10:24, 32; also Acts 9:6).

ekthambeō [ἐκθαμβέω, *1568*]

ekthambeō is a variant of ***thambeō***, above, found in four places, again with the sense of "be amazed." In two of these instances, however, the astonishment may be linked to fear and alarm. (See also Mark 9:15; 14:33.)

ekthambos [ἔκθαμβος, *1569*]

ekthambos is a rare adjectival form found only in Acts 3:11 referring to people's "astonishment" or "wonder" at the healing of the crippled man by Peter and John at the gate of the temple.

ekplēssō [ἐκπλήσσω, *1605*]

The verb ***ekplēssō*** means "to be astonished, amazed" in fourteen contexts, mostly in reaction to the authority of Jesus' teaching (cf. Matt. 7:28; 13:54; 19:25; 22:33; Mark 1:22; 6:2; 10:26; 11:28; Luke 2:48; 4:32; 9:43). The people react similarly when Jesus heals a deaf mute (cf. Mark 7:37). See also Acts 13:12.

existēmi [ἐξίστημι, *1839*]

existēmi is a verb largely synonymous with the entries above, found seventeen times in all, with the primary sense of "be amazed, astonished" in over half these contexts.

The word describes amazement at the miracles and authority of Jesus in Matt. 12:23; Mark 2:12; 5:42; 6:51; Luke 2:47; 8:56. Other such expressions of astonishment at the power of God are found in Acts 2:7, 12; 8:13; 10:45; 12:16. See also Luke 24:22; Acts 8:11ff.; 9:21.

AMBASSADOR

OT Words

ṣîr [**צִיר, 6735**]

ṣîr is a noun found twelve times, denoting an "ambassador" or "messenger" in about half of these (cf. Prov. 13:17; 25:13; Isa. 18:2; 57:9; Jer. 49:14; Obad. 1).

lûṣ [**לוּץ, 3887**]

The noun ***lûṣ*** is found in nearly thirty places and has the primary sense of "one who scorns or mocks." In 2 Chr. 32:31, however, the term denotes "ambassadors" sent from Babylon to Jerusalem.

NT Words

presbeuō [πρεσβεύω, *4243*]

presbeuō is a rare verb meaning "to act as an ambassador." It is found only twice, in 2 Cor. 5:20; Eph. 6:20, both referring to Paul as a representative of the gospel of Christ.

presbeia [πρεσβεία, *4242*]

presbeia is a rare noun derived from ***presbeuō***, above. It is found only twice and means "message" in the sense of a "delegation" in Luke 14:32; 19:14.

See Also: → ANGEL → ELDER

AMEN

OT Words

'āmēn [**אָמֵן, 543**]

'āmēn is an adverbial form transliterated "amen" with the underlying sense of "so be it." It is an affirmation of truth or of the purposes of God, with which one either wholeheartedly agrees or which one accepts stoically as God's will — even though the outcome may be painful. It is commonly uttered as a response of grateful praise to God.

As an expression of praise to God, ***'āmēn*** is recorded in 1 Chr. 16:36; Neh. 5:13; 8:6; Pss. 41:13; 72:19; 89:52; 106:48. The term is a response of resignation to the will of God in Num. 5:22. As an affirmation of truth, ***'āmēn*** occurs throughout the rehearsing of the divine sanctions of the law covenant in Deut. 27:15ff., where the people of Israel recognize by their affirmation the rationale for this brand of divine justice. See also Jer. 11:5; 28:6; as well as 1 Kgs. 1:36 where the "amen" signifies a rejoicing in the purposes of God.

NT WORDS

amēn [ἀμήν, *281*]

The New Testament dynamic equivalent to the Hebrew, ***amēn***, likewise indicates the solemn affirmation of the divine will and purpose in about one-third of the nearly 150 occurrences of the term. The remaining uses of the term yield the adverbial meaning "truly."

The sense of "truly" indicates an affirmation of genuineness or sincerity and is found throughout the gospel narratives (e.g., Matt. 5:18; 18:13; Mark 8:12; Luke 13:35; John 3:3ff.; 5:19ff.; 8:51).

The "amen" also expresses worship and praise of God's person and majesty (cf. Rom. 1:25; 9:5; 11:36; Eph. 3:21; 1 Tim. 1:17; 6:16ff.; Rev. 1:6ff.; 5:14; 7:12; 19:4; 22:20ff.). It also concludes a blessing or benediction (e.g., Rom. 15:33; 16:20ff.; 1 Cor. 16:24; 2 Cor. 3:14; Gal. 6:18; Eph. 6:24; Phil. 4:20ff.; Col. 4:18; 1 Thess. 5:28; Heb. 13:21; 1 Pet. 5:11ff.; Jude 25).

"Amen" is also a metaphorical name for Christ in Rev. 3:14.

AMETHYST

OT WORDS

'aḥlāmāh [אַחְלָמָה, **306**]

In Exod. 28:19 and 39:12, ***'aḥlāmāh*** designates the amethyst in the third row of the precious stones set on the breastpiece attached to the ephod of the high priest's garments. There were twelve stones in all, one for each of the tribes of Israel.

NT WORDS

amethystos [ἀμέθυστος, *271*]

amethystos is a rare noun found only in Rev. 21:20 denoting an "amethyst," a rare gemstone and one of the twelve foundation stones of the wall surrounding the heavenly Jerusalem.

ANATHEMA → CURSE

ANCHOR

NT WORDS

ankyra [ἄγκυρα, *45*]

The noun ***ankyra*** is found in four places, denoting a ship's "anchor" in Acts 27:29ff. It is used metaphorically in Heb. 6:19 for the certainty of God's promises in salvation, an anchor for the soul.

ANGEL

OT WORDS

mal'āk [מַלְאָךְ, **4397**]

The principal word for "angel" in the Old Testament is ***mal'āk***, although the word itself primarily means "messenger." This term refers to both the human and the divine, as outlined below.

In the first instance, ***mal'āk*** refers to messengers in the natural, human sense (approximately forty times). These can be ordinary people sent to convey a message of one sort or another (cf. Gen. 32:3; Josh. 6:17; Judg. 11:12; 1 Sam. 16:19; 2 Sam. 2:5; 1 Kgs. 19:2; 2 Kgs. 14:8). The term can also indicate a prophet as messenger (cf. Isa. 42:19; 44:26) as well as a priest (cf. Mal. 2:7). And although he is hardly an ordinary human being, ***mal'āk*** also refers to the messianic prophet of the new covenant (cf. Mal. 3:1).

Secondly, the term refers to heavenly messengers, or angels. ***mal'āk*** occurs about one hundred times with this general meaning. Included here is the phenomenon known as the "interpreting angel," who appears, literally, as "the angel (who speaks with Zechariah)" throughout the first six chapters of that book. This angelic figure is cast in the role of mediator and interpreter of the visions given to the prophet by God (cf. also Dan. 8 and 9, where the archangel Gabriel brings a revelation to Daniel, though the term ***mal'āk*** is not used).

In addition to the above, there is the theologically significant "angel of the Lord." This is a theophanic manifestation — a divine being who embodies the person and authority of God himself. There are about seventy references to the "angel of the Lord" or the "angel of God" (e.g., Gen. 22:11, 15 [to Abraham]; Josh. 5:13ff. [to Joshua]; Judg. 6 [to Gideon]; Judg. 13 [to Samson's parents]; Zech. 3 [to Zechariah in a vision]). Every occurrence of the phrase "angel of the Lord (or God)" carries with it an important connotation, since his appearance consistently initiates or advances a stage in God's plan of salvation, whether in blessing or judgment.

NT WORDS

angelos [ἄγγελος, *32*]

angelos is a common New Testament term occurring nearly 190 times with the predominant sense of "angel" (i.e., divine messenger).

Angels are mediators of divine revelation in relation to the birth of Christ in Matt. 1:20ff.; 2:13ff.; Luke 1:28ff.; 2:9ff.; to the birth of John the Baptist in Luke 1:11ff. They also function this way in John's vision of the heavenly realms (cf. Rev. 1:1; 22:6; and in particular as divine messengers to the seven churches in Asia Minor, cf. Rev. 1:20; 2:1, 8, 12, 18; 3:1, 5, 7, 14).

General references to angels include those in Matt. 4:6; 18:10; 22:30; Luke 4:10; Rom. 8:38; 1 Cor. 6:3; Heb. 1:4ff.; 13:2. Angels are depicted as instruments of divine judgment and redemption in a number of places (cf. Matt. 13:39ff.; 28:2ff.; Mark 13:25; Luke 16:22; John 1:51; Acts 5:19; 12:7ff.; Rev. 7:1ff.; 8:2ff.; 9:1ff.; 12:7ff.; 14:6ff.; 15:1ff.; 16:1ff.; 17:1ff.; 20:1). Angelic beings form part of the entourage of Christ at his final appearing (cf. Matt. 16:27; Mark 8:38; Luke 9:26).

angelos is also translated "messenger" in certain contexts: Human messengers are indicated in Luke 7:24; Jas. 2:25. Prophetic "messengers" who foreshadow the coming of the Messiah are found in Matt. 11:10; Mark 1:2; Luke 7:27 (all quotations from Mal. 3:1). "Messengers of Satan" are mentioned in 2 Cor. 12:7. "Fallen angels" are indicated in Jude 6; Rev. 12:7.

Additional Notes

angelos in the New Testament and ***mal'āk*** in the Old both refer to human and divine messengers. The only significant difference is that there is no reference to the angel of the Lord in the New Testament — because the person of Jesus Christ in the new covenant embodies, or fulfills, the angel of the Lord figure who acts as a precursor of the Messiah in the old covenant.

ANGER, ANGRY

OT Words

'aph [אַף, 639]

This noun occurs approximately 270 times and usually means "anger" or "wrath" (both human and divine). The verb from which ***'aph*** is derived (*'ānaph*) means "to breathe or snort with anger." The root meaning of ***'aph*** is thus "nose," "nostril," or "face," and the word conveys that meaning in about fifty places. In eight of these instances, the meaning "nose," etc. is specifically linked to the notion of divine anger (cf. Exod. 15:8; 2 Sam. 22:9, 16; Job 4:9; Ps. 18:8, 15; Isa. 65:5; Ezek. 38:18). The word indicates human anger about forty times. Most frequently, however, ***'aph*** indicates the anger of God (approximately 170 times). Divine anger is directed sometimes at pagan rulers and people for their disdain of God (e.g., Pharaoh and Egypt, Exod. 15:8; Balaam, Num. 22:22; the nations, Isa. 63:3; Babylon, Jer. 51:45). It usually focuses, however, on the people of Israel for their consistent violation of obligations to God under the terms of his covenant with them (e.g., Isa. 5:25; 10:25; Jer. 4:8; 15:14; 23:20; Lam. 1:12; Ezek. 20:8, 21; Hos. 8:5). It is also significant to note that the anger of God against the remnant of his people is never ultimate, because he is determined to save them in spite of their sin (e.g., Mic. 7:18).

ḥēmāh [חֵמָה, 2534]

This noun is synonymous with ***'aph*** (see above); it is derived, however, from the verb ***yāḥam*** (→ CONCEIVE), whose root meaning is "to be hot." Thus the primary meaning for ***ḥēmāh*** is "anger" or "fury" — even though the literal meaning of "heat" (or more accurately, "fever") is found only in Hosea 7:5. It can also mean "venom" or "poison." (→ VENOM) The literal meaning of ***ḥēmāh*** gives way, therefore, to the dominant metaphorical one of "anger," and the word occurs with this meaning about 120 times.

Like ***'aph***, above, ***ḥēmāh*** also refers to both human and divine anger. And, like ***'aph***, it refers to the latter more than the former. ***ḥēmāh*** indicates human anger approximately twenty times — including, for example, reference to the fury of King Xerxes and Haman in the book of Esther (cf. 1:12; 2:1; 3:5; 5:9; 7:7, 10). The book of Proverbs also cites human anger as a negative attribute to be avoided (cf. Prov. 6:34; 15:1, 18; 16:14, 19, etc.).

In referring to the wrath of God, this term also distinguishes between divine anger towards the heathen (e.g., Isa. 59:20; 63:6; Jer. 10:25; 25:15, 16; Nah. 1:2) and God's fury at his own rebellious people (e.g., Lam. 2:14; 4:11; Ezek. 9:8; 20:8, 13). And, again, there is the inference that God's anger with his people will not be absolute (cf. Ezek. 24:13; Isa. 51:22).

qāṣaph [קָצַף, 7107]; *qeṣeph* [קֶצֶף, 7110]

Once again these terms refer to both human and divine anger. ***qāṣaph*** indicates the former on ten occasions, and the latter twenty-two times. ***qāṣaph*** does not, however, refer to God's anger against the heathen, but only to God's anger against Israel for her rebellion. These contexts also suggest that God will not be angry with his people forever (cf. Isa. 54:9; 57:16).

The usage of ***qeṣeph*** (the noun derived from ***qāṣaph***) is identical with that of the words discussed above. It applies most frequently to the anger of God (twenty-seven times) rather than to human anger (twice only). In addition, ***qeṣeph*** refers both to God's anger against the nations (cf. Isa. 34:2; Jer. 10:10; 50:13) and against his disobedient people (e.g., 2 Kgs. 3:27; 2 Chr. 24:18; Zech. 7:12). The transitory nature of God's anger giving way to mercy and compassion is again noted (cf. Isa. 54:8; 60:10; Jer. 32:37).

ḥārāh [חָרָה, 2734]; ḥārôn [חָרוֹן, 2740]

The usage and meaning of ***ḥārāh*** is essentially the same as all the terms above. The only minor difference is that ***ḥārāh*** indicates the process of "burning" with anger. Again the distinction is drawn between human and divine anger; but in this case the distribution is fairly even: the anger of human beings is referred to about forty times; the anger of God some thirty times. Divine anger against the nations is registered three times (cf. 2 Sam. 22:8; Ps. 18:7; Hab. 3:8), and the rest of the occurrences note God's displeasure with his own people, either individually or corporately.

The derived noun ***ḥārôn*** refers exclusively to the wrath of God (forty occurrences). In eight instances divine anger is directed against the nations (cf. Exod. 15:7; 1 Sam. 28:18; Pss. 2:5; 69:24; Isa. 13:9, 13; Jer. 49:37; 51:45). The remaining references apply to Israel as the object of God's fury, two of which should be noted particularly. The first of these is Jer. 30:24, where God promises a renewed bond between God and Israel after his anger has been vented upon them. Hos. 11:9 also describes God's determination to redeem Israel, in spite of her sin, and notwithstanding the fierceness of his rage. God will not allow this anger to interfere with his ultimate program of redemption for his people. Both these texts (and see also Ps. 85:3) reinforce the general impression gleaned throughout our discussion here that God's anger against his chosen people — the faithful remnant — is never, in spite of its severity, absolute.

ka'as [כָּעַס, 3707]; ka'as [כַּעַס, 3708]

The verb ***kā'as*** occurs about fifty times and means "provoking to anger." It frequently refers to Israel provoking Yahweh through her constant idolatry. It occurs forty-four times with this meaning (e.g., Deut. 4:25; 1 Kgs. 14:9; 2 Kgs. 17:11; Jer. 7:18; Ezek. 8:17). See also some more implicit references to this phenomenon (e.g., 1 Kgs. 15:30; 16:2; 2 Kgs. 23:26). In these cases it is the evil of wicked kings that acts as the catalyst for divine rage. The context makes it clear, however, that idolatry is the key element in God's disaffection with these leaders and with the people in general.

The derivative noun ***ka'as*** (occurring twenty-one times) is similar, although its more general overall meaning is "provocation," "vexation," or "grief." There are, however, several instances where it also refers to provoking God to anger by the idolatrous worship of the Israelites (cf. Deut. 32:19; 1 Kgs. 15:30; 2 Kgs. 23:26; Ezek. 20:28). In addition, Ps. 85:4 records the psalmist's prayer for God's wrath toward his people to cease, on the basis of his mercy.

rāgaz [רָגַז, 7264]

This verb means to evoke mental turmoil or agitation of various kinds. Only in a few instances does it mean "anger." Job 12:6 refers to the provocation of God; Ps. 4:5 describes the anger of human beings; Ezek. 16:43 describes the provocation of God in the face of Israel's sin; and, finally, 2 Kgs. 19:27ff. and Isa. 37:28ff. refer to God's anger at Sennacherib, the Assyrian king.

regaz [רְגַז, 7266 (Aramaic)]

regaz is a rare Aramaic noun found only in Dan. 3:13 denoting the "rage" of King Nebuchadnezzar.

za'am [זַעַם, 2195]

The noun ***za'am*** is found in about twenty places, meaning "anger," "indignation," and having primary reference to the wrath of God poured out on people as a judgment for sin (cf. Pss. 38:3; 78:49; Isa. 10:5; 30:27; Jer. 10:10; Ezek. 21:31; Dan. 8:19; Nah. 1:6; Hab. 3:12; Zeph. 3:8). Human "anger" is described in Jer. 15:17; Hos. 7:16.

NT Words

orgē [ὀργή, *3709*]

The noun ***orgē*** occurs around forty times in a variety of contexts, meaning "anger," "wrath" throughout.

Divine "wrath" to be poured out on wicked humankind at the end of the age is indicated in Matt. 3:7; Luke 3:7; 21:23; Rom. 9:22; Eph. 5:6; Col. 3:6; 1 Thess. 2:15; Rev. 11:18; 14:10; 16:19; 19:15. The death of Christ removes such wrath, as noted in Rom. 5:9; 1 Thess. 1:10; 5:9. In particular, the "wrath" of the Lamb (i.e., the heavenly Christ) is described in Rev. 6:16ff.

Jesus' anger at his skeptical audience's hardness of heart is noted in Mark 3:5. Human anger is referred to in Eph. 4:31; Col. 3:8; 1 Tim. 2:8; Jas. 1:19ff.

orgizō [ὀργίζω, *3710*]

The verb ***orgizō*** is found eight times with the meaning "to be angry" throughout. Human anger is in view for most of the contexts (cf. Matt. 5:22; 18:34; 22:7; Luke 14:21; 15:28; Rev. 11:18). In Eph. 4:26 there is an exhortation "to be angry" without sinning. Rev. 12:17 mentions the dragon's wrath at the symbolic woman, the mother of the universal child-king (i.e., the Messiah).

parorgizō [παροργίζω, *3949*]

parorgizō is a rare verb found only twice with the meaning "to anger," "provoke to anger." Rom. 10:19 describes God provoking his people to anger with another nation. Eph. 6:4 contains the injunction to fathers not to anger their children.

cholaō [χολάω, *5520*]

cholaō is a rare verb found only in John 7:23 with reference to the Pharisees "being angry" at Jesus for healing a man on the Sabbath.

orgilos [ὀργίλος, *3711*]

orgilos is a rare adjective found only in Titus 1:7 denoting the vice of being "prone to anger" or "quick-tempered."

thymos [θυμός, *2372*]

thymos is a noun occurring eighteen times with the meaning "wrath" or "anger" throughout.

The wrath of God aimed at the wicked is noted in Rom. 1:18; Rev. 15:1, 7; 16:1. Metaphorical references to the "cup, or wine of God's wrath" are found in Rev. 14:10; 16:19; 18:3; 19:15 (cf. "the winepress of God's wrath" in Rev. 14:19). The "anger" of the devil is indicated in Rev. 12:12.

Human anger is depicted as a vice to be shunned in 2 Cor. 12:20; Gal. 5:20; Eph. 4:31; Col. 3:8. See also Heb. 11:27.

Additional Notes

Given the number of synonyms for "anger" in the New Testament, it is impossible to precisely identify any one of them as a dynamic equivalent for any of the corresponding Old Testament terms. There is, however, a significant overlap between the two groups of words. For example, the major New Testament terms for "anger" also preserve the distinction between God's anger and human anger. With regard to the latter, see particularly the discussions of ***orgē*** and ***thymos***, as well as their related verbs.

As in the Old Testament, the New Testament addresses the matter of God's wrath with an emphasis on the anger of God towards both the nations and his own people for their rejection of him. Such anger, however, was qualified when the people of God were subject to its effect — since God never intended to allow his anger full sway. It was limited by his mercy and redemptive purpose. Further, when the nations are subject to divine wrath in the Old Testament, it is not expressed in terms of a consummate fury.

The use of ***orgē*** and ***thymos*** is particularly significant in the New Testament, for these words express the divine anger in absolute terms. ***thymos*** is used in Rev. 14:10, 19; 15:1, 7; 16:1 to allude to the fact that all wicked people will be exposed to the wrath of God for eternity. ***orgē*** is also used this way (cf. Rev. 6:16, 17; 14:10; 16:19; 19:15). Note also Rev. 11:18, which refers to the great day of the wrath of God and the Lamb.

Such an eschatological expression of anger is found not only in Revelation, but also throughout the rest of the New Testament. Jesus' teaching on God's anger in future (as well as present) judgment is found in the gospels (e.g., Luke 21:23; Matt. 3:7; Luke 3:7). Paul also writes about it in Rom. 5:9; 2:8; 12:19; 9:22; Eph. 2:3; 5:6; Col. 3:6; 1 Thess. 5:9.

It is clear, then, that the anger of God against all who oppose him will be consummated on all who oppose him on the final day of judgment when Christ returns. The anger of Yahweh under the old covenant will pale into relative insignificance by comparison with the magnitude of his wrath poured out on all those who are found outside of a saving relationship with his Son.

See Also: ➞ WRATH

ANGUISH

OT Words

ṣar [צַר, 6862]

This noun describes "deep distress" or "anguish" as the result of traumatic circumstances, either at a personal or national level. There are approximately twenty-five occurrences of the term with this connotation. Other translations for ***ṣar*** include "affliction" and "distress." It can also mean "enemy" (approximately seventy times), although in one or two contexts there is some ambiguity as to whether it refers to the agony of suffering or a personal foe (e.g., Zech. 8:10).
(➞ AFFLICT)

When ***ṣar*** refers to inner turmoil, there are a number of significant features to note. First of all, ***ṣar*** is used to indicate anguish in situations that are undefined (e.g., Job 7:11; 15:24; Pss. 4:1, 2; 66:14; 119:143).

Secondly, anguish is precipitated in response to God's judgment against his people for disobedience (cf. Deut. 4:30; 2 Chr. 15:4; Ps. 107:6, 19; Isa. 5:30; Hos. 5:15). In Hosea, the prophet records that the people's affliction will cause them to turn back to God. Also, in Ezek. 30:16, anguish is prescribed as a divine judgment for the land of Upper Egypt, which is representative of Israel's traditional enemies.

In the third place, harassment from Israel's enemies leads to considerable distress for God's people (cf. Ps. 60:11; Isa. 25:4; 63:9). In Isa. 63, the context is an oracle where the kindness of Yahweh is under review. Here the anguish of God's people has been removed by the intervention of the "angel of his presence." This is an oblique reference to God himself, since this title may be identified with the person of the "angel of the Lord" who is everywhere attested in the Old Testament as a divine figure.

In the fourth instance, God is described as a haven, a place of refuge for those suffering the agony of difficult circumstances (cf. Pss. 32:7; 59:16; 102:2). God himself consistently responds in mercy to the affliction of his people by intervening directly on their behalf and alleviating their distress. This is evident in Ps. 106:44, which refers back to the compassionate divine response in Exod. 2:24 where God responds to the anguish of Israel in their Egyptian captivity by implementing his rescue plan.

The corresponding related verbs ***ṣārāh*** and ***ṣārar*** have much the same emphasis.

ṣûqāh [צוּקָה, 6695]

This word only occurs three times in the Old Testament. On each occasion the connotation is negative: Prov. 1:27 cites anguish as one of the painful consequences of rejecting wisdom; Isa. 8:22 likewise warns that great distress will come as a result of God's people rejecting him and his ways. Later on, the prophet again declares that great turmoil will be in store for Israel if she persists in maintaining her alliance with Egypt (Isa. 30:6).

ḥûl [חוּל, 2342 (Verb)]; *ḥîl* [חִיל, 2427 (Noun)]

These terms have the root meanings to "whirl," "dance," or "writhe." The latter meaning is the relevant one here since it not only indicates the inner turmoil of someone in distress, but also frequently refers to the anguished writhing of a woman in labor.

In the general sense of the term, ***ḥîl*** refers to the anguish of Israel as well as that of her enemies. In the first place, the distress of God's people consistently stems from divine judgment on their rebellion against their God (cf. Mic. 1:12; Jer. 4:19; 23:19; Joel 2:6). Secondly, the enemies of Israel also suffer anguish as part of God's judgment against them for their wickedness (cf. Deut. 2:25; Ezek. 30:16 [Egypt]; Isa. 23:5 [Tyre]; Jer. 51:29 [Babylon]; Zech. 9:5). The psalmist refers metaphorically to the writhing of the natural elements in anguish at the terror of God's judgment on the earth (cf. Ps. 97:4).

Through the metaphor of a woman (or women) in labor, ***ḥîl*** is sometimes used symbolically to indicate the anguish of Israel as part of her punishment from God (cf. Isa. 26:17; Mic. 4:10). It is also used to indicate the agony of a pagan nation for the same reason (e.g., Babylon, Isa. 13:8). Finally, the same image can express not punishment, but blessing, as in Isa. 66:8 where Israel is explicitly declared not to have suffered in childbirth. This reference is located within an oracle of hope and blessing in which the nation is promised a complete transformation by God.

The noun ***ḥîl*** occurs much less frequently in the Old Testament, yet its six occurrences preserve that balanced emphasis between the anguish experienced by Israel and by the nations. In Exod. 15:14, Philistia, for example, is threatened by God with inevitable anguish as a consequence of Israel's entry into Canaan. The remaining occurrences all utilize the metaphor of a woman's anguish in labor: Ps. 48:6 refers to the agony of the nations this way; and Jer. 50:43 singles out Babylon in a similar fashion. Jer. 6:24; 22:23; and Mic. 4:9 all speak of Israel's anguish as a sign of God's anger toward them.

NT Words

stenochōria [στενοχωρία, *4730*]

stenochōria is a noun found in four contexts denoting "anguish" or "distress" in each case. The "anguish" of the wicked is noted in Rom. 2:9. The "anguish" or "distress" borne of persecution is indicated in Rom. 8:35; 2 Cor. 6:4; 12:10.

synechō [συνέχω, *4912*]

synechō is a verb found in twelve places, communicating the underlying sense of being caught in difficult circumstances — both physical and emotional.

The term is translated "to be taken sick, or afflicted with sickness" in Matt. 4:24; Luke 4:38; Acts 28:8. The meaning "to be hard-pressed" in an emotional sense, indicating a state of anxiety or anguish, is evident in Luke 12:50; Phil. 1:23.

synochē [συνοχή, *4928*]

synochē is a rare noun found only twice, with the meaning "distress" or "anguish" in Luke 21:25; 2 Cor. 2:4.

odynaō [ὀδυνάω, *3600*]

The verb ***odynaō*** is found in four places with the consistent meaning "to suffer anguish," "be sorrowful" (cf. Luke 2:48; 16:24, 25; Acts 20:38).

Additional Notes

The New Testament words discussed above do not allude to women in labor. However, with the exception of ***odynaō***, all of the above Greek terms do still adopt a metaphorical sense in which "anguish" is an extension of the word's literal meaning. All references to such emotional and physical distress include both the godly and the wicked. (→ TRAVAIL)

Concerning the terms ***synechō*** and ***synochē***, Jesus himself was in anguish over his approaching death (cf. Luke 12:50). Phil. 1:23 records Paul's distress over conflicting desires, namely, whether to remain alive in service for Christ or to die and be with him in glory. Paul also records his own anguish over the lamentable spiritual condition of the Corinthian church (cf. 2 Cor. 2:4).

stenochōria is noteworthy in the sense that while it carries basically the same meaning as the other terms, Paul uses it distinctively in a number of contexts: In Rom. 8:35 he writes in triumphant hope that the love of God in Christ will ultimately preserve his people from all distress and anguish. Then, in the Corinthian correspondence, he first of all commends his own personal anguish as an illustration of the sufficiency of God's power in his life. Secondly, he boasts about his suffering and distress in 2 Cor. 12:10, because it demonstrates a paradoxical strength in weakness, through submission to God's will and purpose.

Both ***stenochōria*** and ***synochē*** also refer to the anguish of the wicked who come under judgment. The former term is found in Rom. 2:9, and the latter in Luke 21:25 with this connotation. ***odynaō*** also indicates the anguish of the wicked in the parable of the rich man and Lazarus, where the former is condemned to the fires of hell for his selfishness and lack of compassion for Lazarus the beggar.

These terms for anguish in both the Old and New Testaments illustrate the reality of such suffering for the godly and wicked alike. Yet their use also makes it clear that the anguish of God's people will not last forever — unlike the fate of the wicked. However, for those who truly love God, there will be genuine turmoil and distress over the presence of sin in their lives and in the life of the community of God's people. It will come either as a consequence of personal sin, or as the result of a concern for sin in the life of others (the latter of which even Jesus was not spared).

See Also: → AFFLICT

ANNOUNCE

NT WORDS

anangellō [ἀναγγέλλω, *312*]

anangellō is a verb occurring eighteen times with the underlying meaning "tell" in the sense of "announce," "make known," "report."

The action of "making known," "announcing (information)" is indicated in several places, with reference to spreading the news of Jesus' miraculous signs in Mark 5:14, 19; the deeds of God in Acts 14:27; 15:4; the "whole counsel of God" in Acts 20:27; and "reporting" to the authorities in Acts 16:38. See also Rom. 15:21.

The phenomenon of the "revealing," "announcing" of all things by the Messiah is indicated in John 4:25. In related contexts, spiritual truth is said to be "revealed" to the believer by the Holy Spirit (cf. John 16:13ff.; 1 Pet. 1:12). See also 1 John 1:5.

See Also: → REPORT → TELL

ANOINT, ANOINTING

OT WORDS

sûk [**סוּךְ, 5480**]

This word occurs nine times and generally means "anointing," but in a purely non-ritual way. It refers to the use of oil or perfume in a general context as well as for cosmetic and medicinal purposes. The mundane use of olive oil, for example, is mentioned in Deut. 28:40 and Mic. 6:15 in a context of divine judgment, where the substance is denied to Israel as a punishment for her wickedness. ***sûk*** is used in the sense of cosmetic application in Ruth 3:3; Dan. 10:3; 2 Sam. 12:20; 14:2; and to mean "ointment" in 2 Chr. 28:15 and Ezek. 16:9.

māshaḥ [**מָשַׁח, 4886**]

This is the verb the Old Testament employs universally to convey the theologically significant phenomenon of anointing (applied primarily to three classes of people — prophets, priests, and kings).

There is only one explicit mention of a prophet being anointed with oil, and that is Elisha, whose commissioning is recorded in 1 Kgs. 19:16. Another perspective on this issue is associated with the operation of the Spirit of God in the Old Testament. More frequently, the anointing ceremony is linked to the installation of the Israelite priests (including the high priest) and the monarchy. Anointing of priests in general is recorded in Exod. 28:41; 29:7; Lev. 7:36; Num. 3:3, with the ritual commissioning of the high priest receiving a like emphasis in Exod. 30:30; 40:13; Lev. 6:20; 8:12; 16:32; Num. 35:25. Associated with the installation of the priests is the ritual anointing of the tabernacle itself, as well as its contents. The altar is sanctified by this means (Exod. 29:36; 40:10; Lev. 8:11; Num. 7:10, 84, 88); as is the wash-basin (Exod. 40:11); some of the grain offerings (Exod. 29:2; Lev. 2:4, 7, 12; Num. 6:15); the tabernacle vessels (Num. 7:1); the holy of holies (Dan. 9:24), and the tabernacle itself (Num. 7:1). (→ SPIRIT)

References to the anointing of the kings of Israel and Judah are also quite common. There are about thirty-five altogether, ranging through the books of Samuel, Kings and Chronicles, commencing with the anointing of Saul in 1 Sam. 9:16 and 10:1. Included among these are two references to the anointing of kings in the Psalms, one of which is a messianic hymn (Ps. 45:7). Isa. 61:1 describes the messianic servant king who claims an anointing from God himself as the seal upon his earthly mission. In the Gospels, Jesus himself claims to be this figure as he cites this text from Isaiah in his first public sermon in Luke 4:18ff.

It is clear that the phenomenon of ritual anointing carried a very great significance for the people of Israel in the old covenant. It was by this procedure that God ratified the offices of prophet, priest, and king as his divinely ordained channels of revelation to his people in that age.

māshîaḥ [מָשִׁיחַ, 4899]

The term ***māshîaḥ***, which is translated "Messiah" or "anointed one," indicates a very important concept in the Old Testament — namely the idea that such a person has been specifically chosen by God for a special purpose. This is true in both a collective as well as an individual sense, although the individual concept of the Messiah tends to dominate in the Old Testament.

The collective idea of messianism is first of all illustrated in 1 Chr. 16:22, where a warning is issued to Gentile kings not to touch the "anointed ones" of Yahweh, not to harm his prophets. This is actually part of a quotation from Ps. 105:1–15, which celebrates Israel's conquest of Canaan and the victory over her enemies There is some ambiguity as to whether this text refers to the prophets as a group within Israel or to the population as a whole. Exod. 19:6 would seem to support the latter, since it identifies Israel as a "nation of priests." Whatever the precise meaning of 1 Chr. 16:22 may be, the point is that God clearly intends his people to play a central role in his plan of salvation. The fundamental idea in this context is that they have been anointed for the task. Pss. 28:8 and 84:9 may also refer to Israel collectively as the anointed of Yahweh, although the point cannot be made with certainty. Hab. 3:13 falls into the same category. The issue is raised when discussing the messianic figure of the servant in Isa. 40–66. Is he to be understood corporately or individually? Although it is not possible to provide a detailed answer to that question here, the weight of the biblical evidence would suggest that an individual identity is foundational. There are, however, also elements of a corporate identity that cannot be overlooked. (→ SERVANT)

Other uses of ***māshîaḥ*** relate primarily to the office of kingship. Of the thirty-six occurrences of the term, twenty-six of these refer to royal figures. These include Saul and David throughout 1 and 2 Samuel (sixteen times). Then there are eight references to kings as "anointed ones" in the Psalms, including the well-known messianic profile recorded in Ps. 2:2. Isa. 45:1 refers to Cyrus the Persian as Yahweh's "anointed," indicating that even a pagan ruler may have a messianic function in God's purposes. In this case, Cyrus was the king who issued the decree to release the people of Israel from captivity in 539 B.C. — which was part of God's plan of deliverance for his people. Dan. 9:25, 26 also refer to the figure of a royal messiah who will carry out God's ultimate plan of salvation for his people. Exegesis of this difficult passage is often disputed. It may be said, however, that an individual interpretation of the "anointed one" in Dan. 9 that points forward to Jesus Christ is not without strong exegetical warrant. (→ COVENANT)

māshîaḥ is also applied specifically to the office of the high priest in Lev. 4:3, 5, 16; 6:22; 1 Sam. 2:35. There is no specific reference to any prophet as ***māshîaḥ*** in the Old Testament.

The comments on the verb ***māshaḥ*** (see above) apply equally to the related noun ***māshîaḥ***. It is clear that the offices of prophet, priest, and king constitute an old covenant phenomenon of prime importance. It is these people, individually and collectively, who function as the vehicles of divine revelation and purpose. They are set apart for their task by the anointing of God himself. The New Testament also makes it clear that Jesus Christ himself is the ultimate fulfillment of the old covenant messianic prototype.

mishḥāh [מִשְׁחָה, **4888**]

This term occurs twenty-two times and refers exclusively to the oil of anointing used for ritual purposes associated with the priesthood in old covenant worship. It is limited to the books of Exodus (thirteen times) and Leviticus (eight times), with one reference in Numbers (4:16).

NT Words

aleiphō [ἀλείφω, *218*]

aleiphō is a verb found nine times meaning "anoint." Its use in the New Testament is entirely non-ceremonial.

"Anointing" is associated with personal ablutions during periods of fasting (cf. Matt. 6:17). "Anointing with oil" is also indicated in the context of administering medicinal aid (cf. Mark 6:13; Jas. 5:14). The process of "anointing" in the context of embalming a body in preparation for burial is noted in Mark 16:1. In several places, Mary, the sister of Lazarus, is identified as the one who "anointed" the feet of Jesus with perfume, indicating a bathing or pouring action.

chriō [χρίω, *5548*]

chriō is a verb found five times with the meaning "anoint," primarily in the sense of "commission" or "consecrate."

Christ is described as having been "anointed" with the Spirit of God as an indispensable prerequisite for his ministry. This phenomenon is depicted as a supernatural investiture (cf. Luke 4:18; Acts 4:27; 10:38). 2 Cor. 1:21 specifically notes the action of God in "consecrating" his apostles for ministry. Heb. 1:9 affirms that God "has anointed" his Son with "the oil of gladness," equipping him for ministry.

enchriō [ἐγχρίω, *1472*]

enchriō is a rare variant form of ***chriō***, above, found only in Rev. 3:18 and meaning to "anoint" one's eyes by applying medicinal ointment to them.

epichriō [ἐπιχρίω, *2025*]

epichriō is another rare variant form of ***enchriō*** and ***chriō***, above, denoting the action of "anointing" in applying moistened clay to the eyes. The term is found only in John 6:9, 11 with reference to Jesus' healing of a blind man.

myrizō [μυρίζω, *3462*]

myrizō is a verb occurring only in Mark 14:8. It refers to the action of the unnamed woman who "anointed" (i.e., poured expensive perfume onto) the head of Christ as an act of devotion. Jesus interpreted the act as a symbolic preparation of his body for burial.

chrisma [χρίσμα, *5545*]

chrisma is a rare noun found only in 1 John 2:20, 27 with reference to the "anointing" of the Holy Spirit for ministry.

Additional Notes

The term ***chrisma*** is a dynamic equivalent for ***mishḥāh***. What is of interest in the New Testament, however, is its close association with the anointing of the Holy Spirit, referred to metaphorically in 1 John 2:20, 27. What emerges from this observation is the realization that, while the use of ***chrisma*** may be infrequent (it occurs only in 1 John 2), the phenomenon of Spirit anointing is far more widespread than the use of the term would indicate. If one compares the experience of the judges in the Old Testament, for example, in their receiving the Spirit of Yahweh for particular service, it is clear that this constitutes an anointing of the Spirit even though the term ***māshaḥ*** (or its derivatives) is not employed. The theological association of ***māshaḥ*** with the offices of prophet, priest, and king has already been discussed above. Add to this the phenomenon of the ministry of the Holy Spirit in the New Testament, and a similar observation may be made. Even though the term ***chrisma*** is used only in John's first epistle, the anointing of the Holy Spirit as such is the characteristic experience of the church community in the first century A.D. after the ascension of Jesus Christ back to his heavenly realm. It is evident that the Holy Spirit could only come after Jesus had ascended to the Father (cf. John 16:7). Once Jesus had left the earth, it was clearly God's intention that his Spirit would come upon his people in a way hitherto not experienced. That this process may be deemed an anointing is beyond doubt. Thus the significance of the phenomenon goes far beyond the actual occurrence of the term. God has always communicated his power and authority for service in his kingdom to his people through the Spirit, and he always will.

ANSWER

OT Words

'ānāh [עָנָה, 6030]

This word is very common in the Old Testament and has two primary meanings. It most frequently means (over three hundred times) to "respond" or "answer." Within that broad range of texts, it is possible to see a number of perspectives on both human and divine responses.

The large majority of occurrences of *'ānāh* refer simply to ordinary human discourse where responses are made in mundane circumstances. The remaining texts indicate particular kinds of responses given in particular circumstances.

In the first place, *'ānāh* refers to the testimony of witnesses in judicial contexts, indicating responses at both an individual and corporate level. Several references in the Pentateuch specify the importance and function of the Israelite witness in a court of law (cf. Num. 35:30; Deut. 19:16). The nation itself is given a "song of witness" by God to remind them that they will sin against him during their lifetimes, as will the generations to follow (cf. Deut. 32). Moses reminds the people in Deut. 31:21 that this song will "testify" against them. David also declares in 2 Sam. 1:16 that the soldier who killed Saul has brought judgment on himself through his own testimony. Several verses in the Prophets bear out the tragedy of Israel's rebellion against God when the testimony of the nation's sin is brought into the open (cf. Isa. 3:9; 59:12; Jer. 14:7; Hos. 5:5; 7:10). In a slightly different context, Samuel requests in his farewell speech that the people of Israel would testify against him before the Lord if he has done anything improper during his time as their spiritual leader (1 Sam. 12:3). Finally, Prov. 25:18 condemns the person who bears false witness.

Not surprisingly, the psalmist utters impassioned pleas to God to hear him and respond with mercy and compassion during difficult times. *'ānāh* is the word used in these specific requests for God to either hear or respond (cf. Pss. 4:1; 13:3; 27:7; 55:2; 60:5; 69:13ff.; 86:1; 102:2; 108:6; 119:145; 143:1ff.). The psalmist also expresses his conviction that God will indeed answer him favorably (cf. Pss. 17:6; 20:6; 22:2; 38:15; 86:7; 91:15; 119:26; 138:3).

The nature of God's response to human beings is also significant in the usage of this term. In some instances, for example, God's response brings painful judgment or reproof (cf. Job 38:1; 40:1; Jer. 23:35, 37; Ezek. 14:4, 7). It must be recognized, however, that these texts specifically refer only to God's verbal response, which leads to judgment. There are innumerable other Old Testament contexts in which the divine response brings punishment to both Israel and the nations, but where the term *'ānāh* is not employed (→ AGE). It is interesting to observe that, more often than not, the very lack of response from God is in itself a punishment — a loss of divine counsel. These texts usually center on the problem of people calling upon God and receiving no response (cf. 1 Sam. 8:18 [warning to Israel]; 1 Sam. 28:6 [Saul]; Ps. 18:4 [the enemies of God]; Mic. 3:4 [Israel]). On occasion, the reverse is also true — God calls to his people but they refuse to answer him. This also brings judgment on them (cf. Isa. 50:2; 65:12; 66:4; Jer. 7:13; 35:17).

God's response to the needs of his people in particular, and to those of humankind in general, is also multifaceted. *'ānāh* is used, for example, to denote God's answer to David's intercession in 1 Chr. 21:28 whereby the plague judgment on Israel is brought to an end. The psalmist constantly affirms God's gracious response to his pleas (cf. Pss. 22:21; 34:4; 99:8; 118:5, 21). The prophets are also convinced that God will respond ultimately in mercy and grace to his people, notwithstanding his punishment of them (cf. Isa. 30:19; 41:17; 58:9; 65:24; Hos. 14:8; Jer. 33:3; 42:4). Hos. 2:21, 22 describes Yahweh's response to Israel as one that will result in the transformation and renewal of the nation after the completion of her time of punishment in exile. In the book of Zechariah there is an interesting use of *'ānāh* relating to the response of the heavenly intermediary who communicates to the prophet aspects of the meaning of the visions he has experienced. The references make it clear that this figure is none other than the angel of the Lord, who functions as a divine figure and also gives interpretive comments to Zechariah, including words of comfort and hope (cf. Zech. 1:10, 12; 3:4; 4:5, 6; 6:5). The theme of these visions is essentially the judgment of Israel in exile, followed by her redemption and renewal by God in her return to the land. Zech. 10:6 and 13:9 encapsulate this aspect of God's saving response to his people by emphasizing that he will answer them by renewing and restoring them to that relationship of covenant intimacy with him as their God and the Israelites as his people.

shûb [שׁוּב, 7725]

This verb occurs very frequently in the Old Testament and is commonly translated "return" or "repent" (over one thousand times). (→ REPENT → RETURN)

However, in a small number of instances (twenty-eight times) it means to "respond," "reply," or "answer" (lit. "to cause an answer to return"). Almost all of these references are concerned with ordinary human discourse. On several occasions the term is used to indicate a human being's direct response to God (i.e., Moses in Exod. 19:8; Job in Job 40:4).

rîb **[רִיב, 7379]**

This term assumes virtually a technical meaning in the Old Testament with regard to legal defense or dispute. It constitutes a specialized "answer" in a particular context that is primarily covenantal and judicial. For this reason it is best dealt with elsewhere. (→ LAWSUIT)

massā' **[מַשָּׂא, 4853]**

Once again, this word indicates a specialized sense of "answer." It has the primary meaning of "oracle" or "utterance," and it is best dealt with under those headings. (→ ORACLE → UTTER)

'āmar **[אָמַר, 559]**

'āmar is a very common verb found over 5,300 times with the primary senses of "say," "speak," plus a wide variety of nuances including the meaning "answer." There is a great deal of overlap between these three senses.

Examples of people "answering" people include Josh. 4:7; 2 Chr. 10:10; Jer. 5:19; Ezek. 21:7; Zech. 13:6. Commonly, answers are specifically given in response to questions (e.g., Judg. 8:18; 2 Sam. 1:8; Esth. 5:4; Jer. 22:9). Specific response or answer to the call of God is noted in 1 Sam. 3:4ff., as is the response to God's questioning in Isa. 39:4; Ezek. 37:3.

Elsewhere, God "answers" human beings, in particular as a response to prophetic inquiry (cf. Isa. 6:11; Zech. 1:19).

NT Words

apokrinomai **[ἀποκρίνομαι, *611*]**

The common verb ***apokrinomai*** occurs 250 times with the consistent meaning "to answer."

Christ gives answers to questions in various contexts (e.g., concerning John the Baptist in Matt. 3:15; 11:4; about himself in John 1:48; about eternal life in John 3:5ff.; from his disciples in John 6:70; 14:23). In addition, he responds to questions in the course of explaining the significance of his parables (cf. Matt. 12:48; 13:37). Jesus also "answers" various challenges (e.g., from his disciples showing lack of faith, cf. Mark 9:19; from religious leaders, cf. Mark 12:28ff.; from unbelievers or hostile Jewish leaders, cf. Matt. 12:39, 15:3; Mark 11:30ff.; Luke 5:22; John 5:17ff.; 8:19, 49; 18:5, 20ff.; from Satan, cf. Matt. 4:3; and from his accusers at trial [i.e., he gave no answer], cf. Matt. 27:12ff.).

Examples of people responding to other people include Matt. 20:13; Luke 3:16; John 1:21; Acts 3:12; Col. 4:6. People also answer Christ in the context of a confession of belief and faith (cf. John 1:49; Saul on the road to Damascus, cf. Acts 22:8). Other examples of this usage include Matt. 8:8; 25:37; Mark 9:17; John 16:31; Acts 9:13.

Luke 1:19 records the angels' "answer" to the inquiries of human beings.

apokrisis **[ἀπόκρισις, *612*]**

apokrisis is a noun derived from ***apokrinomai***, above. In each of the four contexts where it is found, it means "answer." In Luke 2:47; 20:26 people express their amazement at the answers Jesus gave to their questions. In John 1:22 people question John the Baptist, asking him for an answer as to his identity. John 19:9 records Jesus' refusal to give an answer to his accusers at his trial.

antapokrinomai **[ἀνταποκρίνομαι, *470*]**

antapokrinomai is a rare variant verb of ***apokrinomai***, above, with the meaning "to answer back" — to reply in contradiction to the speaker. It is found only in Luke 14:6; Rom. 9:20. The latter reference affirms that such a stance may not be taken against God.

chrēmatismos **[χρηματισμός, *5538*]**

chrēmatismos is a rare noun found only in Rom. 11:4 denoting an "answer" from God.

hypolambanō **[ὑπολαμβάνω, *5274*]**

hypolambanō is a verb occurring four times. It expresses the meaning "to answer" in the context of Jesus responding to a question by telling the story of the good Samaritan.

apologeomai **[ἀπολογέομαι, *626*]**

The verb ***apologeomai*** is found in eleven places with the primary meaning of "answer for oneself" in the sense of "making a defense" in a judicial context (cf. Luke 12:11; 21:14; Acts 19:33; 25:8; 26:1ff.; Rom. 2:15; 2 Cor. 12:19).

apologia [ἀπολογία, *627*]

apologia is the noun derived from ***apologeomai***, above, found eight times in all, with the meaning "defense," in a judicial context, where one has to "answer for oneself" (cf. Acts 22:1; 25:16; 1 Cor. 9:3; 2 Tim. 4:16). In 1 Pet. 3:15; Phil. 1:7 the context is that of the defense of the gospel.

Additional Notes

As is clear from the New Testament article above there are a number of Greek terms that function as dynamic equivalents to the Hebrew ***'ānāh*** to a greater or lesser degree. In terms of theological significance, it is true that the words ***apologia*** and ***apologeomai*** are more closely linked to the Hebrew ***rîb*** rather than ***'ānāh***. However, as discussed above, the latter term is used to convey the idea of testimony that results in the outpouring of divine wrath and punishment. In this sense, the meaning of ***'ānāh*** is linked to the semantic field of ***rîb*** without being a precise synonym. It is also worth noting that only one text in the New Testament indirectly refers to divine testimony or judgment against human beings. In Rom. 2:15, Paul implies that God will judge the effects of his law on the hearts of humankind, whether the thoughts of their hearts accuse or defend (***apologeomai***) them. The remaining uses of ***apologia*** and ***apologeomai*** have almost exclusive reference to a defense at the human level (viz. the defense of the gospel).

ANTICHRIST

OT Words

qeren [**קֶרֶן, 7161**]

qeren is the standard Hebrew term for "horn" in the Old Testament, found in nearly eighty contexts and referring to both literal and symbolic horns. (→ HORN)

In relation to the person of the antichrist, there is one particular set of references to "horn(s)" that is especially significant. It is found in Dan. 8:3ff., where mention is made of the "horn" growing out of the symbolic goat representing the ruler of Greece, Alexander the Great. Other "horns" grow up, and eventually one emerges that is more destructive than the others. This horn represents the vicious anti-Semitic ruler, Antiochus Epiphanes, who led a fierce campaign of terror and persecution against the Jewish people in the first half of the second century B.C. This "horn" constitutes a classic Old Testament prototype of the satanic figure of the antichrist, the "man of lawlessness," portrayed as the archenemy of the people of God in the new covenant age.

NT Words

antichristos [ἀντίχριστος, *500*]

The term ***antichristos*** occurs five times and denotes the archetypal enemy of Christ and his people, the embodiment of satanic opposition to Jesus Christ. The usage denotes not just one person, but rather the spirit of such a one indwelling all those who deny that Jesus is the incarnation of God in human form (cf. 1 John 2:18ff.; 4:3; 2 John 7).

ANXIETY → CARE

APOSTLE, APOSTLESHIP

OT Words

shālaḥ [**שָׁלַח, 7971**]

The term "apostle" or "apostleship" does not exist as such in the Old Testament. However, the root meaning of this term can refer to a person or persons "being sent away," "commissioned," or "appointed" to a specific task. The verb ***shālaḥ*** is by far the most significant term in this regard. It occurs nearly 850 times and usually means to "send" or "send away."

Sometimes ***shālaḥ*** refers to God as the sending or commissioning agent, and other times it refers to human beings fulfilling this role. The latter is more frequent as far as people being commissioned or authorized by other people is concerned. In these contexts, however, it is the presence of divine authority behind the human activity of "sending" that is most significant. In each case, the human figure or group of people acts as a vehicle for the advancement of God's redemptive purposes, to bring about either blessing or judgment.

There are a number of such examples. Joseph declares to his brothers in Gen. 45:5 that God had sent him down to Egypt before them in order to preserve the lives of many people on account of the current famine. Clearly Joseph is including the families of his brothers, as well as his father Jacob. Joseph's sense of a divinely ordered destiny is very clear at this point.

Moses provides us with another clear example of God commissioning a human being to accomplish his purpose. Explicit references to God sending Moses to confront Pharaoh and to lead the people of Israel out of Egyptian bondage are found, for example, in Exod. 3:13–15; 4:28; 5:22; 7:16; Deut. 34:11. And it is not only Moses' experience as the divinely-appointed leader of the exodus that is emphasized, but also his role in commissioning the twelve spies to explore the land of Canaan prior to the Israelite invasion (cf. Num. 13:2, 16, 17). Underlying his role here is the fact that God had raised Moses up and sent him to carry out the divine plan. The same applies to Joshua, Moses' successor, whom God appointed to lead the people into the promised land. Joshua's initiatives in spying out the cities of Jericho and Ai, for example (cf. Josh. 2:1; 6:17, 25; 7:2), were grounded in the realization that God had chosen and appointed him for that task.

The period of the judges also provides us with examples of the phenomenon of divine "sending." God calls Gideon to deliver his people from the oppression of the Midianites. Gideon is left in no doubt that it is God who sends him on this mission (cf. Judg. 6:14). Then, under the anointing of the Spirit of God, Gideon sends out his own messengers in the course of his career as judge in Israel (cf. Judg. 6:35; 7:24). Note also Jephthah's actions in Judg. 11:17, 28 in this light. The emerging monarchy in Israel is also controlled by divine initiative, as see clearly when God sends Samuel to anoint Saul as king in 1 Sam. 9:16; 10:2.

It is in the prophetic writings of the Old Testament, however, that the phenomenon of God sending out his chosen servants with words of comfort or warning or threats of punishment is most prominent. One of the most powerful examples of this is the mission of the Suffering Servant, depicted throughout the latter portion of the book of Isaiah (i.e., chs. 40–66). This messianic figure is described as one who is sent by God to accomplish the divine plan of salvation for the people of God (cf. Isa. 42:19; 61:1). Other references also implicitly indicate this figure as one sent by God (cf. Isa. 48:16; 55:11), a savior for his people (Isa. 19:20). Isaiah, too, submits to the call of God and offers himself for service as one willing to be sent by divine appointment (cf. Isa. 6:8). Both Jeremiah and Ezekiel are also keenly aware that God has sent them to the people of Judah to warn them of impending divine judgment (cf. Jer. 25:4, 15, 16, 27; 26:12, 15; Ezek. 3:6). In the postexilic period, the prophet Haggai is also self-consciously aware of the same reality (cf. Hag. 1:12).

Dire warnings are also sounded in the Old Testament against those who would presume to speak in God's name when in fact God has neither spoken to nor sent them. These are referred to as false prophets and their offense is a capital one in the eyes of God (cf. Jer. 27:15; 28:15; 29:9, 31; Ezek. 13:6). Israel was equally culpable, in God's eyes, for rejecting the genuine prophets that had been divinely authorized and sent to them (cf. Jer. 26:5; 43:1, 2; Zech. 7:12; 2 Chr. 36:15).

One unusual feature of divine commissioning in the Old Testament is the fact that God does not choose only his own people. Balaam is one classic illustration of God choosing and sending a pagan messenger to bring words of comfort to his own people (cf. Num. 22:10, 37; 24:12). It is clear from the context of these passages that the divine initiative underlies the abortive attempt of Balak, the Moabite king, to have the people of Israel cursed through Balaam (cf. also Cyrus in this regard in Isa. 45).

Finally, there are also clear indications that God does not use only human agents as part of his redemptive plan. The appearances of the "angel of the Lord" are clearly under the control of God, who sends this divine figure amongst his people to guard, admonish, and comfort them (cf. Exod. 23:20). Linked with this figure is the Messianic Servant himself, whose coming is anticipated by the prophet Malachi through the prophet Elijah, who is sent by God (cf. Mal. 3:1; 4:5). Many commentators agree that the person of John the Baptist fulfills the elements of this prophecy.

NT Words

apostolos [ἀπόστολος, *652*]

The noun ***apostolos*** occurs in about eighty contexts with the consistent meaning of "apostle," a divinely appointed messenger or representative.

References to the twelve apostles chosen by Christ can be found in Matt. 10:2; Mark 6:30; Luke 17:5; Acts 1:2; 15:2ff.; 1 Cor. 15:7ff.; Gal. 1:17ff.; Eph. 2:20; 1 Pet. 1:1; 2 Pet. 1:1; Jude 17; Rev. 21:14.

Other references to "apostles" as divinely appointed messengers and representatives of Christ are found in Luke 11:49; John 13:16; Acts 11:1; 2 Cor. 8:23; Eph. 3:5; Phil. 2:25; 1 Thess. 2:6. The unique apostleship of Paul is indicated in Rom. 1:1; 1 Cor. 1:1; 2 Cor. 1:1; Gal. 1:1; Eph. 1:1; Col. 1:1; 1 Tim. 1:1; 2 Tim. 1:1; Titus 1:1. The office of "apostle" in the church is noted in 1 Cor. 12:28ff.; Eph. 4:11; Rev. 18:20. Self-styled (i.e., false) apostles are referred to in 2 Cor. 11:5, 13; 12:11; Rev. 2:2. In Heb. 3:1 Jesus is described as the supreme "apostle."

apostolē [ἀποστολή, *651*]

apostolē is a noun found in four places, denoting the "office of an apostle," or "apostleship" (cf. Acts 1:25; Rom. 1:5; 1 Cor. 9:2). See also Gal. 2:8.

Additional Notes

In spite of the fact that there is no direct equivalent of the terms ***apostolos*** and ***apostolē*** in the Old Testament, the concept of commissioning and sending is very much in evidence. The Old Testament data provide a foundation for the emergence of Jesus Christ, his twelve apostles, and all subsequent disciples, in the new covenant age. The notion of God choosing a particular person, or group of people, and sending them into the world among his people Israel (and beyond) as vehicles for the advancement of his kingdom is fundamental to the old covenant era. It is also clear that there are false apostles in the Old Testament. But whether it is the messianic figure of the servant, or anyone else chosen by God for a particular function, the common denominator between these people and Jesus and his followers is that all have been chosen by God and commissioned by him to do his will. That is the underlying principle of "apostolic calling" that is common to the entire scriptural revelation.

APPARITION

NT Words

phantasma [φάντασμα, *5326*]

phantasma is a rare noun, found only twice, denoting an "apparition" or "ghost" in Matt. 14:26; Mark 6:49.

APPEAL

OT Words

qārā' [קָרָא, **7121**]

This common Old Testament verb has a number of meanings including "call," "meet," "read," "name," "befall." It occurs 730 times, and in the large majority of instances the dominant sense is that of "calling," or "crying out." It can also mean "appeal" — as it does in about ninety contexts. ***qārā'*** conveys the idea of "appeal" in two specific areas — in the worship of God, and in pleading to him for help in times of distress.
(➠ CALL ➠ MEET ➠ READ)

qārā' gives expression to what is virtually a technical phrase for worship in the Old Testament — "to call upon God" or "to call upon the name of the Lord." Underlying this expression is the human appeal to God to give heed to their expression of praise, a plea for help or to accept a sacrificial offering. This is especially true of the patriarchal age where such appeals to the person of Yahweh are synonymous with an expression of worship (cf. Abraham in Gen. 12:8; 13:4; 21:33 and Isaac in Gen. 26:25, as well as the godly generation at the time of Seth [Gen. 4:26]). The phrase is also found in a negative sense in Isa. 43:22, where the prophet records God's displeasure at Israel's failure to "call upon" him. It is precisely Israel's failure to make an appropriate appeal to the person of Yahweh that places them in jeopardy — their failure to worship God with a right heart attitude. Conversely, in Jer. 29:12 there is a magnificent promise of renewal given to the people of Judah. In this text God guarantees to transform and renew them so that they will indeed be able to respond to him with devoted hearts ready to express their praise and worship in an appropriate way. Significantly, as elsewhere in Scripture, it is the divine initiative that will provoke the people to do this. Such an action will not originate with human beings.

In the second place, ***qārā'*** denotes an appeal to God whereby people in distress plead with him for help. This is the most common meaning of "appeal" associated with this verb. Such an attitude is prevalent throughout the Psalms, as in about forty places the psalmist indicates his plight and his subsequent appeal to God for deliverance from his enemies (e.g., Pss. 17:6; 31:17; 69:3; 3:4), from overwhelming sorrow of an undefined nature (e.g., Pss. 88:9; 118:5; 119:145, 146), pleading for divine mercy from the penalty of sin (e.g., Ps. 130:1, 2). The psalmist also uses the expression "to call upon the name of the Lord" as a means of expressing his appeal to God to hear him and accept his ritual act of worship (e.g., Pss. 116:13, 17; 145:18).

At various stages in the history of God's people there is evidence of this kind of appeal being expressed from various quarters. Samson appealed to God to relieve his thirst after killing 1,000 Philistines with the jaw of an ass (Judg. 15:18). Then he made a similar appeal, just before his death, that God would avenge his mistreatment at the hands of the Philistines (Judg. 16:28). Samuel appeals to God to remind the Israelites of their wickedness in asking for a king in the way they did (1 Sam. 12:18). Then Elijah pleads with God to bring the dead son of the Zarephath widow back to life (1 Kgs. 17:21). Later on, the same prophet makes a solemn appeal to God to vindicate his name by igniting the altar saturated with water on Mt. Carmel (1 Kgs. 18:24). The prophet Isaiah appealed to God on behalf of King Hezekiah, who was stricken with a deadly illness. As a consequence, another fifteen years were added to the king's life, and God verifies this promise with a sign (2 Kgs. 20:11). King David, similarly, makes an appeal to God to bring the severe plague judgment on his people to an end (1 Chr. 21:26).

This concept is also found in the prophetic literature. In Zech. 13:9 we read of God's promise to answer the appeal of his people when they call on his name and renew their covenant relationship with him. Similar thoughts are expressed in Jer. 33:3, where Yahweh assures the people of Judah that he will answer their appeal to him. Even though they must pass through a terrible period of judgment, he promises to renew and restore them to the land of Canaan. Isaiah also exhorts the people of Israel to seek God and make their appeal known to him while he is still near (Isa. 55:6). The clear inference is that he will respond favorably to such a plea.

NT Words

epikaleō [**ἐπικαλέω,** *1941*]

epikaleō is a verb found in around thirty contexts with the primary senses of "be called (i.e., named)," "call upon." (→ CALL)

In several places, however, ***epikaleō*** expresses the sense of "appeal" in the judicial context of Paul's appeal to Caesar (cf. Acts 25:11ff.; 26:32; 28:19).

Additional Notes

The semantic range of both Old and New Testament terms in this case is somewhat similar. Both ***epikaleō*** and ***qārā'*** mean "appeal" in a defined set of circumstances, although the New Testament term occurs less frequently. In Acts, for example, ***epikaleō*** is used for both Paul's legal appeal to Caesar (see above) as well as an expression of worship, "calling upon the name of the Lord." This latter sense is found in Acts 9:14, 21, where Ananias' testimony concerning the newly converted Saul of Tarsus refers to the latter's prior obsession of arresting all those who "call upon the name of God." The context indicates that Jewish converts to Christianity are in view. Such believers, it is implied, had dedicated their lives to God through the person of Jesus Christ in a way that rankled the infamous Pharisee prior to his conversion. See also Acts 22:16; Rom. 10:12, 13.

Returning to the sense of legal appeal, there is another text in 2 Cor. 1:23 that utilizes ***epikaleō*** with an appeal to God in view. Here Paul invokes God's name and appeals to him as a witness in order to add weight to his claim that his failure to return to Corinth was motivated by a genuine concern for the Corinthians.

APPEAR, APPEARING

OT Words

rā'āh [**רָאָה, 7200**]

This common Hebrew verb occurs over 1,300 times with the primary meaning "see." In about 100 of these contexts, the verb means "appear." This meaning is in fact derived from the passive (i.e., Niphal) form of the verb "to be seen" (i.e., "to appear"). There are three different categories of "appearing" in the Old Testament.

The first of these relates to inanimate objects or natural phenomena. Some of these are theologically significant, some less so. With regard to the latter, there are some twenty references that indicate the appearing (or "non-appearing") of mundane objects — for example, the mountaintops in Gen. 8:5; grass in Prov. 27:25; mildew in articles of clothing in Lev. 13:57; poles inserted into the rings at the side of the ark of the covenant in 1 Kgs. 8:8. On the other hand, the appearance of other phenomena has a profound impact and carries great significance for those who witness it. The appearance of the rainbow in Gen. 9:14, for example, is of great comfort and significance to Noah and his surviving family since it confirms to them the promise that God had made, never to inundate the earth with floodwater again. Ezek. 10:1 describes the vision of that prophet in which the throne of God appears before him in the heavenly divine council. Such an image conveys a great deal of comfort to Ezekiel and the people of Judah in exile, for it testifies to them that Yahweh, their God, is still in sovereign control of their destiny — even though they are experiencing his hand of chastisement (cf. also Ezek. 10:8 in this regard). In a slightly different sense, but still in the sphere of the inanimate, the sins of human beings are said to appear in order to make their condemnation before God undeniable (cf. Jer. 13:26; Ezek. 21:24; Isa. 47:3).

The concept of "appearing" in the Old Testament can also relate to human beings. While in some instances the context is mundane and without great importance, in other cases there are significant observations to be made — when human beings appear before God, for instance. In Exod. 34:23, for example, it is laid down that all Israelite men must appear before the Lord three times a year at the tabernacle as part of their ritual obligation under the terms of the covenant (cf. also Exod. 23:17; Deut. 16:16). A similar injunction is given to the entire nation in Deut. 31:11. In a related context, Yahweh required a mandatory sacrifice during the Feast of Unleavened Bread when he issued the command "No one shall appear before me empty-handed" (cf. Exod. 23:15; 34:20). Isa. 1:12 records an instance where the people's appearance before the Lord in worship was totally unacceptable on account of their hypocritical formalism and hardness of heart. Finally, there is the account of Hannah's devotion to God in presenting her firstborn son Samuel to the Lord in the tabernacle. 1 Sam. 1:22 records Hannah's words to her husband, and they literally read (referring to Samuel): ". . . I will take him so that he may appear before the Lord . . ." In each of these instances, the concept of human beings appearing before God is set squarely within the framework of worship. Such appearances before Yahweh must be accompanied by genuine devotion to him — otherwise those acts of worship will not be accepted and will incur divine displeasure.

The final aspect of "appearing" in the Old Testament relates to God himself, and it is here that we find the most theologically significant occurrences of the term ***rā'āh*** with this meaning. Firstly, when it is said of God that he appears before human beings, the clear inference is that it is a theophanic vision. This is the experience of Abraham (cf. Gen. 12:1; 17:1; 18:1; Exod. 6:3); Isaac (cf. Gen. 26:2, 24); Jacob (cf. Gen. 35:1, 9; 48:3); Moses (cf. Exod. 3:16; 4:15); the Levitical priests (cf. Lev. 9:4); Samuel (cf. 1 Sam. 3:21); David (cf. 2 Chr. 3:1); Solomon (cf. 1 Kgs. 3:5; 9:2; 11:9; 2 Chr. 1:7; 7:12). In each case, the appearance of God was for the specific purpose of revealing his will to selected key individuals for the advancement of his redemptive plans for his chosen people. In other contexts, the appearance of God signifies the anticipation of messianic fulfillment (cf. Ps. 102:16; Mal. 3:2).

God also appears to his people in a cloud, but the purpose of most of these appearances is to bring judgment against them for one reason or another. One of the most notable examples of this is the execution of Korah and his followers as a consequence of their rebellion against Moses, recorded in Num. 16:19, 42 (cf. also Exod. 16:10; Num. 14:10; Lev. 16:2; Deut. 31:15). In Lev. 9:23, however, the Lord appears to the assembled Israelites in the "glory cloud" as a sign that he had accepted the offerings that the priests had made on their behalf. Even here, however, one might argue that the appearance of the Lord in the cloud is a sign of his judgment against their sin, symbolized in the fiery consumption of the sacrificial offerings.

In addition, the appearance of God is sometimes expressed through the phenomenon of the "angel of the Lord." On five occasions the verb ***rā'āh*** is used in this connection. Exod. 3:2 records the presence of the angel of the Lord before Moses in the burning bush. There is no doubt here that this being is a divine figure — a genuine theophany. Then, in the book of Judges, the angel of the Lord appears to Gideon (cf. Judg. 6:13) and to the mother of Samson (Judg. 13:3, 10, 21). In each case, similar to other contexts discussed above, the appearance of the angel of the Lord is for the express purpose of equipping, and the angel promises the recipients of the vision that God will use them through his power to rescue Israel from their oppressors.

Whatever the context in which human beings appear before God, or vice-versa, it is therefore clear that such a visitation or confrontation relates very closely to the plans and purposes of God for his people. This is the case whether it involves worship, the blessing of salvation, or even judgment.

gālāh [**גָּלָה, 1540**]

This verb means primarily "to uncover" (i.e., reveal one's nakedness), "reveal," "remove," or "carry away." However in its passive sense, as with ***rā'āh***, above, there are a number of instances where it means "appear." In line with the sense of "reveal," ***gālāh*** in these passages conveys the underlying connotation of revelation. For example, Gen. 35:7 records the appearance of God to Jacob; 1 Sam. 2:27 indicates that God had appeared to this people while they were in Egypt; Isa. 40:5 predicts that the glory of the Lord shall be revealed (i.e., that it will one day appear to the people of Israel, cf. also Isa. 53:1). From a negative perspective, there are several powerful metaphorical expressions of Israel's sins, which are described as being laid bare or exposed; that is, they appear in the sight of God (cf. Ezek. 13:14; 23:29; Hos. 7:1). In short, the usage of ***gālāh*** is very similar to that of ***rā'āh***.

NT Words

phainō [**φαίνω, *5316***]

The verb ***phainō*** is found in about thirty contexts with the dual senses of "appear," "shine" throughout. (➟ SHINE)

The meaning "appear" is found in a variety of contexts. There is reference, for example, to an angel of the Lord appearing to Joseph bringing news of the birth of the Messiah and accompanying circumstances (cf. Matt. 1:20; 2:13, 19). The appearance of the sign of the final coming of the Son of Man is noted in Matt. 24:30. The appearance of the star indicating the birthplace of the Messiah in Bethlehem is recorded in Matt. 2:7. Mark 16:9 records the appearance of the resurrected Christ before Mary Magdalene. Matt. 23:26ff. describes the phenomenon of self-righteousness Pharisees appearing as hypocrites.

Other uses of ***phainō*** with this meaning include Matt. 13:26; Luke 9:8; Rom. 7:13; 2 Cor. 9:8; Heb. 11:3; Jas. 4:14; 1 Pet. 4:18.

epiphainō [**ἐπιφαίνω, *2014***]

epiphainō is a verb found in only four places. In three of these it expresses the meaning "appear." Acts

27:20 mentions the non-appearance of the sun and stars in the context of bad weather. Titus 2:11 speaks of the appearance of the grace of God for salvation; and Titus 3:4 refers to the appearance of God's goodness and kindness.

anaphainō [ἀναφαίνω, *398*]

anaphainō is another rare variant form of ***phainō***, above, with the meaning "appear" in reference to the coming kingdom of God in Luke 19:11.

phaneroō [φανερόω, *5319*]

The verb ***phaneroō*** occurs about sixty times with the consistent meanings of "reveal" (i.e., cause to appear), "appear" throughout.

The passive sense "to be revealed" is found in a number of places, occurring with reference to God's work in the lives of human beings (cf. John 9:3); the righteousness of God (cf. Rom. 3:21); the love of God (cf. John 4:9); eternal life through God's word (cf. Titus 1:3); the life of Jesus in the bodies, lives of believers (cf. 2 Cor. 4:10ff.; Col. 3:4); and the mystery of Christ and the gospel, communicated to the saints (cf. Col. 1:26; 1 Tim. 3:16; 2 Tim. 1:10; 1 Pet. 1:20; 1 John 1:2). The revelation of Christ to Israel is indicated in John 1:31; and to the world at large at the end of the age in 1 Pet. 5:4; 1 John 2:28; 3:2.

The active meaning "to reveal" (in the sense of "cause to appear") is found in relation to Christ's glory during his earthly ministry (cf. John 2:11). John 17:6 affirms that Christ reveals God's name to God's people. Rom. 1:19 declares that God reveals himself to humankind. The sense of "make clear, plain" is also evident in the use of this term (cf. 2 Cor. 11:6; Col. 4:4; 1 John 2:19).

The specific sense of "appear" is noted in the context of the risen Christ showing himself to his disciples prior to his ascension to heaven (cf. Mark 16:12ff.; John 21:1, 14). All believers are set to "appear" before the judgment seat of Christ as indicated in 2 Cor. 5:10. Heb. 9:26; 1 John 3:5, 8 affirm that Jesus "has appeared" to take away sin once and for all. The phenomenon of "becoming visible" in the glare of light is indicated in Eph. 5:13.

phaneros [φανερός, *5318*]

phaneros is an adjective found in around twenty contexts with the meanings "apparent," "evident" (in the sense of being clearly recognized) in about half of these texts.

General reference to all things being "made evident" on the day of judgment is indicated in Luke 8:17. The general knowledge of God as Creator is said to "be made plain" to all people in Rom. 1:19. Humankind's work on the day of judgment will also "be made plain" to God as noted in 1 Cor. 3:13. See also 1 Cor. 14:25 for a related usage. Gal. 5:19 declares that the works of the flesh are "plain" (i.e., "apparent"). See also Acts 4:16.

epiphaneia [ἐπιφάνεια, *2015*]

epiphaneia is a noun found six times, with the meaning "appearing" in all but one of these places, referring solely to the manifestation of Jesus Christ at his return to earth at the end of the age (cf. 1 Tim. 6:14; 2 Tim. 1:10; 4:18; Titus 2:13).

emphanizō [ἐμφανίζω, *1718*]

The verb ***emphanizō*** means "appear," "reveal" in about half of the ten contexts in which it occurs.

The meaning "appear" in the sense of "show oneself in public view" occurs in Matt. 27:53. It is also predicated of Christ, who now "appears" in heaven to intercede before God on behalf of his people (cf. Heb. 9:24).

emphanizō also expresses the meaning "reveal" in the sense of "make oneself known," and is applied to Christ in John 14:21ff., where it is claimed he will "manifest" himself to those who love him, along with God the Father.

Additional Notes

From the discussion of all the above terms it is evident that the range of emphases within the meaning "appear" in both ***rā'āh*** and ***gālāh*** closely approximates that of the New Testament Greek terms as well. The dominant emphasis in both Testaments is the revelation of the Godhead. The differences reflect the distinctions in the stages of redemptive history: Under the old covenant God revealed himself and appeared before his people in various guises, namely through theophanic visions, dreams, the glory cloud, and the angel of the Lord, to name the most prominent. In the new covenant era, however, it is in the person of Jesus the Messiah that the revelation of God comes to its fullest expression, along with the appearance of the Holy Spirit. It is in the person of Christ and all that he represents that the fulfillment of all the old covenant revelatory phenomena is realized.

See Also: → COMING → REVEAL → SHINE → SHOW

APPEARANCE

OT Words

mar'eh **[מַרְאֶה, 4758]**

This Hebrew noun is derived from the verb ***rā'āh*** (→ APPEAR) discussed above. Its principal meaning is "appearance" or "vision," and it occurs approximately one hundred times (half of which are concentrated in the books of Ezekiel and Daniel). Not surprisingly there is little, if any, difference in emphasis from that of ***rā'āh.***

In non-theological contexts, ***mar'eh*** refers to the external form or appearance of animals (cf. Gen. 41:2ff.); people of both sexes (cf. Gen. 12:11; 24:16; 29:17; 1 Sam. 16:7; 17:42; 2 Sam. 11:2; 14:27; Esth. 1:11; 2:2ff.; Song 2:14; 5:15); and even skin disease (cf. Lev. 13:3ff.).

The majority of the remaining occurrences of ***mar'eh*** are found in significant theological contexts that emphasize the revelation of God and his redemptive purposes for Israel. They are located primarily in prophetic contexts in the books of Ezekiel and Daniel. In the visionary material of Ezekiel 1, 8 and 10, ***mar'eh*** is used eighteen times. The object of the prophet's attention here is the extraordinary vision of the heavenly throne room in which the "appearance" of cherubim, the mysterious wheels supporting the divine throne, fire, and the equally mysterious human-like form from which it emanates, overwhelm him. Such a vision underscores for Ezekiel, and for the people of Judah in captivity, the fact that their God is still in sovereign control and that they need not despair. Similarly, Daniel receives a series of heavenly visions in which the nations of the world are doomed to destruction as a consequence of the emerging power of the kingdom of God. The appearance of certain phenomena within the visions, as well as the visions themselves, leave a profound impression on Daniel (cf. Dan. 8:15, 16, 26, 27; 9:23; 10:1, 6, 18). In spite of the fact that Daniel does not receive an exhaustive revelation in these visions, he is given sufficient insight so as to derive real hope for the people of God from them.

Once again, there is no doubt that the phenomenon of the divine appearance or vision in the Old Testament serves to advance the understanding of God's purposes for his people.

See Also: → FACE

APPOINT, APPOINTED

OT Words

yā'ad **[יָעַד, 3259]**

The primary meaning of this verb is "appoint," with other connotations of gathering by appointment and meeting by appointment. It occurs about thirty times with this meaning, describing both human beings and God.

On the human level, ***yā'ad*** refers to a mutually agreed time or place between people of varying stations in society (cf. 2 Sam. 20:5; Amos 3:3; Josh. 11:5; Neh. 6:2, 10; Job 2:11).

As far as divine appointment is concerned, there are a number of significant texts to note. Firstly, there are references that indicate God's determination to destroy the enemies of his people, literally by divine appointment — including the destruction of Philistia (Jer. 47:7), Edom (Jer. 49:19), and Babylon (Jer. 50:44). In Mic. 6:9, such an appointment has Israel herself in view. Here God is described as having appointed a rod for the punishment of his people.

On a much less somber note, there are several texts in the Pentateuch that speak of God's plan to meet with his people for the purpose of imparting aspects of his will for their lives. The context clearly suggests that their meetings are by definite design on God's part — that they are literally divinely ordained appointments when the people of Israel must come together before God to hear his will (cf. Exod. 25:22; 29:43; Num. 10:3, 4).

Finally, there is a third category of texts that bring the spheres of human and divine appointments together. In a negative context, Num. 14:35 and 16:11 describe, for example, the gathering together of Korah and his Levitical followers for the purpose of rebelling against Moses, and therefore against God. It is clear that this was predetermined on their part, an appointed time for insurrection. By way of contrast, 1 Kgs. 8:5 (and the parallel text in 2 Chr. 5:6) gives an account of the Israelites assembling for worship and sacrifice around the ark of the covenant in the temple just prior to its installation in the holy of holies. Again, the implication of ***yā'ad*** here is that such a gathering takes place according to a regular pattern of worship under the terms of the covenant — a divinely appointed gathering.

pāqad **[פָּקַד, 6485]**

This verb has a number of meanings, one of which is "to appoint." ***pāqad*** occurs about three hundred times — it means "appoint" in about twenty of these places. (→ VISIT → NUMBER)

Some of these texts refer to the ritual appointment of priests and Levites (cf. Num. 1:50; 3:10; 4:27; Neh. 7:1; 12:44); others indicate military-style appointments (cf. 1 Sam. 29:4; 2 Kgs. 7:17). A much more specific meaning for ***pāqad*** is found in contexts where the appointment of overseers (cf. Gen. 39:4, 5; 41:34) or governors (cf. 2 Kgs. 25:23; Jer. 40:5ff.; 41:2, 10, 18) is in view.

On a more explicitly theological plane, ***pāqad*** is used metaphorically to refer to the judgment of God against Jerusalem (e.g. Jer. 51:27). Such punishment is an explicit divine appointment. In Lev. 26:16, a curse is threatened against Israel in the event of her violating her covenant obligations to God. In a more positive example, Jeremiah is informed that his position of authority over the nations will be gained solely by divine appointment — Yahweh will set him as his representative over the nations, to bring them messages from God of both blessing and hope.

'āmad [עָמַד, 5975]

This common verb has the primary meaning "stand" (approximately 520 occurrences). However in a few instances (about twenty), ***'āmad*** means "appoint" — mostly in the history of the Chronicler and the books of Ezra-Nehemiah. They refer almost exclusively to the ritual appointment of priests and Levites (cf. 1 Chr. 15:16, 17; 2 Chr. 8:14; 11:15, 22; 20:21; 29:25; 31:2; 35:2; Ezra 3:8, 10; Neh. 13:30) or to civil or military positions (cf. Neh. 7:3; 2 Chr. 19:5; 25:5). Nehemiah is also slanderously accused of appointing prophets in Jerusalem in Neh. 6:7.

nāṣab [נָצַב, 5324]

This verb is a synonym of ***'āmad***, "to stand." In several contexts, however, ***nāṣab*** means "to set over (someone)" (i.e., "to appoint"). Examples of this usage are found in Ruth 2:5, 6; 1 Sam. 19:20; 22:9; 1 Kgs. 4:7; 9:23; 2 Chr. 8:10. In each case the context reflects a human agency rather than a divine one. The texts in Ruth and Samuel refer to civil appointments; whereas the Kings and Chronicles references have military or royal appointments in view.

sûm [שׂוּם, 7760]

This common verb occurs about six hundred times in the Old Testament, with the principal meanings of "put," "place," and "set," along with various synonyms. One of these synonyms carries the sense of "appoint" and is found in a number of contexts (approximately twenty). The underlying meaning associated with ***sûm*** in this regard is "to set over (someone or something)" in the sense of establishing or setting in place. Both humans and God are seen as "agents of appointing" in the use of this term.

As far as divine appointing is concerned, there are several examples to note. It is Joseph's testimony in Gen. 45:9 that God had appointed him lord over all Egypt. Then there is reference to God appointing the people of Israel, by his sovereign choice, as his own possession (cf. Isa. 44:7). Solomon is declared to be God's chosen appointee for the throne of Israel (cf. 1 Kgs. 10:9). Then, on a non-personal level, God appoints cities of refuge as a haven for those who commit unintentional manslaughter (cf. Exod. 21:13). Divine appointment is also highlighted in the plague on Egyptian livestock when God establishes a time for Pharaoh to release his people from captivity. Pharaoh refuses and so the plague is carried out (cf. Exod. 9:5). In 2 Sam. 7:10 God promises to appoint David a place in which he and the people of Israel will find rest in the land of Canaan.

On the human level, ***sûm*** refers to the activity of military appointment in 1 Sam. 8:11; 2 Sam. 17:25; 23:23; 2 Kgs. 10:24; 1 Chr. 11:25. In the period of the Egyptian captivity, reference is made to the appointment of Moses over the Hebrews (Exod. 2:14), and to the appointment of Hebrew foremen by their Egyptian overlords (Exod. 5:14). And, prior to that period, Potiphar appointed Joseph over his household (cf. Ps. 105:21). Hos. 1:11 contains a prophecy that is distinctly messianic in its thrust as the prophet refers to the reunited people of Israel appointing a single ruler over themselves.

nātan [נָתַן, 5414]

nātan is one of the most frequently occurring verbs in the Old Testament (approximately two thousand times). It means primarily to "give," "put," "set," and in regard to the latter two meanings it is virtually synonymous with ***sûm***, above. Like ***sûm***, ***nātan*** also means "appoint" in a number of instances, with both a human and divine sense. Concerning the former, for example, Gen. 41:41 refers to Pharaoh appointing Joseph over the land of Egypt as his chief representative; and in 2 Kgs. 23:5 reference is made to the kings of Judah appointing pagan priests for service throughout the land. ***nātan*** is also used to describe God's initiative in ordering the affairs of his people. In 1 Sam. 12:13, Samuel himself declares to the people of Israel that God has appointed a king over them. 1 Kgs. 1:48 records King David's prayer of thanks in which he praises God for allowing him to see the one whom God had appointed to be his successor on the throne — that is, Solomon. Then in Jer. 1:5, a very significant text, God declares to Jeremiah that he had appointed him to be a prophet before he was even born.

ṣāwāh [**צָוָה, 6680**]

This verb occurs about 450 times and generally means "command." However, in a handful of references it is translated "appoint." 1 Sam. 25:30 refers to God's appointment of King Saul over Israel; 1 Kgs. 1:35 refers to Solomon's appointment as king over Israel; and 2 Sam. 6:21 also refers to a divine appointment — that of David as ruler in Israel. On a slightly different level, 2 Sam. 17:14 describes God's intention (lit. "appointing") to destroy Absalom by frustrating the sound advice of Ahithophel in the eyes of the rebel king.

'āsāh [**עָשָׂה, 6213**]

'āsāh is another example of a common verb which has a more narrow meaning in a small number of texts. ***'āsāh*** occurs over 2,500 times and has a whole range of meanings centering on the two primary senses of "do" and "make."

'āsāh is translated "appoint" in several ritual contexts where the appointment of the following is in view: priests (1 Kgs. 12:31; 13:33; 2 Chr. 2:17); a feast (1 Kgs. 12:32, 33); a sacrifice (Num. 28:6); and a festival day (Ps. 118:24).

menāh [**מְנָה, 4483** (Aramaic)]

menāh is an Aramaic verb that means "appoint" (to public office) in Ezra 7:25; Dan. 2:24, 49; Dan. 3:12.

NT Words

histēmi [ἵστημι, *2476*]

histēmi is a common verb with the principal meaning of "stand" in almost all of the nearly 160 occurrences of the term. In Acts 17:31, however, this term is translated "appoint" with reference to God "having appointed" a day in which he will judge the world.

kathistēmi [καθίστημι, *2525*]

kathistēmi is a verb found in about twenty places with the underlying senses of "placing someone in authority over" or "making someone ruler over," which leads to the primary translation of "appoint."

The appointment of a household manager is indicated in Matt. 24:45ff.; 25:21ff.; Luke 12:42ff.; elders are appointed to church congregations as noted in Titus 1:5; deacons are likewise appointed to their tasks in Acts 6:3. Acts 7:10 refers to the appointment of Joseph as governor of Egypt. Heb. 7:28; 8:3 make reference to men "being appointed" as high priests. See also Luke 12:14; Acts 7:35 for metaphorical usage of the term.

tithēmi [τίθημι, *5087*]

tithēmi is a common verb found in nearly 100 contexts with the dominant meanings "put," "set," plus related nuances. One of these nuances is that of "appoint" or "ordain." John 15:16 speaks of Christ "appointing" (i.e., setting aside) believers to bring forth spiritual fruit in their lives, demonstrating the indwelling power of God. 1 Thess. 5:9 makes reference to God "appointing" or "ordaining" his people — not for wrath, but for salvation. Paul refers to his being "appointed" by God as an apostle and preacher of the gospel.

tassō [τάσσω, *5021*]

tassō is a verb found in eight places with the meanings "appoint," "ordain" in the sense of "set aside for a special purpose."

General reference to a soldier "set under authority" is found in Luke 7:8. The phenomenon of "being appointed, or ordained" to eternal life is noted in Acts 13:48. Governments are declared to "be appointed" by God in Rom. 13:1. Acts 22:10; 28:23 make reference to "being set aside" for particular gospel service.

protassō [προτάσσω, *4384*]

protassō is a rare verb found in Acts 17:26 with reference to God "having ordained beforehand" the boundaries of human earthly kingdoms.

apokeimai [ἀπόκειμαι, *606*]

apokeimai is a verb expressing the meaning "to appoint" in Acts 9:27, where it is affirmed that people are "appointed once to die and then the judgment."

cheirotoneō [χειροτονέω, *5500*]

cheirotoneō is a rare verb found only twice, expressing the meaning "to appoint (to the office of elder)" in Acts 14:23; and also "assign (a particular ministry to)" in 2 Cor. 8:19.

procheirizomai [προχειρίζομαι, *4400*]

procheirizomai is a rare middle verb, found only in Acts 22:14; 26:16, with reference to God "ordaining" or "appointing" Saul at the point of his conversion to gospel proclamation and ministry.

horizō [ὁρίζω, *3724*]

horizō is a verb found in eight places, with all but one referring to the sovereign divine action of "appointing," "determining" Jesus Christ as the Savior and Redeemer of the world, through his action of a sacrificial death on the cross (cf. Luke 22:22; Acts 2:23; 10:42; 17:31). Christ is also described as one "appointed" by God to exercise judgment on the world. See also Rom. 1:4. Heb. 4:7 also makes reference to God "setting aside" (i.e., determining, appointing) a particular day for the final judgment.

anadeiknymi [ἀναδείκνυμι, *322*]

anadeiknymi is a rare verb referring to the action of Jesus in "choosing" or "appointing" seventy of his followers to undertake an evangelistic mission to the towns of Judea (cf. Luke 10:2). Acts 1:24 refers to God "choosing," "appointing" a replacement in the apostolic band for Judas Iscariot.

poieō [ποιέω, *4160*]

poieō is a common verb found in nearly 600 contexts with the predominant sense of "do," "make," plus a broad range of related meanings. In one context, ***poieō*** denotes God "having appointed" Christ as "the apostle and high priest" of his people (cf. Heb. 3:2).

Additional Notes

Because of the wide variety of both Hebrew and Greek terms that mean "appoint" and overlap in meaning, it is very difficult to assign precise dynamic equivalence to any two of them. However, taken overall, the usage of these terms is consistent in both Testaments, in that the process of "appointing" functions at both the human and divine level in very similar ways. It is God who appoints priests and Levites, for example, for service in the Old Testament; and in the New Testament it is God also who appoints pastors and elders in the church through the Holy Spirit, the Spirit of Christ. Judgment on the nations as well as on his people is appointed (or ordained) by God in the Old Testament; and in the New Testament the final judgment is appointed by Christ on the authority of God the Father. God appoints his people, Israel, to be his own unique possession in the Old Testament; and it is God who likewise appoints (or ordains) people to eternal life in the new covenant era. Appointing in civil and military contexts is also found in both Testaments.

What is clear is that the sovereignty of God is affirmed throughout the Scriptures by the process of his appointing people to carry out his will, and by places and events that reflect his redemptive purpose. That is true whether one looks to the Old or the New Testament; and it is also true that, in Jesus Christ, God's own divine appointing reaches its climax.

See Also: → COVENANT

APPREHEND

OT Words

lākad [לָכַד, 3920]

This verb occurs approximately 120 times, and its basic meanings are "capture," "take hold," which in most cases may also be translated as "apprehend."

The great majority of contexts in which ***lākad*** is found relate to the literal capture of cities, towns, and people. This is the case in the Former Prophets, the extended accounts of God's dealings with this people from the conquest of the land to the exile, where reference to the capture of armies and cities in Canaan accounts for about half the incidence of ***lākad***. In this broad context ***lākad*** refers to the effectiveness of God's intention and power in enabling his people to accomplish what he required of them in ridding the land of Canaanite influence. Sadly, because of the people's lack of faith in God, the task was never fully completed. There was always some residual Canaanite influence, therefore, that proved a stumbling block to Israel and led them constantly into idolatry. Other references to capture refer not to Israel's successes, but to God's judgment against her, namely their destruction and capture by her enemies (e.g., 2 Kgs. 18:10 [the overthrow of the northern kingdom by the Assyrians]; Jer. 38:28 and Lam. 4:20 [the capture of Jerusalem by the Babylonians]).

lākad is also used to signify "apprehending" or "overtaking" in a slightly different sense: Josh. 7, for example, reports the sins of Achan in stealing from the plunder of Jericho. In Josh. 7:16–18 reference is made to Achan and his family being "taken by lot." The sense here is that God apprehended him by a divine judgment, through the casting of lots. In a positive sense, the same phenomenon is recorded in 1 Sam. 10:20, 21, where Saul is "chosen" (i.e., taken by lot) to be king over Israel.

Non-literal uses of ***lākad*** are found in Pss. 35:8; 59:12; Prov. 5:22; 16:32; 11:6; Job 5:13; 36:8 and Eccl. 7:26, where the common thought is that the sinner shall be "apprehended" or "overtaken" in his sin.

Apart from the metaphorical use of ***lākad***, it is clear that the use of this verb to indicate "capture" or "apprehending" reinforces both the positive and negative aspects of God's plan of salvation for his people in the old covenant. Blessing for Israel involves the destruction and defeat of her enemies; judgment against her for sin signifies exactly the opposite — namely defeat at the hands of her enemies.

'āḥaz [אָחַז, 270]

This term has the primary meaning of "seize," "take hold of," and occurs about seventy times. Nearly half of these references may also be translated "apprehend" and, like ***lākad***, above, ***'āḥaz*** has both a literal and nonliteral sense in this regard.

At the literal level of meaning, ***'āḥaz*** refers principally to deeds of valor whereby the Israelites were able to subdue (i.e., "apprehend") their enemies. References here are concentrated in the period of the judges and the reign of David (cf. Judg. 1:6; 12:6; 16:3, 21; 20:6; 2 Sam. 4:10; 6:6; 20:9).

Metaphorically speaking, ***'āḥaz*** refers mainly to the painful experience of suffering and anguish which overwhelms the victims of adverse circumstances. In the main, the contexts reveal that the source of such agony is the judgment of God against the sin of the nations (cf. Exod. 15:14; Ps. 48:6, 7; Jer. 49:24; Isa. 13:8) and against the sin of his people (cf. Isa. 5:29; Jer. 13:21). There is also reference to the suffering of God's people in general, who are seized by the weight of their anguish in the face of oppression from their enemies (cf. Ps. 119:53; Isa. 21:3; 33:14). Finally, ***'āḥaz*** with this meaning has a positive connotation when referring to the state of the godly in Israel, who are overwhelmed by the intimacy and security of their relationship with their God (cf. Pss. 73:23; 139:10).

NT Words

katalambanō [καταλαμβάνω, *2638*]

katalambanō is a verb found in fifteen contexts with the meanings "take," "overcome."

In several places where the term is translated "take," the thought of "seize" or "apprehend by force" is indicated (cf. Mark 9:18). Elsewhere, ***katalambanō*** is translated "seize" in the sense of "take by surprise" (cf. 1 Thess. 5:4). In John 8:3, 4 mention is made of the woman "caught," or "apprehended," in the very act of adultery.

piazō [πιάζω, *4084*]

piazō is a verb translated "seize" or "arrest" (i.e., apprehend by force) throughout most of the twelve occurrences of the term.

The action of "arresting," or at least attempting to arrest in a judicial sense, is indicated in John 7:30ff., 44; 8:20; 10:39; 11:57 — all with respect to Christ. See also Acts 12:4; 2 Cor. 11:32.

The meaning "capture" is evident in Rev. 19:20 in relation to the satanic "beast."

Additional Notes

It is not possible to pinpoint precise semantic equivalence between these Greek and Hebrew terms. Taken together, however, the sense of ***lākad*** and ***'āḥaz***, alongside ***katalambanō*** and ***piazō***, present a consistent perspective in both Testaments. There is no doubt that the emphasis on apprehending the literal enemies of Israel in the Old Testament is reflected in the apprehending of the devil and his angels in the New (the archenemies of new covenant believers). Similarly, the phenomenon of pagans in the old covenant being apprehended or overtaken in their sin is repeated in the experience of unbelievers in the new. Finally, the positive experience of apprehending the blessings of the old covenant climaxes in the new covenant with the laying hold of the blessings found in Christ.

APPROACH

OT Words

qārēb [קָרֵב, 7131]

qārēb is a participial form of ***qārab*** (→ DRAW) found eleven times. It is used nominally in several different contexts to refer to "the one who comes near (i.e., approaches)."

Several references contain dire warnings of instant death for any person who "approaches" the sacred, forbidden area of the tabernacle and is not authorized to do so — namely those who are neither priests nor Levites (cf. Num. 1:51; 3:10, 38; 17:13; 18:7). Conversely, the ceremonial rituals of those priests and Levites who may legitimately "approach" or "come near" the temple are noted in Ezek. 40:46; 45:4.

Other general references to physical "approach" are found in 1 Sam. 17:41; 2 Sam. 18:25; 1 Kgs. 4:27. See also Deut. 20:3.

qārôb [קָרוֹב, 7138]

qārôb is an adjective meaning "near" for almost all of the nearly eighty occurrences of the term. However, in Ezek. 42:13; 43:19 it refers to priests as "those who approach the Lord."

qerābāh [קְרָבָה, 7132]

qerābāh is a rare noun denoting those who "draw near to (i.e., approach) God" in a general sense in Ps. 73:28; Isa. 58:2.

——— NT WORDS ———

engizō [ἐγγίζω, *1448*]

The verb ***engizō*** occurs around forty times with the meanings "draw near," "approach" in the majority of these instances in a variety of contexts.

The act of "drawing near," "approaching" in a physical, geographic sense is indicated in relation to coming to Jerusalem in Matt. 21:1; Mark 11:1; Luke 19:41. Other general references with this sense include Luke 7:12; 15:25; Acts 9:3. Other references to approaching people are found in Luke 12:33; 15:1; 18:40.

Elsewhere, ***engizō*** denotes the "approaching" of various times, seasons, and significant events (e.g., harvest, cf. Matt. 21:34); ceremonial festivals (cf. Luke 22:1); the fulfillment of God's promise to Abraham (cf. Acts 7:17); Christ's suffering and death (cf. Luke 21:8); the final day of judgment (cf. Luke 21:20; Rom. 13:12; Heb. 10:25; Jas. 5:8 [re the return of Christ]; 1 Pet. 4:7). In addition, reference to the imminent approach of the kingdom of God is indicated in Luke 10:9ff.

A general exhortation to "draw near to" God is found in Jas. 4:8, with a promise that he will reciprocate. In Heb. 7:19 the believer is guaranteed the right to approach God, on the basis of the person and work of Christ.

aprositos [ἀπρόσιτος, *676*]

aprositos is a rare adjectival form found only in 1 Tim. 6:16. It refers to the light surrounding the being of God, which is "unapproachable."

See Also: → ACCESS

APPROVE, APPROVED

——— NT WORDS ———

dokimazō [δοκιμάζω, *1381*]

dokimazō is a verb occurring nearly thirty times. It expresses the meanings "approve," "prove" with several related nuances.

The meaning "approve" in the sense of "examine," "impact" is indicated in relation to cattle in Luke 14:19; the value of people's ministry to be tested by fire at the last judgment in 1 Cor. 3:13; self-examination in 2 Cor. 13:5; Gal. 6:4. In 1 John 4:1, believers are exhorted to "test" the spirits to see whether they are of God.

The capacity for "approving" ("discerning") what pleases God in relation to his law and will is noted in Rom. 2:18; 12:2; Eph. 5:10; Phil. 1:10; 1 Thess. 5:21 (cf. Rom. 14:22 in relation to what is morally right).

The "approving" of people for ministry in the sense of deeming them worthy of commendation is indicated in 1 Cor. 16:3; 1 Tim. 3:10.

The status of being "approved" by God is mentioned in 1 Thess. 2:4 in the context of gospel ministry; and in 1 Pet. 1:7 in relation to one's life work, to be tested by fire at the final judgment.

apodeiknymi [ἀποδείκνυμι, *584*]

apodeiknymi is a verb found in four contexts, with the meaning "exhibit," "put on display" in all but one of these. In Acts 2:22, it means to "approve" in the sense of "attest," "accredit" with reference to Jesus Christ as one "approved," "attested" by God among the people of Israel.

dokimos [δόκιμος, *1384*]

dokimos is an adjectival form derived from ***apodeiknymi***, above, with the meaning "approved" in several different senses. It occurs seven times.

The state of being "approved," "commended" by human beings refers to one's acceptability and worthiness for gospel ministry in Rom. 14:18; 16:10. 1 Cor. 11:19; 2 Cor. 10:18 refer explicitly to those who are "commended" by God.

dokimos also refers to those who "have been approved," that is, to those who have been subject to assessment and deemed satisfactory (cf. 2 Cor. 13:7). Similarly, Jas. 1:12 affirms that those who "have stood the test" will receive the crown of life in the state hereafter.

Finally, 2 Tim. 2:15 describes a worker in the word of God as one who is "approved," who demonstrates competence in accurately teaching its content.

ARCHANGEL

——— NT WORDS ———

archangelos [ἀρχάγγελος, *743*]

archangelos is a rare noun occurring only twice with reference to the archangel in general in 1 Thess. 4:16; and to Michael in particular in Jude 9.

See Also: → ANGEL

ARISE

OT Words

qûm **[קוּם, 6965]**

The basic meaning of this common verb (occurring over six hundred times) is "to stand." There are, however, a number of synonymous nuances that also constitute legitimate translations. The most common of these are "rise," "arise," and "raise." Within this semantic range, two levels of meaning may be noted — one is literal, the other metaphorical.

In the literal sense, ***qûm*** refers to the actions of standing or rising up from a seated position in mundane contexts. This accounts for over ninety percent of references, and these are concentrated in the Pentateuch and Former Prophets. There are, however, a number of instances where such an action, particularly when predicated of Yahweh, carries a specific theological connotation. This is especially the case when ***qûm*** is used as an imperative, usually translated "Arise . . . !" For example, God commands Abraham in Gen. 13:17 to get up and walk through the land of Canaan to which he has brought him, and that he has promised as an inheritance to his descendants. Similar injunctions are given to Jacob (cf. Gen. 31:13; 35:1) and much later to Moses, whom God commands to rise up and lead the Israelites through the wilderness to the land he has promised them (cf. Deut. 2:13, 24; 9:12; 10:11). Joshua also receives the same instructions when he finally approaches and subsequently enters Canaan (cf. Josh. 1:2; 8:1). These instructions focus on the task of leading the people to complete the conquest God had promised to accomplish on their behalf. God commands Gideon to arise and eradicate the inhabitants of the land in Judg. 7:9, 15. God also commands Elijah to arise and go to a widow in Zarephath for a divine appointment; and he directs Jonah towards Nineveh to bring that city a warning of judgment (Jonah 1:2; 3:2). God also directs his servants to arise and bring messages of impending punishment to those who have rebelled against him, as in 2 Kgs. 1:3, where Elijah is instructed by God to arise, go, and meet the messengers of King Ahaziah, in order to denounce this northern ruler and pronounce sentence upon him for his idolatry. Similarly, God instructs Jeremiah to go to the potter's house in order to bring an indictment against the people of Judah for their rejection of Yahweh (cf. Jer. 18:2).

Such literal commands are not only given directly by God, but are also given by Israel's leaders to those under their charge. For example, Deborah instructs Barak, her army commander, to arise and destroy the Canaanite city of Hazor (cf. Judg. 5:12). Later on in Israel's history, David instructs his son Solomon to arise and build the temple of the Lord (cf. 1 Chr. 22:19).

Apart from the imperative use of ***qûm***, there are several significant occurrences of this term used in an active verbal sense to describe the action of rising up in order to do something important in relation to God's plans for his people. A number of these texts refer to the failure of God's enemies to thwart his purposes by attacking or harassing the Israelite nation. The inevitable consequence of such attempts is that God overthrows these enemies. The Song of Moses and Miriam, for example, praises God for the destruction of the Egyptian army at the Red Sea, rejoicing in the downfall of those who had risen up against the Lord and his people (cf. Exod. 15:7). Similar testimony to such victory over all opposition to Israel from the surrounding nations who "rise up against" God is recorded in Deut. 33:11; 2 Sam. 18:31; 22:40, 49; Pss. 18:39, 48; 44:5; 92:11. In addition to these texts that describe the historical vanquishing of Israel's enemies, there are also pleas directed to God to overthrow all who "rise up against" his people (cf. Pss. 3:1; 74:23; 7:6; 9:19; 10:12; 44:26; 74:22; 82:8).

A slightly different perspective emerges when ***qûm*** is used in a "causative" sense to mean "raise" or "raise up" (i.e., to cause to arise or emerge). Here the contexts cited contain both a positive and negative emphasis. Positively, God is said to "raise up" deliverers for his people including the judges (cf. Judg. 2:16, 18; 3:9, 15); priests (cf. 1 Sam. 2:35); prophets (cf. Deut. 18:15, 18); the messianic shepherd king (cf. Jer. 23:4, 5; 30:9); as well as David's royal descendants in general (cf. 2 Sam. 7:12). God also promises to "raise up" or restore the Jerusalem temple (cf. Amos 9:11) as well as Jerusalem itself (cf. Isa. 44:26; 58:12; 61:4). Negatively, God is also seen to raise up nations in order to bring judgment against his people (cf. Hab. 1:6; Deut. 28:7; Isa. 29:3). Returning to the positive connotation of ***qûm*** with respect to the divine initiative, this term is occasionally translated "establish." The reference here is to the setting up (or raising up) of a covenant that will determine God's relationship to Israel. Yahweh is their Savior and Redeemer, and his people are bound to their God in faith, love, and obedience (cf. Gen. 6:18; 9:9, 11, 17; 17:7, 19, 21; Exod. 6:4; Lev. 26:9; Num. 30:14; Ezek. 16:60, 62; Deut. 8:18; 29:13; 28:9; 2 Sam. 7:25). Less frequently, though with equal significance, ***qûm*** is used in a metaphorical sense to refer either to God's "arising" or to the emergence of a person who will function as an agent of God's purposes. In each case, while the use of the word is metaphorical or symbolic, it is nonetheless real, and of genuine redemptive historical significance. For example, Num. 24:17 refers to the rising of a "scepter" in Israel, a messianic symbol. From the perspective of judgment against Israel, God is sometimes said to rise up against his people (cf. Amos 7:9; Ps. 76:9; Isa. 28:21; 33:10). Finally, there are several texts that exhort Israel to "arise" or "wake" in order to appropriate the deliverance God has provided for them (cf. Isa. 51:17; 52:2; 60:1).

It is clear from this overview that the use of ***qûm*** in the sense of "arise" has profound theological connotations.

This usage shows God to be constantly on the alert, ready to meet the needs of his people at his appointed time and implement the next step in his plan of salvation. Such a move will involve either blessing or judgment for the people of Israel — whether from God himself or through his appointed servants. For all those who oppose God and his purposes, however, such a divine "arising" will inevitably bring divine wrath. Sadly, this was not only reserved for the surrounding pagan nations, but was also for Israel herself.

'ûr [עוּר, 5782]

The basic meaning of this verb is "wake" or "awaken," and it occurs about twenty times with this sense. As an extension of this meaning, ***'ûr*** is also translated "raise (up)" "rouse" or "stir" (approximately forty-five times). The majority of contexts are identical with those associated with ***qûm***, above — God takes the initiative in blessing and judgment or commands his servants to act on his behalf.

This is particularly evident in situations where ***'ûr*** is translated "awake" in an imperative sense. It is virtually synonymous with the command "arise." Deborah, for example, is commanded to "awake" and have her general Barak commence battle maneuvers against the Canaanites. The command "arise" (***qûm***) is given to Barak in the very next breath. Similar invocations are made to God to "awake" and take action against the enemies of Israel (cf. Pss. 7:6; 59:4; Isa. 51:9, 17). In every instance, the sense of "arise" is implicit in these texts.

Other texts specifically refer to God raising up designated peoples — either to bring judgment against other nations or against his own people Israel. In the former scenario, God is described, for example, in Zech. 2:13 as rousing himself in order to judge the nations (cf. also Isa. 42:13; Jer. 25:32). More specifically, it is predicated of Yahweh that he will raise many kings and others to attack Babylon (cf. Joel 3:12; Zech. 4:1; Isa. 41:2; 13:17; Jer. 50:9; 51:1, 11); Assyria is also in line for divine destruction along with Babylon (cf. Isa. 41:2). Greece is similarly lined up for judgment (cf. Zech. 9:13), as are Tyre, Sidon, and Philistia (cf. Joel 3:7). In regard to the latter phenomenon, it is Israel herself who becomes the object of divine wrath; for it is God who raises up various nations to punish his people for rebellion against him: for example, Babylon (cf. Jer. 6:22; Ezek. 23:22); Assyria (cf. 1 Chr. 5:26); Philistia and Arabia (2 Chr. 21:16).

In a more positive light, God is said to have raised up (or stirred up) the spirit of Cyrus I, the Persian ruler, to release the people of Judah from their captivity and return them to their homeland in order to rebuild the temple (cf. 2 Chr. 36:22; Ezra 1:1, 5).

zāraḥ [זָרַח, 2224]

zāraḥ is a verb found in eighteen places meaning "rise," "rise up."

The term has primary reference to the "rising" of the sun (cf. Gen. 32:31; Exod. 22:3; Job 9:33; 2 Sam. 23:4; Job 9:7; Ps. 104:22; Eccl. 1:5; Jonah 4:8; Nah. 3:17).

Elsewhere, Yahweh is said "to rise up" from Sinai (cf. Deut. 33:2); and in Mal. 4:2 he is described as the "sun of righteousness" who "rises up" to bring healing to his people. Similarly, Isa. 60:1ff. depicts the glory of God "rising upon" his people. Then, in Ps. 112:4; Isa. 58:10, light is said "to rise" in the darkness.

There is an unusual usage in 2 Chr. 26:19, where leprosy is described as "rising up" (i.e., breaking out) on the forehead of King Uzziah, as a punishment from God.

NT Words

anistēmi [ἀνίστημι, *450*]

anistēmi is a verb found over one hundred times with the primary sense of "arise," "rise (up)," "raise (up)" in a variety of contexts.

Commonly, ***anistēmi*** denotes the act of "rising," "arising" in the sense of "stand, get up." Mundane references include Matt. 9:9; Mark 2:14; Luke 1:39; Acts 1:15; 9:6ff.; 1 Cor. 10:7. The action of "standing up" as the result of a miraculous cure is noted in Acts 9:34; 14:10. See also Acts 13:16. The men of Nineveh are depicted as ones who "will rise up" in judgment against the unbelieving towns of Judea at the last "day" (cf. Matt. 12:41; Luke 11:32). Satan is also said "to rise up" in Mark 3:26. Christ himself is portrayed as "rising up" to rule the Gentiles in Rom. 15:12; and also as a high priest after the order of Melchizedek (cf. Heb. 7:11, 15).

The phenomenon of resurrection frequently describes Christ, whose "rising from the dead" is both prophesied and recorded (cf. Matt. 17:9; 20:19; Mark 9:9ff.; 10:34; Luke 18:33; 24:7, 46; John 20:9; Acts 2:24ff.; 3:26; 13:33ff.; Rom. 14:9). This experience is also predicated of others in Mark 12:25; Luke 9:8, 19; 16:31; John 11:23ff.; Eph. 5:14; 1 Thess. 4:16.

Elsewhere, ***anistēmi*** is translated "to raise up," for example in the context of "rearing" children in Matt. 22:24. God is said "to raise up" his people to eternal life on the day of judgment (cf. John 6:40ff.), and also raises up prophets for his service in Acts 7:37.

exanistēmi [ἐξανίστημι, *1817*]

exanistēmi is a rare variant form of ***anistēmi***, above, found in only three places. In Mark 12:19; Luke 20:28, it refers to a man "raising up" children by the widow of his deceased brother in order to preserve the name of the family line in Israel (i.e., the custom of "Levirate" marriage). In Acts 15:5 the meaning "rise up" is indicated in relation to the "emerging" of a Pharisaical sect.

egeirō [ἐγείρω, *1453*]

egeirō is a verb synonymous with ***anistēmi*** (see above), occurring over 150 times with the senses of "rise," "arise," "raise (up)," and various nuances in different contexts.

The general, mundane sense of "rise," "stand, get up" is indicated in Matt. 2:13; Mark 4:27; John 11:29; Rev. 11:1. The action of "standing up" as a consequence of healing is noted in Matt. 9:5ff.; Mark 2:9ff.; Luke 5:23ff.; John 5:8; Acts 3:6, 7. To "arise" in the sense of "come into public view," "to emerge," is indicated in Matt. 11:11; 24:11, 24; Mark 13:22.

Where God is the subject of this verb, the predominant meaning is that of "raise up." The possibility of God "raising up" children from stones is indicated in Matt. 3:9; Luke 3:8. Luke 1:69 affirms that God "has raised up" a "horn of salvation" for his people. Acts 13:22 records that God "raised up" David as king over Israel. There are a number of references indicating that God has power to raise the dead to life (cf. Matt. 10:8; 11:5; Acts 26:8; 1 Cor. 15:12ff.; 2 Cor. 1:9; 4:14). Christ in particular is the object of divine resurrecting power (cf. Acts 3:15; 5:30; 13:30; Rom. 4:24ff.; 8:11; 1 Cor. 6:14; 15:12ff.; 2 Cor. 5:15; Gal. 1:1; Eph. 1:20; Col. 2:12; 1 Thess. 1:10; 1 Pet. 1:21).

People are said "to rise up" in judgment at the last day in Matt. 12:42; Luke 11:31; and also in the context of armed conflict (cf. Matt. 24:7; Mark 13:8).

The action of "rising" from the dead is predicated of people, largely through the divine power demonstrated by Christ (cf. Matt. 14:2; 27:52; Mark 12:26; Luke 7:14ff.; 9:7; 20:37). More particularly, it is also commonly used with reference to Jesus Christ's own resurrection (cf. Matt. 16:21; 26:32; 27:63ff.; 28:6ff.; Mark 14:28; 16:6; Luke 9:22; John 21:14; 2 Tim. 2:8). In John 2:19ff., this phenomenon is expressed in the metaphor of Jesus vowing "to raise the temple in three days," — referring to his own body.

diegeirō [διεγείρω, *1326*]

diegeirō is a variant form of ***egeirō***, above, found in seven places with the primary sense of "awaken," "rouse from sleep" (cf. Matt. 1:24; Mark 4:38ff.; Luke 8:24; 2 Pet. 1:13; 3:1). In John 6:18 it refers to the "rising" of the sea in a storm.

ginomai [γίνομαι, *1096*]

ginomai is a common verb (occurring over one thousand times) with quite generalized meanings such as "be," "become," "happen (i.e., come to pass)," "come," plus a number of other nuances.

In a few places, ***ginomai*** also expresses the sense of "rise" in the sense of "happen," "come to pass." It is used to denote the coming of persecution (cf. Matt. 13:21; Acts 11:19); of a storm (cf. Mark 4:37); flood (cf. Luke 6:48); famine (cf. Luke 5:14); civil unrest (cf. Acts 19:23; 23:9); and of a dispute (cf. Acts 23:7ff.).

anabainō [ἀναβαίνω, *305*]

anabainō is a verb found in approximately eighty contexts, with the underlying meanings "go up," "come up," plus several related nuances. One of these nuances is "arise," indicated with respect to thoughts "rising" in the heart in Luke 24:38. The smoke of divine judgment "rising out" of the abyss is noted in Rev. 9:2; 19:3. In Rev. 13:1, 11, the two satanic beasts are depicted as "rising" out of the sea and the earth.

synephistēmi [συνεφίστημι, *4911*]

synephistēmi is a rare verb found only in Acts 16:22 with reference to a hostile crowd "rising up against" Paul and his companions to attack them.

eiserchomai [εἰσέρχομαι, *1525*]

eiserchomai is a common verb with the predominant sense of "enter," "go in," "come in" for the large majority of its nearly two hundred occurrences. In Luke 9:46 the meaning "arise" is indicated, in relation to an argument among the disciples as to who is the greatest.

anatellō [ἀνατέλλω, *393*]

anatellō is a verb found in eleven places with primary reference to the "rising" of the sun. In this respect it may be viewed as a dynamic equivalent to the Hebrew term ***zāraḥ***, above.

Reference to God causing the sun to rise is found in Matt. 5:45. Other references to the rising sun are indicated in Matt. 13:6; Mark 4:6; 16:2; Jas. 1:11.

Elsewhere, Luke 12:54 refers to a cloud "rising" in the west; and in 2 Pet. 1:19 metaphorical reference is made to the morning star "rising" in the hearts of God's people.

Additional Notes

The semantic ranges of Old and New Testament vocabulary that translates as "arise . . . ," etc. are roughly parallel. In both the Hebrew and Greek terminology, there is mundane as well as theologically significant usage. In the Old Testament there is no doubt that, when God is the subject of ***qûm*** or ***'ûr***, the phenomenon of a divine arising is very significant indeed since it demonstrates the redemptive activity of God both amongst his own people and beyond. And as we have noted, such activity may result in either judgment or blessing, depending on whether one rejects Yahweh or embraces him in a spirit of devotion.

In the New Testament, this particular emphasis is not given quite the same prominence. Where it does occur, however, with the verbs ***anistēmi*** and ***egeirō***, for example, there is likewise no doubt about its significance. Here, when Christ is the subject of these verbs, the reference is either to his own resurrection (his "arising") from the dead or to his raising others from that state. Such activity clearly springs from none other than a divine being. There is also the dual emphasis in the New Testament concept of "arise" that is both positive and negative. The positive implications of Jesus' own resurrection from the dead have to do with the fulfillment of God's plan of salvation on earth. It is the climax of redemptive history. Negatively speaking, the resurrection of unbelievers from the dead, by the same divine power that raised Jesus, will result in their everlasting torment. The difference in the New Testament evidence here is that such "(a)rising" or "raising" carries eternal consequences as the climax of either blessing or judgment.

See Also: ➟ OFFER

ARK

OT Words

'ārôn [אָרוֹן, 727]

This word occurs about 180 times in the Old Testament. In the overwhelming majority of instances it refers to the sacred covenant box or chest that was housed firstly in the tabernacle, and then in the temple in Jerusalem, in the most holy place behind the veil. It is traditionally referred to as the ark of the covenant. The exceptions to this usage are found in Gen. 50:26, where ***'ārôn*** refers to Joseph's coffin, and also in 2 Kgs. 12:9; 10:11; 2 Chr. 24:8ff., where it indicates a money chest.

In the Pentateuch, the references to ***'ārôn*** focus on the construction of the ark (cf. Exod. 25:10ff.; 35:12; 37:1, 5; Deut. 10:19), the setting up of the ark in the tabernacle (cf. Exod. 40:3, 5, 20, 21), and the ritual ceremony associated with the ark (cf. Lev. 16:2; Num. 3:31; 4:5; 7:89; 10:33, 35; 14:44).

The remaining references to ***'ārôn*** occur almost exclusively in the Former Prophets and Chronicles. The significance of this becomes clear as this narrative portion of the Old Testament unfolds. It is evident in Joshua, for instance, that the ark of the covenant plays a central role in the initial conquest of Canaan by the army of Israel under the command of Joshua. Initially the ark is taken in front of the people as a vanguard to pave the way across a flooded Jordan River so that the whole nation may cross over on dry ground into the land itself (cf. Josh. 3:4 — sixteen occurrences). This is a vivid reminder and repetition of a similar miracle that took place at the Red Sea many years before, when the Israelites were fleeing from the Egyptians. Now, as then, such a miracle was due entirely to the sovereign intervention of Yahweh, whose powerful presence is metaphorically yet truly concentrated in the ark at the Jordan River. Then the sacred covenant box figures prominently in the destruction of Jericho as it is paraded in full view of the city. On this occasion the ark is placed in the midst of the Israelites as they circle Jericho for seven days prior to its eventual destruction (cf. Josh. 6:4ff.).

In the books of Samuel, the ark also features in circumstances that are highly significant for the people of God. For the most part, references to ***'ārôn*** in 1 Samuel indicate a period of harsh discipline for the Israelite people. In 1 Sam. 4 and 5, the ark is first of all captured by the Philistines on account of the Israelites' abuse of the sacred object when they took the person and presence of God for granted in a culpable way. The presence of the ark wreaks havoc in the Philistine cities and they return it to the Israelites. Yet this return is not without tragedy, since seventy Israelites are struck dead by God for having looked into the ark and thus violated its sanctity (cf. 1 Sam. 6:19). King David finally brings the sacred chest to Jerusalem in 2 Sam. 6, but not before tragedy strikes again, when Uzzah the Levite is also executed by God's hand for reaching out and touching the ark when the cart on which it was traveling suddenly lurches (cf. 2 Sam. 6:7).

The significance of the ark of the covenant in Kings and Chronicles is seen primarily in its return to Jerusalem and its investiture in the temple by King Solomon (cf. 1 Kgs. 8; 1 Chr. 13; 15; 16; 2 Chr. 5). On each occasion, both the solemnity of the event and the accompanying jubilation of the king and the people are clearly evident. In the ark of the covenant the people of Israel have their most majestic and potent symbol of the genuine presence of God in their midst.

There is no doubt that all these portions of the Old Testament (and, by implication, the remainder as well) emphasize the central importance of the ark of the covenant in the worship of ancient Israel. This most sacred of objects constituted the most powerful symbolic representation of the person of Yahweh who dwelled and ruled among his people in a manner altogether unparalleled throughout the ancient Near East and indeed in the entire history of the human race.

tēbāh [תֵּבָה, 8392]

This word occurs nearly thirty times in the Old Testament. On almost all occasions it refers to the huge vessel, or ark, built by Noah at God's command in order to preserve him and his family and a remnant of the earth's animal population from destruction in the universal flood recorded in Genesis 6–9. ***tēbāh*** also refers to the vessel used to hide the infant Moses from the Egyptians, by his very courageous and godly parents. The common element here is that ***tēbāh*** indicates an object designed for protection in the face of imminent danger.

NT Words

kibōtos [κιβωτός, *2787*]

kibōtos is a noun found in six places, with reference to both Noah's "ark" at the time of the great flood (cf. Matt. 24:38; Luke 17:27; Heb. 11:7; 1 Pet. 3:20); and also the ark of the covenant in Heb. 9:4; Rev. 11:19.

Additional Notes

The Greek term ***kibōtos*** occurs infrequently in the New Testament (only six times). However, where it does occur there is explicit reference to the phenomena indicated by both ***'ārôn*** and ***tēbāh***. The text in Rev. 11:19 is particularly significant, since here the ark of the covenant is described in a heavenly setting. While the language is clearly symbolic, the reality behind the symbolism is also quite clear. In heaven there is the fulfillment and consummation of all that the Old Testament temple pointed towards — eternal, unbroken fellowship with God in his very presence, where the people of God from all ages will enjoy him without fear of separation. Conversely, for those outside of the kingdom, there will never by any such enjoyment but only the prospect of the wrath of God, who will forever bar them from his presence in glory.

ARM

OT Words

zerôa' [זְרוֹעַ, 2220]

This term occurs approximately ninety times and carries the primary meaning of "arm." The two exceptions to this are found in Num. 6:19 and Deut. 18:3, where ***zerôa'*** refers to the shoulder of the animal carcass that has been presented as an offering by the people. The sense of "arm" carries with it both a literal as well as a metaphorical connotation.

Referring literally to a person's arm(s), ***zerôa'*** is found in about six passages; these are generally without theological significance.

It is the non-literal usage of ***zerôa'*** that is most significant. In these passages, the senses of "arm" are metaphorical, referring basically to the phenomena of power and strength on both the divine and human level. As far as human strength is concerned, there are a variety of contexts to note. In 1 Sam. 2:31, for example, the house of Eli the high priest is condemned by God to gradually decline and then disappear altogether. The specific reference is to Eli's "arm" and the "arm" of his fathers' house being cut off. The meaning is that the strength and vitality of his descendants will decay, and that his entire high-priestly lineage will ultimately become extinct. The fundamental emphasis in the metaphor of the "arm of man" is that it is weak and frail. This is evidently also the case in the remaining instances, where "arm" refers to human strength that is largely ineffective and impotent (cf. 2 Chr. 32:8; Job 22:8, 9; 26:2; 35:9; 38:15; Pss. 10:15; 37:17; 44:3; Jer. 17:5; 48:5; Ezek. 30:21ff.; Dan. 11:6, 15, 22, 31). It is evident, particularly in the prophetic references above, that the weakness and frailty of the human "arm" is due directly to the judgment of God against people.

When divine power is in view, however, through the metaphor of the "arm of God," there is no such weakness. In every single instance, the "arm of God" triumphs — whether referring to the salvation of God's people as a result of the divine conquest of her enemies, or in reference to God's judgment against his people for their rebellion against him. This perspective is frequently indicated, for example, by reference to the "outstretched arm of God" against Egypt, or by some other synonymous expression (cf. Exod. 6:6; 15:16; Deut. 4:34; 5:15; 7:19; 9:29; 11:2; 26:8; 2 Kgs. 17:36; Pss. 77:15; 136:12; Isa. 63:12). In every one of these contexts, it is the "arm of God" that is responsible for the defeat of the Egyptians — and conversely for the salvation of the Israelite people. There are, in addition, other references to the "arm of God" that have spelled disaster for the enemies of Yahweh and his people in general terms (cf. 1 Kgs. 8:42; 2 Chr. 6:32; Ps. 89:10, 13; Isa. 30:30; 48:14).

Then there are references to the "arm of God" in a positive sense, working for the salvation of his people in history, triumphing over their enemies (cf. Deut. 33:27; Isa. 33:2; 40:10; 52:10; 59:16; 62:8; 63:5). And the Israelites are not the sole object of God's mercy in the exercising of the divine "arm." Isa. 51:4, 5 makes it clear, for example, that the "arm of God" will bring justice to the nations, who will, as a result, also wait in hope for their salvation from Yahweh. Judgment against the people of Israel is also clearly expressed through the metaphor of the "arm of God": for example, Zedekiah is given his sentence of condemnation in this way in Jer. 21:5, as are the people generally in Jer. 27:5 and Ezek. 20:33.

Not every occurrence of the "arm" metaphor with respect to God, however, has force or power in view. Isa. 40:11 presents the image of God gathering his people like little lambs into his arms. This is similar to the image recorded in Deut. 33:27, which describes the absolute security and comfort of the "everlasting arms of God." For his people, Yahweh is the ultimate refuge from their enemies.

'ezrôa' [אֶזְרוֹעַ, **248**]

'ezrôa' is a rare variant form of ***zerôa'***, above, found only twice. It refers literally to a man's arm in Job 31:22; and metaphorically to the outstretched "arm" of God in Jer. 32:21, signifying his mighty power.

derā' [דְּרָע, **1872** (Aramaic)]

derā' is a rare Aramaic term denoting the "arms" of silver on the four-metal statue in King Nebuchadnezzar's dream in Dan. 2:32.

NT Words

ankalē [ἀγκάλη, *43*]

ankalē is a rare noun denoting "the arms" of Simeon, who held the infant Jesus on the occasion of the child's consecration in the temple (cf. Luke 2:28).

brachiōn [βραχίων, *1023*]

brachiōn is a noun found in only three places denoting metaphorically the "arm" of God in each case, indicating his mighty power (cf. Luke 1:51; John 12:38; Acts 13:17).

enankalizomai [ἐναγκαλίζομαι, *1723*]

enankalizomai is a verb occurring four times with reference to Jesus "taking little children into his arms" in order to bless them (cf. Mark 9:36; 10:16).

Additional Notes

As is evident from the above discussion of ***brachiōn***, the New Testament term for "arm," the principal features of the Old Testament usage are also reflected here. Though the occurrence of ***brachiōn*** is less frequent than ***zerôa'***, the theological perspective is very similar.

It is also clear in relation to ***enankalizomai*** that the element of compassionate concern for little children shown by Jesus in the New Testament matches the attitude manifested by God towards Israel in the Old. In both cases, the tenderness of God towards those who display an attitude of trusting dependence towards him will result in immeasurable peace and comfort. In Jesus' case, it is his commendation of the children's attitudes of innate trust and dependence that is designed to provoke his adult audience into a similar attitude in their own relationship with God.

Thus the "arm of God" in a metaphorical sense encapsulates the idea of both divine power in redemption as well as divine compassion. It is an image which is given powerful symbolic expression in the Old Testament; and it also emerges with similar force in the New, if less frequently.

See Also: → HAND → SHOULDER

ARMS, ARMOR, TO ARM

OT Words

māgēn [מָגֵן, **4043**]

This word occurs about sixty times with the basic meaning of "shield." However, since the shield was the basic element of the ancient Near Eastern soldier's battle defense, it may be understood to represent the whole of his armor. This is evident in the metaphorical use of ***māgēn***, which accounts for about forty of the sixty references. The literal use of the term is found primarily in the historical narratives of Kings and Chronicles and does not bear much significance in a theological sense (sixteen occurrences).

With the metaphorical use of this word, however, there are a number of significant aspects to note. In the first instance, ***māgēn*** is used to refer to God as Abraham's "shield" in Gen. 15:1. The context indicates beyond doubt that this image refers to the unique sovereign protection that God is offering to the patriarch, along with the covenant promises relating to Abraham's posterity and the land of Canaan. Similar affirmations of blessing and protection for Israel with this allusion to God as the shield of his people are found in Deut. 33:29; 2 Sam. 22:3, 31, 36; Pss. 3:3; 7:10; 28:7; 33:20; 35:2; 59:11, 12; 84:9, 11; 89:18; 115:9ff.; 119:114; 144:2. In every instance, the metaphor of the divine shield brings a profound sense of comfort and assurance to this people, particularly in the face of extreme difficulty.

In the Prophets, ***māgēn*** is used metaphorically in various contexts. In Isa. 21:5, the commanders of Babylon are told to oil their shields. It is clearly a call to arm themselves for battle. In this case, the oracle (i.e., 21:1–10) describes the imminent destruction of that nation.

Perhaps one of the best known prophetic oracles of judgment directed against a foreign nation is found in Ezek. 38, 39, where the destruction of Gog and Magog is portrayed in graphic detail. Once again, preparation for battle is described with reference to armor — shields and helmets in particular (38:4, 5). Then, after their catastrophic overthrow by Yahweh, the people of Israel will own all of their armor, using it for fuel. The portrait is one of complete and utter annihilation (cf. 39:9). The fate of Egypt is similarly indicated with reference to these people carrying their shields, only to be defeated in battle (cf. Jer. 46:3, 9). Note also Ezek. 27:16 in reference to Tyre.

It is not only Gentile nations, however, who experience the wrath of God in this way. Similar reference is made to the city of Kir (southern Babylonia) "uncovering her shield" in preparation for the attack on Jerusalem as part of God's threatened judgment against his own people. It is likewise a preparation for armed conflict. In the allegorical description of Israel's rebellion against Yahweh in Ezekiel 23, reference is made to the armor of Israel's enemies as they make their assault on the people of Jerusalem (Ezek. 23:24).

It is clear that these references to "shield," both in the context of preparation for battle and also the promise of divine protection, demonstrate the all-powerful influence of God upon the affairs of humankind. Whether God is comforting his own people with his protection, or summoning nations to arms in order either to destroy them or use them to punish his people, his plans are being implemented with absolute effectiveness.

nesheq [נֶשֶׁק, 5402]

There are only ten occurrences of this word, with all but one bearing the meaning "weapons" or "armor" in a general sense (in Ps. 140:7 ***nesheq*** is translated "battle"). Of these, four are found in historical narrative with no particular significance; they are used simply in a descriptive sense (cf. 1 Kgs. 10:25; 2 Kgs. 10:2; 2 Chr. 9:24; Neh. 3:19). Job 39:21 also contains a descriptive use of the term, referring to the actions of a horse in battle confronting the weapons of the enemy. There is another interesting use of the term in Job 20:24, where ***nesheq*** refers metaphorically to the "iron weapon" of God as an instrument of punishment. In this instance it is Zophar who assumes (wrongly) that Job is the hapless sufferer of such treatment at the hands of God on account of the man's sin. A similar connotation is found in Isa. 22:8, where the futility of Israel's weaponry in the face of divine judgment is made clear. On this occasion, however, there is no doubting the guilt of God's people. Finally, reference to the weapon of Gog and Magog is again found in Ezek. 39:9, 10. In this case, as with ***māgēn***, above, it is these weapons that will be used for firewood after the destruction of this pagan kingdom by direct divine intervention. It is therefore clear that ***māgēn*** and ***nesheq*** have similar meanings.

ḥalîṣāh [חֲלִיצָה, 2488]

This word only occurs twice; and on each occasion it refers to soldiers' armor (cf. Judg. 14:19; 2 Sam. 2:21).

ḥālaṣ [חָלַץ, 2502]

ḥālaṣ is a verb with the primary dual senses of "deliver," "arm" (i.e., prepare for war) throughout the forty or so contexts in which the term occurs.

(→ DELIVER)

The meaning "to arm for war" is indicated in Num. 31:3ff.; 32:20ff.; Deut. 3:18; Josh. 6:7ff.; 1 Chr. 12:23ff.;

2 Chr. 17:18. The nominal sense of "army" is evident in 2 Chr. 20:21; and in 2 Chr. 28:14; Isa. 15:4 it refers to "armed men."

ḥāmûsh [חָמוּשׁ, **2571**]

ḥāmûsh is an adjectival form with the meaning "armed" in the context of people ready to fight. It is found four times (cf. Exod. 13:18; Josh. 1:14; 4:12; Judg. 7:11).

kelî [כְּלִי, **3627**]

kelî is a noun with a broad range of meanings found about three hundred times. Predominant senses include "article," "implement," "utensil," "instrument."

The term can also mean "armor" (cf. 1 Sam. 14:1, 6; 17:54; 31:9ff.; 2 Sam. 18:15; 2 Kgs. 20:13; 1 Chr. 10:9ff.; Isa. 39:2).

mad [מַד, **4055**]

mad is a noun found twelve times with the dual senses of "clothing," "armor" — though the former meaning predominates. In 1 Sam. 17:38ff. ***mad*** denotes the "armor" of King Saul. (→ CLOTHING)

ḥagôrāh [חֲגוֹר, **2290**]

ḥagôrāh is a noun referring to military "arms" in 2 Kgs. 3:21, and to a "warrior's belt" in 2 Sam. 18:11; 1 Kgs. 2:5.

NT Words

hoplon [ὅπλον, *3696*]

hoplon is a noun found in six places, four of which explicitly refer to "arms" or "weapons." John 18:3 indicates literal weaponry. Rom. 6:13 makes reference to the spiritual "armor" of light; 2 Cor. 6:7 speaks of the "armor" of righteousness; and 2 Cor. 10:4 describes the "(spiritual) weapons" of divine "warfare."

hoplizō [ὁπλίζω, *3695*]

hoplizō is a rare verb found only in 1 Pet. 4:1 referring to the symbolic act of "arming" ourselves with the Christ-like attitude of willingness to suffer for righteousness' sake.

panoplia [πανοπλία, *3833*]

panoplia is a noun denoting "armor" in all three occurrences of the term. In Luke 11:22 the literal "armor" of a soldier is indicated. However, Eph. 6:11, 13 both refer to the metaphor of "the armor of God" — weaponry used in the spiritual warfare waged by the believer.

kathoplizō [καθοπλίζω, *2528*]

kathoplizō is a rare verb, found only in Luke 11:21 with the meaning "to supply with arms, or weapons."

Additional Notes

Like the Old Testament terms ***māgēn*** and ***nesheq***, ***hopla*** and ***panoplia*** in the New Testament also refer literally as well as metaphorically to "weapons" or "arms." In the New Testament as in the Old, there is an emphasis on the metaphorical use of these terms. In the case of ***panoplia***, the emphasis is a wholly positive one. With ***hopla*** there is a dominant positive emphasis as well. In addition, however, there is a negative connotation associated with the word in Rom. 6:13, where Paul refers to parts of the body being used as "instruments" (plural) of unrighteousness. In all other instances (see above), the metaphorical use of the word is wholly positive and very significant as a means of encouraging the believer in his struggle against satanic opposition.

There is, therefore, a progression in thought associated with the idea of "weapons" from the Old to the New Testament. The Old Testament frequently refers to literal weaponry, but also uses it as a powerful metaphor — particularly with reference to God as "shield" giving absolute protection to his people. In the old covenant there was both a physical as well as a spiritual element in that guarantee. When we come to the New Testament, however, the "armor of God" as it is referred to in Eph. 6:10ff. is completely spiritual in nature — though nonetheless real and effective against the enemy. Significantly, there is a specific Old Testament precedent, in Isa. 59:16ff., for the Pauline description of the divine armor in Ephesians 6. Although the words for armor are not found there, the phenomenon is certainly present. Such a bequeathing of divine protection for the people of God, both corporately and individually, has been made possible in the new covenant only by the outpouring of the Spirit of God in the wake of the finished work of Jesus Christ in accomplishing our salvation.

ARMY

OT Words

ḥayil [חַיִל, **2428** (**2429** Aramaic)]

ḥayil is a common noun occurring nearly 250 times with a variety of meanings centered on the dual senses of "strength," "ability" as well as "wealth," "riches" — though the former is far more prominent.

Included in this field of meaning is the sense of "army." (→ ABILITY → RICH)

References to "armies" of men include those of Egypt (cf. Exod. 14:9; Jer. 37:5; Ezek. 17:17); Babylon (cf. 2 Kgs. 25:5; Jer. 32:2; 34:1, 7, 21; 39:1ff.; Ezek. 29:18ff.); Persia (cf. Neh. 2:9); and the "kings of the North and South" (Dan. 11:7, 13, 25ff.). Other general references to military forces include 1 Kgs. 20:19ff.; 1 Chr. 11:26; 2 Chr. 13:3; Isa. 43:17; Ezek. 27:10ff. The Aramaic form of the noun is rare, found only in Dan. 3:20, denoting the army of Babylon.

ḥayil is also found in metaphorical contexts such as Ezek. 37:10, referring to the "army" of the nation of Israel depicted as a resurrected host of corpses, given "new life" by God in being brought back to the land of Israel from captivity. Ezek. 38:4, 15 make reference to the "armies" of "Gog and Magog," a possible symbolic reference to the forces of Babylon — though this is by no means a universally accepted interpretation. In Joel 2:11, 25 ***ḥayil*** most likely portrays a terrible locust plague as a punishment from God, depicted in terms of the invading "army" of Yahweh.

ṣābā' [צָבָא, 6635]

ṣābā' is a very common noun occurring around 450 times with the predominant sense of "host(s)," plus the allied senses of "war," "army." The meanings "host" and "army" often overlap. Dominant in the usage of ***ṣābā'*** is its link with the divine name to form the title "Lord of Hosts." (→ GOD → WARFARE)

General references to "army," "host" include Gen. 21:22; Judg. 4:2ff.; 1 Sam. 12:9; Ps. 68:12. Particular mention of the people of Israel as "the army of God" is made in Exod. 6:26; 12:41. The armies of Egypt and Assyria are noted in Exod. 7:4; 2 Chr. 33:11 respectively, as is the army of Israel in 2 Sam. 10:7; 1 Kgs. 1:25; 2:32ff.; Ps. 44:9.

Particular mention of "the army of the Lord" is made in Josh. 5:14ff., a likely reference to combined forces of heavenly beings in company with the army of the Israelites, all under the command of Yahweh.

ma'arākāh [מַעֲרָכָה, 4634]

ma'arākāh is a noun found in twenty contexts with the primary meanings "battle," "army."

Reference to the "field of battle" is found in 1 Sam. 4:2; "battle lines" are mentioned in 1 Sam. 4:12; 17:48. The "battle" as such (i.e., military confrontation) is recorded in 1 Sam. 4:16.

The "armies" of Israel and Philistia, designated as ranks of soldiers, as well as the assembly of companies, are indicated in 1 Sam. 17:8, 10, 20ff.; 23:3. And the Israelites are described as "the armies of the living God" in 1 Sam. 17:26, 36.

gedûd [גְּדוּד, 1416]

The noun ***gedûd*** is found in over thirty contexts with the principal meaning of "troop," "band," denoting groups of soldiers functioning as "guerrilla units, or bands" engaged in military raids or sorties (cf. Gen. 49:19; 1 Sam. 30:8, 15, 23; 2 Sam. 3:22; 4:2; 2 Kgs. 5:2; 6:23; 13:20ff.; 24:2; Ps. 18:29).

In addition, ***gedûd*** specifically refers to the "army" of Israel in 2 Chr. 25:9ff. Elsewhere, the term also denotes "bands of robbers" in Hos. 6:9, 7:1.

NT Words

strateuma [στράτευμα, *4753*]

strateuma is a noun occurring eight times, meaning "army" as well as "soldiers," "men of war."

References to "armies" include those in Matt. 22:7; Rev. 9:16. ***strateuma*** also refers to the apocalyptic armies of the heavenly Christ-king and those of the evil one (cf. Rev. 19:14, 19).

In addition, "soldiers" are mentioned in Luke 23:11; Acts 23:10, 27.

stratopedon [στρατόπεδον, *4760*]

stratopedon is a rare noun occurring only in Luke 21:20 with reference to "armies" that will surround Jerusalem.

parembolē [παρεμβολή, *3925*]

parembolē is a noun found in ten contexts, referring primarily to "army barracks" in Acts 21:34ff.; 22:24; 23:10, 16, 32. Heb. 13:11 makes specific reference to "foreign armies."

ARRANGE

OT Words

'ārak [עָרַךְ, 6186]

'ārak is a verb occurring nearly eighty times with the primary meanings of "arrange," "set, put in order" in a variety of contexts.

General references to "arranging" things include Josh. 2:6; Prov. 9:2. In particular, wood "laid out" in preparation of sacrificial offering is indicated in Gen. 22:9; Lev. 1:7; 1 Kgs. 18:33. The careful "arranging" of the sacrificial animal on the altar is noted in Lev. 1:8, 12; 6:12. In other ceremonial contexts, the perpetual bread-offering to Yahweh is set out in Exod. 40:23; Lev. 24:8. In prophetic contexts, a table "laid out" for idolatrous worship and feasting is indicated in Isa. 65:11; Ezek. 23:41. Elsewhere, and more commonly, battle lines are "drawn up" for battle in Judg. 20:20ff.; 1 Sam. 17:2ff.; 2 Sam. 10:8ff.; 1 Chr. 19:9ff.; Jer. 6:23; 50:9, 14; Joel 2:5.

Where God is the subject of this verb, he is said to "arrange" (i.e., "make provision for") every detail of the covenant promises given to David in 2 Sam. 23:5. Then, Yahweh is said to "arrange" (i.e., "prepare") a victory meal in the presence of his defeated foes (cf. Ps. 23:5). Then, in Isa. 30:33, "Topheth," a metaphor for a place of fiery torment, is said to "have been prepared" for the King of Assyria.

ARRIVE

OT Words

bô' **[בּוֹא, 935]**

bô' is a common verb occurring nearly 2,500 times with the primary meanings "come," "bring," "enter," "go," plus a wide variety of associated nuances.

One of these nuances expresses the meaning "arrive at" in the sense of "come to," with each reference designating a geographic location, usually a town or city (e.g., Gen. 35:6; Exod. 15:27; Deut. 1:19; Judg. 9:31; Ruth 1:19; 1 Sam. 15:5; Isa. 35:10; Jer. 20:6; Ezek. 17:12).

NT Words

katantaō **[καταντάω, *2658*]**

katantaō is a verb found thirteen times meaning "arrive at," "come to" — designating a geographic location in most cases (cf. Acts 16:1; 18:19ff.; 20:15; 21:7; 25:13; 26:7ff.; 27:12; 28:13). See also 1 Cor. 10:11; 14:36 for "non-geographic" usage. (→ ATTAIN)

katapleō **[καταπλέω, *2668*]**

katapleō is a rare synonym with ***katantaō***, above, found only in Luke 8:26 and also denoting "geographic arrival."

erchomai **[ἔρχομαι, *2064*]**

erchomai is another common verb with the primary sense of "come" in most of the nearly 650 occurrences of the term, along with various nuances. Occasionally, the meaning "come to," in the sense of "arrive at or in" a particular destination is indicated (cf. Matt. 17:24; Mark 9:33; 10:46; Luke 2:51; John 12:1; Acts 13:13; 17:1; 20:14; 28:16).

paraginomai **[παραγίνομαι, *3854*]**

paraginomai is another synonymous term for the entries listed above. It occurs nearly forty times with the primary meaning "to come." However, in several places the term denotes the action of "arriving at" a particular location (cf. Luke 11:6; Acts 9:26; 13:14; 14:27; 15:4; 1 Cor. 16:3).

ARROW

OT Words

ḥēṣ **[חֵץ, 2671]**

The noun ***ḥēṣ*** occurs around fifty times, denoting "arrow(s)" as a weapon. The term is used both literally and metaphorically.

Literal references to "arrows" as a weapon are found in 1 Sam. 20:20ff.; Ps. 127:4; Prov. 7:23; Isa. 5:28; 37:33; Jer. 51:11; Ezek. 39:3 9.

Metaphorical usage of the term is indicated in contexts where God is said to shoot "arrows" to defeat his enemies (cf. Num. 24:8; Deut. 32:23, 42; 2 Sam. 22:15; Pss. 7:13; 18:14; 64:7; 144:6). Conversely, there is reference to the wicked who direct their "arrows" against the godly in order to harass and persecute them (cf. Pss. 11:2; 64:3). The tongue is also described as a "deadly arrow" in Jer. 9:8. The "arrows" of God are also depicted as instruments of divine punishment, a chastisement for his disobedient people as well as the nations (cf. Job 6:4; Ps. 38:2; Ezek. 5:16; Zech. 9:14). In particular, the "Suffering Servant" figure is portrayed in Isa. 49:2 as an "arrow" fashioned by Yahweh for the purpose of bringing judgment against the nations.

ḥāṣāṣ **[חָצָץ, 2687]**

ḥāṣāṣ is a rare variant of ***ḥēṣ***, above, found only in Ps. 77:17, referring to lightning bolts as "arrows" coming from God.

resheph **[רֶשֶׁף, 7565]**

The noun ***resheph*** is found seven times, usually denoting "thunderbolt," "coals," "burning heat." In Ps. 76:3, however, the term refers to the "flaming arrows" of God's enemies destroyed by him along with other weapons of war.

ASCEND → ARISE

ASHAMED

OT Words

bôsh **[בּוֹשׁ, 954]**

This is one of several terms for "shame" in the Old Testament and occurs about one hundred times. In the majority of these instances, ***bôsh*** refers to "shame" either as a direct consequence of sin and therefore the inevitable result of divine punishment, or as something from which God's people will be delivered. It can be applied in an individual or a corporate sense, and it can refer either to Israel or to the surrounding pagan nations.

At the individual level, Ezra expresses great shame before God when confronted with the phenomenon of Israelite intermarriage with foreign women (cf. Ezra 9:6). He is also ashamed to accept the offer of an escort from the Persian king prior to his return from exile because it would reflect poorly on his faith in God (or lack thereof, cf. Ezra 8:22). The psalmist, on the other hand, prays that God will keep him from being put to shame as a result of his enemies gaining the better of him (cf. Pss. 25:2, 20; 31:1, 17; 71:1). And, as a corollary to this, he beseeches God to put his enemies to shame and thereby bring judgment on them (cf. Pss. 6:10; 25:3; 31:17; 35:4, 26; 40:14; 70:2; 71:13; 83:17; 86:17; 97:7; 109:28; 129:5). The book of Proverbs denounces the one who brings shame either to himself or others (cf. Prov. 10:5; 12:4; 14:35; 17:2; 19:26; 29:15).

In the Prophets, "shame" is applied both to Israel and to the nations. As far as Israel is concerned, her shame is intimately bound up with her rejection of Yahweh and the ultimate judgment of invasion — firstly by Assyria, and then later at the hands of the Babylonians (cf. Mic. 3:7; Hos. 4:19; 10:6; Ezek. 16:52; 36:32; Jer. 9:19; 12:13; 14:3, 4; 15:9; Isa. 1:29; 65:13; 66:5). In these contexts, the shaming of Israel is seen as divine retribution and chastisement. As a corollary to this, it is precisely Israel's lack of shame for her sin that precipitates the onset of divine punishment (cf. Jer. 6:15; 8:12). But the references in this context are not all negative, for it is the mercy and compassion of God that counterbalance his justice. The result is a promise to his people that they will be delivered from their shame, after their time of punishment has passed (cf. Isa. 45:17; 49:23; 50:7; 54:4; Jer. 31:19; Ezek. 16:63; Joel 2:26, 27; Zeph. 3:11). And what is more, these texts imply that the people of God will be truly ashamed of their sin and will experience a profound transformation of spirit. Note also Zech. 13:4, where there is a vision of national cleansing from sin and where it is said that the prophets will be ashamed of their prophesying.

The shame of the nations is also a common theme found in the Prophets. As with Israel, such shame is designated as the inevitable consequence of the outpouring of divine wrath. This applies to Moab (cf. Isa. 48:13), who will be ashamed of their gods since they will be unable to nullify the judgment of Yahweh. This is both a statement against the people of Moab and a mockery of their deities. This shame also applies to Hamath (cf. Jer. 49:23); Babylon (cf. Jer. 50:12; 51:47); Sidon (cf. Isa. 23:4); all idol makers (cf. Isa. 45:16); evildoers (cf. Pss. 44:7; 53:5); and pagan nations in general (cf. Isa. 41:11; 42:17; 44:9, 11; Ezek. 32:30). In the case of the apostate nations, their shame is unremitting. Unlike Israel, these people will not have their shame removed. It must be recognized, however, that such a judgment does not mean that there will be no faithful remnant redeemed from the nations. This "shaming" refers only to those who steadfastly and continually refuse to put their faith in the God of Israel. The context of Scripture makes it quite clear elsewhere that there will be a chosen number of believers taken from the nations.

bûshāh [בּוּשָׁה, 955]

This is a rare feminine form of ***bôsh*** that occurs only four times. It refers twice to the shame of Israel (Ps. 89:45; Ezek. 7:18), once to the shaming of Edom (Obad. 10), and once to the shame of Israel's enemies (Mic. 7:10). Its meaning is exactly the same as that of ***bôsh***.

bōshet [בֹּשֶׁת, 1322]

Another noun derived from ***bôsh***, ***bōshet*** is also identical in meaning and emphasis. ***bōshet*** occurs about thirty times. About one-third of these references point to the sin and punishment of Israel as the root cause of her shame (cf. Ezra 9:7; Isa. 30:3, 5; 42:17; Jer. 2:26; 3:24, 25; 7:19; Dan. 9:7, 8; Mic. 1:11; Zeph. 3:19). The altar to Baal is twice referred to as a shameful thing (cf. Jer. 11:13; Hos. 9:10). On both occasions it is the people of God who are indicted for committing such blasphemy. The shame of the wicked is also in view: for example, Sennacherib and the Assyrian rout (cf. 2 Chr. 32:21); the Babylonians (cf. Hab. 2:10). There are, however, far fewer instances in the prophetic books where ***bōshet*** refers to the shaming of the nations. Again, the psalmist employs this term to invoke shame upon his enemies in the name of Yahweh (cf. Pss. 35:26; 40:15; 70:3; 109:29; 132:18). The psalmist also refers to his own shame before his enemies (cf. Ps. 44:15), as does Jeremiah in his lament (cf. Jer. 20:18). The shamelessness of the wicked is also noted in Zeph. 3:5.

Finally, and positively, there are two references to Israel being delivered from her shame, coming to repentance for her sin, and experiencing a divine transformation of her attitude towards God in renewed devotion to him (cf. Isa. 54:4; 61:7).

kālam [כָּלַם, 3637]

Of the forty occurrences of this word found in the Old Testament, a significant number of them refer to the evoking of shame among individuals or groups of people in a general sense without special theological significance (cf. 1 Sam. 25:7, 15; Job 11:3; 19:3; Judg. 18:7; Prov. 25:8; 28:7; Ruth 2:15; 2 Sam. 10:5; 19:3; 1 Chr. 19:5). On the other hand, there are texts that do emphasize that certain people are ashamed as a consequence of their wrongdoing before God. 2 Chr. 30:15, where the Levites are said to be ashamed on account of their failure to celebrate the Passover for so long, is a good example of this. In Ezra 9:6, Ezra is ashamed of his people's sin. Distinctive uses of ***kālam*** are also found in several places. In Ezek. 16:27, for example, shame at the lascivious conduct of Israel is expressed — not by God, but by the Philistine nation. Such a reaction only serves to amplify the shameful condition into which Israel herself had fallen. Then the psalmist issues his complaint against God for putting his people to shame (cf. Ps. 44:9). In addition, God himself exhorts his sinful people to be ashamed (cf. Ezek. 36:32).

Other references link ***kālam*** to ***bôsh***, ***bûshāh***, and ***bōshet***, above. The punishment of King Jehoiakim in Jer. 22:22 illustrates this very well, since his shame is the direct consequence of his turning away from God and results in his utter rejection by God. Likewise, Isa. 45:16 records that shame is the direct result of God's chastising hand on idol makers. And Isa. 41:11 declares that all the enemies of Israel will be ashamed. Then, Jer. 6:15 refers to Israel's shameless attitude in regard to her sin — the very opposite of a repentant heart. This is also indicated in Jer. 3:3; 8:12.

In a positive sense, by way of contrast to the above, ***kālam*** is also used to refer to Israel's deliverance from sin whereby she will display a truly penitent heart and express shame at her previous behavior (cf. Jer. 31:19; Ezek. 16:54, 61; 43:11). Then, Isa. 50:7 records the confident hope of the servant of Yahweh that he will not be ashamed, because he does put his trust in God.

Finally, as with the previous terms, ***kālam*** is also used by the psalmist to express his fervent prayer that God will bring all his enemies into shame and despair.

kelimmāh [כְּלִמָּה, 3639]

This is the noun derived from ***kālam***, above, and expresses an identical meaning and emphasis, although it is not quite as frequently used (approximately thirty times).

The psalmist expresses his feeling of shame when confronted and persecuted by his enemies (cf. Pss. 44:15; 69:7, 19); reproaches his enemies for their blaspheming of Yahweh by turning "my glory into shame" (Ps. 4:2); and also prays for their humiliation and shaming (cf. Pss. 35:26; 71:13; 109:29).

Israel's shame is also laid bare in Isa. 30:3; Jer 51:51; and her arrogance and shamelessness are noted in Mic. 2:6. The same positive contrast is also reflected in the use of ***kelimmāh*** to describe Israel's deliverance from shame (Isa. 61:7; Ezek. 34:29) and her genuine repentance that evokes shame for her sinfulness (Ezek. 16:54, 63; 39:26; Jer. 3:25). There is also a divine exhortation for Israel to be ashamed (Ezek. 16:52).

The shame of the pagan nations is likewise indicated by the use of this term (cf. Ezek. 32:24, 25, 30; 36:7, 15).

ḥāphēr [חָפֵר, 2659]

ḥāphēr is another synonym for ***bôsh*** and ***kālam*** (see above). It occurs seventeen times and is found in contexts that are identical to those in which the other two verbs are found. There are six instances in the Psalms, for example, where ***ḥāphēr*** is used to invoke shame upon the enemies of Yahweh (cf. Pss. 35:4, 26; 40:14; 70:2; 71:24; 83:17). Israel's shame and disgrace as the result of her sinfulness are cited in Jer. 15:9; Mic. 3:7; Isa. 33:9. Then, in a positive sense, God's transforming power leads Israel to become ashamed and ultimately leads to her repentance (cf. Isa. 1:29).

It is not, however, only a matter of Israel being ashamed of her sinfulness. Rather, there is also the guarantee that God will preserve her from shame by renewing his covenant relationship with his people (cf. Isa. 54:4). All those who look to him with appropriate reverence and awe will likewise be spared shame and degradation (cf. Ps. 34:5).

NT Words

aischynomai [αἰσχύνομαι, *153*]

aischynomai is a verb found five times with the meaning "to be ashamed." The term is used positively in Luke 16:3 to refer to a person's shame at the prospect of having to beg. Elsewhere it is used negatively. In 1 Pet. 4:16 there is the exhortation "not to be ashamed" for suffering as a Christian. Phil. 1:20; 1 John 2:28 both refer to a desire not to be ashamed on the day of judgment. See also 2 Cor. 10:8.

epaischynomai [ἐπαισχύνομαι, *1870*]

epaischynomai is a variant form of ***aischynomai***, above, with the sense of "be ashamed" throughout all eleven occurrences of the term.

Mark 8:38; Luke 9:26 both contain the solemn declaration that Christ "will be ashamed" at the last judgment of those who "are ashamed" of him and his teaching during this life. Paul affirms in Rom. 1:16; 2 Tim. 1:12 that he is "not ashamed" of the gospel of Christ, and he exhorts others to be of the same mind in 2 Tim. 1:8. The attitude of "being ashamed" of one's sinful past is indicated in Rom. 6:21. Heb. 2:11 declares that Christ is "not ashamed" to call his people his "brothers"; and Heb. 11:16 declares that God is "not ashamed" to be called the God of his people.

kataischynō [καταισχύνω, *2617*]

kataischynō is another variant form of the entries listed above, with the meanings "to shame," "put to shame," "disgrace," "dishonor," in several different contexts.

The general meaning "put to shame" in the sense of "embarrass," "humiliate" is indicated, for example, in Luke 13:17; 1 Cor. 11:22; 2 Cor. 7:14; 9:4; 1 Pet. 3:16. Where God is the subject of the verb, he is said to "shame" both the wise and strong of this world (cf. 1 Cor. 1:27).

The negative use of ***kataischynō*** in Rom. 5:5 indicates that the hope of the gospel does "not put the believer to shame"; and those who believe in Christ will likewise "not be put to shame" (cf. Rom. 9:33; 10:11; 1 Pet. 2:6).

The meaning "dishonor" or "disgrace" is indicated in 1 Cor. 11:4, 5, where it is affirmed that men who pray and prophesy with their heads covered, and women who do so with their heads uncovered, serve to "dishonor" their heads. This suggests that they act inappropriately in worship and thereby fail to bring glory to God.

aischynē [αἰσχύνη, *152*]

The noun ***aischynē*** is found in six places with the predominant sense of "shame," "disgrace" in an oral sense (cf. 2 Cor. 4:2; Phil. 3:19; Jude 13; Rev. 3:18). In Heb. 12:2 the shame denoted is that which Christ was prepared to suffer himself on our behalf. More positively, ***aischynē*** expresses "humility" in Luke 14:9.

entrepō [ἐντρέπω, *1788*]

entrepō is a verb found in nine places, expressing in three of these contexts the sense of "to be ashamed" (i.e., humiliated, disgraced, cf. 1 Cor. 4:14; 2 Thess. 3:14; Heb. 12:9).

entropē [ἐντροπή, *1791*]

entropē is a rare noun denoting "shame," (i.e., "humiliation," "embarrassment") found only in 1 Cor. 6:5; 15:34.

anepaischyntos [ἀνεπαίσχυντος, *422*]

anepaischyntos is a rare adjectival form found only in 2 Tim. 2:15, referring to a preacher of the word who "has no need to be ashamed," for he knows how to accurately interpret the word of God.

atimazō [ἀτιμάζω, *818*]

atimazō is a verb synonymous with the entries listed above, occurring six times with the meanings "put to shame," "suffer shame," "dishonor."

The sense of "treat shamefully" (i.e., mistreat cruelly) is indicated in Luke 20:11. The action of "dishonoring" Christ and God the Father is noted in John 8:49; Rom. 2:23. Acts 5:41 speaks of "suffering shame" for the name of Christ. Rom. 1:24 refers to the "dishonoring" of one's body through immorality; and Jas. 2:6 to the "shameful despising" of the poor.

atimoō [ἀτιμόω, *821*]

atimoō is a rare variant form of ***atimazō***, above, found only in Mark 12:4 with the meaning "treat shamefully" (i.e., cruelly).

atimia [ἀτιμία, *819*]

atimia is a noun found in seven contexts with the consistent sense of "shame," "dishonor" throughout.

The term is used adjectivally in Rom. 1:26 to denote "shameful" sexual relations. The meaning "shame" or "dishonor" in a personal sense is indicated in 1 Cor. 11:14; 15:43; 2 Cor. 6:8; 11:21. The same meaning is applied in non-personal contexts to household utensils with the sense of "menial" or "common."

paradeigmatizō [παραδειγματίζω, *3856*]

paradeigmatizō is a rare verb occurring only twice, with the meaning "to put to open shame" or "hold up to contempt." It is found in Matt. 1:19 in relation to Joseph's unwillingness to publicly disgrace Mary, his betrothed, after finding out she was pregnant. It is also found in Heb. 6:6 in relation to Christ being publicly disgraced as a consequence of his death by crucifixion.

hybrizō [ὑβρίζω, *5195*]

The verb ***hybrizō*** is found in five contexts with the predominant meaning to "treat cruelly, or shamefully" in the contexts of physical assault (cf. Matt. 22:6; Luke 18:32; Acts 14:5; 1 Thess. 2:2).

Additional Notes

There is no doubt that the semantic range of meaning covered by the Old Testament terms for "shame" is much the same as, if not identical to, that of the New Testament Greek expressions. Both sets of terms contain references to the shame of the wicked, to shame as the appropriate accompaniment to genuine repentance, to the invocation of shame upon the enemies of God and his people.

In addition, however, there is one distinctive use of the idea of "shame" that is found in the Old Testament only by implication, but which comes to complete fulfillment in the New. In the Old Testament, "shame" is frequently experienced in the very presence of God as part of the divine punishment. The implication is that "shame" is an inevitable accompaniment to the divine initiative of judgment. Then, in the New Testament, believers are clearly warned to devote themselves in faithful submission to Christ, lest they find themselves "ashamed" at the judgment seat of our Lord. In other words, whoever is ashamed of the Lord in this life will him or herself be the object of the Lord's shame on the day of judgment.

ASHES

OT Words

***'ēpher* [אֵפֶר, 665]**

This term occurs approximately twenty times and means "ashes" in both a literal and figurative sense.

Generally speaking, ***'ēpher*** conveys the idea of grief, anguish, sorrow, and self-effacement in a number of contexts. Abraham describes himself as "dust and ashes" in his dialogue with God concerning the fate of the righteous in Sodom and Gomorrah in Gen. 18:27. It is the patriarch's way of expressing humility in the presence of God. This term also frequently refers to personal distress and anguish — for example, Tamar, after being raped by her brother Amnon (cf. 2 Sam. 13:9); Mordecai's anguish, and that of his fellow countrymen, after hearing news of Haman's plot to exterminate the Jewish people (cf. Esth. 4:13); Job's personal agony in Job 2:8; the psalmist's agony in the face of suffering (cf. Ps. 102:9); Jeremiah's lament over the sack of Jerusalem (cf. Lam. 3:16); the mourning of the "international business community" over the destruction of Tyre (cf. Ezek. 27:30).

There are also a few instances in which ***'ēpher*** is used as an expression accompanying genuine repentance — for example, Job (Job 42:6); the king of Nineveh (Jonah 3:6); Daniel (Dan. 9:3). In Jer. 6:26 there is a divine command to repent, issued to the rebellious people of Judah with reference to "ashes." Conversely, ***'ēpher*** is also found in Isa. 58:5, referring to a contrived repentance that lacks any real substance.

In miscellaneous contexts, ***'ēpher*** refers to the destruction of the wicked in a Day of the Lord judgment oracle in Mal. 4:3; to Job's perceived hopelessness and helplessness (cf. Job 13:12; 30:19); and to the futility of the idol worshiper's hope in his gods (cf. Isa. 44:20).

Finally, on two occasions, ***'ēpher*** refers to the literal ashes of the burnt offering in Num. 19:9, 10.

***piyaḥ* [פִּיחַ, 6368]**

piyaḥ is a rare noun found only in Exod. 9:8, 10 denoting "ashes" or "soot" from a furnace.

***dāshēn* [דָּשֵׁן, 1878]**

The verb ***dāshēn*** has the underlying sense of "enrich," plus allied nuances, for most of the twelve occurrences of the term. In addition, ***dāshēn*** is translated "to remove the ashes" in the context of preparing the bronze altar for fresh sacrifices by sweeping it clean of previous animal remains (cf. Exod. 27:3; Num. 4:13).

***deshen* [דֶּשֶׁן, 1880]**

deshen is a noun found in fifteen places with the dual meanings of "ashes" and "choice food," "delicacies."

The meaning "ashes" is evident in ritual contexts denoting the remains of sacrificial animals slaughtered on the altar (cf. Lev. 1:16; 4:12; 6:10ff.; 1 Kgs. 13:3ff.). In Jer. 31:40 the term refers to "ashes" in relation to human remains incinerated in the Kidron Valley outside Jerusalem.

***'āphār* [עָפָר, 6083]**

The noun ***'āphār*** occurs about one hundred times with the primary meaning "dust" for most of the usage. However, in a couple of contexts the term denotes "ashes" in relation to sacrificial offerings (cf. Num. 19:17); and in 2 Kgs. 23:4 it refers to the "ashes" of idolatrous utensils used in the worship of Baal, destroyed in the cleansing of the Jerusalem temple undertaken by King Josiah.

NT Words

spodos [σποδός, *4700*]

The noun ***spodos*** is found in three contexts. It refers to "ashes" sprinkled on sackcloth and one's body as a symbolic expression of anguish and grief in Matt. 11:21; Luke 10:13. In Heb. 9:13 the term denotes the "ashes" of a heifer sprinkled on ceremonially unclean people as a means of purifying them.

tephroō [τεφρόω, *5077*]

tephroō is a rare verb with the meaning "to reduce to ashes" (i.e., by fire) found only in 2 Pet. 2:6 in relation to the destruction of the cities of Sodom and Gomorrah.

Additional Notes

spodos in the New Testament would appear to be an approximate dynamic equivalent to the Hebrew term ***'ēpher***. However, the use of ***'ēpher*** is more varied than its New Testament Greek counterpart. A similar observation may also be made with respect to ***tephroō***.

ASK

OT Words

shā'al [שָׁאַל, 7592]

This is the most common term for "ask" in the Old Testament, and it occurs approximately 170 times. In about half of these instances, requests are made between human beings in a broad variety of contexts that are, for the most part, mundane and without any distinctive theological significance.

On the other hand, most of the remaining texts contain references to requests or petitions made to God in a variety of significant contexts. For example, King David and Solomon both make requests to God. In David's case it is either to ask for divine guidance in the matter of attacking the Philistines and other enemies of Israel (cf. 1 Sam. 23:2, 4; 2 Sam. 5:19, 23; 1 Chr. 14:10, 14; 1 Sam. 30:8) or to ask permission to go up to Hebron in Judah in order to be crowned as king (cf. 2 Sam. 2:1). Solomon's request for wisdom in response to God's extraordinarily generous offer to grant whatever he wanted is well known (cf. 1 Kgs. 3:5). Solomon's desire for wisdom earns him blessing and favor with God (cf. 1 Kgs. 3:10, 11, 13; 2 Chr. 1:11). In contrast, Saul's requests to God for guidance, unlike David's, are characterized by rejection (cf. 1 Sam. 14:37; 28:6). This is undoubtedly part of the divine judgment against Saul for his rejection of God, a circumstance which drives Saul to consult a medium for guidance and to communicate with Samuel from the grave (cf. 1 Sam. 26:6ff.; 1 Chr. 10:13). As a consequence of this flagrant violation of God's law, Saul is virtually executed by God shortly afterwards. In a battle against the Philistines, the Israelite king took his own life after being struck by enemy arrows. Still in the context of the theocratic kingdom, Ahaz, one of the latter Judean kings, is distinguished in biblical history not for the acceptance or rejection of his request to God, but for not making one at all. Isaiah instructs Ahaz to seek a sign from the Lord; and the king refuses to do so. It is a sign of his cowardice and lack of trust, but God gives him the sign anyway (cf. Isa. 7:11ff.).

On a number of occasions, Israel makes requests to God. There is, first of all, the people's request (out of sheer terror) not to have God speak to them from Mt. Sinai (cf. Deut. 18:16). Then, in 1 Sam. 12:13 Israel asks God for a king through the prophet Samuel. This request was illegitimate — not because they asked, but due to the underlying motive that prompted the people to pose it (viz. that they wanted to be just like the other nations). On a more positive note, ***shā'al*** is used to describe Israel asking God which of the tribes would go up to fight against the Canaanites (cf. Judg. 1:1). Judah was subsequently chosen for the task. Israel's experience in the wilderness, however, was not characterized at all by a faithful attitude of dependence upon God. It is recorded in Ps. 78:18ff., for example, that they put God to the test at that time by demanding that he provide them with the food they craved (cf. also Ps. 105:40). Josh. 9:14 also records their failure to consult God as to the real identity of the apparent sojourners in Canaan to whom they gave safe conduct, promising not to slay them. These people turned out to be the inhabitants of nearby Gideon, and ought to have been put to death in accordance with God's instructions to Joshua and the Israelites (cf. Deut. 7). Later on in their history, the Israelites fail to consult God with respect to their political and economic alliance with Egypt (cf. Isa. 30:2). Ironically, there was a period during the time of the judges when Israel's request to God for guidance resulted in a terrible civil war between the Benjaminites and the other tribes (cf. Judg. 20:18, 23, 27). This was a sign of the spiritual bankruptcy of that age. On a final positive note with respect to the nation of Israel, Jer. 50:5 promises that the renewed and redeemed people of God will repent of their sin and will return in tears to ask their way back to Zion and renew the covenant relationship with their God.

On an individual level (apart from the Israelite monarchy), there are a number of significant contexts in which requests are made known to God. Hannah, the mother of Samuel, asks God for a son in her desperate plea to have her barrenness taken away (cf. 1 Sam. 1:17, 20, 27); the mysterious Jabez (cf. 1 Chr. 4:11) asks God to bless him and enlarge his territory, to which God responds favorably. Abimelech makes a request of God on behalf of the fugitive David (cf. 1 Sam. 22:10ff.). The psalmist cites the request of the Messianic King for God to grant him life (Ps. 21:4) and also utters his own plea that he be allowed to dwell in the house of the Lord forever.

Not only do we have the phenomenon of human beings asking God to fulfill their requests (see → COMMAND → COMMANDMENT), but God also makes requests of humans using the term ***shā'al.*** Deut. 10:12 contains the summary statement of Israel's obligations under the covenant, "What does the Lord your God ask of you; but to fear the Lord your God . . . ?" In his confrontation with Job, God demands some answers to the questions he, God, is putting to him (cf. Job 38:3; 40:7). In a passage of scathing sarcasm and indictment against idolatry and idol craftsmen, God affirms that he asked the idols for answers to his questions, but none were forthcoming (cf. Isa. 41:28).

There is one use of ***shā'al*** on a purely human level that is of some significance in relation to the discussion above. Josh. 4:6, 21 refers to children asking their fathers about the significance of the memorial stones commemorating the crossing of the Jordan. This request is to be taken very seriously by Israelite parents as an opportunity to teach their children about the redemptive actions of Yahweh in history on behalf of his people.

It appears, therefore, that the phenomenon of asking God for guidance, blessing, and help of any kind yields two primary responses from God — acceptance or rejection — depending on one's attitude towards and relationship with him. Then, when God makes his requests known to human beings, it is clear that he is asking them for wholehearted, unconditional devotion to him.

she'ēlāh [שְׁאֵלָה, 7596]

Although this nominal form of ***shā'al*** is rare, occurring only fourteen times, its use highlights some of the major theological emphases of the verb. For example it is used to indicate Hannah's successful request for a son in 1 Sam. 1:17, 27; 2:20. It is also found in the book of Esther where the Jewish queen, married to the Persian king Xerxes, requests that he spare her people and bring judgment upon the conspirator Haman. He grants this plea and thus, through an intriguing series of divinely ordained "coincidences," Haman's plot to annihilate the entire Jewish race is foiled. As a consequence, the redemptive purposes of God for his people remain on track (cf. Esth. 5:6–8; 7:2, 3; 9:12). Then, in Ps. 106:15, the psalmist refers to Israel's illegitimate and ungrateful request for meat in the wilderness when God had so generously provided manna.

dārash [דָּרַשׁ, 1875]

This word has some affinity of meaning with ***shā'al,*** above, but is not a full synonym. ***dārash*** occurs about 160 times with the general meanings of "seek," "search out," or "inquire." In the large majority of cases the meanings "seek" and "inquire" overlap, but this is not always easily discernible. In some contexts the meaning of "searching" may be dominant; in other cases, the meaning "inquire" or "ask" may carry the greater weight. The following discussion will concentrate on those texts that would appear to favor the emphasis on "inquiry" or "asking." (→ SEEK)

dārash is found in a number of places where a legal inquiry is in view — where there is a theological problem to resolve within the Levitical system or a matter of criminal trial for violations of the Mosaic covenant (cf. Exod. 18:15; Lev. 10:16; Deut. 13:14; 17:4, 9; 19:18). In each case, those responsible for making a decision are to take that decision with the utmost seriousness.

A number of texts describe a situation where godless kings of Israel and Judah "seek after" or "consult" with idols. Such activity is culpable and judgment is inevitable, as in the case of Amaziah (2 Chr. 25:15, 20) and Ahaziah (2 Kgs. 1:3, 6, 16). Even Saul's sin in consulting the medium of Endor falls into this category (cf. 1 Sam. 28:7; 1 Chr. 10:14). Israel and her leaders are also declared guilty in this respect (cf. Isa. 19:3; Jer. 8:2; 10:21; Zeph. 1:6; Ezek. 14:3; 20:1, 3). The law clearly lays down warnings and prohibitions against such activity (cf. Deut. 12:30; 18:11). Isa. 8:19 also describes the problem in unambiguous terms: How can Israelites dare speak with, consult, or seek advice from pagan gods, and ignore the one, true, and living God?

On a more positive note there are a number of Judean rulers who are commended for their determination to seek God and inquire of him, rather than pagan deities — for example, Jehoshaphat (2 Chr. 17:3, 4; 19:3; 20:3; 18:4, 6, 7; 1 Kgs. 22:5, 7, 8; 2 Kgs. 3:11); Jehu (2 Chr. 34:3, 21, 26); Asa (2 Chr. 14:4; 15:12); Uzziah (2 Chr. 26:5); and Hezekiah (2 Chr. 30:19; 31:21).

Other kings are condemned generally for their failure to make inquiry of God in a proper way — for example, Saul (1 Chr. 10:14; 13:3); Rehoboam (2 Chr. 12:14); and Zedekiah (Jer. 37:7). And Israel generally is also condemned for consulting God in a hypocritical fashion (cf. Isa. 58:2), or for neglecting to consult him at all (cf. 1 Chr. 15:13).

Genuine, legitimate, and commendable inquiries of God are also noted concerning Ben-Hadad of Syria (or Aram) in 2 Kgs. 8:8, when he seeks help and healing from Yahweh through Elisha the prophet. Then Rebekah, Isaac's wife, is moved to inquire of God concerning the twins in her womb (cf. Gen. 25:22).

As mentioned above, there are a number of uses of ***dārash*** that signify the action of "seeking the Lord." Whether this involves actually inquiring of the Lord, or simply the attitude of a godly spirit, is not always clear. One final text, however, is beyond dispute: Ezek. 36:37 contains a marvelous promise to God's people in exile that, one day, access to him will once more be granted to them and they will again be able to communicate freely with him, without hindrance.

she'ēl [שְׁאֵל, 7593 (Aramaic)]

she'ēl is an Aramaic verb occurring six times with the consistent meaning "to ask (of, for)" (cf. Ezra 5:9ff.; 7:21; Dan. 2:10ff., 27).

NT Words

aiteō [αἰτέω, *154*]

The verb ***aiteō*** is found in approximately seventy places with the predominant meanings "ask," "desire" throughout most of the usage.

The underlying sense of ***aiteō*** is that of "making request." General references include Matt. 14:7; 27:58; Mark 6:22; Luke 1:63; John 4:9ff.; Acts 3:14. ***aiteō*** describes requests for money or food in Matt. 5:42; Luke 6:30. 1 Cor. 1:22 declares that Jews "ask" or "make demands" for miraculous signs.

Petitioning God in prayer is also indicated in the semantic range of ***aiteō***, most commonly in relation to material needs (cf. Matt. 6:8; 7:7ff.; Mark 11:24; Luke 11:9ff.; John 11:22; 16:23ff.; Eph. 3:20; Jas. 1:5ff.; 1 John 3:22; 5:14ff.). Incorporated in these references is the willingness of God to grant these requests when they are made with due recognition of his name (i.e., in accord with the divine will and purpose). Allied with these texts are those that contain references to requests made of Christ. In John 14:13ff.; 15:7, 16, Jesus affirms that he will do whatever his people ask of him in his name. Elsewhere, some of his disciples "make an (illegitimate) request" of him that is denied to them (cf. Mark 10:35ff.). In Col. 1:9 the apostle Paul, in prayerful request on behalf of the Colossian believers, "asks" for them to be filled with spiritual knowledge.

apaiteō [ἀπαιτέω, *523*]

apaiteō is a rare verb found only twice. In Luke 6:30 it means "to ask again, a second time." In Luke 12:20 it is used passively in the context of a rich man's soul "being required of him" by God.

erōtaō [ἐρωτάω, *2065*]

The verb ***erōtaō*** occurs about sixty times with the underlying sense of "ask" and includes various nuances such as "ask a question," "beg," "make a request," and "sue for peace."

The action of "asking (with earnestness)" in the sense of "beg," "plead" is indicated, for example, where Jesus is begged to respond to various crisis situations, usually involving a need for healing (cf. Matt. 15:23; Mark 7:26; Luke 4:38; 7:3; John 4:47). "Begging" for money is noted in Acts 3:3. Apostolic exhortations to live for God in accordance with his revealed ways are found in 1 Thess. 4:1; 5:12; 2 Thess. 2:1; 2 John 5.

General references to "asking a question" include John 1:19ff.; 5:12; 9:15ff. In particular, ***erōtaō*** describes questions posed by the hearers of Jesus and by Jesus himself (cf. Matt. 16:3; 21:24; Mark 4:10; Luke 5:3; 20:3; John 9:2; 16:19). In Luke 9:45, the disciples are afraid to ask Jesus questions because of their ignorance and confusion.

References to "making a request" are found in Luke 14:18ff.; John 4:40; 12:21; 19:31, 38; Acts 10:48; 23:18. Jesus himself makes requests of his Father on behalf of his people in John 14:16; 16:23; 17:9ff.

The meaning "sue for peace" is indicated in Luke 14:32.

eperōtaō [ἐπερωτάω, *1905*]

eperōtaō is a variant form of ***erōtaō***, above, occurring about sixty times with the consistent sense of "ask a question."

General references include John 18:7; Acts 5:27; 1 Cor. 14:35. More commonly, the term denotes questions asked of Jesus by his hearers, and of them by him (cf. Matt. 12:10; 22:23, 35ff.; Mark 7:5; 9:11ff.; 10:2, 17; 14:60ff.; 15:2ff.; Luke 2:46; 17:20). Mark 12:34 records the incident where no one dared ask Jesus any more questions in order to save further embarrassment.

Then, in Mark 5:9; Luke 20:40, specific mention is made of Christ's interrogation of a demon.

pynthanomai [πυνθάνομαι, *4441*]

pynthanomai, found in twelve places, is synonymous with the entries listed above. All but one indicate the meaning "ask" in the sense of either "demand" or "inquire" (cf. Matt. 2:4; Luke 15:26; 18:36; John 4:52; 13:24; Acts 4:7; 10:18, 29, 33; 21:33; 23:19ff.).

exetazō [ἐξετάζω, *1833*]

exetazō is a rare verb found in only three places with the meaning "make an inquiry" in Matt. 10:11; and "ask a question" in John 21:12. See also Matt. 2:8, where the translation "search diligently" presupposes stringent inquiries being made.

anakrinō [ἀνακρίνω, *350*]

anakrinō is a verb found sixteen times in all with the primary meaning of "examine," as well as the subsidiary senses of "ask," "judge." (➠ EXAMINE ➠ JUDGE)

parakaleō [παρακαλέω, *3870*]

parakaleō is a verb occurring around one hundred times with the dual meanings "to comfort" and "plead with" (i.e., ask in earnestness, beg, exhort). This latter sense predominates. (➠ COMFORT)

General references to the action of "pleading" and associated nuances include Matt. 18:29; Acts 13:42; 16:9; 21:12; 2 Cor. 2:8; 9:5; Phlm. 9, 10. Urgent appeals to Christ for healing are made in Matt. 8:5; 14:36; Mark 1:40; 5:23; 8:22. Paul "pleads with" God for the removal of his "thorn in the flesh" in 2 Cor. 12:8. Demons "beg" Christ to send them into a herd of swine in Matt. 8:31ff.; Mark 5:10ff.; Luke 8:32. There are numerous strong appeals for God's people to maintain a vital, faithful, and dependent relationship with him in their Christian life (e.g., Acts 11:23; 15:32; Rom. 12:1; 15:3; 1 Cor. 1:10; Eph. 4:1; Phil. 4:2; 1 Thess. 4:1; 2 Thess. 3:12; 1 Tim. 6:2; Titus 2:6; Heb. 3:13; 13:19ff.; 1 Pet. 2:11; 5:1; Jude 3). Then, in Acts 2:40; 2 Cor. 5:20, people are "urged" to be reconciled to God.

In Matt. 26:53 Christ declares his capacity "to make an appeal" to his Father to rescue him from the cross, should he so desire.

Additional Notes

Broadly speaking, the New Testament and Old Testament usage with respect to "asking" or "making requests" is approximately the same. The Hebrew terminology, however, does not differentiate between persons of equal or unequal standing making requests of one another, as is the case with the Greek terms.

What is clear is that both the Old and New Testaments emphasize the fundamental importance of making our requests to God with the right attitude. The Old Testament clearly indicates that failure to do this brings inevitable judgment. It is often the people of Israel who are guilty of such an offense. In stark contrast, Jesus always makes requests of his Father in the most appropriate way. This is particularly noticeable in John's Gospel, where Jesus' requests to God relate to the ongoing divine plan of salvation to which Jesus is fully committed. In John 14:16, for example, Jesus asks that the Father send his promised Holy Spirit, the Counselor — the one to whom is committed the divine task of carrying on and applying the work of Jesus. Then, in John 16:26, the work of the Holy Spirit is implied when Jesus promises his disciples that they will be able to ask the Father anything in the name of the Son. As Jesus models himself, the God-honoring request will be made in an attitude of humble submission to God. Although Jesus is indeed the equal of God in essence, he never spoke to his Father or made requests of him in prayer during his earthly life in any way other than with the greatest respect. Such an attitude is likewise commended to us. We are also encouraged to make our requests known to him with reverent boldness (cf. Phil. 4:6; Heb. 10:19). If such an attitude is evident, then the Scriptures make it clear that God will honor those requests. As a consequence, the redemptive purposes of God are advanced. Jesus provides us with the supreme example of just such an attitude.

See Also: ➠ REQUEST ➠ REQUIRE ➠ SEEK

ASLEEP

OT Words

shākab [**שָׁכַב, 7901**]

This term occurs around two hundred times but only means "sleep" in a physiological sense in approximately one-third of these contexts. For the remaining occurrences of ***shākab***, the contexts divide fairly evenly between "sleeping" as a euphemism for sexual intercourse (approximately fifty times) and "sleep" as a euphemism for death (approximately sixty times).

The references to "sleep" in the ordinary, natural sense are distributed throughout the whole of the Old

Testament. In some cases ***shākab*** is translated "lie down" yet, by and large, sleeping is implied in these contexts. In narrative contexts such as the Former Prophets, the term is used without any special significance. In Job, however, sleep (or rather, lack of it) is referred to in a context of Job's own suffering and despair. In some ways it is likened to a death experience (cf. Job 3:13; 7:4; 14:12; 21:26; 27:19). Ecclesiastes also refers to loss of sleep as a result of anxiety and stress (cf. Eccl. 2:23).

As a euphemism for death, ***shākab*** is found in the books of Kings and Chronicles, for example, as a universal technical expression for recording the deaths of the kings of Israel (North) and Judah (South). The expression simply states ". . . slept with his fathers." In prophetic contexts, the word is used with similar overtones in certain instances, where divine judgment is declared to be the cause of one's "lying" or "sleeping" (i.e., in death). This is predicated of Egypt and her allies (cf. Ezek. 32:19, 21, 32); Meshech and Tubal (cf. Ezek. 32:27); Babylon (cf. Isa. 43:17); Israel (cf. Isa. 50:11); and Judah (cf. Lam. 2:21).

More significant still is the way in which ***shākab*** is used metaphorically and euphemistically to refer to the action of sexual intercourse. The contexts indicated are both appropriate (i.e., within the confines of marriage) and inappropriate (i.e., adultery, promiscuity, fornication, and idolatry) — and it is the latter that predominates in the Old Testament. For example, the incestuous activity of Lot's daughters (cf. Gen. 19); the lecherous attentions of Potiphar's wife towards Joseph (cf. Gen. 39:7ff.); David's adultery with Bathsheba (cf. 2 Sam. 11:4); Amnon's rape of Tamar (cf. 2 Sam. 13:14). Such activity is also explicitly linked with idolatry (cf. Ezek. 23:8; Jer. 3:2).

The great importance God attaches to appropriate sexual behavior is indicated by the emphasis given to the subject, particularly in the Pentateuch, where sanctions against fornication in general abound (e.g., Lev. 20:11ff.; 18:22; 19:20; Exod. 22:16; Num. 5:13, 19; Deut. 22:23, 25, 28; 27:20ff.). In each case, ***shākab*** is used to indicate illegitimate sexual intercourse. Legitimate sexual activity within marriage is also referred to by this term (cf. Gen. 30:15, 16; 34:2; Lev. 15:18, 33; 2 Sam. 12:24).

Another interesting use of ***shākab*** that is related to the area of sexual activity is the action of Ruth towards Boaz, prior to their marriage. In Ruth 3:4, 7 the young "heroine" of the story lies down beside Boaz after he falls asleep and "uncovers his feet." This amounts to a proposal of marriage, and shortly thereafter Boaz does indeed take Ruth to be his bride.

shākab therefore conveys significant metaphorical meaning alongside the natural meaning of "sleep." It is in the distinctive areas of death and intimate sexual activity that ***shākab*** reveals its full significance, both positive and negative. Positively, it describes the natural, untainted expression of intimate sexuality within marriage. Negatively, it refers to death as a judgment from God and prohibits promiscuous sexuality that also brings down the wrath of God, swiftly and inevitably.

NT Words

katheudō [καθεύδω, *2518*]

katheudō is a verb with the underlying sense of "sleep," "be asleep." The term is used both literally and metaphorically and occurs around twenty times.

Literal references to "being asleep," "sleeping" include Matt. 8:24; 26:40ff.; Mark 4:27, 38; 14:37ff.; Luke 22:46; 1 Thess. 5:6ff.

katheudō is also used metaphorically to refer to "death" — the "sleep" of death prior to resurrection. Texts include a resurrection miracle performed by Christ, plus the Christian hope of eternal life following physical death (cf. Matt. 9:24; Mark 5:39; Luke 8:52; Eph. 5:14; 1 Thess. 5:10).

koimaō [κοιμάω, *2837*]

koimaō is a verb synonymous with ***katheudō***, above, found nearly twenty times with the meaning "sleep," "fall asleep," "be asleep." Usage is both literal and metaphorical, though the latter predominates.

Literal references include Matt. 28:13; Luke 22:45; Acts 12:6. Elsewhere, ***koimaō*** denotes the action of "falling asleep" with reference to physical death as the precursor to eternal life in glory (cf. Matt. 27:52; John 11:11ff.; Acts 7:60; 13:36; 1 Cor. 7:39 [here, literally translated "dies"]; 11:30; 15:6, 18ff., 51; 1 Thess. 4:13ff.; 2 Pet. 3:4).

exypnizō [ἐξυπνίζω, *1852*]

exypnizō is a rare verb found only in John 11:11 with reference, in a metaphorical sense, to Christ "awakening" Lazarus "from his sleep" — bringing him back to life.

aphypnoō [ἀφυπνόω, *879*]

aphypnoō is a rare verb found only in Luke 8:23 with reference to Christ "falling asleep."

exypnos [ἔξυπνος, *1853*]

exypnos is an adjectival form found only in Acts 16:27 describing the jailer as one "being awoken from sleep."

hypnos [ὕπνος, *5258*]

hypnos is a noun denoting "sleep" in each of the five occurrences of the term. Literal sleep is indicated in Matt. 1:24; Luke 9:32; John 11:13; Acts 20:9. In Rom. 13:11, believers are exhorted to awake from their "sleep." The usage is metaphorical, referring to an obligation to be on one's "spiritual guard" awaiting the "day" of the Lord's return.

Additional Notes

katheudō and ***koimaō*** function as comparable dynamic equivalents of ***shākab.*** There is, however, one significant difference between the Old and New Testament vocabulary here. The Greek terms do not convey the idea of "sleeping" with reference to sexual activity. The parallels are limited to the areas of natural sleep as well as death. ***koimaō*** also emphasizes the peaceful, restful nature of death as "sleep" for believers in Christ with far greater poignancy and detail than does ***shākab*** for godly believers under the old covenant. The difference is accounted for in the person and work of Christ, whose supreme self-sacrifice guarantees that death no longer holds any fears for the genuine believer. A far greater emphasis on the significance of life after death is found in New Testament teaching as a consequence of Jesus Christ's fulfillment of God's redemptive purposes.

See Also: → AWAKE → SLEEP

ASS

OT Words

'ātôn [אָתוֹן, **860**]

This is one of two Hebrew terms for "ass" or "donkey" in the Old Testament; it occurs approximately thirty times. ***'ātôn*** is used either in reference to people's wealth — for example, the patriarchs (cf. Gen. 12:16; 32:15; 45:23; 49:11); Job (cf. Job 1:3, 14); or the animal as a conventional beast of burden. Note, for example, Balaam (cf. Num. 22:21ff.), and Kish, Saul's father (cf. 1 Sam. 9:3ff.; 10:2ff.). Interestingly, Balaam's donkey is the only animal in Scripture to be given the power of speech by God (cf. Num. 22:28ff.).

Theologically speaking, Zech. 9:9 is a text of some significance. An ass is referred to here as the mode of transport for the conquering Messianic King who will enter Jerusalem in triumph. The New Testament makes it clear that Jesus' actions, recorded in Matt. 21:5; John 12:14, 15, when he rode into the city of Jerusalem during the final days of his earthly life, are regarded as the fulfillment of this prophecy in Zech. 9:9. This constitutes further evidence of Jesus' true messianic identity.

ḥamôr [חֲמוֹר, **2543**]

This is a synonym for ***'ātôn***, above. The only difference here is that ***ḥamôr*** occurs three times more frequently than ***'ātôn*** (approximately ninety times; cf. Gen. 12:16; Exod. 22:9ff.; Num. 31:28ff.; Deut. 22:3ff.; Judg. 15:15ff.; 1 Sam. 8:16; 25:18ff.; 1 Kgs. 13:23ff.; Isa. 21:7; Ezek. 23:20). This term is also found in Zech. 9:9 alongside ***'ātôn*** (see above).

NT Words

onos [ὄνος, *3688*]

onos is a noun denoting an "ass" or "donkey" in all six occurrences of the term (cf. Matt. 21:2ff.; Luke 13:15; 14:5; John 12:15).

hypozygion [ὑποζύγιον, *5268*]

hypozygion is a rare synonym for ***onos***, denoting an "ass" or "donkey" in Matt. 21:5; 2 Pet. 2:16.

ASSEMBLE, ASSEMBLY

OT Words

qāhāl [קָהָל, **6951**]

In general, this term carries the meaning of "an assembly," "a gathering," "convocation" or "congregation." It has both a general or non-theological sense as well as a specific theological connotation that is characteristic of both Old and New Testaments.

In the Old Testament there is a variety of usage. The term applies to gatherings of people in a number of different situations: to tribal councils of Simeon and Levi (cf. Gen. 49:6); to the enemies of Babylon (cf. Jer. 50:9); Israel (cf. Ezek. 16:40; 23:24, 46, 47); and Egypt (cf. Ezek. 32:3); to the armies of Pharaoh (cf. Ezek. 17:17); Assyria (cf. Ezek. 32:22, 23); Babylon (cf. Ezek. 27:27, 34); and even to a gathering of the dead (cf. Prov. 21:16).

qāhāl is also used to describe the general gathering of God's people without a specific purpose in mind (Exod. 16:3; Num. 14:5; 16:33, 47; 20:6, 10, 12; 22:4; 1 Chr. 13:2, 4; 2 Chr. 28:14; Ezra 2:64; Ps. 26:5; Prov. 5:14; Jer. 26:17; 44:15).

qāhāl also refers to the gathered people of God, who will be assembled in accordance with the covenant promises that God made to the patriarchs and prophets. Gen. 28:3 and 35:11 repeat to Jacob the promise that God originally gave to Abraham regarding the great nation that would come from him. He is told that a great assembly (***qāhāl***) of nations will come from his descendants. Jacob in turn repeats that same promise to Joseph in Gen. 48:4. Then, in Jer. 31:8, the promise is given to the prophet that a great throng (***qāhāl***) of God's people will be returned from exile. This promise was fulfilled about seventy years later.

In Ps. 89:5 ***qāhāl*** refers to the assembly of the holy ones in the heavenly court.

By far the most extensive use of ***qāhāl*** in the Old Testament relates to the gathering of God's people, Israel, for the purpose of ritual assembly. That is, the people gather together for sacrifice (cf. Lev. 4:13, 14, 21; 16:17, 23; Num. 15:15; Judg. 21:5, 8; 2 Chr. 1:3, 5; 7:8; 29:23, 31, 32); to celebrate festivals and observe ritual ceremonies (cf. Exod. 12:6; 2 Chr. 20:5, 14; 30:2ff., 24:6; Neh. 8:17); to worship (Deut. 23:1, 2, 3, 8; 1 Kgs. 8:14, 22, 55, 65; 1 Chr. 28:8; 29:1, 10, 20; 2 Chr. 6:3ff.; Neh. 13:1; Pss. 22:22, 25; 35:18; 40:9, 10; 149:1; Joel 2:16); and to ratify a covenant (2 Chr. 23:3). There are also general references to the Israelite community (***qāhāl***) in a ceremonial setting (cf. Num. 19:20; 2 Chr. 29:28; 31:18; Ezra 10:1, 8, 12, 14; Neh. 5:13; 8:2; Ps. 107:32; Lam. 1:10; Mic. 2:5).

Outside the realm of the ritual setting, ***qāhāl*** is used to refer to the gathering of the Israelites for war in Judg. 20:2 and 1 Sam. 17:47.

In the final instance we see ***qāhāl*** referring to the assembly of Israel as hearers of divine revelation. Significantly, the majority of these instances refer to Israel as the assembled people of God, receiving the law of the covenant at Mt. Sinai (Deut. 5:22; 9:10; 10:4; 18:16; 31:30). In Josh. 8:35 the context is not that of Sinai, but rather Mt. Ebal in Canaan, where Joshua leads the assembled Israelites in a covenant renewal ceremony. Here they reaffirm the pledge of allegiance to God that they had originally made at Mt. Sinai.

In summary, where ***qāhāl*** is used in the Old Testament in a significant theological context it always has reference to the assembly of God's people in their covenant relationship with him. Thus the ***qāhāl*** of Israel receives revelation from God or acts upon that revelation in worship, ceremonial ritual, sacrifice, and even war.

'ēdāh [עֵדָה, 5712]

This term has a similar range of meaning to that of ***qāhāl***, above. ***'ēdāh*** derives from a verb meaning to "appoint," "meet," "gather," or "assemble" by appointment. The predominant general meaning is that of a congregation or assembly gathered for a particular purpose. The nearest dynamic equivalent in New Testament Greek is the word ***synagōgē*** (see below) from which comes the word synagogue. Like ***qāhāl***, ***'ēdāh*** has a general, non-theological meaning as well as a specific theological one.

Non-theological and non-personal usage include a reference to a "swarm" of bees in Judg. 14:8; and a "herd" of bulls in Ps. 68:30. In Job 16:7, ***'ēdāh*** refers to Job's "household." In Jer. 6:18, ***'ēdāh*** means "witnesses." In the remaining two texts in this category, ***'ēdāh*** refers to "band(s)" of wicked men.

In pointing to the general gathering of God's people, ***'ēdāh*** is found predominantly in the Pentateuch. Here it refers to the wilderness "community" of Israel: Exod. 16:1, 2; 17:1; 34:31; Num. 1:2, 16, 18, 53; 10:2, 3; 13:26; 14 (eight times); 16 (fifteen times); 20 (seven times); 27:2, 3, 14; 32:2, 4; Josh. 9:19, 21, 27; 18:1; 22:16ff.; Pss. 1:5; 111:1; Prov. 5:14.

'ēdāh also refers explicitly to the gathered community of God's people in accordance with the divine promise. Ps. 74:2 refers to the past redemptive action of God in delivering the people (***'ēdāh***) of Israel from Egypt. Secondly, Jer. 30:20 contains the promise to restore the community of Israel after their threatened destruction and exile.

Likewise, Ps. 82:1 uses ***'ēdāh*** to refer to the heavenly court. This usage parallels that of ***qāhāl*** in Ps. 89:5.

Most significantly, ***'ēdāh*** (like ***qāhāl***) refers to the purposeful gathering of the people of Israel.

'ēdāh refers to general ceremonial gatherings in Exod. 12:3ff., 47 (Passover); Lev. 4:13, 15; 8:3, 5; 10:6, 17; 16:5; Num. 3:7; 4:34; 8:19, 20; 15:24–26; 16:3, 9, 10; 19:9; 25:6, 7; 26:2; 1 Kgs. 8:5; 12:20; 2 Chr. 5:6.

'ēdāh refers to gathering for war in Josh. 22:12; Judg. 20:1 (parallel usage to ***qāhāl*** in Judg. 20:2); 21:10, 13, 16.

'ēdāh refers to gathering to hear revelation from God in Exod. 16:9; 34:31; 35:1, 4; Lev. 9:5; 19:2; Num. 27:20.

There are a number of interesting usages of ***'ēdāh*** that indicate the gathering of a group of people for judgment. The meaning varies from "exacting punishment," "receiving punishment," or "adjudicating on judicial matters."

In Lev. 24:14, 16; Num. 15:33, 35, 36; for example, ***'ēdāh*** refers to the community of Israel who were assembled to execute someone by stoning. Then there are a number of references that point to the Israelite community as a legal assembly which hands down a judicial decision (Num. 35:12ff.; Josh. 9:15, 18; 20:6, 9). Finally, there are a few references that point to various assembled peoples awaiting punishment from God: Job 15:34 (the "company" of the godless); Ps. 7:7 (the assembled peoples); 106:17 (the company of Abiram); Hosea 7:12 (Ephraim "flocking together").

As with ***qāhāl***, ***'ēdāh*** means an assembled group of people in various contexts, both theological and non-theological. The dominant reference is to the congregation of Israel. Moreover, the phenomenon of the covenant makes its presence felt in the usage of the term ***'ēdāh***: both blessing and judgment are experienced by God's people in a number of different circumstances. Both ***qāhāl*** and ***'ēdāh*** are synonymous in that regard. The only significant variation in the semantic range of these two terms is that ***'ēdāh*** carries a non-personal strand of meaning as well (cf. 2:1.)

'aṣārāh [עֲצָרָה, 6116]

This word is used in the Old Testament to indicate a sacred assembly in two senses. First of all, it refers to a legitimate ritual assembly of God's people under the terms of the Mosaic law (cf. Lev. 23:36; Num. 29:35; Deut. 16:8; 2 Chr. 17:9; Neh. 8:18; Joel 1:14; 2:15). In the second place, it indicates either an idolatrous gathering (cf. 2 Kgs. 10:20; Isa. 1:13) or one which is characterized by a spirit of rebellion against the law covenant (cf. Jer. 9:2; Amos 5:21)

Once again, the perspective of the covenant underlies the usage of this term.

qāhal [קָהַל, 6950]

This is the verbal root associated with the noun discussed under ***qāhāl***, above. ***qāhal*** occurs approximately forty times and carries the same breadth of meaning and significance as does ***qāhāl***. The contexts in which they are found are virtually identical.

yā'ad [יָעַד, 3259]

yā'ad is a verb translated variously as "meet," "gather together," "assemble," with the underlying sense of setting a specific time or place for a gathering. (→ APPOINT → MEET)

zā'aq [זָעַק, 2199]

zā'aq is a verb found in approximately seventy contexts with the predominant sense of "cry," "call out." The allied sense of "summon" (to an assembly) is also indicated in this usage. (→ CRY)

regash [רְגַשׁ, 7284 (Aramaic)]

regash is an Aramaic verb with the meaning "assemble (together)," found only three times in Dan. 6:6, 11, 15.

miqrā' [מִקְרָא, 4744]

The noun ***miqrā'*** occurs twenty-three times with the almost exclusive sense of the "sacred assembly" of Israelites gathered together for ceremonial rituals and festivals according to the requirements of the Mosaic law covenant (cf. Exod. 12:16; Lev. 23:2ff.; Num. 10:2; 28:18ff.; 29:1, 7, 12; Isa. 1:13; 4:5).

mô'ēd [מוֹעֵד, 4150]

mô'ēd is a noun occurring around 220 times with the predominant sense of "congregation" or "meeting," signifying primarily the "gathered assembly" of the Israelite people. The term ***mô'ēd*** is most frequently linked to the tabernacle, described as the "tent of meeting" or "tent of the congregation" — the place where the gathered community of Israel came to worship. ***mô'ēd*** is also translated "festival," "appointed time," signifying ritual occasions that possess a specific and significant purpose for the people of God. (→ FEAST)

References to the "tent of meeting" dominate the usage of ***mô'ēd*** (e.g., Exod. 27:21; 29:10ff.; 40:2ff.; Lev. 4:4ff.; 16:16ff.; Num. 1:1ff.; 4:30ff.; 18:4ff.; Josh. 18:1; 1 Kgs. 8:4; 1 Chr. 6:32; 2 Chr. 1:3ff.). The term refers to the leaders of the congregation of Israel in Num. 16:2. ***mô'ēd*** also denotes "meeting places" (i.e., synagogues) in Ps. 74:8; and see also Lam. 2:6.

There is a general description of an "assembly" in Lam. 1:15 — most likely a reference to the invading Babylonian army.

NT Words

synerchomai [συνέρχομαι, *4905*]

synerchomai is a verb found in around thirty contexts, signifying the action of "coming together" with several different nuances. One of these is "gathering together," the "assembling" of a group of people for particular purposes (e.g., Mark 3:20; 14:53; Luke 5:15; Acts 1:6; 2:6; 5:16; 10:27; 28:17). In particular, 1 Cor. 11:17ff.; 14:23ff. refer explicitly to "coming together" for worship.

ekklēsia [ἐκκλησία, *1577*]

The noun ***ekklēsia*** occurs over one hundred times, meaning "church," with the sense of a gathered community of God's people assembled for worship. The word has only a few exceptional "secular" uses.

General references to the "church" as the new covenant community of believers include Matt. 18:17; Acts 2:47; 8:1ff.; 15:38; Rom. 16:1ff.; 1 Cor. 11:16ff.; 14:4ff.; 2 Cor. 8:18ff.; Eph. 3:10; Phil. 3:6; Col. 4:15ff.; Jas. 5:14. In particular, Acts 7:38 makes reference to the old covenant community of God's people as "the church in the wilderness." And Heb. 12:23 refers to "the assembly of the first-born, enrolled in heaven."

Elsewhere, specific references to "the church(es) of God" are found in Acts 20:28; 1 Cor. 1:2; 10:32; 11:22; 15:9; 2 Cor. 1:1; Gal. 1:3; 1 Tim. 3:5; 2 Thess. 1:4. ***ekklēsia*** refers to the letters to the seven churches of Asia in Rev. 1:4, 11, 20; 2:1ff.; 3:1ff.; 22:16. Christ is depicted as head of the church, his "body," in Eph. 1:22; Col. 1:18, 24. ***ekklēsia*** is also used metaphorically of the church, portrayed as a community "wedded" to Christ and the object of his love and devotion (cf. Eph. 5:23ff).

ekklēsia is also found in several places with the "profane" sense of a "crowd" or "mob" in Acts 18:22; 19:32ff.

panēgyris [πανήγυρις, *3831*]

panēgyris is a rare noun, found only in Heb. 12:22, denoting the company of countless angels in "joyful assembly."

synagōgē [συναγωγή, *4864*]

synagōgē denotes the place where Jewish people gathered for worship and instruction from the Hebrew Scriptures. The synagogue also served as the initial focus and location for Jewish evangelism by the early apostles. The synagogue constitutes a meeting place for the gathering of God's people for worship. The term is found only in the New Testament, though the origin of the synagogue dates most likely from the time of the return from captivity in Babylon. There is, however, no scholarly consensus on this matter.

synagōgē is found about sixty times in the New Testament. The synagogue itself as a place of worship is indicated, for example, in Matt. 6:2ff.; 23:34; Mark 13:9; Luke 12:11; Acts 6:9; 9:2; 17:1, 10. It is the place where Jesus preached his first public sermon (cf. Luke 4:15ff.); and where he often taught during the course of his public ministry (cf. Matt. 4:23; Mark 1:21ff.; Luke 6:6; John 6:59; 18:20).

The term is also used metaphorically in Rev. 2:9; 3:9 with reference to the "synagogue of Satan," indicating a spiritually corrupt, or apostate, congregation.

synagōgē is also translated "assembly" in Jas. 2:2, indicating an explicitly Christian gathering.

aposynagōgos [ἀποσυνάγωγος, *656*]

aposynagōgos is an adjective denoting "one who is expelled from the synagogue," or "excommunicated." It is found three times (John 9:22; 12:42; 16:2).

archisynagōgos [ἀρχισυνάγωγος, *752*]

archisynagōgos is a noun occurring nine times denoting "the ruler of the synagogue." This is the position held by Jairus (Mark 5:22ff.; Luke 8:49); Crispus (Acts 18:8); and Sosthenes (Acts 18:17). Other references include those in Luke 13:14; Acts 13:15.

episynagōgē [ἐπισυναγωγή, *1997*]

episynagōgē is a rare noun found only twice. In 2 Thess. 2:1 it denotes the hope of God's people in anticipating "their being gathered together" with him in glory on the last day. Heb. 10:25 contains the exhortation to believers not to neglect "the gathering (assembling) of themselves together" for worship.

Additional Notes

In the New Testament, the term ***ekklēsia*** is used almost exclusively to refer to the new covenant people of God as the "church" in a number of senses. In the context of these references it is clear that ***ekklēsia*** functions as a true dynamic equivalent for the Old Testament ***qāhāl***.

In the first instance, ***ekklēsia*** refers to the local communities of believers in the New Testament — the churches. The term is found with this meaning nineteen times in Acts; five times in Romans 16; thirty times in the Corinthian correspondence; eighteen times in Revelation 1–3; as well as in the remaining epistles: Gal. 1:2, 13, 22; Phil. 4:15; Col. 4:15, 16; 1 Thess. 1:1; 2:14; 2 Thess. 1:1, 4; 1 Tim. 5:16; Phlm. 2; 3 John 6, 9, 10. There is also one reference in the gospels (Matt. 18:17).

It is clear from all these references that ***ekklēsia*** generally refers to the gathered community of believers.

One interesting usage of the term is found in Acts 7:38, where in his defense before the Sanhedrin Stephen refers to the ***ekklēsia*** (i.e., assembly) in the wilderness. This further identifies ***ekklēsia*** with the Hebrew term ***qāhāl***.

In the second place, ***ekklēsia*** refers to the church in the New Testament in a more general theological sense. The meaning is that of the "people of God in congregation." (cf. Eph. 3:10, 21; Heb. 2:12; Jas. 5:14; Rev. 22:16). In addition, there are three specific references to the "church of God" (Phil. 3:6; 1 Tim. 3:5, 15). And finally, in Heb. 12:23, there is an intriguing reference to the "church of the first-born, whose names are written in heaven," which suggests a possible parallel to the heavenly ***qāhāl*** mentioned in Ps. 89:5.

Next, there are a number of significant references to ***ekklēsia*** as the body of Christ in the Pauline epistles (Eph. 1:22; 5:23ff.; Col. 1:18, 24).

The usage of ***ekklēsia*** in the New Testament, therefore, builds upon and complements the portrait of the assembled people of God as depicted by the term ***qāhāl*** in the Old Testament. The emphasis of both ***ekklēsia*** and ***qāhāl*** is on the community of believers in special relationship to God and, by implication, to one another. The fact that ***ekklēsia*** refers to this community as the body of Christ suggests the fulfillment of a relationship that began with the ***qāhāl*** of Israel under the old covenant.

In the New Testament, ***synagōgē*** is almost universally translated as "synagogue," the traditional place of worship for both Jews and Jewish Christians. The usage of ***synagōgē*** in the Gospels and Acts focuses on the synagogue as a center for worship, although the term also implies the idea of the community. Within this broad context there are some significant observations to be made.

synagōgē can refer to a place of worship in a purely descriptive sense, without theological significance (Matt. 6:2, 5; 12:9; 23:6, 34; Mark 1:23; 3:1; 12:39; Luke 7:5; 8:41; 11:43; 20:46).

Other uses of ***synagōgē*** in the Gospels and Acts reflect some significant perspectives on this Jewish-Christian phenomenon of the first century A.D.

In the first place, the synagogue is frequently referred to in the Gospels as the place where Jesus teaches (cf. Matt. 4:23; 9:35; 13:54; Mark 1:21; 6:2; Luke 4:15ff.; 6:6ff.; John 6:59; 18:20); preaches (Mark 1:39; Luke 4:44); and heals (Luke 4:33ff.). In a couple of places, these activities are combined. Luke 6:6–11, for example, records the healing of the man with the withered hand in the synagogue. The miracle is performed during one of Jesus' teaching sessions there. A similar combination of teaching and healing is also recorded in Luke 13:10–13, where the crippled woman is also healed in the synagogue. This phenomenon is repeated in the book of Acts, where the first-century apostolic missionaries (Paul in particular) also use the synagogue as a venue for their preaching and teaching ministry (cf. Acts 9:20; 13:4, 14ff., 42–43; 14:1ff.; 18:26). Acts 15:21 refers to the synagogue as the place where the law of Moses was read every Sabbath.

The significant parallel between these uses of ***synagōgē*** and the Old Testament terms for the assembled people of God is evident from the above discussion. In the New Testament, the synagogue functions as the primary location for the communication of God's word to his people through Jesus his Son and the preachers of the apostolic age. In the Old Testament, the assembled congregation (both ***'ēdāh*** and ***qāhāl***) heard God's word directly through the prophets. Although the term ***synagōgē*** contains the idea of the "place of assembly," the concept of the assembly itself is clearly present in the term as well. In Rev. 2:9 and 3:9, ***synagōgē*** refers specifically to the congregations of Smyrna and Philadelphia as "synagogues of Satan." While this is a negative reference, the explicit meaning of "assembly" rather than "place of assembly" is unambiguous.

Finally, ***synagōgē*** is referred to in the New Testament as a place of punishment and legal pronouncement. The synagogue is a location for judicial process in Luke 12:11 and 21:12. Then, Matt. 10:17 and Mark 13:9 both refer to the synagogue as the place where floggings are carried out. This suggests a possible parallel to the Old Testament phenomenon of trial and judgment, where the "community" of Israel itself formed the location for judicial process (cf. Num. 15:33ff.; 35:12ff.; Josh. 9:15ff.).

It is therefore apparent that there are no significant differences in meaning between the terms ***'ēdāh*** and ***qāhāl***, or between the New Testament terms ***synagōgē*** and ***ekklēsia***. Central to all four terms is the underlying phenomenon of a people who are bound together by a formal and intimate covenant relationship with their God. Such a relationship is essential for the community of God's people.

See Also: → GATHER → MULTITUDE

ASSURANCE, ASSURE

NT Words

plērophoria [πληροφορία, *4136*]

plērophoria is a noun occurring four times, meaning "full assurance, conviction" in matters relating to the believer's hope of salvation (cf. Col. 2:2; 1 Thess. 1:5; Heb. 6:11; 10:22).

hypostasis [ὑπόστασις, *5287*]

hypostasis is a noun found in five contexts, most of which indicate the meaning "confidence," "assurance."

Heb. 3:14 speaks of the believer's confidence in Christ; and in Heb. 11:1 "assurance" is linked with the definition of faith. See also 2 Cor. 9:4; 11:17.

See Also: → FAITH → GUARANTEE → PERSUADE → TRUST

ASTONISH → AMAZE

ASTRAY → ERR

ATONEMENT

NT Words

katallagē [καταλλαγή, *2643*]

katallagē is a noun derived from ***katallassō*** (→ RECONCILE), found in four places with the meaning "reconciliation." However, in each instance it is clear from the context that such "reconciliation" of sinners with God has come about only as a result of Christ's work of atonement through his death on the cross (cf. Rom. 5:11; 11:15; 2 Cor. 5:18, 19).

See Also: → RECONCILE → PROPITIATION

ATTAIN

NT Words

katantaō [καταντάω, *2658*]

katantaō is a verb found in thirteen places with the primary meaning "come to." In most of these contexts, the sense is that of reaching, or arriving at, a particular destination. (→ ARRIVE) In two places, however, the meaning "come to" carries the additional sense of "attain" — "to come to the point of experiencing." In Eph. 4:12 the aim is to "attain to the unity of the faith"; and in Phil. 3:11 the apostle's goal is "to attain (i.e., experience) the resurrection from the dead."

katalambanō [καταλαμβάνω, *2638*]

The verb ***katalambanō*** is found in fifteen contexts, expressing the underlying sense of "lay hold of," "take," "apprehend"; plus other related nuances. One of these nuances is "attain" or "obtain," as in Rom. 9:30 in relation to the Gentiles "obtaining" righteousness. 1 Cor. 9:24 refers to believers striving to "obtain" or "win" the prize of eternal life. (→ APPREHEND; → OBTAIN) In addition, ***katalambanō*** indicates the sense of "attain to understanding" or "comprehend," "understand" in relation to perceiving spiritual truth (cf. Acts 10:34; Eph. 3:18).

ATTEND

OT Words

qāshab [קָשַׁב, **7181**]

qāshab is a verb found approximately fifty times with the sense of "listen to," "give heed to," "hear," "attend to" (i.e., give attention to). The psalmist pleads for God to give attention to (or heed) his cry or prayer (cf. Pss. 17:1; 55:2; 61:1; 66:19; 86:6; 142:6). There are also exhortations to a son to be attentive to his father's instruction or teaching (cf. Prov. 4:1, 20; 5:1; 7:24).

NT Words

prosechō [προσέχω, *4337*]

The verb ***prosechō*** occurs about twenty times with the meanings "beware," "give heed to," or "give attention to." The latter sense is indicated in contexts where particular care is advised in specific circumstances — for example, in the public reading of Scripture (cf. 1 Tim. 4:13); the appropriate response to the word of the prophets (2 Pet. 1:19); and, negatively, in a refusal to give heed to Jewish myths or human traditions (Titus 1:14).

See Also: → CONTINUE → HEAR

AUTHORITY

OT Words

memshālāh [מֶמְשָׁלָה, **4475**]

This is a general Hebrew term for "dominion," "rule," or "kingdom" and occurs seventeen times. There are several levels of meaning associated with this noun.

First of all, there is a metaphorical reference to the "rule" of the sun and moon in the created order by which the light of day and night is to be governed (cf. Gen. 1:16; Ps. 136:8, 9).

Secondly, ***memshālāh*** refers to earthly kingdoms with their rulers. These include Solomon (cf. 1 Kgs. 9:19; 2 Chr. 8:6); Hezekiah (cf. 2 Kgs. 20:13; Isa. 39:2); Seleucus I Nicator, contemporary of Ptolemy I of Egypt (cf. Dan. 11:5); Nebuchadnezzar (Jer. 34:1); and the kingdom of the Medes (cf. Jer. 51:28). There is also a reference to the authority of Eliakim, the chief adviser to King Hezekiah who appointed him in place of Shebna, who had been disgraced (cf. Isa. 22:21).

Lastly, the dominion or kingdom of God is referred to in Pss. 103:22; 114:2; 145:13. ***memshālāh*** here is not simply the earthly locations of the divine kingdom (viz. Israel), but also the nature and quality of God's rule. In Mic. 4:8 there is also reference to the restored kingdom of Judah. This is in the context of Micah 4 — a direct reference to the divine initiative in bringing the exiled Jewish people back to their homeland. The ultimate fulfillment of this promise would not take place in human history. The return to Canaan, however, is a sure indicator that God is in the process of bringing that promise to fulfillment at the end of time. And it was in the first coming of the Messianic King that this promise reached its final stage of fulfillment. His next return will be the climactic one, when his rule over the entire kingdom of God's people will be revealed in its full eternal glory.

shallît [שַׁלִּיט, **7989** (**7990** Aramaic)]

This term occurs fourteen times in the Old Testament. It is similar to ***memshālāh***, above, but refers primarily to the ruler and the authority attached to him. ***shallît*** does not indicate the location or physical extent of that rule.

shallît is actually the form of both a Hebrew and Aramaic term with identical spelling (hence the two Strong's numbers indicated above). The first number refers to the Hebrew ***shallît***, the second to the Aramaic term.

The Hebrew ***shallît*** is used in Gen. 42:6 where Joseph is referred to as the governor (or ruler) of Egypt. Then Eccl. 7:19 and 10:5 refer to earthly rulers in general terms. Eccl. 8:8 refers to the power of human beings (or the lack thereof) in relation to the wind.

In the Aramaic portions of Ezra and Daniel, ***shallît*** is found in several contexts. Ezra 4:20 refers to the rule of Jerusalem in a negative way in the letter issued by Artaxerxes I forbidding the rebuilding of the Jewish capital. Then, in Ezra 7:24, ***shallît*** refers to the lack of authority of the treasurers of the Trans-Euphrates region, who were in fact forbidden to withhold any material assistance form Ezra and other Jewish leaders responsible for the refurbishing and maintenance of the Jerusalem temple. Dan. 2:10 refers to rulers, or kings in general, and 2:15 indicates Arioch as the king's commander. Dan. 4:17, 25, 26, 32 and 5:21 record Nebuchadnezzar's praise for the Most High God of Heaven as the most powerful deity in the universe. And, finally, Dan. 5:29 records that Belshazzar promoted Daniel to "third highest ruler (***shallît***) in the kingdom."

shālat [שָׁלַט, **7980**]

This is the verbal form of ***shallît*** (Hebrew) and occurs in only eight places. With some variation, it means to "rule." Neh. 5:15 refers to the economic oppression within Jerusalem and Judea, talking of leading officials "lording it" over the general population in the post-exilic community. Similarly, in Eccl. 8:9, the writer laments the fact that in the society of his day there is abundant evidence of people oppressing others. In both these cases, the connotation of "rule" is a negative one. In Esth. 9:1 there are two occurrences of ***shālat***, both referring to the overpowering of their enemies. In this context, ***shālat*** implies conquest. On two other occasions in Ecclesiastes the word refers simply to "power" or "ability" (cf. Eccl. 5:19; 6:2), and also to one's control over a business empire (cf. Eccl. 2:19). Finally, there is a reference to the dominion power or rule of sin in Ps. 119:133, where the psalmist pleads with God not to allow such wickedness to overpower him.

tōqeph [תֹּקֶף, **8633**]

tōqeph is a rare noun found only three times, meaning "(royal) authority" in Esth. 9:29; "(royal) power" in Esth. 10:2; "(royal) strength" in Dan. 11:17.

NT Words

exousia [ἐξουσία, *1849*]

exousia is a noun found in approximately one hundred contexts with the predominant sense of "authority" or "right," and "power." "Authority" constitutes the inherent "right" and principal foundation of "power"; and the exercise of "power" is evidence of a duly grounded "authority." "Power" and "authority" are neutral in and of themselves. It is the moral contexts from which these phenomena derive that determine whether "power" and "authority" are good or evil. The scriptural context makes it clear that all "power" and "authority" derives from God — and may be justly utilized, or abused. In any case, God will in the end judge their use or abuse. The meanings "power" and "authority" often overlap, although there is no one English term that describes the fusion of these two senses.

General references to "authority" include Luke 19:17; Rom. 9:21. Civil authority or jurisdiction is indicated in Luke 23:7; John 19:10; Acts 9:14; 26:10ff. Such authority is specifically said to be granted by God in John 19:11; Rom. 13:1ff. A soldier recognizes his obligation to submit to a superior "authority" in Matt. 8:9; Luke 7:8. Civil authorities, or magistrates, are noted in Luke 12:11; Titus 3:1. References to "heavenly authorities" in general are found in Col. 1:16; Eph. 3:10; 1 Pet. 3:22.

In particular, God's "authority" in general terms is indicated in Acts 1:7; Jude 25. General references to "authority" given to human beings by God include Matt. 9:8; Eph. 1:21; and apostolic "authority" is evident in 2 Cor. 10:8; 13:10.

Elsewhere, Christ's "authority" is both implicitly and explicitly declared to be given by God. Explicit indications of Christ's God-given authority are noted in Matt. 28:18; Col. 2:10. In particular, Christ affirms that he has been given authority to forgive sin in Matt. 9:6; Mark 2:10; 6:7; Luke 5:24; to exorcise demonic spirits in Matt. 10:1; Mark 1:27; Luke 9:1; and to execute divine judgment in John 5:27.

General references to God's power are found in Acts 8:19; and in Rev. 6:8; 9:3, 10; 12:10; 16:9 such power is manifested in the execution of divine judgment on sinful humanity. See also Luke 12:5. Divine power is said to be given to Christ in John 10:18; 17:2, and to angels in Rev. 14:18. John 1:12 affirms that God gives power to his people to become his "adopted" children. Such a "power" is linked with "right" or "privilege."

Luke 22:53; 1 Cor. 15:24, Eph. 2:2; 6:12; Rev. 13:2ff.; 17:12ff. refer to evil, or demonic, power. Christ destroys such power (cf. Col. 1:13; 2:15).

exousia can also mean "right." 1 Cor. 9:4ff.; 2 Thess. 3:9 make reference to the "right" to derive material support from one's ministry in the gospel. In Rev. 22:14 the saints in heaven are given the "right" to access the tree of life.

epitagē [ἐπιταγή, *2003*]

epitagē is a noun found seven times with the meaning "command," "commandment" in all but one context. (→ COMMANDMENT) In Titus 2:15 the term denotes the "authority" associated with the pastoral office.

exousiazō [ἐξουσιάζω, *1850*]

exousiazō is a verb meaning "have power, authority over."

The exercise of royal power or authority is indicated in Luke 22:25. In 1 Cor. 6:12 Paul declares that he will not "be enslaved" by anything (i.e., brought under its power). 1 Cor. 7:4 makes several references to the principle or "rule" that the husband does not have power (or rule) over his own body, but over rather his wife, and vice-versa.

katexousiazō [κατεξουσιάζω, *2715*]

katexousiazō is a variant form of ***exousiazō***, above, with the meaning "exercise authority" or "wield power" over. It is found only twice (cf. Matt. 20:25; Mark 10:42).

authenteō [αὐθεντέω, *831*]

authenteō is a rare verb, found only in 1 Tim. 2:12 with reference to the apostle's refusal to allow a woman "to have authority over" a man.

Additional Notes

The semantic range of these Greek and Hebrew terms, taken as a whole, is roughly the same. Of the Greek words referred to above, ***exousia*** and ***exousiazō*** are the richest in meaning and are the closest dynamic equivalents of ***shālat***, ***shallît***, and ***memshālāh***.

Given the fact that the Hebrew terms together provide both a positive and negative perspective on the question of authority, it is worth noting that ***authenteō***, by and large, carries a negative connotation of "self-rule" or "domineering." By way of contrast, ***exousia***, ***exousiazō*** are largely positive in describing authority, both human and divine.

It is also noteworthy that both Old and New Testament terms for "authority," such as ***memshālāh*** and ***exousia*** respectively, have significant spiritual emphases. The principle of God as the ruling power behind the earthly powers and authorities is present in both eras. However, with the coming of Christ in the new covenant age, there is no doubt that ***exousia*** reflects a heightened sense of spiritual authority — foreshadowed in the old covenant and fulfilled in the new.

See Also: → RULE

AVENGE, AVENGER

OT WORDS

nāqam [נָקַם, 5358]; *nāqām* [נָקָם, 5359]; *neqāmāh* [נְקָמָה, 5360]

These three terms may be considered together since they are virtually synonymous. All three words mean "revenge," "vengeance," or "avenge." The verbal form ***nāqam*** has only a slightly different meaning.

Beginning with ***nāqam***, we note that it occurs approximately thirty times, with the predominant emphasis on divine vengeance against both Israel and the Gentile nations. The large majority of these texts reflect this perspective. For example, in 1 Sam. 24:12, David calls on God to avenge the wrongs done to him by Saul. On several occasions God also threatens Israel with his vengeance for covenant violations against him. In these contexts divine vengeance is equated with divine justice and is seen as God's holy response to his people's disobedience (cf. Ezek. 24:8; Lev. 26:25; Ps. 99:8; Jer. 5:9, 29; 9:9; Pss. 8:2; 44:16). There are also a number of references to God enacting vengeance against the enemies of Israel — both for their own wickedness and also for the way in which they treat the people of Israel (e.g., Edom [Ezek. 25:12]; Midian [Num. 31:2]; Nineveh [Nah. 1:2]; Egypt [Jer. 46:10]; Babylon [Jer. 50:15; 51:36]; Philistia's vengeance on Israel will lead to her punishment by God [Ezek. 25:15]; the enemies of God in general [Isa. 1:24; Deut. 32:43]). There are also examples of individuals or groups of people who exact revenge which may be directly or indirectly linked to divine vengeance. Samson, for example, calls upon God to avenge his mistreatment at the hands of the Philistines (cf. Judg. 15:7; 16:28). During the time of Esther, the Jewish exiles exact vengeance on their enemies in the Medo-Persian empire. This is clearly a divine providential judgment even though the name of God is not mentioned in the book (cf. Esth. 8:13). Then there is Saul's solemn oath to avenge himself against the Philistines. Once again, such an action advances the purposes of God in ridding the land of the enemies of his people (cf. 1 Sam. 14:24).

Finally, revenge takes place at a purely human level. In the context of the Deuteronomic law, vengeance is sometimes equated with or linked to a call for justice (cf. Exod. 21:20, 21); but in a general sense it is a procedure that is forbidden (cf. Lev. 19:18). Sometimes vengeance is taken for purely selfish motives (cf. Lamech's boast in Gen. 4:24, and Saul's plan to avenge himself against the Philistines in 1 Sam. 18:25 in order to try and bring about David's demise).

The use of the noun ***nāqām*** (seventeen occurrences) has an almost exclusive reference to divine vengeance, either against Israel or the Gentile nations. There are five references in the former category (cf. Lev. 26:25; Deut. 32:35; Ezek. 24:8; 25:12, 15) and eleven in the latter (cf. Deut. 32:41, 43; Judg. 16:28; Ps. 58:10; Isa. 34:8; 35:4; 47:3; 59:17; 61:2; 63:4; Mic. 5:15). One unique use of this noun is found in Prov. 6:34, where it describes the vengeance of a jealous husband.

neqāmāh is a synonym for ***nāqām*** and occurs twenty-four times. This term, however, refers almost exclusively to the exacting of divine vengeance against the enemies of God and his people. The list of nations in this regard is very similar to those above: Midianites (Num. 31:3); Ammonites (Judg. 11:36); David's enemies (2 Sam. 22:48; Ps. 18:47); the wicked in general (Pss. 79:10; 94:1; 149:7); Egypt (Jer. 46:10); Babylon (Jer. 50:15, 28; 51:6, 11, 36); Edom (Ezek. 25:14); the Philistines (Ezek. 25:17). The prophet Jeremiah pleads for God to take vengeance on his persecutors (cf. Jer. 11:20; 20:12), who also plot to take revenge on him (cf. Jer. 20:10). Then Jeremiah laments the vengeance taken by the Babylonians on his own people (cf. Lam. 3:60). Finally, 2 Sam. 4:8 records Recab's vengeance on Ish-Bosheth, Saul's son — he cut off his head for daring to attempt to wrest the throne of Israel away from David. David then executes Recab and his accomplice for taking the law into their own hands.

yāsha' [יָשַׁע, 3467]

yāsha' is a common verb found in approximately two hundred contexts with the primary meanings "save," "deliver," "help." (→ SAVE)

In several places, however, ***yāsha'*** is also translated "avenge," "take revenge" (cf. 1 Sam. 25:26, 31, 33).

NT Words

ekdikeō [ἐκδικέω, *1556*]

The verb ***ekdikeō***, meaning "avenge," "take revenge" predicated of God with respect to his enemies in Rev. 6:10; 19:2, is found in six places. Believers are enjoined in Rom. 12:19 not to avenge themselves against their enemies, that being God's prerogative alone. In Luke 18:3ff. the sense of ***ekdikeō*** is that of "vindicate," through a plea for justice against one's adversary.

ekdikos [ἔκδικος, *1558*]

ekdikos is an adjectival form derived from ***ekdikeō*** (see above) denoting "one who takes revenge." It occurs only twice. In Rom. 13:4 the term describes a God-ordained ruler as "an agent of (divine) wrath" (lit. "one who takes revenge on God's behalf"). In 1 Thess. 4:6, God himself is described as "an avenger" — one who initiates punishment against the wicked.

ekdikēsis [ἐκδίκησις, *1557*]

ekdikēsis is a noun occurring ten times with the meaning "vengeance," "revenge" and related nuances.

In Luke 18:7, 8, mention is made of God "vindicating" his elect (lit. "taking revenge" on their behalf) against their enemies. The phrase "days of vengeance" is found in Luke 21:22 denoting a period of divine punishment. Rom. 12:19; Heb. 10:30 contain the declaration that "vengeance" belongs to God. "Vengeance" in the sense of "punishment" is indicated in 2 Thess. 1:8; 1 Pet. 2:14. See also Acts 7:24; 2 Cor. 7:11.

Additional Notes

It is evident that there is a consistent emphasis throughout Old and New Testaments in the usage of these terms. The Hebrew term ***nāqam*** and its derivatives function as dynamic equivalents to the Greek verb ***ekdikeō*** and its derivatives. Although there may not be exact correspondence in meaning between the three terms in each group, the overall significance and range of meaning for the concept of "avenge" in each of the Testaments is much the same — divine vengeance directed at both the people of God and the enemies of God's people. This vengeance is never arbitrary but is always linked to the justice of God as an appropriate, be it painful, response to a violation of his commands and requirements. This is especially the case with God's people, who enjoy an enormous privilege under the terms of the covenant. In a very real sense, those who reject God and his purposes after having received knowledge and blessing from him through the covenant will face a much more severe punishment. This was true of Israel in the old covenant, and is even more so in the new. An even more terrible vengeance awaits those who, having known the person of Jesus Christ, turn their backs on him in rejection and denial. Their fate will be worse than those who suffered similar divine wrath under the old covenant. The universal scriptural principle is thus apparent: the greater one's privilege and blessing, the greater one's responsibility in devotion to God and Christ.

AVOID

NT Words

ekklinō [ἐκκλίνω, *1578*]

ekklinō is a rare verb meaning "avoid," found in Rom. 16:17 referring to opponents of the gospel message, whom Paul instructs the Roman believers to avoid. The sense of "turn away from" is indicated in Rom. 3:12; 1 Pet. 3:11.

ektrepō [ἐκτρέπω, *1624*]

ektrepō is a verb synonymous with ***ekklinō***, above, with the primary meaning "turn aside, turn away from" (1 Tim. 1:6; 5:15; 2 Tim. 4:4; Heb. 12:13). In 1 Tim. 6:20, it is translated "avoid" in the context of Paul's admonition to Timothy to "keep away from" godless chatter.

paraiteomai [παραιτέομαι, *3868*]

paraiteomai is a verb found in nine contexts. For the most part it is translated "refuse," "have nothing to do with." In two places, it means "avoid": 2 Tim. 2:23 contains the injunction to "avoid" senseless controversies; and in Titus 3:10 there is an admonition to "avoid" any troublemaker in the church who refuses to accept rebuke.

periistēmi [περιΐστημι, *4026*]

periistēmi is a verb translated "shun," "avoid" in 2 Tim. 2:16; Titus 3:9 in relation to stupid, foolish, or profane talk.

See Also: → TURN

AWAKE

OT Words

qûṣ [קוּץ, **6974**]

qûṣ is a verb occurring about twenty times with the sense of "awake" in several different contexts.

Literal references to "waking up" or "awaking" include 1 Sam. 26:12; 2 Kgs. 4:31; Pss. 3:5; 17:15; 73:20; 139:18; Prov. 23:35; Isa. 29:8; Jer. 31:26.

qûṣ is also used metaphorically of Yahweh in Pss. 44:23; 59:5, where the psalmist pleads with God to "wake up" and take action on behalf of his people. Elsewhere, the term is used metaphorically to refer to resurrection, where people "wake up" or "rise" from the dead (cf. Isa. 26:19; Dan. 12:2). Conversely, reference to "not waking up" is equated with "dying" (cf. Jer. 51:57). See also Joel 1:5; Hab. 2:19.

yāqaṣ [יָקַץ, **3364**]

yāqaṣ is a verb found eleven times referring to "awakening," "waking up" (from sleep).

Literal references include Gen. 41:7, 21; Judg. 16:14ff.; 1 Kgs. 3:15; 18:27. God is said metaphorically to "wake up" in Ps. 78:65. See also Hab. 2:7.

See Also: → ARISE → ASLEEP

AWE → FEAR

AX

OT Words

garzen [גַּרְזֶן, **1631**]

This word occurs only four times in the Old Testament. In Deut. 19:5 it is found in a piece of civil legislation under the covenant, where legal provisions are made for a person who accidentally kills someone with an ax in the process of felling trees. In another legal context, Deut. 20:19 records the prohibition against felling fruit trees around a besieged city with an ax for the purpose of eating their fruit. 1 Kgs. 6:7 refers to the fact that no ax was used in the construction of Solomon's temple. The only occurrence of ***garzen*** in a prophetic context occurs in Isa. 10:15, where the term is found in a metaphor of divine judgment against the king of Assyria.

qardōm [קַרְדֹּם, 7134]

Here is another rare term, found only five times in the Old Testament. Judg. 9:48 records that Abimelech, the renegade "king," cut wood with an ax in order to burn the tower in Shechem along with about 1,000 men and women who had taken shelter there. Shechem had turned against Abimelech and he was taking his revenge. 1 Sam. 13:20ff. refers to the Israelite dependence on the Philistines' superior "iron technology" at this point in time. The people of Israel were forced to go to their enemy in order to have their axes and other agricultural implements sharpened, because there were no blacksmiths in Israel. In Ps. 74:5 there is a probable reference to the use of axes in the Babylonian destruction of Jerusalem in 587 BC. Babylon is not mentioned by name here, but the context suggests the identification. Jer. 46:22 does, however, mention Babylon by name — this time in reference to her assault against Egypt, in which axes are used.

ma'aṣād [מַעֲצָד, 4621]

ma'aṣād is a rare noun denoting "ax" in Jer. 10:3.

magzērāh [מַגְזֵרָה, 4037]

magzērāh is a rare noun denoting "axes" only in 2 Sam. 12:31.

megērāh [מְגֵרָה, 4050]

megērāh is a noun denoting "saws" for stonecutting in 2 Sam. 12:31; 1 Kgs. 7:9; 1 Chr. 20:3; as well as "axes" in 1 Chr. 20:3.

kashîl [כַּשִּׁיל, 3781]

kashîl is a rare noun found only in Ps. 74:6, also referring to "axes."

ḥereb [חֶרֶב, 2719]

ḥereb is a common noun found approximately four hundred times with the primary sense of "sword." However, in Ezek. 26:9 it denotes "axes." (→ SWORD)

NT Words

axinē [ἀξίνη, *513*]

axinē is a rare noun denoting an "ax," found only in Matt. 3:10; Luke 3:9.

Additional Notes

While ***axinē*** is rare in the New Testament, both occurrences of the word refer to John the Baptist's indictment of the Jewish society of his day. The ax laid "at the root of the trees" is a powerful warning directed at any who do not respond appropriately to John's call for genuine repentance.

There is no exact parallel usage of the two Hebrew terms in the Old Testament. Although ***qardōm*** and ***garzen*** are both found in contexts of judgment against Gentile nations, there is no indication of similar "ax" judgments against Israel.

B

BABE

OT Words

taph **[טַף, 2945]**

This term occurs approximately forty times and means "child" in the majority of cases. ***taph*** usually includes infants as well as preadolescent children. The word always refers to children as family members.

In the majority of instances, ***taph*** indicates the children of Israelite families: the patriarchal families of Joseph's brothers (cf. Gen. 43:8; 45:19; 46:5; 47:12, 24; 50:21); Israelite children during the Egyptian captivity (cf. Exod. 10:10, 24) and Exodus (cf. Exod. 12:37); children of the Transjordan tribes of Reuben, Gad, and half of Manasseh (cf. Num. 32:16ff.; Deut. 3:19; Josh. 1:14); Danite children (cf. Judg. 18:21); children of Jabesh Gilead (cf. Judg. 21:10); children of families returning to Canaan with Ezra (cf. Ezra 8:21); children of remnant families under the protection of Gedaliah (cf. Jer. 40:7; 41:16; 43:6). In all of these cases, children are mentioned in connection with their families and as being under their protection.

However, in several contexts the children of Israelite families are singled out for special treatment, either good or bad. In two striking instances, for example, Israelite children are punished along with their parents. First of all there is the capital punishment handed down to Dothan, Korah, and Abiram and their entire families for their rebellion against Moses (cf. Num. 16:27). Then, secondly, in Ezekiel's vision of the apostasy of the people of Jerusalem, there is the anticipated slaughter of those inhabitants, along with their children. Both of these incidents result from a specific divine judgment.

The safety of Israelite children is also threatened in several places. For example, the people of Israel complain bitterly at the border of Canaan that they will be overtaken by the inhabitants of that land and taken captive along with their children (cf. Num. 14:3). Haman's edict (cf. Esth. 3:13) also threatens the very existence of all Jewish families.

Conversely, however, there are also indications that Israelite children are sometimes spared the judgment decreed for their parents. The most striking example of this is the promise that all children of Israelite families of the wilderness generation, aged nineteen years and younger, would inherit the land of promise, rather than their parents (Num. 14:31 — but note also Num. 14:29–35 as a whole). In this case ***taph*** also applies to children over the age of maturity, and not merely to preadolescents.

Children of pagan peoples are also mentioned in the Old Testament, but by and large they figure in contexts of divine judgment where they are destroyed or taken captive along with their parents — Moabite children (cf. Deut. 2:34); Canaanite children (cf. Deut. 3:6). Pagan children outside the land of Canaan were also taken as slaves, if their families did not resist the Israelites (cf. Deut. 20:14). The children of Shechem, whose fathers were slain by Simeon and Levi, and who were themselves taken captive along with their mothers, also suffered a terrible fate (cf. Gen. 34:29). An interesting distinction, however, is made between Midianite boys and girls in Num. 31:17, 18. In this chapter, divine judgment is invoked against the Midianites for leading the Israelites into idolatry. All the males — men and boys (lit. "males among the children") were to be killed along with all the women who had known a man sexually. However, all the virgin girls (lit. "female children") were to be spared — presumably because they were innocent of any immorality at the Peor incident (cf. Num. 25).

It would appear that special favor and protection attached to the children of God's people under the old covenant, whereas divine judgment fell on the children of the pagan nations, along with their parents.

'ôlēl **[עוֹלֵל, 5768]**

A synonym for ***taph*** (see above), ***'ôlēl*** occurs about half as frequently in the Old Testament. The meaning of ***'ôlēl*** is also similar. General references to the well-being of young children, for example, are found in Pss. 8:2 and 17:14, where the indications are that they are blessed by God both spiritually and materially.

The majority of references to ***'ôlēl***, however, are negative. The suffering and destruction of Israelite children is mentioned in 1 Sam. 22:19 (Saul's slaughter of priests and their families at Nob); 2 Kgs. 8:12 (the prediction of Hazael's slaughter of Israelite children and their families); Job 3:16 (Job's lament for stillborn children); Jer. 6:11; 9:21; 44:7; Lam. 1:5; 2:11, 19, 20; 4:4; Mic. 2:9 (all refer to God's judgment on the children and families of Judah and Israel). Pagan children also bear the brunt of divine judgment (cf. 1 Sam. 15:3 [Amalekites]; Ps. 137:9 [Babylonians]; Hos. 13:16 [Samaritans]; Nah. 3:10 [Assyrians]).

'ôlēl is also paired with and distinguished from the term ***yônēq***, which means "suckling child" or "infant at the breast" (see below). This pairing occurs several times (cf. 1 Sam. 15:3; 22:19; Ps. 8:2; Jer. 44:7; Lam. 2:11; 4:4) and clearly indicates that ***'ôlēl*** (and also, by implication, ***taph***) designates a "child " or "children" between infancy and puberty.

yônēq **[יוֹנֵק, 3243]**

This term is a participial form of the verb ***yānaq***, which means "to (give) suck" and refers to a child at the breast. (→ NURSE) It occurs eleven times in this form and is translated either as "suckling child" or "infant (i.e., at the breast)." General references to infants are found in Num. 11:12; Song 8:1; Joel 2:16.

For the most part, however, suckling children share in divine judgment and suffering along with the rest of their families (cf. Deut. 32:25; 1 Sam. 15:3; 22:19; Jer. 44:7; Lam. 2:11; 4:4).

There are, however, two striking exceptions to this usage. One is found in Ps. 8:2, where the psalmist declares that God ordains praise even from the mouths of infants and children. The other reference forms part of the idyllic prophetic portrait of the consummation of Israel's rest and prosperity when the Messianic King will finally come into his kingdom — Isa. 11:8 refers to the infant playing near the cobra's lair without being in the slightest danger.

NT Words

brephos **[βρέφος,** ***1025*****]**

brephos is a noun found in eight contexts with the meanings "babe" (baby); "infant"; "(young) child."

In Luke 1:41ff., ***brephos*** refers to the baby in Elizabeth's womb — John the Baptist, the forerunner of Christ. In Luke 2:12ff., the term refers to the newly-born "infant" Jesus. Elsewhere, Luke 18:15; Acts 7:19; 1 Pet. 2:2 refer to "newly-born infants." 2 Tim. 3:15 refers to one's "(early) childhood."

nēpios **[νήπιος,** ***3516*****]**

nēpios is a synonym for ***brephos***, above, again denoting "babe," "infant," "little child" throughout the fourteen occurrences of the term.

nēpios denotes "little children" in general (cf. Rom. 2:20; Gal. 4:1ff.).

More commonly, ***nēpios*** is used metaphorically to indicate "little children," "infants" as suitable recipients of divine revelation — those who have a childlike devotion to, and trust in, God (cf. Matt. 11:25; Luke 10:21). See also Matt. 21:16. The expression "babes in Christ" denotes immature believers in 1 Cor. 3:1; Eph. 4:14; Heb. 5:13. The simile "like, as a child" is found in 1 Cor. 13:11.

Additional Notes

As observed in the New Testament entry above, there is a considerable overlap and similarity of meaning between the various Greek and Hebrew terms for children and infants. However, it is also clear that the New Testament use of ***nēpios***, particularly, carries with it a distinctive metaphorical level of meaning that is absent in the Old Testament. ***nēpios*** is used almost exclusively to indicate a childish immaturity in the lives of God's people in the new covenant age.

See Also: → CHILD

BACK

NT Words

nōtos **[νῶτος,** ***3577*****]**

nōtos is a rare noun found only in Rom. 11:10 with reference to people "bending their backs."

opisthen **[ὄπισθεν,** ***3693*****]**

opisthen is an adjectival form translated "behind" or "after" in most of the seven occurrences of the term. However, in Rev. 5:1 it denotes the reverse side or "back" of a scroll sealed with seven seals of divine judgment.

BAD → AFFLICT → EVIL → WICKED

BAG

OT Words

kîs **[כִּיס, 3599]**

This word only occurs five times and means "bag" or "purse." ***kîs*** refers three times to a bag containing weights for scales used in the sale of merchandise (Deut. 25:13; Prov. 16:11; Mic. 6:11). In each of these contexts it is clear that God's demand for honesty in business dealings is a primary ethical consideration among his people. Failure to use fair and true weights in business will bring divine judgment. The other two texts refer to the bag as a container for money (Prov.

1:14; Isa. 46:6). The latter passage indicts God's people for illegitimate use of their gold in idolatrous worship.

kelî **[כְּלִי, 3627]**

kelî is a common noun found in about three hundred places, with various meanings including "implement," "container," "instrument," and "weapon," as well as "(household) goods," "baggage." Specific reference to the latter sense is found in 1 Sam. 10:22; 25:13; 30:24; Ezek. 12:3ff.

ṣerôr **[צְרוֹר, 6872]**

ṣerôr is a noun found in seven places, with the meanings "bundle," "bag." The latter sense is found in three places, denoting "bag" in the general sense of "pouch" or "container" (Job 14:17; Prov. 7:20; Hag. 1:6).

ḥārîṭ **[חָרִיט, 2754]**

ḥārîṭ is a rare noun denoting a "bag" or "purse" in 2 Kgs. 5:23; Isa. 3:22.

NT Words

glōssokomon [γλωσσόκομον, *1101*]

glōssokomon is another rare noun denoting "bags" or "purses" used for carrying money. It is found only in John 12:6; 13:29.

ballantion [βαλλάντιον, *905*]

ballantion is a noun found only in Luke 12:33 with reference to a "money bag."

pēra [πήρα, *4082*]

The noun ***pēra*** is found in six places, all denoting a "traveling bag" for taking one's personal possessions on a journey (Matt. 10:10; Mark 6:8; Luke 9:3; 10:4; 22:35, 36).

BALANCE

OT Words

mō'zenayim **[מֹאזְנַיִם, 3976]**

This word is the standard term for "scales" or "balances" in the Old Testament. It has a literal as well as a metaphorical meaning.

Where the literal meaning is envisaged, there is once again a preoccupation with God's demand that his people use honest scales and not defraud their fellow Israelites (Lev. 19:36; Prov. 11:1; 16:11; 20:23; Ezek. 45:10; Hos. 12:7; Amos 8:5; Mic. 6:11). Wherever Israel fails in this area, she will be condemned for her dishonesty. Jer. 32:10 is the one occurrence that describes a literal business transaction in a neutral sense.

At the metaphorical level, there are two references in Job that express the writer's desire to have his life adjudicated in the balance by God himself (Job 6:2; 31:6). The psalmist metaphorically alludes to the insignificance of human beings when he is found to be nothing when "laid in the balance." In Isa. 40:12, 15 there are two metaphorical references to the incomparable power of God — God alone is able to weigh the hills in a balance, and the mountains on a scale.

Finally, in Ezek. 5:1 the literal and the symbolic combine as the prophet is commanded to shave his head and beard and then weigh the hair on a set of scales. The message for the people of Judah was one of condemnation. The hair would be weighed and then divided into three sections, each of which would indicate one aspect of God's judgment against the people of Judah in general and the city of Jerusalem in particular.

qāneh **[קָנֶה, 7070]**

The noun ***qāneh*** is found nearly sixty times with the predominant meanings "reed," "stalk," or "branch." In Isa. 46:6, however, ***qāneh*** refers to a "balance" (i.e., a set of scales) used to weigh precious metals.

NT Words

zygos [ζυγός, *2218*]

zygos is found in six places and refers mostly to a "yoke" in both a literal and metaphorical sense. However, in Rev. 6:5 it denotes a "pair of scales" or a "balance" held by the rider of the black horse and symbolizing economic ruin for humankind — a judgment from God.

BAND

OT Words

môsēr **[מוֹסֵר, 4147]**

This word is a participial noun derived from the verb ***'āsar.*** (➡ BIND) It means "band(s)," "bonds" or other kinds of restrictive bindings such as "chains" or "fetters." Although it occurs relatively infrequently in the Old Testament, the contexts in which it is found are of interest — first in the Wisdom literature, and then in the Prophets.

In Job 39:5, God makes metaphorical allusion to the unrestrained behavior of the wild donkey with the question: "Who untied his ropes?" In context, the clearly intended answer is that the omnipotent Creator God has given the creature its freedom.

môsēr occurs three times in the Psalter. One of these refers to the vain pretensions of the rebellious nations opposed to God. These people imagine that they can single-handedly free each other from what they see as God's despotic rule. They express their futile intention to "throw off their chains," at which time God mocks them. They can only expect his divine judgment, since they are powerless against him (Ps. 2:3). Then, Pss. 107:14; 116:16 refer to the redemptive actions of God in rescuing his people from the grip of their enemies by loosing or breaking their "bonds." Similar imagery is found in the Prophets, where on three occasions God's deliverance of his people is described in terms of breaking the bonds that tie them. Isa. 52:2 is a divine exhortation to Israel to free herself from the chains around her neck. They are not called to save themselves by their own effort, for the context clearly indicates that God has initiated the process of deliverance. Rather, this is a call to appropriate by faith what has been made possible by God's intervention on their behalf. Jer. 30:8; Nah. 1:13, however, specifically declare God's intention to shatter the bonds that other nations have inflicted on them. In Jer. 30 it is the Babylonians that are under divine judgment, and in Nah. 1 it is the Assyrians.

There are two other references that describe not God's deliverance of his people, but rather a judgment against them. Isa. 28:22 contains a warning to Israel to stop mocking God through her idolatry or her "chains will become heavier." Then, in Jer. 27:2, the prophet is instructed by God to make and wear a yoke with "straps" or "ropes" on it in order to show the inhabitants of Judah that their subjection to the Babylonians is imminent.

'abōt [עֲבֹת, 5688]

'abōt is roughly synonymous with ***môsēr***, above, though there is a distinctive aspect in its usage. ***'abōt*** is the noun derived from the verb *'abāt*, to "wind" or "weave," and it occurs approximately twenty-five times in the Old Testament. It means "rope" or "foliage" with the underlying connotation of that which is braided or woven.

The idea of braiding is explicitly indicated in Exod. 28 and 39, where there are a number of references to braided chains of golden cord which are part of the high priest's clothing.

There are literal references to new ropes in Judg. 15, 16 where the Philistines try to bind Samson — at first unsuccessfully, and then finally, with success, thanks to the persistence of Delilah.

In Ezek. 19:11; 31:3, 10, 14, ***'abōt*** indicates the foliage of large trees, presumably to emphasize the interweaving of their thick branches. The context is a symbolic allusion to the nation of Israel (19:11) and to Assyria (31:3ff.)

'abōt is also used as a synonym for ***môsēr*** (see above) in Ps. 2:3, and as a substitute for that term in Ezek. 3:25 (cf. note on Jer. 27:2 above).

Isa. 5:18 indicts the people of Israel for carrying sin around with them as one draws a cart with ropes.

And finally, by way of contrast, Hos. 11:4 alludes to the tender love God has demonstrated to his people by leading them out of Egypt and through the wilderness with "cords of human kindness."

ḥarṣubbôt [חַרְצֻבּוֹת, 2784]

This rare term, derived from a verb meaning to "wind or twist powerfully," occurs only twice. On both occasions, ***ḥarṣubbôt*** is used metaphorically. Firstly, in Ps. 73:4 it refers to one's "struggles" or "pangs" (in death), presumably to that which "binds" one's mind with fear. Sadly for the psalmist, he observes that such bondage appears to be absent in the wicked. Then Isa. 58:6 refers to God's desire to rid his people of the practice of cruelty and selfishness by "loosing the cords of injustice."

qesher [קֶשֶׁר, 7195]

There are fourteen occurrences of this word, meaning "conspiracy" or "treason." The underlying sense here is that of "binding together," mainly for the purpose of conspiracy. This is also one of the meanings of the related verb ***qāshar***. (→ BIND)

The following texts all indicate treason of a political nature against the rulers of both Israel and Judah: 2 Sam. 15:12, Absalom against David; 1 Kgs. 16:9ff., Zimri against Elah; 2 Kgs. 11:14, Jehoiada against Athaliah; 2 Kgs. 12:20, court officials against Joash; 2 Kgs. 14:19, the people of Jerusalem against Amaziah on account of his idolatry; 2 Kgs. 15:15, Shallum against Zechariah; 2 Kgs. 15:30, Hoshea against Pekah.

qesher also refers to Hoshea's conspiracy against Shalmaneser, the Assyrian king, which led to the Assyrian invasion and destruction of the northern kingdom of Israel (cf. 2 Kgs. 17:3ff.). This particular conspiracy led to horrific consequences for the Israelite people.

Several references in the Prophets also indicate that Israel herself was guilty of conspiracy or treason against God. In Isa. 8:12, for example, the context indicates that Isaiah had warned Israel not to form an alliance with Assyria. The Israelites regarded such a warning as treason against the national interest. But God is encouraging the prophet not to be concerned about this particular disobedience — for the people demonstrate their treason against God in this situation by condemning the very man whom God had raised up to declare his word to the nation. Jer. 11:9; Ezek. 22:25 both refer to a conspiracy among God's people against God and his covenant law. Such a rebellious attitude leads inevitably to the downfall of the Judean nation.

NT Words

speira [σπεῖρα, *4686*]

speira is a noun found seven times, referring to a "band" or "regiment" of soldiers in Matt. 27:27; Mark 15:16; John 18:3, 12; Acts 10:1; 27:1.

Additional Notes

As the New Testament has a variety of words for "band," so the Old Testament terminology has both literal and metaphorical meanings. It is also worth noting that there is a considerable degree of similarity in meaning between these groups of words. Of particular interest is the association of the Hebrew term ***qesher*** with the idea of "conspiracy" (binding people together secretly for the purpose of destroying a common enemy). This is used with a largely negative connotation in the Old Testament. The roughly corresponding Greek term, ***syndesmos*** (→ BOND), also carries the idea of a binding together of people for a common cause. ***syndesmos***, however, occurs primarily in a positive sense, referring to the spiritual bonds of fellowship that characterize the body of Christ, the fellowship of all believers. It is also used once in a negative sense, with reference to an individual — Simon Magus — who is described in Acts 8:23 as one in bondage to sin. In broad terms one may observe that ***qesher*** and ***syndesmos*** share the common perspective of "binding together." In the former, however, the "binding together" is negative, whereas in the latter the sense is generally positive. Positively, ***syndesmos*** refers to the spiritual bonds of fellowship that characterize the body of Christ — his people. Negatively, it suggests binding together for evil purposes, referred to in the New Testament, for example in the case of Simon Magus, as the "bond of iniquity" (cf. Acts 8:23). The idea of "conspiracy," while not precisely matching the sense of "bond," is certainly linked to it at its fundamental level of meaning.

See Also: → BOND

BAPTISM, BAPTIST, BAPTIZE

OT Words

tābal [**טָבַל, 2881**]

The primary sense of this verb is "to dip." Of the fifteen occurrences in the Old Testament, six refer to the ceremonial practices — the rest are found in nonritual contexts.

In relation to Israelite ceremonial practices, ***tābal*** indicates first of all the action of the priest in dipping his finger into the blood of the sacrificial bull prior to the sprinkling of the altar of incense for the forgiveness of priestly sins (cf. Lev. 4:6, 17; 9:9). A similar action is also performed in Lev. 14:16, where the priest's finger is dipped into oil and sprinkled before the Lord as part of the ceremony of cleansing for the person infected with certifiable skin disease. The priests also dip small birds and other objects in blood for the purposes of ritual sprinkling for cleansing as part of that same ceremony (cf. Lev. 14:6). A house infected by mildew is also cleansed by that same ritual dipping and sprinkling (cf. Lev. 14:51). In Num. 19:18, a bunch of hyssop is to be dipped in water for the ceremonial purification of those who have been ritually contaminated by exposure to a corpse.

Then, in a related sense, there is the action prescribed by God for the people of Israel in Egypt to escape the divine judgment against Egypt and to then escape from captivity. Exod. 12:22 commands the people to dip hyssop into the blood of the slaughtered lamb (or kid) and daub the doorway and lintel with the blood in order to escape the angel of death, who would come to slay all the firstborn in Egypt. This historical action, while not formally part of Israelite worship, certainly prefigured the subsequent ceremonial ritual that would celebrate God's deliverance of his people from the clutches of their Egyptian captors.

The remaining non-ceremonial uses of ***tābal*** describe the action of dipping in various narrative contexts — for example, Ruth and Boaz (cf. Ruth 2:14); Joseph's brothers with Joseph's coat (cf. Gen. 37:31); Jonathan, son of Saul (cf. 1 Sam. 14:27); Naaman in the Jordan River (cf. 2 Kgs. 5:14); Hazael's murder of Ben Hadad by suffocation (cf. 2 Kgs. 8:15); Moses' blessing on Asher (cf. Deut. 33:24); the priests on the edge of the Jordan River (cf. Josh. 3:15).

The only other use of ***tābal*** is found in a poetic context in Job 9:31, where Job gives vent to his despair, imagining that God will "plunge (i.e., dip) him in the ditch" and abandon him.

NT Words

baptisma [βάπτισμα, *908*]

baptisma is a noun occurring around twenty times, meaning "baptism." It indicates submerging or immersing people in water for ritual purposes.

John's "baptism" of repentance is indicated in Matt. 3:7; 21:25; Mark 1:4; 11:30; Luke 3:3; 7:29; 20:4; Acts 1:22; 10:37; 13:24; 18:25; 19:3ff.

References to the "baptism" of Christ are metaphorical when denoting his suffering and death on the cross (cf. Matt. 20:22ff.; Mark 10:38ff.; Luke 12:50).

Elsewhere, ***baptisma*** denotes the baptism of believers performed in the name of Christ, depicted metaphorically as a baptism into his death and resurrection (cf. Rom. 6:4; Col. 2:12).

General references to baptism include Eph. 4:5; 1 Pet. 3:21.

baptismos [βαπτισμός, *909*]

baptismos is a variant form of ***baptisma***, above, found only four times, denoting "washing" in the sense of a purification ritual for sacred utensils (cf. Mark 7:4, 8); and also for priestly purification and preparation for service in the temple (cf. Heb. 6:2; 9:10).

baptistēs [βαπτιστής, *910*]

The noun ***baptistēs*** signifies "baptizer" (i.e., "one who baptizes"). The term is used in the New Testament exclusively as a surname for John, the forerunner of Christ — John the Baptist (cf. Matt. 3:1; 11:11ff.; 14:2ff.; 17:13; Mark 6:24ff.; 8:28; Luke 7:20ff.; 9:19).

baptizō [βαπτίζω, *907*]

The verb ***baptizō*** is found about ninety times in the New Testament, with a very significant theological sense. Its root meanings are "dip," "immerse," "submerge" in water, and it is found in the context of John the Baptist's ministry of "baptizing" for the forgiveness of sin, as well as Christian baptism. The latter usage has to do both with Christ's own personal trauma surrounding his death, as well as with the ritual applied to his followers signifying their spiritual union with him through the symbolism of immersion in water. The ritual of baptism is also associated with the outpouring of the Holy Spirit.

References to "baptizing" for the confession of sin in relation to the ministry of John the Baptist include Matt. 3:6ff.; Mark 1:4ff.; Luke 3:7ff.; 7:29ff.; John 1:25ff.; 3:23ff.; 10:40; Acts 19:3ff. Some of these references describe John baptizing Jesus. In reality, Christ needed no baptism to cleanse him from sin, because by nature he was perfect. However, his submission to John's baptism indicates the divine intention for him to be identified with human beings.

baptizō is used passively and metaphorically in relation to Christ "being baptized," or suffering in the course of his crucifixion and death (cf. Matt. 20:22ff.; Mark 10:38ff.; Luke 12:50). Jesus' own ministry of baptism is indicated in John 3:22; 4:12, though it is clear that it is the disciples, not Christ, who actually perform the rite. Then there is Christ's promise to "baptize" his followers with the Holy Spirit (cf. Luke 3:16; John 1:33; Acts 1:5; 11:16).

The followers of Christ are commanded to baptize disciples in the name of the Father, Son, and Holy Spirit (cf. Matt. 28:19). In Acts 2:38, Peter exhorts his large audience "to repent and be baptized." In other very significant contexts, salvation applied through the expression of saving faith is attested by the sign of baptism (cf. Mark 16:16; Acts 2:41; 8:12ff., 36ff.; 9:18; 10:47ff.; 16:15, 33; 18:8; 19:5; 22:16). The apostle Paul's ministry of baptism is noted in 1 Cor. 1:13ff.

baptizō also denotes the act of "ritual bathing, or washing," referring to the Pharisaic tradition whereby one could maintain ceremonial purity (cf. Mark 7:4). It also refers to the tradition of "washing" prior to taking a meal (cf. Luke 11:38).

"Being baptized" into Christ, symbolizing the believer's identification with him in his death and resurrection, is indicated in Rom. 6:3; Gal. 3:27.

The phenomenon of Israel "being baptized" into Moses in the cloud and the sea is noted in 1 Cor. 10:2. ***baptizō*** is used metaphorically here to refer to Israel's dependence upon and submission to Moses as their spiritual leader and deliverer. The "cloud" refers to the divine mode of guidance through the wilderness; and the "sea" refers to the miraculous deliverance of Israel from the pursuing Egyptian army at the Re(e)d Sea. In both cases it is Moses who functions as the people's prophet, mediator, and leader, chosen and appointed by God for that purpose. The parallel with Christian baptism is clear. Just as the Israelites identified themselves with God though Moses, so Christian believers identify themselves with God through Christ, in the sacrament of baptism.

Baptism is the "mechanism" by which the Holy Spirit constitutes all believers as members of the "one body" of Christ (cf. 1 Cor. 12:13).

There is also a cryptic reference to the practice of "baptizing" people on behalf of the dead in 1 Cor. 15:29. This is not mentioned or explained anywhere else in the New Testament.

baptō [βάπτω, *911*]

baptō is a rare variant form of ***baptizō***, above, found in only three contexts. It means to "dip" or "immerse," but without the ritual or theological significance of ***baptizō***. Luke 16:24 refers to the "dipping" of the finger in water, and John 13:26 denotes the "dipping" of bread into a dish. Rev. 19:13 contains a metaphorical use of ***baptō*** in relation to a robe "dipped" in blood, worn by the Messiah-King going into battle.

embaptō [ἐμβάπτω, *1686*]

embaptō is a variant verb of ***baptō***, above, found only three times. In each context, the action indicated is that of "dipping" one's hand into, or "dipping" bread into, a dish associated with eating a meal (cf. Matt. 26:23; Mark 4:20; John 13:26).

Additional Notes

It is evident from the above analyses of both ***tābal*** and ***baptizō*** that there is a considerable correspondence of meaning and significance between the two terms. Where ***tābal*** occurs in a ceremonial context, the idea of atonement and/or cleansing is paramount. Similarly, ***baptizō*** (etc.) in the New Testament also describes the cleansing and forgiveness of the genuine disciple of Christ. John's baptism of repentance, and Jesus' own personal "baptism of fire," followed by the phenomenon of Spirit baptism and the associated symbol of water baptism, focus on two things: cleansing from sin, and being made ready to enter into the presence of God as members of his kingdom. The Hebrew term ***tābal*** clearly anticipates that reality in the Old Testament, while the use of ***baptizō*** (etc.) points to its fulfillment in the New.

BARE → NAKED

BARLEY

OT Words

se'ōrāh [שְׂעֹרָה, 8184]

There are approximately thirty references to barley grain in the Old Testament. Along with wheat, this grain was one of the most common sources of food in the ancient Near East. Egyptian barley crops are mentioned in Exod. 9:31, for example, and the land of Canaan is described in Deut. 8:8 as being rich in wheat and barley. The barley harvest constitutes an important background in the book of Ruth, against which the divinely ordered events in the lives of Ruth and Boaz are played out.

NT Words

krithē [κριθή, *2915*]

krithē is a rare noun found only in Rev. 6:6 with reference to "barley" grain, priced at three measures for a penny.

krithinos [κρίθινος, *2916*]

krithinos is a rare adjectival form derived from ***krithē***, above, referring to loaves "made of barley" in John 6:9, 13.

BARN

OT Words

'ôṣār [אוֹצָר, 214]

This noun derives from the verbal root ***'āṣar***, "to lay up, store up." (→ SHUT) ***'ôṣār*** means "treasure(s)," "stores" as well as the places where they are stored (i.e., "treasury" or "storeroom"). The word is used in both a literal and a metaphorical sense and occurs approximately eighty times.

The literal use of ***'ôṣār*** predominates, meaning "treasure" in over half the texts. Of these, there are approximately thirty instances where ***'ôṣār*** refers to the treasures of the Jerusalem temple (or tabernacle), as well as to the storehouses containing these riches within the temple precincts. And, in some instances, ***'ôṣār*** implies both the treasure itself as well as the storeroom containing it. (→ TREASURE)

References to ***'ôṣār*** as the "storehouse" or "treasury" of the temple are found mainly, though not exclusively, in the books of Kings and Chronicles (cf. 1 Chr. 9:26; 28:12; 2 Chr. 32:27; Neh. 13:12, 13). The storehouse or treasury of the tabernacle is also mentioned in Josh. 6:19, 24. ***'ôṣār*** also combines the images of temple treasure and treasury, where no precise distinction is made (cf. 2 Kgs. 14:14; 18:15; 20:13; 1 Chr. 26:20ff.; 27:25; 29:8; 2 Chr. 8:15; Neh. 7:70, 71).

'ôṣār also has a metaphorical level of meaning. Job 38:22, for example, refers to the divine "storehouse" of the snow and hail. Here God is confronting Job, challenging him to compare his knowledge and wisdom with those of his Creator. In the wake of such a confrontation, Job is duly penitent and humbled (cf. also Jer. 10:13; 7:16). In a spirit of praise and worship, the psalmist also mentions the "storehouses" of the Creator where he lays up the waters of the deep and from which he dispatches the wind (cf. Pss. 33:7; 135:7). The writer of Proverbs refers to the blessing gained from an intimate acquaintance with (Lady) Wisdom. Whoever loves Wisdom will have their treasuries filled (Prov. 8:21). The context here clearly suggests that this constitutes a rich spiritual inheritance, leading to everlasting peace and joy. Finally, ***'ôṣār*** has a negative connotation in Jer. 50:25, where it refers to God's "armory," his storehouse of weapons, from which he will select the means to inflict his judgment and wrath against the land of Babylon.

megûrāh **[מְגוּרָה, 4035]**

megûrāh is a rare noun, denoting a "barn" as a storage place for food in Hag. 2:19; Ps. 34:4.

'āsām **[אָסָם, 618]**

'āsām is a term denoting "storehouse," "barn," found only in Deut. 28:8; Prov. 3:10.

—————— NT Words ——————

apothēkē [ἀποθήκη, *596*]

apothēkē is a noun denoting "barn," "storehouse" for grain, food, or other goods (cf. Matt. 3:12; 6:26; 13:30; Luke 3:17; 12:18, 24).

BARREN

—————— OT Words ——————

'āqār **[עָקָר, 6135]**

Barrenness is a very significant theological concept in the Old Testament. Although the verb ***'āqār*** itself only occurs eleven times, the majority of references relate to the entire scope of God's redemptive purposes in both the old and new covenants.

The first three references to barrenness relate to the wives of the patriarchs — Sarai, Rebekah, and Rachel. Each woman's infertility has a direct bearing on the plans and purposes of God, for in each case it is a prelude to God's blessing them with children.

In the first instance, Gen. 11:30 records the fact that Abram's wife Sarai was barren. It is interesting to note here that this comment is made in the genealogical listing of Abraham's descendants, immediately preceding the initial covenant promise given to Abraham in Gen. 12:1ff. The subsequent removal of Sarah's barrenness through the birth of Isaac (cf. Gen. 21:1ff.) testifies to God's power and graciousness in overcoming what was, humanly speaking, an insurmountable barrier. Similarly, the reference to Rebekah's barrenness in Gen. 25:21 is significant in that it is the catalyst for her husband Isaac's prayer. Once the prayer is uttered, God answers it promptly by enabling Rebekah to become pregnant. The sons born to her, Jacob and Esau, form the next link in the covenantal lineage, when God chooses Jacob as the heir to the promise. The third patriarchal wife, Rachel, also experiences a period of barrenness in a time of severe testing, as she stands by and watches rival wife Leah, and maidservants Bilhah and Zilpah, all give birth to sons before her (cf. Gen. 29:31). Finally, God releases her from her agony, and Rachel gives birth to Joseph (cf. Gen. 30:23). Once again, the significance of a woman's barrenness is bound up with the plans and purposes of God, who withholds fertility from these key women in the history of salvation for a period of time, and then grants them the capacity to bear children. It is difficult to escape the conclusion that the theme of barrenness is a deliberate ploy in the divine plan to enhance the impact of the births of those children whose roles in the purposes of God for his people are of central importance.

Other references to barrenness reinforce this important idea. In Exod. 23:26; Deut. 7:14, God promises the Israelites that barrenness will never be found among them, provided they remain obedient and faithful to the laws that God has laid before them. Then there are the examples of Manoah's wife and Hannah. In the case of the former, this unnamed lady, the mother of Samson, received a visitation from the angel of the Lord who promised her a son. Interestingly, the angel's remarks in Judg. 13:3 affirm the woman's barrenness while at the same time giving her a guarantee that she will soon bear a son. Hannah's case is very similar, except that in the narrative describing her own personal trauma of infertility, and her sheer delight in having her prayer for a son answered, the word ***'āqār*** is not found (cf. 1 Sam. 1; 2:5). There is no doubt, however, that the phenomenon of barrenness is very much to the fore. Indeed, her sterility is specifically declared to be from the hand of God, for in 1 Sam. 1:5 the text reads: ". . . for the Lord had closed her womb." The subsequent opening of Hannah's womb leads to the birth of Samuel, one of the centrally important political, prophetic, and priestly figures of the Old Testament. This is a good illustration of the maxim that thematic word studies are not always and only restricted to passages containing particular key words.

The psalmist also recognizes that God's removal of the trauma of barrenness is part and parcel of God's redemptive purposes for his people. This is expressed in Ps. 113:9 as one element in the redemptive activity that God undertakes on behalf of his people, Israel: "He settles the barren woman in her home as a happy mother of children."

One prophetic text that builds on this theme is found in Isa. 54:1, where the prophet urges the barren woman who never bore a child to burst into a song of praise to God for having resolved her dilemma by granting her children. Again, the context here is one of eschatological fulfillment: that is, the certain hope that God will accomplish the salvation of his people, which will one day result in their perfect transformation. Among other things, this will result in the elimination of barrenness. Whether this is to be interpreted literally, symbolically, or both is hard to say. It is clear, however, that God's action of removing barrenness for certain women among his people is a distinct pointer to the powerful theological symbol of divine renewal and transformation for his people as a whole.

NT Words

steira [στεῖρα, *4723*]

steira is an adjectival form found in five contexts meaning "barren." In four of these places, the term denotes women who have not been able to conceive and bear children (cf. Luke 1:7, 36; 23:29; Gal. 4:27).

Additional Notes

The clear link between old and new covenant terminology becomes clear as both ***'āqār*** and ***steira*** are compared in their respective contexts.

Paul's citation of Isa. 54:1 in Gal. 4:27 leaves the reader in no doubt that the theme of barrenness in the old covenant has powerful theological significance in the new. The continuity between the Old and New Testaments is undeniable. Removal of barrenness signifies God's promise guaranteeing eternal release for his people from the bondage of sin through the transforming ministry of the indwelling Spirit of God.

BASKET

OT Words

dûd [**דּוּד, 1731**]

This is a rare term, occurring only six times. Only three of these mean "basket." 2 Kgs. 10:7 describes the gruesome episode of the slaughter of the seventy princes of the dynasty of Ahab, whose heads were placed in baskets by their executioners on the orders of Jehu. Ps. 81:6 refers poetically to the deliverance of the Israelite people from their enslavement in Egypt. The reference here is to their hands being delivered "from the baskets" in that country. Finally, Jer. 24:1, 2 records the vision given to the prophet in which the Israelite people are symbolically represented by two baskets of figs — one good, the other bad.

The remaining uses of ***dûd*** refer to Levitical cooking utensils. In 1 Sam. 2:14 the word is translated "kettle"; and "cauldrons" in 2 Chr. 35:13. There is also a poetic reference in Job 41:20 to the smoke from the nostrils of the Leviathan pouring out like smoke from a boiling "pot."

sal [**סַל, 5536**]

This noun occurs fourteen times and means "basket." In the majority of contexts, ***sal*** refers to the baskets containing offerings of unleavened bread and cakes to fulfill the requirements for the consecration of the Levitical priests (cf. Exod. 29:3, 23, 32). The term also refers to the ceremonial baskets containing unleavened bread for the Nazarite ordination ritual in Num. 6:15, 17, 19.

Gen. 40:16–18 also refers to baskets — the three white baskets featured in the dream of the baker in Pharaoh's court at the time of Joseph. These baskets were perched on the baker's head and contained all kinds of baked goods that the birds came to feed on. The dream signified the baker's imminent execution by Pharaoh.

Finally, in Judg. 6:19 ***sal*** refers to the basket that Gideon used to carry the meal prepared for his visitor, the angel of the Lord.

tenē' [**טֶנֶא, 2935**]

tenē' is a noun found four times, with the meaning "basket" in each case, denoting a hand-held container for carrying goods (cf. Deut. 26:2ff., 17).

kelûb [**כְּלוּב, 3619**]

kelûb is another rare term denoting "basket," found only twice, referring to containers of summer fruit (cf. Amos 8:1, 2).

NT Words

kophinos [κόφινος, *2894*]

kophinos is a noun found in six contexts, all referring to the large "baskets" used to collect the scraps of food left over after the miraculous feeding of thousands of people performed by Christ as a demonstration of his divine power (cf. Matt. 14:20; 16:9; Mark 6:43; 8:19; 9:17; John 6:13).

spyris [σπυρίς, *4711*]

spyris is a synonym for ***kophinos***, above, also denoting a "basket," most likely made of reeds, and plaited. ***spyris*** is found five times and usually refers to the baskets used to collect food scraps after Christ's feeding miracle, as recorded in Matt. 15:37; 16:10; Mark 8:8, 20. In Acts 9:25, ***spyris*** refers to the "basket" used to lower the apostle Paul down the wall of the city of Damascus, allowing him to escape the clutches of a hostile crowd.

sarganē [σαργάνη, *4553*]

sarganē is a rare synonym for ***spyris***, above, found only in 2 Cor. 11:33, referring to the "basket" Paul used to escape from his enemies in Damascus.

BATTLE → WARFARE

BEAR (VERB)

OT Words

nāśā' [**נָשָׂא, 5375**]

This very common verb is found over 650 times in the Old Testament. Its root meaning is to "bear" or "carry," with a number of derivative meanings such as "lift up," "forgive," "suffer," "take," "exalt," and "weep" (i.e., "lift up one's voice"). ***nāśā'*** does not mean "bear" in the sense of "beget," however. (→ BEGET)

The mundane literal sense of "carry" is evident in approximately eighty occurrences of ***nāśā'***. It is found, for example, in Gen. 47:30, where Jacob instructs his son Joseph to carry his body out of Egypt after his death and back into Canaan, to be buried alongside his ancestors there. There are also a number of places in the Pentateuch and Former Prophets where ***nāśā'*** is used to indicate the ark of the covenant being carried by the priests and Levites.

nāśā' also refers to the phenomenon of intercession, where the high priest Aaron is said to "bear" the names of the tribes of Israel before the Lord, and also to "bear" their guilt when he appears before God in the holy of holies (Exod. 28:12, 29ff.). ***nāśā'*** has both a literal and theological force here, since the very garments worn by the high priest represent the people of Israel before Yahweh. Aaron literally "carries" the people of Israel into God's presence through his ceremonial clothing, and there God accepts the priestly offering for the people as a whole, that they might again be made acceptable in his sight. Elsewhere, ***nāśā'*** clearly indicates the idea of "bearing the people's guilt" — in the sense of making atonement on their behalf. For example, Lev. 16:22 refers to the scapegoat in the Day of Atonement ceremony bearing the iniquities of the nation. Similarly, Lev. 10:17 refers to the effect of the sin offering in "making atonement" or "bearing the guilt" of the community. The vocation of the Suffering Servant also involves a substitutionary atonement on behalf of the people to whom he is sent to minister by God. In Isa. 53:4, 12 the words: "Surely he has borne our grief . . ." and "He bore the sin of many . . ." leave the reader in no doubt as to the import of his actions.

nāśā' also means "forgive" in a general sense. It is reasonable to argue that the idea of "bearing guilt," in the sense of removing sin, is inherent in the concept of forgiveness. In this sense, "forgiveness" is an extension of the meaning "bear," where someone's guilt is concerned. Examples of this usage of ***nāśā'*** are found in Pss. 25:18; 32:5; 85:2; Gen. 50:17; Exod. 10:17; 32:32; Num. 14:19; 1 Sam. 15:15; 25:28; Mic. 7:18.

The concept of "bearing one's guilt" is also found with a negative connotation in the use of ***nāśā'***. In several contexts, the term is used to refer to those whose sinful actions lead inevitably to them "bearing their (own) guilt" with painful, often disastrous consequences (cf. Ezek. 14:10; 18:19; 44:10, 12, 13; Lev. 19:8; 20:17, 19, 20; Num. 5:31; 14:34; 18:1, 23).

nāśā' also indicates suffering leading to repentance in one or two contexts where the meaning "bear" is evident. Jer. 31:19 mentions Israel having borne the disgrace of her youth and being duly ashamed and humiliated by it. Then, in Mic. 7:9, there is again the recognition that the people will bear God's wrath because of their sin. But the text affirms that God will not ultimately abandon them — there is the hope that restoration and forgiveness will follow after their time of punishment.

In one instance, the metaphorical sense of ***nāśā'*** of "carry" or "bear" refers to God's deliverance of his people from captivity in Egypt. Exod. 19:4 refers to God "bearing" his people on the wings of eagles, so that they might be spared and come into an intimate relationship with him through the revelation of the covenant at Sinai through Moses.

A far more common meaning of ***nāśā'***, however, is to "lift up." It occurs with several shades of meaning, as well as a mundane literal one.

In the first instance, ***nāsā'*** indicates a worshipful attitude of devotion to Yahweh (cf. Pss. 25:1; 63:4; 86:4; 123:1; 134:2; 143:8; Isa. 24:14; 40:26; 52:8). In all of these references, the focus is on "lifting up" one's eyes, one's soul, one's hands, or one's voice (and similar expressions) to God. Negatively, the term also refers to "lifting up" one's attention to idols (cf. Ezek. 18:6, 12).

Secondly, the phenomenon of God "lifting up" a banner or flag to the nations points to the powerful proclamation of God's plan of salvation both to his own people and to Gentile nations the world over (cf. Isa. 5:26; 11:12; 49:22). Included in this perspective as well are the references to God "lifting up his hand" to demonstrate his solemn intention to grant Israel possession of the land he had promised them (Ezek. 20:28, 42; 47:14), and to deliver his people (cf. Isa. 10:26; Ezek. 20:6).

In the third place, the idea of God "lifting up his hand" or "raising a sign" can be negative. In certain contexts, this expression indicates the inevitability of God's judgment. Some places refer to Israel's punishment (cf. Ezek. 20:23; 36:7; Jer. 4:6; 6:1), and others refer to imminent divine judgment against foreign nations such as Babylon (e.g., Jer. 50:2; Isa. 13:2).

Fourthly, ***nāsā'*** describes prophetic inspiration whereby the prophet is declared to be "lifted up" by the spirit of God, prior to receiving his revelation (cf. Ezek. 3:14; 8:3; 11:1, 24; 43:5).

In the fifth place, ***nāsā'*** refers to personal grief in the phrase "to lift up one's voice" (cf. Judg. 21:2; Ruth 1:9, 14; 1 Sam. 11:4; 24:16; 30:4; 2 Sam. 3:32; 13:36).

Finally, there is reference to the "lifting up" or exaltation of the kingdom of God on earth during the old covenant. Reference is made, for example, to God's exaltation of the Davidic kingdom (cf. 1 Chr. 14:2); to the extolling of the Suffering Servant (cf. Isa. 52:13); to the exaltation of God himself on the heavenly throne (cf. Isa. 6:1); and then to the anticipated establishment of God's kingdom on the Day of the Lord when Mic. 4:1 states that this kingdom "will be exalted above the hills."

'ānāh [עָנָה, 6030]

'ānāh is a common verb, found over three hundred times, meaning "answer," "hear," plus related senses. In three places, however, ***'ānāh*** denotes the sin of "bearing" false witness (i.e., telling lies).

sābal [סָבַל, 5445]

sābal is a verb found in nine places with the meanings "bear," or "carry" in most of these contexts.

sābal denotes God "carrying" or "sustaining" his people in their old age (cf. Isa. 46:4). Isa. 46:7 refers to the idolatrous practice of literally "carrying" one's idols to a place of worship. Isa. 53:4, 11 both refer to the messianic "Suffering Servant's" redemptive action of "bearing" the sins of the people for whom he died. Lam. 5:7 refers to the admission that the exiled people of Jerusalem and Judah "had borne" the iniquities of their forefathers.

NT Words

bastazō [βαστάζω, *941*]

The verb ***bastazō*** means "bear," "carry" throughout the usage.

References to "bearing" or "carrying" people include Matt. 3:11; Mark 14:13; Luke 10:4; John 20:15; Acts 3:2; 21:35; Rev. 17:7 (cf. Gal. 6:17). Matt. 8:17 refers to sorrows "borne" by the messianic Suffering Servant (cf. Isa. 53:4). Exhortations to "bear one another's burdens" are found in Rom. 15:1; Gal. 6:2. The "bearing" of children in the womb is indicated in Luke 11:27. In the context of the spread of the gospel, the task of "bearing" or "carrying" the name of Christ to the Gentiles is indicated in Acts 9:15. John 19:17 describes Christ as literally "carrying" his cross to his place of execution. In Luke 14:27, the expression "to carry one's cross" is used symbolically to indicate a person's desire to identify with the sufferings of Christ.

The meaning "bear" in the sense of "receive" is found in connection with the appropriating of the teachings of Christ (cf. John 16:12).

bastazō is also translated "support" in relation to a tree's root system "bearing" or "supporting" the branches (cf. Rom. 11:18).

Elsewhere the meaning "bear" signifies "to endure," "tolerate." The Ephesian congregation is commended for refusing to "tolerate" evil men in Rev. 2:2, and for "enduring" persecution in Rev. 2:3.

pherō [φέρω, *5342*]

The verb ***pherō*** occurs around sixty times with the primary sense of "bring." A few contexts indicate the meaning "bear," or "carry."

The capacity of a branch to "bear" fruit is indicated in John 15:2ff. in both a literal and metaphorical sense. The literal phenomenon of "fruit bearing" is used as an analogy for the manifestation of godly character in the life of the believer, brought about by the Holy Spirit.

The meaning "bear" is found in Heb. 13:13 in reference to sharing in the disgrace Christ experienced as a means of identifying with him in his suffering.

pherō is also predicated of God when he is said to "endure," or "bear," wickedness with patience (cf. Rom. 9:22).

anapherō [ἀναφέρω, *399*]

anapherō is a variant of ***pherō***, above, found twelve times with the senses of "offer up" (i.e., sacrifices), and "carry" or "bear."

Luke 24:51 affirms that Christ was carried up to heaven by angels. In Heb. 9:28; 1 Pet. 2:24, Christ is declared to "have borne" the sins of many people in his atoning death on the cross.

ekpherō [ἐκφέρω, *1627*]

ekpherō is a verb found in nine places, with the primary meaning "carry out." The term refers to the literal, physical removal of dead bodies from a house in Acts 5:6ff.; and to the impossibility of "carrying out" anything of this world into the next (cf. 1 Tim. 6:7).

hypopherō [ὑποφέρω, *5297*]

hypopherō is a rare verb found three times with the meaning "bear up" in the sense of "patiently endure." God's promise to enable his people to "bear up" under trials and tribulation is noted in 1 Cor. 10:13. In 2 Tim. 3:11; 1 Pet. 2:19, general references are made to "enduring" various trials.

karpophoreō [καρποφορέω, *2592*]

karpophoreō is a verb found in eight places with the universal sense of "bear, bring forth fruit."

The term is used literally in Matt. 13:23; Mark 4:20, 28. It refers metaphorically to the manifestation of godly virtue in Luke 8:15; Rom. 7:4; Col. 1:10. There is a negative usage in Rom. 7:5, where the impact of sinful passion aroused by the law in the life of the believer are portrayed as "bearing fruit for death." Then, in Col. 1:6, mention is made of the gospel "bearing fruit" throughout the world.

phoreō [φορέω, *5409*]

phoreō is a verb found five times, with the meanings "wear" and "bear."

Rom. 13:4 refers to the civil ruler as one who "bears the sword of justice." 1 Cor. 15:49 refers to God's people "bearing" both the image of man as a created being and also the image of the man in heaven.

stegō [στέγω, *4722*]

The verb ***stegō*** is found six times with the meaning "bear" in the sense of "endure," "suffer." General references to "enduring" or "forbearing" are found in 1 Cor. 9:12; 1 Thess. 3:1ff. Love is said "to endure all things" in 1 Cor. 13:7.

anechomai [ἀνέχομαι, *430*]

anechomai is a verb found nearly twenty times with the meaning "endure," "bear with," "forbear."

Most commonly, ***anechomai*** expresses the sense of "bear with someone" (i.e., be patient with) in Matt. 17:17; Luke 9:41; 2 Cor. 11:1, 19ff.; Eph. 4:2; Col. 3:13; Heb. 13:22.

Elsewhere, ***anechomai*** is translated "bear," "endure persecution" (cf. 1 Cor. 4:12; 2 Thess. 1:4). Then 2 Tim. 4:3 mentions the refusal of people to "bear" or "endure" sound teaching.

dysbastaktos [δυσβάστακτος, *1419*]

dysbastaktos is an adjective found only twice, with the meaning "hard to bear." Both Matt. 23:4; Luke 11:46 refer to intolerable burdens the religious leaders placed on the Israelite people.

Additional Notes

nāśā' is the major Hebrew word meaning "bear," and it has a fairly broad semantic field. In relation to the various Greek terms, it would seem that the verb ***bastazō*** would constitute the closest dynamic equivalent to ***nāśā'***, since the range of meaning is fairly close to that of the Hebrew term. The other Greek terms may occasionally approximate the meanings attached to ***nāśā'***, but not as frequently as ***bastazō***.

The concepts of "bear" or "carry," plus associated meanings, carry considerable theological weight in the Old and New Testaments alike. Particularly significant is the emphasis on substitutionary atonement for sin, which is undoubtedly a major theme of the Scriptures, embodied in the sacrificial worship of the old covenant and culminating in the person and work of Jesus Christ, the ultimate fulfillment of the Suffering Servant of Yahweh.

See Also: → ABLE → BEGET → CARRY → ENDURE → EXALT → LIFT → TAKE → WEAR → WITNESS

BEAR (NOUN)

OT Words

dōb [דֹּב, **1677**]; *dôb* [דּוֹב, **1678** (Aramaic)]

There are eleven references to the "bear" in the Old Testament, four of which refer to the animal in a literal, narrative context. ***dōb*** (***dôb***) occurs three times in relation to David's exploits as a youth when he killed one with his bare hands (cf. 1 Sam. 17:34–37). Two bears emerge from the woods to maul a group of youths who persist in mocking the prophet Elisha. Such an attack was unleashed upon these youngsters at the command of Elisha, who called a curse down upon them in the name of the Lord (cf. 2 Kgs. 2:24).

The remaining occurrences of ***dōb*** (***dôb***) are found in metaphorical contexts. 2 Kgs. 2:24 records, for example, the words of Hushai, who persuades Absalom to delay his final assault on David in hiding, on the grounds that his father would be highly dangerous, "like a bear robbed of her cubs." Prov. 17:12; 28:15 use the metaphor of the bear to symbolize a situation that leads to pain and distress. On a much more positive note, Isa. 11:7 depicts an idyllic vision of harmony where predator (bear) and prey (cow) live together in peace. In several other poetic contexts, the metaphor of the bear is used to indicate divine judgment. Lam. 3:10; Hos. 13:8; Amos 5:19 all refer to Israel growling "like bears" as they suffer God's judgment in misery. Finally, Dan. 7:5 contains the Aramaic term ***dōb*** to refer to the second visionary beast that "looked like a bear," commonly interpreted as representing the kingdom of Persia. This beast, along with all the others in Dan. 7, is subject to destruction in accordance with the plan and judgment of God.

It would appear that, in a majority of cases, the curse of the "bear" carries a distinctive theological significance as a symbolic indicator of divine judgment — in both narrative and prophetic contexts.

NT Words

arkos [ἄρκος, *715*]

arkos is a rare term found only in Rev. 13:2 with symbolic reference to a "bear," — part of the makeup of the satanic beast that came up out of the sea.

BEAST

OT Words

ḥay, ḥayyāh [**חַי, חַיָּה, 2416**];
ḥēwā' [**חֵיוָא, 2423** (Aramaic)]

This common term is found over 450 times in the Old Testament. ***ḥay*** and ***ḥayyāh***, respectively, are the masculine and feminine forms of the noun which can also be used adjectivally. As a noun it means "life," "living thing," "animal," "(wild) beast." As an adjective it means "living" or "alive."

The Aramaic equivalent, ***ḥēwā'***, is also found in a number of contexts.

Of the 450 occurrences of ***ḥay*** and ***ḥayyāh***, only about ninety of them refer to "beasts" or "animals." The term ***ḥay*** is found fairly frequently with this meaning in the first nine chapters of Genesis, for example. There are references to animal life in the creation account in chapter 1. Adam's naming of the beasts is then highlighted in Gen. 2:19–20. Animals are paired together for future mating purposes and given refuge from the flood in Noah's ark. Distinctions between clean and unclean animals are made in Lev. 5:2; 11:2, 27, 47.

The connotation of "wild beast" is found quite frequently in the Old Testament with significant theological overtones in a number of contexts. Lev. 26:6, for example, contains the divine promise to Israel to rid the land of wild beasts if they devote themselves to God by keeping his law. Conversely, in Lev. 26:22, there is the divine threat to send wild animals against the people if they disobey God. In 1 Sam. 17:46, David throws out a contemptuous challenge to Goliath, declaring that God will destroy the Philistines and hand them over to the wild beasts of the land. Wild beasts are also frequently used as vehicles of divine judgment in the Prophets (cf. Jer. 12:9, 16; Ezek. 5:17; 14:15; 33:27; Hos. 2:12; 13:8). In these texts, the objects of divine wrath are the people of Israel and Judah. Ezek. 29:5; 32:4; 39:39:17; Zeph. 2:14 all refer to wild beasts being used to demonstrate God's wrath against the nations. Following a similar theme, there is a reference in Isa. 56:9 to wild beasts who are called upon to witness the sins of Israel against God. Then, from an entirely different perspective, wild animals are mentioned in Ezek. 34:5, 8 as those who harass the people of God — the result of wholesale neglect by Israel's leaders. Their sin lies in abandoning their "flock" to "wild animals" — presumably enemy nations who prey on the people. Finally, in this regard, there are at least two places where God's promise to transform and renew his people includes references to "wild animals." Ezek. 34:25, 28 contains God's promise to protect his people from such attacks, assuring the people of Judah that he will provide a good shepherd for them. Then, in Hos. 2:18, there is a promise of a divine covenant renewal that involves not just his people but the whole creation as well. God undertakes to make a new covenant with the "beasts of the field."

The equivalent Aramaic form ***ḥēwā'*** is found in Dan. 2:38; 4:12ff.; 5:21; 7:3ff. — all of which refer literally to "beasts" with the exception of the last text, which describes a symbolic creature.

Finally, there is the unique reference to the mysterious "living creatures" that surround the heavenly throne in Ezekiel's vision of the heavenly court in Ezek. 1. These are known as cherubim but in the book of Ezekiel the term ***hay*** is used. They function in the Old Testament as the messengers of God and the guardians of his throne (Ezek. 1:5, 13, 14, 15; 10:15, 17, 20).

behēmāh [בְּהֵמָה, 929]

behēmāh is a noun found approximately two hundred times, meaning "beast," "cattle," with considerable overlap between these two meanings.

behēmāh is generally translated "beast" in contexts where animals are spoken of as distinct from human beings (cf. Gen. 6:7; 7:2ff.; Exod. 8:17ff.; Lev. 7:21ff.; 20:15ff.; Num. 8:17; Deut. 4:17; 1 Sam. 17:44; Ezra 1:4; Job 12:7; Ps. 135:8; Isa. 18:6; Jer. 19:7; Ezek. 14:13ff.; Joel 1:20; Jonah 3:8).

NT Words

zōon [ζῷον, *2226*]

The noun ***zōon*** occurs about twenty times with the senses of "beast," "living creature."

The term denotes animals that have been slaughtered for sacrifice in Heb. 13:11. Then, in 2 Pet. 2:12; Jude 10, ***zōon*** refers metaphorically to false teachers as "irrational beasts." Most commonly, ***zōon*** refers to the "living creatures" (four in all) that guard the throne of God in Revelation. These "living creatures" are most likely cherubim, as illustrated in the visions of the prophet Ezekiel (cf. Ezek. 1; 10). They are found in Rev. 4:6ff.; 5:6ff.; 6:1ff.; 7:11; 14:3; 15:7; 19:4.

thērion [θηρίον, *2342*]

The noun ***thērion*** occurs about fifty times with the consistent meaning "beast," in both literal and metaphorical contexts.

General references to "wild beast(s)" or "beasts of prey" include Mark 1:13; Acts 10:12; 11:6; Heb. 12:20; Jas. 3:7; Rev. 6:8. In Acts 28:4ff., ***thērion*** specifically denotes a "viper."

The term is also used metaphorically as a term of abuse against the citizens of Crete, described as "beasts" in Titus 1:12. Elsewhere, ***thērion*** denotes the satanic "beast" sent to effect judgment on wicked humankind in Rev. 11:7. It also denotes the satanic "beasts" from sea and earth, members of the so-called "unholy trinity" who mimic the person and role of Christ and the Holy Spirit respectively (cf. Rev. 13:1ff.; 14:9ff.; 15:2; 16:2, 10, 13; 19:10; 20:4, 10). Similarly, ***thērion*** makes reference to the dragon, the great satanic opponent set against God the Father, as a "beast" with seven heads and ten horns (cf. Rev. 17:7ff.).

ktēnos [κτῆνος, *2934*]

The noun ***ktēnos*** occurs four times denoting "beast(s)" in the senses of "cattle" (Rev. 18:13); "animals" in general in 1 Cor. 15:39; "horses" in Acts 23:24; and "donkey" in Luke 10:34.

tetrapous [τετράπους, *5074*]

tetrapous is a term denoting "beast" or "animal," emphasizing their characteristic of having four feet. It is found in only three places (cf. Acts 10:12; 11:6; Rom. 1:23).

sphagion [σφάγιον, *4968*]

sphagion is a rare noun, found only in Acts 7:42 denoting a "beast" marked out for ritual sacrifice or slaughter.

thēriomacheō [θηριομαχέω, *2341*]

thēriomacheō is a rare verb found only in 1 Cor. 15:32 with the meaning "to fight against wild beasts."

Additional Notes

It is interesting to observe that while the semantic range of the Hebrew ***ḥay*** and ***ḥayyāh*** is reasonably broad, the three Greek terms ***zōon***, ***thērion***, and ***ktēnos*** are all fairly close in meaning to the Hebrew. In this sense, the meaning and significance of New Testament references to animals and beasts match those of Old Testament quite closely.

See Also: → CATTLE → CREATE → LIFE

BEAT

OT Words

pāshat [פָּשַׁט, 6584]

This verb occurs about forty times in the Old Testament but has only an indirect relation to the idea of beating. Its primary meaning is to "strip off." On four occasions, however, it indicates "flaying" or "skinning." In Lev. 1:6; 2 Chr. 29:34; 35:11 ***pāshat*** refers to the flaying or skinning of sacrificial animals. In Mic. 3:3 it refers to the cruel treatment of the Israelite population by their leaders, who "tear the skin" off the people. The fundamental idea of beating is included here, but the meaning of ***pāshat*** in this sense has a quite specific focus in only a few texts.

nākāh [נָכָה, 5221]

This is a common verb occurring about five hundred times throughout the Old Testament. The primary meaning of the term is to "beat," "smite," "strike" — mostly (though not exclusively) with fatal consequences wherever the objects of the "beating" are personal. In only about five percent of the occurrences of ***nākāh*** are the objects of the abuse inanimate.

About half of the occurrences of ***nākāh*** involve either murder or assault upon individuals with no particular theological significance other than demonstrating human sin.

The remaining texts refer either to God's punishment upon his own people or to his judgment of the nations for their rebellion against him or against the people of Israel. Such references include the few significant places where inanimate objects are involved.

The plague judgments on Egypt constitute the single most important group of texts in this regard. Exod. 7–11 contain significant references to God striking the land of the Egyptians with a series of plagues in order to force Pharaoh and the Egyptians to recognize that Yahweh alone is God, and to gain release for the Israelites from their bondage. Exod. 9:31, 32, for example, refer to God striking the Egyptian crops with hail and destroying them. See also Exod. 7:20, 25; 8:17.

There are two broad categories for the dominant use of ***nākāh***, where people and nations are involved.

The first of these is the group of texts in which ***nākāh*** indicates God's judgment against pagan nations for their rebellion against him. Egypt is a clear example of this, as noted above. God declares in Exod. 3:20 that he will reach out his hand and strike Egypt. The climax to this terrible series of plague judgments is the Passover, when God will strike down all the firstborn in the land (cf. Exod. 12:12). This major act of divine judgment is referred to elsewhere (cf. Num. 3:13; 8:17; 33:4; Pss. 135:8; 78:51; 136:10; 1 Sam. 4:8). The nations of Canaan also come under this category. They are consistently targeted as objects of divine wrath, to be struck down and slaughtered by the Israelites as part of God's judgment against them (cf. Deut. 7:2; 20:13; Josh. 10 [passim]; 11:8, 11ff.; Judg. 1:4ff., 10, 12, 17; 3:29; 7:13; 8:11; 14:19; 15:8). In particular, the Philistines constitute one of Israel's most formidable enemies in the land, and there are numerous references to these people as the objects of God's judgment, to be struck down and slain. For example, David's bold challenge to Goliath in this regard is especially significant (cf. 1 Sam. 17:46), as are David's brave actions in this regard (cf. 1 Sam. 6:19; 7:11; 23:2; 2 Sam. 1:1; 5:24; 23:10, 12; 1 Chr. 14:16; 18:11). Judgments against other nations such as Midian (cf. Judg. 6:16); Amalek (cf. 1 Sam. 15:3); Egypt (cf. Jer. 46:13); Moab (cf. Judg. 3:29); Syria (cf. 2 Sam. 8:3, 5), in addition to others, are similarly described. One especially striking example here is the overthrow of Haman's plot (cf. Esth. 7:1ff.) to destroy the entire Jewish people. A decisive victory against the Persian Empire is recorded in Esth. 9:5.

The second major category of texts involving the use of ***nākāh*** with personal objects concerns God's punishment of his own people, whom he also strikes in his anger. These texts are found predominantly, though not exclusively, in the Prophets. Jer. 2:30, for example, refers to God's punishment of his people, which appears to have had no salutary effect on them. God declares that he has beaten his children in vain (cf. also 5:3). Similar judgments against the rebellious people of Judah are referred to in Jer. 20:4; 21:6. Other instances of God punishing his people through "smiting" them are found in Ezek. 9:7; Amos 4:9; Zech. 13:7. Outside the Prophets, references to such treatment include 1 Kgs. 14:15; 2 Kgs. 9:7; Num. 11:33; 14:12; Deut. 28:22, 28, 35.

Two other texts that are related to these categories are found in the prophecy of Isaiah, in two of the so-called Suffering Servant songs (Isa. 50:6; Isa. 53:4). Here the Messianic Servant of Yahweh is portrayed as enduring a series of beatings. In Isa. 50:6 the Servant willingly submits to his tormentors, to those who beat his back. Isa. 53:4 refers to the Servant's rejection by God as he submits to divine beating and affliction. There is little doubt that, in the light of New Testament teaching, this experience foreshadows Jesus' own suffering on the cross.

ḥābat [חָבַט, 2251]

This is a rare verb in the Old Testament occurring only five times. The primary meaning is that of "beating out" or "threshing." Four of these texts refer to a literal agricultural harvesting (cf. Deut. 24:20; Ruth 2:17; Judg. 6:11; Isa. 28:27); while the remaining one refers metaphorically to God's deliverance of his people from exile (cf. Isa. 27:12). The idea here is that God will "harvest" his people from captivity, ushering in a return to Jerusalem.

nāgaph [נָגַף, 5062]

Here is another synonym for ***nākāh*** (see above), found approximately fifty times in the Old Testament with the basic meaning to "smite" or "strike."

On an individual level there are a number of instances where ***nāgaph*** refers to personal attack, whether accidental (cf. Exod. 21:22) or deliberate (cf. 2 Chr. 21:18; Judg. 20:35; 1 Sam. 25:38; 26:10; 2 Sam. 12:15). These latter references all relate to divine punishment for sin and indicate fatal blows. In 2 Sam. 12:15, the death of David's child born to Bathsheba relates to his sin of adultery with her.

Like ***nākāh***, ***nāgaph*** usually refers to divine judgment against the nations, both in Israel and elsewhere. In the case of Israel's chastisement, there are several explicit references to God striking his people for their rebellion against him (e.g., Exod. 32:35; 1 Sam. 4:10; 2 Chr. 13:15; 2 Chr. 21:14). On the other hand, God also meted out similar treatment to the enemies of Israel who opposed his will (cf. Exod. 12:23, 27; Josh. 24:5; Zech. 14:12, 18; Deut. 28:7; 2 Chr. 20:22; 2 Sam. 10:15, 19). ***nāgaph*** also refers to divine punishment as a specific prelude to special blessing. Isa. 19:22 refers to God striking Egypt with a plague. But, immediately following the announcement of that judgment, God promises to heal the nation, which will lead to their turning to him.

dāphaq [דָּפַק, 1849]

The verb ***dāphaq*** is found three times, with the meaning "knock (on the door)" suggesting a heavy action such as "beating" or "pounding" (cf. Judg. 19:22; Song 5:2).

kātat [כָּתַת, 3807]

kātat is a verb occurring about twenty times with the primary sense of "beat" or "crush (by beating)."

The term is used passively with reference to human and animals testicles that have been "crushed" (cf. Lev. 22:24).

kātat also describes the destruction of the golden calf at Sinai by "crushing," "pounding," or "grinding" to dust (cf. Deut. 9:21). Similar acts of destruction are indicated with respect to other idol images in 2 Chr. 34:7; Mic. 1:7.

The action of "beating" or "crushing" one's enemies is noted in Ps. 89:23; Jer. 46:5.

In significant theological contexts, ***kātat*** denotes the action of "beating" (i.e., fashioning) one's weapons into agricultural tools as an eschatological sign of imminent peace, the end of warfare (cf. Isa. 2:4; Joel 3:10; Mic. 4:3).

miqshāh [מִקְשָׁה, 4749]

miqshāh is a noun in the form of a passive participle found ten times. It denotes metal work that has literally been "beaten"— that is, fashioned, hammered, or sculpted.

The usage is exclusive to Israel in the context of tabernacle furniture. ***miqshāh*** refers first of all to the golden cherubim having been "fashioned" on top of the ark of the covenant (cf. Exod. 25:18; 37:7). The construction of the golden lampstand is similarly described in Exod. 25:31, 36; 37:17, 22; Num. 8:4, as are ceremonial silver trumpets in Num. 10:2.

shāḥat [שָׁחַט, 7820]

shāḥat is a verb found in five places, a passive participle with the meaning "beaten," in the sense of "fashioned," "sculpted," identical to ***miqshāh***, above. The term refers exclusively to shields of "beaten" gold in 1 Kgs. 10:16, 17; 2 Chr. 9:15, 16.

NT Words

derō [δέρω, *1194*]

The verb ***derō*** is found fifteen times with the primary sense of "beat," or "strike," in the context of giving someone a beating.

General references to this action are found in Matt. 21:35; Mark 12:3ff.; Luke 12:47ff.; Acts 5:40; 22:19; 2 Cor. 11:20. Christ is subject to such treatment in Luke 22:63; John 18:23. 1 Cor. 9:26 refers to the actions of a boxer who practices his art by "beating" the air.

typtō [τύπτω, *5180*]

The verb ***typtō*** is synonymous with ***derō***, above, found in fourteen places with the meaning "beat," "strike," as in giving a beating (cf. Matt. 24:49; Luke 12:45; Acts 18:17; 21:32). The specific act of "striking" is indicated in Matt. 27:30; Mark 15:19; Luke 6:29; 22:64; Acts 23:2ff. The phrase "beat one's breast" is found in Luke 18:13; 23:48, expressing a penitent humility.

rhabdizō [ῥαβδίζω, *4463*]

rhabdizō is a rare verb with the meaning "to beat with rods," found only in Acts 16:22; 2 Cor. 11:25.

Additional Notes

While there are similarities between the various Hebrew and Greek terms for "beat" or "strike," there are not precise parallels. The Old Testament tends to focus on the aspect of God's judgment in the idea of "beating" or "striking" those who disobey or oppose him. Such treatment applies equally to Israel and the nations. Such a perspective is not found in the New Testament usage.

BEAUTIFUL, BEAUTY

OT Words

***nā'āh* [נָאָה, 4998]**

A rare verb, ***nā'āh*** is only found on three occasions in the Old Testament. The meaning "beautiful" is derived here from the underlying sense of "that which is befitting, desirable, or suitable." The psalmist records in Ps. 93:5 that holiness "adorns" the house of God and thus makes it very attractive for the devout worshiper of Yahweh. The lover describes his beloved's cheeks as "beautiful" with earrings. And then the prophet Isaiah describes the feet that bring the good news of the gospel of peace to God's people as "beautiful on the mountains."

***yāphāh* [יָפָה, 3302]**

This verb is also rare, occurring only eight times, but with the specific meaning "to be beautiful" or "to adorn." It relates to personal beauty in the Song of Songs (4:10; 7:1, 6) where the lover expresses his delight at the beauty of his beloved. ***yāphāh*** is also used in Jer. 4:30 to indicate beauty associated with putting on finery. Ps. 45:2 refers to the "excellent" appearance of the king.

Allegorical references to the beauty of Israel and Assyria are found in Ezek. 16:31 and 31:7, respectively. These descriptions apply collectively to the people of those nations.

Jer. 10:4 contains a non-personal use of ***yāphāh***, referring to the adorning of idols with silver and gold.

***yāpheh* [יָפֶה, 3303]**

This is the more common adjectival form of ***yāphāh***, occurring about forty times. Once again there is a dual focus on personal and non-personal beauty, with the latter category being largely allegorical.

Various individuals are singled out for their attractiveness — Sarai (cf. Gen. 12:11); Rachel (cf. Gen. 29:17); Joseph (cf. Gen. 39:6); David (cf. 1 Sam. 16:12); Absalom (cf. 2 Sam. 14:25); Abishag (cf. 1 Kgs. 1:3, 4). The lover and the beloved also exchange mutual affirmations of one another's attractiveness in the Song of Songs.

The attribution of personal beauty is dominant in the usage of ***yāpheh***, but the metaphorical non-personal sense is also found in a number of contexts. One of the most significant of these is found in Ps. 48:2, where Mt. Zion is praised for its beautiful situation. There is little doubt that the beauty of this sacred place of worship is affirmed precisely because it is where the person of Yahweh may be found and worshiped. The second significant non-personal use of ***yāpheh*** is in Eccl. 3:11, which states that God has made everything beautiful in its time. The whole of creation is in view here, and the affirmation in this context clearly reflects the author's appreciation for the wonder of the universe, notwithstanding the difficulties he faces in gaining an understanding of its purposes — an important theme analyzed throughout the book of Ecclesiastes.

***yophî* [יְפִי, 3308]**

This is the noun derived from ***yāphāh***, above, and is identical in meaning with the adjective ***yāpheh***. ***yophî*** occurs eighteen times and has the same dual emphasis on personal and non-personal beauty. Both Zion and Jerusalem are declared beautiful in Ps. 50:2 and Lam. 2:15, respectively. The beauty of Israel is declared in the allegorical description of Ezek. 16:14, 15, 25. Affirmations of individual beauty are found in Esth. 1:11; Ps. 45:11; Ezek. 28:12, 17.

***tō'ar* [תֹּאַר, 8389]**

The noun ***tō'ar*** occurs fifteen times with the general meaning "that which is good-looking," "of fine form and shape." The specific sense of "beautiful" or "handsome" is applied to people in Gen. 29:17; 39:6; Deut. 21:11; 1 Sam. 16:18; 25:3; 1 Kgs. 1:6; Esth. 2:7. Isa. 53:2 refers to an absence of any "beauty" in the disfigured form of the Suffering Servant. Jer. 11:16 also applies ***tō'ar*** to fruit described as "beautiful" in shape and texture.

***tôb* [טוֹב, 2896]**

tôb is a common adjectival form with the general sense of "good" and related nuances throughout its approximately six hundred occurrences. Occasionally, ***tôb*** refers to "beautiful" women, as in 2 Sam. 11:2; Esth. 2:7.

***tiph'eret* [תִּפְאֶרֶת, 8597]**

tiph'eret is a noun found approximately fifty times meaning "beauty," "glory," plus associated nuances.

The sense of "beauty" is often synonymous with that of "splendor." Royal "splendor," for example, is indicated in Isa. 13:19. Isa. 64:11 refers to the Jerusalem temple as the "beautiful house." The "beauty" of the human form used in the construction of pagan idols is indicated in Isa. 44:13.

Other uses of ***tiph'eret*** are symbolic: for example, the term is used metaphorically to designate the fallen "splendor" of the corrupt nation of Israel in Isa. 28:1, 4; Lam. 2:1. The "Lord of hosts" is depicted metaphorically as a "wreath of beauty" for the remnant of his people on the Day of the Lord (cf. Isa. 28:5). A "beautiful" crown is prepared for the head of Yahweh's chosen bride (i.e., Israel) in the allegorical tale in Ezek. 16:12 (cf. also Ezek. 23:42). Isa. 52:1 describes "beautiful garments," which denote godly character in the people of Yahweh.

hadārāh **[הֲדָרָה, 1927]**

hadārāh is a noun found five times, expressing "beauty" or "splendor," referring to the "beauty" of God's holiness (cf. 1 Chr. 16:29; 2 Chr. 20:21; Pss. 29:2; 96:9).

NT WORDS

hōraios [ὡραῖος, *5611*]

hōraios is an adjectival form meaning "beautiful." It describes the "beautiful" appearance of whitewashed tombs (cf. Matt. 23:27) and constitutes the name "Beautiful," given to one of the gates of Jerusalem (cf. Acts 3:2, 10). The feet of those who preach the gospel are described as "beautiful" in Rom. 10:15 (cf. Isa. 52:7).

See Also: ➞ DELIGHT IN ➞ GLORIFY ➞ GLORY ➞ GOOD ➞ SPLENDOR

BED

OT WORDS

mishkāb **[מִשְׁכָּב, 4904]**

This is the noun derived from ***shākab*** (➞ LIE), "to lie down," and occurs about fifty times. ***mishkāb*** means "bed," but with a dual connotation. While it is translated "bed" in the majority of cases, the term refers not only to the literal place where one sleeps but is also a euphemistic reference to sexual intercourse (usually translated "lying").

Just over half the occurrences of ***mishkāb*** mean "bed" (approximately thirty times), and most of these are found in the Pentateuch, Former Prophets, and Psalms. It is, however, this derivative connotation of sexual intercourse that calls for further comment. In Lev. 18:22, ***mishkāb*** indicates the detestable practice of sodomy. Such homosexual activity is condemned in Scripture and constitutes a capital offense (cf. Lev. 20:13). Certain instances of sexual intercourse result in ceremonial impurity (cf. Num. 31:17, 18, 35). The act of adultery is specifically in view in Gen. 49:4; Prov. 7:17. One group of texts calls for special mention in this regard. In Isa. 57:7, 8 and Ezek. 23:17, the idolatrous activity of Israel in worshiping foreign deities is described in graphic terms as "bedding down" with their "lovers" (i.e., their gods). Such actions are designated as spiritual adultery and are particularly heinous in the light of the unique covenantal relationship between Yahweh and his people. The Old Testament makes it very clear that the bond existing between Israel and her God is equated with marriage. Worship of foreign deities, therefore, is a gross betrayal of trust on Israel's part and the charge of adultery in a spiritual sense is rightly laid at the feet of God's people.

Finally, ***mishkāb*** refers three times to death in terms of being laid on a bed — twice in Isa. 57:2 and Ezek. 32:25, and once in 2 Chr. 16:14, where the term refers to a funeral bier.

mittāh **[מִטָּה, 4296]**

The noun ***mittāh*** occurs about thirty times with the meaning "bed," "couch" (cf. Gen. 47:31; Exod. 8:3; 1 Sam. 19:13ff.; 1 Kgs. 17:19; 2 Chr. 24:25; Esth. 1:6; Ps. 6:6; Song 3:7; Ezek. 23:41; Amos 6:4).

yāṣûa' **[יָצוּעַ, 3326]**

The noun ***yāṣûa'*** is found eleven times, meaning "bed" in a literal sense in Job 17:13; Pss. 63:6; 132:3. The expression "to defile the bed . . ." signifies an action of adultery or sexual impropriety (cf. Gen. 49:4; 1 Chr. 5:1).

'eres **[עֶרֶשׂ, 6210]**

'eres is a noun found in ten contexts with the (literal) meaning "bed" or "couch" (cf. Job 7:13; Pss. 6:6; 132:3; Prov. 7:16; Song 1:16; Amos 3:12; 6:4).

maṣṣā' **[מַצָּע, 4702]**

maṣṣā' is a rare noun denoting a literal "bed" in only six contexts (cf. Dan. 2:28ff.; 4:5ff.; 7:1).

NT WORDS

klinē [κλίνη, *2825*]

klinē occurs ten times, with the literal sense of "bed" (cf. Matt. 9:2ff.; Mark 4:21; 7:30; Luke 5:18; 8:16; 17:34; Acts 5:15; Rev. 2:22).

koitē [κοίτη, *2845*]

The noun ***koitē*** means "bed" in two places. It is literal in Luke 11:7; and Heb. 13:4 contains the injunction "to keep the marriage bed undefiled." Here the exhortation relates to maintaining sexual fidelity in marriage.

BEFALL

OT Words

qārā' [קָרָא, 7122]

The verb ***qārā'*** means "befall," "happen to" in several different contexts.

Gen. 42:4, 38 indicates an anticipation of harm; and Deut. 31:29; Jer. 32:23; 44:23 refer to calamity in the context of divine judgment. The outworking of events still to come is noted in Gen. 49:1 (cf. also Deut. 22:6). Exod. 1:10 refers to an anticipated war. Similarly, disaster is anticipated in Lev. 10:19; Isa. 51:19.

qārāh [קָרָה, 7136]

qārāh is a partial synonym for ***qārā'***, above, occurring about thirty times with the meanings "befall," "happen to" in about half these contexts.

The recounting of experience in general terms is indicated in Gen. 42:29; Esth. 4:7; Eccl. 2:14ff.; 9:11. The experience of harm is indicated in Gen. 44:29. 1 Sam. 28:10 contains a promise that punishment will not happen or take place. Isa. 41:22; Dan. 10:14 record the anticipation of future events.

māṣā' [מָצָא, 4672]

māṣā' is a common verb occurring about 450 times, with the primary meaning "find" plus a variety of related nuances. Included in these nuances is the sense of "befall," "happen."

Deut. 31:17ff. indicates the anticipation of trouble in relation to divine judgment. Num. 20:14; Josh. 2:23; Judg. 6:13 recount difficult experiences.

'ānāh [אָנָה, 579]

'ānāh is a verb found four times, translated "befall," "happen" in Prov. 12:21, affirming that no evil "befalls" the righteous. In Ps. 91:10, the same is true of the psalmist.

See Also: ➠ HAPPEN

BEG, BEGGAR

OT Words

shā'al [שָׁאַל, 7592]

shā'al is a verb occurring around 170 times with the underlying meaning "to ask" as well as a number of related nuances. One of these nuances is "to beg," found in Ps. 109:10; Prov. 20:4, in relation to people seeking food.

NT Words

epaiteō [ἐπαιτέω, *1871*]

epaiteō is a rare verb found only in Luke 16:3 with the meaning "to beg" (i.e., for a living).

prosaiteō [προσαιτέω, *4319*]

prosaiteō is a variant form of ***epaiteō***, above, found in three places. It also expresses the sense of "to beg (for a living)" (cf. Mark 10:46; Luke 18:35; John 9:8).

ptōchos [πτωχός, *4434*]

ptōchos is an adjective occurring about thirty-five times with the primary sense of "poor." There is occasional overlap in meaning with the sense of "beggars" (e.g., Luke 16:20ff.).

See Also: ➠ AFFLICT ➠ ASK ➠ POOR

BEGET

OT Words

yālad [יָלַד, 3205]

This common term occurs approximately five hundred times in the Old Testament and is the usual word for giving birth. In the overwhelming majority of cases ***yālad*** is used in its natural, literal sense — referring to the cycle of human procreation so dear to the mind and culture of the ancient Hebrews.

In a few places, however, the use of ***yālad*** is atypical, or at least unusual, and calls for further comment. In Deut. 32:18, during the so-called "Song of Moses," Israel is condemned for rejecting Yahweh. Such rebellion is described in terms of their deserting the Rock who "fathered" them. This is a clear indication of the intimate nature of Israel's relationship with Yahweh; the term "Rock" can refer to no one else in this context. ***yālad*** in this text points to the origins of Israel as being entirely dependent on the creative power and initiative of God himself. This is an additional perspective on the manner in which Israel's relationship with God is described in the Old Testament. Yahweh is here portrayed as the Israelites' spiritual father. Elsewhere, of course, the bond is described in marital terms. In both cases, the nature of the union is one of intimate dependence, a reality that Israel only infrequently recognized throughout her long history. A similar situation is envisaged in Ps. 2:7, where the psalmist describes the anointed one of God as "begotten" by him. This psalm is traditionally understood as messianic in nature, anticipating the incarnation of Jesus Christ and illuminating our understanding of the unique relationship that exists between Father and Son.

At a less sublime though nonetheless significant level, Hos. 5:7 condemns Israel's idolatry in a striking way. The prophet denounces the people of God for having given birth to illegitimate children. This is a colorful, metaphorical way of alluding to their idolatrous and adulterous relationship with the Canaanite deities of the land. It is a relationship fraught with spiritual perils, and the reference to "illegitimate children" only serves to heighten the terrible consequences for Israel that such rebellious behavior will entail.

nēphel [נֵפֶל, 5309]

This noun occurs only three times in the Old Testament and indicates "stillbirth" or spontaneous abortion (cf. Job 3:16; Ps. 58:8).

tā'am [תָּאַם, 8382]

tā'am is a verb found in six contexts, with the underlying sense of "be joined together." In Song 4:2; 6:6 the term means "to give birth to twins" with reference to sheep.

NT Words

gennaō [γεννάω, *1080*]

gennaō is a verb occurring about one hundred times with the primary meanings "beget," "give birth to."

This term is commonly employed in genealogical listings referring to the origin of successive generations, especially in relation to the earthly lineage of Jesus Christ (cf. Matt. 1:1ff.). See also Acts 7:8, 20, 29.

The general sense of "to be born" is indicated in relation to Christ in Matt. 2:1ff.; Luke 1:35; John 18:37. Other general references include Matt. 19:12; Mark 14:21; Luke 1:57; Acts 22:3; Gal. 4:23; Heb. 11:23.

The metaphorical sense of "to be born illegitimately" (i.e., as the result of an immoral liaison) is indicated in John 8:41. Elsewhere, the phrase "bear children for slavery" is a symbolic reference to Israel's condition under the bondage of the old covenant (cf. Gal. 4:24, 29). John 9:23 refers to "being born in sin." The expression "to become one's spiritual father" is found in connection with Paul's relationship to his converts in 1 Cor. 4:15; Phlm. 10.

The most significant metaphorical usage of ***gennaō*** is found in the expression "to be born again," which indicates a new spiritual sensitivity to the movement of the Spirit of God, producing saving faith in Christ and leading to membership in the kingdom of God (cf. John 1:13; 3:3ff.). The expression "to be born of God" indicates a similar reality (cf. 1 John 2:29; 3:9; 4:7; 5:4, 18). In addition, "being born of God" describes the process by which Christ the Son came to have a filial relationship with God the Father, indicated by the statement: "You are my son, today I have begotten you" (cf. Acts 13:33; Heb. 1:5; 5:5).

The state of "being born blind" in a literal, physical sense is noted in John 9:2, 19ff.

anagennaō [ἀναγεννάω, *313*]

anagennaō is a rare verb found three times with the meaning "to be born again," referring to one's spiritual awakening to the word of God through his Spirit (cf. 1 Pet. 1:3, 23).

genesis [γένεσις, *1083*]

genesis is a rare noun derived from ***gennaō*** (see above), occurring twice and denoting the "birth" of Christ in Matt. 1:18; Luke 1:14.

monogenēs [μονογενής, *3439*]

monogenēs is a noun found in nine contexts denoting an "only child."

General references to an "only child" include Luke 7:12; 8:42; 9:38. References to Christ as the "only begotten" Son of God the Father are found in John 1:14, 18; 3:16ff.; Heb. 11:17; 1 John 4:9.

gennētos [γεννητός, *1084*]

gennētos is a rare adjective denoting "that which is born of woman" (i.e., children) (cf. Matt. 11:11; Luke 7:28).

artigennētos [ἀρτιγέννητος, *738*]

artigennētos is a rare adjectival variant of ***gennētos***, above, found only in 1 Pet. 2:2 denoting "newborn" babies.

apokyeō [ἀποκυέω, *616*]

apokyeō is a rare verb found only twice with the symbolic meaning "to bring forth" in relation to the process by which sin ultimately results in death in Jas. 1:15. Positively, Jas. 1:18 refers to the action of the divine will whereby God "has brought us forth" by the word of truth — he has constituted his people as his children through faith and trust in him.

ektrōma [ἔκτρωμα, *1626*]

ektrōma is a rare noun found only in 1 Cor. 15:8 referring metaphorically to the atypical origin of Paul's apostolic authority as one who had an "untimely birth."

tiktō [τίκτω, *5088*]

The verb ***tiktō*** occurs about twenty times with the underlying sense of "to bring forth," referring literally to the begetting of children and the cultivation of plants. It also has a metaphorical usage.

Literal references to "giving birth" to children include the birth of Jesus the Messiah (Matt. 1:21ff.; 2:2; Luke 1:31, 57; 2:6ff.; Heb. 11:11 [cf. also Gal. 4:27]). Heb. 6:7 refers to the "bringing forth" of plants.

tiktō is used metaphorically in Jas. 1:15 to indicate that desire "gives birth" to sin. And in Rev. 12:2ff. there is a symbolic reference to the birth of Christ.

prōtotokos [πρωτότοκος, *4416*]

prōtotokos is an adjective found nine times with the meaning "firstborn" throughout. A general reference to "firstborn" children is found in Heb. 11:28.

With reference to Christ, Mary's "firstborn" son is indicated in Luke 2:7; Heb. 1:6. In a spiritual sense he is designated as the "firstborn" among many in Rom. 8:29. Col. 1:15 affirms that Christ is the "firstborn" of all creation; and Col. 1:18; Rev. 1:5 both declare that he is also the "firstborn" from the dead.

Heb. 12:23 makes reference to the "firstborn" enrolled in heaven, speaking of the saints.

Additional Notes

It is evident that the various New Testament terms for giving birth have a profound spiritual dimension. In this regard, the focus of the term ***yālad*** can be said to match that of the New Testament vocabulary at least in a minimal way. Although the spiritual sense of "giving birth" receives a far greater emphasis in the New Testament, it could be argued that the Old Testament anticipates this.

See Also: ➡ DEATH ➡ DIE ➡ NATION ➡ PEOPLE

BEGIN, BEGINNER, BEGINNING

OT Words

ḥālal [חָלַל, 2490]

The verb ***ḥālal*** has a broad range of meanings, including "begin." Other meanings are "pollute," "defile," and "profane." Of the approximately 170 occurrences of ***ḥālal***, about one-third of them mean "begin."

One particular aspect of the meaning of ***ḥālal*** is worthy of comment — the occasions on which God is said to initiate certain activity. There are ten such references, and they indicate God's determination to initiate either blessing on, or judgment against, his people.

In regard to the latter, 2 Kgs. 10:32; 15:37; Jer. 25:29 all refer to God commencing judgment against his people for their sin. Then, God declares his intention in 1 Sam. 3:12 to begin specific judgment on the house of Eli for the high priest's failure to restrain the wickedness of his sons, Hophni and Phinehas.

God is also said to initiate specific blessings on his people. Deut. 3:24; 2:25 affirm the initial actions of God as he begins to pave the way for Israel's entry into the land of promise. At the outset, this involves the removal of barriers to entry into Canaan. In Deut. 3:24 Moses recognizes that God truly has begun to make his intentions clear and to fulfill his promises concerning Canaan. Deut. 2:25, more specifically, declares that God has begun to instill fear into the hearts of the Canaanites so that the conquest of the land will be much easier to accomplish. Finally, in this regard, God declares in Deut. 2:31 that he has begun to give Sihon, the king of the Moabites, into the hands of the Israelites. God then immediately commands the people to go and begin to possess the land of Moab. This verse demonstrates the balance of divine initiative and human responsibility that is so often emphasized throughout Scripture.

Josh. 3:7 indicates God's determination to reveal Joshua to the people of Israel as his appointed successor to Moses. From this point on, God accordingly begins to exalt Joshua in the eyes of the people. Finally, in Judg. 13:5, the Spirit of the Lord begins to move in the life of Samson so that he can begin to rid the land of the Philistines.

rē'shît [רֵאשִׁית, 7225]

This term occurs approximately fifty times in the Old Testament, meaning "first," "chief," and "beginning." The meaning "beginning" is found in about a third of the occurrences. Unique among these is the reference in Gen. 1:1 to the beginning of all things when God created the heavens and the earth. ***rē'shît*** also refers to the beginning of human institutions such as kingdoms or regal periods (cf. Gen. 10:10; Jer. 26:1; 27:11; 28:1; 49:34); to the origins of virtues such as knowledge and wisdom (cf. Ps. 111:10; Prov. 1:7; 8:22); and also to the origins of sinful behavior (cf. Mic. 1:13). Other references to "beginning" are found in Gen. 49:3; Deut. 11:12; 21:17; Job 8:7; 42:12; Prov. 17:14; Eccl. 7:8; Isa. 46:10.

teḥillāh [תְּחִלָּה, 8462]

This term is synonymous with ***rē'shît***, above, and carries the predominant meaning of "beginning." It is found twenty-two times in the Old Testament and is translated "beginning" on fifteen occasions (cf. Gen. 13:3; 41:21; Ruth 1:22; 2 Sam. 21:9, 10; 2 Kgs. 17:25; Ezra 4:6; Neh. 11:17; Prov. 9:10; Eccl. 10:13; Isa. 1:26; Dan. 9:21, 23; Hos. 1:2; Amos 7:1). In the remaining texts, ***teḥillāh*** is translated "at the first" or "first time" (cf. Gen. 43:18, 20; Judg. 1:1; 20:18; 2 Sam. 17:9; Dan. 8:1).

NT Words

archomai [ἄρχομαι, *756*]

The verb ***archomai***, meaning "begin," occurs about eighty times.

The translation "begin," in the sense of "be the first to do something," is indicated in relation to Jesus' preaching activity in Matt. 4:17; to his teaching the crowds in Matt. 11:7; Mark 4:1; 12:1; Luke 7:24; 11:29; and to showing his disciples that he must die in Matt. 16:21; Mark 10:32. See also Matt. 12:1; Mark 11:15; Luke 3:23; John 13:5; Acts 1:1.

Other general uses of "begin" include Matt. 14:30; 26:74; Mark 2:23; Luke 5:21; Acts 2:4; 18:26; 27:35. The expression "judgment begins at the house of God" is found in 1 Pet. 4:17.

enarchomai [ἐνάρχομαι, *1728*]

enarchomai is a rare variant of ***archomai***, above, with the meaning "begin" in Gal. 3:3; Phil. 1:6.

proenarchomai [προενάρχομαι, *4278*]

proenarchomai is another rare variant of ***archomai***, above, with the sense of "to make a beginning already, or before" (cf. 2 Cor. 8:6, 10).

archē [ἀρχή, *746*]

The noun ***archē*** is found in about sixty contexts with the primary meaning "beginning," with a variety of nuances.

The translation "beginning," with reference to the creation of the world, is indicated for example in Matt. 19:4, 8; Mark 10:6; 13:19; John 8:44; 2 Thess. 2:13; Heb. 1:10; 2 Pet. 3:4. Specific reference to Christ's pre-existent state with God before creation as "the beginning" is indicated in John 1:1ff.; Col. 1:18. In Rev. 1:8; 21:6; 22:13 Christ is described as "the Alpha and the Omega" — the "beginning" and the "end."

General, non-specific references to "beginning" include Luke 1:2; John 15:27; Acts 11:15; Heb. 7:3; 1 John 2:7, 13ff.; 3:8ff.

The meaning "beginning" in the sense of "commencement" is used metaphorically to describe the beginnings of trials at the end time as birth pangs in Matt. 24:8; Mark 13:8. References to the "commencement" or "beginning" of the gospel of Christ are found in Mark 1:1; Phil. 4:15; 1 John 1:1.

BEHEAD

OT Words

kārat [כָּרַת, 3772]

kārat is a common verb found about three hundred times with the underlying meanings "cut off," "cut down" in both a literal and metaphorical sense. In 1 Sam. 17:51; 31:9, ***kārat*** is used to indicate the "beheading" of an enemy. (→ CUT)

NT Words

apokephalizō [ἀποκεφαλίζω, *607*]

apokephalizō is a verb meaning "to behead." It is found in five places, all in the context of the execution of John the Baptist (cf. Matt. 14:10; Mark 6:16, 27; Luke 9:9).

pelekizō [πελεκίζω, *3990*]

pelekizō is a rare verb found only in Rev. 20:4, referring to believers who "were beheaded" for their faith in Christ. The term literally means "to cut off with an ax."

BEHOLD → APPEAR → SEE

BELIEF, BELIEVE, BELIEVER

OT Words

'āman [אָמַן, 539]

This verb is found approximately one hundred times in the Old Testament. With only several minor exceptions, the meaning of ***'āman*** centers on the concepts of "belief," "faith," and "trust" — terms that are by and large synonymous. (→ FAITH → TRUST)

'āman means to "believe" in about fifty contexts. The majority of these (approximately forty) convey the idea of "belief" in conjunction with "faith" and "trust" — such that the translations "believe," "have faith," and "trust" are virtually interchangeable. About half the uses of ***'āman*** refer to belief or trust in God, while the other half indicate belief or trust in people and, in two cases, in animals.

With respect to belief in God, several examples stand out. Gen. 15:6 contains the profoundly significant statement that Abraham believed God and it was credited to him as righteousness. This belief on Abraham's part indicated a wholehearted commitment to, and trust in, the person of God — rather than a mere intellectual assent to a particular proposition. Num. 20:12 refers to Moses' act of disobedience in the wilderness when he struck the rock to bring forth water, rather than merely speaking to it as God had commanded. God's admonition of Moses centers on the fact that the latter did not believe in or trust God sufficiently to honor him in this situation. Deut. 9:23 refers to Israel's rebellion against God in failing to enter the land. The charge leveled against them is that they failed to believe God — that is, they failed to put their faith and trust in him. 2 Chr. 20:20 records Jehoshaphat's charge to the people of Jerusalem and Judah to believe in the Lord their God. It is a call to have faith and trust in him. In a more positive light, Exod. 14:31 records the Israelites' worship of God after their deliverance from the Egyptians at the Re(e)d Sea. The text says they believed the Lord and his servant, and the meaning is clear. As a result of their deliverance, the people's faith and trust in Yahweh, and in Moses, was renewed and restored. Then, in Isa. 7:9 the prophet confronts a nervous and doubting Ahaz and exhorts him not to waver in his belief in God by failing to trust him at this time of crisis in the face of an Assyrian attack. Other references that reflect a similar perspective are found in 2 Kgs. 17:14; Pss.78:22, 32; 106:24; 116:10; 119:66; Exod. 4:5, 31; Exod. 19:9; Num. 14:11; Jonah 3:5; Deut. 1:32; Isa. 28:16.

Even in contexts where ***'āman*** refers to belief in people, a like emphasis is found. Believing in people is equivalent to putting faith in them (cf. Gen. 45:26; Exod. 4:1, 8, 9; Judg. 11:20; 1 Sam. 27:12; 2 Chr. 32:15; Mic. 7:5; Hab. 1:5).

There are, however, a few exceptions to this observation, for ***'āman*** may also be understood as "believing" only in the sense of granting intellectual assent to a particular point of view (cf. 1 Kgs. 10:7). Also, in 2 Chr. 9:6, the Queen of Sheba is forced to concede that the reports of Solomon's wisdom and wealth were quite true, even though she previously had refused to believe them. Other examples are found in Jer. 40:14; Lam. 4:12; Job 29:24.

The predominant usage of ***'āman*** in the Old Testament testifies to the phenomenon of "belief" in an active sense, incorporating the elements of "faith" and "trust," whether referring to God or human beings.

NT Words

pisteuō [πιστεύω, *4100*]

The verb ***pisteuō*** occurs around 250 times with the underlying meaning "believe." Included in this usage is the very significant nuance of "have faith, put one's trust in" the person of Christ, as the means by which God applies salvation to his people.

pisteuō most commonly means "believe" in reference to saving faith in Christ. Examples of this meaning include Matt. 8:13; Mark 9:24; Luke 22:67; John 1:7; 3:15ff., 36; 4:39ff.; 6:29ff.; 7:38ff.; 11:25ff.; 16:27ff.; Acts 2:44; 4:4, 32; 11:17, 21; 15:5ff.; Rom. 1:16; 4:24; 10:4ff.; 1 Cor. 1:21; Gal. 2:16; Eph. 1:13; 1 Thess. 2:10ff.; 1 Tim. 3:16; 1 Pet. 1:8; 2:6; 1 John 3:23; 5:1ff. The serious consequences of not believing in Christ are noted in John 10:26. References to Abraham's "belief" (i.e., his saving faith) in God as a model of genuine saving trust are found in Rom. 4:3ff., 11, 17ff.; Gal. 3:6, 22; Jas. 2:23.

Jesus commands belief in the gospel in Mark 1:15; John 10:38; 14:1. The need to believe in God for answer to prayer is expressed in Matt. 21:22; Mark 11:23ff. Luke 1:45; 24:25; John 2:22 refer to believing in the prophetic word of God. Heb. 11:6; Jas. 2:19 address the need to believe in God. The command not to believe false teaching is found in Matt. 24:26.

General references to "believe" with the sense of "accept as true," both positive and negative, are found in Matt. 21:32; Mark 16:13; 1 Cor. 11:18; 13:7.

apisteō [ἀπιστέω, *569*]

apisteō is the negative form of ***pisteuō***, above, found seven times with the meaning "not to believe," or "have no faith," "be unfaithful." The sense of "refuse to believe" in the gospel and/or the true significance of Christ and his works is found in Mark 16:11, 16; Acts 28:24. See also Luke 24:11, 41. The sense of "be unfaithful" to Christ and the gospel is indicated in Rom. 3:3; 2 Tim. 2:13.

apeitheō [ἀπειθέω, *544*]

apeitheō is a negative variant of ***peithō*** (→ TRUST) meaning "not to believe" and "be disobedient." The two occasionally overlap in meaning.

A refusal to believe in Christ is indicated in John 3:36; Acts 14:2; 17:5; 19:9; Rom. 15:31; 1 Pet. 2:7. The refusal to obey the word or truth of the gospel is indicated in Rom. 2:8; 10:21; 11:30ff.; Heb. 3:18; 11:31; 1 Pet. 2:8; 3:1, 20; 4:17.

See Also: → FAITH → FAITHFUL → PERSUADE → TRUST

BELLY

OT Words

gāḥôn [גָּחוֹן, **1512**]

This is a rare term, occurring only twice in the Old Testament. In Gen. 3:15, ***gāḥôn*** refers to the belly of the serpent. The context makes it clear that this is a reference to the utter humiliation of the serpent by God, who condemns the beast for his role in deceiving Adam and Eve. The second reference is found in Lev. 11:42, where the law forbids the consumption of animals that crawl on their bellies.

beten [בֶּטֶן, **990**]

This word occurs approximately seventy times in the Old Testament. The majority of references (about fifty) indicate the meaning "womb." Literal references to the physical womb are found in Judg. 3:21, 22; Song 7:2; Hab. 3:16. The remainder of texts containing the term ***beten*** all use the word in a metaphorical sense (cf. Job 15:2; 32:18, 19; Ps. 31:9; Prov. 13:25).

NT Words

koilia [κοιλία, *2836*]

The noun ***koilia*** is found in approximately twenty places, with the meanings "belly" and "womb" evenly divided throughout the usage. (→ WOMB)

Matt. 12:40 refers to the "belly" of a great fish, citing the story of Jonah. The term is also used metaphorically, indicating the "belly" as the seat of human emotions (though it is best translated "heart," cf. John 7:38).

Elsewhere ***koilia*** refers to the "stomach" (cf. Matt. 15:17; Mark 7:19; Luke 15:16; 1 Cor. 6:13; Rev. 10:9, 10). In Rom. 16:18; Phil. 3:19 ***koilia*** implies the sense of "gluttony."

See Also: → WOMB

BELOVED

OT Words

yedîd [יְדִיד, **3039**]

yedîd is the construct form of the adjective ***yādîd***. It means "beloved" and is used largely, though not exclusively, in poetic contexts.

yedîd occurs only nine times, with all but one of these texts referring to God's people as "beloved" in his sight. Deut. 33:12 describes Benjamin as "beloved of the Lord" in the contexts of Jacob bestowing his final blessings on his children. Ps. 45:1 contains the title *shîr yedîdôt* — "a wedding song," but which literally translates "song of the beloved." God's people are described as his "beloved" in general terms in the following passages: Pss. 60:5; 108:6; 127:2; Isa. 5:1. Jer. 11:15 refers to Israel as the "beloved" of God. But what is particularly striking here is the context in which such a term of affection is used, for it occurs in the midst of an oracle damning Israel for her idolatrous rebellion against Yahweh. A very similar expression is used in much the same way in the following chapter (cf. Jer. 12:7), where God announces his intention to deliver his "beloved" into the hands of her enemies because she has rejected him. In this case, the term used for "beloved" is *yedîdût*, a derivative of ***yedîd*** that occurs only once in the Old Testament.

Finally, ***yedîd*** is used in an impersonal sense only once, where in Ps. 84:1 the dwelling place of God is described as "lovely."

dôd [דּוֹד, **1730**]

This is a more common term for "beloved" that occurs about thirty times in the Old Testament with this meaning. The term is also translated "uncle" in seventeen occurrences.

dôd is found almost exclusively in the Song of Songs, where on all but four occasions it is used by the woman to refer to her beloved. Twice he uses it to describe her (cf. Song 2:17; 4:10), and twice the mysterious group of onlookers known as "the chorus" uses it to refer to them both (cf. Song 1:4; 5:1).

NT Words

agapētos [ἀγαπητός, *27*]

agapētos is an adjectival form occurring around sixty times with the meaning "(dearly) beloved," "well-loved."

God designates Christ as "my beloved Son" (cf. Matt. 3:17; 12:18; 17:5; Mark 1:11; 9:7; Luke 3:22; 9:35; 2 Pet. 1:17). In 1 Cor. 4:17, Paul refers to Timothy as his "beloved son" since he was converted under the apostle's ministry. In Luke 20:13, ***agapētos*** refers to a person in the parable, though in reality it is applied to Christ as the Son of God.

People are deemed "highly esteemed" or "beloved" in general contexts in Acts 15:25; Rom. 16:5ff.; Eph. 5:1; 6:21; 1 Tim. 6:2. Rom. 1:7; 11:28 designates people as "beloved of God."

The term "beloved" is also a form of address or greeting in Rom. 12:19; 1 Cor. 10:14; 2 Cor. 7:1; Phil. 2:12; Phlm. 2; Heb. 6:9; 1 Pet. 2:11; 2 Pet. 3:14ff.; 1 John 4:1ff.; Jude 3, 17, 20.

See Also: → LOVE

BENEFIT, BENEFACTOR → FAVOR → GOOD → GRACE

BERYL

OT Words

tarshîsh **[תַּרְשִׁישׁ, 8658]**

tarshîsh is a noun occurring eight times denoting the precious stone "beryl" or "chrysolite." There is some vagueness in the identification of this particular stone. The translation of Hebrew and Greek terminology in relation to gemstones is often imprecise.

Literal references to this precious stone are found in relation to the gemstone settings representing each of the twelve tribes of Israel on the high priest's breastpiece attached to the ephod (cf. Exod. 28:20; 39:13). This was an important part of the high priest's apparel when he appeared before Yahweh in the holy of holies on the Day of Atonement representing the entire nation of Israel, offering sacrifice for their sins of the past year.

The use of ***tarshîsh*** in Song 5:14 is metaphorical, alluding to the new bride's perception of the beauty of her lover. Similarly, it is symbolic in Ezek. 28:13, denoting the beauty of the king of Tyre prior to his fall from heaven.

Dan. 10:6 mentions "beryl" or "chrysolite" in relation to the appearance of the angelic "man dressed in linen" (probably the angel of the Lord) in Daniel's vision.

This precious stone is also observed in the appearance of the cherubim, the guardians of Yahweh's "chariot throne" in the vision of the prophet Ezekiel (cf. Ezek. 1:16; 10:9).

NT Words

bēryllos [βήρυλλος, *969*]

bēryllos is a rare noun found only in Rev. 21:20, denoting a "beryl" as the key component of the eighth gate of the heavenly city of Jerusalem.

BESEECH → ASK

BESIEGE → SIEGE

BETRAY → DELIVER

BETROTH

OT Words

'āras **[אָרַשׂ, 781]**

This term is relatively rare in the Old Testament, occurring only eleven times. However, its usage is very significant in that it gives us a key insight into the phenomenon of marriage and betrothal in ancient Israelite culture.

Most of the occurrences of ***'āras*** are found in the Deuteronomic legislation of the Pentateuch. Deut. 20:7 refers to a situation in which an Israelite is betrothed to a woman, but has not yet married her. In this case he is not required to go to war, lest he die in battle and someone else marry her. Deut. 28:30 contains a curse concerning the loss of one's betrothed to another. The curse relates to Israel's violation of her responsibilities and obligations under the Mosaic covenant. One of the consequences of such disobedience for the people of God would be the shattering of the intimate connection between betrothal and marriage. In ancient Israel, betrothal was considered a binding promise prior to the consummation of marriage. Though betrothed couples were not granted the rights of marriage, they were considered as good as married. The breakdown of a betrothal was thus viewed with the greatest seriousness — hence the tragedy of Deut. 28:30. Israel's rebellion against Yahweh would result in men loving their promised "brides-to-be" and seeing them ravished by another. One assumes, in the context of Deut. 28, that these "others" would be the soldiers of foreign armies.

Exod. 22:16 and Deut. 22:28 record similar circumstances in which a virgin is seduced, and then required to marry the man involved. In Exod. 22:16 it is a matter, one assumes, of mutual attraction; whereas in Deut. 22:28 the rape of a virgin woman is involved. In both cases marriage is the required outcome for both parties. The key distinction here is that the woman in both cases is not betrothed. If she had been, then the consequences of premarital intercourse with another man would have been far more serious. Deut. 22:23ff. records the legislative requirements covering such a situation. Two separate sets of circumstances are in view here. In Deut. 22:23, the penalty for a man sleeping with a betrothed woman whom he meets in a town is death — the same penalty as for proven adultery (cf. Deut. 22:22). In this case both the man and the woman are to die. Interestingly, the rationale for the woman's execution is that she did not scream for help, presumably because she had willingly consented to intercourse. The rationale for the man's sentence is equally interesting in that he is condemned for taking another man's wife — even though the woman was not yet technically married. This demonstrates the very close link between betrothal and marriage in the old covenant law. Secondly, Deut. 22:25, 27 record the event of a man meeting a woman who is betrothed, and raping her when the two are in the country. In this case only the man is to be executed, for the woman is judged to be defenseless when she screams for help, since no one hears her and comes to her aid. In this case no blame attaches to the woman. There is no doubt from these observations just how seriously God viewed betrothal and its implications for marriage as a sacred institution in the life of his people.

Two other texts remain to be considered. In 2 Sam. 3:14ff. David calls for Michal to be given to him as his wife. Previously he had betrothed her for the price of 100 Philistine foreskins paid to her father Saul (cf. 1 Sam. 18:27). There is no doubt that David was justified in making his claim; the only problem here is that, in the interim, Michal had married Paltiel, son of Laish. Michal, however, is simply taken from Paltiel and given to David. The narrative does not address any question of impropriety here. What is clear, notwithstanding the anomaly in question, is that the link between betrothal and marriage in very close indeed.

Finally, in Hos. 2:19, 20 we have one of the most sublime images of Yahweh's love for his people in the whole of Scripture. Here God declares his intention to take Israel back as his betrothed, despite her having rejected him completely, and after a period of severe chastening. Israel's idolatry is portrayed in Hosea as damnable adultery against God and is symbolically represented through the life experience of Hosea, who is required to marry the woman Gomer, who in turn would form a number of adulterous relationships and bear him children of adultery. The healing process initiated by God is described in terms of God taking Israel back, promising to "re-betroth" her forever, in an intimate relationship of righteousness and justice, love and compassion. There is no doubt that "re-marriage" is in view, since the language anticipates the inauguration of new covenant blessing. The marriage between God and Israel in the old covenant is paralleled and developed in the new covenant through the powerful metaphor of Christ and his bride, the church, portrayed most fully in the book of Revelation (cf. Rev. 21).

ḥāraph [**חָרַף, 2778**]

ḥāraph is a verb occurring around forty times with the primary meaning "reproach." However, in Lev. 19:20 it means "betrothed" in relation to sexual misconduct with a slave girl promised in marriage to another man.

NT Words

mnēsteuō [μνηστεύω, *3423*]

mnēsteuō is a rare verb found three times, used only in the passive sense of "be promised in marriage" (i.e., betrothed). It is used only in relation to Mary the mother of Christ, as one "betrothed" to Joseph (cf. Matt. 1:18; Luke 1:27; 2:5).

harmozomai [ἁρμόζομαι, *718*]

harmozomai is a rare verb found only in 2 Cor. 11:2, used metaphorically in relation to the apostle Paul's action in "betrothing" the Corinthian congregation to Christ as their (corporate) spiritual Lord.

Additional Notes

It is interesting that the reference to betrothal in the account of Mary and Joseph's experience in Matt. 1:18ff. reinforces the meaning of the Old Testament ***'āras***. Joseph's response to Mary's apparent promiscuity, prior to the revelation given him by angelic visitation, is admirable. On the surface, she was guilty of a capital offense, but Joseph's love for her overrode this; hence his desire to "put her away quietly." Of course, the subsequent revelation of Mary's miraculous conception by the Holy Spirit dispelled all such fears. However, the solemnity of betrothal and its implications under the law were certainly not lost on Joseph.

The implications for maintaining "fidelity" in our relationship with Christ as head of the church are also important. Unfaithfulness in our relationship with Jesus Christ will be regarded in exactly the same way as Israel's idolatry and unfaithfulness towards Yahweh was viewed under the old covenant. Indeed, the penalty is much more severe.

See Also: → MARRIAGE

BETTER → GOOD

BEWAIL → MOURN

BIER

OT Words

***'ārôn* [אָרוֹן, 727]**

This term basically means "chest" or "box." It is found approximately 180 times in the Old Testament, and on almost every occasion it refers to the sacred chest containing the scrolls of the Decalogue and other holy items that were kept in the holy of holies in the tabernacle and the temple. It is normally translated "ark."

On one occasion, however, it refers to the coffin containing Joseph's remains that were carried from Egypt back to Canaan at his request. His bones were eventually buried at Shechem in a plot of land bought by Jacob, his father, from the sons of Hamor, the father of Shechem (cf. Josh. 24:32). ***'ārôn*** refers elsewhere to a chest used to collect money from the people as gifts to the temple treasury (cf. 2 Kgs. 12:9, 10; 2 Chr. 24:8–11).

NT Words

***soros* [σορός, *4673*]**

soros is a rare noun found only in Luke 7:14, denoting a "bier" — that is, a funeral carriage on which the dead were transported to their place of burial.

BIND, BINDING

OT Words

***'āsar* [אָסַר, 631]**

This verb occurs approximately sixty times in the Old Testament with the basic meanings "tie," "bind," "imprison." ***'āsar*** is used both literally and metaphorically.

At the literal level, ***'āsar*** refers to prisoners in varying contexts being bound with ropes or chains. Among these, Samson is mentioned frequently (cf. Judg. 15:10ff.; 16:7ff.), along with Joseph and others in Egypt (cf. Gen. 39:20; 40:3, 5; 42:16). In its participial form, ***'āsar*** is actually translated "prisoners" in several contexts (cf. Ps. 146:7; Eccl. 4:14; Isa. 49:9; 61:1). Other literal references to prisoners being bound are found in the historical accounts of the fall of the northern kingdom of Israel (cf. 2 Kgs. 17:4, Hoshea); Pharaoh Neco's campaign against Judah (cf. 2 Kgs. 23:33, Jehoahaz); Assyria's campaign against Judah (cf. 2 Chr. 33:11, Manasseh); Nebuchadnezzar's campaign against Jerusalem (cf. 2 Chr. 36:6, Jehoiakim; 2 Kgs. 25:7, Zedekiah). ***'āsar*** is also used with reference to "tying up" (i.e., preparing) chariots (cf. 1 Kgs. 18:44; Gen. 46:29; Exod. 14:6; 2 Kgs. 9:21; Jer. 46:4); and, on one occasion, ***'āsar*** refers to the binding of a festal offering prior to sacrifice (cf. Ps. 118:27).

'āsar is also used metaphorically in the sense of a "vow." Here the idea is that one "binds" one's soul to a specific promise or cause. Num. 30 contains all the instances of ***'āsar*** used in this way. This chapter formalizes the legal principles and procedures to be adopted when Israelites make vows for service and worship of Yahweh (cf. Num. 30:2ff.). ***'āsar*** can also symbolize the phenomenon of divine judgment. For example, foreign kings are condemned to be bound with chains in Ps. 149:8, and Hos. 10:10 refers to God's people being bound by him in judgment. Although expressed symbolically, these judgments are nonetheless very real.

***'esār* [אֱסָר, 632]**

This is the noun derived from ***'āsar***, above, and has the metaphorical sense of "vow." It is found only in Num. 30:2–15.

***ḥābash* [חָבַשׁ, 2280]**

ḥābash is a synonym for ***'āsar*** (see above), occurring about thirty times with the meaning "bind" in both a literal and metaphorical sense.

In its literal sense, ***ḥābash*** refers to the binding of turbans on the heads of the priests in Exod. 29:9; Lev. 8:13. It is also used this way in Ezek. 24:17, where the prophet is commanded to keep his turban fastened and not display his grief publicly after the sudden death of his wife. ***ḥābash*** is also used to indicate preparation for riding. In the following texts it is translated "saddle" with reference to riding asses: Gen. 22:3; Num. 22:21; 2 Sam. 17:23; 19:26; 1 Kgs. 2:40; 13:13ff.; 2 Kgs. 4:24; Judg. 19:10; 2 Sam. 16:1.

Metaphorically, ***ḥābash*** is used in several places to indicate God's divine healing of his people, where he promises to "bind up" their wounds (cf. Isa. 30:26; Ezek. 34:16; Hos. 6:1; Ps. 147:3). ***ḥābash*** also describes the healing ministry of the Suffering Servant in Isa. 61:1. The term can be used negatively, for example to refer to God's refusal to "bind up" (i.e., heal) the arm of a pharaoh which he has broken in judgment against him (cf. Ezek. 30:21). The term is used in similar fashion in Isa. 3:7, where God declares that he will not heal (i.e., "bind up") his people on account of their sinful rebellion against him.

dābaq [**דָּבַק, 1692**]

This term, meaning "cleave," occurs about fifty times. In about half these instances it refers to the idea of intimate association, of "bonding" in a metaphorical sense. The following contexts are in view: marriage (cf. Gen. 2:24); devotion to God (cf. Ps. 119:31; Deut. 11:22; 10:20; 13:4, 5; 30:20; Josh. 22:5; 23:8; 2 Kgs. 18:6); devotion to individuals (cf. Ruth 1:14; 2 Sam. 20:2; 1 Kgs. 11:2; Gen. 34:3); interrelationship of parts of the body (cf. Job 19:20; 29:10; 31:7; Ps. 102:5, 6; Lam. 4:4); sinful associations or the consequences of sin (cf. Josh. 23:12; Deut. 28:60; 2 Kgs. 3:3; 5:27).

qāshar [**קָשַׁר, 7194**]

Like the terms above, ***qāshar*** has both a literal and a metaphorical level of meaning in the idea of "binding." This term is found in forty-four places in the Old Testament.

The literal level of meaning accounts for about a quarter of the occurrences of ***qāshar***. Deut. 6:8 and 11:18, for example, talk about the divine requirements of literally tying portions of the law to one's forehead as a means of continually focusing on the centrality of the covenant in the life of the people of Yahweh (cf. also Prov. 3:3; 7:3). Then there are references to tying scarlet thread around the hand of the baby Zerah (cf. Gen. 38:28), and binding the scarlet cord to the widow Rahab's house (cf. Josh. 2:18, 21). Neh. 4:6 refers to the "joining together" of the reconstructed wall of Jerusalem.

The metaphorical sense of ***qāshar*** indicates "conspiracy" — a joining together, or bonding, in intimate association for an illicit purpose. This is the dominant meaning of the verb. Examples of this are found in various contexts: Saul's accusations against his people (cf. 1 Sam. 22:8), and in particular against the priests of Nob (1 Sam. 22:13); conspiracies associated with kings of the divided monarchy (cf. 1 Kgs. 16:9ff. [Zimri]; 1 Kgs. 15:27 [Baasha]; 2 Kgs. 15:10 [Shallum]; 2 Kgs. 15:25 [Pekah]; 2 Kgs. 15:30 [Hoshea]; 2 Kgs. 21:23 [Ammon]; Neh. 4:8 [against Nehemiah]; 2 Sam. 15:31 [Ahithophel]).

There is one striking positive use of ***qāshar*** in 1 Sam. 18:1, where the word describes the intimate bond of friendship between David and Jonathan.

rākas [**רָכַס, 7405**]

rākas is a rare verb meaning "to bind, tie (up)," used literally in Exod. 28:28; 39:21.

ṣārar [**צָרַר, 6887**]

ṣārar is a verb found approximately sixty times with two spheres of meaning — "to be an enemy," "harass," "cause distress," and "to bind," "tie up," "be bound, tied up." (→ DISTRESS → ENEMY) In Prov. 26:8, ***ṣārar*** literally refers to a stone being "tied up" in a sling. Isa. 8:16 contains a metaphorical reference to "binding up the testimony" among the people of Israel, signifying a legal obligation to keep God's law. See also Prov. 30:4 for another metaphorical usage.

'ālam [**אָלַם, 481**]

'ālam is a verb found nine times with the meaning "bind," "tie up" in the context of harvesting sheaves of grain in Gen. 37:7.

kephat [**כְּפַת, 3729** (Aramaic)]

kephat is a verb occurring four times with the meaning "to bind (with rope)." It is used exclusively with reference to the tying up of Daniel's three friends prior to their being cast into the fiery furnace (cf. Dan. 3:20ff.).

'āqad [**עָקַד, 6123**]

'āqad is a rare synonym for ***kephat***, above, found only in Gen. 22:9 and referring to "binding" Joseph with rope.

NT Words

deō [δέω, *1210*]

deō is a verb found in approximately forty contexts meaning "bind," "tie up," plus associated nuances — both literal and metaphorical.

The literal sense of "bind" or "tie up" is found in connection with people (cf. Matt. 12:29; 14:3; Mark 3:27; 15:1; John 11:44; Acts 9:2; 21:11ff.); bundles of weeds (cf. Matt. 13:30); and a donkey (cf. Matt. 21:2; Mark 11:2ff.; Luke 19:30). Satan is also said to be bound by angels in Rev. 20:2. See also Rev. 9:14. The state of imprisonment is described as "being in bonds" in Col. 4:3.

Other uses of ***deō*** are metaphorical. In Matt. 16:19; 18:18, the sense of "bind" indicates a "bringing into subjection, under control." Acts 20:22 specifically mentions being brought under the control of the Holy Sprit. Luke 13:16 refers to bondage, the affliction of suffering, as the expression of satanic control. Several texts refer to "being bound" by the law, or being under legal obligation (cf.

Rom. 7:2; 1 Cor. 7:27, 39). The latter text refers explicitly to the bond of marriage. ***deō*** is used negatively in 2 Tim. 2:9, which affirms that the word of God is "not bound," that is not restricted, in its effect.

katadeō [καταδέω, *2611*]

katadeō is a rare variant of ***deō***, above, meaning "to bind (i.e., dress)" a wound, found only in Luke 10:34.

desmeuō [δεσμεύω, *1195*]

The verb ***desmeuō*** is found in two places with the meaning "bind," "tie up." It refers literally in Acts 22:4 to tying people up in order to restrict their movement. In Matt. 23:4 it is used metaphorically to refer to Jewish religious leaders who "tie up heavy burdens" (make intolerable demands) and impose them callously onto the common people.

proteinō [προτείνω, *4385*]

proteinō is a rare synonym for ***deō*** and ***desmeuō***, above, meaning "tie up" (with rope). It is found only in Acts 22:25.

anathematizō [ἀναθεματίζω, *332*]

anathematizō is a verb occurring four times with the meaning "to bind oneself under a solemn oath" in Acts 23:12ff.

Additional Notes

Considering the relatively large number of words used to express the idea of "binding" with various shades of meaning throughout both Old and New Testaments, the overlap in meaning between Hebrew and Greek terms is considerable. It is, however, impossible to argue for an exact parallel between any two terms, notwithstanding the significant metaphorical uses of these terms in both and old and new covenant settings. It is clear throughout the entire scriptural record, however, that the concepts of intimate devotion to God and his law are of highest priority. The importance of being bound to God in faith and obedience is given universal emphasis in Scripture.

BIRD

OT Words

'ôph [**עוֹף, 5775**]

This, one of the two general terms for "bird" in the Old Testament, occurs about seventy times. The references are mostly prosaic and without particular significance. Birds are referred to in the creation account (cf. Gen. 1:2); the flood narrative (cf. Gen. 6–9); in relation to ritual worship (cf. Lev. 1:14; 7:26; 11:13ff.; 17:13; 20:25; Deut. 14:19, 20); and several times throughout the Former Prophets and Wisdom writings.

In the Prophets, however, birds are mentioned rather frequently (twenty times), and they are almost always associated with God's judgment against either his people or the nation. In reference to Israel, judgment is described in terms of an absence of bird life in the land (cf. Jer. 4:25; 9:10; Hos. 9:11), or as an abandoning of the people's bodies to the "birds of the air and the beasts of the earth" (cf. Ezek. 29:5; 32:4 [Egypt]; Ezek. 38:20 [Gog]). Hos. 2:18 specifically mentions a positive restoration and renewal of God's covenant with "the birds of the air," in anticipation of new covenant renewal.

ṣippôr [**צִפּוֹר, 6833**]

This term is synonymous with ***'ôph***, above, and is found about forty times in the Old Testament. ***ṣippôr*** is used mostly in a mundane sense, like ***'ôph***, in literal contexts (cf. Gen. 7:14); in contexts of ritual sacrifice (cf. Lev. 14:4ff., 49ff.; Deut. 4:17; 14:11); and in poetic contexts (cf. Pss. 8:8; 107:7; 84:3).

In several places in a prophetic context, however, ***ṣippôr***, like ***'ôph***, conveys images of blessing and judgment. In Isa. 31:5, for example, the image of birds hovering over Jerusalem conveys the idea of God protecting and delivering his people just as he did at the time of the Passover. Ezek. 39:4, 17 also records the graphic image of God handing over the remains of Gog and Magog to the ravenous "birds of the air."

'ayit [**עַיִט, 5861**]

'ayit is a noun denoting a "bird of prey" in eight contexts (cf. Gen. 15:11; Job 28:7; Isa. 18:6; 46:11; Jer. 12:9; Ezek. 39:4).

ṣephar [**צְפַר, 6853** (Aramaic)]

ṣephar is the Aramaic equivalent of ***ṣippôr***, above, denoting "birds" in four places (cf. Dan. 4:12ff., 33).

NT Words

peteinon [πετεινόν, *4071*]

peteinon is a noun denoting "bird" in a general sense in fifteen contexts (e.g., Matt. 6:20; Mark 4:4; Luke 8:5; 9:58; Acts 10:12; Rom. 1:23; Jas. 3:7; 1 Cor. 15:39).

orneon [ὄρνεον, *3732*]

orneon is a noun found in three places denoting "birds" (cf. Rev. 18:2; 19:17, 21).

BIRTH → BEGET

BIRTHRIGHT

OT Words

bekôrāh **[בְּכוֹרָה, 1062]**

This is the feminine form of the noun ***bekôr*** (firstborn) and occurs nine times in the Old Testament with the meaning "birthright." The most famous example of this phenomenon in Scripture is found in the narrative concerning the twin brothers Jacob and Esau. Esau was duped by Jacob into forfeiting his birthright in exchange for a pot of stew — an action which he came to regret very much, but one which had irreversible consequences for Esau (cf. Gen. 25:31ff.; 27:36). Then, in Deut. 21:17, the legal conditions surrounding the principle of primogeniture in Israel are spelled out in the Mosaic legislation. Finally, 1 Chr. 5:1–2 mentions Reuben's loss of his birthright when he defiled his father's bed by sleeping with Bilhah, his father's concubine (cf. Gen. 35:22).

NT Words

prōtotokia **[πρωτοτόκια, *4415*]**

prōtotokia is a rare noun denoting the "birthright" of Esau, who foolishly sold it to his brother Jacob for a hearty meal (cf. Heb. 12:16).

BISHOP

NT Words

episkopos **[ἐπίσκοπος, *1985*]**

The noun ***episkopos*** is found six times with the consistent meaning "bishop," or "overseer." The term exclusively denotes one who is given the spiritual charge (i.e., oversight) of a local congregation or group of congregations (cf. Acts 20:28; Phil. 1:1; 1 Tim. 3:2; 2 Tim. 4:22; Titus 1:7; 3:15). In 1 Pet. 2:25, ***episkopos*** refers to Christ as the supreme "overseer" of our souls.

This term, though distinctive in its usage, is functionally synonymous with the spiritual offices of both "pastor" and "elder."

BIT → BRIDLE

BITE

OT Words

nāshak **[נָשַׁךְ, 5391]**

This is an interesting verb with the principal meaning "bite," but it is also associated with the phenomenon of usury. The derivative noun ***neshek*** has this meaning. ***nāshak*** occurs fifteen times in the Old Testament and is translated "bite" on twelve of these occasions. The remaining three texts carry the sense of "charging interest" (or usury). (→ INTEREST)

For the most part, "biting" in the Old Testament is connected with serpents, and the phenomenon is also linked to God's judgment against his people. In Num. 21:6, 8, 9, for example, God sends venomous serpents into the midst of his people as a punishment for their rebellious attitude against him. Many Israelites are subsequently bitten and die. After the people seek the Lord in repentance, he provides them with a means of healing in the form of a bronze snake mounted on a pole. Anyone who gazes upon it after being bitten will be healed and survive. In Amos 5:19; 9:3; Jer. 8:17 the venomous bites of serpents are cited as a divinely ordained means of judgment against God's people for their sin.

In contexts that are distinctly poetic or metaphorical, ***nāshak*** is used in various ways. Prov. 23:32, for instance, talks about the effect of too much wine in terms of a serpent's bite. Eccl. 10:8, 11 mournfully discusses the misfortune of snake bites as part of life's inevitable "hard knocks" that have no explanation. Jacob's son, Dan, is described in Gen. 49:17 as a "viper" — one who will bring justice for his people by "biting the horse's heels so that its rider stumbles backward." This suggests enemy riders invading the territory of Dan. In Mic. 3:5 the reference to the prophets "biting with their teeth" is a metaphorical allusion to their oppression of the people — the context favors this interpretation. Finally, in Hab. 2:7, the translation "bite" may also combine with the sense of "creditors," in that it is these very creditors who will "bite" those to whom they have lent money.

NT Words

daknō **[δάκνω, *1143*]**

daknō is rare verb used metaphorically with the meaning "bite" in the sense of "tear people apart" with unkind words or vicious slander. It is found only in Gal. 5:15.

BITTER, BITTERNESS

OT Words

mar **[מַר, 4751]**

mar is used both as an adjective and as a noun, and it occurs nearly forty times in the Old Testament. The meaning "bitter" or "bitterness" gives rise to a number of slightly differing perspectives within the semantic range of this term.

One common element that consistently merges in the use of ***mar*** is the idea of "anguish." For example, in Gen. 27:34, Esau cries out in great bitterness, which indicates a deep anguish at having lost his birthright to Jacob. Then there is Naomi's anguish in response to the tragic losses of her husband and two sons. She even asks to be renamed Marah — which means "bitterness" (cf. Ruth 1:20). Hannah is described in the grip of a "bitterness of spirit" in anguish at her barrenness (cf. 1 Sam. 1:20). Mordecai cries out in bitter anguish at the news of Haman's plot to exterminate the Jewish people (cf. Esth. 4:1). ***mar*** is similarly used in the book of Job (cf. Job 3:20; 7:11; 10:1; 21:25). Such a "bitterness of soul" also afflicts Hezekiah during his illness (cf. Isa. 38:15, 17); the prophet Ezekiel after he receives the message of judgment from God that he must pass on to the exiles in Babylon as well as to those remaining in Jerusalem (cf. Ezek. 3:14); as well as the people of God in general, for whom such anguish is to be the inevitable consequence of God's judgment upon them (cf. Isa. 5:20; Jer. 2:19; 4:18; Amos 8:10; Zeph. 1:14)

mar also refers to the bitter taste of the water in Exod. 15:23, where the Israelites encountered an undrinkable spring in the wilderness before God miraculously sweetened it. Num. 5 refers to bitter water associated with the trial by ordeal for a woman suspected by her husband of adultery. There are probably elements of both literal and symbolic bitterness associated with this ritual (cf. Num. 5:18ff.).

mārar [מָרַר, 4843]

mārar is the verbal form from which ***mar***, above, is derived. It occurs fourteen times and has the predominant sense of experiencing and causing bitterness in the sense of anguish and great distress. Naomi experiences such an emotion after tragically losing her husband and sons, and she attributes the experience to the hand of God (cf. Ruth 1:13, 20). David and his men are likewise devastated after finding their headquarters at Ziklag destroyed and their families taken captive by the Amalekites (cf. 1 Sam. 30:6). The Shunammite is cast into anguish at the death of her son (cf. 2 Kgs. 4:27). The Israelites also experience bitterness and anguish in Egypt because of their oppressive enslavement by the Egyptians (cf. Exod. 1:14). Isaiah weeps bitterly over the fate of Jerusalem (cf. Isa. 22:4); and Zech. 12:10 refers to the people's bitter mourning and repentance over their sins.

mārôr [מָרוֹר, 4844]

mārôr is a rare noun found three times denoting the "bitter herbs" of the Passover meal in Exod. 12:8; Num. 9:11. In Lam. 3:15 the term denotes the emotion of "bitterness" as a reaction to the destruction of Jerusalem in 587 B.C.

merōrāh [מְרֹרָה, 4846]

merōrāh is a rare variant form derived from ***mārar***, above. It denotes the "bitterness" of grapes in Deut. 32:32 — a metaphorical usage signifying gross immortality. The term designates "bitter things" — that is, vicious slander, in Job 13:26. In Job 20:14 the meaning indicated is "venom" in relation to poisonous snakes.

tamrûr [תַּמְרוּר, 8563]

tamrûr is a rare noun denoting "bitterness" in three places. It refers to the "bitterness" or "anguish" of a deep sorrow in Jer. 6:26; 31:15; and the "bitterness" of the provocation Israel brought against Yahweh in Hos. 12:14.

mamrôr [מַמְרוֹר, 4472]

mamrôr is a rare noun denoting "bitterness" as a powerful negative emotion in Job 9:18.

mārrāh [מָרָּה, 4787]

mārrāh is another rare noun, found only in Prov. 14:10 and denoting "bitterness" — the absence of all happiness and joy.

memer [מֶמֶר, 4470]

memer is a rare noun denoting "bitterness" in the sense of anguish, found only in Prov. 17:25.

NT Words

pikros [πικρός, *4089*]

pikros is a rare adjective describing "bitter" or "brackish" water in Jas. 3:11 and "bitter" jealousy in Jas. 3:14.

pikrainō [πικραίνω, *4087*]

pikrainō is a verb found six times with the meaning "to embitter," "make bitter, sour." The sense of "embitter" is found in connection with an injunction to husbands not to embitter their wives (i.e., treat them harshly, cf. Col. 3:19). The meaning "make bitter" is found in relation to water made unfit for drinking (cf. Rev. 8:11). The term means to "turn (the stomach) sour" in Rev. 10:10.

pikria [πικρία, *4088*]

pikria is a rare noun denoting "bitterness" in the sense of "anger," "disillusionment" in Acts 8:23; Rom. 3:14; Eph. 4:31; Heb. 12:15.

pikrōs [πικρῶς, *4090*]

pikrōs is a rare adverbial form with the meaning "bitterly" in the context of weeping with great anguish, inconsolable grief (cf. Matt. 26:75; Luke 22:62).

Additional Notes

The theme of "bitterness" has similar emphases in both Old and New Testaments, both literally and metaphorically. This is particularly so in reference to bitterness as the consequence of specific divine judgment.

BLACK, BLACKNESS

OT Words

shāḥōr [שָׁחוֹר, **7838**]

This term is quite rare, occurring only six times as an adjective meaning "black." In Lev. 13:31, 37 it refers to black body hair. Song 1:5 alludes to the dark skin of the Shulamite, and 5:11 to the black hair of her lover. Zech. 6:2, 6 describes black horses.

'aphēlāh [אֲפֵלָה, **653**]

This noun is the feminine form of ***'ōphel*** (→ DARK), which translates "darkness." ***'aphēlāh*** occurs ten times in the Old Testament. The relationship of "blackness" to "darkness" is obvious, but ***'aphēlāh*** conveys an extra metaphorical, symbolic connotation that deserves some attention.

In every instance, with one exception, ***'aphēlāh*** is linked with some aspect of the judgment of God. Exod. 10:22 speaks of the plague of darkness — one of the ten plagues that God visited on the Egyptians for refusing to let his people out of slavery. Prov. 4:19 refers in a general sense to the way of the wicked as "darkness." Deut. 28:29 affirms that the affliction of blindness will come upon the people of God for violating their covenant obligations under the Mosaic law. As a consequence they will be forced to grope about in darkness. This will be just one of the many curses which God will bring down upon them for their disobedience.

The prophets pronounce similar judgments, all of which focus on darkness as the consequence of the people's sin (cf. Isa. 8:22; 59:9; Jer. 23:12; Joel 2:2; Zeph. 1:15). While some of these punishments are symbolic rather than literal, the judgment of God is very real. Underlying the metaphor of darkness — if literal blindness is not in view — is the reality that the people of God will be confused, with no direction, destitute, and lonely. This is the clear implication of the darkness that will be thrust upon them. Finally, in a positive sense, ***'aphēlāh*** is used in Isa. 58:10 to indicate that darkness will be removed from God's people if they repent of their sin and refrain from oppressing their fellow Israelites.

Prov. 7:9 contains the sole reference to literal darkness. ***'aphēlāh*** refers here to the dark night in which the adulteress appears. Though the darkness is literal, the symbolism of this context in which the prostitute plies her immoral trade is also worthy of note.

'arāphel [עֲרָפֶל, **6205**]

This term is a broad synonym for ***'aphēlāh***, above, but with a distinctive emphasis that renders it unique. ***'arāphel*** means "(a thick) darkness" or "dark cloud" and occurs fifteen times.

As does ***'aphēlāh***, ***'arāphel*** indicates darkness as evidence of God's judgment against his people — an inevitable consequence of their rebellion against him. This is reflected in the following texts: Jer. 13:16; Ezek. 34:12; Joel 2:2; Zeph. 1:15; Isa. 60:2. Implicit in all these references is the threat of spiritual blindness that will come upon Israel. This is especially so in Isa. 60:2.

In the remaining texts, however, there is the unique reference to the "thick darkness" where God dwells. This is almost certainly indicative of the so-called "glory cloud" that was associated with the theophanic revelation at Mt. Sinai, and it is this phenomenon that is referred to in Exod. 20:21; Deut. 4:11; 5:22; 2 Sam. 22:10. Closely associated with this is the phenomenon of the cloud that descended first upon the tabernacle and later upon the temple, surrounding the ark of the covenant in the holy of holies (cf. 1 Kgs. 8:12; 2 Chr. 6:1). These last two references use the term ***'arāphel*** to indicate that the cloud associated with the tabernacle/temple is identical to the phenomenon witnessed by Moses and the Israelites at Mt. Sinai. This "thick darkness" is, therefore, the theophanic manifestation of God's dwelling place.

qādar [קָדַר, **6937**]

qādar is a verb found in seventeen places meaning to "be, grow dark," "mourn." (→ MOURN) There is, however, some overlap in meaning here, with the metaphorical sense of people's hearts "growing dark" with sadness (mourning).

1 Kgs. 18:45; Jer. 4:28 refer to the sky "growing dark (or black)" with clouds. A similar phenomenon is stated of stars and the sun when they are said to lose their light in Ezek. 32:7ff.; Joel 2:10; 3:15; Mic. 3:6. See also Job 6:16.

NT Words

melas [μέλας, *3189*]

melas is an adjective describing the color "black" in Matt. 5:36 (human hair); Rev. 6:12 (darkening of the sun); and Rev. 6:5 (one of the four "apocalyptic" horses of John's vision).

Additional Notes

See Also: → CLOUD → DARK

BLADE → GRASS

BLAME, BLAMELESS

NT Words

mōmaomai [μωμάομαι, *3469*]

mōmaomai is a rare verb meaning "to blame," "find fault with" in 2 Cor. 8:20. In 2 Cor. 6:3, however, the term is used negatively to mean "be blameless," "without fault."

amōmos [ἄμωμος, *299*]

amōmos is an adjective found in nine places with the consistent sense of "blameless," "without fault." This status is God's intention and purpose for his chosen people (cf. Eph. 1:4; 5:27; Phil. 2:15; Col. 1:22; 2 Pet. 3:15; Jude 24). The saints in heaven are described as "flawless" in Rev. 14:5. Heb. 9:14; 1 Pet. 1:19 both affirm the person of Christ as one "without blemish."

amemptos [ἄμεμπτος, *273*]

The adjective ***amemptos*** is synonymous with ***mōmeomai*** and ***amōmos*** (see above), meaning "blameless," "faultless."

Luke 1:6; Phil. 3:6 refer to those who live "blameless" lives in accordance with God's ordinances. Heb. 8:7 describes the hypothetical "blameless" nature of the first covenant. "Blameless" lives are clearly indicated as God's purpose for his people in Phil. 2:15; 1 Thess. 3:13.

anaitios [ἀναίτιος, *338*]

anaitios is a rare adjective synonymous with ***mōmeomai***, ***amōmos***, and ***amemptos***, above, denoting those who are "blameless" or "without guilt" under the law (cf. Matt. 12:5, 7).

anepilēmptos [ἀνεπίλημπτος, *423*]

The adjective ***anepilēmptos*** is found in three places denoting those who are "without reproach," "blameless" in their lifestyle — a prerequisite for those who aspire to positions of leadership in the church (cf. 1 Tim. 3:2; 5:7; 6:14).

anenklētos [ἀνέγκλητος, *410*]

anenklētos is an adjective found in five places meaning "blameless," or unable to be accused. Such is the moral destiny of the people of God, made possible by the work and person of Christ (cf. 1 Cor. 1:8; Col. 1:22). It is also the quality required of spiritual leaders in the local congregation of believers (cf. 1 Tim. 3:10; Titus 1:6, 7).

amemptōs [ἀμέμπτως, *274*]

amemptōs is an adverbial form found only twice, meaning "blameless," "without fault" — a characteristic of true believers (cf. 1 Thess. 2:10; 5:23).

See Also: → BLEMISH → INNOCENT

BLASPHEME, BLASPHEMY, BLASPHEMER, BLASPHEMOUS

OT Words

nā'aṣ [נָאַץ, **5006**]

This verb means "to speak or regard with contempt," and thus it means "to blaspheme" when the object of contempt or rebellion is God. ***nā'aṣ*** occurs twenty-five times, and about half of the occurrences indicate blasphemy against God — either implicitly or explicitly.

In Num. 14:11, 23 God declares his anger at Israel for their rebellion against him in the wilderness. This provocation is a form of blasphemy against him. Similarly, in Num. 16:30, Korah's rebellion against the authority of Moses is again cited as a provocation, a rebellion against God, and thus may be deemed blasphemous. Here it constitutes a capital offense. Then, David's adultery with Bathsheba and his subsequent murder of Uriah, her husband, brings a severe rebuke from God. In 2 Sam. 12:14 Nathan declares, as a rationale for the divine censure, that the king's actions have given opportunity for the enemies of God's people to blaspheme his name. The sins of Hophni and Phinehas, the sons of Eli, also result in God giving them a death sentence. They blasphemed God by treating the Levitical ritual offerings with contempt (cf. 1 Sam. 2:17). Other general references to the people of God blaspheming his name include Deut. 31:20; Isa. 60:14; 52:5; Jer. 23:17; Ps. 74:18.

ne'āṣāh **[נְאָצָה, 5007]**

ne'āṣāh is the noun derived from ***nā'aṣ***, above, and it is found only in 1 Kgs. 19:3 and Isa. 37:3. The context here concerns Sennacherib's diatribe against the nation of Israel and against Yahweh himself when the Assyrian king besieged the city of Jerusalem in 701 B.C. Hezekiah, the Judean king at the time, reports to Isaiah that this day is one of "distress, rebuke, and disgrace." The latter term translates ***ne'āṣāh*** and refers to the blasphemous attack by Sennacherib's representative against the person of God and his people (cf. 2 Kgs. 18:17ff.).

gādaph **[גָּדַף, 1442]**

gādaph, a synonym for ***nā'aṣ***, above, is found only seven times in the Old Testament. All but one of these references indicate blasphemy against God. 2 Kgs. 19:6, 22 and the parallel passage in Isa. 37:6, 23 refer to the slanderous discourse of Sennacherib's messenger against God at the siege of Jerusalem (see above). Ezekiel also uses this term to refer to the Israelite nation's blasphemous rejection of God in the past (Ezek. 20:27). The Deuteronomic legislation in Num. 15:30 specifies the death penalty for blasphemy.

nāqab **[נָקַב, 5344]**

nāqab is a verb found twenty-five times with two strands of meaning, one of which is "to blaspheme," "curse."

The capital offense of "blaspheming" God, or bringing his name into disrepute, is indicated in Lev. 24:11, 16. Elsewhere, ***nāqab*** means "to bring a curse upon someone" (cf. Num. 23:8, 25; Job 5:3; Prov. 11:26; 24:24).

NT Words

blasphēmia **[βλασφημία, *988*]**

blasphēmia is a noun occurring about twenty times with the consistent meaning "blasphemy," "slander."

General references to blasphemy include Matt. 15:19; Mark 3:28; 7:22; John 10:33; Rev. 2:9. The "slandering" of people is condemned in Eph. 4:31; Col. 3:8; 1 Tim. 6:4. Blasphemy against the devil, equivalent to cursing him, is noted in Jude 9.

Explicit blasphemy against God is indicated in Matt. 12:31; Mark 2:7; Rev. 13:1ff.; 17:3. In Matt. 26:65; Mark 14:64; Luke 5:21, Jesus is wrongfully accused of such an offense. Matt. 12:31 mentions "blasphemy" against the Holy Spirit. This is designated as the unforgivable sin — the hardness of heart resulting from a persistent refusal to acknowledge God's rightful place in one's life. Here, in the case of the Pharisees, such a crime also involves attributing the work of God to the devil.

blasphēmeō **[βλασφημέω, *987*]**

blasphēmeō is a verb found in about forty places, meaning "to speak blasphemy (against)," "slander," "speak scornfully (of someone)."

General references to the blaspheming of God are found in Mark 3:28; Acts 26:11; Rom. 2:24; 1 Tim. 1:20; Jas. 2:7; Rev. 13:6ff.; 16:21. The blaspheming of idols is noted in Acts 19:37. Such activity is wrongfully attributed to Jesus in Matt. 9:3; 26:65; John 10:36. The blaspheming of the Holy Spirit is indicated in Mark 3:29; Luke 12:10 (see the discussion under ***blasphēmia***, above).

Matt. 27:39; Mark 15:29; Luke 22:65; Acts 13:45; Rom. 3:8; 1 Cor. 4:13; Titus 3:2; 1 Pet. 4:4, 14 all refer to scornful and mocking speech. See also 2 Pet. 2:10; Jude 8ff.

The word of God is said to "be defamed," or "discredited," in Titus 2:5, as is the Christian way of life in 2 Pet. 2:2.

blasphēmos **[βλάσφημος, *989*]**

blasphēmos is an adjective meaning "blasphemous," as well as a noun denoting a "blasphemer."

Stephen, the first Christian martyr, is wrongfully accused of blasphemous speech against God in Acts 6:11ff. 1 Tim. 1:13 refers to Paul's pre-Christian activity as a blasphemer. More generally, ***blasphēmos*** refers to "abusive" speech in 2 Tim. 3:2; 2 Pet. 2:11.

Additional Notes

The entire scriptural record consistently portrays the concept of blasphemy against God. In both Testaments, this particular sin is viewed with utmost seriousness. The sin of speaking or acting contemptuously with respect to other persons is also indicated, but both the Hebrew and Greek terminology emphasize blasphemy against God and Christ.

See Also: → REPROACH

BLEMISH

OT Words

mûm **[מוּם, 3971]**

A specific Hebrew term meaning "blemish," ***mûm*** occurs approximately twenty times and is found mostly in the legislative sections of the Pentateuch. References to physical blemishes or imperfections on

Israelite people are mentioned in Lev. 21:17ff. These physical flaws bar those afflicted from worshiping at the tabernacle while the conditions persist. Lev. 22:20ff.; Deut. 15:21; 17:1 refer to prohibited offerings in which the prospective animals for sacrifice are to be rejected because of certain physical imperfections. In a unique use of ***mûm***, Num. 19:2 refers to a red heifer "without blemish" as the required sin offering for the Israelite community. See below under ***tāmîm*** for a full discussion of the phrase "without blemish."

mûm also refers to physical beauty in terms of the absence of blemish. This is predicated, for example, of Absalom (cf. 2 Sam. 14:25); the Shulamite's lover and husband in Song 4:7; and the Israelite youths deported to Babylon from Israel by Nebuchadnezzar at the very end of the sixth century B.C. (Dan. 1:4).

This group included Daniel and his three friends Hananiah, Mishael, and Azariah.

On three occasions ***mûm*** indicates "blemish" in a moral sense. First, Deut. 32:5 refers to God's people as "tarnished" or "blemished" by their sin against God. In Job 11:15, Zophar declares to Job that if he puts away sin that is in his hand, he will be able to lift up his face "without blemish" (i.e., without shame). And finally, Prov. 9:7 mentions that whoever rebukes a wicked person will incur "abuse" from him or her.

tāmîm **[תָּמִים, 8549]**

The adjective ***tāmîm*** means either "without blemish" or "blameless," depending on the context in which it is found. It occurs about ninety times in the Old Testament with an approximately equal emphasis on the ritual and moral spheres.

tāmîm is used to mean "without blemish" in the pentateuchal legislative sections, and in Ezekiel it refers to animal sacrifices that are flawless. The term is applied to lambs (e.g., Exod. 12:5; Lev. 14:10; 23:12; Num. 6:14; 28:9; 29:17–36; Ezek. 46:4); rams (e.g., Exod. 29:1; Lev. 5:15; Num. 6:14; Ezek. 45:23); bullocks (e.g., Lev. 4:3; Ezek. 45:18); goats (e.g., Ezek. 45:22; Lev. 4:23, 28); and heifers (e.g., Num. 19:2). Such an emphasis in the legislation of the covenant reinforces the absolute prerequisite of flawless animal specimens for sacrifices.

In the realm of moral attributes, ***tāmîm*** frequently refers to people as "blameless." Alternative, additional translations are "perfect," "upright." When ***tāmîm*** is applied to people in this sense, it does not refer to sinless perfection — rather, it signifies that those who are "blameless" are wholeheartedly devoted to God and desire to live in obedient submission to him. Such an attitude is predicated of Noah (cf. Gen. 6:9) and David (cf. 2 Sam. 22:24). Abraham is commanded to walk blamelessly before God in Gen. 17:1. Joshua exhorts the Israelite tribes to serve God blamelessly — that is, with a genuine heartfelt sincerity (cf. Josh. 24:14). The psalmist writes that those who live blamelessly before God are favored by him (Pss. 15:2; 18:32; 37:18; 84:11; 119:1). The writer of Proverbs makes a similar claim (cf. Prov. 2:21; 11:5; 28:10, 18).

tāmîm is also applied to God, and in these contexts it is clear that this description refers to a literal and absolute perfection. The work and actions of God are described in this way (cf. Deut. 32:4; 2 Sam. 22:31; Ps. 18:30), as is his law (cf. Ps. 19:7) and his knowledge (cf. Job 36:4; 37:16).

teballûl **[תְּבַלּוּל, 8400]**

teballûl is a rare noun found only in Lev. 21:20 denoting a "blemish" in the sense of a "physical defect."

NT Words

mōmos [μῶμος, *3470*]

mōmos is a rare noun found only in 2 Pet. 2:13 with reference to the "blemishes" (i.e., disgraceful behavior) of false teachers.

Additional Notes

The Hebrew terminology for "blemish" "blame," "blameless" in the Old Testament conveys a ritual as well as a moral perspective. The translation "blemish" is reserved largely for Levitical offerings and physical imperfections in general, whereas the concepts of "blame" and "blamelessness" are solely moral attributes. All the terms listed above communicate both the ceremonial and moral sense.

See Also: → BLAME → PERFECT

BLESS, BLESSED, BLESSING

OT Words

bārak **[בָּרַךְ, 1288]**

The phenomenon of "blessing" in the Old Testament is rich and varied in its expression. The most common term is this verb ***bārak***, along with its derivative noun ***berākāh*** (see below). ***bārak*** occurs about three hundred times in the Old Testament and is translated "bless" on almost every occasion.

Inherent in the idea of blessing is the invocation of special favor on a person or object that is held in high esteem. The object of blessing in the Old Testament may be either divine or human, or that which belongs to either God or human beings.

Where God is the object of human blessing, the context is invariably one of worship and praise. When people bless God, they offer him praise for who he is and what he has done on behalf of those he loves. ***bārak*** is used this way about eighty times, with the majority of texts occurring in the Psalms. Elsewhere, the same emphases are observed. In Gen. 14:20, for example, Melchizedek blesses the God of Abraham for having delivered him from his enemies. Jethro, the Midianite priest, blesses Yahweh for having delivered the Israelites from Egypt. The women of Bethlehem praise God on Naomi's behalf for not leaving her without a descendant in the wake of her husband's death. The birth of Obed evokes this ascription of blessing to God (cf. Ruth 4:14). Ezek. 3:12 provides a slightly different perspective on ascribing praise to God. Here, the prophet is taken up by the Spirit into the heavenly throne room of God. Ezekiel's immediate response is to utter a cry of wonder: "May the glory of the Lord be praised (i.e., blessed) in his dwelling place!" This blessing is a response to a revelation of God's glory, rather than an expression of gratitude for what God has done. However, in making this distinction, it needs to be noted that the character and person of God are never divorced from each other in Scripture. In every instance, praise and blessing are given to God because of who he is and what he has done. God's character is always evident in his actions, and his actions are always consistent with his character. Blessing is never given to God in any mystical sense that separates his being from his involvement in human affairs, particularly those of his chosen people. In Ezek. 3:12, for instance, the context makes it clear that the glory of God is intimately linked with the fortunes of God's people as he communicates his message of judgment and hope to the prophet. The Psalms are very good examples of the way in which blessing is given to God in response to both his character and his actions. Note the following references in this regard: Pss. 96:2; 104:1, 35; 72:15, 18, 19; 106:48; 16:7, 8; 26:12; 63:4, 5; 115:18; 145:1, 2, 10, 21.

Human objects of divine blessing receive a greater amount of attention in the usage of ***bārak***. The bestowal of blessing upon the people of Israel, and also upon people and nations beyond the borders of Canaan, is a major theme in the Old Testament. Of primary importance here is the phenomenon of covenant blessing, given first of all to the patriarchs throughout the book of Genesis. Abraham is the most prominent recipient of such blessing. God promises to grant him descendants too numerous to count and a land for them to dwell in. God also promises to enable his descendants to be a blessing to nations all over the world. These blessings, given in the form of promises, are then handed down repeatedly to Abraham's son Isaac, and to Isaac's son Jacob (cf. Gen. 12:2, 3; 17:16; 18:18; 22:17; 26:24; 28:14; 30:27; 48:3, 9). The implications of these blessings and promises are laid down for the people of Israel in the detailed legislation of the Mosaic covenant, especially in the books of Leviticus, Numbers, and Deuteronomy. Deut. 28 is particularly significant in this regard, for this chapter repeatedly mentions blessings that will come to Israel, provided the people maintain their obedience and devotion to God (Deut. 28:3–6). The people of Israel are constantly reminded that their obligation to serve their God is grounded in the fact that he has blessed them in a uniquely wonderful way by granting them deliverance from Egypt (Deut. 2:7; 7:13; 8:10; 12:7; 15:6, 15 — this last verse is quite specific on this matter). References to God blessing his people Israel are found throughout the Old Testament (e.g., Num. 6:23; Deut. 26:15; 1 Sam. 25:14; 2 Sam. 6:18; 7:29; 2 Chr. 31:10; Pss. 29:11; 66:8; 132:15; Isa. 51:2; Hag. 2:19). The reference in Hag. 2:19 is particularly significant in that the promised blessing anticipates a new era in the relationship between God and his people that is elsewhere taken up as the promise of a new covenant.

Not only are the blessings of God granted to Israel, but the Old Testament also makes it clear that divine favor is extended to Gentile people as well. One of the most significant passages in this regard is Isa. 19:23–25. In these verses God promises to bless Israel, along with Egypt and Assyria — all three of whom God will draw together to worship him. The intent of the divine blessing is quite clear — God will perform a work of inner spiritual renewal within these two pagan nations, two of Israel's "classic" enemies. God's blessing is also poured out on the household of Potiphar, the captain of the Egyptian guard in Gen. 39:5, because of the kindness he extended to Joseph. While these two passages are the only ones in which ***bārak*** specifically indicates divine blessing upon the nations, these are not the only places where blessing to the nations is intended in the Old Testament. (See below under Additional Notes.)

Finally, ***bārak*** also indicates the invocation of blessing between people — whether it be a solemn pronouncement of favor in the name of the Lord or merely an exchange of greetings. It is used in this way about fifty times.

The pronouncement, invocation, or pleading for blessing has a tangible as well an intangible element. When one blesses God, it is invariably in the context of an attitude, if not a ritual, of worship and devotion to Yahweh. Such a blessing is wholly intangible, yet nonetheless real. When coming from people who are genuinely devoted to God in their hearts, such praise delights the heart of God.

Divine blessing in the old covenant does indeed have a tangible aspect in that all such blessing focuses on the possession and enjoyment of the land. But the intangible, yet very substantial, spiritual blessing is also very much in evidence — the joy of being in an intimate personal relationship of favor with one's God.

berākāh [בְּרָכָה, 1293]

berākāh is the noun derived from ***bārak***, above, which occurs approximately seventy times. The range of meaning for ***berākāh*** is very close to that of ***bārak***. However, one difference is that ***berākāh*** is not linked specifically to ascriptions of praise to God. Rather, the term largely reflects the bestowing of blessing by God upon his people — for example, to Abraham and his descendants (cf. Gen. 12:2; 28:4); to David and his lineage (cf. 2 Sam. 7:29); to Joshua and the Israelites (cf. Josh. 8:34); and to his people in general (cf. Deut. 11:26; 28:2, 8 [note here that the blessings are contingent upon obedience]; Pss. 3:8; 21:3, 6; 24:5; 129:8; 133:3). Two passages call for a special comment in this regard. Isa. 44:3 and Ezek. 34:26 both indicate that God will bring about blessings for his people that amount to a thoroughgoing transformation — both literal and spiritual. From the context of these two passages, it may be argued that such favor represents an anticipation of new covenant blessing.

Like ***bārak***, ***berākāh*** also indicates the presence of blessing or favor between individuals, emphasizing the solemn invocation of God's blessing upon the recipient. Jacob blessing his sons is one example (cf. Gen. 49:25ff.); as is the blessing Moses gives to Naphtali (cf. Deut. 33:23). In a negative context, ***berākāh*** also refers to Esau's loss of blessing when he squanders his birthright to his brother Jacob (cf. Gen. 27:12, 35, 36) and tries in vain to regain it.

'āshar [אָשַׁר, 833]

This is a comparatively rare verb that occurs about sixteen times in the Old Testament. The root meaning of ***'āshar*** is to "go straight on," "advance," or "lead." It is, however, translated "to pronounce (or make) blessed" in about half of these instances. Zilpah pronounces herself blessed in Gen. 30:13 after the birth of her son, Asher. Solomon is declared blessed in Ps. 72:17, as are the "noble wife" in Prov. 31:28; the "Beloved" in Song 6:9; the godly man in Ps. 41:2; and those who embrace wisdom in Prov. 3:18. Mal. 3:12 also notes that all nations who witness God's work of renewal among his people Israel will call her blessed.

'ashrê [אַשְׁרֵי, 835]

This term functions as an adjective and, as with ***'āshar*** above, affirms the blessed state of all those who submit themselves to God in obedient devotion to him. It occurs about forty times in the Old Testament, mostly in the Psalms and Proverbs (e.g., Deut. 33:29; 2 Chr. 9:7; Pss. 1:1; 34:8; 84:4ff.; 119:1ff.; Prov. 8:32ff.; 29:18; Isa. 32:20; Dan. 12:12).

berak [בְּרַךְ, 1289 (Aramaic)]

berak is the Aramaic equivalent for the Hebrew ***bārak*** (see above). It occurs five times with the meaning "bless" or "praise" in all but one of these contexts. This action of "blessing," or praising, God is indicated in Dan. 2:19ff.; 3:28; 4:34.

NT Words

eulogeō [εὐλογέω, *2127*]

The verb ***eulogeō*** is found in about forty places with the primary sense of "bless," often equated with the actions of "praise," "give thanks."

The meaning "bless" in the sense of "give thanks" is indicated in relation to thanking God for food (cf. Matt. 14:19; Mark 6:41; 14:22; Luke 9:16; 24:30); and for the cup of the Lord's Supper (cf. 1 Cor. 10:16). See also Luke 1:64; 2:28, 34; Jas. 3:9.

eulogeō also expresses the meaning "blessed" in the sense of "happy," "joyful." It is predicated of Christ in Matt. 21:9; 23:39; Mark 11:9ff.; Luke 13:35; 19:38; John 12:13; of God's people in Matt. 25:34; Luke 1:28, 42. Such blessing is also indicated in the context of receiving the gift of salvation (cf. Gal. 3:9; 1 Pet. 3:9) and the fulfillment of the covenant promises (cf. Heb. 6:14).

Elsewhere, ***eulogeō*** conveys the sense of "giving a spiritual blessing." Christ is said to do this to his people in Mark 10:16; Luke 24:51; Acts 3:26. Similarly, God provides spiritual blessings for his people in Christ (Eph. 1:3). Such blessing is also provided by Melchizedek for Abram (Heb. 7:1, 6ff. [citing Gen. 14]). Invoking a blessing on someone through prayer is indicated with respect to one's enemies in Luke 6:28; Rom. 12:14; 1 Cor. 4:12

(cf. also 1 Cor. 14:16). Blessing through the covenant promises is also invoked in Heb. 11:20ff.

eneulogeō [ἐνευλογέω, *1757*]

eneulogeō is a rare variant form of ***eulogeō***, above. It is found only twice and used in the passive voice. The meaning "be blessed" is found in the context of receiving the promises of the Abrahamic covenant in relation to the nations of the world (cf. Acts 3:25; Gal. 3:8).

eulogētos [εὐλογητός, *2128*]

eulogētos is an adjectival form found eight times with the meaning "blessed." It is used as a title, "the blessed (One)," predicated of God in Mark 14:61. The ascription of praise "blessed be God" is found in Luke 1:68; Rom. 1:25; 9:5; 2 Cor. 1:3; 11:31; Eph. 1:3; 1 Pet. 1:3.

eulogia [εὐλογία, *2129*]

The noun ***eulogia*** occurs sixteen times and means "blessing."

Blessing associated with belonging to Christ is indicated in Rom. 15:29; Eph. 1:13. The blessing of the Abrahamic covenant associated with the fulfillment of divine blessing to the Gentiles (i.e., the spread of the gospel) is noted in Gal. 3:14. The "cup of blessing" associated with the Lord's Supper, commemorating the significance of his shed blood, is mentioned in 1 Cor. 10:16. Blessing from God in a general sense is indicated in Heb. 6:7; 12:17; Jas. 3:10; 1 Pet. 3:9.

Blessing in the sense of "praise" is attributed to the heavenly Christ in Rev. 5:12, 13, and to God in Rev. 7:12.

makarizō [μακαρίζω, *3106*]

makarizō is a verb found three times with the meaning "call someone blessed," "count someone happy" (cf. Luke 1:48; Jas. 5:11).

makarios [μακάριος, *3107*]

makarios is an adjective found in fifty places with the meaning "blessed," "happy."

The term is commonly used by Christ. He promises a state of "blessedness," "happiness" to all who live out the virtues of godly living as expressed in the "Beatitudes" (cf. Matt. 5:3ff.; Luke 6:20ff.). Christ also offers blessings to those who follow him and who genuinely seek after God in Matt. 11:6; 13:16. In Matt. 16:17, Peter is declared "blessed" when he acknowledges the true identity of Jesus as the Christ, the Son of God. See also Luke 1:45; 11:27ff.; 23:29; John 13:17; 20:29; Acts 20:35. Such blessing, or happiness, is also promised to servants who are faithful to their masters (cf. Luke 12:37ff.). God is described as "blessed" in 1 Tim. 1:11; 6:15 (i.e., worthy to be praised).

Blessings in the spiritual sphere are affirmed for those whose sins are forgiven (cf. Rom. 4:7ff.); and for those who will enjoy eternal life in glory (cf. Rev. 14:13; 19:9; 20:6; 22:7, 14). See also Rom. 14:22; Jas. 1:12, 25; 1 Pet. 3:14; 4:14; Rev. 1:3.

makarismos [μακαρισμός, *3108*]

The noun ***makarismos*** denotes "blessing" in Rom. 4:6, 9; Gal. 4:15.

Additional Notes

The terms associated with the phenomenon of blessing in both Old and New Testaments have almost identical meanings. No single term for "bless" (and associated senses) in either Hebrew or Greek may be said to be full dynamic equivalents.

The frequency or location of particular words in Scripture does not always equate with the limits of the concept indicated by those words. And so, even though the term ***bārak*** does not refer very frequently to the nations in the Old Testament, this does not mean that blessing on the nations is a phenomenon limited to those texts alone. The reality of blessing in Scripture is not limited to those texts in which the specific terminology for blessing is found.

BLIND, BLINDNESS

OT WORDS

'iwwēr [עִוֵּר, 5787]

Blindness in the Old Testament is both a physical and a spiritual affliction. The term ***'iwwēr*** is an adjective, and it is the primary word used to describe this condition. It occurs twenty-five times in the Old Testament.

There are eight places in which ***'iwwēr*** is translated with the purely physical sense of "blindness," most of which are found in the Pentateuch. Exod. 4:11 refers to physical blindness as coming under the sovereign control of God. Lev. 19:14; Deut. 27:18 both reflect the compassion for blind people (as well as for those with handicap of deafness and dumbness) that is clearly evident in the Mosaic legislation. Blind people, however, were not permitted to personally approach the altar or the sanctuary area for worship or sacrifice (cf. Lev. 21:18). And any animal that was blind was not permitted as a sacrificial offering (Deut. 15:21). In relation to this, Mal. 3:8 condemns the Israelites in the postexilic period for offering up blind animals to God. Finally, 2 Sam. 5:6ff. refers to the blind people in the city of

Jebus, whom the inhabitants scornfully maintained would be able to rebuff the attempts of David and his men to capture the city. They were proved wrong.

The majority of occurrences of *'iwwēr*, then, indicate blindness in a figurative sense. On at least five occasions, however, a literal sense may also be present. Ps. 46:8; Isa. 29:18; 35:5; 42:7, 16 all make promises relating to the restoration of sight to the blind. The similarity here is that all these passages reflect the scenario of what might be called a "messianic charter," referring to the healing ministry of the so-called Suffering Servant of Yahweh. This Servant figure comes in the person of Christ, whose healing ministry literally gave back sight to the blind — both physically and spiritually.

The figurative sense of blindness, or spiritual dullness and hardness of heart, is found primarily in the Prophets. The one exception is Deut. 28:29, where judgment for Israel's sin is described in terms of the people groping about in darkness just like the blind. Their curse is that they will lose their way, in a spiritual sense, for having rejected God. Much the same perspective is found in the Prophets (cf. Isa. 42:18; 56:10; 59:10; Lam. 4:14; Zeph. 1:17). It is not a hopeless picture, however, for Jer. 31:8 describes the "blind" in Israel as objects of "imminent" divine grace. The context of Jer. 31 makes it clear that these people will soon have their sight restored — that is, they will be returned to the land and renewed in their relationship with Yahweh.

kāhāh [כָּהָה, 3543]

The rare verb ***kāhāh*** occurs only eight times in the Old Testament and means "to grow dim, faint." In a few places it refers to failing eyesight (cf. Isaac in Gen. 27:1); to eyes dim (or blind) with grief (cf. Job in Job 17:7); and to healthy eyesight (affirming that Moses' eyesight was not dim in Deut. 34:7). ***kāhāh*** is used in a theologically significant sense only in Zech. 11:17. It refers here to God's act of judgment on the wicked, whereby their right eyes will be "totally blinded."

'āwar [עָוַר, 5786]

'āwar is a verb found five times with the meaning "to blind," "put out the eyes."

Literal reference to the blinding of King Zedekiah, who had his eyes put out at the sack of Jerusalem, is found in 2 Kgs. 25:7; Jer. 39:7; 52:11.

The term is also used metaphorically in Exod. 23:8; Deut. 16:19 referring to the "blinding" impact of bribes on civil officials, who as a consequence engage in injustice and corruption.

sanwērîm [סַנְוֵרִים, 5575]

sanwērîm is a rare noun found in three places denoting literal "sudden blindness" in Gen. 19:11; 2 Kgs. 6:18 as a consequence of divine judgment.

NT Words

typhloō [τυφλόω, *5186*]

typhloō is a rare verb found three times with the meaning "to make blind."

John 12:40 cites the divine judgment against Israel whereby God "blinded their eyes" (cf. Isa. 6:10), a symbolic reference to the reality of a withdrawal of genuine spiritual understanding and insight.

Similarly, in another context, Satan is said to "have blinded the minds" of unbelievers to the truth of the gospel (cf. 2 Cor. 4:4).

typhlos [τυφλός, *5185*]

The adjective ***typhlos*** occurs around fifty times with the meaning "blind," "blind man."

There are a number of references to blind men who experienced healing at the hands of Jesus (cf. Matt. 9:27ff.; 20:30; Mark 8:22ff.; 10:46ff.; Luke 18:35; John 9:1ff.). Other general references allude to "the blind" as a class of people (e.g., Matt. 11:5; 15:30ff.; 21:4; Luke 6:39; 14:13; John 5:3; 9:39; 10:21).

Elsewhere ***typhlos*** denotes those who are "spiritually blind" (cf. Rom. 2:19; 2 Pet. 1:9; Rev. 3:17). In particular, Jesus denounces hypocritical, self-righteous Pharisees who were a hindrance to God's people attaining true godliness (cf. Matt. 23:14ff.).

In Acts 13:11, Elymas the sorcerer is afflicted with blindness as a judgment from God.

Additional Notes

The phenomenon of blindness throughout the Bible in a metaphorical sense is most frequently associated with spiritual dullness, insensitivity, or hardening brought on by the judgment of God. It is therefore necessary to consider this particular affliction within the broader context of hardening and hardness of heart. (→ HARD)

BLOOD

OT Words

dām [דָּם, 1818]

dām is the standard term for "blood" in the Old Testament, occurring a little over three hundred times. It is found everywhere in narrative, legislative, poetic, and prophetic contexts. It is used both literally and symbolically and gives rise to significant theological perspectives on the phenomenon of blood in the Old Testament.

At the literal level, for example, there are references to the blood of a goat into which Joseph's brothers dipped his ornamental coat in order to deceive their father Jacob into believing that Joseph was dead (cf. Gen. 37:31). Then there was the first plague judgment on Egypt when Moses turned the River Nile into blood (cf. Exod. 7:17ff.).

In the ritual legislation of the Old Testament it is significant, but not really surprising, to discover that nearly half the occurrences of the term ***dām*** (approximately 130) are found in the Sinaitic legislation (viz. Exodus — Deuteronomy) and in Ezekiel. The emphasis on blood sacrifices is a very strong one indeed, lying at the very heart of the sacrificial system of the ancient Israelites. ***dām*** is certainly used in its literal sense in this context, but the symbolism associated with it is very potent.

There are a number of perspectives to note here. Exod. 12, for example, records the ritual slaying of the lamb (or kid) immediately prior to the final "Passover plague" when the all the firstborn in Egypt were to be slain by the avenging angel of Yahweh. The blood of the lamb is of the greatest significance here — its presence on the doorposts and lintels of the Israelite houses would act as a protection against the plague. Upon seeing the blood, the angel of death would "pass over" and leave those houses unaffected by the divine punishment (Exod. 12:7, 13, 22, 23). Blood sacrifices are of central importance in the consecration ceremony for the Aaronic priesthood (cf. Exod. 29:12, 16, 20, 21; Lev. 8:15ff.; 9:9ff.); in the covenant renewal ceremony, described in Exod. 24:6, 8; in the general ritual requirements prescribed under the Mosaic covenant (cf. Lev. 1:5ff.; 3:2, 8, 13; 4:5–30; 6:27ff.; 7:2–33; 12:4ff.; 14:6, 14, 25, 51, 52; Num. 18:17; 19:4, 5). Of particular importance in this regard is the Day of Atonement ritual when the high priest's sprinkling of the blood in the holy of holies atones for the sins of the entire Israelite population for that year preceding the festival (cf. Lev. 16:14, 15, 18, 19, 27). There are also the specific sanctions against the eating of blood (cf. Lev. 17:4–14; Deut. 12:16, 23, 27); and also against the abuse of revenge killing (cf. Num. 35:19ff.; Deut. 19:6–13; Josh. 20:3ff.). This particular legislation is aimed at preventing the "avenger of blood" exacting revenge for the death of a close relative when that death was caused by accidental means (i.e., manslaughter). These provisions are directed not towards the murderer, whose just punishment was death (cf. Gen. 9:4–6), but rather towards the accidental manslayer who deserved to be protected. The book of Ezekiel also refers to the atoning effect of sacrificial blood in the prophet's vision of the new temple (cf. Ezek. 43:18, 20; 44:7, 15; 45:19). The key verse, which provides a rationale for the entire ceremonial process of blood sacrifice in worship, is Lev. 17:11 — which states that the life of the creature is in the blood. Here is the supreme symbol of life that God designated as the vehicle for cleansing and purification in the Old Testament. It achieves its consummate purpose and fulfillment, of course, in the sacrifice of Jesus Christ, God's anointed Son.

The term "blood" is also used as a symbolic metaphor for murder in a number of places (cf. 2 Sam. 3:27, 28; 1 Kgs. 2:5, 9, 31, 32; 9:7, 26 — all narrative contexts in the period of the united monarchy); also in poetic contexts (cf. Pss. 79:3, 10; 94:21; 106:38; Prov. 1:11, 16, 18; 6:17; 28:17). In a related sense, ***dām*** also indicates the legal guilt that attaches to murder, a concept clearly evident in phrases such as "blood upon his head" (1 Kgs. 2:33; 2 Sam. 4:11). Such expressions are quite common in the Prophets and refer frequently to Israel's bloodguilt, literally as murderers and those who sacrifice their own children to pagan deities, and to moral iniquity as well (cf. Isa. 59:3, 7; Jer. 2:34; 7:6; 22:3, 17; Lam. 4:13, 14; Ezek. 18:10, 13; 23:37, 45). It also refers to the guilt of other nations in the same way — for example, Nineveh (cf. Nah. 3:1); Babylon (cf. Hab. 2:8, 12, 17); and Israel's enemies in general (cf. Zech. 9:7, 11).

dām is also used in contexts of divine judgment against wickedness and rebellion in general, whereby it is declared that God will "require their blood" (or some similar expression) as a consequence. This is predicated of Israel (cf. Isa. 9:5; Ezek. 14:19; 24:8; 28:23; Zeph. 1:17) and of her enemies (cf. Ps. 78:44; Jer. 46:10 [Egypt]; Jer. 48:10 [Moab]; Jer. 51:35 [Babylon]; Ezek. 21:32 [Ammon]; Ezek. 38:22; 39:17ff. [Gog and Magog]; Isa. 34:3, 6, 7 [the nations in general]).

In a positive sense, Joel 3:19 refers to the fact that God will pardon the bloodguilt of his people.

NT Words

haima [αἷμα, *129*]

The noun ***haima*** noun occurs around one hundred times, denoting "blood" in various contexts.

The phrase "flesh and blood" is a metaphorical expression referring to "humanity" in generalized contexts (cf. Matt. 16:17; John 1:13; 1 Cor. 15:50; Gal. 1:16; Eph. 6:12; Heb. 2:14).

General references to "blood" in a literal, physiological sense include Mark 5:25; Luke 8:43ff.; John 19:34. In particular, Acts 15:20, 29; 21:25 rehearse the old covenant law forbidding the consumption of blood. The "shedding of blood," denoting murder and killing, is indicated in general contexts in Matt. 27:4ff.; Luke 13:1; Acts 2:19; 20:26; Rom. 3:15; Rev. 19:2. In particular, the slaughter of the Hebrew prophets is described thus (cf. Matt. 23:30ff.; Luke 11:50ff.; Acts 5:28); as is the suffering of martyrs who likewise had their blood shed (cf. Heb. 12:4; Rev. 6:10; 17:6; 18:24). In addition, the "shedding of blood" takes place in the context of "divine judgment" (cf. Rev. 8:7ff.; 14:20; 16:3ff.).

Undoubtedly the most theologically significant usage of ***haima*** occurs in contexts where the "blood of Christ" is the dominant motif. Christ's "blood" of the new covenant is symbolized by the Passover cup, given new significance just prior to his own death (cf. Matt. 26:28; Mark 14:24; Luke 22:20; 1 Cor. 10:16; 11:25ff.). Elsewhere, Christ is said to purchase the salvation of his people with his own "blood" — through his atoning self-sacrifice on the cross (cf. Acts 20:28; Rom. 3:25; 5:9; Eph. 1:7; 2:13; Col. 1:14, 20; Heb. 9:12ff.; 10:19, 29; 1 Pet. 1:2, 19; 1 John 1:7; Rev. 1:5; 5:9; 12:11; 19:13). The "blood" of the old covenant sacrifice is deemed ultimately ineffective. For it is the blood of Christ that secures forgiveness of sins and lasting peace with God (cf. Heb. 9:13ff.; 10:4ff.). General references to the sacrificial blood of the old covenant are found in Heb. 11:28; 13:11.

The metaphorical expression "to drink the blood of Christ" denotes the dedication of one's life to follow him and obey his teaching (cf. John 6:53ff.).

References to "the moon turning to blood" reflect a cosmic catastrophe, the dissolution of the celestial bodies, heralding the end of time (cf. Acts 2:20; Rev. 6:12).

haimatekchysia [αἱματεκχυσία, *130*]

haimatekchysia is a rare noun found only in Heb. 9:22, denoting the "shedding of blood" and affirming the necessity of such blood-letting as the divinely ordained means of forgiveness for sin under the terms of the old covenant law.

haimorroeō [αἱμορροέω, *131*]

haimorroeō is a rare verb found only in Matt. 9:20, meaning "to suffer from a hemorrhage, a flow of blood."

Additional Notes

The symbolism of "blood" runs very deep — both in the Old Testament and the New. The terms ***dām*** and ***haima*** are rich in complexity and significance, both positive and negative. Of primary importance is the role of blood in the Levitical ritual sacrifices, and its indispensability in the process of atonement under the old covenant. The New Testament also clearly indicates the supreme significance of blood — not the blood of sacrificial animals, but rather the all-pervasive, eternal effectiveness of the shed blood of Christ, offered freely on our behalf. It is this phenomenon of substitutionary atonement through the medium of blood sacrifice that lies at the heart of God's redemptive actions on behalf of his people.

BLOT OUT

OT Words

māḥāh [מָחָה, 4229]

This verb occurs approximately forty times and means "wipe," "wipe out," or "blot out." It is closely linked to the sense of "destroy," and is used most frequently in this sense. (→ DESTROY)

māḥāh conveys the idea of "blotting out" or "destruction" in several different contexts. It refers to the extermination of the entire animal and human population at the time of the flood (cf. Gen. 6:7; 7:3, 4). It also refers to the destruction of the wicked and the blotting out of God's enemies in general (cf. Ps. 9:5; Exod. 17:14; Deut. 25:19). There are one or two metaphorical uses of ***māḥāh*** in this regard that are particularly striking — the invoking of a curse upon the enemies of God and his people that their sins would never be blotted out (cf. Neh. 4:5; Ps. 109:14; Jer. 18:23). Similarly, there is the express wish that the names of their enemies be blotted out of God's "book of life" (cf. Ps. 69:28). Such a fate is also decreed by God for those Israelites who flagrantly disobey him (cf. Exod. 32:33). Interestingly enough, Moses himself volunteers to have that same penalty applied to him, if by it his own people could be spared. But God refuses his offer (Exod. 32:32–33). Deut. 29:20 and 9:14. imply that such a fate will also befall any of God's people who arrogantly and deliberately turn away from him to worship idols. God's judgment on Israel for their sin as a nation is also sometimes expressed as an intention to "blot out" or "destroy" (cf. 2 Kgs. 21:13; Ezek. 6:6).

In a positive sense, ***māḥāh*** indicates the process of "blotting out" or "removing" one's sin. David prays passionately for this to happen in Ps. 51:1, 9. God declares in Isa. 44:22 that he has blotted out the sins of his servant people, Israel. Isa. 43:25 also declares that such actions are fully consistent with God's character; but in this particular instance God is still going to exact vengeance on his people for their idolatry. Finally, Nehemiah pleads that God will remember his good works and not blot them out (cf. Neh. 13:14).

NT Words

exaleiphō [ἐξαλείφω, *1813*]

The verb ***exaleiphō*** occurs in five contexts with the meaning "blot out," "wipe away."

Acts 3:19 refers to "blotting out" sin, and Col. 2:14 alludes to this. Rev. 3:5 records God's promise never to "blot out" the names of his faithful people from the book of life. Rev. 7:17; 21:24 refer to the "wiping away" of tears.

Additional Notes

māḥāh and ***exaleiphō*** share a considerable similarity of meaning when used in metaphorical contexts in reference to sin and judgment.

BLOW (NOUN)

OT Words

tigrāh **[תִּגְרָה, 8409]**

tigrāh is a rare noun denoting a "blow" dealt by God's hand in Ps. 39:10, signifying the chastening of his servant.

makkāh **[מַכָּה, 4347]**

makkāh is a noun found in about fifty contexts with the predominant meanings "wound," "plague." In Jer. 14:17, however, it is translated "blow" in regard to God's punishment of his people in Judah.

NT Words

rhapisma [ῥάπισμα, *4475*]

rhapisma is a noun found in three places meaning to strike someone with the hand, to strike them with a "blow." Mark 14:65; John 18:22; 19:3 all describe the actions of some officials of the high priest in assaulting Jesus at the time of his trial.

BLOW (VERB)

OT Words

nāshab **[נָשַׁב, 5380]**

This is a rare verb, occurring only three times and only twice with the meaning "blow." Isa. 40:7 is a metaphorical reference to the breath of God blowing on the grass and flowers, causing them to wither and fall. Ps. 147:18 refers to God causing his wind to blow. The psalm celebrates God's sustaining his creation.

nāshaph **[נָשַׁף, 5398]**

This term is also rare, being found on only two occasions in the Old Testament. Exod. 15:10 refers to the divine miracle at the Re(e)d Sea where God blew over the waters, causing them to separate. ***nāshaph*** is used metaphorically in Isa. 40:24, where it refers to the destruction of world leaders as a consequence of the divine wind (or breath) blowing on them.

tāqa' **[תָּקַע, 8628]**

The verb ***tāqa'*** occurs about seventy times and expresses the action of "sounding," "blowing" (a trumpet) in a number of different contexts.

Blowing the trumpet as a summons to ritual service, worship, or celebration is indicated in Num. 10:3ff.; Ps. 81:3; Isa. 27:13. Trumpets are "sounded" as a prelude to the destruction of Jericho in Josh. 6:4ff.; and as a call to arms, to engage in battle (cf. Judg. 3:27; 6:34; 7:18ff.; 1 Sam. 13:3; Jer. 4:5; Ezek. 7:14). Trumpets are also "sounded" to bring an end to battle in 2 Sam. 2:28; 18:16. In Zech. 9:14, the trumpet is "sounded" by Yahweh himself as a sign of the apocalyptic end of the age when the kingdom of God will triumph over all opposition.

Trumpets are also sounded to warn of an enemy invasion (cf. Ezek. 33:3ff.; Hos. 5:8; Joel 2:1, 15; Amos 3:6); and as a signal for the commencement of coronation ceremonies (cf. 1 Kgs. 1:34ff.; 2 Kgs. 9:13; 11:14; 2 Chr. 23:13). See also 2 Sam. 20:1, 22; Neh. 4:18; Isa. 18:3; Jer. 6:1.

ḥāṣar **[חָצַר, 2690]**

ḥāṣar is a verb found eleven times meaning to "blow," "sound" a trumpet. It is synonymous with ***nāshab***, above.

ḥāṣar refers to blowing a trumpet for ritual purposes such as worship and festival ceremonies in 1 Chr. 15:24; 2 Chr. 5:12ff.; 7:6; 29:28; and as a call to battle in 2 Chr. 29:28.

pûaḥ **[פּוּחַ, 6315]**

pûaḥ is a verb found in fifteen places with the underlying sense of "breathe out," "speak." In two contexts, however, the meaning "blow" is evident. The wind "blows" in Song 4:16; and in Ezek. 21:31 ***pûaḥ*** signifies the metaphorical "blowing" of Yahweh upon his people in judgment.

nāphaḥ **[נָפַח, 5301]**

nāphaḥ is a verb occurring twelve times with the dual meanings of "breathe," "blow." (→ BREATHE)

The action of "blowing" on a fire to fan it and increase its intensity is indicated in Job 20:26; Isa. 54:16; Ezek. 22:20. In a metaphorical context, the act of "blowing" on Israel with fire denotes the outpouring of divine judgment on God's people (cf. Ezek. 22:21). The similar action of Yahweh "blowing away" the economic gains of his people as a judgment against them is indicated in Hag. 1:9.

NT Words

pneō [πνέω, *4154*]

pneō is a verb found in eight contexts referring to the "blowing" of the wind (cf. Matt. 7:25ff.; Luke 12:55; John 3:8; 6:18; Acts 27:40; Rev. 7:1).

hypopneō [ὑποπνέω, *5285*]

hypopneō is a rare variant of ***pneō***, above, found only in Acts 27:13 referring to the "gentle blowing" of the wind.

BOAST, BOASTFUL

OT Words

hālal **[הָלַל, 1984]**

This verb is one of the primary terms in the Old Testament for "praise." It occurs 165 times and is translated "boast" or "glory in" on about twenty occasions. The relationship between the concepts of praising and boasting is quite a close one. Praise is usually a direct expression of appreciation or worship, depending on whether God or other people are being addressed. However, boasting is an indirect attribution of worth. One boasts about something or someone. While boasting carries negative connotations, it is also found in contexts that are both edifying and positive.

Positively, ***hālal*** is translated "boast" or "glory in" the following contexts: Ps. 34:2; Isa. 41:16; 45:25; Jer. 4:2 all testify to the fact that the people of God, and even the nations, are committed to boast about God, to glory in his gracious deeds on their behalf. Jer. 9:23, 24 exhorts various kinds of people not to boast about their wisdom, power, or wealth, but rather to glory in their God, in his gracious and compassionate character.

Then, in negative contexts, boasting is depicted in several ways. It is considered foolhardy, for example, in 1 Kgs. 20:11, where Ahab warns the Syrian king Ben Hadad II not to boast too much about his ability. Ahab then proceeds to defeat him in battle. Psalms and Proverbs also address the folly of boasting — whether it be through boasting of one's wealth (cf. Ps. 49:6); in one's evil ways (cf. Ps. 52:1); of one's ability to face tomorrow (cf. Prov. 27:1); or even about one's faith in idols (Ps. 97:7). In every single case here, the boasting is done without recognizing the part that God plays in shaping people's lives and purposes. To boast about anyone or anything apart from God is to court disaster. The only appropriate object of praise or boasting is the person and character of the living God.

gābāh **[גָּבַהּ, 1362]**

This term means "be high," "exalt," and it occurs about thirty times in the Old Testament. In about half of these contexts ***gābāh*** contains the specific idea of "being proud, haughty" or "exalted (in a positive sense)." The remaining texts refer only to being raised high in a physical sense.

In regard to haughtiness, or boasting, the proud hearts of Uzziah and Hezekiah are described in 2 Chr. 26:16; 32:25. The women of Jerusalem are declared to be haughty (cf. Isa. 3:16). Similarly, the arrogance of the northern kingdom of Israel is referred to in Ezek. 16:50. Edom's boasting is condemned in Obad. 4. Common to all these passages is the inevitability of judgment from God as a consequence of such an attitude. One particularly savage indictment of arrogant boasting is found in Ezek. 28:2, 5, 17, where the King of Tyre is condemned for his pride. The language here is reminiscent of the serpent's arrogance in the garden of Eden. The consequence of such boasting is a terrifying punishment from God leading to Tyre's ultimate destruction. Jeremiah solemnly warns God's people not to boast — otherwise divine judgment will certainly follow (cf. Jer. 13:15).

Like ***hālal***, above, ***gābāh*** can also indicate an exaltation that is wholly positive in its thrust. For example, the Suffering Servant is said to be highly exalted by God in Isa. 52:13. This amounts to an elevation to the status of deity. In Zeph. 3:11 God promises renewal to the people of Judah, whereby their pride and boasting will be eliminated. Then, Jehoshaphat's heart is described as being "lifted up" in an attitude of worship to God. This is a wholly positive "exalting" of one's soul (cf. 2 Chr. 17:6). Job declares that the righteous will be exalted (cf. Job 36:7). Finally, in Isa. 5:16 the exaltation of the Lord of Hosts is starkly juxtaposed with the humiliation of arrogant human beings.

yāhîr **[יָהִיר, 3093]**

This is a rare term, an adjective meaning "haughty," "proud," that is found only twice. Prov. 21:24 condemns the scornful person who is proud and haughty (***yāhîr***). Then Hab. 2:5 describes the coming Babylonian invader as an arrogant man.

pā'ar **[פָּאַר, 6286]**

pā'ar is verb found fourteen times with the meanings "glorify," "boast" throughout — though the latter meaning occurs only twice. Judg. 7:2 records the "boasting" of the Israelite tribes in their own achievements. There is metaphorical use of the term in Isa. 10:15.

NT Words

kauchaomai [καυχάομαι, *2744*]

kauchaomai is a verb occurring around forty times with the senses of "glory in," "boast about," "rejoice in." These three meanings overlap to some degree. This term indicates both positive and negative connotations of boasting.

"Boasting" about one's faithful observance of Jewish law as a means of gaining right standing before God is an attitude condemned in Rom. 2:17, 23. 2 Cor. 5:12 condemns boasting in one's self-righteousness. 1 Cor. 1:29 warns against boasting in the presence of God. Vain or arrogant boasting is noted in 2 Cor. 11:12, 16ff.; 30; Gal. 6:13; Eph. 2:9; Jas. 4:16.

In positive contexts, 1 Cor. 1:31; 10:13ff.; Gal. 6:14 speak of "boasting" in the goodness of God. Phil. 3:3 refers to "rejoicing" or "boasting" in Christ. Similarly, "rejoicing" (or boasting) in one's growth in grace, as a blessing from God, is indicated in 2 Cor. 7:14; 9:2; 2 Thess. 1:4. Paradoxically, Paul "boasts" of his own weakness in 2 Cor. 12:9.

Other general references to boasting are found in 1 Cor. 3:21; 2 Cor. 10:16; 12:1ff.; Jas. 1:9.

katakauchaomai [κατακαυχάομαι, *2620*]

katakauchaomai is a rare variant of ***kauchaomai***, above, meaning "boast" in Rom. 11:18; Jas. 3:14. Both texts warn against "vain boasting."

kauchēma [καύχημα, *2745*]

kauchēma is a noun found eleven times meaning "boasting" or "rejoicing in."

Boasting from a purely human perspective, and therefore illegitimate in God's sight, is indicated in 1 Cor. 5:6. By way of contrast, legitimate "boasting" or "rejoicing in" the goodness of God is referred to in 2 Cor. 1:14; 5:12; 9:3; Phil. 1:26; 2:16; Heb. 3:6. Other general references include 1 Cor. 9:15ff.; Gal. 6:4.

kauchēsis [καύχησις, *2746*]

kauchēsis is synonymous with ***kauchēma***, above, denoting the act of "boasting" or "rejoicing" in twelve contexts.

Boasting in one's righteousness is rendered null and void on the principle of faith in Rom. 3:27. Vain, arrogant boasting is indicated in Jas. 4:16.

Positively expressed, "rejoicing" in one's ministry in Christ is noted in Rom. 15:17; 2 Cor. 1:12. 1 Cor. 15:31 speaks of "boasting" or "rejoicing" in Christ. "Rejoicing" in the spiritual growth and maturity of one's flock, or congregation, and one's fellow workers, is a characteristic of the apostle Paul's letters in 2 Cor. 7:4, 14; 8:24; 11:10; 1 Thess. 2:19. See also 2 Cor. 11:17.

megalaucheō [μεγαλαυχέω, *3166*]

megalaucheō is a rare verb found only in Jas. 3:5 with reference to the tongue, which "boasts of great things."

alazōn [ἀλαζών, *213*]

alazōn is a rare noun found only twice, denoting "those who boast" with arrogance and insolence (cf. Rom. 1:30; 2 Tim. 3:2).

alazoneia [ἀλαζονεία, *212*]

alazoneia is a rare noun denoting "arrogant boasting, or pride," found only in Jas. 4:16; 1 John 2:16.

Additional Notes

As with boasting in the Old Testament, there is a like emphasis in the New that distinguishes between legitimate boasting or glorying in the person and character of God and Jesus Christ, and the selfish arrogant pride of human beings that is universally condemned in Scripture.

See Also: → GLORIFY → GREAT

BOAT

OT Words

'oniyyāh **[אֳנִיָּה, 591]**

This term is used exclusively in the Old Testament to refer to ships. It occurs about thirty times and is found in a literal sense on most occasions.

From a purely historical perspective, it is interesting to note the number of times ships are mentioned in connection with Tarshish. Scholars consider this to be a reference to a distinct port, possibly located in Spain. The phrase "ships of Tarshish" is often translated as "trading ships," referring simply to large sea-going vessels involved in international maritime trade (cf. 1 Kgs. 22:48; 2 Chr. 9:21; Ps. 48:7; Isa. 2:16; 23:1, 14; 60:9; Ezek. 27:25). Other references point to ships going to Tarshish (cf. 2 Chr. 9:21; 20:36; Jonah 1:3). Another distant destination referred to in relation to ships is the port of Ezion-Geber, today associated with the resort town of Eilat at the north-eastern end of the Red Sea (1 Kgs. 22:48; 2 Chr. 20:36).

NT Words

ploion [πλοῖον, *4143*]

The noun ***ploion*** is found about seventy times with the consistent literal meaning "ship," "boat" (e.g., Matt. 4:21ff.; Mark 1:19; 6:15ff.; Luke 5:2ff.; John 6:17ff.; 21:3ff.; Acts 21:2ff.; Jas. 3:4; Rev. 8:9; 18:17, 19).

ploiarion [πλοιάριον, *4142*]

ploiarion is a diminutive form of ***ploion*** (see above) found in five places, denoting "a small boat," "little ship" in Mark 3:9; 4:36; John 6:22ff.; 21:8.

skaphē [σκάφη, *4627*]

skaphē is a rare synonym for ***ploion*** and ***ploiarion***, above, designating a "ship" or "boat" in Acts 27:16; 30, 32.

BODY

OT Words

nephesh **[נֶפֶשׁ, 5315]**

This common Hebrew term has a broad semantic range. (→ LIFE → MIND → SOUL) In several instances, however, ***nephesh*** denotes a "corpse" or "dead body," with which Israelites were forbidden to come in direct contact, lest they become ceremonially unclean (cf. Lev. 21:11; Num. 6:6; 9:6ff.; 19:11).

mût **[מוּת, 4191]**

The common verb ***mût*** occurs around 850 times meaning "die," "slay," plus the nominal senses of "death," "the dead." Infrequently, the term denotes a "dead body" or "corpse" (cf. Num. 19:16; 2 Kgs. 8:5).

nebēlāh **[נְבֵלָה, 5038]**

nebēlāh is a noun occurring about fifty times denoting a "carcass" or "corpse" (both human and animal).

nebēlāh refers to animal carcasses (which render God's people unclean if they touch them and which they are forbidden to eat) in Lev. 5:2; 11:8ff.; Deut. 14:8.

Human corpses, or remains, are indicated in Deut. 21:23; 28:26; Josh. 8:29; 1 Kgs. 13:22ff.; 2 Kgs. 9:37; Ps. 79:2; Isa. 5:25; Jer. 7:33; 16:18; 26:23; 36:30.

gewîyāh **[גְּוִיָּה, 1472]**

gewîyāh is a noun found thirteen times, denoting a "body" which is either alive or dead.

Human "bodies," denoting individual persons subject to slavery, are indicated in Gen. 47:18; Neh. 9:37. The "bodies" of cherubim (i.e., heavenly creatures, guardians of the throne of God) are described in Ezek. 1:11, 23. Similarly, the "body" of the angelic man dressed in linen is described in Dan. 10:6.

The "carcass" of a lion is mentioned in Judg. 14:8ff.; as are human "corpses" in 1 Sam. 31:10ff.; Ps. 110:6; Nah. 3:3.

gûphāh **[גּוּפָה, 1480]**

gûphāh is a rare noun denoting human "remains" or a "corpse" in 1 Chr. 10:12.

geshem **[גֶּשֶׁם, 1655]**

geshem is a noun found five times, denoting the human "body" in all but one of these contexts.

Literal references to the human body include Dan. 3:27ff.; 4:33; 5:21. The term is also used metaphorically to denote the "body" of the fourth beast of Daniel's apocalyptic vision, a beast destroyed by the blazing fire of God's judgment (cf. Dan. 7:11).

peger **[פֶּגֶר, 6297]**

The noun ***peger*** occurs around twenty times and is a synonym for all seven of the words above. ***peger*** denotes both human and animal carcasses.

Animal remains are indicated in Gen. 15:11. Human carcasses are indicated in two major contexts. The first is in Num. 14:29ff., where the bodies of Israelites lying in the wilderness represent the outworking of God's judgment against his people for their sin. Elsewhere, and more commonly, the laying out of the "bodies" (i.e., the corpses) of all of God's enemies (including his own people) is a sign of their destruction under the hand of God (cf. 1 Sam. 17:46; 2 Kgs. 19:35; 2 Chr. 20:24ff.; Isa. 14:19; 34:3; 37:36; 66:24; Jer. 31:40; 33:5; 41:9; Ezek. 6:5; 43:7; Amos 8:3).

NT Words

sōma [σῶμα, *4983*]

sōma is a noun found in approximately 150 contexts meaning "body," with a variety of nuances and several different contexts.

General references to the human body include Matt. 5:29ff.; 6:22ff.; 26:12; Mark 5:29; Luke 11:34ff.; 12:22ff.; Rom. 1:24; 4:19; 1 Cor. 5:3; 9:27; 12:22ff.; 2 Cor. 5:6ff.; Gal. 6:17; Col. 2:23; Jas. 2:26; Jude 9. The term "body" can also indicate the whole person, or being (cf. Rom. 12:1; 1 Cor. 6:13ff.; Eph. 5:28; Heb. 10:22). A reference to animal carcasses is found in Heb. 13:11.

The other significant literal sense of ***sōma*** is that of "(human) corpse," used in general contexts such as John 19:31; Matt. 14:12. "Bodies" undergoing the miracle of resurrection are indicated in Matt. 27:52; Acts 9:40; 1 Cor. 15:35ff. In particular, references to the "body" of Christ removed from the cross are found in Matt. 27:58ff.; Mark 15:43ff.; Luke 23:52ff.; John 19:38ff.

Other uses of ***sōma*** are metaphorical. For example, the "body of Christ" is represented by the bread of the Passover meal, a "body" about to be broken to the cross (cf. Matt. 26:26; Mark 14:22; Luke 22:19; 1 Cor. 10:16; 11:24ff.). The phrase "body of Christ" also functions as a summary expression for Christ's atoning sacrifice (cf. Rom. 7:4; Eph. 2:16; Col. 1:22; Heb. 10:5, 10; 1 Pet. 2:24); and as a metaphor for the whole community of God's people (cf. 1 Cor. 12:27; Eph. 4:4, 12ff.; 5:30; Col. 2:19). John 2:21 refers to the "body of Christ" as a temple. And, finally, the expression is equated with the church in Eph. 1:23; 5:23.

Elsewhere, the term "body" symbolizes the totality of the people of God in Rom. 12:4ff.; 1 Cor. 10:17. And the expression "sinful body" symbolizes the finite, fallen aspect of the nature of humankind in Rom. 6:6; 7:24; 8:10ff.; Phil. 3:21; Col. 2:11.

sōmatikos [σωματικός, *4984*]

sōmatikos is a rare adjective found only twice, meaning "bodily" in the sense of relating or pertaining to a bodily form. Luke 3:22 describes the Holy Spirit descending on Jesus in the "bodily" form of a dove. 1 Tim. 4:8 refers to "bodily" exercise.

sōmatikōs [σωματικῶς, *4985*]

sōmatikōs is an adverb, related to ***sōmatikos***, above, found only in Col. 2:9 with reference to the fullness of the Godhead dwelling "bodily" in Christ.

syssōmos [σύσσωμος, *4954*]

syssōmos is an adjectival form found only in Eph. 3:6 affirming that Gentile believers are members "of the same body" (i.e., of Christ, the church).

chrōs [χρώς, *5559*]

chrōs is a rare noun denoting the "surface of one's body" in Acts 19:12.

ptōma [πτῶμα, *4430*]

ptōma is a noun found in five places with the meaning "dead body," "corpse," or "carcass." Matt. 24:28 refers to a carcass (whether human or animal is uncertain). Human corpses are noted in Mark 6:29; Rev. 11:8ff.

See Also: → FLESH

BOIL

OT Words

sheḥîn [שְׁחִין, **7822**]

sheḥîn is a noun found thirteen times denoting a "boil" — a skin eruption, inflammation (cf. Lev. 13:8ff.). The plague of "boils" in Egypt is noted in Exod. 9:9ff. A similar outbreak of boils is threatened in the curse sanctions of the covenant in Deut. 28:27, 35. Legislation concerning the ritual status of those suffering from boils is found in Lev. 13:18ff. General references to boils are found in 2 Kgs. 20:7; Job 2:7; Isa. 38:21.

bāshal [בָּשַׁל, **1310**]

The verb ***bāshal*** is found in around thirty places, meaning "to boil" in the context of cooking in about half these occurrences. Most commonly, ***bāshal*** indicates the action of "boiling" meat with water in ritual contexts (e.g., Exod. 12:9; 16:23; Lev. 6:28; 8:31; 1 Sam. 2:13ff.). Non-ritual, or profane, usage is indicated in 1 Kgs. 19:21; 2 Kgs. 4:38; Ezek. 24:5; 46:20; Zech. 14:21. Elsewhere, the term refers to the prohibition against boiling a kid goat in its mother's milk (cf. Exod. 23:19; 34:26; Deut. 14:21). In addition, ***bāshal*** is found in rare contexts where cannibalism was practiced among the people of Yahweh, citing those who "boiled" their offspring for eating (cf. 2 Kgs. 6:29; Lam. 4:10).

bā'āh [בָּעָה, **1158**]

bā'āh is a verb with the meaning "to boil (water)" in Isa. 64:2.

rātaḥ [רָתַח, 7570]

The verb ***rātaḥ*** means "to boil" in relation to cooking meat in Ezek. 24:5. In Job 41:31, the term is used metaphorically to depict Yahweh's action in "making the waters (of the ocean) boil" like a pot.

BOLD, BOLDNESS, BOLDLY

OT Words

bāṭaḥ [בָּטַח, 982]

bāṭaḥ is a verb occurring around 120 times meaning "trust," "have confidence." In Prov. 28:1, the term is translated "bold," depicting the righteous.

NT Words

tharreō [θαρρέω, *2292*]

tharreō is a verb found in six places with the meaning "be bold, confident."

The sense of "be confident of, have confidence in" is indicated in relation to one's intimate relationship with God being characterized by peace (cf. 2 Cor. 5:6ff.; Heb. 13:6). 2 Cor. 7:16 speaks of "having confidence" in one's friends in Christ. Having confidence, or being bold in the presence of people, is noted in 2 Cor. 6:1ff.

parrēsiazomai [παρρησιάζομαι, *3955*]

parrēsiazomai is a verb found nine times with the meaning "to speak boldly" in the context of preaching the gospel (cf. Acts 9:27ff.; 13:46; 14:3; 18:26; 19:8; 26:26; Eph. 6:20; 1 Thess. 2:2).

parrēsia [παρρησία, *3954*]

parrēsia is a noun found in thirty places meaning "boldness," "confidence" in about half of these contexts. It is also used adverbially in several places with the sense of "boldly."

"Boldness" or "confidence" in preaching is indicated with respect to apostolic preachers in Acts 4:13, 29ff.; 28:31; 2 Cor. 3:12; Eph. 6:19; Phil. 1:20.

2 Cor. 7:4 refers to "having confidence" in fellow believers. The same state of mind is also noted in relation to the day of judgment in 1 John 4:17; and to Christ and one's salvation in Eph. 3:12; 1 Tim. 3:13; Phlm. 8; Heb. 3:6; 10:19, 35; 1 John 2:28; 3:21; 5:14.

The adverbial meaning "boldly" describes preaching in Acts 2:29; and approaching God in prayer in Heb. 4:16.

tolmaō [τολμάω, *5111*]

tolmaō is a verb found eighteen times with the primary meaning "to dare." The related senses of "to be bold," "show boldness" are indicated in 2 Cor. 10:2; 11:21. In Phil. 1:14 the demonstration of boldness is specifically related to speaking the word of God without fear.

apotolmaō [ἀποτολμάω, *662*]

apotolmaō is a rare variant of ***tolmaō***, above, found only in Rom. 10:20.

tolmēroterōs [τολμηροτέρως, *5112*]

tolmēroterōs is a rare adverbial form found only in Rom. 15:15 with the meaning "very boldly."

BOND

OT Words

'esār [אֱסָר, 632]

'esār is a noun found eleven times referring to a "pledge" — a solemn binding oath or vow made before the Lord (cf. Num. 30:2ff.).

māsōret [מָסֹרֶת, 4562]

māsōret is a rare noun found only in Ezek. 20:37, denoting the solemn "bond" or "oath" of the covenant into which Yahweh would bring his people anew, resulting in severe punishment for their violation of the covenant vow first enacted at Sinai.

môsēr [מוֹסֵר, 4147]

môsēr is a noun meaning "bonds" — "ropes" or "chains" — that restrict the movement of people in captivity. Less commonly, it can also describe a "pledge" (i.e., a solemn bond or oath).

There is a general reference to "ropes" or "chains" in Job 39:5. Ps. 2:3 records the impotent threats from the enemies of God and his people to cast off their "chains."

In other metaphorical contexts, God is said to deliver his people from their "bonds" (i.e., chains) in Pss. 107:14; 116:16; Isa. 52:2; Jer. 30:8; Nah. 1:13. In Isa. 28:22, God warns his people against disobedience lest their "bonds" be made strong. See also Jer. 27:2.

Jer. 2:20; 5:5 record the action of Israel breaking away from her "bonds," or her obligations to Yahweh under the terms of the old covenant, and becoming ensnared by idolatrous worship.

NT Words

desmos [δεσμός, *1199*]

desmos is a noun found about twenty times with the underlying meaning "bonds" signifying restriction of movement in the literal sense of "chains," and the metaphorical sense of "imprisonment" or "crippling disease."

Literal references to "chains" include Luke 8:29; Acts 26:29; Col. 4:18; 2 Tim. 2:9. "Chains" broken by divine power are noted in Acts 16:26, and prisoners are released by the civil authorities in Acts 22:30.

A metaphorical reference to the satanic "bondage" of a crippling disease from which a woman was healed by Jesus is noted in Luke 13:16. Other metaphorical references to "imprisonment" include Acts 20:23; 23:29; 26:31; Phil. 1:7, 13ff.; Phlm. 10ff.; Heb. 10:34; 11:36. There is another symbolic usage of ***desmos*** in Jude 6, which mentions "eternal chains" that keep fallen angels bound in darkness until the judgment day.

desmios [δέσμιος, *1198*]

The noun ***desmios*** is found in sixteen places referring to a "prisoner" as one who is "kept in bonds, chains" (cf. Matt. 27:15ff.; Mark 15:6; Acts 16:25ff.; 28:16ff.; Eph. 3:1; 4:1; 2 Tim. 1:8; Phlm. 1, 9; Heb. 13:3).

syndesmos [σύνδεσμος, *4886*]

syndesmos is a noun found four times with the largely metaphorical sense of "bond," or that which "binds" people together for good or ill.

Acts 8:23 refers to the evil desire for power that had overtaken Simon the magician who tried to buy the gift of the Holy Spirit. Peter rebuked him as one who was "captive to sin" (lit. "in the bond of iniquity"). Eph. 4:3 enjoins believers to maintain the "bond of peace," or the spirit of unity that will maintain their strong fellowship. There is a similar expression in Col. 3:14 — "the bond of perfect harmony."

In Col. 2:19, ***syndesmos*** refers to the "ligaments" of the human body that give it a uniform structure and function. The context is a metaphorical description of the importance of the unity of the body of Christ, the fellowship of Christian believers.

halysis [ἅλυσις, *254*]

halysis is a noun found eleven times referring to "chains" as a means of restricting one's movement in several different contexts.

Chains restraining the Gadarene demoniac are noted in Mark 5:3ff.; Luke 8:29. Acts 12:6ff.; 21:33; 28:20; Eph. 6:20; 2 Tim. 1:16 refer to prisoners' "chains." In Rev. 20:1, the angel holds "chains" to restrain the activity of Satan, who will be released for a short time prior to the final judgment.

See Also: → SERVANT

BONDAGE

NT Words

katadouloō [καταδουλόω, *2615*]

katadouloō is a verb found four times meaning to "bring into bondage, slavery." It is used literally in 2 Cor. 11:20 and figuratively in Gal. 2:4 in relation to the old covenant law.

See Also: → SERVANT → SERVE

BONDSERVANT → SERVANT

BONE

OT Words

'eṣem [עֶצֶם, **6106**]

This word is found approximately 120 times in the Old Testament with the dominant meaning "bone." The term is used in several senses.

Occasionally, ***'eṣem*** refers in a metaphorical sense to the intimacy of kinship within a family. The Hebrew phrases in which ***'eṣem*** is found with this meaning are literally rendered "bone of one's bone," "one's bone and flesh," ". . . of one's bone." The closest English expression is the rendering "one's flesh and blood." One of the most striking examples of this usage is found in Gen. 2:23 where Adam exclaims in joy and delight concerning the woman God has given him as his partner and companion: "This is now bone of my bones and flesh of my flesh" (cf. also Judg. 9:2; 2 Sam. 5:1; 19:12, 13; Gen. 29:14; 1 Chr. 11:1).

'eṣem is also used in about twenty passages to refer to human skeletal remains. Joseph's remains (i.e., his "bones") are given the greatest possible honor, when after his death, in accordance with his own request, they are solemnly taken out of Egypt and buried in Canaan (cf. Gen. 50:25; Exod. 13:19; Josh. 24:32). Other literal references to human remains or bones are found in the following places: Num. 19:18; 1 Sam. 31:13; 2 Sam. 21:12ff.; 1 Kgs. 13:2, 31; 2 Kgs. 13:21; 23:14ff.; 1 Chr. 10:12; Jer. 8:1; Amos 2:1; 6:10. Perhaps the most notable reference to human bones in the Old Testament is found in Ezekiel's vision of "dry bones" that symbolize the people of God, lifeless and desperate in an alien land. God then brings the skeletal remains back to life, putting flesh on his people and bringing them back from the dead. The vision relates, of course, to God's promise to bring his people back out of captivity and restore them to the land of their forefathers (cf. Ezek. 39:1–11).

'eṣem also refers to the human body, not only in the physiological sense but also, and more frequently, in the sense of "one's whole being." This usage is found principally in the Wisdom sections of the Old Testament (cf., e.g., Job 2:5; 4:14; 21:24; 30:17; 33:19; Pss. 6:2, 3; 31:10, 11; 38:3; Prov. 3:8; 14:30; Eccl. 11:5; Jer. 20:9).

'eṣem refers to animal bones as well. Exod. 12:46 and Num. 9:12 both mention the ritual requirement that the bones of the sacrificial Passover lamb must never be broken. Ezek. 24:2 refers to the "choice bones" of sacrificial animals.

gerem [גֶּרֶם, 1634]

gerem is a noun found in five places. It denotes a "bone" in three of these. Animal bones are noted in Job 40:18; and general references to human bones are found in Prov. 17:22; 25:15.

'āṣam [עָצַם, 6105]

'āṣam is a verb found twenty times with the dominant sense of "be numerous, strong." However, in Jer. 50:17 it is translated "to crush the bones," metaphorically depicting the terrible fate of the people of God at the hands of Nebuchadnezzar, king of Babylon.

NT Words

osteon [ὀστέον, *3747*]

osteon is a noun found in five places with the meaning "bones."

The "bones" of corpses are noted in Matt. 23:27; and also in Heb. 11:22 in the context of burial. Elsewhere, "bones" in the literal, physiological sense are indicated in Luke 24:39; John 19:36. The term is also used metaphorically in the sense of "body" in Eph. 5:30.

Additional Notes

It is evident that there is a much wider usage of the term "bone" in the Old Testament than in the New. Yet one important parallel is found in John 19:36, where the apostle affirms that the absence of broken bones in the body of Christ on the cross is a typological fulfillment of the Passover lamb in Exod. 12:46; Num. 9:12, whose bones were not to be broken in the course of its ritual slaughter.

BOOK

OT Words

sēpher [סֵפֶר, 5612]

Though translated "book" in many instances in the Old Testament, the word ***sēpher*** literally means "scroll." ***sēpher*** is probably related to the verb ***sāphar*** (→ TELL), which means to "recount" or "relate," and is found approximately 160 times. For the purposes of this discussion, the term "book" will be used, bearing in mind the above qualification.

The phenomenon of writing books in the Old Testament is seen at several levels. In the first instance, ***sēpher*** refers to the "book of the law" (and variations thereof) as the sacred record of God's revelation to Moses on Mt. Sinai. It is used this way approximately fifty times. In Exod. 24:7, the "book of the law" denotes the summary of that whole body of legislation, plus the events that immediately precede its transmission on Sinai and then follow on to the covenant renewal ceremony. Most scholars are agreed that Exod. 19–24 constitutes the limits of this "book" within a book. This same concept is then referred to some eleven times in the book of Deuteronomy, with the book itself being indicated by the use of ***sēpher*** in this context. The phrase "book of the law" is also found five times in Joshua, where the context in 1:8 and 8:34 suggests that the Deuteronomic legislation is in view; whereas 8:31 refers back to Exod. 20:25 concerning the altar of uncut stones. In any case, what is clear is that some of the traditions of the pentateuchal material were already extant by the time of Joshua. In Josh. 23:6, this phrase alludes to legislation from the Decalogue (Exod. 20:1ff.; Deut. 5) and Deut. 7. Finally, Josh. 24:26 refers to Joshua recording the events surrounding the people's recommitment to the divine covenant in the "book of the law of God." This suggests that Joshua himself supplemented the Sinaitic traditions that were already available to the people in his day.

Other references to "the book of the law" are found in 2 Kgs. 22; 2 Chr. 34 during the revival under King Josiah, when this "book," presumably the book of Deuteronomy, was rediscovered in the temple. Neh. 8 also records Ezra's reading and interpretation of the "book of the law" to the postexilic community. Here it is not clear exactly what Ezra had in his hands when he read to the people — whether it was the whole of the Mosaic covenant law, or only selected portions of it. Certainly Neh. 8:14–15 specifically refers to Exod. 23:16 and Lev. 23:37ff., though one cannot accurately determine what exactly Ezra had with him from the Mosaic legislation.

sēpher also refers to a number of extra-canonical sources that were utilized by the authors or editors of Samuel-Kings and Chronicles. These almost certainly refer to the prophetic traditions contained in the royal archives in Jerusalem, and there are about twenty references to such "books."

The mention of the "book of life" is also worthy of note. The phrase occurs with reference to Moses' extraordinary offer to have himself struck out of this divine record and bear the punishment for the golden calf incident instead of the people (Exod. 32:32). Other references to the "book of life" are found in Ps. 69:28 and possibly Mal. 3:16 as well.

Some occurrences of ***sēpher*** also indicate that sacred Scripture is in view. Frequent mention is made of God's instructions to the prophets to write down in a book what he has just communicated to them, or revelation previously given (cf. Jer. 25:13; 30:2; 36:2–18; 45:1; 51:60, 63; Dan. 12:1, 4; Nah. 1:1).

sēpher can also refer to: "letters" (i.e., correspondence); a divine lawsuit oracle (cf. Isa. 30:8); the archives of the Persian Empire (cf. Esth. 6:1; 10:2); deeds of purchase (cf. Jer. 32:10–16); and to a bill of divorce (cf. Isa. 50:1; Jer. 3:8).

sephar [סְפַר, **5609** (Aramaic)]

sephar is the Aramaic equivalent of ***sēpher*** (see above) denoting "book(s)" or "scrolls" in each instance.

"Books" in the sense of archival records or chronicles are indicated in Ezra 4:15; 6:1. Ezra 6:18 refers to the "book of Moses" (i.e., the law covenant). "Books" containing legal indictments are mentioned in the context of divine judgment against the wicked in Dan. 7:10.

NT Words

biblos [βίβλος, *976*]

biblos is a noun found thirteen times denoting a "book" (or "scroll") in a variety of contexts.

The genealogical records of Christ are indicated in Matt. 1:1. Matt. 12:26 refers to the covenant law of Moses. The prophet Isaiah is noted in Luke 3:4; and the Psalter in Luke 20:42; Acts 1:20. The prophetic writings in general is indicated in Acts 7:42; and in Rev. 22:19 the book of Revelation is explicitly indicated. Acts 19:19 refers to magic books and occult manuscripts.

The "book of life," which contains all the names of God's people destined for glory, is specifically mentioned in Phil. 4:3; Rev. 3:5; 13:8; 20:15.

biblion [βιβλίον, *975*]

biblion is a noun found about thirty times, a diminutive form of ***biblos***, above, denoting "book" (or "scroll"). It can also refer to a "document" or "bill."

General references to "books" are indicated in John 21:25; Rev. 1:11; 6:14. In the context of John's vision in the book of Revelation, ***biblion*** refers to the "scroll" containing the expression of divine judgment and condemnation of sin, a document fastened with seven seals that only Christ, the Lamb of God, is able to open (cf. Rev. 5:1ff.). The "book" of Revelation itself is indicated in Rev. 22:7ff. Metaphorical reference to the "book of life" (see above) is indicated in Rev. 17:8; 21:27. The "book" containing the legal indictment of the wicked, to be used at the last judgment, is noted in Rev. 20:12.

Elsewhere, ***biblion*** denotes the "book" of Isaiah the prophet in Luke 4:17ff.; John's gospel in John 20:30; and the law covenant in Gal. 3:10; 2 Tim. 4:13; Heb. 9:19; 10:7. Then, Matt. 19:7; Mark 10:4 both refer to a "bill of divorce" that constituted a legal document in biblical times.

biblaridion [βιβλαρίδιον, *974*]

This noun is a diminutive of ***biblion***, above, meaning "little book" or "scroll." ***biblaridion*** occurs four times and is found exclusively in Revelation, where the angel hands over a "little book" to the apostle which he is commanded to eat. This book symbolizes and contains the judgment of God against the godless nations of the world (cf. Rev. 10:2ff.).

Additional Notes

Both the Hebrew term ***sēpher*** and the Greek word ***biblos*** (and its derivatives) conveys a broad variety of emphases under the term "book" or "scroll." Both Testaments use these terms that reveal a "secular" as well as a "sacred" perspective. Common to both Old and New Testaments is the significant emphasis on books and writings that testify to an authoritative divine origin. The New Testament affirms this of the old covenant Scriptures throughout, and it also clearly indicates that the teachings of the apostles and Paul (and, by implication, the other writings) are all to be accorded that same respect.

BORDER

OT Words

gebûl [גְּבוּל, **1366**]

This term occurs around two hundred times in the Old Testament and has the predominant meaning of "border" in the sense of a national boundary. About half of these occurrences refer to the national boundaries of Israel and are concentrated in the Pentateuch and Joshua (cf. Num. 20:16ff.; 21:13ff.; 34:3ff.; Josh. 13–19). See also Ezek. 47:13; 48:1ff.; Mic. 5:6. Then, in Ps. 74:17, ***gebûl*** refers to the "boundaries" or "borders" of the earth. The term also indicates the "borders" or "boundaries" of other nations (cf. Isa. 15:8; Ezek. 27:4).

The other meaning assigned to ***gebûl*** is that of "boundary stone," referring to the pillars of stones that marked out the designated boundaries of each tribal allotment, or each parcel of land belonging to individual clans. The covenant legislation forbade altering the position of or removing the boundary stone of one's neighbor. To do so invited the judgment of God (cf. Deut. 19:14; 27:17; Prov. 22:28; 23:10).

qāṣeh [קָצֶה, **7097**]

qāṣeh is a noun occurring around ninety times with the predominant meaning "end," as well as a variety of related senses. In one context the term is translated "border" with reference to the eastern border of Jericho in Josh. 4:19.

gābal [גָּבַל, **1379**]

gābal is a verb found five times, expressing the actions of "set a boundary," "form a border." Specific references to geographic borders or boundaries are found in Josh. 18:20; Zech. 9:2.

NT Words

kraspedon [κράσπεδον, *2899*]

kraspedon is a noun denoting the "border" of a garment — the "fringe" or "hem" (cf. Matt. 9:20; 14:36; 23:5; Mark 6:56; Luke 8:44).

BORN → BEGET

BORROW

OT Words

lāwāh [לָוָה, **3867**]

This verb occurs twenty-five times in the Old Testament, but on only five occasions does it mean "borrow." The charging of interest (or possibly excessive interest) to another citizen in ancient Israelite society was forbidden. Neh. 5:4 refers to the poverty-stricken in the postexilic community who are groaning under the weight of their fellow Israelite creditors. This plight of the poor brings an angry response from Nehemiah, who condemns the practice whereby the disadvantaged in the land are being forced to borrow from their fellow Israelites. In Deut. 28:12, the principle is laid down that Israel may lend to other nations, but not borrow from them. Ps. 37:21 indicts the wicked who, among other things, borrow but do not repay. Prov. 22:7 reflects on the awful predicament of the borrower in relation to his creditor. Finally, Isa. 24:2 refers to both the borrower and the lender who will suffer an equal fate as God threatens judgment on a wicked world.

The other primary meaning of ***lāwāh*** is "to lend." (See under → LEND for further discussion of this term.)

shā'al [שָׁאַל, **7592**]

shā'al is a verb found approximately 170 times with the meaning "ask," "inquire," plus several related nuances. One of these nuances is the sense of "to borrow." It is used in relation to animals in Exod. 22:14; and to personal property in 2 Kgs. 4:3; 6:5.

'ābat [עָבַט, **5670**]

'ābat is a verb found four times with the meaning to "lend" in Deut. 15:6, 8; and "borrow" in Deut. 15:6.

NT Words

daneizō [δανείζω, *1155*]

daneizō is a verb found four times with the meaning "to borrow" in Matt. 5:42; and "to lend" in Luke 6:34, 35. All contexts suggest the borrowing and lending of money.

BOSOM

OT Words

ḥêq [חֵיק, **2436**]

This word refers generally to that part of the body bounded by the arms and the chest. The translation "bosom" conveys a number of connotations. ***ḥêq*** is variously translated "lap," "arms," "breast," "embrace." In this regard, the term suggests varying degrees of intimacy.

The most intimate use of ***ḥêq*** relates to the description of husbands lying in the embrace of their wives or concubines (cf. Gen. 16:5; 12:8; Mic. 7:5; Deut. 13:6; 28:54, 56), and men lying in the embrace of a prostitute (cf. Prov. 5:20). The word also refers to the arms of a mother embracing her child (cf. 1 Kgs. 17:19; Lam. 2:12), the tender arms of God in a metaphorical sense (cf. Num. 11:12; Isa. 40:11), and even the arms of a man carrying his favorite animal (cf. 2 Sam. 12:3). ***ḥêq*** also indicates the "lap" where a mother places her child (cf. Ruth 4:16), and also to the mother's breast (cf. 1 Kgs. 3:20 — except that here the children are recently deceased). ***ḥêq*** also refers simply to one's chest (cf. Exod. 4:6, 7; Ps. 74:11).

In addition, ***ḥêq*** can be used metaphorically to refer to a person's heart (cf. Ps. 89:50; Prov. 6:27; Eccl. 7:9), or to the secret state of a person's heart (cf. Prov. 17:23; 21:14). Finally, ***ḥêq*** refers to the "laps" of his people in the context of God punishing them for their sin (cf. Isa. 65:6, 7; Jer. 32:18).

NT Words

kolpos [κόλπος, *2859*]

The noun ***kolpos*** primarily denotes that part of the human body between the arms. The translation "bosom" is somewhat archaic. The translations "lap" or "breast" are more contemporary, as noted in Luke 6:38; 16:22ff.; John 13:23. The term is used metaphorically in John 1:18 to denote the "lap" of the Father.

Additional Notes

The concept of "bosom" (in its various senses) is rich in meaning throughout both Old and New Testaments as it suggests varying levels of intimacy. However, only in the Old Testament use of ***ḥêq*** is there a negative connotation of the concept in terms of God's judgment upon his people.

BOTTOM, BOTTOMLESS → DEEP → DOWN

BOUNTY, BOUNTIFULLY → BLESS → GRACE

BOW (VERB)

OT Words

kāra' [כָּרַע, **3766**]

This verb occurs approximately thirty times with various shades of meaning associated with bowing or falling down at the knees, both literally and metaphorically.

The literal sense of "bow down" is found in various contexts of worship, including the adoration of God (cf. 2 Chr. 29:29; 7:3; Pss. 22:29, 30; 72:9; 95:6; Isa. 45:23), and also prostration before idols (cf. 1 Kgs. 19:18). In a related context, Mordecai refuses to bow down to Haman in recognition of the authority granted him by King Xerxes (cf. Esth. 3:2, 5). This is in marked contrast to the other leading citizens of Susa, who did acknowledge Haman in this way (Esth. 3:2). Reference is then made to Solomon in prayer with ***kāra'*** translated "kneeling" (cf. 1 Kgs. 8:54), and likewise Ezra in Ezra 9:5. Kneeling of a different sort is indicated in 2 Kgs. 1:13, where the captain of Ahaziah's military embassy begs Elijah on bended knee not to slay him and his men. Gideon's men are also described as "bending down on their knees" to drink from the spring at En Harod (cf. Judg. 7:5, 6). Sisera's death is described in Judg. 5:27 in terms of him "falling down" after being dealt a mortal blow by Jael, the wife of Heber the Kenite. The pregnant wife of Phinehas also passes away in tragic circumstances when, after hearing of the deaths of her husband and Eli her father-in-law and the capture of the ark of the covenant by the Philistines, she "falls down," commences her labor, and then dies as she gives birth.

kāra' is also used metaphorically in various contexts. It refers to the "crouching" of Judah like a lion in Gen. 49:9; and of Israel in Num. 24:9. It also refers to the humiliation of pagan deities, such as Bel and others, who must "bow down" when carried on the backs of their animal transports. Then there were those situations in which the judgment of God brought about the downfall of those who opposed him: Ps. 20:8 records the "bringing down" of the enemies of God in defeat; Isa. 10:4 indicts rebellious Israelites by declaring that God will make them bow down before their captors. Similarly, Isa. 65:12 cites the judgment of God upon his wicked people who shall all "bow down" for slaughter (cf. also Ps. 78:31). ***kāra'*** also refers to a condition of misery and wretchedness in the sense of "being brought low" (cf. Ps. 17:13; Judg. 11:35 [re Jephthah's daughter]).

gāhar [גָּהַר, **1457**]

This is a rare verb occurring only three times. In the first instance, a position of prayer is indicated in 1 Kgs. 18:42 when Elijah bows down with his face between his knees and prays for rain. In 2 Kgs. 4:34, 35, ***gāhar*** refers to the action of Elisha "stretching himself out" upon the body of the Shulamite widow's son as the prelude to the boy's resurrection from the dead. (→ STRETCH)

shāḥāh [שָׁחָה, **7812**]

shāḥāh is a verb found about 170 times with the dominant sense of "worship" plus the related sense of "bow (down)." There is considerable overlap in meaning here, since the classic position for worship is in fact a prostrate one. (→ WORSHIP)

The meaning "bow down" is found in a number of contexts. As a mode of social greeting, this position is indicated in Gen. 18:2; 23:7; 33:3ff.; Exod. 18:7; Ruth 2:10. Bowing before angelic visitors is indicated in Gen. 19:1. ***shāḥāh*** signifies an attitude of submission or enslavement to one's captors in Isa. 51:23. Prostrating oneself before others also expresses deep respect and reverence. The passage in Gen. 37:7ff. reveals an attitude that borders on "human worship." Other references include Gen. 27:29; 48:12; Exod. 11:8; 1 Sam. 25:23; 2 Sam. 9:8; 1 Kgs. 1:31; 2 Kgs. 4:37; 1 Chr. 21:21.

Exod. 20:5; 23:24; Lev. 26:1 prohibit "bowing down" to pagan idols; and the practice of bowing down to such idols is indicated in Num. 25:2; Judg. 2:12ff.; 2 Chr. 25:14.

qādad [קָדַד, 6915]

qādad is a verb found fifteen times with the dominant sense of "bow one's head" and "bow down," primarily in the context of worshiping God.

The action of "bowing one's head" in worship of Yahweh is noted in Gen. 24:26, 48; Exod. 4:31; 12:27; 34:8; 1 Chr. 29:20; 2 Chr. 20:18; 29:30; Neh. 8:6. Bowing the head as a mark of respect to others is indicated in Gen. 43:28; 1 Sam. 24:8; 1 Kgs. 1:16, 31.

Num. 22:31 describes "bowing down" or "falling prostrate" before the angel of the Lord in fear and reverence.

kāphaph [כָּפַף, 3721]

The verb ***kāphaph*** occurs five times with the meaning "bow down." It is used primarily in the passive voice with the underlying sense of "being cast down," or overwhelmed with grief (cf. Pss. 57:6; 145:14; 146:8). In the two latter references, the psalmist is raised up and consoled by God. Isa. 58:5 denotes a man "bowing his head" in grief. ***kāphaph*** also indicates the action of "bowing down" to God in worship (cf. Mic. 6:6).

NT Words

kamptō [κάμπτω, *2578*]

This verb occurs four times with the meaning to "bow down" in worship, with primary reference to the worship of God (cf. Rom. 14:11; Eph. 3:14; Phil. 2:10). Rom. 11:4 uses ***kamptō*** in a negative sense to refer to those who, at the time of the prophet Elijah, "had not bowed the knee to Baal."

klinō [κλίνω, *2827*]

klinō is a verb found seven times with the meaning "bow," "bow down" in two of these contexts.

Luke 24:5 refers to the disciples "bowing down" in fear when first confronted by the angels announcing that Jesus had risen from the dead. John 19:30 depicts Christ as "bowing" his head at the point of death on the cross.

gonypeteō [γονυπετέω, *1120*]

gonypeteō is a verb occurring four times with the underlying sense of "bow the knee," or kneel down, fall on one's knees — either in an act of worship or in order to make a special plea.

A man falls on his knees before Jesus to plead for healing for his son (cf. Matt. 17:14). Similarly, a leper "bows down" to Jesus, begging for healing in Mark 1:40. In Mark 10:17 a man "kneels before" Jesus and asks him what the requirements are for inheriting eternal life. Matt. 27:29 records the action of those who mock Christ on the cross by "falling on their knees" pretending to worship him.

Additional Notes

The Hebrew verbs ***kāra'*** and ***shāḥāh*** embrace a range of meanings and emphases similar to the Greek terms above. These Hebrew terms refer to both literal and metaphorical "bowing down" — including the act of religious worship, the falling down of individuals in various circumstances, as well as the metaphorical sense of being forced down or buffeted by the judgment of God. The Old Testament appears to offer a richer, more varied use of this concept of "bowing" than does the New.

BOW (NOUN)

OT Words

qeshet [קֶשֶׁת, 7198]

This word means "bow" and is used in both a literal and metaphorical sense when referring to the weapon of war. ***qeshet*** is used with this meaning nearly eighty times in the Old Testament. On four occasions, however, it refers to the "rainbow." (→ RAINBOW)

Literal references to the "bow" as a weapon of war are predominant in the Old Testament (approximately fifty times).

The metaphorical usage of ***qeshet***, though not as frequent (approximately twenty times), has a distinctive theological significance. For example, there are a number of references to God "breaking the bow." The context of each indicates that this expression points to the power of God triumphing over all opposition to his will and purpose, through the destruction or punishment of these opponents. In this regard, the wicked in general are singled out (cf. Ps. 37:15); as are the nations in general (cf. Ps. 46:10), the nation of Elam (cf. Jer. 49:35), and even Israel herself (cf. Hos. 1:5). In Hos. 2:18, however, the phrase "breaking the bow" is used in a profoundly positive sense when it refers to God's intention to abolish all hostility in the land of Israel and usher in a new era of universal peace. This particular guarantee is located within the framework of the divine promise to inaugurate a new, permanently enduring covenant with his people that will result in a renewed intimacy between God and his people that will never be broken (cf. Hos. 2:14–23).

NT Words

toxon **[τόξον,** ***5115*****]**

toxon is a rare noun found only in Rev. 6:2 denoting a "bow" as a weapon.

BOWL

OT Words

mizraq **[מִזְרָק, 4219]**

This term refers almost exclusively to the sacred bowls of the tabernacle and temple used for sprinkling purposes in the ritual offerings and sacrifices. It occurs with this meaning about thirty times (e.g., Exod. 27:3; Num. 7; 1 Kgs. 7:40ff.; 2 Kgs. 12:13; 1 Chr. 28:17; 2 Chr. 4:8ff.).

On three occasions, however, ***mizraq*** has a different sense. Amos 6:6 refers to the inhabitants of Israel drinking wine by the bowlful, as a symptom of their spiritual complacency, which will lead to their inevitable judgment. Then, in Zech. 9:15, God's people are described as being filled like bowls with wine — on this occasion as a sign of their great joy, a celebration of their preservation by God and the victory over their enemies. Finally, Zech. 14:20 describes Jerusalem and Judah as a place where every cooking pot will be marked "holy to the Lord," just like the sacred bowls in front of the altar in the holy place. It is a metaphorical way of alluding to the divine process of renewal and purification that will take place on the consummation of the Day of the Lord.

sēphel **[סֵפֶל, 5602]**

sēphel is another rare noun found in two places denoting a "bowl" — a utensil for eating and drinking (cf. Judg. 5:2; 6:38).

gullāh **[גֻּלָּה, 1543]**

gullāh is a noun found fourteen times denoting a "bowl" or "bowl-shaped" object in most of these contexts.

A general reference to a "bowl" is found in Eccl. 12:6. The "bowl" of the temple lampstand, functioning as the receptacle for lamp oil, is noted in Zech. 4:2, 3.

gullāh also denotes the "bowl-shaped" features at the top of the pillars of Solomon's temple (cf. 1 Kgs. 7:41ff.; 2 Chr. 4:12ff.).

menaqqît **[מְנַקִּית, 4518]**

menaqqît is a noun designating ceremonial "bowls" or "cups" used for ritual purposes in the tabernacle and temple. It is found in four places (cf. Exod. 25:29; 37:16; Num. 4:7; Jer. 52:19).

saph **[סַף, 5592]**

saph is a noun occurring in about thirty places, about a third of the time denoting a "bowl" or "basin."

The domestic "bowl" (or "basin") is noted in Exod. 12:22; 2 Sam. 17:28. Ceremonial ritual vessels in the temple are indicated in 1 Kgs. 7:50; 2 Kgs. 12:13; Jer. 52:19.

NT Words

phialē **[φιάλη,** ***5357*****]**

phialē is a noun fond in twelve places denoting a "(broad, shallow) bowl" — all in the context of John's vision of the heavenly city in the book of Revelation. In this sense, all occurrences are symbolic. Golden "bowls" filled with incense are noted in Rev. 5:8. "Bowls" filled with the wrath of God are noted in Rev. 15:7; 16:1ff.; 17:1; 21:9.

Additional Notes

The phenomenon of "bowl" in the Old Testament is also closely linked with that of "cup." It is with the Old Testament use of ***kôs*** that one sees an intimate connection with the phenomenon of divine judgment and blessing mirrored in the Greek terms ***phialē*** and ***potērion***. (→ CUP).

See Also: → CUP

BOX

NT Words

alabastron **[ἀλάβαστρον,** ***211*****]**

alabastron is a noun found in four places meaning a "box" or "flask" made of alabaster designed to carry perfume (cf. Matt. 26:7; Mark 14:3; Luke 7:37).

BOY → CHILD → SERVANT

BRANCH

OT Words

ṣemaḥ [צֶמַח, **6780**]

While this word means "sprout" or "branch," it also refers to various kinds of vegetation in different contexts. *ṣemaḥ* is found twelve times in the Old Testament, and of these occurrences only five have distinctive theological significance.

ṣemaḥ refers to "vegetation" in Gen. 19:25; "crops" in Ps. 65:10; "bud" in Isa. 61:11; "stalk" in Hos. 8:7. It is used metaphorically of the nation of Egypt in Ezek. 17:9, referring to her military campaign of expansion as "new growth," and also to Israel's "youth" in terms of a "plant of the field."

It is, however, in the translation of *ṣemaḥ* as "branch" that its most significant theological usage is found. In five separate texts the term refers metaphorically (but clearly) to the messianic ruler whom God will raise up as "the Branch," the ultimate deliverer and redeemer of his people. Isa. 4:2 speaks of "the branch of the Lord"; Jer. 23:5 refers to "a righteous branch" from the lineage of David; Jer. 33:15 mentions "the branch of righteousness"; Zech. 3:8 affirms that the servant of Yahweh will be named "the Branch"; and, finally, Zech. 6:12 refers to the messianic figure whose name is "the Branch."

dālîṯ [דָּלִית, **1808**]

This term means "branch" or "bough" and is found only eight times in the Old Testament, and only in the plural. It is used in an exclusively metaphorical sense, referring variously to Israel as "olive tree branches" (cf. Jer. 11:16); "vine branches" (Ezek. 17:6, 7; 19:11); and "cedar branches" (cf. Ezek. 17:23); and to Assyria as "branches" (of a cedar tree) (Ezek. 31:7, 9, 12).

zemôrāh [זְמוֹרָה, **2156**]

This is another rare noun that occurs only five times in the Old Testament with the meaning "branch" or "shoot." It is used both literally and symbolically.

zemôrāh refers to literal branches in Num. 13:23 and Ezek. 15:2. On two occasions it is used metaphorically to refer to idolatrous practices adopted by Israelites. In Isa. 17:10 **zemôrāh** refers literally to the "shoot of a strange one" — a probable reference to an idolatrous cult. In Ezek. 8:17, apostate inhabitants of Jerusalem are depicted putting "the branch to their nose" in the temple in Jerusalem. This is undoubtedly a ritual ceremony associated with some form of idolatry, although it is attested nowhere else in the Old Testament.

Finally, this word is found in Nah. 2:3 where Israel's destruction by the Assyrians is referred to as "the ruining of her vines." However, the context makes it clear that it is God's intention to punish Nineveh and rehabilitate the land, to "restore the glory of Jacob."

qāneh [קָנֶה, **7070**]

qāneh is a noun found in approximately sixty places with the meanings "stalk," "reed," "branch." The latter meaning is found solely in relation to the construction of the ceremonial lampstand of both the tabernacle and temple, the "branches" of which were made of beaten gold (cf. Exod. 25:32ff.; 37:17ff.).

qāṣîr [קָצִיר, **7105**]

qāṣîr is a noun found in around fifty contexts with the dominant sense of "harvest." However, in a few places the meaning "branch" is indicated. Job 14:9 denotes the "branches" of a tree. Ps. 80:11 mentions the "branches" of a vine, referring metaphorically to the prosperity of the people of Israel. Then, in Job 18:16; 29:19, the term denotes "branches," as symbols of a person's life-force threatened with destruction.

nēṣer [נֵצֶר, **5342**]

nēṣer is a noun used metaphorically in four contexts denoting a "branch" with different connotations.

Isa. 11:1 refers to the coming messianic ruler as a "branch" (i.e., a descendant from the line of Jesse). More generally, Dan. 11:7 equates a "branch" with a dynastic lineage. Isa. 14:19 depicts the King of Babylon as a "rejected branch." Isa. 60:21 designates the people of Yahweh as the "branch" of his planting in the land of Canaan.

'ānāph [עָנָף, **6057**];
'anaph [עֲנַף, **6056** (Aramaic)]

'ānāph is a verb found seven times denoting "bough" or "branch."

Literal references to "tree branches" are found in Lev. 23:40; Mal. 4:1; Ps. 80:10. In Ezek. 17:8, 23; 31:3; 36:8, symbolic "branches" denote aspects of human kingdoms of which the "tree" is the dominant symbol.

The Aramaic equivalent of this term is identical in form and also denotes "branches" as symbolic components of a human kingdom — the Babylonian realm of King Nebuchadnezzar (cf. Dan. 4:12ff.).

sārîg [שָׂרִיג, 8299]

sārîg is a noun denoting "branches" of a tree or vine, found three times in Gen. 40:10ff.; Joel 1:7.

pe'ōrāh [פֻּארָה, 6288]

This noun is synonymous with ***'ānāph*** (see above) and is found in seven places denoting "branches" as components of political kingdoms such as Assyria, again symbolized through the metaphor of the "tree" (cf. Ezek. 31:5ff.).

shibbōlet [שִׁבֹּלֶת, 7641]

shibbōlet is a noun found sixteen times with the primary sense of "ear (of grain)." However, in Zech. 4:12 the term denotes the "branches" of an olive tree in the vision of the prophet. These refer symbolically to the two anointed servants of Yahweh — the king and high priest who serve to advance his redemptive purposes.

NT Words

klados [κλάδος, *2798*]

klados is a noun found eleven times and translated "branch" throughout.

Literal references to "branches" include Matt. 13:32; 21:8; Mark 4:32; 13:28; Luke 13:19.

klados also signifies "branches" in a symbolic sense referring to the people of Israel in Rom. 11:16ff.

klēma [κλῆμα, *2814*]

klēma is a noun found in four places, all of which use the term metaphorically to denote true followers of Christ as "branches" who derive their life from him, the vine (cf. John 15:2ff.).

stoibas [στοιβάς, *4746*]

stoibas is a rare noun occurring only in Mark 11:8 denoting a "branch" or "leafy limb."

baion [βαΐον, *902*]

baion is another rare noun found only in John 12:13 referring to "branches" of a palm tree.

Additional Notes

The various Hebrew terms for "branch" (and associated meanings) have a considerable theological significance in the Old Testament with respect to the destiny of the land of Israel and the people of God. The term *ṣemaḥ* is undoubtedly the most significant of these, indicating as it does the phenomenon of the messianic ruler who will "sprout" from the lineage of David. The New Testament takes up this theme, principally in the person of Christ with the "vine" metaphor in John 15 (cf. ***klēma***) and in identifying the descendants of Israel in this way (cf. ***klados***) in Rom. 11.

BRASS, BRONZE

OT Words

neḥōshet [נְחֹשֶׁת, 5178]

This word is the standard term for "brass," "copper," or "bronze" in the Old Testament. ***neḥōshet*** occurs approximately 130 times, and in almost all cases it refers literally to the brass utensils of the tabernacle (e.g., Exod. 27:2ff.; 35:5ff.; 38:2ff.), and temple (e.g., 1 Kgs. 7:14ff.; 2 Kgs. 16:14ff.; 25:7ff.; 1 Chr. 18:8; 2 Chr. 1:5; 4:1ff.). ***neḥōshet*** also refers to the serpent of bronze that Moses had erected in the wilderness as a means of healing the Israelite people of their snake bites (cf. Num. 21:9). Workmen in brass, or coppersmiths, are described in Gen. 4:22; Exod. 31:4; 35:32; 1 Kgs. 7:14; 2 Chr. 2:14.

There are, however, several instances where ***neḥōshet*** is used in a symbolic sense. Ezek. 1:7 records the vision of the prophet in which he sees four living creatures whose legs and feet gleamed like burnished bronze (cf. also the angelic figures in Ezek. 40:3; Dan. 10:6). Then, in Ezek. 22:18, 20; 24:11, "bronze" is used metaphorically (along with other metals) in association with the diverse process of purging the people of Israel of their sins. This metal is part of the "dross" that God will "leach" out of his people. The prophet's eighth vision in Zech. 6:1 refers to mountains of bronze. Finally, ***neḥōshet*** occurs in the expression "the sky over your head will be like brass," referring to the drought conditions that God will bring upon his people if they fail to obey him under the terms of the Deuteronomic covenant (cf. Lev. 26:19; Deut. 28:23).

neḥāsh [נְחָשׁ, 5174 (Aramaic)]

This, the Aramaic equivalent of ***neḥōshet***, above, is found nine times in the book of Daniel. In Dan. 2:32ff., for example, ***neḥāsh*** refers to the bronze belly and thighs of the composite metal statue in the dream of Nebuchadnezzar (cf. also Dan. 4:15ff.; 5:4, 23; 7:19).

neḥûshāh [נְחוּשָׁה, 5154]

The noun ***neḥûshāh*** denotes "brass" or "bronze" in most of the ten contexts in which it is found.

The simile "like brass" is used in relation to the earth to refer to the divine judgment of infertility (cf. Lev. 26:19).

"Bronze" is used in connection with the construction of a bow (i.e., a weapon) in 2 Sam. 22:35; and of arrows in Job 20:24; Ps. 18:34. The term is also used metaphorically in Job 40:18; Isa. 45:2 to express great strength; and in Mic. 4:13 it indicates powerful weaponry. In Isa. 48:4 the term describes stubbornness.

neḥûshāh is also translated "copper" in Job 28:2, referring to the metal obtained from smelting ore.

NT Words

chalkos [χαλκός, *5475*]

chalkos is a noun found in five contexts denoting the metal "bronze," "brass" in various forms such as "money" in Matt. 10:9; Mark 6:8; 12:41; a "gong" (i.e., musical instrument) in 1 Cor. 13:1; and the metal itself in Rev. 18:12.

chalkeos [χάλκεος, *5470*]

chalkeos is a rare adjective meaning "brazen," or "made of brass," referring to idols and found only in Rev. 9:20.

chalkion [χαλκίον, *5473*]

chalkion is a rare noun denoting a "bronze vessel, utensil" found only in Mark 7:4.

chalkolibanon [χαλκολίβανον, *5474*]

Here is another rare noun denoting "burnished, polished bronze." It is used metaphorically in Rev. 1:15; 2:18 as a means of describing the glistening feet of the heavenly Christ in John's apocalyptic vision.

Additional Notes

It is interesting to observe the parallel images in Ezek. 1 and Rev. 1 and 2. The brass-like features of the mysterious heavenly creatures in Ezekiel's vision bear a close resemblance to the features of Jesus Christ in the opening chapter of Revelation (cf. ***chalkolibanon***, above).

BREAD

OT Words

leḥem **[לֶחֶם, 3899]**

This is a common term in the Old Testament, occurring around three hundred times and meaning "bread" on virtually every occasion, although it is sometimes translated "food" or "meat."

It is in the historical sections of the Old Testament that the literal rendering "bread" occurs most frequently, although ***leḥem*** in its plain sense is commonly found in both the wisdom and prophetic literature as well. The particular kind of bread-like substance known as "manna" is found in Exod. 16:4, 8, 12, 29, 32; Neh. 9:15; Job 24:5; Ps. 105:40. (→ MANNA) Bread for ceremonial usage in the tabernacle is mentioned in Lev. 3:11, 16; 7:13; 8:26ff.; 21:6ff.; 22:7ff.; 23:14ff.; 1 Sam. 21:3–6, and for the temple in 1 Chr. 9:32; 23:29; 2 Chr. 4:19; 13:11. ***leḥem*** also refers to "food" in a general sense in Num. 15:19; Deut. 8:3, 9; 10:18; Pss. 104:14; 105:16; 132:15; 136:25; 146:7; 147:9; Prov. 6:8; 9:17.

In a metaphorical sense, ***leḥem*** is occasionally used in the phrase "bread of affliction" (cf. Deut. 16:3; Pss. 80:5; 102:9; 127:2). In these contexts the implication is that the people of God are either being chastised for their sinfulness or suffering persecution. Either way, their suffering is expressed through this particular metaphor. In two passages ***leḥem*** refers to wickedness or moral corruption in the phrases "bread of wickedness" (cf. Prov. 4:17) and "bread of deceit" (cf. Prov. 20:17). Finally, ***leḥem*** refers on one occasion to spiritual wisdom as something of great value to "eat." In Prov. 9:5, Lady Wisdom invites her hearers to come and eat her "bread," which leads to acquiring genuine godly wisdom.

maṣṣāh **[מַצָּה, 4682]**

This term is found about fifty times in the Old Testament and refers exclusively to "unleavened bread," which was a formal requirement for ritual offerings under the Mosaic law covenant. For any grain offering involving bread, yeast was a forbidden ingredient.

Any loaves, cakes, or wafers offered up to God could only be made, therefore, with unleavened dough. Penalties for violation of this principle were severe. The majority of the references to ***maṣṣāh*** are found in the Pentateuch (thirty times; e.g., Exod. 12:8ff.; Lev. 2:4ff.; Num. 6:15ff.; Deut. 16:3ff.; Judg. 6:19ff.; Ezra 6:22; Ezek. 45:21). (→ YEAST)

ḥāmēṣ **[חָמֵץ, 2557]**

ḥāmēṣ is a noun occurring eleven times that denotes "leavened bread" (i.e., made with yeast), as well as "leaven" itself.

Leavened bread is prohibited as food during the Passover festival (cf. Exod. 12:15; 13:3ff.; Deut. 16:3). It is also forbidden as an accompaniment to blood sacrifice (cf. Exod. 23:18). However, it is permitted as an element of a thank or peace offering (cf. Lev. 7:13).

NT Words

artos [ἄρτος, *740*]

The noun ***artos***, meaning "bread," occurs about one hundred times. Literal references to "bread" as food include Matt. 4:3ff.; 14:17ff.; 16:5ff.; Mark 3:20; 8:24ff.; Luke 4:3ff.; 9:13ff.; John 6:5ff.; 13:18; Acts 2:42ff.; 20:7ff.; 2 Cor. 9:10.

The "bread of the presence," or ceremonial bread displayed in the temple, is described in Mark 2:6; Luke 6:4; Heb. 9:2.

artos also refers to "manna," the staple food miraculously provided by Yahweh for his people during their sojourn in the wilderness (cf. John 6:31).

"Bread" in a metaphorical sense is indicated in John 6:32ff., where Jesus claims to be the "bread of life," or God's provision from heaven to meet humankind's deepest spiritual need for reconciliation with God and intimate fellowship with him. In this passage Christ claims that he fulfills the spiritual significance of the manna, given by his Father to the Israelites in the wilderness.

Christ gives new significance to the bread of the Passover meal in the company of his disciples (cf. 1 Cor. 10:16ff.; 11:23, 26ff.). This bread symbolizes his broken body that hung on the cross, metaphorically signifying his agony and suffering.

azymos [ἄζυμος, *106*]

azymos is the dynamic equivalent of the Hebrew term ***ḥāmēṣ*** (see above), denoting "unleavened bread" and used only in ritual contexts. The Feast of Unleavened Bread is the festival that followed Passover and lasted for seven days (cf. Matt. 26:17; Mark 14:1, 2; Luke 22:1; Acts 12:3; 20:6). The Day of Unleavened Bread, or Passover, is noted in Luke 22:7.

Additional Notes

The idea of "bread" in the New Testament has profound theological significance — whether one is speaking of the spiritual realities of Jesus Christ as the "bread of life" (***artos***) or about the spiritual condition of holiness indicated by the metaphor "unleavened bread" (***azymos***). In the Old Testament we only have the earthly realities of "bread" and "food" (with a few exceptions), and the theological significance of "bread" is only made clear by the fulfillment of new covenant revelation with the coming of the Messiah.

BREAK

OT Words

shābar [שָׁבַר, **7665**]

This verb means "to break," "break into pieces," with the derived sense of "shatter" or "destroy." ***shābar*** occurs about 150 times in the Old Testament and has both a literal and a metaphorical sense.

In the literal sense, ***shābar*** refers to the action of breaking or smashing into pieces. In Exod. 9:25, for example, the effect of the plague of hail in Egypt was to smash every tree in the field. Moses' anger at the idolatry of the Israelites at Sinai led him to smash the tablets of stone inscribed with the Ten Commandments (cf. Exod. 34:1; Deut. 10:2). The demolition of pagan idols is frequently alluded to in this way (cf. 2 Kgs. 11:18; 18:4; 23:14; 2 Chr. 23:17; 34:4; Isa. 21:9; Jer. 43:13; Exod. 23:24; Deut. 7:5). There is also the instruction in Num. 9:12 to not break any of the bones of the Passover lamb. This particular aspect of the Passover ritual comes to fulfillment in the New Testament with Jesus' own body on the cross. John 19:36 declares that not one bone of his body was broken. Judg. 7:20 refers to Gideon and his band of 300 soldiers blowing the trumpets and breaking the clay pitchers as a prelude to the rout of the Midianites.

At the metaphorical level, ***shābar*** is used in a number of significant contexts. Common expressions utilizing this term focus on the theme of the destruction of a particular world power, leader, or the wicked in general. Expressions such as "breaking the yoke of . . ."; "breaking the arms of . . ." are found in relation to Babylon (cf. Isa. 14:5; Jer. 28:2ff.); Assyria (cf. Nah. 1:13); Egypt (cf. Ezek. 30:21ff.); Elam (cf. Jer. 49:35); and the wicked in general (cf. Pss. 10:15; 37:15, 17). Sometimes the particular nations or rulers in view are simply described as being "broken" or "destroyed" — for example, Assyria (cf. Isa. 14:25; Ezek. 31:12); Moab (cf. Jer. 48:4); Greece (cf. Dan. 8:8); Babylon (cf. Jer. 51:8); Egypt (cf. Ezek. 32:28); Alexander the Great (cf. Dan. 11:4); the "little horn" (cf. Dan. 8:25); Seleucus IV (cf. Dan. 11:20). All of these nations come under the judgment of God, for he always initiates "breaking" them. Even Israel does not escape (cf. Hos. 1:5). The phrase "breaking the yoke of . . . "is also used to refer to Israel's violation of her covenant obligation. In Jer. 5:5, for example, Israel is indicted for having "broken the yoke" of her relationship with Yahweh.

Yet another metaphorical use of ***shābar*** is observed in the expression "to break the staff of bread." This refers to God's judgment of famine, which is one of the curse sanctions of the Mosaic covenant and is applied particularly to the nation of Israel (cf. Ps. 105:16; Ezek. 4:16; 5:16; 14:13; Lev. 26:26).

On a positive note, one of the most poignant expressions of divine comfort and compassion for the people of God is found in Isa. 42:3, where it is said of the Servant of Yahweh that he "will not break even a bruised reed." Furthermore, the expression "breaking the yoke of . . ." emerges yet again in Jer. 30:8. But this time the reference is to God delivering his people from the yoke of their bondage to sin. This thought is coupled with the text in Hos. 2:18, which declares that God will abolish (lit. "break") the bow and sword in the land of Israel, and bring about a transformation from war to peace.

bāqa' [בָּקַע, 1234]

This verb is found about fifty times in the Old Testament with various meanings, including "break," "break through," or "break out." It is used with these meanings thirteen times. ***bāqa'*** is found first of all in 2 Sam. 23:16, where three of David's "mighty men" break through the Philistine lines (cf. also 1 Chr. 11:18; 2 Kgs. 3:26). Then, 2 Chr. 21:17 relates the incident where Philistines and Arabs invade (i.e., break into) Judah and Jerusalem and plunder the king's palace. The invasion and sack of Jerusalem is described in several places in terms of the city being "broken up" (i.e., destroyed) by the Babylonian army (cf. 2 Kgs. 25:14; Jer. 39:2; 52:7; Ezek. 26:10).

This term is also used in Gen. 7:11 to describe the "breaking up" of the fountains of the deep that contributed to the complete inundation of the whole earth at the time of Noah. Isa. 35:6 also mentions water in conjunction with ***bāqa'***. But this time it refers to water "breaking out" into the wilderness in order to give it new life. In both cases, it is the divine initiative that lies behind the process — once for judgment, and once for blessing. Isa. 58:8 also contains the promise of blessing for God's people — this time in relation to light breaking forth over the land as an indicator of God's intended transformation and spiritual renewal of his people.

Finally, ***bāqa'*** is found in Job 32:19 in a metaphorical sense, likening Job's inner agitation to new wine threatening to burst out of new wineskins.

rā'a' [רָעַע, 7489]

The verb ***rā'a'*** occurs nearly one hundred times with the primary meanings "be evil, wicked," with various nuances. In several places, however, the meaning "to break, or shatter" is indicated, as in Job 34:24; Ps. 2:9 with respect to God's judgment on his enemies. Isa. 24:19 describes the physical shaking of the earth as a consequence of an earthquake in terms of the earth being "broken up." Metaphorical reference to the "breaking" of iron is indicated in Jer. 15:12 in relation to the conquest of a military opponent.

deqaq [דְּקַק, 1855 (Aramaic)]

deqaq is an Aramaic verb found ten times with the consistent meaning "break in pieces," "shatter." It refers firstly to the rock in the dream of Nebuchadnezzar that shattered the four-metal statue (cf. Dan. 2:34ff., 45). General reference to the strength of iron, in that it is capable of "shattering" all things, is noted in Dan. 2:40. The capacity of the kingdom of God to "break in pieces" all other kingdoms is noted in Dan. 2:44

The ferocious fourth beast in Daniel's vision "breaks to pieces" its opponents all over the world (cf. Dan. 7:7, 19, 23). Dan. 6:24 refers to lions "breaking the bones" of their victims.

nāphaṣ [נָפַץ, 5310]

nāphaṣ is a verb occurring about twenty times, meaning "shatter," "break in pieces," plus related nuances.

The literal sense of "smashing" clay jars is noted in Judg. 7:19; Jer. 22:28. The metaphorical sense of "dashing into pieces" — describing the destruction of the enemies of God and his people — is evident in Ps. 2:9; Jer. 48:12; 51:20ff. See also Ps. 137:9.

pārar [פָּרַר, 6565]

The verb ***pārar*** occurs in around fifty contexts with the predominant sense of "break," plus related nuances.

The meaning "break" in the sense of "render null and void" is used in relation to the covenant of Yahweh through its violation by the people of God (e.g., Gen. 17:14; Lev. 26:15; Num. 15:31; Deut. 31:16ff.; Ezra 9:14; Ps. 119:126; Isa. 24:5; Jer. 11:10; 31:32; Ezek. 16:59; 44:7). Conversely, Yahweh's guarantee never to break his covenant with this people is indicated in Lev. 26:44; Judg. 2:1 (cf. also Zech. 11:14). However, Zech. 11:10ff. notes that Yahweh "revoked" a covenant with the nations — referring probably to an "arrangement" guaranteeing their security. The impossibility of "breaking God's covenant" with the day and night is noted in Jer. 33:20; as is the covenant with David (cf. Jer. 33:21). The "breaking" of a vow is indicated in Num. 30:12ff.; and the "breaking" of a treaty with one's ally is described in 1 Kgs. 15:19; Isa. 33:8; Jer. 14:21; Ezek. 17:15ff.

Elsewhere, ***pārar*** is translated "break into," "tear apart," with reference to overwhelming someone with pain and suffering in Job 16:12.

nātaṣ [נָתַץ, 5422]

nātaṣ is a verb occurring about forty times with the underlying meaning "break down" and various senses such as "throw," "pull," "cast," "tear down."

The meaning "tear down," "destroy" is indicated in relation to the destruction of pagan altars (cf. Exod. 34:13; Deut. 7:5; 12:13; Judg. 6:28ff.; 2 Kgs. 10:27; Ezek. 16:39); the walls of Jerusalem (cf. 2 Kgs. 25:10; Jer. 39:8; 52:14); and the nations (cf. Jer. 1:10; 18:7; 31:28). The "pulling down" of houses is indicated in Lev. 14:45; Isa. 22:10; Ezek. 26:12; of a tower in Judg. 8:9; Ezek. 26:9; and of a city in Judg. 9:45; Jer. 4:26.

NT Words

klaō [κλάω, *2806*]

klaō is a verb found in fifteen places with the consistent meaning "to break bread" in two contexts. Christ uses the word in the Lord's Supper, symbolizing the suffering he would endure on the cross (cf. Matt. 26:26; Mark 14:22; Luke 22:19; 1 Cor. 10:16; 11:24). The other use of the term is found in the context of eating a meal (cf. Matt. 14:19; 15:36; Mark 8:6, 19; Luke 24:30; Acts 2:46; 20:7, 11; 27:35).

ekklaō [ἐκκλάω, *1575*]

ekklaō is a verb found three times with the meaning "break off" in relation to branches, referring solely to the metaphorical scenario of God "cutting off" some of the Israelites from the stock of the people of God, so that Gentiles may be grafted in (cf. Rom. 11:17ff.).

kataklaō [κατακλάω, *2622*]

kataklaō is a rare variant of ***klaō*** and ***ekklaō***, above, indicating the action of "breaking" loaves of bread in preparation for eating (cf. Mark 6:41; Luke 9:16).

lyō [λύω, *3089*]

lyō is a verb found in forty places with the primary sense of "loose," "release." However, in several contexts the verb is translated "to break."

Matt. 5:19 refers to "breaking" the commandments of God. Jesus is wrongly accused of "breaking" the Sabbath in John 5:18; 7:23. ***lyō*** is used negatively in John 10:35, asserting that Scripture "cannot be broken." See also Acts 13:43; 27:41.

lyō is used metaphorically in Eph. 2:14 to describe how the work of Christ "breaks down" the wall of hostility between Jew and Gentile.

syntribō [συντρίβω, *4937*]

syntribō is a verb found in eight places with the meanings "break in pieces," "shatter." It is used literally with reference to chains in Mark 5:4; to a flask, or pot in Mark 14:3; Rev. 2:27. In John 19:36 there is the affirmation that the Messiah would never suffer a broken bone.

diarrēgnymi [διαρρήγνυμι, *1284*]

diarrēgnymi is a verb found five times with the meaning "break," "tear." The "breaking" of chains is literally indicated in Luke 8:29, where the Gadarene demoniac tears off his fetters. Luke 5:6 refers to "breaking" fishing nets.

katagnymi [κατάγνυμι, *2608*]

katagnymi is a verb occurring five times with the literal meaning to "break" a leg in John 19:31ff.

synthlaō [συνθλάω, *4917*]

synthlaō is a rare verb with the meaning "break in pieces," "crush," found only in Matt. 21:44; Luke 20:18 in relation to the fate of those who attempt to confound the messianic "stone" of God's appointing.

synthryptō [συνθρύπτω, *4919*]

synthryptō is a rare verb fond only in Acts 21:13 and translated "break one's heart" with grief.

dioryssō [διορύσσω, *1358*]

The verb ***dioryssō*** means to "break in" in the sense of "burgle" a house (cf. Matt. 6:19ff.; 24:43; Luke 12:39).

klasis [κλάσις, *2800*]

klasis is a rare noun denoting the "breaking of bread," or sharing a meal (cf. Luke 24:35; Acts 2:42).

Additional Notes

The concept of "breaking" in the New Testament is a rich and varied one. Given the broad overlap of meanings of the words above, it is very difficult, if not impossible, to ascertain any precise or dynamic equivalents in the Hebrew terminology. However, the two terms ***shābar*** and ***bāqa'*** cover quite a broad semantic field between them. It is worth noting that there is some definite overlap in meaning between ***shābar*** and the Greek verbs ***klaō***, ***ekklaō***, ***lyō***, ***syntribō***, ***synthlaō***, and ***katagnymi***. The association of ***katagnymi*** with the breaking of a bruised reed (cf. Matt. 12:20) renders its link with ***shābar*** in Isa. 42:3 (see discussion above) highly significant.

See Also: → TRANSGRESSION

BREAST

OT Words

shad **[שַׁד, 7699]**

shad is the primary term for "(female) breast" in the Old Testament, and it occurs about twenty times. There are a number of perspectives attached to the use of the word.

First of all, there are several references to "breasts" in the context of nursing infants (cf. Ps. 22:9; Song 8:1; Joel 2:16) or children just weaned (cf. Isa. 28:9). Job 3:12 also refers to the patriarch's own infancy, to the day of his birth when he was nursed by his own mother — a day which he curses. Gen. 49:25 contains a similar image, referring to "blessings of the breast and womb" in describing the blessing of fertility that God promises to bestow on the tribe of Joseph.

In the context of divine judgment, ***shad*** symbolically indicates God's severe punishment for his people's rebellion against him. In Ezek. 23:34 the nation of Judah is portrayed allegorically as a prostitute who will tear her breasts in an act of self-mutilation when she experiences the punishment that God will hand down to her. Hos. 2:2 refers to God's warning to Israel to "remove the adulteries from between her breasts" if she wants to avoid his severe punishment for her persistent idolatry. Similarly, in Hos. 9:14 Israel's punishment for her idolatrous rejection of Yahweh will be "wombs that miscarry and breasts that are dry." In all three of these passages, it is significant that the metaphor of adultery or promiscuity is always linked to the sin of idolatry. This is an inevitable equation, given the fact that the relationship between Yahweh and Israel is consistently viewed throughout the Old Testament in terms of a marital union. Further evidence of Israel's idolatry is given graphic allegorical expression in Ezek. 23:3, 21, where the people of Israel and Judah are described as shameless prostitutes who offer their bodies to their lovers (i.e., foreign deities). See also Isa. 32:12 for another perspective on this theme of divine judgment, incorporating this term in a symbolic sense.

Finally, in a much more positive context, ***shad*** also refers to a woman's breasts to symbolize undefiled sexuality. This is especially true in the Song of Songs where, in 1:13; 4:5; 7:3, 7, 8; 8:10, the breasts of the woman beloved by her newlywed husband are enjoyed and admired by him. The setting of the Song is one of idyllic, undefiled physical love where such behavior is perfectly appropriate and pure, as it is conducted within the boundaries of God-ordained marriage. A similar reference to the innocence of a woman come of age is found in Ezek. 16:7, where Israel is allegorically portrayed as a beautiful young maiden whose breasts had formed and who was ready to be betrothed to her God.

ḥāzeh **[חָזֶה, 2373]**

ḥāzeh is a noun denoting the "breast" of animals in the context of ritual sacrifice, in particular the so-called "wave offering." It occurs thirteen times (cf. Exod. 29:26ff.; Lev. 7:30ff.; 8:29; 9:20ff.; 10:14ff.; Num. 6:20; 18:18).

ḥadî **[חֲדִי, 2306** (Aramaic)**]**

ḥadî is a rare Aramaic noun found only in Dan. 2:32 denoting the "breast" (or "chest") of silver of the metal statue in King Nebuchadnezzar's dream.

dad **[דַּד, 1717]**

dad is a noun found four times denoting a woman's "breasts" (cf. Prov. 5:19; Ezek. 23:3, 8, 21).

NT Words

stēthos **[στῆθος,** ***4738*****]**

stēthos is a noun signifying the "breast" or "chest" in a general sense. It is found in five contexts. The phrase "beating one's breast" as a sign of mourning is indicated in Luke 18:13; 23:48. References to "breast" in a general sense are found in John 13:25; 21:20; Rev. 15:6.

mastos **[μαστός,** ***3149*****]**

mastos is a noun found in three places denoting a woman's "breasts" in the context of nursing one's children (cf. Luke 11:27; 23:29). Rev. 1:13 refers to the "breast" (or "chest") of the heavenly Christ in the apocalyptic vision of the apostle John.

BREASTPLATE

OT Words

shiryôn, shiryān **[שִׁרְיוֹן, שִׁרְיָן, 8302]**

These two terms are very similar in meaning, being translated "(coat of) armor" and "breastplate" respectively. They are rare, however; occurring only seven times (***shiryôn***, four times; ***shiryān***, three times).

shiryôn is found only in narrative contexts. In 1 Sam. 17:5 it refers to Goliath's coat of armor, and later in the same chapter (17:38) the term describes the coat of armor Saul gave to David but which David declined to wear. 2 Chr. 26:14 refers to King Uzziah equipping his entire army with weapons and "coats of armor." Similarly, Nehemiah provides weapons and armor for the standing militia of postexilic Jerusalem appointed to guard the city walls during their reconstruction. In all of these contexts, ***shiryôn*** implies armor that covers the upper part of the torso — hence conveying the idea of a breastplate.

shiryān is more specifically translated "breastplate." In 1 Kgs. 22:34; 2 Chr. 18:33 it is used in the account of Ahab's bizarre death, when a random enemy arrow pierces one of the joints in his breastplate. The term is used metaphorically in Isa. 59:17, 18, where ***shiryān*** refers to the "breastplate of righteousness" worn by Yahweh. Such a description indicates that God "arms" himself in order to carry out his plans of salvation — in blessing for his people and in judgment on his enemies.

ḥōshen [חֹשֶׁן, 2833]

The noun ***ḥōshen*** occurs twenty-five times and refers to a "breast plate" or "breastpiece" worn only by the high priest.

This breastpiece is the sacred garment of the high priest wrapped around the ephod (priestly apron). The twelve stones representing the twelve tribes of Israel were mounted on this breastpiece that the high priest brought with him into the presence of Yahweh on the Day of Atonement (cf. Exod. 25:7; 28:4, 15ff.; 29:5; 35:9, 27; 39:8ff.; Lev. 8:8).

NT Words

thōrax [θώραξ, *2382*]

The noun ***thōrax*** denotes a "breastplate." Metaphorical reference to spiritual defense against satanic attack (i.e., the "breastplate" of righteousness) is found in Eph. 6:14; as is reference to the "breastplate" of faith and love in 1 Thess. 5:8. Rev. 9:9, 17 refer to the "breastplates" worn by the demonic locust-like creatures of John's apocalyptic vision, bent on destruction of the wicked.

Additional Notes

The New Testament references to "breastplate" are all symbolic. Of especial significance is Paul's reference to the "breastplate of righteousness" in Eph. 6:14, which parallels the Isa. 59:18 reference to the armor of God. The point of the parallel, of course, is that the believer has access to the limitless reserves of divine strength and protection.

BREATH, BREATHE

OT Words

neshāmāh [נְשָׁמָה, 5397]

This term is found around twenty-five times in the Old Testament with the dominant meaning "breath" — both literal and metaphorical.

The most common use of ***neshāmāh*** is found in relation to the physical "breath of life" in creation (cf. Job 27:3; 33:4; Ps. 150:6; Isa. 2:22; 42:5). Gen. 2:7 records the creative initiative of God in instilling life in and for the very first time. Gen. 7:22 records the destruction in the flood of all who had the "breath of life." Similar references to the destruction of human life are found in Deut. 20:16; Josh. 10:40; 11:11, 14; 1 Kgs. 15:29; 17:17.

neshāmāh also conveys the idea of divine judgment when it refers to the breath of God in terms of a "blast of his breath." This judgment is directed primarily at the enemies of God (cf. 2 Sam. 22:16; Job 4:9; Ps. 18:15; Isa. 30:33).

On two occasions ***neshāmāh*** suggests a spiritual entity, in the sense of a soul or spirit derived from God (cf. Job 32:8; Prov. 20:27). (→ SPIRIT → SOUL)

rûaḥ [רוּחַ, 7307]

rûaḥ is a common noun occurring about four hundred times with the predominant meanings "spirit" and "wind." The term also denotes "breath," though in some places there is genuine ambiguity as to whether it actually means "spirit" or "breath."

rûaḥ indicates the "breath of life" imparted by God to all creatures at creation (cf. Gen. 6:17; 7:15; Job 12:10; Ps. 104:29; Eccl. 3:19). See also Job 9:18. Elsewhere, the phrase is metaphorical. God imparts the "breath of life" as a means of raising his people from the dead (cf. Ezek. 37:5ff.). This context indicates that such a symbolic "resurrection" constitutes returning the Israelites to their land at the conclusion of the exile. This is also one of the contexts where ***rûaḥ*** may be translated either "spirit" or "breath."

Other metaphorical senses of ***rûaḥ*** include the "breath of God's nostrils," or simply the "breath of God," both in the context of divine judgment (cf. 2 Sam. 22:16; Job 4:9; Ps. 18:15; Isa. 30:28; 33:11). Ps. 33:6 also mentions the "breath of God's mouth," a mechanism for the creation of the cosmos; and in Isa. 11:4 the same phrase constitutes an instrument of divine judgment against the wicked.

nāphaḥ **[נָפַח, 5301]**

nāphaḥ is a verb found twelve times, with the primary sense of "blow." In Gen. 2:7, however, it indicates the divine action of "breathing" the breath of life into man's nostrils. In Ezek. 37:9 God commands the prophet to "breathe" upon the bodies of his people lying in the valley, that they might live. Here the prophet is designated as the agent of divine inbreathing.

NT Words

pnoē [πνοή, *4157*]

pnoē is a rare noun denoting the "breath" of life that God gives to all creatures (Acts 17:25). It denotes "wind" in Acts 2:2.

pneuma [πνεῦμα, *4151*]

pneuma is a common noun denoting "spirit," referring to both human beings and God. (→ SPIRIT) However, in Rev. 11:11; 13:15 the term indicates the "breath" of life imparted by God to those who are both dead and inanimate.

empneō [ἐμπνέω, *1709*]

empneō is a rare verb translated "breathe out" in the metaphorical sense of "voicing a desire" to destroy all Christian disciples of the early church. It is found in Acts 9:1 in relation to Saul the Pharisee's dire threats against the followers of Christ.

emphysaō [ἐμφυσάω, *1720*]

emphysaō is a rare verb found only in John 20:22 in relation to Christ "breathing on" his disciples so that they might receive the Holy Spirit.

BRIBE

OT Words

kōpher **[כֹּפֶר, 3724]**

kōpher is a verb with various meanings throughout the seventeen occurrences of the term. It most commonly denotes a "ransom," "price of a life" (i.e., a monetary substitute for human sacrifice, which was otherwise forbidden under the law). However, in one or two places it denotes a "bribe" — Samuel denies ever taking a "bribe" in 1 Sam. 12:3; and in Amos 5:12 the Israelite nation is denounced for engaging in such a practice.

shōḥad **[שֹׁחַד, 7810]**

The noun ***shōḥad*** is found twenty-three times and means "gift," or "bribe," though these two meanings occasionally overlap.

The Mosaic law forbids the acceptance of "bribes." Severe sanctions are imposed on those who accept them (cf. Exod. 23:8; Deut. 16:19; 27:25; 1 Sam. 8:3; Job 15:34; Ps. 26:10; Prov. 17:8, 23; 1 Sam. 1:23; Isa 5:23; Ezek. 22:12; Mic. 3:11). Elsewhere, it is declared that God never accepts bribes (cf. Deut. 10:17; 2 Chr. 19:7). Blessing from God is offered to those who abstain from taking bribes (cf. Ps. 15:5; Isa. 33:15).

BRIDE, BRIDEGROOM

OT Words

kallāh **[כַּלָּה, 3618]**

This term is found just over thirty times in the Old Testament with the dual meanings "daughter-in-law" and "spouse," or "bride." (→ DAUGHTER-IN-LAW)

The meaning "bride" attaches to ***kallāh*** in half the contexts in which it is found. In Song 4:8–5:1, the term refer six times to the newlywed bride of the "lover" with overwhelming delight and passion.

The remaining uses of ***kallāh*** are metaphorical in various contexts. Isa. 49:18; 61:10; 62:5 speak of Israel's relationship with God in terms of her being his bride. Jer. 2:32 indicts the people of God for rejecting Yahweh as their husband. The heinous nature of Israel's betrayal of God is expressed here with the question: "Does a maiden forget her jewelry, a bride her wedding ornaments? Yet my people have forgotten me." Hos. 4:13, 14 expresses Israel's idolatrous rejection of her God in a similar vein by predicting that spouses of Israelite men will commit adultery. This is a clear metaphorical allusion to the nation's idolatry that is consistently expressed in the Old Testament. Remaining uses of ***kallāh*** emphasize the inevitable judgment of God that will follow such a rejection by his people. Jer. 7:34; 16:9; 25:10; 33:11 all clearly state that the sound of the bride's voice will be banished from the land; and Joel 2:16 likewise indicates that marriages will not be consummated: "Let the bridegroom leave his room and the bride her chamber." The contexts here clearly signify judgment against God's people.

See Also: → DAUGHTER-IN-LAW → FATHER → HUSBAND → MARRIAGE

ḥātān **[חָתָן, 2860]**

ḥātān is a noun denoting primarily a "bridegroom" (or "husband") and "son-in-law." (→ SON-IN-LAW)

General references to a "bridegroom" include Ps. 19:5; Isa. 61:10; 62:5; Joel 2:16. In Jer. 33:10 there is the promise that the "voice of the bridegroom" will be restored to Israel. Jer. 7:34; 16:9; 25:10 confirm the banishment of the bridegroom's voice from the land as a covenant curse.

The phrase "bridegroom of blood" is a metaphorical reference to Moses in Exod. 4:25ff. when his wife, Zipporah, dramatically circumcised her son as a means of preventing a fatal assault on her husband by the angel of the Lord.

NT Words

nymphē [νύμφη, *3565*]

nymphē is a noun occurring eight times denoting both a "bride" and a "daughter-in-law."

(➡

John 3:29 contains a literal reference to a "bride." The term is more commonly used metaphorically, denoting the church as a "bride," the people of God in glory, joined to Christ her "bridegroom" (cf. Rev. 21:39; 22:17).

nymphios [νυμφίος, *3566*]

nymphios is a dynamic equivalent for ***ḥātān*** (see above) denoting a "bridegroom" throughout the sixteen occurrences of the term.

The "bridegroom" is cited several times throughout the teaching and parables of Christ (cf. Matt. 9:15; 25:1ff.; Mark 2:19; Luke 5:34, 35). Other literal references to a "bridegroom" are found in John 2:9; Rev. 18:23.

In John 3:29 the use of ***nymphios*** is metaphorical. Here Christ anticipates the heavenly spiritual union of himself (the "bridegroom") with his people, the church (the "bride").

Additional Notes

Of particular interest here is the comprehensive way in which in both Old and New Testament perspectives on the phenomenon of marriage coalesce. The relationship of husband and wife — God and Israel, Christ and the church — receives a great deal of attention in the Bible. Understanding God and Christ as "husband" to Israel and the new covenant community of believers as "bride" to God and Christ is fundamental to a right understanding of the nature of our relationship with God.

BRIDLE

OT Words

meteg **[מֶתֶג, 4964]**

This word is rare, occurring only five times with the meaning "bit" or "bridle." It is used mostly in a metaphorical sense. In 2 Sam. 8:1 it forms part of the name of a Philistine town which David conquered (Meteg-Ammah, the "Bridle of Ammah"). In 2 Kgs. 19:28; Isa. 37:29 the term forms part of God's judgment against the nation of Assyria when it is said of that people that they will be led back to where they came from with God's "bridle" in their mouth. Ps. 32:9 sounds a warning to God's people not to be like the horse and mule who require a bridle in order to be controlled; for better is the attitude of willing submission to his ways. Finally, Prov. 26:3 uses the metaphor of a "bridle for the donkey" as a symbolic parallel to the kind of discipline that God metes out to those who are foolish.

resen **[רֶסֶן, 7448]**

This synonym for ***meteg***, above, is also rare, occurring only four times. Once again, usage here is metaphorical. Job 30:11 describes Job's lament that now that he has been afflicted by God, his enemies throw off all restraint against him (lit. "they let loose the bridle"). Job 41:13 refers to the Leviathan beast's capacity to resist control by human beings by refusing to be tamed by the bridle. Ps. 32:9 contains both ***resen*** and ***meteg***. Finally, Isa. 30:28 refers to God's judgment against the nations, using the metaphor of "a bridle in the jaws of the people" to lead them astray.

NT Words

chalinos [χαλινός, *5469*]

chalinos is a rare noun denoting a horse's "bit" and "bridle." Reference to a horse's "bit" is found in Jas. 3:3; and to a horse's "bridle" in Rev. 14:20.

chalinagōgeō [χαλιναγωγέω, *5468*]

chalinagōgeō is a rare verb with the metaphorical sense of "bridle," or keep in check, restrain. Jas. 1:26 notes the dangers of "not bridling" one's tongue. "Bridling" the whole body is a metaphor for mature self-control in Jas. 3:2.

BRIGHT, BRIGHTNESS

OT Words

bāhîr **[בָּהִיר, 925]**

bāhîr is a rare verb found only in Job 37:21, meaning "to be bright" in relation to brilliant light.

nōgah **[נֹגַהּ, 5051]**

nōgah is a noun with the underlying sense of "brightness" throughout its nineteen occurrences.

General references to the "brightness" of light include 2 Sam. 22:13; Isa. 60:19; 62:1; Joel 2:10; 3:15. The "brightness" of divine radiance is indicated in Ps. 18:12; Isa. 60:3; Amos 5:20; Hab. 3:4. In particular, the brightness of a theophany is described in Ezek. 1:4, 13, 27ff.; 10:4. Isa. 4:5 refers to the "brightness" of fire. In Hab. 3:11 ***nōgāh*** signifies the "flash" of a spear.

NT Words

lampros [λαμπρός, *2986*]

lampros is an adjective denoting that which is "bright," "splendid" in most of the nine occurrences of the term. The explicit sense of "bright" in relation to the brilliance of angelic clothing is evident in Acts 10:30; and in relation to one of the titles for the heavenly Christ — the "bright and morning star" (Rev. 22:16).

lamprotēs [λαμπρότης, *2987*]

lamprotēs is a rare noun found only in Acts 26:13 denoting the "brightness" or "brilliance" of the sun.

See Also: → LIGHT → SHINE → WHITE

BRIMSTONE

OT Words

gophrît [**גָּפְרִית, 1614**]

This term is rare, occurring only seven times. It consistently means "brimstone" or "(burning) sulfur," and is in each context, either implicitly or explicitly, the instrument of God's punishment on the wicked. Gen. 19:24 describes the classic judgment of God against the cities of Sodom and Gomorrah. Deut. 29:23 likens the land of Israel to a mass of brimstone or burning sulfur as a consequence of their rejection of God — just like Sodom and Gomorrah. Job 18:15 uses ***gophrît*** in a general sense to describe God's judgment against the wicked (cf. also Ps. 11:6 in this light). Isa. 30:33 mentions "burning sulfur" as a metaphor of divine judgment against Assyria, as does Isa. 34:9 against Edom, and Ezek. 38:22 against Gog.

NT Words

theion [θεῖον, *2303*]

theion is a dynamically equivalent term for ***gophrît*** (see above), also denoting "brimstone" or "burning sulfur." It refers to the discharge of molten lava and sulfurous gases associated with volcanic eruption, and it is used primarily in the context of divine judgment against the wicked.

Yahweh literally hurls "burning sulfur" against the cities of Sodom and Gomorrah in response to their flagrant sexual perversity (cf. Luke 17:29, citing Gen. 19:24).

The remaining usage of ***theion*** is metaphorical. In Rev. 9:17ff. an emission of "burning sulfur" comes from the mouths of demonic horse-like creatures, symbolizing their capacity to hand out pain and destruction to humankind. Then, the hand of God hurls "burning sulfur" against the wicked in Rev. 14:10. The ultimate fate of the wicked is to be cast into the lake of "burning sulfur" described in Rev. 19:20; 20:10; 21:8.

theiōdēs [θειώδης, *2306*]

theiōdēs is a rare adjective, found only in Rev. 9:17 and meaning "of brimstone" or "of sulfur" in relation to the color of the demonic horses.

Additional Notes

There is little doubt that ***gophrît*** functions as the dynamic equivalent of ***theion***, given the very similar theological implications of the terms in both Testaments.

BRING, BROUGHT

OT Words

bô' [**בּוֹא, 935**]

This verb is one of the most common Hebrew terms in the Old Testament. In all its various forms it is found nearly 2,500 times. Its basic meanings are "go" and "come," but it also means "bring" in about 550 places. The underlying sense of ***bô'***, "to bring," is causative (i.e., "to cause to go," or "cause to come"), and involves the primary idea of moving or transferring objects, people, or even ideas from one location or context to another.

The concept of "bringing" is a complex one, as it may be paired with any number of prepositions (e.g., bring to, bring in, bring on, bring up, bring out, bring against, bring forth, bring down, etc.) with as many different senses. (→ COME → ENTER → VISIT)

NT Words

pherō [φέρω, *5342*]

The verb ***pherō*** means to "bring," along with related nuances, throughout the approximately sixty occurrences of the term.

The meaning "bring" in the sense of "fetch" or "carry" — indicating movement toward the speaker — is noted generally in Matt. 14:18; John 4:33; Acts 4:34. The phenomenon of "bringing glory" into the heavenly city is indicated in Rev. 21:24ff. People are brought to Christ for healing in Mark 1:32; 9:17ff.; Luke 5:18.

The action of "bringing a charge or accusation against someone" is indicated in John 18:29; Acts 25:7; 2 Pet. 2:11. Grain is said to "be brought forth" from good soil in Mark 4:8, as is fruit in John 12:24; 15:2ff.

epagō [ἐπάγω, *1863*]

The verb ***epagō*** means "to bring upon" — to cause something evil to happen to someone. In Acts 5:28 the religious leaders of Jerusalem expressed the fear that the preaching of the gospel by the early Christians would "bring the blood of Christ upon the nation of Israel."

2 Pet. 2:1 refers to the hand of God "bringing" swift destruction upon false teachers. 2 Pet. 2:5 refers to the ancient flood that God "brought upon" the wicked world during the time of Noah.

katagō [κατάγω, *2609*]

katagō is another variant of the entries above, meaning "bring" in a variety of contexts, with several nuances.

The action of "bringing" ships to land, or putting in at a port, is indicated in Luke 5:11; Acts 27:3; 28:12. Acts 9:30; 22:30; 23:15, 28 describe "bringing (people) down" in the sense of "transport on a journey." Rom. 10:6 refers to the attempt to "bring Christ down," to disparage or denigrate his authority and status.

proagō [προάγω, *4254*]

Although ***proagō*** usually means "go before," in three of its eighteen occurrences it signifies "to bring (someone) out, or before" and refers to Paul's appearances before several different audiences (cf. Acts 12:6; 16:30; 25:26).

prosagō [προσάγω, *4317*]

prosagō means to "bring, or lead to." In Luke 9:41 it describes how a boy is brought to Christ for healing; in Acts 16:20 it refers to Paul and Silas being arraigned before the Philippian magistrates. 1 Pet. 3:18 denotes the action of Christ in "bringing" his people to God — reconciling them with him, through his death on the cross.

trephō [τρέφω, *5142*]

trephō is a verb found eight times with the primary sense of "feed," "nourish." However, in Luke 4:16 it refers to Jesus having been "brought up" (i.e., raised as a child) in Nazareth.

anatrephō [ἀνατρέφω, *397*]

anatrephō is a variant of ***trephō,*** above, meaning "bring up" in the sense of "raise, nurture" (a child). It refers to Moses in Acts 7:20ff.; and to Paul in Acts 22:3.

ektrephō [ἐκτρέφω, *1625*]

ektrephō is a rare variant of ***anatrephō***, above, found in three places. Eph. 6:4 enjoins fathers to "bring up" their children to love and fear the Lord.

See Also: → BEAR (VERB) → BEGET → LEAD → OFFER

BROAD, BREADTH

OT Words

rāḥāb [רָחָב, **7342**]

This adjective occurs twenty-one times in the Old Testament, and in over half of these contexts ***rāḥāb*** is translated in the literal sense of "wide" or "broad." It refers, for example, to the land of Canaan (cf. Gen. 34:21; Exod. 3:8; Judg. 18:10); to the city wall of Jerusalem (cf. Neh. 12:38); to Babylon as a place of judgment for Israel (cf. Isa. 22:18); and to the walls of Babylon (cf. Jer. 51:58).

The remaining uses of ***rāḥāb*** are metaphorical. In Ps. 119:45 the psalmist declares that he will walk "at large" (i.e., in freedom), such is the effect of the law of God upon him. Then in Ps. 119:96 the writer affirms the "broad" (i.e., limitless) nature of God's commandments. In Isa. 33:21 ***rāḥāb*** refers to the broad rivers of Israel in a metaphorical description of the land of Canaan under the effect of a thoroughgoing divine renewal. In a contrasting scenario, ***rāḥāb*** also refers to the "broad" and deep cup of God's wrath which the people of Judah are forced to drink in the time of Ezekiel (cf. Ezek. 23:32). For other metaphorical uses of ***rāḥāb*** see also Job 11:9; 30:14.

rōḥab [רֹחַב, **7341**]

This term occurs approximately ninety times with the exclusively literal sense of "breadth" or "width" throughout the Old Testament. The term occurs mainly in relation to the tabernacle and temple measurements in Exodus and Kings/Chronicles (cf. Exod. 25:10ff.; 1 Kgs. 6:2ff.; 2 Chr. 3:3ff.). It is also found in the description of Ezekiel's visionary temple (cf. Ezek. 40:6ff.; 41:1ff.; 42:2ff.; 43:13ff.). Then, in 1 Kgs. 4:29, Solomon's wisdom is described in terms of its great "breadth."

rāḥab **[רָחַב, 7337]**

This is the verbal form of ***rāḥāb***, which is translated "to enlarge." (→ ENLARGE)

NT Words

eurychōros **[εὐρύχωρος, *2149*]**

eurychōros is a rare adjective denoting "broad" or "wide," used metaphorically in Matt. 7:13 to describe the way to eternal destruction.

platynō **[πλατύνω, *4115*]**

platynō is a verb found three times with the meaning "to enlarge," "widen," or "make wide." In Matt. 23:5 the term describes the phylacteries worn by the religious leaders of the Jews. It is used symbolically in 2 Cor. 6:11ff. in a plea to "widen" one's heart, or cultivate a generous spirit.

platos **[πλάτος, *4114*]**

platos is a noun denoting "breadth," "width." It is used in Eph. 3:18 to depict the extent of God's love. In Rev. 20:9; 21:16 it describes the dimensions of the heavenly city of Jerusalem.

BROOK → RIVER

BROTHER, BROTHERLY

OT Words

'āḥ **[אָח, 251]**

This common term occurs just under six hundred times. The predominant meaning in almost five hundred of these texts is "brother." Extensive reference is made, for example, to the brothers of pre-patriarchal figures in Gen. 4, as well as to fraternal relationships within the patriarchal families in the Abraham, Isaac, and Jacob narratives (cf. Gen. 20–29). Joseph and his brothers are frequently mentioned in Gen. 37–50. Legislation concerning fraternal relations within Israel is detailed throughout Leviticus, Numbers, and Deuteronomy. ***'aḥ*** occurs frequently in the Former Prophets, particularly in the books of Chronicles.

The next most common meaning of ***'aḥ*** is "brother" in the non-familial sense of "fellow-countryman." This is quite common in the civil legislation sections of the pentateuchal law code (cf. Lev. 18–25), and it is also found in Josh. 2; Neh. 10–13. In the Prophets ***'aḥ*** is used this way, for example, in Isa. 66:20; Jer. 12:6; 13:14; 22:18; 29:16; Ezek. 11:15; 18:10, 18; Hos. 13:15; Amos 1:9–11; Mic. 5:3; 7:2; Mal. 2:10. In all of the above passages the term "fellow countrymen" is found in either a context of blessing or judgment from God.

Less common is the meaning "relative(s)," found in the following texts: Gen. 13:8; 31:23ff.; Deut. 18:2, 7; 2 Chr. 5:12; Obad. 10, 12.

NT Words

adelphos **[ἀδελφός, *80*]**

adelphos is a noun found about 350 times, translated "brother" and used both literally and metaphorically.

Literal references to "brother" in a familial sense are found, for example, in Matt. 1:2, 11; 12:46ff.; Mark 1:16ff.; 6:17ff.; Luke 8:19ff.; John 1:40ff.; 11:21ff.; Jude 1.

"Brother" in the sense of a friend or fellow countryman is indicated in Matt. 5:22ff.; Luke 6:41ff.; Acts 7:23ff.; 10:23; Rom. 11:25.

More commonly, the term "brother" constitutes a form of address for fellow believers (e.g., Acts 3:17ff.; 23:1ff.; Rom. 7:1ff.; 1 Cor. 1:10ff.; 2 Cor. 8:18ff.; Gal. 5:11ff.; Eph. 6:21ff.; Col. 1:1ff.; 4:7ff.; 1 Thess. 2:1, 9; Heb. 3:12; Jas. 1:9; 1 Pet. 5:12; 1 John 2:7ff.; Rev. 1:9). Significantly, the term "brothers" is recorded as being used by Christ with reference to his followers (cf. Heb. 2:11ff.).

pseudadelphos **[ψευδάδελφος, *5569*]**

pseudadelphos is a rare variant of ***adelphos***, above, denoting a "false brother," or one who professes to be a Christian but whose life contradicts his testimony (cf. 2 Cor. 11:26). Gal. 2:4 contains the additional observation that such "false brethren" are also guilty of false teaching.

adelphotēs **[ἀδελφότης, *81*]**

adelphotēs is a rare noun meaning "brotherhood" or "brethren" in the sense of the community of believes in general terms (cf. 1 Pet. 2:17; 5:9)

Additional Notes

Apart from the meaning of "brother" in a filial sense, there is a possible overlap in meaning between ***'aḥ*** and ***adelphos*** in the idea of the relationship between believers. The concept of "believers" is, of course, a distinctly new covenant phenomenon. However, the use of the Hebrew ***'aḥ*** for "fellow-countrymen" foreshadows this idea. In several Old Testament contexts, the concept of Israelite "fellow countrymen" clearly suggests partnership or sharing in the blessings God bestowed upon his people through the Mosaic covenant (cf. Josh. 22:4, 7, 8; Deut. 3:20; Hos. 13:15; Isa. 66:20).

BRUISE

OT Words

rāṣaṣ **[רָצַץ, 7533]**

This term occurs nineteen times with the various meanings "bruise," "crush," "beat," and "oppress." The dominant sense of ***rāṣaṣ*** is "oppress." (→ OPPRESS)

rāṣaṣ is translated "bruised" or "broken" three times with reference to a reed. In 2 Kgs. 18:21; Isa. 36:6 the field commander of the Assyrian army scoffs at the inhabitants of Jerusalem for placing their trust in Egypt, which he refers to as a "bruised (broken) reed," giving them no support whatsoever.

shûph **[שׁוּף, 7779]**

This term is rare, occurring only three times in the Old Testament. The meaning "bruise" has been traditionally associated with this verb in Gen. 3:15. However, the precise meaning is very difficult to pinpoint. ***shûph*** is derived from an Arabic word meaning "rub off," "rub away," or "grind." However, the fact that the verb appears only three times in the Old Testament makes the precise translation of this term difficult to determine. Its association with injury to the serpent's head and the heel of the woman's seed is the focus of interest. The meaning "crush" or "strike" may well be appropriate. The overall context of Scripture definitely suggests that the injury to the serpent (or the person of Satan) is a mortal one. Rev. 12:9 identifies the serpent with the devil; and the work of Christ on the cross as the triumphant "seed of the woman" is interpreted as inflicting the evil one with a mortal wound (cf. Col. 2:13ff.). The context of Gen. 3, however, does not distinguish a precise meaning for ***shûph***, although a general sense may be affirmed.

Comparing Gen. 3:15 with Job 9:17 may provide a helpful insight. The language used in Job is also metaphorical. In this context, ***shûph*** refers to the effects of a storm upon the writer; perhaps "crush" or "break," rather than "bruise," is the best translation. Ps. 139:11 does not clarify the matter as both "bruise" and "crush" are inappropriate here since the context rules out the idea of a "crushing" darkness. Rather, the thought is one of "hiding" or "concealing" — the latter translation is much to be preferred.

mā'ak **[מָעַךְ, 4600]**

mā'ak is a rare verb with no one distinctive meaning. In Lev. 22:24 it refers to animal testicles that are "bruised" and thus unsuitable for sacrifice.

NT Words

syntribō [συντρίβω, *4937*]

syntribō is the one New Testament term translated "bruise" as well as "break," "shatter," plus related nuances. It occurs eight times.

Matt. 12:20 cites the Old Testament promise, referring to the coming Messiah's gentleness, that he will not break a reed that is "bruised" (cf. Isa. 42:1ff.). ***syntribō*** also refers to those who are "brokenhearted" in Luke 4:18.

The term refers literally to the "tearing apart" of chains in Mark 5:4 (cf. also Luke 9:39). The meaning "shatter" or "break" is applied to a pot of expensive perfume in Mark 14:3 (see also Rev. 2:27). John 19:36 refers to the promise in Ps. 34:20 that not one of the bones of the Messiah would be "broken." Rom. 16:20 describes how God will "crush" Satan under his feet.

See Also: → CRUSH

BUILD, BUILDER, BUILDING

OT Words

bānāh **[בָּנָה, 1129]**

This is a fairly common term in the Old Testament, occurring around four hundred times. The primary meaning, "build," is virtually the universal translation — although it is also used occasionally in a metaphorical sense.

In a literal sense, ***bānāh*** refers to the construction of houses (e.g., Deut. 20:5; 1 Kgs. 22:39; Hag. 1:8); of cities (e.g., 1 Kgs. 16:34 [Jericho]; 2 Kgs. 15:17 [Elath]; 2 Kgs. 8:5 [Upper Beth Horon]; 1 Chr. 8:12 [Ono and Lod]; 1 Kgs. 9:17 [Gezer]; 1 Kgs. 12:25 [Shechem]; 1 Kgs. 15:17 [Ramah]); of altars, both legitimate and illegitimate (e.g., Judg. 6:24; Num. 23:1, 29; Josh. 22:23; Deut. 27:6; 1 Sam. 7:17; 2 Sam. 24:25; 2 Kgs. 16:11; 1 Chr. 21:22; 2 Chr. 33:5; Ezra 3:2); and of towers and fortifications (e.g., 2 Chr. 26:6; 32:5; Isa. 5:2; Jer. 52:4). Undoubtedly the most significant building project in the entire Old Testament is the construction of Solomon's temple. There are approximately eighty references to this, the most magnificent building activity in the history of God's people (cf. 2 Sam. 7; 1 Kgs. 6–9; 2 Chr. 2–6; 1 Chr. 14:1; 17:25; 22).

Linked with temple building is the less common though very powerful symbolic pattern of divine building activity. 2 Sam. 7 is a key text in this regard. In response to David's request, God refuses to allow him to build the temple. There is a remarkable "turning of the tables," however — for God promises in the same breath to "establish a house for David" (cf. 7:11). While the word ***bānāh*** is not used here, the inference that God will "build the house" is perfectly clear. What is being promised is an unbroken dynastic succession from the Davidic lineage. In the parallel text in 1 Chr. 17:4ff. God does in fact promise to "build a house."

There are other passages in which ***bānāh*** is used with reference to God nurturing and renewing his people. Note, for example, Ps. 102:16, where it is said that God will "build up" Zion. Ps. 89:4 refers to God "building up" his throne. Prov. 9:1 alludes to the symbolic "building" of Lady Wisdom's house. More specifically, in the following texts God promises to "build up" his people, as opposed to "tearing them down": Jer. 24:6; 33:7; 1:10; 18:9; 31:28. In all of the above contexts, the underlying thought is that God establishes his people and his kingdom, making them secure and granting them a firm foundation in relationship with him. And that intimate, covenant relationship is the foundation of the divine building process — an activity that will guarantee the security of his chosen people for all eternity.

bānāh is also used nominally to denote a "builder" in a number of places (cf. 1 Kgs. 5:18; 2 Kgs. 12:11; Ezra 3:10; Ps. 18:22; Ezek. 27:4).

benāh [בְּנָה, **1124** (Aramaic)]

benāh is the Aramaic verbal equivalent of ***bānāh*** (see above) occurring some twenty times, with the meanings "build," "rebuild."

Ezra 4:12ff. contains an account of the rebuilding of the temple. See also Ezra 5:2ff.; 6:3ff. in this regard. King Nebuchadnezzar claims to have built the city of Babylon in Dan. 4:30.

binyān [בִּנְיָן, **1146**]

binyān is a noun derived from ***bānāh*** (see above) with the underlying sense of a "structure" or "building." The term denotes a "building" with reference to the temple precincts of the prophet Ezekiel's vision (cf. Ezek. 41:12ff.; 42:5). It also denotes a "wall" in Ezek. 40:5; 42:1, 10. (→ WALL)

NT Words

oikodomeō [οἰκοδομέω, *3618*]

oikodomeō is a verb found in approximately thirty contexts indicating the action of "building" in both a literal and metaphorical sense. The term is also translated nominally as "builder." General references to the act of "building" are found, for example, in Matt. 7:24ff.; Mark 12:1; Luke 6:48ff.; 17:28. References to the construction of the temple are found in John 2:20; Acts 7:47ff.

oikodomeō is used metaphorically in Matt. 16:18, where Christ promises Peter to build his (i.e., Christ's) church on the rock, referring to himself as the foundation of the worldwide community of believers. Elsewhere, Jesus promises to "rebuild" the temple in three days, referring to his own person as the resurrected Messiah (cf. Matt. 26:61; Mark 14:50). See also Matt. 27:40; Mark 15:29. In other contexts, ***oikodomeō*** is translated "edify," "build up" (i.e., to strengthen and nurture one's faith) (cf. Acts 9:31; 1 Thess. 2:11; 1 Pet. 2:5). True love is said to produce this effect in 1 Cor. 8:1 (cf. also 1 Cor. 14:4). Similarly, the task of "building" one's gospel ministry in the sense of developing and maintaining it is noted in Rom. 15:20 (cf. also Gal. 2:18).

oikodomeō in the sense of "builder" is also used metaphorically to refer to the unbelieving leaders of God's people throughout history who rejected the servants of Yahweh including, ultimately, Christ himself (cf. Matt. 21:42; Mark 12:10; Luke 20:17; Acts 4:11; 1 Pet. 2:7).

anoikodomeō [ἀνοικοδομέω, *456*]

anoikodomeō is a rare variant of ***oikodomeō***, above, meaning "rebuild." It is found only in Acts 15:16 citing the prophecy of Amos 9:11, 12, where God promises "to rebuild the fallen tent of David" — to restore the kingdom of Israel to his people.

epoikodomeō [ἐποικοδομέω, *2026*]

epoikodomeō is another variant of ***oikodomeō***, above, signifying "to build up," "build upon." It is found in eight contexts, all metaphorical. The meaning "build up" in the sense of encouraging or strengthening one's faith is indicated in Acts 20:32; Col. 2:7; Jude 20. In 1 Cor. 3:10ff. this term means to "build upon," in the sense of developing and furthering one's gospel ministry. In particular, Eph. 2:20 speaks of the church "(having been) built on" the foundation of Christ and the apostles.

synoikodomeō [συνοικοδομέω, *4925*]

Here is another rare variant of ***oikodomeō***, above, signifying to "build together." It is found only in Eph. 2:22 and is used passively to indicate the continuing spiritual process of believers "being built together" into the community of God's people worldwide, joined together by the spirit of God in Christ.

kataskeuazō [**κατασκευάζω,** ***2680***]

The verb ***kataskeuazō*** is found thirteen times and means to "prepare" or "build." The underlying sense for both of these meanings is that of "to make ready," "construct." Jesus is designated indirectly as "the builder" (lit. "one who builds") of the "house," referring to the church, the community of God's people in Heb. 3:3. God is described as the ultimate "builder" in Heb. 3:4. Heb. 9:2 refers to the "building" or "construction" of the tabernacle, and Heb. 11:7; 1 Pet. 3:20 refer to Noah's ark.

oikodomē [**οἰκοδομή,** ***3619***]

oikodomē is a noun derived from ***oikodomeō***, above, found in eighteen contexts and denoting a "building" in both a literal and metaphorical sense.

Literal references to the temple "buildings" are found in Matt. 24:1; Mark 13:1ff.

The metaphorical sense of "building up" or "edification," in the sense of the spiritual maturing of one's faith, is indicated in Rom. 14:19; 15:2; 1 Cor. 14:3ff.; 2 Cor. 10:8; 12:19; 13:10; Eph. 4:12, 16, 29.

The expression "God's building" is an indirect metaphorical reference to the church community of God's people, both in the earthly and heavenly contexts (cf. 1 Cor. 3:9; 2 Cor. 5:1; Eph. 2:21).

technitēs [**τεχνίτης,** ***5079***]

technitēs is a rare noun denoting a "builder," designating God as the "builder" of the heavenly city in Heb. 11:10. (→ CRAFTSMAN)

Additional Notes

The Greek term ***oikodomeō*** (and its derivative terms) and the Hebrew ***bānāh*** may be understood as dynamically equivalent concepts. While it is true that no one Greek term precisely matches the breadth of usage of the single Hebrew term, the similarity in the range of meaning of this group of synonyms is demonstrably close. Both the Old and New Testaments affirm the profound theological significance of God's "building" activity, culminating in the person and work of the Lord Jesus Christ.

BULL

OT Words

par [**פַּר, 6499**]

par means "bull" throughout the nearly 130 occurrences of the term.

General references to this beast are found in Gen. 32:15; Pss. 50:9; 69:31; Jer. 50:27. Bulls for ritual sacrifice are indicated in Num. 23:1; Judg. 6:25ff.; 1 Sam. 1:24ff.; 1 Kgs. 18:23ff.; Job 42:8; Ps. 51:19; Isa. 1:11. In particular, bulls are sacrificed at the priestly consecration ceremony (cf. Exod. 29:1ff.; Lev. 4:3ff.); and slaughtered for the sin offering (cf. Lev. 8:2, 14; 16:3ff.; Ezek. 43:19; 46:6ff.); for the burnt offering (cf. Lev. 23:18; Num. 7:15ff.; 28:11ff.; Ezek. 45:18ff.); and also for the coronation of Solomon (cf. 1 Chr. 29:21).

In Ps. 22:12, ***par*** refers metaphorically to "bulls" surrounding the psalmist, indicating a situation of danger.

NT Words

tauros [**ταῦρος,** ***5022***]

tauros is a rare noun denoting "bull" or "ox." A bull slaughtered for food is indicated in Matt. 22:4. Slaughter in a general ritual context is noted in Acts 14:13. The "blood of bulls" in a sacrificial sense is indicated in Heb. 9:13; 10:4.

See Also: → CATTLE → OX

BURDEN

OT Words

massā' [**מַשָּׂא, 4853**]

This noun occurs around sixty times in the Old Testament with the meanings "oracle" and "burden."

massā' means "burden" in about half the contexts in which the term is found. It refers literally to the burden or load carried by donkeys (cf. Exod. 23:5) and other beasts (cf. 2 Kgs. 5:17; 8:9). There are also several references to ***massā'*** designating the particular responsibilities of certain Levite clans for carrying the furniture of the tabernacle (cf. Num. 4:15ff.; 2 Chr. 35:3). Special mention is also made of the general prohibition of carrying goods on the Sabbath (cf. Jer. 17:21–27; Neh. 13:15, 19).

The concept of "burden" is also used metaphorically to indicate the demanding nature of Moses' administrative and judicial responsibilities as leader of the people of Israel (cf. Num. 11:11, 17; Deut. 1:12). Likewise, ***massā'*** refers symbolically to the "burden" of guilt in Ps. 38:4, 5; and to the "burden" of oppression on Israel by the King of Assyria (cf. Hos. 8:10).

sōbel [**סֹבֶל, 5448**]

The noun ***sōbel*** denotes a "burden" in all three references, which refer to the removal of a "burden" metaphorically signifying a political oppression eliminated by God (cf. Isa. 9:4; 10:27; 14:25).

sebālāh [סְבָלָה, **5450**]

sebālāh is a noun denoting "burden" in the sense of "forced labor," all in the context of the Egyptian enslavement of the Israelite people (cf. Exod. 1:11; 2:11; 5:4ff.; 6:6ff.).

NT Words

baros [βάρος, *922*]

baros is a noun found six times with the general meaning of "burden" in different contexts.

Reference to the "burden" of a completed day's work is indicated in Matt. 20:12. ***baros*** also denotes an "obligation" under the law described as a "burden" in Acts 15:28 (cf. also 1 Thess. 2:6). 2 Cor. 4:17 refers to a "weight" (i.e., burden) of glory. "Burdens" in the sense of "difficulty," "personal trauma" are noted in Gal. 6:2; Rev. 2:24.

phortion [φορτίον, *5413*]

phortion is a noun denoting "burden" in the primary sense of an obligation under the law, and is found in five contexts. Christ promises his followers a light "burden" when they commit themselves to him (cf. Matt. 11:30). Jesus condemns the religious leaders of the day for imposing unjust, harsh "burdens" on the people of Israel (Matt. 23:4; Luke 11:46). Gal. 6:5 mentions a man's "burden" in reference to his own "responsibility."

epibareō [ἐπιβαρέω, *1912*]

epibareō is a verb found three times with the meaning to "be a burden," or put people to inconvenience (cf. 1 Thess. 2:9; 2 Thess. 3:8).

katabareō [καταβαρέω, *2599*]

katabareō is synonymous with ***epibareō***, above, and found only in 2 Cor. 12:16.

katanarkaō [καταναρκάω, *2655*]

katanarkaō is another synonym for ***epibareō*** and ***katabareō***, above, also signifying to "be a burden" on someone. It is always used in a negative context (cf. 2 Cor. 11:9; 12:13ff.).

See Also: → HEAVY → WEIGH

BURIAL, BURY

OT Words

qeber [קֶבֶר, **6913**]

This term occurs about seventy times with the meaning "sepulcher," "tomb," or "grave." In about fifty of these contexts the reference is to a literal burial place. These include the tomb of Sarah (cf. Gen. 23:4, 6, 9, 20); Joseph's request to be buried in a tomb in Canaan (cf. Gen. 50:5); and the name Kibroth Hattaavah, which means "graves of craving" — the location in the wilderness where the people of Israel committed the sin of gluttony over quail meat and were struck dead by God with a severe plague (cf. Num. 11:34, 35). Various references to the tombs of illustrious members of David's court are found in 2 Samuel (cf. 2:32; 3:32; 4:12; 17:23; 19:37), as is a reference to the tomb of Kish, where his son Saul was finally laid to rest (cf. 2 Sam. 21:14). Kings and Chronicles refer to the tombs of the following people, among others: the unnamed prophet (cf. 1 Kgs. 13:22); Elisha (cf. 2 Kgs. 13:21); and six kings of Judah (2 Chr. 16:14 [Asa]; 2 Chr. 21:20 [Jehoram]; 2 Chr. 24:25 [Joash]; 2 Chr. 28:27 [Ahaz]; 2 Chr. 32:33 [Hezekiah]; 2 Chr. 35:24 [Josiah]).

In the Psalms and the Prophets, references to "tombs" or "graves" are mostly symbolic or metaphorical. Ps. 5:9, for instance, uses ***qeber*** to refer to the wickedness of evildoers, as those whose "throats are open graves." Ps. 88:11 refers to "graves" in the context of death in general. Isa. 14:9 employs the term to indicate God's utter rejection of the satanic spirit of the king of Babylon. He is said to be cast out of his grave. Isa. 53:9 contains the significant reference to the tomb of the suffering Messianic Servant. In Jer. 5:16, ***qeber*** refers to the Babylonians, who are portrayed as lethal enemies of Judah. These opponents of God's people are described as having (arrow) quivers like "open graves." Jeremiah laments the day of his birth and wishes that his father had murdered him while still in his mother's womb, thus making his mother his "grave." On a much more powerful and positive note, Ezek. 37:12ff. refers to the divine miracle of resurrection whereby the people of God are brought out of their graves and given new life. All of this is recorded in the vision of the prophet in Ezek. 37.

qābar [קָבַר, **6912**]

qeber, above, is derived from this verb, which means to "bury" in very similar contexts to those in which ***qeber*** is found. ***qābar*** occurs about 130 times throughout the Old Testament. The overwhelming majority of these occurrences are found in the Pentateuch and historical sections of the Old Testament.

qebûrāh [קְבוּרָה, **6900**]

qebûrāh is a noun found in fourteen places with the meanings "burial," "grave," and "sepulcher." The sense of "grave" is indicated in Ezek. 32:23ff.; Gen. 35:20; 47:30; 2 Chr. 26:23; "burial field" in Ezek. 32:23ff.; "burial" in Eccl. 6:3; Isa. 14:20; Jer. 22:19; and "sepulcher" or "tomb" in Deut. 34:6; 1 Sam. 10:2; 2 Kgs. 9:28; 21:26; 23:30.

NT Words

entaphiasmos [ἐνταφιασμός, *1780*]

entaphiasmos is a rare noun signifying a "burying" or "burial" in the context of preparing the body for burial, specifically Christ's own body (cf. Mark 14:8; John 12:7).

taphē [ταφή, *5027*]

taphē is a term found only in Matt. 27:7 denoting a "burial" place for strangers.

entaphiazō [ἐνταφιάζω, *1779*]

entaphiazō is a rare verb with the meaning "bury" in the sense of "preparing a body for burial," again with reference to Christ (cf. Matt. 26:12; John 19:40).

thaptō [θάπτω, *2290*]

thaptō is a verb that is consistently translated "bury" throughout its eleven occurrences (cf. Matt. 8:21ff.; 14:12; Luke 9:59ff.; 16:22; Acts 2:29; 5:6ff.; 1 Cor. 15:4).

synthaptō [συνθάπτω, *4916*]

synthaptō is a verb used only metaphorically and passively in relation to being "buried together with Christ" in baptism.

Additional Notes

qābar and ***qeber*** are used in the Old Testament in approximately the same way as corresponding Greek terms listed above are used in the New Testament. With reference to Christian baptism, and the theme of "burial" with Christ as a prelude to being "raised to life with him," there is an interesting possibility for comparison with the Ezek. 37 vision of the "valley of dry bones." Here the two Hebrew terms refer metaphorically to the spiritual lifelessness of the people of Israel, whom God by his Spirit raises to life again. Historically, the vision of Ezek. 37 refers to the re-occupation of the land of Canaan after the period of exile in Babylon. It is a powerful prophetic metaphor that anticipates the new covenant experience of resurrection initiated by the power of God through the person of Christ. It is this resurrection that all believers will ultimately share in on the final day of our Lord's return.

See Also: → RESURRECTION

BURN, BURNING

OT Words

bā'ar [בָּעַר, **1197**]

This term occurs about ninety times in the Old Testament, with the principal meaning "burn" (sixty times). The other sense of this verb is to "put away."

bā'ar is used literally in mundane contexts, without special theological significance, on only a relatively few occasions (cf. Judg. 15:5, 14; Job 1:16; Exod. 22:6; Jer. 36:22). On other occasions literal burning is in view, but a special significance may also be noted. For example, in Exod. 3:5 Moses is confronted by a burning bush, but one which is not consumed by fire. Here, fire is clearly theophanic in nature, representing the person and presence of God. On a much larger scale, there is the phenomenon of fire burning on Mt. Sinai in the glory cloud that contains the very presence of God (cf. Deut. 4:11; 5:23). This is arguably the most significant of all Old Testament theophanies, indicating the formal enactment of God's covenant relationship with his people, Israel. Literal burning is also associated with ceremonial ritual (cf. 2 Chr. 4:20; 13:11; Neh. 10:34) and also idolatrous worship (cf. Jer. 7:18; Isa. 44:15; 2 Chr. 28:3). In addition, burning is occasionally used as a specific divine judgment against his people for rebellion against him (cf. Num. 11:1, 3; Ps. 106:18).

Symbolic use of ***bā'ar*** to indicate "burning" is also prevalent in a number of texts. It is used, for example, as a general metaphor for divine anger and judgment against the wicked (cf. Isa. 1:31; Mal. 4:1; Pss. 2:12; 79:5; 89:46); against the Israelites (cf. Lam. 2:3; Ezek. 20:48); and against specific nations such as Assyria (cf. Isa. 10:17; 30:27, 33); Nineveh (cf. Nah. 2:13); Edom (cf. Isa. 34:9); and also Magog, whose identity is not known (cf. Ezek. 39:9).

bā'ar is also used metaphorically in contexts that indicate internal anguish (cf. Ps. 39:3; Jer. 20:9); anger (cf. Esth. 1:12); and lust (cf. Hos. 7:6). Positively, ***bā'ar*** can refer to the act of divine purging, or cleansing by fire (cf. Isa. 4:4); to the divine protection of Israel against suffering (cf. Isa. 43:2); and also to the reality of Israel's salvation, which is portrayed as a "burning torch."

sāraph **[שָׂרַף, 8313]**

This verb, meaning "burn," is a synonym for ***bā'ar***, above, and occurs about 120 times. ***bā'ar*** and ***sāraph*** occur in similar contexts, although ***sāraph*** is predominantly a literal, rather than a metaphorical, term.

In its literal sense ***sāraph*** refers to the burning of ritual sacrifices to Yahweh (cf. Exod. 29:34; Lev. 4:12, 21; 8:17, 32; 9:11; 10:6; 13:55; 19:6; 20:14; 21:9; Num. 19:5; Ezek. 43:21). Like ***bā'ar***, it also refers to idolatrous ritual practices related to burning (cf. Jer. 7:31; 2 Kgs. 17:31). Israel is called upon to destroy all traces of Canaanite religious centers by burning them (cf. Deut. 7:5, 25; 12:3, 31).

In addition, ***sāraph*** occurs in a significant number of contexts to indicate God's judgment by fire for those who rebel against him. This is true concerning Jericho (cf. Josh. 6:24); Hazor (cf. Josh. 11:9ff.); Egypt (cf. Jer. 43:13); Babylon (cf. Isa. 47:14; Jer. 51:32); the cities of Canaan in general (cf. Deut. 13:16); Ai (cf. Josh. 8:28); Achan (cf. Josh. 7:25); Korah, and others who opposed the authority of Moses (cf. Num. 16:39); and against evil people in general (cf. 2 Sam. 23:7). ***sāraph*** is also used in contexts which involve God's judgment against his own people in general terms (cf. Ps. 80:16; Isa. 1:7; Mic. 1:7); and also as the specific object of the invading Babylonian army under Nebuchadnezzar (God's chosen instrument for punishing his people). It is the Babylonians who will destroy the city of Jerusalem by fire (cf. 2 Kgs. 25:9; 2 Chr. 36:19; Jer. 21:10; 32:29; 34:2; 37:8, 10; 38:18; 43:12; 52:13). One of the significant incidents that occurred shortly before the second Babylonian invasion was King Jehoiakim's arrogant rejection of God, demonstrated by his burning the very scroll that Jeremiah had produced containing the message that God had given to the prophet. Positively, ***sāraph*** also refers to the "mini-reformation" launched by King Josiah, in which this ruler had all the visible reminders of Baal worship destroyed by fire (cf. 2 Kgs. 23:15).

sārāph **[שָׂרָף, 8314]**

This noun, derived from the verbal root ***sāraph***, occurs only seven times. On five of these occasions it refers to "fiery serpents," three of which are beasts and two of which are heavenly beings. In the first instance, ***sārāph*** refers to the reptiles that God sent among his people in plague proportions as a punishment for their sin in the wilderness (cf. Num. 21:6). Moses then immediately erects a bronze serpent as a means of obtaining healing for the hapless Israelites (cf. Num. 21:8). Deut. 8:15 refers to the presence of poisonous serpents in the wilderness during Israel's wandering. The other two references are to angelic beings, the "seraphim" or "burning ones" mentioned in the call of Isaiah the prophet (Isa. 6:2, 6).

serēphāh **[שְׂרֵפָה, 8316]**

This is the other nominal form derived from ***sāraph***, and it is found on twelve occasions. A few of these refer to literal burning of no real significance (cf. Gen. 11:3; 2 Chr. 16:14; 21:19). The majority, however, indicate burning as an instrument of divine judgment against, for example, God's own people (cf. Lev. 10:6 [Nadab and Abihu's fiery execution]; Num. 16:37 [the Korahite followers incinerated by fire]; Deut. 29:23; Isa. 64:11). Amos 4:11 is somewhat different in that it refers to a man plucked out of the fire, like a burning stick, and granted protection by God. The remaining references point to God's judgment against the nations (cf. Jer. 51:25; Isa. 9:5).

qāṭar **[קָטַר, 6999]**

qāṭar is a verb with the primary sense of "burn" throughout its nearly 120 occurrences. The use is exclusively ceremonial.

The act of "burning" fat on the altar is indicated in Exod. 29:13. More commonly, the burning of incense is noted in Exod. 30:7ff.; Lev. 2:2ff.; 1 Kgs. 3:3; 13:1ff.; 2 Kgs. 23:5ff.; Isa. 65:3, 7; Hos. 2:13; 11:2; Mal. 1:11. The "burning" of yeast on the altar is forbidden in Lev. 2:11.

General references to the presentation of offerings through fire are found in Exod. 30:20; Num. 5:26; 1 Sam. 2:15ff.; and in relation to the priestly consecration ceremony in Exod. 29:25; Lev. 8:16ff.; 9:10ff.

Legislation covering the presentation of "burnt offerings" is laid out in Lev. 1:9ff.; 3:5ff.; 6:12ff.; 2 Kgs. 16:13ff.; the sin offering in Lev. 4:10; 19:26ff.; 5:12; 16:12; the grain offering in Lev. 6:15; the guilt offering in Lev. 7:5; and the fellowship offering in Lev. 7:31.

yāqad **[יָקַד, 3344]**

The verb ***yāqad*** means to "keep burning perpetually." It is found nine times and is literally applied to the altar fire in the tabernacle sanctuary in Lev. 6:9ff.; and metaphorically to the divine fire of judgment that will burn forever (cf. Isa. 65:5; Jer. 15:14; 17:4).

yāṣat **[יָצַת, 3341]**

yāṣat is a verb with the primary sense of "set on fire" with a view to destruction by burning. It occurs around thirty times (cf. Josh. 8:8ff.; Judg. 9:49; 2 Sam. 14:30ff.; Neh. 1:3; 2:17; Isa. 33:12; Jer. 2:15; 32:29; 49:2; Amos 1:14). The latter text has particular reference to divine judgment.

Metaphorical use of the term is found in contexts where the anger of the Lord is said to "burn" against his enemies, including his own people (cf. 2 Kgs. 22:13ff.; Jer. 11:16; 17:27; 21:14; 43:12; Ezek. 20:47). Similarly, Isa. 9:18 affirms that wickedness "burns" like a fire.

ḥārar **[חָרַר, 2787]**

ḥārar is a verb with the meaning "burn up," "consumed by fire." It occurs eleven times with a primarily metaphorical sense in the context of personal trauma or suffering (cf. Job 30:30; Ps. 102:3). In Isa. 24:6; Ezek. 24:10ff., the context is one of divine judgment. Exod. 15:4ff. contains a literal reference to "burning up."

lāhat **[לָהַט, 3857]**

lāhat is a verb with the principal meanings of "burn up," "set fire to," "kindle fire" Its use is metaphorical throughout the twelve occurrences of the term, indicating the use of fire symbolizing God's judgment (cf. Deut. 32:22; Job 41:21; Pss. 57:4; 83:14; 106:18; Isa. 42:25; Joel 1:19; Mal. 4:1).

NT Words

kaiō [καίω, *2545*]

The verb ***kaiō*** means to "burn," "light a fire." It is used both literally and metaphorically in twelve contexts. Matt. 5:15 refers to "lighting" a candle. Luke 12:35 refers to lamps "burning."

Elsewhere, ***kaiō*** is used in a metaphorical sense. There are numerous "burning" phenomena in the apocalyptic visions of John, including torches before the divine throne (cf. Rev. 4:5); a star (cf. Rev. 8:10); a mountain (cf. Rev. 8:8); and the lake of "burning" sulfur (cf. Rev. 19:20; 21:8). Heb. 12:18 describes the mountain "blazing" with fire (Mt. Sinai), which symbolizes the divine presence. "Burning" is an indication of divine judgment in John 15:6 (cf. also 1 Cor. 13:3). The "burning" of one's heart, indicating an awareness of a strong, inner perception, is indicated in Luke 24:32.

katakaiō [κατακαίω, *2618*]

katakaiō is a variant form of ***kaiō***, above, found in twelve places with the meaning "burn up," "consume by fire."

Acts 19:19 describes the destruction of magic books by fire; and Heb. 13:11 refers to the "burning" of the sin offering.

In metaphorical contexts, ***katakaiō*** indicates the consuming fire of divine judgment against the wicked (cf. Matt. 3:12; 13:30, 40; Luke 3:17; 2 Pet. 3:10; Rev. 8:7; 17:16; 18:8). It also constitutes the symbolic means of testing the believer's life work (cf. 1 Cor. 3:15).

ekkaiō [ἐκκαίω, *1572*]

ekkaiō is a rare variant of ***kaiō***, above, found only in Rom. 1:27 referring to the perverse passion of men "burning with lust" for one another.

pyroō [πυρόω, *4448*]

pyroō is a verb with the meaning "burn," "set on fire" in both literal and metaphorical contexts. It occurs six times.

Literal references to the process of refinement, to "purification by fire" are found in Rev. 1:15; 3:18. Metaphorically, ***pyroō*** signifies to "burn" with lust or passion in 1 Cor. 7:9. The vision of the cosmic elements "on fire," as a sign of the apocalyptic end of the world, is recorded in 2 Pet. 3:12. Eph. 6:16 refers to the "flaming" darts of the devil.

kausis [καῦσις, *2740*]

kausis is a rare noun found only in Heb. 6:8 with the literal meaning "burning," signifying the end of the earth. It is translated "to be burned."

pyrōsis [πύρωσις, *4451*]

pyrōsis is a noun denoting a "burning," "fiery ordeal or trial." The latter meaning is noted in 1 Pet. 4:12; the former in relation to the fiery destruction of the city of Babylon, personified as a whore (cf. Rev. 18:9, 18).

thymiaō [θυμιάω, *2370*]

thymiaō is a rare noun with the meaning to "burn incense" found only in Luke 1:9

Additional Notes

The semantic range of both the Hebrew and Greek terminology for "burning," taken as a whole, is quite consistent — whether in reference to burning as a literal or metaphorical expression of God's wrath; or as an indicator of divine cleansing and purification.

BURNT OFFERING → OFFERING

BUSH

OT WORDS

seneh **[סְנֶה, 5572]**

This rare noun occurs only four times in the Old Testament. It means "bush" and is found on three occasions in the account of the "burning bush" in Exod. 3:2, 3, 4. The remarkable phenomenon associated with this event is twofold. First, although the bush appeared to be ablaze it was not consumed by the fire; and secondly, God himself spoke to Moses through the angel of the Lord.

The final reference is found in Deut. 33:16, where, in the context of a blessing to Joseph, Moses alludes to the "favor of him who dwelt in the burning bush." Clearly, the Exod. 3 encounter is in view here.

NT WORDS

batos [βάτος, *942*]

batos is a noun denoting a "bush" in Mark 12:26; Luke 6:44; Luke 20:37; Acts 7:30, 35.

BUSINESS ➠ SERVE ➠ WORK

BUY, BOUGHT

OT WORDS

qānāh **[קָנָה, 7069]**

This verb occurs about eighty times in the Old Testament with the meaning "get," "acquire" — mostly in the sense of "buy" or "purchase."

It is used in a literal sense in the majority of cases, and for the most part the usage is mundane, referring to the purchase of land (cf. Gen. 25:10; 1 Kgs. 16:24; Neh. 5:8, 16); slaves from foreign lands (cf. Lev. 25:15, 44, 45); and building materials (cf. 1 Kgs. 22:6; 12:12), to mention just a few examples.

There are, however, a number of literal purchases referred to in the Old Testament that are highly significant. Ruth 4, for example, refers to Boaz purchasing the estate of Naomi's deceased husband, Elimelech. As a consequence, he also acquires Ruth as a wife and restores the lineage of Elimelech, guaranteeing him a line of posterity. This illustration from Old Testament history is a profound example of the act of redemption, that quality of selfless compassion and mercy that is perfectly mirrored in the character of God, and also of Jesus Christ, both of whom are described as "Redeemer." Boaz's actions point forward to the work of Jesus Christ, whose sacrificial death on the cross "buys us back" from the grip of sin's penalty, and liberates us so that we may enjoy the rich inheritance God has in store for us, his chosen people. Thus we, too, have direct access to the "family of God." This action of redemption is a very significant theme in the Old Testament. (➠ REDEEM)

Another significant buying transaction is recorded in Jer. 32, where the prophet Jeremiah is instructed to buy some land back from his cousin Hanamel (Jer. 32:9ff.). The purpose of this exercise is to give life to the people of Judah so that one day they will return to the land to resume normal life. Jeremiah's purchase, while a literal transaction, carries with it a powerful symbolism — the promise that one day God will bring the people back to the land to live, where they will resume buying and selling houses and property.

King David's purchase of Araunah's threshing floor in 2 Sam. 24:24 is also highly significant in that this is the eventual site of the temple which Solomon, David's son, would build. 1 Chr. 22:1 needs to be read in conjunction with the Samuel text.

In a more general, metaphorical sense, ***qānāh*** sometimes expresses the meaning "acquire" — not so much in the literal sense of "purchasing" or "buying," but with the implicit idea of redemption. Isa. 11:11 is one example of this usage, where God promises to "reclaim" the remnant of his people from all over the world. Underlying these words is God's determination to regain or "redeem" his people from captivity and exile. In a slightly different context, Prov. 4:5ff. refers to the supreme value of "gaining wisdom" for oneself. The reader is exhorted to "get it" at all costs. "Wisdom" is a quality that reflects living in harmony with God, seeking to serve and obey him and aligning oneself with his ways. Such a quality may never be literally purchased, but one may acquire it just the same through a relationship of faith and trust in God. Note also the exhortations of Lady Wisdom in Prov. 8 in relation to this theme.

shābar **[שָׁבַר, 7666]**

This verb is found about twenty times and means to "buy" in the majority of cases. It is used only in a literal sense. Over half of the references are in the Joseph narrative (cf. Gen. 41:57; 42:2ff.; 43:20, 22; 47:14). On several occasions ***shābar*** also means to "sell" (cf. Deut. 2:28; Amos 8:5, 6; Gen. 42:6).

kārāh **[כָּרָה, 3739]**

kārāh is a verb translated "buy," "purchase" — in relation to food in Deut. 2:6; and to the price of redemption for an unfaithful wife in Hos. 3:2.

miqnah [**מִקְנָה, 4736**]

miqnah is a noun found in fifteen places signifying a "purchase price" — that which is bought with money. It refers to the purchase of slaves in Gen. 17:12ff.; Exod. 12:44; to the purchase of land in the Year of Jubilee (cf. Lev. 25:16; Lev. 27:22; cf. also Jer. 32:11ff.); and finally to the price of release or redemption for slaves in the Year of Jubilee (cf. Lev. 25:51).

NT Words

agorazō [ἀγοράζω, *59*]

agorazō is a verb translated "buy" in its approximately thirty occurrences. (→ REDEEM)

Literal references to "buying" include the purchase of property in Matt. 13:44; 27:7; Luke 14:18; of goods and merchandise in Matt. 14:15; 25:9ff.; Mark 6:36ff.; Luke 9:13; 22:36; John 4:8; 13:29; 1 Cor. 7:30; Rev. 13:17; 18:11; and of a precious pearl in Matt. 13:46.

ōneomai [ὠνέομαι, *5608*]

ōneomai is a rare noun found only in Acts 7:16 with the meaning "purchase" in relation to a tomb.

Additional Notes

There is a distinct connection between the sense of "purchase" and that of "redemption" throughout the Old and New Testaments. ***qānāh***, and ***agorazō*** have both a literal as well as a metaphorical sense. While these terms share a common perspective, however, they are not translated "redeem." (→ REDEEM)

C

CALL, CALLED, CALLING

OT Words

qārā' **[קָרָא, 7121]**

This fairly common verb occurs 730 times with the meanings "call," "meet," and "read." (→ READ)

There are four discernible strands of meaning under the general sense of "call" in regard to this verb: "naming," "crying out," "summoning," and "proclaiming."

qārā' means "naming" in over 200 places. In these cases, it is the normal term used to identify a person, place, or particular phenomenon. For example, Gen. 1:5 refers to God calling the darkness "night." Abraham names his son Isaac (cf. Gen. 17:19), and he also names one of the most significant patriarchal cities, Beersheba (lit. "well of seven"; cf. Gen. 21:31). The act of naming in ancient Israel was not a matter of aesthetics; rather, more often than not, names were given to indicate blessing and divine favor, or cursing and judgment. A few examples of names indicating divine blessing and divine favor include: Noah (Gen. 5:29); Abraham (Gen. 17:5); Isaac (Gen. 17:19); the name of God in association with Solomon's temple (1 Kgs. 8:43); Immanuel — "God with us" (Isa. 7:1); and "wonderful" (Isa. 7:6). Names indicating cursing and judgment include the Valley of Achor (i.e., "disaster"), where Achan was executed for stealing spoil from Jericho in clear violation of the divine command not to touch any of the plunder (Josh. 7:26). The place was so named as a reminder to God's people not to fall into a similar trap again in the future. Then the three symbolic names of Hosea's children indicate judgment against Israel for her rejection of Yahweh: "Jezreel," reminding Israel of the valley where Jehu slaughtered the relatives of Ahaziah, king of Judah, in an unwarranted fashion (Hos. 1:4, see also 2 Kgs. 10:12–14); "Lo-Ruhamah," or "Not-Loved" (Hos. 1:6); and "Lo-ammi," or "Not-My-People" (Hos. 1:9).

Another celebrated instance of naming a child as a symbol of judgment against the people of Israel is found in the story of the son of the unnamed wife of Phinehas — a woman who died in childbirth after hearing of the news of the deaths of her husband and Eli her father-in-law, and of the theft of the ark of the covenant by the Philistines. Before she died, she named the boy "Ichabod," which means "no glory," indicating that the glory of God had left his people with the capture of the sacred covenant chest. The whole incident reflects very poorly on Israel's spiritual life at the time (cf. 1 Sam. 4:21–22).

The second meaning attached to ***qārā'*** in the sense of "calling" is that of "cry out." The term occurs approximately thirty times this way. It refer to both the cries of human beings and the cries of God (cf. 1 Sam. 26:14; Isa. 6:3; 65:12; Lam. 4:15; Zech. 1:14; Lev. 13:45; 1 Sam. 20:38).

More significantly, ***qārā'*** means "summon" (approximately one hundred times), particularly with reference to God calling upon his people, corporately and individually, to follow him in trust and obedience. One of the most significant illustrations of this principle is found in the narrative of 1 Sam. 3, where God summons the boy Samuel to pronounce judgment on the corrupted priestly line of Eli and his sons, Hophni and Phinehas. Throughout the chapter, God's calling of Samuel is seen as irresistible, even though it was not until the third issuing of the "call" or "summons" that Samuel finally was in a position to give heed to the divine message (1 Sam. 3:4ff.). Another interesting use of ***qārā'*** in this regard is the summoning of the Messianic Servant of Yahweh in Isa. 42:6; 49:1 by the Spirit of God. Hos. 11:1 also alludes to an effective divine summons in referring to Israel's exodus from Egypt in the past as a model for God's promised deliverance of his people from exile in the future. From the perspective of the people's response to God, ***qārā'*** is also used as a synonym for worship whereby people "call upon the name of the Lord." This refers to a solemn, worshipful invoking or "calling upon" the divine Person as an expression of thanksgiving or a plea for blessing (cf. Gen. 4:26; 12:8; 13:4; 21:33; 26:35; 2 Kgs. 5:11; Isa. 29:12; 1 Chr. 16:8; Joel 2:32; Zech. 13:9). It is also found in 1 Kgs. 18:26 in reference to idol worship where the prophets of Baal invoke the name of the pagan god Baal on Mt. Carmel in their doomed confrontation with Elijah.

Finally, ***qārā'*** may be translated "call" in the sense of "proclaim." The verb occurs about eighty times with this meaning. It refers to the proclamation of holy festival occasions (cf. Lev. 23:4, 21; 25:10; Exod. 32:5); to royal decrees for fasting (cf. 1 Kgs. 21:9; 2 Chr. 20:3); and to national repentance, for example in Nineveh (cf. Jonah 3:4, 5). ***qārā'*** is also found in the proclamation of judgment against Nineveh (cf. Jonah 1:2; 3:2); and against Judah and Jerusalem (cf. Jer. 2:2; 3:12ff.; 7:2). Then, in Isa. 61:1, the proclamation of liberty to those in bondage is depicted as an element in the "messianic" charter of the Servant of Yahweh.

miqrā' [מִקְרָא, 4744]

This is purely a ceremonial term, referring to the holy assemblies of the Israelites under the terms of the Mosaic covenant. Literally, the word means "convocation," or "a called-out gathering." It is found twenty-three times with this sense (cf. Exod. 12:16; Lev. 23:2ff.; Num. 10:2; 28:18ff.; Neh. 8:8; Isa. 1:13; 4:5).

'āmar [אָמַר, 559]

'āmar is a very common verb found over 5,300 times with the predominant senses of "say," "speak" and several related nuances. Included in these is the meaning "call."

The meaning "call" in the sense of "designate" is found in Isa. 5:20, where judgment is invoked on those who "called" evil good and vice versa. Jerusalem is "called" the "city of perfection" in Lam. 2:15 (cf. also Isa. 19:18). Faithful Israelites are "called" holy (cf. Isa. 4:3).

'āmar is also translated "call" in the sense of "rename" in Gen. 32:28, where Jacob is renamed "Israel." Tophet is "renamed" the "Valley of Slaughter," denoting the place of refuse outside of Jerusalem (cf. Jer. 7:32).

NT Words

kaleō [καλέω, *2564*]

kaleō is a verb found around 150 times indicating the primary sense of "call" with several related nuances in a variety of contexts. It is used of both human beings and God.

Commonly, ***kaleō*** expresses the meaning "call" in the sense of "giving someone or something a name." The "naming" of Jesus is indicated in Matt. 1:21ff.; 2:23; Luke 1:31ff. In particular, he is "called" the "Son of God" in Luke 1:35; "Faithful and True" in Rev. 19:1; and "Word of God" in Rev. 19:13. See also Luke 1:13, 60 in relation to John the Baptist. Peacemakers are called "sons of God" in Matt. 5:9. Reference is made to Abraham being called the "friend of God" in Jas. 2:23. See also John 1:42. Satan is given the alternate name of "Beelzebub" in Matt. 10:25. The naming of places and towns is indicated, for example, in Luke 7:11; 23:33; Acts 1:12; 9:11; Rev. 12:9.

Another common denotation for this verb is that of "summon," "invite." General references to this usage include Matt. 22:3ff.; Luke 14:7ff.; John 2:22; Acts 4:18; 1 Cor. 10:27. With this sense Christ is said to "call" the righteous to repentance in Matt. 9:13; Mark 2:17; Luke 5:32; and he "calls" people to follow him as his disciples in Mark 1:20. See also John 10:3. Elsewhere, God is the subject of ***kaleō*** — for example, Heb. 11:8 refers to God "calling" Abram out of Ur. God also "calls" his people to peace in 1 Cor. 7:15. Paul notes his "calling" to be an apostle in 1 Cor. 15:9, with the implication of divine calling.

Other uses of ***kaleō*** with God as the subject include God "calling" things into existence, or employing his creative power, in Rom. 4:17. Of particular significance are references to God "calling" people into a relationship with himself, initiating the conversion experience (cf. Rom. 8:30; 9:11, 24; 1 Cor. 1:9; Gal. 1:6, 15; Eph. 4:1ff.; 1 Thess. 2:12; 2 Thess. 2:14; 1 Tim. 6:12; 2 Tim. 1:9; Heb. 9:15; 1 Pet. 1:15; 2:9; 5:10). Then, in Rom. 9:25ff. (citing Hos. 2), God is said to "call" his people (i.e., give them a new name) and restore them to divine favor.

The meaning "cry out" is indicated in Matt. 4:21.

epikaleō [ἐπικαλέω, *1941*]

epikaleō is a verb found thirty times with the senses of "call on, upon" and "be called" (i.e., be given a name).

References to "calling upon" the name of the Lord in the contexts of worship and prayer are found in Acts 2:21; 7:59; 9:14; 22:16; 1 Pet. 1:17; Rom. 10:12ff.; 2 Tim. 2:22. "Calling on" the name of Christ is noted in Acts 9:21; 1 Cor. 1:2. Paul exercises his prerogative to "call upon"or "make (legal) appeal to" Caesar in Acts 25:11ff.; 28:19. "Making appeal" to God is noted in 2 Cor. 1:23.

epikaleō also indicates the passive sense of "be called" (i.e., "named") in relation to people in Acts 10:18, 32; 12:12, 25; 15:22. In Heb. 11:16 it is affirmed that God is not ashamed "to be called" the God of his people.

metakaleō [μετακαλέω, *3333*]

metakaleō is a verb found four times with the meaning "to call for" or "summon" individuals (cf. Acts 7:14; 10:32; 20:17; 24:25).

proskaleomai [προσκαλέομαι, *4341*]

The verb ***proskaleomai***, a synonym for ***metakaleō***, above, is found in thirty places with the meaning "to call to," "summon" people for a particular purpose. Jesus "calls" people to himself in Matt. 15:10, 32; 18:2; 20:25; Mark 3:13; Luke 18:16. Acts 2:39 refers to God "calling" people to himself. The Spirit of God is said to "call" Saul and Barnabas into the work of the gospel in Acts 13:2; 16:10.

General references to people "calling others to themselves" are found in Matt. 18:32; Luke 7:19; Acts 5:40; 6:2; 20:1; Jas. 5:14.

synkaleō [συγκαλέω, *4779*]

synkaleō is another synonym for the above entries, meaning "call together," "assemble" in the contexts of summoning people. It is found eight times (cf. Mark 15:16; Luke 9:1; 15:6ff.; 23:13; Acts 5:21; 10:24; 28:17).

phōneō [φωνέω, *5455*]

phōneō is a verb occurring about forty times with the predominant meaning to "call, cry out" as well as to "summon."

The sense of "call, cry out" is indicated, for example, in Matt. 20:32; Mark 15:35; Luke 8:8; 23:46; John 1:48; Acts 16:28; Rev. 14:18.

The action of "summoning" people is indicated in Mark 9:35; 14:12; Luke 19:5; John 2:9; 4:16; Acts 9:41. Jesus' action of "calling Lazarus up from the dead" is noted in John 12:17.

legō [λέγω, *3004*]

legō is a common verb occurring over 1,300 times with the dominant sense of "say," "speak." However, in a number of cases ***legō*** means "call," primarily in the passive sense of "be called," "named."

General references to peoples' names are noted in Matt. 4:18; 10:2; Acts 9:36; and particular reference to the naming of Christ is made in Matt. 1:16; John 9:11; Col. 4:11; Heb. 7:11; 11:24. Rev. 8:11 mentions the naming of the star "Wormwood." See also 1 Cor. 8:5.

Elsewhere, general references to the naming of places include Matt. 27:16; John 4:5; 19:13ff.; Acts 3:2. Other uses of ***legō*** with this sense are found in relation to Gethsemane in Matt. 26:36; to the Passover feast in Luke 22:1; and to the holy place of the temple in Heb. 9:2ff.

There is a metaphorical use of ***legō*** in Eph. 2:11 where Gentiles are "called" the "uncircumcision."

klēsis [κλῆσις, *2821*]

klēsis is a noun derived from ***kaleō*** (see above) found in eleven contexts and denoting the primary sense of "calling" or "vocation."

The meaning "vocation," "call" in a general sense is found in 1 Cor. 7:20.

More significantly the "calling" of God, that is the irresistible summons of God extended to those whom he desires to save, is indicated in Rom. 11:29; 1 Cor. 1:26; Eph. 1:18; 4:1ff.; Phil. 3:14; 2 Tim. 1:9; Heb. 3:1; 2 Pet. 1:10.

klētos [κλητός, *2822*]

klētos is an adjective derived from the verb ***kaleō*** (see above), found eleven times with the meaning "called."

The state of being "called" by God, implying sovereign divine election in the context of salvation, is indicated in Matt. 20:16; 22:14; Rom. 1:6ff.; 8:28; Jude 1; Rev. 17:14. Then, in Rom. 1:1; 1 Cor. 1:1ff., 24, Paul indicates that he was "called" by God to be an apostle.

Additional Notes

qārā' is a rich, multifaceted word that overlaps in meaning with almost all of the New Testament Greek terms discussed above. Both the Old and New Testament terminology focuses to a significant degree on the effectual calling of God. In the old covenant, Israel and her chosen leaders, prophets, and priests were duly called out and summoned by God to serve him faithfully. In the New Testament the situation is the same — except that the effective calling of believers in the new covenant rests upon the foundation of the finished work of Jesus Christ on the cross. In the Old Testament, the spiritual "calling" of the servants and people of Yahweh is nonetheless supremely effective, also initiated by the Spirit of God. In this former age the work of the Messianic Servant of God is not yet fulfilled, but only anticipated. Undoubtedly, the phenomenon of divine calling lies at the heart of God's redemptive activity.

CALVARY

OT WORDS

gulgōlet [**גֻּלְגֹּלֶת, 1538**]

This word occurs only twelve times, and on three occasions it means "skull" or "head." In the rest of the occurrences it means "head" in the sense of "person" when used in a statistical poll or census (cf. Exod. 16:16; 38:26; Num. 1:2, 18ff.; 3:47; 1 Chr. 23:3, 24).

The passages in which ***gulgōlet*** translates "skull" or "head" all refer to circumstances involving a violent death: In Judg. 9:53, the cruel despot Abimelech meets a humiliating end when a woman drops a millstone on his head, cracking his skull and dealing him a mortal wound. 2 Kgs. 9:35 describes the ghastly demise of Queen Jezebel when, after being thrown to the ground from the window of her palace, she is eaten by wild dogs, who leave nothing except her skull, feet, and hands. Finally, in 1 Chr. 10:10, Saul's severed head is hung in the temple of Dagon by the Philistines, who defeated Israel in the battle on Mt. Gilboa — an encounter which saw the death of the first Israelite king.

NT Words

kranion [κρανίον, *2898*]

kranion is a rare noun found only four times. In Luke 23:33 it denotes the location referred to as "the skull," the place of Christ's crucifixion. In Matt. 27:33, Mark 15:22; John 19:17 the same meaning is indicated; but the term ***kranion*** is juxtaposed here with the Aramaic term "Golgotha."

CANDLE, CANDLESTICK → LAMP → LAMPSTAND

CAPTAIN

OT Words

sar [**שַׂר, 8269**]

This term is very common throughout the Old Testament, occurring approximately four hundred times with varying shades of meaning. The principal senses are "commander (military)"; "ruler"; "(chief) official."

With the meaning "military commander," ***sar*** is found predominantly, though not exclusively, in the historical portions of the Old Testament. It is found, for example, about 130 times in the books of Samuel–Kings, with reference to the armies of Saul, David, Solomon, and the rulers of the northern and southern kingdoms of Israel and Judah, respectively. The same meaning also occurs with respect to the Israelite infantry in the Pentateuch (cf. Num. 31:14, 48ff.; Deut. 1:15; 20:9) and Joshua–Judges (cf. Josh. 5:14ff.; Judg. 4:2ff.; 5:15; 10:18). Of particular significance here is the reference in Josh. 5:14ff., where it is evident that this particular "commander" figure is none other than the "angel of the Lord." This theophanic appearance is all the more important as it confirms in the mind of Joshua, to whom the angel appears, that God himself is in total control of the campaign upon which Joshua and the people of Israel are about to embark. This revelation occurs immediately prior to the fall of Jericho.

Other references to "military commands" are found in Gen. 39:1, where Potiphar, the captain of the guard in Pharaoh's prison, is given charge over Joseph. This is a blessing for the young Israelite and for the advancement of God's redemptive purposes amongst his people. Foreign military rulers are also mentioned in the Prophets (cf. Isa. 19:11; 21:5, Zoan in Egypt).

With the meaning "ruler" or "prince," ***sar*** has a fairly broad variety of senses. The term may refer to members of a royal family (cf. 2 Chr. 22:8 [Ahaziah]; 2 Chr. 28:21 [Ahaz]), to the Babylonian royal family (cf. 2 Chr. 32:31), to the royal lineage of David (cf. Jer. 17:25), and to rulers or leaders of Israel and the nations in a general, undefined sense (cf. Pss. 105:22; 119:23, 161; Prov. 8:16; Eccl. 10:7).

Two particular uses of ***sar*** stand out with reference to the meaning "ruler." The first is found in Isa. 9:6, where the extended oracle of the "Immanuel" sign given to King Ahaz of Judah finds a consummate expression in the person of the messianic child — a royal ruler who shall come to be known, among other titles, as the "prince of peace." This royal figure is theologically linked in the prophet Isaiah to the person of the "Servant of Yahweh." And, in Isa. 49:7, it is the "princes" or "rulers" of the world who will fall down and worship this messianic ruler who is called up, anointed, and empowered by the Spirit of God. Thus the "Servant of the Lord" is clearly established as a divine royal figure, one who will inaugurate and fulfill God's rule on earth in the hearts and lives of his people.

It is where ***sar*** means "official" that the greatest variety of usage — and ambiguity — is to be found. It would appear that, in the vast majority of cases, "official" may also be rendered "noble" or even "leader." However, the underlying sense is that of a leading official in either a ritual or administrative position. For example, in Gen. 40 ***sar*** is used throughout in an adjectival sense to refer to the "chief" butler and baker in the court of Pharaoh. In Num. 22 it indicates the "nobles" in the entourage of Balak the Moabite king. It refers to "court officials" in Isa. 24–52; 2 Chr. 29:20–32:3; and in Ezra 7:28; 8:20; 9:1; 10:2ff. Nehemiah 3 contains several occurrences of ***sar*** — here the term refers to the chief administrative officers of districts in Jerusalem. "Nobles of the realm" are mentioned frequently in the book of Esther in reference to the court of Ahasuerus (or Xerxes). And, finally, ***sar*** refers in Dan. 10:13–12:1 to high-ranking angelic beings of both the heavenly and demonic realm, who are engaged in spiritual warfare over the fate of both the people of God (Israel) and the nations of Greece and Persia.

On two occasions in the book of Daniel, ***sar*** indicates God himself as the "Prince of princes" (cf. Dan. 8:25) and "prince of the host" (cf. Dan. 8:11). In both instances God is the despised object of the "little horn," Antiochus Epiphanes, the Seleucid ruler of Palestine in the second century B.C., best known for his passionate Hellenism and violent anti-Semitism. His quest, however, is doomed to failure and his subsequent destruction is duly noted in the text.

segānîm **[סְגָנִים, 5461]**

This is the plural form of the Hebrew term ***sāgān*** (→ RULE), which occurs seventeen times and means "prefect" or "official." It is found in Neh. 2:16; 4:14ff.; 5:7ff.; 12:40; Jer. 51:23, 57; Ezek. 23:6, 12, 23; Ezra 9:2; Isa. 41:25.

NT Words

chiliarchos [χιλίαρχος, *5506*]

chiliarchos is a noun occurring about twenty times with literal reference to the commander of 1,000 soldiers, and is translated "captain" or "commander" throughout its usage. This military sense is indicated in Mark 6:21; John 18:12; Acts 21:31ff.; 22:24ff.; 23:10, 15ff.; 24:22; 25:23; Rev. 6:15; 19:18.

stratēgos [στρατηγός, *4755*]

stratēgos is a synonym for ***chiliarchos***, above, denoting the supreme civil officers, commanders (or captains) of the Jerusalem temple (cf. Luke 22:4, 52; Acts 4:1; 5:24, 26); and also refers to "civil magistrates" (cf. Acts 16:20ff.).

kybernētēs [κυβερνήτης, *2942*]

kybernētēs is a noun denoting a ship's "captain" in Acts 27:11; Rev. 18:17.

archēgos [ἀρχηγός, *747*]

archēgos is found only four times in the New Testament. It refers metaphorically to Jesus as the "author" of the Christian's life in Acts 3:15; as the "author" of salvation in Heb. 2:10; and as the "author" of the faith of God's people in Heb. 12:2. Each context indicates Jesus' role and function as the one who provides the foundation and impetus for each phenomenon. The translation "captain" is somewhat archaic in these instances. In Acts 5:31, ***archēgos*** refers to Jesus as "Prince," seated next to God's right hand.

Additional Notes

There is considerable overlap in meaning between the Hebrew term ***sar*** and the corresponding Greek terms ***chiliarchos*** and ***stratēgos***. These two New Testament terms carry both a military as well as a civil connotation. The Hebrew term ***sar*** offers a broader range of meaning, which includes not only the human aspect of leadership and rule in varying military, ritual, and civil contexts, but also an angelic and divine perspective.

See Also: → HEAD → RULE

CAPTIVE, CAPTIVITY

OT Words

gôlāh **[גּוֹלָה, 1473]**

This is the noun of the verb ***gālāh*** (see below), occurring about forty times and meaning "captivity" or "exile." In all but five texts, it refers to the exile and captivity inflicted by the Babylonian army on the kingdom of Judah in the early sixth century B.C. Usage of the term is spread among the books of Ezra (e.g., 1:11; 2:1; 4:1; 6:19ff. 10:6ff.), Jeremiah (e.g., 28:6; 29:1ff.), and Ezekiel (e.g., 1:1; 3:11, 15; 11:24; 25:3), with the actual historical account of the sack of Jerusalem and subsequent "exile" being recorded in 2 Kgs. 24:15, 16. ***gôlāh*** refers either to the phenomenon of the exile or to the exiled people themselves in these passages.

The exceptions to this usage are found in the following texts. The meaning of the term does not change here, but simply the designation of those who are subject to captivity. In Jer. 49:3; Amos 1:15, it is the Ammonites who are threatened by God with inevitable exile and captivity as a punishment for their sin. Interestingly, in the Jeremiah text it is the Ammonite god Molech who is singled out for deportation, as representative of the people of Ammon. Similarly, in Jer. 48:7, Moab (or the god Chemosh) is likewise indicted and sentenced by Yahweh, as is Egypt in Jer. 46:19, and Nineveh in Nah. 3:10.

In all the above instances, the context indicates that such captivity is the direct consequence of rebellion against God. It constitutes the specific divine judgment for that crime.

gālāh **[גָּלָה, 1540]**

This verb means "to carry away into captivity," and approximately sixty of its nearly two hundred occurrences carry that sense. It refers not only to the Babylonian captivity, but also to the Assyrian sacking and removal of the northern kingdom of Israel in 721 B.C. The distribution of ***gālāh*** with respect to the deportation of Israel is concentrated mainly in the books of the Kings (cf. 2 Kgs. 15–18) and Amos (cf. Amos 5:5, 27; 6:7; 7:11, 17). And, concerning the Babylonian captivity, ***gālāh*** occurs several times in the following books: Jer. 1:3; 20:4; 24:1; 29:1ff.; 52:2; Lam. 1:3; 4:22; Ezek. 12:3; 39:28; Ezra 2:1; Neh. 7:6; Esth. 2:6. (→ APPEAR)

shābāh [שָׁבָה, 7617]

This is another synonym for ***gālāh*** and ***gôlāh***, above, but ***shābāh*** has a much broader focus than the period of either the Assyrian or Babylonian captivity. In fact, of the nearly fifty occurrences of ***shābāh***, only a few refer specifically to this era (cf. 1 Kgs. 8:46, 48; Pss. 106:46; 137:3; Jer. 13:17; 50:33; Ezek. 6:9).

In the large majority of cases, ***shābāh*** refers to a multiplicity of situations where the captivity and confinement of both Israelite and pagan peoples are in view. For example, Gen. 34:29 refers to Jacob's sons pillaging the city of Shechem and taking the women captive, in revenge for Shechem's violation of their sister Dinah. See also Gen. 14:14; 31:26 for other instances of capture in the early patriarchal period. There are several incidents of note in the Old Testament where the people of Judah are taken captive (other than in 587 B.C. at the hands of the Babylonians) (cf. 2 Chr. 28:11; Jer. 41:10, 14; 2 Chr. 28:17). Similar references are found with respect to the people of Israel (i.e., the northern kingdom) being captured (cf. Num. 21:1; 2 Kgs. 5:2). Likewise, there are situations where the people of Israel are referred to as the captors (e.g., Deut. 21:10; 2 Kgs. 6:22; 2 Chr. 25:12; Judg. 5:12). In addition, both Egypt and Babylon are threatened with destruction and captivity at the hand of God as a divine punishment (cf. Isa. 14:2; Jer. 43:12). Finally, there is the mission of the Servant of Yahweh, one of whose tasks will be to proclaim liberty for those in bondage or captivity. This may be understood as part of the "messianic charter" of the Servant, whose identity is fulfilled in the person of Jesus Christ (cf. Isa. 61:1). It is significant in this regard that Jesus' first public sermon in the Nazareth synagogue included this reading from the prophet Isaiah, and it was this particular passage that Jesus claimed to have fulfilled in their midst.

shebî [שְׁבִי, 7628]

This noun derived from the verb ***shābāh***, above, occurs about fifty times. ***shebî*** is identical in meaning to ***shābāh***, and it occurs in the same variety of contexts in which captivity is depicted. However, unlike ***shābāh***, this noun focuses much more on Judah's Babylonian captivity (cf. Ezra 2:1; 3:8; 8:35; 9:7; Neh. 1:2, 3; 7:6; 8:17; Isa. 52:2; Jer. 15:2; 20:6; 22:2; Lam. 1:5, 18; Ezek. 12:11). In Amos 9:4 it is the Assyrian invasion of the northern kingdom that is in view.

On two occasions, the use of ***shebî*** is linked with God's promise to deliver his people from captivity (cf. Jer. 30:10; 46:27).

shibyāh [שִׁבְיָה, 7633]

This is another noun derived from ***shābāh***, also meaning "captivity" (cf. ***shebî***, above). It occurs only nine times. There are two references to Israel taking captives (cf. Deut. 21:11; 32:42); as well as several references to the Judean people being captured (cf. 2 Chr. 28:5 [by Aram]; 2 Chr. 28:11 [by Pekah, king of Israel]); and being returned from the captivity (instigated by Pekah, cf. 2 Chr. 28:14, 15). In Neh. 4:4, ***shibyāh*** occurs in a context where a curse is invoked on the enemies of God's people that will result in their inevitable confinement. The Moabites are similarly condemned in Jer. 48:46.

NT Words

aichmalōsia [αἰχμαλωσία, *161*]

The noun ***aichmalōsia*** denotes "captivity" in a spiritual sense in Eph. 4:8; and in a visionary context in Rev. 13:10.

aichmalōteuō [αἰχμαλωτεύω, *162*]

The verb ***aichmalōteuō*** means "to make, take captive" and is found in Eph. 4:8 with reference to Christ's activity in "capturing" his enemies at the point of his ascension. In 2 Tim. 3:6 the term is used metaphorically with reference to false teachers who prey on, harass, and manipulate weak and vulnerable women — this activity is described as "leading them into captivity."

aichmalōtizō [αἰχμαλωτίζω, *163*]

aichmalōtizō is a synonym for ***aichmalōteuō***, above, with the meaning "to take captive" in three contexts. It is used literally in Luke 21:24. Rom. 7:23 contains a figurative usage, referring to the law of his mind "making him captive" to the law of sin. Then, 2 Cor. 10:5 speaks of "taking every thought captive" to obey Christ.

aichmalōtos [αἰχμάλωτος, *164*]

aichmalōtos is a rare noun denoting a "captive" found only in Luke 4:18.

zōgreō [ζωγρέω, *2221*]

zōgreō is a rare verb meaning to "catch," "take captive." In Luke 5:10 the term is used metaphorically to refer to the evangelizing activity of "catching" people for the kingdom of God. 2 Tim. 2:26 refers to "being captured" by the devil to do his will.

Additional Notes

Both Hebrew and Greek terminology for "captive" and "captivity" is significant throughout the Scriptures. The group of Hebrew terms focuses on "captivity" in a generalized sense, involving nations and individuals, Jew and Gentile alike. In particular, it is the emphasis on the two periods of Israel's exile (viz. Assyrian and Babylonian) and the divine promise to rescue them from that predicament that carry the greatest theological weight. The New Testament Greek terminology builds on that foundation, emphasizing the spiritual nature of the human bondage to sin and the crucial role of Jesus Christ in liberating people from this "captivity." Here we have in Scripture a very clear example of a concept that carries fundamentally important insights into the way God has intervened in history, both to bring judgment on people for their sin, and at the same time to guarantee their deliverance. This process is begun in the Old Testament and finds its fulfillment in the New, principally in the person of Christ.

CARCASS → BODY

CARE, CAREFUL

NT Words

merimna [μέριμνα, *3308*]

The noun ***merimna*** denotes "care," "worry," or "anxiety" in six places. In each context, the "cares" of this life are indicated (cf. Matt. 13:22; Mark 4:19; Luke 8:14; 21:34; 2 Cor. 11:28; 1 Pet. 5:7).

merimnaō [μεριμνάω, *3309*]

This verb occurs around twenty times with the underlying sense of "take care," "be careful."

The negative sense of "take no thought for" (i.e., don't be anxious about) is found in Matt. 6:25, 34; 10:19; Luke 12:11, 22ff.; Phil. 4:6.

The meaning "be anxious about" occurs in Matt. 6:27ff.; Luke 10:41 in relation to the necessities of life. It is also used with this meaning in the context of the demands of Christian ministry (cf. 1 Cor. 7:32ff.). See also Phil. 2:20.

In 1 Cor. 12:25 the term means "to care for someone."

melei [μέλει, *3199*]

melei is a verb found in thirteen places with the meaning to "care about" or "care for."

The meaning "care about" (i.e., "have a compassionate interest in") is found in Mark 4:38; Luke 10:40; 1 Cor. 9:9; 1 Pet. 5:7.

By way of contrast, the negative sense of "have no care for" (i.e., pay no attention to) is indicated in Acts 8:17.

epimeleomai [ἐπιμελέομαι, *1959*]

epimeleomai is a rare verb found in three places, a synonym for ***melei***, above, meaning "to take care of" in the sense of to "see to someone's personal needs" in Luke 10:34ff. The responsibility of "caring for" the church of God is indicated in 1 Tim. 3:5.

phrontizō [φροντίζω, *5431*]

phrontizō is a rare verb found only in Titus 3:8, meaning "be careful" in relation to doing good works.

Additional Notes

The English word "care" has a very broad semantic range, represented by a wide variety of Hebrew terms. For a discussion of specific Hebrew terminology consult the entries listed below.

See Also: → FEAR → HASTE → QUAKE → TROUBLE

CARNAL, CARNALLY → FLESH

CARRY → BEAR (VERB) → LEAD → TAKE

CAST

OT Words

nāphal [נָפַל, 5307]

This term occurs about 450 times in the Old Testament, primarily with the meaning "fall." However, in about thirty instances ***nāphal*** is used in a causative sense, which may be translated "cast down" or "overthrow." The literal sense of this verb is "to cause to fall or bring down." (→ FALL)

nāphal is used several times in the context of "casting lots." It is found, for example, in reference to priests and Levites seeking to implement their respective duties, assigning themselves to specific functions and places of service (cf. 1 Chr. 24:31; 25:8; 26:14; Neh. 10:34; 11:1). Lots were also cast in order to ascertain which one of Saul's army had disobeyed his command not to eat anything until the Philistine army had been vanquished. Jonathan, Saul's son, was drawn (cf. 1 Sam. 14:42). The same practice was undertaken on the vessel that Jonah had boarded for Tarshish in the middle of a terrible storm. In this case, lots were cast in order to find out who was responsible for the calamity. Jonah was taken, and his fate was to be thrown overboard and swallowed by a great fish (cf. Jonah 1:7).

The writer of Ps. 22 laments the fact that his enemies cast lots for his clothing as they anticipate his imminent destruction (cf. Ps. 22:18). This psalm is understood as a foreshadowing of the suffering Servant-Messiah at Calvary. The Roman soldiers at the foot of the cross in Matt. 27:35 directly fulfill this prophecy.

Esth. 3:9; 9:24 also refer to casting lots. These two texts record the setting of Adar 12 as the date for implementing Haman's plot to eradicate all Jewish people within the Persian Empire. The plot is foiled and the Jewish people counterattack in spectacular fashion. Finally, this expression occurs in a positive sense in Isa. 34:17, where God is declared to have "allotted" blessings for wild animals in the land of Canaan. This is an allusion to the guarantee that God will transform the land of Canaan, after a period of judgment, from barren wilderness into a region of great fertility and peace.

nāphal also describes the "casting down" of the wicked. In a general sense, God is said to cast down the wicked and thus destroy them (cf. Pss. 73:18; 140:10). This even includes some of God's own people (cf. Jer. 22:7; Ezek. 6:4)

Dan. 8:10 refers to the actions (symbolically expressed) of the "little horn," Antiochus Epiphanes, in "casting down" the starry host. This is a metaphorical allusion to the persecution of Israel by this cruel Seleucid ruler of Palestine in the second century B.C. Then, Dan. 11:12 refers to the destruction of a host of people. This time it is the king of the south (Egypt) that destroys (i.e., "casts down") the king of the north (Syria).

Finally, Isa. 26:19 refers to the earth "casting out" its dead. The context makes it clear that a divine miracle of transformation and resurrection is in view. This text refers in a powerful, symbolic way to God's redemption of his people in the wake of the destruction of her enemies.

yāṣaq [יָצַק, 3332]

The verb ***yāṣaq*** is found in approximately fifty contexts with the primary senses of "pour," "cast."

The meaning "to cast" is found in the context of manufacturing tabernacle and temple furniture, referring to the "casting" of molten metal (cf. Exod. 25:12; 26:37; 37:3, 13; 38:5, 27; 1 Kgs. 7:24ff.; 2 Chr. 4:17).

nātaṣ [נָתַץ, 5422]

The verb ***nātaṣ*** expresses the primary sense of "destroy" in the sense of "pull down," "throw down," "tear down," or "cast down."

The action of "tearing down," including all related nuances listed above, is indicated in relation to the destruction of idol altars (Exod. 34:13; Deut. 7:5; 12:3; Judg. 2:2; 6:28ff.; 2 Kgs. 10:27; 23:7ff.; 2 Chr. 23:17; 31:1); and of houses (Lev. 14:45; Isa. 22:10). Other references include Judg. 8:9; 2 Kgs. 25:10; Jer. 39:8; Ezek. 16:39; 26:9, 12.

In particular, references to prophetic authority given by God as well as divine power itself "tearing down," for the purpose of destroying the enemies of Yahweh and his people, are found in Jer. 1:10; 18:7; 31:28.

hāras [הָרַס, 2040]

hāras is a synonym for ***nātaṣ***, above, meaning "cast down" as well as the related nuances of "overthrow," "throw down," "break down" throughout most of the nearly forty occurrences of the term.

The meaning "cast down" in the sense of "overthrow," "defeat" is indicated in relation to the enemies of God in Exod. 15:7.

Elsewhere, ***hāras*** is translated "cast down" with the underlying sense of "destroy" in a number of contexts. The destruction of pagan altars is in view in Exod. 23:24; Judg. 6:25; as are altars of Yahweh in 1 Kgs. 18:30; 19:10, 14; and cities in battle in 2 Sam. 11:25; 2 Kgs. 3:25; 1 Chr. 20:1; Isa. 14:17. The wicked are said to be "cast down" by the hand of Yahweh in the context of divine judgment in Ps. 28:5. In particular, such treatment is handed down to Assyria in Mic. 5:11; to Babylon in Jer. 50:15; to Tyre in Ezek. 26:4, 12; and to Egypt in Ezek. 30:4. God's people also come under the destructive hand of divine "overthrow" in Lam. 2:2; Ezek. 13:14. See also Prov. 14:1; Isa. 22:19; Jer. 31:40.

In addition there are general references to prophetic power and authority to "pull down," "overthrow" the enemies of God and his people — a power and prerogative that is also assumed by Yahweh himself (cf. Jer. 1:10; 24:6; 31:28; 42:10; 45:4). See also Mal. 1:4.

rāmāh [רָמָה, 7411]

rāmāh is a verb found in twelve places with the predominant meaning "deceive." (→ DECEIVE) In two places, however, it means "throw" or "cast." Exod. 15:1, 21 make reference to the Egyptian horses and riders "being thrown" into the Re(e)d Sea.

sāqal **[סָקַל, 5619]**

The verb ***sāqal*** means "to stone" (i.e., cast stones), primarily as a means of execution. (→ STONE) In 2 Sam. 16:6, 13, however, ***sāqal*** refers to the action of "throwing stones" as a means of harassment.

NT Words

ballō [βάλλω, *906*]

The verb ***ballō*** is found over 120 times with the meaning "cast" or "throw" in a variety of contexts both literal and metaphorical.

The literal, general sense of "throw," "cast" is indicated in relation to various objects in Matt. 3:10; 13:47; Mark 1:16; 11:23; Luke 3:9; John 21:6ff.; Rev. 4:10. In particular, John 8:7, 59 speak of casting stones in the context of public execution. The action of "throwing" people down is indicated in Mark 9:22; 9:42; and "throwing oneself down" is noted in Matt. 4:6. The sense of "throw away," "reject" is indicated in Matt. 5:13; 13:48; 18:9; Luke 14:35. The judicial process of having people "thrown" into prison is indicated in Matt. 5:25; 18:30; Luke 12:58; John 3:24; Acts 16:23ff.; Rev. 2:10. The decision-making process of "casting lots" is indicated in Matt. 27:35; Mark 15:24; Luke 23:34; John 19:24.

Where God is designated as the subject of ***ballō*** he is said to "throw" the wicked into the fire of eternal judgment in Matt. 13:42, 50. Luke 12:49; Rev. 8:5ff. affirm that God "throws" fire on the earth in the process of divine judgment.

In other contexts ***ballō*** is used metaphorically — indicating, for example, the phenomenon that perfect love "casts out" fear (cf. 1 John 4:18). In John's vision in Rev. 12:9ff., the dragon and his angels are "thrown out" of heaven. Elsewhere, the satanic beasts are all "thrown into" the lake of burning sulfur (cf. Rev. 19:20; 20:10ff.), and into the bottomless pits in Rev. 20:3.

rhiptō [ῥίπτω, *4496*]

rhiptō is a verb found eight times, meaning "throw" in most of these contexts.

Matt. 27:5 describes the action of "throwing down" pieces of silver in the temple. A demon "throws down" its hopeless victim to the ground in Luke 4:35. Ship's tackle is "thrown into" the ocean in Acts 27:19; anchors are "cast out" in Acts 27:29. See also Luke 17:2.

apoballō [ἀποβάλλω, *577*]

apoballō is a rare verb describing the action of "throwing aside" one's cloak in Mark 10:50. Heb. 10:35 warns believers not to "throw away" their confidence.

ekballō [ἐκβάλλω, *1544*]

ekballō is a verb found in around 100 places with the underlying meanings "cast," "cast out" in a variety of contexts.

The exorcising or "casting out" of demons is indicated in Matt. 7:22; 9:33ff.; 12:24ff.; Mark 1:34; 3:15ff.; 9:18ff.; Luke 9:40, 49; 11:14ff.

Being "cast into outer darkness," symbolizing eternal punishment, is indicated in Matt. 8:12; 22:13; 25:30. The satanic ruler of the world is "cast out" by God in John 12:31. See also Acts 27:38.

People are "thrown out" of the temple in Matt. 21:12; Mark 11:15; Luke 19:45; John 2:15. Other references to eviction of varying kinds include Matt. 21:39; Mark 12:8; Luke 20:15; John 9:34ff.; Acts 7:58; Gal. 4:30.

God's promise never to "cast out" those who come to Christ in the right spirit is noted in John 6:37.

emballō [ἐμβάλλω, *1685*]

emballō is a rare verb found only in Luke 12:5, citing God's power to "cast people into hell."

kataballō [καταβάλλω, *2598*]

kataballō is a rare verb with the passive sense of "being cast (or thrown) down" in the context of persecution in 2 Cor. 4:9. The accuser of the saints is said to "be thrown down" in Rev. 12:10.

aporiptō [ἀπορίπτω, *641*]

aporiptō is a rare verb found only in Acts 27:43 indicating the action of "throwing oneself overboard."

epiriptō [ἐπιρίπτω, *1977*]

epiriptō is another rare verb, found only in 1 Pet. 5:7 and meaning "to cast" all one's cares on the Lord.

katalyō [καταλύω, *2647*]

katalyō is a verb found twenty times with the primary sense of "destroy," as well as "throw down," "overthrow" (as with the Hebrew verbs ***nātaṣ*** and ***hāras,*** above.

Jesus affirms in Matt. 24:2; Mark 13:2; Luke 21:6 that there will be no stone left standing in the temple that "will not be thrown down" on the day of judgment. See also Acts 5:39.

kathaireō [καθαιρέω, *2507*]

kathaireō is a verb found eleven times with the meanings "take down," "destroy," which may also imply the sense of "cast down," "overthrow." God is said to have "cast down" the mighty from their thrones in Luke 1:52. Similarly, God is said to have "destroyed" (i.e., "overthrown") the Canaanite nations in Acts 13:19. See also Acts 19:27. In 2 Cor. 10:5, Paul refers to "destroying" arguments that seek to discredit the gospel.

Additional Notes

Owing to the great variety of senses and shades of meaning conveyed by the concept of "casting" in both Old and New Testaments, it is impossible to pinpoint any particular dynamic equivalence between any two terms. There is, however, a great deal of overlap in meaning. The Hebrew ***nāphal*** and the Greek ***kathaireō*** clearly indicate that the phenomenon of divine judgment, in which God casts down the wicked, exists in both Testaments. The destruction of the wicked depicted in the Old Testament foreshadows the ultimate fate of the ungodly as described in the New.

See Also: → DEPART → DRIVE → LEAVE → REJECT → THRESH

CATCH

OT Words

ṣûd [צוּד, 6679]

This term is found in about fifteen places and means "hunt" (i.e., catch by hunting).

There are several references to God hunting down his people in order to catch them for judgment. It is predicted in Jer. 16:16 and ruefully acknowledged in Lam. 3:52; 4:18. In a similar way, God savagely indicts the false women prophets in Jerusalem through the prophet Ezekiel for preying on (i.e., hunting down) their fellow countrymen, inciting them to reject God by misrepresenting his purposes, and leading the people astray (cf. Ezek. 13:18, 20). Then the psalmist invokes a curse on the wicked, that they might be hunted down by disaster (cf. Ps. 140:11).

At the purely human level, ***ṣûd*** refers metaphorically to the "ensnaring" or "hunting" activity of the prostitute in Prov. 6:26 as she seduces the morally inept young man — a truly fatal attraction. Then, in Mic. 7:2, ***ṣûd*** describes the utter inhumanity of Israelites towards each other when it refers to men hunting each other down with a view to murder.

ṣûd is used twice in the book of Job: once in Job's brazen charge against God that he hunts him like a lion catching his prey (cf. Job 10:16), and once in reference to God questioning Job about whether he has ever caught the prey of a wild animal in order to feed it (cf. Job 38:39).

Finally, on a prosaic level, ***ṣûd*** refers to hunting laws in the Mosaic legislation (cf. Lev. 17:13), and to Esau hunting for game (cf. Gen. 27:3, 5).

NT Words

harpazō [ἁρπάζω, *726*]

harpazō is a verb found in thirteen places with the underlying sense of "take by force." However, in several places ***harpazō*** expresses the passive sense of "being caught up, away." Paul refers to his visionary experience of "being caught up into heaven" in 2 Cor. 12:2ff. The experience of "being caught up" with the Lord at the end of time is recorded in 1 Thess. 4:17. The child is said to "be caught up" to God in Rev. 12:5.

agreuō [ἀγρεύω, *64*]

agreuō is a rare verb meaning "to catch." It is found only in Mark 12:13 with reference to the attempt by Jewish civil and religious leaders to "catch" or "entrap" Jesus in his words.

thēreuō [θηρεύω, *2340*]

thēreuō is a rare verb, synonymous with ***agreuō***, above, describing the attempt by the enemies of Jesus to "catch" him in his speech in order to discredit him. It occurs only in Luke 11:54.

piazō [πιάζω, *4084*]

piazō is a verb found twelve times with the primary senses of "take," "seize." (→ APPREHEND) In two places, the meaning "catch" is indicated: John 21:3, 10 make reference to catching fish.

See Also: → APPREHEND → CAPTIVE → SEIZE

CATTLE

OT Words

miqneh [מִקְנֶה, 4735]

This noun occurs approximately seventy times with the meaning "cattle" or "flocks." Most of these references are found in narrative contexts, with the majority of them located in Genesis, Exodus, and Numbers. In every instance the usage is literal and indicative of personal wealth. The patriarchs are notable in this regard (cf. Gen. 13:2, 7 [Abraham]; Gen. 26:14 [Isaac]; Gen. 30:29 [Jacob]; Job 1:3 [Job himself]).

bāqār **[בָּקָר, 1241]**

bāqār is a generic term signifying "cattle," "herd of cattle" as a collective noun, as well as "bull," "ox" indicating a particular head of cattle. (→ OX)

References to "herd(s) of cattle" include Gen. 13:5; 24:35; Exod. 34:3; Lev. 1:2ff.; Num. 15:3; Deut. 8:13; 15:19; 2 Sam. 12:2; Neh. 10:36. See also Num. 31:28ff.

bāqār also denotes "bull(s)" in Exod. 29:1; Lev. 4:3; 22:19ff.; Num. 15:8; 2 Chr. 13:9ff.; Ps. 66:15; Ezek. 43:19ff. See also Isa. 65:25.

behēmāh **[בְּהֵמָה, 929]**

behēmāh is another collective noun signifying "cattle" and "beast (of burden)" in most of the nearly two hundred occurrences of the term.

General references to "cattle" include Exod. 12:29; Num. 3:41; 31:9; Deut. 3:7; 28:4; Josh. 8:27; Neh. 9:37; Ps. 107:38; Hag. 1:11. The specific creation of "cattle" by God is noted in Gen. 1:24ff.; 2:20; 3:14; Ps. 50:10. "Cattle" are also preserved in Noah's ark (Gen. 6:20; 7:2ff.; 8:1, 17). Reference to "herds of cattle" is found in Gen. 47:18. Lev. 1:2; 5:2 refer to "cattle" set aside for slaughter.

be'îr **[בְּעִיר, 1165]**

be'îr is a noun found in six places referring to "cattle" (cf. Gen. 45:17; Num. 20:4ff.; Ps. 78:48).

NT Words

thremma [θρέμμα, *2353*]

thremma is a rare noun denoting "cattle" in a general sense, found only in John 4:12.

CAUSE

NT Words

aitia [αἰτία, *156*]

The noun ***aitia*** means "cause," "reason" in several of the twenty occurrences of the term. (→ CHARGE)

Matt. 19:3 refers to the "cause" or "reason" for divorce. The "cause," or legal ground, for capital punishment, is noted in Acts 13:28; 28:18.

aition [αἴτιον, *158*]

aition is a rare variant of ***aitia***, above, denoting the total absence of a "cause" (i.e., reason) for capital punishment in relation to Christ at his trial (cf. Luke 23:22). The absence of a "reason" or "cause" for a riot is noted in Acts 19:40. (→ FAULT)

logos [λόγος, *3056*]

logos is a common term denoting "word," "saying," or "speech" in most of the 331 occurrences of the term. In Matt. 5:32, however, ***logos*** denotes a "cause" (i.e., legal ground) of adultery, validating a divorce.

CEASE

OT Words

ḥādal **[חָדַל, 2308]**

This verb means "stop" or "cease," but also has some variation in usage. ***ḥādal*** is found about fifty times in the Old Testament.

In a number of instances, ***ḥādal*** simply refers to the cessation of a particular activity or phenomenon. For example, Joseph stops counting the supply of corn in Egypt after the seven years of plenty (cf. Gen. 41:49). The inhabitants of Babel stop building their tower after God confuses their language (cf. Gen. 11:8). Naomi stops trying to convince Ruth to return to Moab (cf. Ruth 1:18). Baasha. King of Israel, stops his building program at Rama (cf. 1 Kgs. 15:21).

ḥādal occasionally indicates the cessation or suspension of divine judgment: for example, the plague of hail against the Egyptians (cf. Exod. 9:29ff.); Amos' plea to God to suspend his judgment against Israel (cf. Amos 7:5). The term is also used in contexts of divine judgment: for example, the cessation of all gaiety and celebration as a sign of God's judgment (cf. Isa. 24:8); the eradication of Babylon as a fighting force in the face of God's punishment (cf. Jer. 51:30); Ezekiel's reference to the people of Judah refraining from listening to the voice of God (cf. Ezek. 2:5, 7; 3:11, 27).

ḥādal also functions as an imperative to stop or refrain from doing certain things, whether in a human context (cf. 2 Chr. 25:16; 35:21), or in the context of God warning his people to cease from sinful activity (cf. Isa. 1:16; 2:22).

The term is also used in a metaphorical or abstract way: Judg. 5:7, for example, refers to the "ceasing" (i.e., "breakdown") of village and community life in Israel until Deborah arose as judge. Job 19:14 refers to the grave as a place where trouble or turmoil ceases. In Gen. 18:11, ***ḥādal*** is used in a metaphorical expression in reference to Sarah that literally translates: "it ceased to be with her after the way of women" — meaning that she is well past the age of childbearing.

shābat [שָׁבַת, **7673**]

The verb ***shābat*** occurs around seventy times with the primary sense of "cease," "rest." (→ REST)

The meaning "cease," in the sense of "come to an end," occurs in relation to the divine promise that the natural order of the cosmos "will never cease" (cf. Gen. 8:22). Prov. 22:10 refers to the cessation of quarreling. Josh. 5:12 notes that the supply of manna in the wilderness had come to an end.

The meaning "put an end to" (lit. "cause to cease") is found in relation to disputes in Prov. 18:18; and in Isa. 13:11 the action of God is said to "put an end" to pride.

shābat is also translated "cease" in the sense of "stop" in a general sense in Isa. 14:4; 17:3. Josh. 22:25 mentions the situation in which people might "stop" fearing the Lord. See also 2 Chr. 16:5; Neh. 4:11; 6:3; Job 32:1.

In several contexts, God is indicated as the subject of this term — for example, God promises to "put an end" to immorality in Ezek. 23:27ff. Ps. 46:9 affirms that God causes war to cease. In the context of divine judgment, Yahweh is said to "bring joy to an end" for the people of Jerusalem in Jer. 7:34; 16:9; Lam. 5:15; Ezek. 7:24; 26:13; Hos. 2:11. Similarly, there is the promise to "put an end" to the kingdom of Israel in Hos. 1:4. Jer. 31:36 speaks of the hypothetical "cessation" of the fixed order of the cosmos if God's promises ever fail to come to pass. See also Ezek. 16:41; 30:10.

Dan. 9:27 contains a prophecy concerning the Messiah who will "put an end" to sacrifice (i.e., cause it to cease).

——— NT Words ———

pauō [παύω, *3973*]

pauō is a verb found fifteen times with the meaning "cease" in a variety of contexts.

General references to the action of "ceasing" or "stopping" are found in Acts 20:1; 1 Pet. 4:1. ***pauō*** is also used in relation to the cessation of speaking in Luke 5:4. The miracle of Christ "putting an end" to a storm is recorded in Luke 8:24. 1 Cor. 13:8 contains the promise that tongues "would cease." Luke 11:1 records that Jesus "finished" his praying. Eph. 1:16; Col. 1:9 both refer to Paul's practice of "never ceasing" to pray. Acts 5:42 notes that the apostles "never stopped" preaching the gospel. See also Acts 6:13; 20:31; Heb. 10:2.

dialeipō [διαλείπω, *1257*]

dialeipō is a rare verb found only in Luke 7:45 referring to the actions of a woman who never "stopped" kissing Jesus' feet during a visit to a Pharisee's home.

kopazō [κοπάζω, *2869*]

kopazō is a rare verb found only in Matt. 14:32; Mark 4:39; 6:51. It refers to the wind "ceasing" at the command of Christ.

adialeiptōs [ἀδιαλείπτως, *89*]

adialeiptōs is an adverb meaning "without ceasing," "constantly." It is used in the context of praying in Rom. 1:9; 1 Thess. 2:13; 5:17. See also 1 Thess. 1:3.

——— *Additional Notes* ———

Owing to the variety of meanings and nuances associated with the idea of "ceasing," it is difficult to draw any precise dynamic equivalent between Old and New Testament terms. Since ***ḥādal*** does not exhaust the idea of "cessation" in the Old Testament, other Hebrew terms, such as those for "rest" and "finish," need to be included. The Greek terms cited above that most closely approximate the sense of ***ḥādal*** are ***pauō*** and ***kopazō***.

See Also: → FINISH → REST

CEDAR

——— OT Words ———

'erez [אֶרֶז, **730**]

'erez denotes "cedar" wood and also, less frequently, "cedar tree." It occurs around seventy times.

Lev. 14:4ff., 49ff.; Num. 19:6 refer to cedar wood for ritual offerings. ***'erez*** is used for house construction in 2 Sam. 7:2; 1 Kgs. 6:9ff.; and for temple construction in 1 Kgs. 7:3ff.

The cedar trees of Lebanon are noted in Judg. 9:15; 2 Sam. 5:11; 1 Kgs. 4:33; 9:11; 2 Kgs. 14:9; Ezra 3:7; Ps. 92:12; Isa. 2:13; Ezek. 27:5; Zech. 11:1, 2. Other general references to cedar include Job 40:17; Pss. 29:5; 80:10; Song 5:15; Jer. 22:7; Ezek. 17:3, 22ff.; Amos 2:8.

'arzāh [אַרְזָה, **731**]

'arzāh is a rare noun denoting "cedar work" in construction, found only in Zeph. 2:14.

CERTAIN, CERTAINTY → SAFE → TRUST

CHAFF

——— OT Words ———

teben [תֶּבֶן, **8401**]

This noun is found seventeen times and is translated "straw" on all but two occasions. These two texts refer to "chaff" or "stubble."

teben refers to straw as animal fodder on six occasions (cf. Gen. 24:25, 32; Judg. 19:19; 1 Kgs. 4:28; Isa. 11:7; 65:25). Exod. 5, which describes the Egyptians forcing the Israelites to find their own straw to make bricks instead of supplying them with it (cf. Exod. 5:7–18), frequently uses the word. The word is used metaphorically in Job, once translated as "straw" (cf. Job 41:27) and once as "stubble" (cf. Job 21:18). Finally, ***teben*** is found in Jer. 23:28, where it also refers metaphorically to the word of the false prophet as "straw," in contrast to the truth of God's word (i.e., the "grain").

mōṣ [מֹץ, 4671]

This term is quite rare, occurring only eight times. It is translated as "chaff" on each occasion. All references to ***mōṣ*** are metaphorical, describing the fate of the wicked in being "blown" or "driven away" by God. In most cases ***mōṣ*** refers to the wicked in general (cf. Job 21:18; Pss. 1:4; 35:5; Isa. 17:13; 29:5; 41:15), but in two texts the term refers to Israel's judgment (cf. Hos. 13:3), and to Judah's punishment (Zeph. 2:2).

qash [קַשׁ, 7179]

This synonym for ***mōṣ***, above, is found on sixteen occasions. ***qash*** is consistently translated "chaff" or "stubble." In one case the term refers to literal stubble in connection with Israel's brick-making activities during their Egyptian captivity (cf. Exod. 5:12).

On every other occasion, the term is used metaphorically. In Job, for instance, ***qash*** refers to "chaff" in contexts indicating that which is both useless and fragile (cf. Job 13:25; 41:28, 29). Then, as with ***mōṣ***, ***qash*** refers to God's judgment on the wicked, whom he discards and destroys just like chaff. This punishment is meted out, for example, to the kings of the earth (cf. Isa. 41:2); to Babylon (cf. Isa. 47:14); to Edom (cf. Obad. 18); to Nineveh (cf. Nah. 1:10); as well as to God's own people (cf. Isa. 5:24; Mal. 4:1).

NT Words

achyron [ἄχυρον, *892*]

achyron is a rare noun denoting "chaff," the stalk of produce from which the grain has been harvested, found only in Matt. 3:12; Luke 3:17.

Additional Notes

Although the New Testament use of ***achyron*** is rare, it bears a close affinity with the symbolism of "chaff" in the Old Testament. The Hebrew terms ***mōṣ*** and ***qash*** clearly embrace the idea of divine judgment upon the wicked. Thus the metaphor of "chaff" as a symbol of such judgment is applicable to both old and new covenant eras.

CHAIN → BIND

CHANGE

OT Words

ḥālaph [חָלַף, 2498]

This verb is found about thirty times with the meanings "pass on," "pass through" as well as "change." ***ḥālaph*** is translated "change" in nine of these passages.

In mundane or non-theological contexts, ***ḥālaph*** refers to changing one's clothes in Gen. 35:2; 41:14; 2 Sam. 12:20; and, in the case of Jacob's employment with Laban, to changing his wages (cf. Gen. 31:7, 41).

Isa. 24:5 refers to the disobedience of the nations in violating — "changing," "altering" — the laws of God. Then, in Isa. 9:10, the northern kingdom of Israel boasts that they will be effective in restoring the land, particularly in replacing (i.e., "changing") the trees that have been destroyed. However, God decrees that they will never succeed in doing so. Finally, Ps. 102:26 makes the profound declaration that while the heavens and the earth will be dramatically changed, God will always maintain his control, never changing in the slightest.

ḥalîphāh [חֲלִיפָה, 2487]

This noun is derived from the verb ***ḥālaph*** and occurs ten times with the meaning "change of clothes" (cf. Gen. 45:22; Judg. 14:12, 19; 2 Kgs. 5:22, 23). In 1 Kgs. 5:14 the term refers to the groups of tradesmen sent by Hiram King of Tyre to Solomon, to assist with the construction of the temple. In this verse, ***ḥalîphāh*** refers to the groups of men traveling down from Phoenicia in "shifts." In Ps. 55:19 the psalmist pronounces judgment on his enemies, because they show no intention of "changing" their wicked ways.

mûr [מוּר, 4171]

The verb ***mûr*** is another relatively rare term that means "change" or "exchange." It occurs eight times with this sense. In Lev. 27:10, 33 Israelites are forbidden to exchange animals for sacrifice once they have been passed as ritually acceptable (cf. also Ezek. 48:11). Ps. 106:20 cites Israel's idolatry at the foot of Mt. Sinai when they built a golden calf and worshiped it, thereby "exchanging" the glory of God for a worthless idol (cf. also Hos. 4:7; Jer. 2:11 for a similar indictment). Still on the theme of judgment, Jer. 48:11 contains an unusual metaphor in which Moab's "scent" is described as "unchanged." That is, the nation is still ripe for God's judgment. A similar threat of judgment with respect to the northern kingdom of Israel is found in Mic. 2:4.

hāphak [**הָפַךְ, 2015**]

Although it occurs nearly one hundred times, this verb is translated "change" on only two occasions: Lev. 13:55; Jer. 13:23.

shenā' [**שְׁנָא, 8133** (Aramaic)]

shenā' is an Aramaic verb meaning "change," "alter" throughout most of the twenty or so occurrences of the term.

The terrible consequences of "changing" a royal edict are indicated in Ezra 6:11ff. Dan. 6:8, 15, 17 describe the laws of the Medes and Persians that "can never be changed."

God's power to "change" times and seasons is noted in Dan. 2:21. A "change" or "alteration" of physical appearance is noted in Dan. 3:19ff. See also Dan. 2:9. The "alteration" of a person's countenance is recorded in Dan. 5:6ff.

Dan. 4:16 describes the "changing" of a person's heart.

NT Words

metathesis [**μετάθεσις**, *3331*]

metathesis is a rare noun denoting a "change" in the law in Heb. 7:12.

allassō [**ἀλλάσσω**, *236*]

allassō is a verb found six times with the meanings "change," "exchange." Acts 6:14 refers to "changing" the customs of the law. The perversity of "exchanging" the glory of God for the worship of idols is indicated in Rom. 1:23. The experience of "being changed (i.e., transformed)" at the end of time in preparation for glory is described in 1 Cor. 15:51, 52; Heb. 1:12. See also Gal. 4:20.

metallassō [**μεταλλάσσω**, *3337*]

metallassō is a rare synonym of ***allassō***, above. The term indicates the process of idolatry whereby unbelievers "exchanged" the truth of God for a lie in Rom. 1:25. Rom. 1:26 mentions the morally perverse "exchanging" of heterosexual for homosexual desire.

metatithēmi [**μετατίθημι**, *3346*]

The verb ***metatithēmi*** refers to the "changing" of the priesthood necessitating a corresponding change of the law as noted in Heb. 7:12.

metaballō [**μεταβάλλω**, *3328*]

metaballō is a rare verb referring to "the changing" of one's mind, found only in Acts 28:6.

Additional Notes

Because the Hebrew terminology for "change" encompasses a relatively broad spectrum of meaning, there is a limited degree of overlap in meaning with the New Testament vocabulary (but no full dynamic equivalence). Rom. 1:25, 26, however, contains a clear parallel with the Old Testament in that the Greek word ***metallassō*** suggests the same attitude of idolatry of which Israel was guilty at Mt. Sinai, indicated by the word ***mûr***.

See Also: → EXCHANGE → TURN

CHARGE

NT Words

aitia [**αἰτία**, *156*]

aitia is a noun occurring in twenty contexts with the primary meaning "cause," or "reason," as well as "charge," "accusation." (→ CAUSE)

The meaning "charge" in a legal sense is indicated in a number of places with reference to the accusation against Christ as "the King of the Jews" (cf. Matt. 27:37; Mark 15:26); other contexts recording "(legal) accusation" include Acts 23:28; 25:27. In John 19:4ff. Pilate fails to find any "(legal) grounds" for prosecution against Christ. See also Acts 13:28; 25:18.

aitiōma [**αἰτίωμα**, *157*]

aitiōma is a rare noun denoting a legal "charge" or "complaint" in Acts 25:7.

enklēma [**ἔγκλημα**, *1462*]

enklēma is a rare synonym for ***aitia*** and ***aitiōma***, above, denoting a "(legal) charge" in judicial contexts, found only in Acts 23:29; 25:16.

parangelia [**παραγγελία**, *3852*]

parangelia is a noun denoting a "charge," or "instruction" in Acts 16:24; 1 Tim. 1:18.

adapanos [ἀδάπανος, *77*]

adapanos is a rare adjectival form meaning "free of charge" (i.e., at no cost), found only in 1 Cor. 9:18.

diamartyromai [διαμαρτύρομαι, *1263*]

diamartyromai is a verb meaning "testify" in most of the fifteen occurrences of the term. The term also means "to charge" in the sense of "to give a solemn instruction or exhortation" as found in 1 Tim. 5:21; 2 Tim. 2:14; 2 Tim. 4:1; Heb. 2:6. (→ WITNESS)

diastellomai [διαστέλλομαι, *1291*]

diastellomai is a verb found nine times with the meaning "to charge" in the sense of "issue strict instructions." It is used in the context of Jesus' exhortations to his disciples (cf. Matt. 16:20; Mark 5:43; 9:9). See also Acts 15:24; Heb. 12:20.

embrimaomai [ἐμβριμάομαι, *1690*]

The verb ***embrimaomai*** means to "give a solemn charge, or instruction" and is found in Matt. 9:30; Mark 1:43.

enkaleō [ἐγκαλέω, *1458*]

enkaleō is a verb found in seven places with the meaning "accuse," "lay a charge against" in each of these contexts (cf. Acts 19:38ff.; 23:28ff.; 26:2ff.; Rom. 8:33).

exorkizō [ἐξορκίζω, *1844*]

exorkizō is a rare verb meaning "to charge" or "to issue a solemn injunction" found only in Matt. 26:63.

horkizō [ὁρκίζω, *3726*]

horkizō is a verb found in three places meaning to "give a solemn charge to" (cf. Mark 5:7; Acts 19:13; 1 Thess. 5:27)

See Also: → COMMAND → DISPUTE → INIQUITY → REBUKE → WITNESS

CHARIOT

OT Words

rekeb [רֶכֶב, **7393**]

This noun is found just over one hundred times in the Old Testament, and it is consistently translated "chariot," referring to the classic horse-drawn military vehicle of the day. ***rekeb*** is found throughout the Old Testament, but the term predominates in the historical narratives of the Former Prophets and Chronicles. Almost two-thirds of the occurrences of ***rekeb*** are found in this section of the Old Testament.

There are, in addition, one or two unusual uses of ***rekeb***. The first of these concerns the supernatural manner of Elijah's departure from this world. 2 Kgs. 2:11, 12 record the prophet's transport to heaven in a flaming chariot, indicating that he was one of only two men in Scripture to have the privilege of bypassing natural death (the other was Enoch in Gen. 5:24). Then, shortly after this incident, Elisha is given a divine guarantee that the siege of the city of Samaria by the Arameans would be short lived. The particular assistance from God came in the shape of a heavenly "army" composed of "chariots of fire" (2 Kgs. 6:17).

merkābāh [מֶרְכָּבָה, **4818**]

This is a synonym for ***rekeb***, above, occurring about forty times with a similar distribution throughout the Old Testament. ***merkābāh*** likewise has a predominantly literal, historical sense, although the term also figures in several symbolic, prophetic oracles indicating both divine judgment and salvation (cf. Isa. 66:15; Hag. 2:22; Zech. 6:1ff.).

NT Words

harma [ἅρμα, *716*]

harma is a rare noun found in only four places denoting a "chariot" in each case. Three of these are literal references (cf. Acts 8:28ff.); and a symbolic reference is found in Rev. 9:9.

rheda [ῥέδα, *4480*]

rheda is a rare noun of Latin origin denoting a "chariot," found only in Rev. 18:13.

CHASTEN, CHASTISE, CHASTISEMENT

NT Words

paideuō [παιδεύω, *3811*]

paideuō is a verb found in fifteen places with the sense of "chasten," "chastise" as well as "learn," "instruct." (→ INSTRUCT)

In Luke 23:16, 22, the meaning "chastise" conveys the sense of "flog with a whip," utilized in the context of Christ's pre-crucifixion suffering at the hands of the Romans.

The meaning "to chasten" in the sense of "exercise discipline" or "punish" is used exclusively in the contexts of divine punishment directed towards his people (cf. 1 Cor. 11:32; 2 Cor. 6:9; Heb. 12:6ff.; Rev. 3:19).

paideia [παιδεία, *3809*]

paideia is a noun derived from ***paideuō*** (see above) found in six places with the sense of "chastening" or "discipline" from the Lord (cf. Heb. 12:5ff.).

See Also: → ADMONISH → CORRECT → INSTRUCT

CHERUBIM

OT Words

kerûbîm [**כְּרוּבִים, 3742**]

kerûbîm denotes a "cherub," an angelic being depicted as an attendant of the throne of God. The term is found in the context of the Israelite tabernacle and temple as well as in the visionary contexts of prophetic revelation.

Cherubim are also recorded as the guardians of the way back to the garden of Eden preventing the return of Adam and Eve (cf. Gen. 3:24).

The golden cherubim cast on the lid of the ark of the covenant symbolizing the heavenly guardians of the divine throne are noted in Exod. 25:18ff.; 37:7ff.; Num. 7:89; 1 Sam. 4:4; 1 Kgs. 6:23ff.; 8:6ff.; 2 Chr. 3:10ff.; 5:7. See also Pss. 80:1; 99:1; Isa. 37:16. Cherubim are also embroidered on the tabernacle curtains (Exod. 26:1, 31; 2 Chr. 3:14).

Cherubim are revealed to Ezekiel in the prophet's visionary experience in Ezek. 10:1ff.; 11:22. See also Ezek. 41:18ff.

NT Words

cheroubim [χερουβίμ, *5502*]

cheroubim is the Greek transcription of the Hebrew term ***kerûbîm*** (see above) denoting these creatures as the guardians of the heavenly throne. It is found only in Heb. 9:5.

Additional Notes

The Hebrew term ***kerûbîm*** occurs about eighty times, and on each occasion it refers to these angelic beings — principally in connection with the ark of the covenant in both the tabernacle and the temple. The bulk of the remaining references are found in Ezek. 10, where the prophet is given a vision of the glory cloud abandoning the temple in Jerusalem. In this vision, Ezekiel identifies the heavenly creatures that surround the image of the sapphire throne as cherubim. These cherubim are identified as the same creatures that the prophet saw in his vision by the Kebar River, recorded in Ezek. 1 (although the word ***kerûbîm*** does not occur here). This vision gives the prophet a unique insight into the heavenly reality lying behind the symbolism inherent in the furniture of the Jerusalem temple. The ark of the covenant represents the throne of God in heaven, and Ezekiel witnesses the likeness of that throne in this divine revelation. The context is one of divine judgment against sin, in which God abandons the temple and sends his people into exile.

CHIEF

OT Words

rōʾsh [**רֹאשׁ, 7218**]

This is a common term, occurring nearly six hundred times with various meanings relating to the basic idea of "head" in both a literal and a metaphorical sense. (→ HEAD) As well as referring to the head as part of the human body, ***rōʾsh*** signifies "chief"; "ruler (both civil and military)"; "king"; "(chief) priest"; "Levitical chief"; "prince." It refers to the idea of "chief" in various contexts.

By far the most common usage of ***rōʾsh*** is in regard to civil leadership among the tribes and clans of Israel. It means "chief" or "ruler" in this sense in a number of places (cf. Num. 7:2; 13:3; 25:4; Deut. 1:13ff.; 5:23; Josh. 14:1; 19:51; 22:14; 1 Chr. 5–9; Mic. 3:1, 9; Hab. 3:14). In Judg. 11:8ff., ***rōsh*** describes the office to which Jephthah was appointed by the leaders of Gilead. In this case, Jephthah was appointed a "chief" or "ruler" in both a military and a civil capacity. The biblical term that expresses this function is "judge," which is used as a synonym for ***rōʾsh***. (→ JUDGE)

The use of ***rōʾsh*** to indicate a military chief or commander is found almost exclusively in 1 and 2 Chronicles (e.g., 1 Chr. 11:6; 27:1, 3). Of particular note are the references to the mighty men of David (cf. 1 Chr. 11:10ff.); also the leaders of David's private army (cf. 1 Chr. 12:3–32). Then, in 2 Chr. 13:12, the Judean king Abijah declares that God is the commander-in-chief of the people. See also Num. 14:4; Neh. 9:17 for ***rōʾsh*** with this military connotation.

The other significant element in the meanings associated with ***rōʾsh*** as "chief" is in the ceremonial sphere, where the term refers to the leaders of the priestly and Levitical class. Once again, it is the Chronicler who utilizes this meaning most frequently. See also 1 Chr. 9:33ff.; 2 Kgs. 25:18; Ezra 7:5; Neh. 11:16; 12:7, 24, 46; Jer. 52:24.

rō'sh also refers to kings in the sense of "chief" or "ruler" on a number of occasions — for example, Saul (cf. 1 Sam. 15:17); Rezin of Damascus (cf. Isa. 7:8); Remaliah of Samaria (cf. Isa. 7:9); Gog of Magog (cf. Ezek. 38:2, 3; 39:1).

NT Words

prōtos [πρῶτος, *4413*]

prōtos is an adjectival term with the primary sense of "first" for most of the 100 or so occurrences of the term. In several places it means "chief," referring to the "chief" civil rulers of the Jews in Luke 19:47; Acts 13:50; 25:2; 28:17. Acts 16:12 refers to Philippi as the "chief" or "leading" city of Macedonia. See also Acts 17:4; 28:7; 1 Tim. 1:15.

archipoimēn [ἀρχιποίμην, *750*]

archipoimēn is a rare term denoting Christ as the "chief shepherd," found only in 1 Pet. 5:4.

akrogōniaios [ἀκρογωνιαῖος, *204*]

akrogōniaios is a rare term denoting Christ as the "chief cornerstone" of the heavenly temple in Eph. 2:20; 1 Pet. 2:6. This is a metaphor for Christ's status as the foundation of the kingdom of God.

Additional Notes

There are so many senses associated with the term "chief" in both Old and New Testaments that is impossible to precisely identify true dynamic equivalence between any Greek and Hebrew terms. What is clear is that both the Hebrew and Greek terminology, whether one is talking about a ritual, civil, military, or royal sphere, communicate the inherent authority of leadership.

See Also: ➟ PRIEST ➟ RULE

CHILD, CHILDLESS

OT Words

na'ar [נַעַר, **5288**]

This term means "boy," "lad," "youth," "young man," "servant," and occurs about 230 times throughout the Old Testament. ***na'ar*** is predominantly male in its reference, and translates "child" or "children" in a general sense only infrequently, mostly in the book of Proverbs. With reference to male children, excluding the senses of "young man" or "servant," ***na'ar*** occurs about seventy times.

Reference to specific individuals as "boys" or "lads" constitutes the bulk of the usage of ***na'ar***: for example, Ishmael (cf. Gen. 21:12–20); Benjamin (cf. Gen. 44:22ff.); Moses (cf. Exod. 2:6); Samson (cf. Judg. 13:5ff.); Samuel (cf. 1 Sam. 1:22ff.; 2:17ff.); David (cf. 1 Sam. 17:33ff.); the Shunammite's son (cf. 2 Kgs. 2:19ff.). In Isa. 7:16; 8:4, ***na'ar*** refers to the child of promise in the Immanuel sign given to King Ahaz of Judah by the prophet Isaiah. In the first instance, it is the child born to Isaiah, Maher-Shalal-Hash-Baz, that is in view. However, in this boy there is invested a powerful metaphor that designates him as a symbolic figure anticipating the coming of the messianic ruler who will bring into effect the ultimate deliverance of his people from their bondage to sin and death. The New Testament makes it clear that this Isaianic prophecy comes to full expression in the person of Jesus Christ.

na'arāh [נַעֲרָה, **5291**]

This is the feminine form of ***na'ar*** and is found approximately sixty times meaning "young woman," "maid." (➟ MAID) However, 2 Kgs. 5:2, 4 refers to the little slave girl of Naaman, the Syrian general who came to Elisha in order to find a cure for his leprosy.

yeled [יֶלֶד, **3206**]

Largely synonymous with ***na'ar***, above, ***yeled*** refers to children of both genders in a number of cases. This term is found approximately eighty times with the various meanings "child (male and female)," "son," "boy," "youth."

yeled occurs approximately sixty times meaning "child." For example, it refers to Ishmael (cf. Gen. 21:8ff.); the Israelite children rescued by the courageous Hebrew midwives in Egypt (cf. Exod. 1:17f.); Moses (Exod. 2:3ff.); the child (boy) of the Zarephath widow miraculously brought back to life by Elijah (cf. 1 Kgs. 17:21ff.). See also 2 Kgs. 4:18, 26, 34.

Isa. 9:6 refers to the Messianic King, born to be the Savior and Redeemer of his people (cf. also Isa. 7:14 [***na'ar***]). Isa. 51:4 uses ***yeled*** metaphorically to describe the Israelite people as "children of liars." Similarly, in Hos. 1:2, the offspring born to Gomer are indicted as "children of adultery," representative of the people of Israel who have turned their backs on Yahweh, worshiped pagan idols, and are therefore guilty of gross spiritual adultery against their God and "husband." In a much more positive sense, ***yeled*** refers to Israel as a child dear to the heart of God, in spite of her sin (Jer. 31:20).

Other mundane uses of ***yeled*** in reference to children in general are found in several contexts (cf. Ezra 10:1; Neh. 12:43; Job 21:11; 39:3; Eccl. 4:13, 15; Isa. 29:23).

yaldāh [**יַלְדָּה, 3207**]

This feminine form of ***yeled***, translated as "girl" or "young woman" is found only three times: Gen. 34:4; Joel 3:3; Zech. 8:5.

yāḥîd [**יָחִיד, 3173**]

This is a rare term which carries the force of both an adjective and a noun, meaning "only" or "solitary" and "only one" (i.e., "only child"). ***yāḥîd*** occurs only ten times, six of which refer to an only child. Gen. 22:2, 16 both refer to Isaac as the only son of Abraham, during God's testing of his servant whereby he asked the patriarch to sacrifice the boy on Mt. Moriah. Judg. 11:34 refers to the only daughter of Jephthah, who felt compelled to sacrifice his daughter because of his own oath. Jer. 6:26 and Amos 8:10 both utilize the term ***yāḥîd*** to refer to the people of Yahweh as an"only child," fit for divine judgment, and for whom they would mourn. Finally, Zech. 12:10 contains the profound messianic prophecy that anticipates the agony of Christ on the cross as God's "only son."

'arîrî [**עֲרִירִי, 6185**]

This term is translated "childless" and is found only four times. In Gen. 15:2, Abram is puzzled by the divine promise to make him the father of a great nation, since he is childless. Lev. 20:20, 21 invoke the curse of barrenness on those who engage in illicit sexual intercourse. Jer. 22:30 contains a solemn pronouncement of judgment against King Jehoiachin of Judah for his wickedness. The judgment takes the form of a divine proclamation: "Record this man as if he were childless!" In fact, Jehoiachin did produce offspring, who lived in and beyond the exile, but who never assumed the throne of Judah.

shakkûl [**שַׁכּוּל, 7909**]; ***shākōl*** [**שָׁכֹל, 7921**]

These terms are rare, meaning childlessness — usually through bereavement. They are found in the following texts, all referring to this condition as a specific judgment from God: Isa. 49:20, 21; Jer. 18:21. Other references are metaphorical, indicating a bear robbed of her cubs (cf. 2 Sam. 17:18; Hos. 13:8; Prov. 17:12).

NT Words

teknon [**τέκνον,** ***5043***]

teknon is one of the common terms for "child" or "children" found in about one hundred contexts.

Literal references to children include Matt. 2:18; Mark 10:29; Luke 1:7; 20:31; Acts 7:5; 1 Cor. 7:14; Eph. 6:1ff.; Col. 3:20ff.; 1 Tim. 3:4; Titus 1:6.

Christ referred to his disciples as "children" as a term of endearment (cf. Mark 10:24). Other metaphorical uses of the term include references to Abraham's spiritual descendants as "children" in Luke 3:8; John 8:39. "Children" of wisdom are noted in Luke 7:35. Several texts describe believers as "children" of God (e.g., John 1:12; 11:52; Rom. 8:16ff.; 9:7ff.; Gal. 4:27ff.; Eph. 5:1; 1 Tim. 1:2; 1 John 3:10; 2 John 1). In 1 Cor. 4:14, Paul uses "children" as a term of endearment for his congregation in Corinth. Gal. 4:25 refers to "children" as a symbol for the nation of Israel under the old covenant. The phrase "children of wrath" designates those under divine condemnation in Eph. 2:3. The infant Messiah is described as a "child" in the vision of Rev. 12:4ff.

teknion [**τεκνίον,** ***5040***]

teknion is a diminutive form of ***teknon*** (see above) with the meaning "little child." Each of its nine occurrences refer metaphorically to one's congregation and/or fellow believers under one's pastoral care (cf. John 13:33; Gal. 4:19; 1 John 2:1, 12, 28; 3:7, 18; 4:4; 5:21).

pais [**παῖς,** ***3816***]

The noun ***pais*** means "servant," "child." The former sense is the most common. (→ SERVANT)

General references to "child," including "boy," are found in Matt. 17:18; 21:15; Luke 9:42. In particular, Luke 2:43; Acts 4:27, 30 refer to the "child" Jesus.

paidion [**παιδίον,** ***3813***]

paidion is a diminutive form of ***pais*** (see above) meaning "little child," "young child" throughout its nearly fifty occurrences.

The literal sense of "little child" is indicated in Matt. 2:8ff.; 18:2ff.; 19:13ff.; Luke 1:59, 66, 76; 2:17ff. The term "little children" refers metaphorically to one's congregation in 1 John 2:13, 18.

Elsewhere ***paidion*** denotes "child," "children" in general contexts (e.g., Matt. 14:21; Mark 5:39ff.; 10:13ff.; Luke 11:27; 18:16ff.; John 16:21; Heb. 11:23).

Jesus uses ***paidion***, "children," as a term of endearment for his disciples (cf. John 21:5). It is also a designation for the people of God in Heb. 2:13.

paidarion [**παιδάριον,** ***3808***]

paidarion is another diminutive form of ***pais*** (see above), a rare term denoting "child," "children" in Matt. 11:16; John 6:9.

nēpios [νήπιος, *3516*]

nēpios is found in fourteen places with primary reference to "babies," "infant children." ***nēpios*** is used literally in Matt. 11:25; 21:16; Luke 10:21. It is used metaphorically to refer to "babes in Christ" (i.e., immature believers) in 1 Cor. 3:1; Eph. 4:14; Heb. 5:13 (cf. also 1 Cor. 13:11). The meaning "child" in a general sense is indicated in Gal. 4:1ff.

nepiazō [νηπιάζω, *3515*]

nepiazō is a rare verb with the meaning to "be, act like a child" found only in 1 Cor. 14:20, in relation to spiritual maturity.

teknotropheō [τεκνοτροφέω, *5044*]

teknotropheō is a rare verb found only in 1 Tim. 5:10, meaning "to bring up children."

teknogoneō [τεκνογονέω, *5041*]

teknogoneō is a rare verb with the meaning "to bear children," found only in 1 Tim. 5:14.

enkyos [ἔγκυος, *1471*]

enkyos is a rare adjective indicating the state of pregnancy — "expecting a child" — found only in Luke 2:5 and referring to Mary, the mother of Jesus.

ateknos [ἄτεκνος, *815*]

ateknos is an adjective found in three places with reference to the state of being "without children," "childless" (cf. Luke 20:28ff.).

Additional Notes

Here again it is difficult to identify any precise dynamic equivalents between the Hebrew and Greek terminology for "children." Of all the Hebrew terms discussed above, only ***yeled*** and ***na'ar*** are used both literally and metaphorically. Theologically speaking, the prophecies concerning the messianic child of promise are of the greatest significance. However, the Hebrew terminology does not offer the breadth of perspective that the Greek does.

While the Hebrew usage discussed above clearly indicates that childlessness is by and large a judgment from God, such a perspective is absent from the New Testament.

See Also: → BABE → BARREN → SERVANT → SON

CHOICE, CHOOSE

OT Words

bāḥar [בָּחַר, 977]

This verb occurs about 170 times in the Old Testament with the consistent meaning "choose." About two-thirds of these references indicate choices made by God, and about one-third point to choices made by humans.

bāḥar is found in several different contexts regarding human choice. One significant use of the term has a decidedly negative connotation, in that it refers to Israel choosing to worship idols rather than Yahweh (cf. Judg. 5:8; 10:14; Isa. 40:20; 41:24). ***bāḥar*** also frequently refers to the choosing of men for battle (cf. Exod. 17:9; 1 Sam. 13:2; 1 Kgs. 12:21; 1 Chr. 19:10; 2 Chr. 25:5). ***bāḥar*** is also found in a number of contexts that indicate moral choice of one kind or another. For example, Deut. 30:19 contains Moses' exhortation to the people of Israel to choose life by trusting in Yahweh and obeying his covenant laws. See also Josh. 24:15, 22. Ps. 119:30, 173 emphasize the importance of choosing God's laws and precepts. Exod. 18:25 points out that Moses chose seventy able men to assist him in the task of leading the Israelites and resolving their civil and legal inquiries as well as their disputes. Prov. 3:31 warns against making wrong moral choices while Isa. 65:12; 66:3 both refer to the people of Israel actually falling into that trap. Finally, there is the interesting, though very painful, choice God placed before the people of Israel when they were required to choose a method of divine punishment that God would inevitably bring to bear on account of their sinfulness (cf. 2 Sam. 24:12; 1 Chr. 21:10).

The occurrence of ***bāḥar*** is most significant when the action is predicated of God himself. In particular, ***bāḥar*** is used to indicate the divine selection of Israel as his special people (cf. Deut. 14:2; 1 Kgs. 3:8; Ps. 33:12; Isa. 14:1; 41:8, 9; 43:10; 44:1; Jer. 33:24; Ezek. 20:5). Associated with this choice is the divine designation of Jerusalem as the focal point of God's presence among his people. This is given particular emphasis in the book of Deuteronomy (cf. Deut. 12:5ff.; 14:23ff.; 26:2; 31:11). As a consequence of God choosing this one place in which his name would dwell, Jerusalem assumed the status of Israel's most significant city. While the name "Jerusalem" is not actually found in the Deuteronomy texts, it is clearly implied and confirmed by the broader context of the historical narratives that follow. In this regard see also 1 Kgs. 8:16; 2 Kgs. 23:27; Neh. 1:9; Zech. 1:17; 2:12; 3:2.

The choice of priests as mediators of the old covenant is also clearly understood as a divine prerogative (cf. Num. 16:5, 7; Deut. 18:5; 1 Sam. 2:28; 1 Chr. 15:2; 29:11; Ps. 105:26).

Several individuals are singled out for particular mention as objects of divine favor and choice: for example, David (cf. 2 Sam. 6:21; 1 Kgs. 8:16; Ps. 89:19); Solomon (cf. 1 Chr. 28:5, 10); Zerubbabel (cf. Hag. 2:23); and the Servant of Yahweh (cf. Isa. 49:7). There is a strong messianic element associated with the divine designation of each of these people — especially David and the Servant figure.

The judgment of God is also depicted as something reserved for divine choice — both against his own people (cf. Isa. 66:4); as well as against pagan nations (cf. Jer. 49:19; 50:44).

bāḥîr [בָּחִיר, 972]

bāḥîr is an adjective derived from the verb ***bāḥar*** and refers to the elect of God, his "chosen ones" (cf. 2 Sam. 21:6; 1 Chr. 16:13; Pss. 89:3; 105:6, 43; 106:5, 23; Isa. 42:1; 43:20; 45:4; 65:9ff.).

mibḥār [מִבְחָר, 4005]

mibḥār is a noun found in around twenty places, used adjectivally with the meaning "choice," or "best."

The term is used in relation to tombs (Gen. 23:6); and to trees (Isa. 37:24; Jer. 22:7; Ezek. 24:4ff.).

Other references include Deut. 12:11; 2 Kgs. 3:19; 19:23; Ezek. 31:16.

NT Words

eklegomai [ἐκλέγομαι, *1586*]

eklegomai is a verb occurring about twenty times and meaning "choose."

In the context of divine election, God is said to "choose" his people in Mark 13:20; Acts 13:17; 15:7; Eph. 1:4. In 1 Cor. 1:27ff. God is said to "choose" the foolish things of the world to shame the wise.

Jesus "choosing" his disciples is recorded in Luke 6:13; John 6:70; 13:18; 15:16ff.; Acts 1:2, 24.

Other general references to people exercising choice are found in Luke 10:42; 14:7; Acts 15:22, 25. Acts 6:5 refers to "choosing" deacons in the early church.

epilegō [ἐπιλέγω, *1951*]

epilegō is a rare verb with the meaning "choose" in Acts 15:40 in relation to Paul's choice of a traveling companion.

haireomai [αἱρέομαι, *138*]

haireomai is a rare verb synonymous with ***eklegomai*** and ***epilegō***, above, again meaning "choose" in only three places.

The choice of human beings is indicated in Phil. 1:22. Moses' choosing to side with the people of Israel is recorded in Heb. 2:13. God's elective "choosing" of believers is noted in 2 Thess. 2:13.

hairetizō [αἱρετίζω, *140*]

hairetizō is a rare verb found only in Matt. 12:18 with reference to God having "chosen" his Servant Son.

procheirotoneō [προχειροτονέω, *4401*]

procheirotoneō is a rare verb meaning "choose (beforehand)" in the context of God having already chosen those who would witness the post-resurrection appearances of Christ (cf. Acts 10:41).

eklektos [ἐκλεκτός, *1588*]

eklektos is an adjective meaning "elect," "chosen" throughout its approximately twenty occurrences.

The process of "being chosen" by God in the context of being joined to his people is noted in Matt. 20:16; 22:14. Christ is designated as God's "chosen one" in Luke 23:35; 1 Pet. 2:4ff. Believers are described as a "chosen generation" in 1 Pet. 2:9.

The "elect" (i.e., chosen by God) specifically refers to the body of believers worldwide (cf. Matt. 24:22ff.; Mark 13:20ff.; Luke 18:7; Rom. 8:33; Col. 3:12; 2 Tim. 2:10; Titus 1:1; 1 Pet. 1:2; 2 John 1, 13; Rev. 17:14). "Elect" angels are noted in 1 Tim. 5:21.

eklogē [ἐκλογή, *1589*]

eklogē is a noun denoting "election," referring to God choosing his people. It is found seven times.

The term is used adjectivally in Acts 9:15, where God designates Paul as his "chosen" instrument to preach the gospel.

The phenomenon of divine "election," of God having "chosen" his people according to his redemptive purposes, is evident in Rom. 9:11; 11:5ff., 28; 1 Thess. 1:4; 2 Pet. 1:10.

Additional Notes

The semantic range of the various Greek terms for "choice" is roughly equivalent to that of the single, all-embracing term ***bāḥar*** in the Old Testament.

CHRIST

NT Words

Christos [Χριστός, *5547*]

Christos is the dynamically equivalent Greek term for the Hebrew ***māshîaḥ*** (→ ANOINT), constituting the name and title of Christ. It is found over 550 times, often in connection with the name Jesus (e.g., Matt. 1:1; Mark 1:1; John 17:3; Acts 2:38; Rom. 1:1ff.; 1 Cor. 9:1; Gal. 1:1ff.; Eph. 2:6ff.; Phil. 2:5; Col. 2:6ff.; 1 Tim. 2:5; Titus 2:13; Phlm. 3ff.; Heb. 3:1; 2 Pet. 3:18; 1 John 4:2ff.; Rev. 1:1ff.; 22:21).

The designation "Christ" is also indicated, for example, in Matt. 2:4; 26:68; Mark 9:11; John 4:25; Acts 2:36; Rom. 5:6; 2 Cor. 1:5; Gal. 1:6ff.; Eph. 1:10ff.; Phil. 1:13ff.; Col. 2:2ff.; 1 Tim. 2:7; Heb. 3:6; 1 Pet. 3:16ff.; Rev. 11:15; 20:4.

Elsewhere ***Christos*** occurs with the definite article, thus emphasizing the full significance of Christ's person as "the Messiah" (i.e., the Christ, cf. Matt. 16:16; Mark 8:29; Luke 9:20). Peter confesses that Jesus is indeed "the Christ"; as does Martha in John 11:27. Other occurrences include Matt. 26:63; Luke 3:15; 22:67; John 1:20; 7:41; 20:31; 1 John 2:22; 5:1.

See Also: → ANOINT

CHRISTIAN

NT Words

Christianos [Χριστιανός, *5546*]

Christianos is a rare noun transliterated as "Christian," denoting those who are followers of Jesus Christ. It is found only in Acts 11:26; 26:28; 1 Pet. 4:16.

CHRYSOLITE → BERYL

CHURCH → ASSEMBLE

CIRCUMCISE, CIRCUMCISION

OT Words

mûl [מוּל, **4135**]

This term occurs thirty times and is consistently translated "circumcise." Since ***mûl*** refers to the ritual act of circumcision as required under the Abrahamic and Mosaic covenant stipulations, the majority of these texts are found in the Pentateuch.

The sign of the covenant given to Abraham was expressed through the physical act of circumcision (cf. Gen. 17:10ff.); Abraham then circumcised his son Isaac (cf. Gen. 21:4). Gen. 34:15ff. refers to the circumcision of the Shechemites. Joshua has the entire male population of Israel circumcised before the campaign of conquest begins (cf. Josh. 5:4ff.). See also Exod. 12:44, 48; Lev. 12:3; Jer. 9:25. There is also one occurrence of the derivative noun *mûlōt* in Exod. 4:26.

The remaining occurrences of ***mûl*** are all highly significant theologically, being references to "heart circumcision" — the desired and appropriate spiritual attitude of faithful obedience to God in accordance with the requirements of the Mosaic covenant. In Deut. 10:16; Jer. 4:4 God requires that his people "circumcise their hearts" with respect to him. Such a task was obviously beyond the people's capacity in their own strength. However, in Deut. 30:6 God assures his people that he himself will circumcise their hearts, and thus do for them what they could never do for themselves. Coming as it does in the context of the Deuteronomic covenant renewal ceremony, this promise provides the people of God (both then and now) with the greatest assurance that God's gracious power and mercy lies at the root of our salvation. Nothing we do can ever contribute to our own salvation. A response of faith and obedience is certainly required, but it is a response initiated by God himself.

'orlāh [עָרְלָה, **6190**]

This noun occurs sixteen times and means "foreskin." It is always linked, either implicitly or explicitly, with the act of circumcision (see above), and is therefore commonly translated "circumcision." The contexts in which ***'orlāh*** is used are virtually identical to those associated with ***mûl***, above (cf. Gen. 17:11ff.; Exod. 4:25; Lev. 12:3). Aside from reference to the ritual act of circumcision, ***'orlāh*** refers literally to foreskins in Josh. 5:3; 1 Sam. 18:25, 27; 2 Sam. 3:14.

In contrast to ***mûl***, ***'orlāh*** is also used to indicate "uncircumcision," in the sense that male persons so described still have a foreskin (cf. Gen. 34:14; Jer. 9:25). Fruit is also described as being "uncircumcised" in Lev. 19:23, indicating metaphorically that the fruit is unclean and thus forbidden to eat.

Finally, ***'orlāh*** is used in parallel with ***mûl*** in Deut. 10:16; Jer. 4:4 to refer to "heart circumcision" (see above).

'ārēl [עָרֵל, **6189**]

The adjective ***'ārēl*** refers almost exclusively to those who are uncircumcised, both literally and metaphorically. It is found about thirty times.

Most commonly, the term refers somewhat contemptuously to pagan Gentiles as "uncircumcised" (cf. Judg. 14:3; 1 Sam. 14:6; 2 Sam. 1:20; Ezek. 28:10; 32:19ff.; Isa. 52:1).

This metaphorical usage applies not only to Gentiles, but to Israelites as well. There are several texts in which *'ārēl* refers to those of God's people who are rebellious towards him as "uncircumcised" (cf. Lev. 26:41; Jer. 6:10; 9:26). The term also refers to ceremonial impurity (cf. Exod. 6:12, 30; 12:48; Lev. 19:23).

NT Words

peritomē [περιτομή, *4061*]

peritomē is a noun denoting "circumcision" throughout the nearly forty occurrences of the term.

Literal references to the old covenant rite of circumcision are found in John 7:22ff.; Rom. 2:25ff.; 3:1, 30; 4:9ff.; 1 Cor. 7:19; Gal. 5:6, 11; 6:15; Col. 3:11. The "covenant of circumcision" is indicated in Acts 7:8.

The designation "uncircumcised" is a metaphorical reference to Gentile unbelievers in Gal. 2:7. References to "circumcised believers" (i.e., Jewish Christians) are found in Acts 10:45; Col. 4:11. The term "circumcised" constitutes a metaphorical reference to the Jewish nation in Gal. 2:9. See also Col. 4:11. References to the "circumcision party" — a virtual technical term denoting those strict observers of Mosaic law who prized circumcision as an important element in one's justification before God — are found in Acts 11:2; Gal. 2:12; Titus 1:10.

Reference to spiritual "circumcision," denoting true heart renewal, is made in Rom. 2:29. This condition is clearly distinguished from the mere ritual of circumcision. In Phil. 3:3, genuine followers of Christ are designated as the "true circumcision."

There is a significant usage of ***peritomē*** in Col. 2:11, where the "circumcision of Christ" is indicated. This phrase is generally regarded technically as a "subjective genitive." This grammatical form indicates here that the circumcision mentioned is something performed by Christ and not simply as something belonging to him. The "circumcision" referred to here is the work of salvation accomplished by Christ on the cross. (See the Additional Notes below.)

peritemnō [περιτέμνω, *4059*]

peritemnō is a verb meaning "circumcise" throughout the approximately twenty occurrences of the term, referring to the removal of the foreskin by a sharpened flint.

Literal references to ritual circumcision include Luke 1:59; 2:21; John 7:22; Acts 16:3; 21:21; 1 Cor. 7:18; Gal. 2:3; 5:2ff.; 6:12.

In Acts 7:8; 15:1, 5, 24; 6:13 the desire to be circumcised is linked to the erroneous belief that it is necessary for salvation.

For the metaphorical usage of ***peritemnō*** in Col. 2:11, see ***peritomē***, above.

aperitmētos [ἀπερίτμητος, *564*]

aperitmētos is a rare adjective meaning "uncircumcised" found only in Acts 7:51. The use is metaphorical, referring to those who are "uncircumcised" in heart — possessing an unbelieving heart and a rebellious attitude towards God.

akrobystia [ἀκροβυστία, *203*]

akrobystia is a noun denoting "uncircumcision" — the state of being uncircumcised. It is found in twenty contexts.

References to "uncircumcised men" are found in Acts 11:3. The "uncircumcised" in Gal. 2:7; Eph. 2:11 are unbelievers. See also Col. 2:13 in this regard.

The state of being uncircumcised is indicated in Rom. 2:25ff.; 4:9ff.; 1 Cor. 7:18ff.; Gal. 5:6; 6:15; Col. 3:11.

epispaomai [ἐπισπάομαι, *1986*]

epispaomai is a rare verb found only in 1 Cor. 7:18 with the meaning "to remove the marks of circumcision."

Additional Notes

There is overlap in meaning between the respective Greek and Hebrew terminology for the phenomena of "circumcision" and "uncircumcision." Powerful theological themes are developed in both Testaments with respect to this motif. In both the Old and New Testaments, circumcision indicates a person's rightly-ordered heart attitude toward God as a result of divine forgiveness and transformation. In the New Testament, it is of course Jesus Christ who embodies the supreme significance of spiritual circumcision as the means of purging the believer of his sin and thus rendering him fit for membership in the kingdom of God (cf. Col. 2:11). This is, in effect, the fulfillment of the Old Testament ritual act of circumcision mentioned throughout the old covenant period — and in the Pentateuch in particular. Though no words for circumcision are used, the reference in Ezek. 36:24ff. to the divine action of removing the heart of stone and replacing it with the heart of flesh is tantamount to the same thing. In this regard, dynamic equivalence for the terms ***peritomē***, ***peritemnō***, and ***mûl***, ***'orlāh*** (in part); followed by ***akrobystia***, ***aperitmētos***, and ***'ārēl***, ***'orlāh*** (in part) may be affirmed with reasonable confidence.

Again, what is affirmed both literally and symbolically in the Old Testament is then confirmed and consummated in the New, through the ultimate work of Christ's spiritual circumcision "performed," as it were, on the hearts of all his people by the Spirit of God.

CITY

OT Words

'îr **[עִיר, 5892]**

This common term occurs about one thousand times, meaning "city." Most of these references have no particular theological significance, but simply refer to cities in general, both within and without the borders of Israel.

When ***'îr*** refers to the city of Jerusalem, however, particular theological emphases clearly emerge. In the first instance, Jerusalem is consistently declared in the Old Testament to be the chosen city of God in accordance with his covenant promises. This is the place where God determined to have his name dwell. And it is the Jerusalem temple that constitutes the focal point of God's dwelling place on earth. The narratives of Samuel-Kings and Chronicles consistently emphasize this point. 2 Sam. 5:7, 9, for example, presents the first indication of the significance of Jerusalem by describing the successful capture of the Jebusite stronghold by David and his men. The fortress was renamed the City of David, which subsequently became known as Jerusalem (cf. also 1 Chr. 11:5ff.). The significant point here is that 2 Sam. 5:10 declares that the Lord was with David, implying a special relationship between the king and his God. Solomon, David's son and the builder of the Jerusalem temple, reinforces this perspective in his prayer of dedication in 1 Kgs. 8:16, 44, 48 by affirming that God had chosen this city out of all the cities of Israel in which to place his name. The significance of Jerusalem is also heightened in the Samuel narrative through the account of the ark's eventful journey from the house of Abinadab, then to Obed-Edom's lodging, and finally to the City of David (cf. 2 Sam. 5:10, 12, 16; also 1 Chr. 15:29; 2 Chr. 5:12).

Throughout the remainder of the Samuel-Kings narrative, the status of the city of Jerusalem shifts from a positive evaluation as God's chosen dwelling place to one of condemnation as the focal point of God's judgment against his people for their wickedness. This positive aspect is illustrated, for example, in 2 Kgs. 19:32ff.; 20:6, where God assures Hezekiah that Jerusalem will not be taken by the Assyrians, who have begun to lay siege to it, but will be spared, on account of the covenant promises given to David. As a consequence, Nebuchadnezzar's Assyrian army is slaughtered by the angel of the Lord and the Assyrian king returns to Nineveh a crushed ruler (cf. also Isa. 37:33–35). In time, however, the sins of the nations of Judah increase to the point where God determines to hand over the city of Jerusalem and the whole country to the Babylonians as a climactic judgment upon his people (cf. 2 Kgs. 24:10, 11; 25:2ff.). This theme of judgment is taken up extensively throughout the Prophets, referring to the indictment of the city of Jerusalem (e.g., Isa. 6:6; 19:11; 21:10; 26:6; Jer. 32:25; 33:5; 37:10; 46:8; Ezek. 9:7; 11:6; 43:3).

As a corollary to pronouncing judgment upon the city of Jerusalem, God promises to restore Jerusalem to his people. The striking thing about these promises is that they are regularly found in juxtaposition to the prophetic indictments against the city. So even before the tragedy of the Babylonian invasion takes place, God blends his threats of punishment with his promises of restoration and renewal (cf. Isa. 1:26; 45:13; 62:12; Jer. 30:18; 31:38). In a similar theological context, Daniel prays that God would turn away his wrath from the city of Jerusalem (cf. Dan. 9:16ff.).

For the psalmist, the city of Jerusalem (or Zion) is a place of refuge, for which he praises God (cf. Pss. 46:4; 48:1, 8; 87:3). He is also convinced that God will rescue the city and rebuild the cities of Judah (cf. Ps. 69:35).

In the postexilic period, the reconstruction of the city walls of Jerusalem assumes a marked theological significance during the period of Nehemiah. Nehemiah's rebuilding program constitutes a symbolic resurrection of the kingdom of God in the postexilic period; a program that finds its ultimate fulfillment in the person of Christ who comes to reign, not in an earthly city, but in the heavenly city of Jerusalem (cf. Neh. 2:3ff.; 11:1). It is in the prophecy of Zechariah that this eschatological anticipation of Jerusalem's final glory reaches a climax in the Old Testament. Zech. 14 speaks of a consummate Day of the Lord judgment against the enemies of God's people — enemies who will attack Jerusalem, but who will be repulsed and destroyed. The whole chapter is relevant for this theme, and its fulfillment is given expression in the New Testament, particularly in the books of Revelation and Hebrews (cf. Heb. 12:18ff.).

qiryāh **[קִרְיָה, 7151];**
qiryā' **[קִרְיָא, 7149** (Aramaic)]

qiryāh is synonymous with ***'îr*** (see above) and means "city" throughout its approximately thirty occurrences (cf. Num. 21:28; Deut. 3:4; 1 Kgs. 1:41; Prov. 10:15; Isa. 1:21; Lam. 2:11; Hos. 6:8).

qiryāh also refers to Mt. Zion as the "city of the great King" in Ps. 48:2.

The Aramaic equivalent, ***qiryā',*** denotes the city of Jerusalem in Ezra 4:12ff. The "cities" of Samaria are noted in Ezra 4:10.

qeret **[קֶרֶת, 7176]**

qeret is a general, non-specific term for "city," "town" in Job 29:7; Prov. 8:3; 9:3, 14; 11:11.

NT Words

polis [πόλις, *4172*]

The noun ***polis,*** meaning "city" or "town," occurs about 160 times.

Literal references to "city" include Matt. 2:23; Mark 1:45; Luke 1:26; 10:8ff.; John 4:5ff.; Acts 8:5ff.; 16:12ff.; Rom. 16:23; 2 Cor. 11:26ff.; Jas. 4:13; 2 Pet. 2:6. The "city" of Jerusalem is noted in Matt. 5:35. Rev. 11:2 refers to Jerusalem as the "holy city."

Metaphorical references to the "heavenly city" of Jerusalem are found in Heb. 11:10, 16; 12:22; 13:14; Rev. 3:12; 14:20; 21:2, 10ff.

Metaphorical references to the "city" of Babylon (the symbolic embodiment of godlessness) are found in Rev. 14:8; 17:18; 18:10ff.

Additional Notes

'îr and ***polis*** may be understood as genuine dynamic equivalents. The distinctive significance of ***'îr*** emerges in the analysis of Jerusalem as the divinely designated city where God chooses to dwell among his people. This old covenant perspective is then taken up in the New Testament, where the use of ***polis*** with respect to the heavenly city of Jerusalem constitutes a climactic fulfillment of the theme of God living in eternal fellowship with his people.

CLAY

OT Words

ḥōmer **[חֹמֶר, 2563]**

This term is found on seventeen occasions in the Old Testament, meaning "clay" or "mortar." In several contexts it is used in a straightforward literal or narrative sense, referring to building material (cf. Gen. 11:3; Exod. 1:14; Job 4:19; Nah. 3:14).

The remaining references are all metaphorical. In the book of Job, for example, ***ḥōmer*** ("clay") refers to human frailty (cf. Job 10:9; 13:12; 33:6); trauma (cf. 30:19); wealth (cf. 27:16); and creation (cf. 38:14). The word is also used as a symbol of divine sovereignty, whereby human beings are designated as "clay" and God the divine potter (cf. Isa. 29:16; 45:9; 64:8). ***ḥōmer*** refers to the reality of divine judgment against the Assyrians, who are doomed to be trodden under foot like clay (cf. Isa. 10:16), and also to God's own people, who are described as disfigured clay pots, fit only to be destroyed by God (cf. Jer. 18:4, 6).

ṭîṭ **[טִיט, 2916]**

This synonym for ***ḥōmer,*** above, is found twelve times. ***ṭîṭ*** refers to "clay" or "mud" in a literal sense in Job 41:30; Jer. 38:6. The remaining references are all metaphorical. Like ***ḥōmer, ṭîṭ*** refers to the phenomenon of divine judgment — but only to the enemies of God's people, not to the people of God themselves (cf. 2 Sam. 22:43; Ps. 18:42; Isa. 41:25; 57:20; Zech. 10:5). ***ṭîṭ*** also symbolizes wealth (cf. Zech. 9:3).

ḥasaph **[חֲסַף, 2635** (Aramaic)]

The Aramaic noun ***ḥasaph*** occurs nine times denoting "clay," referring exclusively to the composite elements (iron and clay) of the feet of the statue in King Nebuchadnezzar's vision (cf. Dan. 2:33ff.).

NT Words

pēlos [πηλός, *4081*]

pēlos denotes "clay" in six places, referring to the mixture of dirt and spittle that Jesus applied to the eyes of a blind man, which led to the restoration of his sight in John 9:6ff. Rom. 9:21 refers to the potter's "clay."

CLEAN, CLEANSE, CLEANSING

OT Words

ṭāhôr **[טָהוֹר, 2889]**

This adjective occurs about eighty times, meaning "clean," "pure." Approximately half the time ***ṭāhôr*** refers to ceremonial purity or cleanliness, mostly in the Pentateuch. In these contexts, ***ṭāhôr*** refers to animals that are clean (e.g., Gen. 7:2; 8:20; Lev. 14:4; Deut. 14:11); people (e.g., Lev. 13:17; 15:8; Num. 9:13ff.); places (e.g., Lev. 4:12; 10:14); and sacred objects (e.g., 2 Chr. 13:11; Isa. 66:2).

On several occasions, the meaning "clean" shifts from a merely ceremonial purity to a more elevated moral purity. A classic illustration of this is found in David's confession and plea for forgiveness in Ps. 51:10, where he begs God to create in him a "clean heart." A similar perspective is also found in texts such as Prov. 15:26; 30:12; Eccl. 9:2; Hab. 1:13.

Finally, Ezek. 36:25 combines the sense of ritual cleanliness with that of profound spiritual renewal. The sprinkling of "clean" water here is a divine initiative of spiritual forgiveness and cleansing that is a prelude to the Spirit of God entering the life of a believer — one who is devoted to him in faith and obedience (cf. Ezek. 36:26, 27). It is one of the two great prophetic anticipations of new covenant forgiveness and renewal in the Old Testament (cf. also Jer. 31:31ff.).

tāhēr [טָהֵר, 2891]

tāhēr is the verbal root from which ***tāhôr***, above, is derived. It occurs approximately ninety times and is translated "be clean," "cleanse," or "purify," "to pronounce clean," and "to cleanse oneself." For the most part, like ***tāhôr***, ***tāhēr*** refers to the ritual cleansing associated with the Mosaic covenant legislation, and the bulk of references are found in the Pentateuch. Ritual purification is mainly associated with people, both "lay" Israelites as well as priests and Levites (e.g., Lev. 12:7; 13:6ff.; 14:4ff.; 15:28; Num. 19:12; 8:7, 21). But, also like ***tāhôr***, the cleansing of particular locations is in view as well: for example, houses (cf. Lev. 14:48; 2 Chr. 29:18); the altar in the tabernacle and temple (cf. Lev. 16:19; Ezek. 43:26); the temple itself (cf. 2 Chr. 29:15, 16); and the land of Israel (cf. Ezek. 39:12ff.; 2 Chr. 34:3ff.).

The word also describes the profound spiritual cleansing of divine renewal and forgiveness. ***tāhēr*** indicates that the people of Israel are the objects of God's purifying grace (as does ***tāhôr***). Most of these references relate to the anticipation of new covenant renewal and forgiveness, the fulfillment of which is focused in the person of our Lord Jesus Christ. Note particularly in this regard Jer. 33:8; Ezek. 24:13; 36:25; 37:23; Mal. 3:3; Lev. 16:30. There is also the appeal of David in Ps. 51:2 for God to cleanse him of his sin.

tehār [טְהָר, 2890]

This is a rare noun, occurring only twice, with the meaning "clean," "pure." Both occurrences refer to moral purity (cf. Job 17:9; Prov. 22:11).

tōhar [טֹהַר, 2892]

Similar to ***tehār***, above, this noun is rare — occurring only three times. Once it means "brightness" (Exod. 24:10); and twice it refers to ritual purification in regard to a woman's menstrual flow (cf. Lev. 12:4, 6).

tāhorāh [טָהֳרָה, 2893]

tāhorāh is also a relatively rare noun related to the entries above. It means "cleansing," "purification" and is found on thirteen occasions, all of which relate to ritual purification (e.g., Lev. 12:4ff.; 13:7, 35; Num. 6:9; 1 Chr. 23:28; 2 Chr. 30:19; Ezek. 44:26).

ḥāṭā' [חָטָא, 2398]

ḥāṭā' is a verb meaning "to sin" in most of the nearly 250 occurrences of the term. (→ SIN) In addition, however, ***ḥāṭā'*** also means "purify," "cleanse" in several places — all in a ritual context.

The action of "purifying" or "cleansing" the altar in the tabernacle is recorded in Exod. 29:36; Lev. 8:15; Num. 8:21; 31:23; as the temple altar is cleansed in the prophet Ezekiel's vision (cf. Ezek. 45:18). See also Ezek. 45:18. The ceremonial cleansing of one's person is indicated in Num. 19:13; 31:19ff. Lev. 14:49ff.; Num. 19:12, 19ff. describe the ceremonial purification of houses.

zak [זַךְ, 2134]

zak is an adjective meaning "pure," "clean" throughout the eleven occurrences of the term.

The meaning "pure" is indicated in relation to oil used for ritual purposes in Exod. 27:20; Lev. 24:2. "Pure" frankincense is described in Exod. 30:34; Lev. 24:7.

zak also means "pure," "clean" in a moral sense in Job 8:6; 33:9; Prov. 16:2; 20:11; 21:8. It is also used in relation to doctrine in Job 11:4. See also Job 16:17.

zākak [זָכַךְ, 2141]

zākak is a rare verb found in several places with the sense of "be clean, pure" in relation to the cosmos in Job 15:15; 25:5. It refers to "to cleansing" one's hands in Job 9:30.

zākāh [זָכָה, 2135]

The verb ***zākāh*** means to "be clean, pure" in a moral sense in most of the eight occurrences of the term (e.g., Job 15:14; 25:4; Ps. 51:4).

The meaning "to keep oneself (morally) pure" is indicated in Pss. 71:13; 119:9; Prov. 20:9. See also Isa. 1:16.

bārar [בָּרַר, **1305**]

bārar is a verb found nearly twenty times with the meaning "purify oneself," "show oneself pure" in four of these contexts. The sense of "showing oneself pure" is evident in 2 Sam. 22:27; Ps. 18:26. The action of purifying oneself in a ceremonial context is noted in Isa. 52:11; Jer. 4:11; Dan. 12:10; Zeph. 3:9.

bar [בַּר, **1249**]

bar is an adjective signifying "clean," "pure" in a moral sense in most of the seven occurrences of the term. The "pure" in heart are indicated in Pss. 24:4; 73:1. The commandment of the Lord is deemed to be "pure" in Ps. 19:8. General "cleanness" of heart is noted in Job 11:4.

NT Words

katharos [καθαρός, *2513*]

katharos is an adjective denoting that which is "clean," "pure." It is found in nearly thirty contexts.

References to the "pure in heart," or to those who are morally upright, are made in Matt. 5:8; 1 Tim. 1:5; 2 Tim. 2:22. A "pure" conscience is indicated in 1 Tim. 3:9; 2 Tim. 1:3.

To be "clean" in the sense of being free from moral impurity is indicated in Matt. 23:26; John 13:10; Rom. 14:20; Titus 1:15; Jas. 1:27. The state of righteousness in relation to having been "made clean" is indicated in John 15:3. "Clean" in the sense of "innocent" is the meaning indicated in Acts 20:26.

katharizō [καθαρίζω, *2511*]

katharizō is a verb meaning "cleanse," "purify," plus related senses, throughout the nearly forty occurrences of the term.

The meaning "make clean," "cleanse" is evident in contexts describing Christ's healing ministry. For example, lepers are "healed," or "cleansed," in Matt. 8:2ff.; 11:5; Mark 1:40ff.; Luke 4:27; 5:12ff.; 7:22; 17:17. References to people "healed" or "cleansed" of various diseases are found in Matt. 10:8; Luke 17:14.

The literal sense of "cleanse" in relation to the outside of a cup is used symbolically in Matt. 23:25ff.; Luke 11:39 to denote the superficial cleanliness of the Pharisees and imply their hypocrisy.

God makes a declaration of ceremonial cleanness in Acts 10:15; 11:9. In Acts 15:9 God is said to "cleanse" the heart by faith.

The "purifying" effect of blood in the old covenant ritual sacrificial system is recorded in Heb. 9:22, 25. The process of "cleansing oneself" from (moral) defilement is indicated in 2 Cor. 7:1.

1 John 1:7, 9 affirms that the blood of Christ "cleanses" one from all sin. Eph. 5:26 contains the declaration that Christ "has cleansed" the church by the spiritual application of God's word. In Titus 2:14 Christ is said to "purify" a people for himself. Heb. 9:14 declares that the consciences of believers are "purged" or "purified" by the blood of Christ.

diakatharizō [διακαθαρίζω, *1245*]

diakatharizō is a rare variant of ***katharizō***, above, meaning "clear" in the sense of "clean" (i.e., remove all refuse) in the metaphorical context of Christ preparing his threshing-floor to gather in his "wheat" with his people and burn the "chaff" (i.e., his enemies) (cf. Matt. 3:12; Luke 3:17).

katharismos [καθαρισμός, *2512*]

katharismos is a noun derived from ***katharizō*** (see above) meaning "cleansing," "purification" and found in eight places. Ritual "cleansing" is indicated in Mark 1:44; Luke 2:22; John 2:6; 3:25. Heb. 1:3 refers to Christ "having made purification" for the sins of his people. 2 Pet. 1:9 describes the reality of "being cleansed" from one's sins.

katharotēs [καθαρότης, *2514*]

katharotēs is a rare noun found only in Heb. 9:13 referring to the "(ritual) purification" of the Levitical covenant.

ekkathairō [ἐκκαθαίρω, *1571*]

ekkathairō is a rare verb meaning "to thoroughly cleanse" in the metaphorical context of 1 Cor. 5:7, where the believer is exhorted to rid himself of all "leaven" (i.e., a godless lifestyle). 2 Tim. 2:21 refers generally to people "purifying" themselves from what is ignoble.

hagnos [ἁγνός, *53*]

hagnos is an adjective found in eight contexts with the underlying sense of "pure."

"Pure" in the sense of "chaste" is indicated in 2 Cor. 11:2 with metaphorical reference to the church as

Christ's "bride." The sense of "guiltless" is indicated in 2 Cor. 7:11. General references to moral purity are noted in Phil. 4:8; 1 Tim. 5:22; Titus 2:5; 1 Pet. 3:2. Divine wisdom is described as "pure," or "without corruption, "in Jas. 3:17. See also 1 John 3:3.

hagnotēs [**ἁγνότης,** *54*]

hagnotēs is a rare noun denoting "purity" of life found only in 2 Cor. 6:6.

hagnismos [**ἁγνισμός,** *49*]

hagnismos is a rare noun referring to ritual "purification" only in Acts 21:26.

hagnizō [**ἁγνίζω,** *48*]

hagnizō is a verb meaning "to purify oneself" in a ritual, ceremonial context in John 11:55; Acts 21:24ff. The word has a general moral, spiritual emphasis in Jas. 4:8; 1 Pet. 1:2; 1 John 3:3.

Additional Notes

The Hebrew and Greek terminology relating to the phenomenon of cleansing, both ritual and spiritual, carries similar theological force in both Testaments. The importance of ritual purity — for a variety of reasons, and in a number of different contexts — is duly recognized and emphasized throughout the Bible. The significant difference in the New Testament vocabulary of "cleansing" is that it finds its consummation and fulfillment in the person and work of Christ — a reality which the Old Testament era eagerly anticipates but does not fully experience in a redemptive-historical sense.

CLEAR

NT Words

krystallizō [**κρυσταλλίζω,** *2929*]

krystallizō is a rare verb meaning "to be as clear as crystal," denoting a high degree of brilliance and transparency. It is found only in Rev. 21:11.

lampros [**λαμπρός,** *2986*]

lampros is an adjective meaning "bright" in most of the nine occurrences of the term. However, in Rev. 22:1 the river of the water of life is described as "clear" as crystal.

CLEAVE → JOIN

CLOSE (VERB)

OT Words

'āṣar [**עָצַר, 6113**]

The verb ***'āṣar*** occurs around fifty times with a variety of meanings. Included here is the sense of "close (up)," "shut," found in several places, with God as the primary subject.

God is said to "have closed" the wombs of various women and groups of women (cf. Gen. 20:18; Isa. 66:9). He is also described as "having shut" the heavens and thus prevented rain in Deut. 11:17; 1 Kgs. 8:35; 2 Chr. 6:26; 7:13.

In Neh. 6:10 ***'āṣar*** means being "shut in" (i.e., detained) in one's house. See also Jer. 33:1.

sāgar [**סָגַר, 5462**]

The verb ***sāgar*** is found approximately ninety times with the sense of "shut," "shut up." In several contexts it means to "close up." In Gen. 2:21 God "closes up" the flesh of Adam. See also Judg. 3:22, where a man's flesh is described as "closing over" the sword that pierced him.

kāsāh [**כָּסָה, 3680**]

kāsāh is a common verb found around 140 times with the primary meaning "cover." In one place, the verb describes the earth "closing over" Korah and his fellow conspirators as they lost their lives under divine judgment (cf. Num. 16:33).

'āṣam [**עָצַם, 6105**]

'āṣam is a verb found in twenty contexts with the primary sense of "increase." However, in Isa. 29:10 it refers to "closing" the eyes.

NT Words

kammyō [**καμμύω,** *2576*]

kammyō is a rare verb meaning "close, shut the eyes," found only in Matt. 13:15; Acts 28:27.

ptyssō [**πτύσσω,** *4428*]

ptyssō is a rare verb found only in Luke 4:20 indicating the action of "closing" a book.

CLOTH

NT Words

rhakos [**ῥάκος,** *4470*]

rhakos is a rare noun denoting a piece of woven "cloth" in Matt. 9:16; Mark 2:21.

See Also: → CLOTHING

CLOTHE

OT Words

lābash **[לָבַשׁ, 3847]**

This verb occurs a little over one hundred times in the Old Testament and means "to clothe" or "put on (garments, etc.)," in both a literal and metaphorical sense.

In a little more than half of these contexts, ***lābash*** refers to putting on clothes, as well as to the ceremonial robing of the priests and Levites.

It is in the metaphorical sense of the term, however, that the significance of ***lābash*** in theological terms becomes apparent. One of its most striking uses for example, occurs in Zech. 3:3ff., where the prophet Joshua, the high priest, stands in the presence of Yahweh, covered in filthy clothes. The scene is a courtroom where Satan is anxious to press charges against the people of Israel through the person of the high priest. The climax of the vision comes when God orders that Joshua's filthy clothes be removed and that he be clothed in clean garments. This is a powerful symbolic description of the process of forgiveness and renewal through the intervening grace of God. What is in view here is not simply the standing of Joshua the high priest, but the status of the entire people of God. Similar uses of ***lābash*** are also applied to the Messianic Servant of Yahweh (cf. Isa. 61:10); to the priests of Israel (cf. Ps. 132:16); and to the nation in general (cf. Isa. 51:9; 52:1). In all cases, the salvation of these people is in view.

Other metaphorical uses of ***lābash*** are found in various contexts. The term is used in a positive sense to symbolize God's love for his people (cf. Ezek. 16:10); God's creative power (cf. Isa. 50:3); and even to allude metaphorically to the armor of God (cf. Isa. 59:17). In a negative sense, ***lābash*** describes God's judgment on his people (cf. Jer. 4:30; Ezek. 7:27; 9:2ff.), and on his enemies as well (cf. Ps. 132:18; Ezek. 26:16). More generally, ***lābash*** refers metaphorically to the linen garments of the mediating angel in Daniel's visions (cf. Dan. 10:5; 12:6, 7), and also to the idols of Assyria in the graphic allegory of Ezek. 23.

Finally, ***lābash*** is used in Judg. 6:34 to describe the manner in which the Spirit of God came upon (lit. "clothed") Gideon in order to equip him for the confrontation with the Midianites. A similar use of the term is found in 1 Chr. 12:18; 2 Chr. 24:20.

lebash **[לְבַשׁ, 3848** (Aramaic)]

lebash is an Aramaic verb found in three contexts, all expressing the passive sense of "to be clothed" (cf. Dan. 5:7, 16, 29).

NT Words

amphiennymi [ἀμφιέννυμι, *294*]

amphiennymi is a verb found in four places and meaning "clothe" throughout. The term is used metaphorically in Matt. 6:30; Luke 12:28, where God is said to "clothe" the grass of the field. In Matt. 11:8; Luke 7:25, ***amphiennymi*** is used in the literal sense of a man "clothed" in fine apparel.

endyō [ἐνδύω, *1746*]

The verb ***endyō*** occurs about thirty times with the consistent meaning "to put on clothes," "clothe."

General references to "putting on" clothes are found in Matt. 6:25; Mark 1:6; 15:17ff.; Luke 12:22; 15:22. The "putting on" of royal apparel is noted in Acts 12:21.

The remaining usage of ***endyō*** is metaphorical. The heavenly Christ is described as being "clothed" in a long white robe in Rev. 1:13. The saints are likewise "clothed" in pure white linen in Rev. 15:6. Luke 24:49 refers to being "clothed" with power from on high.

In Rom. 13:12 the term indicates the symbolic action of "putting on" the (spiritual) armor of light. Similarly, Eph. 6:11, 14; 1 Thess. 5:8 describe "putting on" the whole armor of God — spiritual weapons against satanic attacks. ***endyō*** also indicates the act of "embracing" the Lord Jesus Christ as Lord of one's life through faith and repentance (cf. Rom. 13:14; Gal. 3:27). "Putting on" the imperishable nature of immortality, referring to the appearance of the believer in glory, is noted in 1 Cor. 15:53ff.; 2 Cor. 5:3. Eph. 4:24; Col. 3:10ff. describe the act of "putting on" the new person (i.e., embarking on a godly lifestyle).

ependyomai [ἐπενδύομαι, *1902*]

ependyomai is a verb derived from ***endyō*** (see above) and found only in 2 Cor. 5:2, 3 with the passive sense of "be clothed" in the context of the believer's longing to put on heavenly "clothing" after death.

endidyskō [ἐνδιδύσκω, *1737*]

endidyskō is a rare synonym for ***endyō*** (see above) found only in Luke 8:27; 16:19 with the meaning "to wear, put on clothes."

himatizō [ἱματίζω, *2439*]

The verb ***himatizō*** is also synonymous with the entries above, meaning to "be clothed" in Mark 5:15; Luke 8:35.

periballō [περιβάλλω, *4016*]

periballō is a verb found in approximately thirty contexts with the underlying meaning "to clothe," plus several related nuances.

The general sense of "wear," "put on clothes," "dress oneself" is evident in Matt. 6:31; Mark 14:51; 16:5; Acts 12:8. References to "clothing" other people are found in Matt. 25:36ff.; Luke 23:11. See also John 19:2.

Metaphorical reference to the "clothing" of the lilies of the field is found in Luke 12:27. The saints are declared to "be clothed" in white garments in heaven in Rev. 3:5, 18; 4:4; 7:9ff.; 19:8. The heavenly Christ is described as "being clothed" in a robe dipped in blood.

CLOTHING

OT Words

beged [**בֶּגֶד, 899**]

This is the most common word in the Old Testament for "clothes," "clothing," or "garment(s)," and it occurs around 180 times. For the most part it is used in a mundane literal sense throughout the narrative portions of Scripture from Genesis to Nehemiah, and in portions of the Wisdom writings and the Prophets.

Several times in the prophetic books, however, ***beged*** is used in a significant theological sense. This is especially the case in Isaiah. In Isa. 50:9, for example, the term refers metaphorically to the enemies of the Messianic Servant, who are described as wearing out "like a garment." Isa. 51:6 describes the earth and God's enemies in a similar way in a metaphorical allusion to the final Day of the Lord judgment. Their fate is likened to a piece of clothing being consumed by a moth (cf. Isa. 51:8).

The following examples all relate to the symbolic wearing of garments. In Isa. 52:1 the people of God are commanded to put on their "garments of splendor." This is an instruction not to gain their own salvation, but rather to appropriate the salvation God had made available to them. Another similar salvation metaphor is applied to the Messianic Servant in Isa. 61:10, when he rejoices in the fact that God has clothed him with the "garments of salvation." The symbolic wearing of clothing is also predicated of God in two significant contexts. First of all, in Isa. 59:17, Yahweh is described as putting on "garments of vengeance," for the purpose of punishing and avenging his enemies. Then, Isa. 63:1ff. alludes to the same phenomenon with respect to the nations, who must bear the brunt of God's wrath. Finally, on a different note, Isa. 64:6 highlights the futility of attempting to justify oneself in the sight of God by one's own virtuous deeds, since all human righteousness is rejected by God just as one discards "filthy garments" (or rags).

beged is also found in Zech 3:3ff., where re-clothing the high priest Joshua with spotlessly clean garments symbolizes his spiritual transformation and forgiveness by God. (→ CLOTHE)

salmāh [**שַׂלְמָה, 8008**]

This noun is a synonym for ***beged***, above, occurring sixteen times with the literal sense of "clothing" or "garment(s)." ***salmāh*** is found in a variety of contexts: for example, in the Mosaic legislation (cf. Exod. 22:9; Deut. 24:13); in historical narrative (cf. Josh. 9:5; 1 Kgs. 10:25; Neh. 9:21); in Wisdom literature (cf. Job 9:31; Ps. 104:2; Song 4:11); and once in the Prophets (cf. Mic. 2:8).

simlāh [**שִׂמְלָה, 8071**]

This term is also synonymous with ***beged*** and ***salmāh*** (see above) and occurs thirty times in literal, mundane contexts. ***simlāh*** only means "clothing" or "garment(s)." Again the usage is varied: for example, in historical narrative (cf. Gen. 9:23; 44:13; 45:22; Josh. 7:6; Judg. 8:25; Ruth 3:3; 1 Sam. 21:9; 2 Sam. 12:20); once in Proverbs (cf. Prov. 30:4), and several times in Isaiah (cf. Isa. 3:6ff.; 4:1; 9:5).

ketōnet, kuttōnet [**כְּתֹנֶת, כֻּתֹּנֶת, 3801**]

This term means "coat" or "tunic." It may be written two different ways, and the combined usage amounts to about thirty occurrences.

These terms are used literally in every instance. For example, they indicate Joseph's so-called "coat of many colors" (cf. Gen. 37:3, 23ff.). Both ***ketōnet*** and ***kuttōnet***, however, refer mainly to the official tunics worn by the priests and Levites while on duty in the tabernacle — and, one assumes, in the temple later on as well, although neither of these particular words are found in Kings or Chronicles (cf. Exod. 28:4ff.; 29:5, 8; Lev. 8:7; 16:4). Priestly garments are also referred to elsewhere (cf. Ezra 2:69; Neh. 7:70). In Isa. 22:21 Eliakim is given a tunic or cloak which represents the civil office of palace secretary (cf. Isa. 36:3).

lebûsh [**לְבוּשׁ, 3830**]

lebûsh is the noun derived from the verb ***lābash*** (→ CLOTHE) and is found a little over thirty times in the Old Testament — again, with the meaning "clothing" or "apparel." As do the terms above, it refers to "clothing" in a literal sense in varying non-theological contexts: for example, in historical narrative (cf. 2 Sam.

1:24; 20:8; 2 Kgs. 10:22; Esth. 4:2; 6:8ff.); poetry (cf. Job 24:7, 10; 38:9; Pss. 35:13; 45:13; Lam. 4:14); and prophecy (cf. Mal. 2:16).

This term does, however, have a metaphorical sense as well. Prov. 31:25, for example, describes the wife of noble character as one whose "clothing" is that of strength and honor. Isa. 63:1, 2 describes a mighty God whose "clothing" suggests he is both an avenging ruler and a redeeming king.

me'îl **[מְעִיל, 4598]**

me'îl occurs around thirty times meaning "tunic" or "robe." As with the above terms, ***me'îl*** occurs in predominantly literal, non-theological contexts. It is closest in meaning to ***ketōnet*** and ***kuttōnet*** (see above) — particularly with regard to the priestly garments required in the Mosaic legislation (cf. Exod. 28:4, 31, 34; 39:22–26). Elsewhere, ***me'îl*** refers to ordinary apparel (cf. 1 Sam. 2:19; 24:4, 11; 1 Chr., 15:27; Ezra 9:3).

There is one significant metaphorical use of ***me'îl***. Isa. 61:10 refers to the Messianic Servant's "robe of righteousness" that has been given to him by God — a sign of his divine nature.

mad **[מַד, 4055]**

mad is a noun found twelve times in all, with the predominant sense of "(article[s] of) clothing."

The priestly garment of linen breeches is indicated in Lev. 6:10.

Clothes in general are indicated in Judg. 3:16; 1 Sam. 4:12; 2 Sam. 20:8; Ps. 109:18. The term also denotes "armor" in 1 Sam. 17:38ff.; 18:4.

NT Words

himation [ἱμάτιον, *2440*]

himation is a noun found about sixty times, with the predominant senses of "garment," "clothing" plus associated senses.

General references to "garment(s)," "piece(s) of clothing," "clothes" are found in Matt. 9:16ff.; 27:35; Mark 2:21; Luke 5:36; 8:27; 19:35ff.; John 13:4, 12; 19:23, 24; Acts 22:20ff.; Heb. 1:11; Jas. 5:2; 1 Pet. 3:3; Rev. 3:4ff.

The high priest's "clothes" are described in Matt. 26:65. In Mark 9:3 the "clothes" of Christ shine brilliantly white at his transfiguration. In Rev. 19:13, 16, ***himation*** denotes the "garment," or "robe" dipped in blood and worn by the heavenly Christ.

endyma [ἔνδυμα, *1742*]

endyma is a noun found in eight places meaning "garment," "clothing" throughout. References to a "garment" (i.e., an article of clothing) include Matt. 3:4; 22:11, 12. "Clothing" in a general sense is indicated in Matt. 6:25ff.; 7:15; Luke 12:23. Matt. 28:3 describes angelic "clothing," brilliant and gleaming.

esthēs [ἐσθής, *2066*]

esthēs is a noun found in seven contexts with the meanings "robe," "clothing" throughout. The latter sense occurs in Acts 1:10; 10:30; Jas. 2:2, 3.

stolē [στολή, *4749*]

stolē is found eight times with reference to "robes" or "clothing" (see Mark 12:38; 16:5; Luke 15:22; 20:46). In particular, it denotes the heavenly white "robes" of the saints in glory (Rev. 6:11; 7:9, 13, 14).

Additional Notes

There is such an abundance of Hebrew and Greek words for "clothing" that it is virtually impossible to assign any precise dynamic equivalence between individual words. There is, however, one common area of significance worth mentioning. It concerns the use of ***stolē*** to refer to the robes of the glorified saints in heaven. The point of this allusion in the book of Revelation is to emphasize that such redeemed peoples have immediate and unhindered access to the presence of God forever. Such a priestly access in the Old Testament was, of course, temporary and potentially difficult. However, priestly intercession under the old covenant foreshadowed the reality of a so-called new covenant priesthood, where all believers in Christ are granted personal access to God without the need for another mediator. Yet, just as the priestly robes of the old covenant set apart those privileged few in ancient Israel, so the robes mentioned in the new covenant vision of John's Revelation testify to the unlimited access to God that all believers will have. It is characteristic of new covenant blessing that all those who place their faith and trust in Jesus Christ will be clothed in "robes of righteousness," just like the priests of old. And, in the "new heavens and new earth," there will be no restrictions concerning who may have intimate access to the living God through his Son.

CLOUD

OT Words

'ānan **[עָנָן, 6051]**

'ānan is the most common word for "cloud" in the Old Testament, occurring about eighty-five times. About one quarter of these texts refer to clouds in a natural sense — whether in a narrative, poetic, or prophetic context.

There is also a distinctive theological emphasis to be noted — namely that the phenomenon of the cloud in the Old Testament frequently indicates the manifestation of the presence and person of Yahweh. In this sense, the cloud may be understood as a very powerful theophanic symbol, and its significance in the Old Testament is noted in three primary contexts: the wilderness, the Sinai revelation, and the tabernacle/temple.

During the period of Israel's wandering in the wilderness, God often revealed himself to his people through the "pillar of cloud" by day and the "fiery (pillar of) cloud" by night (cf. Exod. 13:21ff.; 14:19ff.; 16:10; Deut. 1:33; Neh. 9:12; Ps. 78:14). This was the means God used both to guide them and to remind them of his unique power and authority, which could never be ignored or disobeyed without severe and painful consequences.

Undoubtedly, Yahweh's appearance to Moses and the Israelites on Mt. Sinai is one of the high points of divine revelation in the Old Testament. The presence of the so-called "glory cloud" on the summit, with the accompanying phenomena of thunder and lightning, emphasized to these people the unique majesty and holiness of their God in a way that would have impressed itself indelibly upon their minds. It was at this time, while he was "in the cloud," so to speak, that God communicated all the details of his covenant law to Moses and the Israelites. The actual account of the theophanic cloud at Sinai is found in Exod. 19–24 (cf. esp. Exod. 19:9, 16; 24:15–18; Deut. 4:11; 5:22).

The appearance of the divine glory cloud is also of the greatest importance during the construction and dedication of the tabernacle in the wilderness, although later, when Solomon finally completed the temple, the presence of the shekinah cloud is no less significant. There are over thirty references to the cloud of God's presence in conjunction with the tabernacle in Exodus, Leviticus, Numbers, and Deuteronomy (cf. Exod. 33:9; 40:34ff.; Lev. 16:2, 13; Num. 9:15ff.; 10:11ff.; 11:25; 12:5ff.; 14:14; 16:42; Deut. 31:15). Each of these references focuses in some way upon the sanctity of the tabernacle in relation to the presence of the glory cloud. Indeed, it is the very presence of that cloud that renders the place holy; without it, there is no holy place or holy of holies. In every instance above, the real presence of Yahweh is symbolized in the cloud — whether it be for the purpose of transmitting the divine law, or punishing the people, or as the means of guiding them through the wilderness. Similar references to the glory cloud are found in relation to the temple (cf. 1 Kgs. 8:11; 2 Chr. 5:13, 14).

The phenomenon of the glory cloud is also referred to in the book of Ezekiel, where the prophet's initial vision in chapter 1 reveals an extraordinary glimpse into the heavenly throne room and temple where Yahweh holds divine council (cf. Ezek. 1:4, 28). In Ezek. 10, the cloud also figures prominently in a vision of judgment, where the prophet is given to understand that the cloud is about to depart from the holy of holies in the Jerusalem temple. This is to be understood as nothing less than God abandoning his people, thus bringing to fulfillment his threatened judgment against them for their rejection of him (cf. Ezek. 10:3, 4).

'āb [עָב, 5645]

Synonymous with ***'ānan***, above, ***'āb*** is found thirty times throughout the Old Testament. ***'āb*** suggests not only clouds in general but also "dark (or thick) cloud mass." The term refers to clouds in their ordinary sense as natural phenomena (e.g., Judg. 5:4; 1 Kgs. 18:44). It is also found frequently in poetic contexts (e.g., Job 20:6; 37:11; Ps. 18:11ff.; Eccl. 11:3, 4).

While ***'āb*** lacks the extensive theological significance of ***'ānan***, it does reveal important insights on at least two occasions. The first is in relation to the Sinai cloud (cf. Exod. 19:9); and the second is in reference to divine judgment, specifically against the nation of Egypt, where God is described as riding "on a swift cloud" in order to bring disaster upon that nation (cf. Isa. 19:1).

shaḥaq [שַׁחַק, 7834]

This term is also translated "cloud," but it has the additional meanings "(fine) dust" and "skies." ***shaḥaq*** is therefore broader in meaning than the other two terms discussed above. Although it occurs twenty times in the Old Testament, it means "cloud(s)" on only about half those occasions — mainly in poetic contexts (cf. Job 35:5; 36:28; Pss. 36:5; 57:10; Prov. 3:20).

NT Words

nephos [νέφος, *3509*]

nephos is a rare noun, used only in Heb. 12:1 in a metaphorical reference to the "cloud" of heavenly witnesses that surrounds all believers as a means of their spiritual encouragement to godliness.

nephelē [νεφέλη, *3507*]

The noun ***nephelē*** denotes a "cloud" throughout the nearly thirty occurrences of the term.

Literal reference to a "cloud" is found in Luke 12:54. Then, a "cloud" is said to take the risen Christ out of the sight of his disciples and up into heaven in Acts 1:9.

In other places ***nephelē*** denotes the theophanic "cloud" of God's presence. From this cloud God commends his son as the one with whom he is well pleased in Matt. 17:5; Mark 9:7; Luke 9:35. Christ is depicted coming at the end of the age in the "clouds" of heaven (cf. Matt. 24:30; 26:64; Mark 13:26; 14:62; Luke 21:27; 1 Thess. 4:17; Rev. 1:7). Reference to the cloud that enveloped Christ and his three disciples on the Mount of Transfiguration is found in Luke 9:34. 1 Cor. 10:1ff. mentions the "cloud," the presence of Yahweh, leading the people of Israel through the desert. Rev. 14:14ff. refers to the cloud "throne" on which the heavenly Son of Man figure sits.

Other metaphorical uses of ***nephelē*** include those in 2 Pet. 2:17; Jude 12; Rev. 10:1; 11:12.

Additional Notes

The New Testament usage of ***nephelē*** makes it clear that the powerful theological significance attached to the phenomenon of "cloud" has carried over from the Old Testament. And it may be argued that the Hebrew term ***'ānan*** functions as a dynamic equivalent for ***nephelē***. The theological impact of the term ***'ānan*** centers on the person and presence of God himself, whereas ***nephelē*** focuses upon the person and work of Christ whenever he is associated with the glory cloud. Arguably, the most significant uses of ***nephelē*** in the New Testament center on the cloud of transfiguration and the clouds attending the final return of Christ. In both instances, these cloud references highlight the divine nature and person of Jesus Christ, for they remind the reader of the theophanic cloud of the old covenant era when God revealed himself to his people through this symbol. What is begun in the old covenant concerning the revelation of Yahweh is brought to climactic fulfillment in the new covenant, in the person of his Son.

See Also: → BLACK

COALS

OT Words

gaḥelet [גַּחֶלֶת, 1513]

This term is found seventeen times in the Old Testament and is translated "coals" in both a natural and a metaphorical sense. The natural sense is found, for example, in Lev. 16:12, in reference to burning coals from the altar of burnt offering, as well as in poetic contexts (e.g., Job 41:21; Prov. 6:28), and prophetic oracles (e.g., Isa. 44:19; Ezek. 1:13; 10:2; 24:11).

The metaphorical use of ***gaḥelet*** is largely taken up with the idea of God's wrath against his enemies, expressed through the symbol of burning coals (cf. 2 Sam. 22:9, 13; Pss. 18:8, 12; 140:10; Prov. 25:22). The term is also used in 2 Sam. 14:7 to refer to a sole descendant or heir.

peḥām [פֶּחָם, 6352]

peḥām is a noun denoting burning "coals" in all three occurrences of the term (cf. Prov. 26:21; Isa. 44:12; 54:16).

NT Words

anthrax [ἄνθραξ, *440*]

anthrax is a rare noun used metaphorically to refer to the experience of guilt. It is found only in Rom. 12:20, where it denotes "burning coals" heaped on the head of one's enemies in response to love being shown to them.

anthrakia [ἀνθρακιά, *439*]

anthrakia is a noun found only in John 18:18; 21:9, denoting a "charcoal fire" in both instances.

COLD

OT Words

qōr [קֹר, 7120]

This noun, translated "cold," occurs only in Gen. 8:22 in reference to the winter season.

qārāh [קָרָה, 7135]

qārāh is the feminine form of ***qōr***, above, indicating coldness in the natural sense of low temperature (cf. Job 24:7; Ps. 147:17; Nah. 3:17).

qar [קַר, 7119]

qar is the adjectival form of ***qōr*** and ***qārāh*** (see above) and occurs only twice, in Prov. 25:25; Jer. 18:14, where only the natural sense is indicated.

NT Words

psychos [ψῦχος, *5592*]

psychos is a rare noun found in three places, denoting in each case the sensation of "(being) cold" (cf. John 18:18; Acts 28:2; 2 Cor. 11:27).

psychros [ψυχρός, *5593*]

psychros is an adjective denoting "cold" in Matt. 10:42; Rev. 3:15, 16.

psychō [ψύχω, *5594*]

psychō is a rare verb found only in Matt. 24:12 with the metaphorical sense "grow cold" in relation to human love for God.

COLT

OT Words

'ayir **[עַיִר, 5895]**

This noun occurs eight times in the Old Testament with the meaning "colt," namely the male offspring of an ass (cf. Gen. 32:15; 49:11; Judg. 10:4; 12:14; Job 11:12; Isa. 30:6, 24; Zech. 9:9). The last of these is the most theologically significant in that it constitutes a prophetic anticipation of the Lord's triumphal entry into the city of Jerusalem at the time of the Passover immediately prior to his own crucifixion. The selection of this humble beast of burden is in line with Jesus' own genuine desire not to present himself as a typical ruler of this world, but rather as one whose kingdom was founded not on self-aggrandizement but on self-sacrificial denial and obedience to God, and in service to humanity (cf. Matt. 21:1ff.).

NT Words

pōlos [πῶλος, *4454*]

pōlos is a noun found twelve times, denoting a "colt" (i.e., the young of a horse or donkey) throughout (cf. Matt. 21:2ff.; Mark 11:2ff.; Luke 19:30ff.; John 12:15).

COME

OT Words

bô' **[בּוֹא, 935]**

This is one of the most common verbs in the entire Old Testament, occurring nearly 2,500 times. Its primary meaning is "go," "come," and it is found just under 2,000 times with this sense. The remaining five hundred occurrences of the term are primarily translated "bring." (→ BRING)

In the majority of instances, then, ***bô'*** has the straightforward sense of "come." However, it sometimes takes on related meanings, including "enter" and "visit" (i.e., God's coming upon his enemies to punish them, and upon his people to bless them). (→ ENTER → VISIT)

While the majority of the occurrences of ***bô'*** are prosaic, there is one area of meaning associated with this term that is highly significant. It has to do with God "coming" to his people in various contexts.

One example of this phenomenon concerns the coming of God among his people in the symbolism of the ark of the covenant. The coming of God among his people is far too broad a theme to be examined simply in a discussion of the verb ***bô'***, but its significance may be noted. For instance, in 1 Sam. 4:5–7, the ark of the covenant comes into the Israelite camp, brought there by the Israelites who believed, wrongly, that they could treat the symbol of Yahweh's dwelling in their midst as a kind of magic charm that would guarantee them victory, simply by its presence. They had failed to consult God on the matter and took him for granted. As a result, the ark was lost to the Philistines in the comprehensive defeat in the ensuing battle. Later, the ark also came to the Philistine cities of Ashdod and Ekron, where havoc and disease came upon them as a judgment for blaspheming God's name (cf. 1 Sam. 5:1ff.). Then, in 1 Chr. 15:29, the arrival of the ark in Jerusalem precipitates a period of great feasting and rejoicing on the part of King David and the people of the city, for there is great joy in the realization that God has finally come to dwell in the place he had chosen for his name. That permanent location (i.e., the temple) would not be built until the time of Solomon. However, prior to the construction of the temple, Solomon also recognized the sanctifying effect of the ark's coming to the palace of David (cf. 2 Chr. 8:11).

Further evidence of the significance of God's "coming" in the Old Testament is seen particularly in the allusion to the coming Day of the Lord, when that time of judgment will result in punishment for his people (e.g., Joel 2:1, 31); punishment against his enemies (e.g., Babylon [cf. Isa. 13:9]); and punishment involving both his people and their enemies. Zech. 14 is particularly significant here, for it is a picture of climactic blessing and judgment. At the end of time, the Day of the Lord will result in hardship for God's people — but they will ultimately be delivered and transformed, and all of their enemies will be destroyed forever. The complex Day of the Lord theme unfolds progressively throughout the Scriptures. Yet it is finally fulfilled in the return of the Messiah. Other significant references to the coming of God in wrath are found, for example, in Pss. 50:3; 96:13; 98:9; Isa. 3:14; 30:27; 35:4; 66:15; Ezek. 43:3.

In a positive light, the coming of God as the Redeemer and deliverer of his people is also clearly indicated in the Old Testament (cf., e.g., Isa. 40:10; 59:20; 60:1; Pss. 24:7, 9; 121:1; Zech. 9:9).

NT Words

Just as there are various Hebrew terms expressing the very common and general sense of "come," so the New Testament has a great variety of terms with this sense and other related nuances. The entry below will deal with some of these, sampling their usage and referring to related entries for further discussion.

erchomai [ἔρχομαι, *2064*]

erchomai is a common verb meaning "come" in a variety of contexts throughout the approximately 650 occurrences of the term. (→ ARRIVE)

The "coming" of people is found in the context of traveling in Matt. 2:2ff.; John 4:5ff.; Rom. 15:22ff. Elsewhere, "coming" with a specific purpose is illustrated in relation to the Queen of Sheba's visit to Solomon (Luke 11:31); to people seeking healing from Christ (Mark 1:40; 2:3; Luke 8:47); and to those seeking baptism from John the Baptist (Luke 3:12). People come to Jesus to seek salvation (John 6:37); as well as spiritual nourishment (cf. John 6:35; 7:37). John 3:21 speaks of those "coming" to the light of God for true spiritual illumination. John 6:44ff.; 65 speak of God enabling people to "come" to him. There are blessings available for the one who "comes" in the name of the Lord.

A variety of contexts refer to the "coming" of various inanimate objects. ***erchomai*** describes the appearance of a star over the place where Christ was born in Matt. 2:9. It also refers to the "coming" of faith in relation to the gospel in Gal. 3:23ff.; to the arrival of the Day of the Lord (cf. Acts 2:20); and similarly to the "coming" of the final judgment of the Lord (cf. Matt. 9:15; Mark 2:20; Luke 21:6; John 4:21ff.; 5:25). The "arrival" of the hour of Christ's suffering on the cross is noted in John 12:23; 17:1. The "coming" of a light to the world with reference to the incarnation of Christ is indicated in John 1:9, 29ff.; 3:19. The "coming" of the wrath of God is noted in Col. 3:6; 1 Thess. 1:10; Rev. 6:17. God's voice is described as "coming out" of a cloud to commend his son in Mark 9:7; John 12:28.

Christ's "coming" to earth in regard to his carrying out the divine plan of salvation is noted in a variety of contexts. He is said to come to earth in the Father's name (cf. John 5:43). General references to his redemptive "coming" are found in Mark 1:7; 10:45; Luke 19:10; John 1:11; 4:25; 12:47; 16:28; 1 Tim. 1:15. His "coming" to call sinners to repentance is noted in Matt. 9:13; Mark 2:17; Luke 5:32. He "comes" to bring judgment on the earth as noted in Matt. 10:34ff.; Luke 12:36ff.; John 7:27; 9:39. John 12:13ff. affirms Jesus' "coming" as the king of Israel. John 14:23 affirms that Christ and the Father "come" to believers in order to establish intimate relationships with them. Christ's "coming" in the flesh is understood as the revelation of himself as the true Messiah in 1 John 4:3; 2 John 7. Jesus' "coming" in his final glorious return to earth at the end of time is noted in Matt. 16:27; Luke 21:27; Acts 1:11; 1 Cor. 11:26; Rev. 1:7.

In one or two places, the "coming" of Christ relates to his return to heaven on his ascension from earth. This is described as the "coming into his kingdom" in Matt. 16:28; Mark 9:1.

Several places describe the "coming" of God's kingdom to earth (cf. Matt. 6:10; Luke 11:2; 22:18). Then, in John 16:8, Christ declares that the Holy Spirit "will come" to earth, sent by him on the authority of God the Father. This will take place, however, only after Jesus' return to his heavenly glory, for the purpose of convicting the world of sin.

eperchomai [ἐπέρχομαι, *1904*]

eperchomai is a variant of ***erchomai***, above, meaning "come," along with a number of related nuances.

The miraculous conception of Mary with the Christ child is described in terms of the Holy Spirit "coming upon" her in Luke 1:35. In addition, the baptism of the Holy Spirit is depicted in terms of the Spirit "coming upon" the disciples of Christ in Acts 1:8 (cf. also Acts 8:24). The meaning "overcome" in a physical sense is indicated in Luke 11:22. The "coming" of the Day of the Lord (the final judgment) is indicated in Luke 21:26, 35. See also Jas. 5:1; Acts 13:40. The "coming ages" is another expression indicating the consummation of God's plan of salvation in Eph. 2:7. "Come" in the mundane sense of "arrive" is indicated in Acts 14:19.

proserchomai [προσέρχομαι, *4334*]

proserchomai is another variant of ***erchomai***, above, meaning "come," "draw near" in a variety of contexts throughout the nearly ninety occurrences of the term.

The literal mundane sense of "coming" in relation to people is illustrated in Matt. 4:3; Mark 12:28; Luke 9:12; John 12:21; Acts 7:31.

There are a number of references to people "drawing near" to God's throne of grace in prayer (cf. Heb. 4:16; 7:25; 10:22; 11:6 [cf. also 1 Pet. 2:4]). Heb. 10:1 refers to worshipers "drawing near" to God through their sacrifices. Heb. 12:22 speaks of the people of God "drawing near" to the heavenly Mt. Zion.

Matt. 28:2 mentions an angel "coming" from heaven in order to roll back the stone from Jesus' grave.

ginomai [γίνομαι, *1096*]

ginomai is a very common verb found over one thousand times meaning "be," "become," "happen," plus a variety of other related nuances. One of these nuances is "come."

The meaning "come,"or "arrive," is evident in relation to evening in Matt. 14:23; Mark 4:35; John 6:16; to morning in Matt. 27:1; to a particular time of day (cf. Mark 15:33; Luke 22:14); and also in the context of travel (cf. Acts 9:3; 21:17).

A number of phenomena are described as emanating from God. The voice of God is said to "come" from a cloud for the purpose of commending his son (cf. Luke 9:35 [see ***erchomai***, above]). Acts 7:31 describes God's voice "coming" to Moses from out of the burning bush. See also Acts 10:13. Grace and truth are declared to "have come" through Jesus Christ in John 1:17.

ginomai also means "come upon" in several contexts. The Holy Spirit is said to "come upon" Jesus in Luke 3:22. Acts 2:43; 5:5ff. record fear "coming upon" people. The blessing of God is said to "have come upon" the Gentiles through Christ Jesus.

hēkō [ἥκω, *2240*]

hēkō is another synonym for the preceding entries meaning "come" throughout the nearly thirty occurrences of the term.

The mundane sense of "come," "arrive" is illustrated in the context of travel, as noted in Matt. 8:11; Mark 8:3; Luke 13:29; John 4:47; Acts 28:23. The "coming" of the end of the world is indicated in Matt. 24:14; as are the final days of this age in Luke 19:43. John 2:4 records the preordained "hour" (i.e., coming) of Christ's suffering.

The meaning "come upon" in the sense of "happen to" is indicated in Matt. 23:36; Rev. 18:8 in relation to the judgment of God "coming upon" unbelievers. 2 Pet. 3:10 affirms that the Day of the Lord "will come" as a surprise.

The action of "coming" with a specific intention or purpose is noted in relation to people worshiping God in Rev. 15:4; and to those coming to God seeking salvation in John 6:37. In relation to the person of Christ, Rev. 2:25; 3:3 declare that he "will come" on the day of judgment. In several places Christ is described as "coming" from God in order to accomplish his Father's will (cf. John 8:42; Rom. 11:26; Heb. 10:7ff.; 1 John 5:20).

phthanō [φθάνω, *5348*]

phthanō is a verb found in nine contexts with the meaning "come upon" in the sense of "reach," "touch," or "make an impact on." Matt. 12:28; Luke 11:20 speak of the kingdom of God "coming upon" unbelieving Pharisees. 1 Thess. 2:16 refers to the wrath of God "coming upon" the Gentiles.

See Also: → ARISE → ARRIVE → ASSEMBLE → DEPART → DESCEND → ENTER → LEAVE → PASS → RETURN

COMFORT, COMFORTER

OT Words

nāḥam [נָחַם, **5162**]

This verb has the dual meanings "repent" and "comfort," or "console." The latter meaning is found about sixty times in a number of different contexts.

On a purely human level, ***nāḥam*** refers to the comfort offered by those seeking to console loved ones or close friends at a time of personal trauma — for example, David, in the aftermath of his son Amnon's death (cf. 2 Sam. 13:39); and Isaac, after the death of his mother Sarah (cf. Gen. 24:67). Ruth expresses her gratitude to Boaz for offering her comfort in the provision of food and employment (cf. Ruth 2:13). David offers a message of consolation to Hanum, King of Amnon, on the occasion of his father's death (cf. 1 Chr. 19:2). Job's friends offer him initial comfort at the time of his physical affliction (cf. Job 2:11). In Gen. 27:42 Esau consoles himself with the prospect of killing his brother, Jacob, after the latter had swindled him out of his birthright. Note, in addition, the following references: Gen. 5:29; 37:35; 50:21; Job 42:11; 1 Chr. 7:22.

There are a number of texts that express either the withholding or the granting of divine comfort. The most significant of these relate to the invasion and destruction of both the northern and southern kingdoms of Israel and Judah. At these times it is noteworthy that God both withholds and grants comfort to his people.

The following texts illustrate God's denial of comfort to his people. In Isa. 57:6, for example, there is bitter irony in the question God asks of his people — whether he should take comfort in their grain and drink offerings. The implied answer is a resounding no, since the entire oracle is an indictment of Israel's idolatrous sacrifices to pagan gods. The divine mood is clearly one of anger and, if God receives no comfort, then the people shall certainly be denied it as well. Isa. 51:19 is more explicit — there shall be no divine consolation during the people's experience of God's wrath. The book of Lamentations records the poignant despair of Jeremiah and the people of Jerusalem in the wake of the city's destruction. They are inconsolable, and there is no one to comfort them — not even God (cf. Lam. 1:2ff.).

On the other hand, there are texts that clearly indicate God's determination to extend comfort to his people notwithstanding the fact that he is angry with them and will carry out his judgment against them. This comfort is consistently proclaimed in the Prophets, often in close juxtaposition with the pronouncement of condemnation (cf. Ezek. 14:22, 23; Isa. 49:13; 51:3; 52:9; 66:18; Zech. 1:17; Lam. 2:13).

From a more general perspective, there are those classic expressions of divine comfort that are promised to the people of God and experienced by them (cf. Pss. 23:4; 71:21; Isa. 12:1; 40:1; 51:12). In the Old Testament, it is the figure of the Isaianic Servant of Yahweh that embodies this hope and comfort in a powerful way (cf. Isa. 61:2). It needs to be recognized that the mere occurrences of ***nāḥam*** alone do not exhaust this theme. Indeed, the entire body of Old Testament prophecy, in relation to the coming of God's kingdom and the anticipation of full salvation in the messianic Redeemer-King, brings its own profound consolation to the people of God.

niḥûmîm [נִחוּמִים, 5150]

This plural noun occurs only three times, and twice with the sense of "comfort(s)." In Isa. 57:18 it reflects the same promise of comfort as ***nāḥam***, above. Once again, God determines to offer his people hope of consolation in the wake of their punishment by him. The comfort lies in the divine promise to restore and renew them, both physically and spiritually (cf. also. Zech. 1:13).

tanḥûmîm [תַּנְחוּמִים, 8575]

This word is also rare. Found only three times in the Old Testament, it is synonymous with ***nāḥam***, above. It refers once to divine comfort granted to the psalmist in a time of crisis (cf. Ps. 94:19), and once it refers metaphorically to the "beasts" of Jerusalem that will provide consolation for God's people (cf. Isa. 66:11). This second reference is an indirect indication of comfort derived from God. Jer. 16:7 refers to God withholding "the cup of consolation" from his people in their time of judgment at the hands of the Babylonian army.

NT Words

parakaleō [παρακαλέω, *3870*]

parakaleō is a verb occurring over one hundred times with the primary meanings "exhort" and "comfort."

The meaning "offer comfort" is indicated in several contexts. Such comfort is forthcoming in the face of persecution or catastrophe in Matt. 2:18; 5:4; 2 Cor. 1:4ff. The penitent sinner benefits from such comfort in 2 Cor. 2:7.

There are exhortations to "comfort" or "encourage" one's fellow believers in 1 Thess. 4:18; 5:11.

The passive sense of "be comforted" is indicated in relation to the support received through the faith of one's congregation in 1 Thess. 3:7. The experience of comfort is offered in the aftermath of suffering in Luke 16:25; Acts 20:12. 2 Cor. 7:13 mentions "being comforted" by God.

In 2 Cor. 7:6 God is said to "comfort" the downcast.

paraklēsis [παράκλησις, *3874*]

paraklēsis is a noun derived from ***parakaleō*** (see above) denoting "consolation," "encouragement," "comfort."

Metaphorical reference to the "consolation of Israel" denotes the coming Messiah, who would bring comfort to Israel (cf. Luke 2:25).

The designation "Son of Encouragement" is a name for Barnabas recorded in Acts 4:36.

paraklēsis denotes the literal sense of "(material) comfort" in Luke 6:24.

Elsewhere, this term denotes comfort that is intangible or spiritual. For example, Phil. 2:1 describes the "comfort" and encouragement found in Christ. The spiritual "comfort" of the Holy Spirit is noted in Acts 9:31, as well as that offered by God in 2 Cor. 1:3, 7; 2 Thess. 2:16. "Comfort" derived from the Scriptures is indicated in Rom. 15:4. "Comfort" gained from Christian fellowship is noted in 2 Cor. 7:7, 13; Phlm. 7.

paraklētos [παράκλητος, *3875*]

paraklētos is a rare noun derived from ***parakaleō***, above, referring mainly to the person of the Holy Spirit. A precise translation of ***paraklētos*** is difficult to determine. The underlying sense of the term is that of "one who stands alongside another in order to offer encouragement, comfort." It is generally conceded that the legal connotation of "advocate" also constitutes a likely understanding of ***paraklētos.*** The four contexts in which this term appears (John 14:16, 26; 15:26; 16:7) suggest that the role attributed to the Holy Spirit is that of either "Counselor" or "Advocate." Christ describes the Holy Spirit's mission as one of revealing truth, convicting of sin, and applying the context of Jesus' teaching to the lives of his disciples. Clearly the function of the Holy Spirit is to enable the people of God, individually and corporately, to maintain a vital relationship with God through his personal indwelling presence. Thus the designations "Advocate" and "Counselor," while accurate, are not comprehensive. No one English term expresses the full semantic range of ***paraklētos.***

paramythia [παραμυθία, *3889*]

paramythia is a rare term denoting "comfort" as one of the intended consequences of genuine prophecy for those who listened. It is found only in 1 Cor. 14:3.

paramytheomai [παραμυθέομαι, *3888*]

paramytheomai is a verb found only four times, meaning offer "comfort" or "consolation" in the case of a bereavement in John 11:19, 31, and "encourage" in the general sense of "offer helpful advice" in 1 Thess. 2:11; 5:14.

parēgoria [παρηγορία, *3931*]

parēgoria is a rare noun denoting "comfort" in the sense of "encouragement" found only in Col. 4:11.

Additional Notes

The theme of "comfort" is consistently affirmed throughout both Testaments. This is especially the case in regard to divine comfort. Both Testaments focus on the consolation provided by God: first of all in the context of his relationship with Israel as their redeemer and king, and secondly in the New Testament through the person of his Son, Jesus Christ. The New Testament makes it clear that the Messiah fulfills the promised "consolation to Israel." In this sense, genuine dynamic equivalence exists between ***nāḥam*** and ***parakaleō***; ***niḥûmîm***, ***tanḥûmîm***, and ***paraklēsis.***

COMING (NOUN)

NT Words

parousia [παρουσία, *3952*]

The noun ***parousia*** denotes a "coming" in the primary sense of Christ's return at the end of the age. It is found twenty-four times (cf. Matt. 24:3; 1 Cor. 15:23; 1 Thess. 2:19; 2 Thess. 2:1; Jas. 5:7ff.; 2 Pet. 1:16; 3:4; 1 John 2:28).

parousia also refers to the "coming of the lawless one" (i.e., the antichrist) in 2 Thess. 2:9. Other mundane references to people "coming" include 1 Cor. 16:17; 2 Cor. 7:6ff.; Phil. 1:26; 2 Thess. 2:1, 8ff.

eisodos [εἴσοδος, *1529*]

eisodos denotes the "coming" of Jesus in Acts 13:24.

eleusis [ἔλευσις, *1660*]

eleusis is a rare noun, found only in Acts 7:52, referring to the "coming" of the righteous one — Christ the Messiah.

COMMAND

OT Words

ṣāwāh **[צָוָה, 6680]**

This verb has the primary sense of "charge," or "command," and is found approximately 450 times. Occasionally, ***ṣāwāh*** is translated "appoint." (→ APPOINT)

Of all the occurrences of ***ṣāwāh***, about 350 relate to the specific commands of God to his people. And although the contexts vary, the common emphasis throughout the Old Testament with regard to the divine command centers on Yahweh's sovereign authority as Creator, ruler, and deliverer of his people. Whenever God directs his people, it is with utmost authority. The use of ***ṣāwāh*** in this sense is concentrated primarily in the Pentateuch and the Prophets.

Over half the uses of ***ṣāwāh*** referring to God issuing the command relate to the Mosaic covenant. It is here that the authority of Yahweh is most graphically demonstrated. For example, God begins by giving Moses his commission to confront Pharaoh and demand that the king of Egypt let the Israelite people go free (cf. Exod. 4:26; 7:3ff.). After the deliverance from Egypt, God brings his people to the foot of Mt. Sinai, where he makes known to the Israelites, through Moses, the detail of his covenant law. The content of this revelation is the focal point of approximately half the book of Exodus (i.e., chs. 25–40); the whole of Leviticus; significant portions of Numbers; and virtually the entire book of Deuteronomy. In this section of Scripture, there are many references to God commanding Moses — and by extension the people of Israel — to keep the law of the covenant that God had revealed to them. Some of the more significant texts in this regard are Exod. 19:7; 40:16; Lev. 9:6; 16:34; Num. 1:19;

15:23; Deut. 1:3; 5:12ff.; 6:1, 17ff.; 28:45; 31:5. While the bulk of these references to the divine commands are found in the Pentateuch, they are not restricted to this section of Scripture. Israel's obligation to her God under the terms of the covenant is mandatory, and God leaves his people in no doubt that devotion and obedience to his laws are a strict requirement, not an optional extra (cf. Josh. 7:11; 8:8; 11:12ff.; Judg. 2:20; 1 Kgs. 8:58).

What is also clear is that God commanded his people not only to keep his laws but also to carry out his plan of salvation. He determined the part they must play and bound them to it. The divine command even extended to the animal world, which God required to carry out his plans. For example, God commands ravens to supply Elijah with food by the brook Cherith in the wilderness, as he awaited further developments in God's plan (cf. 1 Kgs. 17:4). Gentiles, too, are under his control (e.g., the widow of Zarephath, whom God commissioned to give hospitality to Elijah in 1 Kgs. 17:9).

In addition, the prophets constantly reinforce the importance of heeding and obeying God's commands. They also warn the people of the serious consequences of neglecting to do so (cf. Jer. 7:22ff.; 11:4, 8; 17:22; 26:8; 32:23; Amos 9:3, 4).

God's commandments are not restricted to the content of the Mosaic covenant. Prior to the time of the Exodus, God had made his requirements very clear, for example, to Adam and Eve in the garden of Eden (cf. Gen. 2:16; 3:11, 17); and to Noah, preceding the flood (cf. Gen. 6:22; 7:5).

Whenever the Old Testament records a divine command, the subject of that instruction always relates either directly or indirectly to the purposes of God in history on behalf of his people. This applies whether God is instructing his people in the matter of the covenant law or directing them to implement aspects of his redemptive purposes. At times this involves punishment as well as blessing. Either way, the impact of the divine command in the Old Testament is universal and profound.

ṣāwāh is also used to refer to various people in authority issuing commands to their subordinates. The term is used this way about one hundred times.

'āmar [אָמַר, **559**]

The verb ***'āmar*** is most commonly translated as "say" or "speak" in the over 5,300 occurrences of the term. There are also a number of other related senses, including that of "command." God is said to issue "commands" to creation (cf. Job 9:7; Ps. 107:25); and to his people (cf. Exod. 8:27; 1 Sam. 16:16; 1 Chr. 21:27; Ps. 106:34; Dan. 2:2). 1 Chr. 21:18 refers to a "command" given by the angel of the Lord.

In the human sphere, people issue "commands," or give orders, as noted in 1 Chr. 21:17; 2 Chr. 29:24ff.; Neh. 13:9; Esth. 1:10, 17.

dābar [דָּבַר, **1696**]

dābar is a common synonym for ***'āmar***, above, again with the primary meaning "say," or "speak." It carries the force of "command" (i.e., "give an order") in a general sense in Exod. 1:17; Num. 16:47. God is said to "issue a command" in Num. 27:23.

NT Words

diatassō [διατάσσω, *1299*]

diatassō is a verb found in sixteen places, meaning "command," "charge."

The meaning "command" in the sense of "give a charge, instruction(s)" is found in Luke 8:55; 17:9ff.; Acts 18:2; 20:13; 23:31; 24:23; 1 Cor. 11:34; 16:1; Titus 1:5.

Acts 7:44 describes God "giving instructions" to Moses on how to construct the tabernacle. In 1 Cor. 9:14, Paul affirms that the Lord "has commanded" that those who preach the gospel should earn their living from the gospel.

epitassō [ἐπιτάσσω, *2004*]

epitassō is a variant form of ***diatassō***, above, found in ten contexts, meaning "command," "charge."

The "giving of orders" in a military context is indicated in Mark 6:27. The household context of a master "giving instructions" to his servant is noted in Luke 14:22. In a civil context, Acts 23:2 records the high priest "issuing instructions" to his servants. In the apostolic context, Paul "gives an instruction" to Philemon in Phlm. 8.

Christ "issues a command" to evil spirits to abandon their victims in Mark 1:27; 9:25; Luke 4:36; 8:31; and in Mark 6:39 he "instructs" the crowd to be seated. In Luke 8:25, he "commands" the natural elements of wind and sea to obey him.

prostassō [προστάσσω, *4367*]

The verb ***prostassō*** is also synonymous with ***diatassō*** and ***epitassō***, above. It is found seven times, meaning "command," "instruct" throughout.

God is said to "issue commands" coming through the old covenant law of Moses in Matt. 8:4; Mark 1:44; Luke 5:14. There is also direct "instruction" from God in Acts 10:33; and in Acts 10:48 Peter "gives instructions" for new converts to be baptized. The angel of the Lord "gives instructions" to Joseph to take Mary his wife home in Matt. 1:24. Matt. 21:6 refers to Christ "instructing" his disciples.

syntassō [συντάσσω, *4929*]

syntassō is a rare variant for the above entries. It is found twice in Matt. 26:19, where Christ "directs" his followers to make preparations for the Passover. Matt. 27:10 cites Jer. 32:6ff. in regard to the Lord's "instruction" to the prophet to purchase the field at Anathoth.

keleuō [κελεύω, *2753*]

keleuō is another synonym for the entries above, indicating the action of "commanding," "directing," or "instructing" people to perform certain actions. Jesus instructs the crowds following him in Matt. 8:18; 14:9, 19; 15:35; and he "commands" a blind man to be brought to him (Luke 18:40). Peter asks Jesus to "command him" to walk on water in Mark 14:28.

General references to people "giving orders" are found in Matt. 18:25; 27:58, 64; Acts 27:43; Acts 4:15. Elsewhere, the "giving of orders" in a judicial context is noted in Acts 12:15; 16:22; 21:33ff.; 22:30; 24:8; 25:6, 17, 21ff.

entellō [ἐντέλλω, *1781*]

entellō is a verb meaning "command," "give orders" throughout the nearly twenty occurrences of the term.

God is said to "give commands" concerning his angels in Matt. 4:6; Luke 4:10; in relation to honoring one's parents in Matt. 15:4; concerning divorce in Matt. 19:7; through Moses in Mark 10:3; John 8:5; and to his son in John 14:31. God also "directs" his servants to be a light for the Gentiles in Acts 13:47. He issues a command with respect to keeping the covenant in Heb. 9:20.

Jesus "gives commands" to his disciples in Matt. 17:9; 28:20; John 15:14, 17. See also Acts 1:2.

Other general references to "giving orders" include Mark 13:34; Heb. 11:22.

parangellō [παραγγέλλω, *3853*]

parangellō is a verb found in about thirty places, with the primary meaning "command."

The meanings "charge," "give a solemn order to" are found in relation to the disciples being forbidden to preach the gospel of Christ in Acts 4:18; 5:28, 40. Paul "instructs" husbands and wives not to separate in 1 Cor. 7:10. Christian converts are commanded in Acts 15:5 to keep the law of Moses and to be circumcised—an order contrary to the gospel and to new covenant practice. Commands are given to evil spirits in the process of their exorcism in Acts 16:18. Instructions relating to godly living and gospel ministry are noted in 1 Tim. 1:3; 4:11; 6:17. See also Acts 16:23; 2 Thess. 3:4ff.

In relation to the ministry of Christ, Jesus "gives instruction" to his disciples in Matt. 10:5; Mark 6:8; Acts 1:4; and to the crowds following him in Mark 8:6. He "commands" his followers to preach the gospel in Acts 10:42; and he "orders" unclean spirits to leave their victims in Luke 8:29. See also Luke 9:21.

Acts 17:30 contains the divine command for all people everywhere to repent.

Additional Notes

While there are many terms for "command" in the New Testament, this concept is mainly expressed in the Old Testament by the one verb, ***ṣāwāh***. Although there are other terms in Hebrew for issuing instructions or laying down precepts, this one word embodies a variety of perspectives and emphases that are more precisely expressed through a number of approximately equivalent Greek terms. For breadth of meaning, the closest dynamic Greek equivalents for ***ṣāwāh*** would most likely be ***diatassō*** and ***entellō***.

COMMANDMENT

OT Words

miṣwāh [מִצְוָה, 4687]

miṣwāh is the noun derived from *ṣāwāh* (→ COMMAND), and occurs around 180 times, meaning "commandment."

As with *ṣāwāh*, the predominant emphasis of ***miṣwāh*** is on the divine precept. ***miṣwāh*** most frequently refers to commandments issued by God, most of which in turn center on the law of the covenant. As one might expect, ***miṣwāh*** occurs most frequently in the Pentateuch (approximately sixty times), and these occurrences are concentrated in the book of Deuteronomy. The most common verb associated with ***miṣwāh*** is the term for "keep." (See → ***shāmar*** under → KEEP.) Note the following sample list of texts: Exod. 16:28; 20:6; Lev. 22:31; Num. 36:13; Deut. 5:10, 29; 7:9, 11; 8:2ff.; 11:8; 13:4; 19:9; 27:1; 30:10.

This distribution of ***miṣwāh*** is not, however, restricted to the Pentateuch. The word appears fifty times in the books of Kings and Chronicles, the majority of which refer to the attitudes — good and bad — of the kings of Israel and Judah towards divine commands issued under the Mosaic covenant (cf. 1 Kgs. 2:3; 3:14; 13:21; 14:8; 2 Kgs. 17:19; 18:6; 1 Chr. 28:7; 2 Chr. 17:4). Similar emphases are found in Ezra and Nehemiah, where ***miṣwāh*** occurs eighteen times (cf. Ezra 7:11; 9:10; Neh. 1:5ff.; 9:13, 14, 34). The Wisdom writings contains a number of references to ***miṣwāh***. More than half of these occur in Ps. 119, a psalm devoted entirely to praise and thanksgiving to God for his covenant law and precepts. In the prophetic literature, ***miṣwāh*** is comparatively rare (occurring only eleven times).

Aside from the reference to God's commandments, ***miṣwāh*** also indicates commands given by people. It is used fifteen times in this way. However, there is a like emphasis here on the law of the covenant, as with God's commands. Several places refer to four kings issuing commands to their people that reflect their intention to uphold the laws of God laid down in the Mosaic legislation. These are David (cf. 2 Chr. 8:14; Neh. 12:24); Solomon (cf. 2 Chr. 8:15); Josiah (cf. 2 Chr. 35:10, 15, 16); Hezekiah (cf. 2 Chr. 30:6, 12).

ṣaw [צַו, 6673]

ṣaw is a noun derived from ***ṣāwāh*** (→ COMMAND), occurring nine ?times with the generalized, vague meaning of "precept" or "command" (cf. Isa. 28:10, 13). The context makes it clear, however, that there is no divine ordinance in view here.

piqqûd [פִּקּוּד, 6490]

The noun ***piqqûd*** occurs around twenty times (in the plural only), denoting the revealed "precepts," "commands," or "ordinances" of God. ***piqqûd*** is found only in the Psalter and most references are in Ps. 119. These "precepts" of Yahweh are the object of the psalmist's delight, both in meditation and practice (e.g., Pss. 19:8; 103:18; 111:7; 119:4, 40, 45, 93ff., 100, 128, 173).

peh [פֶּה, 6310]

peh is a common noun denoting "mouth" in the majority of the nearly five hundred occurrences of the term. There are also several related senses, one of which is "commandment," referring to the instructions or orders uttered by both God and human beings.

General references to "commands" issued by people are found in Gen. 45:21; 2 Kgs. 23:35; Eccl. 8:2. Elsewhere, the "commandments" of Yahweh are in view. Commands governing the fixing of God's created phenomena are noted in Prov. 8:29. The commands associated with his revealed intention and requirements for his people are spoken through Moses (cf. Exod. 17:1; 38:21; Num. 3:39; 9:18ff.; 14:41; 33:2). See also Josh. 17:4; 21:3; 2 Kgs. 24:3. Yahweh gives "instructions" to Balaam in Num. 24:13. Israel's rebellion against God's commands is recorded in Deut. 1:2, 43. Warnings against such rebellion are found in Josh. 1:18; 1 Sam. 12:14. Transgression of the Lord's commands is recorded in 1 Sam. 15:24.

dābār [דָּבָר, 1697]

dābār is a common noun found nearly 1,500 times with the primary meaning "word," along with numerous related senses — one of which is "command," "commandment."

References to the "commandment" of the Lord include Josh. 8:8; 1 Sam. 15:13; 2 Sam. 12:9; Dan. 9:23ff. ***dābār*** is also used to refer to the Decalogue,or the ten "commandments," in Exod. 34:28; Deut. 4:13; 10:4.

Commands issued by military leaders are noted in 1 Chr. 28:21; and by kings in 2 Chr. 31:5; Esth. 1:1, 12, 19; 2:8; 3:15; 4:3; 8:14; 9:1.

NT Words

diatagma [διάταγμα, *1297*]

diatagma is a rare noun found only in Heb. 11:27, referring to the Egyptian king's "edict" or "command" to have all male Hebrew infants slain at birth so as to prevent the expansion of the Israelite people.

entolē [ἐντολή, *1785*]

entolē is a noun denoting "commandment" throughout its nearly seventy occurrences. Its primary usage centers on the commandments of the Mosaic law covenant.

General references to the law given by God include Matt. 5:19; 19:17; 22:36ff.; Mark 7:8ff.; Luke 1:6; 1 Cor. 7:19; 14:35; Heb. 7:5; 9:19; 2 Pet. 2:21; Rev. 12:17; 14:12. In particular, Rom. 7:8ff. mentions the lethal effect of the law on the heart of human beings. Transgressing God's "law" is noted in Matt. 15:3ff. Explicit mention of the Decalogue is made in Mark 10:19; 12:28ff.; Luke 18:20; 23:56; Rom. 13:9; Eph. 6:2. The curse of the "commandments" is declared abolished by the death of Christ in Eph. 2:15. The outmoded uselessness of the old "commandment" in making people perfect, set aside by God in favor of the new covenant, is noted in Heb. 7:18. The importance of keeping God's "commandments," thus demonstrating one's genuine love for him, is indicated in 1 John 2:3ff.; 4:21; 5:3; 2 John 4ff.

Christ's "new command" to his disciples to love one another is recorded in John 13:34; 15:12. General references to the binding nature of the commandments Christ gave to his disciples are found in John 14:15, 21; 15:10. The specific "charge" or "command" given by God to Christ, granting him authority to take up his own life again after death, is recorded in John 10:18 (cf. also John 12:49ff.).

Human "commands" or "instructions" are noted in Luke 15:29; John 11:57; Acts 17:15; Col. 4:10; Titus 1:14.

entalma [ἔνταλμα, *1778*]

entalma is a rare noun denoting the "precepts" or "commandments" of human beings in the sense of "human traditions." The term is found only in Matt. 15:9; Mark 7:7; Col. 2:22, and the connotation is wholly negative. All three references indicate that such traditions are wholly useless in attracting the favor of God.

epitagē [ἐπιταγή, *2003*]

epitagē is a noun denoting the general sense of "command" in seven contexts. General references to the command of God are found in Rom. 16:26; 1 Cor. 7:25; 1 Tim. 1:1; Titus 1:3; 2:15.

References to human commands are found in 1 Cor. 7:6; 8:8.

Additional Notes

The New Testament Greek terminology for "commandment" communicates shades of meaning and perspective that are not represented by separate Hebrew terms. In a broad sense, the Greek noun ***entolē*** corresponds most closely to the Hebrew term ***miṣwāh***. However, those emphases represented by the different Greek terms may also be observed within the semantic range of ***miṣwāh***. This becomes especially significant when one notes that the commands given by Christ are in complete and utter conformity with those issued by God under the old covenant.

See Also: → DECREE → LAW → WITNESS → WORD

COMMIT, COMMISSION → BELIEF → DELIVER → PRACTICE → SIN

COMMON, COMMONLY → DEFILE → UNCLEAN

COMMUNICATE, COMMUNICATION → SPEECH → TALK

COMMUNION → FELLOWSHIP → FRIEND → NEIGHBOR → WALK (VERB)

COMPANY → ASSEMBLE

COMPASS → SURROUND

COMPASSION, COMPASSIONATE

OT Words

ḥûs [חוּס, 2347]

The verb ***ḥûs*** means "have pity, or compassion," "spare."

In the context of divine judgment, God is said to "have had no pity" on his people in Deut. 7:16; Jer. 13:14; Ezek. 5:11; 7:4, 9; 8:18; 9:5, 10; 24:14. God's "having pity, or compassion" on the weak and poor is noted in Ps. 72:13.

Where people are concerned, the absence of pity or compassion shown towards one's enemy is indicated in Deut. 13:8; Jer. 21:7. Similar lack of pity shown towards a person condemned to death or physical punishment is noted in Deut. 19:13, 21; 25:12. See also Isa. 13:18.

The meaning "to spare" in the sense of refraining from killing is noted in 1 Sam. 24:10.

Neh. 13:22; Joel 2:17 contain petitions asking God to "refrain" from punishment, appealing to his compassion. Yahweh is said to "spare" his people from punishment, motivated by his compassion in Ezek. 20:17. Jonah 4:11 records Yahweh's "having pity" on Nineveh.

ḥāmal [חָמַל, 2550]

The verb ***ḥāmal*** means "pity," "spare," "have compassion on," and is found in around forty contexts.

General references to the expression of compassion on the part of people are found in Exod. 2:6; 1 Sam. 23:21; 2 Sam. 12:4; 21:7.

Elsewhere, use of the term is in the negative. Refusal to "spare" a person from judicial punishment is indicated in Deut. 13:8. Refusal to "show compassion" to one's enemies is noted in 2 Chr. 36:17; Jer. 21:7. Other general references to the withholding of compassion are found in Job 27:22; Isa. 9:19. In 1 Sam. 15:3, God instructs the Israelites not to have pity on the Amalekites. The action of "sparing" Agag, their king, and the best of the livestock is noted in 1 Sam. 15:9ff., where compassion may or may not have been present.

God is said to "have compassion" on his people in 2 Chr. 36:15; Joel 2:18. In contrast, there are a number of passages where God refuses to "show pity" toward his people in relation to their inevitable punishment for sin (cf. Jer. 13:14; Lam. 2:17; Ezek. 5:11; 7:4, 9; 9:5, 10).

NT Words

oikteirō [οἰκτείρω, *3627*]

oikteirō is a rare verb found only twice, in Rom. 9:15, is part of the promise that God will have compassion on whom he will have compassion — that is, affirming God's sovereignty in the dispensing of his mercy.

splanchnizomai [σπλαγχνίζομαι, *4697*]

splanchnizomai is a verb found in twelve places with the consistent sense of "have compassion," "be moved with compassion."

People "moved with compassion" for others are noted in Matt. 18:27; Luke 10:33; 15:20.

Christ is depicted as one "moved with compassion" for the crowds following him in Matt. 9:36; 14:14; 15:32; Mark 6:34; 8:2; as well as for those afflicted with illness or incapacity prior to healing (cf. Matt. 20:34; Mark 1:41). See also Luke 7:13. In Mark 9:22, a demon-possessed man pleads for Jesus to have pity and help him.

See Also: → COMFORT → MERCY

COMPLAINT

OT Words

rîb [רִיב, **7378**]

rîb is a verb found about seventy times with the meaning "strive," "argue," or "quarrel," as well as "complain," "make a complaint against."

The action of "complaining" about personal discomfort is noted in Num. 20:3. The meaning "make a complaint against" is indicated in response to a personal wrong (cf. Judg. 21:22); and in a formal legal sense (i.e., lay charges against) in Neh. 5:7.

God's people are said to "complain" against him in a spirit of rebellion and bitterness in Jer. 2:29; and in the context of prophetic bewilderment in Jer. 12:1.

sîaḥ [שִׂיחַ, **7878** (Verb)]

sîaḥ is a verb found twenty times with the primary sense of "tell," "speak." In two places it specifically means "complain" in the context of people bemoaning their anguish of spirit (cf. Job 7:11; Ps. 77:3).

sîaḥ [שִׂיחַ, **7879** (Noun)]

sîaḥ is the noun derived from the verb ***sîaḥ***. It is used fourteen times to denote a "complaint."

References to a "complaint" in the context of Job's calamity are noted in Job 7:13; 9:27; 10:1; 21:4; 23:2. See also Ps. 55:2. "Complaints" made to God in prayer are found in Pss. 64:1; 102:1; 142:2.

'ānan [אָנַן, **596**]

'ānan is a rare verb found only twice with the specific sense of "complain" in both instances. Num. 11:1 speaks of the Israelites complaining against Yahweh, and Lam. 3:39 refers to a man complaining of being punished for his sins.

NT Words

momphē [μομφή, *3437*]

momphē is a rare noun denoting a "complaint" against someone, found only in Col. 3:13.

mempsimoiros [μεμψίμοιρος, *3202*]

mempsimoiros is a rare noun found only in Jude 16 referring to "those who complain or grumble."

See Also: → AVENGE → STRIVE

COMPLETE, COMPLETELY

NT Words

epiteleō [ἐπιτελέω, *2005*]

epiteleō is a verb found thirteen times meaning "perform," "bring to an end," "complete." The sense of human agents "completing," or "finishing," a task is indicated in Rom. 15:28; 2 Cor. 8:6, 11. In Phil. 1:6, God is said to "bring his work of salvation to completion."

artios [ἄρτιος, *739*]

artios is a rare noun found only in 2 Tim. 3:17 referring to a person of God being "complete," or equipped for every good work.

apartismos [ἀπαρτισμός, *535*]

apartismos is a rare noun found only in Luke 14:28 denoting the "completion" of a tower.

See Also: → END → FULFILL → FULL

CONCEAL → HIDE

CONCEIVE

OT Words

hārāh **[הָרָה, 2029]**

This verb occurs forty times in the Old Testament with the consistent meaning "to conceive." On all but five occasions, ***hārāh*** refers to literal conception. It is applied, for example, to Eve (cf. Gen. 4:1, 17); Sarah (cf. Gen. 21:2); Hagar (cf. Gen. 16:4ff.); Rebekah (cf. Gen. 25:21); Leah and Rachel, and Rachel's maidservant Bilhah (cf. Gen. 29:32); Lot's daughters (cf. Gen. 19:36); Hannah (cf. 1 Sam. 1:20); Samson's mother (cf. Judg. 13:3); and Gomer, the wife of Hosea (cf. Hos. 1:3ff.).

hārāh is also used on five occasions to refer symbolically to the lifestyle of the wicked, whose sinful attitudes "conceive" sinful actions in rebellion against God (cf. Ps. 7:14; Job 15:35; Isa. 33:11; 59:4, 13).

yāḥam **[יָחַם, 3179]**

yāḥam is a verb found in nine places with the principal meaning "to mate" in the case of animals (cf. Gen. 30:38ff.; 31:10); and to "conceive" in relation to David's mother in Ps. 51:5.

hārāh **[הָרָה, 2030]**

The noun ***hārāh*** is found sixteen times with the primary sense of being "with child," or pregnant. In three instances it means to "conceive." Such a state is promised to the future mother of Samson in Judg. 13:5ff.; and to the future mother of the Immanuel child in Isa. 7:14 — a classic prophetic anticipation of the Messiah.

hērāyôn **[הֵרָיוֹן, 2032]**

hērāyôn is a rare noun found three times denoting a woman's "conception" in Ruth 4:13; Hos. 9:11. In Gen. 3:16 the term denotes "childbearing" as cursed by God as a consequence of the fall, resulting in increased anguish and pain for womankind in this primary function of her being.

NT Words

syllambanō [συλλαμβάνω, *4815*]

syllambanō is a verb found sixteen times with the meaning "conceive" in about one-third of these contexts. (→ SEIZE)

References to Elizabeth conceiving John the Baptist are noted in Luke 1:24, 36; and to Mary miraculously conceiving Jesus by the mysterious operation of the Holy Spirit in Luke 1:31; 2:21.

katabolē [καταβολή, *2602*]

katabolē is a noun with the primary meaning "foundation" in reference to the foundation of the world. (→ FOUNDATION) However, in Heb. 11:11 this term refers to Sarah's capacity to "conceive," as granted to her by God in fulfillment of his promise to her husband Abraham, leading to the birth of their son Isaac.

Additional Notes

The idea of "conception" in both Old and New Testaments is quite similar, with both a literal and a symbolic emphasis. Of the Greek terms for "conceive," ***syllambanō*** is the closest dynamic equivalent for ***hārāh***.

See Also: → BEGET

CONDEMN, CONDEMNATION

OT Words

rāsha' **[רָשַׁע, 7561]**

rāsha' is found approximately fifty times in the Old Testament and means to "do wickedly," "commit transgression," or "condemn." The latter meaning is found in several different contexts — whether it is condemnation resulting from an accusation that is formal or informal, legitimate or illegitimate.

In the first instance, there is the judicial indictment for various misdemeanors that is outlined under the Mosaic legislation (cf. Deut. 25:1; 1 Kgs. 8:32; Exod. 22:9). Such a process is also alluded to in Job (cf. Job 9:20; 15:6), as well as in Psalms and Proverbs, where sometimes rank injustice and false accusation prevail, resulting in divine judgment against such practices (cf. Ps. 94:12; Prov. 12:2; 17:15). God himself is never guilty of this (cf. Ps. 37:33); and, what is more, he promises his divine resources to those who are falsely condemned, in order that they might rebuff their accusers (cf. Isa. 54:17). Job's companion Elihu is aghast that Job seeks to condemn God, and God himself personally asks Job whether he is condemning him (cf. Job 40:8). Job, in turn, has pleaded previously that God might not condemn him (cf. Job 10:2). And, finally, the Messianic Servant is confident that no charge from God will be laid at his feet, declaring himself to be free from condemnation (cf. Isa. 50:9).

rîb **[רִיב, 7379]**

rîb means "controversy," "dispute," "judge" — all of which bear relation to the idea of "condemnation."

mishpāt [מִשְׁפָּט, **4941**]

As with ***rīb***, above, ***mishpāt*** also means "judgment," which likewise has a close affinity with the concept of "condemnation."

shāphat [שָׁפַט, **8199**]

shāphat is a common verb occurring over two hundred times and meaning "to judge" in about half these contexts. The term is also used nominally, denoting a "judge" in most of the remaining usage. The sense of "to condemn" is found only in Ps. 109:31, where the action of condemning a man to death is indicated.

NT Words

kataginōskō [καταγινώσκω, *2607*]

kataginōskō is a rare verb found only three times with the meaning "condemn" in each case. It refers to Paul's assessment of Peter, who stood "condemned" in the former's sight because the latter had compromised his integrity in the gospel by refusing to have fellowship with Gentile believers out of fear of the so-called "Jewish party," who disapproved of such interaction. In 1 John 3:20, 21 ***kataginōskō*** refers metaphorically to the heart of the believer "condemning" him in the face of sinful action(s) or a sinful attitude.

katadikazō [καταδικάζω, *2613*]

katadikazō is a verb occurring six times and translated "condemn." The act of judicial "condemnation" is indicated both directly and indirectly in Matt. 12:7, 37; Jas. 5:6. In Luke 6:37 the term is used in a general sense, affirming that if one does not condemn others without just cause, then one will escape condemnation from the hand of God.

krinō [κρίνω, *2919*]

krinō is a common verb with the primary meaning "judge" throughout the approximately 110 occurrences of the term. In several contexts, however, the sense of "condemn" is expressed. John 3:17, 18 speak of both the absence and presence of divine condemnation. The culpable action of the Jewish leaders in condemning Christ during his lifetime is indicated in Acts 13:27. Rom. 14:22 describes self-condemnation.

katakrinō [κατακρίνω, *2632*]

katakrinō is a verb found in nineteen places with the predominant sense of "condemn," "pass judgment on," throughout the usage.

The meanings "condemn," "pass judgment on" in circumstances precipitated by moral outrage are noted in Matt. 12:41ff.; Luke 11:31ff.; John 8:10 (cf. also Rom. 8:34).

Such an action is taken against Christ by the spiritual and civil authorities of Jerusalem who sought to be rid of him (cf. Matt. 20:18; Mark 10:33). Christ himself is said to "have condemned" sin in his own body through his death on the cross. The passive sense of "being condemned" describes Judas, who stood morally culpable, aware of his heinous crime in betraying Jesus to the authorities (cf. Matt. 27:3). God is said to have condemned Sodom and Gomorrah to destruction, as recorded in 2 Pet. 2:6.

A number of references depict people "condemned by God" for unbelief (cf. Mark 16:16; 1 Cor. 11:32). Jas. 5:9 contains a warning against being "exposed to divine judgment." Heb. 11:7 refers to Noah having "condemned" the world by his righteousness. In John 8:11, Jesus refuses to "pass judgment" on the woman caught in adultery. "Self-condemnation" is evident in Rom. 2:1; 14:23.

katakrima [κατάκριμα, *2631*]

katakrima is a variant form found in only three places and denoting the universal "condemnation" of humankind brought about by the sin of Adam and Eve (Rom. 5:16, 18). Rom. 8:1 declares that there is no "divine condemnation" for those who are joined to Christ in faith.

katakrisis [κατάκρισις, *2633*]

katakrisis is a rare synonym for ***katakrima***, above, denoting the "condemnation" wrought by the law on humankind in 2 Cor. 3:9. 2 Cor. 7:3 refers to "passing judgment" on someone in general terms.

autokatakritos [αὐτοκατάκριτος, *843*]

autokatakritos is a rare adjective found only in Titus 3:11, denoting one who is "self-condemned."

akatagnōstos [ἀκατάγνωστος, *176*]

akatagnōstos is a rare adjectival form found only in Titus 2:8, denoting noble character that "cannot be condemned."

Additional Notes

There is no significant difference concerning the idea of "condemnation" between the two Testaments. The idea of God bringing condemnation down upon the wicked, both within Israel and beyond, is consistent throughout the Bible. What is distinctive in the New Testament is the finished work of Christ that removes condemnation from his people absolutely, as a consequence of his substitutionary atonement on the cross. What is anticipated through the sacrificial system under the Mosaic covenant is consummated in the new by the finished work of Christ on our behalf.

See Also: → ANSWER → DISPUTE → JUDGE → JUDGMENT → LAWSUIT → PROPITIATION

CONFESS, CONFESSION

OT Words

yādāh **[יָדָה, 3034]**

Of the 100 or so occurrences of this verb, a few are translated "confess." The remainder are translated "praise." The two meanings of this verb are, in fact, related. To praise God, for instance, which is the primary thrust of ***yādāh***, is to acknowledge his intrinsic value and give due recognition to him in an act of thankfulness and worship. Then, to confess one's sin, which is the secondary meaning of this verb, is likewise to acknowledge God's unique value as the only source of forgiveness for one's transgression. And so, by confessing sin to God, one pays tribute to this facet of the divine personality, recognizing that God alone can remove the guilt of one's sin. Failure to confess sin is a refusal to acknowledge God's capacity for forgiveness, and thus a denial of worship due to him.

In 1 Kgs. 8:33ff., the phrase "confess the name of God" is equivalent to seeking forgiveness through the recognition of the majesty of his person (cf. also 2 Chr. 6:24, 26). Several references in the Pentateuch explicitly mention the confession of sin as a necessary prerequisite for forgiveness (cf. Lev. 5:5; 16:21; 26:40; Num. 5:7). The psalmist declares his intention to confess his sins (cf. Ps. 32:5). Ezra finishes confessing sin in Ezra 10:1; as does Nehemiah (Neh. 1:6) and the people of Nehemiah's day (cf. Neh. 9:2, 3); and also Daniel in Dan. 9:4, 20. Note also Prov. 28:13 and 2 Chr. 30:22.

tôdāh **[תּוֹדָה, 8426]**

This is the noun derived from ***yādāh***, and likewise means "praise," or "thanksgiving," and "confession." The sense of ***tôdāh*** is identical with that of ***yādāh***, although only two of the occurrences of ***tôdāh*** translate "confession (of sin)" (Josh. 7:19; Ezra 10:11).

NT Words

homologeō [ὁμολογέω, *3670*]

The verb ***homologeō*** is found about twenty-five times with the underlying sense of "confess" throughout, with several associated nuances.

The meaning "confess" in the sense of "acknowledge" is evident in relation to those confessing Christ before others, whom Christ will likewise confess before God (cf. Matt. 10:32; Luke 12:8). The act of "confessing" Christ as God is indicated in 1 John 2:23; 4:2ff., 15. In John 1:20 John the Baptist refuses to "confess" that he is the Christ. "Confessing" one's sins before God is described in 1 John 1:9. "Acknowledging" the reality of the resurrection is indicated in Acts 23:8. Heb. 13:15 refers to "acknowledging" the name of God.

General references to "identifying" Jesus as the Christ are found in John 9:22; 12:42.

The meaning "confess" in the sense of "profess," "admit," "declare" is found in Paul's "declaration" that he is a believer or follower of the way in Acts 24:14. See also 1 Tim. 6:12. The act of "confessing" Jesus as Lord is recorded in Rom. 10:9ff. The affirmation of "pressing" to know God is indicated in Titus 1:16. See also Heb. 11:13.

exomologeō [ἐξομολογέω, *1843*]

exomologeō is a variant form of ***homologeō***, above, meaning "confess" in all eleven occurrences of the term, with one or two related senses.

"Confessing" one's sins is indicated in Matt. 3:6; Mark 1:5; Acts 19:18; Jas. 5:16. The act of "giving thanks, or praise" to God is indicated in Matt. 11:25; Luke 10:21; Rom. 14:11; 15:9. Paul "declares that Christ is Lord" in Phil. 2:11. In Rev. 3:5 Christ is depicted as "acknowledging" the names of the saints before God.

homologia [ὁμολογία, *3671*]

homologia is a noun found six times denoting both "confession" and "profession."

The "confession" (i.e., declaration) of the gospel is noted in 2 Cor. 9:13; 1 Tim. 6:12, 13; Jesus is described in Heb. 3:1 as the apostle and high priest of our "confession" (i.e., indicating the gospel). See also Heb. 4:14; 10:23 for related contexts.

Additional Notes

Of particular interest here is the phenomenon of "confessing the name." The expression ***yādāh*** is found twice with respect to the person of God (see discussion above). In the New Testament, significant reference is made to "confessing the name of Christ" through the term ***homologeō***. The same attitude of reverence for the name of Jesus in the New Testament is paralleled by the use of ***yādāh*** in the Old Testament. That is, "confessing" the name of Christ is tantamount to "confessing" the name of God. It is Jesus Christ, the Son of God, who perfectly mirrors the character of God in his own divine being. It is therefore entirely appropriate that, in the new covenant, the people of God look to Christ as they confess their sins and find in him their sole hope of forgiveness.

See Also: → PRAISE

CONFIDENCE, CONFIDENT

OT Words

bittāḥôn **[בִּטָּחוֹן, 986]**

This is a rare noun, occurring only three times, meaning "hope" or "confidence." In Isa. 36:4; 2 Kgs. 18:19 ***bittāḥôn*** refers to the supposedly vain confidence Hezekiah has in thinking that the Assyrian siege of Jerusalem will fail. This constitutes a blasphemous attack on God's credibility by the Assyrian king. And, as a consequence, Hezekiah's confidence in God was vindicated, resulting in the collapse of the Assyrian campaign. The other occurrence of ***bittāḥôn*** is found in Eccl. 9:4, where the writer expresses the persistent belief among the living that life does in fact offer some hope or confidence, in spite of all the evil and futility that human beings inevitably experience. To validate this conclusion, one needs to take Eccl. 9:4 in the context of the whole chapter — and, indeed, the entire book.

betaḥ **[בֶּטַח, 983]**

This noun appears in approximately forty contexts. Most of the time it is used adverbially and translated "confidently," "safely," "boldly," or "in safety."

Of considerable significance here is the sustained emphasis in the Old Testament on Israel dwelling confidently, or securely, in the land of Canaan. Approximately half the occurrences of ***betaḥ*** reflect this perspective. In Lev. 25:18, 19 there is the promise that Israel will dwell in the land in safety (i.e., with confidence) if she maintains her devotion and obedience to Yahweh. Israel's security in the land is affirmed in 1 Sam. 12:11; 1 Kgs. 4:25. In the Prophets, the hope is expressed that, after God has completed the harsh discipline imposed upon his people through the Assyrians and Babylonians, there will be a return to the land. The common theme is that the people of God will once again dwell safely in the country of their forefathers. They will be redeemed and transformed by God, and their confidence in him will be renewed (cf. Jer. 23:6; 32:37; 33:16; Ezek. 34:25ff.; Hos. 2:18). Also common to all these texts is the affirmation, both implicit and explicit, that the return to the land is in anticipation of new covenant blessing, which will guarantee eternal rest for the people of God. This confidence will find fulfillment not merely in a return to a physical homeland, but in an eternal spiritual rest that is grounded in an intimate personal relationship with God through his Son, the Lord Jesus Christ.

yārē' **[יָרֵא, 3372]**

This verb is found approximately three hundred times with the consistent meaning "fear" or "be afraid." However, it is the occurrence of ***yārē'*** with the negative that is relevant for our discussion here. The expression "fear not" (and associated renderings) encourages a positive affirmation of trust and confidence in God in about ninety contexts. In each case, faith and confidence in God are grounded in his character of love and compassion, and in his promise to be with his people to comfort, nurture, and protect them (e.g., Gen. 15:1; 46:3; Exod. 14:13; 20:20; Num. 14:9; Deut. 1:21; 31:6, 8; 2 Sam. 9:7; Ps. 23:4; Isa. 4:10, 13, 14; 43:1ff.; Jer. 1:8).

NT Words

pepoithēsis **[πεποίθησις, *4006*]**

pepoithēsis is a noun found six times and means "confidence," "trust."

Confidence (in the sense of certainty) is indicated in 2 Cor. 1:5. Confidence or trust in human nature (i.e., "flesh") is noted in 2 Cor. 8:22; 10:2; Phil. 3:4. Confidence (i.e., hope, trust) in Christ is indicated in 2 Cor. 3:4; Eph. 3:12.

hypostasis **[ὑπόστασις, *5287*]**

hypostasis is a noun denoting "confidence," "assurance" in four of the five occurrences of the term.

"Confidence" associated with boasting is indicated in 2 Cor. 9:4; 11:7. One's "confidence" (i.e., hope of salvation) in Christ is noted in Heb. 3:14.

The "assurance" (i.e., certainty) of things hoped for is part of a definition of faith in Heb. 11:1.

Additional Notes

The concept of "confidence" is intimately associated with "trust" and "hope" (see entries under those headings).

The correlation between Hebrew and Greek usage is reasonably close. ***betaḥ*** is a fairly close dynamic equivalent to ***pepoithēsis***.

See Also: → BOLD → HOPE → TRUST

CONFIRM → ESTABLISH

CONFLICT → FIGHT

CONFORMED

NT Words

symmorphizō [συμμορφίζω, *4833*]

symmorphizō is a rare verb with the meaning "to be conformed to," "become like," found only in Phil. 3:10. It indicates Paul's desire to "become like" Christ by sharing in his suffering.

symmorphos [σύμμορφος, *4832*]

symmorphos is a rare adjectival form of ***symmorphizō*** (see above), denoting that which is "conformed or likened to." Rom. 8:29 speaks of believers whom God had predestined to be "conformed" to the image of his son. Phil. 3:21 refers to the believer's body at death becoming conformed to the body of Christ.

syschēmatizō [συσχηματίζω, *4964*]

syschēmatizō is a rare verb with the sense of "conform oneself to" found only in Rom. 12:2, urging believers "not to be conformed" to ungodly passions.

CONFOUND, CONFUSE, CONFUSION

OT Words

bālal [בָּלַל, 1101]

This verb occurs about forty times in the Old Testament, primarily in the sense of "mingle" or "rise." In all but a handful of texts, ***bālal*** refers literally to the mixing of flour and oil in Levitical offerings. Only twice does it mean "confound" or "confuse" (viz. Gen. 11:7ff.). The context is God's judgment on those who were attempting to build a tower to heaven at Babel by "confusing" their language. As a result people dispersed from Babel, each with their own language, and scattered all over the earth. There are several other Old Testament terms that relate to the idea of "confounding" or "confusing" that should also be understood.
(→ ASHAMED → TROUBLE)

NT Words

akatastasia [ἀκαταστασία, *181*]

akatastasia is a noun found in five contexts with the general sense of "confusion," "disorder." Luke 21:9 refers to "revolutions" in the context of social upheaval and war; as does 2 Cor. 6:5, specifically mentioning "riots." Confusion and disorder in general are noted in 2 Cor. 12:20; Jas. 3:16. 1 Cor. 14:33 affirms that God is not a God of "confusion."

synchysis [σύγχυσις, *4799*]

synchysis is a rare noun found only in Acts 19:29 denoting "confusion" in the sense of civil unrest.

syncheō [συγχέω, *4797*]

syncheō is a verb found in five places with the underlying sense of "confound," "confuse," as well as a few related nuances.

The "bewilderment" of a crowd is indicated in Acts 2:6, denoting a "confused amazement." The newly converted Saul of Tarsus is said to have "confounded" the Jewish population of Damascus by proving that Jesus was the Christ.

The "confusion" of crowds elsewhere points to civil rioting and unrest (cf. Acts 19:32; 21:27, 31).

See Also: → SHAME

CONGREGATION → ASSEMBLE

CONQUER, CONQUEROR → OVERCOME → RULE

CONSCIENCE

NT Words

syneidēsis [συνείδησις, *4893*]

syneidēsis is the sole term in the New Testament denoting the human "conscience" as the created moral faculty for discerning between good and evil.

General references to one's conscience are found in 1 Cor. 10:29; 2 Cor. 4:2; 5:11; Heb. 9:9, 14. A "good, clear conscience" is noted in Acts 23:1; 24:16; 1 Tim. 1:5; 3:9; 2 Tim. 1:3; Heb. 10:2, 22; 13:18; 1 Pet. 3:16, 21. A "seared or defiled conscience" is indicated in 1 Cor. 8:7; 1 Tim. 4:2; Titus 1:15. Rom. 2:15 mentions one's "conscience" working to either excuse or accuse. The condition of having a "weak conscience" is indicated in 1 Cor. 8:10ff. The vindication of one's conscience is noted in Rom. 9:1. 1 Tim. 1:19 refers to "rejecting one's conscience." Acting for the sake of one's conscience, or avoiding morally dubious behavior, is mentioned in Rom. 13:5; 1 Cor. 10:25.

CONSECRATE → DEDICATE → PERFECT

CONSENT

NT Words

synkatatithēmi [συγκατατίθημι, *4784*]

synkatatithēmi is a rare verb found only in Luke 23:5, referring to Joseph of Arimathea's refusal "to consent" (i.e., give approval) to the Sanhedrin's decision to seek the execution of Christ.

syneudokeō [συνευδοκέω, *4909*]

The verb ***syneudokeō*** is found in six places and means "consent," "give approval to." Christ condemns the Pharisees' "approval" of their ancestors killing the prophets in Luke 11:48. Similar culpable "consenting" to evil deeds is noted in Rom. 1:32. Saul's "giving consent" to the execution of Stephen, the first Christian martyr, is indicated in Acts 8:1; 22:20. References to an unbelieving spouse "consenting" to live with his/her partner are found in 1 Cor. 7:12ff.

See Also: → AGREE

CONSIDER

OT Words

bîn [בִּין, **995**]

This term has the basic meanings "understand," "perceive," or "discern," and is found eighty times. In a number of these places ***bîn*** is also translated "consider," with the underlying sense of "reflect on," "ponder," "weigh up in one's mind."

It is used first of all as an imperative. In Deut. 32:7, the people of Israel are instructed to ponder the actions of God in history on their behalf (cf. also Job 37:14). In Ps. 5:1, the writer pleads with God to give attention to his distress. By way of contrast, Ps. 50:22 warns those who ignore God to take careful note of him — otherwise, they shall be punished. A general exhortation to "consider" carefully what one does is found in Prov. 23:1. There are also two instances in the book of Jeremiah where the people of God are called to "consider" the gravity of their sins (cf. Jer. 2:10; 9:17). Similarly, in Isa. 14:16, the prophet exhorts his listeners to "consider" and give heed to the fate of Babylon, as a warning against the sin of rebellion and blasphemy against Yahweh. In a positive sense, Daniel is commanded by God to "consider" and give close attention to the revelation he has just been given. The inference is that God will grant him understanding as he does so (cf. Dan. 9:23).

In Isa. 43:18 God commands his people to no longer consider the past (i.e., to forget it), for God is about to usher in a new era of blessing and restoration. The immediate context here is the divine promise of a return to the land after Israel's captivity.

Moving away from the imperative usage of ***bîn***, we note in Dan. 8:5, for instance, that Daniel is pondering over the meaning of the vision of the ram and the goat. He will soon be given further understanding. In Ps. 119:95, the psalmist declares that he will "consider" God's law. The writer's explicit intention is to honor and obey God's revealed word.

It is clear that while ***bîn*** may be legitimately translated "consider" in these (and other) contexts, there is a very close affinity with the idea of "understanding."

nābat [נָבַט, **5027**]

The primary meaning of this term is "look," and it is found with this sense about eighty times. However, as an extension of this meaning, it is translated "consider" on a handful of occasions. These are all imperatives, and in each case there is an appeal made for God to give heed to the plight of his people (Ps. 13:4; Lam. 1:11; 2:20; 5:1). (→ SEE)

ḥāshab [חָשַׁב, **2803**]

ḥāshab is found approximately 120 times, meaning "reckon," "account," "esteem," "regard." ***ḥāshab*** is also used about thirty times with the related meaning "consider."

One of the best-known uses of this term is found in Isa. 53:3, where the Suffering Servant of Yahweh is described as one who has had no consideration from his own people, no regard, no esteem. Rather, he is considered worthless and dishonorable. Then, in Isa. 53:4, this pathos is deepened by the observation that his people regarded him as afflicted by God. Another significant use of the term is found in Gen. 15:6, where it is said that God regarded or counted Abraham's faith as righteousness. In other words, God considered Abraham to be a righteous man in the light of the faith he demonstrated. Similar uses of ***ḥāshab*** with this meaning are found in Neh. 13:13; Ps. 106:31. With the negative sense of the imputation of guilt, ***ḥāshab*** is found in Lev. 7:18; 17:4.

Other mundane uses of ***ḥāshab*** with the meaning "consider" are found in Num. 18:27; Job 18:3; Isa. 40:15; 2 Sam. 4:2; Num. 23:9.

The meaning "consider," in relation to ***ḥāshab*** must also be compared with the nuances of "impute," "account," and "reckon." (→ ACCOUNT → IMPUTE → RECKON)

NT Words

katamanthanō [καταμανθάνω, *2648*]

katamanthanō is a rare verb found only in Matt. 6:28 referring to Christ's injunction to his listeners not to worry, and hence to "consider" the lilies of the field — to "reflect" on the fact that they are cared for by their Creator without the need for anxiety.

noeō [νοέω, *3539*]

noeō is a verb found in around twenty contexts with the primary sense of "understand." However, in 2 Tim. 2:7 the term expresses the meaning "consider" in the sense of "think over," or "reflect on," referring to Paul's injunction to Timothy to carefully consider the apostle's teaching. (→ UNDERSTAND)

katanoeō [κατανοέω, *2657*]

katanoeō is a verb meaning "consider" in the sense of "perceive," "notice," and "reflect on" in most of the fourteen occurrences of the term.

It refers to the action of "considering," or "noticing," one's own faults (Matt. 7:3; Luke 6:41); as well as another's craftiness (cf. Luke 20:23).

Elsewhere, Christ's advice to his listeners to "ponder" or "reflect on" the birds of the air and the flowers of the field, who have no need to worry, is found in Luke 12:24ff. Paul affirms in Rom. 4:19 that Abraham, while "considering" the aged condition of his own body, had not weakened in his faith. Heb. 3:1 contains an appeal to "reflect on" the person of Christ. See also Heb. 10:24.

anatheōreō [ἀναθεωρέω, *333*]

anatheōreō is a rare verb found only twice. It means "observe" in Acts 17:23, and "consider" in the sense of "reflect on" in Heb. 13:7. This latter reference contains the exhortation to "consider" the lifestyle of one's spiritual leaders and imitate their faith.

analogizomai [ἀναλογίζομαι, *357*]

analogizomai is a verb found only in Heb. 2:3 expressing the admonition to "consider" (i.e., "ponder," "reflect on") the suffering endured by Christ.

logizomai [λογίζομαι, *3049*]

logizomai is a verb found about forty times, translated various ways, with the underlying connotation of mental "reasoning" or "calculating." It often means to "count," "consider," or "reckon."

The meaning "count" in the sense of "consider," or "regard," is found in a number of places. "Regarding" uncircumcision as circumcision, as in the case of Gentiles who were devout followers of the Jewish law, is the meaning indicated in Rom. 2:26. To "consider" someone justified by faith rather than works of the law is a position indicated in Rom. 3:28. This assessment applies especially to Abraham in Rom. 4:3ff.; Gal. 3:6; Jas. 2:23. "Regarding" oneself as dead to sin is a state of mind indicated in Rom. 6:11. Believers "considered" as sheep to be slaughtered are indicated in the context of persecution in Rom. 8:36. In Rom. 9:8, children of Abraham are "reckoned" as children of God. God refuses to "count" the sins of his people against them in 2 Cor. 5:19.

Other occurrences include those in1 Cor. 4:1; 2 Cor. 12:6; Phil. 3:13; 2 Tim. 4:16; Heb. 11:19.

Additional Notes

The meanings associated with the idea "consider" in both Old and New Testaments are similarly complex. There are a number of Hebrew and Greek terms that are broadly synonymous.

See Also: → UNDERSTAND

CONSOLATION, CONSOLE → COMFORT

CONSULT, CONSULTATION → ADVICE → COUNSEL

CONSUME

OT Words

'ākal [אָכַל, **398**]

'ākal occurs approximately 750 times. The primary, literal meaning is "eat." However, the word is used metaphorically about 120 times with the meaning "devour" or "consume" in the sense of "destroy."

'ākal is used this way in several contexts, and the judgment of God figures prominently in the majority of these. There are a number of texts, for example, that speak of the fire of God consuming his people as a judgment against them for their wickedness (cf. Ps. 78:63; Ezek. 15:7; 19:12; Joel 2:3; Isa. 5:24; 29:6; 2 Kgs.

1:10ff.; Amos 7:4; Zech. 9:4; 11:1). Perhaps the most striking examples of ***'ākal*** in this regard are, first of all, the horrifying judgment of God against Korah and those who rebelled against Moses' authority in the wilderness (cf. Num. 26:10); and, secondly, the deaths of Nadab and Abihu in Lev. 10:2.

Other general references to God "consuming" Israel in his wrath are found in Jer. 5:14; 17:27; 21:14; Lam. 2:3; 4:11; Ezek. 7:15; 28:18; Hos. 5:7; 8:14; 11:6; Amos 5:6; Deut. 31:17; Isa. 9:18). This judgment of God is also directed against the pagan nations, who are likewise "consumed" by the wrath of God (cf. Zech. 9:15; 12:6; Deut. 32:22; Ps. 21:9; Isa. 26:11; 51:8; Jer. 29:17; 30:16; Zeph. 1:18). Specific nations are also singled out in this regard — for example, Egypt (cf. Jer. 46:10, 14; Exod. 15:7; Ps. 78:45); Assyria (cf. Isa. 10:17; 30:27; Nah. 1:10; 2:13; 3:15); Moab (cf. Num. 21:28; Amos 2:2, 5; Jer. 48:45); Babylon (cf. Jer. 50:32); Edom (cf. Amos 1:12; Obad. 18); Damascus (cf. Amos 1:4; Jer. 49:27); Ammon (cf. Amos 1:14).

'ākal refers not only to the expression of God's wrath and judgment towards people, but also to humankind's inhumanity towards others. There is reference, for example, to Israel "consuming" or "devouring" her own people through social and economic oppression (cf. Jer. 2:30; Ezek. 19:3, 6; 22:25; Hos. 7:7). The enemies of Israel are also indicted for doing the same to the people of God (cf. Ps. 79:7; Jer. 2:3; 50:17; 52:33; Isa. 9:12).

Finally, this metaphorical use of ***'ākal*** indicates the glory of God as a "consuming" fire in Exod. 24:17; Deut. 5:25; Isa. 33:14.

tāmam [תָּמַם, 8552]

The root meaning of this word is "to finish," or "be complete," and it is found on sixty-five occasions in the Old Testament. In a little less than half of these, however, ***tāmam*** means "consume" or "be consumed," indicating death or destruction resulting from God's judgment against both his people and the wicked in general.

First of all, in regard to God's own people, it is frequently recorded that Yahweh passes judgment against those who spurn his law and thereby despise him. In these cases, God hands down a sentence of death against them, as either a threat (cf. Num. 14:35; Jer. 6:29; 14:15; Ezek. 22:15), or a statement of fact (cf. Num. 32:13; Deut. 2:15; Josh. 5:6). Secondly, the nations in rebellion against Yahweh are also similarly condemned (cf. Pss. 73:19; 104:35; Josh. 8:24; 10:20; Isa. 16:4).

Lam. 3:22 sounds a positive note when Jeremiah records that it is because of the Lord's mercies that the people of Judah and Jerusalem are not "consumed"; notwithstanding the traumas they have just suffered.

kālāh [כָּלָה, 3617]

This noun occurs about twenty times, with the primary sense of "completion," although its meaning is largely negative, indicating "complete destruction," or "annihilation." In this latter sense, several texts suggest the idea of "being consumed" in much the same way as ***'ākal*** and ***tāmam***, above.

Neh. 9:31, for example, mentions that God did not fully "consume" his people (i.e., put an end to them) when he handed them over to the Babylonians for punishment. Isa. 10:31 declares that God will carry out the planned destruction of the land of Israel through the Assyrians. Ezek. 13:13 records the unleashing of God's fury against the false prophets in Jerusalem, who distort his message of judgment against them. Great hailstones and torrents of rain will be poured down on them to consume (i.e., destroy) them. See also Dan. 11:16; Isa. 28:22.

NT Words

analiskō [ἀναλίσκω, *355*]

analiskō is a rare verb found in three places, meaning "consume" in the underlying sense of "destroy." Luke 9:54 mentions destruction by fire. Gal. 5:15 warns believers not to quarrel and thereby be metaphorically "consumed" (i.e., destroyed) by one another. 2 Thess. 2:8 describes the fate of the antichrist (the "lawless one") in terms of the Lord Jesus "slaying" him with the breath of his mouth.

katanaliskō [καταναλίσκω, *2654*]

katanaliskō is a rare variant of ***analiskō***, above, found only in Heb. 12:29 and denoting God as a "consuming" fire in the context of divine judgment.

Additional Notes

There is a clear similarity between the Hebrew and Greek terminology for "consume" in the negative sense of "destruction." All three Hebrew terms discussed above share an affinity of meaning with the New Testament terms ***analiskō*** and ***katanaliskō***.

See Also: → DESOLATE → DESTROY

CONTEND → JUDGE

CONTINUE

NT Words

menō [μένω, *3306*]

menō is a verb found about 120 times with the predominant sense of "abide," "remain," along with several related nuances. One of these nuances is "continue," which overlaps in meaning with "remain" in a number of places.

John 8:31 contains Jesus' exhortation to his disciples to "continue" in his word, to maintain an attitude of respect with constant attention and obedience to it. In John 15:9 Jesus also exhorts his followers to "continue" to cultivate among themselves the love of God as manifested in his own person. Heb. 13:1 contains the exhortation to "let brotherly love continue." Similar references to "continuing" in faith, love, and holiness are made in 1 Tim. 2:15; 2 Tim. 3:14. See also 1 John 2:19. Heb. 7:24 refers to Christ "continuing" forever in his high priestly ministry.

emmenō [ἐμμένω, *1696*]

emmenō is a rare variant form meaning "continue" in three places. The need for "continuing" in the faith is indicated in Acts 14:22, as is the importance of "continuing" to do everything as written in the book of the law in Gal. 3:10. Israel's failure to "continue" to observe the law covenant is recorded in Heb. 8:9.

epimenō [ἐπιμένω, *1961*]

epimenō is another variant of ***menō***, above, meaning "continue," "remain," along with related nuances, in nineteen places.

The practice of "continuing" to ask questions is indicated in John 8:7. Continual knocking on the door is indicated in Acts 12:16. 1 Tim. 4:16 contains an exhortation to "persevere" in living a godly life.

The meaning "continue" in the sense of "remain" is found in relation to: God's grace (Acts 13:43); God's kindness (Rom. 11:22); a sinful condition (Rom. 6:1). Col. 1:23 contains a general reference to "continuing" in the faith.

paramenō [παραμένω, *3887*]

paramenō is another rare synonym for the entries listed above, meaning "continue," "remain" in three places. This state of "continuing" in the priestly office is noted in Heb. 7:23. The desirability of "continuing" in the law of liberty in the gospel, indicating the underlying sense of "perseverance," is noted in Jas. 1:25.

prosmenō [προσμένω, *4357*]

prosmenō is a verb found in seven places with the meaning "remain," "stay." In 1 Tim. 5:5, however, the term describes Christian women who "continue" in prayer night and day.

proskartereō [προσκαρτερέω, *4342*]

The verb ***proskartereō*** has the underlying sense of "continue," along with various nuances, for most of the ten occurrences of the term. It means "continue with," in the sense of "give attention to," or "devote oneself to" in reference to prayer (Acts 1:14; 2:42, 46; 6:4); and to the study of apostolic doctrine (Rom. 12:12; Col. 4:2).

See Also: → REMAIN

CONTRADICT, CONTRADICTION

→ DISPUTE → STRIFE

CONVERT, CONVERSION

NT Words

epistrophē [ἐπιστροφή, *1995*]

epistrophē is a rare noun found only in Acts 15:3, referring to the "conversion" of the Gentiles from their pagan religion to faith in Christ.

See Also: → TURN

CONVICT

NT Words

elenchō [ἐλέγχω, *1651*]

The verb ***elenchō*** means to "convict," "reprove," in addition to associated nuances, throughout the nearly twenty occurrences of the term.

The meaning "be convicted" in relation to sin is indicated in John 8:9; 1 Cor. 14:24; Jas. 2:9. Then, the active sense of "convict" (i.e., of sin) is found in John 8:46; 2 Tim. 4:2. John 16:8 specifically mentions the Holy Spirit's role in convicting the world of sin.

The associated senses of "reprove," "expose," in the context of rebuking people of sin, are found in Matt. 18:15; Luke 3:19ff.; Eph. 5:11; 1 Tim. 5:20; Titus 1:9, 13; 2:15; Heb. 12:5.

exelenchō [ἐξελέγχω, *1827*]

exelenchō is a rare verb found only in Jude 15, referring to "convicting" the ungodly of their lawlessness.

See Also: → CONDEMN → REBUKE

COPY

OT Words

mishneh [**מִשְׁנֶה, 4932**]

The noun ***mishneh*** is found thirty-five times meaning "second" (that which is manifested twice). In two places, it means "copy." Deut. 17:18; Josh. 8:32 refer to the "copy" of the Mosaic law required to be made by Yahweh himself in order to remind the king and people of Israel of their obligations to God under the terms of the covenant.

parshegen [**פַּרְשֶׁגֶן, 6573** (Aramaic)]

parshegen is a rare Aramaic term denoting the "copy" of a letter in Ezra 4:11, 23; 5:6; 7:11; and the "copy" of a decree in Esth. 3:14; 4:8; 8:13.

NT Words

hypodeigma [ὑπόδειγμα, *5262*]

hypodeigma is a noun denoting a "pattern," "example," or "copy" in the six occurrences of the term. Specifically, Heb. 8:5; 9:25 both refer to the tabernacle and temple and their sacred furniture as "copies" of the heavenly realities which they symbolized.

CORD

OT Words

ḥebel [**חֶבֶל, 2256**]

This noun, found sixty times, means "cord" (or "rope," "band") or "(portion of) territory." With the former sense, ***ḥebel*** occurs about twenty times.

Most of the time, ***ḥebel*** refers to "cord(s)" or "rope(s)" in a mundane, literal sense (cf. Josh. 2:15; 2 Sam. 8:2; 1 Kgs. 20:31; Jer. 38:6ff.). There are, however, several instances where ***ḥebel*** translates "cord" in a metaphorical sense, referring to both positive and negative qualities such as "cords of affliction" (cf. Job 36:8); "cords of sin" (cf. Prov. 5:22); "cord of life" (cf. Eccl. 12:6); "cords of deceit" (cf. Isa. 5:18); "cords of human kindness" (cf. Hos. 11:4).

'abōt [**עֲבֹת, 5688**]

'abōt is a noun found in twenty-five contexts with the varying senses of "ropes," "chains," "bonds," and "cords." Literal references to cords (i.e., ropes) for tying someone up are found in Judg. 15:13ff.; 16:11ff.; Job 39:10; Ezek. 3:25; 4:8.

Metaphorical reference to the "cords" of the wicked (i.e., their lifestyle) that condemn them is found in Ps. 129:4, where they are said to be cut by Yahweh.

Elsewhere, mention is made of the symbolic "cords" of love, used by Yahweh to lead the people of Israel through the wilderness (cf. Hos. 11:4).

NT Words

schoinion [σχοινίον, *4979*]

schoinion is a rare noun denoting "cords," "ropes," found only in John 2:15; Acts 27:32.

CORN, CORNFIELD → FIELD → GRAIN

CORNER, CORNERSTONE

OT Words

pinnāh [**פִּנָּה, 6438**]

This term is found nearly thirty times, and is usually translated "corner" or "cornerstone."

pinnāh refers to the literal corners of the altar in the tabernacle and temple (cf. Exod. 27:2; 38:2; Ezek. 43:20; 45:19); and to the corners of towers, gates, and houses in Jerusalem and elsewhere (cf. 2 Kgs. 14:13; 2 Chr. 26:9; Neh. 3:24ff.; Prov. 7:12; 21:9; Jer. 31:38ff.).

In three significant texts, however, ***pinnāh*** refers to the "cornerstone" that God will raise up in the process of establishing his universal kingdom. The description of this kingdom involves several building metaphors, one of which is the "cornerstone." In each case (i.e., Ps. 118:22; Isa. 28:16; Zech. 10:4), a messianic understanding of ***pinnāh*** may be gleaned from both the immediate and wider context of the term itself. This is particularly the case in Zech. 10:4; Isa. 28:16, where the cornerstone is associated with the divine renewal of Judah and Zion, respectively. In both cases, the establishment of this ***pinnāh*** indicates that God's program of redemption, on behalf of his people, will focus on this object. It is this "cornerstone" that finds its ultimate fulfillment in the person of Christ.

miqṣō'a [**מִקְצֹעַ, 4740**]

This term occurs ten times and in each case refers to literal "corners" — of the tabernacle (cf. Exod. 26:24; 36:29); of the visionary temple in Ezekiel's vision (cf. Ezek. 41:22; 46:21ff.); and of the corners of the wall in Jerusalem (cf. Neh. 3:19ff.).

***pē'āh* [פֵּאָה, 6285]**

pē'āh is a common noun found in nearly ninety contexts meaning "side," as well as the senses of "edge," "corner." There is occasionally some overlap of meaning.

The "corner" of the table of the showbread is noted in Exod. 25:26; 37:13. The "corner" of a field, its "edge," or "border," is indicated in Lev. 19:9, 23:22. See also Neh. 9:23; Amos 3:12.

***kānāph* [כָּנָף, 3671]**

kānāph is a common noun found over one hundred times with the predominant sense of "wing." However, the term refers to the "four corners" of the earth in Isa. 11:12, and to the "four corners" of the land of Israel.

NT Words

gōnia [γωνία, *1137*]

gōnia is a noun denoting a "corner" in a variety of contexts. The "corner" of a street is noted in Matt. 6:5.

The "chief cornerstone" of a building, referring metaphorically to the Messiah, is indicated in Matt. 21:42; Mark 12:10; Luke 20:17; Acts 4:11; 1 Pet. 2:7.

The phrase "things done in a corner," in Acts 26:26, indicates secrecy.

The expression "four corners of the earth," denoting universal extent, is recorded in Rev. 7:1; 20:8.

akrogōniaios [ἀκρογωνιαῖος, *204*]

akrogōniaios is a rare noun found only in Eph. 2:20; 1 Pet. 2:6, denoting Christ as the "chief cornerstone" of the temple. This is a metaphorical reference to Christ as the key figure in God's redemptive program for his people.

archē [ἀρχή, *746*]

archē is a noun with the primary meaning "beginning." In two places, however, the term denotes the "corners" of a sheet that the apostle Peter saw in a vision (cf. Acts 10:11; 11:5).

Additional Notes

pinnāh, in the three Old Testament references to "cornerstone," finds a clear dynamic equivalent in the Greek term ***akrogōniaios***. ***pinnāh*** is also similar to the more literal ***gōnia*** in general usage. The fact that the "cornerstone" in Isa. 28:16 is seen explicitly as a cause of stumbling reinforces the idea that this object will bring the judgment as well as the supreme blessing of God. Both these phenomena find their ultimate expression in the person and work of Jesus Christ as depicted in the New Testament.

CORPSE → BODY

CORRECT, CORRECTION

OT Words

***mûsār* [מוּסָר, 4148]; *yāsar* [יָסַר, 3256]**

These two terms are intimately connected with the idea of "chasten," "chastisement," and "instruction." The latter translation includes the elements of correction and discipline.

NT Words

epanorthōsis [ἐπανόρθωσις, *1882*]

epanorthōsis is a rare noun denoting "correction" in the sense of moral reformation, found only in 2 Tim. 3:16 as one of the divinely ordained purposes of Holy Scripture.

See Also: → ADMONISH → CHASTEN → INSTRUCTION

CORRUPT, CORRUPTION, INCORRUPTIBLE

OT Words

***shāḥat* [שָׁחַת, 7843]**

This verb is found approximately 160 times. Although in the majority of references it means "destroy," in about thirty places it means "corrupt," "ruin" (in the sense of "spoil"). (→ DESTROY)

With regard to the sense of "corrupt," ***shāḥat*** is used primarily in a metaphorical sense to indicate moral corruption. It refers particularly to the general wickedness of the nation of Israel. Mention of this is made, for example, at the infamous "golden calf" incident at Mt. Sinai (cf. Exod. 32:7; Deut. 9:12). The Song of Moses refers to Israel's future rebellion against Yahweh, also in terms of her moral corruption (cf. Deut. 32:5). See also Deut. 31:29. Further examples of Israel's corruption in the sight of God are indicated in Hos. 9:9; Judg. 2:19; Zeph. 3:7; Isa. 1:4.

The same is predicated of the nation of Judah (cf. 2 Chr. 27:2; Ezek. 16:47; 20:44; Jer. 6:28; Mal. 2:8). Not only is the fact of Israel's corruption recorded, but also God's warnings to her against such attitudes and behavior (cf. Deut. 4:16, 25). Also indicted for corruption are the wicked in general (cf. Gen. 6:11ff.; Pss. 14:1; 53:1; Prov. 25:26); and the king of Tyre (cf. Ezek. 28:17).

shāḥat is also used in a literal sense in several contexts to indicate that which is "spoiled" or "ruined." Jer. 13:4, for example, refers to the linen belt belonging to Jeremiah that was ruined after being buried under a rock. Although ***shāḥat*** refers here to a literal spoiling, the context leaves no doubt that it symbolizes the moral corruption of God's people. A similar usage is found in Jer. 18:4 with respect to the clay pot. Then, Nah. 2:3 refers to the Assyrian invaders literally spoiling Israel's vineyards. Finally, Mal. 1:14 refers to "corrupted" (i.e., diseased) animals that the people of God were presenting as sacrifices. Such offerings were forbidden under Mosaic law, and the people are condemned for it.

shaḥat [שַׁחַת, 7845]

This is the noun derived from ***shāḥat*** (see above), and it occurs twelve times. Only twice, however, does it refer to "corruption" — once in Job 17:14, where it refers metaphorically to the pain of Job's suffering; and once in Ps. 16:10 to indicate physical decay in the grave. Elsewhere ***shaḥat*** refers to pits, graves, or ditches.

Two other minor terms related to ***shāḥat*** also refer to the idea of corruption: *māshḥat* (Lev. 22:25); and *mashḥît* (2 Kgs. 23:13; Dan. 10:8).

NT Words

phtheirō [φθείρω, *5351*]

phtheirō is a verb found eight times meaning "ruin," "destroy." The sense of "ruin" incorporates the meaning "corrupt" in a number of these contexts. 1 Cor. 15:33 speaks of bad company "corrupting" good morals. The "corrupting" of one's mind and old nature is indicated in 2 Cor. 11:3; Eph. 4:22. The senses "ruin," "destroy" refer to the corrupting of the earth in Rev. 19:2 and the corruption of evil people in Jude 10. See also 2 Cor. 7:2.

diaphtheirō [διαφθείρω, *1311*]

diaphtheirō is a variant form of ***phtheirō***, above. Its underlying sense of "corrupt" is translated in various ways.

The meaning "destroy," "ruin" refers literally to the destructive activity of moths on personal possessions (cf. Luke 12:33). It refers to ships in Rev. 8:9; and to the earth in Rev. 11:18.

The meaning "waste away" refers to the physical deterioration, or corrupting, of one's human form in 2 Cor. 4:16.

The adjectival sense of "corrupt" or "depraved" minds is noted in 1 Tim. 6:5.

kataphtheirō [καταφθείρω, *2704*]

kataphtheirō is a rare variant verb of ***phtheirō***, above, used adjectivally in 2 Tim. 3:8 to refer to "corrupt (i.e., morally depraved) minds." 2 Pet. 2:12 speaks of the hand of God "destroying" evil people.

phthora [φθορά, *5356*]

phthora is a noun derived from ***phtheirō*** (see above) denoting "corruption," "decay" for most of the nine occurrences of the term.

The meaning "decay" in the sense of physical and spiritual corruption in relation to created human existence is noted in Rom. 8:21; Gal. 6:8.

phthora denotes the sense of "perishable," or "subject to corruption" in relation to the human body in 1 Cor. 15:42; 50; and with general reference to all things earthly in Col. 2:22.

Moral "corruption" is indicated in 2 Pet. 1:4; 2:19. 2 Pet. 2:12 indicates the "destruction" of false teachers.

diaphthora [διαφθορά, *1312*]

diaphthora is a variant form of ***phthora***, above, meaning "corruption" or "decay" with the sense of physical decay associated with human corpses. The term is found in only six places, referring to the "decay" of David's body in Acts 13:36. The remaining contexts declare that there is no such corruption associated with the person of Jesus Christ, whose body did not decay because God raised him from the dead (Acts 2:27, 31; 13:34ff.).

aphtharsia [ἀφθαρσία, *861*]

aphtharsia is a term denoting that which is "incorruptible" or "immortal" throughout most of the eight occurrences of the term.

The designation "incorruptible" is equated with the "immortal" state of the renewed body in glory after the resurrection (cf. Rom. 2:7; 1 Cor. 15:42, 50ff.). A general reference to immortality is found in 2 Tim. 1:10, 11.

phthartos [φθαρτός, *5349*]

phthartos is an adjective denoting that which is "corruptible," or "perishable," "mortal," "subject to decay."

Rom. 1:23 refers to mortal human beings. Human nature is described as "perishable" in 1 Cor. 15:53ff.;

1 Pet. 1:23. 1 Cor. 9:25; 1 Pet. 1:18 both speak of "perishable" things in general.

aphthartos [ἄφθαρτος, *862*]

aphthartos is an adjective meaning "incorruptible," "immortal" in seven places. Rom. 1:23; 1 Tim. 1:17 describe God as "incorruptible." The "incorruptible," "immortal" condition of the resurrected believer is noted in 1 Cor. 9:25; 1 Pet. 1:23. The "incorruptible" or "imperishable" inheritance of eternal life is indicated in 1 Pet. 1:4; 1 Cor. 9:25. See also 1 Pet. 3:4.

aphanizō [ἀφανίζω, *853*]

aphanizō is a verb meaning to "make disappear" or "put out of sight." It is translated "corrupt" or "destroy" with general reference to the destructive activity of moths and corrosion in Matt. 6:19, 20.]

Additional Notes

The range of emphases of ***shāḥat*** overlap in part with all the Greek terms discussed above. Both Old and New Testaments emphasize that moral corruption is endemic in humanity. It is found not only among the wicked, but also among the community of the people of God.

What is distinctive about the New Testament usage, however, is that it focuses more broadly and in more detail on corruption than does the Old Testament. This New Testament perspective includes the phenomenon of "incorruptibility" (cf. ***aphtharsia*** and ***aphthartos***), a condition only made possible, in an ultimate sense, by the completed work of redemption in Christ.

See Also: → CHASTEN → DECAY → DESTROY → INSTRUCTION → PIT → REBUKE

COST, COSTLINESS, COSTLY

→ VALUABLE

COUNCIL

OT WORDS

sôd [סוֹד, 5475]

This term is found about twenty times with a mundane sense, as well as a distinctively theological one. ***sôd*** has the two broad connotations of "council" and "counsel," but it is translated in various ways.

With regard to the idea of "council," ***sôd*** is sometimes rendered "assembly." This is the case, for instance, in Jer. 6:11; 15:17, where the word refers to a gathering of young men and a gathering of mockers, respectively. Ezek. 13:9 refers to the false prophets in Israel who are denied a place in the "council" (or "assembly") of God's people. This "council" is probably a gathered group of God's people who enjoy the special privilege of gaining access to genuine divine revelation. It may in fact refer to the body of genuine prophets in Israel. This phenomenon is given more explicit emphasis in Jer. 23:18, 22, where false prophets are condemned for proclaiming lies, since they have not stood in Yahweh's divine "council." This infers that God has an intimate circle of chosen servants gathered around him in order to communicate his revelation to his people. It may be argued that this "divine council" experience is a necessary prerequisite for all genuine prophets of Yahweh. A similar perspective is seen in Pss. 89:7; 111:1; Job 15:8.

sôd refers not only to the phenomenon of a "gathering," "assembly," or "council," but also to the content of what is revealed in such gatherings. This is indicated, for example, in Amos 3:7, where the prophet affirms that God reveals his "plans" (or "counsel") to his servants. See also Ps. 25:14; Prov. 3:32; Job 29:4 in this regard. On the human level, ***sôd*** suggests different meanings in various contexts. Gen. 49:6 refers to Jacob's unwillingness to enter the "intimate circle" of his sons Simeon and Levi, whom he perceives as aggressive and war-like. In Pss. 64:2; 83:3, ***sôd*** refers to the "conspiracy" of the wicked against God's people. Then, on a more positive note, ***sôd*** refers to the sweet "fellowship" that exists between the psalmist and his godly companion in Ps. 55:14 when they meet together. Finally, in Proverbs, ***sôd*** occasionally refers to "confidences" between friends (cf. Prov. 11:13; 20:19; 25:9), and on one occasion refers to the process of "consultation" (cf. Prov. 15:22).

NT WORDS

symboulion [συμβούλιον, *4824*]

symboulion is a noun denoting both a "council" and "counsel" (i.e., advice given). (→ COUNSEL) Reference to a "council," or formal gathering, is found in Matt. 12:14 (describing the Pharisees' determination to be rid of Jesus). The "council" of Festus, the Roman governor of Judea, is noted in Acts 25:12.

synedrion [συνέδριον, *4892*]

synedrion is a noun found about twenty times with the meaning "council." In some contexts, ***synedrion*** is transliterated "Sanhedrin" — the great Jewish council in Jerusalem composed of civil and religious leaders, which was the highest judicial court in the land.

The "Sanhedrin" itself is indicated in Matt. 5:22; 26:59; Mark 14:55; Luke 22:66; John 11:47; Acts 4:15; 5:21ff.; 6:12ff.; 22:30; 23:1ff. The more general sense of "councils" is found in Matt. 10:17; Mark 13:9.

Additional Notes

sôd encompasses both the idea of the location of a gathering — human and divine — as well as the content emerging out of a gathering. The specific phenomenon of the divine council is especially important for understanding the mechanism of prophetic revelation in the Old Testament. The Greek terminology for "council" does not of itself refer to this divine perspective. The phenomenon of God revealing himself to his prophetic mediators is, however, contained in the New Testament — even if this is not indicated by the specific terms for "council." One may argue, for example, that the whole book of Revelation constitutes an extended "divine council" that was given to John the apostle by the Holy Spirit.

See Also: → ASSEMBLY

COUNSEL

OT Words

yā'aṣ **[יָעַץ, 3289]**

This term is found approximately eighty times. In its verbal sense, ***yā'aṣ*** is translated "to counsel" or "to give counsel." However, on about twenty-five occasions, the participial form of the verb is translated as "counselor" (i.e., one who gives counsel).

yā'aṣ is predominantly concerned with human counsel. Examples of this are found in 2 Sam. 16:23; 17:7ff., where Ahithophel offers advice to Absalom; in 1 Kgs. 12:8ff., where Rehoboam consults with his advisers; in Ezek. 18:19 where Jethro advises Moses to seek some judicial and administrative assistance. It is used similarly in the following places: 1 Kgs. 1:12; 2 Chr. 25:17; 32:3; Neh. 6:7; Isa. 7:5; Jer. 38:15; 49:30; Mic. 6:5; Hab. 2:10. As mentioned above, ***yā'aṣ*** is also used in a nominal sense, with the meaning "counselor" in a human sense in all cases except one. Specific individuals are mentioned in this capacity in the following texts: 2 Sam. 15:16 (Ahithophel); 1 Chr. 26:14 (Zechariah); 2 Chr. 22:3 (Athaliah). Groups of counselors are mentioned, for example, in Ezra 4:5; 7:28; Job 3:14; Prov. 11:14; 15:22; Isa. 1:26; 19:11; Ezek. 11:2. These individuals and groups reflect both good and bad counsel.

Isa. 9:6 is the one significant exception to this — one of the names given to the messianic child of promise is "Counselor." This is suggestive of the ministry characteristic of the Holy Spirit in the new covenant era. And, in combination with all the other names given, this further indicates the divine nature of the messianic figure.

In addition to the human sphere of meaning associated with ***yā'aṣ***, there is a less common but highly significant usage that links the act of "counseling" with God himself. Divine counsel is linked to judgment against Judah and the nations (cf. 2 Chr. 25:16 [Amaziah, king of Judah]; Isa. 14:24ff. [Assyria]; Isa. 19:12 [Egypt]; Isa. 23:8ff. [king of Tyre]; Jer. 49:20 [Edom]; Jer. 50:45 [Babylon]). Such "divine counsel" reflects God's judgment on specific acts of rebellion against his name — a reaction that reflects Yahweh's determination to suffer neither insult to his person, nor any breach of his will.

'ûṣ **[עוּץ, 5779]**

This is a rare noun, occurring only twice, and it translates "counsel" on the human plane in Judg. 19:30; Isa. 8:10.

NT Words

boulē **[βουλή, *1012*]**

boulē is a noun found in twelve places denoting "counsel" in the sense of "advice," or "purpose."

The meaning "counsel," denoting the "will" or "purpose" of God, is indicated in Luke 7:30; Acts 13:36; 20:27. In particular, Acts 2:23 speaks of Jesus Christ having been delivered up to death by God's explicit "counsel" or "plan." Eph. 1:11; Heb. 6:17 refer to God's "will" controlling all things.

The "counsel," "purpose," or "plan" of human beings is indicated in Luke 23:51; Acts 4:28; 5:38; 27:42; and 1 Cor. 4:5 refers to the "counsel" of people's hearts.

bouleuō **[βουλεύω, *1011*]**

bouleuō is a verb found ten times meaning "to plan" throughout — all in the context of human determination (cf. Luke 14:31; John 12:10; Acts 5:33; 15:37; 27:39; 2 Cor. 1:17).

symboulos **[σύμβουλος, *4825*]**

symboulos is a rare noun denoting a "counselor" in a general sense in Rom. 11:34, hypothetically questioning who would be the Lord's "counselor."

symboulion [συμβούλιον, *4824*]

symboulion is a noun denoting "counsel" or "advice" in the eight occurrences of the term. The Sanhedrin "takes counsel" (i.e., makes plans) for the purpose of destroying Jesus (cf. Matt. 22:15; 27:1; Mark 3:6; 15:1). See also Matt. 27:7; 28:12.

symbouleuō [συμβουλεύω, *4823*]

The verb ***symbouleuō*** means "to take counsel"; "give counsel"; "to plot" in five contexts. In Matt. 26:4; John 11:53; John 18:14 the object of the Sanhedrin's deliberations or "plans" is the destruction of Jesus. Acts 9:23 records the "plot" to kill Paul. Rev. 3:18 contains the divine "counsel" or "advice" for the members of the congregation at Laodicea to seek after true godliness.

Additional Notes

The concept of "counsel," or "advice" is treated consistently in both Old and New Testaments. The Greek terms ***bouleuō*** and ***symbouleuō*** reflect the emphasis of ***yā'aṣ*** insofar as human counsel is concerned (although there are many more instances of this recorded in the Old Testament than in the New). The one area of difference concerns the Old Testament usage of ***yā'aṣ*** that reflects the initiative of "divine counsel" in judgment against wickedness — this perspective is entirely absent in the New Testament.

COUNT

NT Words

hēgeomai [ἡγέομαι, *2233*]

The verb ***hēgeomai*** is found in thirty places meaning "count," "think," "consider," as well as some related nuances.

The action of "counting" in the sense of "consider," "reckon" is indicated in Phil. 3:7ff., referring to "counting" gain as loss for the sake of Christ. See also Heb. 11:26; Acts 26:2.

hēgeomai means to "judge someone faithful" in 1 Tim. 6:1. "Esteeming" people highly is indicated in 1 Thess. 5:13. To "consider" the blood of Christ as useless is a heinous offense in the sight of God (Heb. 10:29). Other references include 2 Thess. 3:15; Heb. 11:11; 13:7; Jas. 1:2; 2 Pet. 1:13; 2:13.

Referring to Christ, Paul affirms in Phil. 2:6 that the Lord "did not count" equality with God something to be grasped.

See Also: → CONSIDER → NUMBER → RECKON

COUNTRY

NT Words

agros [ἀγρός, *68*]

The noun ***agros*** means "field" throughout the nearly forty occurrences of the term. (→ FIELD)

The sense of "country" (i.e., "countryside") is indicated in Mark 5:14; 15:21; Luke 8:34; 23:26.

patris [πατρίς, *3968*]

patris is a noun found in eight places with the meaning "country," "homeland." References to one's own "homeland" or "country" are found in Matt. 13:54, 57; Mark 6:1, 4; Luke 4:23ff.; John 4:44. Heb. 11:14 refers to people seeking a "homeland," a metaphor for the search after one's "eternal home."

chōra [χώρα, *5561*]

chōra is a noun denoting "country" in the sense of "region," "countryside," "native land" for most of the nearly thirty occurrences of the term. References to "country" denoting "native, or foreign land" are found in Matt. 2:12; Mark 1:5; Luke 15:13; 19:12; Acts 10:39 (Judea); 12:20.

The meaning "region" is indicated in Matt. 4:16; 8:28; Luke 3:1; 8:26; John 11:54; Acts 8:1; 13:49; and "countryside" is noted in Mark 5:10; Luke 21:21.

perichōros [περίχωρος, *4066*]

perichōros is a variant form of ***chōra***, above, denoting "surrounding countryside," "surrounding region" throughout the eleven occurrences of the term (cf. Matt. 3:5; 14:35; Mark 1:28; 6:55; Luke 3:3; 4:14, 37; 7:17; 8:37; Acts 14:6).

oreinos [ὀρεινός, *3714*]

oreinos is a rare adjective found only in Luke 1:39, 65 denoting the "hill country" of Judea.

apodēmeō [ἀποδημέω, *589*]

apodēmeō is a verb found in six places with the meaning "travel to a far country" in most of these contexts (cf. Matt. 21:33; Mark 12:1; Luke 15:13; 20:9).

See Also: → EARTH → FIELD

COURAGE

OT Words

'āmaṣ [אָמַץ, **553**]

This verb has several meanings, the principal ones being "be strong" and "have courage." ***'āmaṣ*** is translated "be strong" on thirty occasions and is used in the imperative a number of times with the meaning "be courageous." Several of these imperatives are divine exhortations directed to Joshua and the people of Israel about to make their entry into Canaan (cf. Deut. 31:6, 7, 23; Josh. 1:6ff.). Joshua himself repeats this exhortation in Josh. 10:25 to the people of Israel, clearly modeling the divine command. David also exhorts his son Solomon (cf. 1 Chr. 22:13; 28:20), as does Hezekiah with respect to the citizens of Jerusalem (cf. 2 Chr. 32:7).

See Also: ➞ BOLD ➞ CONFIDENCE ➞ STRENGTH

COURT

OT Words

ḥāṣēr **[חָצֵר, 2691]**

This noun occurs approximately 160 times with the predominant meaning "court" or "courtyard." It is also translated "village" or "town." ***ḥāṣēr*** refers primarily to the courtyards of both the tabernacle and temple. ***ḥāṣēr*** refers to the tabernacle, for example, in Exod. 27:9ff.; 35:17ff.; 38:15ff.; 39:40; 40:33; Lev. 6:16, 26; 25:31. The books of Kings and Chronicles refer to the courts of Solomon's temple (cf. 1 Kgs. 6:36; 1 Chr. 23:28; 28:6ff.; 2 Chr. 4:9; 23:5; 24:21; 33:5).

The psalmist also refers to the courts of the temple on several occasions (cf. Pss. 65:4; 84:2ff.; 92:13; 100:4; 116:19; 135:2); as do the prophets (cf. Isa. 1:12; 62:9; Jer. 19:14; 36:10). The book of Ezekiel frequently refers to the courts of the temple (mostly found in Ezek. 40–44 in relation to the prophet's visionary temple).

ḥāṣēr also refers to the courtyard of a prison on several occasions (cf. Neh. 3:25; Jer. 32:2ff.; 33:1; 37:21; 38:6ff.).

'azārāh **[עֲזָרָה, 5835]**

This noun occurs only seven times and translates "court(yard)" on only two occasions; both times referring to the courtyard of the priests in Solomon's temple (cf. 2 Chr. 4:9; 6:13).

NT Words

agoraios [ἀγοραῖος, *60*]

agoraios is a rare adjectival form used nominally in Acts 19:38 to denote a "court of law."

aulē [αὐλή, *833*]

aulē is a noun denoting "palace," "hall" in most of the twelve occurrences of the term. In Rev. 11:2, however, the term denotes the "outer court" of the temple in John's apocalyptic vision.

basileion [βασίλειον, *933*]

basileion is a rare noun denoting a "royal court" (or palace) found only in Luke 7:25.

COVENANT

OT Words

berît **[בְּרִית, 1285]**

berît embraces one of the most important theological concepts in the Bible in general, and in the Old Testament in particular. It is found a little over three hundred times and is translated "covenant" in all but a few cases. The underlying sense of ***berît*** is that of a "binding agreement," or "relationship," usually drawn up with a solemn vow. This is particularly the case when the divine covenant between Yahweh and his people is in view; and most of the occurrences of ***berît*** refer to this covenant. The rest refer either to "agreements" or "covenants" between people, or to those made by human beings with God.

In relation to the dominant usage of this term, ***berît*** may be defined as an intimate relationship between God and humankind, sovereignly initiated, maintained and fulfilled by God alone; and involving a commitment to life and death from both God and humankind. The phenomenon of "covenant" permeates the entire Old Testament and constitutes the very essence of Israel's relationship with Yahweh. As might be expected, the term ***berît*** receives the most emphasis in the books of the Pentateuch, where the origins of the people of Israel are documented.

The term "covenant" is mentioned first of all in Gen. 6:18, when God promises to establish his covenant with Noah. This stage of the covenant is concerned with the theme of preservation in regard to Noah, his family, and the future population of the earth (cf. Gen. 8:22–9:16).

The next major development of the covenant theme concerns the patriarch Abraham. The principal references here are Gen. 12; 15; 17. However, the term ***berît*** is found only in Gen. 15:18; 17:2–21.

The term ***berît*** is next linked to Moses, the great prophetic mediator of the Sinai covenant. The obligations and requirements for the Israelite nation that emerge out of the Mosaic ***berît*** testify to the intimate and binding nature of the relationship that God establishes with his people. Such legislation is not peripheral to the life of Israel, but lies instead at its very core. This covenant is integral not only throughout Exodus, Leviticus, and Deuteronomy, but it lies behind all aspects of Israel's life and history until the close of the Old Testament canon. While it is not practical to list every occurrence of ***berît*** that refers to the Mosaic treaty, the following key texts reflect the various elements of the definition mentioned above: Exod. 19:5; 24:8; Lev. 26:9, 15, 42; Deut. 4:13; 29:1ff.; Josh. 23:16; 1 Kgs. 11:11; 2 Kgs. 17:15; Neh. 1:5; 9:8, 32; Isa. 61:8; Jer. 31:31ff.; 33:20; Ezek. 16:8; 20:37; 37:26; Dan. 9:4, 27; Hos. 2:18; 6:7.

The solemn bonding between God and his people lies at the heart of the covenant phenomenon. This bond testifies to God's mercy and compassion in nurturing and redeeming his people, guaranteeing them an intimate relationship with himself as well as the prospect of a blissful life in the land he had given them. All of this, however, was conditional on the people's response of gratitude, obedience, and exclusive loyalty. The terms of the covenant always stemmed from the divine initiative, and always demanded a response of obedience from the Israelite people. One remarkable aspect of the covenant, as far as the Israelites were concerned, was the extraordinary grace and mercy of God that resulted in the endurance of the relationship, notwithstanding the people's frequent violations of their covenant responsibilities.

Another important aspect of this covenant is the promise God gives to David in 2 Sam. 7 with respect to the king's unending royal lineage. The point here is that God promises David a son, who will reign on his throne forever. The promise is distinctly messianic and is fulfilled ultimately in the person of Jesus Christ, who is raised from the dead and subsequently ascends to his Father's right hand in heaven. The event, recorded in Acts 1, is anticipated in Daniel's vision in Dan. 7 where the messianic "Son of Man" returns to the "Ancient of Days" to receive his kingdom in full. Further references to the Davidic covenant are found in Ps. 89:3, 4; Jer. 33:20, 21; 2 Chr. 21:7.

berît is used in the Old Testament not only to refer exclusively to the old covenant, but also in prophecies that anticipate the inauguration of the new covenant age. Several key passages stand out in this regard. One is Jer. 31:31ff., which explicitly mentions a new ***berît*** that will replace the old covenant in its entirety. This new covenant will result in a spiritual internalizing of God's law, complete forgiveness of sins, and universal knowledge of God among his people in a way hitherto unparalleled. And this new covenant, unlike the old, will be eternal and unbreakable. It will herald a new age, characterized by the personal indwelling of the Spirit of God in the lives of his people. This latter perspective is emphasized particularly in Ezek. 36:26, 27. Even though the term ***berît*** is not used here, the new covenant phenomenon is clearly in view (cf. also Ezek. 37:28).

One final text worthy of note in this regard is Dan. 9:27. It reads: "He will confirm a covenant with many for one 'seven.'" The text and context is difficult, and the antecedent of "he" in this verse is grammatically ambiguous. One legitimate reading of this passage, however, indicates that "he" may refer here to the Messiah. If this is the case, we have here an explicit reference to the work of Christ in inaugurating the new covenant age through his death and resurrection.

Wherever ***berît*** is found in the Old Testament, including the instances where only human relationships are in view, it is clear that all such treaties are sealed with a solemn oath (often incorporating a symbolic ritual) that has legally binding force — whether initiated by God or by human beings.

NT Words

diathēkē [διαθήκη, *1242*]

diathēkē is a significant term found approximately thirty times meaning "covenant" throughout, referring to both the old and new covenant bonds. In one or two places it also denotes a human "(last) will and testament."

Reference to the inauguration of the new covenant is noted in Rom. 11:27. See also Eph. 2:12; Heb. 13:20.

New covenant forgiveness is anticipated on the occasion of the Last Supper over which Jesus presides on the eve of his crucifixion. At that meal he affirms that his blood, about to be shed, constitutes the blood of "the covenant" effective for the forgiveness of sins (cf. Matt. 26:28; Mark 14:24). See also 1 Cor. 11:25; Heb. 10:29. Heb. 9:15; 12:24 affirm Christ as the mediator of a new covenant. General references to the "covenant" promises made to the patriarchs of old are found in Luke 1:72; Acts 3:25; Rom. 9:4.

Acts 7:8 refers to the "covenant of circumcision" given to Abraham, and 2 Cor. 3:14; Gal. 3:17; Heb. 8:9; 9:15, 20 refer to the old covenant.

The characteristic and distinctive spiritual nature of the new covenant is recorded in 2 Cor. 3:6.

diathēkē may also be translated "last will" or "testament" in the context of a human disposition. It is found with this meaning first of all in Gal. 3:15. Paul uses ***diathēkē*** to illustrate a binding promise or guarantee on the earthly plane that is mirrored in essence in the divine-human covenant that is likewise binding on both God and humankind. The apostle's primary intention here is to stress the certainty that such promises made by God to his people will never be broken. Such a sense is also indicated in Heb. 9:16, 17.

Reference to both the old and new covenants in an allegorical context is made in Gal. 4:24. The "new covenant" is declared better than the old in Heb. 7:22; 8:6.

The divine promise to establish a "new covenant" that would be characterized by a spiritual internalizing of the law of God in the believer's heart is recorded in Heb. 8:8, 10; 10:16. The "ark of the covenant" is noted in Heb. 9:4; Rev. 11:19.

diatithēmi [διατίθημι, *1303*]

diatithēmi is a verb found in seven places with the primary sense of "make a covenant." The term refers to a person making a last will and testament in Heb. 9:16, 17 (translated here "testator"), as well as to God making a covenant (both old and new) in Acts 3:25; Heb. 8:10; 10:16.

syntithēmi [συντίθημι, *4934*]

syntithēmi is a verb found in four places with the meaning "to enter into an agreement," "make plans." The contexts are all mundane and refer only to human participants (cf. Luke 22:5; John 9:22; Acts 23:20; 24:9).

Additional Notes

The phenomenon of the covenant lay at the very heart of Israel's relationship with God. ***berît*** is rich in connotations linked with the idea of "covenant" — "promise"; "oath"; "(covenant-) sign"; "agreement"; "bond." The phenomenon of "relationship" is fundamental to this concept and underlies every occurrence of the term and every situation where a covenant motif is implied.

In the New Testament, however, the use of the dynamic equivalent ***diathēkē*** is not nearly as extensive. Rather, ***diathēkē*** assumes and builds upon the perspectives of ***berît***.

Thus, there is no discontinuity whatsoever between ***berît*** in the Old Testament and ***diathēkē*** in the New. ***berît*** lays the foundation of the covenant relationship between God and his people. ***diathēkē*** focuses on Christ's work and ministry in the inauguration of the new covenant — the consummation of God's plan of salvation.

See Also: ➟ AGREE

COVER, COVERING

OT Words

kāsāh [כָּסָה, 3680]

The verb ***kāsāh*** means "cover," in the sense of "hide" or "conceal," and its secondary meaning is to "clothe." ***kāsāh*** occurs about 140 times with a fairly even distribution between a literal and metaphorical sense.

In its literal sense, ***kāsāh*** refers to "covering" in a wide variety of contexts: covering one's face (cf. Gen. 38:15); covering the earth with floodwaters (cf. Gen. 7:19, 20); covering the earth with plagues of frogs (cf. Exod. 8:6), and locusts (cf. Exod. 10:5); covering (i.e., drowning) the enemies of God's people in water (cf. Exod. 14:28; 15:5, 10; Josh. 24:7; Ps. 106:11); covering the skin with leprosy or other infectious skin diseases (cf. Lev. 13:12, 13); concealing information from someone (cf. Gen. 18:17); covering various items of the tabernacle and temple (cf. Num. 4:5ff.; Exod. 26:15; 1 Kgs. 7:18, 41, 42; 2 Chr. 5:8); and covering people with various garments — clothing them (cf. Gen. 24:65; Exod. 28:42; 1 Kgs. 11:29; 2 Kgs. 19:1, 2; Isa. 37:1, 2).

Significantly, ***kāsāh*** also refers to the glory cloud that enveloped Mt. Sinai and the tabernacle as the sign of God's indwelling presence in the holy of holies (cf. Num. 9:15; 16:42; Exod. 24:15, 16; 40:34; see also Lev. 16:13). In addition, ***kāsāh*** frequently indicates a metaphorical covering in a similar variety of contexts. There is mention, for example, of shame covering the face of those who are convicted of their sinfulness (cf. Pss. 44:15; 69:7; Jer. 51:51; Obad. 10; Mic. 7:10).

The term likewise refers to the covering of sin in the sense of being forgiven (cf. Pss. 32:1; 85:2; Prov. 10:12), and also in the opposite sense of not being covered, or being overlooked (cf. Ezek. 24:8; Job 31:33). ***kāsāh*** also indicates the covering of God's own people, as well as his enemies, with divine wrath through various means (cf. Isa. 29:10; Ezek. 12:6; 26:19; 30:18; 31:15; 38:9, 16; Num. 16:33; Neh. 4:5; Isa. 26:21; 60:2, 6; Jer. 3:25; 46:8). Conversely, the term also indicates the divine "covering" as an act of mercy and compassion, specifically in the context of the allegorical representation of Israel in Ezek. 16:8ff.

ḥāphāh [חָפָה, 2645]

This word occurs twelve times and is translated "cover" in a literal sense on almost every occasion. Several texts refer to the covering of the head as a response of dismay or anguish, a sign of deep sorrow (cf. 2 Sam. 15:30; Esth. 6:12; 7:8; Jer. 14:3, 4). On one occasion,

ḥāphāh refers metaphorically to the wings of a dove being covered with silver (cf. Ps. 68:13). The remaining texts refer to the interior coverings of the temple buildings (cf. 2 Chr. 3:5ff.).

kesût [**כְּסוּת, 3682**]

This is another comparatively rare noun that refers to "covering" in the sense of "clothing." There are only eight occurrences of the term. All but one of these is literal in its connotation (cf. Gen. 20:16; Exod. 21:10; 22:27; Deut. 22:12; Job 24:7; 31:19; Isa. 50:3). The exception is the metaphorical reference to destruction having "no covering" in Job 26:6.

NT WORDS

kalyptō [καλύπτω, *2572*]

kalyptō is a verb found eleven times meaning "cover," "hide."

A boat is said to be "swamped" (i.e., covered) by waves in Matt. 8:24. The phenomenon of one's sins "being covered" is indicated in Jas. 5:20; 1 Pet. 4:8. 2 Cor. 4:3 refers to the state of spiritual blindness inflicted on unbelievers whose minds "are veiled" (i.e., covered) by sin, impervious to the light of the gospel. See also Matt. 10:26; Luke 8:16; 23:30.

epikalyptō [ἐπικαλύπτω, *1943*]

epikalyptō is a rare variant form of ***kalyptō***, above, found in Rom. 4:7 referring passively to the happy state of the person whose sins "are covered" (i.e., forgiven).

perikalyptō [περικαλύπτω, *4028*]

perikalyptō is another variant of ***kalyptō***, above, found three times meaning "completely cover" or "cover up." The "covering up" of one's face is indicated in Mark 14:65. The ark of the covenant is described as "being covered" with gold in Heb. 9:4. Luke 22:64 refers to the "blindfolding" of Christ.

synkalyptō [συγκαλύπτω, *4780*]

synkalyptō is a rare verb found only in Luke 12:2 with the sense of "cover up," "conceal" in a general sense.

katakalyptō [κατακαλύπτω, *2619*]

The verb ***katakalyptō*** means "to cover (one's head) with a veil," and it is found only in 1 Cor. 11:6, 7.

peribolaion [περιβόλαιον, *4018*]

peribolaion is a noun describing a woman's hair as the "covering" for her head. The term also denotes a "mantle" in 1 Cor. 11:15.

COVET, COVETOUSNESS

OT WORDS

beṣa' [**בֶּצַע, 1215**]

This term is found about twenty times and means "covetous," "greedy for gain." One or two passages commend all those who despise greed and covetousness (cf. Exod. 18:21; Prov. 28:16). For the most part, however, **beṣa'** is used in a negative sense indicating that greed is liable for judgment in the sight of God (cf. Ps. 119:36; Isa. 57:17; Jer. 6:13; Ezek. 33:31).

NT WORDS

pleonexia [πλεονεξία, *4124*]

pleonexia is a noun denoting "covetousness," "greed" throughout the ten occurrences of the term (cf. Mark 7:22; Luke 12:15; Rom. 1:29; 2 Cor. 9:5; Eph. 4:19; Col. 3:5; 2 Pet. 2:3, 4).

pleonektēs [πλεονέκτης, *4123*]

pleonektēs is a noun denoting a "covetous (or greedy) man" in 1 Cor. 5:10, 11; 6:10; Eph. 5:5.

philargyros [φιλάργυρος, *5366*]

philargyros is an adjective denoting those who are "lovers of money" in Luke 16:14; 2 Tim. 3:2.

aphilargyros [ἀφιλάργυρος, *866*]

aphilargyros is an adjective denoting those who are "free from the love of money" (cf. 1 Tim. 3:3; Heb. 13:5).

See Also: → DESIRE → JEALOUS → LUST → PLEASANT

COW

pārāh [**פָּרָה, 6510**]

In the majority of its twenty-two occurrences, **pārāh** refers to a literal cow (Gen. 41:2ff.; 1 Sam. 6:7ff.; Isa. 11:7). Elsewhere, it denotes a young heifer (Num. 19:2ff.). There is also a significant metaphorical usage in Amos 4:1, where the rich women of Samaria are condemned for their self-indulgence and arrogant pride and are described as "cows of Bashan."

CRAFT, CRAFTSMAN

OT WORDS

ḥārāsh [**חָרָשׁ, 2796**]

This term refers both to craftsmen in general and also to specific tradesmen such as "carpenters," "goldsmiths," "engravers," and "masons." ***ḥārāsh*** is found approximately thirty times.

ḥārāsh refers in an entirely positive sense to the various craftsmen employed in the construction of both the tabernacle (cf. Exod. 28:11; 35:35; 28:23), and the temple (cf. 1 Chr. 14:1; 22:15; 29:5) — including the later renovations of the temple during the reforms of Josiah (cf. 2 Kgs. 12:11; 22:6; 2 Chr. 24:12; 34:11). The term is also used negatively to refer to the craftsmen involved in idol construction. Such people were roundly condemned by God (cf. Deut. 27:15; Isa. 40:19ff.; 41:7; 44:11ff.; 45:16; Jer. 10:3, 9; Hos. 13:2).

General references to craftsmen are also found in 1 Sam. 13:9; 2 Sam. 5:11; 2 Kgs. 24:14ff.; Zech. 1:20.

NT Words

technitēs [τεχνίτης, *5079*]

technitēs is a noun denoting a "craftsman" in Acts 19:24, 38; Heb. 11:10; Rev. 18:22.

ergasia [ἐργασία, *2039*]

ergasia is a denoting a "craft" or "business" in Acts 19:25. Elsewhere it refers to the monetary gains derived from business (cf. Acts 16:16, 19; 19:24).

homotechnos [ὁμότεχνος, *3673*]

homotechnos is a rare adjectival form denoting one who was "of the same trade (or business)" in Acts 18:3.

meros [μέρος, *3313*]

The noun ***meros*** usually means "part," "portion" (approximately forty times). However, in Acts 19:27 the term denotes the "trade" or "business" of the idol manufacturers in Ephesus.

CRAFTINESS, CRAFTY

→ DECEIT
→ PRUDENCE

CREATE, CREATION, CREATOR, CREATURE

OT Words

bārā' [בָּרָא, 1254]

bārā' is used fifty times with the predominant meanings "create" or "shape." Whenever it is used in this sense it refers exclusively to divine activity. In the remaining contexts it is translated in various ways — "cut down" (cf. Josh. 17:15, 18; Ezek. 23:47); "mark out" (cf. Ezek. 21:19); or "make fat" (cf. 1 Sam. 2:29).

With regard to divine creative activity, ***bārā'*** is used in several ways. It refers first of all to the creation of the heavens and the earth (cf. Gen. 1:1; 2:4; Pss. 89:12, 13; 148:5; Isa. 40:26, 28; 42:5; 45:8, 18). It also refers to the "new heavens and new earth," the anticipated consummation of God's re-creative activity that will usher out the old order of reality and usher in the new (cf. Ps. 104:30; Isa. 4:5; 41:20; 65:17, 18; Jer. 31:22). Such a fulfillment is closely associated with the new covenant and the coming of the Messiah.

In the second place, ***bārā'*** refers to the creation of people. For example, God created Adam and Eve (cf. Gen. 1:27; 2:3; 5:12); humankind in general (cf. Deut. 4:32; Ps. 89:47; Isa. 45:12; Eccl. 12:1); the universal people of God, as well as Israel in particular (cf. Isa. 43:1, 7, 15; 57:19; Ps. 102:18; Mal. 2:10); and even the nations of Assyria and Babylon, for the purpose of bringing judgment against the people of Israel (cf. Isa. 54:16). One intriguing use of ***bārā'*** in this regard is found in Ezek. 28:13, 15 which refers to the creation of the "Satan-like" spirit which possesses the king of Tyre. The condemnation of the Phoenician ruler in this oracle focuses on the man's inordinate and blasphemous pride. The description of the spirit that indwells him is likened to the angelic being that once was perfect in Eden, but who subsequently rebelled against God and was cast out of his presence.

David also uses ***bārā'*** when he repents of his sin of adultery and murder in Ps. 51. In Ps. 51:10, David pleads with God to create a new heart within him. This is, in effect, a plea for renewal and forgiveness — a prominent feature of the anticipated blessing of the new covenant, promised in the oracles of Isaiah, Jeremiah, and Ezekiel (cf. Isa. 4:4; Jer. 31:31ff.; Ezek. 36:24ff.).

In Isa. 45:7 ***bārā'*** refers to God creating both darkness and disaster — contrasted with God "forming the light" and "bringing prosperity." In other words, this term affirms the absolute sovereignty of God, so that people will worship him as the unique, omnipotent Creator of the universe.

Other uses of ***bārā'*** not directly related to the above are found in Gen. 1:21; Num. 16:30; Isa. 48:17; Amos 4:13.

yāṣar [יָצַר, 3335]

A synonym for ***bārā'***, above, ***yāṣar*** is found approximately sixty times meaning "forming" or "shaping." In its participial form it is often translated "potter."
(→ POTTER)

yāṣar describes both divine and human creative activity. ***yāṣar*** refers to divine activity in several different contexts (as does ***bārā'***). For example, ***yāṣar*** describes the creation, or forming, of the earth (cf. Ps. 95:5; Isa. 45:18; Jer. 33:2); and the creation of human beings, both at the beginning of time and also the shaping of the child in the mother's womb (cf. Gen. 2:7, 8; Jer. 1:5; Pss. 33:15; 94:19; 139:16; Zech. 12:1).

The sense of divine creative activity (i.e., people shaped or formed by God) applies not only to individuals such as the prophet Jeremiah, but also to the people of God and the Servant of Yahweh in powerful metaphorical contexts (cf. Isa. 43:1, 7, 21; 44:2, 21, 24; Jer. 10:16). ***yāṣar*** alludes to the judgment "formed" by God against both this people (cf. Isa. 46:11; Jer. 18:11), and against the enemies of his people — Sennacherib, the Assyrian king, in particular (cf. 2 Kgs. 19:25; Isa. 37:26). Then, in two places, ***yāṣar*** is used as a noun to refer to God as Creator, or Maker (cf. Isa. 45:9, 11).

In Isa. 45:7 ***yāṣar*** refers to God "forming the light." (See the discussion of this text under ***bārā'***, above.)

When found in connection with human activity, ***yāṣar*** refers several times to the shaping of idols (cf. Isa. 27:11; 44:9, 12; Hab. 2:18). Elsewhere it refers to the shaping activity of the potter (cf. 2 Sam. 17:28; Isa. 29:16; 45:9), and once to the production of weapons (cf. Isa. 54:17).

'āsāh [עָשָׂה, 6213]

'āsāh is a common verb found over 2,500 times with the primary senses of "do," "make," as well as a variety of associated nuances. One of these is the nominal (participial) sense of "Maker," referring to Yahweh as the Creator of the world and humankind (cf. Job 4:17; 32:22; Ps. 95:6; Prov. 14:31; 22:2; Isa. 17:7; 51:13; Jer. 33:2; Hos. 8:14).

pā'al [פָּעַל, 6466]

The verb ***pā'al*** is found over fifty times with the primary meanings "do," "make," "work." In Job 36:3, ***pā'al*** is used nominally to denote Yahweh as Job's "Maker" (cf. Job 36:3).

ḥārāsh [חָרָשׁ, 2796]

ḥārāsh is a noun occurring about thirty times with the underlying sense of a "craftsman," referring to "carpenters," "engravers," and "workmen" in general. In Isa. 45:16 the term denotes a "maker" of idols.

nephesh [נֶפֶשׁ, 5315]

nephesh is a common noun found about 750 times with a variety of meanings. Prominent meanings include "person," "soul," "life," "mind," as well as several other associated meanings, including references to "creatures." In each case where ***nephesh*** refers to creatures, it describes animals as the handiwork of God (cf. Gen. 1:21ff.; 2:19; 9:10ff.; Lev. 11:46; Job 12:10).

NT Words

ktizō [κτίζω, *2936*]

ktizō is a verb found in sixteen contexts with the predominant meaning "create."

References to God's creative activity with respect to the cosmos include Mark 13:19; Eph. 3:9; Rev. 4:11; 10:6. 1 Cor. 11:9 specifically mentions God's creation of humankind. Creation effected in and through Christ is indicated in Col. 1:16. See also 1 Tim. 4:3. God is referred to as "Creator" in Rom. 1:25; Col. 3:10.

Believers are described symbolically as God's workmanship "created" in Jesus Christ for good works (cf. Eph. 2:10; 4:24).

Christ is said to have "created" in himself a new man by abolishing the effect of the law through his self-sacrifice (cf. Eph. 2:15).

ktisis [κτίσις, *2937*]

ktisis is a noun derived from ***ktizō***, above, consistently translated "creation," "creature" throughout its nineteen occurrences.

General references to "creation" include Mark 10:6; 13:19; Rom. 1:20; 8:39; 2 Pet. 3:4. The despoiling of "creation" by the impact of sin, placing it in bondage, is noted in Rom. 8:19ff. Included in this context also is the anticipated renewal of creation in the wake of the work of Christ.

"Creation" as the object and context of preaching the gospel is noted in Mark 16:15.

References to "creatures" as the general product of God's creative power are found in Rom. 1:25; Col. 1:23; Heb. 4:13.

Believers are described as a new "creation" in Christ in 2 Cor. 5:17 (cf. also Gal. 6:15). Christ is described as "the firstborn of all creation" in Col. 1:15.

ktisma [κτίσμα, *2938*]

ktisma is a rare noun derived from ***ktizō***, above, denoting a "creature" in a general sense in 1 Tim. 4:4; Rev. 5:13; 8:9. In Jas. 1:18, believers are described as a kind of firstfruits of his creatures.

ktistēs [κτίστης, *2939*]

ktistēs is a rare noun found only in 1 Pet. 4:19, denoting God as "Creator."

dēmiourgos [δημιουργός, *1217*]

dēmiourgos is a rare noun found only in Heb. 11:10, referring to God as the "maker" of the eternal city.

Additional Notes

Broadly speaking, the Hebrew term ***bārā'*** is dynamically equivalent to the Greek verb ***ktizō*** (and its nominal derivatives). Both terms concentrate on the exclusive and distinctive creative activity of God. ***yāṣar***, on the other hand, embraces both divine and human activity.

See Also: → BEAST

CREDITOR → LEND

CROOKED

OT Words

'iqqēsh [עִקֵּשׁ, **6141**]

This word is found eleven times, meaning "crooked," or "(morally) perverse." In all cases except one, ***'iqqēsh*** refers to the wicked in general. The bulk of the references are found in Proverbs (cf. 2 Sam. 22:7; Pss. 18:26; 101:4; Prov. 2:15; 8:8; 11:20; 17:20; 19:1; 22:5; 28:6). Deut. 32:5 refers to the "crookedness" or "perversity" of the people of Israel, whose future rebellion against God is recorded in a song that God instructed Moses to teach the Israelites. This so-called "Song of Moses" in Deut. 32 is a testimony to the inevitable wickedness that will characterize future generations of God's people.

NT Words

skolios [σκολιός, *4646*]

skolios is an adjectival form meaning "crooked," denoting a "curved" path in Luke 3:5. The term also means "crooked" in the sense of "morally perverse," referring to wicked people (cf. Acts 2:40; Phil. 2:15).

CROSS, CRUCIFY

NT Words

stauros [σταυρός, *4716*]

The noun ***stauros*** means "cross" throughout the nearly thirty occurrences of the term.

"Cross" is used as a symbolic term for suffering in contexts where followers of Christ are exhorted to "take up their cross" and follow him, being ready to completely identify with him (cf. Matt. 10:38; 16:24; Mark 8:34; 10:21; Luke 9:23; 14:27).

Literal references to a wooden "cross" are found in relation to the execution of Christ. Simon of Cyrene carries one for Christ to the place of crucifixion (cf. Matt. 27:32; Mark 15:21; Luke 23:26). The "cross" as the instrument of Christ's death is noted in Matt. 27:40ff.; Mark 15:30ff.; John 19:17ff.; Phil. 2:8; Heb. 12:2.

Metaphorically speaking, the "cross of Christ" is the primary symbol of the spiritual effectiveness of the gospel (cf. 1 Cor. 1:17ff.; Gal. 6:12ff.; Eph. 2:16; Col. 1:20; 2:14). The "cross of Christ" is also depicted as the symbolic "stumbling block" for the acceptance of the gospel in Gal. 5:11. Phil. 3:18 refers to the enemies of the "cross of Christ."

stauroō [σταυρόω, *4717*]

The verb ***stauroō*** means "to crucify" throughout the nearly fifty occurrences of the term.

Most of the occurrences refer to Christ's crucifixion (cf. Matt. 20:19; 27:22ff.; 28:5; Mark 15:13ff.; Luke 23:21ff.; 24:7, 20; John 19:6ff.; Acts 2:36; 4:10; 1 Cor. 1:23; 2:8; 2 Cor. 13:4; Gal. 3:1). See also Matt. 23:34; 1 Cor. 1:13; Rev. 11:8.

Gal. 5:24 records a metaphorical use of ***stauroō*** affirming that those who belong to Christ "have crucified" the flesh, determining to put to death ungodly passions and desires.

systauroō [συσταυρόω, *4957*]

systauroō is a variant form of ***stauroō***, above, meaning "to crucify along with," referring to the two criminals executed alongside Christ (cf. Matt. 27:44; Mark 15:32; John 19:32). The term also refers metaphorically to the "old self" of the natural human being "having been crucified" with Christ, so that the new believer would no longer be a slave to sin.

anastauroō [ἀνασταυρόω, *388*]

anastauroō is a verb found only in Heb. 6:6, used metaphorically to describe apostasy as the act of "crucifying afresh" the Son of God.

prospēgnymi [προσπήγνυμι, *4362*]

prospēgnymi is a verb found only in Acts 2:23, describing the death of Christ in terms of wicked people "nailing him to the cross."

See Also: → HANG

CROWD

OT Words

***hāmôn* [הָמוֹן, 1995]**

hāmôn is a noun occurring about eighty times with the predominant meaning "multitude" or "crowd," as well as associated nuances.

The sense of "multitude," denoting a throng or crowd of people, is found in relation to an army or military troops in Judg. 4:7; 2 Chr. 13:8; 14:11; 2 Chr. 20:12ff.; Dan. 11:10ff. "Crowds" of Israelites are indicated in 1 Sam. 14:16; 2 Sam. 6:19; 1 Kgs. 20:13; 2 Kgs. 7:13. References to "throngs" of other peoples are found in 2 Chr. 32:7; Isa. 16:14; 17:12; 29:5ff.; Ezek. 30:10, 15; 32:12ff.; 39:11. Non-specific references to "crowds" include Job 31:34; Ps. 42:4; Isa. 5:13; 13:4.

In another context, ***hāmôn*** refers to "herds" of cattle in Jer. 49:32.

***rōb* [רֹב, 7230]**

rōb is a common noun found approximately 160 times with the underlying sense of "abundance," "greatness." In several contexts ***rōb*** denotes "multitude," or "throng, crowd (of people)" (cf. Gen. 48:16; 2 Chr. 30:13, Ps. 33:16 [a great army]; Prov. 14:28; Zech. 2:4).

NT Words

ochlos [ὄχλος, *3793*]

ochlos is a noun denoting a "crowd" or "throng" of people for most of the 175 occurrences of the term.

Literal references to "crowds" include Matt. 4:25; 15:30ff.; Mark 2:4; 8:1ff.; Luke 5:15ff.; 9:11ff.; John 6:2ff.; 12:9ff.; Acts 13:45; 21:27, 34.

Acts 11:24 refers to a "large company of people" converted under the apostolic preaching of the gospel. The "throng" of the saints in heaven is noted in Rev. 7:9; 17:15; 19:1ff.

ochlopoieō [ὀχλοποιέω, *3792*]

ochlopoieō is a rare verb found only in Acts 17:5 meaning to "gather a crowd."

plēthos [πλῆθος, *4128*]

plēthos is a noun synonymous with ***ochlos*** (see above), denoting a "multitude," "crowd" throughout the nearly thirty occurrences of the term.

References to "crowds" of people include Mark 3:7ff.; Luke 6:17; 19:37; John 5:3; Acts 2:6; 6:5. Acts 5:14 describes the crowds converted under apostolic preaching.

plēthos also denotes the heavenly "host" of angelic beings praising God (cf. Luke 2:13).

epikeimai [ἐπίκειμαι, *1945*]

The verb ***epikeimai*** means "lie on," "lay upon" for most of the seven occurrences of the term. However, in Luke 5:1 the term describes people "crowding in upon" Jesus.

dēmos [δῆμος, *1218*]

dēmos is a noun found four times with the meaning "people" in the contexts of a crowd (cf. Acts 12:22; 17:5; 19:30, 33).

CROWN

OT Words

***'āṭar* [עָטַר, 5849]**

This is a rare verb, occurring seven times and meaning "crown" in most of these contexts, all of them metaphorical. In Ps. 65:11 the psalmist praises God for "crowning" the year with his goodness. Ps. 8:5 refers to God having "crowned" human beings with glory, as those privileged to be at the summit of God's created order. Ps. 103:4 declares God as the one who "crowns" the author with loving-kindness. The poignant poetic metaphor in Song 3:11 describes the "crowning" of King Solomon by his mother, on his wedding day. Isa. 23:8 describes the city of Tyre as one who "bestows crowns" on others (reflecting her high standing among the nations) — but not in the sight of God, for the city is condemned for arrogant blasphemy. In all these cases, "crowning" suggests the idea of being raised to a position of great privilege and blessing.

***'aṭārāh* [עֲטָרָה, 5850]**

This is the most common term for "crown" in the Old Testament, occurring about twenty times. It occurs predominantly in a poetic or prophetic context, with a metaphorical sense in each case (except for several literal references to royal crowns in 2 Sam. 13:20; 1 Chr. 20:2; Esth. 8:15). Zech. 6:11 also refers to a literal crown, as Zechariah the prophet is asked to have a crown made for Joshua the high priest as a symbolic gesture to reunite the priesthood and the monarchy among God's people of the postexilic community. This is a highly suggestive symbolic representation of the coming Messiah, whose ministry will indeed combine the roles of priest and king in the coming kingdom of God.

The remaining uses of ***'aṭārāh*** are metaphorical and found in a variety of contexts. For example, Ps.

21:3 contains an idealized description of God himself crowning a king in Israel.

Then, in the sense of great moral virtue, Lady Wisdom is portrayed in the book of Proverbs as one who gives a "crown of glory" to all those who embrace her in order to gain true godly wisdom. Similar metaphors that present virtue and nobility as a "crown" are found in Prov. 12:4; 14:24; 16:31. In contrast, "crowns" are also powerful symbols of indictment against the rebellious people of Israel — crowns are either removed from the people, or crowns represent particular vices (cf. Isa. 28:1, 3; Lam. 5:16; Ezek. 21:26).

Grandchildren are also described as the "crown" of the aged (cf. Prov. 17:6). Also, the city of Zion (Jerusalem) is described as a "crown of glory" on the occasion of her promised renewal by God in Isa. 62:3.

In a negative sense, ***'aṭārāh*** is used in a symbolic fashion in Ezek. 23:42 to indicate the idolatrous passions of the people of Israel who are portrayed as prostituting themselves before their "lovers" (i.e., foreign deities), who, in turn, cover the people of Israel with their "crowns."

Other general symbolic uses of this term are found in Job 19:9; 31:36.

keter [כֶּתֶר, 3804]

This term is only found on three occasions, each time referring to the royal crown of the Persian kingdom in Esth. 1:11; 2:17; 6:8.

nēzer [נֵזֶר, 5145]

The noun ***nēzer*** denotes consecration or separation. It is translated "crown" in a number of places.

A "diadem" or "crown" is set on the turban of the high priest, a symbol of the supreme consecration of Israel's spiritual leader (cf. Exod. 29:6; 39:30; Lev. 8:9).

nēzer denotes a "royal crown" in 2 Sam. 1:10; 2 Kgs. 11:12; 2 Chr. 23:11; Prov. 27:24. See also Pss. 89:39; 132:11.

NT Words

stephanos [στέφανος, *4735*]

The noun ***stephanos*** denotes a "crown" in all eighteen occurrences, in a number of contexts that are primarily metaphorical.

References to a "crown" of thorns, placed on the head of Christ prior to his crucifixion, are found in Matt. 27:29; Mark 15:17; John 19:2, 5.

The metaphorical sense of "wreath," "crown" refers symbolically to the believer's eternal reward in glory (cf. 1 Cor. 9:25; Phil. 4:1; 1 Thess. 2:19; Jas. 1:12; 1 Pet. 5:4; Rev. 2:10; 3:11; 4:4). See also Rev. 9:7. In particular, 2 Tim. 4:8 refers to the "crown of righteousness."

The crown is the symbol of the supreme authority of the Messianic King, leading the army of heaven against the armies of Satan (cf. Rev. 6:2; and also Rev. 14:14). See also Rev. 12:1.

stephanoō [στεφανόω, *4737*]

stephanoō is a verb found four times with the meaning "to crown." An athlete is crowned with a wreath in 2 Tim. 2:5. Heb. 2:7, 9 speak of Christ "crowned" with glory by God.

diadēma [διάδημα, *1238*]

diadēma is a noun found in three places meaning "crown." Rev. 12:3; 13:1 speak of the crowns worn by the two satanic beasts in John's visions. By contrast, Rev. 19:12 refers to the many "crowns" worn by the messianic King of kings.

Additional Notes

By and large, the Hebrew noun ***'aṭārāh*** and the corresponding Greek terms ***stephanos*** and ***diadēma*** share dynamic equivalence. The Hebrew concept of "crown," however, is broader than the emblem of kingship, honor, and glory that constitutes the New Testament Greek usage. Similar remarks may be made about the usage of ***'āṭar*** and ***stephanoō***, yet one very significant parallel links the respective verbs between the Testaments. ***stephanoō*** is used in Heb. 2:7 in a direct quote from Ps. 8:5 (where ***'āṭar*** is used). Clearly, in the new covenant order of things, Jesus Christ is likewise "crowned" with glory and honor — but in a consummate sense far above that of mortal humankind.

CRUCIFY ➞ CROSS ➞ HANG

CRUSH

OT Words

dāka' [דָּכָא, 1792]

dāka' is a verb found eighteen times meaning "crush," "break in pieces" in a metaphorical sense.

The meaning "crush" is used in general symbolic contexts to denote people being destroyed (cf. Job 4:19; 5:4; 22:9; 34:25; Pss. 94:5; 143:3). The phenomenon of "being crushed" by God is indicated in Job 6:9; 19:2. God's action in "crushing" the wicked, or his enemies, is noted in Pss. 7:2; 89:10; Lam. 3:34.

"Crushing" the poverty-stricken, or defrauding them of whatever meager assets they own, is forbidden under the law (cf. Prov. 22:22). Israel is condemned for such action in Isa. 3:15.

Isa. 53:5, 10 refer to the messianic Suffering Servant "being crushed, or bruised" for the sins of his people.

NT Words

syntribō [συντρίβω, *4937*]

syntribō is a verb found eight times meaning "break," "shatter," "crush." Matt. 12:20 refers to a "crushed" reed. Rom. 16:20 predicts that God will soon "crush" Satan under the feet of his people.

thrauō [θραύω, *2352*]

thrauō is a rare verb found only in Luke 4:18 referring to the spirit-anointed Christ setting free those who are "oppressed," suggesting deliverance for those who are crushed in their spirit.

apothlibō [ἀποθλίβω, *598*]

apothlibō is a rare verb found only in Luke 8:45, meaning "press" or "crush" in the context of a crowd "pressing" in on Christ and his disciples.

See Also: ➡ BRUISE

CRY

OT Words

zā'aq [זָעַק, **2199**]

This term means "cry" in the senses of "cry out," "wail," "weep," "shout," "call." ***zā'aq*** is found in a variety of contexts, and it occurs approximately seventy times.

zā'aq is used predominantly in the context of crying out to God in a number of different circumstances. This term is frequently found in situations of distress or calamity, where the suppliant cries out to God for help (e.g., Exod. 2:23; 1 Sam. 7:8, 9; 8:18; 15:11; 1 Chr. 5:20; 2 Chr. 32:20; Pss. 22:5; 107:13, 19; 142:5; Isa. 30:19). There are also references to people beseeching God for aid and mercy in the face of his judgment against them. In other words, the hand of God's discipline provokes them to cry out to him for mercy and relief (cf. Judg. 3:9, 15; 6:6, 7; Jer. 11:11; 30:15; Lam. 3:8; Ezek. 9:8; Neh. 9:28; Joel 1:14; Mic. 3:4). There are also occasional specific cries to God for repentance (cf. 1 Sam. 12:10; Neh. 9:4).

"Cries" are also uttered in various contexts without specific reference to God, but rather simply as expressions of anguish (cf. 1 Sam. 28:12; 2 Sam. 19:4; Esth. 4:1; Jer. 47:2; Ezek. 27:30; 1 Kgs. 22:32). They are often uttered in response to the judgment of God, which renders the agony even more pathetic (cf. 1 Sam. 4:13; 5:10; Isa. 14:31; 15:4; Jer. 25:34; 48:20; Ezek. 21:12).

Also worthy of note are the contexts in which ***zā'aq*** is used in reference to idol worship, where people — both Israel and the surrounding Gentile nations — cry out to their pagan deities (cf. Judg. 10:14; Isa. 57:13; Jer. 11:12).

zā'aq also refers to "crying out," or "calling" between people in varying circumstances. These occurrences include, for example, Tamar's weeping after being raped by Amnon (cf. 2 Sam. 13:19); Mephibosheth's appeal to King David (cf. 2 Sam. 19:28); and Jephthah's unsuccessful summoning of the Ephraimites to join him in battle (cf. Judg. 12:2). See also Jonah 3:7; Zech. 6:8.

In a number of places, ***zā'aq*** is translated "gather together" in the sense of "being summoned to assembly" (cf. Josh. 8:16; Judg. 4:10ff.; 18:22ff.; 1 Sam. 14:20; 2 Sam. 20:4, 5).

ze'āqāh [זְעָקָה, **2201**]

ze'āqāh is the noun derived from ***zā'aq***, above, and it is found eighteen times with the meaning "cry."

In all but a handful of places ***ze'āqāh*** refers to a cry of anguish or distress, and thus it has a narrower semantic range than its verbal counterpart. However, the contexts in which cries of grief and pain are uttered are similar to the range of texts in which the verbal form ***zā'aq*** is found. The judgment of God causes great distress among the enemies of Yahweh and Israel and evokes such cries, for example, in Sodom and Gomorrah (cf. Gen. 18:20); in Moab (cf. Isa. 15:5, 8; Jer. 48:4, 34); among the nations (cf. Jer. 50:46); in Babylon (cf. Jer. 51:54); and in Tyre (cf. Ezek. 27:28). And Israel herself is not excluded from this phenomenon (cf. Jer. 18:22; 20:16). Neh. 9:9 also notes Israel's cry to God for assistance during her enslavement in Egypt.

Exclamations of sorrow, though not specifically addressed to God, are also found with respect to the poor (cf. Neh. 5:6; Prov. 21:13), and to the distress of Mordecai and the Jews throughout the Persian empire (cf. Esth. 9:31).

Eccl. 9:17 refers to the "cry" of the ruler. In this context, though there is some ambiguity, it would appear that ***ze'āqāh*** indicates "shouts" of abuse.

Finally, ***ze'āqāh*** is used in Isa. 65:19 in the negative sense of an absence of crying. This context is a remarkably positive one of blessing, indicating that the divine transformation of the sinful world of a degenerate humanity into the new heavens and new earth will result in the removal of all traces of crying and grief.

shaw'āh [שַׁוְעָה, 7775]

This term is synonymous with ***ze'āqāh***, above, meaning "cry (of distress)" in each of the eleven occurrences. This word is always used in conjunction with Yahweh, who is the object of the people's cry of anguish. In all but one reference, those who appeal to God for aid are Israelites: Exod. 2:23 (Israel in Egypt); 2 Sam. 22:7; Ps. 18:6 (David); Pss. 34:15; 39:12; 40:1; 102:1; 145:19 (the psalmist and the people of God in general); Jer. 8:19; Lam. 3:56 (Jeremiah). In the last two texts, the catalyst for the anguished cry of the prophet is the judgment of God against the people of Judah — in this case, the Babylonian invasion.

In 1 Sam. 5:12, the cry (***shaw'āh***)of the Philistines is in view. In this context, the Philistines' exclamation of agony is said to ascend to heaven. They are under the punishment of God for having taken the ark of the covenant from the Israelites in battle and placed it in a position of prominence in their own temple.

rinnāh [רִנָּה, 7440]

rinnāh is a noun found approximately thirty times with the predominant sense of "cry" or "shout" in a variety of contexts.

The meaning "cry" is found in the context of urgent pleas to God in prayer (cf. 1 Kgs. 8:28; 2 Chr. 6:19; Pss. 17:1; 61:1; 88:2; 106:44; 119:169; 142:6). In Jer. 7:16; 11:14 the prophet is forbidden to offer up "intercession" on behalf of his people. Jer. 14:12 records God's refusal to hear his people's "cry."

General references to "cry" in the sense of "shout" are found in 1 Kgs. 22:36; Isa. 43:14. "Shouts" of joy are noted in Ps. 126:5ff.; Prov. 11:10; Isa. 48:20. References to "singing" praise to God are found in 2 Chr. 20:22; Pss. 105:43; 126:2; Isa. 35:10; 55:12. See also Isa. 14:7.

shāwa' [שָׁוַע, 7768]

shāwa' is a verb meaning "cry out," "shout" throughout the twenty or so occurrences of the term. The dominant context is that of crying aloud for help.

General reference to "crying out" is indicated in Job 19:7. "Crying out" to God for help is noted in Job 24:12; 30:20; Pss. 18:6; 22:24; 30:2; 88:13; Isa. 58:9; Jonah 2:2. Non-specific crying for help is indicated in Job 30:28. In Ps. 18:41; Lam. 3:8 God refuses to answer humanity's cry for help.

NT Words

kraugē [κραυγή, *2906*]

kraugē is a noun denoting a "sharp cry," "shout(ing)" in each of the six contexts in which it is found. A "cry" of surprise is indicated in Matt. 25:6; a "cry" of support for the innocence of the apostle Paul is noted in Acts 23:9. "Shouting" in the context of unrestrained brawling occurs in a list of vices in Eph. 4:31. Heb. 5:7 refers to the "loud cries" of Christ offered to God in prayer during times of trial in his ministry on earth. The saints in heaven are described as being free from the "crying" of anguish and pain in Rev. 21:4.

kraugazō [κραυγάζω, *2905*]

kraugazō is a verb found seven times meaning "cry out aloud" in each case (cf. Matt. 12:19; 15:22; John 11:43; 18:40; 19:6, 15; Acts 22:23).

boē [βοή, *995*]

boē is a rare noun denoting a "cry" of protest in the face of injustice found only in Jas. 5:4.

boaō [βοάω, *994*]

The verb ***boaō*** means "cry out" throughout its eleven occurrences in a variety of contexts.

General references to "crying out" are found in Acts 17:6; 21:34. "Crying out" in the context of a proclamation is evident in Mark 1:3; Luke 3:4; John 1:23. Gal. 4:27 refers to "crying out" in joy. Jesus' "cry" of anguish on the cross is noted on Mark 15:34. The distressed "cries" of the elect in prayer to God are found in Luke 18. There is a "pleading" with Christ for a miraculous healing from blindness in Luke 18:38. Acts 8:7 contains a "cry" of terror from evil spirits cast out by the power of Christ from people whom they had previously oppressed.

anaboaō [ἀναβοάω, *310*]

anaboaō is a rare variant of ***boaō***, above, found in only three places and meaning "cry out" in Matt. 27:46 in relation to Jesus' cry of anguish on the cross as he experiences the rejection of his Father. In Luke 9:38 a father cries out to Jesus to exorcise the evil spirit from his son.

epiboaō [ἐπιβοάω, *1916*]

epiboaō is another rare variant of ***boaō***, above, denoting the "shouting" of a crowd in Acts 25:24.

krazō [κράζω, *2896*]

krazō means "cry," "cry out" throughout the nearly sixty occurrences of the term in various contexts.

Evil spirits "cry out" in fear of Christ in Matt. 8:29; Mark 1:26; Luke 4:41 (cf. also Acts 16:17). People afflicted with sickness or disability "cry out," seeking healing from Christ in Matt. 9:27; 20:30ff.; Mark 9:24; 10:47; Luke 18:39. "Calling out" in prayer to God is indicated in Rom. 8:15; Gal. 4:26. In Rev. 6:10 the saints "beseech" God for revenge on their enemies. In contrast, Matt. 21:9; Mark 11:9; John 12:13; Rev. 7:10 record "crying out" in praise of God. Jesus' "cry" at the point of his death is recorded in Matt. 27:50. In Mark 15:13, the Jerusalem crowd "cries out" demanding the death of Jesus.

General references to "crying out" include Matt. 15:23; Mark 5:5; John 1:5; Acts 7:57; Rev. 18:18. See also Matt. 14:26ff.; Acts 19:28; Rev. 12:2. A metaphorical reference to stones "crying out" is indicated in Luke 19:40.

anakrazō [ἀνακράζω, *349*]

anakrazō is a variant form of ***krazō***, above, meaning "cry out" in each of the five occurrences of the term. The cry of anguish from those possessed by evil spirits is noted in Mark 1:23; Luke 4:23. In Luke 8:28 the cry comes from the demon itself, struck with terror at the prospect of being confronted by Christ. A cry of fear is recorded in Mark 6:49. Luke 23:18 records the crowd's "clamoring shout" demanding that Pilate release Barabbas, the revolutionary, instead of Jesus.

epiphōneō [ἐπιφωνέω, *2019*]

epiphōneō is a rare variant form meaning "cry, shout out" in relation to a crowd (cf. Luke 23:21; Acts 12:22; 22:24).

Additional Notes

Dynamic equivalence between the Hebrew and Greek terminology for "cry," "crying" as a whole may be affirmed. In both Old and New Testaments, the cries of human beings to God are found alongside the utterances between human beings. ***anaboaō*** and ***krazō*** indicate that Jesus himself cried out to God at the point of surrendering his life to his Father — one instance where the paradox of Jesus' humanity and divinity surfaces in the New Testament text.

See Also: → CALL → SHOUT

CUP

OT Words

kôs [כּוֹס, 3563]

This term is translated "cup" nearly thirty times in the Old Testament, in both a literal and metaphorical sense.

At the literal level ***kôs*** refers, for example, to a wine goblet in the Joseph narrative (cf. Gen. 40:11, 13, 21) and elsewhere (2 Sam. 12:3; Prov. 3:31; Jer. 35:5). It also refers to the cup-like brim of the large bronze washbasin of the Solomonic temple (cf. 1 Kgs. 7:26; 2 Chr. 4:5). This latter usage is in fact a simile — that is, ***kôs*** indicates the brim of the basin as being "like a cup."

It is in the full metaphorical sense of ***kôs*** as a "cup" of both blessing and judgment (or wrath) that the term is most significant. Used in a positive sense, in contexts that indicate divine blessing or favor, ***kôs*** is found three times in the Psalms, and once in Jeremiah. In Ps. 16:5 ***kôs*** is translated "cup," in distinct parallel with the idea of blessed "inheritance," as the God-given privilege of faithful Israelites living in the land. Ps. 23:5 expresses a similar thought, with ***kôs*** meaning "cup" in the sense of "abundant blessings from God." Ps. 116:13 refers to the "cup of salvation," a phrase which likewise indicates the blessings of God bestowed upon his people in the land. It suggests the idea of safety, comfort, and deliverance from one's enemies. Jer. 51:7 refers to Babylon as "a golden cup," a symbolic reference (in context) to the great privilege bestowed upon that empire by God himself (cf. Dan. 2:31ff.).

More frequently, however, ***kôs*** refers symbolically to the outpouring of God's judgment and wrath upon those who rebel against him — the people of God as well as the nations. In this sense, the "cup" of the wicked in general is referred to in Pss. 11:6; 75:8. With regard to this "cup" of God's fury, those who are being punished are described as "having drunk it," "being made to drink it," or "having it poured out (on them)." In each case the effect is the same: they bear the painful consequences of rebellion against God and suffer his anger. This is predicated of the nations (cf. Jer. 25:15, 17, 28); of Edom (cf. Jer. 49:12); of Babylon (cf. Hab. 2:16); and of Israel and Judah (cf. Isa. 51:17, 22; Ezek. 23:31ff.). Jer. 16:7 also refers to "the cup of consolation" being denied to the nation of Judah near the time of her imminent destruction at the hands of the Babylonians. Though the wording is different, the thought underlying the refusal of this "cup" of consolation is virtually identical to God's people drinking the "cup" of his wrath.

NT Words

potērion [ποτήριον, *4221*]

The noun ***potērion*** denotes a "cup" (i.e., a drinking vessel) throughout its nearly thirty occurrences.

Literal references to "cups" in general contexts include Matt. 10:42; 23:25ff.; Mark 7:4; 9:41; Luke 11:39. The "Passover cup" drunk by Jesus and his disciples on the evening prior to his death is indicated in Mark 14:23; Luke 22:17, 20.

The remaining usage of ***potērion*** is metaphorical. The "cup" symbolizing the anticipation of Christ's suffering on the cross denotes the "judgment of God" in Matt. 20:22ff.; 26:39ff.; Mark 10:38ff.; 14:36; Luke 22:42; John 18:11. Specific mention of the "cup" of God's anger is found in Rev. 14:10; 16:19; 18:6. Babylon's "cup of abominations" is noted in Rev. 17:4.

In a positive sense, the "cup of blessing" is mentioned in 1 Cor. 10:16, 21; 11:25ff., denoting the wine drunk at the Lord's Supper, symbolizing the blood Christ shed for the forgiveness of sins.

Additional Notes

The dynamic equivalence between ***potērion*** and ***kôs*** in reference to the "cup" of divine judgment is clear. What is of particular significance is the New Testament's focus on ***potērion*** as one of the most potent symbols of Jesus' suffering on the cross. It highlights the development of a major redemptive-historical theme in Scripture: that is, the progression from God's judgment on the sin of the world, with respect to both his own people and the nations at large, to the narrowing of that judgment on the Messianic Servant himself. It is Jesus Christ who bears in his own person the ultimate "cup" of his Father's wrath, for the sake of his people, and as a substitute in their place. Such a selfless act of mercy and love lies at the heart of the biblical gospel.

CURSE, CURSED

OT Words

'ālāh [אָלָה, 423]

This noun occurs around forty times with the dual, though related, meanings of "oath" and "curse." (→ OATH) ***'ālāh*** is translated "curse" in about half of the occurrences.

Cursing in the Old Testament has a significant theological emphasis when linked with the phenomenon of a solemn oath. In this context, a curse may be defined as the legal punishment or consequence enacted upon those who violate a previously sworn solemn oath, and the biblical writer regards it with the utmost seriousness. One graphic example of this is found in Num. 5:21ff., where legislation is prescribed for a "trial by ordeal" for women suspected by their husbands of having committed adultery. ***'ālāh*** is used in this particular context to refer to the curse that will befall the woman if she is found guilty. The "ordeal" prescribed here is for adultery committed in the past that has not been proven, where there were no witnesses (otherwise, the death sentence would apply). The suspicion of the husband is sufficient to initiate the ordeal and the "curse" envisaged is lifelong infertility and, if necessary, the miscarriage of the unborn child. It is important to note here that the curse follows the taking of an oath by the woman immediately prior to the ordeal (cf. Num. 5:19ff.), provided she is proven guilty in the process.

At a more formal level, ***'ālāh*** refers to the punishment God hands down to all those who violate his commands and laws contained in the Mosaic covenant legislation. Specific curses are directed at the people of God for their disobedience in this area. These are recorded either as a warning for the future (cf. Deut. 29:19, 20, 21); or as the rationale for their present crisis or imminent catastrophe, such as the invasion of the Babylonian army (cf. 2 Chr. 34:24; Jer. 23:10; Dan. 9:11; Zech. 5:3); or as a matter of past history (cf. Neh. 10:29). In a more general sense, covenant curses also extend to the nations of the earth who rebel against God. While these nations never formally entered into a covenant relationship with Yahweh, they are still held accountable for their idolatry and blasphemy against him. In their case, the divine anger they face is the consequence of ignoring the implications of general revelation (not the violation of a formal legal relationship, as is the case with the Israelites). Reference to this kind of curse is found in Isa. 24:16, where the judgment of God against the nations is declared to be the consequence of the divine curse.

'ālāh also designates cursing in a "non-technical" sense, distinct from the covenant context, when referring to swearing or bad language in general (cf. Pss. 10:7; 59:12). In addition, ***'ālāh*** conveys the contempt expressed by the nations towards Israel, as a consequence of her punishment. In this sense, Israel is made an "object of cursing" to the nations. There is, however, no explicit covenantal sense in these particular contexts (cf. Jer. 29:18; 42:18; 44:12).

qelālāh [קְלָלָה, 7045]

This term is largely synonymous with ***'ālāh*** (see above) and occurs approximately thirty times. ***qelālāh*** has both the technical meaning of "curse" (i.e., as a consequence of covenant violation) and the non-technical sense of "curse" (i.e., the invoking of abuse or personal misfortune upon one's enemy).

In the non-technical sense, ***qelālāh*** is found in the following texts where cursing involves the expectation of some impending calamity: Gen. 27:12, 13; Num. 23:5; Judg. 9:57; Neh. 13:2; Ps. 109:17, 18. In other texts, personal abuse is involved (cf. 2 Sam. 16:12; 1 Kgs. 2:8; Prov. 26:2).

qelālāh also indicates specific covenant curses. As with ***'ālāh***, above, ***qelālāh*** is found in contexts in which warnings are given to God's people so that the divine curse may be avoided (cf. Deut. 11:26, 28, 29; 27:13; 28:15, 45; 29:27; 30:1, 19). In fact, this is the dominant context in which ***qelālāh*** is found. Yet in 2 Kgs. 22:19 ***qelālāh*** affirms that the curse of the covenant is an inevitable future reality — but not during Josiah's lifetime. See also Jer. 29:22 for a similar perspective.

qelālāh is also used similarly to ***'ālāh*** in that it, too, refers to Judah and Jerusalem as "objects of cursing" in the eyes of the pagan nations (cf. Jer. 25:18; 26:6; 42:18; 44:8, 12, 22; Zech. 8:13); as is Edom (cf. Jer. 49:13).

Finally, Deut. 21:23 indicates that being hung on a tree after execution for a capital offense symbolized a terrible divine curse. This punishment undoubtedly highlighted the heinous nature of the crime and was intended as a deterrent to others lest they come under the same divine judgment and rejection. It is this very text that the apostle Paul quotes in Gal. 3:13 to indicate the true nature of Christ's own death by crucifixion in becoming a "curse for us."

me'ērāh [מְאֵרָה, 3994]

This is a rare term, occurring only five times. It is translated "curse" on each occasion and refers to the curses of the covenant in Deut. 28:20 in a specific sense, and those in Mal. 2:2; 3:9 in a general sense, arising from the postexilic community's abuse of the ritual system of worship. Cursing in the general sense of personal abuse is found in Prov. 28:27. ***me'ērāh*** is used in Prov. 3:33 to indicate the "curse of the Lord" in the sense of enacting his judgment against the wicked in a non-specific way.

'ārar [אָרַר, 779]

This verb is found on sixty occasions throughout the Old Testament, and it is synonymous in its range of meaning with the three entries above. ***'ārar***, like ***'ālāh*** and ***qelālāh*** above, likewise embraces both the technical and non-technical sense of "curse."

As regards the specific curses of the covenant, ***'ārar*** is frequently listed in the Deuteronomic legislation as an imperative, invoking the judgment and wrath of God upon those who disobey the specific tenets of the Sinai covenant. The texts all commence with the words "Cursed is the man who . . . " (cf. Deut. 27:15ff.; 28:16ff.). An identical statement, with specific reference to the Mosaic law, is found in Jer. 11:3.

There are a number of other passages that invoke the curse and judgment of God upon sin, but these are not explicitly linked to the covenant. They simply represent the divine reaction of judgment against sin in a general sense. This is evident, for example, in the curses associated with Adam and Eve's disobedience in the garden of Eden and the subsequent emergence of a sinful human culture in rebellion against God (cf. Gen. 3:14, 17; 4:11). See also Gen. 9:25 for reference to the curse on Canaan in the aftermath of the flood narrative. Then there is the promise of the divine curse being enacted upon all those who curse God's chosen servants (cf. Gen. 12:3; 27:29; Num. 24:9).

For general declarations of God's curse upon sinners, see also Gen. 5:29; Josh. 6:26; Judg. 5:23; 1 Sam. 26:19; 2 Kgs. 9:34; Ps. 119:21; Jer. 17:5; 48:10. This perspective is also evident in the "trial by ordeal" legislation of Num. 5, where ***'ārar*** refers to the bitter water that "brings a curse" (cf. Num. 5:18ff.). Divine judgment also falls upon the postexilic community in Malachi's day, who are cursed by God for their abuse of the Levitical system of worship, and for their failure to honor God thereby (cf. Mal. 1:14; 2:2; 3:9). In the Malachi texts, although the curses of God in relation to the people's offenses refer to the covenant, they are not "curses of the covenant" in the classical sense of the word.

'ārar also refers to cursing in the non-technical sense of invoking misfortune and/or personal abuse upon one's enemy (cf. Exod. 22:28; Num. 22:6, 12; 23:7; Judg. 21:18; 1 Sam. 14:24, 28; Job 3:8; Jer. 20:14).

There is one final text that is worthy of note, on account of its irony: Judg. 9:23 refers to the curse Joshua placed on the Gibeonites to remain perpetual slaves to the people of Israel. These Canaanites, who were near neighbors, had deceived Joshua and the Israelite tribes into believing they were travelers from a distant land. Joshua and the people of Israel should have slaughtered them in accordance with God's specific instructions in Deut. 7. This was to have been their fate according to the divine curse. Yet, because of the oversight of the Israelites, they escaped.

NT Words

anathema [ἀνάθεμα, *331*]

anathema is a noun found in six places with the underlying sense of a "curse." In most of these contexts the term is used adjectivally with the meaning "accursed." 1 Cor. 16:22; Gal. 1:8, 9 record the apostolic invocation "Let him be accursed," directed against false teachers and the faithless. 1 Cor. 12:3 affirms that no true believer would ever express the invocation "Jesus be cursed." See also Rom. 9:3. Acts 23:14 implies a "curse" by referring to a "solemn oath" taken by those who had sworn to assassinate the apostle Paul, and not to eat until they had accomplished that task.

katathema [κατάθεμα, *2652*]

katathema is a rare variant of ***anathema***, above, denoting a "curse." It is found only in Rev. 22:3, indicating the total absence of anything accursed in heaven.

anathematizō [ἀναθεματίζω, *332*]

anathematizō is a verb found in four places meaning "to curse," or "invoke a curse" in Mark 14:71; and "to bind oneself a solemn oath" in Acts 23:12ff., referring to the attempt to murder Paul.

katathematizō [καταθεματίζω, *2653*]

katathematizō is a rare variant of ***anathematizō***, above, found only in Matt. 26:74 referring to Peter "invoking a curse" in the course of denying his relationship.

ara [ἀρά, *685*]

ara is a rare noun found only in Rom. 3:14, denoting "cursing" in general terms alongside the spirit of bitterness.

katara [κατάρα, *2671*]

katara is a variant of ***ara***, above, denoting the nominal sense of "curse," "cursing" in all but one of the six occurrences. Gal. 3:10, 13 refer to the "curse" of the law. The practice of "cursing" is condemned in Jas. 3:10. The adjectival sense of "cursed" is indicated in Heb. 6:8; 2 Pet. 2:14.

kataraomai [καταράομαι, *2672*]

kataraomai is a verb found in six places and translated "to curse" in each case. The action of cursing people is indicated in Matt. 5:44; Luke 6:28; Rom. 12:14; Jas. 3:9. The wicked who are "cursed" by God are noted in Matt. 25:41. Mark 11:21 mentions the fig-tree "cursed" by Christ.

epikataratos [ἐπικατάρατος, *1944*]

epikataratos is an adjectival form found in three places, meaning "cursed" in each case. All of these contexts refer to "being cursed" by God (cf. John 7:49; Gal. 3:10, 13).

kakologeō [κακολογέω, *2551*]

kakologeō is a verb found four times with the underlying sense of "speak evil of." Matt. 15:4; Mark 7:10 refer to "cursing" one's parents — a capital offense under the Mosaic law. The act of "maligning" someone is noted in Mark 9:39; Acts 19:9.

Additional Notes

To understand the significance of "curse" in the Old Testament, one must consider the relevant terms discussed here as well as the phenomenon of the ***ḥērem*** (→ DESTROY) — the total ban God placed upon the land of Canaan, as the ultimate curse of the old covenant dispensation. However, it may be said that all the curses under the old covenant legislation come to a final expression in the new covenant in two ways. First of all, the curse of the law was only removed once and for all through the sacrificial atoning death of Christ on the cross. And secondly, all those who refuse to repent of their sins and in faith accept the sacrifice of Christ as the only full and adequate payment for their sins can gain no relief from that same divine curse.

See Also: → DESTROY

CUSTOM → TRIBUTE

CUT

OT Words

kārat [כָּרַת, 3772]

This is a common verb with a complex semantic range, occurring nearly three hundred times throughout the Old Testament. The fundamental meaning of ***kārat*** is "cut," but it is translated a number of ways: "to make (i.e., cut) a covenant"—in this context always used with ***berît*** (→ COVENANT); "to cut down"; "to cut off," both in a literal and a metaphorical sense. With this latter symbolic sense, the meaning of ***kārat*** is "destroy," or "remove," or both. The meaning "cut off" is also used frequently in a technical sense to refer to capital punishment, or execution, through the specific sanction of the Mosaic law covenant. (→ DESTROY)

The use of ***kārat*** in connection with the phenomenon of the covenant, or ***berît***, is of the greatest significance for a full appreciation of Old Testament theology. The Old Testament describes entering into a covenant relationship as "cutting (i.e., making) a covenant." This is true whether it is a purely human transaction, a relationship with God initiated by human beings, or whether it is the most significant covenant of all — the divine covenant inaugurated by God with his chosen people.

In regard to the divinely inaugurated covenant process, ***kārat*** designates the various stages of this phenomenon throughout the history of Israel. The only one not specifically described in this way is the covenant with Noah.

kārat is used in relation to the Abrahamic covenant (cf. Gen. 15:18; 1 Chr. 16:16; Ps. 105:9; Neh. 9:8). More frequently, it designates the constituting of the Mosaic covenant in the Pentateuch (cf. Exod. 24:8; 34:10, 27; Num. 13:24; Deut. 4:23; 5:2, 3; 9:9; 29:1, 12, 14, 25; 31:16). It is then used to refer back to this initial Sinai process throughout the remainder of the Old Testament (e.g., 1 Kgs. 8:9; 2 Kgs. 17:15, 35; 2 Chr. 5:10; Jer. 11:10; 31:32; 34:13; Hag. 2:5). The implementation of the Davidic covenant is described this way on three occasions (cf. 2 Chr. 7:18; 21:7; Ps. 89:3). Although the actual phrase "cutting a covenant" is not used in 2 Sam. 7, where the principal features of God's promise to David are enunciated, the actual process of covenant formation is clearly in view.

Not only are the various stages of old covenant implementation described in terms of "cutting," but the anticipation of the new covenant is also described this way. ***kārat*** is used in this connection in Isa. 55:3; 61:8; Jer. 31:31, 33; 32:40; Ezek. 34:25; 37:26; Hos. 2:18. These passages constitute some of the great prophetic high points of Old Testament revelation, as they anticipate the coming of the Messiah and the fulfillment of God's purposes in salvation.

In addition, ***kārat*** is used in contexts that indicate a renewal or reaffirmation of the Mosaic covenant — normally initiated by the people of God, either individually or corporately (cf. Josh. 24:25 [Joshua and the Israelites]; 2 Chr. 29:10 [Hezekiah]; 2 Kgs. 11:17 [Jehoiada]; 2 Chr. 23:3 [Josiah]; Nehemiah 9:38 [the postexilic community]).

Occasionally, ***kārat*** also signifies the intention of God's people to initiate a specific covenant transaction between themselves and God that is not related to the divine covenant. Instances of this usage are found first of all in Jer. 34:8, 15, 18, where Zedekiah and the people of Judah enter into a solemn covenant never to enslave their fellow Hebrew countrymen again. A similar phenomenon is observed in Ezra 10:3, when the Israelite men who had intermarried with women of Canaan in violation of the law vow before God to have their marriages annulled.

There are numerous examples of covenant transactions that are undertaken solely at the human level — for example, 1 Sam. 22:8 (David and Jonathan); Josh. 9:6 (Joshua/Israel and the Gibeonites); Gen. 21:27 (Abraham and Abimelech); Gen. 31:44 (Jacob and Laban); 1 Kgs. 5:12 (Hiram and Solomon); 20:34 (Ahab and Ben-Hadad); Ezek. 17:13 (Nebuchadnezzar and Zedekiah); Hos. 12:1 (Israel and Assyria). See also 1 Sam. 11:1; 2 Sam. 3:12; 5:3; Hos. 10:4.

In certain circumstances, ***kārat*** is used in negative contexts where covenant transactions are forbidden to the people of Israel. This is the case specifically in regard to the Canaanites (cf. Exod. 23:32; 34:12; Deut. 7:2; Judg. 2:2). In addition, Isa. 57:8 refers to the metaphorical idolatrous covenant that Israel entered into with the Canaanite deities.

Finally, ***kārat*** refers to two metaphorical covenant transactions recorded in prophetic contexts. The first is in Isa. 28:15, where Yahweh indicts the arrogant people of Jerusalem for boasting about their "covenant with death," indicating their belief that they were invincible. Then, in Zech. 11:10, there is an intriguing reference to Yahweh revoking the covenant he had made with the nations. In the context of the oracle, it appears that this refers to the withdrawal of God's restraint against punishing the nations for their wickedness, but not to a literal oath of protection.

qāṣaṣ [קָצַץ, **7112**]

This term occurs on fourteen occasions and is translated "cut off" or "cut" (literally) in most contexts. It can refer to cutting off human limbs — hands, thumbs, and toes (cf. Deut. 25:12; Judg. 1:6, 7; 2 Sam. 4:12). Other times it refers to cutting various materials (cf. Exod. 39:3; 2 Kgs. 16:17; 18:16; 24:13; Ps. 46:9; 2 Chr. 28:4).

gāda' [גָּדַע, **1438**]

This is a synonym for ***qāṣaṣ***, above, occurring around twenty times and meaning "cut off," "cut down," and "cut in two." It is used in both a literal and metaphorical sense.

The literal meaning of ***gāda'*** is found in a number of contexts — for example, in reference to cutting down idols (cf. Deut. 7:5; 12:3; 2 Chr. 14:3; 31:1; 34:3, 4, 7; Ezek. 6:6; Amos 3:14); cutting off limbs (cf. 1 Sam. 2:31); a beard (cf. Isa. 15:2); boughs of trees (cf. Isa. 9:10; 10:33).

Metaphorically, ***gāda'*** refers to the destruction of both the enemies of God and the people of God as an indication of divine judgment against them. In these contexts, ***gāda'*** is translated "cut off" or "cut down." Israel, for example, is said to be "cut off" in Judg. 21:6; Lam. 2:3. Pagan nations are similarly said to be "cut off" in Isa. 14:12; 22:25; Jer. 48:25; 50:23; Pss. 75:10; 107:16. Several unusual uses of ***gāda'*** allude metaphorically both to God's judgment against Israel and the nations, and to his assistance to Cyrus of Persia. Zech. 11:10 describes Yahweh cutting the staff called "Favor" in two, referring to God's "covenant with the nations" (see above). Zech. 11:14 refers to God cutting his second staff, named "Union," in two. This indicates the dividing of the nations of Israel and Judah — an action suggestive of his judgment against them. Isa. 45:2 refers to Yahweh cutting bars of iron in two. The context indicates that this is done in order to assist Cyrus in his conquest of the nations, and, more importantly, to make him aware of the uniqueness of Yahweh's power.

nātaḥ [נָתַח, 5408]

This rare verb occurs only nine times and has the literal meaning of "cut up" or "cut in pieces." It refers to the slaughter of sacrificial animals in Exod. 29:17; Lev. 1:6, 12; 8:20; 1 Sam. 11:7; 1 Kgs. 18:23, 33; and to the dissection of a woman in Judg. 19:29; 20:6.

ḥāṣab [חָצַב, 2672]

ḥāṣab is a verb occurring twenty-five times with the principal meaning "cut out" or "hew." (→ DIG)

The action of "hewing," or "cutting" with an ax is indicated in Isa. 10:15. See also Isa. 22:16. 2 Chr. 2:2, 18 speak of "quarrying" for stone. A metaphorical reference to the hand of God "cutting out" a people from Abraham's descendants is found in Isa. 51:1, 9. This metaphor identifies the Israelites as a people created by God alone.

The expression "cut to pieces" denotes a metaphorical judgment by the hand of God, directed against his disobedient people in Hos. 6:5.

The nominal sense of "stone cutters" is indicated in 1 Kgs. 5:15; 2 Kgs. 12:12; 1 Chr. 22:2, 15; 2 Chr. 24:12; Ezra 3:7.

shāsaph [שָׁסַף, 8158]

shāsaph is a rare verb found only in 1 Sam. 15:33 referring to Samuel's action in executing Agag the Amalekite King, "cutting" him to pieces.

NT Words

koptō [κόπτω, *2875*]

koptō is a verb found in ten places with the predominant senses of "lament," "wail." In Matt. 21:8; Mark 11:8, however, the term indicates the "cutting" of branches from a tree. (→ MOURN)

apokoptō [ἀποκόπτω, *609*]

apokoptō is a variant form of ***koptō***, above, meaning "cut off," "mutilate" throughout the nine occurrences of the term. Mark 9:43ff. refers metaphorically to "cutting off" one's hands and feet, symbolizing the need to remove those things that give rise to sin. John 18:10, 26 record the action of Peter who "cut off" the ear of the high priest's servant on the occasion of Jesus' arrest. Acts 27:32 refers to "cutting away" a ship's ropes. In Gal. 5:12 Paul gives vent to his rage and frustration at the false teachers, the so-called "Judaizers," expressing the wish that they should mutilate themselves.

ekkoptō [ἐκκόπτω, *1581*]

ekkoptō is another variant form of ***koptō***, above, meaning "cut off," "cut down," "cut out" for most of the sixteen occurrences.

The literal action of "cutting down" trees is indicated in Matt. 3:10; 7:19; Luke 3:9; 13:7, 9.

The rest of the usage is metaphorical. In Matt. 5:30; 18:8, ***ekkoptō*** refers to the need to symbolically "amputate" one's hands or feet should they cause one to sin — that is, remove those features that produce sinful attitudes and behavior. Rom. 11:22 refers to eternal judgment in terms of being "cut off" from God. Rom. 11:24 describes Gentile believers being "cut out" of a wild olive tree and grafted onto the cultivated olive tree (symbolizing the people of Israel).

katakoptō [κατακόπτω, *2629*]

katakoptō is a rare variant of ***koptō***, above, found only in Mark 5:5, describing the actions of a demon-possessed man "cutting" himself with stones.

dichotomeō [διχοτομέω, *1371*]

dichotomeō is a rare verb found only twice, referring symbolically to the act of divine judgment against the wicked and faithless and describing their fate as "being cut to pieces" (cf. Matt. 24:51; Luke 12:46).

aphaireō [ἀφαιρέω, *851*]

The verb ***aphaireō*** is found in eleven places meaning "take away," "cut off." The latter sense is found in Matt. 26:51; Mark 14:47; Luke 22:50, all referring to Peter's action in "cutting off" the right ear of the high priest's servant.

latomeō [λατομέω, *2998*]

latomeō is a rare verb found only twice, indicating the action of "cutting a tomb from the rock" (cf. Matt. 27:60; Mark 15:46).

laxeutos [λαξευτός, *2991*]

laxeutos is a rare adjective denoting a tomb that had been "cut from the rock" or "cut out of stone."

Additional Notes

There is a close correlation in meaning between the Hebrew and Greek terminology for "cut," and various related meanings. However, the uniqueness of ***kārat*** with respect to covenant making sets it apart from the New Testament terminology.

CYMBAL

OT Words

meṣiltayim [מְצִלְתַּיִם, **4700**]

This term for the musical instrument the "cymbal" occurs thirteen times, mainly in the books of the Chronicles (cf. 1 Chr. 13:8; 15:19ff.; 16:5, 42; 25:6; 2 Chr. 5:12ff.; 29:25; Ezra 3:10; Neh. 12:27).

NT Words

kymbalon [κύμβαλον, *2950*]

kymbalon is a rare noun found only in 1 Cor. 13:1 denoting a "cymbal" that clanged noisily.

D

DAILY

NT Words

epiousios [ἐπιούσιος, *1967*]

epiousios is a rare adjectival form found only in Matt. 6:11; Luke 11:3 referring to God supplying people with their "daily" bread, sufficient for their needs day by day.

ephēmeros [ἐφήμερος, *2184*]

ephēmeros is a rare synonym for ***epiousios*** (see above) found only in Jas. 2:15 with reference to one's "daily" food.

kathēmerinos [καθημερινός, *2522*]

kathēmerinos is another rare adjective denoting the "daily" distribution of food, found only in Acts 6:1.

See Also: → DAY

DAMAGE → LOSE

DAMNATION, DAMNED → CONDEMN → DESTROY → JUDGE → JUDGMENT

DANCE, DANCING

OT Words

rāqad [רָקַד, **7540**]

This verb occurs nine times in the Old Testament with the principal meanings "dance," "skip," "leap," "bound." It is found in both literal and metaphorical contexts, depicting both positive and negative emotions.

rāqad is found in 1 Chr. 15:29, describing David dancing joyfully before the Lord because of the successful return of the ark of the covenant to Jerusalem. Job 21:11 refers to children dancing. Eccl. 3:4 also refers to "a time to dance," indicating that dancing is one of many activities appropriate and relevant to the human experience.

The remaining occurrences of ***rāqad*** are all metaphorical and describe activity that is likened to divine judgment. Ps. 29:6 refers to God's judgment on Lebanon whereby the nation will be made to skip like a calf in fear of its life. Ps. 114:4, 6 allude to Yahweh's judgment against Egypt, specifically depicting God's power over nature — the Re(e)d Sea and then the later parting of the Jordan River on the borders of the promised land of Canaan. Isa. 13:21 depicts the dancing of the satyrs, along with other wild beasts on the site of Babylon, destroyed by the judgment of Yahweh. Joel 2:5 portrays the invading army of the unspecified enemy of Israel (possibly Babylon), leaping or dancing on the mountaintops as Israel herself is about to face divine judgment. Nah. 3:2 refers to the "leaping chariots" of the army of Nineveh — again in a context of judgment against one of Israel's fiercest enemies.

māḥôl [מָחוֹל, **4234**]

This term means "dance," "dancing" and occurs eight times. On all occasions the references are literal.

Ps. 30:11 expresses the psalmist's joy at God turning his mourning into dancing. In a similar vein, the psalmist exhorts the people of God to praise him with dancing (cf. Pss. 149:3; 150:4). Jer. 31:4, 13 record the divine promise of renewal and redemption for the people of Judah and Jerusalem, expressed here in terms of dancing and merrymaking. In contrast, Lam. 5:15 refers to the despair of the inhabitants of Jerusalem in the wake of the Babylonian invasion. Their dancing has turned to mourning.

meḥōlāh [מְחֹלָה, **4246**]

This is a synonym for ***māḥôl***, above, occurring eight times. Once again the usage is entirely literal, except for one reference (cf. Song 6:13).

In Exod. 15:20, Miriam and the women of Israel celebrate the deliverance of God's people from the Egyptians at the Re(e)d Sea with dancing. Exod. 32:19 records Moses' anger at the idolatrous dancing of the Israelites before the golden calf. Judg. 11:34 refers to the tragic daughter of Jephthah coming out of her house in a dance of celebration to meet her father after his victory over the Ammonites. Judg. 21:21 describes the incident involving the "daughters of Shiloh" (i.e., young virgin women dedicated to the perpetual service of Yahweh in the tabernacle at Shiloh) at a festival dance. This provides the occasion for the men of Benjamin to take wives for themselves after the other Israelite tribes had placed a ban on any Benjaminite male taking a wife from any of their families. A number of texts in 1 Samuel refer to the women of Israel celebrating the victory of David over the Philistine giant, Goliath, in song and dance (cf. 1 Sam. 18:6; 21:11; 29:5).

ḥûl [חוּל, **2342**]

ḥûl is a verb found about sixty times with a wide variety of meanings, including to "writhe in pain," particularly in the context of giving birth. On two occasions, however, ***ḥûl*** refers to the activity of "dancing" as recorded in Judg. 21:21ff. in relation to the "daughters of Shiloh" — celibate female attendants dedicated to service for Yahweh, attached to the tabernacle at Shiloh.

kārar [כָּרַר, **3769**]

kārar is a rare verb denoting "dancing" with a whirling motion, describing David's joyful response to the return of the ark to Jerusalem (cf. 2 Sam. 6:14ff.).

ḥāgag [חָגַג, **2287**]

The verb ***ḥāgag*** occurs sixteen times with the primary sense of "celebrating or keeping a ritual festival" in honor of Yahweh. In 1 Sam. 30:16, however, it refers to "dancing" in response to one of David's military victories over the Philistines.

NT Words

choros [χορός, *5525*]

choros is a rare noun found only in Luke 15:25 denoting "dancing" as part of general festivity.

orcheomai [ὀρχέομαι, *3738*]

orcheomai is a verb occurring six times, meaning "to dance" in the context of celebration in Matt. 14:6; Mark 6:22; and with reference to an individual girl in Matt. 11:17; Luke 7:32.

Additional Notes

"Dancing" has a far richer theological sense in the Old Testament than it does in the New.

DANGER, DANGEROUS

NT Words

kindyneuō [κινδυνεύω, *2793*]

kindyneuō is a verb found in four places, meaning to "be in danger" in the context of facing physical danger (cf. Luke 8:23; Acts 19:27, 40; 1 Cor. 15:30).

enochos [ἔνοχος, *1777*]

enochos is an adjective found ten times meaning "in danger of" in the sense of "being liable" to judgment and punishment in a legal forensic sense in Matt. 5:21ff.; 26:66; Mark 14:64; Jas. 2:10. Such "danger" — "liability," or "guilt" in the context of punishment for sin — is indicated in Mark 3:29 in relation to blasphemy against the Holy Spirit; and in 1 Cor. 11:27 in relation to profaning the body and blood of Christ at the Lord's Supper. See also Jas. 2:15.

episphalēs [ἐπισφαλής, *2000*]

episphalēs is an adjective found only in Acts 27:9 denoting a "dangerous" sea voyage.

See Also: → ENSNARE

DARE, DARING

NT Words

tolmaō [τολμάω, *5111*]

tolmaō is a verb meaning "to dare," "be bold" throughout the eighteen occurrences of the term.

The meaning "dare" is used mostly in the negative, indicating the sense of "being unwilling to act through moral conviction, fear, or embarrassment." In order to avoid public humiliation, people often "dared not" ask Jesus any more questions (cf. Matt. 22:46; Mark 12:34; Luke 20:40; John 21:12). Other similar uses are found in Acts 5:13; 7:32; Rom. 15:18; 2 Cor. 10:12; Jude 9.

The positive sense of "be bold," "take courage" is indicated in Mark 15:43; Rom. 5:7; 1 Cor. 6:1; 2 Cor. 10:2; 11:21. In particular, Phil. 1:14 refers to the disciples "being bold" to speak the word of God fearlessly.

tolmētēs [τολμητής, *5113*]

tolmētēs is an adjectival form derived from ***tolmaō*** (see above), found only in 2 Pet. 2:10, denoting people who are "bold" in an arrogant sense.

DARK, DARKNESS

OT Words

ḥōshek [חֹשֶׁךְ, **2822**]

This term means "dark," "darkness," but is also translated "obscurity," or "night" on a couple of occasions. ***ḥōshek*** is found eighty times, in both literal and metaphorical contexts.

First of all, ***ḥōshek*** refers to the primeval darkness of creation both in the creation account of the divine origins of the universe (cf. Gen. 1:2); and in the poetic sections of Scripture (cf. Job 12:22; 26:10; Ps. 104:20).

At a different level, though still alluding to the creative powers of God, ***ḥōshek*** refers to the darkness that indicates the presence of God in terrifying judgment. One of the most striking examples of this phenomenon is the plague of darkness visited by God on Pharaoh and the Egyptians for that king's refusal to free the people of Israel from bondage (cf. Exod. 10:21, 22). See also Ezek. 32:8. Similarly, the term refers to the theophanic cloud of darkness — the "glory cloud" — as the setting for God's pronouncement of judgment against the wicked (cf. 2 Sam. 22:12; Ps. 18:11). Divine presence (implying judgment) is also clearly manifested in the theophanic cloud of darkness on Mt. Sinai (cf. Deut. 4:11; 5:23). In a more positive context, ***ḥōshek*** indicates the protection of God's people from the pursuing Egyptian army through the darkness of night and the presence of the divine glory cloud. Then, in a more conventional sense, darkness functions as a protection for the Israelite spies in Jericho, though clearly God uses the natural darkness as part of his overall plan of protection (cf. Josh. 2:5).

In the metaphorical sense of the term, ***ḥōshek*** contains several significant nuances. Most frequently, darkness is associated with the terrible fate of the wicked at the hand of God (cf. 1 Sam. 2:9; Job 5:14; 12:25; Pss. 35:6; 105:28; Isa. 9:2; 42:7; 49:9; 47:5). The ultimate indicator of the terrifying judgment of God against the wicked is found in the symbol of darkness associated with the coming Day of the Lord (cf. Joel 2:28, 31; Amos 5:18, 20; Zeph. 1:15). The term is also used symbolically to refer to the "way of darkness" in relation to the lifestyle of the wicked (cf. Prov. 2:13). Finally, darkness is the fitting setting for committing sin against God (cf. Ezek. 8:12).

Another frequent use of ***ḥōshek*** is linked with the theme of the "darkness of the soul," suggesting bitter grief and despair at the barrenness of one's relationship with God. This is evident in a general sense, linked to the apparent meaninglessness of human existence (cf. Eccl. 2:13, 14; 5:17; 6:4), or as a consequence of God's judgment against his people (cf. Isa. 5:30). See also Isa. 58:10; 59:9; 60:2; Mic. 7:8; Nah. 1:8.

"Darkness" also refers in a general metaphorical sense to a negative experience of alienation, where one is bereft of the companionship of friends or of God (cf. Job 28:3; 34:22; Ps. 88:12).

Finally, positive references to deliverance from darkness suggest the dispelling of divine judgment and the re-establishment of intimate relationship with God (cf. Pss. 107:10, 14; 112:4; Isa. 60:2).

'ōphel [אֹפֶל, 652]

This term occurs only eight times and conveys the predominantly figurative sense of "darkness," "gloom" linked to the idea of spiritual unreceptiveness or alienation from God.

In Job 3:6, Job invokes the darkness to conceal the day of his birth which he now despises in the light of his present ordeal. Job 10:22 refers to darkness as a symbol for death and chaos. Then, in Job 23:17, ***'ōphel*** describes the darkness of utter loneliness and alienation from God. Job 28:3 refers to the darkness of the mine where gemstones are quarried. ***'ōphel*** also indicates the agony of the writer's soul. Instead of the hoped for justice and blessing from God (viz. the "light"), he perceives only darkness (cf. Job 30:26).

In Ps. 11:2, ***'ōphel*** indicates the cunning of the wicked who shoot in the dark at the "upright in heart." Ps. 91:6 affirms that darkness is the natural environment for the "stalking pestilence" that would afflict the psalmist were it not for the hand of God.

Finally, in a positive sense, ***'ōphel*** in Isa. 29:18 refers to the divine healing of the blind, who shall have the darkness of their eyes removed at the coming of the glorious Day of the Lord.

'aphēlāh [אֲפֵלָה, 653]

Synonymous with ***'ōphel***, above, ***'aphēlāh*** also occurs relatively infrequently — only ten times, with both a literal and a metaphorical sense.

'aphēlāh conveys the literal sense of "darkness" only twice — in Prov. 7:9; and in Exod. 10:22, where it refers to the plague of darkness on Egypt.

The dominant symbolic usage of ***'aphēlāh*** focuses on darkness as the fate of the wicked — Jew and Gentile alike — who act in defiance of God's will (cf. Isa. 8:22; 59:9). In reference to Israel as God's covenant people, this darkness is expressed as a specific judgment of blindness (cf. Deut. 28:29), or as an alienation from Yahweh, a removal of intimacy in relationship with him, a thrusting into darkness (cf. Jer. 23:12). With regard to the latter judgment, ***'aphēlāh*** is occasionally associated with the climactic judgment of the Day of the Lord (cf. Joel 2:2, Zeph. 1:15). Finally, Prov. 4:19 refers to darkness as the distinctive characteristic of the "way" of the wicked.

In a positive sense, this term is found in the context of the bestowal of divine blessing, whereby darkness gives way to light as a consequence of a lifestyle characterized by selfless love and compassion towards others.

ḥāshak [חָשַׁךְ, **2821**]

This is the verbal root from which ***ḥōshek*** (see above) is derived. ***ḥāshak*** is found nineteen times with the meanings "grow dark," "cause to be dark," "hide," as well as other related nuances. As with the majority of Hebrew terms that indicate darkness, ***ḥāshak*** also has both a literal and a metaphorical sense. The various senses of ***ḥāshak*** include all those previously discussed above.

Non-theological or mundane references to growing dark are found in Ps. 139:12; Eccl. 12:2, 3; Amos 5:8. Exod. 10:15; Ps. 105:28 both refer to the plague of darkness in Egypt. In Job 3:9 darkness is invoked upon the day of Job's birth. Darkness as the fate of the wicked is indicated in Job 18:6; Ps. 69:23 (blindness); Isa. 13:10 (Babylon); Ezek. 30:18 (Egypt). Similarly, darkness is the judgment of Yahweh upon his people for violating their covenantal responsibilities (cf. Isa. 5:30; Jer. 13:16; Lam. 4:8; 5:17; Amos 8:9; Mic. 3:6). Finally, Job 38:2 contains a rebuke from God, when he chides Job for his folly in attempting to justify himself at God's expense: "Who is this that darkens my counsel with words without knowledge?"

maḥshāk [מַחְשָׁךְ, **4285**]

This is a noun construct form derived from ***ḥāshak*** (see above), meaning "darkness" (as well as related terms), "hiding place," "grave," and "secrecy." It occurs seven times in the Old Testament.

Pss. 88:6, 18; 143:3 use the term metaphorically to indicate anxiety and despair. Similarly, Lam. 3:6 refers to darkness as a metaphor for the grave. Isa. 29:15 also uses ***maḥshāk*** in a symbolic sense to indicate the nature of the activities of the wicked, who plot their schemes "in the dark" (i.e., in secret).

qādar [קָדַר, **6937**]

Here is another synonym for ***ḥāshak*** (see above). ***qādar*** occurs seventeen times with the primary meanings "to darken" and "to mourn."

Literal meanings associated with the darkness of clouds and other natural phenomena are found in 1 Kgs. 18:45; Job 6:16; Ezek. 32:7; Joel 2:10. The one theologically significant occurrence of ***qādar*** that conveys a metaphorical sense of darkening is found in Mic. 3:6, where it indicates divine judgment against the prophets of Israel for their disobedience (i.e., God will withdraw his revelation, or his voice, from them).

'alāṭāh [עֲלָטָה, **5939**]

'alāṭāh is a noun found in four places denoting "dusk," or "twilight," in Ezek. 12:6ff.; and "thick darkness" associated with a divine revelation in Gen. 15:17.

ṣālal [צָלַל, **6751**]

ṣālal is a rare verb meaning to "grow dark" in connection with encroaching night in Neh. 13:19. The meaning "to cover in shade" is indicated in Ezek. 31:3.

'arāphel [עֲרָפֶל, **6205**]

'arāphel is a noun found in fifteen contexts with primary reference to "thick darkness," denoting the theophanic cloud of the presence of Yahweh (cf. Exod. 20:21; Deut. 4:11; 5:22; 2 Sam. 22:10; 1 Kgs. 8:12; 2 Chr. 6:1; Pss. 18:9; 97:2). In Joel 2:2; Zeph. 1:15, the cloud of "thick darkness" is noted in connection with the Day of the Lord judgment. See also Isa. 60:2.

Other general references to "(clouds of) darkness" include Job 22:13; 38:9; Jer. 13:16.

'êphāh [עֵיפָה, **5890**]

'êphāh is another synonym for the above entries, a rare term denoting "darkness" as the divinely created phenomenon in Amos 4:13. Job 10:22 contains a metaphorical reference to "darkness," symbolizing moral chaos.

NT WORDS

skotizō [σκοτίζω, *4654*]

skotizō is a verb meaning "to darken," "cover with darkness" in both literal and metaphorical contexts.

References to the sun "being darkened" as one of the signs of the impending final day of judgment are found in Matt. 24:29; Mark 13:24; Luke 23:45; Rev. 8:12; 9:2.

Metaphorical usage is indicated in contexts where the eyes, hearts, and minds of unbelievers "are darkened," preventing them from discerning spiritual truth.

skotia [σκοτία, *4653*]

skotia is a noun derived from ***skotizō***, above, occurring sixteen times denoting "darkness" in both literal and metaphorical contexts.

References to the "darkness" of night include Matt. 10:27; Luke 12:3; John 6:17; 20:1. More commonly, ***skotia*** indicates a moral "darkness" that grips the hearts and minds of unbelievers — their natural state of spiritual hostility against and enmity with God (cf. John 1:5; 8:12; 12:35, 46; 1 John 2:9, 11). 1 John 1:5 affirms that there is no such trace of darkness in God; and 1 John 2:8 notes that the age of spiritual "darkness" is passing away and the light of salvation is already shining.

skoteinos [σκοτεινός, *4652*]

skoteinos is an adjectival term denoting the "darkness" of spiritual blindness or moral perverseness, found only in Matt. 6:23; Luke 11:34, 36.

skotos [σκότος, *4655*]

Found over thirty times, ***skotos*** is the most common noun denoting "darkness" in the New Testament. Since this term is predominantly used in a metaphorical sense, its significance is profound where it refers to literal darkness.

The "darkness" of spiritual blindness, preventing people from understanding the truth of the gospel, is noted in Matt. 4:16; Luke 1:79; Acts 26:18; Rom. 2:19; 2 Cor. 4:6; 1 Thess. 5:4.

The "darkness" of moral evil in one's heart is indicated in Matt. 6:23; Luke 11:35; John 3:19; Rom. 13:12; 1 Cor. 4:5; Eph. 5:11; 1 John 1:6.

The phrase "outer darkness" symbolically designates the realm of everlasting punishment in Matt. 8:12; 22:13; 25:30.

The "darkness" that fell on the earth during the crucifixion of Christ immediately prior to his death signifies the judgment of God coming upon his Son, whereby he suffers the divine wrath as a consequence of bearing the sin of the world (cf. Matt. 27:45; Mark 15:33; Luke 23:44).

Reference to the "power of darkness" indicates satanic influence in relation to those who had come to arrest Jesus (cf. Luke 22:53). See also 2 Pet. 2:17; Jude 13.

The phenomenon of the sun "turning black" (i.e., into darkness) to indicate the imminent arrival of the final Day of the Lord judgment is noted in Acts 2:20.

The "darkness" of physical blindness is indicated in Acts 13:11.

The realm of moral "darkness" of satanic origin is indicated in 2 Cor. 6:14; Eph. 5:8; 6:12; Col. 1:13; 1 Thess. 5:5. 1 Pet. 2:9 refers to God's people being "called out of darkness" into the light.

The "darkness" of the theophanic cloud containing the presence of God at Sinai is mentioned in Heb. 12:18.

auchmēros [αὐχμηρός, *850*]

auchmēros is a rare adjective, referring literally to a "dark" place in 2 Pet. 1:19.

zophos [ζόφος, *2217*]

zophos is a noun found in four places denoting the "darkness" of the realm of eternal punishment to which the enemies of God are consigned (cf. 2 Pet. 2:4, 17; Jude 6, 13).

gnophos [γνόφος, *1105*]

gnophos is a rare noun found only in Heb. 12:18, denoting the "darkness" or "blackness" of the theophanic cloud at Mt. Sinai (cf. Heb. 12:18).

Additional Notes

The correspondence in meaning between the New Testament terms ***skotia*** and ***skotizō*** (as well as their related terms) and the Hebrew terms ***ḥōshek*** and ***ḥāshak*** (as well as their derivatives) is quite close. The phenomenon of darkness indicates both the consequences of divine judgment against the wicked and the terrible psychological and spiritual impact of alienation from God in both Old and New Testaments. Both phenomena inspire dread and are profoundly significant in all biblical contexts. Conversely, the removal of darkness is celebrated throughout Scripture as one of the most powerful metaphors of salvation, deliverance, and forgiveness of sin — culminating in the person and work of Jesus Christ.

DART

OT Words

ḥēṣ [חֵץ, 2671]

This noun is reasonably common, occurring about fifty times with the predominant meaning "arrow" or "dart," both literal and symbolic.

ḥēṣ is used literally in the sense of "arrow" (as a weapon) in approximately half the texts where the word occurs. These are found mainly in narrative contexts (e.g., 1 Sam. 17:7; 2 Sam. 22:15; 2 Kgs. 13:15; 1 Chr. 12:2; 2 Chr. 26:15). See also Gen. 49:13; Pss. 45:5; 127:4; Isa. 7:24; 37:33 for usage of the term in poetic and prophetic contexts.

ḥēṣ is also used in significant theological contexts with a variety of metaphorical senses. For example, Num. 24:8 refers to the arrows of Yahweh that will inflict painful judgment against the enemies of God's people (cf. also Deut. 32:23, 42). And the people of Israel will also experience such a punishment for their disobedience towards God (cf. Isa. 5:28; Ezek. 5:16). In Isa. 49:2, ***ḥēṣ*** refers to the Servant of Yahweh as a "polished arrow," an indication that this agent of the Lord is a potent weapon set against the enemies of God and his people. Other uses of this term that point to divine judgment against foreign nations include Jer. 50:4 (Babylon); Ezek. 39:3 (Gog and Magog); Hab. 3:11 (Egypt); Zech. 9:14 (apocalyptic judgment against the nations).

Finally, *ḥēṣ* refers symbolically to a "wound" (Job 34:6) and also is a metaphor for the psalmist's persecution by evil people (cf. Pss. 57:4; 64:3, 7).

shēbet **[שֵׁבֶט, 7626]**

shēbet is a noun found nearly two hundred times with the primary senses of "tribe," "rod," "scepter." In 2 Sam. 18:14, however, it means "dart" — referring either to a "javelin," or to the "shaft" of a spear.

NT Words

belos [βέλος, *956*]

belos is a rare noun referring solely and symbolically to the fiery "darts" of the devil — those demonic weapons designed to destroy the people of God.

Additional Notes

In contrast to the single New Testament occurrence of ***belos***, *ḥēṣ* carries a far greater symbolic weight throughout the Old Testament, with an emphasis on arrows as one of the instruments of God's judgment against his enemies. ***belos*** is significant, however, in that it indicates the fiery arrows of the evil one seeking to destroy the people of God.

DASH

OT Words

nāphaṣ **[נָפַץ, 5310]**

This verb occurs in approximately twenty contexts with the primary meanings "shatter," "dash (to pieces)" and "scatter, disperse," as well as associated senses. The former meaning is more common.

nāphaṣ is translated "disperse" or "scatter" in several contexts (e.g., Gen. 9:19; 1 Sam. 13:11; 1 Kgs. 5:9). Perhaps the most significant usage of the term in this sense is found in Isa. 11:12, where God clearly proclaims his promise to gather his people back to himself from their dispersal in exile.

In a more sobering sense, though no less significant, ***nāphaṣ*** is translated "dash (to pieces)" or "shatter" in a number of contexts. Among these are well-known texts such as Ps. 2:9, where God derides his enemies and declares that he will dash them to pieces for their arrogant and foolish blasphemy. Ps. 137:9 contains the terrible curse against the nation of Babylon, whereby those who dash the children of these people against a rock shall be called "blessed." See also Jer. 51:20, where the Medes are depicted in a similar graphic fashion as those who will be Yahweh's agents of destruction against Babylon. Jer. 13:14; 48:12 contain similar pronouncements of judgment directed against the people of God. Finally, Dan. 12:7 refers to the apocalyptic climax of God's judgment against his people when their suffering will come to an end, heralding the imminent arrival of the eternal age of God's rule among his chosen people.

rātash **[רָטַשׁ, 7376]**

This is a rare verb found only six times, meaning "dash to pieces."

rātash mainly refers to the slaughter of infant children as a terrible judgment from God, either against his own people for their rebellion (cf. Hos. 10:14; 13:16; see also 2 Kgs. 8:12), or against idolatrous pagan nations (cf. Isa. 13:16, 18 [Babylon]; Nah. 3:16 [Nineveh]).

rā'aṣ **[רָעַץ, 7492]**

rā'aṣ is a rare verb meaning "dash" in the sense of "shatter to pieces," referring to Yahweh's conquest of his enemies in Exod. 15:6. Judg. 10:8 refers to the Philistines "shattering" the Israelites for a period of eighteen years.

NT Words

proskoptō [προσκόπτω, *4350*]

proskoptō is a verb found in eight places with the predominant sense of "stumble." In two places, however, the term means "dash" in the context of "striking one's foot against a stone" (cf. Matt. 4:6; Luke 4:11).

See Also: → STRIKE → STUMBLE

DAUGHTER, DAUGHTER-IN-LAW

OT Words

bat **[בַּת, 1323]**

This is a common noun, occurring over five hundred times with the predominant meaning "daughter." In addition to the literal, mundane uses of the term, ***bat*** also has symbolic and theological significance.

In quite a few poetic and prophetic contexts, ***bat*** refers to a nation, city, or people group in the phrase "daughter of . . ." The most frequent of these, and one of the most theologically important, is the expression "daughter of Zion." It is used, for example, as a general symbolic designation for the people of Israel (cf. 2 Kgs. 19:21; Pss. 9:14; 16:1). In a number of contexts this expression indicates God's people under his judgment in relation to their threatened expulsion and exile from the land (cf. Isa. 1:8; 10:32; Jer. 4:31; 6:2; Lam. 1:6; Mic. 1:13; 4:10). Conversely, this phrase also designates the people of Israel and Judah as objects of divine mercy whereby God promises to deliver them from his judgment, to forgive their rebellion against him and renew their covenant relationship with him (cf. Isa. 52:2; Zeph. 3:14; Zech. 2:10). Interestingly, in Mic. 4:8, 13 "daughter of Zion" is used twice in connection with the divine promise of restoration, and in close juxtaposition with the identical phrase in Mic. 4:10, which speaks of God's judgment against them. Finally, Zech. 9:9 refers to the king of the "daughter of Zion" coming on a colt. This is a messianic prophecy, fulfilled in the final days of Jesus' earthly ministry when he entered Jerusalem for the last time (cf. Mark 11:1ff.; John 12:13ff.). The phrases "daughter of Judah" (cf. Lam. 1:15; 2:2, 5) and "daughter of Jerusalem" (cf. Isa. 7:22; Lam. 2:13, 15; Mic. 4:8; Zeph. 3:14; Zech. 9:9) are both synonymous with "daughter of Zion."

Other nations indicated by the use of this expression include Babylon. The phrase "daughter of Babylon" is found exclusively in the context of divine judgment against that people (cf. Isa. 47:1; Ps. 137:8; Jer. 50:2; 51:33; Zech. 2:7). Similarly, the phrase "daughter of Egypt" is found in Jer. 46:11, 24.

Finally, the phrase "daughter of my people" is used sixteen times in the books of Jeremiah and Lamentations to refer to the people of Judah who suffer under the severe hand of God's punishment. Judah is also referred to as "daughter of a foreign god" in Mal. 2:11, where she is indicted by God for her idolatry.

kallāh [כַּלָּה, 3618]

This term is found approximately thirty times, with the predominant meaning "daughter-in-law." ***kallāh*** is also translated "bride" in other contexts.

kallāh is used only in a literal sense with the meaning "daughter-in-law" (e.g., Gen. 11:31; Lev. 18:15; Ruth 1:6; 1 Sam. 4:19; 1 Chr. 2:4). See also Ezek. 22:11; Hos. 4:13, 14.

NT Words

thygatēr [θυγάτηρ, *2364*]

The noun ***thygatēr*** occurs around thirty times with the meaning "daughter," in both literal and metaphorical contexts.

Jesus uses the term as a courteous title for a woman, in the context of a healing (cf. Matt. 9:22; Mark 5:34; 7:26ff.; Luke 8:48).

The literal sense of "daughter" is indicated in Matt. 10:35ff.; Mark 5:35; Luke 1:5; 2:36; 12:53; Acts 2:17; 7:21; 21:9; Heb. 11:24. Reference to "daughters" denoting the "female descendants" of Abraham is found in Luke 13:16.

The expression "daughter of Zion" is a metaphorical reference to the city of Jerusalem and its population (cf. Matt. 21:5; John 12:15).

Similarly, the phrase "daughters of Jerusalem" denotes the female inhabitants of the city in Luke 23:28. Reference to "daughters" in 2 Cor. 6:18 describes women as children of God.

thygatrion [θυγάτριον, *2365*]

thygatrion is a rare diminutive form of ***thygatēr***, above, denoting a "little daughter," found only in Mark 5:23; 7:25.

parthenos [παρθένος, *3933*]

parthenos is a noun denoting a "virgin" throughout the fourteen occurrences of the term. In Acts 21:9 ***parthenos*** expresses the precise nuance of "unmarried daughters" (of Philip the evangelist).

nymphē [νύμφη, *3565*]

The noun ***nymphē*** denotes both a "bride" and "daughter-in-law" in the eight occurrences of the term. The latter meaning is found only in Matt. 10:35; Luke 12:53.

See Also: → BRIDE → MAID → VIRGIN

DAWN

NT Words

diaugazō [διαυγάζω, *1306*]

diaugazō is a rare verb denoting the "dawning" of a day, found only in 2 Pet. 1:19.

epiphōskō [ἐπιφώσκω, *2020*]

epiphōskō is a rare synonym for ***diaugazō***, above, also indicating the "dawning" of a new day in Matt. 28:1; Luke 23:54.

orthros [ὄρθρος, *3722*]

orthros is a noun denoting "daybreak," translated "early in the morning" or "at dawn" in Luke 4:21; John 8:2; Acts 5:21.

See Also: → MORNING

DAY

OT Words

yôm **[יוֹם, 3117]**

This is a common term occurring nearly 2,300 times. The usage of ***yôm*** is largely mundane, referring to "day" as a literal twenty-four-hour period or in a metaphorical sense to indicate an indefinite period of time.

There is, however, one expression containing the term ***yôm*** that has profound theological significance — the Day of the Lord. It is found in this particular form as well as in variations that indicate the same phenomenon (e.g., "in the last days"; "in that day"; "that day").

The phrase "Day of the Lord" occurs about twenty times throughout the Old Testament, with the sense of an ultimate period of divine judgment that includes the final destruction of the wicked, and results in the eternal salvation of God's people. The linguistic context of this expression is frequently characterized by the use of apocalyptic language. What renders this expression even more significant, however, is its application not simply to the final day of judgment, but also to a number of historical events recorded in Scripture that "anticipate" the apocalyptic end of time. As a consequence, a number of incidents in the Bible are referred to as a Day of the Lord judgment. Thus the expression has a somewhat timeless, cyclical application that is not restricted merely to the period immediately prior to the end of this earthly age. The use of this phrase (and similar expressions) in Scripture clearly indicates that history in the Bible is never recorded for its own sake, but as a means of demonstrating that God's purposes in history may be seen as "progressively unfolding," moving towards a climax that has been prepared by God since the beginning of time.

The phrase "Day of the Lord" is found in the following texts: Isa. 13:6, 9 refers to the fierce judgment God has in store for the Babylonians; Jer. 46:10 refers in similar fashion to the fate of the Egyptians, along with the nations in general (cf. also Ezek. 30:3). See also Obad. 15 in regard to the Edomites and the nations. More frequent are the references to Israel herself (cf. Joel 1:15; 2:1, 11, 31; 3:14, where the fate of God's people is clearly depicted). Israel is to be punished for her rebellion against God. It is significant that this judgment recorded in Joel applies specifically to the threat of imminent exile at the hands of either the Assyrians or the Babylonians (depending on the date of the book). Both the Assyrian and Babylonian deportations of Israel (the northern kingdom and Judah respectively) are described in the Old Testament as a Day of the Lord judgment — arguably, the definitive Day of the Lord punishment for God's people under the old covenant.

In Amos 5:18ff. there is tragic irony for the Israelite people: for whereas they are anticipating divine blessing as they await the Day of the Lord, only the dreadful reality of God's wrath (i.e., destruction and exile at the hand of the Assyrians) awaits them. See also Zeph. 1:7, 14; Mal. 4:5. Zech. 14:1ff. refers to the Day of the Lord in an apocalyptic section that graphically depicts both the salvation of God's people and the destruction of the wicked.

The phenomenon of the Day of the Lord, however, is not restricted to the occurrence of that particular phrase. For example, the expressions "in that day" and "in the last days" both occur in Isa. 2–4, one of the most detailed descriptions of the Day of the Lord phenomenon in the Old Testament (cf. Isa. 2:1 ["in the last days"]; 2:11, 17, 20; 3:7, 18; 4:1, 2 ["in that day"]). What is noteworthy in this prophetic oracle is the juxtaposition of divine wrath and mercy. It is clear that the people of Israel will have to endure a time of great trauma and devastation as punishment for disobeying Yahweh. However, it is equally clear that for God's people this coming "day" will also usher in a period of unprecedented moral, spiritual, and physical transformation. Having punished them, God will then cleanse and forgive his people, resulting in complete restoration (cf. Isa. 4:1ff.). This is partially fulfilled within the Old Testament period itself, when the Judean exiles are returned to the land in 539 B.C. during the first year of Cyrus the Persian (cf. Ezra 1).

The expression "in that day" occurs over one hundred times. Its use is concentrated in the Prophets, where it is found most frequently in Isaiah (forty times). Of these occurrences, there is equal distribution in meaning between the negative phenomenon of judgment and the positive phenomenon of blessing (i.e., forgiveness, cleansing, restoration, and transformation). With regard to the latter, Isa. 19:16ff. is a particularly significant example. Here, the promise of salvation is extended to the nations of Egypt and Assyria, as well as to the people of Israel. A similar balance between judgment and blessing in contexts where this phrase is found is also observed in Amos (cf. 2:16; 8:3ff.; 9:11); Micah (cf. 2:4; 4:6; 5:10; 7:11, 12); Zephaniah (cf. 1:10; 3:11, 16); and Zechariah (chs. 12–14). The phrase is also found in Exod. 8:22; 13:8, for example, where references to the plagues on Egypt indicate a foretaste of the final day of judgment against the wicked (cf. also Deut. 31:17; 1 Sam. 3:12; 1 Kgs. 22:25).

The related phrase "that day" occurs over two hundred times, mostly in Isaiah, Jeremiah, Ezekiel, Hosea, Amos, Micah, and Zechariah, where it has a similar meaning and significance to the expressions above.

The phrase "in the last days" is rare, occurring only three times (cf. Gen. 49:1 [Jacob's prophetic blessings to his sons]; Isa. 2:2; Mic. 4:1). The latter two references indicate the anticipated restoration of God's intimate covenant relationship with his people.

NT Words

hēmera [ἡμέρα, *2250*]

hēmera is the most common term for "day" in the New Testament, constituting the clear dynamic equivalent to the Hebrew term ***yôm*** (see above). The term ***hēmera*** signifies "day" in both literal and metaphorical contexts with a variety of nuances.

The meaning "days," signifying a "period," "age," or "time," is indicated with regard to a regnal period in Matt. 2:1; Luke 1:5; Acts 7:45; Rev. 2:13. Jesus' "day," signifying the time of his coming to earth, is noted in John 8:56. The expression "these last days" refers to the period of Christ's incarnation in Heb. 1:2. Reference to "the days" that will usher in the new covenant age is found in Heb. 8:8. The designation "today" denotes the current new covenant age in Heb. 3:13. The "day" of Israel's rebellion in the wilderness is noted in Heb. 13:8. The "days" leading up to the period of final judgment are mentioned in Matt. 9:15; Mark 2:20.

The meaning "day" as a literal twenty-four-hour period is indicated, for example, in Matt. 4:2; Mark 4:35; Luke 2:44; 17:29; John 1:39; Acts 21:10ff.; Rev. 14:11. The forty-day period of Christ's temptation in the wilderness is noted in Mark 1:13; Luke 4:2. The third day after Christ's death — the day of his resurrection — is noted in Matt. 16:21; 27:64; Mark 9:31; Luke 9:22; Acts 10:40; 1 Cor. 15:4. See also Matt. 6:34.

The expression "on that day," as well as variations singular and plural, signifying the consummate time of God's judgment on the earth at the end of time (viz. the Day of the Lord) are found in a number of places. The phrase denotes a time when God will pass a final sentence on the wicked and vindicate the righteous who belong to him in Christ. The negative perspective of "judgment" is found, for example, in Matt. 7:22; 24:19ff.; Mark 13:17ff.; Luke 10:12; 21:22ff.; Acts 2:20; Rom. 2:5, 16; 1 Cor. 1:8; 1 Thess. 5:12ff.; 2 Thess. 1:10; 2 Tim. 1:12; 2 Pet. 3:3ff.; 1 John 4:17; Rev. 10:7. The positive aspect of "blessing" in relation to the day is indicated in Matt. 26:29; Mark 14:25; Luke 6:23; John 16:23ff.; Acts 2:17ff.; 1 Cor. 5:5; Eph. 4:30; Phil. 1:6ff.; Heb. 10:25. Specific reference to the "last day" of divine judgment is found in John 6:39ff.; 12:48; 1 Pet. 2:12.

In other contexts, various references are made to a specific "day" of major significance — for example, the Sabbath day in Luke 4:16; 13:16; 14:5; Acts 13:14; 16:13. In a related context, Heb. 4:4ff. refers to the eschatological "day" of rest, symbolized by the land of Canaan, that anticipates the ultimate heavenly rest for the believer. The "day of unleavened bread" is indicated in Luke 22:7; Acts 20:6. See also Luke 23:54. The "Lord's Day" is noted in Rev. 1:10. Acts 2:1; 20:16 refer to the "day of Pentecost." Other such references include Luke 1:80; Gal. 4:10; 1 Pet. 3:20; Rev. 11:9ff.

Additional Notes

In terms of the Old and New Testament usage of Day of the Lord terminology, what is initiated and developed under the old covenant is brought to fulfillment in the new through the person and work of Jesus Christ, who brings this phenomenon to its triumphant conclusion.

DAZZLING

NT Words

astraptō [ἀστράπτω, *797*]

astraptō is a rare verb denoting the "dazzling" of lightning in Luke 17:24; and the "dazzling" appearance of angelic apparel in Luke 24:4.

exastraptō [ἐξαστράπτω, *1823*]

exastraptō is a verb found only in Luke 9:29 referring to the glistening clothing of Christ that "became dazzling white" during his transfiguration on the mountain.

See Also: → LIGHTNING

DEACON

NT Words

diakonos [διάκονος, *1249*]

The noun ***diakonos*** denotes the general sense of "minister," "servant" in around thirty contexts. In Rom. 16:1, 27; Phil. 1:1; 1 Tim. 3:8, 12, however, the term specifically denotes "deacons" as officers in the early church, entrusted with the day-to-day administration of Christian ministry both to those within and without the community of God's people.

diakoneō [διακονέω, *1247*]

diakoneō is a verb with the general sense of "serve" throughout most of the nearly forty occurrences of the term. However, in 1 Tim. 3:10, 13 the term specifically expresses the meaning "to serve as deacons."

See Also: ➠ SERVE

DEAD, DEADLY

NT Words

nekros [νεκρός, *3498*]

nekros is an adjectival form meaning "dead" throughout the nearly 130 occurrences of the term, but it is used predominantly as a noun in both literal and metaphorical contexts.

General references to "the dead" are found in Matt. 8:22; 22:32; Luke 9:60; 24:5; John 5:25; Rev. 20:5.

More commonly, references to the miraculous "raising or the resurrection of the dead" are found in Matt. 10:8; 11:5; Mark 9:10; 12:25ff.; Luke 7:22; 9:7; 15:24; 20:35ff.; John 5:21; 12:1, 9, 17; Acts 23:6; Phil. 3:11; Heb. 6:2; 11:19. The promise that the Son of Man will be "raised from the dead" is noted in Matt. 17:9; Mark 9:9; Luke 24:46; John 20:9. The reports of Christ's resurrection are found, for example, in Matt. 27:64; 28:7; John 2:22; Acts 3:15; 13:30, 34; 26:23; Rom. 1:4; 6:4, 9; 7:4; 8:11; Gal. 1:1; Eph. 1:20; Col. 2:12; 1 Thess. 1:10; Heb. 13:20; 1 Pet. 1:3, 21; Rev. 2:8. In Rom. 4:17, God is said to give life to the dead.

Christ is designated as "Lord of the dead" in Rom. 14:9. The "dead" are designated as the objects of divine judgment in Acts 10:42; 2 Tim. 4:1; 1 Pet. 4:5; Rev. 11:18; 20:12ff. 1 Cor. 15:12–52 is a significant passage which sets out the supreme significance of Christ's resurrection from the dead as the firstfruits of the general resurrection for believers. The certainty of resurrection from the dead is dependent on the fact of Christ's resurrection, without which there is no hope for believers. See also Col. 1:18; Rev. 1:5. God is designated as the one who "raises the dead" in 2 Cor. 1:9. 1 Thess. 4:16 affirms that "the dead in Christ" shall rise first when Christ returns. See also Rom. 6:13.

The adjectival sense of "dead" refers to the physically deceased in Matt. 23:27; Luke 7:15; Acts 5:10; 20:19; 28:6; Rev. 1:17; 16:13.

Elsewhere, the adjective "dead" refers to bodies that have been fatally affected by sin in Rom. 8:10; 10:9; Eph. 2:1, 5; Col. 2:13. Rev. 3:1 describes the "spiritually dead." Jas. 2:17, 26 affirm that "faith without works is dead." Rom. 7:8 refers to sin "lying dead" apart from the law. Heb. 6:1; 9:14 mention "dead works," or deeds or actions that are ineffective in gaining merit in the sight of God.

nekroō [νεκρόω, *3499*]

nekroō is a rare verb found in only three places, meaning "to be dead" in a literal sense in Rom. 4:19. Col. 3:5 contains the exhortation to "put to death" one's fleshly desires. In Heb. 11:12 the term is used metaphorically, referring to Abraham's physiological inability to father a child — his body "being as good as dead."

thanatoō [θανατόω, *2289*]

thanatoō is a verb found in seventeen contexts with the principal meaning "put to death," "kill."

The meaning "have someone put to death" is indicated in Matt. 10:21; Matt. 13:12; Luke 21:16. See also Rom. 8:36; 2 Cor. 6:9. The plot to have Jesus "put to death" is recorded in Matt. 26:59; 27:1; Mark 14:55.

thanatoō has a metaphorical sense in 1 Pet. 3:18 with reference to believers "being put to death" in the flesh but made alive in the Spirit. Similarly, Rom. 7:4 refers to believers "having died to the law" through being linked to Christ through faith.

thanatēphoros [θανατηφόρος, *2287*]

thanatēphoros is a rare adjectival form denoting "deadly" poison, found only in Jas. 3:8.

thanasimos [θανάσιμος, *2286*]

thanasimos is a rare synonym for ***thanatēphoros***, above, also denoting "deadly" poison in Mark 16:18.

hēmithanēs [ἡμιθανής, *2253*]

hēmithanēs is an adjective found only in Luke 10:30 referring to a man left "half-dead" by robbers on a desolate road.

See Also: ➠ DIE

DEAF

OT Words

ḥērēsh [חֵרֵשׁ, **2795**]

This term, meaning "deaf," occurs nine times and always refers to physiological deafness (cf. Exod. 4:11; Lev. 19:14; Pss. 38:13; 58:4). In addition to the references in the Pentateuch and Psalms there are five occurrences in Isaiah. In four of these (Isa. 29:18; 35:5; 42:18, 43:8), the focus is on deliverance from deafness as one consequence of the fulfillment of God's plan of salvation for his people. Such physical healing was demonstrated in the coming of the Messiah, to which event each of these texts either directly or indirectly alludes. Then, finally, in Isa. 42:19, deafness is attributed to the "servant of Yahweh" — in this case it is a metaphorical allusion to the people of Israel, referring to their spiritual bankruptcy.

—————— NT Words ——————

kōphos [κωφός, *2974*]

kōphos is an adjective found fourteen times in all denoting the disabilities of "dumbness" and "deafness." References to those who are "deaf" include Matt. 11:5; Mark 7:32, 37; Luke 7:22, all in contexts where the power of God in Christ guarantees their healing. In Mark 9:25 Jesus commands a "deaf and dumb spirit" to leave a man it had been controlling.

—————— *Additional Notes* ——————

The New Testament term ***kōphos*** refers to those afflicted with deafness whom Jesus healed during the course of his earthly ministry. In this sense the New Testament consummates in practice what the Old Testament anticipated through the prophets. Curing the deaf, along with other healing miracles, was one sign of the advent of the messianic age, manifested supremely by the coming of Christ.

DEAR

—————— OT Words ——————

yaqqîr [**יַקִּיר, 3357**]

yaqqîr is a rare adjective found only in Jer. 31:20 referring to Ephraim as Yahweh's "dear" son, a term of endearment

See Also: ⟶ BELOVED ⟶ HONOR ⟶ VALUABLE

DEATH

—————— OT Words ——————

māwet [**מָוֶת, 4194**]

This is a noun derived from the verb ***mût*** (⟶ DIE), and it is uniformly translated "death" or "dying." It is found over 150 times and refers almost exclusively to the termination of physical life — either anticipating death or describing the deaths of individuals as having taken place (e.g., Gen. 21:16; Exod. 10:18; Lev. 11:31; Num. 6:7; Ruth 1:17; 1 Sam. 15:23; Esth. 2:7). The psalmist refers to death as something truly distasteful and occasionally links it with Sheol, the place of the dead in the Old Testament (cf. Pss. 6:5; 18:5; 49:15; 55:15; 89:49; 116:3). The author of Proverbs does likewise (cf. Prov. 1:12, 5:5; 7:27). See also Isa. 28:15, 18; 38:18; Hos. 13:14. On a few occasions ***māwet*** is used adjectivally in the sense of "deadly" (cf. 1 Sam. 5:11; Ps. 7:13). And Isa. 25:8 refers to God's promise to swallow up death forever.

môt [**מוֹת, 4193** (Aramaic)]

môt is a rare Aramaic term denoting "death" in connection with judicial execution, found only in Ezra 7:26.

—————— NT Words ——————

thanatos [θάνατος, *2288*]

thanatos is a common noun denoting "death" throughout its nearly 120 occurrences in a variety of contexts.

Literal references to "death" include Matt. 15:4; 26:38; Mark 7:10; Luke 9:27; John 11:4; Rom. 8:38; Phil. 1:20; Heb. 7:23; 11:5; Jas. 1:15; Rev. 9:6. "Death" by judicial execution is noted in Acts 23:29; 28:18. A martyr's "death" is indicated in John 21:19; Rev. 2:10; 12:11. The action of handing someone over to death is noted in Matt. 10:21; Luke 2:26; Acts 22:4; Rev. 2:23.

The record of Christ being condemned to death is found in Matt. 20:18; 26:66; Mark 10:33; Luke 24:20; Acts 13:28; as is the prospect of his death in John 12:33; 18:32. In significant theological contexts the death of Christ is declared to result in justification for the people of God, releasing them from the results of sin and eternal death (cf. Acts 2:24; Rom. 5:10; 6:3ff.; Phil. 2:8; Col. 1:22; Heb. 2:9; 9:15). The significance of Christ's death in relation to the Lord's Supper is indicated in 1 Cor. 11:26.

Metaphorical usage of ***thanatos*** includes references to the "shadow of death" in relation to spiritual darkness in Matt. 4:16; Mark 9:1; Luke 1:79. The "law of sin and death" is mentioned in Rom. 8:2. 1 Cor. 15:26; 54ff. affirm that the last enemy to be destroyed is "death." See also Rev. 21:4; 2 Cor. 4:11.

In other places, "death" signifies the horrifying reality of eternal judgment. The expression "second death" is the most profound symbol of eternal separation from God (cf. Rev. 2:11; 20:6; 21:8). General references to eternal death include John 5:24; Rom. 1:32; Jas. 5:20; 1 John 3:14; 5:16. The abolition of such a death through the work of Christ is indicated in 2 Tim. 1:10; Heb. 2:14ff. See also John 8:51ff. "Death" as the consequence of the "fall" of human beings, in both a literal and spiritual sense, is indicated in Rom. 5:12ff.; 6:16ff.; 1 Cor. 15:21; 2 Cor. 3:7; 7:10. The primary feature of "spiritual death" is alienation from God. The name "Death" is given to the symbolic rider bringing divine judgment to wicked humankind in Rev. 6:8. See also Rev. 20:13.

apagō [**ἀπάγω,** *520*]

apagō is a verb found fifteen times with the primary meaning "to lead away." In a number of places it refers to Christ being "led away" to be crucified. In Acts 12:19 the term specifically indicates King Herod's orders that certain prison guards "be put to death."

epithanatios [**ἐπιθανάτιος,** *1935*]

epithanatios is a rare adjectival form, found only in 1 Cor. 4:9, referring to people "sentenced to death."

anairesis [**ἀναίρεσις,** *336*]

anairesis is a rare noun denoting "death" in the context of the public execution of Stephen, the first Christian martyr, found only in Acts 8:1.

teleutē [**τελευτή,** *5054*]

teleutē is a rare noun, found only in Matt. 2:15, referring to the "death" of King Herod.

Additional Notes

Unlike the New Testament vocabulary, the Hebrew terminology for "death" does not embrace any detailed view of life after death. Death is viewed in the old covenant as an untimely tragedy at worst, and at best as a passing from the state of life into the unknown and mysterious realm of Sheol, or the grave.

See Also: → DIE → KILL

DEBT, DEBTOR

OT Words

mashā'āh [**מַשָּׁאָה, 4859**]

This word only occurs twice in the Old Testament. Once it means "thing" in reference to an undefined loan (cf. Deut. 24:10); and once it indicates a "debt" (cf. Prov. 22:26).

nāshā' [**נָשָׁא, 5378**]

This rare verb occurs only four times, meaning "to lend on interest," "to act as a creditor." It is found in 1 Sam. 22:2; Neh. 5:7; Isa. 24:2. In Ps. 89:22 its extended meaning denotes subjecting someone to tax, or tribute.

neshî [**נְשִׁי, 5386**]

neshî is a noun found only in 2 Kgs. 4:7 referring to monetary "debts."

yād [**יָד, 3027**]

yād is a common term denoting "hand" in the large majority of its occurrences (approximately 1,600 times). In one context, ***yād*** refers to people's "debt" (cf. Neh. 10:31).

ḥôb [**חוֹב, 2326**]

ḥôb is a noun found only in Ezek. 18:7 denoting a "debtor."

NT Words

opheilē [**ὀφειλή,** *3782*]

opheilē is a noun found only twice. It denotes "debt" in Matt. 18:32. In Rom. 13:7 the term refers to "that which is owed" in the context of paying government taxes.

opheilēma [**ὀφείλημα,** *3783*]

opheilēma is a rare synonym for ***opheilē***, above, denoting "that which is due" to someone, in the context of one's wages, in Rom. 4:4. In Matt. 6:12 the term is part of the text of the Lord's Prayer. Its meaning is most likely metaphorical, referring to people's "sins" or "offenses."

opheiletēs [**ὀφειλέτης,** *3781*]

opheiletēs is a noun found seven times referring to a person bound by some obligation or duty. Negatively, the term denotes a "sinner" or an "offender" in Matt. 6:12; Luke 13:4. In Matt. 18:24 it refers to a "debtor" owing a huge sum of money to a creditor.

Positively, ***opheiletēs*** denotes a person under moral obligation in several contexts. In Rom. 1:14 Paul sees himself as "under obligation" to Gentiles on account of the gospel; and in Rom. 8:12 the obligation is to live according to the dictates of the Holy Spirit. Gal. 5:3 affirms that everyone who is circumcised "is bound" to keep the whole law. See also Rom. 15:27.

opheilō [**ὀφείλω,** *3784*]

opheilō is a verb found nearly forty times with the underlying meaning "ought," "owe." The latter sense embraces several nuances.

The literal sense of "owing" money, or being in the grip of debt, is indicated in Matt. 18:28ff.; Luke 7:41; 16:5ff.; Rom. 13:8; Phil. 1:18.

Elsewhere, ***opheilō*** means "being bound by an oath" or "being under a moral obligation." It is found with this meaning in Matt. 23:16, 18, referring to a solemn ritual oath. 2 Thess. 1:3; 2:13 refer to the solemn "obligation" to give thanks to God.

daneion [**δάνειον,** *1156*]

daneion is a rare noun denoting a monetary "debt" in Matt. 18:27.

chreopheiletēs [**χρεοφειλέτης,** *5533*]

chreopheiletēs is a noun denoting a "debtor," in the literal sense of "one who owes money," found only in Luke 7:41; 16:5.

Additional Notes

The metaphorical sense of "debt" or "debtor" is not present in the Old Testament as it is in the New. While the New Testament contains literal references to "debt" and "debtor," the meaning is extended to refer to those under spiritual debt (i.e., obligation) to God and Christ.

DECAY

OT Words

bālāh [**בָּלָה, 1086**]

This term occurs fifteen times, meaning "wear out," "become (or grow) old." The literal sense of growing old is found in Gen. 18:12 in relation to Sarah. Then, in relation to clothes wearing out or rotting away, ***bālāh*** is found in Deut. 8:4; 29:5; Josh. 9:13; Neh. 9:21.

bālāh is also used in the metaphorical sense of "wasting away." In Job 13:28, Job reflects on the pitiable state of humankind. In Ps. 32:3, the psalmist affirms that when he failed to repent of his sin, his body "wasted away" through his groaning. Ps. 49:14 records the fate of the self-righteous who will waste away in the grave (cf. also Ps. 102:26; Isa. 50:9; Lam. 3:4). Finally, in Isa. 51:6, ***bālāh*** refers to the decaying of the whole earth as part of God's final judgment on this present age.

māqaq [**מָקַק, 4743**]

This verb is a synonym for ***bālāh***, above, occurring seven times and meaning "decay," "pine away," "rot (away)." It is used in both a literal and symbolic sense.

In a metaphorical sense, ***māqaq*** is found in Lev. 26:39, where Israel's predicted judgment in exile will result in her "pining away" there. Similarly, Ezek. 24:23; 33:10 describe Judah's fate of suffering in exile. Ps. 38:5 refers to the psalmist's wounds "rotting" or "becoming foul" on account of his foolishness. Isa. 34:4 records the predicted apocalyptic dissolution of the cosmos at the end, when God will destroy the created universe as we know it: "the host of heaven shall rot away . . ." And, finally, ***māqaq*** occurs in Zech. 14:12, in an apocalyptic description of final judgment against those who attack Jerusalem in the last days: ". . . their flesh will rot while they are still standing on their feet. . . ."

There is also a literal use of ***māqaq*** in Ezek. 4:17, alluding to Israel's physical deprivation and even starvation in exile: ". . . they may lack bread and water . . . and waste away . . ."

NT Words

palaioō [**παλαιόω,** *3822*]

palaioō is a verb found in four places with the meaning "grow old," "wear out." The term is used in relation to clothes and bags (or purses) in Luke 12:33; Heb. 1:11. In Heb. 8:13 ***palaioō*** refers metaphorically to the old covenant "becoming obsolete."

diaphtheirō [**διαφθείρω,** *1311*]

The verb ***diaphtheirō*** is found six times, meaning "destroy" with several nuances.

The "decaying," "destructive" effect of moths on material possessions is indicated in Luke 12:33.

2 Cor. 4:16 refers to the "wasting away," the "corruption" of the human frame. 1 Tim. 6:5 refers to human minds "being depraved." The literal "destroying" of ships is indicated in Rev. 8:9; and the destruction of people in Rev. 11:18.

See Also: → CORRUPT → OLD

DECEASE → DIE

DECEIT, DECEITFUL, DECEIVE, DECEIVER

OT Words

mirmāh [**מִרְמָה, 4820**]

This term means "deceit," "guile," "treachery" and occurs about forty times. There are a number of different contexts reflected in the use of ***mirmāh*** that are worth distinguishing.

In the first place, deceit is indicated in a certain number of specific personal relationships (cf. Gen. 27:35 [Jacob deceives Esau]; Gen. 34:13 [the sons of Jacob deceive the Shechemites]; 2 Kgs. 9:23 [Jehu deceives Joram]). Deceit is also generally predicated of the wicked in a number of passages, especially in Psalms and Proverbs (e.g., Job 15:35; 31:5; Pss. 5:6; 43:1; 55:23; Prov. 11:1; 12:5; 26:4). The psalmist also expresses his abhorrence of deceit, which is thoroughly unworthy of the righteous (cf. Pss. 17:1; 24:4; 34:3).

The people of Israel and Judah are also indicted for their treachery and conniving, especially within their own society (cf. Jer. 5:27; 9:6, 8; Hos. 11:12; 12:7; Amos 8:5; Mic. 6:11; Zeph. 1:9).

Two final illustrations of the use of ***mirmāh*** provide a stark contrast. Isa. 53:9 describes the purity of the Suffering Servant when the prophet affirms that "there was no deceit in his mouth." Then, in Dan. 8:25, the cunning deceit of the "little horn" (i.e., Antiochus Epiphanes) is said to be one of his chief characteristics as he desperately strives to destroy the people of Yahweh (cf. also Dan. 11:25).

remîyāh [רְמִיָּה, 7423]

This is a synonym for ***mirmāh***, above. ***remîyāh*** is translated in a number of different ways, including "deceit," "deceitful," "deceitfully," "guile" — accounting for a tenth of the fifteen occurrences. The range of contexts in which ***remîyāh*** is found is similar to that of ***mirmāh***.

General indictments against deceit are found in Job 13:7; 27:4; Pss. 52:2; 78:57; 101:7. Blessing is also indicated for the one in whom no deceit is found (cf. Ps. 32:2). The psalmist pleads for deliverance from a deceitful tongue in Ps. 120:2. Indictments against Israel for their deceitfulness are also recorded in Hos. 7:16; Mic. 6:12.

pātāh [פָּתָה, 6601]

This term is broadly synonymous with ***mirmāh*** and ***remîyāh***, above. ***pātāh*** is found nearly thirty times and has a number of meanings, the principal ones being "entice," "deceive," "persuade."

Specific instances of enticement or deception are found in a variety of contexts. In Exod. 22:16; Job 31:9, 27, physical seduction is in view. Judg. 14:15; 16:5 refer to the beguiling activities of Delilah against Samson. Abner's treachery against David is indicated in 2 Sam. 3:25. See also Jer. 20:10. One very significant and remarkable instance of deception is found in 1 Kgs. 22:20ff., where God places a lying spirit in the mouth of one of his angelic servants in order to deceive King Ahab and bring him to his death at Ramoth-Gilead. This constitutes one of the most bizarre and terrifying judgments of God recorded in the entire Bible.

General indictments against the practice of deception are found in Ps. 78:36; Prov. 1:10; 16:29; 24:28. The danger of being enticed into idolatry is specifically mentioned in Deut. 11:16.

Finally, there are three specific texts that deserve special mention. In Jer. 20:7 the prophet accuses God of deceiving him. This outburst reflects the dire emotional and psychological torment to which Jeremiah had been subjected in the course of his prophetic ministry. Secondly, Ezek. 14:9 is a difficult text that provides for capital punishment for a prophet deceived by God. This verse must be read in its context. In this chapter, the idolatrous population of Judah, including many prophets, is condemned for rejecting Yahweh as the one true and living God. Those who fail to repent of their actions and attitudes in this regard will be executed by God. Therefore, Ezek. 14:9 may be understood as the account of a divine mode of execution involving the deception of an idolatrous prophet. Thirdly, Hos. 2:14 speaks of God's remarkable mercy and compassion towards his people who have rejected him. After pronouncing judgments against them, God promises to entice his people back into an intimate relationship with him. Such a promise is expressed through the metaphor of a lover courting his beloved and speaking tenderly to her.

hātal [הָתַל, 2048]

This verb is comparatively rare, occurring only nine times. It is translated "deceive," "mock."

tālal is used similarly to the three entries above. Specific examples of individuals deceiving or being deceived are recorded in Gen. 31:7 (Laban cheating Jacob); Exod. 8:29 (a warning to Pharaoh against cheating the Israelites). In Judg. 16:10ff., Samson's mocking of Delilah implies deceit.

In Job 13:9, the patriarchal hero asks Zophar whether one can deceive God. The scathing indictmentin Isa. 44:20 lays bare the delusion of the idol worshiper. In Jer. 9:5, the deception practiced by the people of Judah within their own community is condemned.

nākal [נָכַל, 5230]

nākal is also synonymous with the four entries above. ***nākal*** occurs only four times and is translated "beguile," "deceive," or "conspire."

Gen. 38:18 refers to the conspiracy between Joseph's brothers to murder him. Num. 25:18 refers to the condemnation of the Midianites for beguiling Israel into idolatry. Ps. 105:25 describes God turning the hearts of Israel's enemies against his people — enemies who would conspire against them. Mal. 1:14 indicts a worshiper who offers a blemished lamb to Yahweh, thereby attempting to cheat God and depriving him of pure worship.

rāmāh [רָמָה, 7411]

rāmāh is a verb found in twelve places with the primary meaning "deceive," "betray."

The action of people "deceiving" one another is indicated in Gen. 29:25; Josh. 9:22; 1 Sam. 19:17; 28:12; 2 Sam. 19:26; Prov. 26:19; Lam. 1:19. More particularly, ***rāmāh*** indicates the act of "betrayal" in a military context in 1 Chr. 12:17.

tarmît [תַּרְמִית, 8649]

tarmît is a noun occurring six times, denoting in most of these contexts the "deceit" of those who disobey God. A general reference to such people is found in Ps. 119:118. Jer. 8:5 notes such "deceit" in relation to the unfaithful Israelite people. Jer. 14:14; 23:26 speak of the "deceit" of Israelite false prophets. Zeph. 3:13 mentions the removal of a "deceitful" tongue from the remnant of faithful Israelites.

sheqer [שֶׁקֶר, 8267]

sheqer is a noun found over one hundred times, meaning "lie," "lying." It can also mean "deceit," "deceitful," as in the reference to the "deceitful" acquisition of food in Prov. 20:17. Prov. 31:30 refers to the "deceitfulness" of charm.

mashā'ôn [מַשָּׁאוֹן, 4860]

mashā'ôn is a rare noun found only in Prov. 26:26 denoting "deceit" as a general vice.

'āqōb [עָקֹב, 6121]

'āqōb is an adjective found in three places, referring to the human heart being "deceitful" above everything else.

nāshā' [נָשָׁא, 5377]

The verb ***nāshā'*** is found sixteen times with the predominant sense of "deceive" in a variety of contexts.

Gen. 3:13 refers to the serpent "deceiving" Eve. Admonitions not to allow others to engage in deception are found in 2 Kgs. 18:29; 19:10; 2 Chr. 32:15; Isa. 36:14; Jer. 29:8. References to various people being deceived include those in Isa. 19:13; Obad. 7. The act of "deception" is also mistakenly predicated of God in Isa. 37:10; Jer. 4:10. Horror is said to have deceived the hearts of the Edomites along with their pride in Jer. 49:16; Obad. 3. In Jer. 37:9 Yahweh exhorts his people not to deceive themselves into imagining that the Babylonians will not rise against Jerusalem and the land of Judah.

kāḥash [כָּחַשׁ, 3584]

kāḥash is a verb found in approximately twenty contexts with the predominant sense of "lie." It can also mean to "deceive," as in Zech. 13:4, which alludes to the ruse adopted by Jacob in Gen. 27:14ff., whereby he wrapped himself with an animal skin in order to deceive his almost blind father Isaac into thinking that he was his twin brother Esau, who had hairy skin.

NT Words

apatē [ἀπάτη, *539*]

apatē is a noun found in seven places, meaning "deceit," "deception" and used metaphorically throughout.

The "deceitfulness" of riches is indicated in Matt. 13:22; Mark 4:19. Similarly, Eph. 4:22 speaks of the "deceitful" lusts of life, and Heb. 3:13 refers to the "deceitfulness" of sin. 2 Thess. 2:10 indicates the "deception" of wickedness with reference to the wicked.

apataō [ἀπατάω, *538*]

apataō is a verb meaning "deceive" in all five occurrences.

Eph. 5:6 contains an exhortation not to allow unbelievers to deceive God's people with empty words. 1 Tim. 2:14 refers to the serpent "deceiving" Adam and Eve in Eden. The moral and spiritual danger of "deceiving" one's heart is indicated in Jas. 1:26.

exapataō [ἐξαπατάω, *1818*]

exapataō is a synonym for ***apataō***, above, meaning "deceive" throughout.

Rom. 7:11 notes the "deceiving" effect of sin in one's life. The deceptive activities of false teachers are indicated in Rom. 16:18. 1 Cor. 3:18 records warnings against self-deception; and 2 Thess. 2:3 warns against being deceived by false teaching. 2 Cor. 11:3 speaks of the serpent deceiving Eve in the garden of Eden.

phrenapataō [φρεναπατάω, *5422*]

phrenapataō is a rare synonym for the entries above, found only in Gal. 6:3 and referring to the folly of those who "deceive" themselves into thinking they are of importance when in fact they are not.

dolos [δόλος, *1388*]

dolos is a noun denoting "deceit," "stealth," or "craftiness" throughout the twelve occurrences of the term.

"Deceit" is listed as a general vice in Mark 7:22; John 1:47; Acts 13:10; Rom. 1:29; 1 Thess. 2:3; 1 Pet. 2:1; 3:10. 1 Pet. 2:22 affirms that "no deceit" was found on the lips of Christ. See also 2 Cor. 12:16.

The process and action of arresting Christ by "stealth" is noted in Matt. 26:4; Mark 14:1.

dolios [δόλιος, *1386*]

dolios is a rare adjective found only in 2 Cor. 11:13, referring to false teachers as "deceitful workmen."

dolioō [δολιόω, *1387*]

dolioō is a rare verb found only in Rom. 3:13, referring to sinful humanity who "practice deceit" with their tongues.

doloō [δολόω, *1389*]

doloō is a rare variant of ***dolioō***, above, found only in 2 Cor. 4:2 and referring to the apostle Paul's refusal to "handle the word of God deceitfully."

planaō [πλανάω, *4105*]

planaō is a verb found about fifty times, meaning "deceive" in addition to related nuances.

Matt. 24:4; Mark 13:5; Luke 21:8 warn the disciples not to be deceived by others.

The activity of false christs in deceiving many is recorded in Matt. 24:5, 11; Mark 13:6 — except for the elect, as noted in Matt. 24:24.

General references to the activity of "deceiving" are found in John 7:12, 47; 2 Tim. 3:13. Rev. 12:9; 13:14; 19:20; 20:3ff. describe Satan "deceiving" the whole world. See also Rev. 18:23.

General exhortations for believers "not to be deceived" or "be led astray" in relation to spiritual truth and holy living are found in 1 Cor. 6:9; 15:33; Gal. 6:7; 1 John 3:7.

The state of "being deceived" by one's ungodly lifestyle is indicated in Titus 3:3.

The folly of "deceiving oneself" in relation to being without sin is noted in 1 John 1:8.

paralogizomai [παραλογίζομαι, *3884*]

paralogizomai is a rare verb, occurring only twice and meaning "deceive." In Col. 2:4 it refers to the apostolic intention to have the Colossian church well-instructed in the gospel lest they "be deceived" by pagan thinking. Jas. 1:22 warns about "deceiving oneself" in relation to having God's word without acting upon it.

planē [πλάνη, *4106*]

planē is a noun found in ten places meaning "error," as well as the derivative sense of "deceit."

Eph. 4:14 refers to the "deceitful schemes" (lit. "schemes of deceit") of the wicked.

planos [πλάνος, *4108*]

planos is an adjective used primarily in the nominal sense of "deceiver." Matt. 27:63 contains a blasphemous reference to Christ as a "deceiver" — an epithet given to him by his enemies. "Deceivers" in the sense of "impostors," referring to false teachers, are noted in 2 Cor. 6:8; 2 John 7. "Deceitful" spirits of satanic origin are noted in 1 Tim. 4:1.

phrenapatēs [φρεναπάτης, *5423*]

phrenapatēs is a rare noun found only in Titus 1:10 denoting the "deceivers," the false teachers belonging to the so-called fanatical "Jewish circumcision party," whose members opposed the apostolic gospel message of salvation through Christ's sacrifice alone, apart from the law.

Additional Notes

The Hebrew and Greek terminology share a high degree of dynamic equivalence. "Deceit" (and associated nuances) is characteristic not only of individuals, but also of groups of people and nations. There are also frequent warnings against deception in both Testaments, and these are particularly relevant for leaders in the community of God's people — whether they be old covenant prophets or leaders in the new covenant church.

See Also: → LIE → OPPRESS

DECIDE, DECISION → JUDGE

DECLARE, DECLARATION

NT Words

exēgeomai [ἐξηγέομαι, *1834*]

exēgeomai is a verb found in six places, meaning "report," "make a declaration." It is used in relation to narrating events or circumstances in Luke 24:35; Acts 10:8. Acts 15:12, 14; 21:19 record the "declaring" or "reporting" of God's miraculous deeds and signs among his people. Specifically, John 1:18 affirms that God has "made Jesus known" to the world — that is, he has made Christ the subject of a divine declaration.

horizō [ὁρίζω, *3724*]

horizō is a verb found in eight contexts with the primary sense of "ordain," "predetermine" throughout. However, in Rom. 1:4 the apostle affirms that Jesus Christ "was declared" by God to be his Son through his resurrection from the dead.

See Also: → APPOINT → COMMAND → DEMONSTRATION → EXPLAIN → PREACH → TELL

DECREASE

OT Words

mā'aṭ [מָעַט, **4591**]

This verb is found about twenty times and is translated "diminish," "become small" with reference to both size and number.

mā'aṭ occurs most frequently in mundane contexts. It refers to diminished size in Exod. 12:4; 16:17; 30:15; Num. 26:54; 33:54; 35:8. Jer. 10:24 contains a plea for God not to reduce the prophet to nothing in the course of his punishment. And, in Ezek. 29:15, divine judgment is passed on the nation of Egypt whereby it will be reduced to its smallest size in its entire history.

In regard to diminished number, the following texts are noted: Lev. 25:16; 26:22; Num. 11:32; 2 Kgs. 4:3; Jer. 29:6. In Isa. 21:17, divine judgment is also passed on the Arabian archers of Kedar, whose number will be drastically reduced by God himself. In contrast, Ps. 107:38 promises great blessing for God's people in that he will not allow their herds of cattle to "decrease."

In Jer. 30:19, God promises to restore the fortunes of Israel by increasing their number (i.e., ". . . they shall not be few"), multiplying them, and increasing their joy.

NT Words

elattoō [ἐλαττόω, *1642*]

elattoō is a rare verb found in three places with the meaning "decrease" in relation to John the Baptist's declaration that the Christ must "increase" (i.e., become greater) and he must "decrease." In Heb. 2:7, 9 the term refers to human beings, whom God "has made a little lower" than the angels.

See Also: → NEED

DECREE

OT Words

dāt [דָּת, **1881** (**1882** Aramaic)]

This term is translated "decree," "law," "edict" and occurs around twenty times.

Almost all the occurrences of ***dāt*** are found in the book of Esther, referring to the laws, edicts, and customs of the Persian Empire in general, and also to the specific royal decrees which were part of Haman's insidious but unsuccessful plot to destroy the entire Jewish people (cf. Esth. 1:8ff.; 2:8, 12; 3:14, 15; 4:3ff.; 8:13–17; 9:1, 13, 14). The remaining two occurrences are found in Ezra 8:36, again in relation to the decree of the Persian king, and in a poetic reference to the Sinai theophany in Deut. 33:2, where Yahweh is described as shining forth ". . . with flaming fire at his right hand." However, the Hebrew literally reads at this point ". . . a fire of law." The exact meaning of these words remains unknown.

The Aramaic use of the term is identical, signifying both "law(s)" and "decree(s)." References to the "laws" or "decrees" of God's covenant are found in Ezra 7:12ff.; Dan. 6:5; 7:25; and references to the "laws or decrees" of the Medes and Persians are found in Dan. 2:9, 13, 15; 6:8, 12, 15.

te'ēm [טְעֵם, **2942** (Aramaic)]

te'ēm is an Aramaic noun denoting a "command" or "decree." It is used in relation to various decrees issued by the kings of Persia (cf. Ezra 4:19ff.; 6:1, 11; Dan. 3:10; 4:6). In particular, Ezra 5:3, 9ff.; 6:1ff.; 7:13, 21 refer to the decree first issued by King Cyrus of Persia to send the Israelite community back to their land in order to rebuild their temple.

pitgām [פִּתְגָם, **6599**]

pitgām is a rare noun of Persian origin denoting an "edict" or "decree" issued by the Persian ruler Artaxerxes in Esth. 1:20. In Eccl. 8:11 the word indicates a judicial "sentence" for a crime.

ḥēqeq [חֵקֶק, **2711**]

ḥēqeq is a rare noun denoting unjust "laws," noted in Isa. 10:1.

NT Words

dogma [δόγμα, *1378*]

dogma is a noun found in five places denoting "ordinances," "decrees."

Luke 2:1 refers to the "decree" issued by Caesar Augustus for a universal census throughout the Roman Empire — the catalyst for events leading up to the birth of Christ. Caesar's "decrees" in general are noted in Acts 17:17. Acts 16:4 refers to the "ordinances" or "decisions" of the apostolic council. Eph. 2:15; Col. 2:14 refer to the "decrees" or "ordinances" of the law covenant, whose curse and penalty have been abolished through the death of Christ.

See Also: → COMMAND → LAW

DEDICATE, DEDICATION

OT Words

ḥānak [חָנַךְ, **2596**]

ḥānak is a rare verb, occurring only four times, with the meaning "dedicate," "consecrate" in three of those instances. Deut. 20:5 notes the provision made under the law for those intending to go to war for Israel to first of all "dedicate" their new house. 1 Kgs. 8:63 and 2 Chr. 7:5 both refer to the huge peace offerings Solomon made to Yahweh on the occasion of the "dedication," or "consecration," of the temple.

qādash [קָדַשׁ, **6942**]

qādash is a common verb found over 170 times with the predominant meaning "sanctify," "make holy." The word also has the underlying senses of "consecrate," "dedicate."

ḥērem [חֵרֶם, **2764**]

ḥērem is a noun found about forty times with the highly significant sense of "that which is dedicated or devoted to the Lord." It is translated variously in several different contexts.

The meaning "devoted to the Lord" in the context of ritual dedication is used in relation to fields in Lev. 27:21, and to general property in Lev. 27:28; Num. 18:14; Ezek. 44:29.

Elsewhere, and more commonly, ***ḥērem*** means "devoted to destruction" with the underlying sense of "placement under the divine curse or ban." It is used in relation to individuals in Lev. 27:29; and in 1 Kgs. 20:42 divine judicial execution is in view. Josh. 7:12; 22:20 both declare that the Canaanite peoples are placed under "the ban." A similar fate is designated for Canaanite cities in Josh. 6:17, and for the Amalekite people and possessions in 1 Sam. 15:21. See also Deut. 7:26; 13:17. Booty from Jericho, "placed under the ban" (i.e., devoted to the Lord, belonging to him alone) was stolen by the Israelite Achan — a crime for which he lost his life, and which temporarily delayed the ongoing conquest of the land (cf. Josh. 6:18; 7:1ff.).

ḥanukkāh [חֲנֻכָּה, **2598**]

ḥanukkāh is a noun found eight times denoting the "dedication" or "consecration" of the temple altar in Num. 7:10ff., 84ff.; 2 Chr. 7:9; the wall of the rebuilt city of Jerusalem under Nehemiah's supervision in Neh. 12:27; and the "house of David" (i.e., the temple) in Ps. 30:1.

NT Words

enkainizō [ἐγκαινίζω, *1457*]

enkainizō is a rare verb meaning "consecrate" in respect of the old covenant law in Heb. 9:18. The underlying sense is that of "put into effect."

enkainia [ἐγκαίνια, *1456*]

enkainia is a rare noun found only in John 10:22 referring to the "Feast of Dedication," celebrating the cleansing of the temple by Judas Maccabeus in the middle of the second century B.C., following its desecration by Antiochus Epiphanes IV — the cruel, despotic and anti-Semitic Seleucid ruler.

Additional Notes

The "dedication" of the old covenant temple has a close theological connection with the dedication or ratification of the new covenant in the book of Hebrews. The temple embodies the heart of old covenant worship; in the new covenant age it is Christ who inaugurates and consummates worship. Old covenant worship was focused on a building; new covenant worship is focused on a person.

DEED, DEEDS

NT Words

euergesia [εὐεργεσία, *2108*]

euergesia is a rare noun denoting a "good deed" shown to a crippled man who was healed through the apostolic ministry in Acts 4:9.

See Also: → WORK

DEEP, DEPTH

OT Words

ma'amaqqîm [מַעֲמַקִּים, 4615]

This is a rare term, occurring only five times and translated "depths" or "deep." In the Psalms ***ma'amaqqîm*** refers three times in a metaphorical sense to the "deep waters" of anguish and sorrow arising out of persecution (cf. Ps. 130:1). In Isa. 51:10, ***ma'amaqqîm*** refers to Israel's deliverance from Egypt at the Re(e)d Sea where "the waters of the great deep" dried up to allow the Israelite people to pass across on dry land. Then, in Ezek. 27:34, another prophetic oracle of indictment, the term alludes to the destruction of the Tyrian king and Phoenician Empire as a divine judgment against their blasphemous arrogance towards Yahweh. The metaphor of being swallowed up by the "depths of waters" is apt, since the Phoenicians were renowned as seafaring merchants.

meṣôlāh [מְצוֹלָה, 4688]

meṣôlāh is a synonym for ***ma'amaqqîm***, above. The term is found eleven times with the primary sense of "deep" or "depth(s)."

A number of poetic or symbolic references describe the watery destruction of the Egyptian army at the Re(e)d Sea (cf. Exod. 15:5; Ps. 107:24; and see also Zech. 10:11 for a related context). Ps. 68:22 also uses ***meṣôlāh*** in a general metaphorical allusion to deliverance from one's enemies "out of the depths of the sea." See also Pss. 69:2, 15; 88:6. Jonah 2:3 refers to the amazing (and salutary) experience of the reluctant prophet being thrown into the depths of the sea, only to be swallowed by a great fish. Finally, Mic. 7:19 contains the well-known metaphor for forgiveness, where God is said to cast all the sins of his people into the depths of the sea.

taḥtî [תַּחְתִּי, 8482]

This term is used both as an adjective and a noun, meaning "low," "lowest," or "depths," "lower parts," and is found nearly twenty times.

The metaphorical sense is dominant: ***taḥtî*** indicates, for example, the terrible wrath of God in Deut. 32:22, where the divine anger against the sin of his people "burns to the realm of death below" (i.e., the depths of Sheol). See also Ps. 86:13. ***taḥtî*** also indicates a place of judgment in the phrase "depths of the earth" (cf. Pss. 63:9; 88:6), or as a place of testing (cf. Lam. 3:55), and also as the specific location where the wicked shall be judged (e.g., Ezek. 26:20; 31:14ff.; 32:18, 24). The word is also found in Ps. 139:15 in the phrase "depths of the earth," referring to the mystery of the omnipotent Creator fashioning human beings.

tehôm [תְּהוֹם, 8415]

This word is broadly synonymous with the terms discussed above. ***tehôm*** occurs about thirty-five times, meaning "deep," "depth," "primeval ocean," "abyss," "Sheol."

tehôm is frequently associated with the mystery of divine creation, referring to the primeval ocean depths at the beginning of time (cf. Gen. 1:2; Pss. 33:7; 104:6; Prov. 8:24), and to the "fountains of the deep" during the times of the Noahic flood (cf. Gen. 7:11; 8:2). It also indicates the depth of the Re(e)d Sea waters that destroyed the Egyptian army in their vain pursuit of Moses and the Israelites (cf. Exod. 15:5ff.; Ps. 106:9; Isa. 51:10; 63:13).

tehôm is also used to indicate the lowest regions of the earth (or the "abyss"), usually in conjunction with the sea (cf. Job 28:14; 38:16; 41:32); and sometimes with the connotation of anguish and suffering (cf. Pss. 42:7; 71:20). In the context of God's judgment, the abyss signifies the place to which the wicked are condemned.

'āmaq [עָמַק, 6009]

This term is the verbal root of ***ma'amaqqîm***, above. It occurs nine times and basically means "be deep or profound," "make deep." For example, it refers in Ps. 92:5 to the profoundness of God's thoughts. Isa. 7:11 refers to the extent of the sign that God offered to King Ahaz, who refused to make that request of God. Then, in Isa. 29:15, ***'āmaq*** refers to the futility of the wicked, who go to great depths to hide their plans from God. Isa. 30:33 records the preparation of the place of execution for the king of Assyria. Yahweh is the one who prepares the fire pit, deep and wide. There are also two divine injunctions against the citizens of Tyre and Hazor to "dwell in the depths" (cf. Jer. 49:8, 30) as the precursor of God's judgment against them.

tardēmāh [תַּרְדֵּמָה, 8639]

tardēmāh is a noun denoting a "deep sleep," or "trance" (cf. Job 4:13; 33:15; Prov. 19:15). In particular, such "deep sleep" is induced by God upon Adam in the context of the creation of woman in Gen. 2:21; upon Abraham in Gen. 15:12 for the purpose of divine revelation; and in 1 Sam. 16:12 the "deep sleep" is induced as a means of protecting David from the pursuit of Saul and his men.

'āmōq [עָמֹק, 6013]

'āmōq is an adjective meaning "deep" in both a literal and metaphorical sense.

It refers to skin blemishes that appear to be more than "skin deep" in Lev. 13:4ff., 25ff.

On a metaphorical level, ***'āmōq*** refers to the "deep things" of darkness revealed by God in Job 12:22. A person's words and heart are likened to "deep water" in Prov. 18:4; 20:5. In Prov. 22:14; 23:27 both the adulteress and the prostitute are likened to a "deep pit."

meḥqār [מֶחְקָר, 4278]

meḥqār is a rare noun found only in Ps. 95:4, describing "the depths of the earth" as belonging to the hand of God.

NT Words

bathos [βάθος, *899*]

bathos is a noun found in nine contexts, with an adjectival as well as a nominal force.

The term denotes "deep water" in a literal sense in Luke 5:4. "Deep" (i.e., extreme) poverty is indicated in 2 Cor. 8:2.

Metaphorically, ***bathos*** refers in Rom. 8:39 to the unlimited "depth" of the protection offered to believers by the love of God. Similarly, the term denotes the immeasurable "depth" of God's love in Eph. 3:18, and the "depth" of his wisdom in Rom. 11:33. The incomprehensible "deep things" of God are indicated in 1 Cor. 2:10; and by contrast the "deep secrets" of Satan are noted in Rev. 2:24.

bathys [βαθύς, *901*]

bathys is an adjectival form found only three times, denoting a "deep" well in John 4:11; and a "deep" sleep in Acts 20:9.

abyssos [ἄβυσσος, *12*]

abyssos is a term consistently denoting the "abyss" or "bottomless pit" as the symbolic designation for the location and confinement of Satan and demonic spirits (cf. Luke 8:31; Rev. 9:1, 2, 11; 11:7; 17:8; 20:1ff.). In Rom. 10:7, however, the term is a symbolic designation for the "grave."

bathynō [βαθύνω, *900*]

bathynō is a rare verb found only in Luke 6:48, meaning "dig deep" in relation to the foundation of a house.

pelagos [πέλαγος, *3989*]

pelagos is a rare noun denoting the "depth" of the sea in Matt. 18:6.

Additional Notes

The main difference to be noted between the various terms for "deep" in the Old and New Testaments is that the focus in the former is on the negative aspects of either personal suffering or anguish, or the phenomenon of divine judgment. The New Testament, however, emphasizes the infinite depth of God's wisdom, mercy, and love. Such wisdom has come to supreme expression in the person of Christ, who has himself passed through, in a profound literal and spiritual sense, the deepest personal suffering and anguish in order to accomplish God's perfect plan of salvation for his people.

DEFENSE

OT Words

misgāb [מִשְׂגָּב, 4869]

misgāb is a term with the interchangeable senses of "refuge," "shelter," "defense."

NT Words

apologia [ἀπολογία, *627*]

apologia is a noun found in eight places with the underlying sense of a "verbal defense," or a reasoned statement offered as a defense in the face of threatened legal prosecution.

Formal legal "defenses" undertaken by the apostle Paul before his opponents are noted in Acts 22:1; 25:16; 1 Cor. 9:3; Phil. 1:7; 2 Tim. 4:16.

The non-judicial sense of a defense is indicated in 2 Cor. 7:11 in relation to the Corinthian congregation's successful attempt at their "vindication" in the context of a moral dilemma. 1 Pet. 3:15 stresses that believers must be able to offer a "reasoned defense" of their faith to any who might challenge them.

apologeomai [ἀπολογέομαι, *626*]

apologeomai is a verb found in eleven places, meaning "to make, offer a defense," primarily in a judicial setting (cf. Luke 12:11; 21:14; Acts 19:33; 25:8; 26:1, 2, 24). The non-judicial sense of "defending oneself" is indicated in Rom. 2:15; 2 Cor. 12:11.

See Also: → REFUGE → SIEGE

DEFEND

OT Words

***gānan* [גָּנַן, 1598]**

gānan is a verb occurring in eight contexts, referring consistently to the divine guarantee that Yahweh would "defend" the city of Jerusalem against foreign attack (cf. 2 Kgs. 19:34; 20:6; Isa. 31:5; 37:35; 38:6; Zech. 12:8). In Zech. 9:15, Yahweh promises to "shield" or "defend" the inhabitants of Jerusalem.

***shāphat* [שָׁפַט, 8199]**

shāphat is a common verb meaning "judge," in both a verbal and nominal sense, in most of its nearly two hundred occurrences. However, in Ps. 82:3 ***shāphat*** means "defend" in relation to "dispensing justice" for the poor. (→ JUDGE)

***nāṣal* [נָצַל, 5337]**

nāṣal is a verb with the primary senses of "deliver," "rescue" throughout the 200 or so occurrences of the term. In 2 Sam. 23:12, however, ***nāṣal*** refers to the successful "defending" of a field against Philistine attack.

NT Words

amynō [ἀμύνω, *292*]

amynō is a rare verb found only in Acts 7:24, referring to Moses "defending" his fellow countryman against assault by an Egyptian soldier.

DEFILE, DEFILEMENT

OT Words

***tāmēʾ* [טָמֵא, 2930]**

This term is found nearly 150 times, and its primary meaning is "to become unclean," "defile," or "pollute." Defilement manifests itself in three distinct areas: sexual misconduct; ritual uncleanness; and idolatrous practices.

In regard to sexual impurity, ***tāmēʾ*** is found in a number of contexts. For example, Gen. 34:5ff. describes the rape of Dinah, the daughter of Jacob, by the men of Shechem and the subsequent revenge taken on them by Dinah's brothers. Lev. 18:20, 23 specifically prohibit the defiling activities of adultery and bestiality. Num. 5:13ff. describes the ritual ordeal prescribed for a woman suspected of adultery. The process of the ordeal is intended to determine whether or not the woman is guilty of moral defilement, since this particular procedure is carried out only on the basis of the husband's suspicion. Another interesting illustration of the principle of sexual defilement is found in Deut. 24:4, where a woman is forbidden to remarry her first husband, if the woman has subsequently remarried and been divorced a second time (or if her second husband dies). The use of the term ***tāmēʾ*** in this verse suggests that the woman has been defiled by her second marriage (i.e., through a legal form of adultery), as the result of an improper divorce. Therefore, to remarry her first husband under those circumstances compounds the problem even further and is thus forbidden by God. See also Ezek. 18:6, 11, 15; 22:11; 33:16 for further examples.

tāmēʾ is also used to refer to ceremonial impurity, especially in the book of Leviticus (cf. Lev. 5:3; 11–13; 14:36, 46; 15:4ff.; 17:15; 20:25; 22:6ff.). Such defilement precludes those affected from participating in worship or regular social interaction, or even both. Such impurity involves no moral defilement, however, and the ceremonially unclean Israelite is not disciplined beyond the normal period of compulsory separation from the community. Other circumstances that result in ceremonial defilement include leprosy (e.g., Num. 5:13), and various items associated with the Nazirite vow (cf. Num. 6:7). See also 2 Kgs. 23:8ff.

tāmēʾ can also indicate what might be called "religious defilement"—involving activities condemned by God as idolatrous and resulting in the desecration of places such as land and temple, and the corruption of that unique bond between Yahweh and Israel. For example, Lev. 19:31 prohibits any Israelite involvement in occult activity. Lev. 18:25; Ezek. 36:17, 18; Num. 19:7ff.; 35:34 all refer to the defiling of the land of Israel as a result of the people's idolatry. 2 Chr. 36:14 refers to Zedekiah's desecration of the temple through the worship of pagan deities. The prophets Jeremiah and Ezekiel also indict the people of God for their idolatry, which again renders them spiritually unclean and morally culpable before Yahweh (cf. Jer. 2:7, 23; 7:30; 32:34, Ezek. 5:11; 20:7ff.). Then, in Ezekiel and Hosea, the idolatry of Israel is spoken of metaphorically as spiritual adultery against her husband Yahweh (cf. Ezek. 23:7ff.; Hos. 5:3; 6:10; 9:4).

One or two references depict the removal of defilement through expressions of repentance, including a divine promise to cleanse Israel of her spiritual corruption (cf. Isa. 30:22; Ezek. 43:7).

ḥānēph [חָנֵף, **2610**]

ḥānēph occurs nine times and is synonymous with ***tāmē'***, above.

ḥānēph emphasizes general spiritual and moral defilement brought about by varying circumstances. In Num. 35:33 there is a sanction against murder, for shed blood pollutes the land (cf. also Ps. 106:38). In Isa. 24:5, ***ḥānēph*** indicates the moral impurity of the nations. Jer. 3:1ff. refers to the corruption of the land of Judah, again as a consequence of the people's idolatry (cf. also Jer. 23:11).

From a slightly different perspective, the use of ***ḥānēph*** in Mic. 4:11 points to the Babylonian defilement of Jerusalem. In this particular context, the fate of the city is bound up in God's judgment against his people for rejecting him (cf. also Dan. 11:32).

piggûl [פִּגּוּל, **6292**]

This is a rare noun, found only in four places. It means "abomination," in reference to ritually unclean sacrificial meat (cf. Lev. 7:18; 19:7), or to meat that is inherently unclean (cf. Isa. 65:4; Ezek. 4:14).

ḥālal [חָלַל, **2490**]

The verb ***ḥālal*** has two distinctive strands of meaning: "begin"; as well as a variety of senses including "profane," "pollute," "defile," "desecrate" (all of which are synonymous). ***ḥālal*** is found nearly 170 times in a variety of contexts.

The meaning "defile" in a moral sense is found in a number of places. It is used, for example, in relation to a father's bed "defiled" by a son who sleeps with his father's wives or concubines (cf. Gen. 49:4; 1 Chr. 5:1). See also Lev. 21:9. People "defiling" the name of Yahweh by their sinfulness is noted in Lev. 18:21; 19:12; 20:3; 21:6; 22:2; Isa. 48:11; Jer. 34:16; Ezek. 20:9, 14, 22, 39; 36:20ff.; 39:7; Amos 2:7. Mal. 2:10 refers to "defiling" or "profaning" the covenant through disobedience.

The meaning "defile," in addition to the nuances "profane," "render unclean," are also found in ritual contexts. General references to such defilement include Lev. 19:8; 21:4; 22:15; Ps. 89:39. The "defiling" of the altar stone of the tabernacle is noted in Exod. 20:25. The "profaning" of the Sabbath is indicated in Exod. 31:14; Neh. 13:17ff.; Isa. 56:2ff.; Ezek. 20:13ff.; 22:8; 23:38. The tabernacle or temple sanctuary is "defiled" in Lev. 21:12, 23; Ps. 74:7; Ezek. 23:39; 24:21ff.; 25:3; 28:18; 44:7; as are the tabernacle utensils in Num. 18:32. The "defiling" of the land of Israel is noted in Jer. 16:18; Lam. 2:2; Ezek. 7:22ff.

Elsewhere, in the context of divine judgment, God is said to "defile" his inheritance — that is, his people.

tāmē' [טָמֵא, **2931**]

tāmē' is an adjective identical in form to the first entry above, found in approximately ninety places, with the primary meaning "unclean," "defiled" in both a ritual and moral sense (though the former predominates).

Ritual or ceremonial defilement or uncleanness is indicated in relation to food (Lev. 7:19); to offerings (Lev. 7:21; Hag. 2:14); to animals unfit for offering or consumption (Lev. 11:4ff.; 27:11, 27; Num. 18:15; Deut. 14:7ff.); to people rendered unclean through disease (Lev. 13:11, 15, 36, 44ff.; 14:57) and through contact with a corpse (Num. 5:2; 9:6; 19:13; Hag. 2:13); to bodily discharges such as semen or a woman's menstrual flow (Lev. 15:2, 25ff.; 22:4; Ezek. 22:10); to unclean food (Judg. 13:4; Ezek. 4:13; Hos. 9:3); and to the land of Canaan (Josh. 22:19).

Other general references to ceremonial defilement include Lev. 5:2; 10:10; Num. 19:17ff.; Deut. 12:15; 2 Chr. 23:19; Job 14:4; Eccl. 9:2; Lam. 4:15; Ezek. 22:26; 44:23.

The sense of "unclean," "defiled" is also found in metaphorical contexts, denoting unworthiness before God (Isa. 6:5; 64:6); the wicked and godless (Isa. 35:8; 52:1, 11). The land of Judah "defiled" by idolatry is indicated in Jer. 19:13; and the land of Israel, "defiled" by the people's disobedience, is described in Amos 7:17.

gā'al [גָּאַל, **1351**]

gā'al is a verb found eleven times, meaning "defile," "pollute," "desecrate" and used mostly in a metaphorical sense denoting "moral failure," "wickedness" — although the ceremonial sense of ritual defilement is also evident.

Priests returned from the exile who were unable to demonstrate their genealogical connection with former generations are designated "unclean" in a ritual sense in Ezra 2:62; Neh. 7:64. The offering of "defiled," "polluted" food on the altar is recorded in Mal. 1:7, 12.

Elsewhere, in a moral sense, hands "defiled with blood" — denoting unrighteous deeds — are noted in Isa. 59:3. See also Lam. 4:14. The "defiled," or morally bankrupt, city of Jerusalem is indicated in Zeph. 3:1.

Reference to the act of "defiling" oneself by eating unclean food is found in Dan. 1:8.

NT Words

koinoō [κοινόω, *2840*]

koinoō is a verb with the predominant meaning "defile," "pollute" throughout its fifteen occurrences.

The act of "defiling" in a moral sense is described in Matt. 15:11ff.; Mark 7:15ff., where Jesus affirms that it is not what goes into people that defiles them, but rather what comes out of them — their speech and actions. Moral impurity in a general sense is indicated in Rev. 21:27.

In a ceremonial context, the "defiling" of the holy place of the temple is indicated in Acts 21:28. Heb. 9:13 mentions people who are ritually unclean.

koinos [κοινός, *2839*]

koinos is an adjective with the dual senses of "common" and "defiled," "unclean." It is found in twelve places.

The meaning "unclean" in a ritual sense is indicated in relation to unwashed hands in Mark 7:2. General references to that which is unclean are found in Rom. 14:14.

The designation "common" in the sense of "unclean" refers to food shown to the apostle Peter in a vision — an opinion for which God rebuked the apostle (cf. Acts 10:14, 28; 11:8). The term is used in a moral sense in Heb. 10:29, where terrible judgment is threatened for anyone who has treated the blood of Christ's sacrifice as an "unclean thing" (i.e., through unbelief).

The meaning "common" in the sense of something held in common is indicated in Acts 2:44; Titus 1:4; Jude 3.

miainō [μιαίνω, *3392*]

The verb **miainō**, meaning "defile," is found five times. John 18:28 describes the contraction of "ritual uncleanness," with the result of being "defiled." The process of "becoming corrupted or defiled" in a moral sense is mentioned in relation to the wicked (Titus 1:15); as a warning to believers (Heb. 12:15); and in connection with false prophets (Jude 8).

miasma [μίασμα, *3393*]

miasma is a rare noun denoting the moral "defilement" or "corruption" of the world, found only in 2 Pet. 2:20.

miasmos [μιασμός, *3394*]

miasmos is a rare variant of **miasma**, above, found only in 2 Pet. 2:10, denoting a "morally defiling" passion.

molynō [μολύνω, *3435*]

molynō is a verb found three times with the passive sense of "being defiled" in relation to weak consciences in 1 Cor. 8:7. Rev. 3:4 refers to believers who "have not defiled" their garments with sinful corruption. Rev. 14:4 describes the saints who "have not defiled themselves" with women.

molysmos [μολυσμός, *3436*]

molysmos is a rare derivative noun from **molynō** (see above) found only in 2 Cor. 7:1 and denoting moral "defilement" in a general sense.

spiloō [σπιλόω, *4695*]

spiloō is a rare synonym for the entries listed above. Jas. 3:6 describes the tongue as an organ that "defiles" the whole body. Jude 23 speaks of a piece of clothing "stained" by the flesh with reference to ritual contamination.

Additional Notes

In both the Hebrew and Greek vocabulary for "defilement," there is a high degree of semantic equivalence. The New Testament does not significantly develop the Old Testament understanding of moral or ceremonial "uncleanness." The whole of Scripture underscores the importance of the moral and ceremonial purity of God's people. In particular, God demands a lifestyle that is consistent with his own standard of righteousness, whether expressed through the Mosaic law covenant or in the person of his Son, Jesus Christ. In both cases, purity of heart and life claims the highest priority in the life of a child of God.

See Also: ➠ CORRUPT

DEFRAUD

OT Words

bāṣa' [בָּצַע, **1214**]

bāṣa' is a verb found sixteen times with various meanings. However, the underlying sense is that of "to acquire by unjust, violent means." On two occasions, **bāṣa'** means "to make financial gain through fraudulent means" (cf. Ezek. 22:12, 27).

NT Words

aposteréō [ἀποστερέω, *650*]

aposteréō is a verb found seven times with the primary sense of "defraud," "keep back by fraudulent means."

Mark 10:19 lists some of the ten commandments repeated by Christ. One of them is "Do not defraud," a variation on the crime of "stealing." The action of "defrauding," or "acquiring by fraudulent means," is indicated in 1 Cor. 6:7, 8. In Jas. 5:4 ***aposteréō*** means "keep back, withhold by fraudulent means."

pleonekteō [πλεονεκτέω, *4122*]

pleonekteō is a verb found in five contexts with the underlying sense of "gain advantage over" someone in the context of fraudulent acts and motives. Such action is predicated of Satan in 2 Cor. 2:11. Denial of such an action is noted in 2 Cor. 7:2; 12:17, 18. 1 Thess. 4:6 contains a warning against such action.

See Also: ➡ OPPRESS

DELAY

OT Words

'āḥar [אָחַר, 309]

This verb occurs seventeen times meaning "delay" or "tarry," with the associated nuances of "hinder" or "refrain."

'āḥar is found in several narrative contexts with a literal meaning and no particular theological significance (cf. Gen. 24:56; 34:19, Judges 5:28; 2 Sam. 20:5). Note also the command in Exod. 22:29 that forbids any Israelite to withhold or refrain from offering sacrifices to God.

More significant, in a theological sense, is the absence of delay in the dispensing of God's judgment. Deut. 7:10 declares that God will not hesitate in bringing judgment against his people for their sinfulness, as does Hab. 2:3, with respect to the Babylonian invasion of Judah, and also Deut. 23:21, regarding those who refuse to honor their vows before God.

Equally significant though, from a different perspective, is the psalmist's plea in Ps. 40:17 for God to quickly bring him salvation, and not to delay. Similarly, Isa. 46:13 records God's promise not to delay in bringing salvation to Israel; and in Dan. 9:19 Daniel pleads with God not to delay the fulfillment of his promise to restore his people in captivity to their homeland, after seventy years of exile.

māhah [מָהַהּ, 4102]

māhah is a verb found in nine places with the primary sense of "linger," or "delay." It is used with this meaning in narrative contexts in Gen. 19:16; 43:10; Exod. 12:39; Judg. 3:26; 19:28. In Ps. 119:60, the psalmist expresses his intention "not to delay" in keeping the commandments of God.

NT Words

okneō [ὀκνέω, *3635*]

okneō is a rare verb found only in Acts 9:38 with the negative sense of "not to delay."

chronizō [χρονίζω, *5549*]

chronizō is a verb found six places with the meaning "linger," "delay." It is used in the positive sense in Matt. 24:48; 25:5; Luke 1:21; 12:45. Heb. 10:37 refers to the Messiah as one "who will not delay" in his coming.

anabolē [ἀναβολή, *311*]

anabolē is a rare noun found only in Acts 25:17, where it refers to Festus, the Roman governor of Judea, taking "no delay" in establishing his tribunal to hear the defense of Paul.

Additional Notes

The specific concept of "delay" occurs only rarely in the New Testament. Yet where it does occur in a significant theological context — for example, in the parable of the foolish maidens in Matt. 25:5, and of the unwise servant in Matt. 24:48, the certainty of God's coming judgment is made perfectly clear. The apparent delay in that final day of reckoning does not mean it will not happen. The force of the Old Testament usage in this respect reinforces the idea that there will be no ultimate delay in God's dealings with humankind, for either good or ill. The whole of Scripture testifies to that reality.

DELIGHT IN

OT Words

ḥāphēṣ [חָפֵץ, 2654]

This verb occurs about seventy times with the primary meanings "delight in," "take pleasure in," "desire."

ḥāphēṣ relates first of all to physical attraction — for example, Gen. 34:19 speaks of Shechem's delight in Dinah, the daughter of Jacob. Deut. 21:14 refers to legislation addressing an Israelite's desire to take a captive, alien woman as his wife. See also Esth. 2:14.

ḥāphēṣ also relates to the Lord's delight in his chosen people (cf. Num. 14:8; 2 Sam. 24:3; 1 Kgs. 10:9; Pss. 18:9; 22:8). Isa. 62:4 contains a metaphorical allusion to God's redemption of his people in terms of a renewed covenant relationship of intimacy — a renewed "marriage" between Yahweh and his people, together with the land of Canaan. There is a very strong relationship here between the land God had given his people and the people themselves. God also delights in other things, such as his people's genuine heart worship (cf. Ps. 51:19; Jer. 9:24; Hos. 6:6; Mic. 7:18), and his own law (cf. Isa. 42:21).

From a human perspective, ***ḥāphēṣ*** likewise indicates delight in the things of God, such as doing his will or taking pleasure in his law (cf. Pss. 40:8; 112:1; 119:35). The term also refers to personal delight in other people — in a non-sensual way (cf. Esth. 6:6ff.); by way of favor shown (cf. 1 Sam. 18:22); or through the attraction of friendship (cf. 1 Sam. 19:1, David and Jonathan).

From a negative perspective, God rejects formal worship which lacks heart devotion — God "takes no delight" in this. For example, Isa. 1:11 formally indicts Israel for this crime; and Isa. 66:3ff. invokes condemnation for those who "delight" in abominations. See also Ps. 51:16; Isa. 65:12.

ta'anûg [תַּעֲנוּג, 8588]

This is a relatively rare noun, found on only five occasions, meaning "delight," or that which is pleasing to the senses. Prov. 19:10 indicates that living in "delight" is an inappropriate lifestyle for the fool. Song 7:6 refers to the lover's expression of "delight" in the beauty of his beloved. Eccl. 2:8 mentions concubines as a man's "delight." On a different note, Mic. 1:16 refers to the exile of the children of the Israelites — the "delight" of their parents — as a time of great mourning and sorrow (cf. also Mic. 2:9).

'ānag [עָנַג, 6026]

This verb has the primary sense of "delight in" and is found seven times with that meaning. There are several references to delighting oneself in God (cf. Job 22:26; 27:10; Ps. 37:4; Isa. 58:14); and also to delighting oneself in prosperity, as an indicator of God's blessing (cf. Ps. 37:4; Isa. 66:11).

ḥēpheṣ [חֵפֶץ, 2656]

ḥēpheṣ is a noun found around forty times with the meanings "pleasure," "desire," "delight" throughout. Yahweh is said "to take delight" in sacrifices in 1 Sam. 15:22, and in his people in Ps. 16:3. Eccl. 5:4 affirms that God "takes no delight" in fools. A general reference to God taking pleasure is found in Job 22:3.

Human beings are said to "express delight" in the law of the Lord in Ps. 1:2. Ps. 111:2 declares that human beings "take pleasure" in the works of the Lord. Negatively, Eccl. 12:1 declares that the elderly "will find no pleasure" in the days of their youth if they forget their Creator. In Mal. 3:12, the land of Israel is designated a "land of delight."

rāṣôn [רָצוֹן, 7522]

The noun ***rāṣôn*** has a wide range of meanings including "favor," "will," "pleasure," "delight" throughout its nearly sixty occurrences. The sense of "delight" is predicated solely of God.

God is said "to take pleasure, delight" in the city of Zion (cf. Ps. 51:18); in fair business dealings (cf. Prov. 11:2); in the blameless ways of the righteous (cf. Prov. 11:20; 12:22; 16:13); and in the prayers of the upright (Prov. 15:8).

shā'a' [שָׁעַע, 8173]

shā'a' is a verb found nine times in the Psalms with the meaning "delight." Ps. 94:19 refers to the psalmist's "delight" in divine consultation. Then, Ps. 119:16, 47, 70 speak of the psalmist's "delight" in the law of God.

'edenāh [עֶדְנָה, 5730]

'edenāh is a noun found four times denoting the "delights" of sexual pleasure in Gen. 18:12. References to "delights" in general terms are indicated in Ps. 36:8; Jer. 51:34.

sha'ashû'îm [שַׁעֲשׁוּעִים, 8191]

sha'ashû'îm is a noun denoting "delight" for most of the nine occurrences of the term. References to the psalmist's "delight" in the law of the Lord are found in Ps. 119:24, 77, 92, 143, 174. Prov. 8:30, 31 use the word metaphorically to denote the "delight" of God's divine partner in the work of creation.

NT Words

synēdomai [συνήδομαι, *4913*]

synēdomai is a rare verb found only in Rom. 7:22 describing Paul's "delighting" in the law of God.

See Also: → PLEASE

DELIVER, DELIVERANCE

OT Words

nāṣal [נָצַל, 5337]

This verb is found approximately two hundred times in various contexts, meaning "deliver," "rescue," or "snatch away."

nāṣal describes the phenomenon of deliverance from a number of different perspectives. In the first place, ***nāṣal*** indicates deliverance from one's human enemies. Gen. 37:21, for example, describes Reuben's rescue of Joseph from the murderous clutches of his brothers. See also 2 Sam. 19:9. There is a demand for social justice in Jer. 21:12; 22:23, where God, through the prophet, calls for the deliverance of those who are oppressed in Israel.

Far more common is the emphasis on God delivering his people from their enemies. ***nāṣal*** describes this in a general sense concerning Israel (cf. Deut. 23:14; Judg. 8:34; 1 Sam. 12:10; 2 Kgs. 18:30). In particular, God delivers Israel from the enslavement of the Egyptians (cf. Exod. 2:19; 3:8; 6:6; Judg. 6:9; Jer. 15:21); and from other pagan nations, such as Moab (cf. Josh. 24:10); Philistia (cf. 1 Sam. 7:3); Assyria (cf. 2 Kgs. 20:6); and Babylon (cf. Jer. 42:11). God also promises to deliver Jerusalem from those nations who took her into exile. Jerusalem, of course, stands symbolically for the people of God in Judah. This promise is linked with the prospect of a new covenant age foreshadowed by the return of exiled Israelites to their land (cf. Jer. 31:5; 38:6; Mic. 4:10). In a similar context, God delivers a remnant from Israel, which reflects the mercy of God in refusing to abandon his people entirely, notwithstanding their sinfulness (cf. Amos 3:12; Mic. 5:8; Zech. 3:2). ***nāṣal*** also describes the deliverance of Israel from the ravages of her own false prophets and wicked rulers (cf. Ezek. 13:23; 34:10). Jer. 1:8 demonstrates God's intention to rescue and protect his individual servants as well (cf. also 1 Sam. 26:24; 2 Sam. 12:7). The Psalms contain frequent pleas for God to protect and deliver from trouble in general (e.g., Pss. 34:4; 70:1; 144:7, 11); enemies in particular (e.g., Pss. 7:1; 22:8; 35:10; 59:1ff.; 142:6); and from sin and its consequences (cf. Ps. 51:14).

nāṣal is also used to plead for deliverance from God, in the sense of being preserved from his judgment or wrath. Josh. 2:13, for example, records Rahab's plea for deliverance from Yahweh's wrath, which is about to be poured out on Jericho (cf. also Josh. 9:26). Similar pleas are found in Gen. 32:30; 1 Sam. 4:8.

On a more sobering note, the Old Testament prophets also indicate that, in some instances, pleading for deliverance will be in vain because divine punishment is inevitable (cf. Hosea 2:9; 5:14). This theme is also found in Deut. 32:39, where it is affirmed that no one can deliver out of God's hand those whom God has singled out for retribution. In regard to the worship of pagan deities, such pleas for deliverance are utterly vain and only result in the outpouring of divine wrath upon those who engage in such idolatry (cf. Isa. 44:17, 20; 47:14; 57:13; Jer. 7:10).

nātan [נָתַן, 5414]

This common verb occurs nearly 2,000 times with the predominant meaning "give," but it is translated "hand over" or "deliver" in about 180 instances.

In theological terms, the most significant usage of ***nātan*** occurs in contexts where God is said to deliver his people from their enemies. In this sense, ***nātan*** is synonymous with ***nāṣal***, above. Examples of this meaning are found in the following passages, where Israel is the object of God's mercy and protection: Num. 21:34 (Sihon); Deut. 3:2 (Og); Deut. 7:24 (kings of Canaan); Deut. 20:13; Josh. 10:8, 19 (cities of Canaan); 1 Sam. 14:10 (Philistines). Deliverance from various Canaanite peoples is affirmed in Josh. 21:44; Judg. 3:28, and promised in Judg. 4:7, 14; 7:7ff.

There is also a negative aspect to the meaning of ***nātan*** (as with ***nāṣal*** above), where divine justice requires that people be handed over to Yahweh for punishment. For example, Deut. 19:12 stipulates that a murderer must be handed over to the avenger of blood for capital punishment. Isa. 34:2 proclaims that nations in rebellion against God will be delivered up for slaughter. In Lam. 1:14, Jeremiah bewails the fate of the people of Jerusalem who have been handed over by God to the Babylonians and exiled because of their persistent rejection of Yahweh. The inevitable judgment of God against his people is also highlighted in Jer. 43:3; Ezek. 7:21; 11:9; 23:9ff. The traditional enemies of Israel do not escape this fate either — Amnon is to be handed over to God for punishment in Ezek. 21:31; 25:7.

sāgar [סָגַר, 5462]

This term is also synonymous with ***nāṣal*** and ***nātan***, above. ***sāgar*** occurs about ninety times, with the principal meaning "shut," or "shut up." But it is also translated "deliver" or "hand over" in a number of significant contexts.

Deut. 23:15 records legislation concerning handing over a slave to his master. Josh. 20:5 details legislation covering the protection of the manslayer — not the murderer — who is not to be handed over to the "avenger of blood." In 1 Sam. 17:46 David threatens Goliath by saying that God will hand him over to David for punishment that very day. 1 Sam. 23:11ff. refers to the handing over of one's enemies. In this situation it is Saul's attempt to have David delivered over to him that is in view. Ps. 78; Amos 6:8 both refer to handing Israel over to Yahweh for punishment.

mālat [מָלַט, **4422**]

This verb occurs about ninety times with the predominant sense of "escape." In about a third of these instances and in different contexts, ***mālat*** is translated "deliver."

There a number of references to God delivering his people (cf. Pss. 22:5; 107:20). Some texts speak of a divine promise to rescue or deliver Israel (e.g., Isa. 46:4; 49:25; Dan. 12:1; Joel 2:32). In addition, there are promises of deliverance for Jerusalem (cf. Isa. 31:5); and for the prophet Jeremiah, who will not go into exile (cf. Jer. 39:18). There are also promises relating to the protection and deliverance of the innocent or the poor (cf. Job 22:30; Ps. 41:1; Prov. 11:21). Pleas to God for deliverance from one's enemies or from anguish and sorrow are recorded in Job 6:23; Ps. 116:4.

On the other hand, deliverance for the wicked will not be entertained (cf. Eccl. 8:8) — including those among God's people who persist in their rebellion against God (cf. Amos 2:14; 9:1).

Finally, there is one instance where ***mālat*** refers to a woman being delivered of a child (cf. Isa. 66:7).

ḥālaṣ [חָלַץ, **2502**]

The verb ***ḥālaṣ*** is found about forty times with the predominant senses of "deliver," "arm" (i.e., with weapons).

God is said to "deliver" his people from catastrophe (Ps. 81:7); from their enemies (2 Sam. 22:20; Ps. 18:19); from their affliction (Job 36:15); and from trouble (Pss. 50:15; 91:15). Ps. 34:7 affirms that the angel of the Lord delivers those who fear him.

The psalmist appeals to God to "deliver" him from trouble (cf. Pss. 6:4; 60:5; 108:6; 119:153); and from his enemies (Ps. 140:1). A general reference to deliverance from trouble is recorded in Prov. 11:8.

NT Words

anadidōmi [ἀναδίδωμι, *325*]

anadidōmi is a rare verb found only in Acts 23:33, referring to a group of soldiers "delivering" a letter to the Roman governor.

epididōmi [ἐπιδίδωμι, *1929*]

epididōmi is another verb found in eleven places with the principal sense of "give." In Acts 15:30, however, the verb indicates the action of "delivering" a letter.

paradidōmi [παραδίδωμι, *3860*]

paradidōmi is a common verb found in approximately 120 contexts with the meaning "deliver," "betray."

The meaning "deliver" in the sense of "hand over" is evident in the context of arrest and delivering people to the courts (cf. Matt. 5:25; 10:17ff.; Mark 3:11). See also Matt. 24:9. "Handing over" prisoners to the jailers is recorded in Matt. 18:34; Acts 28:17. The Sanhedrin — the Jewish supreme civil court — "hand Jesus over" to Pilate for sentence in Mark 15:1; John 18:30ff. God is said to "hand over" wicked angels to gloomy dungeons to be held for judgment in 2 Pet. 2:4. Pilate's action in "handing Jesus over" to be crucified is recorded in Matt. 27:26; John 19:16. Blood money is "handed over" to Judas in Matt. 26:15ff. for betraying Jesus.

paradidōmi is also translated "betray," a more specific nuance of "deliver," indicating the "handing over" of someone to a terrible fate. General references to "betrayal" include Matt. 10:21; Mark 13:12; Acts 21:11. Christ's "betrayal" into the hands of humans is noted in Matt. 17:22; 20:18ff.; 26:2, 23ff.; 27:18; Mark 9:31; 10:33; 14:41; Luke 9:44; 18:32; 24:2; Acts 3:13. Judas' role in this act of treachery is recorded in Mark 14:10ff.; Luke 22:4, 21ff.; John 6:71; 13:2; 18:5.

The passive sense of the term "be delivered up" is indicated in several contexts (e.g., Matt. 11:27; Luke 10:22). Here all things are said "to be delivered up" by God to Christ, in the sense of committing them to him. Rom. 4:25; 8:32 confirm that Christ "was delivered over to death" by God for our sins.

Other general references to the act of "delivering," in the sense of "hand over," "entrust to," include entrusting money or property to one's servants in Matt. 25:14, 20. The "handing down" of the traditions of the gospel of Christ to future generations is a process indicated in Luke 1:2; Rom. 6:17; 1 Cor. 15:3; 2 Pet. 2:21; Jude 3. God is said to "deliver over" the morally perverse to their lusts in Rom. 1:24ff. The "handing over" of an immoral man to Satan — an action of ecclesiastical discipline — is noted in 1 Cor. 5:5; 1 Tim. 1:20. 1 Cor. 15:24 affirms that Christ "will deliver" the heavenly kingdom to his Father at the end of the age.

eleutheroō [ἐλευθερόω, *1659*]

eleutheroō is a verb found twelve times with the predominant meaning "set free," with the sense of "being rescued, or delivered from."

John 8:32, 36 refer to "setting free" the believer from the darkness of unbelief. Rom. 6:18, 22 affirm the experience of "being set free (i.e., delivered)" from the power and sentence of sin. Positively, Rom. 8:2 affirms that the work of Jesus Christ "sets (people) free" from the law of sin and death. See also Gal. 5:1. Rom. 8:21 declares that creation "will be delivered" (i.e., liberated) from bondage to decay.

exaireō [ἐξαιρέω, *1807*]

exaireō is a verb found eight times with the predominant sense of "set free," "rescue," "deliver."

Acts 7:10 refers to Joseph, whom God "rescued" or "delivered" from his troubles. Acts 7:34 notes that God had intended to set Israel free from the Egyptian bondage. Peter reports that God "had set him free" from prison in Acts 12:11. See also Acts 26:17; 23:27. Gal. 1:4 affirms that Christ's sacrificial death "has rescued" his people from the present evil age.

katargeō [καταργέω, *2673*]

katargeō is a verb with the primary meanings "destroy," "abolish," as well as related nuances, in about thirty places. In Rom. 7:6, however, the term is used passively — affirming that believers "have been released" (i.e., delivered) from the law as a consequence of the redemptive work of Christ.

rhyomai [ῥύομαι, *4506*]

The verb ***rhyomai*** means "deliver" throughout its nearly twenty occurrences.

Matt. 6:13; Luke 11:4 record appeals to God to "deliver" his people from temptation. The act of rescuing from death is indicated in Matt. 27:43; Luke 1:74; Rom. 7:24. Then, the experience of being "rescued" from one's enemies is recorded in Rom. 15:31; 2 Thess. 3:2.

rhyomai is also used in a nominal sense denoting the "deliverer," with reference to the coming Messiah, in Rom. 11:26.

Christ is said to "rescue" his people from the coming wrath in 1 Thess. 1:10. References to God having "delivered" his people from the judgment of sin are found in 2 Cor. 1:10; Col. 1:13. 2 Cor. 1:10; 2 Tim. 4:18; 2 Pet. 2:9 also promise deliverance.

lytrōtēs [λυτρωτής, *3086*]

lytrōtēs is a rare noun found only in Acts 7:35, referring to Moses as the "deliverer" of the Israelites from Egypt.

Additional Notes

Given the number of terms in both Hebrew and Greek that embrace the idea of deliverance, it is impossible to establish any precise equivalence of meaning between any corresponding terms. There is, however, a common emphasis throughout Scripture as a whole. The deliverance of God's people from their enemies, and from any ultimate consequences of their sinfulness in the old covenant, has a distinct parallel in the new. The political, geographic, and military deliverance of Israel with respect to the land of Canaan foreshadows the profound spiritual deliverance of God's people from their bondage to sin under the new covenant, inaugurated and fulfilled by the redemptive work of Jesus Christ. As a corollary to this, divine judgment is poured out upon the wicked in the old covenant, including apostate Israelites. In the new covenant, there is a final judgment reserved for those who ultimately turn their backs on the Savior whom God has graciously provided as a means of escape. Deliverance from the judgment of God is a profound theological concept throughout the whole Bible, as is the negative corollary — a delivering over to divine judgment.

See Also: → REDEEM → SAVE

DELUDE, DELUSION → DECEIT

DEMAND → ASK → INQUIRE

DEMON, DEMONIAC

OT Words

shēd [**שֵׁד**, **7700**]

shēd is a rare noun denoting "demons" to whom apostate Israelites had offered sacrifices (cf. Deut. 32:17; Ps. 106:37).

NT Words

daimōn [δαίμων, *1142*]

daimōn is a noun denoting "demons" in all five occurrences of the term. Matt. 8:31; Mark 5:12 refer to the demons cast out of the Gadarene demoniac by Christ. Luke 8:29 records the impact of the demon on the man he possessed — driving him into the wilderness. Spirits of "demons" are said to perform miracles in Rev. 16:14. Babylon is described as a haunt of "demons" in Rev. 18:2.

daimonion [δαιμόνιον, *1140*]

daimonion is a derivative form of ***daimōn*** (see above) with the consistent meaning of "demon" throughout its sixty occurrences.

"Demons" are driven out by Christ in miracles of exorcism in Matt. 7:22; 12:24ff.; Mark 1:34; 3:15; 7:26ff.; Luke 4:41; 11:14ff. Christ's disciples also drive them out in Mark 6:13; Luke 9:1; 10:17. See also Mark 9:38. References to people possessed by a "demon" or "demons" are found in Matt. 11:18; Luke 4:33ff.; 8:27ff.; 9:42.

Christ is falsely accused of being demon-possessed in Luke 11:15, 18; John 7:20; 8:48ff.; 10:20. Rev. 9:20 refers to pagans worshiping demons. 1 Cor. 10:20ff. describes the sacrifices pagans offered to demons. 1 Tim. 4:1 refers to the teaching of demons. Jas. 2:19 notes that "demons" are said to believe in God.

daimonizomai [δαιμονίζομαι, *1139*]

daimonizomai is a verb with the consistent meaning "be possessed by a demon (or demons)" (cf. Matt. 4:24; 8:16ff.; 9:32; 12:22; 15:22; Mark 1:32; 5:15ff.; Luke 8:36; John 10:21).

daimoniōdēs [δαιμονιώδης, *1141*]

daimoniōdēs is a rare adjectival form, found only in Jas. 3:13 and referring to worldly wisdom being "of the devil."

DEMONSTRATION

NT Words

apodeixis [ἀπόδειξις, *585*]

apodeixis is a rare noun denoting the "demonstration" of the Holy Spirit's power, found only in 1 Cor. 2:4.

endeixis [ἔνδειξις, *1732*]

endeixis is a noun denoting "proof" or "demonstration" in four contexts. Rom. 3:25, 26 speak of Christ's atonement as a "demonstration" of God's justice. The "proof" or "demonstration" of Christian love is noted in 2 Cor. 8:24. A "token" or "proof" of the imminent destruction of the wicked is indicated in Phil. 1:28.

DEN

OT Words

me'ônāh [מְעוֹנָה, **4585**]

me'ônāh is a noun found nine times with the meanings "refuge," "den" throughout, though the latter sense predominates. References to the dens of lions are found in Job 38:40; Pss. 76:2; 104:22; Song 4:8; Amos 3:4; Nah. 2:12. See also Job 37:8.

sōk [סֹךְ, **5520**]

sōk is a noun found four times with the general meaning "dwelling place." The term denotes a lion's "den" in Ps. 10:9; Jer. 25:38.

me'ārāh [מְעָרָה, **4631**]

me'ārāh is a noun found nearly forty times with the predominant sense of "cave." There is one metaphorical reference to "den" in Jer. 7:11, where the prophet refers to the desecration of the temple reduced to the condition of a "den" of robbers.

gōb [גֹּב, **1358** (Aramaic)]

gōb is an Aramaic noun denoting a lion's "den" only in Dan. 6:7, 12ff.

NT Words

spēlaion [σπήλαιον, *4693*]

spēlaion is a noun found six times with the dual senses of "cave," "den." References to "caves" are literal, whereas Matt. 21:13; Mark 11:17; Luke 19:46 all mention Christ's denunciation of those who had desecrated the Jerusalem temple, making it a "den of thieves."

DENY

OT Words

kāḥash [כָּחַשׁ, **3584**]

This verb occurs about twenty times with a number of meanings, all of which are associated with deceit, lying, or denial. ***kāḥash*** is translated "deny" on five occasions, but denial is either directly or indirectly involved in some of the remaining occurrences as well.

In Gen. 18:15, for example, Sarah denies laughing at God's promise that she would bear a child. But this is clearly a lie, for she did indeed laugh. Josh. 7:11 indicates Achan's lie in regard to the booty he had stolen from the plunder taken from Jericho. Here, denial is explicitly in view in the usage of ***kāḥash***. Josh. 24:27 contains a solemn warning regarding the stone of testimony, which will function as a witness against Israel should they ever deny their God in the future. It is explicitly linked with the covenant renewal ceremony depicted in this chapter. Isa. 59:13 indicts Israel for denying Yahweh; and the context clearly indicates that such denial involves rejection, disobedience, and deceit (cf. also Hos. 4:2).

For other uses of ***kāḥash*** in relation to denial, see Lev. 6:2, 3; 19:11; Deut. 33:29; 1 Kgs. 3:18.

NT Words

arneomai [ἀρνέομαι, *720*]

arneomai is a verb with the predominant sense of "deny," with a variety of nuances, throughout the nearly thirty occurrences of the term.

References to "denying" in the sense of "disown" are found regarding those who "deny" Christ, or refuse to recognize him as Lord and bear testimony to him before human beings (cf. Matt. 10:33; Luke 12:9; 2 Tim. 2:12; 1 John 2:22ff.; 2 Pet. 2:21; Jude 4; Rev. 2:13; 3:8). "Denying" God is noted in Titus 1:16. The action of "denying" in the sense of "refusing to acknowledge or admit the truth" is indicated in Matt. 26:70ff.; Mark 14:68ff.; Luke 8:45; 22:57; John 18:25ff. Acts 3:13ff. refers to the Jews "denying" or "disowning" Christ and handing him over to Pilate.

Acts 4:16 describes the impossibility of "denying" a miracle.

The action of "denying" (i.e., rejecting) one's faith is recorded in 1 Tim. 5:8, as is "denying" the power of godliness in 2 Tim. 3:5. The impossibility of Christ "denying" (i.e., "disowning") himself is described in 2 Tim. 2:13.

aparneomai [ἀπαρνέομαι, *533*]

aparneomai is a variant form of ***arneomai***, above, meaning "deny" throughout the fourteen occurrences of the term.

Matt. 16:24; Mark 8:34; Luke 9:23 speak of the importance of "denying" oneself to take up one's cross and follow Christ.

Peter's action in "denying" Christ on the eve of his trial, refusing to acknowledge him as master and friend, is noted in Matt. 26:34ff.; 75; Mark 14:30ff., 72; Luke 22:34, 61; John 13:38.

Luke 12:9 affirms that whoever "denies" Christ before others will be denied before the angels in heaven.

antilegō [ἀντιλέγω, *483*]

antilegō is a verb occurring ten times with the underlying sense of "speak against." It specifically means "deny" in Luke 20:27 where the Sadducees are said to "deny" (i.e., refuse to believe in) the resurrection.

Additional Notes

There is no exact correspondence in meaning between the Old and New Testament terminology for "denial." The Hebrew terms tend to have a broader semantic range than the corresponding Greek words. There is, however, one common feature worth noting — the severe and painful consequences of turning one's back on God. To deny God under the old covenant brought inevitable and sometimes swift retribution. Exactly the same phenomenon is observable in the New Testament. The consequences of denying Jesus Christ, however, are far worse — leading to exclusion from the presence of God forever.

See Also: → DESPISE → REFUSE → REJECT

DEPART, DEPARTURE

OT Words

sûr [סוּר, **5493**]

This verb occurs about 280 times with the dominant meanings "put away," "remove," "turn aside." However, ***sûr*** is also translated "depart" in about eighty instances. About one tenth of these are prosaic, simply indicating movement from one place to another (e.g., Exod. 8:11; Lev. 13:58; 1 Sam. 15:6; Isa. 7:17). In some cases, however, the movement has real significance. For example, in Isa. 52:11 there is the divine exhortation to the people of Israel to leave their country of exile. The cry "Depart!" signals the beginning of the fulfillment of God's promise to bring his people back from exile.

The central importance of the law covenant in the spiritual life of Israel may be observed in various contexts where ***sûr*** indicates the phenomenon of "departing." In Jer. 32:40 God promises to so transform his people that they will never depart (or turn aside) from his law. This text alludes to the coming age of new covenant blessing. Then, the importance of never departing from God's commandments is emphasized in 2 Sam. 22:23. A number of rulers from Israel and Judah are commended for keeping the laws of Yahweh and for never departing from them (cf. 2 Kgs. 18:6 [Hezekiah]; 2 Chr. 20:32 [Jehoshaphat]; 2 Chr. 34:33 [Josiah]). Others are condemned for turning away or departing from the law (e.g., 2 Kgs. 3:3 [Jehoram]; 2 Kgs. 10:29 [Jehu]; 2 Kgs. 14:24 [Jeroboam]). This condemnation extends to the people of Israel and Judah (cf. Ezek. 6:9;

Hos. 9:12; Mal. 2:8). It is this sin that Daniel confesses on behalf of his people in Dan. 9:5.

The term also conveys the metaphorical sense of "departing" in a number of texts. Gen. 49:10 contains the prophetic anticipation of the coming of the Messiah through the blessing of the dying Jacob to his son, Judah. Here is the prophecy that the scepter "will never depart" from Judah — a prediction of a royal posterity. Deut. 4:9 stresses the importance of remembering what God has done for his people, Israel, lest these things "depart" from their hearts and minds. Punishment for the family of David as a consequence of his crimes of adultery and murder is indicated in 2 Sam. 12:10, where God warns that the sword "shall never depart" from his house. It is a terrible prophecy of continual family strife that culminates in the rebellion and death of David's beloved son, Absalom. Ezek. 16:42 gives the assurance that God's anger against his people will be satisfied and his jealous anger "will depart (or turn aside)" from them. In the context of the Wisdom literature of the Old Testament, true wisdom is gained by abandoning or departing from evil (cf. Job 28:28; Pss. 34:14; 37:27; Prov. 3:7; 14:16).

Finally, there are several sobering texts that speak of the terrible reality of God "departing in judgment from" (i.e., abandoning) those who have sinned against him. For example, Judg. 16:20 speaks of God leaving Samson; and the following texts from the Samuel narratives point to the departure of God's Spirit from King Saul, thus depriving him of his divine right to rule (cf. 1 Sam. 16:14, 23; 18:12; 28:15, 16).

mûsh **[מוּשׁ, 4185]**

This comparatively rare verb occurs only about twenty times. ***mûsh*** is translated both as "remove" and "depart," and the usage is fairly evenly divided.

There is the mundane aspect of "departing," found in Exod. 33:11; Num. 14:44; Judg. 6:18; while a symbolic meaning is evident in the remaining texts. Josh. 1:8 contains the divine command to observe the book of the law, to never let it depart from the mouths of his people (cf. also Isa. 59:21). Isa. 54:10 records the promise that God will never depart from his people (cf. also Jer. 31:36). Finally, Prov. 17:13 indicates that evil will never leave a person's house if they return evil for good.

NT WORDS

analyō [ἀναλύω, *360*]

analyō is a rare verb with the meaning "depart" in Phil. 1:23, where Paul expresses his desire to "depart" (i.e., to die) and be with the Lord.

analysis [ἀνάλυσις, *359*]

analysis is the rare noun derived from ***analyō***, above, found only in 2 Tim. 4:6 with reference to Paul's realization that the time for his "departure" (i.e., his execution) is near.

exodos [ἔξοδος, *1841*]

exodos is a noun found in three places referring metaphorically to Jesus' "departure" (i.e., his approaching death) in Luke 9:31, and likewise to Peter's demise in 2 Pet. 2:15. Heb. 11:22 refers to Israel's historical release or exodus (i.e., departure) from Egypt.

aphixis [ἄφιξις, *867*]

aphixis is a rare noun denoting a physical departure (i.e., leaving) in Acts 20:29.

Additional Notes

No precise equivalence between Old and New Testament terminology may be established for the enormous variety of terms embracing the concept of "departing." Consult the entries listed below for a fuller understanding of the significance of this term.

It is clear, however, that the whole of biblical revelation emphasizes the crucial importance of never departing from the revealed will and purpose of God, especially in the light of God's final revelation of himself through the person of his Son, Jesus Christ.

See Also: → DESCEND → FLEE → GO → LEAVE → OFFER → PASS → SAIL → SEPARATE → TURN → WALK

DEPOSIT

NT WORDS

'ērābôn **[עֵרָבוֹן, 6162]**

This is a rare noun, occurring on only three occasions, meaning "pledge" or "earnest" in the sense of a deposit as proof of intent to carry through a transaction. ***'ērābôn*** is found only in Gen. 38:17ff., which contains the bizarre account of Judah's sexual liaison with his daughter-in-law Tamar. She disguised herself as a shrine prostitute, waited for Judah, and succeeded in gaining his attention. When Judah made inquiries of her, she asked what price he would pay her. He offered her a kid goat from his flock. Since he did not have it with him, Tamar asked him for a "pledge," a down-payment until she received her full price. This involved Judah in handing over to her his personal ring, seal, and staff, which Tamar would produce later on as proof that the father of her child was in fact her father-in-law. The catalyst for this remarkable incident was Judah's failure to provide his daughter-in-law with the husband he had promised her — namely Shelah, his sole remaining son.

NT WORDS

arrabōn [ἀρραβών, *728*]

arrabōn is a term originally denoting "earnest money" deposited by the purchaser and forfeited if the purchase was not completed. It was probably a Phoenician word, introduced into Greece. In general usage it came to denote a "pledge" or "earnest" of any sort. In the New Testament it is used only of that which is assured by God to believers. It is predicated of the Holy Spirit, who is described as the divine "pledge" of all future blessedness (cf. 2 Cor. 5:5). In Eph. 1:14, the term refers particularly to their eternal inheritance.

DEPTH → DEEP

DESCEND, DESCENT

OT WORDS

yārad [יָרַד, 3381]

This verb is common throughout the Old Testament, occurring about 350 times with the predominant meaning "come (or go) down." The overwhelming majority of occurrences refer to literal movement downwards.

Those references that are worthy of particular mention all speak of God's intentions and activity. For example, Gen. 18:21 records God's determination to go down and investigate the sinful lifestyle of the cities of Sodom and Gomorrah, with a view to determining their fate. Exod. 3:8 speaks of God's promise to come down and rescue his people from Egypt (cf. Neh. 9:13; Ps. 18:9). The descent of God onto Mt. Sinai carries with it enormous significance as it constitutes the great revelation of God to his chosen people and the occasion of the formal ratification of his unique covenantal relationship with them (cf. Exod. 19:11ff.; and note also Exod. 34:5).

yārad also carries the connotation of divine judgment in several contexts — in particular, God's action in "bringing down" all those who oppose him. That is, he brings about their downfall, whether it be loss of life, military defeat or, as in the case of Israel, the loss of homeland. Ezek. 31:16, for example, speaks of God bringing or casting down the nations into Sheol, or the pit (cf. also Zech. 10:11). The same fate is predicated of God's people (cf. Ezek. 26:20); the king of Tyre (cf. Ezek. 28:8); and the king of Egypt (cf. Ezek. 32:18). Ezek. 32:21ff. contains an extended depiction of several nations whose fate, at the hands of God, lies in the grave.

NT WORDS

katabainō [καταβαίνω, *2597*]

katabainō is a verb found about eighty times with the primary senses of "come down," "descend," with some related nuances.

The literal sense of "descend" occurs in connection with the Spirit of God descending on Christ at his baptism in the form of a dove (cf. Matt. 3:16; Mark 1:10; Luke 3:22; John 1:32ff.). The "descending" of a road is noted in Acts 8:26.

Elsewhere, ***katabainō*** indicates the "coming down" of fire from heaven in Luke 9:54; Rev. 13:13; 20:9. The "pouring down" of rain is noted in Matt. 7:25ff.; and the "descent" of a windstorm in Luke 8:23. The sense of "come down" is also evident in the context of a person's movement or journey in Matt. 8:1; Mark 3:22; Luke 6:17; John 2:12; Acts 7:15; 14:25. Angels "descending" from heaven are noted in Matt. 28:2; John 1:51; 5:47; Rev. 10:1; 18:1; 20:1. John 3:13 refers to the Son of Man "descending" from heaven, referring to his incarnation. In 1 Thess. 4:16 Christ is likewise described as "descending" from heaven, but here it refers to his final return. God is also described as "coming down" to deliver his people from Egypt in Acts 7:34 (cf. Exod. 12, 13).

In metaphorical contexts, ***katabainō*** refers to the bread of God "coming down" from heaven, referring to Christ himself (cf. John 6:33ff., 50ff.). The act of "descending" into the abyss of the dead is noted in Rom. 10:7; Eph. 4:9ff. A sheet of food "descending" from heaven in the vision of the apostle Peter is noted in Acts 10:11; 11:15. God's gifts are said to "come down" to human beings in Jas. 1:17. Rev. 3:12; 21:2, 10 refer to the new Jerusalem "coming down" from heaven. In a pagan context, gods are said to "come down" amongst human beings in Acts 14:11.

katerchomai [κατέρχομαι, *2718*]

The verb ***katerchomai*** expresses the meaning "come down," "descend" throughout the thirteen occurrences of the term.

The literal meaning of "come, go down" in the context of travel predominates (cf. Luke 4:31; 9:37; Acts 8:5; 9:32; 12:19; 13:4; 18:5, 22; 21:10; Acts 27:5). In

Jas. 3:15, there is a metaphorical usage of the term referring to earthly, unspiritual wisdom that "does not come down" from above.

agenealogētos [ἀγενεαλόγητος, *35*]

agenealogētos is a rare adjective found only in Heb. 7:3, denoting Melchizedek as a man "without descent," or without record of mother or father (citing the account of the patriarch Abraham's mysterious priestly royal visitor in Gen. 14).

genealogeō [γενεαλογέω, *1075*]

genealogeō is a rare verb found only in Heb. 7:6 with the sense of "trace one's descent, or ancestry."

DESCRIBE → WRITE

DESERT

OT Words

midbār [מִדְבָּר, 4057]

This is a fairly common term that occurs about 250 times and is almost always translated "desert" or "wilderness." Aside from the physical, geographic sense of wasteland, which is found occasionally in the Genesis patriarchal narratives, the term ***midbār*** yields a number of significant perspectives.

In the first place, the desert is portrayed in the Old Testament as the arena where Israel's faith was tested and tried by Yahweh. It constitutes, for example, the setting for God's deliverance of his people from Egypt and their journeying towards Canaan, the land of promise, through Mt. Sinai. The Israelite exodus and its connection with the wilderness is a dominant theme in the Pentateuch, and to a lesser extent in the Former Prophets. Key texts are found in Exod. 13–15; 17:1; 18:5; 19:1, where movement from Egypt through the wilderness towards Sinai is in view. ***midbār*** is then utilized frequently, with this broad context in mind, in Numbers; Deuteronomy; Joshua; 1 and 2 Samuel; Kings and Chronicles. See also Ezek. 20:10; Amos 2:10 in this regard.

Various other themes emerge from this usage of ***midbār***. Exod. 16:2, 3 refer, for example, to Israel's grumbling in the desert. In Exod. 16:32 there is the record of God providing manna for his people in a miraculous fashion in the wilderness; but there is no record of their gratitude to him for this (cf. Num. 21:5, where their ingratitude towards God is explicitly mentioned). Deut. 8:2 specifically refers to the desert as a place of testing, to see whether or not Israel would keep God's commandments. During the period of Israel's wanderings in the wilderness the people of Yahweh constantly rebelled against him; and their sinful behavior and attitudes in this setting are a recurring theme in the Old Testament (cf. Deut. 9:7; 32:51; Pss. 78:40; 95:8; 106:14; Ezek. 20:13; Hos. 9:10). On a more positive note, the wilderness is also depicted as the place where God, time and again, offered protection for his people (cf. Deut. 8:15ff.; Josh. 24:7; Neh. 9:19, 21; Ps. 78:52; Isa. 63:13). One especially significant text is Jer. 2:2, which describes the wilderness as the place where God formally bound himself to his people. This covenantal bonding adopts the analogy of a marriage in which Yahweh, the bridegroom, pledges himself to his bride, Israel. Initially, Israel's response to God was equally wholehearted. This "honeymoon period" did not last, however, for it was quickly followed by Israel's idolatry, disobedience, and ingratitude (cf. Jer. 2:6, 24; 3:2).

midbār is also used to denote the desert as the location of God's judgment against his people. In Lev. 16:10, 21, 22, the scapegoat is sent away into the wilderness as part of the Day of Atonement ritual. The banishment of this animal symbolizes the eradication and removal of Israel's sin. Num. 14:29ff. is another important text in this regard. Here, the wilderness literally constitutes the place of God's judgment against his people, for they have failed to go up and take the land as directed. As a punishment, they are forced to wander through the desert for forty years. In addition, all those twenty years and older who had left Egypt would die during this period. Only those under twenty years old would survive and enter Canaan as God had promised (cf. also Num. 32:13; Ps. 106:26). This judgment of "wilderness wandering" is repeated metaphorically on Israel at the time of her exile, at the hands of both the Assyrians (721 B.C.) and the Babylonians (587 B.C.). At this time, the people of God are sent away into the "wilderness" of exile as the climactic judgment of God against them for their wickedness (cf. Ezek. 20:35; Hos. 2:3). Included in this punishment is the wasting or desolation of the land of Israel itself (cf. Isa. 64:10; Jer. 4:26; 9:2ff.; 12:12; 13:24; 22:6; Ezek. 6:14). Such a devastation is also predicated of the nations, who constantly oppose Yahweh and treat his people with disdain (cf. Joel 3:19; Zeph. 2:13).

From the perspective of blessing, the wilderness is also depicted as a stage for God's sovereign initiative in salvation. Isa. 40:3 portrays the messianic deliverer emerging from the desert. He is a figure that finds fulfillment in the person of Jesus, and is heralded by the arrival of John the Baptist. Jer. 31:2 refers to Israel finding grace in the wilderness, after God's anger had been poured out on them (cf. also Ezek. 20:17). Then, in Hos. 2:14ff., there is the remarkable divine promise to lead Israel back into the desert, metaphorically speaking, and to restore her to that intimate covenant relationship with God — a union that will last forever and remove all traces of unfaithfulness in the hearts of the Israelite people.

Finally, there is God's promise to transform the desert and make it flourish, as part of the symbolic representation of his overall program of redemption for his people (cf. Ps. 107:35; Isa. 32:16; 35:1, 6; 43:19; Ezek. 34:25).

ṣî [צִי, **6728**]

ṣî is a noun found in five places with the meaning "desert" or "wilderness" throughout, referring to wild animals of the "desert" in Ps. 74:14; Isa. 13:21; 34:14; Jer. 50:39. People dwelling in the "wilderness" are noted in Isa. 23:13.

ḥorbāh [חָרְבָּה, **2723**]

ḥorbāh is a noun denoting "desolation," "places laid waste" for most of the nearly forty occurrences of the term. (→ DESOLATION) In several places ***ḥorbāh*** also denotes "desert," a variation on "waste places."

General references include Ps. 102:6; Ezek. 13:4. Isa. 48:21 describes the "desert," the place through which God led his people from captivity in Egypt to the land of Canaan.

yeshîmôn [יְשִׁימוֹן, **3452**]

yeshîmôn is synonymous with the entries above, denoting a "wilderness" or "desert" in Num. 23:28; Deut. 32:10; Ps. 107:4. The "wilderness" as the theater of God's redemptive dealings with his people is indicated in Pss. 68:7; 78:40; 106:14. The term ***yeshîmôn*** is also used in transliteration with reference to a "wasteland" (cf. 1 Sam. 23:19, 24; 16:13).

NT Words

erēmia [ἐρημία, *2047*]

erēmia is a noun found four times denoting a "wilderness" or "desert" throughout (cf. Matt. 15:33; Mark 8:4; 2 Cor. 11:26; Heb. 11:38).

erēmos [ἔρημος, *2048*]

erēmos is an adjectival form used primarily in the nominal sense of "wilderness," "desert" throughout the fifty occurrences of the term.

John the Baptist's preaching in the "wilderness," preparing for the coming of Christ, is indicated in Matt. 3:1ff.; 11:7; Mark 1:3, 4; Luke 3:2ff.; 7:24; John 1:23. Jesus' temptation by the devil in the "wilderness" is recorded in Matt. 4:1; Mark 1:12ff.

General references to "wilderness" include Matt. 14:13; 24:26; Mark 6:31ff.; Luke 5:16; 15:4; John 11:54; Acts 21:38; Rev. 12:6, 14; 17:3.

John 3:14 refers to Moses lifting up the serpent in the "wilderness" — the serpent that provided the catalyst for divine healing. References to Israel's wandering in the "wilderness" between Egypt and Canaan are found in John 6:31, 49; Acts 7:30ff.; 13:18; 1 Cor. 10:5; Heb. 3:8, 17, emphasizing the divine actions of both blessing and judgment.

Additional Notes

Although there is great significance in the New Testament description of the commencement of Jesus' ministry in the desert, and his subsequent temptation in the wilderness at the hands of Satan, the use of wilderness terminology with a potent theological force is comparatively rare. The arrival of John the Baptist in the desert, and the heralding of the coming Messiah there, constitutes the most significant theological development in the New Testament of the Old Testament wilderness theme. For Jesus Christ, beginning his ministry in the desert, including his baptism and testing, all serve to underscore the powerful symbolism of the desert in his life. Likewise, in a powerfully symbolic way, Jesus' suffering on the cross is a genuine "wilderness" experience, as he removes and eradicates our sin. The parallels with Israel's own experiences under the old covenant are both moving and powerful, and they demonstrate clearly once again the overarching significance of the wilderness theme found throughout the whole of biblical revelation.

See Also: → DRY → PLAIN

DESIRE

OT Words

'āwāh [אַוָּה, **183**]

This noun occurs nearly thirty times with the predominant meaning "desire," signifying "coveting" or "lusting" in the majority of instances. ***'āwāh*** carries both a positive and negative connotation, and refers to both God and human beings.

Num. 11:4, 34 describe Israel's physical craving for meat in the desert and the severe punishment from

God that followed. However, in Deut. 12:20, God also indicates that the time will come when such a restriction will not apply (cf. also Ps. 106:14). Then, in Deut. 5:21, ***'āwāh*** is used in the tenth commandment, which prohibits any form of covetousness or illicit desire. Other illegitimate desires are listed in Prov. 13:4; 21:10. Vain desire is indicated in Amos 5:18, where woe is declared upon those Israelites who desire the coming of the Day of the Lord. Their hope is vain, because they are rebels against God, and they will face inevitable judgment on that day instead of salvation.

Concerning godly desires, Isa. 26:9 forms part of a song in which the people of Judah express their strong desire for God, that their souls may be satisfied. Then, in the Former Prophets, King David is offered the realm of Israel, with a view to rule over all that his heart desires (cf. 2 Sam. 3:21; 1 Kgs. 11:37). See also Eccl. 6:2 for another perspective on the desires that God fulfills.

Finally, in Ps. 132:13, 14, the psalmist notes that Zion constitutes the object of God's desire as a place in which to dwell.

ḥāmad [חָמַד, 2530]

This verb is found on twenty occasions and is translated "desire" or "covet." It is synonymous with ***'āwāh***, above.

ḥāmad is also used to denote coveting in Exod. 20:17; Deut. 5:21 with respect to the tenth commandment. In addition, God forbids his people to covet the gold and silver overlaying the pagan idols from Canaan (cf. Deut. 7:25). Prov. 6:25, 26 issue a somber warning to those who might yield in their desire for the adulteress. As a corollary to the above, punishment for coveting is indicated in the case of Achan, who stole plunder from Jericho in direct violation of God's specific command (cf. Josh. 7:21). Mic. 2:2 also implies judgment against those Israelites who covet the property of others and seize it. Vain desires are also listed in Ps. 39:11; Isa. 1:29. By way of stark contrast, Ps. 19:10 notes that the ordinances of God, his sacred law statutes, are a truly worthy object of desire, for they constitute value that is far greater than fine gold.

Isa. 53:2 uses ***ḥāmad*** in the negative. Here the unattractiveness of the Suffering Servant is graphically depicted in the description of his sufferings. He is one whom people will despise, for there will be nothing about him that will attract the desire of humankind while he remains in his state of humiliation and suffering.

teshûqāh [תְּשׁוּקָה, 8669]

teshûqāh is a rare noun found only three times with the meaning "desire," suggestive of intense longing or craving.

Gen. 3:16 refers to Eve's "desire" for her husband as one of the aspects of the curse placed upon Adam and Eve by God. At first glance it appears that "sexual desire" may be intended; however, the context suggests that this "desire" may well indicate a strong urge to dominate or manipulate her husband — a battle of marital wills. Gen. 4:7 describes how, metaphorically, sin lies in wait for Cain, entertaining a "desire" or "urge" to control him. In Song 7:10, "desire" has an overwhelmingly sexual overtone.

ḥāshaq [חָשַׁק, 2836]

ḥāshaq is a verb found eleven times with the meaning "desire," "set one's heart on."

Sexual "desire" is indicated in Gen. 34:8; Deut. 21:11. God's "desire" for his people, his gracious loving determination to redeem and nurture them, is indicated in Deut. 7:7; 10:15.

Ordinary intent or "desire" to accomplish a task is indicated in 1 Kgs. 9:19; 2 Chr. 8:6.

ḥēpheṣ [חֵפֶץ, 2656]

The noun ***ḥēpheṣ*** occurs about forty times denoting "pleasure," "delight," "desire" in a variety of contexts.

The meaning "desire" in the sense of "want" or "wish" for a particular outcome is indicated in 1 Sam. 18:25; 1 Kgs. 5:8ff.; 9:11; 2 Chr. 9:12, Job 31:16. "Desire" in a general, undefined sense is indicated in 2 Sam. 23:5; Prov. 3:15; 8:11.

ta'awāh [תַּאֲוָה, 8378]

ta'awāh is a noun denoting "desire" or "craving" in both the positive sense of "desire" for good, and the pejorative nuance of "lust."

The deceptive "desire" for all-embracing wisdom to be gained from the tree of the knowledge of good and evil is exposed as a lie in Gen. 3:6ff.

The illegitimate "craving" of personal indulgence is indicated in relation to Israel's desire for food in the wilderness in Num. 11:4; Pss. 78:29ff.; 106:14

General references to morally perverse "desires" are found in Pss. 10:3; 112:10; Prov. 21:25ff.

The positive, godly "desires" of the righteous are noted in Pss. 10:17; 21:2; 38:9; Prov. 10:24; 11:23; 13:12, 19; Isa. 26:8.

NT Words

epithymia [ἐπιθυμία, *1939*]

epithymia is a noun denoting "desire" largely in relation to "inordinate craving" or "lust" as well as legitimate longing.

Christ's "strong desire" to eat the Passover meal with his disciples before his crucifixion is indicated in Luke 22:15.

John 8:44 describes the perverted "desires" of the evil one. References to the immoral "lusts" of the natural human being and the wicked are found in Rom. 1:24; 6:12; 7:7ff.; Gal. 5:16, 24; Eph. 2:3; 4:22; Col. 3:5; 1 Thess. 4:5; 1 Tim. 6:9; 2 Tim. 2:22; 3:6; Titus 2:12; 3:3; Jas. 1:14ff.; 1 Pet. 2:11; 4:2ff.; 2 Pet. 1:4; 2:10, 18; 1 John 2:16ff.; Jude 16ff.

Paul indicates his longing to depart this life and be with God in Phil. 1:23. Other legitimate "desires" are noted in 1 Thess. 2:17.

eudokia [εὐδοκία, *2107*]

eudokia is a noun found nine times with the predominant sense of "good will," "good pleasure." In Rom. 10:1, however, ***eudokia*** denotes Paul's heartfelt "desire" to see his fellow countrymen saved.

epipothēsis [ἐπιπόθησις, *1972*]

epipothēsis is a rare noun denoting "earnest longing" in 2 Cor. 7:7, 11.

epithymeō [ἐπιθυμέω, *1937*]

epithymeō is a verb found in eighteen places meaning "desire," denoting both a legitimate longing as well as a perverse "lusting" or "coveting."

Immoral "lusting" after a woman is noted in Matt. 5:28. "Longing" to gain insight into spiritual truth is indicated in Matt. 13:17; 1 Pet. 1:12. General references to "desire" are found in Luke 15:16; 16:21 in relation to food. See also Rev. 9:6; 1 Tim. 3:1. The "desire" to witness the coming of the Son of Man is noted in Luke 17:22. Christ's "desire" to eat the Passover with his disciples is indicated in Luke 22:15.

Illegitimate "desire" or "coveting" is noted in Acts 20:33; Rom. 7:7; 13:9; 1 Cor. 10:16; Jas. 4:2. Gal. 5:17 refers to the "desires" of the flesh being in conflict with the desires of the Spirit.

oregō [ὀρέγω, *3713*]

oregō is a verb found in three places meaning "desire," with both a positive and negative connotation. 1 Tim. 3:1 affirms that to "desire" the office of bishop is a noble aspiration. 1 Tim. 6:10 refers to the sin of "lusting, craving after" money. The believer's "desire" for a better country (i.e., a heavenly one) is noted in Heb. 11:16.

Additional Notes

The semantic range for "desire" is far too broad in both Hebrew and Greek to draw a comprehensive conclusion about the relationship between the two Testaments concerning this concept. It is clear, however, that desire may be both godly and godless — depending upon one's motivation and the object of one's desire. Unless it is rooted in the person of God and Christ and motivated by a yearning to honor him, desire may be illegitimate and therefore subject to God's judgment.

See Also: → ASK → DELIGHT → JEALOUS → WILL → WILLING → ZEAL

DESOLATE, DESOLATION

OT Words

ḥārēb [חָרֵב, **2717**]

This verb occurs around forty times with the primary meaning "lay waste" in the sense of "making desolate." ***ḥārēb*** also means "to dry up." (→ DRY)

In the large majority of texts, ***ḥārēb*** refers to divine judgment — whether it be destroying Israel's enemies or the people of God themselves. Among the nations that God lays waste are Tyre (cf. Ezek. 26:19); Egypt (cf. Ezek. 29:12); and Edom (cf. Isa. 34:10). General references to the desolation of God's enemies are found in Jer. 50:21; Isa. 42:15; 60:12; Zeph. 3:6. The people of God are likewise not immune from such punishment. Amos 7:9 refers specifically to the desolation of Israel. The prophet Jeremiah warns of the impending desolation of Jerusalem at the hand of God (cf. Jer. 26); as does Ezekiel (cf. Ezek. 6:6; 12:20; 19:7; 26:2). A slight variation on this theme is found in Jer. 2:12, where God invokes a reaction of horror from the heavens at the sins of his people.

The aggression of foreign nations in laying waste their enemies is also indicated by the use of ***ḥārēb***. Assyria is one such example, recorded in Isa. 37:18.

Finally, God will deal with those nations who had made Israel desolate by removing them from his people (cf. Isa. 49:17).

ḥorbāh [חָרְבָּה, **2723**]

This is a noun derived from ***ḥārēb*** (see above). ***ḥorbāh*** also occurs about forty times in the Old Testament with the primary meaning "desolate place," or a "place laid waste." The contexts are very similar to those of ***ḥārēb***.

As expected, the dominant usage of ***ḥorbāh*** also relates to the invoking of divine judgment against both Israel and the enemies of Yahweh. As far as Israel is concerned, Lev. 26:31, 33 prophesy the inevitable devastation of the land and cities of Israel, which will be "made desolate" as a consequence of the people's violation of God's covenant law. Similar judgments against Israel are also found in the following texts: Isa. 5:17; 49:19; Jer. 7:34; 22:5; 44:2, 6, 22; Ezek. 5:14; 33:24; 36:4. Devastation is also prescribed for the enemies of God and his people, including Edom (cf. Jer. 49:13; Ezek. 25:13; 35:4; Mal. 1:4); Tyre (cf. Ezek. 26:20); and Egypt (cf. Ezek. 29:9, 10).

In addition to indicating the phenomenon of divine judgment, ***ḥorbāh*** is also found in the context of God's mercy and blessing, whereby he promises to repair the desolation or devastation of the land of Israel as part of his plan of deliverance and renewal for his people. There is specific mention of this in relation to the renewal of Jerusalem in the wake of the Babylonian exile (cf. Ezra 9:9; Isa. 44:26; 51:3; 58:12; 61:4; Ezek. 36:10, 33). Then, in Dan. 9:2, Daniel himself realizes that the end of the seventy-year desolation of Jerusalem and Judah is near. His reading of Jer. 25 in this regard acts as a catalyst for his prayer which follows — a prayer that beseeches God to bring his promise to fulfillment.

shāmēm [שָׁמֵם, 8074]

This verb is found approximately ninety times throughout the Old Testament. The primary meanings of ***shāmēm*** are "to be desolate (or appalled)"; "to devastate" or "make desolate." It is synonymous with ***ḥārēb*** and ***ḥorbāh***, above.

Once again, divine judgment is at the fore in the usage of this term. Devastation (or desolation) of the land of Canaan is forecast with inevitable certainty as a consequence of the Israelites' disobedience towards God and their rejection of the Mosaic law covenant (e.g., Lev. 26:31ff.; 1 Kgs. 9:8; Jer. 12:11; 33:10; Lam. 1:4; 5:12; Ezek. 6:4; 33:28; Hos. 2:12; Joel 1:17; Amos 7:9; Mic. 6:13; Zech. 7:14). Similarly, the enemies of Israel are also threatened with this devastating punishment: for example, Moab (cf. Num. 21:30); Edom (cf. Jer. 49:17); Babylon (cf. Jer. 50:13); and Egypt (cf. Ezek. 29:12; 32:10ff.). Ps. 69:21 directs the threat against Israel's enemies in general; and Dan. 9:26 implies apocalyptic judgment of desolation against the enemies of God's people.

shāmēm is also used in conjunction with the desolation of Israel brought about by her own enemies (cf. Ps. 79:7; Ezek. 25:3). Jer. 10:25 emphasizes that Israel's enemies who do this will be punished by Yahweh.

The divine promise of renewal or the repair or eradication of desolation is also indicated in certain contexts where ***shāmēm*** is used. Isa. 49:8, 19 is a significant text, linking the prospect of the divine renewal of the land of Israel with the redemptive mission of the Servant of Yahweh. See also Isa. 61:4. In Dan. 9:18, Daniel prays that God might look with mercy on the desolation of Jerusalem, and restore the people to their homeland and their city in accordance with his promise.

Particular mention is made in the book of Daniel of the desolation (i.e., desecration) of the altar in the Jerusalem temple during the period of intense persecution of the Jewish nation at the hands of the infamous Seleucid ruler, Antiochus Epiphanes (c. 170 B.C.) (cf. Dan. 8:13; 9:27; 11:31; 12:11).

An additional semantic element, largely unique to ***shāmēm***, denotes an emotional psychological desolation in various contexts. 2 Sam. 13:20, for example, records the harrowing desolation of Tamar, who was raped by her brother Amnon. The terrible anguish and desolation of Ezra the priestly scribe is recorded in Ezra 9:4, where this leader of the postexilic community of Israel is appalled to discover that many Israelite men had entered into marriage with Gentile women since their return from captivity. Isa. 54:1 promises children for the woman who is desolate and barren. Lam. 3:11 records Jeremiah's desolate lament over the destruction of Jerusalem. For other examples, see Ps. 40:15; Jer. 4:9; Ezek. 20:26; 26:16; 28:19; Dan. 8:27.

shemāmāh [שְׁמָמָה, 8077]

This noun derived from ***shāmēm***, above, occurs about sixty times. The primary meaning of ***shemāmāh*** is "desolation" or "devastation," and the contexts in which it is found are virtually identical to those of ***shāmēm*** (see above).

The desolation of the land of Israel as a consequence of the people's sin is indicated in the majority of occurrences (e.g., Isa. 1:7; 17:9; Jer. 4:27; 9:11; 44:6; Ezek. 6:14; 12:20; 23:33; Joel 2:3; Zeph. 1:13). In Mic. 1:7 there is the prophetic threat that all Israel's idols will be laid waste.

The devastation of the lands or cities of Israel's enemies is also in view as a direct judgment from God: for example, Ai (cf. Josh. 8:28); Babylon (cf. Jer. 25:12; 51:26); Ammon (cf. Jer. 49:2); Egypt (cf. Ezek. 29:9ff.); Edom (cf. Ezek. 35:3ff.); Philistia (cf. Zeph. 2:4); Moab (cf. Zeph. 2:9). Then God decrees universal desolation in Mic. 7:13.

The divine restoration of Israel and the repair of her devastation is indicated in Isa. 62:4; Ezek. 36:34.

Finally, ***shemāmāh*** is used to indicate emotional anguish or desolation at the prospect of the coming judgment of God at the time of the Babylonian exile (cf. Ezek. 7:27).

shô'āh [שׁוֹאָה, 7722]

shô'āh is a noun occurring thirteen times denoting "desolation," "devastation," "destruction" in a variety of contexts.

shô'āh is used adjectivally in certain places to denote ground that is "desolate," or barren, unproductive (cf. Job 30:3; 38:27).

"Desolation" in the sense of "ruin," or "destruction" is indicated in Ps. 35:8; Prov. 3:25; Isa. 47:11 in relation to the fate of the wicked (cf. also Ps. 35:17), and to the threatened "destruction" of the psalmist's soul in Ps. 63:9. The term specifically denotes the divinely instigated "ruin" of the wicked on the Day of the Lord in Isa. 10:3; Zeph. 1:15.

shammāh [שַׁמָּה, 8047]

shammāh is another noun derived from ***shāmēm*** (see above) meaning "desolation" in the sense of "destruction," "devastation" that is brought by Yahweh against both his own people for their rebellion as well against the pagan nations at large (cf. Ps. 46:8; Isa. 5:9; 24:12; Jer. 2:15; 4:7; 25:11; 48:9; 51:29ff.; Hos. 5:9; Joel 1:7; Mic. 6:16; Zeph. 2:15; Zech. 7:14).

yāsham [יָשַׁם, 3456]

yāsham is a verb meaning "become desolate" in relation to the impoverishment of Egypt though famine in Gen. 47:19. Ezek. 6:6 refers to Yahweh "wreaking destruction" on the idolatrous high places of Judah.

shē't [שֵׁאת, 7612]

shē't is a rare noun denoting "ruin" or "desolation," found only in Lam. 3:47 with reference to Yahweh's destruction of Jerusalem through the invasion of the Babylonian army.

NT Words

erēmoō [ἐρημόω, *2049*]

erēmoō is a verb found in five places with the consistent sense of "make desolate," "lay waste," or "bring to ruin."

In Matt. 12:25; Luke 11:17, Christ declares that every kingdom that is divided against itself is guaranteed to "be made desolate, laid waste" by its enemies. God's judgment in "laying waste" the devil and his servants — both individual and corporate — is indicated in Rev. 17:16; 18:17, 19.

erēmōsis [ἐρήμωσις, *2050*]

erēmōsis is a rare term meaning "desolation" in the sense of "desecration," in relation to the pagan altar erected in the Jerusalem temple by the Seleucid ruler, Antiochus Epiphanes (see ***shāmēm,*** above).

It is clear from the occurrences of ***erēmōsis*** in Matt. 24:15; Mark 13:14, where Christ refers to this "abomination of desolation," that this flagrant desecration of the temple functions as an apocalyptic sign, one that will be repeated in the future, signifying the imminence of Christ's return on the final day of God's judgment on the earth. Luke 21:20 refers to the imminent "desolation" (i.e., destruction) of Jerusalem at the hands of the Roman army — an invasion and devastation predicted by Christ during his public ministry.

Additional Notes

The phenomenon of "desolation" is viewed similarly in both the Old and New Testaments, even though the Hebrew terminology is much more extensive. Divine judgment is clearly dominant in the whole semantic range of the Hebrew vocabulary, and the same theme is present in the Greek usage of ***erēmoō*** in the book of Revelation. The "desolation of Jerusalem," noted in Luke 21:20, also draws upon the Old Testament portrayal of the desolation of Israel for maximum theological impact, since the destruction of Jerusalem and the kingdom of Judah at the hands of the Babylonians was such a major catastrophe in the history of Israel. The theme of desolation is, of course, offset by the theme of renewal — whether as the initiative of God in the old covenant that anticipates the new, or as the fulfillment of that divine promise manifested in the person and work of Christ. Renewal, or the removal of desolation, operates at both a corporate as well as an individual level.

See Also: → DESERT → DESTROY

DESPAIR

OT Words

yā'ash **[יָאַשׁ, 2976]**

yā'ash is a verb found six times meaning "despair," in the sense of "be deprived of hope" in 1 Sam. 27:1; Job 6:26; Eccl. 2:20; Isa. 57:10; Jer. 2:25; 18:12.

NT Words

exaporeō [ἐξαπορέω, *1820*]

exaporeō is a rare verb found only in 2 Cor. 1:8; 4:8 with the meaning "despair" in the sense of "give up hope for living."

DESPISE, DESPISER

OT Words

bûz **[בּוּז, 936]**

This is a comparatively rare verb, occurring only eleven times, meaning "despise" or hold in contempt. The bulk of references are found in the Wisdom literature of Proverbs and the Song of Songs.

Prov. 1:7 draws a sharp contrast between wisdom and folly. Whereas the fearful reverencing of God is the foundation of wisdom, the fool despises wisdom and counts it for nothing. Prov. 6:30 mentions contempt for a thief. Folly is also predicated of those who despise their neighbor (cf. Prov. 11:12; 14:21). Prov. 23:22 forbids the despising of one's mother (cf. also Prov. 30:17). Prov. 13:13 warns that despising God's word leads to self-destruction.

Outside Proverbs, Song 8:1 contains the wistful reflection of the beloved that if she were sister to her lover, then she would not be despised for showing affection in public. Then, Zech. 4:10 contains the words: "Who despises the day of small things?" The question here suggests that some of the postexilic community may have held the temple in Jerusalem in low esteem, at least during its reconstruction. Yet on its completion they would still rejoice.

bāzāh **[בָּזָה, 959]**

This verb is synonymous with ***bûz***, above. However, ***bāzāh*** occurs more frequently (approximately forty times) and is found in a wider variety of contexts.

bāzāh is used in a number of places to mean "despise" in the sense of treating someone or something as totally insignificant or worthless. Gen. 25:34, for example, describes Esau's despising his birthright when he gives it to his brother Jacob in return for a bowl of stew. Whenever anyone despises the law of God in such a manner, severe punishment is bound to follow. Num. 15:31 illustrates this in relation to the Israelites in the wilderness. 2 Sam. 12:9 notes how David despised God's law when he committed adultery with Bathsheba and murdered her husband Uriah the Hittite. In 2 Chr. 36:16 Judah's mockery (or despising) of the prophets of Yahweh leads inevitably to exile at the hands of the Babylonians (cf. also Ezek. 16:59; 17:19; 22:8). Prov. 19:16 warns that death will come to those who despise God's word. When God himself is despised and treated with contempt, no less a punishment is in view (cf. 1 Sam. 2:30; Prov. 14:2; Mal. 1:6ff.). Allusions to holding other people in contempt are also quite common — for example, Saul, by his fellow countrymen (1 Sam. 10:27); Goliath, by David (1 Sam. 17:42); Jerusalem, by Sennacherib (2 Kgs. 19:21; Isa. 37:22). See also Neh. 2:19; Esth. 1:17; Ps. 22:6; Ezek. 17:16. In Isa. 53:3 the Suffering Servant of Yahweh is despised by his many enemies — this is a profound prophetic anticipation of the sufferings of Christ on the cross centuries later. In this particular case, ***bāzāh*** indicates a despising amounting to hatred, rather than mere indifference.

When God himself is the subject of ***bāzāh***, two contexts are worthy of note. Firstly, God refuses to despise those whom he loves, and those who worship him with a true heart (cf. Pss. 22:24; 51:17; 69:33; 102:17). Then, as an outworking of his judgment, God causes both the enemies of his people to be despised — for example, Edom (Jer. 41:15; Obad. 2) — as well as the Israelites themselves, on account of their sin (Mal. 2:9).

mā'as **[מָאַס, 3988]**

mā'as is found approximately seventy-five times with a number of meanings, including "despise" (about one-third of its occurrences). Other meanings include "reject," "refuse," which are often linked to the sense of despising. (➠ REJECT)

The contexts in which ***mā'as*** is found are very similar to those of ***bāzāh*** (see above). Whenever God's law is held in contempt, divine punishment inevitably follows (cf. Lev. 26:15, 43; 2 Kgs. 17:5; Isa. 30:12; Ezek. 20:13ff.; Amos 2:4; Jer. 8:9). In Lev. 26:43, 44 it is significant to observe that God's contempt for his people, based on their despising him, will not last forever.

Num. 14:31 records the unusual phenomenon of the Israelites "despising" the land of Canaan. The people failed to enter the land and conquer it as God had instructed them — they therefore treated the land with contempt in that they did not regard it as having the same importance and significance that God did.

Had they done so, they would have trusted in God's promise and not allowed their fear to overwhelm them, thus preventing them from even attempting the conquest. Despising the land, therefore, was equivalent to despising God (cf. also Ps. 106:24).

The despising of God himself is also indicated by the use of ***mā'as***, in 1 Sam. 8:7; 10:9, where Israel chooses a king in a manner that indicates no consideration of God whatsoever.

As ***bāzāh*** above, ***mā'as*** is also found in contexts where God is associated with this attitude. Amos 5:21 states that God despises false worship; Ps. 53:5 affirms that God despises the wicked. In Job 36:5 God is said to despise no one. But it is evident that Elihu here is speaking of God's general attitude towards humankind, in that he holds people responsible for their actions and attitudes. He is obviously not speaking of God's attitude towards those who arrogantly disdain him.

qālal [קָלַל, 7043]

qālal is a verb with a variety of meanings, occurring about eighty times. Prominent among these is the sense of "curse," accounting for around half the occurrences of the term. Other senses include "to be swift," "be trifling, of little account." In three places, ***qālal*** indicates the meaning "despise" in the sense of "treat (someone) with contempt" (cf. Gen. 16:4, 5; 2 Sam. 19:43).

nā'aṣ [נָאַץ, 5006]

The verb ***nā'aṣ*** has the broad meaning "despise," including several different nuances. It occurs in twenty-five places.

The action and attitude of "despising" Yahweh signify "treating him with contempt" in Num. 14:11, 23; 16:30; Deut. 31:20; Ps. 10:13; Isa. 1:4.

Similarly, the "despising" of the Lord's offering (i.e., treating it with contempt) is noted in 1 Sam. 2:17 "Despising the name of the Lord" is equivalent to "blasphemy" in several places. (➡ BLASPHEME) Ps. 107:11 refers to "despising" the words of God in the sense of "rejecting" them. See also Prov. 1:30; 5:12; 15:5; Isa. 5:24; Jer. 23:17 for similar usage.

nā'aṣ also refers to the enemies of God's people "despising" them (viz. treating them with contempt) in Isa. 60:14; Jer. 33:24. Jer. 14:21 contains the prophet's appeal to God not to similarly "despise" his people, for his name's sake.

zûl [זוּל, 2107]

zûl is a rare verb meaning "despise" in the sense of "view with disgust, disdain," referring to the Babylonians' attitude towards the people of Jerusalem (cf. Lam. 1:8).

shā'aṭ [שָׁאַט, 7590]

shā'aṭ is a rare verb found in three places, all referring to the enemies of God's people "despising" them, or viewing them with disdain and treating them contemptuously (cf. Ezek. 16:57; 28:24, 26).

NT Words

exoutheneō [ἐξουθενέω, *1848*]

exoutheneō is a verb found in thirteen places with the general meaning "despise," including several related nuances.

"Despising" others in the sense of "viewing with disdain" is indicated in Luke 18:19; Rom. 14:3, 10; 1 Cor. 1:28. The allied sense of "esteeming people as worthless" is evident in 1 Cor. 6:4. See also 2 Cor. 10:10; 1 Thess. 5:10. The sense of "treat with contempt" is noted in Luke 23:11; 1 Cor. 16:11; Gal. 4:14.

The Old Testament reference to the stone "rejected" by the builders — a messianic allusion — is recorded in Acts 4:11.

kataphroneō [καταφρονέω, *2706*]

kataphroneō is a synonym for ***exoutheneō***, above, meaning "despise" throughout the eleven occurrences of the term.

"Despise" in the sense of "reckon to be of no value or importance" is indicated in Matt. 6:24; Luke 16:13; 1 Tim. 4:12.

The sense of "view with disdain" is indicated in relation to the warning against "despising" little children, keeping them from entering the kingdom of heaven (cf. Matt. 18:10). The same attitude in relation to the mercy of God is indicated in Rom. 2:4. See also 1 Tim. 6:2.

The action of "treating people with contempt" is noted in 1 Cor. 11:22. Treating civil authority with contempt is indicated in 2 Pet. 2:10.

Heb. 12:2 refers to Christ "despising" the shame of the cross, indicating his determination to "set it at naught," emptying it of its potency.

periphroneō [περιφρονέω, *4065*]

periphroneō is a rare verb found only in Titus 2:15 in relation to Paul's exhortation to his young protégé not to allow anyone to "despise" him — that is, to disregard him, or view him as unimportant.

atimos [ἄτιμος, *820*]

atimos is an adjectival form meaning "without honor" in relation to a prophet in Matt. 13:57; Mark 6:4. 1 Cor. 12:23 refers to private parts of the body that are deemed "less honorable." The sense of "being despised" (i.e., held in disrepute) is indicated in 1 Cor. 4:10.

atheteō [ἀθετέω, *114*]

atheteō is a verb with the primary meaning "reject." In Heb. 10:28, however, the term refers to the act of "despising" the law of Moses — "violating" it, or treating it with contempt through disobedience.
(→ REJECT)

Additional Notes

While the Hebrew vocabulary for "despising" embraces both a divine and human perspective, the phenomenon is less complex in the New Testament. The Greek terminology for "despise" focuses on the phenomenon as a highly undesirable attitude to adopt with respect to other people. Only rarely does it refer to despising God or his activity (e.g., Rom. 2:4). In contrast, the Old Testament frequently warns of the serious consequences of despising either God himself or that which he reveals to humankind.

DESTROY, DESTROYER, DESTRUCTION

OT Words

'ābad [**אָבַד, 6**]

This verb is found approximately two hundred times, meaning "perish" and "destroy" (→ PERISH)

The most common usage of ***'ābad*** relates to the destruction of the enemies of God and Israel. In the first instance, this relates specifically to places like Egypt (cf. Exod. 10:7; Deut. 11:4; Jer. 46:8); and the cities of Canaan (cf. Num. 24:19; 33:52; Deut. 9:3); as well as to people such as the Persians who were attacked and destroyed — at least in part — by the Jews throughout the Persian Empire (cf. Esth. 9:6, 12). Jer. 1:10 contains, among other things, the prophet's commission to pronounce the divine judgment of destruction against all who oppose Yahweh and his purposes (cf. also Jer. 12:17; 31:28). General references to this broad theme are found also in Job 12:23; Pss. 5:6; 143:12; Jer. 18:7; 51:55; Ezek. 25:16; Mic. 5:10; Zeph. 2:5.

'ābad also refers to divine judgment on those Israelites who sin under the law. These violations all involve capital punishment (cf. Lev. 23:30; Deut. 7:10, 20, 24; Josh. 7:7). Deut. 28:51, 63 specifically affirms that God invokes such harsh disciplinary measures under the curse sanctions of the covenant. Idol worship is also strictly forbidden under the law, and all who engage in such activity are likewise destroyed (i.e., executed), along with the idolatrous high places (cf. Deut. 12:2, 3; 2 Kgs. 10:19; 19:18; 21:3; Ezek. 30:13). God also uses the Babylonians to eventually destroy Jerusalem and Judah for centuries of willful disobedience against him.

'ābad is also used in contexts where the people of Israel suffer at the hands of her enemies (cf. Haman's plot to destroy the Jews; although this scheme was a spectacular failure, Esth. 3:9, 13; 4:7ff.; 7:4; 8:5, 11; 9:24). Persecution of the godly at the hands of the wicked is recorded in Ps. 119:95. The references in Jer. 23:1; Ezek. 22:27, where the people of Israel suffer terrible treatment from their own leaders — who are cruel and perverse, lacking in compassion and justice — are of particular interest.

'ābad also refers to destruction in the sense of murder or slaughter in 2 Kgs. 11:1; 13:7.

kārat [**כָּרַת, 3772**]

This is a very significant term found about three hundred times with the primary sense of "cut" or "cut off." (→ CUT) In the former sense, ***kārat*** indicates the initiating and ratifying of a covenant bond (i.e., "cut a covenant"). In the sense of "cut off," however, the meaning is most often "destroy." The invocation of the covenant sanction demands, in certain cases, the "cutting off" or execution of the Israelite man or woman who willfully rebels against the law of the covenant. In some contexts, ***kārat*** may also refer to banishment (e.g., Num. 19:13, 20).

kārat describes the "cutting off" (i.e., execution, destruction) of law breakers in Israel for various offenses, whether prescribed or actual — for example, Gen. 17:14 (failure to circumcise); Exod. 31:14 (Sabbath violation); Lev. 18:29 (sexual immorality and idolatry); Ezek. 14:8; Hos. 8:4 (idolatry); Num. 9:13 (failure to keep Passover; but note Josh. 5). See also Exod. 12:15, 19; 30:38; Lev. 7:20ff.; 19:8; 20:3ff.; 22:3; 23:29; Mal. 2:12.

Not only are individuals threatened with being cut off; the punishment is also applied to the nation of Israel under the terms of the covenant curse sanctions, although such destruction is never absolute (cf. Isa. 9:14; 48:19; Jer. 7:28; 44:7ff.; Ezek. 14:13ff.; Zeph. 3:6, 7; Zech. 13:2). Even the destruction of cattle in Israel is included in this category (cf. Lev. 26:22).

Pagan nations are also frequently threatened with and suffer the same fate (e.g., Deut. 12:29; 19:1; Josh. 23:4; Judg. 4:24 — all relating to the land of Canaan). The wicked in general are so designated in Pss. 34:16; 109:13ff.; Isa. 10:7; 29:20; Jer. 47:4; Ezek. 25:13ff.; Amos 1:5, 8; 2:3; Obad. 9ff.; Mic. 5:9ff.; Nah. 1:14ff.; Zeph. 1:3ff.; Zech. 9:6. Linked to the destruction of the nations in this manner is the "cutting off" of pagan idols (cf. Exod. 34:13; Judg. 6:25ff.; Lev. 26:30).

In a positive sense, ***kārat*** is also found in contexts where God promises not to destroy by cutting off — for example, the divine promise to never again destroy the world by floodwaters (Gen. 9:11). See also Num. 4:18; Isa. 48:9; Zech. 14:2 (a promise of preservation for the remnant of God's people).

kārat also refers to the "cutting off" of one's name in Israel as a consequence of having no male descendants (cf. Ruth 4:10; 1 Sam. 24:21; 1 Kgs. 14:10; 21:21; 2 Kgs. 9:8).

The destruction or slaughter of godly individuals at the hands of their enemies is also indicated by the use of ***kārat*** (cf. 1 Kgs. 18:4; Jer. 11:19).

Finally, there is a very important use of ***kārat*** in Dan. 9:26, where the Messiah is prophetically described as one who will be "cut off." This is not an absolute judgment, but a necessary act of atonement in order that God's forgiveness and redemption might be applied to his people.

shāḥat [שָׁחַת, 7843]

This verb occurs about 140 times with the principal meaning "destroy," and the allied senses of "corrupt," "ruin," or "decay."

Destruction by God as a punishment for sin is indicated in a number of contexts where ***shāḥat*** is found. For example, universal destruction is in view in Gen. 6:13, 17. The destruction of Sodom and Gomorrah is described in Gen. 13:10; 18:28ff.; 19:13ff. The terrible fate of the godless nations is also depicted in Exod. 12:23 (Egypt); Jer. 48:18 (Moab); Jer. 51:1, 11, 20 (Babylon); Ezek. 26:4 (Tyre). Israel is also marked out for destruction on account of her rebellion against Yahweh (cf. Num. 32:15; 1 Chr. 21:12; Hos. 13:9); as is Jerusalem (cf. 2 Sam. 24:16; 2 Chr. 36:19); and Judah (cf. 2 Chr. 35:21; 25:16; Jer. 4:7; 6:5; 22:7; Lam. 2:5ff.; Ezek. 5:16; 20:17; 43:3).

In contrast, ***shāḥat*** also occurs in contexts where destruction is either abolished or withheld as a consequence of divine mercy. For example, in Gen. 9:11, 15 God promises to never again destroy the world by flood. There are also a number of divine guarantees not to destroy the Israelite people, even though such a reprieve would not last forever (cf. Deut. 4:31; 2 Kgs. 8:19; 13:23; 2 Chr. 21:7). Occasionally, there are pleas directed to God not to destroy his people (cf. Deut. 9:26; 10:10; Ps. 106:23). God's compassion comes explicitly to the fore in a number of places where he forgoes his threatened destruction of the nation in response to his people's repentance (cf. 2 Chr. 12:7, 12; Ps. 78:38). Sometimes God also cuts short their punishment for the sake of the faithful remnant (cf. Isa. 65:8; Hos. 11:9).

At the human level, attacks on Israel from the surrounding nations are recorded as acts of destruction — for example, the Midianites (cf. Judg. 6:4, 5; 2 Chr. 24:23); Syria (cf. 2 Chr. 24:23); Assyria (cf. Isa. 36:10; 37:12 — threats only). Jer. 12:10 records the destruction of the Israelite people by her own godless and vicious rulers. Finally, 2 Sam. 11:1 records the destruction of the Ammonite nation by the armies of Israel.

There is a metaphorical use of ***shāḥat*** in the book of Proverbs, where immorality is said to bring about self-destruction (cf. Prov. 6:32), and a spiteful tongue brings harmful destruction in its wake (cf. Prov. 11:9).

ḥāram [חָרַם, 2763]

This verb occurs approximately fifty times with the principal meaning "to (utterly) destroy," or "put to the ban," "devote," "exterminate."

In some contexts, ***ḥāram*** indicates capital punishment for any Israelite who violates specific laws — he is to be "utterly destroyed" (cf. Exod. 22:20, Deut. 13:15 [idolatry]). Lev. 27:29 contains a general indictment for such violations where there is no possibility for a remission of sentence (cf. also Judg. 21:11). This condemnation of individuals is extended to the nation as a whole in Jer. 25:9, where ***ḥāram*** depicts God's judgment on Judah at the hands of the Babylonians in terms of total devastation. One positive use of ***ḥāram*** is found in Lev. 27:28, where the term is used in the expression "devoting an offering to the Lord," indicating that the offering may not be redeemed.

ḥāram is also used to depict God's judgment of annihilation upon pagan nations — for example Egypt (Isa. 11:15); all nations (Isa. 34:2); Babylon (Jer. 50:21, 26; 51:3). The destruction of the cities and people of Canaan is frequently alluded to by the use of this term (cf. Num. 21:2, 31; Deut. 2:34 [Heshbon]; Josh. 2:10 [Amorites]; Josh. 6:21 [Jericho]; Josh. 10:1 [Ai]). The general destruction of Canaan is alluded to in Josh. 10:28; 11:11ff.; Judg. 1:17.

In addition, ***ḥāram*** refers to the destruction inflicted by warring nations upon their enemies — for example, Assyria (cf. 2 Kgs. 19:11; 2 Chr. 32:14); Ammon and Moab (cf. 2 Chr. 20:23). In Dan. 11:44 there is a likely symbolic reference to the aggression of Antiochus Epiphanes towards all who oppose him.

Finally, ***ḥāram*** indicates the devoting of plunder to Yahweh — the plunder of Jericho (Josh. 6:18), and the plunder of all nations (Mic. 4:13). The latter text is a metaphorical allusion to the universal dominion of God's kingdom.

ḥērem [חֵרֶם, 2764]

ḥērem is the noun derived from ***ḥāram***, above. The precise sense of this term is difficult to express in one word, but the underlying meaning indicates "that which is devoted" (i.e., to God). It occurs either in the positive sense of being dedicated to him, or in the negative sense of being devoted to destruction, usually as the consequence of an indictment or condemnation by God. The latter sense is more frequent. ***ḥērem*** occurs around twenty times with these meanings.

In its positive sense ***ḥērem*** refers to offerings dedicated to the Lord (cf. Lev. 27:21, 28). Num. 18:14 outlines the privileges of the Aaronic priesthood — they are to be the recipients of "the devoted things" in the land of Canaan (cf. also Ezek. 44:29). However, Josh. 7:1 contains the significant, yet disturbing, example of Achan, who violated "the ban" (***ḥērem***) placed on the plunder of Jericho. This booty had been devoted to Yahweh and was not to be taken by any Israelite. Achan paid for his sin with his life (cf. Josh. 7:11; 22:20; 1 Chr. 2:7; 1 Sam. 15:21).

In a predominantly negative sense, ***ḥērem*** refers first of all to those Israelites "devoted to destruction." Such people were executed under the curse sanctions of the Mosaic law covenant (cf. Lev. 27:29; 1 Kgs. 20:42). The "ban" was also placed on places like Jericho (cf. Josh. 6:17, 18); Edom (cf. Isa. 34:5); and even Israel herself (cf. Isa. 43:20).

Finally, Zech. 14:11 records a vision of renewal in which the curse of total destruction in Jerusalem shall be removed forever.

shāmad [שָׁמַד, 8045]

This verb is synonymous with ***ḥāram*** and ***ḥērem***, above. ***shāmad*** occurs ninety times, and its primary meaning is "destroy" or "annihilate."

First of all, ***shāmad*** refers to the violent destruction of individuals through violent attacks on their person (cf. Gen. 34:30; 2 Sam. 14:7ff.; 21:5).

The predominant usage of this verb centers on both the threat and enacting of punishment handed down by God to all those who oppose his will and rebel against him. It concerns firstly those people of Israel who suffer the covenant curse in this regard as a result of their sin (cf. Lev. 26:30; Deut. 4:3, 26; 7:4; 9:8; 28:20ff.; Josh. 7:12; 23:15). A similar divine judgment is invoked against the apostate kings of the northern kingdom of Israel (e.g., 1 Kgs. 13:34; 15:29; 16:12; 2 Kgs. 10:17, 28). See also Hos. 10:8; Isa. 48:19. In Amos 9:8, however, this punishment will not be absolute — the house of Jacob will be spared. Conversely, Yahweh's annihilation of the enemies of Israel is also indicated by the use of ***shāmad***. In this case, Canaan is specifically indicted (e.g., Deut. 2:21ff.; 7:23ff.; 9:3, 14; Josh. 9:12; 11:14, 20; 1 Chr. 5:25); as are the surrounding nations (cf. 2 Sam. 22:38; Jer. 48:8; Ezek. 25:7; 32:12; Amos 2:9; Mic. 5:14; Hag. 2:2). Yahweh instructs the Israelites to destroy all idolatrous images in Canaan (cf. Num. 33:52; Deut. 12:30).

shāmad also refers to the destructive aggression of various nations towards their enemies (cf. Deut. 2:12; Dan. 11:44). In particular it refers to Haman's murderous, though ultimately vain, plot to destroy the entire race of Jewish people in Esth. 3:6, 13; 4:8; 7:4. In addition, the term refers to the revenge of the Jewish people upon their Persian enemies in Esth. 8:11.

'abaddôn [אֲבַדּוֹן, 11]

This is a rare noun, occurring six times with the meaning "destruction," or "place of destruction." It is used exclusively in a metaphorical sense as a partner for death, Sheol, or the grave (cf. Job 26:6; 28:22; 31:12; Ps. 88:11; Prov. 15:11; 27:20).

shōd [שֹׁד, 7701]

This noun occurs about twenty-five times with the meaning "destruction," "ruin."

It is used, for example, in the poetic context of Job 5:21, 22. In Isa. 13:6; Joel 1:15, ***shōd*** refers to the Day of the Lord judgment against Babylon. And, like terms discussed above, ***shōd*** also indicates divine judgment in the "destruction" of both Israel (cf. Isa. 51:19; Hos. 7:13); and Moab (cf. Jer. 48:3). Finally, ***shōd*** is predicated of both Israel and Judah in Jer. 6:7; Hab. 1:3, where God's people are condemned for their violent and destructive ways.

sheber **[שֶׁבֶר, 7667]**

sheber is found in about forty places, meaning "destruction" in about half of these occurrences.

It is used metaphorically of personal calamity in Prov. 16:8; 17:19; 18:12. The principal focus of the term, however, lies in the phenomenon of divine destruction for both Israel and the nations for their sinfulness. Israel's fate is indicated in this regard in Isa. 51:7; 59:7; Jer. 4:6; 6:1; and the similar destruction of the nations is mentioned in Isa. 15:5; Jer. 48:3, 5; 50:22; 51:54. In Isa. 60:18, however, ***sheber*** has a positive connotation where Israel's deliverance from destruction is in view. Finally, in Lam. 2:11; 3:47, 48; 4:10, ***sheber*** refers to the destruction of Jerusalem at the time of the Babylonian exile.

nātaṣ **[נָתַץ, 5422]**

nātaṣ is a verb found approximately forty times with the underlying sense of "destroy" and the specific meanings "break down," "throw down," as well as related nuances.

Yahweh's instructions to his people to "tear down" the Canaanite altars, or high places, are recorded in Exod. 34:13; Deut. 7:5; 12:3; Judg. 2:2. The action of "tearing down" these altars is noted in Judg. 6:28ff.; 2 Kgs. 10:27; 11:18; 23:7ff.; 2 Chr. 23:17; 31:1ff.

"Breaking in pieces" is indicated in Lev. 11:35 in relation to household utensils.

The "tearing, pulling down" of buildings is indicated in Lev. 14:45; Judg. 8:9, 17; 2 Chr. 36:19; Isa. 22:10. Divine judgment in relation to this action is noted in Jer. 4:26; 33:4; 39:8; 52:14; Ezek. 16:39; 26:9, 12. See also Nah. 1:6. The metaphorical sense of God "tearing someone down," in the context of causing him anguish, is indicated in Ps. 52:5.

The prophetic mandate to "pull, or break down" kingdoms as part of God's program of divine justice, and also involving God himself, is noted in Jer. 1:10; 18:7.

sāphāh **[סָפָה, 5595]**

sāphāh is a verb found in twenty places meaning "destroy" or "consume," primarily with reference to divine judgment. For example, Abraham questions God in relation to any godly inhabitant that may have lived in Sodom: "Will you destroy the righteous along with the wicked?" (cf. Gen. 18:23, 24).

God "destroying" or "consuming" the wicked is indicated in Gen. 19:15, 17; Num. 16:26. Such "destruction" is also predicated of God's people in 1 Sam. 12:25.

"Destruction" by one's enemies is noted in 1 Chr. 21:12.

māḥāh **[מָחָה, 4229]**

māḥāh is a verb with the underlying sense of "destroy," incorporating related nuances such as "wipe out," "obliterate."

God's intention to "blot out" humankind from the face of the earth on account of their sin is indicated in Gen. 6:7; 7:4.

The action of God in "destroying" the wicked is recorded in Gen. 7:23; and his declared intention to do so is found in Exod. 17:14; Deut. 9:14; 25:19.

Moses' extraordinary offer to have his name "blotted out" from the divine record of the godly for the sake of his people the Israelites is indicated in Exod. 32:32, 33. Elsewhere, the expression "to blot out someone's name from under heaven" is indicative of a divine destruction (cf. Deut. 29:20; Pss. 9:5; 69:28). It is also used in relation to Israel's destiny in 2 Kgs. 14:27.

References to being "blotted out" also metaphorically indicate the tragic consequence of having no heirs to carry on the family name in Israel (cf. Judg. 21:17).

Appealing to God to have one's sins "blotted out" is recorded in Ps. 51:1, 9. Divine refusal to do this is noted in Ps. 109:14; and Isa. 43:25 records his promise to act thus. See also Isa. 44:22; Jer. 18:23.

NT Words

apollymi **[ἀπόλλυμι, *622*]**

apollymi is a verb found nearly ninety times with the primary meaning "perish," "lose," "destroy."
(→ LOSE → PERISH)

The meaning "destroy," in the sense of "kill," is indicated in relation to Herod's plan to eradicate the infant Jesus (cf. Matt. 2:13). It is also used in relation to the Pharisees' attempt to have Jesus killed (cf. Matt. 12:14; 27:20; Mark 3:6; Luke 19:47). The prospect of God "destroying" both body and soul in hell is noted in Matt. 10:28. Luke 17:27 refers to the Noahic flood having "destroyed" the inhabitants of the earth.

General references to people being "destroyed" (i.e., killed) are found in Matt. 21:41; 22:7; Mark 9:22; Luke 6:9; Jas. 4:12. Divine judgment on the rebellious Israelites in the wilderness is indicated in 1 Cor. 10:9 with reference to their being "destroyed" by serpents. See also Jude 5.

Christ "destroying" or "eliminating" demons is indicated in Mark 1:24; Luke 4:34. ***apollymi*** also refers to "destroying" property in John 10:10.

God's promise to "destroy" (i.e., render null and void) the wisdom of the wise is recorded in 1 Cor. 1:19.

lyō [λύω, *3089*]

lyō is a verb found about forty times, meaning "loose," "release." Once, in 1 John 3:8, it refers to the Son of God "destroying" the works of the devil.

katalyō [καταλύω, *2647*]

The verb ***katalyō*** means "destroy," in addition to related nuances, for most of the seventeen occurrences of the term.

Christ denies having come to earth in order to "destroy" (i.e., "abolish") the law and the prophets — rather, he came to fulfill them (cf. Matt. 5:17).

Christ prophesies that the temple will be "destroyed" or "thrown down" in Matt. 24:2; 26:61; 27:40; Mark 13:2; 14:58; 15:29; Luke 21:6; Acts 6:14.

A warning against "destroying" the work of God, nullifying its impact, is issued in Rom. 14:20. See also Gal. 2:18.

olothreuō [ὀλοθρεύω, *3645*]

olothreuō is a rare verb found only once, used in a participial form with reference to the angel of death as the "destroyer" of the Egyptian firstborn (cf. Heb. 11:28).

phtheirō [φθείρω, *5351*]

phtheirō is a verb with the predominant sense of "corrupt" for most of the eight occurrences of the term. (→ CORRUPT) However, 1 Cor. 3:17 warns against anyone who might want to "destroy" the temple — God would "destroy" such a person himself.

diaphtheirō [διαφθείρω, *1311*]

diaphtheirō is a variant form of ***phtheirō***, above, occurring six times with the meanings "corrupt" and "destroy." (→ CORRUPT)

Rev. 8:9 refers to "destroying" ships, and Rev. 11:18 to "destroying" the earth.

olethros [ὄλεθρος, *3639*]

olethros is a noun found in four places, denoting "destruction" in each of them.

The "destruction" of the flesh in relation to church discipline is noted in 1 Cor. 5:5. The "destruction" of the wicked, implying eternal judgment, is noted in 1 Thess. 5:3; 2 Thess. 1:9; 1 Tim. 6:9.

apōleia [ἀπώλεια, *684*]

apōleia is a noun denoting "ruin," "destruction" for most of the twenty occurrences of the term.

Eternal "destruction" visited on the ungodly is indicated in Matt. 7:13; Rom. 9:22; Phil. 1:28; 3:19; 1 Tim. 6:19; Heb. 10:39; 2 Pet. 2:1ff. In particular, the final "destruction" of Satan and his minions is indicated in 2 Thess. 2:3; Rev. 17:8, 11.

portheō [πορθέω, *4199*]

portheō is a rare verb meaning "destroy" in relation to Paul's attempt to eradicate the infant Christian church prior to his conversion (cf. Gal. 1:13, 23).

Additional Notes

The semantic field for the concept of "destroy" and "destruction" is a very broad one in both the Old and New Testaments. Because of the variety of both Greek and Hebrew terms that indicate various shades of meaning for "destroy," it is impossible to assign precise equivalence for any two terms. Two significant similarities, however, emerge. Both Testaments emphasize "destruction" as the consequence of a divine judgment against sin — whether it be the transgression of God's own people, or that of the enemies of God. In the Old Testament, this destruction is specifically viewed as the curse sanction of the covenant.

"Destruction" is viewed in both Testaments in a positive light when considered as the process by which evil or sin is eradicated. In the Old Testament, such destruction is directed against people or objects (such as idols). In the New Testament, however, this "destruction" culminates in the eradication of sin and death, and of the devil himself (see esp. the book of Revelation).

It is evident that such a thorough and radical removal of evil from the world can only come about by the sovereign initiative, love, and power of God. Again, what is begun in the Old Testament is brought to perfect fulfillment in the New through the person and work of Jesus Christ — God's supreme agent of destruction.

See Also: → ABOLISH

DETERMINE

OT Words

kālāh [כָּלָה, **3615**]

kālāh is a common verb found about two hundred times with the primary senses of "finish," "consume," "end," as well as a number of related nuances. One of these nuances is "to determine," in the sense of "plan a course of action" (cf. 1 Sam. 20:7, 9; 25:17; Esth. 7:7).

yā'aṣ [יָעַץ, 3289]

yā'aṣ is a verb occurring eighty times with the predominant sense of "advise," "counsel," as well as several related nuances. One of these nuances is the sense of "determine," found only in 2 Chr. 25:16; Isa. 19:17 — both of which speak of divine "determination" in the context of punishment.

ḥāraṣ [חָרַץ, 2782]

ḥāraṣ is a verb occurring twelve times, meaning "decree," "determine" in about half of these occurrences.

Job 14:5 refers to a mortal's days as "determined." Yahweh decrees "destruction" against Israel for rebelling against him in Isa. 10:22, 23; 28:22. Similarly, divine destruction is "decreed" against the enemies of God in Dan. 9:27; 11:36. A more general reference to destruction "determined" by God refers to an indefinite time in Dan. 9:26.

ḥātak [חָתַךְ, 2852]

ḥātak is a rare verb occurring only in Dan. 9:24 with reference to God "having determined" a metaphorical period of seventy weeks as the duration for the outworking of his plan of salvation for his people. The meaning "determined" suggests a precisely-defined period (perhaps symbolic) set in motion by God himself.

NT Words

horizō [ὁρίζω, *3724*]

horizō is a verb found in eight places meaning "determine" in relation to exercising sovereign divine purpose and intent.

The handing over of Christ to death by crucifixion, and his subsequent resurrection and ascension to glory, resulting in his return to heavenly power and authority, are a series of events "determined" or "decreed" by the explicit intention and plan of God, indicated in Luke. 22:22; Acts 2:23; 10:42; 17:31; Rom. 1:4. The divine "determination" of the boundaries and circumstances of humankind is noted in Acts 17:26. In Heb. 4:7, God is said to have "determined" or "set" a certain day for the proclamation of the gospel in a call for repentance and the expression of saving faith.

proorizō [προορίζω, *4309*]

proorizō is a significant verb found in seven places meaning "predetermine," "foreordain," or "predestine" — relating to God's sovereign purposes in relation to humankind.

General references to God's "predetermined" purposes and plan are found in Acts 4:28; Eph. 1:11. The action of God in "predetermining" people for salvation is noted in Rom. 8:29, 30; Eph. 1:5. The secret wisdom of God "decreed" before the beginning of time and now revealed to God's people in Christ is noted in 1 Cor. 2:7.

Additional Notes

The vocabulary for "determine" in both Old and New Testaments most significantly refers to the sovereign purposes of God.

In the Old Testament such purposes are primarily linked to judgment on the wicked, although Israel is also included. However, the Dan. 9 reference to the "seventy weeks" is clearly a broader divine "determination" involving the climactic revelation of the Messiah as the crowning point of God's plan of salvation for his people. However, divine judgment in a negative sense is also implied in the broader context of the outworking of this prophecy.

In the New Testament, the vocabulary expressing the phenomenon of divine "determination," including "predestination" or "foreordination," embraces the entire redemptive plan of God that culminates in the person and work of the Messiah Jesus Christ. In particular, it is Christ's work of atonement and subsequent role as universal judge and King that constitutes the focal point of God's "predetermined" purpose for his people and humankind in general.

See Also: → JUDGE

DETEST → ABHOR → ABOMINABLE

DEVIL

NT Words

diabolos [διάβολος, *1228*]

diabolos is the sole term denoting "the devil" in the New Testament as the prince of demonic beings. This meaning is evident for most of the nearly forty occurrences of the term. (→ DEMON)

A number of references describe the forty-day temptation of Christ at the outset of his public ministry in the hands of the devil (cf. Matt. 4:5ff.; Luke 4:2ff.).

The devil is described as the archenemy of the people of God in Matt. 13:39; Luke 8:12; Eph. 4:27;

6:11; 2 Tim. 2:26; Jas. 4:7; 1 Pet. 5:8; Rev. 2:10; 12:9, 12. He is also described as "the father" of unbelievers in John 8:44; Acts 13:10. See also John 13:2; Eph. 4:27.

The ultimate fate of the devil, as one tormented in the lake of eternal fire, is noted in Matt. 25:41; Rev. 20:10; and implied in 1 Tim. 3:6; 1 John 3:8ff. See also Rev. 20:2.

The devil is described as the great spiritual oppressor of humankind in Acts 10:38; Heb. 2:14; Jude 9.

General reference to "devil" is found in John 6:70.

diabolos is also translated "slanderer" in 1 Tim. 3:11; 2 Tim. 3:3; Titus 2:3.

See Also: ➞ SATAN

DEVOUR ➞ EAT

DEVOUT

NT Words

eulabēs [εὐλαβής, *2126*]

eulabēs is an adjective meaning "devout" in all three occurrences of the term. It describes those who are godly, whose lives are characterized by wholehearted, pure worship of God (cf. Luke 2:25; Acts 2:5; 8:2).

eusebēs [εὐσεβής, *2152*]

eusebēs is an adjectival form synonymous with ***eulabēs***, above, referring to "devout" believers in Acts 10:2, 7; 22:12; 2 Pet. 2:9.

sebomai [σέβομαι, *4576*]

sebomai is a verb meaning "worship" for the majority of the ten occurrences of the term. On three occasions the term is used in the participial nominal sense of "God-fearing ones," the "devout" (cf. Acts 13:43, 50; 17:4, 17).

See Also: ➞ HOLINESS ➞ RIGHTEOUS ➞ SAINT

DIADEM ➞ CROWN

DIE, DEAD, DYING

OT Words

mûṯ [מוּת, **4191**]

This is a common verb, occurring around 850 times. ***mûṯ*** is translated "die," which is the primary meaning of the word; but it can also have the causative sense of "slay" or "put to death." The term is used in a number of different contexts.

mûṯ is first used in the context of the garden of Eden and the account of humankind's rebellion against God. Gen. 2:17; 3:3, 4 warn that those who disobey God will die. The implication is that human beings will experience both a physical and a spiritual demise.

There are also a considerable number of references to death by natural causes, especially in the pentateuchal narratives of the patriarchs (e.g., Gen. 5:5ff.; 9:29; 42:2; 50:5ff.; Exod. 2:25; Num. 6:9; Deut. 2:16; 10:6; Josh. 24:29; Judg. 8:32). Accidental death (i.e., manslaughter) is also mentioned in Josh. 20:9. Reflections on the meaninglessness, or arbitrariness, of death are found in Job and Ecclesiastes (e.g., Job 4:21; 14:10, 14; 36:14; Eccl. 2:16; 4:2; 7:17; 9:3ff.).

The overwhelming majority of texts with the word ***mûṯ*** refer to death as a consequence of specific circumstances. First of all, death is portrayed as a specific judgment of God against the sin of humankind. For example, the flood (Gen. 7:22); the Egyptian plagues, including the death of the firstborn at the final "Passover judgment" (Exod. 9:19; 11:5; 12:30); the slaying of the Egyptian army at the Re(e)d Sea (cf. Exod. 14:30; Lev. 27:29 [Canaanites]); Sennacherib's Assyrian army (2 Kgs. 19:35; Isa. 37:36). General indictments against the wicked, calling for their death, are found a number of times in the Prophets (e.g., Isa. 11:4; 14:30; 51:6; 66:4; Ezek. 28:8, 10). Such a judgment is also directed against God's people (e.g., Num. 26:19; Isa. 22:2; 65:15; Jer. 11:22; 44:12; Ezek. 3:19; Hos. 2:3; 9:16; 13:1; Amos 7:11, 17; 1 Kgs. 14:11; 16:4; 22:37; 2 Kgs. 1:4; 17:26).

Death is also depicted as a divine punishment, whether it be threatened or actual, for the specific crime of violating God's laws. References to death for disobedience in general are found in Exod. 19:12; 28:35; 21:12, 36; 30:20ff.; Lev. 8:35; 10:2, 6; 16:2. Capital punishment is invoked for the following offenses: Sabbath-breaking (cf. Exod. 31:14, 15; 35:2; Num. 15:35, 36); defiling the tabernacle (cf. Lev. 15:31; Num. 1:51; 4:15ff.; 17:13; 19:13); sexual immorality of all kinds (cf. Lev. 19:20; 20:10ff.; Deut. 22:21ff.); idolatry (cf. Lev. 20:2ff.; Deut. 13:5ff.; 17:5ff.); cursing or rebelling against one's parents (cf. Lev. 20:9; Deut. 21:21); blasphemy (cf. Lev. 24:16); grumbling against God (cf. Num. 21:6); and false prophecy (cf. Deut. 18:20; Jer. 28:16). In addition, God invokes death as a punishment against his people for willful disobedience of his law in general (e.g., 1 Sam. 4:11ff. [Hophni and Phinehas]; 1 Sam. 31:5 [Saul]; 2 Sam. 18:15 [Absalom];

Deut. 4:22 [Moses]; Ezek. 18:4ff.). In the book of Proverbs, death is also prescribed for folly on the part of those who despise God and his word (cf. Prov. 5:23; 10:21; 15:10; 19:16).

God also prescribes the slaughter of the Canaanites under the curse sanctions of the Mosaic covenant for their idolatrous rejection of him (cf. Josh. 10:11; 11:7; Judg. 1:7; 3:25; 4:21ff.). The fate of the Philistines, and others, is determined in a similar way (cf. 1 Sam. 14:13, 39ff.; 15:3; 17:35ff.).

Death is also indicated as the consequence of human action and initiatives, such as murder or execution (e.g., Gen. 26:11; 37:18; Exod. 1:16; Judg. 9:49; 1 Sam. 19:11, 15; 22:16ff.; 2 Sam. 11:5; 13:28; 1 Kgs. 21:10).

mût also refers to the death of animals during the course of the Egyptian plagues (cf. Exod. 7:18ff.; 8:13; 9:6ff., 19).

Finally, Job 1:19 mentions death by the hand of Satan.

gāwa' [גָּוַע, 1478]

gāwa' is a verb meaning "die," "perish" throughout the nearly twenty occurrences of the term.

References to people dying as the direct result of God's purpose in judgment are found in Gen. 6:17; 7:21; Josh. 22:20; Zech. 13:8.

General references to "dying" from natural causes are found in Gen. 25:8, 17; 49:33; Num. 20:29; Job 3:11; Ps. 104:29; Lam. 1:19. Fear of dying is indicated in Num. 17:13.

NT Words

thnēskō [θνήσκω, *2348*]

thnēskō is a verb occurring fifteen times with the meaning "die," "be dead."

References to people who are dead include Matt. 2:20; Mark 15:44; Luke 7:12; 8:49; John 11:21, 39ff.; 12:1; 19:33; Acts 14:19; 25:19.

1 Tim. 5:6 refers metaphorically to the pleasure-seeking women who had rendered themselves spiritually insensitive "being dead."

apothnēskō [ἀποθνήσκω, *599*]

apothnēskō is a common verb meaning "die," "be dead," "perish" throughout the more than one hundred occurrences of the term, and in a variety of significant contexts.

General references to "perishing," "dying" are found in relation to animals (Matt. 8:32; Rev. 16:3); and to people (Matt. 9:24; Mark 5:35ff.; Luke 8:52ff.; 20:28ff.; John 6:49ff.; 8:52ff.; Acts 9:37; Rom. 7:2; Heb. 9:27). In particular, people "dying" as a result of divine judgment is mentioned in Rev. 8:11; a judgment that also includes Christ (cf. Mark 15:44). John 12:24; 1 Cor. 15:31 refer to a seed "dying."

The appearance of "death" is noted in Mark 9:26. Resurrection to life is guaranteed to believers after their physical death in John 11:25ff. "Spiritual death" is indicated in John 8:21, 24. The state of being "dead to sin" is predicated of the believer, justified by faith in Christ, in Rom. 6:2ff.

Reference to the principle that it is better for one person to die for the people than for the whole nation to perish, indicating the approaching death of Christ, is found in John 11:50ff. Specific references to the certainty of Christ's coming death are found in John 12:33; 18:32; 19:7.

The redemptive impact of Christ's substitutionary death for the ungodly is indicated in Rom. 5:6ff.; 8:13; 14:9, 15; 1 Cor. 8:11; 15:3; 2 Cor. 5:14, 15; 1 Thess. 4:14; 5:10.

The universal condemnation of the human race to death as the consequence of the sin of Adam is noted in Rom. 5:15; 1 Cor. 15:22.

The impact of the law on an individual brings about that person's death, unless its strangle hold is broken by the grace of God through saving faith (cf. Rom. 7:9; 8:13). In this regard, Gal. 2:10 bears testimony to Paul's experience of "dying to the law." See also 1 Cor. 15:31. 2 Cor. 5:14; Col. 2:20; 3:3 refer metaphorically to the spiritual identification of all believers in the death of Christ, indicating that in him "they all died."

Paul expresses the unthinkable hypothesis in Gal. 2:21 that, "if righteousness could be gained through the law, then Christ died for nothing."

The prospect of living with Christ for eternity leads Paul to the conclusion that "to die" is far better (cf. Phil. 1:21).

synapothnēskō [συναποθνήσκω, *4880*]

synapothnēskō is a rare variant of ***apothnēskō***, above, meaning "to die together with" someone (cf. Mark 14:31; 2 Cor. 7:3). In 2 Tim. 2:11 the term is used metaphorically, affirming that those who "have died" with Christ (i.e., in self-denial) shall also live with him.

teleutaō [τελευτάω, *5053*]

The verb ***teleutaō*** is synonymous with ***thnēskō*** and ***apothnēskō***, above, meaning "to die, be dead" throughout its ten occurrences, mostly concerning people (cf. Matt. 2:19; 15:4; Mark 7:10; Luke 7:2; Acts 2:29; 7:15; Heb. 11:22).

koimaō [κοιμάω, *2837*]

koimaō is a verb with the primary meaning "sleep" throughout the nearly twenty occurrences of the term. It is used both literally and metaphorically. Metaphorically, it denotes the "sleep" of death in Matt. 27:52; John 11:11ff.; Acts 7:60; 13:36; 1 Cor. 11:30; 15:6, 18, 20, 51; 1 Thess. 4:13ff.; 2 Pet. 3:4.

apoginomai [ἀπογίνομαι, *581*]

apoginomai is a rare verb found only in 1 Pet. 2:24 with the metaphorical sense of "being dead" to sin.

Additional Notes

The phenomenon of death and dying is discussed throughout Scripture in such a way that the Old Testament treatment of the theme may be said to provide a foundation which the New Testament subsequently builds on and develops.

From the Hebrew term ***mût***, it may be affirmed that death in the Old Testament is viewed primarily, though not exclusively, as a judgment from God which is a consequence of sinful attitudes and behavior. In addition, it was seen as a means of atoning for sin under the ritual requirements of the old covenant.
(→ SACRIFICE → SLAUGHTER)

The New Testament views death not merely as the destruction of physical life, but also as the separation of the physical body from the human spirit. In that sense, the New Testament perspective on death is more highly developed than that of the Old. For instance, the New Testament makes clear that physical death is not the end of one's existence, but rather the gateway into the realm of eternity, where a person will be judged in accordance with how they have responded to the person of Jesus Christ in this life.

Two kinds of death are described in the New Testament — one physical, and one spiritual. And it is of the utmost importance to recognize the supreme significance of the death of Jesus himself. Christ's death on the cross, which fully atones for the sin of humankind, is the ultimate fulfillment of God's purpose. This substitutionary death fulfills all that the old covenant sacrificial system anticipated, and by it people are declared righteous before God. The Old Testament describes God's wrath against sin and affirms that many died as a consequence of it. The New Testament affirms that the death of one man has freed many from the eternal consequences of their sin, allowing them to escape forever from the wrath of God.

See Also: → DEATH

DIFFER, DIFFERENT, DIFFERENCE
→ DISTINCTION

DIG

OT Words

ḥāphar [חָפַר, 2658]

This verb is found approximately twenty times with the meaning "dig," although in several places it is translated "search out."

In the literal sense, ***ḥāphar*** refers to digging wells (cf. Gen. 21:30; 26:15ff.; Num. 21:18); digging for water (cf. Exod. 7:24); and digging a hole for human excrement (cf. Deut. 23:13).

Metaphorically, ***ḥāphar*** signifies "digging" in a number of different contexts. For example, Job 3:21 speaks of "digging (i.e., searching for) death." Ps. 35:7 refers to a plan to destroy the psalmist by having him thrown into a pit "dug" for his life. Eccl. 10:8 uses the term to indicate meaningless misfortune: ". . . he who digs a pit will fall into it." Jer. 13:7 describes an act of prophetic symbolism whereby the prophet digs out a linen belt buried in the crevice of a rock. The belt has rotted away, signifying the moral and spiritual corruption of the people of Judah.

kārāh [כָּרָה, 3738]

This verb is synonymous with ***ḥāphar***, above. ***kārāh*** occurs sixteen times in both literal and metaphorical contexts.

kārāh refers literally to the "digging" of wells (Gen. 26:25; Num. 21:18); graves (Gen. 50:25; 2 Chr. 16:14); and pits (Exod. 21:33).

The metaphorical usage of ***kārāh*** is also similar to that of ***ḥāphar***. Pss. 7:15; 57:6; Prov. 26:27 all speak of "digging" a trap for the wicked in which they will snare themselves through their own deceit. Ps. 94:13, on the other hand, speaks of divine judgment in which God will dig a pit for the wicked. The persecution of God's people is also indicated by the use of ***kārāh*** — the wicked dig traps for them (cf. Ps. 119:85; Jer. 18:20, 22).

ḥātar [חָתַר, 2864]

Another synonym for ***ḥāphar*** and ***kārāh***, above, ***ḥātar*** occurs seven times. It is translated "dig" or "dig through" in all but one instance. It is used metaphorically in Job 24:16; Amos 9:2. In the book of Ezekiel ***ḥāṯar*** indicates the literal activity of digging, but with a highly significant symbolic meaning (Ezek. 8:8; 12:5ff.). The prophet digs through the wall of the city of Jerusalem and the wall of the outer court of the temple as a prophetically symbolic means of indicating that Judah's exile to Babylon is inevitable.

ḥāṣab [חָצַב, **2672**]

ḥāṣab is a verb meaning "dig" throughout its twenty-five occurrences.

The literal sense of "dig" is used in relation to wells (cf. Deut. 6:11; 2 Chr. 26:10; Neh. 9:25). It also refers to "mining" copper in Deut. 8:9. More commonly, ***ḥāṣab*** refers to the "cutting" or "hewing" of stone from the ground (cf. 1 Kgs. 5:15; 2 Kgs. 12:12; 1 Chr. 22:2, 15; 2 Chr. 2:2, 18; 24:12; Ezra 3:7). The act of "digging out" a tomb is indicated in Isa. 22:16.

ḥāṣab is used metaphorically in Isa. 51:1, which refers to Yahweh "having hewed" his people from the rock — identifying Abraham as a symbolic quarry from which the patriarch's descendants were taken. In addition, the "digging of wells" in Jer. 2:13 denotes the futile action of God's people in cultivating a lifestyle completely alien to God. The context indicates that these "wells" were empty of water, for the people had rejected Yahweh, the bountiful fountain of living water.

qûr [קוּר, **6979**]

qûr is a rare verb indicating the "digging" of wells, found only in 2 Kgs. 19:24.

nāqar [נָקַר, **5365**]

nāqar is a verb with the passive sense of "being dug out" in Isa. 51:1. The use here is metaphorical, indicating Yahweh's action in shaping a people in accordance with his own redemptive purposes, having "dug them out" from the quarry.

NT Words

oryssō [ὀρύσσω, *3736*]

oryssō is a verb found in three places denoting the "digging" of the ground in Matt. 25:18, and digging a pit for a winepress in Matt. 21:33; Mark 12:1.

skaptō [σκάπτω, *4626*]

skaptō is a verb found three times indicating the action of "digging" the ground in Luke 6:48; 13:8; 16:3.

DILIGENCE, DILIGENT

OT Words

ḥārûṣ [חָרוּץ, **2742**]

ḥārûṣ is a participial verb with the nominal sense of "one who is diligent," referring to a person of industry and determination as opposed to one who is lazy and indifferent (cf. Prov. 10:4; 12:24, 27; 13:4; 21:5).

NT Words

spoudē [σπουδή, *4710*]

spoudē is a noun found twelve times with the primary sense of "haste," "diligence." (→ HASTE)

The meaning "diligence" in the sense of "earnest zeal" is indicated in Rom. 12:8, 11; 2 Cor. 7:11, 12; 8:7ff.; Heb. 6:11 — all in the context of living out godly lives.

spoudazō [σπουδάζω, *4704*]

The verb ***spoudazō*** means to "be diligent" in the sense of "strive," "do one's best" in most of the eleven occurrences of the term.

The sense of "striving" to arrange meetings is indicated in 1 Thess. 2:17; 2 Tim. 4:9, 21; Titus 3:12. "Being diligent" in the pursuit of godly living is noted in Gal. 2:10; Eph. 4:3; 2 Tim. 2:15. In particular, Heb. 4:11 exhorts believers to "strive" to enter their heavenly "rest." There is a similar exhortation in 2 Pet. 2:10 for believers to "be zealous" or "diligent" to confirm their call and election.

spoudaios [σπουδαῖος, *4705*]

spoudaios is a rare adjective found only in 2 Cor. 8:22 denoting a "diligent," "earnest" believer.

spoudaioteros [σπουδαιότερος, *4706*]

spoudaioteros is an adverb meaning "diligently" in relation to Onesiphorus's earnest drive to find Paul in Rome.

epimelōs [ἐπιμελῶς, *1960*]

epimelōs is a rare adverb, synonymous with ***spoudaioteros***, above, denoting a woman's "diligent" search for a coin (cf. Luke 15:8).

akribōs [ἀκριβῶς, *199*]

akribōs is an adverb meaning "diligently" in relation to Herod's careful search for the infant Jesus in Matt. 2:8.

exeraunaō [ἐξεραυνάω, *1830*]

exeraunaō is a rare verb found only in 1 Pet. 1:10 referring to the prophets of old who "had searched diligently" concerning the fulfillment of God's plan of salvation embodied in the coming of the Messiah, Jesus Christ.

DIP → BAPTISM

DISCERN, DISCERNMENT

OT Words

shāma' [**שָׁמַע, 8085**]

shāma' is a common verb with the primary meanings "hear," "listen," "obey," as well as other related senses. One of these related meanings is "discern" or "distinguish," as in 2 Sam. 14:17, with reference to "discerning" good and evil; and in 1 Kgs. 3:11, in relation to "discerning" what is right. Both contexts refer to the capacity for moral judgment.

bîn [**בִּין, 995**]

bîn is a verb found about 170 times with the primary meaning "understand," "consider," as well as related nuances. In 1 Kgs. 3:11 the term refers to Solomon's request to God for the ability to "discern" between good and evil.

NT Words

anakrinō [ἀνακρίνω, *350*]

anakrinō is a verb found sixteen times with the principal meanings "judge," "examine." In 1 Cor. 2:14, however, the term refers to the unspiritual person's inability to "discern" spiritual things.

diakrisis [διάκρισις, *1253*]

diakrisis is a rare noun denoting the capacity for "discerning" between good or evil in Heb. 5:14; and for "discerning" spirits in 1 Cor. 12:10. The latter practice required an assessment of whether spirits were godly or demonic.

DISCIPLE

OT Words

limmûd [**לִמּוּד, 3928**]

limmûd is a rare noun referring to Yahweh's "disciples" found only in Isa. 8:16.

NT Words

mathētēs [μαθητής, *3101*]

mathētēs is a noun denoting "disciple" throughout all occurrences of the term (approximately 270).

References to Jesus' twelve disciples include Matt. 5:1; 8:21ff.; 26:17ff.; Mark 8:1ff.; 14:12ff.; Luke 6:13ff.; 19:39; John 1:35ff.; 2:11ff.; 6:11ff.; 18:15ff. The followers of Jesus, the broader circle of his "disciples," are noted in John 13:35; 15:8; 19:38.

Other general references to "disciples" are found in Matt. 10:24; Luke 6:40; 14:26ff. The term specifically refers to the early Christians as "disciples" in Acts 6:1ff.; 9:1, 10; 11:26; 14:20ff.

The "disciples" of John the Baptist are noted in Matt. 9:14; Mark 2:18; Luke 7:18; John 3:25. "Disciples" of Moses are indicated in John 9:28.

mathētria [μαθήτρια, *3102*]

mathētria is a rare feminine variant of ***mathētēs***, above, referring to the "disciple" in Acts 9:36.

mathēteuō [μαθητεύω, *3100*]

mathēteuō is a verb meaning to "make disciples" in Matt. 28:19, referring to Jesus' last instructions to his own disciples. The activity of "making disciples" is indicated in Acts 14:21. In Matt. 27:57 the term is translated "to be a disciple."

DISCIPLINE

OT Words

yāsar [**יָסַר, 3256**]

yāsar is a verb occurring about forty times with the primary senses of "chastise," "instruct," "correct" in the context of discipline.

God's "chastising," "disciplining" his people for their sins, or threatening to do so, is noted in Lev. 26:18, 28; Hos. 7:12; 10:10. See also Pss. 39:11; 94:12; 118:18; Jer. 10:24; 30:11. The psalmist pleads with God not to "chastise" him (cf. Pss. 6:1; 38:1). Parental "discipline" is indicated in Deut. 8:5; 21:18; Prov. 19:18; 29:17. Judicial "punishment" is recorded in 1 Kgs. 12:11; 2 Chr. 10:11, 14.

General references to "correction" or "discipline" are noted in Prov. 29:19.

yākaḥ [**יָכַח, 3198**]

yākaḥ is a verb found in nearly sixty places meaning to "reprove," "rebuke" as well as related nuances. The word is used in contexts of "discipline."

God's intention to "chasten" his "son," with reference to Solomon on one level, and to the Messiah on another, is indicated in 2 Sam. 7:14.

Requests for God to "rebuke" his enemies are noted in 1 Chr. 12:17. The psalmist asks God not to "rebuke" him in Pss. 6:1; 38:1. Such divine "chastening" is indicated in 1 Chr. 16:21; Pss. 94:10; 105:14; Prov. 3:12; Hab. 1:12. The blessings of divine discipline or reproving are noted in Job 5:17. General references to "chastening" or "discipline" include those in Job 33:19; Prov. 9:7.

mûsār [מוּסָר, 4148]

mûsār is a noun found fifty times with the consistent sense of "instruction," "chastisement" or "discipline," "correction."

The "chastisement," "punishment," or "discipline" of Yahweh is indicated in relation to his people in Deut. 11:2; Jer. 2:30; 5:3; 7:28; 17:23; Hos. 5:12. In particular, the divine chastisement poured out on the Suffering Messiah-Servant, resulting in his atoning death for his people, is indicated in Isa. 53:5. For the divine "disciplining" of people in general see Job 5:17; Prov. 3:11; Isa. 26:16.

"Discipline" in a general sense is indicated in Ps. 50:17; Prov. 1:2ff.; 5:12; 12:1; 13:18, 24; 15:10; 16:22. Parental "discipline" is indicated in Prov. 15:5; 22:15; 23:13.

See Also: → CHASTEN

DISEASE

OT Words

ḥolî [חֳלִי, 2483]

This noun occurs twenty-four times, meaning "sickness," "disease" in a number of different contexts.

ḥolî indicates literal, physical illness in a non-theological context in Ps. 41:3; Eccl. 5:17; 2 Kgs. 13:14. Physical disease is mentioned in a number of contexts which clearly suggest a divine initiative or purpose of either blessing or judgment. In Deut. 7:15, for example, God promises to remove all disease from his people if they will obey him. Conversely, God's people are threatened with all kinds of sickness if they disobey God (cf. Deut. 28:59ff.). In Isa. 38:9, Hezekiah's illness is predicated by God — a sickness that is used to teach the king of Judah a valuable lesson in trust and faith. In 1 Kgs. 17:17 the widow of Zarephath's son contracts an illness, subsequently dies, and is then miraculously brought back to life through the prophet Elijah (cf. also 2 Kgs. 8:8, 9).

Elsewhere, God invokes illness and disease upon all who rebel against him. In this case, ***ḥolî*** is found mainly in contexts where the people of God are so punished, including the kings of Israel and Judah — for example, Asa (2 Chr. 16:12); and Jehoram (2 Chr. 21:15ff.). The people of Israel themselves are also afflicted this way (cf. Isa. 1:5), as are the Judean population (cf. Jer. 6:7). In the most significant context where ***ḥolî*** occurs, Isa. 53:3 records the divine initiative reflected in the suffering of Yahweh's Servant-King. This affliction from God was absolutely necessary if his people were to experience full deliverance from their sin, since the suffering Messianic King would bear the divine punishment in their place.

ḥolî is used in a metaphorical sense in Eccl. 6:2, referring to the "affliction" of having a stranger take over one's hard-earned wealth and possessions. In Hos. 5:13 the term describes the sin of Israel as "sickness."

maḥalāh [מַחֲלָה, 4245]

This is a rare noun, occurring only six times and translated "disease" or "sickness."

Literal disease is in view in Prov. 18:14. Illness is prescribed as a divine punishment in 2 Chr. 21:15 against Jehoram, king of Judah. God also promises to spare his people from disease, if they obey him (cf. Exod. 15:26; 23:25). In 1 Kgs. 8:37; 2 Chr. 6:28, Solomon pleads with God to heal his people's diseases when they cry out to him.

madweh [מַדְוֶה, 4064]

madweh is a rare noun referring to the Egyptian "diseases," or "plagues," in Deut. 7:15; 28:60.

taḥalû'îm [תַּחֲלוּאִים, 8463]

taḥalû'îm is a noun denoting "disease" in four of the five occurrences of the term. "Diseases" inflicted on Israel by Yahweh are noted in Deut. 29:22. Other references to "diseases" are found in 2 Chr. 21:19; Ps. 103:3; Jer. 14:18.

NT Words

astheneia [ἀσθένεια, *769*]

astheneia is a noun denoting "disease," "sickness" in most of the twenty-four occurrences of the term.

The "infirmities" in Matt. 8:17 refer symbolically to the "afflictions" or "weaknesses" of God's people borne by the Suffering Servant-Messiah, as cited in Isa. 53:4.

References to people's "diseases," eradicated by the miraculous power of Christ, are found in Luke 5:15;

8:2; 13:11ff.; John 5:5; 11:4. Similarly, "diseases" cured by the apostles are noted in Acts 28:9. Other references to "bodily ailments" are found in Gal. 4:13; 1 Tim. 5:23.

malakia [μαλακία, *3119*]

malakia is a rare noun denoting "disease" in Matt. 4:23; 9:35; 10:1.

nosos [νόσος, *3554*]

The noun ***nosos*** is synonymous with ***malakia***, above, denoting "disease," "sickness" in twelve places (cf. Matt. 4:23ff.; 8:17; 9:35; 10:1; Mark 1:34; 3:15; Luke 4:40; 6:17; 7:21; 9:1; Acts 19:12).

See Also: → SICK → SORROW → WEAK

DISH

OT Words

qe'ārāh [קְעָרָה, **7086**]

This noun occurs seventeen times and is translated "dish" or "plate." It is found exclusively in ritual contexts and refers to the dishes and plates used in the tabernacle (cf. Exod. 25:29; 37:16; Num. 7:13ff.).

ṣallaḥat [צַלַּחַת, **6747**]

ṣallaḥat is a rare noun denoting a "dish" in three places (cf. 2 Kgs. 21:13; Prov. 19:24; 26:15).

NT Words

tryblion [τρύβλιον, *5165*]

tryblion is a noun denoting a household "dish," found only in Matt. 26:23; Mark 14:20.

DISHONESTY

OT Words

beṣa' [בֶּצַע, **1215**]

beṣa' is a noun denoting "unjust profit," or "gain" derived through dishonest means, probably violence, in approximately twenty places (cf. Exod. 18:21; 1 Sam. 8:3; Prov. 1:19; Jer. 6:13; 8:10; 22:17; Ezek. 22:13, 27; 33:3; Mic. 4:13; Hab. 2:9).

See Also: → SHAME

DISHONOR

OT Words

kelimmāh [כְּלִמָּה, **3639**]

The noun ***kelimmāh*** occurs thirty times meaning "shame," "disgrace," "dishonor" throughout. "Shame" or "dishonor" among people in general contexts is indicated in Pss. 4:2; 44:15; Prov. 18:13; Isa. 50:6.

The psalmist invokes "shame" or "dishonor" against his enemies (cf. Pss. 35:26; 69:19; 71:13; 109:29). See also Jer. 20:11. Exposing God's enemies to "shame," "dishonor" is noted in Ezek. 32:24ff.; 36:7. Ps. 69:7 refers to enduring "shame," "dishonor" for the sake of the Lord.

The "dishonor" of God's people, brought on as a result of Yahweh chastising them for their rebellion against him, is recorded in Jer. 51:51; Ezek. 16:52ff.; 36:6; 44:13.

In Ezek. 36:15; 39:26, Yahweh promises to remove from his people the "reproach" or "dishonor" brought against them by the surrounding nations.

qālôn [קָלוֹן, **7036**]

qālôn is a noun synonymous with ***kelimmāh***, above, denoting "shame," "dishonor" for most of the seventeen occurrences of the term. General references include Prov. 3:35; 6:33; 11:2; 13:18; 18:3.

Jer. 13:26; Hos. 4:7, 18 refer to the "shame" or "dishonor" of the people of God, brought about by their sinfulness.

The "shame" of Egypt initiated by Yahweh is noted in Jer. 46:12; as is Assyria's "dishonor" in Neh. 3:5.

qālāh [קָלָה, **7034**]

qālāh is a verb found six times and translated various ways, including "be degraded, dishonored" in the context of excess cruelty in judicial punishment in Deut. 25:3. The "dishonoring" of one's parents is noted in Deut. 27:16.

nemibzāh [נְמִבְזָה, **5240**]

nemibzāh is a rare participial form used adjectivally to refer to that which is "despised," "vile," or "dishonorable" in 1 Sam. 15:9.

'arwāh [עַרְוָה, **6173** (Aramaic)]

'arwāh is a rare Aramaic noun referring to the "dishonor" of the king in Ezra 4:14.

NT Words

atimia [ἀτιμία, *819*]

atimia is a noun found seven times, denoting "dishonor," "shame," and related nuances.

The term is used adjectivally in Rom. 1:26 to refer to "vile" or "shameful" passions. In Rom. 9:21 the term refers metaphorically to vessels constructed for "common" or "menial" use. See also 2 Tim. 2:20.

Personal "shame" or "dishonor" is indicated in 1 Cor. 11:14; 2 Cor. 6:8; 11:21.

The humble condition of the human body, referred to metaphorically as having been "sown in dishonor," is noted in 1 Cor. 15:43.

atimos [ἄτιμος, *820*]

atimos is an adjective found four times referring to people who are "without honor" in Matt. 13:57; Mark 6:4; 1 Cor. 4:10. It also denotes body parts that are "less honorable" than others in 1 Cor. 12:23.

atimazō [ἀτιμάζω, *818*]

atimazō is a verb occurring six times, meaning "to treat shamefully," "dishonor," and "suffer dishonor."

Luke 20:11; John 8:49; Jas. 2:6 refer to treating people shamefully. The experience of believers "suffering dishonor" in the course of persecution is indicated in Acts 5:41. "Breaking the law" is identified with "dishonoring" God in Rom. 2:23. Rom. 1:24 refers to "dishonoring" one's body through sexual impurity.

See Also: → SHAME

DISOBEDIENCE, DISOBEDIENT

OT Words

merî [מְרִי, 4805]

This noun occurs twenty-three times and is usually translated "rebel" or "rebellion." The idea behind the term is that of spurning or rejecting authority, implying a disobedient spirit.

God issues a solemn warning to those Israelites who rebel against the authority of Yahweh (e.g., Num. 17:10). A similar example is found in Deut. 31:27, where Moses acknowledges the rebellious, disobedient spirit of the Israelites (cf. also Neh. 9:17). God also severely indicts King Saul for rebelling against him (cf. 1 Sam. 15:23).

In the book of Ezekiel, ***merî*** refers to the rebellious, disobedient spirit of Judah (cf. Ezek. 2:5ff.; 3:9, 26, 27; 12:2ff., 25; 17:12; 24:3; 44:6).

mārāh [מָרָה, 4784]

Another term translated "rebel," "rebellious," ***mārāh*** incorporates the element of disobedience and occurs around forty times.

mārāh is most commonly found in contexts where rebellion, or disobedience, is predicated of the Israelites against God — first of all in the wilderness period of their existence, prior to their conquest of the land of Canaan. Their disobedience consists primarily in their failure to honor Yahweh as their one and only God and Lord (cf. Num. 20:20; 27:14; Deut. 1:26; 9:7, 23; 31:27; Ezek. 20:8, 13, 21; Ps. 78:10, 17, 40, 56). The second context in which the disobedience of Israel emerges is during their time in Canaan (cf. Pss. 106:7, 43; 107:11). In the third instance, the disobedience of both Israel and Judah against God throughout their entire history is mentioned in several significant contexts (cf. Neh. 9:26; Isa. 63:10; Jer. 4:17; 5:23; Ezek. 5:6; Hos. 13:16).

mārāh also refers to the disobedience of an arrogant son in Deut. 21:18, 20. It is not an actual occurrence, but an item of case law which allows the death sentence in the event of such an act of rebellion against one's parents.

There is a solemn exhortation in 1 Sam. 12:14ff. not to rebel against or disobey God. Destruction is invoked as a threat against those who disobey God's commands (cf. Josh. 1:18; Isa. 1:20). Such a punishment is in fact recorded against an unnamed prophet for doing just that in 1 Kgs. 13:21, 26.

As far as the wicked are concerned, Ps. 5:10 refers generally to their rebellion against God.

Finally, Lam. 1:18ff.; 3:42 record a confession of disobedience and rebellion against God.

NT Words

apeithēs [ἀπειθής, *545*]

apeithēs is an adjective found in six places, all referring to "disobedience."

General references to "disobedient" people are found in Luke 1:17; Titus 1:16; 3:3. Paul acknowledges in Acts 26:19 that he was "not disobedient" to the heavenly vision. Those disobedient to their parents are mentioned in Rom. 1:30; 2 Tim. 3:2.

parakoē [παρακοή, *3876*]

parakoē is a noun denoting "disobedience" in all three occurrences of the term. The "disobedience" of Adam and its terrible impact on the whole human race is noted in Rom. 5:19. Other references to "disobedience" are found in 2 Cor. 10:6; Heb. 2:2.

Additional Notes

The concept of disobedience is expressed fairly consistently throughout both Old and New Testaments. The Hebrew terminology focuses primarily on disobedience as an act of rebellion against God and its terrible consequences. The same emphasis is found in the New

Testament, with the added element of unbelief that is contained in the semantic field of the Greek verb ***apeitheō*** (→ BELIEF), which can mean both "to disobey" and "to be or act as an unbeliever."

See Also: → UNBELIEF

DISPUTE

NT Words

syzētētēs [συζητητής, *4804*]

syzētētēs is a rare noun found only in 1 Cor. 1:20, denoting a "philosopher," or one who "debates," who engages in disputes or discussions concerning human life. In this context the reference is negative, indicating the person who extols only human wisdom and ignores the wisdom of God.

syzēteō [συζητέω, *4802*]

syzēteō is a verb found ten times with the sense of "dispute," "argue," or "debate" in most of these contexts. Specific references to "disputing" or "arguing" include Mark 1:27; 8:11; 9:10ff.; 12:28; Acts 6:9; 9:29. Neutral contexts where "questioning" or "discussion" is involved are found in Luke 22:23; 24:15.

logomachia [λογομαχία, *3055*]

loogomachia is a rare noun found only in 1 Tim. 6:4, denoting "quarrels, or disputes over words" — a practice condemned by the apostle.

diaparatribē [διαπαρατριβή, *3859*]

diaparatribē is a rare noun denoting unprofitable "wrangling," "arguments," or "disputes" as practiced by false teachers, whom Paul denounces as depraved in mind and lifestyle. ***diaparatribē*** is found only in 1 Tim. 6:5.

antilogia [ἀντιλογία, *485*]

antilogia is a noun found four times with the various senses of "opposition," "rebellion" and "strife," or "dispute." The latter meaning is indicated in Heb. 6:16; 7:7.

diakrisis [διάκρισις, *1253*]

diakrisis is a noun denoting "disputes" over various opinions in Rom. 14:1.

See Also: → DISCERN → JUDGE → REASON → STRIVE → THINK

DISSOLVE

OT Words

nātak [**נָתַךְ, 5413**]

nātak is a verb with the primary meaning "pour," "pour out" in most of its nearly twenty occurrences. In several places, however, ***nātak*** is also translated "melt" — dissolved by heat. It is used metaphorically in this sense in the context of divine discipline in Ezek. 22:20ff.; 24:11. (→ POUR)

NT Words

lyō [λύω, *3089*]

lyō is a verb found approximately forty times in all, with the predominant meanings "release," or "loose(n)." (→ DESTROY → RELEASE)

In a couple of places, however, ***lyō*** is also translated "melt" or "dissolve." In 2 Pet. 3:10ff. it refers to the apocalyptic destruction of the cosmos through a fiery heat.

DISTINCTION

NT Words

diastolē [διαστολή, *1293*]

diastolē is a noun found three times meaning "distinction" or "difference." Rom. 3:22 affirms that there is no distinction between any who put their faith in Christ. Similarly, Rom. 10:12 declares that there is no "distinction" in status between Jew and Gentile in their relationship with Christ. 1 Cor. 14:7 mentions the "distinction" between music notes.

DISTRESS, DISTRESSED

OT Words

meṣûqāh [**מְצוּקָה, 4691**]

This is a rare noun occurring seven times, translated "distress" or "anguish."

Job 15:24 refers generally to the distress of the wicked. The psalmist pleads to God to rescue him from his distress — a cry to which God responds positively (cf. Ps. 107:6, 13, 19, 28). Zeph. 1:15 describes the Day of the Lord as a day of distress and anguish.

ṣar [**צַר, 6862**]

This noun occurs approximately one hundred times with various meanings, including "enemy," "adversary." These meanings account for more than half the occurrences of ***ṣar*** (→ ENEMY). However, ***ṣar*** is also found on about twenty occasions with the meanings "trouble," "distress," or "affliction."

ṣar refers first of all to "distress" as the consequence of divine judgment. Deut. 4:30; Isa. 5:30 indicate that the people of Israel will suffer affliction and distress at the time of their exile from the land. There is also reference to Israel's distress during the time of the judges (cf. 2 Chr. 15:4). A general indication of the distress of the wicked is found in Job 15:24.

The suffering of individuals is also evident in the use of this term. For example, David cries out to God for relief from his "anguish" in 2 Sam. 22:7; Pss. 4:1; 66:14; 108:12, as does the anonymous psalmist in Pss. 102:2; 119:43. Job's distress is also mentioned in Job 7:11; 16:19.

On a positive note, there are passages that affirm God as the one who delivers his people from their "distress" (cf. Pss. 106:44; 107:6, 13, 19, 28 [a continuous refrain through the psalm]; Isa. 25:4). Hos. 5:15 implies divine deliverance, but it will be dependent on Israel turning back to the Lord. Then the psalmist expresses his confidence in God as a refuge from trouble and "distress" in Pss. 32:7; 59:16. Isa. 63:9 declares the profoundly comforting truth that God is prepared to identify with his people in their "distress," and thereby offer comfort to them.

ṣārāh [צָרָה, 6869]

This noun is a variant form of ***ṣar*** (see above). ***ṣārāh*** occurs about seventy times and is consistently translated "distress," "trouble," "anguish."

Again, there is an emphasis on trouble or distress as a divine judgment for sin, first of all on the part of his people who suffer disciplinary action from God throughout their entire history (cf. Deut. 31:17ff.; 2 Kgs. 19:3; 2 Chr. 15:6; Neh. 9:37; Isa. 8:22; Jer. 4:31; 6:24). In Zeph. 1:15 there is a significant reference to the distress Judah will suffer as a consequence of the coming Day of the Lord. The sins of the nations also result in their being afflicted by God with emotional and physical turmoil (cf. Ps. 78:49 [Egypt's plagues]; Jer. 49:24 [Syria]; Jer. 50:43 [Babylon]; Hab. 3:16 [Babylon]).

ṣārāh is also found in a number of contexts in which the writer pleads with God for relief from personal trauma (cf. 1 Sam. 26:4; Pss. 20:1; 25:17; 77:2; 143:11; Prov. 1:27; Isa. 33:2; Jer. 15:11). A variation on this is found in Pss. 10:1; 22:11, where the psalmist expresses his anguish at God's perceived inaccessibility in times of difficulty. Emotional distress and anguish of soul are also indicated in Gen. 42:21 (Joseph's brothers) and Ps. 116:3.

By far the most extensive use of ***ṣārāh*** is found in situations where God is affirmed and praised as the one who delivers from trouble and distress (e.g., Gen. 35:3; 1 Sam. 10:19; 2 Sam. 4:9; 1 Kgs. 1:29; 2 Chr. 20:9; Neh. 9:27; Pss. 9:9; 54:7; 81:7; 120:1; 138:7; Prov. 12:7). In Isa. 65:16 there is an intriguing reference to God putting the past troubles of his people out of his mind, clearly indicating that he has forgiven them. Dan. 12:1 refers to an apocalyptic deliverance from persecution. See also Jer. 14:8; 15:11; 16:19; 30:7; Jonah 2:2; Nah. 1:7ff.

In contrast, a couple of texts highlight the impotence of idols to alleviate "personal anguish." One is Isa. 46:7; the other is Judg. 10:14, where divine sarcasm is evident. God declares: "let the idols you have chosen deliver you in the time of your distress."

ṣārar [צָרַר, 6887]

This is the verb from which ***ṣar*** (see above) is derived. ***ṣārar*** occurs about sixty times and is translated in a variety of ways. Two basic senses attached to this verb are "to show hostility towards," "to be at enmity with"; and "to be in distress" or "to cause distress." ***ṣārar*** occurs about twenty times with this latter meaning.
(➠ ENEMY)

ṣārar indicates trouble and distress as a divine judgment — the consequence of sinful attitudes and behavior for two groups of people. Concerning the people of God, in 1 Chr. 21:13 God punishes David and the people of Israel for engaging in an illegitimate census. Jer. 10:18 records the coming of exile and destruction for the nation of Judah — a period of unparalleled anguish and distress — as punishment for the people's sin. See also Judg. 11:7; 1 Sam. 28:15; 2 Chr. 28:22; 33:12; Lam. 1:20; Zeph. 1:17.

ṣārar indicates emotional distress in 2 Sam. 1:26, where David expresses profound grief at the death of his friend Jonathan.

The psalmist pleads with God for deliverance from anguish in Pss. 31:9; 69:17.

ṣûq [צוּק, 6693]

ṣûq is a verb meaning "to distress," "cause anguish" in three of the eleven occurrences of the term. Deut. 28:53ff. refers to the threat of Israel's enemies "bringing distress" to the people of God. (➠ OPPRESS)

māṣôq **[מָצוֹק, 4689]**

māṣôq is a noun derived from ***ṣûq*** (see above) meaning "distress," "anguish" in each of its six occurrences.

Jer. 19:9 refers to "distress" inflicted on the people of God by their enemies. General references to "distress" and "anguish" are found in 1 Sam. 22:2; Ps. 119:143.

mēṣar **[מֵצַר, 4712]**

mēṣar is a rare noun denoting "distress," or "anguish," found only in Ps. 118:5; Lam. 1:3.

yāṣar **[יָצַר, 3334]**

yāṣar is a verb meaning "to be distressed" in the sense of being in a state of desperate fear or anguish. It occurs with this meaning in Gen. 32:7; Judg. 2:15; 10:9; 1 Sam. 30:6. In 2 Sam. 13:2, ***yāṣar*** means to "be tormented."

NT Words

anankē [ἀνάγκη, *318*]

anankē is a noun denoting "distress" or "anguish" in three places (cf. Luke 21:23; 1 Cor. 7:26; 1 Thess. 3:7).

stenochōria [στενοχωρία, *4730*]

stenochōria is a noun denoting "distress," "anguish," or "calamity" — all in the context of the trauma of persecution (cf. Rom. 2:9; 8:35; 2 Cor. 6:4; 12:10).

synochē [συνοχή, *4928*]

synochē is a rare noun denoting "anguish," "distress" in the sense of deep emotional turmoil in Luke 21:25; 2 Cor. 2:4.

basanizō [βασανίζω, *928*]

basanizō is a verb found in twelve places meaning "to torment," in the sense of "cause great pain, and distress."

Matt. 8:6 refers to the "distress" and pain of a terrible illness. Matt. 8:29; Mark 5:7; Luke 8:28 refer to Christ "tormenting" demons. 2 Pet. 2:8 notes Lot's "torment" or "distress" in response to the lawless deeds of the citizens of Sodom. The "distress" or "pain" of women in childbirth is indicated in Rev. 12:2.

Inflicting pain, distress, or torment in the context of punishment is indicated in Rev. 9:5; 11:10. In particular, Rev. 14:10; 20:10 refer to God "tormenting" the wicked.

basanismos [βασανισμός, *929*]

basanismos is a noun found in six places, denoting "torment," or the terrible anguish of distress in the context of divine punishment against the wicked (cf. Rev. 9:5; 14:11; 18:7, 10, 15).

basanos [βάσανος, *931*]

basanos is a noun denoting the "torment," "terrible anguish," or "distress" of eternal punishment in Luke 16:23, 28. Matt. 4:24 refers to the "painful torments" of disease.

See Also: → AFFLICT

DIVIDE

OT Words

ḥālaq **[חָלַק, 2505]**

ḥālaq occurs sixty-five times and is translated "divide," "share," "allot" (as well as related senses) in about two-thirds of its occurrences.

There are a number of significant references to dividing the land among the tribes of Israel, allotting to each tribe their God-given inheritance in Canaan (cf. Num. 26:53; Josh. 13:7; 14:5; 18:2ff.; 19:51; Neh. 9:22; Ps. 60:6). Joel 3:2 contains an image of judgment in which the land of Canaan has been divided up by Israel's enemies, and God determines to punish them for their aggression towards his people. Amos 7:17; Mic. 2:4 both refer to judgment against Israel, in which her enemies will divide up the land. In Zech. 14:1 a climactic Day of the Lord judgment is professed against the nations which will result in, among other things, the division of the plunder for the people of Judah. An associated use of ***ḥālaq*** concerns the formation of priestly divisions in Israel, which were determined by lot (i.e., they were "divided" into groups) (cf. 1 Chr. 23:6; 24:3ff.; 2 Chr. 23:18).

ḥālaq also frequently refers to the "dividing" or "sharing" of spoils, plunder, or booty (cf. Gen. 49:27; Exod. 15:9; Josh. 22:8; Judg. 5:30; Ps. 68:12; Prov. 16:5; Isa. 9:3; 33:23). In particular, in 2 Sam. 6:19 David "distributes" cakes and fruit to the Israelite people after the successful transfer of the ark of the covenant to Jerusalem. This action is a highly significant symbol of a king dividing the spoil of victory among his people. Isa. 53:12 describes one aspect of the victory of the Suffering Servant in terms of his "dividing the spoil with the many." This constitutes a powerful prophetic anticipation of the victory of Christ, a victory of profound spiritual significance, since the "spoil" amounts to freedom from the curse of sin and death, accomplished by the substitutionary atonement of the Servant.

There are also a number of miscellaneous uses of *ḥālaq*. For example, Job 27:17 refers to dividing wealth; Prov. 17:2 to the sharing of an inheritance; Dan. 11:39 to the invasion and dividing of Canaan by the unidentified "king of the north." Ezek. 5:1 refers to the dividing of the prophet's hair, which is part of an act of prophetic symbolism predicting the destruction of Jerusalem. Finally, Ps. 22:8 contains a prophetic anticipation of the dividing of Christ's clothing by the Roman soldiers immediately prior to his crucifixion.

shāsa' [שָׁסַע, 8156]

This rare verb occurs only nine times, meaning "divide," "cleave," "split in two."

shāsa' is always used literally. It is found in a ritual context with reference to the "cleaving" or "dividing" of the animal carcass (cf. Lev. 1:17). In Judges it refers to Samson's extraordinary feat of strength in "tearing apart" a lion (cf. Judg. 14:6). Finally, ***shāsa'*** refers to cloven-hoofed animals in Lev. 11:3, 7, 26; Deut. 14:6, 7.

nāḥal [נָחַל, 5157]

This verb occurs about sixty times and is usually translated "inherit." (→ INHERIT) However, in several contexts ***nāḥal*** also means "divide" in the sense of distributing an inheritance. The following examples refer exclusively to the division of Canaan for the purpose of assigning it to the entire population of Israelites: Num. 34:17, 18, 29; Josh. 19:51.

ḥāṣāh [חָצָה, 2673]

ḥāṣāh is a verb meaning "divide," "separate" for most of the fifteen occurrences of the term.

The act of "dividing" or "separating" people into smaller units is indicated in Gen. 32:7; 33:1; Num. 31:42; Judg. 7:16; 9:43.

Exod. 21:35 describes "dividing" the price of a sale or the booty from a battle. Elijah's miracle in "dividing" the water of the Jordan is recorded in 2 Kgs. 2:8, 14. "Dividing" the nation of Israel into two kingdoms is noted in Ezek. 37:22.

pāras [פָּרַס, 6536]

pāras is a verb meaning "divide" or "split in two," referring almost exclusively to animals with "split (or cloven) hoofs."

bāqa' [בָּקַע, 1234]

bāqa' is a verb found about fifty times meaning "break," with a number of related senses.
(→ BREAK)

bāqa' is also translated "divide," referring to the miracle of the parting of the Re(e)d Sea when Yahweh granted the Israelites a miraculous escape from the Egyptians (cf. Exod. 14:16, 21; Neh. 9:11; Ps. 78:13; Isa. 63:12).

pālag [פָּלַג, 6385]

pālag is a verb found in four places referring to the "dividing" of the earth in Gen. 10:25; 1 Chr. 1:19, in the context of the earth's expanding population.

NT Words

aphorizō [ἀφορίζω, *873*]

aphorizō is a verb found in nine places with the primary meaning to "separate." In two of these contexts the underlying sense is that of "divide," referring to the "separating" of the wicked and the righteous in Matt. 13:49; 25:32.

diaireō [διαιρέω, *1244*]

diaireō is a verb found in only two places, meaning "divide" in the sense of "distribute." A man's inheritance is "divided" between his sons in Luke 15:12. The Holy Spirit is said to "apportion" ("distribute") gifts to all believers in 1 Cor. 12:11.

diadidōmi [διαδίδωμι, *1239*]

diadidōmi is a verb found five times, meaning "divide" in the sense of "distribute." Luke 11:22 refers to the "dividing" or "distribution" of the spoils of war. "Distributing" money to the poor is noted in Luke 18:22; Acts 4:35; as is the "distribution" of food to the masses in John 6:11.

merizō [μερίζω, *3307*]

merizō is a verb found fifteen times with the underlying meaning "divide," including the dual senses of "split," and "distribute."

Matt. 12:25ff.; Mark 3:24ff. refer to "dividing" a kingdom, signifying its breakup or disintegration leading to obliteration. The "distribution" of food is noted in Mark 6:41; and the "dividing" of an inheritance in Luke 12:13. The capacity of God to "distribute" or "assign" a measure of faith is indicated in Rom. 12:3. See also 1 Cor. 7:17. 1 Cor. 1:13 refers to the impossibility of Christ "being divided."

diamerizō [διαμερίζω, *1266*]

diamerizō is synonymous with ***merizō***, above, meaning "divide" in the sense of "part."

The "parting" or "dividing" of Christ's garments by Roman soldiers at his crucifixion is recorded in Matt. 27:35; Mark 15:24; Luke 23:34; John 19:24.

Luke 11:17; 12:52ff. affirm that a kingdom or house "divided" against itself, that is, experiencing internal dissension and strife, will collapse. See also Luke 11:18.

Luke 22:17 refers to the "dividing," or "sharing," of the Passover cup.

merismos [μερισμός, *3311*]

merismos is a rare noun, referring metaphorically to the powerful penetration and impact of the word of God in the life of the believer as a "dividing" of the soul and spirit.

schizō [σχίζω, *4977*]

schizō is a verb found eleven times with the primary sense of "to bear." There is also, however, the associated metaphorical sense of "divide," found in Acts 14:4; 23:7, referring to two contrasting points of view held by two opposing groups of people within a community — a people "divided."

See Also: → SEPARATE

DIVINATION, DIVINE (VERB)

OT Words

qesem [**קֶסֶם, 7081**]

qesem is a noun denoting "divination" or "witchcraft" in most of the eleven occurrences of the term (cf. Num. 22:7; 23:23; Deut. 18:10; 1 Sam. 15:23; 2 Kgs. 17:17; Jer. 14:14; Ezek. 13:6, 23; 21:21).

qāsam [**קָסַם, 7080**]

qāsam is a verb consistently translated "to practice divination, witchcraft," including the participial nominal sense of "diviner," "soothsayer."

Prohibitions against practicing witchcraft are given to the people of Israel in Deut. 18:10, 14. God condemns such practices in Isa. 44:25; Jer. 27:9; 29:8; Ezek. 13:9, 23; 22:28; Mic. 3:6ff.

References to these practices by Israelites include 1 Sam. 28:8 (King Saul and the witch of Endor); 2 Kgs. 17:17; Isa. 3:2; Mic. 3:11; Zech. 10:2. Pagan practitioners of divination are mentioned in Josh. 13:22; 1 Sam. 6:2; Ezek. 21:21ff.

miqsam [**מִקְסָם, 4738**]

miqsam is a rare synonym for ***qesem***, above, denoting "divination" in Ezek. 12:24; 13:7.

nāḥash [**נָחַשׁ, 5172**]

nāḥash is a verb found eleven times with the broad sense of "practice divination," including several related nuances.

The process of "learning by divination" is noted in Gen. 30:27; 44:5, 15. Yahweh forbids Israel to engage in such practices in Lev. 19:26; Deut. 18:10. The act of "watching for an omen" is indicated in 1 Kgs. 20:33. The "practicing of sorcery" is recorded in connection with the horror of child sacrifice in 2 Kgs. 17:17; 21:6; 2 Chr. 33:6.

NT Words

pythōn [πύθων, *4436*]

pythōn is a rare noun literally denoting the name "Python," referring to the dragon in Greek mythology that guarded the oracle at Delphi. In the New Testament it is found only in Acts 16:16, referring to the Philippian girl who had a "spirit of divination" (i.e., spirit of Python), which Paul subsequently cast out.

DIVINE (ADJECTIVE)

NT Words

theios [θεῖος, *2304*]

theios is an adjective found three times denoting "divine" power in 2 Pet. 1:3; and his "divine" nature in 2 Pet. 1:4. See also Acts 17:29.

See Also: → GOD

DIVISION

OT Words

ḥaluqqāh [**חֲלֻקָּה, 2515**]

ḥaluqqāh is a rare noun denoting a "subdivision" of a family group or unit in Israel in 2 Chr. 35:5.

maḥalōqāt [**מַחֲלֹקֶת, 4256**]

maḥalōqāt is a noun found approximately forty times meaning "division," referring to various groups of people within the Israelite community.

The "divisions" or "allotments" of the land of Canaan assigned by Yahweh through Joshua to the tribes of Israel are recorded in Josh. 11:23; 12:7; 18:10. The "divisions" of the Israelite priests assigned to various responsibilities are indicated in 1 Chr. 23:6; 26:1ff.; 28:13; 2 Chr. 5:11; 2 Chr. 8:14; 31:15ff.; 35:4, 10. Israelite army "divisions" are listed in 1 Chr. 27:1ff.; 28:1.

miphlaggôt [**מִפְלַגּוֹת, 4653**]

miphlaggôt is a rare noun denoting Israelite priestly "divisions" set aside for ritual service in the temple in 2 Chr. 35:12.

peluggāh [**פְּלֻגָּה, 6392** (Aramaic)]

peluggāh is a rare Aramaic noun found only in Ezra 6:18 denoting Israelite priestly "divisions," specific Levitical groupings for particular ritual service.

NT Words

diamerismos [**διαμερισμός,** *1267*]

diamerismos is a rare noun found only in Luke 12:51 denoting "division" in the sense of "strife."

dichostasia [**διχοστασία,** *1370*]

dichostasia is a noun found in two places referring to "divisions" in the sense of "quarreling," "dissension" in Rom. 16:17; Gal. 5:20.

schisma [**σχίσμα,** *4978*]

schisma is a noun found eight times denoting "division" in the sense of "dispute," "argument" in John 7:43; 9:16; John 10:19. In particular, Paul exhorts the Corinthian congregation not to engage in "factional arguments or disputes" in 1 Cor. 1:10; 11:18; 12:25.

DIVORCE

OT Words

gārash [**גָּרַשׁ, 1644**]

This verb occurs about fifty times meaning "drive out," "cast out," and related nuances. (→ DRIVE) On four occasions, however, ***gārash*** refers to the action or state of divorce. Lev. 21:7, 14 prohibit a priest from marrying a divorced woman. Lev. 22:13 refers to the divorced (or widowed) daughter of a priest, who is legally entitled to care and provision in her father's house. Finally, Num. 30:9 refers to the binding vow of a widow or divorced woman.

kerîtût [**כְּרִיתוּת, 3748**]

This is a rare noun, occurring only four times. It is translated "divorce," "bill of divorce," and each occurrence is theologically significant.

Deut 24:1, 3 refers to the provision of the Mosaic law covenant whereby a woman who is divorced from her husband may not remarry him if she takes a second husband who then either dies or subsequently divorces her.

The remaining two uses of ***kerîtût*** are symbolic, referring to the divorce (i.e., breakdown of the covenant relationship) between Yahweh and Israel. Isa. 50:1 affirms that God sent Israel away with a bill of divorce because of her constant acts of treachery against him. Jer. 3:8 also refers to Israel's bill of divorce that God gave to her, alluding to the past action of God at the time of the Assyrian invasion and conquest of the northern kingdom. Yet the kingdom of Judah has taken no notice of this warning from Israel's past history. What lies at the heart of the divine "divorce proceedings" is the spiritual adultery of his people — their idolatrous worship of other gods, which constituted a grave breach of the nation's covenantal "marriage" vows of exclusive allegiance to Yahweh.

NT Words

apolyō [**ἀπολύω,** *630*]

apolyō is a common verb found in nearly ninety places with the primary senses of "release," "let go," "dismiss." (→ RELEASE)

In several places, however, ***apolyō*** refers to the action or process of "divorcing" one's wife (Matt. 1:19; 5:31ff.; 19:3ff.; Mark 10:2ff.; Luke 16:18).

apostasion [**ἀποστάσιον,** *647*]

apostasion is a noun found only in Matt. 5:31; 19:7; Mark 10:4, denoting a "bill of divorce" in each case.

Additional Notes

Although Hebrew words for "divorce" are used rarely in the Old Testament, it is a very significant concept. At the heart of Israel's relationship with Yahweh is the demand God placed upon his people for exclusive loyalty and devotion to him. Israel's relationship with God is characterized, from at least one perspective, as an intimate bond that may be appropriately described as a marriage union. Idolatry is often portrayed as spiritual adultery in the Old Testament — a sin which constituted (and continues to constitute) one of the most serious threats to the relationship between God and his people. The great blessing for God's people, however, lies in the fact that God never intended this divorce to be absolute, but always planned to be reconciled to his people. The fulfillment of this plan, whereby the community of Israel would be forgiven their sin and cleansed from their adulterous practices, was anticipated in the Old Testament by the promise of a new covenant (cf. Jer. 31:31ff.; Ezek. 36:24ff.). That new covenant was brought into being and fulfilled by the work of Jesus Christ, who perfectly accomplished the forgiveness and cleansing of all God's people — past, present, and future. Significantly, one of the most sublime symbolic portrayals of Jesus Christ in the New Testament is found in Rev. 21:1ff., where he is presented as the heavenly bridegroom coming to claim his spotless bride — the church, the community of all believers. In heaven there will never again be any divorce or separation from God.

DO, DONE

Both the Hebrew and Greek vocabularies for the concept of "doing" cover a broad range of meaning. For full discussion of the relevant vocabulary, consult the entries listed below.

See Also: → APPOINT → CREATE → EXECUTE → KEEP → MAKE → OFFER → PRACTICE → PREPARE → WORK

DOCTOR → TEACH

DOCTRINE

NT Words

didachē [διδαχή, *1322*]

didachē is a noun found thirty times to mean "doctrine," "teaching." The "teaching" of Christ during his public ministry is indicated in Matt. 7:28; 22:33; Mark 1:22, 27; 4:2; 12:38; John 7:16ff.; 18:19.

The "teaching" of the Pharisees is noted in Matt. 16:12, and the apostolic "teaching" of the early church in Acts 2:42; 5:28; 17:19. In particular, the "teaching" of the Lord is mentioned in Acts 13:12; and the "teaching" of Christ in 2 John 9.

The liberating "teaching" of the gospel in general terms is noted in Rom. 6:17; 16:17; Titus 1:9; 2 Tim. 4:2; 2 John 10. See also 1 Cor. 14:6; 14:26. In contrast, strange or heretical "teaching" is indicated in Heb. 13:9; Rev. 2:14, 15, 24.

didaskalia [διδασκαλία, *1319*]

didaskalia is a synonym for ***didachē*** (see above) denoting "doctrine," or "teaching" throughout the nearly twenty occurrences of the term.

The necessity for "sound teaching," based on the apostolic doctrine of the gospel tradition, is indicated in 1 Tim. 1:10; 4:6, 13ff.; 5:17; 6:1ff.; 3:10ff.; 4:3; Titus 1:9; 2:1ff. There is also one reference to demonic teaching or "doctrines" in 1 Tim. 4:1.

logos [λόγος, *3056*]

logos is a common term denoting "word" as well as various nuances throughout the 331 occurrences of the term. In Heb. 6:1, however, ***logos*** is translated "doctrine," or "teaching" in relation to "the elementary teaching of Christ."

See Also: → LEARN → TEACH

DOG

OT Words

keleb [כֶּלֶב, **3611**]

This noun occurs approximately thirty times and is consistently translated "dog" in both a literal and metaphorical sense.

Literal, mundane references to the animal are found in Exod. 11:7; 22:31; Judg. 7:5; 1 Kgs. 14:11; Job 30:1; Pss. 59:6ff.; 68:22; Prov. 26:11ff.; Eccl. 9:4; Isa. 66:3. There are also a number of significant references to dogs attacking and killing human beings and licking up human blood. This gruesome activity is always associated with God's specific judgment on the wicked, especially apostate, idolatrous rulers of Israel and Judah — for example, Jezebel (cf. 2 Kgs. 9:10, 36; 1 Kgs. 21:23); Ahab (cf. 1 Kgs. 21:19, 24; 22:38); Baasha (cf. 1 Kgs. 16:4); and Jeroboam 1 (cf. 1 Kgs. 14:11). See also Jer. 15:3.

Metaphorically, ***keleb*** is also used as a term of contempt for a male prostitute (cf. Deut. 23:18). "Dog" is also used as a general term of abuse and describes those who engage in despicable acts of wickedness or who come from a despised group of people (cf. 1 Sam. 17:43; 24:14; 2 Sam. 3:8; 9:8; 16:9; 2 Kgs. 8:13; Ps. 22:16, 20; Isa. 56:10, 11).

NT Words

kyōn [κύων, *2965*]

kyōn is a term translated "dog" in each of the five occurrences of the term. Literal references to "dogs" are found in Matt. 7:6; Luke 16:21; 2 Pet. 2:22. The term is also used metaphorically in Phil. 3:2; Rev. 22:15, describing people who are ceremonially impure as "dogs." It also has the underlying sense of "moral perversity."

kynarion [κυνάριον, *2952*]

kynarion is a diminutive form of ***kyōn*** (see above) referring to "dogs" in the literal sense in each of the four occurrences of the term in Matt. 15:26, 27; Mark 7:27ff.

DOMINION

OT Words

māshal [מָשַׁל, 4910]

This verb occurs about seventy times and is translated "rule," "have dominion over." ***māshal*** is generally used in a literal sense, but several texts indicate a metaphorical usage as well.

In its literal sense, ***māshal*** means "to rule" in a variety of contexts. Of these, several are of relatively minor importance. They include the sense of rule in the context of a domestic head of a household (cf. Gen. 24:2); the harsh rule imposed on Israel by foreign powers (cf. Isa. 52:5); and non-specific moral rule, authority, or control (cf. Prov. 6:7; 12:24; 16:32; 19:10).

māshal can also convey the idea of political and/or civic rule — for example, it refers to the civic rulers of Israel, the city elders, tribal leaders (cf. Judg. 14:4; 15:11; 2 Chr. 23:20; Isa. 3:4; Jer. 51:46; Lam. 5:8). The Wisdom literature also contains important maxims for the proper godly exercise of political and civic authority (cf. Prov. 23:1; 28:15; 29:12; Eccl. 9:17; 10:4). See also Gen. 37:8; 45:8, 26; Deut. 15:6. ***māshal*** can also express royal dominion in general (cf. Josh. 12:2; 9:2; 2 Sam. 23:2; Neh. 9:37; Pss. 105:20ff.; 106:41). Of particular interest is Gideon's refusal to accept the position of king offered to him by the tribes of Israel on the occasion of his miraculous victory over the Midianites (cf. Judg. 8:22, 23).

The theocratic rule of kings in Israel and Judah, especially through the Davidic dynasty, is also important. Of greatest significance here is the covenant promise given to David in 2 Chr. 7:18 whereby God guarantees to preserve his dynastic rule over Israel forever. This promise finds its fulfillment in the person of Christ. There is also the divine guarantee never to renege on this covenant promise to David (cf. Jer. 33:26). See also 1 Kgs. 4:24; 2 Chr. 9:26 with reference to Solomon.

The phenomenon of royal dominion and rule is also closely associated with messianic prophecies in the Old Testament that focus on the great ruler to come as one who will have divine authority and power. Such is the case with the prophecy relating to the royal status of the Suffering Servant of Yahweh in Isa. 49:7. Similar promises relating to the emergence of a Messianic King are found in Jer. 30:21; Micah 5:2, both of which (as does Isa. 49:7) anticipate the coming of Jesus Christ. Zech. 6:13 also highlights the coming of a ruler; but this text focuses on the dual aspects of the messianic ruler as one who will exercise a priestly as well as a royal authority.

The direct rule of Yahweh over his people and the nations is also indicated by the term ***māshal*** (cf. 1 Chr. 29:12; 2 Chr. 20:6; Job 25:2; Pss. 22:28; 59:13; 89:9; Isa. 40:10).

māshal is also found in negative contexts where the punitive judgment of God is in view, whether against the rulers of godless nations or against rebellious rulers of Israel and Judah, including Babylon (cf. Isa. 14:5); Moab (cf. Isa. 16:1); Egypt (cf. Isa. 19:4); the unnamed kings of the north and south (cf. Dan. 11:3ff., 39, 43); the rulers of Israel (cf. Isa. 28:14); and Jehoiachin (cf. Jer. 22:30).

The final illustration of the literal use of ***māshal*** may be found in Ps. 8:6, where the writer refers to humankind's "cultural mandate" to rule the earth, given to them at the very beginning of creation (cf. reference to Gen. 1:26, 28 in ***rādāh***, below).

In its metaphorical sense, ***māshal*** refers to the rule of the sun over the day (cf. Gen. 1:18); the husband's tyrannical "rule" over his wife, as a consequence of his rebellion against God (cf. Gen. 3:16); the potential threat of sin's dominion over one's life (cf. Cain in Gen. 4:7).

shelēt [שְׁלֵט, 7981 (Aramaic)]

This is an Aramaic term found only in Daniel. ***shelēt*** occurs seven times and is translated "rule," "have power over."

Dan. 2:38, 39 refer symbolically to the rule of pagan kings in the empires of Babylon and Greece. Daniel is the most powerful civic officer in the kingdom of Babylon, second only to Nebuchadnezzar (cf. Dan. 2:48). See also Dan. 5:7, 16. Finally, ***shelēt*** refers to the "power" of both fire (cf. Dan. 3:27), and lions (cf. Dan. 6:14).

rādāh [רָדָה, 7287]

This verb occurs nearly thirty times and is translated "rule," "have dominion over." ***rādāh*** is synonymous with ***māshal*** and ***shelēt***, above.

rādāh indicates humankind's dominion over creation in Gen. 1:26, 28. God's mandate here gives humankind a privileged position to rule over all of creation and also the solemn responsibility of exercising that control and authority in accordance with God's explicit instructions. It is not a dominion invested in human authority — it is derived from God alone. Human beings act as God's vice regents over the created world.

rādāh also refers in a general sense to the exercise of authority over people — either legitimate or illegitimate. For example, in Lev. 25:43, 46, Israelites are forbidden to enslave their poverty-stricken countrymen and "rule over" them harshly (cf. also Lev. 25:53). Jer. 5:31 indicts the illegitimate priestly rule in Israel, inspired by the false prophets of the day. Ezek. 34:4 condemns the cruelty of Israel's civil rulers. Foreign political rule over Israel is also indicated by this term (cf. Lev. 26:17; Neh. 9:28). This foreign control is understood in the Old Testament as an outworking of the covenant curse. ***rādāh*** also refers to civil authority in Israel (cf. 1 Kgs. 5:16; 9:23; 2 Chr. 8:10).

Regarding the idea of dominion in a military political sense, ***rādāh*** is found in contexts where God promises Israel dominion over her enemies (Num. 24:19), including guarantees that he will punish them for their rebellion against him — for example, Babylon (cf. Isa. 14:6); Egypt (cf. Jer. 5:13); and the Canaanites (cf. Judg. 5:13).

Finally, ***rādāh*** refers specifically to the theocratic rule of Israel within the land of Canaan (cf. 1 Kgs. 4:24), where Solomon's dominion is mentioned. Ps. 72:8 invokes the universal dominion of Israel's king in an ideal, poetic setting. Ps. 110:2 is a prophetic anticipation of the coming Messianic King, fulfilled in the person of Jesus.

sholtān [שָׁלְטָן, 7985 (Aramaic)]

sholtān is an Aramaic term found in nine places with the consistent meaning "dominion" or "rule." Human "dominion" in the context of royal power is indicated in Dan. 4:22; 6:26; 7:6, 12, 26. All these contexts make it clear that such power is derived from God alone. Dan. 4:3, 34; 7:14, 27 specifically refer to the everlasting "dominion" of the divine kingdom.

NT Words

kratos [κράτος, *2904*]

kratos is a noun found in twelve places with the primary sense of "power" or "strength." In several places, however, the term also denotes the "dominion" or "rule" of God — all in the context of invoking such divine authority (cf. 1 Pet. 4:11; 5:11; Jude 25; Rev. 1:6; 5:13).

kyrieuō [κυριεύω, *2961*]

kyrieuō is a verb with the principal meaning "have dominion, power over," "be Lord over" throughout its nine occurrences.

The exercise of human royal dominion or authority is indicated in Luke 22:25. Death is declared to no longer have dominion over Christ in Rom. 6:9. Similarly, sin is declared to no longer exercise any dominion over the believer, who has passed from law to grace. The binding effect of the power or "dominion" of the law is noted in Rom. 7:1. Rom. 14:9 declares that Christ "is Lord of both the dead and the living" (cf. Rom. 14:9). See also 2 Cor. 1:24; 1 Tim. 6:15.

katakyrieuō [κατακυριεύω, *2634*]

katakyrieuō is a variant form of ***kyrieuō***, above, found in four places meaning "exercise dominion, rule over" in the sense of "lord (it) over someone." Such an attitude and action is predicated of the Gentiles in Matt. 20:25; Mark 10:42. The denial of a "domineering stance" towards the members of one's congregation is noted in 1 Pet. 5:3. The meaning "overpower" is found in Acts 19:16.

kyriotēs [κυριότης, *2963*]

kyriotēs is a noun derived from ***kyrieuō*** (see above) denoting "dominion," "civil authority" in a general sense in only four places (cf. Eph. 1:21; Col. 1:16; 2 Pet. 2:10; Jude 8).

See Also: → KINGDOM → RULE

DOOR

OT Words

delet [דֶּלֶת, 1817]

This noun occurs about ninety times meaning "door," "gate."

The majority of occurrences of this term are literal and mundane, with ***delet*** referring variously to the doors of houses (e.g., Gen. 19:6; Exod. 21:6; Josh. 2:19; Isa. 26:20); doors of the tabernacle (e.g., 1 Sam. 3:15); doors of the temple (e.g., 1 Kgs. 16:31ff.; 1 Chr. 22:3. 2 Chr. 4:9; Ezek. 41:23ff.); gates of Jerusalem (e.g., Neh. 3:1ff.; 6:1; 7:1, 3); and gates of the city (e.g., Deut. 3:5; Josh. 6:26; 16:3; 1 Sam. 21:13; 23:7; Ezek. 38:11).

delet is also used in a small number of metaphorical contexts to refer, for example, to the "door" of the womb (Job 3:10); the "door" of the sea (Job 38:8ff.); the "doors" of heaven (Ps. 78:23); and the "doors" of Lebanon (Zech. 11:1).

petaḥ [פֶּתַח, 6607]

This term occurs nearly 160 times and is synonymous with ***delet*** (see above), meaning "door," "entrance," "gate."

Like ***delet***, above, ***petaḥ*** has an almost exclusively literal sense. But ***petaḥ*** frequently refers to the doors of both the tabernacle and the temple. ***petaḥ*** refers to the portable sanctuary of the Israelites in a number of places (cf. Lev. 1, 3, 4, 8, 10, 12, 14ff.; Num. 3, 4, 6, 10, 11, 12, 16; Deut. 31:15; Josh. 19:5; 1 Sam. 2:22, 1 Chr. 9:21). Concerning the doors of the temple, ***petaḥ*** is used about twenty times (e.g., 1 Kgs. 6:8ff.; 2 Chr. 4:22, Jer. 26:10; Ezek. 8:3, 7, 8; 10:19; 40:11, 13, 38, 40; 42:2ff.; 46:3). It also refers to the "gates of the city" in the book of Judges; 1 Kgs. 14:27; 2 Kgs. 10:8; 23:8; Jer. 1:15. Ps. 24:7 contains a poetic reference to the city gates opening to the conquering king. The remaining occurrences all indicate the entrance ways to houses of various kinds (e.g., Gen. 19:6; Exod. 12:22ff.; Judg. 19:27; 2 Sam. 11:9; Neh. 3:20; Job 31:9; Prov. 9:14). In particular, the door of Noah's ark is mentioned in Gen. 6:16.

In Hos. 2:15 ***petaḥ*** is used metaphorically in the context of God's promise to help the people of Israel by making the Valley of Achor into a "door of hope." Achor was associated with the terrible punishment God inflicted on Achan for having taken some of the forbidden plunder of Jericho for himself, and causing the conquest of Canaan to temporarily falter (cf. Josh. 7:26).

saph **[סַף, 5592]**

saph is a term found about thirty times meaning "door," "threshold" in about half these instances.

The "threshold" of a house is indicated in 1 Kgs. 14:17; and that of the tabernacle and temple in 2 Kgs. 12:9; 22:4; 23:4; 1 Chr. 9:19; 23:4; Isa. 6:4; 35:4; Ezek. 40:6ff.; Amos 9:1.

NT Words

thyra [θύρα, *2374*]

The noun ***thyra*** designates a "door" or "gate" throughout its nearly forty occurrences.

Literal references to "doors" include Matt. 6:6; 25:10; Mark 11:4; 15:46; Luke 11:7; John 10:1ff.; 18:16; Acts 3:2; 12:6; 16:26ff.

Elsewhere, ***thyra*** refers metaphorically to a "door" of opportunity for ministry in 1 Cor. 16:9; 2 Cor. 2:12; Col. 4:3. The "door" of the heavenly kingdom is indicated in Rev. 3:8; 4:1; and similarly, Jas. 5:9 refers to the symbolic "doors" of heaven, at which the judge of all the earth stood ready to pronounce his judgment.

DOUBLE

OT Words

kāphal **[כָּפַל, 3717]**

This is a rare verb, occurring only five times, meaning "double" or "double over." All but one reference is found in a ritual context.

In Exod. 26:9, ***kāphal*** refers to the coupling or doubling of curtains in the front of the tabernacle. Exod. 28:14; 39:9 describe the folding or doubling of the high priest's breastpiece. Ezek. 21:14 refers metaphorically to the inevitable slaughter of the Babylonians through the prophetic symbol of the sword being "doubled" (i.e., brought down twice in an action of slaying an opponent).

mishneh **[מִשְׁנֶה, 4932]**

This noun occurs thirty-five times with the principal meaning "second," "double," as well as associated senses. (→ SECOND)

Gen. 43:12, 15 refer to "double the money"; Exod. 16:5, 22 refer to "twice as much manna." Job 42:10 describes the double blessing that God bestowed on Job after his testing, granting to him double the material benefits he had enjoyed prior to his suffering. Isa. 61:7 refers to a promised double portion of blessing to Israel (cf. also Zech. 9:12). ***mishneh*** indicates double divine punishment for Judah on account of their rebellion against God in Jer. 16:18, while in Jer. 17:18 the prophet invokes "double disaster" on his tormentors.

shenayim **[שְׁנַיִם, 8147]**

shenayim denotes the number "two," as well as related senses throughout its more than 750 occurrences. Several places indicate the meaning "double." "Double payment" rendered as a restitution for stolen goods is noted in Exod. 22:4ff. See also Deut. 21:17. In 2 Kgs. 2:9 Elisha requests a "double" portion of Elijah's spirit.

kephel **[כֶּפֶל, 3718]**

kephel is a rare noun meaning "double" in Isa. 40:2, referring to Isaiah's recognition that Israel had received "double" payment for all her sins from the Lord's hands.

NT Words

diplous [διπλοῦς, *1362*]

diplous is an adjective meaning "double" in 1 Tim. 5:17, referring to elders worthy of "double honor." Rev. 18:6 refers to the divine sentence passed on Babylon, who will receive "double repayment" for her sins.

diploō [διπλόω, *1363*]

diploō is a verb signifying "to double," "to repay or render twofold" (cf. Rev. 18:6).

dipsychos [δίψυχος, *1374*]

dipsychos is a rare adjective referring to those who are "double-minded," signifying emotional and spiritual immaturity (cf. Jas. 1:8; 4:8).

DOUBT, DOUBTLESS

NT Words

diakrinō [διακρίνω, *1252*]

diakrinō is a verb found over twenty times with the primary meaning "judge," "discern." (→ JUDGE) In several places ***diakrinō*** also means "to doubt," referring in Matt. 21:21; Mark 11:23 to the importance of "not doubting" the power of God. Jas. 1:6; Rom. 14:23 affirm that the person who doubts is condemned. See also Jude 22.

distazō [διστάζω, *1365*]

distazō is a rare verb meaning "doubt" in relation to the wavering of one's faith and trust in God and Christ (Matt. 14:31; 28:17).

DOVE, TURTLEDOVE

OT Words

yônāh [יוֹנָה, **3123**]

This term, translated "dove" or "pigeon," is found about thirty times in both a metaphorical and literal sense.

Literal references to doves are found in narrative contexts in Gen. 8:8ff.; 2 Kgs. 6:25; Jer. 48:28. There are also a number of references to doves or pigeons as sacrificial birds (for both the burnt offering and the sin offering) in the ritual sections of the Pentateuch (cf. Lev. 1:14; 5:7, 11; 12:6, 8; 14:22, 30; 15:14, 29; Num. 6:10).

yônāh is also found in a number of metaphorical contexts. In Ps. 55:6, the psalmist wishes for "wings of a dove" to escape from his trials (cf. also Ps. 68:13). The Song of Songs expresses in several places the delight of the lover and his beloved for one another. Each admires the other's physical beauty, remarking among other things that their eyes are "like doves" (cf. Song 1:15; 4:1; 5:12); the term "dove" is also used an expression of endearment (cf. Song 2:14; 5:2; 6:9). Conversely, ***yônāh*** is also used in contexts that suggest deep anguish, usually with the expression "moan like doves." It is used, for example, in the case of King Hezekiah at the time of his illness (cf. Isa. 38:11); of Israel's despair at her divine punishment (cf. Isa. 59:11); and of Judah's anguish in similar circumstances (cf. Ezek. 7:16). See also Nah. 2:7 in relation to the nation of Assyria. In Hos. 7:11, Ephraim (i.e., Israel) is described as being "silly," "like a dove," for turning to Egypt for support and help.

tôr [תּוֹר, **8449**]

This is a relatively rare term occurring only fourteen times. ***tôr*** is synonymous with ***yônāh*** (see above), meaning "dove" or "turtledove."

tôr is found primarily in ritual contexts, referring to the turtledove as a sacrificial animal. In Gen. 15:9, for example, the turtledove forms part of a very solemn and significant animal sacrifice, in which God reaffirms his covenant promise to Abraham and prophesies the future enslavement of his descendants in Egypt for a period of about four hundred years, followed by their release. Then, as with ***yônāh***, ***tôr*** indicates a sacrificial bird either as a burnt offering, or sin offering, or both (cf. Lev. 1:14; 5:7, 11; 12:6ff.; 14:22, 30; 15:29; Num. 6:10). Other literal references are found in Song 2:12; Jer. 8:7.

tôr is used metaphorically in Ps. 74:19, where the psalmist pleads with God not to hand over his "dove" (i.e., his people) to wild beasts.

NT Words

peristera [περιστερά, *4058*]

peristera is a noun found ten times with the meaning "dove."

Literal references to "doves" include Matt. 10:16; 21:12; Mark 11:15; John 2:14, 16. The term also refers symbolically to the form of a dove that settled upon Christ after his baptism at the outset of his public ministry, indicating his Father's personal stamp of approval (cf. Matt. 3:16; Mark 1:10; Luke 3:22; John 1:32).

In Luke 2:24 ***peristera*** refers to "pigeons."

trygōn [τρυγών, *5167*]

trygōn is a rare noun denoting "turtledoves" in Luke 2:24.

DOWN

NT Words

katō [κάτω, *2736*]

katō is an adverbial form meaning "down" in half of the eleven occurrences of the term. In vain, Satan commands Christ to "throw himself down" from the pinnacle of the temple in Matt. 4:6; Luke 4:9. John 8:6 describes Jesus "stooping down" to write in the dust. The act of "falling down" is noted in Acts 20:9.

DRAG → DRAW

DRAGON

NT Words

drakōn [δράκων, *1404*]

drakōn is a noun found thirteen times denoting a "dragon." The term has exclusive metaphorical reference to the devil in his most potent guise, and is found only in the book of Revelation (cf. Rev. 12:3ff.; 13:2ff.; 16:13; 20:2).

See Also: → SERPENT

DRAW

OT Words

shālaph [**שָׁלַף, 8025**]

This verb occurs twenty-five times, meaning "draw out." ***shālaph*** refers almost exclusively to the "drawing" of a sword in situations of armed military conflict or deeds of individual valor. One prominent example of this is found in the David and Goliath narrative of 1 Sam. 17:51, where the young warrior "draws" his sword and cuts off the Philistine giant's head. Other occurrences are found in Num. 22:23; Josh. 5:13; Judg. 8:10; 9:54; 20:2ff.; 1 Sam. 31:4; 2 Sam. 24:9; 2 Kgs. 3:26; 1 Chr. 21:5, 16.

shā'ab [**שָׁאַב, 7579**]

This term means "draw water" and occurs nineteen times, in both literal and symbolic contexts.

The physical "drawing" of water is mentioned in Gen. 24:11ff.; Deut. 29:11; Josh. 9:21ff.; Ruth 2:9; 1 Sam. 7:8; 2 Sam. 23:16; 1 Chr. 11:18; Nah. 3:14.

shā'ab is used metaphorically in 1 Sam. 12:3 to refer to the promise of Israel "drawing water" from the wells of salvation.

māshak [**מָשַׁךְ, 4900**]

This verb occurs nearly forty times with the meanings "draw," "drag," "seize." ***māshak*** includes the actions of "drawing" (i.e., pulling), "drawing (lifting) out," "drawing the bow," "drawing out" (i.e., prolonging and/or attracting). ***māshak*** has these meanings in about half of its occurrences.

In the sense of "lifting out," ***māshak*** is found in Gen. 37:28, where Joseph is pulled out of a pit; and also in Jer. 38:13, where the prophet is lifted out of a well. Job 41:1 refers to the impossibility of lifting Leviathan out of the ocean with a hook. In Deut. 21:3 ***māshak*** indicates the "drawing" or "leading" of a heifer by the yoke. The word is used metaphorically in Hos. 11:4 to describe how God "led" or "drew" Israel in the past with cords of compassion.

The meaning "attraction" is found in Judg. 4:7, for example, where Sisera is "lured" or "drawn" into battle to face defeat at the hands of the Israelites. Song 1:4 records the intimate attraction between the two lovers. Jer. 31:3 contains a significant reference to the attraction between God and his people — Yahweh affirms his deep love for them, maintaining that he "has drawn" them to him with loving-kindness.

The "drawing" of a bow is mentioned in 1 Kgs. 22:34 (the random slaying of King Ahab); 2 Chr. 18:33; Isa. 66:19.

Finally, ***māshak*** means "drawing out" or "prolonging" in Job 24:22; Ps. 85:5.

nāgash [**נָגַשׁ, 5066**]

This is a fairly common verb that occurs 125 times meaning "draw near" or "approach," in a variety of contexts.

Most common is the mundane sense of "approaching," referring to physical proximity. This usage is found predominantly in the Pentateuch and Former Prophets (e.g., Gen. 18:23; Exod. 34:30ff.; Deut. 20:2; Josh. 8:11; Ruth 2:14; 1 Sam. 9:18; 2 Sam. 11:21; 1 Kgs. 18:21ff.; 2 Kgs. 4:27; Jer. 42:1.)

More significantly, the book of Exodus refers to those who "draw near" to God on Mt. Sinai, where he meets with Moses and imparts to him the details of the law covenant intended for the whole of the Israelite people (cf. Exod. 19:22; 20:21; 21:6; 24:2). Other significant references to ***nāgash*** in this sense are found in Jer. 30:21, for example, where the promise is given of a Messiah who will "draw close" to God. Isa. 29:13 contains an indictment of false worship in which people draw near to God with lip service only. See also Lev. 21:21; Deut. 21:5; 1 Kgs. 18:36; 2 Chr. 29:31; Isa. 45:20.

In a related sense, ***nāgash*** also describes priests "drawing near" to the altar in solemn preparation for their divine service (cf. Exod. 28:43; 30:20; Num. 4:19; 8:19).

Other uses of ***nāgash*** include "drawing near," for the purpose of sexual relations (Exod. 19:15); approaching the civil courts for legal judgment (Deut. 25:1); the nations "drawing near" to God for judgment (Isa. 41:1; 50:8; Joel 3:9); and "assembling," or "drawing near" for battle (Judg. 20:23; 1 Sam. 17:16; 2 Sam. 10:13; 11:20; 1 Chr. 19:14; Jer. 46:3). In addition, prophets are said "to approach" the intended recipient of God's revelation in order to convey that divinely received message (cf. 1 Kgs. 20:13, 22, 28). Finally, the command to stay away (i.e., not to draw near) is expressed in several contexts: disobedient Levitical priests are banned from approaching God in order to serve him (cf. Ezek. 44:13); and the avenging angel is forbidden to "approach" anyone who has the mark of God's preservation on their forehead (cf. Ezek. 9:6). See also Isa. 65:5.

qārab **[קָרַב, 7126]**

This term is synonymous with ***nāgash*** (see above), occurring about 280 times with the principal meaning "draw (come) near," "offer." As with ***nāgash***, ***qārab*** is found in a variety of contexts. (→ OFFER)

With the mundane sense of "approaching," referring to physical proximity, ***qārab*** is found primarily in narrative sections of the Pentateuch and Former Prophets (e.g., Gen. 12:11; Exod. 14:10; Lev. 10:4ff.; Deut. 1:22; Josh. 10:24; 2 Sam. 15:5; 1 Kgs. 2:7; Ps. 32:9; Jonah 1:6).

"Drawing near" for legal assistance or to make important decisions is mentioned, for example, in Num. 27:1; 36:1; Josh. 17:4, where God himself adjudicated the case of the daughters of Zelophehad through Moses and granted these women their full inheritance in Canaan. See also Esth. 5:2; Ezek. 9:1.

qārab also indicates "approaching" someone for the purpose of sexual relations (cf. Gen. 20:4; Lev. 18:6, 14, 19; 20:16; Isa. 8:3; 26:17; Ezek. 18:6).

Another significant use of ***qārab*** involves the phenomenon of "drawing near" to God. For example, in Exod. 16:9 Israel is commanded to "approach" God to receive her judgment for sin. Similarly, in Num. 16:5 Korah is summoned to "appear" before God to receive his punishment for rebelling against Moses. See also Josh. 7:14ff., concerning Achan; and Isa. 34:1; 41:1, 5; 48:16, where the nations are summoned to God for the same purpose — to hear sentence passed upon them. Jer. 30:21 contains the promise of the Messiah, who will "draw near" to God. Other examples of ***qārab*** with this sense are found in Lev. 9:5ff.; Deut. 4:11; 5:23ff.; 1 Sam. 14:36; Job 31:37. ***qārab***, like ***nāgash*** above, is also used in a negative sense (cf. Exod. 3:5, where God commands Moses not to approach the burning bush because it is ground made sacred by the presence of God).

"Approaching" the altar is also indicated by the use of ***qārab***; and again the ritual context of priestly service predominates (cf. Exod. 40:32; Num. 3:6; 16:40; Ezek. 44:15ff.). See also Lev. 21:17.

"Assembling" for battle is likewise indicated by ***qārab*** in Deut. 20:2, 10; Josh. 8:5; Judg. 20:24; 1 Sam. 17:48.

Finally, there are two distinctive uses of ***qārab*** that are not matched by that of ***nāgash***. Several texts refer to someone's time drawing near, whether it be their death — for example, Jacob (cf. Gen. 47:29); Moses (cf. Deut. 31:14); David (cf. 1 Kgs. 2:1); humankind in general (cf. Job 33:22) — or inevitable judgment from God (cf. Lam. 4:18; Ezek. 22:4). See also Gen. 27:41. ***qārab*** is also used in situations where the writer pleads for God to draw near (e.g., Ps. 69:18; Isa. 5:19; Lam. 3:57).

In a metaphorical use of ***qārab*** in Ps. 91:10, the psalmist affirms that no disaster will approach his tent if he fully commits himself to God and his service.

rûq **[רוּק, 7324]**

rûq is a verb found nineteen times with the predominant sense of "empty," "draw."

rûq commonly refers metaphorically to Yahweh "drawing his sword" with a view to punishing his enemies, including his own rebellious people (cf. Exod. 15:9; Lev. 26:33; Ezek. 5:2, 12; 12:14). See also Ps. 35:3; Ezek. 30:11.

dālāh **[דָּלָה, 1802]**

The verb ***dālāh*** means "draw" in relation to literally drawing water from a well in Exod. 2:16, 19. In Prov. 20:5 the sense is metaphorical, referring to "drawing out" a man's purpose from his mind like drawing water from a well.

NT Words

anabibazō **[ἀναβιβάζω, *307*]**

anabibazō is a rare verb found only in Matt. 13:48 referring to people "drawing" or "pulling" a boat to shore.

helkō **[ἕλκω, *1670*]**

helkō is a verb found eight times with the meaning "draw," "drag."

In literal contexts, the term refers to the "drawing (i.e., unsheathing)" of a sword (cf. John 18:10). The "dragging" or "hauling" in of a net full of fish is indicated in John 21:6, 11. The physical action of "dragging" people away is noted in Acts 16:19; 21:30. See also Jas. 2:6.

Metaphorically, ***helkō*** also describes the divine act of "drawing people" to God — causing them to come to him in faith and trust (cf. John 6:44; 12:32).

exelkō [ἐξέλκω, *1828*]

exelkō is a rare variant of ***helkō***, above, found only in Jas. 1:14 and referring symbolically to people "being dragged away (i.e., lured)" by their own lust.

syrō [σύρω, *4951*]

syrō is a synonym for the entries above, meaning "draw," "drag" in literal contexts. John 21:8 describes the disciples "dragging" a net full of fish. Elsewhere, the term denotes the physical "removal" or "dragging" of people from one location to another.

spaō [σπάω, *4685*]

spaō is a rare verb found only in Mark 14:47; Acts 16:27, referring to "drawing" a sword.

anaspaō [ἀνασπάω, *385*]

anaspaō is a rare variant of ***spaō***, above, referring to "drawing or pulling up" an animal or person that had fallen into a well in Luke 14:5. In Acts 11:10, the sheet laden with food in Peter's vision is "drawn up" into heaven.

antleō [ἀντλέω, *501*]

antleō is a verb referring to the "drawing of water" in John 2:9; 4:7, 15; and to the miraculous "drawing" of wine from a jar that had been filled with water in John 2:8.

engizō [ἐγγίζω, *1448*]

engizō is a verb found around forty times meaning "draw near," as well as associated nuances.

The action of "drawing near" to a physical location is indicated in Matt. 21:1; Mark 11:1; Luke 7:12; 15:1; 18:35; 19:29; 19:41; Acts 9:3.

The meaning "approach," in the context of the coming harvest season, is indicated in Matt. 21:34.

The meaning "be at hand" in the temporal sense of "draw near" in relation to a particular significant event, is indicated in Matt. 26:45ff.; Mark 14:42; Luke 21:8; 22:1; Acts 7:17; Heb. 10:25; Jas. 5:8. This is particularly the case in relation to the coming of the kingdom of God (cf. Mark 1:15; Luke 10:9ff.).

The process of "drawing near" to God through the person and work of Christ is indicated in Heb. 7:19. See also Jas. 4:8.

See Also: ➡ COME

DREAM

OT Words

ḥalôm [חֲלוֹם, **2472**]

This noun occurs sixty-five times with the meaning "dream." It has an exclusively literal sense but refers to both ordinary and prophetic dreams.

ḥalôm is used in a mundane sense in Job 20:8; 33:15; Ps. 73:20; Eccl. 5:3, 7; Isa. 29:7.

In a prophetic context, ***ḥalôm*** refers to dreams that point to the future purposes of God, both immediate and more distant. In the first instance, this term indicates dreams that are given by divine agency to those other than vocational prophets — for example, Abimelech (Gen. 20:3ff.); Jacob (Gen. 31:10, 11); Laban (Gen. 31:24); Joseph (Gen. 37:5ff.); the Egyptian cupbearer and baker (Gen. 40:5ff.); Pharaoh (Gen. 41:7ff.); and Nebuchadnezzar (Dan. 2:1ff.). Joel 2:28 speaks of the coming of new revelation through the Spirit of God. Although this prophecy is recorded in a canonical prophet's work, the dreams and visions referred to will be experienced by ordinary lay people. See also Judg. 7:13ff.; 1 Sam. 28:6; 1 Kgs. 3:5, 15.

Secondly, dreams are also given by God to those with special prophetic calling. For example, Num. 12:6; Deut. 13:1ff. refer to the general prophetic phenomenon of dream revelation from God. Dan. 1:17 also affirms that Daniel's ability to both receive and interpret dreams is only possible through the wisdom of God, granted solely by God himself. By way of stark contrast, Jer. 23:27; 27:9; 29:8; Zech. 10:2 refer to the dreams of lying prophets, which are products of their own delusions and not from God.

ḥēlem [חֵלֶם, **2493** (Aramaic)]

This is an Aramaic term, the noun equivalent to the Hebrew ***ḥalôm*** (see above). Meaning "dream, "***ḥēlem*** occurs more than twenty times, only in the book of Daniel.

ḥēlem refers almost exclusively to the dreams that God gave to Nebuchadnezzar (cf. Dan. 2:4–45; 4:5ff.; 5:12), including Daniel's God-given ability to interpret those dreams. Through those dreams, God conveyed to Daniel his saving purposes for his people Israel, and also conveyed to Nebuchadnezzar the certain destruction of not only the Babylonian Empire, but also of all human empires opposed to Yahweh. Finally, in Dan. 7:1 ***ḥēlem*** refers to the apocalyptic vision of the four beasts.

ḥālam **[חָלַם, 2492]**

This is the verbal root from which the noun ***ḥalôm*** (see above) is derived. ***ḥālam*** occurs about thirty times, and is translated "dream" in the majority of instances. Again, a distinction is made in the usage of this term between ordinary dreams and dreams with distinct prophetic significance; although the latter predominate. The ordinary use of ***ḥālam***, for instance, is found in Ps. 126:1; Isa. 29:8.

There is a considerable degree of overlap between the usage of ***ḥālam*** and ***ḥalôm*** in contexts where the dreams have genuine prophetic significance. For example, ***ḥālam*** is found in the following texts: Gen. 28:12; 37:5ff.; 40:5, 8; 41:11; Deut. 13:1ff.; Jer. 23:25; 29:8; Judg. 7:13; Dan. 2:1; Joel 2:28.

NT Words

onar **[ὄναρ, *3677*]**

onar is a noun denoting "dream" in all six occurrences of the term, most of which indicate divine presence and intention in the dream and have to do with protecting the infant Jesus and those who were venerating him (cf. Matt. 1:20; 2:12ff.). Matt. 27:19 refers to the disturbing dream of Pilate's wife, which moved her to warn her husband to have nothing to do with Jesus.

enypnion **[ἐνύπνιον, *1798*]**

enypnion is a rare noun denoting "dreams," found only in Acts 2:17.

enypniazō **[ἐνυπνιάζω, *1797*]**

enypniazō is a verb found only twice, designating the experience of "dreaming" in Acts 2:17; Jude 8.

DRINK

OT Words

mishteh **[מִשְׁתֶּה, 4960]**

This noun occurs about fifty times meaning "feast," "banquet," "drink." (→ FEAST) However, ***mishteh*** in the latter sense of "drink" is rare, occurring only five times (Ezra 3:7; Dan. 1:5ff.).

shēkār **[שֵׁכָר, 7941]**

This noun is translated "strong drink," "strong wine," referring to alcoholic beverage of some potency. It is also very likely that ***shēkār*** refers to "beer." The term occurs about twenty times and has a literal meaning throughout.

The use of ***shēkār*** is forbidden in two contexts within the life of ancient Israel: First of all, priests were forbidden to use "intoxicating liquor" while on duty in the tabernacle (cf. Lev. 10:9). Secondly, "alcoholic drink" was also forbidden to all those who undertook a Nazirite vow (cf. Num. 6:3; Judg. 13:4).

"Liquor" also formed part of the drink offering in Num. 28:7; and it was served at the fellowship meal eaten in the presence of God in the tabernacle (cf. Deut. 14:26). In addition, "alcoholic beverages" were absent from the diet of the Israelites in the wilderness (cf. Deut. 29:6).

The moderate consumption of ***shēkār*** is enjoined in Prov. 20:6; 31:5; but Isa. 5:11, 22 condemn its abuse. Isa. 28:7 condemns the debauchery of Israelite priests and prophets in this regard. See also Isa. 56:12; Mic. 2:11; 1 Sam. 1:15.

Finally, alcoholic beverages were administered as a palliative in the case of terminal illness or overwhelming distress (cf. Prov. 31:6).

shātāh **[שָׁתָה, 8354]**

This common verb translates "drink," "be (get) drunk." ***shātāh*** occurs around two hundred times and has both a literal as well as a metaphorical sense.

Throughout the Pentateuch, "drinking" in a mundane, literal sense is referred to about fifty times, and a significant number of these occurrences relate to the hardship of thirst in the wilderness — a need to which God responded in a miraculous way. Throughout the remainder of the Old Testament there are approximately 150 references to drinking in the ordinary sense, spread fairly evenly over the various forms of literature contained there.

Drinking alcoholic beverage to excess, or getting drunk, is indicated in Gen. 9:21; 1 Kgs. 16:9; 20:16. In an interesting use of the term, God invokes "drunkenness" on the nations in Jer. 25:27ff. as part of their punishment. The intention is that they will be driven to drink as they contemplate the terror of facing God's wrath, referred to here as "the cup of God's wrath."

There are also various metaphorical uses associated with the idea of drinking in the Old Testament. Prominent here is the use of ***shātāh*** in reference to "drinking the cup of God's wrath," which means to experience fierce punishment from God as a consequence of one's sin. This is indicated in a general sense in Ps. 75:8; then various pagan nations also partake of this bitter "cup" — for example, Edom (Jer. 49:12); Babylon (Hab. 2:16); and the wicked in general (Job 21:20). Even God's people do not escape such a punishment when their actions call for it — for example, Jerusalem (Isa. 51:17, 22); Judah (Ezek. 23:32). Other symbolic actions associated with the verb ***shātāh*** include the drinking of blood in Ezek. 39:17ff., a passage describing the symbolic but very real annihilation of the enemies of God and his people. Drinking the blood of one's enemies is a way of symbolically describing a consummate victory over them. See also Num. 23:24 in this regard.

shākar [שָׁכַר, 7937]

This verb occurs nineteen times with the primary meaning "be (get) drunk." It is also used both literally and symbolically.

In the literal sense of being intoxicated, ***shākar*** is found in Gen. 9:21; 43:34; 1 Sam. 1:14; 2 Sam. 11:13; Song 5:1; Hab. 2:15; Hag. 1:6.

Metaphorically, ***shākar*** refers to the state of being "drunk" with blood as a symbolic depiction of God's judgment on his enemies (cf. Deut. 32:42; Isa. 49:26). The term is also used in expressions that seek to describe the emotional and psychological response of those who are confronted by the wrath and judgment of God. Various nations, including the Israelites, are described as being "drunk (with fear and, or shock)" as they face the wrath of Yahweh — for example, Moab (cf. Jer. 48:26); Babylon (cf. Jer. 51:39, 57); Edom (cf. Lam. 4:21); Nineveh (cf. Nah. 3:11); the nations at large (cf. Isa. 63:6; Jer. 25:27); and Judah and Jerusalem (cf. Isa. 29:9).

shāqāh [שָׁקָה, 8248]

shāqāh is a verb that means "drinking" in most of the nearly eighty occurrences of the term.

The "drinking" of wine is indicated in Gen. 19:32ff.; Esth. 1:7; Song 8:2; Jer. 35:2; Amos 2:12. "Drinking" water is noted in Gen. 21:19; 24:14ff.; Prov. 25:21; Exod. 32:20; Num. 5:24ff.; Judg. 4:19; 1 Sam. 30:11; 1 Chr. 11:17. God's miraculous prevision of water for his people is indicated in Ps. 78:15; Isa. 43:20. Giving water to animals to drink is recorded in Gen. 29:2ff.; Exod. 2:16ff.; Num. 20:8; Ps. 104:11.

"Drinking" in the metaphorical sense of enjoying the blessings of God is indicated in Ps. 36:8. In contrast, the psalmist refers to God "giving his people wine to drink" in the context of handing out punishment (cf. Pss. 60:4; 80:5; Jer. 8:14; 9:15; 23:15). In a similar context, God is said to force the nations to drink the cup of the wine of his wrath in Jer. 25:15, 17. See also Hab. 2:15.

mashqeh [מַשְׁקֶה, 4945]

mashqeh is a noun derived from ***shāqāh*** (see above) denoting "drink" in most of the seven contexts of the term. General usage is indicated in Lev. 11:34; 1 Kgs. 10:21; 2 Chr. 9:20; Isa. 32:6.

shetāh [שְׁתָה, 8355 (Aramaic)]

shetāh is an Aramaic verb meaning "to drink" in the context of King Belshazzar's blasphemous use of the sacred utensils of the Jerusalem temple, taken by his predecessor, Nebuchadnezzar, at the sack of the city (cf. Dan. 5:1ff., 23).

shikkôr [שִׁכּוֹר, 7910]

shikkôr is an adjective denoting the state of "drunkenness" throughout its thirteen occurrences (cf. 1 Sam. 1:13; 25:36; 1 Kgs. 16:9; 20:16; Job 12:25; Ps. 107:27; Prov. 26:9; Isa. 19:14; 24:20; 28:1ff.; Jer. 23:9; Joel 1:5).

NT Words

poma [πόμα, *4188*]

poma is a rare noun denoting "drink" in a general sense in Heb. 9:10. 1 Cor. 10:4 refers to the "supernatural drink" provided by God for his people in the wilderness.

posis [πόσις, *4213*]

posis is a noun found in three contexts denoting "drink" in a general sense in Col. 2:16; Rom. 14:17. John 6:55 refers to Christ's blood as "drink," symbolizing spiritual nourishment for the believer alongside his flesh, designated as "food."

sikera [σίκερα, *4608*]

sikera is a rare noun denoting "strong drink," found only in Luke 1:15. It constitutes the dynamic equivalent for the Hebrew term ***shēkār*** (see above).

pinō [πίνω, *4095*]

pinō is a verb found in approximately seventy places meaning "to drink," used both literally and figuratively.

Literal references to "drinking" include Matt. 6:25; 11:18ff.; 24:38; 27:34; Mark 2:16; 15:23; Luke 1:15; 5:30ff.; 12:19; John 4:7ff.; Acts 9:9; 23:12; 1 Cor. 11:22. "Drinking" the cup of the Lord's Supper is indicated in 1 Cor. 10:21; 11:25ff.

A significant metaphorical usage of ***pinō*** is found in Matt. 20:22ff.; 26:42; Mark 10:38ff., with reference to Christ "drinking the cup" that will be given to him. This refers to his approaching arrest, trial, and crucifixion. Luke 22:30; John 18:11 refer to eating and drinking in the heavenly kingdom of Christ as a metaphor for enjoying his fellowship.

Christ asks his disciples "to drink" the cup of the Passover meal with him, signifying his blood of the covenant which is soon to be poured out for the forgiveness of the sins of many people (cf. Matt. 26:27ff.; Mark 14:23ff.). See also John 6:53ff.

Associated with Christ's request for drinking water from the Samaritan woman is his own "offer" to the woman. He affirms that if she "drinks" the water he gives to her she will never thirst again. This is the "water of life," a symbol for everlasting peace with God gained through Christ. (cf. John 4:14). See also John 7:37. In the context of judgment, Rev. 14:10 declares that the wicked will be forced "to drink" the wine of God's wrath. See also Rev. 16:6; 18:3.

1 Cor. 10:4 refers to Israel "drinking" the water provided by Yahweh in the wilderness.

methyō [μεθύω, *3184*]

methyō is a verb found seven times with the primary meaning "to be drunk" as a consequence of taking excessive amounts of wine (cf. Matt. 24:49; John 2:10; Acts 2:15; 1 Cor. 11:21; 1 Thess. 5:7). Metaphorical usage of the term is found in Rev. 17:2 in relation to the kings of the earth having got "drunk" on the immorality of the "Babylonian whore," symbolizing the kingdom of Babylon. The same symbolic whorish figure is said "to be drunk" with the blood of the martyrs.

potizō [ποτίζω, *4222*]

potizō is a verb found fifteen times, meaning "provide water," "give to drink" throughout.

The act of "giving a drink of water" to someone is indicated in Matt. 10:42; 25:35ff.; 27:48; Mark 9:41; 15:36; Rom. 12:20. The act of "watering" animals is noted in Luke 13:15. The "giving of milk to drink" is indicated in 1 Cor. 3:2.

The remaining use of ***potizō*** is metaphorical. The act of "watering" in 1 Cor. 3:6ff. refers to the cultivation and enrichment of one's ministry. Believers are said to "have been made to drink" of the one Spirit, signifying their spiritual union with Christ on the occasion of their baptism. Rev. 14:8 refers to Babylon "making the nations drink the wine of her adulteries."

hydropoteō [ὑδροποτέω, *5202*]

hydropoteō is a rare verb found only in 1 Tim. 5:23, referring to "drinking water."

Additional Notes

When comparing the Old Testament phenomenon of "drinking" with that of the New, the divine provision of water in the wilderness parallels the person of the Messiah, presented as the living water. This imagery illustrates the progressive unfolding of one aspect of God's plan of salvation — meeting the deep needs of God's people, commencing with the physical and culminating in the spiritual. The other significant parallel lies in comparing the action of "drinking the cup of God's wrath" in the old covenant context with the sharing of the "maddening wine" of Babylon's adultery, and her own "cup" from God in the book of Revelation. The terrible fate of the harlot Babylon in the Apocalypse of John is one of the ultimate representative symbols of the eternal destiny of the wicked, foreshadowed by the experience of all those nations. These included Israel and Judah in the old covenant era, who tasted the wrath of God for their sins.

DRIVE

OT Words

gārash [גָּרַשׁ, 1644]

gārash is translated "drive out," in addition to associated meanings, and it occurs about fifty times.

In the sense of "drive out," or "expel," ***gārash*** is used in a number of contexts. There are a number of passages, for example, that have no particular significance (e.g., Num. 22:6, 11; Judg. 9:41; 11:2, 7; 1 Kgs. 2:27; Job 30:5; Ps. 34:1; Mic. 2:9). Some passages reveal God's judgment on sin — for example, Adam and Eve's expulsion from the garden of Eden (cf. Gen. 3:24); and Cain's exile from his fellow human beings (cf. Gen. 4:4). Of particular significance for the outworking of God's plan of salvation for his people under the old covenant is God's determination to drive out the Canaanites from the land of promise (cf. Exod. 23:28ff.; 34:11; Josh. 24:12, 18; Judg. 6:9; 1 Chr. 17:21; Pss. 78:55; 80:8). Within this broad plan, however, there is a so-called "reversal theme," whereby God does not completely expel the Canaanites. He does this because of Israel's unwillingness to obey him and engage the inhabitants of the land in battle (cf. Judg. 2:3ff.).

At a broader level, ***gārash*** is used in contexts where divine judgment against the nations at large is in view. Where it is said that God drives the nation away, casting it aside, the destruction of that people is implied — for example Assyria (Ezek. 31:11); and the Philistines (Zeph. 2:14). Similar judgment is also invoked against Israel, whereby God determines to drive them out of the land of Canaan, as punishment for their idolatry and rebellion against him (cf. Hos. 9:15).

nādaḥ [**נָדַח, 5080**]

This verb occurs about fifty times and means "drive out," "drive away."

In its literal sense, **nādaḥ** indicates the action of physical removal (cf. 2 Chr. 13:9; Ps. 5:10; Jer. 23:2). Neh. 1:9; Isa. 27:13 refer to those Israelites who are cast out of their land.

There are also a number of texts that refer to God driving his people into exile as a punishment for their sin (cf. Deut. 30:1; Jer. 8:3; 24:9ff.; 29:18; Ezek. 4:13; Dan. 9:7). There are also passages that include a promise of restoration along with the fact of exile (cf. Jer. 16:15; 23:3, 8; 29:14; 30:17; 32:37; 46:28).

As far as the nations are concerned, God determines to drive away those people who rebel against him (cf. Joel 2:20; Jer. 49:5 [Ammon]).

nādaḥ is also found in a number of metaphorical contexts. Isa. 8:22, for example, outlines the terrible consequences of the nation of Israel's preoccupation with occult phenomena: they will be driven into outer darkness, symbolizing their alienation from God. The following texts refer to Israelites being driven or compelled to worship pagan deities — a capital offense under the Mosaic law covenant: Deut. 4:19; 13:5ff.; 30:17ff. See also 2 Kgs. 17:21 in this regard.

dāqar [**דָּקַר, 1856**]

dāqar is a verb found in eleven places with the primary sense of "drive, thrust through" with a spear or sword, usually resulting in a fatal wound (cf. Num. 25:8; Judg. 9:54; 1 Sam. 31:4; 1 Chr. 10:4; Isa. 13:15; Zech. 13:3). In Zech. 12:10 the action of "piercing through" is predicated in relation to the prospective death of the Messiah. (→ PIERCE)

hādaph [**הָדַף, 1920**]

hādaph is a verb meaning to "drive out" in the sense of "expel," "push aside" for most of its eleven occurrences.

Yahweh's "driving out" of the enemies of Israel from their presence is indicated in Deut. 6:19; 9:4; Josh. 23:5. See also Jer. 46:15. He also promises to "drive out," "oust" a high official (Shebna) from his position in Jerusalem (cf. Isa. 22:19). To "push aside," "drive away" is noted in 2 Kgs. 4:27. See also Ezek. 34:21.

tāqa' [**תָּקַע, 8628**]

tāqa' is a common verb found about seventy times with the predominant meaning "blow" in relation to a musical instrument. In a couple of places, however, **tāqa'** means "drive" in relation to a violent stabbing, an action leading to a fatal injury (cf. Judg. 3:21; 2 Sam. 18:14). (→ BLOW)

ṭā'an [**טָעַן, 2944**]

ṭā'an is a rare verb found only in Isa. 14:19 in relation to "driving" a sword through people (i.e., piercing them with a sword).

yānāh [**יָנָה, 3238**]

yānāh is a verb found in around twenty places with the primary meaning "to oppress." (→ OPPRESS) However, in Ezek. 46:18 the term indicates the action of "dispossessing" in relation to the messianic prince's refusal to "drive the people out" of their land inheritance in Canaan.

nāhag [**נָהַג, 5090**]

nāhag is a verb occurring about thirty times with the principal senses of "lead away," "carry off." There is also the related meaning "drive," signifying the "driving" of carts or chariots in Exod. 14:25; 2 Sam. 6:3; 2 Kgs. 9:20; 1 Chr. 13:7; and the "driving" or "herding" of cattle in 1 Sam. 30:20; 2 Kgs. 4:24; Job 24:3.

ṭerad [**טְרַד, 2957** (Aramaic)]

ṭerad is an Aramaic term meaning "drive away" in the sense of "banish," referring to King Nebuchadnezzar's banishment from human society on the occasion of his divinely inflicted insanity.

minhāg [**מִנְהָג, 4491**]

minhāg is a rare noun derived from **nāhag** (see above) denoting the furious "(chariot) driving" of King Jehu in 2 Kgs. 9:20.

NT Words

ekballō [ἐκβάλλω, *1544*]

ekballō is a verb with the primary meaning "cast out," "throw out." The sense of "drive out" is virtually synonymous. (→ CAST)

ekdiōkō [ἐκδιώκω, *1559*]

ekdiōkō is a rare verb meaning "persecute" in Luke 11:49. In 1 Thess. 2:15 the term is translated "drive out," referring to Jews persecuting the early Christians.

elaunō [ἐλαύνω, *1643*]

elaunō is a verb found five times with the meaning "drive" in a couple of different contexts. Luke 8:29 refers to a man possessed by a demon "being driven" into the wilderness by that evil spirit. Jas. 3:4 refers to large ships "being driven" by fierce winds. 2 Pet. 2:17 mentions false teachers symbolically depicted as "mists driven by a storm."

exōtheō [ἐξωθέω, *1856*]

exōtheō is a rare verb indicating God's redemptive action in "driving out" the pagan peoples of Canaan. It is found with this meaning only in Acts 7:45. In Acts 27:39, the term expresses the sense of "run aground" with reference to a boat.

pherō [φέρω, *5342*]

pherō is a verb found about sixty times with the primary meanings "bear," "carry," "bring," as well as related nuances. Acts 27:15, 17 refers to a ship "being driven along" by a storm wind.

DROWN

OT Words

tāba' [טָבַע, **2883**]

tāba' is a verb found ten times with the primary meaning of "sink (down)." In Exod. 15:4, however, the term signifies the "drowning" of the Egyptian armies in the Re(e)d Sea.

NT Words

katapinō [καταπίνω, *2666*]

katapinō is a verb found seven times with the primary meaning "to swallow." In Heb. 11:29 the related sense of "drown" is indicated in connection with the Egyptian army that was "swallowed up" by the waters of the Re(e)d Sea.

katapontizō [καταποντίζω, *2670*]

katapontizō is another rare verb meaning "to be drowned" in connection with the preferred punishment prescribed by Christ for any who prevented little children from coming to faith in him.

DRUNK, DRUNKENNESS

OT Words

sābā' [סָבָא, **5433**]

This verb is rare, occurring six times. ***sābā'*** means "drink heavily" (i.e., to excess), but in its participial form as a noun it means "drunkard" (cf. Deut. 21:20; Prov. 23:20, 21; Isa. 56:12; Ezek. 23:42; Nah. 1:10). In every context, the connotation of ***sābā'*** is negative — those who are so affected are under the direct or indirect judgment of God.

shikkôr [שִׁכּוֹר, **7910**]

This is an adjectival form, derived from ***shākar***. (→ DRINK) It means "drunk," "drunkard" and occurs thirteen times.

In its literal sense, ***shikkôr*** is found in 1 Sam. 1:13; 25:36; 1 Kgs. 16:9; 20:16; Job 12:25; Ps. 107:27; Prov. 26:9. In the following texts, ***shikkôr*** is used in similes. Isa. 19:14; 24:20 speak of God's judgment against the nations, causing them to act in total confusion and shame, just like a drunkard. Isa. 28:1, 3 refers in similar fashion to Israel. Finally, in Jer. 23:9, as a consequence of God's judgment, the prophet feels like a drunken man (cf. also Joel 1:15).

NT Words

methyskō [μεθύσκω, *3182*]

methyskō is a form of ***methyō*** (→ DRINK) with the specific meaning "get drunk," "become intoxicated," found only in Luke 12:45; Eph. 5:18; 1 Thess. 5:7.

methysos [μέθυσος, *3183*]

methysos is a rare noun, a variant form denoting a "drunkard" and found only in 1 Cor. 5:11; 6:10.

methē [μέθη, *3178*]

methē is a noun found only three times, signifying the state of "drunkenness" in Luke 21:34; Rom. 13:13; Gal. 5:21.

paroinos [πάροινος, *3943*]

paroinos is an adjective denoting the vice of those "given to drunkenness," a characteristic forbidden to those aspiring to the office of elder (cf. 1 Tim. 3:3; Titus 1:7).

oinophlygia [οἰνοφλυγία, *3632*]

oinophlygia is a rare synonym for ***methē*** and ***paroinos***, above, found only in 1 Pet. 4:3 denoting the vice of "drunkenness" in relation to orgies and debauchery.

See Also: → DRINK

DRY

OT Words

yābēsh [יָבֵשׁ, **3001**]

This verb occurs about eighty times and is translated variously "dry," "be (make, become) dry," "wither," "dry up."

With the sense of "dry up," ***yābēsh*** is found, for example, in Gen. 8:7, 14; 1 Kgs. 17:7; Job 8:12; 14:11. Of particular significance are the allusions to the drying up of the Re(e)d Sea through the miraculous dividing of her waters (cf. Josh. 2:10; Zech. 10:11), and also to the similar miracle at the Jordan River when the Israelites entered the land (cf. Josh. 4:3; 5:1; Ps. 74:15). Other important uses of ***yābēsh*** are noted in contexts where the judgment of God results in the withering of her land. Various nations are in view — for example, Moab (Isa. 15:6); Egypt (Isa. 19:5); Babylon (Jer. 50:38); Israel (Hos. 9:16; Amos 1:2; 4:7; Joel 1:10); and Judah (Jer. 12:4). Two texts are particularly worthy of note: Ezek. 17:9, 10 contains an allegorical allusion to the punishment of Judah in exile as the withering of a newly planted vine. This refers to the rebellion of Zedekiah against Babylon, an action that precipitated the invasion of Judah (cf. also Ezek. 19:12). Ezek. 37:11 refers metaphorically to "dried bones," symbolically indicating the hopeless spiritual condition of the people of God in exile, cut off from God. This situation was to be miraculously reversed, however, when God gave "life" back to his people by restoring them to the land.

With the meaning "withered hand," "withered arm," ***yābēsh*** is found in 1 Kgs. 13:4; Zech. 11:17.

yābēsh is also found in a number of other metaphorical contexts. In Job 15:30; 18:16; Ps. 129:6, the withering of God's enemies is in view. In Ps. 22:15, the psalmist refers to his strength being dried up — a prophetic psalm anticipating the sufferings of the Messiah.

ḥārēb [חָרֵב, 2717]

This verb occurs forty times, meaning "lay waste," "dry," "dry up." ***ḥārēb*** is translated "dry," "dry up" in the contexts listed below. (→ DESOLATE)

Literal references to "drying up" are found in Gen. 8:13; Judg. 16:7, 8; 2 Kgs. 19:24; Ps. 106:9; Isa. 37:25; 50:2; 51:10. Divine judgment on the nations is indicated for Egypt, threatened with the drying up of the Nile (Isa. 19:6); for Babylon, threatened with the drying up of her water resources (Jer. 51:36); and similarly for Assyria (Hab. 1:4). Hos. 13:15 refers to the desolation of the land of Israel, whose "fountain shall be dried up."

yabbāshāh [יַבָּשָׁה, 3004]

This noun is derived from the verb ***yābēsh*** (see above). ***yabbāshāh*** occurs fourteen times and means "dry land," "dry ground."

yabbāshāh has an exclusively literal meaning in all but one text. Gen. 1:9, 10; Jonah 1:9 refer to the divine creation of dry land. Then, the crossing of the Re(e)d Sea on dry ground is referred to in Exod. 14:16, 22; 15:9; Neh. 9:11; Ps. 66:11. Josh. 4:22 refers to the crossing of the Jordan River on dry ground. See also Exod. 4:9; Jonah 1:13; 2:10. Isa. 44:3 contains a prophetic anticipation of the renewal of the land, where streams will be poured on the dry ground, accompanied by the promise of the pouring out of the Spirit of God on his people.

ḥārābāh [חָרָבָה, 2724]

ḥārābāh is synonymous with ***yabbāshāh*** (see above), derived from the verb ***ḥārēb*** (see above). The term occurs eight times and is also translated "dry land," "dry ground."

Gen. 7:22 records the perishing of all dry land animals in the flood. Exod. 14:21 refers to the dry land of the Re(e)d Sea bed. Josh. 3:17; 4:18 refer to the dry bed of the Jordan River after a similar miracle. And 2 Kgs. 2:8 records Elijah's duplication of a similar miracle at the Jordan River, which he crosses on dry ground just before he is taken into heaven. Ezek. 30:1 points to the "drying up" of the Nile River as a divine judgment against Egypt; and Hag. 2:6 refers to a prediction of general divine judgment in which God will shake the dry land, earth, and sea.

ṣîyāh [צִיָּה, 6723]

This noun occurs sixteen times and is translated "dry land," "wilderness," "drought."

There is a literal reference to "drought" in Job 24:19, and to wilderness in general in Job 30:3; Ps. 63:1. Three significant allusions to Israel's wilderness wandering are found in Jer. 2:6; Pss. 78:17; 105:41. See also Ps. 107:35; Isa. 53:2.

Isa. 35:1; 41:18 contain divine promises of renewal for the land of Israel whereby God undertakes to transform the "barren wilderness" into fertile land, symbolizing the spiritual renewal and transformation of the people.

ṣîyāh is also used to refer to divine judgment, with the desolation of the nations in view: Babylon (cf. Jer. 50:12; 51:43); the unidentified enemy from the north (cf. Joel 2:20); and Nineveh (cf. Zeph. 2:13). Likewise, a similar fate is in store for both Israel (cf. Hos. 2:3), and Judah (cf. Ezek. 19:13).

yeshîmôn [יְשִׁימוֹן, 3452]

This is another synonym for ***yabbāshāh***, ***ḥārābāh***, and ***ṣiyyāh***, above. ***yeshîmôn*** occurs thirteen times and is translated "wilderness," "desert," "desolate, dry place."

The term ***yeshîmôn*** is often transliterated Yeshimon in the following texts: Num. 21:20; 23:28; 1 Sam. 23:19ff.; referring to the Judean wilderness. General references to "wilderness" are found in Deut. 32:28; Ps. 107:4. Ps. 68:7 alludes to the divine protection of God's people in the "wilderness," and Pss. 78:40; 106:14 allude to Israel's rebellion in the "desert." In Isa. 43:19, 20 God promises to transform the "desert" into fertile fields.

yabbeshet **[יַבֶּשֶׁת, 3006]**

yabbeshet is a rare noun denoting "dry land" in a general sense in Exod. 4:9. It also denotes "dry land" as the result of God's creative power in Ps. 95:5.

ṣîyôn **[צִיּוֹן, 6724]**

ṣîyôn is a rare noun denoting "dry ground" or "desert" in Isa. 25:5; 32:2.

ṣāmaq **[צָמַק, 6784]**

ṣāmaq is a rare verb referring to the "drying up" or "shriveling" of a woman's breasts in Hos. 9:14.

NT Words

xēros [ξηρός, *3584*]

xēros is an adjective found seven times referring to the "dry land" of the bed of the Re(e)d Sea over which the people of Israel crossed during their miraculous escape from Egypt.

xēros also refers to limbs that are "withered" (i.e., "dried up," rendered lame by disease) (cf. Matt. 12:10; Luke 6:6ff.). See also John 5:3.

xērainō [ξηραίνω, *3583*]

xērainō is a verb found in sixteen places meaning "wither," "dry up."

Matt. 13:6; Mark 4:6; Luke 8:6; John 15:6; Jas. 1:11; 1 Pet. 1:24 all refer to grass or plants that "wither" or "dry out" in the heat. When Christ utters a curse against a fig tree in Matt. 21:19ff.; Mark 11:20ff., the tree "withers" — a symbolic act of judgment against his people.

Elsewhere, ***xērainō*** indicates the "cessation" of a woman's chronic hemorrhage as the result of Christ's healing, literally the "drying up" of her blood flow (cf. Mark 5:29). Rev. 16:2 refers to the "drying up" of the Euphrates River in the visionary judgment of the "sixth bowl."

anydros [ἄνυδρος, *504*]

anydros is an adjective denoting the state of being "dry," "without water" in four places. "Dry," or "waterless" places are noted in Matt. 12:43; Luke 11:24. "Waterless" springs are mentioned in 2 Pet. 2:17; clouds "without water" are indicated in Jude 12.

See Also: → HEAT

DUE → OWE

DUMB

OT Words

'ālam **[אָלַם, 481]**

This verb occurs nine times, and on all but one occasion is translated "be dumb," "put to silence."

In Ps. 31:18 there is a call for lying lips to "be silenced." Ps. 39:2, 9 affirm that "silence," "dumbness" is brought about by the chastening hand of God. Isa. 53:7 refers to the "silent" suffering of the Messianic Servant of Yahweh. Ezek. 3:26 contains an act of prophetic symbolism whereby Ezekiel is temporarily "struck dumb" by God so that the people of Judah will initially be denied a rebuke from God as part of their judgment. The following three texts all speak of the removal of dumbness from the prophet, which acts as a prelude to uttering divine revelation: Ezek. 24:27; 33:22; Dan. 10:15. The temporary affliction of "speechlessness" would appear to heighten the impact of what God was about to reveal.

'illēm **[אִלֵּם, 483]**

'illēm is an adjective found six times, consistently referring to the state of "muteness." It indicates people who are "dumb" "mute," or deprived of speech in Exod. 4:11; Ps. 38:13; Prov. 31:8. Isa. 35:6 records the anticipated divine renewal of the world in which, among other things, those who are "dumb" shall receive back their voices and render praise to God. Isa. 56:10 refers to "dumb" dogs; and "dumb" idols are noted in Hab. 2:18.

NT Words

alalos [ἄλαλος, *216*]

alalos is an adjective found in three places, all referring to the condition of speechlessness. The "dumb" are designated in Mark 7:37 as the objects of Christ's miraculous power when they are given back their voices. Mark 9:17, 25 both refer to demonic spirits who afflict their victims with muteness and who are designated as "dumb" spirits.

aphōnos [ἄφωνος, *880*]

aphōnos is another adjectival form meaning "dumb" or "voiceless" in four places, referring not to people but to idols (1 Cor. 12:2); to a lamb "dumb" before its shearer (Acts 8:32); and the "dumb" ass associated with Balaam which was given a voice by God to rebuke the pagan seer (cf. 2 Pet. 2:16 [citing Num. 22:21–30]). The term is also translated "without meaning" in 1 Cor. 14:10.

kōphos [κωφός, *2974*]

kōphos is an adjective meaning "dumb," "speechless" (i.e., without voice, mute) throughout its twelve occurrences. ***kōphos*** is also translated "deaf." (→ DEAF)

A "mute" demoniac is noted in Matt. 9:32ff.; 12:22; Luke 11:14. Christ's healing of the "dumb" is recorded in Matt. 12:22; 15:30ff. The "mute" condition of Zechariah the priest, father of John the Baptist, is indicated in Luke 1:22.

See Also: → SILENCE

DUNG

OT Words

dōmen [**דֹּמֶן, 1828**]

This noun is rare, occurring only six times. ***dōmen*** is translated "dung," but always in reference to corpses. As such it is always found in contexts where the judgment of God has taken place, and it symbolizes divine disdain for the persons concerned — for the body of Jezebel (cf. 2 Kgs. 9:37); and for the bodies of Sisera, and Jabin, leaders of the Midianites (cf. Ps. 83:10). Jer. 8:22; 9:22; 16:4 refer to the exposure of the bodies of Israel and Judah to the elements, leading to their decomposition as a mark of God's anger against his people. In Jer. 25:33 a similar indictment is handed down to all nations who rebel against Yahweh.

ṣô'āh [**צוֹאָה, 6675**]

ṣô'āh is a term denoting human "excrement" ("dung") in 2 Kgs. 18:27; Isa. 36:12.

'ashpôt [**אַשְׁפּוֹת, 830**]

'ashpôt is a noun denoting the "Dung" Gate, one of the ten listed gates of Jerusalem in the book of Nehemiah (cf. Neh. 2:13; 3:13, 14; 12:31).

NT Words

koprion [κόπριον, *2874*]

koprion is a rare noun found in Luke 14:35 referring to a "manure pile." See also Luke 13:8.

DUST

OT Words

'āphār [**עָפָר, 6083**]

This term occurs about one hundred times and translates variously as "dust," "dry, loose earth," "ashes."

With the literal meaning "dust," ***'āphār*** is found in a number of places (e.g., Gen. 3:19; Exod. 8:16, 17; Lev. 14:41ff.; Num. 5:17; Deut. 9:21; 2 Sam. 16:13; 1 Kgs. 20:10; Ezek. 24:27). Gen. 2:7; Isa. 40:12 refer to "dust" as the medium God used for the creation of the first man, although some would argue that ***'āphār*** refers to "(clumps of) earth." (cf. also Gen. 26:15).

'āphār means "ashes" in Num. 19:17; 23:10; 2 Kgs. 23:4ff. The text in 2 Kings refers to the time of the Josianic reformation, where the ashes of pagan idols symbolically indicate their total destruction.

Much more significant is the metaphorical sense of ***'āphār***. First of all, "dust" is often symbolically linked to "death" and "the grave (Sheol)" (cf. Job 17:16; 21:26; 40:13; Ps. 22:15, 29; Eccl. 3:20; 12:7). In Dan. 12:2, the context clearly indicates that "sleep in the dust of the earth" is a prelude to resurrection.

Dust is also referred to symbolically as "serpent's food" (cf. Gen. 3:14; Isa. 65:5; Mic. 7:17). In all these texts ***'āphār*** highlights the punishment inflicted by God, leading to humiliation.

'āphār is also used in the phrase "as the dust of the earth," or similar expressions, to indicate the innumerable posterity promised by God to Abraham in the covenant blessing given to the patriarch (cf. Gen. 13:16; 28:14; Num. 23:19; 2 Chr. 1:9).

The phrases "treading in the dust," or "casting to the dust," allude metaphorically to divine judgment. They apply, for instance, to Moab (cf. Isa. 25:12); to Babylon (cf. Isa. 41:2; 47:1); to Tyre (cf. Ezek. 26:12; 27:30); and to the enemies of God in general (cf. Isa. 26:5). Linked to this phenomenon is a theme of "reversal," whereby God raises his people from the dust, from a position of abject humiliation and defeat, to one of glorious victory and conquest (cf. Isa. 26:19; 52:2ff.). Isa. 49:23 is particularly noteworthy in this regard in that here the rulers of the nations "lick the dust off the feet" of the Messianic Servant — a symbolic depiction of their utter defeat and humiliation. Social evils are also alluded to in Amos 2:7, where it is recorded that the poor are "trampled into the dust" by cruel and heartless overlords.

The best-known symbolic action for the expression of humiliation and anguish is that of covering oneself with "dust and ashes," often expressed in the context of repentance before God (cf. Gen. 18:27; Josh. 7:6; Job 2:12; 42:6; Lam. 2:10; 3:29; Mic. 1:10).

'ābāq **[אָבָק, 80]**

This is a rare term occurring only six times meaning "dust," "powder."

In Exod. 9:9, ***'ābāq*** refers to the plague of boils in Egypt, occasioned by "dust." The remaining texts all speak metaphorically of "dust" in relation to the judgment of God poured out on all who oppose him. Deut. 28:24 refers to rain turning to "dust"; Isa. 5:24 refers to judgment against Israel; and in Isa. 29:5 the destruction of Israel's enemies is in view, whereby God will "grind them into dust."

NT Words

chous, choos [χοῦς, χόος, *5522*]

chous is a rare noun found only twice, referring literally to "dust" in Mark 6:11. Rev. 18:19 refers to throwing dust over one's head as a sign of mourning.

koniortos [κονιορτός, *2868*]

koniortos is a synonym for ***chous***, above, denoting "dust" in the expression "to shake the dust off one's feet" as a symbolic gesture of rejection, curse, and denial for most of the five occurrences of the term (cf. Matt. 10:14; Luke 9:5; 10:11; Acts 13:51). See also Acts 22:23.

DWELL, DWELLING

OT Words

yāshab **[יָשַׁב, 3427]**

This is a common term occurring about 1,200 times. ***yāshab*** is translated a number of ways, but the primary meanings are "dwell," "inhabit," "sit," with several related nuances.

Mundane references to living or dwelling in a particular location are very common throughout the Old Testament: especially in the Pentateuch, the Former Prophets; and the prophets Isaiah, Jeremiah, and Ezekiel (e.g., Gen. 4:16; 14:7; Exod. 15:14ff.; Num. 21:1, 31ff.; Deut. 2:4ff.; Josh. 2:15; Judg. 21:9ff.; Ruth 2:23; 1 Sam. 23:14; 2 Sam. 14:28; 2 Kgs. 16:6; Isa. 9:2; 58:12; Jer. 8:16; Ezek. 28:25ff.).

There are also a number of contexts where the literal use of ***yāshab*** gives rise to some significant theological emphases. The first of these relates to Israel dwelling in the land of Canaan, which is indicated in a general sense in Lev. 20:22; 25:10; 26:32, and several times throughout the book of Numbers. The anticipation of the Israelite people living in the land is referred to in Num. 33:50ff.; 35:2ff., 32, 34. These and other texts reveal God's specific promise and guarantee to Israel that they will live in the land he has given to them (cf. Deut. 11:31; 12:10, 29; 17:14; 19:1; 30:20). The conquest of Canaanite territory, followed by the occupation (i.e., ***yāshab***) of that land, is recorded in Josh. 19:47, 50; 21:43; 24:13ff. These last two references both affirm that God had given his people the entire land in which they would dwell — and yet, paradoxically, the people failed to complete that task. The point here is that God in principle had given them the land in its entirety. The problem, however, lay with the people's unwillingness to appropriate that principle by faith and carry out the task — hence their ongoing problems in the land. These difficulties are highlighted, for instance in Judg. 1:19ff., which affirms that the Israelites could not gain a place to dwell in many regions within Canaan.

Another significant use of ***yāshab*** relates to the tabernacle and temple as the "dwelling place" of God. Though employed in the literal, physical context of Old Testament worship, ***yāshab*** has a powerful symbolic sense nonetheless, in that the earthly habitation of God in the holy of holies is directly linked to the heavenly realm of God's person and majesty (cf. Heb. 9:1ff.). The following texts are relevant in this regard: 2 Sam. 7:2; 5, 6; Pss. 113:8; 123:1; 132:14. Ps. 80:1; Isa. 37:16 refer to God dwelling on the "throne" (i.e., "seat" or "cover") of the ark of the covenant, between the cherubim. Linked to this is the phrase in Solomon's prayer at the temple dedication, "Hear from your dwelling place and forgive!" (cf. 1 Kgs. 8:13, 27, 30, 39, 43, 49). This repeated refrain makes an undeniable allusion to the very profound link between the earthly symbolism of the ark of the covenant and the heavenly reality to which it points. Furthermore, there are a number of texts which affirm that true comfort and lasting peace are granted to those "who dwell in the house of Yahweh." This is a clear symbolic reference to the spiritual blessing enjoyed by those who are granted an intimate relationship with God (cf. Pss. 23:6; 27:4; 84:4; 91:1; 101:6, 7; 140:13; Isa. 32:18).

Finally, in this regard, the Old Testament also alludes to God's "dwelling place" in Zion. Zion refers primarily to the city of Jerusalem and its inhabitants, as the center of God's kingdom on earth (cf. Ps. 9:11; Isa. 10:24, 30:19).

yāshab is also found in contexts in which divine judgment against the nations results in the destruction and removal of both people and their houses (i.e., their dwelling places): for example, Babylon (cf. Isa. 13:20); Egypt (cf. Jer. 44:13); Edom (cf. Jer. 49:18; Ezek. 35:9);

Philistia (cf. Zeph. 2:5; Zech. 9:5). The same punishment is also handed down to Judah (e.g., Jer. 2:15; 4:7, 9; 8:16; 34:22; Ezek. 12:1; Joel 2:1). As a corollary to the latter phenomenon, God promises healing for the land itself, and also that the exiled people of Judah will return to the land (cf. Jer. 23:8; 32:7; Ezek. 28:6; 36:10, 28; 37:25; Hos. 12:9; Joel 3:20; Zech. 2:4; 12:6; 14:11).

shākan [שָׁכַן, 7931]

This verb occurs about 130 times with the principal meaning "dwell" and associated nuances.

In its literal sense, ***shākan*** refers first of all to ordinary dwellings in a number of contexts (e.g., Gen. 14:13; 25:18; 35:22; Judg. 8:11; Job 15:28; 30:6; Ps. 68:6; Prov. 2:21).

Of particular interest is the Old Testament focus on the tabernacle and temple as the "dwelling place" of God among his people. The physical reality of the shrine of Yahweh carried with it a profound symbolism whereby a literal edifice pointed to an eternal, heavenly reality (cf. Exod. 25:8; 29:46; Num. 5:3; Josh. 22:19; 1 Kgs. 6:13). In Deut. 12:11; 14:23; 16:2, Yahweh indicates his intention to choose a place for his name to dwell, anticipating the selection of Jerusalem. In Ezek. 43:7, 9, in the context of the vision of Ezekiel's temple, there is a focus on the holy of holies as the place of God's dwelling. Linked with the emphasis on the temple is the theme of Yahweh's dwelling on Mt. Zion, a term that refers to the mount on which the temple was built as well as to Jerusalem and its inhabitants (cf. Ps. 69:36; Isa. 8:18; Joel 3:17, 21). In a general sense, the land of Canaan itself is designated as the place of God's dwelling in Num. 35:34.

With reference to the Israelites themselves, ***shākan*** indicates their dwelling in the land of Canaan in accordance with God's promise (cf. Num. 14:30; Deut. 33:28; 2 Sam. 7:10; 1 Chr. 17:9; Pss. 37:3; 37:29; 78:55).

shākan is also used to refer to the theme of divine judgment. On account of their sinfulness, the homes and lands of the nations will be destroyed, making them uninhabitable — for example, Babylon (cf. Isa. 13:20ff.; Jer. 50:39); Moab (cf. Jer. 48:28); Edom (cf. Jer. 49:16). The same punishment is also handed down to Judah, for the same reasons (cf. Jer. 17:6; Mic. 4:10). Then, conversely, there is also the divine promise of return to and renewal of the land for God's people to dwell in (cf. Isa. 34:17; Jer. 23:6; 33:16; Zech. 2:10ff.; 8:3, 8).

mishkān [מִשְׁכָּן, 4908]

This noun is derived from ***shākan*** (see above) and occurs about 140 times with the principal meaning "tabernacle." (→ TABERNACLE) However, ***mishkān*** is also translated "dwelling," "dwelling place" in a number of other contexts.

General mundane uses of the term are found in Job 39:6; Pss. 49:11; 78:28; Isa. 22:16. God's dwelling place is mentioned in 2 Chr. 29:6. Divine judgment on the Babylonians is described in Jer. 51:30, whereby their homes are destroyed. Similar judgment is handed out to the people of Judah at the hands of the Babylonians themselves (cf. Jer. 9:19; Ezek. 25:4). Divine restoration of the land of Canaan is in view in Jer. 30:18. In Ezek. 37:27 Yahweh promises to restore the intimacy of the covenant relationship between himself and his people: "My dwelling place shall be with them" (cf. also Isa. 54:2). Finally, Job 18:21; 21:28 refer metaphorically to the dwellings of the ungodly.

môshāb [מוֹשָׁב, 4186]

This noun is derived from ***yāshab*** (see above) and occurs about forty times. ***môshāb*** is translated primarily as "dwelling place."

In a general, mundane sense, ***môshāb*** is found in a number of places (e.g., Gen. 10:30; 36:43; Exod. 12:20, 40; Lev. 7:26; 25:29; Num. 24:21, 2 Sam. 9:12; 1 Chr. 4:33; Ps. 107:4, 7; Ezek. 48:15).

môshāb also refers to Canaan as the "dwelling place" of God's people (cf. Num. 15:2). In relation to God, the term indicates Zion as his dwelling place (cf. Ps. 132:13). In Ezek. 6:6, 14 divine judgment is pronounced on Judah in terms of the destruction of her dwellings (i.e., her cities) at the hands of the Babylonian invaders. Again, by way of contrast, there is a promise of divine renewal and restoration of the land after the exile, whereby God's people will be returned to their homes (cf. Ezek. 34:13). Additionally, Ezek. 37:23 refers to the renewal of intimacy between Israel and God.

NT Words

oikeō [οἰκέω, *3611*]

oikeō is a verb occurring nine times, meaning "to dwell" throughout, largely in a metaphorical sense.

Sin is described as "dwelling" in the life of believers in Rom. 7:17ff.; underscoring their ongoing struggle. Conversely, the person of the Holy Spirit is said to "dwell" in the heart of the believer in 1 Cor. 3:16. 1 Cor. 7:12ff. refers to an unbelieving spouse being content to "live" with their believing partner. 1 Tim. 6:16 mentions God who "dwells" in unapproachable light.

katoikeō [κατοικέω, *2730*]

katoikeō is a verb found in nearly fifty places, meaning "live" or "dwell" throughout.

Literal references to "living," "dwelling" in various localities include Matt. 2:23; 4:13; Luke 13:4; Acts 1:19; 2:5ff.; 7:2ff.; 9:22ff.; 19:10ff. References to people "dwelling" on earth include Rev. 3:10; 6:10; 8:13; 13:8ff.; 14:6; 17:2ff.

All other uses of ***katoikeō*** are metaphorical. Demons "dwelling" in their human hosts are noted in Matt. 12:45; Luke 11:26. God is said to "dwell" in the tabernacle and temple in Matt. 23:21; Heb. 11:9 — though in an absolute sense God can never truly "dwell" in houses made by human beings (cf. Acts 7:48; 17:24ff.). Christ "dwelling" in the hearts of believers is mentioned in Eph. 3:17. Col. 1:19; 2:9 affirm that God "dwells" in his fullness in the person of Christ. The Holy Spirit is said to "dwell" in the believer in Jas. 4:5. The phenomenon of righteousness "dwelling" in the new heavens and the earth is described in 2 Pet. 3:13.

enoikeō [ἐνοικέω, *1774*]

enoikeō is another variant of ***oikeō*** (see above) indicating the phenomenon of a spiritual inhabiting or "indwelling."

References to the Holy Spirit "indwelling" the believer are found in Rom. 8:11; 2 Tim. 1:14. The phenomenon of God "living" among his people is noted in 2 Cor. 6:16; as is the word of Christ in Col. 3:16. See also 2 Tim. 1:5.

synoikeō [συνοικέω, *4924*]

synoikeō is a rare verb meaning "to live together with" in relation to husbands and wives, found only in 1 Pet. 3:7.

menō [μένω, *3306*]

menō is a common verb found 120 times with the predominant senses of "stay," "remain," with related nuances, including the meaning to "live," "dwell" in literal general contexts (e.g., Luke 1:56; 8:27; John 1:39; Acts 18:3; 28:16, 30).

Elsewhere, the meaning "dwell" is metaphorical. John 14:10 refers to God "dwelling" in Christ. The Spirit of God is said to "dwell" in the believer in John 14:17.

skēnoō [σκηνόω, *4637*]

skēnoō is a verb found in five places with the underlying meaning "to live in a tent." It is translated "to dwell" with reference to Christ "living" among men in John 1:14. In this text the use of this particular term draws a theological connection between the glory cloud of the ancient tabernacle and its redemptive-historical fulfillment in the person of Christ, who embodies and incarnates the divine glory cloud; hence the significance of the possible translation here: of "and the Word . . . tabernacled among us." References to those who "dwell" in heaven with God are found in Rev. 12:12; 13:6; 21:3.

Additional Notes

Aside from the mundane usage associated with the concept of "dwelling" in both Old and New Testaments, there is a significant amount of overlap (in a theological sense) between the Hebrew and Greek vocabulary associated with this idea.

In the Old Testament there is a great deal of emphasis on Canaan in general, and on the phenomenon of the tabernacle/temple in particular, as the dwelling place of God on earth. The permanent location of the temple in Jerusalem gave rise to the terminology of Mt. Zion as the focal point of God's kingdom on earth. Crucial importance was attached to this by the old covenant people of God, whose very existence as a nation was defined by the intimate presence of their God among them. He dwelled in their midst in a manner unique among the nations.

This phenomenon of God's dwelling place in the midst of his people is given an ultimate fulfillment in the New Testament through the person and work of Christ and the coming of the Holy Spirit. No longer is there to be any holy place in a physical sense for the people of Yahweh. Rather, the ongoing covenant relationship found fulfillment not in any physical, earthly place or institution, but in a person. God dwelling among his people found supreme expression in the incarnation of the Messiah, born of a virgin. It is Jesus Christ who constitutes the chief cornerstone of the heavenly temple, and those joined to him by faith are the temple itself. When Jesus ascended to heaven, he sent the Holy Spirit to carry on the spiritual work of joining others to the ever-growing community, or dwelling place, of God's people.

See Also: → SOJOURN

DYSENTERY

NT WORDS

dysenterion [δυσεντέριον, *1420*]

dysenterion is a rare term denoting "dysentery," mentioned only in Acts 28:8.

E

EAGLE

OT Words

nesher **[נֶשֶׁר, 5404]**

This noun occurs twenty-six times and means "eagle" or "vulture." ***nesher*** is used primarily in a metaphorical sense, although it is found twice in the Pentateuch, referring literally to eagles as unclean birds, unfit for eating (cf. Lev. 11:13; Deut. 14:12).

In the first instance, ***nesher*** is found in contexts where the general metaphorical sense of swiftness and majestic flight is in view, symbolized by the eagle (e.g., Job 9:26; Prov. 23:5; Jer. 48:40; Lam. 4:19; Obad. 4).

nesher is also used to indicate divine power or enabling. In Exod. 19:4, Israel's successful escape from Egypt is depicted in terms of God delivering his people "on the wings of an eagle." See also Isa. 40:31.

With respect to God himself, ***nesher*** is used allegorically in Ezek. 17:7 to refer to Yahweh as a "great eagle" who nourishes his people. In addition, God's nurture of his people is compared with the devotion of an eagle guarding its young (cf. Deut. 32:11). Conversely, Deut. 28:49 contains a prophetic anticipation of the nations of Assyria and Babylon being sent by God as a judgment against his people, coming against Israel "as swift as the eagle flies." See also Jer. 4:13; Ezek. 17:3; Hos. 8:1; Hab. 1:8.

In other contexts, ***nesher*** refers to a number of different phenomena. In 2 Sam. 1:23; Ps. 103:5, the symbol of the eagle refers to the vigor of youth. Mic. 1:16 indicates the despair of God's people in the face of his judgment through the phrase "bald as the eagle" — a reference to the people shaving their heads in anguish. Ezek. 1:10; 10:14 describe the cherubim, the heavenly guardians of God's throne who manifest four faces, one of which is an eagle.

neshar **[נְשַׁר, 5403** (Aramaic)**]**

neshar is the rare Aramaic equivalent of ***nesher*** (see above) denoting "eagles," "feathers" in Dan. 4:33; and "eagles'" wings in Dan. 7:4.

NT Words

aetos **[ἀετός, *105*]**

aetos is the dynamic equivalent of ***nesher*** (see above), referring to "eagles" as birds of prey in Matt. 24:28; Luke 17:37. Rev. 4:7; 12:14 refer to "eagles" in the visions of the apostle John.

Additional Notes

The occurrence of ***aetos*** in the New Testament is rare; but where the term does occur it overlaps with the Old Testament usage of the Hebrew term ***nesher***. As indicated above, ***aetos*** is also used in a context of divine judgment, and of special interest is the text in Rev. 12:14, where the woman is given eagle's wings so that she might escape the clutches of the dragon, who wants to destroy her and the son she bears. There is no doubt that the child referred to in Rev. 12 is the Messiah; and there is also no doubt that the allusion to God rescuing his people from Egypt on "eagle's wings" in Exod. 19:4 is clearly in view. The deliverance of Israel from bondage, and the ultimate deliverance of God's people from the power of sin through the person and work of Jesus Christ, are two events that are intimately related. The former is a symbolic foreshadowing of the latter; and the metaphor of "the eagle's wings" symbolizes the common theme and the supreme effectiveness of God's redemptive purposes demonstrated in both Testaments.

EAR

OT Words

'ōzen **[אֹזֶן, 241]**

This noun occurs around 180 times meaning "ear," as well as "hearing." ***'ōzen*** is used literally and metaphorically in relation to both human beings and God.

In its literal sense, ***'ōzen*** refers to the ear as the organ of hearing in about half of its occurrences, spread fairly evenly throughout the Old Testament. Most of the literal occurrences of ***'ōzen*** are prosaic, but there are several instances where the usage is significant. Exod. 21:6; Deut. 15:17, for example, both refer to the ceremonial ritual whereby a slave indicates his willingness to enter into life service with his master by allowing his ear to be pierced with an awl. The underlying theme is that of devotion to one's master; and this attitude is supremely demonstrated in the person of Jesus Christ, who determined to submit himself wholly without question to the will of his Father. In Hebrews 10:5–7 the writer quotes Ps. 40:6–8, referring to the "piercing of the ear" in Exod. 21 and Deut. 15. Then, in Exod. 29:20; Lev. 8:23, 24, the right ears of the high priest, Aaron, and his sons are daubed with ram's blood as part of their solemn ordination ritual (cf. also Lev. 14:14).

In a number of contexts ***'ōzen*** indicates "hearing the Lord" or "hearing his word" and focuses on the importance of obeying God (e.g., Deut. 5:1; 31:28; 1 Chr. 28:8; Isa. 30:21; 2 Kgs. 23:2; Neh. 8:3; Isa. 32:3; 35:5). In a negative context, this term refers to an inability to comprehend what God has done for his people — an implicit judgment by God who has not given his people "ears to hear" (cf. Deut. 29:4).

'ōzen is also closely linked to the phenomenon of revelation, where God speaks in the ears of his people, as a prophet (cf. 1 Sam. 9:15; Isa. 50:4, 5; Ezek. 40:4; 44:5; 2 Sam. 7:27). In Isa. 55:3 God promises to renew his covenant with his people if they "incline their ear" to him. God also speaks judgment in the ears of his servants in response to the rebellion of his people (cf. Isa. 5:9; 22:14; Jer. 2:2ff.; Ezek. 3:10).

In a metaphorical sense, ***'ōzen*** also refers anthropomorphically to the "ears of God," indicating God's keen awareness of what happens among his people. For example, Num. 11:1, 18; 14:28 all refer to the Israelites grumbling in the wilderness, which brings God's punishment upon them. A similar divine response is found in 2 Kgs. 19:28; Isa. 37:29. God refuses to hear his people in Ezek. 8:18 because of their sin. Conversely, whenever Israel humbles herself and turns from her sin, God is perfectly willing to hear the prayers of his people (cf. 2 Chr. 7:15; Pss. 10:17; 34:15).

Pleas are also frequently directed to God to "incline his ear" and give help (e.g., 2 Sam. 22:7; 2 Kgs. 19:16). Solomon pleads with God to "let his ears be attentive to the prayers of his people" (cf. also Neh. 1:6, 11). The psalmist also frequently makes such pleas to God — for example, in Pss. 17:6; 31:2; 86:1, 2; 116:2 (cf. also Isa. 37:17; Lam. 3:56; Dan. 9:18).

Finally, ***'ōzen*** is used in reference to Israel's "deafness," or rather their unwillingness to hear the voice of God — often in association with their "blindness" or their refusal to see. As a consequence, they come under the judgment of God (e.g., Isa. 42:20; 43:8; Jer. 5:21; 7:21, 26; 25:4; Ezek. 12:2; Zech. 7:11). The same "spiritual disability" also describes the nations in Mic. 7:16.

NT Words

ous [οὖς, *3775*]

The noun ***ous*** is found nearly forty times meaning "ear," used in both literal and metaphorical contexts.

Literal references to the human "ear" include Matt. 11:15; Mark 4:9; 7:33); Luke 1:44; 4:21; 8:8; 22:50; Acts 7:57; 11:22; 1 Cor. 2:9; Rev. 2:7ff.; 3:6ff.; 13:9. A symbolic reference to the human ear is found in 1 Cor. 12:16. The term ***ous*** also refers to a person's "ear," indicating spiritual perception or understanding. Lack of such understanding is indicated in Matt. 13:15; Mark 8:18; Acts 28:27; Rom. 11:8. In particular, Acts 7:51 refers to the "uncircumcised ears" of people who offer resistance to the prompting of the Holy Spirit. Conversely, the capacity for such discernment is noted in Matt. 13:16.

ous also refers anthropomorphically to the "ears" of the Lord of Hosts, who becomes aware of human injustice in Jas. 5:4. The "ears" of the Lord are also declared to be open to the prayers of the righteous in 1 Pet. 3:12.

ōtion [ὠτίον, *5621*]

ōtion is a rare diminutive form of ***ous*** (see above) found only in Matt. 26:51; Mark 14:47; Luke 22:51; John 18:10, 26, and referring exclusively to the "ear" of the high priest's servant cut off by the sword of the apostle Peter.

akoē [ἄκοη, *189*]

akoē is a noun occurring around twenty times with the primary sense of "hearing" and the associated senses of "fame," "report," "audience." In Mark 7:35; Acts 17:20, the term refers literally to the human ear. In 2 Tim. 4:3 the term refers metaphorically to "itching ears," denoting an indiscriminate curiosity for strange doctrine.

Additional Notes

The Old and New Testament terminology for "ears" and "hearing" are very similar. Greek distinguishes the terms ***ous*** (and ***ōtion***) and ***akoē*** with respect to the ear as the organ of hearing, and the sense of hearing, respectively; whereas the Hebrew term ***'ōzen*** covers both elements. In both instances, however, the concept of human beings "giving ear" to God is paramount. Both Old and New Testaments stress the importance of not merely listening to God, but also of carrying out his commands without question. God's judgment of those who fail to hear him and act upon his word is a universal biblical theme. It is Jesus in the New Testament who issues those solemn words in an ultimate call to faithful attention to and dependence upon God: "He who has an ear, let him hear. . . ." In contrast, the Old Testament frequently alludes to the "ears of God," attentive to his people in both blessing as well as judgment. Only Jas. 5:4 in the New Testament alludes to the "ears of the Lord of hosts" in the context of human sinfulness.

See Also: ➡ HEAR ➡ REPORT

EAR OF CORN

NT Words

stachys [στάχυς, *4719*]

stachys denotes a literal "ear of corn" or "head" of grain in Matt. 12:1; Mark 2:23; 4:28; Luke 6:1.

See Also: → GRAIN

EARLY

OT Words

shākam [שָׁכַם, 7925]

This verb occurs approximately sixty-five times meaning "to rise early," "start early," and it is used both literally and metaphorically.

shākam is found nearly fifty times meaning "early in the morning," mostly in the historical portions of the Old Testament (e.g., Gen. 19:2; 28:18; Exod. 8:20; 24:4; Num. 14:40; Josh. 3:1; 6:12, 15; Judg. 7:1; 19:5ff.; 1 Sam. 1:19; 9:26; 2 Sam. 15:2; 2 Kgs. 3:22; 2 Chr. 36:15). See also Job 1:5; Ps. 127:2; Prov. 27:14, Song 7:12. The sense of all these occurrences is mundane. One notable exception to this is found in Isa. 5:11, where rising early is associated with the degenerate lifestyle of the people of God, whom God condemns for excessive drinking and drunkenness that occupies them from early morning until late into the night.

shākam also refers anthropomorphically to God "rising early" to address his people about their spiritual condition. While God persistently and constantly speaks to them through his servants the prophets, they refuse to listen to him (cf. Jer. 11:7; 25:3, 4; 26:5; 29:19; 32:33; 35:14; 44:3).

There are two other metaphorical uses of ***shākam***, both of which are found in Hosea. Hos. 6:4 refers to Israel's fickle and shallow love for God that is likened to early morning dew and mist that evaporates and disappears. Secondly, Hos. 13:3 refers to God's judgment against the idolatry of his people, for which crime they shall be dispelled, like the early morning dew.

See Also: → MORNING

EARTH

OT Words

'ereṣ [אֶרֶץ, 776]

This is a common term, occurring over two thousand times. ***'ereṣ*** means "earth," "country," and "land."

In the sense of "earth" ***'ereṣ*** is mostly literal, although it is used in a metaphorical sense as well. ***'ereṣ*** refers to the earth generally as the product of God's creation, the arena for both human and divine activity. This is especially the case throughout Gen. 1–11, where ***'ereṣ*** is the focal point of God's creative endeavors and of subsequent judgment and blessing (cf. Gen. 1:1ff.; 2:1ff.; 4:12, 16; 6:4ff.; 7:3ff.; 8:1ff.; 9:1ff.; 10:8ff.; 11:1ff.). Of particular interest is the flooding of the entire earth (chs. 6–8), a classic indicator of God's terrible judgment on the sin of humankind. Elsewhere, the use of ***'ereṣ*** in this general sense is largely mundane (e.g., Gen. 14:22; 28:14; Exod. 8:22; 31:17; Lev. 11:2ff.; Num. 12:3; Deut. 3:24; 5:8; Josh. 2:11; Judg. 5:4; 1 Sam. 2:10; 2 Sam. 7:23). ***'ereṣ*** is used about seventy times this way in the Pentateuch and Former Prophets; over 200 times in the Prophets; and about 250 times in the Writings. There is, however, one other significant use of the term in this general sense of "earth" — when it refers to the earth as the sphere or arena of God's covenant blessing to Abraham (cf. Gen. 12:3; 13:16; 18:18; 22:18; 26:4; Deut. 7:6; 14:2; 28:1; 2 Chr. 1:9). In particular, 2 Sam. 7:9 constitutes part of God's covenant promise to David, indicating that his name will be great throughout the whole earth.

The literal use of ***'ereṣ*** can also indicate the earth more particularly as the place inhabited by human beings. In this regard, the phrase "peoples (or nations) of the earth" is found in a number of contexts. Firstly, God's people are chosen from among the nations of the earth and are regarded as unique; they are intended ideally to be blessed by God and to be a blessing to others (cf. Deut. 7:6; 28:10; Josh. 4:24; 1 Kgs. 8:43, 53, 60; Ps. 148:11). The phrase is then used in respect of God's judgment on his people, whom he scatters among the nations of the earth (cf. Deut. 28:64). Thirdly, it expresses the divine intention that the knowledge of God might come to the nations of the earth (cf. 2 Chr. 6:33; Ps. 67:4; Dan. 4:1; 6:25; Zeph. 3:20). This phrase also indicates God's judgment against the pagan peoples of the earth (cf. Job 12:24; Ps. 98:9; Isa. 34:1; Ezek. 31:12; Mic. 1:2; Zech. 12:3). Finally, these words refer to the people of the earth in general terms (cf. Isa. 42:5; 2 Chr. 32:19).

'ereṣ also indicates the idea of the earth being owned by God and being under his sovereign control. The words "the earth is the Lord's" (or similar phraseology) express such a meaning. In Exod. 9:29, for example, God's judgment on the Egyptian nation is intended as a revelation to them that Yahweh is supreme and unique as the God of creation and the whole earth. Then, Deut. 10:14; Ps. 24:1 also bear testimony to Israel that their God is in total control of the entire creation

— it is his (cf. also Exod. 19:5; Josh. 3:11, 13; 1 Sam. 12:8; Pss. 47:7; 82:8; 83:18; Isa. 54:5; 66:1, 22; Zech. 14:9).

'ereṣ also commonly refers to the earth as "ground" — the surface of the ground, or under the ground (e.g., Gen. 37:10; Exod. 10:3ff.; Num. 11:31; 26:10; Deut. 11:6; Josh. 5:14; Judg. 3:25; 6:37; 1 Sam. 5:3; 24:8; 2 Sam. 12:16, 20; Ezek. 1:15ff.; Dan. 4:15, 35). There are about fifty references with this meaning; and a significant number of them indicate bowing down to the earth (or ground), either in fear or worship or both.

'ereṣ also refers to earth as "soil" or "dust." In some contexts it is used in conjunction with sprinkling of dust over one's head — the classic expression of mourning (1 Sam. 4:12; 15:32; 2 Sam. 1:2; Neh. 9:1). See also Exod. 8:17; 20:24; 2 Kgs. 5:17.

There are also several contexts in which ***'ereṣ*** is used in a metaphorical sense. The "earth," for example, is referred to as a witness against the sins of God's people (cf. Deut. 4:26; 30:19; 31:28; Isa. 1:2; Jer. 6:19, Mic. 1:2). All of these texts are connected with ***rîb*** (i.e., lawsuit) oracles, in which God brings an indictment against his people for breach of covenant. The phrase "the way of all the earth" is a euphemism for dying (cf. Josh. 23:14; 1 Kgs. 2:2). And, finally, there is the theme of the "new heavens and the new earth" — God's promise of a transformed reality, a new sublime order of existence (cf. Isa. 65:17; see also Isa. 35).

The second principal meaning of ***'ereṣ*** is "country." ***'ereṣ*** means "country" in the general sense of one's homeland in approximately fifty contexts (e.g., Gen. 36:6; Num. 20:17; Deut. 3:14; Josh. 2:3; Judg. 12:12; 1 Kgs. 4:19; 2 Kgs. 3:20; 1 Chr. 8:8; 2 Chr. 6:32; Prov. 25:25; Isa. 13:5; Jer. 4:16; Ezek. 20:38). On occasions, specific nations are mentioned — for example, Amalek (Gen. 14:7); Edom (Gen. 32:6); Moab (Ruth 1:1ff.); Philistia (1 Sam. 6:1); Ammon (1 Chr. 20:1); Babylon (Isa. 39:3).

'ereṣ also frequently refers to the country of Canaan, or Israel. It can indicate Canaan as the land promised to Abraham and his descendants (cf. Gen. 20:1; 24:62; 30:25; 32:9; Jer. 2:7; Ezek. 20:42; 34:15). Otherwise, the term may refer to the homeland of the Israelites without specific reference to the promise given to Abraham (e.g., Lev. 16:9; 24:22; Num. 15:13; Deut. 4:43; Josh. 7:2; 22:10; Ezek. 47:8; Jonah 1:8). Israel is also referred to as a country under the judgment of God (cf. Isa. 1:7).

The phrase "a far country" also refers to three phenomena: the location of Israel's enemy (cf. Jer. 10:22); the location of Israel's punishment in exile (cf. Jer. 22:26; 23:8; 31:8); and the location of God's judgment against his foes (cf. Jer. 46:10; 50:9).

Finally, ***'ereṣ*** is translated "country" in reference to either a rural district or region of the plain (cf. Lev. 25:31; 2 Chr. 26:10; 28:18; Neh. 12:28; Jer. 48:21).

'adāmāh [אֲדָמָה, 127]

'adāmāh is a common noun meaning "earth," "land," "ground" throughout its more than two hundred occurrences.

Literal references to "earth" in the sense of "the ground" are found in Gen. 1:25; 2:5; 3:19; 4:2ff.; 7:4; Exod. 8:21; 20:24; Num. 16:30ff.; Deut. 26:2; 2 Sam. 17:12; 2 Chr. 4:17; Neh. 10:35; Ps. 105:35; Prov. 12:11; Isa. 28:24; Dan. 12:2.

The phrase "face of the earth" — denoting the broad expanse of the world as the dwelling place of human beings — is found in Num. 12:3; Deut. 6:15; 7:6; 1 Sam. 20:15; 1 Kgs. 13:34; Isa. 23:17; Jer. 25:26. God is said to form every bird and animal from out of "the ground" in Gen. 2:19.

The ground is said to be cursed on account of the sin of humankind in Gen. 3:17; 5:29; 8:21 (cf. also Gen. 4:11). "Holy ground," denoting the site of a divine revelation, is indicated in Exod. 3:5.

The "earth" as the dwelling place of human beings is indicated in Deut. 4:10; 12:1; 14:2; Isa. 24:21; Amos 3:2. ***'adāmāh*** also denotes "granules of earth" or "dust" in 2 Sam. 1:2; Neh. 9:1.

The meaning "land" is evident in a number of contexts. The "land" of Canaan is God's gift to his people in Gen. 28:15; Exod. 20:12; Lev. 20:24; Num. 11:12; Deut. 4:40; 5:16; 11:9, 21; 28:11ff.; 30:20; Josh. 23:13ff.; 1 Kgs. 8:34; 2 Chr. 6:25; Jer. 16:15; 35:15.

Reference to Canaan as the Israelites' "own land" is found in Ezek. 36:24; 37:21; 38:18ff.; Amos 5:2; 7:11.

General references to "land" as "country" are found in Gen. 47:20ff.; 2 Kgs. 17:23; Ps. 49:11; Isa. 7:16; Dan. 11:39; Jonah 4:2. Another reference to the "land" of Canaan is found in Isa. 1:7. The "land" of Judah is specifically mentioned in Isa. 19:17; Jer. 12:14; Ezek. 12:19; as is the "land" of Israel in Ezek. 7:2; 11:17; 12:22; 18:2; 33:24; 37:12. Canaan is described as Yahweh's "land" in Zech. 9:16.

yabbeshet [יַבֶּשֶׁת, 3007 (Aramaic)]

yabbeshet is a rare Aramaic noun referring to "earth" as the sphere of humankind's habitation in Dan. 2:10.

'ara' [אֲרַע, **772** (Aramaic)]

'ara' is an Aramaic noun denoting "earth" in a variety of contexts.

"Earth" in contrast to "heaven" is indicated in Ezra 5:11; Jer. 10:11; Dan. 6:27; 7:23. The term also refers to "earth" designating the "whole world" in Dan. 2:39; 4:1, 10, 11, 20, 22, 35; 6:25. References to "earth" as "ground" in which trees take root are found in Dan. 4:15, 23. Dan. 7:4 refers to the "ground" as the surface of the earth. See also Dan. 7:17.

NT Words

gē [γῆ, *1093*]

gē is a dynamic equivalent for both ***'ereṣ*** and ***'adāmāh*** (see above), found nearly two hundred times with the principal meanings "earth," "land," "ground."

gē refers to "land" in the sense of "country" in a number of places, indicating the land of Israel or Judah in Matt. 2:6, 20ff.; John 3:22. See also Matt. 27:45; 15:33; Luke 4:25; Acts 7:11ff.; 13:19; Heb. 11:9. References to other "lands," including the tribal regions of Zebulun and Naphtali near Galilee, are noted in Matt. 4:15. See also Matt. 9:26; 10:15; 11:24; Heb. 8:9; Jude 5 The meaning "land" in contrast to "sea" is indicated in Mark 4:1; 6:47, 53; Luke 5:24; John 6:21.

The "earth" as the sphere of God's punishment is indicated in Luke 21:23ff.; Rom. 9:28; Rev. 6:10; 7:1ff.; 8:7; 9:1ff.; 14:18ff.; 16:1ff.; and as the sphere of his authority in Rom. 9:17; 1 Cor. 10:26; Rev. 5:13; 11:4.

The "earth" is also designated as the sphere of God's punishment of Satan (cf. Rev. 12:4ff.); and also the domain of the "unholy trinity" in Rev. 13:3ff.

The "earth" as the place of Jesus' ministry is noted in John 12:32; 17:4.

gē also refers to the earth in the general sense of "the world" as a whole in Matt. 5:5; 10:34; Luke 11:31; Acts 1:8.

God is designated as Lord of the earth in Matt. 11:25; Luke 10:21; Acts 17:24; and as the creator of the earth in Acts 4:24; 14:15; Col. 1:18; Heb. 1:10; 2 Pet. 3:5; Rev. 14:7.

"Earth" is contrasted to "heaven" in Matt. 5:18; 6:10; 16:19; 18:18; 24:35; 28:18; Mark 13:27ff.; Luke 2:14; 16:17; Eph. 3:15; Jas. 5:12.

References to the "new heavens and the new earth" are found in 2 Pet. 3:13; Rev. 21:1.

The term also denotes "ground" with reference to the surface of the earth in Matt. 10:29; 13:5ff.; 25:25; Luke 24:5; John 8:6ff.; Acts 9:4. It refers to "soil" in Mark 4:8, 20ff.; Luke 8:8, 15; Jas. 5:18. In particular, 1 Cor. 15:47 refers to Adam as "the first man from the earth."

Eph. 4:9 indicates the "lower parts of the earth," with probable reference to the realm of the dead.

epigeios [ἐπίγειος, *1919*]

epigeios is an adjectival form found in six places, meaning "earthly."

The meaning "earthly" in the sense of "belonging to the earth" indicates that which is wicked or sinful in Jas. 3:15; Phil. 3:19. "Earthly" matters in a neutral sense are noted in John 3:12. "Earthly, or terrestrial bodies," referring possibly to geological features such as mountains, oceans, and valleys, are noted in 1 Cor. 15:40. The human body is described symbolically in 2 Cor. 5:1 as an "earthly house."

oikoumenē [οἰκουμένη, *3625*]

oikoumenē refers to the "world" in the sense of the "(universally) inhabited earth" throughout its fifteen occurrences.

The "world" as the arena of gospel preaching is noted in Matt. 24:14; Rom. 10:18.

General references to the "world" as the "universally inhabited earth" are found in Luke 2:1; 4:5; Acts 11:28; 17:6; 19:27; 24:5; Heb. 1:6; Rev. 3:10; 12:9; 16:14.

The "world" as the sphere of divine judgment is indicated in Luke 21:26; Acts 17:31.

See Also: → DUST → WORLD

EARTHEN, EARTHLY, EARTHY

OT Words

ḥeres [חֶרֶשׂ, **2789**]

This term is found on sixteen occasions and translated "earthen" (i.e., made of clay) or "potsherd" (i.e., piece of broken pottery). It always refers to vessels of clay, in both a literal and metaphorical sense.

In its literal sense, ***ḥeres*** refers first of all to clay pots for culinary purposes, either for cooking or as water jars (cf. Lev. 6:28; 11:33; 14:5, 50; 15:12; Num. 5:17; Jer. 19:1; 32:14). On one occasion it also means "potsherd" in a literal sense when referring to Job picking up a piece of broken pottery to scrape his sores and relieve the discomfort (cf. Job 2:8).

The remaining occurrences of ***ḥeres*** are all metaphorical. Ezek. 23:34, for example, speaks of God breaking the (clay) pot of his wrath upon the people of Judah. Lam. 4:2 describes the people of Jerusalem and Judah in the aftermath of the Babylonian invasion as worthless as clay pots. This metaphor refers to their overwhelming sense of loss and shame. The wicked are similarly described in Prov. 26:23; Isa. 45:9. Ps. 22:15 also employs the "broken pottery" metaphor but indicates the utter weakness of the writer, who is in torment. This psalm anticipates the suffering of the Messiah. Isa. 30:14 refers to breaking pottery as part of a symbolic depiction of divine judgment against Israel. Finally, Job 41:30 describes the underbelly of the leviathan metaphorically as "pieces of broken pottery."

NT Words

ostrakinos **[ὀστράκινος, *3749*]**

ostrakinos is a rare adjective found only twice. In 2 Tim. 2:20 it refers to household vessels "made of earth," or "clay." In 2 Cor. 4:7 it refers metaphorically to the believer's human frailty as "earthen vessels," the fragile "containers" that enjoy the treasure, the blessings of the gospel.

choikos **[χοϊκός, *5517*]**

choikos is a rare adjective found three times referring to the original man created by God as a man "of the earth" (cf. 1 Cor. 15:47ff.).

EARTHQUAKE

OT Words

ra'ash **[רַעַשׁ, 7494]**

This noun derives from the verb ***rā'ash***, "to shake," "tremble," "quake." (→QUAKE →TREMBLE) ***ra'ash*** occurs seventeen times and is variously translated "earthquake," "shaking," "trembling," and several associated meanings.

Where ***ra'ash*** is translated "earthquake," the contexts are both literal and metaphorical. 1 Kgs. 19:11, 12, for example, refer to an earthquake experienced by Elijah as a sign given by God immediately prior to him speaking to the prophet. Then, Amos 1:1; Zech. 14:5 refer to an earthquake at the time of Uzziah and Jeroboam II, possibly as a divine judgment against his people. What is implicit in these two texts, however, is quite explicit in Isa. 29:5, where God threatens an earthquake upon his people in Jerusalem and Judah as part of their punishment for rebellion against God. Finally, in Ezek. 3:12, 13 there is a metaphorical reference to an "earthquake" as part of God's revelation to the prophet in the vision of the mysterious angelic beings in the heavenly throne room.

NT Words

seismos **[σεισμός, *4578*]**

seismos is a noun denoting an "earthquake" in most of the fourteen occurrences of the term.

Literal references to "earthquakes" as recorded historical phenomena are found in several places, all of which depict these events as divine indicators of a particularly significant point in time. They took place, for example, at the death of Christ in Matt. 27:54; and at the moment of his rising from the dead in Matt. 28:2. Acts 16:26 records that an earthquake shook the foundation of the prison holding the apostle Peter, thus allowing him to escape.

Elsewhere, earthquakes are depicted as future indicators of divine judgment, one of the signs that will characterize the last days before the return of Christ (cf. Matt. 24:7; Mark 13:8; Luke 21:11). In the book of Revelation, earthquakes are depicted as one of the catastrophic manifestations of divine wrath poured out against wicked humankind (cf. Rev. 6:12; 8:5; 11:13; 16:18). See also Rev. 11:19.

Additional Notes

Earthquakes in the New Testament are for the most part literal, with an accompanying potent symbolism. Earthquakes are usually associated with God's specific judgment against wicked people, particularly in the book of Revelation. They also function as signs from God, indicating the final day of divine judgment when God will bring his purposes in salvation and condemnation to an absolute climax. In this regard, the earthquake at the time of Jesus' death on the cross (Matt. 27:54) is particularly significant. Earthquakes in the Old Testament era also function as powerful indications of God's presence and purpose, especially at times of divine intervention in the affairs of his people — both to demonstrate his displeasure and wrath at their sin and to remind them of his awesome power and holiness. Once again, the Old Testament phenomenon anticipates and prepares for the New.

EASE, EASED → LIE (VERB) → REST

EAST

OT Words

mizrāḥ **[מִזְרָח, 4217]**

This term means "east(ward)," in association with the place of sunrise, and occurs about seventy times.

There are a number of occasions in which ***mizrāḥ*** is associated with the eastward orientation of the tabernacle (cf. Exod. 27:13; 38:13). In addition, the term refers to the east gate, or east side, of the temple (cf. 1 Chr. 26:14, 17; 2 Chr. 5:12; 31:14; Neh. 3:29). 2 Chr. 29:4 indicates the assembling of the priests and Levites on the east side of the temple as a prelude to the ritual reforms of King Hezekiah. There are also two references to the eastward orientation of the tribes of Israel in the desert (cf. Num. 2:3; 3:38). In the latter reference it is the location of the campsite of Moses and Aaron, towards the sunrise, that is in view.

In a theologically significant sense, the east is the direction from which God will bring judgment on his people and the nations surrounding Israel (cf. Isa. 41:2, 25; 46:11). The east is also the direction from which God will release his people from captivity (cf. Isa. 43:5; Zech. 8:7). In a related though metaphorical sense, the east is also depicted as the region to which sin shall be removed, absolutely (cf. Ps. 103:12).

About half the occurrences of ***mizrāḥ*** refer to the east in a variety of mundane, miscellaneous contexts (e.g., Num. 32:19; Deut. 3:17; Josh. 12:1, 3; Judg. 21:10; 1 Kgs. 7:25; Jer. 31:40; Zech. 14:4).

qādîm [קָדִים, 6921]

This term is synonymous with ***mizrāḥ***, above, but includes the additional sense of "east wind." ***qādîm*** is also found about seventy times.

qādîm is found in a number of significant passages in the latter portion of Ezekiel's prophecy relating to the visionary temple described in Ezek. 40ff. It refers to the east gate or side of this temple, which is the entrance through which the glory cloud of Yahweh returns from the east (cf. Ezek. 43:1ff.). See also Ezek. 10:1; 40:6ff.; 42:15; 41:14.

Such a return, however, did not literally take place in history; the second temple was never reinvested with the glory cloud. The return of this cloud in Ezek. 43 symbolizes and anticipates the coming of the Messiah described in John 1:14 as the full embodiment, or incarnation, of the shekinah glory of Yahweh. In the later portions of this temple vision, the east side or gate of the sanctuary is closely associated with the movements of the prince, an unambiguous messianic figure (cf. Ezek. 45:7; 46:12). Earlier in Ezekiel's prophecy it is the east gate of the temple (i.e., the Jerusalem temple) that is identified as the point of departure for the glory cloud. This signifies Yahweh's abandonment of the most holy place and his people at the Babylonian destruction of the city and temple in 587 B.C.

Other references to easterly direction are also found in this section of Ezekiel's prophecy — the eastward orientation of the altar (Ezek. 43:17); and the direction of the water flowing out from below the temple threshold (Ezek. 47:1ff.). These two references are also significant in the context of the relationship of the east gate to both the departure and return of the divine glory cloud. See also Ezek. 47:18; 48:10, 16ff.

Literal references to the east wind are found in Gen. 41:6; Exod. 10:13; Job 38:24; Jonah 4:8. In Exod. 14:21 it is the east wind sent by God that separates the waters of the Red Sea.

Metaphorical references to the east wind are found in contexts where such a natural phenomenon symbolizes the coming of divine judgment (e.g., Jer. 18:17; Isa. 27:8; Ezek. 17:10; Hos. 13:15).

qedem [קֶדֶם, 6924]

This term is synonymous with ***qādîm***, above. It occurs about eighty times and means "east(ward)" or "east side" on about fifty occasions.

General references to easterly direction are quite frequent (e.g., Gen. 2:8, 14; 3:24; 4:16; 28:14; Num. 34:3ff.; Josh. 7:2; Judg. 6:3; 1 Kgs. 4:30; Job 1:3; Ezek. 25:4; 39:11).

References to the eastern side of the tabernacle and temple are found in Exod. 27:13; 38:13; Lev. 1:16; 1 Kgs. 7:39. ***qedem*** also occurs in Ezekiel in significant contexts. The "East" is the location of sun worship, practiced by rebellious Israelites about to be punished by God (Ezek. 8:16). Then there is the eastern side of Jerusalem, identified as the location for the departure of the glory cloud from the temple (Ezek. 11:23). The eastern side of the prince's land allocation is also indicated in Ezek. 45:7.

NT Words

anatolē [ἀνατολή, *395*]

anatolē is a noun denoting the direction "east" throughout most of its ten occurrences.

Matt. 2:1 refers to the "east" as the direction from which the wise men had come in order to pay homage to the infant Jesus. The star which had been the initial indicator of the birth of Christ to the magi was first seen by them in "the east" (cf. Matt. 2:2, 9). Other references to the east include Matt. 8:11; 24:27; Luke 13:29; Rev. 7:2; 16:12; 21:13.

Additional Notes

The "east" in the Old Testament refers to this geographic orientation as the place from which God brings judgment and deliverance, as well as the place to which he directs or focuses his judgment. This is true for both his own people and the nations at large.

This perspective is not quite as dominant in the New Testament, though it is implied in texts such as Luke 1:78, which indicates the "rising sun" (i.e., place of the east) as a metaphor for Christ, the focal point of God's redemptive purposes.

EASTER → PASSOVER

EAT, EATING

OT Words

'ākal **[אָכַל, 398]**

This common verb occurs over 850 times meaning "eat," as well as associated senses of "devour," "consume."

'ākal refers to the ordinary sense of eating in most of the occurrences of the term. There are, however, several particular contexts of interest. In Gen. 2:16, 17, and throughout Gen. 3, there is the profound significance of Adam and Eve eating the forbidden fruit, in direct violation of God's command, with disastrous consequences for themselves and the entire human race. In Exod. 12 there is the powerful symbolism of the Passover meal, eaten in haste just prior to the exodus from Egypt. In the book of Leviticus there are over eighty references to partaking of food associated with sacrificial meals. Included here also are prohibitions and sanctions against eating prohibited, unclean food; eating blood; and the practice of cannibalism (cf. Lev. 17:10–14; 26:29, 38). See also Deut. 15:23; 28:53, Jer. 12:9; Lam. 2:10; Ezek. 5:10.

'ākal is also used in a number of contexts where the phenomenon of "consuming" or "devouring" symbolically expresses the outpouring of divine wrath. In the first instance, fire is often associated with the phenomenon of "consumption," whereby God brings punishment against both his enemies and his own people and destroys them in the process. This fate concerning the enemies of Yahweh is illustrated, for example, in Num. 21:28; Isa. 26:11; Jer. 48:45; Amos 1:4ff., Zech. 9:4, 15. In Zeph. 1:18, the consuming fire of God's wrath is associated with the Day of the Lord judgment. The same fate is also predicated of God's people (cf. Lev. 10:2; Num. 11:1; 16:35; Isa. 5:24; Jer. 5:14; Lam. 4:11). Other references to God "devouring" his people in judgment, apart from fire, are found in Ezek. 7:15; Joel 1:4, 19, 20. Eating as a symbolic action of God's specific judgment against Israel and Judah is found in Ezek. 3:1ff.; 4:9ff.; Hos. 2:12; 5:7; Isa. 1:20. The "devouring" of God's enemies is also in view in Isa. 24:6; 31:8; Jer. 15:3; Ezek. 39:17ff.

In more general contexts, the phenomenon of Yahweh as a "consuming fire" indicates the holiness and awe of his person and presence (cf. Exod. 3:2; Deut. 4:24; 6:25; Ps. 50:3; Isa. 10:17; 30:27).

bārāh **[בָּרָה, 1262]**

This rare verb occurs only seven times, and in five of these contexts it means "eating." All references are to the literal consumption of food (2 Sam. 3:35; 12:17; 13:6, 10). Lam. 4:10 refers to the horrors of cannibalism associated with the siege of Jerusalem at the time of the Babylonian invasion when Israelite women ate their own children.

NT Words

esthiō **[ἐσθίω, *2068*]**

esthiō is a verb found about sixty times, meaning "to eat" and used only in the present tense form. ***esthiō*** is to be compared with ***phagō*** (see below).

Mundane references to people "eating" include Matt. 9:11; 12:1; Mark 1:6; 7:2ff.; Luke 5:30ff.; 7:33ff.; 17:27ff.; Rom. 14:2ff.; 1 Cor. 9:7, 13; 11:22, 34; 2 Thess. 3:10ff.

1 Cor. 8:7, 10 refer to "eating" food offered to idols, and in 1 Cor. 10:25ff. there is a reference to consuming food that may possibly have been so presented.

"Eating" the various items of the Lord's Supper (i.e., the bread and the wine), in remembrance of Christ's death and resurrection, is indicated in 1 Cor. 11:26ff.

In Heb. 10:27 the use of ***esthiō*** is metaphorical, referring to the fury of God's wrath that will "consume" his enemies.

phagō **[φάγω, *5315*]**

phagō is an alternate form of ***esthiō*** (see above), used in tenses other than the present (***esthiō*** is used exclusively in the present). ***phagō*** is found nearly one hundred times and is translated "to eat" throughout.

Mundane references to "eating" food include Matt. 6:25; 15:32ff.; Mark 6:31ff.; 8:1ff.; Luke 4:2; 7:26; John 4:31ff.; 6:23ff.; Acts 10:13ff.; Rom. 14:21ff.; 1 Cor. 8:8, 13; 15:32; 2 Thess. 3:8. Eating food sacrificed to idols is noted in Rev. 2:14, 20. Jesus eats the Passover meal with his disciples in Matt. 26:17, 26; Mark 14:12ff.; Luke 22:8ff.; John 18:28. Other references to eating the Lord's Supper include 1 Cor. 11:20ff. The manna miraculously provided by God for his people in the wilderness, described as "bread from heaven," is noted in John 6:31, 49. See also 1 Cor. 10:13. In John 6, however, there is a distinctive play on words employed by Christ, who compares and contrasts the literal "heavenly bread" (i.e., manna) with the true "spiritual bread from heaven," or his own person and teaching that is eternally satisfying to those who partake of it (cf. John 6:49ff.).

phagō is used metaphorically in Jas. 5:3, referring to the spiritually harmful effect of wealth on those who idolize it as something that will "eat" their flesh. Elsewhere, the term refers to "eating" the fruit of the tree of life in the heavenly Jerusalem, symbolically designating the purification of its inhabitants (cf. Rev. 2:7). See also Rev. 2:17. Rev. 10:10 refers to the apostle John "eating" the scroll of judgment against humankind, handed to him by the angel in his vision. The destruction of the Babylonian "whore" in Rev. 17:16 is recorded in terms of her flesh being "devoured." See also Rev. 19:18.

trōgō [τρώγω, *5176*]

trōgō is a rare synonym of ***esthiō***, above, found six times and meaning "to eat." Most of these occurrences are metaphorical, referring in John 6:54ff. to "eating" the flesh of Christ — an allusion to the spiritual significance of the Passover bread (or meal) when consumed in an attitude of genuine faith. John 6:58 refers to "eating" the Passover bread. Matt. 24:38 speaks of "eating" in a mundane, literal sense.

geuomai [γεύομαι, *1089*]

geuomai us a verb found in twenty places meaning "taste." The mundane sense of "eating" food is indicated only in Acts 23:14.

bibrōskō [βιβρώσκω, *977*]

bibrōskō is a rare verb found only in John 6:13, referring to the physical act of eating.

katesthiō [κατεσθίω, *2719*]

katesthiō is a synonym for ***phagō*** and ***esthiō*** (see above), with the primary meanings "devour," "eat" in both literal and metaphorical contexts — though the latter usage predominates. The literal meaning "devour" is found in the contexts of birds consuming seed in Matt. 13:4; Mark 4:4; Luke 8:5.

The remaining use of ***katesthiō*** is metaphorical. The "devouring" (i.e., "buying up") of widows' houses by callous religious leaders is indicated in Matt. 23:14; Mark 12:40; Luke 20:47. The sense of "devour," denoting the act of "destroying," is used in relation to the enemies of God and his people (cf. Rev. 11:5; 12:4; 20:9). Zeal for the temple is said to "consume" Christ in John 2:17. The apostle John's symbolic "eating" of a scroll is recorded in Rev. 10:9. See also 2 Cor. 11:20; Gal. 5:15.

korennymi [κορέννυμι, *2880*]

korennymi is a rare verb indicating "eating one's fill," "sating oneself," found only in Acts 27:38; 1 Cor. 4:8.

synesthiō [συνεσθίω, *4906*]

synesthiō is a variant form of ***esthiō***, above, meaning "to eat with someone" in all five occurrences of the term (cf. Luke 15:2; Acts 10:41; 11:3; 1 Cor. 5:11; Gal. 2:12).

brōsis [βρῶσις, *1035*]

brōsis is a noun denoting "food," "meat" for most of its eleven occurrences. However, in 1 Cor. 8:4 it designates "eating" food offered to idols.

Additional Notes

The Hebrew term ***'ākal*** occurs in a number of contexts which express God's anger and judgment against both his enemies and his own people with powerful symbolism. ***'ākal*** has no single Greek equivalent but embraces the whole range of New Testament terminology that deals with "eating."

These various terms for "eating" in the New Testament do not carry as much theological weight as does ***'ākal*** in the Old Testament. The one notable exception is the reference to eating the Lord's Supper, which consummates the symbolic significance of the Passover meal in Exod. 12 in the person of Christ. Linked to this are the metaphorical references to feeding on the body of Christ in John 6 (see ***trōgō***, above), which derive their spiritual significance from Israel feeding on manna in the wilderness.

It is evident that the phenomenon of "eating" (as well as associated nuances) throughout Scripture carries powerful symbolic significance with respect to the judgment of God, in both a positive as well as a negative sense.

See Also: ➞ FOOD ➞ TASTE

EDGE, EDGED

OT WORDS

peh [פֶּה, 6310]

This noun is found thirty-five times, meaning "edge (of the sword)." In each instance, slaughter is implied (cf. Gen. 34:26; Exod. 17:13; Num. 21:24; Deut. 13:15; Josh. 8:24; Judg. 3:16; 18:27; 1 Sam. 15:8; 2 Sam. 15:14; Jer. 21:7).

qāṣeh **[קָצֶה, 7097]**

This term occurs about ninety times, but is translated "edge" on only six occasions (cf. Exod. 13:20; Num. 33:6 [of the wilderness]; Exod. 26:5; 36:12 [of the tabernacle curtain]; Num. 33:37 [of the land of Edom]; Josh. 13:27 [of the Sea of Galilee]).

qāṣāh **[קָצָה, 7098]**

qāṣāh is related to ***qāṣeh***, above, occurring thirty-five times, but meaning "edge" on only three occasions. Both Exod. 28:7 and 39:4 refer to the extremities of a piece of clothing; and Judg. 3:16 refers to the two edges of a sword.

sāphāh **[שָׂפָה, 8193]**

sāphāh is a verb found over 170 times with a variety of meanings. The most common of these is "lip"; as well as the senses of "bank," "language," "speech." The meaning "edge" is also evident in a number of places, referring to the "edge(s)" of the tabernacle curtains in Exod. 26:4, 10; 36:11, 17. It also designates the "edge" of the altar as portrayed in the vision of Ezekiel's temple in Ezek. 43:13. (→ LANGUAGE → LIP)

NT Words

stoma [στόμα, *4750*]

stoma is a noun found nearly eighty times with the predominant sense of "mouth." (→ MOUTH) However, in Luke 21:24; Heb. 11:34, ***stoma*** denotes the "edge" of a sword.

distomos [δίστομος, *1366*]

distomos is a rare adjective referring to a "two-edged" sword in Heb. 4:12; Rev. 1:16; 2:12.

EDIFICATION, EDIFY

NT Words

oikodomē [οἰκοδομή, *3619*]

oikodomē is a noun found in eighteen contexts with the primary meaning "building" in both a literal and metaphorical sense. (→ BUILD) The meaning "edification" in the sense of "being built up, strengthened in one's faith" is indicated, for example, in Rom. 14:19; 15:2; 1 Cor. 14:3ff., 12, 25; 2 Cor. 10:8; 12:19; 13:10; Eph. 4:12; 16.

Symbolic references to the people of God as his "building" are found in 1 Cor. 3:9; 2 Cor. 5:1; Eph. 2:21.

oikodomeō [οἰκοδομέω, *3618*]

oikodomeō is a verb with the principal meaning "to build" in most of its approximately thirty occurrences, used in both literal and metaphorical contexts. (→ BUILD)

The meaning "to edify," in the sense of "build up, encourage, nurture one's faith," is evident in relation to the church in Acts 9:31; 1 Cor. 4:4; 1 Pet. 2:5; and to the individual in 1 Cor. 8:1; 14:4, 17; 1 Thess. 5:11.

See Also: → BUILD

EIGHT, EIGHTEEN, EIGHTH

OT Words

shemînî **[שְׁמִינִי, 8066]**

This term translates the ordinal form of the numeral "eight." It is found approximately thirty times with this meaning. It primarily refers to offerings made on the eighth day — for example, the eighth-day assembly (cf. Num. 29:35; Neh. 8:18); including the day of the temple dedication (cf. 2 Chr. 7:9); the eighth-day Sabbath (cf. Lev. 23:39). Other eighth-day offerings in general are found in Lev. 14:10, 23; 23:36; Num. 6:10; Ezek. 43:27. The eighth-day rite of circumcision for infant boys in mentioned in Lev. 12:3.

Finally, a number of references specify the eighth in a series of various phenomena, with no particular significance (e.g., Exod. 22:30; Num. 7:54; 1 Kgs. 6:8; 1 Chr. 24:10; Zech. 1:1).

shemōneh **[שְׁמֹנֶה, 8083]**

This numerical term for "eight" occurs over one hundred times in the Old Testament. No special significance attaches to this usage, except that Gen. 17:12; 21:4 refer to the rite of circumcision that is required to be performed on eight-day-old baby boys. The following examples are noted concerning the number eight: the ages of the prediluvian patriarchs (Gen. 5); the size of armies opposed to Israel (2 Sam. 8:13); the duration of foreign oppression during the period of the Judges (Judges 3:14); the dimensions of the temple (1 Kgs. 7:10); the regal years of Israelite kings (2 Kgs. 22:1, 3).

NT Words

oktō [ὀκτώ, *3638*]

oktō is a term denoting the cardinal number "eight," "eighteen" in nine places. Reference to the first eight-day period of an infant boy's life leading to his ritual circumcision is noted in Luke 2:21. A period of eight days is indicated in Luke 9:28; John 20:26. 1 Pet. 3:20 refers to the eight members of Noah's family saved from the flood. Luke 13:4 mentions the "eighteen" people killed in the collapse of the Tower of Siloam. See also Luke 13:11, 18; John 5:5; Acts 9:33.

ogdoos [ὄγδοος, *3590*]

ogdoos is the term for the ordinal number "eighth" in five places. The "eighth" day in relation to the ritual of circumcision is noted in Luke 1:59; Acts 7:8. See also 2 Pet. 2:5; Rev. 17:11; 21:20.

oktaēmeros [ὀκταήμερος, *3637*]

oktaēmeros is a rare adjectival form of ***ogdoos***, above, found only in Phil. 3:5 with reference to Paul's claim to Jewish orthodoxy in respect of his being circumcised on the "eighth" day.

ELDER, ELDEST

OT Words

zāqēn **[זָקֵן, 2205]**

This is a common noun, also used adjectivally, that translates "elder," referring to age as well as to civil authority in ancient Israelite society. ***zāqēn*** occurs approximately 170 times. The nominal usage of the term is predominant.

Old age is indicated primarily in mundane contexts (e.g., Gen. 18:11; Josh. 6:21; 1 Sam. 28:14; Ps. 119:100; Eccl. 4:13). The following texts, however, are of particular interest. In Isa. 65:20, old age is seen as a blessing in the prophet's vision of a renewed earth. In Lam. 2:21 there is much agonizing over the death of the elderly in Jerusalem. In Ezek. 9:6, the elderly are not spared the wrath of God as a result of their idolatrous practices. Finally, Joel 2:28 contains the classic prophetic reference to the anticipated coming of the Holy Spirit, when old men shall dream dreams of God's great work of redemption.

In reference to civil authority, ***zāqēn*** is used over one hundred times to indicate the office of "elder" in Israel. There are a variety of contexts to note. General references to elders are found, for example, in Exod. 3:16; Num. 11:16ff.; Deut. 5:23; 1 Kgs. 8:1. Elders are involved in a number of ritual contexts such as the covenant renewal ceremony described in Josh. 24:31; the public anointing of David as king over all Israel in 1 Sam. 5:3; and the ceremonial return of the ark to Jerusalem in 2 Chr. 5:2ff. Elders are also present with Moses on Mt. Sinai in Deut. 24:9. Deut. 19:12; 21:2ff.; 22:16ff. allude to their distinctive legal function. Elders are also marked out for divine judgment as a consequence of their abuse of office and neglect of God's laws in Isa. 3:14 (cf. also Ezek. 8:12; Lam. 1:19). In Joel 2:16, God calls the elders of Israel to repentance. Then, in Isa. 24:23, the elders of Israel will witness the universal reign of Yahweh in a visionary oracle depicting the victory of God's kingdom over the nations of the world.

gādôl **[גָּדוֹל, 1419]**

gādôl is a common adjectival form meaning "great," "large," as well as related nuances, throughout the more than five hundred occurrences of the term. The meaning "elder" is also evident in several contexts.

References to the "elder" brother in a literal sense are found in Gen. 10:21; 27:42; 1 Kgs. 2:22. Likewise, Gen. 29:16; 1 Sam. 18:17 refer to "elder" sisters.

In Ezek. 16:46, 61; 23:4 ***gādôl*** is symbolic, denoting Samaria (i.e., the northern kingdom of Israel) as the "elder" sister of Judah.

sîb **[שִׂיב, 7868** (Aramaic)**]**

sîb is an Aramaic term denoting the "elders" of the Jews in all five occurrences of the term (cf. Ezra 5:5ff.; 6:7ff.).

NT Words

presbyteros [πρεσβύτερος, *4245*]

presbyteros is the predominant term for "elder" in the New Testament, found nearly seventy times.

The term refers primarily to the "elders" as one section of the civil and ritual leadership of first-century Judean society, comprising also the priests, scribes and Pharisees (e.g., Matt. 15:2; 26:47ff.; 27:1ff.; Mark 7:3ff.; 11:27; 14:43ff.; Luke 7:3; 22:52; Acts 4:15ff.; 6:12; 25:15).

presbyteros also refers to the "elder" brother in the parable of the prodigal son, cf. (cf. Luke 15:25). See also John 8:9.

The term also denotes "old men" in Acts 2:17; 1 Tim. 5:1. See also 1 Tim. 5:2 and the "elders" of the local church in Acts 11:30; 15:2ff.; 1 Tim. 5:17ff.; Titus 1:5; Jas. 5:14; 1 Pet. 5:1ff.; 2 John 1; 3 John 1. The heavenly "elders" that surround the throne of God and Christ are indicated in Rev. 4:4, 10; 5:5ff.; 7:11ff.; 11:16; 14:3; 19:4.

sympresbyteros [συμπρεσβύτερος, *4850*]

sympresbyteros is a rare variant of ***presbyteros***, above, denoting a "fellow elder," found only in 1 Pet. 5:1.

presbyterion [πρεσβυτέριον, *4244*]

presbyterion is another rare variant of ***presbyteros***, above, denoting the "council of the elders" of the Jewish people in Luke 22:66; Acts 22:5; 1 Tim. 4:14.

Additional Notes

The office of elder is found throughout both Testaments of Scripture. The Hebrew term ***zāqēn*** highlights the civil and legal office of God-ordained authority in Israelite society, the old covenant people of God. In the New Testament, the term ***presbyteros*** is used similarly, with the focus not on a geographic, linguistic, ritual or socio-political entity, but on the God-ordained spiritual leadership of local congregations of believers. Elders in new covenant churches carry a solemn, spiritual authority with clearly defined qualities of character that are prerequisite to office. Such characteristics are rarely alluded to in the Old Testament, with the notable exception of Exod. 18:21. It is clear, however, that the establishment of God's rule over his people, whether in the old or new covenant era, involves the important agency of eldership.

ELECT, ELECTION

NT Words

eklektos [ἐκλεκτός, *1588*]

eklektos is an adjective found in approximately twenty places with the predominant meaning "elect" or "chosen" throughout. (→ CHOOSE)

References to the "elect" denoting the "chosen people of God" are found in Matt. 20:16; 24:22ff.; Mark 13:20ff.; Luke 18:7; Rom. 8:33; Col. 3:12; 2 Tim. 2:10; Titus 1:1; 1 Pet. 1:2. In particular, "elect" individuals chosen by God include angels in heaven in 1 Tim. 5:21; and the Messiah, under the guise of the "chief cornerstone" of the temple, in 1 Pet. 2:4ff. See also 1 Pet. 5:13; 2 John 1, 13.

eklogē [ἐκλογή, *1589*]

eklogē is a noun denoting the phenomenon of divine "election" in Rom. 9:11; 11:5ff., 28; 2 Thess. 1:4; 2 Pet. 1:10.

See Also: → CHOICE

EMBRACE → GREET

EMERALD

OT Words

nōphek [נֹפֶךְ, 5306]

This term means "emerald" four times in the Old Testament. It refers to one of the precious stones in the high priest's breastplate (cf. Exod. 28:18; 39:11). The translation of terms such as this for specific gemstones, however, is not always definitive. ***nōphek*** also refers to one of the precious stones in the coronet of the pre-existent spirit of the king of Tyre in the garden of Eden, as seen in Ezek. 28:13. There is one other reference to emeralds as part of the valuable commodities purchased by the king of Tyre from Edom (cf. Ezek. 27:16).

bāreqet [בָּרֶקֶת, 1304]

This term occurs three times, denoting (as ***nōphek***, above) the precious stones of the high priest's breastplate. ***bāreqet*** is the last gem mounted in the first row (cf. Exod. 28:17; 39:10); and is also listed among the gems belonging to the primeval spirit of the Tyrian king in Ezek. 28:13.

yahălōm [יַהֲלֹם, 3095]

This term also occurs three times and possibly refers to a "diamond." The contexts are identical to those of ***nōphek*** and ***bāreqet***, above (viz. Exod. 28:18; 39:11; Ezek. 28:13).

NT Words

smaragdos [σμάραγδος, *4665*]

smaragdos is a rare noun found only in Rev. 21, referring to the "emerald" that is one of the precious stones adorning one of the twelve gates of the heavenly city — each gate representing one of the twelve tribes of Israel.

smaragdinos [σμαράγδινος, *4664*]

smaragdinos is the rare adjectival form derived from ***smaragdos***, above, found only in Rev. 4:3 and relating the likeness of the rainbow encircling the throne of God to an "emerald," the semi-translucent precious stone of a light green hue.

EMPTY

OT Words

rûq [רוּק, 7324]

This verb has the basic sense of "pour, draw out," as well as "empty (out)," "make empty." ***rûq*** occurs nineteen times overall, but only seven times with meanings relating to emptying.

The literal sense of "empty out" is found in Gen. 42:35 and Eccl. 11:3. ***rûq*** also occurs in Isa. 32:6, referring to those who are hungry whom the Lord leaves "empty." The context here is one of divine judgment.

rûq is used metaphorically in a number of contexts. In Jer. 48:11, 12 it is God who "empties out" the object of his wrath (viz. Moab), implying an action of divine destruction. Hab. 1:17 refers to the unrestrained activity of wicked nations who continually "empty their nets," thereby destroying other people. The prophet's complaint here is that God is seemingly uninterested in remedying this injustice. Zech. 4:12 refers to the empowering of the Spirit of God with respect to his chosen servant, king, and high priest. The two olive trees here represent priest and king respectively, and these trees "empty out" the golden oil that fills the lampstand, which in turn bears witness to the light of God's person and presence among his people and in the world at large.

rêq [רֵיק, 7386]

This is the adjectival form of ***rûq***, above, and occurs fourteen times in the Old Testament. ***rêq*** means "empty," "vain." Literal emptiness is indicated in Gen. 37:14; 41:27; Judg. 7:16; 2 Kgs. 4:3.

Metaphorically, ***rêq*** refers to God's purifying and painful judgment against his people in Ezek. 24:11, which describes the prophet's symbolic action of placing the empty cooking pot on the fire, so that all its impurities may be burned off (see also Neh. 5:13). Isa. 29:8 refers to the nations that will suffer gnawing pangs of hunger (lit: ". . . those who awake empty"), again as a direct consequence of God's judgment against them. References to those who are "empty" in the sense of being "vain" or "idle" are found in Deut. 32:47; Judg. 9:4; 2 Sam. 6:20; 13:7; Prov. 12:11; 28:19.

rêqām [רֵיקָם, 7387]

This is a synonym for ***rêq***, above, and occurs with approximately the same frequency (e.g., Gen. 31:42; Exod. 3:21; Deut. 15:13; 1 Sam. 6:3; 2 Sam. 1:22; Ps. 7:14; Isa. 55:11; Jer. 50:9).

'ārāh [עָרָה, 6168]

'ārāh is a verb found in fifteen places. It means to "uncover," as well as a number of related senses, including that of to "empty." (→ UNCOVER)

The literal sense of to "empty" in the sense of "pour out" liquid from a container is indicated in Gen. 24:20; as is the act of "emptying" the contents from a chest (cf. 2 Chr. 24:11).

NT Words

kenoō [κενόω, *2758*]

kenoō is a verb found in five places with the underlying metaphorical sense of "to render null and void," "be in vain." In several places ***kenoō*** is translated "to empty" with these symbolic meanings.

Rom. 4:14 affirms that if eternal life were ever to be gained through obedience to the law, faith would be rendered "null and void," or "emptied" of its effect and importance. Similarly, 1 Cor. 1:17 claims that the cross of Christ would run the risk of "being emptied of its power," should the preaching of the gospel ever be grounded in human wisdom, and be received accordingly by its hearers as mere folly. Of particular significance is the statement in Phil. 2:7 that Christ "emptied himself" by taking the form of a man and becoming a servant of humankind in accordance with God's purposes.

This "emptying" centers on the willingness of Christ to voluntarily put aside his status as a heavenly, divine figure and to assume a full human identity so that he might accomplish God's redemptive purpose in gaining salvation for humankind. (See the Additional Notes below.) See also 1 Cor. 9:15; 2 Cor. 9:3, which mention the futility of boasting, "to render it void."

kenos [κενός, *2756*]

kenos is an adjectival form derived from ***kenoō***, above, found eighteen times with the primary sense of "vain," "futile." In several places, however, ***kenos*** also means "empty-handed," or lacking in property and/or wealth (cf. Mark 12:3; Luke 1:53; 20:10, 11).

Additional Notes

The phenomenon of "emptying" has a similar import throughout both Testaments. In the New Testament context, the reference to Christ "emptying himself" suggests an ultimate self-denial. With the Old Testament perspective on "emptying" as an act of divine judgment, however, Paul's use of the term ***kenoō*** in Phil. 2:7 assumes a heightened significance. It appears that our Lord's "emptying himself" is not simply an action of self-denial, but another symbolic expression signifying Jesus Christ's willingness to adopt the form of a human being in order to implement his Father's redemptive purposes — a reference, therefore, to the Son's voluntary submission to a divine judgment. Such an "emptying" becomes the prerequisite for the final ordeal on the cross, the climax of God's profound judgment on sin that was wholly borne by Christ himself.

ENABLE → STRENGTH

ENACT

NT Words

nomotheteō [νομοθετέω, *3549*]

nomotheteō is a rare verb found only twice. In Heb. 7:11 it refers to "providing" the law to the Israelite people at Sinai. In Heb. 8:6 it refers to "enacting" or "establishing" the new covenant on better promises, indicating its superiority over the old.

ENCOUNTER → MEET

ENCOURAGE, ENCOURAGEMENT

OT Words

ḥāzaq [**חָזַק, 2388**]

ḥāzaq is a verb occurring nearly three hundred times, meanings "be strong," "strengthen," as well as several related senses.

In several places, ***ḥāzaq*** also means "encourage," indicating the offering of emotional and moral support to Joshua in Deut. 1:38; 3:28. See also 2 Chr. 35:2; 2 Sam. 11:25; Isa. 41:7.

NT Words

protrepō [προτρέπω, *4389*]

protrepō is a rare verb found only in Acts 18:27, meaning "to encourage" in the context of exhorting fellow believers.

See Also: → COMFORT

END, ENDING

OT Words

qēṣ [**קֵץ, 7093**]

This noun occurs about seventy times. It derives from a term that means "extremity"; and ***qēṣ*** is translated "end" in the majority of instances with a variety of senses.

First of all, ***qēṣ*** indicates an "end" in the general sense of a "termination" or "finish." In several texts the term refers to destruction brought about by God as punishment for sin, "the end of . . ." (cf. Gen. 6:13 [the end of all flesh]; Jer. 51:13 [Babylon]; Ezek. 7:2ff.; 21:25; Lam. 4:18 [Judah]; Ezek. 21:29 [the wicked in general]; Amos 8:2 [Israel]). Other references include Ps. 119:96 (the end of perfection); Eccl. 4:8 (no end of toil); Eccl. 12:8 (no end of making books).

In a number of contexts, ***qēṣ*** simply refers to an "end" or "termination" in a purely chronological sense. These uses are mostly mundane (e.g., Gen. 8:6; Exod. 12:41; Num. 13:25; Deut. 9:11; Judg. 11:39; 2 Sam. 14:26; 1 Kgs. 2:39; Job 16:3; Jer. 34:14; Ezek. 29:13; Hab. 2:3). Of distinct significance, however, is the reference in Isa. 9:7 to the kingdom of God "having no end" (i.e., of eternal duration).

There are also a couple of references to "end" in the sense of a particular destiny (cf. Job 6:11; Ps. 39:4). And, in a related sense, ***qēṣ*** also refers to "end" as the point of eschatological consummation. This is the case in the book of Daniel particularly, where the phrase "time of the end" anticipates the consummation of the kingdom of God both on earth and in the eternal age (cf. Dan. 8:17, 19; 11:27, 35, 40; 12:4, 6, 9, 13).

kālāh [**כָּלָה, 3617**]

This noun occurs about twenty times, with the basic sense of "end" in about half of these texts. In most contexts, destruction is in view.

In the following texts, God's restraining mercy is in view in that he undertakes not to destroy (i.e., "make an end of") his people altogether at the time of the Babylonian invasion of the land of Judah: Jer. 4:17; 5:10, 18; 30:11; 46:28; Ezek. 20:17. Neh. 9:17 alludes to the past in this regard; and in Ezek. 11:13 the prophet pleads with Yahweh to spare his people from such an absolute destruction through an impassioned question: "Ah, sovereign Lord! Will you completely make an end of the remnant of Israel?"

Then, in a related context, Isa. 10:23 indicates Yahweh's decree to "make an end" of his people on account of their sin against him. This refers to the impending Assyrian invasion of Israel, the northern kingdom. Other references point to a similar divine judgment on the nations at large (cf. Jer. 30:11; 46:28; Nah. 1:8, 9; Zeph. 1:18).

'ephes [**אֶפֶס, 657**]

This term occurs about forty times, but only translates "end" in the sense of "extremity" in the phrase "ends of the earth," which occurs in about a third of these contexts (e.g., Deut. 33:17; 1 Sam. 2:10; Ps. 22:7; Prov. 30:4; Isa. 45:22; Jer. 16:19; Mic. 5:4; Zech. 9:10).

tāmam **[תָּמַם, 8552]**

This verb is found on about sixty occasions with the sense of "be at an end," "come to an end" in a number of contexts.

In a purely mundane chronological sense, ***tāmam*** is found in Gen. 47:18; Jer. 1:3.

The phenomenon of "coming to an end" in the sense of divine judgment is expressed in Num. 14:35; Jer. 44:12, 27, where God's people are the object of his wrath. The enemies of God are similarly in view in Ps. 9:6.

Finally, ***tāmam*** expresses the idea of "finality" or "conclusion" in Deut. 31:24, 30; 34:8; 2 Sam. 20:18; Job 31:40. Of particular note is the thought expressed in Ps. 102:27 that God has no end. In Lam. 3:22, genuine comfort is offered to God's people in distress when the writer declares that the mercies of Yahweh never come to an end. Then, in Dan. 9:24, God declares through the angel Gabriel to Daniel that he, Yahweh, will put an end to the sin of his people.

kānāph **[כָּנָף, 3671]**

kānāph is a noun occurring around one hundred times with the primary meanings "wing," "skirt," in the majority of instances, as well as several related nuances. It also means "end" in several places.

Reference to the "ends" of the earth in the sense of its far-flung "corners" is found in Job 37:3; 38:13; Isa. 11:12; 24:16. The distant "ends," or "corners," of the land of Israel are noted in Ezek. 7:2.

tenûk **[תְּנוּךְ, 8571]**

tenûk is a noun found eight times denoting the "tip" or "extremity" (i.e., "end") of the ear lobes of the priests and high priests in Exod. 29:20; Lev. 8:23ff.; 14:14.

qāṣāh **[קָצָה, 7098]**

qāṣāh is a noun signifying the "end" or "extremity" of various objects or phenomena in most of the thirty-five occurrences of the term.

In the context of the design and construction of the tabernacle, ***qāṣāh*** frequently refers to the physical extremities (or ends) of various pieces of furniture and other trappings — for example, the ark of the covenant (cf. Exod. 25:18, 19; 36:7); the carved golden cherubim (cf. Exod. 37:8); the curtains (cf. Exod. 26:4; 36:11); the bronze altar (cf. Exod. 27:4); the breastpiece of the ephod (cf. Exod. 28:23ff.; 39:4, 16ff.).

Similarly, 1 Kgs. 6:24 refers to the "extremities" or "ends" of the cherubim mounted on the ark housed in Solomon's temple.

The "ends" of the earth are indicated in Job 28:24; Ps. 19:6; Isa. 40:28; 41:5, 9; Jer. 49:36. See also Ezek. 15:4.

NT Words

telos **[τέλος, *5056*]**

telos is a noun denoting an "end" for most of the nearly forty occurrences of the term in various contexts.

In a temporal sense, ***telos*** denotes the "end" of the age, the time when God will consummate his redemptive purposes for humankind that will include both the judgment of the wicked and the salvation of the righteous — all to take place when Christ returns for the last time (cf. Matt. 24:6, Mark 13:7; Luke 21:9; John 13:1; 1 Cor. 1:8; 15:24; Heb. 3:14; 6:11; 1 Pet. 4:7; Rev. 2:26; 21:6; 22:13). The kingdom of God and Christ is described as a kingdom "without end" in Luke 1:33.

In more mundane contexts, ***telos*** refers to "end" as the termination or completion of a particular circumstance or event (cf. Matt. 26:58). More significantly, 2 Cor. 3:13 refers to the "end" of the radiance (i.e., its fading) on Moses' face on Mt. Sinai, a phenomenon that the Israelites were prevented from seeing. See also Heb. 7:3.

The meaning "end" in the sense of "destruction" is used in relation to Satan and his kingdom in Mark 3:26; 2 Cor. 11:15; Phil. 3:19; 1 Pet. 4:17. See also Heb. 6:8.

"End" in the sense of "consequence" is indicated in Rom. 6:21 in relation to eternal death as the result of sin, and in relation to eternal life as the result of faith and sanctification in Rom. 6:22; 1 Pet. 1:9.

telos also refers to Christ as the "end" or "fulfillment" of the law in Rom. 10:4.

synteleō **[συντελέω, *4931*]**

synteleō is a variant form of ***telos***, above, found seven times meaning "to bring to an end," "finish," or "complete." Matt. 7:28 refers to Jesus "completing" his discourse to the multitude. The "accomplishment" of Jesus' miracles is indicated in Mark 13:4. The "ending" of the days of Christ's temptation by the devil is noted in Luke 4:2, 13. See also Acts 21:27.

synteleia **[συντέλεια, *4930*]**

synteleia is a noun derived from ***synteleō***, above, found six times and meaning "end" in the sense of "consummation." All references denote the "end" of the world, anticipating the climax of divine judgment, embracing both eternal destruction and life in glory (cf. Matt. 13:39ff.; 24:3; 28:20; Heb. 9:26).

peras [πέρας, *4009*]

peras is a noun found in four places, three of which indicate the meaning "end" as part of the expression "the uttermost ends of the earth" (cf. Matt. 12:42; Luke 11:31; Rom. 10:18).

akron [ἄκρον, *206*]

akron is a noun found in four places meaning "end," "tip" or "point."

In two places, the term refers to the remote corners of the earth, or "the ends" of the earth (cf. Matt. 24:31; Mark 13:27). Luke 16:24 refers to the "tip" of a finger; and Heb. 11:21 to the "end" of a staff.

See Also: ➡ FINISH ➡ FULFILL ➡ LAST

ENDEAVOR

NT Words

spoudazō [σπουδάζω, *4704*]

spoudazō is a verb found twelve times, meaning "endeavor" in the senses of "be eager, diligent," "make every effort" to do something. General references include Gal. 2:10; 1 Thess. 2:17; 2 Tim. 2:15; 4:9, 21. In particular, the term constitutes an appeal to "do one's best," to present oneself as one approved in the art of explaining/interpreting God's word (cf. 2 Tim. 2:15). Eph. 4:3 contains the exhortation "to make every effort" to maintain the unity of the Spirit; in Heb. 4:11 the same exhortation is expressed in relation to believers entering their eternal rest; and in 2 Pet. 1:10 with reference to making one's calling and election sure. See also 2 Pet. 3:14.

See Also: ➡ SEEK

ENDURE, ENDURING

NT Words

menō [μένω, *3306*]

menō is a common verb found in 120 places with the primary meanings "remain," "abide," "dwell." The sense of "endure" or "last" is also evident in 1 Pet. 1:25 in relation to the word of God enduring forever.
(➡ REMAIN)

hypomenō [ὑπομένω, *5278*]

hypomenō is a variant form of ***menō***, above, found in eighteen contexts with the primary meanings "endure," "bear patiently."

References to the perseverance of believers who "stand firm (i.e., endure) to the end" are found in Matt. 10:22; 24:13; Mark 13:13. See also Jas. 5:11. The exhortation "to be patient" under persecution is found in Rom. 12:12; Heb. 12:7. Christ himself is said to "have endured" much persecution, including death on the cross. "Suffering, or enduring affliction, persecution" is indicated in 2 Tim. 2:10ff.; Heb. 10:32; Jas. 1:12. The virtue of love is said to "endure" all things in 1 Cor. 13:7.

tropophoreō [τροποφορέω, *5159*]

tropophoreō is a rare verb found only in Acts 13:18, referring to God "enduring" the ill-conduct of his people in the desert for forty years.

See Also: ➡ BEAR (VERB) ➡ PATIENCE ➡ SUFFER

ENEMY

OT Words

'āyab [אָיַב, **340**]; ***'ōyēb*** [אֹיֵב, **341**]

The verb ***'āyab***, meaning "to be an enemy," occurs only once — in Exod. 23:22. Far more common is the participial noun ***'ōyēb***, meaning "enemy," which occurs nearly three hundred times. There are a number of significant contexts to note.

In the first instance, ***'ōyēb*** refers in a general sense to the enemies of God and his people, throughout the entire course of Israel's history. It refers to enemies such as Egypt (e.g., Exod. 15:9); Canaanite people in general (e.g., Lev. 26:34ff.; Deut. 12:10); Philistia (e.g., 1 Sam. 14:24, 27); and also in preexilic contexts (cf. Isa. 1:24; Mic. 7:10); as well as during the period of exile (cf. Jer. 31:16; Lam. 3:46); and the Persian period (cf. Esth. 8:13; 9:1ff.). Enemies are also referred to in nonspecific contexts (e.g., Exod. 23:4; Num. 24:18; Deut. 1:42; 1 Sam. 24:19; Job 13:24; Prov. 16:7). Also, in general terms, Israel is described as the enemy of other nations (cf. Num. 23:11; Judg. 16:23; 1 Sam. 29:8).

More significantly, there are a considerable number of references to the enemies of Israel being destroyed by God through the agency of his people. All of these events signify great encouragement for the people of God. Key references include Gen. 22:17 where, in the context of the covenant promise to Abraham, Yahweh solemnly declares to the patriarch that his descendants will take possession of the cities of their enemies.

1 Sam. 12:11 refers to the overthrow of Israel's enemies during the period of the judges (Gideon, Barak, Jephthah, and right up to the time of Samuel himself), again indicating Yahweh's sovereign protection of his people, in spite of their sinful rejection of him. 2 Sam. 5:20 records David's victory over the Philistines at the outset of his reign — a victory that David attributes directly to God himself.

In God's covenant promise to David in 2 Sam. 7:9, 11, Yahweh guarantees to remove all of David's enemies from before him.

Ps. 110:1 contains the well-known prophetic promise concerning the enemies of David's "Lord." This is one of the great messianic prophecies of the Old Testament, pointing forward to the time when all the enemies of God's people will be crushed. The one who will preside over such a victory will be "David's Lord," the coming messianic ruler, the King of kings. Other texts to note in this regard are Num. 10:35; Deut. 30:7; Josh. 10:13; 23:1; Judg. 8:34; 2 Sam. 3:18; Isa. 62:8.

In a related context, a number of texts speak of the deliverance of God's people from their enemies (cf. Num. 10:9; Josh. 21:44; 2 Sam. 7:1, 11; 2 Kgs. 17:39). Of particular significance in this regard is the promise in Ezek. 39:27, where Yahweh undertakes to bring spiritual renewal to his people after he has delivered them from the countries of their enemies. Similar promises of rescue from captivity and one's enemies are found in Mic. 4:10; 5:9; Zeph. 3:15. As a corollary to this perspective, there are also contexts in which God openly expresses his wrath against his enemies (e.g., Isa. 9:11; 42:13; 59:18; 66:6, 14; Nah. 1:2, 8).

God directs his wrath not only against the enemies of God's people, but also against Israel herself on account of her sin (e.g. Isa. 63:10; Lam. 2:5). Related to this is the observation that the enemies of God's people are victorious over them because of Israel's sin. In the majority of texts, the rationale for such tragic circumstances for Israel is the outworking of the covenant curse. See particularly Lev. 26:16, 17, 25, 38; Deut. 28:7, 25, 31, 48, 53ff. Other references with the same emphasis are found in 2 Kgs. 21:14; Jer. 12:7; 15:9; 20:4ff.; Lam. 1:9ff.; Hos. 8:3; Amos 9:14.

Finally, ***'ōyēb*** is found in contexts where Israel pleads for deliverance from her enemies (cf. 1 Sam. 12:10; 20:16), as does the psalmist (e.g., Pss. 3:7; 9:3ff.; 42:9; 56:9; 68:1).

ṣar [צַר, 6862]

This noun occurs around one hundred times and means "enemy" in a little over half of these contexts. ***ṣar*** is a synonym for ***'ōyēb***, above, and the various emphases are almost identical.

Like ***'ōyēb***, ***ṣar*** refers in a general sense to the enemies of God (cf. Deut. 32:27; Job 19:11), and to the enemies of God's people (cf. Josh. 5:13; 1 Chr. 12:17; Ezra 4:1; Neh. 4:11; Pss. 74:10; 119:139; Jer. 50:7).

This term also refers to the destruction of Yahweh's enemies, whether they are referred to as Yahweh's own enemies (cf. Num. 24:8; Deut. 32:41; Ps. 78:66; Isa. 1:24; 64:2; Jer. 46:10; Nah. 1:2), whom he destroys; or the enemies of God's people, whom he also destroys (cf. Gen. 14:20; Num. 10:9; Pss. 60:12; 78:42; 108:13; Jer. 30:16). There are also references to God delivering his people from their enemies (cf. Ps. 136:24; Mic. 5:9).

As with ***'ōyēb***, ***ṣar*** is also used to indicate that God's people have suffered or will suffer defeat at the hands of their enemies on account of the people's sin (cf. 2 Sam. 24:13; Neh. 9:27; Pss. 44:10; 78:61; Isa. 63:18). In particular, Ps. 89:42; Lam. 1:5ff.; 2:17 all indicate that Israel's enemies have defeated her as a consequence of Yahweh invoking the curse of the covenant against his people, for Yahweh hands his people over to their enemies as a consequence of their disobedience against him (cf. Isa. 9:11; 26:11; Ezek. 39:23; Amos 3:11).

Finally, ***ṣar*** is also found in contexts where pleas are forthcoming for divine help against the enemies of God's people (cf. Deut. 33:7; Esth. 7:4; Ps. 27:12).

ṣārar [צָרַר, 6887]

ṣārar is the verbal root from which ***ṣar*** (see above) is derived. ***ṣārar*** occurs about sixty times and means "to be at enmity with" only once. In the remaining occurrences it is participial and means "enemy," functioning as a noun.

Yahweh promises to destroy the enemies of his people if his people obey him (cf. Exod. 23:22). This text constitutes the sole verbal usage of ***ṣārar***.

In general terms, the enemies of God are referred to in Pss. 10:5; 74:4, 23. In Isa. 11:13, certain destruction is decreed for Yahweh's enemies who mistreat his people. Esth. 3:10 refers to Haman as the enemy of the Jews (cf. also Esth. 8:1; 9:24). The psalmist also utilizes the term in reference to his own enemies who afflict him (cf. Ps. 6:7); and pleads for God to resist them (cf. Ps. 7:14). See also Pss. 8:2; 23:5; 31:11; 42:10; 69:19.

śānē' [שָׂנֵא, 8130]

śānē' is a common verb, meaning "to hate" in most of the nearly 150 occurrences of the term. In several places, the term is used in a participial nominal form with the related sense of "enemy." Literal references to the "enemies" of Israel are found in Exod. 1:10; 2 Chr. 1:11; Esth. 9:16. One's individual "foes" are noted in Prov. 25:21; 27:6.

NT WORDS

echthros [ἐχθρός, *2190*]

echthros is an adjectival term with the nominal sense of "enemy" or "foe" throughout the thirty or so occurrences of the term with a variety of nuances, both literal and spiritual.

The meaning "enemy" in the general sense of one's personal adversary is evident in Matt. 5:43ff.; 13:25ff.; Mark 12:36; Rom. 12:20; Luke 6:27, 35; Gal. 4:16; 2 Thess. 3:15; Rev. 11:5. The sense of "enemy" as one who opposes everything that is right is indicated in Rom. 5:10.

echthros also denotes the "enemies" of God's people, Israel, in Luke 1:71, 74. See also Rom. 11:28; Rev. 11:12.

In spiritual contexts, this term also refers directly and indirectly to Satan as the great "enemy" of God's people (cf. Luke 10:19).

In a related context, ***echthros*** denotes the defeat of the "enemies" of Christ in Acts 2:35; 1 Cor. 15:25; Phil. 3:18; Heb. 1:13; 10:13. Unbelievers are designated as "enemies" of God in Rom. 5:10; Col. 1:21; Jas. 4:4.

Metaphorically, ***echthros*** denotes "death" as the last enemy to be destroyed in 1 Cor. 15:26.

Additional Notes

Throughout the Old Testament, the terminology for "enemy" centers on the antagonism between Yahweh and his enemies, Yahweh and the enemies of Israel (which are essentially the same), and also between Yahweh and his own people, whom he designates as his enemy whenever they rebel against him.

One distinctive difference between the enemies of Yahweh and Israel under the old covenant and those mentioned in the new is that the former almost always manifested themselves as nations. Their opposition against God and his people was almost exclusively political and military. It is not that the enmity against God lacked a spiritual dimension in the Old Testament, but rather that it expressed itself as an earthly political reality in keeping with the external aspect of the old covenant era.

When we come to the new covenant age and the ministry of Jesus Christ, the enmity against God and the one who perfectly represents him is portrayed more in terms of demonic spiritual opposition to God and his kingdom. All who are enemies of God and Christ thus partake of that satanic spirit of opposition, whether they be human beings or the very forces of Satan, including the devil himself.

It is the heart of the gospel that demonstrates the ultimate victory of Christ over the enemies of God and his people — a conquest that is essentially and consummately spiritual in nature.

ENMITY

OT WORDS

'êbāh [**אֵיבָה, 342**]

This noun occurs five times and is translated "enmity" or "hatred."

Though infrequently used, ***'êbāh*** does occur in Gen. 3:15, a key verse that anticipates the spiritual warfare between the satanic spirit that dwelled in the primeval serpent in the garden of Eden and the seed of the woman that finds its fulfillment in the person of Jesus Christ. As well as having a profound spiritual dimension, the significance of such "enmity" between good and evil has inevitable consequences for the whole outworking of human history. Such hostility anticipates the perpetual struggle throughout history between the genuine people of God and all who oppose him and his purposes.

In Num. 35:21, ***'êbāh*** indicates hostility towards another human being, where murder committed in anger constitutes a capital offense. Interestingly, the context refers to manslaughter, which indicates accidental death (that is, hostility was not a factor). In this instance, the guilty party may seek protection in a city of refuge.

Finally, Ezek. 25:15 speaks of divine judgment against Philistia, who acted with hostility or enmity towards Israel. A similar intention is expressed towards Edom in Ezek. 35:5.

NT WORDS

echthra [ἔχθρα, *2189*]

echthra is a variant form of ***echthros*** (→ ENEMY) found in only six places with the predominant sense of "enmity" or "hatred." It most commonly refers to "enmity" with God, as in Rom. 8:7; Eph. 2:16; Jas. 4:4. "Hostility" among individuals is noted in Luke 23:12. The vice of "hatred" is indicated in Gal. 5:20.

Additional Notes

In general, the phenomenon of "enmity" in Scripture is identical to the idea of "enemy" (→ ENEMY).

The significance of Gen. 3:15, however, must not be overlooked. The enmity described in this verse is foundational to understanding the origin of human misery and suffering. Satan's hatred of God and his determination to destroy the divine creation motivate him to deceive the woman in the garden. As a consequence of that deception, humankind is plunged into the chaos of rebellion against, and alienation from, God and fellow human beings. It is this enmity that Jesus Christ came to both confront and destroy. Jesus' death and resurrection guarantee our deliverance from that terrible state of hostility, despair, and alienation. The gospel transforms that ancient hostility and enmity into peace, joy, and total reconciliation between humankind and God.

ENGRAVE

OT Words

pittûaḥ **[פִּתּוּחַ, 6603]**

This noun occurs eleven times and is translated "engraving" or "carving," always in reference to the Israelite sanctuary and worship.

In its literal sense, ***pittûaḥ*** refers first of all to those craftsmen working on the temple who were skilled in engraving (cf. 2 Chr. 2:7, 14). Secondly, it refers to the engraving of the names of the twelve tribes of Israel on the onyx stones attached to the ephod of the high priest (cf. Exod. 28:11, 21; 39:6, 14, 30), as well as to the engraving "holy to the Lord" on the gold plate of the high priestly turban. The carvings of cherubim on the walls of the temple are indicated in 1 Kgs. 6:29. Still with reference to the temple, ***pittûaḥ*** refers to the destruction of the carvings in the sanctuary at the time of the Babylonian invasion in Ps. 74:6.

In a metaphorical context, Zech. 3:9 refers to God engraving the "stone," or, most likely, the golden plate, fastened to the turban of the high priest with the inscription "holy to the Lord." This is in the context of one of the visions given to Zechariah that contains a symbolic description of God's forgiveness and spiritual renewal of his people. Although metaphorical in the context of the prophecy of Zechariah, this usage of ***pittûaḥ*** is based on the literal ceremonial ritual involving the high priestly garments found in Exod. 28 (especially Exod. 28:36).

NT Words

entypoō **[ἐντυπόω, *1795*]**

entypoō is a rare verb found only in 2 Cor. 3:7 and meaning "engrave," referring to the old covenant law that had been "engraved" in letters on stone tablets. Paul refers to this as a ministry of death.

Additional Notes

The phenomenon of engraving in the Old Testament is clearly focused on the ceremonial arena, with the Hebrew term ***pittûaḥ*** referring exclusively to the temple and the high priestly garments. Though this term is not used in the exodus narratives to describe the engraving of the law on the two tablets of stone at Mt. Sinai, Paul mentions it in 2 Cor. 3:7. The theological parallel here between the ritual engraving of the Mosaic law covenant on stone and the "engraving" of the Holy Spirit on the hearts of his people is clear in 2 Cor. 3. The other references to engravings in the tabernacle and temple, particularly in regard to the gold plate on the high priest's turban, are also designed to anticipate the ultimate spiritual reality of God dwelling in the hearts of his people. This is only made possible by the finished work of Christ on the cross and his subsequent role as our eternal high priest, who stands before the throne of God, interceding on our behalf.

See Also: → INSCRIPTION

ENJOIN → COMMAND

ENJOY

OT Words

rāṣāh **[רָצָה, 7521]**

rāṣāh is a verb with the dominant senses of "accept" or "be pleased with," as well as associated nuances throughout the nearly sixty occurrences of the term. One of these nuances is the meaning "to enjoy," found in four places. In the prophecy of the period of the seventy-year exile in the Pentateuch traditions, the land of Israel is said to "enjoy" its Sabbaths over that period (cf. Lev. 26:34, 43). The actual "enjoying" of those "Sabbath rests" by the land of Judah is indicated in 2 Chr. 36:21.

bālāh **[בָּלָה, 1086]**

bālāh is a verb found sixteen times with the primary meaning "grow old." There is one occurrence of the meaning "enjoy," in Isa. 65:22, referring to the divine promise given to the people of Israel that they will one day "enjoy" the work of their hands.

NT Words

tynchanō **[τυγχάνω, *5177*]**

tynchanō is a verb occurring thirteen times with the predominant meaning "to obtain," "attain." The meaning "enjoy" is found only in Acts 24:2, referring to the Roman province of Judea "having enjoyed" (i.e., experienced) a long period of peace under the jurisdiction of Governor Felix.

apolausis [ἀπόλαυσις, *619*]

apolausis is a rare noun found only twice, denoting the "enjoyment" of the pleasures of sin in Heb. 11:25. 1 Tim. 6:19 refers to the blessings of God given to his people for their "enjoyment."

ENLARGE

OT Words

rāḥab [רָחַב, 7337]

This verb occurs twenty-five times with the principal meaning "enlarge," "make large," or "grow large."

In its literal sense, ***rāḥab*** refers to God's covenant promise to enlarge the borders of the land of Canaan (cf. Exod. 34:24; Deut. 12:20; 19:8; 33:20). In a completely different context, ***rāḥab*** also refers to the increasing size of the rooms in the upper stories of the visionary temple of Ezekiel (cf. Ezek. 41:7).

The other uses of this term are non-literal. Isa. 54:2, for example, contains a metaphorical exhortation to the people of God to "enlarge the place" of their tents, referring to the future glory of Zion that will contain innumerable inhabitants. Then, in Amos 1:13, there is a metaphorical reference to the expansionist policies of countries who wish to enlarge their empires. Other various metaphorical uses of ***rāḥab*** are found in Ps. 18:36; Isa. 5:14.

See Also: → GREAT → INCREASE

ENLIGHTEN → LIGHT

ENRICH → RICH

ENSLAVED → SERVE

ENSNARE

OT Words

yāqōsh [יָקֹשׁ, 3369]

This verb is quite rare, occurring only eight times and meaning "entice," "ensnare," "set a trap" in all but one of these contexts. The usage is entirely metaphorical.

In Deut. 7:25, Israel is declared to be ensnared by idolatry. Ps. 141:9 contains the psalmist's plea that God would keep him from the snares of evildoers. Prov. 6:2 warns of the danger of being ensnared by your own words (cf. also Eccl. 9:12). Isa. 8:14 declares that Yahweh will be a stumbling block and a snare to both houses of Israel, to all of his people who oppose and rebel against him (cf. also Isa. 28:13). Jer. 50:24 points to the same fate for Babylon.

NT Words

pagideuō [παγιδεύω, *3802*]

pagideuō is a rare verb found only in Matt. 22:15 with reference to the plans of the Pharisees seeking to "ensnare" or "trap" Jesus in his speech.

emplekō [ἐμπλέκω, *1707*]

emplekō is a rare verb found only twice, referring to the "entangling" or "ensnaring" of the soldier in civilian affairs in 2 Tim. 2:4. 2 Pet. 2:20 speaks of the danger of "becoming entangled" or "being trapped" in the corruption of the world.

ENTER, ENTRANCE

OT Words

bô' [בּוֹא, 935]

This is a common verb, occurring nearly 2,500 times with a variety of meanings associated with the primary senses of "go," "come," and "bring," as well as a host of derivative nuances. It is translated "enter" approximately 150 times in the Old Testament. On about half of these occasions, ***bô'*** is used in mundane contexts referring to entering a house, town, country, and so on with no special significance. In a number of contexts, however, the term carries some theological significance.

In some places ***bô'*** refers to entering certain places that carry a special significance, such as Noah and the ark (cf. Gen. 7:13). More significant is the phenomenon of people entering the tabernacle or tent of meeting in order to stand before Yahweh (cf. Exod. 33:9). What is true of the tabernacle is of course also true of the temple. And so entering the Israelite sanctuary for worship is also a significant phenomenon of the old covenant (cf. Deut. 23:8; 2 Chr. 30:8; Pss. 100:4; 143:2; Ezek. 44:16). In Jer. 7:2 people are condemned for entering the temple and engaging in false worship. Reference is also made to Levites entering the service of the tabernacle or temple itself (cf. Num. 4:3, 23ff.; 2 Chr. 3:16).

On a slightly different note, entry into the tabernacle/temple is prohibited for a variety of reasons, including physical defects or ceremonial uncleanness (cf. Deut. 23:1; 2 Chr. 23:19); illegitimate birth (cf. Deut. 23:2); and Gentile birth (cf. Deut. 23:3, Ezek. 44:9).

bô' is also used to refer to the significant phenomenon of entering the land of Canaan. There is, first of all, reference to entering the land in order to conquer the cities of Canaan in accordance with God's command (cf. Josh. 8:19; Judg. 18:9). Not all the Old Testament material devoted to the phenomenon of entering and possessing the promised land contains the word ***bô'***, and so the full significance of the phenomenon must always be recognized apart from the occurrence of this single term.

There are a number of contexts in which the action of entering the land reveals a number of distinctively negative connotations. For example, Num. 20:24 refers to Aaron being denied entry into Canaan on account of his rebellion against Yahweh. Jer. 2:7 contains an indictment against Israel for entering the land in order to defile it by her idolatry. Reference is also made to God's people being denied entry to the land as a divine punishment (cf. Ps. 95:11; Ezek. 13:9; 20:38). Related to this theme are references to the enemies of Israel entering (i.e., invading) the land as a consequence of God's judgment against his people (cf. 2 Chr. 32:1; Jer. 1:15; Ezek. 7:22). In Obad. 1:11, 13 the enemies of God's people enter Jerusalem in order to destroy it, but they themselves are punished for gloating over Judah's plight.

At a metaphorical level, ***bô'*** signifies both God entering into covenant relationship with his people (cf. Ezek. 16:8) and the people of Israel entering into covenant relationship with him (cf. Deut. 29:12; 2 Chr. 15:12; Jer. 34:10). The word suggests here the general "engaging" of an intimate bond between God and human beings without specifying the dynamics of that relationship.

bô' is also used metaphorically to indicate God "entering into" judgment against his people on account of their sin (cf. Job 22:4; 34:23; Ps. 143:2). In a number of contexts there is a very close correlation between the people's rebellion against Yahweh and his consequent "entry" into judgment against them, understood as the invocation of the covenant curse (cf. Isa. 3:14; Jer. 9:21). On a positive note, Hos. 11:9 records God's solemn covenant promise to never again "come in wrath" against (i.e., devastate) the northern kingdom. Num. 5:24, 27 describes the curse "entering" the unfaithful wife as the consequence of her ritual ordeal identifying her as an adulteress, though no one had either witnessed the act or gained evidence to indict her. The penalty is lifelong infertility.

Finally, ***bô'*** refers to the entry of the Sprit of God into the mind of the prophet, in order to communicate the divine word (cf. Ezek. 2:2; 3:24). The term also indicates the life-giving entry of the Spirit of God which brings new life and spiritual transformation to his people (cf. Ezek. 37:5).

mābô' [**מָבוֹא, 3996**]

mābô' is a noun derived from ***bô'*** (see above) found about twenty times, meaning "coming, going down" or "entrance."

1 Chr. 9:19; 2 Chr. 23:13; Jer. 38:14 refer to the "entrance" of the Jerusalem temple; Ezek. 42:9; 44:5; 46:19 to the entrance to the temple of Ezekiel's vision; and 2 Chr. 23:15; 2 Kgs. 11:16 to the entrance of the royal palace in Jerusalem. Prov. 8:3; Ezek. 26:10 refer to the "entrance" to a city.

NT Words

eiserchomai [**εἰσέρχομαι, *1525***]

eiserchomai is a common verb with the predominant meanings "enter," "go, come in" throughout the nearly two hundred occurrences of the term.

Mundane references to "entering" various places include those in Matt. 6:6; 24:38; Mark 1:21; 11:11; Luke 1:9; 7:44ff.; 10:5ff.; 24:3; John 18:28; 20:5ff.; Acts 1:13; 5:7ff.; 9:6; 10:25ff.; 23:16; 1 Cor. 14:23ff.; Jas. 2:2. The phenomenon of "entering the temple" in a visionary context is indicated in Rev. 15:8.

Elsewhere, ***eiserchomai*** indicates the process of "entering" the kingdom of heaven (cf. Matt. 5:20; 7:13). In particular, "entering" into the heavenly kingdom is said to be dependent on doing God's will in Matt. 7:21; on having one's name in the Lamb's book of life in Rev. 21:27 (cf. also Rev. 22:14); on adopting a childlike stance of faith in Matt. 18:3; Mark 10:15; Luke 18:17; and it is likened to "entering" a banquet in Luke 14:23. Barriers to such an entry include an idolatrous attachment to wealth (cf. Matt. 19:23ff.; Mark 10:23ff.; Luke 18:25); and lack of repentance and faith in Jesus Christ (cf. also John 3:5, 14). "Entering" into eternal life is noted in Matt. 18:8ff.; Mark 9:43ff. Jesus' exhortation to "enter" the kingdom of heaven by the narrow door of faith and repentance is found in Luke 13:24. Reference to Jesus as the gate of the sheepfold designates him as the sole entry point to salvation in John 10:9. Rom. 11:25 mentions the full number of Gentiles "coming into," or "entering into" their salvation. The meaning "enter into" in the sense of "share in" is indicated in Matt. 25:23.

The action of evil spirits "entering into" a herd of pigs is described in Mark 5:13. Other references to demons "entering into" people include Mark 9:25;

Luke 8:30ff. In particular, Satan is said to "enter into" Judas Iscariot, enticing him to betray Christ in Luke 22:3; John 13:27.

The experience of three disciples "entering into" the theophanic cloud associated with Jesus' transfiguration is indicated in Luke 9:34.

Luke 24:26 mentions Christ "entering into" his glory after his resurrection. In significant related contexts Jesus is said to "have entered into" the inner sanctuary of the heavenly temple to both offer himself as a sacrifice and to mediate on behalf of his people before God as our great high priest (cf. Heb. 6:19ff.; 9:12, 24ff.). Metaphorical reference to savage wolves "entering into" the flock of God's people in Acts 20:29 emphasizes the ever-present danger of false teachers infiltrating the Christian community.

References to sin "entering" the world include Rom. 5:12.

A highly significant group of texts describes the ancient Israelites' failure "to enter their rest," that is, the land of Canaan. Such a failure was precipitated by their lack of saving faith in God. A parallel warning is then issued to Christian believers, who are exhorted to maintain their faith in, and sole dependence on, Christ for their salvation, lest they too fail "to enter their rest," which in context clearly denotes eternal rest with God and Christ in heaven (cf. Heb. 3:11, 18, 19; 4:1ff.; 3ff., 10ff.).

The heavenly Christ is said to "enter into" fellowship with believers in Rev. 3:20.

The breath of life is said to "enter into" martyred saints, thus bringing them back to life, in Rev. 11:11.

syneiserchomai [συνεισέρχομαι, *4897*]

syneiserchomai is a rare variant of ***eiserchomai***, above, denoting the action of "entering" with other people. It is found in John 6:22 in connection with Jesus and his disciples on the Sea of Galilee. See also John 18:15.

pareiserchomai [παρεισέρχομαι, *3922*]

pareiserchomai is another rare variant of ***eiserchomai***, above, expressing the sense of "infiltrating" in relation to false teachers making inroads into Christian congregations in order to deceive them (cf. Gal. 2:4).

eisporeuomai [εἰσπορεύομαι, *1531*]

eisporeuomai is synonymous with ***eiserchomai*** (see above), and means "enter," "go, come in" throughout the eighteen occurrences of the term.

The mundane sense of "entering" into various places and locations is indicated in Matt. 15:17; Mark 1:21; 5:40; 6:56; 11:2; Luke 8:16; 11:33; 19:30; 22:10; Acts 3:2; 8:3; 28:30.

Elsewhere ***eisporeuomai*** refers to those things that "enter into" a person's body, such as food and drink (cf. Mark 4:19; 7:15ff.).

In Luke 18:24 Christ laments how hard it is for a rich person to "enter" the kingdom of God.

anabainō [ἀναβαίνω, *305*]

anabainō is a verb with the predominant sense of "go, come up" for almost all of the nearly eighty occurrences of the term. However, in 1 Cor. 2:9 ***anabainō*** refers to God's revelation to his people by his Spirit, which transcends the normal human senses. In particular, it is literally affirmed that "nothing has entered into the heart of human beings" to indicate the true reality of God's revelation prepared for them.

embainō [ἐμβαίνω, *1684*]

embainō is a verb found in eighteen places with the exclusive sense of "board (a boat)," that is, to get into or enter it (cf. Matt. 8:23; 9:1; 13:2; 14:22; 15:39; Mark 4:1; 5:18; 6:45; 8:10ff.; Luke 5:3; 8:22, 37; John 6:17, 24; 21:3; Acts 21:6).

epibainō [ἐπιβαίνω, *1910*]

epibainō is a rare variant of ***anabainō*** and ***embainō***, above, found in only six places and meaning "enter" in the sense of "arrive in (a province)" in Acts 20:18; 25:1. In Acts 27:2 the term refers to "boarding (a boat)."

eiseimi [εἴσειμι, *1524*]

eiseimi is a rare verb found only four times with reference to people "entering" the temple in Acts 8:3; 21:6. Specifically, in Heb. 9:6, ***eiseimi*** refers to the priests continually "entering" the temple precinct to conduct their ministry.

eisodos [εἴσοδος, *1529*]

eisodos is a rare noun found in five places and is variously translated as "coming," "visit," "welcome," and "entry." Heb. 10:19 speaks of the believer's unique privilege in "gaining entry" into the very presence of God, that is, into the most holy place, through the sacrificial blood of Christ.

2 Pet. 1:11 refers to the believer receiving a rich "welcome" (i.e., implying an entry) into the eternal kingdom of God.

Additional Notes

As with the Hebrew usage, the New Testament Greek vocabulary for "enter" is largely mundane and without special significance. One point of interest may be noted, however, in the usage of the Greek noun ***eisodos***, which signifies a believer's entrance or access into the very presence of God as well as entrance into the consummated divine kingdom. In both cases, the New Testament makes it clear that such entry, or access, is only made possible through the ministry of the Holy Spirit, which in turn is founded on the completed work of Christ. It is this reality which is anticipated in the Old Testament prophetic promises centering on the outpouring of the Spirit of God, who "enters" the people of God under the sovereign initiative and power of Yahweh himself. It is clear that entrance into God's kingdom is wholly dependent on the gracious sovereign purposes of God in redemption.

ENTICE, ENTICING

OT Words

sût **[סוּת, 5496]**

This verb occurs eighteen times, meaning "entice" in the sense of "incite," "allure" or "urge on" in about half of those contexts.

There are a number of texts that involve Yahweh himself in these circumstances. In Job 2:3, for example, Satan "incites" God against Job, hoping to get Job to curse God and die. 1 Sam. 26:19 points to a hypothetical instance of God inciting Saul against David. In 2 Sam. 24:1 Yahweh incites David against his people, resulting in David taking an illegitimate census. The context clearly suggests that this is a punishment against the people of Israel. Thus, David's action is a catalyst for this judgment to take place. In the parallel account in 1 Chr. 21:1, the agency of enticement is said to be Satan. This may be seen as a complementary, rather than a contradictory, perspective, with God permitting the satanic temptation to be the instrument of his judgment against David and Israel.

With regard to people enticing or inciting each other, a number of texts are noteworthy. Deut. 13:6 cites the instance of enticement to commit idolatry, which constitutes a capital offense under the Mosaic law covenant in ancient Israel. 1 Kgs. 21:25 refers to Jezebel inciting her husband Ahab to do evil in the eyes of the Lord, and in 2 Chr. 18:2 Ahab incites Jehoshaphat to go up and attack Ramoth-Gilead.

pātāh **[פָּתָה, 6601]**

This verb occurs about thirty times, meaning "entice."

Concerning enticement among people, the following texts are relevant. Judges 14:15; 16:5 refer to the seductive and persuasive manner of Delilah, who entices Samson into capture by the Philistines. Prov. 1:10 warns against being enticed or deceived by sinners; and Prov. 16:29 reflects a similar context.

Divine involvement in enticing or inciting human beings is also reflected in the usage of ***pātāh.*** 1 Kgs. 22:20ff. tells the story of Yahweh enticing Ahab to his death through the agency of a lying spirit (cf. also 2 Chr. 18:19ff.). In a starkly contrasting situation there is a metaphorical, though nonetheless real, allusion to Yahweh enticing or alluring his wayward people back into an intimate relationship with himself in Hos. 2:14. The metaphor the prophet uses here is that of a lover courting his beloved, wooing her for her hand in marriage.

NT Words

deleazō **[**δελεάζω, *1185*]

deleazō is a rare verb found in only three places, meaning "seduce," "entice," indicating an inciting to sin in each case. Jas. 1:14 contains a general recognition that people are "enticed" into sinning by innate sinful desire. 2 Pet. 2:14, 18 condemn false teachers for "enticing" others into doctrinal error and immorality.

Additional Notes

The Hebrew words ***sût*** and ***pātāh*** function as broad dynamic equivalents to the Greek term ***deleazō***, where enticement to various kinds of wickedness is in view, since the latter term has a wholly negative connotation. ***sût*** may be closer to the meaning of ***deleazō*** than ***pātāh***, since ***sût*** also has a primarily negative connotation of incitement to evil.

ENTIRE

OT Words

tāmîm **[תָּמִים, 8549]**

This is an adjectival form of the verb ***tāmam*** (→ END) and is found meaning "complete" or "entire" on only six occasions. ***tāmîm*** is more commonly translated "perfect" or "without blemish." (→ PERFECT)

The literal meaning "entire" or "whole," with respect to physical objects or living things, is found in Lev. 3:9 in reference to sacrificial portions of meat, and in Ezek. 15:5 concerning wood from a vine.

tāmîm also refers to the entirety of specific periods of time — for example, entire weeks (Lev. 23:15); or an entire year (Lev. 25:30). See also Josh. 10:13, which records the amazing miracle of the sun standing still for one whole day, allowing Joshua to wreak vengeance on the Amorite coalition of kings that had attacked him and lost.

Finally, Prov. 1:12 refers metaphorically to the fate of the innocent being swallowed "whole" by the wicked, as if by the grave.

See Also: → PEACE → WHOLE

ENVY

NT Words

phthonos [φθόνος, *5355*]

phthonos is a noun found nine times, denoting the emotion and attitude of "envy" or "jealousy" throughout. "Envy" is the dominant emotion motivating the Jewish leaders who sought to have Jesus handed over to the Roman courts in Matt. 27:18; Mark 15:10. "Envy" is listed among a number of vices in Rom. 1:29; Gal. 5:21; 1 Tim. 6:4; Titus 3:3; 1 Pet. 2:1. Phil. 1:15 affirms that some false teachers preach Christ out of "envy."

phthoneō [φθονέω, *5354*]

phthoneō is a rare verb found only in Gal. 5:26, meaning "to be envious" (of someone).

See Also: → JEALOUS

EPISTLE

OT Words

'iggeret [אִגֶּרֶת, **107**]

This rare noun is translated "letter" in the sense of "epistle" or "correspondence" on ten occasions. The contexts are all literal.

2 Chr. 30:1, 6 mentions Hezekiah's "letters" to the tribes of Israel and Judah, calling on them to celebrate the Passover in Jerusalem. In Neh. 2:7ff., Nehemiah requests "letters" of safe conduct from King Artaxerxes of Persia to the governors of the land beyond the river (i.e., the nations surrounding, and including, the postexilic colony of Judah). Neh. 6:5, 17, 19 refer to "correspondence" sent by a coalition of Judah's enemies to Nehemiah in order to intimidate him. Finally, Esth. 9:26, 29 refer to Mordecai's "letters" sent to the Jews throughout the Persian kingdom, enjoining them to celebrate the feast of Purim every year, commemorating their victory over those who had conspired to destroy them.

NT Words

epistolē [ἐπιστολή, *1992*]

epistolē is a noun found approximately twenty times, meaning "letter" or "epistle" in the natural sense of a written correspondence (cf. Acts 9:2; 15:30; 22:5; Rom. 16:22; 1 Cor. 5:9; 16:3; 2 Cor. 3:1; 7:8; Col. 4:16; 1 Thess. 5:27; 2 Thess. 2:2, 15; 3:14ff.; 2 Pet. 3:1, 16).

The term is also used metaphorically in 2 Cor. 3:2 to denote the Corinthian congregation as his "letters of recommendation" bearing testimony to the world of their worthy spiritual qualifications.

Similarly, 2 Cor. 3:3 refers to the Corinthian believers as a "letter" from Christ "written" by the Spirit of God. This is a metaphorical description of the spiritual transformation of a person from pagan to believer.

EQUAL, EQUALITY

OT Words

tākan [תָּכַן, **8505**]

tākan is a verb found in eighteen places with the primary meaning "to weigh" or "measure." In several places, the term is used metaphorically to indicate being "just" or "unjust" in relation to God. This meaning is derived from the phenomenon of "fairness," "equality." The charge of God as "unjust" is untenable and rejected (cf. Ezek. 18:25, 29; 33:17, 20).

NT Words

isos [ἴσος, *2470*]

isos is an adjective found in eight places, meaning "equal" in about half these occurrences.

The sense of equality of status in relation to wage earning is indicated in Matt. 20:12. Christ's equality with his father in the sense of his standing, authority, and person is indicated in John 5:18; Phil. 2:6. Equality of measurement is noted in Rev. 21:16.

isotēs [ἰσότης, *2471*]

isotēs is a rare noun denoting "equality" in the context of shared material prosperity in 2 Cor. 8:14. In Col. 4:1 the meaning "equality" carries the sense of "fairness" in relation to the just treatment of slaves.

ERR

OT Words

tā'āh [תָּעָה, **8582**]

This verb occurs around fifty times with the primary meanings "err," "wander," "go astray" in the sense of "losing one's direction," both geographically and ethically.

tā'āh refers literally to wandering or moving about in a nomadic sense, particularly during the patriarchal period of early Israelite history (cf. Gen. 20:13; 21:14; 37:15; Exod. 23:4; Job 38:41).

tā'āh also occurs in a number of metaphorical contexts. A number of references speak of going astray in an ethical or moral sense, first of all in relation to humankind in general (cf. Ps. 58:3; Prov. 10:17; Isa. 30:28); and then to God's people in particular (cf. Pss. 95:10; 107:4; Isa. 3:12; 9:16; 29:24; 53:6; Ezek. 44:10, 15). In addition, there is an expressed exhortation as well as a determination not to wander from God's ways in the following texts: Ps. 119:110; Prov. 7:25; Ezek. 14:11. More specifically, several passages indict God's people for being led away into idolatry and moral evil (cf. 2 Kgs. 21:9; 2 Chr. 33:9; Jer. 23:13; Hos. 4:12; Amos 2:4; Mic. 3:5). In Jer. 23:32; 50:6 God's anger is directed at those responsible for leading his people astray. Emphasis is also laid on the fact that God causes people to wander or go astray as a sign of judgment, whether it be literally (cf. Job 12:24; Ps. 107:40) or metaphorically—making them morally inept (cf. Isa. 9:14 [Egypt]; Isa. 63:17 [God's own people]).

Finally, Isa. 35:8 speaks of God's grace and mercy in preserving his people and keeping them from going astray.

***shāgāh* [שָׁגָה, 7686]**

shāgāh is a verb occurring about twenty times with the underlying meaning "err," "go astray," primarily in the sense of "commit sin," "transgress the moral law of God."

The meaning "commit sin unintentionally" is indicated in Lev. 4:13. Other references to "straying" from the commandments of God are found in Num. 15:22; Ps. 119:10; Ezek. 45:20.

General references to "erring," "going astray" in a moral sense are found in 1 Sam. 26:21; Job 6:24; 19:4; Prov. 5:23; 19:27; 20:1; 28:10; Isa. 28:17.

NT Words

***planaō* [πλανάω, *4105*]**

planaō is a verb occurring about fifty times, meaning "err" with the nuances "lead astray," "go astray" in a moral sense.

Matt. 18:12, 13 refer literally to sheep "going astray" (i.e., getting lost); Heb. 11:38 refers to people.

The meaning "err" in the sense of "be mistaken, wrong" is found in Matt. 22:29; Mark 12:24, 27.

Warnings against "being led astray" in a moral sense are found in Matt. 24:4; Mark 13:5; Luke 21:8. See also Titus 3:3. Likewise, the meaning "be deceived" is found in 1 Cor. 15:33; Gal. 6:7; Jas. 1:16.

Similarly, the practice of "deceiving," "leading (people) astray" in the sense of morally corrupting them is indicated in Matt. 24:5, 11; Mark 13:6; John 7:12; 1 John 2:26; Rev. 12:9; 13:14; 19:20; 20:3, 8, 10. See also Matt. 24:24; John 7:47.

The sense of "going astray" indicating disobedience against God is noted in Heb. 3:10. The danger and practice of "wandering" from the truth is noted in Jas. 5:19; 1 Pet. 2:25; 2 Pet. 2:15.

***apoplanaō* [ἀποπλανάω, *635*]**

apoplanaō is a rare variant of ***planaō***, above, found only twice. It means "lead astray" in the context of "wandering" from the faith (cf. Mark 13:22; 1 Tim. 6:10).

***astocheō* [ἀστοχέω, *795*]**

astocheō is a rare synonym for ***planaō*** and ***apoplanaō***, above, meaning "erring," or wandering, in the context of abandoning the faith in 1 Tim. 6:21. In 2 Tim. 2:18, ***astocheō*** refers to "wandering away" from the truth.

ERROR

OT Words

***meshûgāh* [מְשׁוּגָה, 4879]**

meshûgāh is a rare noun, found only in Job 19:4, denoting "error" in a general moral context.

***shegāgāh* [שְׁגָגָה, 7684]**

shegāgāh is a noun occurring nineteen times with the predominant sense of "ignorance" in the context of sinning unwittingly. In Eccl. 5:6; 10:5, however, ***shegāgāh*** denotes a "mistake" or "error" in both a ritual and civil context.

NT Words

***planē* [πλάνη, *4106*]**

planē is a noun found in ten places, meaning "error" or "deceit."

"Error" in the sense of "fraud" or "deception" is indicated in Matt. 27:64; "delusion" in 2 Thess. 2:11; and "false doctrine" in 1 John 4:6.

planē denotes "error" in the sense of moral perversion in Rom. 1:27; 2 Pet. 2:18; 3:17; Jude 11; 1 Thess. 2:3; and the general sense of "sin" in Jas. 5:20.

The "deceit" of false teaching is indicated in Eph. 4:14.

agnoēma [ἀγνόημα, *51*]

agnoēma is a rare noun, found only in Heb. 9:7, denoting the Jewish people's "errors" or "sins."

ESCAPE

OT Words

pālît, pālêt, pālēt [פָּלִיט, פָּלֵיט, פָּלֵט, **6412**]

This form ***pālît*** (or ***pālêt***) occurs about twenty times, meaning "one who has escaped" (i.e., an escapee).

First of all, ***pālît*** refers literally to those who have escaped from captivity (cf. Gen. 14:13; 2 Kgs. 9:15; Ezek. 33:21); or who are fugitives for a variety of reasons (cf. Num. 21:29; Judg. 12:4; Isa. 66:19; Ezek. 24:26ff.; Obad. 14).

More particularly, this term also refers to those whom God will prevent, or has prevented, from escaping in the context of his judgment against them (cf. Jer. 42:17; 44:14; Lam. 2:22; Amos 9:1). In all instances, these latter references focus on the climactic periods of divine judgment involving both Assyrian and Babylonian attacks on the nation of Israel. Conversely, there are several instances where ***pālît*** indicates those who escape Yahweh's judgment on account of his mercy (cf. Jer. 44:28; Ezek. 6:8, 9; 7:16). Isa. 66:19 refers to the "fugitives" among the nations, whom God will use to proclaim his glory and his name among those nations.

Metaphorically, ***pālît*** also refers to fugitives from the nations as those who are in spiritual darkness in Isa. 45:20.

The form ***pālēt*** means "escaped one" or "fugitive." In Jer. 50:28 ***pālēt*** denotes Jewish "fugitives" from the land of Babylon (i.e., "those who escape"). Similarly, Jer. 44:14 refers to "fugitives" from Egypt. Jer. 51:50 then refers to those who have escaped from Egypt.

mālat [מָלַט, **4422**]

This verb occurs around one hundred times with a number of meanings associated with the idea of flight or escape. ***mālat*** is translated "escape" in about forty of these contexts. Sometimes the semantic boundary between escape and flight is not clear-cut. The references listed below, however, clearly indicate "escaping" as a rescue or removal from perilous situations both physical and spiritual.

The following examples refer to literal escape. Judg. 3:29 records the destruction of the Moabite army, none of whom escaped, at the hand of Ehud. David's escape from Saul is described in 1 Sam. 19:10; 23:13; 27:1. See also 1 Sam. 22:20; 1 Kgs. 20:20; 2 Kgs. 19:37; Esth. 4:13; Isa. 20:6; Jer. 41:5; Dan. 11:41.

As with ***pālît***, above, ***mālat*** also refers to divine intervention in the fate of those whom God prevents from eluding his judgment. 1 Kgs. 18:40, for example, mentions Elijah's refusal to allow the apostate Israelite priests of Baal to escape execution. Then, Jer. 32:4 records Zedekiah's inevitable punishment for violation of his oath. This last king of Judah was to be tortured by the Babylonians and would die in captivity. See also in this regard Jer. 38:18; 46:6; 48:8; Ezek. 17:15, 18. Finally, Zech. 2:7 contains a divine exhortation to escape and flee from the land of Babylon since it is God's time to deliver his people and bring them out of their captivity.

In a metaphorical sense, ***mālat*** indicates escape from spiritual and/or physical torment in Job 19:20; Ps. 124:7; Eccl. 7:26.

See Also: → FLEE

nāṣal [נָצַל, **5337**]

nāṣal is a verb with the dominant sense of "deliver," "rescue" throughout the nearly two hundred occurrences of the term. In Deut. 23:15, however, ***nāṣal*** refers to a slave who "has escaped" from his master.

NT Words

pheugō [φεύγω, *5343*]

pheugō is a verb occurring about thirty times with the primary meaning "to flee." In three places, however, ***pheugō*** expresses the explicit sense of "escape." Matt. 23:33 refers to "escaping" from the sentence of hell. "Escaping" the edge of the sword is indicated in Heb. 12:25. Failure to "escape" the judgment of God is noted in Heb. 12:34.

apopheugō [ἀποφεύγω, *668*]

apopheugō is a variant form of ***pheugō*** (see above) meaning "escape," "escape from." References to "escaping" the corruption of the world are found in 2 Pet. 1:4; 2:20. 2 Pet. 2:18 mentions those who had barely "escaped" from the error of false teachers.

diapheugō [διαφεύγω, *1309*]

diapheugō is a rare verb found only in Acts 27:42, denoting the action of "escaping" from the perils of shipwreck.

ekpheugō [ἐκφεύγω, *1628*]

ekpheugō is another variant form of ***pheugō***, above, found eight times and meaning "escape."

References to "escaping" the judgment of God are found in Luke 21:36; Rom. 2:3; Heb. 2:3. The fear of prisoners "escaping" is noted in Acts 16:27. Paul's experience of "escaping" from his persecutors is recorded in 2 Cor. 11:33.

diasōzō [διασώζω, *1295*]

diasōzō is a verb occurring eight times, meaning "save," "preserve" as well as "escape." Acts 27:44; 28:1, 4 refer to an "escape" from physical danger.

ekbasis [ἔκβασις, *1545*]

ekbasis is a rare noun denoting the "way of escape" God promises to believers so that they will not be compelled to commit sin (cf. 1 Cor. 10:13).

ESTABLISH

OT Words

kûn [**כּוּן, 3559**]

This term occurs around two hundred times with the principal meaning "prepare" and "establish," as well as a number of related nuances. ***kûn*** means "establish" in about a third of these instances.
(→ PREPARATION)

The meaning "establish," in the sense of "determine" or "set," with Yahweh as the agent of establishing, is found in a variety of contexts, mostly metaphorical. For example, Ps. 9:7 refers to God's throne, established by him for judgment; Ps. 37:23 affirms that the steps of a righteous man are determined by God. Other references with this usage are found in Ps. 99:4; Prov. 4:26; 16:3. Prov. 24:3 speaks of a house "established" by wisdom and understanding, with the implicit inference that God is behind it.

The use of the term with the idea of "build (up)" or "make secure," again with Yahweh as the agent of establishing, is also found in various contexts. The establishing of the tabernacle is referred to in Exod. 15:17; as is Zion, the city of God, in Pss. 48:8; 87:5. At a metaphorical level, there are references to establishing the righteous (cf. Ps. 7:9); God's love (cf. Ps. 89:2); one's children (cf. Job 21:8; Ps. 102:28); the work of our hands (cf. Ps. 90:17). Most significant in this regard are the number of texts that refer to the establishing of the theocratic kingdom of Israel (cf. 1 Sam. 13:13; 2 Sam. 5:12; 7:12ff.; 1 Kgs. 2:12, 24, 45, 46; Ps. 89:4; Isa. 2:2; 54:14; Jer. 30:20; Mic. 4:1). In all these passages, and elsewhere, the underlying factor that accounts for the emergence of the nation of Israel on earth is the power and authority of Yahweh, who intervenes in human history on behalf of his chosen people in order to carry out his redemptive purposes.

Finally, ***kûn*** is translated "establish" in the sense of "created (by God)," referring to God's people (Deut. 32:6); and to the created order of the universe, earth, moon, and stars (Ps. 8:3). See also Pss. 24:2; 119:90; Prov. 3:19; Isa. 45:18; Jer. 10:12; 51:15.

qûm [**קוּם, 6965**]

This is a common verb with the primary meaning "stand," and related senses. ***qûm***, however, is translated "establish" (in a predominantly literal sense) about thirty times.

Significantly, the term refers to Yahweh's promise and initiative in establishing his covenant with humankind. Specifically, this process is initiated with Noah (cf. Gen. 6:18; 9:9, 11, 17); Abraham (cf. Gen. 17:7, 19); Isaac (cf. Gen. 17:21); Jacob (cf. Ps. 78:5); the Servant of Yahweh (cf. Isa. 49:8); and the people of Israel in regard to the land of Canaan (cf. Exod. 6:4; Lev. 26:9; Deut. 8:18; 29:13). In addition, Ezek. 16:60 refers to God's promise to establish an everlasting covenant with his people, in spite of their rebellion against him and after punishing them for their sin. Deut. 28:9 refers to establishing a people holy to the Lord, on condition of their obedience.

In a related context, God's promise to establish David and the kingdom of God on earth, for David and his sons forever, is referred to in 1 Sam. 24:20; 2 Sam. 7:25; 1 Kgs. 9:5; 2 Chr. 7:18.

qûm also means "establish" in the sense of "being made certain and secure." The following examples are noted: Lev. 25:30 (concerning perpetual ownership of a house in Israel); Num. 30:13, 14 (concerning a vow); Deut. 19:15 (concerning a legal charge on the basis of two or three witnesses). See also 1 Sam. 1:23; Ps. 119:38.

yāsad [**יָסַד, 3245**]

yāsad is a verb meaning "to found," "lay a foundation," "establish" for most of the forty or so occurrences of the term. The "founding" or "establishing" of a nation is indicated in Exod. 9:18.
(→ FOUNDATION)

The divine creative activity of "founding" the earth is indicated in Pss. 24:2; 78:69; 89:11; Prov. 3:19. Similarly, God's initiative in "establishing" his law is recorded in Ps. 119:152. Yahweh is said to "have founded" (i.e., established) the city of Zion in Isa. 14:32. The action of "establishing" (i.e., setting up) a defense against one's enemies is indicated in Ps. 8:2.

NT WORDS

stērizō [στηρίζω, *4741*]

stērizō is a verb found thirteen times with the primary senses of "establish," "strengthen."

The meaning "establish" in the context of "strengthening" one's faith is indicated in 1 Thess. 3:2, 13; 2 Thess. 3:3; 1 Pet. 5:10.

In 2 Thess. 2:17, ***stērizō*** is translated "establish" with the sense of "grounding" one's heart in good works. See also Jas. 5:8. 2 Pet. 1:12 depicts believers as "established" in the truth.

stereoō [στερεόω, *4732*]

stereoō is a variant form of ***stērizō***, above, referring to churches being "established" or "strengthened" in their faith in Acts 16:5.

histēmi [ἵστημι, *2476*]

histēmi is a common verb found nearly 160 times with the predominant sense of "stand." (→ STAND) In several instances, however, the meaning "establish" is also indicated.

Rom. 10:3 refers to the Israelites seeking to "establish" their own righteousness apart from God's. The term specifically refers here to their futile attempt to "bring into being" or "create" that righteousness. Heb. 10:9 speaks of Christ setting aside the sacrifices of the old covenant in order to "establish" the second, more perfect, sacrifice of his own. That is, he removed the sin of his people once and for all. 1 Thess. 3:2 refers to the ministry of Timothy in "establishing," or "strengthening," his congregation in their faith.

bebaioō [βεβαιόω, *950*]

bebaioō is a verb found nine times with the sense of "confirm" in most of these contexts. The meaning "establish" is also found in the context of "strengthening" one's faith in Col. 2:7. The "establishing" or "strengthening" of one's heart by grace is indicated in Heb. 13:9.

ETERNAL

qedem [קֶדֶם, **6924**]

qedem is a noun occurring nearly ninety times, meaning "east," "old," as well as related nuances. In Deut. 33:27, however, ***qedem*** is used adjectivally to denote God as "eternal."

NT WORDS

aiōn [αἰών, *165*]

aiōn is a noun found in nearly 130 places with the primary senses of "world," "ever," as in the expression "forever and ever." In two contexts, ***aiōn*** indicates the meaning "eternal." Eph. 3:11 refers to the "eternal" purpose of God's redemptive plans that culminate in Christ. Then, 1 Tim. 1:17 refers to God as the "eternal" king. (→ EVER → WORLD)

aiōnios [αἰώνιος, *166*]

aiōnios is an adjectival form derived from ***aiōn***, above, with the principal meanings "eternal," "everlasting."

The meaning "eternal" in the sense of "unending" is found in relation to the judgment of hell fire in Matt. 18:8; 25:41. "Eternal" destruction is indicated in 2 Thess. 1:9; Heb. 6:2; Jude 7.

In particular, "eternal" or "everlasting" life, the blissful state of unbroken fellowship with God in heaven, is noted in Matt. 19:16, 29; Mark 10:17; Luke 10:25; 18:18; John 5:39; 6:27ff.; 12:25; Acts 13:46ff.; Rom. 2:7; 5:21; 6:22; Gal. 6:8; 1 Tim. 6:12; Titus 3:7; 1 John 3:15; Jude 15.

Mark 3:29 refers to the "eternal" sin of blasphemy against the Holy Spirit. The sense of "eternal" here denotes a transgression of which there can be no forgiveness.

God is described as the source of "eternal" life in John 17:2; Rom. 2:7; 1 John 2:25; 5:11ff. Christ is also designated as the source and giver of eternal life in John 3:15ff.; 4:14; 5:24; 6:40; 10:28; Rom. 6:23; 1 Tim. 1:16; Heb. 5:9; 9:12; 1 John 1:2.

Other uses of ***aiōnios*** include references to the "eternal" weight of glory in 2 Cor. 4:17. See also 2 Tim. 2:10; 1 Pet. 5:10. Unseen "eternal" things are noted in 2 Cor. 4:18. "Eternal" comfort derived from God is indicated in 2 Thess. 2:16. 1 Tim. 6:16 refers to God's "eternal" dominion. The believer's "eternal" inheritance is noted in Heb. 9:15; the "eternal" covenant in Heb. 13:20; the "eternal" kingdom of God in 2 Pet. 1:11; and the "eternal" gospel in Rev. 14:6. ***aiōnios*** also denotes the Spirit of God as "eternal" in Heb. 9:14.

aidios [ἀΐδιος, *126*]

aidios is a rare adjectival variant of ***aiōnios***, above, denoting God's "eternal" power in Rom. 1:20; and the "eternal" chains of confinement in Hades in Jude 6.

See Also: → AGE → EAST
→ EVERLASTING → OLD

EUNUCH

OT Words

sārîs **[סָרִיס, 5631]**

This noun is found about forty times meaning "eunuch," or a castrated male, usually holding an office in the courts of kings as a leading official, and sometimes placed in charge of the royal harem. ***sārîs*** is also translated "official" or "officer." However, the distinctive sense of the term is only conveyed in a few passages.

The literal sense of "officer" is found in Gen. 37:36; 39:1 in reference to the captain of the guard in Potiphar's house, and also in Gen. 40:2, 7 with regard to Pharaoh's butler and baker. See also 1 Sam. 8:15; 1 Kgs. 22:9; 2 Kgs. 8:6; 1 Chr. 28:1; Jer. 29:2; 52:25.

In a number of passages it is difficult to determine whether the distinctive sense of "eunuch" is intended, or only the general meaning of "(court) official" (cf. 2 Kgs. 9:32; 20:18; Isa. 39:7). In Isa. 56:4 ***sārîs*** refers to those godly servants of Yahweh who keep the Sabbath.

The distinctive sense of "eunuch" is clearly indicated in Esth. 2:3, 14, 15; 4:4, 5 in reference to Hegai, the eunuch in charge of the harem of Ahasuerus. This meaning is also possible (though not certain) in Esth. 1:10ff.; 2:21; 6:2, 14; 7:9. Finally, Isa. 56:3 utilizes the term to refer to one who is infertile.

NT Words

eunouchos [εὐνοῦχος, *2135*]

eunouchos is a noun denoting a "eunuch" in all eight occurrences of the term. The word refers generally to people who are sterile in a sexual sense in Matt. 19:12 and have chosen to remain celibate in their service of the kingdom of God. In Acts 8:27ff. the term refers to the Ethiopian "eunuch" — a high official in the royal court of that country. Men such as this were incapable of fathering children, and so a likely position for this Ethiopian official was as head of the royal harem.

eunouchizō [εὐνουχίζω, *2134*]

eunouchizō is a rare verb found only in Matt. 19:12, meaning "to make a eunuch" in both passive and reflexive senses. The sense indicated is that of "castrate," "remove a man's manhood."

EVANGELIST

NT Words

euangelistēs [εὐαγγελιστής, *2099*]

euangelistēs is a noun denoting the office of "evangelist," or a messenger bearing the good news of the gospel (cf. Acts 21:8; 2 Tim. 4:5).

EVENING

OT Words

'ereb **[עֶרֶב, 6153]**

This term occurs around 140 times with the principal meaning "evening" in reference to nighttime. The predominant sense is mundane and literal.

Examples of this general literal usage are found in Gen. 1:5ff. in association with creation (cf. also Gen. 8:11; 19:1; Exod. 16:6ff.; Ruth 2:17; 1 Sam. 14:24; 2 Sam. 1:12; 1 Kgs. 19:16; 2 Kgs. 16:15; Eccl. 11:6; Ezek. 12:4, 7).

The literal sense of "evening" is also found in association with ceremonial ritual and sacrifice (cf. Exod. 27:21; 30:8; Lev. 6:20; Deut. 16:4, 6; 1 Chr. 16:40; 2 Chr. 2:4; 18:34; Ps. 141:2; Ezek. 46:2). Dan. 8:14, 26 predict the length of discontinued evening sacrifices in relation to a campaign of persecution instigated against the Jewish people by the "little horn," identified by Bible scholars as the Seleucid ruler Antiochus IV (Epiphanes).

'ereb is used poetically in Job 4:20; Pss. 55:17; 65:8; Prov. 7:9; Hab. 1:8; Zeph. 3:3; Zech. 14:7.

nesheph **[נֶשֶׁף, 5399]**

nesheph occurs twelve times and means "twilight" or "evening" on all but two of these occasions. The literal sense is found in 1 Sam. 30:17; 2 Kgs. 7:5, 7; Job 24:15; Prov. 7:9; Isa. 5:11, and it is used poetically in Job 3:9; Isa. 21:4; 59:10; Jer. 13:16.

NT Words

hespera [ἑσπέρα, *2073*]

hespera is a noun found three times, denoting "evening" in the literal sense of the period after sunset (cf. Luke 24:29; Acts 4:3; 28:23).

opsia [ὀψία, *3798*]

opsia is synonymous with ***hespera*** (see above), also denoting "evening" in its natural sense in fifteen contexts (e.g., Matt. 8:16; 14:15; 27:57; Mark 1:32; 4:35; John 6:16; 20:19).

opse [ὀψέ, *3796*]

opse is a rare variant of ***opsia*** (see above) denoting "evening" in Mark 11:19; 13:35.

EVER, EVERLASTING, FOREVER

OT Words

'ôlām **[עוֹלָם, 5769]**

'ôlām is a common noun found over four hundred times with the predominant meaning "(for)ever," "everlasting," along with several related nuances. The underlying sense is that of a long, or perpetual, duration of time.

The phenomenon of "living forever" without the specific motif of a heavenly eternity, which is made explicit primarily in the New Testament, is common (e.g., Gen. 3:22; Neh. 2:3). One Old Testament context, however, does suggest that "everlasting life" may be linked to heavenly realities (i.e., Dan. 12:2).

God's covenant with humankind in general and his people in particular, is described as "everlasting" in Gen. 9:16; 17:7, 13ff.; 2 Sam. 23:5; 1 Chr. 16:17; Pss. 105:8ff.; 111:9; Isa. 24:5; 55:3; 61:8; Jer. 32:40; 50:5; Ezek. 16:60; 37:26 (cf. also Hos. 2:19). In particular, Sabbath observance is described as an "everlasting" covenant in Exod. 31:16; Lev. 24:8.

The everlasting bond of an intimate friendship is indicated in 1 Sam. 20:42 in relation to David and Jonathan's mutual vow.

The promised inheritance of the land of Canaan for the people of God, characterized as one that will last forever, is noted in Gen. 13:15; 17:8; 48:4; Exod. 32:13; Lev. 25:32ff.; Josh. 14:9; Jer. 25:5. The word of God is described as everlasting in Isa. 40:8, as is the salvation offered by him in Isa. 45:17; 51:6ff.

The title or description of God as "everlasting" is recorded in Gen. 21:33; Isa. 40:28 (cf. also Deut. 32:40 Isa. 30:8; 60:20; 63:16; Jer. 10:10).

The covenant name "Lord" or ***YHWH*** (→ GOD) is designated as a name that is to be given to God "forever" in Exod. 3:15.

The temple is described as a place in which God will dwell forever in 1 Kgs. 8:13; 9:3; 2 Chr. 6:2 (cf. also Ezek. 43:9).

Israelite festival days, designated to be observed in perpetuity (i.e., "forever"), are recorded in Exod. 12:14ff. Similar perpetual observation is demanded of ritual practices in worship (e.g., Exod. 27:21; 28:43; 29:9; 40:15; Lev. 3:17; 7:34ff.; 16:31ff.; 23:14ff.; Num. 10:8; 18:8ff.; 28:13; 2 Chr. 2:4).

By way of contrast, the sense of "never" is found, for example, in Exod. 14:13; Judg. 2:1; 2 Sam. 12:10; Ps. 30:6; Joel 2:27.

The rule or reign of God is depicted as lasting "forever" in Exod. 15:18; Pss. 9:7; 10:16; 45:6; 145:13; Isa. 9:7; Mic. 4:7. God's love and mercy are said to endure "forever" in 1 Chr. 16:34; 2 Chr. 5:13; Ezra 3:11; Pss. 18:50; 29:10; 103:17; Jer. 31:3; 33:11; as is his glory in Pss. 104:31; 118:3ff.; 136:1ff. References to Israel's blessing from God that will last forever are found in Deut. 5:29f.; 12:28 — all in relation to a prosperous lifestyle in the land of Canaan. Elsewhere, God's "everlasting" righteousness is mentioned in Dan. 9:24. The Israelite monarchy is described as an institution that will last "forever," including references to the eternal throne of God, in 1 Sam. 13:13; 2 Sam. 7:13ff.; 1 Chr. 17:12ff.; 28:7ff.; 1 Kgs. 1:31; 2:45; 9:5; 2 Chr. 13:5.

Other general references to "forever" are found in Exod. 19:9; Deut. 29:29; Josh. 4:7; 1 Sam. 3:13; 2 Kgs. 5:27; Pss. 9:5; 33:11; Eccl. 1:4; Isa. 32:14; Jer. 35:6; Jonah 2:6.

Ascriptions of praise to God as one to be blessed "forever" are found in 1 Chr. 16:36; 29:10; Neh. 9:5; Pss. 30:12; 41:13; 72:19.

God declares to David's "Lord" that he will be a priest "forever" after the order of Melchizedek in Ps. 110:4 — a distinctly messianic prophetic context that is fulfilled in the person of Jesus Christ (cf. Heb. 7ff.).

'ālam [עָלַם, 5957 (Aramaic)]

'ālam is an Aramaic noun occurring twenty times in all with the primary senses of "ever," and the adjectival meaning "everlasting."

The term is found in the formal salutation offered to Babylonian and Persian kings: "O king, live forever" (cf. Dan. 2:4; 3:9; 5:10; 6:6, 21).

It also occurs in the offering of praise to God whose name deserves to be glorified "forever and ever" (cf. Dan. 2:20). See also Dan. 6:6.

God's kingdom is affirmed as an "everlasting" dominion in Dan. 2:44; 4:3, 34; 7:14, 18, 27.

'ad [עַד, 5703]

'ad is a noun, also used adjectivally, found nearly fifty times as a synonym for ***'ôlām*** and ***'ālam***, above, denoting the primary sense of "ever," used in the expression "forever (and ever)," as well as "everlasting."

The rule or reign of God is said to be "everlasting" in Exod. 15:18; Pss. 10:16; 45:6.

'ad is used as a title for God in Isa. 9:6, referring to him as "Everlasting Father" and the "Eternal Rock" in Isa. 26:4. The meaning "forever" in the sense of "unending, continuing existence" is indicated in 1 Chr. 28:9; Job 19:24; Pss. 21:4, 6; 45:17; 132:12; Isa. 30:8; 65:18; Dan. 12:3; Mic. 4:5; Hab. 3:6. In particular, the eternally unending punishment of the wicked, lasting "forever and ever" (the latter "ever" translating ***'ad***) is indicated in Pss. 9:5; 92:7. The identical expression is used in relation to the person of God himself in Pss. 48:14; 52:8.

The fear of the Lord is said to endure "forever" in Ps. 19:9; as does his "righteousness" in Pss. 111:3; 112:3, 9.

The meaning "ever" in the sense of "constantly," "continual," "always" in the context of praising God is indicated in Ps. 61:8. See also Pss. 83:17; 111:10; 145:1ff.

NT Words

aiōn [αἰών, *165*]

aiōn is a noun with the primary meanings "world," "age," and "ever" throughout the nearly 130 occurrences of the term. (→ WORLD) The latter meaning is found primarily in the expressions "forever," "evermore," denoting the unending passage of time. The meaning "ever" is linked to "forever" in the sense of unending duration (cf. Luke 1:33; Heb. 1:8; 13:8; 2 John 2; Jude 13, 25; Rev. 18:6; 14:11; 20:10).

In particular, the phenomenon of "living forever," in the context of eternal life, is indicated in John 6:51, 58.

In John 8:35, Christ the Son is said to continue "forever" (cf. also John 12:34; Rev. 1:18). He is also declared as a priest "forever" in the order of Melchizedek in Heb. 5:6; 6:20; 7:17ff. John 14:16 affirms that the Holy Spirit will remain with his people forever. The ascribing of blessing or glory to God "forever" is indicated in Rom. 1:25; 9:5; 11:36; 2 Cor. 11:31; Gal. 1:5; Phil. 4:20; 2 Tim. 4:18; 1 Pet. 4:11; 2 Pet. 3:18; Rev. 1:6; 5:13; 7:12 (cf. also Heb. 13:21). The everlasting reign of Christ is indicated in Rev. 11:15.

The phenomenon of the punishment of the wicked lasting "forever" is indicated in Rev. 14:11; 15:7; 19:3; 20:10.

The contrasting negative meaning of "never" is indicated in John 4:14; 8:51ff.; 10:28; 11:26; 13:8.

See Also: → ETERNAL

EVIDENCE, EVIDENT, EVIDENTLY

NT Words

tekmērion [τεκμήριον, *5039*]

tekmērion is a rare noun denoting the "convincing proofs" or "evidence" provided by Christ to people of the region that he had indeed risen from the dead (cf. Acts 1:3).

dēlos [δῆλος, *1212*]

dēlos is an adjective meaning "clear," "evident" in two places.

The meaning "apparent," "obvious" in the impersonal expression "it is evident that . . ." is indicated in 1 Cor. 15:27; Gal. 3:11.

katadēlos [κατάδηλος, *2612*]

katadēlos is a rare adjectival form, an intensive form of ***dēlos***, above, meaning "thoroughly plain or evident" in Heb. 7:15.

prodēlos [πρόδηλος, *4271*]

prodēlos is another rare adjectival variant of ***dēlos***, meaning "obvious," "evident" as a description of the sins of humankind in 1 Tim. 5:1; and also as a designation of good deeds in 1 Tim. 5:25. The general sense of "clear" or "evident" in the expression "it is clear that . . ." is indicated in Heb. 7:14, explaining that Jesus Christ was a direct descendant from the tribe of Judah.

EVIL, EVILDOER

OT Words

ra' [רַע, **7451**]

This noun, in both masculine and feminine forms, is found approximately 650 times and means "evil" or "wickedness" in the large majority of occurrences. There are, however, quite a number of differing nuances in a variety of contexts, which render this term semantically complex.

To begin with, "evil" is sometimes employed as a negative moral category that stands starkly opposed to "goodness" or "holiness" — for example, Gen. 2:9, 17 refer to "the tree of the knowledge of good and evil" (cf. Gen. 3:5, 22; Deut. 1:39; 1 Kgs. 3:9; Jer. 18:20; Amos 5:14; Hab. 1:13).

Many texts express the idea of "evil" in the sense of "immorality" or "vice." Evil in this sense is predicated of people and circumstances in the following examples: Gen. 6:5 (Noah's generation); Gen. 39:9 (Joseph's refusal to sleep with Potiphar's wife); Num. 14:27, 35 (the wicked congregation of Israel); 2 Sam. 13:14 (Amnon's rape of Tamar); Esth. 7:6 (Haman's wicked plot to destroy the Jews); Prov. 6:24 ("Madame Folly," the personification of evil); Prov. 11:19 (a death sentence for the one who pursues evil); Jer. 9:3 (an evil, corrupt lifestyle as the consequence of having no intimate relationship with God). See also Deut. 1:35; Ps. 107:34; Eccl. 12:14; Isa. 5:20; Hos. 7:2; Jonah 3:8; Mic. 7:3; Zech. 7:10.

"Evil" is also used in the sense of divine punishment. There are a number of significant contexts in this regard. Exod. 32:14, 22 speak of Yahweh "changing his mind" concerning the terrible judgment he had in store for his people after they had worshiped the golden calf (cf. also Exod. 33:4). Deut. 29:21 speaks of the terrible, evil consequences of the divine curse of the covenant, which God invokes against his people for their violation of his law. Other references to the covenant curse in this regard are found in Deut. 31:17; Josh. 23:15; Judg. 2:15; Ezra 9:13; Neh. 13:18; Isa. 3:9; Jer. 1:14; 11:8ff.; 36:3; 42:10; 44:21; Dan. 9:14; Amos 9:4. In other contexts, ***ra'*** refers to divine punishment for wrongdoing in a general sense (cf. 2 Sam. 12:11; 17:14; Ps. 54:5; Prov. 16:4; 21:12). And, finally, there are several passages in which Yahweh's judgment against the nations is in view (cf. Isa. 47:11; Jer. 49:37; 51:60).

ra' also indicates "evil" in the sense of violating the divine covenant. In most cases idolatry or immorality is in view, although more generalized rebellion against God is sometimes intended by the use of the term in the phrase "doing what is evil in the sight of God" (e.g., Deut. 9:18; Judg. 2:11; 3:7; 10:6; 13:1; 1 Sam. 15:19; 2 Sam. 12:9; 1 Kgs. 11:6; 2 Kgs. 3:2; 21:2; Ezek. 20:43).

General divine condemnation for evil is also found in a number of places (e.g., 1 Sam. 12:17; 2 Kgs. 21:6, 9; Neh. 9:28; 13:7; Isa. 66:4; Jer. 2:3). Then, 2 Chr. 7:14 contains the classic expression of repentance whereby whole nations turn away from their wicked ways and back to God. In another well-known passage, Ps. 51:4 contains David's sublime confession of his sin.

There are, in addition to the above, a variety of contexts containing the term ***ra'***, each expressing "evil" in a distinctive way. Evil is referred to as disaster or misfortune, for example, in Gen. 19:19; 44:34; Judg. 20:41; 1 Sam. 6:9. It is also used in connection with the demonic spirit world (cf. Judg. 9:23; 1 Sam. 16:14ff.; 18:10; 19:9). On a more prosaic level, ***ra'*** signifies as evil those things which are unfavorable, or which merit disapproval (e.g., Gen. 37:2; Lev. 27:10; Num. 13:19; Deut. 22:14ff.; 2 Sam. 19:35). Ill treatment and despicable behavior are also designated as "evil" (e.g., Gen. 50:17; Deut. 30:15; 1 Sam. 24:11, 17; 2 Kgs. 8:12). Gen. 50:20 contains a significant affirmation of God's sovereignty in this regard, where Joseph acknowledges that while his brother's persecution of him was intended as evil, God had intended it for noble purposes, resulting in Joseph's rise to power in Egypt and the rescue of Jacob and his family from starvation in Canaan.

More frequent are references to "evil" in the sense of calamity or awful circumstances (e.g., Deut. 7:25; 1 Sam. 25:17ff.; 2 Sam. 5:14; Esth. 7:7; Job 2:10, 11; Pss. 23:4; 90:15; Eccl. 2:21; Ezek. 7:5; Dan. 9:12; Mic. 1:12). In a related sense, Exod. 5:19 refers to the desperate circumstances of the Israelite slaves in Egypt which are described as "evil."

Finally, ***ra'*** describes disobedience or rebellion against God as "evil" (cf. Jer. 18:10; Ezek. 33:11; 36:31; Zech. 1:4). In Nah. 1:11 such action is referred to as "plotting evil against God."

rā'a' [רָעַע, 7489]

rā'a' is a verb occurring nearly one hundred times, meaning "to be wicked, evil," "act wickedly," "do evil," along with related nuances and the nominal sense of "evildoer."

The meaning "to act wickedly," "do evil, wrong" is evident in Gen. 19:7; Lev. 5:4; Num. 11:11; Deut. 26:6; Judg. 19:23; 1 Sam. 2:25; 1 Kgs. 14:9; 1 Chr. 16:22; Pss. 37:8; 119:115; Prov. 24:8; Isa. 1:16; 65:25; Jer. 4:22. The sense of "harming" someone is indicated in Gen. 31:7. God is charged with "having done evil to" or "afflicted" his people in Exod. 5:22ff.; Ruth 1:21; 1 Kgs. 17:20; Ps. 44:2; and he determines to so "afflict" his people on account of their rebellion against him in Jer. 25:29; 31:28; Mic. 4:6; Zech. 8:14. References to "evildoers" or the "wicked" include Job 8:20; Pss. 22:16; 64:2; Prov. 17:4; Isa. 1:4; 14:20; Jer. 20:13.

rōa' [רֹעַ, 7455]

rōa' is a noun synonymous with ***ra'***, above, denoting "evil," "wickedness" in most of its nineteen occurrences.

The "wickedness" of Israel's actions is noted in Deut. 28:20; Isa. 1:16; Jer. 4:4; 21:12; 23:2, 22; 25:5; 26:3; 44:22; Hos. 9:15. References to moral "evil" are found in 1 Sam. 17:28. In particular, the "evil deeds" of the wicked are noted in Ps. 28:4.

NT Words

kakos [κακός, *2556*]

kakos is an adjectival form found in approximately fifty places as a clear dynamic equivalent for the Hebrew terms ***rā'*** and ***rōa'*** (see above), meaning "evil," "wicked," used both adjectivally and nominally. The term denotes "wicked people" in a general sense in Matt. 21:41; Phil. 3:2; Titus 1:12; Rev. 2:2.

kakos is used adjectivally to refer to a "wicked" servant in Matt. 24:48; and to "evil" thoughts in Mark 7:21. In 2 Cor. 5:10, the term refers to the good or "bad" done in the body which will be adjudicated at the judgment seat of Christ.

kakos denotes "evil" in a moral, nominal sense in Matt. 27:23; Mark 15:14; Luke 16:25; John 18:23; Acts 9:13; Rom. 1:30; 9:11; 12:17ff.; 13:3ff.; 1 Cor. 10:6; Col. 3:5; 1 Thess. 5:15; 1 Tim. 6:10; Heb. 5:14; Jas. 1:13; 1 Pet. 3:9ff. The meaning "harm" in the sense of "physical injury" is indicated in Acts 28:5; and in the sense of "hurt" in a psychological, emotional context.

kakia [κακία, *2549*]

kakia is a noun derived from the adjectival ***kakos*** (see above), denoting "evil," "wickedness" in the generalized sense of "moral depravity" throughout the eleven occurrences of the term (cf. Matt. 6:34; Acts 8:22; Rom. 1:29; 1 Cor. 5:8; 14:20; Eph. 4:31; Col. 3:8; Titus 3:3; Jas. 1:21; 1 Pet. 2:1, 16).

kakōs [κακῶς, *2560*]

kakōs is an adverbial form found in sixteen places with the primary meaning "ill," "sick." However, in Acts 23:5, the term occurs in the context of an injunction not to speak "evil" of a civil ruler. (→ SICK)

kakoō [κακόω, *2559*]

kakoō is a verb found in seven places, meaning to "ill-treat," "harm" in three of these contexts (cf. Acts 7:6; 18:10; 1 Pet. 3:13).

ponēros [πονηρός, *4190*]

ponēros is an adjectival form synonymous with ***kakos*** and ***kakia***, above, found nearly eighty times with the meaning "evil," "wicked."

"Evil" in the sense of "harm, injury" is indicated in Matt. 5:11.

The general sense of moral "evil" is evident in Matt. 5:37ff.; 7:11ff.; Mark 7:22ff.; Luke 3:19; John 3:19; 7:7; Rom. 12:9; Eph. 5:16; 1 Thess. 5:22; Jas. 4:16.

ponēros is used nominally to denote the devil as "the evil one" in Matt. 13:19, 38; John 17:15; Acts 19:12ff.; Eph. 6:16; 1 John 2:13ff.; 3:12; 5:18ff.

ponēros also denotes wicked people in general in Matt. 13:49; Luke 6:45; Acts 17:5; 1 Cor. 5:13; "evil" (i.e., "immoral") thoughts are noted in Matt. 15:19; Jas. 2:4; "evil" spirits in Luke 7:21; 8:2; the current "evil" age in Gal. 1:4; Eph. 6:13; an "evil" conscience in Heb. 10:22.

The adjectival sense of "wicked" or "evil" describes people in Matt. 16:4; 18:32; 25:26; Luke 11:29; 19:22; Heb. 3:12.

phaulos [φαῦλος, *5337*]

phaulos is an adjective found in four places, denoting "(moral) evil" in a nominal sense in John 3:20; 5:29. The adjectival sense of "evil," "wicked" is found in Titus 2:8; Jas. 3:16.

kakopoios [κακοποιός, *2555*]

kakopoios is an adjectival form used nominally in only five places, denoting "evildoer," "those who do practice evil" (cf. John 18:30; 1 Pet. 2:12ff.; 3:16; 4:15).

kakopoieō [κακοποιέω, *2554*]

kakopoieō is a verb meaning "to do wrong," "harm" in the general sense of "moral evil" in 1 Pet. 3:17; 3 John 11. Mark 3:4; Luke 6:9 refer to "doing harm" on the Sabbath.

Additional Notes

The Hebrew term ***ra'*** (and related forms) has a complex semantic range that incorporates the senses of the two primary Greek terms, ***kakos*** and ***ponēros***, as well as their derivative forms. In a general sense it may also be affirmed that the phenomenon of "evil," with its large variety of nuances, is similar in force in both Testaments. Yet ***ra'*** is predominantly linked to the concept of evil both as active rebellion against Yahweh and as the severe punishment or curse that results from such disobedience. While there are generalized, non-specific references to "evil," the dominant theological perception of evil under the old covenant centers on the violation of the legal code of the Mosaic covenant and the ensuing painful consequences. In the New Testament usage of ***kakos*** and ***ponēros*** there is not as much of an emphasis on "evil" in the sense of either God's judgment or humankind's wickedness against God. Of the approximately 150 references to "evil" in the New Testament, only a handful specifically relate to these themes (cf. Matt. 13:48; Rom. 2:9; 2 Cor. 5:10; 2 Tim. 4:4; 1 Pet. 3:12; Rev. 16:2). Although the New Testament emphasizes God's judgment against the wicked, it does not always express this with the vocabulary that translates "evil." Here, again, we see that theological emphases are not restricted to word usage alone. The divine consummation of judgment on evil is not observable solely by the consideration of specific vocabulary.

See Also: → WICKED

EXALT, EXALTED

OT WORDS

rûm [רוּם, 7311]

This verb occurs around two hundred times with the primary meaning "lift up," "exalt" in both a literal and metaphorical sense, though the latter sense predominates.

The literal meaning "exalt," with the idea of "raising high" or "lifting high" is found in Gen. 7:17 in regard to the ark; and in Exod. 7:20; 14:16 in relation to Moses' rod or hand (cf. also Exod. 17:11; Num. 20:11). Exod. 29:27 refers to the "raising" of the wave offering. 2 Kgs. 2:13 mentions Elisha "lifting up" Elijah's mantle; and Isa. 40:9 refers to the "lifting" of one's voice (cf. also Isa. 58:1; Ezek. 21:22).

"Exaltation" is commonly linked to the person of God, especially in the context of worship. A number of texts refer to the practice of "exalting," or praising, God (e.g., Exod. 15:2; Neh. 9:5; Pss. 18:46; 46:10; 108:5; Isa. 25:1). In a related context, Isa. 52:13 speaks of the "exalting" of the Servant of Yahweh. Similarly, mention is also made of God "exalting" his chosen servants (e.g., 1 Sam. 2:10 refers to the exaltation of the "horn of God's anointed"). This is a messianic prophecy linked to the conquest of the enemies of Yahweh, both in a spiritual as well as a physical sense (cf. also in this regard Pss. 75:10; 89:17, 19; 148:14). Then, 2 Sam. 22:49 refers to God "exalting" David above his enemies. Other relevant texts are 1 Kgs. 14:7; 16:2; 1 Chr. 25:5. General references to God "exalting" his people are found in 1 Sam. 2:7, 8; Pss. 9:13; 18:48; 27:6.

A variety of passages speak of the exalting of various human emotions, qualities, and actions, both good and bad. For example, the manifestation (or exalting) of pride is condemned in Deut. 8:14; 17:20; Ps. 66:7; Isa. 14:13; Dan. 11:12, 36; Hos. 13:6. The "lifting up" of one's hands in rebellion is also mentioned in 1 Kgs. 11:27, where Jeroboam is set to take over the throne from King Solomon. Ps. 12:8 deplores the exalting of evil among humankind. In a positive vein, Neh. 9:6 mentions the "lifting of one's face" in the context of prayer and communion with God.

Finally, in Balaam's oracle of blessing, there is a metaphorical exaltation of the kingdom of Israel (cf. Num. 24:7). Linked to this is the reference to the exaltation of Israel's enemies over his people as a part of God's punishment against Israel in Lam. 2:17.

gādal [גָּדַל, 1431]

This term is found over one hundred times with the primary sense of "becoming great," as well as a number of related meanings. ***gādal*** is translated "exalt" in the sense of "making great (or highly esteemed)" in about thirty places.

God is said to "exalt the name" of his servants, granting them a great reputation. This is said of Joshua (cf. Josh. 3:7; 4:14), of David (cf. 2 Sam. 7:26; 1 Chr. 17:24), and of Solomon (cf. 1 Chr. 29:25; 2 Chr. 1:1). The exaltation of humankind in general is spoken of in Job 7:17. Reference to the "exalting" (or honoring) of God's people is found in Zech. 12:7.

"Exalting" the name of the Lord and his law is indicated in Pss. 35:27; 40:16; 138:2; Isa. 42:1; Ezek. 38:23.

References to selfish boasting, or exalting oneself, are found in Job 19:5; Ps. 35:26; Jer. 48:26; Ezek. 35:13. Dan. 8:11, 25; 11:36. The references in Daniel are noteworthy here, in that they focus on the blasphemous and cruel activities of the "little horn," the antecedent of the antichrist who is the epitome of arrogance and self-centeredness in the visions of Daniel.

gābah [גָּבַהּ, 1361]

This verb occurs over thirty times, meaning "being high" or "exalted" in a number of different senses.

Positively speaking, ***gābah*** refers to the "exalting" or "lifting" of one's heart in the sense of devotion or courage with reference, for example, to Jehoshaphat's devotion to God in 2 Chr. 17:6. By way of contrast, the "lifting" of one's heart in pride and arrogance is indicated in the case of Uzziah (2 Chr. 26:16); Hezekiah (2 Chr. 32:25); the King of Tyre (Ezek. 28:2); Pharaoh (Ezek. 31:10); and Edom (Obad. 4).

The "exalting" of kings is mentioned in Job 36:7, as is exalting the Lord in Isa. 5:16, and the Servant of Yahweh in Isa. 52:13.

Ezek. 21:26 refers to the exalting of the lowly in Israel, but the context is one of divine judgment against the people of God — for at the same time, those who are "exalted" (i.e., the arrogant and the proud) will be bought low.

sāgab [שָׂגַב, 7682]

sāgab is a verb found in twenty places with the varying senses of "to be high," "be exalted" as well as several related nuances. References to God "being exalted" on high in his unique majesty are found in Job 36:22; Ps. 148:13; Isa. 2:11, 17; 12:4; 33:5.

NT Words

hypsoō [ὑψόω, *5312*]

hypsoō is a verb found in approximately twenty places meaning "to exalt," "lift on high."

The state of "being exalted, lifted up" to heaven is indicated in Matt. 11:23; Luke 10:15. The arrogant act of "exalting oneself" is indicated in Matt. 23:12; Luke 14:11; 18:14.

God's action in "exalting" the poor and downtrodden, "lifting" their fortunes, is noted in Luke 1:52. See also 2 Cor. 11:7; Jas. 4:10; 1 Pet. 5:6. The significant parallel between Christ "being lifted up" on the cross and Moses "lifting up" the serpent in the wilderness (and healing the plague-ridden Israelites) is indicated in John 3:14; 8:28; 12:32ff. The point of this comparison is to emphasize the unique effectiveness of Christ's substitutionary atonement, removing the sins of his people once and for all in a supreme act of spiritual healing. As a sequel to this phenomenon, Acts 2:33; 5:31 refer to Christ being "exalted" at the right hand of God after his ascension to heaven.

The sense of God "exalting" his people in Egypt carries the underlying meaning of "to make great" in Acts 13:17.

hyperypsoō [ὑπερυψόω, *5251*]

hyperypsoō is a rare variant of ***hypsoō***, above, denoting God's action in "highly exalting" his Son, Jesus Christ, granting to him the name that is greater than any other name.

hyperairō [ὑπεραίρω, *5229*]

hyperairō is a rare verb found in three places. The meaning "be exalted," in the sense of being affected by a supreme feeling of elation, is indicated in 2 Cor. 12:7, referring twice to the apostle Paul's experience of a heavenly vision. The arrogant and idolatrous action of "exalting oneself" before God, seeking to supplant him, is predicated of the "man of lawlessness" in 2 Thess. 2:4.

Additional Notes

The Hebrew and Greek terms reflecting the idea of "exaltation" are reasonably close parallels. The phenomenon of "exaltation" carries both positive and negative connotations throughout the Bible. In a theological sense, the emphasis on exalting the name of Yahweh in the Old Testament finds its consummation in the New through the experience of Christ being literally lifted up on a cross. It also finds a supreme expression through the sublime spiritual exaltation or elevation of the name of Christ by God the Father as a direct consequence of our Lord's substitutionary death and resurrection on our behalf.

See Also: → BEAR (VERB)

EXAMINATION, EXAMINE

OT Words

ḥāqar [חָקַר, 2713]

This verb occurs approximately thirty times with the primary meaning "search (out)," "examine." ***ḥāqar*** has both a literal and a metaphorical sense.

There are a number of texts in which ***ḥāqar*** indicates a formal legal inquiry or examination. For example, Deut. 13:14 describes the legal process of ascertaining whether or not a town is guilty of idolatry. Job 29:16 refers to Job's "legal examination" on behalf of the poor. See also Prov. 18:17; Eccl. 12:9; Job 32:11.

A geographic search or reconnaissance mission is in view in Judg. 18:2; 2 Sam. 10:3; 1 Chr. 19:3; Job 28:3. Ezek. 39:14 reports a "visionary" search for dead bodies in Israel as the result of the victory over Gog and Magog.

ḥāqar is used metaphorically of God "examining" the phenomenon of wisdom in Job 28:27, or the foundations of the earth in Jer. 31:37. God also "examines" the hearts of human beings in Pss. 44:21; 139:1, 23; Jer. 17:10. Lam. 3:40 expresses the people's desire for repentance.

NT Words

anakrisis [ἀνάκρισις, *351*]

anakrisis is a rare noun denoting the "(judicial) examination, or investigation" of Paul before King Agrippa in Acts 25:26.

anakrinō [ἀνακρίνω, *350*]

anakrinō is a verb found in sixteen places, meaning to "examine," as well as several related nuances.

The act of "examining" a person in a judicial sense is indicated in Luke 23:14; Acts 4:9; 12:19; 28:18; 1 Cor. 9:3. In a similar context, the meaning "judge" is indicated in 1 Cor. 4:3. See also 1 Cor. 14:24. The citizens of Berea are commended for their eagerness to "search," or "examine" the Scriptures in Acts 17:11.

The divine prerogative of "judging" or "examining" a person is acknowledged by Paul in 1 Cor. 4:4.

anetazō [ἀνετάζω, *426*]

anetazō is a rare verb meaning "to examine" in a judicial context in Acts 22:29.

dokimazō [δοκιμάζω, *1381*]

dokimazō is a verb found nearly thirty times, with the principal meanings "prove," "approve," "discern."

In several places, however, the meaning "examine" is evident. (→ APPROVE)

The action of "examining" one's newly-acquired oxen is noted in Luke 14:19. The exhortation to let a person "examine" himself or herself prior to taking the Lord's Supper is recorded in 1 Cor. 11:28. Another exhortation to "test" or "examine" oneself to see if one is holding to the faith is noted in 2 Cor. 13:5. See also Gal. 6:4; 1 Thess. 5:21. The "testing" or "examining" of potential deacons to determine their suitability for office is indicated in 1 Tim. 3:10. The charge to "test" or "examine" the spirits to see whether they are of God is found in 1 John 4:1.

peirazō [πειράζω, *3985*]

peirazō is a verb found in approximately forty contexts with the predominant meaning "tempt" or "test." In one context, however, ***peirazō*** means "examine." 2 Cor. 13:5 contains the exhortation to "examine" oneself to see whether one is still holding to the faith. (→ TEMPT)

Additional Notes

The concept of "examination" (and associated meanings) receives consistent emphasis throughout Scripture. Both Hebrew and Greek words reflect a literal as well as a metaphorical sense, focusing on judicial procedure as well as on divine investigation. The significance of God examining the hearts of human beings with a view to judging them is a consistently biblical theme.

See Also: → PROVE → REQUIRE → SEEK

EXAMPLE

NT Words

deigma [δεῖγμα, *1164*]

deigma is a rare noun found only in Jude 7, referring to the cities of Sodom and Gomorrah as a solemn "example" of immorality and the object of divine judgment — a "lifestyle" to be scrupulously avoided.

deigmatizō [δειγματίζω, *1165*]

deigmatizō is a rare verb found only in Col. 2:15, referring to Christ having destroyed the powers of darkness through his death and "having made a public example" of them through their destruction.

hypodeigma [ὑπόδειγμα, *5262*]

hypodeigma is a noun derived from ***deigmatizō*** (see above), meaning "example" with several different nuances. It is found six times.

Christ's action of washing his disciples' feet is described as an "example," a pattern of behavior for his disciples to follow, in John 13:15. By way of a negative counter example, 2 Pet. 2:6 refers to the cities of Sodom and Gomorrah as a terrible "example" — a warning to those who followed the same example of ungodliness. A warning against falling into the same "pattern" of disobedience as demonstrated by the ancient Israelites in the wilderness is indicated in Heb. 4:11. There, Heb. 8:5; 9:23 both refer to the earthly tabernacle/temple as a "copy" of the heavenly sanctuary. Finally, Jas. 5:10 refers to the prophets who served as an "example" to the people of God of suffering and patience.

typos [τύπος, *5179*]

typos is a noun found fifteen times with the primary meaning "example," as well as "type," "pattern." (→ TYPE)

hypotypōsis [ὑποτύπωσις, *5296*]

hypotypōsis is a variant form of ***typos*** (see above) found only twice, meaning "example" in 1 Tim. 1:16 in relation to Christ setting a perfect example of patience to his followers. 2 Tim. 1:13 contains Paul's exhortation to Timothy to follow the "example" or "pattern" of the sound words of the apostle's teaching.

hypogrammos [ὑπογραμμός, *5261*]

hypogrammos is a rare noun found only in 1 Pet. 2:21, referring to Christ having left an "example" for his followers to keep.

EXCEED, EXCEEDINGLY

NT Words

perisseuō [περισσεύω, *4052*]

perisseuō is a verb found nearly forty times with the principal meaning "abound," as well as related nuances. (→ ABUNDANCE)

The meaning "exceed" in the sense of "be greater than" is indicated in Matt. 5:20, referring to the need for a person's righteousness to "exceed" that of the Pharisees.

EXCEL, EXCELLENT

OT Words

'addîr [**אַדִּיר, 117**]

This adjectival term means "majestic," "noble," "famous," and is translated "excellent" on four occasions. ***'addîr*** occurs around thirty times overall.

Ps. 8:1, 9 describe the name of God as "excellent." Excellence is predicated of the saints in Israel in Ps. 16:3. And God is acclaimed as more excellent than the mountains in Ps. 76:4.

yāqār [יָקָר, 3368]

yāqār is an adjective, occurring about forty times overall, meaning "valuable" or "precious." The term is twice translated "excellent" — once in Ps. 36:7, where the psalmist attributes excellence to the character of God, and then in Prov. 17:27, which refers to a person of understanding having an excellent spirit.

gā'ôn [גָּאוֹן, 1347]

gā'ôn means "majesty," "pride" (in both a good and bad sense) as well as "excellence." The latter meaning is found in approximately a quarter of the nearly fifty occurrences of the term.

For example, "excellence" is predicated of Yahweh in Exod. 15:7 for his deliverance of the Israelites from the Egyptians. Job 37:4 refers to the excellence of God's voice. Isa. 4:2 describes the fruit of Canaan as "excellent," in a vision of renewal for the remnant of Israel on the Day of the Lord (cf. also Isa. 60:15; Nah. 2:2).

In Isa. 13:19, with reference to arrogant pride, it is the "excellence" of Babylon that God will overthrow. For the same attitude, Israel will suffer a similar fate at the hand of Yahweh in Ezek. 24:21; Amos 6:8; 8:7.

yatîr [יַתִּיר, 3493 (Aramaic)]

This is an Aramaic adjectival term found on eight occasions, five of which indicate the idea of "excellence" or "preeminence." All are found in the book of Daniel.

Dan. 2:31 refers to the "excellence" of the image seen by Nebuchadnezzar in his dream. Dan. 4:36 refers to the "excellence" of Nebuchadnezzar's reign. Dan. 5:12, 14; 6:3 mention Daniel's "excellent" spirit of knowledge and wisdom in relation to his gift of dream interpretation from God.

NT Words

hyperballō [ὑπερβάλλω, *5235*]

hyperballō is a verb found five times, meaning "surpass," denoting the underlying sense of "excel," "be exceedingly great" on three of these occasions. 2 Cor. 3:10 speaks of the glory of the new covenant that "surpasses" the glory of the old. In Eph. 3:19, the love of Christ is said to "surpass" all human knowledge. 2 Cor. 9:14 speaks of the "surpassing" grace of God indwelling the lives of the Corinthian congregation, describing it as something of exquisite excellence. In the remaining texts, ***hyperballō*** is used adjectivally to refer in Eph. 1:19 to the "immeasurable" or "excellent" greatness of God's power; and in Eph. 2:7 to the "immeasurable" riches of God's grace.

hyperbolē [ὑπερβολή, *5236*]

hyperbolē is a noun derived from ***hyperballō*** (see above) found in eight places, with an adjectival and adverbial sense as well as a nominal one.

The meaning "exceedingly," or "beyond measure," is used in relation to the divine commandment that provoked a sinful response in the apostle Paul (cf. Rom. 7:13). Gal. 1:13 refers to Saul persecuting the early Christians "violently," or with excessive force. 2 Cor. 1:8 refers to the "exceedingly" great force of the apostle's affliction. 2 Cor. 4:7 refers to the "all-surpassing" power of God; and 2 Cor. 4:17 to the glory of God that "far outweighs" everything else.

hyperbolē is translated nominally in 2 Cor. 12:7 with reference to "the abundance" of revelations given to the apostle Paul.

diaphoros [διάφορος, *1313*]

diaphoros is an adjectival form found in two places, meaning "excellent." Heb. 1:4 refers to the name of Christ that is "more excellent" than that of the angels. In Heb. 8:6 the ministry of Christ in the new covenant is described as "more excellent" than that of the old covenant.

kratistos [κράτιστος, *2903*]

kratistos is an adjective found in four places with the superlative sense of "most excellent" used as a title, a form of address for royalty or nobility (cf. Luke 1:3; Acts 23:26; 24:3; 26:25).

prōteuō [πρωτεύω, *4409*]

prōteuō is a rare verb found only in Col. 1:18, meaning "to be preeminent" in the sense of holding the primary place of power and status.

philoprōteuō [φιλοπρωτεύω, *5383*]

philoprōteuō is a rare variant of ***prōteuō***, above, found only in 3 John 9, meaning "to love to have the preeminence," or to strive for a position of excellence.

EXCHANGE

OT Words

temûrāh [תְּמוּרָה, 8545]

This term occurs only six times and refers to that which is exchanged (i.e., an exchange or substitute) on all but one of these occasions.

Lev. 27:10, 33 cites legislation covering an exchange of ritual offerings. Ruth 4:7 refers to the ancient custom of a commercial transaction involving the exchange of a sandal by the initiating party. The lack of profit from a business transaction is the subject of Job 20:18.

mûr [**מוּר, 4171**]

mûr is a verb found fourteen times with the primary meaning "exchange," "change."

Lev. 27:10, 33 mention an Israelite worshiper "exchanging" animals in order to sacrifice. Ps. 106:20; Jer. 2:11 refer to the idolatrous people of Israel who had "exchanged" the glory of God for images of idols. Ezek. 48:14 contains the injunction directed to the Levites not to "exchange" or sell the portion of land assigned to them, since it was holy ground. All of these details are contained within Ezekiel's visionary revelation of the new temple and the transformed land of Israel.

NT Words

antallagma [ἀντάλλαγμα, *465*]

antallagma is a rare noun found only twice. Matt. 16:26; Mark 8:37 both contain the poignant question posed by Christ "What shall a person give in exchange for their soul?"

metallassō [μεταλλάσσω, *3337*]

metallassō is a rare verb, found only twice in Rom. 1:25, 26, referring first to the idolatrous action of men who had "exchanged" the truth of God for a lie in their idols; and secondly to the immorality of women who also had "exchanged" natural sexual relations for unnatural.

See Also: → CHANGE

EXCUSE

NT Words

apologeomai [ἀπολογέομαι, *626*]

apologeomai is a verb found eleven times, meaning "answer," "excuse," "defend." The former meaning is predominant. (→ ANSWER)

The meaning "excuse" is found in Rom. 2:15, referring to the phenomenon of a person's conscience "excusing" him. In 2 Cor. 12:19 the apostle asks his readers whether they think he and his companions were "defending" themselves.

anapologētos [ἀναπολόγητος, *379*]

anapologētos is a rare adjective found only twice (Rom. 1:20; 2:1), referring to godless people who are "without excuse" in feigning ignorance of God.

paraiteomai [παραιτέομαι, *3868*]

paraiteomai is a verb found nine times, meaning "excuse," "refuse." (→ REFUSE)

Luke 14:18, 19 refer to a man "making excuses" in refusing an invitation to a feast and also requesting to "have himself excused" from such an obligation.

prophasis [πρόφασις, *4392*]

prophasis is a noun occurring seven times, meaning "pretext" in most of these contexts. John 15:22, however, mentions people "having no excuse" for their sin.

EXECUTE

OT Words

'āsāh [**עָשָׂה, 6213**]

This is one of the most common verbs in the Old Testament, occurring over 2,500 times. The dominant sense of ***'āsāh*** is "do," "make." But it also means "execute" in about twenty-five places.

In most cases where ***'āsāh*** indicates the sense of "execute," divine judgment or justice is in view. With regard to the former, the judgment of God is invoked against Egypt (Exod. 12:12; Ezek. 30:19); Moab (Ezek. 25:11); Philistia (Ezek. 25:17). Judgment is also said to fall on the persecutors of the godly Israelites in Ps. 119:84; on the heathen nations in Ps. 149:7, 9; Mic. 5:15; and on his own people for their sin in Ezek. 5:8, 10, 15; 11:9; 16:41. In Hos. 11:9, God is said to refrain from repeating his "execution" against Israel.

"Execution" involving the administration of divine justice is also found in a number of texts. Mic. 7:9 refers to the vindication of God's people. In Deut. 10:18, God is said to "execute" (i.e., defend) the cause of the fatherless and the widow. Jer. 23:5; 33:15 indicate that the Davidic "branch," the coming Messianic King, will "execute" justice in the land.

A number of passages also cite the demand for carrying out or executing human justice (cf. Isa. 16:3; Jer. 7:5; 22:3; Ezek. 45:9). 1 Kgs. 6:12 records God's injunction to Solomon to render obedience to him through the "execution" (i.e., carrying out) of his decrees.

shāphat [**שָׁפַט, 8199**]

This term normally means "judge" or "lead, rule as judge." But on two occasions it means "execute" in the sense of carrying out just and merciful judgments against one's neighbor (cf. Zech. 7:9; 8:16).

NT Words

poieō [**ποιέω,** *4160*]

poieō is a common verb found nearly six hundred times with the predominant meanings "do," "make," with a variety of related senses, including "to execute." John 5:27; Jude 15 mention the Son of God's divine authority to "execute (i.e., pass) judgment" on the wicked.

EXERCISE

NT Words

gymnasia [**γυμνασία,** *1129*]

gymnasia is a rare noun denoting physical "exercise" found only in 1 Tim. 4:8.

exousiazō [**ἐξουσιάζω,** *1850*]

exousiazō is a verb found four times with the underlying sense of "have power, rule over." Luke 22:25 refers to the Gentile rulers "exercising authority" over their people.

EXHORT, EXHORTATION

NT Words

parakaleō [**παρακαλέω,** *3870*]

parakaleō is a common verb with the primary meanings "beseech," "comfort," as well as "exhort" and some related nuances. (→ COMFORT)

The meanings "beseech" and "exhort" are related in contexts where pleas are made in order to produce a certain response or avoid a course of action. The sense of "urge" is indicated in Luke 3:8; Acts 2:40; 11:23; Rom. 12:8; 1 Thess. 2:11; 1 Tim. 2:1; 2 Tim. 4:2; Titus 2:6, 15; Heb. 3:13; 1 Pet. 5:1, 12. In particular, "exhortations" are frequently made in the name of the Lord Jesus (cf. 1 Thess. 4:1; 2 Thess. 3:12).

paraklēsis [**παράκλησις,** *3874*]

paraklēsis is a noun derived from ***parakaleō***, above, found in approximately thirty places, with the principal meanings "comfort," "consolation," and "exhortation." (→ COMFORT) There is, however, some overlap in meaning between all these senses in several contexts. The meaning "exhortation" in the context of teaching and preaching the word of God is evident in Acts 13:15; Rom. 12:8ff.; 1 Tim. 4:13. The related sense of "encouragement" is found, for example, in Acts 15:31; Rom. 15:4; 1 Cor. 14:3; Heb. 12:5. See also 2 Cor. 8:17 for the meaning "appeal," "exhortation" in a general context.

paraineō [**παραινέω,** *3867*]

paraineō is a rare verb found only twice, meaning "urge," "exhort" in Acts 27:9, 22.

protrepō [**προτρέπω,** *4389*]

protrepō is a rare verb found only in Acts 18:27, meaning "exhort" or "encourage" in relation to welcoming friends.

See Also: → COMFORT

EXILE

OT Words

gālāh [**גָּלָה, 1540**]

gālāh is a verb found nearly two hundred times with a variety of meanings including "uncover," "remove," "appear," "captive," "reveal." (→ APPEAR → CAPTIVE → REVEAL → UNCOVER)

gālāh is also used nominally to refer to those in captivity, or "exiles" (cf. 2 Sam. 15:19; Jer. 29:17).

The meaning "be taken into exile" is synonymous with "be carried into captivity" (cf. Isa. 49:21; Jer. 13:19; 29:1ff.; Lam. 1:3; Amos 1:5ff.; 7:11ff.).

EXORCIST

NT Words

exorkistēs [**ἐξορκιστής,** *1845*]

exorkistēs is a rare noun found only in Acts 19:13, denoting itinerant Jewish "exorcists."

EXPECT, EXPECTATION

NT Words

ekdechomai [**ἐκδέχομαι,** *1551*]

ekdechomai is a verb found eight times with the predominant meaning "to wait for." In 1 Cor. 16:11, however, the verb indicates the sense of "expect" in the context of anticipating someone's return. (→ WAIT)

ekdochē [**ἐκδοχή,** *1561*]

ekdochē is a rare noun derived from ***ekdechomai***, above, meaning "prospect" or "expectation" in the context of a terrible anticipation of judgment.

prosdokaō [προσδοκάω, *4328*]

prosdokaō is a verb found eighteen times, meaning "wait for," "look for," "expect." There is occasionally some overlap in meaning.

The meaning "expect" is found in the context of John the Baptist's question of Jesus, asking him if he is the Messiah, or if they should "expect" someone else (cf. Matt. 11:3; Luke 7:19ff.).

The general sense of "expecting" or "looking for" someone is indicated in Matt. 24:50; Luke 3:15; 12:46; Acts 3:5. In Acts 28:6, after Paul had been bitten by an adder, his companions "were expecting" him to swell up.

prosdokia [προσδοκία, *4329*]

prosdokia is a rare noun derived from ***prosdokaō***, above, found only in Luke 21:26; Acts 12:11, meaning "expectation," "anticipation," and, in the former text, "foreboding."

apokaradokia [ἀποκαραδοκία, *603*]

apokaradokia is a rare noun meaning "eager or anxious expectation, or longing." It is used metaphorically in Rom. 8:19, referring to the "eager expectation" of creation for the revealing of the final day when God's people will experience the climax of their redemption. Phil. 1:20 refers to Paul's "eager expectation" of his salvation.

See Also: → HOPE → WAIT

EXPLAIN

OT Words

bā'ar [בָּאַר, **874**]

This is a rare verb, occurring only three times and meaning "declare," "make plain, clear," or "explain."

Deut. 1:5 refers to Moses "declaring" or "explaining" the law he had received from God on Mt. Sinai. Deut. 27:8 speaks of Yahweh instructing Moses to clearly write the words of the law covenant on the memorial stones set up at Mt. Ebal. In Hab. 2:2 God instructs the prophet to write the vision he had been given onto clay tablets with clarity, so that anyone could read it easily.

NT Words

phrazō [φράζω, *5419*]

phrazō is a rare verb found only twice, meaning "explain" in Matt. 13:36; 15:15, referring to the disciples' request to Jesus to "explain" the parable of the weeds to them.

See Also: → EXPOUND → TELL

EXPOSE

NT Words

elenchō [ἐλέγχω, *1651*]

elenchō is a verb occurring eighteen times, meaning "convict," "rebuke," "expose." (→ CONVICT → REBUKE)

The meaning "expose" is used mainly in the context of bringing people's sin to light (cf. John 3:20; Eph. 5:11).

See also Eph. 5:13, where the general sense of "exposing" hidden objects to the light is indicated.

EXPOUND

NT Words

ektithēmi [ἐκτίθημι, *1620*]

ektithēmi is a rare verb found in several places, meaning to "expound" in the sense of "explain" or "interpret." The activity of "expounding" the word of God is indicated in Acts 18:26; 28:23. In Acts 11:4 ***ektithēmi*** means "explain."

epilyō [ἐπιλύω, *1956*]

epilyō is a rare verb found only once, meaning "expound" in the context of Jesus "explaining" the significance of his teaching to his disciples.

diermēneuō [διερμηνεύω, *1329*]

diermēneuō is a verb found in six places, meaning "expound," "interpret" throughout. Luke 24:27 refers to Jesus' response to his disciples in "expounding" or "interpreting" for them the christological focus of the entire Old Testament canon, which points unambiguously to him as its fulfillment.

EXTORT, EXTORTION, EXTORTIONER

NT Words

harpagē [ἁρπαγή, *724*]

harpagē is a noun found three times, denoting the crime of "extortion" by illegal and oppressive means as perpetrated by the religious leaders of the Jewish people against the poor and powerless in that society (cf. Matt. 23:35; Luke 11:39). The "plundering" of property is indicated in Heb. 10:34.

harpax [ἅρπαξ, *727*]

harpax is an adjectival form found five times, translated nominally as "extortioners" in Luke 8:11, and as "robbers" in 1 Cor. 5:10, 11; 6:10. See also Matt. 7:15, where the term refers metaphorically to false prophets as "ravenous" wolves.

See Also: → OPPRESS → SPOIL → STEAL

EYE

OT Words

'ayin [עַיִן, **5869**]

This common noun occurs nearly nine hundred times in the Old Testament, with the predominant meanings "eye," "sight." About half of this usage is rich, diverse, and complex, with a number of perspectives that reflect significant aspects of God's character and purpose in relation to his chosen people, as well as to his enemies. In these contexts, ***'ayin*** reflects a predominantly metaphorical sense.

With reference to people, the "opening of one's eyes" brings a realization of sinfulness. This is evident in Gen. 3:5, 7, for example. In contrast, Judg. 17:6; 21:25 refer to the attitude that denies the presence of sin in one's life: "everyone did what was right in their own eyes." Ps. 19:8 refers to the impact that Yahweh makes on the lives of his people, "enlightening" their eyes. There are also several examples of God opening his people's eyes in miraculous ways. For example, in 2 Kgs. 6:17 God permits the servant of Elisha to catch a glimpse of the heavenly army in the treetops encircling the city of Samaria — a sign that God will deliver the city from the besieging Arameans. See also 2 Kgs. 6:20. Divine illumination and understanding are given to God's people in Ezra 9:8 (cf. also. Prov. 29:13). Opening the eyes of the blind is also declared to be part of the Servant of Yahweh's mission in Isa. 42:7 (cf. also Isa. 35:5).

By far the most significant usage of ***'ayin*** is in contexts where the "eyes of God" or "the sight of God" are spoken of anthropomorphically, focusing on matters that grab God's attention and act as catalysts for both his mercy and judgment. Gen. 6:8, for example, contains the striking observation that Noah found grace in the eyes of the Lord — Noah and his family constituted the remnant of the human race who survived the universal flood, gave humanity a second start, and facilitated the ongoing development of God's plan of salvation for his people.

Yahweh's gaze of favor on the righteous, on those who fear him, is mentioned in Pss. 33:18; 34:15. In Jer. 24:6, God declares that he will "set his eye" on them for good, as part of his promise to renew and transform his disobedient people. Amos 9:4, 8, on the other hand, illustrate divine justice and judgment against the people of Israel for their sin, when Yahweh declares that he will set his eye against them for evil. In one of the most striking examples of this phenomenon in Scripture, Zech. 3:9 refers to the "seven eyes of God" on the stone attached to the high priest Joshua's turban. Through this "redemptive gaze" directed at the stone, Yahweh accepts the high priestly offering on behalf of his people on the Day of Atonement, and thereby removes their sin in a single day. It is a distinctive prefiguring of the atoning work of Christ on the cross (cf. also Zech. 4:10; Lev. 16; Exod. 28:36ff.). As a consequence, the people are renewed in their relationship with him. One poignant metaphor that expresses God's unique and intimate relationship with Israel is the phrase "the apple of his eye," an expression that alludes to the great delight Yahweh takes in his people. This is found in Ps. 17:8; Zech. 2:8, where God issues a terrifying warning of destruction against those nations who would dare to touch his people, "the apple of his eye."

In contrast, God is also said to "hide his eyes" from his people, as a sign of judgment against them (cf. Isa. 1:15, 16). In Isa. 29:10, the eyes of the prophets (presumably the false ones) are said to be closed by God. And, in Hos. 13:4, such is the sin of the Israelites that all compassion will be hidden from his eyes, and divine judgment will be inevitable. Such judgment is expressed in even stronger terms in Ezek. 5:11; 7:4, 9; 8:18; 9:10, where the prophet affirms that God's eye will not spare his people from punishment. However, Ezek. 20:17 also states that the divine "eye" did in fact spare them during their time of wandering in the wilderness. The point to note here is that Yahweh's punishment of his people is never enacted in an absolute sense — there is always an accompanying promise of deliverance, forgiveness, and renewal.

Similarly, the phenomenon referred to as "the sight of God" commonly expresses the same duality of blessing and curse. In Exod. 33:6, for example, God finds Moses favorable in his sight; as he does the Israelite people themselves in Exod. 33:13ff.; 34:9 (cf. also Num. 11:11ff.; Judg. 6:17). Lev. 10:19 speaks of offerings made in the sight of God.

The texts that describe doing both good and evil "in the sight of God," actions which lead to covenant blessing and curse respectively, are of particular significance here. The former is indicated, for example, in Exod. 15:6; Deut. 6:18; 12:25; 2 Sam. 15:2; 1 Kgs. 3:10; 14:8; 22:43; 2 Kgs. 10:30; Jer. 34:15. In addition to these examples, blessings conditional on doing good in the sight of God are indicated in 1 Kgs. 11:38. Related to this perspective is the observation that Yahweh will do what is "good in his sight," i.e., what is in accord with his purpose in salvation (cf. 2 Sam. 10:12; 2 Kgs. 3:18). The corollary to this is "doing what is evil in God's sight." General references to such activity are found in Deut. 4:25; 9:18; Judg. 10:6; 13:1; 1 Sam. 12:17; Isa. 65:12; Jer. 18:10. Especially noteworthy in this regard are David's murder of Uriah the Hittite (2 Sam. 12:9); Solomon's idolatry (1 Kgs. 11:6); Saul's rejection of Yahweh (1 Sam. 15:19); and David's confession (Ps. 51:4). Israel's idolatry as a constant evil in the sight of God is also frequently mentioned, mostly in the books of Kings and the parallels in Chronicles (e.g., 1 Kgs. 11:33; 14:22; 15:26; 16:9; 21:20; 2 Kgs. 3:2; 14:24; 17). See also Jer. 7:30; 32:30; 52:2. Further development of this perspective on "doing evil in the sight of God" is found in passages where God's eyes are said to be directed towards those who are wicked as a prelude to their judgment (cf. 2 Sam. 22:8; 2 Kgs. 19:16; Job 24:23; Pss. 5:6; 66:7; Jer. 32:19). In addition, God is said to shut people's eyes as a punishment, blinding them to godly, spiritual realities (cf. Isa. 44:18; 59:10).

Pleas are also directed to God that he might open his eyes towards his people, and the temple, as a prelude to hearing and accepting their prayers of repentance (cf. 1 Kgs. 8:29, 52; 2 Chr. 6:20, 40; 9:3; Neh. 1:6; Ps. 17:2). Tied in with this theme is the promise of Yahweh in Zech. 9:8; 12:4 to keep his eyes on (i.e., keep watch over) his people in order to protect them.

In addition to being used with respect to God in an anthropomorphic sense, *'ayin* is also found in a number of significant texts emphasizing human response, whether it be towards God or towards other people. For example, Pss. 25:15; 123:1ff. speak about lifting one's eyes to God in prayerful worship. In the book of Proverbs, *'ayin* is used metaphorically. It describes the "eyes" as the focus of the human heart, or inner being (cf. Prov. 3:4ff.; 4:21; 23:26; 27:20; 30:17). Secondly, it indicates a profoundly conceited assessment of oneself as being right or smug "in one's own eyes" (cf. Prov. 12:15; 16:2; 21:2; 28:11; 30:12). See also Isa. 2:11; 5:15, 21; 10:12. The Song of Songs refers to "eyes" in the context of mutual attraction between the lover and his beloved (cf. Song 1:15; 4:1; 5:12; 6:5; 7:4; 8:10). Finally, *'ayin* is used in the book of Lamentations in a poetic sense to refer to God's people copiously weeping in Jerusalem in the wake of the destruction of their city (cf. Lam. 1:16; 2:11; 3:48).

NT Words

ophthalmos [ὀφθαλμός, *3788*]

ophthalmos is the predominant term for "eye" in the New Testament. It is used both literally and metaphorically and is found in approximately one hundred contexts.

References to the "eye(s)" in the literal, physiological sense are found in Matt. 5:29; 13:15ff.; Mark 8:18; Luke 2:30; 24:31; John 4:35; 11:37ff.; Acts 9:8; 26:18, 27; 1 Cor. 12:16ff.; Gal. 3:1; 4:15; Heb. 4:13; 1 John 1:1; Rev. 1:7; 3:18; 21:4.

The expression "before one's eyes" indicates the sense of "from one's heart or mind" as a response to something observed, like the fear of God (cf. Rom. 3:18).

Metaphorical references to the "eye(s)" as an instrument of spiritual perception are evident in Rom. 11:8, 10; 1 Cor. 2:9; Eph. 1:18; 1 John 2:11. "Eyes full of adultery" are noted in 2 Pet. 2:14. The vice of the "lust of the eyes" is noted in 1 John 2:16. The phrase "twinkling of an eye," indicating the briefest moment of time, is found in 1 Cor. 15:52.

Anthropomorphic references to the "eyes of the Lord" are found in 1 Pet. 3:12; and in the visionary context of John's revelation in Rev. 1:14; 2:18; 5:6; 19:12. See also Rev. 4:6ff.

monophthalmos [μονόφθαλμος, *3442*]

monophthalmos is a rare adjectival form derived from ***ophthalmos***, above, denoting the disability of having only "one eye" (cf. Matt. 18:9; Mark 9:47).

omma [ὄμμα, *3659*]

omma is a rare term denoting a "human eye," found only in Mark 8:23.

trymalia [τρυμαλιά, *5168*]

trymalia is a rare noun denoting "the eye" of a needle in Mark 10:25; Luke 18:25.

trypēma [τρύπημα, *5169*]

trypēma is a rare variant of ***trymalia***, above, denoting the "eye" of a needle in Matt. 19:24.

Additional Notes

The terms for "eye," "(eye)sight" in the Old Testament are used in a variety of rich and complex ways.

There is not the same degree of diversity or complexity in the New Testament. In the Old Testament, the phenomenon of "eyes" and "sight," when applied to the person of God, yields significant insights into the divine character and plan of salvation. Reflection on the "eyes" of Yahweh teaches us that the actions of his chosen people, as well as those outside of the covenant, can never escape the scrutiny of his "gaze" — whether it be for good or ill. Nothing can be hidden from him. We also discover from this usage that the "eyes of God" are indeed the gateway, in an anthropomorphic sense, to the heart of his own being. Such "eyes" are capable of expressing both compassion and delight as well as terrifying wrath and judgment. Of all the biblical metaphors that relate to the person and character of God, this is one of the most potent and illuminating.

EYE SALVE

NT Words

kollourion [κολλούριον, *2854*]

kollourion is a rare noun denoting the medicinal "eye salve" produced by the city of Laodicea, as noted in Rev. 3:18.

EYEWITNESS

NT Words

autoptēs [αὐτόπτης, *845*]

autoptēs is a rare noun denoting an "eyewitness" to the ministry of Christ in Luke 1:2.

epoptēs [ἐπόπτης, *2030*]

epoptēs is a rare synonym for ***autoptēs***, above, denoting "eyewitnesses" to the majesty of Christ through his miraculous signs in 2 Pet. 1:16.

F

FACE

OT Words

***pānîm* [פָּנִים, 6440]**

pānîm is a common plural noun form found in approximately 2,100 contexts. In about 400 of these contexts it means "face," "countenance." (→ PERSON → PRESENCE → VISION)

In a literal sense, ***pānîm*** refers to a person's physical countenance (cf. Gen. 4:5, 6; 31:21; Lev. 13:41; Num. 12:14; Deut. 1:17; Ruth 2:10; 1 Sam. 16:12; 2 Sam. 19:4; 1 Kgs. 19:13; Esth. 7:8; Job 4:15; Ezek. 27:35; Dan. 5:6). In Exod. 34:28ff., the word refers to Moses' shining face, gleaming with reflected glory after his prolonged meeting with God on Mt. Sinai. ***pānîm*** also refers to the faces of angels and cherubim (cf. Isa. 6:2; Ezek. 1:10; 10:14). In Ezek. 41:14 the term refers to the "face" of the temple — that is, its front wall.

pānîm is also commonly found with the verb "fall," with several different connotations. For example, Gen. 17:17 refers to Abraham falling on his face laughing. In 1 Sam. 17:49 Goliath falls down on his face, dead. David and Jonathan fall on their faces weeping together in 1 Sam. 20:41. The Philistine idol Dagon is cast down on its face by the power of Yahweh in 1 Sam. 5:3, in mockery of the Philistines' attempt to usurp his power. There are also a number of contexts in which "falling on one's face" expresses the posture of worship or prayer before God (e.g., Gen. 17:3, Josh. 5:14; Isa. 49:23; Ezek. 1:28; 3:23; 11:13). Num. 22:31 records the intriguing incident of Balaam falling down in reverence before the angel of the Lord. ***pānîm*** is also found in the phrase "lifting one's face to God (in prayer)" (e.g., Ezra 9:6; Isa. 38:2; Lam. 2:19; Dan. 9:4). To "fall on one's face" also expresses an attitude of reverence towards someone in authority or to someone deemed worthy of honor in the eyes of the beholder (cf. 1 Sam. 24:8; 2 Sam. 9:6 [Mephibosheth bowing before King David]; Dan. 2:46 [Nebuchnadezzar paying honor to Daniel]).

The expression "the face of the Lord" is an anthropomorphism for the person of God. For example, in Exod. 33:20 God declares that no one may see his face and live. 1 Chr. 16:11 enjoins people to seek God's face at all times. 2 Chr. 30:9 expresses Yahweh's promise to turn his face in blessing to his people when they repent. See also Gen. 19:13; Num. 6:25, 26; Ps. 24:6; 1 Kgs. 1:23; 2 Chr. 7:14; Dan. 10:6.

There are a number of metaphorical uses of the term ***pānîm***. The term refers in a number of texts to the physical surface of the earth and expanses of water (e.g., Gen. 1:2; 2:6; 7:18; 11:8, 9; Exod. 10:5; 16:14; Deut. 7:6; 1 Sam. 20:18; 1 Kgs. 13:34; Isa. 23:17; Jer. 8:2; 25:26; Dan. 8:5; Zech. 5:3).

pānîm also refers to the "face" of people, indicating their whole being. The term is used in the first, second, and third person (i.e., "my face," "your face," etc.) (e.g., Gen. 30:33; 50:18; Exod. 10:20; 14:19, 25; Deut. 25:2, 9; 2 Sam. 3:13).

pānîm is also used in the expression "to hide one's face," in the context of fearing God (cf. Exod. 3:6; Job 13:4; Ps. 13:1). This expression is also predicated of God, and in this instance it expresses God's judgment against those who oppose him (e.g., Deut. 31:17; Ps. 30:7; Isa. 6:2; Ezek. 39:29; Mic. 3:4). In several instances the psalmist pleads with God not to hide his face from him (cf. Pss. 27:9; 102:2; 143:1). Further to the theme of divine judgment on rebellion, God is also said to "set his face against" those who do rebel against him (cf. Lev. 17:10; 26:17; Ps. 34:16; Jer. 44:11; Ezek. 14:8). In Ps. 51:9, David pleads with God to hide his face from the royal sin of adultery and murder.

The expression "face to face," when predicated of an encounter with God, signifies an intimate communion with the person of Yahweh (cf. Gen. 32:30 [Jacob]; Exod. 33:11 [Moses]; Deut. 5:14 [Sinai theophany]). In Ezek. 20:35, however, the context is one of divine judgment, where God is said to have confronted his people in the desert "face to face."

Finally, ***pānîm*** occurs in the phrase "set one's face . . . ," an expression that implies determination of purpose (e.g., Isa. 50:7 [predicated of the suffering servant of Yahweh]; Ezek. 4:3; 6:2; 28:21; 38:2).

***mar'eh* [מַרְאֶה, 4758]**

This noun occurs about one hundred times with the primary meaning "appearance," "vision." However, ***mar'eh*** is also translated "countenance" (i.e., "face") in a limited number of contexts. (→ APPEARANCE → VISION)

mar'eh refers literally to the face of an angel in Judg. 13:6. See also 1 Sam. 17:42; 2 Sam. 14:27; Esth.

2:2ff.; Song 5:15; Dan. 1:13, 15. Isa. 52:14 contains the prophetic anticipation of the crucifixion of the Messiah, expressed in a reference to the "marred countenance" of the suffering servant.

NT WORDS

prosōpon [πρόσωπον, *4383*]

prosōpon is a noun occurring nearly eighty times with underlying reference to the front of the human head, translated for the most part "face," "countenance." (→ PERSON)

Literal references to the human face include those in Matt. 6:16; 17:6; Mark 14:65; Luke 5:12; 17:6; Acts 20:25; 1 Cor. 14:25; 2 Cor. 11:20; Jas. 1:23; Rev. 4:7; 7:11; 9:7. The expression "face to face," indicating a personal confrontation, is found in Acts 25:16; 1 Thess. 3:10; 2 Cor. 10:1; Gal. 2:11, in a human setting. It is also found in the context of a human being in the presence of the Lord in 1 Cor. 13:12 (cf. also 2 Cor. 3:18).

Occasionally the term is used as a synonym for one's person, translated as the personal pronoun "you" in Matt. 11:10; Mark 1:2; Luke 7:27, and as "him" in Luke 10:1.

The metaphorical sense of "appearance" is indicated with reference to the "sky" in Matt. 16:3; Luke 12:56.

The transfigured "face" of Christ on the mountain before his disciples Peter, James, and John is described in Matt. 17:2; Luke 9:29; as is the "face" of Stephen, the first Christian martyr, at the point of his death in Acts 6:15. Reference to Moses' "face" is found in 2 Cor. 3:7. Other references to the "face" of Christ include 2 Cor. 4:6; Rev. 10:1.

The "face" (i.e., surface) of the earth is referred to in Luke 21:35; Acts 17:26; Rev. 20:11.

Anthropomorphic references to the "face" of God are found in Matt. 18:10; 1 Pet. 3:12; Rev. 6:16; 22:14. Similarly, the expression "before the face of the Lord" is often simply translated "before the Lord" (e.g., Luke 1:76). Acts 23:19; 2 Thess. 1:9; Heb. 9:24 mention the Lord's "presence."

The expression "set one's face," denoting a determined intention, is noted in relation to Christ in Luke 9:51ff.

prosōpon also denotes a person's "presence" in Acts 2:28; 3:13.

opsis [ὄψις, *3799*]

opsis is a rare term denoting a person's "face" in John 11:44, and the "face" of the heavenly Christ in Rev. 1:16.

eidea [εἰδέα, *2397*]

eidea is a rare noun found only in Matt. 28:3, denoting the dazzling "appearance" of the angel who appeared at the tomb from which Christ had risen from the dead.

stoma [στόμα, *4750*]

stoma is a term with the primary sense of "mouth" for most of its nearly eighty occurrences. In several places, however, ***stoma*** denotes a person's "face." The expression "face to face," indicating friendly social intercourse, is found in 3 John 14; 2 John 12.

Additional Notes

The vocabulary for "face" is used similarly in both Old and New Testaments. ***pānîm*** and ***prosōpon***, for example, both emphasize the distinction between the "face" as part of one's physical features and as a symbolic term for the complete person. This is true for both human beings and God, including references to Christ. References to the "face of God" in the Old Testament carry a greater theological weight, indicating the majestic presence of the God of Israel through the ritual phenomena of ark, tabernacle, and temple. To violate the sanctity of God's presence (i.e., his face) was to court disaster and bring the severe chastisement of God. It is not that the new covenant believer is to fear God any less — rather, the expression the "face of God" in the Old Testament very clearly emphasizes his holy presence, which may never be taken lightly without terrifying consequences.

See Also: → EYE

FADE AWAY

OT WORDS

nābēl [נָבֵל, **5034**]

This verb occurs around twenty-five times and is translated "fade," "fade away" in about half of these contexts. The uses of ***nābēl*** with this meaning are both figurative and literal.

In 2 Sam. 22:46; Ps. 18:45, the term means "fade away" in the sense of "losing heart." In a number of texts ***nābēl*** means "fade" in the sense of "wither" (e.g., Isa. 1:30; Jer. 8:13; Ezek. 47:12). ***nābēl*** also refers to the phenomenon of a flower losing color, or wilting (e.g., Isa. 28:1, 4; 40:7, 8).

NT WORDS

marainō [μαραίνω, *3133*]

marainō is a verb found only in Jas. 1:11, referring to the rich man "fading away" in the middle of his exploits, indicating his inevitable perishing or destruction.

amarantos [ἀμάραντος, *263*]

amarantos is a rare adjectival form found only twice. In 1 Pet. 1:4 the believer's inheritance is described as "unfading," reserved in heaven with complete security. Similarly, 1 Pet. 5:4 refers to the believer's "unfading" crown of glory.

FAIL

OT Words

kālāh **[כָּלָה, 3615]**

This verb means "end," "complete," or "finish." It is found about two hundred times, with these three meanings accounting for half the occurrences of the term. ***kālāh*** is also translated "fail" on eighteen occasions, in a variety of contexts. (→ FINISH)

In most instances, this term expresses the idea of "failing" in the sense of losing function or capacity — for example, eyesight (cf. Job 11:20; Ps. 69:3; Lam. 4:17); strength (cf. Pss. 71:9; 73:26); anger (cf. Prov. 22:28); new growth (cf. Isa. 15:6; 32:10); and a failing spirit that leads to despair (cf. Ps. 143:7). The glory of the nation of Arabia is condemned to "fail" (i.e., die out) in Isa. 21:16. With a slightly different connotation in Lam. 3:22, God's mercy is declared never to fail (i.e., it never ceases to have an effect).

kārat **[כָּרַת, 3772]**

kārat occurs around three hundred times with the primary meanings "cut," "cut down," but it also means "fail" on six occasions. It is used negatively in 2 Sam. 3:29 as a curse on the lineage of Joab: "Let there not fail to be someone who has . . . leprosy . . ." In contrast, the other uses of ***kārat*** in this sense express the opposite — the continuous blessing of unbroken succession for the lineage of Solomon, contingent on obedience to Yahweh (cf. 1 Kgs. 2:4; 8:25; 9:5; 2 Chr. 6:16; 7:18).

The usage of this verb in the sense of "fail" is interesting. Though it occurs infrequently compared with the dominant sense of "cut" or "cut off," the two senses are related. The making (or cutting) of a covenant (in the positive context of divine blessing), and the "cutting off" or destroying of those who violate God's covenant decrees and purposes (in the negative context of judgment) both constitute a significant advancement of the divine purpose. In all six occurrences of ***kārat*** where the sense of "failing" is in view, the expression "let there not fail to be . . ." is utilized in the context of either judgment (against those who violate God's law), or blessing (with God's covenant promises regarding the lineage of David in view). There is clearly a theological consistency in the usage of ***kārat***, whether it refers to "cutting" or "failing."

rāphāh **[רָפָה, 7503]**

This term occurs around fifty times with the dominant sense of "being feeble." ***rāphāh*** is translated "fail" on four occasions: Deut. 31:6, 8; Josh. 1:5; 1 Chr. 28:20. In these texts God promises never "to fail" or "abandon" his people.

nāphal **[נָפַל, 5307]**

nāphal is a common verb meaning "fall," as well as related nuances, for most of its nearly 450 occurrences. However, it also means "fail" in several instances.

In 1 Sam. 17:32, David exhorts Saul not to let anyone's heart "fail" on account of Goliath, the Philistine giant. References to not one of God's promises "failing" are found in Josh. 21:45; 23:14; 1 Kgs. 8:56.

NT Words

ekleipō [ἐκλείπω, *1587*]

ekleipō is a verb found in three only places meaning "fail" in each instance. Luke 16:9 refers to worldly wealth "failing" (i.e., ceasing to exist).

In Luke 22:32 Jesus promises to pray for Peter, that his faith may not fail. Heb. 1:12 affirms that the years belonging to God will never fail (i.e., will never end).

anekleiptos [ἀνέκλειπτος, *413*]

anekleiptos is a rare adjectival form derived from ***ekleipō***, above, found only in Luke 12:33 and referring to one's treasure in heaven that does not fail (i.e., it remains forever).

FAINT

OT Words

yā'aph **[יָעַף, 3286]**

This term occurs nine times and means "be weary" or "faint." The latter sense occurs in four of these contexts. Isa. 40:28 declares that God the Creator never grows faint. Isa. 40:30, 31 affirms that young men will not faint when they wait upon the Lord. Isa. 44:12 refers to physical "faintness" through lack of water. (→ WEARY)

'āṭaph **[עָטַף, 5848]**

This verb is found on fifteen occasions, with the predominant sense of "be feeble," "weakened," or "faint."

The meaning "faint" in the sense of physical weakness is found in Gen. 30:42; Lam. 2:11, 19. ***'āṭaph*** also indicates "faintness" in the sense of emotional and spiritual depression (cf. Pss. 61:2; 102:1; 143:4; Jonah 2:7). In the above contexts, when the one who is suffering faintness and weakness of spirit seeks help, the plea for help is always made to God, the source of all strength.

rākak **[רָכַךְ, 7401]**

rākak is a verb meaning "be faint" in the sense of "timid," "fearful" in four of the eight occurrences of the term. (→ TENDER)

Exhortations not to let one's heart grow faint (i.e., not be overcome with fear) are found in Deut. 20:3; Isa. 7:4; Jer. 51:46. In Job 23:16 the patriarch charges God with having made his heart faint.

mûg **[מוּג, 4127]**

mûg is a verb with the primary sense of "melt," "dissolve" for most of its seventeen occurrences. However, the term signifies "to be fainthearted" (i.e., overcome with fear) in Josh. 2:24. (→ MELT)

'ûph **[עוּף, 5774]**

'ûph is a verb with the principal meaning "to fly" for most of the thirty or so occurrences of the term. In several places it also means "to be faint."

References to people being "faint" with hunger are found in 1 Sam. 14:28, 31. The experience of being "faint" with fear is noted in 2 Sam. 22:11.

pāgar **[פָּגַר, 6296]**

pāgar is a rare verb found only in 1 Sam. 30:10, 21, signifying the state of "fainting" with exhaustion.

dawwāy **[דַּוָּי, 1742]**

dawwāy is a rare adjective found three times, all denoting the condition of "faintness (of heart)" in the context of deep anguish (cf. Isa. 1:5; Jer. 8:18; Lam. 1:22).

dāweh **[דָּוֶה, 1739]**

dāweh is a rare adjectival variant of ***dawwāy***, above, denoting a condition of "faintness" in the context of anguish in Lam. 1:13.

'ālaph **[עָלַף, 5968]**

'ālaph is a verb meaning "to faint" (with exhaustion) in three contexts (cf. Isa. 51:20; Amos 8:13; Jonah 4:8).

NT Words

eklyō **[ἐκλύω, *1590*]**

eklyō is a verb found six times meaning "to faint" throughout.

Matt. 15:32; Mark 8:3 mention people in danger of "fainting" (with hunger). Exhortations not to "faint," or lose heart, are found in Gal. 6:9; Heb. 12:3, 5.

See Also: → SICK → TENDER → WEARY

FAITH

NT Words

pistis **[πίστις, *4102*]**

pistis is the most common term denoting "faith" in the New Testament, with the underlying senses of "belief," "trust," and "conviction" in the person of God and Christ as the only means of salvation, forgiveness of sin, and guarantee of eternal life. In most cases, the meanings "belief" and "faith" are interchangeable.

The designation "faith" in the general sense of belief and trust in Christ or God is indicated in Matt. 17:20; Luke 8:25; Acts 14:9, 27; Rom. 1:8, 17; Eph. 6:16; 1 Thess. 3:2ff.; 1 Tim. 1:19; 2 Tim. 1:13; Titus 2:2; Heb. 10:22; 11:1; Jas. 1:3; 2:14ff.; 1 Pet. 1:5ff.; 2 Pet. 1:5.

The exercise of faith in Christ as a prerequisite for healing is noted in Matt. 8:10; 9:29; 15:28; Mark 2:5; 10:52; Luke 5:20; Acts 3:16; and as the specific prerequisite for salvation in Acts 3:22ff.; Rom. 5:1ff.; 10:17; 1 Cor. 15:14ff.; Gal. 2:16, 20; 3:2ff.; Eph. 1:15; 2:8; Phil. 3:9; Rev. 14:12. Related to this is the corresponding quality of faith in God under the old covenant (cf. Rom. 4:5ff.; Gal. 3:7; 1 Tim. 3:13; Heb. 11:2ff.). Heb. 4:2 notes that this quality was totally lacking in the Israelite people when they first approached the borders of Canaan. Non-specific references to "faith" include those found in Matt. 23:23; Acts 6:5; Rom. 1:5; 14:1; 1 Cor. 13:1, 13; 2 Cor. 5:7.

Specific references to "the faith" as a designation for Christianity as a system of belief centered on the person of Christ are found in Acts 13:8; 14:22; 2 Cor. 13:5; Gal. 1:23; Eph. 4:13; Phil. 1:25ff.; Col. 1:23; 2:7; 1 Tim. 1:2; 4:1; 2 Tim. 4:7; Titus 1:13; Jas. 2:1; Jude 3; Rev. 13:10. See also Eph. 4:5. "Faith" is described specifically as a gift of God in 1 Cor. 12:9.

pistis denotes "assurance" in the sense of the conviction of a certain outcome in relation to salvation in Acts 17:31.

The attribute of "faithfulness" is predicated of God in Rom. 3:3; and is listed as a fruit of the Spirit in Gal. 5:22.

The specific sense of "belief" in the truth of the gospel is indicated in 2 Thess. 2:13.

oligopistos [ὀλιγόπιστος, *3640*]

oligopistos is a rare adjective found only in Matt. 6:30 denoting doubting believers as people "of little faith."

Additional Notes

The phenomenon of "faith" is intertwined in the Old Testament with the related phenomena of "belief" and "trust" — as far as these attitudes toward God are concerned. One cannot understand any of these in isolation from the other two. Throughout the Old Testament, the vocabulary for "faith" is more commonly translated "belief" or "trust." The adjectival sense of "faithful" is more frequent, especially in relation to the character of Yahweh.

See Also: ➞ BELIEF ➞ FAITHFUL ➞ TRUST

FAITHFUL, FAITHLESS

OT Words

'ēmûn [אֵמוּן, **529**]

This term is the masculine (and much rarer) form of the noun ***'ĕmûnāh*** (see below). ***'ēmûn*** occurs only five times, meaning "faith" or "trust."

In Deut. 32:20, God condemns Israel for her faithlessness. Prov. 13:17 contains a commendation for a faithful (i.e., trustworthy) messenger (cf. also Prov. 14:5; 20:6). Isa. 26:2 contains a prophetic anticipation of the righteous (i.e., faithful) nation of Israel returning to Jerusalem.

'emûnāh [אֱמוּנָה, **530**]

This is a derivative form of ***'ēmûn***, above, occurring about fifty times — again with the dominant sense of "faith" and "trust." Underlying this is the sense of "truthfulness" when ***'emûnāh*** is predicated of Yahweh.

"Faithfulness," a characteristic of the divine nature, is the inherent element of divine truth. God's faithfulness is integrally bound up with absolute truthfulness; and ***'emûnāh*** is sometimes translated "truth" (➞ TRUE). Examples of this particular usage are found in Deut. 32:4; Pss. 33:4; 89:1ff.; 119:30, 75, 86, 90, 138. Isa. 25:1 refers to Yahweh's plan as faithful and sure, and in Lam. 3:23 the prophet Jeremiah extols the faithfulness of God, who will be true to his promises to his people and shower his mercy upon them. Associated with this characteristic of God is the "faithfulness" of the Messianic Servant of Yahweh in Isa. 11:5.

On the human level, faithfulness is portrayed as a human quality deserving of reward or approval from God (cf. 1 Sam. 26:23; Prov. 12:22). Hab. 2:4 records the truth that the righteous shall live by their faith (i.e., trust in God).

"Faithfulness" also describes honest dealings in business transactions. For example, in 2 Kgs. 12:15 such a virtue is predicated of those handling the financial matters relating to the restoration of the temple (cf. also 2 Kgs. 22:7; 2 Chr. 31:12ff.; 34:12).

'āman [אָמַן, **539**]

'āman is a verb found in more than 100 contexts with a variety of meanings. The most common of these meanings are "to believe" and the adjectival sense of "faithful." (➞ BELIEF)

The meaning "faithful" in the sense of "devoted to one's duty" is evident in relation to Moses in Num. 12:7; to a faithful priest in 1 Sam. 2:35; to David in 1 Sam. 22:14. Other references with this meaning include 2 Sam. 20:19; Neh. 13:13; Prov. 25:13. God is described as "faithful" in the sense of honoring his covenant promises in Deut. 7:9; Isa. 49:7. See also Jer. 42:5.

Specific references to people deemed "faithful" to God include Neh. 9:8; Pss. 12:1; 31:23; 101:6; Hos. 11:12. The meaning "faithful" in the sense of "morally upright" is indicated in relation to the city of Jerusalem in Isa. 1:21, 26.

NT Words

pistos [πιστός, *4103*]

pistos is the standard adjectival term in the New Testament for "faithful," found about seventy times.

The meaning "faithful" in the sense of "devoted to duty" is predicated of servants in Matt. 24:45; 25:21ff.; Luke 12:42; 16:10ff.; 1 Cor. 4:2; 1 Tim. 3:11; 1 Pet. 5:12, and of Moses in Heb. 3:5.

Believers who are "faithful" are described in Acts 16:15; 1 Cor. 4:17; Eph. 1:1; 6:21; Col. 1:2, 7; 4:7ff.; 2 Tim. 2:2; Titus 1:6; Rev. 1:5; 2:10ff.; 3:14; 17:14. See also Gal. 3:9; 1 Tim. 1:12. God is described as "faithful," implying the consistent honoring of his promises, in 1 Cor. 1:9; 10:13; 2 Cor. 1:18; 1 Thess. 5:24; 2 Tim. 2:13; Heb. 10:23; 11:11; 1 John 1:9. He is described as the "faithful" Creator in 1 Pet. 4:19.

References to "faithful" or "sure" sayings are found in 1 Tim. 1:15; 2 Tim. 2:11; Rev. 22:6.

Jesus Christ is described as a "faithful" high priest in Heb. 2:17; and as a "faithful" son to his Father in Heb. 3:2; and he is given the name "Faithful" in Rev. 19:11.

apistos [ἄπιστος, *571*]

apistos is an adjective found in around twenty contexts meaning "unfaithful," "faithless," "unbelieving" throughout. (→ UNBELIEF)

Additional Notes

The faithfulness of God in the Old Testament is frequently, if not universally, cited in relation to the plans and purposes of God. Yahweh is consistently portrayed as a God of absolute integrity, true to his word and thoroughly dependable. Such a perspective is likewise observable in the New Testament.

FALL, FALLEN

OT Words

nāphal [נָפַל, 5307]

This verb is found approximately four hundred times with the primary sense of "fall" and associated nuances. ***nāphal*** has both a literal and figurative meaning.

In its literal sense, ***nāphal*** refers to falling in a variety of ways. It means "fall" in the sense of "descend" or "come upon"— such as sleep, for example as a prelude to the theophanic revelation to Abraham (cf. Gen. 15:12); or the "fire of the Lord" (cf. 1 Kgs. 18:38); or to the action of falling upon someone in order to seize them (e.g., Gen. 43:18; Judg. 16:30). It also commonly means "stumble over, into" (e.g., Gen. 14:10; Deut. 22:8; 1 Sam. 5:4; Isa. 9:10; Dan. 11:19); or "drop to the ground" (cf. Lev. 11:32; Josh. 6:5 [the walls of Jericho]; 2 Sam. 4:4).

The phrase "fall on one's face" also occurs in a number of contexts where laughing (e.g., Gen. 17:17); or crying (e.g., Gen. 33:4; 50:1) is concerned. More common and more significant, however, are the references to falling on one's face to worship God (e.g., Gen. 17:3; Num. 20:6; Josh. 5:14; Ezek. 1:28; Dan. 8:17); or to falling down in fear and terror of him (cf. Lev. 9:24; Josh. 7:6, 10; 13:20; Ezek. 9:8; 11:13). The phrase is also used to indicate respect of other persons (e.g., Gen. 44:4; 50:18; Ruth 2:10; 2 Sam. 1:4; 2 Kgs. 4:37).

There are, in addition, a number of contexts in which ***nāphal*** is used in a figurative sense. "Falling" may indicate, for instance, being overwhelmed by a strong emotion such as sadness and anger (e.g., Gen. 4:5, 6 [Cain]); or fear (e.g., Exod. 15:16; Josh. 2:9; Ps. 55:4; Dan. 10:7). The phenomenon of the judgment of the Lord "falling" on those who curse God is very significant. Such an experience is predicated first of all of the nations at large (e.g., Isa. 24:20; Jer. 25:34); as well as Lebanon (cf. Isa. 10:34); Babylon (cf. Isa. 21:9; 47:11; Jer. 50:15); Assyria (cf. Isa. 31:8; 37:7); Egypt (cf. Isa. 46:12; Ezek. 29:5); and Moab (cf. Jer. 48:44). A similar judgment also awaits the people of God who are disobedient. Judah is indicted (cf. Jer. 6:15; 9:22; Isa. 3:8; Ezek. 5:12; 11:10; Lam. 1:7); as well as Israel (cf. Amos 3:4, 8:14; Hos. 7:16; Zech. 11:2). Lucifer, too, is declared to "have fallen under" the judgment of God in Isa. 14:12. In a more general sense, ***nāphal*** also refers to "falling" in relation to major catastrophe (cf. 2 Kgs. 14:10; Ps. 5:10).

Finally, the literal and figurative sense merge in the usage of ***nāphal*** when referring to "falling" in the sense of "perish" (e.g., Exod. 32:28; Judg. 3:25; 1 Sam. 4:10; 1 Kgs. 22:20), which occasionally incorporates the experience of "falling by the sword" (i.e., perishing in battle) (cf. Num. 14:29; Josh. 8:24; Judg. 4:16; 2 Sam. 3:29).

pāga' [פָּגַע, 6293]

A term occurring about fifty times with the primary sense of "meet" or "encounter," ***pāga'*** also means "fall upon" in contexts of hostility on twelve occasions. For example, Exod. 5:3 refers to the threat of the wrath of God falling upon the Israelites, invoked as the rationale behind the people's request to Pharaoh to let them go into the wilderness to sacrifice to Yahweh. See also Judg. 8:21; 1 Sam. 22:17; 2 Sam. 1:15; 1 Kgs. 2:25ff.

kāshal [כָּשַׁל, 3782]

kāshal is synonymous with ***nāphal***, above, and occurs nearly seventy times with the primary meaning "fall," or "stumble." Again, both the literal and figurative senses of this term merge.

kāshal primarily refers to "falling" or "stumbling" in the context of God's judgment. Such a "stumbling" may be understood as literal and/or figurative, in the sense of military defeat. Either way, it is viewed as the consequence of divine judgment for various groups of people. For example, God's enemies in general are threatened in this way (cf. Jer. 20:11; 46:12; Dan. 11:14ff.); as are the people of Israel (cf. Lev. 26:37; Isa. 59:10; Hos. 4:5); and Judah (cf. 2 Chr. 25:8; Jer. 6:21; Mal. 2:8; Lam. 1:14). Specific indictments involving "stumbling" and "falling" are also directed at Assyria (cf. Nah. 2:5); Egypt (cf. Jer. 46:6); and Babylon (cf. Jer. 46:16).

The figurative use of ***kāshal*** also indicates moral failure (e.g., Prov. 4:12ff.; 24:16, 17; Isa. 59:14). Related to this is the sense of being brought down by God (i.e., ruined) in a non-specific way (cf. Jer. 8:12; Ps. 64:8).

mappelet [מַפֶּלֶת, 4658]

A rare noun derived from ***nāphal*** (see above), ***mappelet*** occurs eight times, and is translated "fall" or "ruin" in all but one of these contexts. It refers literally to a "fall" in the sense of "overthrow" or "ruin" in Ezek. 26:15, 18; 27:27 in reference to Tyre — again in the context of God's judgment. Prov. 29:16; Ezek. 31:13, 16; 32:10 describe a "fall" in the metaphorical sense of a moral and spiritual collapse.

NT Words

piptō [πίπτω, *4098*]

piptō is the most common verb meaning "fall," "fall down," and is found in approximately ninety places.

The meaning "fall down" in relation to the act of worshiping the Christ child is noted in Matt. 2:11. The same action in connection with worshiping Satan is indicated in Matt. 4:9 — a response that the devil failed to elicit from Christ in the wilderness. Matt. 17:6 describes the disciples' veneration of Christ on the "Mount of Transfiguration." References to other people "falling down" to worship Christ include those in Mark 5:22; Luke 17:16. In 1 Cor. 14:25; Rev. 7:11; 19:4 the same action is performed to worship God. The action of "falling down" to worship the heavenly Christ is indicated in Rev. 4:10; 5:8. Mundane references to "falling" are found in relation to rain (Matt. 7:25ff.); birds (Matt. 10:29; Mark 4:4ff.; Luke 8:5ff.; John 12:24); people stumbling (Matt. 15:14; 17:15); and people begging for mercy (Matt. 18:26ff.; Luke 5:12). See also Mark 9:20; Luke 6:49; John 11:32; Acts 9:4; 27:34; Rom. 14:4; Heb. 11:30.

Stars "falling" from heaven and mountains "falling" onto a desperate humanity as a sign of the dissolution of the cosmos at the end of time are described in Matt. 24:29; Luke 23:30; Rev. 6:16; 8:10; 11:16; 18:2. Satan is also described as "falling" in the context of his expulsion from heaven (Luke 10:18). Christ himself "fell" on his face in Gethsemane, praying that his Father might remove the threat of imminent crucifixion from him (Matt. 26:39; Mark 14:35).

The metaphorical context of Luke 20:18 indicates that everyone who "falls" on the stone will be broken. The "stone" here refers to the Messiah, who will destroy those who reject him. The action of "falling" is equated with the act of "rejecting." See also Acts 15:16. The meaning "to fall" in the sense of "commit apostasy" is noted in Rom. 11:11; Heb. 4:11. The "fall" (i.e., eternal destruction) of Babylon is noted in Rev. 14:8.

The fate of "falling" in battle is noted in Luke 21:24. The action of "falling down" dead is indicated in Acts 5:5, 10; 20:9; 1 Cor. 10:8; Heb. 3:17.

apopiptō [ἀποπίπτω, *634*]

apopiptō is one of the rare variants of the term ***piptō*** (see above), found only in Acts 9:18 referring to the scale-like substance that "fell" from the eyes of a blind man healed by Jesus.

ekpiptō [ἐκπίπτω, *1601*]

ekpiptō, a variant form of ***piptō***, above, also means "fall" in six places. Reference to stars "falling" from heaven as one of the signs of cosmic dissolution at the end of time is found in Matt. 13:25. The effect of scorching heat on plants, resulting in the "dropping" of the flower, is noted in Jas. 1:11; 1 Pet. 1:24. Acts 12:7 describes chains "falling off" the hands of prisoners.

Gal. 5:4 refers to those who "have fallen" from grace. See also Rev. 2:5 for a similar context.

empiptō [ἐμπίπτω, *1706*]

empiptō is a verb found seven times meaning "fall among," "fall into."

Literal references to beasts "falling into" a pit are found in Matt. 12:11; Luke 14:5; and to a man who "fell among" thieves in Luke 10:36. 1 Tim. 3:6ff. warns believers against "falling into" satanic temptation.

Finally, Heb. 10:31 declares that it is a terrible thing to "fall into" the hands of the living God.

epipiptō [ἐπιπίπτω, *1968*]

epipiptō means "fall upon," "fall," with several related nuances throughout most of its thirteen occurrences.

The operation of the Holy Spirit who "fell" on those listening to the word of God resulted in their conversion in Acts 10:44; 11:15. See also Acts 8:15. The phenomenon of fear "falling upon" people is described in Luke 1:12; Acts 19:17.

The action of people "embracing" one another with the literal sense of "falling upon their neck" is indicated in Luke 15:20; Acts 20:10, 37. The phenomenon of "falling into" a trance is indicated in Acts 10:10. See also Rom. 15:3.

katapiptō [καταπίπτω, *2667*]

katapiptō is a rare verb found only twice, meaning "fall down" in both places. In Acts 26:14 Paul relates how he and his companions "had fallen" to the ground in the wake of his revelation of Christ on the road to Damascus. In Acts 28:6, Paul's traveling companions expected him "to fall down" dead after being bitten by a poisonous snake.

parapiptō [παραπίπτω, *3895*]

parapiptō is a rare verb found only in Heb. 6:6, referring to those who "fall away," or "commit apostasy."

peripiptō [περιπίπτω, *4045*]

peripiptō is a rare verb referring to "falling among" thieves in Luke 10:30.

prospiptō [προσπίπτω, *4363*]

prospiptō is a verb meaning "fall down before (someone)" throughout most of its eight occurrences.

Prostrating oneself in fear is an action noted in Mark 3:11; 5:33; Luke 8:28, 47; Acts 16:29. Mark 7:25 refers to a woman who fell down at Jesus' feet, imploring him to heal her daughter. Luke 5:8 refers to Peter acting this way in order to express sorrow at his own unbelief.

aphistēmi [ἀφίστημι, *868*]

aphistēmi is a verb meaning "draw away," "depart" in most of its fifteen occurrences. However, in Luke 8:13 the term refers to those who hear the word of God with initial eagerness but then "fall away" from the faith in a time of temptation.

Additional Notes

Apart from the purely literal sense of "falling," "falling" in a figurative sense has a great deal of theological weight in both the Old and New Testaments. In the Old Testament, the concept of "falling" under the judgment of God is prevalent in a significant number of contexts — referring to nations as well as individuals stumbling in a moral or a military sense. The New Testament takes the idea a step further by describing the terrible state of apostasy or "falling away" of those who turn their backs on Jesus Christ. While the Old Testament does not use the term "falling away" in precisely the same sense as the New, the same phenomenon is present in the sense that the people of Israel frequently abandoned their God by turning their backs on him in rebellion and disobedience. The consequences for God's people were terrible: they forfeited the land of promise for seventy years and incurred many harsh judgments from God. In the new covenant era, however, rejection of God's Son carries far more serious consequences. (→ REBEL)

See Also: → GUILT → INIQUITY → TRANSGRESSION → TRESPASS

FALSE, FALSEHOOD

NT Words

pseudēs [ψευδής, *5571*]

pseudēs is an adjectival form found in only three places, denoting "false" witnesses in Acts 6:13; and "liars" (i.e., those who bear false witness) in Rev. 2:2; 21:8.

pseudōnymos [ψευδώνυμος, *5581*]

pseudēs is a rare adverb found only in 1 Tim. 6:20 denoting knowledge that is "falsely named."

See Also: → LIE → VAIN

FAME

NT Words

phēmē [φήμη, *5345*]

phēmē is a rare noun occurring only twice and denoting "fame" in the sense of "news," or a "report" that emerged in the wake of Jesus raising the synagogue ruler's daughter from the dead (cf. Matt. 9:26). A general "report" of Jesus' unique activity and ministry is indicated in Luke 4:14.

akoē [ἄκοη, *189*]

akoē is a noun occurring nearly twenty-five times, meaning "hearing" in most of these contexts. In several contexts, however, ***akoē*** signifies the "fame" of Christ in relation to his performing miraculous signs, as noted in Matt. 4:24; 14:1; Mark 1:28. (→ HEAR)

See Also: → SPREAD

FAMILY

OT Words

bayit [בַּיִת, 1004]

This common noun means "house," with a number of associated nuances. However, on nearly sixty occasions it means "household" in the sense of "family." ***bayit*** with this meaning is exclusively literal.

bayit refers to family in the mundane sense of "household members" (cf. Gen. 31:37; Exod. 1:1; Lev. 16:17; Deut. 15:20; 1 Sam. 25:17; 1 Kgs. 4:7; Prov. 31:15.ff.).

bayit also indicates "family" in the sense of descendants, both present and future — for example in Gen. 18:19, where God determines to preserve Abraham and his descendants after him in accordance with his covenant promise.

There are several contexts in which families or households are portrayed both as the objects of divine favor and blessing (cf. Lev. 16:17; Deut. 14:26; Josh. 2:18; 2 Sam. 6:3); and as the objects of God's wrath (cf. Deut. 6:22; Josh. 7:14ff. [Achan and his family]).

mishpāḥāh [מִשְׁפָּחָה, 4940]

A term largely synonymous with ***bayit*** (see above), ***mishpāḥāh*** occurs around three hundred times with the primary sense of "family," "clan," or "tribe."

Most frequently, the usage of ***mishpāḥāh*** with this sense is mundane (e.g., Gen. 10:15; Exod. 6:14ff.; Lev. 25:10ff.; Numbers [around ninety times]; Deut. 29:18; Joshua [around forty times]; 1 Sam. 20:6). In Amos 3:1, the nation of Israel is referred to as a "family."

As with ***bayit***, above, ***mishpāḥāh*** refers to families as objects of God's blessing. Notable examples are Gen. 12:3, in which the descendants of Abraham, that is his "family," are made beneficiaries of God's covenant promises. In Jer. 3:14 God promises to return the families of Judah to their homeland. Jer. 31:1 contains God's promise to forgive and renew his people, whereby he will once again become the God of all the families of Israel, and they shall be his people. In Amos 3:2 there is symbolic reference to the family of God, indicating the unique relationship that Yahweh sustained with his people under the covenant.

Conversely, families are also subject to the wrath of God. Judah is indicted through this metaphor (cf. Jer. 2:4; 8:3; 33:24); as is the nation of Israel (cf. Mic. 2:3; Ezek. 20:32). In Jer. 10:25, the prophet pleads with God to judge those pagan tribes who have decimated the people of God. In association with this particular theme, there is a distinctive usage of ***mishpāḥāh*** that depicts clans or families as the instruments of God's wrath. For example, Jer. 1:15 refers to the Babylonian clans who will invade the land of Judah, as does Jer. 25:9.

NT Words

oikos [οἶκος, *3624*]

oikos is a common noun occurring over one hundred times with the primary meanings "house," "home."

In several places, however, the sense of "household" or "family" is indicated. The "house of David," denoting the ruler's lineage, is indicated in Luke 1:27, 69; 2:4; as is that of Jacob in Luke 1:40; the "house of Israel" in Acts 2:36; 7:42; Heb. 8:10; and the "house of Judah" in Heb. 8:8. General references to a "household" or "family" are indicated in Luke 11:17; Acts 10:2; 1 Cor. 1:16; 1 Tim. 3:5, 12; 2 Tim. 1:16; Heb. 11:7. In reference to the community of believers, ***oikos*** denotes the "household" or "family" of God in 1 Tim. 3:15; 1 Pet. 4:17.

patria [πατριά, *3965*]

patria is a rare noun found in three places. It refers to the "lineage" or "family" of David in Luke 2:4; the "families" of the earth in Acts 3:25; and a general reference to a "family" in Eph. 3:15.

Additional Notes

The Hebrew vocabulary for "family" designates not only household members in the narrow sense, but also larger units such as tribes and clans, and even, though more infrequently, entire nations.

Considerable significance is attached to family groupings in the Old Testament for a number of reasons. The family is an object of both divine mercy and wrath. The catalyst for God's blessing or curse is the divine covenant; and in the Old Testament it is the people of God, the covenant nation of Israel (including regenerate Gentiles who have been brought into God's family), who are the focus of God's blessing as well as his judgment.

In the New Testament, however, the concept of "family" as a theologically significant term moves from the ethnic, sociological, and earthly plane to the heavenly sphere of the family of God. For in this new covenant age, God's people all over the world anticipate the hope of eternal fellowship with the family of God, of one day enjoying an intimate relationship with their "brothers and sisters" along with their Lord and Savior and heavenly Father. This will not take place in an earthly locality, but in the new heavens and the new earth in glory forever.

FAMINE

OT Words

***rā'āb* [רָעָב, 7458]**

rā'āb is a noun occurring ninety times, with the sense of "famine" or "(extreme) hunger" in both a literal and a metaphorical sense.

"Famine" is literally indicated in a large number of texts without special theological significance (e.g., Gen. 47:4ff.; Ruth. 1:1; 2 Kgs. 4:38; Neh. 5:3; Ps. 33:19). Extreme hunger is described in Exod. 16:3; Jer. 32:9.

In other contexts, famine is often indicated as a divine punishment or covenant curse resulting from violation of God's covenant laws. The most significant of these texts is Deut. 28:48, where famine is threatened as one of the inevitable consequences for God's people should they rebel against him. It is described as a certain punishment. Evidence for the fulfillment or outworking of this curse is abundant, especially in the prophets (e.g., Isa. 5:13; 51:19; 2 Sam. 24:13; 1 Kgs. 8:37; Jer. 11:22; 16:4; 21:7ff.; 32:24ff.; 44:12ff.; Lam. 2:19; 5:10; Ezek. 5:12ff.; 12:16; 14:13, 21). Conversely, in two passages the removal of famine is designated as a divine blessing (cf. Ezek. 34:29; 36:29ff.).

There is also one significant metaphorical usage of ***rā'āb*** in Amos 8:11, where God promises to send a "famine of hearing the words of the Lord" upon his people, denying them divine revelation for an undesignated period of time. Some commentators understand this as the 400 years of prophetic silence from the time of the prophet Malachi to the coming of John the Baptist.

***kāphān* [כָּפָן, 3720]**

kāphān is a rare synonym for ***rā'āb*** (see above) found only twice, denoting a "famine" in Job 5:22; 30:3.

NT Words

***limos* [λιμός, *3042*]**

limos is the Greek dynamic equivalent for ***rā'āb*** (see above), denoting "famine," "hunger" in twelve places. Specific references to "famine" are noted as evidence that the world's end is nigh in Matt. 24:7; Mark 13:8; Luke 21:11; Rev. 18:18.

General references to "famine" or "(extreme) hunger" are found in Luke 4:25; 15:14ff.; Acts 7:11; 11:28; Rom. 8:35; 2 Cor. 11:27; Rev. 6:8.

Additional Notes

"Famine" is nowhere near as widespread in the New Testament as it is in the Old. The depiction of famine as the outworking of the divine covenant curse is absent in an explicit sense, although there are suggestions of this meaning in Rev. 6:8; 18:8.

FAR

OT Words

***rāḥaq* [רָחַק, 7368]**

This verb occurs about sixty times with the primary sense of "be far off, away," with a number of related meanings.

In a few places ***rāḥaq*** refers to being "distant" or "far from" in a literal physical sense (e.g., Gen. 21:16; Exod. 8:28; Deut. 12:21; Josh. 3:16; Judg. 18:22; Job 5:4).

The meaning "keep away, far from," in the sense of "have nothing to do with," is found in the context of exhortation to keep away from the evil effects of sin (cf. Exod. 23:7; Job 11:14; 21:16; 22:23; Prov. 4:24; Ezek. 43:9). Related to this is the condition of being far away from God — that is, out of fellowship with him (cf. Pss. 55:7; 119:50; Isa. 59:9, 11; Jer. 2:5; Lam. 1:16; Ezek. 8:6; 44:16.

In Isa. 29:13, God laments through the prophet that the hearts of his people are "far from" him, that their worship is vain and superficial.

As a consequence of this neglect on the part of his people, God punishes them by removing them "far from" him (cf. Jer. 27:10; Ezek. 11:16). The psalmist, for his part, pleads with God not to abandon (i.e., go far away from) him in Pss. 22:11, 19; 35:22; 38:21; 71:12. And in Prov. 30:8, the writer also asks God to keep falsehood and lies "far from him."

rāḥaq is also used to describe God removing our sins "far from" us (cf. Ps. 103:12), as far as the east is from the west. Joel 2:20 records God's promise to remove Israel's enemy far from her, as does Isa. 49:19. In a similar vein, God's deliverance is not far off (cf. Isa. 46:13; 54:14).

***rāḥôq* [רָחוֹק, 7350]**

This is an adverbial form of ***rāḥaq*** (see above), occurring about seventy times and meaning "far off."

The predominant usage is mundane, referring simply to remote distance (e.g., Gen. 22:4; Exod. 2:4; Josh. 9:6ff.; 1 Sam. 26:13; Ezra 3:13; Ps. 139:2; Isa. 5:26).

There are also references to God "being far away" as part of the outworking of his judgment. Ps. 22:1, for example, records the classic cry of the psalmist, "My God, my God, why have you forsaken me?" — anticipating the agony of Christ on the cross, who experienced God's abandonment in a uniquely painful way. The psalmist then asks: "Why are you so far from saving me?" See also Ps. 119:155; Prov. 15:29; Jer. 12:2; 23:23.

In contrast, Jer. 30:10 records God's promise to save his people from afar, or to bring them back from captivity (cf. also Jer. 46:27).

NT Words

makros [μακρός, *3117*]

makros is a rare adjective meaning "far" in the sense of "distant" countries in Luke 15:13; 19:12.

makran [μακράν, *3112*]

makran is an adverb meaning "far," "far off," "far away."

The meaning "far off" in the sense of "some distance away" is indicated in Matt. 8:30.

The state of "not being far" from the kingdom of heaven is noted in Mark 12:34 in reference to one's spiritual proximity to peace with God. The contrary sense of being "far away" from God is indicated in several places, each of them affirming that such people would be brought near to Yahweh through faith and repentance (cf. Acts 2:39; Eph. 2:13, 17). God is described as being "not being far away" from his people in Acts 17:27.

The sense of "far away" in a physical, literal sense is indicated in Luke 7:6; 15:20; John 21:8; Acts 22:21.

See Also: → LENGTH

FAREWELL

NT Words

chairō [χαίρω, *5463*]

chairō is a verb with the primary sense of "rejoice," as well as related nuances, for most of its nearly eighty occurrences. However, in 2 Cor. 13:11 ***chairō*** expresses the salutation "farewell" or "goodbye."

apotassomai [ἀποτάσσομαι, *657*]

apotassomai is a verb found six times, meaning "bid farewell," "take leave" in most of these contexts. Such farewells are found in Mark 6:46; Luke 9:61; Acts 18:18ff.; 2 Cor. 2:13.

FARM

OT Words

'ikkār [**אִכָּר, 406**]

'ikkār is a noun found seven times denoting "one who works the fields," or a farmer (cf. 2 Chr. 26:10; Isa. 61:5; Jer. 14:4; 31:24; 51:23; Joel 1:11; Amos 5:16).

NT Words

geōrgos [γεωργός, *1092*]

geōrgos is a noun found in nineteen places with the primary sense of "tenant," suggesting the sense of hired land workers. However, in two places the term specifically denotes a "farmer" (cf. 2 Tim. 2:6; Jas. 5:7).

See Also: → FIELD

FAST, FASTING

OT Words

ṣôm [**צוֹם, 6685**]

The noun ***ṣôm*** occurs about twenty times, meaning "fast" in the context of literally abstaining from food and drink in the ritual sphere of Israelite worship.

Appropriate, legitimate fasting is indicated in the majority of texts where ***ṣôm*** is used (e.g., Ezra 8:21; Neh. 9:1; Ps. 69:10; Isa. 58:6; Jer. 36:6; Dan. 9:3). On the other hand, illegitimate fasting is indicated in Isa. 58:3ff.; Joel 1:14; 2:12, where it is not accompanied by genuine love for God.

ṣûm [**צוּם, 6684**]

This term is synonymous with ***ṣôm*** (see above), the verbal root from which ***ṣûm*** is derived. ***ṣûm*** is found approximately 230 times. Again, the context is uniformly a ritual one.

Genuine fasting is again indicated in most contexts (e.g., Judg. 20:26; 1 Kgs. 21:27; Ezra 8:23; Neh. 1:4). Illegitimate fasting is mentioned only in Isa. 58:4; Jer. 14:12, with the latter occasion bringing down the judgment of God.

NT Words

nēsteia [νηστεία, *3521*]

nēsteia is a noun denoting the practice of "fasting" in eight places (cf. Matt. 17:21; Mark 9:29; Luke 2:37; Acts 14:23; 1 Cor. 7:5; 2 Cor. 6:5; 11:27). In particular, Acts 27:9 refers to the "fast" associated with the Day of Atonement festival.

nēsteuō [νηστεύω, *3522*]

nēsteuō is a verb found around twenty times with the consistent meaning "to fast."

Jesus' own "fasting" in the wilderness prior to the beginning of his public ministry is noted in Matt. 4:2.

Elsewhere, ritual "fasting" is indicated in Matt. 6:16ff.; 9:14ff.; Mark 2:18ff.; Luke 5:33ff.; 18:12; Acts 10:30; 13:2ff.

nēstis [νῆστις, *3523*]

nēstis is a rare noun denoting "fasting" in the sense of "refraining from eating" and is translated "hungry" in Matt. 15:32; Mark 8:3.

FATHER

OT Words

'āb [אָב, 1]

This common noun occurs over 1,200 times. The primary sense of ***'āb*** is "father," but it also refers to secondary paternal relationship and beyond (viz. "grandfather" and/or "ancestor," "forefather"). ***'āb*** also embraces the concept of tribal or national head or founder. Only those uses of the term that have particular significance or interest will be discussed here, and not the occurrences of "father" in the mundane, biological sense.

Although the fatherhood of God is predominantly a New Testament phenomenon, this description of God is found in the Hebrew Scriptures in several places. Ps. 68:5, for example, refers to God as "father of the fatherless and protector of widows." 1 Chr. 29:10 cites God as the father of Israel. Ps. 89:26 mentions God as the father of his chosen servant. Isa. 9:6 contains the classic divine name of the messianic child of promise; "Everlasting Father." Mal. 2:10 describes God as the "Father of all humanity." See also Jer. 3:4, 19; Isa. 63:16; 64:8.

With reference to the patriarchs, Abraham is described as the "father" of the Israelite nation in accordance with the covenant promises given to him by God (e.g., Gen. 17:5; Exod. 3:6; Isa. 51:2). Concerning Jacob, see Isa. 58:1. The role of the father as spiritual head of the household, who guides and nurtures his children, is indicated in Proverbs (cf. 1:8; 3:12; 4:1, 3; 6:20; 10:1; 13:1; 15:5).

The concept of one's "fathers" (i.e., ancestors) is very common, occurring in around 550 contexts. The following phrases containing this term reflect significant Old Testament themes.

The land of the "fathers" (i.e., Canaan) constitutes one of the major elements of the old covenant promises. Of the many references to this motif, the following are among the most significant. Deut. 1:8 designates the land of Canaan as the fulfillment of this promise to the "fathers" of that current generation who now stood on its border. Josh. 1:6 reminds the people of the promise to their "fathers," again as they are on the verge of entering the land. In 2 Chr. 6:25 Solomon prays that God will restore the people to the land he had given to their "fathers" after the people have served their time in exile and confessed their sin. 2 Chr. 33:8 contains the promise that God will let his people continue living in the land of their "fathers," if they will turn from their sin. See also Jer. 7:7; 25:5; 35:15 in this regard. Jer. 16:15; 30:3; Ezek. 36:28; 37:25 likewise record the promises of God to restore his people to the land given to their forefathers. In Jer. 24:10 God threatens to remove his people from the land of their fathers if they continue in their sin, which is the curse of the covenant.

The people of Israel inherited the land of Israel from their fathers, in accordance with the covenant promises (cf. Num. 33:54; 34:14; 36:3, 4, 7; Josh. 1:6; 14:1; Ezek. 47:14). There is also the account of Naboth's vineyard in 1 Kgs. 21:3ff., in which this godly Israelite man refused to sell his inherited portion of land (i.e., from his "fathers") to King Ahab.

The covenant itself was made under solemn obligation with the "fathers" of Israel (cf. Deut. 4:31; 7:12; 8:18; 29:25; 31:16; Judg. 2:1, 20; 1 Kgs. 8:21). It was this covenant that the people of Israel despised, the covenant made with their ancestors so long before (cf. 2 Kgs. 17:5; Jer. 11:10). 2 Chr. 15:12 refers to the covenant renewal undertaken by the people of Judah during the reign of Asa, to reforge the relationship with the God of their fathers. In contrast, Jer. 31:32ff. details the uniqueness of the promised new covenant that would be quite unlike the previous covenant God made with the forefathers of his people.

The phrase "God of our (your, their) fathers" is a unique declaration of the status of Israel as the people of Yahweh, the God who spoke to them in a unique, intimate relationship with him (cf. Exod. 3:13ff. [God's revelation to Moses]; Deut. 1:11; 4:1; Josh. 18:3; 1 Chr. 29:20; Deut. 26:7; Josh. 24:17; 1 Kgs. 8:53; Ezra 7:27).

One of the great tragedies of the old covenant era was the terrible consequences of "the sins of the fathers," which led to the destruction and loss of the land of Canaan for seventy years. This phenomenon is referred to specifically in a number of places (cf. Num. 14:18; Exod. 20:5; Deut. 5:9; Lev. 26:39, 40; 1 Kgs. 14:22; Neh. 9:2; Jer. 14:20; Lam. 5:7; Ezek. 20:4, 27ff.; Dan. 9:16; Zech. 1:2ff.).

Finally, the phrase "going to one's fathers" is a euphemism for death and burial, along with the phrase "lie with your fathers" (cf. Gen. 15:5; Deut. 31:16; 2 Sam. 7:12). This expression occurs frequently throughout Kings and Chronicles with respect to the rulers of those nations (approximately forty times) (e.g., 1 Kgs. 2:10 [death of David]; 1 Kgs. 11:43 [death of

Solomon]). See also 1 Kgs. 14:31; 2 Kgs. 8:24; 2 Chr. 9:31; 33:20.

NT Words

patēr [πατήρ, *3962*]

patēr is the Greek dynamic equivalent of the Hebrew term ***'āb*** (see above) and is translated "father" throughout its more than four hundred occurrences.

References to one's biological father predominate (e.g., Matt. 2:22; 10:37; 19:5; Mark 7:10ff.; Luke 1:59ff.; 15:12ff.; Acts 16:1; Eph. 5:31; 6:2ff.; 1 Tim. 5:1; Heb. 12:7ff.).

patēr, like its Hebrew equivalent ***'āb***, also signifies "father" in the sense of "ancestor," with references to Abraham (Matt. 3:9; Luke 1:73; 16:24; John 8:39; Rom. 4:11ff.; Jas. 2:21); to David (Mark 11:10; Luke 1:32); and to Israel's ancestors in general (Matt. 23:30; Luke 11:47ff.; John 4:12; Acts 3:22; Rom. 9:5; 1 Cor. 4:15; Heb. 1:1). References to God as the "Father" of his people are found in Matt. 5:16, 45; 10:29ff.; Mark 11:25ff.; Luke 11:2; Acts 1:4ff.; Rom. 8:15; Eph. 3:14; Eph. 2:11; 1 Thess. 1:3; Titus 1:4; 1 Pet. 1:2; 2 Pet. 1:17. The designation "Father" in the context of the relationship between God and Christ his Son is indicated, for example, in Matt. 11:27; 16:17; 18:19; 26:39ff.; Mark 14:36; Luke 2:49; 24:49; John 1:14, 18; 3:35; 4:23; 5:17ff.; 6:32ff.; 8:16ff.; 12:26ff.; 14:2ff.; 15:1ff.; 16:3ff.; 17:1ff.; Rom. 15:6; Gal. 1:1ff.; Eph. 1:2, 3; Col. 1:3; 1 Pet. 1:3; 1 John 2:22ff.; Rev. 2:27; 3:5, 21; 14:1. The term "Father" also occurs with the other persons of the Godhead (viz. Son and Holy Spirit) in Matt. 28:19; Mark 8:38. Luke 9:26 refers to God as the "Father" of the Son of Man.

apatōr [ἀπάτωρ, *540*]

apatōr is a rare adjective found only in Heb. 7:3 referring metaphorically to Melchizedek as one "without father or mother," whose parents are not recorded in any genealogy.

patroparadotos [πατροπαράδοτος, *3970*]

patroparadotos is a rare adjectival form found only in 1 Pet. 1:18, referring to ways "inherited from one's fathers."

Additional Notes

Although it is not frequently mentioned, the idea of the "fatherhood of God" clearly exists in the Old Testament. The concept does not reach theological maturity until the advent of Jesus, as the messianic Son of God, in the New Testament era. God is portrayed as the Father of his people in at least an "embryonic" sense in the Old Testament. As with many other key biblical concepts, this idea progressively unfolds from the old to the new covenant age.

One of the important aspects of this concept is the uniqueness of the relationship that God sustains with his people — a phenomenon that holds true and is applicable for both eras of divine revelation. The intimate bond that existed between Yahweh and his people in the Old Testament prefigures and anticipates Jesus' unique relationship with his Father in the New.

FATHER-IN-LAW

OT Words

ḥām [**חָם, 2524**]

This is a rare term occurring only four times, meaning "father-in-law" (cf. Gen. 38:13, 25; 1 Sam. 4:19, 21).

ḥātan [**חָתַן, 2859**]

ḥātan is a verb found approximately thirty times, with the underlying sense of becoming a son-in-law. In the participial form it also has the sense of "mother-in-law" or "father-in-law." The latter meaning is indicated in the majority of instances (e.g., Exod. 3:1, 18; Num. 10:29; Judg. 1:16; 19:4ff.; 1 Sam. 18:21ff.; 1 Kgs. 3:1).

NT Words

pentheros [πενθερός, *3995*]

pentheros is a noun meaning "father-in-law," found only in John 18:13 with reference to the high priest Caiaphas' relative.

FATHERLESS

OT Words

yātôm [**יָתוֹם, 3490**]

This noun occurs approximately forty times and is consistently translated "fatherless child" or "orphan."

Those who suffered the misfortune of losing their parents in ancient Israel, and who were unable to care for themselves, were granted a special place in the Mosaic covenant. The law of Moses consistently emphasizes the needs of those children and makes provisions for their ongoing support. General legislative clauses guaranteeing protection and care for the fatherless are found in Exod. 22:22; Deut. 14:29; 24:17, 19, 20, 21; 26:12, 13; 27:19. God's care of and favor towards orphans is also indicated in Deut. 10:18; 16:11, 14; Ps. 10:4, 18; Jer. 49:11; Hos. 14:3.

Abuse of the fatherless is mentioned in Job 6:27; Ps. 94:6, and condemned in Isa. 10:2; Jer. 5:28; Ezek. 22:7. In the latter instances it is God's people who are guilty of such offenses; and so there are strong exhortations to care for the fatherless (cf. Ps. 82:3; Isa. 1:17; Jer. 7:6; 22:3).

A divine curse is also pronounced on the wicked, resulting in their being made fatherless (cf. Exod. 22:24; Ps. 109:9, 12; Isa. 9:17; Mal. 3:5).

NT Words

orphanos [ὀρφανός, *3737*]

orphanos is a rare adjectival form denoting "those who are without fathers" (i.e., orphans) in John 14:18; Jas. 1:17.

FATNESS → BLESS

FAULT, FAULTLESS

OT Words

zākāh [זָכָה, **2135**]

This verb means "be clean," "pure," "without blemish" — and hence also "to be without fault." ***zākāh*** is found eight times and is a synonym for "righteous" in Job 15:4; 25:4. God is described as "faultless in judgment" in Ps. 51:4. Moral purity ("without blemish") is in view in Ps. 73:13; Prov. 20:19; and in Isa 1:16 ***zākāh*** is used as a moral imperative from God to his people to rid themselves of their evil deeds, by making themselves clean. See also Mic. 6:11.

ḥāṭā' [חָטָא, **2398**]

ḥāṭā' is a common noun denoting "sin," as well as related nuances, for most of its nearly 250 occurrences. One of these associated meanings is that of "fault," found only in Exod. 5:16, where Pharaoh charges that the "fault" for failure to make bricks without straw lay with the Israelite people.

me'ûmāh [מְאוּמָה, **3972**]

me'ûmāh is a pronoun with the indefinite sense of "anything" for most of its thirty or so occurrences. In 1 Sam. 29:3, however, ***me'ûmāh*** denotes "fault" in the sense of a "moral flaw."

NT Words

aition [αἴτιον, *158*]

aition is a noun found four times meaning "fault" (i.e., crime) in Luke 23:4, 14, 22; and denoting a "reason" in Acts 19:40.

amemptos [ἄμεμπτος, *273*]

amemptos is an adjective found five times meaning "blameless," or "without fault, guilt" in relation to the law (Luke 1:6; Phil. 3:6); and in the sight of God (Phil. 2:15; 1 Thess. 3:13). In Heb. 8:7 ***amemptos*** means "faultless" in the sense of "without defect" — which does not describe the first (i.e., old) covenant.

memphomai [μέμφομαι, *3201*]

memphomai is a rare verb meaning "find fault" (i.e., attribute blame) in Rom. 9:19; Heb. 8:8.

elenchō [ἐλέγχω, *1651*]

elenchō is a verb occurring seventeen times with the primary meanings "rebuke," "reprove." In Matt. 18:15, however, it is translated "to show someone's fault to them," or to expose their fault or blame.

See Also: → PERFECT → REBUKE

FAVOR, FAVORED

OT Words

rāṣôn [רָצוֹן, **7522**]

rāṣôn is a noun found in nearly sixty contexts meaning "pleasure," "delight," "desire," "will," and "favor" throughout. (→ DELIGHT → WILL)

"Favor" in the general sense of a person's "goodwill" is indicated in Prov. 11:27; 14:35; 16:15; 19:12.

Elsewhere, ***rāṣôn*** denotes divine "favor," or "benevolence," "goodwill," or "kindness" (cf. Deut. 33:23; Pss. 5:12; 30:5ff.; 106:4; Prov. 8:35; 12:2; 18:22; Isa. 60:10; Mal. 2:17).

NT Words

charitoō [χαριτόω, *5487*]

charitoō is a rare verb found only twice. In Luke 1:28 it is used adjectivally to refer to Mary as one "favored" by God. In Eph. 1:6, God is said "to have freely granted" grace to his people through the person of Christ his Son.

See Also: → GRACE

FEAR

OT Words

yārē' [יָרֵא, **3372**]

yārē' is a common verb, with the dominant sense of "to fear," "be afraid." ***yārē'*** reflects the sense of both being terrified and standing in awe of God, as well as the fear of human beings and other earthly phenomena.

The concept of a mortal fear or terror of Yahweh is quite common. For example, Moses experiences the fear of God by the burning bush (Exod. 3:6); as do the people of Israel at Mt. Sinai (cf. Deut. 5:5). See also in this regard Gen. 28:17; 1 Sam. 28:20; 2 Sam. 6:9; Ezek. 11:8; Zech. 9:5. The terror of Yahweh's judgment provides a motivation for obedience to his commands in Deut. 13:11; 17:13; 19:20.

God often utters the command "Fear not . . ." to his people, usually at significant points of divine-human revelation, in order to comfort them — for example, to Abraham (Gen. 15:1); Hagar (Gen. 21:17); Isaac (Gen. 26:24); Jacob (Gen. 46:3); Gideon (Judg. 6:33); and Daniel (Dan. 10:12). In Isa. 7:4, Yahweh exhorts Ahaz not to fear the kings of Aram and Israel. Similarly, in Jer. 1:8, there is the divine injunction to the prophet not to be afraid of his enemies. See also in this regard Ezek. 2:6; Jer. 42:11. The same exhortation also occurs at a purely human level (e.g., Gen. 35:17; 1 Sam. 4:20; 1 Kgs. 17:13; 2 Kgs. 1:15; 25:24).

As well as referring to a sense of terror, ***yārē'*** also indicates "fear" in terms of an awesome reverence of God. Such an attitude is in fact explicitly required of God's people under the terms of the Mosaic covenant (cf. Lev. 19:14; 25:17; Deut. 4:19; 6:2, 13, 24; 31:12; Josh. 24:14). The psalmist also frequently exhorts his readers to fear God in this way (e.g., Ps. 33:8). Likewise, even the pagan nations are included among those who fear God (cf. Isa. 25:3; Jer. 32:39; Jonah 1:9, 16), including those who shall turn back to God in fear of him as a result of his chastising them (cf. Mic. 7:17).

In contrast, Yahweh forbids his people to fear or reverence any other gods (cf. Judg. 6:10; 2 Kgs. 17:35ff.). And if such an attitude does evidence itself, severe punishment will follow. One prime example of this is Israel's destruction and exile at the hands of the Assyrians in 721 B.C., largely because Israel "feared" other gods (cf. 2 Kgs. 17:7). Israel's failure to fear Yahweh drew the wrath of God upon them (cf. Judah's failure in this regard in Jer. 3:8; 5:22; 44:10; Hosea 10:3 [Israel's failure]; Mal. 3:5).

yārē' also refers to the fear (or terror) of other people (e.g., Gen. 19:30; Exod. 2:14; Deut. 2:4; 7:19; Josh. 9:24; Judg. 4:18; Ruth 3:11; 1 Sam. 31:4; 1 Kgs. 1:50ff.; Jer. 26:21). Note in particular the Canaanites' fear of the Israelites in Deut. 28:10 as a sure sign that Yahweh was on Israel's side and would fight on their behalf in order to secure the conquest of the land of Canaan; Saul's sin in fearing the people of Israel rather than God (cf. 1 Sam. 15:24); and also the Israelites' cowardly fear of Goliath (1 Sam. 17:11, 24).

yārē' is also used to indicate a lack of "respect," or "reverence," for other people. For example, lack of such respect for Moses on the part of Miriam and Aaron leaves them both subject to God's anger (Num. 12:8). Then, in 2 Sam. 1:14, lack of respect for Saul cost an Amalekite refugee his life as he was executed by King David for having assisted in the death of the former Israelite king.

Finally, ***yārē'*** is found in commands to God's people not to fear others because God is with them. In Deut. 1:21, 29, for example, Yahweh commands his people not to fear the Canaanites, for the land has been given to Israel. See also Deut. 3:2; 7:18; 31:6; Josh. 8:1; 10:8; 2 Sam. 9:7 in this regard. In Isa. 37:6, God instructs Hezekiah not to fear Sennacherib, the Assyrian king, for similar reasons (viz. Yahweh will bring about his destruction). Underlying such commands, of course, is the reality that Yahweh's presence and protection of his people guarantees their security, notwithstanding his temporary judgments against them. This absence of fear is a wonderful blessing (cf. Pss. 23:4; 118:6; Isa. 35:4). The divine admonition to "fear not, for I am with you . . ." is a promise of divine comfort, assurance, and redemption (e.g., Isa. 41:5; 43:1, 5; 44:2; 51:7; Jer. 23:4 30:10; 42:11; Zeph. 3:16; Zech. 8:13, 15).

'êmāh [אֵימָה, 367]

'êmāh is a relatively uncommon noun, occurring seventeen times and meaning "fear" in the sense of "terror," "dread."

Gen. 15:12 describes the terror of God in Abraham's vision; and Josh. 2:9 contains Rahab's confession that the Canaanites are terrified of Israel and their God. See also Job 9:34; Ps. 88:15. Terror is also the accompaniment to divine judgment (cf. Exod. 15:16; 23:27; Deut. 32:25, where the focus is on terrorizing the Canaanites who will flee before the invading Israelites).

'êmāh also describes fear of other people (Ezra 3:3; Job 33:7; Prov. 20:2; Isa. 33:18); of Leviathan (Job 39:20; 41:14); and the terror of death (Ps. 55:4).

yir'āh [יִרְאָה, 3374]

This is the noun derived from the verb ***yārē'*** (see above), and translated "fear" in almost every context. ***yir'āh*** occurs around forty times, and is synonymous with ***'êmāh*** (see above).

yir'āh indicates, first of all, the "fear of God" as an attitude of reverential awe and worship (cf. Exod. 20:20; 2 Chr. 19:9; Neh. 5:9, 15). In Jer. 32:40, this fear of God is cited as one consequence of new covenant blessing. Isa. 11:2, 3 depict the fear of God resting on the Suffering Servant of Yahweh (i.e., the messianic "branch"). A number of texts in Proverbs affirm that the fear of the Lord prolongs life (e.g., Prov. 1:29; 8:13; 10:27; 19:23). See also Jonah 1:16; Job 22:4.

Negatively, ***yir'āh*** is also used to describe the fear of God being absent (e.g., Gen. 20:11; Job 6:14; Isa. 63:17).

As with ***'êmāh*** above, ***yir'āh*** also indicates fear as an accompaniment to, or the result of, divine judgment (cf. Isa. 7:25; 30:13; John 1:10).

paḥad [פַּחַד, 6343]

Synonymous with ***'êmāh*** and ***yir'āh***, above, ***paḥad*** occurs approximately fifty times.

paḥad often describes the terror of God related to his judgment. Such terror will fall upon the nations (cf. Isa. 24:17; Jer. 48:43; 49:5), as well as on his own people, when they are judged for their rebellion against him (cf. Deut. 28:67; also Jer. 30:5; Lam. 3:47). Such fear is also associated with the coming of the Day of the Lord (cf. Isa. 2:10, 19, 21). The terror of the ungodly before God is mentioned in a general way in Ps. 14:5.

paḥad also refers to the terror of Yahweh that will be inflicted upon his enemies — for example, the Canaanites (cf. Deut. 2:25; 11:25); the pagan neighbors of Judah (cf. 2 Chr. 17:10); the nations at large (cf. 2 Chr. 20:29); and the Persians at the time of Queen Esther (cf. Esth. 8:17; 9:2, 3). While the name of God is never mentioned in the book of Esther, this fear of the Jewish people is tantamount to the same thing.

The absence of the fear of God in the wicked is mentioned in Ps. 36:1; and the fear of God in the sense of reverential awe or worship is described in Ps. 36:1.

môrā' [מוֹרָא, 4172]

môrā' is a noun derived from the verb ***yārē'*** (see above), found thirteen times meaning "fear," "terror." The "fear" of human beings felt in the animal world is noted in Gen. 9:2. Deut. 11:25 describes the "fear" inspired by the Israelite army invading the land of Canaan.

môrā' also denotes an "act of terror" perpetrated by God against the nation of Egypt in Deut. 4:34; 26:8; Jer. 32:21. See also Deut. 34:12.

"Fear" inspired by God against his enemies is indicated in Ps. 9:20; and such a response is also invoked in the people of Israel as an appropriate attitude to cultivate in the presence of Yahweh (cf. Isa. 8:13). Other references to the "fear" of God include Ps. 76:11; Mal. 1:6; 2:5. See also Isa. 8:12.

deḥal [דְּחַל, 1763 (Aramaic)]

deḥal is an Aramaic verb meaning "to fear, be afraid," as well as the adjectival sense "terrible," "terrifying" throughout its six occurrences.

The "terrifying" aspect of the image in Nebuchadnezzar's dream is noted in Dan. 2:31. The fourth beast of Daniel's vision in Dan. 7:7, 19 is described as "dreadful" or "terrible."

Dan. 4:5 records that Daniel's dream had "made him afraid." "Fearing" the Babylonian king is indicated in Dan. 5:19; and "fearing" God in Dan. 6:26.

gûr [גּוּר, 1481]

gûr is a verb with the predominant sense of "sojourn," "dwell," as well as related nuances, throughout its nearly one hundred occurrences. The meaning "to fear," "be afraid" is also evident in several contexts.

The "fear" of Gentile nations in the face of Israel's presence in Canaan is noted in Num. 22:3.

General references to "being afraid" of human beings are found in Deut. 1:17; 18:22; 32:27; 1 Sam. 18:15; Job 19:29; 41:25.

Exhortations to "fear" God in the sense of "standing in awe" before him are noted in Pss. 22:23; 33:8. Hos. 10:5 describes apostate Samaritans "trembling (before)," "being afraid of" a pagan idol.

NT Words

phobos [φόβος, *5401*]

phobos is a noun denoting "fear," "terror" throughout its nearly fifty occurrences.

General references to the emotion of "fear" or "terror" in a human context are found in Matt. 14:26; Rom. 8:15; 1 Cor. 2:3; Eph. 6:5; 1 Pet. 3:14. 1 John 4:18 affirms that perfect love casts out "fear." In particular, "fear" of the Jews is indicated in John 7:13; 19:38; 20:19; and the "fear" of death in Heb. 2:15. See also Rev. 18:10, 15.

Expressing "fear" in the presence of an angel is recorded in Matt. 28:4; Luke 1:12; 2:9. The emotion of "fear" in response to a miraculous sign is indicated in several contexts — for example, on the occasion of Christ's resurrection (Matt. 28:8); and in response to Christ's miracles (Mark 4:41; Luke 5:26; 8:37). See also Acts 2:43.

Luke 21:26 describes "fear" or "terror" at the signs of the world's end.

Experiencing the "fear" of God is indicated in Acts 5:5, 11; 9:31; 19:17; 2 Cor. 5:11; 7:1, 5; Phil. 2:12; Rev. 11:11. The absence of the "fear" of God is recorded in Rom. 3:18.

"Fear" in the sense of "reverence," or "respect," in the context of paying respect to civil authorities, is indicated in Rom. 13:7. "Reverence" for Christ is noted in Eph. 5:21; 1 Pet. 3:15; and "respect" for one's master in 1 Pet. 2:18.

phoberos [φοβερός, *5398*]

phoberos is a rare adjective found in only three places, meaning "fearful," "terrible." The "fearful" prospect of falling under divine judgment is noted in Heb. 10:27, 31. The "terrifying" impact of the Sinai theophany on Moses is indicated in Heb. 12:21.

ekphobos [ἔκφοβος, *1630*]

ekphobos is a rare adjective meaning "very (much) afraid," found only in Mark 9:6; Heb. 12:21. Both texts speak of humanity's fear in the face of a divine revelation.

aphobōs [ἀφόβως, *870*]

aphobōs is an adverb found only four times, meaning "without fear."

Serving God "without fear" is indicated in Luke 1:74; as is speaking the word of God "without fear" in Phil. 1:14. False prophets acting "without fear" are depicted in Jude 12. See also 1 Cor. 16:10.

phobeō [φοβέω, *5399*]

phobeō is a verb found nearly one hundred times with the principal meanings "to fear," "be afraid."

Divine exhortations for people "not to fear" in the face of theophanic revelations include those in Matt. 1:20; 28:5ff.; Mark 5:36; Luke 1:13; 2:10; John 6:20; Rev. 1:17. See also Matt. 10:26ff.; John 12:15; Heb. 11:23.

General references to people "being afraid" include Matt. 2:22; Luke 19:21; John 19:8; Acts 5:26; 2 Cor. 12:20; Gal. 2:12; 1 John 4:18. In particular, Matt. 27:54; Mark 4:41; Luke 2:9; 8:35; 9:34; John 6:19 record people's fear at the manifestation of signs and miracles.

Luke 1:50; Acts 10:2, 22; Col. 3:22; 1 Pet. 2:17; Rev. 14:7 describe the positive phenomenon of expressing "fear" towards God. In contrast, Luke 12:5 contains a warning "to fear" God, who is able to cast one into hell. See also Luke 23:40. An exhortation to "fear" the civil authorities for their power to wield the sword in judicial execution is noted in Rom. 13:4.

The meaning "to respect" is indicated in the context of a wife's appropriate attitude to her husband in Eph. 5:33.

eulabeia [εὐλάβεια, *2124*]

eulabeia is a rare noun denoting "godly fear," found only in Heb. 5:7; 12:28.

deilia [δειλία, *1167*]

deilia is a rare noun found only in 2 Tim. 1:7 denoting "fear" or "timidity."

deilos [δειλός, *1169*]

deilos is an adjective found only three times, meaning "fearful," "afraid." In Matt. 8:26; Mark 4:40, Christ rebukes his disciples for being "afraid" and having no faith. Rev. 21:8 refers to the "cowardly."

entromos [ἔντρομος, *1790*]

entromos is an adjectival form meaning "trembling with fear," found only in Acts 7:32; 16:29; Heb. 12:21.

Additional Notes

The phenomenon of "fear" in both the Old and New Testaments reflects common emphases as far as attitudes to God are concerned — whether one is talking about the terror of God or worshipful reverence. The Old Testament, however, places a greater emphasis on the terror of God as a consequence of divine punishment because of the dominant theme of retribution for violation of covenant obligation. In the old covenant, the fear of Yahweh resulted from the onset of physical catastrophes such as military defeat, disease, invasion, and slaughter from enemy forces — experiences that were often repeated many times over. The New Testament, however, focuses on the ultimate punishment of eternal separation from God, which by definition is a non-repeatable phenomenon. This theme is highlighted in the book of Revelation and in certain parts of Jesus' teaching in the Gospels — both by explicit mention of the terms for "fear" as well as by implication from the contexts.

FEAST

OT Words

ḥag **[חַג, 2282]**

This noun occurs around sixty times with the principal meaning "festival," or "feast," and is associated almost exclusively with the Levitical calendar commemorating the redemptive actions of Yahweh on behalf of his people.

ḥag usually refers to those memorial festivals celebrating Yahweh's redemptive actions on behalf of his people (viz. Passover; Weeks [or Harvest]; tabernacles). All such festivals are compulsory celebrations, specifically included in the Mosaic legislation. Deut. 16:16; Isa. 29:1 mention all three festivals. Instructions to celebrate the Passover feast are found, for example, in Exod. 12:14; 23:15; Lev. 23:6; Num. 28:17; 2 Chr. 30:13, 21. Similarly, the harvest feast is indicated in Exod. 23:16; 34:22; Deut. 16:10, as is the Feast of Tabernacles in Lev. 23:34; Num. 29:12; Deut. 16:13ff. In Zech. 14:16ff., punishment is prescribed for those nations who do not go up with the people of God to Jerusalem to keep the Feast of Tabernacles.

Abuse of the festival requirement is mentioned in 1 Kgs. 12:32, 33, where Jeroboam sets up an idolatrous, illegitimate eighth month feast in mimicry of the Levitical feast of the seventh month. Similarly, in Hos. 2:11, Yahweh indicts Israel for abusing the sacred festivals through a sinful lifestyle. See also Amos 5:21; 8:10; Mal. 2:3.

Isa. 30:29; Ezek. 45:17 refer to feasts in general.

mô'ēd [מוֹעֵד, 4150]

This term has a variety of meanings and is derived from the verbal root ***yā'ad*** (→ MEET), signifying "to meet together," "assemble." ***mô'ēd*** occurs around 220 times and is translated "feast" on about twenty occasions, with exclusive reference to the ritual festivals of the Israelite calendar. Passover is mentioned in 2 Chr. 30:22; 31:3; tabernacles in Hos. 12:9. Other references to the major festivals of the Israelite calendar include Lev. 23:2; Num. 10:10; 1 Chr. 23:31; 2 Chr. 8:13; Ezra 3:5; Isa. 1:14; Ezek. 36:38; Hos. 9:5.

mishteh [מִשְׁתֶּה, 4960]

mishteh is a noun denoting a "banquet" or "feast," derived from the verb ***shātāh***, "to drink." (→ DRINK) ***mishteh*** occurs around fifty times, and is used both literally and metaphorically.

mishteh refers to feasting as a social occasion in Gen. 19:3; 21:8; Judg. 14:10ff.; 1 Sam. 25:36; Job 1:4, 5; Isa. 5:12; Jer. 16:8. It indicates royal banquets in the book of Esther (e.g., Esth. 1:3ff.; 2:18; 5:4ff.; 6:14; 7:2ff.). In addition, Esth. 8:17; 9:17ff. refer to feasting associated with the celebration of (implicit) divine deliverance from the attacks of the Persian population.

Only in 1 Kgs. 3:15 does ***mishteh*** refer to feasting associated with sacrificial offering.

In a metaphorical sense, ***mishteh*** signifies the feasting of a joyful heart in Prov. 15:15. More significantly, Isa. 25:6 records the symbolic phenomenon of feasting on the occasion of God's victory over his enemies (viz. an apocalyptic victory banquet). See also Jer. 51:39.

ḥāgag [חָגַג, 2287]

A relatively rare verb, ***ḥāgag*** occurs sixteen times with the principal meaning "holding, keeping a feast," again in association with worship. See also Exod. 5:1; 12:1 (Passover); Lev. 23:14 (all major festivals); Lev. 23:39, 41.

NT Words

heortē [ἑορτή, *1859*]

heortē is a noun found nearly thirty times meaning "feast," "festival" throughout, indicating specific celebrations in the Jewish religious calendar.

The Feast of Passover is indicated in Matt. 26:5; 27:15; Mark 14:2; 15:6; Luke 2:41; John 2:23; 6:4; 11:56; 12:12, 20. The Feast of Tabernacles is noted in John 7:2ff.

General references to an unidentified feast are found in John 5:1; Col. 2:16.

heortazō [ἑορτάζω, *1858*]

heortazō is a rare verb found only in 1 Cor. 5:8, exhorting the people "to celebrate the festival" of Passover in sincerity and truth.

deipnon [δεῖπνον, *1173*]

deipnon is a noun denoting a "banquet," "feast," or "meal" in both a ritual and non-ritual sense. The term occurs sixteen times. The sense of "banquet" or "feast" is found in Matt. 23:6; Mark 6:21; Luke 14:12ff.

Ritual "festivals" are in view in Mark 12:39; Luke 20:46; John 13:2ff.; 21:20. The Lord's "supper" is mentioned in 1 Cor. 11:21. An ordinary "meal" is indicated in John 12:2.

Rev. 19:9, 17 refer metaphorically to the marriage "supper" of the Lamb at the end of time.

dochē [δοχή, *1403*]

dochē is a rare synonym for ***heortē*** (see above), denoting a "banquet," "feast" in a general context, found only in Luke 5:29; 14:13.

agapē [ἀγάπη, *26*]

agapē is a common term denoting "love," "affection" throughout its nearly 120 occurrences. In particular, ***agapē*** denotes a "love feast" in Jude 16.

Additional Notes

There is a progressive development of the significance of feasting from a primarily literal one in the Old Testament to a predominantly spiritual one in the New Testament. The vocabulary of "feasting" in the old covenant centers largely on the Israelite ritual festivals, where fellowship and sharing meals among Levitical priests and lay Israelites at the physical level undoubtedly symbolizes spiritual fellowship and intimacy with Yahweh. In the New Testament, it is clear that the parables of Jesus that focus on feasting and celebration also speak of intimate fellowship with God. In the book of Revelation, the greatest feast of all (viz. the "wedding supper of the Lamb") is the culmination of all that the ritual festivals of the Mosaic covenant anticipate, namely eternal peace and fellowship with God and his Son in glory.

See Also: → MARRY

FEEBLE → POOR → SICK → WEAK

FEED

OT Words

'ākal **[אָכַל, 398]**

This verb is very common in the Old Testament and has the dominant sense of "eat," "devour." With the causative (Hiphil) sense of "feed," however, it is found approximately twenty times.

In the literal sense of "feed," meaning "providing for or giving food (to people)," ***'ākal*** occurs in 1 Kgs. 22:27; 2 Chr. 18:26. The meaning "feed on" is also indicated in Lam. 4:5; Dan. 11:26.

The remaining usage of ***'ākal*** in this sense is metaphorical. Ps. 80:5 refers to God's people being "fed with the bread of tears" (i.e., punishment), indicating the bringing about of a certain emotion or state of mind. Similarly, Isa. 49:26 refers to Yahweh "feeding" his enemies with their own flesh, as an expression of his wrath against them. The theme of "feeding" as punishment is also taken up in the context of Yahweh enacting the curses of the covenant against his people for their rejection of him (cf. Jer. 9:15; 23:15). ***'ākal*** is also used positively in Isa. 58:14, to refer to Yahweh rewarding his people's obedience by allowing them to "feed" on the blessing of the Abrahamic covenant.

rā'āh **[רָעָה, 7462]**

This term occurs around 170 times and means "feed" in both a literal and metaphorical sense. Firstly, ***rā'āh*** refers to the pasturing or grazing of animal herds; and secondly to shepherding or pastoring in the metaphorical sense.

The literal meaning of pasturing flocks is found, for example, in Gen. 29:7; 37:2ff.; Exod. 34:3; 1 Sam. 17:15; Job 1:14; Isa. 5:17. In Isa. 11:7; 65:25, ***rā'āh*** refers to the literal activity of pasturing, but the context is also profoundly symbolic, for both of these texts describe an idyllic picture of harmony and peace that will characterize the restoration and renewal of the earth. These scenes anticipate the ushering in of the future messianic age.

The metaphorical sense of "feeding" (i.e., shepherding) God's people (i.e., his flock) is found in 2 Sam. 5:2; 1 Chr. 11:2; Ps 78:1, where this role is predicated of King David in relation to the people of Israel. Similarly, Ezek. 34:23; Mic. 5:4 refer to the messianic "Davidic" shepherd whom God will provide for this purpose. See also 1 Chr. 17:6; 2 Sam. 7:7. Related to this theme is the idea of Yahweh as the shepherd of his people, as one who "feeds" them (cf. Ps. 28:9; Isa. 40:11; Ezek. 34:13ff.). In addition, Yahweh promises good shepherds who will feed Israel with knowledge and understanding (cf. Jer. 3:15; 23:15).

In Hos. 4:16, Israel's sin hampers Yahweh's shepherding role. There are also references to Israel's evil shepherds, who are not "feeding" God's people with love and compassion (cf. Jer. 23:2; Ezek. 34:2, 3, 10).

rā'āh also refers metaphorically to divine punishment on the wicked — death shall be their shepherd (i.e., shall feed on them) (cf. Ps. 49:14; Hos. 9:2; Zech. 11:4, 7).

kûl **[כּוּל, 3557]**

This verb occurs about forty times and means "nourish," "sustain," "feed."

The literal sense of "feed" (i.e., provide food for) occurs in Gen. 45:11; 50:21; 2 Sam. 19:32; 2 Sam. 20:3; 1 Kgs. 17:4; 18:4; Neh. 9:1.

Zech. 11:16 illustrates a metaphorical use of ***kûl***, where, as a judgment against the wickedness of his people, Yahweh will raise up a worthless shepherd who will fail to feed them.

NT Words

boskō [βόσκω, *1006*]

boskō is a verb found nine times meaning "feed" in both a literal and metaphorical sense in most of these contexts.

The description of animals "feeding" is recorded in Matt. 8:30; Mark 5:11; Luke 8:32; 15:15.

Christ's injunction to Peter to "feed my sheep" has the metaphorical sense of "nurture God's people in the word" (cf. John 21:15, 17).

poimainō [ποιμαίνω, *4165*]

poimainō is a verb meaning "feed," "tend," "rule" throughout its eleven occurrences.

The literal meaning "tending" cattle or sheep includes the responsibility of "feeding" them, among other things (cf. Luke 17:7; 1 Cor. 9:7). Christ's figurative exhortation to Peter to "feed my sheep" is an injunction to attend to the spiritual needs of his people (cf. John 21:16). See also Acts 20:28; 1 Pet. 5:2; Rev. 7:17.

trephō [τρέφω, *5142*]

trephō is a verb meaning "feed," "nourish" throughout its eight occurrences. References to God "feeding" his creatures are found in Matt. 6:26; Luke 12:24. Rev. 12:6, 14 refer to the divine "nourishing" of the symbolic woman in the wilderness. Matt. 25:37 mentions "feeding" people. See Jas. 5:5 for another symbolic usage.

psōmizō [ψωμίζω, *5595*]

psōmizō is a rare verb, expressing the sense of "feeding" someone in Rom. 12:20.

Additional Notes

Both the Hebrew and Greek vocabulary for feeding can be either literal and metaphorical. In the latter sense, "feeding" in both Testaments, especially when predicated of God, is primarily concerned with the process of nurturing and rendering comfort to those under God's care.

See Also: → DRINK → FILL

FEEL, FEELING

OT Words

mûsh [**מוּשׁ, 4184**]

This rare verb occurs only three times, with the literal sense of "touch," "feel" (cf. Gen. 27:21; Judg. 16:26; Ps. 115:7).

māshash [**מָשַׁשׁ, 4959**]

māshash is another rare verb, meaning "grope," "feel," "search." ***māshash*** occurs nine times (cf. Gen. 27:12; 31:34ff.). In Exod. 10:21, the thick darkness of the Egyptian night plague is so impenetrable that it may be "felt." Deut. 28:29 contains the covenant curse whereby Israel will "grope" in the dark like a blind person as a result of her punishment from Yahweh. See also Job 5:14; 12:25.

NT Words

ginōskō [γινώσκω, *1097*]

ginōskō is a common verb found over two hundred times with the primary meaning "to know," as well as a variety of related senses. In Mark 5:29 ***ginōskō*** is translated "feel," referring to the woman healed of her hemorrhage when she "felt" that the disease had left her body.

psēlaphaō [ψηλαφάω, *5584*]

psēlaphaō is a verb found in four places meaning "feel," "touch," or "handle" with one's hands (cf. Luke 24:39; Acts 17:27; Heb. 12:18; 1 John 1:1).

FELLOW

NT Words

anēr [ἀνήρ, *435*]

anēr is a common noun occurring over two hundred times with the principal meaning "man," "husband." In Acts 17:5, however, ***anēr*** refers to wicked "fellows," troublemakers inciting a civil riot.

See Also: → MAN → FRIEND

FELLOWSHIP

OT Words

ḥābar [**חָבַר, 2266**]

This term occurs about thirty times, with the predominant sense of "join (together)," "unite." However, it is translated once as "fellowship" in Ps. 94:20, which poses the rhetorical question as to whether wicked rulers can ever have fellowship with God. The implied answer is, understandably, in the negative. (→ JOIN)

ḥābēr [**חָבֵר, 2270**]

This is the adjectival form of ***ḥābar*** (see above), occurring eleven times, with the dominant sense of "compassion." ***ḥābēr*** does, however, indicate the idea of close bonding or intimate "fellowship" in Judg. 20:11, where all the Israelites came together against the city of Gibeah, "united as one person."

NT Words

koinōnia [κοινωνία, *2842*]

koinōnia is a noun denoting "fellowship," "communion" throughout most of its twenty occurrences. It emphasizes the worth of Christian community bound together by faith and trust in Christ (cf. Acts 2:42; 1 Cor. 1:9).

In particular, ***koinōnia*** refers to the "participation," the "communion" made possible through the symbolic meal signifying the body and blood of Christ in 1 Cor. 10:16; Gal. 2:9; 1 John 1:3ff.

A general reference to "fellowship" in the sense of a "partnership" is found in 2 Cor. 6:14; Phil. 1:5. The bond of "fellowship" between the believer and the Holy Spirit is indicated in 2 Cor. 13:14; Phil. 2:1; the "fellowship" or "sharing" of Christ's sufferings in Phil. 3:10; and the "sharing" of one's faith in Phlm. 6.

koinōnos [κοινωνός, *2844*]

koinōnos is a variant of ***koinōnia***, above, denoting a "partner," or one who shares in a bond, commitment, or common task.

The murderous "partnership" of godless Israelites who had brought about the death of prophets is indicated in Matt. 23:30.

Various "partnerships" are referred to: business comrades (Luke 5:10); fellow-worshipers (1 Cor. 10:18); demon-worshipers (1 Cor. 10:20); partners in Christ's sufferings (2 Cor. 1:7); gospel ministry (2 Cor. 8:23; Phlm. 17); suffering in persecution (Heb. 10:33).

Being a "partaker" of divine glory is indicated in 1 Pet. 5:1; and a "partaker" of the divine nature in 2 Pet. 1:4.

koinōneō [κοινωνέω, *2841*]

koinōneō is a verb found in eight places signifying the action of "making oneself a partner," "sharing in."

"Sharing in" the spiritual blessings of God's people is indicated in Rom. 15:27. The act of "sharing" material goods with the teachers of God's word is noted in Gal. 6:6. "Entering into a partnership" of gospel ministry is indicated in Phil. 4:15. A warning against "participating" in another person's sin is recorded in 1 Tim. 5:22. The privilege of "sharing in" Christ's sufferings is noted in 1 Pet. 4:13. See also Rom. 12:13; 2 John 11.

synkoinōneō [συγκοινωνέω, *4790*]

synkoinōneō is a synonym for ***koinōneō***, above, found in only three places. A warning to "take no part in" the works of darkness and the sins of others is found in Eph. 5:11; Rev. 18:4. Phil. 4:4 refers to "sharing" one's trouble .

FEMALE

NT Words

thēlys [θῆλυς, *2338*]

thēlys is an adjectival form found in five places used nominally to denote a "woman" or "female."

The designation "female," referring to God's creative work in bringing the woman Eve into the world, is noted in Matt. 19:4; Mark 10:6. In Gal. 3:28 Paul affirms, among other things, that there is neither male nor "female" in Christ Jesus — there is a complete equality of status. In Rom. 1:26, 27, ***thēlys*** denotes "women" in the generalized context of those leading immoral, sexually promiscuous lifestyles, which brings down the wrath of God.

See Also: → WOMAN

FEVER

OT Words

qaddaḥat [קַדַּחַת, **6920**]

qaddaḥat is a rare noun, occurring only twice and meaning "fever" in the context of illness as a consequence of a divine curse for the violation of the Mosaic law covenant (Deut. 28:22; Lev. 26:16).

NT Words

pyretos [πυρετός, *4446*]

pyretos occurs six times, denoting the medical condition of a "fever" in each case (cf. Matt. 8:15; Mark 1:31; Luke 4:38, 39; John 4:52; Acts 28:8).

pyressō [πυρέσσω, *4445*]

pyressō is a rare verb found only twice, meaning "to be sick with fever" in Matt. 8:14; Mark 1:30.

FEW

OT Words

me'at [מְעַט, **4592**]

This adverb has the primary sense of "little," or "small," and "few," thus describing diminution of quantity, size, and number. (→ LITTLE) ***me'at*** means "few" in approximately twenty contexts. In some cases, there is ambiguity in the translation between "few"(in number) and "small" (in quantity) (e.g., Num. 26:56; 33:54; 35:8).

References to small numbers of people include those in Deut. 7:7; 26:5 28:62; 1 Chr. 16:19, all of which refer to the Israelite people. Jer. 42:2 mentions the small size of the Judean remnant remaining in the land after the fall of Jerusalem.

Other general references include 1 Sam. 17:28 (sheep); Job 15:11 (comforts from God); Ezek. 5:3 (strands of hair).

NT Words

oligos [ὀλίγος, *3641*]

oligos is an adjective meaning "few," "little," "small" for most of its nearly forty occurrences.

The meaning "few," denoting "a small number," is used in relation to people in Matt. 7:14; 22:14; Luke 13:23 in the context of the comparatively small number who find true salvation and peace with God. In particular, Noah and his family are described as the "few" who were saved from the great flood in 1 Pet. 3:20. Other general references include Matt. 9:37; Mark 6:5; Rev. 3:4.

"Few" is used in a non-personal way in Matt. 15:34; Mark 8:7; Luke 10:2; 12:48; Acts 17:4; Rev. 2:14, 20.

See Also: → LITTLE

FIDELITY → FAITH

FIELD, CORNFIELD

OT Words

sādeh [**שָׂדֶה, 7704**]

sādeh is quite a common noun that occurs over three hundred times, with the primary meanings "field," "land" in the sense of both cultivated land and undeveloped countryside (i.e., plains).

sādeh is generally used in a mundane sense, referring to fields (e.g., Gen. 27:3ff.; Exod. 10:15; Num. 19:16; Deut. 11:5; Josh. 8:24; Eccl. 5:9; Isa. 36:2; Jer. 6:12; Ezek. 7:16). In particular, Deut. 28:3 speaks of covenant blessings that will result in fertile fields, while Deut. 28:16 refers to the curse of the covenant, which results in an agricultural wasteland.

Fields as personal property are also indicated in a number of contexts. In Jer. 32:7ff., the prophet purchases a field in response to Yahweh's instruction as a symbolic indicator that one day in the future, after a time of punishment, Judah will be renewed. Exod. 23:11, 16 refer to Israelite personal property, giving instruction as to how those fields are to be managed by the people of God under Mosaic law. See also in this regard Lev. 19:9; 23:22; 27:16ff.; Deut. 5:21; 24:19. Fields are sometimes designated as burial plots, particularly in the case of the patriarchs Sarah, Abraham, and Joseph (cf. Gen. 23:9ff.; 25:9, 10; 49:29ff.; 50:13; Josh. 24:32). Other references to fields as personal property include those in Ruth 2:2ff.; 1 Sam. 6:14; 2 Kgs. 8:3ff.; 9:25; Neh. 5:3.

In addition, references to a "plowed field" (or similar metaphor) indicate the consequences of a judgment against God's people at the hand of their enemies, since it signifies the wasting of the land of Canaan (cf. Jer. 26:18; Ezek. 33:27; Joel 1:10; Mic. 1:6; 2:4; 3:12). Ezek. 36:30 contains a promise of renewed agricultural fertility as part of the sign of renewed covenant blessing.

karmel [**כַּרְמֶל, 3759**]

karmel is a noun denoting a "fruitful, fertile field" for most of its thirteen occurrences (cf. Isa. 10:18; 32:15ff.; Jer. 48:33). It also refers to the "fertile land" of Canaan in Jer. 2:7; 4:26.

bar [**בַּר, 1251** (Aramaic)]

bar is an Aramaic term found seven times, denoting "field" in the sense of "open countryside" (cf. Dan. 2:38; 4:12ff.).

NT Words

agros [ἀγρός, *68*]

agros is a noun signifying "field" throughout its nearly forty occurrences.

agros refers to a "field" as a plot of agricultural land, cultivated or uncultivated, in Matt. 6:28ff.; 13:24ff.; 27:7ff.; Mark 13:6; Luke 12:28; 15:15, 25; Acts 4:37.

chōra [χώρα, *5561*]

chōra is a noun found nearly thirty times with the primary senses of "country," "region," "land" throughout. In two places, the term denotes a "field" ready for harvesting (cf. John 4:35; Jas. 5:4).

chōrion [χωρίον, *5564*]

chōrion is a diminutive form of ***chōra***, above, denoting a "field" in the ten occurrences of the term (cf. John 4:5; Acts 1:18; 4:34; 28:7). Acts 1:19 specifically refers to the "field of blood."

sporimos [σπόριμος, *4702*]

sporimos is a noun found three times denoting a "field of corn" in Matt. 12:1; Mark 2:23; Luke 6:1.

geōrgion [γεώργιον, *1091*]

geōrgion is a rare noun found only in 1 Cor. 3:9, referring to the sphere and object of God's work of redemption among people as his "field."

See Also: → EARTH → REGION → SOW → VINEYARD

FIERCE, FIERCENESS

NT Words

anēmeros [ἀνήμερος, *434*]

anēmeros is a rare adjective found only in 2 Tim. 3:3, denoting false teachers as "fierce" (or "savage") — one moral flaw in a long list of vices.

chalepos [χαλεπός, *5467*]

chalepos is a rare adjectival form describing the Gadarene demoniac as "fierce" (i.e., frightening in behavior and appearance) in Matt. 8:28.

See Also: → ANGER → FEAR → ZEAL

FIERY → BURN → REFINE

FIG

OT Words

te'ēnāh [תְּאֵנָה, **8384**]

te'ēnāh is a noun occurring about forty times that refers to the fruit of the fig tree, as well as to the fig tree itself. ***te'ēnāh*** is both literal and metaphorical in its usage.

Literal fruit is indicated in Gen. 3:7; Num. 13:23; 20:5; 2 Kgs. 20:7; Neh. 13:15; Isa. 38:21.

Figs and fig trees in the Old Testament symbolize both blessing and judgment. They indicate security and prosperity in the land of Canaan (cf. 2 Kgs. 18:31; Isa. 36:16; Mic. 4:4; Zech. 3:10). In Joel 2:22; Hag. 2:19 they signify promised renewal, after the inflicting of divine judgment. In contrast, the deprivation of figs and fig trees is often a clear sign of Yahweh punishing his people for their covenant disobedience (cf. Jer. 5:17; 8:13; Hos. 2:12; Joel 1:12; Amos 4:9; Hab. 3:17). Rotten figs are also symbolic of divine judgment (cf. Jer. 24:1ff.; Hos. 9:10; also Nah. 3:12).

NT Words

sykon [σῦκον, *4810*]

sykon is a noun denoting "figs" in four contexts, all of them literal (cf. Matt. 7:16; Mark 11:13; Luke 6:44; Jas. 3:12).

olynthos [ὄλυνθος, *3653*]

olynthos is a rare noun occurring only in Rev. 6:13, referring to an "unripe fig."

Additional Notes

Figs and fig trees are much more prevalent in the Old Testament than in the New. Jesus cursing the barren fig tree in Mark 11:14 sums up in one climactic verse all that the Old Testament "fig (tree) symbolism" anticipates by way of divine judgment against the people of Yahweh. In short, Jesus' words represent a devastating indictment against the faithlessness and godlessness of that Jewish generation among whom he lived and worked. There is little doubt that this curse relies for its full impact on the hearers' knowledge and understanding of Old Testament symbolism involving this particular fruit so common in the ancient Near East.

FIG TREE

NT Words

sykē [συκῆ, *4808*]

sykē is a term denoting a literal "fig tree" in each of the sixteen contexts in which it is found (cf. Matt. 21:19ff.; 24:32; Mark 11:13ff.; 13:28; Luke 13:6ff.; John 1:48ff.; Jas. 3:12; Rev. 6:13).

FIGHT, FIGHTING

OT Words

lāḥam [לָחַם, **3898**]

lāḥam is found nearly 180 times, meaning "to fight," as well as the derivative senses of "do battle," "make war."

With human beings as the subject, ***lāḥam*** refers to literal fighting in general (as in battle) in a number of contexts (e.g., Exod. 1:10; Num. 21:21ff.; Isa. 19:2; 37:8; Jer. 41:12). With Israel or Israelite leaders as its subject, ***lāḥam*** refers to warfare against the Canaanites (cf. Josh. 10:25; 19:47; Judg. 1:1ff.; 10:18); the Midianites (cf. Judg. 8:1); the Ammonites (cf. Judg. 11:4ff.); the Philistines (i.e., David and Goliath — 1 Sam. 17:9ff.); the Amalekites (cf. 1 Sam. 15:18); and also against one another in civil war (cf. Judg. 12:3, 4).

The use of ***lāḥam*** is more significant when Yahweh is its subject. In these contexts, God functions as the divine warrior who fights against his enemies on behalf of his people. First of all, there is the divine promise to fight for Israel against the peoples of Canaan (cf. Deut. 1:8; 3:22; 20:4). This is followed by the record of

Yahweh's confrontation with these people (cf. Josh. 10:14; 23:3; Judg. 11:32). Egypt also falls victim to Yahweh as divine warrior (cf. Exod. 14:14, 25).

This same theme continues in the prophetic writings. Yahweh promises to destroy the enemies of Israel by fighting against them (cf. Isa. 10:32 [Assyria]). Zech. 10:5; 14:3 contain the apocalyptic vision of the heavenly army of Yahweh uniting with the armies of Israel and Judah against their foes. Dan. 10:20 records the vision of a heavenly battle between the angel of the Lord and the demonic prince of Persia.

Conversely, Yahweh also declares his intention to fight against his own people for rejecting him (cf. Isa. 63:10; Jer. 21:5; 34:22).

When ***lāḥam*** has a human subject, there are a number of contexts in which the enemies of Israel fight against the people of God — for example, the Ammonites (cf. Judg. 11:20); the Philistines (cf. 1 Sam. 4:9; 13:5; 31:1); the Arameans (or Syrians) (cf. 1 Kgs. 20:1); the Babylonians (cf. Jer. 21:2; 32:24; 37:8, 10). Then, in Jer. 1:19, Yahweh promises to protect the prophet from his own people, who will fight against him, for they have even turned against God.

The psalmist pleads with God to fight against his enemies for him (cf. Ps. 35:1). There is a metaphorical reference to "fighting" in Pss. 56:2; 109:3, wherein the psalmist is suffering opposition and persecution from his enemies.

NT Words

agōn [ἀγών, *73*]

agōn is a noun found six times, meaning "conflict," "fight," in both literal and metaphorical contexts.

General references to "conflict" among people are found in Phil. 1:30; Col. 2:1; 1 Thess. 2:2. Metaphorical references to "fighting the good fight" in relation to living out the Christian life are found in 1 Tim. 6:12; 2 Tim. 4:7. The Christian life is described as a "race" in Heb. 12:1, with the underlying inference of a struggle.

agōnizomai [ἀγωνίζομαι, *75*]

agōnizomai is a verb found seven times, meaning "to strive," "fight," and used both literally and metaphorically.

An exhortation to "strive" to enter the narrow door that leads to salvation is found in Luke 13:24.

A general reference to people "fighting" in a physical sense is found in John 18:36. The athlete's "striving" for self control is noted in 1 Cor. 9:25. The apostle Paul's "toiling" in the context of gospel ministry is indicated in Col. 1:29. Paul describes "laboring earnestly" in prayer in Col. 4:12. The stance of "fighting the good fight" in relation to the struggle of Christian living is indicated in 1 Tim. 6:12; 2 Tim. 4:7.

athlēsis [ἄθλησις, *119*]

athlēsis is a rare noun denoting the "struggle" with suffering, found only in Heb. 10:32.

pykteuō [πυκτεύω, *4438*]

pykteuō is a rare verb found only in 1 Cor. 9:26 meaning "to fight" as a boxer.

machomai [μάχομαι, *3164*]

machomai is a verb found four times meaning "strive," "quarrel." References to people "arguing," "quarreling" among themselves are found in John 6:52; Acts 7:26; 2 Tim. 2:24. Jas. 4:2 refers generally to "fighting."

thēriomacheō [θηριομαχέω, *2341*]

thēriomacheō is a rare verb meaning "to fight with wild beasts," found only in 1 Cor. 15:32.

machē [μάχη, *3163*]

machē is a noun derived from ***machomai*** (see above) denoting "fighting," "quarreling" in four contexts. Three of these contexts indicate "quarreling" among believers. In 2 Cor. 7:5 ***machē*** denotes "fighting" in the probable sense of "physical harassment" in the context of persecution.

theomachos [θεομάχος, *2314*]

theomachos is a rare adjectival form describing those "who fight against God."

Additional Notes

With one or two exceptions, the overwhelming usage of the Hebrew term ***lāḥam*** focuses on physical fighting or combat. Such confrontation takes place on earth both among human beings, and between Yahweh and his enemies, and occasionally includes his own people. The reason for this physical focus is clear, since the world of the ancient Israelite is bound up with the destiny of Canaan, and the focus of all conflict centers on the land, either directly or indirectly. In the New Testament, the focus of "fighting" shifts from earthly combat to heavenly spiritual conflict. The real "fight," as far as the new covenant believer is concerned, is not with earthly opponents but with spiritual forces of darkness. Christ has won the decisive battle against such forces on the cross, so that his people might be fully delivered from the power of sin and death.

See Also: → PLEA → STRIVE → WARFARE

FIGURE → ALLEGORY → IMAGE → TYPE

FILL, FILL UP

OT Words

mālē' [מָלֵא, 4390]

This verb occurs around 250 times, with the principal meaning "fill (up)." ***mālē'*** is also translated "fulfill" on approximately thirty occasions. (→ FULFILL)

In the literal sense of "fill," ***mālē'*** indicates the occupation of physical space — for example, oceans filling the earth (Gen. 1:22); and the creation mandate for humans to populate the whole earth (Gen. 1:28; 9:1). The remaining usage is predominantly mundane, referring to filling common household containers and other natural or manmade objects (e.g., Gen. 26:15; Exod. 10:6; Deut. 6:11; 1 Kgs. 18:33; Job 41:7; Ps. 104:24; Ezek. 3:3; Nah. 2:12; Zech. 8:5).

The metaphorical usage of ***mālē'*** accounts for about half of the occurrences of the term and is found in a variety of contexts, referring to both animate and inanimate subjects.

Concerning people, ***mālē'*** refers to the righteous being filled with the blessings of God (e.g., Pss. 107:9; 127:5; Joel 2:24); and the wicked being filled with curses from God (e.g., Ps. 110:6; Prov. 20:17; Ezek. 23:33). As a sign of God's judgment, various places are declared to be "filled" with the slain (e.g., Ezek. 32:5, 6; Jer. 51:5; 41:9; Ezek. 11:6). Skilled workmen are also declared to be filled with the Spirit of God (cf. Exod. 28:3), including the master craftsmen Oholiab and Bezalel, who were assigned to work on the construction of the tabernacle (cf. Exod. 31:3; 35:1). Being filled with wisdom is also related to the filling of the Spirit (cf. Exod. 35:35; 1 Kgs. 7:14).

At the inanimate level, "filling" is predicated of various phenomena. In the sphere of moral evil, for example, Jerusalem is declared to be filled with innocent blood (cf. 2 Kgs. 24:4); and Israel is said to be full of idols (cf. Isa. 2:8; Jer. 16:18). Jer. 51:5 declares Babylon to be full of guilt before Yahweh; Judah is charged with being full of adultery in Jer. 23:10. Similar instances of this kind are also found in Gen. 6:11; 2 Kgs. 21:16; Ezra 9:11; Eccl. 9:3; Ezek. 9:9. Elsewhere, violence is said to fill the earth (cf. Gen. 6:13; Ps. 74:20; Isa. 1:15); as does the love of God (cf. Ps. 119:64); and praise to God (cf. Hab. 3:3). Yahweh promises to fill Zion with righteousness in Isa. 33:5; and the knowledge of the Lord is said to fill the earth in Isa. 11:9. See also Hab. 2:14. Conversely, Isa. 30:27; 34:6 declare that God's wrath will fill the nations. Although these references speak above all of inanimate phenomena, the underlying reference is to people who are either blessed or condemned, depending on the kind of "filling" they experience.

Finally, with regard to the tabernacle and temple, the filling of those structures with the glory cloud, the sacred presence of Yahweh, is described in a number of significant texts (cf. Exod. 40:34, 35; 1 Kgs. 8:10, 11; 2 Chr. 5:13, 14; 7:1, 2; Isa. 6:4; Ezek. 10:4; 43:5; 44:4). Such a filling is of great importance since it foreshadows, in a dramatic, historical, and literal way, the coming of God's Spirit to dwell in the heart of every believer in the new covenant age to signal the fulfillment of God's kingdom on earth. Such a coming is foreseen by the prophet Haggai in Hag. 2:7, who records the divine promise to fill the postexilic temple with a splendor that will exceed the glory of Solomon's temple. It is, in fact, a prophecy of the coming of the Messiah. (→ FULL)

sāba' [שָׂבַע, 7646]

sāba' is a synonym for ***mālē'*** (see above), meaning "satisfy" and "fill." (→ SATISFY)

In its literal sense, ***sāba'*** indicates "filling to satisfaction" in regard to food. The term is commonly found in contexts describing the blessings of the old covenant whereby Yahweh guarantees for his people the provision of abundant food (i.e., he will "fill" them . . .) in the land of Canaan (cf. Deut. 6:11; 8:10, 12; Neh. 9:29; Ps. 37:19; Isa. 44:16; Jer. 44:17); and also during the period of Israel's stay in the wilderness (cf. Pss. 78:29; 81:16; 105:40). Other more general references to being provided (i.e., "filled") with food include those in Deut. 14:29; Ruth 2:14; Job 31:31; Ps. 132:15; Prov. 12:11. In a judgment context according to the covenant curse, God's people are deprived of food (viz. they are not to be filled) (cf. Lev. 26:26; Ezek. 7:19; Mic. 6:14; Hos. 4:10).

On a metaphorical level, ***sāba'*** refers to "filling" as spiritual satisfaction (Pss. 17:15; 104:28; 107:9; Jer. 50:19); as old age (i.e., "full of days") (1 Chr. 23:1; 2 Chr. 24:15); and as grieving (i.e., full of sorrow) (Ps. 88:3).

"Filling" is also found in contexts where the judgment of God is in view. For example, in Ezek. 32:4 the beasts of the earth are set to gorge (i.e., fill) themselves on the Egyptians; and in Ezek. 39:20 the same will happen to the conquered foes of Israel at the hands of the Israelite army. In Hab. 2:16, the prophet records that Yahweh's enemies will be filled with shame.

melō' [מְלֹא, 4393]

This noun, which is also used adjectivally, means "full," "fullness" in the majority of the approximately forty contexts in which it is found.

The literal sense of ***melō'*** refers to the fullness of physical space, and occurs in mundane contexts (e.g., Exod. 16:33; Lev. 16:12; Judg. 6:38; Ezek. 41:8).

The metaphorical sense of this term refers first of all to the abundance (i.e., fullness) of earthly riches (e.g., Deut. 33:16; Ps. 24:1). Then, as a prelude to divine judgment, it is found in passages in which all inhabitants of the earth (i.e., all that fill it) are summoned to listen to the indictment of the people of Israel by Yahweh himself (cf. Mic. 1:2; Isa. 34:1). ***melō'*** also signals the actual invocation of Yahweh's judgment on his people, when her enemies will come and destroy the land of Judah and "all that fills it" (i.e., its inhabitants) (cf. Jer. 8:16; 47:2; Ezek. 12:19; 19:7; 30:12). See also Amos 6:8; Ezek. 32:15.

NT Words

plēroō [πληρόω, *4137*]

plēroō is a common verb found in nearly 100 places with the principal meaning "fulfill." Other meanings of ***plēroō*** include "fill," "be full." (→ FULFILL → FULL)

Christ tells the Pharisees "to fill up" the measure of the sins of their forefathers — an exhortation to maintain their hypocritical stance and thereby bring upon themselves the wrath of God (cf. Matt. 23:32).

The state of "being filled" with wisdom is predicated of Christ in Luke 2:40; being "filled" with emotion in John 16:6; Acts 13:52; Rom. 15:13; 2 Tim. 1:4; being "filled with the fullness" of God's Spirit in Eph. 3:19; 5:18; and being "filled" with righteousness in Phil. 1:11. Metaphorical reference to the "filling" of a valley is indicated in Luke 3:5. The "filling" of Ananias' heart with Satan is noted in Acts 5:3.

See also John 12:3; Acts 2:2; 5:28; Rom. 1:29; 15:14; 2 Cor. 7:4; Eph. 4:10; Col. 1:9.

anaplēroō [ἀναπληρόω, *378*]

anaplēroō is a variant form of ***plēroō***, above, found in six places and meaning "fulfill," "fill up" in three of these. (→ FULFILL)

In 1 Thess. 2:16 Paul declares that his Jewish detractors "fill up" their sins by hindering his efforts to evangelize the Gentiles.

symplēroō [συμπληρόω, *4845*]

symplēroō is another rare variant of ***plēroō*** (see above), referring to boats "filling up" with water in Luke 8:23.

empimplēmi [ἐμπίμπλημι, *1705*]

empimplēmi is a verb meaning "fill," "be full" in most of the six occurrences of the term.

Luke 1:53 refers to God "filling" the hungry with good things. Other references to people being "full" with food are found in Luke 6:25; John 6:12. Acts 14:17 refers metaphorically to God "satisfying" or "filling" people's hearts with food and gladness.

chortazō [χορτάζω, *5526*]

chortazō is a verb found in sixteen places with the consistent senses of "satisfy," "fill," "be full," in both a literal and metaphorical sense.

Matt. 5:6; Luke 6:21; 9:17 affirm that those who earnestly desire righteousness "shall be satisfied."

The physical state of "being filled" with food is noted in Matt. 14:20; Mark 6:42; John 6:26; Phil. 4:12; Jas. 2:16. Other references to "feeding" people include those in Matt. 15:33; Mark 8:4; Luke 16:21. Birds "gorged" with flesh are described in Rev. 19:21.

gemizō [γεμίζω, *1072*]

gemizō is a verb with the consistent sense of "fill," "fill up" in each of its six occurrences.

Reference to boats "filling" with water is found in Mark 4:37. A sponge was "filled" with vinegar before it was offered to Christ on the cross is noted in Mark 15:36. "Filling" a house with people is indicated in Luke 14:23. "Filling" baskets with leftover food after Jesus' miraculous feeding of the multitude is recorded in John 6:13. See also John 2:7.

In visionary contexts, ***gemizō*** denotes "filling" a censer with fire from the heavenly altar in Rev. 8:5; and "filling" the temple with smoke in Rev. 15:8.

mestoō [μεστόω, *3325*]

mestoō is a rare verb found only in Acts 2:13, referring to the false claim that the apostles "were full" of new wine, as observers mistook their Spirit-filled state for drunkenness.

plēthō [πλήθω, *4130*]

plēthō is a verb found nearly thirty times with the primary meaning "to fill."

"Filling" a sponge with vinegar and offering it to Christ on the cross to ease his pain is described in Matt. 27:48; John 19:29. "Filling" boats with fish is indicated in Luke 5:7.

The state of "being filled" with the Spirit is indicated in Luke 1:15, 41, 67; Acts 2:4; 4:8, 31, 9:17; 13:9.

plēthō is also used metaphorically to mean "to be filled" with anger (Luke 4:28; 6:11); with awe (Luke 5:26; Acts 3:10); with jealousy (Acts 5:17; 13:45). Acts 19:29 refers to a city "filled" with confusion.

plērōma [πλήρωμα, *4138*]

plērōma is a noun meaning "fullness," "fulfillment" in most of its seventeen occurrences.

The sense of "fullness" indicates that which contains a full measure, something abundant and ample, or vast. The term is used in relation to God's grace (John 1:16); to the blessing of Christ (Rom. 15:29); to God's universal possession (1 Cor. 10:26ff.); to the fullness of his presence (Eph. 1:23); and to the fullness of his being (Eph. 3:19; Col. 1:19). In particular, the "fullness" of Christ's person and authority is indicated in Eph. 4:13. The "fullness" of God's divine nature is said to dwell in Christ in Col. 2:9. The "fullness" of Christ's blessing in relation to the gift of salvation is noted in Rom. 15:29.

A significant use of ***plērōma*** is found in Rom. 11:12, 25, where it is translated "fullness" in relation to the Gentiles. It signifies the full extent of their conversion from paganism to faith in Christ in accordance with his redemptive purposes, and constitutes a catalyst for God's intent to redeem "all Israel." In the broader context of New Testament teaching on the end times, the "fullness of the Gentiles" signals the ushering in of the climactic new heavens and the new earth.

Love is said to be the "fulfillment" of the law in Gal. 4:4.

There is another use of ***plērōma*** in Gal. 4:4; Eph. 1:10 — texts containing the phrase the "fullness of time." In these contexts, "fullness" denotes "fulfillment," referring to the completion of God's redemptive purposes founded on the person of Christ.

Additional Notes

While there is a reasonable degree of similarity between the Old and New Testament vocabulary for "filling," the only comparison worthy of note is the usage of the various terms relating to the "filling" of either blessing or curse. Fullness of blessing under the old covenant primarily focused on material prosperity, whereas, under the new covenant, fullness of blessing centers primarily on spiritual values. The same is true for the phenomenon of the fullness of judgment. In the new covenant, God's judgment against his people falls on his Son, so that their salvation might be complete. All those who remain outside of Christ's sphere of salvation, however, will still have to bear the full brunt of God's wrath on the final day of judgment.

FILTH, FILTHY

OT Words

ṣô' [צוֹא, **6674**]

This adjective is rare, occurring only twice and meaning "filthy." In Zech. 3:3, 4, Joshua the high priest stands before God and Satan, covered in human excrement from head to foot. This visionary portrait depicts a condition of gross ritual uncleanness, symbolizing spiritual corruption that adheres to the high priest. But he is subsequently cleansed and forgiven by Yahweh himself.

NT Words

perikatharma [περικάθαρμα, *4027*]

perikatharma is a rare noun denoting "filth" or "rubbish" in 1 Cor. 4:13, referring symbolically to the attitude of hatred and disgust directed at the apostle Paul by his enemies.

rhypos [ῥύπος, *4509*]

rhypos is another rare noun denoting "filth" in the literal sense of "dirt" in 1 Pet. 3:21.

rhypainō [ῥυπαίνω, *4510*]

rhypainō is a rare verb found only twice, meaning "to be vile, filthy" in a moral sense in Rev. 22:11.

rhyparos [ῥυπαρός, *4508*]

rhyparos is a rare adjective found only in Jas. 2:2, referring to a poor man's "dirty shabby" clothing.

rhyparia [ῥυπαρία, *4507*]

rhyparia is a noun found only in Jas. 1:21 denoting moral "filthiness."

aischrotēs [αἰσχρότης, *151*]

aischrotēs is a term occurring only in Eph. 5:4, referring to the vice of "obscenity," "moral filth."

See Also: → DEFILE → EVIL

FIND

OT Words

māṣā' [מָצָא, 4672]

This common verb occurs approximately 450 times with the primary sense of "find."

In more than three-quarters of its occurrences, ***māṣā'*** means "find" in the sense of "discover." The usage is literal and predominantly mundane with people as its subject (e.g., Gen. 18:3; Num. 15:32; Deut. 17:2; Ruth 1:9; 2 Sam. 7:27; 2 Kgs. 22:8; Ps. 21:8; Eccl. 3:11; Isa. 10:14; Ezek. 22:30).

Where God is the subject, there are only three instances of divine "discovering" (cf. Gen. 16:7; 18:26ff.; Hos. 9:10). More common are references to people "finding grace, or favor" in the eyes of the Lord, or some similar expression. Significant examples are Noah (cf. Gen. 6:8); Moses (cf. Exod. 33:12ff.); and Israel (cf. Jer. 31:2). See also Gen. 19:19; 32:5; Exod. 34:9; Num. 11:15; 2 Sam. 15:25.

"Finding" favor in the eyes of human beings is also indicated in several places (cf. Gen. 33:8; Judg. 6:17; 1 Sam. 1:18; 2 Sam. 14:22; 1 Kgs. 11:19; Song 8:10).

māṣā' also describes human beings successfully "finding" or "discovering" God (cf. Deut. 4:29; 1 Chr. 28:9; Prov. 8:17, 35; Isa. 55:6; Jer. 29:13ff.). It is also used in a negative sense to describe not being able to find God, clearly suggesting divine judgment (e.g., Hos. 5:6; Amos 8:12).

"Finding" the knowledge of God is mentioned in Prov. 2:5. "Finding" rest is indicated Jer. 6:16; and finding no rest is mentioned in Jer. 45:3, as a consequence of divine judgment.

Num. 32:33 refers to the classic dilemma of the certainty of one's sin leading to "discovery."

shekaḥ [שְׁכַח, 7912 (Aramaic)]

This is an Aramaic verb found eighteen times in Ezra and Daniel, meaning "find" in the sense of the discovery or disclosure of that which has been covered, hidden, or forgotten (cf. Ezra 4:15, 19; 7:16; Dan. 2:25; 5:11ff.; 6:4ff.).

NT Words

heuriskō [εὑρίσκω, *2147*]

heuriskō is a common verb found nearly 180 times meaning "find," in a variety of contexts with a number of different nuances.

The meaning "find" in the general sense of "discover" is indicated in Matt. 2:8ff.; Mark 1:37; Luke 2:12; 11:9; John 1:41ff.; Acts 4:21; Rom. 7:21; 2 Cor. 2:13; 2 Tim. 1:17; Rev. 2:2; 9:6.

The passive sense of "be found" is indicated in relation to Mary's supernatural encounter with the Holy Spirit when it is recorded that she "was found" to be pregnant (cf. Matt. 1:18). Other passive uses include 1 Cor. 15:15; 2 Cor. 5:3; Gal. 2:17; Phil. 2:8; 1 Pet. 2:22; Rev. 5:4; 16:20; 20:11ff.

There is a significant metaphorical usage of "find" in Matt. 10:39; 16:25, with the underlying sense of "take full possession of" in relation to people "finding" true life if they are prepared to deny themselves for the sake of the gospel.

heuriskō means "find" in the sense of "receive" in Luke 1:30, which speaks of Mary "finding favor" with God. Other references to people "finding" such divine favor include those in Acts 7:46; 2 Tim. 1:18; Heb. 4:16. See also Heb. 9:12; 11:5.

The meaning "find" with the sense of "consider," or "make an assessment" of someone, is indicated in Acts 24:5 with reference to Paul's enemies having "found" him to be a troublemaker. See also 1 Cor. 4:2. Rev. 3:2 mentions divine assessment of people.

"Find" has the sense of "measure" in Acts 27:28, in relation to taking soundings in deep water.

aneuriskō [ἀνευρίσκω, *429*]

aneuriskō is a rare variant of ***heuriskō***, above, meaning "to find" as a result of searching. It is found in only two places (Luke 2:16; Acts 21:4).

FINGER

OT Words

'eṣba' [אֶצְבַּע, 676]

'eṣba' occurs around thirty times, with the consistent meaning "finger" in all but a few texts. ***'eṣba'*** is used both literally and metaphorically.

In its literal sense, ***'eṣba'*** refers first of all to the "fingers" of the priest in relation to the ritual sprinkling of blood on the altar (e.g., Exod. 29:12; Lev. 4:6ff.; 8:15; 16:14, 19; Num. 19:4). Then, the binding of the law on one's "fingers" is mentioned in Prov. 7:3. Other general, literal references include Prov. 6:13; Isa. 2:8; 17:8; Jer. 52:21.

Metaphorically, ***'eṣba'*** refers to the "finger" of God as a sign of his power and authority. In Exod. 8:19, for example, the Egyptian magicians are unable to duplicate the plague of gnats, declaring that this is the "finger of God" upon them. Jesus alludes to this incident in Luke 11:20. (See ***daktylos***, below.) Exod. 31:18; Deut.

9:10 refer to the "finger of Yahweh" writing the Ten Commandments on tablets of stone. Ps. 8:3 describes creation as the work of God's "fingers." See also Ps. 144:1; Isa. 59:3.

'eṣba' [**אֶצְבַּע, 677** (Aramaic)]

'eṣba' is the equivalent Aramaic term for ***'eṣba'***, above, denoting "fingers" and "toes" in only three places. Dan. 5:5 describes the "fingers" of a man (in reality, God) writing a message of condemnation against Belshazzar, the last of the Babylonian rulers.

NT Words

daktylos [δάκτυλος, *1147*]

daktylos is the sole dynamic equivalent of the Hebrew term ***'eṣba'*** (see above), occurring eight times and denoting a "finger." References include Matt. 23:4; Mark 7:33; Luke 11:46; 16:24; John 20:25, 27.

John 8:6 refers to Christ using his "finger" to write on the ground. Luke 11:20 contains an anthropomorphic reference to the "finger" of God as the agent of exorcising demons.

FINISH

OT Words

kālāh [**כָּלָה, 3615**]

This verb has a wide range of meanings, one of which is "to finish" in the sense of "complete," "accomplish." ***kālāh*** is found in approximately two hundred contexts and is translated "finish" in about a third of these.

In the sense of "complete," ***kālāh*** is found in Gen. 2:1, 2 indicating that God had finished his work of creation after six days. Other references to physical, literal completion include Gen. 6:16 (the ark); Ruth 2:21ff. (harvest); 2 Chr. 4:11; 7:11; 8:16 (the temple of Solomon).

Other uses of ***kālāh*** indicate "finishing" in the sense of "ceasing a certain activity." Not too fine a distinction may be drawn between "completing" and "finishing" a task; some overlap in meaning is therefore inevitable. Examples of this latter usage include Amos 7:2, where locusts threaten to devour all the crops of Israel in a vision of judgment. Gen. 27:30 refers to Isaac coming to the end of the patriarchal blessing he gave to Jacob (cf. also Gen. 49:33). The Israelites are said to have finished the construction of the tabernacle in Exod. 39:32; 40:33. The conclusion of the Day of Atonement sacrifices is recorded in Lev. 16:20 (cf. also 1 Sam. 13:10; 2 Sam. 6:18; 2 Kgs. 10:25; Ezra 9:1). Deut. 31:24 refers to Moses finishing the task of writing down the law of the covenant. Other references include Josh. 10:20; 19:49ff.; 1 Sam. 10:13; Ezek. 42:15; Jer. 51:63.

tāmam [**תָּמַם, 8552**]

tāmam is a synonym for ***kālāh*** (see above). Although ***tāmam*** occurs around sixty times, it means "finish," in the sense of completing a task, in only six places (cf. Josh. 4:10, 11; 5:8; 2 Sam. 15:24; 1 Kgs. 6:22; 7:22). The latter texts refer to the completion of the temple in Jerusalem. (→ CONSUME)

kālā' [**כָּלָא, 3607**]

kālā' is a verb found in eighteen contexts meaning "shut up," "restrain" with several related nuances. One of these nuances is the sense of "finish," found only in Dan. 9:24 in relation to one of the purposes of the "seventy 'sevens,'" — to "finish" transgression. The sense here is that of "abolishing" transgression.
(→ RESTRAIN)

NT Words

teleō [τελέω, *5055*]

teleō is a verb found twenty-six times with the primary senses of "finish," "fulfill," as well as related nuances.

The meaning "finish" implies "complete (a task)" in Matt. 11:1; 13:53; 19:1; 26:1; 2 Tim. 4:7; Rev. 11:7.

There is an overlap in meaning with "fulfill" in a number of places, where ***teleō*** is translated "finish" in the sense of "accomplish." The contexts here all relate to "completing," or "accomplishing," God's redemptive purposes through Christ's death on the cross (cf. Luke 12:50; 18:31; 22:37; John 19:28, 30).

The meaning "finish" also connotes the sense of "come to an end" in Rev. 15:8; 20:3ff.

teleioō [τελειόω, *5048*]

teleioō is a verb roughly synonymous with ***teleō***, above, meaning "perfect," "make perfect," in most of its nearly twenty-five occurrences. (→ PERFECT)

Several occurrences of the term also denote the act of "finishing." Luke 2:43 refers to a feast "coming to an end," "finishing." In addition, ***teleioō*** means "finish" in the sense of "accomplish," in relation to the redemptive work of Jesus Christ in John 5:36; 17:4; 19:28. Similarly, John 4:34 records Christ's intention to "finish," or "accomplish," the work of his Father. Acts 20:24 refers to Paul "finishing" the course of his ministry.

ekteleō [ἐκτελέω, *1615*]

ekteleō is a rare verb found only twice in Luke 14:29, 30, meaning "finish," "complete" in the context of building a tower.

synteleō [συντελέω, *4931*]

synteleō is a verb found seven times with the primary meaning "finish" in the sense of "bring (a task) to an end" in Matt. 7:28; Luke 4:13. The simple sense of "finish," "come to an end" is indicated in Luke 4:2; Acts 21:27. (→ FULFILL)

dianyō [διανύω, *1274*]

dianyō is a rare verb found only in Acts 21:7, describing Luke's "completing," or "finishing," a sea voyage.

plēthō [πλήθω, *4130*]

plēthō is a verb occurring nearly thirty times, with the dominant sense of "fill." However, in Luke 1:23 it means "finish," or "come to an end" in reference to the completion of Zechariah's priestly duties.

See Also: → FULFILL

FIRE

OT Words

'ēsh [**אֵשׁ, 784**]

'ēsh is a common noun, occurring around four hundred times with the almost exclusive sense of "fire." ***'ēsh*** is used both literally and metaphorically.

'ēsh in its literal sense of "fire" occurs in a number of contexts that are purely mundane (e.g., Gen. 22:6, 7; Judg. 9:15; Ps. 66:12; Isa. 44:16; Jer. 36:23; Ezek. 15:4ff.). Fire is also employed as an agent of military destruction (cf. 1 Sam. 30:1; 2 Sam. 14:30; 1 Kgs. 9:16); as a means of destroying idols (cf. 2 Kgs. 19:18; 1 Chr. 14:12; Isa. 37:19), and also the city of Jerusalem (cf. Neh. 1:3; 2:3, 13, 17). Fire is also frequently associated with Levitical ritual sacrifice (e.g., Exod. 29:14, 34; Lev. 1:7ff.; 2:14; 6:9ff.; Num. 6:18; 2 Chr. 7:1, 3; 35:13). In addition, it constitutes a major feature of Elijah's sacrifice on Mt. Carmel in confrontation with the prophets of Baal.

'ēsh is also used with reference to idolatrous calf worship (e.g., Exod. 32:20, 24). See also Jer. 7:18. Fire is also used in human sacrifice, a ritual absolutely prohibited by Yahweh. Prohibitions against the practice are recorded in Deut. 12:31; 18:10; 2 Kgs. 23:10; and instances of violation are found in 2 Kgs. 16:3; 17:17; 21:6; Jer. 7:31; 19:5; Ezek. 20:31.

One of the more significant common uses of ***'ēsh*** is in the large number of contexts where fire is used as an instrument of divine judgment. Significant examples are found in Gen. 19:24 (the destruction of Sodom and Gomorrah); Lev. 10:1, 2 (the execution of Nadab and Abihu); Num. 16:35 (the deaths of Korah and his family). References to the fiery destruction of Jerusalem and the temple at the hands of the Babylonians are found in Jer. 34:2; 39:8; 52:13; Lam. 2:3, 4; Ezek. 5:4; 16:41; 2 Kgs. 25:9; 2 Chr. 36:19. In certain places, Yahweh also condemns the wicked to a fiery death (e.g., Pss. 11:6; 68:2; Isa. 30:33; 66:15; Jer. 50:32; Ezek. 28:18; Zech. 9:14). Such punishment is also directed towards the people of God for covenant violation (e.g., Ps. 78:21; Isa. 1:7; 30:14; Jer. 4:4; Ezek. 20:47; Hos. 8:14; Mic. 1:4, 7). Finally, in this regard, fire is utilized as a means of destroying all traces of pagan worship and culture (e.g., Deut. 7:25; 9:21; Josh. 6:24; Judg. 1:8).

Metaphorically, ***'ēsh*** is used in contexts where supernatural fire is seen as an accompaniment to theophanic revelation. Particularly significant texts here include Exod. 3:2 (Moses and the burning bush); Exod. 13:21ff. (the pillar of fire in the wilderness, see also Exod. 40:38; Num. 14:14; Deut. 1:33; Neh. 9:12, 19; Ps. 78:19). Exod. 19:18 describes the Mt. Sinai theophany (see also Exod. 24:17; Deut. 4:11ff.; 5:4ff., 22ff.; Ps. 18:12ff., Ezek. 1:4, 13, 27; 10:2ff.). Related to the above are the descriptions of Yahweh as a "consuming fire" (e.g., Deut. 4:24; 9:3; 2 Sam. 22:9, 13; Ps. 50:3; Isa. 30:27; Jer. 15:14).

Other symbolic uses of this term include references to "fire" as strong passion, extortion (e.g., Ps. 39:3; Song 8:6; Jer. 20:9; Lam. 1:13); indications of promised divine deliverance from the fires of judgment (e.g., Zech. 2:5; 3:2); depicting fire as the dwelling place of God (e.g., Ezek. 28:14, 16); symbolizing the Day of the Lord judgment (e.g., Joel 2:30; Zech. 12:6); and refining the people of God through the fire of divine judgment (e.g., Zech. 13:9; Mal. 3:2).

lāhat [**לָהַט, 3857**]

lāhat is a verb found twelve times, meaning "set on fire," "burn (up)," in all but one instance. The usage is predominantly metaphorical.

The meaning "set on fire" is found in contexts depicting the wrath of God (e.g., Deut. 32:22; Ps. 97:3; Joel 1:19; 2:3; Mal. 4:1). The latter prophetic texts mention the phenomenon of fire as part of the Day of the Lord judgment. Ps. 104:4 uses ***lāhat*** in reference to the majesty of Yahweh. Other references include Job 41:21; Ps. 83:14.

nûr [נוּר, **5135** (Aramaic)]

nûr is an Aramaic noun found seventeen times, denoting the "fire" of a furnace in Dan. 3:22ff.; and the visionary "fire" of a divine revelation in Dan. 7:9, 10. Elsewhere the term is used adjectivally, meaning "fiery." All of these occurrences refer to the furnace into which Daniel's three friends had been thrown, and from which they were miraculously rescued (cf. Dan. 3:6ff.).

—— NT Words ——

pyr [πῦρ, *4442*]

pyr is virtually the sole term for "fire" in the New Testament, and it is found over seventy times.

References to literal "fire" are found in Matt. 3:10; Mark 9:22; Luke 22:55; Acts 28:5; Jas. 3:5. In addition, "fire" as the vehicle for a divine theophany is noted in Acts 7:30 in relation to the "burning bush" in the Sinai wilderness where God had appeared to Moses. See also Heb. 12:18. "Fire" in the metaphorical context of divine revelation is indicated in Matt. 3:11; Luke 3:16, with reference to baptism in the Holy Spirit; and in Acts 2:3 in relation to speaking in tongues as a consequence of baptism in the Holy Spirit. The phenomenon of "fire" as a sign accompanying the end of time is noted in Acts 2:19.

More commonly, "fire" is indicated symbolically as the instrument of divine wrath (Matt. 3:12; 25:41; Mark 9:43ff.; Luke 3:17; John 15:6; Heb. 10:27; 2 Pet. 3:7; Jude 7; Rev. 14:10; 16:8; 19:20; 20:9ff.; 21:8); and of divine judgment (1 Cor. 3:13ff.; 1 Pet. 1:7; Rev. 3:18). God himself is described as a "consuming fire" of judgment (Heb. 12:29); and "fire" is associated with the essential being of God (Rev. 1:14; 10:1), and of Christ (Rev. 19:12; 2:18). Other metaphorical references to "fire" include Heb. 1:7; Jas. 3:6; 5:3; Rev. 8:5ff.; 9:17ff.; 17:16.

pyrinos [πύρινος, *4447*]

pyrinos is a rare adjective found only in Rev. 9:17, describing the visionary breastplates of demonic creatures as "fiery."

phlogizō [φλογίζω, *5394*]

phlogizō is a rare verb meaning "to set on fire" found only in Jas. 3:6.

anthrakia [ἀνθρακία, *439*]

anthrakia is a rare noun denoting a "charcoal fire" in John 18:18; 21:9.

—— *Additional Notes* ——

Throughout both Old and New Testaments, fire represents the holiness of God and is a very powerful, almost universal, symbol of judgment on the wicked. The literal fiery judgments of God upon specific people, cities, and nations under the old covenant foreshadow the ultimate and terrible judgment of the Day of the Lord, when Jesus Christ shall return to judge the whole earth.

See Also: → BURN → OFFERING → REFINE

FIRM

—— NT Words ——

stereos [στερεός, *4731*]

stereos is an adjective found in four places meaning "solid," "firm."

2 Tim. 2:19 refers to the "foundation" of God's purposes being in his people's standing "firm." 1 Pet. 5:9 also exhorts people to be "firm" in their faith.

See Also: → STRENGTH

FIRST

—— OT Words ——

ri'shôn [רִאשׁוֹן, **7223**]

This is the standard Hebrew term for the ordinal number "first." ***ri'shôn*** occurs around two hundred times and has both numerical meaning as well as the superlative sense of "best" (i.e., first in degree). The term also means "former." (→ FORMER)

The literal numerical sense is frequently found in dates, such as the first day, month, or year (e.g., Gen. 8:13; Exod. 12:2; Lev. 23:5ff.; Josh. 4:19; Dan. 10:4). It is also used to describe the first occasion of an event (e.g., Gen. 13:4; Num. 10:13; 1 Kgs. 17:13; Isa. 1:26; Dan. 10:12), or the first of a series or sequence (e.g., Gen. 25:25; Exod. 34:1ff.; Lev. 4:4; 5:8). The translation "best" is found in 1 Chr. 18:17; Isa. 41:4; 44:6; Dan. 10:13.

'eḥād [אֶחָד, **259**]

'eḥād is a common noun found in nearly 1,000 places with the predominant meaning "one," denoting the cardinal numeral in the large majority of these contexts. ***'eḥād*** also signifies the ordinal number "first" (i.e., the adjectival sense) in around forty contexts.

The meaning "first" in a temporal sense is indicated, for example, in Gen. 1:5; Exod. 40:2; Lev. 23:24; Num. 1:1; Deut. 1:3; Ezra 3:6; Ezek. 26:1; Hag. 1:1. ***'eḥād*** means "first" in a sequential sense in Exod. 28:17; 39:10; Job 42:14.

qadmay [קַדְמַי, **6933** (Aramaic)]

qadmay is a rare Aramaic adjectival form denoting the ordinal number "first" in a sequential sense in Dan. 7:4, 8.

NT Words

prōtos [πρῶτος, *4413*]

prōtos is the standard adjectival form in the New Testament denoting the sense of "first" for most of the 100 or so occurrences of the term.

The designation "first" in the context of a sequence is indicated in Matt. 10:2; Mark 12:20; John 8:7; 1 Cor. 15:45ff.; Phil. 1:5. In particular the "first" (i.e., old) covenant is discussed in Heb. 8:7ff.; 9:15ff.; Rev. 2:4ff.; 20:5ff.; 21:1, 19.

The meaning "first" in the sense of a "former" state is noted in Matt. 12:45; 27:64; Luke 11:26. The temporal sense of "former" is evident in Matt. 21:31; Acts 1:1.

The state of being "first" in the sense of "most important" is noted in the paradoxical truth affirming that "the first shall be last, and the last first" in Matt. 19:30; Mark 9:35; Luke 13:30. See also Matt. 20:27; Acts 16:12. Matt. 22:38; Mark 12:28ff. refer to the "first" (i.e., the chief) commandment as the requirement to love God with all one's heart. See also Acts 25:2.

The heavenly Christ is described in Rev. 1:17 as "the first and the last," signifying his omnipotent authority (cf. also Rev. 2:8; 22:13).

mia [μία, *3391*]

mia is a dynamic equivalent for the Hebrew term ***'eḥād*** (see above), denoting the cardinal sense of "one" for most of its nearly eighty occurrences. Several contexts, however, indicate the sense of "first."

The meaning "first" in relation to a time sequence is indicated in Matt. 28:1; Mark 16:2; Luke 24:1; John 20:1, 19; Acts 20:7; 1 Cor. 16:2, all with reference to the "first" day of the week.

See Also: → FIRSTFRUIT → HEAD

FIRSTBEGOTTEN → FIRSTBORN

FIRSTBORN

OT Words

bekôr [בְּכוֹר, **1060**]

bekôr is a noun meaning "firstborn," "eldest (child)," referring in most cases to a male child. The term occurs about 120 times.

Most of the usage of ***bekôr*** is literal and mundane (e.g., Gen. 10:15; Exod. 12:12; Lev. 27:26; Deut. 15:19; 2 Kgs. 3:27; Isa. 14:30). More theologically significant uses of the term are found in Exod. 13:2, which requires that all firstborn male children be consecrated to Yahweh. See also Exod. 4:23; Pss. 78:51; 105:36; 136:10, all of which refer to the plague on the Egyptian firstborn. Finally, Exod. 4:22 contains the powerful symbolic reference to Israel as Yahweh's firstborn son (cf. also Jer. 31:9 in this regard).

NT Words

prōtotokos [πρωτότοκος, *4416*]

prōtotokos is an adjective found nine times with the meaning "firstborn" in both a literal and figurative sense.

References to Jesus as Mary's "firstborn" son are found in Matt. 1:25; Luke 2:7; Heb. 1:6. Heb. 11:28 refers to the "firstborn" of Egyptian families destroyed by the avenging angel, a divine judgment precipitating the exodus of the Israelite captives.

In metaphorical contexts, the meaning "firstborn" signifies the person of Jesus Christ, who is described as the "firstborn" of creation in Col. 1:15, the initial representative of a regenerate communion of believers who would continue throughout eternity. Col. 1:18; Rev. 1:5 refer to Christ as the "firstborn" from the dead, the prime example of the resurrected members of his body, the church. See also Heb. 12:23; Rom. 8:29 for related usage.

Additional Notes

The motif of the "firstborn son" is a powerful theological theme that pervades both Old and New Testaments. The significance of the dedication of all firstborn males to Yahweh, as well as the law of primogeniture and the attendant privileges of inheritance, all point forward in a redemptive-historical sense to the unique miracle of the incarnation, in which Jesus Christ is portrayed as the first-begotten of God the Father. This phenomenon expresses a centrally important element of the relationship between the first and second persons of the Godhead.

FIRSTFRUIT

OT Words

rē'shît **[רֵאשִׁית, 7225]**

This term occurs around fifty times and is usually translated "beginning," as well as related senses including "first" and "chief." In approximately one-third of its occurrences, however, ***rē'shît*** means "firstfruits."

In its literal sense, ***rē'shît*** refers to the firstfruits of harvest that are to be given as an offering to Yahweh (cf. Exod. 23:19; Lev. 2:12; Neh. 10:37; Ezek. 20:40; 44:30).

Metaphorically, Israel is referred to as the "firstfruits" of Yahweh's harvest in Jer. 2:3, as is the prince's land portion described in the temple vision of Ezekiel the prophet in Ezek. 48:14.

bikkûr **[בִּכּוּר, 1061]**

A synonym for ***rē'shît*** (see above), ***bikkûr*** occurs around twenty times, meaning "firstfruits" (or the equivalent). Its usage is purely literal.

bikkûr generally occurs in the context of the firstfruits of the harvest, required under the Mosaic law as an offering to Yahweh (e.g., Exod. 23:16; 34:22, 26; Lev. 2:14; Num. 18:13; 2 Kgs. 4:42; Ezek. 44:30). Similar reference is made to baked goods (cf. Lev. 23:17, 20); ripe grapes (cf. Num. 13:20); and the first ripe fig (cf. Isa. 28:4; Nah. 3:12).

NT Words

aparchē **[ἀπαρχή, *536*]**

aparchē is a noun denoting "firstfruits" in eight contexts, and is a dynamic equivalent for the Hebrew term ***rē'shît*** (see above). The usage of ***aparchē*** is metaphorical in all but one of these contexts.

Rom. 8:23 refers to the "firstfruits" of the Spirit in the context of the believer's assurance of salvation as a consequence of the Spirit's indwelling. In other contexts the designation "firstfruits" refers to the initial converts in Asia (Rom. 16:5); and in Achaia (1 Cor. 16:15). In Rev. 14:4 the redeemed people of God, the "144,000," are described in heaven as the "firstfruits" for God and the lamb. See also Jas. 1:18.

In 1 Cor. 15:20, 23 Christ himself is referred to as the "firstfruits" of those who have been raised from the dead, indicating that he is the first of many who would likewise rise from the dead and live with him eternally in glory.

Rom. 11:16 contains the sole literal reference to bread dough offered as "firstfruits" to God in ritual worship.

Additional Notes

Like the term "first-begotten," "firstfruits" is a motif that has significant redemptive-historical implications throughout the Bible. Though relatively uncommon in the Old Testament, it highlights the idea (as does "first-begotten") of that which belongs to God. Ultimately ***rē'shît***, like ***bekôr***, points forward to Jesus Christ as the one supremely dedicated to God, his Father.

FISH

OT Words

dāg **[דָּג, 1709];** ***dāgāh*** **[דָּגָה, 1710]**

These nouns, both masculine and feminine in form, occur about thirty-five times and mean "fish" in a literal sense (e.g., Gen. 1:26, 28; 9:2; Exod. 7:18ff.; Ps. 8:8; Isa. 50:2; Ezek. 29:4, 5; Jonah 1:17; 2:1). ***dāg*** is also used as a name for one of the gates of the city of Jerusalem (e.g., Neh. 3:3; 12:39; Zeph. 1:10).

dawwāg **[דַּוָּג, 1728]**

dawwāg is a rare term, occurring only twice, meaning "fisherman" (cf. Jer. 16:16; Ezek. 47:10).

NT Words

ichthys **[ἰχθύς, *2486*]**

ichthys is the dynamic Greek equivalent for the Hebrew term ***dāg*** (see above), denoting "fish" throughout its twenty occurrences, all of them literal (cf. Matt. 7:10; 17:27; Mark 6:38ff.; Luke 11:11; John 21:6ff.; 1 Cor. 15:39).

ichthydion **[ἰχθύδιον, *2485*]**

ichthydion is a rare diminutive form of ***ichthys*** (see above), denoting "small, little fish" in Matt. 15:34; Mark 8:7.

opsarion **[ὀψάριον, *3795*]**

opsarion is a rare synonym for ***ichthys***, denoting "fish" in five contexts (cf. John 6:9ff.; 21:9ff.).

halieus **[ἁλιεύς, *231*]**

halieus is a noun found in five places denoting a "fisherman" in a literal sense in Matt. 4:18; Mark 1:16; Luke 5:2. Matt. 4:19; Mark 1:17 both contain Jesus' assertion that he would make his disciples "fishers of men" (i.e., evangelists engaged in winning people for Christ).

halieuō **[ἁλιεύω, *232*]**

halieuō is a rare verb found only in John 21:3, meaning "to go fishing."

FLAME, FLAMING

OT Words

lahab **[לַהַב, 3851]**

lahab is derived from a verbal root meaning "to gleam," which gives rise to the two meanings "blade" and "flame." The latter meaning is evident in seven of the twelve contexts in which ***lahab*** is found.

The literal sense of "flame" occurs in Judg. 13:20; Job 41:21, and symbolically refers to the wrath of God in Isa. 29:6; 30:30; 66:15; Joel 2:5. In Isa. 13:8 there is another metaphorical use of ***lahab*** in reference to pain.

lehābāh **[לֶהָבָה, 3852]**

lehābāh is the feminine form of ***lahab*** (see above). It occurs around twenty times, meaning "flame" in the majority of instances.

lehābāh refers literally to "flames" in a destructive sense in Num. 21:28; Pss. 83:14; 105:32. ***lehābāh*** is cited as an instrument of divine judgment in Ps. 106:18; Isa. 5:24; 10:17; 47:14; Jer. 48:45; Joel 1:19; 2:3; Hos. 7:6; Ezek. 20:47; Dan. 11:33. Metaphorically, the term is used in relation to the voice of Yahweh (cf. Ps. 29:7); and to the divine glory protecting his people (cf. Isa. 4:5; 43:2).

labbāh **[לַבָּה, 3827]**

labbāh is a rare noun found only in Exod. 3:2 denoting the "flame" appearing in a desert bush that served as a vehicle for the divine revelation to Moses, commissioning him to lead the people of Israel out of the Egyptian bondage.

shalhebet **[שַׁלְהֶבֶת, 7957]**

shalhebet is a noun found in three places denoting a "flame." The usage is entirely metaphorical. Job 15:30; Ezek. 20:47 both refer to the "flame" of divine wrath in the context of judgment. Song 8:6 refers to the "flame" of jealousy.

lāshôn **[לָשׁוֹן, 3956]**

lāshôn is a common noun signifying a "tongue" for the large majority of its nearly 120 occurrences. However, in one reference, ***lāshôn*** denotes the "flame" of God's wrath directed against his people for their rejection of him (cf. Isa. 5:24). (→ TONGUE)

shebîb **[שְׁבִיב, 7631** (Aramaic)**]**

shebîb is a rare Aramaic term found only twice. It denotes a literal "flame" of fire in Dan. 3:22; and in Dan. 7:9 the term is used metaphorically to describe the throne of God in Daniel's vision as an object of "flaming fire."

lahat **[לַהַט, 3858]**

lahat is a rare noun used adjectivally in Gen. 3:24, referring to the "flaming" sword of the cherubim God posted to guard the way to the tree of life in the garden of Eden after the expulsion of Adam and Eve.

NT Words

phlox **[φλόξ, *5395*]**

phlox is a dynamic equivalent for the Hebrew term ***lahab*** (see above), denoting "flame(s)" in each of its seven occurrences.

Acts 7:30 refers to a literal "flame" in relation to the theophanic fire from which God revealed himself to Moses.

The sense of "flame" in the context of divine judgment is recorded in Luke 16:24. Elsewhere, the expression "flame(s) of fire" refers to one visionary aspect of God and Christ in theophanic revelation (cf. Rev. 1:14; 2:18; 19:12). Similarly, Heb. 1:7 describes the servants of God as "flames of fire," probably denoting heavenly creatures alongside angelic beings.

FLEE

OT Words

bāraḥ **[בָּרַח, 1272]**

bāraḥ is a verb meaning to "flee," "put to flight," and associated nuances, and occurs around sixty times. It is used primarily in a literal sense (e.g., Gen. 16:6, 8; Exod. 14:5; 2 Chr. 10:2; Neh. 6:11; Ps. 139:7; Isa. 48:20; Amos 7:12; Jonah 4:2).

nûs **[נוּס, 5127]**

This term is synonymous with ***bāraḥ*** (see above), occurring approximately 160 times with the consistent meanings "flee," "escape."

The mundane sense of "flee," "run away" is common (e.g., Gen. 14:10; Exod. 4:3; Judg. 1:6; 1 Sam. 4:16; 1 Kgs. 20:30; Isa. 10:3; Amos 5:19).

nûs is also found in contexts where flight from one's enemies is in view. For example, Israel's enemies flee before her (e.g., Deut. 28:7; Josh. 8:5ff.; 10:11ff.; Judg. 8:12; 1 Sam. 17:51; 2 Chr. 14:12); Israel flees before her enemies (e.g., Deut. 28:25; Josh. 7:4; 1 Sam. 17:24; Zech. 2:6); the psalmist pleads for God's enemies to flee from him (cf. Ps. 68:1); and God's enemies flee before him (cf. Prov. 28:1). Isa. 20:6 describes Israel's vain flight to Assyria, her enemy. Israel also flees from the wrath of Yahweh in Amos 2:16; 9:1, and the nations flee from that same wrath in Isa. 24:18; 31:8; Jer. 48:44, 45; 50:28.

In metaphorical contexts, ***nûs*** refers to waters fleeing before the rebuke of Yahweh (cf. Ps. 104:7; Lev. 17:13); and also to sorrow fleeing as a consequence of God redeeming his people (cf. Isa. 35:10; 51:11).

mālaṭ [מָלַט, 4422]

This verb occurs around one hundred times, meaning "flee," "escape" in about half of these contexts.

mālaṭ is often used to describe escape from God's wrath (e.g., Gen. 19:17ff.; 1 Kgs. 18:40; Ps. 124:7; Isa. 20:6; Jer. 41:15) and from God's judgment (e.g., Jer. 32:4; 34:3). The futility of such a flight is highlighted in Jer. 46:6 (Egypt); Jer. 48:8 (Moab); Ezek. 17:15, 18 (the people of God); while Joel 2:32 records a successful escape for all those who call upon the name of Yahweh.

Flight from danger in a general sense is indicated in Judg. 3:26, 29; 1 Sam. 19:10ff.; 22:1; 23:13.

nādad [נָדַד, 5074]

nādad is a verb found nearly thirty times with the primary meanings "flee," "wander away," as well as some related nuances.

The meaning "flee" in the sense of "leave" is indicated in Gen. 31:40, with reference to sleep "fleeing from" the eyes of Jacob.

nādad is also translated "flee" in the sense of "run away from" in Ps. 31:11; Isa. 21:15; Nah. 3:17, all referring to people. References to birds and animals "fleeing" are found in Jer. 4:25; 9:10.

NT Words

pheugō [φεύγω, *5343*]

pheugō is a verb found over thirty times with the consistent meaning "to flee."

The meaning "flee" in the literal sense of "escape (to)" is found in Matt. 2:13; Mark 5:14; 13:14; Luke 8:34; John 10:12ff.; Acts 7:29; Heb. 11:34; Rev. 12:6. Sheep are said to "flee" in John 10:5. The devil is said "to flee" from those who submit themselves to God.

The metaphorical sense of "flee" in relation to "running away from" the judgment or wrath of God is evident in Matt. 3:7; Luke 3:7; Heb. 12:25. An exhortation to "flee" or "shun" immorality is found in 1 Cor. 6:18. A like injunction is directed against idolatry in 1 Cor. 10:14. See also 1 Tim. 6:11; 2 Tim. 2:22. In the context of executing divine wrath, death is said "to flee" from those who seek it (cf. Rev. 9:6). Similarly, at the end of time, elements of the cosmos are said "to have fled away," signifying the dissolution of the heavens and the earth (cf. Rev. 16:20; 20:11).

ekpheugō [ἐκφεύγω, *1628*]

ekpheugō is a variant form of ***pheugō***, above, meaning "escape," "flee" in each of the eight occurrences of the term.

"Escaping" the judgment of God is a course of action indicated in Luke 21:36; Rom. 2:3. Such an escape is denied in 1 Thess. 5:3; Heb. 2:3.

"Fleeing" from a dangerous situation is recorded in Acts 16:27; 19:16; 2 Cor. 11:23.

katapheugō [καταφεύγω, *2703*]

katapheugō is another rare variant of ***pheugō***, above, meaning "to flee (for refuge)" in Acts 14:6; Heb. 6:18.

Additional Notes

As with many other concepts, the literal, physical "flight" of Old Testament times anticipates the spiritual "flight" of the New Testament era. The exhortations of the New Testament writers to flee that which is sinful and godless have a genuine precursor in the Old Testament era. Sadly, for the old covenant people of God as well as for the Gentile nations, such flight from him was vain, since God's righteous character required a punishment against such people when they violated his precepts. However, what gives the new covenant people renewed hope in their flight from judgment and the wrath of God is the reality that the messianic Redeemer has already borne that wrath so that, in one sense, there is now no need to flee. However, believers in Christ may still be waylaid by sin, and therefore the exhortation to flee the devil and all that he represents is an appropriate exhortation. It is, however, not to be a directionless flight in panic — but rather a flight to seek refuge in Christ and his finished work of redemption.

FLESH

OT Words

bāśār [בָּשָׂר, 1320]

This common Hebrew term is translated "flesh" in a variety of contexts and with several distinctive senses. ***bāśār*** is found in approximately 250 contexts and is used both literally and metaphorically.

The dominant literal sense of ***bāśār*** refers to human flesh (i.e., physical body; body tissue) (e.g., Gen. 2:21;

Exod. 4:7; Lev. 13:2ff.; 2 Kgs. 4:34; 5:10; Ps. 16:9; Ezek. 11:3; Dan. 1:15). In describing the ritual act of circumcision, Gen. 17:11ff. refers to the "flesh of the foreskin." The curse of cannibalism, in which parents will eat the flesh of sons and daughters, is mentioned in Lev. 26:29; Deut. 28:53, 55; Isa. 49:26; Jer. 19:9.

bāsār also means "flesh" with reference to blood relationship — for example, Eve as the "flesh" of Adam (Gen. 2:23; cf. also Gen. 37:27; Lev. 18:6; Judg. 9:2; 2 Sam. 5:1; Neh. 5:5; Isa. 58:7).

bāsār also refers to meat or animal flesh in general (e.g., Exod. 16:8; 29:31ff.; Lev. 4:11; Deut. 12:15; 1 Kgs. 17:6). Specific ritual contexts also mention the flesh of animal sacrifice (e.g., Lev. 7:15, 17ff.; 8:17, 31; Num. 18:18; Deut. 12:27; Ezek. 40:43; Hos. 8:13). Lev. 17:11 contains the foundational truth that "the life of the flesh is in the blood."

bāsār also has a number of metaphorical senses (e.g., "flesh" as a symbol for humanity, or mortality). In Gen. 7:21, "all flesh" is destroyed as a consequence of the flood. In Gen. 9:11, God issues a promise to never again destroy all "flesh" by floodwaters. Isa. 40:22 contains the prediction that "all flesh" (i.e., all people) shall see the glory of God. Similarly, Isa. 66:23 claims that "all flesh" shall worship Yahweh. Joel 2:28 issues the promise that God's spirit will be poured out on all flesh. In contrast, Isa. 66:16; Jer. 25:31; Ezek. 21:4ff.; Jer. 45:5 all indicate that God's judgment is to come upon the whole world (i.e., "all flesh"). Similar examples are found in Deut. 5:26; 2 Chr. 32:8; Isa. 40:6; Jer. 32:27; Zech. 2:13.

Other metaphorical uses of ***bāsār*** include "flesh" in the sense of one's personhood, or being (e.g., Pss. 63:1; 84:2; 119:120; Eccl. 5:6); as a euphemism for genitalia (Ezek. 23:20); and as a symbol for all animal life (e.g., Gen. 6:19; 7:15; 9:4). Finally, and perhaps most significantly, ***bāsār*** is employed in the expression "heart of flesh," which indicates a spiritual sensitivity towards God, leading to an attitude of love and devotion towards him (cf. Ezek. 11:19; 36:26). Ezek. 44:7 mentions those who are spiritually hardened towards God, or those who are "uncircumcised in heart and flesh."

she'ēr [שְׁאֵר, **7607**]

she'ēr is a noun found in sixteen places with various meanings including "flesh," "food," as well as related nuances in both literal and metaphorical contexts.

References to "flesh" meaning literal "meat," or "food," are found in Exod. 21:10; Ps. 78:20, 27. Prov. 5:11 refers literally to human "flesh."

Elsewhere, ***she'ēr*** denotes "flesh" metaphorically in the sense of "near kin" or "relative" (Lev. 18:6; 20:19; 25:49; Num. 27:11; Jer. 51:35).

This term also signifies "flesh" in the sense of one's "body" in Ps. 73:26; Prov. 11:17. The expression "eat, tear the flesh" of people signifies economic abuse and social and political injustice (cf. Mic. 3:2, 3).

besar [בְּשַׂר, **1321** (Aramaic)]

besar is the rare Aramaic equivalent of the Hebrew term ***bāsār*** (see above), denoting "flesh" in three places. In Dan. 2:11; 4:12 the term "flesh" signifies "humankind," "mankind." Dan. 7:5 refers to "flesh" in the sense of "meat."

NT Words

sarx [σάρξ, *4561*]

sarx is the most common term for "flesh" in the New Testament, functioning as a clear dynamic equivalent for ***bāsār*** (see above). ***sarx*** occurs about 150 times and means "flesh" throughout, with a number of related senses, both literal and metaphorical.

The expression "flesh and blood" indicates "humankind" or "mankind" in general (cf. Matt. 16:17; 1 Cor. 15:50; Gal. 1:16; Eph. 6:12; Heb. 2:14).

This sense of "humanity" in general is also evident in the meaning "flesh" in John 1:13; 3:6; 17:2; 1 Pet. 1:24. Similarly, Christ's humanity is so indicated in Heb. 5:7. In particular, the Holy Spirit is promised to be poured out on all "flesh" at the end of the age (cf. Acts 2:17). This is a particular reference to all the people of God.

The phrase "one flesh" denotes the result of a union of two people in marriage (viz. husband and wife), constituting an intimate lifelong bonding of two persons (cf. Matt. 19:5ff.; Mark 10:8; 1 Cor. 6:16; Eph. 5:31).

General references to "flesh" as "human beings," "persons," are found in Matt. 24:22; Luke 3:6; Rom. 3:20; 1 Cor. 1:29; Gal. 2:16. In particular, the word of God is said to have become "flesh" (i.e., adopted a full human form) in John 1:14; 1 Tim. 3:16; 1 John 4:2. Specific references to the human body as "flesh" are found in Eph. 5:29; Heb. 9:13; 1 Pet. 3:21. Metaphorical references to "flesh" denoting "human weakness" are found in Matt. 26:41; Phil. 3:3. In Phil. 3:4, however, "flesh" denotes "human accomplishment" in a positive sense.

References to literal human "flesh" are found in Luke 24:39; Rev. 19:18, 21. 1 Cor. 15:39 uses "flesh" in the general sense of a "physical being," with reference to man and animal alike (cf. also Rev. 17:16). ***sarx*** also denotes the human "body" in contrast with the spirit (cf. 2 Cor. 7:1, 5; 12:7). The body of Christ offered up in sacrifice for the sins of the world is designated as his "flesh" in John 6:51. Eating the "flesh" of Christ symbolically indicates the nurturing of one's absolute faith and dependence on him (cf. John 6:52ff.). Other references to the "body" of Christ include Eph. 2:15; Col. 1:22; Heb. 10:20.

sarx also denotes "flesh" in the sense of "sinful human nature" in Rom. 7:5; 8:3ff.; Gal. 3:3; 5:13ff.; Eph. 2:3; Col. 2:11ff.; 2 Pet. 2:10; 1 John 2:16.

"Flesh" also denotes "racial kinship" in Rom. 9:3ff., with reference to the Jewish people. See also Gal. 6:13; Eph. 2:11. Then, similarly, in Gal. 4:23, 29, "flesh" denotes the "principle of human regeneration" (i.e., born in the ordinary human way).

sarkikos [σαρκικός, *4559*]

sarkikos is an adjectival form derived from ***sarx***, above, meaning "fleshly," "carnal" (i.e., belonging to this world) as well as "material," with reference to earthly possessions. The term occurs eleven times.

The meaning "carnal" in the sense of "worldly," denoting a sinful lifestyle, is indicated in Rom. 7:14; 1 Cor. 3:1ff.; 1 Pet. 2:11. "Earthly" wisdom is indicated in 2 Cor. 1:12; and "earthly," "carnal" weapons are indicated in 2 Cor. 10:4. See also Heb. 7:16.

sarkikos refers to "material" blessings in Rom. 15:27; 1 Cor. 9:11.

kreas [κρέας, *2907*]

kreas is a rare noun denoting the "meat," "flesh" of sacrificial animals in Rom. 14:21; 1 Cor. 8:13.

Additional Notes

While there are common elements between the Old and New Testament concepts of "flesh," the Greek term ***sarx*** reflects a broader semantic field than the Hebrew ***bāśār***. However, the Hebrew focus on "flesh," as a symbol of humanity in general, does lay a foundation for a more particularized meaning in the New Testament, where "flesh" indicates varying human attitudes that are largely negative (see above). ***bāśār*** comes closest to this New Testament emphasis when referring to the "heart of flesh"; but only in the sense that this phrase refers to an inner spiritual dimension of humankind. As is clear in the New Testament, the term "flesh" by itself has an almost exclusively negative connotation.

See Also: ➡ BODY

FLIGHT

OT Words

mānôs [מָנוֹס, 4498]

mānôs is a rare noun, found only eight times and meaning "flight," "refuge."

This term refers first of all to a "place of refuge" in 2 Sam. 22:3; Jer. 16:19; Ps. 59:16 (God is the refuge here); Ps. 142:4; Jer. 25:35. It also indicates that flight, as a "way of escape" from the judgment of Yahweh, is impossible (cf. Job 11:20; Amos 2:14). Fleeing in haste is mentioned in Jer. 46:5.

menûsāh [מְנוּסָה, 4499]

This term is also rare and derives from ***mānôs*** (see above), occurring only twice. ***menûsāh*** means "fleeing" or "flight" in Lev. 26:36; Isa. 52:12. In both instances Yahweh's protective hand over his people is in view.

NT Words

phygē [φυγή, *5437*]

phygē is a rare noun derived from ***pheugō*** (➡ FLEE), found only in Matt. 24:20 denoting "flight" in the sense of "escape" from danger.

klinō [κλίνω, *2827*]

klinō is a verb with the primary meanings "lay," "bow (down)" throughout its seven occurrences. However, in Heb. 11:34 it means "rout," "put to flight," referring to one's enemies.

FLOCK

OT Words

ṣō'n [צֹאן, 6629]

This noun is a general term for small cattle, including sheep and goats. ***ṣō'n*** occurs around 250 times, and in about half of these contexts it is translated "flock," with both a literal and figurative sense.

Most frequently it means "flock," referring literally to undesignated animals (cf. Gen. 13:5; 37:2ff.; Exod. 2:16ff.; 1 Sam. 30:20; Ps. 65:13; Isa. 60:7; Jer. 33:12; Ezek. 24:5; Amos 7:15). In addition, it frequently refers to flocks from which offerings to Yahweh are selected (e.g., Lev. 1:2; 27:32; Deut. 8:13; 15:14, 19; Neh. 10:36; Ezek. 3:23). Flocks of sheep and goats are specifically mentioned, for example, in Gen. 21:28; 38:17; Lev. 1:10; 2 Chr. 17:11; Joel 1:18.

ṣō'n also refers metaphorically in a general sense to people or children as "flocks" (cf. Job 21:11; Ps. 77:20; Ezek. 36:37ff.). Specifically, ***ṣō'n*** refers symbolically to the people of Israel, both as those who are protected and redeemed by Yahweh (e.g., Isa. 63:11; Zech. 9:16); as well as those under his judgment (e.g., Zech. 11:17; Jer. 25:34). Other passages refer to the "flock" of Israel, that receives cruel treatment at the hands of their corrupt leaders (i.e., "shepherds) (cf. Ezek. 34:2ff.; Amos 6:14; Zech. 10:2); and the Babylonian armies (cf. Jer. 5:17).

'ēder [עֵדֶר, 5739]

'ēder is a synonym for ***ṣō'n*** (see above), occurring around thirty times meaning "flocks," "herds."

'ēder indicates literal flocks of animals in a general sense (e.g., Job 24:2; Isa. 32:14; Jer. 31:24); as well as herds of cattle, sheep, and goats. (e.g., Gen. 32:16ff.; Song 4:1; Joel 1:18).

'ēder is also used symbolically to refer to the people of Yahweh under his tender care (cf. Isa. 40:11; Jer. 31:10; Ezek. 34:12; Zech. 10:3). In these contexts, Yahweh is portrayed as the compassionate shepherd. However, the "flock" of Yahweh is not immune from his punishment when they stray from him (cf. Jer. 6:3; 13:17; Mic. 5:8).

'ashterôt [עַשְׁתְּרוֹת, 6251]

This rare term is found only four times, meaning "flock" in a literal sense (cf. Deut. 7:13; 28:4, 18, 51).

NT Words

poimnē [ποίμνη, *4167*]

poimnē is a noun found in only four places, denoting a "flock" of herd animals such as sheep or goats in Luke 2:8; 1 Cor. 9:7. The term refers metaphorically to God's people as his "flock" in Matt. 26:31; John 10:16.

poimnion [ποίμνιον, *4168*]

poimnion is a diminutive form of ***poimnē*** (see above), also designating a "flock" in the sense of the people of God in general terms in Luke 12:32. It is also found in Acts 20:28ff.; 1 Pet. 5:2ff., denoting Christian congregations as "the flock" of God under pastoral care.

Additional Notes

The old covenant community of Israel, the "flock" of Yahweh, parallels the faithful followers of Jesus Christ, designated by him as his "flock." The use of this vocabulary makes clear the redemptive-historical continuity of the new covenant community with the old.

FLOOD

OT Words

mabbûl [מַבּוּל, 3999]

mabbûl is found in thirteen contexts, almost all of which refer to the Noahic flood (cf. Gen. 6:17; 7:6ff.; 9:11ff.; 10:1, 32; 11:10), with the possible exception of Ps. 29:10.

ye'ôr [יְאוֹר, 2975]

This term has the predominant sense of "river," and occurs around sixty times. However, ***ye'ôr*** means "flood" on five occasions, all of which are metaphorical. Referring to the hordes of Egypt, Jer. 46:7, 8 refer literally to the Nile in flood. See also Amos 8:8; 9:5, where ***ye'ôr*** again refers to the Nile in flood, but the context is one of God's judgment against Israel.

nāhār [נָהָר, 5104]

Similar to ***ye'ôr*** (see above), ***nāhār*** means "river" on most occasions. ***nāhār*** is found 120 times and is translated "flood" in about twenty instances, again in metaphorical contexts.

The psalmist depicts "floods" rising up and lifting their voices in testimony to the majestic rule of Yahweh (cf. Pss. 93:3; 98:8). In Song 8:7, the beloved declares that many "floods" (i.e., waters) can never drown love. Isa. 59:19; Ezek. 31:15 both refer to the judgment of Yahweh, who will rise up like a "flood" and overwhelm his enemies. See also Jonah 2:3.

naḥal [נַחַל, 5158]

naḥal is a noun found over 140 times meaning "river," as well as "brook," "stream," and also "valley" for most of the usage. However, in several contexts ***naḥal*** denotes a "flood." Ps. 29:10 contains a non-specific reference to the phenomenon of flooding. The term is used metaphorically in Jer. 47:2 to refer to the invading foreign army of Babylonians as a "torrent"; and in 2 Sam. 22:5; Ps. 18:4 it refers to "torrents" of destruction.

sheteph [שֶׁטֶף, 7858]

sheteph is a noun found six times. In Job 38:25ff. it denotes a "flood" in the sense of "torrential rain." Elsewhere, ***sheteph*** is used figuratively, indicating "overwhelming" (i.e., traumatic) circumstances in Ps. 32:6; Dan. 11:22; and "consummate destruction" in Dan. 9:26; Nah. 1:8.

——— NT Words ———

kataklysmos [κατακλυσμός, *2627*]

kataklysmos is a noun found in four contexts denoting the divine judgment of the universal "flood" in the days of Noah (cf. Matt. 24:38ff.; Luke 17:27; 2 Pet. 2:5).

plēmmyra [πλήμμυρα, *4132*]

plēmmyra is a rare noun denoting a literal "flood" in Luke 6:48.

potamos [ποταμός, *4215*]

potamos is a noun occurring sixteen times with the predominant sense of "river." However, on four occasions it denotes a "flood," brought about by torrential rain (cf. Matt. 7:25, 27; Mark 6:48, 49).

See Also: → RIVER → VALLEY

FLOOR → THRESH

FLOUR

——— OT Words ———

sōlet [סֹלֶת, **5560**]

This term occurs around fifty times, meaning "flour" in each instance. ***sōlet*** is found predominantly in ritual contexts, where flour is associated with sacrificial offerings (e.g., Lev. 2:1ff.; Num. 7:13ff.; 15:4ff.; Ezek. 46:14).

qemaḥ [קֶמַח, **7058**]

qemaḥ is a noun denoting "flour" in the literal sense of "ground grain" in all fourteen occurrences of the term (e.g., Gen. 18:6; Num. 5:15; 2 Sam. 17:28; 1 Kgs. 4:22; 2 Kgs. 4:41; Isa. 47:2; Hos. 8:7).

——— NT Words ———

semidalis [σεμίδαλις, *4585*]

semidalis is a rare noun found only once, denoting "fine flour" in Rev. 18:13.

aleuron [ἄλευρον, *224*]

aleuron is a rare term also denoting "flour," found only in Matt. 13:33; Luke 13:21.

FLOW

——— OT Words ———

zûb [זוּב, **2100**]

zûb means "flow," "discharge," "gush out," and occurs about forty times.

The term refers first of all to bodily discharges from men (e.g., Lev. 15:2ff.; 22:4; Num. 5:2); and women (cf. Lev. 15:19, 25). It is clear in these contexts that a woman's menstrual flow renders her ceremonially unclean. Pss. 78:20; 105:41; Isa. 48:21 all refer to water flowing (or gushing) from the rock in the wilderness, whereby Yahweh miraculously satisfied his people's thirst.

In a metaphorical sense, ***zûb*** also indicates the economic prosperity of Canaan, described as "a land flowing with milk and honey" (e.g., Exod. 3:8; Lev. 20:24; Num. 16:13, 14; Deut. 6:3; 31:20; Josh. 5:6; Jer. 11:5; Ezek. 20:6).

nāzal [נָזַל, **5140**]

nāzal is a verb roughly synonymous with ***zûb*** (see above), occurring sixteen times. ***nāzal*** means "flow," "flow out," "flow down" in half of these contexts. Literal meanings are found, for example, in Ps. 78:16; Jer. 9:18; Song 4:16; Isa. 48:21. In a metaphorical sense, "flow" indicates material prosperity in Num. 24:7.

nāhar [נָהַר, **5102**]

nāhar is a rare verb, occurring six times. In three of these occurrences it means "flow" in a metaphorical sense. Isa. 2:2; Mic. 4:1 both speak of all nations "flowing to" the mountain of the Lord's temple. Jer. 51:44 records the same verb in the negative. The underlying sense is that of "being attracted to."

zôb [זוֹב, **2101**]

zôb is a noun found thirteen times with the consistent meaning "flow" in the sense of "bodily discharge." The term is found exclusively in Lev. 15:2–33, referring to the male "discharge" of semen and to the female menstrual "flow (of blood)."

FLOWER

——— OT Words ———

ṣîṣ [צִיץ, **6731**]

This noun occurs fifteen times, and on most occasions ***ṣîṣ*** means "flower," "blossom."

ṣîṣ refers, for example, to the almond blossom that sprouts on Aaron's rod in Num. 17:8. Other flowers in a general sense are mentioned in 1 Kgs. 6:29ff.; Isa. 40:8. Metaphorical references are found in Job 14:2 (of humankind); Isa. 28:1 (of Israel). See also Ps. 103:15; Isa. 40:6, 7.

peraḥ **[פֶּרַח, 6525]**

peraḥ is synonymous with *ṣîṣ* (see above), and occurs approximately the same number of times with the same meanings. Most frequently, ***peraḥ*** refers to the flowers of hammered gold placed on the furniture of the tabernacle and temple (cf. Exod. 25:31ff.; 37:17ff.; 1 Kgs. 7:49). It also refers to the "blossoming" of Aaron's rod (cf. Num. 17:8). Metaphorical uses of the term are found in Isa. 5:24; 18:5; Nah. 1:4.

niṣṣāh **[נִצָּה, 5328]**

niṣṣāh is a rare term denoting "flower blossom" and found only in Job 15:33; Isa. 18:5.

NT Words

anthos [ἄνθος, *438*]

anthos is the sole term for "flower" in the New Testament, found only four times (cf. Jas. 1:10ff.; 1 Pet. 1:24).

FLY

OT Words

'ûph **[עוּף, 5774]**

'ûph means "to fly," with associated nuances, in the majority of contexts in which it is found. The term occurs around thirty times and is employed more in a metaphorical sense than in a literal one. However, literal references to flying birds are found in Gen. 1:20; Deut. 4:17; Ps. 91:5. Isa. 6:2 mentions flying seraphim in the call vision of the prophet.

"Flying" is predicated symbolically of Yahweh in 2 Sam. 22:11; Ps. 18:10; and also of God's mode of protecting Jerusalem in Isa. 31:5. Other metaphorical uses of ***'ûph*** include Hos. 9:11, which speaks of Ephraim's (i.e., Israel's) glory "flying away," as a consequence of divine judgment. Similar references to "flying" creatures, which play a part in God's punishment of those who oppose and reject him, are found in Hab. 1:8; Isa. 14:29; 30:6. Of special interest is the image of the "flying scroll" in Zech. 5:1, 2, which symbolizes divine judgment against the nation of Judah. See also Job 5:7; 10:8; Ps. 55:6; Isa. 60:8; 11:14.

dā'āh **[דָּאָה, 1675]**

dā'āh is a rare verb that occurs only four times. The term means "fly" on each occasion, and only in a metaphorical sense. In three of these texts "flying" is linked to the image of the eagle, which in turn symbolizes the judgment of Yahweh (cf. Deut. 28:49; Jer. 48:40; 49:22). See also Ps. 18:10.

zebûb **[זְבוּב, 2070]**

zebûb is a rare term denoting the insect the "fly" in Eccl. 10:1; Isa. 7:18.

'ārōb **[עָרֹב, 6157]**

'ārōb is a noun occurring nine times, meaning "swarms of flies" in relation to one of Yahweh's plague judgments against Egypt (cf. Exod. 8:21ff.; Pss. 78:45; 105:31).

NT Words

petomai [πέτομαι, *4072*]

The verb ***petomai*** is found in five places and means "to fly" in each context, all of them metaphorical. Rev. 4:7; 12:14 refer to a "flying" eagle, the latter text denoting the wings of an eagle bearing the mother of the messianic Christ child away from the clutches of the satanic dragon. Rev. 8:13; 14:6 refer to "flying" angels. Rev. 19:17 speaks of "flying" birds attacking the corpses of Satan's armies.

FOAM

NT Words

aphrizō [ἀφρίζω, *875*]

aphrizō is a rare verb meaning "to foam (at the mouth)" in relation to a demon-possessed man in Mark 9:18; Luke 9:39.

epaphrizō [ἐπαφρίζω, *1890*]

epaphrizō is a rare noun found only in Jude 13, referring to false teachers depicted metaphorically as "casting up the foam" of their own shame.

FOE → ENEMY

FOLLOW

OT Words

'aḥar **[אַחַר, 310]**

'aḥar embraces a number of grammatical categories. It is an adverb, a conjunction, a preposition, and also has verbal and nominal functions. When used verbally, ***'aḥar*** is often found in conjunction with specific verbs. The primary meanings of ***'aḥar*** are "after" and "behind," in both a temporal and spatial sense. In all its various syntactic forms, the term is common in the Old Testament, occurring over seven hundred times. However, with its verbal sense of "follow" (as well as associated meanings), ***'aḥar*** occurs about eighty times.

The literal meaning "follow after," in the temporal, chronological sense of "following on from," is found in Gen. 41:31; Jer. 42:16, for example, with reference to the famine in Egypt. See also Num. 16:25.

The meaning "follow after," but with the spatial sense of physical pursuit, is more frequent. Examples of this meaning are found in Exod. 23:2; 1 Sam. 13:7; 2 Sam. 7:8; 1 Kgs. 20:19; Ps. 45:14; Ezek. 10:11.

Other uses of ***'aḥar*** incline to non-literal connotations. For example, the term means "follow," in the sense of "give one's allegiance to," in a number of contexts. Positively, ***'aḥar*** refers to those who willingly follow God himself (cf. Num. 14:24; 32:12; Deut. 1:36; Josh. 14:8, 9; 2 Kgs. 18:6). Negatively, it refers to those who refuse to do so — the disobedient generation of Israelites who refused to enter the land of promise on the first occasion (cf. Num. 32:11). Exhortations to follow Yahweh are found in 1 Sam. 12:14, 20, as is a warning against failing to do so in 1 Kgs. 9:6. Israel is also frequently condemned and indicted by God for "following after the Baals" in idolatrous apostasy (cf. Deut. 4:3; Josh. 22:16; 1 Sam. 15:11; 1 Kgs. 18:18; 2 Chr. 25:27). Prohibitions against such activity are declared in Deut. 7:4; 12:30; Josh. 22:18. On the human level, good and bad allegiances are also defined as "following after" certain individuals — for example, Judg. 9:3 (Abimelech); Ruth 1:16 (Naomi); 2 Sam. 2:10 (David); 2 Sam. 17:9 (Absalom).

rādaph [רָדַף, 7291]

This verb occurs in about 140 contexts and is consistently translated "follow after," "pursue," or "chase."

In the literal sense of physical pursuit, ***rādaph*** is found in a number of contexts. In the arena of battle, for example, opposing forces pursue (i.e., follow after) each other, or the visitor chases the vanquished (e.g., Gen. 14:14ff.; 35:5; Exod. 14:4; 15:9; Deut. 1:44; Josh. 2:5; Judg. 1:6; 1 Sam. 7:11; 1 Kgs. 20:20; Isa. 30:6; Jer. 39:5; Nah. 1:8).

Pursuit is also mentioned in non-military contexts such as in Deut. 19:6, where the likely scenario of the "avenger of blood" following after the murderer is described. See also Josh. 20:5; 2 Kgs. 5:21; Ps. 119:150. ***rādaph*** is also found in passages where divine judgment is in view, in that Yahweh and/or his punishment follows after those who rebel against him (e.g., Deut. 28:22; 2 Sam. 24:13; Jer. 29:18; Hos. 8:3; Ezek. 35:6).

rādaph also occurs in various metaphorical contexts, particularly where "following after" virtuous qualities is praised, and devoting oneself to vice is condemned. As far as the former practice is concerned, Deut. 16:20, for example, contains the command to follow after justice, and Ps. 38:20 to pursue goodness. See also Ps. 23:6; Isa. 51:1 in this regard. The dangers of following after particular forms of evil or vice are mentioned in Prov. 11:19; Hos. 12:1; Isa. 5:11.

yālak [יָלַךְ, 3212]

This common term is found over one thousand times with the primary meanings "go," "walk," as well as associated senses, which include "follow." With this latter sense, however, ***yālak*** is only found seven times. The literal sense of physically following someone is mentioned in Gen. 24:5ff.; 1 Sam. 30:21. The word means "following," in the sense of "giving one's allegiance to," in 1 Kgs. 18:21; 19:20.

regel [רֶגֶל, 7272]

regel is a common noun found in nearly 250 places with the primary sense of "foot" throughout. However, in four places the term is used in a participial sense designating "those who follow (after someone)" (cf. Exod. 11:8; Judg. 8:5; 1 Kgs. 20:10; 2 Kgs. 3:9).

NT Words

akoloutheō [ἀκολουθέω, *190*]

akoloutheō is a verb found about ninety times with the consistent meaning "to follow." It is used in a variety of contexts, with a number of nuances.

The meaning "follow after" with the underlying sense of "become devoted, attached to," involving a solemn commitment to a person, is evident in the disciples' relationship to Christ, their leader (cf. Matt. 4:20, 25; Mark 1:18; 2:14ff.; Luke 5:27ff.; John 1:37ff.).

Christ's command to his disciples to "follow" him is recorded in Matt. 9:9; 19:21; John 12:26; 21:19, 22. Exhortations concerning such a "following" are found in Matt. 10:38; 16:24; Mark 8:34; Luke 9:23; 18:22.

Such an action is also predicated of the crowds who "followed after" Jesus. But this following was motivated largely by curiosity, the desire to witness miraculous signs and, for some, the need for healing — rather than by a genuine commitment to him (cf. Matt. 4:25; 8:1, 10, 22; John 6:22). There is one exception, noted in Matt. 21:9; Mark 11:9, where crowds had followed him to Jerusalem in order to offer him praise — though this would be short lived. It must also be noted that of those whom Jesus had healed, many chose to "follow" him with wholehearted devotion (cf. Luke 9:11; 18:43).

A promise to "follow" Jesus, offering him a solemn lifelong commitment, is given in Matt. 8:19; Luke 9:59. Such promises, however, were inevitably halfhearted (but compare John 13:36ff.).

Mundane references to people "following" others include those in Matt. 8:23; Luke 22:10; John 18:15. See also Matt. 12:8, 9; Acts 13:43.

Metaphorical references to Christ's sheep "following" him denote his people in John 10:4, 5, 27. Elsewhere, 1 Cor. 10:4 mentions the supernatural rock (viz. Christ), from which they drank, that "followed" the people of Israel through the wilderness. Rev. 6:8 mentions Hades "following" the rider Death. Rev. 14:4 refers to the martyrs in heaven who always "follow" the Lamb (i.e., Christ) with great devotion. Reference to the deeds of the saints in heaven "following" them is found in Rev. 14:13. In Rev. 19:14 the armies of heaven "follow" the messianic rider on a white horse, who is their heavenly leader victorious against the forces of Satan.

exakoloutheō [ἐξακολουθέω, *1811*]

exakoloutheō is a rare variant of ***akoloutheō***, above, meaning "follow" in all three occurrences of the term. 2 Pet. 2:15 refers to false teachers who had "followed the way of Balaam" (i.e., lived according to the dictates of greed). 2 Peter 1:16 contains the denial that Peter and the other apostles had ever "followed" cleverly devised fables in their proclamation of the gospel. 2 Pet. 2:2 warns of the danger of "following" the way of immorality as practiced by the false teachers.

epakoloutheō [ἐπακολουθέω, *1872*]

epakoloutheō is another rare variant of ***akoloutheō***, above. It is found in 1 Pet. 2:21, exhorting believers to "follow" the example of Christ's suffering.

parakoloutheō [παρακολουθέω, *3877*]

parakoloutheō is another variant of ***akoloutheō***, above. It is found in 1 Tim. 4:6, where Paul affirms that Timothy had "followed" (i.e., devoted himself to) good biblical teaching throughout his life.

synakoloutheō [συνακολουθέω, *4870*]

This rare variant of ***akoloutheō*** (see above) is found only twice, in Mark 5:37; Luke 23:49. In these texts, ***synakoloutheō*** means to "follow" in the sense of "accompany (someone)."

diōkō [διώκω, *1377*]

diōkō is a verb found nearly fifty times with the primary sense of "persecute." (→ PERSECUTE) In several places, however, there is some overlap in meaning with the sense of "follow," "pursue." An exhortation not to "follow after" false messiahs is found in Luke 17:23.

Rom. 9:30 contains the affirmation that Gentiles "did not pursue" righteousness. In the following verse it is claimed, by way of contrast, that Israel had indeed "pursued" righteousness — but one that was unattainable by law. Exhortations to "pursue" peace are found in Rom. 14:19; Heb. 12:14; 1 Pet. 3:11. Similarly, 1 Cor. 14:1 contains an injunction to "follow" (i.e., pursue) the way of love. See also 1 Thess. 5:15; 1 Tim. 6:11; 2 Tim. 2:22.

katadiōkō [καταδιώκω, *2614*]

katadiōkō is a rare variant of ***diōkō***, above, found only in Mark 1:36 with the literal sense of "following after," or "pursuing," someone.

mimētēs [μιμητής, *3402*]

mimētēs is a noun found seven times with the predominant meaning "follower," or "imitator," throughout.

Paul exhorts his readers to be "imitators" of him in 1 Cor. 4:16; 11:1. See also 1 Thess. 1:6; Phil. 3:17; Heb. 6:12. Eph. 5:1 contains an exhortation to be an "imitator" of God. 1 Thess. 2:14 calls the Thessalonian congregation to become "imitators" of the Judean churches in their suffering.

Additional Notes

There is a great deal of similarity between the Hebrew and Greek vocabulary for "follow (after)." In both Testaments, the ideal of devoting oneself to God and the pursuit of holy and righteous living is held up as being of first importance. Following after Yahweh under the old covenant involved the godly Israelite or Gentile convert in wholehearted submission to the law of the covenant. In the new covenant, the pursuit of holiness lies in gaining an ever-increasing Christlikeness through dependence upon the Spirit of God. The negative corollary to this pattern involves recognizing the dire consequences of "following after" pagan deities in the old covenant age, which led to severe punishment at the hands of Yahweh. Similar apostasy under the new covenant will lead to a far worse judgment, since it involves willful rebellion against the very

Son of God, the supreme manifestation of divine saving grace.

FOLLY

OT Words

'iwwelet **[אִוֶּלֶת, 200]**

This term is found exclusively in the Wisdom writings of the Old Testament and mostly in Proverbs. ***'iwwelet*** is consistently translated "foolishness," "folly," and occurs twenty-five times.

The primary sense of ***'iwwelet*** may be expressed as moral ineptitude or weakness, a failure to live up to God's standards in accordance with his covenantal precepts. Examples of this usage are found in Ps. 38:5; Prov. 5:23; 14:1, 8, 17ff.; 15:2, 14; 22:15; 26:4ff.; 27:22. Folly is a characteristic that inevitably brings down the wrath of God. In the Old Testament it is a moral defect rather than an intellectual disability and is portrayed as the antithesis of a godly lifestyle.

nebālāh **[נְבָלָה, 5039]**

nebālāh is a synonym for ***'iwwelet*** (see above). It is also consistently translated "folly," with clear overtones of stupidity, disgrace, and sexual immorality. The term occurs thirteen times.

The sense of "folly" as an expression of sexual immorality is found in several contexts — for example, Shechem's rape of Dinah (Gen. 34:7); and the brutal rape of the Levite's concubine (Judg. 20:6). Capital punishment is prescribed in Israel for the "folly" of engaging in prostitution in Deut. 22:21. See also Judg. 19:23; 2 Sam. 13:12; Jer. 29:23.

nebālāh also refers to folly in the sense of shameful rebellion against God (cf. Achan's sin in Josh. 7:15). Isa. 9:17; 32:6 refer to "vile speech" as folly in a similar way.

Nabal, the husband of Abigail, is mentioned in 1 Sam. 25:25 as a man of "folly" (i.e., reflected in his name) with a base and perverse character.

siklût **[סִכְלוּת, 5531]**

siklût is another term that is roughly synonymous with ***nebālāh*** and ***'iwwelet***, above. ***siklût*** is unique, however, in its distinctive usage as the direct and specific contrast to wisdom. ***siklût*** also means "foolish," "folly," and this suggests an attitude of senselessness, perversity, or futility. The term is found seven times, and only within the book of Ecclesiastics (cf. Eccl. 1:17; 2:3, 12, 13; 10:1, 13). In Eccl. 7:25 "folly" is equated with insanity. ***siklût*** is to be shunned just as fervently as wisdom is to be embraced.

NT Words

anoia **[ἄνοια, *454*]**

anoia is a rare noun denoting "folly" in the sense of "moral ineptitude," "senselessness," of minds closed to the truth.

aphrosynē **[ἀφροσύνη, *877*]**

aphrosynē is a noun found four times denoting "folly" as one of several vices listed as characteristic of the human heart. In 2 Cor. 11:1, 17, 21 Paul uses this term as hyperbole, referring to his hypothetical "foolishness" in the face of his detractors.

FOOD

OT Words

leḥem **[לֶחֶם, 3899]**

A common noun throughout the Old Testament, ***leḥem*** occurs around three hundred times with the predominant meaning "bread." (→ BREAD) ***leḥem*** is also translated "meat" and "food," with the latter sense occurring about twenty times. These two meanings sometimes overlap.

Food in general is indicated, for example, in Deut. 10:18; 1 Kgs. 5:9; Prov. 27:27; Ezek. 48:18. Yahweh is also referred to as a provider of food (e.g., Pss. 78:25; 136:25; 147:9).

In relation to Israelite worship, ***leḥem*** refers to the food offered to Yahweh in sacrifice in Lev. 3:11, 16, and also to food for the priests as part of their divinely ordained provision in Lev. 22:7.

'ōkel **[אֹכֶל, 400]**

'ōkel is derived from the verbal root ***'ākal***, "to eat," and occurs around fifty times. (→ EAT) The term is translated "food" in about one-third of these contexts. The meaning is literal and mundane (e.g., Gen. 41:35ff.; 44:1, 25; Job 38:41; Prov. 13:23).

ma'akāl **[מַאֲכָל, 3978]**

This noun is also derived from ***'ākal*** (→ EAT) and occurs around thirty times. ***ma'akāl*** is generally translated "meat," but it also refers literally to "food" on five occasions. See Gen. 2:9; 3:6; 6:21; Lev. 19:23; Prov. 6:8.

'oklāh **[אָכְלָה, 402]**

'oklāh is a noun found in eighteen places with the dominant meaning "food." The verbal sense of "eat" is also indicated in several places.

The general sense of "food" is indicated in Gen. 1:29ff.; 6:21; 9:3; Lev. 25:6. The verbal sense of "eat," "devour" is evident in Lev. 11:39; Jer. 12:9. Food specifically provided by God for his people to eat is mentioned in Exod. 16:15.

The atrocity of offering children up as "food" for idols is indicated in Ezek. 23:37. In the context of divine judgment, God is said metaphorically to hand Egypt over to the beasts and birds for "food" (cf. Ezek. 29:5). The context signifies the destruction of that nation. See also Ezek. 34:5ff.; 35:12, where references to "food" and "being devoured" also relate to the oppression of the poor by the corrupt elite of Israel's leaders, and also to foreign harassment. In Ezek. 39:4, the sense of "being devoured" refers also to the consequence of divine judgment — in this case the nation of Magog is indicated.

***māṭʻam* [מַטְעָם, 4303]**

māṭʻam is a noun found in eight places, and in six of these it denotes "tasty, savory food" (cf. Gen. 27:4ff., 14ff., 31). In Prov. 23:3, 6, the term refers to "delicacies," or luxury foods.

***māzôn* [מָזוֹן, 4202]**

māzôn is a rare noun denoting "food" in the sense of "provisions," found only in Gen. 45:23; 2 Chr. 11:23.

***biryāh* [בִּרְיָה, 1279]**

biryāh is a noun denoting "food" in a general sense in 2 Sam. 13:5ff.

***ṣêdāh* [צֵידָה, 6720]**

ṣêdāh is a noun found ten times with the primary meaning "food" in the sense of "provisions" (cf. Gen. 42:25; 45:21; Exod. 12:39; Josh. 1:11; 9:11; Judg. 7:8; 20:10; 1 Sam. 22:10; Ps. 78:25). In addition, ***ṣêdāh*** signifies "wild game" in the context of hunting for food in Gen. 27:3.

***ṭereph* [טֶרֶף, 2964]**

ṭereph is a noun found over twenty times with the predominant meaning "prey." In several instances, however, it denotes "food" in a general sense (Ps. 111:5; Prov. 31:15; Mal. 3:10).

***patbag* [פַּתְבַּג, 6598]**

patbag is a term denoting "food" associated with the royal table. It occurs ten times (cf. Dan. 1:5ff.; 11:26).

***ṣayid* [צַיִד, 6718]**

ṣayid is a noun found in nineteen contexts with the predominant sense of "game" or "prey." In several places, however, "food" or "provisions" are indicated (e.g., Josh. 9:5, 14; Neh. 13:14; Job 38:41).

NT Words

***trophē* [τροφή, *5160*]**

trophē is a general term for "food," found in sixteen places (e.g., Matt. 3:4; 6:25; Luke 12:23; John 4:8; Acts 2:46; 27:33ff.; Heb. 5:12ff.; Jas. 2:15).

***diatrophē* [διατροφή, *1305*]**

diatrophē is a rare variant of ***trophē***, above, found only in 1 Tim. 6:8, also denoting "food" in a general sense.

***brōsis* [βρῶσις, *1035*]**

brōsis is a noun found eleven times, denoting "food" in both a literal and metaphorical sense in most of these occurrences.

"Food" in a general sense is indicated in John 6:27a; Rom. 14:17; 2 Cor. 9:10; Col. 2:16.

brōsis also denotes "food" in the metaphorical sense of "spiritual nourishment," intimately associated with the person of Christ and his teaching in John 6:27b. In particular, Christ declares that his flesh is "food" in John 6:55, indicating that genuine spiritual life is dependent on "nourishing" oneself on his body — on believing in and committing oneself wholly to Christ.

***brōma* [βρῶμα, *1033*]**

brōma is a noun found seventeen times, denoting "food" in both a literal and symbolic sense throughout.

General references to "food" include those in Matt. 14:15; Mark 7:19; Rom. 14:20; 1 Cor. 6:13; 1 Tim. 4:3; Heb. 9:10. In particular, ***brōma*** denotes the food God supernaturally supplied to his people in the wilderness (1 Cor. 10:3).

Elsewhere, the sense of "food" is metaphorical. Christ affirms in John 4:34 that his "food" is to do the will of his Father. In this context, "food" denotes the innermost desire of his being, his fundamental purpose in life. In 1 Cor. 3:2, "solid food" signifies teaching from the word that is instrumental in maturing people in their faith.

FOOL, FOOLISH, FOOLISHNESS

OT Words

***'ewîl* [אֱוִיל, 191]**

'ewîl derives from an unused verbal root meaning "to be perverse." It is found approximately thirty times and is consistently translated "fool," "foolish (person)" "folly." The essence of *'ewîl* and other terms (see below) denotes not intellectual deficiency, but moral perversity.

The translation "fool" in a general sense is found in Job 5:23; Prov. 11:29; 20:3; Isa. 19:11; 35:8. *'ewîl* also indicates a "fool" in the sense of one who violates God's laws (e.g., Ps. 107:17; Prov. 10:8; Jer. 4:22); and one who despises wisdom (e.g., Prov. 1:7; 12:15; 15:5). Fools are also contrasted with the righteous in Prov. 10:21; 14:9.

kesîl [כְּסִיל, 3684]

kesîl is a noun derived from a rarely used verb meaning "to be foolish." ***kesîl*** occurs around seventy times and is a synonym for ***'ewîl*** (see above), consistently translated "fool" or "foolish."

A number of texts refer to fools in a general sense (e.g., Pss. 49:10; 94:8; Prov. 8:5; 17:10ff.; 26:1ff.; Eccl. 2:15, 16; 6:8; 9:17; 10:15).

kesîl also specifically indicates fools who despise wisdom and knowledge (e.g., Prov. 1:22; 14:7; 23:9; 29:11); who violate God's laws (e.g., Prov. 10:18, 23; 13:19); and who are contrasted with the wise (e.g., Prov. 3:35; 13:16; Eccl. 2:14; 4:13; 10:2, 12). Fools are also depicted as those who will suffer harm (e.g., Prov. 13:20; 18:7; 19:29).

nābāl [נָבָל, 5036]

This noun is synonymous with ***'ewîl*** and ***kesîl***, above, occurring approximately twenty times and translated "fool," "foolish."

General, non-specific usage is indicated in Ps. 39:8; Prov. 17:7; Isa. 32:5. The sense of "foolish," as in "without understanding," is found in Deut. 32:21; Job 2:10; Ezek. 13:3. ***nābāl*** indicates lawlessness in 2 Sam. 3:33; Job 30:8. The term means "foolish" in the sense of "sinful," or "corrupt," in Deut. 32:6; 2 Sam. 13:13; Ps. 74:18, 22; Isa. 32:6; Jer. 17:11. Ps. 14:1 contains the classic outburst of folly: "The fool has said in his heart, 'There is no God.'" In 1 Sam. 25:4ff., the name Nabal is given to a man whose very nature epitomizes that of a fool.

sākal [סָכַל, 5528]

sākal occurs eight times and is translated "be foolish," "act foolishly," "play the fool."

sākal indicates a general sense of "foolish" only in Gen. 31:28. "Acting foolishly," in the sense of disobeying God, is described in 1 Sam. 13:13; 2 Sam. 24:10; 2 Chr. 16:9; 21:8. "Playing the fool" is indicated in 1 Sam. 26:21. Finally, ***sākal*** refers to the action of "turning into foolishness" two unrelated phenomena. First, in 2 Sam. 15:31, David prays that the advice of Ahithophel to Absalom may be turned into "folly." Then, in Isa. 44:25, Yahweh judges the false prophets by turning their messages into nonsense.

sekel [סֶכֶל, 5529]

sekel is a rare noun found only in Eccl. 10:6, denoting "fools" who are found in many high places.

petî [פֶּתִי, 6612]

petî is a noun denoting "simplicity" as well as the adjectival sense of "simple." The precise sense of this term is ambiguous, indicating simplicity either as a "naïve ignorance" or as "moral ineptitude" that inclines to wickedness.

The sense of "simplicity" as "naïve ignorance" is indicated in Pss. 19:7; 119:130 — a condition that is remedied through instruction in God's word, resulting in both wisdom and understanding. Ps. 116:6 affirms that God preserves the "simple."

In the book of Proverbs, however, ***petî'*** signifies those who are "simple" in the sense of "morally inept," with a tendency towards evil (cf. Prov. 7:7; 8:5; 14:15; 19:25). The transformation of "the simple" from morally inept to living in a way that is godly and prudent, is indicated in Prov. 1:4; 21:11. The indictment of "the simple" is evident in Prov. 1:22, 32; 14:8; 22:3; 27:12. Exhortations to "the simple" to abandon their foolishness are found in Prov. 9:4ff., 16.

NT Words

aphrōn [ἄφρων, *878*]

aphrōn is a noun found in eleven places denoting a "fool," and is always used as a term of reproach to describe those who are morally and spiritually corrupt at worst, or naïvely stupid at best.

Jesus designates hypocritical and self-righteous Pharisees as "fools" in the worst sense of spiritual and moral corruption in Luke 11:40. He similarly denounces the rich "fool" in the parable in Luke 12:20.

The designation "fool" in the sense of naïve ignorance or stupidity is found in Rom. 2:20; 1 Cor. 15:36; 2 Cor. 11:16ff.; 12:6, 11; Eph. 5:17; 1 Pet. 2:15.

mōros [μωρός, *3474*]

mōros is an adjective found in thirteen contexts with the meanings "foolish," "stupid" throughout.

The sense of "foolish," denoting "senseless stupidity," is indicated in relation to Jesus' indictment of the Pharisees in Matt. 5:22; 23:17ff. Similarly, Paul exhorts his fellow believers to avoid engaging in "foolish" controversies or arguments in 2 Tim. 2:23; Titus 3:9. People lacking spiritual discernment are described as "foolish" in Matt. 7:26; 25:2ff.

In several contexts ***mōros*** is used hyperbolically, referring for example to the "foolishness" of God in 1 Cor. 1:25 as that which is "wiser than human wisdom." The point here is that God's wisdom is infinitely superior to that of human beings. 1 Cor. 1:27 claims that God has chosen the "foolish" things of the world (viz. things, people deemed worthless) to shame the wise (viz. the self-sufficient, the arrogant). The experience of becoming "fools" for the sake of Christ and the gospel is noted in 1 Cor. 3:18; 4:10.

mōrainō [μωραίνω, *3471*]

mōrainō is a rare verb meaning "become fools" in Rom. 1:22, referring to ungodly people who had wholly turned their backs on God and his revealed moral code. 1 Cor. 1:20 affirms that God "has made foolish" the wisdom of the world — that is, he has nullified it.

mōria [μωρία, *3472*]

mōria is a noun derived from ***mōrainō***, above, denoting "folly," "foolishness" in each of the five occurrences of the term.

The message of the gospel is said to be "folly" in the eyes of unbelievers (i.e., nonsense fantasy) in 1 Cor. 1:18, 23. Similarly, in 1 Cor. 1:21 there is the ironic affirmation that God chose to save people through the "folly" of preaching. In 1 Cor. 2:14 the gifts of the Spirit are said to be "folly" to the unspiritual person — that is, incapable of being understood. 1 Cor. 3:19 declares that the wisdom of the world is "folly" to God — that is, despised by him as of no account.

anoētos [ἀνόητος, *453*]

anoētos is an adjective meaning "foolish" throughout the six occurrences of the term, in several different contexts.

The designation "foolish" implies "lack of spiritual insight or perception" in Luke 24:25; Rom. 1:14; Gal. 3:1, 3. 1 Tim. 6:9 refers to "foolish" (i.e., senseless, morally questionable) desires. See also Titus 3:3 for a similar sense.

asynetos [ἀσύνετος, *801*]

asynetos is an adjectival term found five times, signifying people as "foolish" who are "without understanding," "lacking spiritual insight" (Matt. 15:16; Mark 7:18; Rom. 1:21, 31; 10:19).

Additional Notes

There is a notable consistency between the Old and New Testament concepts of "fool," "foolishness." Both Hebrew and Greek terminology stress that folly is invariably linked with perverse, immoral behavior. And while the rational element is not entirely absent from the vocabulary, it is significantly less prevalent than the moral perspective. Fools and foolishness are condemned throughout the Bible — not because people are intellectually deficient, but because they are in a state of rebellion against God.

See Also: → FOLLY

FOOT, FEET, FOOTSTOOL

OT Words

regel [רֶגֶל, 7272]

regel is a fairly common term, occurring around 250 times, with the predominant meanings "foot," "feet." It is used both in a literal as well as a symbolic sense.

In a mundane, literal sense, ***regel*** refers first of all to the feet of human beings (e.g., Gen. 18:4; Exod. 21:24; Judg. 4:15; 2 Sam. 4:4; 2 Kgs. 4:37; Ezek. 3:24). Then, in ritual contexts, the requirement for priestly footwashing as a ritual cleansing is indicated (cf. Exod. 29:20; 30:19, 21; 40:31). In addition, the practice of placing blood on the foot as part of the sacrificial priestly ritual is prescribed in Lev. 8:23, 24; 14:14ff. Ps. 22:16 refers to the piercing of one's feet — though symbolic in this context, it has a profoundly literal fulfillment in the experience of Christ on the cross. Literal references to the feet of animals are found in Gen. 8:9; Lev. 11:24, 42; Ezek. 32:13. The soles of the feet are mentioned in Deut. 28:65; Josh. 1:3; 2 Sam. 14:25. The feet of cherubim are mentioned in 2 Chr. 3:13, referring to the carved figures of Solomon's temple; and in Isa. 6:2; Ezek. 1:7 they are indicated in the context of prophetic revelation.

The metaphorical sense of ***regel*** refers primarily to the idea of "rule" or "dominion" — for example in Pss. 8:6; 47:3, where the phrase "under one's feet" suggests human dominion initiated by God himself. Allied to this is the action of "treading under foot," predicated of

Yahweh with reference to his enemies in Isa. 41:2; Lam. 3:4. The term ***regel*** is also used anthropomorphically of God (cf. Exod. 24:10; Ps. 18:9; Nah. 1:3; Zech. 14:4); and in Ezek. 43:7 such a reference points to the dwelling place of God. In a related figurative sense ***regel*** also denotes a "footstool" in Ps. 99:5, referring symbolically to God's throne. Isa. 66:5 depicts the earth as God's "footstool."

regel is a euphemism for genitalia in Exod. 4:25; Ruth 3:4ff.

kēn [**כֵּן, 3653**]

kēn means "foot" in the sense of "base," or "pedestal," and occurs nine times with these meanings. All but one of these occurrences refer to the pedestal of the large bronze sea (i.e., basin) in the tabernacle (cf. Exod. 30:18, 28; 31:9; 35:16; 38:8; 39:39; 40:11; Lev. 8:11). The remaining reference is to the base of the smaller, moveable washbasin in the temple in 1 Kgs. 7:31.

raglî [**רַגְלִי, 7273**]

This noun derived from ***regel*** (see above) means "footman" or "man on foot." ***raglî*** occurs about twelve times with these meanings (cf. Exod. 12:37; Judg. 20:2; 1 Sam. 4:10; 1 Kgs. 20:29; Jer. 12:5).

hadōm [**הֲדֹם, 1916**]

This term occurs only six times, but in each instance the reference is theologically significant.

hadōm refers first of all to the "footstool" of Yahweh, symbolically indicating victory over his enemies (cf. 1 Chr. 28:2; Pss. 99:5; 132:7; Lam. 2:1; Isa. 66:1). Then, in Ps. 110:1, ***hadōm*** refers metaphorically to victory over one's enemies. Again, it is a conquest initiated by Yahweh, and here it constitutes a prophetic anticipation of victory by the Messianic King — a victory clearly attested by the New Testament in reference to Jesus Christ.

kebesh [**כֶּבֶשׁ, 3534**]

kebesh is a rare noun found only in 2 Chr. 9:18, denoting a golden "footstool" attached to a throne.

NT Words

pous [πούς, *4228*]

pous is the most common term for "foot" in the New Testament, occurring about ninety times and referring to the feet of both human beings and beasts. ***pous*** also signifies a "footstool" in several metaphorical contexts.

Literal references to the feet of people include those in Matt. 15:30; Mark 7:25; Luke 24:39; John 11:2, 44; Acts 5:2; 14:10; 1 Tim. 5:10. In particular, Jesus' action in washing his disciples' feet as a gesture of servanthood is described in John 13:5ff. With regard to the literal usage of ***pous***, a significant number of references denote the feet of Christ. See also 1 Cor. 15:21ff.; Eph. 6:15. Matt. 7:6 refers to the feet of animals.

In the book of Revelation ***pous*** designates "feet" in a number of visionary contexts — for example, the "feet" of the heavenly Christ (cf. Rev. 1:15, 17; 2:18); the feet of angelic beings (Rev. 10:1, 2; 19:10; 22:8); the feet of the saints (Rev. 11:11; 12:1); and the feet of the sea beast — the satanic counterfeit messiah (Rev. 13:2).

In particular, Matt. 4:6; Luke 4:11 (citing Ps. 91:11, 12) refer to God's protection of his Son, lest "he strike his foot against a stone."

The translation "footstool" is used metaphorically in several places to denote the vanquished enemies of God (cf. Matt. 5:35; Mark 12:36; Luke 20:43; Acts 2:35; Heb. 1:13; 10:13). In Acts 7:49, the Lord's "footstool" refers to the earth, the whole world. In Rom. 16:20, ***pous*** is also translated "feet," but the context implies the messianic conquest of Satan, and reducing him to the status of a "footstool." See also Eph. 1:22; Heb. 2:8. The expression "shake the dust off one's feet" is a literal action that symbolically represents rejection (cf. Matt. 10:14; Mark 6:11; Luke 9:5; Acts 13:51).

The designation "feet" is sometimes used metaphorically to denote the whole person with reference, for example, to "guiding one's feet into the way of peace" (cf. Luke 1:79). Acts 22:3 refers to Paul's pre-Christian vocation as a Pharisee, "sitting at the feet" of Gamaliel, his mentor.

basis [βάσις, *939*]

basis is a rare noun denoting a person's "feet" miraculously healed of paralysis, found only in Acts 3:7.

pezeuō [πεζεύω, *3978*]

pezeuō is a rare verb meaning "to walk on foot," found only in Acts 20:13.

hypopodion [ὑποπόδιον, *5286*]

hypopodion is a noun found nine times, meaning "footstool" throughout. Matt. 5:35; Acts 7:49 refer to the earth as God's "footstool" (i.e., symbolizing his sovereignty over all nations). Specific references to the vanquished enemies of God as his footstool are found in Matt. 22:44; Mark 12:36; Luke 20:43; Acts 2:35; Heb.

1:13; 10:13. Most of these references are citations of Old Testament texts. See also Jas. 2:3.

See Also: → FOUNDATION

FORBID

OT Words

ḥālîlāh **[חָלִילָה, 2486]**

This is an imperative form of the verb ***ḥālal***, meaning "to begin," "profane," "pollute" (→ BEGIN) which functions as an interjection or expression of passionate intensity, and is translated "God forbid (that . . .)!" or "far be it (from me) . . . !"

ḥālîlāh is first of all an expression of incredulity, predicated of God that he would never engage in a particular action or activity (e.g., Gen. 18:30; 1 Sam. 2:30). Elsewhere, the term is used with reference to people, not God (e.g., Gen. 44:7, 17; Josh. 22:29; 1 Sam. 12:23; 2 Sam. 20:20; 21:3).

NT Words

kōlyō [κωλύω, *2967*]

kōlyō is a verb occurring about twenty times with the senses of "hinder," "forbid," "prevent" throughout.

The meaning "forbid" with the underlying sense of people expressing a negative command is indicated in Mark 9:38ff.; Luke 9:49ff.; 23:2; 1 Cor. 14:39; 1 Tim. 4:3; Acts 10:47.

The Holy Spirit is said to "have forbidden" the apostle Paul to enter Asia in Acts 16:6.

Jesus exhorts his disciples not to "hinder" little children from coming to him in Matt. 19:14; Mark 10:14; Luke 18:16. He also denounces Jewish lawyers for "hindering" those seeking to enter the kingdom of heaven by keeping knowledge of the truth from them (cf. Luke 11:52). Heb. 7:23 refers to priests "being prevented" by death from continuing in office. Other occurrences of the meaning "hinder" or "prevent" include those in Acts 8:36; 1 Thess. 2:16.

FORCE

OT Words

'ānāh **[עָנָה, 6031]**

'ānāh has the general sense of "afflict" or "humble." However, on five occasions it means "force," indicating violent sexual assault (cf. Judg. 20:5; 2 Sam. 13:12ff.). (→ AFFLICT)

NT Words

bebaios [βέβαιος, *949*]

bebaios is an adjective found in nine places with the primary meanings "sure," "firm." In Heb. 9:17, ***bebaios*** refers to a last will and testament being "in force" only on the death of the testator.

biazō [βιάζω, *971*]

biazō is a rare verb meaning "to endure, suffer violence" in the cause of the kingdom of heaven (Matt. 11:12). Luke 16:16 refers to people "forcing their way" into the kingdom of heaven.

harpazō [ἁρπάζω, *726*]

harpazō is a verb found thirteen times with the predominant meaning "seize" or "catch," with several nuances.

In several places, ***harpazō*** also means "take by force." Matt. 11:12 refers to people "taking the kingdom of heaven by force." The meaning here is unclear, but it may suggest feverish human attempts to gain favor with God. John 6:15 records the Jewish crowd's abortive attempt to "take Jesus by force" and make him king over them. See also Acts 23:10.

See Also: → STRENGTH

FOREHEAD

OT Words

mēṣaḥ **[מֵצַח, 4696]**

mēṣaḥ is translated "forehead" or "brow" in all but one of the thirteen contexts in which it is found.

In Exod. 28:38 the "forehead" of Aaron the high priest is mentioned in relation to the sacred plate worn around his turban with the expression "holy to the Lord" engraved on it. This plate is the symbolic repository of all guilt associated with the sacrificial gifts of the Israelite people; and therefore these gifts may be consecrated and rendered acceptable to Yahweh when the high priest stands before God so attired. In Ezek. 9:4, the foreheads of the faithful remnant in Jerusalem are marked in order to preserve them from the inevitable divine slaughter of apostate Israelites who had capitulated to idolatrous worship of pagan deities. See also 1 Sam. 17:49; 2 Chr. 26:19, 20.

The metaphorical expression "forehead(s) of brass" refers to stubbornness or stoic resistance in Isa. 48:4; Jer. 3:3; Ezek. 3:7ff.

gibbēaḥ **[גִּבַּחַת, 1371]**

gibbēaḥ is a rare noun denoting a man's bald "forehead" in Lev. 13:41.

NT Words

metōpon [μέτωπον, *3359*]

metōpon is a noun meaning "forehead" in all eight occurrences of the term — all of which are found in the visionary context of the book of Revelation.

Rev. 7:3; 9:4 mention the seal of God on the "foreheads" of his protected people. Similarly, Rev. 14:1; 22:4 refer to the name of God the Father branded on the "foreheads" of the elect 144,000.

Conversely, Rev. 13:16; 14:9 refer to the mark of the beast, placed on either the right hand or "the forehead" of all those who worshiped the satanic figure. See also Rev. 20:4.

Similarly, Rev. 17:5 mentions the title "mystery, Babylon the great, the mother of harlots" written on "the forehead" of the symbolic woman epitomizing all moral evil.

FOREIGN ➠ ALIEN

FOREKNOW, FOREKNOWLEDGE

NT Words

proginōskō [προγινώσκω, *4267*]

proginōskō is a verb found in five contexts meaning "to know beforehand," "foreknow," "foreordain." Acts 8:29; Rom. 11:2 speak of God "foreknowing" those whom he has redeemed. 1 Pet. 1:20 affirms that Christ was "foreordained" (i.e., chosen by God) prior to the foundation of the world. The sense of "knowing someone beforehand" is indicated in Acts 26:5; 2 Pet. 3:17.

prognōsis [πρόγνωσις, *4268*]

prognōsis is a rare noun derived from ***proginōskō***, above, denoting divine "foreknowledge" in Acts 2:23; 1 Pet. 1:2. Both of these contexts imply divine election.

See Also: ➠ DETERMINE

FOREST

OT Words

ya'ar **[יַעַר, 3293]**

ya'ar is a noun found nearly sixty times with the consistent literal meaning "forest," "wood(s)" (e.g., Deut. 19:5; Josh. 17:15ff.; 1 Kgs. 7:2; 2 Kgs. 2:24; Ps. 96:12; Eccl. 2:6; Isa. 7:2; Jer. 5:6; Ezek. 20:46ff.; Hos. 2:12; Amos 3:4; Mic. 3:12; Zech. 11:2).

FOREVER ➠ EVER

FOREWARN ➠ WARN

FORGET

OT Words

shākaḥ **[שָׁכַח, 7911]**

shākaḥ occurs around one hundred times and means "forget" on virtually every occasion.

Most common is the usage indicating normal human "forgetfulness" (e.g., Gen. 27:45; Deut. 24:19; Job 24:20; Ps. 119:39; Eccl. 2:16; Isa. 23:15, 16; Jer. 20:11; 44:9). Within this broad category, there are also a significant number of texts that reflect the grave danger of God's people "forgetting" either God himself, or what Yahweh has done for them by way of redemptive activity in the past. Such "forgetfulness" is apt to bring the wrath of God down on them (e.g., Judg. 3:7; 1 Sam. 12:9; Ps. 44:20; Jer. 2:32; 50:6; Ezek. 22:12; Hos. 2:13). Specific warnings against such "forgetfulness" are prevalent, especially in the book of Deuteronomy (e.g., Deut. 4:9, 23; 6:12; 8:11ff.; 9:7; 25:19; 32:18; 2 Kgs. 17:38; Ps. 78:7; Prov. 2:17; Isa. 17:10; 51:13). Prov. 3:1; 4:5 record the father's plea to his son not to forget God's law.

In relation to God himself, such intellectual and psychological weakness is, of course, impossible. In this sense, God never "forgets" (e.g., Deut. 4:31; Ps. 9:12, 18; Isa. 49:15; Jer. 50:5). This observation notwithstanding, the psalmist nevertheless beseeches God "not to forget" (cf. Pss. 10:12; 74:19, 23; see also 1 Sam. 1:11 in this regard). The psalmist also claims that his people "have not forgotten" God or his covenant (cf. Pss. 44:17; 119:83, 141, 153); and he himself promises "not to forget" (cf. Ps. 119:16, 61, 93, 109).

In Hos. 4:6, the prophet records that God will indeed "forget" his people on account of their sin. This "forgetting" is not a sign of weakness (see preceding paragraph), nor is it expressed in an absolute sense. Rather, it suggests a temporary abandonment of his people for the purpose of punishing them. There are also occasional cries of anguish to God, asking why he has apparently "forgotten" his people (e.g., Pss. 13:1; 42:9; Isa. 49:14; Lam. 5:20).

nāshāh [נָשָׁה, 5382]

nāshāh is a verb found in six places, meaning to "forget" in most of these. All contexts are literal, signifying the psychological phenomenon of omitting things from one's memory (cf. Gen. 41:51; Job 39:17; Lam. 3:17). In particular, Isa. 44:21 affirms that Yahweh could never forget his chosen Servant.

NT WORDS

epilanthanomai [ἐπιλανθάνομαι, *1950*]

epilanthanomai is a verb found in nine places meaning "forget" throughout, with several different nuances.

"Forgetting" in the sense of "failure to do something" is indicated in Matt. 16:5; Mark 8:14, in relation to providing food.

The impossibility of God "forgetting" or "overlooking" the needs of his creation is noted in Luke 12:6; as is his determination not to "forget" or "overlook" the service of the saints in Heb. 6:10.

Phil. 3:13 refers to Paul's determination to "forget" (i.e., put aside from his mind) what lies behind him.

Heb. 13:2 contains an injunction not to "forget" (i.e., neglect) to show hospitality to strangers; and Heb. 13:16 contains a more generalized exhortation not to "forget" (i.e., neglect) to do good.

Jas. 1:24 describes the phenomenon of a person looking into a mirror and then "forgetting" what he looks like — that is, failing to recall the image in his memory. See also Jas. 1:25.

eklanthanomai [ἐκλανθάνομαι, *1585*]

A rare variant of ***epilanthanomai***, above, ***eklanthanomai*** means "forget" in the sense of "fail to recall" in Heb. 12:5.

FORGIVE, FORGIVENESS

OT WORDS

sālaḥ [סָלַח, 5545]

sālaḥ is a verb consistently translated "forgive," "pardon," and is found approximately fifty times.

Pleas to God for forgiveness are found in Exod. 34:9; Num. 14:19; 1 Kgs. 8:30ff.; 2 Kgs. 5:18; Ps. 25:11; Dan. 9:19; Amos 7:2. The Mosaic law covenant makes provision for the granting of forgiveness for Israelite worshipers after appropriate sacrificial offerings have been made (cf. Lev. 4:20ff.; 5:10ff.; 6:7; 19:22; Num. 15:25ff.). However, mere sacrifices alone do not automatically guarantee forgiveness — an appropriate spirit of repentance must also be in evidence (cf. 2 Chr. 7:14; Isa. 55:7; Jer. 5:1; 36:3). Other references to God granting forgiveness are found in Num. 14:20; 30:5, 8; Ps. 103:3. However, God refuses to forgive deliberate, calculated acts of rebellion against him (cf. Deut. 29:20; 2 Kgs. 24:4; Jer. 5:7). In Lam. 3:42, God's refusal to forgive is not absolute. He only refused in the sense that he did not withdraw the threatened punishment of the Babylonian invasion. Jer. 31:34; 33:8; 50:20 promise complete forgiveness in the coming new covenant age.

selîḥāh [סְלִיחָה, 5547]

selîḥāh is a rare noun found three times, denoting "forgiveness" as a quality intimately associated with the person and character of God, who is willing and ready to offer it to his people (cf. Neh. 9:17; Ps. 130:4; Dan. 9:9).

nāsā' [נָשָׂא, 5375]

nāsā' is a common verbal form, occurring over 650 times with a variety of meanings centering around the concepts of "bear," "lift up," "carry." ***nāsā'*** is also found eleven times with the derived sense of "forgive."

Literal requests for forgiveness from another person are recorded in Gen. 50:17; Exod. 10:17. Pleas to God for forgiveness are found in Exod. 32:32; Num. 14:19; 1 Sam. 25:28; Ps. 25:18. Interestingly, Isa. 2:9 contains a plea for God not to forgive, issued in the context of the anticipation of the final Day of the Lord judgment on all of Yahweh's enemies, including those who are apostate.

sallāḥ [סַלָּח, 5546]

sallāḥ is a rare adjectival form found only in Ps. 86:5, depicting God as one who is "forgiving," or "willing to forgive."

NT WORDS

aphiēmi [ἀφίημι, *863*]

aphiēmi is a common verb occurring nearly 150 times with the meaning "to leave," with a variety of associated senses. (→ LEAVE → ALLOW) This term is also translated "forgive" in about one-third of its occurrences.

A plea for God to "forgive" is found in Matt. 6:12a; Luke 11:4a; Acts 8:22. However, people who do not forgive one another will not be offered forgiveness themselves (cf. Mark 11:26). God's action of "forgiving" is noted in Matt. 6:15; Mark 3:28; Jas. 5:15; 1 John 1:9; 2:12.

References to the act of human forgiveness, including the requirement to forgive, are found in Matt. 6:12b; 18:21ff.; Mark 11:25; Luke 11:4b; 17:3.

Jesus' right to forgive sin is recorded in Matt. 9:2, 6; Mark 2:5ff.; Luke 5:20ff.; 7:49. At his crucifixion, Jesus asks God his Father to "forgive" those who were tormenting him (cf. Luke 23:34).

General references to the act of "forgiving" are found in Matt. 9:5; 12:31; Rom. 4:7.

The sin of blaspheming the Holy Spirit is designated as the one sin that will not be forgiven, as noted in Matt. 12:31ff.; Luke 12:10.

aphesis [ἄφεσις, *859*]

aphesis is the noun derived from ***aphiēmi*** (see above), denoting "forgiveness (of sin)" in all but one occurrence.

One of the specific purposes for which Jesus was to die, the forgiveness of people's sins, is recorded in Matt. 26:28; Acts 5:31.

John's baptism was designed as a ritual of repentance leading to forgiveness of sin, as noted in Mark 1:4; Luke 3:3.

Those who blaspheme against the Holy Spirit are denied "forgiveness" (cf. Mark 3:29). Heb. 9:22 affirms that without the shedding of blood there can be no "forgiveness" of sins.

References to the "forgiveness of sins" for the people of God, granted through the person of Christ, are found in Luke 1:77; 24:47; Acts 10:43; 13:38; 26:18; Eph. 1:7; Col. 1:14; Heb. 10:18. Exhortations to repent and be baptized for the "forgiveness" of sins are found in Acts 2:38.

aphesis denotes "release" for captives in Luke 4:18.

charizomai [χαρίζομαι, *5483*]

charizomai is synonymous with ***aphiēmi***, above, and found around twenty times, meaning "freely give" and "forgive." This term refers primarily to the act of forgiving in a human context, as indicated in Luke 7:42ff.; 2 Cor. 2:7, 10; 12:13; Eph. 4:32a; Col. 3:13. This term also refers to God's act of "forgiving" the sin of his people in Eph. 4:32; Col. 2:13. (→ GIVE)

apolyō [ἀπολύω, *630*]

apolyō is a verb found in nearly ninety places with various meanings including "let go," "release," "divorce," "send," and "forgive." The latter use is rare, found only in Luke 6:37 with an injunction to "forgive" so that forgiveness might be received back.
(→ DIVORCE → RELEASE → SEND)

Additional Notes

The phenomenon of "forgiveness" in Scripture, as with all other motifs that are complex and multi-faceted, cannot be comprehensively understood simply by an analysis of the vocabulary for "forgiveness." Rather, a broad range of semantic material in both Old and New Testaments must be considered before a viable grasp of the subject can be obtained. However, as far as these specific terms for "forgiveness" go, a consistency of usage is observable throughout Scripture. "Forgiveness" is something that may be obtained from God, flowing freely as it does from his being. But this comes about only after the satisfaction of his justice and the response of a penitent, contrite heart. The miracle of divine "forgiveness" and grace, however, emerges from the fact that through the system of sacrifice for sins under the old covenant and the imparting of the gift of faith and repentance, God himself provides the ultimate sacrifice for sin and the foundation of absolute "forgiveness" in the person of his Son, Jesus Christ. While God's grace and "forgiveness" are clearly evident in the Old Testament, it is not until the coming of Christ that the full scope of such mercy becomes apparent. God demands repentance from his people, but even that response is initiated by the action of his sovereign grace. From that perspective, all of us as the people of God find ourselves eternally indebted to his kindness which leads to our "forgiveness."

See Also: → PROPITIATION

FORM

OT Words

tōhû [תֹּהוּ, **8414**]

This term is found twenty times and is translated "vain," "vanity," "formlessness," "without form," "confusion." The meaning "without form" or "formless" occurs only twice. Gen. 1:2 refers to the "formless" mass of the earth prior to its creative shaping by the divine word. Jer. 4:23 uses it metaphorically to describe the prophetic anticipation of divine judgment, referring to the desolation of the land that will be "formless" and empty in the face of God's wrath.

tabnît [תַּבְנִית, **8403**]

tabnît occurs around twenty times and is translated "pattern" in most instances. However, on three occasions in the book of Ezekiel it means "form." In Ezek. 8:3 it refers to the hand of Yahweh taking hold of the prophet just prior to him receiving revelation from God. Ezek. 8:10 refers to the idolatrous "forms" of animals, and Ezek. 10:8 mentions the form of a human hand under the wings of the cherubim in the vision of the heavenly throne room.

tō'ar [תֹּאַר, 8389]

tō'ar is a rare term, meaning "form" in only three of its fifteen occurrences. 1 Sam. 28:14 refers to the "form" of Samuel coming up from the grave to condemn Saul. In Isa. 52:14; 53:2, ***tō'ar*** refers to the "form" of the Suffering Servant; again, the sense of "appearance" is dominant.

tō'ar, however, also refers to "form" or "appearance" in an indirect way, indicating the sense of "beautiful" (cf. Gen. 29:17; Deut. 21:11; 1 Sam. 25:3; Esth. 2:7); and "handsome" (cf. Gen. 39:6; 1 Sam. 16:18; 1 Kgs. 1:6) in reference to women and men, respectively. See also Gen. 41:18, 19; Judg. 8:18; Lam. 4:8.

yāṣar [יָצַר, 3335]

yāṣar means "to form," or "fashion," and refers mainly to the divine action of forming or fashioning (i.e., creating). ***yāṣar*** occurs approximately sixty times.

In a literal sense, this term refers to "forming" in the context of divine, fiat creation of the earth itself (cf. Isa. 45:18; Jer. 33:2; Ps. 95:5); of human beings (cf. Gen. 2:7, 8; Zech. 12:1); of animals (cf. Gen. 2:19; Ps. 104:26); and of other inanimate phenomena (e.g., Ps. 74:11; Isa. 45:7; Jer. 10:16; Amos 4:9). ***yāṣar*** also indicates God's fashioning of his own people (cf. Isa. 29:11; 43:17, 21; 44:2, 21; 49:5; Jer. 1:5). A couple of texts also portray Yahweh as having planned judgment against the wicked, including his own people (cf. Isa. 37:26; 46:11; Jer. 18:11).

On the human level, ***yāṣar*** indicates the activity of people who form (i.e., shape, create) idols (cf. Isa. 44:9, 10; Hab. 2:18). Significantly, Isa. 43:10 contains Yahweh's denial that any god was formed either before or after him. For other uses of shaping or "forming" by human agency, see also Ps. 94:20; Isa. 29:16; 54:17.

NT Words

morphē [μορφή, *3444*]

morphē is a rare noun found three times, meaning "form" in each case. Mark 16:12 records Jesus' appearance to two of his disciples in another "form" after his resurrection. This change of "form" relates to a noticeable difference in the body of Christ, transformed by his experience of resurrection. Phil. 2:6 refers to Jesus being in the "form" of God, denoting the divine aspect of his dual nature. Then, Phil. 2:7 declares that Jesus took upon himself the "form" of a servant — that is, he assumed a fully human nature, marking him out as a true man.

morphōsis [μόρφωσις, *3446*]

morphōsis is a rare variant of ***morphē***, above, found only twice. The expression "form of knowledge" is found in Rom. 2:20, designating the "embodiment" of knowledge as revealed in the law. 2 Tim. 3:5 contains the apostolic warning against fellowship with godless men who hold merely to the "form" of religion but deny its power. This "form" denotes the "outward ceremony or ritual" of worship, without the accompanying heart devotion.

morphoō [μορφόω, *3445*]

morphoō is a rare verb found only in Gal. 4:19, used passively with reference to Christ "being formed" in his congregation as followers come to a Christlike spiritual maturity.

plassō [πλάσσω, *4111*]

plassō is another rare verb found only twice, meaning "to form" with the underlying senses of "mold," or "shape." Rom. 9:20 refers to the literal action of the potter "molding" his artistic creation. 1 Tim. 2:13 declares that Adam "was formed" (i.e., fashioned, created) by God prior to Eve.

plasma [πλάσμα, *4110*]

plasma is a rare derivative noun from ***plassō*** (see above), found only in Rom. 9:20 with the generalized sense of "that which is formed" by its maker, denoting (from the context) an earthen pot fashioned by the potter.

eidos [εἶδος, *1491*]

eidos is a noun found five times denoting "sight," "appearance," "form" with the underlying sense of "external appearance, or shape."

In Luke 3:22 the Holy Spirit is said to descend upon Jesus in the "form" (i.e., appearance, shape) of a dove. On the Mount of Transfiguration the "form" or "appearance" of Jesus' face is said to undergo a profound transformation, revealing a glimpse of his heavenly nature (cf. Luke 9:29). John 5:37 affirms that no one has ever seen the "form" of God, referring to his "essence," his true spiritual "shape" (the reference here is entirely non-material). In 1 Thess. 5:22 there is an exhortation to abstain from every "form" or "kind" of evil. See also 2 Cor. 5:7.

See Also: → APPEARANCE → IMAGE → PATTERN → VISION

FORMER

OT Words

ri'shôn **[רִאשׁוֹן, 7223]**

ri'shôn occurs around two hundred times with the primary meaning "first," as well as the derived sense of "former." The latter meaning is found in about thirty contexts.

With reference to a previous time ***ri'shôn*** is found, for example, in Gen. 40:13; Num. 6:12; 1 Kgs. 13:6; Dan. 11:42. Indicating previous persons, ***ri'shôn*** occurs in Num. 21:26; Neh. 5:15; Jer. 34:5. The meaning "former" in the sense of "former way, or manner of doing things" is found in 2 Kgs. 17:34, 40.

ri'shôn also indicates various other phenomena. For example, Ps. 89:49 refers to the "former" loving-kindness of Yahweh; Hag. 2:3, 9 mention the "former" glory of the Solomonic temple; and Ps. 79:8; Isa. 65:7 mention God's dealing with the "former" sins of his people. Yahweh promises that he will not remember the "former things" (i.e., sins) against his people (cf. Isa. 65:17; 43:18 [an instruction for the people to forget their past]). See also Isa. 41:22; 43:9; 46:9; Isa. 61:4; Eccl. 1:11.

NT Words

prōtos [πρῶτος, *4413*]

prōtos is a common adjective found over one hundred times with the predominant sense of "first," as well as several related nuances throughout. In one context ***prōtos*** denotes "the former things" as having passed away, signifying the end of the earthly age (cf. Rev. 21:4).

proteros [πρότερος, *4387*]

proteros is a comparative adjectival form meaning "former" in three places. Eph. 4:22 refers to the "former" (i.e., previous) way of life of his Ephesian parishioners. The sense of "previous" is also evident in the phrase "former days" in Heb. 10:32. 1 Pet. 1:14 refers to the passions of one's "former" ignorance.

FORNICATION

OT Words

zānāh **[זָנָה, 2181]**

This verb means "to commit fornication," "play the harlot." In its participial form, ***zānāh*** is translated nominally as "harlot," "fornicator," and occurs around one hundred times.

In its nominal form, ***zānāh*** means "harlot," "fornicator" (e.g., Gen. 34:31; Judg. 11:1; Isa. 23:15; Joel 3:3; Amos 7:17). The literal sense of "playing the harlot" (i.e., with a prostitute) is found, for example, in Gen. 38:24; Lev. 21:7; Num. 25:1; Deut. 22:21; 23:18.

zānāh also reflects a significant metaphorical usage when referring to Israel and Judah "playing the harlot." In this sense, the term highlights the people's unfaithfulness to Yahweh, for they have committed spiritual adultery by becoming idolatrous in their worship of pagan deities (e.g., Exod. 34:15ff.; Deut. 31:16; Judg. 8:27, 33; Ps. 106:39; Jer. 2:20; 3:1ff.; Ezek. 16:5ff.; 23:3ff.; Hos. 2:5; 3:3; Mic. 1:7). The term is also predicated of Jerusalem in Isa. 1:22.

zenûnîm **[זְנוּנִים, 2183]**

A noun plural form derived from ***zānāh*** (see above), ***zenûnîm*** is translated "fornication," "adultery," or "prostitution." ***zenûnîm*** occurs twelve times.

"Fornication" in the sense of prostitution is indicated in Gen. 38:24. All other uses of ***zenûnîm*** are metaphorical, as "fornication" refers to spiritual adultery, which in turn equates with idolatry. Every reference is to Israel, except for Nah. 3:4, which alludes to Assyria (cf. 2 Kgs. 9:22; Ezek. 23:11, 29; Hos. 1:2; 2:2, 4; 4:12; 5:4).

zenût **[זְנוּת, 2184]**

This term is synonymous with ***zenûnîm*** (see above). ***zenût*** occurs nine times and is translated "fornication," "prostitution," with symbolic reference to the idolatry of Israel through the metaphor of adultery (cf. Num. 14:33; Jer. 3:2, 9; 13:27; Ezek. 23:27; 43:7, 9; Hos. 4:11; 6:10).

taznût **[תַּזְנוּת, 8457]**

Another synonym for ***zenûnîm*** and ***zenût***, above, ***taznût*** occurs twenty times and refers to "fornication," "harlotry," as idolatry through the figure of spiritual adultery. The term occurs only in the book of Ezekiel (cf. Ezek. 16:15ff.; 23:7ff.).

NT Words

porneia [πορνεία, *4202*]

porneia is a noun occurring around twenty-five times with the general meaning "fornication," expressing the underlying sense of "sexual immorality" in a variety of contexts.

porneia denotes the vice of "sexual immorality" in the context of marriage in Matt. 5:32; 19:9; John 8:41; Acts 15:20, 29; 1 Cor. 5:1; 6:13, 18; 7:2. A specific reference to "sexual immorality" outside the confines of a marital context is found in Rev. 2:21.

General references to "immorality," implying "moral perversity" and signifying more than marital infidelity, are found in Matt. 15:19; Rom. 1:29; 1 Cor. 5:1; 6:13, 18; 7:2; Gal. 5:19; Eph. 5:3; Col. 3:5; Rev. 9:21.

porneia expresses the sense of "sexual immorality" in a number of metaphorical contexts in the book of Revelation with reference to the symbolic woman "Babylon," portrayed as a prostitute. In these contexts, her "sexual immorality" denotes the sin of "idolatry," frequently described through the symbol of moral impurity. It is the sin of idolatry that most distresses God as it challenges and undermines his unique authority and majesty in the hearts of those who commit such sin (cf. Rev. 14:8; 17:2, 4; 18:3; 19:2).

pornos [πόρνος, *4205*]

pornos is a noun found ten times with the general sense of an "immoral person" throughout, referring both to sexual misconduct as well as to moral perverseness in general. References to "immoral men," denoting people who are sexually immoral, are found in 1 Cor. 5:9ff.; Eph. 5:5; Heb. 13:4; Rev. 22:15 (implied).

General references to "the immoral" in the broad sense of "the morally perverse" are found in 1 Cor. 6:9; 1 Tim. 1:10; Heb. 12:16; Rev. 21:8.

pornē [πόρνη, *4204*]

pornē is a variant of ***pornos***, above, denoting a "(female) prostitute" in both literal and metaphorical contexts. The term occurs twelve times. Literal references to a "harlot" or "prostitute" include those in Matt. 21:31ff.; Luke 15:30; 1 Cor. 6:15ff.; Heb. 11:31; Jas. 2:25.

The godless city of Babylon is depicted metaphorically as a "whore" in Rev. 17:1ff.; 19:2, denoting her rank idolatry and opposition against God.

porneuō [πορνεύω, *4203*]

porneuō is a verb found eight times meaning "to practice, indulge in immorality" in a sexual sense in 1 Cor. 6:18f.; 10:8; Rev. 2:14, 20. In Rev. 17:2; 18:3, 9 ***porneuō*** signifies the committing of adultery in a metaphorical sense, with reference to the peoples of the earth engaging in morally culpable business with the archetypal evil nation Babylon. Such symbolic "adultery" most likely takes the form of idolatry — a practice universally evident throughout the nations of the world and frequently equated with "immoral living" (symbolically speaking) in the prophetic canon of Scripture.

ekporneuō [ἐκπορνεύω, *1608*]

ekporneuō is a rare verb found only in Jude 7, referring to the citizens of Sodom and Gomorrah who had "given themselves over to sexual immorality."

Additional Notes

The phenomena of fornication and associated practices, both literal and metaphorical, are clearly attested throughout both Old and New Testaments. What is preserved in both Hebrew and Greek vocabulary is the equation of idolatry and spiritual adultery. The book of Revelation is the exclusive source of this imagery in the New Testament, while in the Old Testament it is a theme characteristic of the prophetic writings. The powerful imagery of the Apocalypse in this regard draws directly on the equally powerful imagery of the Old Testament prophets. Idolatry as spiritual adultery all but destroyed the spiritual fiber of the Israelite nation, and severely damaged their relationship with Yahweh. The practice's potential for similar damage to the people of God under the new covenant is also great.

FORSAKE

OT Words

'āzab [עָזַב, 5800]

'āzab occurs approximately two hundred times with the primary meaning "forsake," or "leave." One significant concept that underlies the usage of this term is that of "abandonment," particularly in regard to Israel's neglect and rejection of their covenant obligations towards God.

Theologically speaking, the idea of "forsaking" one's covenant responsibility, in the sense of abandoning or neglecting it, is of prime importance. It is predicated of God negatively in that he never abandons his responsibility and always keeps his promises with regard to his people (e.g., Gen. 24:7; Deut. 31:6, 8; Josh. 1:5; 1 Kgs. 6:13; Ezra 9:9; Isa. 42:16). However, it is also predicated of Yahweh when he abandons his people, albeit temporarily, as punishment for violating the terms of the covenant and hands them over to the curse sanctions of the law (e.g., Deut. 31:17; Isa. 17:2, 9; 54:7; Jer. 12:7).

In regard to the Israelite people themselves, ***'āzab*** is frequently employed to indicate their "abandonment," their "rejection" of God (e.g., Deut. 28:20; 2 Kgs. 21:22; 2 Chr. 13:11; Ezra 8:22; Isa. 1:4; Jer. 2:17). It is something they are warned against doing in Josh. 24:20; 1 Chr. 28:9. The Israelites' wholesale "abandoning" of the covenant is referred to in Jer. 22:9; Dan. 11:30. The practice of idolatry as an inevitable consequence of "abandoning" God is cited in Judg. 2:12, 13; 10:6; 1 Sam. 12:10; 1 Kgs. 9:9; 19:10; 2 Kgs. 22:17; 2 Chr. 34:25; Jer. 1:16; Hos. 4:10. Israel is also condemned for "abandoning," "forsaking" the commandments of Yahweh — that is, for disobeying them (cf. 2 Kgs. 17:16; Ezra 9:10; Jer. 9:13).

'āzab is also used quite frequently to refer to "forsaking" in the sense of "(physically) leaving behind," whether referring to people (e.g., Gen. 50:8; Exod. 2:20; Isa. 10:3); to objects and animals (e.g., 2 Sam. 5:21; 1 Chr. 14:12; Jer. 14:5); or to places (e.g., Lev. 26:43 [the land]; Jer. 51:9 [Babylon]; Zeph. 2:4 [Gaza]). To "leave" or "forsake" in the sense of putting aside physical and psychological dependence is given a special significance in Gen. 2:24, which describes the essence of a rightly-ordered marriage — that a man "leave" his father and mother and be united with his wife. See also Gen. 44:22; Isa. 10:14.

nāṭash **[נָטַשׁ, 5203]**

A synonym for ***'āzab*** (see above), ***nāṭash*** occurs about forty times and means "forsake," "abandon," "leave" in nearly half of these contexts.

Such an action is predicated of Israel when they are said to "abandon" Yahweh through the violation of his covenant (cf. Deut. 32:15; Jer. 15:6).

Yahweh is also depicted as "abandoning" his people in response to their rebellion against him, a divine response in line with the sanctions of the covenant (cf. 2 Kgs. 2:14; Ps. 78:60; Isa. 2:6; 32:14; Jer. 7:29; 23:39; Amos 5:2). However, in 1 Sam. 12:22; Ps. 94:14, Yahweh promises not to ultimately "abandon" his people on account of his promises. 1 Kgs. 8:57; Ps. 27:9 contain pleas for God not to "abandon" his people.

Prov. 1:8; 6:20 contain definite commands not to "abandon" or neglect the teaching of one's parents.

NT Words

apostasia [ἀποστασία, *646*]

apostasia is a rare noun denoting "apostasy," or rebellion against God, and found only twice. Acts 21:21 contains the accusation against Paul, charging him with inciting Jewish people literally to "teach rebellion" against Moses, dissuading them from having their children circumcised. 2 Thess. 2:3 refers to the anticipated "apostasy" or "rebellion" of the last days when many would abandon the faith.

Additional Notes

There is a measurable consistency in the usage of Hebrew and Greek terminology for the concept of "forsaking" or "abandoning," especially where it involves rebellion against God. The Old Testament, however, places much greater emphasis upon the phenomenon. The dire physical consequences of abandoning or rejecting Yahweh are clearly and frequently spelled out for the people of Israel. The curses of the covenant constitute a significant incentive for not disobeying God. Such consequences acquire a terrifying spiritual dimension under the new covenant, where such apostasy threatens to remove one forever from the presence of God.

See Also: ➠ LEAVE

FORTY

OT Words

'arbā'îm **[אַרְבָּעִים, 705]**

The number "forty" occurs about 140 times in various contexts. Some contexts reflect mundane usage such as age; population count; size of herds, armies; dimensions of buildings; duration of monarchical rule. Other contexts, however, indicate that the number forty may be understood variously as a period of divine judgment, testing, blessing, or revelation in theologically significant contexts.

Examples of the theologically significant use of the number forty in contexts of judgment include the forty-day duration of the Noahic flood (cf. Gen. 7:4, 12, 17; 8:6); and the forty-year period of Israel's wandering in the wilderness (e.g., Exod. 16:35; Deut. 1:3; 29:5; Josh. 5:6; Ps. 95:10). Moses spent forty days and nights on Mt. Sinai receiving the law covenant from God (cf. Exod. 24:18; 34:28; Deut. 9:9, 11; 10:10). In the book of Judges, the Israelite confederation suffered forty years of harassment at the hands of the Philistines (cf. Judg. 13:1). Forty-year periods of rule are also characteristic of Israel's premonarchic period when Eli, for example, judged Israel for that length of time (cf. 1 Sam. 4:8). David and Solomon also ruled Israel for forty years each (cf. 1 Kgs. 2:11; 11:42). Other significant uses of the number forty include those in Josh. 14:7; Ezek. 4:6; 29:12.

NT Words

tessarakonta [τεσσαράκοντα, *5062*]

tessarakonta is the dynamic equivalent for ***'arbā'îm*** (see above), denoting "forty" in approximately twenty places.

The significant reference to Jesus' forty-day period of temptation in the desert is found in Matt. 4:2; Mark 1:13; Luke 4:2. Other notable symbolic references to the number forty are found in Rev. 7:4; 14:1ff., in relation to the metaphor of the 144,000 constituting the elect of God. See also Rev. 11:2; 13:5; 21:17. References to Israel's forty-year wandering in the wilderness are found in Acts 7:36, 42; Heb. 3:9, 17.

Other mundane references to the number forty include those in John 2:20; Acts 1:3; 4:22; 23:13, 21; 2 Cor. 11:24.

FOUL → DEFILE

FOUNDATION, LAY A FOUNDATION

OT Words

yesôd **[יְסוֹד, 3247]**

yesôd refers to a "foundation," or "base," and occurs twenty times.

In its literal sense, ***yesôd*** refers to the base of the altar associated with the sacrificial altar of Israelite worship (cf. Exod. 29:12; Lev. 4:7, 18ff.; 4:34; 5:9; 8:15; 9:9); to "building foundations" (cf. Job 4:19); and to the "Foundation Gate" in Jerusalem (cf. 2 Chr. 23:5). There is also a semi-metaphorical usage of the term in reference to the "foundation" of Jerusalem being destroyed (cf. Ps. 137:7; Ezek. 13:14); and also to the divine destruction of the "foundation" of Egypt (cf. Ezek. 30:4).

Metaphorically, ***yesôd*** refers to the destruction of the "foundation" of the wicked (viz. their false hope) in Job 22:16, as well as to the eternal establishment of the righteous, placing them on a firm "foundation" forever (cf. Prov. 10:25).

môsād **[מוֹסָד, 4144];** ***mûsādāh*** **[מוּסָדָה, 4146]**

Both the masculine and feminine forms of this noun mean "foundation." ***mûsādāh***, the feminine, is more common than the masculine ***mûsād.*** Together, these two terms occur thirteen times. ***mûsād*** refers metaphorically to the foundations of the mountains (Deut. 32:22); to the foundations of the earth at creation (Prov. 8:22); and to the shaking of those foundations (Ps. 82:5). Similarly, ***mûsādāh*** indicates the foundations of the earth at the moment of creation (e.g., Isa. 40:21); and also the phenomenon of the shaking of the foundations of heaven as a consequence of the anger of God (cf. 2 Sam. 22:8, 16; Ps. 18:7, 15; Isa. 24:18). ***mûsādāh*** refers to the "foundation of many generations" in Isa. 58:12 in reference to the rebuilding of Jerusalem. The usage of these terms is consistently metaphorical.

yāsad **[יָסַד, 3245]**

yāsad is the verb from which ***yesôd*** and ***mûsād*** (see above) are derived. ***yāsad*** occurs around fifty times and has the dominant sense of "to found" (i.e., establish or begin), with the related meaning "lay a foundation."

The meaning "lay the foundation of" is predicated of the city of Jericho, for example, in the sense of rebuilding it, which is related to a divine curse (cf. Josh. 6:26; 1 Kgs. 16:34). It is also found with reference to the temple of Solomon and the postexilic temple (cf. 1 Kgs. 5:17; 6:37; 2 Chr. 31:7; Ezra 3:6, 10, 11, 12; Isa. 44:28; 54:11; Hag. 2:18; Zech. 4:9; 8:9). There is a significant metaphorical usage of this expression in Isa. 28:16, where Yahweh's "laying a foundation stone" in Zion constitutes a prophetic anticipation of the coming of the Messiah.

The "laying of the foundation" of the earth is alluded to in Job 38:4; Pss. 24:2; 78:9; 104:5; Prov. 3:19; Isa. 48:13; 51:13; Zech. 12:1.

The meaning "found" in the sense of "establish" is predicated of Egypt in Exod. 9:18; and of Zion in Isa. 14:32.

massad **[מַסַּד, 4527]**

massad is a rare noun found only in 1 Kgs. 7:9 denoting the "foundation" of the temple.

'ōsh **[אֹשׁ, 787** (Aramaic)**]**

'ōsh is an Aramaic term, found only three times, denoting the "foundation" of the second temple, rebuilt after the Israelite people returned from captivity (cf. Ezra 4:12; 5:16; 6:3).

mûsād **[מוּסָד, 4143]**

mûsād is a rare variant of ***mûsād***, above, found only twice and denoting the "foundation" of Solomon's temple in 2 Chr. 8:16. In Isa. 28:16 ***mûsād*** refers metaphorically to the coming Messiah, who would constitute a "sure foundation," a cornerstone of the temple laid down by God himself. The context here and that of the New Testament (see below) suggests clearly that such a "foundation stone" constitutes the central figure in God's redemptive plan to reestablish his kingdom on earth, ultimately through the person and work of his Son Jesus Christ.

mākôn **[מָכוֹן, 4349]**

mākôn is a noun found in seventeen places with the primary meaning "place," "dwelling place." In Ps. 104:5, however, ***mākôn*** is used metaphorically to denote the "foundations" of the earth, set in place by God himself. (➡ PLACE)

NT Words

themelios [θεμέλιος, *2310*]

themelios is a noun found sixteen times with the consistent meaning "foundation."

Literal references to the "foundations" of a house are found in Luke 6:48ff.; to the "foundation" of a tower in Luke 14:29; and to the "foundations" of a prison in Acts 16:26.

Elsewhere, ***themelios*** is used in metaphorical contexts. The "foundation" of a man's ministry is indicated in Rom. 15:20; 1 Cor. 3:10ff. In particular, Jesus Christ is depicted as the "foundation" of gospel ministry in 1 Cor. 3:11; and in Eph. 2:20 the household or family of God is said to be built on the "foundation" of the apostles and prophets, with Christ himself as the chief cornerstone.

In 1 Tim. 6:19, ***themelios*** denotes a "foundation" in the sense of a "spiritual guarantee" of eternal life. Heb. 6:10 refers to the "foundation" of repentance in the sense of a "fundamental set of teachings" as prerequisite for a godly life. See also 2 Tim. 2:19.

Heb. 11:10; Rev. 21:4, 19 refer to the "foundations" of the heavenly city.

katabolē [καταβολή, *2602*]

katabolē is a synonym for ***themelios*** (see above) meaning "foundation" and found exclusively in the expression "foundation of the world."

For the most part, the contexts of this expression all relate to the "beginning of creation" as the starting point for God's redemptive purposes and revelation that would ultimately culminate in the person of Christ (cf. Matt. 13:35; 25:34; John 17:24; Heb. 4:3; 9:26; 1 Pet. 1:20; Rev. 17:8). In particular, Eph. 1:4 refers to God having chosen his people from "before the foundation or creation of the world." Similarly, Rev. 13:8 mentions the Lamb's book of life inscribed with the names of the elect, again "before the foundation of the world." See also Luke 11:50.

themelioō [θεμελιόω, *2311*]

themelioō is a verb found six times meaning "found," "ground," "establish," as well as "lay a foundation." The sense of "setting a foundation," both literal and metaphorical, is common to each reference.

Matt. 7:25; Luke 6:48 both refer to the efficient "founding," or erection, of a house that can withstand the impact of wind and rain. Eph. 3:17 mentions believers being "grounded" in love. Col. 1:23 refers to the blessing of a steadfast, or well-grounded, faith. 1 Pet. 5:10 contains the promise that God will "establish" his people in their faith. Finally, Heb. 1:10 affirms that God "has laid the foundation of the earth" at the beginning of time.

FOUNTAIN

OT Words

'ayin [עַיִן, **5869**]

'ayin is a common term found nearly nine hundred times, with the large majority of occurrences referring to "eye," "eyesight." However, ***'ayin*** also means "fountain," or "spring," in about ten instances.

Ground water, in the form of a spring, is mentioned in Num. 33:9; Deut. 8:7; 1 Sam. 29:1; 2 Chr. 32:3; and in Gen. 16:7 ***'ayin*** indicates a spring in the wilderness. Prov. 8:28 refers to oceans as "fountains of the deep." The name "Fountain Gate," in relation to the city of Jerusalem, occurs in Neh. 2:14; 3:15; 12:37.

ma'yān [מַעְיָן, **4599**]

A noun derived from ***'ayin*** (see above), ***ma'yān*** occurs around twenty times and is consistently translated "fountain," "well," or "spring(s)."

ma'yān refers to the fountains of the great deep in Gen. 7:11; 8:2. There are also numerous references to ground springs or wells (e.g., Lev. 11:36; Josh. 15:9; 1 Kgs. 18:5; 2 Chr. 32:4; Pss. 74:15; 104:10).

In Ps. 87:7, the psalmist writes that all his "springs" are found in Yahweh — a symbolic reference to one who is in intimate relationship with his God. Other metaphorical uses of the term include references to the staining of sinfulness (cf. Prov. 25:26); and to a woman's virginal purity prior to the consummation of marriage (cf. Song 4:12, 15). ***ma'yān*** also refers to both judgment (cf. Hos. 13:15 [Israel's "well" will dry up]); and blessing (cf. Isa. 12:3; 41:18; Joel 3:18).

NT Words

pēgē [πηγή, *4077*]

pēgē is a noun found twelve times meaning "fountain," "well," "spring" throughout, both in a literal and metaphorical sense.

A pathological menstrual hemorrhage is described in relation to a woman's illness as a "flow" (lit. "fountain of blood") in Mark 5:29.

Literal references to a "well" or "spring" are found in John 4:6; Jas. 3:11ff.; Rev. 8:10; 14:7; 16:4.

Elsewhere, ***pēgē*** is used metaphorically to denote a "spring of water" that symbolizes the spiritual life force emanating from Christ that will guarantee its possessor an unbroken relationship with God throughout eternity (cf. John 4:14). The heavenly consummation of the "springs of living water" is found in Rev. 7:17; 21:6. Both texts indicate that these "springs" constitute the visionary symbolic source of eternal life.

FOUR

OT Words

'arba', 'arbā'āh [אַרְבַּע, אַרְבָּעָה, **702**]

This term occurs around three hundred times. In all but fifty of these instances (such as when combined with "ten" to equal "fourteen"), ***'arba'*** is translated "four."

In the large majority of cases, throughout all the literary genres of the Old Testament, the usage of ***'arba'*** is mundane — referring to age, population, size, time, and measurement.

In the prophetic writings, however, ***'arba'*** does occasionally have some distinctive theological significance. For example, Isa. 11:12 mentions the "four corners of the earth" from which God's people will be regathered out of exile. In Dan. 8:8; 11:4, the "four winds of heaven" symbolize the universal dominion of the nations. The number "four" may also be understood as a symbolic indicator of divinely initiated punishment. Here again, the phrase "four winds of heaven" is utilized in a couple of contexts — for example, against Edom (cf. Jer. 49:36), and Judah (cf. Zech. 2:6). Other uses of the number "four" in contexts of judgment are found in Jer. 15:3; Ezek. 1:2; 14:2; Zech. 1:18; 6:1, 5.

'arba' is also a symbol of divine majesty and perfection in Ezek. 1:5ff., where the four living creatures (i.e., cherubim) constitute the four "supports" for the throne of Yahweh. This number is also symbolic of complete divine renewal in Ezek. 37:9, where there is a plea for God's Spirit to come from "the four winds" to breathe new life into the moribund people of God.

NT Words

tessares [τέσσαρες, *5064*]

tessares is an adjectival form denoting the number "four" in about forty places.

The expression "four winds" denotes the full extent of the world in a geographic sense (cf. Matt. 24:31; Mark 13:27).

Mundane usage is indicated, for example, in Matt. 13:27; Luke 2:37; John 11:17; Acts 10:11; 27:29.

The usage of the term in the book of Revelation is entirely symbolic. The number "four" suggests completeness or entirety — for example, the "four living creatures" surrounding the throne of God indicate a complete symbolic protection (Rev. 4:6ff.; 5:6ff.; 6:1ff.; 7:11; 14:3; 15:7; 19:4). The "four winds" symbolically denote the universal extent of divine judgment in Rev. 7:1.

The number 144,000 symbolically indicates the entirety of God's people in Rev. 7:4; 14:13. Rev. 9:13ff. mentions the "four angels" set aside as instruments of divine judgment against wicked humankind. See also Rev. 20:8.

FOWL

→ BIRD

FOX

OT Words

shû'āl [שׁוּעָל, **7776**]

shû'āl is a rare term, occurring only seven times and meaning "fox" on each occasion. Literal references to the animal are found in Judg. 15:4; Neh. 4:3; Ps. 63:10; Lam. 5:18. ***shû'āl*** also refers symbolically to the activity of false prophets in Judah who prey upon the people of God like foxes (cf. Ezek. 13:4). The term is also found in Song 2:15, where "the little foxes" may represent those factors that mar the relationship between husband and wife.

NT Words

alōpēx [ἀλώπηξ, *258*]

alōpēx is a rare noun found only three times, referring to literal "foxes" in Matt. 8:20; Luke 9:58. In Luke 13:32 Jesus refers to Herod the tetrarch (i.e., Antipas) as a "fox," indicating that he is a crafty, deceitful, and dangerous man.

FRANKINCENSE

OT Words

lebônāh [לְבוֹנָה, **3828**]

lebônāh refers to the pale-colored, milky sap that is extracted from the bark of the Boswellia tree that grows in southern Arabia and India. It is a highly fragrant substance, prized for its qualities as a perfuming agent. The English word "frankincense," used to translate ***lebônāh***, derives from an Old French expression meaning "pure incense." This term derives from the corresponding Hebrew ***lābān***, meaning "white(ness)." (→ WHITE) ***lebônāh*** occurs around twenty times.

Frankincense was widely used throughout the ancient Near East. In the Old Testament period it was utilized by the Israelite people as an integral part of their ritual worship of Yahweh. ***lebônāh*** was a major ingredient of the incense mixture prepared and used by the Levites for their ceremonial and sacrificial offerings to God.

In Exod. 30:1–10, God gives instructions for the construction and use of the altar of incense in the tabernacle. Later in the chapter (Exod. 30:34ff.), the recipe for incense itself is given, which includes frankincense as well as four other fragrant spices. The significant factor here is that this mixture is sacred, and the recipe must not be made up for any Israelite's personal enjoyment. Expulsion from the Israelite community is the penalty for any breach of this command. 1 Chr. 9:29 records the particular responsibility of the Levites for taking care of the frankincense, oil, and spices (cf. also Neh. 13:5, 9).

Lev. 2:1, 2, 15, 16 give further instructions for mixing frankincense and oil as the necessary accompaniment to the grain offering, which was itself also offered along with the burnt offering (cf. Lev. 6:15). The use of frankincense and oil with the grain offering was normally associated with praise and thanksgiving to God (cf. Isa. 60:6; Jer. 17:26), although Jer. 41:5 records an instance of such an offering being rendered in connection with mourning and sorrow.

There were also prohibitions restricting the use of frankincense in certain circumstances. In Lev. 5:11, for example, ***lebônāh*** is forbidden to be offered in conjunction with the bloodless sin offering of fine flour — an offering reserved for only the poorest in Israel. There is a similar restriction laid down in Num. 5:15, where frankincense is forbidden to be used in conjunction with the grain offering for jealousy.

In Lev. 24:7, another piece of ceremonial legislation requires that frankincense be placed on the table of the presence, along with the twelve loaves of bread, each Sabbath. This table is part of the sacred furniture found in the holy place that adjoins the holy of holies (or most holy place) in the tabernacle. This bread, along with the frankincense (by implication), is declared to represent a lasting covenant between Israel and her God.

The improper use of frankincense is also described in the Old Testament. Isaiah refers to God's condemnation of thank offerings containing frankincense that are performed with illegitimate motives (Isa. 43:23), or even in circumstances of idolatrous worship (Isa. 66:3). Jer. 6:20 contains a similar indictment.

On a different note, ***lebônāh*** is also used in the poetic context of the Song of Songs. Song 3:6 refers to the perfumed fragrance of frankincense and myrrh associated with Solomon's carriage in the wedding procession. In Song 4:6, 14 the same combination of perfumes is associated with the woman on her wedding night. In both instances here, the respective partner sings the praises of the other, delighting in their mutual attraction symbolized by these fragrant substances.

The use of this word in the Old Testament has an unmistakable connection with the law of Moses in relation to the ceremonial worship of God. There are clear prescriptions for the specific use of ***lebônāh***, along with definite restrictions on its improper use. Its poetic usage in the Song of Songs highlights the sublime beauty and attraction of the intimacy of marriage.

NT Words

libanos **[λίβανος, *3030*]**

libanos is the dynamic equivalent of the Hebrew term ***lebônāh*** (see above). Its occurrence in the New Testament is rare. In Matt. 2:11 frankincense is one of the three gifts brought by the magi to the infant Jesus, along with gold and myrrh. In Rev. 18:13, this fragrant perfume is found among the list of wares traded by the nations of the world with Babylon.

Additional Notes

Matt. 2:11 contains the well-known reference to the gifts of the magi presented to the infant Jesus: gold, frankincense, and myrrh. The symbolic meaning of these gifts is heightened when their significance is measured against the backdrop of the Old Testament period. Gold is everywhere recognized as the appropriate gift for a king; while frankincense and myrrh may point forward to the priestly role Jesus would assume after his resurrection and ascension to heaven. The role of frankincense in the Israelite sacrifices under the old covenant reinforces this perspective. There is no doubt that Jesus is portrayed not only as the messianic King, but also as the great high priest of the new covenant age (cf. Heb. 7–9). Such a priestly role has an intimate connection with the Levitical priesthood under the old covenant. (→ GOLD)

FREE, FREEDOM

OT Words

ḥophshî **[חָפְשִׁי, 2670]**

This is the adjectival form of the rare verb ***ḥāphash***, "to be free" (see below). ***ḥophshî*** occurs around twenty times and is translated "free" in various senses.

Literal, physical freedom from slavery is indicated in Exod. 21:5, 26ff.; Deut. 15:12ff.; 1 Sam. 17:25; Jer. 34:9ff.; Job 3:19. Job 39:25 mentions freedom for wild animals, as Isa. 58:6 refers to freedom for the oppressed.

nedābāh [נְדָבָה, 5071]

nedābāh is a noun found in nearly thirty contexts with the primary meaning "freewill, or thank offering." This term is also used adverbially with the sense of "freely," "willingly," in 2 Chr. 35:8. In particular, Ps. 110:3 refers to God's people offering themselves "freely" or "willingly" to him. In Hos. 14:4 God declares that he will love his people "freely." (→ OFFERING)

ḥāphash [חָפַשׁ, 2666]

ḥāphash is a rare verb meaning "to be free." It is found only in Lev. 19:20, used in the negative with reference to a female slave.

pātaḥ [פָּתַח, 6605]

pātaḥ is a common verb meaning "open," in addition to related nuances, for most of its nearly 150 occurrences. In Ps. 105:20, however, ***pātaḥ*** means to "set (someone) free" in relation to Pharaoh's liberation of Joseph from prison.

ḥuphshāh [חֻפְשָׁה, 2668]

ḥuphshāh is a rare noun derived from ***pātaḥ***, above, found only in Lev. 19:20 referring to granting "freedom" to a slave.

NT Words

eleutheros [ἐλεύθερος, *1658*]

eleutheros is an adjectival form occurring nearly twenty-five times with the predominant meaning "free," with several different nuances.

The meaning "free" is evident in Matt. 17:26 in relation to the non-payment of taxes, that is, being "exempt" from payment. "Freedom" from slavery in a literal sense is indicated in 1 Cor. 7:21; 12:13; Gal. 3:28; Eph. 6:8; Col. 3:11; Rev. 6:15; 13:16; 19:18. The state of being "set free" from spiritual bondage through the agency of Christ is indicated in John 8:33ff.; Rom. 6:20; 1 Cor. 7:22.

Freedom from the law is indicated in Rom. 7:3; 1 Cor. 7:39 in relation to the marriage bond being dissolved by death, thus setting the surviving party free to remarry.

The state of freedom in the gospel, in relationship with Christ, is noted in 1 Cor. 9:1, 19; 1 Pet. 2:16. The metaphorical designation of "free woman" is applied to Sarah, Abraham's wife, in Gal. 4:22ff. — a description identifying Sarah as a woman sealed through the gift of a son, favored by God as the recipient of covenant blessing.

eleutheroō [ἐλευθερόω, *1659*]

eleutheroō is a verb found seven times, meaning "to set free" and conveying the significant nuance of being liberated from the power of sin through the person and work of Christ.

In John 8:32, 36 Jesus declares that he, the Son, who embodies ultimate truth, "will make free" any who put their trust in him. Rom. 6:18, 22; 8:2 contain the significant statements that believers "have been set free" from sin and death through the person of Christ in his redemptive work. Rom. 8:21 offers a similar expression of truth, claiming that the creation itself "will be set free" from its bondage to decay. Gal. 5:1 also affirms that Christ "has set his people free" from enslavement to sin.

eleutheria [ἐλευθερία, *1657*]

eleutheria is the noun derived from ***eleutheros*** and ***eleutheroō***, above, denoting "liberty," "freedom" throughout its eleven occurrences.

eleutheria denotes "liberty" or "freedom" in the context of deliverance from the bondage of sin and death (cf. Rom. 8:21; Gal. 2:4; 5:1). Elsewhere, "liberty" denotes "freedom of conscience" in 1 Cor. 10:29; 1 Pet. 2:16.

In 2 Cor. 3:17, ***eleutheria*** denotes "freedom" in the general sense of a lifestyle liberated by the indwelling Holy Spirit in the life of the believer, a "freedom" to serve God wholeheartedly. See also Gal. 5:13 for a similar context. Such a "freedom" is identified in Jas. 1:25; 2:12 as the "law of liberty."

False "freedom" proclaimed by false teachers is indicated in 2 Pet. 2:19.

apeleutheros [ἀπελεύθερος, *558*]

apeleutheros is a rare variant of ***eleutheros***, above, found only in 1 Cor. 7:22, referring to the Lord's "freedman" — a metaphorical reference to the paradox of the believer's standing before God. Only as a "slave" to God in Christ does one become truly "free."

dōrean [δωρεάν, *1432*]

dōrean is an adverbial form found in nine places with the underlying sense of "freely," with several nuances.

The meaning "freely" in the sense of "without payment or costs" is indicated in Matt. 10:8; 2 Cor. 11:7; 2 Thess. 3:8, with literal reference to monetary concerns. Rev. 21:6; 22:17 use "freely" in a metaphorical sense to refer to God offering to all his people free access to the water of life in the heavenly city.

In order to emphasize the limitless generosity of God's grace, Rom. 3:24 affirms that the people of God are justified "freely" by that grace — that is, as an unmerited gift.

dikaioō [δικαιόω, *1344*]

dikaioō is a verb meaning "to justify" throughout its nearly forty occurrences. However, in one context, Rom. 6:7, ***dikaioō*** is translated passively "to be freed" in relation to being liberated from sin.

See Also: → GIFT → WILL

FRIEND, FRIENDSHIP

OT Words

'āhab [**אָהַב, 157**]

This term is found over two hundred times with the primary meaning "to love," with both God and human beings as its object. However, in a handful of contexts, ***'āhab*** in a related sense also indicates the action of "being a friend" or "showing friendship."

In terms of friendship with other people, ***'āhab*** is found, for example, in Esth. 5:10, 14; Prov. 18:24; Jer. 20:4; Zech. 13:6. 2 Sam. 19:6 refers to friends as those who demonstrate love. Both 2 Chr. 20:7 and Isa. 41:8 refer to Abraham as "the friend of God."

rēa' [**רֵעַ, 7453**]

rēa' is translated variously as "neighbor," "friend," "companion" in the sense of an intimate acquaintance. The term occurs in nearly 200 contexts, with the above meanings reflected in the great majority of instances. The translation "friend" occurs about fifty times.

"Friend" in the sense of a male companion is indicated, for example, in Gen. 38:12; Exod. 32:27; 1 Kgs. 16:11; Job 2:11; 42:7, 10. Friendship on a more intimate level is found in Exod. 33:11, for example, where the Lord speaks to Moses as to a friend, face-to-face.

See also in this regard Jer. 3:1, 20; Hos. 3:1. At a less intimate level, Judg. 7:13ff.; 1 Sam. 14:20; 1 Kgs. 20:35; Zech. 3:8 refer to "friends" in the sense of "comrades" or "colleagues."

Non-specific usage of ***rēa'*** is found in Job 6:14, 27; Ps. 38:14; Prov. 6:3; 19:4, 6; Song 5:1; Lam. 1:2; Mic. 7:5.

mērēa' [**מֵרֵעַ, 4828**]

A rare term derived from ***rēa'*** (see above), ***mērēa'*** occurs on seven occasions, meaning "companion" or "friend" (cf. Gen. 26:26; Judg. 14:11, 20; 15:2, 6; 2 Sam. 3:8; Prov. 19:7).

rē'eh [**רֵעֶה, 7463**]

rē'eh is a rare term, synonymous with the entries above, denoting a "friend" in all three occurrences (cf. 2 Sam. 15:37; 16:16; 1 Kgs. 4:5).

NT Words

philos [φίλος, *5384*]

philos is a noun occurring about thirty times with the consistent meaning "friend."

The meaning "friend" in the sense of a "genuine companion" is predicated of Christ in his relationship with the outcasts of Jewish society (cf. Matt. 11:19; Luke 7:34).

References to "friends" in general human relationships are found in Luke 7:6; 11:5ff.; 14:10ff.; 16:9; John 3:29; 15:13; Acts 10:24; 19:31; 27:3. Jesus refers to his disciples as his "friends" in Luke 12:4; and also all those who devote themselves to him (cf. John 15:14ff.). In Jas. 2:23 Abraham is designated the "friend of God." Caesar's "friend" in John 19:12 denotes one who is a loyal citizen of the empire, and obedient to the emperor.

In a metaphorical context, ***philos*** denotes the secular, godless person as a "friend" of the world.

philia [φιλία, *5373*]

philia is a rare variant of ***philos***. It is found only in Jas. 4:4 and equates enmity with God with "friendship" with the world.

hetairos [ἑταῖρος, *2083*]

hetairos is a noun meaning "friend," found in Matt. 20:13; 22:12; 26:50. The sense here denotes the polite form of address "Sir."

FRUIT, FRUITFUL

OT Words

perî [**פְּרִי, 6529**]

perî occurs around 120 times and is consistently translated "fruit," both in the literal sense of "produce (of the ground)" and "children," as well as the figurative meaning "consequences."

Fruit from trees is commonly indicated (e.g., Gen. 1:11ff.; Lev. 19:23ff.; Ps. 105:35; Song 4:13; Isa. 65:21; Ezek. 17:8, 9; 47:12). Harvest produce, especially from the land of Canaan, is also described as "fruit" in a number of places (e.g., Lev. 25:19; Num. 13:20ff.; Deut. 1:25; 26:2, 10; 28:33ff.; Ps. 107:34; Jer. 2:7; Ezek. 36:30; Amos 9:14; Zech. 8:12; Mal. 3:11). The latter texts here from the prophetic writings associate abundant produce from the land with the promise of divine renewal.

"Fruit of the womb," a symbolic reference to children, is also a significant element in the usage of ***perî***. It is used positively as a sign of blessing from God when children are granted in abundance (cf. Deut. 7:13; 28:4, 11; 30:9; Ps. 132:11; Mic. 6:7); and also as a sign of divine judgment, when children die young or are slaughtered (cf. Deut. 28:18; Ps. 21:10; Isa. 13:18; Hos. 9:16). The horrendous practice of devouring one's children during times of siege is mentioned in Deut. 28:53; Lam. 2:20.

The metaphorical use of this term is also significant. The remnant of God's people is described as "fruit," for example, in 2 Kgs. 19:30; Isa. 4:2. ***perî*** also indicates both the blessed consequences of righteous and holy living (cf. Ps. 1:3; Jer. 17:8; Prov. 11:30; 13:2); as well as the consequences of a sinful lifestyle (cf. Prov. 1:31; 18:21; Hos. 10:13; Mic. 7:13). In Jer. 17:10; 21:14; 32:19, the term "fruit" signifies one's lifestyle and moral character in a general, non-descriptive sense.

Other various uses of the term are found in Prov. 8:19; 31:16, 31; Song 4:16; Hos. 14:8.

tebû'āh **[תְּבוּאָה, 8393]**

This term is broadly synonymous with ***perî*** (see above), and refers primarily to produce of the earth in terms of "harvest," "increase," "fruit." ***tebû'āh*** also has a metaphorical sense of "fruit" in relation to a person's deeds. The word is translated "fruit" about thirteen times — approximately one-third of its total usage.

"Fruit" in the sense of produce of the land is indicated in Lev. 25:3, 21; Deut. 22:9; 33:14; Josh. 5:12; 2 Kgs. 8:6. The metaphorical sense of the term as "lifestyle" is mentioned in Prov. 10:16; 18:20.

qayiṣ **[קַיִץ, 7019]**

qayiṣ occurs around twenty times and means "summer fruit" on nine occasions, referring also to the season of summer itself.

Literal "fruit" is referred to in 2 Sam. 16:1, 2; Isa. 16:9; Jer. 40:10, 12; 48:32; Mic. 7:1. In Amos 8:1, 2, ***qayiṣ*** is used metaphorically to indicate Israel's sin.

pārāh **[פָּרָה, 6509]**

pārāh is a verb meaning "to be fruitful," "bear fruit" throughout its nearly thirty occurrences.

The exhortation "be fruitful" in the sense of "have a large number of children" is found in Gen. 1:22; 8:17, directed by God to key figures in his creation (Adam and Noah). Similar divine exhortations are found in Gen. 35:11; 48:4. Yahweh also promises to make Abraham "very fruitful"—to grant him a great many descendants (cf. Gen. 17:6). Similar promises are made to the people of Israel in Lev. 26:9; Ps. 128:3; Jer. 23:3; Ezek. 36:11 — all of them constituting promises of the Abrahamic covenant. Other admonitions "to be fruitful" in an exclusively human context are found in Gen. 28:3. A mundane reference to a "fruitful" vine is found in Isa. 32:12.

"Fruitfulness" in the sense of possessing many children is indicated in Gen. 47:27; 49:22, with reference to key figures among the emerging people of Israel. Such a blessing is also predicated of the descendants of Israel in Exod. 1:7; Ezek. 19:10.

'ēb **[אֵב, 4** (Aramaic)**]**

'ēb is a rare Aramaic noun denoting "fruit" in a literal sense in Dan. 4:12, 14, 21.

yebûl **[יְבוּל, 2981]**

yebûl is a noun found thirteen times, meaning "fruit," "crops," or "produce." "Produce" or "crops" are indicated in Lev. 26:4, 20; Deut. 11:17; 32:22; Judg. 6:4; Pss. 78:46; 85:12; Ezek. 34:27; Hag. 1:10. There is one specific mention of vine "fruit" in Hab. 3:17.

karmel **[כַּרְמֶל, 3759]**

karmel is a noun occurring thirteen times with the nominal meaning "fertile, or fruitful land" in Isa. 10:18; 16:10; 29:17; 32:15ff., denoting cultivated fields in a general sense. Jer. 2:7; 4:26 refer to the "fertile land" of Canaan; and Moab is also described this way in Jer. 48:33.

zimrāh **[זִמְרָה, 2173]**

zimrāh is a rare noun found only in Gen. 43:11 denoting "choice fruits or produce" from the land of Canaan.

NT Words

karpos [καρπός, *2590*]

karpos is a noun found nearly seventy times meaning "fruit," in several different contexts with differing nuances.

karpos is used metaphorically to denote "fruit" in the sense of "moral characteristics" in Matt. 3:8, 10; 7:16ff.; Luke 3:8ff. "Fruit" in the sense of "tangible results of gospel ministry" such as conversions and spiritual maturity in the lives of believers is indicated in Rom. 1:13. "Fruit" in a literal sense is indicated, for example, in Matt. 12:33; 21:19ff.; Mark 4:7ff.; Luke 6:43ff.; 12:17; John 12:24; 1 Cor. 9:7; Jas. 5:17ff. Children are designated as "fruit" of the womb in Luke 1:42. See also Acts 2:30.

The metaphorical expression "to harvest crops (or fruit) for eternal life" denotes cultivating a godly lifestyle that will lead to the enjoyment of eternal peace with God (cf. John 4:36). In a similar context, ***karpos*** also denotes "fruit," referring to those spiritual characteristics that derive from a relationship of faith and trust in the person of Christ (John 15:24ff.). The metaphor of "fruit" is here linked to the metaphor of a "vine," referring to Christ himself. A listing of "fruit" (i.e., virtues) as the produce of the work of the Spirit in the life of the believer is found in Gal. 5:22. See also Eph. 5:9; Phil. 1:11; Heb. 12:11; Jas. 3:17ff. for a similar usage.

In other contexts, praising God is the "fruit" of one's lips (cf. Heb. 13:15). Rev. 22:2 refers to the tree of life in the heavenly city that yielded its "fruit" for the healing of the nations.

karpophoros [καρποφόρος, *2593*]

karpophoros is a rare adjectival form found only in Acts 14:17, referring to "fruitful" seasons that result in a good harvest.

karpophoreō [καρποφορέω, *2592*]

karpophoreō is a verb found eight times, meaning "to bear fruit," "be fruitful" in predominantly figurative contexts.

The literal sense of "bearing fruit" in relation to the production of crops is indicated in Mark 4:28.

The rest of the usage is figurative. The nurturing of godly virtues as a result of exposure to the word of God is described as the process of "bearing fruit" in Matt. 13:23; Mark 4:20; Luke 8:15. Similarly, the phenomenon of the gospel "bearing fruit," acting as a catalyst for genuine godliness, is indicated in Col. 1:6, 10. See also Rom. 7:4, 5 for a similar context.

akarpos [ἄκαρπος, *175*]

akarpos is an adjective found six times meaning "unfruitful," usually in a figurative sense.

The meaning "unfruitful" in Matt. 13:22; Mark 4:19 expresses the sense of "unproductive," in reference to spiritual maturity extinguished by the cares of the world. Both of these contexts concern the parable of the sower.

1 Cor. 14:14 refers to an "unfruitful" mind in the context of praying in tongues. The meaning here focuses on the inability of the mind to grasp the meaning of an unknown language.

"Spiritual ineffectiveness" is indicated by the term "unfruitful" in 2 Pet. 1:8; Titus 3:14. Eph. 5:11 speaks of the "unfruitful" works of darkness, denoting deeds that have no positive value whatsoever.

References to trees "without fruit" are found in Jude 12.

gennēma [γέννημα, *1081*]

gennēma is a rare noun found nine times meaning "generation," "fruit," "harvest" throughout.
(➠ GENERATION)

gennēma denotes the "fruit" of the vine, referring to wine drunk by Christ and his disciples at the Passover feast (cf. Matt. 26:29; Mark 14:25; Luke 22:18).

2 Cor. 9:10 refers to a "harvest" of righteousness, signifying significant growth in godliness in the life of the believer.

In Luke 12:18 ***gennēma*** denotes "produce" or "grain," signifying the fruits of a person's labor.

opōra [ὀπώρα, *3703*]

opōra is a rare noun found only in Rev. 18:4, meaning "fruit" in a figurative sense, denoting "material wealth" which the city of Babylon yearned for but failed to acquire.

Additional Notes

Similar metaphors for "fruit" are found throughout both Testaments. The Old Testament often refers to lifestyle, both righteous and wicked, as "fruit" — although the specific causal agent giving rise to someone's spiritual and moral makeup is not mentioned. What is clear, however, is that godly lifestyle is consistent with a rightly-ordered covenant relationship with God; whereas ungodly living indicates an absence of such a bond. In the New Testament, the phenomenon of "fruitfulness" in the sense of godly characteristics is specifically declared to originate from the presence of the Holy Spirit in the life of the believer. Conversely, godless living or the "fruit of the flesh" (mostly referred to as "works of the flesh," or "acts of the sinful nature") imply either the absence of the Spirit of God in that person's life or a surrender to the temptations of one's sinful nature.

FULFILL, FULFILLMENT

OT Words

mālē' **[מָלֵא, 4390]**

mālē' is a common verb occurring around 250 times with the primary sense of "fill," as well as the derivative sense of "fulfill" and related meanings including "consecrate," "accomplish." ***mālē'*** means "fulfill" on about twenty occasions

In the literal sense of "fulfill," ***mālē'*** conveys the idea of "complete" — for example, in reference to the completion of Rebekah's pregnancy (Gen. 25:24); completing the days of purification (Lev. 12:46); completing the period of a vow (Num. 6:5, 13); bringing one's plans to completion (Ps. 20:4, 5); completing the days of a siege (Ezek. 5:2). See also Gen. 50:3; Jer. 44:25; 2 Sam. 7:12; Lam. 4:18.

The word also occurs with the classic meaning "fulfill," in the sense of a realization of a prophetic decree or promise (e.g., 1 Kgs. 2:27; 8:15; 2 Chr. 6:4, 15; 36:21).

NT Words

plēroō [πληρόω, *4137*]

plēroō is a verb found nearly one hundred times meaning "fulfill," "fill," "be full," as well as related nuances.

The phenomenon of "fulfilling" prophecy is indicated in a number of places with reference to the climactic realization of God's redemptive purposes in the person of Jesus Christ (e.g., Matt. 1:22; 2:15ff.; Mark 1:15; 15:28; Luke 4:21; 24:44; John 13:18; 17:12ff.; Acts 3:18; 13:27). See also Jas. 2:23.

In addition to fulfilling prophecy, ***plēroō*** also denotes the "fulfilling" of the requirements of the law, made possible solely through the sacrifice of Christ, enabling his people to live godly lives through the indwelling Holy Spirit (cf. Rom. 8:4).

The meaning "fulfill" with the sense of "complete" is indicated in Matt. 3:15 in relation to Jesus' desire to "fulfill" all righteousness in his baptism. There are also mundane references to "fulfilling," or "completing," a task (cf. Acts 12:25). Jesus' declared intention to "fulfill" the law and the Prophets by bringing their purposes to completion is indicated in Matt. 5:17.

The action of "fulfilling" the law in relation to believers obeying its terms is noted in Rom. 13:8; Gal. 5:14.

eklēroō [ἐκπληρόω, *1603*]

ekplēroō is a rare variant of ***plēroō***, above. It is found only in Acts 13:33, referring to God "fulfilling" his covenant promises to raise up Jesus for the salvation of his people.

anaplēroō [ἀναπληρόω, *378*]

anaplēroō is another rare variant of ***plēroō***, above, meaning "fulfill" in Matt. 13:14, where Jesus declares that the inability to understand the message of his parables is a direct consequence of the fulfillment of the prophecy recorded in Isa. 6:9ff. Gal. 6:2 contains Paul's injunction to "fulfill" the law of Christ by bearing one another's burdens.

plērophoreō [πληροφορέω, *4135*]

plērophoreō is a verb found six times with a variety of meanings. Luke 1:1 refers to the things "most certainly believed." Rom. 4:21; 14:5 both allude to the state of mind of "being completely or fully convinced." In 2 Tim. 4:5, Paul's injunction to Timothy to "fulfill his ministry" means "discharging" or "carrying it out." In 2 Tim. 4:17 ***plērophoreō*** is translated "to preach completely or fully" in relation to the gospel.

plērōma [πλήρωμα, *4138*]

plērōma is a noun found seventeen times with the dominant meaning "fullness" throughout. However, in Mark 8:20 the term refers to love as "the fulfilling" of the law.

ekplērōsis [ἐκπλήρωσις, *1604*]

ekplērōsis is a rare noun found only in Acts 21:26 with reference to the "completion" or "accomplishing" of the days set aside for the performance of a vow.

teleō [τελέω, *5055*]

teleō is a verb found twenty-six times meaning "fulfill," "complete," "finish," "accomplish" for most of the usage. There is some overlap in meaning between these senses.

Luke 12:50 refers to the prospect of Christ's baptism "being accomplished, or completed." Luke 18:31 refers to Jesus' claim that everything prophesied about him as the Son of Man "will be fulfilled (i.e., accomplished)" in Jerusalem. Luke 22:37; John 19:28 contain similar claims. John 19:30 records Christ's last word on the cross, ***teleō***, translated "It is finished" and referring to the work of salvation given him by his Father to accomplish. Other references to the "fulfilling" of prophecy include those in Acts 13:29; Rev. 10:7; 17:17.

The sense of "fulfilling (or keeping) the law" is indicated in Rom. 2:27. See also Jas. 2:8.

synteleō [συντελέω, *4931*]

synteleō is a variant form of ***teleō***, above, found seven times with the predominant sense of "finish" or "end." In Mark 13:4, however, the term denotes the "fulfilling" of the signs of the end times.

teleioō [τελειόω, *5048*]

teleioō is a verb with the synonymous meanings "fulfill," "accomplish," "finish," "perfect," "complete" throughout most of its nearly twenty-five occurrences.

Jesus' determination to "fulfill" or "accomplish" the tasks given to him by God is indicated in John 4:34; 5:36; and the completion of that redemptive work is noted in John 17:4; 19:28.

teleiōsis [τελείωσις, *5050*]

teleiōsis is a rare noun meaning "fulfillment" in relation to the word of the Lord spoken by the angel Gabriel to Mary, promising her that she would be the mother of the Messiah, the Christ child.

See Also: → FILL → FINISH → PERFECT

FULL

OT Words

mālē' [מָלֵא, **4392**]

mālē' has both an adjectival and a verbal sense. The verb ***mālē'*** means "fill" or "fill up," as well as "fulfill." As an adjective, ***mālē'*** means "full" and occurs about sixty times.

In its primary literal sense, ***mālē'*** refers to fullness in its quantitative sense — a full measure (e.g., Gen. 41:37; Num. 7:13ff.; Deut. 6:11; 2 Sam. 23:11; 2 Kgs. 4:4; Ps. 144:13; Eccl. 1:7; Ezek. 37:1; Amos 2:13).

In addition, ***mālē'*** means "full" in a metaphorical sense with reference to non-tangible phenomena — for example, wisdom (cf. Ezek. 28:12); divine blessing (cf. Deut. 33:23); God's wrath (cf. Ps. 75:8; Isa. 51:20; Jer. 6:11); justice (cf. Isa. 1:21); and lies (cf. Nah. 3:1). Deut. 34:9 refers to Joshua being "full of the Spirit of God."

sābēa' [שָׂבֵעַ, **7649**]

This adjectival form of ***sāba'*** (→FILL) occurs ten times and is translated "full" in the sense of "filled to capacity," or "satisfied," in both a positive and a negative sense.

sābēa' refers to old age by describing various people as "full of years" — for example, Abraham (Gen. 25:8); Isaac (Gen. 35:29); David (1 Chr. 29:28); Job (Job 42:17). See also 1 Sam. 2:5; Prov. 27:7.

In a metaphorical sense, like ***mālē'*** (see above), ***sābēa'*** indicates the fullness of the blessing of the Lord in Deut. 33:23. Job describes himself as being full of shame in Job 10:15. See also Job 14:1; Prov. 19:23.

NT Words

plērēs [πλήρης, *4134*]

plērēs is an adjective with the consistent meaning "full," "filled up" throughout its seventeen occurrences.

The literal sense of "full" is indicated in relation to baskets of food scraps in Matt. 14:20; 15:37; Mark 6:43; 8:19; and to the ripe ear of grain in Mark 4:28. A diseased man is described as "full" of leprosy in Luke 5:12.

Luke 4:1 refers to Jesus being "full" of the Holy Spirit prior to his temptation in the wilderness. Christ is also described as being "full" of grace and truth in John 1:14.

Believers are depicted as "full" of the Holy Spirit in Acts 6:3ff.; 7:55; 11:24. Other contexts refer to people being "full" of a particular quality. Dorcas is described as a woman "full of good works" (Acts 9:36); Elymas the sorcerer as one "full of deceit" (Acts 13:10); a crowd as "full of wrath" (Acts 19:28). See also 2 John 8.

plēroō [πληρόω, *4137*]

plēroō is a verb with the primary sense of "fulfill," "fill" for the majority of the ninety occurrences of the term. In addition, ***plēroō*** also means "be full" in several places. Matt. 13:48 refers to a net "full" of fish. John 15:11; 16:24; 1 John 1:4; 2 John 12 all contain the wish that people's joy "may be made complete" (lit. "full"). (→ FILL → FULFILL)

mestos [μεστός, *3324*]

mestos is an adjective found eight times with the consistent meaning "full," in both personal and impersonal contexts.

A bowl "full" of vinegar is noted in John 19:29; a net "full" of fish in John 21:11.

People "full" of hypocrisy are indicated in Matt. 23:28; those "full" of envy in Rom. 1:29; and those "full" of adultery in 2 Pet. 2:14. The human tongue is designated as "full" of evil in Jas. 3:8. Conversely, divine wisdom is said to be "full" of mercy; and the Roman believers are said to be "full" of goodness.

gemō [γέμω, *1073*]

gemō is a verb found in eleven places with the consistent meaning "to be full."

Christ condemns the Pharisees for "being full" of greed and wickedness in Matt. 23:25; Luke 11:39. In a similar context, the Pharisees are likened to whitewashed tombs in Matt. 23:27. The mouth of the wicked is said "to be full" of cursing and bitterness in Rom. 3:14.

Elsewhere, ***gemō*** is found in the figurative context of the book of Revelation. The heavenly creatures surrounding the throne of God are described as "being full of eyes," both front and back, in Rev. 4:6, 8. Rev. 5:8 refers to bowls "full of incense" held by the twenty-four elders surrounding the throne. See also Rev. 15:7; 17:3ff.; 21:9.

See Also: → FILL

FURNACE

OT Words

'attûn [אַתּוּן, **861** (Aramaic)]

This is an Aramaic term that occurs ten times and means "furnace" on each occasion. All references are found in Dan. 3:6ff.

kûr [כּוּר, **3564**]

This noun occurs nine times and means "furnace" or "forge." ***kûr*** derives from an unused root meaning "to dig through."

kûr refers to a literal furnace in Prov. 17:3; 27:21. More commonly, it refers metaphorically to the circumstances of suffering as a "furnace" (cf. Deut. 4:20; Isa. 48:10; Jer. 11:4; Ezek. 22:18ff.).

kibshān [כִּבְשָׁן, **3536**]

kibshān is synonymous with both ***'attûn*** and ***kûr*** (see above), and is also rare, occurring only four times. It refers to a literal "furnace" in Exod. 9:8, 10; and in Gen. 19:28 it refers to the destruction of Sodom and Gomorrah as being "like a furnace." Exod. 19:8 also refers to the smoke on Mt. Sinai, "like a furnace."

tannûr [תַּנּוּר, **8574**]

tannûr occurs fifteen times and is translated "furnace," "fire-pot," "oven," with both literal and symbolic force.

In its literal sense, ***tannûr*** refers to a "furnace" or "oven" in Exod. 8:3; Lev. 2:4; 7:9; 11:35; 26:26; Neh. 3:11; 12:8. In Gen. 15:17 it signifies a "fire-pot" that forms part of a theophanic revelation to Abraham. The fire-pot itself symbolizes the person of Yahweh.

Metaphorically, ***tannûr*** indicates the "furnace" as a symbolic vehicle for the expression of God's wrath against his people for their sin (cf. Isa. 31:9; Hos. 7:4ff.; Mal. 4:1); and against the wicked in general (cf. Ps. 21:9). See also Lam. 5:10.

NT Words

kaminos [κάμινος, *2575*]

kaminos is a noun found four times denoting a metaphorical "furnace" of fire. It refers to a "fiery furnace" of eternal torment in Matt. 13:42, 50; Rev. 9:2. In Rev. 1:15, the feet of the heavenly Christ are likened to those refined in a furnace.

G

GAIN

OT Words

beṣa' [בֶּצַע, 1215]

This term refers to "profit" or "gain" — that which is acquired, both justly and unjustly, although the latter negative sense predominates. **beṣa'** occurs around twenty times.

beṣa' occasionally indicates the sense of "advantage," and is usually expressed through the question: "What profit is there if . . ." (cf. Gen. 37:26; Job 22:3; Ps. 30:9; Mal. 3:14).

Meaning "gain," **beṣa'** also refers to the spoils of war (cf. Judg. 5:19; Mic. 4:13). The remaining usage of this term refers largely to the culpable practice of soliciting "unjust gain," or bribes, to satisfy one's greed. For example, the sons of Samuel are corrupted by this practice (cf. 1 Sam. 8:3), as are the people of Israel and Judah, including the civil and spiritual leaders of God's people (cf. Isa. 56:11; 57:17; Jer. 6:13; 8:10; Ezek. 22:13; 33:31; Hab. 2:9). The practice is condemned in general in Prov. 1:9.

yā'al [יָעַל, 3276]

yā'al is a verb found over twenty times with the primary meanings "to profit, gain."

The meaning "profit" or "gain" in the general sense of "procure a favorable outcome" is indicated in 1 Sam. 12:21; Job 21:15; 35:3. The specific sense of "obtaining a material profit" is evident in Prov. 10:2; 11:4; Isa. 30:5ff.; Jer. 12:13.

The negative sense of "being good for nothing" (i.e., making no gain) is found in Isa. 44:9ff.; Jer. 2:8.

Isa. 57:12 declares that one's own righteousness brings no spiritual profit or benefit. Similarly, Jer. 2:8ff.; Hab. 2:18 affirm that idolatrous worship "brings no profit" to those who practice it. See also Jer. 16:19; 23:32.

yitrôn [יִתְרוֹן, 3504]

yitrôn is a noun denoting "profit" or "gain" in four occurrences of the term, all in the book of Ecclesiastes. All of these contexts clearly imply that no "gain" or "profit" may be had from one's vocational labor in life (cf. Eccl. 1:3; 2:11; 3:9; 5:16).

NT Words

kerdainō [κερδαίνω, *2770*]

kerdainō is a verb meaning "to gain," "acquire" throughout most of its seventeen occurrences.

References to "gaining the whole world," in the sense of becoming materially prosperous, at the expense of one's spiritual life are found in Matt. 16:26; Mark 8:36; Luke 9:25.

"Gaining" someone, in the sense of winning him or her over to a renewed relationship, is indicated in Matt. 18:15; 1 Pet. 3:1. In particular, 1 Cor. 9:19ff. affirms Paul's desire to "win" or "gain" more converts.

References to "gaining" or "acquiring" money are found in Matt. 25:17ff.; Jas. 4:13.

In Phil. 3:8 Paul refers to "gaining" Christ, or making his eternal salvation secure.

kerdos [κέρδος, *2771*]

kerdos is a rare noun derived from **kerdainō**, above, denoting "gain" in the sense of "material wealth" in Phil. 3:7; Titus 1:11. **kerdos** is used figuratively in Phil. 1:21 in Paul's affirmation that to live is Christ and to die is "gain," or a decided advantage over physical life.

porismos [πορισμός, *4200*]

porismos is a rare noun denoting "gain" in the sense of "monetary remuneration" in 1 Tim. 6:5; and referring to "spiritual benefit" in 1 Tim. 6:6.

diapragmateuomai [διαπραγματεύομαι, *1281*]

diapragmateuomai is a rare verb found only in Luke 19:15, denoting the action of "gaining" a living through business.

peripoieō [περιποιέω, *4046*]

peripoieō is another rare verb referring to deacons "gaining" a good reputation for themselves.

ophelos [ὄφελος, *3786*]

ophelos is a noun found only three times, always as part of the question "What profit is it?" or "What good is it?" (cf. 1 Cor. 15:32; Jas. 2:14, 16).

ōpheleō [ὠφελέω, *5623*]

ōpheleō is a verb meaning "to be advantageous," "to be of value" in several of its nineteen occurrences.

Like the derivative noun ***ophelos***, above, ***ōpheleō*** occurs in the question "What does it profit a person . . . ?" in Matt. 16:26; Mark 8:36; Luke 9:25.

The sense of "bringing or gaining spiritual benefit" is found in John 6:63; 1 Cor. 13:3; 14:6; Gal. 5:2; Heb. 4:2; 13:9.

See Also: → WORK

GANGRENE

NT Words

gangraina [γάγγραινα, *1044*]

gangraina is a rare noun found only in 2 Tim. 2:17 denoting "gangrene" in a figurative context. Here the impact of foolish talk is likened to the spreading condition of rotting flesh.

GARDEN

OT Words

gan [גַּן, **1588**]

gan means "garden" in both a literal and figurative sense, although the natural meaning is dominant. The term occurs around forty times.

gan refers first of all to the garden of Eden during the period of creation, where it is depicted as the setting for humankind's probation and subsequent act of rebellion against God (cf. Gen. 2:8ff.; 3:1ff.). Ezek. 36:35 also describes the renewed the land of Canaan as resembling the garden of Eden, as does Isa. 51:3. Ezek. 28:13 also refers to this primeval paradise, describing Eden as the dwelling place of the blasphemous spirit of the king of Tyre, whose origins are clearly intended to be seen as satanic. The context of the whole section, Ezekiel 26–28, lends support to this perspective on the Tyrian ruler.

Mundane usage of the term is found in a number of texts (e.g., Deut. 11:10; 1 Kgs. 21:2; 2 Kgs. 25:4; Neh. 3:15; Jer. 52:7). This includes the use of the word in the simile "like a garden," as found in Isa. 58:11; Jer. 31:2; Lam. 2:6; Joel 2:3.

Finally, ***gan*** is used metaphorically in the Song of Songs to refer to the virginal purity of the bride on her wedding night prior to the consummation of her marriage. The beloved describes herself as a "garden" and invites her husband to enter (cf. Song 4:12ff.; 5:1; 6:2).

gannāh [גַּנָּה, **1593**]

gannāh is the derivative feminine form of ***gan***, above, occurring twelve times.

gannāh refers to "gardens" in a mundane sense (cf. Job 8:16; Eccl. 2:5; Jer. 29:5, 28; Amos 4:9; 9:14), and is also used as a simile in the expression "like a garden" (e.g., Num. 24:6; Isa. 1:30; 61:11). Finally, and significantly, ***gannāh*** denotes "gardens" as places of idolatrous worship frequented by the people of Israel, for which they shall be judged (cf. Isa. 1:29; 65:3; 66:17).

NT Words

kēpos [κῆπος, *2779*]

kēpos is a noun found in five contexts. It denotes a "garden" in a general sense in Luke 13:19. John 18:1, 26; 19:41 refer to the garden of Gethsemane where Jesus was betrayed and arrested.

GARMENT → CLOTHING

GATE

OT Words

sha'ar [שַׁעַר, **8179**]

sha'ar means "gate" in a variety of contexts, both literal and figurative. The term occurs around 370 times.

sha'ar occurs most frequently in contexts where the city or town gate is indicated. The sense is usually mundane (e.g., Gen. 19:1; Exod. 20:10; Deut. 5:14; Josh. 2:5ff.; Judg. 9:35ff.; 1 Sam. 4:18; 2 Kgs. 23:8; Ps. 127:5; Prov. 1:21; Isa. 22:7). However, in several places the "gate" of the city is cited as the location of the "civil court," or "center of administration" for the ancient Israelite town or city (e.g., Deut. 21:19; Ruth 4:1ff.; 2 Chr. 18:9; Isa. 29:21). Amos 5:10ff. refers to the abuse of justice at the city "gate"; and in Zech. 8:16 there is an exhortation to act justly "in the gate." In two places, ***sha'ar*** refers to the "gates" of a house (cf. Deut. 6:9; 11:20). Exod. 32:26, 27 refer to the "gates" of the Israelite camp.

In a number of places, ***sha'ar*** refers to the "gates" of Jerusalem, both in a physical, literal sense (e.g., 2 Chr. 25:23; Neh. 1:3; 2:3ff.; 3:1ff.; 12:25ff.; Isa. 60:11; Jer. 1:15; Mic. 1:9; Zeph. 1:10; Zech. 14:10), as well as in a metaphorical one (e.g., Pss. 87:2; 100:4; 122:2). Lam. 1:4; 2:9 refers to the destruction of the "gates" of Jerusalem.

The "gates" of the tabernacle are mentioned in Exod. 27:16; 35:17; 38:15ff.; 40:8, 33; Num. 4:26, as are those of the Jerusalem temple in 2 Kgs. 15:35; 1 Chr. 22:3; 2 Chr. 8:14; Jer. 26:10; Ezek. 8:3ff. ***sha'ar*** also refers to the "gates" of the visionary temple in Ezekiel's prophecy (e.g., Ezek. 40:3ff.; 42:15; 44:1ff.; 47:2; 48:31).

sha'ar is also used metaphorically in various contexts. The expression "gate of one's enemies" is used as a metaphor for conquest — for example, it indicates a divine promise of victory over one's enemies in Gen. 22:17; 24:60. Ps. 118:19 refers to the "gates of righteousness," pointing out how one may enter into an attitude of praise and worship to God. ***sha'ar*** is also used in expressions containing life and death images. The "gate of heaven" is mentioned in connection with Jacob's theophanic vision at Bethel (cf. Gen. 28:17). Pss. 9:13; 107:18 refer to the "gates of death," or a near-death experience. Similarly, Isa. 38:10 refers to the "gates of Sheol," indicating a situation of hopeless despair.

NT Words

pylē [πύλη, *4439*]

pylē is the dynamic equivalent for ***shā'ar*** (see above), denoting a "gate" in all ten occurrences, in both a literal and figurative sense. Literal references to the "gate" of a city are found in Luke 7:12; Acts 9:24; 12:10; Heb. 13:12. The temple gate known as "Beautiful" is noted in Acts 3:10.

pylē is also used metaphorically, denoting a "gate" as a symbolic access point to the dual destinies of eternal blessing and judgment. Matt. 7:13 refers to the "narrow gate," that leads to eternal life with God, and also to the "wide gate," that leads to destruction. The same "narrow gate" is found in Matt. 7:14, Luke 13:24. In Matt. 16:18 Jesus declares that the "gates of hell" shall not prevail against his church.

pylōn [πυλών, *4440*]

pylōn is a variant form of ***pylē***, above, also denoting a "gate" in both a literal and figurative sense.

The "gates" of domestic residences are noted in Luke 16:20; Acts 10:17; 12:13ff. See also Matt. 26:71. City "gates" are indicated in Acts 14:13.

In Rev. 21:12ff.; 22:14 there are several allusions to the "gates" of the heavenly city.

Additional Notes

The usage of the terminology for "gate" or "gates" throughout Scripture is fairly uniform. In particular, the metaphorical sense of "gate" indicates access to situations either of hope or despair, life or death. Even in the literal use of the term with reference to Jerusalem and the tabernacle and temple, there is the clear sense of the people of God being able to gain access to the person and presence of Yahweh.

GATHER, GATHERING

OT Words

'āsaph [אָסַף, 622]

This fairly common verb occurs around one hundred times meaning "gather," "assemble." ***'āsaph*** is found in a variety of contents.

The literal meaning "gathering" is predominant. With the sense of "collect," ***'āsaph*** refers to the gathering of food (Gen. 6:21; Num. 11:32); the harvesting of produce (Exod. 23:10ff.; Lev. 23:39; Deut. 11:14; Ruth 2:7; Isa. 17:5; Jer. 40:10); and miscellaneous gathering (Num. 19:9; 2 Kgs. 22:4; 2 Chr. 34:9; Eccl. 2:26; Jer. 9:22; Ezek. 24:4).

'āsaph also conveys the ideas of "assembling" or "bringing together." The literal meaning is once again dominant, but not always without significance. The "gathering" of flocks, for example, is mentioned in Gen. 29:3ff. More significantly, people are "gathered together" for a variety of purposes. "Assembling" or "gathering" for war, for example, is quite a common phenomenon (cf. Gen. 34:30; Josh. 10:5; Judg. 3:13; 1 Sam. 13:5; 2 Sam. 6:1; 1 Kgs. 10:26). In particular, Isa. 13:4 speaks of Yahweh "mustering" a divine army in order to inflict a climactic Day of the Lord judgment against the nations of Babylon. Then, in Hos. 10:10; Zech. 14:2, God "marshals" the nations against his own people, as a sign of judgment against them. In Josh. 24:1; Neh. 8:1, 13 the people of God "gather together" for the purpose of renewing their covenant obligation to Yahweh. The prophets occasionally refer to Yahweh bringing his people back (i.e., "gathering" them) from captivity as a sign of their deliverance and renewing their intimate relationship with him (cf. Isa. 49:5; Ezek. 11:17; Mic. 2:12; 4:6). In addition, Zeph. 3:8 describes Yahweh "gathering" the nations together in order to bring judgment on them. Similarly, there is a "gathering" of the armies of Israel in Ezek. 39:17 in order to "feast" on the vanquished armies of Gog and Magog. There are also several references to God's people "assembling" in order to express their penitence before Yahweh (cf. Neh. 9:1; Joel 1:14; 2:16). Other miscellaneous "gatherings" of people are recorded in various places (e.g., Gen. 29:22; Exod. 3:16; Lev. 26:25; Deut. 33:5; Judg. 9:6; 1 Sam. 5:8; Ezra 3:1; Ps. 47:9; Jer. 8:14; Ezek. 38:12; Amos 3:9).

Finally, ***'āsaph*** is found in the expression "to be gathered to one's fathers, or people," which is a metaphor for the stark reality of death — for example, Isaac (Gen. 35:29); Jacob (Gen. 49:29); Aaron (Num. 20:24); and Moses (Deut. 32:50). See also Judg. 2:10; 2 Kgs. 22:20.

qābaṣ **[קָבַץ, 6908]**

qābaṣ is synonymous with ***'āsaph*** (see above) and also means "gather (together)," "assemble." The term occurs about one hundred times with these meanings.

With the literal sense of "collect," or "store," ***qābaṣ*** refers to food (Gen. 41:35, 48); to spoil (Deut. 13:16); and to idols (Mic. 1:7). Metaphorical references are found in Ps. 41:6; Prov. 28:8.

The predominant meaning of ***qābaṣ*** is to "gather" in the sense of "assemble," and it refers exclusively to people in various contexts. The "assembling" of God's people for worship is noted in Ps. 102:22; they "gather" to express repentance before God in 1 Sam. 7:5; Ezra 10:1ff.; and they are also "assembled" for war (cf. Josh. 9:2; Judg. 9:47; 12:4; 1 Sam. 28:1; 2 Sam. 2:25; 1 Kgs. 11:24; 2 Chr. 25:5).

In a significant number of texts, God is said to "gather" both his own people and the nations abroad for the purpose of both blessing and judgment. Yahweh promises to deliver his people by "gathering" them out of the land of their captivity (e.g., Deut. 30:3, 4; Ps. 107:3; Isa. 11:2; Jer. 23:3; 29:14; 31:8; Ezek. 11:17; 36:24; 37:21; Hos. 1:11; Mic. 4:6). Isa. 40:11 refers metaphorically to Yahweh "gathering" his people like "lambs in his arms" for the purpose of protecting them. Conversely, the divine "assembling" of the nations is primarily for the purpose of bringing judgment upon them — for example, Babylon (Isa. 48:14); Ammon (Jer. 49:5); the nations (Joel 3:2); Gog and Magog (Ezek. 39:17). Such a divine "gathering" is not limited to the nations either, for Israel and Judah are also "assembled" by God to face his wrath and punishment for violation of their covenant obligations (cf. Ezek. 16:37; 22:19ff.). See also 1 Kgs. 18:19, where the Israelite prophets of Baal are assembled for punishment for their apostasy.

lāqaṭ **[לָקַט, 3950]**

lāqaṭ is a verb found in nearly forty places meaning "to gather," "glean," "collect," mostly in a literal sense.

References to "gathering" or "collecting" food are found in Exod. 16:4ff.; Lev. 19:9ff.; 23:22; Num. 11:8; Judg. 1:7; 2 Kgs. 4:39; Ps. 104:28; Isa. 17:5. See also Gen. 31:46; 47:14; 1 Sam. 20:38; Song 6:2; Jer. 7:18 for references to "gathering" various objects. Judg. 11:3 refers to "gathering" people together.

In Ruth 2:2ff. ***lāqaṭ*** refers to "gleaning," or collecting remnants of the grain harvest — a provision under Mosaic legislation for the maintenance of the poor.

In Isa. 27:12 there is a metaphorical reference to Yahweh "gathering up" the people of Israel one by one from their captivity in exile to their repatriation in the land of Canaan.

qāshash **[קָשַׁשׁ, 7197]**

qāshash is a verb found seven times denoting the action of "gathering" straw for making bricks in Exod. 5:7, 12; and sticks for fuel in Num. 15:32ff.; 1 Kgs. 17:10, 12. God also commands his people to "gather together," or assemble, in Zeph. 2:1.

bāṣar **[בָּצַר, 1219]**

bāṣar is a verb with the predominant adjectival sense of "fortified" (in relation to cities) throughout most of its nearly forty occurrences. However, in several places, ***bāṣar*** denotes "gathering" grapes (cf. Lev. 25:5, 11; Deut. 24:21; Judg. 9:27; Jer. 6:9; 49:9; Obad. 5).

'āgar **[אָגַר, 103]**

'āgar is a rare verb with the general sense of "gathering" food, found only in Deut. 28:39; Prov. 6:8; 10:5.

kānas **[כָּנַס, 3664]**

The verb ***kānas*** occurs eleven times and means "gather" in several different contexts.

The "gathering together" of people is indicated in 1 Chr. 22:2; Esth. 4:16. In particular, Yahweh is said to "gather" the outcasts of Israel with a view to returning them to the land of Canaan (cf. Ps. 147:2; Ezek. 39:28). In Ezek. 22:21, the divine "gathering" is for the purpose of judgment. The "gathering" or "collecting" of food is noted in Neh. 12:44.

God is said to "gather" the water of the seas in Ps. 33:7.

Eccl. 2:8 refers to a person "gathering," or "accumulating," wealth. See also Eccl. 2:26; 3:5.

dāgar **[דָּגַר, 1716]**

dāgar is a rare verb found only in Isa. 34:15; Jer. 17:11, referring to birds "gathering" their young for protection and nurture.

qāwāh **[קָוָה, 6960]**

qāwāh is a verb found about fifty times with the predominant meanings "wait," "look for." In Gen. 1:9, 10, however, the term refers to God "gathering together" the waters under heaven into one place.

kenash **[כְּנַשׁ, 3673** (Aramaic)**]**

kenash is a rare Aramaic verb found only in Dan. 3:2, 3, 27, with reference to people "assembling" or "gathering together."

'ārāh [אָרָה, 717]

'ārāh is a rare verb denoting "gathering" or "picking" fruit and spices in Ps. 80:12; Song 5:1.

NT Words

synagō [συνάγω, *4863*]

synagō is a dynamic Greek equivalent for most of the Hebrew terms listed above. It is found in approximately sixty contexts meaning "to gather (together)," "assemble" as well as the corresponding passive sense "be gathered."

Matt. 2:4; 13:2; Mark 5:21 refer to "gathering" or "calling" people together in mundane senses.

Matt. 3:12; Luke 15:13; John 6:12; 15:6 refer to "gathering" produce, or material goods.

Christ's action in "gathering" people to himself for the purpose of making them his own is indicated in Matt. 12:30; 25:32; Luke 11:23; John 11:52.

In several contexts, "gathering wheat" is equated with the final assembling of believers in glory (cf. Matt. 13:30; Luke 3:17).

As in the Old Testament, people often "gather" or "assemble" for a specific purpose — for example, to worship (Matt. 18:20; Acts 20:7; 1 Cor. 5:4); to plot to kill Jesus (Matt. 26:3; Acts 4:27); to see and hear Jesus speak (Mark 2:2); to attempt to humiliate Jesus in public (Mark 7:1); to force the disciples to stop preaching (Acts 4:6); to gather against the Lord (Acts 4:26); to wait to receive the Holy Spirit (Acts 4:31); to hear the preaching of the word of God (Acts 13:44); to hear about the spread of the gospel (Acts 14:27); and to face God on the great and final day of battle (Rev. 16:14ff.; 19:19; 20:8). See also Rev. 19:17.

Vultures "gather" around a corpse prior to feeding on it in Luke 17:37.

episynagō [ἐπισυνάγω, *1996*]

episynagō is a variant form of ***synagō***, above, occurring nine times and meaning "gather together" throughout.

Jesus expresses the desire to "gather his children together," as a hen gathers her chickens under her wings, referring to the wayward people of Jerusalem (cf. Matt. 23:37; Luke 13:34). The prospect of God "gathering together" his elect from all over the world is noted in Matt. 24:31; Mark 13:27.

Mundane references to people "gathering together" include those in Mark 1:33; Luke 12:1.

episynagōgē [ἐπισυναγωγή, *1997*]

episynagōgē is the noun derived from ***episynagō***, above, found only twice. In 2 Thess. 2:1 it signifies the prospect of "being gathered" to the Lord in glory. Heb. 10:25 contains an admonition to believers not to abandon their "assembling together" for worship.

syllegō [συλλέγω, *4816*]

syllegō is a verb found eight times, meaning "gather," "pick," and used exclusively in relation to fruit and plants.

"Gathering" or "picking" grapes is noted in Matt. 7:16; and figs in Luke 6:44. Matt. 13:28ff. refer to "harvesting" weeds.

systrephō [συστρέφω, *4962*]

systrephō is a rare verb found only in Acts 28:3, referring to Paul "gathering" some firewood.

trygaō [τρυγάω, *5166*]

trygaō is a rare verb, synonymous with ***syllegō*** (see above), found only three times. It signifies "gathering" or "harvesting" grapes in a literal sense in Luke 6:44; and metaphorically in Rev. 14:18, 19 (referring to "harvesting" both the righteous and the wicked).

synathroizō [συναθροίζω, *4867*]

synathroizō is a verb found only three times, meaning "to gather, call together" people (cf. Luke 24:33; Acts 12:12; 19:25).

Additional Notes

"Gathering" in both Old and New Testaments displays a distinctive theological significance when referring to God assembling people for the purposes of both judgment of blessing. In the Old Testament, the assembling of the nations for temporal punishment anticipates the ultimate Day of Judgment referred to in the book of Revelation, in which a harvesting or gathering metaphor is specifically employed to indicate climactic spiritual punishment (cf. Rev. 14). Conversely, the ultimate spiritual salvation of God's people as depicted in the New Testament is also foreshadowed by the divine gathering of the old covenant people of God out of the land of exile, and their repatriation in the land of Palestine. In the case of Israel and Judah, such a temporal deliverance was of course preceded by severe disciplinary measures that included losing the land of promise. In short, the temporal punishments and salvation of "gathered peoples" under the old covenant anticipate the supremely spiritual blessings and judgments of those "assembled peoples" in the new covenant age.

See Also: → ASSEMBLE

GENEALOGY

OT Words

yāḥas **[יָחַשׂ, 3187]**

yāḥas is a reflexive verb that means "reckon genealogically" or "enroll on a genealogical record." It occurs twenty times.

yāḥas is found exclusively in the postexilic works of Ezra, Nehemiah, and the Chronicler, and in all cases refers to the genealogical recording of the Israelite tribes (e.g., 1 Chr. 4:33; 5:1, 7, 17; 7:5ff.); all Israel (cf. 1 Chr. 9:1; Neh. 7:5); Levitical families, listed in reference to their ritual responsibilities (cf. 1 Chr. 9:22; 2 Chr. 31:16ff.); and priestly genealogies, demanded as prerequisite for the right to commence service in the reconstructed postexilic temple (cf. Ezra 2:62). See also Ezra 8:1ff.; Neh. 7:64.

NT Words

genealogia [γενεαλογία, *1076*]

genealogia is a rare noun found only twice, denoting a "genealogy" in the sense of a "record of family descent" (cf. 1 Tim. 1:4; Titus 3:9).

genealogeō [γενεαλογέω, *1075*]

genealogeō is a rare verb found only in Heb. 7:6 meaning "to trace one's family lineage."

agenealogētos [ἀγενεαλόγητος, *35*]

agenealogētos is a rare adjective found only in Heb. 7:3, describing Melchizedek as a priest-king "without genealogy" — that is, there is no record of his parentage.

GENERATION

OT Words

tôledôt **[תּוֹלְדוֹת, 8435]**

This term occurs about forty times and means "descendants"; "generations"; "genealogies." On a number of occasions, however, notably in the book of Genesis, ***tôledôt*** is a technical term for a narrative section listing the descendants of, and in most cases containing historical details relating to, key figures in the creation and patriarchal narratives. It is normally translated "These are the generations of . . . ," or more colloquially in modern English, "This is the account of . . ." (Gen. 2:4; 5:1; 6:9; 10:1, 32; 11:10, 27; 25:12, 13, 19; 36:1, 9; 37:2). The one non-personal reference here is Gen. 2:4, in which the "heavens and the earth" are the subjects of the "generations."

The remaining uses of ***tôledôt*** all refer either to genealogical listings of Israelite tribes (e.g., Exod. 6:16; Num. 1:20ff.; Ruth 4:18; 1 Chr. 5:7; 7:2ff.); or to Israelite priests (cf. 1 Chr. 9:34; 26:31).

NT Words

genea [γενεά, *1074*]

genea is a noun found about forty times with the primary meaning "generation," denoting a "natural grouping of family descent," as well as associated nuances.

Matt. 7:11 lists the "generations" in a stylized genealogy tracing the descent of Jesus Christ from the very origins of the Israelite people of God.

"Generation" in the sense of a community of people living at the same period of time, at the national or local level, is noted in Matt. 11:16; 12:39ff.; 23:36; Mark 8:12, 38; 9:19; Luke 7:31; 9:41; 11:29ff.; Acts 2:40; Phil. 2:15; Heb. 3:10 (all of which refer to a wicked and unbelieving generation).

The term is used in a neutral sense in Matt. 24:34; Luke 1:48ff.; 16:8; Acts 8:33; 13:36; 14:16; 15:21; Eph. 3:5.

genesis [γένεσις, *1078*]

genesis is a rare noun denoting the "genealogy" of Jesus Christ in Matt. 1:1.

gennēma [γέννημα, *1081*]

gennēma is a noun found in nine places meaning "generation" in the sense of that which is born or begotten. It is used metaphorically in Matt. 3:7; 12:34; 23:33; Luke 3:7 to refer to hypocritical, self-righteous Pharisees as a "brood" of vipers.

GENTILES

NT Words

ethnos [ἔθνος, *1484*]

ethnos is a noun found over 160 times with the dominant meanings "Gentiles," "nations" throughout. (→ NATION)

The term "Gentile" denotes pagan peoples in Matt. 4:15; Luke 22:25; Acts 14:2; Rom. 2:14; 1 Cor. 5:1; Gal. 2:2ff.; 1 Pet. 4:3.

ethnos refers to the Romans in Matt. 20:19; Mark 10:33; Luke 18:32; Acts 4:27.

The Gentile nations are the objects of divine mercy and saving revelation in Luke 2:32; Acts 21:19ff.; Rom. 1:13; 9:24; 15:9ff.; Col. 1:27; 2 Tim. 4:17. In particular, they are said to be the recipients of the Holy Spirit in Acts 10:45; 11:1, 18; Eph. 2:11; 3:6ff. Similarly, the Gentiles are also said to receive the "light" of the gospel in Acts 13:47ff.; and their conversion is noted in Acts 15:3ff.; 26:23; Rom. 11:11ff.

The expression "times of the Gentiles" refers to the time when the world will come to an end and God's final judgment is imminent (cf. Luke 21:24). Similarly, the phrase "fullness of the Gentiles" refers to the time when the greatest number of pagan peoples will be brought into the kingdom of God (cf. Rom. 11:25).

ethnikos [ἐθνικός, *1482*]

ethnikos is a rare noun denoting a "pagan, or Gentile man," found only in Matt. 6:7; 18:17.

ethnikōs [ἐθνικῶς, *1483*]

ethnikōs is a rare adverbial form meaning "like a Gentile" (i.e., after the custom of the Gentiles), found only in Gal. 2:14.

hellēn [Ἕλλην, *1672*]

hellēn is a noun found nearly thirty times denoting those of Greek nationality. In the New Testament the "Greeks" are synonymous with the Gentiles (e.g., John 12:20; Acts 14:1; 18:4; Rom. 1:14ff.; 2:9ff.; 10:12; 1 Cor. 1:22ff.; Gal. 2:3; Col. 3:11).

See Also: → NATION

GENTLE, GENTLENESS

NT Words

epieikēs [ἐπιεικής, *1933*]

epieikēs is a rare adjectival form meaning "gentle" in relation to a kindly, patient disposition of spirit (cf. 1 Tim. 3:3; Titus 3:2; Jas. 3:17; 1 Pet. 2:18).

ēpios [ἤπιος, *2261*]

ēpios is a rare synonym for ***epieikēs***, above, meaning "gentle" in 1 Thess. 2:7; 2 Tim. 2:24.

epieikeia [ἐπιείκεια, *1932*]

epieikeia is a rare variant form of ***epieikēs*** (see above) denoting the "gentleness" of Christ in Acts 24:4.

GET

NT Words

ktaomai [κτάομαι, *2932*]

ktaomai occurs seven times in all with the meaning "possess" in Luke 18:12; "acquire" or "buy" in Acts 1:18; 8:20; 22:28. See also Matt. 10:9; Luke 21:19; 1 Thess. 4:4.

Additional Notes

The concept of "get" covers a broad range of words in Hebrew and Greek. To understand how it is used in Scripture, consult the entries listed below.

See Also: → DESCEND → ENTER → FIND → GAIN → INHERIT → LEAVE → OBTAIN → POSSESS → PROVIDE → RECEIVE

GHOST

OT Words

gāwa' [**גָּוַע, 1478**]

gāwa' is a verb found nearly twenty-five times with the fundamental meaning "to die." Occasionally the term is translated "to breathe one's last" or "give up the ghost," although there is considerable overlap in meaning (e.g., Gen. 25:8, 17; 35:29; 49:33; Job 14:10; Ps. 104:29).

NT Words

ekpneō [ἐκπνέω, *1606*]

ekpneō is a rare verb found three times with reference to Christ "breathing his last" (lit. "giving up the ghost") on the cross.

ekpsychō [ἐκψύχω, *1634*]

ekpsychō is rare synonym for ***ekpneō***, above, referring to people "breathing their last," or "giving up the ghost" in Acts 5:5, 10; 12:23.

Additional Notes

With reference to the third person of the Godhead, the title "Holy Ghost" is equivalent to "Holy Spirit." (→ SPIRIT)

GIFT, GIVING

OT Words

mattānāh [**מַתָּנָה, 4979**]

This noun is derived from ***nātan***, "to give" (→ GIVE) and means "gift." ***mattānāh*** occurs seventeen times.

In the first instance, the term indicates "gift" in the sense of that which is freely bestowed (i.e., among people) — for example, Abraham gives gifts to the sons of his concubines (Gen. 25:6); and gifts are given to the poor (2 Chr. 21:3; Esth. 9:22); also Ezek. 46:16, 17.

mattānāh also refers to gifts given to God as an act of worship (cf. Exod. 28:38; Lev. 23:38; Num. 18:29; Deut. 16:17; Ps. 68:18). Ezek. 20:26, 31, 39 refer to the perverse, vile "gifts" of child sacrifice to Yahweh.

God's gift as something freely bestowed upon his people is indicated in Num. 18:6, 7, where the Levites are described as being God's gift to his people for the purpose of serving him in the tabernacle. Finally, Prov. 15:27; Eccl. 7:7 refer to gifts in the sense of "bribes."

mattān [מַתָּן, 4976]

A synonym for ***mattānāh***, above, ***mattān*** is found on five occasions. "Gifts" among people in general terms are mentioned in Prov. 18:16; 19:6; 21:14. Gen. 34:12 refers to a marriage "gift"; and in Num. 18:11 the wave offering is indicated as God's "gift" of sustenance for the priests and Levites through the people of Israel.

mattāt [מַתָּת, 4991]

A synonymous term for both ***mattānāh*** and ***mattān*** (see above), ***mattāt*** means "gift" on six occasions. God's "gifts" to humankind of food and drink, as well as labor, are mentioned in Eccl. 3:13; 5:19. 1 Kgs. 13:7 refers to a "gift" in the sense of "reward." Our "gift" to God in the form of an act of worship is indicated in Ezek. 46:5, 11. Prov. 25:14 refers to "gift" in a general sense.

shōḥad [שֹׁחַד, 7810]

shōḥad is a noun found twenty-three times, denoting a "gift," "reward," or "bribe."

The meaning "bribe" in relation to a corrupt legal transaction is indicated in Exod. 23:8; Deut. 16:19; 1 Sam. 8:3; Ps. 15:5; Prov. 17:23; Isa. 1:23; 5:23; Ezek. 22:12; Mic. 3:11. God is said to have never taken a "bribe" in Deut. 10:17; 2 Chr. 19:7.

The presentation of a "gift" is noted in 1 Kgs. 15:19; 2 Kgs. 16:8. The sense of "gift" or "bribe" is possible in Prov. 6:35.

Isa. 45:13 refers to a hypothetical "reward" offered to God.

nādān [נָדָן, 5083]

nādān is a rare noun denoting a "gift," a "monetary payment," offered to one's "lovers" in Ezek. 16:33. The sense here is metaphorical, alluding to Israel's compulsive worship of idol deities — her "lovers."

NT Words

dōron [δῶρον, *1435*]

dōron is a noun found nineteen times with the primary meaning "gift" in a variety of contexts.

"Gifts" presented to the Christ child are noted in Matt. 2:11.

Offering a "gift" at the altar in the context of worship is noted in Matt. 5:23ff.; Luke 21:1, 4; Heb. 5:1; 8:3ff.; 9:9; 11:4. A non-ritual reference to a "gift" is found in Rev. 11:10.

In an intangible spiritual sense, ***dōron*** refers to saving faith as the "gift" of God in Eph. 2:8.

dōrea [δωρεά, *1431*]

dōrea is a variant form of ***dōron***, above, denoting a "gift" in all eleven occurrences of the term. The usage of ***dōrea*** is entirely spiritual. References to salvation and eternal life as "the gift" of God are found in John 4:10; Rom. 5:15, 17; 2 Cor. 9:15; Heb. 6:4.

The "gift" of the Holy Spirit as the accompaniment to personal conversion is noted in Acts 2:38; 10:45; 11:17. See also Acts 8:20. Then, the divine "gift" of grace is indicated in Eph. 3:7; 4:7.

dōrēma [δώρημα, *1434*]

dōrēma is a rare synonym for ***dōron*** and ***dōrea***, above, denoting the "gift" of salvation in Rom. 5:16; and a "gift" in the general sense of God's goodness to humankind in Jas. 1:17.

doma [δόμα, *1390*]

doma is a noun found four times meaning "gifts" in a general, tangible sense in Matt. 7:11; Luke 11:13; Eph. 4:8; Phil. 4:17.

charisma [χάρισμα, *5486*]

charisma is a noun denoting a "spiritual gift" throughout its seventeen occurrences.

The meaning "spiritual gift" as given by God in a general sense is indicated in Rom. 1:11; 11:29; 12:6; 1 Cor. 1:7; 7:7; 2 Tim. 1:6; 1 Pet. 4:10. Specific "gifts" granted by the Spirit of God are noted in 1 Cor. 12:4, 9, 28ff.; 1 Tim. 4:14.

charisma denotes the "free gift" of salvation in Rom. 5:15, 16; 6:23.

merismos [μερισμός, *3311*]

merismos is a rare noun denoting the "gifts" of the Holy Spirit in Heb. 2:4.

Additional Notes

In order to understand the full significance of "gifts" in both Old and New Testaments, other terms such as "blessing" and "offering" must also be considered. This is especially true when God's gift to humankind is in view, whether it is applied to his own covenant people, or to those outside of that special unique relationship.

See Also: ➡ BLESS ➡ OFFERING

GIRDLE

OT Words

ḥagôr **[חֲגוֹר, 2289]**

This term occurs four times and means "girdle," "belt," or "sash." Three of these occurrences refer to this article of clothing in a mundane sense (cf. 1 Sam. 18:4; 2 Sam. 20:8; Prov. 31:24). Ezek. 23:15 refers to the "belts" of the Babylonian nobility, symbolizing pagan deities in the allegory of the two sisters (Israel and Judah), depicting their apostasy.

ḥagôrāh **[חֲגוֹרָה, 2290]**

A synonym for *ḥagôr* (see above), *ḥagôrāh* occurs five times and is translated "girdle" or "belt" in a literal sense in 2 Sam. 18:11; 1 Kgs. 2:5; Isa. 3:24.

'abnēt **[אַבְנֵט, 73]**

'abnēt refers exclusively to the linen "belt" attached to the tunics of the priests and high priest. The term occurs nine times, and each reference is located in ritual contexts that relate to the investiture and service of the Israelite priests (cf. Exod. 28:4, 39; 29:9; 39:29; Lev. 8:7, 13; 16:4; Isa. 22:21).

NT Words

zōnē **[ζώνη, *2223*]**

zōnē is the dynamic equivalent for the Hebrew terms listed above, denoting a "belt" in most of the eight occurrences of the term. Most of these refer to the literal item of clothing (cf. Matt. 3:4; 10:9; Mark 1:6; 6:8; Acts 21:11). In Rev. 1:13; 15:6 ***zōnē*** denotes the golden "sashes" worn by the heavenly Christ and angelic beings.

GIRL

OT Words

na'arāh **[נַעֲרָה, 5291]**

na'arāh indicates a "girl," "young woman" (either married or unmarried) in a general sense, with the extended meanings "maidservant," "concubine," or "prostitute." ***na'arāh*** occurs about sixty times, predominantly in narrative contexts.

In regard to young women of marriageable age who are virgins, ***na'arāh*** refers to Rebekah, the wife of Isaac, in the account of their meeting and betrothal (cf. Gen. 24:14ff.). It also similarly refers to Dinah, the daughter of Jacob (cf. Gen. 34:12ff.); to the daughter of Pharaoh (cf. Exod. 2:5); to Ruth (cf. Ruth 2:5ff.); to the servant girls of Boaz (cf. Ruth 2:22ff.); to the young virgins of Jabesh-Gilead (cf. Judg. 21:12); and to the concubine of the wandering Levite (Judg. 19:3ff.). See also Esth. 2:2ff.

na'arāh also refers to servant girls in general (cf. 1 Sam. 9:11; 25:42; Job 4:5; Prov. 9:3; 27:27; 31:15), and to the little girl in the service of Naaman, the Syrian general (cf. 2 Kgs. 5:2ff.).

There is also some interesting Mosaic legislation concerning young women who are about to be given in marriage and whose virginity is put to the test (cf. Deut. 22:15ff.). If the young woman is found not to be a virgin, she is to be executed. The Deuteronomic legislation also prescribes certain procedures to be followed in the case of young women, betrothed or single, who are forcibly violated (cf. Deut. 22:22ff.).

In Amos 2:7, ***na'arāh*** is used in a prophetic context and most likely refers to a prostitute, who is used by a father and son alike.

yaldāh **[יַלְדָּה, 3207]**

yaldāh is a noun found only three times, denoting a "girl" or "young woman" in each case. Gen. 34:4 refers to a "young woman" of marriageable age. Joel 3:3 refers to a "girl" working as a prostitute. Young "girls" playing in the street are noted in Zech. 8:5.

NT Words

korasion **[κοράσιον, *2877*]**

korasion is a term denoting a "girl" in each of the eight occurrences of the term (cf. Matt. 9:24ff.; 14:11; Mark 5:41ff.; 6:22ff.).

paidion **[παιδίον, *3813*]**

paidion is a diminutive form of ***pais*** (➡ CHILD) denoting a "(young) child" in most of its nearly fifty occurrences. However, in Mark 5:39ff. ***paidion*** denotes the "young girl" brought back to life by Jesus.

paidiskē **[παιδίσκη, *3814*]**

paidiskē is another variant of ***pais*** (➡ CHILD), denoting a "servant girl" for most of its thirteen occurrences (cf. Matt. 26:69; Mark 14:66ff.; Luke 12:45; 22:56; John 18:17; Acts 12:13; 16:16). In Gal. 4:22ff. ***paidiskē*** refers metaphorically to Hagar as the "slave woman," in contrast to Sarah as the "free woman" — symbolizing two contrasting destinies. Sarah alone is the beneficiary of the covenant promise given to Abraham, whose wife was the one chosen by God to bear the child of promise. (→ CHILD)

See Also: → MAID

GIVE

OT Words

nātan **[נָתַן, 5414]**

A common verb occurring nearly two thousand times, ***nātan*** is translated "give" in over half of these contexts. The semantic range of ***nātan*** is quite broad. (→ DELIVER → PAY → SET)

nātan is found predominantly in three contexts: where "giving" is predicated firstly of God to human beings, then human beings to one another, and finally human beings to God.

In the first instance, God is said to "give" food to human beings in the garden of Eden (cf. Gen. 1:29; 9:3), and food to his ritual servants the Levites (cf. Lev. 6:17; 7:3; 10:14). He also feeds (i.e., gives food to) his people in the wilderness (cf. Num. 11:18; Ps. 78:24), including water (cf. Num. 21:16; Isa. 43:20). Yahweh also gives revelatory signs to his people — for example, the Emmanuel sign (Isa. 7:14; 9:6); and the person of the Suffering Servant as a sign of new covenant blessing (cf. Isa. 42:6; 49:8). See also 1 Kgs. 13:3.

In relation to the theme of covenant, Yahweh gives Abraham the promise of a son (Gen. 17:16); and he gives the Israelites the law of the covenant (e.g., Exod. 24:12; Deut. 9:11; 10:4; Ps. 99:7; Ezek. 20:11; Neh. 9:13). ***nātan*** is used in the Pentateuch and Former Prophets in relation to Yahweh giving his people the land of promise (cf. Gen. 12:7; 15:7, 18; Exod. 6:4; 20:12; Lev. 14:34; Num. 10:29; Deut. 1:36; Josh. 1:2ff.; 1 Kgs. 8:48). Elsewhere, the same phenomenon is referred to, for example, in Neh. 9:8; Ps. 105:11; Jer. 3:19; Ezek. 11:15; Amos 9:15. In addition to the land itself, God also gives blessing in the land (e.g., Deut. 11:14; 12:15, 21; Ruth 1:6). God gives the people the tribal allotments in Canaan through Moses and Joshua (cf. Josh. 13:8ff.; 14:3ff.; 15:13), as well as cities for the Levites to live in (cf. Num. 35:2ff.; Josh. 21:2ff.).

Divine judgment is also predominant in the use of this term — for example, Yahweh often gives his people over to judgment, "into the hands" of their enemies (e.g., Deut. 28:32; Judg. 2:14; Isa. 47:6; Jer. 20:4, 5; Ezek. 7:21; 16:39). Conversely, Yahweh is also declared to have given his enemies over to his own people (cf. Deut. 31:5; Josh. 6:16; 24:8, 11; Judg. 7:7ff.; 8:3ff.; 1 Sam. 14:10ff.; Ps. 18:40). God's judgment on the nations is also described in terms of him giving the nations over for slaughter (cf. Isa. 34:2; Ezek. 39:4, 11).

In other general contexts, God is said to give mercy to his people (cf. Gen. 43:14; Exod. 11:3; Neh. 1:11); to appoint (i.e., give) people to office (cf. Exod. 31:6; Num. 3:9; Zech. 3:7); to give deliverance to his people (cf. Judg. 15:18; Ps. 18:35); to give his people a king (cf. 1 Sam. 8:6); and to give "rest" to his people — to protect them from their enemies or give them victory over their enemies (cf. 1 Kgs. 8:56).

In the second place, on the purely human level, ***nātan*** is found in a variety of contexts. In Gen. 3:6, Eve gives the forbidden fruit to her husband, Adam. Capital punishment, or the giving of life for life, is also indicated (e.g., Exod. 21:23). The practice of giving a wife in marriage is mentioned in Gen. 16:3; 24:41; 1 Sam. 18:17ff.; 1 Kgs. 2:35, as is the giving of one's daughter in marriage (cf. Judg. 21:1). The giving of love in the marriage relationship is indicated in Song 7:12. In regard to the law of the covenant, financial compensation (i.e., "giving back") for misdemeanors under the law is mentioned in Exod. 21:32; 22:17; as is restoration of property (cf. Exod. 22:29; Lev. 6:5). Giving freely to the poor is commended under the law (cf. Deut. 15:10). Prov. 4:12; 29:15 also commend fathers for giving good teaching and wisdom to their children.

Finally, as far as people giving to God is concerned, tithing is mentioned (Gen. 14:20; Exod. 30:14; Lev. 23:38; Num. 31:41), including the tithing of one's firstborn (cf. Num. 8:16). Ransom to the Lord is also indicated in Exod. 30:12; Num. 3:51. Offerings to God given as atonement for sin are mentioned in Lev. 5:16; and Lev. 17:11 emphasizes that blood is given by God to make atonement for sin.

There are also a number of metaphorical uses of ***nātan*** — for example, Yahweh gives human beings the shield of salvation (2 Sam. 22:36); God gives a "lamp" to David, or a royal descendant (1 Kgs. 15:4); and a "nail in the temple" for his people, or a place of security (Ezra 9:8; Eccl. 12:11). He gives "life" back to his people when he brings them back from exile (cf. Ezra 9:9); and gives Israel as a "light" to the nations (cf. Isa. 49:6).

NT Words

didōmi **[δίδωμι, *1325*]**

didōmi is a common verb found in approximately four hundred places with the predominant meaning "to give" throughout, in a variety of contexts and with a variety of nuances.

The "granting" of a certificate of divorce is indicated in Matt. 5:31; 19:7.

Mundane references to "giving" among people include those in Matt. 5:42; Mark 6:37; Luke 6:38; John 4:12; Acts 20:35.

"Giving" praise or glory to God is indicated in Luke 18:43; John 9:24; Acts 12:23; Rom. 4:20. Heb. 7:4 mentions Abraham "giving" Melchizedek a tenth of the plunder from the victory over the Canaanite kings. People are said to "give" glory to the God of heaven in Rev. 11:13.

Requests for God to "give" his people their daily needs are found in Matt. 6:11; Luke 11:3. There are also other references to people requesting God to "grant" them their requests (e.g., Matt. 7:7).

In particular, some of the disciples ask Christ to "grant" them the privilege of sitting next to him in glory in Mark 10:37.

God "gives" various things to his people, including civil authority (Matt. 9:8); spiritual power over unclean spirits (Matt. 10:1; Mark 6:7); insight into spiritual realities (Matt. 13:11ff.; Mark 4:11; 13:11; Luke 8:10; John 3:27); knowledge of salvation (Luke 1:77); the kingdom of God (Luke 12:32); power to become children of God (John 1:12); the law to Moses (citing the Sinai narrative traditions, John 1:17); manna from heaven (John 6:31ff., again with reference to the wilderness narratives of the Pentateuch); the Holy Spirit as another counselor for his people (John 14:16; Acts 11:17); peace to his people (John 14:27); repentance to Israel (Acts 5:31); the covenant of circumcision to Abraham (Acts 7:8); and rain from heaven (Acts 14:17).

General references to God "giving" the Holy Spirit to his people include those in Acts 15:8; 1 John 3:24; 4:13; Rom. 5:5; 1 Cor. 12:7; 2 Cor. 1:22. In a related sense, God is also said to "give" gifts to his church through the Spirit (1 Cor. 12:8; Eph. 4:11), as well as "grace" (cf. 1 Cor. 3:10; Gal. 2:9; Eph. 3:7, 8; 2 Tim. 1:9); and love (cf. 1 John 3:1). 1 John 5:11 declares that God "has given" his people eternal life

Divine refusal to "give" is noted in Matt. 12:39; Luke 11:29, with reference to a sign.

White robes are given to the saints in heaven (cf. Rev. 6:11). Jesus takes to himself the prerogative of "giving the keys of the kingdom" to Peter his disciple in Matt. 16:19.

Jesus is said to "give his life as a ransom for many" (Matt. 20:28; Mark 10:45; 1 Tim. 2:6), and to "give" his people eternal life (John 10:28). Gal. 1:4 affirms that Christ "gave himself" for the sins of his people. Eph. 4:8 affirms that he "gave" gifts to people.

God himself is said to "give" divine authority to his Son in Matt. 21:23; 28:18 (cf. also Mark 11:28); to "give" him the throne of David his ancestor (Luke 1:32); to "give" all things into his hand (John 3:35; 13:3). See also John 5:22ff.; 10:29; 18:11. In particular, John 17:2ff. refers to the people God had given to him. 1 Pet. 1:21 declares that God "gave" glory to Jesus after raising him from the dead. John 3:16 records that God "gave" his Son to a lost world, that it may be redeemed and forgiven.

In non-personal contexts, Matt. 24:29; Mark 13:24 refer to the light "given off" by the sun and moon.

The devil promises to "give" Jesus all the kingdoms of the world if he will fall down and worship him (Matt. 4:9; Luke 4:6).

Satanic beings "are given" power to harm humankind in Rev. 9:5; 16:8. See also Rev. 13:2ff. The sea and hell are said to "give up" the dead in Rev. 20:13.

epididōmi [ἐπιδίδωμι, *1929*]

epididōmi is a verb found twelve times with the primary senses of "give," "hand over (to)."

The literal act of "giving," or "handing" something over to someone, is indicated in Matt. 7:9ff.; Luke 4:17; 11:11ff.; 24:30, 42; John 13:26.

paradidōmi [παραδίδωμι, *3860*]

paradidōmi is a common verb meaning "betray," "deliver up (to)" in most of its 135 occurrences, with the underlying sense of "give over." (→ DELIVER)

In several places, the explicit sense of "give over (to)" is indicated where God's judgment on the morally perverse results in him "giving them over" to their immorality in a permanent state of alienation from him (cf. Rom. 1:24ff.). Similarly, Eph. 4:19 refers to the wicked "giving themselves over" to every kind of immorality.

Elsewhere, the use of ***paradidōmi*** is positive. In Gal. 2:20, Paul affirms that Christ "gave himself" for him; and Eph. 5:2, 25 declares that Christ "has given himself up" for his church, speaking of his supreme self-sacrifice.

charizomai [χαρίζομαι, *5483*]

charizomai is a verb found over twenty times with the predominant sense of "forgive." The term also means "give" in several places. (→ FORGIVE)

Luke 7:21 refers to Jesus "giving (sight) back" to the blind.

The meaning "give (up)," "grant," in the sense of "hand (someone) over," or "deliver," is found in Acts 3:14; 25:11, 16. See also Phlm. 22.

God is said to "have freely given" his people all things in Christ in Rom. 8:32; 1 Cor. 2:12. Specifically, Gal. 3:18 declares that God "gave" Abraham the covenant promise of land and progeny. Phil. 2:9 affirms that God "has given" to Christ a name that is above every name.

dōreō [δωρέω, *1433*]

dōreō is a rare verb found three times, meaning "give," "grant."

Mark 15:45 refers to Pilate "granting" Jesus' body to Joseph of Arimathea. 2 Pet. 1:3ff. declares that God "has granted" much spiritual blessing to his people.

GLAD, GLADLY, GLADNESS

NT Words

hēdeōs [ἡδέως, *2234*]

hēdeōs is an adverb found only five times meaning "gladly," "with pleasure" in the context of human emotion (cf. Mark 6:20; 12:37; 2 Cor. 11:19; 12:9, 15).

See Also: → JOY → REJOICE

GLASS

NT Words

hyalos [ὕαλος, *5194*]

hyalos is a rare noun found only twice. In Rev. 21:18, 21 it denotes "glass" in a simile referring to the heavenly Jerusalem as a city "clear as glass."

hyalinos [ὑάλινος, *5193*]

hyalinos is a rare adjectival form derived from ***hyalos***, found only in Rev. 4:6; 15:2 referring to a visionary sea "of glass."

GLORIFY

OT Words

kābēd [כָּבֵד, **3513**]

This verb occurs around one hundred times with a variety of meanings. In approximately half of these contexts ***kābēd*** means "to glorify" or "honor," "bring honor to."

When used in relation to people, ***kābēd*** means to "bring honor to" — for example, Shechem (Gen. 34:19); parents (Exod. 20:12); Balaam (Num. 22:15, 17, 37); Samuel (1 Sam. 9:6); and David (2 Sam. 6:22). Ps. 91:15 refers to God "honoring" his faithful servants, and Jer. 30:19 refers to God "honoring" his people. The Suffering Servant is also "honored" by God in Isa. 49:5.

When predicated of God, ***kābēd*** means "to honor" in the sense of "glorify" (e.g., Exod. 14:4; Deut. 28:58; Judg. 13:17). In Lev. 10:3, on the deaths of Nadab and Abihu, Moses says to Aaron that such an incident results in God "drawing glory" (or honor) to himself. In 1 Sam. 2:30 God declares that those who "honor" him, he "will honor." Ps. 22:23 contains the command to "glorify" God, as does Isa. 24:15. And, in the context of worship, Pss. 50:14, 23; 86:9, 12; 87:3 all contain similar commands. In contrast, Isa. 29:13; 43:23 condemn those who offer "honor" to God under false pretenses through bogus worship.

For other uses of ***kābēd*** with this meaning, see Lam. 1:8; Dan. 11:38; Prov. 4:8; Isa. 43:20.

pā'ar [פָּאַר, **6286**]

This is a comparatively rare term, occurring only fourteen times. In half of these contexts ***pā'ar*** means to "glorify," "honor."

pā'ar is predicated of Yahweh, who "will be glorified," in several contexts. In Isa. 44:23, his glory will be displayed in Israel; Isa. 49:3 indicates that God's glory will be manifested in the Servant figure. Isa. 60:21; 61:3 indicate that God "will be glorified" through his plan of redemption on behalf of his people.

In Isa. 55:5; 60:7, 9 such a quality is predicated of God's people, who "will be honored" by Yahweh.

NT Words

doxazō [δοξάζω, *1392*]

doxazō is a verb constituting a dynamic equivalent of the Hebrew terms listed above. ***doxazō*** occurs about sixty times with the dominant meanings "glorify," "give glory, praise to," in a variety of contexts.

References to people "glorifying" God or "giving praise" include those in Matt. 5:16; Luke 5:25ff.; Acts 4:21; 11:18; Rom. 15:6ff. In particular, praise to God is offered in the aftermath of healing received from Christ (cf. Luke 17:15; 18:43). And, in Luke 23:47, the Roman centurion who witnessed the death of Christ "praised" God by declaring that Jesus was innocent. See also 2 Cor. 9:13; Gal. 1:24; 1 Pet. 2:12; 4:16. In Luke 4:15 people "offer praise" to Jesus.

Matt. 6:2; Mark 2:12 refer to people "giving praise" to other people.

doxazō is used passively in relation to the coming of the Holy Spirit, who would not be revealed until Christ "was glorified," or received his heavenly, glorious status at the right hand of the Father upon returning to heaven (cf. John 7:39). See also John 12:16, 23.

Other references to God "glorifying," or "giving supreme honor to," his Son include those in John 8:54; 11:4; 12:28; 17:1; Acts 3:13. Conversely, God is said "to be glorified" in and through his Son in John 13:31ff.; 14:13; 15:8; 17:1ff.; 21:19; 1 Pet. 4:11. See also Heb. 5:5. Rom. 1:21 describes the refusal of human beings to "glorify" or "honor" God.

God is said "to glorify" those whom he has chosen — to grant them the status of a heavenly citizen freed forever from the penalty of sin and death (cf. Rom. 8:30). See also 1 Pet. 4:14.

endoxazō [ἐνδοξάζω, *1740*]

endoxazō is a rare variant of ***doxazō***, above, found only twice and used passively in both places. 2 Thess. 1:10, 12 refer to Christ "being glorified" in his saints, or receiving honor and praise for redeeming them.

syndoxazō [συνδοξάζω, *4888*]

syndoxazō is another rare variant of ***doxazō***, above, found only in Rom. 8:17 and referring to the believer's certain hope of "being glorified" with him.

Additional Notes

Throughout the Old and New Testaments, the significance of the terminology for "glorify," "honor" centers on the unique value and esteem of the one and only God and his people. To glorify God is to acknowledge his majesty and power, and indeed all of those qualities that set him above the created order. When predicated of human beings, the usual sense is that of "honor," which suggests exactly the same thing, but on the plane of mortality. While God alone may be uniquely glorified, human beings may also honor their fellow human beings by acknowledging some particular character trait. But this is based on the acknowledgment that all such qualities are subject to the initiative and shaping of the eternal God, who is Creator of all things.

See Also: → PRAISE

GLORY

OT Words

kābôd [כָּבוֹד, 3519]

kābôd means "glory" in most of the 200 contexts in which it is found. Associated with the meaning "glory" is the idea of "honor," which is found approximately thirty times.

kābôd refers predominantly to the glory of Yahweh, in a number of contexts. The term is used in a general, non-specific way in Exod. 29:43; Lev. 9:6; Num. 14:2; Ps. 104:31; Isa. 3:8. Most common are the references to the glory of God reflected in the Shekinah glory cloud, revealed at Sinai (cf. Exod. 24:10, 17; Deut. 5:24); in the tabernacle (cf. Exod. 40:34; Num. 14:10; 20:6); and in the Jerusalem temple (cf. 1 Kgs. 8:11; 2 Chr. 7:1ff.; Ps. 26:8). The phenomenon is also associated with the pillar of cloud in the wilderness, mentioned in Isa. 58:8 with reference to Israël's release from captivity, where the glory of the Lord is said to be the rear guard. In Ezek. 10:4, 18, 19; 11:22, 23 the prophet speaks of the glory cloud abandoning the temple in Jerusalem; and in Ezek. 43:2ff.; 44:4 he mentions the same cloud returning — not to the Jerusalem temple, but to the new temple of the prophetic vision which is defined in a profound eschatological sense. Finally, the symbol of the glory cloud over Mt. Zion in Isa. 4:5 represents the eschatological anticipation of the new heavens and earth, which will usher in the eternal age of peace and joy.

Hag. 2:3 refers to the former glory of Solomon's temple in the memory of those who witnessed the dedication of the reconstructed temple of the postexilic period. Then, in Hag. 2:9, the future glory of this postexilic edifice is linked with the coming of the Messiah (cf. also Isa. 40:5; 4:2).

The glory of God is also depicted as filling the earth in Num. 14:21; Ps. 72:19; Isa. 6:3; Hab. 2:14. Associated with this is the theme of God's glory among the nations (cf. 1 Chr. 16:24; Isa. 66:19; Ezek. 39:21); and the declaration of that glory by the heavens (cf. Ps. 19:1).

The glory of God is also incorporated in the theme of judgment in several contexts — in Exod. 16:7 against the Israelites; and in Num. 16:19 against Korah, who rebelled against the authority of Moses. In 1 Sam. 4:21, 22, the glory of God departs from Israel when the ark of the covenant is captured by the Philistines. That predicament gives rise to the name "Ichabod" (i.e., "no glory") for the child born to Phinehas' wife, who dies in childbirth.

Other miscellaneous references to the glory of God include that in Ps. 3:3, where such glory is claimed by the psalmist in worship: "God is my glory . . ." Ps. 24:7ff. refers to Yahweh as the king of glory. The glory of God's name is invoked in Ps. 79:9; Isa. 43:7; Mal. 2:2. Isa. 42:8; 48:11 refer to God's jealous glory, which he refuses to give to anyone else. A vision of the glory of God in divine council is depicted in Ezek. 1:28; 3:23; 8:4; 9:3.

The term "glory" is also used in relation to people; and more commonly means "honor" — for example, of Joseph (cf. Gen. 31:1; 45:13); of Aaron (Exod. 28:2, 40); of royalty (Esth. 1:4); of human beings (Ps. 8:5); and of Jacob (Isa. 17:14). Hos. 4:7 contains the divine promise that Yahweh will change the glory of his people into shame.

tiph'eret [תִּפְאֶרֶת, 8597]

tiph'eret occurs about fifty times with the dominant senses of "glory" and "beauty," as well as associated nuances. The meaning "glory" is found in about half of these contexts, although there is occasional overlap in meaning between "glory" and "beauty." The underlying sense of ***tiph'eret*** is that of "honor" and "majesty" in relation to "glory," and it is used in relation to both God and human beings.

Glory is attributed to human beings in Judg. 4:9; Prov. 20:29; 19:11; and predicated of Israel in Isa. 46:13. The glory of Jerusalem is affirmed in Jer. 33:9; Zech. 12:7, as is the glory of the temple in 1 Chr. 22:5; Isa. 60:7; 64:11. Ezek. 24:25 notes that the glory of the people will be taken from them. The context here is one of judgment, and the reference is to the temple. Ps. 78:61 mentions the glory of God being sent into the hands of the enemy; again the context is one of judgment and ***tiph'eret*** refers to the ark of the covenant.

Glory is attributed to God in general terms in 1 Chr. 29:11; Ps. 71:8; Isa. 60:19; 63:13, 15; Jer. 13:11.

hādār [הָדָר, 1926]

hādār is a noun meaning "glory," "majesty," "honor," as well as associated nuances, throughout its thirty occurrences.

The "glory" or "majesty" of God is indicated in 1 Chr. 16:27; Pss. 29:4; 96:6; 104:1; 111:3; Isa. 2:10, 19ff.; Mic. 2:9.

God is said to bestow "honor" (i.e., a position of the highest privilege in God's created order) on human beings, synonymous with a state of glory in Ps. 8:5. Similarly, Pss. 21:5; 45:3 affirm that God imparts "majesty" (i.e., a glorious status) to his appointed king.

The "glory" of the saints is indicated in Ps. 149:9, denoting their solidarity with God, who is victorious over all their foes.

hôd [הוֹד, 1935]

hôd is a synonym for ***hādār*** (see above), also meaning "glory," "honor," "majesty," as well as related nuances, in the more than twenty occurrences of the term. There is some overlap in meaning between these three senses.

The "glory" or "majesty" of God is noted in 1 Chr. 16:27; 29:11; Job 37:22; Pss. 8:1; 104:1; 111:3; 148:13; Hab. 3:3. ***hôd*** is also used adjectivally in Isa. 30:30 to denote the "majestic" (or "glorious") voice of God. The "majesty" of Solomon is indicated in 1 Chr. 29:25.

God issues a sarcastic challenge to Job in Job 40:10, asking the patriarchal figure to clothe himself with "glory" and splendor.

The "glory" of God's chosen king is noted in Ps. 45:3, as is the royal "majesty" of the one who rebuilds the temple of the Lord. See also Jer. 22:28; Dan. 11:21.

ṣebî [צְבִי, 6643]

ṣebî is a noun found about thirty times meaning "glory," as well as related nuances, in about half of these contexts.

The "glory of Israel" in 2 Sam. 1:19 is depicted as "slain," referring to the death of King Saul in battle.

In a general context, Babylon is described as the "glory" of pagan kingdoms (i.e., the most notable, or powerful) in Isa. 13:19. In Isa. 23:9, Yahweh determines to bring down the "glory" of the nations. See also Ezek. 25:9.

"Glory" is ascribed to God in Isa. 24:16; 28:5.

ṣebî is used adjectivally in Isa. 28:1, 4 to refer to the "glorious" beauty of Israel (Ephraim); and to Canaan as the "most glorious" of all lands in Ezek. 20:6, 15 (cf. also Dan. 11:16, 41, 45).

NT Words

doxa [δόξα, *1391*]

doxa is the dynamic equivalent of ***kābôd*** (see above), denoting "glory" in most of its nearly 170 occurrences in a variety of contexts and with different nuances.

The "glory" of world kingdoms (their wealth, power, and prestige) is indicated in Matt. 4:8; Luke 4:6, in the context of Satan's temptation of Jesus in the wilderness.

The created "glory" of the universe is indicated in 1 Cor. 15:41; 1 Pet. 1:24; and the "glory" of the heavenly realm in 1 Cor. 15:43; Col. 3:4. Heb. 2:7ff. declares that God has crowned human beings with "glory" and honor, and also includes the implicit crowning of Christ with such "glory." "Glory" in the sense of "beauty" is indicated in relation to Solomon in Matt. 6:29; Luke 12:27; and in the sense of a literal radiance in relation to Moses' transfigured face after his meeting with God on Mt. Sinai in 2 Cor. 3:7.

The heavenly "glory" of God is indicated in Matt. 16:27; Mark 8:38; Luke 2:9; 1 Thess. 2:12; 2 Thess. 1:9; as is that of Christ upon his return to earth in Matt. 24:30; Mark 13:26; Luke 9:26; 21:27. Christ's own heavenly "glory" is glimpsed on the Mount of Transfiguration in Luke 9:31ff. Jesus' miracles are also described as a manifestation of his "glory" in John 2:11.

doxa is also used adjectivally to denote the "glorious" throne of God in Matt. 19:28.

General references to "the glory" of God include those in John 11:4; Acts 7:2; Rom. 1:23; 3:23; 1 Cor. 10:31; 2 Cor. 3:18; 4:6; Rev. 21:23. In particular, the expression "glory of God" refers to the "glory cloud" in the heavenly temple (see ***kābôd***, above).

The "glory" of the new covenant is indicated in 2 Cor. 3:10ff.

"Glory" is ascribed to God in Luke 2:14; John 9:24; Rom. 11:36; Eph. 1:12ff.; Phil. 4:20; 1 Tim. 1:17; 1 Pet. 1:7; 2 Pet. 3:18; Jude 25; Rev. 1:6; 4:9ff.; 5:12ff.; 19:1.

Jesus Christ is declared to be the embodiment of divine glory in Luke 2:32; John 1:14; Phil. 2:11; Col. 1:27; Heb. 1:3; 3:3. Such glory was anticipated by the prophet Isaiah (cf. John 12:41). God is said to "give glory" to Christ his Son in 1 Pet. 1:21. "Glory," denoting the privileged state of heavenly intimate relationship with God in Christ, is indicated in John 5:44; Rom. 9:4, 23; 2 Thess. 2:14; 1 Tim. 2:10; 1 Pet. 5:1. In particular, 1 Pet. 5:4 describes the believer's "crown of glory."

Human "glory" in the sense of pride, power, accomplishment, and status is noted in John 7:18; Phil. 3:19; 1 Thess. 2:6 — all with negative connotations.

Jesus' explicit claim for "divine glory" is found in John 17:5, 22. 2 Cor. 4:4 also refers to the "glory" of Christ. New Testament churches are depicted as the "glory of Christ" in 2 Cor. 8:23. Christ is said to receive "glory" from God the Father in 2 Pet. 1:17.

Believers striving for "(heavenly) glory" in their desire to know and serve God forever are noted in Rom. 2:7; 8:18.

A women's hair is said to be her "glory" in 1 Cor. 11:15, denoting her "crowning beauty."

endoxos [ἔνδοξος, *1741*]

endoxos is a rare adjectival form found only four times. Luke 7:25 refers to the "glorious" (i.e., beautiful, gorgeous) clothing worn by the rich. Luke 13:17 refers to "glorious" things done by Christ (i.e., his miracles). Believers are said to be "held in honor" in 1 Cor. 14:10. Eph. 5:27 describes the "glorious" or "splendid" state of the church.

Additional Notes

Among the many references to the glory of God in the Old Testament, a central core of texts anticipate the coming of the Messiah, whose new covenant glory is the supreme embodiment of that which has been revealed in the old. The prime example of this messianic anticipation in association with the phenomena of Yahweh's glory is the glory cloud phenomenon in all its manifestations, particularly in connection with the temple. Associated with this is the theme of the divine glory that expresses judgment against both the people of God and the nations.

See Also: → BOAST → JOY → PRAISE

GNASH, GNASHING

OT Words

ḥāraq [חָרַק, **2786**]

A rare verb, ***ḥāraq*** is found only on five occasions, meaning "gnash" or "grind" (the teeth), conveying deep anguish or despair. Job 16:9; Lam. 2:16; Ps. 35:16 all refer to one's enemies gnashing their teeth at the biblical writer. It is also predicated of the wicked in Pss. 37:12; 112:10.

NT Words

brychō [βρύχω, *1031*]

brychō is a rare verb indicating "gnashing" one's teeth in anger in Acts 7:54.

brygmos [βρυγμός, *1030*]

brygmos is a noun denoting "gnashing" of teeth, all in the context of people expressing anguish in eternal torment (cf. Matt. 8:12; 13:42, 50; 22:13; 24:51; Luke 13:28).

trizō [τρίζω, *5149*]

trizō is a rare verb found only in Mark 9:18, meaning "to grind" one's teeth in the context of a demonic possession.

GO

NT Words

poreuomai [πορεύομαι, *4198*]

poreuomai is a common verb with the mundane sense of "go," as well as some metaphorical usage, for most of its nearly 150 occurrences. The meaning "go," with the underlying sense of "walk," "make a journey (short or long)" is found, for example, in Matt. 2:8ff.; 11:4ff.; Mark 16:12; Luke 1:39; 9:51ff.; John 8:1; Acts 5:20; 19:21; Rom. 15:24ff.; 1 Cor. 10:27; 1 Tim. 1:3. See also 1 Pet. 3:19.

The specific sense of "depart," "go away" (i.e., on an errand, or journey) is found in Matt. 25:41; John 4:50; 8:11; Acts 5:41; 8:36ff. Of special note is Christ's intention to "leave" this world in order to facilitate the permanent coming of the Holy Spirit into the world (cf. John 16:7, 28). See also Acts 1:10ff.; 1 Pet. 3:22.

In particular, see Christ's command to his disciples to "go and make disciples of all nations," in the context of their lifelong mission (Matt. 28:19; Mark 16:15). See also Acts 28:26.

The metaphorical sense of "walk" indicating a lifestyle of "living in obedience to God's commands" is evident in Luke 1:6. See Acts 14:16 for the meaning "to live according to one's own ways." The specifically negative sense of "living" contrary to God's ways is found in 1 Pet. 4:3; 2 Pet. 2:10; 3:3; Jude 16ff.

The exhortation and blessing "go in peace" is found in Luke 8:48; Acts 16:36.

hypagō [ὑπάγω, *5217*]

The verb ***hypagō*** is synonymous with ***poreuomai*** (see above), meaning "go," "get away," as well as related nuances, throughout its nearly eighty occurrences.

Mundane references to "go" in the sense of "go away," "leave" include those in Matt. 5:24; 19:21; Mark 2:11; Luke 19:30; John 7:3. The coming and "going" of the wind is indicated in John 3:8.

Commands to "get away (from)" are found in Jesus' dismissal of Satan in the wilderness in Matt. 4:10; Luke 11:8. See also Matt. 16:23. Matt. 8:32 describes Jesus exorcising a demon-possessed man.

The meaning "go" in the sense of "travel" is indicated in Matt. 5:41; Mark 10:52; John 9:7. See also Rev. 13:10; 16:1. Jesus commands his disciples to "go one's way" when he sends them on their mission in Luke 10:3. The benediction "go in peace" is found in Jas. 2:16.

John 8:14, 21; 13:3, 33; 14:28; 16:5, 10, 17 describe Jesus "going" to his death and then to heaven back to his Father after resurrection. In stark contrast, the satanic beast is said to "go away" to eternal damnation in Rev. 17:8, 11.

Moral confusion is indicated in 1 John 2:11, which speaks of people who walk in darkness and do not know where they "are going."

proagō [προάγω, *4254*]

proagō is a verb found in eighteen places with the primary meaning "go before."

Matt. 2:9 describes the progress of the star from the east "going before" the Magi to the place of Jesus' birth.

Mundane references to the physical spatial movement of "going before" are found in Matt. 14:22; 21:9; 26:32; Mark 6:45; 10:32; 14:28; 16:7.

The temporal sense of "go before" is evident in Matt. 21:31, referring to harlots and tax-collectors who will go into heaven before the hypocritical Pharisees.

Additional Notes

The concept of "go" in English covers a broad range of words in Hebrew. To understand how it is used in Scripture, consult the entries listed below.

See Also: → BRING → COME → DESCEND → ENTER → FINISH → FLEE → FULFILL → JOURNEY → LEAD → LEAVE → OFFER → PASS → SURROUND → WALK

GOAL → MARK

GOAT

OT Words

gedî [גְּדִי, **1423**]

gedî occurs about sixteen times and is consistently translated "kid" or "young goat" (e.g., Gen. 27:9, 16; 38:17ff.). The ritual requirement, "You shall not boil a kid in its mother's milk" is found in Exod. 23:19; 34:26; Deut. 14:21. See also Judg. 6:19; 1 Sam. 10:3; Isa. 11:6.

sā'îr [שָׂעִיר, **8163**]

This term occurs about sixty times and is translated "kid" or "goat" in most of these contexts.

sā'îr is found in a number of contexts referring to a ritual offering (e.g., Lev. 4:23ff.; 10:16; 9:3ff.; Num. 7:16ff.; 2 Chr. 29:13; Ezek. 43:22, 25. In Lev. 16:5ff., ***sā'îr*** refers to the goats for the Day of Atonement ceremony, and to the scapegoat who was to bear the sin of the Israelites by being led out into the wilderness and abandoned there.

There is also reference to the symbolic "goat," representing the king of Greece (i.e., Alexander the Great) in Dan. 8:21.

'attûd [**עַתּוּד, 6260**]

A synonym for ***gedî*** and ***sā'îr***, above, ***'attûd*** also means "goats" in most of the thirty or so contexts in which it is found. Mundane references are found, for example, in Deut. 32:14; Prov. 27:26; Jer. 50:8; Ezek. 27:21. Sacrificial goat offerings are indicated in Num. 7:17ff.; Pss. 50:9, 13; 66:15; Isa. 1:11.

In a metaphorical sense, ***'attûd*** indicates divine judgment through a sacrificial slaughter, that includes goats (cf. Isa. 34:6; Ezek. 39:18), referring to the destruction of Gog, Magog, and the nations. Ezek. 34:17 contains a symbolic reference to "he-goats" as part of God's people.

ṣāphîr [**צָפִיר, 6842**]

A synonym for all of the above terms, ***ṣāphîr*** means "goat" on five occasions. Goat offerings are mentioned in 2 Chr. 29:21; Ezra 8:35. Dan. 8:5, 8, 21 refer to the "he-goat" of Daniel's vision, representing the king of Greece.

tayish [**תַּיִשׁ, 8495**]

Another synonym for the above terms, ***tayish*** means "goat" in four contexts. Three uses are mundane (cf. Gen. 30:35; 32:14; 2 Chr. 17:11); and one is metaphorical (Prov. 30:31).

'ēz [**עֵז, 5795**]

'ēz is a noun denoting a "female goat" in approximately seventy contexts. The term also denotes a male goat in two places.

Non-ceremonial references to "she-goats" include those in Gen. 27:9; Exod. 25:4; Num. 31:20; Deut. 14:4; Judg. 13:15ff.; 1 Sam. 16:20; 1 Kgs. 20:27; Prov. 27:27; Song 6:5.

In the ritual use of ***'ēz***, goats are selected for sacrificial worship of Yahweh (cf. Gen. 15:9). In particular, Mosaic law prescribed selection criteria for goats before they could be sacrificed (cf. Exod. 12:5; Lev. 1:10; 4:23, 28; 23:19; Num. 7:16ff.; 15:24ff.; 29:11ff.). Such ritual offerings are described in Lev. 3:12; 5:6; 9:3; 16:5; 2 Chr. 29:21; 35:7; Ezek. 43:22; 45:23.

'ēz denotes a "male goat" in Dan. 8:5, 8 in the visionary revelation given to Daniel. Here a goat constitutes a symbolic depiction of the kingdom of Greece led by Alexander the Great.

NT WORDS

eriphos [ἔριφος, *2056*]

eriphos is a rare noun found only three times, denoting "goats" in general in Luke 15:29; and a "kid goat" in Matt. 25:32, 33.

tragos [τράγος, *5131*]

tragos is a rare noun found only in Heb. 9:12 referring to the sacrificial blood of "goats."

GOD

OT WORDS

'ēl [**אֵל, 410**]

This is the most general, inclusive name for God. It is also found, for example, in ancient Ugaritic literature of the fourteenth century B.C. to refer to the chief god of the Canaanite pantheon, and it is one of the most ancient titles for deity in the ancient world. The word itself derives from a root term meaning "power," "strength," or "might." It is certainly used this way in the Hebrew Scriptures, especially in combination with other titles (e.g., Gen. 17:1; 28:3; 35:11; Josh. 3:10; 2 Sam. 22:31; Neh. 1:5; Pss. 78:10; 139:17; Isa. 9:16; Ezek. 10:5; Dan. 9:4; Hos. 11:9; Mic. 7:18). ***'ēl*** occurs around 250 times.

'elōhîm [**אֱלֹהִים, 430**]

This is a plural form of ***'ēl*** and occurs approximately 2,600 times. The most common meaning is "God"— of humankind in general, of Israel in particular, and as Creator of the cosmos. In approximately 200 contexts, however, it refers to idol deities, or "gods" (e.g., Exod. 23:24; Deut. 7:14; Josh. 24:20; 1 Kgs. 9:9; Ezra 1:7; Ps. 95:3; Isa. 42:17; Jer. 2:11; Dan. 5:23). In a significant number of these instances, it is Israel's culpable attachment to foreign gods that brings about her downfall as a nation, in relation to both kingdoms of the north and south. It is possible that the very word ***'elōhîm***, plural in form but singular in meaning, conveys the idea of plurality within the Godhead with reference to the God of Israel. God is not only "One" in an absolute sense, but also contains "within himself," so to speak, a plurality of characteristics and personhood.

YHWH [**יהוה, 3068**]

This name is often referred to as the "tetragrammaton," the combination of the four consonants ***YHWH***. Such is Jewish respect for this name of God that the word was never given a vowel pointing, and therefore never pronounced. When this divine name is encountered in the biblical text, a substitute term is read, most commonly *adonai*, meaning "Lord" or "master." As far as English translation is concerned, the name ***YHWH*** was conventionally rendered "Jehovah" or, more recently, "Yahweh," which represents an educated guess as to what the name may have sounded like. In modern translations of the Scriptures, however, this name is rendered "Lord" — most often standing alone, but occasionally in combination with other terms. The name Yahweh, or Lord, occurs over 6,500 times in the Old Testament.

The most significant feature of the name ***YHWH*** is its distinctiveness as the uniquely revealed name of Israel's covenant God. Exod. 3:14ff. records the occasion on which God declared himself to Moses, identifying himself as the great "I AM," who raised up Moses for the purpose of delivering his people from Egyptian slavery. The designation "I am who I am" bears a relationship to the archaic form of the verb "to be, become, happen." And therefore this name of God, the "Lord," signifies God's ever-present, all-pervading power and majesty as the God who rescued his chosen people from captivity and entered into solemn covenant relationship with them at Mt. Sinai during their period of wilderness wandering from Egypt to Canaan. And so this name for God, since it represents a bond of solemn intimacy between Israel and her Maker, is a uniquely distinctive divine name in the Scriptures.

The name ***YHWH*** actually occurs about 180 times throughout the book of Genesis, prior to Exod. 3:14. Exod. 6:3 informs the reader that God has appeared to Abraham and his descendants by the name "God Almighty" (see ***'ēl shadday***, below), but had not made himself known to them as "Lord." The uniqueness of God's revelation to Moses lay not in the mere knowledge or articulation of the name ***YHWH***, but rather in the divinely given insight that ***YHWH*** is the ever-present, all-powerful God, the redeemer of his people, and the one who keeps his solemn promises pledged under the oath of the covenant. Such a revelation had not been imparted to the patriarchal predecessors of Moses — they had only had the promise.

The names that follow are significant names for God that reflect particular aspects or characteristics of his person.

YHWH ṣebā'ôt [יהוה צְבָאוֹת, 6635]

This title, translated "Lord of hosts," occurs around two hundred times, mainly in Isaiah, Jeremiah, and the postexilic prophets. It is found occasionally in the Former Prophets, Chronicles, and Psalms. This phrase combines the divine name with the term "hosts" and may also be translated "Lord almighty."

The name "Lord of hosts" is found in association with the ark of the covenant (cf. 1 Sam. 4:4; 2 Sam. 6:2); as well as the temple (cf. Hag. 1:14; 2:7; Zech. 7:3); and Mt. Zion (cf. Isa. 8:18; 24:23). The "divine warrior" motif is often linked with this title in conjunction with the armies of Israel (cf. 1 Sam. 17:45; Ps. 46:11; Isa. 1:24). The "Lord of hosts" often refers to God in the role of establishing his kingdom on earth (cf. Isa. 9:7; Zech. 8:3; 14:16); and the eschatological renewal of the kingdom of Israel (cf. Mic. 4:4; Zech. 1:17). The title also reflects the judgment and wrath of God (e.g., Isa. 9:19), whether it be directed against the enemies of Israel (e.g., Isa. 10:26; 13:4; 19:12; Nah. 2:13; Zech. 8:2), or against his own people (cf. Jer. 6:6; 8:3; 11:22).

Occasionally the divine name is combined with the title ***'elōhîm*** (see above), to give a compound phrase "Lord God of hosts." The meaning is essentially the same. God is thus described as the divine warrior of Israel (2 Sam. 5:10); as the transcendent God of heaven (cf. Ps. 80:14); as the one who will judge his people for their sin against him (cf. Isa. 10:23; Jer. 35:17; Amos 3:13); and as the one who will punish his enemies (cf. Jer. 46:10; 49:5; 50:31).

The significance of the term "hosts" is debated. Given that these two titles often allude to the judgment of God, and that this judgment involves military assaults, the term "hosts" may refer to the heavenly armies of Yahweh, involving angelic beings. Some contexts, on the other hand, suggest the armies of Israel themselves (cf. 1 Sam. 17:45). The meaning behind the name probably combines these two senses, indicating that Yahweh is the omnipotent sovereign ruler of all human destiny, with a special regard for his own chosen people.

'ēl 'elyôn [אֵל עֶלְיוֹן, 5945]

This title defines God as "God most high," or "most high God." The name ***'elyôn*** derives from the verb ***'ālāh***, "to go up" (→ OFFER), and refers to God as supremely exalted and lofty. For example, Gen. 14:18ff. refers to Melchizedek as priest of God most high (cf. also Dan. 3:6; Num. 24:16; Deut. 32:8; Dan. 5:18, 21).

Occasionally the word "God" is omitted (cf. 2 Sam. 22:14; Dan. 4:17ff.; Pss. 21:7; 78:17, 56; Isa. 14:14; Dan. 7:18ff.).

'ēl shadday [אֵל שַׁדַּי, 7706]

shadday refers to God as "almighty." The derivation of the term ***shadday*** is unknown, but it may be connected to the verb ***shādad*** (→ SPOIL), "devastate," "destroy" — hence the popular translation "almighty" (cf. Gen. 17:11; 35:11; Exod. 6:3; Num. 24:4, 16; Ruth 1:20, 21; Ps. 68:14; Isa. 13:6; Joel 1:15).

ṣûr [צוּר, 6697]

This title, "rock," symbolizes God's utter steadfastness, his unchangeable character and dependability. The following texts refer to God as the rock of salvation, in relation to Israel (e.g., Deut. 32:15, 18; 2 Sam. 22:47; Pss. 89:26; 95:1). God the rock, as a refuge or shelter, is found in Pss. 62:7; 94:22; Isa. 17:10.

qādôsh [קָדוֹשׁ, 6918]

God as the "holy one" (i.e., of Israel) emphasizes that characteristic that sets him apart from all that is tainted with imperfection. It also indicates his "otherness," his unimpeachable, unapproachable purity. Yet the title also suggests, paradoxically, his unique relationship with Israel, his chosen people. He alone is their holy God (cf. 2 Kgs. 19:22; Ps. 89:18; Isa. 5:19; Hab. 3:3). Israel's sin in rebelling against the "holy one" of Israel is cited in Ps. 78:41; Isa. 1:4; 5:24; 30:11; 31:1; 37:23. In Ezek. 39:7 the uniqueness of the "holy one" is made known to his people. See also Jer. 50:29; Isa. 17:7; 60:14; 29:23; 41:14; 54:5.

'ēl gibbôr [אֵל גִּבּוֹר, 1368]

This title, "mighty God," indicates God's power and greatness (cf. Isa. 9:6; 10:21; Jer. 32:18).

ṣaddîq [צַדִּיק, 6662]

This term designates God as "righteous." This is not so much a name as an affirmation of God's pristine purity (cf. Exod. 9:27; 2 Chr. 12:6; Pss. 129:4; 145:17; Lam. 1:18).

melek [מֶלֶךְ, 4428]

melek denotes God as "king." Again, this is not a name but a proclamation of his status as ruler of all creation (e.g., Pss. 24:8, 10; 29:10; 89:18; Isa. 6:5; 43:15; Jer. 10:10; 48:15; Zech. 14:9, 16, 17; Mal. 1:14).

'āb [אָב, 1]

'āb signifies God as "Father." This is a name for God, demonstrating his intimate love and concern for his people (cf. Pss. 68:5; 89:26; Isa. 9:6; Mal. 2:10).

shāphat [שָׁפַט, 8199]

shāphat denotes God as "judge." Here is another description of God, rather than a name as such, which focuses on the guarantee of true justice for his people (cf. Gen. 18:25; Pss. 50:6; 75:7; Isa. 33:22).

gā'al [גָּאַל, 1350]

gā'al signifies God as "redeemer." This name is often associated with the personal pronouns "my," "our," "your" (cf. Ps. 78:35; Isa. 41:14; 43:14; 49:7; 60:16; 63:16; Jer. 50:34).

yāsha' [יָשַׁע, 3467]

yāsha' denotes God as "savior," a name similar to that of "redeemer" (cf. 2 Sam. 22:5; Isa. 43:3; 45:21).

pālat [פָּלַט, 6403]

pālat depicts God as "deliverer" — one who rescues from distress and trouble (cf. 2 Sam. 22:2; Pss. 18:2; 70:5).

māgēn [מָגֵן, 4043]

māgēn signifies God as "shield" — a name that describes God as one who offers supreme protection (cf. Gen. 15:1; Deut. 33:29; 2 Sam. 22:3; Pss. 28:7; 115:9ff.).

'ōz [עֹז, 5797]

'ōz denotes God as "strength." God empowers his people for service and performs mighty deeds of deliverance on their behalf (cf. Exod. 15:2; 2 Sam. 22:23; Pss. 18:2; 46:1; 140:7; Isa. 12:2; Hab. 3:19).

NT Words

theos [θεός, *2316*]

theos is the one Greek term (occurring nearly 1,350 times) that functions as the broad dynamic equivalent for the Hebrew terms ***'elōhîm*** and ***YHWH*** (see above). The former denotes the general expression for God as Creator and omnipotent deity, the latter constitutes the covenant name "Lord," the divine suzerain, initiator of the intimate bond with his people Israel. While ***theos*** is not used with as many different titles as are the Hebrew names for God, ***theos*** does convey a number of significant nuances in a variety of contexts.

The designation "God" as the one true and living deity, without any other qualifying title or attribute, is indicated, for example, in Matt. 1:23; 19:26; Mark 2:7; Luke 1:37; John 1:18; 3:16ff.; Acts 15:4ff.; Rom. 1:18, 25ff.; 8:28; Gal. 3:6; Eph. 4:6; Col. 1:15; 1 Tim. 2:15; Heb. 3:12; Jas. 2:19; 1 Pet. 2:17; 1 John 4:8ff.; Rev. 19:1ff.

Specific references to God the Spirit are found in Matt. 3:16; John 4:24; Rom. 8:9; 15:19; 1 Cor. 2:14; 2 Cor. 3:3; Eph. 4:30; 1 John 4:2.

The full title "the Lord your God" (as well as variations on the pronoun) suggests the link with the Old Testament title of Yahweh the Lord (of the covenant) (e.g., Matt. 4:7; Mark 12:29ff.; Luke 1:32; Acts 3:22; 7:37; Rev. 4:8; 11:17). This perspective is reinforced in reference to the deity as the God of Abraham, Isaac, and Jacob (cf. Acts 3:13; 5:30; 7:32; 22:14).

God is described as one who lives among his people in his "house" (i.e., the temple) in Matt. 12:4; 21:12; Mark 2:26; Luke 6:4. In 2 Cor. 10:16; Eph. 2:22; Heb. 10:21, the "dwelling place of God" refers symbolically to the spiritual community of the people of God. In particular, the heavenly temple of God is noted in Rev. 11:1, 19; 21:3, 22. God as supreme ruler is indicated in the expression "kingdom of God," depicting him as the unparalleled monarch ruling over the dominion of human beings and the hearts of his people (e.g., Matt. 12:28; Mark 1:14ff.; 4:26ff.; Luke 10:9ff.; John 3:3ff.; Acts 8:12; 1 Cor. 4:20; Eph. 5:5; Rev. 12:10). This phenomenon is also evident in relation to Jesus' position of authority at "the right hand of God" in Mark 16:19; Acts 2:33; 7:56; Col. 3:1; Heb. 10:12; 12:2. God's throne designates his infinite power and authority in Rev. 22:3.

The fatherhood of God is affirmed in relation to Jesus Christ, depicted as the "Son of God" in many places (e.g., Matt. 14:33; 27:40ff.; Mark 1:1; 15:39; Luke 1:35; John 3:18; 19:7; Acts 9:20; Rom. 1:4; Gal. 2:20; Heb. 4:14; 1 John 3:8; 5:10ff.). This is emphasized in particular in Jesus' cry from the cross "My God, why have you abandoned me?" (cf. Matt. 27:46; Mark 15:34). Explicit references to God as Father are found in John 8:42; Rom. 1:7; 1 Cor. 1:3; 2 Cor. 1:3; 11:31; Gal. 1:1ff.; Eph. 1:3; Phil. 2:9ff.; Col. 1:3; Titus 1:4; Jas. 1:27; Rev. 2:18. God is also the consummate "lawgiver," the one who reveals his precepts to human beings (cf. Matt. 15:4; Mark 7:8).

The title "most high God" is found in Mark 5:7, emphasizing the unique, supreme status of God as a transcendent, omnipotent deity (cf. also the title ***'ēl 'elyôn***, under OT entry above, for further discussion).

The phrase "the word of God" also confirms that God is the one who communicates with humankind (cf. Mark 7:13; Luke 3:2; Acts 4:31; Heb. 4:12; 13:7; 1 Pet. 1:23; Rev. 1:12). In particular, Christ is described as the incarnation of the Word of God in John 1:1, 12ff.; 10:35. In related contexts, God is said to have spoken by the mouth of his prophets (cf. Acts 3:21). God is described as Creator in Mark 10:6ff.; 13:19; Acts 14:15; 17:24; Heb. 11:3; Rev. 3:14.

God is described as savior in Luke 1:47; Jude 25. God's role as universal judge is indicated in Heb. 12:23; 13:4.

GODLINESS, GODLY

OT Words

ḥāsîd **[חָסִיד, 2623]**

This term occurs four times with reference to those who are "holy," "good," or "godly," who are committed to living their lives in conformity with God's will (cf. Pss. 4:3; 12:1; 32:6; Mal. 2:15). (→ RIGHTEOUS)

NT Words

eusebeia [**εὐσέβεια,** *2150*]

eusebeia is a noun occurring fifteen times with the predominant sense of "godliness," "piety," denoting devotion to God characterized by a life of conformity to his will, or godly living.

This virtue of "piety," "godly living" is indicated in Acts 3:12; 1 Tim. 2:2; 4:7ff.; 6:3ff., 11; Titus 1:1; 2 Pet. 1:3ff.

2 Tim. 3:5 refers to false believers who merely adopt the form of "godliness" but deny its power.

eusebēs [**εὐσεβής,** *2152*]

eusebēs is a rare adjective found in four places with the consistent sense of "devout" or "godly" (cf. Acts 10:2, 7; 22:12; 2 Pet. 2:9).

eusebōs [**εὐσεβῶς,** *2153*]

eusebōs is a rare adverbial form (see above) found only twice, with the sense of "godly," "devout" in 2 Tim. 3:12; Titus 2:12.

GOLD, GOLDEN

OT Words

zāhāb **[זָהָב, 2091]**

zāhāb occurs around four hundred times and means "gold," or "golden," with reference to the precious metal. ***zāhāb*** can indicate monetary wealth or simply color and is used both literally and metaphorically.

The term refers literally to gold as a valuable metal in Gen. 2:11ff.; Josh. 7:21ff. In Exod. 31:4; 2 Chr. 2:7 it refers to workers or craftsmen in fine gold. ***zāhāb*** refers to gold in terms of the personal wealth of Abraham (Gen. 13:2); the Queen of Sheba (1 Kgs. 10:2ff.); and

Solomon (1 Kgs. 10:14ff.). Isa. 2:7 refers to the national wealth of Israel, as does Zech. 14:14.

The offering of gold in the context of worshiping God is recorded in Exod. 25:3; 32:2ff.; Ezra 8; Neh. 7:70ff. In contrast, gold is used in idolatrous worship in 1 Kgs. 12:28; Ps. 135:15; Isa. 2:20; 40:19; 46:6; Jer. 10:4; Hos. 8:4. A divine prohibition against constructing such idols is found in Exod. 20:23.

The use of gold in the construction of the tabernacle, temple, and its furnishings is mentioned in a number of places (cf. Exod. 25:11–31:4; 36:13–40:26; Lev. 8:9; Num. 7; 1 Kgs. 6:7; 2 Chr. 3:4). See also Zech. 4:2, 12; Ezra 1.

zāhāb is also used in several places in a metaphorical sense — for example, the law of the Lord is said to be more valuable than gold (cf. Pss. 19:10; 119:72, 127). Prov. 22:1 declares that favor is better than gold. Babylon is depicted as a symbol of idolatry in Jer. 51:7, likened to a golden cup (cf. also Ezek. 16:17; Hos. 2:8).

dehab [דְּהַב, 1722 (Aramaic)]

dehab is an Aramaic noun denoting the precious metal "gold," throughout its approximately twenty-five occurrences.

The articles of "gold" housed within the Solomonic temple are noted in Ezra 5:14; 6:5; Dan. 5:2ff.

Ezra 7:15ff. refers to "gold" provided by King Artaxerxes for the returning exiles led by Ezra back to the land of Israel. The precious metal (along with silver) was allocated to enable the Judean exiles to rebuild their temple in Jerusalem.

Dan. 2:32ff. mentions the metal statue of King Nebuchadnezzar's dream, composed of various metals including a "head of gold." Similarly, Dan. 3:1ff. describes the "image of gold" constructed by Nebuchadnezzar as a means of coercing a response of devotion and worship from the people of his realm.

Literal references to a chain of "gold" are found in Dan. 5:7, 16, 29. Idols of "gold" are noted in Dan. 5:4, 23.

pāz [פָּז, 6337]

pāz is a noun found nine times, denoting literal "fine, or pure gold" in Job 28:17; Pss. 19:10; 21:3; 119:127; Prov. 8:19; Isa. 13:12; Lam. 4:2. In Song 5:11, 15, ***pāz*** is used metaphorically to describe an element of a man's handsome physique as "gold."

ketem [כֶּתֶם, 3800]

ketem is a synonym for the terms above, denoting "gold" as a precious metal in Job 28:16ff.; 31:24; Ps. 45:9; Prov. 25:12; Isa. 13:12; Lam. 4:1; Dan. 10:5. In Song 5:11, the term is used symbolically to denote a man's hair as "finest gold."

ḥārûṣ [חָרוּץ, 2742]

ḥārûṣ is a passive participial form, found eighteen times with the nominal sense of "gold" in a third of these contexts (cf. Ps. 68:13; Prov. 3:14; 8:10, 19; 16:16; Zech. 9:3).

NT Words

chrysos [χρυσός, *5557*]

chrysos is the dynamic Greek equivalent term for the Hebrew entries listed above, denoting the precious metal "gold" throughout its approximately twenty occurrences (cf. Matt. 2:11; 10:9; 23:16ff.; Acts 3:6; 17:29; 1 Cor. 3:12; 1 Tim. 2:9; Heb. 9:4; Jas. 5:3; 1 Pet. 1:7ff.; Rev. 9:7; 17:4; 18:12ff.; 21:18ff.).

chryseos [χρύσεος, *5552*]

chryseos is the adjectival form derived from ***chrysos***, above, with the consistent meaning "golden," "of gold" throughout the eighteen occurrences of the term.

Literal references are found in 2 Tim. 2:20; Heb. 9:4.

The remaining usage of ***chryseos*** is metaphorical, found exclusively in the book of Revelation. The "golden" lampstand of the heavenly temple scene is noted in Rev. 1:12, 20; 2:1; the "golden" altar in Rev. 8:3; 9:13. The "golden" belt wrapped around the heavenly Christ is indicated in Rev. 1:13, also worn by angels in Rev. 15:6. Crowns of "gold" worn by the elders surrounding the throne of God are depicted in Rev. 4:4 (cf. also Rev. 14:14). "Golden" bowls full of incense, depicting the outpouring of God's wrath, are noted in Rev. 15:7. See also Rev. 17:4; 21:15.

GOOD, GOODNESS

OT Words

ṭôb [טוֹב, 2896]

A somewhat vague term, ***ṭôb*** occurs approximately six hundred times, both in verbal and nouns with the adjectival meanings "good," "pleasing," "prosperous," "favorable," as well as the nominal sense of "goodness" and other associated nuances.

ṭôb indicates "goodness" in the sense of "perfection" or "completeness" in Gen. 1:4ff. as God's assessment of his creative endeavors. Other examples of this sense are found in Pss. 136:1; 145:9, which point to the goodness of God. Neh. 9:13 refers to the "good statutes" of God given at Sinai. See also Ps. 119:39.

"Good" in the sense of high quality is indicated, for example, in reference to gold in the land of Eden (Gen. 2:12); cattle (Gen. 18:7); trees (2 Kgs. 3:25); figs (Jer. 24:2); the intelligence of Abigail (1 Sam. 25:3). The fertility of Canaan is also described this way (e.g., Exod. 3:8; Num. 14:7; Josh. 23:13ff.; 1 Kgs. 14:13).

The sense of "goodness" as a moral or spiritual virtue is found in Gen. 2:17; 3:5 in reference to the "tree of the knowledge of good and evil." Several texts emphasize that which is "good" in accordance with the covenant law of Yahweh, mediated through Moses (e.g., Neh. 6:19; Ps. 52:3; Amos 5:14; Mic. 6:8). Indictments against those who fail to do good are recorded in Pss. 14:1, 3; 53:1, 3; Eccl. 7:20.

tôb also refers to physical beauty, indicating those who are "fair," or "beautiful" — for example, a young woman (Gen. 24:16); Moses (Exod. 2:2); Saul (1 Sam. 9:2); Bathsheba (2 Sam. 11:2); and Queen Esther (Esth. 1:11).

Material blessing from God is also described as that which is "good" (cf. Gen. 50:20; 1 Sam. 24:19; Ps. 107:9). This is especially the case where covenant blessings concerning the land of Canaan are in view (e.g., Num. 10:29; Deut. 30:15; Josh. 21:45; 2 Sam. 7:28; Jer. 24:6; 33:9ff.).

Other miscellaneous uses of ***tôb*** indicating that which is "good" include the blessing of God in a general sense (e.g., Pss. 23:6; 118; Jer. 21:10; Amos 9:4); kindness (cf. 2 Sam. 3:13); God's protection (cf. Ezra 7:9; 8:18; Neh. 2:8); that which is pleasing to the Lord (cf. 1 Kgs. 14:13); and that which brings comfort (cf. 2 Kgs. 20:19).

yāṭab [יָטַב, 3190]

This verb means "to do, go well," "do good," "please." ***yāṭab*** occurs around one hundred times.

"Doing well," that is, acting in accordance with God's character, is mentioned in Gen. 4:7 in relation to the warning God gives to Cain after the murder of his brother Abel. "Doing good" in a general sense is referred to in Lev. 5:4; Ps. 36:3; Jer. 10:5. The action of "pleasing" is indicated in Gen. 45:16; Josh. 22:30; as is treating someone kindly in Gen. 12:16; Ruth 3:10. "Doing good," or "blessing," is also predicated of God in Gen. 32:12; Deut. 8:16; Josh. 24:20; Judg. 17:3.

ṭûb [טוּב, 2898]

ṭûb is a variant noun from ***tôb*** (see above), found over thirty times with the nominal sense of "goodness," as well as the adjectival sense of "good" throughout most of the usage.

The general sense of "good things" in relation to "material prosperity" is indicated in Gen. 45:23; Deut. 6:11; Ezra 9:12; Neh. 9:25; Job 21:16; Isa. 1:19.

Exod. 33:19; Ps. 25:7 refer to the "goodness" of God in relation to his nature. Elsewhere, the "goodness" of God refers explicitly to the blessings he bestows on his people — the material blessings promised under the old covenant (cf. Neh. 9:25; Pss. 27:13; 128:5; Isa. 63:7; Jer. 2:7; 31:12ff.; Hos. 3:5). The psalmist requests "good" judgment from God in Ps. 119:66.

NT Words

agathos [ἀγαθός, *18*]

agathos is an adjectival form that constitutes a general dynamic equivalent for ***tôb*** (see above). The dominant meaning is "good" in a broad sense, used both adjectivally and nominally with a variety of nuances throughout its nearly one hundred occurrences.

The nominal meaning "good" in the sense of "that which is morally upright," including people, is indicated in Matt. 5:45; 12:35; John 5:29; Rom. 2:10; 7:13, 18; 9:11; Eph. 6:8. Elsewhere, "good" denotes "ultimate spiritual benefit" in Rom. 8:28; 2 Cor. 5:10; Heb. 9:11; 10:1; and also "well-being" in relation to people in Rom. 15:2; 1 Thess. 5:15. The adjectival sense of "good," denoting that which is "of high quality" is found in Matt. 7:11; Luke 1:53; 11:13; John 1:46; Gal. 6:6; Jas. 1:17. Such an attribute is predicated of the divine commandment in Rom. 7:12.

Elsewhere, "good" indicates the sense of "healthy" in relation to non-personal phenomena — to a tree (Matt. 7:18); soil (Luke 8:8); and conscience (1 Tim. 1:5).

The adjectival sense of "virtuous" in relation to both deeds and people is indicated in Matt. 19:17; 25:21ff.; Luke 6:45; John 7:12; Acts 9:36; Rom. 5:7; 2 Cor. 9:8; Eph. 2:10; Titus 1:16. In particular, Christ is said to be "good" in Mark 10:17ff.; Luke 18:18, as is God in Mark 10:17ff.; Luke 18:19.

agathōsynē [ἀγαθωσύνη, *19*]

agathōsynē is a rare noun found four times, indicating the virtue of "goodness" in the sense of "(moral) uprightness of heart" in Rom. 15:14; Gal. 5:22; Eph. 5:9. See also 2 Thess. 1:11.

agathopoieō [ἀγαθοποιέω, *15*]

agathopoieō is a verb found eleven times, meaning "to do good" throughout. There are a couple of nuances to note.

"Doing good" in the sense of performing an act of kindness for someone is indicated in Mark 3:4; Luke 6:9, 33ff.

"Doing good" is also predicated of God in the sense of "bestowing material blessing" on his people in Acts 14:17.

agathopoieō also means "doing good" in the sense of "living righteous lives" in accordance with God's precepts in 1 Pet. 2:15ff.; 3:6, 17; 3 John 11.

agathoergeō [ἀγαθοεργέω, *14*]

agathoergeō is a rare variant of ***agathopoieō***, above, meaning "do good" in the general sense of "acting uprightly," found only in 1 Tim. 6:18.

kalos [καλός, *2570*]

kalos is an adjective found over one hundred times with the general meaning "good," as well as a variety of nuances.

The sense of "excellent," "choice," "of high quality" is indicated in Matt. 3:10; 13:24ff.; Luke 3:9; John 2:10; 1 Tim. 4:4; 2 Tim. 2:3.

kalos denotes that which is "morally upright," primarily in relation to "good works" (cf. Matt. 5:16; Mark 7:27; John 10:32ff.; Rom. 14:21; 1 Thess. 5:21; 1 Tim. 5:4, 25; Titus 3:8; Heb. 10:24). The description "good" is applied to the law of God in this sense in Rom. 7:16ff.; 1 Tim. 1:8.

"Fertile" soil is indicated in Matt. 13:23; Mark 4:8; Luke 8:15.

kalos is also used adverbially in the sense of "well"; "better" in Matt. 17:4; 18:8ff.; Mark 9:42ff.; 1 Cor. 5:6; 1 Tim. 3:13.

"Good" in the sense of "beautiful," "admirable" is evident in Matt. 26:10; Mark 14:6; 1 Tim. 3:1.

Christ is referred to as the "good" shepherd in John 10:11ff., indicating his tender care for and love of his people.

kalos is used nominally in Heb. 5:14; Jas. 4:17 to denote "good" in contrast with "evil" in a moral sense.

Heb. 13:18 refers to a "good" conscience (in the sense of "clear").

kalōs [καλῶς, *2573*]

kalōs is the adverbial form of ***kalos***, above, meaning "well" or "good" throughout most of its nearly forty occurrences.

The action of "doing good or well" in the sense of that which is "noble," "intrinsically valuable," is noted in Mark 7:37; Luke 6:27; 1 Cor. 7:37ff.; Heb. 13:18; 2 Pet. 1:19.

kalōs means "well" in the sense of "accurately" in Matt. 15:7; Mark 7:6; John 4:17; Acts 28:25.

kalōs means "well" in the sense of "skillfully" in Mark 12:28. See also Gal. 5:7; 1 Tim. 3:4. Speaking "well" of someone in the sense of commending them is indicated in Luke 6:26.

eu [εὖ, *2095*]

eu is an adverbial form occurring six times meaning "well" or "good" throughout. In most of these contexts ***eu*** denotes the commendation "Well done!" (cf. Matt. 25:21ff.; Luke 19:17). Mark 14:7; Acts 15:29 both indicate "doing good" in the sense of doing what is morally upright. The meaning "well" in the sense of "prosperous" is noted in Eph. 6:3.

eupoiia [εὐποιΐα, *2140*]

eupoiia is a rare noun found only in Heb. 13:16, denoting the action of "doing good" in the sense of acting generously, kindly toward others.

aretē [ἀρετή, *703*]

aretē is a noun found five times denoting "virtue," "good(ness)" in Phil. 4:8; 2 Pet. 1:3ff.

See Also: → KINDNESS

GOODS

OT Words

rekûsh [רְכוּשׁ, 7399]

This term occurs around thirty times with the primary sense of "property" in the sense of "goods and possessions."

rekûsh means "possessions" in a mundane, literal sense in Gen. 12:5; 13:6; 14:11ff.; Num. 16:32; 1 Chr. 28:1; Ezra 1:4. ***rekûsh*** can also indicate an abundance of possessions in the sense of great wealth (e.g., Gen. 15:14; 2 Chr. 20:5; Dan. 11:13).

ḥayil [חַיִל, 2428]

ḥayil is a noun found about 250 times with the primary meanings "army," "host," "strength," as well as a number of related nuances. One of these is "wealth" or "riches," overlapping with the sense of "goods" in a number of places. (→ RICH)

nekas **[נְכַס, 5232]**

nekas is a rare Aramaic noun denoting "goods," "property" in Ezra 7:26.

qinyān **[קִנְיָן, 7075]**

qinyān is a noun found ten times meaning "goods," "property" in Gen. 36:6; Josh. 14:4; Ps. 105:21; Ezek. 38:12ff.

NT Words

hyparxis [ὕπαρξις, *5223*]

hyparxis is a rare noun denoting "goods," "property," in Acts 2:45.

bios [βίος, *979*]

bios is a noun found eleven times with the primary meaning "life" or "living." In 1 John 3:17, however, it denotes "goods" in the sense of "possessions."

skeuos [σκεῦος, *4632*]

skeuos is a noun denoting a "vessel," "container" for most of the twenty or so occurrences of the term. However, in Mat. 12:29; Mark 3:27; Luke 17:31 it refers to a person's "goods" or "possessions."

hyparchonta [ὑπάρχοντα, *5224*]

hyparchonta is the most common New Testament noun denoting "goods," "property," "possessions." It occurs fourteen times (cf. Matt. 19:21; 24:47; Luke 11:21; 12:15, 44; 16:1; 19:8; Acts 4:32; 1 Cor. 13:3; Heb. 10:34).

ousia [οὐσία, *3776*]

ousia is a rare term denoting "goods," "property" in Luke 15:12, 13.

GOSPEL, GOOD NEWS

OT Words

besôrāh **[בְּשׂוֹרָה, 1309]**

A rare noun, ***besôrāh*** occurs six times and means "tidings," "news." With the sense of "information," it is found in 2 Sam. 4:10; 18:20ff. "Good news" is indicated in 2 Kgs. 7:9 with the report of the lifting of the siege of Samaria from the Arameans.

bāsar **[בָּשַׂר, 1319]**

bāsar occurs around twenty-five times meaning "bear, bring news," "preach, proclaim good news."

In 1 Sam. 4:17 ***bāsar*** refers to bringing bad news, with the report of the tragic deaths of Hophni and Phinehas, sons of Eli, and the capture of the ark of the covenant by the Philistines. By contrast, good news is reported in 1 Sam. 31:9 (the death of Goliath); 2 Sam. 18:19 (the death of Absalom — at least from Israel's perspective, if not from David's). See also 2 Sam. 4:10; 1 Kgs. 1:42.

The "preaching" of salvation is mentioned in Pss. 40:9; 96:2; Isa. 40:9; 41:27; 52:7; 61:1; Nah. 1:15. And, in a related sense, Ps. 68:11 proclaims news of God's deliverance of his people through victory over his enemies.

NT Words

euangelion [εὐαγγέλιον, *2098*]

euangelion is the distinctive New Testament Greek term for the "gospel," the good news of the consummation of God's plan of salvation, forgiveness for sin and promise of eternal life and peace with God gained through the sacrifice of Jesus Christ. The term occurs nearly eighty times and is used with several distinctive nuances.

The "gospel" of the kingdom (of God), emphasizing the omnipotent rule or control of God over his people, is noted in Matt. 4:23; 24:14; Mark 1:14.

The message of the "gospel" in an unqualified sense is described in Matt. 26:13; Mark 8:35; 16:15; Acts 15:7; Rom. 10:16; 1 Cor. 4:15; 15:1; Gal. 1:11; Eph. 1:13; Phil. 1:5ff.; Col. 1:5; Rev. 14:6.

References to the "gospel of (Jesus) Christ" are found in Mark 1:1; Rom. 1:16; 15:19; 1 Cor. 9:12; 2 Cor. 2:12; Gal. 1:7; 1 Thess. 3:2; 2 Thess. 2:14. Acts 20:24 mentions the "gospel of the grace of God," emphasizing the merciful expression of divine compassion in effecting the salvation of his people.

General references to the "gospel of God" are found in Rom. 1:1; 15:16; 2 Cor. 11:7; 1 Thess. 2:2; 1 Pet. 4:17; to the "gospel of his (i.e., God's) Son" in Rom. 1:9; and to the "gospel of peace" in Eph. 6:15. In a negative context, Paul condemns Jewish false teachers who are proclaiming a "false gospel" and deceiving many (cf. Gal. 1:6).

The phrase "mystery of the gospel" in Eph. 6:19 refers to the hidden nature of God's plan of salvation prior to the revelation of Jesus Christ, now proclaimed by the apostle Paul.

euangelizō [εὐαγγελίζω, *2097*]

euangelizō is the verb corresponding to ***euangelion***, above, found nearly sixty times with the primary meaning "preach the gospel" throughout most of the usage (approximately fifty occurrences) — for example, Matt. 11:5; Luke 4:18; 8:1; Acts 8:25; 14:21; 2 Cor. 11:7; Gal. 1:11; 4:13; Heb. 4:2, 6; 1 Pet. 1:12; 4:6; Rev. 14:6. Then Gal. 1:8ff. refers to the "proclamation" of a false gospel.

euangelizō is also translated to "bring, preach good news" (cf. 1 Thess. 3:6).

In many of these contexts, however, the sense of "gospel" is implied (cf. Luke 1:19; 2:10; 16:16; Acts 8:12; Rom. 1:15; 1 Cor. 1:17; 9:16ff.; 15:1ff.).

In addition, ***euangelizō*** is also simply translated "to preach." In Acts 5:42; 8:35; 17:18, Jesus is the direct object of the verb.

"Preaching the word" is indicated in Acts 8:4; 15:35. "Preaching" Christ is noted in Eph. 3:8. See also Gal. 1:23; Eph. 2:17.

Additional Notes

The consistency of meaning and usage between the Hebrew terms ***bāsar*** and ***besōrāh*** and the Greek ***euangelion*** and ***euangelizō*** is noteworthy. In the New Testament, of course, the proclamation of gospel tidings centers on the finished work and person of Jesus Christ, who consummates God's plan of redemption for his people. However, in the Old Testament that same emphasis on the divine plan of redemption is also observable in the proclamation of news in Psalms and the Prophets, especially Isaiah. God's plan of salvation for Israel clearly revolves around deliverance from their earthly enemies. Such deliverance on an earthly, physical scale constitutes the typological anticipation of a redemption, a deliverance, that totally transcends the physical, human realm. The proclamation of God's deliverance in the old covenant age looks forward to the eternal, irreversible salvation from the power of sin and death won by Christ through his death and subsequent resurrection and ascension.

GOVERNMENT

OT Words

misrāh [מִשְׂרָה, 4951]

misrāh is a rare noun denoting the "government," "rule," or "dominion" promised by Yahweh to the messianic child born to the virgin woman in Isa. 7:6. That child was named Maher-Shalal-Hash-Baz, and he foreshadowed the Christ child (cf. Isa. 9:6, 7).

See Also: → GOVERNOR → DOMINION

GOVERNOR

NT Words

hēgemōn [ἡγεμών, *2232*]

hēgemōn is a noun found around twenty times with the predominant meaning "governor." General references to "governors" as civil rulers are found in Matt. 10:18; Mark 13:9; 1 Pet. 2:14. Specifically, Matt. 27:2ff. mentions the Roman governor Pontius Pilate, and Acts 23:24ff. refers to Felix, another Roman governor.

hēgemoneuō [ἡγεμονεύω, *2230*]

hēgemoneuō is a rare verb meaning "to be governor," found only in Luke 2:2; 3:1.

ethnarchēs [ἐθνάρχης, *1481*]

ethnarchēs is a rare synonym for ***hēgemōn***, above, denoting the "governor" of Damascus in 2 Cor. 11:32.

See Also: → RULE

GRACE, GRACIOUS

OT Words

ḥēn [חֵן, 2580]

This noun occurs approximately seventy times with the predominant meanings "grace," "favor," and when predicated of Yahweh it indicates the free and unconditional granting of his blessing.

In relation to "grace" or "favor" emanating from God, ***ḥēn*** frequently occurs in the expression "to find favor with God, or in his sight." Such favor is extended for instance, to Noah (Gen. 6:8); Joseph (Gen. 39:21); Moses (Exod. 33:12); and the people of God in the wilderness (Jer. 31:2). Zech. 4:7 records God's shout of "Bless it!" (lit: "Grace to it!"), directed at the capstone on the occasions of the completion of the postexilic temple as witnessed during the vision of the prophet Zechariah. Zech. 12:10 contains a messianic prophecy, a promise that God will pour out a spirit of grace and supplication on the descendants of David, who will look mournfully on the one they have pierced.

When the same expression is applied to people by others, on the human level, it has the force of "to please someone," or "make a favorable impression on them" (e.g., Gen. 18:3; 39:4; Exod. 11:3; Ruth. 2:10; Esth. 2:15). It is used negatively in Deut. 24:1 to refer to a wife who is not approved by her husband.

Other general usage of ***ḥēn*** is found in Prov. 13:15; 22:1; 22:11; Eccl. 9:11.

ḥānan [חָנַן, **2603**]

ḥānan is a verb found nearly eighty times meaning "to be gracious," "show mercy, favor."

In general contexts, God is said to "be gracious," or "deal graciously with" people in Gen. 33:11; Exod. 33:19; 2 Kgs. 13:23. Pleas for God to "be gracious or merciful" are noted, for example, in Pss. 4:1; 6:2; 26:11; 51:1; 86:16; 123:3; Isa. 32:2.

The injunction "God be gracious to . . ." is evident in Gen. 43:29; Num. 6:25.

Deut. 7:2 refers to God refusing to "show mercy" to the enemies of his people; and also to the Israelites in Isa. 27:11. Amos 5:11 records the hope that God may "show mercy" to the northern kingdom of Israel. See also Mal. 1:9.

General references to people "being gracious," "showing favor" to others are found in Deut. 28:50; Ps. 112:5; Prov. 19:17.

NT Words

charis [χάρις, *5485*]

charis is the dynamic Greek equivalent for the Hebrew term ***ḥēn***, above, found about 150 times. ***charis*** denotes "favor," "grace," as well as a variety of related nuances, throughout the usage. The large majority of occurrences indicate "grace" originating from God. This "grace" denotes the limitless kindness and mercy of God that is freely given to human beings undeserved.

The blessing of finding "favor" with God is noted in Luke 1:30; Acts 7:46. Jesus is explicitly said to have found "favor" with both God and human beings in Luke 2:52.

Specific references to the "grace of God" granted to human beings include those in Luke 2:40; John 1:16; Acts 4:33; 11:23; Rom. 1:5; 2 Cor. 6:1; Jude 4. In particular, God's "grace" is indicated as the specific catalyst initiating a person's salvation in Rom. 3:24; 4:16; 5:15ff.; 11:5; Gal. 5:4; Eph. 1:7; 2:5ff.; Titus 2:11; 3:7.

Reference to Christ as the incarnate Word of God, "full of grace and truth," indicates that his being was full of divine goodness and favor intended for the blessing of God's people (John 1:14, 17; 1 Pet. 1:13). Divine "grace" is also predicated of Jesus Christ in Acts 15:11; Gal. 1:6; 2 Tim. 2:1.

The "grace of God" is noted as part of a benediction in Rom. 1:7; 1 Cor. 1:3; 2 Cor. 8:9; Gal. 1:3; Eph. 1:2; Phil. 1:2; Col. 1:2; 1 Thess. 1:1; 1 Tim. 1:2; Heb. 13:25; 1 Pet. 1:2; Rev. 1:4; 22:21.

"Grace" in the sense of "divine enabling, or gift" is indicated in Rom. 12:3ff.; 1 Cor. 3:10; Eph. 4:7; Heb. 2:9; 1 Pet. 4:10. "Favor" in the sense of "goodwill" among people is indicated in Acts 2:47; 7:10. "Favor" in the sense of an "act of kindness" is indicated in Acts 25:3; 2 Cor. 8.

See Also: → MERCY

GRAIN

OT Words

shibbōlet [שִׁבֹּלֶת, **7641**]

shibbōlet occurs sixteen times meaning "ears of corn, grain" in most cases.

The term occurs literally in Gen. 41:5ff. in the context of the dreams of Joseph (cf. also Ruth 2:2). ***shibbōlet*** is used metaphorically in Job 24:24; Isa. 17:5.

qāmāh [קָמָה, **7054**]

qāmāh is also rare, occurring eight times and meaning "standing corn, grain." Literal references are found in Exod. 22:6; Deut. 16:9; Judg. 15:5; Isa. 37:27. ***qāmāh*** is used metaphorically in Isa. 17:5; Hos. 8:7 — both in contexts of judgment against Israel, where harvesting of grain symbolizes punishment.

dāgān [דָּגָן, **1715**]

This noun is used more frequently than ***shibbōlet*** and ***qāmāh*** (see above), occurring about forty times and meaning "corn," "grain."

Abundance of corn, or grain, is cited as a blessing from God in Gen. 27:28; Deut. 7:13; Ps. 65:9. Jer. 31:12 promises renewed blessing, involving the divine provision of grain in the land (cf. also Ezek. 36:29). Hos. 2:8, 9 mentions God providing Israel with grain and then withdrawing it because of her idolatry.

Deprivation of grain often comes under the category of covenant curse (cf. Deut. 28:51; Joel 1:10, 17 — an aspect of the Day of the Lord judgment). In Hag. 1:11, grain is withheld from the postexilic community as a consequence of their failure to rebuild the temple immediately upon their return from exile.

Grain is also mentioned as part of the priestly food allowance decreed under the Mosaic law (cf. Num. 18:12; Deut. 18:4); and is prescribed as a ritual offering or tithe (cf. Deut. 12:17; 14:23).

In several texts, Canaan is referred to as a "land of grain and wine" (cf. Deut. 33:28; Isa. 36:17).

ḥiṭṭāh [חִטָּה, **2406**]

ḥiṭṭāh occurs thirty times and means "wheat."

The wheat harvest is mentioned in Gen. 30:14; Exod. 34:22; Ruth 2:23; Joel 1:11. The reference in Joel indicates the loss of a harvest due to divine judgment. Wheat crops are indicated in general terms elsewhere (e.g., Exod. 9:32; Deut. 8:8; 2 Sam. 4:6; Jer. 12:13; Ps. 81:16; Song 7:2; Ezek. 4:9).

NT Words

kokkos [κόκκος, *2848*]

kokkos is a noun denoting "grain" in all seven occurrences of the term. It refers to a "grain" of mustard seed in Matt. 13:31; 17:20; Mark 4:31; Luke 13:19; 17:6. John 12:24 refers to a "kernel" of corn, and 1 Cor. 15:37 to a "grain" of an indeterminate kind.

GRANT ➡ GIVE

GRAPE

OT Words

'ēnāb **[עֵנָב, 6025]**

'ēnāb is a noun occurring around twenty times with the principal meaning "grape(s)." References to the literal fruit are found in Gen. 40:10ff.; Lev. 25:5; Num. 6:13; Deut. 23:24; Isa. 5:2ff.; Jer. 8:13; Amos 9:13. Metaphorically, ***'ēnāb*** refers to Israel in Hos. 9:10, where the people of God are likened to "grapes" in the wilderness as discovered by Yahweh.

'eshkôl **[אֶשְׁכּוֹל, 811]**

This term occurs only ten times, meaning "cluster" in reference to various kinds of fruit. "Grapes" are indicated in about half of these contexts. Literal fruit is indicated in Gen. 40:10; and in Num. 13:23 the first harvesting of the promised land is described when the spies pick a huge cluster of grapes as evidence of the land's fertility. In Deut. 32:32; Isa. 65:8, ***'eshkôl*** is used metaphorically to refer to Israel's sinful lifestyle.

bōsēr **[בֹּסֶר, 1155]**

This rare noun is found four times and refers to "unripe, or sour grapes" (cf. Isa. 18:5). Jer. 31:29, 30; Ezek. 18:2 refer to the ancient proverb about sour grapes setting one's teeth on edge.

semādar **[סְמָדַר, 5563]**

semādar is another rare noun, found several times only in the Song of Songs, referring to a "tender grape" or "grape blossom" (cf. Song 2:13, 15; 7:12).

NT Words

staphylē [σταφυλή, *4718*]

staphylē is a rare noun found only three times, denoting "grapes" in each context (cf. Matt. 7:16; Luke 6:44; Rev. 14:18).

GRASS

OT Words

'ēseb **[עֵשֶׂב, 6212]**

'ēseb means "herb," "grass," and is found about thirty times. The latter meaning is indicated in about half of these instances.

Grass in general is referred to in Deut. 29:23; 2 Kgs. 19:26; Ps. 72:16; Amos 7:2. In Amos, ***'ēseb*** describes a vision of a locust plague consuming the grass of the land of Israel. ***'ēseb*** refers to food for cattle in Deut. 11:15; Ps. 104:14. ***'ēseb*** is also used metaphorically in Pss. 92:7; 102:4, 11; Isa. 37:7, where the wicked are said both to sprout and wither "like grass."

ḥāṣîr **[חָצִיר, 2682]**

Synonymous with ***'ēseb***, above, ***ḥāṣîr*** is translated "grass" in most contexts.

Mundane usage is found in 2 Kgs. 19:26; Ps. 147:8. ***ḥāṣîr*** means "grass" as food for cattle and horses in 1 Kgs. 18:5; Ps. 104:4. Metaphorical uses of ***ḥāṣîr*** are found in Pss. 37:2; 90:5; Isa. 37:27; 40:6ff.; 51:12. Isa. 35:7 describes the land of Israel in an eschatological vision of renewal, in which "grass" — one of the symbols of renewal — is replenished in the land.

deshe' **[דֶּשֶׁא, 1877]**

This term is also synonymous with ***'ēseb*** and ***ḥāṣîr***. ***deshe'*** occurs fifteen times and means "grass" on half of these occasions. The usage is entirely literal.

"Grass" in general is indicated in Gen. 1:11, 12; Deut. 32:2; 2 Sam. 23:4; and is designated as "food" for animals in Job 6:5; Prov. 27:25; Isa. 15:6; Jer. 14:5.

yereq **[יֶרֶק, 3418]**

yereq is a noun denoting "(green) vegetation" in five of the six occurrences of the term. Num. 22:4 explicitly refers to "the grass of the field."

dete' **[דְּתֵא, 1883** (Aramaic)**]**

dete' is a rare Aramaic term denoting "grass" in a general sense, found only in Dan. 4:13, 15.

NT Words

chortos [χόρτος, *5528*]

chortos is a noun denoting "grass" throughout most of its fifteen occurrences (cf. Matt. 6:30; 14:19; Mark 6:39; Luke 12:28; John 6:10; Jas. 1:10ff.; 1 Pet. 1:24; Rev. 8:7; 9:4).

GRAVE

OT Words

qeber [קֶבֶר, 6913]

qeber occurs around seventy times and is translated "grave," or "tomb," in most contexts.

With regard to tombs, ***qeber*** refers firstly to the resting places of the patriarchs (e.g., Gen. 23:4ff.; 49:30; 50:5, 13); then the kings (e.g., 2 Chr. 21:20; 24:25); and also to the tombs of the fathers (e.g., 2 Chr. 35:24; Neh. 2:3, 5). See also Judg. 16:31; 1 Kgs. 13:22.

qeber also refers to burial sites, commonly translated "grave" (e.g., Exod. 14:11; 2 Sam. 19:37; Ps. 88:5, 11; Isa. 53:9; Jer. 26:23; Ezek. 32:22).

Various metaphorical senses are also evident in the use of this term. For example, 1 Kgs. 14:13 speaks of death, through the symbol of the "grave"; Ps. 5:9 speaks of moral perversity, designating the throats of the wicked as an "open tomb." In a significant use of the term in Ezek. 37:12, the prophecy of the resurrection of the Judean population to "new life" is symbolized by their anticipated release from Babylonian captivity — that is, from their "grave."

she'ôl [שְׁאוֹל, 7585]

This term is transliterated directly into English as "Sheol," but its primary meaning is "grave," depicting the abode of the dead in the Old Testament. The term is primarily used euphemistically for the experience of death and dying and occurs around seventy times.

The translation "grave" in the sense of the experience of death is found in a number of places (e.g., Gen. 37:35; 2 Sam. 22:6; 1 Kgs. 2:6; Pss. 18:5; 139:8). Num. 16:30, 33 records the execution of Korah and his associates, who rebelled against Moses' authority. Hence, their "going down to Sheol" was a terrifying divine judgment against them. Other instances of divine judgment in which this phrase occurs include Pss. 9:17; 31:17; Ezek. 31:16; Amos 9:2. See also Prov. 5:5; 7:27; 9:18; Isa. 28:15.

By way of positive contrast, a number of texts contain a "reversal" of the burial theme — people being brought up from Sheol (cf. Pss. 30:3; 49:15; 86:13). In Hos. 13:14 God promises to redeem Israel from the grave.

qebûrāh [קְבוּרָה, 6900]

qebûrāh is a rare noun, occurring only fourteen times and meaning "grave" or "tomb" in most instances (cf. Gen. 35:20; Deut. 34:6; 2 Kgs. 9:28; 23:30; Ezek. 32:24). The sense of "burial" is found in Eccl. 6:3; Isa. 14:20; Jer. 22:19.

NT Words

mnēmeion [μνημεῖον, *3419*]

mnēmeion is a noun denoting a "grave" or "tomb" throughout its nearly forty occurrences. All the references are literal (e.g., Matt. 8:28; 27:52ff.; 28:8; Mark 5:2ff.; 16:2ff.; Luke 11:44ff.; 24:2ff.; John 11:17, 31, 38; 19:41ff.; 20:1ff.; Acts 13:29).

mnēma [μνῆμα, *3418*]

mnēma is a variant form of ***mnēmeion***, above, denoting a "grave" or "tomb" in each of its seven occurrences (cf. Mark 5:5; Luke 8:27; 23:53; 24:1; Acts 2:29; 7:16; Rev. 11:9).

taphos [τάφος, *5028*]

taphos is a synonym for ***mnēmeion*** and ***mnēma***, above. It is found in seven places, denoting "tombs," "graves" throughout (cf. Matt. 23:27ff.; 27:61ff.; 28:1). In Rom. 3:13, ***taphos*** is used symbolically to denote the mouth of the ungodly as an "open grave" that produced poisonous, libelous speech.

GREAT, GREATNESS

OT Words

gādôl [גָּדוֹל, 1419]

A common adjective that also has nominal force, ***gādôl*** occurs around five hundred times with the predominant meaning "great." Though translated "great" in the majority of instances, a variety of nuances underlie that meaning — greatness of magnitude, number, intensity, and status.

When predicated of natural phenomena and living things including human beings, the four nuances of "great (ness)," listed above, come into play.

With regard to greatness of intensity, ***gādôl*** is used in a variety of contexts, such as in the realm of natural phenomena. For example, greatness is imputed to lights in the sky (Gen. 1:16); darkness (Gen. 15:12); strength (Judg. 16:5); and storms (Jonah 1:10, 12). The term also refers to the intensity of slaughter in military conflict (cf. Josh. 10:10; Judg. 11:33; 1 Sam. 4:10). In the realm of emotions, ***gādôl*** describes the intensity of, for example, pain and punishment (Gen. 4:13); anguish (Gen. 27:34; Exod. 11:6); mourning (Gen. 50:10); and rejoicing (Neh. 8:17; Ezek. 9:9). Terrible sin is also thus described — for example, idolatry (Exod. 32:21, in the golden calf incident; Ezek. 8:6); moral and ritual violation (1 Sam. 2:17); blasphemy (Neh. 9:26); and covenant rebellion (Jer. 16:10; Ezek. 9:9).

Greatness of magnitude or size is also commonly referred to — for example, sea creatures (Gen. 1:21; Jonah 1:17); the inhabitants of Canaan (Deut. 1:28; 9:2; Num. 13:28); mighty nations (Jer. 50:41); visions (Dan. 10:8); assemblies of people for worship (1 Kgs. 8:65); court room judgments (Neh. 5:7); sacrifices and sacrificial feasts (Judg. 16:23; Ezek. 39:17); riches (1 Sam. 17:25; Dan. 11:28); and a symbolic horn of power (Dan. 8:8, 21).

When applied to people's social, military, ritual, or civic standing, ***gādôl*** refers, for example, to people's importance (cf. Gen. 10:21; Jonah 1:2; Deut. 1:17; Jer. 16:6; 42:1); to leaders, princes, and rulers such as Saul (2 Sam. 3:38), David (2 Sam. 5:10), Naaman (2 Kgs. 5:1), and Mordecai (Esth. 10:3); and also to one's name or reputation (cf. 2 Sam. 7:19; Isa. 36:13; Dan. 12:1).

In relation to numerical strength, ***gādôl*** refers, for example, to the great numbers of Israelite people in accordance with the covenant of promise (e.g., Gen. 12:2; 17:20; 21:18; Exod. 32:10; Deut. 4:6; 26:5); and to the nations in general (cf. Deut. 9:1; 23:9; Jer. 28:8; 50:9).

gādôl is also used extensively to refer to God and his attributes. In relation to himself, there are frequent allusions to God as "great and terrible" (cf. Deut. 7:21; Neh. 1:5; Dan. 9:14). The ascription of praise "Great is the Lord . . ." is frequently mentioned in the Psalms (e.g., 48:1; 77:13; 86:10; 95:3; 135:5; see also Isa. 12:6; Jer. 10:6; 32:18). "Greatness" is also predicated of God's work of redemption (Exod. 14:31) and his divine power, especially in regard to his acts of salvation and deliverance on behalf of his people Israel (cf. Exod. 32:11; Deut. 7:19; 10:21; 11:7; Josh. 24:17; Judg. 15:18; 1 Sam. 19:5; Neh. 1:10). God's omnipotence is also indicated in Exod. 18:11; Deut. 4:37. And, in Jer. 27:5; 32:17, such all-encompassing divine power is cited with reference to the creation of the cosmos. The "greatness" of God's name is closely related to his person and presence (cf. Josh. 7:9; 1 Kgs. 8:42; Ps. 76:1; Ezek. 36:23; Jer. 44:26; Mal. 1:11); to his great mercy (cf. 1 Kgs. 3:6; Pss. 86:13; 108:4; 145:8); and to his compassion (cf. Isa. 54:7). The "greatness" of the revelation of God's person in theophanic signs also constitutes a significant use of the term ***gādôl*** — for example, fire on Sinai (cf. Deut. 4:36; 18;16); the voice of Yahweh at Sinai (cf. Deut. 5:22, 25); the glory cloud (cf. Ezek. 1:4); thunder (cf. 1 Sam. 7:10); and earthquake (cf. Ezek. 3:12, 13).

The "greatness" of God's judgment and signs against those who oppose him are also indicated by this term — for example, the plagues against Egypt (cf. Gen. 12:17; Exod. 6:6; 7:4); and plagues in general as a manifestation of the covenant curse (cf. Deut. 28:59). God's judgment against his people for their willful rejection of him also brought about their great destruction, as in the Babylonian invasion of Judah in the sixth century B.C. (cf. Jer. 6:1, 22; 10:22; 26:18; 51:54).

The great severity of divine punishment against God's people is also indicated in Dan. 9:12, as is God's wrath (cf. Deut. 29:28; 2 Kgs. 3:27; Jer. 21:5; 36:7; Zech. 7:12).

Finally, the greatness of the Day of the Lord as the ultimate manifestation of God's judgment is indicated in Joel 2:11, 31; Zeph. 1:14; Mal. 4:5.

rab [רַב, 7227]

rab is partially synonymous with ***gādôl***, above, occurring approximately five hundred times and translated "many," "much," "great," in the majority of texts. The meaning "great" is found in about a third of these contexts.

Greatness of intensity is indicated particularly in regard to evil and wickedness (cf. Gen. 6:5; 18:20; 1 Sam. 12:7; Ps. 25:11; Eccl. 2:21; Jer. 13:9; Joel 3:13).

Greatness of size is mentioned in relation to a number of phenomena — for example, the great deep (Gen. 7:11); the plague (Num. 11:33); the empire (Esth. 1:20); the power of a nation (Dan. 11:3); and riches (Gen. 13:6; 2 Sam. 3:22; Isa. 54:13).

The status of important people is likewise described through the use of ***rab*** in Isa. 53:12.

Magnitude of number is also predicated of nations and people in Josh. 17:14ff.; 1 Kgs. 3:8; Ezek. 17:17; Isa. 13:4; Lam. 1:1. Large congregations are also mentioned in Ezra 10:1; Pss. 35:18; 40:9; as are large numbers of descendants in Job 5:25.

rab is also used to describe the "greatness" of God in a variety of contexts — for example, in relation to himself (Ps. 147:5; Prov. 26:10); and to describe his characteristics such as mercy (Num. 14:18; Neh. 9:17; Joel 2:13; Jonah 4:2; 1 Sam. 24:14; Ps. 119:156; Dan. 9:18); his goodness (Neh. 9:35; Ps. 145:7; Isa. 63:7); his faithfulness (Lam. 3:23); and his hatred of sin (Hos. 9:7). The "greatness" of his royal prerogative as king is also indicated in Ps. 48:2.

rōb [רֹב, 7230]

The noun ***rōb*** occurs around 160 times and means "abundance," "multitude." However, ***rōb*** also means "great," "greatness" about twenty times, with that underlying sense of abundance.

rōb refers generally, for example, to a great army (2 Chr. 24:24); to the strength of a horse (Ps. 33:17); to a person's folly (Prov. 5:23); to taxes (Prov. 16:8); to the sin of Judah (Jer. 13:22); and to the pagan wisdom of Tyre (Ezek. 28:5). 2 Chr. 30:13 refers to a great assembly, and 2 Chr. 30:24 refers to a great number of priests.

When predicated of God, ***rōb*** refers to his great mercy (Neh. 13:22); his great power (Job 23:6; Ps. 66:3; Isa. 40:26; 63:1); and his great majesty (Exod. 15:7).

rābab [רָבַב, 7231]

rābab is a verb found seventeen times with the underlying sense of "be, become great," and related nuances.

The meaning "to multiply" in the numerical sense of "increase" is indicated in Gen. 6:1; Job 35:6.

The term means "to be many" (i.e., numerically large) in 1 Sam. 25:10; Pss. 3:1; 104:24; Isa. 22:9; Jer. 5:6; 46:23.

The sense of "be great" denoting quantitative increase (i.e., "abound") is evident in Ps. 4:7; Eccl. 5:11.

gādal [גָּדַל, 1431]

gādal is a verb meaning to "make great," "magnify," as well as associated nuances, throughout its over 100 occurrences. God's promise to "make Israel a great nation" is found in Gen. 12:2. Similarly, Yahweh is said to "magnify," "exalt" his people (Josh. 3:7; 4:14); King Solomon (1 Chr. 29:25); and the law of the covenant (Isa. 42:21).

The meaning "become great" is noted in relation to an outcry against the sin of Sodom and Gomorrah in Gen. 19:13; and to the accumulation of wealth in Gen. 24:35.

The status of "being great" in relation to reputation and authority is indicated in Gen. 48:19; Eccl. 2:9.

gādal also signifies the process of "growing up" in Gen. 21:8, 20; Exod. 2:8; Judg. 13:24; 2 Sam. 12:3.

The affirmation of God himself, and God's name, as "great" is recorded in 2 Sam. 7:22; 1 Chr. 17:24; Pss. 34:3; 40:16; 69:30. Yahweh is said to "reveal his greatness" in Ezek. 38:23.

The action of "magnifying oneself," "making oneself great" is noted in Ps. 35:26. In particular, such a stance is indicated in the context of rebellion against God (e.g., Jer. 48:26; Ezek. 35:13; Dan. 8:4ff.).

NT Words

megas [μέγας, *3173*]

megas is the predominant adjectival term signifying "great" in the New Testament, with a variety of nuances in a number of contexts. ***megas*** occurs nearly two hundred times.

The designation "great" in the sense of "abundant" is noted in relation to joy (Matt. 2:10; Luke 2:10; Acts 15:3); to the "light" of salvation (Matt. 4:16a); and to faith (Matt. 15:28).

The meaning "great" in relation to a position of "supreme importance," "honor," or "standing" is evident in connection with the kingdom of God (Matt. 5:19; 20:26); and the law commandments (Matt. 22:36ff.). "Greatness" in the sight of God is indicated in Luke 1:15, 32. General references to "great men" include that in Mark 10:42. God is described as the "great" king in Matt. 5:35. Conversely, Acts 19:27ff. refers to the Greek goddess Diana. Jesus Christ is designated as our "great God and Savior" (Titus 2:13) and as our "great high priest" (Heb. 4:14). Rev. 17:5 refers to the symbolic incarnation of evil, "Babylon the Great" (cf. also Rev. 18:10ff.).

megas indicates physical enormity in Matt. 8:24; Mark 4:37; Luke 21:11; Rev. 6:12. Rev. 20:1 refers to God's "great white throne."

The meaning "great" in the qualitative sense of "supreme," "to a large extent," is indicated with reference to the destruction of a house (Luke 6:49); to persecution and distress (Luke 21:23; Acts 8:1); to the Day of the Lord (Acts 2:20; Jude 6; Rev. 6:17); to the power of God (Acts 4:33; 8:10); to signs and miracles (Acts 6:8; 8:13; Rev. 13:13); and to fear (Rev. 11:11).

megas also signifies "great" in the sense of "loud" in Matt. 24:31; Mark 1:26; 5:7; Luke 4:33; 17:15; John 11:43; Acts 7:57; Rev. 1:10; 10:3.

polys [πολύς, *4183*]

polys is another common adjectival form found over 350 times, denoting the primary senses of "many," "much." (→ MUCH) The term also means "great" in about sixty places, with a variety of nuances.

The meaning "great" in the sense of "loud" is indicated in relation to mourning in Matt. 2:18.

polys means "great" in the sense of "numerically large" in Matt. 4:25; Mark 3:7ff.; Acts 11:21; Rev. 19:6. "Abundant" is the sense attached to "great" in Matt. 5:12 in relation to one's reward in heaven.

The sense of "supreme," implying that which is best, is found in the designation "great glory" (Matt. 24:30); in relation to "violence" (Acts 24:7); and to God's love (Eph. 2:4). Acts 22:28 uses ***polys*** to emphasize quantity, or size.

megethos [μέγεθος, *3174*]

megethos is a rare noun denoting the "greatness" of God's power in Eph. 1:19.

GREEK → GENTILES

GREET, GREETING

NT Words

aspazomai [ἀσπάζομαι, *782*]

aspazomai is a verb found in sixty places with the dominant sense of "greet."

"Greeting" one's fellow believers is indicated in Matt. 5:47; Acts 21:7; 1 Pet. 5:13. Exhortations to do so are found in Rom. 16:3ff.; 2 Cor. 13:12; Phil. 4:21ff.; Col. 4:15; 1 Pet. 5:14. "Extending a greeting" to a household is indicated in Matt. 10:12.

References to "greeting" people in general contexts are found in Mark 9:15; Luke 1:40; Acts 25:13.

aspazomai also denotes the action of "calling out" or "addressing" someone. The soldiers' mocking salutation of Christ, "Hail, King of the Jews" is recorded in Mark 15:18.

The term is translated "take leave of" or "say goodbye" in Acts 20:1, implying the act of embracing in the ritual of farewell.

aspasmos [ἀσπασμός, *783*]

aspasmos is the noun derived from ***aspazomai***, above, denoting "greetings" throughout the ten occurrences of the term (cf. Matt. 23:7; Mark 12:38; Luke 1:29, 41ff.; 11:43; 20:46). In particular, 1 Cor. 16:21; Col. 4:18; 2 Thess. 3:17 refer to Paul writing his own greeting.

chairō [χαίρω, *5463*]

chairō is a verb with the predominant meaning "to rejoice" throughout its nearly eighty occurrences. However, in Acts 15:23; 23:26; Jas. 1:1, the term denotes the expression of a formal greeting in literary correspondence.

GRIEF, GRIEVE

OT Words

ḥolî [חֳלִי, **2483**]

ḥolî is a noun denoting "sickness," "disease," for most of its twenty-four occurrences. (→ SICK)

In several instances, ***ḥolî*** also denotes "grief" or "suffering," concerning the messianic Suffering Servant whose fate is depicted in Isa. 53:3, 4.

'ādab [אָדַב, **109**]

'ādab is a rare verb meaning "to grieve," "cause grief," found only in 1 Sam. 2:33.

'āṣab [עָצַב, **6087**]

'āṣab is a verb found seventeen times with the consistent sense of "grieve," "cause pain."

The term is used anthropomorphically of God in three places. In Gen. 6:6, the sin of humankind is said to "have grieved" his heart, causing him deep pain. In Ps. 78:40; Isa. 63:10, the nuance of "anger" is present, referring to Israel's rebellion against Yahweh in the wilderness which had "grieved" him.

In Gen. 34:7, "grieve" has the sense of "experience strong indignation." The general sense of "being emotionally distressed" is indicated in Gen. 45:5; 1 Sam. 20:3, 34; Neh. 8:10ff.; Isa. 54:6. The more severe nuance of "mourning" is evident in 2 Sam. 19:2.

NT Words

syllypeō [συλλυπέω, *4818*]

syllypeō is a rare verb with the passive sense of "be grieved," referring to Christ's "distress" at the hardness of people's hearts, found only in Mark 3:5.

See Also: → SORROW

GRIND

OT Words

ṭāḥan [טָחַן, **2912**]

This verb is rare, occurring eight times and meaning "grind," "crush."

Exod. 32:20; Deut. 9:21 refer to the "grinding" or "crushing" of the golden calf; manna is "ground" by the Israelites in Num. 11:8; and "mill grinding" is indicated in Judg. 16:21. See also Job 31:10; Isa. 47:2. Two further metaphorical uses are recorded: Eccl. 12:3 refers to teeth as "grinders," and Isa. 3:15 refers to the economic exploitation of the poor in Israel with the phrase "grinding the face of the poor."

NT Words

alēthō [ἀλήθω, *229*]

alēthō is a rare verb found only twice, indicating the action of "grinding" at a mill (cf. Matt. 24:41; Luke 17:35).

trizō [τρίζω, *5149*]

trizō is a rare verb found only in Mark 9:18, denoting the action of "grinding" one's teeth in anguish and suffering.

GROAN, GROANING

OT Words

'anāḥāh [**אֲנָחָה, 585**]

This noun refers to "sighing," "groaning" as an expression of grief or physical distress. ***'anāḥāh*** occurs eleven times (cf. Job 3:24; Pss. 6:6; 102:5; Isa. 21:2; Jer. 45:3; Lam. 1:22). Both Isa. 35:10; 51:11 refer to the dispelling of all "groaning" as a consequence of God redeeming his people from captivity and bringing them back to the land.

ne'āqāh [**נְאָקָה, 5009**]

A rare term synonymous with ***'anāḥāh***, above, ***ne'āqāh*** occurs four times meaning "sighing," "groaning" as evidence of great anguish on each occasion (cf. Exod. 2:24; 6:5; Judg. 2:18; Ezek. 40:24).

'ānaḥ [**אָנַח, 584**]

'ānaḥ is a verb found twelve times meaning "groan," "sigh" in contexts of pain as well as grief.

"Groaning" as a consequence of trauma is indicated in relation to Israel's expression of pain in their Egyptian bondage in Exod. 2:23. A similar reference is found in Prov. 29:2. "Groaning" is attributed to cattle in Joel 1:18.

The sense of "mourn" underlying the meaning "groan" is evident in Isa. 24:7. The "groaning" of God's people in exile after the destruction of Jerusalem is indicated in Lam. 1:4ff.; signifying their "anguish." Ezek. 9:4 refers to those citizens of Jerusalem who "groaned" over the sins committed by their apostate fellow countrymen, a groaning undergirded by a sense of both "distress" and "shame." See also Ezek. 21:6.

NT Words

stenazō [στενάζω, *4727*]

stenazō is a verb roughly equivalent in meaning to the Hebrew terms listed above. ***stenazō*** means "groan" or "sigh" in most of its six occurrences.

In Mark 7:34, Jesus "sighs" before restoring the hearing of a deaf man, suggesting his "distress" over the plight of the disabled man before him.

In Rom. 8:23; 2 Cor. 5:2, 4 the people of God are said to "groan" under the limitations of their earthly existence while they eagerly await the liberation of life with God and Christ in glory.

anastenazō [ἀναστενάζω, *389*]

anastenazō is a rare variant of ***stenazō***, above, denoting the "deep sighing" of Jesus as he laments the spiritual decline of his own generation in Mark 8:12.

systenazō [συστενάζω, *4959*]

systenazō is another rare variant of ***stenazō***, above. It is found only in Rom. 8:22 and refers to creation "groaning" like a woman in labor.

stenagmos [στεναγμός, *4726*]

stenagmos is a rare noun derived from ***stenazō*** (see above), found only twice. Stephen's speech in Acts 7:34 refers to the "groaning" of the Israelites during their bondage in Egypt. In an unusual use of the term in Rom. 8:26, ***stenagmos*** denotes the "groanings" of the Holy Spirit, symbolically alluding to the Spirit's identification with the believers he indwells, interceding with God the Father on their behalf.

GROUND, GROUNDED

NT Words

edaphos [ἔδαφος, *1475*]

edaphos is a rare noun found only in Acts 22:7, referring to Saul falling to the "ground" when confronted by the heavenly Christ.

edaphizō [ἐδαφίζω, *1474*]

edaphizō is a rare verb found only in Luke 19:44, meaning "throw to the ground" in the context of the threatened destruction of Jerusalem.

themelioō [θεμελιόω, *2311*]

themelioō is a verb occurring six times, meaning "to ground" in the sense of "fix" or "establish" in Eph. 3:17; Col. 1:23. The former text speaks of believers being "grounded" in love for Christ; the latter refers to being "grounded" in the faith.

chamai [χαμαί, *5476*]

chamai is a rare adverbial form found only twice, meaning "on to the ground" in a directional sense (cf. John 9:6; 18:6).

See Also: → EARTH

GROW

OT Words

gādal [גָּדַל, 1431]

This verb occurs over one hundred times with the underlying sense of increasing in magnitude, power, or status. ***gādal*** is translated "grow" on twenty occasions, although this sense is interwoven with the idea of "increasing," or "becoming great." It generally applies to people. (→ GREAT)

With the sense of increasing in stature or size, ***gādal*** refers to people — for example, to Isaac (Gen. 21:8, 20); Esau and Jacob (Gen. 25:27); Moses (Exod. 2:10, 11); Samson (Judg. 11:2); and Samuel (1 Sam. 2:21). It also refers to human hair in Num. 6:5, and to plants in Jonah 4:10. See also 2 Sam. 12:23; 1 Kgs. 12:8ff.; Ps. 144:12.

There is also a metaphorical use of the term in relation to the growth or increase of guilt (cf. Ezra 9:6).

ṣāmaḥ [צָמַח, 6779]

ṣāmaḥ is a verb found more than thirty times with the primary meanings "grow," "spring up."

References to plants "growing," "springing up" include those in Gen. 2:5, 9; Exod. 10:5; Deut. 29:23; Ps. 147:8; Isa. 55:10; 61:11; Ezek. 17:6.

The "growing" of body hair is indicated in Lev. 13:37; Judg. 16:22; 1 Chr. 19:5; Ps. 104:14; Ezek. 16:7.

ṣāmaḥ is used metaphorically in Job 5:6, referring to trouble "sprouting" or "springing up" from the ground. The same is said of "faithfulness" in Ps. 85:11, and of "righteousness" in Isa. 45:8. Ps. 132:17 refers to Yahweh "making a horn sprout for David," signifying the divine intention to bring forth the messianic ruler from the lineage of David. See also Jer. 33:15; Ezek. 29:21. Isa. 42:9; 43:19 refer to "new things springing up," signifying the promise of new covenant blessings to come.

sāphîaḥ [סָפִיחַ, 5599]

sāphîaḥ is a noun found in five places denoting, generally speaking, "that which grows by itself," in agricultural contexts (cf. Lev. 25:5ff.; 2 Kgs. 19:29; Isa. 37:30).

'ālāh [עָלָה, 5927]

'ālāh is a common verb with the primary senses of "come, go up," "offer," as well as numerous related nuances throughout its nearly nine hundred occurrences.

On occasion, however, ***'ālāh*** is also translated "grow," "spring up" in relation to grass (Deut. 29:23); fruit trees (Ezek. 47:12); and finally to the physical maturing of the Messianic Servant of Yahweh (Isa. 53:2).

NT Words

auxanō [αὐξάνω, *837*]

auxanō is a verb found about twenty times meaning "grow (up)," "increase," both literally and metaphorically, in a variety of contexts.

References to plants "growing," "increasing" (in size) are found in Matt. 6:28; 13:32; Mark 4:8; Luke 12:27; 13:19.

The physical development (i.e., growth) of a child is indicated in Luke 1:80 (i.e., John the Baptist) and Luke 2:40 (Jesus).

The sense of "increase" in importance is indicated in relation to Jesus in John 3:30. In Acts 6:7; 12:24; 19:20 the meaning "increase" signifies a growth in impact or effect in relation to the preaching of God's word. This sense is applied to people in Acts 7:17, referring to the numerical expansion of the Israelites in Egypt. The "growth" or "expansion" of the early church is indicated in 1 Cor. 3:6ff.

The metaphorical sense of "increase" is found in 2 Cor. 9:10 in relation to people's righteousness; to faith 2 Cor. 10:15; and to knowledge in Col. 1:10. The concept of the spiritual community of God's people "growing" into a holy temple in the Lord is indicated in Eph. 2:21. See also Eph. 4:15; Col. 2:19; 1 Pet. 2:2; 2 Pet. 3:18 for similar contexts.

synauxanō [συναυξάνω, *4885*]

synauxanō is a rare variant of ***auxanō***, above. It is found only in Matt. 13:30 and refers to weeds and plants "growing together."

hyperauxanō [ὑπεραυξάνω, *5232*]

hyperauxanō is another rare variant of ***auxanō***, above, found only in 2 Thess. 1:3 with reference to the faith of the Thessalonian congregation "growing abundantly."

anabainō [ἀναβαίνω, *305*]

anabainō is a dynamic equivalent for ***'ālāh*** (see above) with the similar meanings "come, go up," "ascend," as well as a variety of nuances. In two places, the term means "spring up," "grow" in relation to thorns (Mark 4:7); and mustard seed (Mark 4:32).

mēkynō [μηκύνω, *3373*]

mēkynō is a rare verb meaning "sprout," "grow up" in relation to seed in Mark 4:27.

See Also: → FRUIT

GUARANTEE

OT Words

'ārab **[עָרַב, 6148]**

'ārab is a verb with the underlying meaning "to give a solemn promise or undertaking." It is variously translated "to make, receive a pledge," "to give a guarantee or security," "to act as a guarantor" in about half of its nearly twenty occurrences.

The sense of "act as a guarantor" or "guarantee safety" is indicated in a personal context in Gen. 43:9; 44:32; Job 17:3; Ps. 119:122; Prov. 6:1.

Prov. 11:15; 17:18; 20:16; 22:26, 27:13 refer to "offering, putting up security, or guarantee" for someone in a tangible or monetary sense.

'ērābôn **[עֵרָבוֹן, 6162]**

'ērābôn is the noun derived from ***'ārab***, above, denoting a tangible "pledge," "security," or "guarantee" offered as a down payment on an agreed remuneration. It is found only three times, in Gen. 38:17ff.

NT Words

engyos [ἔγγυος, *1450*]

engyos is a rare term found only in Heb. 7:22, designating Jesus Christ as the "guarantee" (i.e., the pledge) of a better covenant.

arrabōn [ἀρραβών, *728*]

arrabōn is the Greek equivalent for ***'ērābôn*** (see above), found in only three places and denoting the Holy Spirit's outpouring in the hearts of new covenant believers as the "guarantee" (i.e., deposit, down payment) of one's eternal inheritance in the kingdom of heaven (cf. 2 Cor. 1:22; 5:5; Eph. 1:14).

GUARD

OT Words

shāmar **[שָׁמַר, 8104]**

This common verb occurs nearly five hundred times with the primary meanings "keep," "watch," and the associated senses of "keep watch over" or "guard." This latter meaning, "guard," is found around thirty times.

In the sense of "keep watch," for the purpose of barring exit or entry, ***shāmar*** occurs, for example, in Gen. 3:24 where the flaming cherubim guard the entrance to the garden of Eden in order to prevent people from regaining access to the tree of life in paradise. See also 2 Kgs. 9:14 for a similar use with respect to guarding the city of Ramoth Gilead.

shāmar also conveys the idea of "guard" in the sense of "watching over" or "protecting." For example, God guarding the feet of his faithful ones (1 Sam. 2:9); men guarding the ark of the covenant (1 Sam. 7:1); and guarding a house (2 Sam. 15:16), a palace (2 Kgs. 11:6), or a harem (Esth. 2:3). Great significance is attached to the solemn task of guarding the temple (cf. 2 Kgs. 11:7; 12:7; Ezek. 40:45; Neh. 3:29; Zech. 3:7).

The psalmist pleads for God to guard his life (cf. Pss. 25:20; 140:4). God is also said to watch over the city (cf. Ps. 127:1) and to guard the paths of justice, ensuring that justice is served (cf. Prov. 2:8).

tabbāḥ **[טַבָּח, 2876]**

The noun ***tabbāḥ*** is found approximately thirty times and refers primarily to "guards" in a vocational sense — those who have charge of property and/or prisoners, or who serve as personal bodyguards to a ruler, king, or high government official.

Potiphar is often referred to as the captain of the guard in the Egyptian military bureaucracy (cf. Gen. 37:36; 39:1; 40:3ff.; 41:10).

tabbāḥ also refers to the imperial guards or bodyguards of the Babylonian rulers — for example, Nebuzaradan in 2 Kgs. 25:8; Jer. 40:1; 43:6; 52:12ff. See also 2 Kgs. 25:10ff.; Jer. 39:9ff.

rûṣ **[רוּץ, 7323]**

A verb with the primary sense of "run" (approximately seventy times), ***rûṣ*** is also translated "guard" when used in its participial form. It has this meaning in fourteen contexts.

Temple guards are mentioned, for instance, in 2 Kgs. 11:14ff.; 2 Chr. 12:10, 11; and 2 Kgs. 10:25 refers to a military guard.

mishma'at **[מִשְׁמַעַת, 4928]**

mishma'at is a rare noun denoting a "group of guards" (i.e., bodyguards) employed in the service of King Saul (1 Sam. 22:14), and King David (2 Sam. 23:23).

mishmār **[מִשְׁמָר, 4929]**

mishmār is a noun found over twenty times with the predominant sense of "prison," or "custody" (i.e., place of judicial confinement). In several places it also means "guard" (cf. Neh. 4:9, 22ff.; 7:3; 12:25; Ezek. 38:7). See also Job 7:12.

mattārāh [**מַטָּרָה, 4307**]

mattārāh is a noun signifying "guard" in the expression "court of the guard" in most of its sixteen occurrences. This expression constitutes the equivalent of a "prison" (cf. Neh. 3:25; Jer. 32:2ff.; 33:1; 37:21; 38:6, 13, 28; 39:14ff.). See also Neh. 12:39.

NT Words

koustōdia [κουστωδία, *2892*]

koustōdia is a noun of Latin origin denoting a "unit of guards" (i.e., a watch). The term is found only three times, referring in each case to the Roman guards assigned to watch over the tomb where Christ was buried (cf. Matt. 27:65ff.; 28:11).

phylax [φύλαξ, *5441*]

phylax is a noun denoting a "prison guard or sentry," found only three times (cf. Acts 5:23; 12:6, 19).

phylassō [φυλάσσω, *5442*]

phylassō is a verb meaning "guard," "keep watch over," "keep under guard," as well as the general sense of "keep," "obey." (➞ KEEP)

Luke 2:8 refers to "keeping watch over" a flock of sheep.

Luke 8:29 refers to an outcast demoniac "being kept under guard." The "guarding" of prisoners is indicated in Acts 12:4; 23:35; 28:16.

The precaution of "guarding" one's house and property is indicated in Luke 11:21.

diaphylassō [διαφυλάσσω, *1314*]

diaphylassō is a rare variant of ***phylassō***, above. It is found only in Luke 4:10 and means "to guard" in relation to the divine promise that God will give his angels the task of "watching over," or protecting, his people.

phroureō [φρουρέω, *5432*]

phroureō is a verb found only four times, expressing the literal sense of "guarding" the city of Damascus in 2 Cor. 11:32. The rest of the usage is metaphorical. Gal. 3:23 refers to believers "being guarded" under the law until faith "released" them from that confinement. Phil. 4:7 affirms that the peace of God "will guard" (i.e., protect) the hearts and minds of believers in Christ. In 1 Pet. 1:5, believers are said to "be guarded" through faith in readiness for their future salvation in glory.

GUARDIAN

NT Words

epitropos [ἐπίτροπος, *2012*]

epitropos is a rare noun found in three places denoting both a "steward" and a "guardian." The latter sense is indicated only in Gal. 4:2, referring to legal "guardians" placed as supervisors of those who have not yet become eligible for their inheritance. The sense of "steward" may also imply a role of guardianship or care for members of a family, or a household (cf. Matt. 20:8; Luke 8:3).

GUEST

OT Words

qārā' [**קָרָא, 7121**]

qārā' is a common verb occurring 730 times with the meanings "call," "cry," "meet," as well as related senses.

In several places ***qārā*** is used nominally to denote "guests." The form of the verb is a passive participle in each case, thus meaning "those who are called or invited" to share another's hospitality (cf. 1 Kgs. 1:41, 49; Prov. 9:18; Zeph. 1:7). (➞ LODGE)

NT Words

katalyō [καταλύω, *2647*]

katalyō is a verb found seventeen times with the predominant meanings "destroy," "cast down," but in Luke 9:12; 19:17 it has the meaning "to lodge as a guest." Although this meaning appears unrelated, ***katalyō*** also has the sense, outside the New Testament, of "to unloose, untie." The meaning "lodge as a guest" probably developed from the practice of prospective guests at a lodging place untying the straps from their beasts of burden (i.e., unharnessing them) prior to their entry.

katalyma [κατάλυμα, *2646*]

katalyma is a rare noun denoting an "inn" or a "guest room," found only in Mark 14:14; Luke 2:7; 22:11.

anakeimai [ἀνάκειμαι, *345*]

anakeimai is a verb with the underlying meaning "lie down, recline at a table." The contexts all indicate the partaking of hospitality. ***anakeimai*** occurs fourteen times. In Matt. 22:10ff.; 26:7; Luke 7:37; 22:27, ***anakeimai*** has the explicit sense of "sharing a meal as a guest."

GUIDE

OT Words

***nāḥāh* [נָחָה, 5148]**

A verb with the primary sense of "lead" (twenty-four times), ***nāḥāh*** is also translated "guide" on six occasions. There is an overlap of meaning here.

nāḥāh means "guide" in the sense of moral instruction (Prov. 11:3); family nurture (Job 31:18); and guidance by God (Pss. 73:24; 78:72; Isa. 58:11).

Job 38:32 refers to God "guiding" the stars, in the sense of directing their path.

***nāhal* [נָהַל, 5095]**

nāhal is a comparatively rare verb, occurring ten times with the primary meanings "guide" (four times) and "lead" (three times). Again, there is overlap in meaning.

Exod. 15:13 refers to Israel being guided by God through the wilderness into Canaan — a literal, historical deliverance. The psalmist then pleads for God's guidance in Ps. 31:3. Isa. 49:10 promises renewal, in which God will guide his people by springs of water, leading them to profound refreshment and spiritual renewal. Isa. 51:18, in contrast, refers to the lack of (spiritual) guidance among God's people which led to their severe punishment from God.

***kûn* [כּוּן, 3559]**

kûn is a common verb found over two hundred times, with the primary meanings "prepare," "establish," as well as a variety of related nuances. One of these nuances is the meaning "to direct," in the context of Yahweh "directing" (i.e., guiding) the paths or steps of people — indicating the reality of God's concern for humankind (cf. Prov. 16:9; Jer. 10:23).

NT Words

hodēgos [ὁδηγός, *3595*]

hodēgos is a noun found in five contexts denoting a "guide" or "leader" throughout. Matt. 15:14; 23:16, 24 refer to the Pharisees as "blind guides," condemned by Jesus for their hypocrisy. Acts 1:16 describes Judas Iscariot as the "guide" who had led the Jewish authorities to arrest Jesus. Rom. 2:19 refers to a "guide" to the spiritually blind.

kateuthynō [κατευθύνω, *2720*]

kateuthynō is a verb found in three places meaning "guide," "direct." Each context is metaphorical. Luke 1:79 refers to John the Baptist as a future "guide" for God's people into the way of peace. 1 Thess. 3:11 refers to God as one who "directs" or "guides" the circumstances of his people. 2 Thess. 3:5 contains an appeal to God to "direct" the hearts of the congregation to the love of God.

See Also: → LEAD

GUILE → DECEIT

GUILTLESS → INNOCENCE

GUILT, GUILTY

OT Words

***'āsham* [אָשַׁם, 816]**

This verb is found in about thirty contexts, with the dominant sense of "being guilty," along with the related senses of "trespassing" or "offending."

The primary context of this term is located in the judicial arena of the Mosaic covenant, where individual Israelites as well as the nation and groups within the nation are singled out for condemnation should their actions violate the sacred statutes of the divine covenant.

In the Pentateuch, the use of ***'āsham*** is tied to guilt, requiring that certain judicial or ritual sanctions be imposed upon any of God's people should they violate the covenant code of behavior (e.g., Lev. 4:13, 22, 27; 5:2; 6:4; Num. 5:6, 7). All of these texts refer to mandatory offerings that must be made in the event of any party or parties being found guilty under the legal code.

Moral guilt under the law is also indicated by the use of ***'āsham***, especially where Israel's idolatry is concerned — for that sin is the source of her greatest guilt (cf. Ezek. 22:4; Hos. 4:15; 5:15; 10:2; 13:1).

Other general references to moral guilt are found in Prov. 30:10; Ezek. 25:12; Ps. 34:21; Jer. 2:3; Zech. 11:5.

***'āshām* [אָשָׁם, 817]**

'āshām is the noun that derives from ***'āsham*** (see above) and refers predominantly to the Levitical guilt (or trespass) offering in this ritual context. ***'āshām*** occurs about forty times.

'āshām is most frequently found in Leviticus meaning "guilt offering." It is with this particular sacrifice that the requirement of restitution (one-fifth, or twenty percent) is associated (cf. Lev. 5:6ff.; 6:6, 17; 7:1ff.; 14:12ff.; 18:21, 22). See also Num. 6:12; 1 Sam. 6:3ff.; Ezek. 40:39; 42:13; 44:29; 46:20. Most significantly, Isa. 53:10 refers to the profound self-sacrifice of the messianic Suffering Servant who willingly allows himself to be made an offering for sin (i.e., guilt).

***'āshēm* [אָשֵׁם, 818]**

This adjective is rare, occurring only three times. On each occasion moral guilt is intended (cf. Gen. 42:21; 2 Sam. 14:13; Ezra 10:19).

NT Words

enochos [ἔνοχος, *1777*]

enochos is an adjective found ten times, meaning "liable to," "guilty of" in relation to peoples' deeds that were open to judicial indictment (cf. Matt. 5:21, 22; 26:66; Mark 3:29; 14:64; Jas. 2:10). It also has a spiritual connotation in 1 Cor. 11:27, where those who partake of the Lord's Supper in an unworthy way are deemed "guilty" of despising the body and blood of the Lord.

See Also: ➡ TRANSGRESS

GULF

NT Words

chasma [χάσμα, *5490*]

chasma is a rare noun found only in Luke 16:26, denoting the great "gulf" that was fixed between heaven and hell in the story Jesus told of Lazarus and the rich man.

H

HADES

OT Words

she'ôl [שְׁאוֹל, 7585]

The term ***she'ôl*** occurs around sixty times and may be consistently translated "grave" or transliterated "Sheol." The meaning is the same in both instances — referring to the place of the departed human spirit after physical death.

The term is commonly found in the phrase "go down to Sheol," which is a Hebraic euphemism for "to die." The following texts describe the natural process of dying: Gen. 37:35; 42:38; 44:29ff.; 2 Sam. 22:6; 1 Kgs. 2:6ff.; Job 7:9; Pss. 30:3; 88:3; Ezek. 31:15; Eccl. 9:10. Isa. 57:9 describes deliberate killing. Also evident is the truth that the timing of one's death is entirely subject to divine control (cf. 1 Sam. 2:6).

Other texts indicate that divine judgment rests on those who "go down to Sheol" — for example, Korah and his fellow conspirators (Num. 16:33). See also Pss. 55:15; 141:7; Prov. 5:5; Ezek. 31:16; Amos 9:2.

The fear of the grave (and death) is indicated in Ps. 116:3 (cf. also Prov. 27:20). Associated with this fear is the "power of the grave" that grips the heart of human beings and controls their fate (cf. Prov. 30:16; Isa. 5:14). In stark contrast to this is the prophetic anticipation in Ps. 16:10 of Yahweh's preservation of the Messiah from the confines of death and the grave.

Deut. 32:22 refers metaphorically to Sheol as the place which provides the "arena" for the reception and expression of divine anger; but see also Job 14:13.

General references to Sheol also indicate that it is the resting place of the dead (e.g., Ps. 6:5); and more particularly the resting place, or fate, of the wicked (cf. Pss. 9:17; 49:14; Isa. 14:9ff.; 28:15ff.).

Pss. 49:15; 86:13; Jonah 2:2 contain assurance for godly worshipers of Yahweh that he, Yahweh, will preserve them from the power of the grave (i.e., from death). One significant text in this regard is Hos. 13:14, where Yahweh promises to redeem his people from the power of the grave — to grant them newness of life in a renewed intimate relationship with himself. In so doing he mocks the impotence of both death and the grave and anticipates the similar triumphant assertion of Paul in 1 Cor. 15:55.

NT Words

hadēs [ᾅδης, *86*]

This word is a genuine dynamic equivalent for the Hebrew term ***she'ôl***, above. ***hadēs*** functions both as a name and as a noun derived from the significance of that name. Hades refers firstly to the god of the underworld in classical Greek mythology. This usage does not appear in the New Testament canon, but the noun derived from that name does. Hades, in the biblical context, also refers to the realm of the dead (i.e., "hell" or the "grave"). ***hadēs*** occurs ten times in the New Testament.

In some of these contexts, "hell" or "grave" denotes divine judgment. The terrible fate of Capernaum is one such example — this village is cast down to hell as a consequence of rejecting the Messiah (cf. Matt. 11:23; Luke 10:15). Similar punishment is handed out to the rich man in Luke 16:23. It is also the universal fate of the wicked in Rev. 20:13, 14. Other texts, such as Matt. 16:18, refer literally to the "gates of hell" being impotent before the infinitely greater power of Christ and his church, against which this power of death will never prevail. In a similar vein, Rev. 1:18 refers to Christ's utter supremacy over the kingdom of death (cf. also Rev. 6:8).

Finally, Acts 2:27, 31 refer to God's sovereign power over hell (or Hades) in that the Messiah, of whom David spoke, will never be abandoned by God to the grave, and his body will not suffer corruption. Such a reference is, of course, a prophetic reflection on the resurrection of Christ.

Note: In 1 Cor. 15:5, the best reading is "death" (***thanatos*** → DEATH) rather than "grave" (***hadēs***).

Additional Notes

While the Old Testament contains occasional references to Sheol as the place or consequence of God's judgment on the wicked, all the New Testament occurrences of ***hadēs*** refer to this place as the realm where God's judgment is inflicted on the wicked. In contrast, most of the usage of ***she'ôl*** is neutral in the sense that it is not explicitly connected with divine punishment.

See Also: → HELL

HAIL

OT Words

bārād **[בָּרָד, 1259]**

bārād occurs nearly thirty times meaning "hail," or "hailstones." The term is used predominantly in the context of divine judgment. It is found, for example, in the narrative of the plague judgments against Egypt (cf. Exod. 9:18ff.; 10:5ff.) as well as in the poetic rehearsals of that judgment in Pss. 78:47ff.; 105:32. Hail is also used as a means of punishment against the Amorites in Josh. 10:11; as a general expression of divine punishment in Ps. 18:12; Isa. 30:30; and as a specific judgment against Israel in Isa. 28:2, 17; Hag. 2:17. In Job 38:22; Ps. 148:8, hail is depicted as a natural phenomenon, a product of creation.

NT Words

chalaza **[χάλαζα, *5464*]**

This is a rare term in the New Testament, occurring only three times. It is found only in the book of Revelation, and each occurrence refers solely to sending hail as an expression of divine wrath. In Rev. 8:7, hail forms part of the "first trumpet" judgment. In Rev. 11:19, it constitutes an element of the "seventh trumpet" judgment, a climactic Day of the Lord phenomenon issuing from the heavenly throne room. It is also found in Rev. 16:21 as part of the "seventh bowl" judgment (cf. also Rev. 11:19).

HAIR

OT Words

sē'ār **[שֵׂעָר, 8181]**

This noun occurs approximately thirty times with reference to human or animal hair, or to a garment made of hair.

In regard to human hair, ***sē'ār*** in Lev. 13:3ff.; 14:8 refers to the condition of one's body hair during and after the incidence of infectious skin diseases, including leprosy. Other references include those in Ps. 68:21, Song 4:1; Ezek. 16:7. In Isa. 7:20, shaving the feet constitutes a divine judgment against the King of Assyria. Shaving the head is indicated in Lev. 14:9, and in Num. 6:5 such hair removal is prohibited under the terms of the Nazirite vow of consecration to Yahweh. After the completion of the vow, however, the head may be shaved — as indicated in Num. 6:5. Note also the shaving of Samson's hair, and its consequences in Judg. 16:17ff. See also 2 Sam. 14:26; 2 Kgs. 1:8. Ezra 9:3 records the tearing of one's hair as a sign of anguish — the priestly teacher of the law reacts thus upon hearing of the returned exiles' sin of intermarriage with Gentiles.

Gen. 25:25; Zech. 13:4 mention garments of animal hair.

pera' **[פֶּרַע, 6545]**

This noun is rare, occurring only twice. ***pera'*** refers to human hair in relation to the Nazirite vow in Num. 6:5, and in Ezek. 44:20 in relation to the ritual requirements of the Zadokite priests.

NT Words

thrix **[θρίξ, *2359*]**

This term also refers to human and animal hair. ***thrix*** is found in about a dozen contexts. Animal hair is indicated in Matt. 3:4; Mark 1:6. Human hair in a general sense is referred to, for example, in Matt. 5:36. In a number of instances, ***thrix*** is used in a metaphorical expression that indicates a greatly reassuring divine protection, whereby it is declared that the person in distress or danger will not lose a "single hair on his head." The inference, of course, is that God is watching over his people (cf. Luke 12:7; 21:18; Matt. 10:30; Acts 27:34). The word is also found in texts where a devout or penitent women washes Jesus' feet with her hair — constituting an act of worship (cf. Luke 7:38, 44; John 11:2).

komē **[κόμη, *2864*]**

The sole reference here is to a woman's hair as a symbol of her glory in 1 Cor. 11:15.

HALF

OT Words

ḥaṣî **[חֲצִי, 2677]**

This term is quite common, indicating the measure "half" in about one hundred contexts, with several different dimensions in view.

In terms of quantity, half measures are indicated, for example, in reference to a half-district of Jerusalem (Neh. 3:9); half of a kingdom (Esth. 5:3, 6); half of the land of Canaan (Josh. 13:25); and even half a child (1 Kgs. 3:25).

Numerical halving is most commonly referred to in relation to the tribes of Israel (e.g., Num. 32:33; 34:14ff.; Deut. 3:12; Josh. 1:12; 14:2ff.; 1 Chr. 2:52ff.

Measuring by half in a linear sense is of particular concern in both the construction of the tabernacle (cf. Exod. 25:10ff.; 26:16; 37:1ff.), and in the linear dimensions of Ezekiel's visionary temple (cf. Ezek. 40:42; 43:17). Half measures in various weight categories are also indicated in Num. 15:9ff.; 28:14.

Of particular interest is the expression "time, times and half a time," found in Dan. 12:7. Commentators agree that it may be understood as a symbolic expression of "eschatological time" with a distinct finite frame of reference, but none agree as to its precise meaning — except to note its association with the apocalyptic consummation of history and redemption.

NT Words

hēmisys **[ἥμισυς, *2255*]**

This word refers to the product of that which is equally divided into two, whether of physical matter or time. ***hēmisys*** is rare, occurring only five times. It is the direct dynamic equivalent of the Hebrew term *ḥaṣî*.

Mark 6:23 refers to half of the kingdom belonging to King Herod. Luke 19:8 indicates Zacchaeus' offer to give away half of his wealth to the poor. Three references in the book of Revelation (11:9, 11; 12:14) recall the prophetic formula in Dan. 12:7 (the first two indirectly, the latter specifically). (see *ḥaṣî*, above.) Rev. 11:9, 11 refer to the symbolic period of three and a half days. In Rev. 11:9, this time refers to the period during which the bodies of the two witnesses are exposed; and after which the Spirit of God resurrects them. Rev. 12:14 rehearses the precise formula of Dan. 12:7, referring to "a time, times and half a time" during which the visionary woman is protected by God from the serpent. One can only assume that this eschatological, apocalyptic formula shares the same point of reference in both Old and New Testament, indicating that God's timing in bringing about the completion of his redemptive work will be perfect and precise.

HALLELUJAH

OT Words

halalû yāh **[הַלְלוּ יָהּ, 1984]**

This expression of praise to God is derived from the verb ***hālal*** (→ PRAISE) which is translated primarily "praise" in about 120 contexts, with the associated senses of "glory" and "boast." The actual expression ***halalû yāh*** is found about twenty-five times in the Psalter (cf. Pss. 104:35; 105:45; 106:1; 111:1; 112:1; 113:9; 115:18; 116:19; 117:1ff.; 135:1ff.; 148:1ff.; 149:1ff.; 150:1ff.). See also Jer. 20:13.

NT Words

hallēlouia **[ἀλληλουϊά, *239*]**

A term of praise directed to God in an attitude of thanksgiving for his greatness and goodness, ***hallēlouia*** is a transliteration of the Hebrew phrase ***halalû yāh***, above. This term is rare in the New Testament, being found only a few times in Rev. 19:1, 3, 4, 6. On each occasion the term is heard from the mouths of the saints in heaven, as well as from the twenty-four elders and the four creatures before the divine throne.
(→ PRAISE)

HALLOW → HOLINESS

HAND

OT Words

yād **[יָד, 3027]**

This noun is very common, occurring about 1,400 times meaning "hand" in the majority of cases. ***yād*** refers both to the literal physical part of the body, as well as to the metaphorical senses of "strength" "power," "instrument," or "authority." The term is predicated of both human beings and God.

The literal, mundane sense of "hand" as part of the human limb is very common (cf. Gen. 3:22; Exod. 4:2; Deut. 1:25; Josh. 5:13; Judg. 3:21; 2 Sam. 4:12; Esth. 3:10; Song 5:14). Occasionally, ***yād*** refers to the hands of heavenly beings and angels (cf. Isa. 6:6; Ezek. 1:8); or to the hands of an idol (e.g., Dagon in 1 Sam. 5:4). Ps. 22:16 refers to the piercing of the psalmist's hands as a prophetic, symbolic anticipation of the sufferings of Christ on the cross.

Other contexts refer to the practice of putting one's hands upon the sacrificial animal prior to its slaughter (e.g., Lev. 1:4; 3:2ff.; Lev. 24:14; Num. 8:12). This action is also linked to the ceremony of priestly consecration to ritual office (cf. Lev. 8:14ff.). Deut. 12:11ff. also indicates offering one's hands.

In another literal context, the phrase "lay one's hands on . . ." indicates physical assault (cf. Esth. 3:6; 8:7; Jer. 11:21).

The metaphorical sense of ***yād*** is far more common, and is applied to both God and human beings. A significant number of texts refer to the "hand of God" in various contexts. Basically, this concept refers to divine power and authority. For example, in regard to his people, Yahweh is said to "lift up his hand" against them as punishment for their rebellion against him (cf. Ezek. 44:12). Sometimes "the hand of the Lord" was against them (e.g., Exod. 16:3; Lev. 26:25; Judg. 2:15; Ruth 1:13; Isa. 5:25; Ezek. 20:15). The covenant curse is in view in Exod. 16:3; Lev. 26:25. In a related sense, Yahweh is said to deliver his people "into the hands of . . . (their enemies)" as a punishment for their sin. This is particularly true at the time of the judges (cf. Judg. 2:14; 3:8ff.); and the exile of both Israel and Judah (cf. Hos. 2:10; Ps. 106:41; Jer. 20:4ff.; 32:25ff.; Ezek. 11:9; 39:23; Ezra 9:7). The "hand of Yahweh" is also stretched out against the enemies of his people in judgment — for example, the Canaanites (cf. Deut. 2:15; Josh. 7:7; Judg. 1:4); the Philistines (cf. 1 Sam. 5:6ff.; Ezek. 25:16); Egypt (cf. Exod. 3:20; 7:4ff.; Isa. 11:15); and enemies in general (cf. Isa. 9:12, 17; Mic. 5:9).

"The hand of the Lord" is also referred to in regard to the prophetic endowment of the Spirit of God in preparation for the prophet to receive the divine word. This specific usage, however, is restricted to the prophet Ezekiel (cf. Ezek. 1:3; 3:14; 8:14; 37:1; 40:1).

Other general references to the "hand of God/Yahweh" include his bringing Israel out of captivity "with a mighty hand" (Ezek. 20:34); David pleading with God to "stay his hand of judgment" (2 Sam. 24:16); and God's "good hand of mercy" (Ezra 8:18ff.; Neh. 2:18). See also Exod. 15:17; 1 Sam. 4:8; Prov. 3:27; Eccl. 2:24. God's "hands" are also indicated in contexts referring to divine creativity (e.g., Job 10:8; Ps. 119:73; Prov. 31:31; Eccl. 2:11; Isa. 19:25; 64:8); as well as divine protection (e.g., Job 12:10; Pss. 10:14; 73:23; Eccl. 9:1; Jer. 31:32). Note especially the cry of the psalmist in Ps. 31:5, anticipating the climax of Jesus' death on the cross: "Into your hands, I commit my spirit."

Still in the context of divine initiative, there are a number of references to Yahweh delivering his people "out of the hands of (their enemies)" — for example, Egypt (cf. Exod. 13:3; Deut. 1:27; Judg. 6:9); Philistia (cf. 1 Sam. 7:13, 14); and enemies in general (cf. 1 Sam. 12:11; Ezek. 13:23). See also Pss. 18:1; 31:15; 71:4.

Similar statements are also found concerning the "hand(s)" of human beings, or human authority or instrumentality. There is the exercise of human authority derived from God — for example, Moses stretching out his hand against Egypt (cf. Exod. 7:19; 8:5ff.; 10:12, 21). A general sense of human instrumentality is indicated by the phrase "by the hand of . . ." — for example, murder (cf. Gen. 4:11; 9:5; Exod. 21:20); or political or civic authority (cf. Gen. 41:35; 1 Sam. 23:17). References to one being "delivered out of the hand of . . . ," without a specific connection to divine initiative, are found for example in Exod. 2:19; Num. 35:25; Dan. 8:7. Human productivity is indicated by the phrase "the work(s) of (one's) hands" (cf. Deut. 2:7; 4:28; Job 1:10; Ps. 90:17; Jer. 10:9). All of these contexts are positive in their connotation. However, other passages refer to the works of one's hands with a decidedly negative emphasis, such as the construction of idols (e.g., Isa. 2:8; 37:19; Jer. 1:16; Mic. 5:13). Other references are made to the plans and purposes of the ungodly, including Israelites as well as Gentiles, through the phrase "the hands of the wicked" (e.g., Ps. 40:4; Prov. 11:21; Isa. 1:15; Jer. 22:3). Human arrogance is indicated by the expression "raise one's hand against God" (e.g., Job 15:25). Accountability is also indicated through the expression "to require (something) at (someone's) hand," such as in Ezek. 33:6ff., where the prophet is appointed as a watchman over his people.

Finally, there is the theme of rendering praise to God in the expression "lift up one's hand" (i.e., in worship) (cf. Gen. 14:22; Deut. 32:40; Ps. 28:2).

NT Words

cheir [χείρ, *5495*]

The term means "hand" in a physical sense, as well as conveying the metaphorical ideas of human and divine help or agency. ***cheir*** also refers to divine power and authority in determining the destinies of various people, in much the same way as the Hebrew term ***yād*** (see above). ***cheir*** occurs around 180 times.

The literal, mundane sense of "hand" is found, for example, in Matt. 8:15; Mark 1:31; Luke 6:1; John 11:21; Acts 12:7; 1 Cor. 4:12; Phlm. 9; 1 John 1:1. The physical sense of "hand(s)" is also found in contexts where Jesus performs miracles with his hands (e.g., Matt. 8:3; Mark 6:2; Luke 4:40; 5:13), as do his disciples (cf. Acts 3:7; 5:12; 9:12; 19:11).

cheir is also found in other literal expressions such as "to lay hands on (someone)" in the sense of physical assault or arrest (cf. Mark 14:46; Luke 21:2). In relation to Jesus, it is recorded that no person could lay hands on him, in this sense, during his ministry prior to his appointed time of arrest (cf. John 7:44; 10:39). This same phrase is also used in conjunction with the ceremony of initiation for the Holy Spirit's anointing (cf. Acts 8:17; 19:6); and also for the rite of ordination for ministry (cf. Acts 13:3 [Saul and Barnabas]; 1 Tim. 4:14; 2 Tim. 1:6; Heb. 6:2). 1 Tim. 2:8 also records lifting up one's hands in worship.

In the numerous metaphorical expressions in which the term ***cheir*** is found, there is a focus on both divine and human agency. First of all, there is the idea of the "hand(s) of God" as the instrument of divine judgment against humankind (e.g., Matt. 3:12; Luke 3:17); and against his people (cf. Rom. 10:21). See also 1 Pet. 5:6; Heb. 10:31. Acts 7:35 describes the "hand of God, or the angel" as the instrument of divine deliverance. This term is also found with reference to the hands of theophanic figures in the visions of the book of Revelation — for example, the hands of Christ (cf. Rev. 1:16ff.; 6:5); of the angel (cf. Rev. 8:4; 10:2; 14:14; 20:1, 4); and of the Babylonian "whore" (cf. Rev. 19:2). The concept of the "hand of the Lord" is also used positively in the context of divine favor. Most notable of these is Luke 23:46, where Jesus on the cross repeats the words of Ps. 31:5, "Into your hands I commit my spirit" in fulfillment of that prophetic cry. See also Luke 1:66; John 10:28; Acts 11:21. The motif of the authority of God is also conveyed by the use of this phrase in John 3:35; 13:3.

cheir also conveys human power and authority in being delivered over "into the hands of (one's enemies)." It is predicated of Jesus in his betrayal (cf. Matt. 17:20; 26:45; Mark 9:31; 14:41; Luke 9:44; 24:7), and in his crucifixion (cf. Acts 2:23). It also occurs in reference to the Herodian persecution of the early church in Acts 12:1; and to Paul's being handed over to the Romans in Acts 28:17.

cheir also refers to the phenomenon of creativity: firstly of God in creation (cf. Heb. 1:10; 2:7); and secondly of human beings in Acts 7:41; 19:26. This latter sense is wholly negative, however, for the reference is to idol making.

HANDKERCHIEF

NT Words

soudarion **[σουδάριον, *4676*]**

A rare term found only four times, ***soudarion*** indicates a "cloth" or "handkerchief" used for personal hygiene and as a cloth wrapping. In Luke 19:20, the term refers to a wrapping for a sum of money hidden away. Acts 19:12 refers to "handkerchiefs" used in connection with Paul's healing miracles. John 11:44 refers to the cloth binding around the face of Lazarus at the time of his burial (see also John 20:7 concerning Jesus' body in the tomb).

HANDLE

OT Words

tāphas **[תָּפַשׂ, 8610]**

This verb is found on approximately seventy occasions and has several meanings. The most prominent of these is to "take." Other related senses are "hold," "catch," and "handle." This latter meaning is found in eight of these passages.

tāphas is used, for example, in Gen. 4:21 to indicate the handling or playing of a musical instrument. In Jer. 2:8 the word is also used in the sense of "deal with (i.e., handling) the law." The context is one of condemnation. Israelite priests who knew the law intimately did not have a personal knowledge of Yahweh. In other words, their "handling" of the law was in God's eyes wholly inept and useless. Other references to "handling" include "handling" (i.e., using) military weapons (Ezek. 21:11; 38:4; Amos 2:15; Jer. 46:9); agricultural tools (Jer. 50:16); and an oar (Ezek. 27:29).

NT Words

psēlaphaō **[ψηλαφάω, *5584*]**

This a rare term, occurring four times and meaning "handle," "touch," "feel" in all but one of these contexts.

In Luke 24:39, Jesus invites his disciples to "touch" or "handle" him, to verify that he has a physical body after his resurrection. Heb. 12:18 denies that the new Jerusalem can be physically handled or touched like the ancient Mt. Sinai. 1 John 1:1 emphasizes the fact that John and the other disciples physically touched and handled the incarnate word of life in the person of Jesus Christ.

doloō **[δολόω, *1389*]**

This word occurs only once, in 2 Cor. 4:2, in reference to handling the word of God deceitfully.

HANDSOME → BEAUTIFUL

HANG

OT Words

tālāh **[תָּלָה, 8518]**

tālāh means "hang" in reference to both objects and people. In the case of people, it refers to the mode of execution. ***tālāh*** occurs about twenty-five times and is used both metaphorically and literally.

Referring to execution, ***tālāh*** is found in Gen., 40:19; 41:13; Esth. 2:23; 6:4; 7:9ff.; 8:7; 9:13ff.; Lam. 5:12. In Deut. 21:22ff., this form of execution is linked to a covenant curse sanction for capital offenses. Other references to judicial hanging are found in Josh. 8:29; 10:26; 2 Sam. 4:12; 21:12, in the context of military-style executions. 2 Sam. 18:10 refers to the "accidental" death of Absalom, whose hair got caught in the branches of a tree and who suffered death by hanging. Despite the unusual circumstances of his passing, in the context of the narrative Absalom's death is clearly intended to be understood as a judicial divine sentence.

In metaphorical contexts, ***tālāh*** conveys divine creative omnipotence in reference to "hanging the earth on nothing" (cf. Job 26:7). The hanging of certain objects is indicated in Ps. 137:2; Song 4:4; Ezek. 27:10, 11. Finally, there is a symbolic allusion to the glory of God "hanging" on Eliakim the priest in relation to his service in the temple (cf. Isa. 22:24).

ḥānaq **[חָנַק, 2614]**

This is a rare verb that occurs only twice. In 2 Sam. 17:23, ***ḥānaq*** refers to Ahithophel's suicide by hanging, and in Nah. 2:12 the term indicates the death of animals by strangulation.

NT Words

kremannymi [**κρεμάννυμι,** *2910*]

This is an uncommon verb occurring only seven times, meaning to "hang" in both a literal and metaphorical sense.

The meaning "hanged" in reference to execution is found in Luke 23:39, concerning the criminals who died with Jesus on the cross. In Acts 5:30; 10:39, ***kremannymi*** refers to Jesus himself. Gal. 3:13 quotes the covenant sanction from the book of Deuteronomy: "Cursed is every one who is hung on a tree" (Deut. 21:23). Matt. 18:6 describes the "ideal" punishment for those who hinder little children from entering the kingdom of God — having a millstone hung around their neck and being cast into the sea.

Matt. 22:40 contains the following affirmation from the teaching of Jesus: "On these two commandments hang all the law . . ." Here, ***kremannymi*** is used metaphorically to indicate "hang" in the sense of "derive significance from," or "depend on."

In Acts 28:4, ***kremannymi*** refers to the snake hanging from Paul's arm on the beach in Malta.

perikeimai [**περίκειμαι,** *4029*]

This term means "be hanged" in two of the five contexts in which it occurs (Mark 9:42; Luke 17:2). Both texts refer to the fate of those who actively turn people away from belief and trust in Christ (see ***kremannymi***, above).

apanchō [**ἀπάγχω,** *519*]

This word occurs only in Matt. 27:5, where it refers to Judas going out and hanging himself.

HAPPEN

NT Words

symbainō [**συμβαίνω,** *4819*]

symbainō has an underlying literal sense of "go, come, or walk together," with the extended meaning to "happen," "come to pass." The term occurs eight times, with the sense of "happen" in six of these. Mark 10:32; Acts 3:10; 20:19; 1 Cor. 10:11; 1 Pet. 4:2 all contain ***symbainō*** with the idea of "happen to," "befall." In Luke 24:14 it means to "take place."

See Also: → BEFALL

HAPPY → BLESS

HARD, HARDEN

OT Words

qāsheh **[קָשֶׁה, 7186]**

qāsheh is an adjective found about forty times with various meanings and the underlying senses of "hard," "severe," "obstinate." ***qāsheh*** means "hard" in about a quarter of the contexts in which it is found.

Meaning "hard" in the sense of "harsh," "severe," ***qāsheh*** is found in Exod. 1:14; 6:9; Deut. 26:6, in relation to the suffering of the Israelite people in Egypt. Isa. 14:3 speaks of the promise of release from harsh bondage in exile. 1 Kgs. 12:4; 2 Chr. 10:4 speak of "harsh service" during the reign of King Solomon. See also 2 Sam. 2:17. "Hard," with the idea of "difficult to resolve or understand," is the meaning found in Exod. 18:26 in regard to Moses' civil and judicial responsibilities. Finally, Ps. 60:3 refers to the "hard" circumstances that Yahweh imposed upon Israel as the result of her sinfulness.

ḥāzaq **[חָזַק, 2388]**

This verb form occurs nearly three hundred times with the predominant idea of "be strong," as well as a number of associated senses. One of these meanings is "to harden," found in about thirteen passages. The underlying sense here is to "render impervious to," or "make unyielding." With two exceptions, all occurrences of the term ***ḥāzaq*** with this connotation are found in the context of the hardening of Pharaoh's heart so that he would not free the Israelites from their captivity in Egypt (cf. Exod. 4:21; 7:13, 22; 8:19; 9:12, 35; 10:20, 27; 11:10; 14:4, 8). Exod. 14:17 refers to the hardening of the hearts of the Egyptian people; and Josh. 11:20 speaks of the Hivites hardening their hearts. Significantly, in the large majority of cases, the agent of "hardening" is specifically declared to be Yahweh himself.

qāshāh [קָשָׁה, 7185]

qāshāh is the verbal form of ***qāsheh*** (see above), and occurs about thirty times, meaning "harden" in about half of these contexts.

References to Yahweh hardening the heart of Pharaoh are found in Exod. 7:3; Deut. 2:30. In Prov. 9:1; Jer. 7:26; 19:15, ***qāshāh*** is used in the expression "to harden one's neck," signifying an attitude of stubbornness (cf. also 2 Kgs. 17:14; Neh. 9:16ff.). Prov. 28:14 warns against hardening one's heart, as does Ps. 95:8.

NT Words

sklēros [σκληρός, *4642*]

This adjective is found six times, and in five of these occurrences ***sklēros*** means "hard." With the sense of "harsh," "stern," "severe," ***sklēros*** is found in Matt. 25:24, referring to a master, and in Jude 15 it indicates the nature of words coming from the mouths of the ungodly. ***sklēros*** occurs in John 6:60 meaning "difficult to understand," referring to the response of Jesus' disciples to his teaching concerning himself as the "bread of life." In Acts 9:5; 26:14, ***sklēros*** means simply "difficult," concerning Jesus' response to Saul during his conversion experience on the road to Damascus, when Jesus said to him: "It is hard for you to kick against the goad."

sklērotēs [σκληρότης, *4643*]

sklērotēs occurs only once, referring to the hardheartedness of the Jewish people in Rom. 2:5.

pōrōsis [πώρωσις, *4457*]

This noun is rare, occurring only three times. ***pōrōsis*** primarily denotes a "hardening," hence the translation "hardness." The meaning suggests a dullness of perception with an underlying intention or unwillingness to accept what is otherwise plain. Therefore, the conditions of "stubbornness" and "blindness" are also indicated (e.g., Mark 3:5). Here Jesus expresses his anger at the hardheartedness of the Pharisees in their response to his healing the man with the withered hand. In Rom. 11:25 the term means "blindness," with reference to the Jews' refusal to believe in Christ and his work. Here it is associated with hardness of heart. See Eph. 4:18 for a similar usage.

pōroō [πωρόω, *4456*]

pōroō is the verb from which the noun ***pōrōsis***, above, derives. Like ***sklēros*** and ***sklērotēs***, above, it refers primarily to hardening, associated with hardheartedness and spiritual blindness. It occurs six times.

Mark 6:52; 8:17 refer to the disciples' hardness of heart, indicating their failure to understand the significance of Jesus' miracles and his teaching at this specific point in time. John 12:40 indicates God's action in hardening the hearts of unbelieving Jews (cf. also Rom. 11:7). In 2 Cor. 3:14, Paul mentions the curse of spiritual blindness that will remain on unbelievers until the Spirit of God removes the veil of unbelief that leaves them devoid of spiritual understanding.

sklērynō [σκληρύνω, *4645*]

sklērynō is the verb form associated with ***sklēros*** and ***sklērotēs***, above, and is synonymous with ***pōroō*** and its associated forms. ***sklērynō*** occurs six times.

Acts 19:9; Rom. 9:14 indicate the divine judgment of hardening on those who refuse to heed the message of the gospel. The remaining occurrences of ***sklērynō*** are found in the book of Hebrews, which solemnly warns its readers to guard against hardening their hearts and turning away from allegiance to Christ (cf. Heb. 3:8, 13, 15; 4:7).

HAREM

There is no specific term for "harem" in the Old Testament. It is expressed in Hebrew as "house of the women" (*bēt hanāshîm*); and is found only five times, in the book of Esther, in reference to the harem of King Xerxes (Ahasuerus) (cf. Esth. 2:3, 8, 9, 13, 14). No equivalent concept is found in the New Testament.

HARLOT

OT Words

zānāh [זָנָה, 2181]

This noun occurs about one hundred times, with the principal senses of "fornication," "harlot" (i.e., prostitute), and "harlotry" (i.e., prostitution). ***zānāh*** is used both metaphorically and literally.

zānāh is used frequently to indicate the activity or career of prostitution (e.g., Gen. 34:31; Josh. 2:1; 6:17ff.). There are a number of covenant sanctions in the Mosaic law against this practice (cf. Lev. 19:29; 21:7ff.). Deut. 22:21 records that prostitution is a capital offense under the law. Other references to the practice are found in Judg. 2:17; 8:27; 11:1; 16:1; 1 Kgs. 3:16; Prov. 6:26.

Another common use of ***zānāh*** is the metaphorical allusion to Israel's acts of "adultery" against God. In these contexts, Israel is accused of harlotry in relation to her idolatrous worship of pagan deities. In effect, Israel's covenant vows of fidelity to God constitute symbolic "marriage" vows to Yahweh her "husband." Thus the worship of idols constitutes blatant "marital unfaithfulness," which comes under the usage of the term ***zānāh***. There is a general reference to this sin in Lev. 17:7; 20:6. ***zānāh*** is also used in reference to the infamous incident of worshiping the "golden calf" in Exod. 34:15ff. Deut. 31:16 rehearses Israel's prospective ritual prostitution in the form of a covenant lawsuit — the "Song of Moses." See also 1 Chr. 5:25; Ps. 73:27; Isa. 1:21; Jer. 2:20; Ezek. 6:9; Amos 7:17; Mic. 1:7 Hos. 1:2. Ezek. 16:5ff. contains a particularly vivid description of Israel's prostitution in the so-called allegory of the two sisters, referring to the depraved practices of both Israel and Judah.

A metaphorical use of ***zānāh*** depicts nations other than Israel as harlots — Tyre (Isa. 23:15ff.) and Nineveh (Nah. 3:4).

NT Words

pornē [πόρνη, *4204*]

pornē occurs twelve times with the sole meaning "prostitute." As with the Hebrew term ***zānāh***, above, ***pornē*** has both a literal and a metaphorical sense. ***pornē*** refers to the moral crime of fornication, whether for economic gain or for passion. Metaphorically, the word refers to those who commit idolatry.

The literal sense of ***pornē*** is indicated in Matt. 21:13ff.; Luke 15:30; Heb. 11:30; Jas. 2:5. In 1 Cor. 6:15, 16, however, the term points to the spiritual harm done to one's relationship with Christ as a consequence of sexual immorality with a prostitute. Rev. 17:1, 5, 15, 16; 19:2 all refer allegorically to Babylon as the "great whore," the universal biblical symbol for crass idolatry.

Additional Notes

The Hebrew and Greek terms ***zānāh*** and ***pornē*** constitute genuine dynamic equivalents. The thematic movement of the equation between idolatry and spiritual adultery from Yahweh to Christ is important to note. Both terms reveal a powerful allegorical component in their respective usage (cf. Ezek. 16 and Rev. 17), and both reflect the seriousness of this offense before God.

HARM → EVIL

HARMLESS

NT Words

akeraios [ἀκέραιος, *185*]

This rare term occurs only three times, meaning "harmless." Matt. 10:16 signifies the desirable attitude and manner of "gentleness" and "non-hostility," through the simile "harmless as doves." Paul expresses a similar thought in Rom. 16:19: "(be) harmless concerning evil" (cf. also Phil. 2:15).

akakos [ἄκακος, *172*]

This is another rare term that means "without evil, or harm, or guile" — that is, "harmless." ***akakos*** only occurs twice. Rom. 16:18 refers to those who are "without guile," or void of harmful intent toward others. Heb. 7:26 refers to Jesus as our high priest, who is totally innocent of any deceitful attitude or action.

HARP

OT Words

kinnôr [**כִּנּוֹר, 3658**]

kinnôr indicates a "harp" or "lyre," a stringed musical instrument that is plucked with the fingers. ***kinnôr*** is derived from a verbal root meaning "to want." It is found in about forty texts. The usage is entirely literal. In Gen. 4:21, ***kinnôr*** (harp) is used representatively, along with "flute," to refer to all instruments of that time. See also Gen. 31:27; 1 Sam. 10:5; 1 Kgs. 10:12; Job 30:31; Isa. 5:12; Ezek. 26:13. 1 Sam. 16:16, 23 refer to David's skill with the harp. Levitical musicians playing the harp in worship are indicated, for example, in 1 Chr. 15:16ff.; 25:1ff.; 2 Chr. 5:12; 20:28; Neh. 12:27. The term is also found frequently in the Psalms (e.g., Pss. 33:2; 57:8; 108:2; 137:2; 150:3).

NT Words

kithara [κιθάρα, *2788*]

kithara is found four times, indicating the harp as a musical instrument in a general sense (cf. 1 Cor. 14:7); and as a heavenly instrument used in singing praises to God in glory (cf. Rev. 5:8; 14:2; 15:2).

HARVEST

OT Words

qāṣîr [**קָצִיר, 7105**]

This term occurs around fifty times with the primary sense of "harvest," whether in reference to the process of harvesting or to the produce of harvest, the crop itself. ***qāṣîr*** is used both literally and metaphorically.

As a literal phenomenon, the process of harvesting is indicated in a number of places — in Gen. 8:22, for example, where the divine promises associated with the Noahic covenant guarantee the continual cycle of sowing and harvesting. See also Josh. 3:1; Judg. 15:1; 1 Sam.

6:13; Job 5:5; Prov. 6:8. Gen. 45:6 refers to famine in Egypt, to the absence of harvest. Lev. 19:9; 23:2; Deut. 24:19 refer to the practice of leaving some harvest grain for the poor. Mosaic legislation required that the Israelites could not harvest their crops right to the edges of their land, but must leave some stalks standing for the poor to glean. See also Lev. 25:5. There are also a number of references to the failure of harvest as a divine judgment (cf. Isa. 16:9; 17:11; Jer. 50:20; Joel 1:11; Amos 4:7).

qāṣîr also refers literally to the ritual feast of harvest in thanksgiving to Yahweh, in which the firstfruits of the crop are given to God out of gratitude for his provision (cf. Exod. 23:16; 34:22). Lev. 23:10 then indicates the obligatory offering of the firstfruits of the harvest to be made by the Israelites upon entry to Canaan.

Finally, the metaphorical indication of harvest as a time of divine judgment is found in reference to Babylon (Jer. 51:53); Judah (Hos. 6:11); and the nations in general (Joel 3:13).

qāṣar [**קָצַר, 7114**]

This verb also occurs about fifty times, and in the majority of texts it means "reap" in the context of harvesting.

The practice of leaving standing grain for the poor to harvest, or glean, is indicated in Lev. 19:9; 23:22; Deut. 24:19; Ruth 2:3ff. The bountiful reaping of harvest as a sign of divine blessing is mentioned in Isa. 37:30. "Barren reaping," or famine, as a sign of divine judgment is found in Jer. 9:22. The required offering of firstfruits after the initial reaping of the crop in the land of Canaan is set down in Lev. 23:10 (cf. also Lev. 25:5, 11). General references to reaping are found in 1 Sam. 6:13; 8:12; 2 Kgs. 19:29; Isa. 17:5.

"Reaping" in a metaphorical sense is indicated in a number of places as the consequence of one's actions, whether good (cf. Ps. 126:5); or bad (cf. Job 24:6; 4:8; Prov. 22:8). Hos. 10:12 contains an admonition to reap a spiritual harvest of blessing by devoting oneself in righteousness to Yahweh. The "reaping" of punishment from God in the context of the exile of Israel and Judah is mentioned in Jer. 12:13; Hos. 8:7; 10:13; Amos 9:13; Mic. 6:15.

NT Words

therismos [θερισμός, *2326*]

therismos occurs thirteen times with the exclusive meaning "harvest," in a metaphorical sense. The term is found, for example, in Matt. 9:37, 38; Luke 10:2; John 4:35, with reference to the gathering of converts to Christ. There is also a symbolic reference to "harvest" as the eschatological time of the final judgment when the righteous will be gathered to hear of their eternal blessing, and the ungodly of their doom (cf. Matt. 13:30, 39; Mark 4:39; Rev. 14:15).

Additional Notes

Both Old and New Testaments refer to "harvest" in a consistently symbolic sense. As well as the literal sense of "harvest," the Hebrew terms ***qāṣar*** and ***qāṣîr*** both indicate the metaphorical reaping of divine judgment and blessing (although judgment predominates). "Harvest" is not used literally in the New Testament, but only with the idea of reaping divine judgment or blessing. Significantly, it is the person and work of Christ that functions as the catalyst for gathering both citizens of the kingdom of God and those who will be condemned to eternal separation from God. "Harvesting" in the New Testament is a profoundly eschatological concept — one which is already anticipated in the Old Testament.

HASTE, HASTEN

OT Words

māhar [**מָהַר, 4116**]

māhar is found with the predominant sense of "hasten," "hurry" in about fifty contexts.

The literal sense of "hasten," or "move quickly," occurs in a number of places (e.g., Gen. 18:6; Exod. 10:16; Josh. 4:10; Judg. 13:10; 1 Sam. 4:14; 2 Sam. 15:14; 1 Kgs. 22:9; Isa. 49:17; Jer. 9:18; Nah. 2:5; Hab. 1:6). This includes the irreverent and sinful request to Yahweh to hurry his work along.

Metaphorically, ***māhar*** means to "hasten after," "lust after," or "be attracted to." Ps. 16:4 points to this attraction to other gods. Other texts refer to a "hastening" after evil in general terms (cf. Prov. 1:16; 6:18; Isa. 59:17). One reference to "hasten" describes a rapid onset of terrible circumstances for the country of Moab, as a judgment from God (cf. Jer. 48:16).

mehērāh [**מְהֵרָה, 4120**]

This noun occurs about twenty times with the underlying sense of "haste," or "speed," with a number of related adverbial and adjectival senses.

As an adverb, ***mehērāh*** means "quickly," "hastily" with reference to motion (cf. Num. 16:46; Josh. 8:19; 10:6; Judg. 9:54; 1 Sam. 20:38; 2 Kgs. 1:11). In Isa. 5:26, the term refers to the speed of divine judgment.

The other significant area of meaning associated with this term is that of "quickly" in the sense of "shortness of time." Examples of this usage include Deut. 11:17 — a warning from Yahweh against perishing quickly from the land of promise as a consequence of the people's disobedience. Ps. 31:2 contains a prayer for speedy deliverance, and Ps. 37:2 a plea for Yahweh to quickly destroy the wicked. See also Joel 3:4 for a similar desire with regard to Tyre and Sidon. See also Josh. 23:16; Eccl. 4:12; Isa. 58:8; Jer. 27:16.

bāhal [בָּהַל, 926]

bāhal is a verb found in about forty places with the primary senses of "trouble" or "terrify," and "to make haste," as well as several related senses. ***bāhal*** occurs in ten contexts with the meaning "hasten."

The literal sense of "make haste" in regard to quick action is indicated in 2 Chr. 35:21; Esth. 6:14; 8:14. The literal meaning "speedily," concerning shortness of time, is found in Esth. 2:9; Prov. 20:25; 28:22; Eccl. 5:2; 7:9; 8:3; Zeph. 1:18.

ḥippāzôn [חִפָּזוֹן, 2649]

This is a rare term found only three times, all with the sense of "hastily," "hurriedly," "in hurried flight." ***ḥippāzôn*** occurs only with reference to the time of the Passover and exodus from Egypt. Exod. 12:11; Deut. 16:3 refer to the hurried eating of the Passover meal; and Isa. 52:12 describes the hurried departure from Egypt.

NT Words

spoudē [σπουδή, *4710*]

spoudē is a noun with several meanings including "earnestness," "diligence," and also "haste." The term occurs twelve times but only means "haste" on two occasions, both of which are literal (Mark 6:25; Luke 1:39). Both texts refer to hurried action.

speudō [σπεύδω, *4692*]

speudō is the verbal root form of ***spoudē*** (see above). The term occurs six times, and all but one translate "make haste" or "hurry" in the literal sense of quick action (cf. Luke 2:16; 19:5, 6, Acts 20:16; 22:18). In 2 Pet. 3:12, ***speudō*** refers to the "hastening of the Day of the Lord" as the result of an eager anticipation of the final consummation of God's plan of redemption.

tacheōs [ταχέως, *5030*]

tacheōs is an adverb occurring ten times, meaning "hastily," "quickly." In regard to quick or hurried action, the term is found in Luke 14:21; 16:6; John 11:31; 1 Cor. 4:19. Concerning shortness of time, ***tacheōs*** occurs in Phil. 2:19; 2:24; 2 Thess. 2:2; 1 Tim. 5:22; 2 Tim. 4:9. Gal. 1:6 refers to Paul's anguish over the Galatian congregation's rapid deserting of the Lord after their conversion experience.

HATE, HATRED

OT Words

sānē' [שָׂנֵא, 8130]

sānē' is a fairly common verb with the primary meaning "hate." It occurs about 150 times.

In general, ***sānē'*** means "to bear great ill will or animosity" towards other people or against certain phenomena. In particular, ***sānē'*** indicates hatred towards the enemies of God's people, those who despise the children of Israel (cf. Gen. 24:60; Lev. 26:27; Num. 10:35). Deut. 30:7 refers to those enemies who hate Israel, who in turn will be cursed by God for their stand against his people. See also Esth. 9:1, 5; 2 Sam. 22:18; Pss. 34:21; 129:5. The psalmist offers a lament to Yahweh in the face of the hatred of his enemies (cf. Pss. 9:13; 18:17; 35:19; 69:14; 86:17). Several texts indicate an interpersonal animosity or hatred among individuals (cf. Gen. 26:27; 37:4ff.; Deut. 19:4; Judg. 20:5; 2 Sam. 5:8; 1 Kgs. 22:8; Job 8:22; Prov. 25:17).

sānē' also refers to those who hate evil of various kinds (cf. Exod. 18:21; Ps. 97:10; Eccl. 3:8). Prov. 8:13 indicates that to fear the Lord is to hate all evil; and Amos 5:15 contains a divine exhortation to hate evil and love that which is good.

sānē' also refers to those who hate God (cf. Exod. 20:5; Deut. 5:9; 32:41; 33:11; 2 Chr. 19:2; Ps. 21:8). For all such people, there will be terrible consequences. Prov. 8:36 declares that all who hate God love death; and in Ps. 139:21 the psalmist expresses his hatred of all those who hate God. ***sānē'*** also refers to those who hate all manner of goodness (cf. Ps. 120:6; Prov. 1:22; Eccl. 2:17; Mic. 3:2).

The Mosaic law contains explicit prohibitions against hating one's neighbor, for which sin there are severe penalties (cf. Lev. 19:17; Deut. 19:11; 21:16ff.; 22:13ff.; 24:3).

Yahweh is also frequently declared to hate sin, and in particular all those whose lifestyle demonstrates rebellion against him (cf. Deut. 12:31; Pss. 5:5; 11:5; 45:7; 101:3). His animosity is also directed against those who engage in false worship, denying God his just sacrifices (cf. Isa. 61:8; Amos 5:2; Zech. 8:17). See also Ps. 119:104; Hos. 9:15.

Finally, ***sānē'*** is used in a non-literal sense to indicate a failure to act in one's best interest — for example, Prov. 13:24, which declares that he who spares the rod "hates" his son.

NT Words

miseō [μισέω, *3404*]

miseō occurs about forty times with the exclusive sense of "hate." For the most part it occurs with a literal meaning, indicating animosity towards people, God, or particular attitudes. The term is also used in a non-literal sense, though this is rare.

The literal meaning of bearing ill will towards another person or persons is found in the majority of texts (e.g., Matt. 5:43, 44; 6:24; Luke 1:71; John 7:7; 17:14; Titus 3:3; 1 John 2:9ff.; Rev. 17:16). The world's hatred for the people of God is expressed in Luke 1:71; John 7:7; 15:18; 17:14; 1 John 3:13. Matt. 10:22; 24:9; Mark 13:13; Luke 21:17 describe suffering hatred for the cause of the gospel.

In Luke 14:26, a non-literal use of ***miseō*** refers to "hating one's father and mother . . ." This is a hyperbolic and symbolic use of the verb. Our love for God, for Christ, and for the cause of the gospel should so exceed all other loyalties that, compared with our earthly love for those in our family, our love for the Lord should make our mortal attachment to our loved ones seem like hatred. Explicit malice towards our families is, of course, in no way intended.

John 12:25 describes "hating one's life in order to save or keep it." A similar perspective is found in Luke 14:26. Hate in this text is not literal malice towards oneself, but rather indicates symbolically the most sublime expression of selflessness, expressed hyperbolically as "hatred." Eph. 5:29 also contains a strong expression of self-denial defined as hate.

Hatred of God, an attitude predicated of the wicked, is mentioned in John 15:24, as is the attitude of hating that which is good in John 3:20.

miseō also indicates hatred of sin in Heb. 1:9; Jude 23; Rev. 2:6, 15. Rom. 7:15 mentions the apostle Paul's personal dilemma in which he wrestles with conflicting desires of hatred of sin and an attraction to that which is evil. The paradox of God's attributes and decrees is revealed in Rom. 9:13, where he declares that he loved Jacob, but hated Esau.

stygētos [στυγητός, *4767*]

This term is only found in Titus 3:3, meaning "hateful," or bearing malice against one another.

theostygēs [θεοστυγής, *2319*]

A variation of ***stygētos*** (see above), ***theostygēs*** occurs only once and refers to "God-haters" in Rom. 1:30.

HAUGHTY → PRIDE

HAVEN

OT Words

māḥôz [**מָחוֹז, 4231**]

māḥôz occurs only once, in Ps. 107:30, and means "haven" as a place of refuge and rest, provided by Yahweh.

ḥôph [**חוֹף, 2348**]

This rare term occurs seven times, meaning "seashore" or "coast," and also has the extended senses of "haven" or "refuge" — a safe harbor for people and ships. Gen. 49:13 contains two references to a safe haven for Zebulun, the Israelite tribe located on the coast. Other references to a safe haven on the seashore of Canaan are found in Deut. 1:7; Josh. 9:1; Judg. 5:17; Jer. 47:7; Ezek. 25:6.

NT Words

limēn [λιμήν, *3040*]

limēn is a rare term, occurring only three times in Acts 27:8, 12, indicating a safe haven or harbor, a refuge from storms.

HAY → GRASS

HEAD

OT Words

rō'sh [**רֹאשׁ, 7218**]

rō'sh is a common term found in nearly 600 contexts with the primary meaning "head" in both a literal and metaphorical sense, as well as a number of related meanings.

In Gen. 2:10, ***rō'sh*** indicates the "head" or source of a river. The literal sense of a human head as part of the body is found in a variety of contexts. Mundane references are found in Gen. 40:16; Lev. 13:12; Num. 5:18; Deut. 21:12; 1 Sam. 17:51; Ezek. 5:1; Jer. 48:37. The ritual of patriarchal blessing, whereby the father places his hand on the head of his son, is recorded of Jacob and his sons in Gen. 48:14ff.; 49:26. The head of the high priest is anointed as part of the ceremony of his ordination (cf. Exod. 29:6ff.; Lev. 8:9, 12). As part of the Nazirite vow, one is forbidden to shave his head during the course of the vow (cf. Num. 6:5ff.; Judg. 13:5; 1 Sam. 1:11). The practice of laying hands on the head of a man condemned to death is recorded in Lev. 24:14 (cf. also Num. 25:4). The practice of anointing the heads of kings as part of their coronation is indicated in 1 Sam. 10:1; 2 Kgs. 9:6.

In a slightly different context, ***rō'sh*** refers to the head of an idol in 1 Sam. 5:4. Elsewhere the term refers to the "heads" (i.e., leaders) of various groups of people — for example, tribal chiefs (cf. Exod. 6:14; Num. 1:4; 7:2; Deut. 1:15; Josh. 19:51; 1 Kgs. 8:1); civil and judicial leaders (cf. Exod. 18:25; Num. 13:3; Josh. 24:1); royalty (cf. Josh. 11:10; 1 Sam. 15:4; Isa. 7:4); judgeship (cf. Judg. 11:11); high (or chief) priests (cf. 2 Chr. 24:6; Neh. 12:7; Jer. 52:24).

Heads of animals are also indicated in the use of this term, referring to the preparation and process of ritual offering (e.g., Exod. 12:9; Lev. 1:4ff.; 4:4ff.; 16:21; Num. 8:12).

In an inanimate sense, ***rō'sh*** refers to the "head" or highest point of certain objects — for example, of mountains (cf. Gen. 8:5; Exod. 19:20; Num. 14:40; Isa. 30:17); towers (cf. Gen. 11:4); a ladder (cf. Gen. 28:12); and buildings (cf. Exod. 28:32; 1 Kgs. 7:17ff.). These two latter texts refer to the tabernacle and temple. Ps. 118:22 speaks of the chief cornerstone of the temple, in reference to the coming Messiah.

rō'sh is used metaphorically in a number of contexts. For instance, Gen. 3:15 mentions the "head of the serpent," a reference to Satan upon whose head the seed of the woman will inflict a mortal wound. The term "head" also refers generally to a position of superiority over others (cf. Deut. 28:44). This word is also found in the expression "lift up one's head," which describes one's restoration to a position of honor (cf. Gen. 40:13; Pss. 3:3; 24:7; 27:6; 83:2). Significantly, in Ps. 110:7 this phrase describes the coming to power of the messianic ruler.

The phrase "blood upon one's head" indicates a sign of guilt (cf. Josh. 2:19; 2 Sam. 1:16; 1 Kgs. 2:32; Ezek. 33:4). Sprinkling dust upon one's head indicates an attitude of humility, or anguish over committing an offense, or in the face of overwhelming catastrophe (cf. Josh. 7:6; Lam. 2:10; Ezek. 27:30). The general phrase ". . . upon one's own head" conveys the idea of receiving just punishment for one's misdeeds, usually indicating personal guilt, as in the expression "blood upon one's head" (see above) (cf. 1 Sam. 25:39; Ps. 7:16; Ezek. 9:10; 11:21; Joel 3:4, 7; Obad. 15; Prov. 25:22). Occasionally the sense is wholly positive, as in Isa. 35:10; 51:11, where the expression "joy upon one's head" describes the happy consequence of the blessing of salvation.

qādad [קָדַד, 6915]

This verb occurs fifteen times meaning "to bow the head," "bow down," — either as an act of worship to Yahweh, or in deference to one's superior.

With regard to the worship of Yahweh, ***qādad*** is found in Gen. 24:26; 43:28; Exod. 4:31; 12:27; 34:8; Num. 22:31; 1 Chr. 29:20; Neh. 8:6. Acts of deference towards one who is reckoned to be one's superior are recorded, for example, in 1 Sam. 24:8, where David bows down to Saul. See also 1 Sam. 28:14; 1 Kgs. 1:31.

NT Words

kephalē [κεφαλή, *2776*]

This noun is found approximately eighty times with the principal meaning "head." As with its Hebrew dynamic equivalent (see ***rō'sh***, above), ***kephalē*** conveys a varied range of nuances associated with the concept of "head," both literal as well as metaphorical. The literal meaning is self-explanatory, but the metaphorical sense refers to "headship," suggesting that which is supreme, whether it be in the civil, ritual, or familial sphere of human relationships. In the New Testament, ***kephalē*** has a particular significance regarding the standing of Jesus Christ as head of the church, functioning both as its divine founder and ongoing sustainer, through the person of the Holy Spirit.

With the literal meaning of a human head ***kephalē*** is found, for example, in Matt. 5:36; 10:30; Mark 6:24ff.; Luke 7:38ff.; John 13:9; Acts 18:18. Matt. 8:20; Luke 9:58 refer to Christ having nowhere to lay his head — that is, having no permanent home. John 19:2; Matt. 27:29 refer to the wounds inflicted on Jesus' head prior to his crucifixion. John 19:30 refers to Jesus bowing his head at the point of death, as an act of submission to his Father.

The metaphorical usage of ***kephalē*** is quite extensive. The phrase "blood upon one's head" constitutes a symbolic reference to one's condemnation and guilt (cf. Acts 18:6). To "heap coals of fire upon one's head" is an action cited in Rom. 12:20 which alludes to the aggravation of personal guilt as a consequence of rendering to one's enemy good for evil.

kephalē also refers to the phenomenon of "headship," from both a human and divine perspective. Within the sphere of the family, for example, 1 Cor. 11:3 speaks of a fundamental divine ordering: the head of man is Christ; the head of woman is man, and the head of Christ is God (cf. Eph. 5:23). 1 Cor. 11:5, 10 maintains that a woman uncovering her head amounts to a dishonoring of her head, violating her symbolic submission to both her husband and to Christ. The argument is also adduced (1 Cor. 11:7) that because the man is "then head of his wife" and made in the image of God, his head is not to be covered. The term ***kephalē*** here is used symbolically to refer not to respective values of man and woman in the sight of God, but rather to their relative functions in the divinely ordered sphere of family and worship.

kephalē also conveys a divine perspective on headship. For example, reference to Jesus Christ as the chief cornerstone, the one rejected by the builder, is interpreted by the gospel writers as a fulfillment of the Old Testament prophecy in Ps. 18:22 (cf. Matt. 21:42; Mark 12:10; Luke 20:17). References to Christ as head of the church are found in Eph. 1:22; 4:15; 5:23; Col. 1:18; 2:19. In addition, Christ is depicted as the head of all rulers in the kingdom of God, the supreme figure of universal authority (cf. Col. 2:10).

Significant metaphorical usage of the term ***kephalē*** is also found throughout the book of Revelation. The visionary head of Christ is depicted, for example, in Rev. 1:14 (cf. also Rev. 10:1). Rev. 14:14 refers to the head of the "Son of man"; and Rev. 19:12 speaks of the head of the messianic white rider, who has many crowns on his head. Rev. 4:4 refers symbolically to the heads of the heavenly creatures around God's throne (cf. also Rev. 12:1). Heads of locusts are also depicted in the apocalyptic vision of judgment in Rev. 9:7. Similarly, the head of the dragon (i.e., Satan) is described in Rev. 12:3, and the head of the sea beast (i.e., the false messiah, antichrist) in Rev. 13:1. The head of the scarlet woman, the great "whore of Babylon," symbolizing all the godless nations of the world, is also mentioned in Rev. 17:3ff. Those who witness the destruction of the city of Babylon in this context are described as sprinkling dust on their heads — a sign of anguish at the fall of the great city (cf. Rev. 18:19).

Additional Notes

The meanings of the Hebrew and Greek terminology for "head" and "headship" overlap significantly. This is especially the case when one compares the usage of ***rō'sh*** and ***kephalē*** in the area of authority, both divine and human. The various offices of human authority and rule anticipate or reflect a divine pattern, especially considering the nature of Israelite worship and theocracy. Headship inherent in the priestly, civil, and regal spheres of Israelite society finds its eschatological and messianic fulfillment in the person of Christ. The New Testament makes it abundantly clear that the authority of Jesus as head of the church has very significant implications for the life of God's people in the fundamental spheres of marriage and family.

HEAL, HEALING

OT Words

rāphā' **[רָפָא, 7495]**

This verb occurs around seventy times with the dominant meaning "heal" in both a figurative and literal sense. Healing is predicated of both God and human beings and relates to groups and individuals alike. In a small number of texts, ***rāphā'*** is used as a noun meaning "physician."

Miraculous healing by the hand of God is found in Gen. 20:17; Exod. 15:26; Deut. 32:39; 2 Chr. 30:20. In Num. 12:13, Moses successfully pleads with Yahweh to cleanse Miriam from her leprosy. A promise of healing is given in 2 Kgs. 20:5, 8; and in Ps. 6:2 the psalmist begs for healing. Divine refusal to heal, as part of the covenant curse, is noted in Deut. 28:27, 35.

Physical healing of an indeterminate or general nature, without the mention of any agency, is recorded in Exod. 21:19; Lev. 13:18, 37; 2 Kgs. 8:29; Job 5:18. The noun "physician" is found in Gen. 50:2, and healing at the hands of a physician is indicated in 2 Chr. 16:12.

The metaphorical use of ***rāphā'*** is found in a variety of contexts — for example, in 1 Kgs. 2:21, 22 the water is "healed" in the sense of making it potable. The healing, or restoration and renewal, of the land of Canaan occurs in a number of places (cf. 2 Chr. 7:14; Ps. 60:2; Isa. 19:22). In Ezek. 47:8ff. a spectacular vision of renewal describes the divine promise to bring about a transformation of Canaan through the "healing" effect of the river flowing out from under the sanctuary of the visionary temple.

rāphā' also indicates healing in the sense of personal renewal (cf. Pss. 41:4; 147:3; Eccl. 3:3). Isa. 6:10; 30:26 both speak of heart renewal, or conversion. Especially significant is the use of this term to indicate the forgiveness of sin through the vicarious suffering of the Messiah in Isa. 53:5. Similar references to such divine healing are found in Jer. 3:22; 8:11; 30:17; 33:6; Hos. 6:1; 7:1; 11:3; 14:4. A plea for healing in the sense of renewal, possibly forgiveness, is found in Jer. 17:14. See also Lam. 2:13.

Ezek. 34:4; Zech. 11:16 refer to healing in the sense of being cared for from a negative perspective — Israel's leaders have sorely neglected the people and failed to "heal" and nurture them.

marpē' [מַרְפֵּא, 4832]

marpē' is found fifteen times with the underlying sense of "health," "healing," as well as the meaning "incurable" when used in the negative. The term is used in both a literal and metaphorical sense.

The literal sense of "health" is indicated in Jer. 8:15. ***marpē'*** occurs with the negative in 2 Chr. 21:18, referring to "incurable disease." Also, Jer. 14:19 expresses the vain hope for healing in the light of God's judgment upon his people.

Metaphorically speaking, health, in the sense of peace of mind, is indicated in Prov. 12:18; 16:24; and the promised blessing of renewal in the same sense is found in Jer. 33:6; Mal. 4:2.

'arukāh [אֲרֻכָה, 724]

This is a rare noun, occurring only six times and meaning "healing," "soundness," "health" in four of these instances. Divine healing in the sense of spiritual renewal is indicated in Isa. 58:8; Jer. 30:17; 33:6. Jer. 8:22 refers to Israel's poor health, or her sinful condition.

NT Words

therapeuō [θεραπεύω, *2323*]

therapeuō occurs around forty times with the principal sense of "heal," "cure."

Literal use of this term in reference to Jesus' healing miracles is frequently found in the Synoptic Gospels. Cure from physical illness is mentioned, for example, in Matt. 4:23; 12:10; Mark 1:30; 6:13; and healing from demonically induced sickness in Matt. 8:16; 12:22; Luke 6:18. Other references to healing include that in Matt. 17:16, where the disciples are unable to cure the demon-possessed boy. Luke 8:43 mentions the woman with hemophilia with no medical hope of a cure; Jesus subsequently heals her. In Acts 4:14; 5:16 the crippled man at the gate of the temple is miraculously cured through the agency of Peter and John. The healing ministry of Philip is cited in Acts 8:7; as is Paul's healing activity on Malta in Acts 28:9.

Finally, Rev. 13:3, 12 records the counterfeit healing of the sea beast, mimicking the resurrection of Christ.

iaomai [ἰάομαι, *2390*]

iaomai is synonymous with ***therapeuō***, above, and occurs approximately thirty times.

iaomai refers to the healing ministry of Jesus, both in regard to physical illness (cf. Matt. 8:8; Mark 5:29; Luke 5:17; John 4:47; Acts 10:38); as well as to demonic oppression (cf. Luke 9:42). See also Luke 4:18.

iaomai also refers to God's regenerating activity, but in contexts that indicate a withholding of divine healing. Matt. 13:15 speaks of God's judgment on Israel's hardness of heart and applies that judgment to unbelieving Jews in Jesus' day, stating that in the face of persistent unbelief their hearts will be hardened lest they turn and be healed (cf. also John 12:40; Acts 28:27). In contrast, 1 Pet. 2:24 cites the saving power of the cross of Christ, specifically the wounds he bore by which his people have been healed (cf. Isa. 53:5).

Further examples of physical healing are mentioned in Acts 3:11; 9:34, with reference to Peter and John; and in Acts 28:8 (Paul). In Heb. 12:13, healing is indicated in the sense of spiritual soundness; and Jas. 5:16 records a prayer for healing.

sōzō [σώζω, *4982*]

This verb has the virtually exclusive meaning "save," but sometimes refers to the action of healing, with the translation "make whole" on sixteen occasions. The ideas of "saving" and "healing" are closely linked in these texts. (→ SAVE)

In relation to Jesus' healing ministry, ***sōzō*** refers to physical illness (cf. Matt. 9:21ff.; Mark 5:23ff.; 6:56; 10:52; Luke 8:48, 50; 17:19; 18:42). Luke 8:36 refers to Jesus curing demon possession. ***sōzō*** is also found in connection with the healing activity of Peter and John in Acts 4:9; and of Paul in Acts 14:9. See also Jas. 5:16.

diasōzō [διασώζω, *1295*]

diasōzō occurs eight times, meaning "save" or "escape" in all but two of these texts, where it means "heal" (Matt. 14:36; Luke 7:3). Both refer to the healing work of Christ.

Additional Notes

The semantic range of both the Hebrew and Greek vocabulary for "healing" is much the same. Both Testaments emphasize the phenomenon of divine healing — at the hand of Yahweh in the Old, and by Jesus Christ in the New. Both Testaments also attach great importance to the concept of healing as spiritual renewal, lending a non-personal aspect to the Hebrew vocabulary for "healing" in regard to the land. This motif of land renewal is transcended in the New Testament, where healing is only applied to individuals. The land of Canaan, as the supreme symbol of old covenant "rest," finds fulfillment not in an earthly location, but in the person of Christ the Messiah. Hence healing in the new covenant naturally centers around the healing work of Christ, who is the only one capable of effecting a complete healing and personal transformation on both the physical and spiritual plane.

HEAR, HEARING

OT Words

***shāma'* [שָׁמַע, 8085]**

This is a common term in the Old Testament, occurring around 1,150 times. The primary meanings of ***shāma'*** are "hear," "listen," with a number of associated senses.

The literal sense of "hear" as "auditory perception" occurs in a variety of contexts. With God as the object of hearing, see Gen. 3:8, 10; Num. 7:89; 24:16; Ezek. 2:2. Significant in this regard is the voice of Yahweh on Mt. Sinai (cf. Exod. 19:9; Deut. 4:12, 36). See also Isa. 6:8. With God as subject, Yahweh hears the complaints of his people (Exod. 16:8; Deut. 1:34); he hears his people swear allegiance to him (Deut. 5:28); and he overhears their complaints (Num. 12:2; 14:27). With the object of information from human sources, ***shāma'*** is found in Gen. 35:22; Exod. 18:1; Judg. 7:15; and with other people as the object of hearing, this term occurs in Gen. 37:22; Lev. 5:1; Num. 11:10; Song 2:14. ***shāma'*** is also used to describe hearing various sounds — for example, the sound of ritual celebration (Josh. 6:20); the trumpet for royal anointing and coronation (2 Sam. 15:10); the noise of cattle (Jer. 9:10); the wings of cherubim (Ezek. 1:24); and the sound of people cheering and weeping (Ezra 3:13). Deut. 4:28 mentions the utter inability of idols to hear anything whatsoever. ***shāma'*** also conveys the sense of "listen," or "give heed, or attention to." In a number of contexts, people constitute the object of such "hearing." For instance, Gen. 3:17 refers to Adam's sin in giving heed to Eve's sinful offer of fruit from the forbidden tree. A number of texts refer to Pharaoh's refusal to listen to Moses' instruction to let the Israelites go free and leave Egypt, a refusal that leads to God hardening Pharaoh's heart (cf. Exod. 7:4, 13; 8:15; 9:12; 11:9). The importance of giving careful attention to the words of one's parents is recorded in Gen. 49:2; Deut. 21:18; Prov. 1:8; 4:1, 10; 5:7; 7:24. See also Gen. 4:23; 27:13; 16:2; Job 31:35.

God is often described as one who pays close attention to, and listens carefully to, his people and their need. In particular, the following passages indicate the divine response of mercy as Yahweh hears his people crying to him: Exod. 2:24; 3:7; 6:2; Num. 20:16; 2 Sam. 22:7; 1 Kgs. 9:3. In Ps. 6:8, God is said to hear his people cry. See also Gen. 16:11; 21:17; 29:33; Deut. 9:19. Conversely, several texts indicate God's refusal to listen to his people because of their sin (cf. Deut. 1:45; 3:26; Ezek. 8:18). There are numerous requests made of God to hear the cry of his people and respond with compassion. Solomon prays for such a response in 1 Kgs. 8:28ff.; as does Nehemiah in Neh. 1:6. Such pleas are commonly found in the Psalter (e.g., Pss. 4:1; 5:3; 18:6; 28:2; 64:1; 119:49; 143:1). See also Dan. 9:17, 19.

A particularly significant usage of ***shāma'*** occurs when Yahweh is made the object of such careful listening — that is, when his people are instructed to pay very close attention to what he has to say. For example, the Israelites are commanded to heed God's voice (cf. Exod. 15:26; Isa. 46:3; 1 Sam. 3:9ff.; Jer. 2:4; 10:1; Ezek. 2:8); and to pay close attention to his law (cf. Deut. 5:1; 6:3, 4; Josh. 3:9; Eccl. 5:1; Isa. 28:3; 30:21). Similarly, the nations are commanded to hear the word of the Lord (Isa. 1:10; 18:3; 34:1; 43:9). In a sustained metaphor, the mountains of Israel are instructed to hear the voice of God in the context of a promised renewal of the land and return form exile in Ezek. 36:1, 4. In Mic. 6:2, the mountains of the earth are called upon to give heed to the accusation of Yahweh against his people. Lev. 26:14 warns against not giving heed to God's words. Isa. 6:10 threatens an inevitable divine curse whereby Israel will be afflicted with a hardness of heart so that they will be unable to hear the Lord and respond in repentance. Specific indictments against Israel are issued for their failure to take heed of Yahweh and his word (cf. Ezek. 3:7; 20:8; Hos. 9:17). In a tragically poignant context, Amos 8:11 declares that there will be a "famine of hearing the word of God" in Israel as a consequence of the people's sin.

It is clear that the sense of ***shāma'***, indicating a careful listening to God and giving heed to him, is tantamount to the idea of obeying him. ***shāma'*** is also found with this meaning in a number of contexts. For example, Abraham's obedience towards God is mentioned in Gen. 22:18; 26:5. In Josh. 24:10, the people of Israel promise to obey God in a ceremony of covenant renewal. The importance of obeying God's covenant word through his spoken revelation is indicated in Exod. 19:5; 23:22; 24:7; Jer. 7:23; 11:4; Hag. 1:12. A specific warning against disobeying God is found in Deut. 11:28. Punishment for failing to obey the voice of Yahweh is explicitly cited in a number of places — for example, during the period of the judges (cf. Judg. 2:2, 20; 6:10); against King Saul for his disobedience (cf.

1 Sam. 15:9); and against Israel for hers (cf. Isa. 30:9; Jer. 7:28; Dan. 9:11). See also Jer. 3:13, 25.

There is also a judicial sense associated with the use of ***shāma'*** when the term refers to "hearing" legal disputes in Deut. 1:16, 17. In a related context, Isa. 1:2 calls for heaven and earth to witness the indictment against Israel and "hear" the account of her sins.

Finally, ***shāma'*** means "hear about" in the sense of "gain knowledge of." This is predicated of people, concerning their awareness of God and his acts of salvation on their behalf (cf. Num. 14:4, 15; Josh. 2:10; Ruth 1:6). ***shāma'*** in this sense also refers to people's knowledge of others — for example, when Eli hears about the wickedness of his sons (1 Sam. 2:22); and when the Queen of Sheba learns of Solomon's great wisdom and knowledge (1 Kgs. 10:1ff.). See also Num. 21:1. Such awareness is also predicated of the nations hearing about God's deeds and being afraid (cf. Josh. 9:1; 10:1).

'ānāh [עָנָה, 6030]

'ānāh occurs over three hundred times with the primary sense of "answer." In about forty places the term means "hear," although the contexts suggest the common idea of response.

Occasionally, ***'ānāh*** conveys the literal sense of "hear" as auditory perception — as in 1 Sam. 7:9, where God hears the voice of his people. In 1 Kgs. 18:26, the prophets of Baal plead in vain for their idol god to hear; and in response, Elijah pleads, successfully, for Yahweh to hear (i.e., respond to) his plea to ignite the offering on the altar.

'ānāh also conveys the idea of "hear" in the sense of "listen to," or "heed." In a negative context, God is said not to hear his people because of their sin (cf. 1 Sam. 8:18ff.; Mic. 3:4). Pleas are also directed towards God in a number of places — that he might give heed and listen. The psalmist gives many such pleas (cf. Pss. 4:1; 13:3; 20:1; 38:15; 69:13). Yahweh is also affirmed as one who does in fact give careful attention to his people (cf. Pss. 3:4; 119:26; Isa. 41:17; Jonah 2:2; Zech. 10:6).

'āzan [אָזַן, 238]

'āzan is synonymous with ***shāma'*** and ***'ānāh***, above. This terms occurs around forty times and constitutes the verbal root form of the noun ***'ōzen*** (→ EAR). ***'āzan***, therefore, has the underlying sense of "give ear to," and thus the meanings "hear," "listen to," "be obedient."

In the literal sense of "listen, give heed to," ***'āzan*** is found in contexts where people give and receive the instruction to listen (e.g., Gen. 4:25; Judg. 5:3; Job 34:2; Ps. 49:1). God also commands attention in order to convey a message of condemnation against his people (cf. Isa. 28:23; 32:9; Jer. 13:15; Hos. 5:1). People give heed to God's commandments (cf. Exod. 15:26; Job 32:11). The psalmist also pleads with God to give heed to his people (cf. Pss. 5:1; 17:1; 55:1; 140:6). In Deut. 1:45 God is the subject, and here ***'āzan*** indicates Yahweh's refusal to listen to his people on account of their sin. Conversely, in Ps. 77:1 God does give careful attention to the psalmist's plea. Then, in Deut. 32:1; Isa. 1:2, God commands that elements of the created order will pay close attention to his testimony against Israel. In Isa. 1:10, the nations are also given a divine instruction to hear the word of Yahweh.

NT Words

akouō [ἀκούω, *191*]

This is a common New Testament verb, occurring around 450 times with the primary sense of "hear," as well as associated senses such as "listen," "give heed to," "comprehend."

With people as subject, ***akouō*** refers to the literal sense of hearing as auditory perception in a number of contexts. For example, aural witness is very important to the life of Jesus (cf. John 3:32; 1 John 1:1), and to his teaching ministry (Matt. 21:45; Mark 6:2; Luke 5:1; John 9:40). As part of the record of Saul's conversion experience, Acts 9:4ff.; 22:7; 26:14 all refer to his hearing the voice of Jesus en route to Damascus. Rom. 10:14 affirms the indispensability of hearing the word of the Lord in order to be saved. Jesus' miraculous restoration of hearing to the deaf is recorded in Matt. 11:5; Mark 7:37. Various references are also made to hearing the voice of God or angels in episodes of divine visitation (cf. Luke 2:20; Acts 10:46; 2 Cor. 12:4; Rev. 5:11; 10:8; 11:12; 14:2). See also Acts 2:6ff.

akouō also has the sense of "hearing about," such as news or information. General references in a mundane sense are found, for example, in Matt. 12:24; Luke 1:58; Acts 7:12; 23:16; 1 Cor. 11:18; Gal. 1:23; 2 Thess. 3:11; Jas. 5:11. Mark 6:55; John 12:18 also refer to people hearing about Jesus and his miracle working. John the Baptist hears about the ministry of Jesus in Matt. 11:2. Paul's delight in hearing about the faith of his fellow believers is noted in Col. 1:4; Phlm. 5.

Hearing in the sense of "understanding" is also indicated in the usage of ***akouō***. Specific blessings that result from genuine spiritual understanding (viz. "hearing") are mentioned in Matt. 13:16; Mark 4:20; Luke 11:28; John 5:24. This includes hearing that leads to conversion (cf. Acts 4:4; 10:44; 18:8; Eph. 1:13). In the Sermon on the Mount, Jesus says, "You have heard that it was said . . ." several times (cf. Matt. 5:21ff.). This new legislation transcends the mere outward formality of the old covenant law, and here Jesus expounds the true inner requirement of divine law, contrasting the external mode of the Mosaic law code.

As with the Hebrew terminology in the Old Testament, ***akouō*** also conveys the idea of "listen carefully, pay heed to." Its predominant usage in the New Testament focuses on the importance of carefully heeding the teaching of Jesus. Note the expression: "He who has ears to hear, let him hear . . ." in Matt. 11:15; Rev. 2:7ff.; 3:6ff.; 13:9. See also Matt. 17:5; Mark 9:7; Luke 16:29; Acts 2:22. In Mark 12:29, Jesus cites the command of Deut. 6:4: "Hear, O Israel, the Lord our God, the Lord is one." Other related contexts stress the importance of hearing the word of God in worship (cf. Acts 13:44); hearing the law of Moses (cf. Gal. 4:21); heeding the words of the apostle Paul (cf. 2 Tim. 1:13); and hearing God's voice and obeying him (cf. Heb. 3:7, 15; 4:7). Negative connotations are also associated with the use of ***akouō***. Failing to hear (i.e., understand, or give close attention to) the word of God in the proclamation of the gospel leads inevitably to spiritual dullness, and hardness of heart (cf. Matt. 13:13, 15; Mark 4:12; Acts 28:27). This is a central theme of the parable of the sower (cf. Luke 8:12ff.), where the seed falling on the path symbolizes the terrible reality of non-productive hearing. See also John 8:47; Rom. 11:8. Conversely, keen hearing in the sense of acute spiritual perception constitutes a profound blessing (cf. Matt. 13:16; 1 Cor. 2:9).

Jesus is also portrayed as the unique "hearer" of God's word (cf. John 8:40; 15:15); and thanks his heavenly Father for hearing him (cf. John 11:41).

Infrequently, God is portrayed as the subject of this verb, as one who has heard the groans and pleas of his people and has responded to them with mercy and grace (cf. Acts 7:34; 1 John 5:14).

akoē [ἄκοη, *189*]

akoē is the noun derived from ***akouō***, above. It occurs about twenty-five times, meaning "hearing" in about half of these contexts

There is a literal reference to the process of hearing as a means to true spiritual understanding in Matt. 13:14; Rom. 10:17; Gal. 3:25; 1 Thess. 2:13.

'akoē is also found in contexts of judgment, where God's people have become "hard of hearing" and are placed under divine judgment (cf. Acts 28:26; Heb. 5:11).

Mundane references to hearing as auditory perception are found in 1 Cor. 12:17; 2 Pet. 2:8.

Additional Notes

The semantic range of the Hebrew and Greek vocabulary for "hearing" is very similar. In both cases, the importance of hearing the word of God and responding to it appropriately is emphasized with forcefulness and clarity. It is also clear that the focus of true spiritual "hearing" comes to a climax in the person of Christ, whose very person and work fulfills that which was anticipated in the old covenant era.

HEART

OT Words

lēb [לֵב, 3820]; *lēbāb* [לֵבָב, 3824]

These two synonymous terms are commonly found throughout the entire Old Testament. Together, ***lēb*** and ***lēbāb*** occur about 850 times (***lēb*** occurs about twice as frequently as ***lēbāb***). Almost without exception, the two nouns mean "heart" in every case, with a number of very significant metaphorical connotations. ***lēb*** and ***lēbāb*** rarely refer to "heart" as the physical organ of the body — rather they refer to the inner person, the mind, understanding, and underlying attitudes of human beings, all subsumed under the metaphorical term "heart." In addition, the term is used anthropomorphically of God. It also refers occasionally to inanimate objects.

With regard to persons, ***lēb*** and ***lēbāb*** signify the heart as the seat of a person's inner being, guiding motivation, or moral conscience. Perhaps the broadest sense of this terminology occurs in those contexts where ***lēb*** refers to "heart" in the sense of "in one's own mind," or even "to oneself" (cf. Gen. 17:17; 24:45; Num. 16:28; 1 Kgs. 12:26; Neh. 5:17). Ps. 14:1 defines the fool as one who says "in his or her heart" there is no God. See also Eccl. 3:18; Ezek. 14:4. ***lēb*** signifies one's mind and predisposition. For example, 1 Kgs. 3:9; Ps. 57:7 point to the desire for an understanding heart to serve God. Prov. 3:3, 5 contains the exhortation: "Trust the Lord with all your heart, and do not lean on your own understanding." A negative predisposition towards evil is also indicated in the use of this term (cf. Jer. 23:26; Ezek. 6:9), as in the following texts where the human heart is depicted as evil (cf. Gen. 6:5; 8:21; Prov. 10:20; Isa. 32:6; Jer. 3:6; 17:19; Ezek. 20:16). See also

1 Kgs. 11:3; Isa. 29:13; Jer. 17:5, which refer to people's hearts turning away from God.

lēbāb also refers to one's mind and predisposition, in both a positive and negative sense. Positively, for example, it refers to serving God with all one's heart (Deut. 11:13); taking God's law to heart gladly (cf. Deut. 4:9; 5:29; 11:18); and praising him with wholehearted devotion (cf. Pss. 86:12; 111:1). The indispensable prerequisite of seeking and loving God with all one's heart is indicated in Deut. 4:29; 1 Sam. 7:3; 1 Kgs. 2:4; Ezra 7:10; Ps. 86:11; Jer. 29:13. This is emphasized particularly in the great commandment of Deut. 6:5 (cf. also Deut. 10:12; Josh. 22:5; 1 Kgs. 8:48; Joel 2:12). Another indispensable criterion for gaining favor with God is circumcision of the heart — a powerful metaphor expressing the sovereign work of divine grace in transforming a person's predisposition towards God, resulting in fervent devotion towards him (cf. Deut. 10:16; 30:6; Pss. 24:4; 73:1). Closely related to this motif is the usage of ***lēb*** in the following texts that refer to the divine promise of a renewed heart to serve and live for Yahweh. These all allude to the anticipation of new covenant blessing (cf. Jer. 31:33; 32:39; Ezek. 11:19; 36:26).

The negative corollary of this phenomenon is the "uncircumcised" heart that indicates an attitude of hardhearted indifference towards, or rebellion against, God. Both ***lēb*** and ***lēbāb*** are used in this way — ***lēb*** in Jer. 9:26; Ezek. 44:7, 9; with allusions to the condition also in Ezek. 3:7; 28:2; Hos. 13:6; Obad. 3; and ***lēbāb*** in Lev. 26:41; Jer. 4:4; with similar allusions in Deut. 8:14; 29:18; 1 Sam. 6:6; 1 Kgs. 11:12ff.; 2 Kgs. 10:31; Ps. 101:5. Of particular interest here is the role played by God in this process, especially in regard to Pharaoh's hardness of heart. ***lēb*** is the predominant term used in this context. The exodus narrative of the plague judgments against Egypt is the primary setting for this motif. Here Yahweh is specifically declared to be the agent of hardening concerning the heart of Pharaoh, resulting in his continual refusal to free the Israelites from their captivity (cf. Exod. 4:21; 7:3, 13, 14; 9:12; 10:1, 20, 27; 11:10; 14:4, 8). At other times during this period Pharaoh is also declared to have hardened his own heart (cf. Exod. 8:15, 32; 9:34); or the hardening is indicated in a passive sense with no mention of any direct agency (cf. Exod. 7:22; 8:19; 9:7). Other references to the divine agency in bringing about a hardening of the heart are found in Isa. 6:10; 63:17; Ezra 6:22; 1 Sam. 6:6. Warnings and commands against hardening one's heart are also found in a couple of contexts, both utilizing the term ***lēbāb*** (cf. Deut. 15:7; Ps. 95:8).

Both ***lēb*** and ***lēbāb*** also refer to the "heart" as the seat of a person's will and the center of emotions. Concerning the heart as the seat of the will, ***lēb*** occurs in Exod. 25:2; 35:22; 2 Chr. 29:31 — all dealing with motivation for the freewill offering. Elsewhere, ***lēb*** indicates the "heart" as a kind of "true, inner self" (cf. Exod. 31:6; Judg. 16:15; 1 Sam. 1:13; Job 33:3; Pss. 26:2; 119:11). The predominant theme of these contexts is a positive inclination of the human heart towards God and his saving purposes. In addition, ***lēb*** indicates "heart" in reference to one's emotional makeup or constitution (cf. Gen. 42:8; 2 Sam. 14:1; Neh. 2:2; Ps. 16:9; Song 3:11; Lam. 3:65). ***lēbāb*** also reflects these meanings in a number of contexts — for example, in reference to the inner self (cf. Gen. 20:5; 1 Kgs. 8:19; Job 17:11; Ps. 139:23); and to one's emotional makeup (cf. Lev. 26:36; Deut. 19:6; 20:8; Isa. 1:5; 30:9; Jer. 15:16). Negative emotions such as "fear" are sometimes associated with this term in relation to people's hearts (cf. Josh. 2:11; Isa. 13:7; 19:1; Isa. 21:4); as is the case with ***lēb*** as well (cf. Deut. 28:65; Josh. 14:8; 1 Sam. 4:13; Isa. 35:4).

lēb and ***lēbāb*** also commonly refer to the worship of God with one's whole heart and whole being (cf. Lam. 3:41; Ps. 20:4 [both with ***lēbāb***]; and 1 Kgs. 8:23; 18:37; 2 Kgs. 23:3; Pss. 9:1; 19:14; 97:11; 119:10, 34 [all with ***lēb***]). Related to this idea is the desire to renew one's relationship with God after committing sin through a plea for a "clean heart" (***lēb***). See Ps. 51:10, as part of David's classic prayer of repentance for his adultery with Bathsheba. See also Pss. 34:18; 51:17.

References to the physical organ of the heart (i.e., ***lēb***) are found in Exod. 28:29ff.; 1 Sam. 25:37; 2 Sam. 18:14; 2 Kgs. 9:24.

When predicated of Yahweh, the terms ***lēb*** and ***lēbāb*** are used exclusively in an anthropomorphic sense to indicate his own true inner being, the divine essence, which is indicative of his own will and purpose. Although there are only a few references with this rather specialized meaning, they are all highly significant. For instance, ***lēb*** refers in Gen. 8:21 to Yahweh's divine intention to preserve the created order after the judgment of the Noahic flood. That is, God said "in his heart" that he would never again destroy humankind as he had just done by means of universal inundation. In that same context, Gen. 6:6 records God grieving in his heart over the sin of humankind. And in 1 Kgs. 9:3; 2 Chr. 7:16 the mention of God's heart signals his capacity to care and demonstrate his compassionate love. ***lēbāb*** is similarly used in 1 Sam. 2:35 with reference to the choice of Samuel as being in full accord with Yahweh's will and purpose. 1 Sam. 13:14 refers to God's choice of David as king as a "man after his own heart."

lēb and ***lēbāb*** are also used to refer to inanimate objects — for example, ***lēb*** indicates "the heart of sea" (i.e., the very midst) in Exod. 15:8; Ps. 46:2; Ezek. 27:27. Deut. 4:11 refers to the "heart of the heavens" in alluding to the extent of the supernatural fire of theophany on Mt. Sinai. ***lēbāb*** is used only once in this way, in Jonah 2:3, to refer to the "heart (i.e., depths) of the sea."

NT Words

kardia [καρδία, *2588*]

kardia occurs around 160 times as a true dynamic equivalent for the Hebrew terms ***lēb*** and ***lēbāb***, above. ***kardia*** likewise refers primarily to the heart as the center of the human will, mind, emotion, and soul or spirit. Like its Hebrew counterparts, it is found in a number of different contexts. But unlike ***lēb*** and ***lēbāb***, ***kardia*** does not refer at all to the heart as a physical organ, and is therefore wholly metaphorical in its usage.

With reference to the human heart as the center or seat of inner being and passions, ***kardia*** is found in a variety of contexts. 1 Cor. 14:25, for example, refers to the secrets of the heart, and in Luke 2:19, 51, the heart is indicated as the location of one's deepest thoughts. The "pure in heart" are singled out as blessed by God (cf. Matt. 5:8f.; 1 Tim. 3:5; 2 Tim. 2:22; Jas. 4:8; 1 Pet. 1:22); as are those whose hearts are obedient to God (cf. Rom. 6:17). The "forgiving" heart is likewise commended in Matt. 18:35. Blessing is also indicated in a heart that rejoices (cf. John 16:22; Acts 2:26). The orientation of one's heart will determine whether one will have lasting spiritual "treasure" or merely temporary earthly riches. The ideal of humility is perfectly modeled in the "heart" of Jesus in Matt. 11:29.

Exhortations concerning the human heart are also found in connection with this term. Jesus exhorts his disciples not to let their hearts be troubled in John 14:1. Paul expresses a strong desire that believers receive encouragement in their hearts in serving the Lord (cf. 2 Thess. 2:17; Col. 2:2); and that they demonstrate gratitude in their hearts towards God (cf. Col. 3:16). Peter urges his readers to sanctify their hearts in 1 Pet. 3:15. By far the most profound exhortation is the command to love the Lord God with all one's heart in Matt. 22:37; Mark 12:30; Luke 10:27, where Jesus cites Deut. 6:4 from which this all-embracing commandment is drawn.

kardia is also found in contexts where the human heart is viewed in a negative light. For example, Luke 1:51 speaks of the vain imagination of the human heart. The wickedness of the human heart is cited in Matt. 9:4; 12:34; 13:15; Mark 7:21; the sin of lust in one's heart is indicated in Matt. 5:28; Rom. 1:24. There are also solemn declarations that the human heart may constitute the object of satanic invasion, as in the case of Judas (cf. John 13:2) and Ananias (cf. Acts 5:3). Finally, Jesus declares that in many cases the heart of his people is far removed from God (cf. Matt. 15:8; Mark 7:6).

In more general terms, the human heart is portrayed as the object of the knowledge of God in Luke 16:15, and as the object of divine blessing in 1 Cor. 2:9. ***kardia*** also refers to the heart as the "mind" of human beings, where reasoning takes place (cf. Mark 2:6; Luke 5:22; 2 Cor. 9:7).

Another significant aspect of the meaning of ***kardia*** is reflected in the concept of the heart as the receptor of divine revelation. There are a number of contexts that demonstrate this usage. For example, in the parable of the sower, the various soils represent various attitudes of the human heart that will either inhibit growth and spiritual blessing or promote it (cf. Matt. 13:19; Mark 4:15; Luke 8:12, 15). In the new covenant, the law of God is written on the heart of the believer (cf. Heb. 8:10; 10:16; Rom. 2:15). The great miracle of conversion is sometimes described as the opening of the heart of faith in the life of a new believer — for example, Lydia (Acts 16:14) and the Ethiopian eunuch (Acts 8:3). See also Mark 11:23; Acts 15:9. Eph. 3:17 affirms that Christ dwells in the heart of the believer by faith. Such a phenomenon is evidently a new covenant manifestation of the old covenant motif of "heart circumcision" (cf. Rom. 2:29). Conversely, the New Testament also refers to the phenomenon of a hardened heart (cf. Mark 3:5; 6:52; 8:17; 2 Cor. 3:15; Rom. 1:21; John 12:40). The curse of the "uncircumcised heart" is also alluded to here. See also 2 Cor. 3:3; Luke 24:25; Eph. 4:18. Heb. 3:8, 12, 15; 4:7 issue a solemn plea not to harden one's heart against the promptings of God's Spirit. For as Gal. 4:6 also declares, the human heart is the location (metaphorically speaking) of the indwelling Spirit of God in the life of the believer (cf. also Rom. 10:8).

HEAT

OT Words

ḥōm [חֹם, 2527]

ḥōm occurs fourteen times and is uniformly translated "heat," "hot." The term is used both literally and metaphorically.

Literally, ***ḥōm*** refers first of all to the "heat of the day" (cf. Gen. 8:22; 18:1; 1 Sam. 11:9, 11; 2 Sam. 4:5;

Neh. 7:3; Job 6:17; 24:19; Isa. 18:4 [twice]; Jer. 17:8); and then to hot bread in 1 Sam. 21:6. It also indicates the retaining of body heat in Hag. 1:6.

Metaphorically, ***ḥôm*** indicates the "heat" of sexual arousal, which refers symbolically to Babylon's profligate lifestyle, probably in relation to her crass idolatry (cf. Jer. 51:39).

ḥōreb [חֹרֶב, 2721]

ḥōreb is also comparatively rare, occurring about sixteen times with the dominant, and mostly literal, senses of "heat," "dry," "drought." "Drought," for example, is indicated in Gen. 31:40; Jer. 50:28; Hag. 1:11; "heat of the day" is mentioned in Isa. 4:6; 25:4; Jer. 36:30; and the meaning "dry" occurs in Judg. 6:37 in relation to Gideon's fleece. The one metaphorical use of the term indicates the feeling of intense pain as "heat" in Job 30:30.

ḥāmam [חָמַם, 2552]

ḥāmam is synonymous with ***ḥôm*** (see above), being the verbal root from which ***ḥôm*** is derived. ***ḥāmam*** occurs thirteen times and conveys the adjectival and nominal meanings "hot," "heat," "warm."

The meaning "hot" is found in Exod. 16:21 with reference to the sun. Body heat is then mentioned in 1 Kgs. 1:2; 2 Kgs. 4:34; Eccl. 4:11. The warmth of fire is indicated in Isa. 44:15; 47:14; as is the warmth of clothing in Job 31:20. See also Job 39:14. ***ḥāmam*** is used metaphorically in several passages with reference to the "heat" of passion — for example in Ps. 39:3, where the psalmist speaks of his heart burning within him. Isa. 57:5; Hos. 7:7 refer to the "heat" of sexual passion in the context of idolatrous worship, probably in association with cult prostitution.

NT Words

kausōn [καύσων, *2742*]

This noun is rare, occurring only three times with the sense of the "burning heat" of the day (cf. Matt. 20:12; Luke 12:25; Jas. 1:12).

kauma [καῦμα, *2738*]

kauma is also rare, occurring only twice with the literal sense of "heat of the day" in Rev. 7:16 and the "scorching heat" of divine judgment in Rev. 16:9.

thermē [θέρμη, *2329*]

This term is found only in Acts 28:3, referring to the scorching heat of fire.

See Also: → ANGER

HEAVEN

OT Words

shāmayim [שָׁמַיִם, 8064]

This term is found about four hundred times with the primary meaning "heaven(s)" in the sense of "sky," or "firmament," as the realm of stars, and as the dwelling place of God.

With the sense of "heavens" as the created firmament, ***shāmayim*** is found in Gen. 1:8ff., 15ff.; 2:1, 4. Outside the Genesis account, it refers to the sky as the product of divine creation (cf. Exod. 20:11; Deut. 4:32; 2 Kgs. 19:15; Neh. 9:6; Pss. 8:1, 3; 33:6; Prov. 8:27; Isa. 37:16). "Heaven" as the realm of the stars is mentioned in Gen. 15:5; 22:17; Deut. 1:10; Josh. 10:13; Nah. 3:16. General references to "heavens" as "sky" or "air" are found in Gen. 2:20; 6:17; Deut. 4:17; Job 28:21; Ps. 8:8; Jer. 4:25; Ezek. 29:5; Hos. 2:18. Isa. 65:17 refers to the divine creation of the "new heavens and new earth."

In contexts linked with the person of Yahweh, ***shāmayim*** refers to "heaven" (and earth) as the possession of God (cf. Gen. 14:22). In addition, heaven is the location from which divine judgment emanates. Gen. 19:24 refers to the terrible fate of Sodom and Gomorrah, destroyed by "fire from heaven." See also 1 Sam. 2:10; 2 Sam. 22:8, 14; 2 Kgs. 1:10ff.; Job 1:16; Ps. 76:8; Lam. 2:1. Conversely, heaven is also a source of divine blessing. Neh. 9:15 refers to God supplying "bread from heaven" during the period of wandering in the wilderness.

Frequently, ***shāmayim*** indicates heaven as the dwelling place of God. General references to the God of heaven are found in Gen. 24:3; Ezra 1:2; Neh. 1:4; Deut. 3:24; 10:14; 26:15; Ps. 2:4; Eccl. 5:2. 1 Kgs. 22:19 specifically mentions the divine council as the "dwelling place" of God, in connection with his heavenly throne. In a related context, Solomon alludes to the heavenly realm of God during his prayer at the dedication of the temple. In 1 Kgs. 8:30ff., the expression "Hear from heaven, your dwelling place, and forgive" occurs about ten times as a recurring refrain in the king's prayer. The "morning star" (translated "Lucifer" in the Latin Vulgate version), in reference to the spirit of the Babylonian king, is declared to have fallen from heaven in Isa. 14:12 as judgment for his arrogance.

shāmayim also refers to "heaven" as the visible universe, an all-inclusive general term indicating the sphere of created reality. For example, in Exod. 17:14; Deut. 25:19, God calls for the destruction and removal of the Amalekite people from "under heaven." Deut. 29:20; 2 Kgs. 14:27 refer to the blotting out of one's name "under heaven." All nations "under heaven" are alluded to in Deut. 2:25; 4:19. Deut. 4:26; 30:19; 31:28; 32:1; Isa. 1:2 call "heaven and earth" as witnesses against the people of Israel in a divine lawsuit.

Other uses of ***shāmayim*** include a reference to the "opening of the heavens" in Ezek. 1:1, as a prelude to the imminent revelation of prophecy. In regard to the onset of torrential rain, Gen. 7:11; 8:2; Deut. 28:12; Judg. 5:4 all refer to the opening of the "windows of heaven." Great height is in view in Gen. 11:4, where the Tower of Babel is said to "reach up to heaven." The "four winds of heaven" are mentioned in Dan. 8:8. The phrase "host of heaven" refers to the idolatrous worship of the stars in 2 Kgs. 17:16; 21:3, 5; 23:4, 5; Jer. 19:3; Zeph. 1:5; and the title "queen of heaven" is applied to the Babylonian goddess in Jer. 7:18; 44:17ff.

Finally, in the context of praise to God, Ps. 19:1 affirms that "the heavens declare the glory of God" (cf. also Pss. 50:6; 97:6). The injunction to "let the heavens rejoice" is found in Pss. 96:11; 148:4; Isa. 49:13.

NT Words

ouranos [οὐρανός, *3772*]

ouranos occurs around three hundred times with the primary meaning "heaven(s)" in both a natural and spiritual sense. The natural connotation of the term conveys the idea of the expanse of the sky and everything in it (i.e., all celestial bodies), the universe. The spiritual sense of ***ouranos***, on the other hand, refers to the dwelling place of God and his heavenly court beyond the created order of things, in addition to a number of related meanings.

In reference to the created phenomenon of "the heavens" or "sky," ***ouranos*** is found in a number of contexts. General references to "sky" as the created order are found in Mark 4:32; Luke 12:56; Acts 4:24; Col. 1:16; Heb. 1:10; 11:12; Jas. 5:18; 2 Pet. 3:5; Rev. 10:6. The dissolution of the heavens as evidence of the impending apocalyptic end of the universe is indicated in Jesus' discourse on the signs of the end of the age in Matt. 24:29; Mark 13:25. See also 2 Pet. 3:10, 12, and the spectacular imagery of Rev. 6:13, 14; 8:10; 9:1; 20:11 in this regard. In a related context, the passing away of heaven and earth is also cited in Matt. 24:35; Mark 13:31. See also Luke 16:17; 21:23. The establishment of a "new heavens and new earth" is mentioned in 2 Pet. 3:13; Rev. 21:1. Luke 4:25 refers to drought as the closing of the heavens. Mark 13:27 refers to the uttermost ends of the heavens and the earth. The term "heaven" is used as a synonym for "world" in Acts 2:5; 4:12; Col. 1:23; Rev. 5:13. The concept of heaven also denotes the rule or kingdom of God among humankind, as in the phrase "kingdom of heaven." General references to this phenomenon are found in Matt. 5:19; 11:11; 19:14; 21:25; and the phrase is also found in the context of Jesus' parables (cf. Matt. 8:11; 13:24, 31ff.; 18:23). Matt. 13:11 refers to the mysteries of the kingdom of heaven. References to the authority of the kingdom of heaven are found in Matt. 16:18; 18:18; and Matt. 28:18 affirms that all power in heaven and earth is given to Jesus by his Father.

A number of contexts also speak about how to enter the kingdom of heaven and enjoy its profound benefits. There are a number of prerequisites for gaining entry into this kingdom — repentance (cf. Matt. 3:2; 4:17; 10:7); righteousness (cf. Matt. 5:20; 7:21); and obedience linked to faith (cf. Matt. 19:23). Possession of the kingdom is guaranteed to those who are "poor in spirit" and "persecuted because of righteousness" (cf. Matt. 5:3, 10). Rewards in the kingdom of heaven are spoken of in Matt. 5:12; Luke 6:23; as are "treasures in heaven" in Matt. 6:20; 19:21; Mark 10:21; Luke 12:33; 18:22.

"Heaven" is also alluded to as the domain of God, or his dwelling place. For example, in Luke 20:4, the question is asked whether John's baptism is from heaven, or from human beings. At the baptism of Jesus by John the Baptist, God's voice "from heaven" is heard confirming the identity and authority of Jesus as his Son (cf. Matt. 3:17; Mark 1:11; Luke 3:22). On the same occasion, the Spirit of God descends from heaven in the form of a dove (cf. Matt. 3:16; Mark 1:10; John 1:32). Other references to the divine voice from heaven are found in John 12:28; Acts 2:2; 2 Pet. 1:18; Acts 11:9; Heb. 12:25; Rev. 14:2, 13; 18:4; 21:3. Jesus looks to his Father in heaven in an attitude of prayer in Matt. 14:11; Mark 6:41; Luke 9:16; John 17:1. Phenomena related to heaven include "manna" or "bread from heaven" (Luke 15:7); "light from heaven" (Acts 9:3; 22:6); divine wrath from heaven (Rom. 1:18); wonders in heaven (Acts 2:19; Rev. 3:12; 4:1, 2; 10:1ff.; 12:1ff.; 13:6; 19:1, 11); an "open heaven" (John 1:51; Acts 10:11); signs from heaven (Like 21:11); and "sin against heaven" (Luke 15:18ff.). Paul speaks of his visionary experience of the "third heaven" in 2 Cor. 12:2, and of angels from heaven in Gal. 1:8 (cf. also Rev. 18:1; 20:1).

John 3:31; 6:38, 42 describe Christ's coming into the world as his coming from heaven. With reference to the conclusion of Jesus' earthly ministry, mention is made of him ascending, or being carried into, heaven (Luke 24:51; John 3:13; Eph. 4:10; Heb. 4:14). The return of Christ at the end of the age is frequently anticipated, when he will descend from heaven (cf. 1 Thess. 1:10; 4:16; 2 Thess. 1:7). Jesus' return is also depicted as the appearing of the Son of Man "in heaven" (cf. Matt. 24:30; 26:64; Mark 14:62).

God is described as "Lord of heaven" in Matt. 11:25; Luke 10:21; Acts 17:24. This is also implied through reference to the "God of heaven" in Rev. 11:3; 16:11, 17. God is referred to as "Father in heaven" in Matt. 5:16, 45; 10:32; 16:17; 6:9; Mark 11:25; Luke 11:2.

ouranos also refers to the "heavenly throne," the heart of God's authority and majesty (cf. Mark 16:19). Heb. 9:23, 24 indicate that the real temple in heaven is represented by the earthly temple and its furniture, such as the ark of the covenant. See also Acts 7:49, where ***ouranos*** refers to heaven as the throne of God. In related contexts, heaven is the origin of the judgment of divine fire (Luke 9:54; 17:29); and the place where the names of God's people are written down (cf. Luke 10:20; Heb. 12:23). Finally, heaven is also the place from which Satan fell like lightning in Luke 10:18.

ouranios [οὐράνιος, *3770*]

This adjectival term occurs only six times and means "heavenly" or "coming from heaven."

ouranios refers to the "heavenly Father" in Matt. 6:14, 26, 32; 15:13; the "heavenly host" in Luke 2:13; and a "heavenly vision" in Acts 26:19, where Paul makes his defense before Agrippa.

epouranios [ἐπουράνιος, *2032*]

epouranios is a synonym for ***ouranios*** (see above), meaning "heavenly" in an adjectival sense about twenty times.

This term is found, for example, in Matt. 18:35 with reference to the "heavenly Father." "Heavenly things" that concern ultimate spiritual realities are indicated in John 3:12; Phil. 2:10. Heb. 8:5 refers to the tabernacle as the shadow of true heavenly realities; and Heb. 9:23 mentions the heavenly realities to which the earthly temple pointed. Stars and planets are described as heavenly or celestial bodies in 1 Cor. 15:40. "Heavenly (i.e., post-resurrection) bodies" of human beings are contrasted with earthly human existence in 1 Cor. 15:48, 49.

Eph. 1:3, 20 refer to the "heavenly" realm of the supra-terrestrial sphere in reference to the position granted to Christ; and Eph. 2:6 refers to our position as believers with the Lord. Godly heavenly powers are mentioned in Eph. 3:10 in contrast to the dark, evil powers of Eph. 6:12. In a similar context, the heavenly kingdom of God is mentioned in 2 Tim. 4:18; Heb. 11:16; as is the heavenly Jerusalem in Heb. 12:23. See also Heb. 3:1; 6:4, which describe one's heavenly calling and gift, respectively.

ouranothen [οὐρανόθεν, *3771*]

This adverb is rare, found only twice in Acts 14:17; 26:13 and meaning "from heaven." The former reference indicates rain from heaven; the latter, light from heaven.

Additional Notes

Both Greek and Hebrew vocabulary indicate "heaven" as the dwelling place of God in terms of his kingdom and his unique power, majesty, and authority. This theme permeates both Old and New Testaments, with the latter emphasizing the divine prerogatives exercised by Jesus Christ on his Father's behalf.

HEAVY, HEAVINESS

OT Words

kābēd [כָּבֵד, 3513]

kābēd is a verb with adjectival force, meaning "(to be) heavy," as well as a number of associated nuances. The term is found approximately twenty times with this meaning. The other dominant sense of ***kābēd*** is that of "honor" or "glorify." (→ GLORIFY)

In literal contexts, ***kābēd*** signifies "heavy" in the sense of weighing a lot — for example, 1 Sam. 4:18 speaks of the heaviness of Eli's body fat, and 2 Sam. 14:26 refers to the weight of Absalom's hair.

The remaining usage of ***kābēd*** is largely metaphorical. For example, in a number of contexts the term signifies "to make heavy" in the sense of "harden," or "make insensitive." This is particularly evident in the case of the Egyptian Pharaoh at the time of the exodus. Exod. 8:32; 9:7, 34; 10:1 refer to the hardening of his heart in refusing to release the Israelites from captivity. A similar phenomenon is predicated of the Israelites in 1 Sam. 6:6, where they are likened to the Egyptians at the time of the exodus. See also 1 Sam. 6:10. Significantly, such a hardening is declared not to be true in the case of Yahweh, whose ear is never "heavy," but always ready to listen (cf. Isa. 59:1).

The sense of "harsh" or "severe" is indicated in a number of places where ***kābēd*** occurs in the formula: "The hand of the Lord was heavy against . . ." 1 Sam. 5:11 is an example of this usage, where the Philistines constitute the object of Yahweh's wrath. See also Ps.

32:4. A synonymous phrase, "the yoke of Yahweh was heavy against," is also applied to the people of Israel as an instance of divine punishment in Isa. 47:6. See also 1 Kgs. 12:10; 2 Chr. 10:10 in this regard. Similarly, the practice of "heavy bondage" in the sense of harsh treatment of slaves is indicated in Neh. 5:18. "Heaviness" is also predicated of grief (Job 6:3; Lam. 3:7); and of sins and iniquities (Ps. 38:4; Isa. 24:20).

NT Words

bareō [βαρέω, *916*]

bareō is found on six occasions with the sense of "be heavy," "weight down," "be a burden." Referring to sleepiness (i.e., "heavy eyes"), the term is found in Matt. 26:43; Mark 14:40; Luke 9:32. 2 Cor. 1:8 tells of Paul being burdened with great trials and difficulties, as does 2 Cor. 5:4, where the apostle is likewise "burdened," or "weighed down," with trouble and sorrow. 1 Tim. 5:16 speaks of a responsibility that the church ought not to be burdened with — the support of widows where there are family members who would be capable of looking after them. The point here is that the support and care of such women who are truly destitute and alone should constitute the legitimate "burden" of the church.

barys [βαρύς, *926*]

barys is the adjectival form of ***bareō*** (see above). This term occurs six times, meaning "heavy," "weighty," "burdensome." It is used metaphorically in all but one of these contexts.

Matt. 23:4 condemns the Pharisees for binding heavy burdens on others without showing any compassion towards them. Similarly, Matt. 23:23 accuses those same Jewish leaders of neglecting the "weighty" matters of the law, or those that are significant and of central importance. In 2 Cor. 10:10 Paul records that many in the church thought that his letters lacked substance (i.e., were not "weighty"). Acts 25:7 refers to the serious (i.e., "weighty.") charges laid against Paul. And in 1 John 5:3, John affirms that God's laws are not burdensome (i.e., "weighty").

adēmoneō [ἀδημονέω, *85*]

This rare verb is found in only three places, meaning "being heavy" with anguish, sorrow, or grief. It is used of Jesus in the garden of Gethsemane in Matt. 26:37; Mark 14:33, and of Epaphroditus in Phil. 2:26.

See Also: ➡ SORROW

HEBREW

OT Words

'ibrî [**עִבְרִי, 5680**]

'ibrî means "Hebrew" as both an adjective and noun. The word derives etymologically from the name Eber, listed as the grandson of Shem in the so-called "table of nations" in Gen. 10:21ff., and in several other genealogical listings (cf. Gen. 11:14ff.; 1 Chr. 1:18ff.; 5:13; 8:12, 22; Neh. 12:20). The term "Hebrew" is therefore a patronymic from the name Eber and designates the patriarchs (as the founders of the Israelite nation), as well as that nation itself (i.e., the descendants of the patriarchs).

'ibrî occurs around thirty times and refers, for example, to Abram (Gen. 14:13); Joseph (Gen. 39:14, 17; 41:12); the land of the Hebrews (Gen. 40:15); the Israelites (Gen. 43:22; Exod. 3:18; 5:3; 7:16; 1 Sam. 4:6ff.; 13:3); the Israelite midwives (Exod. 1:15); and Israelite men and women in general (Exod. 1:16, 19; 2:1, 13; Jonah 1:9). ***'ibrî*** is also found in the context of legislation applying to a Hebrew (i.e., Israelite) slave (cf. Exod. 21:2; Deut. 15:12).

NT Words

Hebraios [Ἑβραῖος, *1445*]

This term is rare in the New Testament, occurring only five times. ***Hebraios*** refers in all cases to the Jewish people or nation in distinction from others (cf. Acts 6:1; 2 Cor. 11:22; Phil. 3:5 [twice]; Acts 13:25).

HEDGE

OT Words

sûk [**שׂוּךְ, 7753**]

sûk is a rare verb found on only three occasions, meaning "to make a hedge, or fence." All three occurrences are metaphorical. Job 1:10; 10:11 refer to "setting a hedge about" someone in the sense of protecting, or equipping, him. Hos. 2:6 points to Yahweh placing a "hedge" around his people, or putting up a barrier around them, so as to prevent escape from their imminent divine punishment.

mesûkāh [**מְשׂוּכָה, 4881**]

This noun is derived from ***sûk*** (see above) and is also rare. ***mesûkāh*** is only found twice. It metaphorically indicates a lazy lifestyle that merely impedes one's progress, like a hedge placed in one's way (cf. Prov. 15:9). In Isa. 5:3 it refers to Yahweh removing his protective "hedge" around his people as a punishment, anticipating the inevitability of exile.

NT Words

phragmos [φραγμός, *5418*]

This noun signifies a "hedge," "fence," and occurs only four times. ***phragmos*** refers three times to a literal hedge in the parables of Jesus (cf. Matt. 21:33; Mark 12:1; Luke 14:23), and once to the "wall of partition" in Eph. 2:14 that kept Jews and Gentiles separate. In this latter context, ***phragmos*** indicates first of all the literal, physical partition in the temple that strictly divided worship areas for Jews and God-fearing Gentiles. It also alludes metaphorically to the barrier that prevented Gentiles from participating in the blessings of the new covenant age. The person and work of Jesus Christ have broken down this barrier.

See Also: → WALL

HEED → ATTEND → HEAR → SEE

HEEL

OT Words

'āqēb [**עָקֵב, 6119**]

This term occurs around thirteen times, meaning "heel" in reference to people and animals, as well as the related sense of "footprint" (i.e., "mark of a heel") in all but two of these contexts.

Literal references to a human heel are found in Gen. 25:26; Job 18:9; Jer. 13:22. Concerning animals, Gen. 49:17; Judg. 5:22 both refer to horses' hooves. See also Song 1:8. Human footsteps are indicated in Pss. 56:6; 89:51.

'āqēb is also found in several metaphorical contexts. Ps. 41:9 employs the expression "lift up one's heel against . . . ," which conveys opposition and hostility. This particular text refers to betrayal by a friend. Gen. 3:15 contains the highly significant expression relating to the "bruising of the heel" of the woman's seed. Here it points to the lesser injury sustained by the woman's child from the attack by the serpent. The latter will be destroyed, but the seed of the woman will overcome the assault. It is a veiled allusion to the cosmic battle between Christ and Satan, in which the former will achieve a consummate victory. ***'āqēb*** is used anthropomorphically in Ps. 77:19, where it signifies the "footsteps" of God.

NT Words

pterna [πτέρνα, *4418*]

The only occurrence of this term in the New Testament is found in John 13:18, where Jesus refers to Judas opposing him (i.e., lifting up his heel against him) on the occasion of the Last Supper, prior to his crucifixion.

HEIFER

OT Words

'eglāh [**עֶגְלָה, 5697**]

'eglāh refers mostly to a "young cow" or "calf" in a variety of contexts, including that of ritual sacrifice. The term occurs around fourteen times and is used both literally and symbolically.

As a literal sacrificial offering, the heifer is designated in Gen. 15:9; Deut. 21:3ff.; 1 Sam. 16:2. The term is also found in Hos. 10:5 in reference to a Samaritan calf-idol. As part of one's personal property, the heifer is mentioned in Isa. 7:21; Jer. 50:11.

'eglāh is used symbolically in Judg. 14:18 to refer to a newlywed woman, the wife of Samson. Other metaphorical uses of the term are found in Jer. 46:20, where Egypt is described as a "fair heifer," and in Hos. 10:11, where Israel is described as a "heifer."

NT Words

damalis [δάμαλις, *1151*]

damalis occurs only once, in Heb. 9:13, referring to the ritual offering of a heifer.

See Also: → COW

HEIGHT

OT Words

mārôm [**מָרוֹם, 4791**]

mārôm is found in about fifty contexts as both an adjective and a noun. In over half of these contexts the usage is adjectival, indicating that which is "high" in both a literal, physical sense and in the metaphorical sense of "proud," as well as related meanings. As a noun, ***mārôm*** signifies first of all the title "most high," as applied to Yahweh. The term also means "height" or "high places." In several instances it has the adverbial sense of "above" or "(on) high."

In a literal sense, ***mārôm*** refers to high elevation. Examples of this usage are found in 2 Kgs. 19:23; Ps. 148:1; Isa. 37:24; Jer. 31:12; 49:16; Ezek. 17:23; 34:14; Obad. 13, which describe mountains. See also Judg.

5:18; Prov. 8:2; Isa. 26:5. Jer. 17:12 also mentions God's high throne.

The adverbial sense of ***mārôm*** indicates that which is "on high" in a number of different contexts. First of all, the term refers to God's dwelling place as being "on high," as in heaven (cf. Job 16:19; Ps. 68:18; Isa. 33:5; Jer. 25:30; Lam. 1:13). Pss. 7:7; 102:19 refer symbolically to Yahweh ruling from the holy of holies in the temple as ruling "from on high." Other adverbial uses of this term indicate, for example, lifting up one's eyes "on high" in prayer to God (cf. 2 Kgs. 19:22; Isa. 40:26). Similar contexts are indicated in Ps. 92:8; Isa. 24:21; 57:1.

The title "most high" with reference to God is found in Ps. 56:2; and Mic. 6:6 refers to the "exalted God."

Jer. 51:53 mentions the high point, or "height," of the strength of Babylon.

qômāh [**קוֹמָה, 6967**]

qômāh is found in about forty contexts. The term refers primarily to the physical dimensions of "height" of buildings, people, and other natural phenomena. For example, ***qômāh*** refers to the height of Noah's ark (Gen. 6:15); the ark of the covenant (Exod. 25:10); the great altar (Exod. 27:1; 37:1); the tabernacle courtyard (Exod. 27:18; 38:18); the altar of incense (Exod. 30:2; 37:25); the table of the showbread or presence (Exod. 37:10); and the altar of burnt offering (Exod. 38:1). 1 Kgs. 6:2, 10, 23, 26 refer to the height of Solomon's temple. See also 1 Kgs. 7:15ff.; 2 Kgs. 25:17 with regard to the height of the temple furnishings. 1 Kgs. 7:2 refers to the height of Solomon's palace. Ezek. 40:5 describes the height of the wall of the prophet's visionary temple.

qômāh also refers to the height of people (1 Sam. 16:7; Song 7:7; Isa. 10:33); the height of trees (2 Kgs. 19:23; Isa. 37:24; Ezek. 31:3ff.); and that of vines (Ezek. 17:6; 19:11).

rûm [**רוּם, 7312**]

rûm is a rare term, found only six times as both a noun and an adjective, indicating "high" in the sense of "haughty" or "proud" (cf. Prov. 21:4; Isa. 2:11, 17; 10:12; Jer. 48:29). In one metaphorical context in Prov. 25:3, ***rûm*** depicts the "height" of heaven.

NT Words

hypsos [ὕψος, *5311*]

hypsos occurs six times and refers to "height" or "high" as both a measurement and the exalted position of rank, in relation to God and human beings.

The phrase "on high," indicating a heavenly origin, is found in Luke 1:78 concerning a visitation of God. In Luke 24:49, Jesus promises the gift of the Holy Spirit as a divine endowment after the risen Christ ascends into heaven and returns to his Father. Concerning the ascension of our Lord, Eph. 4:8 refers to Jesus ascending "on high" and taking captivity captive — a probable reference to Christ's destruction of his spiritual enemies through his atoning death on the cross.

In Paul's prayer for the Ephesians, he attempts to describe the character of Christ's love and asks that they may know the height of that love along with its other "dimensions" (cf. Eph. 3:18).

Rev. 21:16 describes the height of the wall of the heavenly city. In Jas. 1:9, the writer refers to an "exalted" standing of social privilege.

hypsōma [ὕψωμα, *5313*]

This term is also rare, found only twice. On both occasions it means "height" or "elevation" in a metaphorical sense. Rom. 8:39 indicates that which can never separate one from the love of Christ — "neither height nor depth nor anything else in all of creation." 2 Cor. 10:5 speaks of every "high thing," in the sense of arrogance or pride, that opposes the knowledge of God.

HEIR

OT Words

yārash [**יָרַשׁ, 3423**]

yārash is a verb that means "inherit," "possess" in the majority of its 230 or so contexts. In eight of these texts, however, ***yārash*** conveys the nominal sense of "heir" — one who inherits an estate from a testamentary disposition. (→ INHERIT)

In Gen. 15:3, 4 there are three references to Abram as heir to the covenant promises of Yahweh. In Gen. 21:10 Sarah, wife of Abraham, denies Ishmael the rights of inheritance. See also 2 Sam. 14:7; Prov. 20:23; Jer. 49:1, 2.

NT Words

klēronomos [κληρονόμος, *2818*]

klēronomos occurs about fifteen times and means "heir" in the conventional sense of one who receives his allotted property from an inheritance. It also conveys the same meaning in a messianic sense, referring to Christ as one who benefits from his status as God's son. It is most commonly applied to believers as heirs with Christ.

The conventional sense of "heir" is observed in Matt. 21:38; Mark 12:7; Luke 24:14; Gal. 4:1. In Rom. 4:14, ***klēronomos*** refers to Abraham as the "heir" of the world, identifying him as the recipient of the covenant promises.

In the metaphorical, spiritual sense, believers are described as heirs of God and co-heirs with Christ (Gal. 4:7; Rom. 8:17; 1 Pet. 3:7). Gal. 3:29; Heb. 6:17 add that believers are heirs according to the promise (i.e., of the covenant). Heb. 11:7 describes Noah as the "heir of righteousness"; and in Jas. 2:5 believers are designated "heirs of the kingdom." Finally, in Heb. 1:2 ***klēronomos*** indicates that Christ is the divinely appointed "heir of all things."

synklēronomos [συγκληρονόμος, *4789*]

This term is a partial synonym for ***klēronomos*** (see above), emphasizing the phenomenon of a shared inheritance. ***synklēronomos*** is translated "joint heir," "fellow heir" and occurs only four times, always with a spiritual sense. In Rom. 8:17 believers are described as "joint heirs" with Christ; and Eph. 3:6 includes Gentiles in this designation. Heb. 11:9 refers to Abraham, Isaac, and Jacob as fellow heirs of the covenant promise. Then 1 Pet. 3:7 indicates that husband and wife are "heirs together" of the gift of life.

Additional Notes

The common theological motif that lies at the heart of both Old and New Testament vocabulary for "heir" is the promises of the divine covenant. Though the specific Hebrew and Greek terms for "heir" occur relatively infrequently, the contexts in which they are found carry a very significant theological weight. Inheriting the promises of Yahweh is one of the most powerful and poignant incentives for devoting oneself to God in both Old and New Testaments. As with so many other motifs and promises in Scripture, what begins in the old covenant as an earthly, material inheritance or blessing finds its supreme spiritual fulfillment in the person and work of Christ the Messiah in the new covenant age.

See Also: → INHERIT

HELL

OT Words

hinnōm [**הִנֹּם, 2011**]

hinnōm is found on eleven occasions and is the name given to the steep, rocky valley located in the southwest of Jerusalem with Mt. Zion to the north, and the so-called "hill of evil counsel" to the south. It is mentioned for the first time in Josh. 15:8; 18:16 merely as a geographic location without further comment (cf. also Neh. 11:30).

2 Kgs. 23:10 mentions King Josiah of Judah who desecrated Topheth — an area located in the southeastern corner of the Valley of Hinnom — as part of a program of reformation so that no Israelite would be able to sacrifice their children to the Ammonite god, Molech. Such had been the practice during the reigns of Manasseh (cf. 2 Kgs. 21:6) and Ahaz (cf. 2 Chr. 28:3). The prophet Jeremiah explicitly condemns this gross idolatry in Jer. 7:31, 32; 19:2–6; 32:35.

Isa. 30:33 refers to Topheth as a "fire pit," prepared as a place of fiery execution for the King of Assyria. Although Hinnom is not explicitly mentioned here it is assumed, for Topheth is everywhere else associated with this valley in the Old Testament. Such an association with fire and burning in the context of divine punishment is carried over into the New Testament term for "hell."

NT Words

geenna [γέεννα, *1067*]

geenna is the Greek equivalent for the Hebrew *gê(ben)-hinnōm*, the Valley of Hinnom, which became the site of a rubbish dump for the city of Jerusalem, where all refuse was burned. The original Valley of Hinnom had been infamous as a place where Israelite kings sacrificed their children to the god Molech (see ***hinnōm***, above).

In the New Testament, ***geenna*** is translated "hell," a place reserved for the eternal fiery destruction of the wicked. Jesus refers to it as such in Matt. 5:22, 29, 30; 10:28; 18:9; 23:15, 33; Mark 9:43ff.; Luke 12:5. See also Jas. 3:6.

HELMET

OT Words

kôba' [**כּוֹבַע, 3553**]; ***qôbā'*** [**קוֹבַע, 6959**]

kôba' is rare, occurring only six times and translated "helmet" in every case. In all but one instance the usage is literal, referring to a helmet as part of the soldier's conventional armor (cf. 1 Sam. 17:5; 2 Chr. 26:14; Jer. 46:4; Ezek. 27:10; 38:5). In Isa. 59:17 ***kôba'*** is used metaphorically, or anthropomorphically, to refer to the "helmet of Yahweh," symbolizing God's protection of people in order to bring them salvation.

An alternate spelling of the term, ***qôbā'***, is found in 1 Sam. 17:38; Ezek. 23:24.

NT Words

perikephalaia [περικεφαλαία, *4030*]

This term is only found twice, in Eph. 6:17; 1 Thess. 5:8. In both texts the use is metaphorical, referring to the "helmet of salvation" as a symbol of the Christian's hope, and drawing on the use of the equivalent Hebrew term (see ***kôba'***, above) in Isa. 59:17.

HELP, HELPER

OT Words

'āzar [**עָזַר, 5826**]

'āzar occurs around eighty times with the predominant verbal sense of "help." In a few contexts the term is used nominally, indicating a "helper."

'āzar frequently refers to Yahweh as the one who helps his people. General references to this phenomenon are found in Gen. 49:25; 1 Sam. 7:12; 2 Sam. 18:3. The psalmist acknowledges and praises God for his help (cf. Pss. 28:7; 118:7), particularly in delivering his people from their enemies (cf. Pss. 37:40; 46:5). See also 1 Chr. 5:20; 12:18 in this regard. Elsewhere, explicit divine promises are given with respect to helping and sustaining God's people, through the person of the messianic Suffering Servant (cf. Isa. 49:8; 50:7). See also Isa. 41:10ff.; 44:2. Yahweh is also affirmed as one who helps the poor (cf. Pss. 10:14; 72:12). Appeals to God for help are found, for example, in 2 Chr. 14:11; Pss. 30:10; 79:9. God also withdraws help from the wicked (cf. Jer. 47:4; Ezek. 30:8).

In addition to appeals to the one true and living God, Deut. 32:38 contains an appeal to pagan deities for help — but the context here is one of deriding and scorning these idols. No genuine request for such help is being made.

From the viewpoint of people helping people, Josh. 1:14; 10:4ff.; 2 Sam. 21:17; 1 Kgs. 1:7 all refer to Israelites helping their fellow countrymen. 2 Sam. 8:5; 1 Kgs. 20:16 refer to Gentiles helping other Gentiles, and Ezra 8:22 refers to Gentiles assisting Israelites, although in this latter context Ezra is ashamed to ask for such help. As with idols, the uselessness of the people of God seeking help from pagans is made clear in Isa. 30:7.

yāsha' [**יָשַׁע, 3467**]

This term is quite common, occurring in about two hundred contexts with the primary sense of "save," "deliver," accounting for well over half of the occurrences. There are, however, several places where this verb is translated "help." (→ SAVE)

The theme of Yahweh helping his people is mentioned in Prov. 20:22. Ps. 12:1 contains a plea to God for help. Exod. 2:17; 2 Sam. 10:11 refer to people assisting other people, and 2 Sam. 14:4; 2 Kgs. 6:26, 27 refer to people requesting aid from others. In Deut. 28:31, there is no one to help in a situation of dire need.

'ēzer [**עֵזֶר, 5828**]

'ēzer is the nominal form derived from ***'āzar*** (see above), and is found in approximately twenty contexts with the consistent sense of "help" or "helper."

In general terms, God is affirmed as the helper of his people, for example, in Exod. 18:4; Deut. 33:26; Pss. 33:20; 115:9ff.; 146:5. Specifically, God is one who aids his people against their enemies (cf. Deut. 33:7). The psalmist begs God for help in Ps. 20:2. Isa. 30:5 declares the futility of Israel seeking help from pagan nations such as Egypt, while Hos. 13:9 depicts Israel's utter helplessness without God. Of particular significance for human beings is the recognition that woman was created specifically to be man's unique companion and helper (cf. Gen. 2:18, 20).

'ezrāh [**עֶזְרָה, 5833**]

'ezrāh is a synonym for ***'ēzer*** (see above) and occurs around twenty-five times.

"Help" in a general sense is indicated in Job 31:21; Nah. 3:9. The anguish of "helplessness" is indicated in Job 6:13; Isa. 10:3; 20:6; Lam. 4:17. God's help is both sought (e.g., Pss. 22:19; 40:13; 60:11; 108:12) and recognized with gratitude when offered to his people (e.g., Pss. 27:9; 46:1; 63:7; 94:17). Conversely, the anticipation of help for Israel coming from pagan nations is declared to be futile (cf. 2 Chr. 28:21; Jer. 37:17). And, in Isa. 31:1, Israel is condemned for seeking help from Egypt.

NT Words

boētheō [βοηθέω, *997*]

This verb occurs eight times, meaning "help," "bring help" in all instances.

In 2 Cor. 6:2 Paul quotes from Isa. 49:8, affirming that God had extended help to his people in former times. Acts 16:9 records an angelic plea from the "man of Macedonia" for Paul to come and bring help to the Macedonian church.

In reference to the person and work of Christ, several places in the gospels record pleas to Jesus for help (cf. Matt. 15:25; Mark 9:22, 24). Heb. 2:18 mentions Jesus' ability to help his people as their great high priest.

Acts 21:28 refers to a plea for Jews to help ruin the ministry of Paul. And in Rev. 12:14, in a spectacular vision of spiritual and earthly conflict, the earth comes to the help of the woman under attack from the dragon.

antilambanō **[ἀντιλαμβάνω,** ***482*****]**

This verb is rare, occurring only three times and meaning "help" or "support" in two of these contexts. Luke 1:54 records that God's help is given to Israel; and Acts 20:35 contains Paul's exhortation for believers to help the weak.

syllambanō **[συλλαμβάνω,** ***4815*****]**

syllambanō means "to take," "seize," or "conceive" in the majority of its sixteen occurrences. On two occasions it means "help." Luke 5:7 refers to help being given to pull in a huge catch of fish. Phil. 4:3 records Paul's request to the Philippians to help those who labor in the gospel.

synantilambanō **[συναντιλαμβάνω,** ***4878*****]**

This term is also rare, occurring only twice. In Luke 10:40 it refers to Martha's demand for her sister Mary to help her. In Rom. 8:26 Paul indicates that the Spirit of God helps us in our weakness.

boēthos **[βοηθός,** ***998*****]**

boēthos is found only in Heb. 13:6, where it refers to the Lord as our helper.

HEN

OT Words

barburîm **[בַּרְבֻּרִים, 1257]**

This term only occurs in 1 Kgs. 4:23, in the plural, and refers to "fatted fowl" as part of King Solomon's daily provisions of food. Thus it may refer to "hens" as female game birds.

NT Words

ornis **[ὄρνις,** ***3733*****]**

ornis is also a rare term, referring to a "hen" only in Matt. 23:37; Luke 13:34.

HERALD

OT Words

kārôz **[כָּרוֹז, 3744** (Aramaic)**]**

This is an Aramaic term found only in Dan. 3:4, where it indicates a civic messenger proclaiming a royal decree.

bāsar **[בָּשַׂר, 1319]**

The verb ***bāsar*** means "to publish tidings," "bring (good) news," and in its participial form it has the nominal sense of "messenger," "herald." In Isa. 40:9, the term has the explicit sense of "herald," or one who brings good news of God's salvation to Zion.

See Also: → GOSPEL → PROCLAIM

HERB

OT Words

'ēseb **[עֵשֶׂב, 6212]**

'ēseb is found about thirty times, meaning "herb," "grass."

"Herb" in the traditional sense of plant or vegetation is found, for example, in Gen. 1:11ff.; Exod. 3:18; 9:3, 22ff.; 10:15; Isa. 37:27; 42:15; Jer. 12:4. Sometimes ***'ēseb*** is translated "grass" (e.g., Deut. 29:23; Job 5:25; Ps. 72:16; Amos 7:2; Mic. 5:7). The different meanings of ***'ēseb*** overlap, and it is not always possible to clearly distinguish between the senses of "plant," "grass," "herb," or "vegetation."

deshe' **[דֶּשֶׁא, 1877]**

deshe' is synonymous with ***'ēseb*** (see above), but not as common. ***deshe'*** is found on fifteen occasions and also demonstrates the same overlap in meaning between the senses of "herb," "grass," "plant," or "vegetation." See, for example, Gen. 1:11, 12; Deut. 32:2; 2 Sam. 23:4; 2 Kgs. 19:26; Job 6:5; Isa. 15:6; Ps. 23:2.

yārāq **[יָרָק, 3419]**

yārāq is a rare synonym for terms 1 and 2 above, occurring only five times, of which three refer specifically to garden herbs. (cf. Deut. 11:10; 1 Kgs. 21:2; Prov. 15:7.

NT Words

lachanon **[λάχανον,** ***3001*****]**

lachanon occurs four times and refers to "herbs" or "shrubs" (cf. Matt. 13:32; Mark 4:32; Luke 11:42; Rom. 14:2).

botanē [βοτάνη, *1008*]

botanē is found only in Heb. 6:7, where it refers to green herbs or vegetation.

HERD

OT Words

'ēder [עֵדֶר, **5739**]

'ēder refers to "herd(s)" or "flock(s)" of animals and birds and is found approximately thirty times.

'ēder refers to flocks in general, without specifying the type of animal (Job 24:2; Ps. 78:52; Isa. 17:2; Jer. 6:3; Ezek. 34:12); to flocks of sheep (Gen. 29:2ff.; Judg. 5:16; 1 Sam. 17:34; Song 4:2; Mic. 2:12); to herds of cattle (Gen. 32:16ff.; Prov. 27:23); and herds of goats (Song 4:1; 6:5ff.; Joel 1:8; Zeph. 2:14).

'ēder is also used metaphorically to indicate the people of Israel as a "flock" (e.g., Jer. 13:17, 20; Mic. 4:8; Zech. 10:3).

bāqār [בָּקָר, **1241**]

bāqār commonly indicates large bovine animals such as the ox, heifer, bull, calf, cow, and occurs around two hundred times. In about fifty of these contexts, the term refers to the herding of these animals.

The herding of cattle in general is indicated, for example, in Gen. 13:5; 47:17ff.; Exod. 10:9; 1 Sam. 11:5; 1 Chr. 27:29; Isa. 65:10; Jer. 3:24. Setting aside or selecting cattle from the herd for a ritual offering is mentioned in Lev. 1:2ff.; 27:32; Num. 11:22; Deut. 12:6; 16:2; Neh. 10:36.

NT Words

agelē [ἀγέλη, *34*]

agelē refers exclusively to a "herd" (of pigs), and is found eight times (cf. Matt. 8:30ff.; Mark 5:11, 13; Luke 8:32, 33).

HERESY, HERETICAL

NT Words

hairesis [αἵρεσις, *139*]

This noun occurs nine times with the predominant sense of "sect." However, in 2 Pet. 2:1, the word refers to "(destructive) heresies" perpetrated by false teachers within the church, whose punishment from God will be swift and inevitable. (→ SECT)

hairetikos [αἱρετικός, *141*]

hairetikos is directly related to ***hairesis*** (see above) and occurs only once, in Titus 3:10. The term refers to a person who is a schismatic, who divides a congregation with false teaching. Such a one is to be isolated from the community.

HERITAGE → INHERIT

HEW → CUT

HIDE

OT Words

sātar [סָתַר, **5641**]

This verb is found in about eighty places, with the primary meanings "hide," "conceal" in both the active and passive sense.

When predicated of God, ***sātar*** refers to the action of divine concealment in a number of different contexts. God is said to "hide his face" from his people in the context of judgment against them (e.g., Deut. 31:17ff.; Pss. 13:1; 44:24; Isa. 8:17; 64:7; Ezek. 39:23ff.; Mic. 3:4). In contrast, Ps. 22:24 affirms that Yahweh has not hidden his face from the afflicted one. Ezek. 39:29 contains the promise that God will cease to hide his face from his people, signifying an end to judgment. Conversely, a handful of texts refer to humankind's attempt to hide their faces from God (cf. Exod. 3:6 [Moses]; Job 13:20; Isa. 59:2). Job 34:22 declares that it is impossible to hide from God.

sātar is also found in contexts in which pleas are made to God for various reasons. Such requests are all found in the Psalter where, for example, the psalmist pleads with God not to hide his face from the people (cf. Pss. 27:9; 69:17; 102:2; 143:7). Then, in Ps. 51:9, David pleads with God to hide his face from his servant's sin. Pss. 64:2; 17:8 express pleas for Yahweh to hide the writer from his enemies. And Ps. 119:19 contains the plea for God not to hide his commandments from sojourners.

Conversely, a number of texts indicate humankind's attempt to hide from God — which is ultimately impossible to reach or sustain (cf. Exod. 3:6; Job 34:22). The following texts all explicitly affirm the futility of trying to hide either from God personally or to conceal something from him: Isa. 29:15; Jer. 23:24; Amos 9:3. On the other hand, a few texts indicate the terrible possibility of being hidden from God as a divine punishment for sin (cf. Gen. 4:14; Isa. 59:2).

With respect to the divine initiative in a positive context, Ps. 27:5; Isa. 49:2 affirm the comforting fact that God protects his own by hiding them from their enemies.

In contexts where people are involved, ***sātar*** refers to concealment in a variety of contexts — for example, the concealment of adultery (Num. 5:13); hiding information from one's family (1 Sam. 20:2); hiding from danger (Prov. 27:12). Hiding from other people is mentioned in Deut. 7:20; 1 Kgs. 17:3; Ps. 54:1; Jer. 36:19.

sātar is used metaphorically in Isa. 28:15 — the Israelites have deluded themselves into imagining they can take refuge (viz. hide) in falsehood and thus escape judgment from Yahweh.

ḥābā' [חָבָא, 2244]

A synonym for ***sātar*** (see above), ***ḥābā'*** means "hide," "conceal," and occurs around thirty times.

The futility of hiding from God is referred to in Gen. 3:8ff.; Amos 9:3. However, in Isa. 49:2, Yahweh is said to hide his Servant in order to protect him.

In general contexts, ***ḥābā'*** frequently indicates the action of people hiding from others in order to protect themselves (cf. Gen. 31:27; 1 Sam. 23:23; 1 Kgs. 18:4, 13; Isa. 42:22; Dan. 10:7).

tāman [טָמַן, 2934]

tāmam also means "hide," "conceal" in the majority of its thirty occurrences.

tāmam refers to concealing things, in various contexts (Gen. 35:4; Deut. 33:19; Josh. 7:21ff.; Ps. 35:7; Jer. 13:4ff.); to concealing people (e.g., Josh. 2:6; Job 40:13); and to concealing sin (Job 31:33). Isa. 2:10 also refers to the futility of attempting to hide from God in order to escape judgment. Several other texts refer to the wicked concealing a trap for the people of God (cf. Pss. 35:7ff.; 140:5; Jer. 18:22).

'ālam [עָלַם, 5956]

'ālam is another synonym for the preceding three terms, likewise signifying the actions of hiding or concealing. The term is found in about thirty contexts with these meanings.

Humankind's vain attempt to hide from God is recorded in Job 42:3; Eccl. 12:14; Job 6:16. Lev. 20:4 refers to the culpable action of the person who merely hides his eyes from the practice of child sacrifice and does not put the perpetrator of the act to death.

Yahweh's hiding himself from his people as an act of judgment against them is indicated in Ps. 10:1; Isa. 1:15 (cf. also 2 Kgs. 4:27). And, as a corollary to this phenomenon, Ps. 55:1; Lam. 3:56 refer to the plea for Yahweh not to hide himself from his people.

Elsewhere ***'ālam*** refers generally to "hiding" in Lev. 5:2; Num. 5:13; 2 Chr. 9:2.

kāsāh [כָּסָה, 3680]

kāsāh is a fairly common verb that is translated "cover," as well as related senses, in most of its 150 contexts. Two of these related meanings are "hide," "conceal."

The prospect of Yahweh hiding his will and purpose from his people is raised in Gen. 18:17, where God deliberates as to whether he will hide anything from his servant Abraham. The psalmist affirms that he has neither hidden sin in his heart (cf. Ps. 32:5), nor concealed the righteousness of God there (cf. Ps. 40:10). Ps. 143:9 refers to the psalmist hiding in God for security.

In Deut. 13:8, the command is given not to hide anyone who is guilty of a capital offense under the law. General references to hiding or concealing are found in Gen. 37:26; Prov. 10:18; 11:13; 12:23.

mistār [מִסְתָּר, 4565]

This noun is derived from ***sātar*** (see above), and means "hiding place," or that which is secret. ***mistār*** occurs ten times.

"Hiding places" of the wicked are mentioned in Pss. 10:8; 17:12; 64:4 (cf. also Jer. 49:4); and the futility of hiding in secret places from the Lord is declared in Jer. 23:24. Jer. 13:17 refers to the prophet's intention of weeping in "secret (i.e., hidden) places" because of the people's pride.

mistār is used metaphorically in Isa. 45:3, where Yahweh promises to give to Cyrus treasure stored in "hidden places." Then, in Lam. 3:10, God is likened to a lion hiding in "secret places."

NT Words

kryptō [κρύπτω, *2928*]

This verb means "to hide," "conceal," "keep secret." ***kryptō*** occurs in sixteen contexts.

The concealing of persons is indicated in Heb. 11:23, which cites the incident of the baby Moses hidden in the reeds of the Nile (cf. Exod. 2). John 8:59; 12:36 refer to Jesus hiding himself in order to avoid premature arrest or containment by the crowd. The concealment of various objects is described in Matt. 5:14; 13:44; 25:25; Rev. 2:17. 1 Tim. 5:25 contains the reassuring observation that good deeds cannot remain hidden (presumably from God, although this is not made explicit).

As a manifestation of divine judgment, divine mysteries are kept secret, or hidden from human view, in Matt. 13:35. Similarly, understanding is hidden from the disciples in Luke 18:34, and from the people of Jerusalem in Luke 19:42. Rev. 6:15, 16 again affirm the futility of seeking to hide from the judgment of God.

Finally, in a profound symbolic context, Col. 3:3 refers to the life of the believer being hidden with Christ.

apokryptō [ἀποκρύπτω, *613*]

This term is synonymous with ***kryptō*** (see above) and is found six times meaning "hide," "conceal."

The physical concealment of money is indicated in Matt. 25:18 — the only literal use of ***apokryptō***. The term is used metaphorically in Matt. 11:25; Luke 10:21, where divine wisdom is hidden from the "wise" and given to "babes," or those who readily submit to the authority of God and obey him unquestioningly. Then, in 1 Cor. 2:7; Eph. 3:9; Col. 1:26, Paul declares that the secret wisdom of God, kept hidden for centuries, has now been made available to believers through the ministry of Christ and the Holy Spirit.

enkryptō [ἐγκρύπτω, *1470*]

A rare synonym with the preceding two verbs, ***enkryptō*** is found only in Matt. 13:33; Luke 13:21, referring to the parable in which a woman hid yeast in three measures of flour.

kalyptō [καλύπτω, *2572*]

kalyptō is found on seven occasions and means "cover," as well as "hide," "conceal." The latter sense is only specifically mentioned in 2 Cor. 4:3, where the phenomenon of "veiling" is indicated. This infers that the truth of the gospel is hidden from the hearts and minds of those who continue to reject it. The sense of "cover" in Jas. 5:20; 1 Pet. 4:8 overlaps with that of "hide."

lanthanō [λανθάνω, *2990*]

lanthanō means "be hidden" in three of the six contexts in which it occurs.

Mark 7:24 refers to the inability of Jesus to remain hidden from the public in a house in the region of Tyre and Sidon. Luke 8:47 points to the woman suffering from hemophilia who could not remain hidden in her approach to Jesus. Acts 26:26 then refers to King Agrippa's awareness of the significance of Jesus Christ's death, resurrection, ascension, and the emergence of the Christian community of believers. Paul claims here in his public defense that nothing was hidden from the king.

apokryphos [ἀπόκρυφος, *614*]

This adjectival form is also rare, occurring only three times and meaning "hidden" or "kept secret." Col. 2:3 refers to Jesus Christ as the one in whom is hidden all treasures of wisdom and knowledge. Mark 4:22; Luke 8:17 affirm the desirability of bringing into public view that which may have been hidden away, such as a lamp on a lampstand.

HIGH

OT Words

gābōah [גָּבֹהַּ, **1364**]

gābōah means "high," "tall," in a physical, literal sense as well as conveying the symbolic idea of "haughty" or "proud." This term is found in approximately forty places.

The literal meaning "tall," "high" is evident in a number of contexts — for example, in relation to towers (cf. Isa. 2:15; Jer. 51:58); walls (cf. Deut. 3:5; 28:52); gallows (cf. Esth. 5:14; 7:9); mountains or hills (cf. Ps. 104:18; Isa. 30:25; Ezek. 17:22); and the temple altar (cf. Ezek. 41:22). Tall people are indicated in 1 Sam. 9:2; 16:7 (i.e., Goliath). In a technical sense, "high hills" are often linked with idolatrous Baal worship (cf. 1 Kgs. 14:23; 2 Kgs. 17:10; Jer. 2:20; 3:6; 17:2).

The designation "high" in the sense of "proud" is found in 1 Sam. 2:3; Job 41:34; Isa. 5:15; 10:33; Ezek. 21:26. Civic officials are described as "high" in Eccl. 5:8 in relation to their rank. Ps. 138:6 describes Yahweh as "high" in the sense of "exalted."

'elyôn [עֶלְיוֹן, **5945**]

As an adjective, ***'elyôn*** refers to that which is "high" or "exalted" in terms of position or rank. As a noun, it is used of God, meaning "most high," and also of monarchs. ***'elyôn*** occurs around fifty times.

The divine title "most high" occurs in a number of places (e.g., Gen. 14:18ff.; Num. 24:16; Deut. 32:8; 2 Sam. 22:14; Pss. 7:17; 82:6; Isa. 14:14; Lam. 3:35).

The literal sense of "high," "higher," or "highest" in relation to physical objects is evident in the following contexts — referring to, for example, a basket (Gen. 40:17); a gate (2 Kgs. 15:35); a pool (Isa. 7:3); a house

(Neh. 3:25); and the elevated chambers of the temple (Ezek. 42:5).

'elyôn is also found in contexts where "high" refers to rank or authority. For example, Deut. 26:19; 28:1 refer to Israel as "high" above the nations. Ps. 89:27 declares David to be "the highest" (i.e., the most exalted) of the kings of the earth. In Ps. 97:9 the writer proclaims God as "most high over all the earth."

mārôm **[מָרוֹם, 4791]**

This term is synonymous with ***gābōah*** (see above), meaning "height," "elevated place," in a literal sense. The metaphorical use of ***mārôm*** suggests the idea of pride in an adjectival and adverbial sense. ***mārôm*** occurs around fifty times.

The literal sense of "height" is evident, for example, in Judg. 5:18; 2 Kgs. 19:23; Eccl. 10:6; Isa. 22:16; Jer. 31:12; Ezek. 17:23. The concept of the "high places" of heaven is found in Job 25:2; Pss. 102:19; 148:1.

There are various adverbial expressions linked with this term — for example, "from above" (cf. 2 Sam. 22:17; Isa. 32:15); "haughtily," "proudly" (cf. 2 Kgs. 19:22; Ps. 73:8); and "on high," indicating both a human position of authority (e.g., Job 5:11; 31:2; Ps. 7:7), and Yahweh's position in heaven (e.g., Pss. 68:18; 92:8; Jer. 17:12; Mic. 6:6; Isa. 33:5; 24:18; 40:26).

NT Words

hypsēlos **[ὑψηλός, *5308*]**

hypsēlos is an adjective indicating that which is "high," "lofty" in a literal sense. It is also used metaphorically to describe people and things as "exalted" in the sense of an eminent rank or position. The term occurs eleven times.

The literal sense of "high" in relation to a mountain is found in several places (cf. Matt. 4:8; 17:1; Mark 9:2; Luke 4:5; Rev. 21:10). Rev. 21:12 also refers to the high wall of the heavenly city of Jerusalem.

The designation "highly esteemed" (i.e., among people) is found in Luke 16:15, in a negative context of judgment against human pride. Similarly, Rom. 12:16 contains the injunction not to be proud, or haughty.

In relation to God, ***hypsēlos*** refers to his "high (i.e., uplifted) arm" in Acts 13:7. This is a reference to divine power with respect to God's action in delivering his people from their Egyptian bondage.

hypsistos **[ὕψιστος, *5310*]**

hypsistos is a superlative adjectival form, referring literally to the "highest" places or regions and also to the rank of God as "most high," or "highest." The word is found thirteen times.

As a title for God, ***hypsistos*** occurs in Mark 5:7; Luke 1:32, 33, 76; 6:35; 8:28; Acts 7:48; 16:17; Heb. 7:1.

The term also designates heaven as the "highest (of all regions)" (cf. Matt. 21:9; Mark 11:10; Luke 2:14; 19:38). These texts all express praise to God through the person of Christ.

HIGH PLACE

OT Words

bāmāh **[בָּמָה, 1116]**

This term commonly indicates "high place" as a technical term for a raised ritual shrine. The context is usually, though not exclusively, the Israelite idolatrous worship of Canaanite deities. ***bāmāh*** also refers to literal high places in a geographic sense. The term occurs around one hundred times.

"High places" as sites for idol worship were forbidden and condemned by God under the terms of the Mosaic covenant. ***bāmāh*** is used quite frequently to refer to these places, especially in the Former Prophets and the larger prophetic writings (e.g., Lev. 26:30; Num. 22:41; 1 Kgs. 11:7; 12:31ff.; 2 Kgs. 15:4; 21:3ff.; Isa. 16:12; Jer. 7:31; Ezek. 6:3; Hos. 10:8; Amos 7:9). During the reign of Hezekiah (715–686 B.C.), ritual reforms were undertaken and the high places were removed (cf. 2 Kgs. 18:4; 2 Chr. 32:12; Isa. 36:7). In a few places, ***bāmāh*** designates the "high place" as a legitimate Israelite shrine for the worship of Yahweh (e.g., 1 Sam. 9:12ff.; 10:5, 13; 1 Kgs. 3:2, 3, 4).

In a purely geographic sense, "high places" (of the earth) are indicated in Deut. 32:13; 2 Sam. 22:34; Isa. 58:14; Ps. 18:33; Jer. 26:18; Amos 4:13; Mic. 1:13. The term also refers to "heights" in relation to the heavenly realm in Isa. 14:14.

HIGH-MINDED → PRIDE

HIGHWAY → WAY

HILL → MOUNT

HINDER, HINDRANCE → FORBID

HIRE, HIRED → REWARD

HOLD (NOUN) → PRISON

HOLD (VERB)

OT Words

'āḥaz [אָחַז, 270]

'āḥaz occurs around seventy times with the meanings "hold," "grasp," "take hold of," and related senses.

With the literal sense of "take hold of" ***'āḥaz*** is found, for example, in Gen. 25:26, where Jacob takes hold of Esau's heels at birth. In Exod. 4:4, Moses takes hold of the serpent's tail. 2 Sam. 6:6 refers to Uzzah taking hold of the ark of the covenant; and in 1 Kgs. 1:51 Adonijah takes hold of the horns of the altar. The more violent sense of "seize," in relation to grasping other people, is evident in Judg. 12:6; 2 Sam. 2:21; 4:10; Ps. 137:9. The gentler sense of "hold" (holding in one's hand, or embracing) is found in Ruth 3:10; Ps. 73:23; Song 3:4.

In a metaphorical sense, ***'āḥaz*** refers to strong emotions taking hold of a person — for example, fear (cf. Exod. 15:14; Isa. 33:14); anger (cf. Ps. 119:53); anguish (cf. Job 30:16; 2 Sam. 1:9; and pain (cf. Jer. 13:1; Isa. 13:8).

ḥāzaq [חָזַק, 2388]

ḥāzaq is a common verb, occurring approximately three hundred times with the primary meaning "be strong," "strengthen," as well as many different related senses. One of these related senses is "hold," or "take hold of." ***ḥāzaq*** is found about forty times with this meaning.

The action of taking hold of someone with implied force is demonstrated in a number of places — for example, the tearing of clothes as the result of physical grasping (1 Sam. 15:27; 2 Sam. 1:11); and Amnon's rape of Tamar (2 Sam. 3:11). See also 1 Kgs. 1:50; Isa. 4:1; Zech. 14:13.

ḥāzaq also describes the experience of being seized by strong emotions, such as anguish (Jer. 6:24); dismay (Jer. 8:21); and fear (Jer. 49:24).

ḥāzaq is also translated "hold" in the sense of "retain," "keep back" in Exod. 9:2, describing Egyptians enslaving the Israelite people. See also Jer. 50:33.

Non-violent "holding" in the sense of "grasping" is in view in Neh. 4:17, 21; Ps. 35:2; Jer. 6:23; 50:42 in relation to weapons. Judg. 16:26; Isa. 41:13; 42:6; 45:1 describe taking hold of someone's hand. In the Isaiah texts here, it is Yahweh who is depicted as taking hold of the hand of his people.

Metaphorically, ***ḥāzaq*** also conveys the idea of "laying hold of" in the sense of "devoting oneself to." 1 Kgs. 9:9 describes devotion to pagan deities; and in Isa. 64:7 it is God himself who is the object of devotion. In a related context, this term is translated "hold fast to" in the sense of "cherish," or "nurture," in several places. Job 2:3, 9, for example, speaks of holding fast to integrity; Isa. 56:2 commends the practice of maintaining the observance of the Sabbath; and in Isa. 56:4, 6 similar commendations are given to those who hold fast to the covenant.

NT Words

echō [ἔχω, *2192*]

echō primarily means "have," as well as a number of related senses, in the approximately six hundred contexts in which it is found. On seven occasions, however, ***echō*** is translated "hold," with various nuances.

Matt. 21:26; Mark 11:32 record that the Israelite population "held" (i.e., considered) John the Baptist to be a prophet. The same is predicated of Jesus in Matt. 21:46. In Acts 20:24, Paul does not consider (lit. "hold") his own life as precious to himself. 1 Tim. 3:9 contains the exhortation to "hold to" (i.e., believe in) the mystery of the faith; and in 2 Tim. 1:13 a similar injunction is given with respect to the pattern of sound teaching. ***echō*** is translated "hold" in the sense of "possessing" in 2 Tim. 3:5.

katechō [κατέχω, *2722*]

This verb is found in about twenty places meaning "keep," "take possession," "hold." With the latter meaning and several related senses, ***katechō*** occurs nine times.

The meaning "take hold of," in the sense of "seize," is found in Matt. 21:38 with respect to persons. Metaphorically speaking, ***katechō*** is translated "hold," in the sense of "hold down," or "suppress," in relation to the stifling of truth in the human consciousness. More commonly ***katechō*** reflects the idea of "holding fast (i.e., clinging tenaciously) to" a number of things such as the word of the gospel (1 Cor. 15:2); that which is good (1 Thess. 5:21); confidence in Christ (Heb. 3:6); and one's confession of faith (Heb. 10:23). 2 Thess. 2:6, 7 refer to holding back, or restraining, the man of lawlessness.

krateō [κρατέω, *2902*]

krateō occurs around fifty times and is translated "hold" in a variety of contexts with several nuances.

Two predominant meanings are "take hold of" in the sense of "grasp," or "seize"; and "hold fast to," signifying "remain true to" or "observe."

The idea of "grasp" or "seize" is primarily literal in the following texts, where the following objects are laid hold of — for example, sheep (Matt. 12:11); a hand (Mark 1:31); seven stars in the hand of Christ (Rev. 2:1); and the four winds of heaven, by angelic hands (Rev. 7:1). People are also seized upon in the following passages — for example, John the Baptist (Matt. 14:3, Mark 6:17); a servant (Matt. 18:28); and a young man wearing a linen cloth (Mark 14:51). An unsuccessful attempt to seize Jesus is made in Mark 12:12. But, in the garden of Gethsemane, Jesus is finally arrested (Matt. 26:48ff.; Mark 14:44ff.). Heb. 6:18 encourages believers to grasp the hope of salvation set before them.

krateō also reflects the meaning "hold fast to" in the sense of "observe." Mark 7:3ff., for example, reports the Pharisees' strict observance of the traditions of the elders. 2 Thess. 2:15 contains Paul's exhortation to hold fast to the apostle's teaching. See also Heb. 4:14; Rev. 2:14, 15; 3:11.

Reflecting the idea of restraint, Acts 2:24 refers to the impossibility of death "holding" Jesus.

epilambanō [ἐπιλαμβάνω, *1949*]

This term occurs around twenty times with the primary sense of "take." In about half of these contexts, however, ***epilambanō*** is translated "take hold of."

In Luke 20:20, 26, ***epilambanō*** refers to taking hold of Jesus' words. Luke 23:26; Acts 16:19; 21:30, 33 describe "seizing" people. "Seeking after" eternal life is described in 1 Tim. 6:12, 19. And Heb. 8:9 refers to God "taking hold of" the hand of his people to lead them out of Egypt.

HOLE

OT WORDS

ḥôr [חוֹר, 2356]

ḥôr is a rare noun that is translated "hole" in seven places, in a variety of contexts. It refers, for example, to hiding places (1 Sam. 14:11); caves (Nah. 2:12; Job 30:6); a hole in a chest (2 Kgs. 12:9); a "hole" in the wall (Song 5:4); and an eye socket (Zech. 14:12).

NT WORDS

phōleos [φωλεός, *5454*]

phōleos is a rare term, occurring only twice. Matt. 8:20; Luke 9:58 refer to a fox's hole, or lair.

HOLINESS, HOLY

OT WORDS

qādôsh [קָדוֹשׁ, 6918]

qādôsh is an adjectival form found in approximately 120 contexts with the prominent senses of "holy," "holy ones," designating those places and people set aside by Yahweh for his specific purposes.

Such "holy" places include the tabernacle and temple (Lev. 6:16; 7:6; Pss. 46:4; 65:4; Eccl. 8:10; Ezek. 42:13). Not only are the places "holy," but also the sacrifices and offerings (Lev. 21:6, 8; Num. 5:17); and the priests themselves (Lev. 21:7).

Israel is also designated a "holy" nation in Exod. 19:6; Lev. 11:44; 19:2; Num. 16:3; Deut. 7:6; 14:21; Dan. 8:24.

Those who take the Nazirite vow are declared to be "holy" (Num. 6:5ff.). "Holy" days are noted in Neh. 8:9ff. — in particular the Sabbath in Isa. 58:13.

God declares himself to be "holy" in Lev. 20:26; and is described as such in Josh. 24:19; 1 Sam. 2:2; Pss. 22:3; 99:3ff.; Isa. 6:3; 30:11ff.; 49:7; Jer. 51:5; Hos. 11:9.

qōdesh [קֹדֶשׁ, 6944]

qōdesh is a common noun that also has adjectival force. It conveys the primary sense of "holiness," "sanctity," "consecration," implying that which is set apart for the service of Yahweh. The term refers both to God and to the human realm, and is found about four hundred times.

As an adjective, ***qōdesh*** refers to that state which results from the sanctifying presence of Yahweh. It describes holy ground (Exod. 3:5; Josh. 5:15); God's holy dwelling, the tabernacle (Exod. 15:13); and heaven (Deut. 26:15; Ps. 20:6; Jer. 25:30). In addition, ***qōdesh*** refers to the Holy Spirit of God (Ps. 51:11; Isa. 63:10ff.); and the holy name of Yahweh (Lev. 20:3; Ps. 103:1; Ezek. 36:20ff.; Amos 2:7). The anthropomorphic "holy arm of Yahweh" is mentioned in Isa. 52:10.

In a greater number of contexts, ***qōdesh*** as an adjective also describes as "holy" that which is set apart for Yahweh's service or purpose. Such things include the Israelite assembly (cf. Exod. 12:16; Lev. 23:3ff.; Num. 28:18ff.); ritual feasts (cf. Lev. 23:2); the Sabbath (cf. Exod. 16:23; Neh. 9:14; Isa. 58:13); the temple (cf. Pss. 5:7; 11:4; Mic. 1:2; Hab. 2:20); priestly garments (cf. Exod. 28:2ff.; 29:29; Lev. 16:4); food in the sanctuary (cf. Exod. 29:34; 1 Sam. 21:4; Ezra 2:63); vessels from the sanctuary (cf. Num. 31:6; Josh. 6:19; 1 Kgs. 8:4), including the furniture (cf. Exod. 29:37; 30:29; 40:9); the anointing oil or incense (cf. Exod. 30:25, 31ff.; Num.

35:25); the ritual offerings (cf. Exod. 30:10; Lev. 4:6; 6:17; 7:1, 6; 14:13); tithes (cf. Lev. 27:30); and the priests themselves (cf. Lev. 21:6; Ezra 8:28). The divine covenant is also described as "holy" in Dan. 11:28, as are the people of Israel (Exod. 22:31; Ezra 9:2; Isa. 62:12; Dan. 12:7).

Jerusalem is described as the "holy city" in Neh. 11:1, 18; Isa. 48:2; Dan. 9:24. And Zion is declared to be the holy hill (Pss. 2:6; 3:4; 15:1; 43:3). The temple mount is referred to as the "holy mountain" of Yahweh (Isa. 48:1; 56:7; Ezek. 20:40; Dan. 9:16; Joel 2:13; Zeph. 3:11). In connection with the sanctuary itself, ***qōdesh*** refers back to the "holy place" (e.g., Exod. 28:43; Lev. 6:30; Num. 28:7; 1 Kgs. 8:10); and the "most holy place" (e.g., Exod. 26:33ff.; 28:29ff.; Lev. 16:2ff.; Ezek. 41:4; 44:13).

As a noun, ***qōdesh*** refers to holiness as a characteristic of Yahweh (cf. Exod. 15:11; Pss. 29:2; 89:35; Jer. 23:9; Mal. 2:11). The "way of holiness" (Isa. 35:8) is described as part of the anticipated new heavens and new earth. The term also designates, in a general ceremonial sense, the "holy" as distinct from the "unclean" (cf. Lev. 10:10; Ezek. 44:23). Nominally, ***qōdesh*** also indicates the "holy place," or Yahweh's sanctuary in general terms (e.g., Exod. 36:3ff.; Num. 3:28ff.; Ps. 20:2; Lam. 4:1; Ezek. 41:21; Dan. 8:13; Zeph. 3:4). The term also refers to the "holy things" associated with keeping God's commands (cf. Lev. 22:7ff.; Deut. 12:26; 26:13; Ezek. 22:26); and to the "holy district" as depicted in Ezekiel's vision of the new Jerusalem in Ezek. 45:6; 48:20.

qādash [קָדַשׁ, 6942]

qādash is the verbal root from which ***qōdesh*** (see above) is derived. ***qādash*** occurs around 150 times and is translated "to sanctify" (i.e., make holy) in most of the contexts in which it occurs. The term also expresses a number of associated meanings, such as "dedicate," "consecrate," "set apart," — but the root meaning "sanctify" underlies them all.

With the traditional meaning "sanctify," in the sense of "set apart as holy" with Yahweh as the instigator of the process, ***qādash*** refers to the sanctification of the Sabbath (Gen. 2:3; Exod. 20:11; Ezek. 20:12); the temple (1 Kgs. 9:3); the tabernacle (Exod. 29:43, 44); the people of Israel (Exod. 31:13; Lev. 20:8; Num. 3:13); and individuals such as the prophet Jeremiah (Jer. 1:5).

More common than the divine action of sanctifying is the divine command to sanctify, whereby Yahweh requires his people to appropriately prepare themselves for worship and service. Such a command is given with respect to the firstborn (Exod. 13:2; Deut. 15:19); the assembly of Israel (cf. Joel 2:16; Exod. 19:10ff.); the Sabbath (cf. Exod. 20:8; Deut. 5:12; Neh. 13:22); the ritual offerings (cf. Exod. 28:38; 29:27); the people of Israel (cf. Lev. 11:44; 20:7; Josh. 3:5; 1 Sam. 16:5); the altar (cf. Exod. 29:31); the tabernacle (cf. Exod. 30:29; 40:9ff.; Lev. 8:10); the temple (cf. 1 Kgs. 8:64); and the high priest (cf. Lev. 8:12).

qādash also designates the people's act of sanctifying, usually translated "dedicate," and the context is uniformly one of ritual worship of Yahweh. Such dedicating is predicated of the "holy things" belonging to God (cf. Lev. 22:3); of one's personal property to Yahweh (cf. Lev. 27:14ff.; Judg. 17:3); of gifts to Yahweh (cf. 2 Kgs. 12:18); thank offerings (cf. Ezra 3:5); and a fast (cf. Joel 1:14; 2:15).

The meaning "sanctify" is also used of God in the sense of honoring him (e.g., Isa. 8:13; 29:23). Israel's failure to do so is indicated in Num. 20:12; 27:14; Deut. 32:51. Yahweh is also said to sanctify himself, meaning that he shows himself holy through his people (cf. Isa. 5:16; Ezek. 20:41; 28:22, 25). Ezek. 36:23; 38:16; 39:29 refer to the nations seeing the holiness of Yahweh through the punishment of his people.

miqdāsh [מִקְדָּשׁ, 4720]

miqdāsh is a participial form derived from the verbal root ***qādash*** (see above), and is consistently translated "sanctuary," referring to the sacred enclosure of the tabernacle, temple, and the visionary temple of Ezekiel.

Reference to the tabernacle is found in general terms in Exod. 15:17; Lev. 12:4; 16:33; Num. 3:38; Josh. 24:26. The command to revere the sanctuary is recorded in Lev. 19:30; 26:2; and the defiling of the sanctuary is mentioned in Lev. 20:3; Num. 19:20.

miqdāsh refers to the temple in 2 Chr. 26:18; 29:21; 30:8; 36:17. David's instruction to Solomon to build the temple is found 1 Chr. 22:19; 28:10. Pss. 68:35; 78:69; Isa. 60:13 describe the sanctuary, or the temple, as God's possession. In Ezek. 9:6 there is the prophetic anticipation of divine judgment beginning at the Jerusalem temple, as a consequence of the defilement of that sanctuary (cf. Jer. 51:51; Lam. 1:10; Ezek. 5:11; 23:38). The Lord himself is described as a sanctuary for his people in Isa. 8:14; Ezek. 11:16. ***miqdāsh*** is also found in the context of the renewal and restoration of the temple in Ezekiel's vision (cf. Ezek. 37:26, 28; 43:21; 44:11ff.; 45:3, 4; 47:12; 48:10).

ḥāsîd [חָסִיד, **2623**]

ḥāsîd refers to individuals who are godly, faithful, and holy, commonly designated as "saints," "faithful," "holy one(s)," "godly one(s)." ***ḥāsîd*** occurs around thirty times.

David and Moses are both referred to as "godly" in Ps. 89:19 and Deut. 33:8, respectively. See also the psalmist in Ps. 86:2.

1 Sam. 2:9; 2 Chr. 6:41; Pss. 16:10; 30:4; 145:10; Prov. 2:8 depict "the godly" as "saints" in general terms. 2 Sam. 22:26; Ps. 18:25 refer to those who are faithful and loyal. Mic. 7:2 reveals the absence of godly people on earth.

NT Words

hagios [ἅγιος, *40*]

hagios is an adjective that commonly refers to those persons and things that are "holy" in the sense of being set apart for divine redemptive purposes. When predicated of God, ***hagios*** refers to his purity of character and is applied as part of the designation for the third person of the Godhead, the Holy Spirit. ***hagios*** is commonly translated "saint" with reference to the people of God. The term occurs around 230 times.

References to the Holy Spirit abound in the New Testament in connection with this term (e.g., Matt. 1:18ff.; Mark 1:8; Luke 1:15, 67; John 20:22; Acts 1:2ff.; 13:2ff.; Rom. 5:5; 1 Cor. 2:14; Eph. 1:13; 1 Thess. 5:26; Heb. 6:4; 1 Pet. 1:12; 1 John 5:7; Jude 20).

Concerning "holy things" in general contexts, ***hagios*** occurs in Matt. 7:6; Rom. 12:1; 2 Pet. 1:18. In particular, the "holy" city of Jerusalem is indicated in Matt. 4:5; 27:53 in the earthly sense, whereas in Rev. 21:2, 10; 22:19 it is spoken of with reference to the heavenly city of Jerusalem to be revealed at the end of the age with the return of Christ. Matt. 24:15; Acts 21:28; Eph. 2:21 refer to the holy place in the temple. In addition, "holy" angels are mentioned in Matt. 25:31; Mark 8:38; Luke 9:26; Rev. 14:10.

"Saints" in general are also commonly designated by the term ***hagios*** (e.g., Matt. 27:52; Acts 9:13, 32; Rom. 12:13; 1 Cor. 6:2; 2 Cor. 9:1; Eph. 2:19; Phil. 1:1; Col. 1:2, 12; 2 Thess. 1:10; 1 Tim. 5:10; Heb. 6:10; Rev. 5:8; 19:8).

Various other contexts also use the term "holy" to describe Jesus, as the "holy one of God" (cf. Mark 1:24; Luke 1:35; Rev. 3:7); the apostles (cf. Eph. 3:5; Rev. 18:20); the prophets (cf. Luke 1:70; Acts 3:21; Rev. 22:6); the covenant (cf. Luke 1:72); God as "holy Father" (cf. John 17:11); the Scriptures (cf. Rom. 1:2); the commandments (cf. Rom. 7:12; 2 Pet. 2:21); children (cf. 1 Cor. 7:14); the church (cf. Eph. 5:27); God's people (cf. Col. 1:22; 1 Pet. 1:16; 2:9); a kiss of greeting (cf. 1 Thess. 5:26; 1 Cor. 15:20); and holiness as a characteristic of God (cf. 1 Pet. 1:16; Rev. 4:8; 6:10).

hagiazō [ἁγιάζω, *37*]

This is the verb from which the adjective ***hagios*** is derived (see above). ***hagiazō*** is found in about thirty contexts and means "to sanctify" in most of these. The translation of ***hagiazō*** will occasionally vary — for example, "consecrate," or "be, make holy." But the underlying sense of "sanctify," or to set apart people and things for the service of God, remains.

The process or action of sanctifying, in general contexts, is illustrated in Matt. 23:17; 1 Cor. 7:14; 1 Tim. 4:5; 2 Tim. 2:21; Rev. 22:11. The action and attitude of "sanctifying the name of God," or maintaining a holy reverence towards him, is evident in Luke 11:2; Matt. 6:9, where Christ begins his paradigm prayer: "Our Father in heaven, holy be your name . . ." 1 Pet. 3:15 speaks of "sanctifying" Christ as Lord, or treating him with reverence.

The other uses of ***hagiazō*** all relate explicitly to the actions of God and Christ. For instance, Jesus "consecrates" himself for the sake of his disciples (cf. John 17:19); and also sanctifies his church (cf. Eph. 5:26) and his disciples, setting them apart for ministry (cf. John 17:17). God is declared to have sanctified the person and mission of Christ (John 10:36); and also his people (Acts 20:32; Heb. 3:11; 10:10; 1 Thess. 5:23; 1 Cor. 6:11).

hagiasmos [ἁγιασμός, *38*]

hagiasmos is a noun derived from ***hagiazō*** (see above) and is translated "sanctification," or "holiness." The term occurs ten times.

"Godly living" is signified by the use of this term in Rom. 6:19; Heb. 12:14; 1 Tim. 2:15; 1 Thess. 4:7. Sanctification is designated as the fruit or consequences of one's salvation in Rom. 6:22; 1 Thess. 4:3. Paul, in 1 Cor. 1:30, declares that God has made Jesus our sanctification. The process of sanctification by the Spirit of God is affirmed in 2 Thess. 2:13; 1 Pet. 1:2.

hosios [ὅσιος, *3741*]

hosios is an adjective describing people and things as "holy," or morally and religiously pure. The term occurs six times.

The title "holy one" is applied to David in Acts 2:27; 13:35 (cf. Ps. 16:8–11) as a ruler who anticipated the coming of Christ. In Rev. 16:5, the same title is applied to God (cf. also Rev. 15:4). The adjective "holy" is also applied to Christ as our great high priest in Heb. 7:26. The "holy and sure blessings of David," given to him by God for his faithfulness, are referred to in Acts 13:34. 1 Tim. 2:8 describes "lifting holy hands" as an appropriate attitude for prayer. Titus 1:8 lists holiness as an indispensable character trait for a prospective pastor or elder.

hosiotēs [ὁσιότης, *3742*]

hosiotēs is a rare noun, occurring only twice and meaning "holiness." In Luke 1:75 the term is found together with "righteousness" (→ RIGHTEOUS), indicating that the coming of Christ was intended to bring about an attitude of renewed faith and obedience towards God in the lives of the people of God. Eph. 4:24 refers to the new nature of all believers in Christ who have been re-created in righteousness and holiness for the same purpose.

hagiōsynē [ἁγιωσύνη, *42*]

This term is a synonym for both ***hosiotēs*** and ***hagiasmos*** (see above). ***hagiōsynē*** occurs only three times. In Rom. 1:4, the word is applied to the Spirit of God (viz. "Spirit of holiness"), who was instrumental in bringing Jesus back from the dead. 2 Cor. 7:1 exhorts believers to holiness of life (cf. also 1 Thess. 3:13).

hagiotēs [ἁγιότης, *41*]

hagiotēs occurs only once, in Heb. 12:10, and refers to the divine holiness which is the ultimate purpose for which the Lord disciplines us throughout our lives.

Additional Notes

In the Hebrew and Greek vocabulary for "holiness," there are two main strands of meaning. On the one hand, "holiness" indicates moral and spiritual purity, supremely reflected in God the Father and Jesus Christ his Son, and intended for all believers committed to an intimate relationship with Christ. On the other hand, the concept of "holiness" has a functional nuance, whereby people, places, and objects are "sanctified" or "set apart" for specific purposes in relation to the worship and service of God and Christ. The personal holiness demanded of God's people in the Old Testament is fully realized in the person of Jesus Christ.

HOME → HOUSE

HONEST, HONESTY → HONOR

HONEY, HONEYCOMB

OT Words

debash **[דְּבַשׁ, 1706]**

debash is found in approximately fifty contexts and is translated "honey" throughout, including one reference to "honeycomb."

Honey as a food, in a literal sense, is found in a number of contexts (e.g., Gen. 43:11; Exod. 16:31; Lev. 2:11; Judg. 14:18ff.; Isa. 7:15; Ezek. 3:3). In Prov. 24:13, ***debash*** refers to "honeycomb."

debash is also used in a metaphorical sense to indicate abundant fertility. There are a number of references, for example, to Canaan as a "land of milk and honey" (e.g., Exod. 3:8, 17; Lev. 20:24; Num. 13:27; 16:13, 14; Deut. 8:8; Josh. 5:6; Ezek. 20:6, 15). General fertility is alluded to in Job 20:17; Ezek. 16:13, 19. In reference to the desirability of God's word, Ps. 119:103 declares that the words of Yahweh are "sweeter than honey."

nōphet **[נֹפֶת, 5317]**

nōphet refers to the honeycomb and also to the honey dropping from it. The term is found five times. Prov. 24:13; 27:7 refer to honey as food. Ps. 19:10 refers to the attractiveness of God's word as "sweeter than the honeycomb." Prov. 5:3 describes the seductive words of an immoral woman as "honey" dripping from her lips. In a markedly different context, the woman admired by her lover in the Song of Songs is complimented for having "honey and milk" under her tongue (cf. Song 4:11).

ṣûph **[צוּף, 6688]**

A rare term, found only twice, ***ṣûph*** refers to honeycomb in a metaphorical sense. In Ps. 19:10, it refers to the desirability of God's law as sweeter than the honeycomb. In Prov. 16:24, ***ṣûph*** likens pleasant words to a honeycomb.

NT Words

meli [μέλι, *3192*]

This term is rare, occurring only four times. ***meli*** signifies honey as food in Matt. 3:4; Mark 1:6. In Rev. 10:9, 10 it refers to the sweet honey taste of the angelic scroll given to John to eat, which afterwards turns sour in his stomach.

HONOR

OT Words

yeqār **[יְקָר, 3366]**

yeqār is a relatively uncommon noun, occurring about twenty times with the primary senses of "honor," "splendor," evident in the majority of these contexts. (→ PRICE)

"Honor" in the sense of royal splendor is mentioned in Esth. 1:4. With the underlying idea of glory or prestige, ***yeqār*** is translated "honor" in Ps. 49:12, 20. "Honor" as deference, esteem, or recognition is indicated in Esth. 1:20, where wives are commanded by royal decree to give honor to their husbands. Esth. 6:3ff. records the bestowal of dignity or recognition upon Mordecai, and in Esth. 8:16 the same honor is awarded to the Jewish people.

hādar **[הָדַר, 1921]**

hādar is a rare verb that is translated "honor" in the sense of "give deference to" or "give respect to" in two of the seven contexts in which it is found (Lev. 19:15; Lam. 5:12).

NT Words

timē [τιμή, *5092*]

This noun occurs around forty times and refers predominantly to "honor" that is given in recognition of one's service or rank. It can also refer to the "price" or "value" of a person or thing. (→ PRICE)

1 Tim. 1:17; 6:16; Rev. 4:9, 11; 7:12; 19:1 refer to ascribing honor to God in the context of praise or worship. Likewise, "honor" to Christ is indicated in Heb. 2:7, 9; 3:3; 2 Pet. 1:17; Rev. 5:12, 13.

In the context of honor among people, ***timē*** refers to respect or recognition in a number of places — for example, showing deference or honor to one's wife (cf. 1 Pet. 3:7; 1 Tim. 4:14); granting double honor for elders (cf. 1 Tim. 5:17); and bestowing parts of the body with honor (cf. 1 Cor. 12:23, 24). See also Rom. 2:7; 12:10; Acts 28:10; 1 Tim. 6:1. Respect for government authority ordained of God is commanded in Rom. 13:7.

timē also has the sense of "value" as "worth" in Rom. 9:21, where high value is set on a beautiful pot. Merely human regulations have no value in restraining sexual immorality, as affirmed in Col. 2:23.

Rev. 21:24 refers to the glory and honor of the redeemed kings of the earth brought into heaven. Similarly, Rev. 21:26 describes carrying the glory and honor of the nations into the heavenly city.

timaō [τιμάω, *5091*]

timaō is the verb from which ***timē*** (see above) is derived. It is found approximately twenty times and signifies primarily the action of "honoring" in a number of different contexts. It can also mean "to price."

Honoring God in the sense of worshiping and reverencing him in a right spirit is affirmed in John 5:23. This attitude is perfectly illustrated by Jesus' honoring his heavenly Father in John 8:49. Conversely, in John 12:26, God is said to honor his faithful servants. Hypocritical worship, or mere lip service, is condemned by Christ in Matt. 15:8 (cf. Isa. 29:13; Mark 7:6).

God's people are required to give honor to their parents (Matt. 15:4, 6; 19:19; Mark 7:10; 10:19; Luke 18:20; Eph. 6:2); and also to widows, who are to be treated kindly and with respect (cf. 1 Tim. 5:3). Respect for the king or emperor is also demanded in 1 Pet. 2:17.

See Also: → GLORIFY → HEAVY

HOOK

OT Words

ḥakkāh **[חַכָּה, 2443]**

ḥakkāh is a rare noun, occurring three times and referring to "fish hooks." Job 41:1 mentions the impossible task of catching the beast Leviathan with a fish hook. Isa. 19:8; Hab. 1:15 describe catching fish with hook and net.

ḥāḥ **[חָח, 2397]**

This word is also translated "hook," but it is used in contexts other then fishing. ***ḥāḥ*** is also rare, being found in only seven texts.

Hooks (or bracelets) as jewelry are mentioned in Exod. 35:22. Hooks placed through the nose as a means of forcible detention and leading into captivity are noted as a punishment against Israel (2 Kgs. 19:28; Ezek. 19:4, 9); and also against pagan nations (Isa. 37:29; Ezek. 29:4; 38:4).

NT Words

ankistron [ἄγκιστρον, *44*]

This word is found only in Matt. 17:27 with reference to a fish hook.

HOPE

OT Words

Underlying the phenomenon of "hope" in the Old Testament is the overlapping motif of "trust." (→ TRUST)

yāḥal **[יָחַל, 3176]**

yāḥal occurs approximately forty times and means "wait (for)," "hope (for)." With the meaning "wait," the sense is most often an expectant anticipation, thus the underlying sense of "hope" in expectation of a particular result. ***yāḥal*** means "hope" in about half of the contexts in which it occurs. (→ WAIT)

Putting one's hope in God is a common theme expressed in the Psalms (e.g., Pss. 31:24; 33:18, 22; 38:15; 42:5, 11; 43:5; 71:14; 130:7; 131:3; 147:11). See also Lam. 3:24. Similarly, the psalmist expresses his hope in God's law as a means of sustaining his intimate relationship with Yahweh (cf. Pss. 119:43, 49, 74, 81, 114, 147; 130:5). Hoping in Yahweh's mercy and compassion is the prophet Jeremiah's means of gaining consolation from his grief at the destruction of Jerusalem and the temple in Lam. 3:21.

Placing hope in the "arm of Yahweh" is a metaphorical expression for trusting in divine power that will bring certain victory (cf. Isa. 51:5). Ezek. 19:5 alludes metaphorically to a lost hope of victory, in human terms.

sābar **[שָׂבַר, 7663]**

sābar occurs eight times, meaning "wait (for)" "hope (for)" in three of those occurrences.

Esth. 9:1 records the plan in which the enemies of the Jewish people in exile hoped to utterly destroy them. The plan was ultimately foiled. In Ps. 119:166, the psalmist hopes for salvation from Yahweh. And Isa. 38:18 expresses the impossibility of hoping for God's faithfulness after death.

tiqwāh **[תִּקְוָה, 8615]**

This noun is found in about thirty contexts, meaning "hope" or "expectation" in most of them.

Hope in general human terms is indicated in Job 4:6; Prov. 19:18; 23:18; 24:14. Specifically, Naomi expresses hope for a husband in Ruth 1:12. Job 5:16; Ps. 9:18 mention the non-specific hope of the poor.

Hopelessness, the very antithesis of genuine expectation, is expressed in the context of divine judgment against the godless (cf. Job 8:13; 11:20; Prov. 10:28; 11:7, 23), and also against the nation of Israel (Ezek. 37:11).

When directed towards God, hope is viewed in terms of an anticipated deliverance (cf. Jer. 29:11; 31:17; Hos. 2:15; Zech. 9:12).

tôḥelet **[תּוֹחֶלֶת, 8431]**

A rare noun, ***tôḥelet*** is consistently translated "hope" in the six contexts in which it is found. ***tôḥelet*** indicates hope in the Lord (Ps. 39:7); hope of the righteousness which ends in gladness (Prov. 10:28); and the hopelessness of the wicked, or the hope that perishes (Prov. 11:7; Lam. 3:18). The remaining general references are found in Job 41:9; Prov. 13:12.

bittāḥôn **[בִּטָּחוֹן, 986]**

Another rare noun, ***bittāḥôn*** refers to "confidence," "hope" in three passages (cf. 2 Kgs. 18:19; Eccl. 9:4; Isa. 36:4), all of which relate to human confidence.

miqweh **[מִקְוֶה, 4723]**

This noun occurs twelve times and is translated "hope" in four of these contexts. Hope for Israel, in spite of her sins, is expressed in Ezra 10:2. As a title for Yahweh, the phrase "hope of Israel" occurs in Jer. 14:8; 17:13. Jer. 50:17 refers to Yahweh as the "hope of their fathers."

NT Words

elpis **[ἐλπίς, *1680*]**

In virtually all of the approximately fifty contexts in which this noun is found, it is translated "hope," with a number of underlying emphases. ***elpis*** indicates that the Christian hope is not based on mere wishful thinking, but on a certain outcome of blessing that is grounded in the finished redemptive work of Jesus Christ.

The believer's explicit hope in God's finished work of salvation through Christ constitutes the dominant usage of ***elpis*** (e.g., Rom. 5:5; 1 Cor. 9:10; 2 Cor. 3:12; Eph. 1:18; Phil. 1:20; Col. 1:23, 27; 1 Thess. 5:8; Heb. 3:6; 1 Pet. 3:15; 1 John 3:3). Related to this theme is the Christian hope of resurrection from the dead (Acts 23:6), and also hope in the promises of God for salvation (cf. Acts 26:6, 7; Rom. 4:18; 8:20).

Other uses of the term indicate the hope of sharing God's glory (cf. Rom. 5:2); hope as a Christian virtue (cf. Rom. 5:4; 1 Cor. 13:13). See also 2 Cor. 1:7; 1 Thess. 2:19; Gal. 5:5. The tragedy of the unbeliever who has no hope is cited in Eph. 2:12; 1 Thess. 4:13.

elpizō **[ἐλπίζω, *1679*]**

This verb form has the same sense of "hope" as ***elpis*** (see above), its nominal derivative. The action of hoping has nothing to do with a speculative desire. It is, rather, a fully confident anticipation of deliverance, won through the person and work of Christ. ***elpizō*** occurs about thirty times.

The confident hope or expectation of salvation is illustrated in Matt. 12:21; Luke 24:21; Acts 26:7; Rom.

8:24; 2 Cor. 1:10; 1 Tim. 4:10; 5:5; 1 Pet. 1:13. Note also Paul's affirmation of a "hypothetical hopelessness," if Christ had not risen from the dead, in 1 Cor. 15:19. The classic definition of faith as "... the assurance of things hoped for" is found in Heb. 11:1.

False hope in earthly riches is indicated in 1 Tim. 6:17, as is trust in the Mosaic law for salvation in John 5:45.

There is also a mundane usage of ***elpizō*** in relation to general human circumstances in Luke 6:34; Rom. 15:24; Phil. 2:23; 1 Tim. 3:14.

HORN

OT Words

qeren **[קֶרֶן, 7161]**

qeren is translated "horn" in almost all of the eighty contexts in which it is found. The term has both a literal and figurative sense.

Literal ram's horns are noted in Gen. 22:13; Josh. 6:5. See also the vision of the ram and goat in Dan. 8:3, 5, where the horns of these animals symbolize royal and military power. See also Zech. 1:18ff. ***qeren*** also refers to the horns of the altar in both the tabernacle and the temple (cf. Exod. 27:2; 30:2ff.; 37:25ff.; Lev. 4:7, 18ff.; 1 Kgs. 1:50; Ps. 118:27; Jer. 17:1; Ezek. 43:15, 20). The horns of an unknown animal, akin to an ox or bull, are mentioned in Deut. 33:17; Ps. 22:21. 1 Sam. 16:1, 13; 1 Kgs. 1:39 refer to the horn of anointing. See also Ezek. 27:15; 1 Kgs. 22:11.

The figurative usage of ***qeren*** embraces the idea of strength or power in several contexts. As a general term for "strength," the term is found in 1 Sam. 2:1; Ps. 75:4, 5, 10 in relation to people. Divine strength is indicated in Ps. 112:9. The expression "horn of . . ." indicates royal power in relation to pagan, earthly kingdoms — for example, Moab (Jer. 48:25); Media/Persia (Dan. 8:20); Greece (Dan. 8:21). The same expression is also applied to Israel in Lam. 2:3; Ezek. 29:21.

The term "horn" also indicates a coming messianic ruler, as expressed in Hannah's song in 1 Sam. 2:16; Ps. 89:17. In Ps. 132:17, a "horn" is said to "sprout for David." In each case, the catalyst for such a phenomenon is divine initiative and power.

NT Words

keras [κέρας, *2768*]

keras occurs eleven times and is translated "horn" on each occasion in a variety of contexts, with all but one occurring in the book of Revelation.

The messianic "horn of salvation" is depicted in Luke 1:69. In the apocalyptic vision of John, ***keras*** refers to the "horns of the lamb" (i.e., Jesus Christ) (Rev. 5:6); and the horns of the golden altar (Rev. 9:13). In two central visions of this book, horns refer figuratively to the satanic forces of evil and darkness — in reference to the "unholy trinity" of the dragon, sea beast, and earth beast (Rev. 12:3; 13:1 [twice]; 13:11). See also Rev. 17:3, 7. Horns are also mentioned in connection with the ten kings associated with the destruction of Babylon, the "great harlot" (Rev. 17:12, 16).

HORNET

OT Words

ṣir'āh **[צִרְעָה, 6880]**

This term is rare, occurring only three times and referring to "hornets" in a metaphorical sense, indicating a supernatural host sent by Yahweh to drive out the Canaanite nations before Israel (cf. Exod. 23:28; Deut. 7:20; Josh. 24:12).

HORSE

OT Words

sûs **[סוּס, 5483]**

sûs is the standard term for "horse" in the Old Testament, occurring about 140 times.

As personal property, or livestock holdings, horses are mentioned in Gen. 17:17; Exod. 9:3; Deut. 17:16; 1 Kgs. 4:26ff.; 10:25ff.; Ezra 2:66. Non-specific general usage of ***sûs*** is found in Gen. 49:17; Job 39:18; Ps. 20:7; Prov. 26:3; Isa. 63:13; Jer. 12:5.

sûs is also frequently found in military contexts, referring to cavalry forces (e.g., Exod. 14:9; Deut. 20:1; Josh. 11:4ff.; 2 Sam. 15:1; 2 Kgs. 7:6ff.; Ps. 33:17; Isa. 30:16; Ezek. 17:15; Hos. 1:7; Amos 4:10; Hab. 1:8).

sûs is used as a title in Neh. 3:28; Jer. 31:40 in reference to the horse gate, one of a number of gates situated around the wall of Jerusalem.

Visionary horses of fire are described in several contexts of supernatural divine revelation. 2 Kgs. 2:11, for example, describes Elijah being transported to heaven in a chariot drawn by fiery horses. Zechariah's visions also contain several references to these creatures (cf. Zech. 1:8; 6:2ff.; 9:10).

The metaphorical use of this term in reference to "lusty stallions" indicates Israel's sinful passion for idolatry (cf. Jer. 5:8; Ezek. 23:20).

NT Words

hippos [ἵππος, *2462*]

hippos is the Greek equivalent of the Hebrew term ***sûs*** (see above), and occurs sixteen times.

hippos is used generally in Jas. 3:3; Rev. 14:20; 18:13. In the remaining usage, entirely in the book of Revelation, ***hippos*** designates the visionary horses of the apocalypse in a number of contexts. Rev. 6:2ff., for example, refers to the horses and their riders, symbolizing divine judgment. Rev. 9:7, 9, 17 refer to the demonic horses of fiery plague judgment. Rev. 19:18 affirms that the horses of the conquered armies of the antichrist will be destroyed. Rev. 19:11, 21 describe the messianic King of kings riding on the white horse, symbolizing God's victorious army conquering the forces of evil. There is also a retinue of white horses following the white rider in Rev. 19:14.

HOSANNA

OT Words

yāsha' [יָשַׁע, **3467**]

yāsha' is a common verb meaning "to save." It is used in the expression *hôshî'ēnû nā',* which means "save us, we (or I) pray," and from which the English word "hosanna" is derived.

NT Words

hosanna [ὡσαννά, *5614*]

This Greek term is the transliterated equivalent of the Hebrew phrase *hôshî'ēnû nā'* (see ***yāsha'***, above). This word is also rare in the New Testament, occurring six times. In each case, it is used by the Jerusalem population as a cry of adulation directed at Jesus Christ during his triumphal entry into Jerusalem in the last week of his earthly life and ministry (cf. Matt. 21:9 [twice], 15; Mark 11:9, 10; John 12:13).

HOT

OT Words

ḥārāh [חָרָה, **2734**]

ḥārāh is a verb found in about ninety contexts, meaning "to be hot (with)," "burn," "kindle," referring to the idea of getting angry.

The idea of being or getting "hot" with anger, directed towards people, is found in Exod. 32:19, for example, where Moses becomes enraged at Israel for their idolatry. See also Judg. 9:30. ***ḥārāh*** is found in Exod. 32:11; Judg. 2:14; 3:8; 10:7 in the context of Yahweh's anger against his people.

The action of kindling one's anger is indicated in the cause of Yahweh against his people (e.g., Num. 11:10; Deut. 6:15; Josh. 7:1; 2 Sam. 6:7; 2 Kgs. 13:3; Ps. 106:40; Isa. 5:25). It is also evident in the context of human anger (cf. Num. 22:27; 24:10; 1 Sam. 17:28). In 1 Sam. 11:6, it is the Spirit of Yahweh who ignites the anger of Saul. Isa. 45:24 refers to people being incensed at God.

ḥāmam [חָמַם, **2552**]

ḥāmam occurs thirteen times and in most contexts means "be (grow) hot," "be (grow) warm" in the literal sense of being heated either by the sun or by another person or animal. In the remaining instances, ***ḥāmam*** has the metaphorical sense of "getting angry."

With the literal sense of getting warm, ***ḥāmam*** is found in several contexts: warming by the sun (cf. Exod. 16:21); warmth from another person (cf. 1 Kgs. 1:2; Eccl. 4:11); and heat from various objects (cf. Job 31:20; Isa. 44:15, 16; 7:14).

The surging of anger within one's heart is recorded in Ps. 39:3. Growing hot with passion for idol worship is noted in Isa. 57:5; Hos. 7:7.

NT Words

zestos [ζεστός, *2200*]

zestos is a rare adjective, found only three times in Rev. 3:15, 16 with reference to the Laodicean congregation's lack of fervor or zeal in the practice of their Christian faith. Their condemnation by the risen Christ rests on the fact that they are "lukewarm" in their commitment to him — "neither cold nor hot."

HOUR

OT Words

shā'āh [שָׁעָה, **8160** (Aramaic)]

shā'āh is an Aramaic term that occurs only five times in the book of Daniel. Although the word has the sense of "hour," all the contexts in which it is found suggest that it refers not to the literal time period of sixty minutes, but instead means "immediately," or "for a brief period of time." See Dan. 3:6, 15; 4:19, 33; 5:5.

NT Words

hōra [ὥρα, *5610*]

This term is fairly common in the New Testament, occurring around one hundred times. ***hōra*** means "hour" in a variety of contexts, referring both to literal periods of times as well as to specific occasions and moments of great import.

With the literal sense of sixty-minute intervals, ***hōra*** occurs in Matt. 26:40; Mark 14:37; Luke 22:59;

Acts 5:7; 19:30. In Rev. 18:19, with reference to the destruction of Babylon in one hour, the term probably indicates symbolic time. ***hōra*** is also used to indicate the specific time of day (e.g., Matt. 20:5ff.; Mark 6:35; Luke 12:39, 46; John 19:14; Acts 10:30; Rev. 11:13). Occasionally, ***hōra*** is found in the expression "the same hour," meaning "immediately" (cf. Matt. 8:13; 9:22; Luke 2:38; Acts 16:18).

The most significant use of ***hōra*** is in contexts where it means a "time," or "period of time" that is of special import. The translation "hour" is retained in these texts — for example, the hour of Jesus' trial in Gethsemane (Mark 14:35); the hour of incense, in reference to worship (Luke 1:10); the hour of Jesus' earthly destiny in reference to his arrest and crucifixion (Luke 22:53; John 2:4; 7:30); the hour of Jesus' suffering (John 12:27; 13:1); the hour for the Son of Man to be glorified (John 12:23; 17:1); the last hour, in an eschatological sense (1 John 2:18; Rev. 14:7, 15).

HOUSE

OT Words

bayit **[בַּיִת, 1004]**

A common term found throughout the Old Testament (approximately 1,700 times), ***bayit*** primarily refers to "house" in the sense of "dwelling," as well as other related meanings. The word also indicates a "household" or "family" in a number of different contexts.

A brief sampling of the references to "household" or "family" includes Gen. 12:1; Exod. 6:14; Lev. 16:6ff.; Deut. 6:22; 1 Kgs. 21:29; Job 1:10. The family or "house" of Israel is referred to in Exod. 40:38; Lev. 10:6; Josh. 21:45; Ruth 4:11; 2 Sam. 1:12; Isa. 5:7; Ezek. 9:9; Hos. 1:4; Mic. 1:5. The "house of Judah" is indicated in 2 Sam. 2:4; 1 Kgs. 12:24; Neh. 4:16; Jer. 5:11; Ezek. 4:6; Hos. 1:7; Zech. 8:13. Reference is made to the "house of David" in 1 Sam. 20:16; 1 Kgs. 12:19; 2 Kgs. 17:21; Neh. 12:37; Isa. 7:2; Zech. 12:8. A related sense is that of "lineage," mentioned in Exod. 2:1 with reference to the descendants of Levi, and in Ezra 2:59 concerning the need for verification of one's priestly lineage.

Mundane references to "house" or "dwelling" can be found in Gen. 17:3ff.; Exod. 3:22; 20:17; Deut. 6:9; Ruth. 1:8; 1 Kgs. 2:33; Eccl. 2:4; Song 3:4; Isa. 65:24. References to a palace are found in Esth. 1:8, 9; Jer. 38:11.

The nation of Egypt is referred to on occasion as the "house of bondage," (e.g., Exod. 13:3, 14; Deut. 5:6; 6:12; Josh. 24:17; Judg. 6:8.

"The house of the Lord" is used frequently to designate the tabernacle, or temple (e.g., Exod. 23:19; Deut. 23:18; Judg. 9:18; 1 Kgs. 8:10, 11; 2 Kgs. 11:3ff.; Ps. 23:6; Isa. 37:1; Ezek. 40:47; 47:1; Hos. 8:1; Joel 1:9; Mic. 4:1). ***bayit*** also refers to the house of an idol in Judg. 9:46; Jer. 43:12, 13; Dan. 1:2.

NT Words

oikos [οἶκος, *3624*]

oikos occurs around one hundred times and is consistently translated "house," "household" in a variety of contexts with a similar range of meaning as its Hebrew dynamic equivalent, ***bayit*** (see above).

Indicating an ordinary home or dwelling, ***oikos*** is found in Matt. 9:6; 23:38; Mark 2:1; Luke 22:54; John 7:53. The term also refers to a palace in Matt. 11:8.

oikos refers to the nation of God's people in the expression "house of Israel" in Matt. 10:6; 15:24; Luke 1:33; Acts 2:36; 7:42; Heb. 8:8, 10. The "house of David" also refers to God's people in Luke 1:69; 2:4.

In relation to the temple, the expression "house of God" occurs in Mark 2:26; Luke 6:4; John 2:17; Acts 7:47; Heb. 3:2, 5. See also Matt. 21:13; Mark 11:17; Luke 19:46, where Jesus refers to God's designation of the temple as "My house . . ."

oikos also refers to family or household (cf. Luke 12:52; Acts 7:10; 10:22; 1 Cor. 1:16; 1 Tim. 3:4, 12; 2 Tim. 1:16). In Luke 13:35, the term "house" refers to the city of Jerusalem. And the phrase "house of God" in Heb. 10:21; 1 Pet. 2:5; 4:17 refers to the people of God.

oikia [οἰκία, *3614*]

oikia is a synonym for ***oikos***, above, occurring with nearly the same frequency (found in about ninety places). It is likewise translated "house," "household" in a variety of contexts.

In reference to "house" as a literal dwelling ***oikia*** is found, for example, in Matt. 2:11; 7:24ff.; Mark 1:29; Luke 17:31; Acts 12:12. It designates a "household" in Mark 3:25; Luke 18:29; John 4:53; 1 Cor. 16:15; Phil. 4:22; 2 Tim. 3:6. Jesus refers to the heavenly dwelling as "my Father's house" in John 14:2.

HOWL

OT Words

yālal **[יָלַל, 3213]**

yālal occurs around thirty times and is consistently translated "to wail" or "howl."

Indicating a cry of anguish on the part of nations, ***yālal*** refers to the howling of Babylon (Isa. 13:6; Jer. 5:18), and Moab (Isa. 15:2; 16:7; Jer. 48:20, 31, 39; 49:3). See also Isa. 23:1ff.; Jer. 47:2. The wailing of the rulers of Israel is noted in Isa. 52:5, as is that of rebels against Yahweh in Isa. 65:14. Metaphorically, the wailing of the city gate is depicted in Isa. 14:31.

In the face of divine judgment, the wailing of Israel is frequently alluded to in the prophetic writings (cf. Jer. 4:8; 25:34; Hos. 7:14; Joel 1:5, 11; Amos 8:3; Zeph. 1:11; Zech. 11:2). Similarly, the howling of individual prophets is indicated in Ezek. 21:12; 30:2; Joel 1:13; Mic. 1:8.

NT Words

ololyzō [ὀλολύζω, *3649*]

ololyzō is found only in Jas. 5:1, where it refers to the rich being called upon to "howl" in anguish over the miseries that will come upon them.

HUMBLE

OT Words

'ānî [עָנִי, **6041**]

'ānî is an adjective that is translated "poor" in all but one of its eighty occurrences. The exception is Zech. 9:9, where the Messianic King is depicted as a "lowly" (humble) rider on a colt entering the city of Jerusalem. This scene prophetically anticipates the triumphal entry of Jesus into Jerusalem, a week before his crucifixion (cf. John 12:15). (→ POOR)

shāphāl [שָׁפָל, **8217**]

The adjective ***shāphāl*** occurs around twenty times with the primary meaning "low (in height)" and the metaphorical sense of "low in station," or "humble." This latter meaning is evident in about half of the contexts in which ***shāphāl*** is found.

The sense of "lowly" or "humble" in regard to one's station or rank is found in Job 5:11; Ps. 138:6; Prov. 16:19, 29:23; Isa. 57:15; Ezek. 17:14; 21:26. The majority of these references offer commendation for a humble spirit. In a couple of places, however, ***shāphāl*** indicates a state of humiliation inflicted by Yahweh for rebellion against him — by Egypt (Ezek. 29:15), and by the faithless priests in the postexilic community (Mal. 2:9).

kāna' [כָּנַע, **3665**]

kāna' is a verb occurring around forty times with the primary senses of "to humble," "be humbled," with a number of related meanings in differing contexts. (→ SUBJECT)

In Lev. 26:41, ***kāna'*** refers to the humbling of Israelites with "uncircumcised" hearts.

More commonly, ***kāna'*** indicates the humbling of oneself before God in a positive sense (1 Kgs. 21:20; 2 Kgs. 22:19; 2 Chr. 12:6ff.; 32:26; 34:27). 2 Chr. 7:14 records the classic condition of blessing that will be forthcoming from Yahweh only if the people humble themselves before him.

'ānāw [עָנָו, **6035**]

'ānāw is another adjective that indicates "humility" as well as "meekness," "poverty." ***'ānāw*** occurs approximately thirty times, with the related meanings "humble" and "meek" evident in twenty of these contexts.

In reference to meekness, this trait is predicated of Moses (Num. 12:3), and of the people of God (Pss. 22:26; 37:11; Isa. 29:19; 61:1; Zeph. 2:3). Amos 2:7; 8:4 affirm that the abuse of the meek will merit divine judgment.

'ānāw also indicates that Yahweh shows favor to the humble (e.g., Prov. 3:34; 16:19; Isa. 11:4), and that the humble are easily taught by God (cf. Ps. 25:9). In addition, it is the humble, and those who are afflicted and thus have a spirit of dependence upon God, whom Yahweh promises to watch over (cf. Pss. 9:12; 10:12, 17; 34:2; 69:32; 149:4).

NT Words

tapeinoō [ταπεινόω, *5013*]

As do the Hebrew equivalents of this term, discussed above, the verb ***tapeinoō*** refers to the action of humbling or being humbled, as well as a number of related meanings in a variety of contexts. The term also describes the literal action of "lowering the height" of an object. ***tapeinoō*** occurs around seventeen times.

Christ commends the attitude of humbling oneself in Matt. 18:4; 23:12; Luke 14:11; 18:14. Paul refers to his experience of being humbled in 2 Cor. 11:7; Phil. 4:12. And, in 2 Cor. 12:21, he affirms that God had specifically humbled him. Exhortations to humble oneself before God are found in Jas. 4:10; 1 Pet. 5:6. The voluntary humbling of Jesus Christ to the will of his Father is recorded in Phil. 2:8.

tapeinos [ταπεινός, *5011*]

tapeinos is the adjectival form derived from ***tapeinoō*** (see above), and means "lowly in heart" (i.e., humble) and "of low status." The word occurs eight times.

The quality of lowliness or humility of heart is predicated of Christ (Matt. 11:29); of Paul (2 Cor.

10:1); and of believers (Jas. 1:9; 4:6; 1 Pet. 5:5). Lowliness of one's status or rank is indicated in Luke 1:52; 12:16; 2 Cor. 7:6.

tapeinophrosynē [ταπεινοφροσύνη, *5012*]

tapeinophrosynē is a noun related to ***tapeinoō*** and ***tapeinos***, above, meaning "humility (of heart and mind)," "lowliness (of heart and mind)." It is found seven times.

Acts 20:19; Eph. 4:2; 1 Pet. 5:5; Phil. 2:3; Col. 2:18; 3:12 refer to the virtue of humility. A "show" of humility is mentioned in Col. 2:23, in relation to corrupted human traditions of worship.

tapeinōsis [ταπείνωσις, *5014*]

tapeinōsis is a noun that indicates one's low or humble status, or humiliation, and occurs four times. It is found in connection with Mary, the mother of Christ, in Luke 1:48. Christ's own humiliation, anticipated through the sufferings of the Servant of Yahweh, is indicated in Acts 8:33. Phil. 3:21 refers to the transformation of our "lowly" bodies at the end of the age. Jas. 1:10 refers to the humiliation of the rich.

HUNDRED

OT Words

mēʾāh [**מֵאָה, 3967**]

This numeral is common in the Old Testament, referring to "one hundred," as well as to multiples of that number in various contexts — for example, age (cf. Gen. 5:3ff.; 11:10ff.; Josh. 24:29; Isa. 65:20); periods of time in years (cf. Gen. 6:3; Dan. 8:14); days (cf. Ezek. 4:5); various measurements in cubits (cf. Exod. 27:9; 1 Kgs. 7:2; Ezek. 40:19ff.); weight (cf. 1 Sam. 17:7); size of military units (cf. Deut. 1:5; Exod. 14:7; 1 Sam. 22:2; 2 Kgs. 3:26); the tribes of Israel (cf. Num. 1:21ff.; 3:1ff.; 4:1ff.); and number of animals (cf. Gen. 32:14; 1 Kgs. 4:23). Other general references to this numeral are found in Ezra 1:10ff.; Neh. 7:8ff.; 1 Kgs. 9:14; 11:3; 18:22; Deut. 22:19; Esth. 1:1.

NT Words

hekaton [ἑκατόν, *1540*]

This Greek numeral refers to the number "one hundred" as well as the concept of "hundred times," indicating abundant increase. ***hekaton*** occurs seventeen times.

In regard to substantial increase, the expression "hundredfold," or hundred times, is found in the parable of the sower, where Christ refers to the powerful spread of God's word in the world, symbolized by the abundant crop sown in the fertile soil of spiritually receptive hearts (cf. Matt. 13:8, 23; Mark 4:8, 20). In reference to number of animals, ***hekaton*** is found in Matt. 18:12; Luke 15:4; John 2:11. Similarly, with reference to people, the term occurs in Mark 6:40; Acts 1:15; Rev. 7:4; 14:13. In Matt. 18:28 ***hekaton*** refers to money, and in Rev. 21:17 to the wall of the heavenly Jerusalem.

hekatontaplasiōn [ἑκατονταπλασίων, *1542*]

This numerical adjective occurs only three times (Matt. 19:29; Mark 10:30; Luke 8:8), all of which indicate the concept of a "hundred times" as a measure of abundant increase.

HUNGER → FAMINE

HUNT, HUNTING

OT Words

ṣayid [**צַיִד, 6718**]

This noun refers to hunting as well as to the food or game hunted. ***ṣayid*** occurs around twenty times.

ṣayid refers to the "hunter" (Gen. 10:9 [twice]; 25:27); to game hunted and caught (Gen. 25:28); to the activity of hunting (Gen. 27:30; Lev. 17:13; Job 38:41); and to provisions, presumably from hunting (Josh. 9:5; Neh. 13:15).

ṣûd [**צוּד, 6679**]

This verb form occurs around twenty times and is translated "hunt" in most of the contexts in which it is found.

The hunting of game is described in Gen. 27:3ff., Lev. 17:13; Josh. 9:12; Job 38:39. Human beings are the object of hunting in Job 10:16; Ps. 140:11, and the hunters in Ezek. 13:18, 20; Mic. 7:2. Hunting undertaken by Yahweh in order to exercise his punishment for sin is indicated in Jer. 16:16; Lam. 3:52; 4:18.

HURT → EVIL

HUSBAND

OT Words

ʾîsh [**אִישׁ, 376**]

ʾîsh is one of the several words for "man" in the Old Testament. The term occurs over 1,500 times. On about seventy occasions, however, ***ʾîsh*** is translated "husband," referring to human relationships either literally or symbolically. This usage is illustrated, for example, in Gen. 3:6, 16; Lev. 19:20; Num. 5:13; Judg. 13:6ff.; Ruth 1:3ff.; 2 Sam. 3:15, 16; Jer. 6:11; Ezek. 16:32.

ba'al **[בַּעַל, 1167]**

ba'al means "owner," "lord," or "master," and is found approximately eighty times. However, on ten occasions it is translated "husband."

In most of these contexts, the translation "husband" is a generic term, referring to no one in particular (cf. Exod. 21:22; Deut. 22:22; 24:4; Prov. 31:11; Joel 1:8). Isa. 54:5; Jer. 31:32, however, portray Yahweh as husband to Israel.

ḥātān **[חָתָן, 2860]**

This noun occurs nineteen times and is translated "law," "bridegroom," and "husband." The two latter meanings are found in half of these contexts (cf. Exod. 4:25, 26; Ps. 19:5; Isa. 61:10; 62:5; Jer. 7:34; 16:9; 25:10; 33:11; Joel 2:16).

NT Words

anēr [ἀνήρ, *435*]

This term is usually translated "man." ***anēr*** occurs around two hundred times, but the meaning "husband" is found in about fifty places.

Matt. 1:16; Luke 2:36; John 4:16ff.; Acts 5:9, 10 refer to specific husbands. "Husbands" in general are referred to in Mark 10:12; Rom. 7:2, 3; 1 Cor. 7:2ff.; Gal. 4:27; Eph. 5:23, 33. Christ is declared to be "husband" to the church in Eph. 5:25ff.

Additional Notes

The metaphorical sense of the term "husband" underscores the unique intimacy of the relationship between God and his people. The Old Testament emphasizes the symbolic covenantal relationship with Yahweh as the bridegroom of Israel, while the New Testament portrays Christ as bridegroom to the church — fulfilling the old covenant metaphor.

HUSKS

NT Words

keration [κεράτιον, *2769*]

keration occurs only once and refers to the fruit or pod of the carob tree. These pods are shaped like horns and sweet tasting, and are a traditional food for fattening pigs. The term is used in the parable of the lost son (cf. Luke 15:16), where he is reduced through poverty to eating these pods, or "husks."

HYENA

OT Words

'î **[אִי, 338]**

'î refers to a howling beast, probably either a hyena or a jackal. The term occurs three times (cf. Isa. 13:22; 34:14; Jer. 50:39).

HYMN

NT Words

hymnos [ὕμνος, *5215*]

hymnos only occurs in Eph. 5:19; Col. 3:16, where it refers to singing hymns in the context of worship.

hymneō [ὑμνέω, *5214*]

hymneō refers to the activity of singing hymns — that is, psalm singing, or singing praise to God. It occurs four times. Jesus and his disciples sing in Matt. 26:30; Mark 14:26, probably a selection from Pss. 113–118. See also Acts 16:25; Heb. 2:12.

See Also: → SING

HYPOCRISY, HYPOCRITE

OT Words

ḥānēph **[חָנֵף, 2611]**

This noun occurs thirteen times and refers to people who are "profane," "godless," or "hypocritical" (cf. Job 8:13; 17:8; 36:13; Prov. 11:9; Isa. 9:17; 33:14). The term also refers to those who mock with malicious intent (cf. Ps. 35:16).

NT Words

hypokrisis [ὑπόκρισις, *5272*]

This term refers to the practice of dissimulation or hypocrisy, with the Pharisees being the target of Christ's public condemnation during his earthly ministry. ***hypokrisis*** occurs seven times and is translated "hypocrisy" in all but one text, Jas. 5:12, where is is translated as "condemnation." It is also found in Matt. 23:28; Mark 12:15; Luke 12:1; Gal. 2:13; 1 Tim. 4:2; 1 Pet. 2:1.

hypokritēs [ὑποκριτής, *5273*]

hypokritēs occurs twenty times and is consistently translated "hypocrite." ***hypokritēs*** always comes from the mouth of Christ, and is largely directed at the Pharisees (cf. Matt. 6:2, 5, 16; 15:17; 16:3; 22:18; 23:13ff.; Mark 7:6; Luke 11:44; 12:56; 13:15). Matt. 7:5; 24:51; Luke 6:12 express general condemnation of hypocrites.

HYSSOP

OT Words

'ēzôb [אֵזוֹב, 231]

'ēzôb refers to the large plant that was used as a medicinal herb in the ancient Near East, and also for Israelite ceremonial ritual. The term occurs ten times.

Bunches of hyssop were used during the Passover deliverance in Egypt to daub sacrificial blood on the doorposts and lintels of Israelite houses (cf. Exod. 12:22). Lev. 14:4, 6, 49ff.; Num. 19:6, 18 refer to the use of hyssop in the Israelite ceremonial ritual of ceremonial cleansing. General references to hyssop are found in 1 Kgs. 4:33; Ps. 51:7.

I

IDLE

OT Words

rāphāh **[רָפָה, 7503]**

rāphāh occurs around fifty times with the predominant sense of being feeble or weak. In two instances the term means "to be idle" (Exod. 5:8, 17). Here the Egyptian overlords lay false charges of idleness at the feet of the oppressed Israelite people.

'aṣlût **[עַצְלוּת, 6104]**

This term occurs only in Prov. 31:27 and is translated "idleness" in the phrase "bread of idleness," indicating a lazy lifestyle.

remîyāh **[רְמִיָּה, 7423]**

This adjectival form occurs around fifteen times and has the primary sense of "deceitful." However, in three texts it means "idle," or "lazy" (cf. Prov. 12:24, 27; 19:15).

NT Words

argos [ἀργός, *692*]

argos is an adjective occurring six times with the primary sense of "idle," "lazy" in all but one of these contexts. Matt. 12:36 refers to an "idle (i.e., careless) word." Matt. 20:3, 6 speak of idleness in the work place. Paul condemns "idle busybodies" in 1 Tim. 5:13, and refers to Cretans as "lazy gluttons" in Titus 1:12.

IDOL, IDOLATRY

OT Words

ṣelem **[צְלֵם, 6755** (Aramaic)**]**

ṣelem is an Aramaic term with the root meaning "image," with the underlying sense of "statue," or "idol." All seventeen occurrences of the term are found in Dan. 2–3. In Dan. 2, ***ṣelem*** refers to the giant statue composed of four metals, though it is uncertain whether an idol is specifically indicated here. In Dan. 3, however, there is no doubt that ***ṣelem*** refers to an idol statue, since people were forced to worship it.

ṣelem **[צֶלֶם, 6754]**

This Hebrew term means "idol," "image" throughout its usage. It refers to idolatrous images in Num. 33:52; 1 Sam. 6:5, 11; 2 Kgs. 11:18; Ezek. 7:20; 16:17; Amos 5:26.

pesel **[פֶּסֶל, 6459]**

pesel is consistently translated "graven image" in the thirty or so texts in which it is found.

The making and worshiping of idols is prohibited in the second commandment (cf. Exod. 20:4; Lev. 26:1; Deut. 4:16ff.). And a resulting punishment for idol worship is indicated in Deut. 27:15; Nah. 1:14.

Acts of blatant idolatry are recorded in Judg. 17:3ff.; 2 Kgs. 21:7; Isa. 40:19ff.; 42:17; 48:5; and the futility of idol worship is indicated in Isa. 44:9ff.; 45:20; Jer. 10:14; 51:17; Hab. 2:18.

'elîl **[אֱלִיל, 457]**

'elîl is found on twenty occasions and is consistently translated "idol" in most of these contexts.

Idol worship is prohibited in Lev. 19:4; 26:1, and the shame and futility of such a practice is described in Ps. 97:7; Isa. 2:8. Isa. 2:18; 19:1, 3; Ezek. 30:13 describe Yahweh destroying idols.

General references to idolatry are also found in 1 Chr. 16:26; Ps. 96:5; Isa. 2:20; 10:10; 31:7.

gillûl **[גִּלּוּל, 1544]**

gillûl is another common term for "idol," occurring around fifty times. The contexts are both negative and positive.

Ezek. 20:7, 18 prohibit the worship of idols. Yahweh vows to destroy the idols of his people (Lev. 26:30; Ezek. 6:4ff.), along with those of Egypt (Ezek. 30:13) and Babylon (Jer. 50:2). Frequent indictments are brought down against Israel for their idol worship (e.g., Deut. 29:16; Ezek. 8:10; 16:36; 22:3ff.). These indictments include specific charges against kings, such as Ahab (1 Kgs. 21:26) and Manasseh (2 Kgs. 21:11), as well as the Levites in Israel's early history (Ezek. 44:10, 12). As a contrast to divine judgment and condemnation, Yahweh promises to cleanse his people of their sin of idolatry in Ezek. 36:25; 37:23.

hebel **[הֶבֶל, 1892]**

This term occurs approximately sixty times and most commonly refers to that which is "vain" in the sense of "futile." On several occasions, however, ***hebel*** refers to "idols," an extended meaning of the concept of "vanity" or "futility," in that those objects of worship that are utterly without sense or value.

In Jer. 8:19; Ps. 31:6; 1 Kgs. 16:13, 26, ***hebel*** signifies the provoking of Yahweh to anger by idol worship. The root meaning of ***hebel*** is alluded to in Jer. 14:22; Zech. 10:2 where idols are denounced as worthless and full of deceit. Jonah 2:8 indicates that those who cling to idol worship will forfeit the grace of God that could otherwise be theirs.

'āṣāb [עָצָב, 6091]

'āṣāb is another synonym for the terms discussed above, occurring seventeen times and meaning "idol," "image."

'āṣāb generally refers to the practice of idolatry in 1 Sam. 31:9; 2 Sam. 5:21; 1 Chr. 10:9; Pss. 115:4; 135:15; Isa. 46:1.

'āṣāb also refers to Israel's culpable idol worship (2 Chr. 24:18; Ps. 106:36ff.; Hos. 4:17). Hos. 8:4; 13:2 anticipate Israel's destruction and punishment as a consequence of their idolatry.

'āṣāb is also found in contexts indicating the inevitable destruction of idols by the hand of Yahweh (cf. Isa. 10:11; Jer. 50:2; Mic. 1:7; Zech. 13:2).

semel [סֶמֶל, 5566]

This term is rare, found in only five places with the sense of "idol," "image," or "statue."

semel occurs first of all in Deut. 4:16, in a prohibition against making idols. 2 Chr. 33:7 mentions idol worship in relation to the reign of Manasseh. 2 Chr. 33:15 then refers to the subsequent ritual reform during which Manasseh has the idols removed from Jerusalem and the temple. Ezek. 8:3, 5 record Ezekiel's visionary observation of the rampant idolatry in Jerusalem prior to the fall of the city in 587 B.C.

NT Words

eidōlon [εἴδωλον, *1497*]

eidōlon is translated "image," "idol" and occurs eleven times.

A review of Israel's past sin of idolatry is recorded in Acts 7:41. Commands to abstain from idolatry are found in Acts 15:20; 1 John 5:21. The abhorrence of idols is indicated in Rom. 2:22; 2 Cor. 6:16.

The use of ***eidōlon*** in 1 Cor. 8:4, 7; 10:19ff. introduces an important distinction. On the one hand, in 1 Cor. 8 idols are dismissed as nonentities. However, the context of 1 Cor. 10:19 indicates that behind the facade of the idol lies the real world of demonic power.

The powerful influence of idols over those who engage in such worship is indicated in 1 Cor. 12:2; Rev. 9:20; while 1 Thess. 1:9 cites deliverance from idolatry, that was of profound significance for the Thessalonian converts to Christianity.

eidōlothyton [εἰδωλόθυτον, *1494*]

eidōlothyton refers not so much to idols themselves, but to that which was offered to idols in sacrificial worship. The term occurs ten times.

In Acts 15:29; 21:25, ***eidōlothyton*** refers to "food offered to idols" from which Gentile believers are required to abstain. General references to the subject of eating food offered to idols are found in 1 Cor. 8:1ff.; 10:19, 28. Allusion to Israel's past sin in engaging in this practice is found in Rev. 2:14. The same sinful activity is mentioned in regard to the church at Thyatira (cf. Rev. 2:20).

eidōlolatrēs [εἰδωλολάτρης, *1496*]

This term is found on seven occasions and is always translated "idolater." Paul issues a command to the Corinthian church not to associate with idolaters within the congregation (cf. 1 Cor. 5:10, 11). The eternal doom of idolaters is mentioned in 1 Cor. 6:9; Eph. 5:5; Rev. 21:8; 22:15.

eidōlolatria [εἰδωλολατρία, *1495*]

This general term for idolatry is found on fourteen occasions.

1 Cor. 10:14 contains a command to shun idols. Idolatry is one of the fruits of the sinful person (cf. Gal. 5:20). In Col. 3:5, covetousness is equated with idolatry. Idolatry is also declared as characteristic of the pagan lifestyle in 1 Pet. 4:3.

kateidōlos [κατείδωλος, *2712*]

kateidōlos occurs once, referring to the city of Athens as "full of idolatry" in Acts 17:16.

Additional Notes

The Hebrew and Greek vocabulary for "idolatry," and related concepts, are very similar. Both Testaments emphasize the abhorrence of idol worship, forbidding such practices and condemning those who engage in them. The Hebrew term ***ḥebel*** and the Greek ***eidōlon*** are parallel in that both of them point to the futility of idol worship, primarily because the gods are in fact nonentities. However, 1 Cor. 10 makes it clear that there is a real demonic power lying behind the facade of the idol itself. It is this bondage to the satanic spirit realm that constitutes the real danger, for it condemns the practitioner of idolatry to eternal damnation — a fate that is only hinted at in the Old Testament context where idolaters are indicted by Yahweh and threatened with destruction. In this sense, the New Testament consummates the pattern indicated throughout the Old.

See Also: ➠ IMAGE

IGNORANCE, IGNORANT

OT Words

shegāgāh **[שְׁגָגָה, 7684]**

shegāgāh refers to committing sin unintentionally or inadvertently, and occurs in a number of different contexts. With this underlying sense, ***shegāgāh*** occurs around twenty times and is mostly translated adverbially as "inadvertently," "unintentionally," "unwittingly," or "through ignorance."

shegāgāh refers to the general incidence of unintentional sin by the Israelites, requiring a sacrificial offering to receive forgiveness (cf. Lev. 4:2, 22, 27; 5:18; 22:14; Num. 15:24ff.).

On the occasion of accidental (i.e., unintentional) manslaughter, Josh. 20:3, 9 provide a way of escape for the manslayer, who is given the opportunity of fleeing to a city of refuge in order to escape the "avenger of blood" (usually the nearest relative of the deceased).

NT Words

agnoeō [ἀγνοέω, *50*]

agnoeō occurs around twenty times with the principal meaning "be ignorant" in the sense of not knowing or understanding.

Luke 9:45 records the disciples' failure to understand the words of Jesus, and Acts 13:27 records the people of Jerusalem's failure to recognize Jesus' true identity as Messiah. Paul observes the Athenians' folly in worshiping an "unknown" God in Acts 17:23.

General references to being ignorant or "not knowing" are found, for example, in Rom. 1:13; 6:3; 1 Cor. 10:1; 14:38; 2 Cor. 1:8; 1 Thess. 4:13. Rom. 10:3 mentions the ignorance of the Jews in failing to acknowledge that righteousness comes from God. Destruction of ignorant false teachers is indicated in 2 Pet. 2:12. 1 Tim. 1:13 refers to Paul having acted in ignorance and unbelief prior to his conversion. Heb. 5:2 indicates that the ignorant and wayward are dealt with gently by the high priest, who is himself beset with human weakness.

agnoia [ἄγνοια, *52*]

agnoia refers to the state of ignorance and is found in only four contexts. Acts 3:17 speaks of the ignorance of the Jewish people in bringing about the death of Jesus. Acts 17:30 refers to God having overlooked times of human ignorance under the old covenant.

The culpable ignorance of the Gentiles due to their hardness of heart is cited in Eph. 4:18. 2 Pet. 1:14 offers a similar perspective.

Additional Notes

The problem of ignorance appears to operate on two levels throughout Scripture. On the one hand, there is the Old Testament phenomenon of "unwitting" or "inadvertent" transgression, committed as it were "through ignorance." Such actions were forgivable through the ritual of a sacrificial offering. On the other hand, the New Testament evidence suggests in several places that the ignorance of unbelievers, Gentiles, and false teachers in the context of their unbelief is culpable and liable to divine judgment. It is also apparent in the context of Heb. 5:2 that human ignorance is dealt with gently by the Levitical high priest because he is subject to the same weakness as those who approach him to intercede for them before God. The ultimate high priest is the risen Christ — who understands our own ignorance, and yet who is without any weakness whatsoever in this regard.

IMAGE

OT Words

massēkāh **[מַסֵּכָה, 4541]**

massēkāh is a noun derived from the verb ***nāsak*** (➠ POUR), "to pour (out)," "to cast a molten image." Hence ***massēkāh*** means "molten or cast image or idol."

References to the casting of idolatrous images are found in Exod. 32:4, 8; Deut. 9:12, 16; Judg. 18:14ff.; 2 Kgs. 17:16; Neh. 9:18. The practice is prohibited in Exod. 34:17; Lev. 19:4; Hos. 13:2. Yahweh commands his people to destroy the molten images of Canaan in Num. 33:52. Several texts refer to the divine curse directed against those who make molten images (cf. Deut. 27:15; Isa. 42:17; Nah. 1:14; Hab. 2:18). In the context of ritual renewal and reformation, 2 Chr. 34:3ff. records Josiah's destruction of Judah's cast idols; and Isa. 30:22 speaks of Israel's future disposal of her idols as a consequence of her spiritual transformation by Yahweh.

maṣēbāh **[מַצֵּבָה, 4676]**

This term occurs around thirty times and is usually translated "pillar." In the majority of contexts, the underlying sense is that of an idolatrous image.

The worship of such pillars, or images, originating in the Canaanite culture, is strictly forbidden in the Mosaic law (cf. Exod. 23:24; Deut. 16:22). Yet as was the case with other forms of idolatry, Israel became ensnared by this practice (cf. 1 Kgs. 14:23; 2 Kgs. 17:10; Hos. 10:1). Commands to destroy these objects are found in Exod. 34:13; Lev. 26:1; Deut. 7:5; 12:3. The removal and destruction of such images is mentioned in the regnal accounts of reforming kings of Israel and Judah (cf. 2 Kgs. 3:2; 10:26, 27; 18:4; 23:14; 2 Chr. 14:3; 31:1. Hos. 10:2).

terāphîm **[תְּרָפִים, 8655]**

terāphîm refers to household idols or images used in worship. The word is found fifteen times.

References to household idols in general are found in Gen. 31:19, 34ff.; 1 Sam. 19:13ff.; Zech. 10:2. In the context of worship, ***terāphîm*** are mentioned in Judg. 17:5; 18:14ff.; Ezek. 21:21. 1 Sam. 15:23 refers to Saul's idolatry, presumably in relation to his household idols. One aspect of Josiah's reform program involves the removal of such idols from Judah (cf. 2 Kgs. 23:24). In a broader context of renewal, Hos. 3:4 indicates that such images will be thrown away by Israel as a consequence of the people's spiritual renewal.

temûnāh **[תְּמוּנָה, 8544]**

This noun refers in a general way to the "form," "image," or "likeness" of any person or object. ***temûnāh*** occurs ten times, and in most contexts refers to the likeness or image of an idol. Reference is also made, however, to the likeness of God in one or two contexts that are not idolatrous.

A number of texts contain the absolute prohibition against any attempt to construct a physical likeness of Yahweh (cf. Exod. 20:4; Deut. 4:16, 23, 25; 5:8).

temûnāh also refers to the likeness or image of God which came to Moses as a unique privilege in the form of a theophany (cf. Num. 12:8; see also Job 4:16; Ps. 17:5).

Deut. 4:12, 15 make the point that the form or image of God is not revealed to his people in any way except his voice.

ṣelem **[צֶלֶם, 6754]**

ṣelem carries the significant sense of "image" in Gen. 1:26, 27; 9:6, in the context of God making human beings in the "image," or "likeness," of God. See also Gen. 5:3, which refers to "likeness."

NT Words

eikōn **[εἰκών, *1504*]**

This term occurs around twenty times and has the predominant sense of "image," "figure" "likeness." ***eikōn***, however, refers not primarily to the false images of idolatry, but rather to images of people, as well as to heavenly realities including the person of Christ, in whose image believers have been created anew.

In a general, non-theological sense, ***eikōn*** designates the image of Caesar on Roman coins (cf. Matt. 22:20; Mark 12:16; Luke 20:24).

In relation to the phenomenon of idolatry, ***eikōn*** refers firstly to idolatrous images as the characteristic of pagan worship in Rom. 1:23. Then, the term refers to the idolatrous image of the sea beast set up by the earth beast as the supreme object of worship for all people of the earth in Rev. 13:14ff.; 14:9ff.; 16:2.

In contrast, ***eikōn*** is also found in reference to the image of Christ in Rom. 8:29; 1 Cor. 15:49; 2 Cor. 3:18; Col. 3:10. These texts make the point that the ultimate divine purpose for all believers is for them to be conformed to the "image" of Christ, to his person and character. Furthermore, Christ is declared to be the perfect image of God the Father in 2 Cor. 4:4; Col. 1:15. Human beings also portray the image and glory of God, as the supreme manifestation of divine creative activity (cf. 1 Cor. 11:7).

In Heb. 10:1, ***eikōn*** refers to the ritual law of temple worship as the mere image (or form) of the heavenly reality of good things to come in the new heavens and new earth.

charaktēr **[χαρακτήρ, *5481*]**

This term is found only in Heb. 1:3, where it refers to the "express image" or "very stamp" of the nature found in Christ that reflects the essential glory of God.

See Also: → IDOL

IMAGINE, IMAGINATION

OT Words

yēṣer **[יֵצֶר, 3336]**

yēṣer is a noun found in nine places, with the primary meaning "imagination" in the sense of "device" or "innermost thoughts of one's heart," both with a positive and a negative connotation.

Human "imaginings" are described as "evil" in the days of Noah (Gen. 6:5; 8:21). In a neutral context, ***yēṣer*** refers to the "innermost thoughts" of human beings in Deut. 31:21; 1 Chr. 28:9; 29:18.

sherîrût [שְׁרִירוּת, **8307**]

sherîrût is found in ten contexts with the principal meaning "imagination" in the negative sense of ideas, plans, and thoughts that are opposed to the purposes of God (cf. Deut. 29:19; Jer. 3:18; 7:24; 9:14; 11:8; 13:10; 23:17). All of these references imply the arrogant, stubborn, self-centeredness of the human heart that refuses to recognize God's right to rule one's life.

NT Words

meletaō [μελετάω, *3191*]

This verb occurs only in Acts 4:25, meaning "imagine" in the sense of "conspire." Such an attitude is predicated of the Gentiles, who conspire in vain to overthrow the purposes of God — that is, they "imagine" vain things against him.

dianoia [διάνοια, *1271*]

dianoia occurs only once, meaning "imagination" in the sense of "vain, stubborn thinking" in Luke 1:51.

dialogismos [διαλογισμός, *1261*]

dialogismos occurs only in Rom. 1:21 and refers to the vain imagination or futile thinking of Gentiles in their darkened minds.

IMITATE, IMITATOR

NT Words

mimeomai [μιμέομαι, *3401*]

mimeomai is found four times, meaning "follow" or "imitate." Paul's direction to the Thessalonian congregation to imitate his way of life is found in 2 Thess. 3:7, 9. The writer to the Hebrews calls upon his readers to imitate the faithful examples of their spiritual mentors in Heb. 13:7. John instructs his readers not to imitate that which is evil in 3 John 11.

IMMANUEL

OT Words

'immānû'ēl [עִמָּנוּאֵל, **6005**]

This word is only found in Isa. 7:14; 8:8, where it constitutes the name assigned to the son born of the virgin, and means "God with us." ***'immānû'ēl*** (i.e., Emmanuel) specifically refers to the son born to the "prophetess," the unnamed wife of the prophet Isaiah (see ***Emmanouēl***, below).

NT Words

Emmanouēl ['Εμμανουήλ, *1694*]

This term only occurs in Matt. 1:23, where it refers to the infant Jesus as the direct fulfillment of the sign given to the prophet Isaiah (Isa. 7:14; see ***'immānûēl***, above).

IMMEDIATELY → SUDDEN

IMMORTAL, IMMORTALITY

OT Words

'ôlām [עוֹלָם, **5769**]

There is no specific term for immortality in the Old Testament. The term ***'ôlām*** does convey the meanings "everlasting," or "perpetual" — but not in the sense of an infinite state of being, beyond death in the heavenly presence of God. At best, the term ***'ôlām*** only hints at such a state of being, but it certainly anticipates the New Testament use of the term which is, by contrast, quite sparse.

'ôlām occurs frequently in the Old Testament, over four hundred times. It refers to the Abrahamic covenant as "everlasting" (e.g., Gen. 17:13, 19) as well as to the old covenant in general, and additionally, to ceremonial ordinances that are to be observed in perpetuity (cf. Exod. 12:14; 29:9; Lev. 6:22; Num. 18:8).

The Sabbath is also to be observed as a perpetual covenant (cf. Exod. 31:16). ***'ôlām*** indicates the idea of "forever" only in the sense of "lifelong" (e.g., Exod. 21:6; Deut. 15:17). The land of Israel is designated as the perpetual inheritance of the people of Israel (cf. Josh. 14:9). In Ezra 3:11, God's mercy is said to endure forever, as is his salvation in Isa. 51:6. The promised new covenant is declared to be everlasting in Ezek. 16:60; 37:26.

Other significant uses of ***'ôlām*** suggest or anticipate the new covenant concept of everlasting life or "immortality." For example, Gen. 3:22 indicates, in a negative sense, the immortality of eternal judgment hypothetically conferred on those who would eat of the fruit of the tree of life after human beings had disobeyed God in the garden of Eden. Prov. 8:23 points to the "eternal" origin of wisdom personified. 2 Sam. 7:13 declares that the royal lineage of David would rule forever. Dan. 12:2 contains the prediction that the dead shall one day rise again to either everlasting life or death.

NT Words

eis tōn aiōna [εἰς των αἰῶνα, *165*]

This phrase is the New Testament Greek equivalent for the Hebrew *'ôlām* (see above). The phrase is translated "ever," "forever" (and "never" in negative contexts). ***eis tōn aiōna*** is found about thirty times.

Regarding the concept "forever," Luke 1:55 refers to the perpetuity of the Abrahamic covenant. In John 6:51 there is the promise of eternal life for those who eat the "living bread" offered by Christ. John 8:35 refers to Christ's eternal existence as one who lives forever. Similarly, 2 Cor. 9:9 affirms that God's righteousness lasts forever. Heb. 1:8 refers to God's "everlasting" throne. Heb. 5:6; 6:20; 7:17ff. mention Jesus Christ as a priest "forever" after the order of Melchizedek (cf. Gen. 14). 1 John 2:17 records the promise that he who does the will of God remains forever (cf. also. 2 John 2).

The meaning "never" is also frequently used to describe the positive blessing of eternal life as a negative — that is, to never die, or never hunger or thirst (cf. John 10:28; 8:51, 52; 11:26).

athanasia [ἀθανασία, *110*]

athanasia is one of the several specific New Testament Greek terms for immortality. It occurs three times. 1 Cor. 15:53, 54 speak of the ultimate "re-clothing" of the perishable human nature with an immortal, undying nature. 1 Tim. 6:16 affirms that God alone possesses immortality as one of his innate perfections.

aphtharsia [ἀφθαρσία, *861*]

aphtharsia occurs seven times, and in all but one of these contexts is translated "immortality," "imperishable," emphasizing both never-ending life and ultimate purity in that eternal state.

Rom. 2:7 indicates that those who with patient, godly living strive for immortality will be granted eternal life. 1 Cor. 15:42, 50ff. affirm that in the process of becoming immortal, the believer will discard the old earthly nature and assume a nature that will not only be eternally enduring (i.e., ***athanasia***, see above), but also incorruptible or imperishable (i.e., ***aphtharsia***). Eph. 6:24 contains the phrase "loving . . . imperishably," which is usually translated "undying love" with reference to the believer's devotion to Christ. 2 Tim. 1:10 declares that immortality is an inevitable consequence of the light of the gospel.

aphthartos [ἄφθαρτος, *862*]

aphthartos is the adjectival form derived from ***aphtharsia***, above, and is found in six contexts. The term is translated "incorruptible" and "immortal." Rom. 1:23; 1 Tim. 1:17 refer to God as incorruptible. 1 Cor. 9:25 refers to the "imperishable" wreath as the "prize" for the believer who perseveres to the end (cf. also 1 Pet. 1:4). 1 Cor. 15:52 speaks of the dead in Christ being raised incorruptible. 1 Pet. 1:23 affirms that believers have been born of the "imperishable seed" of the word of God. 1 Pet. 3:4 contains a metaphorical reference to the "imperishable jewel" of a quiet spirit.

See Also: → PROSTITUTE

IMMUTABLE → UNCHANGEABLE

IMPART → GIVE

IMPEDIMENT

NT Words

mogilalos [μογιλάλος, *3424*]

mogilalos occurs only in Mark 7:32, referring to a man who was afflicted with deafness and a speech impediment. This man was brought to Jesus, who subsequently cured him.

IMPENITENT → REPENT

IMPOSSIBLE

OT Words

pālā' [פָּלָא, **6381**]

pālā' is a verb that conveys the primary sense of that which is "wonderful" or "marvelous," as well as "hard," or "difficult." In five contexts, ***pālā'*** suggests something "too hard" (i.e., "impossible") to accomplish or conceive of.

Gen. 18:14 poses the question, "Is anything too hard for Yahweh?" Jer. 32:17 affirms that nothing is too hard for the Lord. Judicial cases "too difficult" for the people to decide for themselves must be arbitrated before the judges of the day (cf. Deut. 17:8; Jer. 32:27).

"Unfulfilled lust," in the sense of it being impossible to act upon, is indicated in 2 Sam. 13:2 in relation to Amnon's rape of his sister Tamar — an action fueled by his frustrated desire for her.

NT Words

adynateō [ἀδυνατέω, *101*]

This verb is rare, occurring only twice and meaning "be impossible," indicating utter inability or lack of strength or power. In both instances, however, the context positively stresses what is possible. In speaking of faith in Matt. 17:20, Jesus answers his listeners that if their faith is genuine, nothing they desire to do will be impossible for them. Luke 1:37 contains the declaration that with God nothing is impossible.

adynatos [ἀδύνατος, *102*]

adynatos, an adjective, is more common than the verb form, ***adynateō***, from which it derives (see above). ***adynatos*** occurs ten times, meaning "impossible" in the sense of "impotent," "powerless," or "disabled."

Human impotence is indicated in Matt. 19:26; Mark 10:27; Luke 18:27, affirming that what is impossible with human beings is possible with God. Acts 14:8 refers to a disabled man for whom walking was impossible. Rom. 8:3; Heb. 10:14 refer to the law's utter inability to bring about the permanent removal of sin. Heb. 6:4 contains the sobering warning that for those who have resolutely and absolutely turned their backs on God, there is no possibility of restoration to repentance. And finally, Heb. 11:6 declares the impossibility of pleasing God without the exercise of faith.

anendektos [ἀνένδεκτος, *418*]

This term occurs only in Luke 17:1 with the idea that temptation to sin will certainly emerge, but those through whom the incitement comes will be held responsible. The sense of "impossible" is expressed negatively. The verse literally reads: "It is impossible for offenses not to come, but woe . . ."

IMPRISON → PRISON

IMPUTE

OT Words

ḥāshab [**חָשַׁב, 2803**]

ḥāshab is a verb occurring around 120 times with the root meanings "count," "reckon," or "impute," with a number of associated senses.

With Yahweh as the agent of imputation, the following texts illustrate this usage of ***ḥāshab***. Righteousness is imputed to Abraham on account of his faith in Gen. 15:6. Lev. 7:18 declares that flawed offerings are refused by Yahweh — that is, they are not credited or imputed to the worshiper's benefit. According to Lev. 17:4, failure to present one's sacrificial animal for offering in the prescribed way will result in severe punishment for the worshiper, who is "reckoned" to be guilty of bloodshed. In Isa. 40:15, the Gentile nations are reckoned by Yahweh to be utterly insignificant in their opposition to him. They are considered as dust on the scales. In Job 13:24; 19:11; 33:10, Job mistakenly believes that God counts him as his enemy.

In other contexts, it is not Yahweh but human agency that is involved in the process of imputation. 2 Sam. 19:19 contains Shimei's plea to King David not to "hold" him guilty. In Neh. 13:13, a group of Levitical scribes is considered, or reckoned, to be trustworthy. Prov. 17:28 refers to the reckoning or imputation of wisdom. Other general references to this process are found in 2 Sam. 4:2; 1 Kgs. 10:21; Ps. 44:22.

NT Words

logizomai [λογίζομαι, *3049*]

logizomai is a fairly close dynamic equivalent for the Hebrew term ***ḥāshab***, above. ***logizomai*** is found approximately forty times and is translated "reckon," "count," "impute." There is an underlying rational element to all the meanings associated with this verb, including the sense of "to reason" in a number of contexts.

Paul poses the question in Rom. 2:26 as to whether those who are uncircumcised will be reckoned by God as circumcised if they keep the law of God. The exercise of faith is imputed as righteousness to those who so believe (cf. Rom. 4:3ff., 22ff.; Gal. 3:6; Jas. 2:23), with Abraham as the paradigm for imputed righteousness. In a corollary context, 2 Cor. 5:19 declares that God was in Christ reconciling the world to himself, not imputing the sins of human beings against them. As a consequence, believers are "to reckon" themselves as dead to sin, as stated in Rom. 6:11.

Other general occurrences of ***logizomai*** indicate that wages are "reckoned" as a person's due (cf. Rom. 4:4). In a metaphorical sense, talking about the realities of persecution, believers may often be "considered" as sheep to be slaughtered.

ellogeō [ἐλλογέω, *1677*]

ellogeō is a rare synonym for ***logizomai*** (see above), occurring only twice and meaning "impute," "set to one's account." Rom. 5:13 affirms that where there is no law, sin is not imputed. In Phlm. 18, Paul asks Philemon to charge to the apostle's account any money owed him by Onesimus, his servant.

Additional Notes

The Greek term ***logizomai*** most closely approximates the meaning of ***ḥāshab*** in the Old Testament. Paul uses ***logizomai*** in Rom. 4:3, for example, to express the imputation of righteousness to Abraham on account of his faith (from the citation of Gen. 15:6). Thus ***logizomai*** and ***ḥāshab*** both convey the important concept of the imputation of righteousness to God's people. God does this in order to justify those whom he has called into intimate relationship with himself throughout history.

INCENSE

OT Words

qetōret **[קְטֹרֶת, 7004]**

qetōret is a common term for incense associated with sacrifices and ritual offerings under the Mosaic covenant. It is found in about sixty contexts (e.g., Exod. 25:6; Lev. 4:7; 16:12ff.; Num. 7:14ff.; 16:40ff.; 1 Sam. 2:28; Ps. 141:2). Isa. 1:13 refers to the illegitimate use of incense in hypocritical worship, and Ezek. 8:11; 23:41 refer to the incense of idolatrous worship.

qāṭar **[קָטַר, 6999]**

qāṭar is a verb with the primary meaning "burn," used exclusively in a ritual context. It means both "to burn or offer sacrifices" as well as "to burn incense." ***qāṭar*** occurs around 120 times, with the latter meaning observed in about seventy of these contexts (cf. Exod. 30:7, 8; Lev. 2:2; 1 Kgs. 3:3; 2 Kgs. 12:3; 15:4, 35; 17:11; 23:5, 8). In addition to legitimate uses of incense, there are a number of contexts in which incense is used in idolatrous worship (cf. Isa. 65:3, 7; Jer. 1:16; 18:15; 44:3ff.; Hos. 2:13; Mal. 1:11).

qiṭṭēr **[קִטֵּר, 7002]**

This term, derived from ***qetōret*** (see above), occurs only once. In Jer. 44:21 it refers to incense offered by Jerusalem and Judah in idolatrous worship to the Canaanite deity, the "Queen of Heaven."

NT Words

thymiama **[θυμίαμα, *2368*]**

thymiama is found in six contexts, meaning "incense" and "odor." Luke 1:10 refers to the "hour of incense," which indicates the occasion of ritual worship. Luke 1:11 mentions the "altar of incense" located in the holy place before the veil of the holy of holies; and Rev. 5:8; 8:3, 4 indicate the "golden bowls full of incense," depicting the heavenly reality to which the earthly altar of incense points. In Rev. 18:13, "incense" is included in the inventory of the merchants of the earth in the context of the destruction of the great harlot, the city of Babylon.

thymiaō **[θυμιάω, *2370*]**

thymiaō occurs only once, in Luke 1:9. It refers to the customary ritual of the priest Zechariah, in offering incense at the altar in the Jerusalem temple.

thymiatērion **[θυμιατήριον, *2369*]**

thymiatērion is found only in Heb. 9:4, referring to the golden altar of incense in the earthly tabernacle/temple.

See Also: → FRANKINCENSE

INCREASE

OT Words

rābāh **[רָבָה, 7235]**

rābāh is a common verb, found around three hundred times with the underlying senses of becoming large, great, or numerous. The other two common meanings associated with ***rābāh*** are "multiply" and "increase," which are virtually synonyms.

In terms of theological impact, the most significant usage of ***rābāh*** concerns Yahweh's covenant promise to Abraham and his descendants to greatly increase, or multiply, their progeny. Several texts refer to this promise given to Abraham (cf. Gen. 16:10; 17:2, 20; 22:17; Exod. 32:13; Josh. 24:3; Isa. 51:2). The promise is also repeated to Jacob (Gen. 35:11; 48:4); and also to the people of Israel in the land (cf. Lev. 26:9; Ps. 107:38; Deut. 1:10; 30:5). Yahweh gives this promise again in Ezek. 37:26, as part of the anticipated new covenant blessing. In a similar vein, there is the divine promise to repopulate the land after the exile and to return the people of Israel to their homeland (cf. Jer. 23:3; 33:22; Ezek. 36:10).

In a negative context, Yahweh determines to multiply signs and wonders against Egypt (cf. Exod. 7:3; 11:9). Divine judgment against Israel and Judah is also in view in Ezek. 16:25ff.; 23:19, where their idolatry is declared to be increasingly promiscuous. In another context of judgment, Yahweh expresses bitter sarcasm against Israel when he urges them to go to Gilgal and sin with increasing frequency (cf. Amos 4:4). As a result of the fall, women will experience an inevitable increase in pain in childbirth (cf. Gen. 3:16).

Aside from situations where blessing and judgment are in view, ***rābāh*** occurs in the context of the so-called "cultural mandate," where God commands Adam and Eve to produce many offspring and so increase their number on earth (cf. Gen. 1:22, 28). This command is then repeated to Noah's family.

Various other phenomena are described increasing — for example, floodwaters (cf. Gen. 7:17, 18); the price of food (cf. Lev. 25:16); wealth (cf. Prov. 13:11; Ezek. 28:5; Hos. 10:1); one's anger (Job 10:17); human knowledge (cf. Dan. 12:4). In Ezra 9:6, Ezra acknowledges that the sins of the people have increased alarmingly. The psalmist is convinced that God will once again increase his honor (cf. Ps. 71:21).

tebû'āh [תְּבוּאָה, **8393**]

tebû'āh is a term that has the underlying sense of "increase" with respect to produce of the field (i.e., crops) in a predominantly literal sense. Metaphorically, it is used once to imply gaining increase in wisdom. ***tebû'āh*** occurs around forty times.

Concerning "increase" in regard to "produce," or "crops," ***tebû'āh*** is found in a number of different contexts. Gen. 47:24, for example, refers to a twenty percent tax on the harvest of the Egyptian people to be given to Pharaoh. Lev. 19:25 cites the required practice of not eating the produce of one's fruit trees until the fifth year of the fruit harvest. In this way, one's harvest will be increased (cf. Lev. 19:25). Harvesting the rich (i.e., increased) produce of the land is indicated in Lev. 23:39; 25:3, 7, 12. Under the law, the Israelites were required to present tithes and offerings from the abundance (i.e., the increase) of their harvest (cf. Num. 18:30; Deut. 14:22, 28; 26:12; 2 Chr. 31:5; Prov. 31:5). In several places, the blessings of increased productivity of the land are recognized as coming from the hand of Yahweh (cf. Deut. 16:15; Ps. 107:37; Isa. 30:23; Ezek. 48:18). General references to "increase" in the harvest are found in Job 31:12; Prov. 14:4; Eccl. 5:10.

Conversely, Neh. 9:37 describes the reversal of the economic prosperity for Israel in that the rich yield (i.e., increase) of the people's crops will go to the foreign kings whom Yahweh has placed over his people because of their sin.

In a metaphorical sense, ***tebû'āh*** refers to the "yield (increase) of one's lips" in Prov. 18:20. Here it is implied that the wisdom of one's speech will bring great satisfaction. Conversely, the term is found in the context of divine judgment in Jer. 12:13, where ***tebû'āh*** refers to a "harvest" (increase) that will be shameful for the people of Judah. The sense here is that the people's sinful rebellion will gain them nothing but emptiness, futility, and hopelessness — the consequence of God's fierce anger against them.

tarbît [תַּרְבִּית, **8636**]

tarbît is a noun derived from ***rābāh*** (see above) that conveys the idea of "increase" in the sense of financial gain or interest (i.e., usury). ***tarbît*** occurs six times.

Lev. 25:36 prohibits charging interest on a loan. The culpable practice of gaining wealth unjustly through charging unjust and excessive interest is described in Prov. 28:8; Ezek. 18:13; 22:12. By contrast, Ezek. 18:8, 17 describes the laudable practice of refusing to lend at interest with the intent of personal gain.

marbît [מַרְבִּית, **4768**]

marbît is a noun also derived from ***rābāh*** (see above), occurring five times. In these instances, ***marbît*** is translated "increase" only twice. In Lev. 25:37 it refers to the prohibition against deriving personal financial gain from the poor by selling food at inflated prices. The text literally reads: "You must not sell him food at a profit (i.e., increase)." 1 Sam. 2:23 describes the curse of God placed on the high priest Eli's descendants, referred to here as the "increase of his house," all of whom shall die by the sword. The remaining uses of ***marbît*** refer to numerical greatness (cf. 1 Chr. 12:29; 2 Chr. 30:18); and to the greatness of wisdom in Solomon (cf. 2 Chr. 9:6).

yāsaph [יָסַף, **3254**]

yāsaph is a common verb form occurring nearly 350 times, meaning "add," "increase," as well as the idea of repeating actions or "to do again." The distinctive sense of "add," or "increase," is found in approximately fifty contexts.

In Gen. 30:24 there is a plea for God to increase the number of children. A number of texts refer to the law's requirement to increase the restitution of money or property by twenty percent to a party wronged by theft or negligent loss through the "guilt offering" (cf. Lev. 5:16; 6:5; Num. 5:7). See also Lev. 22:14. Lev. 27:13ff. refers to increasing the price of redeeming an offering by twenty percent.

Num. 36:4 cites a divine amendment to the Mosaic law code whereby Israelite women must marry within their own tribe to prevent tribal inheritances from disappearing through intermarriage with other Israelite tribes.

Various other contexts reflect additional usage of the term ***yāsaph***. Deut. 5:22; 12:32 cite the prohibition against adding to (or increasing) the word of God. There is the promise of increased blessing from Yahweh in Ps. 115:14; as well as the anticipated divine blessing in increasing the borders of Canaan in Isa. 26:15. To increase one's sin will bring the inevitable wrath of God (cf. 1 Sam. 12:19; Ezra 10:10; Job 34:7). Ezek. 5:16 records the increase of Yahweh's judgment against sin. See also 1 Kgs. 12:11; 2 Kgs. 20:6; Prov. 1:5; 9:9; Eccl. 1:18; Jer. 45:3.

yebûl [יְבוּל, 2981]

yebûl is a synonym for ***tebû'āh*** (see above), conveying the idea of "increase" as abundant produce or harvest from the land. The term is found thirteen times.

Lev. 26:4 declares that God's blessing on the land in granting abundant increase or harvest is contingent on the people's covenant obedience. General references to the blessing of abundant harvest are found in Pss. 67:6; 85:12; Ezek. 34:27; Zech. 8:12.

In contrast, God promises as a consequence of disobedience that the land will not "yield her increase" (produce a harvest; cf. Lev. 26:20; Deut. 11:17; 32:22; Hag. 1:10). General references to the destruction of Canaan's produce are found in Judg. 6:4; Ps. 78:14.

sheger [שֶׁגֶר, 7698]

sheger is a term that refers to the offspring of animals as their "increase." ***sheger*** occurs five times (cf. Exod. 13:12; Deut. 7:13; 28:4, 18, 51).

NT Words

auxanō [αὐξάνω, *837*]

auxanō is a verb occurring around twenty times with the primary meanings "grow" and "increase." ***auxanō*** refers to growth or increase in the size of plants, or population, and the metaphorical sense of spiritual growth in believers. (→ GROW)

In reference to natural phenomena, ***auxanō*** indicates the physical growth of plants in Mark 4:8 in relation to the good seed which fell on fertile ground in the parable of the sower. Acts 7:17 refers to the increase of the Israelite population in Israel prior to their enslavement.

Other occurrences of ***auxanō*** refer to increase in status or importance. In John 3:30, John the Baptist defers to the person of Christ. The increase of God's word as it spreads throughout Jerusalem and Judea is recorded in Acts 6:7; 12:24. The increase in spiritual growth and knowledge of God, all of which is accomplished by God, is indicated in 1 Cor. 3:6, 7; 2 Cor. 9:10; Col. 1:10. Increase in faith is mentioned in 2 Cor. 10:15 in relation to the Corinthian congregation.

perisseuō [περισσεύω, *4052*]

perisseuō is normally translated "abound," "be in abundance," and occurs around forty times. However, in Acts 16:5 the term explicitly refers to the increase in the number of believers in the Galatian region.

prokoptō [προκόπτω, *4298*]

prokoptō is found on six occasions meaning "advance," "promote," and "increase." The latter meaning occurs in two contexts. Luke 2:52 refers to Jesus increasing in wisdom and stature and in favor with God and human beings. 2 Tim. 2:16 contains a warning against godless chatter, which will lead to an increase in ungodliness.

prostithēmi [προστίθημι, *4369*]

prostithēmi is found in eighteen places with the primary sense of "add." In Luke 17:5, however, the term is translated "increase," as the apostles ask the Lord to increase their faith.

pleonazō [πλεονάζω, *4121*]

This term is synonymous with ***perisseuō*** (see above) and occurs ten times. ***pleonazō*** is translated "abound" in most cases, but the underlying meaning is that of "increase."

The increasing influence of both sin and grace is referred to in Rom. 5:20. Rom. 6:4 contains the question that indicates profound misunderstanding of the gospel: "Shall we sin that grace may abound (i.e., increase)?" The abundant increase of grace in the life of the Corinthian church is mentioned in 2 Cor. 4:15. Increase in godliness is indicated in Phil. 4:17, as is increase in love in 1 Thess. 3:12; 2 Thess. 1:3.

endynamoō [ἐνδυναμόω, *1743*]

endynamoō occurs eight times with the principal meaning "be strong," or "endow with strength." In Acts 9:22 it indicates the sense of increasing in strength, denoting this as characteristic of Saul, the zealous Pharisee, in his persecution of Christians.

INDEBTED → DEBT → OWE

INDIGNATION → ANGER

INFIRMITY → DISEASE

INHABIT → DWELL

INHERIT, INHERITANCE

OT Words

***yārash* [יָרַשׁ, 3423]**

yārash is a fairly common verb that has the principal meanings "possess," "inherit," as well as the opposite sense of "dispossess," and "disinherit," with a number of related nuances. ***yārash*** occurs in about 230 contexts, meaning "inherit" in approximately twenty of these places. The meaning "possess," when associated with the land of Canaan, clearly implies the right of inheritance by virtue of the divine covenant promises.

Through the divine covenant, Abraham and his wife Sarah are promised an heir (cf. Gen. 15:3, 4). Likewise, the promise of inheriting the land of Canaan through the Abrahamic covenant is indicated in Gen. 15:7, 8; 28:4; Lev. 20:24; Deut. 16:20; 2 Chr. 20:11; Ezra 9:12; Ezek. 33:24. This same promise is issued through the renewal of the covenant in the wake of the exile (cf. Isa. 60:21).

Lev. 25:46 legitimates the acquisition of male and female slaves from the surrounding nations as a right of inheritance for Israelites.

The divine promise of the righteous (those who fear God) inheriting the earth is cited in Pss. 25:13; 37:9, 22, 29, 34; Isa. 54:3. Then, in a context of anticipated eschatological fulfillment, the phrase "inheriting the holy mount of Yahweh" is synonymous with the promise of inheriting the entire land (cf. Isa. 57:13; 65:9).

The threatened divine curse of disinheritance from the land for rebellion against Yahweh is cited in Num. 14:12; Jer. 8:10.

***nāḥal* [נָחַל, 5157]**

This verb more specifically relates to the notion of inheritance than does *yārash*, above. ***nāḥal*** occurs around fifty times and is translated "inherit" in the majority of contexts in which it is found. The underlying sense of ***nāḥal***, as with ***yārash***, is that of acquiring Canaan through an inherited right of possession granted by Yahweh.

The divinely ordained privilege of Israel to "inherit" the land of Canaan through the covenant promises is expressed in Exod. 23:30; 32:13; Deut. 1:38; 12:10; 19:3; 31:7; Josh. 1:6; Jer. 3:18. Yet that continuing right of inheritance is dependent on obedience (cf. 1 Chr. 28:8). The tribal inheritance of Canaan is determined by lot, a process that is described in a number of places (cf. Num. 26:55; 32:18ff.; 33:54; 34:13ff.; Josh. 13:32; 14:1; 16:4; 17:6; 19:9). In Ezek. 46:18, in the vision of a renewed land, the messianic prince will not deprive the people of Israel of their own inheritance, but will assign his own portion of the land as the inheritance for his sons.

Ps. 69:36 contains the promise of inheriting Zion, a poetic symbol of the land of Canaan with Jerusalem at its heart. The Levitical inheritance is not in land, but is Yahweh alone. That is, the Levites will not receive a specific allotment of tribal land along with the other tribes. Instead they will receive part of the tithe to Yahweh for their own use, including food and other material gifts (cf. Num. 18:20ff.).

nāḥal also refers to the legitimate acquisition of foreign slaves by Israelites as a "right of inheritance" from generation to generation (cf. Lev. 25:46).

There is a plea in Exod. 34:9 for Yahweh to take the Israelite people as his "inheritance," notwithstanding their sin. Then, in Zech. 2:12, Judah is designated as Yahweh's inherited portion of the land, which he will take up again in the eschatological vision of the renewal and reconstruction of Jerusalem.

Other uses of ***nāḥal*** are noted in the following contexts: the practice of inheriting the parental home (Judg. 11:2) as that which is denied to Jephthah; and inheriting a seat of honor (1 Sam. 2:8). The word of God is described as a precious inheritance in Ps. 119:111. Blessing and honor are declared to be the inheritance of the wise in Prov. 3:5; 28:10. In contrast, wind and folly constitute the inheritance of the fool (cf. Prov. 11:29; 14:8; Jer. 16:19).

***naḥalāh* [נַחֲלָה, 5159]**

naḥalāh specifically denotes the phenomenon of "inheritance" in almost all of the 200 or so contexts in which it is found.

There are general references to family inheritance in Gen. 31:14; Num. 27:10; Ruth 4:5; 1 Kgs. 21:3; Prov. 19:14; Mic. 2:2.

naḥalāh again refers to Canaan as the inheritance granted to Israel by Yahweh, through the covenant promise given to Abraham and his progeny (cf. Num. 16:14; Deut. 4:21; Josh. 11:23; 13:7; Judg. 21:24; 2 Sam. 20:19; 1 Kgs. 8:36; Ps. 105:11). In Josh. 14:13, Hebron is given to Caleb as a specific inheritance, a reward for his faithful example of leadership in the early stages of Israel's conquest of Canaan. In contexts of divine judgment, the defiling of the land by God's people is seen as a desecration of Yahweh's inheritance (Jer. 2:7; 16:18). Furthermore, Lam. 5:2 declares that God's punishment of his people has involved him in handing over the "inheritance" of Canaan to strangers (cf. also Ps. 79:1).

In the context of blessing, Jer. 12:15 affirms that Yahweh will return his people to the land, restoring them to their inheritance. Then, in Ezekiel's vision of renewal, the land is reallocated to the people of Yahweh as a restored inheritance (cf. Ezek. 45:1; 47:14; 48:29). The land inheritance of the messianic prince is likewise indicated in Ezekiel's vision (cf. Ezek. 46:16ff.).

naḥalāh also refers (as do ***yārash*** and ***nāḥal***, above) to the unique inheritance of the Levites. While they are denied land "inheritance" in the ordinary sense, they are in fact given an allotment of several cities throughout the land in which to live (cf. Num. 18:20; Deut. 10:9). In addition, the Levites receive a tithe from the people as their inheritance in return for their sanctuary service (cf. Num. 18:21).

The people of Israel are designated as Yahweh's "inheritance" in a number of places (cf. Deut. 4:20; 32:9; 1 Sam. 10:1; Ps. 78:62; Isa. 19:25; Mic. 7:14). When Israel and Judah rebel against him, Yahweh punishes his "inheritance" by handing them over to their enemies (cf. Isa. 47:6; Jer. 12:7ff.). Other references to Israel as Yahweh's "heritage" are found in Ps. 94:14; Joel 2:17; 3:2.

Other uses of ***naḥalāh*** include a reference to divine punishment as the "heritage" of the wicked (cf. Job 20:29). Ps. 2:8 affirms that the nations are to be given as the "inheritance" of God's son. Children are deemed as a "heritage" from the Lord in Ps. 127:3.

yerushāh [יְרֻשָּׁה, 3425]

yerushāh is a noun derived from ***yārush*** (see above), and is found fourteen times with the consistent meaning "heritage," "inheritance," or "possession" (i.e., by right of inheritance).

Mt. Seir is granted to Esau as an inherited possession in Deut. 2:5. The land of Moab is denied to the Israelites as an inheritance or possession in Deut. 2:9 (cf. also Deut. 2:19). Several passages depict the land of Canaan as the "inheritance" given by God to his people, Israel (cf. Deut. 2:12; 3:20; Josh. 1:15; 12:6, 7; 2 Chr. 20:11). In a related context, ***yerushāh*** refers to the necessity of the Benjaminite tribe maintaining their continuing "heritage," and not being blotted out from Israel (cf. Judg. 21:17).

yerushāh also refers to King David's descendants as the "heritage" of those who fear God's name (i.e., children given by God to those who truly reverence the name of the Lord [cf. Ps. 61:5]).

Jer. 32:8 indicates that the field of Anathoth belongs to Jeremiah's inheritance in the land of Benjamin.

NT Words

klēronomeō [κληρονομέω, *2816*]

klēronomeō is found in eighteen contexts and is consistently translated "inherit," and in one instance "obtain by inheritance."

Matt. 5:5 says, "Blessed are the meek for they shall inherit the earth." Heb. 12:16, 17 record the incident of Esau rejecting his birthright and afterwards pleading to inherit this blessing again, but to no avail.

The blessing of inheriting eternal life is indicated in Matt. 19:29; Mark 10:17; Luke 10:25; 18:18; Heb. 1:14; Rev. 21:7. Similarly, Matt. 25:34 refers to the blessed destiny of all believers in inheriting the kingdom of God for eternity. Heb. 1:4 affirms that Jesus Christ has obtained by inheritance a more excellent name than the angels.

klēronomeō is also used in a number of negative contexts. The following groups of people do not inherit the kingdom of God: the unrighteous (cf. 1 Cor. 6:9ff.; Gal. 5:21); "flesh and blood" (i.e., mere mortal human beings) (cf. 1 Cor. 15:50); "the son of the slave-woman" (i.e., those outside of God's chosen people) (cf. Gal. 4:30).

klēroō [κληρόω, *2820*]

klēroō occurs only once, in Eph. 1:11, where it refers to the believer's inheritance of salvation having been obtained in and through the person of Christ.

klēronomia [κληρονομία, *2817*]

klēronomia is a noun derived from ***klēronomeō*** (see above) and is consistently translated "inheritance." The term occurs fourteen times.

klēronomia refers to inheritance as a human legacy (cf. Matt. 21:38; Mark 12:7, 13; Luke 20:14; Acts 7:5). The term also refers to the inheritance of the land of Canaan as promised to Abraham, in Heb. 11:8.

klēronomia also refers to the "inheritance" of salvation, which is the destiny of those who are sanctified by God's grace and true servants of Jesus Christ (cf. Acts 20:32; Col. 3:24). Gal. 3:18 refers to this inheritance being accessed not through the law, but by means of grace. Heb. 9:15 affirms that the guarantee of the promised eternal inheritance is made certain by Christ's mediatorial role under the new covenant; and 1 Pet. 1:4 refers to the imperishable inheritance of eternal life. Similarly, Eph. 1:14, 18 indicate that it is the Holy Spirit who is the guarantee of our eternal inheritance.

The sole negative context for ***klēronomia*** is found in Eph. 5:5, which declares that no idolatrous or immoral person has any inheritance in the kingdom of God.

klēros [κλῆρος, *2819*]

klēros refers to that which is obtained by lot, and the process of casting lots, in most of the thirteen contexts in which it is found. On two occasions, however, ***klēros*** refers to the inheritance of salvation to be enjoyed by the people of God (cf. Acts 26:18; Col. 1:12).

Additional Notes

The range of words referring to "inheritance" in both Old and New Testaments is quite broad. However, it is clear that the primary focus in the Old Testament is on the phenomenon of "land inheritance" (i.e., the land of Canaan) as promised through the divine covenant promises given to Abraham and his descendants. "Inheritance" in the Old Testament manifests itself primarily in material terms. In the New Testament, "inheritance" takes on the aspect of blessing that moves from the earthly to the spiritual plane. No longer does "inheritance" focus on the land of Canaan, but rather on the heritage of the eternal promise of salvation. This consummates the kingdom of God that began with a finite earthly manifestation under the old covenant, but that concludes with an infinitely enduring heavenly, spiritual reality.

INIQUITY

OT Words

'āwōn [עָוֹן, 5771]

'āwōn is a common term that designates sin in general terms as "iniquity," and also denotes the guilt of iniquity, or the consequences of iniquity. ***'āwōn*** occurs around two hundred times. (→ SIN → WICKED)

As a general term for sin against God, ***'āwōn*** is found in a variety of contexts. Iniquity is predicated, for example, of the Canaanites (Gen. 15:16); of the "fathers of Israel" (Exod. 20:5; Deut. 5:9; Isa. 14:21); and of the people of Israel (Lev. 16:21; Isa. 1:4; Ezek. 14:4). Prayer for divine punishment to fall upon those guilty of iniquity is offered in Neh. 4:5; Ps. 69:27; Jer. 18:23. On the other hand, prayer for the forgiveness of iniquity is mentioned in Exod. 34:9; Num. 14:19; 2 Sam. 24:10; Ps. 25:11; Dan. 9:16. In related contexts, the confession of iniquity is found in Lev. 26:40, 43; Neh. 9:2; Ps. 51:2; Jer. 14:20; Dan. 9:13. Yahweh responds to these prayers by being willing to forgive the iniquity of his people (cf. Num. 14:18; Ps. 78:3, 8; Mic. 7:18, 19; Ps. 103:3). Jer. 31:34; 36:31; 33:8 contain a divine promise of absolute forgiveness under the new covenant. The motif of forgiveness is extended by the intercessory, substitutionary death of the Suffering Servant of Yahweh, who was bruised for the iniquities of his people (cf. Isa. 53:5, 6, 11).

The guilt associated with the practice of iniquity is another significant component of the usage of ***'āwōn***. General references to such guilt are found in Gen. 44:16; 1 Sam. 20:8; Hos. 5:5. Israel's guilt before Yahweh is indicated in Jer. 2:2; 3:13; 30:14; Ezek. 9:9. Guilt is also associated with flawed sacrificial offerings in Exod. 28:38, 43. Isa. 6:4 declares that guilt can be removed by divine pardon.

Finally, ***'āwōn*** is found in contexts that describe the consequences brought about by committing iniquity. In general terms, Yahweh punishes his people for their iniquity (cf. Lev. 18:25; Josh. 22:20; 1 Sam. 3:3; Jer. 14:10; Hos. 8:13; Amos 3:2). Wicked inhabitants of the earth are also similarly punished for their sinful actions (cf. Isa. 13:11; 26:21; Jer. 25:12). The punishment of Cain is described in Gen. 4:13; and the individual's responsibility for his own iniquity is made clear in Jer. 31:30; Ezek. 18:17ff. The concept of "bearing iniquity" is also indicated by ***'āwōn***. It refers to suffering the consequences of one's iniquity, normally accomplished through the offering of sacrifice (cf. Lev. 5:1; 10:17; 16:22; Num. 5:31; 15:31; Lam. 5:7; Ezek. 4:4; 44:10).

'āwen [אָוֶן, 205]

'āwen is a synonym for ***'āwōn***, above. It occurs less frequently, around eighty times, and is usually translated "iniquity" or "wickedness."

General references to the fact of human wickedness are found in Job 22:15; 34:22; Ps. 7:14; Isa. 59:4. Jer. 4:14; Ezek. 11:2; Hos. 6:8 observe iniquity in Israel.

Those guilty of iniquity are said to be hated by God in Ps. 5:5; Isa. 1:13; and await an inevitable doom (cf. Pss. 92:7; 94:23; Isa. 10:1; Mic. 2:1).

The psalmist makes a number of passionate requests in this regard — a plea for Yahweh to keep one from iniquity (cf. Pss. 28:3; 119:133); for God to punish those who commit iniquity (cf. Pss. 56:7; 59:5); and for divine protection against the wicked (Ps. 64:2).

'āwel [עָוֶל, 5766]

'āwel is another synonym for ***'āwōn*** and ***'āwen*** (see above). It too refers to "iniquity," "unrighteousness," or "wickedness." ***'āwel*** is found approximately forty times.

Human wickedness or iniquity is indicated in general terms in Job 6:30; 15:16; Ps. 58:2.

Specific instruction not to act unjustly (i.e., "in iniquity") is given in Lev. 19:15, 35; 2 Chr. 19:7; and Yahweh is said to abhor those who act in this way (cf. Deut. 25:16; Ps. 53:1).

Terrible consequences for those who indulge in iniquitous lifestyles are predicted in Prov. 22:8. Israel's iniquity comes under divine judgment in Isa. 59:3; Hos. 10:13; Mic. 3:10; Hab. 2:12. As far as individuals are concerned, one's responsibility for one's own sin is clearly evident in Ezek. 3:20; 18:24, 26; 33:13ff. The iniquity of the city of Tyre is mentioned in Ezek. 28:18, characterized particularly by the spirit of arrogant pride and blasphemy in the person of the Tyrian king.

Yahweh is declared to be utterly free of all iniquity in Deut. 32:4; Ps. 92:15; Zeph. 3:5.

In a positive context, Zeph. 3:13 refers to the divine cleansing of the remnant of Israel from her iniquity.

'āwāh [עָוָה, 5753]

'āwāh is synonymous with the entries above but occurs much less frequently (about twenty times). ***'āwāh*** refers to "iniquity" in a general sense, but with the underlying sense of that which is twisted or perverse.

Acts of such wrongdoing are mentioned in general terms in 2 Sam. 19:19; Esth. 1:16. And committing such iniquity leads to divine punishment (cf. 2 Sam. 7:14), and despising by other people (cf. Prov. 12:8). Jer. 3:21; 9:5 refer to Israel's perverse iniquity. Such iniquity is confessed in 2 Sam. 24:17; 1 Kgs. 8:47; 2 Chr. 6:37; Ps. 106:6; Dan. 9:5.

NT Words

anomia [ἀνομία, *458*]

anomia means "lawlessness" (literally, "without law"), and is translated "iniquity," "wickedness," indicating the violation of God's law. ***anomia*** occurs thirteen times.

1 John 3:4 equates sin and lawlessness. The utter incompatibility of righteousness and iniquity is affirmed in 2 Cor. 6:14. Matt. 24:12 indicates the growth of iniquity in a person's heart. Those who are guilty of persistent, unrepentant iniquity are to be removed from the kingdom of God (cf. Matt. 13:41). Heb. 1:9 declares Jesus Christ's hatred of iniquity. And Jesus' command for "evildoers" to leave him on the Day of Judgment is recorded in Matt. 7:23. Jesus levels the charge of iniquity against the Pharisees in Matt. 23:38. 2 Thess. 2:7 makes it clear that the mystery of iniquity is at work in the world; yet is fully subject to God's control.

In a positive context, Rom. 4:7 guarantees blessing for those whose iniquities are forgiven. Christ's role in redeeming his people from iniquity is portrayed in Titus 2:14. Then there is God's refusal to remember the sins of his people as a consequence of Christ's work (Heb. 8:12).

adikia [ἀδικία, *93*]

adikia is a synonym for ***anomia*** (see above), and refers likewise to the action of violating God's law. ***adikia*** occurs twenty-five times and is translated "iniquity," "unrighteousness," in most of these contexts.

Divine wrath against iniquity and wickedness is indicated in Rom. 1:18; 2:8; 3:5; 2 Thess. 2:10, 12; 2 Pet. 2:13. Paul also declares in Rom. 1:29 that iniquity is characteristic of all unbelievers. Acts 8:23 affirms that iniquity brings about a profound moral and spiritual enslavement. An unjust judge is specifically mentioned in one of Jesus' parables in Luke 18:6. Judas' monetary reward for his iniquitous act of betrayal is mentioned in Acts 1:18. Luke 13:27 contains a terrible pronouncement against all "workers of iniquity," to be issued by Christ on the final day of judgment. Other general references to iniquity are found in 1 Cor. 13:6; 2 Cor. 12:13; 2 Tim. 2:19; Jas. 3:6; 2 Pet. 2:15; 1 John 5:17.

In contrast, John 7:18; Rom. 9:14 declare that the persons of God and Christ are absolutely free of iniquity. With respect to human sinfulness, Heb. 8:12 declares God's determination to be merciful toward the iniquity of his people. 1 John 1:9 contains the divine promises to cleanse his people from iniquity on the basis of the finished work of Christ. Rom. 6:13 commands us not to use our bodies as instruments of iniquity.

INJURY → EVIL

INK

OT Words

deyô **[דְּיוֹ, 1773]**

deyô is found only in Jer. 36:18 with reference to Baruch copying the words of Jeremiah in ink onto a scroll.

NT Words

melas [μέλας, *3188*]

melas is the direct equivalent of the Hebrew term ***deyô***, above, and occurs three times, all with reference to writing in ink (cf. 2 Cor. 3:3; 2 John 12; 3 John 13).

INN

OT Words

mālôn **[מָלוֹן, 4411]**

This term is found eight times and consistently refers to "inn" or "place of lodging" (cf. Gen. 42:27; 43:21; 2 Kgs. 19:23; Isa. 10:29; Jer. 9:2).

NT Words

xenia [ξενία, *3578*]

xenia occurs only twice and refers in both contexts to a place of lodging. Acts 28:23 refers to Paul's lodgings in Rome, where he was under house arrest. In Phlm. 22, Paul requests his prospective host to provide him with a guest room on his arrival.

katalyma [κατάλυμα, *2646*]

katalyma is synonymous with ***xenia*** (see above) and refers to either an inn or guest room. The term is found three times. Mark 4:14; Luke 22:11 refer to the guest room requested by the disciples of Jesus for the celebration of the Passover. Luke 2:7 refers to the lack of accommodation for Joseph and Mary in Bethlehem.

pandocheion [πανδοχεῖον, *3829*]

pandocheion is found only in Luke 10:34, referring to the inn in the parable of the good Samaritan.

INNOCENCE, INNOCENT

OT Words

nāqî **[נָקִי, 5355]**

nāqî is an adjectival term translated "innocent" in the majority of the forty or so contexts in which it occurs. The underlying sense is that of freedom from guilt or exemption from punishment, as well as freedom from obligation, though this latter sense is not embraced by the translation "innocent."

In the sense of "free from blame," ***nāqî*** refers to Joseph's brothers as "innocent" in Gen. 44:10. See also Josh. 2:17, 19; 2 Sam. 14:9. In the case of death occasioned by the goring of a bull, the animal itself is to be slain, but the owner is declared "innocent" (i.e., he is not held responsible).

nāqî also refers to the "innocent" as a class of people in Job 4:7; 9:23; Ps. 15:5. Exod. 23:7 contains the command not to falsely accuse the innocent. In regard to the crime of killing innocent people, or "shedding innocent blood," there are severe warnings against such actions in Deut. 19:10, 13; 27:25. Instances of the crime are recorded in 1 Sam. 19:5; 2 Kgs. 21:16; Isa. 59:7; Jer. 2:34; Joel 3:19; Jonah 1:14. Deut. 21:9 contains the command to purge the guilt of shedding innocent blood; and a plea for forgiveness for the crime is found in Deut. 21:8.

nāqāh **[נָקָה, 5352]**

nāqāh is the verbal root from which ***nāqî*** (see above) is derived. This term has the basic meanings "to be, or declare innocent," "to be free from guilt," "to be exempt from punishment." ***nāqāh*** occurs about forty times.

nāqāh is sometimes used in the negative sense of "not to be held innocent" — for example, in the case of blasphemy (cf. Exod. 20:7; Deut. 5:11); of visiting the sins of the fathers onto the third and fourth generations of those that hate Yahweh (cf. Exod. 34:7; Num. 14:8); of adultery (cf. Prov. 6:29; 11:21). See also 1 Kgs. 2:9; Job 9:28; Nah. 1:3.

General references to ***nāqāh***, indicating freedom from guilt or innocence of a crime, are found in Num. 5:31; Judg. 15:3. Num. 5:28 is a unique context in which innocence of adultery is to be proven by a ritual ordeal.

In the plea for forgiveness in Ps. 19:12, the sense is that of rendering one innocent.

NT Words

athōos [ἀθῷος, *121*]

athōos is an adjective occurring only twice, meaning "innocent," "guiltless." With reference to taking innocent blood, Matt. 27:4 indicts Judas with respect to Jesus, and Matt. 27:24 involves Pilate's claim to be innocent of the blood of Christ.

anaitios [ἀναίτιος, *338*]

anaitios is an adjective occurring only twice, meaning "innocent." Matt. 12:5, 7 refer to priests and the "innocent" in Israel.

amemptos [ἄμεμπτος, *273*]

amemptos is a synonym for ***athōos*** and ***anaitios***, above, occurring five times with the underlying sense of "blameless," "faultless," "innocent."

This quality is predicated of Zechariah and Elizabeth (Luke 1:6); and of believers (Phil. 2:15; 1 Thess. 3:13). In Phil. 3:6 it is Paul who, prior to his conversion, was accounted "blameless" or "innocent" in the eyes of Jewish law and tradition. Heb. 8:7 offers the hypothesis that if nothing had been wrong with the first covenant (i.e., if it had been "innocent"), then God would not have sought to replace it with another. But that first covenant was in fact defective and needed to be superseded if full salvation was to be awarded to the people of God.

amemptōs [ἀμέμπτως, *274*]

amemptōs is the adverbial form of ***amemptos***, above. It is translated "blameless" or "innocent" in 1 Thess. 5:23.

anenklētos [ἀνέγκλητος, *410*]

anenklētos is another synonym for the entries above and is also translated "blameless," "innocent," with the particular underlying sense of "beyond reproach," unable to be rightfully accused of wrongdoing. ***anenklētos*** occurs five times.

1 Cor. 1:18; Col. 1:22 declare that true believers will be kept blameless on the final judgment day. Such a quality is also a requirement for elders and deacons (cf. 1 Tim. 3:10; Titus 1:6, 7).

anepilēmptos [ἀνεπίλημπτος, *423*]

This term is a precise synonym for ***anenklētos*** (see above), and is found on three occasions. 1 Tim. 3:2 lists a "blameless" or "innocent" lifestyle as an indispensable quality for appointment to the office of elder or deacon. Similarly, such a virtue is declared to be the desired goal of all of God's people in 1 Tim. 5:7. 1 Tim. 6:14 contains the apostle Paul's charge to Timothy to remain "beyond reproach" in carrying out his pastoral duties.

amōmētos [ἀμώμητος, *298*]

This term occurs twice, meaning "blameless," "irreproachable" in Phil. 2:15; 2 Pet. 3:14, describing God's people in general.

INQUIRE

OT Words

biqqēsh [בִּקֵּשׁ, **1245**]

This is an intensive form of the verbal root ***bāqash*** (→ SEEK), translated primarily "to seek" and occurring 225 times. In three places, however, ***biqqēsh*** means "inquire," "make inquiries." The act of "inquiring of the Lord," or seeking divine guidance, is mentioned in 2 Sam. 21:1. Esth. 2:23; Dan. 1:8 indicate the action of "making inquiries."

biqqēr [בִּקֵּר, **1239**]

biqqēr is another intensive verb form, derived from the root ***bāqar*** (→ SEEK). ***biqqēr*** refers to the action of "seeking," though it occurs far less frequently than ***biqqēsh*** (see above). ***biqqēr*** occurs seven times and may be translated "inquire," "make inquiries (i.e., investigate)" in four of these contexts.

Lev. 27:33 refers to the practice of "investigating" whether a tithe offering is good or bad, once it had been accepted for sacrifice — something that was not permitted under the law. See also Prov. 20:25. King Ahaz chose the bronze altar of the temple as the vehicle for "making inquiries" of Yahweh (cf. 2 Kgs. 16:15). See also Ps. 27:4.

NT Words

pynthanomai [πυνθάνομαι, *4441*]

pynthanomai occurs twelve times, and in each of these contexts it may be translated "ask" or "inquire of," with the aim of finding out certain information.

In Matt. 2:4, Herod makes inquiries concerning the whereabouts of Christ's birth. Peter inquires of Jesus as to who would betray him in John 13:24. Acts 4:7 describes the Sanhedrin's inquiry, set up to investigate the preaching activity of Peter and John. In Acts 21:33 the Roman commander makes an inquiry concerning Paul's claim to be a Roman citizen in the wake of the Jerusalem riot that saw the apostle taken into custody. See also Luke 15:26; 18:26; John 4:52; Acts 10:18, 29; 23:19ff.

akriboō [ἀκριβόω, *198*]

akriboō occurs only twice, meaning "to inquire, or investigate diligently" in Matt. 2:7, where Herod tries to find out from the wise men what time the star in the east had appeared.

zēteō [ζητέω, *2212*]

zēteō commonly indicates "to seek" and occurs over one hundred times with that meaning. Twice, however, *zēteō* expresses the sense of "inquire after" in the sense of gaining information — once by Jesus from the disciples (John 16:19), and once by Ananias from the newly converted Saul of Tarsus (Acts 9:11).

See Also: → ASK

INSCRIBE, INSCRIPTION

OT Words

***pittûaḥ* [פִּתּוּחַ, 6603]**

pittûaḥ connotes the idea of that which is engraved or inscribed, an "inscription" or "engraving." The term occurs eleven times and refers in most instances to the inscriptions associated with the high priest's apparel.

The names of the children of Israel are inscribed on the gold setting of the ephod (Exod. 28:11, 21; 39:6, 14); and on the diadem of the high priest's turban is found the inscription "holy to the Lord" (cf. Exod. 28:36; 39:30; Zech. 3:9). General references to engraving on the walls and furniture of the temple are found in 1 Kgs. 6:29; 2 Chr. 2:7, 14.

***ḥāqaq* [חָקַק, 2710]**

ḥāqaq is a verb that has the root meanings "cut," "decree," "inscribe." In a number of contexts it refers to the authority of a law or decree, and hence is often translated "scepter," indicating the symbol of power and civil authority. It can also refer to one who issues a decree, such as a "governor" or "ruler."

Concerning the specific action of inscribing, ***ḥāqaq*** refers to writing words in a book in Job 19:23; Isa. 30:8. In Isa. 49:16, Yahweh is portrayed as having inscribed his people on the palms of his hands as a sign of their spiritual renewal. Ezek. 4:1 refers to the prophet drawing (i.e., inscribing) the likeness of a city on a mud brick in order to graphically portray the imminent destruction of the city of Jerusalem. Ezek. 23:14 refers to portraits of Israel's Babylonian deities drawn on a wall.

NT Words

***epigraphē* [ἐπιγραφή, *1923*]**

epigraphē is a noun that indicates a "superscription" or "inscription," and occurs five times. Matt. 22:20 refers to Caesar's superscription on a coin (also Mark 2:16; Luke 20:24). Mark 15:16; Luke 23:38 refer to the inscription placed over the head of Jesus as he hung on the cross: "This is the king of the Jews."

See Also: → WRITE

INSOLENCE, INSOLENT

OT Words

***zādôn* [זָדוֹן, 2087]**

zādôn is a noun with the underlying sense of "pride." However, in the majority of the eleven contexts in which the term is found, ***zādôn*** may be translated "insolence," "insolent" in the sense of "arrogant pride," or "presumption" (e.g., 1 Sam. 17:28; Prov. 13:10; 21:24). ***zādôn*** describes the insolence of the nations (Jer. 49:16); of Edom (Obad. 3); of Babylon (Jer. 50:31, 32); and also of Judah and Jerusalem (Ezek. 7:10). Deut. 17:12 refers to the insolent, arrogant refusal to abide by the instructions of a priest or judge, which constitutes a capital offense.

***zēd* [זֵד, 2086]**

zēd is the adjectival form of ***zādôn*** (see above) and means "insolent," with the accompanying sense of "arrogant," "proud," or "presumptuous." ***zēd*** occurs thirteen times.

Insolent people in general are referred to in Ps. 119:21, 78; Prov. 21:24; Jer. 43:2; Mal. 3:15. The psalmist notes in particular that insolent people frequently rise up against him (cf. Pss. 86:14; 119:51, 69, 85, 122). Divine punishment of the insolent and the arrogant is recorded in Isa. 13:11; Mal. 4:1.

NT Words

***hybristēs* [ὑβριστής, *5197*]**

hybristēs occurs only twice. In Rom. 1:30 it indicates the vice of "insolence" as characteristic of the wicked who refuse to acknowledge God's rightful place in their lives. 1 Tim. 1:13 refers to Paul's practice of "insulting" God prior to his conversion, when he actively and aggressively persecuted Christians — implying insolence towards both God and humankind.

See Also: → SHAME

INSPIRATION

NT Words

***theopneustos* [θεόπνευστος, *2315*]**

theopneustos is found only in 1 Tim. 3:16, literally meaning "God-breathed." The term refers to the divine origin of the Scriptures as coming not from the initiative of human beings, but from God. The translation "inspiration" is misleading in a way, for it suggests the idea of "taking breath into . . . ," whereas what is indicated is the product of God's "breathed-out word." However, this popular meaning the of term (viz. "inspiration") to describe the divine foundation of the sacred writings remains, notwithstanding the looseness of the translation of ***theopneustos.***

INSTANT → SUDDEN

INSTRUCT, INSTRUCTION, INSTRUCTOR

OT Words

yāsar **[יָסַר, 3256]**

yāsar is a verb occurring about forty times with the dominant sense of "chasten," "chastise," in about half of these contexts. However, ***yāsar*** is also translated "instruct" or "correct." The underlying sense of "admonition," however, remains throughout.

The exercise of instruction, in the sense of divine discipline, is mentioned in a number of contexts. It is predicated, for example, of Israel (Deut. 4:36; 8:5; Jer. 30:11; Isa. 8:11; Ezek. 23:48); of the psalmist (Ps. 16:7); of Jerusalem (Jer. 6:8); and of Jeremiah himself (Jer. 10:24).

Parental instruction (i.e., discipline) of children is indicated in Deut. 21:18; Prov. 19:18; 29:17; 31:1. 1 Chr. 15:22 describes instruction in music. Job 4:3 refers to Job as "instructor" in a general sense.

yārāh **[יָרָה, 3384]**

yārāh occurs around eighty times, and in over half of these contexts it means "teach" or "instruct."

yārāh refers to teaching or instruction given by God to various people — for example, to Moses (cf. Exod. 4:12ff.); to the Israelites receiving the law (cf. Exod. 24:12); and to Israel during the reign of Solomon (cf. 1 Kgs. 8:36; 2 Chr. 6:27). The craftsmen Oholiab and Ahisamach were given ability by the Spirit of God to teach their skills to others (cf. Exod. 35:34). Similarly, Israelite priests are given knowledge of divine origin for the purpose of instructing the people in the law of the covenant (cf. Lev. 10:11; Deut. 24:8; 2 Kgs. 12:2; 2 Chr. 15:3; Ezek. 44:23); as are the judges in Israel (Deut. 17:11). God himself is referred to as a teacher in Job 36:23; Isa. 28:9, 26; 30:20.

yārāh is also found in contexts where instruction is requested by people from various sources, primarily from God himself (e.g., Pss. 27:11; 119:33). Significant references to this phenomenon are found in Isa. 2:3; Mic. 4:2, where the peoples of the earth are said to seek Yahweh in Jerusalem so they might derive instruction from him. See also Judg. 13:8; Job 6:24.

yārāh refers to teachers in general in Prov. 5:13, and Samuel promises to teach the people in 1 Sam. 12:3. Ps. 45:4 refers to instruction by the king, and Prov. 4:4, 11 to teaching given by a father to his son. False teaching from a false prophet is indicated in Mic. 3:11; and the uselessness of an idol as a teacher is affirmed in Hab. 2:18.

mûsār **[מוּסָר, 4148]**

mûsār is a participial noun from the verb ***yāsar***, above, meaning "instruction," "correction," with the underlying sense of discipline or chastening in a significant number of contexts. ***mûsār*** occurs around fifty times.

Divinely initiated instruction, or discipline, is indicated in Job 36:10. The people of Israel and Judah refuse or reject such discipline in Jer. 17:23; 32:33, leading to the consequence of severe punishment. Prov. 5:12 refers to people despising God's instruction. Ps. 50:17 indicates that the wicked hate such instruction, as do fools (Prov. 1:7).

The book of Proverbs commonly emphasizes the great value of heeding instruction, which is subsumed under the guise of "embracing wisdom" (cf. Prov. 1:2ff.; 4:13; 8:23). Such wisdom is understood to be ultimately derived from God. Likewise, Proverbs stresses the importance of a father's instruction to his son (cf. Prov. 1:8; 4:1; 13:1). This book also lays down two contrasting principles in relation to this phenomenon: Prov. 5:23 declares that lack of instruction leads to death (cf. also Prov. 13:18); whereas Prov. 10:17 affirms that heeding instruction will lead to life.

NT Words

katēcheō **[κατηχέω, *2727*]**

katēcheō is found in eight contexts with the consistent meaning "to instruct," "teach" (cf. Acts 21:21, 24).

Luke writes to Theophilus to convince him of the truthfulness of the elements of the Christian faith in which he has been instructed (cf. Luke 1:4). Acts 18:5 records Apollos' instruction in the "way of the Lord." Rom. 2:18 indicates that Jewish people have been instructed in the law. In 1 Cor. 14:19, Paul mentions his desire to instruct others clearly in gospel truth. Gal. 6:16 expounds the principle that the teachers of God's word derive financial support from those they teach.

paideuō **[παιδεύω, *3811*]**

paideuō is a dynamic equivalent of the Hebrew term ***yāsar***, above, indicating the sense of "chasten," "chastise," as well as the meaning "instruct." ***paideuō*** occurs fifteen times and is translated "instruct," "learn" in about a third of these contexts. Acts 7:22 indicates that Moses was instructed in all of the knowledge of the Egyptians. Acts 22:3 mentions the fact that Paul was educated (i.e., instructed) at the feet of the great rabbinical scholar Gamaliel. 1 Tim. 1:20 records that Paul had to discipline Hymenaeus and Alexander so that they would "learn" not to blaspheme. In 2 Tim. 2:25, Paul advises Timothy to instruct, or correct, his opponents gently. Titus 2:12 affirms that the grace of God "teaches" the people of God to renounce ungodliness.

symbibazō [συμβιβάζω, *4822*]

symbibazō is found in six contexts and has the underlying sense of bringing or joining together, both literally and metaphorically. The term is translated "join together," and by extension "prove," "conclude"; and, in one instance, "instruct." 1 Cor. 2:16 poses the question: "Who has known the mind of the Lord so as to instruct him?" Clearly no one is capable of achieving such insight, since no one is capable of grasping the totality of the divine mind — a perspective suggested by the usage of ***symbibazō.***

paidagōgos [παιδαγωγός, *3807*]

paidagōgos is a term referring to a tutor, or schoolmaster (i.e., one who instructs). This role was performed by trusted slaves whose job it was to teach and supervise the moral development of young boys in both Greek and Roman culture. In the New Testament, ***paidagōgos*** occurs only three times. In 1 Cor. 4:15, it refers to the countless spiritual instructors in the service of the Corinthian congregation. In Gal. 3:24, 25, ***paidagōgos*** is used metaphorically of the law, depicted as a harsh "tutor" for God's people, until true freedom came along in the person of Christ.

paideia [παιδεία, *3809*]

paideia is a term that indicates the entire process of nurturing, educating, and disciplining, applied to believers as well as to children. It is found six times and is translated "instruction" in 2 Tim. 3:16 in reference to the Scriptures, being suitable among other things, for instruction (or training) in righteousness.

paideutēs [παιδευτής, *3810*]

paideutēs occurs only twice, referring to an "instructor" of the foolish in Rom. 2:20, and in Heb. 12:9 to earthly fathers who disciplined their children (lit., ". . . our fathers whom we have as instructors").

INSTRUMENT

OT Words

kelî [כְּלִי, **3627**]

kelî is a noun with a number of senses that relate to "articles" or "implements" of various kinds, including the nondescript designation "things." ***kelî*** occurs over three hundred times, and the translation "instrument" is found around twenty times.

Musical instruments relating to Israelite worship are mentioned, for example, in 1 Chr. 15:16; 2 Chr. 5:13; 29:26; 34:12; Neh. 12:36; Amos 6:5. In reference to weapons as instruments, ***kelî*** is found in Isa. 54:16; Ps. 7:13. Ritual instruments for slaying sacrificial animals are indicated in Ezek. 40:42. (→ UTENSIL)

nāgan [נָגַן, **5059**]

nāgan is a verb referring to the activity of playing stringed musical instruments. It occurs fifteen times.

1 Sam. 16:16ff.; 23; 18:10; 19:9 refer to David as a skilled player of the lyre, or the harp. Pss. 33:3; 68:25; Isa. 38:20 refer to playing instruments in the context of worship.

mēn [מֵן, **4482**]

This term is rare, found only in Pss. 45:8; 150:4 with reference to stringed instruments. In Ps. 150:4, the music is played in the context of worship of Yahweh.

'āsôr [עָשׂוֹר, **6218**]

'āsôr is one of the terms for the number "ten" and also has the ordinal sense of "tenth." ***'āsôr*** occurs fifteen times and refers to the ten-stringed harp, used in the musical expression of worship of Yahweh (cf. Pss. 33:2; 92:3; 144:9). See also 2 Kgs. 3:15; Ezek. 33:32.

shālîsh [שָׁלִישׁ, **7991**]

shālîsh is another ordinal number, indicating literally a "third." The term occurs around twenty times, and is mostly translated "captain," or "military commander." Only in 1 Sam. 18:6 does it have a different meaning, that of "musical instrument," possibly a stringed instrument with a triangular shape.

môrag [מוֹרַג, **4173**]

môrag occurs three times and refers to a "threshing sledge," or an instrument of threshing (cf. 1 Sam. 24:22;

1 Chr. 21:23). In Isa. 41:15, ***môrag*** refers to Israel as a "threshing sledge," to be used by Yahweh as an instrument of divine punishment against the nations.

NT Words

hoplon [ὅπλον, *3696*]

hoplon refers to a tool, implement, or instrument in both literal and metaphorical contexts. The term is found six times.

Indicating weaponry, ***hoplon*** is found in John 18:3 with reference to the armed mob coming to arrest Jesus. In 2 Cor. 10:4 it refers to spiritual weapons, and in 2 Cor. 6:7 it speaks of the weapons of righteousness. Rom. 13:12 mentions believers putting on the "armor of light." Rom. 6:13 urges believers to yield members of their bodies to God as instruments of righteousness, not wickedness.

INTEGRITY

OT Words

tōm [**תֹּם, 8537**]

tōm occurs around twenty times and refers to "integrity" of character. The term suggests that which is whole, complete, and transparently free of duplicity. The meaning "integrity" is evident in the majority of these contexts.

With reference to Abimelech, the Philistine king, ***tōm*** speaks of his "integrity of heart" — in this context indicating a clear conscience. ***tōm*** also expresses the idea of integrity in relation to honest motives and moral uprightness (e.g., 2 Sam. 5:11; Pss. 7:8; 25:21; 26:1; 101:2; Prov. 2:7; 13:6; 20:7; 1 Kgs. 9:4).

yōsher [**יֹשֶׁר, 3476**]

yōsher is translated "integrity," "uprightness" in most of the fourteen contexts in which it occurs. The dominant sense is that of "integrity of the heart."

This quality is predicated of people in general (Job 33:23; Prov. 2:13); of Israel (Deut. 9:5); of David (1 Kgs. 9:4; 1 Chr. 29:7); and of Elihu (Job 33:3). The psalmist pleads with God for integrity of heart to preserve him in Ps. 25:21; and in Ps. 119:7 praise is given to God through the psalmist's integrity of heart, or morally upright heart. Godly living, defined as "paths of integrity," is depicted in Prov. 4:11; 14:2. Writing with integrity is indicated in Eccl. 12:10.

tummāh [**תֻּמָּה, 8538**]

tummāh is synonymous with ***tōm*** (see above), from which it is derived. ***tummāh*** means "integrity" in all of the five contexts in which it is found (cf. Job 2:3, 9; 27:5; 31:6; Prov. 11:3).

NT Words

aphthoria [ἀφθορία, *90*]

aphthoria occurs only in Titus 2:7, meaning "integrity" in the sense of a godly lifestyle consistent with one's teaching.

See Also: → BLAME

INTEND, INTENT → PURPOSE

INTERCEDE, INTERCESSION

OT Words

pālal [**פָּלַל, 6419**]

pālal occurs around eighty times and means "to pray." In about fifty of these contexts, ***pālal*** indicates the specific sense of interceding in prayer.

pālal refers to intercessory prayer as Moses intercedes for the people of Israel in Num. 11:2; 21:7; Deut. 9:20. 1 Sam. 2:25 poses the question: "If a man sins against the Lord, who can intercede for him?" Samuel also intercedes for Israel (1 Sam. 7:5; 12:19, 23); as does Solomon (1 Kgs. 8:28ff.) on the occasion of the dedication of the temple. Ezra does likewise in his intercessory prayer in Ezra 10:1ff.; as does Daniel (Dan. 9:4, 20). In contrast, God commands Jeremiah not to intercede for the people of Judah on account of the heinousness of their sin (cf. Jer. 7:16; 11:14; 14:11).

Other references to the act of intercession are found in 1 Kgs. 13:6; 2 Kgs. 4:33; 2 Chr. 30:18; Jer. 37:3; Job 42:8ff.

pāga' [**פָּגַע, 6293**]

There are a number of meanings attached to this verb. The most common of these are "encounter," "meet," "fall upon." ***pāga'*** occurs in about fifty places, and in seven of them it means "make intercession on behalf of," or "ask on behalf of."

In Gen. 23:8, Abraham "pleads with" a Hittite land owner to allow him to buy a cave in order to bury his wife Sarah. See also Jer. 15:11; 36:25 for the use of ***pāga'*** with this sense.

Isa. 53:12 contains a very significant use of ***pāga'***, in which the self-sacrifice of the messianic Suffering Servant serves to "make intercession" for the wicked. In the absence of anyone else to intercede on behalf of his people, in order to grant them deliverance, God declares his intention to do so himself in Isa. 59:12. In Jer.

7:16, the prophet is forbidden by Yahweh to make intercession for the people of Jerusalem and Judah (but see also Jer. 27:18).

NT Words

entynchanō [ἐντυγχάνω, *1793*]

entynchanō means "intercede," "make intercession for," and "petition" in five contexts.

Acts 25:24 refers to the Jewish people petitioning Festus (the Roman procurator who succeeded Pontius Pilate in Judea), complaining of the evangelistic activities of the apostle Paul. Elsewhere, intercession is spoken of as the ministry of the Spirit of God in making the needs and requests of the saints known to God (cf. Rom. 8:27). Rom. 11:2 refers to Elijah pleading with God against Israel (cf. 1 Kgs. 19:10, 14). Rom. 8:34; Heb. 7:25 speak of the high priestly mediatorial role of Christ in heaven, who intercedes at God's right hand on our behalf.

hyperentynchanō [ὑπερεντυγχάνω, *5241*]

This verb is a variation of ***entynchanō***, above. ***hyperentynchanō*** occurs only in Rom. 8:26, where it refers to the Spirit of God interceding for his people when they find it very difficult to pray in times of suffering.

enteuxis [ἔντευξις, *1783*]

enteuxis is a rare noun derived from ***entynchanō*** (see above) and occurring twice. In 1 Tim. 2:1 it refers to the need for Timothy, as an elder, to pray for all people, making intercession for them before God. In 1 Tim. 4:5, ***enteuxis*** refers to consecrating God's created order through prayer, as well as through the word of God.

INTEREST

OT Words

nāshāh [נָשָׁה, **5383**]

nāshāh occurs thirteen times meaning "to make a loan," as well as "to exact, or lend at interest." The latter sense is found in about half of these contexts.

In the Mosaic legislation, there is a prohibition against lending money to the poor at interest (cf. Exod. 22:25). In Neh. 5:7, charges are laid against Israelites who had lent money to their fellow countrymen at interest. On the other hand, Neh. 5:10, 11 record the care taken by Nehemiah and his associates to avoid such a violation. Those who lend at interest are listed among people whom Yahweh will punish (cf. Isa. 24:2).

neshek [נֶשֶׁךְ, **5392**]

neshek is the most common noun for "interest," occurring twelve times and deriving from the verb form ***nāshak*** (see below).

Taking interest from the poor is a forbidden practice in Israel (cf. Exod. 22:25; Lev. 25:36, 37). Likewise, no Israelite may charge their fellow countrymen interest, though foreigners are exempt from this restriction (cf. Deut. 23:19). Ps. 15:5; Ezek. 18:8, 17 point out that observance of this principle brings blessing. Elsewhere, however, it is also made clear that abuse of this principle brings great loss and judgment (cf. Prov. 28:8; Ezek. 18:13; 22:12).

nāshak [נָשַׁךְ, **5391**]

nāshak is translated "bite" in all but two of the fifteen contexts in which it is found. In Deut. 23:19, 20, it refers to the prohibited practice of lending at interest to a fellow Israelite.

nāshā' [נָשָׁא, **5378**]

nāshā' has the sense of both lending with interest as a creditor and of being in debt. The term occurs four times.

In 1 Sam. 22:2; Isa. 24:2, ***nāshā'*** refers to being in debt. Neh. 5:7 mentions the illegal practice of Israelite officials exacting interest from their fellow countrymen. Ps. 89:22 refers to the practice of subjecting another to tribute (i.e., tax) — an extended application of the meaning "interest."

mashā' [מַשָּׁא, **4855**]

mashā' occurs only twice, and on both occasions it refers to exacting or lending with interest. Such a practice is condemned in Neh. 5:7; but in Neh. 5:10 it is deliberately set aside in recognition of the requirements of the Mosaic law that prohibit Israelites from taking interest from their countrymen.

NT Words

tokos [τόκος, *5110*]

tokos occurs only in Matt. 25:27; Luke 19:23. Both of these texts refer to the parable of the lazy servant, who failed to invest his master's money left in his trust. The man simply buried it in the ground, and he was condemned for doing so. The point is made that at least he could have left the money with the bankers to gain interest.

INTERPRET, INTERPRETER, INTERPRETATION

OT Words

peshar [פְּשַׁר, **6591** (Aramaic)]

peshar is an Aramaic term found exclusively in Daniel, occurring about thirty times. The word is consistently translated "interpretation," specifically relating to dreams or visions experienced by Nebuchadnezzar (cf. Dan. 2:4ff., 24ff.; 4:6ff.), and Belshazzar (cf. Dan. 5:7ff.), kings of Babylon.

pēsher [פֵּשֶׁר, **6592**]

pēsher is the Hebrew term corresponding to the Aramaic ***peshar*** (see above), but which is found only in Eccl. 8:1, referring to the interpretation, or explanation, of things in general.

pātar [פָּתַר, **6622**]

pātar is another related term that means "to interpret," used exclusively in the context of dreams. The particular usage of ***pātar*** centers on the dreams experienced by the chief butler and baker of Pharaoh's household, and which were interpreted by Joseph (cf. Gen. 40:8; 41:8ff.).

pitrôn [פִּתְרוֹן, **6623**]

pitrôn is a noun derived from ***pātar*** (see above) and likewise means "interpretation" in all five contexts in which it occurs, referring to the dream episodes of Pharaoh's butler and baker at the time of Joseph's imprisonment (cf. Gen. 40:5, 8, 12, 18; 41:11).

mēlîṣ [מֵלִיץ, **3887**]

mēlîṣ is a participial form, derived from the verb ***lûṣ*** (→ SCORN), which occurs fourteen times and has a variety of meanings, one of which is "interpret." ***mēlîṣ*** is translated "interpreter" on two occasions: once in Gen. 42:23, referring to language translation, and again in Job 33:23 referring to divine interpretation from an angel.

sheber [שֶׁבֶר, **7667**]

sheber occurs about fifty times with the primary meanings "breaking," "crushing." In Judg. 7:15, however, the term refers to the interpretation of a dream (i.e., its breaking, or decoding).

targēm [תַּרְגֵּם, **8638**]

targēm is a passive participial form that occurs only in Ezra 4:7, referring to the interpretation, or more precisely to the translation, of Aramaic into Persian.

NT Words

methermēneuō [μεθερμηνεύω, *3177*]

This verb form occurs seven times and has the primary sense of "translate" (from one language to another).

methermēneuō refers to the translation of the Hebrew term ***Emmanoyēl***, which is "God with us" (→ IMMANUEL) in Matt. 1:23, and that of the Aramaic command *Talitha kûm* (i.e., "Little girl, arise,"), which was uttered by Jesus in raising Jairus' daughter from the dead in Matt. 5:41. Mark 15:22 refers to Golgotha, which is translated "place of the skull." Jesus' cry from the cross, *Eloi, Eloi lama sabachthani* is translated "My God, my God, why have you forsaken me?" in Mark 15:34. In John 1:4, the term Messiah is translated "Christ." Acts 4:36 records that the name Barnabas means "son of encouragement"; and in Acts 13:8 Elymas is translated "magician."

hermēneuō [ἑρμηνεύω, *2059*]

hermēneuō is a synonym for ***methermēneuō***, above, occurring four times with the primary sense of "translate." In John 1:38 the meaning "teacher" is given for the term "Rabbi," and Cephas is translated "Peter" in John 1:42. John 9:17 indicates that the name of the Pool of Siloam means "sent." And the mysterious figure of Melchizedek, mentioned in Heb. 7:2 (citing Gen. 14:18), is to be understood as the "king of righteousness."

diermēneuō [διερμηνεύω, *1329*]

diermēneuō is another synonym for ***methermēneuō*** and ***hermēneuō***, above, occurring six times. However, in addition to the meaning "translate," it has the expanded sense of "interpret," signifying "to expound, or explain."

In Luke 24:27, for example, Jesus interprets for his disciples all things concerning himself as the fulfillment of all that is in the Hebrew Scriptures. In Acts 9:38, the name Tabitha is translated "Dorcas." Then, in 1 Cor. 12:30; 14:5, 13, 27, ***diermēneuō*** refers to the "interpretation" of speaking in tongues.

hermēneia [ἑρμηνεία, *2058*]

hermēneia is a noun derived from ***hermēneuō*** (see above), and signifies "interpretation" of that which has been expressed or spoken by others. It only occurs twice, in 1 Cor. 12:10; 14:26, and on both occasions refers to interpreting words spoken in tongues.

epilysis [ἐπίλυσις, *1955*]

epilysis is only found in 2 Pet. 1:20, where it refers to an individual's interpretation (lit. "unraveling" or "unloosing") of prophecy. The point of the text is to deny that any prophecy of Scripture ever came about by a "private interpretation" (i.e., from the prophet himself). Rather, all prophecy originates from God, through the Spirit, who mediates that revelation through the human author.

Additional Notes

The phenomenon of interpretation in both Old and New Testaments is largely dependent on divine illumination or initiative. This is true whether it concerns the true meaning of dreams, for which understanding men like Joseph and Daniel were totally dependent on God, or whether it involves the understanding of tongues in the congregation at Corinth. Divine insight is also indispensable in the accurate application of Old Testament prophecy to the new covenant age.

INVISIBLE

NT Words

aoratos [ἀόρατος, *517*]

This adjectival form occurs five times and is translated "invisible" in each case. 1 Tim. 1:17; Heb. 11:27 refer to the invisible God. Rom. 1:20 declares that the invisible aspects or qualities of God's being have been made plain through creation. Concerning the person of Christ, Col. 1:15, 16 indicate that he is the revealed image of the invisible God, and in him all things visible and invisible were created by God through and for him.

INVITE

OT Words

qārā' [**קָרָא, 7121**]

qārā' is a common verb, found 730 times with the dominant sense of "call," "proclaim," or "cry (out)." In several contexts, however, it means "invite."

1 Sam. 9:13, 22, 24 refer to those who had been invited to a sacrificial feast immediately prior to Saul's anointing as king. And, in another context, Absalom invites all the sons of David, his father, to join him in a feast (cf. 2 Sam. 13:23). Similarly, Queen Esther invites Haman to a royal banquet in Esth. 5:12.

NT Words

kaleō [καλέω, *2564*]

kaleō is a term occurring around 150 times with the primary meaning "call." In one text, however, ***kaleō*** is translated "invite" as a particular application of the meaning "to call." In the parable of the marriage feast in Matt. 22:9, an invitation is given to all and sundry to come to the banquet.

phōneō [φωνέω, *5455*]

phōneō occurs around forty times and is usually translated "call (out)," or "crow" (i.e., of a cock). However, in Luke 14:12 it is translated "invite" in the negative context of not inviting someone to come to a feast.

antikaleō [ἀντικαλέω, *479*]

This term occurs only in Luke 14:12 and signifies "to offer an invitation" in return for receiving one, again in the context of a banquet.

IRON

OT Words

barzel [**בַּרְזֶל, 1270**]

barzel is the most common term for "iron" in the Old Testament, occurring around seventy times. General references to iron as a metal are found in Num. 31:22; Deut. 8:9; Josh. 22:8; Isa. 60:17; Ezek. 27:2. In more specific contexts, iron is designated as material for various implements such as tools (cf. Deut. 27:5; Josh. 8:31; 1 Kgs. 16:7; Isa. 10:34); weapons in general (cf. 1 Sam. 17:7; Amos 1:3); a murder weapon (cf. Num. 35:16); an ax head (cf. Deut. 19:5; 2 Kgs. 6:6); chariots of iron (cf. Josh. 17:16ff.; Judg. 1:19; 4:3); iron nails for the construction of the temple (cf. 1 Chr. 22:3; 29:2); and sacred vessels of iron (cf. Josh. 6:19, 24). Iron workers are mentioned in 2 Chr. 2:7; 24:12. Isa. 24:12 refers particularly to those workers in iron who manufacture idols.

The term ***barzel*** also has a significant metaphorical usage. It is found, for example, with reference to drought in the phrase "heavens like iron" in Lev. 26:19; Deut. 28:23. Jer. 1:18 refers to an "iron pillar" as a symbol for toughness in the face of adversity. The phrase "iron neck" in Isa. 48:4 suggests stubbornness. See also Jer. 6:28; Ezek. 22:18 for a similar usage in this regard. The phrase "iron furnace" symbolizes the terrible period of Israelite slavery in Egypt (cf. Jer. 11:4; 1 Kgs. 8:51; Deut. 4:20).

There are a number of contexts in which ***barzel*** is associated with the phenomenon of divine judgment (e.g., Ps. 2:9), where the phrase "rod of iron" is suggestive of such judgment. Deut. 28:48; Jer. 28:13, 14 refer to the "yoke of iron" that will be placed on the people of Israel as punishment for her rebellion against God. It indicates that Israel will be subjected to foreign domination and harassment. See also 1 Kgs. 22:11.

parzel [**פַּרְזֶל, 6523** (Aramaic)]

parzel is the Aramaic equivalent of the Hebrew term ***barzel*** (see above). It occurs twenty times and is found exclusively in the book of Daniel. Dan. 2:33ff. refers to the iron portion of the visionary statue in Nebuchadnezzar's dream. Dan. 4:15, 23 refer to the "band of iron" fastened around the stump of the tree in Nebuchadnezzar's second dream that foretold the imminent onset of the Babylonian ruler's insanity. "Gods of iron" are mentioned in Dan. 5:4, 23. And Dan. 7:7, 19 speak of the "iron teeth" of the unnamed fourth beast of Daniel's vision of successive world empires from Babylon to Rome.

NT Words

sidērous [**σιδηροῦς,** *4603*]

sidērous is an adjectival term that signifies "made of iron," or "iron." It occurs five times. Acts 12:10 refers literally to an "iron gate." Rev. 2:27; 12:5; 19:15 refer to the "rod of iron" as a symbol of divine power and authority. Rev. 9:9 mentions the "iron breastplates" of the visionary locusts, symbolizing the ravages of a divinely initiated plague against a godless humanity.

sidēros [**σίδηρος,** *4604*]

sidēros occurs only in Rev. 18:12, referring to implements of iron owned by merchants.

kaustēriazō [**καυστηριάζω,** *2743*]

kaustēriazō signifies "to sear with a hot iron" and is found only in 1 Tim. 4:2, where it is used metaphorically to refer to hardened liars whose consciences have been seared by their deceit.

ISLAND

OT Words

'î [**אִי, 339**]

'î is a noun referring to "islands" in approximately thirty different contexts. It is often a synonym for the Gentile nations.

"Islands" are referred to as the homes of various nations in Gen. 10:5; Esth. 10:1; Ps. 72:10; Isa. 20:6; Jer. 2:10; Ezek. 27:3; Dan. 11:18. Exhortations to the island peoples to rejoice at the kingship of Yahweh, the God of Israel, are found in Ps. 97:1; Isa. 24:15; 42:10, 12. Yahweh's sovereignty over the islands and nations of the world is indicated in Isa. 40:15; Zeph. 2:11. In a similar vein, Yahweh's judgment on the "islands" is explicitly declared in Isa. 59:18; Ezek. 39:6. And, in Ezek. 26:15, 18; 27:35, the "islands" tremble at the news of the punishment handed out to the nation of Tyre. These "islands" also await the just rule of the Messianic Servant in Isa. 42:4; and that of Yahweh in Isa. 51:5. Isa. 66:19 says that Yahweh is to have his glory declared to the "islands." And, finally, there is a promise of deliverance and restoration from exile in Isa. 11:11, where the remnant of the people of Yahweh are to be gathered from the "islands of the sea," mentioned alongside the nations that held Israel captive. See also Jer. 31:10.

NT Words

nēsos [**νῆσος,** *3520*]

nēsos occurs nine times and consistently indicates the meaning "island." Various islands are mentioned in conjunction with Paul's missionary journey (cf. Acts 13:6; 27:26; 28:1, 7, 9, 11). The apostle John's banishment to the island of Patmos is indicated in Rev. 1:9. In the context of apocalyptic divine judgment against a sinful world, Rev. 6:14; 16:20 refer to every island on earth being removed from its place.

nēsion [**νησίον,** *3519*]

nēsion is a diminutive of ***nēsos***, above, occurring only once, in Acts 27:16, and indicating a "small island."

ITCH

OT Words

neteq [**נֶתֶק, 5424**]

neteq refers to an infectious skin lesion or eruption usually associated with leprosy. It is translated "itch" in regard to the irritation produced by the disease. ***neteq*** occurs fourteen times. All of the references are found in Leviticus (cf. Lev. 13:30ff.; 14:54). The context described is one in which provisions are laid down for diagnosis of the disease and quarantine regulations, followed by ritual procedures to be adopted in order to declare a person free of infection, or "clean."

gārāb [**גָּרָב, 1618**]

gārāb occurs three times and refers to an itching disease characterized by festering sores (cf. Lev. 21:20, 22; Deut. 28:29).

NT Words

knēthō [κνήθω, *2833*]

knēthō is found only in 2 Tim. 4:3, where it refers to people having "itching ears." The term refers to those refusing to countenance sound teaching, only listening to what they want to hear.

IVORY

OT Words

shēn [שֵׁן, 8127]

shēn is found on more than fifty occasions and is translated for the most part "tooth," "teeth." However, in ten instances ***shēn*** refers to "ivory."

Raw ivory is mentioned in 1 Kgs. 10:22; Ezek. 27:15. The material is also mentioned in connection with the construction of a throne (cf. 1 Kgs. 10:18; 2 Chr. 9:17); of beds (cf. Amos 6:4); of houses (cf. 1 Kgs. 22:39; 2 Chr. 9:21; Amos 3:15); of palaces (cf. Ps. 45:8); and of boat fittings (cf. Ezek. 27:6, 15).

Metaphorically, "ivory" refers to the bodies of both the lover and the beloved in Song 5:14; 7:4.

NT Words

elephantinos [ἐλεφάντινος, *1661*]

elephantinos occurs only in Rev. 18:16, with reference to articles of ivory.

J

JAILER

NT Words

desmophylax [δεσμοφύλαξ, *1200*]

This term is rare, occurring only three times with the meaning "jailer" or "prison keeper" on each occasion. All occurrences are found in Acts 16, with reference to the jailer of Paul and Silas in Philippi (Acts 16:23, 27, 36).

See Also: ➡ GUARD

JAR

OT Words

nēbel [נֶבֶל, **5035**]

This noun occurs around forty times and refers to a container, including the translations "pitcher," "bottle," "skin," and "jar" in about half of these contexts.

References to bottles (lit "skins") of wine are found in 1 Sam. 1:24; 10:3; 25:18; 2 Sam. 18:1. Metaphorically, rain is indicated as the "water jars of the heavens" in Job 38:27.

General references to jars or containers are found, for example, in Isa. 22:24 (liquids, drinks); Isa. 30:14. Judgment on Moab is indicated when it is declared that all their jars will be broken (Jer. 48:12).

baqbûk [בַּקְבּוּק, **1228**]

This term is found only three times and refers to a "jar," "bottle," or "flask." 1 Kgs. 14:3 refers to a jar of honey. In Jer. 19:1, 10, the prophet is commanded to buy a pottery jar and then smash it as a symbol of God's impending judgment on Jerusalem.

kad [כַּד, **3537**]

kad refers to a large portable jar, or pitcher. The term is found eighteen times.

Water jars are mentioned in Gen. 24:14ff., 43ff.; 1 Kgs. 18:33; Eccl. 12:6. Food storage jars are indicated in 1 Kgs. 17:12ff. Judg. 7:16ff. mentions jars in a nonspecific sense.

ṣappaḥat [צַפַּחַת, **6835**]

ṣappaḥat occurs seven times and refers on each occasion to a receptacle or jar for storing water (cf. 1 Sam. 26:11ff.) or oil (cf. 1 Kgs. 17:12).

NT Words

keramion [κεράμιον, *2765*]

keramion is rare in the New Testament, occurring only twice. In both instances the term indicates a jar or pitcher of water (cf. Mark 14:13; Luke 12:10).

hydria [ὑδρία, *5201*]

hydria is likewise a rare form, found only three times in John 2:6, 7; 4:28 — all with reference to large stone water jars.

JASPER

OT Words

yāshphēr [יָשְׁפֵה, **3471**]

yāshphēr refers to the precious stone jasper. It is mentioned twice in Exodus in the context of the twelve precious gems mounted on the high priestly ephod, representing each of the twelve tribes of Israel (cf. Exod. 28:20; 39:13). The term is also found in Ezek. 28:13 in reference to the metaphorical covering of the primeval spirit of the king of Tyre with precious stones in the garden of Eden. The allusion here is difficult to identify, but it may well be a symbolic description of the guardian cherub, who was created perfect but fell victim to pride and blasphemy and was cast down to the earth from the heavenly mount of God.

NT Words

iaspis [ἴασπις, *2393*]

iaspis occurs four times, and only in the book of Revelation. Rev. 4:3 likens the appearance of the divine figure on the heavenly throne to jasper; while Rev. 21:11, 18, 19 liken the appearance of the heavenly city of Jerusalem to that of jasper and other precious metals and stones.

JEALOUS, JEALOUSY

OT Words

qannā' [קַנָּא, **7067**]

qannā' is the adjectival form derived from the verbal root ***qānā'*** (see below), and is translated "jealous" in each of the six contexts in which it is found. The term refers only to God as being jealous, indicating the divine determination to tolerate from his people no respect for, or worship of, any other deity besides himself. ***qannā'*** signifies the fierce determination of God to tolerate no rival whatsoever. Thus every single occurrence of this term is found in the context of a prohibition against idol worship (cf. Exod. 20:5; 34:14 [twice]; Deut. 4:24; 5:9; 6:15).

qānā' [קָנָא, 7065]

This verb is found in approximately thirty contexts with the primary sense of "be jealous," "envy," or "provoke to envy, jealousy." ***qānā'*** predicates jealousy of both human beings and God.

With regard to the human emotion of jealousy, ***qānā'*** occurs in a variety of contexts. Concerning other people, ***qānā'*** indicates being jealous of someone else's wealth or property (e.g., Gen. 26:14; Ps. 73:3); of their status (e.g., Isa. 11:13); of other women bearing children (e.g., Gen. 30:1); and of others' gifts and abilities (e.g., Gen. 37:11). Being jealous of one's wife, or suspecting her of adultery, is also evident in Num. 5:14, 30. In the wisdom writings, the command is issued not to be jealous of evildoers (e.g., Ps. 37:1; Prov. 3:31; 23:17). While the preceding texts convey a negative aspect to jealousy, there is a positive emphasis evident elsewhere. For instance, Num. 25:11, 13; 1 Kgs. 19:10, 14 refer to jealousy for the honor of Yahweh, in which Phinehas and Elijah both execute enemies of Yahweh motivated by jealousy (or zeal) for his name. The two men are commended for their actions.

qānā' is also used to describe the jealousy of God. For example, God is provoked to jealousy by his idolatrous people in Deut. 32:16, 21; 1 Kgs. 14:22; Ps. 78:58. Yahweh expresses jealousy for his holy name in Ezek. 39:25, and also for his own land. This latter reaction results in his extending mercy to his people (cf. Joel 2:18; Zech. 1:14; 8:2).

In addition there is one metaphorical, allegorical usage of ***qānā'*** in Ezek. 31:9, in which the trees of Eden are envious of the great cedar in Lebanon.

qin'āh [קִנְאָה, 7068]

qin'āh is the principal noun form derived from ***qānā'*** (see above), occurring around forty times. The meanings for ***qin'āh*** are essentially the same — jealousy, or zeal — which are predicated of both human beings and God in a number of contexts.

In regard to jealousy as it affects other people, Num. 5:14, 30 refer to a husband's jealousy of his wife, suspecting her of infidelity. In addition, Num. 5:15, 18, 25 refer to the "offering of jealousy," associated with the husband's suspicion, that occasions the ritual trial for adultery described in this chapter. ***qin'āh*** indicates jealousy of one's neighbor (Eccl. 4:4); and Edom's envy of Judah (Ezek. 35:11, cf. also Isa. 11:13). Prov. 6:34 affirms that jealousy makes people furious. The destructive effect of jealousy on the human soul is alluded to in Eccl. 9:6; Job 5:2; Prov. 14:30.

As with the verb form ***qānā'***, ***qin'āh*** also refers to people's zeal for the honor of Yahweh that motivates them to take extreme measures. The example of Phinehas in Num. 25:11 has already been mentioned (see ***qānā'***, above); but note also Jehu's eradication of the remainder of Ahab's dynasty in 2 Kgs. 10:16ff. as an outworking of his jealousy for the honor of Yahweh. A similar attitude towards the temple in Jerusalem is expressed in Ps. 69:9.

With regard to the expression of divine jealousy, God's emotion here is often linked with anger, particularly in regard to those who commit idolatry (e.g., Deut. 29:20; Ps. 79:5). In Ezek. 8:3, the idolatrous cult associated with the Jerusalem temple provokes Yahweh to jealous wrath against the people of the city and Judea, leading to the destruction of both city and temple and their deportation at the hands of the Babylonian army. Another significant text in this regard is Ezek. 16:38, 42, where there is a metaphorical and allegorical representation of Yahweh as the betrayed "husband" of Israel who has cheated on him through her adultery, or her idolatrous attraction to other gods. Such treatment brings down upon Israel the wrath of her "husband," God (cf. also Ezek. 23:25).

Another aspect of Yahweh's jealousy towards his people results in anger and judgment against the nations who have mistreated them (cf. Ezek. 36:6; 38:19; Zeph. 1:8; 3:8; Zech. 1:14; 8:2).

qannô' [קַנּוֹא, 7072]

qannô' is a rare adjectival variant of ***qannā'*** (see above) occurring only twice, in Josh. 24:19; Nah. 1:2. On both occasions this term refers to the divine trait of jealousy, whereby Yahweh tolerates no challenge or rival to his person, nor any neglect of his precepts.

NT Words

parazēloō [παραζηλόω, *3863*]

parazēloō occurs four times and is translated "provoke to jealousy" on each occasion. In Rom. 10:19, Paul cites the text of Deut. 32:21, where Yahweh issues the threat that he will make his people jealous of a pagan people far less significant than they. The context is one of covenant curse invoked against Israel. Similarly,

Rom. 11:11, 14 state that as a result of Israel's sins, salvation has come to the Gentiles, with the consequence that Israel is provoked to jealousy against them. 1 Cor. 10:22 alludes to the familiar theme of God being driven to jealousy as a result of idolatrous attitudes and actions on the part of his people.

zēlos [ζῆλος, *2205*]

zēlos occurs nine times and means both "zeal" and "envy" or "jealousy." In John 2:17 the two senses overlap, where Jesus' anger boils over at the moneychangers in the temple, reminding his disciples of Ps. 69:9 — "Zeal for your house will consume me."

The remaining usage of ***zēlos*** focuses on jealousy among human beings — for example, Acts 13:45 records the envy of the Jews against Paul and Barnabas. In Rom. 13:13 there is an exhortation to refrain from the expression of jealousy and other vices. Jealousy is also indicated as one of the besetting sins of the Corinthian congregation (cf. 1 Cor. 3:3; 2 Cor. 12:20). See also Gal. 5:20; Jas. 3:14, 16. In a positive sense, Paul expresses his jealousy for the well-being of the Corinthian congregation whom he had established in their faith (cf. 2 Cor. 11:2).

zēloō [ζηλόω, *2206*]

zēloō is the verb form from which ***zēlos*** (see above) is derived. ***zēloō*** occurs twelve times and is translated "to be jealous" in five of these contexts. This term also has the sense of "be zealous." (→ ZEAL)

Concerning the human action depicted in the use of this term, Acts 7:9 refers to the jealousy of Joseph's brothers towards their precocious younger sibling (cited from Gen. 39ff.). Acts 17:5 records the jealousy of the Thessalonian Jews towards Paul's success in convincing Jewish people that Jesus was the Messiah. 1 Cor. 13:4 declares that genuine love is wholly devoid of any jealousy. Jas. 4:2 declares that coveting is a vice to be avoided — here the idea of coveting overlaps with the sense of being jealous.

Additional Notes

The attitudes and actions of jealousy have both positive and negative connotations. When predicated of Yahweh in the Old Testament, this trait focuses on God's determination to tolerate no rival for worship in the form of pagan deities. Failure to be exclusively devoted to Yahweh triggers an inevitable reaction of divine wrath. The central concept lying behind this phenomenon is that of sovereign divine uniqueness and exclusivity.

This same idea assumes a positive sense when the expression of jealousy is directed by Yahweh toward his people. In this context, Yahweh's "jealousy" serves to guarantee his people's ultimate deliverance and security, notwithstanding the harsh divine discipline they had to endure from time to time.

This dual aspect of divine jealousy is also mirrored to a certain extent in the human emotion. When motivated by a concern for oneself, human jealousy is a negative trait that brings much suffering and emotional trauma. However, a positive aspect to the emotion can emerge when jealousy is motivated by a concern for others, such as the apostle Paul's jealous devotion to the Christian congregations he was privileged to found by divine enabling. Such jealousy leads one to devote a great deal of effort to preserve and safeguard the object of affection.

The one significant difference between human and divine jealousy is that the latter trait never impacts negatively on the person of God. God's moral perfection guarantees a perfectly wholesome and just expression of jealousy. In effect, it is an ardent zeal for maintaining the integrity of his person in the face of created humanity in general, and of his people in particular.

JESTING → LAUGH

JESUS

NT Words

Iēsous [Ἰησοῦς, *2424*]

Iēsous is the Greek equivalent of the Hebrew term ***yeshû'āh***, which means "(God is) salvation." (→ SALVATION) The name Jesus occurs almost one thousand times in the New Testament and refers almost exclusively to Christ, the Son of God. The angel of the Lord revealed this name directly to his mother Mary (cf. Matt. 1:21).

The name ***Iēsous Christos*** or "Jesus Christ" (→ CHRIST) occurs around two hundred times and is found in a number of settings, such as in the genealogical listings of his Davidic ancestry (cf. Matt. 1:1); in significant events of his earthly life including his birth (cf. Matt. 1:18); and as a formal introduction to his person at the beginning of the majority of New Testament books outside the gospels.

In other contexts, the name ***Iēsous Christos*** is associated with his person and work. For example, John 1:17 describes Jesus Christ as the source of grace and truth. See also Rom. 5:15, 17, 21; 6:23; Gal. 2:16; Phil.

1:11. References to Jesus' divine authority and power are found in relation to forgiveness (Acts 2:38); and in association with his miracles (Acts 3:6; 4:10; 16:18). Rom. 6:11 declares Jesus Christ to be the sole means of gaining a personal relationship with God. He is the Lord of the universe (Phil. 3:20) and the Lord of glory (Jas. 2:1). The goal of sanctification and its realization in the lives of believers are bound up with the person of Jesus Christ. He is also declared, for example, to be co-creator with God (1 Cor. 8:6); the founder of our faith (1 Cor. 3:11; Eph. 2:20); the one who rose from the dead (2 Tim. 2:8; 1 Pet. 1:3; 3:21); our great high priest (1 Pet. 2:5); the ruler of the heavenly kingdom (2 Pet. 1:11); the full incarnation of God in human form (1 John 4:2; 2 John 7); the one whose blood cleanses his people from all their sin (1 John 1:7). The above list is by no means exhaustive.

Use of the name ***Iēsous*** by itself, especially in the gospels, usually designates the activity and actions of our Lord during his earthly life. The name "Jesus" occurs approximately six hundred times in the four gospels. Other New Testament occurrences of "Jesus" refer to aspects of his person and work. For example, Acts 1:11 affirms that the risen Jesus will return to earth in the same way he left to ascend into heaven. "Jesus" is the authoritative name under heaven before whom all people will one day bow (cf. Phil. 2:10). Jesus is declared to be the Savior of the world (Acts 13:23; 1 Thess. 1:10); and a man attested by God with mighty works and signs (Acts 2:22; 10:38). He is also said to be the Christ (Acts 5:42; 17:33; 18:28); the crucified Christ (Acts 2:36); the risen Christ in heaven (Acts 7:55).

References to Jesus as Lord are found in Acts 19:13; 20:21; Rom. 4:24; 1 Thess. 4:1. Jesus is also identified as our high priest (Heb. 4:14; 6:20); as the guarantor of a better covenant (Heb. 7:22); as the mediator of the new covenant (Heb. 12:24); and as the pioneer and perfecter of our faith (Heb. 12:2). These references form an extensive, though not exhaustive, listing of the name of "Jesus" in the New Testament.

See Also: → SALVATION

JEW

OT Words

yehûdî **[יְהוּדִי, 3064]**

yehûdî is derived patronymically from the term *yehûdāh* (i.e., Judah) and is translated "Jew" or more precisely "man from, or inhabitant of Judah." The term occurs around eighty times, and is used only from the exilic period onward. Previously, the inhabitants of Judah were referred to generally as "Israelites" or "sons of Israel."

Mundane usage of the term in a narrative context is found, for example, in 2 Kgs. 16:6; 25:25; Neh. 1:2; Esth. 3:10; 4:3ff.; 8:1ff.; 9:1ff.; Jer. 32:12; 52:28ff. In the prophetic context of Zech. 8:23, it is recorded that people will be drawn to the faith of the Jewish people, and Gentiles will take hold of the robe of a Jew, wishing to accompany him in worship of Yahweh.

NT Words

Ioudaios **[Ἰουδαῖος, *2453*]**

Ioudaios refers to a Jew, a person belonging to the Jewish race. The term occurs around two hundred times.

Mundane usage in narrative description is found in Matt. 28:15; Mark 7:3; Luke 7:3; John 3:1. The magi in Matt. 2:2 refer to Jesus as "King of the Jews"; the same title is used in Jesus' trial before Pontius Pilate (cf. Matt. 27:11; Mark 15:2ff.; Luke 23:3; John 18:33). The crowd mocks Jesus with this title (Matt. 27:29); and a sign with this ascription is placed on the cross above Jesus' head (cf. Matt. 27:37; Mark 15:26; Luke 23:38; John 19:19ff.). During the earthly ministry of Jesus, Jewish people were often hostile towards him (cf. John 2:18; 5:16ff.; 6:41; 7:1; 10:31ff.; 19:7). John 4:9 mentions the Jews' hatred of Samaritans.

Jewish opposition to the missionary enterprise of the apostle Paul is frequently alluded to in the book of Acts (cf. Acts 9:23; 13:45; 14:19; 20:3; 21:27; 23:12; 25:7). The early Christians were likewise despised by the Jewish community on the whole (cf. Acts 14:2; 17:1). Ironically, the Jewish people were initially the sole targets, or recipients, of Paul's gospel preaching (cf. Acts 11:19; 13:5; 17:7). According to Paul, genuine "Jewishness" requires the process of "heart circumcision" to take place — that is, renewal of one's heart attitude to God as revealed in the person of Christ (cf. Rom. 2:29). Rom. 10:12; Gal. 3:28 make it clear that there is no distinction between Jew and Gentile believers in the sight of God, who accepts all who call upon him in genuine faith, Jew and Gentile alike.

JEWEL, JEWELRY

OT Words

kelî **[כְּלִי, 3627]**

kelî is a term with a somewhat generalized semantic range throughout most of its three hundred occurrences. The word conveys the general idea of a utensil, implement, or tool. It also refers to nondescript items such as "things." However, on about twenty occasions, ***kelî*** refers to jewelry or jewels.

There are a number of texts in which ***kelî*** refers to precious metals such as gold or silver (cf. Gen. 24:53; Exod. 35:22; Num. 31:50ff.; Ezek. 16:17, 39). In particular, Exod. 3:22, 11:2, 12:35 refer to the precious stones taken as "plunder" from the Egyptians when the Israelites escaped from their enslavement in Egypt.

Jewelry is mentioned in a non-specific sense in 2 Chr. 20:25; Prov. 20:15; Song 1:10; Isa. 61:10; Ezek. 23:26.

ḥalî [חֲלִי, 2481]

ḥalî is a rare term, found only in Prov. 25:12; Song 7:1 with reference to ornamentation or jewelry in a general sense.

ḥelyāh [חֶלְיָה, 2484]

ḥelyāh is a term derived from ***ḥalî*** (see above) and occurs only in Hos. 2:13, in a metaphorical reference to Israel's "jewelry" worn as a means of making herself attractive to her lovers, or her idols.

JOIN

OT Words

ḥābar [חָבַר, 2266]

ḥābar is a verb that conveys the ideas of "join," "join together," "unite," as well as associated senses. ***ḥābar*** occurs around twenty times.

The phenomenon of people joining together is illustrated in Gen. 14:3, which speaks of a local Canaanite militia combining forces against an enemy. Similarly, ***ḥābar*** also indicates people joining together in a political alliance (cf. 2 Chr. 20:35ff.; Ps. 94:20; Dan. 11:6, 23).

ḥābar also describes sewing together materials such as curtains in the context of the tabernacle furnishings (cf. Exod. 26:3ff.; 36:10ff.).

ḥābar is also found in Eccl. 9:4, meaning "join with," or to be in the same company. Here hope is offered to the one who is joined with the living. In a negative sense, ***ḥābar*** is found in Hos. 4:17 to describe Israel being joined together with idols.

lāwāh [לָוָה, 3867]

lāwāh occurs twenty-five times, and in about half of these contexts means "join," "be joined to," "join oneself to" in a number of different contexts.

(→ LEND)

In a spiritual, emotional sense, ***lāwāh*** conveys the idea in Gen. 29:34 of being joined to one's spouse, referring to Leah's claim on her husband Jacob after bearing him three sons.

lāwāh also indicates the people of God joining together to worship Yahweh in a ritual setting (cf. Num. 18:2ff.; Isa. 14:1; 56:3, 6). Jer. 50:5; Zech. 2:11 speak of the Israelite people joining themselves to Yahweh through a solemn covenant oath. Esth. 9:27 refers to the Jewish people in exile, joining together to commemorate their victory over the Persian attempt to annihilate them, in the inaugural celebration of the Purim festival. Ps. 83:8 speaks of a military coalition of pagan nations.

ṣāmad [צָמַד, 6775]

ṣāmad is found five times, and on three of these occasions means "to join, bind oneself to" in the sense of intimately identifying with idolatrous worship. Num. 25:3, 5; Ps. 106:28 speak of the Israelite idolatry with the Baal of Peor, for which crime Yahweh invoked a terrible plague judgment on his people.

dābaq [דָּבַק, 1692]

dābaq occurs around fifty times and conveys the primary sense of "cling to," "cleave" in about half of these contexts. This is a meaning closely related to the sense of "join together."

The idea of "cleaving" to one's partner in marriage embraces the phenomenon of being joined together in intimacy, as indicated in Gen. 2:24, where God inaugurates marriage between Adam and Eve. In a negative context, Josh. 23:12 communicates Yahweh's stern warning to his people against "cleaving" in marriage to the Canaanite peoples around them.

dābaq also describes the phenomenon of "cleaving" or intimate bonding in the context of Israel's covenant relationship with Yahweh. In a number of places the people of God are "joined together" with him in an attitude of worship, obedience, and service (cf. Deut. 10:20; 11:22; 13:4; 30:20; Josh. 22:5; 23:8).

In a literal physical sense, ***dābaq*** signifies the fastening or joining together of the dorsal plates and fleshy hide of the ridges of the "Leviathan" creature in Job 41:17, 23.

yāḥad [יָחַד, 3161]

A rare verb form, ***yāḥad*** occurs only three times, meaning "join," "unite." Gen. 49:6 speaks of "joining together" in the sense of an association with people. Ps.

86:11 contains a plea for God to keep the psalmist's heart "joined together," that is, undivided, in its devotion to the name of Yahweh. Isa. 14:20 reflects a negative context of judgment whereby the king of Babylon is denied funeral rites along with other heads of state: "You will not join them in burial . . ."

NT Words

syzeugnymi [συζεύγνυμι, *4801*]

syzeugnymi is only found twice, and in both of these texts refers to the process of being joined together in marriage — a lifelong bond that may not be broken (cf. Matt. 19:6; Mark 10:9).

kollaō [κολλάω, *2853*]

kollaō occurs eleven times and means "join together with" in over half of these contexts.

In the context of employment in Luke 15:15, the prodigal son "joins himself to" the owner of a swineherd in order to obtain work feeding the pigs and so avoid starvation.

kollaō is also used in the context of worship. 1 Cor. 6:17 mentions a spiritual union with God, being joined to him. Acts 5:13 records that no one initially dared to "join together with" the early Christians in worship, out of fear at the signs performed by the apostles. Then Acts 9:26 explains that Paul's attempt to "join together with" the disciples in Jerusalem was thwarted at first, on account of their fear of him. Acts 17:4 speaks of Jewish converts in Thessalonica who "joined together with" Paul and Silas in fellowship.

In another quite different context, 1 Cor. 6:16 spells out the sobering consequences of "joining oneself together with" a prostitute in becoming one in body with her.

proskollaō *[προσκολλάω, 4347]*

proskollaō occurs only three times, and on each occasion refers to the institution of marriage in which a man leaves his father and mother and is joined to his wife. The idea here is one of intimate union (cf. Matt. 19:5; Mark 10:7; Eph. 5:31).

synarmologeō [συναρμολογέω, *4883*]

This is a rare term, occurring only twice and meaning "to be joined together." The underlying sense is that of a perfect fit. Eph. 2:21 speaks metaphorically of the new covenant community of God's people as a building whose cornerstone is Jesus Christ. It is this "building" that is perfectly built, or "joined together," as an appropriate symbolic expression for the perfection of the church. Similarly, ***synarmologeō*** also describes the body image of the church in Eph. 4:16, referring to Christ as the one from whom the whole body is (perfectly) joined together.

Additional Notes

Both Hebrew and Greek terminology for "join" indicate the phenomenon of intimate bonding in several key contexts. It is the "joining together" of man and wife in marriage that constitutes such a powerful symbol for the joining together of Yahweh and his people in solemn covenant relationship. Marriage is a truly apt metaphor for the symbolic union of Yahweh and Israel. Just as the crime of marital unfaithfulness is so damaging to the marital bond, so is Israel's idolatrous worship of foreign deities to the covenant relationship with her God, her spiritual husband. A renewed relationship with God is spoken of frequently in terms of a new marital relationship between Yahweh and Israel. This solemn metaphor of covenant intimacy is taken over into the New Testament where the people of God, the new covenant church community, are likewise portrayed as being in spiritual union with Christ — joined together with him by the grace of God through the instrument of faith. This phenomenon has very powerful implications for both the old and new covenant communities of believers.

JOINT

OT Words

yāqa' [יָקַע, **3363**]

yāqa' is a verb occurring eight times, with the primary meaning "to hang." In Gen. 32:25, however, ***yāqa'*** means "out of joint" in reference to the angelic opponent of Jacob immobilizing the hip joint of the patriarch at the river Jabbok.

debeq [דֶּבֶק, **1694**]

debeq is a rare term, found only three times. In two of these contexts, ***debeq*** refers to the open joint of a breastplate in a soldier's armor (cf. 1 Kgs. 22:34; 2 Chr. 18:33). In Isa. 41:7, ***debeq*** refers to solder associated with metal sculpture — in this case, of an idol.

pārad [פָּרַד, **6504**]

This verb occurs around twenty-five times and is consistently translated "separate," "divide." However, in Ps. 22:14, ***pārad*** is rendered "out of joint," referring to the bones of the psalmist, who is in great distress. This passage anticipates the suffering of the Messiah. (→ SEPARATE)

ḥammûq [חַמּוּק, 2542]

ḥammûq occurs only in Song 7:1, where it refers to the curved thighs of the young woman, the newlywedded wife of her husband who is adoring her physical beauty. "Joint" in this context refers to the upper leg or thigh.

NT Words

synklēronomos [συγκληρονόμος, *4789*]

synklēronomos refers to a "joint heir" or "fellow heir." It occurs only four times. Rom. 8:17 speaks of believers as "joint heirs" with Christ, as does Eph. 3:6, with particular reference to Gentile converts. Heb. 11:9 cites Isaac and Jacob as "fellow heirs" of the covenant promise given to their father and grandfather Abraham.

haphē [ἁφή, *860*]

haphē occurs only in Eph. 4:16; Col. 2:19, referring to physical joints of the human body. The context of each occurrence, however, is metaphorical, for in both Ephesians and Colossians, Paul uses the metaphor of the human body to illustrate the ideal harmony of believers in union with Christ as "members" of his body, the church.

harmos [ἁρμός, *719*]

harmos is found only in Heb. 4:12, referring, as does ***haphē***, above, to the joints of the human body. In this context, ***harmos*** is used metaphorically to indicate the impact of the word of God on the human heart as that which penetrates to the "joints and marrow," to the very depths, of the soul.

JOT

NT Words

iōta [ἰῶτα, *2503*]

iōta occurs only in Matt. 5:18. It refers to the tenth letter of the Hebrew alphabet — the *yod*, which is the smallest Hebrew character. Jesus affirms here that not one "jot" will disappear from the law until all is fulfilled in him.

JOURNEY

OT Words

derek [דֶּרֶךְ, 1870]

This is a common noun throughout the Old Testament, found nearly seven hundred times with the predominant meaning "way," "road," or "path." However, in around twenty contexts, ***derek*** is translated "journey," assuming the common sense of travel in a narrative context (e.g., Gen. 24:21; Exod. 8:27; Num. 11:3; Deut. 1:2; Josh. 9:13; Judg. 4:9). (→ WAY)

nāsa' [נָסַע, 5265]

nāsa' is a verb that occurs around 150 times and has the dominant sense of "set out on a journey."

The meaning "journey" in the sense of "migrate" is indicated in Gen. 11:2. The common meaning "journey" in the sense of "travel" is found in Gen. 12:9; 13:11; 35:5; Judg. 9:17. Gen. 33:12 refers to the intention to travel.

There are a number of passages in which ***nāsa'*** indicates the process of journeying or traveling undertaken by the Israelite people at the express intention and initiative of Yahweh. Specifically, these texts all relate to the period of deliverance from Egypt where the Israelite people travel out from Egypt and journey through the wilderness before arriving at Shittim, east of the Jordan, ready to cross the river and enter the land of promise (cf. Exod. 12:37; 40:37; Num. 9:17ff.; 21:10ff.; Deut. 1:7, 9, 40; 2:1, 24; Josh. 3:1).

massa' [מַסַּע, 4550]

massa' is the noun form derived from ***nāsa'*** (see above) and occurs twelve times, meaning "journey" in most of these contexts.

"Journey" in the common sense is indicated in Gen. 13:3. The journeying of the Israelites in the wilderness by divine command and guidance is cited in Exod. 17:1; 40:36, 38; Deut. 10:11; Num. 10:2, 6, 12; 33:1, 2.

mahalak [מַהֲלָךְ, 4109]

mahalak is a rare noun from the verb ***hālak***, meaning "to go, walk." (→ WALK) It occurs only four times and means "journey," or "walk," on each occasion — Neh. 2:6 (indicating lengthy travel from Persia to Jerusalem); Ezek. 42:4; Jonah 3:3, 4.

NT Words

hodos [ὁδός, *3598*]

hodos occurs around one hundred times and is commonly translated "way" in the sense of "road," "path," or "route." On five occasions, however, the term is translated "journey." In Matt. 10:10; Mark 6:8; Luke 9:3; 11:6 the ordinary sense of travel is indicated. Luke 2:44; Acts 1:12 refer to a short journey of a day's travel.

apodēmeō [ἀποδημέω, *589*]

apodēmeō is found on six occasions and signifies the action of traveling on a journey abroad. All occurrences are found in the parables of Jesus (cf. Matt. 21:33; 25:14, 15; Mark 1:21; Luke 15:13; 20:9).

apodēmos [ἀπόδημος, *590*]

This is the noun derived from ***apodēmeō*** (see above) and occurs only once, in Mark 13:34, again referring to a journey abroad.

hodoiporeō [ὁδοιπορέω, *3596*]

Occurring only once, ***hodoiporeō*** refers to a literal journey in Acts 10:9.

poreuomai [πορεύομαι, *4198*]

poreuomai is a common verb that normally means "go," "walk," or "come" in about 150 contexts. In one text, however, it indicates the specific action of taking a journey. Acts 9:3 speaks of Saul taking his fateful journey to Damascus, during which he was miraculously converted.

diaporeuomai [διαπορεύομαι, *1279*]

diaporeuomai is a rare variant of ***poreuomai***, above, and is found only five times, meaning "to pass, go through" in all but one of these contexts. In Rom. 15:24, a participial form of this verb refers to Paul's anticipated journey to Spain.

propempō [προπέμπω, *4311*]

This verb form occurs nine times and has the primary sense of "to send, or bring forward on a journey." The contexts are all literal, and all except one relate to the travels of the apostle Paul (cf. Acts 15:3; 20:38; 21:5; Rom. 15:24; 1 Cor. 16:6, 11; 2 Cor. 1:16; Titus 3:13; 3 John 6).

JOY, JOYFUL

OT Words

sāmaḥ [**שָׂמַח, 8055**]

sāmaḥ occurs around 150 times with the primary meanings "to be glad," "rejoice," with a number of associated forms in a variety of contexts which refer overwhelmingly to the human response of rejoicing.

sāmaḥ indicates first of all the emotion of rejoicing in the general sense of feeling good (cf. Prov. 13:9; Eccl. 10:19). The term also signifies rejoicing with the idea of being satisfied or content with someone (cf. Judg. 9:19; Prov. 10:1; Eccl. 3:20); and causing others to be glad (cf. Deut. 24:5). ***sāmaḥ*** also describes being glad in one's heart towards other people (cf. Exod. 4:14; Prov. 15:20; Song 1:4).

In a number of contexts ***sāmaḥ*** conveys the attitude of rejoicing in Yahweh for who he is and what he has done. For example, Lev. 23:40; Deut. 12:7; 27:7 speak of rejoicing in the divine provision of wealth. Ps. 118:24 records the psalmist's joy at God's creation, and in Ps. 19:8 he rejoices at the provision of the law of the Lord. See also 1 Kgs. 5:7; Ezra 6:22; Neh. 12:43.

Rejoicing in Yahweh's salvation and acts of deliverance is commonly attested by the use of ***sāmaḥ*** — for example, joy at the slaying of Goliath (1 Sam. 19:5); joy in the anticipation of a victorious Messianic King (Isa. 9:3); and joy at victory over the enemies of God's people (2 Chr. 20:27). General references to joy in Yahweh's salvation are found in 1 Sam. 2:1; Pss. 14:7; 53:6; Isa. 25:9; Joel 2:21, 23; Zech. 2:10.

sāmaḥ also indicates the mood of rejoicing in the person of God and his attributes, particularly in the context of worship (cf. 1 Chr. 16:10, 31; 2 Chr. 29:36; Pss. 5:11; 33:21; 119:74; 149:2).

Other examples of the uses of ***sāmaḥ*** include Ezek. 25:6; 35:14; Obad 12, where the malevolent glee of pagan nations brings down divine wrath upon them. Yahweh also warns his people not to rejoice in the face of divine judgment (cf. Ezek. 7:12; Hos. 9:1).

The one instance where ***sāmaḥ*** indicates a divine response is negative — Isa. 9:17 declares that God does not rejoice over a sinful people.

sāmēaḥ [**שָׂמֵחַ, 8056**]

sāmēaḥ, derived from ***sāmaḥ***, above, is an adjectival form occurring around twenty times with the meanings "joyful," "glad," "merry," all referring to human response.

The emotion of joy as "gladness of heart" in a general sense is recorded in 1 Kgs. 1:40; 2 Chr. 3:13; Ps. 113:9; Prov. 15:13; Isa. 24:7. Deut. 16:15 indicates joy as a response to God's provision. Other texts refer to a joyful response to the goodness of God (1 Kgs. 8:66; 2 Chr. 7:10; Ps. 126:3). Eccl. 2:10 speaks of having joy or pleasure in one's work. Prov. 2:14 cites the perverseness of being joyful in wrongdoing.

simḥāh [**שִׂמְחָה, 8057**]

simḥāh is the noun derived from ***sāmaḥ*** (see above), occurring around one hundred times and consistently translated "joy" or "gladness."

Joy in the general sense of "gladness of heart" is indicated in Gen. 31:27; 1 Kgs. 1:40; Prov. 10:28; Eccl. 2:1ff.; Song 3:11ff.

Most occurrences of ***simḥāh*** signify joy at several aspects of God's person and work. Firstly, joy in worship of Yahweh is indicated, for example, in 1 Chr. 15:16; 2 Chr. 23:18; Neh. 8:12; Isa. 29:19; Jer. 33:11. The psalmist also expresses his joy in the Lord (cf. Pss. 4:7; 30:11; 43:4; 63:8; 100:2). See also Deut. 28:47.

simḥāh refers to the gladness expressed at the Lord's provision in the context of ritual festivals — for example, in Num. 10:10; 1 Chr. 29:22 (Solomon's enthronement); Ezra 3:12ff. (the rebuilt temple); and Neh. 12:27 (the rebuilt wall of Jerusalem). 1 Sam. 18:6; Esth. 8:16ff.; 9:19ff. refer to rejoicing at God's victory over the enemies of his people. Likewise, delight over his salvation is expressed in Isa. 35:10; 55:12; 61:7; Jer. 31:7, with particular reference to the people's return to the land. There is one example of "ill-fated" joy expressed by the Philistines at the supposed victory of Dagon over Samson in Judg. 16:23.

In a negative context, Yahweh removes joy and gladness from his people as a judgment against them (cf. Isa. 16:10; Jer. 7:34; 16:19; 25:10). That punishment is extended to the peoples of the earth in Isa. 24:11; Jer. 48:33. In another context, Edom's joy at Israel's destruction will earn God's wrath (cf. Ezek. 35:15; 36:5).

Again, the divine response of joy is limited to just one passage, Zeph. 3:17, where Yahweh rejoices over his people as their victorious warrior king.

rānan [רָנַן, 7442]

rānan occurs around fifty times and means "sing, or shout for joy" in the majority of contexts in which it is found. It also simply means "rejoice" in several places.

Most occurrences of ***rānan*** indicate the expression of joy in response to Yahweh and what he has done. There is, for example, rejoicing in God for delivering his people from their enemies (cf. Deut. 32:43; Jer. 51:48; Zeph. 3:14); and for bringing justice on earth (cf. 1 Chr. 16:33; Ps. 67:4). Shouting and singing for joy is recorded as a response of praise to Yahweh in worship (cf. Pss. 98:4; 132:16; Isa. 65:14); and in particular as a response of gratitude for his salvation (cf. Pss. 20:5; 51:14; 95:1; Isa. 26:19). This response comes from the surrounding nations as well as from the people of God (cf. Isa. 24:14; 42:11).

rinnāh [רִנָּה, 7440]

rinnāh is a noun derived from ***rānan*** (see above), occurring in about thirty contexts. The term has the sense of "a shout," "a cry," or "singing." In about half of these instance, ***rinnāh*** signifies a shout of joy.

Shouts of joy, reflecting a general gladness of heart, are recorded in Ps. 126:5, 6; Prov. 11:10. Singing in praise of Yahweh is mentioned (2 Chr. 20:22; Pss. 147:1; 105:43); as is shouting for joy in worship (Pss. 42:4; 107:22). Ps. 126:2; Isa. 35:10; 51:11 refer to shouting over God's salvation of his people; and Isa. 44:23; 49:13; 55:12 allude metaphorically to the mountains singing for joy at the salvation of Israel. Ps. 118:15 refers to shouts, or songs, of joy at Yahweh's victory over his enemies.

renānāh [רְנָנָה, 7445]

renānāh is another noun derived from ***rānan*** (see above), occurring only four times. On each occasion it refers to a cry, or shout, for joy. In Job 3:7 the cry is non-specific; in Job 20:5 it is the short-lived cry of the wicked. Pss. 63:5; 100:2 refer to joyful praise for God.

śûs [שׂוּשׂ, 7797]

The verb ***śûs*** occurs around thirty times with the dominant sense of "rejoice." ***śûs*** expresses the joy of both God and human beings.

As far as the human expression of joy is concerned, ***śûs*** is used similarly to the terms above. People express joy in the Lord's salvation (cf. Ps. 35:9; Isa. 61:10). General rejoicing in Yahweh is indicated in Pss. 68:3; 70:4. Isa. 66:14 records delight in God's victories over his enemies. In addition, there is rejoicing over God's recreation of his city and people in Isa. 65:18; 66:18; and a metaphorical instance of the land rejoicing in the renewal of the earth in Isa. 35:1. In Ps. 119:14, 162, the psalmist takes his delight in God's law.

śûs is also used to describe rejoicing or exalting in one's strength (Job 39:21); and Job 3:22 contains an unusual example of rejoicing in the approach of death, predicated of those gripped by misery and despair. Lam. 1:21 refers to the enemies of God's people rejoicing over the destruction of Jerusalem. In the same book Edom is exhorted, with distinct sarcasm, to rejoice at Jerusalem's demise, for this delight will be very short lived since Yahweh will soon destroy this nation for taking such delight in the misery of his people (cf. Lam. 4:21).

When predicated of God, ***śûs*** refers to Yahweh rejoicing in doing good for his people (cf. Deut. 28:63;

30:9; Jer. 32:41; Zeph. 3:17). Yahweh is said to rejoice over the city of Jerusalem, which he has restored, in Isa. 65:19. And he is also shown rejoicing over his people as a bridegroom adores his bride in Isa. 62:5.

sāsôn **[שָׂשׂוֹן, 8342]**

sāsôn is a noun derived from ***sûs*** (see above), found in approximately twenty places with the primary sense of "joy," "rejoicing."

The psalmist pleads for God to fill him with the joy of salvation (cf. Ps. 51:8, 12); his joy in the Lord is given expression in Ps. 105:43, as is his delight in the law of the Lord in Ps. 119:111. See also Jer. 15:16. Joy in the salvation delivered by God is expressed in Jer. 31:13; Isa. 35:10; 51:3, 11. The three Isaiah texts here refer to the people's delight in returning to Jerusalem. Still with reference to Jerusalem, Jer. 33:9 declares that this city is a joy to God. Alongside the visions and prophecies of the eschatological renewal of Jerusalem and the land, there is also renewed joy in the worship of Yahweh, as stated in Jer. 33:11; Zech. 8:19.

Ps. 45:7 contains a metaphorical expression for the emotion of joy or delight, as the Messianic King is anointed with the "oil of gladness." This "oil of gladness" is also bestowed on those Israelites who mourn for Zion (Isa. 61:3). In contrast, God removes joy as a judgment against his people in Jer. 7:34; 16:9; Joel 1:12.

māsôs **[מָשׂוֹשׂ, 4885]**

māsôs is another noun derived from ***sûs*** (see above), synonymous with ***sāsôn*** (see above), and occurs seventeen times. ***māsôs*** is consistently translated "joy," "rejoicing."

Gladness of heart is expressed in non-specific contexts in Job 8:19; Isa. 24:11; 32:13, 14; 60:15. Ps. 48:2; Isa. 24:8 express joy in worshiping Yahweh; and joy as a result of divine renewal is expressed in Isa. 65:18; 66:18. In a negative context, joy is withdrawn from the people of God as a punishment for their sin in Lam. 5:15; Ezek. 24:25; Hos. 2:11.

gîl **[גִּיל, 1523** (Verb)**]**

gîl is a verb occurring about forty times with the primary meanings "rejoice," "be glad."

A general reference to rejoicing is found in Prov. 23:24, which declares that a father with a righteous son has great joy. Prov. 24:17 contains an exhortation not to rejoice over the misfortune of one's enemy. Song 1:4 speaks of rejoicing in the happiness of others. Rejoicing over the harvest is indicated in Isa. 9:3.

Other texts depict God as the object of people's gladness. The following passages refer to the joy of those who worship Yahweh: Pss. 2:11; 32:11; Isa. 29:19; Joel 2:23; Hab. 3:18. Rejoicing in God's salvation is alluded to in Pss. 9:14; 14:7. God's creation and re-creation are likewise phenomena that evoke delight (cf. Ps. 118:24; Isa. 35:2; 65:18). In turn, the creation itself is symbolically depicted as rejoicing in Yahweh's lordship (cf. Pss. 96:11; 149:2).

gîl also expresses God's delight in rejoicing over his people, for whom he has gained the victory (cf. Zeph. 3:17).

gîl **[גִּיל, 1524** (Noun)**]**

gîl is the noun derived from the verb ***gîl***. The noun and verb are used in virtually the same way and have identical meanings. ***gîl*** occurs ten times.

gîl refers to gladness of heart (Ps. 45:15); joy in praising God (Pss. 43:4; 65:12); and the removal of joy as a divine judgment (Isa. 16:10; Jer. 48:33; Hos. 9:1; Joel 1:16). See also Job 3:22; Prov. 23:24.

'ālaṣ **[עָלַץ, 5970]**

This verb form is quite rare, occurring only eight times. ***'ālaṣ*** consistently means "rejoice."

Rejoicing in general is indicated in Prov. 11:10; 28:12. Most of the other uses of ***'ālaṣ*** focus on rejoicing in the person and work of Yahweh (cf. 1 Sam. 2:1; Pss. 5:11; 9:2; 68:3; 1 Chr. 16:32). In Ps. 25:2, the psalmist pleads with God not to let his enemies rejoice over him.

'ālaz **[עָלַז, 5937]**

'ālaz occurs sixteen times meaning "rejoice" or "exult" in most of these contexts. The usage here is very similar to that of ***'ālaṣ*** (see above).

'ālaz describes gladness and merriment (Prov. 23:16; Jer. 15:17); specific praise for and rejoicing in Yahweh (Pss. 28:7; 68:4; 149:5; Hab. 3:18); and the exultation of the wicked (Ps. 94:3; Jer. 50:11; 51:39). Coupled with this latter phenomenon, Jer. 11:15 declares the practice of rejoicing in corrupted worship of Yahweh to be inappropriate and utterly unacceptable. Divine judgment, in the form of denying a spirit of rejoicing, is handed down to Sidon in Isa. 23:12.

Yahweh exults over the conquest of Shechem as part of his plan to give the land of Canaan to his people (cf. Pss. 60:6; 108:7).

'allîz **[עַלִּיז, 5947]**

'allîz is the adjectival form of ***'ālaz*** (see above) and occurs seven times meaning "joyful," "jubilant."

Jubilation at the anticipated victory of Yahweh over the Babylonians is described in Isa. 13:3. In several of these texts, joy is noted among various peoples immediately prior to their being exposed to the wrath of Yahweh. This joyfulness tinged with arrogance and godlessness is expressed by Jerusalem (cf. Isa. 22:2); Tyre (Isa. 23:7); and Assyria (Zeph. 2:15). As a consequence of divine judgment upon the nations, Isa. 24:8 records the stifling of those who are jubilant.

NT Words

chairō [χαίρω, *5463*]

chairō is a verb found on approximately seventy occasions with the sense of "rejoice," "be glad" in the majority of contexts in which it occurs. ***chairō*** is used in a whole range of situations in which the emotion of joy is evoked. Predominant in the usage of this term is the focus on rejoicing over the redemptive deeds of God that come to fruition in the gospel in the person of the Messiah, Jesus Christ.

A general feeling of delight and well-being is noted, for example, in Luke 23:8; John 3:29; Rom. 12:15. Rejoicing at God's fulfillment of his promise to provide a messianic deliverer for his people is noted in Matt. 2:10 (the reaction of the magi at seeing the divinely-guided star); in John 8:56 (Jesus' claim that Abraham rejoiced at seeing his day); and in Luke 1:14. Frequently, joy is expressed at the prospect of heaven and eternal life (cf. Matt. 5:12; Luke 6:23; John 4:36; Rom. 12:12). Delight in God's goodness to his people is noted (Acts 11:23; Rom. 16:19; 2 Cor. 7:7), as is joy in the faithfulness of believers (Col. 2:5; 1 Thess. 3:9; 2 John 4; 3 John 3). As a corollary to this, rejoicing in the repentance of sinners is described in 2 Cor. 7:9. In Acts 8:39; 13:48; Rev. 19:7, salvation is the focus of people's delight. Paul declares in 1 Cor. 13:6 that love rejoices in righteousness, and he rejoices at the spread of the gospel in Phil. 1:18. Joy is found even in traumatic circumstances — for example, in Acts 5:41; Col. 1:24; 1 Pet. 4:13, which contain evidence of joy experienced in the midst of persecution on account of the gospel, as well as an exhortation to so rejoice. Similarly, 2 Cor. 6:10 records the apostle Paul's joy in the midst of sorrow.

Regarding the person and work of Christ, the joy of the Jewish people in witnessing the miracles of Jesus is noted (cf. Luke 13:17; 19:37). The disciples rejoice at the Lord's resurrection in John 20:20. The apostle Paul exhorts his readers to rejoice in the Lord in Phil. 3:1; 4:4, 10. In the parable depicting the immeasurable value of the kingdom of God, joy is expressed in the discovery of the lost sheep, a symbol of that infinite value (cf. Matt. 18:13; Luke 15:5).

In a number of negative contexts, wicked people express an evil delight — for example, those who are anticipating the destruction of Jesus Christ through his betrayal at the hands of Judas (cf. Mark 14:11; Luke 22:5). And in Rev. 11:10 the wicked rejoice over the death of the two prophets.

chara [χαρά, *5479*]

chara is the noun derived from ***chairō*** (see above). It occurs around sixty times and is consistently translated "joy," "gladness." The range of contexts is quite similar to that of ***chairō***.

Regarding the person and work of God, ***chara*** denotes joy at Yahweh's fulfillment of his promise concerning the Messiah, the birth of Christ (cf. Luke 2:10; Matt. 2:10; Luke 1:14). Joy in receiving God's word is highlighted in Matt. 13:20; Mark 4:16; Luke 8:13. Experiencing the power of God also results in great joy (cf. Luke 10:17; Acts 8:8). The indwelling of the Holy Spirit causes joy (cf. Acts 13:52; Rom. 14:17; 15:13); and joy itself is a fruit of the Spirit (Gal. 5:22). Joy is also found in relationship with Christ (cf. John 15:11; 17:13; 1 Pet. 1:8); and the greatest delight is experienced by those who are party to the resurrection of Jesus (cf. Matt. 28:8; Luke 24:52). Christ himself has a deep, inner joy in anticipating his ascension to the Father (Heb. 12:2).

In more general contexts, joy is a reward for service (Matt. 25:21; Heb. 13:17). There is joy in heaven over every sinner that repents (cf. Luke 15:7, 10). John 16:21 refers to joy in childbirth. Fellowship yields joy (Rom. 15:32; 2 Cor. 1:24); as does affliction (2 Cor. 8:2); and prayer (Phil. 1:4). There is joy in discovering the riches of the kingdom (Matt. 13:44), and in perseverance (cf. Col. 1:11). Paul signals his joy in seeing spiritual growth within his congregations (cf. Phil. 1:25; 1 Thess. 2:19); as does John (3 John 4).

agalliaō [ἀγαλλιάω, *21*]

agalliaō occurs eleven times and signifies a heightened degree of gladness, meaning "to rejoice greatly," "exult."

This term also refers frequently to the person of God and Christ. In general terms, ***agalliaō*** refers to rejoicing in God as Savior (Luke 1:47), and to rejoicing in the Holy Spirit (Luke 10:21, predicated of Jesus). See also Acts 2:26. Similarly, exultation in regard to Christ is noted in 1 Pet. 1:18. The Philippian jailer rejoices at his salvation in Acts 16:34. Jesus speaks of Abraham's delight at "seeing" the day of Christ in John 8:56. 1 Pet. 4:13 mentions rejoicing in sharing in the sufferings of Christ. Rejoicing at the prospect of heaven is found in Matt. 5:12; 1 Pet. 1:6; Rev. 19:7.

agalliasis **[ἀγαλλίασις, *20*]**

agalliasis is the noun derived from ***agalliaō*** (see above), occurring only five times with the sense of "joy," "exultation."

Luke 1:14, 44 refer to joy at the anticipated birth of Christ. Acts 2:46 speaks of the joy in the fellowship of the early church. God anoints Christ his Son with the "oil of gladness" (Heb. 1:9). And Jude 24 affirms joy in the presence of God.

skirtaō **[σκιρτάω, *4640*]**

skirtaō is a rare verb found only three times, meaning "leap for joy." It refers twice to the baby in Elizabeth's womb (John the Baptist), who leapt for joy at the greeting of Mary (cf. Luke 1:41, 44). ***skirtaō*** is also found in Luke 6:23, where Jesus exhorts his followers to leap for joy at the prospect of reward in heaven for suffering for the gospel.

euphrosynē **[εὐφροσύνη, *2167*]**

euphrosynē is found only twice and means "gladness" or "joy." In Acts 2:28, joy is experienced in the presence of God. In Acts 4:17, joy in people's hearts is bestowed by a caring God, who meets all of our needs.

JUDGE

OT Words

shāphat **[שָׁפַט, 8199]**

shāphat is a verb depicting a very important activity and function in Old Testament revelation. ***shāphat*** denotes the judicial process of judging in a formal legal sense as well as the informal practice of discernment. It is an action predicated of both God and human beings.

There are a number of contexts in which ***shāphat*** is predicated of God. In several places, the formula "May the Lord judge between . . ." (plus variations) is used to invoke the judging activity of Yahweh (cf. Gen. 16:5; 31:53; Exod. 5:21; Judg. 11:21; 1 Sam. 24:12, 15). The majority of these settings, however, focus on the negative aspect of divine judging as punishment. General references to divine retribution in this sense are found in 1 Sam. 3:13; 2 Sam. 18:19; Ps. 51:4. Yahweh is said to not only bring judgment on his people for their sinfulness (cf. Jer. 2:35; Ezek. 7:3, 8, 27; 11:10; 16:38; 20:35; Amos 2:3); but also on the nations and the earth as a whole (cf. Pss. 58:11; 96:13; Isa. 66:16; Jer. 25:31; Ezek. 38:22; Joel 3:2). Eccl. 3:17 contains the affirmation that God shall judge the righteous and all the wicked.

In more positive contexts, there are pleas for God to judge his servants rightly (cf. Lam. 3:5; 1 Kgs. 8:32; Pss. 7:8; 35:24), including the judging of heavenly beings (cf. Job 21:22; Ps. 82:1). The perfect judgment of Yahweh is indicated in Jer. 11:20, as is that of the Messianic Servant of Yahweh (cf. Isa. 11:4; 16:5). Finally, Yahweh judges the nations as a prelude to peace and salvation (cf. Isa. 23:4; 51:5; Mic. 4:3).

Likewise, the phenomenon of judging is frequently depicted as a human activity. The primary context in this regard is the judicial role of the civic leader in Israelite society. Moses' role as judge in ancient Israel is the earliest formal illustration of this office (cf. Exod. 18:13ff.), which was subsequently expanded to include many more of these officials (cf. Exod. 18:22, 26; Deut. 16:18; 25:1).

The unique role of the judge during the period of Israelite occupation and settlement in Canaan is described in detail in the book of Judges. These leaders were unique in the sense that their function was not only judicial, but also military. They served as Spirit-filled deliverers of the Israelite tribes, rescuing and liberating them from the clutches of various Canaanite tribal peoples. Their legal, judicial function is implied rather than being explicitly described in the text in most cases, although that function can never be set aside (cf. Judg. 3:10; 4:4; 10:2ff.; 12:7ff.; 15:20; Ruth 1:1; 1 Sam. 4:18; 7:6ff.). This is a role also assigned to the civic assembly in Israel (cf. Num. 35:24); and, on occasion, to the prophet (cf. Ezek. 20:4; 22:2; 23:36). In addition, Yahweh commands people to judge justly (cf. Isa. 1:17; Zech. 7:9; 8:16; Lev. 19:15). Illustrations of Israel's failure to do so are found in Isa. 1:23; Jer. 5:28; Mic. 3:11; Dan. 9:12.

Other examples of ***shāphat*** depicting the practice of judging are found in 1 Sam. 8:6, 20, where the Israelites ask God for a king to judge (i.e., govern) the people. King Solomon fulfills this request ideally when, in 1 Kgs. 3:9, he asks God that he might be enabled to judge (i.e., govern) his people wisely (cf. also 1 Kgs. 3:28). In a negative context, Ezek. 23:24 depicts the nations as instruments of Yahweh's judgment against Israel.

In a somewhat unusual use of the term ***shāphat***, the people of Israel are exhorted to plead their case before Yahweh (Isa. 43:26).

shōphēṭ [שֹׁפֵט, 8199]

shōphēṭ is the participial form of ***shāphaṭ*** (see above), consistently used as the noun "judge" in the sixty contexts or so in which it is found. ***shōphēṭ*** is likewise predicated of both God and human beings.

In relation to God, ***shōphēṭ*** depicts Yahweh as judge of the whole earth in Gen. 18:25; Judg. 11:27; Isa. 33:22.

When speaking of human beings, ***shōphēṭ*** refers to the role of judge in an informal general context, including the idea of "ruler" (cf. Gen. 19:9; Exod. 2:14; Ps. 148:11; Isa. 40:23; Hos. 7:7; Amos 2:3). ***shōphēṭ*** refers predominantly to the civil, judicial offices of early premonarchic Israel (cf. Num. 25:5; Deut. 1:16; 25:2; Josh. 8:33; Judg. 2:11ff. [the primary, "official" description of this period]; Ruth 1:1; 1 Sam. 8:1; 2 Sam. 7:11; 2 Kgs. 23:2; Isa. 1:26; Mic. 7:3).

dîn [דִּין, 1777]

dîn is a verb foccurring around twenty times with the primary meaning "to act as a judge" in a formal, judicial sense. ***dîn*** refers predominantly to Yahweh.

In this sense, ***dîn*** indicates God handing down formal judgment on his people for their rebellion against him (cf. Ps. 50:4; Isa. 3:13); on the nations (Ps. 110:6), for the same reason; and likewise on the enemies of Israel (cf. Gen. 15:14). ***dîn*** also refers to the righteous mode of God's judgment on the world (Ps. 9:8), and on his people (Pss. 72:2; 96:10; Jer. 22:16). Yahweh is said to "make an adjudication" on behalf of his people in several contexts — for example, leading to the blessing of a son for Rachel (Gen. 30:6); resulting in their vindication (Pss. 54:1; 135:14); and giving rise to Israel's deliverance (cf. Deut. 32:36).

dîn is also predicated of human beings in reference to the judicial role of civic leadership in Israel (cf. Gen. 49:16). These leaders are also exhorted to carry out their function in a righteous manner (cf. Jer. 5:28; 21:12; Zech. 3:7).

'elōhîm [אֱלֹהִים, 430]

'elōhîm is the Hebrew term that most commonly designates the person of God in the sense of creator and ruler of the cosmos. ***'elōhîm*** is translated "God" in reference to the one true and living deity approximately 2,600 times (→ ***GOD***). It also occurs approximately 250 times referring to "gods" in the sense of lifeless idols. However, on five occasions the term may refer to the civic authorities, or judges, in Israel (cf. Exod. 21:6; 22:8, 9 [twice]). 1 Sam. 2:25 also contains the term *'elōhîm*, but there is more ambiguity here as to whether God himself or an Israelite judge is in view.

pālîl [פָּלִיל, 6414]

pālîl is a rare term synonymous with ***shōphēṭ*** (see above), occurring only three times, with reference to the judges or civil authorities in Israel (Exod. 21:22; Job 31:11); and referring to the enemies of Israel as judges (Deut. 32:31).

dayyān [דַּיָּן, 1781]

dayyān is a rare term, occurring only twice and referring to God as judge of his people (cf. 1 Sam. 24:15; Ps. 68:5).

NT Words

krinō [κρίνω, *2919*]

krinō is the predominant New Testament term designating the judicial function of "judging." This verb occurs around ninety times, though not exclusively in formal judicial settings. ***krinō*** refers to the act of judging predicated of human beings, Christ, and God.

As far as human beings are concerned, the contexts of judicial function involving the use of ***krinō*** are varied. There are instructions not to judge unjustly or in hypocritical self-righteousness (cf. Matt. 7:1; Rom. 2:1, 3; 14:3ff.). John 18:31; Acts 4:19 allude to the civil function of Jewish judges. Matt. 7:2 affirms the principle that our criteria in judging others will be applied in the same measure by God towards us. The valid right of church leaders to judge those within the church is spelled out in 1 Cor. 5:3, 12. Matt. 19:28; Luke 22:30 refer to the anticipated heavenly privilege of judging the twelve tribes of Israel, as well as angels (1 Cor. 6:2ff.). Gentile judges are mentioned in 1 Cor. 6:1, 6.

In "non-judicial" contexts, ***krinō*** refers to judging in the sense of passing an opinion or considering an issue (cf. Col. 2:16; 1 Cor. 10:29; Acts 13:46; 1 Cor. 10:15; 2 Cor. 5:14). It also expresses the idea of judging in the sense of one who exercises discernment, whether it be commendation (cf. Luke 7:43), or condemnation (cf. Luke 19:22; Rom. 2:27; 2 Thess. 2:12).

When speaking of Christ as the agent of judging, ***krinō*** indicates in John 3:17; 12:47 that his mission lay not in "judging" (i.e., condemning) the world, but in rescuing it. Then, John 5:22, 30; 8:26 affirm that all divine judgment is given to the Son by God. 2 Tim. 4:1 declares that Christ's act of judgment will be consummated at his appearing. John 8:16; Rev. 19:11 declare that Christ's judgment is perfect.

krinō also refers to God as the agent of judging. Such divine action is universal in its effect and includes his people as well as the nations (cf. John 8:50; Heb. 10:30; Acts 7:7; 1 Cor. 5:13). The phenomenon of divine judgment at the end of time is highlighted with respect to "the evil ruler of this world" (John 16:11; Rev. 18:8, 20) and to the world in general on the great day of judgment (Acts 17:31; Rom. 3:6; 1 Pet. 4:5; Heb. 13:4; Rev. 11:18). God is also said to judge his people in the sense of chastising them, to avoid their ultimate condemnation (1 Cor. 11:32). Several texts also declare that God judges justly (cf. 1 Pet. 2:23; Rev. 16:5; 19:2).

kritēs [κριτής, *2923*]

kritēs is the noun derived from ***krinō*** (see above), and is translated "judge" in all seventeen occurrences. Like the verb from which it is derived, ***kritēs*** refers to a judge in a judicial as well as a general, non-judicial sense (i.e., one who passes an opinion or a judgment on someone else).

In the context of society, and of Israelite society in particular, ***kritēs*** refers to a judge or judicial officer in Matt. 5:25; Luke 12:58; and in Acts 24:10, where Felix the governor of Judea is mentioned. In a non-specific sense, ***kritēs*** refers to a judge in Matt. 12:27; Acts 18:15; Jas. 2:4. Acts 13:20 refers to "the judges" as that unique Spirit-anointed class of military and civil leaders during the early period of Israelite settlement in Canaan.

When referring to God, ***kritēs*** refers to him as the judge of the living and the dead in Acts 10:42; Heb. 12:23. 2 Tim. 4:8 portrays God as the righteous judge; and Jas. 5:9 utilizes the term "judge" as a title for God.

dikastēs [δικαστής, *1348*]

dikastēs is a rare synonym for ***kritēs***, above, occurring only in Acts 7:27, 35, referring to a judge in a general sense and not in a formal, official capacity.

anakrinō [ἀνακρίνω, *350*]

anakrinō is a variant form of ***krinō*** (see above), occurring sixteen times with the primary meanings "examine," or "judge," reflecting the sense of investigation, interrogation, and estimation, and other related nuances.

anakrinō indicates "examination" in a judicial sense with Jesus before Pilate (Luke 23:14); and with Peter and John before the Sanhedrin (Acts 4:9). ***anakrinō*** is also used in a non-judicial sense (Acts 12:19; 1 Cor. 9:3. 1 Cor. 14:24); and in the sense of "search" or "inquiry," when the Bereans are commended for examining the Scriptures in Acts 17:11.

anakrinō means "accusation" in Acts 24:8; 28:18, where Paul is accused by the Jews and the Romans, respectively. ***anakrinō*** also means "spiritual discernment" (1 Cor. 2:14, 15); "judging" in a judicial sense (1 Cor. 4:3, 4); and "questioning" (1 Cor. 10:25, 27).

diakrinō [διακρίνω, *1252*]

diakrinō is another variant form of ***krinō*** (see above) with several senses including "discerning," "interpreting," "doubling," and "judging." Of its approximately twenty occurrences, the term is translated "to judge" on four occasions. 1 Cor. 11:31; Jas. 2:4 refer to the process of "judging" in a general, informal sense. 1 Cor. 6:5; 14:29 indicate the practice of making a judgment within the church among believers.

JUDGMENT

OT Words

mishpāt [מִשְׁפָּט, **4941**]

mishpāt is a common noun derived from ***shāphat*** (→ JUDGE), found in around 400 contexts. ***mishpāt*** has a variety of meanings, but the majority of these center around the phenomena of "judgment" and "justice." This term has considerable theological significance in the Old Testament.

As far as human judgment, or justice, is concerned, the usage of ***mishpāt*** is quite varied. In the sense of doing what is right in the sight of God, the term is rendered "justice" in Gen. 18:19; Ezek. 18:5. In the sense of a "legal entitlement," ***mishpāt*** is translated "justice" in Lev. 19:15; Deut. 16:18. The command to execute justice is found in 1 Kgs. 10:9; Isa. 1:17. The anticipated "just" rule of the messianic ruler is indicated in Jer. 33:15. Perverting justice is prohibited in Deut. 16:19; 27:19, and perversion of justice is found in 1 Sam. 8:3; Mic. 3:9. The ritual symbols of the process of judgment, such as the breastpiece of the high priest's apparel, are mentioned in Exod. 28:15, 29, 30. In related contexts, ***mishpāt*** refers to God's will in the so-called ascertaining of judgment of the Urim and Thummim in Num. 27:21. Exod. 28:30 refers to the high priest bearing the judgment of God on behalf of the people (i.e., being responsible for making decisions for the Israelites as their mediator in the presence of God).

References to legal court procedures are found in 2 Kgs. 25:6; Jer. 39:5; Ezek. 23:45, where ***mishpāt*** means "sentence," or a judicial indictment or punishment. See also Deut. 21:22. Num. 27:5 refers to a "legal case" that is brought to court for adjudication. The "judgment" of a civil court is mentioned in Num. 35:12; Deut. 1:17;

25:1; Judg. 4:5; 2 Sam. 15:2. ***mishpāt*** also refers to the place of judgment, such as the "hall of judgment" in 1 Kgs. 7:7. In addition, ***mishpāt*** refers to legal "ordinances" in Josh. 24:25; 2 Sam. 8:15; and to legal rights or privileges in Isa. 10:2; 40:27; Deut. 21:17; Jer. 32:8; and to a "cause," i.e., a plea for right judgment from God, 1 Kgs. 8:49; Pss. 9:4; 35:23.

mishpāt also means "judgment" with the specific sense of "wise discernment" in 1 Kgs. 3:11, where Solomon selflessly requests this gift from God. 1 Kgs. 3:28 refers to this unique wisdom of Israel's wisest king in the affair of the disputed infant. Jer. 23:5 speaks of the anticipated wise judgment of the coming ruler, the messianic "branch."

mishpāt refers extensively to the person and work of Yahweh. The perfection of God's justice or judgment is indicated in Gen. 18:25; Pss. 97:2; 119:7; Isa. 9:7; 42:1; Jer. 4:2; Hos. 2:19. Many references speak of the binding obligation of all divine ordinances, judgments, or precepts of the law covenant on the people of Israel (e.g., Exod. 21:1; Lev. 26:43ff.; Num. 29:6ff.; Deut. 4:1; 30:16; 1 Kgs. 8:58; 2 Kgs. 17:27; Ps. 10:5; Isa. 26:8; Ezek. 5:6ff.; 20:11ff.). Failure to uphold these statutes will result in divine judgment (***mishpāt***) against his people, for their rebellion against him (cf. Isa. 3:14; Jer. 1:16; Hos. 6:5); and the outpouring of his wrath against his enemies (cf. Deut. 32:41; Isa. 34:5 [Edom]; Jer. 51:9 [Babylon]). Pss. 1:5; 9:7; Eccl. 11:9; 12:4 indicate divine judgment at the time of the end.

Particular mention may be made of the use of ***mishpāt*** in relation to the messianic "Servant of Yahweh" in the so-called "Servant Songs" of Isaiah. Isa. 42:3, 4 speak of the Servant establishing or bringing forth perfect divine justice, which will become a light for the Gentiles (cf. Isa. 51:4). Then Isa. 49:4 depicts the Servant possessing a just "cause" (***mishpāt***) before Yahweh; and Isa. 53:8 points to the Servant bearing the divine judgment (***mishpāt***) or curse on the people's behalf.

shephet [שֶׁפֶט, 8201]

shephet is a noun also derived from ***shāphat*** (→ JUDGE). It occurs sixteen times, usually referring to God's judgment.

Divine acts of judgment on behalf of the Israelites are noted in Exod. 6:6; 7:4; 12:12; Num. 33:4, all of which speak of the plagues against Egypt as the prelude to Israel's release from captivity. Several texts indicate Yahweh's judgment against his people — for example, against King Joash (2 Chr. 24:24); Israel (cf. Ezek. 5:10, 15; 11:9; 16:41); and a specific action against Jerusalem (Ezek. 14:21).

shephet also refers to Yahweh enacting his judgment against pagan nations — for example, Egypt (Ezek. 30:14, 19); Moab (Ezek. 25:11); and Sidon (Ezek. 28:26).

The one text that speaks of judgment from a nonspecific human perspective occurs in Prov. 19:29, where ***shephet*** is translated "condemnation."

shephôt [שְׁפוֹט, 8196]

A rare synonym for ***shephet*** (see above), ***shephôt*** also means "judgment," "acts of judgment" in two places (cf. 2 Chr. 20:9; Ezek. 23:10). In both places the judgment is directed against the Israelite people. In the Chronicles text, the punishment indicated anticipates the people's rebellion against Yahweh.

dîn [דִּין, 1779 (1780 Aramaic)]

dîn is both an Aramaic and Hebrew noun meaning "judgment." The Hebrew form ***dîn*** has a few additional nuances other than the translation "judgment." However, the underlying sense of "judgment" is common to both terms.

The Aramaic form ***dîn*** is found five times in Ezra and Daniel. Ezra 7:26 refers to the Persian edict of "capital punishment" for any who dared to disobey the law of Ezra's God. In Dan. 4:37, ***dîn*** refers to the "just" ways of God. Dan. 7:10, 26 indicate the divine condemnation and punishment of the little horn. Then, in Dan. 7:22, judgment is pronounced by Yahweh in favor of his people against the little horn, whereby they are to receive the kingdom of God.

In Hebrew, ***dîn*** also refers to "judgments," but with some additional related senses. The term is found twenty times and is predicated of both God and human beings.

In regard to human beings, ***dîn*** refers in a general sense to justice, or rather the absence of it, in Jer. 5:28. The term indicates a "legal right" in Deut. 17:8; Prov. 29:7; 31:5; Isa. 10:2. It indicates judgment in a judicial sense in Esth. 1:13; Job 19:29; 35:14; Ps. 9:4; Jer. 22:16; Prov. 20:8. When pointing to the person of God, ***dîn*** indicates judgment pronounced from heaven in Ps. 76:8, and the maintenance of the "cause" of the afflicted in Ps. 140:12.

pelîlāh [פְּלִילָה, 6415]

pelîlāh is derived from ***pālîl*** (→ JUDGE) and occurs just once, referring in Isa. 16:3 to the granting of justice.

pelîlîyāh [פְּלִילִיָּה, **6417**]

Also occurring only once, and derived from ***pālîl*** (→ JUDGE), ***pelîlîyāh*** indicates the pronouncement of a legal decision or judgment in Isa. 28:7.

NT Words

krisis [κρίσις, *2920*]

krisis is the principal noun derived from ***krinō*** (→ JUDGE), occurring around fifty times with the primary sense of "judgment," as well as several related nuances in a variety of contexts. Again, it is a term that refers to both human and divine actions.

When referring to human beings, ***krisis*** indicates "judgment" in the legal sense of judicial condemnation for crimes (cf. Matt. 5:21; 1 Tim. 5:24; Jas. 2:13). Pharisaical neglect of justice is indicated in Matt. 23:23; Luke 11:42. John 7:24 commands that righteous judgment be executed.

When divine judgment is in view, ***krisis*** is found in a number of contexts. God's righteous judgment in a general sense is indicated (2 Thess. 1:5; Rev. 16:7; 19:2); as is his judgment against human beings (John 3:19; Heb. 9:27; 2 Pet. 2:9, 11). References to the great day of judgment are found in Matt. 10:15; 11:22, 24; John 5:29; 12:31; 1 John 4:17; Rev. 14:7. Damnation for the wicked is threatened and invoked on the wicked — on the Pharisees (Matt. 23:33; Mark 3:29); the ungodly (Jude 15); and on Babylon (Rev. 18:10).

Judgment is also a function assigned to Christ (John 5:30; 8:16), whose judgment is perfect; and in a negative sense to the archangel Michael, from whom no judgment may be personally directed against the devil.

krima [κρίμα, *2917*]

krima is another noun derived from ***krinō*** (→ JUDGE). It also embraces the sense of "judgment," but with the dominant emphases on judicial sentencing, condemnation, and penal judgment. ***krima*** occurs thirty times in reference to God and human beings.

In the context of human judgment, ***krima*** has a general meaning in Matt. 7:2; 1 Pet. 4:17; and also refers to judicial condemnation (Rom. 13:2); to a lawsuit (1 Cor. 6:7); and to capital punishment (Luke 23:40). Luke 24:20 refers to the condemnation of Jesus under the jurisdiction of Pilate.

Judgment attributed to God in the sense of assessment is indicated in John 3:1. His decrees or statutes are mentioned in Rom. 11:33; Heb. 6:2. Divine condemnation is directed against the Pharisees (Matt. 23:14; Mark 12:40; Luke 20:47); against evil doers (Rom. 2:23; 5:16; Gal. 5:16; Jude 14); and against those who abuse the Lord's Supper (1 Cor. 11:29, 34) In reference to the judgment of Christ, John 9:39 speaks of action that is both redemptive and punitive.

The task of judgment is committed to heavenly beings in Rev. 20:4.

praitōrion [πραιτώριον, *4232*]

This term (derived from the Latin *praetorium*) refers to the governor's residence (or palace) or headquarters of the Roman commander-in-chief. The ***praitōrion*** was used as a civil court, and thus the usual translation "hall of judgment." It is found seven times in relation both to the place of Jesus' trial (Matt. 27:27; Luke 15:16; John 18:28, 33; John 19:9); and to the setting for Paul's trial and imprisonment (Acts 23:35; Phil. 1:13).

kritērion [κριτήριον, *2922*]

kritērion refers to the means of judgment, or to the process of coming to a judicial decision—a "case." It is found only three times.

1 Cor. 6:2 refers to the competency of the Corinthian congregational leaders to "try" cases of church discipline. Here ***kritērion*** is translated in a verbal mode. In 1 Cor. 6:4, ***kritērion*** indicates the actual "cases" of disciplinary matters coming before the church. In Jas. 2:6, ***kritērion*** refers to the "courtroom" itself.

bēma [βῆμα, *968*]

bēma refers to the official seat of a judge or to the tribunal, or court itself. ***bēma*** occurs thirteen times, with all but three of these referring to judgment of some kind.

The judgment seat of Pilate is indicated in Matt. 27:19; John 19:13 in a literal sense; and in spiritual contexts Rom. 14:10 mentions God's judgment seat and 2 Cor. 5:10 refers to the judgment seat of Christ. The tribunal of Gallio, proconsul of Achaia, is indicated in Acts 18:12, 16, 17, as is that of Festus, governor of Judea, in Acts 25:6, 10, 17.

aisthēsis [αἴσθησις, *144*]

aisthēsis occurs once, referring to judgment in the sense of "discernment" in Phil. 1:9.

dikē [δίκη, *1349*]

dikē is found four times meaning "judgment" in the sense of a judicial sentence (Jude 7; Acts 25:15; 2 Thess. 1:9) or principle of justice (Acts 28:4).

gnōmē [γνώμη, *1106*]

gnōmē occurs nine times and means "judgment" in most of these contexts. The underlying sense is that of one's mind, advice, or opinion.

Acts 20:3 records Paul's "decision" to travel through Macedonia. In 1 Cor. 1:10, Paul exhorts the Corinthian congregation to be united in "mind." Rev. 17:13 records the one "purpose" of the ten horns of the symbolic beast ridden by the Babylonian harlot, giving their authority to the satanic beast (cf. Rev. 12; 13).

In the remaining contexts, ***gnōmē*** means "opinion" in Paul's Corinthian correspondence (cf. 1 Cor. 7:25, 40; 2 Cor. 8:10). The notion of "consent" is referred to in Phil. 1:14.

dikaiōma [δικαίωμα, *1345*]

dikaiōma occurs ten times and means "ordinance," "justification." It also means "judgment" on two occasions. In Rom. 1:32 ***dikaiōma*** indicates the divine decree, whereby God's judgment of eternal condemnation will be poured out on those whose lifestyles embody the very antithesis of holiness. Rev. 15:4 speaks of the revelation of God's "judgments," which will bring forth worship from the nations. The term here suggests that God's righteous acts of deliverance throughout history are in view. The force of ***dikaiōma*** clearly indicates a divine initiative and source.

dikaiokrisia [δικαιοκρισία, *1341*]

dikaiokrisia is only found in Rom. 2:5, which speaks of the revelation of God's righteous judgments.

Additional Notes

There is a very broad range of terminology denoting "judgment" and its many related senses in both Old and New Testaments. The human institutions of judicial practice and informal assessment of another's thoughts and actions clearly reflect the divine sphere of judgment. Human decisions concerning the destiny of evil doers, or the righteous, should therefore reflect the divine ideal of rightly assessing people's attitudes and actions. God of course does this perfectly, and that absolute purity of justice and discernment is conveyed to the person of Christ, who likewise exercises perfect judgment on behalf of the Father. Human beings do not carry out his task of just, or righteous, judgment perfectly. There is thus much injustice and poor exercise of judicial function among people — at every level, whether formal or informal. Not until the consummation of this age will this state of affairs be fully rectified; and that will be accomplished by the person of Christ himself, who will return as the perfectly just judge of heaven and earth. Thus all "judgment," in the broadest possible sense, can be said to culminate in him.

JUST, JUSTICE → JUDGMENT → RIGHTEOUS

JUSTIFICATION

NT Words

dikaiōsis [δικαίωσις, *1347*]

dikaiōsis is one of the two nouns derived from ***dikaioō*** (→ JUSTIFY). While the latter term is fairly common in the New Testament, this corresponding noun only occurs twice, in Romans. ***dikaiōsis*** refers in Rom. 4:25 to the resurrection of Christ in conjunction with his death as the ground for our justification. It is this concrete expression of divine grace that results in the acquittal of people's guilt and the declaration of their righteousness in his sight. In Rom. 5:18, the same term indicates that Christ's one act of righteousness (i.e., his death and resurrection, considered as one event) leads to our justification as an antidote to the one trespass of Adam that brought humankind into the bondage of sin and death.

dikaiōma [δικαίωμα, *1345*]

dikaiōma is also derived from ***dikaioō*** (→ JUSTIFY). However, of the ten contexts in which ***dikaiōma*** is found, only Rom. 5:18 explicitly refers to justification as the "free gift" following many sins. This free gift is the finished work of Christ in his death and resurrection, as indicated by the context of Romans 5.

See Also: → JUDGMENT → RIGHTEOUS

JUSTIFY

OT Words

ṣādaq [צָדַק, **6663**]

ṣādaq occurs around forty times and means "justify," "declare righteous," as well as related nuances in a variety of contexts.

When predicated of human beings, ***ṣādaq*** refers to the affirmation or declaration of righteous behavior. Judah speaks this way of his daughter-in-law in Gen. 38:26. See also Job 4:17; 15:14; 25:4. ***ṣādaq*** also indicates the idea of justifying oneself, in the sense of clearing oneself of guilt, or attempting to do so — for example, the brothers of Joseph (Gen. 44:16); and Israel's fruitless attempt to vindicate herself (Isa. 43:26). See also Jer. 3:11; Ezek. 16:51, 52. ***ṣādaq*** also refers to the action of acquittal in a judicial sense (cf. Deut. 25:1; Prov. 17:15; Isa. 5:23). Job 13:18 refers to "being vindicated" before God; and the assertion of one's righteousness is made in Job 32:2; 34:5; 40:8. Ps. 82:3 commends doing what is right and just. Ps. 19:9 affirms that Yahweh is righteous. In Ps. 51:4, David declares that God's treatment of him for his sin was just. Similarly, the psalmist in Ps. 143:2 denies that one is righteous before God. In the midst of his traumatic dilemma, Job denies that God is right (cf. Job 27:5).

When speaking of God, ***ṣādaq*** indicates the action of justifying in the sense of acquittal (cf. 1 Kgs. 8:32). 2 Chr. 6:23 refers to Solomon's plea to Yahweh in this respect during his prayer of dedication for the Jerusalem temple. In Isa. 50:8, the Messianic Servant boldly affirms that God is the one who vindicates or acquits him. It is this same "Suffering Servant" in Isa. 53:11, who, by his substitutionary death, brings about the justification of many in causing them to be declared righteous.

NT Words

dikaioō [δικαιόω, *1344*]

dikaioō is a close dynamic equivalent for the Hebrew verb ***ṣādaq*** (see above). This Greek term for "justify" occurs in about forty contexts, and it may also be translated "declare righteous." ***dikaioō*** usually refers to God's action.

On the rare occasions that ***dikaioō*** refers to the practice of justifying in the human arena, it refers either to justifying oneself, as in Luke 10:29 concerning the lawyer's motive in asking Jesus the question, "Who is my neighbor?"; or to declaring that God's way is right (i.e., "justifying" him, cf. Luke 7:29). In a unique metaphorical reference to the commendation of godly living, wisdom is said to be justified by her deeds (Matt. 11:19) and her children (Luke 7:35).

Elsewhere, "justifying" is an action wholly predicated of God. For example, 1 Tim. 3:16 declares that Jesus is justified by God in the Spirit. In relation to human beings being declared righteous by God, there is the absolute statement in Rom. 8:33 that it is God who justifies. Matt. 12:37 indicates that God uses one's words as a means of either condemnation or acquittal (i.e., justification).

Similarly, it is by the actions of human beings that God will evaluate their standing before him. In Luke 18:14, for example, it is the repentance of the tax collector in Jesus' parable that brings about his justification.

Rom. 2:3 affirms that, by keeping the law perfectly, one will be justified before God. However, it is clear that no mere mortal is able to do so (Rom. 3:20; Gal. 3:11; 5:4 [implied]). As a corollary to this reality, Rom. 4:2 declares that Abraham was justified not by his works, but by his faith and trust in God. Hence, faith and trust in Christ in the new covenant era become the criterion by which one is declared righteous before God (cf. Acts 13:39; Rom. 3:26ff.; 4:5; 5:1; Gal. 2:16; 3:8, 24). The overarching ground of justification is divine grace, as affirmed in Rom. 3:24; Titus 3:7, in relation to which faith is an instrument of justification, as is the blood of Christ (cf. Rom. 5:9). The divinely applied sequence in the application of redemption has the divine calling immediately preceding the believer's justification.

A special note is appropriate in relation to the teaching of Jas. 2:21–25. Here, James is affirming by way of a corollary argument what is implicit in the teaching of the apostle Paul. James wants to emphasize that faith, without the accompanying evidence of good works, is not true faith at all. Here he claims that Abraham and Rahab (for example) were justified by their works. This is not to contradict the Pauline doctrine of justification by grace through faith alone. Rather, James is declaring that faith must be accompanied by, not replaced by, works, if that faith is to be a genuine means of one's justification.

Additional Notes

This term has crucial theological weight in both Old and New Testaments in relation to the way in which people are reconciled to God, and vice versa. There is a considerable overlap in meaning and significance between the ideas of "justify," "(to be) righteous," "justification," and "righteousness."

See Also: → RIGHTEOUS → JUSTIFICATION

K

KEEP, KEEPING

OT Words

shāmar [שָׁמַר, 8104]

A common verb, ***shāmar*** occurs about 450 times with the primary meanings "keep" or "guard," along with other associated senses.

Meaning "keep" in the sense of "tend," or "take care of," ***shāmar*** is found in Gen. 2:15 with reference to Adam and Eve tending the garden of Eden. Gen. 30:31; Hos. 12:12 refer to caring for flocks of animals. Taking care of the royal palace is indicated in 2 Sam. 15:16; 20:3. God is said to take care of Israel in Ps. 121:3ff.; Jer. 31:10. The latter text occurs in the context of Yahweh's promised renewal of Israel.

More commonly, ***shāmar*** refers to "keeping" in the sense of "guarding," or "watching over." General references to this action are found in 1 Sam. 19:11; Neh. 2:8. Gen. 3:24 records the action of God in posting an angelic sentry to guard the way to the tree of life after Adam and Eve's expulsion from the garden. Keeping watch over the tabernacle and its furnishings was the responsibility of the Levites (cf. Lev. 8:35; Num. 1:53; 18:3ff.; 1 Sam. 7:1). Similar attention was given to the temple as well (cf. 1 Kgs. 14:27; 2 Kgs. 11:7; 1 Chr. 23:32; Neh. 11:19; Ezek. 40:45, 46; Zech. 3:7). Josh. 10:18 mentions guarding prisoners.

An extension of the meaning "guard" is that of "protect." In the sphere of divine activity, ***shāmar*** indicates protection by God in Gen. 28:15, 20; 1 Sam. 2:9; Ps. 146:9; Prov. 3:26. The psalmist pleads with God for protection (cf. Pss. 12:7; 16:1; 86:2; 140:4). Closely related to this meaning is the experience of being preserved by God (cf. Josh. 24:17; 1 Kgs. 3:6; Pss. 37:28; 41:2). ***shāmar*** is also used in Exod. 23:20 to indicate the angel of the Lord protecting the Israelites in their wilderness journey. See also Ps. 91:11; Job 2:6. In the "Aaronic blessing" of Num. 6:24, Yahweh is invoked as one who will "bless and keep" his people, or protect and watch over them. Handing over money to one's neighbor for protection or safekeeping is indicated in Exod. 22:7. In a metaphorical context, ***shāmar*** refers to being preserved by discretion (Prov. 2:11), and by wisdom (Prov. 4:6). Used participially, ***shāmar*** has the nominal sense of "keeper," or one who protects — a "minder." For example, Gen. 4:9 records Cain's question of Yahweh: "Am I my brother's keeper?" See also 1 Sam. 17:22; 28:2. The latter text refers to David's "bodyguard." In Esth. 2:3, 14ff., ***shāmar*** refers to the keeper of the harem.

shāmar also has the sense of "obey," primarily with reference to keeping God's laws and statutes. God himself is described as one who keeps his own covenant obligations perfectly (cf. 1 Kgs. 8:23ff.; Neh. 1:5; 9:32; Dan. 9:4; Deut. 7:8ff.). Conversely, the servants of God are also required to keep their solemn obligations under the terms of the covenant — for example, Abraham (Gen. 17:9ff.); Israel at Mt. Sinai (Exod. 19:5), and also at the border of Canaan (Josh. 1:7). See also Ezek. 17:14. The failure of Shimei to keep his covenant oath is recorded in 1 Kgs. 2:43. Blessings for those who keep God's covenant are affirmed in Ps. 103:18. General instructions to "keep" the way of the Lord are given in Gen. 18:19; Judg. 2:22; 2 Sam. 22:22; Ps. 37:34; Prov. 8:32. Specific instructions to keep the commands of Yahweh are given in Gen. 26:5; Exod. 15:26. The law of the covenant is explicitly in view in this regard in Exod. 20:6; Deut. 4:2ff.; 5:1, 10; 6:2ff.; 7:11ff.; 26:16ff.; 28:13, 15, 45, 48; Josh. 22:5; 1 Kgs. 2:3; 8:58; 2 Kgs. 17:13; Ezek. 11:20; 36:37; 37:24. Deut. 12:1 records the obligation of keeping the law of the Lord, laid on the Israelites for as long as they live in the land. A clear intention and desire to keep the law of God is expressed in Ps. 119:17, 44, 55ff., 101, 106. Faithful obedience to Yahweh's commands is recorded in 1 Kgs. 11:34; Job 23:11; Pss. 18:21; 119:167, 168. More commonly, however, the people's failure to keep the divine law covenant is recorded — for example, Saul (1 Sam. 13:13ff.); Solomon (1 Kgs. 11:10, 11); Judah (2 Kgs. 17:19); and the postexilic community of Israel (Neh. 1:7). Frequent reference is made to Israel's failure in this regard (e.g., Ps. 78:10, 56; Jer. 16:11; Amos 2:4; Mal. 2:9; 3:7). Related to this meaning is the idea of obedience with respect to keeping the divinely ordained festivals including Passover (cf. Exod. 12:17ff.; 13:10; 23:15); and the Sabbath day (cf. Exod. 31:13ff.; Lev. 19:3, 30; 26:2; Deut. 5:12; Isa. 56:2ff.).

Other less significant aspects of the use of ***shāmar*** include "keep" in the sense of "store (away)" — including grain (Gen. 41:35); meat (1 Sam. 9:24); and wealth (Eccl. 5:13). ***shāmar*** also refers to the idea of "restrain," "enclose," as in keeping cattle (cf. Exod. 21:29). ***shāmar*** indicates "keep" in the sense of "abstain," "keep away from" sexual relations (1 Sam. 21:4); and ritual uncleanness (Deut. 23:9). In Josh. 6:18, the Israelites are commanded to refrain from taking the plunder of Jericho, or that which was devoted to Yahweh.

ḥāgag [חָגַג, 2287]

This verb has particular reference to keeping or observing festivals of the Israelite ritual calendar in the majority of contexts in which it is found. ***ḥāgag*** occurs sixteen times.

General references to holding or observing the feasts of Yahweh are found in Exod. 5:1; Isa. 42:4; Nah. 1:15. The specific commands to keep or observe the three major Israelite festivals of Passover, Weeks (i.e., Pentecost, in New Testament times), and tabernacles are recorded in Lev. 23:14, 39, 41; Num. 29:12; Deut. 16:15; Zech. 14:16, 18.

'āsāh [עָשָׂה, 6213]

'āsāh, one of the most common verbs in the Old Testament, means "do" or "make" and is found in over 2,500 contexts. In about thirty of these, ***'āsāh*** means "keep."

The primary usage of ***'āsāh*** with this meaning has to do with keeping or celebrating Israelite ritual feasts (e.g., 2 Kgs. 23:21; 2 Chr. 30:1ff.; 35:16, 18). It refers to Passover (Exod. 12:47; Num. 9:2ff.; Deut. 16:1); the Feast of Weeks (Deut. 16:10); Purim (Esth. 9:21, 27); and the specific dedication of the rebuilt wall of Jerusalem (Neh. 12:27). ***'āsāh*** also expresses the requirement to keep the Sabbath (Exod. 31:16; Deut. 5:15).

Other uses of ***'āsāh*** with this meaning include those in 1 Chr. 4:10, where Jabez prays to be kept, or preserved, from evil, and in Esth. 3:8, where the exilic Israelite community in Persia is accused of failing to keep (i.e., obey) the laws of King Xerxes.

'ābad [עָבַד, 5647]

'ābad occurs around three hundred times with the primary sense of "serve," "labor," "work." It means "keep" in only two places. In Exod. 6:5 it refers to the Israelites being kept in bondage by the Egyptians. In Exod. 13:5, Yahweh commands the Israelites to keep or commemorate their day of release from Egyptian captivity.

nāṣar [נָצַר, 5341]

nāṣar is found approximately sixty times with the principal meaning "keep" in the sense of "watch over," "guard," as well as other related nuances.

The meaning "keep" in the sense of "maintain" is indicated in Exod. 34:7, where Yahweh is said to maintain covenant fidelity in love towards his faithful people. An exhortation to maintain wisdom is found in Prov. 3:21.

nāṣar also conveys the sense of "preserve," "watch over," or "protect." Such actions are predicated of God with respect to his people in Pss. 31:23; 32:7; Isa. 26:3; 49:6; Deut. 32:10. Yahweh promises to protect (i.e., keep) his Messianic Servant in Isa. 42:6; 49:8. Ps. 25:21 expresses the desire that integrity and righteousness will protect the writer. God is said to keep, or watch over, one's soul in Prov. 24:12, and to keep (i.e., guard) the paths of justice in Prov. 2:8. The psalmist pleads with God to protect him in Pss. 12:7; 64:1; 140:1; and also asks that God may guard his lips (cf. Ps. 141:3). Prov. 2:11; 4:6, 13 promise that understanding and wisdom will keep (i.e., guard) the one who pursues them.

nāṣar is also translated "keep" in the sense of "observe," "obey." Affirmation of God's people keeping the divine covenant is indicated in Deut. 33:9; Ps. 25:10. Other references to keeping God's commandments are found in Pss. 78:7; 105:45; 119:22, 33; Prov. 3:1; 28:7. Commands to keep to the teaching of one's parents are expressed in Prov. 6:20; 23:26.

Keeping or "tending" a fig tree is mentioned in Prov. 27:18.

ḥāsak [חָשַׂךְ, 2820]

ḥāsak has the underlying sense of "withhold," or "restrain" (i.e., keep from . . .). It is translated this way with related senses in about thirty contexts.

Meaning "keep" in the sense of "prevent," ***ḥāsak*** refers to God preventing people from committing sin — for example, Abimelech, king of Egypt (Gen. 20:6); and David (1 Sam. 25:39). In Ps. 19:13, the psalmist pleads with God to keep him from sinning.

ḥāsak also means "keep back" in the sense of "withhold." For example, Gen. 22:12, 16 refer to Abraham's refusal to keep Isaac back from being sacrificed. Potiphar's generosity in not keeping back anything from Joseph is indicated in Gen. 39:9. 2 Sam. 18:16 speaks of Joab restraining David's troops from pursuing the army of Absalom. Prov. 11:24 refers to keeping back one's wealth and coming to poverty.

ḥāsak means "keep" in the sense of "preserve" in Job 33:18, which records Elihu's affirmation that God preserves his soul from the pit.

nāṭar [נָטַר, 5201]

nāṭar is found in eight contexts and means "keep," "preserve," "maintain" in all but one of these. ***nāṭar*** is also used in a participial form to refer to a "keeper."

nāṭar is translated "to be angry" (lit., "keep anger") with respect to God in Jer. 3:12; Ps. 103:9, where there is the affirmation that God will not always be angry. Jer. 3:5 asks of Yahweh: "Will he be angry forever?" Nah. 1:2 claims that Yahweh will maintain his wrath against his enemies.

In a poetic context, Song 1:6; 8:11, 12 refer to the "keeper" of vineyards.

mānaʿ [מָנַע, 4513]

mānaʿ occurs approximately thirty times and means "to withhold," including the senses of "keep back," "keep from," "restrain," "hinder."

A variety of contexts containing this term indicate the action of "withholding" or "keeping back." In Gen 30:2, the claim is made that God has kept Rachel from bearing children to this point in time. Ps. 84:11; Prov. 3:27 make the point that nothing good is withheld from the godly. Num. 24:11 contains Balak's claim that Yahweh has kept Balaam from being rewarded. Withholding manna from the people of Israel is noted in Neh. 9:20, as is the withholding of food from Job in Job 22:7. Job 38:15 records that light is withheld from the wicked. As an explicit indicator of divine judgment, Jer. 3:3; Amos 4:7 record that Yahweh withholds rain from his people; and Jer. 5:25 makes the general observation that blessing is withheld from Israel because of their sin. Joel 1:13 mentions withholding offerings from the Jerusalem temple as one example of Israel's rebellion against Yahweh. On the level of general admonition, Prov. 23:13 commands parents not to withhold discipline from their children.

In the sense of "hinder" or "prevent," ***mānaʿ*** is translated "keep" in several contexts. Num. 22:16 records the instruction sent to Balaam through the messengers of Balak (king of Moab) not to allow anything to keep him from responding to the king's request to invoke a curse on the people of Israel. In 1 Sam. 25:26, 34 David recognizes that God has kept him from shedding the blood of Nabal through the intervention of the man's wife, Abigail. God commands Jeremiah to refrain from weeping in Jer. 31:16.

mānaʿ is also translated "keep" in the sense of "hold back." Prov. 1:15 speaks of keeping one's foot (back) from the grave (cf. also Jer. 2:25). The writer of Ecclesiastes affirms that no pleasure was held back from him in his quest for life's meaning (cf. Eccl. 2:10). Jer. 42:4 states that no revelation from God will be kept from the prophet. See also Jer. 48:10; Ezek. 31:15.

NT Words

tēreō [τηρέω, *5083*]

tēreō is a verb found seventy-five times and means "keep" in the sense of "obey," "preserve," as well as associated nuances.

The meaning "obey" is found primarily in the context of keeping the commandments of God (cf. Matt. 19:17) and Christ (cf. Matt. 28:20; John 14:15 [implied]). Acts 15:5 expresses the requirement to keep the law of Moses. See also 1 Tim. 6:14. In addition, affirmations of obedience to such commandments are found in John 8:51ff.; 14:21; 17:6; Jas. 2:10; 1 John 2:3; 5:2; Rev. 1:3; 3:8; 12:17; 14:12; 22:7. Conversely, refusal or failure to obey is indicated in Mark 7:9, with reference to the Pharisees. In John 9:16, Jesus is falsely accused of failing to keep the Sabbath. See also John 14:24; 1 John 2:4.

tēreō also means "keep" in the sense of "guard," "watch over." Matt. 27:36, 54 refer to guarding Jesus on the cross. Acts 12:5ff. refers to Peter being kept in prison, and Acts 24:23 refers to Paul in prison. Used participially, ***tēreō*** means "keeper" or "guard" in relation to those watching over Jesus' tomb.

tēreō expresses the idea of "keep" with the sense of "preserve" in a number of different contexts. Keeping the faith is indicated in 2 Tim. 4:7. ***tēreō*** refers to believers being kept or preserved for the coming of the Lord, the eternal inheritance for the people of God (1 Thess. 5:23; 1 John 5:18; Jude 1; 1 Pet. 1:4). Jude 21 contains the commandment to keep oneself in the love of God. In Rev. 3:10, the risen Christ promises to keep the church at Philadelphia safe from the "hour of trial" that will come upon the whole world. This is in response to their faithful endurance in obedience to his command. Several texts also indicate God's intention to preserve the wicked for the day of judgment (cf. 2 Pet. 2:4, 9; 3:7; Jude 13). The command to keep oneself pure is found in 1 Tim. 5:22; Jas. 1:27; and the instruction to maintain the unity of the Spirit in Eph. 4:3.

At a more mundane level, ***tēreō*** also refers to the action of preserving good wine (John 2:10), and perfume (John 12:7).

2 Cor. 11:9 speaks of Paul keeping himself from being a financial burden to the Corinthian congregation.

poieō [ποιέω, *4160*]

The verb ***poieō*** is common, occurring about six hundred times with the primary sense of "do," "make."

However, in Matt. 26:18, ***poieō*** is translated "keep" in reference to Jesus' intention to observe the Passover with his disciples.

phylassō [φυλάσσω, *5442*]

phylassō occurs around thirty times with the primary meaning "keep," as well as a number of related nuances that render the term a close synonym of ***tēreō*** (see above).

With regard to the commands or statutes of God, ***phylassō*** is translated "keep" with the underlying sense of "obey." 1 Tim. 5:21; 6:20 refer to the command to keep the divine laws. Obedience is acknowledged in Matt. 19:20; Mark 10:20; Luke 18:21; Acts 21:24; Rom. 2:26; Gal. 6:13. The blessing for keeping these laws is affirmed in Luke 11:28. Conversely, an indictment for failing to keep them is found in Acts 7:53.

phylassō is also translated "keep watch over" or "protect" in Luke 2:8, in the context of caring for sheep. John 17:12 refers to Jesus protecting his disciples. In 2 Thess. 3:3 Paul assures his Thessalonian congregation that God will protect them from the evil one. 2 Pet. 2:5 records the historical observation that God protected Noah from the effects of the flood.

phylassō also means "keep," as in "guard." The experience of being kept under guard in chains is mentioned in relation to the Gadarene demoniac (Luke 8:29); and in relation to imprisonment (Acts 12:4; 23:35; 28:16). Luke 11:21 refers to guarding one's property. The exhortation to be on guard is indicated in Luke 12:15, where Jesus warns against cultivating such an attitude. In 2 Tim. 4:15, Paul warns his readers to be on their guard against Alexander the coppersmith, who did him a great deal of harm. Similarly, Peter warns his readers against lawless men in 2 Pet. 3:17.

phylassō is also translated "keep" in the sense of "retain." In John 12:25, Jesus declares that the one who "hates" his life in this world will retain it for eternal life. Acts 22:20 refers to retaining articles of clothing.

The idea of "refrain from" is also evident in the usage of this term. ***phylassō*** occurs in Acts 25:25 with reference to Gentile converts being required to refrain from, or keep themselves from, ritual uncleanness. 1 John 5:21 expresses the command to keep oneself from idol worship.

phylassō also refers to "keeping" in the sense of "preserving." In 2 Tim. 1:12, Paul communicates his assurance that God is able to preserve (or guard) the salvation promised to him. Jude expresses a similar assurance that God will keep him from falling away and thereby preserve him for the day of judgment (cf. Jude 24).

diaphylassō [διαφυλάσσω, *1314*]

diaphylassō is found only in Luke 4:10 meaning "to guard," referring to the angelic protection of the Messiah.

katechō [κατέχω, *2722*]

katechō occurs in about twenty places, meaning "keep" in the sense of "hold fast," "secure," "hold back" in about half of these contexts.

The sense of "hold back" is evident in Luke 4:42, where the crowds attempt to prevent Jesus from leaving them. Rom. 1:18 speaks of the wicked attempting (in vain) to hold back (i.e., suppress) the truth of divine revelation in their own lives. 2 Thess. 2:6, 7 describe the restraining of the antichrist, the lawless one, who will be held back by God until the time is right for his appearing.

katechō also conveys the sense of "holding fast," or "keeping with passionate conviction." ***katechō*** refers to holding fast to God's word (Luke 8:15); the traditions of the gospel (1 Cor. 11:2); belief in the gospel (1 Cor. 15:2); and our hope in Christ (Heb. 3:6, 14; 10:23).

In Phlm. 13 ***katechō*** conveys the sense of "retain," referring to Paul's desire to keep Onesimus, the runaway slave, as an assistant in the work of the gospel. However, he recognized that it was best to return Onesimus to his master Philemon.

diatēreō [διατηρέω, *1301*]

diatēreō occurs only twice. Luke 2:51 refers to Jesus' mother keeping in her heart the insights she had gained from her son's encounter with the chief priests and elders in the Jerusalem temple. Acts 15:29 refers to the Jerusalem church leaders' instructions to recent Gentile converts to keep away from ritual and moral uncleanness.

heortazō [ἑορτάζω, *1858*]

heortazō is found only in 1 Cor. 5:8 and refers to keeping the feast of the Passover in sincerity and truth.

phroureō [φρουρέω, *5432*]

phroureō occurs four times, referring to the process of "guarding" or "confirming." In 2 Cor. 11:32 it refers literally to King Aretas placing the city of Damascus under guard in order to seize the apostle Paul. The remaining references are metaphorical, with a spiritual application. In Gal. 3:23, Paul speaks of Christians being kept or confined under the law of Moses before their conversion to Christ, when they were freed from the law. Phil. 4:17 refers to the peace of God guarding or preserving our minds in Jesus Christ; and 1 Pet. 1:5 indicates believers being guarded or preserved by God's power through faith in Christ.

Additional Notes

The Hebrew and Greek vocabulary for "keeping" is complex and multi-faceted, with a broad semantic range. What is particularly significant from a theological and redemptive-historical viewpoint is the dynamic that emerges from the Old Testament and finds its fulfillment in the New concerning God "preserving" his people in various circumstances, whether it be on their journey through the wilderness, or in the land of Canaan. The concept of preservation is also evident in Yahweh's "keeping watch" over his Servant in the Isaianic prophecy. The two primary Hebrew verbs that convey these perspectives are ***shāmar*** and ***nāṣar.***

In the New Testament, the "preservation" of the saints does not revolve around a guarantee of material blessing, as was the case under the old covenant. Rather, the hope of the believer is centered on Christ and the eternal life he has procured for all who believe and trust in him. In particular, the verbs ***tēreō*** and ***phylassō*** convey the thought that God has determined to "preserve" his people for the final day of judgment so that they will be guaranteed their eternal inheritance in Christ. This hope is the consummate fulfillment of salvation, to which the earthly blessings of prosperity in Canaan and all other material benefits of the old covenant pointed. As God "kept" his people of old, so he will "keep" his people in the last days of the new covenant age, guaranteeing their eternal salvation based on the finished work of Christ.

See Also: → JOIN → SHEPHERD → SILENCE → SUBJECT

KEEPER

OT Words

shāmar **[שָׁמַר, 8104]**

This common verb form occurs around five hundred times and is translated "keep," "guard," "protect," as well as a number of related meanings. In about twenty places, however, ***shāmar*** is used nominally to indicate a "keeper," "guard," or "protector."

With the sense of "protector," ***shāmar*** occurs in Gen. 4:9 where Cain responds to Yahweh's question as to Abel's whereabouts: "Am I my brother's keeper?" 1 Sam. 17:20 mentions the "keeper" of the flock.

shāmar refers to a "keeper" or "guard" in a number of contexts — to a keeper of baggage or supplies (1 Sam. 17:22); a bodyguard (1 Sam. 28:2); the keeper of a wardrobe (2 Kgs. 22:14; 2 Chr. 34:2); the keeper of the harem (Esth. 2:3, 8, 15); and the keeper of the royal forest (Neh. 2:8). In relation to the temple, Neh. 3:29 refers to the keeper of the east gate, and Jer. 35:4 refers to the keeper of one of the temple doors.

sar **[שַׂר, 8269]**

sar is a common term, indicating one who is in charge, such as a "prince," "leader," or "captain." The term occurs over four hundred times. On three occasions, however, ***sar*** also refers to a "keeper" in the sense of a "prison guard" (Gen. 39:21–23) in relation to Joseph's incarceration in Egypt in Potiphar's prison.

nāṭar **[נָטַר, 5201]**

nāṭar is a rare verb form, occurring only nine times with the principal meanings "keep," "guard." However, on three occasions it is used participially as a noun to refer to the "keeper" of the vineyard in Song 1:6; 8:11, 12.

NT Words

desmophylax [δεσμοφύλαξ, *1200*]

This term is rare, occurring only three times with reference to a "keeper of the prison," or a jailer (cf. Acts 16:23, 27, 36).

See Also: → SHEPHERD → GUARD → JAILER

KEY

OT Words

maphtēaḥ **[מַפְתֵּחַ, 4668]**

maphtēaḥ is a rare noun, occurring only three times with reference to a key in the literal sense of an opening device (Judg. 3:25; 1 Chr. 9:27). In Isa. 22:22, ***maphtēaḥ*** refers metaphorically to the "key" of the house of David being placed on the shoulder of Eliakim the high priest as a symbol of his spiritual authority over Israel.

NT Words

kleis [κλείς, *2807*]

kleis occurs six times and refers to "key" only in a metaphorical sense, but with powerful symbolism in each context. In Matt. 16:19, Jesus promises to give Peter the "keys" of the kingdom as a sign of his apostolic authority. In Luke 11:52, the ***kleis*** refers to the "key" of knowledge which the Israelite lawyers had removed and deprived many people of the opportunity to enter into the kingdom of heaven. The supreme spiritual authority of Jesus the Messiah-King is indicated by the risen Christ holding the "keys" to death and Hades (Rev. 1:18), and the "key of David" (Rev. 3:7). In Rev. 9:1; 20:1, ***kleis*** refers to the "key" of the bottomless pit as one of the symbols for the place of eternal punishment.

Additional Notes

The Hebrew and Greek vocabulary for "key" is limited to just two terms functioning as dynamic equivalents. While both ***maphtēaḥ*** and ***kleis*** occur infrequently, there is considerable significance in the reference to the "key of the house of David" given to the high priest Eliakim in Isa. 22:22 — a motif that is specifically cited in Rev. 3:7 in relation to the risen Christ, who is described as holding the "key of David." The source of the allusion in Rev. 3:7 is undoubtedly the passage in Isaiah 22, and the dominant theme in both texts is that of authority. In Isa. 22:22, it is a high priestly authority that is in view, and in Rev. 3:7 the supreme authority of the heavenly Christ. The fact that the key is said to belong to David suggests that it embodies messianic significance. Therefore, the authority of the high priestly "key of David" in the Old Testament finds its consummate counterpart in the authority of the one who supremely embraces the office of both king and priest as the King of kings and the great high priest of the people of God of all ages.

KICK

OT Words

bā'at **[בָּעַט, 1163]**

bā'at occurs only in Deut. 32:15, meaning "kick" and referring metaphorically to the people of Israel, likened to an animal who kicked as it grew older and fatter, indicating Israel's increasing neglect and disdain of her God.

NT Words

laktizō [λακτίζω, *2979*]

laktizō occurs only once, referring to the action of "kicking" in a metaphorical sense. In Acts 26:14, Christ uses the term in Saul's vision on the occasion of his conversion. The Lord questions the persecutor of his people and makes the point that it is hard for Saul "to kick against the goads." The allusion is to an ox that tries to break free of the yoke and only succeeds in kicking against the iron spikes of the plow.

KID

OT Words

gedîyāh **[גְּדִיָּה, 1429]**

gedîyāh is found only in Song 1:8, where it indicates "kids," or young female goats.

se'îrāh **[שְׂעִירָה, 8166]**

se'îrāh is only found in two contexts, and on each occasion it refers to the ritual sacrifice of a female kid goat as a sin offering (cf. Lev. 4:28; 5:6).

See Also: → GOAT

KIDNEYS

OT Words

kelāyôt **[כְּלָיוֹת, 3629]**

kelāyôt occurs around thirty times and refers to the physical organ of the kidneys as well as to the heart of human emotion and volition. In the latter instance ***kelāyôt*** is translated "heart."

In its literal sense, ***kelāyôt*** refers to kidneys most commonly in relation to the physical organs of slaughtered sacrificial animals — for example, bullocks (cf. Exod. 29:13; Lev. 8:25; 7:4; 8:16); rams (cf. Exod. 29:22; Lev. 8:25; 9:19); a goat (cf. Lev. 3:15); a calf (cf. Lev. 9:10); an unspecified animal (Lev. 3:4, 10); and humans (Job 16:13).

The metaphorical sense of ***kelāyôt***, the "heart," is found in Job 19:27; Pss. 7:9; 16:7; 26:2; 73:21. In Jer. 11:20; 17:10 it is said that Yahweh tries people's hearts. See also Jer. 12:2; 20:12; Lam. 3:13. ***kelāyôt*** is translated "inward parts" (Ps. 139:13) and "inmost being" (Prov. 23:16), with these two latter expressions denoting the essence of one's being, synonymous with the metaphorical sense of "heart."

KILL

OT Words

nākāh **[נָכָה, 5221]**

This verb form is common and occurs around five hundred times, with the primary meanings "strike," "kill," as well as a number of associated senses.

nākāh incorporates the sense of "strike" in the context of humans slaying other humans. General references to this kind of killing are found, for example, in Gen. 14:5ff.; 36:35; Exod. 2:11ff.; Judg. 12:4; 2 Sam. 17:2; Jer. 41:2. Saul's attempted murder of David is recorded in 1 Sam. 20:33, and Amnon's slaying by Absalom is found in 2 Sam. 13:28. David's infamous murder of Uriah the Hittite is described in 2 Sam. 11:15, 21. Gen. 4:15 refers to Cain's fear of being killed.

At a more formal level, legislation against and penalties for murder are found in Exod. 21:12; 22:2; Lev. 24:17; Num. 35:16ff.; Deut. 27:24. Similarly, legislation for accidental killing or manslaughter is indicated in Num. 35:11, 15; Deut. 19:4; Josh. 20:3ff.

nākāh also refers to the conflicts between nations which involve mass killing. In this regard the victories of Israel over her enemies are indicated, for example, in Num. 21:24, 35; Deut. 1:4; 4:46; 1 Sam. 13:4; 1 Sam. 17:9, 25ff.; 2 Sam. 8:3ff.; 1 Kgs. 11:15; 2 Kgs. 20:20. The divinely-instigated "ban" or ***ḥērem*** (→ ***DEDICATE*** → ***DESTROY***) against the Canaanite peoples involves the command to slaughter them in a wholesale fashion (cf. Deut. 7:2; 13:15; Josh. 7:5; 8:21ff.; 12:1ff.; Judg. 1:4ff.; 11:21). Conversely, the victories of Israel's enemies over Israel herself also involve a great deal of killing (cf. Judg. 3:13; 1 Kgs. 15:20; Jer. 20:4). In regard to Gentile nations, Dan. 8:7 refers metaphorically to the slaughter of the Persian enemies by the Greek military forces by describing a goat slaughtering a ram.

nākāh also means "destroy" in the sense of "slay" or "kill," wholly in the context of bringing judgment against the wicked. Such punishment is invoked against Israel for her rebellion against Yahweh (cf. Num. 11:33; 14:12; Isa. 5:25; Ezek. 7:9; 9:5ff.); and also against particular Israelites — for example, Zimri (Num. 25:14ff.), for bringing a Midianite woman into the Israelite camp; and Uzziah (2 Sam. 6:7), for handling the ark of the covenant. An exceptionally significant illustration of such treatment is found in Isa. 53:4, where the Messianic Servant is said to be put to death by God — not because he himself is guilty of sin, but because he bears the sin of his people. Such a prediction anticipates the death of Christ on the cross. Divine destruction of the nations for their wickedness is indicated, for example, against the Philistines (cf. 1 Sam. 5:2; 6:19); Assyria (cf. Isa. 37:36); Egypt (cf. Jer. 43:11); and the world at large (cf. Isa. 11:4). Other instances of such punishment include the plague judgments against Egypt (cf. Exod. 3:20; 9:15). The most significant of these was the Passover plague, in which all firstborn sons in Egyptian households were slain by the avenging angel (cf. Exod. 12:12ff.; Num. 3:13; Pss. 78:51; 105:36; 136:10).

nākāh refers to the slaughter of animals as the penalty for killing a person (cf. Lev. 24:21). Lev. 24:18ff. refers to compensation being given to the owner of an animal that has been slain by accident at the hands of a third party.

hārag [הָרַג, 2026]

hārag occurs around 150 times and has the primary senses of "slay," "kill," "murder," used only to refer to people.

General references to killing individuals are found in Gen. 4:8; 34:25; Judg. 9:5; 20:5; 2 Sam. 3:30; 12:9; 1 Kgs. 2:5. Legislation prescribing the penalty for murder is found in Exod. 21:14. The command not to slay the innocent is found in Exod. 23:7. Pss. 10:8; 94:6 refer to the wicked slaying the innocent. ***hārag*** also refers to an intent to kill, rather than to the act itself (cf. Gen. 27:41, 42; 37:20; Exod. 2:14, 15; Num. 22:29; Judg. 16:2; 1 Sam. 16:2; 1 Kgs. 18:12ff.; Neh. 6:10). One of the most significant examples of this phenomenon is Haman's abortive plot to have all Jews in Persian captivity killed — a plan which failed spectacularly, resulting in the slaughter of many of the Persian people (cf. Esth. 3:13; 7:4; 8:11; 9:6ff.).

hārag is also found in numerous contexts in which killing is the outcome of divine judgment. Most striking is the example of the Passover slaughter in Exod. 13:15, where the angel of death slays the firstborn male of every Egyptian household in response to Pharaoh's refusal to release the Israelite people from captivity. Other incidents of divine slaughter include that in 1 Kgs. 19:1, 10, referring to Elijah's execution of the prophets of Baal on Mt. Carmel. Similar judgment is invoked against Moab (cf. Amos 2:3); Midian (cf. Num. 31:7, 8; Isa. 14:19); Tyre (cf. Ezek. 26:6ff.); the Canaanite kings (cf. Ps. 136:18); and the whole earth (cf. Isa. 26:21; 27:1). Even the people of Yahweh do not escape episodes of capital punishment. Judah is treated thus in 2 Chr. 36:17 at the hands of the Babylonians (cf. also Lam. 2:2); as is Israel in the wilderness in Ps. 78:31, 34, and at the hands of the Assyrians in Ezek. 23:10 (cf. also Hos. 6:5; Amos 4:10; 9:1). There is a prayer for God's enemies to be slain in Jer. 18:21. Divine intent to kill is expressed in Exod. 4:23; 32:27. In contrast, Ezek. 37:9 contains the divine promise to resurrect the "slain" nation of Israel.

Capital punishment is specifically provided for in Lev. 20:15 for the sin of bestiality. The process of execution is indicated in Deut. 13:9; 2 Sam. 4:12; Ezek. 9:6.

The Israelite "ban" (*ḥērem*) against Canaan, in which many local inhabitants are slain, is recorded in Josh. 8:24; 10:11; Judg. 7:25; 8:17ff. In another military context, David's slaughter of the Syrian army is recorded in 2 Sam. 10:18.

In a metaphorical context, anger is said to kill the fool in Job 5:2; Prov. 1:32.

shāḥat [שָׁחַט, 7819]

shāḥat occurs around eighty times and consistently means "kill," "slay," referring to both people and animals.

In the context of sacrifice, ***shāḥat*** indicates the horrendous practice of child sacrifice to idols (Isa. 57:5; Ezek. 16:21; 23:39). Gen. 22:10 also refers to its intent and preparation. Here Abraham is restrained from slaying his son Isaac only by the last-minute intervention of God.

In regard to animal sacrifice, ***shāḥat*** is used in a variety of contexts — a bull is slaughtered for a burnt offering (Exod. 29:20; Lev. 1:5); an offering of dedication (Exod. 29:11, 16; 1 Sam. 1:25); as a sin offering (Lev. 4:4, 15; 8:11; 16:15); and as a fellowship offering (Lev. 9:18). A calf is offered as a burnt offering in Lev. 9:8, 12. A goat is slain for a sin offering in Lev. 4:24, 29; 9:15; 16:15; 2 Chr. 29:24. Lev. 3:13 records the slaying of a goat for a fellowship offering. In similar contexts, a lamb is slain for a sin offering (Lev. 4:33; 14:13, 25); and specifically for the Passover (2 Chr. 30:15; 35:1, 6, 11; Ezra 6:20). A ram is slain for a burnt offering in Lev. 8:19, 23. Various animals are slain for a cleansing ritual in a number of contexts: birds (Lev. 14:5, 6, 50, 51); a red heifer (Num. 19:3); rams and lambs (2 Chr. 29:22). General, non-specific slaughter for offering is indicated in Lev. 17:3; 22:28.

Non-ritual slaughter of animals is indicated in Gen. 37:31, where a goat is killed for the purposes of deceiving Jacob into believing that his son Joseph has been slain by a wild animal. Joseph's brothers had dipped Joseph's coat in the blood of the goat. Flocks and herds are slain for food in Num. 11:22; 1 Sam. 14:32, 34; Isa. 22:13. A lamb is slain in preparation for a Passover meal in Exod. 12:6, 21. See also Isa. 66:3.

shāḥat is also used to refer to slaying people in Judg. 12:6, where a civil war is waged against Ephraim. In Jer. 41:7 murder is in view; and ***shāḥat*** is found in the context of divine judgment in Num. 14:16; 1 Kgs. 18:40; 2 Kgs. 10:7, 14; 25:7; Jer. 39:6; 52:10.

mût [מוּת, 4191]

mût is a common verb occurring around 850 times with the primary sense of "die." However, on about 200 occasions it is causative, meaning "kill" or "slay," or "put to death."

The sense of killing people, "murder," is found in several contexts (e.g., 2 Sam. 13:28; 1 Kgs. 16:10; 1 Chr. 19:18; Ps. 59:1; 1 Kgs. 15:28). Intent to murder is expressed in 1 Sam. 19:1ff.; 20:33; and the attempted murder is expressed in 1 Kgs. 11:40; Gen. 37:18.

mût also refers to killing as an aspect of divine judgment. Such punishment is meted out to the enemies of Yahweh in 1 Sam. 15:13; 2 Sam. 8:2; Isa. 11:4; 14:30. In particular, the exercise of the "ban" against the Canaanite tribes, involving their slaughter, is mentioned in Lev. 27:28. In 1 Sam. 2:25, the pronouncement of execution is recorded against the wicked sons of Eli, Hophni and Phinehas, and carried out in 1 Sam. 3:11. In other contexts, ***mût*** indicates the anticipated certainty of such a judgment. For instance, Isa. 14:30 records the certainty of God slaying the survivors of Philistia; and a similar threat is made against the apostate of Israel in Isa. 65:15. See also Num. 14:15; Jer. 52:27. In similar contexts, the divine intention to implement capital punishment is expressed in Exod. 16:3; 17:3; Num. 16:13; Judg. 13:23. Interestingly, Gen. 18:25 records Abraham's conviction that God would never slay the righteous along with the wicked.

Execution at the hands of human beings is referred to in 2 Kgs. 11:15; 2 Sam. 21:9; Esth. 4:11. The intent to execute is found in Jer. 26:15; 38:4; 1 Sam. 11:12. Lev. 20:4 refers to Israel's failure to put to death those who practice child sacrifice — an omission for which they themselves would be held responsible.

This use of ***mût*** is also associated with legislation to execute under the Mosaic covenant, commonly expressed in the passive sense of ". . . be put to death." Capital punishment is prescribed under divine law for a number of offenses including murder (cf. Exod. 21:12ff.; Lev. 24:17, 21; 24:21; Num. 35:30); false prophecy (cf. Deut. 13:5); illicit sexual relationships (cf. Lev. 19:20; 20:10ff.); rebellion against God's authority (cf. Josh. 1:18); sacrilege against Yahweh (cf. Exod. 19:12; Num. 1:51; 3:10, 38; 35:16ff.); idolatry (cf. Deut. 13:9; Lev. 20:2); Sabbath violation (cf. Exod. 31:14, 15; 35:2; Num. 15:35); and occult practices (cf. Lev. 20:27). Before a verdict of guilty could be handed down for these and similar crimes, there had to be credible evidence from at least two or three witnesses (cf. Deut. 17:6).

mût is also used metaphorically. Job 5:2 affirms that jealousy slays the simple. Prov. 21:25 warns that the craving of the sluggard will kill him. Ps. 34:21 declares that evil will slay the wicked. In Hos. 2:3, there is the allegory of Yahweh's intention to slay Israel the "prostitute" with thirst, as punishment for her "adultery," or her idolatrous worship of pagan deities.

rāṣaḥ [רָצַח, 7523]

rāṣaḥ is another synonym for the preceding terms. It occurs around forty times meaning "kill," "murder," "slay" as well as the passive sense of "put to death."

The action of murder is indicated in Judg. 20:4; 1 Kgs. 21:19; Ps. 94:6; Hos. 4:2; 6:9, and the intent to murder is found in Jer. 7:9. The divine prohibition against murder is enshrined in the sixth commandment, "do not kill" (Exod. 20:13; Deut. 5:17). ***rāṣaḥ*** refers to the act of execution (i.e., being put to death) in Num. 35:30.

rāṣaḥ also occurs in a participial form meaning "manslayer," or one who unintentionally causes the death of another human being. References to this misdemeanor are found in Num. 35:11ff.; Deut. 4:42; 19:3ff.; Josh. 20:3ff. In order to allow the "manslayer" to escape retribution from the family and friends of the one slain unintentionally, "cities of refuge" are provided as a safe harbor for such offenders. These cities are mentioned in Josh. 21:13ff.; Num. 35:6ff. Scripture also makes it clear that such refuges are not for murderers, who were to be put to death following due judicial process.

The participial usage of ***rāṣaḥ*** also refers to those "who kill with intent," and thus is a synonym for "murderer" (cf. Num. 35:16ff.; Deut. 22:26; 2 Kgs. 6:32; Job 24:14; Isa. 1:21).

ṭābaḥ [טָבַח, 2873]

ṭābaḥ is a rare synonym for the preceding terms, occurring eleven times with the meanings "kill," "slay," "slaughter."

In non-ritual contexts, ***ṭābaḥ*** refers to the slaughter of animals for food (e.g., Gen. 43:16; 1 Sam. 25:11; Prov. 9:2). Exod. 22:1 refers to the slaughter of an animal in a non-specific context. In Deut. 28:31, the slaughter of an ox is seen as an outworking of the covenant curse in the event of Israel's disobedience — it was a significant economic loss for the owner of the beast.

ṭābaḥ also refers to killing people as an action of the wicked (Ps. 37:14); and as an intended action against the prophet Jeremiah (Jer. 11:19).

Divine judgment resulting in the slaughter of rebellious Israelites is also in view in the usage of ***ṭābaḥ***. In Lam. 2:21, the savage judgment of Yahweh is recorded against the inhabitants of Jerusalem. See also Jer. 25:34. In Ezek. 21:10, Babylon is described as the instrument of Yahweh's judgment against Israel. Jer. 51:40 records Yahweh's threat against Babylon, promising that they will be led away "like lambs to the slaughter."

qāṭal [קָטַל, 6991]

This is a rare verb occurring only three times, with the sense of "kill," "slay." Job 13:15 cites Job's fear that God will slay him. The actions of a murderer are indicated in Job 24:14; and the psalmist pleads with God to slay the wicked in Ps. 139:9.

NT Words

phoneuō [φονεύω, *5407*]

phoneuō is a verb occurring about twelve times with the consistent meaning "kill," in the sense of "murder" or "slay."

General references to killing others are found in Jas. 4:2; 5:6. The murder of the prophets in earlier Israelite history is recorded in Matt. 23:31, 35.

Reaffirmation of the sixth commandment prohibiting murder is found in Matt. 5:21; 19:18; Mark 10:19; Luke 18:20; Rom. 13:9; Jas. 2:11.

apokteinō [ἀποκτείνω, *615*]

This verb is the most common New Testament term for "kill," "slay," "put to death." ***apokteinō*** occurs around eighty times.

The meaning "kill," in a general sense, is found in a number of places. Matt. 10:28; Luke 12:4 contain Jesus' exhortation to his listeners not to fear those who can kill the body, but the one who can cast both body and soul into hell. Accidental catastrophe is indicated in Luke 13:4, which describes the death of eighteen people when the tower in Siloam fell on them. Other general references are found in Mark 3:4, John 8:22; Rev. 13:10.

The action of execution, or being put to death, is also evident in the usage of ***apokteinō*** — or, more accurately, the anticipation of that procedure. The term is used in reference to Jesus' approaching death as he predicts his suffering to come (cf. Matt. 16:21; 17:23; Mark 8:31; 9:31; 10:34; Luke 9:22; 18:33). ***apokteinō*** is also used in reference to the plot to kill Jesus (cf. Matt. 26:4; Mark 14:1; Luke 13:31; John 7:1, 19, 20, 25; 11:53). Two passages refer back to Jesus' execution (cf. Acts 3:15; 1 Thess. 2:15).

apokteinō also anticipates the execution or violent death of John the Baptist (cf. Matt. 14:5; Mark 6:19);

Lazarus (cf. John 12:10); and the disciples of Jesus (cf. Matt. 24:9; John 16:2). The book of Revelation mentions the prospective deaths of the wicked at the hands of God (cf. Rev. 2:23; 6:8; 9:15, 18; 11:5, 13; 19:21).

apokteinō also has the specific sense of "murder" in a number of places. In the parables of Jesus, for example, it refers to vineyard tenants who slay the servants of the owner (cf. Matt. 21:35; Mark 12:5); and also the owner's son (cf. Matt. 21:38, 39; Mark 12:7, 8; Luke 20:14, 15). See also Matt. 22:6. The New Testament also speaks of the callous way in which many of Israel's prophets had been murdered by their own people in the past (cf. Matt. 23:37; Luke 11:47, 48, 49; 13:34; Acts 7:52; Rom. 11:3). During Paul's lifetime, several attempts were made to kill him (cf. Acts 21:31; 23:12, 14; 27:42). See also Rev. 2:13; 11:7; 13:15.

apokteinō is also used metaphorically. Paul speaks of himself being put to death by the effect of sin and the law in his life (Rom. 7:11). Similarly, Paul refers to the lethal impact of the law (2 Cor. 3:6). Eph. 2:16 refers to Christ slaying the enemy of sin and death.

thyō [θύω, *2380*]

This term is translated "kill" in the sense of "sacrifice," or "slaughter," in all but one context. ***thyō*** occurs thirteen times.

The slaughter of animals is in view for a festive celebration in Matt. 22:4; Luke 15:23, 27, 30; Acts 10:13; 11:7. The sacrifice of the Passover lamb is mentioned in Mark 14:12; Luke 22:7; and Jesus' sacrifice as "our Passover Lamb" is referred to in 1 Cor. 5:7.

There is a non-specific use of ***thyō***, "to kill," in reference to the action of a thief in John 10:10.

diacheirizomai [διαχειρίζομαι, *1315*]

diacheirizomai is rare, occurring only twice and indicating the act of killing. Acts 5:30 refers to Jesus being slain and hung on a "tree" (i.e., a cross). Acts 26:21 describes the abortive attempt of a Jewish mob to kill the apostle Paul.

thanatoō [θανατόω, *2289*]

thanatoō is found on eleven occasions and is usually translated "put to death," both literally and metaphorically.

In reference to literal slaying, several texts indicate the actions of children in having their parents put to death (cf. Matt. 10:21; Mark 13:12; Luke 21:16). The plot to have Jesus put to death is recorded in Matt. 26:59; 27:1; Mark 14:55. 1 Pet. 3:18 speaks of Jesus having been put to death in the flesh but made alive by the Spirit.

In a metaphorical context, ***thanatoō*** refers to putting to death sinful misdeeds, which, if undertaken by the Spirit, will lead to life (cf. Rom. 8:13). In an illustration of hyperbole, Rom. 8:36 describes the extreme suffering of the apostle Paul in terms of "being killed all day long . . ." (cf. also 2 Cor. 6:9). Rom. 7:4 speaks of the believer "dying to the law" through the body of Christ.

anaireō [ἀναιρέω, *337*]

anaireō occurs around twenty times meaning "kill" in the sense of "slay," "put to death" on all but one occasion, where it signifies "abolish" (cf. Heb. 10:9).

Matt. 2:16 refers to slaying infants according to Herod's decree to have all male children below the age of two put to death as an attempt to get rid of the Christ child, whom he viewed as a potential claimant to the Jewish throne. Other references to the act of murder are found in Acts 7:28; 12:2; 5:36.

anaireō also conveys the meaning "to execute" in several contexts, such as the death of Stephen, the first Christian martyr (cf. Acts 22:20); the thieves on the cross alongside Christ (cf. Luke 22:32); and the death of Jesus Christ himself (cf. Acts 2:23; 10:39; 13:28). Acts 26:10 also speaks of Christians persecuted for their faith by Saul of Tarsus, who voted for their execution.

anaireō is also found in contexts where the intent to kill is expressed, as is the case with ***apokteinō*** (see above). Examples of this usage are found in relation to the plot to kill Paul (cf. Acts 9:23, 29; 23:15, 21, 27; 25:3); and also Jesus (cf. Luke 22:2). Acts 5:33 refers to the intention to have Peter and other apostles killed. Acts 16:27 mentions the attempted or threatened suicide of the Philippian jailer.

sphazō [σφάζω, *4969*]

Another synonym for the preceding terms, ***sphazō*** also means "kill," "slay," where a violent death is in view. This verb is found ten times.

sphazō, with the sense of "murder," is found in 1 John 3:12 (twice) in regard to Cain killing his brother Abel. In Rev. 6:4, in relation to the universal judgment of God against wickedness, ***sphazō*** indicates slaughter with the sword.

The sense of "put to death," or "execute," is also evident in the usage of ***sphazō***. It is used in Rev. 5:6, 9, 12; 13:8 to refer to Christ as the Lamb of God; and in Rev. 6:9; 18:24 to refer to Christian martyrs.

sphazō is also found in a metaphorical context in Rev. 13:3, indicating the "fatal wounding" of the sea beast. As the satanic counterpart to the Son of God in this "unholy trinity" in Rev. 12 and 13, the sea beast mimics the resurrection of Christ from the dead in his recovery from this fatal assault.

KIN, KINSMAN

OT Words

***qārôb* [קָרוֹב, 7138]**

qārôb is primarily an adjective, meaning "near" in the sense of place or time. It is found in eighty contexts, and in eight of these ***qārôb*** is also translated nominally, meaning "kin," "kinsman," "kinsfolk" (i.e., family relatives).

In the sense of "nearest relative," ***qārôb*** is translated "kin" in Lev. 25:25 in regard to their function of redeeming property. In Num. 27:11 it refers to the recipient of an inheritance; and in the book of Ruth to the one who will exercise the right of marrying the wife of his deceased brother (or nearest relative) in order to raise up children to carry on his name in Israel (cf. Ruth 2:20; 3:12). The celebrated marriage of Boaz and Ruth illustrates this phenomenon of the so-called "Levirate marriage."

qārôb refers generally to "kin" in Lev. 21:2; 2 Sam. 19:42; Job 19:14; Ps. 38:11.

***gā'al* [גָּאַל, 1350]**

This term occurs around one hundred times and is utilized as a verb with the sense of "redeem" in about half of these contexts. However, in its participial form *gō'ēl,* it is translated nominally as "redeemer," "kinsman," and "kinsman-redeemer" on about ten occasions. These terms carry significant theological weight in reference to both God and human beings.

The meaning "kinsman" or "relative" in a general sense is indicated in Num. 5:8; Ruth 2:20; 1 Kgs. 16:11.

gō'ēl in the sense of "kinsman-redeemer" is found exclusively in the book of Ruth. Here Boaz is identified as a "kinsman-redeemer" who is in a position to take Ruth as his wife and raise up children for Naomi, who had lost her husband Elimelech and both her sons, one of whom was the husband of Ruth. These references to Boaz are found in Ruth 3:9, 12, 13; 4:14. Ruth 4:1, 3, 6, 8 refer to a relative closer to Naomi than Boaz. However, this man declines the offer given to him by the latter, therefore freeing Boaz to marry Ruth.

***she'ēr* [שְׁאֵר, 7607]**

she'ēr is a noun occurring sixteen times. About half of these texts refer to "flesh" in the sense of the human body, or food. ***she'ēr*** means "kin" in eight places.

she'ēr refers generally to "kin" or near relative in Lev. 21:2; Jer. 51:35. Intimate sexual relationships with such close relatives are expressly forbidden in Lev. 18:6, 13; 20:19. In Lev. 25:49, ***she'ēr*** refers to a blood relative capable of acting as a redeemer to buy back a poverty-stricken member of the family. In Num. 27:11, the term refers to the nearest relative qualifying to receive an inheritance.

***sha'arāh* [שַׁאֲרָה, 7608]**

sha'arāh occurs only in Lev. 18:17 to refer to a near kinswoman or female relative with whom sexual relations are forbidden.

***môdā'* [מוֹדָע, 4129]**

môdā' is a rare synonym for *gō'ēl* as "kinsman," or "relative" (see ***gā'al,*** above). It occurs only in Ruth 2:1, in reference to Boaz, and in Prov. 7:4, where the term refers metaphorically to insight as a "kinswoman."

NT Words

***syngenēs* [συγγενής, *4773*]**

syngenēs occurs twelve times and exclusively means "kin," "kinsman." General references are found in Mark 6:4; Luke 2:44; 14:12; 21:16; John 18:26; Acts 10:24; Rom. 9:3; 16:7, 11, 21. In Luke 1:36 the term refers to Elizabeth, mother of John the Baptist and cousin of Mary, mother of Jesus.

Additional Notes

The literal and metaphorical meanings of ***qārôb,*** ***gā'al,*** and *gō'ēl* highlight one of the major features of the divine character, that of "kinsman-redeemer." Boaz is the most significant and extended human example of this sociological phenomenon in ancient Israel (cf. Ruth. 3:4). The office of "kinsman-redeemer" is one that carried profound significance for the people of Israel, in that it guaranteed the preservation of the family line in the event of the premature passing of a husband who had not fathered children during his lifetime. While this was not the sole function of the "kinsman-redeemer" in ancient Israel, it was one of the most important, since it became a means of rescuing Israelite families from extinction — a fate that gave rise to much grief and anguish.

Significantly, the function of the "kinsman-redeemer" was extended, in a spiritual sense, to the person of Yahweh, as one who rescued his people and preserved their status as his chosen ones, promising them an intimate and unique relationship with him forever. That role was ultimately fulfilled in the person of Christ. And although the specific term "kinsman-redeemer" was not used of him, the general term "redeemer" was. (→ REDEEM)

KIND (NOUN)

OT Words

mîn [מִין, 4327]

mîn is the Hebrew term that indicates "kind" in the biological sense of "species." The term is found in approximately thirty contexts.

Species of vegetation are mentioned in Gen. 1:11, 12. Animal species are likewise mentioned at their point of creation in Gen. 1:21ff., and also at the time of the flood (cf. Gen. 6:20; 7:14). Some insects are permitted as food under the law (cf. Lev. 11:22); whereas a number of bird species are not (cf. Lev. 11:14ff.). See also Ezek. 47:10.

kil'ayim [כִּלְאַיִם, 3610]

kil'ayim is a rare term, occurring four times, that indicates "kind" in the general sense of "diverse or mixed variety." In Lev. 19:19, three practices are forbidden to Israel, namely, crossbreeding; sowing a mixed variety of seed in a field; and weaving clothing made of two different kinds of thread. Similarly, Deut. 22:9 forbids sowing a vineyard with two different kinds of seed.

NT Words

genos [γένος, *1085*]

genos is a noun with a fairly broad range of meaning emphasizing diversity of species, nationality, and other phenomena. ***genos*** occurs around twenty times. The translation "kind" is evident in eight of these contexts.

The meaning "kind" in the general sense of "diverse phenomena" is evident in Matt. 17:21; Mark 9:29, where Jesus claims that this kind of demon can only be cast out through prayer and fasting. Various kinds of languages are mentioned in 1 Cor. 12:10, 28; 14:10. With respect to nationality, Paul refers to people of his own kind, or his own race, in Gal. 1:14; Phil. 3:5; 2 Cor. 11:26.

See Also: → NATURAL

KIND (ADJECTIVE), KINDNESS

NT Words

philanthrōpia [φιλανθρωπία, *5363*]

philanthrōpia occurs only twice, meaning "kindness." In Acts 28:2, the inhabitants of Malta show kindness to the shipwrecked party that includes the apostle Paul. Titus 3:4 speaks of the kindness of God.

chrēstos [χρηστός, *5543*]

chrēstos occurs seven times, meaning "kindness" in three of these contexts. Luke 6:35 refers to God's kindness to the ungrateful. Rom. 2:4 speaks of the riches of God's kindness. Eph. 4:32 contains the Pauline exhortation to be kind to one another.

chrēsteuomai [χρηστεύομαι, *5541*]

chrēsteuomai is found only in 1 Cor. 13:4, where Paul declares that "love is kind."

chrēstotēs [χρηστότης, *5544*]

chrēstotēs occurs ten times and in all but one of these contexts is translated "kindness." The kindness of God is spoken of in Rom. 2:4, where Paul declares that such benevolence is intended to lead one to repentance (cf. Rom. 11:22; Titus 3:4). In Eph. 2:7, Paul affirms that God's kindness is supremely demonstrated to us in the person of Jesus Christ. 2 Cor. 6:6; Col. 3:12 refer to the virtue of human kindness, and Gal. 5:22 describes such a virtue as a fruit of the Spirit.

See Also: → MERCY

KINDLE → LIGHT

KING

OT Words

melek [מֶלֶךְ, 4428]

melek is the standard term for "king" throughout the Old Testament, occurring about 2,500 times. ***melek*** refers to human royalty as well as to Yahweh's position as king over creation and the heavenly realms.

General references to kings are found in Job 3:14; 36:7; Pss. 2:10; 102:15; 144:10; Prov. 8:15; 29:14; 31:3; Eccl. 2:8; 4:13; 8:2ff.; Hos. 8:10; Amos 7:1; Mic. 4:9. Gentile kings of the earth are mentioned in Isa. 14:18; 24:21.

Specific references to pagan kings are found in a wide variety of contexts, including a coalition of Canaanite rulers confronting Abraham in Gen. 14:1ff. Other Canaanite kings are mentioned frequently in the conquest narratives of Joshua and Judges (cf. Josh. 2:3; 8:1ff.; 10:1ff.; 12:1ff.; Judg. 3:10ff.; 4:2ff.; 8:5ff.; 11:12). The Egyptian Pharaoh is frequently referred to as well (cf. Gen. 40:1ff.; Exod. 1:8; 6:13). Specific divine judgment against the rulers of Egypt is indicated in Jer. 46:17, 25; Ezek. 29:2, 3; 30:22ff. The kings of Persia are indicated throughout the books of Ezra, Nehemiah, and Esther. Assyrian rulers are cited throughout the prophecy of Isaiah in particular (cf. Isa. 7:17ff.; 8:4ff.; 36:1ff.; 37:4ff.; also Jer. 50:17; Nah. 3:18). Isa. 30:33 refers to specific divine judgment being enacted against the Assyrian king. The judgment of Yahweh is also invoked against the king of Tyre (Ezek. 28:12ff.), and against the ruler of Babylon (Isa. 14:4; Jer. 50:18; 51:11). The book of Daniel contains a graphic symbolic description of the defeat of the kings (and nations) of Media, Persia, Greece, and Egypt (cf. Dan. 2:24ff.; 7:1ff.; 8:20ff.; 10–12).

In other contexts, the king of Babylon is cited as the instrument of divine judgment against Israel for her rejection of Yahweh (cf. Jer. 21:7ff.; 22:11ff.; 25:9ff.; 32:4; 34:1ff.; 39:1; 52:4; Ezek. 17:12; 19:9).

The record of the kings of Israel and Judah is very extensive, indicated first of all in the charter of Israelite kingship. It is outlined in Deut. 17:14ff. and commences in detail with the reign of Saul (1 Sam. 10ff.), followed by David (1 Sam. 16ff.), and Solomon (1 Kgs. 2ff.), together with the reigns of the Israelite kings (1 Kgs. 12 — 2 Kgs. 17), and those of Judah (1 Kgs. 12 — 2 Kgs. 25). The Chronicler's two books supplement the narrative of Samuel-Kings, but deal exclusively with the southern kingdom of Judah. Outside of the Former Prophets and the Chronicler's history, divine judgment against the rulers of Judah is also invoked (Jer. 17:19ff.; 19:3ff.; 25:18; 34:8; 36:1ff.; 52:10ff.), as is punishment against the king of Israel (Hos. 10:15).

In several places, significant mention is made of a king as the anointed servant of Yahweh, or "messiah." Such a privilege is extended even to a pagan king such as Cyrus of Persia, who is described in Isa. 45:1 as Yahweh's "messiah," the ruler who issued the decree to release the people of Israel from their exile in Babylon. Jer. 23:5; 30:9 record the promise of the coming Messianic King from the lineage of David, and in Ezek. 37:22, 24 there is the prophetic anticipation of the same Davidic Messianic King who will rule over a united and renewed Israelite kingdom. Zech. 9:9 envisages the future Messianic King coming to reclaim the city of Jerusalem riding on a donkey. All of these prophecies find their fulfillment in the person of Christ.

In addition to the figure of the messianic ruler of Israel, there is a unique reference in Gen. 14:18 to Melchizedek, priest of God most high and king of Salem, who came out to meet and bless Abram after his battle with the coalition of Canaanite rulers. This mysterious priest-king thereafter disappears from the pages of the Old Testament, and is interpreted in the book of Hebrews as the typological antecedent of Jesus Christ's high priestly ministry — as one without beginning or end, an eternal high priesthood.

There are also a number of references to Yahweh as king in a variety of contexts. For example, Ps. 24:7 describes him as the "king of glory." Jer. 10:10; Ps. 29:10 refer to God as the eternal king. Yahweh is described as the "great king"in Pss. 48:2; 95:3ff.; Mal. 1:14. He is then described as the "king of Israel" in Pss. 89:18; 149:2; and "king of the earth" in Ps. 47:7; Jer. 10:7; Zech. 14:9. God's absence from Zion is described in Jer. 8:19 as the absence of "her king," the outworking of divine judgment against his people. Yahweh is described as the king on his throne in Isa. 6:5, in a vision of the divine council.

Other references to Yahweh's kingship are found in 1 Sam. 2:10; Pss. 2:6; 44:4; 47:2, 6; 68:24; Zech. 14:16, 17.

NT Words

basileus [βασιλεύς, *935*]

basileus is the dynamic equivalent for the Hebrew term ***melek*** (see above) and is likewise consistently translated "king." ***basileus*** occurs around 120 times and refers to human kingship as well as to the royal office of God and Christ.

General references to kings in the New Testament are found in Matt. 10:18; 17:25; Mark 13:9; Luke 21:12; Acts 4:26; 9:15; 1 Tim. 2:2; Rev. 1:5; 6:15. In 1 Pet. 2:13, 17 believers are commanded to render obedience to earthly kings. In Rev. 17:2, 10, 18; 18:9; 19:18, 19, kings of the earth are depicted as objects of divine wrath on account of their wickedness. Conversely, Rev. 21:24 cites the regenerate kings of the earth among the citizens of heaven. Kings are also frequently mentioned in the parables of Jesus (cf. Matt. 18:23; 22:2, 11, 13; Luke 14:31).

A number of specific royal figures are also cited such as Herod (cf. Matt. 2:1ff.; Mark 6:14, 22ff.; Acts 12:1), Agrippa (cf. Acts 25:13ff., 24; 25:26; 26:2ff.); Aretas of Damascus (cf. 2 Cor. 11:32); the demonic king, Apollyon (Rev. 9:11); as well as kings from the Israelite theocracy such as Saul (Acts 13:21), the king of Egypt (Heb. 11:23), and the mysterious Melchizedek (Heb. 7:12).

Christ's role and position as "king of the Jews" is frequently indicated throughout the New Testament. There is the affirmation first of all that Jesus Christ is the fulfillment of the Messianic King figure of Old Testament prophecy. This is made clear on the occasion of

Jesus' triumphal return to Jerusalem (cf. Matt. 21:5; Luke 19:38; John 12:13, 15). Jesus' action fulfills to the letter the prophecy contained in Zech. 9:9 (see ***melek***, above). During Jesus' trial, Pilate asks him, "Are you the king of the Jews?" (cf. Matt. 27:11; Mark 15:2ff.; Luke 23:3; John 18:33), to which Jesus replies in the affirmative (cf. John 18:37ff.). The sign on the cross testifying to Jesus' status as king of the Jews is deliberately placed there at the behest of Pilate (cf. Matt. 27:37; Mark 15:26; Luke 23:38; John 19:19). The soldiers, who had no idea of the truth of the words they uttered in scorn: "Hail, King of the Jews!" use this title to mock Christ during his pretrial ordeal (cf. Mark 15:18; John 19:3).

In an interesting corollary to this context, John 6:15 records Jesus' refusal to be made king, on the grounds that it was not yet his time to do so. Christ's kingship is then given explicit expression in 1 Tim. 6:15, which contains the titles, "Lord of Lords," and "King of kings," as does Rev. 17:14; 19:16.

Believers are declared to be "kings" reigning with Christ, pointing to their spiritual, royal status in union with him (cf. Rev. 1:6; 5:10).

Additional Notes

The Hebrew and Greek vocabulary designating kingship has significant theological weight in both Testaments. The emergence of kingship in human society is viewed, without specific comment, as a natural consequence of the increasing complexity and sophistication in human social and political development. However, when the phenomenon of kingship arises in Israel, it is clear that it is no accident. Deut. 17:14ff. records the details of Yahweh's charter for kingship in Israel, and while there was notable impropriety in the way Israel asked for a king (cf. 1 Sam. 8–12), the fact of Israel being provided with a ruler was never in doubt.

As the history of the Israelite monarchy unfolds in the Old Testament, it becomes increasingly evident that this institution is required by Yahweh to reflect his own position as Israel's "true king." However, it becomes equally evident that the Israelite monarchy fails to live up to the standard of righteousness and loyalty demanded by God in respect of the covenant relationship established by Yahweh between himself and the king. Consequently, Israelite kingship bore the brunt of divine wrath throughout most of its existence.

The exception to this wholesale failure was David, who, while he himself was not impeccable in his personal behavior, nevertheless received the accolade as a king after God's own heart. Throughout the course of the Israelite theocracy and the ministry of the prophets who interpreted and challenged it, both before and after the Babylonian exile, it is clear that David is held up as the ideal theocratic ruler. And it is through the person of David that the portrait of an ideal messianic ruler is consistently presented to the people of God.

Consequently, the New Testament consistently refers to Jesus Christ as the fulfillment of the Davidic Messianic King, whose ministry as the Son of God includes the role of "king of Kings" and "Lord of Lords."

At the heart of this phenomenon lies the theme of Yahweh as king. His rule over the earth and its peoples is symbolized through the theocratic kingship in Israel and consummated on earth through the person of his son, Jesus Christ, who perfectly mirrors the kingly rule of God in human form.

KINGDOM

OT Words

mamlākāh [מַמְלָכָה, 4467]

mamlākāh occurs around 120 times with the primary meaning "kingdom." It also conveys the sense of "dominion" or "reign" in some cases. ***mamlākāh*** applies to both human dominion as well as to the kingdom of God, though the latter is only referred to explicitly in 1 Chr. 29:11.

In a general sense, references to earthly, human kingdoms are found in Gen. 10:10; 20:9; Num. 32:33; Deut. 3:4ff.; Isa. 14:16. Jer. 1:10; 18:7, 9 refer to the prophet Jeremiah's mission to both destroy kingdoms and raise them up. See also Deut. 28:25; 1 Sam. 10:18; 2 Kgs. 19:15, 19; Ps. 68:32; Isa. 37:16; Jer. 15:4. Zeph. 3:8; Hag. 2:22ff. mention the wrath of God being poured out on such kingdoms. ***mamlākāh*** also refers specifically to Canaanite kingdoms in Josh. 11:10; 2 Chr. 17:10; Ps. 135:11. 1 Sam. 23:2 likewise refers to these kingdoms coming under the judgment of Yahweh.

In relation to the nation of Israel, ***mamlākāh*** is found in a number of contexts designating Israel as a kingdom. In anticipation of the Israelite monarchy, Deut. 17:18, 20 details the divine charter of the Israelite monarch who will rule over that kingdom. ***mamlākāh*** refers to the kingdom of Saul (1 Sam. 13:13; 28:17; 2 Sam. 3:10), the dominion of David (1 Sam. 24:20; 2 Sam. 3:28; 5:12; 2 Chr. 13:5), and that of his son Solomon (1 Kgs. 2:46; 9:5; 11:11). References to the northern kingdom of Israel are found in 2 Chr. 11:1; Amos 9:8. In the latter text, divine judgment is threatened against Israel, but the punishment is not an absolute one. Similarly mention is made of the southern kingdom of Judah in 2 Chr. 14:5; 17:5. In Lam. 2:2, the people of Jerusalem mourn over the divine destruction of that kingdom. The people of Israel themselves are spoken of in Exod. 19:6 as a kingdom of priests.

The messianic kingdom of Israel is prophesied as eternally enduring (2 Sam. 7:12ff.) as part of the blessings promised to David's posterity under the terms of the Davidic covenant. The ruler of this kingdom is likewise anticipated in the celebrated Immanuel prophecy of Isa. 9:7. This same kingdom is spoken of in metaphorical terms in Ezek. 37:22, where the prophet Ezekiel speaks of the idealized reunification of Israel and Judah in his vision of renewal for the people of God.

malkût [מַלְכוּת, 4438]

malkût is a term synonymous with ***mamlākāh*** (see above), and is translated "kingdom" in about fifty of the ninety or so contexts in which it is found. The underlying concept of ***malkût*** is that of royal dominion or power, and it is applied both to human beings and God.

Earthly kingdoms in general are mentioned in Num. 24:7; Jer. 10:7. ***malkût*** also refers explicitly to the kingdoms of Greece (Dan. 8:22; 11:2); Persia (Ezra 1:1; Esth. 1:2ff.; 3:6; 5:3, 9:30; Dan. 10:13); Egypt (Dan. 11:9); and Babylon (Dan. 1:20).

The Israelite kingdom is alluded to in a number of contexts. The Judean or southern kingdom is mentioned as such (2 Chr. 11:17), as is the dominion of Saul and Jonathan (1 Sam. 20:31; 1 Chr. 12:23), and Solomon's kingdom (1 Kgs. 2:12; 2 Chr. 1:1). In 1 Chr. 17:11, the anticipation of Solomon's rule is incorporated as part of the Davidic covenant promise. The Davidic kingdom itself is mentioned in 1 Chr. 11:10; 14:2. The kingdom of David's messianic son who will rule forever (symbolized by Solomon, though not fulfilled in him) is mentioned in 1 Chr. 17:14; 22:10; 28:5, 7; 2 Chr. 17:18.

General references to the kingdom of God are found in Ps. 103:19, where it is described as all-powerful. In Ps. 145:11, 12 it is spoken of as a glorious kingdom. And Ps. 145:13 affirms the kingdom of God as everlasting.

mamlākût [מַמְלָכוּת, 4468]

This is another synonym for ***mamlākāh*** and ***malkût***, above. ***mamlākût*** occurs nine times and refers exclusively to earthly dominion.

mamlākût refers to the kingdom of the Canaanite ruler Og of Bashan (Josh. 13:12, 20, 31), and to that of his contemporary, Sihon of the Amorites at Heshbon (Josh. 13:21, 27). Both of these kingdoms were still unconquered by the time of Joshua's death.

The kingdom of Israel under the control of Saul is mentioned in 1 Sam. 15:28; 2 Sam. 16:3. However, these two texts reflect the historical circumstances which led to the kingdom being taken from Saul on account of his rebellion and disobedience towards God. Hos. 1:4 refers to the threatened end of the kingdom of Israel.

In Jer. 26:1, ***mamlākût*** is actually translated "reign" in reference to the late Judean ruler Jehoiakim (609–597 B.C.).

melûkāh [מְלוּכָה, 4410]

melûkāh is a participial form of the verb ***mālak*** (to rule) and means "kingdom" and the related senses of "kingship" or "royal office." ***melûkāh*** occurs around twenty times.

melûkāh refers to the kingdom of Israel in several contexts — to the newly inaugurated kingdom under Saul (1 Sam. 10:16; 11:14; cf. 1 Sam. 14:47; 18:8); to the kingdom under Solomon (1 Kgs. 2:15, 22); and to the kingdom under Rehoboam (1 Kgs. 12:21). 1 Kgs. 11:35 refers to the transferal of the "kingdom"—ten of the twelve tribes—from Rehoboam to Jeroboam. Rehoboam retained control only over Judah and Benjamin. This action by God resulted in the division of the unified Israelite dominion under Saul, David, and Solomon into northern and southern kingdoms. 1 Chr. 10:14 refers to the kingdom of Israel being given to David by Yahweh after Saul had been, in effect, put to death by God. The office of kingship in Israel is mentioned in 1 Sam. 10:25.

The kingdom of God is expressed as a principle of dominion in Ps. 22:28; Obad. 21.

malkû [מַלְכוּ, 4437 (Aramaic)]

malkû is an Aramaic noun synonymous with the Hebrew terms discussed above. ***malkû*** occurs about sixty times and is translated "kingdom" in the large majority of these instances, principally in the book of Daniel.

As far as human dominion is concerned, ***malkû*** refers to a number of pagan kingdoms in Daniel — for example, the Persian kingdom (Dan. 2:39; 5:31; 6:1ff.; also mentioned in Ezra 7:13, 23), the Babylonian kingdom (Dan. 4:18ff.; 5:7ff.); the kingdom of Greece (Dan. 2:39); and the kingdom of Rome (Dan. 2:40ff.; 7:23, 24), although this identification of Rome is not universally acknowledged. In addition, Dan. 2:37 refers to the principle of royal dominion that God gives to Nebuchadnezzar. Dan. 4:17, 32 likewise indicate that God gives this same principle to human beings in general.

malkû also refers to the kingdom of the Son of Man as an everlasting dominion (Dan. 7:14, 18, 22). Such a kingdom is clearly identified with the kingdom of God (Dan. 2:44; 4:3, 34; 6:26; 7:27).

NT Words

basileia [βασιλεία, *932*]

basileia is the only Greek term for "kingdom," occurring around 150 times and consistently translated as such. Two particularly significant phrases containing the term ***basileia*** are "kingdom of heaven" and "kingdom of God." These phrases are functionally synonymous and both refer to the dominion of God on earth and incorporate the heavenly realm as well. This kingdom is brought to a climax through the person and work of Jesus Christ, and maintained through the indwelling presence of the Holy Spirit in the lives of believers. The phrase "kingdom of heaven" is frequently associated with the parables of Jesus.

General references to the kingdom of heaven are found in Matt. 5:19, 20; 7:21; 10:7; 18:1ff.; 19:12, 14; 19:23; 23:13. The kingdom of heaven requires repentance as a prerequisite for entry (cf. Matt. 3:2; 4:17). This realm is the destiny of the "poor in spirit" (cf. Matt. 5:3; Luke 6:20); and those who are persecuted (cf. Matt. 5:10). The consummation of the kingdom of heaven is destined to take place at the end of the age (Matt. 8:11). Matt. 13:11 affirms that this kingdom is a repository of mysteries, accessible only by divine grace. In Matt. 16:19, the authority of the kingdom is said to be vested in the symbol of the apostolic "keys." In the parables of Jesus in Matthew's gospel, the consistent refrain "the kingdom of heaven is like . . ." opens each symbolic story (cf. Matt. 13:24, 31, 33, 44ff.; 18:23; 20:1; 22:2; 25:1).

In several contexts, references to the "kingdom of God" are very similar to those made in relation to the "kingdom of heaven." For example, the consummation of the kingdom of God is also destined to take place at the end of this world (cf. Mark 14:25; Luke 21:31; 22:30; Rev. 12:10). Similarly, the secrets of the kingdom of God are given to the disciples as an act of divine grace, so that they might understand them (cf. Mark 4:11; Luke 8:10). The phrase, "the kingdom of God is like . . ." is also found at the outset of Jesus' parables, but much less frequently than the corresponding formula in relation to the "kingdom of heaven" parables in Matthew's gospel (cf. Mark 4:26; Luke 13:29).

Other aspects of the "kingdom of God" are indicated in varying contexts. The priority of the kingdom is demanded in Matt. 6:33. It is said to be victorious over the demonic kingdom in Matt. 12:28; and the power of the kingdom is indicated explicitly in Mark 9:1; 1 Cor. 4:20. The kingdom of God is also declared to be essentially one of righteousness and peace (cf. Rom. 14:17), which cannot be inherited by mere human effort (cf. 1 Cor. 15:50). In this regard, access to the kingdom of God is only possible on the basis of the "new birth," as Jesus explains in John 3:3ff.; thus making it difficult to enter, as indicated in Mark 10:24; Luke 18:24. It is an everlasting kingdom (cf. Luke 1:33; Heb. 12:28); and God calls his people to enter in (cf. 1 Thess. 2:12). Jesus himself expresses the desire for God's kingdom to come (i.e., in its fullness) in the prayer he taught his disciples (cf. Luke 11:2; also Matt. 26:29). General references to the kingdom of God are found in Matt. 13:43; 19:24; Mark 1:15; 12:34; Luke 7:28; 18:29; Acts 1:3; 19:8; Gal. 4:11; Heb. 1:8. It is spoken of as the inheritance of God's people in Matt. 25:34; Luke 18:16 (of little children); but denied to the world in Eph. 5:5. The "gospel of the kingdom" is mentioned in Matt. 4:23; 9:35; Mark 1:15; Luke 4:43; 8:1; 16:16.

References to the kingdom of the world from a purely human perspective are found in Mark 3:24; Luke 4:5; 12:32; Heb. 11:33; Rev. 16:10; 17:12ff.

The New Testament also refers to the divine kingdom as belonging to Jesus Christ (cf. John 18:36; Col. 1:13; 2 Tim. 4:1; 2 Pet. 1:11; Rev. 11:5). While Jesus is viewed as God's appointed ruler, he also recognizes that he holds it "in trust," so to speak, from his Father. 1 Cor. 15:24 affirms that Christ will hand the kingdom back to the Father, once his work of redemption is completed.

Additional Notes

The vocabulary for "kingdom" in the Old Testament is quite varied, and yet it is clear that dominion and rule in the human sphere is provided for by God himself. In the case of his people Israel, the theocratic kingdom established in the land was designed to ideally reflect the reality of the heavenly kingdom. In the course of Israel's history, however, the reality fell far short of the ideal. Thus the kingdom of Israel is targeted for destruction as a consequence of the people's rebellion against God. That destruction was never intended to be absolute, however, for the prophets consistently testified to the hope of a renewed kingdom promised by God. Such a kingdom would not be realized in an earthly political sense, but would assume a profound spiritual quality. It is this eternal, spiritual kingdom, ushered in by Jesus Christ in the New Testament, that is the focus of the term ***basileia***, illustrating the fulfillment of the kingdom of God motif that originated with the theocratic kingdom of Israel in the Old Testament.

KISS

OT Words

nāshaq **[נָשַׁק, 5401]**

nāshaq occurs around thirty times with the primary meaning "kiss." This custom is practiced in a variety of contexts.

Kissing as a greeting custom is indicated in Gen. 27:26ff.; 29:11; 31:28, 55; Exod. 4:27; 2 Sam. 14:33; 20:9; 1 Kgs. 19:20; Job 31:27. In several places, the customary kiss of greeting is accompanied by profound emotion, such as at the reunion of Jacob and Esau (Gen. 33:4); at the reuniting of Joseph and his brothers (Gen. 45:15); at the final parting of Joseph and his father Jacob, just prior to the latter's death (cf. Gen. 50:1); and also at the parting between Naomi, Ruth, and Orpah (Ruth 1:9, 14). See also 1 Sam. 20:41.

The kiss of passion is indicated in Prov. 7:13, where the naive young man is embraced by the prostitute who seduces him. In Song 1:2, the beloved expresses the desire to be embraced by her lover (cf. also 8:1).

In one ritual context, "kissing" is depicted as an aspect of worshiping the messianic Son of God (Ps 2:1). It also forms part of an idol worshiping ceremony in 1 Kgs. 19:18; Hos. 13:2. Kissing forms part of the ritual anointing of Saul by the prophet-judge, Samuel (1 Sam. 10:1).

In a metaphorical context, Ps. 85:10 declares that righteousness and peace will kiss each other.

NT Words

phileō [φιλέω, *5368*]

phileō is a verb that occurs approximately thirty times, with the predominant meaning "love." On three occasions, however, it refers to Judas' kiss of betrayal when he effectively handed Jesus over to his enemies through this action (cf. Matt. 26:48; Mark 14:44; Luke 22:47). (→ LOVE)

philēma [φίλημα, *5370*]

philēma is a noun derived from ***phileō*** (see above) with the exclusive sense of "kiss." It is found in seven places.

Luke 7:45 indicates kissing in the context of a social greeting. In a number of places in the Pauline correspondence, the apostle refers to the kiss of greeting among believers, exhorting his readers to engage in it (cf. Rom. 16:16; 1 Cor. 16:20; 2 Cor. 13:12; 1 Thess. 5:26; 1 Pet. 5:14).

Judas' kiss of betrayal with respect to Jesus is mentioned in Luke 22:48.

kataphileō [καταφιλέω, *2705*]

kataphileō is a verb related to ***phileō*** (see above), but with the exclusive sense of "kiss." ***kataphileō*** occurs six times.

kataphileō refers to the action of kissing not merely as a kiss of greeting, but as an action filled with emotions such as devotion, joy, sadness, and treachery — but not sexual passion.

Matt. 26:49; Mark 14:45 mention Judas' kiss of treachery against Jesus. Luke 7:38 describes the action of the sinful woman, who was overcome by her sins and came to express her devotion to Christ by kissing his feet and anointing them with expensive perfume. Luke 15:20 describes the emotional reunion of the rebellious son with his father in Jesus' parable, as the father threw his arms around his son and kissed him on his return. Paul's farewell to the Ephesian elders was likewise an emotional parting when the leaders of the church wept and kissed him (cf. Acts 20:37).

KNEE

OT Words

berek **[בֶּרֶךְ, 1290]**

berek is translated "knee" in each of the twenty-five places in which it is found, in both literal and metaphorical contexts.

In reference to a person's anatomy, ***berek*** is found in Gen. 48:12; Judg. 16:19; 2 Kgs. 4:20; Job 3:12; Ps. 109:24; Isa. 66:12; Ezek. 47:4. Deut. 28:35 refers to the affliction of boils on the knees as an element of the divine covenant curse against sin.

The posture of kneeling down is also indicated in a number of contexts, such as for prayer, referring to Solomon (1 Kgs. 8:54), Elijah (1 Kgs. 18:42), and Ezra (Ezra 9:5). The posture is also used for worship of Yahweh (cf. Isa. 45:23; 1 Kgs. 19:18 refers to all of those who had not bowed the knee to Baal); and for pleading for one's life (cf. 2 Kgs. 1:13).

In metaphorical contexts, ***berek*** is found, for example, in Gen. 30:3, where the expression "bear upon one's knee" refers to the process of giving birth. Job 4:4;

Isa. 35:3 indicate the process of making someone stronger and giving one encouragement and strength in the expression "strengthen one's knees." Then, in the context of divine judgment, the mental state of fear and anguish in those who are being punished is indicated in the expression "knees weak as water" (Ezek. 7:17; 21:7); and "knees tremble" (Nah. 2:10).

NT Words

gony **[γόνυ, *1119*]**

gony occurs twelve times in all and refers to worship, or an act of deference, in most of these contexts.

gony is utilized in the expression "bow the knee" three times with specific reference to worship. In Rom. 11:4, Paul refers to those in Israel who in the past had not "bowed the knee" to Baal. Rom. 14:11; Phil. 2:10 indicate the worship of God and Christ respectively through the phrase "bow the knee." See also Mark 15:19; Luke 5:8; Eph. 3:14.

In the remaining contexts, ***gony*** is used in the verbal sense of "kneel down," with reference to prayer in Acts 7:60; 9:40; 20:36; 21:5; Luke 22:41. (See discussion below on KNEEL.) Heb. 12:12 also mentions "feeble knees" in reference to weakness of spirit.

KNEEL

OT Words

bārak **[בָּרַךְ, 1288];** ***berak*** **[בְּרַךְ, 1289** (Aramaic)**];** ***berek*** **[בֶּרֶךְ, 1290]**

bārak is a verb most commonly translated "bless" However, on four occasions, the term is translated "kneel." (→ BLESS)

There is a mundane reference in Gen. 24:11 to camels kneeling down. In 2 Chr. 6:13; Ps. 95:6, ***bārak*** refers to the posture of kneeling in prayer. Dan. 6:10 refers to this action with the Aramaic term ***berak***.

kāra' **[כָּרַע, 3766]**

kāra' occurs approximately thirty times and is usually translated "bow," "bend or kneel down."

kāra' refers literally to the action of kneeling down to drink (cf. Judg. 7:5, 6); and to give birth (cf. 1 Sam. 4:19; Job 39:3). In several contexts, such action also indicates the worship of Yahweh (cf. 2 Chr. 7:3; 29:29; Ps. 22:29; Isa. 45:23). See also 1 Kgs. 19:18. Bowing down as a means of paying homage is also indicated in Esth. 3:2, 5.

kāra' is used metaphorically in several contexts, including "kneeling, bowing down" for slaughter, indicating divine judgment against Israel (cf. Isa. 65:12); as a euphemism for sexual intercourse (cf. Job 31:10); and alluding to submission to the pagan gods Bel and Nebo (Isa. 46:1, 2). Ps. 20:8 refers to the collapse of Yahweh's enemies as they are "brought to their knees."

NT Words

gonypeteō **[γονυπετέω, *1120*]**

gonypeteō occurs only four times. On each occasion, it refers to people paying homage to Jesus. In Mark 10:17, a rich young man kneels before Jesus and asks what he must do to inherit eternal life. People fall on their knees, begging Jesus to bring healing — a man begs Jesus to heal his demon-possessed son in Matt. 17:14; and a leper begs for healing in Mark 1:40. See also Matt. 27:29.

KNIFE

OT Words

ma'akelet **[מַאֲכֶלֶת, 3979]**

ma'akelet occurs only four times, referring to a "knife" or "knives." Literal reference to a knife as an implement is found in Gen. 22:6, 10 in relation to Abraham's (attempted) sacrifice of his son Isaac; and also in Judg. 19:29. A metaphorical reference to "knives" is found in Prov. 30:14 in regard to the cruelty of the wicked.

sakkîn **[שַׂכִּין, 7915]**

sakkîn occurs only in Prov. 23:2, referring to the action of "putting a knife to one's throat," if one gives in to gluttony while eating at the table of a ruler.

ḥereb **[חֶרֶב, 2719]**

ḥereb is the common term for "sword" in the Old Testament. However, on several occasions it may also mean "knife." (→ SWORD)

All references indicate the use of a knife as a mere cutting implement, rather than as a weapon of war (cf. Josh. 5:2, 3, where circumcision is in view). 1 Kgs. 18:18 indicates self-mutilation on the part of Baal worshipers on Mt. Carmel. See also Ezek. 5:1, 2.

KNOCK

OT Words

dāphaq **[דָּפַק, 1849]**

In Song 5:2, ***dāphaq*** refers to the woman's lover knocking at her door.

NT Words

krouō **[κρούω, *2925*]**

krouō occurs nine times and means "knock at the door (or gate)."

In a literal context, ***krouō*** refers to Peter knocking on the door of John Mark's family home after his miraculous escape from prison (cf. Acts 12:13, 16).

The remaining usage of ***krouō*** is metaphorical. In reference to petitionary prayer, if one "asks and knocks," God will hear and answer (cf. Matt. 7:7, 8; Luke 11:9, 10). In the context of a parable, Luke 12:36 illustrates the same principle. Those who place themselves outside of a saving relationship of faith and trust in God are denied entry into the kingdom of God, symbolized by a narrow door. In this context, persistent "knocking at the door," once the "owner" has closed it, is fruitless (cf. Luke 13:25). The risen Christ's offer to the congregation at Laodicea is to "open the door" of their lives when he "knocks," so that he might enter and have fellowship with them (cf. Rev. 3:20).

KNOW

OT Words

yāda' [יָדַע, 3045]

yāda' is a common verb form, occurring around one thousand times with the primary sense of "know," and a number of different nuances. In many contexts, the theological weight of the term is considerable. The phenomenon of "knowing" is predicated of both human beings and God.

In contexts where human knowledge is in view, ***yāda'*** may be understood in a variety of ways. There is first of all the recognition that "knowing" involves the state of "moral awareness." For example, Gen. 3:5, 22; Isa. 7:15 speak of "knowing good and evil." Knowing sin in one's life, in the sense of being made aware of its existence, is indicated in Lev. 4:28; 1 Sam. 12:17; Ps. 51:3; Jer. 14:20; Ezek. 20:4. In positive contexts, Exod. 18:20; Ps. 119:152 refer to knowing the law of the covenant and its obligations. Similarly, Prov. 1:2; Eccl. 1:17 speak of knowing wisdom; and Ps. 25:4 refers to knowing the ways of God.

yāda' also indicates "knowing" in the essence of physical awareness or perception, such as Adam and Eve knowing they were naked (Gen. 3:7); the people of Israel knowing the character of Yahweh and his deeds (cf. Lev. 23:43; Deut. 4:39; Josh. 2:9; 1 Sam. 17:47). See also Exod. 2:4; Deut. 9:2; 1 Sam. 3:20; Neh. 2:16.

yāda' also has a specific sexual connotation with the sense of "knowing" serving as a euphemism for sexual intercourse (cf. Gen. 4:1, 17; 24:16; Num. 31:17ff.; Judg. 11:39; 1 Sam. 1:9). It also refers to the act of sodomy in Gen. 19:8; Judg. 19:22, 25.

At a less intimate level, ***yāda'*** also indicates the "knowing" of physical acquaintance (e.g., Deut. 9:24; 1 Sam. 10:11; Job 42:11).

In other contexts, where ***yāda'*** is negated, there are significant uses of the term indicating ignorance (i.e., not knowing). Where ignorance of Yahweh is concerned, such lack of knowledge is culpable in the sight of God (e.g., Exod. 5:2; 1 Sam. 2:12; Ps. 79:6; Isa. 1:3; 45:5; Jer. 4:22; 5:4; 9:6; Hos. 5:4). The term also refers to ignorance of other gods (cf. Deut. 11:28; 28:64; Jer. 7:9; 44:3), and to divine judgment (cf. Judg. 16:20; Isa. 44:18). Ignorance of one's sin is indicated in Prov. 4:19; Eccl. 5:1; and ignorance of wisdom in Prov. 14:33.

Great importance is placed in the Old Testament on knowing God, and ***yāda'*** refers to this knowledge in varying degrees of intimacy. For example, Yahweh frequently says to both Israelites and Gentile peoples: "You shall know that I am the Lord your God," as well as variations on that claim (cf. Exod. 6:7; 16:6; Deut. 4:35; Isa. 49:23 [predicated of the Servant of Yahweh]; Jer. 24:7). This formula is found with particular frequency in the prophet Ezekiel, occurring about fifty times (e.g., Ezek. 6:7; 7:4; 11:10; 16:62; 20:38ff.; 25:5ff.; 30:8ff.; 35:4ff.; 36:11; 37:6). Such knowledge is given to Pharaoh (Exod. 7:5, 17; 8:10, 22; 9:14; 10:2), in the context of the plague judgments enacted by Yahweh against the nation of Egypt; as well as to all the peoples of the earth (1 Kgs. 8:60; Isa. 37:20; 49:26).

Jer. 31:34; Hos. 2:20 express the desire to know God intimately, for example, in the context of the promise of new covenant blessing and renewal. See also Dan. 11:32; Ps. 36:10. Moses expresses this desire in Exod. 33:13. Knowing God's name is indicated in Pss. 9:10; 83:18; Isa. 52:6; Jer. 16:21. The conviction of knowing God as Savior is mentioned in Job 19:25 in Job's classic confession: "I know that my Redeemer lives . . ." See also Isa. 60:16. Yahweh is recognized as Creator in Isa. 41:20.

When predicated of God, ***yāda'*** refers to divine knowledge in a number of significant contexts. First of all, God is said to "know" in the sense of "sovereignly choose" in accordance with his plan of redemption. The objects of such knowledge include Abraham (Gen. 18:19); the prophet Jeremiah (Jer. 1:5), who was "known" by God prior to his birth; and the people of Israel (Amos 3:2). God is also said to "know" in an absolute sense — that is, he is omniscient. Such knowledge allows God to access every thought, motive, and attitude in the human heart, whether good or evil (cf. Deut. 2:7; 1 Kgs. 8:39; Ps. 139:1; Isa. 37:28; Jer. 12:3). Objects of this omniscient awareness include Moses (cf. Deut. 33:17; 34:10); the Israelites (cf. Exod. 3:7;

Deut. 32:22; Amos 5:2; Hos. 13:5); Pharaoh (cf. Exod. 3:19); and David (cf. 1 Chr. 17:18).

With respect to God, ***yāda'*** is also causative, in that God is declared to "make himself known" — for example, to the prophets (Num. 12:6); to the Egyptians (Isa. 19:2); and to the nations (Ezek. 20:9). See also Exod. 6:3, where God declares that he did not reveal himself as Lord to Abraham, Isaac, and Jacob in the same way as he had to Moses.

yeda' [יְדַע, 3046 (Aramaic)]

This is the Aramaic form of the Hebrew verb ***yāda'*** (see above), meaning "know." ***yeda'*** is commonly found with the passive sense of "known," and occurs around forty times.

In the book of Ezra, ***yeda'*** is found in the context of official state correspondence between the Persian king and the civic leaders of neighboring nations. For example, the term forms part of the introduction to a royal decree, beginning with the phrase, "Be it known that . . ." (cf. Ezra 4:12, 13; 5:8). It also has the sense of "inform" (i.e., to make known) in the same setting (cf. Ezra 4:14, 16; 5:10; 7:24); as well as the meaning "know" in the sense of "learn" (Ezra 4:15), with respect to the laws of Yahweh.

Elsewhere, ***yeda'*** is also included in the formula "Be it known that . . ." as part of the introduction to a royal decree in the book of Daniel (cf. Dan. 3:18). In other contexts, ***yeda'*** is also translated "make known" in the sense of "inform" (Dan. 2:5ff.; 4:6, 9; 5:8, 15ff.). The meaning "acknowledge," in the context of "knowing God" as the ruler of human kingdoms, is found in Dan. 4:32; 5:21. Knowing in the sense of "being aware" is indicated in Dan. 2:8; 4:9, 17ff.; 5:22ff.; 6:10, 15; and with the sense of "understanding" in Dan. 2:21.

When Yahweh is the subject of ***yeda'***, it refers to his omniscience in Dan. 2:22. Secondly, the term indicates the profoundly significant meaning "making known" — referring to the interpretation of revelatory dreams and visions to Daniel which outline the destiny of earthly kingdoms in their inevitable destruction, and the heavenly destiny of his people in the eternal, indestructible kingdom of the most high God (cf. Dan. 2:23, 28ff., 45; 7:16).

dēa' [דֵּעַ, 1843]

dēa' is a noun derived from ***yāda'*** (see above). It occurs only twice, in Job 36:3; 37:16, referring to knowledge.

dē'āh [דֵּעָה, 1844]

dē'āh is another noun derived from ***yāda'*** (see above) also translated "knowledge." ***dē'āh*** occurs six times.

The concept of knowledge belonging to God, in an absolute sense, is indicated in 1 Sam. 2:3; Job 36:4; Ps. 73:11.

dē'āh is also translated "knowledge" in the sense of knowledge of, or about God, in Isa. 11:9; 28:9; Jer. 3:15.

da'at [דַּעַת, 1847]

da'at is the most common noun derived from the verb ***yāda'*** (see above), and is consistently translated "knowledge," with several related nuances such as "understanding," "discernment," and "wisdom." ***da'at*** is found in ninety contexts.

Knowledge in a general sense is indicated referring to craftsmen (Exod. 31:3; 35:31; 1 Kgs. 7:14); to human learning (Eccl. 1:16; 2:21; 7:12; Dan. 1:4); and to the knowledge of both God and human beings (Ps. 94:10; Isa. 47:10; Eccl. 12:9). Job 15:2; 33:3; 38:2 speak of the absence of knowledge.

da'at specifically indicates humankind's knowledge of God (cf. Num. 24:16; Job 21:14; Ps. 139:6; Isa. 33:6; Hos. 6:6). Lack of the knowledge of God on the part of Israel is spoken of in Isa. 5:13; Hos. 4:1, 6.

In relation to ethical standards, ***da'at*** refers to the knowledge of right living, wisdom, and understanding in Gen. 2:9, 17; Prov. 1:29; 2:6; 8:9ff.; 12:1; 13:16; 23:12. Prov. 1:7 defines the beginning of knowledge as the fear of the Lord.

da'at also refers to the knowledge of God in its subjective sense of knowledge belonging to God. Job 10:7; Isa. 48:4 speak of God knowing a person's heart and thoughts. The divine spirit of knowledge is said to belong to the Messianic Servant in Isa. 11:2; 53:11. The knowledge of Yahweh in the sense of his omniscience is indicated in Isa. 40:14.

nākar [נָכַר, 5234]

nākar occurs approximately fifty times, meaning "know" as well as other related senses such as "acknowledge," "recognize" in about half of these contexts.

"Know" in the sense of "recognize" is the meaning evident in Gen. 27:23, 33; 42:7, 8; Ruth 3:14; 1 Kgs. 18:7; Prov. 20:11; Lam. 4:8. The contexts here involve human recognition only. The sense of acknowledging others is also evident in the use of ***nākar*** (cf. Gen. 38:26; Deut. 21:17; Isa. 61:9; 63:16). Acknowledgment of Yahweh is also in view (cf. Dan. 11:39).

With reference to divine knowledge, Job 34:25 refers to God knowing the deeds of human beings; and Jer. 24:5 refers to God acknowledging the exiles from Judah.

NT Words

ginōskō [γινώσκω, *1097*]

ginōskō is one of the most common verbs in the New Testament, conveying the sense of "knowing" in a variety of contexts, and a whole range of associated senses. This spectrum of meaning closely approximates that of the Hebrew vocabulary for "know," "knowledge."

The meaning "know" in the general sense of "be aware" is found in a number of places (e.g., Matt. 6:3; 24:50; Mark 8:17; Luke 2:43; John 12:9; Acts 19:35; Rom. 7:7; 2 Cor. 2:4; Phil. 1:12; 2 Tim. 1:18; Jas. 1:3; 1 John 3:19; Rev. 2:23). It functions as a euphemism for sexual intercourse in Matt. 1:5.

Another significant aspect of the usage of ***ginōskō*** lies in the meaning "understand." It refers to understanding the law of God (Rom. 7:1); the mind of God (1 Cor. 2:16); the mysteries of heaven (Matt. 13:11; Mark 4:11; Luke 8:10); and the spiritual aspects of God's revealed truth (John 7:17; 14:20; 8:28, 32; 2 Tim. 3:1; 2 Pet. 1:20). From a negative viewpoint, Jesus points out Nicodemus' failure to understand spiritual truth in John 3:10. General lack of spiritual understanding is indicated in John 8:27; 10:6; 1 Cor. 2:14.

With regard to the person of Christ as the object of humanity's knowledge, ***ginōskō*** is found in a variety of contexts. Knowing Christ in the sense of having a relationship of faith and trust in him, based on a recognition of his divine person, is indicated, for example, in John 10:14, 15, where Jesus declares that his followers (i.e., his "sheep") know him and he knows them. In Phil. 3:10, Paul affirms his desire to know Christ and the power of his resurrection. Other references to this knowledge include those in John 14:17; 2 Cor. 8:9; Eph. 3:19; Heb. 8:11; 1 John 2:3ff., 13ff. There is also an intriguing reference in Acts 19:15 to an evil spirit knowing, or recognizing, Jesus.

Concerning God as the object of knowledge, ***ginōskō*** refers to knowing him personally in John 17:3; 17:25; Gal. 4:9; 1 John 4:7. 1 John 4:2 speaks of knowing God as the Spirit of truth. Rom. 1:21 also refers to people knowing God, but only in a superficial sense of merely acknowledging his existence. In contrast, several references indicate the world's ignorance of God — that is, they have not known him (cf. John 16:3; 17:25; 1 Cor. 1:21; 1 John 3:1; 4:8; 5:20).

When predicated of God, ***ginōskō*** indicates the absolute knowledge of every thought and desire of the human heart (cf. Luke 16:15; 1 Cor. 3:20; 1 John 3:20). 1 Cor. 8:3 speaks of the reality of being known by God through loving him. Similarly, ***ginōskō*** refers to Christ knowing our inner being in intimate, omniscient detail (cf. John 2:25; 5:42; 6:15; 16:19; 21:17). A stark contrasting perspective is found in Matt. 7:23, where Jesus declares that he will inform unbelievers on the day of judgment that he never knew them.

epiginōskō [ἐπιγινώσκω, *1921*]

epiginōskō is a synonym for the more common ***ginōskō*** (see above). ***epiginōskō*** likewise has the primary sense of "know" in a variety of contexts, with several related meanings. The term occurs around forty times.

Where human knowledge is concerned, ***epiginōskō*** refers to the state of being aware, or realizing (cf. Acts 22:29; 25:10; Rom. 1:32; 2 Cor. 13:5). It also has the sense of "acknowledge" (1 Cor. 14:37; 16:18; 2 Cor. 1:14); "understand" (1 Cor. 1:13); and "being acquainted with" the way of righteousness (2 Pet. 2:21). Quite a few texts reflect the meaning "know," in the sense of "recognize" — for example, Matt. 7:16, 20 contain Jesus' affirmation that people shall be known or recognized by their "fruit," or their actions. See also Matt. 14:35; Mark 6:33; Luke 1:4; Acts 3:10; 12:14; 19:34. Luke 24:16 refers to the Emmaus disciples being kept from initially recognizing Jesus — a little later they finally recognize him (cf. Luke 24:31).

epiginōskō also indicates the extent and nature of Christ's knowledge. Matt. 11:27 declares that no one knows the Father except the son. Mark 2:8; Luke 5:22 indicate that Christ knows intimately the hearts, minds, and thoughts of people. The sense of "be aware" is evident in Mark 5:30, where Christ realizes that power has left him when a sick woman touched the hem of his garment.

epignōsis [ἐπίγνωσις, *1922*]

epignōsis is a noun derived from ***epiginōskō*** (see above) and refers to knowledge of moral and ethical values as well as of sin. It also refers to intimate acquaintance with God. The term occurs around twenty times.

Concerning a person's knowledge of God, ***epignōsis*** refers to knowledge of the Son (Eph. 4:13); knowledge of God's will (Phil. 1:9; Col. 1:9; 2 Pet. 1:2, 3); and knowledge of the mystery of Christ (Col. 2:2; 2 Pet. 1:8; 2:20). See also Eph. 1:17; Col. 1:10; 3:10. Rom. 1:28 refers to absence of the knowledge of God, as Paul declares that the wicked refuse to acknowledge God. In Rom. 10:2 the Israelites are said to exhibit zeal for God, but it is not based on knowledge.

Knowledge of sin is expressed in Rom. 3:20, and knowledge of the truth in 1 Tim. 2:4; 2 Tim. 2:25; 3:7; Titus 1:1; Heb. 10:26.

gnōsis [γνῶσις, *1108*]

gnōsis is another noun derived from ***epiginōskō*** (see above), a synonym for ***epignōsis*** (see above). ***gnōsis*** is translated "knowledge," with particular reference to understanding and appreciation of the spiritual truths of the Christian faith. ***gnōsis*** occurs around thirty times.

gnōsis is concerned primarily with human knowledge. Luke 1:77; 11:52; Rom. 15:14; 1 Cor. 8:7; 12:8 express the knowledge of salvation. Rom. 2:20 refers to knowledge gained from the law. Rom. 11:33; 2 Cor. 4:6; 10:5 mention human knowledge of God; and 2 Cor. 2:14; Phil. 3:8; 2 Pet. 3:18 speak of the knowledge of Christ.

A number of references point to knowledge in an unspecified way (e.g., Rom. 15:14; 1 Cor. 13:2, 8; 2 Cor. 6:6; 8:7; Eph. 3:19; 2 Pet. 1:5, 6). 1 Cor. 14:6 speaks of spiritual truth, and Col. 2:3 cites knowledge that is derived from Christ.

gnōstos [γνωστός, *1110*]

gnōstos is an adjective derived from ***ginōskō*** (see above) and is translated "known" in most of its fifteen occurrences.

Several texts speak of people known to one another (cf. Luke 2:44; 23:49; John 18:15, 16; Acts 1:19). ***gnōstos*** is also used in contexts where people are made aware of certain information by others (cf. Acts 2:14; 4:10; 13:38; 28:28). God is also said to "make known" (i.e., reveal) his plan of salvation in Acts 15:18. The human being's potential knowledge of God is indicated in Rom. 1:19, where it is said that what can be known about God is evident to humans in general, although the ungodly deny God's existence.

agnoeō [ἀγνοέω, *50*]

agnoeō is a verb expressing the negative sense of "not to know," or "be ignorant," "not understand." ***agnoeō*** is found in twenty-five contexts.

Mark 9:32; Luke 9:45 refer to Jesus' disciples' failure to understand that Jesus was to be betrayed and lose his life. The unbelief of the Jewish population in Jerusalem led to their failure to understand Jesus' real nature (cf. Acts 13:27).

agnoeō also refers to people acting in ignorance in 1 Cor. 14:38; 2 Cor. 2:11. Acting ignorantly in unbelief is mentioned in 1 Tim. 1:13; 2 Pet. 2:12. The Athenians' ignorant worship of idols, specifically adoration of "the unknown God," is indicated in Acts 17:23. Ignoring righteousness that comes from God is mentioned in Rom. 10:3.

The meaning "be unaware" is also evident in the usage of ***agnoeō*** (cf. Rom. 6:3; 7:1; 1 Cor. 12:1; 2 Cor. 1:8). Rom. 2:4 speaks of the contempt shown towards the riches of God's kindness when people are unaware that God's goodness is intended to lead to repentance.

agnoeō is also translated "be unknown" in Gal. 1:22, referring to the fact that Paul was unknown to the Galatian churches.

In a nominal usage of ***agnoeō*** in Heb. 5:2, the writer refers to God dealing gently with those who are ignorant.

agnōsia [ἀγνωσία, *56*]

agnōsia occurs only twice, meaning "ignorance," or "lack of knowledge." 1 Cor. 15:34 refers to some having no knowledge of God, and 1 Pet. 2:15 speaks of the ignorance of foolish people.

gnōrizō [γνωρίζω, *1107*]

gnōrizō is found in about twenty contexts, meaning "make known," "gain knowledge of."

When referring to God, ***gnōrizō*** indicates revealing (i.e., making known) his divine purposes in several contexts: he reveals his purposes to angels concerning Jesus' birth (cf. Luke 2:15); and he also reveals the mystery of his will (cf. Eph. 1:9; 3:3, 5; 6:19); his wisdom (cf. Eph. 3:10); his wrath (cf. Rom. 9:22); and the riches of his glory (cf. Rom. 9:23; Col. 1:27). See also Acts 2:28. Similarly, Christ makes known the teaching of his Father to his disciples (cf. John 15:15; 17:26).

The meaning "gain knowledge of," in reference to human beings, is indicated in 2 Cor. 8:1, where the grace of God is the object of that knowledge. Gal. 1:11 claims that the knowledge of the gospel is not something gleaned from human beings.

The idea of "making known" or "informing" is indicated in Eph. 6:21; Col. 4:7, 9. In Phil. 4:6, believers are exhorted to make their requests known to God. 2 Pet. 1:16 refers to Peter making his readers aware of the power and coming of the Lord Jesus Christ.

anagnōrizomai [ἀναγνωρίζομαι, *319*]

anagnōrizomai occurs only in Acts 7:13, meaning "make known," or "recognize."

oida [οἶδα, *1492*]

oida is a verb in the perfect tense, meaning "know," "understand," with various nuances. It is predicated of both human beings and God and occurs in about three hundred contexts. (→ *SEE*)

In reference to God, ***oida*** indicates his knowing all things, including our need (cf. Matt. 6:8, 32; Luke 12:30); and the mind of the Spirit (cf. Rom. 8:27). Such knowledge is similarly predicated of Christ, who knows everything in the hearts and minds of his hearers (cf. Matt. 9:4; John 8:55), including his enemies (cf. Luke 6:8; John 13:11; Mark 12:15; Matt. 27:18). Christ is also one who knows perfectly his Father's mind and intention for his people (cf. John 11:22; 13:18); as well as God's will for his own life, in relation to his approaching death (cf. John 13:1). Jesus is aware of the truth of God's revelation to him (cf. John 5:32; 12:50); and knows the Father intimately (cf. John 7:29; 8:14). The omniscience of Christ in general is indicated in John 16:30; 18:4; 19:28; 21:17.

oida is also commonly used in the context of human knowledge. The primary sense is that of "being aware." General references to this phenomenon are found, for example, in Luke 8:53; John 4:10; 21:15ff.; Acts 3:17; Phil. 1:19. ***oida*** refers to human awareness or knowledge of, for example, the Scriptures (cf. 2 Tim. 3:15); the uniqueness of Jesus' person and work (cf. John 7:28; 1 Cor. 2:2; 2 Tim. 1:12); the truth of the gospel (cf. John 19:35; 21:24); spiritual truth (cf. Rom. 5:3; Gal. 2:16; 1 Thess. 1:4); the power of God in Christ (cf. Mark 2:10; 5:33; Acts 12:11); and personal knowledge of God (cf. 1 John 5:19).

To "know" in the sense of "believe in" is indicated with reference to the coming of the Messiah (John 4:25, 42); to the resurrection of Jesus (John 11:24; Rom. 6:9); to the return of Christ (cf. 1 John 3:2); and to the assurance of salvation (1 John 5:13). See also Rom. 8:28; 1 Cor. 8:4.

oida also refers to one knowing in the sense of "being (personally) acquainted with" (cf. John 6:42; Acts 3:16; 7:18). John 10:4 speaks of sheep knowing their shepherd, referring to the followers of Jesus. This kind of knowledge is even predicated of demons, who are described as knowing (i.e., recognizing) Christ as the Son of God (cf. Mark 1:24, 34; Luke 4:34ff.).

A number of contexts indicate the negative sense of ***oida***. Matt. 13:14, for example, refers to those who will not understand the teaching of Jesus, as a consequence of divine judgment on them. John 15:21; 1 Thess. 4:5; 2 Thess. 1:8 refer to those who have no saving knowledge of God. Several texts point to the ignorance of human beings in a number of ways — for example, in respect of the timing of the Day of the Lord (cf. Matt. 24:36; Mark 13:22ff.); the person of Christ (cf. John 1:31; 9:30); and spiritual matters (cf. 1 Cor. 5:6; 6:2ff.). See also Matt. 20:22; Mark 10:38; Luke 23:34; John 4:22; Rom. 8:26. In addition, people deny a saving relationship with Christ (i.e., refuse to know him) (Matt. 25:12; Luke 13:27); and deny acquaintance with Christ, in the case of Peter's rejection of Jesus (Matt. 26:70ff.; Mark 14:68ff.; Luke 22:34, 57, 60).

epistamai [ἐπίσταμαι, *1987*]

epistamai, a form of the verb ***ephistēmi*** (→ ***STAND***), means "know," "understand." ***epistamai*** occurs thirteen times and is used only in reference to human knowledge.

The sense of "know" or "be aware" is indicated in Acts 18:25; 19:25; 20:18; 22:19; 26:26. Acts 19:15 refers to "knowing" in terms of personal acquaintance.

epistamai means "understand" in Acts 10:28; 15:7. It is otherwise used negatively — for example, with respect to Peter's denial of Jesus (Mark 14:68); our ignorance of tomorrow (cf. Jas. 4:14); the ignorance of false teachers (1 Tim. 6:4; Jude 10); and Abraham's ignorance of his destination when God called him to leave Ur of the Chaldees (cf. Heb. 11:8).

synesis [σύνεσις, *4907*]

synesis occurs seven times and means "knowledge" in respect of various phenomena, including human knowledge of Christ (cf. Col. 2:2; Eph. 3:4); and of God (cf. Col. 1:9); and spiritual understanding (2 Tim. 2:7). Loving God with all one's understanding is indicated in Mark 12:33. 1 Cor. 1:19 affirms that worldly understanding will be destroyed by God. Luke 2:47 records people's amazement at the boy Jesus' prodigious understanding of the law.

phaneros [φανερός, *5318*]

phaneros is an adjectival form signifying "made known," "manifest." It occurs around twenty times.

That which is known about God is referred to in Rom. 1:19. Information is made known as Paul witnesses in prison (cf. Phil. 1:13); about the secrets of one's heart (cf. 1 Cor. 14:25); and about one's earthly service on the day of judgment (cf. 1 Cor. 3:13). See also Acts 7:13. In two places, Jesus instructs those whom he has just healed not to make him known (Matt. 12:16; Mark 3:12).

See Also: → UNDERSTANDING

L

LABOR → WORK

LACK → NEED

LADDER

OT Words

***syllām* [סֻלָּם, 5551]**

This term occurs only in Gen. 28:12, where it refers to the ladder seen in Jacob's vision at Bethel, on which angels were ascending and descending. It is a visual reminder of the covenant promises made to Abraham in respect of the land of Canaan and the innumerable number of descendants promised to him. Jacob was the direct inheritor of those promises.

LAKE → SEA

LAMB

OT Words

***kibsāh* [כִּבְשָׂה, 3535]**

kibsāh occurs six times and is translated "ewe lamb," "lamb."

In mundane contexts, ***kibsāh*** refers to "lambs" as members of animal flocks (cf. Gen. 21:28).

In ritual contexts describing sacrifices, ***kibsāh*** refers to a lamb being selected as a guilt offering for the ceremony of ritual cleansing after recovery from infectious skin disease (cf. Lev. 14:10). A lamb is also to be selected as a burnt offering at the conclusion of the Nazirite period of separation (cf. Num. 6:14).

***seh* [שֶׂה, 7716]**

seh is a general word for a herd animal. The term refers to a "lamb," as well as "sheep," "cattle," and "goats." ***seh*** is found in fifty contexts, referring to "lamb(s)" on sixteen occasions. All of these contexts have to do with ritual offering.

seh indicates a lamb to be selected for a burnt offering (Gen. 22:7, 8; Isa. 66:3; Ezek. 45:15); a free-will offering (Lev. 22:23; Num. 15:11); for the Passover festival (Exod. 12:3ff.); and for a sin offering (Lev. 5:7; 12:8). Isa. 53:7 refers to a lamb being led to the slaughter — a metaphorical, prophetic allusion to the future suffering of the Messianic Servant of Yahweh, Jesus Christ. ***seh*** also indicates the lamb to be selected for "redeeming" every "firstborn donkey," or obtaining the release of the latter through the sacrifice of the former. The law normally required that all firstborn animals be given over to the Lord, and would therefore be sacrificed in due course. Donkeys were excepted from this law, and could instead be redeemed, because of their importance as pack animals (cf. Exod. 13:13; 34:20).

***keseb* [כֶּשֶׂב, 3775]**

keseb occurs thirteen times and is translated "sheep," "lamb." The latter meaning is found in four of these contexts. ***keseb*** is most likely a transposition of the term ***kebes*** (see below).

keseb indicates a lamb as an animal of the flock (Gen. 30:40); as the object of a fellowship offering (Lev. 3:7), and a sin offering (Lev. 4:35); and also as an illegitimate sacrifice (Lev. 17:3).

***kebes* [כֶּבֶשׂ, 3532]**

kebes is the most common term for "lamb" in the Old Testament, occurring around one hundred times.

Non-ritual, mundane use of the term is found, for example, in Prov. 27:26; Isa. 5:17.

Far more common is the ritual use of ***kebes*** in a variety of contexts. A lamb is prescribed for a burnt offering (Exod. 29:38ff.; Lev. 23:12, 18; Num. 15:5; Ezra 8:35); for a sin offering (Lev. 4:32; 9:3; 23:19); for a Sabbath offering (Num. 28:9); for a purification ritual (Lev. 12:6; 14:10ff.); for offering at the dedication of the tabernacle (Num. 7:15ff.); for the purification of the temple (2 Chr. 29:21ff.); and for the coronation of Solomon (1 Chr. 29:21). In a slightly different context, a lamb was prescribed for the ritual enacting of the Nazirite vow, intended as a guilt offering in anticipation of an inadvertent violation of the vow through coming in contact with a dead person (cf. Num. 6:12). Similarly, at the conclusion of this vow, a lamb was likewise to be offered in sacrifice (cf. Num. 6:14). On the occasions of various key festivals, lambs figured prominently in the quota of animals to be sacrificed — including Passover (Num. 28:19; 2 Chr. 35:7); the Feast of Weeks, or Pentecost (Num. 28:27, 29); the Feast of Trumpets (Num. 29:2ff.); the Feast of Tabernacles

(Num. 29:13ff.); and the Day of Atonement (Num. 29:8ff.).

Isa. 1:11 records a divine attitude of contempt towards sacrifice involving a lamb, which is offered without devotion to God.

Isa. 11:6 contains a symbolic description of a renewed earth, transformed as a consequence of the mission of the messianic deliverer — the Davidic "branch," — in which the wolf shall lie down with the lamb. ***kebes*** is used in a general symbolic way in Jer. 11:19; Hos. 4:16.

kar **[כַּר, 3733]**

kar is a noun denoting a "lamb" in the majority of its sixteen occurrences (cf. Deut. 32:14; 1 Sam. 15:9; 2 Kgs. 3:4; Ps. 37:20; Isa. 16:1; 34:6; Jer. 51:40; Ezek. 27:21; 39:18; Amos 6:4).

NT Words

arēn **[ἀρήν, *704*]**

arēn occurs only in Luke 10:3, where it is used metaphorically. Here Jesus sends out the disciples "like lambs in the midst of wolves."

amnos [ἀμνός, *286*]

amnos is a rare term for "lamb," occurring four times. In John 1:29, 36 it is used by John the Baptist in reference to Jesus Christ as the "lamb of God," who takes away the sin of the world. In Acts 8:32 the Ethiopian eunuch reads Isa. 53, which speaks of the Messiah's docile submission to his tormentors — "as a lamb before its shearers is dumb." 1 Pet. 1:19 speaks of the efficacy of the blood of Christ as that "of a spotless lamb."

arnion [ἀρνίον, *721*]

arnion is a diminutive form of ***arēn*** (see above), occurring around thirty times and meaning "lamb." ***arnion*** refers exclusively to Christ as the Lamb who is King (i.e., the risen king in heaven) in the book of Revelation (cf. Rev. 5:6ff.; 7:9ff.; 12:11; 13:8ff.; 14:1ff.; 19:7ff.; 21:14, 22ff.; 22:1ff.).

The exception to this usage is found in John 2:15, where Jesus instructs Peter to look after his disciples, saying "feed my lambs."

Additional Notes

There is a profound symbolism attached to the Hebrew terminology for "lamb" in the context of ritual sacrifice and worship, which is carried over explicitly into the New. The idea of a spotless lamb as a substitutionary sacrifice for the sin of the worshiper is a paradigm for forgiveness in the Old Testament ceremonial sphere. The theological significance of such a sacrifice is captured perfectly in the figure of Jesus Christ, whose designation by John the Baptist as the "lamb of God" is perhaps the most sublime metaphor of the supreme efficacy of Christ's death in the New Testament. There is perhaps no more succinct phrase than this, that conveys the intention of the biblical writers to describe the divine means of forgiveness for sin that originates with a literal animal sacrifice under the old covenant and is consummated by the death of the Messiah on the threshold of the new covenant age.

LAME

OT Words

pissēaḥ **[פִּסֵּחַ, 6455]**

pissēaḥ is found in fourteen contexts meaning "lame" in both a literal and metaphorical sense.

In a literal sense, ***pissēaḥ*** refers to lameness as a physical disability in people who were consequently refused access to worship in the tabernacle (Lev. 21:18; cf. also 2 Sam. 5:6, 8; 9:13; Job 29:15). ***pissēaḥ*** also refers to physically disabled animals, which are entirely unsuitable for sacrifice (cf. Deut. 15:21; Mal. 1:8, 13). Offering such animals to Yahweh was prohibited, and if they were indeed offered up, it constituted a gross offense under the law covenant. General reference to lame animals is made in Isa. 33:23.

In metaphorical contexts, ***pissēaḥ*** refers to the lame who are granted healing by God in the vision of a redeemed creation (cf. Isa. 35:6). Jer. 31:8 likewise refers to the restoration of the people of Israel, including the lame, to their homeland in Canaan.

nākeh **[נָכֶה, 5223]**

nākeh is a rare term, referring twice to the lameness of Mephibosheth, who was crippled in both feet (cf. 2 Sam. 4:4; 9:3). ***nākeh*** derives from the verb ***nākāh***, "to strike," "smite." (➡ BEAT ➡ STRIKE) Thus the literal meaning of ***nākeh*** is "stricken," or "smitten," which is then translated as "lame" (in an extended sense), with respect to Mephibosheth.

NT Words

chōlos [χωλός, *5560*]

chōlos is an adjectival form (occurring fifteen times) that refers primarily to the physical condition of lameness.

In Jesus' ministry of miracle working, the healing of the lame was a prominent feature (cf. Matt. 11:5; 15:30ff.; Mark 9:45; Luke 7:22; John 5:3). Likewise, the apostles continued with their own healing ministry after the ascension of Christ (cf. Acts 3:2, 11; 8:7; 14:8). Luke 14:13, 21 refer generally to the lame or crippled.

chōlos is used metaphorically in Matt. 18:8, where Jesus refers to the consequences of "cutting off one's limbs." The declared intention is that it is better to enter heaven "maimed" than to be thrown into hell with all hands and feet intact — emphasizing the necessity of self-denial and turning from sin. Heb. 12:13 refers to spiritual healing through the metaphor of deliverance from lameness.

LAMENT, LAMENTATION → MOURN

LAMP

OT Words

nēr **[נֵר, 5216]**

nēr is found in approximately fifty contexts and is translated "lamp" primarily in reference to lighting in the tabernacle and temple. ***nēr*** is also used symbolically in other places.

With regard to the tabernacle, ***nēr*** refers to "lamps" in Exod. 25:37; 27:20; 30:7ff.; 35:14; 37:23; 39:37; 40:4, 25; Lev. 24:2ff.; Num. 4:9; 8:2ff.; 1 Sam. 3:3. Similarly, lamps in the temple are mentioned in 1 Kgs. 7:49; 1 Chr. 28:15; 2 Chr. 4:20ff.; 13:11; 29:7, and in Zech. 4:2 as part of a temple vision.

Metaphorically, ***nēr*** refers to the "lamp" of the wicked being snuffed out (cf. Prov. 13:9; 20:20). God is also referred to as one's guiding lamp (cf. 2 Sam. 22:29; Prov. 6:23; Ps. 119:105). Ps. 132:17 mentions a "lamp" as a symbol for the spiritual enlightenment that will come as the consequence of the coming of the Messianic King, descended from the line of David. See also 1 Kgs. 15:4.

NT Words

lampas [λαμπάς, *2985*]

lampas occurs in nine contexts and means "lamp," "torch," in both a literal and metaphorical sense.

Torches for lighting one's way at night are indicated in Matt. 25:1ff.; John 18:3; Acts 20:8.

lampas refers metaphorically in Rev. 4:5 to fiery lamps illuminating the throne of God in heaven. In Rev. 8:10, ***lampas*** refers to a star falling from heaven, blazing like a torch.

lychnos [λύχνος, *3088*]

lychnos is a synonym for ***lampas*** (see above). It occurs in fourteen places and is likewise translated "lamp."

Mundane usage is indicated in Matt. 5:15; Mark 4:21; Luke 8:16; 11:33, 36; 12:35; 15:8. See also Rev. 18:23; 22:5.

In metaphorical contexts, ***lychnos*** refers first of all to the eye as the "lamp of the body" in Matt. 6:22; Luke 11:34. Scripture is depicted as a guiding "lamp" in 2 Pet. 1:19. In Rev. 21:23, the Lamb of God is described as the "lamp" of the heavenly city. John 5:35 depicts John the Baptist as a "shining lamp."

LAMPSTAND

OT Words

menôrāh **[מְנוֹרָה, 4501]**

menôrāh is a term that refers almost exclusively to the lampstand fashioned and used in the tabernacle and temple for worship of Yahweh. ***menôrāh*** occurs around forty times.

menôrāh refers to lampstands in the tabernacle (Exod. 25:31ff.; 35:14; 37:17ff.; 39:37; 40:4, 24; Num. 3:31; 4:9; 8:2ff.); and in the temple (cf. 1 Kgs. 7:49; 1 Chr. 28:15; 2 Chr. 4:7, 20; 13:11; Jer. 52:19; Zech. 4:2, 11). The latter reference in Zechariah indicates the lampstand in a visionary sanctuary. The sole mundane use of ***menôrāh*** is found in 2 Kgs. 4:10.

nebrashtāh **[נֶבְרַשְׁתָּה, 5043** (Aramaic)**]**

nebrashtāh is an Aramaic term for "lampstand," found only in Dan. 5:5 with reference to the lampstand in the royal palace of Babylon. The message of judgment against Belshazzar from the hand of Yahweh appeared on the wall near this lampstand.

NT Words

lychnia [λυχνία, *3087*]

lychnia occurs in twelve contexts, referring mostly to the "lampstand" of the temple, in its earthly as well as its heavenly location. In addition, ***lychnia*** refers to a "lampstand" or "candlestick" in a mundane sense (cf. Matt. 5:15; Mark 4:21; Luke 8:16; 11:33).

Regarding the use of ***lychnia*** with reference to the lampstands in the temple, Heb. 9:2 lists it among a general description of the Solomonic temple furniture. The remaining references to ***lychnia*** are found in the book of Revelation. In Rev. 1:12, 13, 20, the apostle John records his vision of the risen Christ standing among seven golden lampstands. The heavenly throne room of the celestial temple is in view here, of which the earthly sanctuary is but a pale shadow (cf. Heb. 9:1, 2). Rev. 2:1 makes further allusion to this phenomenon. Rev. 2:5 indicates that the church at Ephesus, in view of its failings, is in danger of having its lampstand removed from the heavenly sanctuary. This reference links the function of the lampstands to the spiritual vitality of the seven churches to whom John is writing.

Additional Notes

The lamp is a significant theological motif that bridges both Old and New Testaments. The correlation between ***menôrāh***, in its reference to the lampstands of the earthly Israelite sanctuaries, and ***lychnia***, in its indication of the heavenly lampstands, makes it clear that the literal light bearing function of the physical lampstands of the tabernacle and temple has a profound symbolism for the spiritual understanding of these items. There is a clear link between the ritual use of the lampstand and the impact that the people of Israel were intended to have on the surrounding nations. God's people were intended to be a beacon for the nations, in order to attract them to Yahweh, although Israel fell far short of that ideal. However, it is in the person of Christ that the true importance of the "lampstands" is brought to fulfillment. Jesus Christ is indeed the "light of the world," who will draw the nations to himself and fulfill that element of God's redemptive purposes through the ongoing testimony and witness of his church. Such a ministry is vindicated in the vision of the apostle John, who sees Christ himself standing among the lampstands (cf. Rev. 1:12), clearly identifying himself with that light. It is also clear from the threat to the church at Ephesus (cf. Rev. 2:5), that the body of believers was grossly negligent of its light-bearing function, and therefore in danger of losing their ministry.

LAND ➡ EARTH

LANGUAGE

OT Words

lāshôn **[לָשׁוֹן, 3956]**

lāshôn means "language," "speech," with the related sense of "tongue." ***lāshôn*** occurs around 120 times, with these meanings evident in the majority of cases.

The literal phenomenon of different human languages is evident, for example, in Gen. 10:5, 20, 31; Deut. 28:49; Neh. 13:24; Isa. 11:15; Jer. 5:15; Ezek. 3:5ff.; Dan. 1:4.

lāshôn likewise indicates human speech, or language in general. Examples of this usage are found in Exod. 4:10; Josh. 10:21; Ps. 45:1. In particular, ***lāshôn*** refers to divine judgment against "perverse speech" (Prov. 10:31), and also against false prophecy (Jer. 23:31). ***lāshôn*** also refers to flattery (cf. Pss. 5:9; 12:3); speaking evil (cf. Ps. 10:7; Isa. 39:3); slander (cf. Ps. 15:3); deceit (cf. Ps. 52:4; Zeph. 3:13); and lying (cf. Ps. 78:36; Mic. 6:12). In much more positive contexts, ***lāshôn*** refers to praising God (cf. Pss. 51:14; 119:172); and kind speech (cf. Prov. 31:26). In addition, ***lāshôn*** refers to prophecy, namely language or speech prompted by Yahweh, through the "tongue" of his servant (cf. 2 Sam. 23:2).

lishān **[לִשָּׁן, 3961** (Aramaic)**]**

lishān is the Aramaic term corresponding to the Hebrew ***lāshôn*** (see above). ***lishān*** occurs seven times, with the consistent meaning "language." Specifically, the diverse languages of humankind are indicated by the use of this term (cf. Dan. 3:4, 7, 29; 4:1; 5:19; 6:25; 7:14).

sāphāh **[שָׂפָה, 8193]**

sāphāh is a noun found on approximately 120 occasions, with the principal meaning "lip(s)." In six of these contexts, however, ***sāphāh*** means "language" in the sense of "human language." (➡ LIP)

Universal human language is indicated in Gen. 11. In Gen 11:7 God intervenes to confuse the language of all the people so that they spread out over the whole earth, forcing the human population of the day to comply with his command to fill the whole earth. Isa. 19:18 refers to the language of Canaan. Human language in general is mentioned in Zeph. 3:9.

lā'az **[לָעַז, 3937]**

lā'az is found only in Ps. 114:1, meaning "strange language."

NT Words

dialektos **[διάλεκτος,** ***1258*****]**

dialektos is the sole term in the New Testament referring to the phenomenon of language. It occurs six times and is translated "language," "tongue," "speech."

Acts 1:19 refers to the language of Aramaic in the expression *akeldama*, indicating the "field of blood" where Judas threw away the thirty pieces of silver gained as the price of betraying Jesus Christ to the Jewish authorities. Specific human languages are indicated in Acts 2:6, 8 on the occasion of the Pentecost miracle, where many nations simultaneously heard the sermon of Peter in their own tongue. The Hebrew language is referred to in Acts 21:40; 22:2, where Paul's speech to the Jerusalem crowd is recorded; and also in Acts 26:14 in Christ's words to Saul during his conversion experience on the road to Damascus.

LARGE → GREAT

LAST

OT Words

'aḥarît [אַחֲרִית, 319]

'aḥarît is a noun form occurring around sixty times with the primary meanings "end," "latter," "last." In a number of significant prophetic contexts, the term indicates the final period of human history in which God's plan of redemption will come to fruition.

One significant phrase containing the term ***'aḥarît*** is the expression "in the last days," or "in the days to come," indicating a connection with the divine plan of redemption. The prophetic contexts containing this expression are quite varied. For example, it refers to the future destiny of the sons of Jacob and the Messianic King who will come from his line (cf. Gen. 49:1, 8); to the restoration of the people of God "in the last, latter days" (Deut. 4:30; Hos. 3:5); to the restoration of the enemies of Yahweh during this period of time, including Moab (Jer. 48:47) and Elam (Jer. 49:37); and to invoking divine judgment upon the people of Israel during their history (cf. Deut. 31:29; Ezek. 38:16). There will also be in this eschatological time period a renewal of worship on the "mountain of the house of the Lord" (cf. Isa. 2:2; Mic. 4:1).

'aḥarît also means "end" in the sense of latter days or last, final destiny. Note in Num. 23:10; Jer. 29:11; 31:17 the blessed "end" of the Israelite people in God's plan for their future. Conversely, this term also expresses a threatened "end" of God's people on account of their rebellion against Yahweh in their past and current experience (cf. Deut. 32:20; Jer. 12:4; 23:20; 30:24; Lam. 1:9). There is also a prediction of this "end" in Deut. 32:29. With regard to the enemies of Israel, their final "end," or doom, is also clearly spelled out — for example, Amalek (Num. 24:20); the wicked in general (Ps. 73:17); and Persia and Greece (Dan. 8:19, 23).

Mundane usage of ***'aḥarît*** is found in Deut. 11:12, Job 42:12; Prov. 5:11.

'aḥarôn [אַחֲרוֹן, 314]

'aḥarôn is an adjectival form related to ***'aḥarît*** (see above), occurring about twenty times meaning "last," "latter." In a number of other contexts it has the adverbial sense of "after(wards)." It is also translated "last" in a few significant theological contexts.

The mundane sense of "latter," in non-prophetic contexts, is indicated in Exod. 4:8; Deut. 24:3. In addition, the meaning "last," in the mundane sense of a final position, is found variously, for example, in Num. 2:31; Ruth 3:10; 2 Sam. 23:1; 1 Chr. 29:29; 2 Chr. 26:22; Neh. 8:18; Dan. 8:3. ***'aḥarôn*** also means "afterwards," as an ordinary temporal adverb (cf. Deut. 13:9; 1 Kgs. 17:13).

The nominal use of ***'aḥarôn*** meaning "last" is found in a number of texts with reference to Yahweh as "the first and the last" (cf. Isa. 41:4; 44:6; 48:12). The underlying emphasis here is on Yahweh's uniqueness as the one true and living God, whose eternal nature is in stark contrast to the nonentity of idols.

There is one very significant use of ***'aḥarôn*** with the adjectival sense of "latter" in Hag. 2:9. Yahweh declares that the glory of this "latter" house (viz. the reconstructed postexilic temple) shall be greater than the glory of the former (i.e., the Solomonic temple). This "latter" glory anticipates the coming of the Messiah.

NT Words

eschatos [ἔσχατος, *2078*]

eschatos is an adjectival form occurring around fifty times, with the predominant meaning "last" in both a temporal and spatial sense, as well as referring to that of lowest status.

In the sense of "last," indicating the final element in a significant series, personal or impersonal, ***eschatos*** is found in a number of places. Matt. 5:26; Luke 12:59 record, for example, the "last penny" of a debt. 1 Cor. 15:52 refers to the "last trumpet" as the prelude to the return of Jesus Christ at the end of the age. And, in 1 Cor. 15:26, Paul declares that the "last enemy" to be destroyed is death. With reference to people, ***eschatos*** is found in 1 Cor. 15:8, referring to Paul as "the last of the apostles." The term also refers to Christ, who is described in 1 Cor. 15:45 as "the last Adam." Finally, in this particular sense, ***eschatos*** occurs in Rev. 1:11, 17; 2:8; 22:13, where the risen Christ refers to himself as "the first and the last." Other mundane references to "last" in this sense are found in Matt. 20:8ff.; John 7:37; 8:9.

eschatos also indicates the meaning "last" in the sense of a final stage in a process. For example, in Matt. 12:45, Jesus declares that if a man, having had demons removed from his person, does not have that spiritual void replaced by the Spirit of God (by implication), then his "last state" will be worse than the first. See also Matt. 27:64; 2 Pet. 2:20. Then, in Rev. 15:1; 21:9, the "last seven" angelic plagues of judgment against the earth are declared to be the completion of God's wrath against the wickedness of humankind.

Perhaps the most significant use of ***eschatos*** in this sense is found in the expression "the last day," indicating the final stage of divine judgment against humankind (cf. John 6:39ff.; 11:24; 12:48). Similarly, the phrase "in the last days" refers to the final period of human history before the consummation, resulting in eternal blessing for the righteous and condemnation for the wicked (cf. Acts 2:17; 2 Tim. 3:1; Heb. 1:2; Jas. 5:3; 1 Pet. 1:5, 20; 2 Pet. 3:3; 1 John 2:18; Jude 18).

eschatos also means "last" in the sense of rank, or status. Commonly, reference is made to the reversal of status in the sight of God with the declaration, "the first shall be last, and the last shall be first" (cf. Matt. 19:30; Luke 11:26).

Additional Notes

The Hebrew and Greek terminology for "last" or "end" is particularly noteworthy, in that terms such as ***'aḥarît*** and ***'aḥarôn***, when relating to the plan and purposes of God in history, both imply that the fulfillment of such a plan is wholly under divine control and inevitably certain. Such an outcome is assured, whether it refers positively to the blessing of Israel and the nations, or negatively to the judgment of both Israel and the nations.

What is therefore viewed as a distant hope in the Old Testament is brought into sharp focus in the New through the person of the Messiah, Jesus Christ, who is identified as the consummate agent of God's redemptive plan. New Testament references to the "last days" (and associated expressions) make it clear that the fulfillment of such a plan is intimately bound up with the person and work of Christ, who is viewed both as Savior and judge.

LAUGH

OT Words

ṣāḥaq [צָחַק, 6711]

ṣāḥaq means "laugh," "make sport of," "mock." The term is found thirteen times, meaning "laugh" or "mock" in about half of these contexts.

The meaning "laugh," with the underlying sense of incredulity or amazement, is found in Gen. 17:17; 18:12ff. in relation to Abraham and Sarah's reactions at learning they will have a child in their old age. ***ṣāḥaq*** also expresses the idea of laughing in the sense of mocking or joking in Gen. 19:14.

ṣeḥōq [צְחֹק, 6712]

ṣeḥōq is the noun derived from ***ṣāḥaq*** (see above). The term is only found twice, but is translated with verbal force on each occasion and refers to the action of "laughing to scorn," or "scoffing." In Gen. 21:6, Sarah fears she will be an object of ridicule for having a child in her old age. Ezek. 23:32 indicates that Judah will be scorned by the nations for her idolatrous rejection of Yahweh.

lā'ag [לָעַג, 3932]

lā'ag is a verb occurring around twenty times with the primary sense of "mock," "laugh to scorn," or "ridicule."

General references to people mocking are found in 2 Chr. 30:10; Job 21:3; Prov. 30:17. In more significant contexts, Sennacherib is mocked (metaphorically speaking) by the city of Jerusalem in 2 Kgs. 19:21; Isa. 37:22. Then, in Neh. 2:19; 4:1, the returned exiles are jeered by their hostile neighbors as they rebuild the city walls of Jerusalem. Jeremiah is mocked by his enemies in Jer. 20:7. Israel is scorned by her neighbors in Ps. 80:6. And the psalmist anticipates some of the suffering of Christ on the cross when he experiences the mocking of the crowd in Ps. 22:7.

lā'ag is also predicated of Yahweh, when he is said to scorn the nations in Pss. 2:4; 59:8 for their vain attempts to overthrow his plans. God's wisdom is said to mock the fools who reject him (cf. Prov. 1:26). Job 9:23 records a charge illegitimately leveled at God, when the patriarchal figure wrongly accuses God of mocking the innocent in their suffering.

sāḥaq [שָׂחַק, 7832]

sāḥaq has a broader semantic range than the terms discussed above. This verb is translated in a variety of senses, such as "play," "laugh," "scorn," "rejoice," as well as a number of related meanings. ***sāḥaq*** occurs about forty times and is translated "laugh," "scorn" in about half of these contexts.

The meaning "mock" or "scorn" is indicated in general contexts such as 2 Chr. 30:10; Ps. 52:6; Prov. 29:6; Hab. 1:10; Eccl. 3:4. In Lam. 1:7, the enemies of

Jerusalem are said to mock her. In several metaphorical contexts, in the book of Job, mocking is predicated of a donkey (Job 39:7); an ostrich (Job 39:18); a horse (Job 39:22); and the mysterious Leviathan (Job 41:29). In Job 29:24, ***sāḥaq*** is translated "laughed" or "smiled."

sāḥaq is also predicated of Yahweh, indicating divine mocking or laughter. In Pss. 2:4; 59:8, Yahweh is said to scoff at the nations who plot against him. See also his mocking of the wicked Ps. 37:13; Prov. 1:26.

NT Words

katagelaō [καταγελάω, *2606*]

katagelaō occurs three times and is translated "laugh to scorn" on each occasion. Matt. 9:24; Mark 5:40; Luke 8:53 refer to the incident where the crowd mocks Jesus for his claim that the dead girl before him, Jairus' daughter (whom he was about to bring back to life), was only sleeping.

gelaō [γελάω, *1070*]

gelaō occurs only twice and refers to the action of laughing in a non-specific context. Luke 6:21 refers to one of the Beatitudes, "Blessed are you that weep now, for you shall laugh." The converse is recorded in Luke 6:25: "Woe to you that laugh now, for you shall mourn and weep." The thought here is that only those who truly appreciate the seriousness of their rebellion against God and mourn over their sin will enjoy ultimate happiness and laughter, through a relationship of faith and trust in Jesus Christ.

gelōs [γέλως, *1071*]

gelōs is the noun derived from ***gelaō*** (see above). It is found only in Jas. 4:9, where sinners are exhorted to turn their "laughter" into mourning, humbling themselves before God. The thought here is essentially the same as that expressed by ***gelaō*** in Luke's gospel (see above).

eutrapelia [εὐτραπελία, *2160*]

eutrapelia occurs only once, in Eph. 5:4, where it refers to the vice of "levity" or "course jesting."

LAW

OT Words

tôrāh [תּוֹרָה, 8451]

tôrāh is a term that has profound theological importance throughout the entire Old Testament. It occurs over two hundred times and is uniformly translated "law," though in a variety of contexts. The heart of the term's significance lies in Yahweh's revelation of his purposes and principles for the Israelite people through the prophetic ministry of Moses, who acted as the mediator for the divine revelation of the law covenant.

tôrāh indicates the law(s) of Yahweh in both general and specific contexts. Gen. 26:5, for example, refers to the laws of God in a pre-Mosaic context as a general expression of his will and purpose for his chosen people. In other general contexts, ***tôrāh*** refers to principles of behavior that are clearly derived from God's ordinances, but are not explicitly declared as God's law. See, for example, Prov. 1:8; 3:1; 4:2; 6:20; 7:2, which refer to the "law" of one's godly parents (or community leaders) which may not be lightly cast aside.

The Sinaitic law covenant constitutes the primary context for the use of ***tôrāh***. Exod. 18:20, for instance, refers to the Mosaic law covenant in summary fashion, indicating the sum total of divine legislation and its binding obligation on the people of Yahweh. In a number of places, ***tôrāh*** refers to the specific Sinai revelation, including the stone tablets, with the explicit sense of "law" (cf. Exod. 24:12; Lev. 26:46; Neh. 9:13ff.; Isa. 24:5; Mal. 4:4). ***tôrāh*** also indicates the covenant law as a means of implementing judicial decisions or solving disputes (cf. Exod. 18:16; Deut. 17:11; 2 Chr. 19:10; Hag. 2:11).

Specific uses of the expressions "this law," "the law," constitute a general summary statement of Yahweh's covenant requirements given to Moses, and are very common. General references to this phenomenon are found in Exod. 13:9; Deut. 1:5; 4:8; Josh. 1:7; 1 Kgs. 2:3; Ezra 3:2; Isa. 1:10; Dan. 9:13. In particular, Josh. 8:32 refers to a copy of the Mosaic law made by Joshua for the purpose of ongoing covenant renewal. Deut. 17:18, 19 mention the duty of the Israelite king to keep a copy of the law and obey it as a model for the people to follow. There are also numerous references to the "book of the law (of Moses)" (e.g., Deut. 30:10; 31:9, 11, 24, 26; Josh. 1:8; 8:31, 34; 24:26; 2 Kgs. 22:8ff.; Neh. 8:1ff.; 9:3). The psalmist frequently expresses delight in and reverence for the law (cf. Pss. 1:2; 119:18, 34, 92, 113, 174). Isa. 42:4 refers to the law of the Suffering Messianic Servant, which is arguably identical with the law covenant of Yahweh.

In relation to the above expressions, there are a number of texts in which Yahweh speaks personally, referring to "my law(s)" (e.g., Exod. 16:28; Pss. 78:1; 89:30; Isa. 51:4, 7). One of the most significant occurrences of this usage is found in Jer. 31:33, where God's law is said to be placed on the hearts of his people, in anticipation of new covenant blessing. See also Hos. 4:6; Amos 2:4; Zeph. 3:4, where God's laws are spoken of in the third person. In several "negative" contexts, the laws of Yahweh are said to be profaned or rejected by the people of Israel and Judah (cf. Jer. 6:19; 9:13; 16:11; 44:10; Ezek. 22:26; Hos. 8:1).

In regard to particular kinds of law, ***tôrāh*** indicates regulations applying to foreigners entering the land of Israel (cf. Exod. 12:49; Num. 15:16); to the ritual law, encompassing the whole spectrum of sacrificial offerings (cf. Lev. 6:9, 25; 7:1, 37; Num. 19:2; 1 Chr. 16:40); the appointment and service of priests and Levites (cf. 2 Chr. 30:16; Neh. 12:44); and Ezekiel's visionary temple (cf. Ezek. 43:12; 44:5, 24). There are also laws relating to personal purification, ceremonial cleanness and uncleanness (cf. Lev. 12:7; 13:59; 15:32; Num. 19:14). Laws in relation to trial by ordeal for suspected adultery on the part of a wife are found in Num. 5:29, 30. Laws regulating the Nazirite vow of holiness are found in Num. 6:13, 21.

There are also several references to the curse sanctions of the law in case of disobedience (cf. Deut. 27:26; 28:58, 61; 29:21; Dan. 9:11).

ḥōq [חֹק, **2706**]

ḥōq occurs around 120 times with the principal meanings "statute," "ordinance." ***ḥōq*** is synonymous with the idea of "law" and refers specifically to those things that are prescribed. ***ḥōq*** is used primarily to refer to the details of the divine law covenant, issued by Yahweh as the conditions or decrees by which his people shall live. ***ḥōq*** also refers in one or two contexts to human statutes.

In regard to statutes of human origin, ***ḥōq*** is found in Gen. 47:26 with reference to Joseph's decree for Egypt, requiring the country to provide one-fifth of the produce of the land for Pharaoh's use. 1 Sam. 30:25 also refers to David's decree concerning the equal sharing of plunder among his men.

ḥōq refers primarily to divinely ordained statutes, in a number of contexts. There are, for example, the divine decrees concerning creation (cf. Job 28:26; Prov. 8:29; Jer. 31:34). Exod. 12:24 contains regulations for the Passover ritual. The stipulations of the Sinaitic law covenant given to the people through Moses are referred to in a number of contexts (cf. Exod. 18:16; Lev. 10:11; 26:46; Num. 30:16; 1 Chr. 22:13; Ezra 7:10, 11; Neh. 9:13, 14). In other general contexts, ***ḥōq*** also refers to non-Sinaitic decrees, where exhortations are made to keep these statutes of Yahweh (cf. Exod. 15:25; 1 Chr. 16:17).

In particular contexts where Mosaic law is in view, ***ḥōq*** refers to the Levitical ordinances of the law. For example, Exod. 30:21 refers to ceremonial washing and cleansing. The priestly share of the people's offering to Yahweh is described in Lev. 6:18ff.; 10:15; Num. 18:8, 11, 19. There are decrees and ordinances under the covenant which relate specifically to the requirements for Israel's lifestyle in the land of Canaan (cf. Deut. 4:1, 5ff., 40ff.; 5:1; 6:17ff.; 7:11; 12:1; 17:19). Specific references to the statutes of Yahweh are also indicated in a number of contexts — for example, the promise of blessing (cf. 1 Kgs. 3:14; 8:58; Ps. 105:45); threatened judgment for disobedience (cf. 2 Kgs. 17:15; Isa. 24:5; Amos 2:4; Ezek. 11:12); repentance for sin (cf. Neh. 1:7; Zech. 1:6); and praise to God for his statutes (cf. Ps. 119:5, 8, 64, 112).

On occasions of covenant renewal, ***ḥōq*** refers to the divinely given stipulations of the law, to which the people of Yahweh pledged their allegiance (cf. Josh. 24:25; 2 Chr. 34:31).

mishpāṭ [מִשְׁפָּט, **4941**]

mishpāṭ is an important term in Old Testament theology in that it reflects a number of concepts and meanings that lie at the heart of God's purposes for his people, as well as referring to his own divine attributes. ***mishpāṭ*** occurs over four hundred times and is translated primarily "justice," or "judgment" (both human and divine) in about three hundred of these contexts. Additional connotations include "ordinance," "law," "custom," "right." (→ JUDGMENT)

dāt [דָּת, **1881** (**1882** Aramaic)]

dāt is another noun that means "law," "decree," "command." It occurs around thirty-five times. ***dāt*** is identical in both its Hebrew and Aramaic form, with the Hebrew usage (approximately twenty occurrences) more frequent than the Aramaic (around fifteen occurrences).

In Hebrew, ***dāt*** refers solely to the decrees or laws of human beings and is found almost exclusively in the book of Esther — for example, the decree of King Artaxerxes (Ezra 8:36); of Xerxes (Esth. 1:8); the laws of the Jewish exiles in the Persian Empire (Esth. 3:8); as well as those of the Medes and the Persians (Esth. 1:13, 19; 2:8; 3:14ff.; 4:3, 8ff.; 8:13ff.; 9:1, 14). Customary regulations for beauty preparation are found in Esth. 2:12.

In Aramaic, ***dāt*** refers to the decrees or laws of God, as well as to those of human origin. With respect to the former, ***dāt*** indicates the law of God in general terms in association with the Mosaic law covenant (cf. Ezra 7:12ff.; Dan. 6:5; 7:25). Concerning human legislation, the decree of Nebuchadnezzar is mentioned in Dan. 2:9, 13, 15; and the laws of the Medes and the Persians in Dan. 6:8, 12, 15.

NT Words

nomos [νόμος, *3551*]

nomos is the only term in the New Testament that refers to the concept of "law" in a variety of contexts. It has both a general and specific usage relating primarily to the law established by God and brought to fulfillment in Christ. ***nomos*** occurs around two hundred times and refers exclusively to the law of God.

In general terms, ***nomos*** indicates the law of God in relation to the pentateuchal traditions and their application throughout the Old Testament. General references to this law include those in Matt. 12:5; Luke 2:2; 24:44; John 18:31; Acts 6:13; Rom. 3:28; 7:12ff.; 8:4; 1 Cor. 9:8; Gal. 5:14; Eph. 2:15; Jas. 2:8.

More particularly, ***nomos*** refers to the Torah (i.e., the Pentateuch) as distinct from the Prophets in a canonical sense (cf. Matt. 7:12; Luke 16:16; John 1:45; Acts 13:15). The Jewish privilege of being instructed in the law is noted in Rom. 2:18, 20, as is their condemnation for violating the law in Rom. 2:23, 25. In a broader context, the condemnation on people brought by the law through the knowledge of sin is made clear in Rom. 3:19, 20; 4:15; 5:20; 1 Cor. 15:56; Gal. 3:10ff.; Jas. 2:12. Similarly, "the law of sin" is said to be at work in the human heart in Rom. 7:23, 25, although Rom. 8:32 declares that believers are set free from that law by the "law" of the Spirit. The obligation of obedience to God "under the law" is indicated in 1 Cor. 9:20; Gal. 3:23, 24; 4:4ff.; 5:3; Heb. 9:22. Laws relating to marriage for the believer are noted in Rom. 7:2ff.; 1 Cor. 7:39.

In distinctively positive contexts, there is divine approval expressed for keeping the law in Rom. 2:27. Rom. 3:21 affirms that the righteousness of God is manifested apart from the law; and Rom. 6:14, 15; 7:6 declare that Christians are not under the curse of the law, but under grace. Heb. 8:10; 10:16 refer to the law of God as written on the hearts of believers. Christ's fulfillment of the law is indicated in Matt. 5:17, 18; John 15:25; Rom. 10:4.

In addition to the above, ***nomos*** refers to the divine law, revealed in the Old Testament, as God's source of judicial assessment for his people in particular, and for humankind in general. These contexts are all found in Rom. 2. The judgment of humankind in general by the law is indicated in Rom. 2:12. Rom. 2:13 affirms that doers of the law will be justified. Finally, Rom. 2:15 declares that the law is written on the hearts of the Gentiles.

nomodidaskalos [νομοδιδάσκαλος, *3547*]

nomodidaskalos occurs only three times, referring to a "teacher of the (Mosaic) law" (cf. Luke 5:17; Acts 5:34; 1 Tim. 1:7).

anomōs [ἀνόμως, *460*]

anomōs is an adverbial expression that signifies "without the law," indicating lack of knowledge of the law, ignorance of its demands. ***anomōs*** occurs only twice, in Rom. 2:12.

Additional Notes

The use of various terms for "law" constitutes a very significant theological phenomenon in both Old and New Testaments. The Mosaic law covenant focused on divine legal statutes that were primarily external in nature, in that they were inscribed initially on stone tablets and later committed to writing in much more detail. When we come to the New Testament, however, there is a dramatic change in the administration of divine law, for in the new covenant era the law is no longer viewed as an external written code, but as an obligation written on the human heart. The catalyst for this new application of divine law is the person of Christ the Messiah, who lived a life in perfect conformity to the law. Consequently, after his death, resurrection, and ascension, the promised Holy Spirit came and inaugurated the new age of spiritual understanding and awareness of God's law "written on the heart." This was a direct fulfillment of prophecies such as Ezek. 36:24ff.; Jer. 31:31ff., which clearly spelled out that a time was coming when God's people would receive a new spiritual awareness of their profound obligation of lifelong obedience and service to their God and Savior.

See Also: → COMMANDMENT → WITNESS → WORD

LAWFUL

NT Words

exesti [ἔξεστι, *1832*]

exesti is a verb form which is translated impersonally "it is lawful." ***exesti*** occurs around thirty times, and in the majority of contexts it is concerned with appropriate or inappropriate behavior in response to the demands of God's law. The appropriate behavior is that which conforms to the principles of the law. Conversely, inappropriate behavior has to do with that which is not permitted under the law. In some cases, however, what is expressed as "not lawful" is a contradiction — not of God's law, but of the misguided Pharisaic interpretation of the law. It is this latter illegality that Jesus and the disciples were sometimes accused of by the Pharisees and others of the Jewish religious hierarchy.

The ascription "not lawful," in accordance with Pharisaic tradition, is recorded in Matt. 12:2; Mark 2:24; Luke 6:2; John 5:10. Such a designation is also predicated of Mosaic ritual legal requirements (cf. Matt. 12:4 Mark 2:26; Luke 6:4). Unlawful behavior, in violation of the moral law, is indicated in Matt. 14:4; 27:6; Mark 6:18. A general sense of illegality, unrelated to the law of God, is referred to in Matt. 20:15; John 18:31; Acts 16:21; 22:25.

Occasionally, ***exesti*** is found in the context of an inquiry, for example "Is it lawful?" in Matt. 12:10; Mark 3:4; Luke 6:9; 14:3, where Jesus is asked: "Is it lawful to heal on the Sabbath?" A similar question is asked with reference to divorce (cf. Matt. 19:3; Mark 10:2), and paying taxes to Caesar (cf. Matt. 22:17; Mark 12:14; Luke 20:22).

The positive affirmation of lawful behavior, behavior that is in full accord with God's law, is illustrated in Matt. 12:12 concerning doing good on the Sabbath, and 1 Cor. 6:12; 10:23, where Paul expresses his liberty in Christ, declaring that all things are lawful for him.

LAWGIVER

NT Words

nomothetēs [νομοθέτης, *3550*]

nomothetēs occurs only in Jas. 4:12, with reference to God as "lawgiver" and judge.

LAWSUIT

OT Words

rîb [רִיב, 7379]

rîb is a noun occurring around sixty times with the basic sense of "strife," "quarrel," or "dispute," and a number of related nuances as well. Included in these nuances are several references to the "lawsuit," a formal, legal indictment brought by Yahweh against his people for violation of their covenant obligations towards him under the law. In other words, Israel's disobedience of Yahweh's laws constituted a formal "breach of contract" and warranted the invocation of the covenant sanctions against them. It is against this backdrop that the canonical prophets voiced their condemnation of Israel's sins and the accompanying invocation of divine judgment. The nations are also condemned and "indicted" on one occasion for their wicked rejection of his person and authority. The prophets functioned in these contexts as a kind of "prosecuting attorney," commissioned by Yahweh to press charges against his people.

Outside of the prophetic writings, ***rîb*** indicates a lawsuit, or legal dispute, when speaking of the Levitical judicial system as indicated in the Pentateuchal traditions. In this context, the term ***rîb*** often indicated a plea for compensation and/or justice.

References to lawsuits in a non-prophetic legal context are found in a number of places — for example, in Deut. 17:8, where difficult legal disputes are in view; and in Exod. 23:3, 6, referring to the lawsuit of a poor man. Deut. 21:5 mentions the responsibility of Levitical judges to resolve disputes and lawsuits (cf. also Ezek. 44:24). Deut. 25:1 refers to the Israelite judicial process involving the management of a lawsuit. Other relevant texts include 2 Sam. 15:2, 4; 2 Chr. 19:8, 10; Job 31:35.

References to lawsuits in prophetic contexts are not as numerous but far more significant in a theological sense. For example, Isa. 41:21 refers to Yahweh's legal challenge to the idols, an example of divine "tongue-in-cheek" sarcasm. ***rîb*** refers to legal proceedings against the nations (Jer. 25:31); and against Israel (Hos. 4:1; 12:2; Mic. 6:2). As indicated above, these "lawsuits" are all conveyed by the canonical prophets, who were functioning as Yahweh's "prosecuting attorneys."

LAWYER

NT Words

nomikos [νομικός, *3544*]

nomikos is a noun derived from the principal term for "law" in the New Testament, ***nomos***. (→ LAW) ***nomikos*** occurs nine times and has the principal meaning "lawyer," in the sense of one who is trained in the interpretation of the Mosaic law and is responsible for teaching that law to the people of Israel.

nomikos refers to the lawyers whom Jesus confronted during his earthly ministry. In all of these situations, such people were antagonistic towards Christ, seeking (unsuccessfully) to trap him in debate (cf. Matt. 22:35; Luke 10:25; 14:3); or rejecting him outright (cf. Luke 7:30). Elsewhere, they suffer the sting of Jesus' rebukes, as Jesus castigates them for the huge barriers they place in the way of those who genuinely seek after God (cf. Luke 11:45, 46, 52).

A positive general reference to a lawyer is found in Titus 3:13; and in Titus 3:9, ***nomikos*** is translated by the adverbial phrase "about the law," in the context of fruitless wrangling over legal matters.

LAY → PUT

LAZY → IDLE

LEAD (VERB)

OT Words

nāhal [**נָהַל, 5095**]

nāhal is a verb occurring ten times, meaning "lead," "guide" in the majority of these contexts.

The physical sense of "leading" a retinue of people and cattle is indicated in Gen. 33:14. That is, it is an action predicated of human beings. Leading or guidance in a moral sense is indicated in Isa. 51:18.

The remaining usage of ***nāhal*** focuses on divine leading and guiding. Exod. 15:13, for example, speaks of Yahweh leading his people through the wilderness towards the promised land. Other references speak of Yahweh's leading or guiding his people in the sense of protecting and nurturing them (cf. Pss. 23:2; 31:3; Isa. 40:11; 49:10).

nāḥāh [**נָחָה, 5148**]

nāḥāh occurs around thirty times and is translated "lead," or "guide," predicated of both human beings and God.

In literal, physical contexts, ***nāḥāh*** refers to the action of "leading" in the sense of "bring up," "bring forth" in Ps. 108:10, and in Num. 23:7, where Balaam is "led" from Aram to Moab by Balak, the Moabite king.

In contexts where Yahweh is the agent of leading or guidance, emphasis is placed on his role as the leader, guiding his people in the wilderness after their exodus from Egypt (cf. Exod. 13:17, 21; 15:13; 32:34; Deut. 32:12; Neh. 9:12, 19; Pss. 77:20; 78:14, 53, 72; 107:30). See also Gen. 24:27, 48; Job 38:32; Ps. 60:9. In a negative context, Job speaks metaphorically of God leading the nations away, in order to bring them down. Moral guidance from Yahweh is indicated, for example, in Job 31:18; Pss. 5:8; 23:3; 43:3; 67:4; Prov. 6:22. God is said to lead his people to comfort and security (cf. Pss. 61:2; 139:10; Isa. 57:18; 58:11); and also in the way of salvation (cf. Ps. 139:24).

nāhag [**נָהַג, 5090**]

nāhag is found in approximately thirty contexts meaning "lead" or "drive," as well as a number of associated senses.

The sense of "leading" when predicated of human beings is indicated in Exod. 3:1, with reference to Moses leading his flock in the desert, and in 1 Chr. 20:1 concerning Joab and his army (cf. also Isa. 20:4; 2 Chr. 25:11). Isa. 11:6 describes a scene of universal renewal, where a little child will lead wild animals around without danger.

nāhag refers to God leading and guiding his people in Pss. 48:14; 78:52; 80:1; Isa. 49:10; 63:14.

yālak [**יָלַךְ, 3212**]

yālak is a common verb form that is usually translated "go," "walk," "come," and occurs nearly one thousand times. However, in several places ***yālak*** conveys the sense of "lead," where Yahweh is the predominant agent of that action.

The primary context for this meaning of ***yālak*** is Yahweh's leading the Israelites in the wilderness (cf. Deut. 8:2, 15; 29:5; Pss. 106:9; 136:16; Isa. 48:2; 63:13; Jer. 2:12; Amos 2:10). Josh. 24:3 refers to Abraham's experience of being led by God.

The sole reference to ***yālak*** indicating leading by a human agency is found in 2 Kgs. 6:19, where Elisha leads the blinded Arameans to Samaria.

NT Words

anagō [ἀνάγω, *321*]

anagō is a verb found nearly twenty-five times meaning "lead," "bring up" for most of the usage.

References to the Spirit "leading Jesus up" into the wilderness to be tempted by the devil are found in Matt. 4:1; Luke 4:5. Other references to people "being brought or led up" to various places are found in Luke 2:22; Acts 9:39; 12:4.

Rom. 10:7; Heb. 13:20 refer to God having brought Jesus up from the dead.

agō [ἄγω, *71*]

agō is a verb occurring around seventy times and is usually translated "bring," "lead," in a variety of contexts.

Meaning "to (physically) lead or bring," ***agō*** refers to both human beings and animals. Matt. 21:2; Mark 11:2; Luke 19:30 refer to the colt being led to Jesus for the ride into Jerusalem. Many texts refer prophetically to the disciples of Jesus being led before councilors to be persecuted (cf. Mark 13:9, 11; Luke 21:12; Acts 5:21, 27; 6:12; Acts 18:12). People are led to Jesus for healing in Luke 4:40; 18:40. Jesus is led from Caiaphas' house to the governor's palace in John 18:28. Other general references to "leading" are found in Luke 4:29; 23:32; John 1:42; Acts 9:2; 17:15. A metaphorical reference to the death of the Messiah is made in Acts 8:32, where his demise is likened to a sheep being led to the slaughter.

agō also refers in a number of places to God leading. Jesus' temptation experience at the outset of his public ministry commences with the Holy Spirit leading him into the wilderness (cf. Luke 4:1). Rom. 8:14; Gal. 5:18 describe the sons of God as those who are led by the Spirit of God. John 10:16 speaks of Jesus bringing his flock together from other peoples, leading them towards himself. A more indirect reference is found in Rom. 2:4, where Paul affirms that the kindness of God is intended to lead to repentance.

agō also refers to the activity of Satan. Luke 4:9 observes that the devil led Jesus to the pinnacle of the temple in order to tempt him.

eispherō [εἰσφέρω, *1533*]

eispherō occurs seven times and is translated "lead into," "bring into." The specific sense of "lead," however, occurs only twice, referring to the petition of the Lord's Prayer ". . . lead us not into temptation" (cf. Matt. 6:13; Luke 11:4).

hodēgeō [ὁδηγέω, *3594*]

hodēgeō occurs five times and is translated "lead," "guide."

There is a metaphorical reference to the spiritual bankruptcy of the Pharisees in Matt. 15:14; Luke 6:39, where they are referred to as "blind guides," who will ultimately lead others who are spiritually blind into eternal destruction. John 16:13 refers to the ministry of the Holy Spirit, who will guide believers into all truth. Similarly, Rev. 7:14 speaks of the Lamb on the throne guiding the saints to springs of living water. In Acts 8:31, the Ethiopian eunuch, reading Isaiah 53, responds to Philip's question with his own, saying: "How can I [understand], unless someone guides me?"

apagō [ἀπάγω, *520*]

apagō is a verb derived from ***agō*** (see above) that means "lead away," with particular emphasis on being taken to trial or punishment, both literally and metaphorically. The term occurs fifteen times.

Metaphorical reference to the narrow path that leads to eternal destruction is found in Matt. 7:13, 14.

Physical leading away is indicated in Matt. 26:57; 27:2, 31; Mark 14:44, 53; 15:16; John 18:13, referring to Jesus being led away to the various authorities at the time of his arrest, as well as to his death. Luke 13:15 mentions beasts of burden being led away to water.

Spiritual blindness is indicated in 1 Cor. 12:2, where Paul refers to the heathen background of the Corinthian believers, citing their being "led astray by dumb idols."

exagō [ἐξάγω, *1806*]

exagō is another verb derived from ***agō*** (see above). ***exagō*** has the primary sense of "lead, bring out" and occurs thirteen times.

Physically leading people out is indicated in a general sense (Luke 24:50; John 10:3; Acts 5:19; 16:37, 39; 21:38); and refers to Jesus in particular (Mark 15:20) when he is taken away to be crucified.

With God as the agent of leading, ***exagō*** refers to Israel being led out of Egyptian captivity in Acts 7:36, 40; 13:17; Heb. 8:9. In Acts 12:17, it refers to Peter's deliverance from prison.

cheiragōgeō [χειραγωγέω, *5496*]

cheiragōgeō means "to lead by the hand" and is found only in Acts 9:8; 22:11, where it refers to the newly-converted Saul being led by the hand into Damascus.

LEAF

OT Words

'āleh [עָלֶה, 5929]

'āleh is a noun meaning "leaf" or "branch (of leaves)." It occurs thirteen times, both in a literal and metaphorical sense.

Literal usage is found in Gen. 3:7; 8:11; Neh. 8:15, with ***'āleh*** also referring to "leaf," "leaves" in metaphorical contexts (cf. Lev. 26:36; Job 13:25). A healthy spiritual condition is likened to a "green leaf," or "a leaf that does not wither" (cf. Ps. 1:3; Prov. 11:28; Jer. 17:8). Conversely, spiritual degeneration is likened to a "fading, or withered leaf" in Isa. 1:30; 34:4; 64:6; Jer. 8:13.

Ezek. 47:12 refers to the leaves of the tree of life, which constitute a source of spiritual healing for the people of God.

'ophî **[עֳפִי, 6074** (Aramaic)]

'ophî is an Aramaic term for "leaf," occurring only three times (Dan. 4:12, 14, 21) with reference to the leaves of the tree in Nebuchadnezzar's dream, symbolizing the kingdom of the Babylonian ruler.

NT Words

phyllon [**φύλλον,** *5444*]

phyllon is the sole New Testament term for "leaf" and is found on five occasions. Matt. 21:19; 24:32; Mark 11:13; 13:28 refer literally and metaphorically to the leaves of a fig tree, illustrating Israel's spiritual vitality, or lack thereof. In Rev. 22:2, ***phyllon*** refers to the leaves of the tree of life, located in the heavenly Jerusalem — leaves designated for the healing of the nations.

LEAP

OT Words

zānaq [**זָנַק, 2187**]

zānaq is found only in Deut. 33:22, where it refers metaphorically to the tribe of Dan as a lion's cub that leaps forth from Bashan.

pāzaz [**פָּזַז, 6339**]

pāzaz occurs only twice, meaning "leap." It is found only in 2 Sam. 6:16, describing King David leaping and dancing before the Lord on the occasion of the return of the ark to Jerusalem.

dālag [**דָּלַג, 1801**]

dālag is found in five contexts with the consistent meaning "leap," "leap over," in a metaphorical sense. Ps. 18:29; 2 Sam. 22:30 refer to the psalmist "leaping over a wall" as a sign of spiritual victory granted by God. Song 2:8; Isa. 35:6 refer to gazelles leaping, predicated of the woman's lover in the former text, and of those healed of their lameness in the latter. Zeph. 1:9 refers to divine punishment being invoked on those who "leap over the threshold," indicating a desire to commit violence against members of that household.

NT Words

skirtaō [**σκιρτάω,** *4640*]

skirtaō occurs only three times, and on each occasion it means "leap for joy." In Luke 1:41, 44, ***skirtaō*** refers to Elizabeth's baby, John the Baptist, leaping in her womb. Luke 6:23 refers to the joy of true followers of Christ, who will leap for joy upon his return.

exallomai [**ἐξάλλομαι,** *1814*]

exallomai is found only in Acts 3:8, referring to the lame beggar who had been cured by Peter and John, and who immediately afterwards leapt up and walked into the temple.

hallomai [**ἅλλομαι,** *242*]

hallomai occurs three times, meaning "leap up" on two of these occasions. Acts 3:8; 14:10 refer to miraculous cures of crippled men, both of whom leapt to their feet immediately when they were healed. John 4:14 contains a related meaning for ***hallomai***, that of "spring up," referring to water as a symbol for the indwelling Spirit of Christ in the heart of a believer.

ephallomai [**ἐφάλλομαι,** *2177*]

ephallomai occurs only in Acts 19:16, referring to the evil spirit cast out of a man by seven Jewish exorcists (the sons of Sceva), who leapt upon those men and overpowered them.

LEARN

OT Words

lāmad [**לָמַד, 3925**]

lāmad occurs around ninety times and means "learn," "instruct," or "teach" in virtually all of these contexts. (→ TEACH) The sense of "learn," with the idea of acquiring knowledge, is found approximately twenty times.

In the sphere of human activity, ***lāmad*** signifies learning to fear Yahweh as one significant intention of the Mosaic law covenant given to Israel (cf. Deut. 4:10; 14:23; 17:19; 31:12, 13). In a related context in Deut. 5:1, ***lāmad*** also refers to learning the law in order to obey Yahweh. Similarly, learning righteousness is indicated in Isa. 26:9; as is learning God's statutes in Ps. 119:7. Isa. 1:17 contains an exhortation to learn to do good. See also Isa. 2:4; Mic. 4:3; Jer. 12:16; Ezek. 19:3, 6.

The Israelites are also warned against learning the abominable practices of the Canaanites (cf. Deut. 18:9; Ps. 106:35; Jer. 10:2).

leqaḥ [**לֶקַח, 3948**]

leqaḥ is a noun signifying "learning," or "teaching." ***leqaḥ*** occurs nine times, but the sense of "learning" is found specifically only in Prov. 1:5; 9:9. Here ***leqaḥ*** refers to the positive learning of the wise person. (→ TEACH)

NT Words

manthanō [μανθάνω, *3129*]

manthanō is the principal verb in the New Testament meaning "learn." It occurs around twenty-five times. The underlying sense, like that of ***lāmad*** (see above), is that of increasing one's knowledge.

Where the learning of men and women is concerned, ***manthanō*** indicates that the true meaning of devotion to God lies in learning mercy, not sacrifice (cf. Matt. 9:13). ***manthanō*** refers to learning in a number of contexts: learning doctrine (Rom. 16:17; 1 Cor. 4:6; 14:31; Phil. 4:9; 2 Tim. 3:14); learning from Christ, the master teacher (Matt. 11:29; cf. also Eph. 4:20); learning from God the Father (John 6:45; Col. 1:7); learning in a general sense (Acts 23:27; Phil. 4:11; 1 Tim. 2:11; Titus 3:14; Rev. 14:3); and learning from the object lesson of the fig tree (Matt. 24:32; Mark 13:28). In John 7:15, the degree of Jesus' great learning is questioned.

Heb. 5:8 declares that Christ learned obedience through what he suffered.

paideuō [παιδεύω, *3811*]

paideuō is found thirteen times and has the principal meaning "chasten," "chastise." (→ CHASTEN) However, in 1 Tim. 1:20, the term signifies "to learn," referring to Paul's disciplinary action against Hymenaus and Alexander, that they might learn not to blaspheme.

See Also: → DOCTRINE

LEAST

OT Words

ṣā'îr [צָעִיר, **6810**]

ṣā'îr is an adjectival form that means "young(er)," "little" in the majority of its twenty or so occurrences. In two of these texts, however, ***ṣā'îr*** means "least" in the sense of "weakest" or "most insignificant" (cf. Judg. 6:15; 1 Sam. 9:21). Both texts refer to the relative impotence or lack of status of the tribes of Manasseh and Benjamin. (→ YOUNG)

qāṭān [קָטָן, **6996**]

qāṭān is an adjective that means "small," "younger," "youngest" in most of its approximately one hundred occurrences. However, in about ten of these instances, ***qāṭān*** is translated "least" in the sense of the lowliest in status, or rank (cf. 2 Kgs. 18:24; Isa. 36:9; Jer. 6:13; Jer. 8:10; 31:34; 42:1, 8; 44:12; Jonah 3:5).

NT Words

elachistos [ἐλάχιστος, *1646*]

elachistos is a superlative form of the adjective *elachys* ("short"), with the primary meaning "least," as well as "smallest," "very little." ***elachistos*** occurs thirteen times.

The meaning "least (in rank)"is found in Matt. 2:6 with reference to Bethlehem, as the least among the towns of Judah. Matt. 5:19 refers to the least of the commandments; and Paul describes himself as the least of the apostles in 1 Cor. 15:9. See also Matt. 25:40ff.

elachistos also means "least" in the sense of "very little." Luke 16:10; 19:17 point to the quality of being faithful in "very little." See also Luke 12:26; 1 Cor. 4:3; Jas. 3:4.

1 Cor. 6:2 refers to legal cases that are "trivial," or "least," in the sense "of little consequence."

elachistoteros [ἐλαχιστότερος, *1647*]

elachistoteros is a comparative form of ***elachistos*** (see above), meaning "last of all," "very least." It occurs only in Eph. 3:8, where Paul refers to himself as the "very least" of the saints.

mikros [μικρός, *3398*]

mikros is an adjectival form meaning "small," "little." However, six of the thirty contexts in which this term is found indicate the sense of "least."

The meaning "least," in the sense of "smallest," is found in Matt. 13:32. The sense of "least (in rank)" is indicated in Luke 9:48; Acts 8:10; Heb. 8:11. Matt. 11:11; Luke 7:28 refer to those who are designated "least in the kingdom of heaven."

LEAVE, LEFT (VERB)

OT Words

yāṣā' [יָצָא, **3318**]

yāṣā' is a common verb found over one thousand times with the general meanings "go out," "come out," as well as a large variety of related nuances. One of these nuances is "to leave," again evident in a number of contexts.

The meaning "leave" in the sense of "go out," in the context of physical travel, departure, movement away from, is evident in Gen. 9:10; 24:11; Exod. 11:8; 12:22. A prohibition against "leaving" one's house on the Sabbath is found in Exod. 16:29. ***yāṣā'*** refers metaphorically to living water "leaving" (i.e., flowing out from) Jerusalem in Zech. 14:8. The sense of "go away from" (i.e., abandon) is evident in Gen. 45:1. Exod. 21:3 refers to the act of "accompanying" someone. Exod. 21:2ff. speaks of a slave "leaving" or "not leaving" his master (i.e., being set free or not set free). See also Lev. 25:54.

nûaḥ [נוּחַ, 5117]

nûaḥ is a verb with a number of meanings, the principal one being "rest." Alongside this sense, ***nûaḥ*** is also translated "leave," "abandon" in a number of contexts. The term occurs over 140 times, meaning "leave" in about a third of these contexts.

When this action is predicated of people, ***nûaḥ*** signifies "to leave" with a variety of nuances. The action of "leaving" in a general sense is indicated in 1 Kgs. 7:47; Ps. 17:14; Isa. 65:15; Ezek. 41:11. The sense of "leave behind" is found in 2 Sam. 16:21; 20:3, referring to David's concubines whom he left behind in Jerusalem after fleeing from Absalom.

See also Gen. 42:23; Jer. 43:6. The meaning "leave" is noted in 2 Sam. 16:11; 2 Kgs. 23:18. ***nûaḥ*** means "leave" in the sense of "bequeath one's estate" in Eccl. 2:18. Eccl. 10:4 contains the concept of "abandon."

God is also said to "leave," primarily in the sense of "abandon." Num. 32:15 refers to Yahweh abandoning his people in the wilderness for their sin. In Ezek. 16:39, he abandons them on account of their idolatry. Ps. 119:121; Jer. 14:9 contain pleas for God not to abandon his servants.

yātar [יָתַר, 3498]

yātar is a verb that is translated principally as "leave," or "remain," with a number of associated senses. ***yātar*** occurs over one hundred times.

yātar is used primarily in the passive voice, "to be left" (i.e., "remain").

Where human beings are concerned, ***yātar*** signifies "to be left alone" in Gen. 32:24; 1 Sam. 30:19. The idea of "being left" or "remain" is indicated in a general sense in Exod. 16:19; Judg. 9:5; 1 Sam. 2:36; 1 Kgs. 9:20. Isa. 4:3 refers to the survivors in Zion as holy (i.e., "those who are left"). ***yātar*** is also found in ritual contexts where remains of sacrificial offerings are said "to be left" (cf. Lev. 2:10; 10:12). Lev. 22:30 records the command that none of the thank offering must be left uneaten. Josh. 11:11 notes that none were left alive after the sack of the city of Hazor. Isa. 1:8 refers to Zion as "abandoned." See also Josh. 18:2; Ruth 2:14; 1 Kgs. 19:14; Ps. 106:11.

Other uses of ***yātar*** are found in 1 Kgs. 15:18; Jer. 27:18ff., where silver and gold are said to be left in the temple treasury. 1 Kgs. 17:17 records the death of the widow's son in Zarephath, mentioning that "no breath was left" in him.

Speaking of God, ***yātar*** refers to Yahweh's promise to leave no remnant of his people behind in exile (cf. Ezek. 39:28). See also Jer. 44:7. Ezek. 6:8; 12:16 also refer to Yahweh's intention to preserve (i.e., leave) a remnant of his people.

shā'ar [שָׁאַר, 7604]

shā'ar is a synonym for ***yātar*** (see above), occurring around 120 times with the primary meanings "leave," "remain."

In the human sphere, ***shā'ar*** is also predominantly passive in nature, with the sense of "be left." General references to this usage are found in Gen. 32:8; Num. 11:26; Deut. 28:55; 1 Kgs. 15:29. The survival of Noah and his family after the flood is indicated in Gen. 7:23. Exod. 14:28 records that no Egyptians are left alive after drowning in the Re(e)d Sea. Likewise, no Amorites are left alive in Heshbon as a result of the Israelite offensive (cf. Num. 21:35; Deut. 2:34). Similarly, the initial Israelite conquest of Canaanite cities left no citizens of Ai alive (cf. Josh. 8:17; 10:28ff.; 11:8ff.; Judg. 4:16). See also 1 Kgs. 16:11; 2 Kgs. 10:11ff.

Other general uses of ***shā'ar*** include impersonal references to animals, for example, in the context of the Egyptian plagues. No frogs were left in the Nile River (Exod. 8:11), no flies were left in the land of Egypt (Exod. 8:31), nor did any locusts remain (Exod. 10:19). Then, in a ritual context, Num. 9:12 requires that none of the Passover lamb be left uneaten. Dan. 10:17 contains a metaphorical allusion to lifelessness — Daniel declares that no breath is left in him after seeing the vision of the angel of the Lord (implied).

shā'ar is also predicated of Yahweh. Lev. 26:39 refers to those of God's people left in enemy lands, who will waste away. Deut. 28:62 states that few of God's people will be left in Canaan because of their disobedience. Conversely, several places refer to Yahweh's action in leaving a faithful remnant in the land — for example, 1 Kgs. 19:18 refers to 7,000 Israelites who refuse to bow the knee to Baal. Ezra 9:8 indicates that Yahweh has returned a remnant to the land from exile. Isa. 11:11 refers to the faithful remnant of God's people in exile. In Zeph. 3:12, Yahweh promises to leave a godly remnant in Jerusalem.

NT Words

aphistēmi [ἀφίστημι, *868*]

aphistēmi is a verb found fifteen times with the predominant sense of "depart from," "leave."

Literal references to physical departure or leaving are found in Luke 2:37; Acts 12:10; 15:38; 22:29.

In particular, the devil is said to leave Jesus after concluding in vain his efforts to tempt him to sin (cf. Luke 4:13). In another context, Jesus anticipates the words of the Father to the unrighteous standing before him on the day of judgment. "Depart (i.e., leave, get away) from me, you workers of iniquity" (cf. Luke 13:27).

In 2 Cor. 12:8, Paul beseeches God for the mysterious thorn in the flesh "to leave" him.

1 Tim. 4:1 mentions those who "abandon" the faith, and a warning against doing so is indicated in Heb. 3:12. See also 2 Tim. 2:19.

aperchomai [ἀπέρχομαι, *565*]

aperchomai is a common verb found over 120 times with the predominant general senses of "go," "depart," "leave," as well as associated nuances.

Literal references to people "leaving," or going their way, include those in Matt. 21:29; 27:5; Mark 5:20; Luke 1:23; 22:4; John 4:3; Acts 10:7; Jas. 1:24.

Elsewhere, ***aperchomai*** refers to disease "leaving" a person (i.e., the experience of healing) (cf. Mark 1:42; Luke 5:13).

exerchomai [ἐξέρχομαι, *1831*]

exerchomai is another common verb form, a partial synonym for ***aphistēmi***, above, found over two hundred times with the primary meanings "to, come out," "depart," "leave," as well as related senses throughout the occurrences of the term.

The literal meaning "leave," or go one's way, is evident, for example, in Matt. 9:31; Luke 4:42; 9:4ff.; John 13:31; Acts 18:23; 20:1.

References to an evil spirit "coming out of" a man are found in Matt. 12:43; 17:18; Mark 9:26; Luke 4:36; 8:29.

The meaning "get away from" is found in Luke 5:8 in the context of a command.

Luke 8:46 records Jesus' remark that power "had left" him.

metabainō [μεταβαίνω, *3327*]

metabainō is a verb found twelve times meaning "to leave" in most of these occurrences.

The meaning "leave" in the literal sense of "depart," "go one's way" is indicated in Matt. 8:34; 11:1; 12:9; 15:29; John 7:3; Acts 18:7.

John 13:1 refers to Jesus' recognition that his time had come to "leave" this world, as he faced his inevitable crucifixion.

ekporeuomai [ἐκπορεύομαι, *1607*]

ekporeuomai is a verb found about thirty-five times meaning "proceed," "go out," as well as "leave" or "depart" in several contexts.

The literal sense of "leaving" is indicated in Mark 6:11; 10:46; 11:19.

exeimi [ἔξειμι, *1826*]

exeimi is a rare verb with the literal meaning "leave" or "depart" in Acts 13:42; 17:15; 20:7.

anachōreō [ἀναχωρέω, *402*]

anachōreō is a verb meaning "leave," in the sense of "set out on a journey," for most of its fourteen occurrences (cf. Matt. 2:12ff., 22; 14:13; John 6:15). See also Matt. 9:24; 27:5.

apochōreō [ἀποχωρέω, *672*]

apochōreō is a rare variant of ***anachōreō***, above. It is found only three times, meaning "leave," "go away," "depart." Matt. 7:23 records the divine command to the wicked on the day of judgment: "Depart from me you evil doers." Luke 9:39 refers to a demonic spirit "leaving" a person. Acts 13:13 refers to John Mark "leaving" the apostle Paul and returning to Jerusalem.

aphiēmi [ἀφίημι, *863*]

aphiēmi is a verb meaning "leave," with various related meanings, as well as "forgive," "persist," also with several nuances. The underlying sense of "leave," however, is predominant in the use of the term. ***aphiēmi*** occurs around 150 times and refers to the actions of both God and human beings.

Where people are concerned, ***aphiēmi*** indicates the action of leaving, in the sense of departure, in a number of general contexts (cf. Matt. 4:22; 18:22; John 4:3). In addition, the devil is said to leave Christ in Matt.

4:11, after failing to succeed in tempting him. Then, in the context of healing, sickness is said to leave the afflicted in Matt. 8:15; Mark 1:31; Luke 4:39.

The meaning "leave behind" is also evident in the use of ***aphiēmi***. Objects, for example, are in view in Matt. 5:24; John 4:28. People constitute the object of this action in Matt. 22:25; Mark 12:19ff.; 14:50; Luke 17:34. John 14:27 contains the promise of Jesus to leave his people peace after his return to glory. In a metaphorical context, the writer to the Hebrews exhorts his readers to leave behind elementary doctrines and strive for spiritual maturity in Heb. 6:1.

The idea of abandonment is also quite frequent in the semantic range of ***aphiēmi***. The disciples of Christ are said to have left all to follow the Lord (cf. Matt. 19:27, 29; Mark 1:18; 10:28; Luke 5:11). In the context of divorce, Paul teaches that the believing wife should not abandon her unbelieving husband if he consents to live with her. Matt. 26:56; Mark 14:50 refer to the followers of Jesus abandoning him at his arrest. Rom. 1:27 speaks of people abandoning natural sexual relations with one another for unnatural ones. Jesus promises never to abandon his followers in John 14:18. The church at Ephesus is rebuked for abandoning their first love for Christ in Rev. 2:4.

aphiēmi is also used passively in the sense of "be left" (or "remain") in the context of Jesus' prophecy of destruction regarding the temple. In Matt. 24:2; Mark 3:2; Luke 21:6, he declares that a time will come when no stones of the temple shall be left standing on each other. A similar prophecy is made with respect to the walls of Jerusalem in Luke 19:44.

Regarding the actions of God, ***aphiēmi*** occurs in Acts 14:17, where it is said that God does not leave himself without a witness in the world. In Heb. 2:8, the writer declares that God leaves nothing outside of his control.

kataleipō [καταλείπω, *2641*]

kataleipō is found in about twenty-five places, meaning "leave," "leave behind," "abandon" in most of these contexts.

The action of "leaving behind" in a physical sense is found with regard to places (Matt. 4:13; Heb. 11:27); to one's flock (Luke 15:4); to people in general (Matt. 16:4; Luke 10:40; Titus 1:5); to a deceased man leaving behind a wife but no children (Mark 12:19; Luke 20:31); and to leaving one's parents in order to marry (Matt. 19:5; Mark 10:7; Eph. 5:31).

kataleipō also refers to the action of leaving in the sense of "abandon." Luke 5:28 mentions Levi, who left everything to follow Christ. In Acts 2:31, it is declared that David was not abandoned to Hades. False teachers are condemned in 2 Pet. 2:15 for having abandoned the way of truth.

enkataleipō [ἐγκαταλείπω, *1459*]

enkataleipō is found nine times, and on all but one occasion the term means "abandon."

The cry of Jesus Christ on the cross: "My God . . . why have you abandoned me?" signified the consummate agony of his temporary separation from God (Matt. 27:46; Mark 15:34). Acts 2:27 records the words of David, confident that God would not abandon his soul to Hades. Abandonment by one's friends is indicated in 2 Cor. 4:9; 2 Tim. 4:10, 16. The writer to the Hebrews warns his readers against "abandoning" their practice of meeting together regularly in Heb. 10:25. The words of Jesus, promising never to abandon his followers, are recorded in Heb. 13:5. The one exception to this usage is found in Rom. 9:29, which cites Isa. 1:9, reflecting on the fact that God had graciously "left" a sufficient number of descendants to ensure the continuity of the people of Israel.

apoleipō [ἀπολείπω, *620*]

apoleipō occurs six times and means "leave," "remain," with the former sense found only in 2 Tim. 4:13, referring to Paul's cloak that he left behind in Troas, and in Jude 6, indicating the evil angels who had left their place in the heavenly realm.

See Also: ➠ CEASE ➠ FORSAKE

LEFT (ADJECTIVE)

OT WORDS

semô'l [שְׂמֹאול, **8040**]

semô'l is an adjectival form occurring around fifty times, meaning "left," "left hand," "left side."

General references to "left" in a directional sense are found in Gen. 13:9; Exod. 14:22; Deut. 2:27. 2 Kgs. 23:8; Isa. 9:20; Ezek. 1:10 mention the "left-hand side."

Gen. 48:13; Judg. 7:20; Song 8:3; Ezek. 39:3; Dan. 12:7 refer literally to the "left hand" as part of the human body. Metaphorically, ***semô'l*** is used in this sense to refer to the "left hand" of Lady Wisdom, containing riches and honor, in Prov. 3:16.

The phrase "not knowing their right hand from their left" indicates moral and spiritual ignorance in

Jonah 4:11. Note also the context of keeping the law of God, where the people of Israel are commanded "to turn neither to the right nor the left" (cf. Josh. 1:7; 23:6; 2 Kgs. 22:2).

NT Words

aristeros [ἀριστερός, *710*]

aristeros is an adjective found in only three places, all referring to the direction "left." Matt. 6:3 refers metaphorically to the attitude of giving with pure motive, "not letting your left hand know what your right hand is doing." Luke 23:33 indicates placing two criminals next to Christ on the hill of Golgotha, one on his right and one on his left. 2 Cor. 6:7 refers metaphorically to God's weapons of righteousness in both one's left and right hands.

euōnymos [εὐώνυμος, *2176*]

euōnymos is a synonymous with ***aristeros*** (see above) and occurs ten times.

Matt. 20:21, 23; Mark 10:37, 40 describe being seated on the right and left of Jesus' throne in heaven. The placement of thieves on the left side of Jesus at his crucifixion is indicated in Matt. 27:38; Mark 15:27. See also Acts 21:3; Rev. 10:2. Significantly, placing "goats" on the "left-hand side" of Christ in Matt. 25:33, 41 indicates that they (i.e., the wicked) are destined for judgment.

LEAVEN → YEAST

LEG, LEGS

OT Words

kerā'ayim [כְּרָעַיִם, **3767**]

kerā'ayim is from ***kāra'*** (→ KNEEL) and occurs nine times and means "legs." The majority of these contexts indicate the legs of sacrificial animals (cf. Exod. 12:9; 29:17; Lev. 1:9ff.; 4:11; 8:21; 9:14). The remaining references speak of the legs of insects and a lion (cf. Lev. 11:21; Amos 3:12).

shôq [שׁוֹק, **7785**]

shôq refers to the upper leg or thigh of an animal as well as to the legs of people. The term occurs around twenty times.

Concerning sacrificial animals, ***shôq*** refers to the thigh (or shoulder) of the beast which is set aside for the officiating priest as his share (cf. Exod. 29:22, 27; Lev. 7:32ff.; 8:25ff.; 9:21; 10:14ff.; Num. 6:20; 18:18). See also 1 Sam. 9:24. Deut. 28:35; Isa. 47:2 refer literally to human legs. Other metaphorical references are found in Judg. 15:8; Ps. 147:10; Prov. 26:7; Song 5:15.

shāq [שָׁק, **8243** (Aramaic)]

This Aramaic term for "leg" is found only in Dan. 2:33, referring to the legs of the metal statue in Nebuchadnezzar's dream.

NT Words

skelos [σκέλος, *4628*]

skelos is found only three times, referring to the legs of Jesus and the two men crucified with him at Golgotha. John 19:31, 32, 33 state that the legs of the two criminals were broken by the Roman soldiers in order to hasten death. But, on coming to Jesus, they found him already dead, so they did not break his legs.

LEGION

NT Words

legiōn [λεγιών, *3003*]

legiōn is translated "Legion" and occurs only four times. Three times it refers to the symbolic name of the demon-possessed man exorcised by Jesus, "Legion," indicating that he had a multitude of evil spirits within him (cf. Mark 5:9, 15; Luke 8:30). In Matt. 26:53, Jesus affirms that, should he so desire, God would send to his aid "twelve legions of angels" to deliver him from the cross.

LEND, LENDER

OT Words

lāwāh [לָוָה, **3867**]

lāwāh occurs twenty-five times and means "join," "borrow," "lend," in about equal proportion. The specific sense of "lend" is indicated in seven contexts.

Deut. 28:12 speaks metaphorically of Israel "lending" her wealth to the nations as part of the prospective covenant blessing to be laid on her. Deut. 28:44, however, refers to the alien "lending" to an Israelite as part of a "curse" scenario, illustrating Israel's poverty. Pss. 37:26; 112:5; Prov. 19:17 all speak of the generosity of the one who lends to the poor. Prov. 22:7 affirms that the borrower is the slave of the lender. Isa. 24:2 refers to divine judgment that will be poured out on the borrower and "lender" the world over, along with the devastation of many other people and institutions.

'ābat **[עָבַט, 5670]**

'ābat occurs four times, meaning "lend," in Deut. 15:6, 8. The first reference speaks of Israel lending to the nations out of her abundant wealth; the latter text speaks of Yahweh's requirement for Israelites to be generous to the poor, lending to them freely.

NT Words

daneizō [δανείζω, *1155*]

daneizō is found only four times. Three times it refers to the action of lending, and once to borrowing. Luke 6:34, 35 speak of the practice of lending, referring firstly to such a practice among pagans. The latter text contains Jesus' exhortation to his followers to lend freely to their enemies, expecting nothing in return.

See Also: → INTEREST

LENGTH

OT Words

'ōrek **[אֹרֶךְ, 753]**

'ōrek is the standard Old Testament term for "length" in the senses of both time and measurement. It is found in about one hundred contexts.

In terms of length as a measurement of space, ***'ōrek*** refers to Noah building the ark (cf. Gen. 6:15); to Abraham measuring the land of Canaan (cf. Gen. 13:17); to the construction of the tabernacle and its furniture (cf. Exod. 25:10–39:9, throughout); and to the temple dimensions and its furniture (cf. 1 Kgs. 6:2–7:27, throughout). See also 2 Chr. 3:3–6:13. The same holds true for the renewed temple in Ezekiel's vision (cf. Ezek. 40:7–43:17; 46:22). See also Zech. 2:2; Ezek. 45:1ff.

With regard to length of time, ***'ōrek*** is found in the phrase "length of days," alluding to long life — the reward for loving and obeying God (cf. Deut. 30:20; also Job 12:12; Ps. 91:16; Prov. 3:16).

NT Words

mēkos [μῆκος, *3372*]

mēkos is found only three times, meaning "length" in the metaphorical allusion to the infinite dimensions of the love of Christ (Eph. 3:18; Rev. 21:16 [twice]).

LEOPARD

OT Words

nāmēr **[נָמֵר, 5246]**

nāmēr occurs six times, and on each occasion refers to a leopard, or leopards, either in a poetic context (cf. Song 4:8); or a symbolic one (cf. Isa. 11:6; Jer. 5:6; 13:23; Hos. 13:7; Hab. 1:8).

nemar **[נְמַר, 5245** (Aramaic)**]**

nemar is the Aramaic term for "leopard," one of the beasts in Daniel's vision (cf. Dan. 7:6).

NT Words

pardalis [πάρδαλις, *3917*]

pardalis is found only in Rev. 13:2, referring to the leopard-like beast that emerged from the sea. This is the satanic beast that served as a counterfeit to the true Messiah.

LEPER

OT Words

ṣāra' **[צָרַע, 6879]**

ṣāra' describes people who suffer from infectious skin diseases, including leprosy. ***ṣāra'*** is generally translated "leper," though the term does not necessarily indicate that the sufferer has the specific disease leprosy. ***ṣāra'*** is also used adjectivally, meaning "leprous." The term occurs around twenty times.

References to "leper(s)" include those in Lev. 13:45; 14:2ff.; 22:4; Num. 5:2; 2 Kgs. 5:1; 15:5; 2 Chr. 26:21ff. The adjectival meaning "leprous" is found in Exod. 4:6; Lev. 13:44; 2 Sam. 3:29.

NT Words

lepros [λεπρός, *3015*]

lepros is the equivalent Greek term for the Hebrew ***ṣāra'*** (see above) and occurs nine times. All occurrences of ***lepros*** are found in the Synoptic Gospels and refer primarily to lepers who were cured by Christ (cf. Matt. 8:2; 10:8; 11:5; Mark 1:40; Luke 7:22; 17:12). Luke 4:27 refers to Naaman the Syrian, who was cured of his leprosy during the ministry of Elisha the prophet. Two references to Simon the leper are found in Matt. 26:6; Mark 14:3.

LEPROSY

OT Words

ṣāra'at **[צָרַעַת, 6883]**

ṣāra'at is the standard Old Testament term for a malignant skin disease, including the affliction of leprosy. ***ṣāra'at*** occurs about thirty-five times, and is consistently translated "leprosy" (→ LEPER). ***ṣāra'at*** is found, for example, in Lev. 13:2ff.; 14:3, 7, 32ff.; Deut. 24:8; 2 Kgs. 5:3ff.

NT Words

lepra [λέπρα, *3014*]

lepra is the equivalent Greek term for the Hebrew ***ṣāra'at*** and is translated "leprosy" in all four contexts in which it is found. All references indicate people who were cured of this disease by the direct intervention of Christ (cf. Matt. 8:3; Mark 1:42; Luke 5:12, 13).

LESS → LITTLE

LETTER

OT Words

nishtewān [נִשְׁתְּוָן, **5406** (Aramaic)]

nishtewān is an Aramaic term that occurs only twice, referring in Ezra 4:7, 11 to letters sent to Artaxerxes of Persia, and return correspondence from Artaxerxes to Ezra the scribe.

'iggerā' [אִגְּרָא, **104** (Aramaic)]

'iggerā' is an Aramaic synonym for ***nishtewān,*** above. It occurs only three times in the book of Ezra, referring likewise to letters between the enemies of the Jews and the kings Artaxerxes and Darius of Persia (cf. Ezra 4:8ff.; 5:6).

'iggeret [אִגֶּרֶת, **107**]

'iggeret is the corresponding Hebrew term to the Aramaic ***'iggerā'*** (see above). ***'iggeret*** occurs ten times and refers to written correspondence. The letters of Hezekiah to the people of Judah are mentioned in 2 Chr. 30:1, 6. International correspondence between Persia and the territories of the "land beyond the river" is noted in Neh. 2:7ff.; 6:5, 17ff. (cf. also Esth. 9:26, 29).

NT Words

epistolē [ἐπιστολή, *1992*]

epistolē is a term indicating "letter," or "epistle," occurring around twenty times.

General references to literary correspondence are found in Acts 9:2; 15:30; Rom. 16:22. The letters of Paul are indicated in 1 Cor. 5:9; 2 Cor. 7:8; Col. 4:16; 2 Thess. 2:2, 15; 2 Pet. 3:16; as are the letters of Peter in 2 Pet. 3:1. Letters of recommendation are noted in 2 Cor. 3:1, 2; 10:9ff. 2 Cor. 3:3 refers to the Corinthian congregation as a "letter from Christ."

See Also: → BOOK

LIBERTY → FREE

LIE (NOUN), LIAR

OT Words

kāzab [כָּזַב, **3576**]

kāzab is found in sixteen contexts with the consistent meanings "lie," "tell a lie," "be a liar" in most contexts.

With reference to God, it is firmly denied that he is susceptible to such a practice (cf. Num. 23:19; Ps. 89:35). In a related context, Hab. 2:3 affirms that a revelation from God will not lie.

Where people are concerned, there is the exhortation in 2 Kgs. 4:16 not to lie. Job 6:28 records a determination not to lie. General references to those who do lie are found, for example, in Job 24:25; Ps. 78:36; Prov. 30:6; Isa. 57:11; Ezek. 13:19; Mic. 2:11.

kāzāb [כָּזָב, **3577**]

kāzāb is the noun derived from ***kāzab*** (see above) and refers consistently to "lies," "falsehood." ***kāzāb*** occurs approximately thirty times.

General references to lies uttered by human beings are found in Judg. 16:10, 13; Ps. 4:2; Prov. 6:19; 30:8; Isa. 28:17; Dan. 11:27; Hos. 7:13; 12:1; Zeph. 3:13. Divine judgment on such people is indicated in Ps. 5:6; Ezek. 13:6ff., 19.

Lies are sometimes equated with idolatry or false gods (cf. Ps. 40:4, Isa. 28:15; Ezek. 21:29; Amos 2:4).

shāqar [שָׁקַר, **8266**]

shāqar is found only six times and is translated "lie" or "deal falsely (i.e., deceptively)" in all but one of these contexts.

The idea of deceiving or dealing falsely with someone is indicated in Gen. 21:23; Isa. 63:8. Such practice is denied in Ps. 44:17 and prohibited in Lev. 19:11. 1 Sam. 15:29 affirms that God does not lie, and Ps. 89:33 contains the promise that he will not do so.

sheqer [שֶׁקֶר, **8267**]

sheqer, a noun derived from ***shāpar*** (see above), is synonymous with ***kāzāb*** (see above) and is translated "lie," "lying," "deception," "deceit." The term occurs in about one hundred contexts.

References to the lies of human beings in general are found in Exod. 5:9; 2 Sam. 18:13; 1 Kgs. 22:22; Ps. 27:12; Prov. 6:17; Jer. 14:14. The eighth commandment prohibits lying (cf. Exod. 20:16). ***kāzāb*** refers to false charges (Exod. 23:7); deceit (Prov. 20:17); and swearing falsely (Lev. 6:3ff.; Jer. 5:2; 7:9; Zech. 5:4; Mal. 3:5). The psalmist pleads for deliverance from lies in Ps. 120:2.

Falsehood and idolatry are also equated (cf. Isa. 28:15 [implied]; 44:20; Jer. 10:14; Hab. 2:18).

kaḥash **[כַּחַשׁ, 3585]**

kaḥash is another noun synonymous with ***kāzāb*** and ***sheqer***, above. The term occurs six times and is translated "lies," "lying" in all but one of these contexts.

Ps. 59:12; Hos. 7:3; 10:13; 11:12 all refer to the lying habits of the people of Israel, for which they were punished. Nah. 3:1 refers to the deception of the Ninevites and likewise anticipates the coming judgment of Yahweh.

NT Words

pseustēs [ψεύστης, *5583*]

pseustēs is a noun that consistently refers to "liars,"or those who are deceptive and totally untrustworthy. ***pseustēs*** occurs ten times.

The devil is referred to as a "liar" and the "father of lies" in John 8:44. General references to people as liars are found in Rom. 3:4; 1 Tim. 1:10; Titus 1:12. 1 John 2:4; 4:20 indicate that those who profess to know God, but who do not show love to others, show themselves to be liars; as are those who deny that Jesus is the Christ (cf. 1 John 2:22). More blatantly, failure to acknowledge our sinfulness and failure to believe in Jesus as sent by God create the impression that God himself is a liar.

pseudēs [ψευδής, *5571*]

pseudēs is the adjectival form derived from ***pseudomai*** (see below) and is translated "lying," "deceitful," "false." ***pseudēs*** occurs three times. Acts 1:13 refers to "false witnesses" who wrongly accused Stephen, the first Christian martyr, of blasphemy. Rev. 2:2 describes false prophets in the church at Ephesus. Rev. 21:8 contains a nominal use of ***pseudēs***, in which "liars" are included in the list of the wicked set aside for judgment.

pseusma [ψεῦσμα, *5582*]

pseusma occurs only in Rom. 3:7 and refers to "falsehood" as a hypothetical moral failing on the part of Paul.

apseudēs [ἀψευδής, *893*]

apseudēs is an adjective virtually identical with ***pseudēs***, above. The term occurs only in Titus 1:2 and is translated as an adjectival clause, "who cannot lie," predicated of God.

pseudos [ψεῦδος, *5579*]

pseudos is a noun found in nine contexts, meaning "lie" or "lying."

Lying is a natural expression of Satan's character (John 8:44). ***pseudos*** refers to the embodiment of the evil one in the person of "the lawless one" in 2 Thess. 2:9, 11. Rom. 1:25 refers to the fundamental attitude underlying the sin of idolatry — exchanging the truth of God for a lie. Rev. 21:27; 22:15 refer to those who utter lies as having no part whatever with the people living in the heavenly city. Eph. 4:25 contains the exhortation to put away all lying or deceit from one's character. 1 John 2:21, 27 affirm the absolute truth of the teaching given by God in Christ — that is, there is no lie in it.

pseudomai [ψεύδομαι, *5574*]

pseudomai is a verb consistently translated "to lie" and occurs twelve times.

The lying activity of individuals is indicated in Matt. 5:11; Acts 5:3, 4; Rev. 3:9; 1 John 1:6. Paul's strong denial of any lying is recorded in Rom. 9:1; 2 Cor. 11:31; Gal. 1:20; 1 Tim. 2:7. Exhortations to keep from speaking lies are found in Col. 3:9; Jas. 3:14. The impossibility of deceit residing in God is affirmed in Heb. 6:18.

LIE (VERB), LIE DOWN

OT Words

shākab **[שָׁכַב, 7901]**

shākab is a verb meaning "lie," "lie down," in a number of contexts, including the euphemistic "lie with," referring to the act of sexual intercourse. In addition, the action of "lying down" is associated with sleep. (→ ASLEEP)

In addition to the above, ***shākab*** is also translated "to lie with," in association with the phenomenon of death. The expression commonly used to convey this is the euphemism "to lie with one's fathers" (cf. Gen. 47:30; 2 Sam. 7:12; 2 Kgs. 13:9; 24:6). ***shākab*** also means "to lie down (dead)" (cf. Judg. 5:27; Job 21:26; Lam. 2:21; Ezek. 32:21). This is also predicated of animals (cf. Num. 23:24). Isa. 50:11 expresses the idea of lying down in sorrow. A symbolic lying down is indicated in Ezek. 4:4ff.

rāba' **[רָבַע, 7250]**

rāba' occurs only three times and is translated "to lie down," with reference to copulation, on each occasion. In Lev. 18:23; 20:16, bestiality is condemned outright and is designated a capital offense under the law. Lev. 19:19 contains a law which forbade owners of cattle from breeding their stock with different species.

'ārab [אָרַב, 693]

'ārab occurs around forty times and signifies "to lie in wait for," "ambush."

Lying in wait with a malicious intent to capture or harm others is indicated, for example, in Deut. 19:11; Judg. 9:32ff.; 1 Sam. 22:8; Ps. 10:9; Prov. 1:18; Mic. 7:2. Lam. 4:19 records this action with respect to Yahweh, who does so as a judgment against his people.

In the context of a military ambush, ***'ārab*** is found in a number of contexts — for example, in Joshua's campaigns against Ai (Josh. 8:2ff.), and Gibeah (Judg. 20:29ff.). Saul's ambush of Amalek is recounted in 1 Sam. 15:5. Such forays against Ammon, Moab, and Edom, recorded in 2 Chr. 20:22, are set by Yahweh himself. See also Ezra 8:31.

rābaṣ [רָבַץ, 7257]

rābaṣ is found in about thirty contexts meaning "lie down" in the sense of "stretching oneself out."

rābaṣ has the mundane, literal sense of "lying down" in Job 11:19; Ps. 23:2; Song 1:7, with regard to people. Animals are described in this position in Gen. 29:2; Exod. 23:5; Deut. 22:6; Isa. 13:20.

In metaphorical contexts, ***rābaṣ*** refers to sin crouching down, ready to pounce (Gen. 4:7); and to lions in a similar position (Gen. 49:9; Ezek. 19:2). Divine punishment against his people, in the context of divine curse, is said to fall upon any who violate his law (cf. Deut. 29:20). Then, in the context of promised divine renewal concerning the transformation of the earth, the wolf will lie down with the lamb in undisturbed harmony (cf. Isa. 11:6ff.). Similarly, the people of Yahweh are described as lying down in a fertile land as a consequence of the earth's divine renewal (cf. Ezek. 34:14; Zeph. 2:7; 3:13).

NT Words

katakeimai [κατάκειμαι, *2621*]

katakeimai means "lie down," "recline." The former sense applies to those who are prostrate with illness or disability, the latter to those who are reclining at a meal table. ***katakeimai*** occurs eleven times.

Mark 1:30; 2:4; Luke 5:25; John 5:3, 6; Acts 9:33; 28:8 refer to those who are lying down, stricken with illness or infirmity. Mark 2:15; 14:3; Luke 5:29; 1 Cor. 8:10 describe guests reclining at a meal.

keimai [κεῖμαι, *2749*]

keimai is found in fifteen contexts with the basic sense of "lie (down)" or "lay" that includes a variety of literal and metaphorical contexts with both an active and passive force.

General references to the action of lying down, or the position of lying down, are indicated, for example, in Matt. 28:6; Luke 23:53, concerning the body of Christ lying in the tomb, dead. Luke 2:12, 16 describe the infant Jesus lying in a manger. Jesus' grave clothes are said to lie in the tomb in Luke 24:12; John 20:5ff. See also John 21:19.

Metaphorical usage of ***keimai*** is evident, first of all, in the context of divine judgment. With respect to the wickedness of Jewish society at the outset of Jesus' public ministry, John the Baptist indicates in Matt. 3:10; Luke 3:9 that "the ax is laid at the root of the trees." In 2 Cor. 3:15, Paul declares that a veil of spiritual darkness "lies" over the minds of unbelievers. 1 John 5:19 affirms that the world "lies" in the power of the evil one.

Secondly, in more neutral and positive contexts, 1 Cor. 3:11 states that no other foundation is possible for gospel ministry other than that which is already laid, that of Jesus Christ himself. 1 Tim. 1:9 states that the law has been laid down for the wicked. In Rev. 21:16, the heavenly city is described as being laid out like a square. Finally, ***keimai*** refers in Matt. 5:14 to a city set on a hill.

enedreuō [ἐνεδρεύω, *1748*]

enedreuō is the dynamic Greek equivalent for the Hebrew term ***'ārab*** (see above), occurring only twice. ***enedreuō*** means "to lie in wait for" in the sense of "trap," "ambush." In Luke 11:54, the Pharisees and scribes are said to "lie in wait" for Jesus, seeking to trap him in his speech with a view to accusing him of wrongdoing. Acts 23:21, on the other hand, refers to the abortive attempt of a group of fanatical Jews to ambush the apostle Paul.

LIFE, LIVE, LIVING

OT Words

ḥay [חַי, 2416]

ḥay is a common adjectival term in the Old Testament that also functions as a noun and occasionally manifests a verbal sense as well. The primary senses of ***ḥay*** are "life," "living," "alive," in numerous contexts. The term occurs around five hundred times.

In the sphere of human beings and animals, ***ḥay*** refers to the "living" in both an adjectival and nominal sense. "Living creatures" are indicated, for example, in Gen. 1:20ff.; 6:19; Lev. 11:10; Num. 16:18. A general nominal designation, "the living," is found in Ruth 2:20; 1 Sam. 25:29; Eccl. 7:2; Isa. 36:11; Ezek. 26:20. The adjective "(a)live," "living" is used with respect to people in 1 Sam. 15:8; 2 Sam. 12:18; Ps. 55:15, and to sacrificial animals in Lev. 16:20, 21 — in particular, to the "scapegoat" designated for the Day of Atonement ritual.

"Life" in general is indicated by the use of ***ḥay*** in Gen. 3:14; Exod. 1:14; Deut. 6:2; Job 3:20; Ps. 23:6; Prov. 10:16; Eccl. 2:17; Lam. 3:53. It is also mentioned in contrast with death (cf. Deut. 30:19; Job 33:22; Isa. 8:19; Jer. 8:3; Jonah 4:3). The "breath of life" is found in Gen. 2:7; 6:17; 7:22; and the "tree of life" in Gen. 2:9; 3:22; Prov. 3:18; 11:30. The concept of "everlasting life" is rare in the Old Testament, but ***ḥay*** is used in this expression in Dan. 12:2.

ḥay is also used verbally, meaning "live." It is predicated of people in general (Lev. 25:36; Deut. 4:10); and also of God in a number of places that contain the expression "as the Lord lives," or "as surely as I live" (cf. 1 Sam. 1:26; 2 Sam. 4:9; Job 27:2; Isa. 49:18; Jer. 4:2; Ezek. 5:11; Hos. 4:15). Job 19:25 affirms that God lives as the patriarch's redeemer.

ḥay describes the Lord adjectivally in the phrase "the living God" (cf. Josh. 3:10; 1 Sam. 17:26; Ps. 42:2; Isa. 37:4; Jer. 10:10; Hos. 1:10).

nephesh [נֶפֶשׁ, **5315**]

nephesh is another common term in the Old Testament that has a wide variety of meanings, including "soul," "mind," "heart," "person," "body," as well as "life." ***nephesh*** refers to the various aspects of human life and personality, and creaturely existence in general. The Hebrew language does not refer separately to the spiritual, physical, and emotional aspects of human beings with distinctive vocabulary. ***nephesh*** indicates a holistic view of humankind, referring to the unity of a human being through a single term. Accordingly, this makes the precise translation of this word very difficult in certain circumstances. ***nephesh*** occurs about 750 times, and the meaning "life" may be attributed to it in about 100 of these contexts. ***nephesh*** may also be translated adjectivally (i.e., "living") in a number of contexts. ➡ MIND ➡ SOUL

Where animals are concerned, ***nephesh*** refers to their "life" as a general designation of their existence (cf. Gen. 1:20; Prov. 12:10). It is also used adjectivally in the phrase "living creature" (cf. Gen. 1:24).

With regard to human beings, ***nephesh*** also signifies "life" as a general designation of existence (cf. Gen. 9:5; 19:19; Exod. 21:23; Deut. 24:16; 2 Sam. 4:8; 1 Kgs. 1:12, Job 2:4; Ps. 34:12; Lam. 2:18). The term also refers to life as an animating principle in the statement that "the life of the creature is in the blood" (cf. Lev. 17:11, 14; Deut. 12:23). In particular, ***nephesh*** refers to the "life" of God's people in Isa. 43:4; Jer. 4:30; 11:21; 38:16; 34:21. In Jer. 31:8, life is contrasted with death.

ḥāyāh [חָיָה, **2421**]

ḥāyāh is a verb with the basic meanings "to live," "be alive," as well as several related senses. The term occurs around 270 times.

When used in the context of human society, ***ḥāyāh*** refers generally to the fact of living in Gen. 27:40; 42:18; 2 Kgs. 14:17; Eccl. 6:6; Jer. 38:17. The term is also used to state the attainment of a certain age, "he lived . . . years" (cf. Gen. 5:3ff.; 9:28; 11:11ff.; Job 42:16). ***ḥāyāh*** can also be translated "to keep alive," "let live," or words to the same effect (cf. Gen. 45:27; Exod. 1:17ff.; Num. 4:19; Deut. 6:24; Josh. 2:13; Judg. 2:14). In Jer. 49:11, the preservation of life is specifically declared to be undertaken by God. In related contexts, there are pleas for God to preserve one's life (cf. Ps. 143:11; Isa. 38:16).

Concerning the people of God, ***ḥāyāh*** refers to their living in the land with a high quality of life as a reward for their obedience. In Deut. 4:1; 5:33; 8:1; 30:16, this quality of living is declared to be contingent on their obeying the laws of Yahweh. See also Ps. 119:17, 77, 93; Prov. 4:4; Ezek. 18:19; Amos 5:4ff. for related usage. There is also a clear affirmation of life evident in expressions such as "Long live the king!" (cf. 1 Kgs. 1:31, 34; 2 Kgs. 11:12; Nah. 2:3, Ps. 72:15).

In several metaphorical contexts, Yahweh is declared to be the one who brings his people back to life from the dead (cf. 1 Sam. 2:6; Ps. 30:3). Arguably, the most spectacular illustration of this theme is found in Ezekiel's vision of the dry bones, resurrected from the dead and symbolizing Israel's return to the land after their seventy-year captivity in Babylon (cf. Ezek. 37:5ff.; also Hos. 6:2).

ḥayā' [חֲיָא, **2418** (Aramaic)]

ḥayā' is the Aramaic verb corresponding to the Hebrew ***ḥāyāh*** (see above). ***ḥayā'*** is found six times in the book of Daniel and means "to live," "keep alive."

Most occurrences of ***ḥayā'*** are found in the expression "Long live the king!" referring to Nebuchadnezzar (cf. Dan. 2:4; 3:9); Belshazzar (cf. Dan. 5:10); and Darius (cf. Dan. 5:6, 21). The meaning "keep alive" is found in Dan. 5:19.

NT Words

psychē [ψυχή, *5590*]

psychē is found in about one hundred contexts with the primary sense of "life," "soul." With regard to the meaning "life," ***psychē*** indicates the animating principle (or breath) of life that God gives to both humans and animals. (→ SOUL)

When referring to human beings, ***psychē*** refers to "life" in a general sense (Matt. 2:20; 6:25; Mark 3:4; Luke 12:22, 23; John 12:25; Acts 20:24; Rom. 16:4). Phil. 2:30 speaks of risking one's life for the sake of Christ. Peter's promise to lay down his life for Jesus is recorded in John 13:37. In John 15:13, Jesus refers to the greatest act of love, that of laying down one's life for one's friend.

In reference to Christ, ***psychē*** also refers to his life, given as a ransom for many (cf. Matt. 20:28; Mark 10:45). In John 10:11ff.; 1 John 3:16, Christ is said to lay down his life for his "sheep" (i.e., his people).

zōē [ζωή, *2222*]

zōē is another of the crucial New Testament terms for "life." ***zōē*** refers to life that is of the highest quality, having reached the fullest potential in the people of God through the finished redemptive work of Christ. In a large number of cases, it refers to "eternal life" — not only to heavenly reality, but also to that quality of life initiated by the Spirit of God at conversion. ***zōē*** occurs around 130 times.

Concerning human life, ***zōē*** refers first of all to life of the highest quality, as God had intended it (cf. Matt. 7:14; Luke 12:15; John 6:33; Acts 2:28; 11:18; Rom. 6:4; 2 Cor. 2:16; 1 Pet. 3:7). Rev. 2:7; 22:2, 14 refer to the "tree of life."

In relation to life as embodied in the person of Christ, ***zōē*** refers to several aspects of this phenomenon. Jesus is the "bread of life" (John 6:48); the "resurrection and the life" (John 11:25); and "the way, the truth and the life" (John 14:6).

"Eternal life" is implied in Matt. 18:8ff.; Mark 9:43; and made explicit in John 17:3; Acts 13:46. Enquiries about eternal life are made in Matt. 19:16; Mark 10:17; Luke 10:25; 18:18; as are promises of such in Matt. 19:29; Mark 10:30; Luke 18:30; John 3:15, 16; Rom. 6:22; 1 Tim. 1:16; Titus 1:2; Jas. 1:12; 1 John 2:25. Certainty of the resurrection to life is indicated in John 5:29. Jesus is noted as the source of eternal life in John 10:28. The "book of life" is referred to in Phil. 4:3; Rev. 3:5; 13:8; 17:8; 20:12, 15; 21:27. Eternal life is granted by God in Rom. 2:7; 6:23; 1 John 5:11, 20, and brought about by the work of Christ (cf. Rom. 5:17ff.; 8:2, 6; Gal. 6:8; 2 Tim. 1:10). The water of (eternal) life is indicated in Rev. 21:6; 22:1, 17.

bios [βίος, *979*]

bios is a noun meaning "life," "living" in eight contexts.

Referring to "living" in the sense of the sum total of one's possessions, ***bios*** is found in Mark 12:44; Luke 21:4 with respect to the generosity of the impoverished widow who gave all she had to the temple treasury. Similarly, the term is also found in regard to the inherited wealth of the "prodigal son" (cf. Luke 15:12, 30).

"Life" in general is indicated by the term ***bios*** in Luke 8:14, with reference to the "pleasures of life." In 1 John 2:16 ***bios*** designates the "pride of life." Leading a quiet life is indicated in 1 Tim. 2:2; 2 Tim. 2:4.

apsychos [ἄψυχος, *895*]

apsychos is an adjectival form meaning "lifeless." It occurs only in 1 Cor. 14:7, with reference to "lifeless" instruments such as the flute or harp.

zaō [ζάω, *2198*]

zaō is the verb from which ***zōē*** is derived (see above), and likewise sometimes means "live," "be alive" in a normal sense. Usually, however, ***zaō*** describes living a life that fulfills the potential God has intended for those who live for him, both here on earth and for eternity. This term is predicated of both God and human beings. The participial form is also used in a nominal or adjectival sense, "living." ***zaō*** occurs around 130 times.

The meaning "to live" refers to people in a variety of contexts. Matt. 4:4; Luke 4:4 declare that human beings shall live by the word of God alone. A number of people are miraculously "restored to life" through the power of Christ — for example, Jairus' daughter (cf. Matt. 9:18; Mark 5:23); and the son of a royal official (cf. John 4:50ff.). To live with the highest quality of life, implying eternal life, is indicated in Luke 10:28; Rom. 1:17. Other texts anticipate the experience of eternal life (cf. John 6:58; 11:25; Rom. 8:3; Rev. 20:4).

With respect to this life, ***zaō*** refers to living in direct dependence on God and his power (Acts 17:28; 2 Cor. 13:14). Gal. 5:25 refers to living by the Spirit, and Heb.

10:38 to living by faith. ***zaō*** refers to living for the glory of God (Rom. 6:10; 14:8; Gal. 2:19); and for Christ's glory (2 Cor. 5:15; Gal. 2:20; Phil. 1:21). The ideal of living by the righteousness of the law as a means to life is put forward in Rom. 10:5; Gal. 3:11.

zaō also indicates the process of living with respect to Jesus Christ, who is said to live in dependence on God in John 6:57. Gal. 2:20 declares that Christ lives in us. And Heb. 7:25 affirms that Christ lives in the presence of his Father to make intercession for us.

Similarly, this term is also applied to God. Rom. 14:11 records the divine affirmation, ". . . as I live." In Rev. 4:9; 10:6; 15:7, God is portrayed as living forever on his throne.

In a nominal sense, ***zaō*** refers to people in general as "the living," usually in contrast with "the dead" (cf. Matt. 22:32; Mark 12:27; Luke 20:38; Acts 10:42; Rom. 14:9; 2 Tim. 4:1; 1 Pet. 4:5).

As an adjective, ***zaō*** indicates "the living God" — for example in Matt. 16:16, in the context of Peter's confession. See also Matt. 26:63; Acts 14:15; Rom. 9:26; 2 Cor. 3:3; 6:16; 1 Thess. 1:9; 1 Tim. 3:15; Heb. 3:12; 10:13; Rev. 7:2. Human beings are described likewise as "living beings" in 1 Cor. 15:45. The adjectival form of ***zaō*** is also used in relation to the person of Christ, describing him, for instance, as "living water" (John 4:10, 11; 7:38; Rev. 7:17) and "living bread" (John 6:51).

zōogoneō [ζωογονέω, *2225*]

zōogoneō occurs only twice, meaning "to preserve life" in both instances. Luke 17:33 refers to those who by "losing" their life (i.e., in self-denial) will in fact "preserve" it for eternity. Acts 7:19 refers to the cruel edict of the Egyptian Pharaoh at the time of Israel's enslavement, who passed an edict requiring all Israelite parents to expose their infant male children, leaving them for dead (lit., that they might not be kept alive).

politeuomai [πολιτεύομαι, *4176*]

politeuomai basically means "to live one's life" in accordance with a particular set of high moral values, or as a good citizen. This term only occurs twice and refers in both cases to living one's life worthy of the calling of God. Acts 23:1 refers to Paul's claim that he has lived before God with a clear conscience. Phil. 1:27 contains the exhortation to live a life worthy of the gospel of Christ.

syzaō [συζάω, *4800*]

syzaō means "to live (together) with" and occurs three times. Rom. 6:8; 2 Tim. 2:11 promise that believers will one day live with Christ in glory. 2 Cor. 7:3 refers to the spirit of Christian community and fellowship whereby believers are said to live together.

eirēneuō [εἰρηνεύω, *1514*]

eirēneuō means "to be, live in peace" (i.e., with others) and is found in only four places (cf. Mark 9:50; Rom. 12:18; 2 Cor. 13:11; 1 Thess. 5:13).

makrochronios [μακροχρόνιος, *3118*]

makrochronios is adjectival in form but has the verbal sense of "live long." It is found only in Eph. 6:3, where it refers to the promise of living long on the earth, made to those who honor their parents.

anazaō [ἀναζάω, *326*]

anazaō occurs five times and is translated on each occasion "to come alive," "come to life again," or "revive," in both a literal as well as a metaphorical sense.

With literal reference to the resurrection, Rom. 14:9 declares that Christ came back to life in order to be Lord of both the dead and the living. Rev. 20:5 refers to the rest of the dead (i.e., the wicked) being brought back to life after the completion of Christ's thousand-year reign.

In metaphorical contexts, ***anazaō*** refers first of all to the prodigal son returning to his father, viewed by the latter as a return to life "from the dead," so to speak (cf. Luke 15:24, 32). In Rom. 7:9, Paul declares that when the law was given, sin "came back to life" within him and he "died" (i.e., became a slave to sin).

tryphaō [τρυφάω, *5171*]

tryphaō is found only in Jas. 5:5, meaning "live in luxury."

Additional Notes

The phenomenon of "life" and "living" has a very extensive profile in both Old and New Testaments.

The Old Testament vocabulary describing the high quality of life that was offered to Israel by Yahweh as a reward for their consistent devotion to him and obedience to his laws is significant (see ***ḥāyāh***, above, in particular). The blessed ideal of life in Canaan was held out constantly to the people as an incentive for remaining faithful to Yahweh in every area of life. Sadly, that ideal was rarely realized.

In the New Testament, the idea of "life" (apart from mundane usage) undergoes significant development. The concept of "everlasting life" is relatively rare in the

Old Testament, and where it did occur, or was implied, it referred primarily to living in the land. In the New Testament, however, terms such as ***zōē***, and ***zaō*** in particular, clearly indicate a new quality of life that transcends the earthly sphere. These point to an eternally enduring, sublime level of existence that is associated intimately with the person and work of Christ, and is obtained through the means of saving faith in him. In short, it is this ideal, consummate level of existence, in union with God and Christ, that is typologically anticipated by the ideal of a peaceful and abundant life in the land. The land, of course, exemplified old covenant "rest"; and the new and radically superior quality of life offered by Christ in the new covenant is characterized by the believer's hope of eternal rest in the heavenly kingdom of God.

LIFT

OT Words

rûm [רוּם, 7311]

rûm is a verb found in about two hundred contexts with the primary meanings "rise," "lift (up)," "exalt," as well as a number of associated nuances. The term is used in both the active and passive voice. The meaning "lift up" is found in about sixty of these contexts. (➡ EXALT ➡ RISE)

With a literal sense of "lift up" or "raise," ***rûm*** indicates the lifting of one's hand in oath-taking (Gen. 14:22), and as a sign of divine power (Exod. 17:11). See also 1 Kgs. 11:26; Mic. 5:9. The term also refers to lifting one's voice (i.e., shouting) in praise to God in 1 Cor. 15:16; Ezra 3:12; 2 Chr. 5:13; Isa. 40:9. See also Gen. 39:15. Lifting up the rod as a symbol of divine power and authority is cited in connection with Moses' leadership and miracle working — in connection with the plagues of Egypt (Exod. 7:20; 14:16); and with the provision of water from the rock (Num. 20:11).

Metaphorically, ***rûm*** also refers to lifting one's heart in pride against God (cf. Deut. 8:14; 17:20; Isa. 2:12 [implicit]); and to lifting one's face to God in prayer (cf. Ezra 9:6).

Where God is in view, ***rûm*** refers to the divine action of lifting up the humble and poor so as to restore them to dignity (cf. 1 Sam. 2:8). Ps. 9:13 refers to the psalmist's plea that God will lift him up from the gates of death. Yahweh is said to lift up the head of the psalmist in Ps. 27:6. In Isaiah's call vision, the prophet sees God lifted upon his throne (cf. Isa. 6:1).

NT Words

epairō [ἐπαίρω, *1869*]

epairō is translated "lift up" in a number of contexts, most of them in a literal sense. The term occurs around twenty times.

The sense of "lift up one's eyes" (i.e., "look") is indicated in Matt. 17:8; Luke 6:20; 16:23; 18:13; John 4:35; 6:5; 17:1. To "lift one's voice" or "shout" is refereed to in Luke 11:27; Acts 2:14; 14:11; 22:22. Luke 24:50 describes Jesus lifting up his hands to bless his disciples, and in 1 Tim. 2:8 the action signifies an attitude of prayer. See also Luke 21:28. The rebellion or treachery of Judas against Christ is in view in John 13:28, where ***epairō*** is used in the expression "to lift one's heel against," symbolically describing that action of betrayal. Acts 1:9 refers to Jesus being "lifted up" into heaven before the very eyes of his followers.

See Also: ➡ ARISE ➡ BEAR (VERB) ➡ EXALT

LIGHT, BRING OR GIVE LIGHT

OT Words

'ôr [אוֹר, 215; 216]

In form, ***'ôr*** functions both as a noun and a verb. The nominal sense of this term means "light," referring to all manner of literal, physical phenomena, and also to the metaphorical sense of "enlightenment." ***'ôr*** is predicated of both human beings and God and occurs in this form about 120 times. As a verb, ***'ôr*** is translated "give light," "shine," "illuminate," as well as associated nuances, in a variety of contexts.

As a noun, ***'ôr*** refers to light in general terms, such as "daylight," "moonlight" (Judg. 16:2; 1 Sam. 14:36; 2 Sam. 23:4; Neh. 8:3; Amos 8:9). The light of the heavenly luminaries (i.e., sun and moon) is indicated in Gen. 1:5, 8; Ps. 136:7; Eccl. 12:2; Isa. 13:10; Jer. 31:35; Ezek. 32:8. Undifferentiated, created light is cited in Gen. 1:3, 4; Job 26:10; 38:23; Isa. 45:7; Zech. 14:7. Ps. 78:14 refers to the glory cloud in the wilderness as a guiding light for the Israelites. ***'ôr*** also refers to "lightning" in Job 36:32, 37:3.

'ôr is also evident in a number of metaphorical contexts. The absence of moral enlightenment is indicated in Job 12:25, referring to those "without light." Positively speaking, ***'ôr*** also mentions light as equivalent to the path of righteousness. Job 24:13, 16, for example, refer to those who rebel against the light. Isa. 5:20 draws the contrast between light and the evil of moral darkness. Isa. 42:16 affirms that Yahweh gives the light of understanding to the spiritually blind.

In a related sense, *'ôr* also points to light as an animating principle of existence. For example, Job 18:5 declares that the "light of the wicked" is snuffed out. The "light of life," as derived from the person of God, is indicated in Job 33:30. Prov. 13:9 refers to the light of the righteous.

'ôr is also frequently mentioned in connection with the person of God: The "light of his countenance" is mentioned in Pss. 4:6; 44:3; 89:15. God is also described as "light," the source of ultimate guidance (Pss. 27:1; 43:3; 119:105; Isa. 2:5; Mic. 7:8). Prov. 6:23 cites the divine guiding light reflected through the instrument of the law. The light of divine revelation, signifying the coming of the messianic ruler, the Servant of Yahweh, is indicated in Isa. 9:2. The light of divine salvation is directed towards the Gentile nations in Isa. 42:6; 49:6; 51:4; 60:1 — again through the ministry of the Suffering Servant. The "light" of God's person is also associated with the Day of the Lord in Amos 5:20.

With its verbal sense, ***'ôr*** means "to give, shed light" in a physical sense. It refers, for example, to the emission of light from sun and moon in Gen. 1:15, 17; and to daylight in Gen. 44:3; 1 Sam. 29:10. The shedding of light from the pillar of cloud in the wilderness as a guide for the tribes of Israel is referred to in Exod. 13:21; 14:20; Neh. 9:12, 19; Ps. 105:39. Similarly, light from the lampstands in the tabernacle is indicated in Exod. 25:37; Num. 8:2.

In metaphorical contexts, Yahweh is said to shine the light of his face on his servants (cf. Num. 6:25; Pss. 31:16; 67:1; 80:3), and also to give the light of his revelation to his people (cf. Pss. 118:27; 119:30; Prov. 29:13).

mā'ôr [מָאוֹר, **3974**]

mā'ôr is a participial form of the verb ***'ôr*** (see above) with the nominal sense of "light" or "luminary." The term occurs around twenty times.

mā'ôr refers to physical light from sun and moon in Gen. 1:14, 15, 16; Ps. 74:16; Ezek. 32:8. It also indicates the light from the tabernacle lampstands (cf. Exod. 25:6; 27:20; Lev. 24:2; Num. 4:9, 16).

Where God is concerned, ***mā'ôr*** refers to the light of his countenance in Ps. 90:8.

nehārāh [נְהָרָה, **5105**]

nehārāh occurs only in Job 3:4, where it refers to "daylight" as part of Job cursing the day of his birth: "May no light shine upon it."

nehôr [נְהוֹר, **5094** (Aramaic)]

nehôr is the Aramaic equivalent of ***nehārāh*** (see above). It also is rare, occurring only three times in the Aramaic portion of Daniel. In all three places, ***nehôr*** refers to "light" in the sense of wisdom and understanding. It is predicated of God in Dan. 2:22, and of Daniel himself in Dan. 5:11, 14.

NT Words

phōs [φῶς, *5457*]

phōs is a noun found approximately seventy times, with the consistent meaning "light." It indicates physical light from natural sources, as well as supernatural light revealed from heaven. In addition, ***phōs*** conveys a distinctive metaphorical sense of "light," associated both with the person of God and the abstract phenomena of moral and spiritual truth.

phōs means "light" in a mundane sense (cf. Matt. 10:16; Luke 12:3; Eph. 5:13) where daylight is mentioned. Firelight is indicated in Mark 14:54; and lamplight in Luke 8:16; Acts 16:29; Rev. 18:23.

phōs refers to the supernatural light of Christ's transfiguration (Matt. 17:2); to heavenly light at Saul's conversion (Acts 9:3; 22:6ff.); to angelic light (Acts 12:7); and to the light of the heavenly city (Rev. 21:24; 22:5).

phōs is also used in metaphorical contexts relating to light and the person of God. First of all, reference is made to the light of God's salvation for the Gentiles, anticipating the coming of the Messiah (cf. Matt. 4:16; Luke 2:32; Acts 13:47; 26:18). Divine light is depicted as the source of eternal life, represented supremely by Jesus (cf. John 1:4ff.; 3:19ff.; 11:10; 12:35ff.; 2 Cor. 4:6; 1 Pet. 2:9; 1 John 2:8ff.). In this connection, Jesus is described as "the light of the world." 1 Tim. 6:16; Jas. 1:17; 1 John 1:5, 7 refer to the light of God, indicating the essence of his being (i.e., as unapproachable).

Metaphorical usage of ***phōs*** also extends to the human sphere. The believer's "armor of light" is indicated in Rom. 13:12. The people of God are described as "children of light" in Eph. 5:8; 1 Thess. 5:5 (cf. also John 5:35; Col. 1:12). In related contexts, God's people are depicted as the "light of the world" in Matt. 5:14; Rom. 2:19. In more general contexts, "light" is the equivalent of moral uprightness, or godliness (cf. Matt. 5:16; 6:23; Luke 11:35; 2 Cor. 6:14).

phōteinos [φωτεινός, *5460*]

phōteinos is an adjective signifying "full of light," "bright." It occurs four times. Three of these occurrences are found in Matt. 6:22; Luke 11:34, 36, where the body is said to be "full of light" if the eyes are sound. Matt. 17:5 refers to the bright cloud overshadowing Christ and his disciples on the mountain of his transfiguration.

phengos [φέγγος, *5338*]

phengos is a noun, found only three times, meaning "light." In Matt. 24:29; Mark 13:24 it refers to moonlight; and in Luke 11:33 to the light of a lamp.

haptō [ἅπτω, *681*]

haptō conveys the meaning "to light a lamp or fire." It occurs only four times (cf. Luke 8:16; 11:33; 15:8; 22:55).

phōtizō [φωτίζω, *5461*]

phōtizō is a verb occurring around ten times, meaning "give, shed light," "enlighten," "illuminate," in both literal and metaphorical contexts.

The literal meaning "give, shed light" is found in Luke 11:36 with reference to a lamp, and in Rev. 21:23 with reference to the effect of the glory of God in the heavenly city. See also Rev. 22:5.

With symbolic reference to illuminating people's hearts and minds with the "light" of revealed truth, ***phōtizō*** occurs in John 1:9; 1 Cor. 4:5; Eph. 1:18; 2 Tim. 1:10; Heb. 6:4; 10:32.

phōtismos [φωτισμός, *5462*]

phōtismos is the noun derived from ***phōtizō*** (see above). It occurs only in 2 Cor. 4:4, 6, referring to the "light of the knowledge of the gospel," denied to the unbelieving Jews, but given to all true believers.

epiphauskō [ἐπιφαύσκω, *2017*]

epiphauskō occurs only in Eph. 5:14, referring to the action of the risen Christ in giving the "light" of new life to all those who died in him and awoke from death.

phōstēr [φωστήρ, *5458*]

phōstēr is a noun meaning "light" in the sense of the radiance emanating from the glory of God. It occurs only twice: once in Phil. 2:15, where it refers to believers who shine as lights in the world (i.e., radiating God's glory in their lives); and once in Rev. 21:11, referring to the heavenly city of Jerusalem, radiating light from the glorious presence of God within her walls.

Additional Notes

The phenomenon of "light" as revealed throughout both Testaments of Scripture constitutes a highly significant theological motif when described in relation to the persons of God and Christ. Though the vocabulary for "light" is wide ranging in both Greek and Hebrew, the underlying impact of light (in both verbal and nominal senses) on people in both covenant eras is quite similar.

As far as "light" in the Old Testament is concerned, its association with the person of Yahweh reinforces the unique holiness of his being in theophanic revelation. Such revelation results in Yahweh being viewed as a literal guiding light for his people in some contexts (e.g., the pillar of cloud in the desert) and as the source of ultimate truth and righteousness in others (e.g., through the law of Moses). The "light" of Yahweh is also seen as a symbolic vehicle for expressing favor and blessing towards his people. The ritual lightning seen in tabernacle and temple expresses one of God's primary purposes for his people, that they might reveal the "light" of God's glory and truth to the nations around them, and thereby attract such people to the God of Israel.

In the New Testament, the significance of "light" in association with the person of God continues, except that here that function is transformed in the person of Christ. Jesus Christ's own claims with respect to divine light are profound, and particularly his claim to be the "light of the world." In this context, the New Testament makes it plain that the "light" of Yahweh offered to the Israelites and to the nations, especially through the figure of the Messianic Servant in the prophecy of Isaiah, now comes to a supreme focus in the person of Christ. It is now through the person of the Son of God, as the "light of the world," that people will be drawn into the kingdom of God. Climactically, the book of Revelation indicates that "light" is the dominant feature of the heavenly city, a place where no darkness can intrude. Both Testaments demonstrate that the light of God, signifying perfect righteousness, utterly displaces all darkness. This phenomenon signifies, conversely, the presence of evil. In this sense, all "light" associated with God and his Son has a powerful underlying redemptive significance.

See Also: → APPEAR → BURN → LAMP → SHINE

LIGHTNING

OT Words

bārāq [בָּרָק, 1300]

bārāq occurs around twenty times and is translated "lightning" in most of these contexts, with reference to the meteorological phenomenon of natural origin as well as that brought about by divine intervention.

Lightning as a natural, created phenomenon is indicated in Job 38:35; Ps. 135:7; Jer. 10:13; 51:16. In other contexts, ***bārāq*** refers to lightning as a phenomenon specifically produced by Yahweh for particular purposes, such as judgment against his enemies (cf. 2 Sam. 22:15; Ps. 18:14). Elsewhere, lightning accompanies divine theophany, such as took place at Mt. Sinai (cf. Exod. 19:16; Pss. 77:18; 97:4; 144:6); and also in the revelation granted to the prophets Ezekiel (cf. Ezek. 1:13) and Daniel (cf. Dan. 10:6).

bārāq is also found in metaphorical contexts, where it is used as part of the simile, "like lightning." It is principally applied to the shine of weapons and the "sword of Yahweh" (cf. Ezek. 21:10, 15, 28; Nah. 2:4; Zech. 9:14).

lappîd [**לַפִּיד, 3940**]

lappîd is a noun that refers primarily to a "torch," occurring in fourteen places. (→ TORCH) Once, however, in Exod. 20:18, ***lappîd*** refers to lightning at Mt. Sinai.

bāzāq [**בָּזָק, 965**]

bāzāq occurs only in Ezek. 1:14 and refers, in a simile, to a "flash of lightning."

NT Words

astrapē [ἀστραπή, *796*]

astrapē is a noun that occurs eleven times with the sense of "lightning," "flash of lightning," in all but one of these contexts.

Matt. 24:27; Luke 17:24 refer to lightning in general terms. ***astrapē*** also likens the appearance of Christ's divine glory to lightning (Matt. 28:3). In Matt. 10:18, Jesus declares that he saw Satan fall like lightning from heaven. In two places in the book of Revelation, ***astrapē*** refers to flashes of lightning as part of a vision of the heavenly throne room of God, the source of divine judgment (cf. Rev. 4:5; 11:19). In addition, the Apocalypse of John records the occurrence of lightning as an accompaniment to God's punishment of the wicked on earth (cf. Rev. 8:5; 16:18).

LIKEN

OT Words

dāmāh [**דָּמָה, 1819**]

dāmāh is a verb meaning "liken," "compare," or "resemble" in six places.

For the most part, ***dāmāh*** is used in a question posed by Yahweh to his people, asking them to whom "he may be likened" (or compared) (cf. Ps. 89:6; Isa. 40:18, 25; 46:5). See also Lam. 2:13.

NT Words

homoioō [ὁμοιόω, *3666*]

homoioō is a dynamic equivalent for ***dāmāh*** (see above), meaning "liken," "compare" throughout its fifteen occurrences.

The passive sense "be compared with" is evident in Matt. 7:24, 26 in relation to the comparison between those who heed the words of Jesus and those who do not.

Matt. 13:24; 18:23; 25:1; Mark 4:30; Luke 13:20 ask what the kingdom of heaven may be compared to. See also Matt. 11:16; Luke 7:31.

LIKENESS → IMAGE

LILY

OT Words

shûshan [**שׁוּשַׁן, 7799**]

shûshan is a noun that is translated "lily" in all of the fifteen contexts in which it is found. The term, however, is predominantly metaphorical in its usage, and where it does refer to genuine lilies, literal flowers are not indicated.

The tops of the stone pillars in the temple, as well as the brim of the huge metal basin for ritual washing, were cast in the form of lilies (cf. 1 Kgs. 7:19ff.; 2 Chr. 4:5). The titles of two Psalms include a probable reference to the "tune of lilies" (cf. Pss. 45:1; 69:1).

shûshan metaphorically indicates the Shulammite woman's beauty in the Song of Songs (cf. Song 2:1, 2; 7:2); and also that of her lover (cf. Song 5:13). The expression "browse among the lilies" is also found in this poetic work, a symbolic reference to intimate lovemaking (cf. Song 2:16; 4:5; 6:2, 3).

Part of Israel's renewed splendor is referred to as the "blossoming of a lily" (Hos. 14:5).

NT Words

krinon [κρίνον, *2918*]

krinon is found only twice in the New Testament, both times in connection with Jesus' description of God's care for his creation, "Consider the lilies of the field . . ." (cf. Matt. 6:28; Luke 12:27).

LINEN

OT Words

***shēsh* [שֵׁשׁ, 8336]**

shēsh is usually translated "(fine) linen." It occurs around forty times.

In reference to "fine linen" as clothing material, ***shēsh*** indicates the dress of high office for Joseph in the court of Pharaoh (Gen. 41:42). Linen was also used extensively in the construction of the tabernacle, and most of the occurrences of ***shēsh*** are found in this context (cf. Exod. 25:4; 26–28). Linen also adorned the Persian palace of King Xerxes (cf. Esth. 1:6). "Fine linen" is also the primary material from which the priestly garments were fashioned (cf. Exod. 28:5ff.; 39:2ff.). Prov. 31:22 refers to "fine linen" as belonging to the "wife of noble character."

shēsh is used metaphorically in Ezek. 16:10, 13, with reference to Yahweh clothing his young "bride," Israel, in "fine linen." See also Ezek. 27:7.

***bad* [בַּד, 906]**

bad is a synonym for ***shēsh*** (see above), and is likewise translated "linen" in all nineteen contexts where it is found.

bad refers to the linen clothing of the Levitical priests (Exod. 28:42; 39:28; Lev. 6:10; 16:4, 23, 32; 1 Sam. 22:18), to the garments of Samuel (1 Sam. 2:18); and of David (2 Sam. 6:14; 1 Chr. 15:27). The rest of the occurrences of ***bad*** refer to the angelic figure conveying the terms of Yahweh's judgment against his people, as well as to the divine message of salvation and hope. This visionary being is consistently described as "the man clothed in linen" in both Ezekiel and Daniel (cf. Ezek. 9:2, 3, 11; 10:2, 6, 7; Dan. 10:5; 12:6, 7).

***pishteh* [פִּשְׁתֶּה, 6593]**

pishteh is found in fifteen places and is translated both "linen" and "flax."

With reference to linen material or clothing in general non-priestly contents, ***pishteh*** occurs in Lev. 13:47ff.; Deut. 22:11; Jer. 13:1. Two references to priestly linen garments are found in Ezek. 44:17, 18.

References to "flax" are found in Josh. 2:6; Judg. 15:14; Prov. 31:13; Isa. 19:19; Hos. 2:5, 9; Ezek. 40:3.

***bûṣ* [בּוּץ, 948]**

bûṣ also refers to "white linen" material for the purposes of clothing as well as ornamentation. The term occurs seven times (e.g., 1 Chr. 4:21; 2 Chr. 2:14; 3:14; Esth. 1:6; 8:15; Ezek. 27:16).

***'ētûn* [אֵטוּן, 330]**

'ētûn refers to Egyptian linen material and occurs only in Prov. 7:16.

***sādîn* [סָדִין, 5466]**

sādîn refers to linen garments in general and occurs only four times (cf. Judg. 14:12, 13; Prov. 31:24; Isa. 3:23).

NT Words

***sindōn* [σινδών, *4616*]**

sindōn occurs six times and indicates a "linen cloth" used both as a garment (cf. Mark 14:51, 52); and as a shroud for wrapping the body of Jesus (cf. Matt. 27:59; Mark 15:46; Luke 23:53).

***byssos* [βύσσος, *1040*]**

byssos is derived from the Hebrew ***bûṣ*** (see above), and refers to linen produced from a species of Egyptian flax. The term only occurs in Luke 16:19; Rev. 18:12.

***othonion* [ὀθόνιον, *3608*]**

othonion refers exclusively to the pieces of linen cloth, or "linen strips," used to wrap the bodies of the deceased prior to burial. In the New Testament, this term is found on five occasions, referring only to the funerary garments of Jesus (cf. Luke 24:12; John 19:40; 20:5ff.).

***linon* [λίνον, *3043*]**

linon occurs only twice, indicating "flax" in Matt. 12:20 and "linen" in Rev. 15:6, with reference to the clothing of angels.

***byssinos* [βύσσινος, *1039*]**

byssinos is the adjectival form of ***byssos*** (see above), but is translated nominally in all three contexts in which it is found. "Fine linen" in Rev. 18:16 refers to the garb of the city of Babylon. In Rev. 19:6, the "bride of the Lamb" is depicted as one "dressed in fine linen," metaphorical clothing that represents her imputed righteousness — for the immediate context says that such clothing was "given her to wear." Rev. 19:14 describes the armies of heaven as clothed in "fine linen."

LION

OT Words

***'aryēh* [אַרְיֵה, 738]**

'aryēh occurs around eighty times and is consistently translated "lion" in both a literal and metaphorical sense.

'aryēh refers to literal lions in Judg. 14:5ff.; 1 Sam. 17:34ff.; 1 Kgs. 13:24ff.; 2 Kgs. 17:25ff.; 1 Chr. 11:22. A visionary depiction of lions is recorded in Isa. 11:7; 35:9; 65:25; Ezek. 1:10; 10:14. Lions are also depicted as motifs on temple furniture in 1 Kgs. 7:29; 10:19.

'aryēh is also used metaphorically in several contexts. The simile "as, or like a lion" is found in Gen. 49:9; Num. 23:4; Isa. 31:4; Amos 3:12; 5:19; Zeph. 3:3. In particular, the king of Babylon is thus described (Jer. 4:7; 5:6); as is a Judean ruler, probably Zechariah (Ezek. 19:6); and also Assyria (Joel 1:6, or possibly Babylon; Nah. 2:11). Yahweh is also likened to a lion in Jer. 49:19; 50:44; Hos. 11:10; Amos 3:8.

lābî' [לָבִיא, 3833]

lābî' is a synonym for ***'aryēh***, above, occurring fourteen times and meaning "lion" in a number of different contexts. The majority of these are metaphorical.

The people of Israel are likened to lions in Gen. 49:9 (Judah); Num. 23:4; 24:9; Deut. 33:20 (Gad); Ezek. 19:2 (the northern kingdoms of Israel). The nations are similarly described in Isa. 5:29; Joel 1:6; Nah. 2:11, 12 (Assyria).

Yahweh is also depicted as a lion turning on his people, in judgment, as a lion turns upon his prey (cf. Hos. 13:8). The psalmist refers to his enemies symbolically as lions in Ps. 57:4.

General allusions to lions are made in Job 4:11; 38:39; Isa. 30:6.

shaḥal [שַׁחַל, 7826]

Another synonym for ***'aryēh*** and ***lābî'***, above, ***shaḥal*** occurs in seven contexts and likewise refers to lions, primarily in a metaphorical sense. General references to lions are found in Job 4:10; 10:16; 28:8; Ps. 91:13; Prov. 26:13. ***shaḥal*** also refers to Yahweh as one waiting to "pounce" on his people as a lion prepares to devour his prey.

kephîr [כְּפִיר, 3715]

kephîr is one of the more common terms for "lion" in the Old Testament and occurs about thirty times.

Judg. 14:5 refers literally to a lion, in relation to one of Samson's exploits. General references to lions are found in Job 4:10; 38:39; Ps. 34:10; Prov. 19:12; 20:2; Amos 3:4; Mic. 5:8.

Enemies of the psalmist are also depicted as lions (Pss. 35:17; 58:6), as are the enemies of Yahweh (Isa. 31:4; Jer. 51:38; Ezek. 3:2). These enemies include Yahweh's own people, who have rebelled against him (Isa. 5:29). The removal of all enmity between beasts of prey and their victims is depicted in the description of universal restoration in Isa. 11:6, where the lion is said to lie down with the lamb.

Metaphorical references to Israel as a "lion" are noted in Ezek. 19:2ff.

Yahweh is depicted as a lion about to tear his prey in the context of judgment against Israel in Hos. 5:14. See also Ezek. 41:19.

layish [לַיִשׁ, 3918]

layish occurs only three times, each time referring to a "lion" in a general sense (cf. Job 4:11; Prov. 30:30; Isa. 30:6).

NT Words

leōn [λέων, *3023*]

leōn is the only term for "lion" in the New Testament and is found in nine contexts.

leōn is used metaphorically in 2 Tim. 4:17 to indicate the narrowness of Paul's escape from the attacks of his enemies, when he testifies that he was "delivered from the lion's mouth." Heb. 11:33 refers to the exploits of the old covenant heroes of faith who, among other things, "stopped the mouths of lions."

The book of Revelation contains various metaphorical references to lions — as part of the physiognomy of the cherubim (Rev. 4:7); demonic creatures inflicting torment on human beings (Rev. 9:8, 17); the satanic sea beast (Rev. 13:2). The voice of the angel of the Lord in Rev. 10:3 is also described as "like the roar of a lion."

Two other significant uses of ***leōn*** remain. One occurs in 1 Pet. 5:8, where Satan is described as a "roaring lion" seeking his prey among humankind. The other is in Rev. 5:5, where the risen Christ is described as the "lion of the tribe of Judah," recalling the prophetic designation of that tribe in Gen. 49:9.

Additional Notes

The vocabulary for "lion" throughout the Bible is primarily metaphorical. Particularly significant are the few references in the Old Testament to Yahweh as a lion, primarily in the context of one bringing terrible judgment against his people, for their rebellion against him, and against the nations, for their own wickedness.

That same perspective of judgment is carried over into the New Testament, though the usage of ***leōn*** is primarily negative. However, the references to both Christ and Satan as "lions" indicate the dual application of the allusion. In the case of the latter, the lion image applied to the devil signifies his extensive cunning and power. In regard to the former, the reference to Christ as the "lion of the tribe of Judah" indicates that his power is triumphant over that of the evil one. The whole context of the book of Revelation makes that victory clear. In addition, Rev. 5:5 indicates a prophetic fulfillment of the somewhat vague predication made for the tribe of Judah in Gen. 49:9. Such a link lends weight to the interpretation that the "lion-like" nature of Yahweh spans both Testaments and describes his triumph over all his enemies, including some of his own people. This victory is consummated in the person of his Son, Jesus Christ the Messiah.

LIP, LIPS

OT Words

sāphāh **[שָׂפָה, 8193]**

sāphāh is a term with the primary meaning "lips" (occurring mostly in the plural), in both a literal and metaphorical sense. Although ***sāphāh*** has numerous other meanings, they generally relate to phenomena pertaining to boundaries or perimeters — for example, "border," "edge," "bank" (of rivers etc.), "shore," "brim." (→ SHORE) ***sāphāh*** is also translated "language," "speech," which is much more closely related to the primary sense of "lips." (→ SPEECH) ***sāphāh*** occurs around 180 times, with the meaning "lip" in about half of these contexts.

The literal sense of "lips" is found in a number of places. They are used to utter vows (Lev. 5:4; Num. 30:12; Deut. 23:23), and for prayer and praise to God (Pss. 17:1; 40:9; 119:13). In Isa. 29:13, however, such worship is declared to be false. The lip as part of the facial anatomy is mentioned in Lev. 13:45; 2 Kgs. 19:28; Song 4:3; 5:13; Isa. 6:7; Ezek. 24:17.

General references to speaking (i.e., "uttering with one's lips") are found in a number of different contexts, predominantly in Proverbs (cf. Num. 30:6; 1 Sam. 1:13; Job 2:10; Ps. 16:4). In particular, ***sāphāh*** refers to deceit or lying (Ps. 34:13; Prov. 12:22; Isa. 59:3); sinful speech (Prov. 4:24; 19:1); speaking truth (Prov. 8:7; 10:32; 12:19); and the speech of a wholesome godly life (Prov. 20:15; 22:18; 23:16).

sāphām **[שָׂפָם, 8222]**

sāphām is a derivative form of ***sāphāh*** (see above) and occurs only four times, with literal reference to lips in Lev. 13:45; Ezek. 24:17, 22. Mic. 3:7 refers to seers and diviners "covering their lips," or being reduced to silence.

NT Words

cheilos [χεῖλος, *5491*]

cheilos occurs only seven times and is translated "lips" with reference to speaking in six of these contexts. (→ SHORE)

Matt. 15:8; Mark 7:6 refer to the false worship of the Jewish people, in Jesus' quotation of the passage from Isa. 29:13, "These people honor me with their lips, but their hearts are far from me . . ." Deceitful speech is indicated in Rom. 3:13; and 1 Pet. 3:10 warns against such expression. True worship of God as the appropriate "fruit of (one's) lips" is indicated in Heb. 13:15. Foreign languages are mentioned in 1 Cor. 14:21.

LISTEN → HEAR

LITTLE

OT Words

me'at **[מְעַט, 4592]**

me'at is a noun form that occurs around one hundred times, meaning "little," "far," indicating primarily smallness of quantity, number, and time. ***me'at*** also functions as an adjective.

With regard to "little" in terms of quantity, general references are found in Deut. 28:38; 1 Sam. 14:29; Prov. 6:10; Ezek. 5:12; Dan. 11:34; Hag. 1:6. Small quantities of food and water are noted in Gen. 18:4; 43:2; 44:25. Progress by degree, expressed by the phrase "little by little," is indicated in Exod. 23:30; Deut. 7:22 in the context of the Israelites gradually driving the Canaanites from the land. Smallness of stature is indicated in Eccl. 9:14.

In regard to periods of time, ***me'at*** expresses the sense of "few" (cf. Gen. 47:9 [days]; Lev. 25:52 [years]).

The expression "very soon" is found in Isa. 10:25; 26:20, where it is said that Yahweh's anger against Israel will quickly come to an end. Likewise, Isa. 29:17 affirms that Yahweh will very soon renew his land and people. See also Jer. 51:33.

"Few" in number is another meaning evident in the usage of ***me'at*** (cf. Num. 13:18; Deut. 7:7; Josh. 7:3; 2 Chr. 29:34; Neh. 2:12. Isa. 1:9 refers to a few survivors left in Israel as a small remnant.

qāṭān **[קָטָן, 6996]**

qāṭān is an adjectival form occurring around one hundred times that is translated "small," "little" in most of these contexts. The remaining usage indicates the sense of "young." (→ YOUNG)

qāṭān refers generally to "little" in the sense of smallness of stature (Gen. 19:11; 1 Sam. 20:35; Song 2:15; 8:8); and in the sense of weight (i.e., "light") (cf. Deut. 25:13).

The meaning "small," or "little (in importance)" is indicated in Exod. 18:22, 26; Deut. 1:17 in the context of legal cases. See also 1 Sam. 15:17; Esth. 1:20; Jer. 8:10; Amos 7:5; Obad. 2. Zech. 4:10 refers to the day of "small things."

The meaning "few" (in number) is found in 1 Chr. 26:13 in relation to the family clans of Israel. See also 1 Sam. 9:21; Isa. 60:22.

NT Words

mikros [μικρός, *3398*]

mikros is an adjectival form found in thirty places, with the primary senses of "small," "little," and associated nuances, with reference to size, time, and quantity.

References to "little" in term of smallness of stature are found in Matt. 10:42; 18:6ff.; Mark 9:42; and Luke 17:2, in relation to children. Luke 19:3 refers to Zacchaeus' short stature. Tiny seeds are mentioned in Matt. 13:32; Mark 4:31. "Little" in the sense of "powerless" is indicated in Luke 12:32.

The meaning "least," in terms of rank or importance, is indicated in general terms in Acts 8:10; Heb. 8:11; Rev. 11:18; 19:5, 18. Concerning the kingdom of God, Jesus declares that the "least" in that kingdom is greater than John the Baptist (cf. Matt. 11:11; Luke 7:28). Then, there is the paradoxical statement of Christ that the one who considers himself "least" among his brethren is in fact the greatest (Luke 9:18).

"Little" in relation to quantity is the sense expressed in 1 Cor. 5:6; Gal. 5:9, concerning the harmful effect of even a little leaven, symbolizing the presence of a sinful attitude.

The phrase "a little longer," with reference to time, is found in John 7:33; 12:35; Rev. 6:11. In Rev. 20:3, there is the declaration that Satan will be set free from his bondage "for a short time," prior to his final doom.

mikron [μικρόν, *3397*]

mikron is an adjectival variant of ***mikros*** (see above) with essentially the same meanings ("small," "little") with reference to quantity, time, and distance.

Referring to distance, ***mikron*** is translated "a little farther" in Matt. 26:39; Mark 14:35. In regard to quantity, 2 Cor. 11:1 refers to a "little foolishness." Concerning time, the phrase "a little while" is indicated in Matt. 26:73; Mark 14:70; Heb. 10:37; and in John's gospel the occurrences of ***mikron*** all refer to the "little while" that will take effect before the return of Christ.

oligos [ὀλίγος, *3641*]

oligos is an adjective synonymous with the preceding entries. It likewise indicates "small," "little" in regard to quantity, size, and time. ***oligos*** occurs around forty times.

The sense of "few" (in number) is found in Matt. 7:14; Luke 13:23, with reference to those who have been saved. 1 Pet. 3:20 refers to Noah and his family as the few who had been rescued from the flood. Jesus notes in Matt. 9:37 that only a few laborers are available for the harvest of souls. The expression "many are called but few are chosen" is found in Matt. 22:14. See also Matt. 15:34; 6:5; Mark 8:7.

With regard to "little" in the sense of quantity, ***oligos*** occurs in Matt. 25:21ff., referring to the fact that he who is faithful in "little" will be entrusted with greater things. Luke 7:47 declares that he who is forgiven little, loves little. See also 1 Tim. 5:23.

A "little distance" is mentioned in Mark 1:19; Luke 5:3.

The phrase a "little while" is found in several contexts (cf. Mark 6:31; Acts 26:28; Heb. 12:10). Jas. 4:14 utilizes it in regard to the brevity of life. Peter mentions the same in regard to suffering in 1 Pet. 5:10. And Rev. 12:12 mentions the fact that the devil's time is short.

elachistos [ἐλάχιστος, *1646*]

elachistos is a superlative adjectival term (from *elachys*, meaning "short") that means "least," "very little." It refers to size and importance and occurs in about ten contexts.

Concerning that which is "least" in size, ***elachistos*** is used in a general away in Luke 12:26. In Luke 16:10; 19:7, the principle is expounded that he who is faithful in little will be faithful over much. The town of Bethlehem is described as being "by no means least" among the rulers of Judah (from the prophecy in Mic. 5:2). Jas. 3:4 refers to a rudder that is "very small."

elachistos also refers to that which is least in importance. Matt. 5:19 refers to the least important commandment. The least of Jesus' "brothers" is referred to in Matt. 25:40, 45.

The most trivial of legal cases is mentioned in 1 Cor. 6:2, and Paul describes himself as the least of the apostles in 1 Cor. 15:9.

brachys [βραχύς, *1024*]

brachys is an adjective that means "little" in several different senses. ***brachys*** occurs seven times, and in three of these contexts it expresses the sense of "a little while" (cf. Luke 22:58; Acts 5:34; Heb. 2:7, 9). John 6:7 refers to a little amount of bread. Acts 27:28 uses the term in a spatial sense with the phrase "a little farther." ***brachys*** is also translated "briefly" in Heb. 13:22.

See Also: ➠ YOUNG

LOCUST

OT Words

'arbeh **[אַרְבֶּה, 697]**

'arbeh occurs around twenty times and is consistently translated "locust," or "grasshopper." The term is used both literally and metaphorically.

In its literal sense, ***'arbeh*** refers to the locust invasion of Egypt as one of the ten plagues visited on that land by Yahweh, in order to force Pharaoh to release the Israelite people from their captivity (cf. Exod. 10:4, 12ff.; Ps. 105:34). The locust is also an insect that is declared "clean," and thus able to be eaten, under the terms of the Mosaic law covenant (cf. Lev. 11:22). ***'arbeh*** also refers generally to the locust as a plague insect, sent by God as one outworking of the curse of the covenant (cf. Deut. 28:38; 1 Kgs. 8:37; 2 Chr. 6:28; Ps. 78:46; Joel 1:4; 2:25).

In metaphorical contexts, ***'arbeh*** refers to "locusts" as a simile for great numbers of men or soldiers (cf. Judg. 6:5; 7:12; Jer. 46:23). ***'arbeh*** is also used in different similes in Job 39:20; Ps. 109:23; Prov. 30:27; Nah. 3:15, 17.

sol'ām **[סָלְעָם, 5556]**

sol'ām occurs only in Lev. 11:22 and refers to a species of edible locust called a "katydid."

ḥāgāb **[חָגָב, 2284]**

ḥāgāb is a synonym for ***'arbeh*** (see above) and occurs five times. Lev. 11:22; Eccl. 12:5 refer to "grasshoppers" (or "locusts") in general. In 2 Chr. 7:13, they are referred to as the instruments of Yahweh's punishment upon the land of Israel. The simile "like grasshoppers" indicates smallness of size (Num. 13:33), and numerical greatness (Isa. 40:22).

gēb **[גֵּב, 1357]**

gēb occurs only in Isa. 33:4, referring to the leaping movement of locusts.

NT Words

akris **[ἀκρίς, *200*]**

akris is the only term for "locusts" in the New Testament, occurring four times. Twice it refers literally to locusts as part of John the Baptist's diet (cf. Matt. 3:4; Mark 1:6). Rev. 9:3, 7 refer symbolically to the demonic creatures, released from the abyss of hell, who had the appearance of huge, grotesque locusts.

LODGE, LODGING

OT Words

lûn **[לוּן, 3885]**

lûn is a verb that means "lodge," or "spend the night," in about half of the ninety contexts or so in which it is found. ***lûn*** also means "to murmur." (➠ MURMUR)

The literal sense of "lodging" is found in Gen. 19:2; Num. 22:8; Josh. 3:1; Judg. 18:2; 19:4ff.; Ruth 1:16; 2 Sam. 17:8; 1 Kgs. 19:9; Neh. 4:22; Song 7:11; Isa. 21:13; Jer. 14:8.

lûn also expresses an impersonal sense of "to leave overnight," in several contexts. Lev. 19:6 indicates the requirement that any food left over from a fellowship offering must be burned up by the third day. Similarly, no sacrificial meat offered up on the first day of the Passover Feast is to be left overnight (cf. Deut. 16:4). Deut. 21:23 contains the statute that the body of an executed criminal must not be left on the site of execution overnight.

mālôn **[מָלוֹן, 4411]**

mālôn is a noun derived from ***lûn*** (see above) and means "lodging place," "inn." The term occurs nine times (cf. Gen. 42:27; 43:21; Exod. 4:24; Josh. 4:3, 8; 2 Kgs. 19:23; Isa. 10:29; Jer. 9:2).

melûnāh **[מְלוּנָה, 4412]**

melûnāh is a noun derived from ***mālôn*** (see above). It refers to a "hut" or "lodging place" in Isa. 1:8; 24:20.

NT Words

kataskēnoō **[κατασκηνόω, *2681*]**

kataskēnoō means "lodge" or "dwell." In three of the four contexts in which it is found, it refers to birds "making their nests" (i.e., "lodging") in trees (cf. Matt. 13:32; Mark 4:32; Luke 13:19). In Acts 2:26, ***kataskēnoō*** refers metaphorically to David "dwelling" in hope, in fellowship with God.

aulizomai **[αὐλίζομαι, *835*]**

aulizomai occurs only twice and indicates Jesus "lodging" or "spending the night" in Bethany (Matt. 21:17) and on the Mount of Olives (Luke 21:37).

xenizō [ξενίζω, *3579*]

xenizō is found in ten contexts, and in the majority of these it means "to lodge," and also "to offer hospitality."

References to "lodging" as a guest in someone's house are found in Acts 10:6, 18, 23, 32; 21:16; 28:7. Heb. 13:2 contains the instruction not to neglect offering hospitality to strangers.

xenia [ξενία, *3578*]

xenia is the noun derived from ***xenizō*** (see above). It occurs only in Acts 28:23; Phlm. 22, meaning "lodging" or "guest room."

xenodocheō [ξενοδοχέω, *3580*]

xenodocheō is a verb derived from ***xenizō*** (see above) and means "to entertain strangers as guests." It occurs only in 1 Tim. 5:10.

LONG, LENGTH, LENGTHEN

OT Words

'ārak [אָרַךְ, **748**]

'ārak is a verb meaning "to be long," "lengthen," "prolong," in a variety of contexts. The term occurs about thirty times.

'ārak indicates length of time in a number of ways. The meaning "to be long" is found firstly in the context of Yahweh's promise to grant his people a lengthy stay in the land of Canaan, providing they kept his law (cf. Exod. 20:12; Deut. 4:40; 5:16, 33; 6:2; 11:9; 17:20). Conversely, should the people prove disobedient, Yahweh threatens that their time there will prove very short (cf. Deut. 4:26; 30:18). See also Num. 9:19ff.; Prov. 28:2.

'ārak is also translated "to lengthen" in respect of time. 1 Kgs. 3:14 contains Yahweh's promise to lengthen the period of royal rule as a reward for obedience to him. In Isa. 53:10, God promises a long life for the Suffering Servant. See also Eccl. 7:15; 8:12. In contrast, Eccl. 8:13 warns of a shortened life in the event of lifelong wickedness.

'ārak also means "lengthen" in regard to physical dimensions, such as the furrows of a field (cf. Ps. 129:3). Metaphorically, Isa. 54:2 speaks of lengthening the cords to one's tent with reference to the future renewal and glory of Zion. In Ezek. 31:5, ***'ārak*** refers to the lengthening of tree branches in the sense of "growing long."

'ōrek [אֹרֶךְ, **753**]

'ōrek is the noun derived from ***'ārak*** (see above), with the consistent meaning "length," used predominantly in the sense of linear distance, and also with regard to length of time.

'ōrek refers to physical length in a number of places, including Noah's ark (cf. Gen. 6:15); the land of Canaan (cf. Gen. 13:17); the furniture of the tabernacle (cf. Exod. 25:10, 17; 25:23; 26:2ff.; 27:1ff.; 30:2; 36:9ff.; 37:1ff.; 38:1, 18); the breastpiece of the priests (cf. Exod. 39:9); Solomon's temple (cf. 1 Kgs. 6:2ff.; 7:2, 6, 27); and Ezekiel's visionary temple (cf. Ezek. 40:7ff.; 41:2ff.; 42:2ff.; 43:16, 17), including the sacred district belonging to the prince (cf. Ezek. 45:1ff.). See also Zech. 2:2.

'ōrek also expresses length of time. For example, long life is promised in the land in return for obedience to Yahweh (cf. Deut. 30:20). General references to long life are found in Job 12:12; Pss. 21:4; 91:16; Prov. 3:2, 16. In Ps. 23:6, ***'ōrek*** is translated "forever."

'ārōk [אָרֹךְ, **752**]

'ārōk is the adjectival form derived from ***'ārak*** (see above) and is translated "long," "longer." The term only occurs three times and refers to length of time in 2 Sam. 3:1; Jer. 29:8. Job 11:9 refers metaphorically to the limits of the Almighty, deemed to be "longer than the earth and broader than the sea."

NT Words

makros [μακρός, *3117*]

makros is an adjectival form that is translated "long," "far." The term occurs five times and means "long" in three of these places, all referring to the "long" self-righteous prayers of the Pharisees (cf. Matt. 23:14; Mark 12:40; Luke 20:47).

mēkos [μῆκος, *3372*]

mēkos is a noun that occurs only three times, meaning "length." Eph. 3:18 refers metaphorically to the immeasurable "length, breadth, and height" of the love of Christ. In Rev. 21:16, ***mēkos*** (twice) refers to the length of the heavenly city of Jerusalem.

LONG FOR → DESIRE

LONG-SUFFERING

OT Words

'erek [אֶרֶךְ, **750**]

'erek is an adjectival form derived from ***'ārak*** (→ LONG) meaning "long-suffering," indicating a slowness to anger, or patience. The term occurs around fifteen times with this meaning.

'erek is commonly predicated of Yahweh in reference to his patient toleration of his people's weaknesses, despite their provocation of him (cf. Exod. 34:6; Num. 14:18; Neh. 9:17; Pss. 86:15; 103:8; 145:8; Jer. 15:15; Joel 2:13). It is true with respect to other nations as well (cf. Jonah 4:2; Nah. 1:3, where the Assyrian nation is in view). However, the reference in Nah. 1:3 also indicates that Yahweh's "slowness to anger" does not mean that he will overlook sin and fail to ultimately judge the guilty.

'erek also refers to the virtue of "long-suffering," or patient endurance, on the part of human beings (cf. Prov. 14:29; 15:18; 16:32; Eccl. 7:8).

NT Words

makrothymia [μακροθυμία, *3115*]

makrothymia is a dynamic equivalent for the Hebrew term ***'erek*** (see above), and is likewise translated "patience," "long-suffering," with the same emphasis on patient endurance in the face of provocation.

The explicit patient forbearance of God is indicated in Rom. 2:4; 9:22; 1 Pet. 3:20; 3:15, in the face of human sinfulness. As with ***'erek*** in the Old Testament, there is no suggestion in the usage of ***makrothymia*** that God ever waives punishment for sin. Such forbearance is also predicated of Christ in 1 Tim. 1:16.

Elsewhere, ***makrothymia*** refers to the virtue of "long-suffering" or "patience" in God's people. ***makrothymia*** is included in a list of other such godly characteristics in 2 Cor. 6:6; Gal. 5:22; Eph. 4:2; Col. 1:11; 3:12. Paul declares that Timothy is aware of the apostle's patient perseverance in suffering in 2 Tim. 3:10, and he exhorts him to do likewise in 2 Tim. 4:2. See also Heb. 6:12.

makrothymeō [μακροθυμέω, *3114*]

makrothymeō is the verb form embodying the attitude to "be patient," "have patience," "be long-suffering." The term occurs nine times.

In one of Jesus' parables, the servant who would subsequently be condemned as ungrateful and wicked initially begs his master to be patient with him and allow him time to pay his massive debt (cf. Matt. 18:26). Another servant then approached this first servant and begged him to also be patient in allowing a much smaller debt to be repaid over time (cf. Matt. 18:29). Abraham is declared in Heb. 6:15 to have "patiently endured" and so obtained the promise of covenant blessing. Love is said "to be patient" in 1 Cor. 13:4. Exhortations to be "patient (in suffering)" are found in 1 Thess. 5:14; Jas. 5:7, 8.

makrothymeō also speaks of divine forbearance and long-suffering in Luke 18:7; 2 Pet. 3:9.

LOOK → SEE

LOOSE → RELEASE

LORD

NT Words

kyrios [κύριος, *2962*]

The term ***kyrios*** is found around seven hundred times in the New Testament and usually refers to Jesus Christ as God incarnate. The title "Lord," when applied to the Messiah, signifies his divine nature. As the New Testament Greek equivalent of the Hebrew term ***YHWH***, normally transliterated as Yahweh (→ GOD), it transfers to the person of Christ all those characteristics that the Hebrew title attributes to the person of God. In approximately five hundred places, ***kyrios*** refers to Jesus as "Lord," "the Lord Jesus," "the Lord Jesus Christ," or "Jesus Christ our Lord" (including slight variations in word order).

The term ***kyrios*** is also used in the expression "angel of the Lord" on twelve occasions (cf. Matt. 1:20, 24; 2:13, 19; 28:2; Luke 1:11; 2:9; Acts 5:19; 7:30; 8:26; 12:7, 23). Only in Matt. 1:24 is the definite article used to specify "*the* angel of the Lord" as the divine messenger to Joseph, instructing him to take Mary as his wife.

kyrios explicitly refers to God as "the Lord" in a number of places. Many of these are quotations from Old Testament sources — for example, Matt. 22:37 (Deut. 6:4ff.); Luke 3:4 (Isa. 40:1ff.); Luke 4:12 (Deut. 6:16); Acts 7:33 (Exod. 3:5); Rom. 10:16 (Isa. 53:1); Heb. 8:8 (Jer. 31:31); Heb. 10:30 (Ps. 135:14). God is described as "the Lord of heaven and earth" in Matt. 11:25. The Day of the Lord is indicated in Acts 2:20. Jas. 5:4 affirms that God is "Lord of hosts." He is declared the "Lord of the harvest" in Matt. 9:30; Luke 10:2. The title "Lord God" is frequently cited in the book of Revelation (cf. Rev. 4:8, 11; 11:17; 15:3ff.; 16:7; 18:8; 19:1, 6; 21:22; 22:6). Other general references to God as Lord are found in Mark 16:20; Luke 1:16; Acts 2:21; Rom. 4:8; Heb. 1:10.

At the human level, ***kyrios*** indicates an "overlord," or "master" (cf. Matt. 6:24; 18:34; Mark 13:35; Luke 12:36; Acts 16:16; Gal. 4:1; Col. 4:1; 1 Pet. 3:6).

despotēs [δεσπότης, *1203*]

despotēs is found on ten occasions and refers to a "lord," or "master," at both the human and divine level.

despotēs refers to God by the title "sovereign Lord," in the context of prayer offered to him (cf. Luke 2:29; Acts 4:24; Rev. 6:10).

Human overlords or masters are indicated in 1 Tim. 6:1, 2; 2 Tim. 2:21; 1 Pet. 2:18, and Paul exhorts those who are in service to pay due respect to their masters.

In 2 Pet. 2:1; Jude 4, ***despotēs*** refers to Jesus Christ as "Master," whom false teachers have denied.

See Also: → GOD

LOSE, LOSS

OT Words

'abēdāh **[אֲבֵדָה, 9]**

'abēdāh is a rare noun, occurring only four times and referring to "a lost thing," or "that which was lost," in the context of one's personal possessions (cf. Exod. 28:9; Lev. 6:3, 4; Deut. 22:3).

'ābad **[אָבַד, 6]**

'ābad is a verb that is commonly translated "perish," "destroy." It occurs about 160 times with those meanings. On ten occasions, however, ***'ābad*** means "lose," in both an active and passive sense.
(→ DESTROY)

1 Sam. 9:3, 20 refer to the lost donkeys of Kish, the father of Saul. Lost hope on the part of the people of Israel is indicated in Ezek. 19:5; 37:11. See also Eccl. 3:6.

Metaphorically speaking, ***'ābad*** refers to the people of Israel as "lost sheep" in several places (cf. Ps. 119:176; Jer. 50:6; Ezek. 34:4, 16).

shekôl **[שְׁכוֹל, 7908]**

shekôl is a rare noun, occurring only three times. On two of these occasions it refers to the "loss of children" (i.e., their death), as a judgment to be brought down on the king of Babylon (cf. Isa. 47:8, 9).

NT Words

apollymi [ἀπόλλυμι, *622*]

apollymi is found in nearly ninety contexts and is translated variously as "destroy," "perish" (→ DESTROY → PERISH), and associated meanings, including "lose," "be lost." These two latter meanings constitute about a quarter of the usage of ***apollymi***. ***apollymi*** has an adjectival, as well as a verbal, sense.

With reference to people, ***apollymi*** signifies "to lose" one's life in Luke 17:33; John 12:25, with the corollary that he will "find" it. Only a life characterized by self-denial and humility will lead to real life in the sight of God. See also Luke 9:25. In 2 John 8, the apostolic writer warns against loss of reward. In another context, Jesus affirms that those who demonstrate genuine love and compassion to the needy will not lose their reward (cf. Matt. 10:42; Mark 9:41).

There is also an adjectival sense evident in the usage of ***apollymi*** in a number of contexts. A lost sheep is indicated in Luke 15:4; and a lost coin in Luke 15:8. See also John 6:12. In the story of the prodigal son, the wayward youth is described as one who was "lost" and then found again (cf. Luke 15:24). With the exception of John 6:12, the preceding references all refer to the joy of rediscovery following a period in which an object, animal, or person was deemed to be lost. Matt. 10:6; 15:24 refer to the "lost sheep of Israel," the object of Jesus' mission and concern. More seriously, 2 Cor. 4:3 declares that the gospel is hidden to those who are "lost," who are therefore liable to destruction.

apollymi also means "lose" in relation to the ministry of Christ. John 6:39; 18:9 record that Jesus should lose nothing of what the Father had given him. The one exception to this was Judas Iscariot, who betrayed Jesus (cf. John 17:12). The mystery of divine providence is evident here — Judas was accountable for his action, even though he was "destined to be lost."

zēmioō [ζημιόω, *2210*]

zēmioō means "to lose," "suffer loss," and is found in six contexts. Matt. 16:26; Mark 8:36; Luke 9:25 refer to Jesus' question, "What will it profit a man if he gains the whole world, but loses his own life?" Paul refers to the judgment of Christ on those who will "suffer loss" for their service, but who themselves will be saved (cf. 1 Cor. 3:15). In Phil. 3:8, Paul declares that he gladly "suffered the loss" of all that he had in order to gain Christ. See also 2 Cor. 7:9.

zēmia [ζημία, *2209*]

zēmia is the noun derived from ***zēmioō*** (see above) and is translated "loss," or "damage." It is found in four places. Acts 27:10, 21 refer to "damage" to a ship. In Phil. 3:7, 8, Paul affirms that everything associated with his former life as a Pharisee was "loss," or utterly worthless, compared with the joy of knowing Christ.

apobolē [ἀποβολή, *580*]

apobolē is a rare noun, found only in two places. Acts 27:22 indicates that there will be no "loss" of life on the ship containing Paul and his companions on the way to Rome. Rom. 11:15 refers to God "casting off" or "rejecting" the Jewish people for their denial of Christ.

LOT

OT Words

gôrāl [גּוֹרָל, **1486**]

gôrāl is consistently translated "lot(s)." The term refers to those implements (probably flat stones) used for determining God's will on a "yes/no" basis, a judicial discrimination, and other matters requiring selection (e.g., land inheritance, priestly duties, etc.). ***gôrāl*** occurs around eighty times in a number of different contexts.

In a ritual context, lots are cast for the selection of the sacrificial goat, as well as for the "scapegoat," for the Day of Atonement ceremony in Lev. 16:8ff. In contrast, lots are also cast in an occult, pagan ceremony in Esth. 3:7; 9:24 to determine the day of assault upon the Jews in the Persian Empire (a plot instigated by Haman the Agagite that failed in a spectacular manner). See also Obad. 11. 1 Chr. 25:8; Neh. 10:34 refer to casting lots for priestly duties.

In the context of property acquisition, lots are cast for the division of the land of Canaan, with Joshua allocating set portions of the land to the various Israelite tribes (cf. Num. 26:55, 56; 33:54; 36:2; Josh. 14:2; 15:1; 16:1; 17:1; 18:6ff.; 19:1, 10ff.; 21:4ff.; Judg. 1:3). In a similar manner, the Levitical cities were so determined (cf. 1 Chr. 6:54ff.; 24:5ff.). See also Neh. 11:1. Lots were also used as selection criteria for the makeup of the Israelite army (Judg. 20:9). In Ps. 22:18, the psalmist records that lots were cast for his clothes, after a period of terrible persecution. Such an event anticipates the experience of Christ himself (cf. Matt. 27:35).

There is one metaphorical use of ***gôrāl*** in Jer. 13:25, where Yahweh declares that the scattering of his people into exile is their "lot," one decreed for them because they have rejected him.

Other general references to the "lot" are found in Ps. 16:5; Prov. 1:14; 16:33; Isa. 17:14; 34:17; Dan. 12:13.

NT Words

klēros [κλῆρος, *2819*]

klēros is a noun referring to objects that were used in casting or drawing lots — either a stone of some sort, or a small piece of wood. ***klēros*** is translated "lot," "allotment," "inheritance." Thus the term connotes both the means of casting lots and the process of allotment itself. ***klēros*** is used both literally and metaphorically and is found twelve times with these meanings.

Reference to the physical casting of lots is found in Matt. 27:35; Luke 23:34; John 19:24, in regard to Jesus' clothing at the time of his crucifixion.

klēros also refers to an "(allotted) place, or share" in ministry, as in the case of Judas Iscariot, who is mentioned in Acts 1:17 as having had a legitimate place in the apostolic band of Jesus' disciples. In the aftermath of Judas' betrayal of Jesus and the subsequent death, burial, resurrection, and ascension of Christ, Acts 1:25, 26 refers to the one who would take "the (allotted) place" of Judas in that continuing ministry. It was Matthias, who was subsequently chosen "by lot" to assume that position. Acts 8:21 cites the case of one, Simon the sorcerer, who was refused a "share" or "place" in the apostolic ministry because of his greed.

Acts 26:18 records the words of the risen Christ who spoke to Saul during his conversion experience on the road to Damascus, promising the Gentiles a "share" or "lot" in the spiritual inheritance of God's people. Similarly, Col. 1:12 refers to the spiritual "inheritance" of the saints of God.

lanchanō [λαγχάνω, *2975*]

lanchanō is a verb meaning "to be chosen by lot," "obtain by lot," "to cast lots." It occurs only four times. Luke 1:9 refers to Zechariah, the father of John the Baptist, being "chosen by lot" to burn incense in the temple. John 19:24 describes the Roman soldiers casting lots for the clothing of Christ at his crucifixion, as the fulfillment of the prophecy recorded in Ps. 22:18. Acts 1:17 refers to Judas Iscariot as "having been allotted" a place in the apostolic band of Christ. 2 Pet. 1:1 uses the term ***lanchanō*** to indicate those who have "received" a faith as precious as the apostle's. The underlying thought is of granting a spiritual allotment, or a share in the blessing of eternal life and peace with God.

LOUD → SHOUT

LOVE

OT Words

'āhab [אָהַב, **157**]

'āhab is a common verb that is translated "to love" in the majority of the approximately two hundred contexts in which it is found. The objects of love are varied, including love of family, friends, strangers, and the physical necessities of life such as food and drink. The term also indicates sexual love. ***'āhab*** refers to love for God and his people, his law and other godly characteristics, as well as ungodly vices. The action and attitude of love is also predicated of God, who is said to love his people and all who express their dependence on him, as well as the virtues of justice and righteousness.

In the human sphere, ***'āhab*** indicates love for one's family in several places. ***'āhab*** expresses love for a son (Gen. 22:2; 37:3; Prov. 13:24); love for one's wife (Gen. 24:67; 29:30; Deut. 21:15; 1 Sam. 1:5; Eccl. 9:9); and affection for the family in particular (Exod. 21:5).

One aspect of the usage of ***'āhab*** is concerned with the expression of love in the context of sexual attraction. General references to this are found in Gen. 34:3; 2 Sam. 13:1; Song 1:3ff.; 3:1ff. ***'āhab*** also refers to the celebrated love of Samson for Delilah (Judg. 16:4).

Expressions of love for a number of virtues are associated with the use of ***'āhab*** — for example, truth (cf. Zech. 8:19); discipline and knowledge (cf. Prov. 12:1); wisdom (cf. Prov. 29:3); righteousness (cf. Prov. 15:9); and other virtues in general (cf. Prov. 22:11). In contrast, ***'āhab*** also refers to an attraction for evil and vice. Mic. 3:2 refers to such an attitude in general. ***'āhab*** refers to love of transgression and strife (Prov. 17:19); love of false prophecy (Jer. 5:31); and the attraction for idolatry (Isa. 1:23; Hos. 12:7). In particular, the love of idolatry is universally condemned in the Old Testament (cf. Jer. 2:5; 8:2; Ezek. 16:33; 23:5ff.; Hos. 2:5ff.; 9:1), especially where the people of God are concerned.

Love for God is another significant aspect of the meaning of ***'āhab.*** The great commandment, whereby love for Yahweh is commanded as the expression of an all-consuming devotion from his people, is mentioned in Deut. 6:5; 10:12; 11:1; 13:3; 30:6; Josh. 22:5. Similar expressions of love from the people of God are indicated in Exod. 20:6; Deut. 5:10; 7:9; Neh. 1:5; Dan. 9:4. Showing love for God's law is commended, for example, in Ps. 119:47ff., 113, 127, 132, 140, 159ff. Expressing joy at the salvation wrought by God is noted in Pss. 40:16; 70:4. The love of God's name is noted in Ps. 69:36; Isa. 56:6. An exhortation to love God is also found in Ps. 31:23.

Other objects of human love are illustrated in the command to love one's neighbor in Lev. 19:18, as well as the command to show love for the alien and the stranger in Lev. 19:34. The love of one's friends and colleagues is indicated in 1 Sam. 16:21; 18:1; 1 Kgs. 5:1; Job 19:19; Prov. 17:17; as well as the love for one's ruler, or king in 1 Sam. 18:28. A mundane reference to love of food is found in Gen. 27:4, 14.

The most significant context in which Yahweh is said to love is in the expression of God's love for his people. Affirmation of divine love, rooted in the historical actions of God's redemptive purposes, is recorded in Deut. 4:37; 10:15; Ps. 78:68; Jer. 31:3; Hos. 11:1; Mal. 1:2. Then there is the present declaration of God's love, and his promise of continuing devotion towards the people of Israel (cf. Deut. 7:13; Ps. 97:10; Prov. 3:12; Isa. 43:4; Hos. 14:4). On occasions, God's love for individuals is explicitly declared, as is his love for Solomon in 2 Sam. 12:24.

Yahweh's loving concern for the stranger is also expressed (Deut. 10:18); as is his love of virtues such as justice (Pss. 37:28; 99:4; Isa. 61:8) and righteousness (Ps. 45:7).

In a metaphorical personification of divine virtue, "wisdom," depicted as a noble lady, is said to love those who love her (Prov. 8:17, 21).

'ahabāh [אַהֲבָה, 160]

'ahabāh is the noun derived from ***'āhab*** (see above), and expresses the action and attitude of "love" in all of the forty contexts in which it occurs. ***'ahabāh*** conveys the sense of human love between men and women. It is also a general designation for affection in less intimate relationships. The term also expresses God's love for his people.

The expression of human love is indicated in various contexts. At the most intimate level, sexual desire is evident in a man's love for his wife (cf. Gen. 29:20; Prov. 5:19). Sensual attraction to women in general is indicated in 2 Sam. 1:26; and illicit lust is found in Amnon's obsession with his half-sister Tamar (2 Sam. 13:15). The love between a man and a woman is celebrated in the Song of Songs (cf. Song 2:4ff.; 3:5; 8:4ff.). At a lesser level of intimacy, ***'ahabāh*** signifies a man's love for his friend, as demonstrated in the friendship of David and Jonathan. Mic. 6:8 contains the command to love mercy and kindness.

Love as a general attribute is indicated in Prov. 10:12; 15:17; Eccl. 9:1. Israel's love for God is explicitly declared in Jer. 2:2.

'ahabāh refers also to God's love for his people (cf. Deut. 7:8; 1 Kgs. 10:9; 2 Chr. 2:11; 9:8; Isa. 63:9; Jer. 31:3; Hos. 3:1; Zeph. 3:17). Conversely, in Hos. 9:15 the prophet declares that God's love has been withdrawn from Israel because of their sin.

ḥābab **[חָבַב, 2245]**

ḥābab is a verb that occurs only in Deut. 33:3, referring to Yahweh's fervent love for his people.

ra'yāh **[רַעְיָה, 7474]**

ra'yāh is found in ten contexts, and in nine of these in the Song of Songs it constitutes a term of endearment, "my love," spoken by the lover to his beloved female companion and subsequently his wife (cf. Song 1:9, 15; 2:2, 10, 13; 4:1, 7; 5:2; 6:4).

NT WORDS

agapaō [ἀγαπάω, *25*]

agapaō occurs around 140 times and is consistently translated "to love," in a variety of contexts. Such an action and attitude is predicated of human beings, God, and Christ. Human love, as indicated by ***agapaō*** in positive contexts, is a noble affection. It is characterized by a concern, not for oneself, but for others. Yet on other occasions it refers to the love of that which is evil and unprofitable. When God and Christ are said to love, ***agapaō*** conveys the idea of a deep, limitless compassion that is given through the supreme self-sacrificial actions of Christ on the cross in association with the mercy and kindness of God.

Where ***agapaō*** refers to the love of human beings, several contexts indicate the mandatory nature of its expression. For example, there is the command to love one's neighbor (Matt. 5:43ff.; 19:19; 22:39; Mark 12:31ff.; Luke 6:27; Rom. 13:9; Gal. 5:14); and the command to love one another (John 13:34; 15:12, 17; 1 Thess. 4:9; 1 John 3:23; 2 John 5). Affirmations of love for each other are found in Rom. 13:8; 1 Pet. 1:22; 1 John 2:10; 3:18. See also Luke 7:42. The command to love God with all one's heart is recorded in Matt. 22:37; Mark 12:30; Luke 10:27. Declaration of love for Christ is indicated in Eph. 6:24. God is the object of human love in Rom. 8:28; 1 Cor. 2:9; Jas. 1:12; and God's love for us is the ground of our love for others (cf. 1 John 4:19). See also 1 John 5:2.

Other references to ***agapaō*** in the human sphere include that in John 3:19, where unbelievers are declared to love darkness rather than light. Similarly, John 12:43 refers to those who love the praise of human beings rather than God. The illegitimate love of money is noted in 2 Pet. 2:15. Paul affirms a love for his congregation in 2 Cor. 12:15 and mentions the importance of a man's love for his wife in Eph. 5:28; Col. 3:19.

Love displayed by Christ is noted in a number of different contexts. There is, for example, his deeply compassionate regard for individuals such as the rich young ruler (cf. Mark 10:21); Martha (cf. John 11:5); and his disciples (cf. John 13:23; 21:7). Jesus' love for his own people is expressed in John 13:1; 14:21, 23; 15:9; Gal. 2:20; Eph. 5:25; Rev. 1:5; 3:9. In particular, Eph. 5:2 emphasizes the self-sacrificial nature of that love. Love for his Father is noted in John 14:31; 15:9. Jesus' question of Peter, "Do you love me?" is found in John 21:15, 16. Heb. 1:9 indicates Christ's love of righteousness.

With respect to God, ***agapaō*** refers to his love for the world (John 3:16); for his Son (John 3:35; 10:7; 17:24); and for his people in particular (John 17:24; Rom. 8:37; Eph. 2:4; 2 Thess. 2:16; Heb. 12:6; 1 John 4:10). See also Rom. 9:13, where God's love for Jacob is expressed as a predestined choice, at the expense of Esau his brother, who is described (with a sense of hyperbole) as one "hated" by God.

agapē [ἀγάπη, *26*]

agapē is the noun derived from ***agapaō*** (see above) and also means "love," with the same emphases and nuances as the verb. ***agapē*** occurs around 120 times.

As a human attitude and emotion, ***agapē*** indicates "love" in a generalized sense in Matt. 24:12; Rom. 12:9; 13:10; 1 Cor. 8:1. In Gal. 5:22, "love" is listed first among the fruit of the Spirit. The underlying essence of ***agapē*** as a supremely self-sacrificing love is indicated in 1 Cor. 13:4, 8, 13; 1 John 4:10, 18; 2 John 6 (cf. also 2 Cor. 6:6; 8:7ff.). One of the great illustrations of ***agapē*** love is giving up one's life for a friend (John 15:13). See also 1 John 3:16; 1 Cor. 14:1. Paul expresses his love for his Corinthian congregation in 1 Cor. 16:24; 2 Cor. 2:4. The reality of the love of Christ controlling our lives is indicated in 2 Cor. 5:14. Mutual love for one another is noted in John 13:35. In a negative context, Luke 11:42 records Christ's censure of the Pharisees for their neglect of the love and justice of God. Similarly, 1 John 2:15; 3:17 declare that those who love the world cannot love God.

In relation to the believer, ***agapē*** refers to love given by God and shaped by the Spirit of Christ as the guiding principle of Christian living. It is a common theme, expressed both in the Pauline correspondence and other general epistles (e.g., Eph. 1:15; Phil. 1:9; Col. 1:4; 1 Tim. 1:5; Heb. 6:10; 1 Pet. 4:8; 1 John 2:5). In Rev. 2:4, the Ephesian church is rebuked for having abandoned her first love (i.e., love for Christ).

When predicated of Christ, ***agapē*** indicates his love as impregnable and unassailable (cf. Rom. 8:35, 39); and surpassing knowledge (cf. Eph. 3:19). John 15:9, 10 contain the command to abide in the love of Christ.

In regard to love as a quality of the divine being, ***agapē*** is found in a number of places. John 15:10 affirms Christ abiding in God's love. Paul declares in Rom. 5:5 that God's love is poured out into our hearts. That love makes us alive with Christ (cf. Eph. 2:4; 3:17; 1 John 4:9) and makes us his children (cf. 1 John 3:1). See also Gal. 5:6. The unique quality of divine love is strikingly illustrated in Rom. 5:8, which states that Christ died for us while we were still sinners. God is described as "love" in 1 John 4:8, 16, and he is given the title "God of love" in 2 Cor. 13:11. The benediction, ". . . love of God," is found in 2 Cor. 13:14; 2 Thess. 3:5; 2 John 3; Jude 2.

phileō [φιλέω, *5368*]

phileō is a verb synonymous with ***agapaō*** (see above), which is also translated "to love," but not usually with that same sublime quality of unselfishness as indicated by ***agapaō***, except perhaps when predicated of God. ***phileō*** indicates the action of "loving" as a strong desire to act, or to express affection to another person.

In regard to human beings, ***phileō*** often indicates the meaning "love" in the sense of "like to do." Such is the case with the Pharisees, who are described in Matt. 6:5 as "loving" to show their piety in public. They also "love" to have the place of honor in public and private gatherings (cf. Matt. 23:6), and they generally have a great fondness for recognition (cf. Luke 20:46).

In terms of "love" as affection, ***phileō*** is found in John 15:19; Titus 3:15. Love for one's family is indicated in Matt. 10:37. The paradoxical statement "he who loves his life will lose it . . ." is found in John 12:25. Peter expresses his love for Christ in John 21:15, 16, 17, using the verb ***phileō***, not ***agapaō***. In John 21:17, when Jesus asks Peter for the third time if he loves him, he uses ***phileō*** rather than ***agapaō***, as he did on the first two occasions.

phileō expresses divine love in John 5:20, where God is said to love the Son, and in John 16:27, which indicates God's love for his people.

With regard to love expressed by Jesus, ***phileō*** indicates the great affection he has for individuals — for example, Lazarus (cf. John 11:3, 36), and John (cf. John 20:2). Rev. 3:19 affirms that Jesus loves his people, but that he will also chasten them.

philadelphia [φιλαδελφία, *5360*]; ***philadelphos*** [φιλάδελφος, *5361*]

philadelphia occurs six times and means "brotherly love," "love of the brethren" (cf. Rom. 12:10; 1 Thess. 4:9; Heb. 13:1; 1 Pet. 1:22; 2 Pet. 1:7). The variant form ***philadelphos*** occurs in 1 Pet. 3:8 with the same meaning.

See Also: → BELOVED → MERCY

LOVER

NT Words

philautos [φίλαυτος, *5367*]; ***philēdonos*** [φιλήδονος, *5369*]; ***philotheos*** [φιλόθεος, *5377*]; ***philoxenos*** [φιλόξενος, *5382*]; ***philagathos*** [φιλάγαθος, *5358*]

These New Testament terms, each of which occurs only once or a few times, all refer to people as "lover(s) of . . ." In each case, the reference is to those people who are passionately devoted to the object of their affection.

philautos refers to "lovers of self," ***philēdonos*** to "lovers of pleasure," ***philotheos*** to "lovers of God," ***philoxenos*** to "lover of hospitality," "given to hospitality," and ***philagathos*** to "lovers of good men."

LOW, BRING LOW, HUMILIATE

OT Words

shāphēl [שָׁפֵל, **8213**]

shāphēl is a verb that occurs around thirty times with the primary meaning "to be, bring low," with the underlying sense of "humiliate." In most of these contexts, it is God who is the subject of the verb.

Yahweh's action in bringing low or humiliating is indicated in a general sense in 1 Sam. 2:7. More commonly, Yahweh is said to bring down low those who are proud (cf. 2 Sam. 22:28, 29; Job 40:11; Pss. 18:27; 75:7; Isa. 2:11ff.; 10:33; 13:11; 25:12; Ezek. 21:26). In Isa. 26:5; 32:19, it is the proud city that is brought low by God. Ezek. 17:24 refers to bringing down the lofty tree, a symbol of human pride. Ps. 147:6 declares that it is Yahweh who brings down the wicked. In Isa. 40:4, the prophet proclaims that every hill will be "brought low," — a symbolic reference to the removal of all obstacles to the victory march of Yahweh as conquering king.

dālal [דָּלַל, **1809**]

dālal is a verb meaning "bring low" in the sense of "cause great anguish or distress," both emotional and physical. ***dālal*** is translated this way in five of the nine contexts in which it is found, all in the passive voice.

Israel is said to be brought low by the Midianite oppression in Judg. 6:6, resulting in great anguish. The psalmist pleads for God's compassion on behalf of his people in Ps. 79:8 so as to combat their state of distress, for they had been "brought low." See also Ps. 142:6. Ps. 116:6 praises God for saving the psalmist when he was "brought low." In the context of divine judgment, Isa. 17:4 declares that "the glory of Jacob will be brought low."

shēphel [שֵׁפֶל, 8216]

shēphel occurs twice, referring to a position of "lowliness" or "low estate." The psalmist is grateful for God's love in Ps. 136:23, for it is he who remembers his people in their "low estate." Eccl. 10:6 notes the humiliation of the rich who sit in a "low place," while those who are foolish enjoy a great reputation.

See Also: → HUMBLE

LOWLINESS → HUMBLE

LOYAL, LOYALTY → MERCY

LUKEWARM

NT Words

chliaros [χλιαρός, *5513*]

chliaros occurs only in Rev. 3:16, referring to the "lukewarm" spirit of devotion to Christ in the Laodicean church. For such an attitude, they will have to endure being "vomited out" of God's mouth if there is no change in their condition.

LUST

OT Words

'āwāh [אָוָה, 183]

'āwāh is a verb that expresses the underlying idea of strong desire, and is translated "lust," "desire," "covet," "long for." ***'āwāh*** occurs around twenty times.

With human desire in view, ***'āwāh*** refers to a strong craving for meat, food, and drink, which may be appropriate or inappropriate. Legitimate appetite for such things is indicated in Deut. 12:20; 14:26; 1 Sam. 2:16; 2 Sam. 23:15; 1 Chr. 11:17. Conversely, a sinful desire for such things arises from a spirit of ingratitude towards God. Such was the case with the Israelites in the wilderness (cf. Ps. 106:14; Num. 11:4, 34). Illegitimate, or evil, desire is spoken of in a general sense in Prov. 13:4; 21:10, 26. "Lusting after" or "coveting" someone else's wife is prohibited in the tenth commandment, recorded in Deut. 5:21.

In other contexts ***'āwāh*** is translated "desire" in the sense of expressing a longing, such as a yearning to rule over all that one desires (cf. 2 Sam. 3:21; 1 Kgs. 11:37). See also Eccl. 6:2. Ps. 45:11 records the king yearning for his bride. Isa. 26:9 indicates the prophet's longing for his God.

In two places, ***'āwāh*** refers to Yahweh's intense desire. Job 23:13 affirms that God gets what he wants. Ps. 132:13, 14 record Yahweh's desire to obtain Zion as his dwelling place.

'awwāh [אַוָּה, 185]

'awwāh is a noun derived from ***'āwāh*** (see above) and is found in seven places meaning "lust," "desire." In all but one of these contexts, the desire is wholesome and positive.

Deut. 12:15, 20, 21 refer to Israel's desire, or craving, for meat, which God indicates they may indulge within their own towns or territory. Deut. 18:6 refers to the legitimate desire of a Levite to come to the divinely designated sanctuary whenever he wishes. 1 Sam. 23:20 records the incident where King Saul is invited by the Ziphites to come "whenever he likes" to have David surrendered to him. Hos. 10:10 speaks of Yahweh's desire to come against his people to punish them for their rebellion against him.

The sole negative use of ***'awwāh*** occurs in Jer. 2:24, where the people of Israel are condemned by Yahweh for lusting after idols.

ta'awāh [תַּאֲוָה, 8378]

ta'awāh is another noun derived from ***'āwāh*** (see above), again with the principal meanings "desire," "lust." The term occurs twenty times.

In negative contexts, ***ta'awāh*** refers to the desires of the wicked in Pss. 10:3; 112:10, and to the "fatal desire" of the sluggard in Prov. 21:25. Eve's unlawful longing for the forbidden fruit is indicated in Gen. 3:6. Israel's gluttonous craving for meat in the wilderness brings the judgment of Yahweh down on them (cf. Num. 11:4; Pss. 78:9, 30; 106:14).

Desire is also expressed in positive contexts. Prov. 10:24; 11:23; 13:19; Isa. 26:19 affirm that the desire of the righteous will be granted. Ps. 10:17 declares that the legitimate desire of the afflicted for justice will be heard by God. Yahweh grants the king the desire of his heart (cf. Ps. 21:2). Ps. 38:9 expresses a yearning for comfort from God.

NT Words

epithymeō [ἐπιθυμέω, *1937*]

epithymeō occurs around twenty times and is translated variously as "desire," "long for," "covet," as well as "lust." **epithymeō** refers to desires that are both legitimate and illegitimate.

With reference to human craving, **epithymeō** indicates lusting as perverted sexual desire. In Matt. 5:28, Jesus equates lusting after a woman as equivalent to adultery. 1 Cor. 10:6; Jas. 4:2 express warnings against illegitimate craving. In Gal. 5:17, the "lusting" of the sinful nature is opposed to the Spirit of God.

Elsewhere, **epithymeō** has the sense of "long for." Matt. 13:17; 1 Pet. 1:12 refer to the Old Testament prophets' yearning for revelation from God. Longing for the coming of the days of the Son of Man is expressed in Luke 17:22. A legitimate aspiring to the office of elder is noted in 1 Tim. 3:1. The translation "covet" is found in Acts 20:33, and Rom. 7:7; 13:9 record commands against this attitude. General craving for food is indicated in Luke 15:16; 16:21.

epithymeō is used once with respect to Jesus (Luke 22:15), who expresses a desire to celebrate the Passover with his disciples.

epithymia [ἐπιθυμία, *1939*]

epithymia is the noun derived from **epithymeō** (see above), and is likewise translated "desire," "craving," "lust," "longing." The term occurs around forty times.

When referring to the desires of human beings, **epithymia** occurs almost entirely in negative contexts. Generalized cravings that choke out, or prevent, fruitful spiritual life and service are mentioned in Mark 4:19; 1 Tim. 6:9; 2 Tim. 2:22; Jas. 1:5; Jude 16, 18. The desires of the wicked are condemned in John 8:44; Rom. 1:24; 6:12; and the vice of coveting is noted in Rom. 7:7, 8; Col. 3:5. The "lusts" of the sinful nature are listed in Rom. 13:14; Gal. 5:16, 24; Eph. 2:3; 4:22; 1 Thess. 4:5; Titus 2:12; 1 Pet. 2:11; 4:3; 2 Pet. 2:10, 18; 1 John 2:16. The noble desire to be with Christ is indicated in Phil. 1:23.

orexis [ὄρεξις, *3715*]

orexis is found only in Rom. 1:17, where it refers to the perverted "lusting" or "passion" of men for each other.

pathos [πάθος, *3806*]

pathos is a participial form of **paschō** (→ SUFFER) occurring in only three places and meaning "impure passions," or "lust," with reference to sexual desire (cf. Rom. 1:26; Col. 3:5; 1 Thess. 4:5).

hēdonē [ἡδονή, *2237*]

hēdonē is a noun denoting "(illicit) passion" in a general sense, in five contexts (cf. Luke 8:14; Titus 3:3; Jas. 4:1, 3; 1 Pet. 2:13).

epipotheō [ἐπιποθέω, *1971*]

epipotheō is a verb that expresses the basic meaning "yearn," "(earnestly) desire," in positive contexts. **epipotheō** occurs nine times.

Paul's longing to make contact with his congregation is expressed in Rom. 1:11; Phil. 1:8; 1 Thess. 3:6; 2 Tim. 1:4. See also Phil. 2:26; 2 Cor. 9:14. The believer's intense desire to enter the realm of heaven after a life of suffering is indicated in 2 Cor. 5:2. Peter exhorts his readers to long for "pure spiritual milk" in 1 Pet. 2:2. Finally, Jas. 4:5 refers to the "jealous yearning" of God for the spiritual welfare of his people.

See Also: → PLEASE

LUTE, LYRE

OT Words

kinnôr [כִּנּוֹר, **3658**]

kinnôr refers to a stringed instrument that may be identified either as a "lyre" or "harp." The term occurs around forty times (e.g., Gen. 4:21; 1 Sam. 10:5; 16:16, 23; 1 Kgs. 10:12; Job 21:12; Pss. 33:2; 71:22; 108:2; Isa. 23:16). In particular, this instrument is associated with Levitical musicians in the context of ritual worship (cf. 1 Chr. 25:1ff.; 2 Chr. 5:12; 29:25).

qîtārōs [קִיתָרֹס, **7030** (Aramaic)]

qîtārōs is an Aramaic term that indicates a musical instrument — probably a "lyre," or "harp" (cf. Dan. 3:5, 7, 10, 15).

nēbel [נֵבֶל, **5035**]

nēbel is another term referring to a stringed instrument, indicating a "harp," "lyre," or the antiquated English word "psaltery." With this meaning, **nēbel** occurs around twenty-five times. **nēbel** also refers to a vessel made of animal hide, usually translated "[wine]skin" or "pitcher." (→ JAR)

General references to this instrument are found in 1 Sam. 10:5; 2 Sam. 16:1; 1 Kgs. 10:12; Pss. 33:2; 71:22; 144:9; 150:3; Isa. 5:12. Like ***kinnôr***, above, ***nēbel*** is also found in the context of ritual worship (cf. 1 Chr. 15:16ff.; 16:5; 25:1, 6; 2 Chr. 5:12; 20:28; 29:25).

pesantērîn [פְּסַנְתֵּרִין, **6460** (Aramaic)]

pesantērîn is another Aramaic term referring to the stringed instrument the "psaltery." The word occurs only four times (cf. Dan. 3:5, 7, 10, 15).

NT Words

kithara [κιθάρα, *2788*]

kithara is found in only four places, referring to a harp on each occasion. 1 Cor. 14:7 indicates the harp in a literal sense. The book of Revelation refers to harps in three places, accompanying the singing of the saints in heaven, praising God (cf. Rev. 5:8; 14:2; 15:2).

M

MAD, MADNESS

OT Words

shāga' **[שָׁגַע, 7696]**

shāga' is a verb occurring seven times meaning "to be mad," as well as the nominal sense of "madman."

Deut. 28:34 refers to the people of Israel being driven mad as a consequence of their disobedience towards Yahweh, an element of the covenant curse sanctions (cf. also Hos. 9:7). David's feigned insanity in 1 Sam. 21:14, 15 earns him the reputation of a madman from Achish, King of the Philistines. The prophet Elisha is referred to as a madman in 2 Kgs. 9:11. Jer. 28:26 mentions madmen who prophecy illegitimately.

shiggā'ôn **[שִׁגָּעוֹן, 7697]**

shiggā'ôn is a rare noun derived from ***shāga'*** (see above) with the sense of "madness." Deut. 28:28 refers to madness as an aspect of the covenant curse, to be brought down upon the Israelites for their rejection of Yahweh. The same punishment will be enacted against the wicked by Yahweh on the great day of judgment, as indicated in Zech. 12:4. In 2 Kgs. 9:20, the term is used metaphorically to indicate Jehu's chariot driving as "madness"(i.e., "furious").

hôlēlāh **[הוֹלֵלָה, 1947]**

hôlēlāh is a term for "madness" that is found only four times, all in the book of Ecclesiastes. This "madness" is contrasted with wisdom as an inevitable element of human existence (cf. Eccl. 1:17; 2:12; 7:25; 9:3).

hālal **[הָלַל, 1984]**

hālal is a verb that is commonly translated "praise," "shine (of divine glory)," "boast," and occurs 165 times. However, on several occasions, the term also means "to act like a madman," or "behave as a fool."

Such an action is predicated of David in 1 Sam. 21:13. Laughter is equated with madness in Eccl. 2:2. In Eccl. 7:7, oppression is said to render the wise man "foolish," or "mad." Isa. 44:25 affirms that Yahweh "makes fools" of diviners. Jer. 25:16; 51:7 declare that the nations will be driven insane by God on account of their wickedness. Then, in Jer. 50:38, judgment is pronounced against Babylon because of her "madness" over her idols.

lāhah **[לָהַהּ, 3856]**

lāhah is a rare verb, found only twice. In Prov. 26:18, the participial form is translated nominally as "madman," or one "who shoots flaming arrows" at his neighbor by deceiving him, and then says he is only joking.

NT Words

mainomai **[μαίνομαι, *3105*]**

This verb occurs in five contexts and means "to be mad, rave like a madman." Jesus is accused of such in John 10:20, as is the servant girl, Rhoda, in Acts 12:15 when she initially reported Peter's miraculous escape from prison. Paul is likewise accused of speaking like a madman in his defense before the governor Festus. See also 1 Cor. 14:23.

mania **[μανία, *3130*]**

mania is the noun derived from ***mainomai*** (see above) and is found only in Acts 26:24, where Festus asserts that Paul's great learning has led him into "madness."

anoia **[ἄνοια, *454*]**

anoia occurs only twice and conveys the sense of "folly" or "madness" in both contexts. In Luke 6:11, the term refers to the anger of the Pharisees directed towards Jesus after he had got the better of them in a confrontation, healing a crippled man on the Sabbath. ***anoia*** thus has the connotation of a "mad" rage or fury here. 2 Tim. 3:9 refers to the "folly" of false teachers, similarly suggesting a "madness of folly."

paraphronia **[παραφρονία, *3913*]**

paraphronia is found only in 2 Pet. 2:16, referring to the "madness" of the prophet Balaam who was restrained by the rebuke of the donkey, supernaturally effected by the hand of Yahweh. The "madness" of the prophet refers to Balaam's insatiable greed.

MAGIC, MAGICIAN

OT Words

ḥartōm **[חַרְטֹם, 2748]**

ḥartōm is a noun referring to a "magician," "diviner," or "astrologer" imbued with occult powers. ***ḥartōm*** occurs eleven times, primarily with reference to the magicians of the Egyptian court of Pharaoh at the time of Joseph and the Exodus (cf. Gen. 41:8, 24; Exod. 7:11, 22; 8:7, 18, 19; 9:11). Dan. 1:20; 2:2 refer to the magicians in the court of Nebuchadnezzar, the king of Babylon.

kāshaph **[כַּשָּׁף, 3784]**

kāshaph refers to "sorcerers," or those who practice witchcraft and sorcery. The term occurs six times.

Egyptian and Babylonian sorcerers are indicated in Exod. 7:11; Dan. 2:2. The practice of sorcery is forbidden to any Israelite in Deut. 18:10. It is said to have been practiced by the Judean king, Manasseh, in 2 Chr. 33:6. Divine judgment against "sorcerers" is alluded to in Mal. 3:5.

kashāph **[כַּשָּׁף, 3786]**

kashāph is a variant form of ***kāshaph***, above, and only occurs in Jer. 27:9 with reference to "sorcerers" and other occult practitioners in the court of the corrupt Judean monarchy on the eve of the Babylonian invasion of the kingdom.

qāsam **[קָסַם, 7080]**

qāsam is a verb indicating the practice of magic or divination, occurring around twenty times.

Such a practice is forbidden to all Israelites in Deut. 18:10, 14; violators are condemned and subject to severe punishment in Isa. 3:2; 44:25; Ezek. 13:9. ***qāsam*** refers to the Israelite practice of divination (1 Sam. 28:8; 2 Kgs. 17:17; 21:21ff.; Jer. 27:9; 29:8; 22:28; Mic. 3:6ff.; Zech. 10:2); and to the custom of pagan nations (cf. Josh. 13:22; [Balaam]; 1 Sam. 6:2 [Philistia]).

In Ezek. 13:23 Yahweh promises to deliver his people from such occult activity.

'ānan **[עָנַן, 6049]**

'ānan is a verb that means "practice magic, divination" in most of the eleven contexts in which it is found.

Lev. 19:26; Deut. 18:10, 14 specifically prohibit the practice. 2 Kgs. 21:6; 2 Chr. 33:6 record that it was practiced in Israel; and God condemns and acts in judgment against it in Isa. 2:6; 57:3; Jer. 27:9; Mic. 5:12.

NT Words

magos [μάγος, *3097*]

magos is found in six contexts meaning "wise man," or "sorcerer," indicating a scholarly class highly trained in astrology and other occult arts. In Matt. 2:1, 7, 16, ***magos*** refers to the wise men who followed the star in the east leading to the birthplace of the infant Jesus in Bethlehem. Acts 13:6, 8 refer to the Jewish sorcerer, or magician, on the island of Cyprus.

pharmakos [φαρμακός, *5333*]

pharmakos occurs only in Rev. 22:15, where it refers to sorcerers among a whole group of the wicked who are cast outside the heavenly kingdom.

manteuomai [μαντεύομαι, *3132*]

manteuomai is found only in Acts 16:16, where the term (in its participial form) refers to the slave girl possessed by an evil spirit that gave her powers of "fortune telling," or "soothsaying."

mageuō [μαγεύω, *3096*]

mageuō occurs only in Acts 8:9, where it refers to the occult skills of Simon, who "practiced magic arts."

MAGISTRATE

NT Words

archōn [ἄρχων, *758*]

archōn is a noun occurring around twenty times with the principal meaning "ruler" or "commander." It is a general term for a civil, spiritual leader. However, on one occasion, the term refers to a civil magistrate (cf. Luke 12:58).

See Also: → RULE

MAGNIFY

NT Words

megalynō [μεγαλύνω, *3170*]

megalynō is a verb occurring eight times meaning "magnify," "enlarge."

Matt. 23:5 refers to priests "enlarging" their phylacteries. There are a number of references to the Lord being praised or "magnified" (cf. Luke 1:46; Acts 10:46; 19:17; Phil. 1:20). ***megalynō*** also refers to faith "increasing" in the life of believers in 2 Cor. 10:15. Acts 5:13 refers to the apostles being "held in high honor."

In the one context where God is the subject of ***megalynō***, Luke 1:58 declares that God "had shown great mercy" to Elizabeth, the mother of John the Baptist. The noun "mercy" is unqualified, thus the sense of ***megalynō*** here is "to manifest, or show greatness."

See Also: → GLORIFY → GREAT

MAID, MAIDEN

OT Words

shiphḥāh [שִׁפְחָה, 8198]

shiphḥāh occurs around sixty times with the primary sense of "maid," with various associated nuances.

The meaning "maid" in the sense of a female household servant is indicated, for example, in Gen. 12:16; 16:1ff.; 30:4ff.; 33:1ff.; Exod. 11:5; 1 Sam. 1:18; 2 Sam. 14:6ff.; 2 Kgs. 4:2; Ps. 123:2; Eccl. 2:7; Isa. 14:2; Joel 2:29.

In a number of contexts, ***shiphḥāh*** also refers to female slaves, often translated "bond maidens" (cf. Lev. 19:20; Deut. 28:68; 2 Chr. 28:10; Esth. 7:4; Jer. 34:9ff.).

'āmāh [אָמָה, 519]

'āmāh is a synonym for ***shiphḥāh*** (see above), also occurring around sixty times with the similar root meaning "maid" or "maidservant."

'āmāh indicates female household servants in Gen. 20:17; 21:10ff.; Exod. 2:5; 23:12; Deut. 5:14; 12:12; Ruth 3:9; 1 Sam. 1:11; 25:24ff.; 2 Sam. 6:20, 22; 1 Kgs. 1:13, 17; Neh. 7:6, 7; Job 31:13; Ps. 86:16; Nah. 2:7.

The meaning "slave woman" is found in Gen. 21:12, 13; Exod. 21:7, 20, 26ff.; Lev. 25:44; Deut. 15:17.

na'arāh [נַעֲרָה, 5291]

na'arāh occurs around sixty times meaning "maiden" or "young girl" in several different contexts.

The majority usage of ***na'arāh*** conveys the sense of "maiden," "young girl" in general non-specific contexts (cf. Gen. 24:14ff., 55ff.; Deut. 22:15ff.; Judg. 19:3ff.; 1 Sam. 9:11; Job 41:5).

More specifically, ***na'arāh*** refers to a "young girl" in 1 Kgs. 1:2ff., a companion for King David in his old age. Esth. 2:2ff. refers to a "young girl" as a member of the royal harem of Xerxes, the Persian king. In Amos 2:7, ***na'arāh*** indicates a "young girl" as a prostitute.

Elsewhere, ***na'arāh*** refers to young girls as "maidservants," or female domestic slaves (cf. Exod. 2:5; Ruth 2:5ff.; 3:2; 1 Sam. 25:42; 2 Kgs. 5:24; Esth. 4:4; Prov. 9:3; 27:27; 31:15).

'almāh [עַלְמָה, 5959]

'almāh is a noun found in seven contexts meaning "virgins," referring to young women of marriageable age who are chaste, or to a "young woman" or "young girl" in general contexts.

The meaning "virgin" is most likely indicated in Gen. 24:43; Ps. 68:25 — a probable reference to temple virgins who dedicated themselves to lifelong celibacy in the service of Yahweh. See also Song 6:8.

Exod. 2:8 refers generally to "young girl(s)" in relation to Moses' sister Miriam, although she is not named here. See also Prov. 30:19; Song 1:3.

There is an intriguing reference in Isa. 7:14 to a "young woman" or "virgin." The precise meaning ***'almāh*** here depends largely on the identification of the young woman in this Isaianic prophecy. Traditional understanding of the verse as a messianic prophecy designating Mary as the mother of the Christ child gave prominence to the translation "virgin." Notwithstanding the validity of this prophetic perspective, when one seeks to understand the identity of the ***'almāh*** in relation to the eighth-century B.C. setting of the passage, the matter is not quite so straightforward. Isa. 7:3 makes clear that Isaiah has a son named Shear-Jashub, but the mother is not named. Who, then, is the woman referred to in 7:14 ? If she is Shear-Jashub's mother, then ***'almāh*** here cannot mean "virgin." On the assumption that the child born to the prophetess in Isa. 8:3, named Maher-Shalal-Hash-Baz, is a fulfillment of 7:14, two likely possibilities emerge. Either the mother of Shear-Jashub and Maher-Shalal is the same woman, or Isaiah's first wife has died, and the prophetess (cf. 8:3) is his new wife. Only if the second possibility holds true, can the translation "virgin" be maintained as likely. Since neither of these two hypotheses can be proved, it would seem best to translate ***'almāh*** as "young woman," allowing the inherent ambiguity of the term to stand.

This in no way detracts from the traditional understanding of this verse as a messianic prophecy that ultimately points forward to the miraculous conception given to Mary the mother of Christ. At the same time there is the need to affirm the partial fulfillment of the prophecy during the time of King Ahaz, signified by the birth of Maher-Shalal-Hash-Baz. Translating ***'almāh*** as "young woman" serves both levels of fulfillment in this context.

NT Words

korasion [κοράσιον, *2877*]

korasion is found in eight places and consistently refers to "girl" or "maiden" in generalized contexts. Matt. 9:24, 25; Mark 5:41, 42 refer to Jairus' daughter, whom Jesus brought back to life, as a "young girl." Similarly, ***korasion*** refers to the daughter of Herodias as a "young girl" (Matt. 14:11; Mark, 6:22, 28).

paidiskē [παιδίσκη, *3814*]

paidiskē occurs twelve times and refers consistently to female domestic servants as "maids" in Matt. 26:69; Mark 14:66ff.; Luke 12:45; 22:56; John 18:17; Acts 12:13.

Elsewhere, ***paidiskē*** means "slave girl" in both a literal sense (e.g., Acts 16:3), and also metaphorically (Gal. 4:22, 23, 30, 31). In Galatians, Paul alludes to Ishmael, the son of Hagar, a female slave belonging to Sarah the wife of Abraham. Paul is speaking symbolically of Ishmael's descendants as those Jews who were still under bondage to the Mosaic law, or "children of the slave woman"; and also to believing Jews and Gentiles, or Christian believers, as "children of the free woman," or spiritual descendants of Isaac, the child of promise.

See Also: → VIRGIN

MAIMED

NT Words

anapēros [ἀνάπηρος, *376*]

anapēros is found only twice, referring both times to those who are "maimed," whom Jesus healed of their physical disabilities (cf. Luke 14:13, 21).

kyllos [κυλλός, *2948*]

kyllos occurs four times and is synonymous with ***anapēros*** (see above). It likewise refers to those who are "maimed," referring to severe physical disability (cf. Matt. 15:30, 31; Matt. 18:8; Mark 9:43).

See Also: → LAME

MAJESTY

OT Words

hôd [הוֹד, **1935**]

hôd occurs around twenty times and is consistently translated "glory," "honor" with the sense of "majesty" apparent in many of these contexts. (→ GLORY)

gedûllāh [גְּדוּלָּה, **1420**]

gedûllāh is found in twelve contexts and is variously translated "greatness," "great honor," "dignity," or "great things." The majority of cases indicate the greatness of God. But ***gedûllāh*** also refers to the greatness of human beings — for example in Esth. 1:4, where the term indicates the "majesty" of King Xerxes of Persia.

gē'ût [גֵּאוּת, **1348**]

gē'ût is a noun derived from the verb ***gā'āh*** (→ RISE) meaning "to rise up," "be exalted." On two occasions, ***gē'ût*** refers to the "majesty" of God, indicating his position of glorious exaltation (cf. Ps. 93:1; Isa. 26:10).

rebû [רְבוּ, **7238** (Aramaic)]

rebû is an Aramaic term found only five times, in the book of Daniel. It refers to the "greatness" or "majesty" of King Nebuchadnezzar (Dan. 4:22, 36; 5:18, 19); and once to the greatness of all human kingdoms that will be handed over to the saints of Yahweh (cf. Dan. 7:27).

NT Words

megaleiotēs [μεγαλειότης, *3168*]

megaleiotēs occurs only three times, with the underlying sense of "greatness." In Luke 9:43, Jesus' healing of the demon-possessed boy gave rise to the people's reaction of astonishment at the "majestic power" of God. A similar comment is made by Peter in his second letter, where he refers to the disciples as eyewitnesses of the "majesty" of Jesus Christ during his lifetime. In a quite different context, Acts 19:27, ***megaleiotēs*** refers to the "majesty" or "greatness" of the Ephesian goddess, Artemis.

megalōsynē [μεγαλωσύνη, *3172*]

megalōsynē is a noun that explicitly refers to the divine "majesty." It occurs in three places only. In Heb. 1:3; 8:1, the term is used as a title for God, the "Majesty on high," or "in heaven." In Jude 25 it is used as an ascription of praise to God: ". . . to the only God . . . be glory, majesty . . ."

See Also: → GLORIFY → PRIDE

MAKE

OT Words

'āsāh [עָשָׂה, **6213**]

'āsāh is a common verb, occurring over 2,500 times with the basic sense of "do," "make" in a large variety of contexts. (→ CREATE → PRACTICE → PREPARATION)

'āsāh is predicated of God in a large variety of contexts. By far the most predominant usage of this term relates to the creative activity of Yahweh in the context of "making" the heavens and the earth, and all aspects of the cosmos (cf. Gen. 1:7, 16; 2:2ff.; Exod. 20:5; Pss.

33:6; 104:24; 124:8; Prov. 20:12; Eccl. 3:11; Isa. 37:16; Jer. 16:12; Amos 4:13; Jonah 1:9). This includes, of course, "making" humankind (cf. Gen. 1:26; 2:18; 5:1; Pss. 119:73; 139:15). In the context of the divine promise to renew the cosmos, ultimately ridding it of all imperfections, Isa. 66:22 contains the guarantee that Yahweh "will make the new heavens and the earth." ***'āsāh*** refers to Yahweh "making a feast" in Isa. 25:6, symbolizing the ultimate celebration of his people on the consummation of the Day of the Lord, when he will renew the heavens and the earth.

'āsāh also refers to God "making a people for himself," a promise that expresses the miracle of divine election and redemption in relation to the nation of Israel (cf. 1 Sam. 12:22; Isa. 43:7; 44:2; 46:4). Gen. 12:2 refers to Yahweh "making a great nation" (i.e., Israel) in the light of the covenant promise to Abraham. See also Num. 14:12; Deut. 9:14; Ps. 86:9. Another related motif is found in 2 Sam. 7:11, where Yahweh promises to "make David a great house," referring to an unbroken line of descendants culminating in the Messiah. In another metaphorical context, Yahweh promises in Ezek. 37:19, 22 to "make one stick (out of two)" in reference to reuniting the people of Israel.

'āsāh also refers to divine activity in Isa. 45:7, where Yahweh is said to "make peace." Isa. 63:12, 14 refer to Yahweh "making a name for himself."

With reference to human activity, ***'āsāh*** occurs in a large number of contexts. It refers to the manufacture of various items such as coverings for Adam and Eve (Gen. 3:7); flint knives (Josh. 5:2); weapons (1 Sam. 8:12); clothes (Prov. 31:22, 24); books (Eccl. 12:12); and jewelry (Song 1:11). The preparation of food in relation to "making a feast" is indicated in Gen. 21:8; 27:9; Judg. 14:10; Esth. 1:3. ***'āsāh*** also refers to "making war" (Deut. 20:20; Josh. 11:18), and "making peace" (Josh. 9:15). In Num. 21:8, God commands Moses to make a bronze serpent to bring healing to the Israelites who were savaged by a plague judgment from Yahweh.

'āsāh is also used in connection with Israelite worship. It refers to making an altar for the worship of Yahweh (Gen. 35:1; Exod. 20:24; 30:1; Deut. 16:21); a sanctuary (Exod. 25:8ff.; 36:8ff.); sacred furniture (cf. Deut. 10:1ff.; Jer. 51:20; Ezek. 40:17ff.; 41:18ff.); incense (Exod. 30:37); and instruments for worship (Num. 10:2). ***'āsāh*** refers to the preparation of offerings for worship in Ezek. 43:27.

Specific commands not to make (construct) idols are found in Exod. 20:23; Lev. 26:1; Deut. 5:8; and a curse sanction for those who do so is laid down in Deut. 28:15. Frequent references to Israel violating this instruction are indicated, for example, in Exod. 32:8; Deut. 9:16, 21; Ps. 106:19 (with reference to the golden calf incident at Sinai). See also Deut. 4:25; 8:12; Judg. 17:3ff.; Isa. 2:8; 31:7; 44:15ff.; Jer. 2:28; Ezek. 7:20; 16:31; Hos. 8:4; 13:2.

sûm [שׂוּם, 7760]

sûm occurs about six hundred times with the primary meanings "put," "set," "make." The latter meaning is found around 120 times.

As with the verb ***'āsāh*** (see above), ***sûm*** refers to the "making" activity of both God and human beings.

When predicated of God, ***sûm*** refers to him "making" in a variety of contexts with the general sense of "bringing about a particular effect." For example, in a context of judgment, Yahweh makes the land of Babylon the refuge of owls (Isa. 14:23); the city of Jerusalem a object of scorn (Jer. 19:8); and threatens to make Israel like a wilderness (Hos. 2:3). See also Isa. 42:15; Jer. 25:9; 29:22; Lam. 3:45; Amos 8:10; Nah. 1:14; Zech. 12:2. In the context of God's creative activity, Job 38:19 refers to Yahweh "making clouds" as the garment for the sea. In Pss. 44:13; 80:6 the psalmist laments the fact that Yahweh has made him an object of scorn to his neighbors. Ps. 147:14 affirms God as one who makes peace. In the context of divine renewal, where Yahweh is depicted as one who effects a total transformation of the earth, Isa. 43:19 contains God's promise "to make a way in the wilderness." Isa. 51:3 declares that Yahweh will make Zion's wilderness like the garden of Eden. See also Isa. 41:18; 49:11; 60:15; Hag. 2:23. In a slightly different context, Exod. 14:21 refers to Yahweh's majestic power in dividing the Re(e)d Sea to allow the people of Israel to pass across. The writer declares: "He made the sea dry land" (cf. also Isa. 51:10).

sûm is also translated "make" with the sense of "place (or put) someone in a position of authority." For example, Gen. 45:9 refers to God making Joseph the lord of Egypt. See also Deut. 1:13; Ps. 18:43; 105:21; 1 Kgs. 10:9.

In a few places, ***sûm*** is translated "make" in the sense of "fashion," or "create." In Gen. 13:16, for example, God promises to make the children of Abraham like the dust of the earth. See also Gen. 32:12; Deut. 10:22 for a similar wording of that promise. Gen. 21:13; 46:3 refer to the divine promise to "make a nation," with Israel in view.

In 2 Sam. 7:23 God is said "to make a name for himself"; and in 2 Sam. 23:5 David affirms that God has made an everlasting covenant.

With reference to human action, ***sûm*** is likewise translated "make" in a variety of contexts. Gen. 47:26; 1 Sam. 30:25 refer to making laws. Judg. 8:33 mentions making idols.

sûm is also found in contexts where human beings take responsibility for placing others in positions of leadership and authority. For example, in Gen. 27:37, Isaac declares to Esau that he has made Jacob lord over him; and in Judg. 11:11, the people of Gilead made Jephthah leader, or ruler, over them. See also Gen. 47:6; 1 Sam. 8:1, 5; 18:13; 2 Sam. 17:25.

sûm is also translated "make" in a number of contexts, with the underlying sense of "bringing about" a certain effect. For example, Ps. 52:7 refers to the plight of the man who refused to make God his refuge. Isa. 14:17 refers to the Babylonian king who "made the world like a desert"; and Isa. 28:15 refers to the one who makes lies his refuge. See also 1 Kgs. 19:2; Ps. 91:9; Jer. 2:7; 4:7; 10:22.

NT Words

poieō [ποιέω, *4160*]

poieō occurs around six hundred times with the primary meanings "do," "make" in a variety of contexts. It is a close dynamic equivalent of ***'āsāh*** and ***sûm*** (see above).

When predicated of people, ***poieō*** refers to the action of "making" in a number of ways. With the sense of "build," "fashion," or "construct," ***poieō*** is found, for example, in Matt. 17:4; Luke 9:33, where Peter offers to make shelters for the heavenly figures that appeared on the Mount of Transfiguration. ***poieō*** also refers to making clothes (Acts 9:39); and building a fire (John 18:18). The fashioning of idols is referred to in Acts 7:43; 19:24; Rev. 13:14; and reference to the construction of the tabernacle is found in Acts 7:44; Heb. 8:5. Food preparation is alluded to in Luke 5:29; 14:13.

Elsewhere, ***poieō*** means "make" with the underlying sense of "bringing about" a particular effect, or change, in the state of a person or object. For instance, Jesus declares to his disciples in Matt. 4:19; Mark 1:7 that he will make them "fishers of men." In Matt. 12:33 he also refers to making the fruit tree good or bad. In Matt. 21:13; Luke 19:46; Mark 11:17; John 2:16, Jesus accuses a crowd of Jewish business people of making the temple a "den of thieves." Luke 6:9 refers to making friends, and Matt. 23:15 to making a proselyte. In relation to miraculous healing, Acts 3:12 records the incident in which Peter and John make the lame man walk. There is an exhortation to "make straight the paths" of the coming Messianic King in Matt. 3:3; Mark 1:3; Luke 3:4 (cf. Isa. 40:3). In Rom. 13:14, Paul exhorts his readers to make no concession to one's sinful nature.

Other general references to the action of "making" are found in Matt. 5:36; Mark 3:12; 6:21; Rom. 15:26; Jas. 3:18; 1 Tim. 2:1.

In relation to God "making," ***poieō*** is likewise found in numerous contexts. Matt. 19:4; Mark 10:6 speak of God making (i.e., creating) humankind in the divine image, as male and female.

Related to this theme is the reference to God making all things new, in Rev. 21:5, and the creation of the new heavens and the new earth in Acts 4:24; 17:24; Heb. 1:2; Rev. 14:7. Heb. 8:9 refers to God making a covenant with Israel. Rev. 1:6; 5:10 mention God fashioning his chosen people into an eternal kingdom. In regard to his son, God declares (through Peter) that he has made Jesus Lord (cf. Acts 2:36). In 2 Cor. 5:21, God is said to have made him who knew no sin to be sin on our behalf; and in Acts 2:36, Peter affirms that God has made Jesus Lord.

poieō is also predicated of Christ. In a number of places, Jesus is said to have made the deaf hear (cf. Mark 7:37); made water into wine (cf. John 4:46); made the blind see (cf. Mark 8:25); and made a man whole (cf. John 5:11, 15; 7:23).

In relation to other aspects of his ministry, Christ is described as the one who makes Jew and Gentile one, in a bond of peace (cf. Eph. 2:14, 15). Those Jews who opposed him at every stage of his career accused Jesus of "making himself equal with God," and thus wrongly charged him with blasphemy (cf. John 5:18; 10:33; 19:7). Ironically, in reality, Jesus' own signs manifested his true divine nature — but unbelieving Jews would not, or could not, see it. See also John 2:15; 4:1; 9:6.

In addition, the satanic beast of Revelation is said to make war on the saints of God in Rev. 11:7; 12:17; 19:19. In Rev. 13:13, he makes fire come down from heaven.

See Also: → COVENANT → FREE → GIVE → HASTE → INTERCESSION → PAY → SET

MAKER → CREATE

MALE

OT Words

zākār [זָכָר, 2145]

zākār is a noun occurring about eighty times, meaning "male." It applies to both men and animals.

In relation to human beings, ***zākār*** refers to the male of the human species as created by God (cf. Gen. 1:27; 5:2); to male children (Gen. 17:10ff.; Lev. 6:18; 12:2; Num. 31:17; Isa. 66:7); and priests (Lev. 6:29; 7:6; 2 Chr. 31:19). General references to males are found in Gen. 34:15; Exod. 12:48; Lev. 15:33; Num. 1:2; Deut. 4:16; Josh. 5:4; Judg. 21:11; 1 Kgs. 11:15. And, in Ezra 8:3ff., there are numerous references to the male leaders of Israelite families returning to the homeland from captivity.

Concerning animals, ***zākār*** refers to the male creatures that constituted half of the animal population in Noah's ark (cf. Gen. 6:19; 7:3, 9, 16). Year-old male animals suitable for sacrifice are mentioned in Exod. 13:15; Lev. 1:3; 3:1; Deut. 15:19. General references to male animals are found in Exod. 13:12; Mal. 1:14.

'îsh [אִישׁ, 376]

While ***'îsh*** almost always means "man" (→ MAN), on two occasions it is translated "male." Gen. 7:2 refers to the seven pairs of clean animals (i.e., male and female) that were taken on board the ark at the time of the flood, and also to the male and female pairs of all other (i.e., unclean) creatures (for the purposes of procreation after the flood had passed).

zākûr [זָכוּר, 2138]

zākûr is actually a passive participial form of the verb ***zākar*** ("to remember"). However, it is used as a synonym for ***zākār*** (see above) and is translated "male" (i.e., men), on four occasions. In three places (cf. Exod. 23:17; 34:23; Deut. 16:16), ***zākûr*** is found in the context of Yahweh's command that all Israelite males present themselves before him three times a year in Jerusalem at the three major ritual festivals of Passover; Tabernacles (or Ingathering); and Harvest (or Weeks). In Deut. 20:13, Yahweh issues the command to put to the sword all men (i.e., males) who live in the Canaanite cities he hands over to his people for destruction.

NT Words

arsēn [ἄρσην, *730*]

arsēn is an adjectival term, occurring nine times and meaning "male" on each occasion. It is used predominantly, however, as a noun.

Matt. 19:4; Mark 10:6 refer to God fashioning the human species as male and female from the beginning of creation. Luke 2:23 refers to firstborn male children as holy to the Lord.

Rom. 1:27 (twice) alludes to males (i.e., men) committing shameless acts with one another that bring down the wrath of God upon them. Gal. 3:28 declares that no distinction in status is made between male and female, since all believers are one in Christ. Rev. 12:5, 13 refer to the male child borne by the woman who is pursued in vain by the dragon who seeks to destroy the child. The context clearly suggests that the male child is the infant Christ child; the woman is his mother Mary; and the dragon is Satan himself.

MALICE, MALICIOUS → EVIL → WICKED

MAN

OT Words

'ādām [אָדָם, 120]

'ādām occurs around 550 times with three primary meanings "man," "humankind," "human being." The latter sense is most commonly associated with this term in the Old Testament.

With reference to "humankind," ***'ādām*** is used as a general designation for the unique last-fashioned creature of God, made in the divine image (cf. Gen. 1:26ff.; 5:2; 9:6; Zech. 12:1). Other uses of ***'ādām*** in this sense, without explicit reference to the image of God, occur in Job 34:15; Ps. 8:4; Prov. 3:4; Isa. 45:12. References to "men" as a general designation of male humanity are indicated in Gen. 6:1ff.; Num. 16:29; Deut. 4:28; 32:8; Job 7:20; Ps. 12:1; Prov. 8:4. ***'ādām*** commonly indicates "man" as a human being, in the sense of "humankind" (cf. Exod. 4:11; Lev. 7:21; Num. 3:13; Deut. 8:3 ["man does not live by bread alone"]; Eccl. 12:13 [". . . the whole duty of man (viz. fearing god)"]; Isa. 2:9; Ezek. 10:8).

'ādām also has the sense of "man" as an individual, a particular human being in a specific context. For example, the prophet Ezekiel is frequently referred to as a "son of man," a phrase which implies that Yahweh has called this ordinary human being to an extraordinary function. It is a title that is taken up by Jesus Christ in the New Testament gospel narratives (cf. Ezek. 2:1ff.; 11:2; 16:2; 17:2; 21:19; 25:2; 37:2ff.). See also Dan. 8:17. ***'ādām*** also refers to individual Israelite males (Lev. 1:2; 13:2; Num. 5:6; 16:32); and to undesignated male individuals (Pss. 58:11; 94:10; Eccl. 9:3; Isa. 44:13; Jer. 33:5; Ezek. 36:12). Jonah 4:11 refers to male citizens of Nineveh.

'ādām is also used in a nondescript way to refer to "persons," and it is often translated in this sense as "anyone," "someone," or "no one" (cf. Judg. 18:28; Neh.

2:10; Jer. 2:6; Eccl. 1:3; 2:12, 18ff.; 3:21; 6:10ff.). In the book of Ecclesiastes, ***'ādām*** means "man" with the proverbial notion of "everyman."

The use of ***'ādām*** as a personal name is indicated clearly and explicitly in Gen. 4:1; and in one case it means "hypocrite" or "godless man" (Job 34:30).

'îsh [אִישׁ, 376]

'îsh is broadly synonymous with ***'ādām*** (see above) and occurs about 1,500 times. However, ***'îsh*** also means "man" as "male" (in contrast to "female"), as well as "husband," "human being," and "man," indicating humankind in general.

With the sense of "man" as "male," ***'îsh*** is found in Gen. 2:23, 24; Num. 5:16; Esth. 4:11; Hos. 3:3. The term is translated literally as "husband" in Gen. 3:6, 16; 16:3; Lev. 19:20; Num. 5:12; Ruth 2:11. Hos. 2:2, 7 also refer metaphorically to Yahweh as husband to Israel.

'îsh is commonly translated "man" in the sense of "individual" or "person(s)" (cf. Gen. 4:1; 6:9; Exod. 2:1; 1 Sam. 17:10; 1 Kgs. 12:22; Job 1:8; Ps. 5:6; Isa. 53:3 ["man of sorrows"]). Zech. 6:12 refers to the "man whose name is the branch" — a messianic prophecy.

'îsh also means "one," "someone," "anyone" to refer to undesignated individuals (cf. Gen. 11:3; Exod. 35:23; Lev. 7:8; Num. 19:18; Josh. 1:5; Neh. 3:28; Isa. 3:5; Jer. 7:5; Ezek. 1:11).

'îsh means "humankind" in Deut. 1:17; Job 12:10, and "man" as "human being" in Exod. 19:13; Eccl. 4:4; 6:2; 7:5.

'enôsh [אֱנוֹשׁ, 582]

'enôsh is also synonymous with ***'îsh*** and ***'ādām*** (see above), meaning "man" as an individual person, "men" as a general collective term, and also "humankind." ***'enôsh*** occurs approximately fifty times.

Meaning "man" as an individual human being, ***'enôsh*** occurs in Job 9:2; 32:8; Ps. 9:20; Isa. 56:2. The sense of "mankind" is indicated in Deut. 32:26; 2 Chr. 14:11; Job 7:17; 33:12; Pss. 8:5; 103:15; Isa. 33:8. Man as "mortal man" is the sense of the term in Job 4:17. General references to "people" are found in Pss. 56:2; 66:12; Isa. 13:12; 24:6.

The personal name of Enosh is found in Gen. 5:6ff.; 1 Chr. 1:1.

NT Words

anthrōpos [ἄνθρωπος, *444*]

anthrōpos is the most common term for "man" in the New Testament and has a broad spectrum of senses alongside the primary meaning "man." ***anthrōpos*** occurs about five hundred times.

The meaning "man" or "men" in the sense of "humankind" is indicated in Matt. 4:4; Mark 2:27; Luke 2:14, 52; John 1:4; 5:41; Acts 4:12; 17:26; Gal. 1:11; 1 Thess. 2:15; 2 Pet. 1:21. Specifically, ***anthrōpos*** refers to the "wickedness of men" (Rom. 1:18); to "the wisdom of man" (1 Cor. 2:5); and to the destruction of "one third of humankind" (Rev. 9:15).

The title "Son of man" is a title adopted by Christ, borrowed from the designation given to the prophet Ezekiel (and also occasionally to Daniel), signifying our Lord's genuine incarnation and identification with humankind. This usage accounts for approximately one-fifth of the total occurrences of ***anthrōpos*** (cf. Matt. 8:20; 9:6; 24:27; Mark 2:10; 13:34; Luke 5:24; John 1:51; 5:27; Rev. 1:13; 14:14 [implied]).

"Men," in the general sense of "people," is the meaning indicated, for example, in Matt. 4:19; 6:1; Mark 1:13; Luke 5:10; 6:22; John 4:28; Acts 4:13; Rom. 12:18; 1 Cor. 4:9; 2 Cor. 5:11; Heb. 9:27.

In a number of contexts, ***anthrōpos*** is translated "men" with the underlying sense of ordinary human beings, or those who are mortal (cf. Acts 14:15; Rom. 2:9; Gal. 1:1; Heb. 1:1; 7:8). Phil. 2:7 describes Jesus as one made "in the likeness of men," emphasizing the genuineness of his humanity. Col. 2:8 refers to "human traditions" (i.e., the traditions of men). Rev. 13:18 refers to the number 666 as "man's number."

anthrōpos also means "one," "someone" with the underlying sense of "man," or "person" — an unspecified individual, not necessarily or exclusively male (cf. Matt. 7:9; Mark 7:11; Luke 15:4; John 1:9; John 3:27; Acts 4:17; Rom. 10:5; 2 Cor. 3:2; Gal. 3:12; 1 Tim. 6:16; Jas. 1:19). Note, in particular, Paul's exhortation in 1 Cor. 11:28, "let a man examine himself" prior to taking part in the Lord's Supper. John 3:4 also illustrates this usage with regard to Nicodemus' question of Jesus: "How can a man be born again?" In Rom. 3:28, Paul teaches that "one is justified by faith."

The translation "man," "men" may also refer to specific individuals in various contexts. For example, the Roman centurion declares to Jesus in Matt. 8:9; Luke 7:8 that he is "a man under authority." At Jesus' trial the Roman procurator, Pontius Pilate, parades him before the crowd and declares: "Behold the man!" Rom. 5:12 draws a contrast between Adam and Christ by affirming that just as sin entered the world through "one man" (i.e., Adam), so also did righteousness emerge through the ministry of "one man" (i.e., Jesus Christ). A similar truth is expressed in Rom. 2:15; 1 Cor. 15:21,

45. "The man of lawlessness," the final incarnation of a satanic personage prior to the return of Christ, is referred to in 2 Thess. 2:3. See also Mark 1:23; 5:2; John 1:6; Acts 4:9; 2 Tim. 3:17.

In the Pauline correspondence, ***anthrōpos*** also refers variously to "man" in the sense of the innermost self, or the old self (e.g., Rom. 6:6; 7:22; Eph. 3:16). The "old man," or the old, corrupt sinful nature prior to conversion, is mentioned in 2 Cor. 4:16; Eph. 4:22; Col. 3:9. Such a nature is cast off when the "new nature" replaces it. This "new man" is fashioned in believers by the ministry of the Holy Spirit (cf. Eph. 2:15; 4:24).

anēr [ἀνήρ, *435*]

anēr means "man" in the sense of "male" in various contexts, and it is also commonly translated "husband." ***anēr*** occurs around two hundred times.

References to a "husband" in narrative contexts are found in the Gospels and Acts (cf. Matt. 1:16; Mark 10:2; Luke 1:34; John 4:16ff.; Acts 5:9, 10). Instruction regarding the appropriate godly conduct of a husband towards his wife is indicated in Rom. 7:2, 3; 1 Cor. 7:2ff.; 11:3; 14:35; Eph. 5:22ff.; Col. 3:18, 19; 1 Pet. 3:1, 5, 7). See also 1 Tim. 3:2; 5:9; Titus 1:6; 2:5. In 2 Cor. 11:2; Eph. 5:22ff.; Rev. 21:2, ***anēr*** is used metaphorically in relation to Christ's role as the "husband" of his "bride," the church.

anēr also refers to "man" in the general sense of "person," as in Matt. 7:24, 26, which refers to the wise and foolish man in Christ's parable. No specific individual is in view. Likewise, in Rom. 4:8, Paul affirms the blessed state of the man whose sin will not be counted against him.

The meaning "man," "men," in the sense of "male individual(s)" or "group of men" is found in Matt. 12:41; Mark 6:20, 44; Luke 1:27; 8:41; Acts 1:10ff.; 8:2, 12; Rom. 11:4; 1 Cor. 11:3ff.; 13:11; 1 Tim. 2:8; Jas. 1:8.

anēr also means "man" in the sense of "mankind," as in relating to the human species, or "humankind" (cf. John 1:13). In addition, this term conveys the concept of "manhood," the quality of being a man (cf. Eph. 4:3).

See Also: → CHILD → YOUNG

MANGER

NT Words

phatnē [φάτνη, *5336*]

phatnē occurs four times and means "manger" or "stall" in each case. Luke 2:7, 12, 16 all refer to the "manger" as the place where the infant Jesus was laid after his birth. ***phatnē*** refers literally to a feeding trough for animal use, which is the meaning indicated in Luke 13:15.

MANNA

OT Words

mān [מָן, **4478**]

mān is the term that is used to describe the bread-like or wafer-like substance that Yahweh provided for the Israelites during their forty-years in the wilderness. It was a miraculous provision of food that is translated "manna" in English. The expression "manna" approximates the Hebrew for "What is it?" — which expresses the Israelites' initial inability to comprehend the nature of this strange food. It is described as tasting like coriander seed mixed with honey.

mān occurs seventeen times (cf. Exod. 16:15, 31ff.; Num. 11:6ff.; Deut. 8:3, 16; Josh. 5:12; Neh. 9:20; Ps. 78:24).

Manna in the Old Testament prefigured "the bread of life" in the New Testament — a phenomenon embodied in the person and work of Jesus Christ. It refers to the eternally satisfying and enriching effects of his life and teaching upon those who embrace him in faith and repentance. (→ BREAD)

MANNER → WAY

MANSLAYER → SLAUGHTER

MANTLE → CLOTHING → ROBE

MANY → MUCH

MARANATHA

NT Words

maranatha [μαρανάθα, *3134*]

maranatha is an expression that occurs only in 1 Cor. 16:22, translated as the invocation "Our Lord, come!"

MARBLE

OT Words

shayish [שַׁיִשׁ, **7893**]

shayish is found only in 1 Chr. 29:2, referring to either "marble" or "alabaster" as part of the inventory of building materials provided for the construction of Solomon's temple.

shēsh [שֵׁשׁ, **8336**]

shēsh occurs about forty times and refers primarily to "white linen." But on three occasions it refers to "marble" — twice in relation to the building materials of the palace of the Persian king Xerxes (cf. Esth. 1:6); and once to indicate symbolically the physical beauty of the legs of the "lover" in Song 5:15 as affirmed by his "beloved."

NT Words

marmaros [μάρμαρος, *3139*]

marmaros occurs only in Rev. 18:12, referring to "marble" as part of the inventory of the merchandise belonging to the nations of the world who traded with the city of Babylon, now earmarked for total destruction.

MARK

OT Words

tāw [תָּו, **8420**]

tāw is found in only three contexts. The meaning "mark" is most clearly indicated in Ezek. 9:4, 6 where, in the vision of Ezekiel, Yahweh commands a mark to be placed on the foreheads of those who grieve and lament over the idolatrous worship of the leaders of Jerusalem and those who follow them. The number of this faithful remnant is not indicated, though only they will be spared from the inevitable slaughter of the Jerusalem population at the hands of the Babylonian army. This is the judgment prophesied in Ezek. 9. The remaining reference to ***tāw*** is found in Job 31:35, where it indicates Job's "signature" to his "defense," which he desires to bring before God one day, to vindicate his perceived moral failure in the eyes of his detractors.

qa'aqa' [קַעֲקַע, **7085**]

qa'aqa' is found only in Lev. 19:28, where it refers to the forbidden practice of marking one's body with a tattoo.

NT Words

skopos [σκοπός, *4649*]

skopos is found only in Phil. 3:14, where it refers to Paul's desire to strive for the "mark," or "goal," of a heavenly calling into the eternal presence of God, based on Christ's finished work of redemption.

charagma [χάραγμα, *5480*]

charagma is a term denoting a physical "mark," "stamp," or "brand." It occurs nine times and is found on all but one occasion in the book of Revelation, where it refers to the "mark of the beast" (or antichrist), placed on the foreheads or hands of those who worshiped him (cf. Rev. 13:16ff.; 14:9ff.; 15:2; 16:2; 19:20; 20:4). See also Acts 17:29.

stigma [στίγμα, *4742*]

stigma occurs only once, in Gal. 6:17, where it refers to the "marks" or "scars" on the body of Christ as a consequence of his crucifixion.

See Also: → SIGN

MARKET, MARKETPLACE

NT Words

agora [ἀγορά, *58*]

agora is a noun found in ten contexts, referring to "market," "marketplace," where people would gather to buy and sell in towns and cities (cf. Matt. 11:16; 23:7; Mark 6:56; 7:4; 12:38; Luke 7:32; 11:43; 20:46; Acts 17:17). In Matt. 20:3, the marketplace is also designated as a location where employment is sought. In Acts 16:19, it is cited as the location of the municipal courts, where Paul and Silas were taken in Philippi.

MARRIAGE

OT Words

ḥātan [חָתַן, **2859**]

ḥātan is a verb occurring around thirty times with the underlying sense of making oneself related by marriage as an "in-law" to the father or mother of one's husband or wife. In its participial sense, ***ḥātan*** refers to "father-in-law" (cf. Exod. 3:1; 4:18; 18:1ff.; 10:29; Judg. 1:16; 4:11; 19:4ff.); "mother-in-law" (Deut. 27:23); and son-in-law (1 Sam. 18:21ff.).

The practice of entering into marriage is indicated by ***ḥātan*** in Gen. 34:9; Deut. 7:3; Josh. 23:12. Ezra 9:14 mentions the sin of illegitimate marriage with Canaanite women, with terrible consequences for those Israelite men guilty of the crime. All of these marriages were subsequently annulled. Finally, political marriage alliances are indicated in 1 Kgs. 3:1; 2 Chr. 18:1.

'ônāh [עוֹנָה, **5772**]

'ônāh is found only in Exod. 21:10, with reference to "conjugal, or marriage rights" to be granted to a man's second wife, should he choose to take one.

NT Words

gamos [γάμος, *1062*]

gamos means "wedding banquet," "marriage feast," and occurs sixteen times. The term is frequently found in Jesus' parables concerning the celebratory feast at the end of the age described in terms of a wedding banquet (cf. Matt. 22:2ff.; 25:10; Luke 12:36). In Matt. 22:11, ***gamos*** is used in conjunction with ***endyma*** to describe a wedding garment. General references to marriage feasts in a literal sense are found in Luke 14:8; John 2:1, 2. Heb. 13:4 refers to the sanctity of the marriage bed. Rev. 19:7, 9 refer to the consummate eschatological feast of the "marriage supper of the Lamb."

See Also: → MARRY

MARRY

OT Words

yābam [יָבַם, **2992**]

yābam is a verb, found in only three places, that refers to the distinctive Israelite custom of performing "levirate marriage"—when a deceased man's eligible brother takes his sister-in-law as his own wife, if there are no children from the previous marriage. The purpose of the practice is to allow for the continuity of the dead man's lineage in Israel (cf. Gen. 38:8; Deut. 25:5, 7).

bā'al [בָּעַל, **1166**]

bā'al is a verb that has both verbal and nominal meanings. In its nominal sense, ***bā'al*** refers to a "husband," "wife," or "master." In its verbal sense, however, the term indicates the act of marrying (cf. Deut. 24:1; Prov. 30:33). The term is also used metaphorically with respect to Yahweh's relationship with Israel in Isa. 62:4, 5. Mal. 2:11 also refers to Israel's practice of "marrying," but on this occasion the reference is to her unholy alliance with foreign idols.

lāqaḥ [לָקַח, **3947**]

lāqaḥ is a common term with the primary sense of "take," in numerous contexts. One of these refers to "take in marriage," and ***lāqaḥ*** occurs four times with this meaning (cf. Gen. 19:14; Num. 12:1 [twice]; 1 Chr. 2:21).

NT Words

gamiskō, gamizō [γαμίσκω, γαμίζω, *1061*]

gamiskō and ***gamizō*** are variant forms of the same verb, which means "to give in marriage." These terms are found in only six contexts. Matt. 24:38; Luke 17:27; 1 Cor. 7:38 speak of marriage in the natural, human context. Mark 12:25; Matt. 22:30; Luke 20:35 refer to the denial of marriage status to heavenly beings such as angels, and the resurrected saints in glory.

gameō [γαμέω, *1060*]

gameō is the more common New Testament term signifying "to marry," "give in marriage." In the majority of cases, the term relates to the human custom of marriage (cf. Matt. 5:32; 19:9ff.; 22:25ff.; 24:38; Mark 6:17; 10:11ff.; Luke 14:20; 16:18; 17:27; 20:34; 1 Cor. 7:9ff.; 1 Tim. 4:3; 5:11ff.). Then, in three contexts, like ***gamizō*** (see above), ***gameō*** refers to the denial of marriage status to angels and resurrected saints in heaven (cf. Matt. 22:30; Mark 12:25; Luke 20:35).

epigambreuō [ἐπιγαμβρεύω, *1918*]

epigambreuō occurs only in Matt. 22:24 and refers to a man marrying the childless widow of his brother who has recently died. This verb is the New Testament dynamic equivalent of the Hebrew term ***yābam*** (see above) that signifies the custom of levirate marriage in ancient Israel. Matt. 22:24 is actually citing and summarizing the Mosaic legislation dealing with this custom.

Additional Notes

One of the most intriguing aspects of marriage in Scripture is the continuity of its significance, spanning both Old and New Testaments. In particular, it is not the actual human institution of marriage that is of primary concern, but rather its metaphorical aspect when applied to the unique relationship between Yahweh and his people Israel.

When considering the theological impact of the marriage metaphor in relation to Israel and Yahweh, not only is the usage of specific "marriage" vocabulary relevant to the discussion, but also the usage of such terms as "husband" and "bride," which further expand the perspective of this phenomenon. In short, the symbolic depiction of the intimate covenant relationship between God and Israel as a "marriage" lays a solid foundation for understanding Israel's solemn commitment to Yahweh, in terms of his demands for absolute loyalty and obedience in return for his love and protection. It also explains why Yahweh gets so angry with his people when they turn their back on him and worship other gods, since this idolatry is tantamount to an act of spiritual adultery. Hence, Yahweh's response constitutes that of a betrayed husband whose wife has cheated and spurned him. (→ ADULTERER → BRIDE → HUSBAND)

The theological continuity of this motif also finds expression in the depiction of Christ's relationship with his church (his people), which is also described as a marriage bond. Here, however, one aspect of this metaphor differs markedly from the old covenant perspective on this theme. In the new covenant age, such is the completeness of Christ's redemptive work that the "marital bond" of the new covenant is deemed to be unbreakable and irrevocable (cf. Jer. 31:31ff.; Rev. 21:1ff.). This means that God will never again "divorce" his people, as he did of old (cf. Jer. 3:8 and → DIVORCE), and that all those who truly belong to him will never fall away.

Such a perspective enhances the solemnity of human marriage, which is a divinely created institution providing for the greatest degree of intimacy possible between two human beings, male and female. It is the spiritual aspect of marriage between God and Israel, Christ and the church, that gives all of God's people in all ages great hope for the life hereafter.

MARTYR → WITNESS

MARVEL → WONDER

MASTER

OT Words

'ādôn **[אָדוֹן, 113]**

'ādôn is a common noun occurring around three hundred times with the predominant meanings "lord," "master" in several different contexts. (→ GOD)

In a number of places, ***'ādôn*** refers to the owner of a slave, or servant — usually the master of a household (cf. Gen. 24:9ff.; 39:2; Exod. 21:4; Deut. 23:15; Judg. 19:11ff.; 1 Sam. 25:10, 17ff.; Job 3:19; Prov. 30:10; Isa. 24:2; Amos 4:1; Zeph. 1:9; Mal. 1:6).

'ādôn also refers to a king or ruler as "lord," or "master." David is frequently referred to this way (cf. 2 Sam. 14:12ff.; 18:28ff.; 19:20ff.; 1 Kgs. 1:2ff.); as is Saul (cf. 1 Sam. 16:16; 24:10ff.; 2 Sam. 2:5); Eglon, king of Moab (Judg. 3:25); and the king of Assyria (Isa. 36:8). See also Gen. 40:1; 1 Kgs. 20:4ff.; 2 Kgs. 9:7; Isa. 19:7; Jer. 37:20; Dan. 1:10. ***'ādôn*** is also used to refer to Joseph as the "ruler" of Egypt in the sense of an "administrative head" (cf. Gen. 45:8ff.).

The title "lord" or "master" is also given to one's superior, whether in a social, military, or ritual context. Joseph's brothers refer to their (unrecognized) sibling this way in Gen. 42:10. Ruth refers to Boaz as her "lord" in Ruth 2:13. Joshua refers to Moses this way in Num. 11:28. The title refers to Elijah and Elisha in 1 Kgs. 18:7ff.; 2 Kgs. 6:5ff., respectively. See also Num. 32:25. Similarly, the term "lord" is offered as a polite form of address to a male relative (cf. Gen. 31:35; 32:4ff.; Exod. 32:22).

Finally, ***'ādôn*** signifies "lord" or "master" as a form of address to a theophanic figure, a heavenly being in human form. Joshua thus addresses the angelic "commander of the Lord's army" (Josh. 5:14), as the prophet Zechariah addresses the interpreting angel in his visions (cf. Zech. 4:4ff.). See also Gen. 19:2.

NT Words

kyrios [κύριος, *2962*]

kyrios is the most common term in the New Testament for "Lord," in relation to the divine title given to Jesus Christ. It occurs nearly seven hundred times in this context.

However, on several occasions ***kyrios*** refers to "master" in the sense of "slave owner," "master of the household" (cf. Acts 16:16, 19; Eph. 6:5, 9; Col. 3:22; 4:1). The term also refers once to the Lord Christ as our "Master in heaven" in Eph. 6:9. Matt. 6:24; Luke 16:13 refer in a general sense to one's "master," of whom there can only be one — God or money — for a person can serve only one master.

epistatēs [ἐπιστάτης, *1988*]

epistatēs is a term of address, "Master," indicating one who has a position of authority and leadership. It occurs only six times and is used of Jesus Christ by his disciples on all occasions except one (cf. Luke 5:5; 8:24, 45; 9:33, 49). In Luke 17:13, a group of lepers addresses Jesus this way.

despotēs [δεσπότης, *1203*]

despotēs is another term meaning "lord" and "master," in ten contexts. Some contexts refer to either God or Christ. In other contexts, ***despotēs*** refers to human overlords (cf. 1 Tim. 6:1, 2; 2 Tim. 2:21; Titus 2:9; 1 Pet. 2:18).

See Also: → CAPTAIN → TEACH

MASTER BUILDER

NT Words

architektōn [ἀρχιτέκτων, *753*]

architektōn is used only once, in 1 Cor. 3:10, to refer to Paul's description of himself as a skilled "master builder," equipped by God for the task of founding churches.

MEAL → FLOUR

MEAN (ADJECTIVE)

OT Words

ḥāshōk **[חָשֹׁךְ, 2823]**

ḥāshōk occurs only in Prov. 22:29 with the sense of "mean," conveying the idea of "obscure," or "insignificant," describing certain kinds of people.

NT Words

asēmos [ἄσημος, *767*]

asēmos is found only in Acts 21:39 with reference to Tarsus as "no mean city" — a city of considerable significance.

MEANING → UNDERSTANDING

MEASURE

OT Words

middāh **[מִדָּה, 4060]**

middāh is a noun occurring around forty times with the primary meanings "measure," "measurement," or "size" in a variety of contexts.

General indications of measurement in various dimensions are referred to in a number of places. Linear measurement is indicated in Lev. 19:35; 1 Kgs. 6:25; 2 Chr. 3:3. Distance is in view in Josh. 3:4. Measurements of quantity are recorded in 1 Chr. 23:29; Job 28:25; and time measurement is indicated in Ps. 39:4.

middāh also indicates "size." Exod. 26:2, 8; 36:9, 15 refer to the tabernacle curtains being one size. References to people of great size or stature are found in Num. 13:32; 1 Chr. 11:23; 20:6; Isa. 45:14. In relation to the temple construction, ***middāh*** refers to its stones being cut "to size" in 1 Kgs. 7:9, 11, and to the size of the moveable washbasin in 1 Kgs. 7:37. Similarly, the detailed description of Ezekiel's visionary temple includes its general dimensions or size in relation to its various components (cf. Ezek. 40:10ff.; 41:17; 43:13; 45:3; 46:22; 48:16).

In addition, ***middāh*** is used adjectivally in Jer. 31:39; Ezek. 40:3, 5; 42:16ff.; Zech. 2:1 with reference to a "measuring line."

mesûrāh **[מְשׂוּרָה, 4884]**

mesûrāh occurs only four times meaning "measure," and in all cases refers to measurements of quantity (cf. Lev. 19:35; 1 Chr. 23:29; Ezek. 4:11, 16).

mādad **[מָדַד, 4058]**

mādad is a verb occurring around fifty times with the consistent meaning "to measure" as well as other nuances such as "divide," "pour into."

References to measuring physical quantities, such as food, are found in Exod. 16:18; Ruth. 3:15. A metaphorical use of ***mādad*** is found in Isa. 65:7, where Yahweh is said to take payment for their sin and "pour [it] into" the laps of his people.

Most commonly, ***mādad*** refers to measuring dimensions, in both literal and metaphorical contexts. Measuring pastureland for Levitical cities is indicated in Num. 35:5. A considerable part of the description of Ezekiel's visionary temple is devoted to describing the measurements of its various structures (cf. Ezek. 40:5ff.; 41:1ff.; 42:15ff.). Included in this section also is the measurement of the holy district surrounding the temple (Ezek. 45:3); and the extent of the river flowing from underneath the temple (Ezek. 47:3ff.). Elsewhere, dividing up, or measuring, the land of Canaan for conquest is predicated of Yahweh in Pss. 60:6; 108:7. Other general references to measuring are found in Deut. 21:2; 2 Sam. 8:2; Isa. 40:12.

'êphāh **[אֵיפָה, 374]**

'êphāh is a noun depicting a dry measure of quantity. It is transliterated "ephah" and equals about three-fifths of a bushel, or twenty-two liters. ***'êphāh*** occurs around forty times.

'êphāh is used in connection with various grain products, often in connection with ritual offerings — for example, flour (cf. Lev. 5:11; 6:20; Num. 28:5; Judg. 6:19; 1 Sam. 1:24); barley (cf. Num. 5:15; Ruth 2:17); and unspecified grain (cf. 1 Sam. 17:17; Ezek. 45:13, 24). A "short ephah," or a dishonest, inaccurate measure, is referred to in Mic. 6:10. A metaphorical use of ***'êphāh*** is found in Zech. 5:6ff., where an ephah is depicted as a container for the collective sin of Israel in Zechariah's vision.

se'āh **[סְאָה, 5429]**

se'āh is another technical term signifying a dry measure of quantity. It is transliterated "seah" and is equal to approximately one-third of an ephah. ***se'āh*** occurs nine times and refers literally to measures of various grains in each instance (cf. Gen. 18:6; 1 Sam. 25:18; 1 Kgs. 18:32; 2 Kgs. 7:1, 16, 18).

kōr [**כֹּר, 3734**]

kōr likewise constitutes a technical term for a dry measure of quantity (transliterated "cor"). It is the largest unit of measure found in the Hebrew Scriptures, equivalent to ten ephahs. ***kōr*** is found in eight places and refers to a literal measure in each case, primarily of grain (cf. 1 Kgs. 4:22; 2 Chr. 2:10; 27:5; Ezra 7:22; Ezek. 45:14). 1 Kgs. 5:11 also refers to a "cor."

mēmad [**מֵמַד, 4461**]

mēmad is only found in Job 38:5, meaning "dimensions," or "measurement," and speaking metaphorically of God's creative activity in establishing the dimensions of the earth.

NT Words

metron [μέτρον, *3358*]

metron has very little reference in the New Testament to literal or physical dimension. Rather, the term is translated "measure," with the sense of "criterion," or "standard," and also "quantity" in a metaphorical or spiritual sense.

metron indicates the sense of "criterion," or "standard," in Matt. 7:2; Mark 4:24; Luke 6:38. All these texts speak of the principle of just judgment whereby the "measure" (i.e., standard) someone applies to others will be used against that person on the day of judgment.

metron means "measure" in various contexts, with the underlying non-literal sense of quantity. Matt. 23:32 refers to Jesus' caustic exhortation to the hypocritical Pharisees to "fill up the measure of the sin" of their forefathers. Luke 6:38 refers to the "measure" of one's spiritual reward. The provision of the Spirit "not by measure" (i.e., without limit) is mentioned in John 3:34. "Measure," in the sense of "portion," is indicated in Rom. 12:3 with reference to the believer's faith; and in Eph. 4:17 with reference to God's grace made possible by the work of Christ. See also 2 Cor. 10:13. Eph. 4:13 speaks of the "measure of fullness" in metaphorical reference to the maximum spiritual impact of the spirit of Christ in the life of the believer.

There is one reference to the linear measure of a cubit in Rev. 21:7.

hyperperissōs [ὑπερπερισσῶς, *5249*];
ametros [ἄμετρος, *280*]

These two terms are both adverbs meaning "beyond measure," or "limitless." ***hyperperissōs*** occurs only in Mark 7:37, with reference to "astonishment beyond measure." ***ametros*** refers in 2 Cor. 10:13, 15 to unlimited boasting, which Paul denies ever having done.

choinix [χοῖνιξ, *5518*]

choinix occurs only in Rev. 6:6, signifying a "measure of wheat." In fact, the term refers to a dry measure of approximately one liter.

metreō [μετρέω, *3354*]

metreō is the verb form from which the noun ***metron*** is derived (see above). ***metreō*** means "to measure" with the underlying sense of "to judge by," "rule," or "standard," as well as the physical sense of spatial measurement.

The sense of judging by a criterion or standard is indicated in Matt. 7:2; Mark 4:24; Luke 6:38, all of which refer to the principle of judgment, whereby the standard one uses is the standard one receives. 2 Cor. 10:12 speaks of measuring or comparing oneself with others in a vain, self-centered way.

Rev. 11:1, 2 contains the divine instruction to the apostle John to measure the temple of God and the altar in a visionary experience. In Rev. 21:15ff., the interpreting angel sets out to measure the heavenly city of Jerusalem.

MEAT → FOOD

MEDIATE, MEDIATOR

NT Words

mesitēs [μεσίτης, *3316*]

mesitēs is the sole term utilized in the New Testament (six times in all) to convey the precise sense of mediator. It is used in Gal. 3:19, 20 to refer implicitly to Moses as the mediator of the old covenant. In 1 Tim. 2:5; Heb. 8:6; 9:15; 12:24, ***mesitēs*** refers to Christ as the unique mediator of the new covenant.

Additional Notes

There is no specific term for "mediation" or "mediator" as such in the Old Testament, but the concept is universally significant among the old covenant people of God prior to and during the period of their nationhood under Yahweh.

Mediation was formally built into the framework of Yahweh's covenant with Israel; and was primarily effected through the offices of prophet, priest, and king — especially the first two. The opportunity for God's chosen people to inquire of him to seek his will and purpose for them was one of the unique features of Yahweh's covenant with Israel. (→ PRIEST → PROPHECY → SERVANT)

In the New Testament, the ultimate mediation between God and humankind is realized in the person of Jesus Christ, who is described as the sole mediator between God and humankind. Though the term ***mesitēs*** refers explicitly to mediators in only a few contexts, the whole ministry of Christ embraces the phenomenon of mediation in the new covenant revelation.

MEDITATE

OT Words

hāgāh **[הָגָה, 1897]**

hāgāh is a verb with various meanings including "moan," as well as a variety of synonyms indicating verbal utterances (e.g., "utter," "matter," "growl"); "devise," "imagine," and "meditate." ***hāgāh*** occurs twenty-five times, and it means "to meditate" in five of these occurrences.

hāgāh refers to the practice of meditating on the law of God (Josh. 1:8; Ps. 1:2); meditating on God (Ps. 63:6); and meditating of God's work in a general sense (Pss. 77:12; 143:5).

sîaḥ **[שִׂיחַ, 7878]**

sîaḥ is a verb with the primary senses of "meditate," "ponder," and also "talk," or "speak" in a general sense. ***sîaḥ*** occurs twenty times, meaning "meditate" in eight of these contexts.

All uses of ***sîaḥ*** with this sense are found in the Psalms. ***sîaḥ*** refers to meditating on the laws or precepts of God (Ps. 119:15, 23, 48, 78); on the works or actions of God (Pss. 119:27; 143:5; 145:5); and on his promise (Ps. 119:148).

MEDIUM

OT Words

'ôb **[אוֹב, 178]**

'ôb is a noun occurring around twenty times with the primary meaning "medium," or "necromancer," indicating one who possesses the occult art of calling up the dead.

Lev. 19:31 forbids the Israelites to consult with mediums. Divine condemnation for consorting with mediums, which constituted a capital offense in Israel, is indicated in Lev. 20:6; 1 Chr. 10:13. Those who practice necromancy are roundly condemned by God in Lev. 20:27; Deut. 18:11; 2 Kgs. 21:6; 2 Chr. 33:6. 2 Kgs. 23:24; 1 Sam. 28:3, 9 refer to the abolition of mediums in Israel. General references to mediums are found in 1 Sam. 28:7ff.; Isa. 8:19; 19:3.

yidd'ōnî **[יִדְּעֹנִי, 3049]**

yidd'ōnî is a synonym for ***'ôb*** (see above), meaning "wizard," "soothsayer." It is paired with the term ***'ôb*** in virtually every instance.

Israelites are forbidden to make contact with wizards in Lev. 19:36; and if they do so it constitutes a capital offense (cf. Lev. 20:6, 27). Divine condemnation of the practice of wizardry is indicated in Deut. 18:11; 2 Kgs. 21:6. The expulsion of wizards from the land is referred to in 1 Sam. 28:3, 9; 2 Kgs. 23:24. General references to wizards are found in Isa. 8:19; 19:3.

See Also: → DIVINATION

MEEK, MEEKNESS

NT Words

praus [πραΰς, *4239*]

praus is an adjectival form conveying the sense of "meek," indicating an attitude of quiet, reverent, and humble submission to the will and purpose of God. ***praus*** occurs only three times. In Matt. 5:5, those who are "meek" are promised the inheritance of the earth as their reward. Matt. 21:5 refers to Jesus as one who is "meek" (or "humble") riding into Jerusalem on a donkey, in fulfillment of the prophecy found in Zech. 9:9. In 1 Pet. 3:4, the apostle commends the person in possession of a "meek" and quiet spirit, which is precious in the sight of God.

prautēs [πραΰτης, *4240*]

The noun ***prautēs*** occurs twelve times and designates the quality of "meekness," the gentle, quiet spirit of selfless devotion to God that is also translated "gentleness." "Meekness" is the very antithesis of arrogant pride.

"Meekness" appears in lists of Christian virtues in Gal. 5:23; Col. 3:12; 1 Tim. 6:11. A "spirit of gentleness (or meekness)" is referred to in 1 Cor. 4:21; Gal. 6:1. Cultivating an attitude of meekness towards one another is enjoined upon believers in Eph. 4:2; 2 Tim. 2:25; Titus 3:2; 1 Pet. 3:15. The meekness of Christ is alluded to in 2 Cor. 10:1. Jas. 3:13 indicates that the quality of "meekness" originates as a by-product of wisdom in the life of the believer. James also exhorts his readers to receive the word of God with "meekness."

See Also: → HUMBLE

MEET

OT Words

qārā' [קָרָא, 7121]

qārā' is a verb with the primary meaning "meet," in the sense of "encounter," "come together," whether by happenstance or design, in about 100 of its 730 occurrences. It is used predominantly in the context of human encounter, though not exclusively so.

qārā' refers to people "meeting" in a number of contexts. Meetings or appointments by design with specific purpose(s) are indicated in Gen. 14:17; Num. 31:13; Josh. 9:11; Isa. 7:3; Jer. 41:6. For example, God sends Aaron to meet with Moses in the wilderness in order to discover the divine purpose regarding a strategy to force the Egyptian Pharaoh to release the Israelite people from their captivity (cf. Exod. 4:27). In Judg. 4:18ff., Jael goes out to meet with the Canaanite commander, Sisera, in order to assassinate him. Prov. 7:10 depicts the harlot confronting the naive young man in order to seduce him. ***qārā'*** also often indicates meeting for the purpose of greeting someone (Gen. 19:1; Exod. 4:14; 18:7; Num. 22:36; 1 Sam. 13:10; 2 Sam. 6:2.; 1 Kgs. 2:19; 2 Kgs. 10:15). In Judg. 11:31, Jephthah makes a rash vow to the Lord to the effect that he would sacrifice as a burnt offering to the Lord whoever came out of his house to greet him after his victory over the Ammonites. Tragically, it was his only daughter who came out to meet him.

Frequently, ***qārā'*** also means "meet" in the sense of coming out against someone in battle. Examples of this are found in Josh. 8:5, 14, 21; 11:20; Judg. 7:24, where, for example, the Israelites confront the Canaanite peoples. Such a confrontation against the Philistines is in view in Judg. 15:4; 1 Sam. 4:1ff.; 17:48 (David and Goliath). See also 2 Sam. 10:10; 2 Chr. 35:10.

On several occasions, people are said to explicitly "meet" with God. Gen. 18:2 describes the meeting between Abraham and the three mysterious visitors, presumably a theophanic revelation or encounter. The people of Israel are said to meet with Yahweh at Mt. Sinai (cf. Exod. 19:17). Judgment against Israel is in view when the prophet Amos declares, "Prepare to meet your god . . ." (cf. Amos 4:12). Zechariah's encounter with angelic mediators is in view in Zech. 2:3.

On one occasion, ***qārā'*** describes Yahweh meeting with a man, Balaam (Num. 23:16).

pāga' [פָּגַע, 6293]

pāga' occurs around fifty times meaning "meet" or "encounter," as well as associated nuances such as "fall upon," "come upon," "touch." (→ INTERCEDE)

The meaning "meet" with the sense of "encounter" is illustrated in a number of places. A meeting by design or purpose is indicated in Gen. 32:1, where the mysterious opponent of Jacob confronts the patriarch at the river Jabbok for the purpose of challenging him in physical combat. The context strongly suggests that this was an angelic or theophanic visitation. See also Exod. 5:20.

There are also a number of places where ***pāga'*** indicates a meeting by coincidence or "chance" (cf. Exod. 23:4; 1 Sam. 10:5; Amos 5:19). Num. 35:19 refers to the chance meeting between the "avenger of blood" and the murderer he seeks. If such a meeting occurs, then the murderer is to be put to death.

pāga' also conveys the idea of "falling upon" someone with a view to attack, or assault (cf. Josh. 2:16; Judg. 8:21; 18:25; 1 Kgs. 2:25ff.). 1 Sam. 22:15ff. describes just such a confrontation between Saul and the priests of Nob, who were cruelly executed by the Israelite king.

In a metaphorical context, ***pāga'*** conveys the idea of "meeting" with reference to the borders of the Israelite allotments in Canaan "touching" various geographical features or locations (cf. Josh. 16:7; 17:10; 19:11, 22ff.).

yā'ad [יָעַד, 3259]

yā'ad is found in approximately thirty places and is translated "meet" in most of these contexts with various related senses. ***yā'ad*** is used in both divine and human contexts.

Where Yahweh is involved, ***yā'ad*** refers to God meeting his people from the vantage point of the "mercy seat" of the sacred ark of the covenant, or from the lid of this gold-covered chest, mounted with two golden cherubim (cf. Exod. 25:22; 30:16). In addition, Yahweh is said to meet his people at the door of the "inner sanctuary" of the tabernacle (cf. Exod. 29:42, 45; 30:36). Moses also meets with God at the "tent of meeting," referring to the holy place within the tabernacle precincts (cf. Num. 17:4).

In human contexts, ***yā'ad*** indicates the sense of "meet" with a number of nuances. The idea of meeting someone for an appointment is found in Neh. 6:2, 10; Job 2:11; Amos 3:3. Israel is called upon to meet with Moses at the "tent of meeting" prior to breaking camp in the wilderness and setting out (cf. Num. 10:3, 4).

yā'ad also refers to "meeting" in the sense of "gathering." Num. 14:35; 16:11; 27:3 refer to Israel gathering against God in the wilderness, in the context of rebelling against him. Peoples are said to "meet" or "gather" for war (Josh. 11:5; Ps. 48:4). 1 Kgs. 18:5; 2 Chr. 5:6 refer to Israel meeting or gathering for worship.

qārāh [קָרָה, 7136]

qārāh occurs around thirty times meaning "happen," "befall," "meet." The specific sense of "meet" occurs in six of these contexts. (→ BEFALL)

Yahweh is depicted as having met with his people in Exod. 3:18. Num. 23:3, 4, 15, 16 relate to Yahweh's meeting with the pagan seer, Balaam, with the intention of revealing his redemptive plans for his people Israel.

Deut. 25:18 records the incident in which the Amalekites "met" the Israelites during their wilderness wandering, confronting and attacking them.

pāgash [פָּגַשׁ, 6298]

pāgash occurs fourteen times with the exclusive sense of "meet," and with the additional nuances of "encounter," "fall upon."

Where people are concerned, ***pāgash*** refers to meeting, or coming together for a purpose, such as Esau being reconciled to Jacob (cf. Gen. 32:17; 33:8). See also Exod. 4:27; 1 Sam. 25:20; 2 Sam. 2:13; Jer. 41:6.

Two significant contexts contain the term ***pāgash***, signifying God's determination to "meet with" or "fall upon" his people in order to punish them for disobedience against him. Exod. 4:24 records the mysterious action of Yahweh confronting Moses with the intention of killing him for failing to have his infant son circumcised. He is saved only through the intervention of his wife Zipporah, who performs the rite on their son immediately. Hos. 13:8 records Yahweh's threat to fall upon his people Israel to punish them as a wild animal devours his prey.

Several metaphorical uses of ***pāgash*** are also recorded. Job 5:14 declares that darkness "meets" (i.e., comes upon) the wicked, and steadfast love and faithfulness are declared to "meet" in Ps. 85:10. See also Prov. 17:12; 22:2; 29:13; Isa. 34:14.

NT Words

apantaō [ἀπαντάω, *528*]

apantaō is a verb meaning "meet," "go to meet." It occurs seven times.

With the general sense of "meet," in the context of coming face-to-face with someone, ***apantaō*** is found in Matt. 28:9; Mark 5:2; 14:13; Luke 17:12; John 4:51; Acts 16:16. In Luke 14:31, ***apantaō*** means "meet" in the sense of a military confrontation between warring parties.

apantēsis [ἀπάντησις, *529*]

apantēsis is the noun derived from ***apantaō***, above, and is found in four places. It conveys the sense of "meeting" in the context of a social gathering in the parable in Matt. 25:1, 6, where wedding guests come out to meet the bridegroom. Acts 28:15 records a meeting between Paul and a group of Roman believers. In 1 Thess. 4:17, Paul describes the blessed fate of those believers who are alive at the return of Christ, who will be caught up to meet him in the air.

hypantaō [ὑπαντάω, *5221*]

hypantaō is a variant form of ***apantaō*** (see above) meaning "meet" in all five contexts in which it is found. The meeting of Jesus and his friend Martha (sister of Lazarus) is recorded in John 11:20, 30. John 12:18 speaks of the curiosity of the Jewish crowd wishing to meet Jesus as a result of his raising Lazarus from the dead. Matt. 8:28; Luke 8:27 speak of the Gadarene demoniac confronting Jesus near the vicinity of the graveyard where he was living as an outcast.

hypantēsis [ὑπάντησις, *5222*]

hypantēsis is the noun derived from ***hypantaō*** (see above) and is found only in John 12:13, where it refers to the Jerusalem population coming out to meet Jesus with palm tree branches, praising him as the coming King of Israel.

synantaō [συναντάω, *4876*]

synantaō is another variant form of ***apantaō*** (see above) and is found in six contexts. This term is translated "meet" in the same general sense as the other terms (cf. Luke 9:37; 22:10; Acts 10:25; Heb. 7:1, 10). In Acts 20:22, ***synantaō*** is translated "to befall," referring to Paul's ignorance of what will happen to him when he arrives in Jerusalem.

synantēsis [συνάντησις, *4877*]

synantēsis is the noun derived from ***synantaō*** (see above) and occurs only in Matt. 8:34, where it refers to the population of Gadara coming out to meet Jesus, begging him to leave their region.

MELODY → PLAY → SING

MELT

OT Words

mûg **[מוּג, 4127]**

mûg is a verb with the exclusive metaphorical sense of "melt (away)," "dissolve," as well as related nuances in seventeen contexts.

The phenomenon of people's hearts "melting in fear" is indicated in Exod. 15:15; Josh. 2:9, 24; Isa. 14:31; Jer. 49:23; Ezek. 21:15. ***mûg*** also describes apocalyptic images of cosmic dissolution, in which the earth or other natural phenomena "melt" or "dissolve" as a consequence of divine judgment (cf. Pss. 46:6; 75:3; Amos 9:5; Nah. 1:5). See also 1 Sam. 14:16; Ps. 65:10.

māsas **[מָסַס, 4549]**

māsas is a synonym for ***mûg*** (see above) and is likewise translated "melt" or "dissolve" in a predominantly metaphorical sense. ***māsas*** occurs around twenty times.

The figurative sense of people's hearts melting in fear is found in Deut. 1:28; 20:8; Josh. 7:5; 2 Sam. 17:10; Ps. 22:14; Ezek. 21:7, all of which refer to the fear within the people of Israel in the face of their enemies or the judgment of God. Josh. 2:11; 5:1; Isa. 13:7; 19:1; Nah. 2:10 refer to the hearts of Gentile people melting in fear.

māsas also refers to the dissolution or "melting" of the earth in apocalyptic descriptions of divine judgment against the cosmos and the wicked (cf. Pss. 68:2; 97:5; 112:10; Mic. 1:4).

In a more mundane context, ***māsas*** refers to the ropes around the arms of Samson being torn off, described as "melting off his hands" in Judg. 15:14. In Exod. 16:21, manna is said to literally melt away in the heat of the desert sun.

māsāh **[מָסָה, 4529]**

māsāh is a synonym for ***māsas*** (see above) found only four times. In two of these contexts ***māsāh*** conveys the sense of "melt." Josh. 14:8 refers to the hearts of the Israelites "melting" with fear; and in Ps. 147:18 the word of Yahweh is deemed capable of melting snow.

NT Words

tēkō **[τήκω, *5080*]**

tēkō is found only in 2 Pet. 3:12, where it refers to the cosmic dissolution brought about by the ultimate judgment of the Day of the Lord. The text refers to the elements melting with fire.

See Also: → REFINE

MEMBER

OT Words

shophkāh **[שָׁפְכָה, 8212]**

shophkāh occurs only in Deut. 23:1, where it refers to man being forbidden entry to the assembly of the Lord (in worship) on account of his emasculation (literally referring to the crushing of the testicles and the removal of the penis or "male member").

yeṣurîm **[יְצֻרִים, 3338]**

yeṣurîm is a passive participial form of ***yāṣar*** ("to form," "shape") expressed as a plural noun. The term only occurs in Job 17:7, where it refers to the "members" of one's body.

NT Words

melos **[μέλος, *3196*]**

melos is a noun occurring around thirty times with the universal meaning "member," referring primarily to parts of the human body in a literal sense (cf. Matt. 5:29ff.; Rom. 6:13, 19; 7:5, 23; Rom. 12:4ff.; 1 Cor. 12:12ff.; Jas. 3:5ff.).

melos is also used metaphorically to refer to the believer as a "member with Christ," joined to him by faith (cf. 1 Cor. 6:15; Eph. 4:25; 5:30). See also Col. 3:5; Jas. 4:1.

MEMORIAL, MEMORY → REMEMBER

MEND → REPAIR

MERCHANT → TRADE

MERCY, MERCIFUL

OT Words

ḥesed **[חֶסֶד, 2617]**

ḥesed constitutes one of the most significant theological terms in the Hebrew Scriptures. The right understanding of the term is bound up with its relationship to the divine covenant with Israel. When applied to Yahweh, ***ḥesed*** is fundamentally the expression of his loyalty and devotion to the solemn promises attached to the covenant. It is most commonly applied to

God, but it is also used to describe a human quality, as well as expressing human commitment to the covenant. *ḥesed* occurs around 250 times and is usually translated "mercy," "kindness," or "steadfast love" (often translated "lovingkindness" in the older English versions).

With reference to Yahweh, *ḥesed* commonly refers to his "steadfast love," signifying an irrevocable commitment to his promise to fashion a people to serve him, whom he in turn promised to love and protect. A significant number of references explicitly linking *ḥesed* to the covenant warrants the claim that whenever such love is predicated of Yahweh, one may argue that that divine response is motivated by his solemn commitment to his people.

Such steadfast love, for example, is shown to Abraham in Gen. 24:27 (cf. also Mic. 7:20), and to Joseph (Gen. 39:21). It is likewise shown to Israel as an explicit consequence of the divine covenant (cf. Exod. 15:13; Ezra 9:9; Ps. 98:3; Isa. 54:8, 10; 63:7). In particular, this love is expressed to those who love God and keep his commandments (cf. Exod. 20:6; 34:6; Deut. 5:10; 7:9, 12; 1 Kgs. 8:3; Neh. 1:5; Ps. 25:10; Dan. 9:4). 2 Sam. 7:15 expresses God's refusal to take his "steadfast love" from David as he took it from Saul; and David begs God not to take it away from him in Ps. 51:1. David is likewise the beneficiary of this divine love in 2 Sam. 22:51; 2 Kgs. 3:6; Ps. 89:49; Isa. 55:3. God is often praised with the words: "His steadfast love endures forever" (as well as some variations) (cf. 1 Chr. 16:34; Ezra 3:11; Pss. 36:5; 100:5; 106:1; 107:1; 118:1ff.; 136:1–26; Jer. 33:11; Lam. 3:22). Similarly, Yahweh is often said to "abound in steadfast love" (cf. Exod. 34:6; Num. 14:18ff.; Neh. 9:17; Ps. 103:8; Joel 2:13; Jonah 4:2).

With reference to the divine covenant, *ḥesed* indicates Yahweh's "loyalty" or "faithfulness" to his people in Jer. 31:3, where he alludes to that commitment to his people in the past. In Hos. 2:19, Yahweh promises to renew his "betrothal" to the people of Israel on the basis of a new covenant that will never be broken. One of the characteristic features of this new relationship will be God's steadfast love.

Concerning the translation of *ḥesed* with reference to the character of Yahweh, it is difficult, if not impossible, to precisely convey the full meaning of the term with just one English word or phrase. The semantic range of the term is rich and complex. Though the majority of the occurrences of *ḥesed* are translated "steadfast love," there are undeniable elements of "mercy" and "kindness" that underlie each of these occurrences. Further illustrations of this rich ambiguity may be seen in Pss. 6:4; 17:7; 25:7; Mic. 7:18, where any of the above suggestions for the meaning of *ḥesed* would be valid.

As far as the use of *ḥesed* in relation to humankind is concerned, much of the same diversity in the nuance of the term is evident. *ḥesed* indicates "kindness" or "mercy" in general in Job 6:14, and it refers in particular to the sparing of Lot's life through the merciful intervention of angels in Gen. 19:19. See also 1 Sam. 15:6. *ḥesed* also refers to "love" or "kindness" in the noble actions of Boaz in relation to Naomi and her daughter-in-law Ruth (Ruth 2:20); and likewise in the close friendship of David and Jonathan (cf. 1 Sam. 20:8ff.; 2 Sam. 9:1ff.). In the three contexts above, it is clear that such a demonstration of "lovingkindness" reflects a solemn commitment to the relationships concerned — implicit in the case of Boaz, but explicit in the relationship between David and Jonathan. God also commands his people to show "kindness" (or "mercy," or "love") to one's brother in Zech. 7:9. A request for "kindness" to be shown is indicated in Gen. 20:13; 40:14.

In the context of a solemn vow among people, *ḥesed* indicates the quality of "kindness" that is actually requested and required of the parties concerned. In Gen. 47:29, for example, Jacob makes Joseph swear to have him buried in Canaan and not in Egypt. Joseph is asked in this instance to show his father "kindness" in doing so. It is in fact a request for a loyal response to a promise made. See also Gen. 21:23 in this light. Similarly, in Josh. 2:12, Rahab pleads with the spies to treat her "kindly," just as she had treated them. Her merciful action in preventing their discovery by the Jericho authorities forms the basis of a demand for a similar act of "kindness."

There is also in Jer. 2:2 a recognition of Israel's initial "devotion" or "loyalty" to Yahweh in the very early stages of their unique covenant relationship, established at Sinai. Here *ḥesed* refers to Israel's positive response to the demands of that relationship.

raḥam [רָחַם, 7356]

raḥam occurs approximately sixty times with the dominant sense of "mercy" that includes the element of "compassion." *raḥam* is predicated of God in the majority of instances, and when people are in view, it occurs in contexts where Yahweh takes the initiative either to provide it or command his people to manifest it.

With respect to Yahweh, there is a plea for him to show mercy in Gen. 43:14; Ps. 119:77; and a plea for him not to withdraw his mercy in Ps. 40:11. God grants mercy to his people in Deut. 13:17; Isa. 54:7; 63:7; Jer. 42:12. In Hos. 2:19, mercy is depicted as one quality (among others) on which Yahweh's "re-betrothal" of Israel is based. 2 Sam. 24:14; Neh. 9:19, 27ff.; Pss. 51:1; 119:156; Dan. 9:18 affirm the greatness of God's mercy to his people. Lam. 3:22 records that God's mercies are never ending. In a negative context, God withdraws mercy from his people in judgment in Jer. 15:5.

Where people are concerned, God is said to grant mercy or compassion to his people in the sight of their captors in 2 Chr. 30:9; Dan. 1:9. 1 Kgs. 8:30; Neh. 1:11 contain a plea for such. Isa. 47:6 records Yahweh's anger at Babylon for refusing to show his people compassion. God commands his people in Zech. 7:9 to show mercy to their fellow-countrymen.

rāḥam [רָחַם, 7355]

rāḥam is the verb from which the corresponding noun ***rāḥām*** (see above) is derived. ***rāḥam*** occurs in about fifty contexts and has the consistent meaning "to show, or grant mercy, or compassion." The term is predicated of both God and human beings.

Where God is concerned, ***rāḥam*** refers to the divine granting of mercy to his people in a general sense in Exod. 33:19; Deut. 13:17; Isa. 30:18; Ps. 102:13. In particular, there is the promise of renewed mercy from Yahweh in the context of the renewal and restoration of his people Israel. This guarantee of renewed divine compassion, as with ***ḥesed*** (see above), is made against the backdrop of a renewed covenant relationship (cf. Isa. 14:1; Jer. 12:15; 30:18; 31:10; 33:26; Ezek. 39:25). Note especially Isa. 49:10, 13; Hos. 2:1; Mic. 7:19 in this regard. Conversely, Yahweh occasionally threatens withdrawal of his compassion as an element of his judgment against his people for turning their back on him (cf. Isa. 9:17; 27:11; Jer. 13:14). Of particular note in this regard, Hos. 1:6 records naming Gomer's illegitimate daughter "No Mercy" as a symbolic indictment against the Israelite people, who will be denied any access to Yahweh's compassion on account of their sin.

There is an affirmation of divine mercy in Ps. 116:5 and a plea for God to remember mercy in Hab. 3:2.

When predicated of human beings, ***rāḥam*** in 1 Kgs. 8:50, for example, refers to the demonstration of mercy as a consequence of a divine enabling. Prov. 28:13 refers to obtaining or receiving mercy. People's refusal to show mercy or compassion is indicated in Isa. 13:18; 49:15; Jer. 6:23; 21:7; 50:42.

rēḥām [רְחֵם, 7359 (Aramaic)]

rēḥām is the Aramaic equivalent for ***rāḥam*** (see above) and occurs only in Dan. 2:18, where it refers to the "mercy" of the God of heaven. Such mercy is sought by Daniel, along with his three faithful companions, who pleaded with God to show compassion in granting to Daniel knowledge of Nebuchadnezzar's dream and its interpretation, so that they could escape from being executed with the other Babylonian wise men.

ḥemlāh [חֶמְלָה, 2551]

ḥemlāh is a noun found only in two places, both of which refer to the mercy of God. In Gen. 19:16, such mercy is extended to Lot, who is rescued by two angels from the doomed city of Sodom. Isa. 63:9 speaks of Yahweh delivering his people Israel of old in his love and mercy.

ḥāsîd [חָסִיד, 2623]

ḥāsîd occurs in about thirty contexts, with the principal meanings "saint(s)" or "holy (one)." However, on three occasions it conveys the sense of "merciful," referring to Yahweh (cf. 2 Sam. 22:6; Ps. 18:25; Jer. 3:12).

NT Words

eleeō [ἐλεέω, *1653*]

eleeō occurs around thirty times meaning "to have mercy," "show mercy," again with the accompanying senses of "compassion" and "pity."

The practice of "showing mercy" is indicated in Rom. 12:8. The obligation to show compassion or mercy is presented in the parable of the ungrateful servant, who received mercy from his master by canceling a huge debt, but who in turn failed to show the same compassion to a colleague who owed him a pittance (cf. Matt. 18:33).

The remaining uses of ***eleeō*** are found in contexts where the source of mercy is located in God or Jesus Christ. The beatitude of Matt. 5:7 promises that mercy will be extended to those who are merciful to others. On a number of occasions, those who are diseased or disabled plead for mercy from Jesus during his earthly ministry — for example, those who are blind (cf. Matt. 9:27; 20:30ff.; Mark 10:47ff.; Luke 18:38ff.); and lepers (cf. Luke 17:13). See also Matt. 15:22; 17:15; Luke 16:24. Other recipients of divine mercy include the Gadarene demoniac exorcised by Jesus (Mark 5:19); and the apostle Paul (1 Tim. 1:13, 16). Other texts speak of the sovereign divine exercise and initiative of mercy (cf. Rom. 9:15ff., "I will have mercy on whom I will have mercy . . ."; 11:30ff.; 1 Cor. 7:25; 2 Cor. 4:1; Phil. 2:27; 1 Pet. 2:10).

eleos [ἔλεος, *1656*]

eleos is the noun derived from ***eleeō*** (see above) and has the primary sense of "mercy" that also includes "compassion," "kindness," "pity." ***eleos*** occurs in approximately thirty contexts and is likewise predicated of God and human beings.

Concerning human "mercy," God desires this quality to be manifested in the life of his people (cf. Matt. 9:13; 12:7). The crime of neglecting to show mercy, kindness, or compassion to others forms part of Jesus' condemnation of the Pharisees in Matt. 23:23. The practice of showing mercy is mentioned in Luke 10:37; and commendation for doing so is indicated in Jas. 2:13.

As far as God is concerned, his mercy is given to those who fear him (cf. Luke 1:50ff.). The phrase "vessels of mercy" is found in Rom. 9:23, referring to those people whom God has destined to be the recipients of his mercy and grace. The fact of divine mercy being granted to the Gentiles is indicated in Rom. 11:31; 15:9. The invocation of divine mercy is found in Gal. 6:16; 1 Tim. 1:2; Jude 2; 2 Tim. 1:2, 16, 18. Titus 1:4; Heb. 4:16; 2 John 3. Mercy is affirmed as a quality of the divine being in Eph. 2:4; Titus 3:5; Jas. 3:17; 1 Pet. 1:3; Jude 21.

eleēmōn [ἐλεήμων, *1655*]

eleēmōn is an adjectival form from ***eleeō*** and ***eleos***, above, occurring only twice. In Matt. 5:7 it refers to the blessed condition of those who are "merciful" by nature and who will in turn receive mercy from the Lord. Heb. 2:17 refers to Jesus Christ as our merciful and faithful high priest.

oikteirō [οἰκτείρω, *3627*]

oikteirō is a synonym for ***eleeō*** and means "to have compassion or pity on." It is found only in Rom. 9:15 and refers to the divine intervention and expression of compassion towards his chosen people: "I will have compassion on whom I will have compassion. . . ."

oiktirmos [οἰκτιρμός, *3628*]

oiktirmos is the noun derived from ***oikteirō*** (see above) and is translated "mercy" or "compassion" in all five contexts in which it is found.

oiktirmos refers to the "mercies" of God (Rom. 12:1; 2 Cor. 1:13), and similarly to the kindness and compassion of Christ (Phil. 2:1). Mercy as a godly quality is commended to the believer in a list of Christ-like virtues in Col. 3:12. Heb. 10:28 refers to the penal sanction of the Mosaic covenant whereby a person found guilty of a capital offense under the law was put to death "without mercy" on the evidence of two or three witnesses.

oiktirmōn [οἰκτίρμων, *3629*]

oiktirmōn is the adjectival form derived from ***oikteirō*** and ***oiktirmos***, above, occurring in only three places and meaning "merciful." Luke 6:36 contains the injunction to be merciful just as God is merciful; and Jas. 5:11 affirms that God is both compassionate and "merciful."

hilaskomai [ἱλάσκομαι, *2433*]

hilaskomai is only found in two places and is translated "to be merciful" in Luke 18:13 with reference to the prayer of the tax-collector in the parable of Christ: "Be merciful to me a sinner . . ." In Heb. 2:18, ***hilaskomai*** is translated "to make reconciliation, or expiation" for sins with reference to the atoning sacrifice of Christ on the cross.

hileōs [ἵλεως, *2436*]

hileōs is an adjectival term that occurs only twice. In Heb. 8:12 is it translated "merciful," with respect to God's compassionate determination to forgive the sins of his people. However, in Matt. 16:22, the term is translated as an interjection: "Be it far from me."

See Also: → GRACE

MERCY-SEAT → THRONE

MERRY → BLESS

MESSAGE → WORD

MESSENGER → ANGEL

MESSIAH → ANOINT → CHRIST

MIDNIGHT → NIGHT

MIDWIFE

OT Words

***meyalledet* [מְיַלֶּדֶת, 3205]**

meyalledet is a participial feminine noun from the verb ***yālad*** ("to bear," "beget," "give birth to") which means "midwife," indicating one who assists women in giving birth to their children. ***meyalledet*** occurs ten times with this meaning. Gen. 35:17 refers to the midwife attending the birth of Benjamin. His mother Rachel dies in the process. Gen. 38:28 records the presence of the midwife attending the birth of the twin boys Perez and Zerah, sons of Tamar, born in the lineage of Judah. The remaining uses of ***meyalledet*** all refer to the Israelite midwives who courageously defied the edict of Pharaoh to kill all newborn Israelite males (cf. Exod. 1:15ff.), a stance which brought them the tangible blessing of God, who gave them families of their own.

MIGHT → STRENGTH

MILE

NT Words

***milion* [μίλιον, *3400*]**

milion is the sole term for "mile" in the New Testament, occurring only in Matt. 5:41.

MILK

OT Words

***ḥālāb* [חָלָב, 2461]**

ḥālāb is a noun occurring in about forty places meaning "milk" in the majority of these instances.

ḥālāb refers to milk served with a meal or as a refreshment by itself (cf. Gen. 18:8; Judg. 4:19; 5:25). References to milk generally, as a dairy product, are found in Deut. 32:14; Job 10:10; Prov. 27:27; 30:33; Isa. 7:22; 55:1; Ezek. 25:4. In particular, a command was issued under the law covenant that forbade the boiling of a kid goat in its mother's milk (cf. Exod. 23:19; 34:26; Deut. 14:21). Isa. 28:9 refers to human breast milk.

ḥālāb is also used in several metaphorical contexts. It is used as a simile in Gen. 49:12 to refer to teeth that are "white as milk." Song 4:11; 5:12; Lam. 4:7 utilize ***ḥālāb*** as a symbol for physical beauty; and in Song 5:1 the term is associated with the couple's love-making, drinking wine mixed with milk. By far the greatest metaphorical use of ***ḥālāb*** is found in the descriptive phrase referring to the abundant fertility and economic prosperity of Canaan as a "land flowing with milk and honey" (cf. Exod. 3:8, 17; Lev. 20:4; Num. 13:27; 14:8; 16:13ff.; Deut. 6:3; 11:9; 31:20; Josh. 5:6; Jer. 11:5; 32:22; Ezek. 20:6, 15). In Joel 3:18, similar terminology is used to describe the anticipated renewal of the land of Israel in the distant future.

NT Words

***gala* [γάλα, *1051*]**

gala is found in only five contexts in the New Testament, meaning "milk" used in a metaphorical sense in all but one of these places.

In these four texts, 1 Cor. 3:2; Heb. 5:12, 13; 1 Pet. 2:2, "milk" refers to elementary or basic spiritual truths. Only 1 Pet. 2:2 uses the term in a positive sense, referring to the "spiritual milk" that will feed and nourish "infant believers." The other three uses constitute rebukes for believers who have become "stunted" in their growth, failing to move beyond the elementary teachings of the faith to greater maturity where they should be partaking of "solid food." Literal reference to milk is found in 1 Cor. 9:7.

MILL, MILLSTONE

OT Words

***rēḥayim* [רֵחַיִם, 7347]**

rēḥayim is a noun in the "dual" form, derived from the verb ***rēḥeh*** (רֵחֶה) signifying the action of grinding, or pulverizing. ***rēḥayim*** is translated "millstones," as well as "mill," indicating a "pair of millstones," hence the dual form that is suggestive of "two-ness" or a natural pairing phenomenon. ***rēḥayim*** occurs five times.

Exod. 11:5; Num. 11:8 refer to a "mill," whereas the actual "millstones" themselves are referred to in Deut. 24:6; Isa. 47:2; Jer. 25:10.

***rekeb* [רֶכֶב, 7393]**

rekeb is a noun referring to a "chariot," occurring over one hundred times with this meaning. In four contexts, however, ***rekeb*** means "millstone" (cf. Deut. 24:6; Job 41:24). Judg. 9:53; 2 Sam. 11:21 refer to the millstone that killed Abimelech, the renegade son of Gideon, who set himself up as king over a small region in Canaan, only to die an ignominious death at the hands of a woman, who dropped a millstone on his head.

NT Words

***mylos* [μύλος, *3458*]; *lithos* [λίθος, *3037*]**

mylos occurs five times and refers in each case to a "millstone." Matt. 18:6; Luke 17:2 refer to the desired fate of those who cause little children and/or those "young in the faith" to stumble and sin in their Christian walk. That is, it would be better for such deceivers to have a large millstone placed around their necks and be cast into the sea. (Note that ***lithos*** refers to this same phenomenon in Mark 9:42.)

Rev. 18:21 refers to an angel throwing a great stone "like a millstone" into the sea in order to symbolically demonstrate and illustrate the violent overthrow of the city of Babylon through the savage judgment of God. Rev. 18:22 declares that the sound of a millstone would never again be heard in the city of Babylon, indicating, along with other things, the total destruction of that civilization.

mylos describes the situation in Matt. 24:41, whereby two women will be grinding at a "mill." One will be taken up to glory to be with God in heaven; the other will be left behind.

MIND

OT Words

nephesh [נֶפֶשׁ, 5315]

nephesh is a common term in the Old Testament, and it is virtually impossible to translate with any one single English term. It is most commonly translated "person," "soul," "life," or "mind." It conveys both the physical and spiritual aspects of human existence in a variety of contexts.

NT Words

dianoia [διάνοια, *1271*]

dianoia occurs thirteen times in all and means "mind," indicating that faculty as the seat of human reason, understanding, emotion, and will. In most of the contexts in which it is found, ***dianoia*** may also be translated "heart."

The command to love God with all one's "mind" is linked to "heart" and "soul" as well. The clear implication is that one is to love God with one's whole being. It is the greatest command of all (cf. Matt. 22:37; Mark 12:30; Luke 10:27). Linked to this all-embracing command is the observation in Heb. 8:10; 10:16 that God has placed his law within the hearts and minds of his people as part of the essence of the promised new covenant renewal, accomplished through the finished redemptive work of Christ. In these two texts, ***dianoia*** ("mind") is used synonymously with ***kardia*** ("heart"). In fact, Heb. 8:10 speaks of God "placing" his law "in their minds," and "writing" it "on their hearts." In Heb. 10:16, the writer switches the metaphorical images, describing God's promise to "put" his law "on their hearts" and "write" it "on their minds."

dianoia also refers to the human mind in a general sense as the seat of understanding, speaking of the spiritual enlightenment of believing hearts or minds (Eph. 1:18), and the darkening or blinding of the mind of unbelievers (Eph. 4:18). The unregenerate minds (or hearts) of human beings are indicated in Eph. 2:3; Col. 1:2. See also 1 Pet. 1:13; 2 Pet. 3:1; 1 John 5:20.

nous [νοῦς, *3563*]

nous is a noun synonymous with ***dianoia*** (see above) that occurs around twenty times with the sense of "mind" in various contexts.

In Luke 24:45, Jesus is said to open the minds of his disciples so that they could understand the full meaning the Scriptures concerning himself. Here ***nous*** refers to the "mind" as the faculty of reasoning and understanding.

The mind as the seat human volitional, moral, and cognitive expression is indicated in several places (cf. Rom. 14:5; 1 Cor. 14:14ff.; Col. 2:18; 2 Thess. 2:2). In particular, divine judgment is brought to bear on the mind of unbelievers, resulting in the debasing of their minds, rendering these faculties corrupt and futile in the sight of God, on account of their wickedness (cf. Rom. 1:28; Eph. 4:17; 1 Tim. 6:5; 2 Tim. 3:8). ***nous*** also refers to the volitional orientation of the human mind in Rom. 7:23, 25, where Paul declares that while his mind is oriented towards the law of God on the one hand, the effect of sin produces a tension which incites him to work against that divine law principle in his mind. Such tension illustrates the classic battle with sin in the life of the believer.

In more general terms, ***nous*** refers to the "mind" as equivalent to the "heart" — the seat of a person's innermost being: In Rom. 12:2; Eph. 4:23; Phil. 4:7 the renewal of the believer's mind, produced by a divine work of grace, is in view. See also 1 Cor. 1:10; Rev. 13:18.

phronēma [φρόνημα, *5427*]

phronēma refers to the "mind" in the general sense of the volitional and rational center of the human being as well as the "mind" of the Spirit of God. ***phronēma*** occurs in only three contexts. Rom. 8:6 declares that an orientation of the mind that is set on the flesh leads to death, but a focus of the mind on the Spirit leads to life. Rom. 8:7 expands this by adding that the mind set on the flesh is hostile to God. Rom. 8:27

refers to the "mind of the Spirit" as something accessible to the divine searcher of the hearts of humankind.

dipsychos [δίψυχος, *1374*]

dipsychos occurs only in Jas. 1:8, 4:8 as an adjective meaning "double-minded," or "wavering," "uncertain."

metaballō [μεταβάλλω, *3328*]

metaballō is found only in Acts 28:6 meaning "to change one's mind."

noēma [νόημα, *3540*]

noēma is a noun occurring six times meaning "mind," or "thought." "Mind" refers to the center of human reason and volition in 2 Cor. 3:14; 4:4, indicating the hardening or blinding of the minds of unbelievers, including apostate Jews. Phil. 4:7 refers to the peace of God that keeps the mind of believers focused on Christ.

Additional Notes

The concept of "mind" in the Old Testament is difficult to discuss in isolation from other more common terms that relate to the seat of the human intellect, reason, and emotion. In particular, the human "mind" is most frequently linked to the phenomenon of the "heart" or "soul." And in many cases, these three terms are interchangeable in their meaning. Other synonyms, such as "imagination," or (rarely) "spirit," occasionally convey the associated sense of "mind." The Old Testament most commonly treats the concept of the non-tangible "soul," "heart," or "mind" of human beings as aspects of one's integral unity, and not divorced from one's person. As such, language describing the "mind" of human beings tends towards imprecision and diversity.

New Testament Greek vocabulary for the concept of the human "mind" is somewhat more precise and explicit than that of the corresponding Hebrew terminology. A number of terms in the New Testament convey the sense of the "mind" as the human faculty from which one's motives, innermost thoughts, reason, and emotions emerge. Ambiguities remain and meanings overlap, however. For additional perspectives on the concept of "mind," consult the references listed below.

See Also: → ADVICE → HEART → LIFE → IMAGINE → PERSON → REMEMBER → SOUL → SPIRIT → THINK → UNITY

MINGLE → MIX

MINISTER → SERVE

MINSTREL → MUSIC

MINT

NT WORDS

hēdyosmon [ἡδύοσμον, *2238*]

hēdyosmon is the term for the fragrant herb "mint," found only in Matt. 23:23; Luke 11:42, referring to the tithing practices of the Pharisees.

MIRACLE → SIGN

MIRE → CLAY → DUNG

MIRROR

OT WORDS

mar'āh [מַרְאָה, 4759]

mar'āh is a noun referring primarily to "visions" given by God as a means of revelation to his people. It has this meaning in ten of the eleven contexts in which it is found. The exception occurs in Exod. 38:8, where ***mar'āh*** refers to the "mirrors" belonging to the Israelite women who served at the door of the tabernacle. These "mirrors" consisted of highly polished plaques of bronze, which were used in the construction of the ritual washbasins for the tabernacle.

re'î [רְאִי, 7209]

re'î is found only in Job 37:18, where it is used as a simile referring to the skies as "hard as a molten mirror."

NT WORDS

esoptron [ἔσοπτρον, *2072*]

esoptron refers to a "mirror" in only two contexts. Paul uses the term metaphorically in 1 Cor. 13:12, where he likens our earthly spiritual perception to looking in a dull mirror with poor reflections. Jas. 1:23 mentions someone looking at his face in a mirror.

MISCARRY

OT WORDS

shākōl [שָׁכֹל, 7921]

shākōl is a verb with the primary meaning "to make, be bereaved." It occurs twenty-five times, and on four occasions conveys the sense of "miscarry." Exod. 23:26; Hos. 9:14 refer to women losing children through miscarriage; and Job 21:10; Gen. 31:38 refer to animals losing their offspring in the same manner.

In Exod. 21:22, miscarriage is indicated through the reference to a woman literally having her child "leave her (i.e., prematurely)," although the verb used is not ***shākōl***, but ***yāṣā'*** ("to leave, exit"). (→ LEAVE)

MISCHIEF → EVIL

MISERABLE, MISERY

OT Words

'āmāl **[עָמָל, 5999]**

'āmāl is a noun that occurs around fifty times with the predominant meanings "toil," or "trouble." In four of these contexts, however, the term means "misery." General references to human misery in the sense of a condition and feelings of wretchedness are found in Job 11:16; Prov. 31:7. Then Judg. 10:16 refers to the misery of Israel, indicating the wretched condition of the people suffering under the oppression of the Ammonites.

'āmāl is also used adjectivally in Job 16:2, referring to Job's "miserable comforters" who did little but taunt, provoke, and frustrate him.

'āmēl **[עָמֵל, 6001]**

'āmēl is a variant form of ***'āmāl*** (see above), found only in Job 3:20, with reference to the misery of humankind in general terms.

NT Words

eleeinos [ἐλεεινός, *1652*]

eleeinos is an adjectival form derived from ***eleos*** (→ MERCY) that is translated "miserable," "pitiable." It occurs only twice. In 1 Cor. 15:19, ***eleeinos*** refers to the hypothetical miserable condition that would come upon all believers if Jesus Christ had not in fact risen from the dead. Rev. 3:17 refers to, among other things, the miserable condition of the congregation at Laodicea.

talaipōria [ταλαιπωρία, *5004*]

talaipōria means "misery" in the sense of "hardship," "calamity," or "judgment." The term only occurs twice. In Rom. 3:16, ***talaipōria*** refers to the misery wrought by the wicked on their victims; and in Jas. 5:1 it indicates the miseries or calamities that await the rich and powerful who despise God and their fellow human beings. The context here is one of imminent divine judgment against them. (→ SORROW → TROUBLE)

See Also: → DISTRESS → SORROW → TROUBLE

MISS

OT Words

ḥāṭā' **[חָטָא, 2398]**

The verb ***ḥāṭā'*** has the primary sense of "sin," as well as a number of associated senses, in most of its 250 or so occurrences. Inherent in the meaning "sin" is the concept of "missing the mark," or failing to reach the standard set by God. (→ SIN)

There is, however, one instance where ***ḥāṭā'*** is translated "to miss the mark" in a literal sense. Judg. 20:16 refers to skilled Benjamite soldiers who could sling a stone with great accuracy and "not miss."

pāqad **[פָּקַד, 6485]**

pāqad is a verb with a variety of meanings including "to number," "visit," "appoint," or "punish." The term occurs in about three hundred places, and on several occasions it is translated "miss" in a number of differing senses.

1 Sam. 20:6 poses the hypothetical situation of Saul "missing" David at a feast (i.e., "observing his absence"). See also 1 Sam. 20:18 in this regard. "To miss" in the sense of "overlook something" is indicated in 1 Sam. 25:15, 21. Then, in 1 Sam. 25:7, ***pāqad*** conveys the sense of "go missing" with the implication of "being stolen." Similarly, 1 Kgs. 20:39 implies someone "escaping."

MIST

OT Words

'ēd **[אֵד, 108]**

'ēd is a rare noun occurring only twice, meaning "mist," or "fog," in Gen. 2:6, Job 36:27.

NT Words

achlys [ἀχλύς, *887*]

achlys is found only in Acts 13:11, where it refers to "mist" in a metaphorical sense, indicating the temporary blindness experienced by the apostle Paul after his conversion.

MISTRESS

OT Words

geberet **[גְּבֶרֶת, 1404]**

geberet occurs nine times and is translated "mistress," or a female leader of a household. It also refers metaphorically to a queen.

References to a household "mistress" are found in Gen. 16:4ff.; 2 Kgs. 5:3; Ps. 123:2; Prov. 30:23; Isa. 24:2. ***geberet*** is used metaphorically in Isa. 47:5, 7, where it refers to Babylon as "the mistress" of kingdoms, indicating her self-perception as an invincible ruler.

ba'alāh **[בַּעֲלָה, 1172]**

ba'alāh is only found three times. On two occasions it refers to a sorceress, a female medium (cf. 1 Sam. 28:7; Nah. 3:4). The remaining reference is found in 1 Kgs. 17:17, where ***ba'alāh*** refers to a household "mistress."

MITE

NT Words

lepton [λεπτόν, *3016*]

lepton refers to a small copper coin, translated "mite," which was worth only a fraction of a cent. ***lepton*** is found in only three contexts, two of which refer to the classic "widow's mite," the offering of a poverty-stricken woman (cf. Mark 12:42; Luke 21:2). ***lepton*** is also found in Luke 12:59, referring to "the very last mite" demanded by a magistrate from a hapless victim of a lawsuit.

MIX, MIXTURE

OT Words

bālal **[בָּלַל, 1101]**

bālal is a verb occurring around forty times with the primary meanings "mix," or "mingle."

The overwhelming usage of this term is found in ritual contexts with reference to mixing various ingredients in preparation for sacrifice. ***bālal*** refers to cakes mixed with oil (Exod. 29:2; Lev. 7:12); flour mixed with oil (cf. Exod. 29:40; Lev. 2:4ff.; Num. 6:15); and cereal offerings and oil (Lev. 7:10).

There is one metaphorical usage of ***bālal***, where the meaning "mix" refers to Israel. Hos. 7:8 declares that "Ephraim mixes himself with the peoples," implying that the people of Yahweh have contaminated themselves with the idolatrous practices of Gentile nations.

māsak **[מָסַךְ, 4537]**

māsak is a verb occurring five times, meaning "mix" or "mingle" on each occasion. Prov. 9:2, 5; Isa. 5:22 refer to people mixing wine and strong drink. Ps. 102:9 contains a metaphorical usage of the term, with the psalmist declaring that in his suffering he "mixes tears" with his drink. Isa. 19:14 depicts Yahweh as one who has "mixed, or mingled" a spirit of confusion within Egypt.

'ārab **[עָרַב, 6148]**

'ārab is a verb occurring around twenty times with the primary sense of "pledge," or "give a guarantee," in most of these contexts. In two places ***'ārab*** means "mingle oneself." Ezra 9:2; Ps. 106:35 refer to the sin of God's people in "mingling themselves," or intermarrying, with pagan nations around them.

'arab **[עֲרַב, 6151** (Aramaic)]

The Aramaic verb form ***'arab*** is found only three times in the book of Daniel and means "mix," "mingle." Dan. 2:41 (twice), 43 refer to the visionary statue in Nebuchadnezzar's dream, focusing on the feet and toes made of "iron mixed with clay," suggesting an inherent structural weakness.

NT Words

synkerannymi [συγκεράννυμι, *4786*]

synkerannymi means "combine together," "mix." This verb is only found in two places. In 1 Cor. 12:24, God is said to have "combined together" the various parts of the human body to form a integrated whole. Heb. 4:2 indicates the absence of a believing response in the hearts of the ancient people of Israel on the border of Canaan in the wilderness. These people heard the message of the gospel, a divine command and promise to take the land of Canaan, but they refused to "combine" the message with saving faith, to "mix them together."

mignymi [μίγνυμι, *3396*]

mignymi means to "mix," "mingle" and occurs four times. Matt. 27:34 refers to "wine mixed with gall," a potion offered to Christ on the cross, which he tasted but did not drink. Luke 13:1 refers to killing Galilean Jews, slaughtered by the Roman procurator, Pontius Pilate, who is described as having "mingled" their blood with the sacrifices they were offering. Rev. 8:7 describes, in an apocalyptic metaphor, one of the plagues inflicted by an angel on the world population as "hail and fire mixed with blood." In another metaphorical description of heaven, Rev. 15:2 refers to a "sea of glass mingled with fire."

migma [μίγμα, *3395*]

migma occurs only in John 19:39 with reference to a blend of spices — a "mixture of myrrh and aloes" — brought by Nicodemus to prepare Jesus' body for burial after his crucifixion.

MOCK, MOCKER, MOCKING

OT Words

lûṣ [לוּץ, **3887**]

lûṣ is a verb occurring about thirty times with the predominant sense of "mock," "deride," or "scorn." The term is found primarily in the wisdom literature of the Old Testament and is used mostly in a nominal sense. Those described as "mockers" or "scoffers" are depicted in a wholly negative light.

General references to "mockers," or "scoffers," "those who scorn," are found in Ps. 1:1; Prov. 1:22; 3:34; 9:7ff.; 13:1; 14:6ff.; 20:1; 21:11, 24; 22:10; 24:9; Isa. 29:20. Job 16:20 refers to the indignity of being mocked by one's friends. Ps. 119:51 refers to the psalmist being scorned by godless men.

qālas [קָלַס, **7046**]

qālas is found in only four contexts and indicates the action of "mocking" or "scorning" in each one. In 2 Kgs. 2:23, a group of small boys mocks the prophet Elisha. Ezek. 16:31 refers to Israel's idolatrous lifestyle. Yet because the people "scorned" a fee for their depravity, they were not technically prostitutes. However, they were still condemned by Yahweh for their behavior. Ezek. 22:5 declares that Jerusalem will become an object of scorn to the nations near and far. Hab. 1:10 records the arrogance of the Babylonian people who mock, or scoff, at other rulers.

qallāsāh [קַלָּסָה, **7048**]

qallāsāh is a rare noun derived from ***qālas*** (see above) found only in Ezek. 22:4. Yahweh will cause his people to become an "object of scorn," or "laughingstock," to all the nations, as punishment for Israel's sin.

lā'ab [לָעַב, **3931**]

lā'ab is a verb meaning "mock," or "jeer," found only in 2 Chr. 36:16 with reference to the sin of Israel in perpetually "mocking" the prophets, the messengers of Yahweh. Such an attitude provoked the Lord to punish them with great severity by removing them from their homeland.

hātal [הָתַל, **2048**]

hātal is a verb meaning "mock," "deceive." It occurs ten times and means "mock" in four of these contexts. Delilah accuses Samson of mocking her in Judg. 16:10ff. Elijah mocks the prophets of Baal in their futile attempts to invoke the action of their god in 1 Kgs. 18:27.

hatullîm [הֲתֻלִּים, **2049** (Aramaic)]

hatullîm is a noun derived from ***hātal*** (see above) meaning "mockers," or "those who scorn," found only in Job 17:2.

NT Words

empaizō [ἐμπαίζω, *1702*]

empaizō occurs in thirteen contexts meaning "to mock," or "scorn."

The primary usage of ***empaizō*** is found in relation to the Roman soldiers and the Jewish religious and civil authorities mocking Christ (cf. Matt. 20:19; 27:29ff., 41; Mark 10:34; 15:20, 31; Luke 18:32; 22:63; 23:11, 36). See also Luke 14:29.

empaiktēs [ἐμπαίκτης, *1703*]

empaiktēs is a noun derived from ***empaizō*** (see above). It refers to "mockers" or "scoffers" who will appear in the last days prior to the return of Christ, deriding the idea of his return. The word occurs only in 2 Pet. 3:3; Jude 18.

empaigmos [ἐμπαιγμός, *1701*]

empaigmos is another noun derived from ***empaizō*** (see above), with the abstract sense of "mocking." It occurs only in Heb. 11:36, with reference to the persecution suffered by God's people down through the ages, who were scorned by the enemies of God.

chleuazō [χλευάζω, *5512*]

chleuazō is a synonym for ***empaizō*** (see above) and means "mock," "deride," or "jeer." It is found only twice. Acts 2:13 mentions those who mocked the disciples' speaking in foreign languages under the influence of the Holy Spirit. The skeptical crowd believed the disciples to be drunk. Acts 17:32 refers to the Athenians, who mocked Paul for his belief in the resurrection from the dead.

myktērizō [μυκτηρίζω, *3456*]

myktērizō occurs only in Gal. 6:7 with the sense of "mock." It is used in the negative, expressing the serious warning that God is not to be mocked, lest one incur his judgment.

See Also: → LAUGH

MONEY

OT Words

qesîṭāh [קְשִׂיטָה, **7192**]

qesîṭāh is a rare noun, occurring only three times, referring to a "piece of money" of undefined value (cf. Gen. 33:19; Josh. 24:32; Job 42:11).

NT Words

nomisma [νόμισμα, *3546*]

nomisma is found only in Matt. 22:19 and refers to money collected for the purposes of taxation.

chalkos [χαλκός, *5475*]

chalkos refers to various items made of brass, including money. ***chalkos*** occurs five times and indicates money in three of these contexts. See Matt. 10:9; Mark 6:8, where Jesus instructs his disciples not to take any gold, silver, or brass with them on their evangelistic mission. Mark 12:41 refers to the rich placing large sums of money in the temple treasury.

kermatistēs [κερματιστής, *2773*]

kermatistēs means "moneychanger" and occurs only in John 2:14, with reference to the people trading in the Jerusalem temple.

kerma [κέρμα, *2772*]

kerma is a companion term to ***kermatistēs*** (see above) and refers to "coins," or "pieces of money." It occurs only in John 2:15 in the context of trading in the temple.

chrēma [χρῆμα, *5536*]

chrēma is found in seven contexts and means "riches," "money." The sense of "money" as a "sum of money" is found in Acts 4:37; 8:18, 20; 24:26.

philargyria [φιλαργυρία, *5365*]

philargyria occurs only in 1 Tim. 6:10 and refers to the sin of the "love of money" as the root of all evil.

See Also: → SILVER

MONTH

OT Words

ḥōdesh [חֹדֶשׁ, **2320**]

ḥōdesh is the most common term in the Old Testament for "month," found with that meaning in the great majority of the (approximately) 280 contexts in which it is found. ***ḥōdesh*** is a participial form, derived from the verb ***ḥādash*** ("to be new," "renew" → RENEW), and in about twenty instances is translated "new moon." (→ MOON)

Most occurrences of ***ḥōdesh*** meaning "month" are mundane, indicating the dating of various events — for example, the flood (cf. Gen. 7:11; 8:4); the crossing of the river Jordan (cf. Josh. 4:19); the commencement of the Jerusalem temple by Solomon (cf. 1 Kgs. 6:1); and the death of the false prophet Hananiah (cf. Jer. 28:17). The term likewise denotes the duration of events (cf. 1 Sam. 27:7; 2 Sam. 2:11).

In addition, ***ḥōdesh*** is found in contexts in which the dating of divine revelation from God to the prophets is recorded in the prophetic canon. This is particularly true of Ezekiel (cf. Ezek. 1:1; 8:1; 20:1; 24:1; 26:1; 29:1, 17; 30:20; 31:1; 32:1, 17; 40:1). See also Hag. 1:1; 2:1, 20; Zech. 1:1, 7; 7:1.

There is, however, a significant group of texts containing references to particular calendar months that are of distinctive significance for the Israelite people and their ritual worship. The examples listed below reveal an order of "redemptive-historical" significance, beginning with the time of Israel's deliverance from Egypt.

The first month of the "ceremonial calendar" (i.e., Abib, or Nisan, March-April), celebrates Israel's deliverance from her Egyptian enslavement. This great redemptive event was to be formally celebrated every year as the Feast of Passover, or Unleavened Bread, one of the three major festivals of the calendar. Every Israelite male was required to attend (cf. Exod. 12:2; 23:15; 34:18; Lev. 23:5; Num. 9:5; 28:16; 33:3; 2 Chr. 35:1; Ezra 6:19; Ezek. 45:21).

Though not explicitly indicated as taking place in the third month of Sivan (i.e., May-June), the second major Israelite feast is called the Feast of Weeks, or Harvest (Pentecost in the New Testament). It was to be celebrated seven weeks after Passover and thus fell in the third month (cf. Exod. 23:16; Lev. 23:15ff.; Deut. 16:9ff.; Num. 28:26ff.).

The third major ritual gathering is the Feast of Tabernacles (or Ingathering), a harvest festival celebrated in the middle of the seventh month (i.e., Ethanim 15,

September-October). This festival initially commemorated Yahweh's provision for, and protection of, his people during their time in the wilderness. It then continued as a festival of thanksgiving to God for the annual harvest of crops in the land. The Feast of Tabernacles was associated with the Feast of Trumpets (Ethanim 1) and the Day of Atonement (Ethanim 10), which were part of a major week-long celebration. Primary references to this feast in the seventh month, including Trumpets and the Day of Atonement, are found in Exod. 23:16; Lev. 23:33ff.; Num. 29:1ff.; Deut. 16:13ff. See also Lev. 23:24; Num. 29:1ff.; 1 Kgs. 8:2; 2 Chr. 5:3; Ezra 3:1, 6; Neh. 7:73; 8:2, 4; Ezek. 45:25.

The other significant month relating to festivals is the twelfth month of Adar (i.e., February-March). During this period, the Jewish people celebrated the deliverance of their ancestors in Persian exile from the plot to exterminate them during the time of Esther and the reign of Xerxes (Heb. Ahasuerus) in the first half of the fifth century B.C. References to this victory and subsequent celebration are found in Esth. 8:11ff.; 9:1ff. The name of this festival is Purim, derived from the ritual casting of the "lots" (*pûr*, "lot"), which gave rise to the projected date (Adar 13) on which the Jewish people were to be put to the sword (cf. Esth. 3:7, 13). That day, however, saw a most remarkable reversal of fortune, and the Jews gained an overwhelming victory over their enemies. Subsequently, the Feast of Purim took place on Adar 14 (cf. Neh. 9:19). Though the name of Yahweh is not mentioned anywhere in connection with this deliverance, it is clearly celebrated as a divine redemptive act along with the other major festivals of the Jewish calendar.

yeraḥ [יֶרַח, 3391]

yeraḥ is another term for "month" that occurs with far less frequency than ***ḥōdesh***. It is found in thirteen contexts and means "month" in twelve of these.

yeraḥ generally refers to the duration of months (cf. Exod. 2:2; Deut. 21:13; 33:14; 2 Kgs. 15:13; Job 3:6; 7:3; 29:2; 39:2; Zech. 11:8). Only in 1 Kgs. 6:37, 38 does ***yeraḥ*** indicate "month" as a date, or a particular point in time. 1 Kgs. 8:2 refers to the seventh-month Feast of Tabernacles.

yeraḥ [יְרַח, 3393 (Aramaic)]

yeraḥ is the Aramaic equivalent of the Hebrew ***yeraḥ*** (see above), occurring in only two places. Ezra 6:15 refers to a date, the third day of the month of Adar. Dan. 4:29 refers to a twelve-month period.

NT Words

mēn [μήν, *3376*]

mēn is the only term for "month" in the New Testament, occurring eighteen times in all. In most of these occurrences ***mēn*** is used in a durative sense, referring to various lengths of time involving months (e.g., Luke 1:24, 56; 4:25; 7:20; Acts 18:11; 28:11; Gal. 4:10; Rev. 9:5ff.; 11:2; 13:5; 22:2). The majority of contexts in the book of Revelation indicate these periods of time as episodes of divine judgment and chastisement. The exception is Rev. 22:2, which speaks of the tree of life in the heavenly city yielding its fruit each month for the healing of the nations. These periods of time mentioned in Revelation are likely to be non-literal.

In three places ***mēn*** refers to "month" as a point in time, or date. Luke 1:26 refers to the sixth month of Elizabeth's pregnancy (carrying her son, John) as the time of the angelic visitation to Mary, announcing that she would be the mother of the Messianic King, the Son of God. See also Luke 1:36. Rev. 9:15 designates a particular day, month, and year as the time for a savage punitive judgment on a third of humankind. The specific date is not mentioned, and once again a real, though non-literal, phenomenon is in view.

MONUMENT → GRAVE → PILLAR → REMEMBER

MOON

OT Words

yārēaḥ [יָרֵחַ, 3394]

yārēaḥ refers to the moon as a celestial body in conjunction with the sun (cf. Deut. 4:19; Job 25:5; 31:26; Pss. 121:6; 148:3; Eccl. 12:2; Isa. 13:10; 60:19; Ezek. 32:7; Hab. 3:11). In particular, Josh. 10:12, 13 record the miraculous divine restraining of the course of the sun and moon to enable Joshua and the Israelite army to pursue and catch the fleeing Amorite armies. A number of texts explicitly refer to the moon as a product of the divine creation (cf. Pss. 8:3; 104:19; 136:9; Jer. 31:35). Conversely, several texts in the book of Joel describe the destruction of the sun and moon as part of the consummate act of divine judgment to be inflicted on the cosmos on the great Day of the Lord (cf. Joel 2:10, 31; 3:15). In Gen. 37:9, the moon is included in the dream visions of Joseph, given to him by God in anticipation of that young man's rise to fame in the Egyptian court, paving the way for the arrival of his wider family in Egypt, recorded at the beginning of the book of Exodus.

In addition, the moon is also indicated as an illicit object of worship, along with the sun, in Deut. 17:3; 2 Kgs. 23:5; Jer. 8:2.

yeraḥ [**יָרֵחַ, 3391**]

yeraḥ is a noun occurring thirteen times in all. In eleven of these contexts, it means "month." However, ***yeraḥ*** also means "moon" in two places, both in connection with the sun (Deut. 33:14; Isa. 60:20).
(➠ MONTH)

ḥōdesh [**חֹדֶשׁ, 2320**]

ḥōdesh, like ***yeraḥ*** above, is a noun with the primary sense of "month." However, on nine occasions it refers to the "new moon" in literal, mundane contexts (cf. 1 Sam. 20:5, 18, 24; 2 Kgs. 4:23; Ps. 81:3; Isa. 66:23; Ezek. 46:1, 6; Amos 8:5).

lebānāh [**לְבָנָה, 3842**]

lebānāh is a rare term for "moon," occurring only three times. It is used metaphorically in Song 6:10 to refer to the physical beauty of the "lover," describing him as "fair as the moon." The other two references to ***lebānāh*** occur in prophetic contexts that anticipate the eschatological climax of human history. They indicate changes to the moon as a consequence of Yahweh's negative judgment on a sinful world (cf. Isa. 24:23); and the powerful enhancing of the moon's brightness as a consequence of the divine renewal of the cosmos at the end of the age (cf. Isa. 30:26).

NT WORDS

selēnē [σελήνη, *4582*]

selēnē occurs nine times and refers to the "moon" predominantly in the context of the cataclysmic changes to the cosmos that will take place at the consummation of history when Christ shall return in glory. Six of these texts refer to the darkening of the moon along with the destruction of the sun as one of the signs of cosmic dissolution at the end of the age (cf. Matt. 24:29; Mark 13:24; Luke 21:25; Acts 2:20; Rev. 6:12; 8:12). A general reference to the light of the moon is found in 1 Cor. 15:41. Rev. 12:1 refers to the moon in an apocalyptic vision of the Christ child and his mother, who is described as having the moon under her feet. Rev. 21:23 describes the illumination of the heavenly city as a supernatural one, not needing the light of the moon, or the sun.

neomēnia [νεομηνία, *3561*]

neomēnia is found only in Col. 2:16 with reference to a "new moon."

MORNING

OT WORDS

bōqer [**בֹּקֶר, 1242**]

bōqer is a common term in the Old Testament referring to "morning" in the large majority of the 200 or so contexts in which it is found.

The usage of ***bōqer*** is primarily mundane, referring to morning simply as the first part of the day (cf. Gen. 24:54; Exod. 8:20; Num. 22:13; Josh. 3:1; Judg. 6:31; 2 Sam. 17:22; Ps. 73:14; Eccl. 11:6; Isa. 5:11; Ezek. 12:8; Hos. 13:3). In Gen. 1:5ff., the "morning" is depicted as part of the created cycle of the day (i.e., morning and evening).

Elsewhere, ***bōqer*** is utilized in the ritual legislation of the Mosaic covenant, referring to "morning" in the context of daily (morning and evening) sacrifices (cf. Exod. 29:41; Lev. 6:9ff.; 24:3; Num. 9:12ff.; Deut. 16:4; 2 Chr. 31:3; Ezra 3:3; Job 1:5; Ezek. 46:13ff.; Dan. 8:14).

shaḥar [**שַׁחַר, 7837**]

shaḥar is a noun occurring around twenty times with the primary meaning "dawn" or "early morning." Occasionally the term is used adverbially to mean "at dawn." Mundane references are found in the following texts: Gen. 19:15; 32:24ff.; Josh. 6:15; Judg. 19:25; 1 Sam. 9:26; Job 38:12; Neh. 4:21; Amos 4:13; Jonah 4:7.

shaḥar is used metaphorically as well — for example, the eyes of Leviathan are described as being "like the rays of the dawn." The "waking of the dawn" is mentioned in Pss. 57:8; 108:2. The physical beauty of the lover in the Song of Songs is described with the expression "like the dawn." The fallen angel from heaven is described in Isa. 14:12 as "the son of dawn." See also Isa. 58:8; Hos. 6:3.

mishḥār [**מִשְׁחָר, 4891**]

mishḥār is a noun occurring only in Ps. 110:3 with the metaphorical sense of "early morning" or "dawn" in the phrase "womb of the morning," from which renewed youthful vigor will come for the people of Yahweh.

nōgah [**נֹגַהּ, 5053** (Aramaic)]

nōgah is an Aramaic term for "morning" or "daybreak" that is found only in Dan. 6:19.

NT Words

prōi [πρωΐ, *4404*]

prōi is an adverbial form and occurs fourteen times meaning "(early) in the morning," in the natural temporal sense (e.g., Matt. 16:3; 21:18; 27:1; Mark 1:35; 11:20; John 20:1; 21:4; Acts 28:23).

orthros [ὄρθρος, *3722*]

orthros is a synonym for ***prōi*** (see above) and is likewise translated as an adverbial phrase "early in the morning" (cf. Luke 24:1; John 8:2; Acts 5:21).

orthrizō [ὀρθρίζω, *3719*]

orthrizō is the verb from which ***orthros*** (see above) is derived. It is found only in Luke 21:38, meaning "to come early in the morning."

prōinos [πρωϊνός, *4407*]

prōinos is an adjectival form related to the adverb ***prōi***, which has the sense of "in relation to the morning." It is used only in Rev. 2:28 with reference to the "morning star," the promised reward from the ascended Christ in heaven to those who persevere in faithful obedience to Christ to the end.

MORROW → TOMORROW

MORTAL

NT Words

thnētos [θνητός, *2349*]

thnētos is an adjective that is translated "mortal" in the sense of "liable to death and decay." It occurs six times and refers exclusively to our mortal bodies (cf. Rom. 6:12; 8:11; 1 Cor. 15:53, 54; 2 Cor. 4:11; 5:4). All texts except Rom. 6:12 promise that our mortality will be exchanged for immortality in the light of the finished redemptive work of Christ and his resurrection from the dead.

MORTIFY → DEATH

MOST HOLY PLACE → TEMPLE

MOTH

OT Words

'āsh [עָשׁ, **6211**]

'āsh means "grass," and "moth." The latter sense is indicated in seven of its twelve occurrences. All uses are metaphorical. In Job 4:19; 13:28; 27:18, ***'āsh*** describes the fragility and decay of human life and possessions. See also Ps. 39:11; Isa. 50:9; Hos. 5:12.

NT Words

sēs [σής, *4597*]

sēs is found only three times in the New Testament, referring to "moth" in a metaphorical sense on each occasion. Matt. 6:19, 20; Luke 12:33 refer to the corruptibility and transitory nature of human possessions. Jesus exhorts his hearers to build up heavenly wealth that cannot be subject to the process of rot and decay brought on by moth infestation, or loss through theft.

sētobrōtos [σητόβρωτος, *4598*]

sētobrōtos is found only in Jas. 5:2, meaning "moth-eaten" in relation to one's clothes.

MOTHER

OT Words

'ēm [אֵם, **517**]

'ēm occurs over two hundred times meaning "mother," referring to both humans and animals.

In a number of general references, ***'ēm*** refers to "mother(s)" in the sense of the role or institution of "motherhood," with no specific person in view. Gen. 2:24, for example, refers to a man leaving his father and mother in order to marry. Exod. 20:12; Deut. 5:16 command children to honor their father and mother, with a corresponding curse on those who dishonor their parents in Deut. 27:16. Exod. 21:15 lists the killing of one's mother as a capital offense under the law. The cursing of one's parents is also unambiguously condemned (cf. Exod. 21:17; Lev. 20:9; Ezek. 22:7; Mic. 7:6). Lev. 18:7ff.; 20:14ff. lay down explicit provisions whereby sexual intimacy with one's mother or maternal relatives is strictly forbidden, on pain of death or banishment from the community. Apart from the Pentateuch, admonitions to honor one's mother (and father) and obey parental instruction, including teaching from one's mother, are commonly found in the book of Proverbs (cf. Prov. 15:20; 19:26; 20:20; 23:22, 25). Other general references to "mother" in a nonspecific sense are found in Deut. 21:18ff.; Pss. 22:9; 139:13; Song 3:4; Isa. 8:4.

'ēm is also used to refer to particular individuals. Gen. 3:20 depicts Eve as "the mother of all living." Gen. 24:67 refers to Sarah, Isaac's mother. Rahab pleads with the Israelite spies in Jericho to spare her family, including explicit mention of her mother and father, when the city falls to the Israelite army (cf. Josh. 2:13; 6:23). See also Judg. 14:2ff.; Job 1:21; Ruth 1:8; 1 Sam. 2:19; 1 Kgs. 3:7; 2 Kgs. 21:19; Esth. 2:7; Eccl. 5:15; Jer. 20:4.

A handful of texts use ***'ēm*** metaphorically. In Judg. 5:7, Deborah is referred to as a "mother in Israel," or a figure of civil authority. Isa. 50:1 is a difficult text to interpret, though perhaps the term "mother" refers to Israel as Judah's "mother," whom Yahweh had previously "divorced" by sending into captivity at the hands of the Assyrians. Jer. 50:12 (another oblique metaphor) most likely refers to the land of Israel as "mother," who will be disgraced and turned into a desert (cf. also Ezek. 16:3; Hos. 2:2).

In several places ***'ēm*** also refers to the mothers of animals. Exod. 23:19; 34:26; Deut. 14:21, contain the instruction never to boil a kid goat in its mother's milk. See also Lev. 22:7; Deut. 22:6.

NT Words

mētēr [μήτηρ, *3384*]

mētēr is found approximately ninety times meaning "mother" in both a literal and metaphorical sense.

mētēr frequently refers to mothers of specific persons, including a number of references to Mary the mother of Jesus (cf. Matt. 1:18; 2:11ff.; 12:46ff.; Mark 3:31ff.; Luke 2:34, 43ff.; John 2:1ff.; 19:25ff.; Acts 1:14). See also Matt. 14:8; 20:20; Mark 5:40; Luke 7:12ff.; Acts 12:12; Rom. 16:13; 2 Tim. 1:5.

mētēr also refers to "mother" in non-specific, generalized contexts. There is the command to honor one's father and mother in Matt. 15:4; 19:19; Mark 7:10; Luke 18:20; Eph. 6:2. Blessing is promised to those who leave father and mother for the sake of the gospel in Matt. 19:29; Mark 10:29ff. The necessity of leaving father and mother in order to marry is indicated in Matt. 19:5; Mark 10:7, 19; Eph. 5:31. Matt. 10:35ff.; Luke 14:26 affirm that love for one's mother and father is to be subservient to the love of Christ. In confronting the necessity of "new birth," Nicodemus had great difficulty in grasping what Jesus meant. His question in John 3:4 illustrates this: "How can a man enter his mother's womb a second time and be born again?" Paul, in Gal. 1:15, declares that God had called him to be his servant prior to his birth, or literally, "from his mother's womb."

mētēr is also found in metaphorical contexts. In several contexts, Jesus declared that his disciples, and all those who obey the word of God, are his "mother and brothers," that is, his true spiritual family (cf. Matt. 12:48ff.; Mark 3:33ff.; Luke 8:21). Gal. 4:26 mentions the heavenly Jerusalem as the "mother" of the church of Christ. In Rev. 17:5, the city of Babylon is declared to be the "mother of harlots," supreme in her idolatry.

See Also: → NURSE

MOTHER-IN-LAW

OT Words

ḥôtenet **[חוֹתֶנֶת, 2859]**

ḥôtenet is a noun derived from the verb ***ḥātan*** which has the sense of establishing a legal relationship through marriage. In the majority of contexts in which ***ḥātan*** is found, the term indicates the relationship of a "father-in-law." However, ***ḥôtenet*** is the feminine participial form of the verb and is found only in Deut. 27:23, where it refers to the prohibited practice of a sexual liaison with one's mother-in-law, a relationship that will bring down the curse of God on those involved.

ḥamôt **[חָמוֹת, 2545]**

ḥamôt occurs in eleven contexts and is translated "mother-in-law" on each occasion. The term is found almost exclusively in the book of Ruth, with reference to Naomi, the mother-in-law of Ruth (cf. Ruth 1:14; 2:11, 18ff.; 3:1, 6, 16, 17). See also Mic. 7:6 for a general reference to "mother-in-law."

NT Words

penthera [πενθερά, *3994*]

penthera occurs five times and means "mother-in-law" in each instance. The "mother-in-law" of the apostle Peter is specifically mentioned in the context of her illness and subsequent cure by Jesus (Matt. 8:14; Mark 1:30; Luke 4:38). The other references to "mother-in-law" are found in Matt. 10:35; Luke 12:53, indicating that the impact of the gospel on families will inevitably entail some division among family members — between those who believe, and those who do not.

MOUNT, MOUNTAIN

OT Words

har **[הַר, 2022]**

har is a common term, occurring over five hundred times throughout the Old Testament with the primary meanings "mount," "mountain," in the overwhelming majority of contexts.

References to mountains as geological, geographic features in mundane contexts are found in Gen. 7:19ff.; Judg. 6:2; Job 9:5; Ps. 72:3; Song 2:8; Isa. 18:6; 40:4. As the specific product of divine creation, mountains are mentioned in Pss. 90:2; 104:8ff.; Prov. 8:25; Amos 4:13.

Specific mountains are mentioned by name in a number of places in a variety of contexts (Mt. Sinai is a special case and will be discussed in detail below). Mt. Carmel, the site of Elijah's victory over the prophets of Baal, is noted in 1 Kgs. 18:19ff. The account of King Saul's death on Mt. Gilboa is recorded in 1 Sam. 31:1ff.; 2 Sam. 1:6. Other mountains located in Canaan which are mentioned include Mt. Hor (cf. Num. 20:22ff.; 33:23ff.); Mt. Nebo (cf. Deut. 32:49); Mt. Tabor (cf. Judg. 4:6); Mt. Hermon (cf. Deut. 4:48; Josh. 11:17; 12:1ff.). In particular, Mt. Seir is noted in Deut. 2:1ff.; Josh. 24:4. And in Ezek. 35:1ff., an oracle of judgment is delivered against the "mountains of Seir," symbolizing the entire nation of Edom. Mt. Gerizim and Mt. Ebal are the locations selected for a unique ceremony of covenant renewal, whereby two groups of Israelite tribes face each other on each mountain across a valley and rehearse the blessings and curses of the Mosaic law covenant received at Sinai (cf. Deut. 11:29; 27:4, 12ff.; Josh. 8:30ff.; Judg. 9:7).

Mountains are also designated in the Old Testament as sites for the worship of Yahweh. An early example is noted in Gen. 22:2, 14, where Mt. Moriah is the location chosen by God for the "test" sacrifice of Isaac, Abraham's son. This human sacrifice was never intended to take place, and Yahweh effected the substitution of a ram.

The prime example of a mountain location for the worship of Yahweh is Mt. Sinai (or Horeb, as it sometimes referred to), which is extensively referred to throughout the Old Testament. It is first mentioned (as "Horeb") in Exod. 3:1, where Yahweh speaks to Moses in the wilderness through the "burning bush," identifying the mountain as the place to which Moses will one day return to worship him (cf. Exod. 3:12). See also Deut. 1:6, 19; 4:11. The people of Israel make camp in front of the "mountain of God" (cf. Exod. 19:2ff.; 20:18; 24:4ff.). Mt. Sinai is frequently identified as the primary location for the revelation of the divine covenant (cf. Exod. 19:11, 20ff.; 24:16; 34:2ff.; Lev. 7:38; 26:46; Num. 3:1; Deut. 5:4ff.; 22ff.; 9:9ff.; 10:1ff.; Neh. 9). It is also explicitly cited as a place for Israelite worship in Num. 28:6.

Another theologically significant use of the term ***har*** is found in reference to Mount Zion, literally referring to the mountain area on and around which the city of Jerusalem was built. Not only does "Zion" refer symbolically to the city of Jerusalem as a whole, but Mt. Zion is also specifically indicated as the site of Solomon's temple and signifies the heart of Yahweh's kingdom on earth — his throne, or dwelling place. References to Mt. Zion as Yahweh's "holy mountain (or hill)" as a worship site for God's people are found in Pss. 15:1; 24:3; 48:1ff.; 99:9; 125:1. Mt. Zion as the dwelling place of God is explicitly indicated in Ps. 74:2. It is also the center of his kingdom on earth (cf. Isa. 4:5; 8:18; 24:23; Zech. 8:3). In other significant prophetic contexts, Mt. Zion is depicted as a beacon which shall draw the nations to Yahweh, a portent of universal transformation and worldwide salvation (cf. Isa. 2:2ff.; 11:9; 27:13; 56:7; 65:25; 66:20; Jer. 31:23; Mic. 4:1ff.). Mt. Zion is also designated as the site of the renewed worship of the people of Israel after their return from captivity (cf. Ezek. 20:40; Zeph. 3:11). Mt. Zion serves as the location for Ezekiel's visionary temple in Ezek. 40:2; 43:12.

Representing the city of Jerusalem as a whole, Mt. Zion is depicted as an object of desolation, the focus of a divine judgment at the hands of the invading Babylonian armies in Lam. 5:8. Ezek. 11:23 predicts Yahweh's abandonment of the Jerusalem temple as the "glory cloud" stands on top of Mt. Zion, ready to depart to Babylon. Mt. Zion (i.e., Jerusalem) is also depicted as the starting point for the emergence of a godly remnant, who will experience a renewed salvation granted by God (cf. Isa. 37:32; Joel 2:32).

In more generalized contexts, ***har*** refers to mountains as places where the Israelites engage in idolatrous worship (cf. Isa. 57:7; Jer. 3:6; Ezek. 22:9; Hos. 4:13; 10:8). The term "mountain" also refers to the location for the promised renewal of Jerusalem, both in terms of return from exile and also in anticipation of the coming Messianic King (cf. Ezek. 17:22ff.; 34:13ff.; 36:1ff.). In particular, Ezek. 37:22 refers symbolically to the reunification of the land, to one nation reunited on the "mountains of Israel." Mountains are also called upon metaphorically to witness the crimes of the Israelite people in Mic. 6:12.

The phrase "mountains of Israel" is likewise used as a symbol for the nation as a whole in contexts where the people of God are subject to his judgment and wrath (cf. Ezek. 6:2ff.; 33:28). The phrase is also used to designate the site of the defeat of Israel's enemies in Ezek. 39:2ff.

har occurs in the expression "mountain of God" to refer symbolically to the heavenly dwelling place of Yahweh prior to the fall of humankind. It also refers to the original home of the angelic being who was subsequently to be cast out of heaven (lit., "from the mountain of God") for his rebellion against God (cf. Ezek. 28:14, 16).

Zech. 14:4, 5 refer, in apocalyptic imagery, to dividing the Mount of Olives, the site of the ultimate victory of the Messianic King against the nations, and establishing the everlasting kingdom of Yahweh.

tûr [טוּר, **2906** (Aramaic)]

tûr is an Aramaic term occurring only twice and meaning "mountain." In Dan. 2:35, the term refers metaphorically to the worldwide kingdom of God in the context of Nebuchadnezzar's dream, in which the stone that smashed the metal statue grew into a mountain that filled the whole earth. Dan. 2:45 refers to mountain in a generalized context, describing the dynamic "stone" as having been cut from a "mountain" by no human hand.

NT Words

oros [ὄρος, *3735*]

oros is the only term for "mount," "mountain" in the New Testament. It occurs around sixty times.

The natural sense of "mountain" as a geological or geographic location is indicated, for example, in Matt. 17:20; Mark 5:5; Luke 21:21; 1 Cor. 13:2. Mountain locations are often mentioned in association with Jesus' ministry (cf. Matt. 5:1; 14:23; 15:29; Mark 3:13; John 6:3); and in particular, the Mount of Olives (e.g., Matt. 21:1; Mark 11:1; Luke 19:29; John 8:1). Jesus sometimes withdrew to mountain areas to pray (cf. Mark 6:46; Luke 6:12; 9:28). The temple mount was also the location for one of the temptations of Christ initiated by Satan (cf. Matt. 4:5; Luke 4:8).

Occasionally, specific mountain areas are given a particular significance in the New Testament. Matt. 17:1; Mark 9:2; 2 Pet. 1:18 refer to the so-called Mount of Transfiguration, where Jesus provided a glimpse of his essential heavenly glory to his disciples Peter, James, and John. John 4:20, 21 refer indirectly to Mount Gerizim as the central shrine of Samaritan worship. ***oros*** refers in several places to Mt. Sinai — as the place where God spoke to Moses in the burning bush (Acts 7:30); as the place where God revealed to Moses the pattern of the tabernacle to be built as the focal point for Israelite worship (Heb. 8:5); and as the allegorical representation of the old covenant (Gal. 4:24, 25). Heb. 12:18 refers to the historical Mt. Sinai in contrast to "Mt. Zion" in Heb. 12:22, the symbolic designation of the heavenly Jerusalem to which all believers have now come. Similarly, Rev. 14:1; 21:10 indicate "Mt. Zion" as symbolic of the heavenly dwelling place of Christ and his people.

In the apocalyptic imagery of the book of Revelation, the dissolution of the cosmos on the great Day of the Lord includes the destruction of mountains (cf. Rev. 6:14ff.; 8:8; 16:20). See also Rev. 17:9.

Additional Notes

"Mountain" imagery plays a very significant part in shaping the reader's understanding of the true earthly and heavenly (or spiritual) significance of Jerusalem and the temple. The Old Testament use of ***har*** indicates that Mt. Sinai and Mt. Zion, in particular, are of key significance in shaping the Israelite understanding of the location of their God. Sinai was the mountain from which Yahweh issued the law covenant and bound Israel to himself in a solemn oath. It was a place that remained forever sacred in the national consciousness throughout their history as recorded in Scripture. Similarly, Mt. Zion, symbolically embracing both city and temple as the dwelling place of Yahweh on earth, figures prominently in the Hebrew prophetic canon as a location of supreme significance for the people of Israel.

The New Testament term ***oros*** likewise continues to develop the theological significance of the "mountain of God." Although there are fewer references to Sinai and Zion in the New Testament, their occurrences are highly significant. The gospel texts relating to Jesus' transfiguration and the references found in Galatians, Hebrews, and Revelation are especially important.

The consistent development of a "mountain" theme throughout both Old and New Testaments demonstrates the powerful motif of God coming to dwell among humankind. The earthly kingdom of Israel, along with the centrality of Jerusalem and its temple, reflect a corresponding reality in the heavenly realm.

MOURN, MOURNER, MOURNING

OT Words

'ābal [אָבַל, **56**]

'ābal is a verb found in approximately forty contexts with the consistent sense of "mourn," or "lament," applied to the people and metaphorically to inanimate objects. The underlying emotions expressed are those of anguish and sorrow in a number of contexts.

Mourning over the death of close family is indicated in Gen. 37:34; 2 Sam. 13:37; 19:1; 1 Chr. 7:20. In relation to persons other than one's family, Samuel laments for Saul (1 Sam. 15:35; 16:1); and the people of Judah mourn the death of King Josiah (2 Chr. 35:24). Mourning for the dead in general is noted in 2 Sam. 14:2; and mourning for oneself, over one's miserable lot in life, in Job 14:22. Exhortations not to mourn are found in Neh. 8:9; Ezek. 7:12.

Moving away from lamenting for individuals, ***'ābal*** also indicates mourning at a corporate or community level. In the face of judgment from God, Israel mourns over her terrible fate (cf. Exod. 33:4; Num. 14:39; 1 Sam. 6:19; Jer. 14:2; Ezek. 7:27; Amos 8:8). Joel 1:9 specifically mentions the priests who mourn over Yahweh's judgment against the land. Ezra mourns over the sin of the returned exiles in Ezra 10:6. The whole world is said to mourn over the punishment God metes out to the nations (cf. Isa. 24:4, 7). Egyptians are also described as lamenting the judgment of God against their nation (cf. Isa. 19:18.)

'ābal also refers to mourning over inanimate objects. Samaria is said to mourn the loss of its idols (cf. Hos. 10:5). The destruction of the city of Jerusalem is mourned in Neh. 1:4; Isa. 66:10; Jer. 4:28. Daniel mourns over a disturbing visionary revelation in Dan. 10:2.

'ābal is also found in several metaphorical contexts. It is predicted in Isa. 3:26, for example, that the gates of Zion shall mourn over the destruction of Judah and Jerusalem. See also Lam. 2:8. Several texts describe the land of Israel mourning over its terrible fate under the judgment of God (cf. Isa. 33:9; Jer. 12:4, 11; 23:10; Hos. 4:3; Amos 1:2). The earth is said to mourn over the destruction of Judah (Jer. 4:28). Ezek. 31:15 refers to the ocean "deep" mourning over Egypt's destruction.

'ēbel [אֵבֶל, 60]

'ēbel is a noun derived from ***'ābal*** (see above) and is consistently translated "mourning" in the context of death and divine judgment. ***'ēbel*** occurs around thirty times.

In the context of personal bereavement over the death of immediate family members, ***'ēbel*** refers to "mourning" at the passing of one's father (Gen. 27:41; 50:10, 11). Bathsheba mourns over the death of her husband Uriah (2 Sam. 11:27). David laments over the death of his son Absalom (2 Sam. 19:2). In Ezek. 24:17, there is an interesting variation on this theme. Here Ezekiel is forbidden to mourn the death of his wife as a sign to Israel that they in turn will be denied the privilege of mourning over the destruction of Jerusalem when God passes judgment on their land. Outside of the family context, ***'ēbel*** refers in Deut. 34:8 to Israel's mourning at the death of Moses, their leader.

The mourning of God's people in the face of divine judgment for their sin is indicated in Jer. 6:26; 16:7; Amos 5:16; 8:10; Mic. 1:8. Similarly, the Israelite community in Persian exile mourns the approaching calamity of a threatened attack against them in Esth. 4:3. This threat never arrives, however, and they are delivered from their enemies.

Mourning in general terms is mentioned in Job 30:31; Eccl. 3:4; Zech. 7:5. In 2 Sam. 14:2; Eccl. 7:2, 4, ***'ēbel*** is used adjectivally to refer to mourning garments.

In the context of a "thematic reversal," the mourning of God's people is transformed into gladness as a consequence of divine intervention in reality (cf. Esth. 9:22); or in anticipation of Yahweh's act of deliverance and renewal (cf. Isa. 60:20; 61:3; Jer. 31:13; Lam. 5:15).

sāphad [סָפַד, 5594]

sāphad is a synonym for ***'ābal*** (see above). It occurs around thirty times and likewise means "mourn" or "lament."

Mourning over the passing of loved ones is indicated in several places. Abraham mourns for his wife, Sarah (Gen. 23:2); and the passing of Jacob is lamented in Gen. 50:10. Bathsheba mourns the death of her husband Uriah (2 Sam. 11:26). In Ezek. 24:16, Ezekiel is forbidden to mourn the sudden passing of his wife, taken by God (see ***'ēbel***, above).

sāphad also refers to mourning the death of national leaders — for example, Samuel (1 Sam. 25:1; 28:3); Saul and Jonathan (2 Sam. 1:12); King Zedekiah (Jer. 34:3 [predicted]). See also 2 Sam. 3:31; 1 Kgs. 13:29; 14:13; Jer. 49:3. In particular, Zech. 10:10, 12 record the prophetic anticipation of mourning over the slain Messiah.

On the national level, ***sāphad*** refers in a number of contexts to mourning for the Israelite people. Mic. 1:8 indicates the prophet's intention to mourn for the nation in the face of God's judgment against them. Jer. 4:8; Joel 1:13 contain explicit instructions for the people of God to lament over the continuing wrath of Yahweh against them. In contrast, there are a couple of texts that actually forbid the people to lament, denying them the traditional means of expressing their grief as part of their punishment from God (cf. Jer. 16:5; Ezek. 24:23). In addition, Jer. 16:4, 6; 22:18; 25:33 declare that no one shall mourn those Israelites slain in the land as a consequence of the impending Babylonian invasion initiated by God himself.

'ābēl **[אָבֵל, 57]**

'ābēl is another noun derived from ***'ābal*** (see above), translated "mourning" in each of the eight contexts in which it is found.

Jacob's mourning for Joseph, whom he wrongly supposed to be dead, is recorded in Gen. 37:35. In Ps. 35:14, ***'ābēl*** conveys the idea of mourning "like one who laments (the death of) his mother." General references to "mourners" are found in Job 29:25; Isa. 57:14.

Lamenting the prospect of dire calamity is indicated in Esth. 6:12, when Haman realizes that his plan to destroy Mordecai has been thwarted.

'ābēl is used metaphorically in Lam. 1:4, where the "roads to Zion" are said to mourn the loss and destruction of the city of Jerusalem.

Divine comfort is promised to those who mourn in Isa. 61:2, 3.

qûn **[קוּן, 6969]**

qûn is a verb occurring eight times, meaning "to lament," "take up a dirge, or lamentation." 2 Sam. 1:17; 3:33; 2 Chr. 35:25 refer to raising a lament for those who have died. Jer. 9:17 contains a nominal use of ***qûn*** with reference to "mourning women." Ezek. 27:32 refers to the chanting of a funeral lament for the city of Tyre; and in Ezek. 32:16 the same is done for the nation of Egypt.

qînāh **[קִינָה, 7015]**

qînāh is a noun derived from ***qûn*** (see above), occurring in approximately twenty contexts with the consistent meaning "lamentation," or "funeral dirge."

Lamentations for individuals are recorded in 2 Sam. 1:17, for the deaths of Saul and Jonathan, and 2 Chr. 35:25, for the death of King Josiah.

More commonly, laments are indicated with respect to the people of Israel. These are noted for both the northern and southern kingdoms in Israel and relate to the expectation of imminent calamity and destruction as a consequence of the people's sin (cf. Jer. 7:29; 9:10, 20; Ezek. 2:10; 19:1, 14; Amos 5:1; 8:10). Similarly, dirges are also invoked for the nations of Egypt (cf. Ezek. 32:2, 16); and Tyre (cf. Ezek. 26:17; 27:2, 32; 28:12).

qādar **[קָדַר, 6937]**

This verb occurs seventeen times, meaning "to grow black or dark," or "to mourn or lament." The latter sense is explicitly indicated mostly in general contexts (cf. Job 5:11; Pss. 35:14; 38:6). In Pss. 42:9; 43:2, the psalmist is said to mourn in the face of persecution by his enemies. See also Ezek. 31:15.

qādar can also mean "to grow black" in the metaphorical sense of "darkening one's mood," or "going into mourning" (cf. Jer. 8:21; 14:2).

mispēd **[מִסְפֵּד, 4553]**

mispēd is a participial noun form derived from ***sāphad*** (see above). It occurs sixteen times and means "mourning," "lamentation," or "wailing" in each case.

Personal lamentation for the passing of Jacob is indicated in Gen. 50:10. Mourning in the face of anticipated disaster is noted in Esth. 4:3.

National lamenting or wailing over the imminent judgment of Yahweh coming upon his people is invoked in Isa. 22:12; Jer. 6:26; Amos 5:16, 17; Mic. 1:8, 11. Similarly, lamentation is in store for the nation of Moab (cf. Jer. 48:38); and Tyre (cf. Ezek. 27:31). In Joel 2:12, Yahweh urges his wayward people to confess their sin and return to him "with mourning." Zech. 12:10, 11 prophetically anticipates mourning over the death of the coming Messianic King.

Ps. 30:11 sounds a note of hope with the psalmist's affirmation that Yahweh has turned his mourning into dancing.

nehî **[נְהִי, 5092]**

nehî is a noun translated "song of mourning," "wailing," or "lamentation" in each of the seven contexts in which it occurs. All references speak of the mourning associated with the judgment of God to come upon the nation of Israel in the form of invasion and exile at the hands of both the Assyrians (cf. Amos 5:16; Mic. 2:4); and the Babylonians (cf. Jer. 9:10ff.; 31:15).

NT Words

koptō **[κόπτω, *2875*]**

koptō is a verb found in seven contexts, meaning "lament" or "mourn" in five of these places.

Mourning as a social custom is mentioned in a generalized context in Matt. 11:17. The peoples of the earth are said to mourn at the appearing of the Son of Man in glory at the end of the age. The context here suggests that it will involve a cry of dismay or anguish (cf. Matt. 24:30; Rev. 1:7). On the occasion of the death of Jairus' daughter (whom Jesus subsequently bought back to life), the wailing of crowds in the street is noted in Luke 8:52. The wailing of a number of women accompanying Jesus on the way to his crucifixion is noted in Luke 23:27. Rev. 18:9 contains a visionary description of the kings of the earth lamenting the demise of the city of Babylon.

kopetos [κοπετός, *2870*]

kopetos is a noun derived from ***koptō***, occurring only in Acts 8:2 and referring to the "lamentation" made for Stephen at his martyrdom.

thrēneō [θρηνέω, *2354*]

thrēneō is a synonym for ***koptō*** (see above). It is found in only four places, with general references to mourning or lamenting (Matt. 11:17; Luke 7:32; John 16:20). Luke 23:27 refers to people following Jesus and mourning for him on the way to his crucifixion.

klauthmos [κλαυθμός, *2805*]

klauthmos occurs on nine occasions and refers to "wailing," "weeping," or "lamentation" in the context of severe anguish. It is the term used in the expression "wailing and gnashing of teeth," where "wailing" conveys the emotion of stark horror and despair at being denied entry into the eternal kingdom of God (cf. Matt. 8:12; 13:42, 50; 22:13; 24:51; 25:30; Luke 13:28). Lamentation or wailing in a more generalized context is indicated in Matt. 2:18. In Acts 20:37, ***klauthmos*** refers to the weeping of the Ephesian elders as they bade farewell to the apostle Paul.

odyrmos [ὀδυρμός, *3602*]

odyrmos refers to mourning and lamentation, expressing great sadness. The term occurs only in Matt. 2:18; 2 Cor. 7:7.

pentheō [πενθέω, *3996*]

pentheō is a verb occurring eleven times, meaning "mourn" in a number of contexts.

Mourning that expresses sorrow for sin is indicated in Matt. 5:4, for which blessing shall be granted. 1 Cor. 5:2 notes the absence of such an attitude. See also 2 Cor. 12:21; Jas. 4:9 in this regard. Mourning expressed at the death of Jesus is noted in Mark 16:10. Rev. 18:11ff. records the outpouring of lamentation by the nations of the world at the destruction of the city of Babylon.

penthos [πένθος, *3997*]

penthos is the noun derived from ***pentheō*** and is translated "sorrow," "mourning." ***penthos*** is found in only four contexts.

Jas. 4:9 exhorts sinners to mourn for their sin. Rev. 18:7 refers to the arrogant boast of the Babylonian rulers, represented as a class by the metaphor of a "queen," who prides herself on the boast that she will never know any sorrow, or mourning. See also Rev. 18:4. By way of stark contrast, Rev. 21:4 promises the resurrected people of God that mourning shall be abolished forever in the heavenly kingdom.

See Also: → WEEP

MOUSE

OT Words

'akbār [עַכְבָּר, **5909**]

'akbār is a noun referring exclusively to the rodent "mouse," or "rat." It is found in only six contexts. In Lev. 11:29; Isa. 66:17 mice are listed as unclean—totally unfit for human consumption. Those who eat such animals will come under divine condemnation. 1 Sam. 6:4, 5, 11, 18 refer to the five golden mice (or rats) made by the Philistine rulers as part of an offering given to Yahweh, the God of the Israelites, in the hope that this might bring to an end the terrible suffering they had endured while they had the ark of the covenant in their possession.

MOUTH

OT Words

peh [פֶּה, **6310**]

peh is a common noun with a variety of meanings such as "mouth," "command," "edge," "word," "hole." By far the most common of these meanings is "mouth," found in a number of contexts. This sense gives rise, metaphorically, to most of the other nuances of the term listed above. ***peh*** occurs in approximately five hundred contexts, with the sense of "mouth" in about two-thirds of these. (→ COMMANDMENT → EDGE → WORD)

In literal contexts, ***peh*** indicates the mouth of an animal or bird in Gen. 8:11; Num. 22:28; Job 41:21; Ps. 22:21. Frequent references are also made to the mouths of people. For example, the mouth is indicated as the organ of speech in Deut. 23:23; Exod. 4:12. Mundane references are found in Gen. 45:12; Exod. 4:11; Judg. 7:6; 1 Sam. 1:12; 1 Kgs. 19:18; Neh. 9:20; Job 16:10; Song 1:2.

peh commonly refers to the phenomenon of human speech in phrases such as "out of one's mouth . . ." (cf. Exod. 23:13; Num. 30:2; Josh. 6:10; 1 Kgs. 22:13).

See also Judg. 11:36; Job 3:1. In relation to the theme of acceptable worship to Yahweh, the psalmist often refers to people's "mouths" in this context (cf. Pss. 8:2; 17:3; 34:1; 89:5; 119:13). In contrast, there are also references to cursing God, and to false worship coming from the mouths of people (cf. Pss. 10:7; 17:10; Isa. 29:13). Godly parental instruction is also noted as coming from the mouth of one's mother and father (cf. Prov. 4:5; 5:7; 7:24).

The phenomenon of speech from the "mouths of the prophets," as one of the explicit channels of divine revelation to humankind, is another very significant aspect of the usage of ***peh***. Several texts refer to Yahweh placing his word in the mouths of his prophetic servants (cf. Num. 22:38; 23:5ff.; Deut. 18:18; 1 Kgs. 17:24; Isa. 59:21; Jer. 1:9; 5:14; 36:4; Ezek. 3:17; 33:7, 22). One unique use of ***peh*** in this regard is found in Ezek. 3:2ff., where the prophet is commanded in a vision to open his mouth and eat a scroll given to him by Yahweh, for the purpose of communicating a message of divine wrath and judgment to the people of God. Note also the interesting reference in 1 Kgs. 22:22 to the phenomenon of a lying spirit being placed in the mouths of false prophets by Yahweh himself to bring about the death of Ahab, king of Israel, as a punishment for his wickedness.

Other references to human speech in non-prophetic contexts include those in Num. 35:30; Deut. 17:6; 19:15; 2 Sam. 1:16, where testimony "from the mouth of two or three witnesses" is required by law as a prerequisite for the conviction of a person accused of a capital offense. The exhortation to "guard one's mouth," or to speak wisely, is found in Eccl. 5:6. A number of wisdom texts refer to the mouths of righteous people yielding wisdom (cf. Prov. 10:32; 12:6; 14:3; 31:26). Conversely, the mouths of the wicked are said to yield folly (cf. Prov. 10:6; 11:9; 15:2; Isa. 9:17). The phrase "in your mouth" in Exod. 13:9; Deut. 30:14; 31:19 constitutes a metaphorical reference to the law of Yahweh being placed on one's heart and mind as a matter of great import.

Metaphorical uses of ***peh*** in other contexts include the mention of the "mouth" of Sheol opening to swallow the wicked in Isa. 5:14. The ground is also said to open its "mouth" and swallow the blood of Abel, who was murdered by his brother Cain (Gen. 4:11). In the context of a divine execution, Korah the Levite and his followers, who rebelled against Moses, were swallowed up by the ground opening its "mouth" beneath them (cf. Num. 16:30; 26:10; Deut. 11:6). The "mouth" of a well is noted in Gen. 29:2ff.; as is the "mouth" of a cave in Josh. 10:8, 22ff.; and the "mouth" of a sack in Gen. 42:27; 43:12, 21. The "hole," or "mouth," of an ephod, indicating its opening at the top, is indicated in Exod. 28:32; 39:23. The expression "mouth to mouth" (i.e., face-to-face) indicates the intimate relationship that existed between Yahweh and Moses.

The term ***peh*** is also applied metaphorically to the person of Yahweh in the expression or concept of the "mouth of God" or "mouth of the Lord." In a number of contexts this phrase or motif is intimately associated with the phenomenon of divine revelation. Deut. 8:3 declares, for example, that people shall live by every word that comes out of the mouth of God. Deut. 32:1; Isa. 1:20; 48:3; 55:11; Jer. 9:12 affirm that teaching or instruction coming from the mouth of the Lord is normative revelation to which people must give heed. In Josh. 9:14, such a phenomenon amounts to divine guidance. Prov. 2:6 declares that knowledge and understanding come from the mouth of God. In 1 Kgs. 8:15; 2 Chr. 6:14, divine promises are in view. The phrase "the mouth of the Lord has spoken" indicates the revelation of divine glory in Isa. 40:5, and it describes the anticipation of renewed salvation in Mic. 4:4.

The "mouth" of the Messianic Servant also constitutes a powerful revelatory phenomenon in the oracles of the "Suffering Servant." In Isa. 49:2, the mouth of the Servant is depicted as being made like a sword, for judgment and revelation. Isa. 51:16 declares that the Servant receives God's words in his mouth — that is, this Servant is a genuine prophet. In the poignant words of Isa. 53:7, the Servant in the face of death is described as one who "opens not his mouth" before his tormentors — he remains silent in his ordeal.

ḥēk [**חֵךְ, 2441**]

ḥēk occurs around twenty times with the meaning "mouth" in most of these contexts, with several additional nuances such as "tongue" or "taste."

Literal mundane references to the human "mouth" are found in Job 12:11; 20:13; 29:10; 33:2; 34:3; Pss. 119:103; 137:6; Prov. 8:7; Lam. 4:4; Hos. 8:1.

In Prov. 5:3; 8:7, ***ḥēk*** is used metaphorically to refer to speech of two distinctly different types. Prov. 5:3 refers to the mouth of the adulterous woman, which is beguiling, whereas Prov. 8:7 conveys the conviction expressed by the godly author that his mouth will utter truth. In Ezek. 3:26, the prophet is given over to an enforced dumbness from the hand of God, who causes Ezekiel's tongue to "cleave to the roof of his mouth" so that he will be unable to reprove the rebellious people of God.

pum [פֻּם, **6433** (Aramaic)]

pum is an Aramaic term that is translated "mouth" in each of the six contexts in which it is found. It refers in a literal sense to the mouth of King Nebuchadnezzar in Dan. 4:31. ***pum*** also refers to the mouths of a visionary lion and bear (cf. Dan. 6:22; Dan. 7:5; respectively). The "little horn" of Daniel's visions, representing the archenemy of God's people, is described as having a mouth that speaks boastfully (cf. Dan. 7:8, 20). Dan. 6:17 refers to the "mouth" (i.e., entrance) of the den of lions.

NT Words

stoma [στόμα, *4750*]

stoma is a noun found approximately eighty times with the predominant sense of "mouth" in a variety of contexts.

When predicated of human beings, ***stoma*** is most commonly used to signify human speech of various kinds. For example, the mouth is said to reflect in speech what is truly on the hearts of human beings, whether good or evil (cf. Matt. 12:34; 15:11, 18; Luke 6:45; Eph. 4:29; Col. 3:8; Jas. 3:10). See also Rev. 14:5. Other kinds of speech coming from people's mouths include false worship (cf. Matt. 15:8); evidence against wrongdoers (cf. Matt. 18:16; 2 Cor. 13:1); genuine praise to God (cf. Matt. 21:16; Rom. 15:6); confession of the person of Jesus (cf. Rom. 10:9ff); cursing by unbelievers (cf. Rom. 3:14); and preaching the gospel (cf. Eph. 6:19). References to prophetic revelation are found in allusions to the "mouth of the prophets" (cf. Luke 1:70; Acts 3:18ff.); including "the mouth of David" (cf. Acts 1:16; 4:25). There is also reference to the prophetic testimony of the two "heavenly witnesses" in Rev. 11:5. Literal, mundane references to "mouth" are found in Luke 1:64; Acts 11:8.

stoma also refers metaphorically to the "mouth of God." In Matt. 4:4, Jesus cites the affirmation of Deut. 8:3: "Man shall live . . . by every word . . . from the mouth of God." Rev. 3:16 declares that God will vomit out (i.e., spit out of his mouth) those who are lukewarm in their faith in the congregation at Laodicea.

Acts 8:32 refers to the prophecy of Isa. 53:7, declaring that the Messianic Servant would not open his mouth before his tormentors.

With reference to the person of Jesus Christ, ***stoma*** also refers to his "mouth," in the context of his teaching. Luke 4:22 declares that words from Jesus' mouth amazed his hearers. The message, or word of commissioning, to the apostle Paul from the "mouth" of the risen Christ is recorded in Acts 22:14. At his final return, the Lord Jesus Christ will slay his enemies with "the breath of his mouth." 1 Pet. 2:22 declares that no guile is to be found on the lips, or mouth, of Christ. The book of Revelation mentions "the sword of his mouth" as the ultimate weapon of the heavenly Christ, which he will use to judge the wicked (cf. Rev. 1:16; 2:16; 19:15, 21). See also Matt. 5:2; 13:35; John 19:29.

With regard to animals, ***stoma*** refers to the "mouth" of a fish (Matt. 17:27); to "mouths" of lions, both literally and metaphorically (Heb. 11:33; Rev. 13:2ff., respectively); to horses' mouths (Jas. 3:3); to the (symbolic) mouths of the apocalyptic beasts (Rev. 9:17ff.); and also to the mouth of the dragon, the embodiment of satanic opposition to God and his people (Rev. 16:13). See also Rev. 12:16.

Additional Notes

When found in the contexts of divine speech, the vocabulary relating to "mouth" in both Old and New Testaments has a distinctive significance. All references to the "mouth of God," or similar phrases, indicate the absolute authority and integrity of the revelation coming from that source. This power extends to the declarations coming from the "mouths" of the prophets.

The theological weight of divine pronouncement is heightened when one considers the impact of judgment and wrath that proceeded from the mouth of God on both Israelite and Gentile alike.

In the New Testament, the words that come from the mouth of Jesus have that same divine authority and judgment — whether in his earthly ministry or his heavenly rule. The book of Revelation contains a significant number of references to the power and authority of words coming from the heavenly Christ — in particular, to the potent metaphor "the sword of his mouth."

Effective communication by the medium of speech has always been a significant factor in the management and control of people and nations. When predicated of God and Christ, the impact and significance of revelation from their "mouth" cannot be overestimated.

MUCH

OT Words

rab [רַב, **7227**]

rab is a common adjectival form that indicates the three related senses of "much," "many," "great." Of the approximately five hundred occurrences of ***rab***, these meanings constitute the large majority of its usage, with some overlap in meaning. The remaining contexts indicate related nuances of these primary senses. (→ GREAT)

rab in the sense of "many" is found in a wide variety of contexts. The temporal sense of "many" is frequently indicated with reference to "days" (cf. Gen. 21:34; Lev. 15:25; Num. 9:19; Deut. 1:46; Josh. 22:3; 2 Sam. 14:2; 1 Kgs. 18:1; 1 Chr. 7:22; Jer. 13:6; Dan. 8:26; Hos. 4:3). Lev. 25:51 refers to the time span of "many years"; and the indefinite period of "many times" is indicated in Neh. 9:30; Ps. 106:43.

The quantitative sense of "many" is likewise found in a number of varying contexts. It refers, for example, to cattle (cf. Josh. 11:4; Isa. 31:1); and to "lovers," referring symbolically to the idols worshiped by the people of God (cf. Jer. 3:1). Many evils or sorrows are said to come upon people as a divine judgment for their sin. Israel is in view in this regard in Deut. 31:17ff.; as are the wicked in Ps. 32:10. The expression "many waters" indicates in a quasi-poetic way the riverside or ocean shore habitat of various people (cf. Jer. 51:13; Ezek. 17:8; 19:10). In addition, the phrase is used in the context of divine judgment to refer to the overwhelming impact of floodwater (cf. Jer. 51:55; Ezek. 1:24; 26:19).

With reference to people, ***rab*** signifies "many" in a general sense (e.g., Gen. 50:20; Exod. 19:21; Num. 13:20). The designation "many" is also given to wives (cf. Judg. 8:30); children (cf. 1 Sam. 2:5; 1 Chr. 4:27); enemies (cf. Pss. 56:2; 119:157); the wicked (cf. Ps. 37:16); priests (cf. Ezra 3:12); and friends (cf. Prov. 14:20). In particular, references to "many nations" are occasionally found in significant theological contexts where Yahweh calls the nations to gather around him for worship, indicating a divine work of renewal, reconciliation, and transformation (cf. Isa. 2:3; Mic. 4:2ff.; Zech. 2:11; 8:22). See also Deut. 7:1; 15:6; Jer. 25:14; Ezek. 26:3; Mic. 5:8; Hab. 2:8.

rab with the sense of "much" is found primarily in contexts where quantity is in view. For example, it refers to "water" for agriculture (Num. 24:7); seed for planting (Deut. 28:38); gold, wealth (1 Kgs. 10:2; Ps. 19:10; Dan. 11:13; 2 Kgs. 12:10); bronze for temple construction (1 Chr. 18:8); and blood (1 Chr. 12:8). It is also applied to non-tangible phenomena, such as transgression (Amos 5:12), and divine mercy (Pss. 86:15; 103:8).

There is a temporal use of ***rab*** meaning "much" in the sense of "long" in 2 Chr. 1:11, with reference to "long life."

In Num. 16:3, 7, ***rab*** is used in a superlative sense of "too much" or "too far," referring first of all to the unwarranted accusation against Moses that he had exceeded his authority (16:3). In Num. 16:7, Moses makes the same countercharge against his Levitical opponents, accusing them of going "too far" in their challenge against him. It was a challenge that cost them their lives, as they were subsequently executed by Yahweh in a terrible, spectacular fashion when the earth opened up and swallowed them alive.

NT Words

polys [πολύς, *4183*]

polys is a dynamic equivalent for the Hebrew adjective ***rab*** (see above) with the three predominant senses of "many," "much," "great." The term occurs around 350 times, and these senses are dominant. (→ GREAT)

The quantitative sense of "many" accounts for the bulk of the usage of ***polys***. General references to great numbers of people are common (e.g., Matt. 8:1; 20:8; Mark 2:2; 10:31; Luke 1:1; 21:8). In particular, mention is made of many people who come to faith in Christ — John's gospel and the book of Acts emphasize this phenomenon (cf. John 2:12, 8:30; 10:42; Acts 9:42; 11:21; 13:43; 17:12; 19:18). See also John 4:39ff.; Heb. 2:10 in this regard. Mark 14:24 also records Jesus' words at the Last Supper, affirming that his blood would be shed for the forgiveness of many.

The designation "many" is also applied to Pharisees (cf. Matt. 3:7); prophets, both true and false (cf. Matt. 13:17; Matt. 24:11; Luke 10:24; 1 John 4:1; 2 John 7); the wicked (cf. Matt. 7:13, 22); all manner of sick people, including the demon-possessed, who were healed by Jesus (cf. Matt. 8:16; 12:15; Mark 4:27; 7:21; John 5:3), as well as those healed by the apostles (cf. Acts 8:7); the enemies of the gospel (cf. 1 Cor. 16:9); widows (cf. Luke 4:25); angels (cf. Rev. 5:11); and those who are born again (cf. Rom. 8:29). "Many nations" are also indicated in Rom. 4:17, 18 in reference to the fulfillment of the Abrahamic covenant.

polys is used in non-personal contexts with this sense to refer to "many" animals (Matt. 8:30; 10:31; Luke 12:17); numerous parables (Mark 5:9); possessions (cf. Mark 10:22); demons cast out by Jesus (cf. Luke 8:30); gods (cf. 1 Cor. 8:5); sins (cf. Luke 7:47; Rom. 5:16); and members (or parts) of the body (cf. Rom. 12:4; 1 Cor. 12:14). Nondescript reference to "many things" is found in Mark 8:31; Luke 10:41; John 8:26; 21:25; Jas. 3:2. John 20:30 refers to the many signs, or miracles, performed by Jesus during his earthly ministry; Acts 2:43; 5:12 refer to the same phenomena during the apostolic ministry.

With reference to the person and work of Christ, ***polys*** indicates his many good works (John 10:32); the many heavenly mansions he is preparing for his people (John 14:7); and the many crowns placed on his head in his role as the heavenly conqueror of the armies of Satan and his followers (Rev. 19:12). The metaphorical reference to "the sound of many waters" (cf. Rev. 1:5; 14:2; 19:6) indicates the supreme authority of the voice of the heavenly Christ.

In a handful of contexts, ***polys*** refers to "many" in a temporal sense — for example, "many days" (cf. Luke 15:13; John 2:12; Acts 1:5, 16:18); "many years" (cf. Rom. 15:23).

With the sense of "much," ***polys*** likewise reflects a quantitative sense in most of its usage. Various phenomena are indicated: soil (cf. Matt. 13:5; Mark 4:5); water for baptism (cf. John 3:23); grass (cf. John 6:10); money or wealth (cf. Matt. 26:9; Luke 12:19; Acts 16:16); wine (cf. 1 Tim. 3:8; Titus 2:3); and fruit (cf. John 12:24). Nontangible usage includes references to "much murmuring" about the activities of Jesus (cf. John 7:12); tribulation (cf. Acts 14:22; 1 Thess. 1:6; 1 Tim. 6:10; 2 Tim. 4:14); fear and trembling (cf. 1 Cor. 2:3); patience (cf. 2 Cor. 6:4); and fruit in the spiritual sense of evidence of godly virtue through one's relationship with Christ (cf. John 15:5). Luke 12:48 contains the principle ". . . to whom much is given, much is required," indicating the importance of being a good steward of all that God gives, to equip one for kingdom ministry.

In several places, ***polys*** is used in an adverbial sense to indicate a degree of enhancement — "much more," "all the more." For example, Rom. 5:10, 15 refer to the powerful impact of salvation fulfilled in Christ. See also Matt. 6:30; Luke 18:39. In Phil. 1:23, Paul declares that to be with Christ is "far better."

See Also: → INCREASE

MULTIPLY → CROWD → INCREASE

MULTITUDE

OT Words

rōb **[רֹב, 7230]**

rōb is a common noun denoting "multitude," "abundance" with related nuances throughout its nearly 160 occurrences. ***rōb*** is also used adjectivally, meaning "plenty."

References to "multitudes," or great crowds or throngs of people, are found in a number of places, often translated as a comparative expression "as numerous as," "too numerous to count" (cf. Gen. 16:10; Deut. 10:22; 28:62, Josh. 11:4; Judg. 6:5; 1 Sam. 13:5; 1 Kgs. 3:8; 2 Chr. 16:8). In particular, "great numbers" of priests are indicated in 2 Chr. 30:24. See also Esth. 5:11; Prov. 11:14.

The adjectival sense of "plenty" is indicated in Gen. 27:28.

rōb refers to the "abundance," or the great quantity, of chariots (2 Kgs. 19:23; Isa. 37:24); of iron (1 Chr. 22:3); of materials for the construction of the temple (1 Chr. 22:4ff.); of ritual sacrifices (1 Chr. 29:21; 2 Chr. 5:6; Isa. 1:11); of Solomon's wealth (2 Chr. 1:15; 4:18; 9:27); of the wealth of kings (2 Chr. 18:1ff.; 20:25); of men's riches (Ps. 52:7; Ezek. 27:33); of God's love (Isa. 63:7; Lam. 3:32); of God's mercy (Pss. 5:7; 51:1; 69:13; 106:7); and of man's sins (Ps. 5:10; Jer. 30:15; Lam. 1:5; Ezek. 28:18).

rab **[רַב, 7227]**

rab is a common adjectival form found nearly five hundred times with the predominant senses of "many," "great," "much," as well as related nuances. In several places, ***rab*** denotes the nominal sense of "multitude," "crowd," or "throng."

"Multitudes" or "crowds" of people are noted in Exod. 12:38; 23:2; Ps. 109:30.

Great "herds" of cattle are indicated in Num. 32:1.

hāmôn **[הָמוֹן, 1995]**

hāmôn is a noun occurring about eighty times, denoting a "multitude" or "crowd" for most of the usage.

The sense of "multitudes," with reference to an "army," or military "troops," is indicated in Judg. 4:7; 1 Sam. 14:16; 2 Chr. 13:8; 20:2; Ezek. 29:12; 31:2; 32:16ff.; Dan. 11:10ff.

References to the assembled "throng" or "crowd" of Israelites are noted in 2 Sam. 6:19.

General references to a "horde," "throng," or "multitude" of people include those in 1 Kgs. 20:13; Job 31:34; Isa. 5:13ff.; 29:5ff.; Ezek. 7:11ff.

hāmôn also denotes a "herd" of cattle in Jer. 49:32.

NT Words

ochlos [ὄχλος, *3793*]

ochlos is a common noun denoting "crowds," or "multitudes," of people.

References to "multitudes" or "crowds" of people include those in Matt. 4:25; 21:8ff.; Mark 5:21ff.; 8:1ff.; Luke 5:1ff.; John 6:2ff.; Acts 8:6; 14:11ff.

Metaphorical references to the assembled "multitudes" of believers in heaven are found in Rev. 7:9; 19:1, 6. The gathered "masses" of earth's inhabitants are noted in Rev. 17:15.

MURDER ➠ SLAUGHTER

MURMUR

OT Words

lûn **[לוּן, 3885]**

lûn is a verb occurring around ninety times with the dominant meaning "lodge," or "spend the night," as well as a number of related nuances. However, in about fifteen places, ***lûn*** means "murmur," indicating an attitude of grumbling or complaining. In most of these contexts it refers to the people of Israel murmuring against God and Moses in the wilderness, demonstrating the people's distinctive lack of faith and trust in Yahweh (cf. Exod. 15:24; 16:2ff.; 17:3; Num. 14:2, 27ff.; 16:11, 41; 17:5). Josh. 9:18 also records an instance of the people of Israel "murmuring" against their leaders for refusing to slay the Gibeonite spies. (➠ LODGE)

rāgan **[רָגַן, 7279]**

rāgan is a rare verb, found only in three contexts, with reference to "murmuring." Deut. 1:27; Ps. 106:25 refer to Israel murmuring against Yahweh in the wilderness. Isa. 29:24 refers in general to the people of God, who will come to accept instruction from the Lord after being spiritually renewed, or "cured" of their complaining spirit.

telunnāh **[תְּלֻנָּה, 8519]**

telunnāh is the noun derived from ***lûn*** (see above) and is translated "murmurings," that is, grumbling, complaining, in all eight contexts in which it is found. ***telunnāh*** refers exclusively to Israel's complaining against Yahweh in their desert wanderings (cf. Exod. 16:7ff.; Num. 14:27, 17:5, 10).

NT Words

gongyzō [γογγύζω, *1111*]

gongyzō is a verb occurring eight times in all, with the senses of "murmur," "mutter," "grumble."

The general meaning "complain" is found in Matt. 20:11 where, in Jesus' parable, workers are dissatisfied with their wage.

The Pharisees complain forthrightly against Jesus' disciples for keeping company with social outcasts, or "sinners" (cf. Luke 5:30).

The Jewish audience mutters in disbelief at Jesus' teaching concerning his claim to be "the bread of life" (cf. John 6:41, 43). Even his disciples "murmured" at this difficult teaching (cf. John 6:61).

The Pharisees are very disturbed at some people's "muttering" about their official denial of Jesus' messianic identify. Clearly, the impact of Jesus' signs was not lost on a number of his hearers (cf. John 7:32).

A historical reference to the sin of Israel's murmuring in the wilderness is noted in 1 Cor. 10:10.

diagongyzō [διαγογγύζω, *1234*]

diagongyzō is a variant form of ***gongyzō***, above, with reference to the Pharisees' "murmuring" against Jesus. The term occurs only in Luke 15:2; 19:7, where it indicates the religious leaders' indignation and disgust at Jesus for fraternizing with people whom they regarded as the refuse of society.

gongystēs [γογγυστής, *1113*]

gongystēs is a noun, likewise derived from ***gongyzō*** (see above). It is found only in Jude 16 and refers to "grumblers," one of the many godless traits of false prophets and teachers.

gongysmos [γογγυσμός, *1112*]

gongysmos is another derivative noun form from ***gongyzō*** (see above), meaning "murmuring," "complaining." It is found only four times. John 7:12 refers to people "muttering" about Jesus as to whether is a genuine or false teacher. Acts 6:1 records the "complaining" of Greek believers against Jewish Christians for neglecting the widows in the Gentile Christian community. Phil. 2:14; 1 Pet. 4:9 exhort believers to do all things "without complaint."

MUSIC, MUSICIAN

OT Words

mangînāh **[מַנְגִּינָה, 4485]**

mangînāh is found only in Lam. 3:63, with reference to the "mocking songs, or music" of the enemies of Jeremiah.

zemār [זְמָר, **2170** (Aramaic)]

zemār is an Aramaic noun that means "music" (of the instrumental variety), found in only four contexts. In all cases, music accompanying idolatrous worship is indicated (cf. Dan. 3:5, 7, 10, 15).

menaṣṣēaḥ [מְנַצֵּחַ, **5329**]

menaṣṣēaḥ is a noun found in approximately seventy contexts, with the sense of "director of music," or "chief musician" evident in the majority of these occurrences. This is found primarily in the titles of many of the Psalms, which give direction to the "director of music" as to the mode of the psalm's performance — for example, which instruments, or tune, to select (cf. Pss. 4:1; 8:1; 42:1; 45:1; 57:1; 58:1). In other Psalms, no particular instruction is given other than to "dedicate" the piece to the "director of music," identifying it as a Psalm of David in most cases (cf. Pss. 11:1; 40:1; 51:1); or as a Psalm of Korah and his sons (e.g., Pss. 44:1; 46:1; 49:1).

NT Words

mousikos [μουσικός, *3451*]

mousikos is found only in Rev. 18:22 with reference to "musicians."

symphōnia [συμφωνία, *4858*]

symphōnia is found only in Luke 15:25 with reference to music in a general sense.

See Also: ➡ INSTRUMENT ➡ SING

MUSTARD

NT Words

sinapi [σίναπι, *4615*]

sinapi is a noun referring to a "mustard seed." It is found in only five contexts, three of which liken the kingdom of God to a mustard seed (cf. Matt. 13:31; Mark 4:31; Luke 13:19). Like the "mustard seed," a tiny seed from which grows a large tree, so the kingdom of God grows to enormous proportions from the smallest beginnings. In Matt. 17:20; Luke 17:6, the point is made that genuine faith need only be as large as a mustard seed in order to be fully effective.

MYRRH

OT Words

mōr [מֹר, **4753**]

mōr is a noun occurring twelve times, referring to "myrrh," the aromatic resin drawn from the bark of the myrrh tree or shrub that grows in the Arabian desert. Myrrh was used in the production of ritual anointing oil (cf. Exod. 30:23), and also as a luxuriant perfuming oil (cf. Esth. 2:12; Ps. 45:8; Prov. 7:17; Song 1:13; 3:6; 4:6, 14; 5:1, 5, 13).

lōt [לֹט, **3910**]

lōt is found in only two places, indicating "myrrh" in a list of commodities (cf. Gen. 37:25; 43:11).

NT Words

smyrna [σμύρνα, *4666*]

smyrna refers to "myrrh" in only two places. Matt. 2:11 lists it is one of the gifts, along with gold and frankincense, brought by the oriental magi to the Christ child. In John 19:39, myrrh is indicated in combination with bitter aloes as an embalming product intended for the body of Christ.

smyrnizō [σμυρνίζω, *4669*]

smyrnizō is a verb meaning "to mix with myrrh." It is found only in Mark 15:23, referring to the drink offered to Christ on the cross — wine mingled with myrrh, as a form of anesthetic.

MYRTLE

OT Words

hadas [הֲדַס, **1918**]

hadas is the noun signifying "myrtle tree" and is found in six contexts. Three of these are literal references to the tree (cf. Neh. 8:15; Isa. 41:19; 55:13); and three are found in a symbolic context in connection with the visions of the prophet Zechariah (cf. Zech. 1:8, 10, 11).

MYSTERY

OT Words

rāz [רָז, **7328** (Aramaic)]

rāz is an Aramaic term occurring nine times, all in the book of Daniel. In every case it refers to a "secret" or "mystery" in relation to the visionary dreams given to King Nebuchadnezzar. The "mystery" concerned both the content and understanding of the dream of the statue composed of four metals in Dan. 2. Nebuchadnezzar refused to relate the content of the dream to his wise men (including Daniel). He demanded that they relate the dream to him and explain its meaning. Daniel was enabled by God to do both, relying entirely upon the revelation of Yahweh and giving thanks for that divine insight (cf. Dan. 2:18, 19, 27). Dan. 2:28ff.; 4:9 specifically acknowledge that Yahweh alone is able to reveal such "mysteries." Significantly, in each of these contexts the "mystery" involves the unfolding revelation of God's kingdom, which will involve the ultimate destruction of all earthly dominion and the emergence of the eternally enduring and indestructible kingdom of heaven.

NT Words

mystērion [μυστήριον, *3466*]

mystērion is a term found in approximately thirty places, meaning "mystery," or "secret" in each instance. The underlying sense of this term in the majority of contexts refers to that which has been kept secret by God in the past, but which he has now chosen to make plain. The revelation of this "mystery" centers on the appearance of Jesus Christ in human history as the messianic King of kings.

The "mysteries" of the kingdom of heaven are said to be given to Jesus' disciples in Matt. 13:11; Mark 4:11; Luke 8:10. The context of this affirmation by Christ is that the intent of his teaching in parables was first of all to illuminate the spiritual understanding of his followers concerning God's plan of salvation. For those who rejected Christ, however, there would be no such insight, and they would learn nothing from hearing the parables.

Understanding the mystery of God's plan of salvation, whereby Israel's full salvation will only take place when all the Gentile peoples have been saved in accordance with the divine plan, is the goal of the apostle Paul for his readers in Rom. 11:25.

The revelation of the divine mystery centers on the disclosure of Jesus as the Christ — a phenomenon that remained hidden for a long time in the past until now. This climactic "unveiling" of the "mystery" of God's plan of salvation is a common motif in the New Testament writings (cf. Rom. 16:25; 1 Cor. 2:7; 4:1; Eph. 1:9; 3:3ff.; 5:32; 6:19; Col. 1:26ff.; 2:2; 4:3; 1 Tim. 3:9, 16; Rev. 10:7).

The "mysteries of God" in a general sense, implying the understanding of the significance of the person of Christ, are referred to in 1 Cor. 13:2; 14:2.

The "mystery" involving the transformation of our earthly bodies into heavenly ones is indicated in 1 Cor. 15:51.

The "mystery of lawlessness" in 2 Thess. 2:7 refers to the time of the unveiling of the antichrist in the last days prior to the Lord's return.

The term ***mystērion*** also indicates the sense of "mystery" with reference to a riddle, or puzzle. In Rev. 1:20, for example, the "mystery" of the seven stars in the right hand of the heavenly Christ refers to the angels of the seven churches addressed in the opening chapters of the book of Revelation. Rev. 17:5 mentions the "mysterious" title given to the city of Babylon, "Babylon the great, the mother of prostitutes and of the abominations of the earth." See also Rev. 17:7.

Additional Notes

While the use of the Aramaic term ***rāz*** is restricted in the Old Testament to the prophet Daniel, it is undeniably a context of great prophetic significance. The "mystery" surrounding Nebuchadnezzar's vision of the four-metal statue finds its solution in the mysterious stone of divine origin that destroys the statue and fills the whole earth. It is clear that the statue constitutes a symbolic depiction of human dominion, which will be no match for the all-pervading, all-powerful kingdom of God represented by the stone.

The parallels here with the distinctive New Testament use of the term ***mystērion*** are clear. It is the person of Jesus Christ who embodies the fulfillment of the revelation of the divine mystery — the unveiling of God's plan of salvation, the coming of God's kingdom for the whole world, Jew and Gentile alike. Jesus Christ is not only the incarnation of God in human form, but the full embodiment of the divinely ordained Messianic King, first prophesied by the Hebrew canonical prophets of old. These Old Testament figures foresaw the coming of the King, the "mystery" hidden for long ages until now.

N

NAIL

OT Words

***ṣippōren* [צִפֹּרֶן, 6856]**

ṣippōren occurs only twice in the Old Testament — once with reference to the fingernails of a wife from a captive people (cf. Deut. 21:12), and once with metaphorical reference to the "point" of a diamond — the symbolic instrument with which the sins of the Israelite people are engraved upon their hearts (cf. Jer. 17:1).

***yātēd* [יָתֵד, 3489]**

yātēd is a noun occurring around twenty times with primary reference to "nail," "stake," or "peg," used in construction or crafts. It has both a literal and metaphorical sense.

In literal contexts, ***yātēd*** refers to "nails" or "pegs" for the purpose of constructing the Israelite tabernacle (cf. Exod. 27:19; 35:18, 20, 31; 39:40; Num. 3:37; 4:32). In Judg. 4:21, 22; 5:26, ***yātēd*** refers to a "tent peg" used as a murder weapon in the assassination of the Canaanite general Sisera, by Jael, the wife of Heber the Kenite. The term indicates a weaver's "pin" in Judg. 16:14; and a general mundane sense of "nail" is indicated in Ezek. 15:3.

There are also a number of metaphorical contexts in the usage of ***yātēd***. Ezra 9:8, for example, refers to a "nail" given to the Israelite people by God, as a means of securing their position within the holy place of the temple. This symbolic "nail" is a guarantee to the Jewish remnant recently returned from captivity that Yahweh is still vitally interested in an intimate spiritual relationship with them. Isa. 22:23, 25 refer to a like phenomenon. In this context, however, the nail will be "sheared off," indicating God's rejection of his people for their sinful rejection of him.

Similarly, in Isa. 33:20, Yahweh promises to never again remove the "tent pegs" of Jerusalem, a prophecy of ultimate spiritual renewal and security. See also Isa. 54:2 in this light.

Finally, ***yātēd*** refers in Zech. 10:4 to a "tent peg" as an aspect of the emergence of the messianic ruler from the tribe of Judah, who will bring spiritual security to the people of God.

***masmēr* [מַסְמֵר, 4548]**

masmēr is found in only five contexts, all with reference to "nails" used in building construction, such as the temple (1 Chr. 22:3; 2 Chr. 3:9), and the manufacture of idols (Isa. 41:7; Jer. 10:4). Eccl. 12:11 refers to nails in a general sense.

***tephar* [טְפַר, 2953** (Aramaic)**]**

tephar is a rare Aramaic term that means "(finger)nail" or "claw." It is found only twice. Dan. 4:33 refers to the long fingernails of King Nebuchadnezzar that grew like animal claws during his bout of insanity, enacted against him by divine decree. Dan. 7:19 refers to the great bronze "claws" of the nameless fourth beast in Daniel's vision.

NT Words

***hēlos* [ἧλος, *2247*]**

hēlos is found in only one verse in the New Testament, referring twice to the prints of the iron nails used in the crucifixion of Christ, seen in the hands of his resurrection body (cf. John 20:25).

***prosēloō* [προσηλόω, *4338*]**

prosēloō is a rare verb found only in Col. 2:14. Here it refers metaphorically to Christ "nailing" to the cross the legal indictment of the sin of his people. This sin would otherwise have condemned them, had not Christ freely offered himself as a substitutionary atonement for that sin.

NAKED, NAKEDNESS

OT Words

***'ārôm* [עָרוֹם, 6174]**

'ārôm is an adjectival form consistently translated "naked" in all sixteen occurrences.

In all but one context, ***'ārôm*** refers to physical nakedness, or exposing the human body. Gen. 2:25 refers to the nakedness of Adam and Eve — a pure, undefiled state prior to their fall from grace. Nakedness accompanies prophetic revelation with respect to Saul (1 Sam. 19:24); and with reference to Isaiah son of Amoz (Isa. 20:2, 3). Having one's clothes stripped away is designated as an explicit divine judgment in Isa. 20:4; Hos. 2:3; Amos 2:16; and as a sign of a prophetic lament in Mic. 1:8. General references to nakedness are found in Job 1:21; 22:6; 24:7, 10; Eccl. 5:15. Job 26:6 refers metaphorically to Sheol being naked before God.

'êrōm [עֵירֹם, 5903]

'êrōm is an adjective closely related in form to ***'ārôm*** (see above). ***'êrōm*** also means "naked," "nakedness," and is found in ten contexts.

Gen. 3:7ff. refer to Adam and Eve's shameful perception of their nakedness after disobeying God. Nakedness as an evidence or consequence of divine judgment is indicated in Deut. 28:48; Ezek. 16:39; 23:29. With reference to Israel's spiritual vulnerability, Ezek. 16:7, 22 depict the people of Israel as naked, awaiting their "adoption" and eventual "marriage" to Yahweh, their redeeming God. See also Ezek. 18:7, 16, 19.

ma'arōm [מַעֲרֹם, 4636]

ma'arōm is a rare noun, occurring once in 2 Chr. 28:15 with reference to the nakedness of men.

'ārāh [עָרָה, 6168]

'ārāh is a verb occurring in about fifteen contexts with the primary meanings "lay bare," "uncover," as well as a number of associated nuances.

In several of these contexts, ***'ārāh*** indicates the action of "making oneself bare," "being stripped naked," or "exposing one's nakedness," in a sexual context. The latter sense is indicated in Lev. 20:18, 19, which prohibits such conduct with a menstruating woman and with one's paternal and maternal aunt. Yahweh in strips bare his enemies in Lam. 4:21; Hab. 3:13.

In Zeph. 2:14, ***'ārāh*** refers in an impersonal context to "laying bare" (i.e., destroying) the cedar framework of Assyrian houses — an aspect of Yahweh's judgment against that nation.

'eryāh [עֶרְיָה, 6181]

'eryāh is a variant noun derived from ***'erwāh*** (see below). It occurs only five times and means "naked," "bare," "nakedness." In four of these contexts, ***'eryāh*** is used in an adjectival sense, describing the nation of Israel as "bare." There is a metaphorical allusion to her youthful vulnerability prior to her union with Yahweh in Ezek:16:7, 22. Ezek. 16:39; 23:29 refer to her naked condition as a mark of shame, as the prophet declares that Yahweh will hand her over to her pagan "lovers," who will strip her naked and expose her lewdness to the world at large. Similar reference is made to the "nakedness" of the inhabitants of Shaphir, in the Judean foothills, also resulting from divine chastisement.

'erwāh [עֶרְוָה, 6172]

'erwāh is the most common term for "nakedness" in the Old Testament, occurring approximately fifty times.

Nakedness, as a physical condition, is viewed in a universally negative light in Scripture. It was forbidden under the law, for example, for any priest to expose his bare flesh, even inadvertently, on the steps of the altar. Hence, linen undergarments had to be worn while on duty (cf. Exod. 20:26; 28:42). In other contexts, the incidence of nudity gives rise to shame (cf. Gen. 9:22ff.; Isa. 20:4; 47:3; Lam. 1:8).

The remaining uses of ***'erwāh*** are all metaphorical. In Ezek. 23:10, Assyria is said to have "stripped naked" the people of Samaria, referring to the people's utter humiliation at the loss of their land. Likewise, Babylon's anticipated treatment of Judah in similar fashion is indicated in Ezek. 23:29. The "nakedness" of the land of Egypt is mentioned in Gen. 42:9, 12, referring to Egypt's vulnerability to attack.

The most common metaphorical usage of ***'erwāh*** relates to the context of sexuality. The expression "to uncover nakedness" is found about thirty-five times in the book of Leviticus, graphically conveying the meaning "to engage in sexual intercourse" (cf. Lev. 18:6ff.; 20:11, 17ff.). All of these references forbid the practice of illicit sexual activity with one's near relatives, on pain of death (cf. Lev. 18:29). See also Ezek. 22:10. In Ezek. 16:36, 37; 23:18, the expression "to expose one's nakedness" is predicated of Israel in relation to her worship of idols, which is likened to an act of spiritual adultery.

Yahweh is said to have "covered Israel's nakedness," or entered into a solemn relationship with his people, under the guise of a marriage bond (cf. Ezek. 16:8). See also Hos. 2:9.

ma'ar [מַעַר, 4626]

ma'ar is found only twice. In Nah. 3:5 it refers to the judgment of God against the Ninevites, whereby he will "expose their nakedness," or reduce them to abject humiliation in the eyes of the nations around them.

mā'ôr [מָעוֹר, 4589]

mā'ôr is found only in Hab. 2:15, referring generally to the moral perversity of those who gaze on the "nakedness" of their neighbors, having first made them drunk.

NT Words

gymnos [γυμνός, *1131*]

gymnos is an adjectival form occurring fifteen times with the predominant sense of "naked," or "bare."

In the context of those who are vulnerable and destitute, such people are said to be "naked" and in dire need of aid (cf. Matt. 25:36; Jas. 2:15; Rev. 3:17). In the sense of shameful exposure, ***gymnos*** indicates nakedness (Rev. 16:15) and refers metaphorically of the city of Babylon (Rev. 17:16) in the context of God's judgment against that people. Literal references to nakedness in non-judgmental, or neutral, contexts are found in Mark 14:51, 52; John 21:7; Acts 19:6 (although this latter reference speaks of men who had their clothes torn off after being assaulted by a demon-possessed man, resulting in their running away naked and bleeding).

In metaphorical contexts, ***gymnos*** is used first of all in 1 Cor. 15:37 to refer literally to a "bare seed" from which substantial growth will come. The context here deals with the subject of the heavenly bodies of believers, which they will inherit at the resurrection. 2 Cor. 5:3 contains an implied reference to our disembodied souls after death as being "naked," prior to our being "clothed" with our "heavenly bodies." In Heb. 4:13, the writer declares that all people are "laid bare" to God's inscrutable gaze — that is, nothing can be hidden from him.

gymnotēs [γυμνότης, *1132*]

gymnotēs is a noun occurring only three times, meaning "nakedness." It is used in Rom. 8:35; 2 Cor. 11:25 to refer to a state of exposure (i.e., being without clothes), among other trials and tribulations. In Rev. 3:18, "nakedness" is indicated as a shameful condition.

NAME

OT Words

shēm [**שֵׁם, 8034**]

shēm is the most common Hebrew term for "name." It occurs in more than 800 places, with a variety of nuances. ***shēm*** is found in both human and divine contexts.

The literal use of ***shēm*** as a name, a designation to identify people, places, and objects, is varied and common. The term is used, for example, to refer to rivers (cf. Gen. 2:11ff.); to living creatures (cf. Gen. 2:19ff.); to a covenant memorial (cf. Gen. 31:48); to an altar, "The Lord is my banner" (cf. Exod. 17:15); to cities (cf. Gen. 4:17; 11:9; Judg. 1:17); and towns (cf. Deut. 3:14). References to the names of individuals are obviously widespread (e.g., Gen. 3:20; 5:29; 32:28; Deut. 7:24; Josh. 2:1; Judg. 8:3; Ruth 1:2; Job 18:17). In particular, Israelite names predominate with the use of ***shēm*** (cf. Gen. 30:6, 32:28; Exod. 1:1ff.; 2:10; Num. 25:14; Ruth 2:1; 1 Sam. 1:20; 2 Kgs. 22:1; Ezra 2:6; Neh. 10:16). Of special significance are the references to the name "Immanuel" ("God with us") given as a sign to King Ahaz of Judah on the eve of the invasion of the northern kingdom of Israel by Assyria (cf. Isa. 7:14). This name is linked with the name "Maher-Shalal-Hash-Baz" (Isa. 8:3), the son born to Isaiah, who in his symbolic function as a child destined to be "quick to the plunder, swift to the spoil" points to the true Immanuel, the Christ child born to the virgin Mary hundreds of years later. Another significant messianic name is "the branch," applied to the coming Davidic Messiah in Zech. 6:12. See also Exod. 28:11; Ezek. 48:1, 31; Hos. 1:6ff.

shēm is also used in relation to pagan deities, indicating the "names" of gods (cf. Exod. 23:13; Deut. 12:3; Josh. 23:7; Hos. 2:17; Zech. 13:2). The latter two texts refer to the removal of such names from the lips of the people of Yahweh — a consequence of their spiritual rebirth. ***shēm*** is also translated "name" in the sense of "reputation," both good and bad. Such a usage indicates a sign of divine covenant blessing in Gen. 12:2; Deut. 26:19, with reference to the blessing attached to the "name" of Abraham.

Similar reference is made to David (2 Sam. 7:9; 8:13), and to Solomon (1 Kgs. 4:31). General references to the blessing of a good name or reputation are found in Prov. 22:1; Eccl. 7:1. The "name" of Israel as a nation is mentioned in 2 Kgs. 14:27; Ps. 83:4; Ezek. 16:5. A bad reputation, or "evil name," is indicated in Deut. 22:19. Prov. 10:7 affirms that the "name of the wicked" is doomed.

shēm also refers to significant place names. For example, Gen. 28:19 indicates Bethel as the place where Yahweh spoke to Jacob in a vision reaffirming to him the covenant promises given to his grandfather Abraham. Jacob designates "Peniel" as the place where he saw God "face-to-face" (cf. Gen. 32:30). The location of brackish water found by the Israelites in the wilderness is named "Marah" in Exod. 16:31, meaning "bitterness." The initial sacred site in the land of Canaan is designated "Gilgal" in Josh. 5:9, after the men of Israel undertook the ritual of circumcision, which had been neglected during the wilderness wandering. The name signifies the action of "rolling away" Israel's reproach, so that they may enter the land with appropriate ritual purity.

The importance of Israelite family lineage is also indicated in the use of ***shēm*** in Deut. 25:7, which refers to the phenomenon of "Levirate marriage." In this context, the Mosaic law requires a man to marry the wife of his deceased brother, when there are no children from the marriage, so that the surviving brother may have children by his sister-in-law in this special circumstance and thus preserve the "name" of his dead brother in Israel.

Of considerable importance is the use of ***shēm*** in connection with the divine "name," of which there are a great number of occurrences in a wide variety of contexts.

One of the most significant uses of this term is found in the phrase "the name of the Lord" (i.e., Yahweh). In this expression, the "name" of Yahweh indicates his person and character.

It is utilized as an object of human worship or blessing of God, whereby one "calls on the name of the Lord." This is said of Abraham (Gen. 12:8; 13:4; 21:33); and of Isaac (Gen. 26:25). See also Gen. 4:26; Job 1:21; Ps. 7:17. This expression is also found in the context of someone desiring a response from God, an answer to prayer or a call for help (cf. 1 Kgs. 18:24 [i.e., Elijah on Mt. Carmel]; 2 Kgs. 5:11; Ps. 116:4; Joel 2:32; Zeph. 3:9).

To serve "in the name of the Lord" is designated as a priestly prerogative in Deut. 18:5, 7; 21:5. The ritual aspect of the phrase is also indicated in contexts which mention the temple to be built "for the name of the Lord" (cf. 1 Kgs. 3:2; 5:5; 8:17ff.; 1 Chr. 22:7; 2 Chr. 2:1; 6:7ff.). Similarly, Zion is noted as the dwelling place "for the house of the Lord" in Isa. 18:7.

There is the prohibition against "taking the name of the Lord in vain" in Exod. 20:7; Lev. 24:16; Deut. 5:11 — an action that is punishable by death. Likewise, any activity that "profanes the name of the Lord" constitutes a capital offense under the law (cf. Lev. 18:21; 20:3; 22:33; Isa. 52:5; Jer. 34:16; Ezek. 36:20ff.; Amos 2:7).

References to God's people proclaiming "the name of the Lord" as an expression of praise in worship are found in Deut. 32:3; Pss. 102:21; 113:1ff.; 116:17; 122:4; 135:1; Joel 2:26. And Yahweh proclaims his own name this way in Exod. 34:5.

To "speak the name of the Lord" in the context of prophetic ministry is a phenomenon noted in Deut. 18:22; 1 Kgs. 22:16; 1 Chr. 21:19; 2 Chr. 13:18; Jer. 11:21. False prophets also use such an expression, but this is arrogant presumption on their part (cf. Jer. 26:20; Zech. 13:3). Such a phrase is also used in the context of blessing the people of God (cf. 2 Sam. 6:18; 1 Chr. 16:2; Ps. 129:8); and also in uttering a curse (2 Kgs. 2:24).

Other uses of this expression include reference to preparation for a battle in 1 Sam. 17:45, where David comes "in the name of the Lord" to confront the Philistine giant, Goliath. "In the name of the Lord" is found in the context of swearing a solemn oath of friendship between David and Jonathan (1 Sam. 20:42). See also Isa. 48:1; Deut. 10:20; Jer. 12:16. Reference is made in 2 Sam. 6:2 to the ark of the covenant being called "by the name of the Lord."

General references to the "name of the Lord" are found in Josh. 9:9; 1 Kgs. 10:1; Pss. 20:7; 118:10; Prov. 18:10; Isa. 24:15; 30:27; 56:6; Amos 6:10; Mic. 4:5.

References to "Yahweh" as the "name" of God are found in Exod. 6:3; 15:3; Ps. 83:18; Jer. 23:6; 33:2, where the divine majesty, power, and authority are affirmed. In a number of places Yahweh is said to refer to himself with the words "my name" (e.g., Exod. 20:24; Deut. 18:19; Jer. 16:21). In particular, 2 Sam. 7:3; 1 Kgs. 8:18ff. record the divine declaration: "Solomon shall build a house for my name." In Isa. 52:6, there is the promise, "My people shall know my name." Neh. 1:9; Jer. 7:11ff. refer to the phenomenon of the divine presence in the temple, with God indicating that this place bears his name, the place where he has chosen to dwell. References in the third person to "his name" are found in the same context (cf. Deut. 12:5ff.; 14:23; 16:2ff.; 26:2). In Exod. 23:21 Yahweh declares, referring to the "angel of the lord," that "my name is in him," clearly indicating that this angelic figure is a divine being. See also Jer. 14:15; 29:21; Dan. 9:19; Amos 9:12. Oblique reference to the name given to the angel of the Lord is indicated in Judg. 13:17, 18. The phrases "for my name's sake," "for his name's sake" indicate the importance of maintaining Yahweh's honor and integrity in the eyes of his people and the nations at large (cf. Pss. 23:3; 25:11; 106:8; Isa. 48:19; 66:5; Ezek. 20:9, 14, 44; 36:22). Direct expressions of praise to God are noted in the words "your name . . ." (cf. Pss. 8:1; 18:49; 45:17; 63:4; 86:12; Isa. 25:1; Jer. 10:6).

The title "Lord of hosts" is specifically mentioned as a name for Yahweh in Isa. 47:4; 51:15; Jer. 10:16; 31:35; Amos 4:13.

"The name of God" in the context of theophanic revelation assumes a special significance in Exod. 3:13ff., where God reveals his name to Moses as: "I am who I am." This signifies his uniqueness as the creator, sustainer, and deliverer of his people. The name of God is also noted in Deut. 28:58; Mal. 1:14 as something to be feared.

NT Words

onoma [ὄνομα, *3686*]

onoma is a noun found in approximately two hundred places, with the consistent meaning "name." It is used of people, places, and objects, and refers also to both God and Christ.

onoma refers to naming people in mundane literal contexts in Matt. 27:32; Mark 3:16; 5:22; Luke 1:5, 13, 27; 8:41; John 1:6; Acts 5:1. Elsewhere the term refers to the names of the twelve disciples (cf. Matt. 10:2). Luke 10:20; Phil. 4:3; Rev. 3:5, 8 all declare in some way that the names of all believers are recorded in heaven. John 10:3 records that Jesus calls his "sheep" (i.e., his followers) by name. In a metaphorical context, Rev. 21:12ff. declares that the names of the twelve tribes of Israel are written on the gates of the heavenly Jerusalem.

The term "name" also refers to places (e.g., Luke 24:13; Mark 14:32; Luke 1:26; Rev. 3:12); and once it refers to a symbolic star with the name "Wormwood," from which will emanate a catastrophic judgment on humankind (cf. Rev. 8:11).

With reference to Christ, ***onoma*** is found in a variety of contexts. General references to the "name of Jesus" are indicated in Matt. 1:21, 25; Luke 1:31; 2:21; Acts 9:15 (implied); Phil. 2:10. Several texts declare that Jesus is given the name that is above every name (cf. Eph. 1:21; Phil. 2:9; Heb. 1:4); and Rev. 3:12; 19:12ff. record that Christ is given a new name in heaven. The prophetic name of Emmanuel is determined for the Christ child in Matt. 1:23.

Jesus uses the phrase "for my name's sake" in the sense of "for my cause," and it is found primarily in contexts where Jesus warns his followers that they will be hated and persecuted for being associated with him (cf. Matt. 10:22; 24:9; Mark 13:13; Luke 21:12, 17; Acts 9:16; 1 Pet. 4:14; Rev. 2:3). See Rom. 1:5; 1 John 2:12 for use of this expression in the third person.

The expression "in the name of Jesus Christ" is used in the context of baptism in Acts 2:36; 8:16; 10:48. It is also found in contexts where the name of Christ is invoked as a prelude to a miraculous cure (cf. Acts 3:6; 4:10, 30; 16:18). The phrase "in his name" is equivalent to the concept "in him," indicating the person of Christ. It is found in Matt. 12:21 with reference to the Gentiles, who "hope in his name." John 1:12 declares that those who believe "in his name" will be granted the status of children of God. General references to believing in his name are found in John 2:23; 20:31; Acts 3:16; 8:12; 1 John 3:23; 5:3. Similarly, Jesus' own words "in my name" have a similar significance (cf. Matt. 18:5; 24:5; Mark 9:37; 13:6; Luke 9:48; John 14:13, 26; 15:16; 16:23ff.). See also Luke 10:17.

onoma is also applied directly to God. John 12:28; Rom. 15:9; Rev. 15:4 refer to glorifying the name of God. The sanctifying of God's name is enjoined in the Lord's Prayer in Matt. 6:9; Luke 11:2. The practice of baptizing in the name of the Father, Son, and Holy Spirit is mentioned in Matt. 28:19. Mary, the mother of Jesus, affirms that God's name is holy in Luke 1:49. Jesus is said to have come and worked in the name of his Father (cf. John 5:43; 10:25); and he speaks of making known to his disciples the name of his Father in his prayer recorded in John 17:6, 26. The sin of blaspheming the name of God is indicated in Rom. 2:24 and warned against in 1 Tim. 6:1. Rev. 14:1; 22:4 refer to the Father's name and the name of the lamb written on the foreheads of the saints in glory.

As in the Old Testament, the expression "the name of the Lord" is found in a number of significant contexts. The hymn of praise for Christ as he enters Jerusalem in triumph at that fateful Passover festival is recorded in Matt. 21:9; 23:9; Mark 11:9; Luke 13:35; 19:38; John 12:13 — "Blessed is he who comes in the name of the Lord." The guarantee that "he who calls on the name of the Lord shall be saved" is found in Acts 2:21; Rom. 10:13. The practice of baptizing believers "in the name of the Lord (Jesus)" is noted in Acts 8:16; 19:5. Preaching and prophesying "in the name of the Lord Jesus" is indicated in Acts 9:29; Jas. 5:10. Praising the name of the Lord Jesus is mentioned in Acts 19:17. Acts 21:13 refers to Paul's willingness to die "for the name of the Lord Jesus." 1 Cor. 6:11 declares that the believer is justified "in the name of the Lord Jesus Christ." See also Acts 19:13; Col. 3:17; Jas. 5:14 for other uses of the expression.

onoma also refers to the names of evil spirits, such as "Legion" (Mark 5:9; Luke 8:30); Apollyon the demonic ruler of the abyss (Rev. 9:11); the blasphemous name of the sea beast (Rev. 13:1); the name of the earth beast (Rev. 13:17; 14:11); and the name of the city of Babylon, "the mother of harlots . . ." (Rev. 17:5).

onoma is translated "name" in the sense of "reputation" in Rev. 3:1. Here the congregation of Sardis falsely assumes that they have a "name" for being alive. But, in reality, they are spiritually dead.

onomazō [ὀνομάζω, *3687*]

onomazō is the verb from which the noun ***onoma*** (see above) is derived. ***onomazō*** is found in only ten places and is translated "to name" or "call."

onomazō refers to the process of naming individuals (Luke 6:13, 14); to naming Christ in the sense of proclaiming the gospel (Rom. 15:20); to naming believing families in the sense of their spiritual identification (Eph. 3:15; also Eph. 1:21); and to naming the name of the Lord (2 Tim. 2:19) in the sense of confessing him as Savior and Lord.

To "name" in the sense of "mention" is the meaning found in 1 Cor. 5:1; Eph. 5:3, with reference to immorality of varying kinds. Acts 19:13 refers to Jewish exorcists "pronouncing" the name of the Lord Jesus, attempting the exorcism of evil spirits.

In 1 Cor. 5:11, ***onomazō*** conveys the sense of "be called," or "bear the name of" with respect to those who wanted to be known as "brothers" in Christ, but whose sinful lifestyle denied the integrity of their profession.

Additional Notes

The concept of "name" in both Old and New Testaments has a particular significance when applied to the persons of God and Christ. When the name of God or Yahweh is invoked in the Old Testament, such a mention is tantamount to invoking the person of God. This is especially the case when "the name of the Lord" is associated with significant theophanic phenomena such as the "pillar of fire/smoke" in the wilderness, the glory cloud of Mt. Sinai, the Shekinah glory of the tabernacle and temple, or even the city of Jerusalem itself.

In the New Testament, the same dynamic is often evident in the references to "the name of Christ" or variations on that phraseology. To believe in the name of Jesus, for example, is to commit oneself to the person of Christ. Also, to hope in the name of Christ is to find hope in his personal being. There is a profound continuity, therefore, between the persons of Jesus Christ and God. Their respective "names" indicate their equivalent divine essence.

See Also: → CALL

NARROW

OT Words

ṣar **[צַר, 6862]**

ṣar is a noun that has the predominant meaning "enemy," "adversary." However, in two places it conveys the adjectival sense "narrow." Num. 22:26 refers to a narrow path; and in Prov. 23:27 a morally corrupt woman is likened to a narrow well.

'ātam **[אָטַם, 331]**

'ātam is an adjectival form occurring four times, meaning "narrow" in a physical sense, referring to "narrow" or "recessed" windows in the temple of Solomon in 1 Kgs. 6:4, and to the same in Ezekiel's visionary temple in Ezek. 40:16; 41:16, 26.

NT Words

stenos [στενός, *4728*]

stenos is an adjective with the sense of "narrow," found in only three places and referring metaphorically to the "narrow gate" that leads to the heavenly kingdom, as opposed to the "wide gate" that leads to destruction (cf. Matt. 7:13, 14; Luke 13:24).

NATION

OT Words

gôy **[גּוֹי, 1471]**

gôy is a common noun form, occurring around 550 times, with the primary meaning "nation" or "people." The term refers both to the nation of Israel as well as to Gentile nations.

Generalized references to nations without regard for racial or geographic distinctions include Gen. 10:5, 20, 31, 32; Exod. 34:10; Lev. 26:45; Num. 23:9; Deut. 15:6; 32:43; 1 Sam. 8:5; 2 Chr. 32:13; Neh. 13:26; Job 34:29; Prov. 14:34; Isa. 9:1; Jer. 1:5; Ezek. 32:12.

Apart from Israel, a number of specific people groups are designated as nations — for example, Egypt (Gen. 15:14; Exod. 9:24); the descendants of Ishmael (Gen. 17:20); Assyria (Isa. 5:26; Amos 6:14); and Babylon (Jer. 4:7; 5:15; Hab. 1:6); and Canaanite nations (Gen. 29:18; Josh. 23:12; 1 Kgs. 11:2). See also Joel 1:6, which could refer to either Assyria or Babylon, depending on when the prophecy was recorded.

In other contexts, ***gôy*** refers to the conquest of nations by the Israelite kingdom of David (2 Sam. 8:11; 1 Chr. 18:11). Isa. 14:6 refers to nations conquered by Babylon; and the fate of nations overcome by the fallen angel from heaven (i.e., Satan) is noted in Isa. 14:12. General reference to the wickedness of the nations is indicated in Ezek. 5:7; 11:12.

With specific reference to Israel as a nation, as the people of Yahweh, ***gôy*** is found in numerous contexts. It refers, for example, to the nation descended from Abraham as a consequence of the covenant promise (Gen. 12:2; 18:18; 26:4; 35:11); to Israel as a "holy nation" (Exod. 19:6); to Israel as a nation belonging to Yahweh (Exod. 33:13; Ps. 33:12); and to the uniqueness of Israel as a nation (1 Chr. 17:21). God promises to bless his nation, his people (Isa. 26:15). Several texts describe Israel as a sinful, rebellious nation, deserving of punishment (cf. Isa. 1:4; 65:1; Jer. 5:9; 7:28; 9:26; Ezek. 4:13; Mal. 3:9). Further to the theme of punishment, Israel is depicted as either scattered "among the nations" or is threatened with such in Lev. 26:33, 38;

Deut. 4:27; Pss. 44:11; 78:55; Jer. 9:16; Lam. 1:3; Ezek. 11:16; 20:23; 36:19; Hos. 9:17; Mic. 5:8.

The nations are also depicted as the arena for the operation of God's mercy, when in a number of places Yahweh promises to gather Israel from the nations and restore his people to the land (cf. Jer. 29:14; Ezek. 20:41; 28:25; 36:24; 37:21ff.). There is also a plea to Yahweh to save his people from among the nations (1 Chr. 16:24ff.; Ps. 106:47).

gôy refers to "nations" in a general sense, coming from the lineage of Abraham and indicating a worldwide number of people groups promised to him above and beyond the specific promise of God's own chosen people (cf. Gen. 17:4ff.; 21:13). In a negative context, the Canaanite nations are described as coming under the judgment of Yahweh, being evicted from the land by him (cf. Lev. 18:24; 20:23; Deut. 4:38; 11:23; Josh. 23:13; 2 Sam. 7:23; 1 Kgs. 14:24; Pss. 44:2; 80:8). Their destruction by God is indicated in Deut. 31:3; Josh. 23:3ff. Elsewhere, God is said to judge the nations, punishing them and frustrating their attempts to thwart his purposes (cf. Ps. 9:5, 17ff.; Isa. 14:26; 30:28; Zeph. 3:8; Hag. 2:7; Zech. 1:5; 12:9; 14:3). God is also declared to be supremely powerful over the nations in Isa. 40:15ff. and rules them, controlling their destiny (cf. Pss. 22:28; 47:8; Ezek. 26:3). Similarly, Pss. 46:10; 96:3; Ezek. 39:21 affirm Yahweh as "exalted among the nations"; and Jer. 10:7ff. declares God to be "king of the nations." In Isa. 64:2; Jer. 33:9 the nations are said to tremble before Yahweh.

The Gentile nations, however, are not only the objects of God's wrath; they are also the beneficiaries of divine grace. A number of texts declare that the nations will flock to Zion, to Jerusalem, and worship God there (cf. Isa. 60:3, 11; Jer. 3:17; Zech. 8:22; Pss. 22:27; 72:17; 86:9; Isa. 2:2; 66:18; Mic. 4:2; Zech. 2:11). Ps. 67:2 affirms that Yahweh will deliver the nations; and Isa. 11:10 indicates that the nations will seek after the Messiah. Furthermore, the Servant of Yahweh, the Messianic King, is depicted as bringing justice (Isa. 42:1) and light (Isa. 42:6; 49:6) to the nations. See also Isa. 45:1; 49:7. (→ PEOPLE)

NT Words

ethnos [ἔθνος, *1484*]

ethnos is the dynamic equivalent of ***gôy***, found in approximately 160 contexts meaning "nation" and "Gentile" (predominantly in the plural). ***ethnos*** refers to "nation" in a general sense and also indicates a pagan or Gentile people group. (→ GENTILES)

ethnos refers to "nation(s)" in a general sense in Matt. 21:43; 24:7; Mark 11:17; Luke 12:30; Acts 2:5; 17:26. Jesus declares in Matt. 24:9 that his followers will be hated by "all nations." The nations are depicted as the object of divine judgment, including both the righteous and the wicked (Matt. 25:32). Several texts declare that divine judgment or wrath is poured out on the nations (cf. Luke 21:25; Acts 7:7; 13:19; Rev. 11:18; 16:19). The nations are described as inflicting temporary victory over the people of God (cf. Rev. 11:2, 9; 13:7). In the latter context, the rule of the "sea beast," or the satanic counterfeit messiah, is in view. In Rev. 18:23, the nations are said to be deceived by the city of Babylon; and they are depicted as the object of satanic deception in Rev. 20:8.

In a much more positive context, the nations are designated as the object of Christian missionary endeavor, that they might become baptized disciples of Christ (cf. Matt. 28:19). Several texts indicate that the gospel is to be preached to "all nations" (cf. Mark 13:10; Luke 24:47; Rom. 1:5 [implied]; Rev. 14:6). The spiritual blessing of salvation is designated for the nations through the covenant promises to Abraham in Gal. 3:8, 14. Rev. 15:4 affirms that all nations will ultimately worship God; and Rev. 21:24 declares that the redeemed nations shall be illuminated by the heavenly city. Rev. 22:2 refers to the nations receiving healing from the tree of life in the heavenly city.

Israel is described as a nation in Luke 23:2; John 11:48; 18:35; Acts 10:22; 24:2; 26:4; 28:19. Believers in Christ are declared to be a "holy nation" in 1 Pet. 2:9, according to the promise given to the old covenant people of Israel. Rev. 2:26 indicates that believers are to be given power over the nations by Christ. Rev. 5:9; 7:9 record that people "from every nation" are delivered from the penalty of sin and death by means of the death of Christ, which constitutes a ransom for sin. In Rev. 12:5; 19:15, Christ is portrayed as the ruler of the nations.

See Also: → PEOPLE

NATURAL, NATURE

NT Words

physikos [φυσικός, *5446*]

physikos is an adjective that occurs in only three places, meaning "natural," "born of instinct." Rom. 1:26, 27 refer to the sin of homosexuality, where men and women give up "natural" sexual relations for one another and transfer them to members of their own sex — inclinations explicitly forbidden by God. In 2 Pet. 2:12, false teachers are likened among other things to irrational animals, "born of instinct" to be caught and destroyed.

astorgos [ἄστοργος, *794*]

astorgos is an adjectival form that occurs only twice, meaning "heartless," or "inhuman," but literally conveying the sense of "without natural affection" (cf. Rom. 1:31; 2 Tim. 3:3).

physis [φύσις, *5449*]

physis is a noun occurring fourteen times, meaning "nature" or "kind" in several different contexts.

In the first instance, ***physis*** conveys the idea of "nature," meaning that which is created by God. Gal. 2:15, for example, refers to those who are Jewish "by nature," as opposed to people born as Gentiles. Rom. 1:26 refers to the unnatural desires of homosexuality as "contrary to nature."

Similarly, "nature" may refer to that which is in accord with a natural order, without explicit reference to the divine origin of the phenomenon. For instance, Rom. 2:14 refers to Gentiles who do things required by the law "by nature," even though they do not have the law of Moses. The physical or "natural" condition of "uncircumcision" is indicated in Rom. 2:27. The custom of Paul's day dictated that long hair on a man was a shameful thing, something that was contrary to "nature" (cf. 1 Cor. 1:14). Idolatry, in Gal. 4:8, is depicted as a bondage to beings that were "by nature" no gods. Eph. 2:3 declares that all human beings are "by nature" children of wrath, under the judgment of God.

physis also has the adjectival sense of "natural," or that which occurs in the physical world. In Rom. 11:21, 24, the expression "natural branches" refers metaphorically to the people of Israel. In a related context, Rom. 11:24 refers symbolically to "wild olive branches," designating the Gentiles as those branches that are literally "wild by nature."

physis also indicates the sense of "nature" in relation to the person of God. 2 Pet. 1:4 speaks of sharing in the "divine nature," which is the ultimate goal of all believers.

physis refers in Jas. 3:7 to "all kinds of animals (etc.)," where "kind" conveys the sense of "species."

psychikos [ψυχικός, *5591*]

psychikos is an adjective that is found in only five contexts, meaning "natural" with the underlying neutral sense of that which is purely physical, or the negative connotation of that which is devoid of true spirituality in a godly sense.

The neutral sense of ***psychikos*** is indicated in 1 Cor. 15:44, 46, with reference to the human body before the resurrection as a purely "physical" or "natural" entity. 1 Cor. 2:14, however, refers to the "natural" person as one who is unspiritual, unreceptive to the gifts of the spirit of God. Similarly, Jas. 3:15; Jude 19 refer to the unspiritual as those who are impervious to spiritual realities.

NAZIRITE

OT Words

nāzîr [נָזִיר, **5139**]

The term ***nāzîr*** is a noun, occurring sixteen times and referring primarily to the Israelite man or woman who undertakes a special vow of separation or holiness, dedicating him/herself to Yahweh for a specified period, up to and including the whole of one's life. Such a person is referred to as a "Nazirite." The legislation concerning this particular phenomenon is found in Num. 6:2–21. The Nazirite vow is specifically mentioned in Judg. 13:5, 7; 16:17, with reference to Samson, and in Amos 2:11, 12, referring to those who take the vow as a class of devout Israelites.

Elsewhere, ***nāzîr*** may refer simply to "those who are separate from" others, although the precise translation of the term in these contexts is uncertain (cf. Gen. 49:26; Deut. 33:17; Lam. 4:7).

NT Words

nazōraios [ναζωραῖος, *3480*]

It is uncertain whether this term derives from ***nāzîr*** (see above) or is simply an adjective referring to the town of Nazareth. ***nazōraios*** is translated "Nazarene" and is found only twice. Matt. 2:23 contains a cryptic reference to an otherwise unknown Old Testament prophecy referring to the Messiah: "He shall be called a Nazarene." In this context, it is clear that the statement refers to Jesus in relation to Nazareth, the town of his upbringing. In Acts 24:25 Jesus is described as the ringleader of the "Nazarene sect."

All other uses of ***nazōraios*** refer to Jesus "of Nazareth" (cf. Matt. 26:71; Mark 10:47; Luke 18:37; 24:19; John 18:5ff.; 19:19; Acts 2:22; 3:6; 4:10; 6:14; 22:8; 26:9).

See Also: → VINE

NECK

OT Words

ṣawwā'r [צַוָּאר, 6677]

ṣawwā'r is a noun referring to the "neck," of both people and animals. ***ṣawwā'r*** carries both a literal and metaphorical sense. The term is found around forty times.

General references to the necks of people are found in Gen. 27:16; 41:42; Judg. 5:30; Song 1:10; 4:4; 7:4. In particular, several texts indicate the action of falling on someone's neck as an expression of grief and sorrow (cf. Gen. 33:4; 45:14; 46:29). The expression "to put one's feet on the neck of another" signifies the condition of utter humiliation or defeat. See, for example, Josh. 10:24, where Joshua, the leader of the Israelite tribes, performs this action on the five Amorite kings immediately prior to their execution.

The remaining usage of *ṣawwā'r* with respect to people is found in metaphorical contexts. The expression "breaking the yoke from one's neck" signifies release from oppression in Gen. 27:40; Jer. 28:10ff. In Isa. 10:27; 52:2; Jer. 30:8, this motif signifies Yahweh's deliverance of his people from bondage. Conversely, having a "yoke around one's neck" points to the trauma of oppression. In particular, Deut. 28:48; Jer. 27:2ff.; Lam. 1:14; 5:5 refer to this condition as a covenant curse of God who sends the enemies of Israel against his people in judgment, as a consequence of Israel's rebellion against him. See also Ezek. 21:29; Hos. 10:11; Mic. 2:3; Hab. 3:13.

ṣawwā'r means "shoulder" in Neh. 3:5, referring to the people "putting their shoulders" to the task of rebuilding the wall of Jerusalem. The expression "stiff neck" indicates stubbornness or arrogant pride in Ps. 75:5. The phrase "reaching to the neck," in the metaphorical context of an overwhelming flood, refers to the imminent Assyrian invasion of the land of Israel in Isa. 8:8; 30:28.

With reference to the necks of animals, ***ṣawwā'r*** is found in general contexts such as Judg. 8:21, 26; Job 39:19; 41:22.

ṣawwa'r [צַוַּאר, 6676 (Aramaic)]

ṣawwa'r is the Aramaic equivalent of ***ṣawwā'r*** and is found only three times. The term occurs in Dan. 5:7, 16, 29, referring to a chain of gold placed around Daniel's neck by the Babylonian ruler Belshazzar, in recognition of his ability to decipher the mysterious handwriting on the wall.

'ōreph [עֹרֶף, 6203]

'ōreph is a noun occurring around thirty times meaning "neck," or (by extension) "back," and is also translated with the adjectival sense of "stiff-necked," "stubborn," or "proud." The latter meaning predominates in the usage of the term.

'ōreph rarely refers literally to "neck." Lev. 5:8 refers to wringing the necks of turtledoves in preparation for a sacrificial sin offering. See also Prov. 29:1.

The remaining use of ***'ōreph*** is metaphorical. The characteristic of being "stiff-necked" is frequently attributed to the people of Israel (cf. Exod. 32:9; Deut. 9:6, 13; 10:16; 2 Kgs. 17:14; 2 Chr. 36:13; Neh. 9:16ff.; Isa. 48:4; Jer. 7:26; 19:15). The expression "to place one's hand on the neck of one's enemies" signifies gaining victory over one's foe (cf. Gen. 49:8). Job accuses God of seizing him by the neck in Job 16:12.

'ōreph is also translated "back" in the expression "to turn one's back towards," indicating a reaction of fear and flight. It is predicated of Israel's enemies before Israel (cf. Exod. 23:27; 2 Sam. 22:41; Ps. 18:40); and also of Israel before her enemies (Josh. 7:8, 12). Israel is also said to turn her back against God as a sign of rebellion against him (cf. 2 Chr. 29:6; Jer. 2:27; 32:33). Jer. 18:17 declares that God will show his back to his people as a sign of judgment against them.

'āraph [עָרַף, 6202]

'āraph is a verb occurring six times with the principal meaning "to break the neck." In two of these contexts, ***'āraph*** refers to breaking the neck of an animal in the context of worship (cf. Exod. 13:13; 34:20). Deut. 2:4, 6 refer to the slaughter of a heifer through this process as part of a ritual ceremony set down for an unsolved murder. Isa. 66:3 refers to breaking a dog's neck in the context of corrupted, idolatrous worship. The remaining use of ***'āraph*** is found in Hos. 10:2, referring to Yahweh "breaking down" the idolatrous altars of his people.

maphreqet [מַפְרֶקֶת, 4665]

maphreqet is found only in 1 Sam. 4:18, referring to the tragic death of the high priest, Eli, who broke his neck in a fall after hearing of the loss of the ark in battle against the Philistines and the deaths of his two sons.

gargeret [גַּרְגֶּרֶת, 1621]

gargeret is another noun meaning "neck," but it is only used in a figurative sense. ***gargeret*** occurs only four times, all in the book of Proverbs. Prov. 1:9; 6:21 refer to the great value of parental instruction and wisdom, which the reader is exhorted to tie around his neck. Similar instruction is given with respect to the virtues of loyalty, faithfulness, and wisdom in Prov. 3:3, 22.

gārôn [גָּרוֹן, 1627]

gārôn is a noun occurring eight times, meaning "neck," "throat" in both literal and metaphorical contexts.

gārôn refers literally to people's throats that are parched with thirst (Ps. 69:3); praising God (Ps. 149:6); and making no sound (Ps. 115:7). See also Jer. 2:25.

In denouncing his enemies, the psalmist refers to their throats as "open sepulchers" in Ps. 5:9. Arrogant pride is indicated in the hearts of women in Jerusalem who walk around with "outstretched necks." Ezek. 16:11 refers metaphorically to Yahweh placing an ornamental chain around the neck of his people Israel, depicted allegorically as a beautiful young woman ready for marriage.

gārôn is used once in a verbal sense in Isa. 58:1, where the prophet is called upon to "cry aloud" to his people, denouncing their transgressions and sins against God.

NT Words

trachēlos [τράχηλος, *5137*]

trachēlos is the only term for "neck" in the New Testament. It occurs seven times with both literal and symbolic force.

Literal references to "neck" are found in Luke 15:20; Acts 20:37. Both texts indicate people weeping as they embrace a person very dear to them, literally "falling upon their necks."

In metaphorical contexts, Matt. 18:6; Mark 9:42; Luke 17:2 refer to the implied terrible fate set aside for those who cause young believers to stumble in their faith. Such a fate is worse than "having a millstone placed around their neck" and being cast into the sea. Making unfair and unreasonable demands on newly-converted Gentile believers is likened in Acts 15:10 to "putting a yoke on the neck" of these disciples. In Rom. 16:4, Paul praises the courage of those "who risked their necks" for his life.

NECKLACE

OT Words

rābîd [רָבִיד, 7242]

rābîd is a noun found only twice, meaning "chain" or "ornamental necklace" on both occasions. In Gen. 41:42, such a necklace is a symbol of high office, given to Joseph on the occasion of his prestigious appointment as chief advisor to Pharaoh. In Ezek. 16:11, the necklace is an expression of Yahweh's devotion to his people, depicted allegorically as a gift to a beautiful young woman, placed around her neck.

'anāq [עֲנָק, 6060]

'anāq is a rare noun, occurring only three times and referring generally to "chain" or "necklace." In Judg. 8:26, the term indicates the pendants or chains around the necks of camels. Song 4:9 refers to the jeweled necklace belonging to the "beloved." Prov. 1:9 refers metaphorically to the instruction given by parents as a necklace for their children.

'ānaq [עָנַק, 6059]

'ānaq is a rare verb that occurs only twice. In Ps. 73:6 it refers to pride "serving as a necklace" for the wicked. (The other occurrence is in Deut. 15:16, where the term is translated "to give generously" from one's flock.)

hamnîk [הַמְנִיךְ, 2002 (Aramaic)]

hamnîk is an Aramaic term translated "necklace" or "chain." It occurs only three times, all in the book of Daniel, with reference to a promised golden chain to be placed around the neck of the person who could read the cryptic handwriting on the wall of the palace belonging to Belshazzar, ruler of Babylon. The "chain of gold" was awarded to Daniel (cf. Dan. 5:7, 16, 29).

NEED

OT Words

maḥsôr [מַחְסוֹר, 4270]

maḥsôr is a noun that is translated "need," "lack," or "want," in different contexts.

The meaning "need," in the sense of that which is necessary for the maintenance of life in regard to food, is indicated in Deut. 15:18; Judg. 19:20. ***maḥsôr*** is also translated "need" as a synonym for "poverty" in Prov. 6:11; 11:24; 14:23; 21:5, 17; 22:16; 24:34.

maḥsôr is also found in the expression "to be in need of nothing," or "lack nothing," referring to places that are rich and fertile (cf. Judg. 18:10; 19:19). Similarly, Ps. 34:9 refers to those who fear God as having no need, lacking nothing. Likewise, ***maḥsôr*** refers to those who are generous to the poor (Prov. 28:27).

ḥāsar [חָסֵר, 2637]

ḥāsar is a verb found in approximately twenty contexts, with the predominant meanings "to have need of," "be in need," and "to lack."

In several places, the meaning "lack" overlaps with the sense of "to be in need of . . ." For example, Deut. 2:7 speaks of Yahweh's provision for his people during their wilderness wandering, during which time they "lacked nothing," or "had no need of anything" in order to live. Similar divine provision is mentioned in Deut. 8:9; Neh. 9:21; Pss. 23:1; 34:10. The very opposite is indicated in Jer. 44:18; Ezek. 4:17, where the people's idolatry results in the total withdrawal of divine blessing in the form of material provision — the people will "lack" everything and thus be "wholly in need."

At the human level, Prov. 13:25 declares, for example, that the wicked shall "suffer need," or be deprived of food. In contrast, the godly woman of Prov. 31 is depicted as an ideal wife, who will "need for nothing" as she has the devoted trust of her husband.

ḥāsēr [חָסֵר, 2638]

ḥāsēr is an adjectival form derived from *ḥāsar* (see above) that is used in a verbal sense and also means "to have need of," "to be in need of" (i.e., to lack). *ḥāsēr* occurs about twenty times.

The necessity for food is indicated in 2 Sam. 3:29; Prov. 12:9. See also 1 Sam. 21:15; 1 Kgs. 11:22. The meaning "lack," or "to be in need of," is commonly found in the book of Proverbs with reference to people lacking in sense or wisdom (cf. Prov. 6:32; 7:7; 9:4, 16; 10:13, 21; 11:12; 12:11; 15:21; 17:18; 24:30; 28:16; Eccl. 10:3). The opposite perspective is indicated in Eccl. 6:2 with reference to the man who stands in need of, or who lacks, nothing.

ṣōrek [צֹרֶךְ, 6878]

ṣōrek is a verb found only in 2 Chr. 2:16, meaning "to need" in regard to supplying timber from Lebanon for the temple.

ḥashaḥ [חֲשַׁח, 2818 (Aramaic)]

ḥashaḥ is an Aramaic verb that occurs only twice, with both uses indicating the sense "to have need of." Ezra 6:9 speaks of the need of animals for burnt offerings. In Dan. 3:16, Daniel's three Jewish friends make the bold claim that they have no need to defend themselves to King Nebuchadnezzar, since they are determined not to bow down to his idolatrous image.

NT Words

chreia [χρεία, *5532*]

chreia is a noun occurring around fifty times with the primary senses of "need" (i.e., necessity of life) and as part of the expressions "to have need (of)," "to be in need."

The literal sense of "need," indicating a material necessity for life, is found in Acts 2:45; 4:35; 20:34; 28:10; Rom. 12:13; Phil. 2:25; 4:16; Titus 3:14. "Need" in a spiritual sense is indicated in Phil. 4:19; 1 John 3:17.

chreia is also utilized in the expression "to be in need" in a general sense (Eph. 4:28), and with reference to food (Mark 2:25), and healing (Luke 9:11).

The expression "to have need (of)" in a general sense is found in Matt. 21:3; Luke 22:71; John 2:25; 13:29; 16:30; 1 Thess. 1:8. The need to be baptized is indicated in Matt. 3:14. Heb. 10:36 speaks of the need for endurance; and Heb. 5:2 indicates the need of immature believers for a teacher. Matt. 26:65; Mark 14:63 refer to the need for witnesses. Jesus' need of a donkey is mentioned in Mark 11:3; Luke 19:31, 34. Matt. 6:8 makes the claim that God knows what his people need.

The expression "to have no need (of)" refers to material goods (Rev. 3:17); to a physician (Matt. 9:12; Mark 2:17; Luke 5:31); and to a teacher (1 John 2:27). The absence of any need for repentance is noted in Luke 15:7. And in a metaphorical context, Rev. 21:23; 22:5 indicate that there is no need of the sun or moon in the heavenly city. In a quite different symbolic context, Paul deals with the metaphor of the human body in discussing the phenomenon of mutual interdependence in the fellowship of believers. In 1 Cor. 12:21 he records a hypothetical "dialogue" between parts of the human body where one part says to the other: "I have no need of you." The point here is that such independence is both untenable and undesirable where genuine Christian community is in view.

chrēzō [χρῄζω, *5535*]

chrēzō is a verb found in only five contexts, meaning "to have need of."

Matt. 6:32; Luke 12:30 speak of God's knowledge of the needs of his people. Awareness of what others may need is indicated in Luke 11:8; Rom. 16:2. A question of need, as regards letters of commendation, arises in 2 Cor. 3:1.

NEEDLE

NT Words

rhaphis [ῥαφίς, *4476*]

rhaphis is found only three times in the New Testament, and on each occasion it refers to "needle" in the expression "the eye of a needle." The phrase is found in the context of Jesus' warning to the wealthy, affirming hyperbolically that, such is the attraction of worldly riches, it is "easier for a camel to go through the eye of a needle" than for a rich person to enter heaven (cf. Matt. 19:24; Mark 10:25; Luke 18:25).

NEGLECT, NEGLIGENT

OT Words

shālāh [שָׁלָה, **7952**]

shālāh is a rare verb form, found only twice. In 2 Chr. 29:11, Hezekiah exhorts the priests and Levites "not to be negligent" in their duties in the temple. The other reference is found in 2 Kgs. 4:28, where ***shālāh*** is translated "to raise one's hope."

NT Words

ameleō [ἀμελέω, *272*]

ameleō is a rare verb found in only four places, meaning "to neglect," "show negligence," "be negligent." Human negligence is indicated in Matt. 22:5; and Heb. 8:9 refers to divine negligence of Israel — a deliberate act of judicial neglect for the people's violation of their covenant responsibilities towards God. In 1 Tim. 4:14, Paul instructs Timothy not to neglect the gifts of ministry given to him by the Spirit of God. Heb. 2:3 warns of the dire spiritual consequences of neglecting one's salvation in Christ.

paratheōreō [παραθεωρέω, *3865*]

paratheōreō occurs only in Acts 6:1, referring to the Hellenistic believers' complaint that the widows in their community were being neglected in the daily distribution of food.

NEIGHBOR

OT Words

rēa' [רֵעַ, **7453**]

rēa' is a noun that is commonly translated "neighbor" as well as "friend" or "companion." It is also used like a pronoun, with the sense of "(one) another," on a number of occasions, overlapping with the meaning "neighbor." ***rēa'*** occurs approximately two hundred times, and about half of these occurrences indicate the sense of "neighbor." (The meaning "friend" is often a closely related one. (→ FRIEND)

rēa' most commonly indicates a "neighbor," in the sense of one's fellow Israelite, in a variety of contexts. There is the command, for example, not to bear false witness against one's neighbor (Exod. 20:16; Deut. 5:20). The practice of lying to one's neighbor is cited in Ps. 12:2; Prov. 25:18. The command not to covet anything belonging to one's neighbor is recorded in Exod. 20:17; Deut. 5:21. See also Eccl. 4:4. There are numerous principles expressed throughout the Mosaic law that stress the importance of treating one's neighbor kindly and compassionately with fair and just dealings (cf. Exod. 22:7ff.; Lev. 19:13ff.; Deut. 15:2; 24:10; Prov. 3:29; Isa. 41:6). In particular, mercy is required to be shown to "manslayers," or to those who cause the death of their neighbor by accident (cf. Deut. 4:42; 19:4ff.; Josh. 20:5). The command to love one's neighbor as oneself is found in Lev. 19:18.

Sin against or mistreatment of one's "neighbor," one's fellow Israelite, brings down the judgment of God. This general principle is illustrated in 1 Kgs. 8:31; Prov. 11:12; 14:21; 21:10; 24:28; Isa. 3:5; Jer. 19:9; 22:13; Ezek. 22:12. Particular mention is made of the sins of adultery (cf. Lev. 20:10; Deut. 22:24; Job 31:9; Prov. 6:29; Jer. 5:8; Ezek. 18:11; 33:26); and murder (cf. Deut. 22:26; 27:24). Furthermore, Exod. 32:27 refers to the expression of divine judgment against the Israelites for their worship of the golden calf at Sinai, whereby Yahweh issues the command for the Levites to slaughter their fellow Israelite "neighbors."

General references to Israelites as one another's "neighbors" are found in Ruth 4:7; 1 Sam. 15:28; Job 16:21; Ps. 28:3; Jer. 31:34; Zech. 3:10. In 2 Sam. 12:11, ***rēa'*** refers to David's son Absalom as his "neighbor." See also Exod. 11:2; 21:14; Isa. 19:2; Jer. 7:5; 23:30.

re'ût [רְעוּת, **7468**]

re'ût is a feminine form of ***rēa'*** (see above), occurring five times and meaning "mate," "neighbor." The latter meaning is found only twice. Exod. 11:2 refers to the female Egyptian neighbors of Israelite women immediately prior to the Hebrew exodus from that land. Jer. 9:20 refers to "neighbors" in the sense of fellow Israelite women.

qārôb [קָרוֹב, **7138**]

qārôb is an adjectival form occurring around eighty times with the primary sense of "near," as well as related senses. On two occasions the term is used nominally to refer to "neighbors." Exod. 32:27 refers to fellow Israelite countrymen, and Josh. 9:16 mentions the Gibeonites as "neighbors" to Israel in the land of Canaan.

shākēn [שָׁכֵן, **7934**]

shākēn is an adjective that is translated primarily with nominal force in about twenty places meaning "neighbor" in most of these contexts.

The meaning "neighbor" in the sense of one who lives adjacent or nearby is indicated in Exod. 3:22; 12:4; Ruth 4:17; 2 Kgs. 4:3. With the sense of "fellow Israelite," ***shākēn*** means "neighbor" in Jer. 49:10. Elsewhere, the designation "neighbor" refers to people groups living in the surrounding region. For example, Israel's Canaanite neighbors are indicated in Deut. 1:7; Jer. 12:14, depicted as "evil neighbors" whom Yahweh will punish. Cities adjacent to Sodom and Gomorrah (i.e., neighboring cities) are mentioned in Jer. 49:18; 50:40. See also Ezek. 16:26, which refers to the idolatrous Egyptians as "lustful neighbors" to Israel.

General, unspecified uses of the term "neighbor" are found in Pss. 31:11; 44:13; 79:4, 12; 80:6; 89:41; Prov. 27:10; Jer. 6:21.

'āmît [עָמִית, **5997**]

'āmît is a noun found in nine contexts, all with reference to "neighbor" in the general sense of one's fellow Israelite countryman (cf. Lev. 6:2; 18:20; 19:11, 15, 17; 24:19; 25:14ff.; Zech. 13:7). In all but the last of these references, ***'āmît*** refers to one's "neighbor" in the context of treating them in a manner that is just, compassionate, and morally appropriate under the Mosaic law.

NT Words

plēsion [πλησίον, *4139*]

plēsion is a general term for "neighbor," expressing the idea of one's fellow human being. In addition, for Jews, the term indicates any member of the Hebrew race; and for Christians, it refers to fellow believers. ***plēsion*** occurs in seventeen contexts.

The general sense of "neighbor" as one's fellow human being is indicated in Matt. 5:43; 19:19; 22:39; Mark 12:31ff.; Luke 10:27ff.; Rom. 13:9ff.; 15:2. Gal. 5:14; Jas. 2:8.

The other senses of "neighbor" occur much less frequently. Acts 7:27 refers to the "neighbor" of Moses, or his fellow Hebrew, whose beating at the hands of an Egyptian task master he avenged by slaying the latter. Eph. 4:25; Heb. 8:11 refer to one's fellow Christian believers as "neighbors."

perioikos [περίοικος, *4040*]

perioikos is found only in Luke 1:58 and refers to the neighbors of Elizabeth, mother of John the Baptist, in the sense of those who lived near her.

geitōn [γείτων, *1069*]

geitōn is a noun found only four times, meaning "neighbor" in the sense of those who live close by (cf. Luke 14:12; 15:6, 9; John 9:8).

NEPHILIM

OT Words

nephîlîm [נְפִילִים, **5303**]

nephîlîm is a plural noun form transliterated into English as "Nephilim," referring in three places to a race of people characterized by their huge stature. The term literally means "fallen ones"; although they are referred to as "heroes of old." Yet the context in each case makes it clear that this godlessness makes them ripe for divine judgment. The references are found in Gen. 6:4; Num. 13:33 (twice).

NEST

OT Words

qēn [קֵן, **7064**]

qēn is a noun that refers to the "nest" of a bird in half of the thirteen contexts in which it is found. In these cases, the sense is a literal one (cf. Deut. 22:6; 32:11; Job 39:27; Ps. 84:3; Prov. 27:8; Isa. 16:2; Jer. 49:16). The remaining use of ***qēn*** is metaphorical, referring to one's "nest" as a hiding place or refuge (cf. Num. 24:21; Job 29:18; Isa. 10:14; Jer. 49:6; Obad. 4; Hab. 2:9).

qānan [קָנַן, **7077**]

qānan is the verb from which ***qēn*** (see above) is derived, and it is translated "to make a nest." It occurs only five times and refers literally to birds making their nest in Ps. 104:17; Isa. 34:15; Jer. 48:28; Ezek. 31:6. The exception is found in Jer. 22:23, where ***qānan*** refers metaphorically to the people in Jerusalem, upon whom the catastrophic judgment of Yahweh is about to fall, "nesting among the cedars."

NT Words

kataskēnoō [κατασκηνόω, *2681*]

kataskēnoō occurs only twice in the New Testament, referring on both occasions to Jesus' claim that unlike the birds "who make nests," he has nowhere permanent to live (cf. Matt. 8:20; Luke 9:58).

NET

OT Words

reshet [רֶשֶׁת, **7568**]

reshet is a general term for "net," occurring around twenty times in a number of contexts, with a primarily metaphorical sense.

A literal reference to a "net" in the sense of a "trap," or "snare," for birds is found in Prov. 1:17. ***reshet*** is also translated "network" or "grate," referring to the bronze grating laid over the altar of sacrifice in the tabernacle (cf. Exod. 27:4, 5; 38:4).

Metaphorical usage of ***reshet*** is much more common. The term is translated "net" or "snare," indicating the downfall of those who are morally inept or culpable. This is applied to individuals (Job 18:18; Prov. 29:5); and to nations who are then subjected to divine judgment (cf. Ps. 9:15). In particular, the psalmist declares on several occasions that a "net" or "trap" is set by the wicked for their unwary victims (cf. Pss. 10:9; 35:7, 8; 57:6; 140:5). The psalmist also affirms that Yahweh has delivered him from such a "snare" (Ps. 25:15). In Ps. 31:4, the psalmist pleads for deliverance from such a snare.

In corporate contexts, Ezek. 19:8, for example, describes a "net" or "snare" being laid by the nations for Israel. Conversely, Yahweh is occasionally said to set a snare for his people, as judgment against them for their sin (cf. Lam. 1:17; Ezek. 12:13; 17:20; Hos. 7:12). See also Hos. 5:1. The same is done against the nation of Egypt in Ezek. 32:3.

meṣûdāh [מְצוּדָה, **4686**]

meṣûdāh is a noun occurring around twenty times with the primary meanings "castle," "fortress," "hold." However, on several occasions it refers metaphorically to a "net," or "snare," each time indicating the action of Yahweh in placing his people in a situation of bondage or imprisonment. This applies in the literal historical context of Judah's threatened deportation to Babylon (cf. Ezek. 12:13; 17:20); and more generally in Ps. 66:11; Job 19:6. The latter reference here indicates merely the perception of Job, rather than the reality of the situation.

makmōr [מַכְמֹר, **4364**]

makmōr is a noun found in only two contexts, both meaning "net." In Ps. 141:10 the term refers metaphorically to the entrapment of the wicked; and in Isa. 51:20 it refers to snaring an antelope.

mikmōret [מִכְמֹרֶת, **4365**]

mikmōret is a noun related to ***makmōr*** (see above), occurring three times and meaning "net," "dragnet." In Isa. 19:8 the term refers to fishing nets. In Hab. 1:15, 16, ***mikmōret*** metaphorically indicates the actions of the wicked in snaring their victims in "dragnets."

ḥērem [חֵרֶם, **2764**]

ḥērem is a noun occurring around forty times, with two distinct strands of meaning. On the one hand, it refers to persons or objects either "devoted" to Yahweh by way of dedication or sanctification, or set apart (i.e., "devoted") for destruction, cursed by God. (→ DESTROY) In this sense, ***ḥērem*** is very difficult to adequately translate with one corresponding English word. On the other hand, ***ḥērem*** occurs on several occasions meanings "net," "dragnet," or "snare," all in metaphorical contexts that imply the exercise of divine judgment and blessing.

The heart of a wicked woman, for example, is said to be full of snares as a means of waylaying sinners (cf. Eccl. 7:26). Other references to the wicked who ensnare their victims with a net are found in Mic. 7:2; Hab. 1:15ff. Specifically, divine judgment is invoked against the nation of Egypt in Ezek. 32:3 with reference to a "dragnet" ensnaring that nation. Similarly, the nation of Tyre is condemned in Ezek. 26:5, 14, with reference to Yahweh's intention to lay that nation waste by rendering it fit only as a place to spread "fishing nets."

In a wholly positive context of divine renewal, the river from Ezekiel's temple promises to bring life to the Arabah (i.e., southern desert region) and the Dead Sea, making fishing a very profitable enterprise through the use of nets in this new river of life (cf. Ezek. 47:10).

NT Words

amphiblēstron [ἀμφίβληστρον, *293*]

amphiblēstron occurs only twice, both with literal reference to fishing nets (cf. Matt. 4:18; Mark 1:16).

sagēnē [σαγήνη, *4522*]

sagēnē is found only in Matt. 13:47, likening the kingdom of God to a "net" that is thrown into the sea and gathers fish of every kind.

diktyon [δίκτυον, *1350*]

diktyon is a noun found in twelve contexts with exclusive reference to fishing nets as used by Jesus' disciples (cf. Matt. 4:20ff.; Mark 1:18ff.; Luke 5:2ff.; John 21:6ff.).

NEW, NEWNESS

OT Words

ḥādāsh [חָדָשׁ, **2319**]

ḥādāsh is an adjectival form that is also used nominally to refer to that which is "new." The term occurs around fifty times.

ḥādāsh is translated "new" in the sense of "different" with reference to the king of Egypt (Exod. 1:8); in regard to gods (Deut. 32:17; Judg. 5:8); and in the affirmation that there is "nothing new under the sun" (Eccl. 1:9, 10).

More commonly, the meaning "new" is used with the underlying sense of "fresh." Examples of this usage are found with reference to newly harvested grain (Lev. 23:16; Num. 28:26); to houses (Deut. 20:5; 22:8); and to a wife (Deut. 24:5). Further illustrations of this sense of "new" in regard to material goods are indicated in Song 7:13; Josh. 9:3; Job 32:19; Judg. 15:13; 1 Sam. 6:7; 2 Sam. 21:16; 1 Kgs. 11:29ff.; Isa. 41:15. ***ḥādāsh*** refers to singing new songs in praise of Yahweh in Pss. 33:3; 40:3; 96:1; 98:1; 144:9; 149:1; Isa. 42:10. God's mercies are declared to be new every morning in Lam. 3:23.

The description "new" is also applied to spiritual blessings granted by Yahweh. In general terms, "new things" are promised in Isa. 42:9; 43:19; 48:6 in anticipation of new covenant blessing. The promise of the new covenant is itself located in Jer. 31:31, and the accompanying promise of a new spirit from God in the hearts of his people is found in Ezek. 11:19; 18:31; 36:26. There is the promise of a "new heavens and a new earth" in Isa. 65:17; 66:22; and the guarantee of a "new name" given by God in Isa. 62:2.

berî'āh [בְּרִיאָה, **1278**]

berî'āh is found only in Num. 16:30, with reference to Yahweh bringing about "something new." The context refers to the anticipated punishment of those Levites who had rebelled against Moses, in that Yahweh would act in an unprecedented fashion by causing the ground to open up and swallow them alive.

NT Words

kainos [καινός, *2537*]

kainos is an adjectival form occurring in about forty contexts with the exclusive meaning "new" in both mundane and highly significant contexts.

kainos indicates the meaning "new" primarily in the sense of "fresh." With regard to material substances and objects, the term refers to new wine and wineskins (Mark 2:22; Matt. 9:17; Luke 5:38); a new tomb (Matt. 27:60; John 19:41); and a fresh patch of material used to cover a tear in an old wineskin (Mark 2:21; Luke 5:36). See also Matt. 13:52. New tongues, or languages, are indicated in Mark 1:6, 17.

The remaining uses of ***kainos*** are found in passages of distinctive theological significance, especially in relation to the "new" phenomena associated with the coming of the new covenant age as embodied in the person and work of Christ. The wine of the Passover feast as celebrated by Jesus with his disciples on the evening prior to his crucifixion is declared to represent the blood of the "new covenant," which Jesus is soon to inaugurate (cf. Luke 22:20; 1 Cor. 11:25). Paul refers to believers as "ministers of the new covenant" in 2 Cor. 3:6. The new covenant itself, as a fulfillment of the old, is indicated in Heb. 8:8, 13; 9:15. Associated with this centrally important phenomenon is the affirmation of the believer's "new creation" in Christ in 2 Cor. 5:17; Gal. 6:15. The emergence of the "new man," Christ Jesus, who has brought together Jew and Gentile in peace, is indicated in Eph. 2:15. The anticipated fulfillment of "the new heavens and new earth" is noted 2 Pet. 3:13; Rev. 21:1. The emergence of the "new Jerusalem" coming down out of heaven is described in Rev. 3:12; 21:2. Rev. 21:5 refers to making "all things new."

Elsewhere, the "new song" in worship of God and the Lamb is mentioned in Rev. 5:9; 14:3. The "new name" promised to believers is indicated in Rev. 2:17. The "new nature" of the believer is affirmed in Eph. 4:24.

Jesus issues his "new command" to love one another in John 13:34. This command is referred to elsewhere in 1 John 2:7, 8; 2 John 5.

kainos is also translated "new" in the sense of "different" in Mark 1:27; Acts 17:19, where it refers to "new doctrine."

The term is also used adverbially in Matt. 26:29; Mark 14:25, where it is translated "anew," with the sense of "once more" or "again."

kainotēs [καινότης, *2538*]

kainotēs is the noun from which ***kainos*** (see above) is derived. The term occurs only twice, in Rom. 6:4; 7:6. In both contexts, ***kainotēs*** refers to the new quality of life granted to the believer as the consequence of coming to faith in Christ. Rom. 7:6 speaks of the "newness" of life; and Rom. 7:6 refers to the "new life" of the Spirit.

agnaphos [ἄγναφος, *46*]

agnaphos is an adjective found only twice, meaning "new" in both contexts. Matt. 9:16; Mark 2:21 refer to "new" cloth in the sense of material that is unprocessed or "unshrunk."

neos [νέος, *3501*]

neos is an adjective found in approximately twenty places meaning "new," "young(er)." The former meaning occurs in about half of these contexts. The term is occasionally used in a nominal sense. (→ YOUNG)

The meaning "new" in the sense of "fresh" is applied to wine in Matt. 9:17; Mark 2:22; Luke 5:37ff.; and to the covenant in Heb. 12:24, where Jesus is depicted as the mediator of a new covenant.

In metaphorical contexts, ***neos*** refers to the believer's desired spiritual condition in 1 Cor. 5:7, where he is likened to a "new" batch of dough, uncontaminated by the leaven (or yeast) of sinfulness. Col. 3:10 refers to one's "new nature" in Christ. Here the term "nature" is included in the term ***neos*** itself (there is no accompanying noun in the text).

neomēnia [νεομηνία, *3561*]

neomēnia occurs only in Col. 2:16 with reference to the Jewish "new moon" festival.

prosphatos [πρόσφατος, *4372*]

prosphatos is an adjective that occurs only once, in Heb. 10:20, referring to the "new" and living way opened up by Christ to peace with God through his sacrifice on the cross.

Additional Notes

The vocabulary relating to "new" and "newness" in both Old and New Testaments has a great deal of significance in contexts where descriptions of God's redemptive purposes for his people are in view. In particular, references to the promise of a new covenant in the Old Testament prophets are fulfilled in the New Testament. Related to the fulfillment of the new covenant are the accompanying phenomena of the "new heavens and the new earth," anticipated in the prophet Isaiah and realized in the apocalyptic vision of the apostle John in the book of Revelation. In addition, much prophetic attention is given to the promised renewal of Jerusalem and the temple. In the book of Revelation, the image of the new Jerusalem coming down from heaven constitutes a supreme symbol of divine renewal that is anticipated not only in the prophets, but also through the return of the exiles to their homeland and the subsequent rebuilding of the temple and the city.

See Also: → MOON

NIGHT

OT Words

laylāh [לַיְלָה, **3915**]

laylāh is the most common term in the Old Testament for the "night," occurring around two hundred times, with the occasional additional sense of "midnight."

The literal sense of "night" in contrast to "day" is indicated in Gen. 1:5, 14ff.; Exod. 10:13; Lev. 6:9; Deut. 23:10; Josh. 1:8; 1 Sam. 15:11; 2 Kgs. 6:14; Pss. 1:2; 22:2; Jer. 31:35; Amos 5:8.

References to "night" as the setting for divine guidance are indicated in the context of the "pillar of fire" phenomenon that enabled Israel to travel through the wilderness at night (cf. Exod. 13:21; 40:38; Num. 14:14; Deut. 1:33; Neh. 9:12, 19; Ps. 78:14; Isa. 4:5).

Similarly, "night" is indicated as the setting for divine revelation, where Yahweh expresses his plans and purposes to his people (cf. Gen. 20:3; 26:24; 31:24; Judg. 7:9; 1 Sam. 15:16; 1 Kgs. 3:5). Exod. 24:18; Deut. 9:9ff. refer to Moses spending "forty days and forty nights" on Mt. Sinai to receive the revelation of the covenant law from Yahweh.

In a contrasting context, "night" is indicated as the setting for divine punishment on the occasion of the Passover judgment against the nation of Egypt in Exod. 12:12, 29.

In several places, ***laylāh*** is also translated "midnight" (cf. 1 Kgs. 3:20; Ps. 119:62; Job 34:20). Exod. 11:4; 12:29 also mention "night" in connection with the Passover judgment.

lûn [לוּן, **3885**]

lûn is a verb found in around ninety places with the primary senses of "spend the night," "lodge (overnight)," "remain overnight." The additional meaning "murmur" is also indicated in several places. (→ MURMUR)

The literal sense of "spend the night," meaning to lodge somewhere overnight is illustrated, for example, in Gen. 19:2; Num. 22:8; Josh. 4:3; Judg. 19:4ff.; Ruth 1:16; 2 Sam. 12:16; Joel 1:13.

The other meaning of ***lûn***, "to leave, or remain overnight" is found in general contexts (with no reference to lodging), and usually indicates inanimate, non-personal phenomena such as offerings, sometimes in a negative sense (cf. Lev. 19:13; Deut. 16:4; 21:23; Ps. 30:5).

lêlê [לֵילֵי, **3916** (Aramaic)]

lêlê is an Aramaic noun found only five times in the book of Daniel, referring to "night" on each occasion. Four of these contexts refer to Daniel receiving divine revelation in visions at night (cf. Dan. 2:19; 7:2, 7, 13). Dan. 5:30 relates the slaying of Belshazzar, the last of the Babylonian rulers, on the very night the city of Babylon fell to the invading Persian army.

bût [בּוּת, **956** (Aramaic)]

bût is an Aramaic verb that occurs only in Dan. 6:18 with reference to King Darius "spending the night" in his palaces.

NT Words

nyx [νύξ, *3571*]

nyx is the standard New Testament term for "night." It occurs in approximately sixty contexts with both literal and metaphorical connotations.

The dominant usage of ***nyx*** indicates the sense of "night" (in contrast to "day") in literal contexts (e.g., Matt. 2:14; 26:31ff.; Mark 4:27; 14:30; Luke 2:37; John 3:2; 21:3; Acts 5:19; 20:31; 1 Cor. 11:31; 1 Thess. 2:9; 1 Tim. 5:6). See also Rev. 8:12.

Occasionally, ***nyx*** refers metaphorically to the "night" as a period of moral darkness (cf. John 9:4; 11:10; 13:10; Rom. 13:12; 1 Thess. 5:5).

Jesus' fasting in the desert for a period of "forty days and forty nights" just prior to his testing by the devil in Matt. 4:2 may suggest a patterning along the lines of old covenant periods of trial and/or divine revelation, such as Israel's forty-year wandering in the desert and Moses' forty-day and forty-night audience with Yahweh on Mt. Sinai. Another chronological expression, "three days and three nights," is used with respect to the sign of Jonah, referring to the time he spent in the belly of the great fish (cf. Matt. 12:40). This expression relates to the anticipation of Christ's approaching death and resurrection, a period identical with the duration of Jonah's "trial."

The expression "day and night" metaphorically conveys the idea of continuous, unending experience, applicable both to the joys of heaven and the agonies of eternal punishment (cf. Rev. 4:8; 7:15; 12:10; 14:11; 20:10). Rev. 4:8; 7:15; 12:10; 14:11; 20:10 refer to the constancy of doing something "day and night." Rev. 21:25; 22:5 indicate that there will be no night in heaven.

In two places ***nyx*** means "midnight" (Matt. 25:6; Acts 27:27).

dianyktereuō [διανυκτερεύω, *1273*]

dianyktereuō is found only in Luke 6:12, referring to Jesus "spending the whole night" in prayer.

See Also: → EVENING

NOBLE, NOBLEMAN

OT Words

nādîb [נָדִיב, **5081**]

nādîb denotes a person of exalted civil or royal rank, translated variously as "noble," or "prince" (Num. 21:18; 1 Sam. 2:8; Job 12:21; Ps. 47:9; 83:11; Prov. 8:16; Song 7:1; Isa. 13:2).

ḥôr [חוֹר, **2715**]

ḥôr refers to "nobles" in both Israel and Judah, indicating a class of civic and judicial leaders in the Israelite community who play a significant role in the life of that community. The term occurs thirteen times.

For the most part, "nobles" are mentioned in a neutral context, along with other leaders such as "officials" and "elders" (cf. 1 Kgs. 21:8ff.; Neh. 2:16; 4:14, 19; 6:17; 7:5; Eccl. 10:17). See also Isa. 34:12. Neh. 5:7; 13:17 refer to the sins of the nobles; and Jer. 27:20; 39:6, mention their exile and slaughter.

partemîm [פַּרְתְּמִים, **6579**]

partemîm is a rare term, found only three times with reference to "nobleman" in the upper echelons of society (cf. Esth. 1:3; 6:9; Dan. 1:3).

NT Words

eugenēs [εὐγενής, *2104*]

eugenēs is a rare term found in only three contexts. In Luke 19:12 it refers in general terms to a "nobleman." In 1 Cor. 1:26 the term is used adjectivally to describe the Berean Christians as "more noble" than those in Thessalonica. The qualities indicated here are those of purity of motive and devotion to Christ and his word. 1 Cor. 1:26 also records an adjectival usage, referring to nobility of birth.

kratistos [κράτιστος, *2903*]

kratistos occurs only four times in the New Testament. On each occasion it serves as a form of address to men of high political or regal status. Luke 1:3 contains Luke's greeting to a "most noble Theophilus." ***kratistos*** similarly addresses Felix the Roman governor of Judea (Acts 23:26; 24:3); and his successor, Festus (Acts 26:25). ***kratistos*** may also be translated "most excellent" in these contexts.

See Also: → EXCEL

NOISE → SOUND → UPROAR

NORTH

OT Words

***ṣāphôn* [צָפוֹן, 6828]**

ṣāphôn is a common noun in the Old Testament describing the direction "north," as well as derivative senses such as "northern," "northward," "north side." The term occurs in about 150 contexts.

In literal, mundane contexts, ***ṣāphôn*** is translated "northward" in Gen. 13:14; Deut. 2:3; 3:27; Josh. 13:3; 18:12ff.; Judg. 12:1; Dan. 8:4; Zech. 14:4. The adjectival sense of "northern" is indicated in Num. 34:7ff.; Josh. 11:2 with respect to the northern hill country and boundary of the land of Canaan, and in Num. 35:5 with respect to the northern boundary around the Levitical cities. Ezek. 47:15; 48:1 mention the renewed northern boundaries of the land of Israel, expressed in visionary form.

The meaning "north side" in general contexts is indicated in Josh. 8:11ff.; 15:5; Judg. 21:9. With reference to the tabernacle, ***ṣāphôn*** is also translated this way in Exod. 26:20; 26:35; Lev. 1:11; Num. 2:25; as it is in regard to the temple in 2 Kgs. 16:14; 1 Chr. 9:24; 26:14; Ezek. 8:14. ***ṣāphôn*** refers to the "north side" of the sacred portion of the land belonging to the messianic prince (Ezek. 48:10ff.); to the north side of the city (Ezek. 48:16, 17, 30, 31); to the "north side" of Mt. Zion (Ps. 48:2; Isa. 14:13); and to the "north wind" (Prov. 25:23; Song 4:16).

The meaning "north" as a "point of the compass" and a geographic regional direction is indicated in general contexts in Job 26:7; 37:22; Ps. 107:3; Eccl. 1:6; Amos 8:12; Zech. 6:6ff. This meaning is also found in the description of Ezekiel's visionary temple (cf. Ezek. 40:20ff.; 41:11; 42:1ff.; 44:4; 46:9; 47:2) and of Solomon's temple (cf. 1 Kgs. 7:25; 2 Chr. 4:4). Israel's enemy from the north coming in judgment against them is indicated in Isa. 41:25; Jer. 1:14ff.; 4:6; 6:1, 22; 13:20; 15:12; 25:9. In a slightly different context, Ezek. 38:6 describes the attempted destruction of God's people by nations from the north (this fails abysmally). The promised return of Israelite exiles from the north is indicated in Isa. 49:12; Jer. 3:18; 16:15; 31:8; Zech. 2:6. The "enemy from the north" is also used as an instrument of divine judgment against Egypt (cf. Jer. 46:20, 24), Babylon (cf. Jer. 50:3, 9) and Tyre (cf. Ezek. 26:7). A general reference to the divine destruction of the kingdoms from the north is found in Zeph. 2:13. A storm theophany of Yahweh "coming out of the north" is noted in Ezek. 1:4. Reference is made to the "king of the north" in a visionary revelation to Daniel, with the identity of this figure likely to be a member of the Seleucid dynasty ruling during the latter part of the third century B.C. (cf. Dan. 11:6ff., 40, 44).

NT Words

***borras* [βορρᾶς, *1005*]**

borras is found only twice in the New Testament, referring once to the "north" as one of the directions from which people from all over the world will come to participate in the consummate feast of the kingdom of God at the end of the age (cf. Luke 13:29). Rev. 21:13 refers to the three gates situated on the north wall of the heavenly city of Jerusalem.

NOSE, NOSTRIL

OT Words

***'aph* [אַף, 639]**

'aph means "nose," "nostril" in both a literal and metaphorical sense approximately thirty times. ***'aph*** is also translated "anger," and has this meaning for the majority of its usage (around 270 times). (→ ANGER) Though apparently unrelated, there is in fact a semantic relationship between the meanings "nose," or "nostril," and "anger" when the term is applied anthropomorphically to the person of Yahweh.

The nose is referred to generally as part of the human anatomy in Num. 11:20; Prov. 30:33; Song 7:4; Isa. 3:21; Ps. 115:6; Lam. 4:20; Amos 4:10. Gen. 2:7; Job 27:3 declare that God breathed life into the nostrils of Adam at the point of his creation. Part of Israel's fate at the hands of her enemies involved having hooks placed in their noses and being led away into captivity (cf. 2 Kgs. 19:28). Such treatment is also predicated of the Assyrian king as a divine judgment (cf. Isa. 37:29). In the same context, "having one's nose cut off" is cited as part of the horrific punishment to be handed down to the rebellious people of Israel at the hands of their enemies (cf. Ezek. 23:5). Ezek. 8:17 mentions the practice of "putting a branch to one's nose," an action relating to idolatrous worship of a pagan deity.

In poetic contexts, reference is made to the nose of a "behemoth" in Job 40:24 — an unknown creature, possibly an elephant or hippopotamus. Similarly, Job 41:2 refers to the nose of "leviathan," another creature impossible to identify with certainty, although a crocodile may possibly be in view.

In metaphorical (i.e., anthropomorphic) contexts, ***'aph*** refers to "the nostrils" of Yahweh in a number of places. In each of these contexts, the breath or blast of Yahweh's nostrils symbolizes the expression of divine anger against the wicked (cf. Exod., 15:8; 2 Sam. 22:16; Job 4:9; Ps. 18:15). Similarly, the phrase "smoke in my nostrils" in Isa. 65:5 indicates Yahweh's wrath against his people. This is one example of the semantic connection between the dual senses of ***'aph***, "nose," and "anger." See also 2 Sam. 22:9; Ps. 18:8.

NOTE → OBSERVE

NOURISH → FEED

NUMBER

OT Words

mispār **[מִסְפָּר, 4557]**

mispār is a noun occurring around one hundred times with the consistent meaning "number." The usage of ***mispār*** is primarily literal.

Literal references to the "number(s)" of people are found in general contexts in Exod. 16:16; Judg. 7:6; 1 Sam. 6:4; 1 Chr. 7:40. ***mispār*** refers to the "numbers" in relation to the size of the Israelite tribes in Gen. 34:30; Num. 1:2, 18ff.; 3:22ff.; Deut. 32:8; Josh. 4:5. Aside from the requirement to count the Israelite people in the book of Numbers, there is the illegitimate census of Israel's fighting men recorded in 2 Sam. 24:2; 1 Chr. 21:2. The numbering of the tribe of Levi in particular is indicated in 1 Chr. 23:3. Ezra 2:2; Neh. 7:7 record the number of exiles returned from captivity. The phrase "few in number" refers to people in 1 Chr. 16:9; Ps. 105:12. Deut. 4:27 refers to the reduction of people in the land of Canaan as one of the inevitable consequences of divine judgment against the people of Israel.

In relation to animals, several texts refer to the specified number of creatures set apart for ritual sacrifice to Yahweh (cf. Num. 29:21ff.; 1 Chr. 23:31; 2 Chr. 29:32; Ezra 3:4; Job 1:5).

The phrase "without number" (i.e., immeasurable) is used in relation to grain (cf. Gen. 41:49); cedar trees (cf. 1 Chr. 22:4); evils or trials (cf. Ps. 40:12); locusts in plague proportions (cf. Ps. 105:12); and people in general (cf. Judg. 7:12; 2 Chr. 12:3). In particular, Hos. 1:10 refers to countless numbers of Israelites who will be reinstated to the land after their time of judgment. Marvelous deeds of God are said to be "without number" in Job 5:9; as are the years of God in Job 36:26.

mispār also refers to a number of lashes (i.e., flogging) (cf. Deut. 25:2); number of days (cf. Exod. 23:26; Num. 14:34; Ezek. 4:4ff.); number of years (cf. Lev. 25:15ff.); number of cities (cf. 1 Sam. 6:18); and the number of articles of temple furniture returned from exile by Cyrus, king of Persia (cf. Ezra 1:9).

sāphar **[סָפַר, 5608]**

sāphar is a verb occurring around 160 times with a variety of meanings. Primarily, ***sāphar*** means "tell," "declare." In addition, however, ***sāphar*** is translated "number," or "count" in around thirty contexts.
(→ SCRIBE → TELL)

The literal sense of "number" or "count" is indicated in the negative in several contexts. It is applied to people who are declared to be innumerable (cf. Gen. 16:10; 32:12; 1 Kgs. 3:8). In particular, Hos. 1:10 refers to the incalculable number of Israelites in consequence of Yahweh's promise of restoration and renewal. The quantity of grain collected by Joseph in Egypt is declared to be immeasurable (i.e., cannot be counted) in Gen. 41:49. In Jer. 33:22, the host of heaven is described as incalculable. The psalmist affirms that God's deeds cannot be numbered in Ps. 40:5.

In a positive sense, ***sāphar*** is translated "number" or "count" in general contexts in 2 Chr. 2:17; Job 38:37; 39:2; Isa. 22:10; 33:18. A period of seven days is counted for ritual cleansing in Lev. 15:13, 28. A seven-week period of time is counted prior to the Feast of Harvest (or Weeks) in Lev. 23:15ff.; Deut. 16:9. Similarly, legislation for the celebration of Jubilee is laid down in Lev. 25:8, where a forty-nine-year period of time is to be counted prior to the Jubilee year. The counting of Israelite warriors in an illegitimate census taken by David is indicated in 2 Sam. 24:10; 1 Chr. 21:2. In ritual contexts, the numbering of Levites is indicated in 1 Chr. 23:3, the counting of animals marked for sacrifice in 2 Chr. 5:6, and also the counting of various articles of temple furniture in Ezra 1:8.

In a metaphorical context, God is said to "number the steps" of human beings in Job 4:16; 31:4.

mānāh [מָנָה, **4487**]

mānāh is a verb occurring around thirty times with the primary meanings "number," "count."

mānāh means to "number," "count" relating to the promised descendants of Abraham in Gen. 13:16. The psalmist prays that God will teach his people to "number" their days in Ps. 90:12. 2 Sam. 24:1; 1 Chr. 21:1, 17 contain commands to count the people of Israel in a census (cf. also 1 Chr. 27:24). There is likewise a command issued to "muster" (i.e., number) an army in 1 Kgs. 20:25.

mānāh is also used in a negative sense in 1 Kgs. 3:8, where the people of God are deemed too numerous to be counted. Innumerable animals for sacrifice are noted in 1 Kgs. 8:5; 2 Chr. 5:6.

This term is also used metaphorically in Num. 23:10, in relation to the descendants of Jacob. The text notes the impossibility of "counting the dust" of Jacob.

mānāh is used passively in Isa. 53:12, where the Suffering Servant is said "to be numbered" with the transgressors.

sephōrāh [סְפֹרָה, **5615**]

sephōrāh is a rare noun form of ***sāphar*** (see above). It occurs only in Ps. 71:15, where it refers to the great "number" of Yahweh's deeds of salvation.

pāqad [פָּקַד, **6485**]

pāqad is a fairly common verb, occurring in about three hundred contexts, with a variety of senses. Its primary meaning, "to number," accounts for about one-third of the usage. It is also translated "visit," "appoint," "punish," as well as a number of associated nuances. (→ APPOINT → VISIT)

"Numbering" refers almost exclusively to counting the people of Israel as they establish their presence in the land of Canaan (cf. Exod. 30:12ff.; Num. 1:3, 19ff.; 2:4ff.; 26:18ff.; Josh. 8:10; Judg. 20:15ff.). See also 1 Sam. 11:8; 1 Kgs. 20:15, 27; 2 Kgs. 3:6. The Syrian army is numbered in 1 Kgs. 20:26.

Articles of furniture and other materials for establishing the tabernacle are numbered, or counted, in Exod. 38:21ff.

miphqād [מִפְקָד, **4662**]

miphqād is a rare noun derived from ***pāqad*** (see above). It is found on four occasions, twice referring to the "number" of the people of Israel (cf. 2 Sam. 24:9; 1 Chr. 21:5). In the other two occurrences it means "appointment."

miksāh [מִכְסָה, **4373**]

miksāh is a noun occurring only twice. Only in Exod. 12:4 does it mean "number" with respect to the size of Israelite households in Egypt immediately prior to the Passover judgment.

minyān [מִנְיָן, **4510** (Aramaic)]

minyān is a rare Aramaic noun found only in Ezra 6:17 with reference to the "number" of the tribes of Israel.

menā' [מְנָא, **4483** (Aramaic)]

menā' is an Aramaic verb form occurring in five contexts with the sense of "appoint" in four of these. (→ APPOINT) Only in Dan. 5:26 does it mean "number" with reference to the mysterious curse against Belshazzar written on the wall of the Babylonian palace. Here the term ***menā'*** is interpreted, "God has numbered the days of your kingdom and brought it to an end."

NT Words

arithmos [ἀριθμός, *706*]

arithmos is the only noun meaning "number" in the New Testament. It occurs eighteen times exclusively with this sense.

The meaning "number" is found predominantly in literal contexts. It refers to the twelve disciples (Luke 22:3); to the people of Israel (Rom. 9:27); and to the crowd whom Jesus miraculously fed from a meager source of food (John 6:10). In the book of Acts, ***arithmos*** refers to the number of those who believed in Christ after hearing the preaching of the apostles (cf. Acts 4:4; 6:7; 11:21); and also to the increase in the size of the New Testament church (cf. Acts 16:5).

arithmos is also used symbolically in the book of Revelation to indicate the number of the earth beast, given to all his followers (cf. Rev. 13:17, 18; 15:2); the number of Israel's enemies arrayed against them (cf. Rev. 20:8); and the number of the elect, the 144,000 chosen by God as his people (Rev. 7:4). In addition, Rev. 5:11 refers to the countless numbers of angels surrounding the throne of God in heaven.

arithmeō [ἀριθμέω, *705*]

arithmeō is the verb corresponding to the term ***arithmos*** (see above). ***arithmeō*** is found in only three places, meaning "to number." Mark 10:30; Luke 12:7 refer to divine providential care and knowledge, and the hairs of our head being all numbered by God. Rev.

7:9 describes the huge multitude of saints in heaven of whom it is said, "no one could number."

katarithmeō [καταριθμέω, *2674*]

The verb ***katarithmeō*** is found only in Acts 1:17, where it refers to the traitor Judas as one who was originally "numbered" among the twelve apostles of Christ.

logizomai [λογίζομαι, *3049*]

logizomai is a verb occurring about forty times with the primary meanings "reckon," "impute." (→ IMPUTE) However, in Mark 15:28, the term is translated "number" with reference to the quotation from Isa. 53, identifying Jesus as the fulfillment of that prophecy in which the Suffering Servant was to be "numbered with the transgressors."

NURSE

OT Words

yānaq [יָנַק, **3243**]

yānaq is a verb meaning to "to nurse," "suckle" in both literal and metaphorical contexts. ***yānaq*** is found in approximately thirty contexts.

When predicated of women, ***yānaq*** refers to the practice of breast-feeding or nursing one's children (cf. Gen. 21:7; Exod. 2:9; 1 Sam. 1:23; 1 Kgs. 3:21). The term is also used nominally, referring to such women as "nurses" (cf. Gen. 24:59; 35:8; Exod. 2:7; 2 Kgs. 11:2; 2 Chr. 22:11; Isa. 49:23).

yānaq also refers to the action of an infant feeding at the breast of its mother (Song 8:1). More commonly in this regard, ***yānaq*** is also used nominally to refer to the nursing infant (cf. Num. 11:12; Deut. 32:25; 1 Sam. 15:3; 22:19; Job 3:12; Ps. 8:2; Isa. 11:8; Jer. 44:7; Lam. 2:11; 4:4; Joel 2:16).

This term is also applied to animals, indicating female animals with their young. Gen. 32:15 refers to camels this way; Lam. 4:3 refers to jackals.

In metaphorical contexts, ***yānaq*** is predicated of the inhabitants of Jerusalem in Isa. 60:16, who will "nurse" at the "breast" of nations and rulers, indicating God's providential care of his people and their valuable standing among the nations. Shifting the metaphor slightly, Isa. 66:11, 12 refer to the people of Yahweh who will "nurse" at Zion's "breasts." That is, the descendants of Israel will be nourished and enriched in the process of God's promised renewal of his people down through the ages.

NT Words

trophos [τροφός, *5162*]

trophos occurs only in 1 Thess. 2:7 with reference to a "nurse" taking care of her children.

O

OAK

OT Words

'ēlāh **[אֵלָה, 424]**

The term ***'ēlāh*** occurs thirteen times, and in the majority of these instances it refers to the "oak tree."

General references to the oak are found in Gen. 35:4; Judg. 6:11, 19; 2 Sam. 18:9ff.; 1 Kgs. 13:14; 1 Chr. 10:12; Isa. 1:30. Ezek. 6:13 refers to the oak tree as a location for pagan shrines.

'allôn **[אַלּוֹן, 437]**

'allôn is another term for oak tree, occurring eight times (cf. Gen. 35:8; Isa. 2:13; 6:13; 44:14; Ezek. 27:6; Amos 2:9; Zech. 11:2). In Hos. 4:13 ***'allôn*** refers to oak trees as places of pagan ritual worship frequented by Israelites, resulting in severe condemnation by Yahweh.

'allāh **[אַלָּה, 427]**

'allāh is a variant form of ***'ēlāh*** (see above) and is found only in Josh. 24:26.

'ayil **[אַיִל, 352]**

'ayil is a noun that means "ram" in the majority of the 185 occurrences in which it is found. However, in Isa. 1:29 it refers to the sacred "oaks" in which the Israelites had formerly taken delight. This passage affirms that the people of Yahweh will become ashamed of this idolatrous practice.

OATH

OT Words

shebû'āh **[שְׁבוּעָה, 7621]**

shebû'āh means "oath" or "curse," with the underlying sense of a sworn pledge. The term is used in both human and divine contexts. ***shebû'āh*** occurs around thirty times.

In the human context, ***shebû'āh*** refers first of all to taking oaths in general contexts (cf. Gen. 24:8; Exod. 22:11; Lev. 5:4; Num. 30:10ff.; Josh. 2:17ff.; 9:20; Judg. 21:5; 1 Sam. 14:26; Neh. 6:18; Ezek. 21:23). Zech. 8:17 refers to swearing false oaths.

A number of contexts refer to swearing a solemn oath before the Lord, or making a vow (cf. Num. 30:2; 2 Sam. 21:7; 1 Kgs. 2:43; Eccl. 8:2; 9:2). In particular, 2 Chr. 15:15 notes the people of Judah making a vow, rededicating themselves to Yahweh (cf. also Neh. 10:29).

An intriguing usage of ***shebû'āh*** is found in Num. 5:21, which refers to taking an "oath" of cursing in the context of the trial of a woman suspected of adultery. If she is found guilty, the curse pronounced in the oath will fall upon the woman immediately.

shebû'āh is also found in contexts where Yahweh makes an oath. Several texts mention Yahweh's oath to Abraham and his descendants, the covenant promise to grant Abraham a mighty lineage and a land to dwell in (cf. Gen. 26:3; Deut. 7:8; 1 Chr. 16:16; Ps. 105:9; Jer. 11:5). ***shebû'āh*** also means "curse" in reference to the sanctions of the Mosaic law covenant (cf. Dan. 9:11). It is also translated this way in Isa. 65:15, where divine judgment is expressed against apostate Israelites, whose name will be regarded as a curse by future generations.

See Also: → PROMISE

'ālāh **[אָלָה, 423]**

'ālāh is a synonym for ***shebû'āh*** (see above), and it is found in fourteen contexts meaning "oath." ***'ālāh*** is also translated "curse." (→ CURSE)

In the human sphere, ***'ālāh*** refers to oath-swearing in general contexts in Gen. 24:41; 26:28; 1 Kgs. 8:31; 2 Chr. 6:22; Ezek. 17:13ff. Lev. 5:1 mentions a formally sworn oath that is legally binding under the Mosaic law. Ezek. 16:59 refers to Israel despising their commitment to the oath of the covenant with Yahweh.

Deut. 29:12ff. refers to the divine oath of the covenant promise to his people.

shāba' **[שָׁבַע, 7650]**

shāba' is a verb occurring around two hundred times with the primary meaning "to swear." However, on seven occasions this term specifically refers to taking or swearing an oath, all in a human context (cf. Gen. 50:25; Num. 5:19; 1 Sam. 14:27, 28; 1 Kgs. 18:10; 2 Kgs. 11:4; Neh. 5:12). It is clear, however, that the more common translation "to swear" also implies taking an oath. (→ SWEAR)

NT Words

horkos **[ὅρκος, *3727*]**

horkos is a noun that constitutes a dynamic equivalent to the Hebrew term ***shebû'āh*** (see above). ***horkos***

occurs ten times meaning "oath," predicated of both God and human beings.

As far as human beings are concerned, Matt. 5:23 contains the command to fulfill one's oaths made to God. General references to sworn oaths are found in Matt. 14:7, 9; Mark 6:26; Heb. 6:16. An oath equivalent to a curse is indicated in Matt. 26:72 in the context of Peter's third denial of Christ, where the apostle utters an oath following two previous denials of his master, in quick succession. There is an injunction in Jas. 5:12, forbidding believers to swear an oath.

Where God is involved with this phenomenon, Luke 1:73; Heb. 6:17 refer to the oath of the covenant given by God to Abraham. Acts 2:30 mentions the oath sworn to David by God, granting him an unending royal lineage.

anathematizō [ἀναθεματίζω, *332*]

anathematizō is a verb indicating the action of "invoking a curse" and "binding oneself under an oath." The term occurs in four contexts.

Mark 14:71 refers to Peter invoking an oath, or a curse, in denying Jesus. Acts 23:12, 14, 21 refer to a group of Paul's Jewish enemies who "conspired under oath" (unsuccessfully) to assassinate the apostle.

horkōmosia [ὁρκωμοσία, *3728*]

horkōmosia is a noun derived from ***horkos*** (see above). It occurs four times meaning "oath." Heb. 7:20, 21, 28 refer to the divine oath that led to the appointment of the risen Christ as the great high priest. The context also notes that no such divine oath accompanied the inauguration of the Levitical priesthood.

Additional Notes

The significance of taking oaths in both Old and New Testaments is intimately bound up with the phenomenon of the "promise," especially in relation to the divine initiative.

See Also: → PROMISE

OBEDIENCE, OBEDIENT, OBEY

OT Words

shāma' [שָׁמַע, **8085**]

shāma' is a common verb occurring in about 1,150 contexts with the predominant meaning "to hear" or "listen," as well as a number of related nuances. (→ HEAR) One of these nuances is the sense of "obey," evident in about eighty contexts and referring to obedience on both the human and divine plane.

In the human sphere on a person-to-person basis, ***shāma'*** is found in a variety of contexts. A child is required to obey his parents (Gen. 27:8, 13, 43); likewise people are to obey their parents (Gen. 28:7; Jer. 35:14, which refers to the Rechabite clan's faithful adherence to the vows made by their forbears). Failure to obey one's parents is declared an offense punishable by death in Deut. 21:18. A refusal to obey others is indicated in 1 Sam. 8:14; Prov. 5:13. General references to people submitting to others with obedience are found in Josh. 22:22; Isa. 11:4; 1 Sam. 15:24; 1 Chr. 29:23.

Where humankind's relationship to God is concerned, frequent mention is made of the importance of obeying God. General injunctions to obey God are found in Exod. 23:21; Deut. 13:4; 27:10; 1 Sam. 15:22. The general promise of blessing as a consequence of obeying God is indicated in Job 36:11, as is the enjoyment of blessing in Gen. 26:5, with reference to Abraham. More specifically, the promise of blessing under the Abrahamic and Mosaic covenants is contingent upon obeying Yahweh (cf. Exod. 19:5; 23:22; Deut. 11:27; 30:2, 8; Jer. 7:23; 11:4; 38:20; Zech. 6:15). Israel's promise to obey Yahweh is noted in Josh. 24:24 in the context of a covenant renewal ceremony (cf. also Jer. 34:10; 42:6; Hag. 1:12).

shāma' is also found in negative contexts. A refusal to obey God is noted in the case of Egypt (Exod. 5:2), and Judah (Jer. 3:13). Threats of punishment at the hand of God if people disobey the Lord's commands are noted in Judg. 2:2; 1 Sam. 12:15; Jer. 12:17; 18:10. This applies at both the individual and national level. The severe punishment resulting from disobeying God is illustrated in 1 Kgs. 20:36; Neh. 9:17; Job 36:12. In a similar vein, ***shāma'*** refers to the threat of curses under the sanctions of the covenant if one does not render obedience to Yahweh (Deut. 11:28; 28:62; Jer. 9:13; 11:8; 26:13; 42:13). Other texts specifically describe Israel's bitter experience of the covenant curse as a result of disobeying Yahweh (cf. Judg. 6:10; Dan. 9:11; Josh. 5:6; 2 Kgs. 18:12; Jer. 40:3).

shema' [שְׁמַע, **8086** (Aramaic)]

shema' is the Aramaic form of the verb ***shāma'*** (see above) and is found on nine occasions, all in the book of Daniel. In all but one of these, ***shema'*** is translated "hear," but in Dan. 7:27 it refers to an ultimate blessing involving all nations serving and obeying the people of God in the future kingdom of God.

yiqqhāh [**יִקְּהָה, 3349**]

yiqqhāh is found only twice in the Old Testament. Gen. 49:10 refers to the "obedience" of the nations that will be granted to the messianic descendant of the tribe of Judah. Prov. 30:17 promises severe condemnation for anyone who scorns obedience to his mother.

NT Words

hypakoē [**ὑπακοή**, *5218*]

hypakoē occurs fifteen times and is consistently translated "obedience" with respect to both human beings and Christ.

In several places, ***hypakoē*** refers to the "obedience" of faith, or to a positive response of faith and trust in Christ (cf. Rom. 1:5; 15:18 [implied]; 16:26). In Rom. 6:16, ***hypakoē*** refers to obedience leading to righteousness. 1 Pet. 1:2 indicates that believers are destined to live lives of obedience to Christ; and 1 Pet. 1:14 refers to obedient children of God, literally "children of obedience."

hypakoē refers to Christ's obedience in undertaking and carrying out the plan of salvation that God sent him to earth to accomplish (cf. Rom. 5:19; Heb. 5:8). In general terms, the obedience of Christ is recognized and affirmed in Rom. 16:19; 2 Cor. 7:15; 10:5, 6; Phlm. 21.

hypakouō [**ὑπακούω**, *5219*]

hypakouō is the verb from which ***hypakoē*** is derived (see above) and is translated "to obey," "be obedient," in almost every context in which it is found. ***hypakouō*** occurs around twenty times.

Regarding inanimate forces and objects, the wind and waves are said to obey the voice of Christ in his miraculous calming of the storm in Matt. 8:27; Mark 4:41; Luke 8:25 (cf. also Luke 17:6).

In Mark 1:27, demonic spirits are said to obey the command of Christ, and they are compelled to abandon the minds and bodies of those they previously possessed.

Concerning the human response of obedience, Acts 6:7 indicates that many Jewish priests were obedient to the call of the gospel as the number of believers multiplied in the early days of apostolic preaching. In contrast, ***hypakouō*** is used in the negative to indicate a response of unbelief (Rom. 10:16; 2 Thess. 1:8; 3:14). Rom. 6:17; Phil. 2:12 speak of the believer's deliverance from sin so that one becomes obedient to a new standard of righteousness in Christ. Likewise, Paul exhorts his readers not to allow sin to cause them to yield to, or obey, their sinful passions (cf. Rom. 6:12, 16).

Children are enjoined to obey their parents (Eph. 6:1; Col. 3:20), and slaves to obey their masters (Eph. 6:5; Col. 3:22). Heb. 11:8 records Abraham's obedience in his faithful dependence upon God, leading him to leave his homeland in Ur. 1 Pet. 3:6 refers to Sarah's obedience to Abraham, her husband, as characteristic of her life. Heb. 5:9 affirms that obeying Christ will lead to eternal salvation.

hypēkoos [**ὑπήκοος**, *5255*]

hypēkoos is an adjectival form derived from ***hypakoē*** and ***hypakouō*** (see above). ***hypēkoos*** is found in only three places, meaning "obedient." Acts 7:39 uses the term negatively, noting the Israelite people's rejection of Moses in the wilderness, refusing to obey him. 2 Cor. 2:9 refers to Paul's testing the Corinthian congregation, to establish whether they are obedient to their new calling. Phil. 2:8 indicates Christ's humble submission to the will of his Father, becoming obedient to the point of death.

peitharcheō [**πειθαρχέω**, *3980*]

peitharcheō occurs four times with the explicit meaning "obey" in three of these contexts. Acts 5:29 affirms the necessity of obeying God as the primary obligation over all other priorities. Acts 5:32 indicates that those who obey God are recipients of the Holy Spirit. Titus 3:1 contains the apostolic injunction to be obedient to civil rulers and authorities. In Acts 27:21 ***peitharcheō*** is translated "to listen to," but the underlying sense is that of "obey." Paul argues here that his traveling companions should not have ignored his warning not to set sail from Crete so late in the year when the risk of bad weather was much greater.

apeitheō [**ἀπειθέω**, *544*]

apeitheō is a verb occurring sixteen times. Approximately half of these contexts reflect the negative sense of "not to obey," or "be disobedient." In the remaining usage it means "not to believe," "be unbelieving."
(→ UNBELIEVER)

Rom. 2:8 refers to those who do not obey the truth. Similarly, 1 Pet. 2:8; 3:1, 20 refer to those who disobey the word of God; and 1 Pet. 4:17 to those who disobey the gospel of God. In Rom. 10:21, Israel is described as a disobedient people.

peithō [**πείθω**, *3982*]

peithō is a verb found in approximately sixty contexts with the primary meanings "persuade," "trust," as

well as related senses. However, ***peithō*** is translated "obey" in three places. Gal. 5:7 refers to the importance of "obeying" the truth, which the Galatians had ceased to do. Heb. 13:7 instructs people to obey their spiritual leaders, whom God has ordained to act as overseers of his people in local congregations. Jas. 3:3 mentions the bits placed in the mouths of horses as a means of rendering them obedient to their riders.
(→ PERSUADE → TRUST)

See Also: → HEAR → SUBJECT

OBSERVE

OT Words

shāmar **[שָׁמַר, 8104]**

shāmar is a common verb found in approximately 450 contexts, meaning "keep," "give heed to" or "obey" in most of them. The meaning "observe" is included in these primary senses.

NT Words

tēreō [τηρέω, *5083*]

tēreō is a verb occurring seventy-five times with the primary meanings "keep," "keep watch." It is a dynamic equivalent for the Hebrew term ***shāmar*** (see above) and also means "observe" in the broad sense of "keep" or "give attention to."

See Also: → KEEP → WATCH

OBTAIN

OT Words

qānāh **[קָנָה, 7069]**

qānāh is a verb meaning "buy," "acquire," "get." (→ BUY) The latter sense is a very general one that also suggests the meaning "obtain." ***qānāh*** occurs around eighty times with the sense of "obtain," or "get," in about fifteen places.

pûq **[פּוּק, 6329]**

pûq is a verb found in seven contexts. It occurs four times in the book of Proverbs, meaning "obtain" or "get." Prov. 8:35; 12:2; 18:22 speak of the happy condition of obtaining favor from the Lord. Prov. 3:13 refers likewise to the happiness of the person who gets (or obtains) understanding.

nāsag **[נָשַׂג, 5381]**

nāsag is a verb expressing a variety of meaning with the primary sense of "overtake," as well as a number of related nuances. On two occasions ***nāsag*** is translated "obtain," referring to the promised renewal of the people of God and their return to Jerusalem after their time in exile. Isa. 35:10; 51:11 indicate that the people shall obtain gladness and joy upon their return.

NT Words

tynchanō [τυγχάνω, *5177*]

tynchanō is a verb occurring thirteen times in all. The meaning "to obtain" is found in four of these contexts. In Acts 26:22 Paul testifies to having obtained help from God. 2 Tim. 2:10 refers to the hope of the elect, who will obtain salvation in Christ for eternity. Heb. 8:6 speaks of Christ having obtained a ministry that is far superior to that of the old covenant. Heb. 11:35 refers to the hope of the martyrs, who look forward to gaining, or obtaining, a better resurrection.

katalambanō [καταλαμβάνω, *2638*]

katalambanō occurs fifteen times and means "take," "take hold of," "make one's own," "grasp." The meaning "gain," in the sense of "obtain," is found in two of these contexts. Rom. 9:30 refers to the Gentiles having obtained righteousness through faith. 1 Cor. 9:24 speaks of Paul's exhortation to the Corinthian believers to run the race that they might obtain the prize (i.e., of eternal life).

peripoiēsis [περιποίησις, *4047*]

peripoiēsis is a noun that refers to a "possession," "acquiring," "gaining," or "obtaining." The term occurs five times, with the latter sense evident in two places. 1 Thess. 5:9 refers to the obtaining of our salvation through our Lord Jesus Christ; and in 2 Thess. 2:14 Paul speaks of believers obtaining the glory of Christ as a consequence of their calling in the gospel.

epitynchanō [ἐπιτυγχάνω, *2013*]

epitynchanō is a verb with the exclusive sense of "obtain," occurring five times. Rom. 11:7 affirms that Israel failed to obtain the salvation they sought, but that it was gained by the elect. Heb. 6:15 declares that Abraham obtained the promise given to him by God, as did the saints of old (Heb. 11:33). In Jas. 4:2 the point is made that human sinfulness makes it impossible for one to always get (or obtain) what one wants.

See Also: → GET → MERCY

ODOR → SMELL

OFFENSE, OFFEND

NT Words

skandalizō [σκανδαλίζω, *4624*]

skandalizō is a verb found in thirty-five contexts with the underlying sense of bringing about someone's downfall as a consequence of sin. ***skandalizō*** is variously translated "cause to sin," "bring about one's downfall," "fall away," "offend," "take (or give) offense." The latter two meanings are found in seven contexts. (→ SIN)

The meaning "take offense" is found in the context of Jesus' person and ministry. For example, not to take offense at Jesus is considered worthy of praise (Matt. 11:6; Luke 7:23). Conversely, those who do take offense at Jesus for what he does and says are condemned (cf. Matt. 13:57; 15:12; Mark 6:3). The question of taking offense at Jesus' teaching is raised in John 6:61. The meaning "offend" in the context of giving offense to people is found in Matt. 17:27.

See Also: → GUILT → SIN → STUMBLING BLOCK → TRANSGRESS

OFFER

OT Words

'ālāh [עָלָה, 5927]

'ālāh is a common verb form occurring nearly nine hundred times with the primary general sense of "come up," "go up," as well as a number of associated meanings. Included in this is the sense of "offer," found in approximately seventy contexts that are almost exclusively ceremonial.

In the realm of offering sacrifice to God, ***'ālāh*** refers generally to presenting burnt offerings to Yahweh in a number of places (cf. Gen. 8:20; Exod. 24:5; Lev. 17:8; Num. 23:2ff.; Deut. 12:13; 27:6; Josh. 22:23; Judg. 13:16; 1 Sam. 10:16; 2 Sam. 24:22; 1 Kgs. 3:4; 1 Chr. 16:40; Job 1:5; Ps. 51:19; Isa. 57:6; Jer. 14:12). As a test of Abraham's faith, Yahweh commands the patriarch to offer his son Isaac up as a burnt offering in Gen. 22:2, and then substitutes a ram for the boy' s life at the very last moment. Child sacrifice, a practice that was abhorrent to Yahweh, is indicated in 2 Kgs. 3:27. Amos 5:22 records that God rejected illegitimate burnt offerings offered by the Israelite people of the northern kingdom. General references to the priestly ministry of offering are found in 1 Sam. 2:28; 1 Chr. 6:49; Ezra 3:2; Jer. 33:18; Ezek. 43:18.

'ālāh refers to offering incense to Yahweh in 1 Kgs. 13:2. Exod. 30:9 records the command forbidding Israelites to offer unholy incense to God.

2 Sam. 24:12 speaks of God offering a choice to David of three different kinds of punishment for his sin of conducting a census of his fighting men without consulting Yahweh.

'āsāh [עָשָׂה, 6213]

'āsāh is one of the most frequently occurring verbs in the Old Testament, signifying the general sense of "do," or "make," in most of the 2,500 or so places in which it is found. There are a number of derivative meanings associated with these two senses. One of these is "offer," "make a sacrifice," found approximately fifty times in the context of ritual sacrifice.

'āsāh refers to presenting offerings of a general, non-specific nature (Num. 15:14; 2 Kgs. 10:24); and to the presentation of burnt offerings (Lev. 16:24; Num. 6:11; Josh. 22:23; Judg. 13:16). The offering of a bull for a burnt offering is noted in relation to the Passover (Num. 28:20); to the Feast of Weeks (Num. 28:31); and to the Feast of Trumpets (Num. 29:2). Grain is also designated as fuel for a burnt offering in Lev. 6:22. The lamb is set apart as an animal to be offered up as a perpetual burnt offering, either on a daily (cf. Exod. 29:38; Num. 28:4) or monthly (cf. Num. 28:21ff.) basis.

With regard to the sin offering, ***'āsāh*** refers to presenting the bull (Exod. 29:36); doves or pigeons (Lev. 5:10; Num. 6:11); and the goat for the Day of Atonement ceremony (Lev. 16:9). See also Lev. 9:7; 14:9; Num. 6:11.

In relation to the freewill, thank, or peace offering, ***'āsāh*** refers to offering up a bull or lamb (Lev. 22:23), and a ram (Num. 6:17).

rûm [רוּם, 7311]

rûm is a verb found in approximately two hundred contexts with the primary sense of "lift up" or "raise" as well as a number of synonymous meanings. It is also translated "offer" thirteen times with the underlying sense of "make an offering" or "make a contribution" to Yahweh in every case.

Offering silver and bronze to Yahweh, by placing it in the tabernacle treasury, is indicated in Exod. 35:24. Other texts speak of Israelites offering gifts to Yahweh (e.g., Num. 18:29; Ezek. 45:13). In particular, Ezek. 45:1; 48:8ff. require God's people to offer him a portion of the renewed land of Israel, designated as a sacred district. See also Lev. 22:15; Num. 18:19, 24. Offering food to Yahweh as an expression of gratitude for granting the land of Canaan to his people is a mandatory requirement (Num. 15:19ff.). Num. 18:26ff. speaks of offering tithes to Yahweh.

qārab [קָרַב, 7126]

qārab occurs about 280 times with the primary senses of "draw near" or "come near." In approximately one-third of these instances, ***qārab*** is translated "to offer" with the fundamental sense of drawing near to God, in order to present an offering or sacrifice in a variety of contexts.

qārab refers to presenting offerings in a non-specific context (Lev. 17:4ff.; 21:6; 23:8). In a number of places, offering an unblemished animal as a burnt offering is recorded as a mandatory element in the Israelite sacrificial system (cf. Lev. 1:3; 9:2; 22:18ff.; Num. 28:3ff.; 2 Chr. 35:12; 28:19 [Passover]; 28:27 [Feast of Weeks]; 29:8 [Day of Atonement]; 29:13 [Feast of Tabernacles]; Ezek. 46:4).

The remaining uses of ***qārab*** cover the whole range of sacrificial offerings. ***qārab*** is translated "offer," or "present," referring to cereal offerings (cf. Lev. 2:1; 6:14ff.; 23:16); first fruits of the harvest (cf. Lev. 2:12ff.); peace, fellowship, or thank offerings (cf. Lev. 3:1ff.; 7:11ff.); drink offerings (cf. Num. 15:7); sin offerings (cf. Lev. 4:14; 5:8; 14:19; Num. 6:16; Ezek. 43:22ff.; 44:27); the Day of Atonement offerings (cf. Lev. 16:6, 9); guilt offerings (cf. Lev. 7:3); and wave, or heave offerings (cf. Num. 5:25).

qārab is also used in the setting of the Nazirite consecration ceremony, where a votive offering is presented (Num. 6:14). Offering food to Yahweh is indicated in Lev. 21:17; Ezek. 44:15ff.; and presenting offerings at the dedication of the tabernacle is indicated in Num. 7:11.

nûph [נוּף, 5130]

nûph occurs in about forty contexts, meaning "wave," "offer" in the majority of its usage. The setting is predominantly that of ritual sacrifice and offering. (➠ SHAKE)

nûph frequently refers to the role of the Levitical priests, who initially present their offerings to Yahweh by waving them before him immediately prior to the actual sacrifice (cf. Exod. 29:24ff.; Lev. 7:30; 8:27ff.; 9:21; 10:15; 14:12, 24; 23:11ff.; Num. 5:25; 6:20). In Num. 8:11ff., the Levites themselves are presented as a "wave offering" prior to the commencement of their sacrifice. In Exod. 35:12, the people of Israel dedicate, or offer, valuables to Yahweh for the purpose of tabernacle construction.

nādab [נָדַב, 5068]

nādab is found in seventeen contexts and means "offer willingly," "give willingly." The contexts are almost exclusively concerned with sacrifices and offerings gladly given to Yahweh.

Offerings willingly presented by Israelite people are indicated in Exod. 25:21; 35:21, 29; Ezra 1:6; 2:68; 3:5. ***nādab*** also refers to those who willingly offer themselves for service to Yahweh (cf. Judg. 5:2, 9; 2 Chr. 17:16, with reference to Israelite leaders). The open-heartedness of the Israelite laity is also indicated in 1 Chr. 29:5ff., where their generous gifts and offerings for the building of the temple are recorded. In one non-ritual context, ***nādab*** refers to those who "willingly offered" themselves to live in Jerusalem at the time of rebuilding the city in Nehemiah's day (cf. Neh. 11:2).

qerēb [קְרֵב, 7127 (Aramaic)]

qerēb is the equivalent Aramaic term for the Hebrew ***qārab*** (see above) and occurs nine times. ***qerēb*** is translated both "to come near" and "to offer." The latter sense is found only in Ezra 6:10, 17; 7:17, referring in all three cases to sacrifices and offerings presented to Yahweh.

nesak [נְסַךְ, 5260 (Aramaic)]

nesak is the Aramaic equivalent for the Hebrew ***nāsak***. (➠ POUR) It occurs only in Dan. 2:46, meaning "to offer" and referring to Nebuchadnezzar's command to have an offering presented to Daniel for having interpreted the king's dream.

nāgash [נָגַשׁ, 5066]

nāgash is a verb found in 125 contexts with the primary meanings "come near," "bring near," "draw near." In several places, it conveys the sense of people approaching the altar in order to offer sacrifices or present offerings to Yahweh — drawing near to God is equivalent to presenting gifts or offering sacrifices to him (cf. Exod. 32:6; Amos 5:25; Mal. 1:7, 8; 2:17; 3:3).

NT Words

prospherō [προσφέρω, *4374*]

prospherō occurs around fifty times with the predominant senses of "offer," "offer up," "bring to," "present." In approximately half of these contexts ***prospherō***

is translated "offer" with the sense of bringing gifts to God in worship.

Matt. 2:11 records the worship of the magi in offering gifts to the infant Jesus. Offering sacrifices to God in general contexts is indicated in Heb. 11:4, 17 with reference to Abel and Abraham, respectively. Offering one's gift at the temple is noted in Matt. 5:23ff.; 8:4; Mark 1:44; Luke 5:14; Acts 21:26; and priestly activity in this regard is specifically mentioned in Heb. 5:1ff.; 8:3ff.; 9:7; 10:1ff. ***prospherō*** also refers to the offering of Jesus Christ, who gave his own life as a once-for-all sacrifice for the sin of the world (cf. Heb. 9:14, 25ff.; 10:12).

Elsewhere, ***prospherō*** refers to those who offered vinegar to Jesus as he hung on the cross. Heb. 5:7 refers to Jesus offering up prayers to his Father during his life on earth. Acts 8:18 refers to Simon Magus offering money to the apostles, vainly seeking to buy the gift of the Spirit of God from them.

anapherō [ἀναφέρω, *399*]

anapherō occurs twelve times, meaning "bring," "bear," "offer (up)." The latter sense is found in five of these contexts. Heb. 7:27 refers to the sacrifices offered up by the high priest under the old covenant law, and also to the once-for-all sacrifice of Jesus Christ, who offered himself as the substitutionary atonement for the sins of humankind. Jas. 2:21 speaks of Abraham's willingness to offer up his own son Isaac as a sacrifice in response to God's command, even though God never intended to allow the sacrifice to take place. 1 Pet. 2:5 speaks of the believer's destiny to offer up spiritual sacrifices to God through godly living (cf. also Heb. 13:15 in this regard).

See Also: → INCENSE → POUR → SACRIFICE

OFFERING

OT Words

qorbān [קָרְבָּן, 7133]

qorbān is a noun occurring around eighty times and translated "offering" in virtually every instance. The contexts are uniformly ritual, reflecting the whole spectrum of sacrifices and offerings.

qorbān refers to offerings made to Yahweh in a general sense (Lev. 1:2, 10; 17:4; 22:17; 27:9; Num. 15:4; 18:9; 31:50; Ezek. 40:43); to offerings associated with the Passover (Num. 9:7, 13); and to daily offerings (Num. 28:2). ***qorbān*** is also translated "burnt offering" in Lev. 1:3. Other primary offerings indicated by this term include the peace, or thank, offering (cf. Lev. 3:1ff.; 7:13ff.; 29; 22:18); the sin offering (cf. Lev. 4:23ff.; 5:11; 9:7, 15; Num. 15:25); the cereal and grain offerings (cf. Lev. 2:1ff.; 6:20; Num. 5:15); and the firstfruits of the harvest (cf. Lev. 2:12; 23:14).

In addition, ***qorbān*** refers to offering doves in Lev. 1:14. Votive offerings are indicated in Num. 6:14 in association with the Nazirite vow. Throughout Num. 7, ***qorbān*** refers to offerings for the dedication of the tabernacle. Wood is offered for the temple altar fire in Neh. 10:34; 13:31. Ezek. 20:28 refers to idolatrous offerings made by the apostate Israel, invoking the wrath of Yahweh against them.

terûmāh [תְּרוּמָה, 8641]

terûmāh is another noun with the principal sense of "offering," found primarily in the ritual context of worship and devotion to Yahweh. The term occurs in nearly eighty contexts.

The general sense of "offering" is indicated in nonspecific contexts in Exod. 25:2; Lev. 22:12; Isa. 40:20. Such offerings are demanded by Yahweh in Ezek. 20:40; and are laid down in Ezek. 45:13 as part of the renewed cultus in Ezekiel's vision of a renewed temple. Offerings for the tabernacle are recorded in Exod. 25:3; 35:5; 36:3; Num. 31:52; and for the temple in 2 Chr. 31:10ff.; Ezra 8:5. Num. 15:19 refers to offering firstfruits from the produce of the land. Exod. 30:13ff. refers to offering atonement money. In Mal. 3:8 the Israelites are condemned for robbing God in their offerings.

In particular, ***terûmāh*** refers to the "wave offering" presented to the priests and Levites as their allotted portion from the people (cf. Exod. 29:27ff.; Lev. 7:14, 32; Num. 6:20; 15:20ff.; 31:29, 41). In Num. 18:8ff.; Deut. 12:6, 11; Neh. 10:37ff.; 13:5; Ezek. 44:30, this "wave offering" is linked to the people's tithe. ***terûmāh*** also refers to offering or dedicating land to Yahweh in Ezekiel's vision of a renewed and transformed land of Israel (cf. Ezek. 45:1, 6, 7; 48:8ff., 18ff.). The term also indicates a similar offering of land for the priests in Ezekiel's vision (cf. Ezek. 48:10ff.).

minḥāh [מִנְחָה, 4503]

minḥāh is another synonym for the preceding terms, with the primary sense of "offering" in most of the two hundred or so contexts in which it is found. ***minḥāh*** is also translated "present" or "gift" in a nonritual context, although the primary setting for the term is a ritual one.

The general sense of "offering" is indicated in a number of places. For example, Gen. 4:3, 4 record the sacrifices offered by Cain and Abel. 1 Sam. 2:17 describes Hophni and Phinehas, the sons of Eli the high priest, treating the Lord's offering with contempt. The cessation of regular sacrifice in the temple is brought about by the coming messianic ruler of Daniel's vision in Dan. 9:27. See also 1 Kgs. 8:36; Pss. 20:3; 96:8; Isa. 66:20; Zeph. 3:10; Mal. 1:10ff.

minḥāh frequently designates the cereal or grain offering as laid down in the Mosaic ceremonial legislation (cf. Exod. 29:41; Lev. 2:1ff.; 7:9ff.; 14:20ff.; Num. 4:16; 5:15ff.; 7:13ff. [in association with the dedication of the tabernacle]; 15:4ff.; Josh. 22:23ff.; Judg. 13:19ff.; 2 Kgs. 16:13ff.; Neh. 10:33; Jer. 17:26; Joel 1:9ff.; Amos 5:22). The cereal offering is also described in relation to the renewed cultus of the visionary temple of Ezekiel (cf. Ezek. 42:13; 44:29; 45:15ff.; 46:5ff.).

minḥāh also refers to the "evening sacrifice" in Ezra 9:4ff.; Ps. 141:2; Dan. 9:21.

In non-ritual contexts, ***minḥāh*** means "present" or "gift," referring to the material exchange of goods among people (cf. Gen. 32:13, 20ff.; Judg. 3:15ff.; 1 Sam. 10:27; Ps. 45:12; Isa. 39:1). In a number of contexts, the term also refers to "tribute," or "tax," paid to one's ruler or overlord (cf. 2 Kgs. 17:3ff.; Ps. 72:10; Hos. 10:6).

'ōlāh [עֹלָה, 5930]

'ōlāh is a common noun in the Old Testament, designating the "burnt offering," or the foundational sacrifice that undergirds the entire Israelite Levitical system, in virtually every one of its occurrences.

Prior to the period of the tabernacle and the Sinaitic law covenant, ***'ōlāh*** indicates the burnt offering as an expression of thankfulness to God (cf. Gen. 8:20; Exod. 10:25). It also expresses obedience to God, as in the case of Yahweh testing Abraham in Gen. 22:2ff., where he commanded the patriarch to sacrifice his only son Isaac as a burnt offering. The term also serves as a general expression of worship of Yahweh in Exod. 18:12.

The "burnt offering" is by far most commonly found as a ritual requirement, a mandatory sacrifice laid down in the charter of the Mosaic law covenant. It is mentioned in a general sense, for example, in Exod. 20:24; 29:42; Lev. 1:3ff.; 6:9ff.; 23:37; Num. 15:3ff.; 23:3ff.; Deut. 12:6ff.; Josh. 22:23ff.; Ps. 40:6.

In particular, 1 Sam. 15:22; Hos. 6:6; Mic. 6:6 express the principle that obedient devotion to Yahweh is far more acceptable to him than the mere ritual presentation of burnt offerings and sacrifices. There are also a number of contexts indicating that the sacrifice of illegitimate burnt offerings is totally unacceptable to Yahweh (cf. Isa. 1:11; 43:23; Jer. 6:20; 7:21ff.; 14:12; Amos 5:22).

There are, in addition, a number of specific ritual contexts in which ***'ōlāh*** refers to burnt offerings. It refers, for example, to the altar of burnt offering itself (cf. Exod. 31:9; 35:16; 38:1; 40:6, 10, 29; Lev. 4:7ff.); to the ordination and consecration ceremonies for priests and Levites (cf. Exod. 29:18, 25; Lev. 8:18, 21; 9:2ff.; Num. 8:12); to the sin offering (cf. Lev. 4:24, 33; 5:7, 10; 6:25); to the regular daily and monthly offerings (cf. Num. 28:3–15); to the guilt offering (cf. Lev. 7:2, 8); to the purification rituals (cf. Lev. 12:6, 8; 14:13ff.; 15:15, 30); to the Day of Atonement ceremony (cf. Lev. 16:3, 5, 24; Num. 29:7ff.); to offering the firstfruits of harvest (cf. Lev. 23:12, 18); to the Nazirite vow (cf. Num. 6:11ff.); to dedicating the tabernacle (cf. Num. 7:15ff.); to the various ritual festivals such as Passover (cf. Num. 28:16ff.), Weeks or Harvest (cf. Num. 28:26ff.), Trumpets (cf. Num. 29:2ff.), and Tabernacles (cf. Num. 29:12ff.); and to temple worship throughout Israelite history (cf. 1 Kgs. 8:64; 9:25; 2 Chr. 7:1). See also 2 Sam. 24:22ff.; Ezra 3:2ff. Included here are references to the presentation of burnt offerings in Ezekiel's vision of the renewed temple and sacrifices in Jerusalem (cf. Ezek. 40:38ff.; 43:18, 24, 27; 44:11; 45:15ff.; 46:2). "Burnt offerings" are also indicated in the context of the hideous crime of human sacrifice committed by the King of Moab, who sacrificed his firstborn son (2 Kgs. 3:27).

nesek [נֶסֶךְ, 5262]

nesek is found approximately sixty times with the primary sense of "drink offering," or "libation," indicating an offering that is poured out on the altar as an act of worship, whether to Yahweh or to idol deities.

nesek is mentioned once in a pre-Mosaic context as Jacob pours out a drink offering to God at Bethel (Gen. 35:14).

Generally, however, ***nesek*** is found in the ritual context of worship as laid down by the Mosaic covenant. ***nesek*** refers to drink offerings in association with the priestly consecration ceremony (cf. Exod. 29:40ff.); the offering of firstfruits (cf. Lev. 23:13); the Feast of Weeks, or Harvest (cf. Lev. 23:18; Num. 28:31); the Feast of Tabernacles (cf. Lev. 23:37; Num. 29:16ff.); the Passover feast (cf. Num. 28:24); the Nazirite vow (cf.

Num. 6:15, 17); regular offerings on a daily, weekly, or monthly basis (cf. Num. 15:5ff.; 28:7ff.); offerings for "unintentional sins" (cf. Num. 15:24); the Feast of Trumpets (cf. Num. 29:6); and the Day of Atonement (cf. Num. 29:11). These offerings are also linked with temple worship in 2 Kgs. 16:13, 15; 2 Chr. 29:35; Ezek. 45:17; Joel 1:9ff.; 2:4; Ezek. 45:17. Drink offerings are forbidden on the altar of incense in the holy place (Exod. 30:9). 1 Chr. 29:21 refers to their presentation in worship on the occasion of Solomon's coronation.

In several other places, ***nesek*** indicates the offering of libations in idolatrous contexts. For example, the psalmist refuses to offer "libations" of blood to other gods in Ps. 16:4. Israel's idolatrous drink offerings to pagan deities are mentioned in Jer. 19:13; 32:29; Ezek. 20:28, including those to the "queen of heaven," an alternative title for the Babylonian goddess Ishtar (cf. Jer. 7:18; 44:17ff.).

ḥattā't [חַטָּאת, 2403]

ḥattā't is a common noun meaning "sin," "sin offering" in approximately three hundred places. (→ SIN) The latter sense is found in about one-third of these contexts. ***ḥattā't*** is used exclusively in ritual contexts.

General descriptions of the sin offering are found in Lev. 4:3; 5:12; 6:24ff.; 7:7; 10:16ff. Ps. 40:6 notes that obedience to Yahweh is far more important than the mere offering of sacrifices for sin.

In common with other terms for "offering," ***ḥattā't*** is used in a variety of specific contexts all associated with the presentation of the sin offering. These include the priestly consecration ceremonies (cf. Exod. 29:14, 16), including the ordination of Aaron and his sons (cf. Lev. 8:2, 14; 9:2ff.); the consecration of the Levites and their prescribed duties (cf. Num. 8:8, 12; 18:19); offerings for purification (cf. Lev. 14:13ff.); the Nazirite votive offering (cf. Num. 6:11ff.); unintentional sins (cf. Num. 15:24); and regular monthly sins (cf. Num. 28:15).

Particular festivals also provide the context for the sin offering — for example, the Day of Atonement (cf. Exod. 29:36; Lev. 16:3ff.; Num. 29:11); the Passover festival (cf. Num. 28:22); the Feast of Trumpets (cf. Num. 29:5); and the Feast of Tabernacles (cf. Num. 29:16ff.). Sin offerings are also associated with the dedication of the tabernacle (Num. 7:16ff.); Hezekiah's purification of the temple (2 Chr. 29:21ff.); the dedication of the postexilic temple (Ezra 6:17); and the renewed sacrifices of Ezekiel's visionary temple (cf. Ezek. 40:39; 42:13ff.; 44:27ff.; 45:17ff.; 46:20).

tenûphāh [תְּנוּפָה, 8573]

tenûphāh is a synonym for ***terûmāh*** (see above) with the consistent meaning "wave offering" in most of the thirty contexts in which it is found. The usage of this term is predominantly ceremonial.

The "wave offering" is employed in association with the sacrificial gifts of food presented to the Israelite priests as part of the people's contribution to their physical needs — they were a portion of the people's thank offering. The "wave offering" usually consisted of the breast and thigh of the sacrificial animal, which the priests "waved" before the Lord at the altar prior to eating it (cf. Exod. 29:24ff.; Lev. 7:30ff.; 8:27, 29; 9:21; 10:14, 15; Num. 8:11ff.; 18:11, 18). Other types of food presented as a wave offering are noted in Lev. 14:21ff.; 23:15ff.; Num. 6:20.

nedābāh [נְדָבָה, 5071]

nedābāh occurs around thirty times with the predominant meaning "freewill offering," which overlaps with the sense of "thank offering" (see ***tôdāh***, below).

In the context of the Israelite people's contribution of materials for the tabernacle, their freewill offerings are noted in Exod. 35:29; 36:3.

Prescriptions for the correct procedure in presenting the freewill offering are laid down in Lev. 7:16; 22:18ff.; Deut. 23:23; 2 Chr. 31:14; Ezra 1:4; 3:5; 8:28. Freewill offerings are also mentioned in connection with the Feast of Tabernacles (Num. 29:39); the Feast of Weeks (Deut. 16:10); and the central place of worship (Deut. 12:6, 17).

nedābāh refers to "freewill offerings" in a general sense in Lev. 23:38; Num. 15:3; Ps. 119:108. Amos 4:5 notes Israel's abuse of these offerings.

tôdāh [תּוֹדָה, 8426]

tôdāh expresses the idea of "thanksgiving," "confession," or "praise" to God. The word occurs in around thirty contexts, and it is associated (see above) with the general class of "peace, or fellowship offerings" in about half of these instances. (→ THANKSGIVING)

Regulations for presenting the "thank offering" or the "offering/sacrifice of thanksgiving" are laid down in Lev. 7:12ff.; 22:29. Examples of the practice are indicated in connection with King Manasseh in 2 Chr. 33:16; and in the Psalms with reference to worship and thanksgiving to Yahweh (cf. Pss. 50:14, 23; 56:12;

100:1; 107:22; 116:17). In Jer. 17:26; 33:11, offerings of thanksgiving are anticipated by the prophet as part of the process of divine renewal. In Amos 4:5, in contrast, the prophet refers to Israel's abuse of the thank offering. Thank offerings are noted in association with the rebuilding of the wall of Jerusalem in Nehemiah's day.

shelem [שֶׁלֶם, 8002]

shelem indicates the general class of sacrifices known as the "peace offering," or "fellowship offering." The word ***shelem*** is derived from the term ***shālôm***, or "peace." (→ PEACE) The idea behind these offerings is that God's people may draw close to Yahweh in the presentation of this sacrifice. The spiritual benefit gained thereby is one of reconciliation, or peace with God, leading to unrestricted fellowship with him. This offering is unique in that it is the only sacrifice that the offerer himself may partake of, along with the priest who presents it to Yahweh on his behalf. This offering therefore conveys the dual aspects of peace and fellowship and may be translated either way. Because both priest and worshiper partake of the sacrificial animal, the offering takes the form of a fellowship meal. ***shelem*** is found in almost ninety contexts, most of which refer to ritual offerings.

Specific procedures for presenting the peace offering are laid down in Lev. 3:3ff.; 7:11. Other references to these regulations include those in Exod. 20:24; 29:28; Lev. 6:14; 17:5; 19:5; 22:21; Num. 15:8; Deut. 27:7.

General references to the presentation of the fellowship, or peace, offering are found in Exod. 32:6; Lev. 9:22; Josh. 8:31; Judg. 20:26; 1 Sam. 10:8; 1 Chr. 21:26; Prov. 7:14. In particular, Hezekiah's use of this sacrifice during his period of ritual reformation and renewal is indicated in 2 Chr. 29:35; 30:22; 31:2. See also 2 Chr. 33:16. 2 Sam. 6:17ff.; 1 Chr. 16:1ff. refer to David presenting peace offerings to celebrate the ark of the covenant's return to Jerusalem. In 1 Kgs. 8:63ff.; 9:25, Solomon presents these offerings on the completion and dedication of the temple.

The peace offering is also associated with the Feast of Weeks (Lev. 23:19); the Nazirite vow (Num. 6:14ff.); the dedication of the tabernacle (Num. 7 [passim]); and the renewal of the Israelite sacrifices in the vision of Ezekiel's temple (cf. Ezek. 43:27; 45:15ff.; 46:2, 12). Israelite abuse of the peace offering is noted in Amos 5:22.

'isheh [אִשֶּׁה, 801]

'isheh is found in approximately eighty contexts with the exclusive sense of "offering made by fire" (i.e., to Yahweh). It is used exclusively in ritual contexts and is found almost entirely within the Pentateuch. ***'isheh*** is associated primarily with the burnt offering and is synonymous with the term ***'ōlāh*** (see above) in several places.

General references to "offering(s) made by fire" are found in Exod. 29:41; Lev. 10:12ff.; Num. 15:3ff.; Deut. 18:1; Josh. 13:14; 1 Sam. 2:28. ***'isheh*** is used as a synonym for "burnt offering" in Exod. 29:18, 25; 30:20; Lev. 1:9ff.

In the majority of its usage, ***'isheh*** is associated with other specific sacrifices, ceremonies, and festivals. It refers, for example, to the offerings for unintentional sins (cf. Num. 15:25); regular offerings at daily, weekly and monthly intervals (cf. Num. 28:2ff.); the grain offering (cf. Lev. 2:2ff.; 6:17, 18); the "wave" offering (cf. Lev. 7:30, 35), as well as the priestly entitlement to the "bread of the presence" (Lev. 24:7, 9); the fellowship offering (cf. Lev. 3:3ff.; 7:25); the "sin offering" (cf. Lev. 4:35; 5:12); and the guilt offering (cf. Lev. 7:5). Offerings made by fire are also indicated in connection with the ordination of Aaron and his sons (cf. Lev. 8:21, 28; 21:6); and the offerings of the firstfruits of harvest (cf. Lev. 23:13).

Such offerings are also closely associated with the following festivals — Passover (cf. Lev. 23:8; Num. 28:19, 24); Weeks (cf. Lev. 23:18); Trumpets (cf. Lev. 23:25; Num. 29:6); Day of Atonement (cf. Lev. 23:27); and Tabernacles (cf. Lev. 23:36ff.; Num. 29:13, 36).

'āshām [אָשָׁם, 817]

'āshām is the noun derived from the verb ***'āsham*** ("to be guilty" → GUILT) and means "guilt (or trespass) offering" in the majority of the fifty or so contexts in which it is found. The guilt offering is a variant of the sin offering and normally required the sacrifice of a ram or lamb, as well as a mandatory component of restitution. The prescribed "fine" amounted to twenty percent of the value of the animal or property in question (i.e., that which was stolen, slain, damaged, destroyed, or lost), which was to be paid either to the person wronged, or to God himself — in which case the money was given to the priest.

General references to the guilt offering are found in Lev. 6:17; 7:37; Num. 18:9. In 1 Sam. 6:3ff. there is an intriguing incident in which the rulers of the Philistines actually prepare a guilt offering to be presented to Yahweh to accompany the return of the ark of the covenant to Israel in the hope that the terrible disasters inflicted on them by the God of Israel might be removed from them.

Regulations for the guilt offering are laid down in Lev. 5:16ff.; 6:6; 7:1ff.; 14:12ff.; 19:21, 22; Num. 5:7, 8.

The guilt offering is presented in association with the Nazirite vow in Num. 6:12 and in connection with Ezekiel's visionary temple and the renewal of the sacrifices in Ezek. 40:39; 42:13; 44:29; 46:20.

'ashmāh **[אַשְׁמָה, 819]**

'ashmāh is a variant form of ***'āshām*** (see above) and is usually translated "sin," "guilt," or "trespass." However, ***'ashmāh*** is translated "trespass offering" in Lev. 6:5. (→ TRANSGRESS)

debaḥ **[דְּבַח, 1684** (Noun, Aramaic), **1685** (Verb, Aramaic)]

debaḥ is an Aramaic form constituting both a noun and a verb. It occurs only in Ezra 6:3, where the term is used in both its verbal and nominal forms to express the phrase "to offer sacrifices." The context is the decree of Cyrus, king of Persia, when he allows the Israelites to return to their homeland for the specific purpose of rebuilding the temple and reestablishing their worship there.

nedab **[נְדַב, 5069** (Aramaic)]

nedab is an Aramaic verb that is found in only three contexts. It has the underlying sense of "to give freely." Only in Ezra 7:16 does it mean "freewill offering." ***nedab*** is used twice in this verse, once participially as a noun, and once as a verb with the sense of "offer willingly" with respect to the Israelite priests.

mimsāk **[מִמְסָךְ, 4469]**

mimsāk occurs only twice — once in Prov. 23:30 with reference to "mixed wine" in a social context, and once in Isa. 65:11 with reference to the idolatrous presentation of mixed wine to pagan gods (i.e., a drink offering to idols).

pesaḥ **[פֶּסַח, 6453]**

pesaḥ is the standard term for "Passover" in the Old Testament, but on three occasions it refers to "Passover offerings" (cf. 2 Chr. 35:7ff.).

NT Words

eidōlothyton [**εἰδωλόθυτον,** *1494*]

eidōlothyton is a term that consistently conveys the sense of "that which is sacrificed to idols," referring to food in each of the ten contexts in which it is found. The principle of abstaining from such food is laid down by the Jerusalem council in Acts 15:29; 21:25. Paul refers to this contentious practice in 1 Cor. 8:1ff.; 10:19, 28. The term is also found in Rev. 2:14, 20 where it refers to this practice wrongly tolerated by members of the church at Thyatira.

spendomai [**σπένδομαι,** *4689*]

spendomai is a verb found only twice. The sense of the term is metaphorical, indicating the idea of "being offered up" or "poured out as a drink offering." In Phil. 2:17 Paul refers to himself in these terms, indicating the likelihood that he will have to surrender his life for his faith. 2 Tim. 4:6 reinforces this perspective, for here Paul refers to his approaching death (i.e., by execution) in terms of "already being poured out as a drink offering" or "on the point of being sacrificed."

prosphora [**προσφορά,** *4376*]

prosphora is a general term for "offering," with both a literal as well as a metaphorical sense. The term occurs nine times.

Acts 21:26; 24:17 refer to an offering or vow of purification taken by the apostle Paul and some of his associates. Heb. 10:5, 8 refer to old covenant offerings in general, indicating that merely presenting such sacrifices in and of themselves was insufficient as a means of gaining favor with God. Rather, it was only the offering up of Christ himself to God through his death on the cross as an act of substitutionary atonement that accomplished salvation and forgiveness for his people (cf. Eph. 5:2; Heb. 10:10, 14). Heb. 10:18 speaks generally of an "offering" for sin.

holokautōma [**ὁλοκαύτωμα,** *3646*]

holokautōma is a noun with the general meaning "burnt offering" in a literal, ceremonial sense. It is found only in Mark 12:33; Heb. 10:6, 8.

See Also: → GIFT → SACRIFICE

OFFICE

OT Words

kēn **[כֵּן, 3653]**

kēn is a noun with several meanings. It refers first of all to the "base" of the great bronze washbasin in the tabernacle and temple. Secondly, it refers to the general sense of a person's place or position. On two occasions ***kēn*** means "office," with reference to one's station, or position, as an employee. Gen. 40:13; 41:13 speak of Pharaoh's cup bearer, who was restored to his "office" after a time in prison.

pequddāh [פְּקֻדָּה, 6486]

pequddāh is a noun found in around thirty contexts meaning "oversight," or "charge," as well as one charged with a particular responsibility. In this regard, the meanings "office," "official," "officer" are appropriate. The term can also mean "visitation," "punishment." (➞ VISIT)

pequddāh refers to priestly oversight and priestly officials in Num. 4:16; 2 Kgs. 11:18. Royal officials are noted in 1 Chr. 26:30; 2 Chr. 24:11; 26:11. Isa. 60:17 refers to "overseers" in a non-specific context.

NT Words

hierateia [ἱερατεία, *2405*]

hierateia is found only in Luke 1:9; Heb. 7:5, where it refers to the "custom" or "office" of the priesthood.

episkopē [ἐπισκοπή, *1984*]

episkopē occurs only four times, referring twice to divine "visitation" and twice to an "office" or "position of leadership." Acts 1:20 refers to Judas' position of leadership being given to another (Matthias) on account of his betrayal of Christ. 1 Tim. 3:1 refers to the "office" of a bishop as a noble ambition for a Christian man to aspire to.

See Also: ➞ SERVICE

OFFICER

OT Words

sārîs [סָרִיס, 5631]

sārîs refers to an "officer" or "official" in a military context or, more commonly, to one belonging to a royal household. These meanings are indicated in about one-third of the forty occurrences of ***sārîs***. The remaining usage indicates the sense of "eunuch."
(➞ EUNUCH)

sārîs refers to an "officer" or "official" in the context of a royal household (cf. Gen. 40:2, 7; 1 Sam. 8:15; 1 Kgs. 22:9; 2 Kgs. 8:6; 23:11; 24:12ff.; Dan. 1:3, 7ff.). The meaning "officer" is in view in Gen. 37:36; 39:1, with reference to Potiphar, who was captain of the guard in Pharaoh's household court. The sense of "military officer" is explicitly in view in Jer. 52:25.

pāqîd [פָּקִיד, 6496]

pāqîd is a noun found in thirteen contexts with the underlying sense of one who is placed in a position of authority or command. The term may be translated "commander," "officer," "official."

Meaning "government official," ***pāqîd*** refers to the court of the Egyptian pharaoh (Gen. 41:34); and to the court of the Persian ruler, Xerxes (Esth. 2:3). In Neh. 11:9ff., civil officials are appointed by Nehemiah in the rebuilt city of Jerusalem. See also Judg. 9:28. Officers of the royal household of Joash, king of Judah, are mentioned in 2 Chr. 24:11.

Levitical officers are noted in 2 Chr. 31:3 where one, Azariah, is described as the officer in charge of the temple. Similarly, Pashur is cited as chief officer in the temple in Jer. 20:1. See also Jer. 29:6.

pāqîd also refers to military officers or commanders in 2 Kgs. 25:19; Jer. 52:25.

neṣîb [נְצִיב, 5333]

neṣîb refers primarily to a military outpost, or garrison, in the twelve contexts in which it is found. However, 1 Kgs. 4:19 refers to one, Geber, who is described as the sole governor or officer in charge of the land of Gilead.

shōṭēr [שֹׁטֵר, 7860]

shōṭēr is a participial noun form which refers to various kinds of "officers," or "officials" in each of the twenty-five contexts in which it is found.

shōṭēr refers to tribal leaders of Israel as "officers" (Num. 11:16; Deut. 1:15; 29:10; 31:28; Josh. 1:10; 3:2; 8:3; 23:2; 24:1). Deut. 16:18 refers to Israelite judicial officers. Deut. 20:5ff.; 1 Chr. 27:1 refer to Israelite military officers or commanders. Levitical officials of various kinds are referred to in 1 Chr. 23:4; 26:29; 2 Chr. 19:11; 34:13. A non-specific "overseer" or "officer" is mentioned in Prov. 6:7.

pāqad [פָּקַד, 6485]

pāqad is a common verb form with the principal meanings "number," "punish," and "appoint." The term is found in about three hundred contexts.

With the last of these meanings, ***pāqad*** refers to the appointment of various kinds of officers or officials. In Gen. 39:4, 5, Egyptian foremen (or taskmasters) are appointed over the Israelites in captivity. The Babylonian authorities appoint Gedaliah as governor over the state of Judah (cf. 2 Kgs. 25:23; Jer. 40:5ff.).

pāqad is also employed as a participial noun to refer to Israelite military officers in Num. 31:14, 48; 2 Kgs. 11:15.

nāṣab **[נָצַב, 5324]**

nāṣab is a verb that is translated primarily "to set," "set up," "stand" (with transitive force). The term is found in seventy-five contexts.

Occasionally, however, ***nāṣab*** is used participially with nominal force. In these contexts, the term denotes "officers," "officials," or those appointed to an office, as in those Israelite civil officials appointed in Solomon's kingdom (cf. 1 Kgs. 4:5ff., 27; 5:16; 9:23; 2 Chr. 8:10).

NT Words

hypēretēs [ὑπηρέτης, *5257*]

hypēretēs means "officer" or "official" in a number of places. The term is found twenty times, with the sense of "officer" evident in half of these contexts.

hypēretēs most frequently refers to a "legal officer" charged with the responsibility of carrying out the judicial sentence of the courts or the maintenance of law and order, similar to a modern member of the police force. Many of these instances occur in the context of Christ's arrest, trial, and crucifixion (cf. John 7:32, 45, 46; 18:3, 12, 18, 22; 19:6). See also Matt. 5:25; Acts 5:22, 26. In addition, ***hypēretēs*** refers to a "synagogue attendant or official" in Luke 4:20.

praktōr [πράκτωρ, *4233*]

praktōr, a synonym for ***hypēretēs*** (see above), occurs only in Luke 12:58, referring twice in that verse to an "officer" of the jail system.

OFFSPRING

OT Words

ṣe'eṣā' **[צֶאֱצָא, 6631]**

ṣe'eṣā', a noun found in eleven contexts, is a general term for "offspring" in the literal sense of "children" or "descendants." It also refers metaphorically to the "produce" of the earth.

Literal references to one's children or descendants are found in Job 5:25; 21:8; 27:14; Isa. 22:24; 48:19. In particular, Isa. 44:3; 61:9; 65:23 record the promised blessing of Yahweh that will come upon the offspring or descendants of the people of God.

Job 31:8; Isa. 34:1; 42:5 refer metaphorically to the "produce" of the earth.

NT Words

genos [γένος, *1085*]

genos refers to the combined number of individuals of the same nature or kind. It occurs in around twenty contexts, meaning "kind," "family," "race" (or nationality), and "offspring."

With the sense of "children," or "descendants," ***genos*** refers in Acts 17:28, 29 to believers as the "offspring of God." In Rev. 22:16, the risen Christ refers to himself as the "offspring of David."

See Also: → KIND

OIL

OT Words

shemen **[שֶׁמֶן, 8081]**

shemen is the most common term for "oil" (specifically olive oil) in the Old Testament. It occurs in about 170 places in a number of different contexts. ***shemen*** is used both literally and metaphorically.

Mundane, general references to oil are found in 2 Sam. 1:21; 1 Kgs. 5:11; 17:12ff.; 2 Kgs. 4:2ff.; Ezra 3:7; Esth. 2:12; Job 24:11; Prov. 21:17.

The use of oil for anointing is mentioned in several contexts. Special sites, such as Bethel, were anointed with oil to commemorate a special divine revelation (cf. Gen. 28:18; 35:14). The ritual anointing of priests in preparation for their service in the tabernacle is indicated in Exod. 25:6; 29:7, 21; 30:24ff.; Lev. 8:2, 10ff.; 10:7; 21:10ff. ***shemen*** refers to anointing kings with oil, including David (1 Sam. 16:1, 13; Ps. 89:20); Saul (1 Sam. 10:1); Solomon (1 Kgs. 1:39); and the messianic ruler (Ps. 45:7). The non-ritual application of oil, probably as a cosmetic, is noted in Pss. 23:5; 104:15; Mic. 6:15; 2 Sam. 14:2; Deut. 28:40.

Oil was also used as fuel for the lamps in the tabernacle (Exod. 25:6; 27:20; 35:14; 39:37ff.; Num. 4:9). Num. 11:8 refers to oil used for cooking.

In the ritual sphere, oil is designated as a component of offerings and sacrifices (Exod. 29:40; Lev. 2:1ff.; 6:15; 7:10ff.; Num. 7:13ff.; 15:4ff.; 28:5ff.) — all in relation to the tabernacle. ***shemen*** is also designated as such in Ezekiel's vision of the renewed temple (Ezek. 45:14, 24, 25; 46:5ff.). Ezra 7:22 refers to oil as part of the provision for reestablishing and rebuilding the temple in Jerusalem.

The abundance of oil as a sign of blessing in the context of prosperity in the land of Canaan is indicated in Deut. 8:8, and also in Isa. 41:19 as part of the divine promise of renewal for Yahweh's land and people.

In metaphorical contexts, ***shemen*** is found in Ps. 55:21; Prov. 5:3 with reference to words being "softer, or smoother, than oil." Ezek. 16:9 mentions Yahweh anointing Israel with oil. This is a symbolic reference to her cosmetic beautification, indicating the devoted care of a loving God (cf. also Ezek. 16:18ff.). In the context of renewal, Isa. 61:3 refers to God presenting his people with "the oil of joy." Mic. 6:7 refers to "ten thousand rivers of oil," indicating Israel's abundant provision of oil for worship and sacrifice. It is a useless ritual, for his people do not truly love him.

yiṣhār **[יִצְהָר, 3323]**

yiṣhār is a synonym for ***shemen*** (see above), occurring around twenty times with the consistent meaning "oil" (i.e., olive oil). Oil in general, mundane contexts is noted in 2 Kgs. 18:3; 2 Chr. 32:28; Neh. 5:11.

yiṣhār also refers to "oil" as part of the material blessings of the land of Canaan promised by God to his people (cf. Num. 18:12; Deut. 7:13; 11:14). Hos. 2:8 mentions Israel's abuse of this provision, whereby they used oil, and other produce of the land, for idolatrous worship. In a number of prophetic contexts, "oil" is also promised to the people of Yahweh as part of the anticipated divine renewal of the land (cf. Jer. 31:12; Hos. 2:22; Joel 2:19, 24).

Conversely, the withdrawal of oil (among other things) occurs as part of the threatened curse brought against Israel by Yahweh at the hands of the invading armies of Assyria and Babylon (cf. Deut. 28:5; Joel 1:10). In Hag. 1:11, such a punishment is specifically declared as a divine action.

Oil is frequently described as a portion of the Israelites' tithe from the produce of the land (cf. Deut. 12:17; 14:23; 18:4; 2 Chr. 31:5; Neh. 10:37, 39; 13:5, 12).

Zech. 4:14 refers to the high priest Joshua and Zerubbabel, the governor in the postexilic community of Judah, as "those anointed with oil."

meshaḥ **[מְשַׁח, 4887** (Aramaic)**]**

meshaḥ is an Aramaic term for "oil," found only in Ezra 6:9; 7:22 with reference to oil provided by the kings of Persia (Darius and Artaxerxes) to the group of Israelites returning to Jerusalem from the land of their captivity. The oil was explicitly designated for reestablishing the Israelite cultus in Judah, including rebuilding the temple.

mishḥāh **[מִשְׁחָה, 4888]**

mishḥāh refers primarily and specifically to oil that is used for the ceremonial ritual of priestly consecration. It is translated "anointing oil" in most of the twenty-two contexts in which it is found (cf. Exod. 25:6; 29:7, 21; 35:8; 40:9, 15; Lev. 8:2ff.; 10:7; 21:10ff.; Num. 4:16).

NT Words

elaion [ἔλαιον, *1637*]

elaion is the sole term for "oil" in the New Testament, occurring eleven times.

General references to oil as a household commodity are found in Matt. 25:3ff.; Luke 16:6; Rev. 6:6; 18:13. ***elaion*** also refers to oil as a healing ointment, or medication (Mark 6:13; Luke 10:34; Jas. 5:14); and as a cosmetic lotion (Luke 7:46). It is used metaphorically in Heb. 1:9 to refer to God anointing his Son with "the oil of joy."

OINTMENT → PERFUME

OLD

OT Words

bēn **[בֵּן, 1121]**

bēn is a common term in the Old Testament, occurring nearly five thousand times. It usually means "son," or "children." In around 140 places, however, it is translated "old" in the sense of a measure of age, primarily referring to people as ". . . years old" (e.g., Gen. 5:32; 12:4; 17:1; Exod. 7:7; Lev. 27:3ff.; Num. 1:3ff.; 4:23ff.; Josh. 14:7ff.; Judg. 2:8; 2 Sam. 2:10; 2 Kgs. 8:17; 1 Chr. 27:23; Ezra 3:8; Isa. 65:20). ***bēn*** is also used in the context of the ritual act of circumcision, which takes place when the Israelite male infant was "eight days old." Gen. 17:12 describes the covenantal requirement to circumcise, and Gen. 21:4 refers to the circumcision of Abraham's son, Isaac.

'ôlām **[עוֹלָם, 5769]**

'ôlām is a noun that has the primary adverbial sense of "forever" or "everlasting" in most of the contexts in which it is found (over 400). In about twenty of these places, ***'ôlām*** is translated "old."

'ôlām is principally used with this sense in the phrase "of old," conveying the idea of "in, of, from ancient times" (cf. Eccl. 1:10; Isa. 57:11; Jer. 2:20; 28:8; Lam. 3:6; Ezek. 26:20). In particular, the designation "of old" is applied, for example, to the ancient heroes of early humanity (Gen. 6:4); to the "fathers of Israel" (Josh. 24:2); to Jerusalem (Ezra 4:15, 19); to the mercy of God (Ps. 25:6); and to God's ordinances (Ps. 119:152). Several texts refer to the "days of old," speaking of the age of God's great acts of deliverance on behalf of his people (cf. Deut. 32:7; Isa. 51:9; 63:9, 11; Amos 9:11; Mic. 7:14; Mal. 3:4). See also Isa. 46:9.

sêbāh [שֵׂיבָה, 7872]

sêbāh conveys the underlying sense of "old age," as well as associated meanings such as "gray hairs," "hoary head." ***sêbāh*** occurs nineteen times and is specifically translated "old age" in a literal, natural sense in six of these contexts (cf. Gen. 15:15; 25:8; Judg. 8:32; Ruth 4:15; 1 Chr. 29:28; Ps. 92:14).

zāqēn [זָקֵן, 2205]

zāqēn has a nominal, verbal, and adjectival sense, centered on the phenomenon of old age. With its nominal meaning, ***zāqēn*** refers to an "old man," or "elder" — a civil official in Israelite society. (➠ ELDER) In its adjectival and verbal senses, ***zāqēn*** means "old," and "to be(come) old, grow old." The term is found about 180 times, and these two latter meanings are found in approximately fifty of these occurrences.

It is used as an adjective meaning "old," with reference only to age, in Gen. 18:11; Exod. 10:9; Deut. 28:50; Josh. 6:21; Job 42:17; Eccl. 4:13; Isa. 3:5; Ezek. 9:6; Joel 1:2.

The verbal force of ***zāqēn***, also exclusively connected with the process of aging, is illustrated in Gen. 18:12ff.; Josh. 13:1; Ruth 1:12; 1 Sam. 2:22; 12:2; 1 Kgs. 1:1, 15; Ps. 37:25.

zequnîm [זְקֻנִים, 2208]

zequnîm is the plural passive participle of the verb ***zāqēn*** (see above) and is used exclusively as a plural noun form in four places. The term is translated "old age," and it refers twice to Isaac as the son of Abraham "in his old age" (cf. Gen. 21:2, 7); and also to Joseph as the son of Jacob "in his old age" (cf. Gen. 37:3; 44:20).

ziqnāh [זִקְנָה, 2209]

ziqnāh is a noun form derived from ***zāqēn*** (see above), which is used both nominally and adjectivally meaning "old" and "old age." It occurs in only six places (cf. Gen. 24:36; 1 Kgs. 11:4; 15:23; Ps. 71:9, 18; Isa. 46:4).

yāshān [יָשָׁן, 3465]

yāshān is an adjective meaning "old" that qualifies impersonal objects. It occurs only seven times, referring to "old produce" (i.e., agricultural products that are not fresh, having been stored for a time) in Lev. 25:22 (twice); 26:10; Song 7:13. Ezra 3:6; Neh. 12:39 refer to the "old gate" of Jerusalem.

Isa. 22:11 mentions the "old pool," which is probably a reference to the "lower pool" of verse 9. This most likely indicates the Pool of Siloam, a reservoir constructed by King Hezekiah at the end of a tunnel channeling water into Jerusalem from the ancient Gihon spring outside the city.

qedem [קֶדֶם, 6924]

qedem is a noun occurring around ninety times with the predominant meaning "east," as well as associated senses. However, in fifteen contexts ***qedem*** has the adverbial sense "from of old" or "(in times, days) long ago." General references to ***qedem*** with this latter meaning are found in Neh. 12:46; Ps. 78:2; Jer. 46:26.

Reference is also made to Yahweh's redemptive actions on behalf of his people enacted "from of old," or "long ago" (cf. Pss. 44:1; 74:2, 12; 77:5, 11; 143:5; Prov. 8:22; Lam. 1:7; 5:21; Mic. 7:20). In contrast, Lam. 2:17 refers to a decree of divine judgment formulated against the people of Israel "long ago." Mic. 5:2 refers to the promised Messianic King whose origins derived from a time "long ago."

yāshîsh [יָשִׁישׁ, 3453]

yāshîsh is an adjective that refers to those who are "aged," "(very) old." It is found only four times, all in the book of Job (cf. Job 12:12; 15:10; 29:8; 32:6).

NT Words

archaios [ἀρχαῖος, *744*]

archaios is an adjective found in twelve contexts meaning "old," "ancient." It also has the adverbial sense of "from old," or "long ago."

The adverbial sense of ***archaios*** is found in Matt. 5:21; 27:33 with reference to people from former times, "of old." It is used similarly in Acts 15:7, 21 with reference to "days of old."

As an adjective, ***archaios*** is found in Luke 9:8, 19 with reference to "old prophets" in the sense of "former prophets." Mnason of Cyprus is literally described in Acts 21:16 as an "old disciple," yet the term here indicates that he was an "early disciple," or one of the first group. The "old" or "ancient world" is noted in 2 Pet. 2:5 in connection with the generation of Noah's day that was destroyed by the great flood. The "ancient serpent," indicating the guise of Satan, is mentioned in Rev. 12:9; 20:2. In 2 Cor. 5:17, Paul affirms that the "old has passed away . . ." indicating that the former era of the old covenant has gone forever, and that in its place the new has come, inaugurated through the person and work of Christ.

palaios [παλαιός, *3820*]

palaios is an adjective found nineteen times in all, with the consistent meaning "old," in the sense of "worn (out)," "aged," "former."

The meaning "worn (out)" is applied to "old" articles of clothing in Matt. 9:11; Mark 2:21; Luke 5:36. The description "old" in the sense of "aged" is applied to wine bottles (Matt. 9:17; Mark 2:22; Luke 5:37); to wine (Luke 5:39); and also to personal valuables (Matt. 13:52).

The phrase "old man" in Rom. 6:6; Eph. 4:22; Col. 3:9 refers to one's former sinful nature prior to conversion, as does the description "old leaven" in 1 Cor. 5:7, 8. The "old covenant" is referred to in 2 Cor. 3:14 with this nuance of "former," as is the "old commandment" in 1 John 2:7.

presbytēs [πρεσβύτης, *4246*]

presbytēs is a noun derived from ***presbyteros***, meaning "old man." (➡ ELDER) It is found in only three places (cf. Luke 1:18; Titus 2:2; Phlm. 9).

gēras [γῆρας, *1094*]

gēras is a noun found only in Luke 1:36, referring to the "old age" of Elizabeth, mother of John the Baptist.

palaioō [παλαιόω, *3822*]

palaioō is the verb from which the adjective ***palaios*** is derived (see above). ***palaioō*** means "to grow old" and is found in only three places. In Luke 12:33 it refers to money bags "growing old." Heb. 1:11 refers to the heavens and the earth "growing old," or moving to a state of decay. And in Heb. 8:13, the writer refers to the old covenant "growing old," or becoming obsolete, giving way to the emergence of the new covenant age.

gerōn [γέρων, *1088*]

gerōn is a rare adjectival form, occurring only in John 3:4 with reference to a man being "old" in the context of the question Nicodemus asked Jesus, "How can a man be born when he is old?"

gēraskō [γηράσκω, *1095*]

gēraskō is a verb synonymous with ***palaioō*** (see above), meaning "to grow old." ***gēraskō*** is also rare, occurring only twice. In John 21:18 it refers to a man being old; and in Heb. 8:13 the term indicates the process whereby the old covenant is "growing old" and is ready to disappear.

See Also: ➡ ELDER ➡ WEAR

OLIVE, OLIVE TREE

OT Words

zayit [**זַיִת, 2132**]

zayit is a term commonly translated "olive" that occurs in around forty contexts.

zayit refers to "olives" as a fruit (Judg. 15:5; Job 15:33; Mic. 6:15; Hab. 3:17); to an "olive leaf" (Gen. 8:11); to an "olive branch" (Neh. 8:15); to "olive oil" (Exod. 27:20; 30:20; Lev. 24:2; 2 Kgs. 18:32); and metaphorically to children as "olive shoots" (Ps. 128:3).

zayit refers literally to an "olive tree" (Deut. 6:11; 8:8; 24:20; 28:40; Judg. 9:8ff.; 1 Chr. 27:28; Ps. 52:8; Isa. 17:6; 24:13; Amos 4:9; Hag. 2:19). The meaning "olive tree" is also used metaphorically in Jer. 11:16; Hos. 14:6, with reference to Israel. In the vision of the prophet Zechariah in Zech. 4:3; 11:12, Joshua the high priest and Zerubbabel the governor are depicted as two olive trees. ***zayit*** refers to an "olive orchard" in Exod. 23:11; Josh. 24:13; 1 Sam. 8:14; 2 Kgs. 5:26; Neh. 5:11; 9:25.

The plural form of ***zayit*** is used in the title "Mount of Olives" in 2 Sam. 15:30; Zech. 14:4.

NT Words

agrielaios [ἀγριέλαιος, *65*]

agrielaios is found only in Rom. 11:17, 24 with reference to a "wild olive tree."

kallielaios [καλλιέλαιος, *2565*]

kallielaios occurs only in Rom. 11:24 and signifies a "cultivated olive tree," as opposed to the wild variety.

elaia [ἐλαία, *1636*]

elaia is a noun referring primarily to the "olive" as a fruit, incorporated in the title "Mount of Olives." The term is found in Matt. 21:1; 24:3; Mark 11:1; 13:3; 14:26; Luke 19:29, 37; 21:37; John 8:1. A literal "olive tree" is indicated in Rom. 11:17, 24; and a metaphorical usage is found in Rev. 11:4, where the "two witnesses" as anointed servants of God are symbolically described as "two olive trees." Only in Jas. 3:12 does ***elaia*** refer to "olives" as a fruit.

elaiōn [ἐλαιών, *1638*]

elaiōn occurs only in Acts 1:12, where it is translated "Olivet." The term refers to an olive plantation and is an alternative title to the "Mount of Olives."

See Also: → OIL

ONE

OT Words

'eḥād [אֶחָד, 259]

This common term is predominantly translated "one," referring to the numeral "one" as well as to the numerical adjectival sense, which includes the meaning "a certain . . ." ***'eḥād*** is also used as a pronoun meaning "one," "each one," and occasionally "every one." The term is found in nearly one thousand places.

Examples of the general usage of ***'eḥād*** as the numerical adjective "one" are found in Isa. 36:9; Jer. 24:2; Ezek. 4:9, Amos 4:8. Particular illustrations of this meaning include references to Yahweh as the "one God" (cf. Gen. 41:25; Deut. 6:4; Zech. 14:9 ["one Lord"]; Mal. 2:10). References to Yahweh as the "one shepherd," with likely messianic overtones, are found in Eccl. 12:11; Ezek. 34:23; 37:24. Jer. 32:29; Ezek. 11:19 mention the phenomenon of "one heart," a reference to the work of the Spirit of God in renewing the lives of his people.

The "one flesh" principle of marriage is set forth in Gen. 2:24. Exod. 12:49; Lev. 7:7; Num. 15:15ff. describe giving "one law" for the people of God. See also Esth. 4:11, which mentions "one law" given for the Persian people. Num. 7:16, 39 describe individual animals such as bulls and goats designated for ritual sacrifice.

The adjectival use of ***'eḥād*** also indicates time, such as "one day" (cf. Num. 11:26; 1 Sam. 27:1; Isa. 9:14; Zech. 14:7); "one month" (cf. 1 Kgs. 22:13; Zech. 11:8); "one year" (cf. Deut. 24:5; 1 Kgs. 10:14; 2 Kgs. 8:26); and the general designation "one time" (cf. 2 Sam. 23:8). The symbolic "seventieth week" of Daniel's vision, indicating the climax of Yahweh's redemptive timetable in human history, is also designated "one week" in Dan. 9:27.

'eḥād also means "certain" in an undesignated adjectival reference to particular individuals (cf. Judg. 9:53; 13:2; 1 Sam. 1:1; 2 Sam. 18:10; Dan. 10:5).

'eḥād is also used in a pronominal sense. General references to "one" are found in Eccl. 4:11, 12; Dan. 8:9; Obad. 11. ***'eḥād*** refers to "one of his ribs" in relation to the man, Adam (Gen. 2:21); and to the ritual sacrifice of "one of the birds" (Lev. 14:50). The pronoun "one" is found in an extensive list in Josh. 12:12ff., referring to each king of the Canaanite tribes conquered by the Israelites. The phrase "one of us" is found in Gen. 3:22, describing the phenomenon of plurality within the Godhead. The people of God are described as "one" in Gen. 11:6; 34:16; Ezra 3:1; Neh. 8:1. Ps. 53:3; Eccl. 7:28 declare that "no one" is good.

'eḥād is translated "any" in a pronominal sense referring, for example, to "any one" of the commandments (Lev. 4:13, 22ff.), and also to "anything" that contravenes the law of Yahweh (Lev. 5:17). In addition, the sense of "every one," "each one" is indicated in Num. 5:12; Judg. 8:18; Ezek. 1:6; 18:10.

'eḥād also indicates the adjectival sense of "each," with reference to "each man" in 2 Kgs. 15:20.

NT Words

heis [εἷς, *1520*]

heis is the most common term for "one" in the New Testament, designating both the numeral itself and the numerical adjectival sense. It is also, like its dynamic Hebrew equivalent (see ***'eḥād*** above), used as a pronoun. ***'eḥād*** is found in around 250 places.

In relation to the meaning "one" in a numerical adjectival sense, examples of a general usage are found in Matt. 6:27; 12:11; Mark 15:6; Luke 15:10. Other particular instances include references to "one jot of the law" in Matt. 5:18. Matters of import are often prefaced by the phrase "one thing . . ." (cf. Matt. 21:24; Mark 10:21; Luke 10:42; John 9:25; Phil. 3:13; 2 Pet. 3:8). ***heis*** is also translated. "certain" in Matt. 8:19; Mark 14:51 as a general designation for particular individuals.

heis is also used in theologically significant contexts. Eph. 4:5 refers to "one Lord" and to "one faith." ***heis*** describes Christ as "one teacher" (cf. Matt. 23:8); "one master" (cf. Matt. 23:10); and "one shepherd" (cf. John 10:16). God himself is also indicated in expressions such as "one Father" (cf. Matt. 23:9; John 8:44); "one lawgiver" (cf. Jas. 4:12); and "one God" (1 Tim. 2:5; Jas. 2:19). The Holy Spirit is likewise indicated in the phrase "one spirit" in 1 Cor. 12:13; Eph. 2:18; 4:4 (see also 1 Cor. 6:17). Elsewhere, references to "one man" in John 11:50; 18:14; 2 Cor. 5:14; Rom. 5:12, 16 all point to the unique person and redemptive work of Jesus Christ. Rom. 5:16 refers to the "one sin" that entered the world and brought death to all human beings. The expression "one body" is a metaphorical reference to the communion of all believers, found in Rom. 12:4ff.; 1 Cor. 12:12, 20; Eph. 2:16; 4:4; Col. 3:15 (see also 1 Cor. 6:16). Similarly, the expression "one mind" is found in Phil. 2:2.

As a pronoun, ***heis*** is likewise translated "one" in numerous contexts. Examples of a general usage are found in Matt. 5:29; 6:24; Mark 5:22; 9:42; Luke 11:46; John 6:70. ***heis*** refers to "one of the prophets" (Matt. 16:14; Mark 6:15); "one of the scribes" (Mark 12:28); "one of the twelve (disciples)" (Mark 14:43; John 6:71); "one of the four beasts" (Rev. 6:1); and "one of the seven angels" (Rev. 21:9).

Paul refers to all believers being "one in Christ," reflecting a universal spiritual communion with the Savior (cf. Gal. 3:28). The expressions "I and my Father are one" (John 10:30), and "the Lord our God is one" (Mark 12:29, 32; Rom. 3:30; 1 Cor. 8:4, 6; Gal. 3:20) reflect both an adjectival and a pronominal sense of ***heis***. Similarly, in John 17:11, 21ff., the people of God are described as "one." Several texts declare that there is only "one" who is good, namely God himself (cf. Matt. 19:17; Mark 10:18; Luke 18:19).

heis has the negative sense of "none," or "no one," in Acts 4:32; 1 Cor. 6:5. Rom. 3:10 affirms that there are "none" righteous before God. Similarly, ***heis*** is used negatively in John 1:3 to mean "nothing" in the context of divine creation, described as a cooperative venture between God the Father and his Son, the "Word," without whom "nothing was made."

The meaning "every one" or "each one" is evident in Eph. 5:33; Col. 4:6; 1 Thess. 2:11.

See Also: → MAN

ONLY

OT Words

yāḥîd **[יָחִיד, 3173]**

yāḥîd is an adjectival term that also functions as a noun. It refers to an "only child" in most instances. Of the twelve occurrences of the term, eight have this meaning.

Gen. 22:2, 12, 16 refer to Isaac as the "only son" of Abraham. Jephthah's daughter is described as his "only child" in Judg. 11:34. Mourning for an "only son" is mentioned by way of a metaphor in Jer. 6:26; Amos 8:10; Zech. 12:10. A general reference is found in Prov. 4:3.

NT Words

monogenēs **[μονογενής, *3439*]**

monogenēs is the dynamic equivalent of the Hebrew term ***yāḥîd*** (see above). It is translated "only child" (son or daughter), both in relation to ordinary people as well as to Christ as the "only begotten" son of God. ***monogenēs*** is found nine times.

Luke 7:12 refers to the deceased son of a widow from the town of Nain as her "only son." Jairus, a ruler of the synagogue, is recorded as having an "only daughter" in Luke 8:42, whom Jesus raised from the dead. In Luke 9:38, a man whose "only son" is under the control of a demon begs Jesus to heal him.

The remaining uses of ***monogenēs*** refer to Christ as the "only begotten" son of God, indicating that the birth of the Messiah-Redeemer was by natural human procreation, but supernatural or divine in its conception (cf. John 1:14, 18, 36; 3:16, 18; Heb. 11:17; 1 John 4:9). The fact that Jesus Christ is the "only begotten" son of the Father constitutes one of the unique features of the Christian faith, emphasizing the unparalleled distinctiveness of God being found in the form of a man in order to bring about salvation for humankind.

See Also: → ALONE

OPEN

OT Words

pātaḥ **[פָּתַח, 6605]**

pātaḥ is the most common verb in the Old Testament meaning "to open," and it is used in a wide variety of contexts. ***pātaḥ*** occurs approximately 150 times and is used both actively and passively in literal and metaphorical contexts.

Mundane references to the action of opening include those in Gen. 8:6; 41:56; Exod. 2:6; Josh. 10:2; 2 Kgs. 13:17; Jer. 50:26. Song 5:5 (poetic). Neh. 8:5 records the postexilic community of Jerusalem opening the book of the law as part of their renewed worship of God. Job 3:1; 33:2; Ps. 78:2; Dan. 10:16 refer to opening one's mouth with the intention of speaking. In particular, Ezek. 24:27; 33:22 mention the prophet Ezekiel's release from dumbness.

The action of "opening" is sometimes predicated of Yahweh. For instance, Gen. 29:31; 30:22 refer to God "opening the wombs" of Leah and Rachel, enabling them to bear children. On occasion, Yahweh is said "to open up the heavens" in order to provide rain (cf. Deut. 28:12; Ps. 78:23). Ps. 105:41 records the act of God opening the rock in the wilderness in order to provide water for his people. Isa. 53:7 says that the Suffering Servant of Yahweh "opened not his mouth" against his tormentors.

The passive sense of ***pātaḥ***, "to be opened," is found in numerous contexts. For example, the heavens were opened at the time of the universal flood. The same expression is used in Ezek. 1:1 as a prelude to divine revelation. The words "Your ear has not been opened" in Isa. 48:8 relate to Israel's rebellion against God. In Isa. 50:5, the Servant of Yahweh affirms that "my ear has been opened" in relation to his obedient submission to the redemptive plan and purpose of Yahweh. Ezek. 44:2 mentions the east gate of Ezekiel's visionary temple being shut. It would not be opened again until the messianic prince came to offer his sacrifice on behalf of the people (cf. Ezek. 46:12). Zech. 13:1 declares that a fountain in Jerusalem shall be opened for cleansing and renewing the people of God.

pātaḥ is also used metaphorically. For example, Num. 16:32; 26:10 refer to the earth "opening its mouth" and swallowing Korah, his family, and Levitical associates alive, as divine punishment for their rebellion against Yahweh (cf. also Ps. 106:17). Num. 22:28 records that the Lord "opened the mouth of an ass" (i.e., caused it to speak). Deut. 15:8, 11 contain the exhortation to "open one's hand," or to be generous. The privilege of "opening the house of God" is noted in Isa. 22:22, symbolically indicating the priestly exercise of divine authority on earth. Further references to the activity of divine "opening" are anthropomorphic. For instance, there are pleas for God to "open his eyes" in order to see the plight of his people and give them help (cf. 2 Chr. 6:40; Neh. 1:6). Conversely, Job 11:5 contains a plea for God to "open his mouth" and curse his enemies.

Yahweh "opens the graves" of his people in Ezek. 37:12, 13 — a metaphorical description of Yahweh bringing his people back to life by promising to return them to the land of Canaan.

pātaḥ is also occasionally used adjectivally. It refers to "open" eyes, for example (1 Kgs. 8:52); to an "open letter" (Neh. 6:5); and in an indictment against the wicked, the throats of the wicked are likened to an "open sepulcher" (Ps. 5:9; cf. also Jer. 5:16).

pānîm [פָּנִים, 6440]

pānîm is a common plural noun form (sg. ***pāneh***), found in approximately 2,100 contexts with a variety of meanings. Most commonly, ***pānîm*** is translated as the preposition "before," as well as in the nominal senses of "face," "countenance," "presence." On thirteen occasions, however, the term is translated adjectivally as "open" (lit. "on/in the face of the . . ."). All but two of these contexts refer to an "open field" (cf. Lev. 14:7, 53; 17:5; Num. 19:16; 2 Sam. 11:11; Jer. 9:22; Ezek. 16:5; 29:5; 32:4; 32:27; 39:5). Gen. 1:8 refers to the "open firmament, or sky" and Ezek. 37:2 to an "open valley."

peter [פֶּטֶר, 6363]

peter is a noun that is literally translated "firstling," or "firstborn." The underlying meaning, however, is "that which is the first to open the womb." ***peter*** occurs ten times with this sense (cf. Exod. 13:2, 12ff.; 34:19, 20; Num. 3:12; 8:16; 18:15; Ezek. 20:6).

pāṣāh [פָּצָה, 6475]

pāṣāh is a verb that is consistently translated "open." It occurs fifteen times in both literal and metaphorical contexts.

pāṣāh refers to several kinds of speech, conveying the sense of "opening" one's mouth. It refers, for example, to Jephthah's vow (Judg. 11:35, 36); to vain talk (Job 35:16); to verbal attacks (Ps. 22:13), where the psalmist declares that his enemies "open wide their mouths" at him (see also Lam. 2:16; 3:46); and to praise offered to God (Ps. 66:14). In Ezek. 2:8, God commands the prophet in a vision to open his mouth and eat a scroll.

pāṣāh also refers metaphorically to the earth or ground "opening its mouth." Gen. 4:11 refers to the earth opening in this way to swallow the blood of Abel, shed by his brother Cain. The terrifying deaths of Korah and his fellow Levites who rebelled against Moses are noted in Num. 16:30; Deut. 11:6 — the ground "opened its mouth" and swallowed them alive.

pātar [פָּטַר, 6362]

pātar is a verb that occurs in only seven places, meaning "to open," "let out," "free." In four of these contexts, ***pātar*** occurs in a participial form with the adjectival sense of "open." These instances refer exclusively to the carvings of "open" flowers that decorate the walls of Solomon's temple (cf. 1 Kgs. 6:18, 29, 32, 35).

pāqaḥ [פָּקַח, 6491]

pāqaḥ is a verb that is translated "to open" with exclusive reference to opening one's eyes (except for one reference to opening ears) in both a literal and metaphorical sense.

General, mundane references to opening one's eyes are found in Job 27:19; Prov. 20:13. Other literal references to this phenomenon are found in the context of the miraculous or as the result of a special divine enabling. For example, the Shunammite woman's son "opened his eyes" after being raised from the dead by the prophet Elisha (cf. 2 Kgs. 4:35). Other occurrences refer to God miraculously curing blindness — either actual, as in. Ps. 146:8, or as part of the divine program of promised renewal (cf. Isa. 35:5; 42:7). Others are given a special miraculous ability to see (cf. Gen. 21:19; 2 Kgs. 6:17, 20).

Metaphorical uses of ***pāqaḥ*** are found in Gen. 3:5, for example, where Satan promises Eve that if she eats of the fruit of the tree of knowledge of good and evil, she will have her eyes opened and will be like God, knowing good and evil. At another level, Adam and Eve's "eyes were opened" after eating the forbidden fruit, leading to an awareness that they were both naked (cf. Gen. 3:7).

God's eyes, too, are opened in an anthropomorphic sense. For example, Jer. 32:19 speaks of God's eyes always being open to humankind. 2 Kgs. 9:16, Isa. 37:17; Dan. 9:18 contain a plea for God to "open his eyes" and consider the plight of his people (see also Zech. 12:4). Isa. 42:20 refers to the ears of God being open.

piteḥôn [פִּתְחוֹן, 6610]

piteḥôn is a rare noun found in only two places, referring to "opening" one's mouth. Ezek. 16:63 refers to Israel's shameful silence before God, on account of her idolatry. Consequently, the Israelite's will never again "open" their mouth. Ezek. 29:21 speaks of God "opening" the mouth of his people, so that they may testify to his majestic power among the nations.

gālāh [גָּלָה, 1540]

gālāh is a verb found about two hundred times with a variety of meanings. In a few instances, it means "to open." (→ APPEAR → CAPTIVE → REVEAL)

All verbal uses of ***gālāh*** meaning "open" are metaphorical and predicated of God. The eyes of human beings are said to be opened by God in Num. 22:31; 24:4, 16; as are their ears in Job 33:16; 36:10. Ps. 119:18 contains a plea for God to open the eyes of the psalmist so that he may behold the wonder of divine law. See also Job 38:17.

There are two adjectival uses of ***gālāh.*** Prov. 27:25 speaks of the desirability of an "open rebuke" rather than a secret love. Jer. 32:11 refers to the "open copy" of a deed of purchase for a block of land.

pā'ar [פָּעַר, 6473]

pā'ar is found in only four places, meaning "to gape (with an open mouth)." Job 6:10 refers to this action in a literal sense. It refers metaphorically in Job 39:23 to people "opening their mouth" to God, drinking in his words, as it were, like the spring rain. Ps. 119:131 speaks of the psalmist panting "with open mouth," longing for God's commandments. Isa. 5:14 refers to Sheol "opening wide its mouth" as an expression of imminent judgment awaiting enactment on the disobedient and rebellious people of Israel.

NT Words

anoigō [ἀνοίγω, *455*]

anoigō is the most common term in the New Testament meaning "to open." ***anoigō*** occurs about eighty times.

anoigō is used in a literal, mundane sense in Matt. 2:11; 17:27; Luke 12:36; John 10:3; Acts 12:10. The resurrection of the woman Tabitha from the dead through the agency of the apostle Peter is accompanied by the reference to her "opening her eyes" (cf. Acts 9:40). A metaphorical reference to opening the eyes of the blind is found in Acts 26:18 as part of the mission of the Messianic Servant (quoted from Isa. 42:7).

The expression "to open one's mouth" is found in a number of contexts. It is used in the description of Jesus' public teaching ministry (cf. Matt. 5:2; 13:5). Others are also said to open their mouths in order to speak — for example, Philip the evangelist (cf. Acts 8:35); Peter (cf. Acts 10:34); and Paul (cf. Acts 8:14). In a citation from Isa. 53:7, the Messianic Servant's silence before his tormentors is noted in the phrase "he opened not his mouth." In Rev. 13:6, the satanic sea beast is said to open his mouth in order to blaspheme.

Other significant uses of ***anoigō*** describe the action of "opening." In Rev. 3:7, for example, it is used in an absolute sense to indicate the exercise of power and authority. Rev. 3:20 contains the divine injunction "to open the door" of one's heart and life as a prelude to enjoying the intimate fellowship of the indwelling spirit of Christ. The divine challenge "to open the scroll" is recorded in Rev. 5:2ff., and only the lamb of God is capable of doing so. The "opening of the seals" of divine judgment is described in Rev. 6:1ff.; 8:1. In Rev. 9:2, the angelic "star" is given a key to open the bottomless pit of destruction.

anoigō is also used in the passive voice. The heavens are said to be opened by God, for example, in John 1:51; Acts 7:56; 10:11 in relation to divine revelation. In Rev. 4:1; 19:11, John declares that he "saw heaven opened" as a prelude to further visionary revelation. Such a phenomenon is also recorded at the baptism of Jesus (cf. Matt. 3:16; Luke 3:21). The temple in heaven is said to be opened in Rev. 11:19; 15:5; as are the books of judgment in Rev. 20:12.

In the aftermath of Christ's crucifixion, graves are opened by the power of God (cf. Matt. 27:52). God likewise opens prison doors in order to bring about the miraculous release of various apostles (cf. Acts 5:19; 16:26ff.). The healing of the blind was a significant element in the healing ministry of Jesus. Several texts declare that the eyes of the blind were opened (cf. Matt. 9:30; 20:33; John 9:10ff.; 10:21; 11:37). Saul also experienced such a healing at the time of his conversion (cf. Acts 9:8). See also Luke 1:64.

Impersonal metaphorical uses of ***anoigō*** are found in a couple of places. The expression ". . . knock and it shall be opened to you" in Matt. 7:7; Luke 11:9 conveys the truth that the knowledge of God and his way of salvation shall be made available to all those who seriously long for it. 1 Cor. 16:9; 2 Cor. 2:12 refer to a door (of opportunity) being opened for Paul.

anoigō is used adjectivally in Rom. 3:13, referring to the throats of the wicked as "an open grave." Rev. 3:8 speaks of an "open door of opportunity."

schizō [σχίζω, *4977*]

schizō is a verb with the principal sense of "tear," or "divide." It occurs ten times. In Mark 11:10, however, it refers to the heavens being "opened" at the baptism of Christ. The likely underlying meaning is that the heavens were spectacularly "torn apart."

dianoigō [διανοίγω, *1272*]

dianoigō is a variant form of ***anoigō*** (see above), meaning "to open" in both the active and passive voice. The term occurs eight times.

In Mark 7:34, 35, Jesus cures a deaf mute. He commands that the man's ears be opened, and the miraculous restoration immediately follows. Luke 2:23 refers to the sanctity of the firstborn male child, or the male "that opens the womb." Luke 24:31 records the enlightening of the two disciples of Christ on the road to Emmaus, who met the risen Lord but did not initially recognize him. The text records that "their eyes were opened" and they recognized him. Similarly, in Luke 24:45, the Lord "opened their minds" to understand the Scriptures. See also Luke 24:32; Acts 16:14. In Acts 17:3, ***dianoigō*** means "explain" with reference to Paul "opening" the Scriptures in order to demonstrate that Jesus was the Christ.

anaptyssō [ἀναπτύσσω, *380*]

anaptyssō is found only in Luke 4:17, where it refers literally to "unrolling" the scroll of Isaiah by Jesus, hence the translation "he opened the book . . ."

See Also: → KEY

OPPOSE → RESIST

OPPRESS, OPPRESSION

OT Words

lāḥaṣ [לָחַץ, 3905]

lāḥaṣ is a verb found in nineteen places with the primary meaning "oppress," as well as several associated senses, in a variety of contexts.

lāḥaṣ means to "oppress" in the sense of "enslave" in Exod. 3:9; Judg. 6:9, with reference to Israel's oppression at the hands of the Egyptians. The more general sense of "harass" or "mistreat" is found in Exod. 22:21, which contains the command not to oppress an alien. Several references to oppression, or military attack, from the Canaanite nations against Israelite tribes are found in Judg. 2:18; 4:3; 10:12; 1 Sam. 10:18; Ps. 106:42. 2 Kgs. 13:4 refers to the Syrian oppression of Israel. Other general references include Jer. 30:20, where Yahweh threatens punishment against all who oppress the people of God. Amos 6:14 threatens God's military oppression against Israel for their disobedience. See also Ps. 56:1; Isa. 19:20.

laḥaṣ [לַחַץ, 3906]

laḥaṣ is the noun derived from ***lāḥaṣ*** (see above) and occurs in about ten contexts meaning "oppression" or "affliction."

"Oppression" in the sense of "enslavement" is again found with reference to the Egyptian enslavement of Israel in Exod. 3:9; Deut. 26:7. 2 Kgs. 13:4 refers to military harassment or attack with reference to Syria's oppression of Israel. General references to oppression (or harassment) from the enemy are found in Pss. 42:9; 43:2; and oppression in the sense of "adversity" is noted in Job 36:15; Ps. 44:24.

The metaphorical expressions "bread of affliction" and "water of affliction" refer to prison food rations (cf. 1 Kgs. 22:27; 2 Chr. 18:26; 1 Sam. 30:20).

yānāh [יָנָה, 3238]

yānāh is a verb synonymous with ***lāḥaṣ*** (see above). It occurs about twenty times with the primary senses of "oppress," "mistreat," as well as associated meanings.

A number of contexts prohibit the act of oppression. Commands not to oppress, or mistreat, aliens are found in Exod. 22:21; Lev. 19:33. Lev. 25:14, 17 record the commands not to oppress one's neighbor; and Deut. 23:16 declares that no one is permitted to mistreat a slave.

There are likewise a number of references to those who oppress, or mistreat — Jer. 22:3, for example, indicates this in a general sense. Those who oppress or harass Israel in a military sense are indicated in Isa. 49:26; Jer. 25:38. Those who oppress, or take advantage of, the poor are noted in Ezek. 18:12; 22:7, 29. Ezek. 45:8; 46:18 note the abolition of oppression in Israel.

yānāh is also used as a noun, meaning "oppressor" in a military sense (Jer. 46:16; 50:16). Zeph. 3:1 refers to Jerusalem, condemned as a city of "oppressors," or "those who oppress."

'āshaq [עָשַׁק, 6231]

'āshaq is another verb with the primary meaning "oppress" in the sense of "defraud" or "mistreat," "deal harshly with." ***'āshaq*** is found in about forty contexts.

The general meaning "oppress," with the implied sense of willfully mistreating others, is indicated in Job 10:3; Prov. 14:31; Eccl. 4:1 (see also Isa. 23:12).

Elsewhere, ***'āshaq*** is translated "oppress" with the sense of "defraud" in a variety of contexts. The act of oppressing others is frequently deemed a culpable practice under the Mosaic law covenant (cf. Lev. 6:2, 4; 19:13; Deut. 24:14; Prov. 22:16; 28:3; Ezek. 18:18; Zech. 7:10). In particular, Jer. 7:6 affirms that refraining from such maltreatment of the poor in Israel will result in divine blessing and favor. In several places there is divine condemnation of Israel for engaging in the oppression of the poor in the land (cf. Ezek. 22:29; Hos. 12:7; Amos 4:1; Mic. 2:2; Mal. 3:5). Pss. 103:6; 146:7; Jer. 21:12 contain Yahweh's promise to vindicate and deliver those who are oppressed. The psalmist pleads for protection against his oppressors in Ps. 119:121, 122, and he invokes Yahweh to "crush the oppressor" in Ps. 72:4. In 1 Sam. 12:3ff., Samuel poses the question to the Israelite people, "Whom have I oppressed (i.e., defrauded)?"

In other contexts ***'āshaq*** is translated "oppress" with the sense of "military attack" from pagan nations. A number of these references indicate that such oppression is an enactment of the covenant curse against Israel (cf. Deut. 28:29, 33; Jer. 50:33; Hos. 5:11). In addition, 1 Chr. 16:21; Ps. 105:14 refer to God's protection of his people against such oppression from abroad.

rāṣaṣ [רָצַץ, 7533]

rāṣaṣ is a verb meaning "oppress" "crush," as well as associated nuances, in the context of treating people cruelly. ***rāṣaṣ*** occurs nineteen times. (➡ BRUISE)

The general sense of "oppress," "(cruelly) mistreat" is found in 1 Sam. 12:3, 4; Job 20:19; Isa. 58:6. In the context of brutal military attack against Israel, ***rāṣaṣ*** means "oppress" in Deut. 28:33; Judg. 10:18; 2 Chr. 16:10.

dak [דַּךְ, 1790]

dak is an adjective that occurs only four times, referring to those who are "oppressed" or "afflicted" in the general sense of being treated unjustly or cruelly (cf. Pss. 9:9; 10:18; 74:21; Prov. 26:28).

ḥāmôṣ [חָמוֹץ, 2541]

ḥāmôṣ is a noun that occurs only in Isa. 1:17 with reference to "oppression" in general, or possibly to "one who oppresses," or an "oppressor."

nāgas [נָגַשׂ, 5065]

nāgas is a verb that is translated "oppress" in a general sense, "to (cruelly) mistreat," and is also used as a noun (in its participial form) with the various meanings "slave driver," "oppressor."

The meaning "slave driver" is found in the context of Israel's enslavement by Egypt with reference to the Egyptian overseers (cf. Exod. 3:7; 5:6ff.; also Job 3:18; 39:7; Isa. 60:17). In Isa. 3:12; 9:4, ***nāgas*** has the general sense of "oppressor." Isa. 14:2ff.; Zech. 9:8 refer to the "oppressors" of Israel, indicating their military enemies.

In its verbal sense, ***nāgas*** is translated "oppress" with the sense of "mistreat" in Isa. 3:5. Isa. 53:7 mentions the extreme oppression or torment of the "Suffering Servant" of Yahweh.

'oshqāh [עָשְׁקָה, 6234]

'oshqāh is a noun found only in Isa. 38:4, used adjectivally and meaning "oppressed" in the sense of "in distress."

'ashûq [עֲשׁוּק, 6217]

'ashûq is a noun found in only three places with the general meaning "oppression," indicating "mistreatment" or "injustice" (cf. Job 35:9; Eccl. 4:1; Amos 3:9).

'āqāh [עָקָה, 6125]

'āqāh is a noun found only in Ps. 55:3 with reference to the "oppression" perpetrated by the wicked. The inference again is one of unjust or cruel treatment.

'ōsheq [עֹשֶׁק, 6233]

'ōsheq is a noun occurring fifteen times meaning "oppression," primarily with the sense of "extortion" and "(cruel) mistreatment."

The explicit sense of "extortion" is indicated in the translation "oppression" in Lev. 6:4; Ps. 62:10; Eccl. 5:8; 7:7; Jer. 22:17; Ezek. 8:18; 22:7, 12, 29. Extortion is also implied in Isa. 59:13; Jer. 6:6.

"Oppression" in the sense of mistreatment is indicated in Pss. 73:8; 119:134; Isa. 30:12; 54:14.

'ōṣer **[עֹצֶר, 6115]**

'ōṣer is a rare noun found only three times. It is translated "oppression" in the general sense of "affliction" in Ps. 107:39. In Isa. 53:8 it is also translated "oppression" with reference to the torment of the "Suffering Servant" of Yahweh. In this context, it is likely that this "oppression" refers to the injustice he would suffer.

ma'ashaqqôt **[מַעֲשַׁקּוֹת, 4642]**

ma'ashaqqôt is another rare noun, occurring only twice. In Prov. 28:16 it refers to an "oppressor," a ruler who is bent on the cruel exploitation of his people. In Isa. 33:15 the term refers to "oppression" in the general sense of "extortion."

'ārîṣ **[עָרִיץ, 6184]**

'ārîṣ is an adjective that essentially means "terrible," or "ruthless," in the context of people in general, and of rulers who exercise power without any concern for the welfare of their subjects in particular. The term also has a nominal force and the translation "oppressor" or "tyrant" is an apt one in the majority of the twenty contexts in which it is found.

Job 6:23; 15:20; 27:13; Isa. 25:4; 29:5; 49:25 refer to "oppressors" or "tyrants" who are rulers. Isa. 25:3 refers to "ruthless nations."

References to "oppressors" or "ruthless people" in general are found in Pss. 54:3; 86:3; Prov. 11:16; Isa. 13:11; 25:5; 29:20; Jer. 15:21.

Ps. 37:35 speaks of "oppression" in the sense of "ruthless power."

ṣûq **[צוּק, 6693]**

ṣûq is a verb occurring eleven times with the primary meaning "to distress." However, in Isa. 51:13 it is translated twice with the nominal sense of "oppressor" with reference to Babylon. (→ DISTRESS)

'āshôq **[עָשׁוֹק, 6216]**

'āshôq is a noun found only in Jer. 22:3 denoting an "oppressor," or "one who extorts."

NT Words

katadynasteuō **[καταδυναστεύω, *2616*]**

katadynasteuō is a verb found only twice. In both instances it means "to oppress" with the underlying sense of being harassed or tormented. In Acts 10:38 such activity is predicated of the devil. Jas. 2:8 accuses the rich of such behavior towards the poor.

kataponeō **[καταπονέω, *2669*]**

kataponeō is also a rare verb that is found only twice. It means "oppress" in the sense of "treating harshly" (Acts 7:24), and "causing distress" (2 Pet. 2:7).

See Also: → AFFLICT → CRUSH

ORACLE

NT Words

logion **[λόγιον, *3051*]**

logion is a noun related to ***logos***, which is translated "oracle." It occurs only four times. In each instance ***logion*** is linked to the person of God, indicating the "oracles of God" or the "word of God." Acts 7:38; Rom. 3:2 utilize this phrase in relation to the Mosaic law covenant. This meaning is also implied in 1 Pet. 4:11. In Heb. 5:12 ***logion*** may also be understood as the "word" of God. (→ WORD)

ORDAIN → APPOINT

ORDER

OT Words

'ārak **[עָרַךְ, 6186]**

'ārak is a verb expressing the primary meanings "to arrange," "set in order," as well as several other nuances. ***'ārak*** occurs nearly eighty times and has these meanings in more than half of these contexts. (→ TAX)

'ārak means to "arrange" or "set in order" wood on an altar in preparation for ritual sacrifices in accordance with Mosaic law (Lev. 1:7, 8; 1 Kgs. 18:33). See also Gen. 22:9 in relation to Abraham's preparation of his son, Isaac, for sacrifice. In another ritual context, ***'ārak*** refers to laying out pieces of the sacrificial animal in the required order on the altar (cf. Lev. 1:8, 12; 6:12). The placement of the "bread of the presence" in a set order on the table in the holy place is noted in Lev. 24:8. Exod. 40:4, 23 refer to setting the sacred furniture and elements in the tabernacle in order.

In non-ritual contexts, *'ārak* also frequently refers to setting up an army in battle array (i.e., order) (cf. Judg. 20:20ff.; 1 Sam. 4:2; 17:2ff.; 2 Sam. 10:8ff.; 1 Chr. 19:9ff.; 2 Chr. 13:3; 14:10; Job 6:4; Jer. 6:23; 50:9; Joel 2:5). Josh. 2:6 refers to the orderly placement of flax on a roof.

The phrase "order one's cause" is found in Job 13:18; 23:4; 33:5; 37:19, referring to the preparation of a "case" in a judicial sense.

The everlasting covenant Yahweh promised to David is described in 2 Sam. 23:5 as being "ordered (i.e., set out) in precise detail."

***ṣāwāh* [צָוָה, 6680]**

ṣāwāh is a verb with the primary meaning "to command." However, in three places, the term is used in the expression "to set one's house in order," indicating preparations to be made prior to one's death (cf. 2 Sam. 17:23; 2 Kgs. 20:1; Isa. 38:1). (→ COMMAND)

***dibrāh* [דִּבְרָה, 1700]**

dibrāh is the feminine noun form of the term ***dābar***. ***dibrāh*** is found only five times with the somewhat vague, undefined sense of "cause," or "regard." However, in Ps. 110:4 it specifically refers to the priestly "order" of Melchizedek, the messianic forerunner of Christ in relation to his ministry of priestly intercession.

***tāqan* [תָּקַן, 8626]**

tāqan is a verb occurring only three times, in the book of Ecclesiastes. In two of these contexts, the term means "make straight," but in Eccl. 12:9 it refers to the preacher "arranging proverbs with great care," or "setting them in order."

NT Words

***taxis* [τάξις, *5010*]**

taxis is a noun that occurs in nine contexts. In all but one of these, it means "order."

In 1 Cor. 14:40, ***taxis*** refers to "orderly" worship, or that which is carried out in accordance with a set of guiding principles. Paul insists here that worship in the Corinthian congregation be undertaken decently and "in order." Col. 2:5 refers to the "orderly" character of the church at Colossae — that is, he commends them for their disciplined Christian lifestyle.

The remaining uses of ***taxis*** refer to the high priestly "order" of Melchizedek, the forerunner of the person of Christ in his ministry of intercession, patterned after the type or model of the ancient priest king of Salem (cf. Gen. 14:17ff.). These references are all found in the book of Hebrews (cf. Heb. 5:6, 10; 6:20; 7:11, 17, 21). In these contexts, ***taxis*** constitutes a dynamic equivalent for the Hebrew term ***dibrāh*** (see above).

***epidiorthoō* [ἐπιδιορθόω, *1930*]**

epidiorthoō occurs only in Titus 1:5 in relation to Paul's instruction to Titus to "set in order," or "straighten out" those matters left unfinished in the churches of Crete.

ORDINANCE → DECREE

OUTCAST → DRIVE

OUTSTRETCHED → STRETCH

OVEN

OT Words

***tannûr* [תַּנּוּר, 8574]**

tannûr is a noun indicating an "oven" or "furnace" in all fifteen contexts in which it is found.

In Gen. 15:17, ***tannûr*** refers to the presence of the Spirit of Yahweh as a "smoking oven" (or fire pot) in the dream vision of the patriarch Abraham.

Literal references to "oven," as an instrument for cooking, are found in Exod. 8:3; Lev. 2:4; 7:9; 11:35; 26:26. Neh. 3:11; 12:38 refer to the "tower of the ovens," one of the fortified sections of the wall of the city.

tannûr is also used metaphorically to refer to the "oven" as an instrument of divine judgment against the wicked, indicating the terrifying prospect of a fiery death (cf. Ps. 21:9; Isa. 31:9; Mal. 4:1). The people of Jerusalem are also depicted as objects of divine wrath who suffer such a judgment at the time of the destruction of Jerusalem (cf. Lam. 5:10). In Hos. 7:4ff., ***tannûr*** refers to the illicit passion of the people of Israel as a "(burning) oven," inciting them to reject Yahweh in favor of idolatrous worship.

NT Words

***klibanos* [κλίβανος, *2823*]**

klibanos is a rare noun, occurring only twice. Both references indicate an "oven" in the literal sense of an earthen vessel for baking bread (cf. Matt. 6:30; Luke 12:28).

OVERCOME

OT Words

gûd **[גּוּד, 1464]**

gûd is a verb found only twice, in Gen. 49:19, referring to invaders who will "overcome" the tribe of Gad. And, in turn, the Gadites will "overcome" their attackers. The context here implies that "overcome" involves troops engaged in a military assault.

NT Words

nikaō [νικάω, *3528*]

nikaō is a verb occurring twenty-five times with the principal meanings "overcome," "conquer," or "prevail." ***nikaō*** is predominantly used in a metaphorical sense.

In a literal context, ***nikaō*** is translated "overcome" in the sense of being overwhelmed in physical combat by a superior opponent (cf. Luke 11:22).

More commonly, ***nikaō*** means "overcome" in the spiritual sense of "to win a victory." Several contexts are in view. Such an action is predicated of Christ, who is said "to overcome" the world, indicating that he has conquered the satanic opposition inherent in a sinful, fallen humanity (cf. John 16:33; Rev. 5:5). Elsewhere, believers are also said "to overcome," or they are exhorted to do so. The context here is likewise that of a spiritual victory over the sinful snare of a wicked world, promised to those who truly belong to Christ and who persevere in their relationship with him to the end (cf. 1 John 5:4, 5; Rev. 2:7, 11, 17, 26; 3:5, 12, 21). Rom. 12:21 exhorts believers not to be overcome by evil, but to overcome evil with good. 1 John 2:13, 14; 4:4 refer to overcoming the "evil one." Rom. 3:4 refers to "prevailing" in the sense of escaping divine judgment.

hēttaomai [ἡττάομαι, *2274*]

hēttaomai is a rare verb, found in only three places. In two of these contexts it means "overcome." 2 Pet. 2:19, 20 refer to the perils of those who, having made a profession of faith in Christ, are then "overcome" afresh by the corruption of sin.

See Also: ➟ FIGHT ➟ WIN

OVERFLOW

OT Words

ṣûph **[צוּף, 6687]**

ṣûph is a verb occurring only three times, meaning "to flow," "overflow." Deut. 11:4 mentions the waters of the Re(e)d Sea "flowing over" the Egyptian army. Lam. 3:54 contains a metaphorical use of ***ṣûph***, describing the overwhelming nature of the prophet's suffering as he witnesses the destruction of the city of Jerusalem and declares: "The waters flowed over my head . . ." In 2 Kgs. 6:6, ***ṣûph***, is translated "float," with reference to a stick.

shāṭaph **[שָׁטַף, 7857]**

shāṭaph is a verb found in approximately thirty places. It is translated variously as "flow," "overflow," as well as several related shades of meaning in both a literal and metaphorical sense.

The literal meaning "to flow" is found in 2 Chr. 32:4 with reference to a river. Ps. 78:20 speaks of the miraculous flow of water gushing from the rock in the wilderness, supplying the people of Israel with water. ***shāṭaph*** is also used with this meaning in Ezek. 13:11, 13 in relation to torrential rain in the context of divine judgment against his people. A similar judgment is enacted against Gog, the ruler of Magog, in Ezek. 38:22.

The metaphorical sense of "overflow" is found in Pss. 69:2, 15; 124:4 with reference to being overwhelmed with sorrow, torment, or suffering. The same is predicated of the Assyrian army, which will "overflow" (i.e., overwhelm) the entire land of Israel in a devastating military invasion (cf. Isa. 8:8; 10:22; 28:2, 15ff.). In contrast, in Isa. 43:2; 66:2, the people of Israel are said to be protected by Yahweh from the "overflowing (i.e., overwhelming) waters" of destruction at the hands of their enemies. Jer. 47:2 similarly refers to the Egyptian armies attacking and invading the land of Philistia.

See also the apocalyptic context of Dan. 11:10, 22ff. A similar action is predicated of Yahweh in Isa. 30:28, where he is likened to "rushing waters."

shāṭaph means "drown" in Song 8:7, referring to love that can never be overrun by adverse circumstances.

shûq **[שׁוּק, 7783]**

shûq is a rare verb found in only three places, meaning "overflow" in two of these. In Joel 2:24, ***shûq*** refers to an abundance of wine and oil in terms of vats "overflowing." The context is one of economic prosperity promised by Yahweh to his people. The same phrase, "the vats overflow," is used in Joel 3:13, but on this occasion the context is one of divine judgment, declaring the outpouring of God's wrath upon the nations, whose "vats overflow" with wickedness.

mālē' **[מָלֵא, 4390]**

mālē' is a verb that expresses the primary meanings "fill," "(be) full," "fulfill," as well as associated senses in most of the 250 contexts or so in which it is found. However, in Josh. 3:15; 1 Chr. 12:15, ***mālē'*** refers to the banks of the Jordan River "overflowing" in flood.

(→ FILL)

OVERLAY

OT Words

ṣāphāh **[צָפָה, 6823]**

ṣāphāh is a verb that is translated "overlay" or "cover" in almost all of the contexts in which it is found (approximately fifty). ***ṣāphāh*** refers almost exclusively to the process of "overlaying" the furniture of the tabernacle and the temple with gold (cf. Exod. 25:11ff.; 26:29ff.; 30:3ff.; 36:34ff.; 37:2ff.; 1 Kgs. 6:20ff.; 10:18; 2 Chr. 3:4, 10; 9:17). In several places, ***ṣāphāh*** refers to covering furniture with bronze (cf. Exod. 27:2, 6; 38:2, 6; 2 Chr. 4:9). 1 Kgs. 6:15 refers to overlaying the floor of the temple with planks of cypress pine. And 2 Chr. 3:6 refers to "adorning" the temple with precious stones.

tûaḥ **[טוּחַ, 2902]**

tûaḥ is a verb found twelve times that also means "overlay," but it refers primarily to covering walls with plaster (cf. Lev. 14:42ff.) or daubing with whitewash (cf. Ezek. 13:10ff.; 22:28). In one context, ***tûaḥ*** refers to "overlaying" the walls of the temple with silver and gold.

ṣippûy **[צִפּוּי, 6826]**

ṣippûy is another synonym for ***ṣāphāh*** and ***tûaḥ***, above. ***ṣippûy*** is a noun that occurs in five places, all with reference to "overlaying" objects with precious metal. Exod. 38:17, 19 refer to overlaying pillars in the tabernacle with silver. Similarly, the bronze "plating" of the large altar of sacrifice is indicated in Num. 16:38, 39. Isa. 30:22 refers to overlaying idols with silver.

ḥāphāh **[חָפָה, 2645]**

ḥāphāh is a verb found twelve times that means "overlay" and "cover." The latter meaning, however, refers to covering one's head. In 2 Chr. 3:5ff., ***ḥāphāh*** refers to overlaying the temple interior with fine gold. Ps. 68:13 contains a metaphorical reference to the wings of a dove "covered (or overlaid) with silver."

(→ COVER)

NT Words

perikalyptō **[περικαλύπτω, *4028*]**

perikalyptō is found in only three places. This verb means "to cover" or "blindfold (one's face)" in two of these contexts. But in Heb. 9:4 it refers to the ark of the covenant "overlaid" with gold.

OVERLOOK

NT Words

hypereidō **[ὑπερείδω, *5237*]**

hypereidō is found only in Acts 17:30 where it means "overlook," referring to God taking no notice of humanity's ignorance in the past.

OVERSEER, OVERSIGHT → BISHOP → OFFICER → VISIT

OVERTAKE

OT Words

nāsag **[נָשַׂג, 5381]**

nāsag is a verb with the primary meaning "overtake," as well as several other meanings. The term is found in fifty places. (→ AFFORD)

In literal contexts, ***nāsag*** is translated "overtake," with the sense of pursuing and passing those being chased (e.g., Gen. 31:2; Exod. 14:9; Deut. 19:6; Josh. 2:5; 1 Sam. 30:8; 2 Kgs. 25:5; Ps. 18:37; Jer. 39:5; Lam. 1:3). ***nāsag*** is used metaphorically in Hos. 2:7, where Israel is depicted chasing after her idolatrous lovers but not overtaking them.

The sense underlying "overtake" in other metaphorical contexts is "to come upon," or in some cases, "overwhelm." Covenant blessings from the hand of Yahweh are said to "overtake" his people (Deut. 28:2). In contrast, the curse sanctions of the covenant enacted by Yahweh are also said "to overtake" his people (Deut. 28:15, 45). Zech. 1:6 refers to the divine law "overtaking" the people of Israel in past times. In a different setting, the "sword of the enemy" is said to "overtake" (e.g., 1 Chr. 21:12; Jer. 42:16) in the sense of a military defeat. See also Hos. 10:9. In a number of places, various phenomena are said to "overtake" people. The meaning here is clearly that of "overwhelm." This is predicated of "terrors" (Job 27:20); of "iniquities" (Ps. 40:12); and of "burning anger" (Ps. 69:24). See also Isa. 59:9, where righteousness is declared not to have overtaken the people of God. This is a declaration of culpable neglect.

nāgash **[נָגַשׁ, 5066]**

nāgash is a common verb with the principal senses of "draw near," "approach." The term occurs 125 times. In two places, however, ***nāgash*** is translated "overtake." Amos 9:10 contains an exaggerated and untenable claim by the people of God that evil will never "overtake" them. Then, in a context of divine promise and renewal, Amos 9:13 declares that "the plowman shall overtake the reaper."

See Also: → APPREHEND → CATCH → SEIZE → TAKE

OVERTHROW

OT WORDS

hāphak **[הָפַךְ, 2015]**

hāphak is a verb with the primary meanings "turn," "overthrow," and related nuances. The term is found in approximately one hundred places.

hāphak means "overthrow" in almost exclusively literal contexts. In the first place, it is predicated of God as an act of judgment, with the consistent sense of "destroy." The "overthrow" of Sodom and Gomorrah is frequently in view in the usage of ***hāphak*** (cf. Gen. 19:25ff.; Deut. 29:23; Jer. 20:16; Lam. 4:6; Amos 4:11). In addition, Hag. 2:22 records Yahweh's determination to "overthrow" the kingdoms of human beings. Jonah 3:4 refers to the promised destruction of Nineveh that never eventuated. Jonah predicted that the city would be "overthrown" within forty days. But the people repented and the city was spared.

The act of "overthrowing" is also predicated of human beings. 2 Sam. 10:3; 1 Chr. 19:3 clearly indicate that "to overthrow" means "to destroy by military assault."

There is also the general statement in Prov. 12:7 that the wicked are "overthrown" — a reference to their ultimate personal and spiritual demise.

haphēkāh **[הֲפֵכָה, 2018]**

haphēkāh is the noun derived from the verb ***hāphak*** (see above). It occurs only in Gen. 19:29, referring to the overthrow of the cities of Sodom and Gomorrah.

hāras **[הָרַס, 2040]**

hāras is a verb with a number of meanings, all concerned with the act of destroying. In particular, ***hāras*** is translated "throw down," "break down," "destroy," "overthrow." It also has a number of related senses and there is some degree of overlap in meaning. The usage of ***hāras*** is metaphorical as well as literal, and the term is found in approximately forty places.

hāras is predicated of God in several contexts. Yahweh is said to "overthrow" his enemies in Exod. 15:7. The reference is to the Egyptians, and the meaning is that he has destroyed them. In Lam. 2:2 the prophet Jeremiah declares that God has "overthrown" (i.e., thrown down) the stronghold of Jerusalem. Then there is Yahweh's threat to "overthrow" (i.e., throw down) the strongholds of all who oppose him (cf. Mic. 5:11; Mal. 1:4).

More frequently, ***hāras*** refers to human action. Yahweh commands the Israelites in Exod. 23:24 to "utterly overthrow" (i.e., destroy) the cities of Canaan. There is also the divine command "to overthrow (i.e., tear down) the altar of Baal" in the town of Ophrah — a task given to Gideon in Judg. 6:25 (cf. 1 Kgs. 18:30; 19:10ff.). God also gives a general prophetic mandate to Jeremiah "to overthrow" in Jer. 1:10 (cf. also Jer. 31:28; 45:4). Here, ***hāras*** indicates that the preaching of God's word is designed to bring about the destruction of all who oppose the plan and person of Yahweh. General references to "overthrow," by military assault, are found in 2 Sam. 11:25; 2 Kgs. 3:25; Isa. 14:17.

In metaphorical contexts, ***hāras*** refers to a city "overthrown by the mouth of the wicked" (Prov. 11:11; cf. also Prov. 29:4); and to idolatrous Israel being "overthrown" (lit. "thrown down") by her pagan "lovers," or her idols (Ezek. 16:39).

mahpēkāh **[מַהְפֵּכָה, 4114]**

mahpēkāh is another noun derived from the verb ***hāphak*** (see above), meaning "overthrow" in the sense of "destruction." It occurs six times, all with reference to Sodom and Gomorrah (cf. Deut. 29:23; Isa. 1:7 [allusion]; 13:19; Jer. 49:18; 50:40; Amos 4:11).

nāphal **[נָפַל, 5307]**

nāphal is a common verb occurring around four hundred times with the primary meaning "fall," as well as a number of related meanings. On several occasions, ***nāphal*** is translated "overthrow" with the nuance of "to cause to fall." Ps. 106:26 refers to Yahweh's judgment against his people in the wilderness by declaring that he "overthrew" them there. Several texts refer to being "overthrown" in battle, to falling down wounded (cf. Judg. 9:40; 2 Sam. 17:9; 2 Chr. 14:13).

kāshal **[כָּשַׁל, 3782]**

kāshal is a verb synonymous with ***nāphal*** (see above) with the principal meanings "fall," "stumble." It occurs about sixty times. On two occasions ***kāshal*** is translated "overthrow" in the passive voice, with the sense of "being cast down" in battle (cf. Jer. 18:23; Dan. 11:41).

sālaph **[סָלַף, 5557]**

sālaph is a verb occurring seven times meaning "overthrow," "pervert," "subvert." The underlying sense of this term is to "bring to ruin." With this nuance, Job 12:19 refers to God "overthrowing the mighty"; and in Prov. 22:12 he is said to "overthrow the words of the faithless," implying that he frustrates them. Prov. 13:6 declares that sin "overthrows" the wicked.

See Also: → BREAK → DESTROY

OVERTURN → OVERTHROW → TURN

OVERWHELM

OT Words

kāsāh **[כָּסָה, 3680]**

kāsāh is a verb with the primary meaning "cover," as well as related senses. It occurs in approximately 150 places. However, in two places it is translated "overwhelm," with the underlying sense of "engulf." Ps. 78:53 refers to "overwhelming" the enemies of Yahweh by the sea. The allusion is to the drowning of the Egyptian army in the Re(e)d Sea. The psalmist refers to horrors that overwhelm him in Ps. 55:5.

See Also: → FAINT

OWE

NT Words

opheilō [ὀφείλω, *3784*]

opheilō is a verb that occurs about forty times. It is translated "to owe," in the sense of "be under obligation," "be in debt." The contexts for the translation "owe" primarily involve financial indebtedness (cf. Matt. 18:28ff.; Luke 7:41; 16:5ff.; Phlm. 18). In Rom. 13:8, an obligation is laid on believers to avoid financial indebtedness to one another.

The general sense of being under a solemn obligation, bound by an oath, is illustrated in Matt. 23:16ff.

prosopheilō [προσοφείλω, *4359*]

prosopheilō is a rare variant verb form of ***opheilō*** (see above), also translated "to owe" and found only in Phlm. 19.

See Also: → DEBT

OWL

OT Words

kôs **[כּוֹס, 3563]**

kôs is a noun that means "cup." It occurs around thirty times. On three occasions, however, it refers to a species of owl, meaning "little owl" (Lev. 11:17; Deut. 14:16) and an "owl" of the desert (Ps. 102:6).

yanshôph **[יַנְשׁוֹף, 3244]**

yanshôph is a term found in only three places, referring to the "great owl" in Lev. 11:17; Deut. 14:16, and to an "owl" in Isa. 34:11.

qippôz **[קִפּוֹז, 7091]**

qippôz is a rare synonym for ***kôs*** and ***yanshôph***, above, referring to an "owl" only in Isa. 34:15.

ya'anāh **[יַעֲנָה, 3284]**

ya'anāh refers to some kind of unclean bird in eight contexts, although its meaning is not absolutely certain. It may refer to the owl, or possibly to the ostrich (Lev. 11:16; Deut. 14:15; Job 30:29; Isa. 13:21; 34:13; 43:20; Jer. 50:39; Mic. 3:8).

OWNER

OT Words

ba'al **[בַּעַל, 1167]**

ba'al is a general term, referring to a "man," "husband," "master" in the majority of the eighty contexts or so in which it is found. In several places ***ba'al*** also means "owner," often overlapping with the sense of "master."

General designations of an "owner" are found in Job 31:39; Prov. 1:19; Eccl. 5:11ff. Exod. 22:12 refers to the owner of animals. Owners are also mentioned in regard to oxen (Exod. 21:28ff.); to a pit (Exod. 21:34); to a house (Exod. 22:11; Judg. 19:22ff.); and to property (Exod. 22:14ff.).

'ādôn **[אָדוֹן, 113]**

'ādôn is a common noun with the principal meaning "lord," or "master." It occurs over three hundred times. 1 Kgs. 16:24, however, refers literally to "the lord, master of the hill" (i.e., its owner).

qānāh **[קָנָה, 7069]**

qānāh is a verb commonly translated "to buy," "get," "acquire" in the eighty or so contexts in which it occurs. Isa. 1:3, however, refers to an ox that knows its "owner," or knows "the one who bought, or acquired it."

NT Words

nauklēros [ναύκληρος, *3490*]

nauklēros occurs only in Acts 27:11, where it refers to "the owner of a ship."

kyrios [κύριος, *2962*]

kyrios commonly refers to a "lord" or "master" in the New Testament, primarily in the title "Lord," given to Jesus Christ by the authors of Scripture. However, on one occasion it means "owners," referring to those who had possession of the colt chosen by Jesus to carry him into Jerusalem at the beginning of the Passover festival (cf. Luke 19:33).

OX

OT Words

shôr [**שׁוֹר, 7794**]

shôr refers to an "ox" in the majority of its nearly eighty occurrences. It is also occasionally translated "bullock."

General references to "ox" are found in Gen. 32:15; Exod. 20:17; 21:28ff.; Lev. 17:3; Deut. 5:14; Josh. 6:21; Prov. 14:4. Oxen are used for food (Deut. 14:4; Neh. 5:18); and for plowing (Deut. 22:10; 25:4).

Oxen as animals destined for sacrifice are indicated in Lev. 4:10; 7:23; Num. 7:3, Deut. 18:3; 2 Sam. 6:13; 1 Kgs. 1:19. Ps. 106:20 refers to the ox as an idolatrous image.

bāqār [**בָּקָר, 1241**]

bāqār is a generic term for "cattle," as well as a specific designation for "ox." ***bāqār*** is found approximately two hundred times, with the latter sense occurring in around half of these contexts. (→ BULL → CATTLE → HERD)

General references to "ox" are found in Isa. 11:7; 22:13; Amos 6:12. Oxen are also mentioned in connection with people's wealth and possessions (cf. Gen. 12:16; 20:14; Exod. 9:3; 22:1; Judg. 3:31; 2 Sam. 12:2; Job 1:3; 42:12).

Oxen are set aside as sacrifices to Yahweh in Exod. 20:24; Num. 7 (passim); 1 Sam. 15:9ff.; 2 Sam. 24:22ff.; 1 Kgs. 1:9; 8:5, 63; 2 Chr. 35:12. An ox is slaughtered and dismembered in 1 Sam. 11:7 for the purpose of calling the Israelite people to arms. Num. 22:40 records oxen being offered up as a pagan sacrifice. Oxen are depicted as beasts of burden in 2 Sam. 6:6.

'eleph [**אֶלֶף, 504**]

'eleph is another generic term for "cattle," "ox(en)." It occurs only seven times and refers to the latter beasts in Judg. 6:15; Ps. 8:7; Isa. 30:24.

tôr [**תּוֹר, 8450** (Aramaic)]

tôr is an Aramaic term for "ox," "bull." It occurs seven times with special reference to "oxen" in Dan. 4:25, 32, 33; 5:21.

NT Words

tauros [ταῦρος, *5022*]

tauros refers to "oxen" and "bulls." It is found only four times. Matt. 22:4; Acts 14:13 refer to the slaughter of oxen in preparation for a feast. (→ BULL)

bous [βοῦς, *1016*]

bous means "ox" or "cow" in eight contexts, referring to oxen as beasts of burden (Luke 13:15; 14:5, 19; 1 Cor. 9:9; 1 Tim. 5:18), and as animals suitable for temple sacrifice (cf. John 2:14, 15).

P

PAIN

OT Words

kā'ab [כָּאַב, 3510]

kā'ab is a verb with the underlying meaning "to be in pain" in the physical sense of being sore and in the emotional sense of suffering or sorrowing. The term is found in eight places.

References to physical pain are found in Gen. 34:25; Job 5:18; 14:22. Emotional pain, sorrow, or trauma is indicated in Ps. 69:29; Prov. 14:13; Ezek. 13:22.

kā'ab is also used metaphorically to refer to the malicious intent of Israel's new enemies, who have brought them much pain.

mak'ôb [מַכְאוֹב, 4341]

mak'ôb is a noun derived from the verb ***kā'ab*** (see above), meaning "pain" or "sorrow" in both a physical and an emotional sense.

In several contexts, pain or anguish is indicated in a general sense. Mental anguish or emotional pain is referred to in 2 Chr. 6:29; Pss. 32:10; 38:17. In Eccl. 1:18; 2:23, the writer alludes to the pain and frustration of human existence. Physical pain is mentioned in Job 33:19.

The pain and suffering of the people of God is noted in Exod. 3:7 with reference to Israel's torment during their Egyptian enslavement. Isa. 53:4 refers in general to Israel's pain and sorrow. Jer. 30:15; 45:3 record such anguish as being the consequence of Yahweh's judgment on his people. Lam. 1:12, 18 describes the specific anguish of the prophet Jeremiah over the destruction of Jerusalem. The suffering and pain of the "Suffering Servant of Yahweh," in his substitutionary death on behalf of his people, is indicated in Isa. 53:3. Jer. 51:8 refers to the suffering of Israel's enemy, Babylon.

ke'ēb [כְּאֵב, 3511]

ke'ēb is synonymous with ***mak'ôb*** (see above), likewise meaning "pain" and "sorrow" and referring to both mental and physical anguish. ***ke'ēb*** is found in six contexts.

Job 2:13; 16:6 refer to Job's physical and mental pain. ***ke'ēb*** refers to the emotional pain of the psalmist (Ps. 39:2); of Damascus (Isa. 17:11); and of God's people under his judgment (Isa. 65:15; Jer. 5:18).

ḥûl [חוּל, 2342]

ḥûl is a verb with a variety of senses derived from the basic meaning "writhe." Derivative senses include "tremble," "wound," "calve," "give birth to children," frequently with a recurring sense of the accompanying pain. ***ḥûl*** is found twenty-five times.

The emotional pain of grief or anguish is noted in Esth. 4:4; Ps. 55:4; Isa. 23:5; Jer. 5:3. Jer. 4:19 specifically mentions Jeremiah's anguish over the sin of the people of Yahweh.

The expression "writhe in pain" is found in Job 15:20 in a general context. Such "writhing" is also indicated as a divine judgment against the wicked (cf. Jer. 30:23; 51:29; Ezek. 30:16; Joel 2:6; Zech. 9:5).

The pain of childbirth, sometimes in a metaphorical context of divine judgment, is indicated in Isa. 13:8; 23:4; 26:17, 18; 45:10; 54:1; 66:7, 8; Mic. 4:10.

ḥîl [חִיל, 2427]

ḥîl is a noun derived from ***ḥûl*** (see above) meaning "pain," "sorrow," with the underlying sense of "writhing" with these emotions. The primary context for this term is the trauma of childbirth (cf. Ps. 48:6; Jer. 6:24; 22:23; 50:43; Mic. 4:9). Emotional pain in general is indicated in Job 6:10, and "pangs" of fear in Exod. 15:14.

ḥalḥālāh [חַלְחָלָה, 2479]

ḥalḥālāh is another noun that means "pain." It occurs in only four contexts, expressed in each instance as the suffering of mental anguish brought on by the prospect of imminent disaster (cf. Isa. 21:3; Ezek. 30:4, 9; Nah. 2:10).

ḥebel [חֶבֶל, 2256]

ḥebel is a noun found in sixty contexts with a number of different meanings. One of these strands of meaning expresses the sense of "sorrow," "pang," "pain." In three places, ***ḥebel*** refers explicitly to the pain or "pangs" of a woman in the throes of childbirth.

ṣîr [צִיר, 6735]

ṣîr is a noun that refers to "pangs" in relation to a woman's labor in three of its twelve occurrences (cf. 1 Sam. 4:19; Isa. 13:8; 21:3). It also indicates the "pain" of mental anguish in Dan. 10:16.

NT Words

synōdinō [συνωδίνω, *4944*]

synōdinō is a verb found only in Rom. 8:22. It refers metaphorically to the suffering of the world under the curse of sin, likening it to the pain of a woman in labor.

ponos [πόνος, *4192*]

ponos indicates "pain" in each of its three occurrences, all in the book of Revelation. Rev. 16:10, 11 indicate the agony, both physical and mental, of the wicked on earth experiencing the wrath of God in a visitation of a terrible punishment on them. Rev. 21:4 refers to the glorious abolition of all pain and suffering in the eternal kingdom of God.

See Also: → AFFLICT → DISTRESS → SICK → SORROW → TROUBLE

basanizō [βασανίζω, *928*]

basanizō is a verb meaning to "torment," inflicting pain in various contexts. The term occurs twelve times.

The affliction of illness is described as terrible pain in Matt. 8:6.

Elsewhere, ***basanizō*** refers to the tormenting impact of evil spirits in the lives of individuals who were subsequently exorcised by Jesus (cf. Matt. 8:29; Mark 5:7; Luke 8:28).

Rev. 9:5; 14:10; 20:10 refer to inflicting pain in the context of God's terrible judgment on the wicked, including the devil (cf. also Rev. 11:10).

basanizō also refers to the pain of a woman in labor in Rev. 12:2. In this case the woman is a visionary representative of the mother of the Christ child.

ōdin [ὠδίν, *5604*]

ōdin is a noun occurring only four times. It is always used metaphorically. In Matt. 24:8; Mark 13:8, the term refers to the onset of the tribulation in the last days prior to the Lord's return as the beginning of "birth pangs." Similarly, in 1 Thess. 5:3 such a judgment is explicitly defined in terms of a woman's pain in childbirth. Acts 2:24 refers to the miraculous display of divine power in raising Jesus from the dead, defining it as a "freeing from the agony of death."

Additional Notes

The Greek and Hebrew terminology for "pain" is similar. A common motif is that of a woman whose birth pangs at the time of her delivery cause her a great deal of distress. In the Old Testament, this frequently functions as an illustration of the outworking of God's judgment against both his people and the nations. Though the New Testament vocabulary for this phenomenon is scant, it is found in Rom. 8:22. One chief characteristic of life in the heavenly city is the absence of all pain, both physical and mental. The context of the New Testament in general, and the book of Revelation in particular, makes it clear that the removal of pain and all other attendant consequences of sin and evil is entirely dependent on the finished work of Christ.

PALACE

OT Words

'armôn [**אַרְמוֹן, 759**]

'armôn means "palace" or "citadel" in almost all of its thirty or so occurrences. The latter translation refers either to the fortification of the town itself or to key buildings or fortresses within the city, constructed to withstand enemy assaults. The royal palace was probably included in such fortifications.

References to the royal "palace" are found in 2 Chr. 36:19; Isa. 32:14; 30:18; Lam. 2:5, 7. The Jerusalem temple is referred to metaphorically as a "palace" in Ps. 48:3, 13.

More commonly, ***'armôn*** indicates a "fortified citadel" that most likely includes the royal dwelling(s). General references to these are found in Isa. 25:2; 34:13. Jerusalem's fortifications are described in Jer. 17:27; 1 Kgs. 16:18; Amos 2:5; Jer. 6:5. In the case of Jerusalem, the reference is probably to the fortress located on the north side of the temple area. Amos 1:7ff.; 2:2; 3:9ff. refer to the destruction of the citadels of various foreign nations as the consequence of divine judgment. Such punishment is also handed down against the fortified citadels of Israel (cf. Amos 6:8; Hos. 8:14).

bîrāh [**בִּירָה, 1002**]

bîrāh refers primarily to the "palace" as the home of the national ruler. It is found sixteen times. ***bîrāh*** refers to the palace of Solomon in 1 Chr. 29:1, 19. Neh. 2:8; 7:2 may refer to the citadel or fortress that was built as an adjunct to the Jerusalem temple. Elsewhere, ***bîrāh*** refers exclusively to the royal palace of the Persian kings located in Shushan (cf. Neh. 1:1; Esth. 1:2ff.; 2:3ff.; 3:15; 8:1ff.; 9:6ff.; Dan. 8:2).

bîrānît [**בִּירָנִית, 1003**]

bîrānît occurs only twice, in 2 Chr. 17:12; 27:4, with reference to a "fortress," or "fortified palace."

bayit [בַּיִת, **1004**]

bayit is the most common term in the Old Testament for "house," occurring over three thousand times. However, in a number of places ***bayit*** refers to the residence of a king, or a palace (e.g., 2 Sam. 9:11; 11:8; 15:35; 1 Kgs. 9:1; 2 Kgs. 11:16ff.; 2 Chr. 16:2; Ezra 6:4; 9:4; Jer. 36:12; 38:7).

bîtān [בִּיתָן, **1055**]

bîtān is another rare noun, occurring only three times and referring to the "palace" of the Persian king, Artaxerxes (cf. Esth. 1:5; 7:7; 7:8).

NT Words

aulē [αὐλή, *833*]

aulē refers to the uncovered courtyard surrounding a dwelling. By extension, it indicates the courtyards and buildings associated with the temple complex in Jerusalem. The term occurs twelve times.

Specifically, ***aulē*** indicates the dwelling of the high priest, referred to as a "palace" in Matt. 26:3, 58, 69 (implied); Mark 14:54, 66; John 18:5. It also refers in Mark 15:16 to the palace built by Herod the Great (located southwest of the temple area), which is also known as the "Praetorium" (see ***praitōrion,*** below).

praitōrion [πραιτώριον, *4232*]

praitōrion is the term given to the Herodian palace near the Jerusalem temple that was used in the first century A.D. as the palatial residence of successive Roman governors in Judea, including Pontius Pilate during the time of Christ. It served not only as a residence but also as a judicial court, and was the setting for the Roman trial of Jesus. ***praitōrion*** occurs eight times. It is sometimes transliterated as "Praetorium" or "Pretorium" and sometimes rendered "palace" or "hall of judgment" (cf. Matt. 27:27; Mark 15:16; John 18:28ff.; 19:9; Acts 23:35; Phil. 1:13).

See Also: → TEMPLE

PALM

OT Words

kaph [כַּף, **3709**]

kaph is the standard term in the Old Testament for "hand," occurring nearly two hundred times. However, the related sense of "palm of the hand" is comparatively rare, found only six times (cf. Lev. 14:15, 26; 1 Sam. 5:4; 2 Kgs. 9:35; Isa. 49:16; Dan. 10:10).

NT Words

rhapisma [ῥάπισμα, *4475*]

rhapisma is a rare term meaning a "strike," "slap" (with one's hand or the palm of one's hand) (cf. Mark 14:65; John 18:22; 19:3).

rhapizō [ῥαπίζω, *4474*]

rhapizō is the verb from which ***rhapisma*** (see above) is derived, and occurs only twice, referring to the action of striking or slapping with the hand or the palm of one's hand (cf. Matt. 5:39; 26:67).

PALM TREE

OT Words

tāmār [תָּמָר, **8558**]

tāmār is a noun meaning "palm tree" in all forty-two occurrences. Literal palms are indicated in Exod. 15:27; Lev. 23:40; Num. 33:9; Neh. 8:15; Joel 1:12. Jericho is referred to as the "city of palm trees" in Deut. 34:3; Judg. 1:16; 3:13; 2 Chr. 28:15. ***tāmār*** is used metaphorically in Ps. 92:12; Song 7:7, 8.

tōmer [תֹּמֶר, **8560**]

tōmer is a rare noun synonymous with ***tāmār*** (see above), occurring only twice. In Judg. 4:5 it refers to the "palm tree" associated with the female judge, Deborah.

timôrāh [תִּמּוֹרָה, **8561**]

timôrāh is another synonym for ***tāmār*** and ***tōmer***, above, meaning "palm tree" in all nineteen occurrences of the term. The unique feature of ***timôrāh***, however, is that the palm trees indicated are all decorative carvings on the walls of the Jerusalem temple (cf. 1 Kgs. 6:29ff.; 7:36; 2 Chr. 3:5) and on the visionary temple of the prophet Ezekiel (cf. Ezek. 40:16ff.; 41:18ff.).

NT Words

phoinix [φοῖνιξ, *5404*]

phoinix is found only twice, with the literal sense of "palm tree" in each case (cf. John 12:13; Rev. 7:9).

PAPER

NT Words

chartēs [χάρτης, *5489*]

chartēs is found only in 2 John 12, referring to the apostle John's disinclination to communicate with his audience fully in writing, in "paper" and ink.

PARABLE

NT Words

parabolē [παραβολή, *3850*]

parabolē is translated "parable" in most of the fifty occurrences in which it is found. It refers predominantly to the stories Jesus told, which were at the heart of his teaching ministry. These narratives have symbolic content with a profound spiritual application (e.g., Matt. 13:3ff.; 21:33, 45; Mark 4:2ff.; 13:28; Luke 8:4ff.; 12:16, 41; 20:9, 19). See also Heb. 9:9; 11:19.

See Also: → ALLEGORY

PARADISE

NT Words

paradeisos [παράδεισος, *3857*]

The term ***paradeisos*** occurs only three times, all with reference to the heavenly realm, the dwelling place of God. Luke 23:43 contains Jesus' promise to the dying thief on the cross, that he would join him that very day in "paradise." 2 Cor. 12:4 refers to Paul's supernatural transporting to "paradise" (synonymous with the "third heaven" in this context), where he heard words he could not describe or repeat. Rev. 2:7 refers to heaven as the "paradise of God."

PARALYZED

NT Words

paralytikos [παραλυτικός, *3885*]

paralytikos is an adjective occurring ten times that describes physical paralysis, a condition that was frequently cured by Jesus during his teaching ministry. Those who were "paralyzed" and subsequently healed by Jesus are described in Matt. 4:24; 8:6; 9:2, 6; Mark 2:3ff.

paralyō [παραλύω, *3886*]

The verb ***paralyō*** expresses the condition of suffering from paralysis. It occurs in five contexts, with all but one use indicating this sense (cf. Luke 5:18, 24; Acts 8:7; 9:33). Heb. 12:12 refers to "weakness" in the knees.

PARCHMENT

NT Words

membrana [μεμβράνα, *3200*]

membrana occurs only in 2 Tim. 4:13, referring to Paul's "parchments," his personal collection of "books."

PARDON → FORGIVE

PARENTS → FATHER → MOTHER

PART (VERB)

NT Words

meros [μέρος, *3313*]

meros is a noun occurring around forty times, with the general sense of "part" in most of these contexts, but with a variety of nuances.

meros refers to "parts" in the sense of geographic locations, sometimes translated as "districts." The term is used in a general sense in Acts 19:1; 20:2. In Eph. 4:9, ***meros*** is used in the phrase "the lower 'parts' of the earth." Explicit references to various geographic "districts" are found, for example, in Matt. 2:22 (Galilee); Matt. 15:21 (Tyre); Matt. 16:13 (Caesarea); Mark 8:10 (Dalmanutha); and Acts 2:10 (Libya).

meros means "part" in the sense of one's "fate," or "lot," in Rev. 21:8, which describes the "fate" of the wicked in terms of destruction in the "lake of fire."

meros is also translated "part" in the sense of "party" or "group" in a political or theological sense. Acts 23:9 refers to the Pharisaic "party."

The word refers to a "portion" or "section" of the human body (Luke 11:36; Eph. 4:16); to property (Acts 5:2); and to a city (Rev. 16:19).

Matt. 24:51; Luke 12:46 refer to one's "place" or "position." In John 13:8, Peter is threatened with having "no part" in Jesus.

In a more tangible context, ***meros*** is translated "piece" with regard to broiled fish consumed by the risen Christ in the presence of his disciples (cf. Luke 24:42). John 19:23 refers to a "piece" of clothing.

meros is also used adverbially with the sense of "partially," "in part" (cf. Rom. 11:25; 1 Cor. 11:18; 2 Cor. 1:14; 2:5).

See Also: → DELIVER → DIVIDE → INHERITANCE → PIECE → SEPARATE → SHARE

PARTITION → WALL

PARTNER → FELLOWSHIP

PASS

OT Words

'ābar [עָבַר, 5674]

'ābar is a common verb that expresses the general sense of "pass," with a variety of nuances. These shades of meaning are evident through the variety of prepositions that emerge in the translations. ***'ābar*** is found over five hundred times.

The primary use of ***'ābar*** covers the sphere of physical movement. The meaning "pass over," for example, is found in relation to the wind, where it is more accurately translated "blow over" (cf. Gen. 8:1; Job 37:1; Ps. 103:16). The sense of "pass by" in the context of people traveling on a journey is evident in Gen. 37:28; 1 Kgs. 19:8; 2 Kgs. 6:26; Ps. 129:8; Isa. 10:28; Ezek. 5:14. In Gen. 15:17, ***'ābar*** means to "pass, or move between." Similarly, the action of "passing by, or in front of" is found in 1 Sam. 16:8; Lam. 1:12. In particular, Exod. 33:19, 22; 34:6 speak of God's glory passing in front of Moses, and before Israel. See also 1 Kgs. 19:11; Ezek. 16:8. A number of contexts express the idea of "passing on," in the sense of continuing one's travel (cf. Gen. 18:5; Josh. 10:31; Judg. 19:14; 1 Sam. 9:27; 2 Sam. 19:40).

'ābar is most commonly used to refer to physical movement with the meanings "pass over" and "pass through."

In the first instance, ***'ābar*** refers in a number of places to "passing over" or crossing natural barriers such as a river or sea. General references to crossing a river are found, for example, in Gen. 31:21; 32:10; Deut. 2:24; 2 Sam. 17:20. The crossing of the Jordan River by the people of Israel constitutes a key element in the canonical records of Yahweh's redemptive action on their behalf, recorded on many occasions (e.g., Num. 32:29; 35:10; Deut. 2:29; 4:26; Josh. 3:14; 4:1ff.; 2 Sam. 2:29; 1 Chr. 12:15; Neh. 9:11). In addition, Ezek. 47:5 refers to crossing the river flowing from under the temple, as part of the prophet Ezekiel's extraordinary revelation in Ezek. 40–48. Isa. 23:2 records the crossing of the sea.

The second of these predominant meanings of ***'ābar*** refers to "passing through," which is predicated of both God and human beings in the context of traveling, or moving from one place to another with purposeful intent. General references to this action are found in Gen. 12:6; Num. 20:20; Deut. 2:4; Judg. 11:29; Zech. 7:14. The Israelite passage through the land of Canaan is indicated in Num. 14:7. Jer. 2:6 mentions the Israelite people passing through the wilderness on their way to the promised land. The miraculous passage of Israel through the Re(e)d Sea is noted in Num. 33:8; Pss. 66:6; 78:13; 136:14; Isa. 57:1. Dan. 11:40 refers to an army passing through a land in the context of a military invasion.

Exod. 12:12, 23 record the profoundly significant action of God "passing through" the land of Egypt, bringing death to the firstborn males of Egyptian families in a final judgment that broke Pharaoh's resistance in refusing to allow the Israelites to leave his land. (For further discussion of the "passover" judgment on Egypt, see ***pāsaḥ***, below.)

'ābar also refers metaphorically to "passing through." Such a phenomenon is predicated of a divine scourge in Isa. 28:15, 18; Ezek. 5:17; 14:17; Amos 5:17. Similarly, Lev. 26:6 speaks of a sword "passing through" the land of Israel. Again, the context here indicates a divine judgment.

Other uses of the term indicating "passing through" include references to the forbidden practice of human sacrifice, whereby people had their children "pass through" the fire in devotion to their pagan deity. Such a practice is clearly denounced as an abomination to Yahweh and is expressly forbidden in the Mosaic law covenant (cf. Num. 31:23; Deut. 18:10; 2 Kgs. 16:3; 17:17; 23:10; Jer. 32:35; Ezek. 20:26; 23:37).

'ābar also refers to passing time in 1 Kgs. 18:29; Job 17:11; Song 2:11; Gen. 50:14. The meaning "pass away" in the sense of "perish" is found in Job 34:20. Non-personal "movement" is indicated in the matter of an inheritance "passing on" in Num. 27:7, 8.

'adāh [עֲדָה, **5709** (Aramaic)]

'adāh is an Aramaic verb that has the primary sense of "take away" or "remove." It occurs nine times. However, in Dan. 7:14, ***'adāh*** indicates the eternal security of the kingdom of God which Yahweh reveals will never "pass away."

ḥālaph [חָלַף, **2498**]

ḥālaph is a verb found in approximately thirty contexts with the predominant sense of "change," or "renew," as well as associated meanings. In several places this term is also translated "pass," with some varying nuances.

Isa. 2:18 refers, for example, to the abolition of all idols, which will utterly vanish (lit. "pass away"). The phenomenon of armies "sweeping down into . . ." (lit: "passing through") the lands they are about to conquer is noted in Isa. 8:8; 21:1; Hab. 1:11. Job 9:11 refers to God "passing by" him.

ḥalaph [חֲלַף, **2499** (Aramaic)]

ḥalaph is an Aramaic term parallel with its Hebrew counterpart ***ḥālaph*** (see above), meaning "pass over." It occurs only four times, with reference to the punishment of King Nebuchadnezzar for his arrogant pride. This judgment is handed down by God himself, who determines that Nebuchadnezzar will suffer a bout of mental illness when a period of "seven times will pass over him" (cf. Dan. 4:16, 23, 25, 32).

pāsaḥ [פָּסַח, 6452]

The verb ***pāsaḥ*** is explicitly linked with the divine action of "passing over" the land of Egypt to bring a terrifying judgment against Pharaoh and his people for refusing to release the Israelite people from their captivity. The verb occurs seven times, with the explicit sense of "pass over" in Exod. 12:13, 23, 27 in relation to the Egyptian judgment. In a distinctive use of this term in Isa. 31:5, Yahweh promises to protect and deliver Jerusalem by "passing over" it. It is both an allusion to Exod. 12 and also a marked contrast to that allusion. The other senses of ***pāsaḥ*** is "to become lame," "to leap."

NT Words

parerchomai [παρέρχομαι, *3928*]

parerchomai means to "pass," "pass away," "pass by" in around thirty contexts.

The principal meaning ***parerchomai*** is that of "pass away," with the underlying sense of "vanish" or "disappear." It is applied, for example, to the apocalyptic passing of the created heaven and earth at the end of time (cf. Matt. 5:18; 24:35; Luke 16:15; 21:33; 2 Pet. 3:10; Rev. 21:1). Such a passing is also attributed to the old covenant reign of the Mosaic law (2 Cor. 5:17). Conversely, such a passing is denied in the case of the generation of Jesus' day, of whom it is said they "will not pass away" until the ministry of Christ is fulfilled on earth (cf. Matt. 24:34; Luke 21:32; Mark 13:30). Similarly, the teaching of Jesus will not pass away (cf. Mark 13:31; Luke 21:33). See also Jas. 1:10.

The meaning "pass by" in the sense of physical movement or passing is found in Matt. 8:28; Mark 6:48; Luke 18:37; Acts 16:8. A significant use of ***parerchomai*** is found in Matt. 26:39; Mark 14:38 with reference to Jesus' momentary prayer to let the "cup" of his suffering "pass him by."

Mundane references to the passing of time are found in Matt. 14:15; 1 Pet. 4:3.

dierchomai [διέρχομαι, *1330*]

dierchomai is a synonym for ***parerchomai*** (see above), translated "pass," "pass through," mostly with the underlying sense of "walk" or "go." (→ WALK)

The literal sense of "pass through" in the context of traveling or walking is indicated in Matt. 12:43; 19:24; Mark 4:35; Luke 17:11; 19:14; John 4:4; Acts 8:40; 14:24; 19:1. 1 Cor. 10:11 mentions Israel passing through the Re(e)d Sea in their escape from the Egyptian army. In a spiritual context, Heb. 4:14 refers to Jesus "passing through" the heavens and establishing his ministry as our great high priest.

There is one metaphorical use of ***dierchomai*** in Rom. 5:12, which indicates that the disobedience of Adam has caused the "spread" (i.e., passing) of sin and death to all human beings.

diabainō [διαβαίνω, *1224*]

diabainō occurs only three times and is translated "pass through" in Heb. 11:29 in relation to Israel crossing the Re(e)d Sea. It also means to "cross over" in the sense of "traveling, or going across to" in Luke 16:26; Acts 16:29.

diaperaō [διαπεράω, *1276*]

diaperaō is a verb that means "pass, or cross over" in the context of sailing a boat. This sense is found in five of the six occurrences of ***diaperaō*** (cf. Matt. 9:1; 14:34; Mark 5:21; 6:53; Acts 21:2). See also Luke 16:26.

paragō [παράγω, *3855*]

paragō means "pass on," "pass by," "pass away" in the ten places in which it occurs.

The literal sense of "pass by" is found in Matt. 9:9; 20:30; Mark 2:14; 15:21; John 8:59; 9:1. The meaning "pass on" in the sense of "depart" is found in Matt. 9:27. 1 Cor. 7:3; 1 John 2:17 refer to the world "passing away" or "vanishing"; and in 1 John 2:8 the same thing is said of the darkness.

paraporeuomai [παραπορεύομαι, *3899*]

paraporeuomai occurs five times, meaning "pass through" in Mark 2:23; 9:30, and "pass by" in Matt. 27:39; Mark 11:20.

antiparerchomai [ἀντιπαρέρχομαι, *492*]

antiparerchomai occurs only in Luke 10:31, 32, meaning "to pass by on the other side."

metabainō [μεταβαίνω, *3327*]

metabainō is a verb with primary sense of "leave," or "depart." However, in the twelve contexts in which it is found it means "pass from" twice, in the context of the promised transition from death to life (cf. John 5:24; 1 John 3:14).

diodeuō [διοδεύω, *1353*]

diodeuō occurs only in Luke 8:1; Acts 17:1, meaning "pass through," "go through."

aperchomai [ἀπέρχομαι, *565*]

aperchomai is a much more common verb form, meaning "go," "depart" in the majority of the 120 occurrences of the term. However, Rev. 21:4 refers to the former things "passing away," speaking of the demise of the created heaven and earth.

PASSION → SUFFER

PASSOVER

OT Words

pesaḥ [פֶּסַח, **6453**]

pesaḥ is the standard Hebrew term for the "Passover festival," referring to the annual ritual celebration of Yahweh's deliverance of his people from the Egyptians. It occurs about fifty times, referring to the historical setting for the festival (cf. Exod. 12:11, 21ff.); the legislation prescribing the details of the feast (cf. Lev. 23:5; Num. 9:2ff.; Deut. 16:1ff.); and the celebration of the feast itself (cf. Josh. 5:11; 2 Kgs. 23:21ff.; 2 Chr. 30:1ff.; 35:1ff.; Ezra 6:19ff.).

NT Words

pascha [πάσχα, *3957*]

pascha is the dynamic equivalent Greek term for the Hebrew ***pesaḥ*** (see above) and refers about thirty times to the celebration of the Passover festival (cf. Matt. 26:2, 17ff.; Mark 14:14ff.; Luke 22:1ff.; John 2:13; 6:4; 12:1; 13:1; 18:28, 39; Acts 12:4; 1 Cor. 5:7; Heb. 11:28).

PASTOR → SHEPHERD

PASTURE

OT Words

mir'eh [מִרְעֶה, **4829**]

mir'eh is a term referring to a "pasture" as food for grazing animals in all but one of the thirteen contexts in which it is found (cf. Gen. 47:4; 1 Chr. 4:39ff.; Job 39:8; Isa. 32:14; Lam. 1:6; Ezek. 34:14ff.; Nah. 2:11).

mar'îṯ [מַרְעִית, **4830**]

mar'îṯ is a synonym for ***mir'eh***, found in ten places. It is used metaphorically in each of these texts, referring to Israel as "the sheep of God's pasture" (cf. Pss. 74:1; 79:13; 95:7; 100:3; Ezek. 34:31; Jer. 23:1). Other symbolic references to "pasture" are found in Isa. 49:9; Jer. 25:36. See also Hos. 13:6.

re'î [רְעִי, **7471**]

re'î is found only in 1 Kgs. 4:23 with reference to "pasture" as cattle fodder.

nā'āh [נָאָה, **4999**]

nā'āh is a term occurring twelve times that refers to "pastures" in most of the contexts in which it is found. The phrase "pastures of the wilderness" occurs in Ps. 65:12; Jer. 9:10; 23:10; Joel 1:19, 20; 2:22. Amos 1:2 refers to "pastures of the shepherds"; and Ps. 23:2 refers to "green pastures." The phrase "pastures of God" symbolically indicates the land of Canaan in Ps. 83:12.

kar [כַּר, **3733**]

kar refers to "lambs" in the majority of the sixteen contexts in which it is found. In two places, ***kar*** refers to "pastures" or "meadow" as grazing for cattle (cf. Ps. 65:13; Isa. 30:23). (→ LAMB)

NT Words

nomē [νομή, *3542*]

nomē occurs in only two places. John 10:9 mentions "pasture" in the metaphorical context of ample spiritual "nourishment" for those who belong to Christ. The other reference to ***nomē*** is found in 2 Tim. 2:17, where it is used in conjunction with the verb ***echō*** (→ HOLD) to convey the meaning "to spread." The context is that of false teaching, which is said to "spread like gangrene."

PATH

OT Words

'ōraḥ [אֹרַח, **734**]

'ōraḥ means "path" and "way" in the sixty or so contexts in which it is found. (→ WAY)

Literal references to "path" in the sense of a "track," or "road," are found in Gen. 49:17; Job 6:18. The phrase "path of the sea," indicating its "course," occurs in Ps. 8:8; Joel 2:7.

Metaphorical references to "path" are more frequent. The meaning "path" in the general sense of "direction in life" is indicated in Pss. 27:11; 139:3; Prov. 2:19; 3:6; 5:6; Isa. 3:6; 30:11. Job 8:13; Prov. 4:14 specifically refer to the "path of the godless." God is said to watch over the "path" of his people in Job 13:27; 33:11. Ps. 16:11 refers to the "path of life" in the sense of "godly living." With similar force, the phrase "paths of God" is found in Ps. 25:4, 10; Mic. 4:2. The expression "path(s) of justice" is found in Prov. 2:8; Isa. 40:14, and "path(s) of righteousness" is found in Prov. 2:13, 20; 4:18; 15:19.

***mish'ôl* [מִשְׁעוֹל, 4934]**

mish'ôl is found only in Num. 22:24, literally meaning "path" or "track."

***nātîb* [נָתִיב, 5410]**

nātîb is a synonym for ***'ōraḥ*** (see above), occurring around thirty times and meaning "path" in most of these contexts.

The literal meaning "path," in the sense of "road," or "track," is indicated in Judg. 5:6; Job 18:10; 28:7; 30:13; Ps. 142:3. Isa. 43:16 speaks of the "path," or "course," of the sea.

nātîb is also used metaphorically in various contexts. The translation "path" in the sense of "life's directions" is indicated in Job 19:8; Ps. 119:105; Isa. 42:16; Jer. 6:16; Hos. 2:6. Specifically, the "path of wisdom" is referred to in Prov. 3:17; 8:2. And, by way of contrast, the "path" of the wicked is indicated in Prov. 1:15; 7:25; Isa. 59:18. Elsewhere, God is said to be making a "path" for the expression of his anger in Ps. 78:50. The "path" of God's commandments is noted in Ps. 119:35; and the "path" of justice in Prov. 8:20.

***shebîl* [שְׁבִיל, 7635]**

shebîl occurs only twice. In Ps. 77:19 the term refers to the "path" or "course" of the sea. In Jer. 18:15, ***shebîl*** refers metaphorically to the ancient "paths," or the commendable ways of one's godly ancestors.

***ma'gāl* [מַעְגָּל, 4570]**

ma'gāl is a noun found in sixteen contexts with the primary senses of "path," "pathway."

The literal sense of "path" or "track" is found in Ps. 140:5.

More common is the metaphorical sense of "path," generally referring to one's "direction in life." ***ma'ggāl*** refers to one's "path" generally (Prov. 5:21); and to the "path" of the righteous (Prov. 2:9; 4:11; Isa. 26:7). Prov. 4:26 contains an exhortation "to heed the path" one chooses in life. The "paths" of the wicked are indicated in Prov. 2:15, 18; 5:6; Isa. 59:8.

NT Words

***tribos* [τρίβος, *5147*]**

tribos is found in only three places, all with reference to the quotation from Isa. 40:3, citing the prophetic command to prepare for the coming of Yahweh by making straight his "paths." In these contexts, "paths" refers metaphorically to the removal of all obstacles to the coming of the Messiah (cf. Matt. 3:3; Mark 1:3; Luke 3:4).

***trochia* [τροχιά, *5163*]**

trochia is found only in Heb. 12:13, meaning "paths" and referring metaphorically to a godly lifestyle.

See Also: → WAY

PATIENCE, PATIENT

OT Words

***'erek* [אֶרֶךְ, 750]**

'erek is an adjectival term meaning "long suffering," "patient" in all but one of the fifteen contexts in which it is found. In the majority of instances, ***'erek*** refers to God.

Yahweh is said to be "patient" or "long suffering" in the sense of being "slow to anger" in Exod. 34:8; Num. 14:18; Neh. 9:17; Pss. 86:15; 103:8; 145:8; Prov. 14:29; Jer. 15:15; Joel 2:13; Jonah 4:2; Nah. 1:3.

Only Prov. 15:18; 16:32 uses ***'erek*** to describe the human characteristic of "long suffering." Eccl. 7:8 refers to one being "patient" in a general sense.

***ḥûl* [חוּל, 2342]**

ḥûl is a noun referring to "pain," as well as various associated meanings, in most of the sixty or so places in which it is found. However, in Ps. 37:7 it expresses the adverbial sense of "patiently" in the context of waiting in the presence of God. (→ PAIN)

***qāwāh* [קָוָה, 6960]**

qāwāh is a verb that is consistently translated "wait (for)," "look for," and is found approximately sixty times. In Ps. 40:1, it has the sense of "wait patiently" in the context of waiting for God.

NT Words

makrothymeō [μακροθυμέω, *3114*]

makrothymeō is a verb with the primary sense of "have patience," "be patient" in most of the occurrences in which it is found.

With regard to human beings, Matt. 18:26, 29; 1 Thess. 5:14 contain a plea to be patient with others. In Jas. 5:7ff., the apostle exhorts his readers to be patient while awaiting the coming of the Lord. Heb. 6:15 contains an exhortation to be patient in enduring persecution. 2 Pet. 3:9 speaks of God's patient forbearance towards all people. Patience is listed in 1 Cor. 13:4 as a key characteristic of love.

makrothymia [μακροθυμία, *3115*]

makrothymia is the noun derived from ***makrothymeō*** (see above), meaning "long suffering" or "patience" in each of the fourteen places in which it is found.

"Patience," or "long suffering," is predicated of God, as one of his perfections (Rom. 2:4; 9:22; 1 Pet. 3:20); and also of Christ (1 Tim. 1:16; 2 Pet. 3:15). Such a characteristic is also true of genuine believers (cf. 2 Cor. 6:6; Eph. 4:2; Col. 1:11; 3:12; 2 Tim. 3:10; 4:2; Heb. 6:12; Jas. 5:10).

makrothymōs [μακροθύμως, *3116*]

makrothymōs is an adverb, found only in Acts 26:3, with reference to listening "patiently."

hypomonē [ὑπομονή, *5281*]

hypomonē is a noun found in around thirty contexts meaning "patience" or "endurance."

Such a quality is predicated of believers as a key factor in producing spiritual growth and hope for the future (cf. Luke 8:15; Rom. 2:7 5:3; 2 Cor. 12:12; 1 Tim. 6:11; Titus 2:2; Heb. 12:1; Jas. 1:4; 2 Pet. 1:6). Believers are also urged to cultivate patience in the face of persecution (cf. 2 Cor. 1:6; Col. 1:11; Heb. 10:36; Rev. 1:9; 3:10; 14:12). God is likewise described as a God of patience in Rom. 15:5.

anexikakos [ἀνεξίκακος, *420*]

anexikakos is an adjective meaning "patient." It occurs only in 2 Tim. 2:24, with reference to teachers.

See Also: → ENDURE

PATTERN

OT Words

tabnît [תַּבְנִית, **8403**]

tabnît is a noun with the principal meaning "pattern," or "likeness," including the sense of "image," often in the contexts of idolatry. ***tabnît*** occurs twenty times.

The meaning "pattern" is used exclusively with the sense of "design." It refers to the tabernacle itself (Exod. 25:9, 40); to the altar of the tabernacle (Josh. 22:28); and to the temple altar (2 Kgs. 16:10; 1 Chr. 28:12, 19). ***tabnît*** refers to the design of the temple porch, or vestibule (1 Chr. 28:11), and to the pattern of the molded golden cherubim on the ark of the covenant (1 Chr. 28:18).

mar'eh [מַרְאֶה, **4758**]

mar'eh is one of a number of terms meaning "appearance" or "vision." However, in Num. 8:4 ***mar'eh*** refers to the "pattern" of the golden candlestick revealed to Moses by Yahweh during the Sinai revelation of the tabernacle's design. (→ APPEARANCE → VISION)

ṣûrāh [צוּרָה, **6699**]

The term ***ṣûrāh*** is found only in Ezek. 43:11, where it refers four times to the revealed "design" or "pattern" of the visionary temple plan given by the Spirit of Yahweh to the prophet Ezekiel.

NT Words

typos [τύπος, *5179*]

typos is a noun occurring sixteen times with the varying senses of "pattern," "type," "example." The meaning "pattern" is evident in two contexts. Acts 7:44; Heb. 8:5 refer to the "pattern" of the tabernacle as revealed by God to Moses on Mt. Sinai. Then, in Titus 2:7, ***typos*** refers to the "pattern" or "model" of good works that Paul desires Titus to demonstrate to his congregation. (→ EXAMPLE → TYPE)

See Also: → EXAMPLE

PAVEMENT

OT Words

riṣpāh [רִצְפָּה, **7531**]

riṣpāh is a noun occurring eight times with reference to a "pavement" or "floor" in all but one of these contexts. Most of the usage of the term refers to the pavement (floor) of the Jerusalem temple (cf. 2 Chr. 7:3; Ezek. 40:17ff. 42). Esth. 1:6 refers to the highly decorative floor, or pavement, of the Persian palace in Shushan.

NT Words

lithostrōtos [λιθόστρωτος, *3038*]

lithostrōtos is found only in John 19:13 as a title for a place of judgment (or judicial court) at or near the

Praetorium in Jerusalem. The term is usually translated as "the stone pavement," or simply "the pavement."

PAY, PAYMENT

OT Words

shālam **[שָׁלַם, 7999]**

shālam is a verb occurring, over one hundred times with the primary meanings "pay," "reward," "restore," with a number of related nuances. (→ PEACE → REWARD)

The meaning "pay" is indicated first of all in the sense of "to make restitution" for a culpable action against one's neighbor (cf. Exod. 21:36; 22:1–15; Lev. 5:16; Prov. 6:31; Eccl. 5:4ff.).

shālam is also commonly translated "pay" in the context of performing or fulfilling a vow (cf. Deut. 23:21; 2 Sam. 15:7; Job 22:27; Pss. 22:25; 116:14, 18; Prov. 7:14; Eccl. 5:14; Isa. 19:21; Jonah 2:9; Nah. 1:15).

2 Kgs. 4:7 refers to paying one's debt.

shāqal **[שָׁקַל, 8254]**

shāqal is a verb occurring around twenty times with the predominant sense of "weigh." On several occasions, however, it is translated "pay." In. Exod. 22:17; 1 Kgs. 20:39 the underlying sense is that of "make restitution." In Esth. 3:9; 4:7, ***shāqal*** conveys the sense of "give a reward." (→ WEIGH)

nātan **[נָתַן, 5414]**

This common verb occurs nearly two thousand times with the primary meaning "give," as well as a variety of associated senses. However, in several places it means "pay." Exod. 21:19, 22 refer to the practice of paying a legally binding compensation; Num. 20:19 refers to payment in return for "goods and services"; and Ezra 4:13 refers to the payment of taxes.

NT Words

teleō [τελέω, *5055*]

teleō is a verb that expresses the primary meaning "finish," "fulfill," as well as associated meanings. It is found in twenty-six places. On two occasions, ***teleō*** conveys the meaning "pay" in the context of paying taxes (cf. Matt. 17:24; Rom. 13:6). (→ FINISH → FULFILL)

apodidōmi [ἀποδίδωμι, *591*]

The verb ***apodidōmi*** primarily means "pay," in addition to the associated senses of "give," "render," "reward." The term is found in approximately fifty places. (→ REWARD)

apodidōmi is translated "pay" in the sense of repaying a debt in Matt. 5:26; 18:25ff.; Luke 7:42; 12:59; 19:8. In Matt. 5:33, the meaning indicated is that of "fulfilling or performing" a vow. Matt. 20:8; Rom. 2:6 refer to paying wages. In the latter text, it is the spiritual sense of "recompense," the intangible but very real divine payment for deeds done in one's life, whether good or bad. Several texts exhort believers to pay their rightful taxes to the governing authorities (cf. Matt. 22:21; Mark 12:17; Luke 20:25; Rom. 13:7).

dekatoō [δεκατόω, *1183*]

dekatoō occurs only in Heb. 7:6, 9 and refers both to the receiving and "payment" of tithes.

PEACE, PEACEFUL

OT Words

shālôm **[שָׁלוֹם, 7965]**

shālôm is a fairly common term in the Old Testament. It conveys the primary sense of "peace," including a number of related meanings, in approximately 250 places.

shālôm indicates "peace," first of all as the tranquillity of death, a state of restful calm, predicated of godly people (e.g., Gen. 15:15; Exod. 18:23; 1 Kgs. 2:6; 2 Kgs. 22:20).

In a number of places, ***shālôm*** means "peace" as the equivalent or close synonym for "prosperity" in a material sense (cf. Ps. 72:3ff.; Isa. 54:13). Isa. 66:12; Jer. 33:6ff. refer to this kind of peace as the gift of God.

In the majority usage of this term, the translation "peace" expresses the sense of tranquillity, or a state of calm without anxiety or stress (cf. Gen. 26:29; 44:17; Lev. 26:6; 2 Sam. 3:23; Ezra 9:12; Ps. 122:7ff.; Mic. 5:5). In a negative context, Isa. 48:22; 57:21 declare that there is no peace for the wicked. Likewise, the withdrawal of God's peace is viewed as a curse (cf. Jer. 16:5; Lam. 3:17; Ezek. 7:5; 13:16). Then, positively, "peace" is identified as the fruit of righteousness (Isa. 32:17); and as a specific blessing from God (cf. 1 Kgs. 2:33; Ps. 29:11; 85:8; Prov. 3:17; Isa. 52:7; 53:7; Jer. 28:9; Nah. 1:15; Hag. 2:9).

shālôm is also found in formulae such as the greeting "Peace be . . ." (cf. Gen. 43:23; Judg. 6:23; Isa. 57:19). It is also found in the benediction "Go in peace" (plus variations) (cf. Exod. 4:18; Num. 6:26; Judg. 18:6; 1 Sam. 20:42; 2 Kgs. 5:19).

The phenomenon of the "covenant of peace" given by Yahweh is indicated in Num. 25:12, Isa. 54:10; Mal. 2:5. In particular, Ezek. 34:25; 37:26 speak of God's promise to renew the covenant of peace for his people. Josh. 9:15 alone speaks of a humanly initiated "covenant of peace" wherein Joshua makes a treaty with the Gibeonite people not to destroy them but to have them serve as laborers for the Israelite people.

Peace in the sense of "absence of military conflict" is indicated in Deut. 20:10; Judg. 4:17; 1 Kgs. 2:5; 4:24; Eccl. 3:8; Isa. 39:8. Isa. 9:7 refers to the anticipated peaceful rule of the Messianic Servant of Yahweh.

The unique messianic title "prince of peace" is found in Isa. 9:6.

shālam [שָׁלַם, 7999]

shālam is a verb that has the primary sense of "pay," "reward," or "compensate," occurring around 120 times. In eleven of these contexts, however, ***shālam*** is translated "to make peace," "be at peace."
(→ REWARD)

"Making peace" is most frequently indicated in the context of a military or political treaty of peace (cf. Deut. 20:12; Josh. 10:1, 4; 11:19; 2 Sam. 10:19; 1 Kgs. 22:44; 1 Chr. 19:19).

The state of "being at peace" in the context of gaining tranquillity of mind, as well as freedom from anxiety, is indicated in Job 5:23; Prov. 16:7.

shelām [שְׁלָם, 8001 (Aramaic)]

shelām is an Aramaic term meaning "Peace" as a greeting. It occurs four times (cf. Ezra 4:17; 5:7; Dan. 4:1; 6:25).

shālēw [שָׁלֵו, 7961]

shālēw is an adjectival form occurring eight times, with the underlying sense of "being at ease," in the context of both prosperity and peace. The meaning "peaceful" is evident in 1 Chr. 4:40; Job 21:23.

NT Words

eirēnē [εἰρήνη, *1515*]

eirēnē is a close dynamic equivalent to the Hebrew term ***shālôm*** (see above), meaning "peace" in virtually all of its ninety occurrences. As with ***shālôm*** above, ***eirēnē*** is found in a number of varying contexts.

eirēnē indicates "peace" first of all as a blessing, greeting, or farewell salutation to individuals, coming from human beings (cf. Matt. 10:13; John 20:19ff.); from Christ (cf. Mark 5:34; John 20:19; Rev. 1:4); and from God himself (cf. Rom. 1:7; Luke 2:29; 2 Cor. 1:2; Eph. 1:2; Phil. 1:2; Col. 3:15; 1 Thess. 1:1; 2 Tim. 1:2). See also Luke 19:38, where the context is offering praise to God.

eirēnē also refers to "peace" as a state of tranquillity, an absence of conflict among people. It is given as a blessing from God through the person of Christ (cf. Luke 2:14; Rom. 2:10; 15:13). See also Matt. 10:34; Luke 12:51. 1 Cor. 7:15 affirms that God calls his people to manifest such a peace.

The "way of peace" is indicated in Luke 1:79; Rom. 3:17 as a godly lifestyle, a consequence of devotion to God in Christ. The "gospel of peace" is alluded to in Eph. 6:15. The title "king of peace" is noted in Heb. 7:2 (citing Gen. 14:18) as a secondary translation of the name Melchizedek, the mysterious priest king of Salem.

The phrase "at peace" refers to the safety and security of property in Luke 11:21. Peace, with reference to the cessation of military conflict, is indicated in Luke 14:32; Acts 12:20.

As a specific blessing, or gift from Christ, peace is promised to his disciples and all his followers. This peace is unique in that it is everlasting and flawless, unlike any peace offered by the world (cf. John 14:27; 16:33). Similarly, the spiritual peace of reconciliation with God as a direct consequence of saving faith in Christ is affirmed in Acts 10:36; Rom. 5:1; 8:6; Eph. 2:15. Christ is described as the supreme embodiment of peace in Eph. 2:14. Peace is likewise described as a "fruit" of the spirit in Gal. 5:22, and as a characteristic evident in the relationship among believers (cf. Eph. 4:3).

eirēneuō [εἰρηνεύω, *1514*]

eirēneuō is the verb from which the noun ***eirēnē*** (see above) is derived, and it is found in four contexts. On each occasion it means "to live peaceably" or "be at peace" and is used as a command or exhortation (cf. Mark 9:50; Rom. 12:18; 2 Cor. 13:11; 1 Thess. 5:13).

eirēnopoieō [εἰρηνοποιέω, *1517*]

eirēnopoieō occurs only in Col. 1:20, meaning "to make peace" or "reconcile." The context here is the reconciliation of the world to God through the agency of Jesus Christ.

Additional Notes

The terminology of "peace" in both Testaments has both similarities and a significant difference that is evident in the context of the redemptive-historical fulfillment of God's plan of salvation in Christ.

Peace in the Old Testament is defined largely in tangible terms, indicating ease of mind and tranquillity, as well as material prosperity. It also constitutes an element of a greeting or benediction. While these senses do not disappear in the New Testament, there is a significant additional component to the idea of "peace" here.

In the New Testament it is clear that "peace" finds its ultimate expression in an intimate relationship with God, made possible by the saving work of Christ. Indeed, the person of Christ is declared as the embodiment of peace, bringing about the eternally permanent reconciliation between humankind and God.

See Also: ➠ OFFERING ➠ SILENCE

PEARL

NT WORDS

margaritēs [μαργαρίτης, *3135*]

margaritēs is a term referring to "pearls" in each of the nine contexts in which it is found. Matt. 7:6; 13:45ff.; 1 Tim. 2:9; Rev. 18:12 refer literally to precious ornaments. In Rev. 17:4; 18:16; 21:21, "pearls" are indicated in the apocalyptic visions of the apostle John.

PEN

OT WORDS

'ēt [**עֵט, 5842**]

'ēt is a term that occurs only a few times, meaning "pen." It is used literally in Ps. 45:8; Jer. 8:8 to refer to a writing implement. It refers metaphorically to a "pen of iron" inscribing words on lead in Job 19:24.

ḥeret [**חֶרֶט, 2747**]

ḥeret is found in only two contexts. In Exod. 32:4 it refers to an "engraving tool," and in Isa. 8:1 to a common pen for inscribing on a clay tablet.

NT WORDS

kalamos [κάλαμος, *2563*]

kalamos is a noun occurring twelve times, meaning "reed," or "rod" in all but one of these contexts. In 3 John 13, ***kalamos*** refers to an ordinary writing pen. (➠ REED)

PENCE, PENNY

NT WORDS

dēnarion [δηνάριον, *1220*]

The term ***dēnarion*** is of Latin origin and is translated "penny," "pence." It is more often transliterated as "denarius." It was the principal silver coin of the Roman Empire. ***dēnarion*** is found sixteen times, each time referring to literal currency (cf. Matt. 18:28; 20:2ff.; 22:19; Mark 6:37; 12:15; 14:5; Luke 7:41; 10:35; 20:24; John 6:7; 12:5; Rev. 6:6).

PENTECOST

NT WORDS

pentēkostē [πεντηκοστή, *4005*]

pentēkostē is transliterated "Pentecost" in reference to the "fiftieth day" after the Sabbath of the Passover week, or the "day of Pentecost." This is the Greek equivalent of the second of the three great annual Jewish festivals — the Feast of Weeks, or Harvest. ***pentēkostē*** occurs only three times, referring to the festival of Pentecost itself (1 Cor. 16:8) and to the day of Pentecost (Acts 2:1; 20:16).

PEOPLE

OT WORDS

'am [**עַם, 5971**]

'am is a common noun occurring about 1,800 times with the primary sense of "people." There are, however, a number of different nuances associated with the term.

'am frequently refers to "people" in the sense of "nation." ***'am*** refers to undesignated peoples of the earth (e.g., Gen. 11:6; Deut. 10:15; Josh. 4:24; Ezra 3:3; Pss. 2:1; 67:5; Isa. 43:9; Dan. 3:29). It also refers to specific people groups, including the Hittites (Gen. 23:7ff.); Egypt (Exod. 1:9; 8:4ff.); Philistia (Exod. 15:14); the people of Canaan (Ezra 4:4); Gomorrah (Isa. 1:10); Babylon (Jer. 50:41); and Nineveh (Jonah 3:5).

'am frequently refers to Israel as the people of God, in a number of different contexts. References to God's people as "his people" are found, for example, in Gen. 17:14; Exod. 18:1; Lev. 7:20; Deut. 32:9; Ezra 1:3; Ps. 78:20; Isa. 5:21; 11:16. "People" refers explicitly and implicitly to the Israelite nation in the contexts of both judgment and blessing (e.g., Gen. 48:4; Exod. 1:20; 12:33ff.; Lev. 4:3; Num. 11:1; Deut. 3:28; 1 Sam. 12:6; Ps. 68:7; Isa. 9:2; 30:6ff.; 65:3; Ezek. 3:5).

The phrase "people of Israel" is used, for instance, in Num. 21:6; Josh. 8:33; 2 Sam. 24:4; 1 Kgs. 16:21; Ezra 2:2; Neh. 7:7; Ezek. 36:8; Amos 8:2. ***'am*** refers to the "people of God" in Judg. 20:2; 2 Sam. 14:13. The expression "people of the Lord" is found in Num. 16:41; Deut. 27:9; Judg. 5:11; 2 Sam. 1:12; 2 Kgs. 9:6; Ezek. 36:20; Zeph. 2:10.

Most significant, in a theological sense, are the references to "my people," spoken by God in respect of Israel (cf. Exod. 3:7ff.; 7:4; 12:31; Ps. 81:8ff.; Isa. 1:3; 40:1; 53:8; Jer. 2:11; Ezek. 37:12; Amos 7:8; Zech. 8:7). In particular, the account of the deliverance of the Israelites from Egypt incorporates Yahweh's command to Pharaoh through Moses: "Let my people go . . ." (cf. Exod. 5:1; 7:16; 8:1, 20). In particular, this designation is associated with the covenantal identity of the people of Yahweh, expressing an intimate relationship (cf. Exod. 6:7; Lev. 26:12; 2 Sam. 7:10; 1 Kgs. 8:16; Isa. 53:8).

A special use of the expression "my people" is found in the context of the summary formula of the covenant, "I shall be your God and you shall be my people," or slight variations on that wording (cf. Jer. 7:23; 11:4; 24:7; 30:22; 31:33; 32:38; Ezek. 14:11; 36:28; 37:27). In Hos. 1:9ff. there is a "negation" of this formula, where Yahweh declares to Israel: "You are not my people . . ." in the context of divine judgment against them, an enacting of the covenant curse for violation of their covenant responsibilities towards God. Hos. 2:23 records the reversal of this negation in the context of a promised renewal of the covenant with Israel. One extraordinary instance of this usage is found in Isa. 19:25, where Yahweh says of Egypt "(you are) my people" — illustrating the promised new covenant blessing that will be extended to the nations at large beyond the borders of national Israel.

le'ôm [לְאוֹם, 3816]

The noun ***le'ôm*** is synonymous with ***'am*** (see above), meaning "people," or "nation." The term occurs thirty-five times.

In Gen. 35:23, the imminent birth of Jacob and Esau is described in terms of two "people" emerging (viz., Israel and Edom).

General references to "people(s)" or "nations" of the world are found in Gen. 27:29; Pss. 7:7; 44:2; 51:9; 108:3; Isa. 7:13; 60:2. In Ps. 2:1, the "peoples" of the world are said to oppose God; and in several other psalms the "nations" of the world are cited as the object of divine judgment (cf. Pss. 9:8; 47:3; 67:4; 149:7).

Isa. 51:4 refers to Yahweh speaking of Israel as "my people."

gôy [גּוֹי, 1471]

gôy refers to the "nations" of the world — the pagan Gentile nations. ***gôy*** is almost interchangeable with ***'am*** in this respect (see above). ***gôy*** also frequently refers to the "nation" of Israel and is likewise interchangeable with ***'am*** here. It is very difficult to distinguish between ***gôy*** and ***'am*** in terms of the meanings "people(s)" and "nation(s)." As a translation convention, the meaning "people" is far less common for the term ***gôy*** than for ***'am***. In a number of contexts, however, this meaning is discernible as a likely alternative to "nation."

gôy means "people," for instance, in relation to Israel journeying in the wilderness and crossing the Jordan River to occupy the land of Canaan and conquer its inhabitants (cf. Josh. 3:17; 4:1; 5:6, 8; 10:13; Judg. 2:20).

The Hebrew vocabulary for "people(s)" and "nation(s)" is, therefore, largely interchangeable.

NT Words

laos [λαός, *2992*]

laos is a noun occurring around 140 times, meaning "people." As with the equivalent Old Testament terminology, this meaning overlaps with that of "nation" in a number of places.

The meaning "people(s)" with the sense of "Gentiles," or "nation(s)," is indicated in Luke 2:31; Acts 4:21; Rev. 10:11; 11:19; 14:6; 17:15. Acts 15:14 refers to a "people" chosen from out of the Gentiles, for his name (i.e., God's name). See also Rev. 7:9.

The bulk of the usage of ***laos*** refers to the people of Israel, the people belonging to God. References to the people of Israel are found, for example, in Matt. 2:6; 15:8; Mark 7:6; Acts 4:8; 13:17; Rom. 10:21; Heb. 5:3; 7:27; Jude 5. John 18:14 records the significant statement of Caiaphas the high priest that it would be expedient if one man should die for the people (or nation). 1 Pet. 2:9, 10; Rev. 5:9 specifically allude to a people belonging to God. In a more general context, ***laos*** refers to people, focusing on the population of Jerusalem (cf. Matt. 2:4; 21:23; 26:5; 27:25; Luke 1:10, 21; Acts 5:20). Several texts indicate the meaning "people" in the sense of a crowd of Jewish citizens (cf. Luke 18:43; 20:9; Acts 3:11).

There are several significant references to "his people," indicating those who belong to Christ (cf. Matt. 1:21); and those who belong to God in the context of God redeeming his people from their sin (cf. Luke 1:68, 77; 7:16; Rom. 11:2). Also recorded in several places is the expression "my people," referring to those who belong to God — both Jew and Gentile (cf. Rom. 9:25; Rev. 18:4). In 2 Cor. 6:16; Heb. 8:10, these words are found in the context of the writers citing the old covenant formula: "I will be your God and you shall be my people." See also Rev. 21:3.

See Also: → CROWD → GENTILES → NATION

PERCEIVE → KNOW → UNDERSTAND

PERFECT

OT Words

tām **[תָּם, 8535]**

tām is an adjective meaning "blameless." It may also be translated "perfect," but not in the sense of one who is without sin. "Blamelessness" in Scripture is a quality predicated of those who manifest a godly character, moral integrity, or uprightness. In one or two instances, ***tām*** refers to that which is perceived as "perfect" in the sense of "flawless." ***tām*** is found thirteen times.

The attribute of being "perfect," in the sense of one who is morally upright is applied, for example, to Job in Job 1:1, 8; 2:3; 9:21. General references to those who are "blameless," "morally upright" are found in Job 8:20; 9:20, 22; Pss. 37:37; 64:4; Prov. 29:10. The man refers to his beloved partner in the Song of Songs as "perfect," or flawless in beauty (Song 5:2; 6:9).

shālēm **[שָׁלֵם, 8003]**

shālēm is an adjective derived from the verb ***shālam***, meaning "to be at peace," "to make whole," "complete," with the primary sense of "perfect" in the sense of "full," "whole," "complete," "true." ***shālēm*** is found in nearly thirty contexts.

shālēm refers to a "perfect" or "full" measure and weight in the context of a fair and accurate commercial transaction (cf. Deut. 25:15; Prov. 11:1).

shālēm more frequently means "perfect" in the sense of a heart that is "wholly true," or "blameless" in its devotion to the Lord (cf. 1 Kgs. 8:61; 11:4; 2 Kgs. 20:3; 1 Chr. 28:9; 29:9, 19; 2 Chr. 15:17; 16:9; Isa. 38:3).

tiklāh **[תִּכְלָה, 8502]**

tiklāh is a noun that is found only in Ps. 119:96, referring to the psalmist perceiving a limit to all "perfection" in contrast to the unlimited boundaries of God's commandments.

kālal **[כָּלַל, 3634]**

kālal is a rare verb found only in Ezek. 27:4, 11 (three times), meaning to "perfect" or "make perfect" the beauty of the city of Tyre.

kālîl **[כָּלִיל, 3632]**

kālîl is an adjective occurring fifteen times. In most of these contexts it is translated "whole," "complete." In four of these contexts, however, ***kālîl*** means "perfect." In Lam. 2:15, Jerusalem is referred to as the "perfection" of beauty. Ezek. 16:14 contains an allegorical description of Israel as the bride of Yahweh, whose beauty was "perfect" by means of the splendor that God had bestowed on her. The city of Tyre is likewise described as "perfect" in beauty in Ezek. 27:3, as is the spirit of the king of Tyre in Ezek. 28:12. (→ WHOLE)

miklal **[מִכְלַל, 4359]**

miklal is a participial noun form derived from ***kālal*** (see above) meaning "perfection." It is found only in Ps. 50:2, where it refers to Zion as the "perfection" of beauty.

NT Words

teleios **[τέλειος, *5046*]**

teleios is an adjective with the primary sense of "perfect" with a number of related nuances in the nineteen contexts in which it is found.

Matt. 5:48 contains a dramatic command emphasizing the necessity for the believer to emulate divine perfection through cultivating consummate human integrity and virtue.

Matt. 19:21 contains Jesus' command to the rich young ruler to sell all his possessions to the poor if he wants to become "perfect," to align himself in total conformity with God's will.

In Rom. 12:2, Paul describes the will of God as perfect, lacking in nothing.

More commonly, ***teleios*** describes as "perfect" those who manifest a "mature Christian character" (cf. 1 Cor. 2:6; 14:20; Eph. 4:13; Phil. 3:15; Col. 1:28; Heb. 5:14; Jas. 1:4; 3:2).

Finally, the ascription "perfect" is applied to that which is flawless or complete in its expression or construction. This is predicated of the heavenly tabernacle (Heb. 9:11; 1 Cor. 13:10); of every gift from God (Jas. 1:17); and of the law of God (Jas. 1:25). And, in 1 John 4:18, the apostle declares that "perfect love casts out fear."

teleioō **[τελειόω, *5048*]**

teleioō is a verb with the primary meaning "to make perfect," with the senses of "complete," "accomplish," "fulfill."

In John 17:23, Jesus prays that his followers may be brought to "complete" or "perfect" unity. The apostle Paul affirms in 2 Cor. 12:9 that power is "made perfect" in weakness. Heb. 10:14; 11:40; 12:23 refer to the perfecting of the saints through the redemptive work of Christ. Jas. 2:22 refers to the perfecting, or completion, of faith. The work of perfecting love in the life of the believer is noted in 1 John 2:5; 4:12ff. The possibility of attaining to moral perfection is denied in the earthly state in Phil. 3:12. The law is declared powerless to make anyone perfect in Heb. 7:19; 9:9; 10:1. Finally, several texts affirm that Christ has been made perfect through his suffering on behalf of his people (cf. Heb. 2:10; 5:9; 7:28).

katartizō [καταρτίζω, *2675*]

katartizō is a verb that is translated "restore," "mend," "repair," as well as "perfect," "make perfect." The term occurs fifteen times. (→ RESTORE)

katartizō is used adverbially in 1 Cor. 1:10 in the expression "perfectly joined together," referring to Paul's exhortation to the Corinthian congregation to manifest a greater unity of spirit. 2 Cor. 13:11 contains another exhortation to the church at Corinth to "aim for perfection."

holoklēria [ὁλοκληρία, *3647*]

holoklēria is a noun found only in Acts 3:16, referring to the "perfect health" of a crippled man, cured of his affliction through the apostolic healing ministry of Peter and John.

teleiotēs [τελειότης, *5047*]

teleiotēs is a rare noun derived from ***teleioō*** (see above) meaning "perfection." It is found only in Col. 3:14, with reference to the "perfect harmony" among believers, and in Heb. 6:1 referring to the state of "spiritual maturity."

teleiōsis [τελείωσις, *5050*]

teleiōsis is another rare noun derived from ***teleioō*** (see above), also meaning "perfection" in two places. In Luke 1:45, ***teleiōsis*** refers to a "fulfillment" of divine prophecy, literally a "perfecting" of what was spoken from the Lord. Heb. 7:11 refers to the impossibility of gaining spiritual or moral perfection through the ministry of the Levitical priesthood.

akribēs [ἀκριβής, *197*]

akribēs is an adverb found only four times. In Acts 18:26 it refers to the ministry of Aquila and Priscilla, who explained the way of God "more accurately" to Apollos. See also Acts 23:15, 20; 24:22.

See Also: → BLEMISH → COMPLETE

PERFUME

OT Words

nûph **[נוּף, 5130]**

The verb ***nûph*** is translated "wave," "lift up," along with a number of associated meanings. In one text, however, ***nûph*** refers to perfuming one's bed with fragrant spices associated with love-making (cf. Prov. 7:17).

qāṭar **[קָטַר, 6999]**

qāṭar is a verb that is usually translated "burn incense," "offer incense." It occurs nearly 120 times with these meanings. However, Song 3:6 contains a participial usage of ***qāṭar*** with reference to a column of smoke "perfumed" with myrrh.

riqqûaḥ **[רִקּוּחַ, 7547]**

riqqûaḥ occurs only in Isa. 57:9 with reference to "perfume" in a general sense.

See Also: → INCENSE

PERISH

OT Words

'ābad **[אָבַד, 6]**

'ābad is a common verb occurring around two hundred times with the dominant meanings "perish," "destroy." The latter meaning is actually a "causative" sense derived from the former (i.e., "to cause to perish"). (→ DESTROY)

The literal sense of "perish" or "die" is indicated in a number of different contexts. It is first of all predicated of God's people under divine judgment for rebellion against him, under the covenant curse. In particular, it constitutes the inevitable fate of the Israelite people, who will perish in the process of being sent into exile (cf. Lev. 26:38; Deut. 4:26; 8:20; 30:18; Josh. 23:13; Jer. 4:9; 27:10; Ezek. 25:7). The people will also perish on account of their idolatry (cf. Deut. 8:19; Josh. 23:16).

Individuals or groups of people are also said to "perish" at the hand of God — that is, they are executed by him. These include Korah and his family (Num. 16:33); Ahab's dynasty (2 Kgs. 9:8). See also Ps. 2:12; Jer. 6:21; Mic. 4:9; Jonah 3:9. Num. 17:2 expresses the fear of perishing. The enemies of Yahweh are said to perish as a consequence of judgment pronounced on them (cf. Num. 21:30; Judg. 5:31; Pss. 9:3, 6; 37:20; Isa. 41:11; Jer. 51:18 [Babylon]; Amos 1:8 [Philistia]).

General references to people dying or perishing are found in Job 4:7; Ps. 49:10; Prov. 31:6; Jonah 1:6. Such a fate includes the wicked (cf. Pss. 1:6; 37:20; 83:17; Prov. 28:28; Jer. 48:8); as well as the righteous (cf. Eccl. 7:15; Isa. 57:1; Mic. 7:2). Job 4:11 refers to animals perishing.

In Esth. 4:16, Queen Esther expresses a resignation over her fate (presumably at the hand of God, though this is not made explicit). She declares: "If I perish, I perish . . ." before daring to go unbidden to the king of Persia to plead for mercy for her people in the face of the royal edict to destroy the Jews throughout the kingdom.

'ābad also refers to that which is "ruined." This is said of the land of Israel in Jer. 9:12 (cf. also Joel 1:11; Amos 3:15; Jonah 4:10).

'ābad is also used metaphorically in several places. For example, Job utters a curse in Job 3:3, where he expresses a desire to have the day of his birth "perish." Similarly, the meaning "perish" expresses the sense of "disappear" with reference to the wisdom of the wise (Isa. 29:14; Jer. 49:7); to the law of God (Jer. 18:8; Ezek. 7:26); and to truth (Jer. 7:26). See also Amos 2:14.

The Hebrew term ***'ābad*** is identical to the Aramaic form, which refers to pagan deities perishing (Jer. 10:11), and to the threatened demise of Daniel and his friends (Dan. 2:18).

kārat [כָּרַת, 3772]

kārat is a verb with the primary sense of "cut," as well as several other nuances. It occurs around three hundred times. In Gen. 41:36, however, it is used metaphorically to refer to the land of Egypt being kept from "perishing" through storing food.

nāphal [נָפַל, 5307]

nāphal is a common verb occurring about 430 times with the primary meaning "to fall," along with a number of derived senses. However, in Exod. 19:21 ***nāphal*** refers to the threatened fate of the Israelite people "perishing" if they trespassed onto the sacred ground of Mt. Sinai, cordoned off by divine command.

sāphāh [סָפָה, 5595]

The verb ***sāphāh*** means "destroy," "consume," "perish" in approximately half of the twenty occurrences in which it is found. The meaning "perish" is found only in 1 Sam. 26:10; 27:1, where it refers to individuals perishing in battle, or by the hand of another.

dāmāh [דָּמָה, 1820]

dāmāh is a verb with a variety of meanings associated with the senses of "destroy," "perish," in the context of being brought to a final end. ***dāmāh*** occurs sixteen times.

The specific sense of "perish" refers to the death of beasts (Ps. 49:12, 20); to the destruction of Ashkelon (Jer. 47:5); to the king of Samaria (Hos. 10:7); and to the final end of the king of Israel (Hos. 10:15). See also Obad 1:5; Zeph. 1:11.

NT Words

apollymi [ἀπόλλυμι, *622*]

apollymi is a dynamic equivalent for the Hebrew verb ***'ābad*** (see above) with the primary meanings "perish," "destroy," or "lose" in the majority of the ninety or so contexts in which it is found. As with ***'ābad***, the meaning, "destroy" for ***apollymi*** is causative in force with the literal sense of "to cause to perish."
(→ DESTROY → LOSE)

apollymi refers to the body "perishing" (Matt. 5:29, 30); and to people in general (Matt. 8:25; 26:52; Mark 4:38; Luke 13:5; Acts 5:37; Rom. 2:12; 1 Cor. 1:18; 2 Cor. 2:15). In particular, the godless are said to perish in 2 Cor. 4:3; 2 Thess. 2:10; Jude 11, as are the people of God in 1 Cor. 15:18. This fate is predicated of individuals in Luke 11:51; 13:33; 15:17. In several contexts, there are declarations that people are to be spared from spiritual death — they will not perish by virtue of their faith and trust in God and his son (cf. John 3:15, 16; 10:28; 11:50). In 2 Pet. 3:9, the writer reveals God's desire that none should perish but that all should come to repentance.

apollymi is also used impersonally to refer to those things that "perish" or "will perish," in the sense of "being ruined" — including wineskins (Matt. 9:17; Mark 2:22; Luke 5:37); food (John 6:27); gold (1 Pet. 1:17); the beauty of flowers (Jas. 1:11); and heaven and earth (Heb. 1:11; 2 Pet. 3:6).

aphanizō [ἀφανίζω, *853*]

aphanizō is a rare verb found in only five places. It is translated variously as "destroy," "disfigure," "vanish" and once, in Acts 13:41, as "perish." The underlying sense of the term is "to bring about a state of decay," both literal and metaphorical, resulting in either disappearance or destruction.

synapollymi [συναπόλλυμι, *4881*]

synapollymi is found only in Heb. 11:31 and is used negatively, referring to sparing Rahab the harlot's life, for she "did not perish" along with the other citizens of Jericho on account of her faith and trust in Yahweh.

See Also: → CORRUPTION → DIE

PERMIT

NT Words

epitrepō [ἐπιτρέπω, *2010*]

epitrepō is a verb that is variously translated as "let," "allow," "give leave," "permit" — although all of these meanings are virtually interchangeable. ***epitrepō*** occurs nineteen times.

The concept of "permitting" occurs first of all in the context of requesting permission to do something. In Matt. 8:21; Luke 9:57, people ask permission of Jesus to bury their dead before becoming his disciples. Similarly, in Luke 9:61, potential disciples ask permission to say farewell to their families.

More frequently, ***epitrepō*** indicates the action of allowing a certain event, or transaction, to take place. Matt. 19:8; Mark 10:4 refer to Moses allowing divorce to take place in the old covenant era. Mark 5:13; Luke 8:32 relate the incident in which Jesus permitted the evil spirits that had formerly possessed the man to enter a herd of pigs. In John 19:38, Pilate gives permission for Joseph of Arimathea to remove the body of Jesus from the cross. Acts 21:39 refers to Paul's request to be allowed to speak to the Jerusalem crowd (cf. also Acts 26:1; 27:3; 28:16). In 1 Cor. 14:34, Paul refuses to give women permission to speak in church (cf. also 1 Tim. 2:12).

Finally, 1 Cor. 16:7; Heb. 6:3 contain the formulaic expression "If God permits . . . ," or "God willing . . ."

PERSECUTE

OT Words

rādaph [רָדַף, **7291**]

rādaph is a verb found in approximately 140 contexts with the predominant meanings "pursue," "follow," "chase," "persecute." The latter sense of "persecute" is found in about twenty places, although in some of these contexts the meanings "pursue" and "persecute" overlap.

"Persecuting," in the sense of "harass" or "treat cruelly," is found in general contexts such as Job 19:28; Pss. 69:26; 119:161. Deut. 30:7 speaks of the enemies of Israel, who have treated the people of God cruelly. Jer. 15:15; 17:18 refer to the prophet Jeremiah's "persecutors," his fellow citizens in Jerusalem.

The dual sense of "persecute" and "pursue" is evident in the following contexts, where it is very difficult to make a sharp distinction between these two meanings. The psalmist often speaks of his enemies who either "pursue" or "persecute" him — or both (cf. Pss. 31:15; 35:3; 119:84, 86, 150, 157; 142:6; 143:3). Similarly, Lam. 4:19; 5:5 speak of the enemies of God's people, who are treated shamefully and/or pursued relentlessly by the invading Babylonian armies.

murdāph [מֻרְדָּף, **4783**]

murdāph is found only in Isa. 14:6, referring to the relentless "persecution" inflicted on the nations by the kingdom of Babylon.

NT Words

diōkō [διώκω, *1377*]

diōkō is a verb found in around fifty contexts meaning "persecute," "follow," or "pursue." While ***diōkō*** is therefore a clear dynamic equivalent for ***rādaph*** (see above), there is one distinctive difference. Whereas ***rādaph*** demonstrates a significant overlap in meaning between "persecute" and "pursue," there is no such blurring of these meanings in the use of ***diōkō***, with the possible exception of Rev. 12:13. In other words, ***diōkō*** clearly and unambiguously refers to "persecution." (→ FOLLOW)

General references to persecution are found in Matt. 23:34; Gal. 4:29; 6:12. In several places persecution is viewed as a blessing, since it will result in true believers gaining possession of the kingdom of heaven (cf. Matt. 5:10, 44; 23:34; Luke 21:12). Rom. 12:14 exhorts believers to bless those who persecute them. The reality of persecution for the followers of Jesus Christ is indicated in Matt. 10:23; John 15:20; 1 Cor. 4:12; 2 Cor. 4:9; Gal. 5:11; 2 Tim. 3:12. Acts 7:52 speaks of the persecution of Yahweh's prophets by the Israelites of old. Paul refers to his persecution of the first generation of Christians following the resurrection of Christ, prior to his own conversion (cf. Acts 22:4; 26:11; 1 Cor. 15:9; Gal. 1:13, 23; Phil. 3:6).

Jesus himself was persecuted by his fellow countrymen, as recorded in John 5:16. In the divine revelation to Saul (later Paul) at his conversion experience, the risen Christ declares that the zealous Pharisee was in fact persecuting him through the harassment of the Christian community (cf. Acts 9:4, 5; 22:7, 8; 26:14, 15).

ekdiōkō [ἐκδιώκω, *1559*]

ekdiōkō is a rare verb, found only twice and meaning to "persecute" in Luke 11:49, and to "drive out," or "banish" in 1 Thess. 2:15.

diōgmos [διωγμός, *1375*]

diōgmos is a noun derived from ***diōkō*** (see above), occurring only in Matt. 13:21 and referring to "persecution" that comes upon a new "convert," causing him to fall away from the faith.

diōktēs [διώκτης, *1376*]

diōktēs is another noun derived from ***diōkō*** (see above) found only in 1 Tim. 1:13, where Paul admits that he was once a "persecutor."

See Also: → TRIBULATION

PERSEVERE → ENDURE → SUFFER

PERSON

OT Words

nephesh [נֶפֶשׁ, **5315**]

nephesh is a term with a broad semantic range and is virtually untranslatable in English by any one word. ***nephesh*** conveys the unity of a human being as a single, indivisible entity, combining both physical and spiritual qualities in a being created in the image of God. It also refers to non-human creatures. ***nephesh*** occurs over 750 times, meaning "person" in around twenty contexts. (→ FLESH → LIFE → MIND → SOUL)

The meaning "person" in the sense of an individual human being is found in Num. 5:6, with reference to a man found guilty of unfaithfulness to the Lord. ***nephesh*** is also found in the plural and refers to "people" in general in a number of places (e.g., Gen. 14:21; Exod. 16:16; Num. 31:28; 35ff.; Deut. 10:22; Jer. 52:29; Jonah 4:11).

nephesh is also translated "anyone" with reference to persons, interestingly, whose lives have been lost. Num. 31:19; 35:11, 15; Josh. 20:3, 9 refer to persons who have been accidentally slain. Num. 35:30; Deut. 27:25; Prov. 28:17 refer to those who have been murdered. Ezek. 33:6 speaks of anyone who has been slain by the sword.

pānîm [פָּנִים, **6440**]

pānîm is a common plural noun form found in approximately 2,100 contexts with the primary meaning "face" in a significant number of contexts. The meaning "face," especially when used anthropomorphically of the divine being, is a synonym for the "person" of God. (→ FACE)

NT Words

prosōpon [πρόσωπον, *4383*]

prosōpon is a noun found in nearly eighty contexts with the primary sense of "face." However, as with the corresponding Hebrew term ***pānîm*** (see above), it occasionally refers to "the face" of God, or the "person" of God (cf. Matt. 18:10; Luke 1:76; 1 Pet. 3:12; Rev. 6:16; 22:14). ***prosōpon*** also refers to "the presence" (i.e., the person) of God in several places (cf. Acts 2:28; 3:19; 2 Thess. 1:9).

Additional Notes

In addition to the terms listed above, there is often no separate term in Hebrew or Greek for "person," which is often associated with the immediately preceding adjective or participial form.

See Also: → MAN

PERSUADE

OT Words

pātāh [פָּתָה, **6601**]

pātāh is a verb with the primary meanings "entice," "deceive" in the majority of the 320 or so contexts in which the term is found. In Prov. 25:15, however, ***pātāh*** is translated "persuade."

NT Words

peithō [πείθω, *3982*]

peithō is a verb meaning "persuade" in about half of the approximately sixty occurrences in which it is found. (→ TRUST)

The meaning "persuade" indicates, first of all, the sense of inducing someone to change his or her course of action or way of thinking (cf. Matt. 27:20; Acts 14:19; 21:14).

peithō is also used passively in the sense of "being persuaded," or "being convinced" (cf. Luke 16:31; 20:6; Acts 18:4; 26:26; Rom. 8:38; 14:14; 15:14; 2 Tim. 1:5, 12; Heb. 6:9). In Acts 17:4, this passive usage refers to those who come to faith, or who believe. The active sense of "persuading" or "convincing" occurs in Acts 26:28, likewise with reference to coming to faith. Acts 19:8, 26; 28:23; 2 Cor. 5:11 express the active sense of "persuade," referring to the process of convincing people through reasoned debate.

In Acts 13:43, ***peithō*** means "persuade" in the sense of "urge," or an attempted persuasion.

plērophoreō [πληροφορέω, *4135*]

plērophoreō is a verb with the underlying sense of making something fully known — by a process of reasoning, persuasion, or proclamation. ***plērophoreō*** occurs only six times and is translated "to be fully persuaded, or convinced" in two of these contexts. Rom. 4:21 speaks of being fully convinced of God's promises, and Rom. 14:5 refers to being fully persuaded in one's own mind.

anapeithō [ἀναπείθω, *374*]

anapeithō is a derivative verb from ***peithō*** (see above) and is likewise translated "persuade." It is found in Acts 18:13.

peismonē [πεισμονή, *3988*]

peismonē is a noun derived, presumably, from ***peithō*** (see above). It means "persuasion" and occurs only in Gal. 5:8, with reference to a negative enticement to abandon one's faith in Christ alone.

See Also: → ENTICE

PERVERSE, PERVERT

OT Words

'āwāh [**עָוָה, 5753**]

'āwāh is a verb with the fundamental senses of "twist," "distort," "pervert," primarily in the context of committing sin, or doing wrong. ***'āwāh*** is found in seventeen contexts.

The meaning "pervert," in the specific sense of distorting that which is just and right, is found in Job 33:27. And, in Jer. 3:21, the reference is to the people of Judah living a corrupt lifestyle. Prov. 12:8; 1 Sam. 20:30 refer to those who are "perverse," or morally corrupt.

'āqash [**עָקַשׁ, 6140**]

'āqash is a synonym for ***'āwāh***, above. The term occurs five times and is used both verbally and adjectivally, meaning "to pervert" and "perverse," respectively. The contexts all refer to moral corruption or immorality (cf. Job 9:20; Prov. 10:9; 28:18; Isa. 59:8; Mic. 3:9).

'āwat [**עָוַת, 5791**]

'āwat means "pervert," "falsify," or "corrupt" in the majority of the eleven contexts in which it is found.

Job 8:3; 34:12 speak, implicitly and explicitly, of the impossibility of God perverting or corrupting what is right.

Several contexts express the meaning "pervert" in the sense of "dealing deceitfully with" (cf. Ps. 119:78; Lam. 3:36; Amos 8:5).

In Eccl. 1:15, ***'āwat*** is used as an adjective with the sense of "perverse," or "morally corrupt."

lûz [**לוּז, 3868**]

lûz is a verb found in only six places, expressing in its participial form the adjectival meaning "perverse" in the sense of devious, or morally corrupt (cf. Prov. 2:15; 3:32; 14:2). In Isa. 30:12 ***lûz*** is used as a noun, referring to the "perversity" of humankind.

tahpûkāh [**תַּהְפּוּכָה, 8419**]

tahpûkāh is a term used both adjectivally and nominally to refer to people whose lifestyle is perverse, or morally corrupt. ***tahpûkāh*** occurs ten times (cf. Deut. 32:20; Prov. 2:12, 14; 6:14; 8:13; 10:31, 32; 16:28, 30; 23:33).

nāṭāh [**נָטָה, 5186**]

nāṭāh is a common verb with the primary meanings "stretch (out)," "turn," as well as a number of associated nuances. In Prov. 17:23, however, it refers to a wicked man "perverting" the course of justice.

NT Words

diastrephō [διαστρέφω, *1294*]

diastrephō is a verb expressing the primary meaning "pervert," as well as the adjectival sense of "perverse," or "morally corrupt," "crooked" in its participial form. It is found in seven places.

Acts 13:10 records Paul's accusation against Elymas, the Jewish sorcerer — that he perverted the straight paths of the Lord. The remaining usage of ***diastrephō*** is adjectival, referring to those who are morally corrupt, or perverse (cf. Matt. 17:17; Luke 9:41; Acts 20:30; Phil. 2:15). See also Luke 23:2; Acts 13:8.

metastrephō [μεταστρέφω, *3344*]

metastrephō is a verb found in only three places. In two of these, the meaning is "turn (around)"; and in Gal. 1:7 it refers to those who "pervert" the gospel of Christ. The underlying sense is that these people seek to "overturn," the gospel so as to place it on a different foundation than that intended by God.

See Also: → CROOKED

PETITION → ASK → REQUEST

PHILOSOPHER, PHILOSOPHY

NT Words

syzētētēs [συζητητής, *4804*]

syzētētēs is found only in 1 Cor. 1:20 and refers to a learned man trained in the art of sophistry, or eloquent persuasive argument.

philosophos [φιλόσοφος, *5386*]

philosophos is found only in Acts 17:18 with reference to the philosophers among the Epicureans — scholars who formed part of the audience at the Areopagus listening to the apostle Paul.

philosophia [φιλοσοφία, *5385*]

philosophia refers literally to the "love of wisdom." The term occurs only in Col. 2:8, referring to the system of human knowledge that is opposed to the knowledge and wisdom of God.

PHYSICIAN

OT Words

rāphā' [**רָפָא, 7495**]

rāphā' is a verb with the predominant meaning "heal" in most of its seventy or so occurrences. In several of these texts, ***rāphā'*** has the nominal sense of "physician" (cf. Jer. 8:22; Gen. 50:2; 2 Chr. 16:12; Job 13:4).

NT Words

iatros [ἰατρός, *2395*]

iatros is the sole term for "physician" in the New Testament. It is found seven times (cf. Matt. 9:12; Mark 2:17; 5:26; Luke 4:23; 5:31; 8:43; Col. 4:14).

PIECE

OT Words

beter [**בֶּתֶר, 1335**]

beter refers to "part(s)" or "piece(s)" of an animal being prepared for sacrifice (cf. Gen. 15:10; Jer. 34:18, 19).

'agôrāh [**אֲגוֹרָה, 95**]

'agôrah is found only in 1 Sam. 2:36, referring to a "piece" of silver.

pelaḥ [**פֶּלַח, 6400**]

pelaḥ refers to a "portion," "part," or "piece" that is cut or sliced from a larger object. ***pelaḥ*** is found in six contexts, referring to a portion of millstone (Judg. 9:53; 2 Sam. 11:21; Job 41:24); to pieces of a pomegranate (Song 4:3; 6:7); and to a piece of cake (1 Sam. 30:12).

qesîtāh [**קְשִׂיטָה, 7192**]

qesîtāh is a term indicating a "piece of money," or "piece of silver," with an unknown value. It is found in three places (cf. Gen. 33:19; Josh. 24:32; Job 42:11).

pat [**פַּת, 6595**]

pat is a general term referring to "piece(s)" of food, bread, or sacrificial animals. It is found in fifteen places (cf. Gen. 18:5; Lev. 2:6; 6:21; Judg. 19:5; Ruth 2:14; 1 Sam. 2:36; 28:22; 2 Sam. 12:3; 1 Kgs. 17:11; Job 31:17; Prov. 17:1; Ps. 147:17; Prov. 23:8; 28:21; Ezek. 13:19).

nētaḥ [**נֵתַח, 5409**]

nētaḥ occurs thirteen times and is a general term for "piece," referring to portions of sacrificial animals (Exod. 29:17; Lev. 1:6ff.; 8:20; Ezek. 24:4). It is used metaphorically in Ezek. 24:6 to refer to Yahweh's punishment of his people, spoken of in terms of a pot of food to be emptied "piece" by "piece." Judg. 19:29 refers to a human body being cut into pieces.

bādāl [**בָּדָל, 915**]

bādāl is found only in Amos 3:12, indicating a severed "piece" of an ear of a slain animal.

gezer [**גֶּזֶר, 1506**]

gezer is found in only two contexts. In Gen. 15:17 it refers to "pieces" of the animal carcasses laid out by Abraham prior to a revelation from Yahweh. Ps. 136:13 refers to Yahweh dividing the Re(e)d Sea into two "parts" to effect the deliverance of his people from the pursuing Egyptian army.

NT Words

epiblēma [ἐπίβλημα, *1915*]

epiblēma refers to a "piece" of cloth used as a patch sewn on to cover a tear. The term is found four times (cf. Matt. 9:16; Mark 2:21; Luke 5:36).

See Also: → BREAK → CUT → DASH → MEASURE → PART → SILVER → TEAR

PIERCE

OT Words

māḥaṣ [מָחַץ, 4272]

māḥaṣ is a verb with the underlying sense of "wound." It occurs fourteen times and expresses the specific sense of "pierce (through)" in a couple of contexts. (→ WOUND)

The action of piercing one's enemies through with "arrows" is indicated in Num. 24:8. Judg. 5:26 describes the assassination of Sisera, the Canaanite general. Jael slays him with a tent peg, piercing his temple while he lay asleep.

nāqab [נָקַב, 5344]

nāqab is a verb found in twenty-five contexts with several meanings, including "to pierce," "bore," "strike through." ***nāqab*** reflects this latter sense in four places. (→ BLASPHEME)

In 2 Kgs. 18:21; Isa. 36:6, ***nāqab*** refers metaphorically to the nation of Egypt as a "broken reed . . . which will pierce the hand" of those who may lean upon it. See also Hab. 3:14; Job 40:24 for more literal uses of the term.

kārāh [כָּרָה, 3738]

kārāh is a verb meaning "dig" in most of the sixteen occurrences in which it is found. (→ DIG) In Ps. 22:16, however, ***kārāh*** is translated "pierce," with reference to boring the writer's hands and feet — a symbolic anticipation of the future suffering of Christ on the cross.

dāqar [דָּקַר, 1856]

dāqar is consistently translated "thrust through," "strike," or "pierce through" in the context of being fatally wounded in battle. This is the most common meaning of ***dāqar*** in the eleven contexts in which it occurs (cf. Num. 25:8; Judg. 9:54; 1 Sam. 31:4; Isa. 13:15; Zech. 13:3). Jer. 37:10; 51:4 retain the general meaning "wounded." In Lam. 4:9, ***dāqar*** is used metaphorically to refer to the inhabitants of Jerusalem being "struck down" with hunger. Zech. 12:10 refers to the inhabitants of Jerusalem gazing "on the one they have pierced" in solemn repentance for their actions — a prophetic anticipation of Christ's crucifixion.

NT Words

dierchomai [διέρχομαι, *1330*]

dierchomai is commonly translated "to go, pass, walk through" in the forty or so contexts in which it occurs. In Luke 2:35, however, it is translated "pierce" — referring to the sorrow that will come upon Mary the mother of Jesus. Simeon foretells here that a sword will pierce Mary's heart, anticipating the agony of her son's suffering.

nyssō [νύσσω, *3572*]

nyssō is found only in John 19:34, referring to the Roman soldiers "piercing" the body of Jesus on his side as he hung on the cross.

ekkenteō [ἐκκεντέω, *1574*]

ekkenteō is found only in John 19:37; Rev. 1:7. The term is a synonym for ***nyssō*** (see above) and refers in each text to "piercing" Christ on the cross.

peripeirō [περιπείρω, *4044*]

peripeirō is another rare verb meaning "pierce through" in the context of torturing oneself with many sorrows. This describes those who have wandered from the faith, who "have pierced themselves with many sorrows."

diikneomai [διϊκνέομαι, *1338*]

diikneomai is used metaphorically in Heb. 4:12 to refer to the word of God as a two-edged sword that "pierces" deep into the soul and spirit of a person.

See Also: → DRIVE

PIETY → DEVOUT → GOOD → RIGHTEOUS

PILGRIM → SOJOURN

PILLAR

OT Words

'ammûd [עַמּוּד, 5982]

'ammûd is a term that is consistently translated "pillar," or "column," in all of its 110 occurrences. It refers to various kinds of "pillars" and "columns," both literal and metaphorical.

Of considerable theological significance are the references to the "pillar" of cloud and fire, containing the sacred presence of Yahweh, which guided the people of Israel through the wilderness to the promised land (cf. Exod. 13:2ff.; 14:19, 24; Num. 14:14; Neh. 9:12, 19; Ps. 99:7). The pillar of cloud signified the presence of God in the tabernacle (cf. Exod. 33:9ff.; Num. 12:5; Deut. 31:15). Though the term "pillar" is not linked with the "glory cloud" associated with the temple, these two phenomena (i.e., "pillar of cloud" and "glory cloud") are in fact identical. All of these texts refer to the very person and presence of Yahweh. (→ CLOUD)

In another, more literal, context, *'ammûd* refers to "pillars" that constituted the supporting framework of both the tabernacle (cf. Exod. 26:32; 27:10ff.; 36:36ff.; 38:10ff.; Num. 3:36ff.); and the temple (cf. 1 Kgs. 7:2ff.; 2 Chr. 3:16ff.; 4:12ff.; Ezek. 40:49; 42:6).

In more mundane contexts, *'ammûd* refers to the pillars of the Philistine temple in Judg. 16:25ff. Other general uses of the term include those in Judg. 20:40; 2 Kgs. 23:3; Esth. 1:6.

'ammûd is also used metaphorically to refer, for example, to the "pillars" of the earth (Job 9:6; Ps. 75:3); to the "pillars" of heaven (Job 26:11); and to the "pillars" of the house built by Wisdom (Prov. 9:1). See also Song 5:15.

maṣēbāh **[מַצֵּבָה, 4676]**

maṣēbāh means "pillar," primarily in the sense of a memorial stone, for pagan idols. It is found in approximately thirty contexts.

maṣēbāh refers to a stone monument commemorating a sacred place of divine revelation, such as Yahweh's dream given to Jacob at Bethel (cf. Gen. 28:18, 22; 31:13; 35:14). Isa. 19:19 also refers to a memorial pillar set up on the border of Egypt, commemorating Yahweh's deliverance of the Israelite people from Egypt. A pillar also serves as a memorial stone at the tomb of Rachel, set up by her husband Jacob (cf. Gen. 35:20). Pillars serving as covenant memorials are noted in Gen. 31:45ff. with respect to Jacob and Laban. See also Exod. 24:4.

More commonly, ***maṣēbāh*** refers to pillars as pagan shrines or images, which Yahweh forbids Israel either to build or worship (cf. Exod. 23:24; 34:13; Lev. 26:1; Deut. 7:5; 1 Kgs. 14:23; Jer. 43:13; Hos. 3:4; 10:12; Mic. 5:13).

muṣṣāb **[מֻצָּב, 4674]**

muṣṣāb is a participial noun form derived from the verb ***nāṣab*** ("to stand," "set up," "erect"), meaning "pillar" in Judg. 9:6. This is the sole occurrence of the term, and it probably refers to a pagan shrine, located at the city of Shechem.

tîmārāh **[תִּימָרָה, 8490]**

tîmārāh occurs only in Song 3:6; Joel 3:20, with reference to "pillars, or columns" of smoke.

NT Words

stylos [στῦλος, *4769*]

stylos is a term found in only four places, referring metaphorically in each case to a "pillar." Gal. 2:9 refers to Peter, James, and John as reputed "pillars" of the church. 1 Tim. 3:15 describes the church of God as the "pillar" of the truth. Rev. 3:12 declares that the faithful believer will be constituted by the living Christ as a "pillar" in God's temple. In Rev. 10:1, the legs of a powerful angel are likened to "pillars" of fire.

PILLOW

OT Words

kebîr **[כְּבִיר, 3523]**

kebîr is a noun found only in 1 Sam. 19:13, 16, referring on each occasion to a "pillow" of goat's hair.

mera'shāh **[מְרַאֲשָׁה, 4763]**

This term occurs eight times, with the meaning "pillow" as a bolster for one's head in Gen. 28:11; 1 Sam. 19:13, 16; 26:7ff.

NT Words

proskephalaion [προσκεφάλαιον, *4344*]

proskephalaion is only found in Mark 4:38, referring to a "pillow" used by Jesus in the fishing boat belonging to his disciples.

PINNACLE

NT Words

pterygion [πτερύγιον, *4419*]

pterygion is a term found only in Matt. 4:5; Luke 4:9. In each place it refers to the "pinnacle" of the Jerusalem temple, meaning the top of the building. It is here that Satan took Jesus during his period of trial and temptation prior to the commencement of his public ministry.

PIPE

OT Words

ḥālîl **[חָלִיל, 2485]**

ḥālîl is a noun meaning "pipe," or "flute," used solely in the context of musical accompaniment in only six places. The pipe is used by God's people in musical celebration (1 Kgs. 1:40; Isa. 5:12; Isa. 30:29); as part of a funeral procession (Jer. 48:36); and to accompany a band of prophets (1 Sam. 10:5).

ḥālal [חָלַל, **2490**]

ḥālal is a fairly common verb with a broad semantic range, with the primary meanings "begin," "desecrate," "pollute." However, in 1 Kgs. 1:40 ***ḥālal*** refers to the people of Jerusalem celebrating the declaration of Solomon as king by "playing the flute." (→ BEGIN → DEFILE)

ṣantār [צַנְתָּר, **6804**]

ṣantār occurs only in the plural, and only in Zech. 4:12. It refers to the "pipes" of the golden lampstand that supply oil to the lamps themselves.

NT Words

aulos [αὐλός, *836*]

aulos refers to the "pipe" or "flute." It is found only in 1 Cor. 14:7.

auleō [αὐλέω, *832*]

auleō is the verb from which ***aulos*** (see above) is derived. It occurs only three times and means "to play the pipe, flute" (cf. Matt. 11:17; Luke 7:32; 1 Cor. 14:7).

aulētēs [αὐλητής, *834*]

aulētēs is translated "flute player" and is found only in Matt. 9:23; Rev. 18:22.

PIT

OT Words

bôr [בּוֹר, **953**]

bôr refers primarily to "pit," with the extended meanings "well," "dungeon." ***bôr*** occurs about seventy times.

References to "pit" as a well or cistern are found in Lev. 11:36; Deut. 6:11; 1 Sam. 13:6; 2 Sam. 23:15ff.; 2 Kgs. 18:13; Neh. 9:25; Prov. 5:15; Eccl. 12:6; Isa. 36:16; Jer. 6:7. ***bôr*** is also found in Jer. 38:6ff. with this meaning as a place of confinement for the prophet Jeremiah. In addition, ***bôr*** specifically indicates a "dungeon" or "prison" in Gen. 40:15; Exod. 12:29; Isa. 24:22; Jer. 37:16.

bôr also refers to a "pit" as a hole in the ground, built as a trap for wild animals (cf. Exod. 21:33ff.; 1 Chr. 11:22; Ps. 7:15). This may also be the kind of "pit" into which Joseph was cast by his brothers in Gen. 37:20ff.

bôr is also used as a metaphor for the grave (cf. Pss. 28:1; 30:3; 143:7; Prov. 1:12; 28:17; Isa. 38:18; Lam. 3:55; Ezek. 26:20; 31:14ff.; Ezek. 32:22ff.).

pāḥat [פַּחַת, **6354**]

pāḥat is found in ten contexts meaning "pit" in the primary sense of a trap, or snare. Literal references to such a pit are found in 2 Sam. 17:9; 18:17. Jer. 48:28 suggests the meaning "cave" or "gorge." Metaphorical references to "pit" as a trap or snare are found in Jer. 48:43ff.; Lam. 3:47.

shaḥat [שַׁחַת, **7845**]

shaḥat is a synonym for ***bôr*** (see above), meaning "pit" in both a literal sense as well as the metaphorical sense of either a "trap" or the "grave." The latter meaning is dominant. ***shaḥat*** occurs in about twenty contexts.

Prov. 26:27 refers to a literal "pit." More commonly, "pit" is a symbolic reference to the grave (cf. Job 17:4; 33:18ff.; Pss. 16:10; 30:9; 49:9; 55:23; 103:4; Isa. 38:17; 51:14; Ezek. 28:8; Jonah 2:6). ***shaḥat*** is also used metaphorically to indicate a "trap," or "snare" (cf. Job 9:31; Pss. 7:15; 9:15; 35:7; 94:13; Ezek. 19:4, 8).

shîḥāh [שִׁיחָה, **7882**]

shîḥāh refers to a "pit" only in the metaphorical sense of a "trap" or "pitfall," "dug" by one's enemies (cf. Pss. 57:6; 119:85; Jer. 18:22).

shûḥāh [שׁוּחָה, **7745**]

shûḥāh is a variant form of ***shîḥāh*** (see above) meaning "pit," likewise in a metaphorical sense in all but one of its five occurrences.

Prov. 22:14; 23:27 refer to an immoral woman as a deep "pit," or a dangerous trap for the unwary man. ***shûḥāh*** refers to "pits" as traps laid by the enemies of the prophet Jeremiah to ensnare him. The one literal reference is found in Jer. 2:6, referring to the wilderness as a land of desert and pits, as experienced by the Israelite people on their journey to Canaan.

sheḥût [שְׁחוּת, **7816**]

sheḥût is found only in Prov. 28:10, referring metaphorically to a "pit" as the place into which the wicked shall fall.

gûmmaṣ [גּוּמָּץ, **1475**]

gûmmaṣ is found only in Eccl. 10:8 with reference to a "pit" that will cause injury to the one that falls into it.

NT Words

bothynos [βόθυνος, *999*]

bothynos is found only three times. It refers to a "pit" as a trap, dug presumably to capture wild animals, but which may also cause injury to the unwary passerby — whether animal (cf. Matt. 12:11); or human (cf. Matt. 15:14; Luke 6:39).

phrear [φρέαρ, *5421*]

phrear occurs in five contexts, referring to a literal "pit" or "well" in Luke 14:5; John 4:11, 12. In Rev. 9:1, 2 ***phrear*** refers to the bottomless "pit" of Hades (or the underworld), the place of fiery judgment for the wicked.

abyssos [ἄβυσσος, *12*]

abyssos is a synonym for ***phrear*** (see above), translated as "abyss," "bottomless pit," or "deep," and referring in each of the nine occurrences to the realm of the dead, the place of departed spirits (cf. Luke 8:31; Rom. 10:7; Rev. 9:1ff.; 11:7; 17:8; 20:1, 3).

Additional Notes

When a "pit" is referred to metaphorically in both Old and New Testaments, a uniform emphasis on the grave or the realm of the dead is evident. While in the Old Testament it functions merely as a euphemism for the grave, the book of Revelation indicates that the "pit" or "abyss" is a place of terrifying judgment — the abode of demonic spirits. The latter sense is also emphasized in Luke 8:31, which refers to the demons pleading with Jesus himself, not to cast them into the "abyss."

See Also: → GRAVE → WELL

PITCH

OT Words

kāphar [כָּפַר, **3722**]

kāphar is commonly translated "to make atonement," in addition to related senses, in around 100 places. (→ PROPITIATION) However, in Gen. 6:14 it means "to cover with pitch" with reference to Noah's ark.

kōpher [כֹּפֶר, **3724**]

kōpher is a noun derived from ***kāphar*** (see above) meaning "ransom" or "bribe" in most of its seventeen occurrences. In Gen. 6:14, however, it means "pitch," referring to the waterproof sealant applied to Noah's ark.

zephet [זֶפֶת, **2203**]

zephet is a term found in only three places meaning "pitch," or "tar." In Exod. 2:3 it refers to the lining of pitch applied to the basket containing the infant Moses in order to make it watertight. In Isa. 34:9, ***zephet*** is used twice, metaphorically, to refer to the destruction of the land of Edom, describing the transformation of its rivers and land into burning pitch, or asphalt.

ḥānāh [חָנָה, **2583**]

ḥānāh is a verb that is usually translated "to pitch (one's tent)" or "make camp" in the approximately 140 contexts in which it is found. The use is primarily a literal one (cf. Gen. 26:17; Exod. 13:20; Deut. 1:33; Josh. 10:31ff.; 1 Sam. 26:3ff.; 1 Kgs. 16:15ff.; Isa. 29:1; Zech. 9:8).

'āhal [אָהַל, **167**]

'āhal is a rare verb found only three times, meaning to "pitch one's tent" in Gen. 13:12; Isa. 13:20. Gen. 13:18 refers to Abraham moving his tent.

tāqa' [תָּקַע, **8628**]

tāqa' is a verb meaning "blow (a trumpet)" or "fasten" in most of the seventy or so contexts in which it is found. (→ BLOW) However, in three places ***tāqa'*** means "to pitch one's tent" (cf. Gen. 31:25 [twice]; Jer. 6:3).

nāṭāh [נָטָה, **5186**]

nāṭāh is a common verb meaning "stretch (out)," "incline," or "turn," as well as a number of associated senses in the 200 or so contexts in which it is found. However, in a number of places, ***nāṭāh*** refers to "pitching" a tent (cf. Gen. 12:8; Judg. 21:11; 2 Sam. 6:17). Exod. 33:7 refers to pitching the tabernacle; and 1 Chr. 15:1; 2 Chr. 1:4 refer to the tent that was pitched to house the ark of the covenant in Jerusalem. This was not the tabernacle, which at this time was set up at Gibeon, to the northwest of Jerusalem.
(→ STRETCH → TURN)

NT Words

pēgnymi [πήγνυμι, *4078*]

pēgnymi is a verb found only in Heb. 8:2 with reference, metaphorically speaking, to the Lord "setting up" (lit. "pitching") the heavenly tabernacle.

PITCHER → JAR

PITIFUL, PITY → COMPASSION → GRACE → KIND (ADJECTIVE) → MERCY

PLACE (NOUN)

OT Words

māqôm [מָקוֹם, 4725]

māqôm means "place" in almost all of its 400 or so occurrences. There are a number of varying contexts and nuances associated with this term.

In a general sense, ***māqôm*** means "place" in the sense of "position," or geographic location (cf. Gen. 1:9; Deut. 11:24; Josh. 4:18; 1 Sam. 26:5; Eccl. 1:5; 3:20). It also refers to "place" as one's own home (cf. Gen. 31:55; Exod. 16:29; Num. 24:25; Judg. 7:7). Other uses of the term refer more specifically to "places" like cities, towns, memorial sites, including Sodom (cf. Gen. 18:24); and Beersheba (Gen. 21:31). In particular, ***māqôm*** designates "places" as memorials to divine revelation (cf. Gen. 22:14 ["The Lord will provide"]; Gen. 28:19 [Bethel — "house of God"]). See also Gen. 32:30; 35:7; Exod. 17:7; Num. 11:34; Josh. 8:19.

Elsewhere, "places" are designated as "holy" in association with the ritual worship of Yahweh (cf. Lev. 4:12; 6:16ff.; 10:13ff.; Num. 19:9). In particular, 1 Kgs. 8:7, 21ff. refer to the sacred "place" of the ark in the temple (see also Ezek. 42:13). In contrast, Lev. 14:40ff. refers to "places" that are unclean, suitable only for refuse.

Significant theological usage of ***māqôm*** centers primarily on the "place" chosen by Yahweh explicitly for the worship of his name and person. These probably refer to the sacred sites where the tabernacle was located, and ultimately the temple — for example, Shiloh; Nob; Gideon; Jerusalem (cf. Deut. 12:14, 18, 21, 26; 14:23; 15:20; 16:6ff.; 26:2; Jer. 7:12). 1 Kgs. 8:30; Isa. 26:21 refer to his heavenly "dwelling place" (cf. also Jer. 17:12). The phrase "this place" refers to the temple as Yahweh's dwelling place on earth in 1 Kgs. 8:35; Ps. 132:5; Hag. 2:9, as does the expression "his holy place" in Ezra 9:8; Ps. 24:3 (cf. also Isa. 60:13). Ezek. 3:12; 43:7 refer to the place of God's glory, of his throne in the temple, or the holy of holies. (→ HOLINESS) In contrast, ***māqôm*** also refers to "places" of idolatrous Canaanite worship, shrines that were forbidden to Israelites (cf. Deut. 12:2, 13).

In other significant contexts, ***māqôm*** refers to "the place" prepared by God for his people, or the land of Canaan (cf. Exod. 23:20; Num. 10:29; 14:40; Deut. 9:7; 12:5, 11; Josh. 1:3; 1 Sam. 12:8; 2 Sam. 7:10; Jer. 7:3ff.; 16:2ff.). Conversely, ***māqôm*** also indicates "the place(s)" assigned by Yahweh as the setting of Judah's punishment for their rejection of him — that is, the land of Babylon (cf. Jer. 40:12; 45:5; Ezek. 34:12). Not only are foreign lands indicated as the "place" of God's judgment for his people. In addition, the phrase "this place" refers to Jerusalem or the land of Judah as the object of divine judgment, the place from which the people of Yahweh will be expelled (cf. 2 Kgs. 22:16ff.; Jer. 19:3ff.; 24:5; 42:18). Elsewhere, the same expression occurs in contexts where Yahweh promises to bring his people back from exile, back to "this place" (cf. Jer. 29:10; 32:37).

mākôn [מָכוֹן, 4349]

mākôn is a variant form of ***māqôm*** (see above) meaning "place" in the majority of the seventeen contexts in which it is found.

Exod. 15:17 mentions the place belonging to Yahweh on Mt. Zion, anticipating the Jerusalem temple site (cf. also Isa. 4:5; 18:4).

In his prayer of dedication at the "opening" of the temple in Jerusalem, Solomon refers to this grand edifice as "the place" where Yahweh dwells on earth (cf. 1 Kgs. 8:13; 2 Chr. 6:2). In the same prayer, Solomon also pleads for God's attention from his "dwelling place" in heaven (cf. 1 Kgs. 8:39ff.; 2 Chr. 6:30ff.). See also Ps. 33:14.

bāmāh [בָּמָה, 1116]

bāmāh is a term found in approximately one hundred places, consistently translated "high place" in almost every context. The expression "high place" is a technical one, referring to the ritual shrines or platforms associated primarily with Canaanite Baal worship, which the Israelites were forbidden to frequent. In several places, however, they are also mentioned in a "neutral" context.

The Israelites were frequently condemned for erecting their own "high places," and divine judgment was pronounced against them (cf. Lev. 26:30).

Israelite "high places" that were idolatrous are indicated in Num. 22:41; 1 Kgs. 11:7 (Solomon's chief failing); 12:33; 2 Kgs. 12:3; 17:9ff.; 23:5f.; 2 Chr. 11:15; 33:17ff.; Ps. 78:58; Jer. 7:31; 19:5; Ezek. 6:6; Hos. 10:8. Canaanite "high places" marked for destruction are noted in Num. 33:52; Deut. 33:29 (cf. also Isa. 16:12).

A number of "neutral" references indicate the existence of legitimate "high places" set apart for exclusive worship of Yahweh (cf. 1 Sam. 9:12ff.; 10:5, 13). In particular, 1 Kgs. 3:2ff.; 1 Chr. 16:39; 21:29; 2 Chr. 1:3 refer to the "high place" at Gibeon, which was the site of the tabernacle sanctuary during the early years of Solomon's reign.

me'ônāh **[מְעוֹנָה, 4585]**

me'ônāh is a noun occurring nine times. In most of these contexts it means "lair," or "den." (→ DEN) However, in Ps. 76:2 it refers to Zion as the "dwelling place" of Yahweh.

mā'ôn **[מָעוֹן, 4583]**

mā'ôn is a term meaning "habitation," or "dwelling place," in most of the nineteen contexts in which it is found.

References to the "dwelling place" of God in heaven are found in Deut. 26:15; 2 Chr. 30:27; Ps. 68:5; Jer. 25:30; Zech. 2:13. 2 Chr. 36:15; Ps. 26:8 refer to the temple in Jerusalem as the "dwelling place" of Yahweh. Ps. 91:9 speaks of God himself as a "dwelling place" or "refuge." In more mundane contexts, ***mā'ôn*** refers to the "dwellings" or "haunts" of wild animals (cf. Jer. 49:33; 51:37).

ma'amād **[מַעֲמָד, 4612]**

ma'amād is a rare term occurring in only five contexts, with the general sense of one's office, or standing, in the context of official duties. In 2 Chr. 35:15, ***ma'amād*** refers to the official "places" of the Levitical singers required for the celebration of the Passover festival.

'ōmed **[עֹמֶד, 5977]**

'ōmed is a participial noun derived from the verb ***'āmad*** ("to stand"). The term occurs ten times and means "place," "post," or "position" in the context of one's official duties or employment. This meaning is found in half of these contexts, referring to priests (2 Chr. 30:16; 35:10); Levites (Neh. 8:7); King Josiah (2 Chr. 34:31); and civic officials (Neh. 13:11). The remaining texts refer to people "standing." (→ STAND)

NT WORDS

topos [τόπος, *5117*]

topos is a noun meaning "place" in the large majority of the ninety or so contexts in which it is found. There are a number of varying nuances and contexts connected with this term. ***topos*** demonstrates a clear dynamic equivalence with the Hebrew ***māqôm.***

There are a number of references to "place" as a general designation for a geographic location, or position. ***topos*** commonly refers to desert, or arid "places" (cf. Matt. 12:43; 14:13ff.; Mark 1:35; Luke 4:42; 1 Cor. 1:2; Rev. 6:11). Other references to places that are named include Golgotha (Matt. 27:33); Armageddon (Rev. 16:16); and Canaan (Heb. 11:8). The "place" of Jesus' burial is indicated in Matt. 28:6; Mark 16:6; Luke 23:33. Other non-specific references include those in Matt. 14:35; Luke 4:17; John 6:10; Acts 4:31.

topos also refers to the holy "place" of the temple in Matt. 24:15; Acts 6:13, 14; 21:28; and to the holy "place" (i.e., ground) where Moses stood when confronted by Yahweh at the site of the burning bush in the desert of Sinai (cf. Acts 7:33).

Finally, ***topos*** refers to "place" as a heavenly destiny prepared by Jesus for his followers (John 14:2ff.), and to heaven itself (Rev. 12:8). Conversely, Acts 1:25 speaks of the "place" to which Judas had gone, implying the realm of everlasting judgment.

chōrion [χωρίον, *5564*]

chōrion is a noun that means "field" or "piece of land" in most of the ten occurrences in which it is found. However, in two contexts it is translated "place" with reference to the garden of Gethsemane (cf. Matt. 26:36; Mark 14:32).

See Also: → DOOR → HOLINESS → REST → SECRET → TABERNACLE

PLACE (VERB) → PUT

PLAGUE

OT WORDS

nega' **[נֶגַע, 5061]**

nega' means "plague" or "disease" in the majority of its occurrences (approximately eighty).

nega' refers first of all to a "plague" as a disease inflicted by God upon his enemies, notably the kingdom of Egypt (cf. Gen. 12:17; Exod. 11:1). ***nega'*** usually refers, however, to the disease of leprosy, or more likely, "infectious skin disease" (cf. Lev. 13:2ff.; 14:3; Deut. 24:8). ***nega'*** also refers to "mildew" that harms both clothing and dwellings as well (cf. Lev. 13:47ff.; 14:33ff.). Illness in general is indicated in 1 Kgs. 8:37; 2 Chr. 6:28ff.; Ps. 38:11.

negeph **[נֶגֶף, 5063]**

negeph is synonymous with ***nega'*** and has the same sense of "plague" or "disease." Common to all but one of these references, seven in all, is the idea that "plague" or "disease" is inflicted by God as punishment for sin (cf. Exod. 12:13; 30:12; Num. 8:19; 16:46, 47; Josh. 22:17).

maggēphāh **[מַגֵּפָה, 4046]**

maggēphāh is another term, found in twenty-six contexts, that is synonymous with ***nega'*** and ***negeph***, above. As with these terms, ***maggēphāh*** is translated "plague," or "disease." And, like ***negeph*** (see above), it refers primarily to "plague(s)" as a judgment of God directed to both his own people (cf. Num. 14:37; 16:48ff.; 25:8ff.; 26:1; 31:16; 2 Sam. 24:21, 5; 1 Chr. 21:17, 22; Ps. 106:29ff.); as well as to foreign nations (cf. Exod. 9:30; Zech. 14:12ff.).

makkāh **[מַכָּה, 4347]**

makkāh means "wound," "slaughter," and "plague," or "disease" in most of its nearly fifty occurrences. Eleven of these indicate the latter two meanings.

A "plague" is referred to as a judgment of Yahweh on his people Israel in Num. 11:33. "Plague" is designated as one of the elements of the covenant curse in Deut. 28:59ff.; 29:22. Similarly, ***makkāh*** refers to "plague" or "disease" as an expression of divine judgment against pagan nations, including Egypt (cf. 1 Sam. 4:8); Edom (Jer. 49:17); and Babylon (Jer. 50:13).

deber **[דֶּבֶר, 1698]**

deber is another synonym for the entries listed above, found in nearly fifty places with the consistent meaning "plague," or "disease."

deber is used almost exclusively in contexts where plague or disease is a judgment from Yahweh. Such punishment, for example, is handed out against Egypt (cf. Exod. 5:3; 9:3, 15; Ps. 78:50); Babylon (cf. Jer. 27:8); and Sidon (cf. Ezek. 28:23). Plague is also cited as a manifestation of the covenant curse, visited on God's people (cf. Lev. 26:25; Deut. 28:21; 1 Kgs. 8:37; 2 Chr. 6:28; 7:13; 20:9). Pestilence is also prescribed for Israel as punishment for specific sins in a number of places (cf. Num. 14:12; 2 Sam. 24:13ff.; Amos 4:10). In this connection, plague is often associated with the Babylonian invasion of Judah and the subsequent exile (cf. Jer. 14:12; 21:6ff.; 29:17ff.; 32:24, 36; Ezek. 5:12, 17; 14:21; 33:27). Zedekiah, the last king of Judah, is threatened with a plague judgment (among other things) for violation of an oath sworn before God (cf. Jer. 34:17). General references to "plague" or "disease" are found in Ps. 91:3, 6; Jer. 28:8.

In a metaphorical sense, ***deber*** refers to "plagues" of death in Hos. 13:14, describing the terrible dilemma of the Israelite nation from which Yahweh promises to deliver them.

NT Words

mastix [μάστιξ, *3148*]

mastix refers to "disease" in four of the six occurrences of the term. In each of these cases, ***mastix*** refers to diseases that were cured by Jesus (cf. Mark 3:10; 5:29, 34; Luke 7:21). (→ SCOURGE)

plēgē [πληγή, *4127*]

plēgē has three meanings — "wound," "beating," "plague" (i.e., disease). ***plēgē*** is found twenty-one times, meaning "plague" or "disease" in twelve of these contexts (all in the book of Revelation). In each case, the reference is to "disease" that is inflicted by God on a sinful world (cf. Rev. 9:20; 11:6; 15:1, 6ff.; 16:9, 21; 18:4, 8; 21:9; 22:18). Although these references all occur in symbolic contexts, it is clear that they all describe the reality of divine punishment.

Additional Notes

The use of "plague" terminology in both Old and New Testaments is very similar. The Old Testament emphasizes "plague" or "disease" as a specific divine punishment meted out to both Israel and the nations for rebellion against Yahweh. Significantly, the visitation of "plagues" against the people of God constitutes one key manifestation of the covenant curses or sanctions. In addition, the removal of disease in the old covenant era is a key element in the divine program of renewal and redemption promised by God through the message of the prophets.

A similar emphasis is found in the New Testament. Again, the removal of such suffering is highlighted in the person and work of Jesus Christ during his earthly healing ministry. It is also evident that "disease" or "plague" is declared to be the lot of the impenitent wicked, as illustrated (albeit symbolically) in the book of Revelation.

It is the finished redemptive work of Christ that ends the presence of disease in the world.

PLAIN

OT Words

biq'āh **[בִּקְעָה, 1237]**

biq'āh is a term found in twenty contexts meaning "valley" or "plain." There is some overlap in meaning between these two senses, though the latter sense of "plain" would appear to be evident in Gen. 11:2; Neh. 6:2; Isa. 40:2; Ezek. 3:22, 23; 8:4; Zech. 12:11.

'arābāh **[עֲרָבָה, 6160]**

'arābāh is consistently translated "plain" with reference to specific regions, indicating a desert plain, steppe, or wilderness area. ***'arābāh*** occurs in about sixty places.

References to the "plains of Moab" are found in Num. 22:1; 26:3, 63; 31:12; 33:48ff.; 35:1; 36:13; Deut. 34:1, 8; Josh. 13:32. Likewise, the "plains of Jericho" are indicated in Josh. 4:13; 5:10; 2 Kgs. 25:5; Jer. 39:5; 52:8.

'arābāh is usually transliterated "Arabah" in the English text. It refers variously to a desert region, or a wilderness plain (e.g., Deut. 1:1; 4:49; Josh. 3:16; 11:2, 16; 18:18; 1 Sam. 23:24; 2 Sam. 2:29; 2 Kgs. 14:25; Ezek. 47:8).

mîshôr **[מִישׁוֹר, 4334]**

mîshôr refers to a "plain" in the sense of a tableland or plateau, or simply a level area of ground, in the majority of the twenty or so passages in which it occurs.

References to "plain," indicating a plateau or tableland, are found for example in Deut. 3:10; 4:43; Josh. 13:9; 20:8. General designations of a "plain" as a level area of ground are found in 1 Kgs. 20:23ff.; Ps. 27:11; Jer. 21:13. In Isa. 42:16, ***mîshôr*** indicates the removal of obstacles for the coming Messianic King — that is, the rough places will be made "plain" (cf. also Zech. 4:7).

NT Words

pedinos [πεδινός, *3977*]

pedinos is found only in Luke 6:17 with reference to a "plain" or "area of level ground" on which Jesus stood as he ministered to the crowd through miraculous healing and teaching.

See Also: → VALLEY

PLAN

OT Words

dāmāh **[דָּמָה, 1819]**

dāmāh is a verb with the primary sense of "liken," "to be like." (→ LIKEN) However, in 2 Sam. 21:5, ***dāmāh*** is translated "to plan," in the context of a plot attributed to King Saul to destroy the city of Gibeon.

maḥashābāh **[מַחֲשָׁבָה, 4284]**

maḥashābāh is a noun derived from the verb ***ḥāshab*** ("to think," etc.), with the primary meanings "thought" (plus associated senses) and "plan," or "plot." (→ THOUGHT)

With reference to "plan" in the sense of a "plot" or "scheme," Esth. 8:3, 5; 9:25 refer to Haman's plot to exterminate the Jewish population throughout the entire Persian kingdom. General references to the "plans" or "schemes" of the wicked are found in Job 5:12; Ps. 33:10; Prov. 6:18; Isa. 65:2. Jer. 11:19; 18:12, 18 speak of such scheming with reference to God's people in Judah. The plotting of Israel's enemies against the people of God is noted in Jer. 49:30 (Babylon); Ezek. 38:10 (Gog and Magog). See also Dan. 11:24, 25. Plans of a general nature are cited in Prov. 15:22; 16:3; 19:21; 20:18; 21:5.

God's plans for his people are expressed both negatively and positively. Negatively, Yahweh is said in Jer. 18:11 to plan judgment against his people. Positively, he reveals his plan to redeem his people in Jer. 29:11, extending pardon for their sin. God's plan to bring judgment against his enemies is noted in Jer. 49:20; 50:45.

zāmam **[זָמַם, 2161]**

zāmam is a verb found in thirteen places with the primary meanings "to plan," "devise" in almost all of these contexts.

With reference to human purpose and intent, ***zāmam*** means "plan" in Gen. 11:6; Deut. 19:19. The "planning" or "plotting" activity of the wicked is evident in Pss. 31:13; 37:12; Prov. 30:32.

Yahweh's intention to punish the land of Judah is indicated in Jer. 4:28; Lam. 2:17; Zech. 1:6; 8:14. Zech. 8:15 records the divine intention to also bless his people. And, in Jer. 51:12, Yahweh expresses his determination to punish the kingdom of Babylon.

yā'aṣ **[יָעַץ, 3289]**

yā'aṣ is a verb expressing the primary sense of "to counsel" (i.e., give and take) in the large majority of the approximately eighty contexts in which it is found. In several contexts, however, ***yā'aṣ*** is also translated "to plan."

With regard to the purposes of Yahweh, he is said to plan judgment against Assyria and the world at large in Isa. 14:24ff.; 23:9. See also Isa. 19:12.

The planning activity of the wicked is noted in Isa. 32:7, and the planning of human beings in general is evident in Isa. 32:8.

PLANT

OT Words

nāta' **[נָטַע, 5193]**

nāta' is a verb found around sixty times with the principal sense of "plant" in a variety of contexts, used both literally and metaphorically.

In literal contexts, for example, the planting of gardens is indicated in Jer. 29:5, 28. More common is the record of vineyard plantation (cf. Gen. 9:20; Deut. 20:6; Josh. 24:13; Prov. 31:16; Eccl. 2:4ff.; Isa. 5:2; 65:21ff.; Ezek. 28:26; Amos 5:11). The planting of trees is noted in Gen. 21:33; Deut. 6:11. In particular, Israelites are forbidden to plant trees that are linked with Canaanite shrines for idol worship (cf. Deut. 16:21). Isa. 44:14 refers to such planting. General references to planting are found in Eccl. 3:2; Isa. 17:10; 40:24. In a few places, God himself is declared to be involved in the process of planting, for example, the garden of Eden (Gen. 2:8), and trees (Num. 24:6; Ps. 104:16).

In metaphorical contexts, God is frequently declared to be involved in "planting" his people in the land of Canaan. The sense here is clearly that of settling and establishing them there securely (cf. Exod. 15:17; 2 Sam. 17:10; 1 Chr. 17:19; Pss. 44:2; 80:8; Jer. 2:21; 11:17; 12:2). Jer. 31:28; 32:41; 42:10; Amos 9:15 indicate a series of promises whereby Yahweh guarantees to return his people to the land and reestablish them there (i.e., "plant" them) after their term in exile. In Jer. 1:10 the prophet is given, by divine authority, the power to "plant," along with other demonstrations of power (e.g., "to tear up"). Implied here is the prophetic authority to bring down nations as well as to reestablish (i.e., "plant") them. See also Jer. 18:9.

sîaḥ [שִׂיחַ, 7880]

sîaḥ is a term found only four times. On each occasion it refers to "plants" (Gen. 2:5); and "bushes" (Gen. 21:15; Job 30:4, 7).

nēta' [נֶטַע, 5194]

nēta' is a noun derived from the verb ***nāta'*** (see above) and refers to "plants" in each of its four occurrences (cf. Job 14:9; Isa. 5:7; 17:10, 11).

yônēq [יוֹנֵק, 3126]

yônēq is found only in Isa. 53:2, in a metaphorical context, likening the youthful messianic servant king to a "tender plant."

mattā' [מַטָּע, 4302]

mattā' is another noun derived from ***nāta'*** (see above) that means "plantation," or "(act of) planting," as well as "plant" itself. ***mattā'*** has these meaning in all six occurrences of the term (cf. Isa. 60:21; 61:3; Ezek. 17:7; 31:4; 34:29; Mic. 1:6).

netîa' [נְטִיעַ, 5195]

netîa' is a noun that is also derived from the verb ***nāta'*** (see above). It is found only in Ps. 144:12, used figuratively to refer to healthy vigorous sons as "plants."

shātal [שָׁתַל, 8362]

The verb ***shātal*** is synonymous with ***nāta'*** (see above), which is consistently translated "to plant" in each of the ten contexts in which it occurs. The usage of ***shātal*** is entirely metaphorical.

A righteous person is likened to a fruitful tree "planted" by life-giving water (cf. Pss. 1:3; 92:13). Jer. 17:8 notes a similar phenomenon, but in this context the reference is most likely to an Egyptian pharaoh. Other references to "planting," or establishing, powerful nations as kingdoms are found in Ezek. 17:8ff.; 19:10, 13. Hos. 9:13 refers to establishing (or "planting") Israel (presumably this is done by Yahweh).

NT Words

phyteia [φυτεία, *5451*]

phyteia is found only in Matt. 15:13, referring metaphorically to genuine children of God, whom Jesus refers to as viable plants that will remain in the ground and not be "pulled up" for judgment.

phyteuō [φυτεύω, *5452*]

phyteuō is a verb referring to "planting" in each of the twelve contexts in which it occurs. The usage is both literal and symbolic and is predicated of both God and human beings. Literal references to "planting" vineyards and trees are found in Matt. 21:33; Mark 12:1; Luke 13:6; 17:6, 28; 20:9.

In 1 Cor. 3:6ff.; 9:7, ***phyteuō*** indicates the spiritual ministry of "planting," undertaken by apostolic preachers who, in proclaiming the gospel, "sowed the seed" of potential followers of Christ. Matt. 15:13 refers to the divine action of "planting" true children of God.

PLATE

OT Words

ṣîṣ [צִיץ, 6731]

ṣîṣ is a term found in fifteen places with the primary meaning "flower," or "blossom." (→ FLOWER) On three occasions, however, it is translated "plate," referring to the sacred diadem, made of gold, that was attached to the high priestly turban, and on which was inscribed the words "holy to the Lord" (cf. Exod. 28:36; 39:30; Lev. 8:9).

NT Words

paropsis [παροψίς, *3953*]

paropsis is a term found only twice, in Matt. 23:25, with reference to "plate" as a household utensil.

pinax [πίναξ, *4094*]

pinax refers to a "large platter" or "plate." It occurs only five times. Matt. 14:8, 11; Mark 6:25, 28 refer to the platter on which was placed the severed head of John the Baptist. In Luke 11:39, ***pinax*** refers to a common "plate" or "dish."

PLAY

OT Words

nāgan [נָגַן, **5059**]

nāgan is a verb that refers to the action of "playing" a musical instrument. It is found in fifteen contexts. David's skill in this area is mentioned in 1 Sam. 16:16ff.; 18:10. Other general references to skilled musicians are found in 2 Kgs. 3:15; Pss. 33:3; 68:25; Ezek. 33:32.

shā'a' [שָׁעַע, **8173**]

shā'a' is a verb meaning "delight" in the majority of the nine contexts in which it is found. However, in Isa. 11:8 it refers to children "playing." (→ DELIGHT)

See Also: → LAUGH

PLEA, PLEAD

OT Words

dîn [דִּין, **1777** (Verb), **1779** (Noun)]

dîn, as a verb, has the primary sense of "to judge" in most of the twenty-four contexts in which it is found. In two places, however, the verb ***dîn*** is translated "to plead the cause." In Prov. 31:9 it refers to the poor, and in Jer. 30:13 it refers to the people of God, as Yahweh declares that none shall plead their cause.
(→ JUDGE)

dîn is also a noun identical in form to the verb from which it is derived. As a noun it is consistently translated "judgment" or "cause" in the majority of its twenty occurrences. However, it also means "plea," in a judicial context, in Deut. 17:8.

rîb [רִיב, **7378**]

rîb is a verb meaning "strive (against)," "argue," "contend for," or "plead one's cause," mostly in judicial contexts. The underlying sense of the verb involves a resolution or vindication of a conflict from both a divine and human perspective. (→ STRIVE)

The meaning "plead" or "contend for" is found in several contexts. The action of "pleading for" Baal is noted in Judg. 6:31. In 1 Sam. 24:15, David asks God to plead his cause and deliver him from the hand of Saul, his persecutor. Job 13:8 speaks of pleading God's cause. Isa. 1:17 contains the injunction to defend or plead the cause of the orphaned in Israel. The psalmist implores God to plead his cause against his ungodly enemies (cf. Pss. 43:1; 119:154). Yahweh himself is said to defend the cause of the poor (i.e., to vindicate them) in Prov. 22:23, and of his people in Isa. 51:22; Jer. 50:34. In Mic. 7:9, the prophet begs God to plead his cause for him. Ps. 74:22 speaks of Yahweh defending his cause against the wicked.

See Also: → JUDGE

PLEASE, PLEASANT, PLEASURE

OT Words

ḥāmad [חָמַד, **2530**]

ḥāmad is a verb meaning "to covet," "delight (in)," "desire" in most of the twenty-one places in which it is found. In two contexts, it means "to be pleasing or pleasant" in one's sight. Gen. 2:9; 3:6 records the pleasing enticement of the fruit of the forbidden tree, which was a temptation to the woman who succumbed and ate it, along with her husband.

nā'ēm [נָעֵם, **5276**]

nā'ēm is a verb expressing the sense of that which is attractive or pleasant. It is translated "to be pleasant, or beautiful" in most of the eight contexts in which it is found.

The quality of "pleasantness" is ascribed to a land (Gen. 49:15); to the intimacy of a close friendship between David and Jonathan (2 Sam. 1:26); to knowledge in the human soul (Prov. 2:10); to the enjoyment of food taken in secret (Prov. 9:17); and to physical beauty (Song 7:6).

nā'îm [נָעִים, **5273**]

nā'îm is an adjective derived from the verb ***nā'ēm*** (see above) and is usually translated "pleasant," "lovely," or "delightful." ***nā'îm*** occurs thirteen times.

"Pleasant" or "lovely" describes people (2 Sam. 1:23); places or locations (Ps. 16:6); the pleasure of knowing God (Pss. 16:11; 135:3; 147:1); the possession of wisdom (Prov. 22:18); and, metaphorically, spiritual riches (Prov. 24:4). See also Job 36:11.

ḥemdāh [חֶמְדָּה, 2532]

ḥemdāh is a noun that is used adjectivally in most of the twenty-five contexts in which it occurs. It refers primarily to what is seen as "precious" or "valuable." (→ VALUABLE) In several places, however, ***ḥemdāh*** describes the land of Canaan as "pleasant" (cf. Ps. 106:24; Jer. 3:19; 12:10).

ḥemed [חֶמֶד, 2531]

ḥemed is a noun with adjectival force indicating that which is "desirable" or "pleasant." It occurs six times. Isa. 27:2 refers to "pleasant" fields; Amos 5:11 to "pleasant" vineyards.

nō'am [נֹעַם, 5278]

nō'am is a term indicating "beauty," or "pleasantness," in seven contexts. Prov. 3:17 refers to the "pleasant" ways of Wisdom. Prov. 15:26 affirms that the speech of the pure is "pleasing" to God. See also Prov. 16:24.

'ārab [עָרַב, 6149]

'ārab is a verb meaning "to be pleasing," "take pleasure." ***'ārab*** occurs eight times.

In several places ***'ārab*** designates that which is "pleasing" to God. Ps. 104:34 indicates the explicit desire of the psalmist that his meditation may be pleasing to Yahweh. Mal. 3:4 affirms that in the times of Israel's renewal, the offerings of his people will be "pleasing" to Yahweh. Conversely, because of Israel's sin, their offerings are not pleasing to God (cf. Jer. 6:20; Hos. 9:4). Jer. 31:26 indicates that Jeremiah's sleep was "pleasant" for the prophet. Ezek. 16:37 refers to the illegitimate "pleasure" in idolatry taken by a rebellious Israelite nation.

yāshar [יָשַׁר, 3474]

The verb ***yāshar*** describes that which is correctly fashioned or arranged in a literal, physical sense, and also that which is morally right. ***yāshar*** is variously translated as "to be straight," "to direct," "to be upright," "to be correctly fitted." In several places, however, ***yāshar*** is also translated "to please" in a number of different contexts. The prospect of "pleasing God" is noted in Num. 23:27. ***yāshar*** is also used in the sense of sexual attraction in Judg. 14:3ff., where Samson demanded a Philistine woman for his wife because she "pleased" him. The term is also used in the general sense of "please," to give or make a favorable impression (cf. 1 Sam. 18:20, 26; 2 Sam. 17:4; 2 Chr. 30:4). ***yāshar*** is used negatively in 1 Kgs. 9:12.
(→ RIGHTEOUS)

yātab [יָטַב, 3190]

yātab is a verb with the primary meanings "to do well," "to be, do good," as well as a number of other nuances. It occurs over one hundred times and also expresses the sense of "to please" with the idea of "make a favorable impression" in a number of these contexts.

In the context of pleasing people, ***yātab*** is found in Gen. 34:18; 45:16; Deut. 1:23; Josh. 22:30ff.; 1 Sam. 20:13; 2 Sam. 3:36; Neh. 2:6; Esth. 1:21; 2:4, 9; 5:14. In two places, ***yātab*** refers to pleasing God (cf. 1 Kgs. 3:10; Ps. 69:31).

NT Words

arestos [ἀρεστός, *701*]

arestos is an adjective referring to those things that are pleasing. The term occurs four times and expresses this meaning in three of these contexts. John 8:29 speaks of Jesus being committed to do what is "pleasing" to his Father; and 1 John 3:22 refers to the willingness of believers to do what is pleasing to God.

areskō [ἀρέσκω, *700*]

areskō is a verb meaning "to please" in each of the seventeen settings in which it occurs.

The general sense of "pleasing" someone conveys the idea of making a favorable impression on others. This usage is evident in Acts 6:5; Rom. 15:2; 1 Cor. 7:33ff.; 10:33; Gal. 1:10; 2 Tim. 2:4. Rom. 15:3 states that Christ chose not to please himself during his life on earth. The same idea is indicated with respect to human beings pleasing God in 1 Cor. 7:32; 1 Thess. 4:1. The impossibility of unbelievers pleasing God is indicated in Rom. 8:8; 1 Thess. 2:15. Rom. 15:1 records the exhortation not to please oneself (cf. also 1 Thess. 2:4). In Matt. 14:6; Mark 6:22, a unique use of ***areskō*** suggests that Herodias' dancing before her stepfather king Herod may have pleased him in an erotic way.

areskeia [ἀρεσκεία, *699*]

areskeia is a noun derived from the verb ***areskō*** (see above) that occurs only in Col. 1:10, where the believer is exhorted to live a life wholly "pleasing" to God.

euaresteō [εὐαρεστέω, *2100*]

euaresteō is a synonym for ***areskō*** (see above) and occurs only three times, meaning "to please." Heb. 11:5

refers to the patriarch Enoch, who was said to have pleased God. Heb. 13:16 affirms that a selfless concern for other people constitutes a sacrifice that is pleasing to God. Heb. 11:6 claims that it is impossible to please God without the possession of saving faith.

euarestos [εὐάρεστος, *2101*]

euarestos is an adjective derived from ***euaresteō*** (see above) and is consistently translated "acceptable" or "(well) pleasing" in each of the nine contexts in which it occurs.

The majority usage of ***euarestos*** centers on those things that are "pleasing" to God, such as wholehearted service to God (Rom. 12:12; Phil. 4:18; Heb. 13:21); and also service to Christ (Rom. 14:18). 2 Cor. 5:9; Eph. 5:10 contain exhortations to live lives pleasing to God. The obedient submission of children to parents, and slaves to masters, evokes a pleasing response from God in Col. 3:20; Titus 2:9, respectively.

eudokeō [εὐδοκέω, *2106*]

eudokeō is a verb meaning "to be (well) pleased," "please," or "take pleasure in" in most of its twenty-one occurrences.

When predicated of God, ***eudokeō*** refers to God being pleased with his son Jesus, expressed through explicit divine testimony at the outset of, and during, the public ministry of Christ (cf. Matt. 3:17; 12:18; 17:5; Mark 1:11; Luke 3:22; 2 Pet. 1:17). In contrast, God was not pleased with most of the Israelite people during their sojourn in the wilderness en route to the land of Canaan (cf. 1 Cor. 10:5). See also Heb. 10:38. In other contexts, God is said to be pleased with, or to take pleasure in, giving the kingdom to his followers (Luke 12:32); saving people through the preaching of the gospel (1 Cor. 1:21); and revealing himself in his Son (Gal. 1:15; Col. 1:19). But God takes no pleasure in formalized worship or sacrifices (Heb. 10:6, 8).

As far as human beings are concerned, the godless are said to take pleasure in unrighteousness in 2 Thess. 2:12. Paul refers to those who "were pleased" to make a significant contribution to the plight of the poor in Rom. 15:26ff.

hēdonē [ἡδονή, *2237*]

hēdonē refers to "pleasure" in the sense of "passion" or "lust" in an unwholesome sense, as a characteristic of a godless lifestyle. The term occurs five times (cf. Luke 8:14; Titus 3:3; Jas. 4:1, 3; 2 Pet. 2:13).

philēdonos [φιλήδονος, *5369*]

philēdonos is an adjectival form derived from ***hēdonē*** (see above), meaning "lovers of pleasure" (i.e., passion, or lust). It occurs only in 2 Tim. 3:4.

See Also: → CONSENT → DELIGHT → GOOD → JOY → WILL

PLEDGE → PROMISE → VOW

PLENTY → MUCH

PLOT → PLAN

PLOW

OT Words

ḥārash [חָרַשׁ, **2790**]

ḥārash is a verb with two strands of meaning. On the one hand, ***ḥārash*** means "to hold one's peace," "keep silent." On the other hand, it denotes the action of "plowing" in both a literal and metaphorical sense. (→ SILENCE)

The physical process of "plowing" in an agricultural context is indicated in Deut. 22:10; 1 Kgs. 19:19; Job 1:14; Prov. 20:4; Isa. 28:24; Amos 9:13 (cf. also Amos 6:12).

The term is also used metaphorically. The expression "plowed like a field" refers to the condition of Jerusalem's physical destruction by the invading Babylonian army in Jer. 26:18 (cf. also Mic. 3:12). In Judg. 14:18, Samson accuses his Philistine companions of extracting the answer to his riddle unfairly from his bride-to-be when he declares that they had "plowed with my heifer." More generally, the expression to "plow iniquity" refers to a sinful lifestyle (Job 4:8; Hos. 10:13). See also Hos. 10:11; Ps. 129:3.

'ēt [אֵת, **855**]

'ēt is a noun meaning "plowshare" in three of the five contexts in which it occurs (cf. Isa. 2:4; Joel 3:10; Mic. 4:3).

maḥarēshāh [מַחֲרֵשָׁה, **4281**]

maḥarēshāh is a noun derived from ***ḥārash*** (see above), meaning "plowshare." The term is found only in 1 Sam. 13:20.

NT Words

arotron [ἄροτρον, *723*]

arotron is found only in Luke 9:62, referring to a "plow."

arotriaō [ἀροτριάω, *722*]

arotriaō is the verb expressing the action of plowing, and is found only twice (cf. Luke 17:7; 1 Cor. 9:10).

PLUCK

OT Words

tārāph **[טָרָף, 2965]**

tārāph is an adjective found only in Gen. 8:11, referring to a "freshly-plucked" olive leaf that a dove brought back to Noah in the ark.

NT Words

tillō [τίλλω, *5089*]

tillō is a verb found in only three places, meaning "plucking" or "picking" ears of corn (cf. Matt. 12:1; Mark 2:23; Luke 6:1).

See Also: → GATHER → UPROOT

PLUNDER → SPOIL

POISON → VENOM

POMP → SPLENDOR

POOR

OT Words

dal **[דַּל, 1800]**

dal is an adjective occurring around fifty times with the consistent meaning "poor" in most of these contexts, referring to those who are impoverished in a material sense.

References to the "poor" as those individuals or groups of people who are underprivileged in a material, economic sense are found, for example, in Exod. 23:3; 30:15; Lev. 14:21; Judg. 2:15; Ruth 3:10; Job 5:16; Ps. 41:1; Prov. 10:15; 22:9; 1 Sam. 14:30; Jer. 5:4.

dal refers to people designated as "poor" who are the objects of divine grace, whose lot Yahweh restores or promises to restore (cf. 1 Sam. 2:8; Ps. 113:7). The same is said of those who are objects of abuse at the hands of the rich and powerful (cf. Amos 2:7; 4:1; 5:11; 8:6).

'ānî **[עָנִי, 6041]**

'ānî is another adjectival form that describes the "poor" in the literal sense of those who are materially impoverished, as well as those who are "afflicted," or those who find themselves in significant personal trauma. ***'ānî*** is found in eighty contexts.
(→ AFFLICT)

'ānî refers, for example, to those who are "poor" in the literal sense of being impoverished in Exod. 22:25; Lev. 19:10; Deut. 15:11; 24:14ff.; Job 24:4; Ps. 9:18; Prov. 14:21; 31:20.

In several places, Yahweh is described as the one who rescues the poor and takes up their cause (e.g., Ps. 72:12; Jer. 22:16). Conversely, there is condemnation in store from the hand of God for those who oppress the poor (cf. Isa. 3:15; 10:2; 32:7; Amos 8:4).

'ebyôn **[אֶבְיוֹן, 34]**

'ebyôn is a synonym for ***dal*** and ***'ānî***, above, again referring to those who are "poor" or "needy." ***'ebyôn*** is found in twenty-four places.

General references to the "poor" in a literal sense are found, for example, in Exod. 23:6; Deut. 15:4ff.; 24:14; Pss. 49:2; 112:9; Isa. 25:4; Amos 2:6; 5:12.

'ebyôn is also translated "needy," which is largely synonymous with the sense of "poor." However, in certain contexts, the term "needy" may suggest more than simply material, or economic, poverty (cf. Pss. 37:14; 70:5; 82:4; Prov. 14:31; Isa. 14:30; Jer. 22:16; Ezek. 18:16; Amos 8:4ff.).

mûk **[מוּךְ, 4134]**

mûk is a verb meaning "to be, or become, poor," in each of the five occurrences of the term (cf. Lev. 25:25, 35, 39, 47; 27:8).

yārash **[יָרַשׁ, 3423]**

yārash is a common verb found in approximately 230 contexts, with the primary meaning "inherit," "possess." However, in several places ***yārash*** also means "to become destitute or poor" (cf. Gen. 45:11; Prov. 20:13; 23:21; 30:9). (→ INHERIT → POSSESS)

rûsh **[רוּשׁ, 7326]**

rûsh is a verb occurring about twenty-five times, meaning "to be poor." However, it is used mainly in a nominal sense, indicating a "poor man," or "the poor" as a clan of people.

The meaning "to be poor" is evident, for example, in Prov. 10:4; 13:7; Eccl. 4:14. The more common nominal sense is indicated, for example, in 1 Sam. 18:23; 2 Sam. 12:3; Prov. 13:8; Eccl. 5:8.

***miskēn* [מִסְכֵּן, 4542]**

miskēn is a rare noun, found in only three places with reference to a "poor man" (cf. Eccl. 4:13; 9:15, 16).

NT Words

ptōchos [πτωχός, *4434*]

ptōchos is the most common term in the New Testament for "poor." While adjectival in form, ***ptōchos*** is used mainly as a noun. The term is found around thirty-five times.

ptōchos means "poor" in the sense of being economically destitute in Matt. 11:5; 26:11; Mark 14:5; Luke 4:18; 16:20ff.; John 12:5; Rom. 15:26; Gal. 2:10; Jas. 2:2ff.

One interesting use of ***ptōchos*** is found in Matt. 5:3, where Jesus blesses those who are "poor in spirit." The expression refers to the quality of genuine humility, recognizing that one lacks worldly status and honor, which leads to a faithful dependence on God.

penichros [πενιχρός, *3998*]

penichros is an adjective found only in Luke 21:2, with reference to a "poor" widow.

ptōcheuō [πτωχεύω, *4433*]

ptōcheuō is the verb from which the adjective ***ptōchos*** (see above) is derived. It is found only in 2 Cor. 8:9, where it refers to the selfless action of Christ, who "became poor" for our sake, that we might become rich in spiritual relationship with him.

penēs [πένης, *3993*]

penēs is an adjective found only in 2 Cor. 9:9, with reference to "the poor," who benefit from divine giving.

Additional Notes

In the Old Testament, those who are destitute of resources and influence are accorded special privilege under the Mosaic law covenant. Such people are not to be exploited but cared for. This ideal, however, was not maintained in Israel, and the history of the Israelite people records a litany of abuse, exploitation, and deprivation of the poor.

In the New Testament, compassionate concern for the poor is likewise commended. In particular, the references to Christ "becoming poor," by setting aside all his heavenly status to become a man, perfectly illustrate that spirit of dependence upon God that the condition of poverty was intended to instill in those so affected.

See Also: → NEED

PORCH

OT Words

***'ûlam* [אוּלָם, 197]**

'ûlam means "porch" or "vestibule." It occurs over thirty times and refers to porches as architectural features of both Solomon's temple (cf. 1 Kgs. 6:3; 7:6ff.; 1 Chr. 28:11; 2 Chr. 3:4; 29:7; Ezek. 8:16; Joel 2:17) and Ezekiel's visionary sanctuary (cf. Ezek. 40:7ff., 15, 39ff.; 41:15, 25ff.; 46:2, 8).

NT Words

stoa [στοά, *4745*]

stoa is a noun meaning "porch" in each of the four contexts in which it occurs. It refers to the porches of the pool of Bethesda (John 5:2); and to the porches of Solomon's temple (John 10:23; Acts 3:11; 5:12).

See Also: → GATE

POSSESS, POSSESSION

OT Words

***yārash* [יָרַשׁ, 3423]**

yārash is a fairly common verb occurring in around 230 contexts with the primary sense of "possess," as well as associated nuances — a meaning that overlaps with that of "inherit."

The meaning "possess" or "take possession of" is occasionally linked to the phenomenon of "inheriting" the land of Canaan given by Yahweh to his people (cf. Gen. 15:7ff.; 28:4; Pss. 25:4; 37:9ff.; Isa. 60:21; Ezek. 33:4).

Elsewhere, ***yārash*** refers to "possessing" the land in the sense of "taking ownership through occupation and conquest." ***yārash*** refers to the divine promise that Israel will take possession of Canaan (cf. Deut. 1:39; 5:33; 7:1; 17:14; 31:3; Josh. 1:11; Ps. 69:35; Isa. 34:17). Jer. 30:3 contains the promise that Israel will regain possession of the land after the Babylonian exile. Associated with this promise is Yahweh's command to take possession of Canaan (cf. Deut. 1:8, 21; 2:24ff.; 4:1, 14;

Ezra 9:11). Some texts also affirm God's gift of Canaan to his people (cf. Deut. 3:18; 5:31; 11:10ff.; Neh. 9:15; Amos 2:10). The process of taking possession of the land is indicated in Josh. 12:1; 21:43; Judg. 2:6; 11:21; Neh. 9:22ff. Conversely, Israel's failure to fully occupy the land is indicated in Josh. 13:1; 18:3.

General references to "taking possession" in the sense of "acquiring ownership" are found in Num. 13:30; Deut. 4:47; Josh. 24:4; Isa. 14:21; Ezek. 7:24; Hos. 9:6.

ḥasan [חֲסַן, **2631** (Aramaic)]

ḥasan is an Aramaic verb meaning "to possess," "take possession of." It is found only in Dan. 7:18, 22 referring to the people of Yahweh taking possession of the kingdom of God.

'aḥuzzāh [אֲחֻזָּה, **272**]

'aḥuzzāh is a noun meaning "possession" or "property" in each of its nearly seventy occurrences.

'aḥuzzāh refers to the divine promise of the land of Canaan as an everlasting "possession" for the people of Israel in a number of places. Such a possession is mentioned explicitly in Gen. 17:8; 48:4; Lev. 14:34; and implicitly in Num. 32:22, 29, 32; 35:2; Deut. 32:49; Josh. 21:12; 22:4. ***'aḥuzzāh*** also means "possession" in the sense of property in Canaan, granted as an ongoing inheritance (cf. Lev. 25:10ff.; 27:21ff.; Neh. 11:3). In a prophetic context, ***'aḥuzzāh*** refers to the portion of the sacred area given to the Levites and the messianic "prince" as their (inherited) possession in the renewed land of Israel (cf. Ezek. 45:5ff.; 46:6ff.; 48:20ff.). Yahweh himself is referred to as "the possession" of Israel in Ezek. 44:28.

The possession of land in more general contexts is indicated in Gen. 36:43; 47:11; Ps. 2:8.

môrāshāh [מוֹרָשָׁה, **4181**]

môrāshāh is a noun derived from the verb ***yārash*** (see above) and means "possession" in each of the nine contexts in which it is found.

In three of these contexts, ***môrāshāh*** refers to the land of Canaan as the "possession" of his people, given to them by God as their everlasting heritage (cf. Deut. 6:8; Ezek. 11:15; 33:24). In Deut. 33:4, the law of Moses is described as a "possession" for the people of God.

In the context of punishing his people, ***môrāshāh*** refers to the people of God as a "possession" given to their enemies (cf. Ezek. 25:4, 10; 36:2ff.).

NT Words

ktēma [κτῆμα, *2933*]

ktēma is a noun found in only four places, meaning "possession(s)" in the sense of one's property, wealth, and personal belongings (cf. Matt. 19:22; Mark 10:22; Acts 2:45; 5:1).

peripoiēsis [περιποίησις, *4047*]

peripoiēsis is a noun derived from the verb ***peripoieomai*** ("to purchase"), meaning "(purchased) possessions" and found only in Eph. 1:14. In this context it refers to the heavenly inheritance of the people of God, whose salvation has been obtained through the redemptive work of Christ on the cross.

daimonizomai [δαιμονίζομαι, *1139*]

The verb ***daimonizomai*** consistently refers to the state of "being possessed by a demon (or demons)." The term occurs thirteen times and on each occasion refers to persons so afflicted, who were subsequently cured by Jesus (cf. Matt. 4:24; 12:22; Mark 1:32; 5:15ff.; Luke 8:36; John 10:21).

See Also: → INHERIT

POSSIBLE

NT Words

dynatos [δυνατός, *1415*]

dynatos is an adjective with the underlying sense of "powerful," or "mighty," as well as "possible." ***dynatos*** is found thirty-five times, meaning "possible" in nearly half of these. (→ STRONG)

In several places there is the affirmation that with God "all things are possible" (cf. Matt. 19:26; Mark 10:27; Luke 18:27). See also Mark 9:23.

Hypothetical situations are occasionally introduced by the words "if possible . . ." This is illustrated in particular with reference to the elect going astray (cf. Matt. 24:24; Mark 13:22); and to Christ avoiding the cross (cf. Matt. 26:39; Mark 14:35, 36).

POT

OT Words

sîr [סִיר, **5518**]

sîr is a noun with the primary meaning "pot," or "pan," indicating a container for cooking, or for use in the tabernacle or temple. ***ṣîr*** is found about thirty times with this meaning.

References to cooking pots include those in Exod. 16:3; 2 Kgs. 4:38ff. ***sîr*** refers to utensils for use in the tabernacle and temple in Exod. 27:3; 1 Kgs. 7:45; 2 Kgs. 25:14; 2 Chr. 4:11, 16; 35:13; Jer. 52:18ff.; Zech. 14:20, 21.

ṣîr also refers to metaphorical "boiling pot," from which the wrath of Yahweh is to be "poured out" upon his people (cf. Jer. 1:13; Ezek. 11:3; 24:3ff.; Mic. 3:3).

ṣîr is used in a general, non-specific way in Job 41:31; Ps. 58:9; Eccl. 7:6.

pārûr [פָּרוּר, 6517]

pārûr is a term meaning "cooking pot" in only three places (cf. Num. 11:8; Judg. 6:19; 1 Sam. 2:14).

dûd [דּוּד, 1731]

dûd refers to a "boiling pot," "cauldron," or "kettle" in Job 41:20; 1 Sam. 2:14; 2 Chr. 35:13.

maṣrēph [מַצְרֵף, 4715]

maṣrēph means "crucible" (i.e., a refining pot). It is found only twice, in Prov. 17:3; 27:21.

ṣinṣenet [צִנְצֶנֶת, 6803]

ṣinṣenet is found only in Exod. 16:33 with reference to a "pot" or "jar" as a common receptacle.

NT Words

stamnos [στάμνος, *4713*]

stamnos indicates a "pot" or "urn." It is found only in Heb. 9:4, referring to the golden urn containing the manna.

xestēs [ξέστης, *3582*]

xestēs is another term referring to a "pot" as a general household utensil, found only in Mark 7:4.

See Also: → VESSEL

POTTER

OT Words

yāṣar [יָצַר, 3335]

yāṣar is a verb meaning "to form" or "fashion" in the majority of the sixty or so contexts in which it is found. ***yāṣar*** is also used nominally, meaning "potter," in seventeen instances (e.g., 1 Chr. 4:23; Ps. 2:9; Isa. 29:16; 64:8; Jer. 18:2ff.; 19:1, 11; Lam. 4:2; Zech. 11:13).

NT Words

kerameus [κεραμεύς, *2763*]

kerameus is a term referring to a "potter," found in only three places (cf. Matt. 27:7, 10; Rom. 9:21).

POUR

OT Words

shāphak [שָׁפַךְ, 8210]

shāphak is a verb found in 115 contexts with the dominant meaning "pour," "pour out," as well as "to shed." The sense of "pour" is found in nearly two-thirds of the occurrences. ***shāphak*** is used both literally and metaphorically, and in both a secular and ritual contexts.

In secular contexts, ***shāphak*** refers to pouring water on the ground (Exod. 4:9) and to pouring out blood (Lev. 17:13; Deut. 12:16; 15:23), emphasizing the prohibition against drinking blood.

In the context of worship, pouring out water before the Lord is indicated in 1 Sam. 7:6. Exod. 29:12; Lev. 4:7, 18ff.; Deut. 12:27 refer to pouring out blood on the altar. In contrast, Isa. 57:6 refers to pouring out drink offerings to idols.

Other references to pouring include those in Lev. 14:41; Judg. 6:20; 1 Kgs. 13:3; Amos 5:8; 9:6; Zeph. 1:17.

shāphak is also used in a variety of metaphorical settings. In a number of places, the expression "to pour out one's soul" indicates a mood of anguish (cf. 1 Sam. 1:15; Job 30:16; Pss. 22:14; 42:4; 102:1; 142:2; Lam. 2:11ff.). Job 12:21 describes pouring contempt on someone. Ezek. 38:8 refers to Israel's idolatrous rebellion against Yahweh through the expression "to pour out their lust against their lovers."

Yahweh is said to pour contempt on the ungodly in Ps. 107:40. More commonly, Yahweh is said to pour out his wrath on the enemies of his people in Pss. 69:24; 79:6; Jer. 10:25 (cf. also 14:16); Lam. 2:4; Ezek. 21:31; 30:15; Zeph. 3:8. Similarly, divine anger is also poured out on Israel for their sin against God (cf. Isa. 42:25; Jer. 6:11; Lam. 4:11; Ezek. 7:8; 9:8; 14:19; 20:8, 13ff.; 22:22, 31; 36:18; Hos. 5:10). Finally, there are several references to Yahweh "pouring out his spirit" on his people as a seal or sign of the anticipated new covenant blessing (cf. Ezek. 39:29; Joel 2:28, 29; Zech. 12:10).

yāṣaq [יָצַק, 3332]

yāṣaq is a synonym for ***shāphak*** (see above) meaning "pour," "pour out" in about half of the fifty or so occurrences of the term. (→ CAST)

yāṣaq refers to pouring oil in the context of anointing a king — for example, Saul (1 Sam. 10:1) and Jehu (2 Kgs. 9:3ff.). Elsewhere, in a specifically ceremonial context, pouring oil on the head of the high priest constitutes his ritual anointing (Exod. 36:36; Lev. 8:12; 21:10). See also Luke 14:15, 26. Lev. 2:1ff. refers to pouring oil on a cereal offering. Gen. 28:18; 35:14 describe Jacob pouring oil onto the stone that served as a pillow at the location of God's revelation to him at Bethel. In other ceremonial contexts, ***yāṣaq*** refers to pouring blood on the altar (Lev. 8:15; 9:9).

In a unique context, Elijah commands that water be poured on the altar constructed on Mt. Carmel for the contest between Yahweh and the prophets of Baal (cf. 1 Kgs. 18:33). Other general references to pouring include those in 2 Kgs. 3:11; 4:4, 40ff.; Ezek. 24:3.

Two metaphorical uses of ***yāṣaq*** are found in Isa. 44:3. It refers here to Yahweh "pouring water on a thirsty land" in the context of the promised renewal of the land of Canaan. It also refers to Yahweh's guarantee "to pour out his spirit" on his people.

nāsak [נָסַךְ, 5258]

nāsak is a verb meaning "pour," "pour out" in the majority of its twenty-five occurrences in exclusively ceremonial contexts referring to drink offerings.

The presentation, or "pouring out," of a drink offering to Yahweh is indicated in Gen. 35:14; Exod. 30:9; Num. 28:7; 2 Sam. 23:16; 2 Kgs. 16:13; 1 Chr. 11:18. In several other contexts, ***nāsak*** refers to pouring out drink offerings to pagan deities (cf. Jer. 7:18; 19:13; 32:29; 44:17ff.; Ezek. 20:28).

nāba' [נָבַע, 5042]

nāba' is a verb with the principal meaning "pour out," "flow (from)," in metaphorical contexts. The term occurs eleven times. The heavens are said "to pour forth" speech in praise of God in Ps. 19:2, as do the lips of the psalmist in Ps. 119:171. Prov. 15:28 affirms that the wicked "pour out" evil speech from their mouths. Similarly, fools are said to "pour out" folly in their speech in Prov. 15:2. In Prov. 1:23, Wisdom is described as having "poured out" her heart to foolish people, who reject her.

rûq [רוּק, 7324]

rûq is a verb meaning "to empty," "draw out" in most of its nineteen occurrences. In two places, however, ***rûq*** conveys the idea of "pour out," "pour forth." Song 1:3 declares that the name of the beloved male companion of the Shulammite maiden is like perfume "poured out." Mal. 3:10 records Yahweh's refusal to "pour out" blessing on his disobedient people.

nātak [נָתַךְ, 5413]

nātak is a verb meaning "pour," "pour out" in the majority of its twenty or so occurrences. The usage is primarily metaphorical. (➟ DISSOLVE)

Exod. 9:33 mentions rain pouring down on the earth.

In metaphorical contexts, ***nātak*** refers primarily to the outpouring of God's wrath upon his people (cf. 2 Chr. 12:7; 34:21, 25; Jer. 7:20; 42:18; 44:6; Dan. 9:11); and also upon his enemies (cf. Dan. 9:27).

Job 3:24 refers to pouring out one's groanings in heartfelt despair.

yāsak [יָסַךְ, 3251]

yāsak is found only in Exod. 30:32, prohibiting the pouring of the oil of anointing on the bodies of Israelite laymen.

ṣûq [צוּק, 6694]

ṣûq is found in only two contexts, referring metaphorically to "pouring out" (cf. Job 29:6; Isa. 26:16).

zāram [זָרַם, 2229]

zāram is another rare verb found only once, meaning "pour out, down" in relation to clouds pouring down water on the earth (cf. Ps. 77:17).

'ārāh [עָרָה, 6168]

'ārāh is a verb meaning "empty," and "uncover," or "lay bare" However, in two places it means "pour out." Isa. 32:15 speaks of the promised Holy Spirit, who will be poured out upon the land of Canaan and bring about a profound renewal and transformation. Then, in Isa. 53:12, the demise of the Suffering Servant of Yahweh is spoken of in terms of his soul being "poured out to death." (➟ EMPTY ➟ UNCOVER)

nāgar [נָגַר, 5064]

nāgar is a verb referring metaphorically to "pouring out" or "flowing (down)" in most of its ten occurrences.

The outpouring of the "wine" of God's wrath upon the wicked is indicated in Ps. 75:8. Similarly, the anger of Yahweh is vented against Samaria through the "pouring down" of stones in Mic. 1:6. The "pouring down" of water in steep places is noted in Mic. 1:4;

and water is poured (or spilled) on the ground in 2 Sam. 14:14.

dālaph **[דָּלַף, 1811]**

dālaph is a verb occurring only three times, indicating profound sorrow in Job 16:20, with reference to the patriarch "pouring out" tears to God. See also Ps. 119:28; Eccl. 10:18.

NT Words

ekcheō [ἐκχέω, *1632*]

ekcheō is found in nearly thirty contexts meaning "pour out" in about half of these, with two distinctive symbolic motifs. (→ SHED)

ekcheō refers first of all to the outpouring of the Holy Spirit on his people, as a sign of the coming of the new covenant age (cf. Acts 2:17ff., 33; 10:45). Secondly, the term indicates the "pouring out" of the judgment of God upon a wicked world (Rev. 16:1ff.).

katacheō [καταχέω, *2708*]

katacheō occurs only in Matt. 26:7; Mark 14:3, referring on both occasions to a repentant woman pouring ointment on the head of Jesus, thereby expressing her devotion to him.

ballō [βάλλω, *906*]

ballō is a common verb with the principal meaning "throw," or "cast," occurring nearly 130 times. On two occasions, however, it is translated "pour" — once with reference to a woman pouring ointment or perfume over Jesus (cf. Matt. 26:12); and once in regard to pouring water in a basin (cf. John 13:5).

kerannymi [κεράννυμι, *2767*]

kerannymi is another rare verb meaning to "pour," "pour out," "mix" in a wholly symbolic sense. It occurs only in Rev. 14:10; 18:6, with reference to the outpouring of God's wrath upon the wicked.

epicheō [ἐπιχέω, *2022*]

epicheō occurs only in Luke 10:34, with reference to "pouring" oil on wounds to speed their healing.

POVERTY → POOR

POWER → AUTHORITY → STRENGTH

PRACTICE

OT Words

'āsāh **[עָשָׂה, 6213]**

'āsāh is a common verb meaning "do," "make," with a variety of related senses throughout the more than 2,500 occurrences of the term. One of these nuances is that of "commit," in the sense of "make a practice of," "practice."

References to people "committing" (i.e., practicing) sin include those in Lev. 5:17; 18:30; Num. 5:6; Jer. 44:7; Ezek. 3:20. Injunctions not to "commit" sin are found in Lev. 18:26; Deut. 19:20; Prov. 16:12.

ḥāṭā' **[חָטָא, 2398]**

ḥāṭā' is a common verb found nearly 250 times with the predominant sense of "to sin." In particular, this term refers to "committing" sin in several places (cf. Lev. 5:7; 1 Kgs. 14:22; Jer. 16:10; Ezek. 16:51; 33:16).

NT Words

prassō [πράσσω, *4238*]

prassō is a partial dynamic equivalent for the OT entries above, meaning "do," "commit" (i.e., practice) in its nearly forty occurrences.

References to "committing" practices that are an abomination to God are found in Rom. 1:32; 2:2.

General references to "committing" sin are found in Acts 25:11, 25; 2 Cor. 12:21.

See Also: → TRESPASS

PRAISE

OT Words

yādāh **[יָדָה, 3034]**

yādāh is a fairly common verb meaning "praise," "give thanks" in the large majority of its nearly 120 occurrences. Virtually all of these references speak of giving praise to God. (→ CONFESS)

In the context of ritual worship, ***yādāh*** is frequently found in the expression "praise the Lord," either as a cry of praise or describing an act of worship (cf. Gen. 29:35; 2 Chr. 7:6; 20:21; Pss. 7:17; 107:8ff.; 118:19; Isa. 12:4; Jer. 33:11). Similarly, ***yādāh*** indicates "giving thanks" to God (cf. 2 Sam. 22:50; Neh. 12:24; Pss. 18:49; 107:1; 122:4; 136:1ff.).

In one instance, ***yādāh*** conveys the idea of giving "praise" to human beings (cf. Gen. 49:8).

tehillāh [תְּהִלָּה, **8416**]

tehillāh is a noun derived from the verb ***hālal*** (see below), meaning "praise" in each of its nearly sixty occurrences. ***tehillāh*** is used in several different contexts with different nuances, almost all of them linked to the person of God.

In a number of places ***tehillāh*** signifies "praise" in the sense of "glory," or "renown," referring to the person of Yahweh (cf. Exod. 15:11; Deut. 10:21; Ps. 22:3; Isa. 60:6; Jer. 33:9; Hab. 3:3). In Isa. 42:10; 43:21 Yahweh himself speaks of "my praise."

The offering of "praise" to Yahweh is associated firstly with temple worship (Pss. 22:25; 34:1; 65:1; 106:2), and additionally with singing (2 Chr. 20:22; Pss. 40:3; 51:15; 66:2; 106:12; 145:1; 147:1; 149:1).

With respect to the people of God, Deut. 26:19; Zeph. 3:19, 20 record that Yahweh sets his people up in a position of "praise" and "honor" among the nations.

In regard to the nations, Jer. 48:2 declares that the praise of Moab shall be no more.

hālal [הָלַל, **1984**]

hālal is a fairly common verb occurring in 165 contexts with the predominant meaning "to praise," as well as "to glory," "boast."

In the context of "praise" directed towards human beings, ***hālal*** conveys the sense of "commend" (Gen. 12:15; Prov. 12:8), and "admire" (2 Sam. 14:25; 2 Chr. 23:12; Prov. 27:2; 31:28ff.; Song 6:9). In Judg. 16:24, the Philistines praise their god, Dagon, for the capture of Samson.

The exclamation "praise the Lord" is found in numerous contexts (e.g., Pss. 105:45; 111:1; 113:1ff.; 135:1ff.; 148:1ff.; 150:1ff.; Jer. 20:13). References to the Israelite people praising God are found in secular contexts (2 Sam. 22:4; Joel 2:26); and, more commonly, in "ritual" contexts (cf. 1 Chr. 16:4; 2 Chr. 5:13; Ezra 3:10ff.; Neh. 5:13; Pss. 22:22ff.; 119:164, 175; Isa. 62:9).

zāmar [זָמַר, **2167**]

zāmar is a verb occurring forty-five times with the consistent meaning "sing praise(s)" to God (e.g., Judg. 5:3; 1 Chr. 16:9; Pss. 7:17; 57:7ff.; 71:22ff.; 138:1; Isa. 12:5).

shābaḥ [שָׁבַח, **7623**]

shābaḥ is a comparatively rare verb meaning to "praise" to God in less than half of the eleven contexts in which it occurs (cf. Pss. 63:3; 117:1; 145:4). The exclamation "praise the Lord!" is found in Ps. 147:12.

shebaḥ [שְׁבַח, **7624** (Aramaic)]

shebaḥ is an Aramaic verb found in five contexts, meaning "praise" in each one. Dan. 2:23; 4:34, 37 refer to praise given to God; while Dan. 5:4, 23 refer to praise given by Belshazzar to his Babylonian gods.

NT Words

ainos [αἶνος, *136*]

ainos is a rare noun, found only in Matt. 21:16; Luke 18:43 with reference to "praise" offered to God.

aineō [αἰνέω, *134*]

aineō is the verb from which ***ainos*** is derived (see above) and is consistently translated "to offer praise" (to God) in each of the ten occurrences in which it occurs (cf. Luke 2:13, 20; 19:37; 24:53; Acts 2:47; 3:8, 9; Rev. 19:5).

epainos [ἔπαινος, *1868*]

epainos is a noun found in eleven contexts, meaning "praise" in the sense of "commendation" given and received, as well as "adoration" offered to God.

The sense of "commendation," given to human beings by other human beings, is found in Rom. 13:3; 2 Cor. 8:18; Phil. 4:8; 1 Pet. 2:14. 1 Cor. 4:5 mentions "praise" or "commendation" given to human beings by God.

epainos also means "praise" in the context of adoration given to God (cf. Rom. 2:29; Eph. 1:6, 12, 14; Phil. 1:11; 1 Pet. 1:7).

epaineō [ἐπαινέω, *1867*]

epaineō is the verb from which ***epainos*** (see above) is derived, meaning "commend," "offer praise." The term is found in only five places, four of which indicate the human attitude of "commending." Two of these speak of positive commendation (cf. Luke 16:8; 1 Cor. 11:2). In 1 Cor. 11:17, 22, the apostle Paul refuses to commend the Corinthian congregation, on account of their carnality. Rom. 15:11 is the only text in which ***epaineō*** indicates giving praise to God.

ainesis [αἴνεσις, *133*]

ainesis is a noun derived from ***aineō*** (see above), referring to "praise" offered to God in Heb. 13:5.

hymneō [ὑμνέω, *5214*]

hymneō is a verb expressing the underlying sense of "singing." It occurs only four times, referring explicitly to "singing praise" to God in Acts 16:25; Heb. 2:12. It speaks implicitly of "singing praise" to God in Matt. 26:30; Mark 14:26, with reference to "singing hymns."

See Also: ➞ BLESS ➞ CONFESS ➞ GLORY ➞ PRAISE ➞ THANK

PRAY, PRAYER

OT Words

pālal [פָּלַל, 6419]

pālal is a verb found in eighty contexts with the predominant sense of "pray" in almost all of its occurrences.

The action of praying in non-specific contexts as an act of intercession is indicated in Gen. 20:7; Deut. 9:20.

pālal refers to offering prayer to God in Gen. 20:17; Num. 11:2; Deut. 9:26; 1 Sam. 1:10ff.; 1 Kgs. 8:28ff.; 2 Kgs. 6:17; 2 Chr. 6:19ff.; Neh. 2:4; Ps. 5:2; Isa. 37:15; Jer. 29:12; Jonah 2:1. Prayer to God as an explicit act of intercession is found in 1 Sam. 7:5; 1 Kgs. 13:6; Jer. 29:7; 42:2ff. Yahweh actually denies Jeremiah intercessory prayer in Jer. 7:16; 11:14; 14:11. Praying to God as an act of confession is noted in Ezra 10:1; Neh. 1:4ff.; Dan. 9:4, 20.

A few texts describe prayer offered by pagan peoples to their gods (cf. Isa. 16:2; 44:12; 45:20).

tephillāh [תְּפִלָּה, 8605]

tephillāh is the noun derived from ***pālal*** (see above) with the consistent meaning "prayer" in each of its nearly eighty occurrences.

Prayer offered to God is indicated in 2 Sam. 7:27; 1 Kgs. 8:28ff.; Ps. 42:8; Jonah 2:7.

Exhortations to Yahweh to hear one's prayer are noted in Pss. 4:1; 17:1; 54:2; 84:8; 86:1, 6; 88:2; 102:1; 143:1; Dan. 9:17. Several contexts specifically mention prayer that is accepted by God (cf. Pss. 6:9; 66:20; 102:17; Prov. 15:29; Isa. 38:5). Conversely, Jer. 7:16; 11:4; Lam. 3:8, 44 record that prayer is on occasion rejected or denied by God. In a similar vein, Yahweh's anger at the prayers of his wayward people, resulting in his refusal to listen to them, is indicated in Ps. 80:4; Isa. 1:15 (cf. also Ps. 109:7). Intercessory prayer is recorded in Isa. 37:4; Dan. 9:3. The temple is referred to as the "house of prayer" in Isa. 56:7. Prayer in non-specific contexts is indicated in Job 16:17; Ps. 35:13; Prov. 15:8; Hab. 3:1.

ṣelā' [צְלָא, 6739 (Aramaic)**]**

ṣelā' is an Aramaic verb found in only two places, meaning "prayer" in Ezra 6:10; Dan. 6:10.

pāga' [פָּגַע, 6293]

pāga' is a verb with the predominant sense of "encounter," "meet," and "fall" in the majority of its nearly fifty occurrences. Once, in Job 21:15, ***pāga'*** refers to the action of praying to God.

'ātar [עָתַר, 6279]

'ātar is a verb with the primary sense of "entreat" or "petition." In the majority of the twenty contexts in which it is found, ***'ātar*** indicates prayers of intercession and petition offered to God.

Intercessory prayer is indicated in Gen. 25:21; Exod. 8:8ff.; 9:28; 10:17ff.; Judg. 13:8; 2 Sam. 21:14; 24:25. Prayers of petition, of earnest plea, are noted in 1 Chr. 5:20; 2 Chr. 33:13, 19; Ezra 8:23; Job 33:6; Isa. 19:22.

shā'al [שָׁאַל, 7592]

shā'al is a common verb found approximately 170 times with the principal meanings "ask," "inquire," as well as a number of associated nuances. One of these nuances is "to pray," which is found only in Ps. 122:6 — an earnest request to petition God for the peace of Jerusalem. (➞ ASK)

ḥālāh [חָלָה, 2470]

ḥālāh is a verb with a variety of senses grouped around two primary spheres of meaning, "to become sick," and "to ask," or "petition." ***ḥālāh*** is found in seventy-five contexts. Four of these refer to petitioning Yahweh. Zech. 7:2; 8:21, 22 speak of those who plead with God for his favor, praying for his mercy to be extended to them (cf. Zech. 7:2; 8:21, 22; Mal. 1:9).

be'ā' [בְּעָא, 1156 (Aramaic)**]**

be'ā' is an Aramaic verb that is translated "ask," "make a request of," or "petition" in all twelve occurrences of the term. Dan. 2:18; 6:7ff. specifically refer to petitioning Yahweh through prayer.

NT Words

proseuchomai [προσεύχομαι, *4336*]

proseuchomai is the most common verb in the New Testament referring to the activity of praying. It is translated "to pray," "offer prayer" in each of its nearly ninety occurrences.

General references to prayer are found in Matt. 24:20; Mark 11:24ff.; Luke 1:10; Acts 9:11; 22:17; 1 Cor. 11:4ff.; 14:13ff. Other texts allude to the posture of praying, as in Matt. 6:5ff.; 1 Tim. 2:8. A prescribed paradigm for praying is indicated with regard to the "Lord's Prayer," as recorded in Luke 11:2.

Exhortations to pray are found in Mark 13:18; Eph. 6:18; 1 Thess. 5:17; Jude 20. In particular, Jesus exhorts his followers to pray for those who persecute them (cf. Matt. 5:44; Luke 6:28).

proseuchomai also refers to praying for guidance (cf. Acts 1:24); praying for the healing of the sick (cf. Jas. 5:13ff.); and intercessory prayer (cf. Rom. 8:26; Phil. 1:9; Col. 1:3, 9; 4:3; 2 Thess. 1:11; 3:1; Heb. 13:8). Praying as an act of commissioning for ministry, associated with the laying on of hands, is indicated in Acts 6:6; 8:15; 13:3; 14:23. Hypocritical praying is condemned in Matt. 23:14; Mark 12:40; Luke 20:47.

A number of texts refer to Jesus praying (cf. Matt. 14:23; Mark 1:35; 6:46; Luke 3:21; Luke 5:16; 6:12; 9:18). The most dramatic and poignant of these episodes is the agony of Jesus' prayer in the garden of Gethsemane the night before his crucifixion. Matt. 19:13 refers specifically to Jesus praying for the sick in order to bring about their healing (cf. also Paul in Acts 28:8).

proseuchē [προσευχή, *4335*]

proseuchē is the noun derived from ***proseuchomai*** (see above), meaning "prayer" in all thirty-seven occurrences of the term.

General references to prayer are found in Matt. 17:21; Acts 2:42; Rom. 1:9; 1 Cor. 7:5; Eph. 1:16; 1 Pet. 3:7.

Prayer associated with temple worship is recorded in Matt. 21:13; Mark 11:17; Luke 19:46; Acts 3:1. A number of contexts refer to intercessory prayer (cf. Acts 12:5; Eph. 6:18; Phil. 4:6; Col. 4:12; 1 Thess. 1:2; 1 Tim. 2:1; Phlm. 4, 22; Jas. 5:17). In particular, the intercessory prayers of the saints are indicated in Rev. 5:8; 8:3, 4. An exhortation to pray is contained in Col. 4:2. Acts 16:13, 16 refer to a "place of prayer" beside the river in Philippi. There were so few Jews in the city, specifically an insufficient number of men, that a synagogue could not be established. References to Jesus' prayer life are found in Luke 6:12; 22:45.

euchomai [εὔχομαι, *2172*]

euchomai is a verb related to ***proseuchomai*** (see above), but it occurs far less frequently. ***euchomai*** occurs seven times and means "pray," "wish." In five contexts, ***euchomai*** refers to the action of earnest, intercessory prayer (cf. Acts 27:29; 2 Chr. 13:7, 9; Jas. 5:16; 3 John 2).

euchē [εὐχή, *2171*]

euchē is a rare term, found only three times. Twice it refers to a "vow," and once, in Jas. 5:15, to a "prayer" of faith.

enteuxis [ἔντευξις, *1783*]

enteuxis is another rare noun meaning "prayer," referring to intercessory prayer (1 Tim. 2:1) and to prayer in a general sense (1 Tim. 4:5).

deomai [δέομαι, *1189*]

deomai is a verb with the underlying meanings "beseech," "beg," "make a request." These senses account for more than half of its twenty-two occurrences. In nine places, however, ***deomai*** specifically indicates the offering up of intercessory prayer (cf. Matt. 9:38; Luke 10:2; 21:36; 22:32; Acts 4:31; 8:22, 24; 10:2; 1 Thess. 3:10).

deēsis [δέησις, *1162*]

deēsis is a noun derived from ***deomai*** (see above), meaning "prayer," "entreaty" in each of its nineteen occurrences.

Prayer in a general sense is indicated in Luke 5:33; Acts 1:14; Rom. 10:1; 2 Cor. 1:11; 9:14. Prayers of entreaty or "supplication" are mentioned in Eph. 6:18; Phil. 4:6; 1 Tim. 2:1; 5:5; Jas. 5:6. Heb. 5:7 refers to the supplication of Christ. Intercessory prayer is indicated in Phil. 1:4, 9; 2 Tim. 1:3. Prayer associated with worship is noted in Luke 2:37, and prayer heard and accepted by God in Luke 1:13; 1 Pet. 3:12.

See Also: → ASK

PREACH, PREACHING, PREACHER

NT Words

kēryssō [κηρύσσω, *2784*]

kēryssō is a verb meaning "preach." The underlying sense is that of making proclamation after the manner of a herald. ***kēryssō*** is found in approximately sixty contexts.

General references to preaching are found in Mark 13:10; Luke 24:47; Rom. 2:21; 10:8, 14ff.; Gal. 2:2; Col. 1:23; 2 Tim. 4:2; 1 Pet. 3:19.

kēryssō describes the preaching ministry of John the Baptist (Matt. 3:1; Mark 1:4ff.; Luke 3:3; Acts 10:37); Jesus' preaching activity (Matt. 4:17, 23; 11:1; Mark 1:14, 39; Luke 4:18ff.; 8:1); and the apostolic proclamation of the gospel (Matt. 10:7; Mark 3:14; Luke 9:2; Acts 8:5; 19:13; 20:25).

The usage of ***kēryssō*** indicates that Christ is the focus of New Testament preaching (cf. 1 Cor. 1:23; 15:12; 2 Cor. 1:19; 4:5; 11:4; Phil. 1:15; 1 Tim. 3:16).

kēryx [κῆρυξ, *2783*]

kēryx is a noun derived from ***kēryssō*** (see above), occurring only three times and meaning "preacher," again with the underlying sense of a "herald" (cf. 1 Tim. 2:7; 2 Tim. 1:11; 2 Pet. 2:5).

kērygma [κήρυγμα, *2782*]

kērygma is another noun derived from ***kēryssō*** (see above), meaning "preaching" in all eight occurrences of the term. ***kērygma*** refers to the content of the proclamation of God's word in the Old Testament and the gospel of Christ in the New.

kērygma refers to the preaching of Jonah (Matt. 12:41; Luke 11:32); to the "preaching of Jesus Christ" (i.e., Jesus as the content of the preaching) (Rom. 16:25); and to the apostolic preaching of the gospel (1 Cor. 1:21; 2:4; 15:14; 2 Tim. 4:17; Titus 1:3).

euangelizō [εὐαγγελίζω, *2097*]

euangelizō is a synonym for ***kēryssō*** (see above), likewise meaning "preach" in all of the fifty-five contexts in which it occurs. ***euangelizō*** conveys the sense of "proclaiming or bringing the good news" of God's plan of salvation, culminating in the person and work of Christ.

The general sense of preaching the gospel, or bringing good news, is indicated in Luke 1:19; 2:10; Acts 13:32; Rom. 10:15; 1 Thess. 3:6; 1 Pet. 1:12; Rev. 14:6.

euangelizō refers to Jesus' own preaching to his people in general terms (Luke 3:18; 4:18; 7:22; 20:1); and specifically to his proclamation of the kingdom of God (e.g., Luke 4:43; 8:1; Acts 8:12). Matt. 11:5 refers specifically to preaching to the poor.

The apostolic preaching of Christ is indicated in Luke 9:6; Acts 5:42; 8:4, 25, 35; Rom. 1:15; 1 Cor. 1:17; 9:16ff.; 2 Cor. 11:7; Gal. 1:8ff. A variation on this theme is found in Eph. 2:17, which mentions the preaching of peace.

diangellō [διαγγέλλω, *1229*]

diangellō is a verb found in only three places with the underlying sense of "declare." However, in Luke 9:60; Rom. 9:17, ***diangellō*** conveys the specific meaning "preach" or "proclaim" with respect to the kingdom of God and the name of Yahweh, respectively.

katangellō [καταγγέλλω, *2605*]

katangellō is a verb found ten times with the predominant sense of "preach" or "proclaim."

The preaching of the resurrection of Christ is noted in Acts 4:2; 17:3. Proclaiming the gospel, preaching Christ, is indicated in 1 Cor. 9:14; Phil. 1:16, 18; Col. 1:28. ***katangellō*** also refers specifically to "preaching" the word of God (cf. Acts 13:5; 15:36; 17:13; 1 Cor. 2:1); the forgiveness of sins (cf. Acts 13:38); the way of salvation (cf. Acts 16:17; 17:23); the light of the Gentiles (cf. Acts 26:23); and, finally, the declaration of the faith of the Roman believers (Rom. 1:8).

parrēsiazomai [παρρησιάζομαι, *3955*]

parrēsiazomai is a verb with the predominant meaning "to speak boldly." In most of its nine occurrences, ***parrēsiazomai*** conveys the sense of "preaching boldly" in the name of Christ (cf. Acts 9:27, 29; 14:3; 18:26; 19:8; Eph. 6:20; 1 Thess. 2:2).

laleō [λαλέω, *2980*]

laleō is a common verb occurring nearly three hundred times with the dominant sense of "speak." In five of these contexts, the explicit sense of "preaching" the word is indicated (cf. Mark 2:2; Acts 16:6; Acts 8:25; 13:42; 14:25). (→ SPEECH)

See Also: → PROCLAIM

PRECEPT → COMMANDMENT → LAW

PRECIOUS → VALUABLE

PREDESTINE → DETERMINE

PRE-EMINENCE → EXCEL

PREPARATION, PREPARE

OT WORDS

kûn [כּוּן, 3559]

kûn is a common verb, occurring over two hundred times with the two predominant spheres of meaning "establish" and "prepare," in a number of varying contexts and with different nuances. (→ ESTABLISH)

Mundane uses of ***kûn*** include references to "making" (Josh. 1:11; 1 Chr. 12:39; Neh. 8:10); preparing materials for building houses (cf. Prov. 24:27); getting ready for battle (cf. 2 Chr. 26:14; Ps. 7:13; Jer. 46:14;

51:2); and preparing and constructing gallows for an execution (cf. Esth. 6:4; 7:10).

kûn is also found in a number of ritual contexts. Preparations for building the temple are noted in 1 Kgs. 5:18; 6:19; 1 Chr. 22:3ff.; 28:2; 29:2; 2 Chr. 2:9 (cf. also 2 Chr. 29:19; 31:11). Associated with this are the preparations for worship and service in the temple (cf. 1 Chr. 9:32; 22:14). 1 Chr. 15:1ff.; 2 Chr. 1:4 refer to David preparing a place for the ark of the covenant in the temple. 2 Chr. 35:4ff. refers to Josiah's preparation for celebrating the Passover festival. Amos 4:12 contains the solemn injunction, "prepare to meet your God."

In a number of places, God is said to be involved in the activity of preparation. Exod. 23:20 affirms that Yahweh is preparing a place for his people (i.e., the land of Canaan). Ps. 147:8 declares that Yahweh prepares rain for the earth. In Isa. 30:33, Yahweh is said to prepare a place for the slaughter of the wicked in divine judgment. In a metaphorical context, Ezek. 28:13 declares that Yahweh prepared precious stones for the primeval demonic spirit, prior to his fall from grace, in the garden of Eden. Zeph. 1:7 refers to God preparing a metaphorical sacrifice, as a prelude to the exercise of judgment against his people.

'āsāh [עָשָׂה, 6213]

'āsāh is one of the most common verbs in the Old Testament, occurring over 2,500 times, with the predominant sense of "do," "make," as well as a variety of associated meanings. One of these meanings is "prepare," which is found in a handful of contexts.

In a ceremonial context, Num. 15:5ff. speaks of preparing animals for sacrificial offerings. More common are mundane references to preparing food (cf. Esth. 5:8; Ezek. 4:15; Gen. 27:17; Exod. 12:39; Neh. 5:18); and preparing for war (Joel 3:9; cf. also. 1 Kgs. 1:5).

'ārak [עָרַךְ, 6186]

'ārak is a verb found in about eighty contexts with a variety of senses. The prime meanings of ***'ārak*** are "arrange," "set in order," found in more than half of these contexts. The meaning "prepare" is evident in only two places: once in Num. 23:4, with regard to preparing an altar for sacrifice, and once in Ps. 23:5, with reference to Yahweh preparing a table for David in the presence of his enemies. The context here indicates that God is offering protection from David's enemies.

pānāh [פָּנָה, 6437]

pānāh is a verb meaning "turn," "look" in the large majority of the fifteen occurrences of the term. In five of these contexts the meaning "prepare" is evident. Gen. 24:31 speaks of preparing a house for the purpose of offering hospitality. And with reference to the redemptive plan of Yahweh, Isa. 40:3; 57:14; 62:10; Mal. 3:1 refer to the phenomenon of "preparing the way of the Lord," indicating the coming of the Messianic King.

qādash [קָדַשׁ, 6942]

qādash is a fairly common verb, found in around 170 contexts with the predominant sense of "sanctify," "consecrate," "be holy." In four instances, however, ***qādash*** means "prepare" in the context of readying oneself for war (cf. Jer. 6:4; 51:28; Joel 3:9; Mic. 3:5).

kārāh [כָּרָה, 3739]

kārāh is a verb found in only four places, meaning "to prepare" in 2 Kgs. 6:23, with reference to a banquet.

NT Words

hetoimazō [ἑτοιμάζω, *2090*]

hetoimazō is the most common verb in the New Testament meaning "prepare," "make ready." The term occurs approximately forty times in a number of varying contexts.

General references to making preparation in mundane contexts are found in Matt.:22:4; Luke 12:20, 47; 17:8; Acts 23:23; Phlm. 22. In particular, Passover preparation is mentioned in Matt. 26:17ff.; Mark 14:12ff.; Luke 22:8ff. Luke 23:56; 24:1 refer to preparing spices and perfumes for the burial of the body of Christ.

In a more explicit theological context, the mission of John the Baptist to "prepare" the way for the coming of the Messianic King in the person of Jesus Christ is described in Matt. 3:3; Mark 1:3; Luke 1:76; 3:4. The unique privilege of sitting at God's right hand is a prerogative prepared by God alone (cf. Matt. 20:23; Mark 10:40).

hetoimazō refers to preparations undertaken by God alone, including God preparing a people for himself (Luke 1:17); a kingdom for his people (Matt. 25:34); and salvation for his people (Luke 2:31). John 14:2ff.; Heb. 11:16 contain the promise that both Christ and God the Father are preparing a heavenly destiny for their people. 1 Cor. 2:9 refers to the spiritual blessings prepared by God for those belonging to him. Conversely, Matt. 25:41 affirms the terrible reality of the everlasting torment prepared by God for the wicked.

hetoimazō is also used metaphorically in several contexts. In Rev. 8:6, angels prepare to blow the seven trumpets initiating divine judgment on a wicked world (cf. also Rev. 9:15; 16:12). Rev. 9:7 refers to demonic locusts preparing for battle. Rev. 12:6 refers to the place prepared by God as a refuge to protect the woman and her messianic child-king from satanic attack. Rev. 19:7; 21:2 depict the "bride" (i.e., the church) preparing to meet her "husband" (i.e., Christ, the Lamb of God).

proetoimazō [προετοιμάζω, *4282*]

proetoimazō only occurs in two places, meaning "prepare beforehand." Rom. 9:23 speaks of the phenomenon of divine election, describing the "vessels of mercy" (i.e., his people) that he has prepared beforehand for glory. Eph. 2:10 speaks of the good works presented by the people of God, works which God has "prepared beforehand." Both references indicate the saving purposes of God conceived in eternity, prior to the creation of the world.

kataskeuazō [κατασκευάζω, *2680*]

kataskeuazō is a verb occurring thirteen times, meaning "prepare" and "build." Most frequently, ***kataskeuazō*** refers to the task of "preparing" the way of the Lord, or the role of the herald announcing the coming of the Messiah (cf. Matt. 11:10; Mark 1:2; Luke 7:27). Luke 1:17 mentions a people "prepared" by God for his own glory. (→ BUILD)

paraskeuē [παρασκευή, *3904*]

paraskeuē is a noun meaning "preparation." ***paraskeuē*** occurs only six times and refers to the day of "preparation," prior to the Sabbath (i.e., Saturday) at the time of Jesus' trial and crucifixion (cf. Matt. 27:62; Mark 15:42; Luke 23:54; John 19:14, 31, 42).

katartizō [καταρτίζω, *2675*]

katartizō is a verb found in only four places. It has the underlying sense of "making complete or perfect." It is with this sense that ***katartizō*** is used in Heb. 10:5 to refer to God "having prepared a body" for his son Jesus Christ in the context of his perfect submission to his Father's will.

See Also: → READY

PRESENCE

OT Words

pānîm [פָּנִים, 6440]

pānîm is a common plural noun form found in approximately 2,100 contexts. It is used with prepositional force, meaning "before," and also has the nominal meanings "face," "countenance," "sight." The semantic range of ***pānîm*** is very broad, and it means "presence" in a number of instances. There is significant overlap in meaning here with the prepositional sense of "before," which may frequently be rendered "in the presence of." (→ FACE)

With respect to the "presence" of individuals, ***pānîm*** refers, for example, to the presence of Isaac (Gen. 27:30); Pharaoh (Gen. 41:46); Moses (Exod. 33:20); David (1 Kgs. 1:28); Solomon (2 Chr. 9:23); Xerxes (Esth. 8:15); the enemies of the psalmist (Ps. 23:5); and the Israelite assembly (1 Kgs. 8:22; 2 Chr. 6:14; Ps. 116:14).

pānîm most frequently alludes to the presence of God himself — for example, at Mt. Sinai (cf. Ps. 68:8); and in the garden of Eden (cf. Gen. 3:8; 4:16). The expression "my presence," referring to the divine accompaniment to the Israelites in the wilderness, is indicated in Exod. 33:14, 15. Referring to the angel of the Lord, the phrase "angel of his presence" occurs in Isa. 63:9. More particularly, the action of going out from the presence of Yahweh is predicated of Satan in Job 1:12; 2:7. The experience of being cast out from the presence of Yahweh at the time of the Babylonian invasion of Judah and Jerusalem is recorded in 2 Kgs. 24:20; Jer. 23:39; 52:3. In Ps. 51:11, David pleads with God not to be cast out from his presence. Lev. 22:3 speaks of being cut off from the presence of Yahweh as an example of divine punishment.

Other attitudes and emotions experienced in the presence of God include terror (cf. Job 23:15; Ps. 114:7; Isa. 19:1; 64:2; Jer. 5:22); joy (cf. Ps. 16:11); thanksgiving (cf. Ps. 95:2); worship (cf. Ps. 100:2); and living in the presence of God (cf. Ps. 140:13).

NT Words

enōpion [ἐνώπιον, *1799*]

enōpion is a preposition with the principal meaning "before," "in the presence of," "in the sight of." There is a significant amount of overlap between these meanings. ***enōpion*** occurs nearly one hundred times.

The meaning "before," in the sense of "in the presence of," is illustrated with respect to God in reference to the angel Gabriel standing in the presence of God (cf. Luke 1:19); feasting in God's presence (cf. Luke 13:26); the absence of boasting in the presence of God (cf. 1 Cor. 1:29); and the torment of the beast in the presence of God (cf. Rev. 14:10).

The presence of individuals is indicated, for example, in Luke 14:10; 24:43; Acts 27:35; 1 Tim. 5:20. Miracles performed by Jesus in the presence of his disciples are noted in John 20:30. Luke 15:10 affirms that angels in the presence of God rejoice over every sinner who repents.

prosōpon [πρόσωπον, *4383*]

prosōpon is a noun with the predominant sense of "face," "person," occurring in about eighty contexts. In five instances, however, ***prosōpon*** is used with prepositional force to mean "in the presence of." It refers to Pilate (cf. Acts 3:13); and the Sanhedrin (Acts 5:41). Acts 3:19 speaks of refreshment gleaned from the presence of God; 2 Thess. 1:9 refers to the wicked being thrust from the presence of God. Heb. 9:24 describes Jesus appearing in heaven in the presence of God.

parousia [παρουσία, *3952*]

parousia is a noun found in twenty-four contexts, meaning "appearing" or "coming" in most occurrences. In two contexts, however, the term is translated "presence," referring to the physical person of the apostle Paul (cf. 2 Cor. 10:10; Phil. 2:12).

katenōpion [κατενώπιον, *2714*]

katenōpion is a preposition, found in only five contexts with the principal meaning "before," "in the sight of," with reference to God. In Jude 24, however, it means "before his (glorious) presence."

PRESENT (VERB); PRESENT (NOUN)

OT Words

nāṣab [נָצַב, **5324**]

nāṣab is a verb with the primary meanings "stand," "set" in the majority of the seventy-five occurrences of the term. In Exod. 34:2, however, ***nāṣab*** is translated "present oneself" in the context of appearing before Yahweh at Mt. Sinai. (→ STAND)

'āmad [עָמַד, **5975**]

'āmad is one of the most common verbs in the Old Testament meaning "stand," or "set," as well as numerous associated senses in the approximately 520 occurrences of the term. In six of these contexts, ***'āmad*** is translated "to present" in a ceremonial setting.

Lev. 14:11 speaks of the need to present before the Lord a person who has been healed of an infectious disease. Lev. 27:11 refers to presenting animals for sacrifice. In particular, Lev. 16:7, 10 prescribe the presenting or offering of two goats to Yahweh, as principal elements of the offerings for the Day of Atonement ceremony. Lev. 27:8 requires the presentation of a poor man to the priests for a valuation. Num. 3:6 describes the requirement to present the Levites to Aaron in preparation for their worship service in the tabernacle. (→ STAND)

yāṣab [יָצַב, **3320**]

yāṣab is a verb with the dominant meaning "stand," as well as related senses, in the majority of its fifty or so occurrences. The secondary meaning, "present," is found in seven places.

The call to present Joshua before the Lord for his commissioning is indicated twice in Deut. 31:14. The requirement to have the leading officials in Israel presented to Yahweh for a covenant renewal ceremony is recorded in Josh. 24:1. A similar requirement is laid down for the coronation of King Saul in 1 Sam. 10:19. Judg. 20:2 describes the presentation of Israel's tribal leader in the assembly of God's people. In Job 1:6; 2:1, the angelic servants of Yahweh present themselves before him in the heavenly council.

teshûrāh [תְּשׁוּרָה, **8670**]

teshûrāh is a term found only in 1 Sam. 9:7 with reference to a "present" or "gift."

berākāh [בְּרָכָה, **1293**]

berākāh is a term with the primary meaning "blessing" in almost all of the seventy or so contexts in which it is found. However, in 1 Sam. 30:26, ***berākāh*** means "present"—a gift given by David to the elders of Judah from the plunder taken from the Philistines.
(→ BLESS)

nāphal [נָפַל, **5307**]

nāphal is a common verb meaning "fall (down)," "cast (down)," as well as several related senses, in the large majority of its nearly 430 occurrences. In several places, ***nāphal*** is translated "to present," referring to presenting one's requests before God (cf. Jer. 36:7; 42:9; Dan. 9:18).

yāṣag [יָצַג, **3322**]

yāṣag is a verb found in sixteen places with the senses of "set," "made," "put" in the majority of these contexts. In Gen. 47:2, ***yāṣag*** is translated "present" in the context of Joseph's brothers being presented to Pharaoh. (→ SET)

qārab [קָרַב, **7126**]

qārab is a verb with the predominant meanings "offer," "come (near)," "bring," "draw near" in the overwhelming majority of the 280 contexts in which it occurs. In two places it is translated "to present." Lev. 2:8 speaks of a cereal offering presented to the priest; and Lev. 7:35 refers to priests having been presented to Aaron the high priest prior to their service.
(→ OFFER)

shay [שַׁי, **7862**]

shay is a term found in only three places, referring to a "present" or "gift" brought to Yahweh in worship (cf. Pss. 68:29; 76:11; Isa. 18:7).

NT Words

paristēmi [παρίστημι, *3936*]

paristēmi is a verb with the primary meanings "stand," "stand by," "present," as well as several other minor senses, in the forty or so contexts in which it is found. (→ STAND)

Luke 2:22 speaks of Jesus' parents presenting him to the Lord in the temple at the time of his circumcision and consecration. Peter presents the young woman Tabitha alive after raising her from the dead (cf. Acts 9:41). Paul is "presented" (i.e., handed over) to Felix, the governor of Judea, in Acts 23:33. Paul exhorts his readers to present their bodies as living sacrifices to the Lord in Rom. 12:1. Paul's desire to present the Corinthian congregation as a "pure bride" to her "husband," the risen Christ, is recorded in 2 Cor. 11:2 (cf. also Eph. 5:27; Col. 1:22, 28).

pareimi [πάρειμι, *3918*]

pareimi is an intransitive verb with the primary meanings "to be present," "come," in most of the twenty-three contexts in which it occurs.

The meaning "to be present" with reference to people in general, mundane contexts is indicated in Luke 13:1; 2 Cor. 10:2, 11; 11:9; 13:2, 10; Gal. 4:19. Acts 10:33 refers to a group of people being present in the sight of God. The setting here is the house of the Roman centurion, Cornelius. 1 Cor. 5:3 speaks of Paul being absent in body, but "present" in spirit.

paraginomai [παραγίνομαι, *3854*]

paraginomai is an intransitive verb with the principal meaning "to come" in all but one of its nearly forty occurrences. In Acts 4:18 it is translated "to be present" with regard to the presence of the elders in the Jerusalem church who had come to meet with Paul and his missionary companions.

sympareimi [συμπάρειμι, *4840*]

sympareimi is a verb found only in Acts 25:24, meaning "to be present."

enistēmi [ἐνίστημι, *1764*]

enistēmi is a verb that is predominantly utilized as an adjective and a noun, as well as a verb with intransitive force. It occurs sixteen times.

The meaning "present" in the sense of the current age, period of time, or history is found in Rom. 8:38; 1 Cor. 3:22. The adjectival sense of "present" or "current" is indicated in 1 Cor. 7:26 with reference to this "present distress" (i.e., persecution, troubled time). In Gal. 1:4 ***enistēmi*** refers to this "present evil world"; and in Heb. 9:9 to "this present time." 2 Thess. 2:2 refers to the Day of the Lord "being at hand" (i.e., has come; is now present).

histēmi [ἵστημι, *2476*]

histēmi is a verb that is translated "to stand," as well as a number of related senses, in the great majority of its nearly 160 occurrences. In one place, however, ***histēmi*** means "to present" in the context of the benediction of Jude 24, whereby Christ is declared able to "present" us without fault to God himself in glory.

See Also: → GIFT → OFFERING

PRESERVE

OT Words

ḥāyāh [חָיָה, **2421**]

ḥāyāh is a common verb with the dominant sense of "to live," "be alive," as well as related meanings, in its nearly 270 occurrences. In Gen. 19:32ff., however, ***ḥāyāh*** is translated "to preserve" with regard to the perverted desires of Lot's daughters, who conspired to have an incestuous relationship with their father in order to "preserve" the paternal family lineage. (→ LIFE)

sûm [שׂוּם, **7760**]

sûm is a common verb with the predominant general sense of "put," "make," "set," as well as a large variety of derivative meanings in all the places it occurs — around six hundred times. In Gen. 45:7, however, it means "preserve" in the context of Joseph's conviction that God had determined to "preserve" a remnant on earth for his brothers and their descendants.

yātar [יָתַר, **3498**]

yātar is a verb meaning "leave," "remain," as well as related senses, in the approximately one hundred contexts in which it occurs. In Ps. 79:11, however, ***yātar*** means "preserve," where the psalmist beseeches God to "preserve those condemned to die."

NT Words

zōogoneō [ζωογονέω, *2225*]

zōogoneō is a verb found only in two places, meaning "preserve," "(keep) alive." Luke 17:33 contains the famous proverbial truth uttered by Christ: ". . . whoever loses his life will preserve it."

syntēreō [συντηρέω, *4933*]

syntēreō is a verb found in four places, meaning "preserve" in Matt. 9:17 with reference to the preservation of fresh wineskins.

See Also: → DEFEND → DELIVER → KEEP → SAVE

PRESS

OT Words

sāḥat [שָׂחַט, **7818**]

sāḥat is a verb found only in Gen. 40:11 with reference to squeezing or pressing grapes for their juice.

NT Words

apothlibō [ἀποθλίβω, *598*]

apothlibō is a verb found only in Luke 8:45 with the sense of "press in on all sides," referring to people crowding around Jesus.

diōkō [διώκω, *1377*]

diōkō is a verb with the dominant sense of "persecute," with the subsidiary meaning "to follow," occurring in over forty contexts. In Phil. 3:14, however, ***diōkō*** is translated "to press on," indicating Paul's determination to attain eternal life with Christ.

piezō [πιέζω, *4085*]

piezō is a verb found only in Luke 6:38 with reference to a measure of grain (implied), "pressed down" and running over, so as to reflect generosity.

See Also: → CROWD → WINEPRESS

PREVAIL → AUTHORITY → STRENGTH

PREY

OT Words

tereph [טֶרֶף, **2964**]

tereph refers to "prey," indicating wildlife taken by animals for food. It is used both literally and metaphorically. ***tereph*** occurs in twenty-three places and is translated "prey" in most of these. The literal sense of "prey" is indicated in Num. 23:24; Ps. 104:21.

In metaphorical contexts, the predominant symbol is that of a lion taking its prey. In Ezek. 22:25, 27; Job 29:17; Ps. 124:6, references to "the prey" indicate victims who fall prey to the wicked. Isa. 5:29 refers to Israel as the "prey" of the nations, to whom she has been handed over by God as punishment for her sins. Ezek. 19:3, 6 refer to "prey" in regard to the nations conquered by a powerful Israelite monarchy. See also Nah. 2:12, 13; Gen. 49:9; Amos 3:4.

'ad [עַד, **5706**]

'ad is found in only three places. In Gen. 49:27 it refers to the "prey" devoured by a wolf — a metaphorical allusion to the tribe of Benjamin.

See Also: → SPOIL

PRICE

OT Words

miqnah [מִקְנָה, **4736**]

miqnah is a noun found fifteen times, denoting several meanings concerning the exchange of money for goods. It means "bought," as well as "purchase," "price."

The meaning "price" is found only twice, both in Lev. 25:16 with reference to the price one could charge for land sold between the years of Jubilee.

keseph [כֶּסֶף, **3701**]

keseph refers almost exclusively to "money," or "silver," throughout its approximately four hundred occurrences. On two occasions, however, it is translated "price." Lev. 25:50 refers to the price set for the sale of a slave in the years leading up to the Jubilee year. 1 Chr. 21:22ff. refers to the price paid by King David for the threshing floor, which was to be the site for the future temple.

meḥîr [מְחִיר, **4242**]

meḥîr is a noun found in fifteen contexts with the underlying sense of "purchase." In several of these places it refers specifically to the price of certain tangible commodities (cf. Prov. 27:26); and people (cf. Isa. 45:13); as well as intangible qualities such as wisdom (cf. Job 28:15).

***meshek* [מֶשֶׁךְ, 4901]**

meshek occurs only once with the meaning "price," in Job 28:18, where it refers to the "price" of wisdom exceeding that of precious stones.

***yeqār* [יְקָר, 3366]**

yeqār is a noun with the predominant sense of "honor," as well as the secondary meaning "precious (thing)," in all but one of its seventeen occurrences: in Zech. 11:13 it means "price."

NT WORDS

***timē* [τιμή, *5092*]**

timē is a noun with the primary sense of "honor" in the majority of the forty or so contexts in which it is found. However, it means "price" in two places. In Matt. 27:9 it refers to the price of thirty pieces of silver paid by the religious leaders of Judea to Judas for the betrayal of Jesus. 1 Cor. 6:20; 7:23 refer to the truth that all believers have been "bought with a price" (i.e., the sacrifice of Christ in his death and resurrection).

See Also: → REDEEM → VALUABLE

PRIDE, PROUD

OT WORDS

***gā'ôn* [גָּאוֹן, 1347]**

gā'ôn means "excellency," "majesty," "pride," as well as several related senses, in its nearly fifty occurrences. The meaning "pride" is found in about half of these.

When it means "pride," ***gā'ôn*** primarily refers to an arrogant conceit that will incur the wrath of God. Such an attitude is predicated of Israel, for example, in Lev. 26:19; Jer. 13:9; Ezek. 7:24; 16:49, 56; 33:28; Hos. 5:5; 7:10; Amos 6:8. Such pride is also attributed to the nations in Jer. 48:29; Ezek. 30:6, 18; 32:12; Zeph. 2:10; Zech. 9:6; 10:11. Evil men in general are also described this way in Job 35:12; Ps. 59:12; Prov. 8:13; 16:18; Isa. 13:11; 16:6; 23:9.

There is one metaphorical usage of ***gā'ôn*** in Job 38:11, with respect to the "pride" of created forces such as waves.

***ga'awāh* [גַּאֲוָה, 1346]**

ga'awāh is synonymous with ***gā'ôn*** (see above), meaning "pride," "arrogance" in most of its nineteen occurrences.

The pride, arrogance, or haughtiness of the wicked is indicated in Pss. 10:2; 31:18, 23; 73:6; Prov. 14:3; Isa. 9:9; 13:11. In Isa. 16:6; 25:11; Jer. 48:29, the arrogance of Moab is cited and condemned. Zeph. 3:11 explicitly mentions the pride of Israel. In Ps. 36:11, the psalmist pleads with God to keep arrogance away from him. A general reference to pride is found in Prov. 29:23.

***gē'āh* [גֵּאָה, 1344]**

gē'āh occurs only in Prov. 8:13, referring to "pride" as characteristic of evil and perverse speech.

***gē'ût* [גֵּאוּת, 1348]**

gē'ût has the dual sense of "pride" and "majesty." The former meaning is found in three of the eight occurrences of the term, all referring to the pride or arrogance of the wicked — either evil people in general (Ps. 17:10), or Israel in particular (cf. Isa. 28:1, 3).

***zādôn* [זָדוֹן, 2087]**

zādôn is a noun found in eleven places, meaning "pride," "arrogance," "presumptuousness."

The presumptuousness of the false prophet is indicated in Deut. 18:22. General references to human pride are found in 1 Sam. 17:28; Prov. 21:24. In Prov. 11:2; 13:10, it is affirmed that pride brings one shame as well as strife. Several texts declare the harsh reality that pride left unchecked leads to inevitable divine punishment (cf. Jer. 49:16; 50:31ff.; Ezek. 7:10).

***zûd* [זוּד, 2103 (Aramaic)]**

zûd is an Aramaic verb found only in Dan. 5:20 with reference to Nebuchadnezzar's heart being hardened with "pride."

***zēd* [זֵד, 2086]**

zēd is a noun referring to "those who are proud, or arrogant" in almost all of its thirteen occurrences (e.g., Pss. 86:14; 119:21, Prov. 21:24; Isa. 13:11; Jer. 43:2; Mal. 3:15; 4:1).

***gēwāh* [גֵּוָה, 1466]**

gēwāh is found in only three places, referring to the sinful "pride" of human beings (cf. Job 22:9; 33:17; Jer. 13:17).

***gē'eh* [גֵּאֶה, 1343]**

gē'eh is an adjective meaning "proud," or "arrogant," in each of its nine occurrences.

Several texts declare that those who are proud will suffer inevitable divine punishment (cf. Job 40:11, 12; Ps. 94:2; Isa. 2:12). General references to "proud" people are found in Ps. 123:4; 140:5; Prov. 16:19; Jer. 48:29.

gōbah [גֹּבַהּ, 1363]

gōbah is a term meaning "height," "grandeur," and "pride." ***gōbah*** is found in sixteen contexts and means "pride" in four of these, where it points to the pride, or arrogance, of humankind in general (cf. 2 Chr. 32:26; Ps. 10:4; Prov. 16:18; Jer. 48:29).

shaḥaṣ [שַׁחַץ, 7830]

shaḥaṣ is a rare noun found only twice, referring in both instances to the pride of wild beasts (Job 28:8; 41:34).

rāḥāb [רָחָב, 7342]

rāḥāb is an adjective with the primary meaning "broad," "large." The term occurs twenty-one times. In two of these contexts, ***rāḥab*** is translated "proud" with respect to the human heart (cf. Ps. 101:5; Prov. 21:4).

yāhîr [יָהִיר, 3093]

yāhîr is an adjective meaning "proud" in regard to human arrogance. The term is found only twice (cf. Prov. 21:24; Hab. 2:5).

NT Words

hyperēphania [ὑπερηφανία, *5243*]

hyperēphania is a noun found only in Mark 7:22 with reference to the human vice of "pride."

hyperēphanos [ὑπερήφανος, *5244*]

hyperēphanos is an adjective found in only five contexts, meaning "proud." This quality inevitably draws down the judgment of God upon those who manifest it (cf. Luke 1:51; Rom. 1:30; 2 Tim. 3:2; Jas. 4:6; 1 Pet. 5:5).

typhoō [τυφόω, *5187*]

typhoō is a verb meaning "to be proud," or "to be filled with pride." It is found only three times (cf. 1 Tim. 3:6; 6:4; 2 Tim. 3:4).

alazoneia [ἀλαζονεία, *212*]

alazoneia is a noun meaning "pride," "boasting." It occurs only twice, in Jas. 4:16; 1 John 2:16.

See Also: → HIGH

PRIEST, PRIESTHOOD

OT Words

kōhēn [כֹּהֵן, 3548]

kōhēn is the only term in the Old Testament that refers to the office of the Israelite priesthood. The meaning "priest" is found in almost every one of its 750 occurrences. Several classes of priest are distinguished. There are also some references to pagan priests.

Two significant uses of ***kōhēn***, indicating a pre-Aaronic priesthood, are found in Gen. 14:18; Ps. 110:4. The first of these refers to the mysterious Melchizedek, priest king of Salem, designated also as priest of the most high God. Ps. 110 refers to an eternal priest patterned after the order of Melchizedek. That role is embodied and fulfilled in the person and work of Christ, who is explicitly declared to be that unique high priest in Heb. 7:11ff.

References to priests in general contexts are found in Pss. 78:64; 132:9; Isa. 24:2; 28:7; 66:21. In particular, Isa. 61:6 refers uniquely to "priests of the Lord."

Most frequently, ***kōhēn*** refers to the Levitical priests (e.g., Exod. 19:22ff.; Lev. 1:5ff.; 7:5ff.; Num. 3:6ff.; Deut. 26:3ff.; 1 Sam. 22:11ff.; 1 Kgs. 8:3ff.; 2 Chr. 5:5ff.; Ezra 2:61ff.; Neh. 7:63ff.; Hag. 2:11ff.; Mal. 2:1). In the vision of Ezekiel's temple, numerous references are made to the renewed worship of Yahweh, in which the role of the priests figures prominently (cf. Ezek. 40:45ff.; 42:13ff.; 44:15ff.; 46:19ff.; 48:10ff.).

In the context of references to the Levitical priests, ***kōhēn*** also indicates in particular the office of the high priest. For example, ***kōhēn*** refers to Aaron himself as the chosen head of the priestly order from whom all future high priests would emerge (cf. Exod. 29:30; 31:10; 35:19; 38:21; 39:41). Other references to particular high priests include Eli (1 Sam. 2:11); Abimelech (1 Sam. 21:1ff.); Abiathar (1 Kgs. 1:7ff.); Zadok (1 Kgs. 1:25ff.); Jehoiada (2 Kgs. 11:9ff.). See also Lev. 16:32ff., and the reference to the Day of Atonement ceremony; and 1 Sam. 2:35, referring to the promise of a "faithful priest" to replace the flawed, discredited priestly lineage of Eli. See also Ezra 7:5; Hag. 1:1, 12, 14; Zech. 3:1, 8; 6:11, 13.

kōhēn also frequently refers to Israelite priests who function illegally and illegitimately, contrary to the Mosaic law provisions, and who are thereby subject to the sanctions of the law covenant, inviting the anger and judgment of God (cf. Judg. 17:5ff.; 18:4ff.; Jer. 23:11, 33ff.; 32:32; Lam. 4:13ff.; Ezek. 22:26; Hos. 4:4, 9; Mal. 1:6). In particular, 1 Kgs. 12:31ff.; 13:33; 2 Chr. 13:9ff. refer to the priests appointed by Jeroboam for the northern kingdom of Israel, who rapidly degenerated into an idolatrous priestly caste.

Pagan priests are indicated in Gen. 41:45ff.; 46:20; 47:22, 26; Exod. 2:16; 18:1; Jer. 49:3.

The phrase "kingdom of priests" is applied to Israel in Exod. 19:6 as part of their unique designation by Yahweh, identifying them as partners in an intimate relationship with him.

kāhan [כָּהַן, 3547]

kāhan is a verb occurring twenty-three times, with the explicit sense "to serve (God) as a priest" in all but one instance (cf. Exod. 28:1ff.; 41; 29:44; 30:30; 40:13ff.; Lev. 7:35; 16:32; Num. 3:3ff.; Deut. 10:6; Ezek. 44:13; Hos. 4:6). The two latter references in Ezekiel and Hosea refer specifically to Yahweh's rejection of Israelite priests for their disregard of his laws.

kehunnāh [כְּהֻנָּה, 3550]

kehunnāh is derived from ***kāhan*** (see above) and occurs fourteen times, with the consistent sense of "priesthood" or "priestly office" (cf. Exod. 29:9; 40:15; Num. 3:10; 16:10; 18:1, 7; 25:13; Josh. 18:7; 1 Sam. 2:36; Ezra 2:62; Neh. 7:64; 13:29).

kōmer [כֹּמֶר, 3649]

kōmer is found in only three places, referring to "idolatrous priests" (cf. 2 Kgs. 23:5; Hos. 10:5; Zeph. 1:4).

NT Words

archiereus [ἀρχιερεύς, *749*]

archiereus is a common term in the New Testament, designating the office of "chief priest" or "high priest." ***archiereus*** occurs over 120 times, with references to "chief" priests and "high" priests divided fairly equally.

References to "chief priests" — that group of priestly leaders immediately below the rank of "high priest," are found, for example, in Matt. 2:4; 21:15; 27:1ff.; Mark 11:18, 27; 15:1ff.; Luke 9:22; 22:2ff.; John 18:3; 19:15ff.; Acts 5:24; 9:14; 19:14. As a group, along with the elders of the Jewish Sanhedrin, these men were implacably opposed to the person and work of Jesus Christ, whom they regarded as a serious threat to their privileged status in the Jewish community.

The "high priest" is also frequently mentioned (cf. Matt. 26:57ff.; Mark 14:47ff.; Luke 22:50ff.; John 11:49ff.; 18:10ff.; Acts 4:6). Other references to the office of the high priest are found in Heb. 5:1; 7:27ff.; 8:3; 9:7, 25; 13:11.

The most significant theological usage of ***archiereus*** is found in the book of Hebrews, with reference to Christ's heavenly ministry as the great high priest of his people (cf. Heb. 2:17; 3:1; 4:14, 15; 7:26; 8:1; 9:11). In particular, Heb. 5:5, 10; 6:20 speak of Jesus' eternal high priestly ministry as one patterned after the order of Melchizedek, without beginning or end.

hiereus [ἱερεύς, *2409*]

hiereus means "priest" in each of the thirty-two contexts in which it is found. It refers primarily to the ceremonial officials of Jesus' day and is also a metaphor for believers in terms of their intimate relationship with God. ***hiereus*** also refers to Christ's heavenly high priestly ministry.

References to priests as Jewish ministers in the first century include those in Matt. 8:4; 12:4ff.; Mark 1:44; 2:26; Luke 1:5; 5:14; John 1:19; Acts 4:1; 6:7; Heb. 7:23; 9:6; 10:11. There is also one reference to a priest of the cult of Zeus (the patron god of the city of Lystra) in Acts 14:13.

hiereus also refers to the high priestly role of Jesus, whose ministry of intercession is patterned after the priesthood of Melchizedek, the ancient priest king of Salem mentioned in Gen. 14 (cf. Heb. 5:6; 7:1ff.).

hiereus also refers to the saints in heaven as "priests" of God in the eternal kingdom (cf. Rev. 1:6; 5:10; 20:6).

hierōsynē [ἱερωσύνη, *2420*]

hierōsynē means "priesthood" in each of the four contexts where it occurs. On three occasions, ***hierōsynē*** refers to the Levitical priesthood (cf. Heb. 7:11ff.). Heb. 7:24 refers to the eternal "priesthood" of the heavenly Christ.

hierateia [ἱερατεία, *2405*]

hierateia is a synonym for ***hierōsynē*** (see above), found only twice and meaning "priestly office" in both contexts (cf. Luke 1:9; Heb. 7:5).

hierateuma [ἱεράτευμα, *2406*]

hierateuma occurs only twice, referring on each occasion to the body of Christ, the people of God, as a holy and royal "priesthood" belonging to God (cf. 1 Pet. 2:5, 9).

hierateuō [ἱερατεύω, *2407*]

hierateuō is a verb found only in Luke 1:8, meaning "to serve as a priest" and referring to Zechariah, the father of John the Baptist.

Additional Notes

An important redemptive-historical element underlies the ministry of priests throughout Scripture.

Priests were chosen in the Old Testament from the tribe of Levi for the express purpose of acting as mediators between God and his people. Their function was primarily ritual, and their duties were strictly prescribed under the terms of the old covenant. They enabled Israelite people to worship Yahweh correctly, to offer acceptable sacrifices of various kinds, and to have their sins forgiven — all of which was dependent on the attitude of faith exhibited in the heart of the worshiper. Such priests were one of three classes of people (along with prophets and kings) under the old covenant to receive a Spirit anointing from God as a guarantee of their legitimate ministry.

While priests are mentioned as a class of privileged servants of God in the New Testament, however, their ministry is brought to a climactic focus in the person of Christ. It is our Lord himself who is likewise anointed by the Spirit of God as a necessary prerequisite to his public ministry. The supreme distinction, however, between the ministry of the old covenant priesthood and that of Christ in the new, is its eternally unbroken effectiveness. Christ's death on the cross functions as an unrepeatable mediatorial sacrifice that guarantees the certainty of the forgiveness of all who put their faith in that action. Such redemption could only be anticipated under the old covenant — although those who truly trusted in Yahweh were promised salvation. Their sacrifices, however, had to be endlessly repeated. New covenant priesthood, as represented in the person of Christ, constitutes the supreme fulfillment of that which was begun in the old.

PRINCE, PRINCIPALITY ➡ RULE

PRISON, PRISONER

OT Words

bayit [בַּיִת, 1004]

bayit is a common noun form with the primary meaning "house," as well as associated senses in the overwhelming majority of its more than two thousand occurrences. ***bayit*** is also translated "prison" in a handful of places that refer to physical incarceration (cf. Gen. 39:20ff.; 40:3ff.; 1 Kgs. 22:27; Jer. 37:4, 18; 52:11, 31).

'āsar [אָסַר, 631]

'āsar is a verb with the primary sense of "bind" in the majority of the sixty or so contexts in which it is found. It also means "to imprison" (cf. Gen. 42:16; Judg. 16:21, 25). In addition, ***'āsar*** indicates the nominal sense of "prisoner" in Ps. 146:7; Eccl. 4:14; Isa. 49:9.

'āsîr [אָסִיר, 615]

'āsîr is a noun derived from ***'āsar*** (see above) with the consistent meaning "prisoner" or "(those) in bondage, captivity." ***'āsîr*** occurs twelve times (e.g., Gen. 39:20ff.; Pss. 68:6; 79:11; 102:20; Isa. 14:17; Lam. 3:34; Zech. 9:11ff.).

'assîr [אַסִּיר, 616]

'assîr is a variant form of ***'āsîr*** (see above) found in only three places, meaning "prisoner" (cf. Isa. 10:4; 24:22; 42:7).

mishmār [מִשְׁמָר, 4929]

mishmār is a noun derived from ***shāmar***, "to guard." The term occurs around twenty times and means "prison" and "custody," in the contexts of being placed under guard, in nearly half of these contexts (cf. Gen. 40:3ff.; 41:10; 42:17ff.; Lev. 24:12; Num. 15:34). (➡ GUARD)

kele' [כֶּלֶא, 3608]

kele' is a noun found in ten places, meaning "prison," "imprisonment." It generally refers to literal confinement (1 Kgs. 22:22; 2 Kgs. 17:4; 25:27ff.; 2 Chr. 18:26; Jer. 37:15ff.; 52:33). Isa. 42:7, 22 refer to those in prison, who are characterized by spiritual darkness. The context clearly implies that the coming of the messianic servant king will result in the release of these people from their "imprisonment."

masgēr [מַסְגֵּר, 4525]

masgēr is a noun occurring seven times, meaning "prison" in three of these contexts. In Ps. 142:7; Isa. 42:7, the use of ***masgēr*** is most likely a symbolic one, referring to those who are in some kind of spiritual bondage, awaiting deliverance from God. Isa. 24:22 is more ambiguous, suggesting either a literal or metaphorical "imprisonment."

NT Words

phylakē **[φυλακή, *5438*]**

phylakē is a term meaning "prison," "imprisonment" in the large majority of its nearly fifty occurrences.

Literal references to imprisonment are found, for example, in Matt. 5:25; Mark 6:17; Luke 3:20; 23:19ff.; John 3:24; Acts 16:23ff.; Heb. 11:36; Rev. 2:10.

Two significant metaphorical uses of ***phylakē*** are to be noted. 1 Pet. 3:19 refers to the Spirit of Christ in Noah (i.e., by implication), who preached to the "spirits in prison" in the days prior to the great flood. The expression "spirits in prison" refers to those who were held in spiritual bondage by their willful rejection of God. Rev. 20:7 refers to the momentary release of Satan from "his prison," heralding a brief flurry of satanic activity prior to his doom.

desmios [δέσμιος, *1198*]

desmios consistently means "prisoner" in each of its sixteen occurrences (cf. Matt. 27:15ff.; Mark 15:6; Acts 16:25ff.; Eph. 3:1; 4:1; 2 Tim. 1:8; Heb. 13:3).

desmōtērion [δεσμωτήριον, *1201*]

desmōtērion occurs only four times, referring to a "prison" (cf. Matt. 11:2; Acts 5:21, 23; 16:26).

desmophylax [δεσμοφύλαξ, *1200*]

desmophylax occurs in only three places, referring to "the keeper of the prison," or the "jailer" (cf. Acts 16:23, 27, 36).

desmōtēs [δεσμώτης, *1202*]

desmōtēs occurs only in Acts 27:1, 42, referring to "prisoners."

tērēsis [τήρησις, *5084*]

tērēsis is a noun with the underlying sense of "keeping." It occurs only three times and refers to a place of confinement, a prison, in two of these contexts (Acts 4:3; 5:18).

Additional Notes

The terminology for "prison" and associated senses is largely literal in both Old and New Testaments. However, in a small number of significant contexts, the phenomenon of "imprisonment" suggests a bondage to spiritual darkness, resulting in the total absence of an intimate, meaningful relationship with God. Deliverance from such "imprisonment" is a powerful theme in the message of redemption signaled in both Testaments. In the Old Testament, such liberation is given over to the Servant of Yahweh, as part of his redemptive program. This program of spiritual release is brought to fulfillment in the person and work of Christ as revealed in the New Testament.

See Also: ➡ CAPTIVE ➡ GUARD

PRIZE

NT Words

brabeion [βραβεῖον, *1017*]

brabeion is found only twice, meaning "prize." 1 Cor. 9:24 refers to the literal prize given to the athlete who wins the race. In Phil. 3:14, Paul uses the term to refer to his great goal — gaining the "prize" of his reward in heaven through the work of Jesus Christ.

PROCLAIM

OT Words

qārā' [**קָרָא, 7121**]

qārā' is a verb with the primary senses of "call," "cry" in the 730 contexts in which it is found. In addition to these meanings, ***qārā'*** is also translated "proclaim" in a number of places. (➡ CALL ➡ READ)

Where God is involved, ***qārā'*** indicates the proclamation of his name in the presence of Moses in Exod. 33:19; 34:5ff.

All other occurrences of ***qārā'*** with this meaning involve human activity. Public proclamation in various contexts is evident in Exod. 32:5; Judg. 7:3; 2 Kgs. 23:16; Esth. 6:9ff.; Jer. 3:12; 7:2; Joel 3:9; Amos 7:5. In particular, divine judgment is proclaimed against Judah in Jer. 11:6; 19:2; 34:17. Fasts are proclaimed in 1 Kgs. 21:9ff.; Ezra 8:21; Jer. 36:9; Jonah 3:5. Freedom for those in captivity is proclaimed in Isa. 61:1; Jer. 34:8; as is the year of the Lord's favor in Isa. 61:2. The holy festivals of the Jewish calendar, celebrating the redemptive deeds of Yahweh in history, are proclaimed in Lev. 23:2ff.; 21, 27. Also included in the ceremonial sphere is the proclamation of liberty for slaves in the year of Jubilee (cf. Lev. 25:10).

'ābar [**עָבַר, 5674**]

'ābar is a common verb with a variety of meanings derived from the basic sense of "to pass," as well as the prepositions "on, over, by, through." This usage accounts for the large majority of its nearly 550 occurrences. However, on several occasions ***'ābar*** is also translated "proclaim" — once in Neh. 8:15, and three times as a noun, "proclamation." 2 Chr. 30:5 refers to keeping the Passover; and 2 Chr. 36:22; Ezra 1:1 refer to Cyrus' decree to release Israel from her captivity in Persia.

zā'aq [**זָעַק, 2199**]

zā'aq is a verb meaning "cry (out)," "gather (together)," in the majority of the seventy or so occurrences of the term. In Jonah 3:7, the related sense of "issue a proclamation" is indicated in relation to the king of Nineveh's repentant response to Jonah's preaching.

***qôl* [קוֹל, 6963]**
qôl is a common noun meaning "voice," "noise," "sound," in the majority of the approximately five hundred places where it occurs. In 2 Chr. 24:9, ***qôl*** specifically refers to a "proclamation," calling for the payment of a tax provided for under the terms of the Mosaic covenant (i.e., the census tax recorded in Exod. 30:14; 38:26).

***keraz* [כְּרַז, 3745 (Aramaic)]**
keraz is an Aramaic term found only in Dan. 5:29. It means "proclamation" and refers to Belshazzar proclaiming Daniel the third highest ruler in the kingdom.

***bāsar* [בָּשַׂר, 1319]**
This verb form occurs around twenty-five times with the underlying sense of "bringing a message, report (good or bad)," "proclaiming news" (e.g., 1 Sam. 31:9; 2 Sam. 1:20; 18:19ff.; 1 Kgs. 1:42). In particular, several texts speak of proclaiming God's word of salvation — his good news (e.g., Pss. 40:9; 68:11; 96:2; Isa. 41:27; 52:7; Nah. 1:15). Then, Isa. 61:1 refers to the Messiah being anointed by God to "preach (proclaim) good news to the poor."

Additional Notes

The Old Testament Hebrew vocabulary for "proclaim" may be considered in conjunction with the New Testament Greek vocabulary for "preach."

The underlying dynamic for each of these concepts is the public announcement of Yahweh's intention to redeem his people from captivity and bondage. This involved a literal deliverance during the old covenant era, including the proclamation of festivals that celebrated Yahweh's past acts of salvation during their early history. What follows in the New Testament is the consummate spiritual release from sin and death accomplished in the person and work of Jesus Christ.

The "preaching" activity of the new covenant age involves the declaration that the ministry of Jesus Christ fulfills what the "proclamation" of Yahweh's promised liberty for his people anticipated during the old covenant period.

See Also: → PREACH

PROFESS, PROFESSION → CONFESS

→ PROMISE → TELL

PROFIT → GAIN → VALUABLE

PROMISE

OT Words

***dābār* [דָּבָר, 1697]**
dābār is one of the most common nouns in the Old Testament, found nearly 1,500 times with the generalized meanings "word," "matter," "thing," as well as a wide variety of associated senses. One of these nuances is that of "promise," found in four places. ***dābār*** refers to the promises of God given to Moses in respect of the land of Canaan (1 Kgs. 8:56); the covenant promise to David (2 Chr. 1:9); God's promise to Abraham (Ps. 105:42); and promises made by the priests at the time of Nehemiah not to exact interest from their fellow countrymen who were stricken by poverty (Neh. 5:12ff.).

***dābar* [דָּבַר, 1696]**
dābar is a common verb found in over 1,150 contexts with the principal meanings "speak," "say," "talk," as well as a number of related nuances. One of these nuances is the meaning "to promise," found in a variety of contexts.

A number of references indicate Yahweh's promise to grant his people the land of Canaan and other attendant blessings (cf. Exod. 12:25; Deut. 6:3; 9:28; 19:8; 27:3; Josh. 23:5; 1 Kgs. 8:56). Other texts refer to Yahweh's promise to Solomon to allow him to build the temple against the backdrop of the divine promise to David (cf. 1 Kgs. 2:24; 8:20; 2 Chr. 6:10). God's promise to David is noted in 1 Kgs. 9:5; 2 Kgs. 8:19; 2 Chr. 6:16ff. Deut. 26:18 records Yahweh's promise to bestow on his people the unique privilege of being his special possession. God's promise to grant wisdom to Solomon is noted in 1 Kgs. 5:12. General references to Yahweh's promised blessing are found in Deut. 1:11; 15:6; Josh. 23:15; Jer. 32:42; 33:14.

dābar also refers to people making promises to Yahweh in Deut. 23:23. General references to making promises are found in Josh. 9:21; 22:4.

***'āmar* [אָמַר, 559]**
'āmar is one of the most common verbs in the Old Testament, with the primary meanings "say," "speak," "answer," as well as several related senses, in its more than 5,300 occurrences. In a couple of contexts, ***'āmar*** means "to promise," referring to the covenant promise God had

made to David (2 Chr. 21:7); and to Haman's promise to make a substantial donation to the Persian royal treasury in return for the destruction of the Jews (Esth. 4:7).

NT Words

epangelia [ἐπαγγελία, *1860*]

epangelia is a noun that is consistently translated "promise" in the fifty or so contexts in which it is found. ***epangelia*** is usually concerned with promises given by God.

In the context of giving divine promises, ***epangelia*** refers, for example, to the promised coming of the Spirit (Luke 24:49; Acts 1:4; 2:33, 39; Gal. 3:14; Eph. 1:13); and to the covenant promises made to Abraham (cf. Acts 7:17; Rom. 4:13ff.; Heb. 6:15ff.; 7:6; 11:9, 17). In particular, Rom. 9:8ff.; Gal. 3:16ff.; 4:23, 28; Eph. 2:12 indicate that all believers are to be reckoned as spiritual descendants of Abraham. Other contexts speak of the covenant promises given to the patriarchs and the heroes of the faith (cf. Acts 26:6; Rom. 9:4; 15:8; Heb. 11:13, 33, 39). See also 2 Cor. 7:1; Eph. 6:2. Reflections on the promise of heavenly rest are found in Heb. 8:6; 9:15; 10:36.

The promise of the savior, referring to Christ himself, is indicated in Acts 13:23, 32; 2 Cor. 1:20; Gal. 3:22; Eph. 3:6; 2 Tim. 1:1. The promise of Jesus' return is affirmed in 2 Pet. 3:4, 9. Heb. 4:1; 6:12 speak of the promise of entering heavenly rest; and 1 John 2:25 mentions the promise of eternal life.

A general reference to promises made by people is found in Acts 23:21; and a reference is made to an undefined promise in 1 Tim. 4:8.

epangellomai [ἐπαγγέλλομαι, *1861*]

epangellomai is a verb meaning "to promise" in most of the fifteen occurrences of the term.

As with the noun ***epangelia*** (see above), ***epangellomai*** refers primarily to promises made by God. Heb. 10:23 contains a general reference to such activity. A number of texts refer to the covenant promise made to Abraham (cf. Acts 7:5; Rom. 4:21; Gal. 3:19; Heb. 6:13; 11:11). Eternal life is pronounced by God in Titus 1:2; Jas. 1:12. 1 John 2:5. Heb. 12:26 refers to judgment against the wicked, promised by God. Mark 14:11 mentions promises made by people, in general terms.

proepangellomai [προεπαγγέλλομαι, *4279*]

proepangellomai is a verb found only in Rom. 1:2, meaning "to promise beforehand" and referring to God's revelation through the prophets.

homologeō [ὁμολογέω, *3670*]

homologeō is a verb meaning "confess" in the majority of the twenty-four contexts in which it occurs. (→ CONFESS) In Matt. 14:7, however, ***homologeō*** means "to promise."

epangelma [ἐπάγγελμα, *1862*]

epangelma is a noun found in only two places, referring to the promises God has given to his people regarding their hope of a heavenly inheritance (cf. 2 Pet. 1:4; 3:13).

Additional Notes

There is a consistent motif evident throughout Scripture regarding divine promises. Promises in the Old Testament focus on Yahweh's intention to grant his people possession of the land of Canaan, which is at the heart of his plan of redemption. This theme is reemphasized in the various stages of progressive covenant revelation by means of the promises given to Moses and David, which follow the pattern of the original guarantee given to Abraham.

The New Testament builds on the foundational Old Testament promises given by God. Here the focus is on the fulfillment of those promises in the person and work of Christ. He consummates the program of God's redemption, ushering in the climactic stage of the outworking of God's kingdom among his people that will include all nations. Such promises will result in the blessing of eternal life in glory for all who follow Christ and worship him as King in the heavenly kingdom of God.

PROOF, PROVE

OT Words

nāsāh [נָסָה, 5254]

nāsāh is a verb found nearly forty times with the predominant meanings "prove," "tempt."

The meaning "prove" in the sense of "test" is found in contexts where God is said to "prove" his people (cf. Exod. 16:4, 20; Deut. 8:2, 16; 33:8; Judg. 2:22). Some of the Canaanites are left by God to "test" Israel in the land (Judg. 3:1, 4). The Queen of Sheba is said to "have tested" Solomon with hard questions (1 Kgs. 10:1; 2 Chr. 9:1). In Ps. 26:2, the psalmist asks the Lord to "prove," or "test" him. See also Mal. 3:10; Dan. 1:12.

bāḥan [בָּחַן, 974]

bāḥan is a synonym for ***nāsāh*** (see above) meaning "try," "prove," in most of its nearly thirty occurrences.

The process of "being tested" to ascertain one's integrity is indicated in Gen. 42:15ff.

References to God "trying" a person's heart are found in 1 Chr. 29:17; Job 23:10; Pss. 7:9; 17:3; Prov. 17:3; Jer. 11:20; 12:3; 17:10. See also Ps. 26:10. The psalmist exhorts God to "prove" or "test" him (Pss. 26:2; 139:23). Ps. 11:5; Jer. 20:12 speak of God "testing" the righteous. God is said to "have tested" his people in the wilderness (Ps. 81:7). See also Jer. 6:27; 9:7.

Conversely, Ps. 95:9 refers to the Israelites "having put God to the test." See also Mal. 3:15.

NT Words

apodeiknymi [ἀποδείκνυμι, *584*]

apodeiknymi is a verb found only in four places, meaning "show," "approve," and "prove." The latter meaning occurs only in Acts 25:7, referring to Paul's enemies, who were unable to prove charges against him. (→ EVIDENCE → DEMONSTRATION → TEST)

PROPHECY, PROPHESY, PROPHET

OT Words

nābā' [נָבָא, 5012]

nābā' means "to prophesy" in virtually all of the 115 occurrences of the term. Where genuine prophesying is in view, all such activity stems from the direct influence of the Spirit of God (affirmed either explicitly or implicitly).

The prophetic activity of the elders of Israel is noted in Num. 11:5ff., and that of the bands of prophets, including Saul, in 1 Sam. 10:5ff.; 19:20ff. In these cases, ***nābā'*** explicitly indicates the ministry of the Spirit of God.

Elsewhere, ***nābā'*** is used in the context of the court prophets in Israel. For example, 1 Kgs. 22:8 refers to the prophesying of one, Micaiah, against King Ahab of Israel. The term occurs much more frequently in the canonical prophets. Jeremiah and Ezekiel emphasize prophesying against the sinfulness of the people of Judah (e.g., Jer. 19:14; 20:1; 26:9ff.; Ezek. 34:2), as well as against the wickedness of the nations (cf. Ezek. 4:7; 6:2; 13:2; 21:2; 29:2; 36:6; 38:2; 39:1). In a positive context, Ezek. 37:4ff. describes Ezekiel prophesying to the skeletal remains of Israel, leading to the resurrection of those bones to newness of life in a most remarkable vision. Joel 2:28 promises prophecy in the Spirit that will usher in the new covenant age. In Amos 7:12ff., the prophet is forbidden to prophesy by Amaziah, a rival cult priest from the syncretistic northern kingdom of Israel. In the context of the canonical prophets, the role of the Spirit of God in producing such activity is implicit in the usage of ***nābā'***.

nābā' occasionally refers to false prophesying (cf. 1 Kgs. 22:12; Jer. 2:8; 5:31; 14:14ff.; 23:13ff.; 27:14ff.; 29:9).

nābî' [נָבִיא, 5030]

nābî' is the principal noun derived from ***nābā'*** (see above), meaning "prophet" in the approximately three hundred occurrences of the term. As with ***nābā'***, in each case where genuine prophetic ministry is involved, the true prophet is one commissioned, enlightened, and equipped by God as his spokesman or "mouthpiece."

General references to "prophet(s)" are found in Num. 12:6; Exod. 7:1; Deut. 13:1ff.; 1 Sam. 9:9; 1 Kgs. 18:13ff.; Ezek. 2:5. ***nābî'*** refers to men such as Abraham (Gen. 20:7) and Samuel (1 Sam. 3:20), who functioned as prophets in addition to their other roles and responsibilities. Several places mention "bands of prophets," which in 1 Sam. 10:5ff.; 19:20ff. also refer to the prophetic activity of Saul. See also 2 Kgs. 2:3ff.

Deut. 18:15ff. describes a genuine prophet of Yahweh. Deut. 34:10; Hos. 12:13 indicate Moses' unique status as the greatest of the Old Testament prophets.

nābî' also refers to the "court prophets" of the Israelite monarchy — for example, Nathan (cf. 2 Sam. 7:2; 1 Kgs. 1:10ff.); Gad (cf. 2 Sam. 24:11); Elijah (cf. 1 Kgs. 18:36; 19:1); and Elisha (cf. 2 Kgs. 5:3; 6:12; 9:1). There are more frequent references to the canonical prophets such as Isaiah (cf. 2 Kgs. 19:2; Isa. 37:2); Jeremiah (cf. Jer. 1:5; 25:2; 37:2ff.); Habakkuk (cf. Hab. 1:1); Haggai (cf. Hag. 1:1); and Zechariah (cf. Zech. 1:1, 7). The general designation "prophets of Yahweh" is indicated, for example, in 2 Kgs. 17:2, 3; Ezra 9:11; Neh. 9:26; Amos 2:11. Yahweh's phrase "my servants the prophets" is found in Jer. 7:25; 25:4; 26:5; 29:19; Ezek. 38:17; Dan. 9:6ff.; Amos 3:7; Zech. 1:6.

In addition, ***nābî'*** also refers to "false prophets," who are inevitably subject to divine judgment. These include the prophets of Baal (1 Kgs. 18:19ff.; 2 Kgs. 10:19); as well as false and corrupt prophets in Israel, which are frequently mentioned (cf. 1 Kgs. 22:10ff.; Isa. 28:7; Jer. 5:13; 14:14ff.; 23:11ff.; 28:1ff.; Ezek. 13:2ff.; Mic. 3:5; Zeph. 3:14).

nebû'āh [נְבוּאָה, 5016]

nebû'āh is a rare term also derived from ***nābā'*** (see above), meaning "prophecy" in all three occurrences of the term (cf. 2 Chr. 9:29; 15:8; Neh. 6:12).

nebā' **[נְבָא, 5013** (Aramaic)]

nebā' is the Aramaic verb equivalent to the Hebrew ***nābā'*** (see above). It is found only in Ezra 5:1, with reference to the "prophesying" of Haggai and Zechariah.

nebû'āh **[נְבוּאָה, 5017** (Aramaic)]

nebû'āh is the noun derived from ***nebā'*** (see above). It means "prophesying" and is found only in Ezra 6:14.

nebî'āh **[נְבִיאָה, 5031]**

nebî'āh is the feminine form of ***nābî'*** (see above) and is translated "prophetess" in each of the six contexts in which it is found (cf. Exod. 15:20; Judg. 4:4; 2 Kgs. 22:14; 2 Chr. 34:22; Neh. 6:14; Isa. 8:3).

nebî' **[נְבִיא, 5029** (Aramaic)]

nebî' is the Aramaic equivalent of ***nābî'*** (see above), meaning "prophet" in all four occurrences of the term (cf. Ezra 5:1, 2; 6:14).

NT WORDS

prophētēs [προφήτης, *4396*]

prophētēs is the standard term for "prophet" in the New Testament and occurs nearly 150 times. Like the corresponding vocabulary of the Old Testament, ***prophētēs*** (when it refers to genuine prophetic activity) describes those individuals who were raised up and equipped by God to communicate his plan and purposes to his people and to the world at large.

General designations of people as "prophets" are found in Matt. 13:57; Mark 6:4; Luke 4:24. Other general references to Old Testament prophets include those in Matt. 1:22; 2:15ff.; 3:3; John 1:23; 12:38 — all of which refer to revelation as that "which was spoken by the prophets." Luke 1:70; Heb. 1:1; Jas. 5:10 refer to the prophets as God's spokesmen. "The prophets" are referred to as a distinct group of people in the old covenant in Matt. 5:17; 7:12; 23:29ff.; Luke 10:24; 13:28. Rev. 10:7; 11:18 refer to the prophets of old as the servants of God. ***prophētēs*** refers on numerous occasions to the canonical prophets (cf. Matt. 22:40; 26:56; Mark 1:2; Luke 3:4; 24:27, 44; John 1:45; 6:45; Acts 3:18; 8:28ff.; 13:15; Rom. 1:2; Eph. 2:20; 3:5).

Jesus is occasionally referred to as a prophet (Matt. 21:11, 46; Luke 7:16; 24:19; John 4:19); as is John the Baptist (Luke 1:76; 20:6). Groups of itinerant New Testament prophets are noted in Acts 11:27; 13:1; 21:10. Prophets in the new covenant church are indicated in 1 Cor. 12:28ff.; 14:29ff.; Eph. 4:11.

prophēteuō [προφητεύω, *4395*]

prophēteuō is a verb meaning "to be a prophet," "prophesy" in all thirty occurrences of the term.

There are general references to prophetic activity in Matt. 7:22; 26:68; Mark 14:65; Luke 22:64; Rev. 10:11. In John 11:51, Caiaphas prophesies that one man would die for the nation.

John the Baptist represents continuity with the Old Testament prophetic tradition (cf. Matt. 11:13). ***prophēteuō*** refers to the activity of the old covenant prophets, including Isaiah (Matt. 15:7; Mark 7:6) and the prophets in general (1 Pet. 1:10). Prophetic ministry at the time of Christ's appearing is noted in Luke 1:67 with respect to Zechariah, the father of John the Baptist.

Acts 2:17, 18 cite the prophecy uttered in Joel 2:28 regarding the outpouring of the Holy Spirit on all "flesh." Prophetic activity as a consequence of Holy Spirit baptism is noted in Acts 19:6; and the ministry of prophets in the first-century church is referred to in Acts 21:9; 1 Cor. 11:4ff.; 13:9; 14:1ff., 39.

prophēteia [προφητεία, *4394*]

prophēteia is the primary noun meaning "prophecy" in the New Testament. It occurs nineteen times.

The prophecy of Isaiah is indicated in Matt. 13:14. There are a number of references to the gift of prophecy in the new covenant community (cf. Rom. 12:6; 1 Cor. 12:10; 13:2, 8; 14:6, 22; 1 Thess. 5:20; 1 Tim. 1:18; 4:14). The "prophecy of Scripture" in a general sense is indicated in 2 Pet. 1:20ff. Rev. 19:10 speaks of the "spirit of prophecy" in relation to Jesus.

The book of Revelation is itself described as a "prophecy" (Rev. 1:3; 22:7ff.); and the prophesying activity of the visionary prophets in Revelation is noted in Rev. 11:6.

prophētikos [προφητικός, *4397*]

prophētikos is an adjectival form meaning "prophetic." The term is rare, found only twice (Rom. 16:26; 2 Pet. 1:19) in relation to the "prophetic word."

prophētis [προφῆτις, *4398*]

prophētis is the feminine form of ***prophētēs*** (see above). It is found in only two places, meaning "prophetess" (Luke 2:36; Rev. 2:20).

pseudoprophētēs [ψευδοπροφήτης, *5578*]

pseudoprophētēs is a variant form of ***prophētēs*** (see above). It occurs eleven times and means "false prophet."

Matt. 7:15 warns against false prophets. Matt. 24:11, 24; Mark 13:22 predict the emergence of false prophets in the last days. Other references to false prophets are found in Luke 6:26; Acts 13:6; 2 Pet. 2:1; 1 John 4:1. The designation "false prophet" is also applied metaphorically to the third member of the "unholy trinity" in Rev. 16:13; 19:20; 20:10. These texts refer to the dragon, the sea beast, and the earth beast — all satanic counterfeits of the Godhead: Father, Son, and Holy Spirit.

Additional Notes

In both Old and New Testaments, the activity of genuine prophesying is clearly grounded in the person and work of Yahweh. It is God alone who initiates the call of the prophet and communicates with him through the Spirit.

The focus of the prophetic task in the Old Testament is twofold: to indicate the purposes of God in his redemptive plan for his people, and also to warn of the impending wrath of God as a consequence of the sin of both Israel and the nations.

The New Testament alludes to the fulfillment of Old Testament prophecy and also refers to prophecy as one of the spiritual gifts given to the church by the Spirit of God. The fulfillment of old covenant prophecy is clearly seen in God's plan of salvation in the person of Christ.

See Also: → SEER

PROPITIATION

OT Words

kāphar [כָּפַר, 3722]

kāphar is a verb with the predominant sense of "make atonement" as well as several associated nuances relating to the removal of guilt and sin through offering sacrifices. ***kāphar*** refers to the process by which the barrier between Yahweh and his people may be removed, or appeasing God's wrath. For his wrath is the inevitable divine response to the violation of his law. This "appeasement" is synonymous with the concept of "propitiation." Divine wrath is set aside, however, only if the sacrifice of atonement is offered with a true sprit of repentance and sorrow for sin. ***kāphar*** is found in approximately one hundred places. When ***kāphar*** means "to make atonement," it is almost exclusively confined to the context of worship — where reconciliation with Yahweh is sought through sacrificial offering.

General references to atoning sacrifices are found in Exod. 29:33; Lev. 7:7. Dan. 9:24, significantly, notes a "sacrifice of atonement" which anticipates the personal sacrifice of the Messiah.

The actual presentation of offerings for making atonement is indicated in a variety of contexts. ***kāphar*** refers to the "atonement" of the bronze altar (Exod. 29:36ff.) and of the altar of incense (Exod. 30:10). As far as personal guilt for sin is concerned, "atoning sacrifices" are offered for individuals, for example, in Exod. 30:15ff.; Lev. 4:26ff.; 5:6ff.; 14:18ff. In Num. 6:11, this offering is presented as part of the ritual ceremony for the adoption of the Nazirite vow. ***kāphar*** refers to sacrifices for the sins of the priests (Lev. 1:4); the Levites (Num. 8:12); the entire Israelite community or nation (Lev. 4:20; 10:17; Num. 8:19; 16:47; 1 Chr. 6:49; 2 Chr. 29:24; Neh. 10:33; Ezek. 45:7); and the high priest (Lev. 9:7; 16:6ff.). The latter passage is especially significant in that it involves the crucial atoning sacrifices for the ritual leader of the nation as he prepares to offer the sacrifice for the Israelite people on the Day of Atonement. In Ezek. 45:20, such sacrifices are presented for cleansing the prophet's visionary temple.

In a slightly different context, Num. 5:8 refers to an atonement offering of a ram for the purposes of making restitution.

NT Words

hilasmos [ἱλασμός, *2434*]

The noun ***hilasmos*** is found only twice. 1 John 2:2; 4:10 refer to the "propitiation" affected by the sacrificial death of Christ on the cross, whose atoning work eradicated the sin of human beings and appeased the wrath of God.

hilastērion [ἱλαστήριον, *2435*]

hilastērion is found only three times in the New Testament. Each occurrence has a great deal of theological significance and refers to the "atoning sacrifice" of Jesus Christ. It is this sacrifice that paid the penalty for the sins of the people of God in their entirety — past, present, and future. This substitutionary atonement appeased, or "propitiated," the wrath of God once and for all (cf. Rom. 3:25; 1 John 2:2; 4:10).

PROSPER → SUCCEED

PROSTITUTE, PROSTITUTION

OT Words

qedēshāh [קְדֵשָׁה, 6948]

qedēshāh is found in only four places, referring to "cult prostitute(s)" associated with pagan idol worship (cf. Gen. 38:21, 22; Deut. 23:17; Hos. 4:14).

See Also: → FORNICATION

PRO → ALLEGORY

PROVIDE, PROVISION

OT Words

rā'āh [רָאָה, 7200]

rā'āh is a common verb meaning "see," "look," as well as a number of related senses, in the more than 1,300 occurrences of the term. In Gen. 22:8, however, ***rā'āh*** is translated "provide," with reference to God declaring to Abraham that he will provide a ram for the burnt offering in the place of Isaac, his son.

kûn [כּוּן, 3559]

kûn is a verb with the primary meanings "prepare," "establish," along with some related nuances. In seven contexts the term is translated "provide," with reference to food (cf. 1 Kgs. 4:7, 27; Job 38:41; Pss. 65:9; 78:20; Prov. 6:8); and to workers to build Solomon's temple (cf. 2 Chr. 2:7).

NT Words

pronoeō [προνοέω, *4306*]

This verb form occurs only three times with the meaning "provide for" in the sense of "take care of" one's family in 1 Tim. 5:8. Rom. 12:7 refers to "being careful" not to repay evil for evil.

See Also: → BREAD → FOOD

PROVOCATION, PROVOKE → ANGER → DESPISE → ENTICE → JEALOUS → REBEL

PRUDENCE, PRUDENT

OT Words

'ārûm [עָרוּם, 6175]

'ārûm is an adjective that is translated "prudent" in the majority of its eleven occurrences. The underlying sense is that of a wise person skilled in applying that knowledge in his or her life. In most occurrences, ***'ārûm*** indicates "prudence" as a virtue, a godly quality of life (cf. Prov. 12:16, 23; 14:8; 27:12). In the remaining contexts, ***'ārûm*** has the negative connotation of "crafty" (cf. Gen. 3:1; Job 5:12; 15:5).

'āram [עָרַם, 6191]

'āram is the verb from which ***'ārûm*** (see above) is derived. ***'āram*** occurs only five times. Twice it means "to be prudent," "gain prudence" (cf. Prov. 15:5; 19:25). Elsewhere, it means "to be crafty" (cf. 1 Sam. 23:22; Ps. 83:3).

'ormāh [עָרְמָה, 6195]

'ormāh is a noun found in five contexts, meaning "guile," "craftiness," and "prudence." The latter meaning is found in Prov. 1:4; 8:5, 12. See also Exod. 21:14; Josh. 9:4.

See Also: → UNDERSTAND → UNDERSTANDING

PUNISH, PUNISHMENT

OT Words

yāsar [יָסַר, 3256]

yāsar is a verb with the predominant meaning "to chastise," or "punish," in the majority of its more than forty occurrences. Other meanings include "instruct," "correct," with an underlying sense of disciplinary action.

Yahweh metes out punishment on his people in accordance with the curse sanctions of the covenant for their rebellion against him (cf. Lev. 26:18, 28; Jer. 30:11; 31:18; 46:8). General references to divine punishment are found in Pss. 6:1; 38:1; 39:11; 94:10ff.; 118:18.

In the human sphere, punishment is often indicated in the context of the family, where the father takes responsibility for disciplining his children (cf. Deut. 8:5; 21:18; 22:18; Prov. 19:18; 29:17). Punishment is also mentioned in relation to the legal sanctions of the civil code during the reigns of Solomon and his son Rehoboam.

nāqam [נָקַם, 5358]

nāqam is a verb with the predominant sense of "avenge," "take revenge" in most of the thirty-five contexts in which it occurs. (→ AVENGE) In two places, however, the term is translated "punish" in the context of a legal sanction for wrongdoing (cf. Exod. 21:20, 21).

ḥāsak [חָשַׂךְ, 2820]

ḥāsak is a verb meaning "withhold," "spare," "keep back" in the large majority of its approximately thirty occurrences. However, in Ezra 9:13 refers to God punishing his people for their rebellion against him.

'āwōn [עָוֹן, 5771]

'āwōn means "iniquity" in most of the 230 contexts in which it is found. (→ INIQUITY) However, in three places the sense of "punishment" is evident, twice with reference to divine chastisement (cf. Gen. 4:13; Lam. 4:22); and once in the human sphere (cf. 1 Sam. 28:10).

NT WORDS

kolazō [κολάζω, *2849*]

kolazō is a verb found only twice, meaning "to punish," — once in the human sphere of legal action (cf. Acts 4:21); and once in the realm of divine dealings with the wicked (cf. 2 Pet. 2:9).

kolasis [κόλασις, *2851*]

kolasis is the noun derived from ***kolazō*** (see above), found in only two places. ***kolasis*** refers to everlasting punishment in Matt. 25:46 and to punishment in general in 1 John 4:18.

timōreō [τιμωρέω, *5097*]

timōreō is a verb meaning "punish" in the context of procuring a legal sanction against those who violate the law. It is found only in Acts 22:5; 26:11, with reference to Saul's fanatical pursuit of the early Christians prior to his conversion, with a view to bringing them to justice and having them punished.

timōria [τιμωρία, *5098*]

timōria is the noun derived from ***timōreō*** (see above) and is found only in Heb. 10:29, where it refers to the terrible divine punishment that will fall upon all those who spurn the Son of God and renounce their allegiance to him.

epitimia [ἐπιτιμία, *2009*]

epitimia is a term found only in 2 Cor. 2:6, referring to "punishment" arising out of the context of church discipline.

dikē [δίκη, *1349*]

dikē is a noun occurring in four contexts with the underlying sense of a judicial sentence. It refers to such a punishment in Acts 25:15; 28:4. In 2 Thess. 1:9; Jude 7, ***dikē*** refers to the sentence of eternal punishment handed down by God to unbelievers on the day of judgment.

ekdikēsis [ἐκδίκησις, *1557*]

ekdikēsis is a noun with the primary meaning "revenge" or "vengeance" in all but one of the ten occurrences of the term. In 1 Pet. 2:14 it refers to the legal prerogative of the civil authorities to punish those who break the law.

See Also: → STRIKE → VISIT

PURCHASE → BUY

PURE, PURGE, PURIFY → CLEAN → REFINE

PURPOSE

OT WORDS

ḥāshab [**חָשַׁב, 2803**]

ḥāshab is a verb with the primary senses of "devise," or "think," with a number of related meanings, found around 120 times. In several places, it is translated "to make a plan," "devise a purpose," or "determine." In Jer. 49:20; 50:45; Lam. 2:8, ***ḥāshab*** indicates the purposes or plans that God has drawn up for judgment against the nations.

ḥēpheṣ [**חֵפֶץ, 2656**]

ḥēpheṣ means "pleasure," "delight" in most of its approximately forty occurrences. In three places, however, ***ḥēpheṣ*** refers to "purpose" in the general sense of a "matter," "issue," or "subject" in human experience (cf. Eccl. 3:1, 17; 8:6).

yāṣar [**יָצַר, 3335**]

yāṣar is a verb meaning "form," "fashion" in the majority of its sixty or so occurrences. In Isa. 46:11, ***yāṣar*** refers to Yahweh's purpose to control the destiny of the land of Babylon.

NT WORDS

prothesis [πρόθεσις, *4286*]

prothesis is found twelve times, referring mainly to God's "purpose" in his plan of salvation (cf. Rom. 8:28; 9:11; Eph. 1:11; 3:11; 2 Tim. 1:9).

boulēma [βούλημα, *1013*]

boulēma is a term found only twice. In Acts 27:43 it refers to the "plan" or "purpose" to have Paul and the other prisoners killed to prevent their escape from a shipwreck.

protithēmi [προτίθημι, *4388*]

protithēmi is a verb found on only three occasions. In two of these contexts, it refers to the expression of one's purpose, or intent. Rom. 1:13 speaks of Paul's determined purpose to visit the church in Rome. In Eph. 1:9, ***protithēmi*** refers to the expression of God's purpose in the person of Christ in relation to the divine plan of salvation.

See Also: → ADVICE → PLAN → THINK

PURSUE → FOLLOW

PUT

OT Words

sûm **[שׂוּם, 7760]**

sûm is a common verb with a variety of meanings including "make," "set," and "put," which constitute the majority usage of the term in its approximately six hundred occurrences. There is a certain amount of overlap in these meanings. (→ MAKE → SET) The meaning "put" or "place" is found in approximately 160 places.

In a number of contexts, God is indicated as the agent of "putting" or "placing." For example, Gen. 2:8 refers to God putting a man in the garden of Eden. In Gen. 4:15, God is said to put a mark on Cain as a means of preserving his life against possible assassins. Exod. 15:26; Deut. 7:15 mention Yahweh inflicting (lit. "putting") diseases on the nation of Egypt in judgment against that people. The phenomenon of Yahweh putting words in the mouth of his prophet Balaam is indicated in Num. 22:38; 23:5ff. In several highly significant theological contexts, God puts (or places) his name in the land of Canaan (cf. Deut. 12:5, 21), in the temple (cf. 1 Kgs. 9:3), and in the city of Jerusalem (cf. 1 Kgs. 11:36; 14:21; 2 Kgs. 21:4). Such an action is equivalent to Yahweh placing himself among his people.

A number of contexts also refer to human beings "putting," or "placing." References to people being placed in set positions are found in Gen. 33:2; Exod. 2:3; 1 Sam. 11:11. In particular, Gen. 40:15; 1 Kgs. 22:27 mention people being put in prison. Army personnel are put in place in 2 Sam. 8:14; 1 Kgs. 20:24. Exod. 32:27 speaks of putting on a weapon. Exod. 40:3ff.; Num. 4:6ff. refer to putting furniture together for the tabernacle. The process of preparing ritual sacrifices by "putting" various substances onto the offerings is described in Lev. 2:15; 8:26; 9:20; 10:1; Deut. 33:10. Various items of clothing are placed on the priests in preparation for their service (Lev. 8:8ff.). The tablets of the law and the book of the covenant are put into the ark of the covenant (Deut. 10:2ff.; 31:26). Sackcloth is put on to reflect personal grief and anguish (1 Kgs. 20:31; 21:27).

Other contexts refer to putting a hand on someone's thigh in demonstration of a solemn vow (cf. Gen. 47:29) and putting a hand on the head as a sign of blessing (cf. Gen. 48:20). Josh. 10:24 refers to putting one's feet on the necks of one's enemies as a sign of their utter defeat. Num. 21:8ff. describes the powerful symbolic action of Moses putting the bronze serpent on the pole in the wilderness as a means of offering healing to the Israelites stricken with poisonous snake bites.

sāmak **[סָמַךְ, 5564]**

sāmak is a verb found in approximately fifty contexts. It means "lay" (i.e., "put") in about half of these contexts. The meaning "lay" is dominant and is exclusively associated with the laying on of hands, either on sacrificial animals prior to slaughter, or on those people set apart by God for special service.

In the context of ritual worship, ***sāmak*** indicates the action of laying hands on the heads of animals immediately prior to their sacrifice — for example, bulls (cf. Exod. 29:10; Lev. 4:4, 15; 8:14; Num. 8:12); rams (cf. Exod. 29:15, 19; 8:18, 22); goats (cf. Lev. 4:24; 16:21 [Day of Atonement scapegoat]; 2 Chr. 29:23); non-specific animals for burnt offering (cf. Lev. 1:4; 3:2ff.); and non-specific animals for sin offering (cf. Lev. 4:29).

The laying of hands on Levites as part of their commissioning ritual is indicated in Num. 8:10; and Joshua is so commissioned prior to assuming the leadership of Israel (cf. Num. 27:18; Deut. 34:9).

shît **[שִׁית, 7896]**

shît is a verb with several meanings, found in approximately eighty places. In several contexts it means "put." (→ SET)

Gen. 3:15 declares that God will put enmity between Eve and the serpent (i.e., Satan). Ps. 8:6 affirms that God has put all things under his feet. Jacob lays his hands on the heads of his grandsons, Ephraim and Manasseh, as a sign of blessing (Gen. 48:14).

NT Words

apolyō **[ἀπολύω, *630*]**

apolyō is a verb found nearly ninety times with the primary meaning "to release," including the more common senses of "let go," "send away," "put away."

The action of "putting away" refers to divorcing one's wife, or at least the intention to do so (Matt. 1:19; 5:31ff.; 19:3, 7ff.; Mark 10:2ff.; Luke 16:18; 1 Cor. 7:12).

tithēmi [τίθημι, *5087*]

tithēmi is a common verb meaning "put," "set," "lay (down)," as well as several related nuances throughout its nearly one hundred occurrences.

"Put," in the literal, mundane sense of "set (in place)," "place," or "lay," is indicated in relation to objects (Matt. 5:15; Mark 4:21; Luke 8:16; John 19:19); and to the dead body of Christ in the tomb (Mark 16:6; Luke 23:53; John 11:34; 19:42; Acts 13:29). See also Acts 9:40; Rev. 10:2.

More significantly, God "puts" or "places" his Spirit upon his servants (Matt. 12:18). God is said to "place" his enemies under his feet (Matt. 22:44; Mark 12:36; 1 Cor. 15:25). Rom. 9:33; 1 Pet. 2:6 refer to God "laying" a stone in Zion, denoting the emergence of the future messianic ruler.

The "placing" or "setting down" of people in a variety of locations is noted for example, in connection with prison (Matt. 14:3; Acts 5:18); eternal darkness (Matt. 24:51); the market place (Mark 6:56); laying a foundation (1 Cor. 3:10ff.); and bringing people to Jesus for healing (Luke 5:18). See also Acts 3:2.

"Laying" hands on people in the ritual of blessing is recorded in Mark 10:16. Bringing an offering and "placing" it at the feet of the apostles is noted in Acts 4:35ff.; 5:2.

The gesture of Christ "laying down" his life for his people is described in John 10:15ff.; the offer of his disciples to do the same is noted in John 13:37ff. The sublime nature of someone making such a sacrifice is described in John 15:13.

The prerogative of "being appointed" as a preacher of the gospel is indicated in 2 Tim. 1:11. God's action in "appointing" his Son as the heir of all things is indicated in Heb. 1:2.

paratithēmi [παρατίθημι, *3908*]

paratithēmi is a variant form of ***tithēmi***, above, found in nineteen places and meaning "to set, place before."

The meaning "set before" is found in several places, denoting the "telling" of a parable in Matt. 13:24, 31.

The action of "setting food before" people is indicated in Mark 6:41; 8:6ff.; Luke 9:16; 10:8; Acts 16:34; 1 Cor. 10:27.

The meaning "to commit," "entrust" oneself to God, is indicated in 1 Pet. 4:19.

epitithēmi [ἐπιτίθημι, *2007*]

epitithēmi is another variant of ***tithēmi***, above, meaning to "lay on," "put," "lay," throughout most of its nearly fifty occurrences.

The action of Christ "laying his hand on" those who would receive his healing is indicated in Matt. 9:18; 19:13ff.; Mark 5:23, 8:23ff.; Luke 4:40; 13:13. See also John 9:15. In Acts 9:12, 17; 28:8, such healing is effected through human agency.

"Placing one's clothes on" a beast of burden is indicated in Matt. 21:7. The "placing" of crowns on the head of Christ is noted in Matt. 27:29; John 19:2. See also Luke 23:26.

The metaphorical sense of "placing" or "laying" burdens on people is found in Matt. 23:4; Acts 15:10, 28.

"Laying one's hands" on those who are being set aside for ministry as an act of spiritual commissioning is noted in Acts 6:6; 13:3; 1 Tim. 5:22. This is also indicated as a precursor to receiving the Holy Spirit in Acts 8:17.

Acts 28:3 also refers to "placing" or "laying down" objects.

peritithēmi [περιτίθημι, *4060*]

peritithēmi is yet another variant form of ***tithēmi***, above, with the underlying meaning "to set around," "put on," in all eight occurrences of the term.

The action of "setting a hedge around" a vineyard is indicated in Matt. 21:33; Mark 12:1.

A scarlet robe is "placed" around Christ in Matt. 27:28. A sponge filled with vinegar is "placed on" a stick and offered to Christ in Matt. 27:48; Mark 15:36; John 19:29. Mark 15:17 refers to Roman soldiers "placing" a crown of thorns on Christ's head.

apotithēmi [ἀποτίθημι, *659*]

Another variant of ***tithēmi***, above, ***apotithēmi*** has the primary metaphorical sense of "put away, off," "cast aside," in the eight occurrences of the term.

Most of these occurrences consist of exhortations to "put off," "cast aside" sinful attitudes and lifestyles (cf. Rom. 13:12; Eph. 4:22ff.; Col. 3:8; Heb. 12:1; Jas. 1:21; 1 Pet. 2:1).

Acts 7:58 refers to people "laying down" their clothes at the feet of Saul.

epiballō [ἐπιβάλλω, *1911*]

epiballō is a verb form found nineteen times with the primary meanings "lay," "put."

The meaning "put" in the sense of "sew" is found in Matt. 9:16; Luke 5:36, with reference to sewing a new piece of material onto an old one.

epiballō, used with the noun ***cheir*** (→ HAND), is commonly translated "lay hands on" in the sense of "seize," or "arrest" someone (Matt. 26:50; Mark 14:46; Luke 20:19; 21:12; John 7:30, 44; Acts 4:3; 5:18; 12:1; 21:27; 1 Cor. 7:35).

Luke 9:62 refers to "putting" one's hand to the plow.

hypotassō [ὑποτάσσω, *5293*]

hypotassō is a verb found nearly fifty times with the predominant meanings "be subject to," "submit." It also has the active sense of "put under, in subjection to."

1 Cor. 15:27ff.; Heb. 2:8 refer to God "having put all things in subjection" under his feet, and under the feet of Christ (Eph. 1:22).

apekdyomai [ἀπεκδύομαι, *554*]

apekdyomai is a rare verb found in Col. 3:9 that describes the believer "having put off" or "cast aside" the old nature.

See Also: → CLOTHE → DRIVE → REMOVE → SEND → SET

Q

QUAKE

OT Words

rāgaz **[רָגַז, 7264]**

rāgaz is a verb that expresses powerful and sometimes violent human emotion, along with metaphorical references to the trembling or quaking of the earth, often in the face of divine anger or judgment. The term occurs about forty times and is translated variously as "tremble," "rage," "provoke." In six contexts it also means "quake," in a metaphorical sense. (→ TREMBLE)

rāgaz in this sense refers to the quaking, or trembling, of the earth in the face of divine anger or judgment (cf. Ps. 18:7; Isa. 5:25; Joel 2:10; Amos 8:8). See also Prov. 30:21; Isa. 14:16.

rā'ash **[רָעַשׁ, 7493]**

rā'ash is a synonym for ***rāgaz*** (see above), again referring primarily to the trembling, shaking, or quaking of the earth before the presence of God in the context of divine wrath or judgment. ***rā'ash*** is used metaphorically to refer to the disturbing intervention of God in human affairs. ***rā'ash*** occurs thirty times, meaning "quake" or "tremble" in the majority of these contexts. (→ SHAKE → TREMBLE)

rā'ash refers metaphorically to the quaking of the earth in the presence of God's power and majesty (cf. Pss. 68:8; 77:18). See also Isa. 14:16. This phenomenon is also specifically indicated as a consequence of divine anger and judgment against the earth and the nations of the world (cf. Judg. 5:4; 2 Sam. 22:8; Ps. 18:7; Isa. 24:18; Jer. 4:24; 10:10; 51:29; Ezek. 28:15; Joel 2:10; Nah. 1:5); and also against Israel (Jer. 8:16). Ps. 46:3 refers to the psalmist taking refuge in God in the face of the calamity of the quaking mountains.

Ezek. 38:20 refers to human beings quaking in the face of divine judgment.

ra'ash **[רַעַשׁ, 7494]**

ra'ash is the noun derived from ***rā'ash*** (see above) and literally means "earthquake" in about half of the seventeen contexts in which it is found. Other meanings, such as "rushing," and "shaking," suggest a confusion of noise, with one reference to a person quaking with fright.

General references to an earthquake are found in Amos 1:1; Zech. 14:5. As a judgment from God, this phenomenon is found in Isa. 29:6; Ezek. 38:19. The prophet Elijah experiences an earthquake, as recorded in 1 Kgs. 19:11, 12, as part of a revelation from God.

In Ezek. 12:18, the prophet Ezekiel is commanded to "quake with fright" as part of a prophetic symbolic action foreshadowing the coming terror of divine judgment upon the people of God.

ḥārad **[חָרַד, 2729]**

The primary sense of ***ḥārad*** is "to tremble," "be afraid," found in almost all of its nearly forty occurrences. Only in Exod. 19:18 does it refer to the "quaking" of Mt. Sinai as a consequence of the presence of Yahweh there. (→ TREMBLE)

NT Words

seiō **[σείω, *4579*]**

The primary meaning of ***seiō*** is to "shake," or "tremble." It occurs only five times, and in Matt. 27:51 it refers to the shaking of the earth at the precise moment of Christ's death on the cross — an undoubted reference to an earthquake. (→ SHAKE)

See Also: → TREMBLE

QUEEN

OT Words

malkāh **[מַלְכָּה, 4436]**

malkāh is the most common term for "queen" in the Old Testament and occurs thirty-five times.

malkāh refers to the Queen of Sheba (1 Kgs. 10:1ff.; 2 Chr. 9:1ff.); Queen Vashti of Persia (Esth. 1:9ff.); and to Queen Esther, the godly and courageous Jewish consort of the Persian King Xerxes (Esth. 2:22; 4:4; 5:2ff.; 7:1ff.; 8:1, 7; 9:12, 29ff.). Song 6:8, 9 refer to "sixty queens" — a possible reference to the harem of King Solomon.

malkā' **[מַלְכָּא, 4433** (Aramaic)**]**

malkā' is the Aramaic equivalent of ***malkāh*** (see above). It occurs only in Dan. 5:10 and refers to a woman of uncertain identity, perhaps the wife of either Nebuchadnezzar or Nabonidus.

shēgāl **[שֵׁגָל, 7694]**

shēgāl is a rare synonym for ***malkāh*** (see above). It is found only twice and refers to an unidentified royal figure in Ps. 45:9, and to the unnamed Persian queen, wife, or consort of King Artaxerxes in Neh. 2:6.

meleket **[מְלֶכֶת, 4446]**

meleket is another term for "queen." It occurs five times, with exclusive reference to the Babylonian female deity, the "queen of heaven" (cf. Jer. 7:18; 44:17ff.).

gebîrāh **[גְּבִירָה, 1377]**

gebîrāh is another synonym for the entries above, signifying female royalty (cf. 1 Kgs. 11:19; 15:13; 2 Kgs. 10:13; Jer. 13:18; 29:2).

sārāh **[שָׂרָה, 8280]**

sārāh is a rare term for "queen," found only in Isa. 49:23; Lam. 1:1. ***sārāh*** occurs five times and refers elsewhere to ladies of nobility, or princesses.

NT WORDS

basilissa **[βασίλισσα, *938*]**

basilissa is the only term for "queen" in the New Testament and is found in four contexts. Matt. 12:42; Luke 11:31; Acts 8:27 refer to historical figures. Rev. 18:7 refers symbolically to the city of Babylon as the idolatrous self-styled "queen" (i.e., "queen of heaven").

QUENCH

OT WORDS

kābāh **[כָּבָה, 3518]**

kābāh is a verb occurring twenty-four times, meaning "to quench" (i.e., extinguish). It is often used passively or intransitively (i.e., in the sense of "go out," "die out") and is used in both literal and metaphorical contexts.

General references to fires "going out" are found in Prov. 26:20; 31:18. Other references to lamps being extinguished in the tabernacle and temple are found in 1 Sam. 3:3; 2 Chr. 29:7. With reference to the altar fire of ceremonial sacrifice, God gives explicit instructions that such fire was not to be quenched or put out, but must be allowed to burn continually (cf. Lev. 6:12, 13).

The remaining usage of ***kābāh*** is metaphorical. 2 Sam. 14:7 refers to a woman's plea not to let her one "burning coal be quenched"— not to allow her one remaining son to be killed (cf. also 2 Sam. 21:7). Several contexts refer to God's anger against his people being maintained, or "not quenched" (cf. 2 Kgs. 22:17; 2 Chr. 34:25; Isa. 1:9; Jer. 4:4; 7:26; 17:27; 21:12; Ezek. 20:47ff.; Amos 5:6). Such an attitude is also expressed in regard to the enemies of Yahweh (cf. Isa. 34:10; 43:17; 66:24; Ezek. 32:7). Song 8:7 indicates that true love cannot be "quenched." Finally, the gentle rule of the coming Messianic Servant of Yahweh is indicated in the assertion that "he will not even quench a burning wick" (cf. Isa. 42:3).

shābar **[שָׁבַר, 7665]**

shābar is a verb with the predominant meaning "break," as well as associated senses, in the 150 occurrences of the term. In Ps. 104:11, however, it refers to donkeys "quenching" their thirst.

NT WORDS

sbennymi **[σβέννυμι, *4570*]**

sbennymi is a verb occurring eight times meaning "quench," or "extinguish," mostly in metaphorical contexts.

Matt. 25:8 refers literally to lamps being extinguished, or going out.

The remaining usage of ***sbennymi*** is symbolic. Matt. 12:20 alludes to the gentle rule of the Servant of Yahweh, who "will not quench a smoldering wick." ***sbennymi*** refers to the unquenchable fire of the wicked in hell (Mark 9:44ff.); to the shield of faith "quenching" the fiery darts of the devil (Eph. 6:16); and to believers "quenching" raging fire (Heb. 11:34). 1 Thess. 5:19 enjoins the believer not to "quench" the spirit of God.

asbestos **[ἄσβεστος, *762*]**

asbestos is an adjective meaning "unquenchable" in all four occurrences of the term. In each case it refers to the fire of divine judgment (cf. Mark 9:43, 45; Luke 3:17).

QUESTION

OT WORDS

ḥîdāh **[חִידָה, 2420]**

ḥîdāh is a noun found in seventeen contexts with the primary meaning "riddle" or "hard saying." In two places, however, the term refers to "(hard) questions" posed by the Queen of Sheba to King Solomon (1 Kgs. 10:1; 2 Chr. 9:1). ***dābār***, below, is also used in this context.

dābār **[דָּבָר, 1697]**

One of the most common words in the Old Testament, ***dābar*** means "word," "speech," "matter" (and related senses) in its nearly 1,500 occurrences. On two occasions, however, ***dābār*** is translated "question," referring to the questions posed to Solomon by the Queen of Sheba (1 Kgs. 10:3; 2 Chr. 9:2).

NT WORDS

syzēteō **[συζητέω,** ***4802*****]**

syzēteō is a verb that occurs ten times and means "to question" in four of these contexts. (→ DISPUTE)

In Mark 1:27; 9:10; Luke 22:23, ***syzēteō*** means "to question" in a group setting with the sense of "questioning one another." Mark 8:11 refers to Jesus questioning the Pharisees.

logos **[λόγος,** ***3056*****]**

logos is a common New Testament term meaning "word," "saying," "speech," as well as a variety of related senses, in the 331 occurrences of the term. In Mark 11:20, ***logos*** is translated "question," referring to Jesus' inquiry to the spiritual leaders of Israel.

zētēma **[ζήτημα,** ***2213*****]**

zētēma is a noun meaning "question" in a legal context in all five occurrences of the term. The sense of "legal matter" underlies the references to "questions" (cf. Acts 15:2; 18:15; 23:29; 25:19). In Acts 26:3, the sense of ***zētēma*** is less clear, though the translation "question" is possible, along with that of "controversy," with reference to Jewish customs that are difficult to understand.

anakrinō **[ἀνακρίνω,** ***350*****]**

anakrinō is a verb occurring sixteen times, meaning "to question" in six of these contexts. Other meanings include "to judge," "search," or "discern." (→ JUDGE)

The sense of "question" in the context of a legal inquiry or examination is indicated in Luke 23:14; Acts 12:19; 28:18; 1 Cor. 9:3. The action of withholding a question is noted in 1 Cor. 10:25, 27, where Paul advises his readers not to raise questions about pagan religious ceremonies associated either with meat sold in the market or meat served to them in the homes of unbelievers.

eperōtaō **[ἐπερωτάω,** ***1905*****]**

eperōtaō is a verb meaning "ask" in the large majority of its nearly sixty occurrences. On several occasions, however, the term is translated "to question" or "ask a question" in the sense of "interrogate" (cf. Luke 2:46; 23:9; Acts 5:29).

QUICKEN

OT WORDS

ḥāyāh **[חָיָה, 2421]**

ḥāyāh is a verb meaning "live," as well as a number of related senses, in the large majority of its more than 270 occurrences. The sense of "quicken" is linked with these meanings and is illustrated, for example, in the action of God "reviving" his servants (cf. Pss. 71:20; 80:18; 119:25). In addition, the meaning "quicken" is associated with the psalmist's plea for God to "preserve his life" (cf. Pss. 119:37, 40, 88, 107, 149ff.; 143:11). See also Ps. 119:50, 93.

NT WORDS

zōopoieō **[ζωοποιέω,** ***2227*****]**

zōopoieō is a verb that means "to quicken" in the sense of "give life," "make alive" — an action that is largely wrought by the power of God. ***zōopoieō*** is found in twelve contexts.

The senses of "give life," "be made alive," are found almost exclusively in the context of divine power bringing the dead back to life. John 5:21; Rom. 4:17; 1 Cor. 15:22; 1 Tim. 6:13 refer to God "quickening." "Quickening" is a consequence of the movement of God's Spirit in John 6:63; Rom. 8:11; 2 Cor. 3:6; 1 Pet. 3:18.

zōopoieō is also used adjectivally in 1 Cor. 15:45 to refer to Christ as the "last Adam, a life-giving spirit."

In a mundane reference, ***zōopoieō*** refers to seed "coming to life" in 1 Cor. 15:36.

syzōopoieō **[συζωοποιέω,** ***4806*****]**

syzōopoieō is a verb found only twice, with the sense of "quicken together with," or "make alive together with." In Eph. 2:5; Col. 2:13, God makes believers alive together with Christ.

QUIET, QUIETNESS

OT WORDS

shāqat **[שָׁקַט, 8252]**

shāqat is a verb with the predominant sense of "to be at rest," "be quiet," in almost all of the forty or so contexts in which it is found. The latter meaning, "be quiet," is found in approximately half of these, although the meanings often overlap. (→ REST)

The meaning "to be quiet" is found first of all in relation to people who are at peace, living in secure surroundings (cf. Judg. 18:7, 27; 2 Kgs. 11:20). In contrast, ***shāqat*** also refers to those who are ill at ease, or "not quiet" in the sense of not being secure and restful (1 Chr. 4:40). Such a description is also predicated of the earth in Ps. 76:8, although in this context it refers to a fearful quietness awaiting the judgment of God. 2 Chr. 20:30; 23:21; Isa. 14:7 refer to the quietness of a kingdom that is secure and peaceful.

As far as people are concerned, Isa. 30:15; 32:17 indicate the "quietness" of calm trust in Yahweh.

Yahweh is also said to be "quiet" in Ezek. 16:42, referring to the withdrawal of his anger against his disobedient people.

Job 3:3 refers to the state of "being quiet" as a metaphor for death.

nûaḥ [נוּחַ, 5117]

nûaḥ is a verb with the principal sense of "to be at rest." Yet ***nûaḥ*** also means "to be quiet" in a negative context in Job 3:26, where it refers to one's lack of quiet, indicating an uneasy, anxiety-ridden state of mind.

rāgēa' [רָגֵעַ, 7282]

rāgēa' occurs only in Ps. 35:20, meaning "to live quietly."

naḥat [נַחַת, 5183]

naḥat is a noun occurring eight times and meaning "rest" in most of these contexts. However, in Eccl. 9:17, it is used adjectivally to refer to the "quiet words" of the wise.

dāmam [דָּמַם, 1826]

dāmam is a verb found in thirty contexts with the predominant meanings "to be silent, still," as well as other associated senses. One of these is "to be quiet," referring to the calming of the psalmist's soul (cf. Ps. 131:2).

sheqet [שֶׁקֶט, 8253]

sheqet is a noun derived from ***shāqat*** (see above). It is found only in 1 Chr. 22:9, meaning "quiet" and describing the promised tranquillity given to Solomon by God.

shalwāh [שַׁלְוָה, 7962]

shalwāh occurs eight times meaning "prosperity," "abundance." In Prov. 17:1 it refers to "quiet" in conjunction with "peace."

NT Words

katastellō [καταστέλλω, *2687*]

katastellō is a verb found in only two contexts. In Acts 19:35 it refers to "quieting" or "calming" a crowd; and in Acts 19:36 it means to "be quiet" or "be calm."

hēsychazō [ἡσυχάζω, *2270*]

hēsychazō is a verb found on five occasions meaning "to hold one's peace," "rest," as well as associated meanings. In 1 Thess. 4:11 it means "to live quietly," or to live at peace with one's neighbors.

ēremos [ἤρεμος, *2263*]

ēremos is an adjective found only in 1 Tim. 2:2. It means "quiet," in the sense of "peaceful," in regard to one's lifestyle.

hēsychios [ἡσύχιος, *2272*]

hēsychios is an adjectival form occurring only twice, derived from ***hēsychazō*** (see above). It means "quiet" or "peaceful" in 1 Tim. 2:2; 1 Pet. 3:4.

hēsychia [ἡσυχία, *2271*]

hēsychia is a noun derived from ***hēsychazō*** (see above), found in four places. It is translated "silence" or "quietness" and is also used as an adjective. Acts 22:2 refers to the silence of a crowd. The quiet submissiveness of women in the context of public worship is indicated in 1 Tim. 2:11ff. 2 Thess. 3:12 contains the injunction "to work in quietness."

R

RACE

OT Words

mērôṣ **[מֵרוֹץ, 4793]**

mērôṣ is found only in Eccl. 9:11, referring in a general context to the "race" run by athletes.

NT Words

stadion [στάδιον, *4712*]

stadion is a noun referring primarily to the linear measurement of approximately 600 feet, or 185 meters — the standard length of athletic running courses in ancient Greece. In five of the six occurrences of this term in the New Testament, ***stadion*** reflects this meaning. In 1 Cor. 9:24, ***stadion*** refers to the actual running of the race itself.

agōn [ἀγών, *73*]

agōn refers primarily to a "fight" or "conflict." It occurs six times, and on one occasion it refers metaphorically to a "race," or the challenge that life presents to the follower of Christ (Heb. 12:1).

dromos [δρόμος, *1408*]

dromos is found in only three places. In two of these it means "race," referring metaphorically to the course of one's life (cf. Acts 20:24; 2 Tim. 4:7). In Acts 13:25, ***dromos*** refers with the same metaphorical force to one's "course," or "life's work."

RAGE

OT Words

za'aph **[זַעַף, 2197]**

za'aph is a noun occurring six times, meaning "rage," "indignation," or "wrath." Human rage or anger is noted in 2 Chr. 16:10; 28:9; Prov. 19:12. The indignation of God is indicated in Isa. 30:30; Mic. 7:9. In Jonah 1:15, ***za'aph*** refers to the "raging" sea whipped up by a storm.

NT Words

phruassō [φρυάσσω, *5433*]

phruassō is a verb found only twice, occurring both times in Acts 4:25. It means "rage," referring to the pagan nations who oppose God and his ways with a "furious arrogance."

klydōn [κλύδων, *2830*]

klydōn is found in only two contexts. In Luke 8:24 it refers to the "raging" of the stormy waters of the Sea of Galilee. In Jas. 1:6 ***klydōn*** is translated "wave," but the context indicates that it is a wave driven by stormy seas.

See Also: → ANGER → TREMBLE → WRATH

RAIMENT → CLOTHING

RAIN

OT Words

māṭar **[מָטַר, 4305]**

māṭar is a verb found in fourteen contexts, referring to "rain" in a literal as well as a metaphorical sense.

Gen. 2:5; 7:4; Job 28:26 refer to the literal meteorological phenomenon of rain. ***māṭar*** refers in Isa. 5:6; Amos 4:7 to God withholding rain, inflicting drought as a divine punishment.

māṭar refers to the action of Yahweh in various contexts. God's gracious provision for his people is indicated, for example, when he is said to "rain down" bread from heaven in the wilderness (cf. Exod. 16:4; Ps. 78:24). See also Ps. 78:27.

māṭar also refers to divine judgment. In Exod. 9:18, 23, Yahweh is said to "rain down" hail on Egypt, as one of the ten plague judgments on that land. In Gen. 19:24, God rains down fire and brimstone on the cities of Sodom and Gomorrah. Such a punishment is handed down to the wicked in general (Ps. 11:6), and to Gog the king of Magog in particular (Ezek. 38:22).

geshem **[גֶּשֶׁם, 1653]**

geshem is a noun referring to the literal meteorological phenomenon of rain. It is found in thirty-five contexts.

General references to rain are found for example, in 1 Kgs. 18:44ff.; Ezra 10:9ff.; Prov. 25:14; Song 2:11; Isa. 44:14; Ezek. 1:28.

Rain is sent on the earth as an act of divine judgment, resulting in great destruction, in relation to the Noahic flood (Gen. 6:5; 8:2); to Egypt (Ps. 105:32), and to Gog of Magog (Ezek. 38:22). Such punishment is occasionally directed at the people of God (cf. Ezek.

13:11ff.). Rain is also withheld, resulting in the onset of drought, in divine judgment on God's people (1 Kgs. 17:7; Jer. 14:4; Amos 4:7); and on the people of the earth (Zech. 14:17).

mātār **[מָטָר, 4306]**

mātār is a synonym for ***geshem*** (see above) and occurs in almost forty contexts.

General references to rain are found in Deut. 11:1; 32:2; 2 Sam. 23:4; Job 28:26; Ps. 135:7; Prov. 26:1; Isa. 4:6; Jer. 10:13.

Exod. 9:33, 34 refer to rain as a destructive deluge, a punishment from God against Egypt. Other contexts of divine judgment refer to withholding rain, resulting in drought, primarily against the people of Israel (cf. Deut. 11:17; 28:24; 2 Chr. 7:13; Isa. 5:6).

The agricultural and economic benefits of rain as a blessing from the hand of God are described in Deut. 11:4; 28:12; 1 Kgs. 8:36; 2 Chr. 6:27; Job 5:10; Isa. 30:23; Zech. 10:1. 1 Sam. 12:17ff. refers to rain given as a sign from God.

yôreh **[יוֹרֶה, 3138]**

yôreh is found only in Deut. 11:14; Jer. 5:24, with reference to the "early rains" of the autumn season.

malqôsh **[מַלְקוֹשׁ, 4456]**

malqôsh is found on eight occasions, all with reference to the "latter rains" of spring (cf. Deut. 11:14; Jer. 3:3; Hos. 6:3; Joel 2:23; Zech. 10:1).

môreh **[מוֹרֶה, 4175]**

môreh is a synonym for ***yôreh*** (see above), occurring only twice and referring to the "early (autumnal) rain" in Ps. 84:6; Joel 2:23.

NT Words

brechō [βρέχω, *1026*]

brechō is a verb found eight times, meaning "to rain," "send rain" in a literal sense in Matt. 5:45; Jas. 5:17; Rev. 11:6. It also refers to Yahweh causing fire and sulfur to "rain down" upon Sodom and Gomorrah. (→ WASH)

brochē [βροχή, *1028*]

brochē is a noun derived from ***brechō*** (see above), found in only two places and referring to the "rain" that flooded the earth during the days of Noah (cf. Matt. 7:25, 27).

hyetos [ὑετός, *5205*]

hyetos is a synonym for ***brochē*** (see above), indicating literal "rain" on six occasions (cf. Acts 14:17; 28:2; Heb. 6:7; Jas. 5:7, 18; Rev. 11:6).

See Also: → SHOOT

RAINBOW

OT Words

qeshet **[קֶשֶׁת, 7198]**

qeshet is a noun occurring in nearly eighty places, with the primary sense of "bow" as a weapon for hunting. (→ BOW [NOUN]) However, in Gen. 9:13ff.; Ezek. 1:28, ***qeshet*** refers to the "rainbow." The Genesis references speak of the rainbow as the sign of God's covenant promise to Noah to never again send such a flood to cover the earth.

NT Words

iris [ἶρις, *2463*]

iris is a term found only twice, referring to a "rainbow" surrounding the throne of God (Rev. 4:3) and encircling the head of a mighty angel (Rev. 10:1).

RAISE

OT Words

'āmad **[עָמַד, 5975]**

'āmad is a common verb with the primary meaning "to stand," as well as a number of related senses, in the approximately 520 occurrences of the term. Included here is the rare sense of "raise up," found in only two places. Exod. 9:16 speaks of Yahweh "raising up" Pharaoh in order to display his unique power and authority over mere human rulers. A similar motive is indicated in Ps. 107:25, where God is said "to raise up" a stormy wind on the sea to demonstrate his power over creation and to evoke a response of saving faith from merchants in the course of their day-to-day business. (→ STAND)

'ālāh **[עָלָה, 5927]**

'ālāh is another common verb with the primary meanings "come up," "go up," "offer (up)," in its nearly nine hundred occurrences. However, in a handful of contexts it means "raise." In 1 Kgs. 5:13; 9:15, ***'ālāh*** refers to "raising" a levy in conjunction with Solomon's construction of the temple. 2 Chr. 32:5 speaks of Hezekiah "raising" towers upon the wall of Jerusalem to reinforce and protect it from possible invasion and attack from Sennacherib, king of Assyria.

zāqaph [זָקַף, 2210]

zāqaph is a rare verb found only twice, referring to God "raising up" those who are bowed down (cf. Pss. 145:14; 146:8). The contexts here suggest an alleviation of misfortune or perhaps release from oppression.

NT Words

exanistēmi [ἐξανίστημι, *1817*]

exanistēmi is a verb found in three places, meaning "raise up," "rise up." Mark 12:19; Luke 20:28 refer to the custom of "Levirate marriage" whereby a man is charged (under the Mosaic law) with the responsibility of taking his deceased brother's widow and "raising up" children by her. Acts 15:5 refers to people "rising up," or standing up, in order to speak.

exegeirō [ἐξεγείρω, *1825*]

exegeirō is a verb related to ***egeirō*** (see above), meaning "to raise up" in each of its three occurrences. Rom. 9:17 twice refers to the action of God in raising up Pharaoh for the explicit purpose of manifesting his divine power in him. 1 Cor. 6:14 indicates that God will likewise "raise us" up (i.e., from the dead), just as he raised Jesus from death.

synegeirō [συνεγείρω, *4891*]

synegeirō is another verb related to ***egeirō*** (see above), meaning "to raise (up) with," "raise together with." It is found only three times, all with reference to the believer "being raised up together with" Christ from death to the heavenly realm (cf. Eph. 2:6; Col. 2:12; 3:1).

See Also: → ARISE

RAM

OT Words

'ayil [אַיִל, 352]

'ayil is the most common term in the Old Testament referring to the "ram" as personal property, food, as well as a ritual sacrifice. ***'ayil*** occurs around 150 times.

'ayil refers to rams in general (Exod. 25:5; 35:7; Deut. 32:14; Ps. 114:4; Jer. 51:40); to rams as personal property (Gen. 32:14; 2 Kgs. 3:4; 2 Chr. 17:11; Ezek. 27:21); to the flesh of rams designated for food in a mundane context (Gen. 31:38); and to their consumption in a ceremonial setting (Exod. 29:31; Ezek. 39:18). The latter text refers to the symbolic feast celebrating Yahweh's triumph over the enemy nation Magog and its ruler, Gog.

In a significant metaphorical context, Dan. 8:3ff. refers to a ram as the symbolic representation of the kingdoms of Media and Persia.

'ayil most commonly refers to the presentation of rams for ritual sacrifice in Israel. A general reference to this phenomenon is found in 1 Sam. 15:22. Gen. 15:9 describes the sacrifice of a ram as part of the ritual preparation for a theophanic revelation to the patriarch Abraham. Gen. 22:13 records the divinely initiated substitution of a ram for the life of Abraham's son, Isaac.

Under the Mosaic covenant legislation, rams are prescribed for the following ritual ceremonies and festivals: priestly ordination (Exod. 29:1ff.; Lev. 8:21); the dedication of the tabernacle (Num. 7:15ff.); the Day of Atonement ceremony (Lev. 16:3; Num. 29:8ff.); the sin and trespass offering (Lev. 5:16ff.; 9:2; 19:21; Ezra 10:9); the fellowship offering (Lev. 9:18, 19; Num. 6:14ff.); the burnt offering (Num. 23:1ff.; Ezek. 43:23ff.); Passover (Num. 28:19ff.; Ezek. 45:23ff.); and the Feasts of Weeks (Num. 28:27ff.), Trumpets (Num. 29:2ff.), and Tabernacles (Num. 29:13ff.). Yahweh also rejects animal sacrifice when the hearts of the people are perverse (cf. Isa. 1:11; Mic. 6:7).

Other contexts that involve the sacrificial presentation of rams include David's celebration in bringing the ark of the covenant back to Jerusalem (cf. 1 Chr. 15:26); the festival surrounding the acknowledgment of Solomon as king (cf. 1 Chr. 29:21); and the people's celebration of their return from captivity (Ezra 8:35).

dekar [דְּכַר, 1798 (Aramaic)]

dekar is an Aramaic term found in only three places, all referring to rams, designated as part of the sacrificial offerings for the dedication of the reconstructed Second Temple of the postexilic period during the time of Ezra the priest (cf. Ezra 6:9, 17; 7:17).

yôbēl [יוֹבֵל, 3104]

yôbēl is a noun referring to the Jubilee festival in most of its twenty-seven occurrences. However, in five of these contexts it refers to the "ram's horn" trumpets that were sounded on the occasion of the destruction of Jericho (cf. Josh. 6:4ff.).

RANSOM

OT Words

pidyôm [פִּדְיוֹם, 6306]

The noun ***pidyôm*** refers to the payment made in order to "buy back" or "redeem" one's life or property. The term may be translated either "ransom" or "redemption," but the underlying sense is identical. ***pidyôm*** occurs four times.

In Exod. 21:30, the owner of a bull who has failed to restrain his beast, resulting in severe injury or death for a number of people, is deemed liable for capital punishment. However, in payment of a "ransom," or "price of redemption," the man's life may be spared. Other references to "ransom" or "redemption" money are found in Num. 3:49, 51. In Ps. 49:8, the psalmist declares the impossibility of paying an adequate ransom to God for the indefinite maintenance of a human life, since eventually all must pass through physical death.

kōpher [כֹּפֶר, 3724]

kōpher is a noun occurring seventeen times, with the primary meanings "ransom," "bribe." (→ BRIBE)

kōpher refers to a "ransom," or an amount of money paid to redeem a person's life (cf. Exod. 21:30; 30:12; Job 33:24; Prov. 13:8; Isa. 43:3). See also Prov. 21:18. This provision, however, is not possible in the case of a murderer (cf. Num. 35:31ff.). Ps. 49:7 declares (along with the following verse — see above) that it is impossible for people to ransom themselves in the sight of God.

NT Words

lytron [λύτρον, *3083*]

lytron is a rare term, occurring only twice and meaning "ransom." In Matt. 20:28; Mark 10:45, ***lytron*** refers to the "ransom" offered by Jesus Christ for the salvation of many — that is, he gave his life freely as a substitutionary sacrifice for sin.

antilytron [ἀντίλυτρον, *487*]

antilytron is a rare synonym for ***lytron*** (see above), occurring only in 1 Tim. 2:6 and referring to Jesus Christ offering himself as a "ransom" for all.

See Also: → REDEEM

RAVEN

OT Words

'ôreb [עֹרֵב, 6158]

'ôreb is the only term in the Old Testament referring to "ravens." It occurs ten times and refers to that bird species in all but one context (e.g., Gen. 8:7; Lev. 11:15; Deut. 14:14; 1 Kgs. 17:4ff.; Isa. 34:11). Song 5:11 refers to the dark hair of the woman's lover being as black as a raven's.

NT Words

korax [κόραξ, *2876*]

korax is found only in Luke 12:24, referring to "ravens" as an illustration in Christ's exhortation to his hearers not to worry about the necessities of life, which will be provided by God.

REACH

OT Words

nāga' [נָגַע, 5060]

nāga' is a verb found 150 times with the dominant sense of "touch," as well as a variety of associated meanings including the sense of "reach," which is indicated nine times. (→ TOUCH)

The meaning "reach" in the sense of "extend up to" is found in several places, all of them metaphorical. Job 20:6 speaks of human pride reaching up to the clouds. With reference to the imminent invasion of Israel by the Assyrian armies, Isa. 8:8 refers to the coming "flood" that will "reach up to" the neck of the people of Judah. A number of texts contain the expression "reach up to heaven," referring to the ladder Jacob saw in the dream vision at Bethel (Gen. 28:12); to an outburst of human rage (2 Chr. 28:9); to the divine judgment against Babylon (Jer. 51:9); and to Nebuchadnezzar's greatness (Dan. 4:22).

The sense of "reach" also includes the idea of "extend" in the context of linear measurement. 2 Chr. 3:11, 12 refer to the wings of the golden cherubim carved on the cover of the ark of the covenant "reaching" to five cubits.

mātāh [מְטָה, 4291 (Aramaic)]

mātāh is an Aramaic verb found in eight contexts meaning "reach," "come upon." The former sense is found in three places. Dan. 4:11, 20 refer to the tree in Nebuchadnezzar's dream that "reached" to the heavens. Dan. 4:22 refers metaphorically to Nebuchadnezzar's greatness likewise "reaching" to heaven.

NT Words

pherō [φέρω, *5342*]

pherō is a verb occurring around sixty times with the predominant meanings "to bring (forth)," "bear" in the majority of its usage. Twice in John 20:27, however, the term is translated "reach out" (i.e., "stretch out") in the context of Jesus' invitation to the disciple Thomas to feel the scars in his hand and side with his own hands in order to satisfy himself that it was truly the same Jesus who had lived among them, died, and was now risen from the dead.

ephikneomai [ἐφικνέομαι, *2185*]

ephikneomai is a rare verb occurring only twice, in 2 Cor. 10:13, 14. In the first of these texts, the sense of "reach" refers to an opportunity that Paul recognized as "extending" to the Corinthian congregation. In the second of these verses, ***ephikneomai*** expresses the idea of "reach" in the sense of "visit" or "come to."

READ, READING

OT Words

qārā' [קָרָא, **7121**]; ***qerā'*** [קְרָא, **7123** (Aramaic)]

qārā' is a common verb, occurring 730 times with the predominant senses of "call," "cry," "proclaim," as well as several other related nuances. ***qārā'*** can also mean "to read," and it occurs in approximately forty contexts with this sense (including several occurrences of the Aramaic form of the verb). (→ CALL)

Various contexts are associated with the activity of reading. In a number of places, for example, the book of the law covenant is read in the hearing of the Israelite people, in association with either covenant ratification or renewal (cf. Exod. 24:7; Josh. 8:34ff.; Neh. 8:3; 9:3). The people of Judah also hear the newly rediscovered book of the law read at the time of King Josiah, when that sacred work was found during the renovation of the temple (cf. 2 Kgs. 22:8ff.; 23:2). The book of the law is also read during the celebration of the Feast of Tabernacles at the time of Ezra the priest's return to the postexilic community of Judah in the mid-fifth century B.C. (cf. Ezra 8:18). The requirement to give a public reading of the law to God's people is laid down in the Mosaic legislation (Deut. 17:19; 31:11).

Other significant "reading" occasions include the reading of Jeremiah's letter to King Jehoiakim announcing the coming judgments that God is about to inflict upon his people for their rebellion against him (cf. Jer. 36:6ff (cf. also Jer. 29:29). A divine judgment against the kingdom of Babylon is "read" in Jer. 51:63. Dan. 5:8ff. refers to the mysterious handwriting on the wall of the palace in Babylon that so terrified Belshazzar, the last of that nation's rulers. That writing was composed by God himself, and only Daniel was able to give an interpretive "reading" that explained and announced the almost immediate downfall of the Babylonian kingdom at the hands of the Persians.

Mundane references to "reading" include those in 2 Kgs. 5:7; 19:14; Ezra 4:18, 23 (both Aramaic); Esth. 6:1; Isa. 29:11; 37:14.

miqrā' [מִקְרָא, **4744**]

miqrā' is a term primarily signifying an "assembly" or "gathering" in most of its twenty-three occurrences. However, in Neh. 8:8, ***miqrā'*** refers to the "reading" of the law that probably indicated not only the mere reading of the text, but also an explanation of its meaning, an interpretation. (→ ASSEMBLY)

NT Words

anaginōskō [ἀναγινώσκω, *314*]

anaginōskō is the only term in the New Testament meaning "to read." It is found thirty-three times.

General references to the Scriptures being read are found in Acts 13:27; 15:21; 2 Cor. 3:15.

In a number of places, Jesus asks of his audience, "Have you not read . . . ?," inquiring about their knowledge of the (Old Testament) Scriptures (cf. Matt. 12:3ff.; 19:4; 21:16, 42; 22:31; Mark 2:25; 12:10, 26; Luke 6:3; 10:26). Jesus also exhorts the reader of the Scriptures to pay close attention to what he is pointing out (cf. Matt. 24:15; Mark 13:14). Jesus' own reading of the Isaiah scroll in the synagogue at Nazareth is recorded in Luke 4:16. John 19:20 mentions the Jerusalem inhabitants reading the inscription placed above the head of Christ on the cross: "The King of the Jews." The incident of the Ethiopian royal official reading the book of Isaiah is recorded in Acts 8:28ff.

General references to the early church congregations reading the letters of Paul are found in Acts 23:34; 2 Cor. 1:13; Eph. 3:4; Col. 4:16; 1 Thess. 5:27. Acts 15:31 refers to the church at Antioch reading the letter of the Jerusalem council to Gentile believers. A specific blessing is promised to all who read the words of the book of Revelation (Rev. 1:3).

Finally, ***anaginōskō*** refers metaphorically to "reading" the hearts of true believers (2 Cor. 3:2).

anagnōsis [ἀνάγνωσις, *320*]

anagnōsis is the noun derived from ***anaginōskō*** (see above), occurring in only three places and referring literally to "reading." ***anagnōsis*** refers to reading the law and the Prophets (Acts 13:15); to reading the old covenant (2 Cor. 3:14); and to the public reading of Scripture (1 Tim. 4:13).

READY

NT Words

hetoimos [ἕτοιμος, *2092*]

hetoimos is an adjective with the primary meaning "ready" in the sense of "being prepared." It is found in seventeen contexts.

Exhortations to be ready for the coming of the Son of Man are found in Matt. 24:44; Luke 12:40. In 1 Pet. 3:15, the apostle urges his readers to be ready to offer a defense of their faith. Peter professes his readiness to suffer persecution for the sake of Christ in Luke 22:33. Acts 23:15, 21 records the readiness of Paul's enemies to assassinate him. Readiness to attend a feast is a prominent theme in several parables taught by Christ during his earthly ministry (cf. Matt. 22:4, 8; 25:10; Luke 14:17). See also Mark 14:15; 2 Cor. 9:5; 10:6. Finally, God declares his readiness to reveal the climax of redemption for his people at the last day in 1 Pet. 1:5.

See Also: → PREPARATION

REAP, REAPER

OT Words

qāṣar [קָצַר, **7114**]

qāṣar is a verb found in approximately fifty places with the principal sense of "to reap" in the majority of its occurrences. The term is also used nominally, referring to "reaper(s)." ***qāṣar*** can also be translated "to cut short," "shorten." (→ SHORT)

qāṣar refers literally to "reaping" a harvest in a number of places (e.g., Lev. 19:9; Deut. 24:19; 1 Sam. 6:13; 2 Kgs. 19:29; Eccl. 11:4; Isa. 37:30). Failure to reap a harvest is indicative of a judgment from God in Mic. 6:5. Literal references to "reapers" of the harvest are found in Ruth 2:3ff.; 2 Kgs. 4:18; Ps. 129:7; Amos 9:13.

qāṣar is also used metaphorically. Several texts enunciate the principle that if one "sows" iniquity, then one will "reap" trouble, or calamity (cf. Job 4:8; Prov. 22:8; Jer. 12:13; Hos. 8:7). Ps. 126:5 refers to "reaping" shouts of joy. Hos. 10:2, 13 record the blessing of "reaping" the fruit of steadfast love from God after having sown the seed of righteousness in one's life.

NT Words

therizō [θερίζω, *2325*]

therizō is the dynamic equivalent of the Hebrew term ***qāṣar*** (see above), meaning "to reap" in each of its twenty-four occurrences. The use of ***therizō*** is both literal and metaphorical.

Literal references to reaping the harvest are found in Matt. 6:26; Luke 12:24; 19:21ff.; Jas. 5:4.

Metaphorically, ***therizō*** refers to the blessing of reaping a harvest of eternal life (John 4:36ff.; 2 Cor. 9:6); and reaping material benefits in the course of one's ministry (1 Cor. 9:11). Gal. 6:7 affirms the universal principle that one will always reap the consequences of one's actions — good and bad. Illustrating this principle, Gal. 6:8 goes on to affirm that if we "sow" to please our sinful nature, we shall "reap" corruption. Conversely, if we "sow" to please the Spirit of God, we shall "reap" eternal life from the Spirit. See also Gal. 6:9.

Rev. 14:15, 16 refer to divine "reaping," where the earth is said to be harvested. In this context, divine judgment on a wicked earth is indicated.

theristēs [θεριστής, *2327*]

theristēs is the noun derived from ***therizō***, occurring only twice and meaning "reaper" in both instances. In Matt. 13:30, 39, Jesus refers to "reapers" in one of his kingdom parables, whose role is to separate the "wheat" (i.e., the godly) and the "chaff" (i.e., the ungodly). These "reapers" are identified as angels who serve as instruments of divine judgment.

REASON, REASONING

OT Words

yākaḥ [יָכַח, **3198**]

The verb ***yākaḥ*** occurs nearly sixty times with the primary meanings "to rebuke," "reprove," "correct," as well as several associated senses. In three places, however, ***yākaḥ*** is translated "to reason." In Job 13:3; 15:3, the term refers to a person "reasoning," or "arguing his case" with God. In Isa. 1:18 there is a divine invitation to the people of Israel "to reason together" with God — a "reasoning" that is not intended as a debate between equals. Rather, it is used metaphorically as an invitation from God to his people to come and hear his plans and purposes for them, and to submit to his "reasoning," working out his plan of redemption on their behalf. (→ REBUKE)

manda' [מַנְדַּע, **4486** (Aramaic)]

manda' is an Aramaic term found only four times, all in the book of Daniel. ***manda'*** is translated variously as "knowledge," "understanding," "reason." The latter two senses are interchangeable and occur in Dan.

4:34, 36, referring to the reasoning powers of King Nebuchadnezzar.

NT Words

dialogizomai [διαλογίζομαι, *1260*]

dialogizomai is a verb found sixteen times, with the principal meaning "to reason (together)" found in most of these contexts. The underlying sense of ***dialogizomai*** is that of engaging in discussion, questioning, or debate over a difficult question to resolve, from the perspective of the participants.

References to reasoning involving general discussion include those in Matt. 16:7ff.; Mark 8:16ff.; Luke 20:14. Matt. 21:25 refers to the reasoned discussion of the spiritual leaders of Israel earnestly seeking, but failing to find, a solution to the difficult question put to them by Jesus.

dialogizomai also refers to the unbelieving questioning taking place in the hearts and minds of the Pharisees and scribes who witnessed Jesus' healing of the young paralytic. They were skeptical of his intentions and accused him of blasphemy for claiming to have the authority to forgive sins (cf. Mark 2:6ff.; Luke 5:21ff.).

In Mark 9:33, ***dialogizomai*** refers to Jesus' disciples "arguing among themselves" as to who was the greatest.

syllogizomai [συλλογίζομαι, *4817*]

syllogizomai is a rare synonym for ***dialogizomai*** found only in Luke 20:5, referring to the reasoned discussion of the scribes and Pharisees seeking in vain to discover a satisfactory response to the question put to them by Jesus.

dialegomai [διαλέγομαι, *1256*]

dialegomai is a verb found in thirteen places with the primary meanings "to dispute," "argue," "reason with," found in most of these contexts.

dialegomai refers to the disciples "arguing" over who is the greatest among them (cf. Luke 9:46).

Most commonly, ***dialegomai*** refers to Paul "debating" or "reasoning" with the Jews from the Hebrew Scriptures over the identity of Jesus Christ as the Messiah (cf. Acts 17:2, 17; 18:4, 19; 19:8ff.).

Jude 9 contains the enigmatic reference to the archangel Michael disputing with the devil over the body of Moses.

See Also: → DISPUTE → QUESTION
→ THOUGHT

REBEL, REBELLION

OT Words

mārad [מָרַד, 4775]

mārad is a verb found in twenty-five contexts, meaning "rebel" or "revolt."

The act of rebellion against a human king is indicated, for example, in Gen. 14:4; 2 Kgs. 18:7; 24:1, 20; 2 Chr. 13:6; 36:13; Neh. 2:19; 6:6; Jer. 52:3; Ezek. 17:15.

Equal emphasis is given in other contexts to the sin of rebelling against God. Num. 14:9; Josh. 22:19, 29 contain commands and warnings not to rebel against Yahweh. A charge of rebelling against Yahweh is made in Josh. 22:16, and Josh. 22:18 cites the consequences of this rebellion against God. Israel's rebellion against Yahweh, for which they are condemned, is described in Neh. 9:26; Isa. 36:5; Ezek. 2:3; 20:38. Dan. 9:5, 9 refer to confessing rebellion against God.

mārad is used metaphorically in Job 24:13, which speaks of people "rebelling against the light."

mārāh [מָרָה, 4784]

mārāh is a verb expressing the dominant sense of "to rebel," "be rebellious" in the majority of the forty or so contexts in which it is found. There are also a number of related meanings associated with the idea of rebellion.

The primary usage of ***mārāh*** is concerned with acts of rebellion against God in several contexts. Frequent mention, for example, is made of people rebelling against the commandments or words of Yahweh (cf. Num. 20:24; 27:14; Deut. 1:26, 43; Josh. 1:18; 1 Sam. 12:14ff.; Pss. 105:28; 107:11; Lam. 1:18). The action of rebelling against Yahweh himself is indicated with regard to the wicked in general (Ps. 5:10); and in relation to the people of Israel and Judah (Deut. 9:7; Pss. 78:17; 106:7; Isa. 1:20; Jer. 4:17; Lam. 1:20; Ezek. 20:8; Hos. 13:16).

mārāh is also used adjectivally in several places, referring to a rebellious youth acting in defiance of his parents (Deut. 21:18ff.); and to the rebellious attitude of Israel and Judah towards Yahweh (Ps. 78:8; Jer. 5:23).

merî [מְרִי, 4805]

merî is an adjectival form derived from ***mārāh*** (see above), occurring twenty-three times with the primary meaning "rebellious," along with the nominal senses of "rebellion," "rebel."

In most cases, ***merî*** indicates a rebellious attitude towards God. Such an attitude is predicated of Israel (the northern kingdom) in Isa. 30:9; and of Judah in Ezek. 2:5ff.; 3:26ff.; 12:2ff., 25; 17:12; 24:3. See also Ezek. 44:6. Acts of rebellion committed by Israel against God are recorded in Deut. 31:27; Neh. 9:17. King Saul's rebellion against Yahweh is recorded in 1 Sam. 15:23.

A general reference to rebellion is found in Prov. 17:11. Num. 17:10 describes the Levite Korah and his associates as "rebels," referring to their abortive attempt to overthrow Moses as leader of the congregation of Israel, for which action they forfeited their lives.

mārād **[מָרָד, 4779** (Aramaic)]

mārād is an Aramaic adjectival form, found only twice and meaning "rebellious" in Ezra 4:12, 15. It refers here to the city of Jerusalem as "rebellious" in the eyes of the nations around them.

mered **[מֶרֶד, 4777]**

mered is a noun occurring only in Josh. 22:22 with reference to Israel's potential "rebellion" against Yahweh.

merad **[מְרַד, 4776** (Aramaic)]

merad is the Aramaic form of ***mered*** (see above). It occurs only once, in Ezra 4:19, with reference to Jerusalem's perceived attitude of "rebellion" against her overlords.

pāsha' **[פָּשַׁע, 6586]**

pāsha' is a verb occurring around forty times with the primary meanings "rebel" and "transgress." There is a considerable degree of overlap between these two renderings.

References to nations rebelling against other nations are found in 1 Kgs. 12:19; 2 Kgs. 1:1; 3:5ff.; 8:20ff.; 2 Chr. 10:19.

More commonly, ***pāsha'*** refers to the act of rebellion against Yahweh by the kingdoms of Israel and Judah (cf. Isa. 1:2; 43:27; 66:24; Jer. 2:8, 29; 3:13; Ezek. 20:38; Hos. 7:13). Jer. 33:8 contains the promise that Yahweh will forgive his people for their rebellion against him.

pāsha' is also used nominally in Isa. 48:8 to refer to Israel as a "rebel" against Yahweh from the moment of her "birth."

sārāh **[סָרָה, 5627]**

sārāh is a noun found in eight contexts meaning "rebellion," or "revolt," in most of these. Where the sense of "rebellion" is explicit, the contexts speak of turning one's back on God (cf. Deut. 13:5; Isa. 1:5; 31:6; 59:13; Jer. 28:16; 29:32).

sārar **[סָרַר, 5637]**

sārar is a verb occurring in seventeen places, with a consistent nominal (i.e., participial) and adjectival usage. ***sārar*** is usually translated "stubborn." (→ STUBBORN) However, in several places it also means "rebellious," which manifests a certain semantic overlap with the sense of "stubborn." For example, Ps. 6:7 speaks of the nations that are "rebellious," presumably towards God. Rebellious people in general are indicated in Ps. 68:6, 18; and God's people in particular are said to be rebellious in Isa. 30:1; 65:2; Jer. 6:28. Rebels are also designated in Isa. 1:3; Hos. 9:15.

NT Words

parapikrasmos **[παραπικρασμός, *3894*]**

parapikrasmos is a term found only twice. On both occasions it refers to the period of Israel's rebellion against God during her times of wandering in the wilderness (cf. Heb. 3:8, 15).

See Also: → TRANSGRESS

REBUKE

OT Words

yākaḥ **[יָכַח, 3198]**

yākaḥ is a verb found in nearly sixty places, with the principal meanings "rebuke," or "reprove," in about half of these contexts, as well as a number of related senses. ***yākaḥ*** means "rebuke" in the context of both divine and human reproof.

Where God is concerned, the action of "rebuking" involves firstly bringing an accusation — for example, against his people (Gen. 31:42) and pagan rulers (1 Chr. 16:21; Pss. 50:21; 105:14). 2 Kgs. 19:4; Isa. 37:4 express the desire that Yahweh might rebuke the Assyrian commander for his insulting words spoken to the people of Jerusalem and directed against God.

In the second place, God is said to bring a rebuke against people with the underlying sense of chastening, or disciplining, them. In the context of Yahweh's covenant promise to King David, the Lord promises to rebuke David's son as a father would his own child (2 Sam. 7:14). God is then said to rebuke (i.e., chasten) his people in general terms in Job 13:10; 22:4; Jer. 2:19 (cf. also Ps. 50:8). Prov. 3:12 refers explicitly to God's action in rebuking (i.e., disciplining) those he loves. He rebukes the nations in Ps. 94:10. Job 5:10 affirms that the person whom God chastens is a happy person. The psalmist begs God not to rebuke him in his anger (cf. Pss. 6:1; 38:1). See also 1 Chr. 12:17.

The prophet Ezekiel is mute as a sign from God, so that the people of God will be unable to receive a rebuke from the Lord through the prophet, and thus be denied his revelation (cf. Ezek. 3:26). Job 40:2 records the foolhardy attempt of people seeking to rebuke God. General references to people rebuking others are found in Job 6:26; Ps. 141:5; Prov. 9:7ff.; 15:12; 24:25; Amos 5:10.

tôkēḥāh [תּוֹכֵחָה, 8433]

tôkēḥāh is a noun derived from ***yākaḥ*** (see above) with the primary meanings "rebuke," or "reproof," as well as the synonymous senses of "correction," "chastisement." These meanings are found in virtually all of the twenty-eight occurrences of the term.

Rebuke from God in the sense of punishment is noted in a number of contexts. The people of God suffer this (2 Kgs. 19:3; Isa. 37:3; Ezek. 5:15; Hos. 5:9); as does the nation of Philistia (Ezek. 25:17).

Divine rebuke in the sense of discipline or chastising is indicated in regard to human beings (Pss. 39:11; 73:14); in regard to the nations (Ps. 149:7); and in relation to one's children (Prov. 3:11). Such reproof of fools by God is described metaphorically in Prov. 1:23, 25 as coming from Lady Wisdom (personifying that divine attribute).

Ps. 38:14; Prov. 6:23 refer to human rebuke generally. In several places, reproof is said to be rejected, or despised — an attitude described as foolish in the extreme (cf. Prov. 5:12; 10:17; 12:1; 15:10). The acceptance of reproof (Prov. 13:18; 15:5) results in real happiness and contentment.

gā'ar [גָּעַר, 1605]

gā'ar is a verb occurring fourteen times and means "to rebuke" in almost all of these contexts. It is synonymous with ***yākaḥ*** (see above).

People rebuke others, in the sense of "reprove," or "correct," in Gen. 37:10; Ruth 2:16 (an instruction not to rebuke); Jer. 29:27.

The action of divine rebuke, also in the sense of "reprove," is more common. Yahweh is called upon in Zech. 3:2 to rebuke Satan for his attempted condemnation of Joshua the high priest. God is said to rebuke the nations (Ps. 9:5; Isa. 17:13); and insolent people (Ps. 119:21). Inanimate objects are also declared, metaphorically, to bear the brunt of a divine rebuke, such as the Re(e)d Sea (Ps. 106:9); and the sea in general (Nah. 1:4). In Isa. 54:9, Yahweh swears never to rebuke (i.e., to punish) his people again.

ge'ārāh [גְּעָרָה, 1606]

ge'ārāh is a noun derived from ***gā'ar*** (see above), found in fifteen places with the consistent meanings "rebuke," "reproof."

The divine rebuke is most often associated with God's judgment and wrath. It is directed symbolically, for example, at the earth and sea (2 Sam. 22:16; Ps. 18:15; Isa. 50:2). See also Job 26:11. It is also directed at the armies of Yahweh's enemies (cf. Ps. 76:6), as well as at his enemies themselves (cf. Isa. 66:15). God is also said to rebuke his own people (Ps. 80:16; Isa. 51:20). There is also a mysterious divine rebuke of the waters at the point of creation, directing them to their assigned place in the earth (cf. Ps. 104:7).

Where a rebuke derives from human beings, the sense of ***ge'ārāh*** is always that of discipline or chastening. Prov. 13:1 declares that the scoffer ignores a rebuke. The wise "man of understanding" appreciates a rebuke (cf. Prov. 17:10). Rebuke is also given by the wise, as affirmed in Eccl. 7:5.

mig'eret [מִגְעֶרֶת, 4045]

mig'eret is a participial noun derived from ***gā'ar*** (see above) that is found only in Deut. 28:20, referring to Yahweh's promised rebuke for his people should they in future abandon their exclusive loyalty toward him.

NT Words

epitimaō [ἐπιτιμάω, *2008*]

epitimaō is a verb meaning "to rebuke" in the majority of its nearly thirty occurrences. The underlying sense is that of "censure," "reprove."

In the course of Christ's earthly ministry, he was occasionally moved to offer a rebuke in a variety of contexts. For example, he rebukes the storm elements of wind and sea, resulting in immediate calm (cf. Matt. 8:26; Mark 4:39; Luke 8:24). Demons are also subject to his divine rebuke, immediately prior to their exorcism from individuals under their control (cf. Matt. 17:18; Mark 1:25; 9:25; Luke 4:35, 41 [cf. also Luke 4:39]; 9:42). Peter receives a stern rebuke for daring to question Jesus' destiny to face betrayal, death, and subsequent resurrection (cf. Mark 8:31). The apostolic band as a whole earn a rebuke from their Lord in Luke 9:55.

epitimaō also refers to humans giving rebukes in a number of contexts. For example, the disciples rebuke the crowds when they bring children to Jesus in order to be blessed (cf. Matt. 19:13; Mark 10:13; Luke 18:15). In another context, the crowd tries to censure those who continually cry out for Jesus to have mercy on them (cf. Matt. 20:31; Mark 10:13, 48; Luke 18:39 [see also Luke 23:40]). Luke 17:3; 2 Tim. 4:2 contain general exhortations to rebuke one's fellow believer for his sin.

Jude 9 records that Michael the archangel asks the Lord to rebuke Satan for (presumably) wanting to tamper with the body of Moses. And in Luke 19:39, the Pharisees demand (quite inappropriately) that Jesus rebuke his disciples for praising him as the coming Messianic King.

epiplēssō [ἐπιπλήσσω, *1969*]

epiplēssō is a verb found only in 1 Tim. 5:1, where Paul instructs Timothy not to rebuke an older man, but rather to exhort him as a father.

elenchō [ἐλέγχω, *1651*]

elenchō is a verb meaning "rebuke," "reprove" in seven of the seventeen contexts in which it occurs. (→ CONVICT → EXPOSE)

In several places, believers are exhorted to rebuke those who have sinned against them so that they might be restored to fellowship with each other and with God (cf. Matt. 18:15; 1 Tim. 5:20; 2 Tim. 4:2; Titus 1:13; 2:15). John the Baptist rebukes Herod the Tetrarch of Judea for improperly taking Herodias, his sister-in-law, as his wife (cf. Luke 3:19).

elenchō also refers to God, who is said to rebuke (i.e., discipline, chasten) those he loves (cf. Heb. 12:5; Rev. 3:19).

elenxis [ἔλεγξις, *1649*]

elenxis is a noun derived from *elenchō* (see above). It occurs only in 2 Pet. 2:16 and refers to the divine rebuke given to Balaam for his greed through the mouth of his donkey.

elenchos [ἔλεγχος, *1650*]

elenchos is another noun derived from *elenchō* (see above). It is found only in 2 Tim. 3:16 as a variant reading meaning "rebuke," designated as one of the divinely ordained purposes of the "God-breathed" Scriptures.

See Also: → REPROACH

RECEIVE

OT Words

lāqaḥ [לָקַח, 3947]

lāqaḥ is a common verb, occurring around one thousand times with the primary meaning "take," as well as several related senses in most of these contexts. *lāqaḥ* is also translated "receive," or "accept," in about twenty places in a variety of contexts. (→ TAKE)

In a number of contexts, people are involved in "receiving" tangible objects — for example, a gift (cf. Gen. 33:10); a pledge (cf. Gen. 38:20); and tithes for the priests from the Israelite "laity" (cf. Num. 18:28).

People also receive things from the hand of God, both tangible and intangible. For example, Moses receives the tablets of the law covenant from Yahweh (cf. Deut. 9:9); and his people receive instruction or direction from God (cf. Job 22:22; Zeph. 3:7). Receiving, or accepting, the words of a godly parent and living according to them is commended in Prov. 2:1; 4:10. Jer. 9:20 contains a general exhortations to receive God's word and instruction (cf. also Jer. 17:23).

God receives prayer (Ps. 6:9) and also his devoted servants (Ps. 49:15), in the sense of "taking (them) to himself."

lāqaḥ is also used in metaphorical contexts, such as Gen. 4:11, where the ground is said to have received the blood of Abel, bearing testimony to his murder at the hands of his brother Cain. Prov. 8:10 refers to people receiving divine words from Lady Wisdom, the personification of elements of the character of God, in Prov. 1–9.

nāśā' [נָשָׂא, 5375]

nāśā' is a common verb with the primary meanings "bear," "lift," "carry," as well as a number of related senses in the majority of its over 650 occurrences. However, in two places *nāśā'* means "receive." Deut. 33:3 speaks of the people of Israel receiving instruction from Yahweh; and Ps. 24:5 affirms that the righteous person will receive blessing from God. (→ BEAR [VERB])

ḥālaq [חָלַק, 2505]

ḥālaq is a verb found in sixty-five contexts meaning "divide," as well as associated senses. In Josh. 18:2, *ḥālaq* is translated "receive," referring to the fact that seven tribes of Israel had not yet received their inheritance in the land — it had not yet been divided or apportioned among them.

NT Words

dechomai [δέχομαι, *1209*]

dechomai is a verb meaning "to receive" in almost all of its nearly sixty occurrences. This meaning has several distinct connotations.

In a number of places, ***dechomai*** is translated "receive" in the sense of "welcome." General references to "receiving" people in this sense are found in Matt. 10:40ff.; Luke 16:9; John 4:45; Acts 21:17; 2 Cor. 7:15 (cf. also 2 Cor. 11:16); Gal. 4:14; Col. 4:10. The courtesy of welcoming people as guests in one's town is noted in Luke 16:4. Also, Heb. 11:31 refers to Rahab's faith in Yahweh and to her courage in welcoming the Israelite spies into her Jericho home and offering them protection. Mark 6:11; Matt. 10:14; Luke 9:5 mention those who refuse to extend hospitality to the disciples of Jesus during their ministry "tour" of Judea. By refusing to "receive" the members of the apostolic band, such towns would incur divine displeasure. Matt. 18:5; Mark 9:37; Luke 9:48 cite the importance of "receiving" (i.e., welcoming) little children into the kingdom of God unconditionally and without prejudice.

The sense of "receive" as "accept as true" is indicated, for example, in Matt. 11:14, where Jesus affirms, for those willing to "accept" it, that John the Baptist is the "new Elijah" as foretold by the prophet Malachi. Luke 8:13; Acts 8:14; 17:11; 1 Thess. 2:13; Jas. 1:21 indicate the value of receiving (i.e., accepting) God's word as true. 2 Cor. 11:4 warns against "receiving" a different gospel.

"Receiving" also expresses the idea of "discerning" in 1 Cor. 2:14, where it is affirmed that unbelievers do not receive gifts from the Spirit of God because they are incapable of appreciating them.

Other contexts refer to the act of "receiving" in regard to human relationships with God. Acts 7:38, for example, cites Moses as the one who received from God the oracles of the law. In Acts 7:59, Stephen asks God to receive his Spirit at the point of his own death. 2 Cor. 6:1 warns against receiving the grace of God in vain.

In mundane contexts, ***dechomai*** also refers to receiving letters (Acts 22:5; 28:21).

lambanō [λαμβάνω, *2983*]

lambanō is a verb occurring around 260 times, with the two primary meanings "take," "receive." The meaning "receive" is found in a variety of contexts.

(→ TAKE)

lambanō refers literally to "receiving" with the sense of "acquire" or "gain." General references to such activity include those in Matt. 10:8; John 13:30; Acts 3:5, including the oft-quoted maxim "It is more blessed to give than to receive" (cf. Acts 20:35). ***lambanō*** also refers to receiving a wage (cf. Matt. 20:9; John 4:36; 1 Cor. 3:8); a prize (cf. 1 Cor. 9:24); tithes (cf. Heb. 7:8, 9); and civil authority (cf. Acts 26:10; Rev. 17:12).

lambanō indicates receiving blessing from God (cf. John 1:16); a reward (cf. 1 Cor. 3:14); a reward for faithful service to God (Matt. 19:29; Mark 10:30); answers as a result of prayer (Matt. 7:8; Mark 11:24; Luke 11:10; John 16:24; 1 John 3:22 [see also Jas. 4:3]); and even the office of the priesthood (Heb. 7:5). Heb. 11:35 cites the blessing of receiving one's dead back to life. Rev. 2:17 speaks of receiving a new name from the risen Christ in heaven.

With particular reference to the relationship between God and his people Israel, Heb. 11:8 mentions the divine promise to Abraham that his descendants would receive the land of Canaan as an inheritance. Heb. 11:13 refers to the list of old covenant saints who received the promises of God concerning his purposes in salvation. God promises that his new covenant people will receive their promised eternal inheritance (cf. Heb. 9:15, including mention of the "crown of life" in Jas. 1:2).

In negative contexts, ***lambanō*** refers to people receiving punishment for sin (cf. Matt. 23:14; Mark 12:40; Luke 20:47; Rom. 13:2; Heb. 2:2). Rev. 14:9, 11; 19:20 refer to the godless receiving the "mark of the beast" on their hands and foreheads. In contrast, Rev. 20:4 refers to those believers who had not received this demonic "mark," declaring that they came to life and reigned with Christ for 1,000 years.

lambanō also refers to "receiving" a welcome that demonstrates genuine hospitality (cf. Matt. 10:41). In a "negative" context, 2 John 10 enjoins believers not to "receive" any false teacher into one's home. No welcome of any kind is to be extended to them.

As with ***dechomai*** (see above), ***lambanō*** also refers to the act of "receiving" in terms of "accepting as true." This applies, for example, to receiving the word of God in John 17:8. Such a response to God's word is also indicated symbolically in the parable of the sower, where seed sown in fertile ground yields an abundant harvest (cf. Matt. 13:20). A lesser response is indicated in Mark 4:16, where the seed is received joyfully but, as it is sown on rocky ground, the results are only short lived. John 12:48 denounces and condemns those who refuse to receive God's word. Similar references to rejecting (i.e., "not receiving") apostolic testimony to the person of Christ are found in John 3:11, 32; 5:43. But see also John 3:33 for a wholehearted acceptance of such testimony.

Other examples of "receiving" include worshiping Christ as Savior and Lord, implicitly indicated in John 1:12; receiving forgiveness of sins (Acts 10:43; 26:18); and receiving circumcision (John 7:23; Rom. 4:11; 5:11). Acts 20:24 refers to Paul receiving a ministry from the Lord; and Acts 1:5 to receiving the grace of God. The promise of receiving the Holy Spirit is noted in John 7:39 (in relation to this phenomenon, see also John 14:17; 1 John 2:27). There are also distinctive references to the early believers receiving the Holy Spirit in Acts 8:17; 10:47; 19:2 (cf. also Acts 8:19); Rom. 8:15; 1 Cor. 2:12; Gal. 3:2, 14.

Jesus Christ is the one who "receives" a command from the Father (e.g., John 10:18); as well as honor and glory (cf. 2 Pet. 1:17; Rev. 4:11; 5:12); and power (Rev. 2:27). Acts 2:33 declares that Jesus receives the promised Holy Spirit in the first instance from God the Father. In related contexts, Jesus invokes the pouring out of the Holy Spirit on his disciples in John 20:22 with the words "receive the Spirit," as an anticipation of the baptism of the Spirit in Acts 2. Acts 1:8 promises that the disciples will receive power at the coming of the Spirit (cf. also Acts 2:38).

anablepō [ἀναβλέπω, *308*]

anablepō is a verb found in nearly thirty places, meaning "to receive one's sight" in more than half of these occurrences. (→ SEE)

The expression "to receive one's sight" occurs exclusively in contexts where miraculous healing is given to the blind. Matt. 20:34; Mark 10:51ff.; Luke 18:41ff.; John 9:11ff. refer to those so cured during the earthly ministry of Christ. Saul, in the immediate aftermath of his dramatic conversion, was cured of his blindness and received back his sight through the intercession of Ananias (cf. Acts 9:12ff.; 22:13). The phenomenon of people receiving back their sight is also declared by Jesus as one of the irrefutable evidences that the Messiah had indeed come to live among his people (cf. Matt. 11:5; Luke 7:22).

paradechomai [παραδέχομαι, *3858*]

paradechomai is a verb closely related to the term ***dechomai*** (see above), occurring in only five contexts and meaning "receive" in the sense of "accept." Mark 4:20 refers to those who hear the word of God and "receive" (i.e., accept) it as true. Acts 16:21 speaks of customs that Romans are unable to accept. Paul exhorts Timothy in 1 Tim. 5:19 never to accept any charges against an elder except on the advice of two or three witnesses. Everyone whom God lovingly accepts as a son will be disciplined by him (cf. Heb. 12:6). See also Acts 22:18.

apolambanō [ἀπολαμβάνω, *618*]

apolambanō is a variant form of ***lambanō*** (see above), occurring fourteen times and meaning "receive" in the general sense of "get back that which is due." The individual usage of the term is varied.

Luke 6:34 refers to the practice of receiving payment from a debtor. Luke 15:27 speaks of the grateful father in Jesus' parable who gets (i.e., receives) his son back home safely. Luke 16:25 speaks of receiving good things in this life (cf. also Luke 18:30). In Luke 23:41, the penitent thief on the cross beside Jesus admits to receiving due justice for his crime. This same fate awaits the godless, alluded to in Rom. 1:27. Gal. 4:5 cites the blessing of believers who receive adoption as God's children. Col. 3:25; 2 John 8 refer to the blessing granted to the believer in Christ, who will receive eternal life as his reward.

proslambanō [προσλαμβάνω, *4355*]

proslambanō is a variant form of ***lambanō*** (see above), found in fifteen contexts and meaning "take," or "receive." The meaning "receive" is found in seven contexts, all with the sense of "welcome" (cf. Acts 28:2; Rom. 14:1, 3; 15:7; Phlm. 12, 17). (→ TAKE)

paralambanō [παραλαμβάνω, *3880*]

paralambanō is also a variant form of ***lambanō*** (see above). It is found in fifty contexts, with the dominant meanings "take" and "receive." The former meaning is more common. (→ TAKE) The meaning "receive," by and large, expresses the underlying sense of "get," "acquire," or "obtain." It is used in various contexts.

Mark 7:4 refers to the fastidious practices of the Pharisees, who "received" (i.e., observed) many traditions under the law. 2 Thess. 3:6 refers to receiving, or observing, the noble tradition of godly living which Paul commended to his congregation at Thessalonica. 1 Cor. 15:1ff.; Gal. 1:9ff. refer to receiving the gospel (cf. also Phil. 4:9); and 1 Thess. 2:13 refers to receiving the word of God. 1 Cor. 11:23 refers to receiving instructions from the Lord, in the context of Paul laying down the essential elements for the observation of the Lord's Supper. Col. 2:6 refers to receiving Christ as Lord. Col. 4:17 speaks of Paul receiving a ministry from the Lord. Believers are described in Heb. 12:28 as receiving a kingdom that is unshakable. John 1:11 uses ***paralambanō*** in a negative sense, with reference to Jesus not being received (i.e., accepted) by his fellow citizens of Nazareth.

Concerning Jesus, as one who also "receives," John 14:3 speaks of heaven as the place where Christ will one day receive his followers — meaning that he will "take them to himself."

metalambanō [μεταλαμβάνω, *3335*]

metalambanō is another variant form of the verb ***lambanō*** (see above) that occurs six times. Only once, however, does it mean "receive." Heb. 6:7 speaks of land that drinks in the rain falling on it as receiving a blessing from God. (→ SHARE)

metalēmpsis [μετάλημψις, *3336*]

metalēmpsis is a noun derived from ***metalambanō*** (see above), occurring only in 1 Tim. 4:3, with the force of a passive infinitive, "to be received." The context speaks of food which God created "to be accepted or received" with thanksgiving from his people.

lēmpsis [λῆμψις, *3028*]

lēmpsis is a noun derived from ***lambanō*** (see above) with the sense of "receiving." It is an abstract term paired with the term "giving," referring to the generosity of the Philippian church in their relationship with Paul and other churches. ***lempsis*** occurs only in Phil. 4:15.

apodechomai [ἀποδέχομαι, *588*]

apodechomai is a variant form of the verb ***dechomai*** (see above). It occurs in only five places, meaning "receive" in the sense of "welcome," "accept" (i.e., believe to be true). The former sense of "welcome" is found in Luke 8:40, with respect to the crowd's reception of Jesus. Acts 15:4; 18:27; 28:30 refer to extending a welcome in terms of hospitality. Acts 2:41 refers to the believing response of the huge audience that listened to the apostle Peter preaching on the day of Pentecost and "received his word." See also Acts 24:3.

prosdechomai [προσδέχομαι, *4327*]

prosdechomai is another variant form of ***dechomai*** (see above), found fourteen times and meaning in three cases "receive" in the sense of "welcome" (cf. Luke 15:2; Rom. 16:2; Phil. 2:9). (→ WAIT)

eisdechomai [εἰσδέχομαι, *1523*]

eisdechomai, another variant of ***dechomai*** (see above), is found only in 2 Cor. 6:17 and means "receive" in the context of God's promise to "welcome" his people when they come out of captivity in Babylon. This Corinthian text cites the prophetic declaration of Isa. 52:11.

epidechomai [ἐπιδέχομαι, *1926*]

This variant form of ***dechomai*** (see above) is found only twice. It refers to the refusal of Diotrephes to "receive," or "acknowledge," the authority of the apostle John. In 3 John 10, ***epidechomai*** means "receive" in the sense of "welcome."

hypodechomai [ὑποδέχομαι, *5264*]

hypodechomai, as a variant of ***dechomai*** (see above), means "receive," with the sense of "to welcome as a guest," in each of its four occurrences (cf. Luke 10:38; 19:6; Acts 17:7; Jas. 2:25).

anadechomai [ἀναδέχομαι, *324*]

anadechomai is a variant form of ***dechomai*** (see above) which is found in only two places, meaning "receive." In Acts 28:7 it describes the act of "welcoming a guest," and in Heb. 11:17 it refers to Abraham as the one who "received" the covenant promises of God.

komizō [κομίζω, *2865*]

komizō is a verb meaning to "receive" in all but one of the eleven occurrences of the term.

Matt. 25:27 refers to receiving interest from a bank loan. ***komizō*** refers in several places to receiving due recompense — either good or evil — for our actions in this life, from the judgment seat of Christ (cf. 2 Cor. 5:10; Eph. 6:8; Col. 3:25; 2 Pet. 2:13). Receiving the benefits of God's redemptive promises is a blessing indicated in Heb. 10:36 (cf. Heb. 11:39; 1 Pet. 1:9 [referring to salvation itself]; 1 Pet. 5:4 [the crown of glory]). This miracle of Abraham "receiving Isaac back from the dead" — metaphorically speaking — is described in Heb. 11:19.

apechō [ἀπέχω, *568*]

apechō is a verb found eleven times, meaning "receive" in several of these contexts. Matt. 6:2ff.; Luke 6:24 speak of receiving a reward. The privilege of receiving payment, as a gift, is indicated in Phil. 4:18. To receive someone back in the sense of welcoming them back is indicated in Phlm. 15.

dekatoō [δεκατόω, *1183*]

dekatoō is a verb found in only two contexts. It means "to receive tithes" in Heb. 7:6, referring to the gift Abraham gave to Melchizedek, king of Salem (cf. Gen. 14:18ff.). It means to "pay tithes" in Heb. 7:9, referring symbolically to the "tithes paid" by Levi (the great-grandson of Abraham) to one greater than Abraham—Melchizedek, who typologically represents Christ as the eternal high priest.

nomotheteō [νομοθετέω, *3549*]

nomotheteō is a verb meaning "to receive the law" in Heb. 7:11, with regard to the people of God. The term occurs only twice, with the second meaning evident in Heb. 8:6, "to enact." (→ ENACT)

See Also: → ACCEPT

RECKON

OT Words

ḥāshab [**חָשַׁב, 2803**]

ḥāshab is a verb occurring around 120 times with a wide variety of meanings grouped around the underlying phenomenon of rational thought. Such meanings include "reckon," "plan," "think." The meaning "to reckon" includes several different nuances and accounts for about one quarter of the usage of ***ḥāshab***. (→ CONSIDER → PURPOSE → THINK)

ḥāshab means "reckon" with the underlying sense of "impute" in a number of places. In Gen. 15:6; Ps. 106:31, God imputes righteousness to human beings. The spiritual benefit of a ritual offering is "imputed" to the offerer in Num. 18:27. See also Lev. 7:18 for a negative use of ***ḥāshab*** with this sense. In Lev. 17:4, bloodguilt is imputed to a murderer. 2 Sam. 19:19 records the general imputing of guilt to another. Ps. 32:2 affirms that the person to whom the Lord imputes no iniquity is blessed.

The translation "reckon" also includes the meaning "count," "calculate." In Lev. 25:27, the sale price for a piece of property is "reckoned" according to the number of years prior to the year of Jubilee (i.e., every fiftieth year). Similar calculation is made with respect to the sale of a slave (cf. Lev. 25:50ff.). 2 Kgs. 12:15 refers to the calculation of a sum of money.

Finally, ***ḥāshab*** means "reckon" in the sense of "consider," or "regard." For example, Num. 18:30 refers to an offering "considered" to belong to the priest. Neh. 13:13 refers to priests and Levites "regarded" as faithful. In Isa. 53:4, the suffering messianic servant king is "considered" to be afflicted by the hand of God. See also Num. 23:9; Deut. 2:11; 2 Sam. 4:2; Job 18:13; Prov. 27:14; Isa. 5:28; Hos. 8:12.

NT Words

logizomai [λογίζομαι, *3049*]

logizomai is a dynamic equivalent for the term ***ḥāshab*** (see above), occurring about forty times with the underlying sense of logical, rational expression. Meanings include "reckon," "think," "count." The meaning "reckon" conveys several nuances. (→ THINK)

Luke 22:37 refers to Isa. 53:12, declaring that the suffering servant-messiah was to be "reckoned" (i.e., "numbered," or "counted") with the transgressors. This prophecy finds fulfillment in the person of Christ.

More frequently, ***logizomai*** is translated "reckon" with the sense of "consider," or "regard." For example, Rom. 4:4 affirms that wages are to be "considered" as one's due. Rom. 6:11 commands believers to "reckon" (i.e., regard) themselves dead to sin. See also Rom. 2:26; 8:36; 1 Cor. 4:1; Phil. 3:13.

logizomai also means "reckon" with the sense of "impute." In several places, it is affirmed that genuine faith in God is "imputed" as righteousness. Abraham is the classic recipient of such divine favor (cf. Rom. 4:3, 9ff., 22ff.; Gal. 3:6; Jas. 2:23). Rom. 4:5ff., 24 declares this to be true for all believers. 2 Cor. 5:19 declares the person blessed against whom the Lord will not "impute" his sin.

See Also: → NUMBER

RECLINE → SIT

RECOMPENSE → REWARD

RECONCILE, RECONCILIATION

OT Words

kipper [**כִּפֶּר, 3722**]

kipper is a form of the root verb ***kāphar*** (→ PROPITIATION), occurring approximately one hundred times with the dominant sense of "to make atonement." ***kipper*** occurs primarily in ceremonial contexts, and the meaning "make atonement" has the underlying connotation of appeasing Yahweh, being reconciled to him through the presentation of an appropriate offering, with the accompanying attitude of true repentance.

kipper refers generally to "making atonement" (Exod. 29:33; 2 Sam. 21:3); and to sin being purged or cleansed (via expiatory sacrifice) (Isa. 6:7; 22:14). Dan. 9:24 refers to the atoning work of the Messiah in removing iniquity as one of the six purposes of the "seventy sevens" of years given to the people of Israel.

More specifically, atonement is effected with a sin offering presented to Yahweh (cf. Exod. 29:36ff.; Lev. 4:20ff., 35; 5:6, 13; 8:15; 14:19ff.; Num. 15:25ff). The Day of Atonement sin offerings are noted in Lev. 16:6ff. The specific efficacy of blood in the offering for the cleansing of one's sin is indicated in Lev. 17:11.

Burnt offerings also play a role in the process of "making atonement" (cf. Lev. 1:4; 5:10; 9:7; 1 Chr. 6:49; Neh. 10:33; Ezek. 45:17).

On occasions, atonement is effected through both the sin and burnt offering (cf. Num. 6:11 [the Nazirite vow]; 8:12; 2 Chr. 29:24; Ezek. 43:20, 26).

Lev. 5:16ff.; 6:7; 7:7; Num. 5:8 refer to making atonement through the presentation of a guilt or trespass offering.

kipper also refers to making atonement for the purification of the Levites (Num. 8:21); and for the congregation of Israel, by means of incense placed on the altar (Num. 16:46ff.). A strikingly unusual instance of "making atonement" is found in Num. 25:13, where a Levite named Eleazer moves swiftly to execute an Israelite man who brought a Moabite woman illegitimately into the holy assembly of the people. Both of these people are slain by Eleazer, but not before thousands of Israelites are struck down with plague by the hand of Yahweh as a punitive measure. God commends Eleazer's action as an atonement made on the people's behalf, bringing an end to the terrible plague judgment on Israel.

In 1 Sam. 3:14, God refuses to grant atonement for the house and lineage of Eli, the high priest.

kipper means "appeasing" a person with a gift in Gen. 32:20, referring to Jacob's attempt to be reconciled to his brother Esau.

NT Words

apokatallassō [ἀποκαταλλάσσω, *604*]

apokatallassō is a verb found in only three places, all referring to Christ's work of reconciliation in restoring harmony between God and humankind. Eph. 2:16 refers to God's intention to reconcile both Jew and Gentile to himself through the redemptive sacrifice of his son on the cross. A like purpose is also indicated in Col. 1:20, 21.

katallassō [καταλλάσσω, *2644*]

katallassō is a synonym for ***apokatallassō*** (see above) meaning "to reconcile" in each of the five occurrences of the term.

katallassō usually refers to the redemptive work of Christ in bringing about a full reconciliation between human beings and God, through Christ's substitutionary atonement for sinful humanity on the cross, cf. (cf. Rom. 5:10; 2 Cor. 5:18ff.). 1 Cor. 7:18 refers to Paul's instruction concerning wives who separate from their husbands. They must either remain single, or be reconciled to their husband.

diallassomai [διαλλάσσομαι, *1259*]

diallassomai is a verb found only in Matt. 5:24, with reference to Christ's command to be reconciled with one's brother (with whom there is a problem) before offering one's gift to the Lord at the altar.

hilaskomai [ἱλάσκομαι, *2433*]

hilaskomai is a term found only twice in the New Testament, meaning "to make atonement" in the sense of bringing about reconciliation between God and sinful humankind. This meaning occurs in Heb. 2:17 with reference to the saving work of Christ, who turns aside the wrath of God against human beings through his sacrifice on the cross. In Luke 18:13, ***hilaskomai*** means "be merciful."

Additional Notes

The vocabulary for "reconcile," "reconciliation" in both Old and New Testaments is inextricably linked with the process of "making atonement."

The Hebrew term ***kipper*** indicates that one of the primary motives for presenting offerings to Yahweh is to have one's sin removed so that one might be "reconciled" to God. Under the old covenant, the presentation of sin and burnt offerings turned aside divine wrath from the "offerer" and placated Yahweh. Thus, in this context, the phenomena of "atonement" and "reconciliation" are very closely interrelated.

The New Testament Greek vocabulary for "reconciliation" or "atonement," while not abundant, is predominantly linked to the death of Christ. It is his act of substitutionary self-sacrifice that makes reconciliation possible between a holy God and sinful humankind. In suffering the curse for sin, thereby satisfying God's just requirement under the law, Christ effectively turned away his Father's anger from sinful humankind — at least for those who would commit themselves to Christ in faithful dependence upon his atoning sacrifice on their behalf.

What was anticipated in the old covenant sacrificial system was fully accomplished in the new, namely, that the death of Christ fully reconciled God to humankind and humankind to God.

See Also: → ATONEMENT → PROPITIATION

RECOVER

OT Words

nāṣal [**נָצַל, 5337**]

nāṣal is a verb occurring around two hundred times with the predominant sense of "deliver" in most of the occurrences of the term. However, in four places it is translated "recover" in the sense of "reclaim." Judg. 11:26 refers to the recovery of land or territory; and 1 Sam. 30:18, 22 speaks of reclaiming plunder. **nāṣal** is also used metaphorically in Hos. 2:9, referring to God threatening to "take back" material used to cover the nakedness of his people — to withdraw his material blessing from Israel. (→ DELIVER)

shûb [**שׁוּב, 7725**]

shûb is a common verb, meaning "turn," "return," "repent," as well as a number of associated senses, in most of its over one thousand occurrences. One of these related nuances is that of "recover," found in four places. The "recovery" of towns (i.e., their "recapture") is indicated in 2 Kgs. 13:25; 14:28; 16:6. Jer. 41:16 speaks of the "recovery" of hostages. (→ REPENT)

ḥāyāh [**חָיָה, 2421**]

ḥāyāh is a common verb found approximately 270 times with the principal meanings "live," "be alive." Several related nuances include "save," "quicken," and "recover." This latter meaning is found in ten contexts. (→ LIFE → SAVE)

ḥāyāh means "recover" in the sense of "revive" in several contexts. Gen. 45:27 speaks of "reviving" one's spirit from despondency. Samson is said to "recover" his physical strength in Judg. 15:19. People are "revived" (i.e., brought back to life) in 1 Kgs. 17:22; 2 Kgs. 13:21. 2 Kgs. 1:2; Isa. 38:9, 21 refer to "recovery" in the sense of "being healed of disease."

'āṣar [**עָצַר, 6113**]

'āṣar is a verb found in nearly fifty contexts with the dominant senses of "close up," "shut up." Other meanings include "avert," "restrain." In one context, **'āṣar** is translated "recover" in the sense of "to regain power" (cf. 2 Chr. 13:20). (→ CLOSE)

ḥāzaq [**חָזַק, 2388**]

ḥāzaq is a common verb, found nearly three hundred times. It means "to be strong," as well as associated senses, including to "recover," in Isa. 39:1, referring to Hezekiah's recovery from illness. (→ STRENGTH)

NT Words

anablepsis [ἀνάβλεψις, *309*]

anablepsis is a noun found only in Luke 4:18, referring to the mission of the Messianic Servant of Yahweh in giving "recovery of sight" to the blind — a mission espoused by, and embodied in, the person of Christ.

REDEEM, REDEEMER

OT Words

gā'al [**גָּאַל, 1350**]

gā'al is a verb found approximately one hundred times, with the primary meanings "redeem," "redeemer," as well as associated meanings in most of the occurrences of the term. The underlying sense is that of "buy back," used both literally and metaphorically, as well as "rescue," or "deliver."

gā'al refes in Gen. 48:16 to the angel of the Lord "redeeming" (i.e., rescuing) Jacob from harm.

Where Yahweh is affirmed as the agent of redeeming, the sense of "deliver," "rescue," or "save" is universal. For example, God promises to redeem his people from bondage in Egypt (cf. Exod. 6:6); from death (cf. Hos. 13:14); and from their enemies (cf. Mic. 4:10). Yahweh rescues his people from Egypt in Exod. 15:13. General references to God redeeming, or delivering, his people are found in Pss. 72:14; 74:2; 103:4; Isa. 43:1; 52:3; Jer. 31:11; Lam. 3:58. The psalmist utters a plea for God to redeem him in Pss. 69:8; 119:54.

gā'al is also used nominally to refer, first of all, to Yahweh as "redeemer." This name, or title, for God recognizes his role as the deliverer or savior of his people (cf. Job 19:25; Pss. 19:14; 78:35; Prov. 23:11; Isa. 41:14; 48:17; 54:5, 8; 60:16; Jer. 50:34).

gā'al refers less commonly to human beings engaging in the act of "redeeming." In these contexts, the underlying sense is that of "to buy back." A number of provisions in the Mosaic law allowed for personal property to be "redeemed" by one's next of kin, in order to alleviate poverty by repurchasing for them the land they had been forced to sell (cf. Lev. 25:25ff.). A family member of a foreigner's clan also has the right to "redeem" that person from slavery, by paying the price of redemption to regain their freedom (cf. Lev. 25:48ff.).

The above economic and social contexts refer to people's need to either sell themselves as slaves, or sell their property in order to relieve financial hardship. Redeeming persons and property was a right given to family members of the poor, which illustrated the distinctive note of compassion and caring concern that permeated the Mosaic covenant legislation.

Isa. 35:9; 51:10; 62:12; 63:4 refer generally to God's people as "the redeemed," or those who had been delivered by him.

The participial form of *gō'ēl*, ***gā'al*** means "kinsman-redeemer." This expression refers to a near relative who is best placed to "redeem" the person in need. When a woman's husband died, leaving her without children, the widow's brother-in-law (or the next nearest eligible male relative) had the responsibility of taking his sister-in-law as a wife, in order to raise up children to carry on the name of his deceased brother in Israel. This arrangement has been described as "levirate marriage" (from the Latin term *levir*, "brother-in-law"). In the book of Ruth, Boaz honorably assumes this role by marrying Ruth the Moabitess, the daughter-in-law of Naomi (the widow of Elimelech), thus preserving the family line in Israel (cf. Ruth 2:20; 3:9ff.; 4:1ff.).

ge'ullāh [גְּאֻלָּה, 1353]

ge'ullāh is a noun derived from ***gā'al*** (see above). It is found in fourteen places with the primary sense of "redemption," or "right of redemption," in various contexts.

Concerning redemption of land or property, Lev. 25:24 refers to the obligatory provision under the law for repurchasing allotted land for the original Israelite family who had owned it, and who had been forced to sell on account of financial hardship (cf. also Jer. 32:7, 8).

ge'ullāh also indicates the "right of redemption" for persons purchased out of slavery (cf. Lev. 25:48, 51ff.).

Finally, ***ge'ullāh*** refers to the "right of redemption" for reacquiring land along with a wife. The unique recorded instance of such a transaction applied to the land of Elimelech (deceased) and his widow Naomi, along with Naomi's daughter-in-law, Ruth. Both of these women were childless. The request for a "kinsman redeemer" (see ***gā'al*** above) was subsequently taken up by Boaz, who by marrying Ruth also inherited the land of Elimelech (cf. Ruth 4:6, 7).

ge'ullāh is also used with verbal force to mean "redeem" in the sense of "repurchase," or "buy back," in the case of land and houses (cf. Lev. 25:26, 29ff.).

pādāh [פָּדָה, 6299]

pādāh is a synonym for ***gā'al*** (see above) meaning "redeem" in virtually all of its nearly sixty occurrences and in a variety of contexts.

Where human agency is involved, the sense of "redeem" or "buy back" is indicated, for example, in Exod. 13:13; 34:20, where the firstborn of an ass is "redeemed" with a lamb so that the ass will not need to be sacrificed. Exod. 13:13, 15; 34:20; Num. 18:15 affirm that it was compulsory for every firstborn son to be "redeemed" with a monetary offering (i.e., to Yahweh), so as to circumvent the need for human sacrifice, which was forbidden under Mosaic law.

General references to redeeming servants (or slaves) are found in Exod. 21:8; Lev. 19:20. When the firstborn of unclean animals are deemed unsuitable for sacrifice, these are to be redeemed by the one presenting the offering (cf. Lev. 27:27; Num. 18:16). The firstborn of cows, sheep, and goats may not be redeemed, but have to be sacrificed. Finally, anyone devoted to destruction by divine decree, such as the Canaanites, may not be redeemed. They must be executed (cf. Lev. 27:20; Num. 18:15).

In one or two places, ***pādāh*** is translated "redeem" with the sense of "rescue," or "deliver" — again through human agency. 1 Sam. 14:45 records the incident where Jonathan is rescued from the hand of his father, Saul. See also 2 Sam. 4:9.

Where God is in view as the agent of redemption, ***pādāh*** means "deliver," or "rescue." Frequent mention is made, for example, of Yahweh's "redemption" (i.e., deliverance) of Israel from Egypt (cf. Deut. 7:8; 9:26; 13:5; 2 Sam. 7:3; 1 Chr. 17:21; Neh. 1:10; Mic. 6:4). Yahweh likewise affirms his promise to redeem (or rescue) his people from their enemies (Jer. 15:21; Zech. 10:8); and from death (Hos. 13:14). There are pleas for God to redeem (or deliver) his people from their enemies in Job 6:23; Pss. 25:22; 44:26; 69:18; 119:134. General references to Yahweh rescuing, or redeeming, his people are found in Pss. 31:5; 49:15; 78:42; 130:8; Isa. 29:22; Jer. 31:11. Zion is said to be redeemed by Yahweh by means of justice (cf. Isa. 1:27). And references to "the redeemed of the Lord" returning to Zion are found in Isa. 35:10; 51:11.

pedûyim [פְּדוּיִם, 6302]

pedûyim is the passive plural participial form of ***pādāh*** (see above). It occurs only four times, in Num. 3:46ff., referring to a group of additional Israelite males over and above the firstborn Levite males set aside for ritual service in Israel. This extra number is designated ***pedûyim***, or "those to be redeemed" (i.e., "bought back").

pedût [פְּדוּת, 6304]

pedût is a noun derived from ***pādāh*** (see above), found only four times. In three of these contexts, the term refers to the "redemption" (i.e., salvation) Yahweh has granted to his people (cf. Pss. 111:9; 130:7). It also refers to God's capacity to redeem (or to save) in Isa. 50:2.

pidyôm [פִּדְיוֹם, 6306]

pidyôm is another noun derived from ***pādāh*** (see above), meaning "redemption" in the four contexts in which it is found.

In Exod. 21:30, ***pidyôm*** refers to the price of "redemption" paid to a victim's family by the owner of a bull that has taken the life of that person. The payment of "redemption" may be made in lieu of the death penalty.

Num. 3:49, 51 refer likewise to "redemption" money to be received by Moses from those Israelites who exceeded the quota of Levite men who were redeemed by Yahweh for lifelong ceremonial service in the tabernacle, in place of the lives of the Israelite firstborn. On this occasion the money is to be handed over to Aaron, the high priest.

In Ps. 49:8, however, no amount of money can compensate God for a human life willfully taken by another. Such a "redemption" price, therefore, becomes impossible.

qānāh [קָנָה, 7069]

qānāh is the most commonly used term in the Old Testament for the transaction of "buying" or "purchasing." It has this meaning, with several related senses, in the eighty or so contexts in which it is found. Included here is the meaning "redeem," referring in Neh. 5:8 to Nehemiah's claims that he had "bought back" his fellow-countrymen from the Gentiles and brought them again to the land of their ancestors.

NT Words

exagorazō [ἐξαγοράζω, *1805*]

exagorazō is a verb found in only four places. It is translated "redeem" on each occasion, but with two distinct senses.

Gal. 3:13; 4:5 refer to Christ "redeeming" his people from the curse of the law so as to reconcile them to God and remove the impact of divine judgment against them. The underlying sense here would appear to be that of "deliver," or "rescue," rather than "buy back."

In Eph. 5:16; Col. 4:5, ***exagorazō*** occurs in the expression "redeem the time" with the sense of "make the most of every opportunity" to serve the Lord, because the days are evil.

lytroō [λυτρόω, *3084*]

lytroō is a verb meaning "redeem." It is found in three contexts with the sense of "deliver" or "rescue" (as with ***exagorazō***; see above).

Luke 24:21 refers to Christ as the hoped-for redeemer of Israel. Titus 2:14 speaks more particularly of Christ's self-sacrifice, given to "redeem" his people from all iniquity. 1 Pet. 1:18 refers to the unique manner of the believer's redemption, in that they have been "redeemed" or "delivered" from sin and death (implied here) by means of the shed blood of Christ on the cross. Being redeemed "not with perishable things such as silver and gold . . ." has given rise to the translation "ransom" for ***lytroō*** in this text, suggesting that the blood of Christ was the price paid in order to effect the release of his people from the penalty of sin. While this is a possible meaning, the context of the New Testament vocabulary for "redemption" does not give unambiguous support for such a rendering. (See the Additional Notes, below, for further discussion.)

lytrōsis [λύτρωσις, *3085*]

lytrōsis is a noun derived from ***lytroō*** meaning "redemption" in all three occurrences of the term. In each case, the phenomenon of "salvation" (i.e., deliverance) is in view.

lytrōsis refers to the "redemption" of God's people in Heb. 9:12 as having been secured by the blood of Christ. Luke 2:38 mentions the "redemption" of Jerusalem to be ultimately won by the power of God. Luke 1:68 speaks of the God of Israel having gained "redemption" for his people.

agorazō [ἀγοράζω, *59*]

agorazō is a verb with the literal sense of "buy," as in a commercial transaction, in the large majority of its nearly thirty occurrences. In several places, however, the term refers metaphorically to "purchasing" people for God by means of the blood of Christ's atoning sacrifice.

1 Cor. 6:20; 7:23 both contain the expression "bought with a price" — a metaphorical reference to the successful impact of Christ's death on his people being released from the curse of sin and death (cf. also 2 Pet. 2:1).

Rev. 5:9 mentions Christ having "purchased" people for God with his blood — an unambiguous allusion to his substitutionary atonement for sin. See also Rev. 14:3, 4.

apolytrōsis [ἀπολύτρωσις, *629*]

apolytrōsis is a noun closely related to ***lytrōsis*** (see above). It occurs ten times, with the primary meaning "redemption" in the sense of "deliverance." It is synonymous with ***lytrōsis*** in Rom. 8:23; 1 Cor. 1:30; Eph. 1:14; 4:30. "Deliverance," or "release" (i.e., from death) is explicitly indicated in Heb. 11:35. The person of Christ and his shed blood are the sole means of accomplishing salvation for his people (cf. Rom. 3:24; Eph. 1:7; Col. 1:14; Heb. 9:15).

Additional Notes

The vocabulary for "redeem," "redemption" in both the Old and New Testaments speaks about how God declares people righteous in his sight. It is sacrifice for sin that accomplishes forgiveness for the people of God — which culminates in the once-for-all sacrifice of Christ on the cross.

In the Old Testament, the terms ***gā'al*** and ***pādāh***, in particular, and their derivatives, make it clear that "redeeming" often involved the presentation of a monetary payment as a substitute either for human sacrifice (which was forbidden), or for the unacceptable offering of unclean animals. In addition, redemption referred literally to the practice of repurchasing land originally sold by poverty-stricken Israelite families, which could then later be redeemed and returned to its original owners.

The Hebrew vocabulary for "redemption" also refers generally to the salvation or deliverance won for Israel by the explicit redemptive actions of Yahweh on her behalf (e.g., deliverance from Egyptian slavery).

The New Testament terms for "redemption," ***exagorazō*** and ***lytroō***, occur much less frequently and function as dynamic equivalents to the Hebrew terminology. "Redeeming" or "redemption" in the New Testament primarily indicates salvation or deliverance. This redemption is grounded in Christ's sacrificial atonement at Calvary.

The idea of "buying back" is not part of the New Testament concept of "redemption." The translation "ransom" (→ RANSOM) is occasionally used synonymously with "redemption." The problem here is that a "ransom" requires someone to receive the payment in order for release to be obtained. In Old Testament usage, this meaning may be validated in certain circumstances. However, in the New Testament nothing explicit is ever said about God being the recipient of the "ransom" paid by Christ. Of particular relevance here is the usage of the term ***agorazō***, used primarily with reference to the commercial transaction of purchasing goods. As noted in the entry for ***agorazō***, above, there are several references to believers having been "brought with a price" (i.e., with the blood of Christ) and also to Christ "having purchased" people for God with his blood. In both of these contexts, the allusion to "purchasing" is left as a generalized affirmation without reference to God as the recipient of such metaphorical payment. Therefore, the translation "ransom" is harder to justify than the more general term "redemption."

While the Hebrew terminology allows for "repurchasing" and "deliverance" within the semantic field of "redemption," the Greek vocabulary is far less extensive, and more narrowly focused. What is clear is that the substitutionary atonement wrought by Christ is the sole ground upon which the redemption of human beings is accomplished. Principally, it is the salvation or deliverance of sinful human beings that is in view in the usage of New Testament vocabulary for "redeem," "redemption." The motif of "repurchasing," "buying back," in a spiritual sense, is left as a generalized metaphor without necessarily implying a "commercial transaction" between Christ and the Father.

REED

OT Words

qāneh **[קָנֶה, 7070]**

qāneh is a term with the primary meanings "branch," "reed." The latter sense is indicated in around one-third of its nearly sixty occurrences. (→ BRANCH)

Literal references to the reed as a plant include those in Job 40:2; Isa. 19:6; 35:7; 42:3. ***qāneh*** also refers to a "measuring rod" (lit. "measuring reed") in Ezek. 40:3ff.; and to the linear measurement of a "reed" in

Ezek. 40:5; 41:8; 42:16ff. (equivalent to 6 cubits, or about nine feet, or a little under three meters).

qāneh is also used metaphorically in 1 Kgs. 14:15, referring to Israel's punishment at the hand of Yahweh, who will shake the nation "like a reed." Elsewhere Egypt is referred to as a "broken reed," indicating that nation's thorough unreliability (cf. 2 Kgs. 18:21; Isa. 36:6; Ezek. 29:6).

NT Words

kalamos [κάλαμος, *2563*]

kalamos is a noun occurring twelve times with the underlying meaning "reed" in a variety of contexts.

There is reference first of all to the "reed" as a plant (cf. Matt. 11:7; 12:20; Luke 7:24). ***kalamos*** also refers to a "stick" or "staff" in Matt. 27:29ff., 8; Mark 15:19. 3 John 13 refers to a "pen" (lit. a "writing reed"). Rev. 11:1; 21:15, 16 speak of a "measuring rod" (or "measuring reed").

REFINE

OT Words

ṣāraph [**צָרַף, 6884**]

ṣāraph is a verb with the underlying sense of refining or smelting metals. The meaning "refine" is combined with several associated senses such as "smelt," "purge," "try." ***ṣāraph*** is found around thirty times. (→ TEST)

The sense of "refine," referring to purifying through the process of smelting, is indicated in Ps. 12:6 with reference to silver. This process is also referred to metaphorically in Isa. 1:25 where the purging of sin from one's life is described as the "smelting away of dross." ***ṣāraph*** also has a nominal sense in Mal. 3:2, 3, indicating the fire of "the refiner."

General references to God "refining" his people in the sense of "testing" them are found in Ps. 66:10; Isa. 48:10; Jer. 6:29; 9:7; Dan. 11:35.

zāqaq [**זָקַק, 2212**]

zāqaq is a verb found seven times, meaning "refine," "purify," "purge" in most of these contexts.

zāqaq refers to the process of refining gold (Job 28:1; Mal. 3:3); silver (Ps. 12:6); and wine (Isa. 25:6).

zāqaq is also used adjectivally in 1 Chr. 28:18 to refer to "refined" gold, and to "refined" silver in 1 Chr. 29:4.

NT Words

pyroō [πυρόω, *4448*]

pyroō is a verb found six times, meaning "burn" in four of these contexts, with both literal and metaphorical force. In two places, ***pyroō*** refers to metals "refined by fire" (cf. Rev. 3:15 [bronze]; 3:18 [gold]). (→ BURN)

REFRESH

OT Words

sā'ad [**סָעַד, 5582**]

sā'ad is a verb found twelve times, meaning "refresh," "sustain" "uphold."

The meaning "refresh" is concerned principally with the idea of sustaining oneself with food (cf. Gen. 18:5; Judg. 19:5, 8; 1 Kgs. 13:7; Ps. 104:15).

nāphash [**נָפַשׁ, 5314**]

nāphash is a verb occurring only three times, meaning "refresh" in the sense of gaining physical and emotional rest. Exod. 23:12 speaks of the purpose of the fourth commandment, resting on the Sabbath — that God's people may be "refreshed" on that day. Exod. 31:17 refers anthropomorphically to God being "refreshed" when he took rest on the seventh day from his work of creation. 2 Sam. 16:14 refers likewise to the physical and emotional refreshment taken by King David at Mahanaim.

shûb [**שׁוּב, 7725**]

shûb is a common verb with the primary meanings "turn," "return," with a number of associated nuances. In Prov. 25:13, ***shûb*** means "refresh," where a faithful messenger is said to "refresh" the spirit of his masters.

NT Words

anapauō [ἀναπαύω, *373*]

anapauō is a verb with the primary sense of "rest" in most of its twelve occurrences. In 1 Cor. 16:18, however, Paul commends his friends for "having refreshed" his spirit. (→ REST)

synanapauomai [συναναπαύομαι, *4875*]

synanapauomai is found only in Rom. 15:32 with reference to Paul's desire "to be refreshed" in the fellowship of the Roman congregation.

anapsychō [ἀναψύχω, *404*]

anapsychō occurs only twice, in 2 Tim. 1:16, where Paul offers thanks to the household of Onesiphorus who often "refreshed" him through their hospitality.

anapsyxis [ἀνάψυξις, *403*]

anapsyxis is a noun derived from ***anapsychō*** (see above) meaning "refreshing," found only in Acts 3:19 with reference to spiritual refreshment coming from God upon those who turn to him in repentance.

REFUGE

OT Words

miqlāt [מִקְלָט, **4733**]

miqlāt is a noun with the exclusive meaning "refuge," or "asylum," occurring seventy times. The term is found in the context of the protection offered by the Mosaic law covenant to those who were guilty of inadvertent, accidental manslaughter. Such people were offered asylum in selected "cities of refuge" throughout the land of Canaan, to which they could flee after the accidental death of their companion (cf. Num. 35:6ff.; Josh. 20:2ff.; 21:13, 21ff.; 1 Chr. 6:57, 67).

me'ônāh [מְעוֹנָה, **4585**]

me'ônāh is a term found in nine places meaning "den," or "lair," in most of these. However, Deut. 33:27 refers to the everlasting God as one's "refuge."

mānôs [מָנוֹס, **4498**]

mānôs is a noun with the primary meaning "refuge" in most of its eight occurrences. There are several references to Yahweh as a "refuge" for his people (cf. 2 Sam. 22:3; Ps. 59:16; Jer. 16:19). Ps. 142:4; Jer. 25:35 lament the absence of a refuge.

misgāb [מִשְׂגָּב, **4869**]

misgāb is a term found in seventeen contexts meaning "stronghold," "defense," "fortress," as well as "refuge." These terms are more or less interchangeable.

Predominantly, ***misgāb*** refers to Yahweh as a "refuge," "stronghold," or "defense" of his people (cf. 2 Sam. 22:3; Pss. 9:9; 18:2; 48:3; 59:9, 16, 17; 62:2; 94:22; 144:2). Ps. 46:7, 11 speak of the God of Jacob as the people's "refuge."

Isa. 25:12; 33:16; Jer. 48:1 mention literal fortresses, or fortification of a city.

maḥseh [מַחְסֶה, **4268**]

maḥseh is a noun occurring twenty times meaning "refuge," "shelter" in the majority of these contexts.

General references to a "refuge" or "shelter" include those in Job 24:8; Ps. 104:18. God is referred to as a refuge for the poor (Ps. 14:6); and for his people (Pss. 46:1; 62:7ff.; 91:2, 9; 142:5; Prov. 14:26; Isa. 25:4; Jer. 17:17). Isa. 28:15 declares that the people of Israel sought to make lies their refuge — a refuge that is swept away in Isa. 28:17. The glory cloud on Mt. Zion is declared to be a "refuge" in Isa. 4:6.

ḥāsāh [חָסָה, **2620**]

ḥāsāh is a verb found nearly forty times, with the primary meaning "take refuge" in a variety of contexts.

ḥāsāh refers to the futility of taking refuge in idols (Deut. 32:37); and in Egypt (Isa. 30:2). See also Judg. 9:15.

2 Sam. 22:3, 31; Pss. 7:1; 18:2; 71:1; 118:8ff.; Isa. 57:3; Nah. 1:7; Zeph. 3:12 refer to taking refuge in Yahweh. A couple of texts mention people taking refuge under the wings of God or "in the shadow of his wings" (cf. Ruth 2:12; Ps. 36:7, a metaphorical allusion to the security afforded by God's presence in his sanctuary). Isa. 14:32 refers to finding refuge in Zion.

Ps. 17:7 speaks of taking refuge from one's enemies, and Prov. 14:32 of seeking refuge in one's integrity.

sēter [סֵתֶר, **5643**]

sēter is a noun with the principal meanings "secret," "secret place," with a number of associated senses including "hiding place," or "refuge." ***sēter*** is found in nearly forty contexts. (→ SECRET)

God is described as a "hiding place," or "refuge," in Pss. 32:7; 61:4; 91:1; 119:114. Isa. 32:2 refers to a "shelter," "refuge," or "hiding place." General references to these are found in Isa. 16:4; 28:17.

REFUSE

OT Words

mā'ēn [מָאֵן, **3985**]

mā'ēn is a verb meaning "to refuse" throughout the forty or so contexts in which it occurs.

Several texts indicate Pharaoh's refusal to release the people of Israel from bondage in Egypt (cf. Exod. 4:23; 7:14; 8:2; 9:12; 10:3, 4). There is also an occasional reference to the people of God refusing to keep the commandments of God (cf. Exod. 16:28; Neh. 9:17; Ps. 78:10; Jer. 11:10). ***mā'ēn*** refers to Judah's refusal to repent (Jer. 8:5); to know God (cf. Jer. 9:6); and to heed his correction (cf. Jer. 5:3; 25:28). Prov. 1:24 notes a refusal to heed the voice of wisdom.

Other references to people's actions of refusal in a variety of contexts include those in Gen. 48:19; Exod.

22:17; Deut. 25:7; 1 Sam. 28:23; Esth. 1:12; Ps. 77:2; Isa. 1:20; Jer. 31:15; Hos. 11:5.

mā'ôs [מָאוֹס, **3973**]

mā'ôs is a noun found only in Lam. 3:45, referring to the people of Jerusalem and Judah as "refuse" (i.e., "rubbish") in the eyes of the Gentiles. This is a consequence of Yahweh punishing his people by scattering them among the nations.

mā'as [מָאַס, **3988**]

mā'as is a verb found in approximately seventy-five places, meaning "despise," "refuse," "reject." The meaning "reject" may be understood as "refuse to accept or acknowledge." (→ DESPISE)

mā'as refers to the people of Israel refusing to accept (i.e., rejecting) Yahweh as King (cf. 1 Sam. 8:7; 10:19). Elsewhere, God's people are said to reject his laws and decrees (cf. 2 Kgs. 17:15; Isa. 5:24; Jer. 6:19; 8:9; Ezek. 5:6; 20:13ff.; Amos 2:4). Job 34:33 speaks of someone refusing to repent. Isa. 7:15ff. refers to a child knowing how to refuse evil and accept the good. Other references to the act of refusing include those in Ps. 118:22; Isa. 8:6.

God is also described in several contexts as one who refuses. For example, God rejects (i.e., refuses to continue to recognize) Saul as king in 1 Sam. 15:23ff.; 16:1, 7. Elsewhere he is said to reject the people of Israel and Judah from the land, and he subsequently sends them into exile (cf. 2 Kgs. 17:20; Pss. 78:59; 89:38; Jer. 7:29). See also Jer. 2:37.

NT Words

paraiteomai [παραιτέομαι, *3868*]

paraiteomai is a verb found only nine times, with the underlying sense of "have nothing to do with." It is translated "refuse" (twice) in Heb. 12:25 in the context of an injunction not to refuse (or reject) the spoken word of God.

arneomai [ἀρνέομαι, *720*]

arneomai is a verb occurring about thirty times, meaning "deny" in most of these contexts. In two places, however, it is translated "refuse" — in Heb. 11:24, and also in Acts 7:35, with the sense of "reject" in reference to Moses, who was unsuccessfully challenged by the rebellious Levitical family of Korah (cf. Num. 16).

apoblētos [ἀπόβλητος, *579*]

apoblētos is a noun derived from the verb ***apoballō*** (to cast away, off), meaning "that which is refused." It is found only in 1 Tim. 4:4, in the admonition not to refuse, or reject, anything that is created by God.

REGARD → SEE

REGENERATION

NT Words

palingenesia [παλιγγενεσία, *3824*]

palingenesia is a rare term, found only twice in the New Testament meaning "regeneration," or "renewal," but with very significant implications. ***palingenesia*** occurs only in Matt. 19:28 with reference to God's ultimate "renewal" of the cosmos, and in Titus 3:5 in regard to the regeneration effected by the Holy Spirit. The underlying sense of ***palingenesia*** is that of "renewal," "recreation" — a radical change of heart and mind resulting in renewed devotion to God and Christ.

Additional Notes

Though rare in the New Testament with specific reference to "regeneration," the term ***palingenesia*** has very significant overtones in relation to the phenomenon of "conversion," or the "new birth," throughout the entire Bible.

In particular, the phenomenon of "regeneration" in the New Testament is closely aligned to that of "heart circumcision," or the receiving of a "new heart," or "new spirit," in the Old Testament. Deut. 10:16; 30:6 refer to heart circumcision, a spiritual transformation both commanded by God and undertaken by him. In these contexts, his people are but the passive recipients of his sovereign grace and transforming power. Such a renewal is promised to all of his future people in Ezek. 36:24ff., where Yahweh promises to remove one's "heart of stone" and replace it with a "heart of flesh," accompanied by the hitherto unprecedented infilling of the Holy Spirit. A similar transformation is also promised in Jer. 31:31ff., where God solemnly guarantees to establish a "new covenant" with his people, one that will be characterized, among other things, by the wholesale renewal of people's hearts and minds.

Another clear New Testament parallel to the phenomenon of "regeneration" is found in Col. 2:11ff., where Paul speaks of the transformation wrought in the hearts of human beings by the saving work of Christ. Such a work is described in this context as the "circumcision" of the heart performed by Christ. This renewal is likewise implied in John 3:3ff., in Jesus' discussion with Nicodemus. "New birth" is an indispensable prerequisite for entry into the kingdom of God.

REGION

OT Words

ḥebel [חֶבֶל, **2256**]

ḥebel is a noun found in approximately sixty contexts with a variety of meanings, the most frequent of these being "sorrows," "cord," as well as related nuances. In addition, ***ḥebel*** is translated "region," with reference to a geographic district, in Deut. 3:4, 13, 14; 1 Kgs. 4:13.

medînāh [מְדִינָה, **4082**]

medînāh refers largely to the administrative regions, provinces, or districts within a monarch's realm (1 Kgs. 20:14ff.; Neh. 1:3; 7:6; Esth. 1:3; 3:8ff.; Eccl. 5:8; Ezek. 19:8).

NT Words

perichōros [περίχωρος, *4066*]

perichōros is found eleven times, meaning "region (or countryside)," or "surrounding region." It is used exclusively in regard to literal geographic areas in and around the land of Israel (cf. Matt. 3:5; 14:35; Mark 1:28; 6:55; Luke 3:3; 4:14, 37; 7:17; 8:37 [twice]; Acts 14:6).

chōra [χώρα, *5561*]

chōra occurs nearly thirty times, meaning "country" in most of these contexts. ***chōra*** can also mean "region," with an occasional ambiguity between these two meanings. (→ COUNTRY)

References to a geographic region include those in Luke 3:1; John 11:54; Acts 8:1; 13:49; 16:6. Ambiguous references to "region" or "country" are found in Matt. 8:28; Mark 5:1; Luke 8:26.

There is one metaphorical reference to "region" in Matt. 4:16, where ***chōra*** indicates a "region of death," referring to the realm of spiritual darkness.

klima [κλίμα, *2824*]

klima is a noun found only three times, referring to geographic regions (cf. Rom. 15:23; 2 Cor. 11:10; Gal. 1:21).

REGRET → REPENT

REIGN

OT Words

mālak [מָלַךְ, **4427**]

mālak is the primary verb in the Old Testament meaning "to reign," in the sense of "to become king or queen," in almost all of its nearly 350 occurrences. ***mālak*** applies to the reign (or rule) of both God and human beings.

In the human sphere, ***mālak*** means "to reign" (i.e., rule as king) in several different areas.

General, non-specific references to the reign of kings are found in Job 34:30; Prov. 30:22; Isa. 32:1.

References to the reign of kings over the nations at large include those in Gen. 36:31ff.; Josh. 13:10ff.; Judg. 9:8ff.; Esth. 1:1; Isa. 37:38; Dan. 9:1. More commoly, ***mālak*** refers to kings who reign over the nation of Israel (cf. 1 Sam. 11:12ff.; 2 Sam. 5:4ff.; 2 Kgs. 1:17; 8:15ff.; Jer. 33:21). Esth. 2:4, 7; 2 Chr. 22:12 refer to women who reign as queens.

mālak also refers to the process of installing a king, in 2 Sam. 2:9; 1 Kgs. 12:20; Isa. 7:6; Ezek. 17:16; Hos. 8:4 (cf. also Judg. 9:6). Yahweh himself crowns kings in 1 Sam. 15:11, 35; 1 Kgs. 1:43. In Gen. 37:8, ***mālak*** means "reign" in the general sense of "rule over," without reference to a royal figure.

Yahweh is declared to be one who reigns over human beings — over the nations of the world (cf. Exod. 15:18; Pss. 47:8; 93:1; 97:1), as well as over his own people (cf. 1 Sam. 8:7; Ezek. 20:33). God promises to inaugurate his consummate divine rule over Mt. Zion in the fullness of time (cf. Isa. 24:23; 52:7; Mic. 4:7).

Lady Wisdom is described as one who establishes the reign of kings on earth, representing unambiguous divine authority (cf. Prov. 8:15).

malkût [מַלְכוּת, **4438**]

malkût is a noun occurring around ninety times, meaning "kingdom" and "reign," and referring to location and duration of royal rule, respectively. The meaning "reign" accounts for about one quarter of the total usage. (→ KINGDOM)

malkût refers to the reigns of David (1 Chr. 26:31; 29:30); of Solomon (2 Chr. 3:2); of other Israelite and Judean kings (2 Chr. 16:1, 2; 35:19; Jer. 49:34; Dan. 1:1); and of pagan rulers (Ezra 4:5ff.; Neh. 12:22; Esth. 2:16; Jer. 52:31; Dan. 2:1; 8:1).

malkû [מַלְכוּ, **4437** (Aramaic)]

malkû is the Aramaic equivalent of ***malkût*** (see above), occurring nearly sixty times with the same dual sense of "kingdom" and "reign." It has the sense of "reign" in only four places. Ezra 4:24; 6:15; Dan. 6:28 refer to the reign of Darius, king of Persia. Dan. 6:28 refers to King Cyrus (which may well be an alternative name for Darius, though this is not universally agreed upon).

mamlākût [**מַמְלָכוּת, 4468**]

mamlekût is a synonym for ***malkût*** (see above), though it occurs much less frequently. ***mamlekût*** occurs in nine contexts, referring to "kingdom" in all but Jer. 26:1, which mentions the reign of Jehoiakim. (➞ KINGDOM)

mamlākāh [**מַמְלָכָה, 4467**]

mamlākāh is a more common synonym for ***malkût*** (see above), occurring about 120 times. It means "kingdom" in virtually every instance, except for Jer. 27:1; 28:1, which refer to the reign of Zedekiah, the last of the kings of Judah. (➞ KINGDOM)

NT Words

basileuō [βασιλεύω, *936*]

basileuō is a dynamic equivalent for the Hebrew term ***mālak*** (see above). It occurs about twenty times, with the exclusive meaning "to reign" in the sense of "to be king." It is used metaphorically in both human and divine contexts.

basileuō refers to the reign of the Herodian dynasty in first-century Judea in Matt. 2:22. General references to royal rule are found in Luke 19:14, 27.

Luke 1:33 refers to Christ reigning as King; and in 1 Cor. 15:25 the reference to the reign of Christ points to the elimination of all the enemies of God. Rev. 11:15 speaks of the eternal reign of Christ. The heavenly reign of God is affirmed in 1 Tim. 6:15; Rev. 11:17; 19:6.

basileuō is used metaphorically in a number of contexts. All of God's people are said to reign on earth in Rev. 5:10. Similarly, it is said that believers will reign with Christ for one thousand years as a prelude to the eternal kingdom of God and Christ (Rev. 20:4, 6). Rev. 22:5 speaks of the eternal reign of all believers in glory. Rom. 5:14, 17 refer to the "reign of death," as it impacts the whole of the human race. Rom. 6:12 refers to the reign of sin in one's body. 1 Cor. 4:8 employs the phrase "to reign as kings," indicating a rise to a position of power and influence in society.

hēgemonia [ἡγεμονία, *2231*]

hēgemonia is found only in Luke 3:1, referring to the reign of the emperor Tiberius Caesar.

archō [ἄρχω, *757*]

archō is a verb found only twice, referring to those who "reign" (or rule) over the Gentiles (cf. Mark 10:42; Rom. 15:12).

symbasileuō [συμβασιλεύω, *4821*]

symbasileuō is a variant form of ***basileuō*** (see above) meaning "to reign together with." It is found only in 1 Cor. 4:8; 2 Tim. 2:12.

See Also: ➞ RULE

REJECT

OT Words

mā'as [**מָאַס, 3988**]

mā'as is a verb with the primary meanings "despise," "refuse," "reject" in the majority of its approximately seventy-five occurrences. There is a degree of overlap between these senses. (➞ DESPISE ➞ REFUSE)

Where ***mā'as*** means "reject," the underlying meaning is that of "cast off (or away)," "spurn." The term is used in relation to both God and human beings.

On several occasions,Yahweh is declared to have definitely rejected his people on account of their sinfulness (cf. Pss. 78:59; 89:38; Jer. 7:29; 31:37; Hos. 9:17). Yet there are also indications that such a rejection is not absolute (cf. Lev. 26:44; Jer. 14:19; 33:26; Lam. 5:22). Yahweh is also described as having rejected Saul as king over Israel in 1 Sam. 15:23ff.; 16:1. Jer. 2:37 speaks of God having rejected his enemies.

The Israelites are said to have rejected Yahweh as King in 1 Sam. 8:7; 10:19. Several texts also refer to the people of God rejecting the laws and statutes of Yahweh (cf. 2 Kgs. 17:15; Isa. 5:24; Jer. 6:19; 8:9; Ezek. 5:6; 20:16), as well as knowledge of him (Hos. 4:6). Isa. 31:7 describes people "casting away" their idols in a gesture of total rejection.

ḥādēl [**חָדֵל, 2310**]

ḥādēl is a rare adjectival form found only three times. It is translated "rejected" in Isa. 53:3, with reference to the messianic Suffering Servant who was "rejected by men."

NT Words

atheteō [ἀθετέω, *114*]

atheteō is a verb occurring sixteen times and meaning "despise," "reject" in most of these contexts. The

underlying sense is that of "cast aside," or "spurn." ***atheteō*** is predicated only of human beings.
(→ DESPISE)

The Pharisees are said to have rejected the law of God (Mark 7:9), and the purpose of God for their lives (Luke 7:30). Luke 10:16; John 12:48 warn against rejecting the person of Christ. A similar warning with respect to the law of God is found in 1 Thess. 4:8. 1 Tim. 5:12 refers to rejecting one's promise to God, in the sense of casting it aside. Jude 8 refers to false prophets rejecting duly instituted civil authority.

apodokimazō [ἀποδοκιμάζω, *593*]

apodokimazō is a verb found in nine places meaning "reject," or "repudiate," in each of these contexts.

Christ refers to the Old Testament (i.e., Ps. 118:22, 23), indicating that the stone rejected by the builders has now become the chief cornerstone (cf. Matt. 21:42; Mark 12:10; Luke 20:17; 1 Pet. 2:4, 7). This allusion refers to the emerging supremacy of the Messiah, notwithstanding the attempts by an unbelieving people to recognize his true divine authority. In other places, Jesus refers to his imminent arrest and crucifixion by indicating to his disciples that the Son of Man is soon to be "rejected" by the religious authorities in Israel (cf. Mark 8:31; Luke 9:22; 17:25).

Heb. 12:17 speaks of Esau's rejection by God, the divine refusal to grant him afresh the birthright he had despised by handing it over to his brother, Jacob.

REJOICE

OT Words

sāmaḥ [שָׂמַח, 8055]

sāmaḥ is a common verb meaning "to rejoice," "be glad, joyful" in most of its approximately 150 occurrences.

Several injunctions are associated with the usage of ***sāmaḥ***. Lev. 23:40; Deut. 12:12; 16:11ff.; 1 Sam. 11:15 exhort people to rejoice in worship before the Lord. The whole of creation is enjoined to rejoice at God's sovereign rule over the earth (1 Chr. 16:31; Isa. 14:8). ***sāmaḥ*** exhorts people to rejoice in all of life's undertakings in which God has brought blessing — for example, in Prov. 5:18 one is invited to rejoice in one's wife. Prov. 23:15, 24 affirm that a wise son brings joy to his father. Eccl. 3:22; 5:19 declare that it is appropriate to rejoice in one's vocation, for that is the gift of God. See also Deut. 12:7. The psalmist asks God that his enemies not be permitted to rejoice over him (cf. Ps. 35:24). Elsewhere, however, this is exactly what Yahweh allows Israel's enemies to do, as an outworking of punishment against his people (cf. Lam. 2:17; Ezek. 25:6; Obad. 12).

There are also general references to people "rejoicing," in the sense of their being glad in heart or full of joy (cf. Exod. 4:14; Judg. 19:13; 1 Sam. 6:13; Job 21:12; Ps. 118:24; Jer. 20:15).

sāmaḥ also refers to rejoicing in one's salvation (cf. 1 Sam. 2:1; Isa. 25:9); the person of God (cf. Pss. 9:2; 32:11; Joel 2:23; Zech. 10:7); and divine perfections such as goodness and love (cf. 2 Chr. 6:41; Neh. 12:43; Ps. 31:7). A number of texts mention rejoicing in God's redemptive actions on behalf of his people (cf. 1 Sam. 19:5; Pss. 14:7; 66:6; Joel 2:21; Zeph. 3:14; Zech. 2:10). 2 Chr. 20:7 refers to rejoicing over the defeat of one's enemies.

sāmēaḥ [שָׂמֵחַ, 8056]

sāmēaḥ is an adjectival form derived from ***sāmaḥ*** (see above) that also has a verbal force. The term means "to rejoice," as well as "joyful," "happy," "glad in heart." It occurs twenty-three times.

The adjectival sense of "joyful," "happy," referring to an emotional state, is found in Deut. 16:15; 1 Kgs. 4:20; 8:66; Esth. 5:9, 8:15; Ps. 113:9; Prov. 17:22.

The people of Israel rejoice in the coronation of King Solomon in 1 Kgs. 1:40, 45. In contrast, Prov. 2:14 refers to the actions of the wicked, who rejoice in doing evil. See also 2 Kgs. 11:14; Job 3:22; Ps. 35:26; Amos 6:13.

sûs [שׂוּשׂ, 7797]

sûs is a synonym for ***sāmaḥ*** (see above), meaning "to rejoice" in almost all of the twenty-seven times it occurs.

Rejoicing is predicated of God in a couple of contexts. He is said to rejoice over his people (Deut. 28:63; 30:9; Isa. 62:5; Jer. 32:41; Zeph. 3:17); and also over Jerusalem at the time of the renewal of the city (cf. Isa. 65:9).

Where human beings are concerned, rejoicing in the Lord is noted in Pss. 35:9; 40:16; Isa. 61:10; and rejoicing at God's creation in Isa. 65:18. The psalmist declares that he rejoices in the law of God (Ps. 119:14, 162). General references to people rejoicing are found in Job 3:22; 39:21.

sûs is used metaphorically in Isa. 35:1, which refers to the prospect of the desert rejoicing at its transformation wrought by God.

rānan [רָנַן, **7442**]

rānan is a verb meaning "sing," "shout." It is also translated "to rejoice" in several contexts. ***rānan*** occurs approximately fifty times. (→ SHOUT → SING)

Exhortations to rejoice in the redemptive deeds of Yahweh are found in Deut. 32:43; Ps. 20:5. The psalmist exhorts the righteous to rejoice in the Lord in Ps. 33:1. See also Pss. 89:12; 90:14.

gîlāh [גִּילָה, **1525**]

gîlāh is a rare noun derived from ***gîl*** (→ JOY), meaning "rejoicing," "joy." It is found only in Isa. 35:2; 65:18, as the response of the land and people of Israel to their renewal and transformation by Yahweh.

sāḥaq [שָׂחַק, **7832**]

sāḥaq is a verb found in approximately forty places with the primary meanings "laugh," "put to scorn," "make fun of." In Prov. 8:30, 31, however, ***sāḥaq*** is translated "to rejoice," referring to Wisdom (personified as a lady) "rejoicing" at God's side during the divine work of creation. The underlying sense here is that of "take delight in."

NT Words

synchairō [συγχαίρω, *4796*]

synchairō is a variant form of ***chairō*** (→ JOY) meaning "to rejoice with, in." It is found in only six places . Luke 1:58; 15:6, 9; 1 Cor. 12:26; Phil. 2:17, 18 speak of rejoicing together with someone. 1 Cor. 13:6 refers to rejoicing in the truth.

euphrainō [εὐφραίνω, *2165*]

euphrainō is a verb occurring fourteen times, meaning "to be glad," "to rejoice."

The sense of "be glad," in the context of enjoying "the good life," is found in Luke 12:19; 15:23ff. 2 Cor. 2:2 refers to the apostle Paul's gladness in a general sense.

The specific meaning "rejoice" is indicated in Rom. 15:10, with reference to celebrating the salvation wrought by God on behalf of his people. In a similar fashion, ***euphrainō*** is used metaphorically in Rev. 12:12, as an exhortation to the heavens to rejoice. Note also the injunction to God's people in Rev. 18:20 to rejoice over the victory gained over the enemies of God. Gal. 4:27 mentions rejoicing over the gift of children.

Acts 7:41 refers to the people of Israel rejoicing in their idolatry at Mt. Sinai. In Rev. 11:10, the wicked rejoice over the martyrdom of two servants of God.

kauchaomai [καυχάομαι, *2744*]

kauchaomai is a verb found in nearly forty places with the primary meaning "to boast," "to glory (in)." In several of these contexts, the sense of "rejoice" is indicated. Rom. 5:2 speaks of rejoicing in the hope of sharing in God's glory. Paul rejoices in his suffering in Rom. 5:3 and rejoices in God in Rom. 5:11.

See Also: → BOAST → JOY

RELEASE

OT Words

shemittāh [שְׁמִטָּה, **8059**]

shemittāh is a noun derived from ***shāmat*** (see below) meaning "release." It refers to remitting or canceling debts every seven years, often referred to as the Sabbatical "year of release" (cf. Deut. 15:1ff.; 31:10).

shāmat [שָׁמַט, **8058**]

shāmat is a verb occuring nine times and meaning "to release" in one or two contexts.

Deut. 15:2 cites the Mosaic legislation requiring Israelite creditors to release their debtors from their debt every seven years (i.e., in the Sabbatical "year of release"). Deut. 15:3 notes that this legislation does not include foreign debtors who are not entitled to such a remission.

NT Words

apolyō [ἀπολύω, *630*]

apolyō is a verb found about ninety times with the underlying sense of "to release," along with several associated nuances. (→ DIVORCE → FORGIVE → SEND)

The specific meaning "release," in the sense of restoring the liberty of those in prison, or of those held in custody after arrest, is indicated, for example, in Matt. 27:15ff.; Mark 15:6ff.; Luke 23:18ff.; John 18:39; Acts 4:21ff.; Heb. 13:23. Luke 23:16 refers to Pilate's failed attempt to have Jesus released from his custody after scourging. ***apolyō*** means "release" in the non-judicial sense of "let go" in Luke 14:4.

lyō [λύω, *3089*]

lyō is a verb with the primary meaning "loose" in the majority of the approximately forty contexts in which it is found. The underlying sense of ***lyō*** is "untie," or "release." It is translated "release" in about half of the occurrences of the term. (→ BREAK → DISSOLVE)

The meaning "release" in the sense of a judicial remission of a penalty is evident in Matt. 16:19; 18:18.

lyō also refers literally to releasing or untying ropes that bind an animal, such as the colt required by Jesus (Matt. 21:2; Mark 11:2ff.; Luke 13:15; 19:30ff.), or a man (Acts 22:30). Metaphorically, the term refers to releasing bound angels (Rev. 9:14ff.); and also to the temporary "untying" or "loosing" of Satan at the end of time (Rev. 20:3, 7). Luke 13:16 refers to a person's "release" from an illness.

REMAIN

OT Words

yāshab [יָשַׁב, 3427]

yāshab is a common term, found in about 1,200 contexts with the primary sense of "dwell," or "stay," as well as related meanings. One of these related senses is "remain," which occurs about twenty times, although there is also a significant amount of overlap with the sense of "dwell." (→ DWELL)

The meaning "remain," in the sense of "to stay in the same condition or state," is indicated in Gen. 38:11 in relation to widowhood, and in Isa. 32:16 with regard to righteousness.

There is overlap with the sense of "dwell" in Deut. 21:13, where ***yāshab*** refers to remaining in one's house (cf. also Isa. 44:13).

Several texts reflect the general meaning "to remain" in the sense of "staying in the same place" (cf. Josh. 1:14; 1 Sam. 20:19; 23:14; 1 Kgs. 11:16; Jer. 17:25).

Num. 35:28 refers to the provision of the Mosaic law whereby a manslayer (i.e., one who unintentionally takes the life of another as the result of an accident) can flee to a designated city of refuge in order to escape execution at the hands of the family of the deceased. This text exhorts the manslayer to remain in the city of refuge.

shā'ar [שָׁאַר, 7604]

shā'ar is a verb found around 130 times, meaning "remain," "leave," or "be left."

shā'ar means to "be left" in a variety of contexts. General references to such a state are found in Exod. 8:9, 31; 1 Kgs. 22:46; 2 Kgs. 7:13; Zech. 12:14. Josh. 23:4ff. refers to Canaanite nations remaining, or being left, in the land. Several texts mention the remnant of Israel likewise remaining in the land (cf. Ezra 9:15; Jer. 8:3; 24:8; 39:9). Land remaining (or still left) to be conquered is noted in Josh. 13:1ff. Gen. 7:23 describes Noah and his family as the only people "left" alive on the earth after the catastrophic flood. Lev. 25:52 refers to remaining time. Exod. 14:28 declares that no survivors remain of the Egyptian army that pursued Israel in the desert. They were drowned in the Re(e)d Sea (cf. also 2 Kgs. 24:14).

yātar [יָתַר, 3498]

yātar is synonymous with ***shā'ar*** (see above) and is found in a little over 100 contexts, again with the senses of "remain," "leave," "be left over" in most of these occurrences.

The meaning "remain," in the sense of "to be left over," is indicated in Exod. 12:10 — ideally nothing is to be left of the Passover feast the next morning, as all food is to be consumed during the feast itself. The same is required in relation to the fat of the feast, as indicated in Exod. 23:18. See also Exod. 29:34; Lev. 19:6. General references are found in Judg. 7:3; 21:7; Jer. 27:19; Josh. 18:2.

Lev. 27:18 refers to the years "remaining" until the Jubilee (i.e., the fiftieth year following seven cycles of seven years). 1 Kgs. 18:22; Isa. 4:3 refer to those left as a remnant; and Num. 33:55 refers to those nations that remain in Canaan.

yātar is also used nominally in ritual contexts, referring to the "remainder" of an offering being wholly consumed by fire (Exod. 12:10; 29:34; Lev. 7:17); and eaten by the priests (Lev. 6:16; 7:16).

sārîd [שָׂרִיד, 8300]

sārîd is a noun occurring nearly thirty times overall. It means "survivor," or "remnant," and signifyies one who survives, or that which remains or is left over.

In personal contexts ***sārîd*** means "survivor," or one who remains unscathed after a military assault or other catastrophe (cf. Num. 21:35; 24:19; Josh. 10:20; Obad. 14; Isa. 1:9; Jer. 31:2). Joel 2:32 speaks of Yahweh saving those who survive (i.e., the remnant of Israel) and restoring them to Jerusalem.

sārîd is also used in situations where no survivors remain (cf. Deut. 2:34; 3:3; Josh. 8:22; 10:28ff.; 11:8). This fate applies to Israel's enemies (2 Kgs. 10:11; Obad. 18); to those of God's people who attempt to migrate to Egypt contrary to God's intention (cf. Jer. 42:17 [see also Jer. 44:17]); and finally to the people of Judah in exile, being punished by God for violating his covenantal requirements (cf. Lam. 2:2).

sārîd also expresses an impersonal usage in Job 20:21, where food is said to remain (i.e., to be left over). See also Job 20:26.

'āmad [עָמַד, 5975]

'āmad is the regular term for "to stand" in the Old Testament, occurring about 520 times. It also has some associated nuances. Included in these is the meaning "remain," with the underlying sense of "endure," predicated of the new heavens and earth that will remain before the Lord forever (cf. Isa. 66:22). 2 Kgs. 13:6 refers to the Asherah pole that "remained standing" in Samaria. Eccl. 2:9 indicates that the writer's wisdom "remained" with him during his attempt to find meaning in life. See also Jer. 48:11; Dan. 10:17.

'ādaph [עָדַף, 5736]

'ādaph is a verb occurring in nine places meaning "to remain" in the sense of "to be left over (as excess)." It refers to an excess number of Israelite firstborn (Num. 3:46ff.); to food (Exod. 16:18, 23); and also to surplus material "left over" from the construction of the tabernacle (Exod. 26:12, 13). Lev. 25:27 refers to a sum of money as the "balance" of a payment from the sale of a piece of land.

NT Words

menō [μένω, *3306*]

The verb ***menō*** is a common term meaning "abide," "dwell," "remain" in most of its 120 occurrences. There is a degree of overlap between these meanings. However, there are contexts where the sense of "remain" is distinct. (→ ABIDE → DWELL)

The meaning "remain" in the sense of "be preserved" is indicated hypothetically in the case of the city of Sodom in Matt. 11:23; and also literally in regard to the earthly destiny of the disciple, John (John 21:23).

The idea of remaining unmarried is found in 1 Cor. 7:11 (cf. also 1 Cor. 7:20, 24).

More commonly, ***menō*** is translated "remain" in the senses of "stay," "rest on," in several contexts. ***menō*** refers to staying in a house as a guest (Luke 10:7; 19:5; John 2:12; 4:40; Acts 9:43); or more generally, to staying in a particular place (cf. John 8:31; 10:40). John 1:32 refers to the Spirit coming to permanently "rest on" the person of Christ. Paul's determination to "stay" with the Philippian congregation for the purposes of nurturing them is indicated in Phil. 1:25. John 19:31 refers to the Mosaic legislation that forbids allowing bodies to remain on a cross of execution during the Sabbath day.

Where believers are concerned, their state of "remaining" in Christ, referring to their intimate relationship with him, is indicated in John 6:56; 1 John 2:24, 28; 3:6ff. Conversely, unbelievers are said "to remain" in darkness (John 12:46); and 2 Cor. 3:14 affirms that the veil of unbelief remains over their understanding.

menō is also predicated of Christ and God. God's word is said to remain in the heart and life of the believer (1 John 2:24); as is God's love (1 John 3:17). In a negative context, the unbeliever is denied the presence of God's word in his heart (cf. John 5:38). God himself is said to remain faithful (2 Tim. 2:13); and John 12:35 declares that Christ remains forever.

The qualities of faith, hope, and love are said to remain, or endure (1 Cor. 13:13). John 9:41 refers to guilt remaining.

perisseuō [περισσεύω, *4052*]

perisseuō is a verb found in approximately forty places with the predominant sense of "abound." It also has a number of additional nuances, including "to remain" in the sense of "be left over." (→ ABUNDANCE)

The meaning "remain" here is applied exclusively to the food left over after Jesus' miraculous provision of food for the multitude in Matt. 14:20; 15:37; Luke 9:17; John 6:12ff.

perileipō [περιλείπω, *4035*]

perileipō is a verb found only twice, in 1 Thess. 4:15, 17, referring to those who "remain" (i.e., who are still alive) at the time of Christ's return.

diamenō [διαμένω, *1265*]

diamenō is a variant form of ***menō*** (see above) occurring five times in all and meaning "to remain" in the sense of "continue in the same state, or condition." Luke 1:22 refers to Zechariah the priest remaining in his mute condition. Jesus commends his disciples in Luke 22:28 for remaining with him in his trials. Gal. 2:5 speaks of the importance of the truth of the gospel remaining with the Galatians. Heb. 1:11 refers to God remaining unchangeable. 2 Pet. 3:4 also speaks of the unchanging nature of the cosmos since the beginning of creation.

apoleipō [ἀπολείπω, *620*]

apoleipō is a verb translated "leave," or "remain," in the six occurrences of the term.

The meaning "remain" is used impersonally in Heb. 4:6, 9 in the declaration: "There remains a Sabbath rest for the people of God." Heb. 10:26 contains the negative affirmation that "there remains" no sacrifice for sin, once a person actively abandons his relationship with Christ.

loipos [λοιπός, *3062*]

loipos is a noun found approximately forty times, meaning "rest" in several of these contexts. The sense here is "that which remains," or "those that remain." Where people are concerned, ***loipos*** means "the rest" in the sense of "the remainder," "those who are left" (cf. Matt. 22:6; Mark 16:13; Luke 24:9; Acts 2:37; Rom. 11:7; 1 Cor. 7:12; Rev. 12:17; 19:21).

Impersonal phenomena are also included in the usage of ***loipos***, meaning "the rest" or "(the) other things" (cf. Luke 12:26; 1 Cor. 11:34).

epiloipos [ἐπίλοιπος, *1954*]

epiloipos occurs only once, in 1 Pet. 4:2, where it refers to "the rest" (i.e., the remainder) of one's life.

See Also: ➞ ABIDE ➞ CONTINUE ➞ REMNANT ➞ REST

REMEMBER

OT Words

zākar [זָכַר, **2142**]

zākar is the primary verb in the Old Testament meaning "to remember," along with several associated senses. The process of remembering is predicated of both God and human beings — although there is a significant difference between the human and divine elements of this process.

Where God is concerned, the act of remembering is not a psychological phenomenon of recall, as is the case with human beings. Rather, when ***zākar*** is associated with God, divine "remembering" signifies Yahweh's intention to implement the next state of his redemptive plan, whether it be his purpose to bless or (less frequently) bring down judgment.

Examples of divine "remembering" include the predicament of Noah in the midst of the flood, when God "remembered" him and then set in motion the gradual receding of the floodwaters (cf. Gen. 8:1). Ps. 136:23 refers to God remembering his people in general. Of considerable theological import are the references to God remembering his covenant with Abraham and his descendants at strategic points in the history of his people — for example, the captivity in Egypt (cf. Exod. 2:24; 6:5). Other references include those in Lev. 26:45; Pss. 105:8, 42; 106:45; 111:5. Elsewhere, with similar import, God is said to remember the land of Canaan, promised to Israel (cf. Lev. 26:42); and the faithfulness of the house of Israel (Ps. 98:3; Jer. 2:2).

In a negative context, God advises people "not to remember" the former things of old, but to look to the new order of salvation that he will bring to his people (cf. Isa. 43:18, but see also Isa. 46:9). Elsewhere, God promises never to remember the sins of his redeemed (cf. Jer. 31:34; Ezek. 18:22; 33:16). See also Isa. 64:9; Ezek. 3:20. On the other hand, God also promises to remember his people's sin, in other contexts, with a view to punishing them for it — though such disciplinary action is not absolute (cf. Jer. 14:10; Hos. 7:2; 8:13; 9:9).

When the action of "remembering" is linked to human beings, the underlying sense of ***zākar*** is that of "bring to mind," "focus on," or "recall." General references to this process include those in Gen. 40:14; 42:9; Num. 11:5; Job 24:20. Negative uses of ***zākar*** include those in Eccl. 9:15, where no one is said to remember. Ezek. 20:43; 36:31 speak of Israel remembering their sin and being ashamed.

zākar also conveys the sense of "commemorate." The people of Israel, for example, are commanded to "remember" in this way the day they were rescued from Egypt (cf. Exod. 13:3; Deut. 16:3; 24:18ff.). A general reference to God's name being commemorated is found in Ps. 45:17.

There are also a number of references containing a command to remember. ***zākar*** enjoins people to "remember" the Sabbath day, to keep it holy (cf. Exod. 20:8); and to remember the laws and statutes of Yahweh, with a view to obeying them (Num. 15:3ff.; Neh. 1:8; Mal. 4:4). Deut. 6:17 enjoins the Israelites to remember the redemptive deeds of God; and Ps. 103:18 affirms those who do so. There is likewise the general command to remember Yahweh himself (cf. Deut. 8:18; Neh. 4:14; Eccl. 12:1; Jer. 51:50). In several places Israel is condemned for failing to remember Yahweh (cf. Judg. 8:34; Ps. 78:42; Isa. 57:11; Ezek. 16:22, 43). Likewise, those who do so are affirmed (cf. Pss. 22:27; 106:7).

In several contexts, the phenomenon of "remembering" is associated with a plea. There are first of all pleas made to God to "remember," to focus his attention on the plight of the supplicant — those who make such a plea include Samson (Judg. 16:28); Hannah (1 Sam. 1:11); and Nehemiah (Neh. 13:31). Nehemiah also pleads with God to remember the sins of his enemies, in order to judge them (cf. Neh. 6:14; 13:29). In Ps. 20:3, the psalmist beseeches God to remember the offerings of his people. There is a plea for Yahweh to remember his covenant in Jer. 14:21.

***zēker* [זֵכֶר, 2143]**

zēker is a noun derived from ***zākar*** (see above) with the consistent meaning "remembrance," or "memorial," in most of its twenty-three occurrences.

Exod. 3:15 speaks of the covenant name of "the Lord" (i.e., Yahweh) as that by which God is "to be remembered" by all generations of his people.

zēker refers to the "remembrance" of God's signs and wonders (Ps. 111:4); and to the "fame" of his goodness (Ps. 145:7).

zēker is also translated "remembrance" in the sense of a memory. Exod. 17:14; Deut. 25:19 record the divine promise to blot out the memory of the Amalekite nation (cf. also Deut. 32:26). The perishing of the memory of the wicked in general is indicated in Job 18:17; Pss. 9:6; 34:16; 109:15; Isa. 26:14. Conversely, the everlasting remembrance of the righteous is noted in Ps. 112:6; Prov. 10:7.

The meaning "remembrance" in the sense of a memorial or commemoration is also indicated in Esth. 9:28, which refers to the festival of Purim "commemorating" the deliverance of the Jewish people from the hands of the Persians.

In a negative context, Ps. 6:5 declares that there is no remembrance of God in death; and Eccl. 9:5 makes the gloomy observation that there is no remembrance of the dead.

***'azkārāh* [אַזְכָּרָה, 234]**

'azkārāh is another noun derived from ***zākar*** (see above) found in seven places, all with the explicit ritual sense of "memorial portion." This refers to part of the grain offering, usually offered up together with oil and spices. The "memorial portion" was a handful of crushed grain, and was not to be eaten but presented alongside the burnt offering, sin offering, and fellowship offering (cf. Lev. 2:2ff.; 5:12; 6:15; 24:7; Num. 5:26).

***zikkārôn* [זִכָּרוֹן, 2146]**

zikkārôn is a term likewise derived from ***zākar*** (see above), meaning "memorial," or "remembrance," in the majority of its twenty or so occurrences.

A day of "memorial," commemorating the redemptive deeds of Yahweh on behalf of Israel, was to be set aside to remember the Passover deliverance from Egypt (cf. Exod. 12:14; 13:9).

A written "memorial" of the defeat of the Amalekites by the Israelite nation is commissioned by Yahweh in Exod. 17:14 (cf. also Mal. 3:16).

"Memorial" stones set on the shoulder pads of the priestly ephod represent the people of Israel before Yahweh (cf. Exod. 28:12; 39:7). Similarly, the names of the twelve tribes are also inscribed on the high priest's breastpiece as a "memorial" before Yahweh (cf. Exod. 28:29). See also Ezek. 30:16. Memorial stones of another kind are mentioned in Josh. 4:7, referring to the stones set by the Jordan River at the point of the Israelites' miraculous crossing, marking their point of entry into the promised land.

There is a "memorial" of rest indicated in Lev. 23:24, accompanied by a trumpet blast.

The "memorial" offering is mentioned in Num. 5:5, 18; 10:10 (cf. ***'azkārāh***, above).

Finally, ***zikkārôn*** is used in a negative context in Eccl. 1:11; 2:16, where the writer declares that there is "no memory" of one's life work in the minds of one's successors.

NT Words

***mnēmoneuō* [μνημονεύω, *3421*]**

mnēmoneuō is a verb found around twenty times, meaning "remember" in most of these contexts.

Most commonly this term refers to the act of remembering as mental recall (cf. Matt. 16:19; Luke 17:32; John 15:20; Acts 20:31, 35; Eph. 2:11; 2 Thess. 2:5).

Elsewhere, ***mnēmoneuō*** means "remember" in the sense of "be mindful of." Each of the following contexts contain injunctions to exercise such a recall — for example, the poor (Gal. 2:10); Paul's imprisonment (Col. 4:18); the resurrection of Christ from the dead as an essential component of the gospel (cf. 2 Tim. 2:8); one's spiritual leaders (Heb. 13:7); and the fate from which one has been delivered (cf. Rev. 2:5). See also Rev. 3:3.

Where God is concerned, ***mnēmoneuō*** refers once to the divine "remembering" of the sins of the nations of Babylon with a view to punishment (cf. Rev. 18:5).

***mnaomai* [μνάομαι, *3415*]**

mnaomai is a verb found in approximately twenty places meaning "remember," as well as associated senses.

As with ***mnēmoneuō*** (see above), ***mnaomai*** refers primarily to people remembering as an act of mental recall (e.g., Matt. 5:23; 27:63; Luke 16:25; John 2:17, 22; Acts 11:16; 2 Tim. 1:4; 2 Pet. 3:2; Jude 17).

The meaning "remember" also indicates the sense of "be mindful of," with a view to acting in a certain way. The penitent thief on the cross, for example, pleads for Christ to remember him in paradise (cf. Luke 23:42). Paul commends the Corinthian congregation for "remembering" the traditions of the gospel he had passed onto them (cf. 1 Cor. 11:2).

When predicated of God, ***mnaomai*** refers to divine remembering in the anthropomorphic sense of initiating an aspect of his redemptive purposes. Luke 1:54 speaks of God "remembering" to be merciful (cf. also Acts 10:31). Luke 1:72 affirms that God will remember his covenant. Heb. 8:12; 10:17 promise that God will remember the sins of his people no more. God is said to remember Babylon in Rev. 16:19, with a view to punishing her for her sins.

mimnēskō [μιμνήσκω, *3403*]

mimnēskō is a rare verb found in only two places, meaning "remember," "be mindful of." Heb. 2:6 refers to God being mindful of humankind. Heb. 13:3 enjoins believers to remember those who are in prison for the sake of the gospel.

hypomimnēskō [ὑπομιμνήσκω, *5279*]

hypomimnēskō is a verb, a variant of ***mimnēskō***, above, found in six contexts meaning "remember," "bring to remembrance."

The term means mental recall in Luke 22:6. In John 14:26, Jesus declares that the Holy Spirit will "bring to remembrance" in the hearts of true believers all that Jesus had taught.

The meaning "remind" (lit., "cause to remember") is also found in several places. The apostolic writers remind their readers of the need to trust in the salvation won by Christ (cf. 2 Tim. 2:14; 2 Pet. 1:12). Paul reminds Titus of the need to submit to governing authorities (Titus 3:1). See also Jude 5.

anamimnēskō [ἀναμιμνήσκω, *363*]

anamimnēskō is a synonym for ***mimnēskō*** and ***hypomimnēskō***, above, occurring six times and meaning "remember," "bring to remembrance."

The process of mental recall is indicated in Mark 11:21; 14:72; Heb. 10:32. The meaning "remind" in the sense of "bring to remembrance" is indicated in 1 Cor. 4:17, with reference to Timothy reminding the Corinthian church of Paul's ways in Christ (cf. also 2 Cor. 7:15). Paul reminds Timothy to rekindle God's gift to him (2 Tim. 1:6).

anamnēsis [ἀνάμνησις, *364*]

anamnēsis is a noun derived from ***mimnēskō*** (see above). It occurs four times, with the meaning "remembrance."

The instruction to celebrate the Lord's Supper in remembrance of Christ who died on the cross is found in Luke 22:19; 1 Cor. 11:24, 25. Heb. 10:3 declares that ritual sacrifices are an annual reminder of sins under the old covenant.

mneia [μνεία, *3417*]

mneia is a noun found in seven places meaning "remembrance," or "memory," "remembering."

In all but one occurrence of the term, ***mneia*** refers to remembering others in one's prayers (cf. Rom. 1:9; Eph. 1:16; Phil. 1:3; 1 Thess. 1:2; 2 Tim. 1:3; Phlm. 4). In 1 Thess. 3:6, ***mneia*** refers to the fond "memories" of people's generosity.

mnēmē [μνήμη, *3420*]

mnēmē is a noun occurring only in 2 Pet. 1:15, with reference to the apostle's readers being able to "recall" his teaching (lit. "to call these things to remembrance").

mnēmosynon [μνημόσυνον, *3422*]

mnēmosynon is a noun found in only three places, indicating the sense of "memory" or "memorial." Christ commends the woman who anointed his feet with perfume by declaring that this deed will be told the world over as a "memorial" to her (cf. Matt. 26:13; Mark 14:9). The prayers of the Roman centurion Cornelius are described in Acts 10:4 as a "memorial" having ascended to God.

Additional Notes

The vocabulary associated with the act or process of "remembering" is extensive in both Old and New Testaments.

This phenomenon is particularly significant in contexts where Yahweh is the agent of remembering. Here the sense is not that of mental recall of persons, events, places, or objects. Rather, divine "remembering" may be understood as an anthropomorphism, indicating that Yahweh brings to the forefront of his consciousness elements of his redemptive purposes, and proceeds to have them played out in the arena of human history. The objects of God's remembering are always significant people or phenomena — key "players" in his plan of salvation. This is likewise observable in the New Testament.

The exercise of divine remembering does not bring only blessing, but also judgment. This is the case in both Old and New Testament contexts.

In the human sphere, the act of remembering is often mundane, referring simply to the process of mental recall. Due emphasis, however, is often placed on commemorating Yahweh's redemptive deeds in the Old Testament, and on the work of Christ's salvation in the New. The latter phenomenon is especially evident in the celebration of the Lord's Supper, in which the people of God are called upon to "remember" what Christ has done for them.

REMISSION, REMIT → FORGIVE

REMNANT

OT Words

yeter [יֶתֶר, 3499]

yeter is a noun derived from ***yātar*** (→ REMAIN) found in approximately one hundred places, with the primary meanings "rest," "remnant" (indicating that which remains or is left over).

yeter refers generally to people as a "remnant" in Deut. 3:11; 28:54; Josh. 12:4; 13:12; 1 Kgs. 22:46. It also refers to the remnant of the nations in the land of Canaan (cf. Josh. 23:12; 2 Sam. 21:2). See also Hab. 2:8.

she'ērît [שְׁאֵרִית, 7611]

she'ērît is a noun derived from ***shā'ar*** (→ REMAIN). It occurs around sixty-five times and means "remnant," or "remainder," in most of these contexts.

she'ērît refers generally to the remnant of God's people in relation to Israel (2 Kgs. 19:4; 2 Chr. 34:9; Ezra 9:14; Isa. 46:3); and in relation to Judah (Isa. 37:4, 32; Jer. 41:16; Zech. 8:6).

2 Kgs. 19:31; Mic. 2:12; 4:7; 7:18 specifically mention the remnant of Israel as those whom Yahweh will rescue and preserve from their enemies. This remnant is also identified in 2 Kgs. 21:14 as those whom God will punish. Similarly, the remnant of Judah is marked out for divine punishment in Jer. 6:9; 11:23; 44:12. And they too find themselves the object of the mercy of God, who promises to renew and restore them to the land of Israel (cf. Jer. 23:3; 31:7; Zeph. 3:13). Hag. 2:12 refers to the remnant of Judah who are renewed in their obedience to Yahweh.

she'ērît also describes the remnant of foreign peoples as those whom God will destroy. This fate is determined for Moab (cf. Isa. 15:9) and the Philistines (cf. Isa. 14:30; Jer. 25:20; 47:4; Amos 1:8).

she'ār [שְׁאָר, 7605]

she'ār is a noun derived from ***shā'ar*** (→ REMAIN), found approximately twenty-five times and meaning "remnant," or "rest" (in the sense of "remainder") in most of these contexts.

Isa. 10:20ff. refers to the remnant of Israel, those whom God will preserve and renew. Isa. 11:11, 16 refers to those whom Yahweh will return to the land. Isa. 14:22 refers to the remnant of the nations, whom God will destroy (cf. also Isa. 17:3).

she'ār is also used metaphorically in the expression "remnant of Baal," referring to idolatrous people in Jerusalem whom God will destroy (cf. Zeph. 1:4).

NT Words

kataleimma [κατάλειμμα, *2640*]

kataleimma is a noun found only in Rom. 9:27, referring to the "remnant" of Israel that alone will be saved.

leimma [λεῖμμα, *3005*]

leimma is a variant form of ***kataleimma*** found only in Rom. 11:27 with reference to a "remnant" of God's people chosen by grace.

Additional Notes

The "remnant" in both Old and New Testaments describes those on whom the blessings and promises of Yahweh rest. In the Old Testament, the remnant is identified primarily as the faithful people of Israel chosen by God, including a number of Gentile converts. In the New Testament, the remnant still consists of those true believers who are chosen by divine grace. The difference in the latter case is that the remnant is expanded to include a great influx of Gentile believers (cf. the book of Acts). Also, the completed work of Christ renders their eternal salvation absolutely secure.

Even though the New Testament vocabulary for "remnant" is quite scant, this theme is everywhere implied. All genuine followers of Christ are described as his people, his sheep, children of God, co-heirs with Christ — all of which presuppose the sovereign grace of God in bringing about their salvation. This is the marvelous destiny of the faithful remnant.

See Also: → REMAIN

REMOVE

OT Words

sûr [סוּר, 5493]

sûr is a verb occurring around three hundred times with the underlying sense of "put away," "take away," with a variety of associated meanings, including "remove." (→ DEPART → TURN)

sûr is used literally to mean "remove" in Ezek. 21:26, referring to "taking off" the king's turban and crown.

Elsewhere, ***sûr*** indicates the action of "removing" with the sense of "take away" (cf. Gen. 30:35; 48:17). Noah is said to remove the covering of the ark after the flood in Gen. 8:13. Yahweh removes the plague of flies from Egypt (Exod. 8:31). 1 Kgs. 15:12; 2 Kgs. 18:4 refer to removing idols and high places from the land of Israel. Eccl. 11:10 speaks of removing sorrow from one's heart. Ps. 39:10 records a plea for God to remove his scourge from the psalmist (cf. also Ps. 119:29). Judg. 9:29; 1 Kgs. 15:13 refer to removing people from their position or office.

Where God is the subject of ***sûr***, the meaning "remove" conveys the divine intention to expel from his presence those who have rebelled against him — including Judah (cf. 2 Kgs. 23:27; 24:3); Israel (cf. 2 Kgs. 17:18); and Jerusalem (cf. Jer. 32:31). In addition, Yahweh commands his people to "remove" (i.e., put away) violence and oppression from the land in Ezek. 45:9.

nāsag **[נָסַג, 5253]**

nāsag is a verb found in nine contexts meaning "remove" in the literal sense of "move," "displace" in the majority of these occurrences. The meaning "remove" is exclusively associated with the practice of displacing a landmark or boundary stone belonging to others — a practice that was forbidden under the law (cf. Deut. 19:14; 27:17; Prov. 22:28; 23:10; Hos. 5:10).

yāgāh **[יָגָה, 3014]**

yāgāh is a rare verb found only once, in 2 Sam. 20:13, with reference to "removing" a body from the highway.

NT Words

parapherō [παραφέρω, *3911*]

parapherō is a verb found only twice, in the context of Jesus' prayer asking God that, if possible, he could remove from him the cup of suffering involving his ordeal on the cross (cf. Mark 14:36; Luke 22:42).

methistēmi [μεθίστημι, *3179*]

methistēmi is a verb found in five places meaning "remove." In Acts 13:22 it refers to King Saul's expulsion from the throne of Israel by a solemn divine intervention in response to Saul's rebellion against Yahweh.

kineō [κινέω, *2795*]

kineō is a verb found in eight places, with the underlying sense of "move." In Rev. 2:5, however, Christ warns that he will "remove the lampstand" representing the church of Ephesus from its place in the heavenly realm.

metathesis [μετάθεσις, *3331*]

metathesis is a noun occurring three times, referring to the "removal" of created things at the end of this age (Heb. 12:27).

See Also: → DEPART → TRAVEL

REND, RENT → TEAR (VERB)

RENEW, RENEWING

OT Words

ḥādash **[חָדַשׁ, 2318]**

ḥādash is a verb found in ten places meaning "renew," or "repair," in most of these contexts. In several places, the meaning "renew" is equated with that of "repair." (→ REPAIR)

The distinctive idea of "renew" is found with several nuances. The sense of "recreate" is indicated in Ps. 51:10, where David pleads that God will "renew a right spirit" within him. And Ps. 104:30 speaks of God "renewing" the face of the earth (i.e., creating it anew).

ḥādash conveys the sense of "refresh" in Ps. 103:5, which speaks of youth being renewed like that of the eagle.

In Lam. 5:21, the people plead with God to have their days of old "renewed" (i.e., brought back).

ḥālaph **[חָלַף, 2498]**

ḥālaph is a verb occurring about thirty times meaning "change," as well as a number of related senses, including "renew." Twice, in Isa. 40:31; 41:1, ***ḥālaph*** refers to renewing one's strength.

NT Words

anakainoō [ἀνακαινόω, *341*]

anakainoō is found only twice. 2 Cor. 4:16; Col. 3:10 refer to the "renewing" of the believer through the Holy Spirit.

ananeoō [ἀνανεόω, *365*]

ananeoō is a verb found only in Eph. 4:23, describing the "renewing" of the believer's mind.

anakainōsis [ἀνακαίνωσις, *342*]

anakainōsis is a noun derived from ***anakainoō*** (see above), meaning "renewing," "renewal" in only two contexts. Rom. 12:2 describes the "renewing" of the believer's mind. Titus 3:5 speaks of the "renewal" of the believer wrought by the Holy Spirit.

Additional Notes

The phenomenon of "renewing" or "renewal" is closely related to that of "restore," "restoration." (→ RESTORE) The emphasis of the few Old Testament references is on the renewal of one's personal being and the earth. In the New Testament, "renewal" is linked to the heart and mind of the believer — a transformation brought about by the work of the Holy Spirit.

The vocabulary for "renew" is also connected to the motif of recreation (e.g., "the new heavens and the new earth"). This phenomenon is anticipated in the old covenant by the promised restoration of the land of Israel, to which the people of God returned after their exile in Babylon.

RENOUNCE

NT Words

apeipomēn [ἀπειπόμην, *550*]

apeipomēn is a verb found only in 2 Cor. 4:2, which speaks of "renouncing" or "casting aside" deceitful practices in undertaking gospel ministry.

REPAIR

OT Words

ḥāzaq [חָזַק, **2388**]

ḥāzaq is a verb with the predominant sense of "strong," along with a number of associated nuances, in the majority of its nearly three hundred occurrences. Among these additional meanings is that of "repair," which is found in a variety of contexts.

The literal meaning "repair," in the sense of "renovate," is indicated in relation to the Jerusalem temple (2 Kgs. 12:5ff.; 22:5ff.; 2 Chr. 24:4ff.; 2 Chr. 29:3; 34:8ff.). Numerous references to "repairing" (i.e., rebuilding) the walls of Jerusalem are found in Neh. 3:4ff.

ḥādash [חָדַשׁ, **2318**]

ḥādash is a verb found in ten places meaning "repair" and "renew." The former sense is found several times, all with reference to "renovating" or "rebuilding." 2 Chr. 15:8 refers to repairing the main altar in the Jerusalem temple. 2 Chr. 24:4, 12 mention King Joash's renovation and restoration of the temple. Isa. 61:4 refers to rebuilding ruined cities.

bādaq [בָּדַק, **918**]

bādaq occurs only in 2 Chr. 34:10 with reference to "repairing" the temple.

'āmad [עָמַד, **5975**]

'āmad is a common verb with the primary meaning "to stand," occurring around 520 times. ***'āmad***, however, is translated "to repair" in Ezra 9:9 with reference to rebuilding the ruins of Jerusalem.

rāphā' [רָפָא, **7495**]

rāphā' is a verb with the common meaning "to heal," found in approximately seventy contexts. In 1 Kgs. 18:30, however, it refers to "repairing" the altar of the Jerusalem temple. (→ HEAL)

gādar [גָּדַר, **1443**]

gādar is a verb found ten times with the underlying sense of "build a wall," used both literally and metaphorically. In Isa. 58:12, the term is used nominally to refer to the "repairer" of broken walls. Amos 9:11 refers metaphorically to the process of "repairing" the ruins of David's "fallen tent" — alluding to the promised renewal of the city of Jerusalem.

REPAY → REWARD

REPENT

OT Words

nāḥam [נָחַם, **5162**]

nāḥam is a verb occurring around 110 times with the primary meanings "comfort" (plus related senses) and "repent." The latter meaning is found in about half of these contexts, and has several different nuances. (→ COMFORT)

"Repenting" describes the process of changing one's mind. It refers to the people of Israel in Exod. 13:17. More commonly, this sense is applied to Yahweh, though not with literal force. Rather, references to God "changing his mind" are to be understood anthropomorphically, since God in reality never "changes his mind" as do human beings. Such a process, when predicated of the divine being, refers to God's perceived change of direction, thinking, or course of action (i.e., from a human perspective). The actual mechanism of God's "mind" in this context is, humanly speaking, impossible to describe. Such divine "changes of mind" occur in the context of him withholding judgment on his people (cf. Exod. 32:12ff.; 2 Sam. 24:16; Amos 7:3ff.). Yahweh also refuses "to change his mind" (cf. Ps. 110:4; Jer. 4:28; Ezek. 24:24; Zech. 8:14) and promises to "change his mind" with respect to punishing any nation that turns from its wickedness (cf. Jer. 18:8; Jonah 3:9ff.; 4:2).

"Repenting" also expresses the idea of being sorry for a particular action. Human beings express sorrow for sin (Job 42:6; Jer. 31:19); and also refuse to express such regret (Jer. 8:6). As far as God is concerned, this "repenting" denotes a regret that he had created humankind, as expressed in Gen. 6:6ff. in the days of Noah, prior to the great flood. Similarly, Yahweh "regrets" that he had made Saul king over Israel in 1 Sam. 15:11, 35. Num. 23:14; 1 Sam. 15:29 deny any need for God to be sorry for doing wrong. See also Jer. 42:10.

shûb [שׁוּב, 7725]

shûb is a common verb with the predominant sense of "turn," including a wide variety of associated nuances. (→ TURN) One of these nuances is "repent," and it is used exclusively of human beings expressing sorrow for sin, as in 1 Kgs. 8:47. Other texts contain the divine command to repent of one's sin (cf. Ezek. 14:6; 18:30). Related to the idea of expressing sorrow for wickedness is the idea of "turning away" from it. Such an action is predicated of Israel (1 Kgs. 8:35; 2 Chr. 6:26; 7:14; Isa. 59:20; Dan. 9:13); of foreign nations (Jer. 18:8); and of human beings in general (Ezek. 18:20; 33:9ff.).

NT Words

metanoeō [μετανοέω, *3340*]

metanoeō is a verb occurring around thirty-five times, meaning "repent" and referring exclusively to "turning from one's sin."

Matt. 3:2; Mark 1:15; Luke 13:3, 5; Acts 2:38; 17:30; 26:30 contain exhortations to repent. General references to repenting are found in Luke 16:30; 17:3ff.; Rev. 2:22. Luke 10:13; Matt. 11:21 refer to a hypothetical repentance. Matt. 12:41; Luke 11:32 speak of the repentance of the Ninevites under the preaching of Jonah. Luke 15:7ff. declares the joy in heaven at the repentance of a sinful person. ***metanoeō*** also refers to people's refusal or failure to repent (cf. Matt. 11:20; 2 Cor. 12:21; Rev. 2:21; 9:20, 21; 16:9, 11).

metanoia [μετάνοια, *3341*]

metanoia is a noun derived from ***metanoeō*** (see above) found in approximately twenty-five contexts, referring exclusively to renouncing and turning from one's sin (with one possible exception).

The fruit of repentance are indicated in Matt. 3:8; Luke 3:8. John's baptism for repentance is noted in Matt. 3:11; Mark 1:4; Luke 3:3; Acts 13:24; 19:4. General references to repentance are found in Luke 5:32; 15:7; Acts 20:21;. Rom. 2:4; 2 Cor. 7:9, 10; Heb. 6:1; as is the preaching of repentance in Luke 24:47; Acts 26:20. Acts 5:31; 11:18; 2 Tim. 2:5 speak of repentance as the gift of God to both Jew and Gentile alike. In contrast, the impossibility of repentance after apostasy is indicated in Heb. 6:6. 2 Pet. 3:9 indicates God's desire that all people should come to repentance, reflecting his divine benevolence.

One text may imply "repentance" as "a change of mind." Heb. 12:21 refers to Esau's abortive attempt to reclaim the blessing he had voluntarily forfeited to his brother Jacob. Esau sought to "produce a change of mind" (i.e., presumably in his father, Isaac), though such was not forthcoming and he lost the blessing of the firstborn forever.

metamelomai [μεταμέλομαι, *3338*]

metamelomai is a synonym for ***metanoeō*** found in six places. It means "to repent" in several different contexts.

It refers first of all to "changing one's mind" in Matt. 21:29; 27:3. The latter text refers to Judas' decision to return the thirty pieces of silver (the price paid for the betrayal of Jesus) to the religious authorities. This was an action fraught with bitter regret, but it did not constitute godly repentance. Heb. 7:21 speaks of God refusing to "change his mind" in regard to assigning to Christ an eternal priesthood after the order of Melchizedek.

metamelomai is also found in the context of refusing to repent of one's sins (cf. Matt. 21:32).

This term also expresses the attitude of "regret" in 2 Cor. 7:8.

ametamelētos [ἀμεταμέλητος, *278*]

ametamelētos is an adjectival form derived from ***metamelomai*** (see above) found only twice. In Rom. 11:29 it refers to God's call as "irrevocable" (i.e., incapable of being altered). 2 Cor. 7:10 refers to a repentance (i.e., ***metanoia,*** see above) that "leaves no regret."

REPLY → ANSWER

REPORT

OT Words

dibbāh [דִּבָּה, 1681]

dibbāh is a noun occurring nine times meaning "bad report," "slander." The former sense is found with respect to the spies' initial assessment of the land of Canaan (cf. Num. 13:32; 14:36, 37). Gen. 37:2 refers to the "bad report" Joseph brought to his father Isaac concerning his brothers. (→ SLANDER)

shēma' [שֵׁמַע, 8088]

shēma' is a noun meaning "news," "fame," "report" in most of its eighteen occurrences.

There is a prohibition against issuing a "false report" in Exod. 23:1. The meaning "report" in the sense of "news about someone" is indicated in Deut. 2:25; Isa. 23:5; Jer. 50:43.

shemû'āh [שְׁמוּעָה, 8052]

shemû'āh is a synonym for ***shēma'*** (see above), found nearly thirty times and meaning "news," "report," or "rumor."

A "report," in the sense of "news," or "rumor," is indicated in several contexts. 1 Sam. 4:19 reports the capture of the ark of the covenant by the Philistines. 2 Sam. 13:30 reports the death of Absalom. 1 Kgs. 10:7; 2 Chr. 9:6 refer to reports of Solomon's wisdom. Jer. 49:14; Obad. 1 refer to reports from the Lord. A bad report, or bad news, is indicated in Jer. 49:23. See also Jer. 51:46; Isa. 28:19. Isa. 53:1 refers to a "report" in the sense of a message proclaimed publicly.

shāma' [שָׁמַע, 8085]

shāma' is a common verb occurring around 1,150 times with the primary meanings "hear," "listen," "obey." However, in two places it is used in the impersonal expression: "It is reported that . . ." (cf. Neh. 6:6, 7). (→ HEAR → OBEDIENCE)

NT Words

akoē [ἀκοή, *189*]

akoē is a noun found approximately twenty-five times with the primary sense of "hearing," as well as a number of associated meanings, one of which is "report." This meaning is found twice, in John 12:38; Rom. 10:16, where it refers to the message proclaimed by the prophet Isaiah (cf. Isa. 53:1).

apangellō [ἀπαγγέλλω, *518*]

apangellō is a verb with the primary sense of "tell" in the large majority of its fifty occurrences. However, in a number of places it is translated "report," with the underlying sense of "convey a message." There is considerable overlap in meaning with that of "tell" (cf. Acts 4:23; 5:22; 16:36; 23:16ff.; 1 Thess. 1:9). (→ TELL)

See Also: → REPUTATION → TELL

REPROACH

OT Words

ḥerpāh [חֶרְפָּה, 2781]

ḥerpāh is a noun derived from ***ḥāraph*** (see below) with the primary meaning "reproach" in almost all of its approximately seventy-five occurrences. (→ SCORN)

ḥerpāh refers primarily to "reproach" in the sense of "disgrace," or "shame," at all levels. General references to "reproach" in the sense of personal disgrace or shame are found in Gen. 34:14; Pss. 15:3; 69:10; 119:39; Prov. 6:33; Isa. 4:1; 30:5.

In several places, "reproach" is also evident at a corporate level. It is listed as an element of divine punishment against Israel (cf. 1 Sam. 11:2; 17:26; Hos. 12:14); Judah (cf. Jer. 23:40; 29:18; Lam. 5:1; Ezek. 5:14ff.; 16:57); and the heathen nations (cf. Josh. 5:9; Jer. 49:13). This term is also associated with the rejection of Jeremiah, who suffered the "reproach" of his fellow-countrymen (cf. Jer. 15:15). See also Jer. 20:8.

In contexts where divine mercy and compassion are evident, Yahweh is said to remove "reproach" from his people Israel (Isa. 25:8; 54:4; Joel 2:19), and from Judah (Ezek. 36:15, 30; Zeph. 3:18).

ḥāraph [חָרַף, 2778]

ḥāraph is a verb occurring approximately forty times with the principal sense of "reproach," as well as several derivative meanings throughout the majority of its usage. (→ SCORN)

In several places, ***ḥāraph*** indicates the action of reproaching in the sense of "giving insult to." Yahweh himself is the object of reproach in 2 Kgs. 19:16ff.; 2 Chr. 32:7; Isa. 37:4, 17ff. at the hand of Sennacherib, the king of Assyria. See also Prov. 14:31 in this regard. Elsewhere, the psalmist bears the brunt of insult from his enemies (cf. Pss. 69:9; 74:10). Here there is overlap with the sense of "scorn," "mock."

ḥāraph also means "reproach" in the sense of "to attribute blame" (cf. Job 27:6; Prov. 27:11).

kālam [כָּלַם, 3637]

kālam is a verb found in approximately forty contexts with the primary meanings "to put to shame," "be ashamed." In Job 19:3, however, the patriarch attacks Bildad for "reproaching" (i.e., casting blame on) him.

NT Words

oneidos [ὄνειδος, *3681*]

oneidos is a noun found only in Luke 1:25 with reference to Elizabeth (the mother of John the Baptist) rejoicing in her pregnancy, declaring that God had taken away her "reproach" (i.e., shame) among her countrymen.

oneidizō [ὀνειδίζω, *3679*]

oneidizō is a verb occurring eleven times and meaning "reproach" in two distinct senses.

In the first place, ***oneidizō*** is translated "reproach" with the underlying sense of "to cast insult(s)." In this regard, the disciples of Christ are declared blessed on account of people "reproaching" and persecuting them for their faith (cf. Matt. 5:11; Luke 6:22; 1 Pet. 4:14). In other contexts, the thief on the cross reproaches Christ by hurling insults at him (cf. Matt. 27:44), as does the crowd watching his agony (cf. Mark 15:32).

Secondly, ***oneidizō*** means "reproach" in the sense of "rebuke" or "denounce." Christ is said to reproach unbelieving hearers in this manner (cf. Matt. 11:20). Even his disciples are so chastised in Mark 16:14. Rom. 15:3 declares that Christ bore the reproach (i.e., disgrace or rejection) of God on the cross. Jas. 1:5 affirms God's generosity in giving blessings to people, "without reproach" (i.e., without finding fault).

oneidismos [ὀνειδισμός, *3680*]

oneidismos, along with ***oneidos*** (see above), is another noun form derived from ***oneidizō*** (see above), meaning "reproach" in all five occurrences of the term.

Rom. 15:3; Heb. 13:13 refer to the "reproach" (i.e., disgrace, shame) borne by Christ. 1 Tim. 3:7 warns against falling into "reproach" (i.e., disgrace). Heb. 10:33 refers to the "reproach" (i.e., abuse) suffered by believers at the hand of their enemies. Heb. 11:26 speaks of Moses suffering "reproach" or "abuse" for the sake of Christ.

loidoria [λοιδορία, *3059*]

loidoria is a noun derived from the verb ***loidoreō*** (see below), found only three times and meaning "insult" on each occasion (cf. 1 Tim. 5:14; 1 Pet. 3:9 [twice]).

loidoreō [λοιδορέω, *3058*]

loidoreō is a verb found in only four places, meaning "reproach" with the sense of "heap abuse on" (cf. John 9:28; Acts 23:4; 1 Cor. 4:12; 1 Pet. 2:23).

See Also: → BLASPHEME → SHAME

REPROOF, REPROVE → REBUKE

REPUTATION, REPUTE

NT Words

martyreō [μαρτυρέω, *3140*]

martyreō is a verb found in about eighty contexts with the primary meanings "witness," "testify," as well as a number of associated senses. One of these is the meaning "to have a good reputation," "be of good repute," applied to individuals in several contexts (cf. Acts 6:3; 10:22; 22:12; Heb. 11:2; 3 John 12).

martyria [μαρτυρία, *3141*]

martyria is the noun derived from ***martyreō*** (see above) meaning "witness," "testimony" in most of its nearly forty occurrences. In 1 Tim. 3:7, however, it means "of good reputation" with reference to one of the prerequisite qualities of an elder.

dysphēmia [δυσφημία, *1426*]

dysphēmia is a noun found solely in 2 Cor. 6:8, referring to the quality of a "bad reputation."

See Also: → REPORT

REQUEST

OT Words

baqqāshāh [בַּקָּשָׁה, **1246**]

baqqāshāh is a noun derived from ***bāqash*** (→ REQUIRE) with the consistent meaning "request" in all eight occurrences (cf. Ezra 7:6; Esth. 5:3ff.; 7:2ff.; 9:12).

'areshet [אֲרֶשֶׁת, **782**]

'areshet is a rare noun occurring only in Ps. 21:2, referring to the "request" of one's lips.

be'ā' [בְּעָא, **1156** (Aramaic)]

be'ā' is an Aramaic verb meaning "seek" or "(make) request" in each of the twelve contexts in which it is found.

The meaning "to make request" is indicated in Dan. 2:23, 49; 6:7, 11ff.

bā'û [בָּעוּ, **1159** (Aramaic)]

bā'û is an Aramaic noun derived from ***be'ā'*** (see above), found only twice and meaning "request" or "petition" in both cases (cf. Dan. 6:7, 13).

NT Words

aitēma [αἴτημα, *155*]

aitēma is a rare noun, occurring only three times and meaning "request," or "petition." Luke 23:24 refers to Pilate bowing to the pressure of the Jerusalem mob, yielding to their "request" (i.e., demand) that Jesus be crucified. Phil. 4:6; 1 John 5:15 refer to "requests" made known to God in prayer.

See Also: → ASK → PRAY → REQUIRE → SEEK

REQUIRE

OT Words

dārash [דָּרַשׁ, 1875]

dārash is a verb with the common meanings "seek," "inquire" in the majority of its approximately 160 occurrences. In several places, however, the meaning "require" is indicated, and is wholly predicated of Yahweh.

The underlying sense of ***dārash*** with this meaning is that of "calling someone to account" or "holding someone responsible" for a particular course of action. In Gen. 9:5; 42:22; Ezek. 33:6, God holds accountable those who wrongfully take human life. Yahweh also holds his "shepherds" (i.e., spiritual leaders of Israel) accountable for his "flock" (i.e., his people) in Ezek. 34:10. Deut. 18:19 affirms that God will call to account those who do not heed the words of his servants the prophets. In Ps. 10:13, the wicked person denies that God will call him to account.

A second aspect of the meaning "require" is that of "to make a demand on." Deut. 23:21 indicates that God requires his people to keep their vows. God also demands that his people present offerings (cf. Ezek. 20:40) and live justly (cf. Mic. 6:8). See also 2 Chr. 24:6.

bāqash [בָּקַשׁ, 1245]

bāqash is a synonym for ***dārash*** (see above) and occurs 225 times. The primary meaning of ***bāqash*** is "to seek." In addition, the meaning "require" is found in a number of contexts and is predicated of both human beings and God.

In the human sphere, ***bāqash*** indicates the sense of "require" with the idea of "holding one responsible or accountable." Such a usage is illustrated in Gen. 31:39, in relation to payment for the theft or death of a domestic beast. Judah offers to be held responsible for the safe return of Benjamin to his father in Gen. 43:9. Personal accountability for murder is indicated in 2 Sam. 4:11. Ezek. 3:18, 20; 33:8 refer to responsibility for failing to warn a sinner of his impending doom, should he fail to turn to God. The sense of "to make a demand" is found in 1 Chr. 21:3; Neh. 5:12, 18.

Elsewhere, God is said to hold his people responsible for building an idolatrous altar (cf. Josh. 22:23); and in 1 Sam. 20:16 he is said to hold David's enemies to account.

shā'al [שָׁאַל, 7592]

shā'al is a verb with the common meanings "ask," "inquire" in most of its nearly 170 occurrences. In several places, the additional meaning "require" is indicated. The underlying sense of ***shā'al*** in these contexts is that of "make a demand on," or "ask," and it is applied to both God and human beings. (→ ASK)

Where God is concerned, Deut. 10:12 notes that Yahweh requires his people to fear him (cf. also 2 Sam. 3:13). Ps. 40:6 indicates that God does not merely require burnt offerings, but a devoted heart.

Where people are said to "require," the sense is that of "ask" (cf. Ezra 8:22; 2 Sam. 12:20; Ps. 137:3).

NT Words

ekzēteō [ἐκζητέω, *1567*]

ekzēteō is a verb found in seven contexts meaning "require" in two of these. Luke 11:50, 51 refer to God "holding accountable" the present generation of Israelites for killing the prophets in ages past. The reason for such condemnation is that this current generation venerates their forbears, who actually put the prophets to death. The literal sense of this accusation reads: ". . . the blood of the prophets will be required of this generation."

apaiteō [ἀπαιτέω, *523*]

apaiteō is a rare verb, occurring only twice. It means "require" in the sense of "demand" in the parable of the rich fool, where God says to this man: "Tonight your soul shall be required of you" (Luke 12:20).

zēteō [ζητέω, *2212*]

zēteō is a common verb meaning "seek" in most of its nearly 120 occurrences. However, in Luke 12:48; 1 Cor. 4:2 it is used passively to indicate that which is required (i.e., demanded) of faithful servants of God.

See Also: → ASK

RESCUE → REDEEM

RESERVE → GUARD → KEEP

RESIST

OT Words

yāṣab [יָצַב, 3320]

yāṣab is a verb occurring in about fifty contexts with the dominant meaning "to stand," along with a number of related senses. One of these is "to withstand," which is equivalent to the idea of resisting. 2 Chr. 20:6; Job 41:10 refer to the impossibility of withstanding or resisting God.

'āmad [עָמַד, 5975]

'āmad (a synonym for ***yāṣab***, see above) is a common verb, occurring approximately 520 times with the primary meaning "to stand," along with a number of associated senses. As with ***yāṣab***, one of these nuances is "to withstand," which equates with the idea of "resisting."

The impossibility of resisting one's enemies is indicated in Dan. 11:15. The power of two men to resist one single assailant is affirmed in Eccl. 4:12 (cf. also 2 Chr. 26:18). The resistance of the demonic spirit of Persia against the archangel Michael, who eventually overcame his adversary, is indicated in Dan. 10:13.

ḥāzaq [חָזַק, 2388]

ḥāzaq is a common verb, found in approximately 300 contexts, with the predominant meaning "to be strong." Among its numerous related senses is "resist," in the sense of "oppose," or "withstand." 2 Chr. 13:7 records Rehoboam's inability to resist troublemakers within his kingdom.

NT Words

anthistēmi [ἀνθίστημι, *436*]

anthistēmi occurs fourteen times with the sense "to resist" or "withstand."

There is, for example, the injunction by Christ not to resist an evil person in Matt. 5:13. Then there is a strong exhortation to resist the devil in Eph. 6:13; Jas. 4:13; 1 Pet. 5:9. Rom. 9:19 affirms the impossibility of resisting God's will. Rom. 13:2 declares that resisting the civil authorities is equated with resisting God. See also Luke 21:15; Acts 6:10.

The meaning "resist" also includes the sense of "oppose." Acts 13:8 refers to Elymas the magician opposing Paul's ministry. Paul himself opposes Peter for inappropriate behavior towards Gentile believers. See also 2 Tim. 3:8; 4:15.

antipiptō [ἀντιπίπτω, *496*]

antipiptō is a verb found only in Acts 7:51 with reference to "resisting" the Holy Spirit, or opposing his influence in the life of the believer.

antitassomai [ἀντιτάσσομαι, *498*]

antitassomai is a synonym for ***antipiptō*** (see above), occurring five times and meaning "resist" (cf. Acts 18:6; Rom. 13:2; Jas. 5:6). Such action is also predicated of God, who "resists" the proud (cf. Jas. 4:6; 1 Pet. 5:5).

antikathistēmi [ἀντικαθίστημι, *478*]

antikathistēmi is found only in Heb. 12:4 with reference to "resisting" (i.e., withstanding the pressure of) sin to the point of shedding blood.

REST

OT Words

nûaḥ [נוּחַ, 5117]

nûaḥ is a verb with the fundamental meaning "to rest," found in over 140 contexts with a variety of nuances.

The literal meaning "rest" can convey the sense of "come to rest" or "settle" as a physical motion — for example, Noah's ark comes to rest on Mt. Ararat (Gen. 8:4); and locusts settle on the land of Egypt (Exod. 10:4; Deut. 5:14). See also Josh. 3:13; Job 3:13ff.; Isa. 7:9; Dan. 12:13; Hab. 3:16. "Rest" is metaphorical in Ps. 125:3, which declares that the scepter of wickedness shall not rest upon the land of God's people. The fury of God coming to rest on his people is declared in Ezek. 5:13; 16:42. Blessing is said to rest on one's house in Ezek. 44:30.

In addition, ***nûaḥ*** means "rest" in the sense "taking a break from one's labor." Exod. 20:11; 23:12 refer to resting on the Sabbath.

More significantly in a theological sense, ***nûaḥ*** indicates the promise or anticipation of rest given by God that focuses on the land of Canaan as a gift to his people, their "rest" (cf. Exod. 33:14; Deut. 3:20; 12:10; Josh. 1:13; 21:44; 22:4; 23:1; 1 Kgs. 5:4; 2 Sam. 7:1). The phenomenon of "rest" given by God in a more general, non-specific sense is indicated in 1 Sam. 14:3.

Elsewhere, ***nûaḥ*** is found in contexts where the Spirit of God is said to "come to rest" upon the prophet (cf. Num. 11:25ff.; 2 Kgs. 2:15; Isa. 25:10); and also upon the Messianic Servant of Yahweh (cf. Isa. 11:2). This experience is also given to the people of God in Isa. 63:14.

In contrast, a denial of rest (i.e., peace, well-being, or security) is indicated as a judgment of God on those who oppose him, including his people (cf. Isa. 23:12; Lam. 5:5).

nôaḥ [נוֹחַ, 5118]

This noun form, based on ***nûaḥ***, above, is found in only four places and means "rest." It refers in 2 Chr. 6:41 to the "resting place" of Yahweh. Esth. 9:16 refers to the "rest" enjoyed by the Jewish people in exile from the attacks of their Persian enemies, which the people of God were able to successfully repel.

mānôaḥ [מָנוֹחַ, 4494]

mānôaḥ is a noun derived from ***nûaḥ*** (see above), found seven times and meaning "resting place." It is used literally in Gen. 8:9; Deut. 28:65; Ruth 3:1; 1 Chr. 6:31; Isa. 34:14; Lam. 1:3; and metaphorically in Ps. 116:7, indicating rest for one's soul.

menûḥāh [מְנוּחָה, 4496]

menûḥāh, a synonym for ***mānôaḥ*** (see above), is also derived from ***nûaḥ*** (see above). ***menûḥāh*** is found twenty-one times, meaning "rest," "resting place" in a variety of contexts.

General references to a "resting place" are found in Gen. 49:15; Num. 10:33.

The meaning "rest" in the sense of "peace," "security," "comfort" is indicated in Ruth 1:9; 1 Chr. 12:9. The latter text refers to Solomon as a "man of rest" (or peace, i.e., not a warrior). In a negative context, Jer. 45:3 declares that the prophet finds no rest in his agony.

The "rest" promised by God to his people (i.e., the land of Canaan) is indicated in Deut. 12:9; 1 Kgs. 8:56; Ps. 95:11, Isa. 28:12, 32:18. 1 Chr. 28:2 refers to the "house of rest" in describing Solomon's temple in Jerusalem.

In a metaphorical context, ***menûḥāh*** refers to the "resting place" of Yahweh on his throne, symbolized by the ark of the covenant (cf. Ps. 132:8, 14; Isa. 11:10; 66:1).

shābat [שָׁבַת, 7673]

shābat is a verb found in approximately seventy places with the primary sense of "cease."

However, the meaning "rest" is also evident in the usage of the term, associated primarily with the Sabbath rest established by God on the seventh day of creation (cf. Gen. 2:2, 3). Exod. 16:30; 31:12; Lev. 23:32 refer to the Sabbath rest as observed by the people of Israel. Exod. 23:12; 34:21 speak of the obligation of rest imposed by the third commandment of the Decalogue. The Sabbath rest is also applied to the land of Israel in Lev. 25:2; 26:34ff.; 2 Chr. 36:21. These references indicate the seventy-year period of exile as equal to an enforced period of "Sabbath rests" to be given to the land as a consequence of the people's failure to observe those rests during their history of occupation.

shabbātôn [שַׁבָּתוֹן, 7677]

shabbātôn is the noun derived from ***shābat*** (see above), occurring eleven times and referring exclusively to the "rest" of the Sabbath day (cf. Exod. 16:23; 31:15; 35:2; Lev. 16:31; 23:3, 24, 32, 39; 25:4, 25).

shāqat [שָׁקַט, 8252]

shāqat is a verb occurring around forty times, with the primary meaning "to rest" in the senses of "be at ease," "cease from activity." (➡ QUIET)

The meaning "to be at rest" is indicated first of all in the context of freedom from war for the land of Canaan (cf. Josh. 11:23; 14:15; Judg. 3:11, 30; 5:31; 8:28; 2 Chr. 14:1ff.). This state is also predicated of the earth in general in Ps. 76:8; Isa. 14:7; Zech. 1:11. In negative contexts, reference is made to the absence of rest (i.e., a state of anxiety) in Job 3:26; Isa. 57:20.

naḥat [נַחַת, 5183]

naḥat is a noun found in eight contexts with the senses of "rest," "quiet." Eccl. 6:5 refers to the "rest" of the stillborn child. Isa. 30:15 indicates that salvation for Israel involves both repentance and "rest."

rāga' [רָגַע, 7280]

rāga' is a verb occurring thirteen times, meaning "to rest" in four of these contexts. Jer. 31:2 speaks of Yahweh granting rest to Israel. Negatively, Deut. 28:65 declares that Israel will find no rest among the nations. Jer. 47:6 refers metaphorically to the sword "being at ease, or rest." See also Isa. 34:14.

margôa' [מַרְגּוֹעַ, 4771]

margôa' is a noun derived from ***rāga'*** (see above) found only in Jer. 6:16, where God promises that his people will find "rest" for their souls if they return to godly ways.

pûgāh [פּוּגָה, 6314]

pûgāh is a rare noun found only in Lam. 2:18, where the prophet exhorts his people to give themselves no "rest" in beseeching God for mercy in their suffering.

NT Words

anapauō [ἀναπαύω, *373*]

anapauō is a verb found twelve times with the central meanings "give rest," "take refreshment, or one's ease."

Christ promises to give his followers "rest" in Matt. 11:28, indicating total peace and freedom from all pain and trauma. Rev. 14:13 depicts the saints of God enjoying their heavenly rest, totally free from all earthly toil. 1 Pet. 4:14 speaks of the Spirit of God coming to rest on one's life. Taking rest in the sense of physical refreshment, or falling asleep, is indicated in Matt. 26:45; Mark 6:31; 14:41. Taking one's ease in the sense of "relax" and "enjoy" is mentioned in Luke 12:19. Finally, ***anapauō*** expresses the idea of "rest," in the sense of "refresh one's spirit," in 1 Cor. 16:18; 2 Cor. 7:13; Phlm. 7, 20.

anapausis [ἀνάπαυσις, *372*]

anapausis is the noun derived from ***anapauō*** (see above), occurring in five places and meaning "rest."

"Rest," in the sense of "peace," "freedom from guilt, fear," is that state promised by Christ to his followers in Matt. 11:29. Matt. 12:43; Luke 11:24; Rev. 14:11, however, deny rest for the wicked.

In the sense of "cessation from work," ***anapausis*** refers to "rest" in Rev. 4:8, where the saints in heaven are said to never rest from their worship of God.

katapausis [κατάπαυσις, *2663*]

katapausis is a noun derived from ***katapauō*** (see below) meaning "rest," used with reference to the "rest" granted by God to his people in the promised land of Canaan (cf. Heb. 3:11, 18; 4:3, 5), which in turn anticipates the heavenly "rest" prepared by God for those who belong to him (cf. Heb. 4:1ff.). See also Acts 7:9.

katapauō [καταπαύω, *2664*]

katapauō is a rare verb found in only four places, meaning "to rest" in three of these contexts. Heb. 4:4 refers to God "taking rest" on the seventh day, after his creative endeavors of the previous six. Heb. 4:8 speaks of Joshua "giving rest" to the people of God. In Heb. 4:10, ***katapauō*** refers to believers "resting" (i.e., ceasing) from their labors.

epanapauomai [ἐπαναπαύομαι, *1879*]

epanapauomai is another rare verb, occurring in only two places. Luke 10:6 speaks of peace resting upon a gracious host. Rom. 2:17 warns against "resting" (i.e., relying) on the law for one's salvation.

anesis [ἄνεσις, *425*]

anesis is a noun found five times, meaning "rest" or "relief" in all but one of these contexts.

The "resting" of mind and body is noted in 2 Cor. 2:13; 7:5 in the negative sense of "no rest."

Rest or relief from troubles and burdens is indicated in 2 Cor. 8:13; 2 Thess. 1:7.

episkēnoō [ἐπισκηνόω, *1981*]

episkēnoō is a verb found only in 2 Cor. 12:9, where Paul speaks of the power of Christ "resting" upon him.

sabbatismos [σαββατισμός, *4520*]

sabbatismos is a rare noun found only in Heb. 4:9, referring to the "Sabbath rest" remaining for the people of God.

hēsychazō [ἡσυχάζω, *2270*]

hēsychazō is a verb found in five places. It means "to rest" only in Luke 23:56, with reference to resting on the Sabbath.

Additional Notes

The vocabulary for "rest" throughout the Old and New Testaments, in both verbal and nominal senses, is of particular significance when associated with the land of Canaan.

The theology of the land in the Old Testament draws its prime significance from the fact that God had promised on oath to give it to his people as an everlasting inheritance for as long as they remained faithful to and obeyed his law. Throughout the Old Testament, the land of Israel remained the greatest symbol of rest for the people of God. For them, in terms of the covenant ideal, the land of promise guaranteed freedom from foreign oppression, stable government, a just and fair society, and economic prosperity. Failure to adhere to this ideal, however, through persistent violation of covenantal obligation towards Yahweh, would draw down the wrath of God upon his people and result in their removal from the land. This is precisely the scenario that unfolded, when the land of Israel was successively invaded, and the people were sent into captivity in foreign lands at the hands of the Assyrian and Babylonian armies. Thus the people lost their "rest." However, the Old Testament prophets also brought messages of renewed hope and forgiveness, for God intended to bring his people back to the land.

While the "land" is the supreme symbol of rest for the people of God under the old covenant, this is transformed in the new covenant era, where "rest" is transferred from the earthly to the heavenly plane. No longer is "rest" for the people of God to be understood in socio-political or socio-economic realities. Rather, "rest" for believers is to be understood in terms of their eternal inheritance in heavenly glory — the heavenly city of Jerusalem in the context of the new heavens and the new earth. Admission to this new dimension of "rest" is solely determined by one's saving faith in Christ, who is depicted in the New Testament as the sole vehicle by which ultimate, spiritual rest is granted to the believer by God. This perspective emerges most clearly in the book of Hebrews, and also in John's Revelation.

See Also: → LIE (VERB) → REMAIN
→ REMNANT

RESTORATION, RESTORE

OT Words

ḥāyāh **[חָיָה, 2421]**

ḥayāh is the principal verb meaning "live," "have life," as well as related nuances, in most of its nearly 270 occurrences. In one context, ***ḥāyāh*** indicates a resurrection miracle — Elijah restoring the widow's son to life in 2 Kgs. 8:1, 5. (→ RESURRECTION)

bānāh **[בָּנָה, 1129]**

bānāh is a verb with the primary meaning "build" in most of its approximately four hundred occurrences. In two places, ***bānāh*** means "to restore" in the sense of "rebuild," "repair" referring to cities (cf. Judg. 21:23); and the temple altar (2 Chr. 23:16). (→ BUILD)

yesôd **[יְסוֹד, 3247]**

yesôd indicates the "foundation" or "base" of buildings and furniture, especially in relation to the altar in the temple. In 2 Chr. 24:27, ***yesôd*** refers to the rebuilding or restoration of the temple itself.

NT Words

apokathistēmi **[ἀποκαθίστημι, *600*]**

apokathistēmi is a verb with the consistent meaning "to restore" in several distinctive contexts.

The meaning "restore" in the sense of "heal," or "cure," in relation to illness that yields to the divine power of Christ is indicated in Matt. 12:13; Mark 3:5; 8:25; Luke 6:10.

Another nuance of the term is that of "renew" or "transform," describing the ministry of John the Baptist, the new "Elijah," of whom it is said, "he will restore all things."

In Acts 1:6, the question is asked of the risen Christ as to whether he would restore (i.e., return) the kingdom to Israel.

Heb. 13:19 expresses the writer's desire that he be "restored" (i.e., brought back) to his readers.

katartizō **[καταρτίζω, *2675*]**

katartizō is a verb found thirteen times with the primary sense of "to perfect," "mend." In one context, the term refers to the believer's obligation to attempt to "restore" his brother who has fallen into sin, returning him to the congregation as a member in good standing, having (presumably) repented of his sin.

See Also: → RETURN

RESTRAIN

OT Words

kālā' **[כָּלָא, 3607]**

kālā' is a verb with a range of meanings including "shut up," "withhold," "restrain." The term is found in eighteen contexts. The sense of "restrain" has several connotations.

kālā' means "restrain" in the sense of "prevent," or "hinder." Exod. 36:6, for example, declares that the Israelite people are "restrained" from bringing any further offering for the tabernacle. Ezek. 31:15 speaks of God restraining the waters of the deep from flowing.

The sense of "keep back," or "withhold," is indicated in Gen. 8:2, where the rain is said to be restrained (i.e., it stopped falling), by the intervention of God. Ps. 40:9 denies restraining one's lips in praise to God. Ps. 119:101 advocates restraining one's feet from the evil way.

'āṣar **[עָצַר, 6113]**

'āṣar is a verb synonymous with ***kālā'*** (see above), found in nearly fifty places with the primary meanings "shut up," "restrain," "prevent." The underlying sense of the term is that of being under restraint, applied to different situations.

In Gen. 16:2, Sarah perceives that Yahweh has "restrained" (i.e., "prevented") her from bearing a child.

Job 12:15 declares that God prevents the waters of oceans or rivers from flowing.

Elsewhere there are a number of references to God restraining (i.e., halting) the course of a plague (cf. Num. 16:48ff.; 25:8; 2 Sam. 24:21, 25; 1 Chr. 21:22; Ps. 106:30).

kāhāh **[כָּהָה, 3543]**

kāhāh is a verb with the primary sense of "grow weak or dim," found in eight places. In 1 Sam. 3:13, however, it refers to Eil's failure to "restrain" his sons from doing wrong.

māna' **[מָנַע, 4513]**

māna' is a verb found in thirty contexts with the principal meanings "withhold," or "prevent," as well as associated meanings, one of which is "restrain."

Num. 22:16 speaks of the king of Moab's desire to let nothing restrain or prevent the seer Balaam of Peor from coming to him. 1 Sam. 25:26 refers to Yahweh restraining individuals from shedding blood. See also Ezek. 31:15.

NT Words

katapauō [καταπαύω, *2664*]

katapauō is a verb found only four times, and in three of these contexts it means "rest." However, in Acts 14:18, ***katapauō*** refers to "restraining" people from offering sacrifices to Paul and Barnabas. (→ REST)

RESURRECTION

OT Words

ḥāyāh **[חָיָה, 2421]**

ḥāyāh is a common verb meaning "to live," "be alive," as well as having a number of associated senses, including "restore to life" and "revive." The former meaning is found in 1 Kgs. 17:22 with reference to Elijah miraculously restoring the widow's son at Zarephath to life after he had died of an illness. Elisha performed a similar miracle in 2 Kgs. 8:1ff. The meaning "revive" is found in 2 Kgs. 13:21 in relation to "resurrecting" Elisha's skeletal remains. ***ḥāyāh*** has the special sense of "coming to life again" in Ezek. 37, with regard to the skeletal remains of the people of Israel. In this vision, Ezekiel is commanded to preach to these bones, which are subsequently brought back to life by the power of the spirit of God. This vision is a symbolic description of Yahweh's promise to "bring his people back to life" by returning them to the land of Israel after their exile and guaranteeing a profound renewal of both people and land. This phenomenon is alluded to again in Ezra 9:9.

NT Words

anastasis [ἀνάστασις, *386*]

anastasis is a noun meaning "resurrection" in most of its approximately forty occurrences.

General references to the "resurrection for the dead" include those in Matt. 22:23ff.; Mark 12:18ff.; Luke 4:14; 20:27ff.; John 11:24ff.; 5:29; Acts 23:8; 24:15ff.; 2 Tim. 2:18; Heb. 6:2; 11:35.

Acts 1:6; 4:33; Rom. 1:4; 6:5; Phil. 3:10; 1 Pet. 3:21 refer to the resurrection of Christ.

Several texts specifically allude to preaching the reality of the resurrection from the dead (cf. Acts 4:2; 17:32; 23:6; 1 Cor. 15:12ff.).

exanastasis [ἐξανάστασις, *1815*]

exanastasis is a rare variant of ***anastasis*** (see above), found only in Phil. 3:11 with reference to the "resurrection" from the dead.

egersis [ἔγερσις, *1454*]

egersis is another rare term found only in Matt. 27:53, with reference to the resurrection of Christ.

Additional Notes

There is no specific vocabulary for "resurrection" in the Old Testament. However, there is evidence for the phenomenon of restoration to life, as indicated by the use of ***ḥāyāh.***

Another general reference to resurrection from the dead is found in Dan. 12:2ff., using the metaphor of "awakening." (→ AWAKE)

In the New Testament, the concept of "resurrection" goes beyond the image of specific vocabulary for this phenomenon.

In the first instance, there is frequent allusion to the phenomenon of "rising from, or being raised from the dead." The primary focus for this expression is Christ's own resurrection (e.g., Matt. 27:64; 28:7; Luke 24:46; John 20:9; Acts 13:30ff.; Rom. 1:4; 4:24; 6:4ff.; 1 Cor. 15:12, 20; Eph. 1:20; Col. 1:18; 2:12; 2 Tim. 2:8; Heb. 11:19; 13:20; 1 Pet. 1:3, 21). Other references to people rising from the dead include the false assumption that John the Baptist had been resurrected (cf. Matt. 14:2; Mark 6:16; Luke 9:7); Lazarus' rising from the dead (John 12:1, 9); and believers rising from the dead (Eph. 5:14). Other general references include those in Luke 16:30ff.; 20:35; Heb. 11:19.

A second set of expressions, "raised," "raised up," "raised (up) to life" also describe the phenomenon of resurrection, including references to the resurrection of Christ (cf. Matt. 16:21; 17:23; Luke 9:22; Acts 13:33; 1 Cor. 15:16, 17).

RETAIN ➞ HOLD ➞ KEEP

RETURN

OT Words

***shûb* [שׁוּב, 7725]**

shûb is a common verb occurring over one thousand times with the predominant meanings "return," "turn," along with a variety of associated nuances, both literal and metaphorical. (➞ TURN)

The literal meaning "to return" (i.e., go, come back) is indicated in a variety of contexts. General, non-specific usage is illustrated in Ps. 73:10. ***shûb*** refers to people returning, in a directional sense, in Gen. 14:9; 50:14; Exod. 4:21; Lev. 25:10ff.; Num. 14:3; Deut. 20:5ff.; 1 Sam. 7:17; Song 6:13; Dan. 11:9ff. Deut. 3:20; Josh. 1:15; Ruth 1:6ff. refer to the people of God returning to their land. In particular, the promised return of the remnant of Israel to Canaan after their period of exile is noted Isa. 10:21; 35:10; 51:11. See also Lev. 27:24; Eccl. 1:7.

The people of Israel and Judah "return" to God in the sense of recommitting themselves to him in faith, trust, and repentance (cf. Deut. 30:2; 1 Sam. 7:3; 1 Kgs. 8:48; 2 Chr. 6:24, 38; Job 22:23; Jer. 15:19; 24:7; Hos. 6:1). However, in Isa. 19:22 such a return to Yahweh is predicated also of Egypt in a remarkable prophetic passage anticipating divine blessing for the nations. Isa. 44:22; Jer. 3:12; Hos. 14:1; Mal. 3:7 record pleas from Yahweh for his people to return to him. Jer. 23:14, in contrast, records an indictment of those who refuse to return to God with a penitent heart. Hos. 2:7 speaks metaphorically of such a return by Israel to her God, describing it as a return to her "first husband."

shûb means "return" in the metaphorical sense of "come back" in several contexts. The concept of blood returning upon one's head, as a sign of retribution, is noted in 1 Kgs. 2:32. The same is said in relation to wickedness in Esth. 9:25; Ps. 7:16; Joel 3:4, 7; Obad. 15. The kingdom of Israel returns to the house of David (1 Kgs. 12:26); and people return to the dust after their physical death (Ps. 104:29; Eccl. 12:7). See also Eccl. 5:15.

The term ***shûb*** is also used in relation to God "returning." God promises to return to his people and bring them back to the land of Canaan (cf. Jer. 12:15; 29:10; 30:3). See also Deut. 30:3. Jer. 22:27 declares a prohibition against the apostate Israelites returning to the land. The psalmist pleads with God in Ps. 90:13, beseeching him to return to his people.

In addition, ***shûb*** means "restore" in Jer. 33:7, 11, 26, where Yahweh promises to "return" (i.e., restore) the fortunes of Judah and Israel as they once were. Such a restoration is also promised to Egypt in Ezek. 29:14.

***tûb* [תּוּב, 8421 (Aramaic)]**

tûb is an Aramaic verb found in seven contexts meaning "return" in three of these. Dan. 4:34, 36 refer to Nebuchadnezzar's reason "returning" after his episode of divinely-initiated insanity. Ezra 6:5 records the command of Darius, the Persian king, to allow the valuable contents of the Jerusalem temple to be returned to Jerusalem.

NT Words

***anakamptō* [ἀνακάμπτω, *344*]**

anakamptō is a verb meaning "return" in each of its four occurrences. Physical "return" to a geographic location is noted in Matt. 2:12; Acts 18:21; Heb. 11:15. Luke 10:6 refers metaphorically to a greeting of peace "returning" to the disciples in the face of inhospitable fellow countrymen.

***hypostrephō* [ὑποστρέφω, *5290*]**

hypostrephō is a verb that occurs thirty-five times and is translated "return" in each of these, with all but one instance indicating a literal usage.

The literal sense of "return," or "go, come back" is found in Mark 14:40; Luke 1:56; 8:37ff.; 17:15ff.; Acts 8:25ff.; 14:21; Gal. 1:17; Heb. 7:1.

A metaphorical usage of ***hypostrephō*** is found in Acts 13:34, where it is affirmed that no corruption whatever "returns" to the resurrected body of Christ.

***epistrephō* [ἐπιστρέφω, *1994*]**

epistrephō is a verb with the principal meaning "turn," as well as associated nuances. (➞ TURN) In several places, however, the meaning "return" is indicated.

The literal sense of "return," or "to go, come back" is indicated in Matt. 12:44; Luke 2:20; 17:31.

epistrephō refers metaphorically to "returning" in Matt. 10:13, where a greeting of peace "returns" to the one who is not shown any hospitality by an inconsiderate prospective host.

In another literal, though highly significant, context, ***epistrephō*** indicates the "return" of a dead girl's spirit. Luke 8:55 records the resurrection of Jairus' daughter, which manifests the divine power of Christ.

anastrephō [ἀναστρέφω, *390*]

anastrephō occurs twelve times and means "return" in two of these contexts. The literal sense of "come back" is indicated in Acts 5:22. The other reference, found in Acts 15:16, is metaphorical. Here, God promises to return to his people and rebuild David's "fallen tent" (i.e., the ruined kingdoms of Israel and Judah) in an act of profound spiritual renewal (citing Amos 9:11, 12).

epanerchomai [ἐπανέρχομαι, *1880*]

epanerchomai occurs only twice, meaning "to return" in the sense of "come back" in Luke 10:35; 19:15.

REVEAL, REVELATION

OT Words

gālāh [גָּלָה, 1540]

gālāh is a verb occurring around two hundred times with a variety of meanings including "reveal," "uncover," "take captive," along with a number of related senses. The meanings "reveal" and "uncover" overlap in a number of contexts. (→ CAPTIVE)

The sense of "uncover" is largely evident in contexts that speak of "revealing (someone's) nakedness." This expression is a euphemism for "sexual intercourse," which is prohibited under the law in a variety of relationships (cf. Lev. 18:6ff.; Deut. 27:20; 20:11ff.). It is also used as a metaphor for idolatry in Ezek. 16:36ff.; 22:10. See also Gen. 9:21; 2 Sam. 6:20; Isa. 47:3.

Elsewhere, ***gālāh*** is used passively to mean "revealed" in the sense of "made known" or "disclosed." Knowledge or instruction revealed by Yahweh to his servants is indicated, for example, in Deut. 29:29; 1 Sam. 3:7; 2 Sam. 7:27; Isa. 53:1; 56:1; Jer. 11:20; 33:6; Dan. 10:1; Amos 3:7. Isa. 40:5 affirms that the glory of the Lord shall be revealed to all humankind.

In several places, God is said "to reveal himself" (i.e., make himself known) (cf. 1 Sam. 3:21; Isa. 22:14); and also to reveal his traits, such as righteousness (cf. Ps. 98:2). Prov. 11:13; 20:19 observe that people reveal secrets.

In the context of non-personal phenomena, Job 20:27 affirms that the heavens will reveal the iniquity of the wicked and Prov. 26:26 declares that guilt will be revealed (i.e., exposed or uncovered).

NT Words

apokalyptō [ἀποκαλύπτω, *601*]

apokalyptō is a verb occurring about twenty-five times with the exclusive meaning "reveal" in the sense of "uncovering, or laying open what has previously been hidden."

The general, passive use of ***apokalyptō***, referring to that which is revealed, is found in John 12:28 (citing Isa. 40:5); 1 Cor. 14:30. In particular, Matt. 10:26; Luke 12:3 affirm that all shall be revealed in the last days. Similarly, 1 Cor. 3:13 declares that a person's life work will be revealed to God on the day of judgment. The revealing of divine glory at the end of time is described in Rom. 8:18; 1 Pet. 5:1. 2 Thess. 2:3ff. warns that the man of lawlessness will be revealed before the return of Christ.

Where God is concerned, ***apokalyptō*** is found in contexts where he reveals spiritual truth or knowledge to those with a childlike devotion to, and trust in, him (cf. Matt. 11:25; 16:17; Luke 10:21; 1 Cor. 2:10; Eph. 3:5; Phil. 3:15; 1 Pet. 1:12). Rom. 1:17 declares that the righteousness of God is revealed through faith; and 1 Pet. 1:5 affirms that salvation will be revealed in the last time. In contrast, Rom. 1:18 states that the wrath of God is revealed from heaven against all wickedness. Gal. 1:16 declares that God reveals his son to humankind.

Concerning Christ himself, Matt. 11:27; Luke 10:22 declare that he reveals God the Father to humankind. Luke 17:30 says that the Son of Man is to be revealed on the last day.

apokalypsis [ἀποκάλυψις, *602*]

apokalypsis is the noun derived from ***apokalyptō*** (see above), with the consistent meaning "revelation" in each of its eighteen occurrences. All references speak of revelation as that which emanates from God or Christ.

General, non-specific references to revelation include those in 1 Cor. 14:6, 26; Gal. 2:2; Eph. 1:17; 3:3.

apokalypsis refers to giving and receiving revelation in contexts including conveying the light of the gospel to the Gentiles (Luke 2:32); the revelation of the mystery of the gospel (Rom. 16:25); the revelation of God's judgment at the last day (Rom. 2:5); and unveiling the sons of God at the end of time (Rom. 8:19). The revelation of the Lord Jesus Christ himself is indicated in 1 Cor. 1:7; 2 Thess. 1:7; 1 Pet. 1:7, 13 (cf. also 1 Pet. 4:13). Gal. 1:12; 2 Cor. 12:1, 7; Rev. 1:1 refer to the revelation given by Christ to his people. Rev. 1:1 indicates the canonical book of Revelation.

chrēmatizō [χρηματίζω, *5537*]

chrēmatizō is a verb found in nine places, meaning "warn" in most of these contexts. (→ WARN) In Luke 2:26, ***chrēmatizō*** means "reveal" with reference to the godly Israelite, Simeon, to whom God had revealed that he would not die before he had seen the Messiah.

Additional Notes

The phenomenon of "revelation" is not limited to the specific vocabulary with this meaning. The "revelation" of God to his people is seen in the Old Testament through dreams, visions, and theophanies (both aural and visual), primarily expressed through the medium of prophets through the vehicle of the covenant. That revelation culminates in the New Testament in the person of Christ, who constitutes the fulfillment, in an organic sense, of all of the Old Testament prophetic revelation. Thus, divine revelation itself, as that which God intended humankind to know and receive concerning his redemptive plan and purposes, spans the entire canon, from Genesis to Revelation.

The reader is directed to the broad range of entries below to see the enormous volume and range of data relating to this fundamentally significant phenomenon that is unique in the Judeo-Christian tradition. This personal God communicates to his chosen people that which is necessary for them to know to have a rightly-ordered relationship with him.

See Also: → ANOINT → APPEAR → CHRIST → COVENANT → DECLARE → DREAM → GLORY → JUDGMENT → PROPHECY → VISION → WORD

REVENGE → AVENGE

REVERENCE → FEAR

REVILE → REPROACH

REWARD

OT Words

sākār [שָׂכָר, 7939]

sākār is a noun meaning "hire," "wages," "reward" in the majority of its nearly thirty occurrences. The meaning "reward" is found in seven contexts. (→ WAGES)

sākār refers to "rewards" given for service done well (cf. 2 Chr. 15:7; Jer. 31:16). In contrast, Eccl. 9:5 declares there is no reward for the wicked.

Ps. 127:3 describes children as a reward from God. Eccl. 4:9 refers to reward for hard labor. Isa. 40:10; 62:11 speak of God's "reward," indicating his redeemed peoples.

seker [שֶׂכֶר, 7938]

seker is a variant form of ***sākār*** found only twice. The meaning "reward" is evident only in Prov. 11:18, with reference to recognition for a person's righteousness.

shālam [שָׁלַם, 7999]

shālam is a verb found in approximately 120 contexts meaning "be at, or make peace," "repay," "recompense," "reward," as well as associated senses. There is some overlap in meaning between the latter three senses. (→ PEACE)

The meaning "reward," in the sense of God repaying with blessing, is indicated in Ruth 2:12; 1 Sam. 24:19; Prov. 11:31; 13:13; 19:17; 25:22. In other contexts the inference is negative, where God is said to "reward" (i.e., repay) sin by bringing down punishment on those who practice it (cf. Deut. 7:10; 32:41; Judg. 1:7; 2 Sam. 3:39; 2 Kgs. 9:26; Ps. 137:8; Isa. 59:16; 65:6; Jer. 16:18; 32:18; Joel 3:4).

Elsewhere, the practice of human beings "rewarding" (i.e., repaying) evil for good is indicated in Pss. 35:12; 38:20; Jer. 18:20 (cf. also Gen. 44:4; Prov. 20:22).

maskōret [מַשְׂכֹּרֶת, 4909]

maskōret is a noun found in four places, meaning "reward." In Ruth 2:12 it refers to a blessing from God for faithful devotion to him and his people. (→ WAGES)

gāmal [גָּמַל, 1580]

The verb ***gāmal*** occurs approximately forty times, meaning "reward," "recompense," along with associated nuances, in the majority of these contexts. (→ WEAN)

Where human beings are concerned, the sense of "reward" is both positive and negative. In 1 Sam. 24:17; 2 Sam. 19:36, ***gāmal*** refers to repaying, or recompensing, with kindness. 1 Sam. 24:17; 2 Chr. 20:11; Ps. 7:4 refer to "rewarding" with evil.

God also is said to "reward," both with blessing (cf. 2 Sam. 22:21; Ps. 18:20) and with evil, or punishment (cf. Joel 3:4). Ps. 103:10 denies that God does this as fully as the sins of his people deserve.

gemûl **[גְּמוּל, 1576]**

gemûl is a noun derived from ***gāmal*** (see above). It occurs nineteen times and is translated "reward," "recompense" in most of these contexts.

As with the verbal root of this term, ***gemûl*** indicates "reward" from God both as blessing for the godly (cf. Prov. 19:17), and as punishment on the wicked (cf. Judg. 9:16; Ps. 28:4; Isa. 3:11; 35:4; 66:6; Jer. 51:6; Lam. 3:14; Joel 3:4ff.; Obad. 15).

In the human sphere, only Prov. 12:14 speaks of a "reward" in the context of gaining recognition for work well done.

'ēqeb **[עֵקֶב, 6118]**

The noun ***'ēqeb*** occurs in fifteen contexts, primarily as the conjunction "because." However, in Ps. 19:11 it refers to a "reward" (i.e., a blessing) from God.

shûb **[שׁוּב, 7725]**

shûb is a common verb occurring over one thousand times, with the primary meanings "turn," "return." However, in several instances it means "reward," "recompense."

Yahweh is said to "reward" his people with blessing (2 Sam. 22:21, 25; Ps. 18:20, 24); and to "reward" (i.e., repay) them with judgment for sin (Hos. 4:9; 12:2; 2 Chr. 6:23).

Human beings are described as "rewarding" evil for good in Prov. 17:13; 1 Sam. 25:21. Gen. 50:15 speaks of rewarding "evil for evil," as in enacting revenge.

perî **[פְּרִי, 6529]**

perî is a noun with the primary sense of "fruit" in most of its nearly 120 occurrences. However, in Ps. 58:11 it is translated "reward," indicating a blessing from God for the righteous.

nebizbāh **[נְבִזְבָּה, 5023** (Aramaic)**]**

nebizbāh is an Aramaic noun found only in Dan. 2:6; 5:17 with reference to "rewards" promised to Daniel by the kings of Babylon for his remarkable dream-interpreting ability.

NT Words

misthos [μισθός, *3408*]

misthos is a noun found in around thirty contexts and means "reward" in most of these.

misthos often refers to a "reward" as a spiritual blessing from God, whether in a general sense (Matt. 10:41ff.; Mark 9:41; 1 Cor. 9:17ff.; 2 John 8; Rev. 11:18; 22:12); or whether it refers specifically to one's reward in heaven (cf. Matt. 5:12, 46; Luke 6:23, 35; 1 Cor. 3:14). Matt. 6:1 threatens no reward from God. Negatively, as in the Old Testament, "rewards" can also be the recompense for sin (cf. Acts 1:18; 2 Pet. 2:13).

In a few places, ***misthos*** also refers to "reward" as an earthly gain, or payment for labor (cf. Matt. 6:2, 16; Jude 11). See also 1 Tim. 5:18.

apodidōmi [ἀποδίδωμι, *591*]

apodidōmi is a verb found in fifty contexts with the meanings "pay," "repay," and "reward." The underlying sense of the term is "rendering to people what is their due," in both a literal and metaphorical sense.

God is said to "reward" (i.e., give a spiritual blessing) to his people for their godly living (cf. Matt. 6:14ff.). The general sense of spiritual recompense for works done in this life is indicated in Matt. 16:27; Rev. 22:12. The negative sense of God "rewarding" punishment for sin is evident in 2 Tim. 4:14; Rev. 18:6.

In the sphere of human relationships, Rom. 12:17; 1 Pet. 3:9; 1 Thess. 5:15 warn against "rewarding" (i.e., repaying) evil for evil.

antapodosis [ἀνταπόδοσις, *469*]

antapodosis is a term found only in Col. 3:24 with reference to receiving an eternal inheritance as a reward for serving Christ.

misthapodosia [μισθαποδοσία, *3405*]

misthapodosia is a noun occurring only three times, meaning "reward" in the sense of "due recompense" on each occasion. Heb. 2:2 refers to a "reward" for wickedness, reflecting the idea of a "just retribution" from God. Heb. 10:3–5; 11:26 speak positively of reward as a spiritual blessing from God.

misthapodotēs [μισθαποδότης, *3406*]

misthapodotēs occurs only once, in Heb. 11:6, referring to God as the one "who rewards" (i.e., a rewarder of) those who seek him.

axios [ἄξιος, *514*]

axios is an adjective found approximately forty times with the primary meaning "worthy." In Luke 23:41, however, ***axios*** is used as a noun meaning "due reward" in the sense of "penalty for sin."

Additional Notes

The phenomenon of "reward" and its associated senses develops throughout both Testaments of the Scriptures.

In the Old Testament, divine "reward" is viewed primarily in terms of material blessing from God (in positive contexts), or judgment from God (in negative contexts). This is consistent with the perspective of covenant blessing or curse in general, which focuses almost exclusively in the Old Testament on the material aspects of economic prosperity, social equity, and political, military stability (or the reverse in the case of divine judgment) in relation to the land of Canaan.

In the New Testament, "reward" from God is interpreted and viewed almost exclusively, in a spiritual sense. This is consistent with the fulfillment of old covenant blessings and curses in the new covenant concepts of eternal blessing and damnation for the wicked. The "prism" through which such "reward" is focused is the person and work of Christ.

See Also: → BRIBE → GIFT

RICH, RICHES

OT Words

'āshîr [עָשִׁיר, 6223]

'āshîr is an adjectival form which is used nominally as well. It is found around twenty times, with the primary meaning "rich," or "wealthy," in a literal sense.

'āshîr is used as a noun and refers generally to "the rich" in Exod. 30:15; Ps. 49:2; Prov. 14:20; Eccl. 5:12; Isa. 53:9. Adjectival usage is indicated in Ruth 3:10; 2 Sam. 12:1ff.; Ps. 45:12; Jer. 9:23; Mic. 6:12.

'āshar [עָשַׁר, 6238]

'āshar is a verb found in seventeen contexts, meaning "to enrich," "to be, become rich."

General references to God extending wealth to people are found in 1 Sam. 2:7; Prov. 10:22 (cf. also Gen. 14:23). Yahweh is also said to enrich the earth in Ps. 65:9.

General references to human beings bestowing riches on others are found in 1 Sam. 17:25; Prov. 10:4. The state of being rich is described in Job 15:29; Ps. 49:16; Prov. 28:20; Jer. 5:27; Zech. 11:5.

'ōsher [עֹשֶׁר, 6239]

'ōsher is a noun derived from **'āshar**, occurring around forty times with the exclusive meaning "riches," or "wealth."

There are a number of general references to earthly, material wealth (1 Sam. 17:25; Prov. 11:16; 2 Chr. 17:5; Esth. 1:4; Eccl. 4:8; Jer. 17:11). 1 Kgs. 3:11, 13; 10:23; 2 Chr. 1:11ff.; 9:22 speak of the riches of Solomon in particular. Other texts affirm the folly of trusting solely in one's riches (cf. Pss. 49:6; 52:7; Prov. 11:28; Eccl. 5:13ff.). **'ōsher** also refers to "riches" as a gift from God (cf. 1 Chr. 29:12; Eccl. 6:2).

'ōsher also refers metaphorically to the "riches" of Lady Wisdom in Prov. 3:16; 8:18, symbolically indicating the supreme value of gaining wisdom.

hôn [הוֹן, 1952]

hôn is a noun found in approximately thirty contexts, meaning "wealth," "riches" in most of these.

General references to earthly wealth are found in Ps. 112:3; Prov. 10:5; 11:4; 19:4; Song 8:7; Ezek. 27:12, 18, 27, 33.

Prov. 8:18 refers metaphorically to the "riches" of Lady Wisdom.

nekes [נֶכֶס, 5233]

The noun **nekes** is synonymous with the above entries, meaning "(earthly) riches," "wealth" in each of its five occurrences (cf. Josh. 22:8; 2 Chr. 1:11, 12). The riches described in Eccl. 5:19; 6:2 are from God.

ḥayil [חַיִל, 2428]

ḥayil is a noun occurring in about 250 contexts with the primary meanings "army," "host," "strength," as well as a number of associated nuances. In several places, however, **ḥayil** means "wealth," or "riches," in the literal sense of material prosperity (cf. Gen. 34:29; Job 20:15; Ps. 62:10; Isa. 8:4; 10:14; Ezek. 26:12; 28:4, 5).

yitrāh [יִתְרָה, 3502]

yitrāh is a noun found in only two places, meaning "abundance" or "riches" (cf. Isa. 15:7; Jer. 48:36).

NT Words

plousios [πλούσιος, *4145*]

plousios is an adjective found in approximately thirty contexts, also used as a noun, and meaning "rich," "rich person." In addition to its literal use, **plousios** is used metaphorically to indicate spiritual wealth, or an abundance of Christian virtue and spiritual blessing.

The literal sense of "rich person" is indicated, for example, in Matt. 19:23ff.; Luke 12:16; 16:1, 19ff.; Jas. 2:6. It is used adjectivally in Mark 12:41; Luke 19:2; 1 Tim. 6:17; Rev. 3:17.

plousios is used metaphorically to refer to Christ as "rich" in divine attributes (cf. 2 Cor. 8:9); and to designate God as "rich" in mercy (Eph. 2:4). Believers are described as "rich" in faith in Jas. 2:5; Rev. 2:9.

plouteō [πλουτέω, *4147*]

plouteō is a verb occurring twelve times, meaning "to be rich," "to enrich," or "make rich."

Luke 1:53; Rev. 18:3, 15, 19 refer to "the wealthy" as a clan of people.

In metaphorical contexts, the term ***plouteō*** is used adjectivally in Luke 12:21; Rev. 3:17 to indicate that the selfish rich are not "rich" towards God. 1 Tim. 6:9 warns against the desire to be rich. ***plouteō*** also refers to heavenly, or spiritual, "riches" (cf. Rom. 10:12; 1 Cor. 4:8; 2 Cor. 8:9; Rev. 3:18). 1 Tim. 6:18 refers to those who are "rich" in good deeds.

ploutizō [πλουτίζω, *4148*]

ploutizō is a synonym for ***plouteō*** (see above) found in four places, meaning "to make rich," "enrich" in a spiritual sense.

1 Cor. 1:5 refers to being enriched in Christ; and 2 Cor. 6:10 (twice); 9:11 describe the experience of being made rich through spiritual blessings.

ploutos [πλοῦτος, *4149*]

ploutos is a noun found in twenty-two places, meaning "riches."

Literal references to material wealth include those in Matt. 13:22; Mark 4:19; Luke 8:14; Jas. 5:2; Rev. 18:17.

Metaphorically, ***ploutos*** refers to the "riches" of God's kindness (Rom. 2:4); his glory (Rom. 9:23; Eph. 1:18; 3:16; Col. 1:27); and his grace (Eph. 1:7; 2:7). Spiritual "riches" are noted in Col. 2:2; 1 Tim. 6:17; Heb. 11:26; Rom. 11:12. The "riches" of Christ are declared in Eph. 3:8; Phil. 4:19; Rev. 5:12. 2 Cor. 8:2 speaks of the "riches" of people's generosity.

chrēma [χρῆμα, *5536*]

chrēma is a noun found in seven contexts meaning "riches" or "money." The former sense is found in Mark 10:23, 24; Luke 18:24, referring to material abundance. The latter meaning is found in Acts 4:37; 8:18, 20; 24:26.

Additional Notes

The vocabulary for "riches" or "wealth" throughout the Scriptures signifies both literal as well as symbolic prosperity.

The Hebrew terminology for wealth generally indicates literal prosperity. This is consistent with the observation that blessing from God in the old covenant focused primarily on material prosperity.

In the New Testament, "riches" refer to literal wealth as well as to the spiritual blessings of the new covenant that culminate in the person of Christ. New Testament believers are warned against placing too much emphasis on gaining earthly riches — a desire that may prove a hindrance to gaining the blessing of "eternal riches" in glory.

See Also: ➠ GOODS ➠ TREASURE

RIDE

OT Words

rākab **[רָכַב, 7392]**

rākab is a verb found approximately eighty times with the primary meaning "ride," along with several related senses.

rākab refers to chariot riding (Gen. 41:43; 2 Kgs. 9:28; 10:6; 23:30); to riding animals such as camels, horses, and donkeys (e.g., Gen. 24:61; 49:17; Exod. 15:1; Num. 22:22; Judg. 5:10; 1 Sam. 25:20; 2 Sam. 18:9; 1 Kgs. 1:33. Esth. 6:9ff.); and to riding horses in a military context (Isa. 36:8; Jer. 6:23; 50:42; 51:21; Amos 2:15).

Zech. 1:8 refers to an angelic figure riding a red horse in a prophetic vision. Riders on horses in Hag. 2:22; Zech. 12:4 are said to be overthrown by God. Zech. 9:9 predicts that the coming king of Jerusalem will enter the city riding on a donkey. This is in fact a prophetic anticipation of the messianic ruler's entry into Jerusalem. Jesus Christ fulfils this prophecy (cf. Matt. 21:1ff.).

rākab is also predicated of Yahweh, referring metaphorically to his "riding" through the heavens as the "divine warrior," who goes into battle against the enemies of God's people (cf. Deut. 33:26; 2 Sam. 22:11; Pss. 18:20; 45:4; 68:4, 33; Isa. 19:1).

RIGHT

OT Words

yāmîn **[יָמִין, 3225]**

yāmîn is a noun that also functions adjectivally, meaning "right" (as opposed to "left"), "right hand," in most of its nearly 140 occurrences. The latter sense is the more predominant of these two meanings.

Mundane references to one's "right side," or more commonly "right hand," in a directional sense, are illustrated in Gen. 13:9; 48:13ff.; Exod. 29:22; Num. 20:17; Josh. 17:7; Neh. 12:31; Song 8:3. References to the "right shoulder" of the sacrificial animal as the portion belonging to the priests are found in Lev. 8:26; 9:21; Num. 18:18.

In several places, the expression "turning neither to the right (hand, side) or left (hand, side)" is a metaphorical exhortation not to stray from the path of devotion to Yahweh (cf. Deut. 5:32; 17:11, 20; 28:14; Josh. 1:7; 23:6).

More frequently, references to God's "right hand" allude metaphorically, or even anthropomorphically, to the affirmation of divine power and authority (cf. Jer. 22:24; Hab. 2:16). In particular, there is praise for the "right hand" of Yahweh in bringing about victory over his enemies, and/or blessing in the life of his people (cf. Exod. 15:6, 12; Pss. 18:35; 118:15ff.). Several texts point to Yahweh's "right hand" as a source of blessing and strength (cf. Pss. 16:11; 63:8). The messianic ruler is said to occupy a position of divine authority at God's "right hand" in Ps. 110:1, 5. Yahweh promises to uphold and protect at his "right hand" in Isa. 41:10ff. Isa. 48:13 refers to the "right hand" of Yahweh as a mechanism for his creative endeavors.

yemānî [יְמָנִי, 3233]

yemānî is an adjective related to ***yāmîn*** (see above), meaning "right" in the thirty or so contexts in which it is found.

The designation "right" refers several times to daubing parts of the body with animal blood, associated with priestly sacrifice. It is usually the right ear, finger, thumb, and foot that are indicated (e.g., Exod. 29:20; Lev. 8:23ff.).

Ezek. 4:6 refers to lying on one's "right side" in relation to the prophetic symbolism associated with the ministry of the prophet Ezekiel.

Other mundane references include those in 1 Kgs. 7:21, 39; 2 Kgs. 11:11; Ezek. 47:1, 2.

yāman [יָמַן, 3231]

yāman is a rare verb, occurring only four times with the underlying sense of "moving, going to the right" (cf. Gen. 13:9; 2 Sam. 14:19; 1 Chr. 12:2; Ezek. 21:16).

NT Words

dexios [δεξιός, *1188*]

dexios is the only term in the New Testament expressing the direction or position "right." It is adjectival in form, though it is also used as a noun, usually referring to the "right hand." ***dexios*** occurs around fifty times and is used both literally and metaphorically.

Literal, mundane references to "right" in relation to parts of the body are found in Matt. 5:9, 30; 6:3; 27:29, 38; Luke 6:6; Acts 3:7. See also John 21:6; Luke 1:11.

More frequently, and with greater significance, ***dexios*** refers to the "right hand" as a position of honor and authority. It refers to human beings (Matt. 20:21ff.; 22:44; 25:33ff.; Mark 10:37, 40; 12:36), as well as to the "right hand" of Christ himself and that of God as the supreme position of divine honor and authority (cf. Matt. 26:64; Mark 14:62; Luke 20:42; 22:69; Acts 2:25ff.; 7:55ff.; Rom. 8:3; Eph. 1:20; Col. 3:1; Heb. 1:3, 13; 10:12; 12:2; 1 Pet. 3:22). The "right hand" of Christ in heaven is mentioned as part of the opening vision in Revelation (cf. Rev. 1:16ff.). See also Rev. 2:1; 5:1; and also Rev. 10:2.

Rev. 13:16 refers to the mark of the beast placed on the "right hand" and forehead of all who worship him.

Additional Notes

Throughout both Old and New Testaments, references to the "right hand" of God and Christ are significant.

In the Old Testament, the "right hand" of Yahweh emphasizes divine majesty and power. In particular, it highlights the role of Yahweh as the "divine warrior" who conquers the enemies of his people and effects deliverance on their behalf through the agency of his "right hand."

In the New Testament, that same aspect of divine majesty and power is also evident. However, the primary emphasis shifts from the "right hand" of God the Father, Creator, to that of Christ. It is now the "right hand" of Christ that embodies impregnable divine power and authority, combined with the extraordinary privilege of his being seated alongside the "right hand" of his Father. In other words, the unique power and majesty of the divine "right hand" is fulfilled in the combined depiction of Christ the conquering Messiah-King, alongside his Father in glory, who has freely bestowed that eternal glory and majesty on his Son. All believers can now anticipate sharing in the supreme blessings of salvation immortalized in the one who sits enthroned at God's "right hand" in heaven.

RIGHTEOUS, RIGHTEOUSNESS

OT Words

ṣaddîq [צַדִּיק, 6662]

ṣaddîq is the principal adjectival term in the Old Testament indicating the quality of being "righteous" or "just." These two meanings, of which the former predominates, are consistently found in the 200 or so contexts in which the term occurs. ***ṣaddîq*** is also used nominally.

ṣaddîq describes human beings who walk with God and follow his ways, who are morally upright, as "righteous." Noah is characterized thus in Gen. 6:9; 7:1. More commonly, this quality is predicated of a class of people in general references (cf. Gen. 18:23ff.; Exod. 23:7; Deut. 16:19; 1 Sam. 24:17; Isa. 3:10; 26:7). In particular, Hab. 2:4 declares that "the righteous shall live by faith." The paradigm of a righteous man is recorded in Ezek. 3:20ff.; 18:5ff.; 33:12ff. The "righteous" are also commonly contrasted with the wicked (cf. Pss. 1:5ff.; 68:3; Prov. 10:3ff.; 11:8ff.; 29:2ff.; Eccl. 7:15ff.; Ezek. 21:3ff.; Hab. 1:4). Israel's "righteous" standing before God is guaranteed by a solemn divine promise in Isa. 60:21.

ṣaddîq also means "righteous" in the sense of "innocent," in contrast to those who are adjudged guilty (cf. 2 Kgs. 10:9; 2 Chr. 6:23; Isa. 5:23; 29:21; Amos 5:12).

ṣaddîq refers to God as "righteous," indicating his perfection in all moral dimensions and describing him as perfectly just (cf. Exod. 9:27; Deut. 32:4; 2 Sam. 23:3; 2 Chr. 12:6; Ezra 9:15; Neh. 9:8; Pss. 11:7; 145:17; Isa. 41:26; Jer. 12:1; Lam. 1:18; Dan. 9:14; Zeph. 3:5). In particular, Yahweh is described as "the Righteous One" in Isa. 24:16. The Messianic Servant of Yahweh is also described as "righteous" (Isa. 53:11); and as the "righteous branch" (Jer. 23:5).

In a non-personal usage in Deut. 4:8, the law of the covenant is said to be "just."

ṣedeq [צֶדֶק, 6664]

ṣedeq is a noun derived from ***ṣādaq*** (see below), occurring around 120 times with the consistent meanings "righteousness," "justice." As with the adjective ***ṣaddîq*** (see above), there is some overlap in meaning between these two senses. ***ṣedeq*** is also used adjectivally. The meaning "righteousness" here has several significant nuances.

ṣedeq refers to human "righteousness" in the sense of justice, exercising fairness in the judicial sphere. General references to this phenomenon are found in Lev. 19:15; Deut. 1:16; 16:20; Job 8:3; Prov. 1:3; 2:9; 17; Eccl. 3:16; Isa. 1:21. One of the elements of the rule of the coming Messiah, as prophesied in Dan. 9:24, is bringing in everlasting "righteousness," suggestive of a reign that will be absolutely just and fair.

Other aspects of "righteousness" include "integrity, or right standing under the law." General references to ***ṣedeq*** with this nuance include those in Job 6:29; 31:6; Eccl. 7:15; Isa. 26:9. In particular, such "righteousness" before God is noted in Pss. 4:1; 7:8; Isa. 51:7. Such a righteousness is deemed to be part of the calling and ministry of the Suffering Servant of Yahweh in Isa. 42:6. In Hos. 2:19, Yahweh promises his people a new "marriage" characterized, among other things, by "righteousness."

ṣedeq is also used adjectivally to refer to economic practices under the Mosaic law that are required to be "right," or "just," and "fair" (cf. Lev. 19:36; Deut. 16:18; 25:15; Prov. 31:9; Ezek. 45:10). See also Ps. 15:2; Prov. 8:15. Sacrifices are similarly described as "righteous" in Deut. 33:19; Pss. 4:5; 51:19 in the sense of being "legitimate" or "in accordance with the law."

ṣedeq may also possibly indicate "salvation," or "deliverance," as an act of Yahweh on behalf of his people (cf. Isa. 51:15; 62:1ff.).

"Righteousness" is also predicated of God, often as a synonym for "justice," ascribing to him moral perfection and consummately fair justice. General references to this characteristic of Yahweh include those in Job 36:3; Pss. 7:17; 35:24; Isa. 42:21. In several places, Yahweh is described as handing down "righteous" judgment (Ps. 9:4, 8; Isa. 11:4, 5; 58:2; Jer. 11:20). Such justice is also predicated of the coming messianic ruler in Isa. 16:5.

Another adjectival usage of ***ṣedeq*** applies specifically to the laws and statutes given by God to his people, ordinances described as "righteous" (cf. Ps. 119:7, 62, 75, 106, 123, 138, 142, 144, 160, 164, 172).

ṣādaq [צָדַק, 6663]

ṣādaq is a verb occurring around forty times with the predominant meanings "to justify," "make righteous," "declare righteous," in almost the entire usage of the term. There is significant overlap in meaning here between these three senses.

First of all, ***ṣādaq*** means "justify" in judicial contexts, with the sense of declaring someone innocent. General references include those in Gen. 44:16; 2 Sam. 15:4; Job 13:18; 32:2. The specific action of vindicating the innocent (i.e., declaring them "righteous") is expressed in Deut. 25:1; 1 Kgs. 8:32; 2 Chr. 6:23; Isa. 50:8. Condemnation for those who attempt to "justify" (i.e., vindicate) the wicked is indicated in Prov. 17:15; Isa. 5:23. In Exod. 23:7, Yahweh categorically refuses to do just that. One central aspect of the mission of the Suffering Servant is to declare many righteous (i.e., justify them) through his atonement on their behalf (cf. Isa. 53:11).

ṣādaq is also translated "be righteous," in the sense of "being morally upright, innocent, or just." It is used this way with general reference to human beings (Job 4:17; 9:2, 15; 25:4), and to the law of God (Ps. 19:9). In contrast, Ps. 143:2 affirms that no human being is righteous before God in his or her natural condition.

ṣedāqāh [צְדָקָה, 6666]; *ṣidqāh* [צִדְקָה, 6665 (Aramaic)]

ṣedāqāh is synonymous with ***ṣedeq*** (see above), occurring around 160 times and meaning "righteousness," "justice" (with some overlap in meaning).

Arguably the most significant theological usage of ***ṣedāqāh*** occurs in contexts where "righteousness" is understood as the consequence of divine action, whereby a person's "right standing" before God is declared by him through the process of a divine judicial reckoning. The righteousness of Abraham is presented this way in Gen. 15:6 (cf. also Job 33:26; Ps. 106:31). Such righteousness is also declared to be conditional, under the Mosaic law, dependent on one's obedience (cf. Deut. 6:25; 24:13). Deut. 9:4ff.; Isa. 64:6 deny humankind's innate righteousness. God promises to bring "righteousness" (and justice) to Israel as part of the promised renewal of his people, suggesting their renewed standing before him (cf. Isa. 33:5; 45:8). See also Isa. 61:10.

The quality of "righteousness" in the sense of living justly before God and humankind, with integrity, is also indicated in several contexts. It is noted in relation to Abraham (Gen. 18:19), and to people in general (Gen. 30:33; Prov. 11:16). The command of God to live justly and righteously is found in Isa. 56:1; Jer. 22:3. King David claims to be living righteously in 2 Sam. 22:21, 25. The context in this instance, however, is of a man whose heart is genuinely devoted to God — and on that basis he makes his plea, not on the grounds of sinless perfection (cf. also 1 Kgs. 8:32; Job 27:6).

Righteousness is occasionally linked or even closely equated with justice in a number of places (cf. 2 Sam. 8:15; 1 Chr. 18:14; Ps. 106:3; Prov. 8:18; Isa. 5:7; 28:17; Ezek. 14:14; 33:12ff.). In Amos 5:7, condemnation is handed down to God's people for failing to live justly.

The quality of righteousness is also applied to God's decrees in Deut. 33:21.

"Righteousness" is a characteristic frequently applied to God. His "righteous" deeds are acts of covenant faithfulness (1 Sam. 12:7; Pss. 40:10; 51:14; Isa. 46:13). Yahweh executes perfect "justice" (i.e., righteousness) (cf. 1 Kgs. 10:9; Job 37:23; Isa. 58:2). Pss. 11:7; 99:4; 112:3ff.; Isa. 5:16; 59:17; Dan. 9:7 are general ascriptions of praise offered to God for his moral perfection, for his "righteousness."

"Righteousness" is also a quality predicated of the "Servant of Yahweh," the promised messianic ruler who will come to reign with justice (cf. Isa. 9:7; Jer. 23:5ff.).

The Aramaic term ***ṣidqāh*** is found only in Dan. 4:27, with reference to King Nebuchadnezzar being exhorted by Yahweh, through the prophet, to "practice righteousness" in his realm, to rule his people with justice.

yāshār [יָשָׁר, 3477]

yāshār is an adjective occurring about 120 times meaning "right," "righteous," "upright," in the sense of being morally pure, or just.

When applied to people, ***yāshār*** indicates that they are "right" in the sense of being morally correct, in accordance with God's standards (cf. 1 Sam. 12:23; Job 1:1, 8). In particular, such people are described as being "right" in the eyes of God, or in God's sight (cf. Exod. 15:26; Deut. 6:18; 1 Kgs. 14:8; 2 Kgs. 15:3; Jer. 34:15). In contrast, several texts refer to people "doing what is 'right' in their own eyes," and thus drawing down divine condemnation (cf. Deut. 12:8; Judg. 17:6; 1 Kgs. 11:33; 2 Kgs. 16:2).

yāshār also refers to "the righteous" (i.e., the morally upright) as a class of people (cf. Num. 23:10; Pss. 7:10; 11:2; Prov. 3:32; 11:6; Eccl. 7:29; Isa. 26:7; Mic. 2:7). Mic. 7:2 affirms that no one lives uprightly before God.

When predicated of God, ***yāshār*** refers to Yahweh as one who is "right," or morally perfect and supremely just (cf. Deut. 32:4; Ps. 92:15). This adjective also describes God's laws as "right" (and true) (cf. Neh. 9:13; Pss. 19:8; 33:4; 119:37; Hos. 14:9).

yāshar [יָשַׁר, 3474]

yāshar is a verb with the primary sense of "please," "make straight," or "direct," occurring nearly thirty times. However, in several places it means "right" (i.e., morally upright) (cf. 1 Chr. 13:4; Prov. 15:21; Hab. 2:4).

yōsher [יֹשֶׁר, 3476]

yōsher is a noun derived from ***yāshar*** (see above), found fourteen times and meaning "right," "uprightness" in the sense of moral goodness.

The "uprightness" of one's heart is indicated in Deut. 9:5; 1 Kgs. 9:4; Job 33:3; Ps. 119:7; Prov. 2:13; Eccl. 12:10.

mêshār [מֵישָׁר, 4339]

mêshār is a synonym for ***yōsher*** (see above), found in approximately twenty contexts and meaning "justice," "righteousness" in most of these.

1 Chr. 29:17; Isa. 33:15 refer to the "uprightness" of the human heart. In related general contexts, Prov. 8:6; 23:16; Song 1:4; Isa. 26:7 refer to "what is right."

mêshār is also predicated of God, who is said to judge people "justly," or "with justice" in Pss. 9:8; 75:2; 96:10; 98:9; 99:4. In Isa. 45:19, Yahweh is described as one who says "what is right."

nākōaḥ [נָכֹחַ, 5228]

nākōaḥ is an adjectival form that also functions as a noun. It is found four times, meaning "uprightness" in the moral sense in all but one of these contexts (cf. 2 Sam. 15:3; Prov. 8:9; 24:26; Isa. 57:2).

NT Words

dikaios [δίκαιος, *1342*]

dikaios is an adjectival form that is also used nominally, found in approximately eighty contexts with the primary meanings "righteous," "just." There is a clear overlap in meaning between the two in many places.

When predicated of people, ***dikaios*** describes them as "righteous" in the sense of "fair," or "just," indicating their moral purity (cf. Matt. 1:19; 13:17; Acts 10:22; Titus 1:8; Jas. 5:16). There are exhortations to judge "rightly" or "with justice" in John 7:24; Col. 4:1.

dikaios also refers to "the just," indicating that class of people who are godly (cf. Matt. 5:45; 25:37; Luke 1:6; 14:14; Heb. 12:23; 1 Pet. 3:12; Gal. 3:11). Rom. 1:17 contains the declaration that "the just shall live by faith" (citing the Old Testament declaration of Hab. 2:4).

In negative contexts, the attitude of the "self-righteous" is condemned (cf. Matt. 9:13; 10:41; Mark 2:17). And Rom. 3:10 denies that there are any who are truly "righteous" before God in their natural condition.

Christ is also frequently described as one who is uniquely "just," or "righteous," in the sense of being completely innocent of all wrong (cf. Matt. 27:19, 24; Luke 23:47; Acts 3:14; 7:52; 22:14; 1 Pet. 3:18; 1 John 2:1). In John 5:30, his judgment is described as "just."

God is likewise declared to be "righteous" in the sense of "morally perfect," "just" (cf. John 17:25; Rom. 3:26; 1 John 1:9; Rev. 15:3; 16:5ff.). His judgment is likewise deemed "righteous" in 2 Thess. 1:5; 2 Tim. 4:8; Rev. 19:2.

Rom. 5:19 is a significant theological statement whereby, through an act of God, many will be constituted "righteous" in his sight (i.e., justified, declared guiltless before him) as a consequence of the atoning work of Christ. See also Heb. 11:4, where Abel's sacrifice, presented in a wholehearted attitude of faith and trust in God, was the means by which he was approved by God as righteous.

dikaiosynē [δικαιοσύνη, *1343*]

dikaiosynē is the most common term in the New Testament for "righteousness," with all its significant theological connotations. It is found approximately eighty times.

First of all, ***dikaiosynē*** means "righteousness" in the sense of "meeting the demands of God's law." In general terms, Christ's desire to manifest this kind of righteousness is indicated in Matt. 3:15 with regard to his baptism by John. Paul's pre-Christian conversion concept of righteousness under the law is indicated in Phil. 3:6. The phenomenon of the "way of righteousness" is noted in Matt. 21:32; 2 Pet. 2:21. In relation to Christ himself, his righteousness is identified in Rom. 5:21 with his act of obedient submission to death on the cross. References to "our righteousness" in Christ, or "the righteousness of God" in Christ, illustrate the doctrine of imputed righteousness for the believer (cf. 1 Cor. 1:30; 2 Cor. 5:21; 2 Pet. 1:1).

In a more general sense, the meaning "righteousness" indicates the state of being acceptable to God in every way (cf. Matt. 5:30; John 16:8, 10; 2 Cor. 6:14; 2 Tim. 3:16). Phil. 1:11; Heb. 12:11; Jas. 3:18 refer to the "fruits of righteousness" in Christ. Rom. 6:13ff.; 2 Tim. 2:22; 6:11; 1 Pet. 2:24 affirm that attaining such a state is the great goal of all believers. See also Matt. 5:6 in this regard. In addition, Eph. 6:14 contains the apostolic injunction to all believers to don the "breastplate of righteousness." There is also, in contrast, an invalid "righteousness" based on the pursuit of lawful obedience apart from Christ (cf. Rom. 9:31; Titus 3:5).

dikaiosynē also means "righteousness" in the sense of "justification," or the judicial declaration of innocence under the law. The grounds for such an acquittal is the completed redemptive work of Christ on the cross, and the instrument for applying such righteousness to the believer is saving faith in the person of God under the old covenant, and trust in the person of

Christ in the new. The patriarch Abraham is used by the apostle Paul as the classic old covenant illustration of this phenomenon (cf. Rom. 4:3ff.; 5:17; 9:30; 10:4, 6, 10; Gal. 2:21; 3:6; Phil. 3:9; Heb. 11:7; Jas. 2:23).

When applied to the person of God, ***dikaiosynē*** signifies divine righteousness as one of his essential characteristics (cf. Matt. 6:33; Rom. 1:17; 3:5, 21ff.; 10:3; 2 Cor. 9:9; Eph. 4:24; Jas. 1:20). Acts 17:31 speaks of God's perfect judgment of the world through Christ, "in righteousness."

Similarly, in relation to Christ, his love of "righteousness" is indicated in Heb. 1:9. In Rev. 19:11, he is described as the one who judges in righteousness, with perfect justice. The mysterious Melchizedek is given a typological significance through his name, "king of righteousness," anticipating the eternal nature of Jesus Christ's high priestly ministry (cf. Heb. 7:2 [citing Gen. 14]).

dikaioō [δικαιόω, *1344*]

dikaioō is a verb found forty times in the New Testament with the consistent meaning "to justify," with a variety of nuances. With respect to humankind's standing before God, this action is wholly a divine one, with the underlying sense of "declaring righteous" those who have humbled themselves before him, in repentance and faith. And for those living at the time of the earthly ministry of Christ (and afterwards), such a declaration is made for all who so commit themselves to the person of the Messiah. As a consequence, all who regard the person of God and Christ in this manner are adjudged innocent of all guilt under the law of Moses, for that sin has been borne by Christ through his substitutionary death on the cross.

General references to such a declaration by God include those in Luke 18:14; Acts 13:39 (cf. also Rom. 2:13).

Classic references to being justified by grace through faith in the person and work of Christ include those in Rom. 3:20, 24ff.; 4:5; 5:1, 9; 8:30, 33; 1 Cor. 6:11; Gal. 2:16ff.; 3:8, 24; Titus 3:7. The "justifying" of Abraham through his faith, mentioned in Rom. 4:2, applies the identical principle as indicated in each of the above texts. Even though Christ was not the object of the patriarch's trust in his own time and experience, his explicit faith in Yahweh is deemed to be identical in essence. Such was the case with all old covenant believers.

James' teaching on justification requires a point of clarification: for faith to be genuine, James argues that it must be accompanied by good works. James is not contradicting the Pauline perspective here. Rather, he is complementing it by emphasizing good works as the inevitably fruit of genuine faith, and not as the ground of our right standing with God (cf. Jas. 2:21ff.).

Christ himself is "declared righteous," or "justified," "vindicated" by the Spirit of God, who enabled him to validate his claim to the divine nature through his miracles, and ultimately through his resurrection from the dead (cf. 1 Tim. 3:16). Other references to the action of "justifying" or "declaring righteous" include those in Matt. 11:19; Luke 7:35, where "Wisdom" (a personification of a divine attribute) is justified by her deeds.

The act of justifying in the sense of "granting an acquittal" is indicated in Matt. 12:37; Rom. 3:4; 1 Cor. 4:4. Luke 10:29; 16:15 refer to justifying oneself in the sense of "making oneself appear to be in the right." Luke 7:29 refers to "justifying" God in the sense of "acknowledging his ways as right."

dikaiōma [δικαίωμα, *1345*]

dikaiōma is a noun derived from ***dikaioō*** (see above), found ten times and meaning "righteousness," "ordinance," "decree," "justification." This term refers to actions or a state of heart and mind that conform to the law of God.

The usage of ***dikaiōma*** with reference to God's "righteous" decrees, or judgments, is indicated in Luke 1:6; Rom. 2:26. God's "righteous acts" are noted in Rev. 15:4. In Rom. 1:32, the context is that of a divine decree that threatens judgment upon those that flout God's law. ***dikaiōma*** also refers to the "just requirements" of the law in Rom. 8:4.

"Justification" is the explicit meaning of ***dikaiōma*** in Rom. 5:16, referring to the righteous standing before God imputed to his people through the redemptive work of Christ.

The "righteous deeds" of the saints are noted in Rev. 19:8. And the climactic "act of righteousness" performed by Christ that brought life to all humankind is indicated in Rom. 5:18.

Finally, ***dikaiōma*** refers to "regulations" for worship in Heb. 9:1, 10. The sense here is that such regulations are in full accord with the law of ritual worship.

dikaiōs [δικαίως, *1346*]

dikaiōs is an adverbial form occurring five times, derived from the adjective ***dikaios*** (see above) and meaning "righteously," "justly," or "blameless." The term refers to human behavior in Luke 23:11; 1 Cor.

15:34; 1 Thess. 2:10; Titus 2:12. In 1 Pet. 2:23, ***dikaiōs*** refers to God as one who judges "justly."

dikaiōsis [δικαίωσις, *1347*]

dikaiōsis is a rare noun derived from ***dikaioō***. It is found only twice and means "justification" in both cases. ***dikaiōsis*** refers, as do the synonymous terms discussed above, to the judicial declaration of righteousness by God, granted to his people on the basis of Christ's finished work of redemption (cf. Rom. 4:25; 5:18).

euthytēs [εὐθύτης, *2118*]

euthytēs is a term found only in Heb. 1:8, referring to the scepter of "righteousness" belonging to God.

Additional Notes

The vocabulary for "righteousness" in both Testaments refers to moral uprightness (i.e., conformity to the law covenant) as well as to a judicial pronouncement of right standing before God. There is also a close semantic connection between the senses of "righteousness" and "justice."

The principle of a judicial declaration of righteousness remains the same in both Testaments — even though the redemptive work of Christ as the sole prerequisite ground of a person's salvation only becomes evident in the New Testament era. Under the old covenant, such faith and trust in the person, work, and revelation of Yahweh was deemed sufficient as the basis for a declaration of righteousness before God, as if in anticipation of the new covenant manifestation of Jesus Christ.

See Also: → JUDGMENT

RING

OT Words

tabba'at [**טַבַּעַת, 2885**]

tabba'at is a noun occurring approximately fifty times meaning "ring," "signet ring." The primary usage of the term relates to rings associated with the sacred furniture of the tabernacle. Rings were also a symbol of royal authority and an item of jewelry.

In relation to the tabernacle, ***tabba'at*** refers first of all to rings connected with the framework of the structure itself (cf. Exod. 26:24ff.; 36:29ff.). Rings were also attached to the corners of the ark of the covenant as receptacles for poles (cf. Exod. 25:12ff.; 37:3). Similar features applied to the bronze altar (cf. Exod. 27:4ff.; 38:5ff.); as well as to the altar of incense (cf. Exod. 30:4; 37:27); and the priestly breastpiece (cf. Exod. 28:23ff.; 39:16ff.).

The "ring" or "signet ring" of royal authority is noted in relation to the Egyptian Pharaoh (Gen. 41:42); and to King Xerxes (Esth. 3:10ff.; 8:2ff.).

Rings used as personal adornment, or jewelry, are noted in Exod. 35:22; Num. 31:50; Isa. 3:21.

gālîl [**גָּלִיל, 1550**]

gālîl is a noun occurring four times meaning "rings" in Esth. 1:6 in relation to curtains hung in the palaces.

NT Words

daktylios [δακτύλιος, *1146*]

daktylios is a rare noun, found only in Luke 15:22 with reference to an ornament for the hand.

chrysodaktylios [χρυσοδακτύλιος, *5554*]

chrysodaktylios is a variant form of ***daktylios***, occurring only in Jas. 2:2 and indicating "rings" as part of the personal jewelry of the rich.

RINGLEADER

NT Words

prōtostatēs [πρωτοστάτης, *4414*]

prōtostatēs is a noun found only in Acts 24:5, accusing Paul of being a "ringleader" of the sect of the Nazarenes.

RIPE

OT Words

bāshal [**בָּשַׁל, 1310**]

bāshal is a verb found approximately thirty times with the primary meanings "boil," "cook." However, in a couple of places it means "ripen," "be ripe."
(→ BOIL)

The literal ripening of fruit is indicated in Gen. 40:10. Joel 3:13 speaks of the ripening of the harvest, referring symbolically to Israel's readiness to suffer Yahweh's hand of judgment on them.

bakkûrāh [**בַּכּוּרָה, 1073**]

bakkûrāh is a noun found only in Jer. 24:2 with reference to "early ripened" figs.

NT Words

xēraino [ξηραίνω, *3583*]

xēraino is a verb occurring sixteen times with the principal meanings "wither," "dry up." However, in Rev. 14:15, ***xēraino*** refers to the harvest of the earth as "ripe" (i.e., ready for judgment). (→ DRY)

akmazō [ἀκμάζω, *187*]

akimazō is a verb found only in Rev. 14:18 with reference to the grapes of the earth being "ripe" for harvest (i.e., for judgment).

RISE

OT Words

shākam [שָׁכַם, 7925]

shākam is a verb that occurs sixty-five times, meaning "rise (up) early" in most of these contexts.

The mundane meaning "rising early" in the morning is found in Gen. 19:2; Exod. 8:20; Josh. 6:12ff.; Judg. 6:28; 2 Kgs. 3:23; Isa. 5:11.

In Jeremiah, ***shākam*** expresses the literal sense of Yahweh sending his prophets to the people of Judah, "rising up early" to warn them of his coming judgment. The emphasis here is on Yahweh's "persistence" in doing so (cf. Jer. 7:13; 11:7; 25:3ff.; 29:19; 44:4). See also Zeph. 3:7.

'ālāh [עָלָה, 5927]

'ālāh is a common verb, found nearly nine hundred times with the underlying meaning "go up," with a variety of associated senses, including "rise up," "ascend."

The phenomenon of smoke "rising up" is indicated in several places — for example, as a consequence of destructive fire (Judg. 20:38, 40; John 8:20ff.); as an element of theophanic manifestations at Sinai (Exod. 19:18); and in association with the angel of the Lord (Judg. 13:20). ***'ālāh*** also refers to rising clouds (Ps. 135:7); mist (Jer. 10:13; 51:16); and floodwaters (Jer. 47:2).

In Amos 8:8; 9:5 ***'ālāh*** indicates the "rising up" of the land accompanying an earthquake.

In Isa. 14:13, 14, the blasphemous claim of the Babylonian king is said to "rise up" to heaven.

zāraḥ [זָרַח, 2224]

The verb ***zāraḥ*** occurs eighteen times, meaning "arise," "rise up" in the majority of these occurrences.

The rising of the sun is indicated in Gen. 32:31; Job 9:7; Ps. 104:22; Jonah 4:8; Nah. 3:17.

Elsewhere, the usage of ***zāraḥ*** is metaphorical. In Mal. 4:2, the "sun of righteousness" is said to rise with healing on its wings. Isa. 60:1ff. declares that the glory of Yahweh will rise upon his people.

rûm [רוּם, 7311]

rûm is a verb found approximately three hundred times with the principal meanings "lift (up)," "raise," "exalt." (→ EXALT) The meaning "rise" is indicated in Gen. 7:17 in relation to Noah's ark rising high above the earth. In Ezek. 10:4, ***rûm*** refers to the rising up of the glory of the Lord from the cherubim over the ark of the covenant.

gā'āh [גָּאָה, 1342]

gā'āh is a verb meaning "rise up" in Ezek. 17:5 in relation to the rising waters of a river.

mizrāḥ [מִזְרָח, 4217]

mizrāḥ is found in around seventy contexts with the primary sense of "east," or "to the east," and frequently refers to the "rising" of the sun (i.e., as taking place in the east) (cf. Num. 2:3; Deut. 4:41; Josh. 1:15; Ps. 50:1; Isa. 41:25).

See Also: → ARISE

RIVER

OT Words

nāhār [נָהָר, 5104]

nāhār is a noun meaning "river," or "stream," in the 120 occurrences of the term.

Literal references to "rivers" include those that water the garden of Eden (Gen. 2:10ff.); the Jordan River (Ps. 66:6); and the Euphrates, sometimes designated simply as "the river" (cf. Gen. 15:18; Exod. 23:31; Deut. 11:24; Josh. 1:4; 2 Sam. 10:16; 1 Kgs. 4:21; Isa. 27:12; Jer. 21:8; Mic. 7:12). The description "beyond the river" (i.e., the Euphrates) designates the Syro-Palestinian region in the postexilic period in several places (cf. Neh. 2:7, 9; 3:7). See also Isa. 7:20. Other contexts refer to the "rivers" of Egypt (cf. Exod. 7:19; 8:5; Isa. 19:5), Damascus (cf. 2 Kgs. 5:12), as well as various others mentioned in 2 Kgs. 17:6; Ezra 8:15; Ezek. 1:1; Dan. 10:14. General, non-specific references to "rivers" include those in Job 40:23; Pss. 24:2; 105:41; Ezek. 32:14.

nāhār is also used metaphorically in Isa. 66:12, referring to the manifestation of peace "like a river."

nehar **[נְהַר, 5103** (Aramaic)**]**

nehar is the Aramaic equivalent of ***nāhār*** (see above), found fifteen times meaning "river," or "stream." It refers primarily to the postexilic region of Syro-Palestine as "the province beyond the river" (cf. Ezra 4:10ff.; 5:3ff.; 6:6ff.; 7:21ff.). It is also used metaphorically in Dan. 7:10 to refer to the "stream" of fire coming from the throne of God in Daniel's vision.

ye'ôr **[יְאוֹר, 2975]**

This noun, thought to be of Egyptian origin, is found in approximately sixty contexts, meaning "river" in virtually every occurrence. ***ye'ôr*** refers almost exclusively to the Nile River in Egypt (cf. Gen. 41:1ff.; Exod. 1:22; 2:3ff.; 7:15ff.; 8:3ff.; Ps. 78:44; Jer. 46:7ff.; Ezek. 29:3ff.; Zech. 10:11). It also refers to the rivers of Egypt in general terms (2 Kgs. 19:24; Isa. 7:18; 37:25). Other general references to "rivers" are found in Isa. 33:21; Dan. 12:5ff.

naḥal **[נַחַל, 5158]**

This noun is a synonym for the above terms. ***naḥal*** is found in about forty contexts meaning "brook," "river," "valley." In the case of the latter meaning, a river valley is most often in view. (→ VALLEY)

General references to "river(s)" include those in Lev. 11:9ff.; Judg. 4:7, 13; 1 Kgs. 8:65; Ps. 83:9; Eccl. 1:7; Isa. 27:12.

Ps. 78:20 refers to "streams" (of water) flowing from rocks in the wilderness (cf. also Isa. 35:6).

naḥal also refers to a "brook" (i.e., a small stream) in 1 Kgs. 2:37; 17:3ff.; 2 Kgs. 23:6, 12; Ps. 110:7.

naḥal is used metaphorically in Ps. 36:8, referring to the "river" of God's delights. A "gushing stream" is likened to a fountain of wisdom (Prov. 18:4); and also to righteousness (Amos 5:24). The breath of Yahweh is likened to an "overflowing stream" in Isa. 30:28 (cf. also 30:33). Lam. 2:18 refers to tears of anguish flowing down the faces of God's people "like a stream."

In Ezek. 47:5ff., ***naḥal*** refers to the river flowing out from under the temple and rejuvenating all the land through which it flows.

peleg **[פֶּלֶג, 6388]**

peleg is another term for "river," or "stream," found in ten contexts.

Literal references to "streams" of water are found in Ps. 1:3; Prov. 5:16; 21:1; Isa. 30:25; 32:2. Rivers provided by God for the nourishment of the earth are mentioned in Ps. 65:9. "Streams" of tears are noted in Ps. 119:136; Lam. 3:48. ***peleg*** also refers metaphorically to "streams" of oil (Job 29:6); and to the river flowing into the heavenly city of God (Ps. 46:4).

'āphîq **[אָפִיק, 650]**

This noun occurs in nineteen contexts and refers to a "river" or "stream" in around half of these. The remaining occurrences of ***'āphîq*** refer to "valleys" or "ravines" through which rivers flow. (→ VALLEY)

Literal references to "rivers," "springs," or "streams" are found in Pss. 42:1; 126:4; Song 5:12; Ezek. 31:12; 32:6; 34:13; Joel 1:20.

NT WORDS

potamos **[ποταμός, *4215*]**

potamos is a noun found in sixteen places meaning "river," "flood," or "stream" in each of these contexts. General references to "river(s)" are found in Acts 16:13; 2 Cor. 11:26; Mark 1:5.

potamos is used metaphorically in John 7:38, where "rivers" of living water refer to the blessing of eternal peace and satisfaction. Rivers are also mentioned in the apocalyptic visions of Rev. 8:10; 9:14; 12:15ff.; 16:4. The "river" of the water of life is noted in Rev. 22:1, 2.

ROAD → WAY

ROAR

OT WORDS

rā'am **[רָעַם, 7481]**

rā'am is a verb found in twenty-three contexts with the primary metaphorical sense "to thunder," "roar," in relation both to Yahweh and the sea.

In relation to the sea, ***rā'am*** describes the thundering roar made by these vast bodies of water (cf. 1 Chr. 16:32; Pss. 96:11; 98:7).

rā'am also refers to the "roaring" of Yahweh, indicating the action of shouting aloud or roaring like a lion (cf. 1 Sam. 2:10; 7:10; 2 Sam. 22:14; Job 37:4ff.; Pss. 18:13; 29:3).

hāmāh **[הָמָה, 1993]**

hāmāh is a verb occurring around thirty times with a variety of meanings, expressing the underlying sense of making a loud noise in a number of contexts. One of these strands of meaning is "roar," "be in uproar."

"To be in uproar" refers to tumultuous confusion in 1 Kgs. 1:41; Ps. 83:2; Isa. 22:2; 51:15.

The sound of the sea "roaring" is noted in Ps. 46:3; Isa. 17:12; Jer. 6:23; 31:35; 50:42; 51:55.

shā'ag **[שָׁאַג, 7580]**

This verb occurs around twenty times with the primary meaning "to roar" in relation to lions.

The literal sense of lions roaring is indicated in Judg. 14:5; Ps. 104:21; Jer. 2:15. People are described as roaring like lions in Pss. 22:13; 74:4; Isa. 5:29; Jer. 51:38; Ezek. 22:25; Zeph. 3:3.

Yahweh is also described as "roaring," expressing his anger and judgment against sin (cf. Job 37:4; Jer. 25:30; Hos. 11:10; Joel 3:16; Amos 1:2; 3:4, 8).

she'āgāh **[שְׁאָגָה, 7581]**

she'āgāh is a noun derived from ***shā'ag*** (see above). It is found in seven contexts, all with the sense of "roaring."

Roaring in the sense of emitting loud groans of anguish is indicated in Job 3:24; Pss. 22:1; 32:3.

Job 4:10 refers literally to the roaring of lions. And the sound of a lion "roaring" is described in Isa. 5:29; Zech. 11:3. Ezek. 19:7 refers to the "roaring" of an attacking army.

nāham **[נָהַם, 5098]**

nāham occurs in five contexts, meaning "to roar" in three of these. All of these occurrences are metaphorical, referring to those who "roar" like lions (cf. Prov. 28:15; Isa. 5:29); and those who "roar" like the sea (cf. Isa. 5:30). In Prov. 5:11; Ezek. 24:23, ***nāham*** refers to "loud groaning" in the context of mourning or anguish.

naham **[נַהַם, 5099]**

naham is a noun derived from ***nāham*** (see above), meaning "roaring" in both of its occurrences. Prov. 19:12; 20:2 refer to the wrath of a king as being like the roaring of a lion.

nehāmāh **[נְהָמָה, 5100]**

nehāmāh is a synonym for ***naham*** (see above), found only twice and referring metaphorically to the roaring of the sea in Isa. 5:30 and to the tumultuous "roar" of the heart of the psalmist in Ps. 38:8 in the midst of his anguish.

—— NT WORDS ——

mykaomai [μυκάομαι, *3455*]

mykaomai is a verb found only in Rev. 10:3, referring to the loud voice of an angel, which is likened to the "roaring" of a lion.

ēcheō [ἠχέω, *2278*]

This verb is found in two places. Luke 21:25 refers to the "roaring" of the sea; and 1 Cor. 13:1 describes an undefined "noisy" gong.

ōryomai [ὠρύομαι, *5612*]

ōryomai is a verb found only in 1 Pet. 5:8 as a simile, referring to the devil prowling around like a "roaring" lion.

ROB, ROBBERY

—— OT WORDS ——

shakkûl **[שַׁכּוּל, 7909]**

shakkûl is an adjective found in six places with the underlying sense of "bereaved." Two of these contexts refer to a bear "robbed" of her cubs (cf. 2 Sam. 17:8; Prov. 17:12).

pārîṣ **[פָּרִיץ, 6530]**

pārîṣ is a noun found six times, with the fundamental sense of "one who is violent." The term is translated "robber" in Jer. 7:11, referring to profaning the Jerusalem temple as a "den of robbers." A similar implication is indicated in Ezek. 7:22.

—— NT WORDS ——

sylaō [συλάω, *4813*]

sylaō is found only in 2 Cor. 11:8 with reference to Paul metaphorically "robbing" churches by accepting support from them.

lēstēs [λῃστής, *3027*]

lēstēs is a term found in fifteen places meaning "robber," "thief."

Jesus refers to the profaning of the temple in Matt. 21:13; Mark 11:17; Luke 19:46 (cf. also Jer. 7:11). He describes it as a "den of robbers," because of the corrupt activity of those conducting business in the outer court.

General references to "robbers" include those in Matt. 26:55; Luke 10:30ff.; John 10:1, 8; 2 Cor. 11:26.

kleptēs [κλέπτης, *2812*]

This noun occurs sixteen times, meaning "thief" or "robber" (cf. Matt. 6:19ff.; Luke 12:33; John 10:1; 1 Cor. 6:10; 1 Pet. 4:15). In Rev. 3:3; 16:15, the return of Christ is described as being "like a thief."

See Also: → DESTROY → SPOIL → STEAL

ROBE

OT Words

'adderet **[אַדֶּרֶת, 155]**

'adderet is a noun that occurs twelve times with the underlying sense of a "garment," or item of clothing, usually a "robe," "cloak," or "mantle" (cf. Gen. 25:25; 1 Kgs. 19:13, 19; Jonah 3:6; Zech. 13:4).

NT Words

chlamys [χλαμύς, *5511*]

chlamys is found only twice, referring to the scarlet "robe" draped around Christ by the Roman soldiers prior to his crucifixion, in mockery of his claim to be King of the Jews (cf. Matt. 27:28, 31).

See Also: → CLOTHING

ROCK

OT Words

ṣûr **[צוּר, 6697]**

ṣûr is a noun found approximately eighty times with the primary sense of "rock," in addition to a variety of nuances, in a number of different contexts. It is used both literally and figuratively.

ṣûr refers to a "rock" as the site of a theophany in Exod. 33:21ff.; Judg. 6:21. ***ṣûr*** also refers to the "rock" at Horeb/Sinai from which Yahweh miraculously provided water for his people in the wilderness (cf. Exod. 17:6; Deut. 8:15; Ps. 78:20; Isa. 48:21).

In metaphorical contexts, ***ṣûr*** refers to Yahweh as the "Rock" — a divine name symbolizing God's function as savior, redeemer, and refuge (cf. Deut. 32:4, 15, 18, 30ff.; 1 Sam. 2:2; 2 Sam. 22:3, 32, 47; 23:3; Pss. 18:31, 46; 28:1; 61:2ff.; 78:35; 89:26; 92:15; 94:22; 95:1; Isa. 17:10). In contrast, Yahweh is a "rock of offense" to his people who reject him. This rejection leads to their destruction (cf. Isa. 8:14). The term "rock" is also found in Deut. 32:37 with reference to pagan gods.

General references to "rock" include those in Num. 23:9; 1 Sam. 24:2; Ps. 27:5; Prov. 30:9; Isa. 2:9.

sela' **[סֶלַע, 5553]**

sela' is a synonym for ***ṣûr*** (see above), occurring sixty times and meaning "rock." It is also used both literally and figuratively.

sela' refers to the "rock" in the wilderness that miraculously yielded water for God's people (cf. Num. 20:8ff.; Neh. 9:15; Ps. 78:16). Judg. 6:20 refers to a rock as the site of a theophany.

General references to "rocks" include those in Judg. 15:8ff.; 1 Sam. 23:25; Ps. 137:9; Isa. 2:21; Jer. 5:3.

As with ***ṣûr*** above, ***sela'*** also refers to Yahweh as the "Rock," the savior, redeemer, and refuge for his people (cf. 2 Sam. 22:2; Pss. 18:2; 31:3; 42:9; 71:3).

kēph **[כֵּף, 3710]**

kēph is a noun used only in the plural. It is found twice, referring literally to "rocks" (cf. Jer. 4:29; Job 30:6).

NT Words

petra [πέτρα, *4073*]

petra is the principal term for "rock" in the New Testament, found in sixteen contexts.

General references to rocks are found in Matt. 7:24ff.; Mark 15:46; Luke 6:48; Rev. 6:15, 16.

In significant theological contexts, ***petra*** is used, for example, as the name "Rock." Christ takes this title in Matt. 16:18, thereby affirming his divine nature as the foundation of the new covenant church. Christ is also described as the "rock of offense" to unbelievers in Rom. 9:33; 1 Pet. 2:8 — citing the same title used for Yahweh in Isa. 8:14, and indicating the same fate for unbelievers. ***petra*** also refers to Christ as the "Rock" in 1 Cor. 10:4, where Paul identifies Christ as that same "rock" that provided water for Israel in the wilderness.

trachys [τραχύς, *5138*]

This noun is found in only two places, referring to the rocky shoreline where the ship in which Paul was sailing en route to Rome was wrecked (Acts 27:29). In Luke 3:5, ***trachys*** refers to "rough ways (or roads)," indicating a rocky, stony surface.

Additional Notes

The most significant aspect of the vocabulary for "rock" in both Old and New Testaments is the way in which the terms are used as titles for both Yahweh and Christ.

In relation to Yahweh, the title "Rock" connotes all that is ultimately strong, secure, and safe about the person of God. This title is found in contexts where God's people affirm their trust in him in situations of dire need and trauma.

When one turns to the New Testament terminology for "rock," ***petra,*** there is a clear link between the persons of Yahweh and Christ. By attributing the titles "Rock" and "rock of offense" to Christ, the New Testament writers are affirming the divinity of the messianic Son of God. There is no greater hope for new covenant believers in Christ than to know that their ultimate hope, salvation, security, and refuge is found in him alone, in Christ their "Rock."

ROD → SCEPTER

ROLL

OT Words

gālal **[גָּלַל, 1556]**

This verb is found in eighteen contexts, meaning "to roll" in a variety of senses. ***gālal*** is used both literally and metaphorically.

Literally, ***gālal*** refers to rolling a stone (1 Sam. 14:33; Prov. 26:27); rolling away a stone from the mouth of a well (Gen. 29:3ff.); rolling a stone against the mouth of a cave (Josh. 10:18); and also to "rolling" a garment in blood (Isa. 9:5).

Metaphorically, ***gālal*** refers to "rolling away reproach or shame" (Josh. 5:9); to letting justice "roll down" like a stream (Amos 5:24); to Yahweh "rolling down" a mountain as an aspect of his judgment against the kingdom of Babylon (Jer. 51:25); and to the heavens being "rolled together" like a scroll, constituting an apocalyptic image of cosmic disintegration (Isa. 34:4).

pālash **[פָּלַשׁ, 6428]**

pālash is a verb found in only five contexts, meaning "roll," or "wallow," and referring exclusively to repentance. The ritual of rolling or wallowing in ashes is described in Jer. 6:26; 25:34; Ezek. 27:30. Mic. 1:10 refers twice to rolling in dust as an expression of sorrow for sin.

NT Words

apokyliō **[ἀποκυλίω, *617*]**

This term refers exclusively to "rolling away (or back)" the stone across the entrance of the tomb where Christ's body was placed. ***apokyliō*** is found only in Matt. 28:2; Mark 16:3, 4; Luke 24:2.

proskyliō **[προσκυλίω, *4351*]**

proskyliō is a verb related to ***apokyliō***, above, meaning "roll towards." It is found only twice, with reference to "rolling" the stone across the entrance to the tomb containing the body of Christ (cf. Matt. 27:60; Mark 15:46).

helissō **[ἑλίσσω, *1507*]**

helissō is a verb found only in Rev. 6:14, indicating the symbolic process of the heavens and earth vanishing like a scroll that is "rolled up."

ROOF

OT Words

qûrāh **[קוֹרָה, 6982]**

qûrāh is a noun found in only five contexts. It refers to the "roof" of a house in Gen. 19:8. In the remaining contexts ***qûrāh*** means "beam," in relation to the construction of a building.

gāg **[גָּג, 1406]**

gāg is found thirty times, meaning "roof," "rooftop." It usually refers to the "roofs" of houses (cf. Deut. 22:8; 1 Sam. 9:25ff.; Neh. 8:16; Ps. 102:7; Prov. 25:24; Jer. 19:13). The roof of a Philistine temple is indicated in Judg. 16:27, and the roof of Ezekiel's visionary temple in Ezek. 40:13.

ḥēk **[חֵךְ, 2441]**

This term occurs eighteen times with the primary meaning "mouth." In five places, however, it refers to the "roof of the mouth" (cf. Job 29:10; Ps. 137:6; Song 7:9; Lam. 4:4; Ezek. 3:26). (→ MOUTH)

NT Words

stegē **[στέγη, *4721*]**

stegē is found in only three places, referring to the "roof" of a house (cf. Matt. 8:8; Mark 2:4; Luke 7:6).

ROOM

OT Words

māqôm **[מָקוֹם, 4725]**

māqôm is a common noun found around four hundred times with the primary meaning "place." In three contexts it means "room," all with reference to "space" in one's house (cf. Gen. 24:23, 25, 31). (→ PLACE)

rāḥab **[רָחַב, 7337]**

rāḥab is a verb found twenty-five times, meaning "to enlarge." In two places ***rāḥab*** expresses the sense of "make room, or space (for)" (cf. Gen. 26:22; Prov. 8:16).

qēn **[קֵן, 7064]**

qēn is a noun found in thirteen contexts meaning "nest" in all instances except Gen. 6:14, where it refers to "rooms" in Noah's ark. (→ NEST)

NT Words

chōreō **[χωρέω, *5562*]**

This verb occurs twelve times, meaning "receive," "contain." In Mark 2:2, however, ***chōreō*** indicates negatively that there is "no room" for any more people to enter the house where Jesus is teaching.

anagaion [ἀνάγαιον, *508*]

anagaion occurs only twice, referring to the "upper room" where Jesus shared the Passover meal with his disciples (cf. Mark 14:15; Luke 22:12).

topos [τόπος, *5117*]

topos is a noun occurring about ninety times, with the dominant sense of "place." But in Luke 14:22 ***topos*** may be translated "room" in the sense of "space" remaining, in relation to the availability of room left for a banquet.

hyperōon [ὑπερῷον, *5253*]

hyperōon is synonymous with ***anagaion*** (see above), referring to the highest part of a house as an "upper room" (cf. Acts 1:13; 9:37, 39; 20:8).

ROOT

OT Words

shōresh [שֹׁרֶשׁ, **8328**]

shōresh is a noun occurring approximately thirty times meaning "root" in both a literal and figurative sense, although the latter emphasis is dominant.

Literal references to the roots of plants and trees include those in Job 8:17; 14:8; 30:4; Isa. 53:2; Jer. 17:8; Ezek. 17:6ff.; 31:7.

Figurative uses of ***shōresh*** are varied: Deut. 29:18 refers to the "'root' of bitterness," indicating a deep-seated attitude of resentment. The expression "take root" refers to the remnant of Judah being firmly established (cf. 2 Kgs. 19:30; Isa. 37:31). Job 28:9 refers to the "roots" of the mountains, or their deepest places.

In specific relation to people, ***shōresh*** indicates the "'root' of the righteous" in Prov. 12:3, 12 as deep-seated virtue. Conversely, the "'root' of the wicked" in Isa. 5:24 indicates a deep-seated vice. This expression is also attributed to the lineage of the serpent, referring to their anticipated condemnation (cf. Isa. 14:29). Isa. 11:1, 10 refer to the "roots" of Jesse, or the messianic branch, indicating the origins of the Messiah in the lineage of the tribe of David. In a more general context, ***shōresh*** refers to "root" in the sense of a people or lineage — for example, the "root" of the Philistines, who are destined for destruction (cf. Isa. 14:30; cf. also Amos 2:9; Mal. 4:1); and the "root" of Israel (Hos. 9:16).

shōrēsh [שֹׁרֵשׁ, **8330** (Aramaic)]

This Aramaic term is identical in form to the above entry. ***shōrēsh*** occurs only three times, referring to the "roots" of the tree stump in Dan. 4:15, 23, 26 in relation to Nebuchadnezzar's royal status and kingdom.

NT Words

rhiza [ῥίζα, *4491*]

rhiza is a Greek dynamic equivalent for the Hebrew ***shōresh*** (see above), found in seventeen contexts and meaning "root" in both a literal and metaphorical sense.

Literal references to "roots" of plants include those in Matt. 3:10; 13:6; Mark 4:6; 11:20; Luke 3:9.

As with the Hebrew term ***shōresh***, ***rhiza*** manifests a varied figurative usage. Rom. 11:16ff., for example, refers to the "root" of the Israelite people as a remnant. The expression "root of Jesse" is mentioned in Rom. 15:12 (cf. Isa. 11:10); and the phrase "root of David" in Rev. 5:5; 22:16. Both expressions refer to the messianic line of promise through the tribe of Judah and allude to the messianic promises of the Old Testament that utilize the same terminology. ***rhiza*** is also found in the expression "root of bitterness," indicating a deep-seated attitude of resentment in Heb. 12:15 (cf. Deut. 29:18). 1 Tim. 6:10 refers to the love of money as the "root of all evil." ***shōresh*** is also used negatively in Matt. 13:21; Mark 4:17; Luke 8:13, referring to people who have "no root," or no permanent, enduring faith or trust in God and his word.

Additional Notes

Of particular significance in the vocabulary for "root," in both Hebrew and Greek, is the metaphorical reference to the tribe and lineage of David. This tribe was chosen by Yahweh to be the carrier of the promised messianic line. The New Testament makes it clear that messianic prophecy is fulfilled in the person of Jesus Christ. The Hebrew noun ***shōresh*** and the Greek term ***rhiza*** may therefore be designated as full "dynamic equivalent" terms, pointing to the phenomenon of the Messiah, anticipated in the old covenant and fulfilled in the new.

See Also: → UPROOT

ROPE → CORD

ROUSE → ARISE

ROYAL

OT Words

mamlākāh **[מַמְלָכָה, 4467]**

mamlākāh occurs around 120 times with the primary sense of "kingdom." In several places, however, it is used adjectivally to mean "royal." (→ KINGDOM)

"Royal" cities are mentioned in Josh. 10:2; 1 Sam. 27:5; and "royal" families in 2 Kgs. 11:1; 2 Chr. 22:10.

melûkāh **[מְלוּכָה, 4410]**

melûkāh is synonymous with ***mamlākāh***, above, occurring twenty-four times and meaning "kingdom" in most of these contexts. However, as with ***mamlākāh***, ***melûkāh*** is also used adjectivally, meaning "royal." (→ KINGDOM)

"Royal" cities are indicated in 2 Sam. 12:26; 2 Kgs. 25:25; Jer. 41:1; and Isa. 62:3 speaks of a "royal" diadem, or crown.

malkût **[מַלְכוּת, 4438]**

malkût is another synonym for the entries above, found approximately ninety times with the predominant sense of "kingdom." ***malkût*** is also used adjectivally to mean "royal."

malkût refers to "royal" majesty (1 Chr. 29:25); the "royal" house of King Xerxes (Esth. 1:9; 2:16; 5:1); the "royal" crown (Esth. 1:11; 2:17); a "royal" decree (Esth. 1:19); and "royal" apparel (Esth. 5:1; 6:8; 8:15).

NT Words

basilikos **[βασιλικός, *937*]**

basilikos is an adjective found in five places with the underlying sense of "belonging to the nobility." It is translated "royal" in Jas. 2:8 with reference to "royal" law, and in Acts 12:21 it refers to "royal" apparel.

basileios **[βασίλειος, *934*]**

basileios is an adjectival form synonymous with ***basilikos***. It occurs only in 1 Pet. 2:9 and refers to the "royal" priesthood of believers.

RULE, RULER

OT Words

māshal **[מָשַׁל, 4910]**

This verb occurs in about seventy contexts, meaning "to rule," "have dominion over" in most places. ***māshal*** is also used nominally, meaning "ruler," or "governor."

As a verb, ***māshal*** is used in a "non-personal" sense in Gen. 1:18, referring to the sun which God created as the greater light "to rule" over the day. And in Ps. 19:13 the psalmist exhorts his readers not to allow sin "to rule" over their lives.

Much more common is the verbal use of ***māshal*** in personal contexts, referring to the exercising of dominion or authority. In a "non-royal" context, a husband is said "to rule over" his wife (Gen. 3:16). In the sphere of managerial authority, a chief steward is said "to rule over" his master's household (cf. Gen. 24:2; Ps. 105:21). The exercise of parental rule in the family is indicated in Prov. 17:21 (cf. also Gen. 37:8). The nation of Israel is said to "rule over" her enemies (Deut. 15:6); and conversely her enemies are said to "rule over" her (Judg. 14:14). Ruling over one's spirit, an expression of self-control, is noted in Prov. 16:32. Exercising dominion over the poor is alluded to in Prov. 22:7; 28:15.

In the context of royal dominion, the ruling activity of kings is indicated in general contexts in Josh. 12:2ff.; Judg. 8:22ff.; 1 Kgs. 4:21; Neh. 9:37; Isa. 14:5; Jer. 51:46; Ezek. 19:14; Dan. 11:3ff. The rule of Judean and Israelite kings is specifically indicated in Isa. 52:5; Jer. 22:30; 30:21. The anticipated reign of the Messianic King is mentioned in Jer. 33:26; Zech. 6:13. 2 Sam. 23:3 refers to ruling in the fear of the Lord.

māshal also indicates the ruling activity of God over creation (Ps. 89:9); over all people and nations (1 Chr. 29:12; 2 Chr. 20:6; Pss. 22:28; 66:7; 103:19; Isa. 40:10); and over Israel (Ps. 59:13).

māshal is used nominally in several places. Joseph is described as "governor" over Egypt (Gen. 45:8, 26). The rulers of the people of Israel are noted in 2 Chr. 7:18; 23:20. Humankind is declared to be "ruler" over creation (Ps. 8:6). The Philistines are declared to be "rulers" over Israel (Judg. 15:11), in the sense of "lords" or "masters." Mic. 5:2 predicts the coming of the messianic ruler. Job 25:2 mentions the rule of God in relation to his dominion and authority.

memshālāh **[מֶמְשָׁלָה, 4475]**

memshālāh is a noun derived from ***māshal*** (see above), occurring seventeen times and meaning "dominion," "rule." The latter meaning is found four times, with ***memshālāh*** employed in a verbal sense, referring figuratively to the sun and moon as the greater and lesser lights "to rule" the day and night, respectively (cf. Gen. 1:16 [twice]; Ps. 136:8, 9).

mimshāl **[מִמְשָׁל, 4474]**

mimshāl is another noun derived from ***māshal*** (see above), found only three times. It means "rulers" in

1 Chr. 26:6 with probable reference to the "chief stewards" of their masters' household estates.

shālat [שָׁלַט, **7980**]

shālat is a verb found eight times, with the primary meanings "to rule" or "exercise dominion (over)."

shālat refers to God's rule over his people in Neh. 5:15. Esth. 9:1 affirms that the people of God in captivity "exercised dominion" over their enemies in their successful counterattack against the Persian plot to annihilate them. In Ps. 119:133, the psalmist pleads that sin "will not have dominion" over him. See also Eccl. 2:19; 8:9.

shelēt [שְׁלֵט, **7981** (Aramaic)]

shelēt is the Aramaic equivalent of ***shālat*** (see above). It is found in seven places and means "to rule," "make, appoint a ruler."

In Dan. 2:38, Nebuchadnezzar declares that the God of Israel makes rulers of men, who are then said to "rule over" the earth (Dan. 2:39).

The process of "appointing a ruler" is indicated in Dan. 2:48; 5:7, 16 with respect to Daniel's promotion to "governor" over the kingdom of Babylon.

shelēt also means "to have mastery over," "to overpower" (Dan. 6:24).

shallît [שַׁלִּיט, **7990** (Aramaic)]

shallît is an Aramaic adjectival form that has both a verbal and a nominal force. It occurs ten times and means "to rule," "ruler," "officer," "governor."

"Ruling" as kings is indicated in Ezek. 4:20; Dan. 2:10. Daniel is referred to as a "governor" in Dan. 5:29, and mention is made of the king's "officer" in Dan. 2:15.

Dan. 4:17 affirms that God "rules" the kingdoms of human beings.

rādāh [רָדָה, **7287**]

rādāh is a verb found approximately thirty times meaning "to rule," "have dominion over," "have charge of," similar to the entries above. The term refers predominantly to human dominion.

Gen. 1:26ff. refers to humankind having charge of creation. In relation to slaves, Lev. 25:43ff. expresses the command "not to rule" them harshly. Israel is said "to rule" over her enemies (Isa. 14:2); and, in contrast, her enemies are said to "rule over" her as part of the enactment of the divine covenant curse against Israel (cf. Lev. 26:17; Neh. 9:28). Jer. 5:31; Ezek. 34:4 refer to corrupt priestly and civil dominion over the Israelite people. In Ps. 110:2, the psalmist records the divine command to the Messiah-King to rule his people. See also Num. 24:19; 1 Kgs. 4:24; Ps. 72:8; Ezek. 29:5.

rādāh means "to have charge of" in relation to hired workers in 1 Kgs. 5:16; 9:23; 2 Chr. 8:10.

sārar [שָׂרַר, **8323**]

sārar is a verb found in five contexts meaning "to rule," "make oneself a ruler." The latter sense is found in Num. 16:13 (twice). Esth. 1:22 refers to men "being the ruler" in their own homes. General references to "ruling" activity are found in Prov. 8:16; Isa. 32:1.

sar [שַׂר, **8269**]

sar is a common noun derived from ***sārar*** (see above). It occurs over four hundred times with the underlying meaning "one who rules or who has royal, military, civil, or ritual authority," including some references to divine and demonic authorities. Meanings include "ruler," "leader," "chief," "prince." It is difficult to precisely distinguish these various meanings with any degree of certainty, even though the foundational sense of the term is not in doubt.

The term "prince" is used as a general title for a "commander-in-chief," for example, in Gen. 12:15; Exod. 2:14; Num. 22:8ff.; Judg. 7:25; 8:3ff.; 1 Kgs. 9:22; 1 Chr. 19:3. In Isa. 9:6, the title "prince of peace" is applied to the coming messianic child of promise. The titles "prince of the host" (Dan. 8:11) and "prince of princes" (Dan. 8:24) refer to the person of Yahweh. In contrast, the designations "prince of Persia" (Dan. 10:13, 20) and "prince of Greece" (Dan. 10:20) refer to demonic spirit beings who superintend the destiny of those kingdoms. Michael, the "prince of Israel," is specifically indicated as the angelic protector of the people of God (Dan. 10:13, 21).

General references to "rulers" in an unspecified sense include those in Exod. 18:21; Ps. 45:16; Eccl. 10:7; Isa. 19:11; Hos. 3:4; Amos 1:15.

sar also indicates the sense of Israelite military "rulers," referred to as "captains," or "chiefs" (cf. Gen. 21:32; Num. 31:4; Judg. 4:7; 1 Sam. 8:12; Ezra 7:28; Jer. 17:25). Specific mention is made of David's military "leaders" in 1 Chr. 12:21, 34; 13:1; 11:6, 21; 27:1ff.; including Joab (cf. 2 Sam. 24:2; 1 Kgs. 1:19). See also 2 Kgs. 5:1; Esth. 1:3ff.; 2:18.

Civil leaders, rulers, or commanders in Israel are also included in the usage of ***sar*** (cf. Deut. 1:15; 1 Kgs. 5:16; 20:14ff.; Ezra 9:1). In a number of contexts, such leaders or rulers are described as corrupt (cf. Isa. 1:23;

Jer. 1:18; 34:10ff.; Ezek. 11:1; 17:12; Hos. 5:10). Esth. 1:3ff. refers to a similar class of officials in Persia. Other royal "officials" in a non-military context are noted in Gen. 40:2ff.; 47:6. In Babylon, such officials are probably to be understood as "eunuchs" (cf. Dan. 1:7ff.).

In the ceremonial sphere, Israelite levitical "leaders" or "officers" are mentioned in 1 Kgs. 4:2; 1 Chr. 15:5ff.; 24:5ff.; 25:1; Ezra 8:20ff.; 10:5; Ps. 68:21.

In the context of a theophany, ***sar*** refers in Josh. 5:14ff. to the "commander" of the Lord's host — clearly the angel of the Lord.

nāśî' [נָשִׂיא, 5387]

nāśî' is synonymous with ***sar*** (see above), though not as common, and found approximately 130 times. It, too, has a similar underlying sense of "one who is entrusted with authority in ritual, civil, and military matters." Translations include "prince," "captain," "ruler," "chief." Again, it is very difficult to precisely identify its meaning in every instance. ***nāśî'*** also refers to the coming messianic ruler of Israel.

References to the "prince" as one who has marked authority in governing a nation are found in Gen. 17:20; 25:16; Ezek. 7:27; 30:13; 32:29; 39:18. The meaning "prince" also applies to the office of "king" in Ezek. 12:10ff., with reference to Zedekiah, the last king of Israel. Other general references to the "princes" (i.e., kings) of Israel may be found in Ezek. 19:1; 21:12, 25. Gog, the chief "prince" of Meshech, is referred to in Ezek. 38:2ff.; 39:1. Ezek. 34:24; 37:25 refer metaphorically to the messianic ruler as a "prince," coming from the lineage of David. More specifically, the title "prince" is given to the mysterious messianic ruler of Israel depicted in Ezekiel's vision of the renewed temple and land (cf. Ezek. 44:3; 45:7, 16ff.; 46:2ff.).

nāśî' also refers to the civil leaders or rulers of Israel (Exod. 16:22; 34:31; Lev. 4:22; Num. 16:2; 25:14; Josh. 9:15ff.; 1 Kgs. 8:1). Ezra 1:8 mentions the "prince" or "governor" of Judah.

Tribal "leaders," "chiefs," or "princes" of Israel are noted in Num. 1:16, 44; 2:3ff.; 7:2ff.; 10:4; Josh. 22:14. Bedouin tribal "chiefs" may also be indicated in Ezek. 27:21.

nāśî' also refers to Levitical "leaders" or "rulers" (cf. Num. 3:24ff.; 4:34, 46).

nāgîd [נָגִיד, 5057]

nāgîd is another term indicating the general sense of "one who exercises civil, political, or military authority." It occurs around forty times and is commonly translated "ruler," "prince," "leader," with other associated senses, in most of its approximately forty occurrences.

The meaning "ruler," or "prince," in the sense of a military leader, is indicated in a number of contexts. Referring to Saul, ***nāgîd*** is a synonym for "king," as it is elsewhere for David and others. However, ***nāgîd*** in the following contexts suggests Saul as one who has been called to function as a military deliverer much like the judges. Samuel, as the last of the judges, brings this era to a close and is chosen by God to anoint Saul as the first king of Israel (cf. 1 Sam. 9:16; 10:1; 13:14; 2 Sam. 5:2). A similar designation is given to David (1 Sam. 25:30; 2 Sam. 6:21; 7:8; 1 Chr. 5:2; Isa. 55:4); and to Solomon (1 Kgs. 1:35). See also 1 Kgs. 14:7; 2 Kgs. 20:5; 1 Chr. 29:22. In other contexts, ***nāgîd*** refers to tribal military leaders in Israel (1 Chr. 13:1; 2 Chr. 28:7); and to Assyrian "officers" (2 Chr. 32:21).

nāgîd also refers to "chief officers" or "leading officials" of the Levites in 1 Chr. 9:11, 20; 12:27; 26:24; 27:4; 2 Chr. 19:11; 31:12; Neh. 11:11; Jer. 20:1.

The meaning "ruler(s)," "prince(s)" in a general sense is indicated in Ps. 76:12; Prov. 28:16; 2 Chr. 11:1. In particular, Ezek. 28:2 mentions the "prince" of Tyre. The title "prince of the covenant" is noted in Dan. 11:22. The identity of this figure cannot be precisely determined — two possible candidates are the Jewish high priest, Onias III, and Ptolemy IV of Egypt. In Dan. 9:25, however, the title "prince" most likely indicates the messianic ruler linked to the person of Jesus Christ. In contrast, Dan. 9:26 refers to another "prince," who is most likely a pagan king.

rāzan [רָזַן, 7336]

rāzan is a verb found six times with a nominal usage, meaning "prince," "ruler" in general contexts (cf. Judg. 5:3; Ps. 2:2; Prov. 8:15; 31:4; Isa. 40:23; Hab. 1:10).

qāṣîn [קָצִין, 7101]

qāṣîn is a noun occurring twelve times and meaning "ruler," "leader," "commander" in several different contexts.

Josh. 10:24; Judg. 11:6ff.; Isa. 22:3; Dan. 11:18 refer to the "chief," or "commander," of military forces.

The sense of "leader" or "ruler" in general contexts is evident in Prov. 6:7; 25:15; Isa. 3:6ff. Mic. 3:1, 9 speaks of "rulers" in Israel, referring to civil leaders. Isa. 1:10 refers to the "ruler," or "king," of Sodom.

sāgān [סָגָן, 5461]

sāgān is found in seventeen contexts meaning "ruler," or "governor," and referring primarily to leaders in the civil sphere of government. The leaders of Israel are referred to this way in Ezra 9:2; Neh. 2:16; 4:14, 19; 5:7, 17; 7:5; 12:40; 13:11. Similarly, ***sāgān*** refers to the civil rulers of Media (Jer. 51:28), and of Babylon (Jer. 51:57).

Isa. 41:25 refers to "rulers," or "kings," in general. In several places, ***sāgān*** also denotes "rulers" or "commanders" in the military sphere (cf. Jer. 51:23; Ezek. 23:6, 12, 23).

nāsîk [נָסִיךְ, 5257]

nāsîk is a noun occurring six times, meaning "leader," or "ruler," in most of these contexts. It most likely has the sense of a "military commander" (cf. Josh. 13:21; Ps. 83:11; Ezek. 32:30; Mic. 5:5).

NT WORDS

archō [ἄρχω, *757*]

archō is a verb found in only two places, meaning "to rule over," "reign over." Mark 10:12; Rom. 15:12 refer to ruling over the Gentiles.

archōn [ἄρχων, *758*]

archōn is a participial noun derived from ***archō*** (see above), meaning "ruler," "commander," "chief." The term is found in approximately forty contexts.

The general sense of "ruler" is indicated in Acts 3:17; 4:26; 7:27; Rom. 13:8; 1 Cor. 2:6, 8. Matt. 20:25 mentions the rulers of the Gentiles. Luke 12:58 refers to a "ruler" who is a magistrate (cf. also Luke 18:18).

In the religious or ceremonial sphere, ***archōn*** also denotes a "ruler" of the synagogue, as in the case of Jairus (cf. Matt. 9:18ff.; Luke 8:41). Other likely references to synagogue rulers include those in Luke 23:13, 15; 24:20; John 7:48; 12:42; Acts 4:5ff.; 13:27. Luke 14:1 refers to a "ruler" of the Pharisees.

archōn refers to Satan as the "ruler," or "prince," of demons (Matt. 9:34; 12:24; Mark 3:22; Luke 11:15; Eph. 2:2). The title "ruler of this world" is also applied to Satan in John 12:31; 14:30; 16:11.

archōn refers to Christ as "the ruler" of kings in Rev. 1:5.

politarchēs [πολιτάρχης, *4173*]

politarchēs is found only in Acts 17:6, 8, with reference to the "ruler of the city."

poimainō [ποιμαίνω, *4165*]

poimainō is a verb meaning to "feed" or "tend" (animals) in the majority of its eleven occurrences. However, in several of these places, ***poimainō*** means "rule" or "govern." (→ FEED)

Matt. 2:6 refers to the one who will come to "govern" the people of God (i.e., Christ). Rev. 2:21 speaks of the "rule" of Christ in the heavenly kingdom. Rev. 12:5; 19:15 refer to the universal rule of Christ over all nations — a reign characterized by the use of a rod of iron.

proistēmi [προΐστημι, *4291*]

proistēmi is a verb found in eight contexts, meaning "rule," "govern," "watch, or preside over" in most of these.

Rom. 12:8 mentions ruling as a leader in an unspecified way. 1 Thess. 5:12; 1 Tim. 5:17 speak of the "ruling" function of pastors and elders in the church, as those who "watch over" the congregation of God's people. The responsibility of "governing" one's household is affirmed in 1 Tim. 3:4ff., 12.

kathistēmi [καθίστημι, *2525*]

kathistēmi is a verb occurring about twenty times and meaning "to appoint as a ruler," "to watch over" in several of these contexts.

The sense of "to appoint as a ruler" is indicated in Matt. 24:45ff.; 25:21ff.; Luke 12:42ff., all of which refer to a servant placed in authority over his master's household. Acts 7:10 refers to Joseph being appointed as "governor" of Egypt. A general reference to this action is found in Acts 7:27, 35.

hēgeomai [ἡγέομαι, *2233*]

hēgeomai is found in approximately thirty contexts with the primary meanings "think," "consider." However, in several places, the term is used nominally to refer to a "ruler," or "governor."

Luke 22:26 mentions a "leader" or "ruler" in a general sense. Matt. 2:6 refers to the messianic "ruler" of the people of God. Acts 7:10 refers to Joseph as a "governor," or "ruler," of Egypt. In the context of congregational leadership, Heb. 13:7, 17, 24 refer to elders as those "having authority" or "ruling" over their churches.

hēgemōn [ἡγεμών, *2232*]

hēgemōn is a participial noun derived from ***hēgeomai*** (see above), meaning "ruler" or "governor."

The general meaning "ruler," referring to the "kings" of Judah, is indicated in Matt. 2:6.

More commonly, ***hēgemōn*** means "governor." General references to this office are found in Matt. 10:18; Mark 13:9; Luke 21:12; 1 Pet. 2:14. In particular, Matt. 27:2ff.; 28:14; Luke 20:20 refer to Pilate as Roman "governor" of Judea. Felix, one of Pilate's successors, is likewise referred to by his official title of "governor" in Acts 23:24ff.; 24:1.

brabeuō [βραβεύω, *1018*]

This verb is used figuratively and found only in Col. 3:15 in the exhortation: "Let the peace of Christ 'rule' in your hearts." Here ***brabeuō*** expresses the underlying sense of "having the role of greatest influence."

archisynagōgos [ἀρχισυνάγωγος, *752*]

archisynagōgos is found in nine places, meaning "ruler of the synagogue" (cf. Mark 5:22, 35ff.; Luke 8:49; 13:14ff.; Acts 18:8, 17).

kosmokratōr [κοσμοκράτωρ, *2888*]

kosmokratōr is a noun found only in Eph. 6:12, referring to the demonic "rulers" of the present dark age, or spiritual powers of darkness, satanic "authorities" arrayed in opposition against heavenly, angelic "rulers."

See Also: → STANDARD

RUMOR

NT Words

akoē [ἀκοη, *189*]

akoē is a noun found in approximately twenty-five contexts with the fundamental sense of "hearing." It is derived from the verb ***akouō*** and is variously translated as "hearing," "news," "fame," "report," "rumor." (→ HEAR → REPORT)

The meaning "rumor" indicates essentially the same sense as "report," though with the less formal nuance of "hearsay." This usage is illustrated in Matt. 24:6; Mark 13:7, in the context of Jesus' discourse on the signs of the end times where he warns that there will be, among other things, "wars and rumors of war."

See Also: → REPORT

RUN

OT Words

rûṣ [רוּץ, 7323]

rûṣ is a verb that occurs about one hundred times and means "to run" — primarily in the literal, physical sense.

rûṣ indicates the physical action of running in Gen. 18:2ff.; 20:6; 2 Sam. 15:1; 1 Kgs. 18:4; Ps. 19:5; Isa. 40:31; Joel 2:7; Zech. 2:4. The meaning "run away (from)" is indicated in Jer. 49:9; 50:44. Horses are also described as "running" in Amos 6:12. The nations are described in Isa. 55:5 as "running" (i.e., hurrying) towards Yahweh and his people.

rûṣ is also used nominally, meaning "messenger," or "courier," in Job 9:25; Esth. 3:13, 15; 8:10, 14; Jer. 51:31.

Several metaphorical expressions are also associated with this term. Ps. 119:32 speaks of "running" in the path of God's laws (i.e., living a life of obedience). Ps. 147:15 describes God's word as "running" swiftly on the earth (i.e., is swiftly communicated). In Prov. 1:16; Isa. 59:7, wicked people are said "to run" to evil.

shût [שׁוּט, 7751]

shût is a verb found in thirteen contexts, meaning "to run to and fro" in the majority of these.

The underlying sense of this term is that of searching out or investigating. It is applied anthropomorphically to the eyes of God in 2 Chr. 16:9; Zech. 4:10, which are said to run to and fro over the whole earth. It is also predicated of Satan (Job 1:7; 2:2), who is said "to have been roaming to and fro" throughout the earth. The prophet Jeremiah is commanded by God to "run throughout" Jerusalem in search of any person who practices justice (cf. Jer. 5:1). Dan. 12:4; Amos 8:12 refer to people in search of knowledge.

ḥay [חַי, 2416]

ḥay is an adjectival form with the predominant senses of "live," "alive," "living" throughout its nearly five hundred occurrences. (→ LIFE)

In several places, however, ***ḥay*** refers to "running" water in the sense of water that is "fresh" and "flowing" or, metaphorically speaking, "living" water (cf. Lev. 14:5, 6, 50ff.; 15:13; 19:17).

merûṣāh [מְרוּצָה, 4794]

merûṣāh is a noun derived from ***rûṣ*** (see above), found in only four places. It refers to the action of running in 2 Sam. 18:27 (twice). In Jer. 8:6; 23:10, ***merûṣāh*** indicates a literal "running course, or track," but in fact refers to a lifestyle that is evil.

rewāyāh [רְוָיָה, 7310]

rewāyāh is a rare noun, found only in Ps. 23:5 with reference to one's cup "running over" (i.e., overflowing).

NT Words

trechō [τρέχω, *5143*]

trechō is a verb found in twenty contexts, meaning "to run" in most of these. It also has a number of derivative forms (see below).

The literal, physical action of running is indicated in Matt. 27:48; 28:8; Mark 5:6; 15:36; Luke 15:20; 24:12; John 20:2ff.; 1 Cor. 9:24ff.

The meaning "rush" is also indicated in Rev. 9:9, referring to horses rushing headlong into battle.

trechō also has a figurative sense in Gal. 2:2; 5:7; Phil. 2:16; Heb. 12:1, with reference to "running" the race. In these contexts, the metaphorical allusion is to the goal of maintaining one's faith in Christ throughout the whole course of life.

prostrechō [προστρέχω, *4370*]

prostrechō is a variant form of ***trechō***, above, meaning "run towards, up to." It is found only in Mark 9:15; 10:17; Acts 8:30.

episyntrechō [ἐπισυντρέχω, *1998*]

episyntrechō occurs only in Mark 9:25 with the sense of "run together," referring to a crowd.

hypotrechō [ὑποτρέχω, *5295*]

hypotrechō is a verb meaning "to run under the lee." It occurs only in Acts 27:16 in a nautical context, referring to a boat sailing past a shoreline protected from the wind.

syntrechō [συντρέχω, *4936*]

syntrechō is found in only three places, meaning "to run together" in a literal sense in Mark 6:33; Acts 3:11. In 1 Pet. 4:4, the term means "to join together" in the context of participating in a lifestyle — in this case a profligate one.

peritrechō [περιτρέχω, *4063*]

peritrechō is found only in Mark 6:55, meaning "to run through" a neighboring vicinity.

protrechō [προτρέχω, *4390*]

protrechō means "to outrun," "run ahead of," and is found only in Luke 19:4; John 20:4.

eistrechō [εἰστρέχω, *1532*]

eistrechō occurs only in Acts 12:14, meaning "to run" in a directional sense.

katatrechō [κατατρέχω, *2701*]

katatrechō means "to run down" (i.e., towards). It is found only in Acts 21:32.

hyperekchynnō [ὑπερεκχύννω, *5240*]

hyperekchynnō occurs only in Luke 6:38 meaning "to run over," referring generally to the "overflowing" of a measured portion (e.g., of grain).

hormaō [ὁρμάω, *3729*]

hormaō is a verb expressing the sense of "run, or rush violently (together)." It is found in five contexts. Matt. 8:32; Mark 5:13; Luke 8:33 refer to a herd of pigs "rushing headlong" over a cliff to their death, drowning in the ocean. Acts 7:57; 19:29 refer to the violent rushing of a crowd.

epikellō [ἐπικέλλω, *2027*]

epikellō is found only in Acts 27:41, referring to a boat that "ran aground" on a rocky shoreline.

S

SABAOTH ➞ GOD

SABBATH

OT Words

shabbāt **[שַׁבָּת, 7676]**

shabbāt is the primary noun derived from ***shābat*** ("to cease, rest"). ***shabbāt*** occurs around one hundred times with the consistent meaning "Sabbath," referring to the seventh day of rest, consecrated by God at the time of creation. The Sabbath concept was applied not only to days but also to weeks and years, and was enshrined in the Mosaic law covenant as a binding period of mandatory rest from labor. In a redemptive-historical sense, the "Sabbath" day anticipated Israel's "rest" in the land of Canaan and also, ultimately, the heavenly rest of the believer. (➞ REST)

References to the Sabbath as a sacred day (or period) of rest enshrined in the Mosaic law are indicated from several perspectives. Exod. 16:23ff. is in fact a pre-Sinai reference to the requirement of Sabbath observance. The explicit command to observe the Sabbath, in the framework of the Decalogue, is indicated in Exod. 20:8ff.; Deut. 5:12ff.; Neh. 9:14. Other contexts also refer to the command to observe the Sabbath (Exod. 31:13ff.; 35:2ff.; Lev. 16:31; 19:3; 23:3; 26:2; Isa. 56:2ff.; Jer. 17:21ff.; Ezek. 44:24). Violations of Sabbath observance are recorded in Num. 15:32; Neh. 10:31; 13:15; Ezek. 20:12ff.; 23:38; Amos 8:5. Worship on the Sabbath is indicated in Ps. 92:1; Isa. 66:23; Ezek. 46:1ff. Isa. 1:13; Hos. 2:11 refer to corrupt Sabbath worship.

General references to Sabbath observance are found in Lev. 23:11ff.; Num. 28:9ff.; 2 Kgs. 4:23; 11:5ff.; 2 Chr. 2:4; Lam. 2:6.

Lev. 26:34ff.; 2 Chr. 36:21 refer to the land of Israel enjoying its "Sabbath rests" during the seventy-year period of exile, as a compensation for the people's neglect of the Sabbath during their period of occupation.

shabbātôn **[שַׁבָּתוֹן, 7677]**

shabbātôn is a synonym for ***shabbāt*** (see above), occurring eleven times and referring primarily to the "Sabbath rest" that was mandatory under Mosaic law (cf. Exod. 31:15; 35:2; Lev. 16:31; 23:3, 24, 32, 39). Lev. 25:4, 5 refer to the Sabbatical Year of rest prescribed for a plot of land, which must be allowed to lie fallow every seventh year Exod. 16:23 also prescribes "Sabbath rest," although this is a pre-Sinai context.

NT Words

sabbaton **[σάββατον, *4521*]**

sabbaton is the Greek transliteration of the Hebrew ***shabbātôn*** (see above), and it is found in approximately seventy contexts. ***sabbaton*** refers to the "Sabbath day" in the majority of these contexts.

General references to the "Sabbath day" include those in Matt. 24:20; Mark 6:2; 16:1ff.; Luke 23:54; John 5:9ff.; 7:22ff.; Acts 1:12; 1 Cor. 16:2; Col. 2:16.

The remaining usage of ***sabbaton*** focuses on the healing ministry of Jesus, that sometimes took place on the Sabbath, and which drew sharp criticism from the Pharisees. Jesus responded by drawing attention to the Pharisees' own hypocrisy on this issue (cf. Matt. 12:1ff.; Mark 3:2ff.; Luke 6:6ff.; 13:14ff.; 14:3ff.; John 5:16ff.; 9:14ff.). See also Mark 2:23ff.; Luke 6:1ff.; 13:10. Jesus declared himself to be "the Lord of the Sabbath."

Additional Notes

The vocabulary associated with the "Sabbath" in both Old and New Testaments is closely associated with the phenomenon of "rest." (➞ REST)

Jesus' claim to be "Lord of the Sabbath" constitutes an aspect of his divine nature. He self-consciously identifies himself as one who has the right to dictate what is and is not appropriate on this day. Such a prerogative rests within the divine sphere alone. According to the New Testament, the person of Jesus Christ is the consummate embodiment of Sabbath rest — a rest that is found not in a place, but in a person.

SACKCLOTH

OT Words

saq **[שַׂק, 8242]**

saq is a noun referring almost exclusively to "sackcloth" as the traditional ceremonial clothing material associated with mourning or humiliation. ***saq*** is found in approximately forty places.

References to the individual donning sackcloth include those in Gen. 37:34; 2 Sam. 3:31; 1 Kgs. 20:31ff.; Esth. 4:1ff.; Job 16:15; Ps. 30:11; Isa. 3:24; Dan. 9:3.

Nations collectively put on sackcloth — for example, Israel and Judah (cf. Jer. 4:8; 6:26; Lam. 2:10;

Ezek. 7:18; Joel 1:8, 13; Amos 8:10); Moab (cf. Jer. 48:37; 49:3); Tyre (cf. Ezek. 27:31); and Nineveh (cf. Jonah 3:5ff.).

Isa. 50:3 refers metaphorically to sackcloth covering the heavens.

saq also means "sack," or bags made of fibrous material designed to carry merchandise (cf. Gen. 42:25ff.; Lev. 11:32; Josh. 9:4).

NT Words

sakkos [σάκκος, *4526*]

sakkos is a noun found in only four contexts, all with reference to "sackcloth." Matt. 11:21; Luke 10:13 mention the hypothetical repentance of ancient Sodom and Gomorrah "in sackcloth and ashes," had they witnessed the same kinds of miraculous signs given to the towns of Bethsaida and Chorazin, who rejected Jesus outright. Rev. 16:12 refers metaphorically to the darkness of the sun at the end of time, likened to the blackness of "sackcloth." Rev. 11:3 refers to sackcloth worn by the two witnesses, faithful to their Christian testimony to the point of death. In this context, wearing sackcloth expresses penitence for the sin of the people of God, as the two witnesses are identified as the priestly and royal intercessors for the people of God.

SACRED → HOLINESS

SACRIFICE

OT Words

zebaḥ [זֶבַח, **2077**]

zebaḥ is a noun derived from ***zābaḥ*** (see below), which occurs in around 160 places with the predominant sense of "sacrifice" in the context of the Israelite worship. ***zebaḥ*** also refers to illegitimate sacrifice to idols.

Sacrifices in general contexts, describing the worship of Yahweh, are found, for example, in Gen. 31:54; 46:1; Exod. 10:25; 18:12; 1 Sam. 6:15; 2 Sam. 15:12; Ps. 27:6; Prov. 7:14. A renewed purity of sacrificial ritual is anticipated in the prophecies of Jer. 17:26; 33:18. Isa. 19:21 refers to Egyptian people offering sacrifices to Yahweh (cf. also Jonah 1:16).

Sacrifices as offerings commemorating the redemptive deeds of Yahweh in gratitude to him are indicated in general contexts (e.g., Num. 15:13ff.; Deut. 33:19; Josh. 22:26ff.); and during the Passover festival in particular (Exod. 23:18). Neh. 12:43 records the offering of a sacrifice of thanksgiving on the occasion of the completion of the rebuilt walls of Jerusalem in the mid-fifth century B.C. Similarly, sacrifices are offered to Yahweh at the dedication of Solomon's temple (1 Kgs. 8:62, 63; 2 Chr. 7:1ff.); and at King Solomon's coronation (1 Chr. 29:4. See also 2 Chr. 29:31ff.).

Sacrifices prescribed under the Mosaic law covenant, as well as the appropriate mode of sacrifice, are noted in general terms in Exod. 34:15; Deut. 12:6, 11, 27; 1 Sam. 1:21. In particular, frequent mention is made of the sacrifice associated with the peace, or fellowship, offering (Exod. 29:28; Lev. 3:1ff.; 4:26ff.; 7:11ff.; 19:5, 6; Num. 6:17ff.; 7:17ff.; 1 Sam. 10:8; 2 Chr. 33:16). Exhortations to offer right sacrifices to Yahweh are found in Pss. 4:5; 107:22. Sacrificial offerings also form part of the renewed priestly worship in the visionary temple of the prophet Ezekiel (cf. Ezek. 40:42; 44:11; 46:24). Certain parts of the animal carcass offered in sacrifice are presented to the priests as part of their allotted food portion under the law (cf. Deut. 18:3).

In other contexts, ***zebaḥ*** refers to corrupt Israelite sacrificial worship (e.g., 1 Sam. 2:13, 19, 29; Isa. 1:11; 43:23ff.; Jer. 7:21ff.; Hos. 8:13; Amos 4:4; 5:25). Lev. 17:7 records the prohibition against sacrificing to idols; and instances of illegitimate idolatrous sacrifice as practiced by the Israelites are noted in Exod. 34:15; Num. 25:2; Ezek. 20:28; Ps. 106:28. See also 2 Kgs. 10:19ff.

In more general terms, the sacrifices of the wicked are declared to be unacceptable in the sight of God (cf. Prov. 15:8; 21:27; Eccl. 5:1). And formalized sacrifices without either regard or genuine love for Yahweh are likewise rejected by him (cf. Pss. 40:6; 51:6ff.; Hos. 6:6).

Judg. 16:23 refers to pagans sacrificing to their gods.

When predicated of Yahweh, the slaughter of his enemies is metaphorically described as a "sacrifice" in Isa. 34:6; Ezek. 39:17ff. — the latter text describes the destruction of the armies of Gog and Magog.

Dan. 9:27 contains a probable allusion to the person and mission of the Messiah, whose redemptive work will put an end to "sacrifice" and offering. This may refer to the permanent effect of Christ's crucifixion in removing forever the need to offer any further sacrifice for sin.

zābaḥ [זָבַח, **2076**]

zābaḥ is the principal verb in the Old Testament for "offering or presenting sacrifice." It occurs around 130 times with this meaning, in a number of contexts, but its use is focused on the Israelite cultus.

General references to offering sacrifices in worship of Yahweh are found in Gen. 31:54; 46:1; Exod. 3:18; 5:3ff.

— all pre-Sinai contexts. 1 Sam. 1:3, 4, 21 refer to priestly or Levitical sacrificial duties. See also Deut. 18:3.

Divine requirements to offer sacrifices to Yahweh under the terms of the Mosaic covenant are indicated in Exod. 20:24; 23:18; 2 Kgs. 17:36. The practice of offering these sacrifices is noted in Exod. 24:5; Lev. 9:4; 17:5; Deut. 27:7; 33:19; Judg. 2:5; 1 Sam. 2:13ff.; 10:8; 1 Kgs. 1:9; 3:2ff.; 2 Chr. 33:16; Neh. 12:43. The specific context of sacrifice in worship is indicated in Pss. 27:6; 54:6; 107:22; 116:17. Elsewhere, sacrificing to Yahweh at specific festivals or on special occasions is mentioned in relation to the Passover (cf. Deut. 16:2ff.); the dedication of Solomon's temple (cf. 1 Kgs. 8:5, 62ff.; 2 Chr. 5:6; 7:4, 5); covenant renewal (cf. Josh. 8:31); the ark of the covenant's return to Jerusalem (cf. 1 Chr. 15:26); and Solomon's coronation (cf. 1 Chr. 29:21).

Offering sacrifices to idols is prohibited (2 Kgs. 17:35), as is sacrificing blemished animals (cf. Deut. 15:21; 17:1). Instances of idolatrous sacrifice on the part of Israel are indicated in Exod. 32:8; 34:15; Deut. 32:17; 1 Kgs. 12:32; 2 Kgs. 16:4; Ps. 106:37ff.; Isa. 57:7; Ezek. 16:20; 20:28; Hos. 4:13ff.; 13:2. Inappropriate sacrifices not in accordance with the law are rejected by God (cf. 1 Sam. 15:15ff.; Hos. 8:13; Mal. 1:8, 14).

The pagan practice of sacrificing to idols is indicated in Num. 22:40; Judg. 16:23; 1 Kgs. 11:8.

zābaḥ also indicates the non-ritual sense of "slaughter." In Deut. 12:15, 21, it refers to killing animals for food. 2 Kgs. 23:20 refers to the execution (i.e., the slaughtering) of idolatrous Israelite priests. Yahweh is also said to "slaughter" his enemies, referring to the destruction of Gog and Magog (Ezek. 39:17, 19).

ḥag [חַג, 2282]

ḥag is a noun with the predominant meaning "feast." However, on several occasions it also indicates the sense of "sacrifice" that merges with the idea of "feast." Exod. 23:18 speaks of the "festival offerings" dedicated to Yahweh in the three major festivals of Israel's ceremonial calendar. All of these (i.e., Passover; Tabernacles; Harvest) involve the presentation of sacrificial offerings. Other general references to this phenomenon are found in Ps. 118:27; Isa. 29:1. Ritual feasts or festivals included ritual sacrificial offerings as a matter of course. (→ FEAST)

NT Words

thysia [θυσία, *2378*]

thysia is a noun found in approximately thirty places, meaning "sacrifice" in a variety of contexts.

General references to the ritual of sacrifice include those in Phil. 2:17; Heb. 10:26. In Matt. 9:13; 12:7; Mark 12:33; Heb. 10:5, 8, the ritual of sacrifice is subordinated to demonstrating a merciful, compassionate spirit towards others, and a genuine love for God. Metaphorical references to a "sacrifice" of praise to God that is pleasing to him are found in Heb. 13:15, 16.

References to sacrificial ritual under the old covenant are found in Luke 2:24; Acts 7:41, 42; Heb. 11:4. In particular, Heb. 5:1; 7:27; 8:3; 9:9 all refer to the priestly role in offering sacrifices under the Mosaic law. Heb. 10:1, 11 point out that the old covenant was utterly incapable — by deliberate divine intention — of removing sin and making perfect those who offered sacrifices.

The presentation of sacrificial offerings in the New Testament era is noted in Luke 13:1; 1 Cor. 10:18. In the latter text, idolatrous sacrifice is in view.

The superior quality of new covenant offerings is affirmed in Heb. 9:23, speaking of "better sacrifices." In significant metaphorical language, Paul exhorts believers to present their whole lives as "living sacrifices" to God (Rom. 12:1; 1 Pet. 2:5). See also Phil. 4:18. Christ's work of atonement is designated as a "sacrifice" to God in Eph. 5:2, supremely effective in doing away with sin (cf. Heb. 9:26; 10:12).

thyō [θύω, *2380*]

thyō is a verb found fourteen times, referring to the action of "sacrificing" or "slaughtering" for sacrifice in about half of these contexts. (→ KILL)

thyō refers to the sacrifice of the Passover lamb (Mark 14:12; Luke 22:7); pagan sacrifice (Acts 14:13; 1 Cor. 10:20); and to Christ as the lamb sacrificed for the sins of his people (1 Cor. 5:7).

eidōlothyton [εἰδωλόθυτον, *1494*]

eidōlothyton is an adjectival form used nominally with the sense of "that which is offered in sacrifice to idols," usually in reference to food.

Gentile believers are prohibited from consuming food that had undergone such a ritual (Acts 15:29; 21:25). See also Rev. 2:14, 20.

Paul considers that eating such food, however, is a matter for one's individual conscience (cf. 1 Cor. 8:1ff.; 10:28). See also 1 Cor. 10:19.

Additional Notes

There is a significant theological connection between the Old and New Testament vocabulary for "sacrifice." ***zābaḥ*** and ***zebaḥ*** emphasize the importance of sacrifice in the ritual worship of Yahweh as the indispensable prerequisite for gaining access to him, whether it be to seek forgiveness or to thank him for his redemptive deeds or his provision for one's material needs. In terms of worship that was acceptable to Yahweh, sacrifices presented with pure motive were essential for maintaining a positive relationship with God.

The corresponding New Testament vocabulary (viz. ***thyō***, ***thysia***) makes its clear that the biblical writers were aware of the central importance of sacrifice under the old covenant. They were also keenly aware that the ritual sacrifices of the old covenant did not adequately deal with the problem of sin, since the sacrifices had to be continually repeated. Against this backdrop, the central importance of Christ's sacrificial work is underscored in the New Testament as the ultimately effective sacrifice for sin that deals with the guilt of humankind once and for all.

The Old Testament teaching on sacrifice focuses on ritual slaughter and presentation of unblemished animals. The New Testament perspective on sacrifice shifts the focus to the once-for-all atoning sacrifice of Christ the Messiah. Christ is thus viewed metaphorically as the eternally efficient "paschal Lamb," whose sacrifice is described in old covenant terminology. But the reality of its far-reaching impact on restoring lost humankind lies at the heart of a radically new covenant.

See Also: ➡ OFFERING

SAD, SADNESS

OT Words

zā'aph **[זָעַף, 2196]**

zā'aph is a rare verb with the general underlying sense of "be troubled." It is translated "be sad" in Gen. 40:6, referring to the crestfallen countenance of the Egyptian pharaoh's chief baker and butler.

sar **[סַר, 5620]**

sar is a rare verb, found in only three contexts and meaning "sad" or "depressed." It describes the Israelite king Ahab's vexation at failing to get Naboth to sell him his vineyard (cf. 1 Kgs. 20:43; 21:4, 5).

ra' **[רַע, 7451]**

ra' is an adjective occurring about 650 times with the almost exclusive sense of "wicked," "evil," as well as associated nuances. However, in Neh. 2:1, 2 ***ra'*** refers to Nehemiah's "sadness" that is noticed by the Persian king, Artaxerxes.

rōa' **[רֹעַ, 7455]**

rōa' is an uncommon noun, a variant form of ***ra'*** (see above), found nineteen times with the principal meanings "evil," "wickedness." However, in Eccl. 7:3, ***rōa'*** refers to the "sadness" of one's countenance.

kā'āh **[כָּאָה, 3512]**

kā'āh is a rare verb, found only three times, meaning "to be sad, or disheartened" (cf. Ps. 109:16; Ezek. 13:22). In Dan. 11:30, the sense is more that of "being afraid."

NT Words

skythrōpos **[σκυθρωπός, *4659*]**

skythrōpos is a rare adjective found only twice and meaning "sad," describing a facial expression (cf. Matt. 6:16; Luke 24:17).

stygnazō **[στυγνάζω, *4768*]**

stygnazō is a rare verb found only twice. In Mark 10:22 it describes a "falling" countenance, in relation to the rich young ruler who rejected Jesus' call to give away his wealth to the poor, resulting in him becoming sad or dejected. See also Matt. 16:3, where ***stygnazō*** is used metaphorically, referring to the "threatening" appearance of a stormy sky.

SADDLE

OT Words

merkāb **[מֶרְכָּב, 4817]**

merkāb is a noun referring either to a "seat" or "riding saddle" of a chariot, or donkey (cf. Lev. 15:9; Song 3:10); or to a chariot itself (cf. 1 Kgs. 4:26). It occurs only in these three places.

ḥābash **[חָבַשׁ, 2280]**

ḥābash is a verb found in around thirty contexts with the principal meaning "to saddle up" for riding, in about half of these contexts. (➡ BIND)

ḥābash refers exclusively to saddling a donkey for riding in Gen. 22:3; Num. 22:21; Judg. 19:10; 19:26; 1 Kgs. 2:40; 13:13; 2 Kgs. 4:24.

SAFE, SAFETY

OT Words

betaḥ **[בֶּטַח, 983]**

betaḥ is a noun with both adjectival and adverbial force, occurring approximately forty times and meaning "safe," "safety," "safely" in the majority of these contexts.

betaḥ emphasizes living "safely" in the land of Canaan. Promises of such a secure lifestyle for the people of Israel are found in Lev. 25:18, 19; 26:5; Deut. 12:10; 33:28. In Jer. 23:6; Ezek. 34:25; Hos. 2:18, such promises are projected into the messianic age. In Zech. 14:11, ultimate safety, or security, is promised to the people of Yahweh in Jerusalem for the Day of the Lord. Several places refer to the divine promise of a return to Israel from captivity, to once again dwell "in safety" there (cf. Jer. 32:37; 33:16; Ezek. 28:26; 38:8ff.). The reality of living "securely" in Canaan is noted in 1 Sam. 12:11; 1 Kgs. 4:25; Ezek. 39:26.

General references to living "safely" are found in Job 11:18; Prov. 10:9. God grants people safety, or security, in Job 24:23; Pss. 4:8; 78:3; Prov. 1:33; 3:23; Isa. 14:30.

shālôm [שָׁלוֹם, 7965]

shālôm is a common noun found in approximately 240 places with the primary sense of "peace," or "well-being," in the majority of these contexts. There are a number of associated meanings, including that of "safe," found in 2 Sam. 18:29, 32 in relation to David's inquiry after the safety or welfare of his son Absalom. Job 21:9 speaks of houses "safe" from fear.

yāsha' [יָשַׁע, 3467]

yāsha' is a common verb with the underlying meaning "to save," as well as a variety of nuances. One of these is the adjectival sense of "safe," found in Ps. 119:117 with reference to the psalmist's plea to God to keep him "safe" from danger. (→ SAVE)

yēsha' [יֵשַׁע, 3468]

yēsha' is a noun commonly translated "salvation" in the majority of its nearly forty occurrences. In several places, however, ***yēsha'*** expresses the somewhat broader, more generalized sense of "safety" (cf. Job 5:4, 11). In Ps. 12:5, God promises to place the poor and needy in a situation of "safety." (→ SALVATION)

sāgab [שָׂגַב, 7682]

sāgab is a verb found twenty times with the predominant sense of "be high, or exalted." In one or two contexts, ***sāgab*** refers to being set on high by God in a position of safety or security (cf. Job 5:11; Prov. 8:10; Ps. 91:14 [implied]). Prov. 29:25 indicates the general sense of "being safe" in the Lord.

NT Words

diasōzō [διασῴζω, *1295*]

diasōzō is a verb with the underlying meaning "bringing to safety" in the sense of "make well" or "escape." It occurs eight times.

The explicit sense of "bring to safety" is found in Acts 23:24, referring to Paul's safe passage to Felix the governor. Acts 27:44 describes escaping safely to land from a shipwreck.

asphalēs [ἀσφαλής, *804*]

asphalēs is an adjectival form occurring five times meaning "safe," "certain." The sense of "safe" in a nominal sense is found in Phil. 3:1, where Paul refers to his writings as a "safeguard" for the Philippian congregation. Heb. 6:19 refers metaphorically to the hope of the gospel as an anchor that is "safe."

asphalōs [ἀσφαλῶς, *806*]

asphalōs is an adverbial form found three times, translated "safely" in reference to physical security in Mark 14:44; Acts 16:23.

asphaleia [ἀσφάλεια, *803*]

asphaleia is a noun occurring three times, indicating people's "safety" or "security" in general terms in 1 Thess. 5:3. Acts 5:3 speaks of a prison cell "securely locked" (lit. "locked with safety").

See Also: → VICTORY

SAIL

OT Words

nēs [נֵס, 5251]

nēs is the standard term for "flag," "banner," or "ensign" in the Old Testament, found in twenty places. In two of these contexts, ***nēs*** refers to a ship's sail (Isa. 33:23; Ezek. 27:7).

NT Words

pleō [πλέω, *4126*]

pleō is a verb found in five places, meaning "to sail" (cf. Luke 8:23; Acts 21:3; 27:2, 6, 24).

parapleō [παραπλέω, *3896*]

parapleō (a derivative of ***pleō***, above) is found only in Acts 20:16, meaning "to sail by."

apopleō [ἀποπλέω, *636*]

apopleō, also derived from ***pleō***, above, is found four times meaning "to set sail," "sail away" (Acts 13:4; 14:26; 20:15; 27:1).

ekpleō [ἐκπλέω, *1602*]

ekpleō is another variant form of ***pleō***. It occurs three times and means "sail," "sail away" (cf. Acts 15:39; 18:18; 20:6).

hypopleō [ὑποπλέω, *5284*]

hypopleō is a variant of ***pleō*** (see above). It occurs only twice and means "to sail under" (cf. Acts 27:4, 7).

diapleō [διαπλέω, *1277*]

diapleō is found only in Acts 27:5, meaning "sail over, or across."

paralegomai [παραλέγομαι, *3881*]

paralegomai is found in only two places and means "to sail close" (i.e., to the shore) (cf. Acts 27:8, 13).

anagō [ἀνάγω, *321*]

anagō is a verb occurring around twenty-five times with the dual meanings "to bring, lead up," and "to launch, set sail." The latter sense is indicated in Luke 8:22; Acts 18:21; 20:3, 13; 21:1, 2; 27:2, 4, 12, 21; 28:10, 11.

SAILOR

OT Words

shût [**שׁוּט, 7751**]

shût is a verb with the predominant meaning "to go, run to and fro" in most of its thirteen occurrences. However, in Ezek. 27:8, 26, ***shût*** is used nominally to refer to "sailors."

mallāḥ [**מַלָּח, 4419**]

mallāḥ is a noun found in four places, translated "sailor" (cf. Ezek. 27:9, 27, 29; Jonah 1:5).

NT Words

nautēs [ναύτης, *3492*]

nautēs is a noun found three times, meaning "sailor" (cf. Acts 27:27ff.; Rev. 18:13).

SAINT

OT Words

qādôsh [**קָדוֹשׁ, 6918**]

qādôsh is an adjectival form that is also used nominally, with the predominant senses of "holy," "holy one," applied to Yahweh, people, and other phenomena in most of the nearly 120 occurrences. However, in several of these contexts ***qādôsh*** means "saint" or "saints," with reference to the people of Yahweh set apart by him (cf. Deut. 33:3; Job 5:1; Pss. 16:3; 34:9; 89:5ff.; 106:16).

Additional Notes

The vocabulary for "saint(s)" and "holy" is very closely interrelated.

See Also: → HOLINESS

SALT

OT Words

melaḥ [**מֶלַח, 4417**]

melaḥ is a noun that occurs nearly thirty times and means "salt" in various contexts.

There are a number of references to the "Salt Sea," or the Dead Sea (cf. Gen. 14:3; Num. 34:3, 12; Deut. 3:17; Josh. 3:16; 15:2, 5; Josh. 18:19).

A "pillar of salt" is found in Gen. 19:26 — Lot's wife was transformed into one after disobeying God's command not to look back at the fiery destruction of Sodom and Gomorrah. This description of her death may well refer to her being covered in volcanic ash — especially in view of Deut. 29:23, which refers to "salt" in connection with volcanic brimstone.

Salt is noted as an accompaniment to ritual offerings in Lev. 2:13; Num. 18:19; 2 Chr. 13:5; Ezek. 43:25.

Other general references to salt include those in Judg. 9:45; 2 Kgs. 2:20ff.; Job 6:6; Ezek. 4:11. Zeph. 2:9 mentions "salt pits."

NT Words

halas [ἅλας, *217*]

halas is a noun found eight times with reference to "salt" in each case. ***halas*** emphasizes the preserving effect of salt in both a literal sense, in relation to food, as well as in a metaphorical sense, in relation to the wholesome influence of godly people in a sinful world (cf. Matt. 5:13; Mark 9:50; Luke 14:34; Col. 4:6).

halizō [ἁλίζω, *233*]

halizō is the rare verb from which ***halas*** is derived (see above). It is found only twice. In Matt. 5:13, ***halizō*** is used passively to indicate the hypothetical process of salt "having its saltiness restored" (lit: "salt . . . being salted"), something which is in reality impossible. Mark 9:49 refers metaphorically to the terrible fate of the wicked who, as part of their torment, are depicted as being "salted" with fire.

halykos [ἁλυκός, *252*]

halykos is an adjectival form derived from ***halas*** and ***halas***, above. It is found only in Jas. 3:12, where it refers to "salt" water.

analos [ἄναλος, *358*]

analos is an adjectival form derived from the noun ***halas*** (see above). It is found only once, with a "negative prefix," and is translated literally as "unsalted" or "without salt," though in the context of Mark 9:50 it refers to salt "losing its saltiness."

SALUTATION → GREET

SALVATION

OT Words

yeshû'āh [יְשׁוּעָה, **3444**]

yeshû'āh is a noun found in nearly eighty contexts with the principal meaning "salvation," in the sense of "rescue," "deliverance." In the majority of cases God is declared to be the agent of salvation, on behalf of his people.

In a number of places, salvation is declared to be wrought by God (cf. Gen. 49:13; Deut. 32:15; 1 Sam. 2:1; 14:45; 2 Chr. 20:17; Pss. 3:8; 9:14; 44:4; 119:174; Isa. 25:9). In particular, Exod. 14:13 speaks of Israel's deliverance from Egyptian bondage. Isa. 49:6, 8 refer to the salvation of God's people through the agency of the Messianic Servant.

Praise for the salvation God grants to his people is found in Pss. 20:5; 35:9; 68:19; Jonah 2:9. Yahweh himself is declared to be the source of salvation (cf. Exod. 15:2; Pss. 62:1ff.; 89:26; 118:14, 21; Isa. 12:2). 1 Chr. 16:23; Ps. 96:2 contain exhortations to proclaim the salvation wrought by God.

Pleas for divine deliverance are found in Pss. 14:7; 53:6; 88:1; 106:4.

General references to salvation are found in Job 13:16; Ps. 119:155; Isa. 12:3; 59:11.

yeshû'āh is used metaphorically in Isa. 59:17 to refer to "the helmet of salvation" put on by God (see also Isa. 60:18). The metaphorical "cup of salvation" is offered by God in Ps. 116:13.

teshû'āh [תְּשׁוּעָה, **8668**]

teshû'āh is a synonym for ***yeshû'āh***, above, found approximately thirty-five times with the primary senses of "salvation," or "deliverance," brought about by God.

teshû'āh refers to salvation or deliverance explicitly granted by God in Judg. 15:18, describing Samson's victory over the Philistines. 1 Sam. 19:5 cites the deliverance God won for Israel through David's triumph over the Philistine giant Goliath. Salvation for Israel is also indicated in 1 Sam. 11:13; 2 Sam. 19:2; 23:10ff.; 1 Chr. 11:14; Isa. 46:13; 45:17.

Yahweh is closely identified with the salvation he provides for his people through expressions such as "my salvation," "your salvation" (cf. Pss. 38:22; 40:10, 16; 51:14; 71:15; 119:41; Jer. 3:23; Lam. 3:26).

yēsha' [יֵשַׁע, **3468**]

yēsha' is another synonym for ***yeshû'āh*** and ***teshû'āh***, above, found about thirty times with the primary meanings "salvation," "deliverance."

yēsha' refers to salvation wrought by Yahweh for his people in 2 Sam. 22:3, 36, 47; Pss. 18:2, 35, 46; 27:1; 51:12; 85:4; Isa. 17:10; 51:5; 62:11; Mic. 7:7; Hab. 3:13, 18.

1 Chr. 16:35; Pss. 79:9; 85:7 contain pleas to God for salvation. Ps. 95:1 praises God for his salvation.

In a metaphorical context, "garments of salvation" are offered by God to "clothe" his people (Isa. 61:10).

NT Words

sōtēria [σωτηρία, *4991*]

sōtēria is the only New Testament term for "salvation," "deliverance." It occurs fifty times, with these meanings in the large majority of these texts. In each of these contexts, the salvation is predicated of God and/or Christ, either explicitly or implicitly.

General references to "salvation" include those in 2 Cor. 7:10; Phil. 1:19; 1 Thess. 5:8; Heb. 1:14; 6:9; 2 Pet. 3:15. More explicit references to the salvation granted by God to his people are found in Luke 1:77; John 4:22; Acts 4:12; 13:26; Phil. 1:28; 2 Thess. 2:13. In particular, the consummate "day of salvation" is noted in 2 Cor. 6:2. Other references to the salvation to be revealed at the end of time include those in Rom. 13:11; 1 Pet. 1:5, 9.

Particular references to salvation having come to God's people in the person of Christ are found in Luke 2:30; 19:9; 1 Thess. 5:9; 2 Tim. 2:10; 3:15; Heb. 2:3, 10; 5:9; Heb. 9:28; 1 Pet. 1:10; Jude 3. Acts 16:7 refers to the "way of salvation" in connection with the proclamation of the gospel of Christ. God and Christ are praised and glorified as the source of the salvation of their people in Rev. 7:10; 12:10; 19:1.

The gospel is declared to be the power and vehicle of salvation in Rom. 1:16; Eph. 1:13.

Acts 13:47; 28:28 proclaim God's people to be the bearers of the message of salvation to the world at large. Rom. 11:11; Titus 2:11 declare that salvation is to be granted to the Gentiles.

The expression "horn of salvation" refers metaphorically to Jesus Christ the Messiah in Luke 1:69. The "helmet of salvation" is mentioned as part of the believer's spiritual armor in Eph. 6:13.

Additional Notes

The vocabulary for "salvation" must be correlated with that of the verb "save" to appreciate the phenomenon of divine deliverance throughout Scripture.

See Also: → SAVE

SANCTIFY → HOLINESS

SANCTUARY → TABERNACLE → TEMPLE

SAND

OT Words

ḥôl **[חוֹל, 2344]**

ḥôl is the only word for "sand" in the Old Testament. It is found in twenty-three contexts.

Most commonly, ***ḥôl*** refers metaphorically to the sand of the seashore. For example, ***ḥôl*** describes the incalculable number of Israelites descended from Abraham and his family (Gen. 22:17; 32:12; Isa. 10:22; 48:19; Jer. 33:12; Hos. 1:10). More generally, huge numbers of people likened to "sand of the seashore" are noted in Gen. 41:49; Josh. 11:4; Judg. 7:12; 1 Sam. 13:5; 1 Kgs. 4:20; Jer. 15:8. Solomon's abundant wisdom is described this way in 1 Kgs. 4:29. See also Job 5:3; Pss. 78:27; 139:18; Hab. 1:9.

General, literal references to sand include those in Exod. 2:12; Deut. 33:19; Prov. 27:3; Jer. 5:22.

NT Words

ammos [ἄμμος, *285*]

ammos is a noun found in only four places, meaning "sand," or "sandy ground." The literal sense is found in Matt. 7:26. Rom. 9:27; Heb. 11:12 refer to the enormous number of Israelite people as "sand on the shore." Rev. 20:8 uses the same metaphor.

SANDAL

OT Words

na'al **[נַעַל, 5275]**

na'al is found in twenty-two places, all referring literally to "sandals" (e.g., Gen. 14:23; Exod. 3:5; Deut. 25:9ff.; Josh. 5:15; Ruth 4:7ff.; Isa. 11:15; Amos 2:6).

There is an interesting usage in Deut. 25:9, 10, referring to a man refusing to marry the surviving childless wife of his recently deceased brother in order to continue the family line. This custom was known as "levirate marriage" and was sanctioned under the Mosaic law so that the name of the deceased man's family might continue in Israel. In the event of the eligible relative refusing to marry, one of his sandals would be removed, as a symbol of his shame. From that time on, his family would be known as "the Unsandaled."

NT Words

sandalion [σανδάλιον, *4547*]

sandalion occurs only in Matt. 6:9; Acts 12:8, referring to "sandals."

SATAN

OT Words

sāṭān **[שָׂטָן, 7854]**

sāṭān is a noun designating both "Satan," the name of the demonic archenemy of God, and the "adversary." The term is found around thirty times.

The meaning "adversary" signifies an "opponent," or "enemy." In Num. 22:22 it is the angel of the Lord who opposes the pagan seer, Balaam. A military opponent or enemy is indicated in 1 Sam. 29:4; 2 Sam. 19:22.

The name "Satan" has the underlying sense of "accuser," and it refers to Yahweh's chief demonic opponent (cf. 1 Chr. 21:1; Job 1:6ff.; 2:1ff.; Ps. 109:6; Zech. 3:1, 2).

NT Words

Satanas [Σατανᾶς, *4567*]

Satanas is a proper noun used exclusively to refer to "Satan," the prince of demons. The term occurs nearly forty times in various contexts.

Satan is explicitly rebuked by Christ in Matt. 4:10; Mark 8:33; Luke 4:8. His activity is also alluded to in the public ministry of Christ (cf. Matt. 12:26; Mark 3:23ff.; Luke 11:18); and is observed elsewhere as well (Acts 5:3; 1 Cor. 5:5; 2 Cor. 7:5; 1 Thess. 2:18; 1 Tim. 1:20). Luke 22:3; John 13:27 refer to Satan's entrapment of Judas Iscariot; and 1 Tim. 5:5 refers to his entrapment of others.

Satan unsuccessfully seeks to tempt Christ to sin during his period of testing in the wilderness (cf. Mark 1:13). In Luke 10:18, Christ says that he saw Satan fall like lightning from heaven. Deliverance from Satan's power is indicated in Acts 26:18; Rom. 16:20. Rev. 2:13

refers to Satan's throne. "Satan" is also mentioned as the alternate name for the devil in Rev. 12:9; 20:2, 7.

There are metaphorical references to apostate members of a "synagogue of Satan" in Smyrna and Philadelphia in Rev. 2:9; 3:9. See also Rev. 2:24.

Additional Notes

References to "Satan" in the Old Testament are relatively infrequent, but it is clear that he is subservient to the power and purposes of Yahweh. In the New Testament, that position of subservience is rigidly maintained, as he is curtailed by the person of Christ. Satan's inevitable demise is portrayed in Revelation, which demonstrates the utter victory of God and Christ over the evil one. This victory is won through the substitutionary sacrifice of Christ on the cross.

See Also: → DEMON

SATISFY, SATISFACTION

OT Words

***sāba'* [שָׂבַע, 7646]**

sāba' is a rare form occurring around one hundred times, meaning "to satisfy," "fill (up)," as well as associated meanings in a variety of contexts.

In a number of places, ***sāba'*** indicates the state of "being satisfied" with an abundance of food. (→ FILL)

Job 38:27 declares that God "satisfied" the wasteland with rain (cf. also Ps. 104:13). Ps. 91:16 affirms that God satisfies the godly person with long life. Elsewhere, God is said to satisfy his people's thirst in the wilderness (cf. Ps. 107:9); the desires of all his creatures (cf. Ps. 145:16); and his people with his blessing (cf. Ps. 58:11).

sāba' refers to the psalmist's satisfaction with beholding the presence of God in worship (cf. Pss. 17:15; 63:5; 65:4); and to being satisfied with the love and goodness of God (cf. Ps. 90:4; Jer. 31:14; Joel 2:19).

In particular, the "Suffering Servant of Yahweh" is said to be satisfied with his return to life after his suffering (cf. Isa. 53:11).

References to the satisfaction of humankind in general include those in Prov. 12:14; 27:20; Eccl. 1:8; Isa. 58:10; Hag. 2:5.

sāba' is also used metaphorically in Isa. 66:11, referring to God's people being "satisfied" at the breasts of mother Jerusalem. Ezek. 16:20; Hos. 4:10 refer to Israel "not being satisfied" with their lustful idolatry. See also Jer. 46:10; 50:10, where divine judgment on the enemies of Yahweh is spoken of in terms of Yahweh's sword being "satisfied" or "satiated" with the blood of his foes.

***sābēa'* [שָׂבֵעַ, 7649]**

sābēa' is an adjectival form derived from ***sāba'*** (see above). It is found six times and means "full," "satisfied." It is translated "satisfied" only in Prov. 19:23, with reference to being content with life.

***sobā'h* [שָׂבְעָה, 7654]**

sobā'h is a noun derived from ***sāba'*** (see above) that is used both verbally and adjectivally, meaning "full," "be satisfied," or "have enough." It is found six times.

sobā'h refers to having enough, or being satisfied by food, literally (Isa. 56:11; Hag. 1:6), and metaphorically (Ezek. 39:19). The desire for idol worship that was never satisfied is recorded in Ezek. 16:28. See also Isa. 55:2.

***rāwāh* [רָוָה, 7301]**

rāwāh is a verb with the underlying sense of "to have, take, or drink one's fill," and thus, in certain contexts, "to be drunk," "be saturated," or "to water abundantly."

The explicit sense of "satisfy" is found in Prov. 5:19 in relation to the pleasure of loving one's wife, allowing her breasts to "satisfy" one at all times. Jer. 31:14 speaks of God promising to satisfy the priests of Israel with abundant blessing. He also promises to satisfy the weary soul in Jer. 31:25.

See Also: → FILL

SATRAP

OT Words

***'aḥashdarpan* [אֲחַשְׁדַּרְפַּן, 324 (Aramaic)]**

'aḥashdarpan is an Aramaic term referring to a member of the Persian civil bureaucracy, probably indicating a medium level provincial governor or ruler. The term is found in nine places (cf. Dan. 3:2, 3, 27; 6:1ff.).

SAVE

OT Words

***yāsha'* [יָשַׁע, 3467]**

yāsha' is a verb occurring approximately two hundred times with the principal meaning "save" in the majority of these contexts, including various related nuances such as "deliver," "rescue," "preserve."

The action of "saving" is frequently predicated of Yahweh, referring to that which is accomplished as well as to that which is promised. ***yāsha'*** refers generally to divine "saving" activity in the period of the judges (e.g., Judg. 6:36ff.; 7:7; 8:22; 10:1, 12ff.; Neh. 9:27), and elsewhere (e.g., Deut. 33:29; 1 Sam. 4:3; 2 Sam. 22:4; Ps. 18:27; Isa. 25:9; Zech. 9:16). Exod. 14:30 refers particularly to Yahweh having "saved" (i.e., rescued) Israel from her enemies (with respect to Egypt), and 1 Sam. 7:8; 9:16; 2 Sam. 3:18 refer to Israel being "saved" from the Philistines. God also promises to save, or deliver, his people from captivity in Babylon (cf. Jer. 23:6; 30:7ff.; 33:16; 46:27); and to deliver, or save, them from uncleanness, or sin (cf. Ezek. 36:29; 37:23).

yāsha' also refers to Yahweh saving, or preserving, individuals — in general contexts (2 Kgs. 6:27; Job 5:15; Ps. 7:10; Isa. 43:12); in respect of King David (2 Sam. 8:6, 14; Ps. 138:7); and referring to the prophet Jeremiah (Jer. 15:20). 2 Kgs. 19:34; Ps. 69:35; Isa. 37:35 contain the promise to save, or deliver, Jerusalem.

yāsha' is also found in contexts where his people plead for Yahweh to save, or deliver, them from their enemies (cf. Pss. 3:7; 22:21; 44:7; 80:3; 109:26; Isa. 37:10; Jer. 2:27).

In contrast, gods are declared to be utterly impotent to save (cf. Isa. 45:20; Jer. 2:28; 11:12).

yāsha' also refers to human beings "saving" in the sense of "rescuing, or delivering." General references include those in Deut. 22:27; 28:31; Josh. 10:6; 1 Sam. 11:3. In particular, the judges are depicted as having delivered the Israelites out of the hands of their enemies (Judg. 2:16ff.; 3:9, 15; 6:14ff.).

shāmar [שָׁמַר, 8104]

shāmar is a verb found in about 450 places with the predominant meanings "keep," "guard," as well as several associated nuances. One of these nuances is "preserve," with the underlying sense of "save."

The psalmist pleads with God to "preserve" him from calamity (cf. Pss. 16:1; 86:2) and trusts that Yahweh will preserve (i.e., save, protect) him from trouble (Pss. 41:2; 121:7). Wisdom will preserve one's life (cf. Prov. 4:6; 14:3), as will righteousness (cf. Prov. 16:17).

God is also depicted as one who "preserves" his people (cf. Josh. 24:17; 1 Sam. 30:20; 2 Sam. 8:6; Job 10:12; Pss. 97:10; 145:20; Hos. 12:13).

ḥāyāh [חָיָה, 2421]

ḥāyāh is a verb occurring about 270 times, meaning "to live," "be alive" in most of these contexts, as well as a number of related nuances including "to save."

(→ LIFE)

Human beings are declared to be involved in saving the lives of others in Gen. 47:25; Josh. 6:25; Judg. 8:19; 1 Sam. 27:11. Another nuance of ***ḥāyāh*** meaning "save" implies the sense of "allow to live" (cf. Exod. 1:17ff.; Num. 22:33; 31:15).

NT Words

sōzō [σώζω, *4982*]

sōzō is the most common verb in the New Testament meaning "save." The term occurs around 110 times in a variety of contexts, although the most common of these refers to being saved, or delivered, from the penalty of sin and death.

General references to "saving one's life," in the sense of preserving it, are found in Matt. 16:25; Mark 3:4; 8:35; 9:24; Luke 17:33; 1 Tim. 2:15; Jas. 5:15.

The saving work of Jesus Christ is explicitly alluded to in Matt. 1:21; 18:11; Luke 19:10 — referring to Christ as the one who saves his people, or the lost, from their sin. Christ expresses his intention to save the world — sinners — in John 12:47; 1 Tim. 1:15. In other contexts, there is the taunt, directed at Christ on the cross, to "save himself" (cf. Matt. 27:40; Mark 15:30ff.; Luke 23:35ff.). Appeals to Christ for literal physical rescue are found in Matt. 8:25; 14:30.

In relation to the great hope of the believer, a number of texts refer to "being saved" through the work of Christ, or being delivered from the penalty of sin and its terrible consequences (cf. John 3:17; 10:9; Acts 4:12; Rom. 5:9; 10:9; 1 Cor. 1:18, 21; 2 Cor. 2:15; Eph. 2:5, 8; 2 Tim. 1:9; Titus 3:5; Heb. 7:25; 1 Pet. 3:21). In contrast, the impossibility of "being saved" by the law of Moses is indicated in Acts 15:1.

Other contexts indicate the hope and reality of "being saved" by God, in the sense of being delivered from destruction and being granted eternal life (cf. Matt. 24:22; Mark 10:26; 13:20; Luke 7:50; Acts 2:47; 16:30; Rom. 9:27; 11:14, 26; 1 Cor. 3:15; 7:16; 1 Tim. 2:4; 4:16; Jas. 1:21; 5:20; Jude 5). Promises of deliverance or salvation are also found in Matt. 10:22; 24:13; Mark 13:13, contingent on the believer enduring to the end.

diasōzō [διασώζω, *1295*]

diasōzō is a verb occurring eight times and meaning "escape," "bring to safety." It is with this sense that the term is translated "to save" in Acts 27:43, with reference to the plan to save Paul from being assassinated; and in 1 Pet. 3:20, in relation to Noah and his family "having been saved" at the time of the great flood.

See Also: → DELIVER

SAVOR

OT Words

yāsha' **[יָשַׁע, 3467]**

yāsha' is the standard verb meaning "save," and it has this meaning in the majority of its approximately two hundred occurrences. (→ SAVE) However, in several places, ***yāsha'*** is also translated nominally as "savior" (i.e., one who delivers, or rescues), all predicated of Yahweh.

God is described as the savior of David (2 Sam. 22:3); and of Egypt (Isa. 19:20); and of Israel (2 Kgs. 13:5; Ps. 106:25; Isa. 43:3ff.; 49:26; Jer. 14:8; Hos. 13:4).

NT Words

sōtēr **[σωτήρ, *4990*]**

sōtēr is the dynamic equivalent for the nominal use of ***yāsha'*** (see above) in the New Testament. ***sōtēr*** is found in approximately twenty-five contexts and is consistently translated "savior" (as one who saves, delivers, or rescues).

Mary declares God to be "my Savior" in Luke 1:47; and his people declare God to be "our Savior" in Titus 1:3; 2:10; 3:4; 2 Pet. 3:2; Jude 25.

Christ is declared to be the "Savior" of his people Israel (Luke 2:11; Acts 5:31; 13:23); of the world (John 4:42; 1 Tim. 4:10; 1 John 4:14); and of the church (Eph. 5:23). He is described as "our Savior" in 1 Tim. 1:1; 2:3; 2 Tim. 1:10. The title "Savior" in a general sense is recorded in Phil. 3:20.

Additional Notes

All vocabulary associated with the motif of "salvation" in both Old and New Testaments has significant theological weight when predicated of both God and Christ.

In the Old Testament, the great "saving" acts of Yahweh constitute a direct divine intervention in the affairs of humankind. Such actions bring about the fulfillment of God's redemptive purposes on behalf of his people — both Jew and Gentile, corporate and individual. Such deliverance is illustrated in events such as the Noahic flood, the deliverance from Egypt, the miraculous provision of food and water in the wilderness, the conquest of Canaan, and the numerous signs and wonders throughout the period of the old covenant. In this era, salvation was primarily defined and presented in a physical and material way, directed towards the anticipated enjoyment of the promised land of Canaan with attendant economic prosperity, security, and political stability. Because of the sin of the Israelite people, the fullness of old covenant salvation was never enjoyed for a sustained period of time.

With Christ, the new covenant period consummates divine salvation — defined not in material, earthly blessing, but rather in a profound spiritual sense. The salvation of new covenant believers focuses on eternal heavenly and spiritual realities — a blessing granted as a consequence of Christ's atoning sacrifice for sin.

And so both God and Christ are designated as "Savior," fulfilling a process that was begun in the very earliest dealings of God with humankind.

See Also: → REDEEM

SAVOR → SMELL

SAY

OT Words

'āmar **[אָמַר, 559]**

'āmar is among the most frequently occurring verbs in the Old Testament, found over 5,300 times. In most of its occurrences ***'āmar*** means "say," usually in the past tense. A wide variety of associated meanings include the sense of "speak." The usage of ***'āmar*** is divided between the verbal communication of both God and human beings. (→ ANSWER → CALL → COMMAND → PROMISE → TELL)

Instances of divine speech include the following: the creation of the world (cf. Gen. 1:3ff.); expressing the promises of the covenant (cf. Gen. 17:9; 9:12, 17; Deut. 34:4; Exod. 34:1, 27); the self-revelation to Moses (cf. Exod. 3:14); promising blessing to Solomon (cf. 1 Kgs. 3:5); accepting of offering (cf. Gen. 8:21); initiating signs and wonders (cf. Exod. 4:4; 14:14; Num. 21:8); exercising sovereign control over Satan (cf. Job 1:7ff.); issuing commands, or regulations, for worship (cf. Exod. 30:1ff.; Lev. 4:1ff.; Ezek. 44:5); granting military victory to his people (cf. Josh. 6:2; Judg. 1:2; 2 Sam. 5:19); the pronouncing judgment (cf. Gen. 6:13; Exod. 7:14; 1 Sam. 16:1; Hos. 1:6); communicating his word to the prophets (cf. Jonah 1:1; Hab. 2:2; Mic. 2:3; Nah. 1:12; Obad. 1; Hag. 1:1; Zech. 1:7).

Elsewhere ***'āmar*** indicates human verbal discourse (e.g., Gen. 11:3ff.; Deut. 25:7ff.; Ruth 1:8ff.; 1 Sam. 11:1ff.; Ezra 1:1, 2). Eccl. 2:1ff. refers to a man "addressing" his own heart.

Human beings also frequently address God — for example, Abraham (Gen. 18:23ff.) in the context of a theophanic revelation. Talking to God in prayer is illustrated in Ezra 9:6; Neh. 1:5; Pss. 16:2; 27:8; 41:4; 42:9; Amos 7:2ff.

dābar [דָּבַר, 1696]

dābar is another common verb, found over 1,150 times with the senses of "speak," "say," as interchangeable meanings in the large majority of instances. Other related meanings include "promise," "tell," "utter." ***dābar*** refers to the communication of both God and human beings, signifying Yahweh's initiative and process of communicating verbally with humankind, and vice versa. ***dābar*** is also used in the context of natural human discourse. (→ PROMISE → TELL)

Examples of divine speech in contexts where human beings are the recipient of such revelation include communication with the patriarchs (cf. Gen. 8:15; 46:2); with Moses (cf. Exod. 6:2ff.; 40:1; Lev. 4:1; Num. 5:1ff.); and with the people of Israel (cf. Deut. 4:12; Hos. 2:14). Isa. 45:19 records God speaking righteousness; and Isa. 60:6 refers to him speaking in his sanctuary. The angel of God speaks to Jacob in Gen. 35:15.

In other significant contexts, God commands Moses to speak to the people of Israel in relation to regulations for worship (Lev. 1:2; 4:2; 23:2ff.); to other legislation (Num. 5:6, 12; 6:2); and to judgment for sin (Num. 16:24; Ps. 2:5). God also speaks in relation to giving covenant promises to David (1 Kgs. 8:24ff.; Ps. 89:19).

Where human speech is concerned, people speak to God in prayer, including Abraham (Gen. 18:27, 31) and Moses (Num. 27:15). People praise Yahweh for deliverance (2 Sam. 22:1), and in general terms of praise (Ps. 145:21). People also speak wisdom (Ps. 49:3); truth (Prov. 8:7); lies (Ps. 63:11); and a foreign language (Neh. 13:4; Isa. 19:18). See also Gen. 22:7; Judg. 19:3; Eccl. 3:7. In particular, special mention is made of the prophet speaking to others what the Lord has commanded him to say (cf. Num. 23:12; 24:13; Deut. 18:18ff.; Josh. 4:10; Jer. 1:7; Ezek. 20:3; Zech. 7:5).

NT Words

legō [λέγω, *3004*]

legō is the dynamic equivalent of ***'āmar*** (see above). It occurs over 1,300 times with the primary meanings "say," "speak" — again divided in usage between human and divine verbal communication.

The verbal expression of God is illustrated in the context of passing judgment on the wicked (cf. Luke 12:20); speaking to Moses (cf. Mark 12:26); and commending Christ as his Son (cf. Matt. 17:5; 22:44; Luke 3:22).

Christ addresses Satan in rebuke (Matt. 4:7; Luke 4:8). He also speaks to those whom he cures of disease or raises back to life (cf. Matt. 8:13; Mark 10:52; John 11:39; Luke 7:14); to his disciples in the course of their instruction (cf. Matt. 14:16); to the crowds listening to his teaching discourses (cf. Matt. 19:11ff.; Mark 6:4; John 13:31); to those who are prospective disciples (cf. Matt. 8:22; Mark 1:17); and to those he seeks to evangelize (cf. John 4:17). He also personally addresses his Father in prayer (cf. John 11:41; 17:1); and he prays for the forgiveness of those who put him to death (cf. Luke 23:34).

legō also indicates angelic verbal communication with human beings, especially in relation to announcing Christ's birth to Mary (cf. Luke 1:30ff.). See also Luke 1:13; 2:10; Acts 12:8; Rev. 4:1; 17:7. Satan himself also engages Christ in conversation during the time of the latter's "trial" in the wilderness (cf. Matt. 4:3; Luke 4:6).

The phrase "It is said . . ." refers in Heb. 4:7; 11:18 to the authority of Scripture.

In a number of contexts, various individuals address Jesus Christ. For example, people ask him questions in Matt. 8:19ff.; Mark 2:16; Luke 6:2. Peter speaks with the risen Christ in a vision in Acts 10:2. The Pharisees blaspheme against him in Matt. 9:34; Luke 11:15. Judas speaks in order to betray him in Matt. 26:25. A request for salvation is made of him in Luke 23:42.

Ordinary human discourse is indicated in Matt. 20:4, Mark 1:37; Luke 9:9; Acts 2:13.

laleō [λαλέω, *2980*]

laleō is a synonym for ***legō*** (see above), and a dynamic equivalent for ***dābar***, occurring around three hundred times with the primary sense of "speak," "say." Again the usage is divided between divine and human verbal expression.

God is declared to have spoken to Moses (John 9:29); to the patriarchs (Luke 1:55); and to the prophets (Acts 3:21; 23:9; Luke 1:70). In Heb. 1:1, the fulfillment of God's spoken word is expressed in the person of his son, Jesus Christ. The angel of the Lord speaks to Philip the evangelist in Acts 8:26 in order to redirect his ministry.

In the context of Christ's teaching ministry, he speaks to the people of Israel (Matt. 26:47; John 8:12, 30). He also speaks in parables (cf. Matt. 13:33ff.; 22:1; Mark 4:33). Jesus speaks to his Father in prayer in John 17:1.

Human verbal discourse is indicated in Acts 6:10, with reference to speaking godly wisdom; and in Acts 19:6; 1 Cor. 14:5, in relation to speaking in tongues. Acts 4:31 refers to the disciples of Christ speaking the word of God boldly. John 12:41 indicates that Isaiah spoke of Christ. See also Acts 16:13.

phēmi [φημί, *5346*]

phēmi is a synonym for ***legō*** and ***laleō***, a verb with the primary sense of "say" or "declare," found in around sixty places. The contexts often suggest an underlying nuance of a solemn affirmation or declaration borne of deep conviction or divine authority.

In relation Christ speaking, for example, Matt. 4:7 affirms the authority of the written word of God, as Christ's rebuke to Satan. Christ is said to instruct his people in the gospel (Matt. 19:21); and he is involved in teaching his disciples (Matt. 17:26). He is recorded as speaking a prophetic word (Matt. 26:34); and he acknowledges his royal status to Pilate (Matt. 27:11).

References to general human discourse are found in Matt. 13:28; 14:8; Luke 22:58. Instances of preaching are found in Acts 2:38; 7:2; 17:22. Peter affirms his loyalty to Christ in Mark 14:29. A profession of faith in Christ is indicated in John 9:38. The formula "It is said . . ." in relation to the authority of Scripture is indicated in 1 Cor. 6:16.

SAYING

OT Words

dābār [דָּבָר, **1697**]

dābār is a very common noun occurring nearly 1,500 times with the primary meanings "word," "thing," "matter."

However, in several contexts, ***dābār*** is translated "saying" with varying nuances. 1 Sam. 18:8, for example, refers to a proverbial "ditty" or "song" celebrating David's victory over the Philistine warrior, Goliath. ***dābār*** refers also to a "piece of advice" in 2 Sam. 17:4; Esth. 1:21. The root meaning "saying" refers to the recorded "words" or "oracles" of the court prophets (2 Chr. 13:22), and to the "chronicles of the seers" (2 Chr. 33:19). Ps. 78:2; Prov. 1:6 refer to "riddles" or "puzzling words."

SCAPEGOAT

OT Words

'azā'zēl [עֲזָאזֵל, **5799**]

'azā'zēl is found only four times, with reference to the "scapegoat" associated with the Day of Atonement ritual in Lev. 16:8, 10 (twice), 26. The "scapegoat" is actually one of two goats selected for the ritual. One is slaughtered as a sacrifice for sin; the other (i.e., the "scapegoat") is taken away into the wilderness, symbolically bearing the sins of the people, which are thereby removed from the presence of God.

SCARLET

OT Words

tāla' [תָּלַע, **8529**]

tāla' is a verb found only in Neh. 2:3, referring to "being clothed in scarlet."

shānî [שָׁנִי, **8144**]

shānî is a noun occurring around forty times, referring exclusively to the color "scarlet," "crimson," or more precisely the dye of that color obtained from the dried body of an insect. ***shānî*** is found in various contexts.

Gen. 38:28ff.; Josh. 2:18ff. refer to "scarlet thread." Song 4:3; Isa. 1:18 refer metaphorically to scarlet. Isa. 1:18 refers to the people's sins as "scarlet," resulting in gross moral and spiritual contamination.

shānî also refers to "scarlet material" used, for example, in the manufacture of furnishings for the tabernacle (cf. Exod. 25:4; 26:1, 31, 36; 27:16; 28:5ff.; 35:6, 23ff.; 36:8, 35ff.; 38:18; Num. 4:8). It is also used in making the high priestly garments (cf. Exod. 39:1ff.). Lev. 14:4ff., 49; Num. 19:6 refer to scarlet material as a component of an offering for ceremonial cleansing. In mundane contexts, ***shānî*** refers to an item of clothing (cf. 2 Sam. 1:24; Prov. 31:21; Jer. 4:30).

tôlā' [תּוֹלָע, **8438**]

tôlā' is a synonym for ***shānî*** (see above) and is used in conjunction with it, occurring about forty times. ***tôlā'*** likewise refers to the color scarlet, derived from the animal dye. The references are the same as for ***shānî*** (see above). In addition, ***tôlā'*** can be translated "worm." (→ WORM)

NT Words

kokkinos [κόκκινος, *2847*]

kokkinos is the dynamic equivalent of the Hebrew terms ***shānî*** and ***tôlā'***. It occurs six times, all with reference to the color "scarlet."

The Roman soldiers place a scarlet robe on Christ prior to his crucifixion in mockery of his claims to be king of the Jews (cf. Matt. 27:28).

Heb. 9:19 refers to scarlet thread as a component of the offering of consecration for covenant renewal.

Rev. 17:3, 4 mention the scarlet beast in the symbolic description of Babylon, portrayed as a demonic "queen," an idolatrous "prostitute," the epitome of blasphemy against God. Rev. 18:12, 16 refer to scarlet material as merchandise.

Additional Notes

The symbolism of "scarlet" is significant in the Old Testament. Where associated with ritual worship, it constitutes a material symbol for blood, indicating the process of cleansing from sin. This applies by implication to the scarlet material of the tabernacle furnishings and the high priestly garment. Such a phenomenon is then explicitly indicated in connection with the scarlet thread associated with the offering for ceremonial purity.

This symbolism is only mentioned once in the New Testament, alluding to the old covenant sacrifice of cleansing in Heb. 9:19. However, it is evident from the context of Heb. 9 that such a cleansing has been accomplished once for all through the sacrificial blood of Christ. Thus the symbolic force of "scarlet" is linked to the overarching motif of atonement through the shedding of blood in both Old and New Testaments.

SCATTER

OT Words

pûṣ [פּוּץ, 6327]

pûṣ is a verb occurring around seventy times with the primary meanings "scatter," "disperse," with related nuances.

pûṣ refers to people "scattering" in various places — for example, early human society (Gen. 10:18; 11:4); Israelites throughout Egypt (Exod. 5:12); armies in defeat (1 Sam. 11:11; 2 Sam. 18:8; 2 Kgs. 25:5; Jer. 52:8); people in general (1 Sam. 13:8; 14:34); and Israel (1 Kgs. 22:17; 2 Chr. 18:16), who is described as leaderless. Jer. 10:21; 23:1, 2; Ezek. 34:5ff. refer to the people of Judah being scattered by ruthless leaders.

In a number of other contexts, God is depicted as the agent of scattering or dispersing. He scatters early human society abroad (Gen. 11:8, 9), and the sons of Jacob, Simeon and Levi (Gen. 49:7). The scattering of the enemies of Yahweh is recorded in Num. 10:35; 2 Sam. 22:15; Pss. 18:14; 68:1; 144:6; Isa. 24:1; Ezek. 29:12. In several places there is a warning of exile for God's people, when they will be scattered among the nations (cf. Deut. 4:27; 28:64; 30:3; Neh. 1:8; Zech. 13:7). ***pûṣ*** refers to the reality of being scattered in exile (Ezek. 11:16, 17; 20:34, 41); and to the threat of imminent scattering in exile (Jer. 9:16; 13:24; 18:17; Ezek. 12:15; 20:23; 22:15).

In metaphorical contexts, the clouds are said to scatter lightning in Job 37:11; and Job 38:24 declares that the wind is scattered on the earth.

zārāh [זָרָה, 2219]

zārāh is a verb occurring about forty times with the principal sense of "scatter," as well as several associated nuances such as "disperse," "winnow," "spread."

Scattering powder or dust onto water, in the sense of "spreading," or "casting out," is indicated in Exod. 32:20. Similarly, Num. 16:37 refers to scattering spent coals on the ground. See also Isa. 30:22.

The action of "winnowing" grain (i.e., scattering or throwing it to the wind to separate the chaff) is indicated in Ruth 3:2; Isa. 30:24; 41:16; Jer. 4:11. The metaphorical "winnowing" of the evil is noted in Prov. 20:8, 26.

God is declared to be the agent of scattering in a number of contexts. Israel is threatened with dispersal among the nations as the outworking of divine judgment in Lev. 26:33; Ezek. 6:8; 12:14ff.; 20:23; 22:15; 1 Kgs. 14:15; Ps. 44:11; 106:27; Jer. 31:10. A similar fate is handed down to foreign nations who are threatened with scattering to the four points of the compass (cf. Jer. 49:36; Ezek. 29:12; 30:23ff.; 36:19).

God is also said to "winnow" the Israelites (Jer. 15:7), and his enemies (Jer. 51:2).

pā'āh [פָּאָה, 6284]

pā'āh is a verb found only in Deut. 32:36 with reference to Yahweh "scattering" Israel among the nations in divine judgment.

bāzar [בָּזַר, 967]

bāzar is a verb that occurs only twice. It refers to the "scattering" of peoples in Ps. 68:30, and to the "scattering" of plunder and wealth among people in Dan. 11:4.

zāraq [זָרַק, 2236]

zāraq is a verb with the primary meaning "sprinkle." (➡ SPRINKLE) However, in Ezek. 10:2 it is translated "scatter" in relation to the cherubim scattering burning coals over Jerusalem in divine judgment.

bedar [בְּדַר, 921 (Aramaic)**]**

bedar is an Aramaic verb found only in Dan. 4:14, indicating the "scattering" of fruit.

pāzar **[פָּזַר, 6340]**

pāzar is a verb found ten times, meaning "scatter abroad," "disperse." References to Israel being scattered among the nations are found in Esth. 3:8; Jer. 50:17; Joel 3:2. The scattering of God's enemies is indicated in Ps. 89:10. See also Pss. 112:9; 141:7; 147:16; Prov. 11:24; Jer. 3:13.

pārad **[פָּרַד, 6504]**

pārad is a verb occurring around thirty times with the primary meanings "divide," "separate." However, in Esth. 3:8 it refers to the scattering of Israel in exile, and in Ps. 92:9 to the scattering of the enemies of God.

pāras **[פָּרַשׂ, 6566]**

pāras is a verb found in around seventy contexts with the dominant senses of "spread (out)," "stretch (out)." However, it is translated "scatter" in Ps. 68:14 with reference to God scattering pagan kings in the land of Canaan. In Ezek. 17:21 it refers to Israelite survivors scattered in foreign lands.

nāphaṣ **[נָפַץ, 5310]**

nāphaṣ is a verb found in approximately twenty contexts with the principal meaning "shatter," "break in pieces." In two places, however, ***nāphaṣ*** means "scatter," with reference to people dispersing (1 Sam. 13:11). Isa. 11:2 refers to regathering "scattered" Israelites from exile.

pārash **[פָּרַשׁ, 6567]**

pārash is a verb found only five times. It means "scatter" in Ezek. 34:2, describing the "scattered" sheep of Israel in exile.

pûsh **[פּוּשׁ, 6335]**

pûsh is a verb occurring only four times. It means "scatter" in Nah. 3:8, with reference to the "scattered" people of Assyria.

NT Words

diaskorpizō [διασκορπίζω, *1287*]

diaskorpizō is a verb with the primary meanings "scatter," "disperse," "winnow." It is found eleven times.

The meaning "winnow" is expressed in Matt. 25:24, 26. The "scattering" of the flock refers to those who will abandon Christ at the time of his trial (cf. Matt. 26:31; Mark 14:27). God is said to scatter the proud in Luke 1:51. John 11:52 refers generally to the scattering of God's children. See also Acts 5:37.

skorpizō [σκορπίζω, *4650*]

skorpizō is related to ***diaskorpizō***, above, meaning "scatter abroad," "disperse" in all five occurrences. Matt. 12:23; Luke 11:23; John 10:12 all warn that the opponents of Christ will scatter his people. John 16:32 also warns that the followers of Jesus Christ will "scatter" (i.e., abandon him) at the time of his suffering. See also 2 Cor. 9:9.

dialyō [διαλύω, *1262*]

dialyō is a verb found only in Acts 5:36 with reference to the "scattering" of the followers of the false messiah, Theudas.

diaspeirō [διασπείρω, *1289*]

diaspeirō is a verb referring to the "scattering" of the early believers as a consequence of their persecution, found only in Acts 8:1, 4; 11:19.

diaspora [διασπορά, *1290*]

diaspora is the noun derived from ***diaspeirō*** (see above), referring to the "scattering" of believers in the face of persecution in three contexts (cf. John 7:35; Jas. 1:1; 1 Pet. 1:1).

SCENT → SMELL

SCEPTER

OT Words

shēbet **[שֵׁבֶט, 7626]**

shēbet is a noun occurring in about 190 contexts with the dominant meaning "tribe," as well as the associated senses "scepter," "rod," "staff." (→ TRIBE)

Literal references to a "rod" in the sense of a "staff," or "stick," are found in Exod. 21:20; Lev. 27:32; 2 Sam. 7:14; 23:21, indicating it as a weapon, or instrument of corporal punishment. Other references to the "rod" as a means of disciplining children are found in Prov. 10:13; 13:24; 22:15; 23:13ff. In a related but extended context, ***shēbet*** also refers metaphorically to the "rod" as Yahweh's instrument of discipline (cf. Job 21:9; Ps. 89:32; Isa. 10:5; 30:31; Lam. 3:1; Ezek. 20:37; 21:13).

In other contexts, ***shēbet*** refers to the "scepter" as a symbol of royal authority — in reference, for example, to the anticipated royal rule of the Messiah (cf. Gen. 49:10; Num. 24:17). The Messiah will exercise his scepter in the context of achieving victory over his enemies, thus establishing his dominion over them (cf. Ps. 2:9;

Isa. 11:4). The scepter is the symbol of God's royal authority in Pss. 23:4; 45:6. ***shēbet*** also refers to the "staff" of God, indicating his compassionate pastoral care of his people (cf. Mic. 7:14).

The "rod" symbolizes human power and authority in Ps. 125:3; Isa. 9:4; Ezek. 19:11; Amos 1:5, 8; Mic. 5:1; Zech. 10:11.

sharbît [שַׁרְבִיט, **8275**]

sharbît is a noun found in four places, all with reference to the "scepter" of the king of Persia (cf. Esth. 4:11; 5:2 [twice]; 8:4).

NT Words

rhabdos [ῥάβδος, *4464*]

This noun is a dynamic equivalent for the Hebrew term ***shēbet*** (see above), likewise meaning "scepter," "staff," "rod."

rhabdos refers literally to a "staff" for walking, or support, in Matt. 10:10; Mark 6:8; Luke 9:3; Heb. 11:21. It also refers to Aaron's "rod," the symbol of his high priestly authority in Heb. 9:4.

All other uses of ***rhabdos*** are metaphorical. It is translated "rod" and used as a symbol of chastisement in 1 Cor. 4:21. The meaning "scepter" is symbolic of the rule of the Messiah (cf. Rev. 2:27; 12:5; 19:15); and of God's kingdom (Heb. 1:8).

Additional Notes

The "scepter" is of primary theological significance in both Old and New Testaments.

The phenomenon of the royal scepter in the Old Testament is closely linked to the coming of the Messianic King and his universal dominion over his people. Though references to this phenomenon are few, they occur in very significant redemptive-historical contexts. The scepter is a universal symbol of royal authority and power, and it succinctly expresses the essence of messianic dominion over the world.

In the New Testament, the term ***rhabdos*** clearly indicates that the rule of Christ, as the fulfillment of Old Testament prophecy, can be adequately expressed through the powerful symbol of his royal "scepter." It is a symbol that demonstrates the powerful redemptive-historical continuity of the kingdom of God throughout the canon of Scripture.

SCOFF → SCORN

SCORCH

NT Words

kaumatizō [καυματίζω, *2739*]

kaumatizō is a verb found in four places, meaning "scorch" in the sense of "burn with intense heat."

Reference is made in Matt. 13:6; Mark 4:6 to plants "scorched" or "withered" by the sun. Rev. 16:8, 9 refers to "scorching" the wicked — an indication of their fiery torment.

See Also: → BURN

SCORN

OT Words

seḥôq [שְׂחוֹק, **7814**]

seḥôq is a noun derived from ***sāḥaq*** (→ LAUGH), occurring fifteen times with the primary senses of "laugh," "derision," "scorn."

General references to "laughing" include those in Job 8:21; Prov. 14:13; Eccl. 2:2; 7:3, 6; 10:19.

The meaning "laughingstock," indicating those who are mocked or scorned, is found in Ps. 126:2; Job 12:4; Jer. 48:27, 39; Lam. 3:14.

In Jer. 20:7; 48:26, ***seḥôq*** refers to the experience of being scorned, mocked, or held in derision.

lûṣ [לוּץ, **3887**]

lûṣ is a verb with the dominant sense of "mock," "scorn" in its nearly thirty occurrences. It is also translated "interpret" on several occasions. (→ INTERPRET)

"Mocking" or "scorning" among people is indicated in general terms in Job 16:20; Prov. 1:22; 14:6ff.; 19:25ff.; and such activity is condemned by God in Ps. 1:1; Prov. 3:34; Isa. 28:22. The action of "scorning" on the part of godless people is indicated in Ps. 119:51.

God is said to scorn the wicked in Prov. 14:9.

la'ag [לַעַג, **3933**]

la'ag is the noun derived from ***lā'ag*** (→ LAUGH) with the sense of "scorn," "derision" in all seven uses of the term (cf. Job 34:7; Pss. 44:13; 79:4; 123:4; Ezek. 23:32; Hos. 7:16).

ṣeḥōq [צְחֹק, **6712**]

ṣeḥōq is a rare noun found only twice, referring to "laughter" in Gen. 21:6, and to "scornful laughter" in Ezek. 23:32.

qālas **[קָלַס, 7046]**

qālas is a verb found in only four places, meaning "scorn," "mock," "laugh at."

Children are said to "make fun of" Elijah in 2 Kgs. 2:23. Ezek. 22:5 declares that nations will "make fun of" Jerusalem. The action of "scoffing" at kings is noted in Hab. 1:10. "Scorning" payment for idolatrous "prostitution" is indicated in Ezek. 16:31.

misḥāq **[מִשְׂחָק, 4890]**

misḥāq is a participial form with verbal force, found only in Hab. 1:10 with reference to "scoffing" at fortresses.

lāṣôn **[לָצוֹן, 3944]**

lāṣôn is a noun meaning "scorning," or "scoffing." Prov. 1:22 refers generally to people "scorning"; and Prov. 29:8; Isa. 28:14 refer to "scornful people."

lāṣaṣ **[לָצַץ, 3945]**

lāṣaṣ is a participial verb found only in Hos. 7:5, meaning "mockers," or those who scorn, or mock.

ḥerpāh **[חֶרְפָּה, 2781]**

ḥerpāh is a noun derived from ***ḥāraph*** (see below), with the primary sense of "reproach," or "shame," in most of the seventy-five or so occurrences of the term. There is some overlap in meaning, however, with the sense of "scorn."

ḥerpāh means "scorn" in the sense of active mocking or taunting (cf. Neh. 5:9; Pss. 22:6; 79:12; 119:22; Lam. 3:61).

ḥāraph **[חָרַף, 2778]**

ḥāraph is a verb occurring around forty times with the primary meaning "reproach," or "defy," including the sense of "taunt," "mock," or "scorn."

Yahweh is said to be scorned, or mocked, by his enemies (2 Kgs. 19:4, 16, 22ff.). Isa. 37:4, 17, 23ff.; Pss. 74:10; 79:12; 1 Chr. 20:7; Neh. 6:13; Zeph. 2:10 refer to Israel being taunted by her enemies. The psalmist declares that he is "scorned" by his enemies, who despise him (cf. Pss. 42:10; 55:12; 102:8; 119:42). The sin of "casting scorn" upon the poor is indicated in Prov. 17:5.

See Also: → LAUGH

SCORPION

OT Words

'aqrāb **[עַקְרָב, 6137]**

'aqrāb is the only term in the Old Testament referring to the "scorpion." It occurs four times. Literal references to these poisonous creatures are found in Deut. 8:15; Ezek. 2:6. Metaphorically, ***'aqrāb*** refers to a severe mode of punishment, whereby King Rehoboam of Judah threatens to chastise his people with "scorpions" (cf. 1 Kgs. 2:11, 14; 2 Chr. 10:11, 14).

NT Words

skorpios [σκορπίος, *4651*]

skorpios is the dynamic equivalent for ***'aqrāb***, referring to "scorpions" in all five occurrences of the term. Literal references to the animal are found in Luke 10:19; 11:12. Metaphorical references occur in Rev. 9:3, 5, 10, where an aspect of divine punishment on the wicked is likened to the sting of a scorpion.

SCOURGE

OT Words

shôt **[שׁוֹט, 7752]**

shôt is a noun found in eleven places, meaning "whip," or "scourge."

Literal references to the "whip" as an instrument of corporal punishment are found in 1 Kgs. 12:11, 12. Whips used on horses are noted in Prov. 26:3; Nah. 3:2.

The tongue is described metaphorically as a "scourge" in Job 5:21. The "scourge" as an instrument of divine punishment is indicated in Isa. 10:26; 28:15, 18.

shōṭēṭ **[שֹׁטֵט, 7850]**

shōṭēṭ is found only in Josh. 23:13, with reference to a "scourge."

NT Words

mastigoō [μαστιγόω, *3146*]

mastigoō is a verb found seven times, meaning "scourge," or "whip."

Most commonly, ***mastigoō*** refers to "scourging" (or whipping) as a judicial punishment (cf. Matt. 10:17; 20:19; 10:34; Luke 18:33; John 19:1).

The term is used metaphorically in Heb. 12:6 concerning the disciplinary action of God in "whipping" or "scourging" his children.

mastizō [μαστίζω, *3147*]

mastizō is a rare verb found only in Acts 22:25, meaning "scourge" or "whip" in the literal sense of judicial punishment.

mastix [μάστιξ, *3148*]

mastix is a noun that occurs six times, referring to the practice of "scourging," or "flogging," as corporal punishment (cf. Acts 22:24; Heb. 11:36).

phragelloō [φραγελλόω, *5417*]

phragelloō is a verb found only twice, referring to the "scourging" or "whipping" of Christ prior to his crucifixion (cf. Matt. 27:26; Mark 15:15).

phragellion [φραγέλλιον, *5416*]

phragellion is the rare noun derived from ***phragelloō*** (see above), found only in John 2:15 with reference to a "whip."

SCRIBE

OT Words

sôpher [סוֹפֵר, **5608**]

sôpher is the present participial form of the verb ***sāphar*** (→ COUNT). ***sāphar*** has the predominant senses of "tell," "declare," "count," but in about one-third of the occurrences the participial form ***sôpher*** is used, with the sense of "scribe." Scribes constituted part of the educated elite among the civil and ritual leadership of ancient Israel. As the term suggests, "scribes" had responsibility for the preservation, interpretation, and teaching of the written canon of the Hebrew Scriptures, especially the Mosaic law.

References to the Levitical scribes include those in 2 Sam. 8:17; 1 Kgs. 4:3; 2 Kgs. 12:10; 22:3ff.; 1 Chr. 2:55; 2 Chr. 34:13ff.; Isa. 36:3, 22; Jer. 36:20ff. Ezra the scribe is specifically mentioned in Ezra 7:6, 11; 8:9; Neh. 8:1ff.; 12:26.

Esth. 3:12 refers to pagan scribes, who were presumably likewise an educated elite class of "civil servants" or public officials. Scribes are also referred to generally in Isa. 33:18.

sāphēr [סָפֵר, **5613** (Aramaic)]

sāphēr is an Aramaic noun found in six places, meaning "scribe," or "secretary."

sāphēr describes Ezra the Israelite scribe and leader of the postexilic community (Ezra 7:12, 21). Shimshai the Persian scribe, who was opposed to rebuilding the city of Jerusalem, is mentioned in Ezra 4:8ff.

NT Words

grammateus [γραμματεύς, *1122*]

grammateus is the primary term for "scribe" in the New Testament, occurring nearly seventy times. It refers, as does its dynamic Hebrew equivalent ***sôpher***, to the teachers, interpreters, and preservers of the Hebrew Scriptures. In the New Testament, "scribes" are often associated with the priests and/or the Pharisees.

Scribes are specifically referred to in Matt. 2:4; 7:29; 8:19; 12:38; Mark 1:22; 12:35; Luke 5:30; John 8:3; Acts 4:5; 6:12; 23:9. In particular, the scribes bear the brunt of Jesus' wrath on account of their hypocrisy (cf. Matt. 23:13ff.; Luke 11:44).

General references to scribes are found in Matt. 13:52; 1 Cor. 1:20.

SCRIPTURE

NT Words

graphē [γραφή, *1124*]

graphē is a noun with the underlying sense of "writing." However, in the fifty or so occurrences of the term, it refers almost exclusively to "Scripture(s)," or the sacred, canonical writings of the old covenant people of Israel. In at least one place, ***graphē*** also refers to the unique canonical authority of the New Testament "Scriptures."

The Scriptures, or the old covenant canonical writings, are affirmed by Jesus Christ in the course of his teaching ministry (cf. Matt. 21:42; 26:54; Mark 12:10; 14:49; Luke 4:21; 24:27; John 5:39; 7:38).

The Hebrew Scriptures are similarly viewed by the Gospel writers (cf. Matt. 26:56; Luke 24:45; John 2:22; 20:19). They are also declared to be uniquely authoritative, and are quoted by other apostolic writers (cf. Acts 1:16; 8:35; Rom. 1:2; 11:2; 1 Cor. 15:3ff.; Gal. 3:8, 22; 1 Tim. 5:18; 2 Tim. 3:16; Jas. 2:8; 4:5; 1 Pet. 2:6).

General references to the Old Testament Scriptures are found in Acts 17:11; 18:24, 28. 2 Pet. 3:16 mentions the New Testament writings of Paul as "Scripture."

gramma [γράμμα, *1121*]

gramma is a noun occurring fourteen times, with the sense of "writing," "letters," "learning," in most of these. In 2 Tim. 3:15, ***gramma*** refers to the "sacred writings," or the old covenant Scriptures.

Additional Notes

In the Old Testament, there is no specific reference to the canon of Scripture as such. However, the underlying concept of authoritative written revelation is present throughout, whether implicit or explicit. The phenomenon of Scripture, however, is closely related to "the word of God," and "the word of the Lord."

See Also: → WORD

SCROLL → BOOK

SEA

OT Words

yām **[יָם, 3220]**

yām is a common noun, meaning "sea" in the majority of its nearly four hundred occurrences. "Sea" refers to both general and specific bodies of water. Other meanings include the direction "west." (➡ WEST)

yām refers generally to "sea(s)" (Gen. 22:17; Deut. 33:19; Ps. 8:8; Eccl. 1:7; Jer. 6:23; Ezek. 26:3, 17ff.; Hab. 2:4; Zech. 9:4); to the bodies of water created by God (cf. Gen. 1:10, 22ff.; Pss. 33:7; 95:5; Prov. 8:28); and to the shore of the sea (cf. Judg. 7:12; 1 Sam. 13:5; 1 Kgs. 4:29; Jer. 47:7).

yām refers to the Dead Sea (literally, the Salt Sea) (Gen. 14:3; Num. 34:3; Deut. 3:17; Josh. 3:16; 15:2ff.; Ezek. 47:8ff.); and to the Re(e)d Sea (cf. Exod. 10:19; 14:2ff.; 15:4ff.; Num. 33:10, 11; Deut. 1:1, 40; Josh. 24:6; Judg. 11:16; Pss. 106:7ff.; 136:13ff.; Jer. 49:21). A number of texts specifically celebrate Israel's miraculous divine deliverance from the Re(e)d Sea (cf. Pss. 66:6; 68:22; 78:13, 53; Isa. 50:2; 51:10; Hab. 3:14).

The Mediterranean Sea (literally the Great Sea) is referred to in Num. 34:6ff.; Josh. 1:4; 9:1; 15:12, 47; 23:4; Ezek. 47:10ff.; Dan. 7:2; as is the Sea of Galilee (or Sea of Chinnereth), in Num. 34:11; Josh. 13:27.

In the context of ritual worship, ***yām*** refers to the great bronze washbasin in the temple court used for the ritual purification of the priests as a "sea" (cf. 1 Kgs. 7:23ff.; 2 Kgs. 16:17; 25:13, 16; 1 Chr. 18:8; 2 Chr. 4:2ff.; Jer. 27:19; 52:17ff.).

yam **[יַם, 3221** (Aramaic)**]**

yam is a rare Aramaic noun meaning "sea" found only in Dan. 7:2, 3.

NT Words

thalassa **[θάλασσα, *2281*]**

thalassa is the dynamic equivalent of ***yām***, meaning "sea" in the approximately ninety occurrences of the term. General references to the sea are found in Matt. 8:27; 18:6; Mark 4:41; Luke 17:6; Acts 27:38; Rom. 9:27; Heb. 11:2; Jude 13; Rev. 5:13; 7:1ff.; 10:2ff.; 18:17ff. The "seas" as created by God are mentioned in Acts 14:15. Rev. 21:1 contains a vision of the disappearance of the sea in the new heavens and the new earth. The Re(e)d Sea is indicated in Acts 7:36; 1 Cor. 10:1, 2; Heb. 11:29.

A metaphorical reference to a "sea of glass" is found in Rev. 4:6.

SEAL

OT Words

ḥôtām **[חוֹתָם, 2368]**

ḥôtām is a noun occurring fourteen times, meaning "seal" or "signet ring."

General references to the "signet ring" as a form of personal identification are found in Gen. 38:18; Exod. 28:11, 21, 36; 39:6, 14, 30; 1 Kgs. 21:8.

In Hag. 2:23, Zerubbabel is declared to have been fashioned as Yahweh's "signet ring," or his precious possession, stamped as his "personal property." Jer. 22:24 refers symbolically to the signet ring of King Jehoiachin. Song 8:6 alludes to "the seal upon one's heart" — a symbolic reference to undying love.

ḥātam **[חָתַם, 2856]**

ḥātam is a verb found in around thirty contexts, with the predominant meanings "seal," "seal up."

ḥātam means "to seal up" in the sense of "lock, or store away" with respect to goods or property (Deut. 32:34); to sin (Job 14:17); and to the law (Isa. 8:16). Sealing up letters, ready for delivery, is indicated in 1 Kgs. 21:8. Reference to the "sealed fountain" of the beloved in Song 4:12 is a metaphorical allusion to her virginal state prior to the physical consummation of her marriage. The "sealing up" of a divine vision, or revelation, is indicated in Isa. 29:11; Dan. 9:24; 12:4, 9.

ḥātam refers to "setting a seal" on a covenant or treaty document (Neh. 9:38; 10:1); and on a title deed for land (Jer. 32:10ff.).

The process of "sealing" with a royal ring is noted in Esth. 3:12; 8:8ff.

ḥatam **[חֲתַם, 2857** (Aramaic)**]**

This Aramaic verb, synonymous with ***ḥātam***, is rare and found only in Dan. 6:17 with reference to Darius and his officials "sealing up" the mouth of the lion's den to guarantee that Daniel's planned execution will in fact be carried out.

NT Words

sphragizō **[σφραγίζω, *4972*]**

sphragizō is a verb occurring about thirty times meaning "to seal," "set one's seal on," in a number of contexts.

The meaning "to seal" in the sense of "secure," or "lock up," is indicated in Matt. 27:66, with reference to a stone over the entrance to Jesus' tomb. In Rev. 20:3 it refers to Satan being prevented from deceiving the nations.

Elsewhere, the meaning "seal" means "to bind up," so as to prevent disclosure of divine revelation, as in Rev. 10:4; 20:10. "Sealing" the people of God in Rev. 7:3ff. functions as an ultimate measure of protection against divine judgment.

The expression "set one's seal on" is used in several contexts, all of them metaphorical. In John 3:33 this expression serves as a guarantee of truth for particular testimony, the validation of the truth of God. John 6:27 affirms that God sets his seal on Jesus Christ in order to validate his status as the Son of God. God is also said to "set the seal" of his Spirit on the hearts of believers in order to guarantee and preserve their status as belonging to him (cf. 2 Cor. 1:22; Eph. 1:13; 4:30).

sphragis [σφραγίς, *4973*]

sphragis is a noun derived from ***sphragizō*** (see above) meaning "seal" or "signet ring" in all sixteen occurrences and in various contexts.

sphragis is used metaphorically to refer to a "seal" as a sign of a guarantee or validation of circumcision, described in Rom. 4:11 as a "seal" of righteousness. In 1 Cor. 9:2, the Corinthian congregation is designated as a "seal" of Paul's apostleship.

The phenomenon of "sealing" the people of God, identifying them as belonging to him, is indicated in 2 Tim. 2:19. Rev. 9:4 refers to the "seal" of God that protects the saints.

Rev. 5:1ff.; 6:1ff.; 7:2; 8:1 refer to "seals" attached to a scroll. Each of these seals represents an aspect of God's universal judgment on wicked humankind.

katasphragizō [κατασφραγίζω, *2696*]

katasphragizō is a rare variant of the verb ***sphragizō*** (see above), meaning "cover with a seal" and found only in Rev. 5:1, in relation to the visionary scroll of John's revelation.

Additional Notes

The principal significance of the vocabulary for "seal," both as a noun and a verb, lies in its distinctive usage as a symbol for personal identification and authentication of one's status. In particular, it is the "sealing" of the people of God with respect to their relationship with both Yahweh and Christ in the old and new covenant eras, respectively, that yields the unique theological connotation of these terms.

The practice of "sealing" to validate one's social, political, or ritual standing in society is a very ancient one. What is especially significant in the biblical worldview is that God takes this cultural motif and applies it to the unique covenant relationship that he establishes with the nation of Israel. The various literal and metaphorical contexts where God's "seal" is indicated provide a glimpse of the multi-faceted and complex nature of the relationship between Yahweh and his people. Whatever the precise context, the "seal" of Yahweh marks out the individual, or group, concerned as being of special value to God.

In the New Testament it is the Spirit of God who is given to believers as the "seal" (i.e., the irrevocable guarantee) of their unique saving relationship with God, in and through the person of Jesus Christ. In particular, the "sealing" of the saints in the book of Revelation depicts their blessed heritage of eternal fellowship with God in heaven, in a powerful symbolic context. This in turn alludes back to a similar phenomenon in the prophecy of Ezekiel (cf. Ezek. 9), whereby the godly citizens of Jerusalem who grieve and lament over the apostasy of their fellow countrymen are spared the terrible slaughter that will soon be handed down by God to that largely apostate generation. In short, it is the "seal" of God in Christ, applied by the ministry of the Spirit, that guarantees the believer freedom from the guilt and punishment of sin. It is this ultimate "sealing" that is anticipated in the Old Testament traditions.

SEARCH

OT Words

tûr **[תּוּר, 8446]**

tûr is a verb occurring around twenty times, meaning "search (out)," "spy out" in most of these contexts.

The meaning "search out" in the context of looking for a place to rest is found in Num. 10:33. Similarly, ***tûr*** means "search out" in the sense of "spy out" or "undertake a reconnaissance" with reference to the land of Canaan at the hands of the Israelite tribal leaders (cf. Num. 13:2ff.; 14:6ff.; 34ff.). This task is said to be undertaken by Yahweh himself in Ezek. 20:6. Judg. 1:23 also refers to "searching out" the land. Similarly, Yahweh is said to have searched out a way through the wilderness through the pillar of cloud in Deut. 1:33.

tûr is also used metaphorically, meaning "to search out" or "seek" for ways to cheer oneself in Eccl. 2:3.

ḥāphar **[חָפַר, 2658]**

ḥāphar is a verb found in about twenty places with the primary sense of "dig." (→ DIG) However, in a couple of contexts ***ḥāphar*** is translated "search for," "search out" (cf. Deut. 1:22; Josh. 2:2, in the context of explorating the land of Canaan).

ḥāqar [חָקַר, **2713**]

ḥāqar is a verb found in approximately thirty places with the primary sense of "search" in a variety of contexts, with several different nuances.

Human beings "search" in the sense of "examine," or "make inquiry," in Deut. 13:4; Job 5:27; 13:9; Eccl. 12:9. Lam. 3:40 contains the exhortation "to examine one's ways." In a literal, physical context, ***ḥāqar*** is translated "search out" in relation to the land of Canaan in Judg. 18:2; 2 Sam. 10:3. Ezek. 39:14 refers to searching for dead bodies after battle.

ḥāqar is also used in the context of divine examination, as God "searches" the heart of humankind (cf. Ps. 139:1, 23; Jer. 17:10).

ḥāphas [חָפַשׂ, **2664**]

ḥāphas is a verb which occurs over twenty times, with the sense of "search," "search out," in over half of these contexts.

The literal sense of "searching" for property is noted in Gen. 31:35; 44:12. Other objects of "searching" include missing persons (1 Sam. 23:23) and persons guilty of idolatry (cf. 2 Kgs. 10:23). Yahweh is said to "search out" sinful people for judgment in Amos 9:3; Zeph. 1:12.

In metaphorical contexts, people "search out," or "examine," the hearts of human beings. Prov. 2:4 speaks of "searching after" wisdom.

beqar [בְּקַר, **1240** (Aramaic)]

beqar is an Aramaic verb found in five places, meaning "search for," or "inquire."

Ezra 4:15, 19 refer to searching for records in the Persian archives confirming Jerusalem as a rebellious city. Similarly, the search for records of Cyrus' decree to send Israelites back to Canaan to rebuild the temple is noted in Ezra 5:17; 6:1. See also Ezra 7:14.

See Also: ➞ SEEK

SEASON ➞ TIME

SEAT

OT Words

kappōret [כַּפֹּרֶת, **3727**]

kappōret is a significant term occurring nearly thirty times, referring exclusively to the lid or cover of the ark of the covenant, made of pure gold. ***kappōret*** is translated in the older English versions as "mercy seat," while a more modern rendering is "atonement cover." At both ends of the ***kappōret*** were two sculpted golden cherubim, facing each other with outstretched wings. This golden "seat" or "cover" symbolized the throne of Yahweh, the earthly representation of a heavenly reality, assigned to occupy the most sacred space in the whole of God's kingdom on earth — the holy of holies in the central shrine of Israel's tabernacle and temple. The appropriateness of the designation "mercy seat" lies in the fact that a faithful devoted worshiper of Yahweh may obtain mercy and forgiveness through the offerings of the high priest, once a year, during the Day of Atonement ceremony. It was only at this time that the "mercy seat" was exposed to the high priest in order that forgiveness for sin might be obtained for that year for the people of Israel.

kappōret refers almost exclusively to the "atonement cover" or "mercy seat" of the tabernacle (cf. Exod. 25:17ff.; 26:34; 38:6ff.; 40:20; Lev. 16:2, 13ff.; Num. 7:89). The same item of furniture in the Solomonic temple is noted only in 1 Chr. 28:11.

kissē' [כִּסֵּא, **3678**]

kissē' is a noun occurring around 140 times with the primary sense of "throne." In the majority of cases, it refers to the seat of human royalty as well as to that of divine royal authority. (➞ THRONE)

In a number of places, the term "throne" refers to God's heavenly "seat" of authority, which can be understood metaphorically as a reference to the "seat" or "throne" of God, associated with the ark of the covenant in the Israelite tabernacle or temple (cf. Pss. 9:7; 11:4; 45:6, 8; 103:19; Isa. 6:1; Jer. 3:17; 17:12; Ezek. 10:1; 43:7; Zech. 6:13).

Elsewhere, the meaning "seat" is indicated in mundane, literal references to a bench, or chair, on which people sit (cf. 1 Sam. 2:8; 4:13, 18).

Prov. 9:14 refers metaphorically to "seat" as the location of judicial or civic authority.

môshāb [מוֹשָׁב, **4186**]

môshāb is a participial noun derived from ***yāshab*** (i.e., "to live," "dwell" (➞ DWELL), which means "dwelling," "habitation" in most of the forty or so occurrences of the term. There are, however, a number of places where ***môshāb*** also means "seat."

The literal sense of "seat" as the place where one sits is found in 1 Sam. 20:18, 25; 1 Kgs. 10:5; 2 Chr. 9:4. In Job 29:7 the term indicates the site of public office, with reference to the "seat" in the square.

Metaphorically, Ps. 1:1 refers to "the seat" of sinners, indicating their lifestyle, or ethos. Ezek. 28:2 refers to "the seat" of the gods, or their dwelling place.

shēbet [שֶׁבֶת, 7675]

shēbet is a noun found in four places, with the explicit sense of "seat" that is equated with a "throne," only in 1 Kgs. 10:19.

NT Words

bēma [βῆμα, *968*]

bēma is a noun occurring thirteen times with the predominant sense of "judgment seat" or "throne" in contexts where justice is administered from this vantage point — both human and divine.

The "judgment seat" of Pontius Pilate during the time of Christ is indicated in Matt. 27:19; John 19:13. The divine "judgment seat" of Christ, before which all believers will stand, is noted in Rom. 14:10; 2 Cor. 5:10.

bēma refers to "the throne" of Herod Agrippa (Acts 12:21), and to the Roman "tribunal" (i.e., the official Roman court of justice) in Acts 25:17; 18:12ff.; 25:6, 10.

kathedra [καθέδρα, *2515*]

kathedra is a rare noun found only three times meaning "seat," or "chair." It refers literally in Matt. 21:12; Mark 11:15 to the seats of the moneychangers in the temple. A metaphorical usage is found in Matt. 23:2, referring to "the seat" of Moses, which signified his position of leadership in Israel. This "seat" is now occupied by the Pharisees, the religious leaders of Israel at the time of Jesus Christ.

prōtokathedria [πρωτοκαθεδρία, *4410*]

prōtokathedria is a noun occurring four times, referring to the "best seats" (i.e., seats of chief honor) in the synagogues, that were the prime choice of the Pharisees and other religious leaders of the day (cf. Matt. 23:6; Mark 12:39; Luke 11:43; 20:46).

Additional Notes

In the contexts where "seat" refers metaphorically, in both Testaments, to the place where Yahweh and Christ exercise their divine authority and justice, this vocabulary (especially ***kappōret*** and ***bēma***) is highly significant. The powerful symbolism of the "atonement cover" or "mercy seat," associated with the ark of the covenant, suggests the very throne room of Yahweh where he administers both mercy and judgment.

This divine prerogative is carried over into the New Testament, where the "judgment seat" of Christ constitutes a redemptive-historical consummation of divine judgment and mercy. Such a judgment will serve to distinguish, in an ultimate sense, between the godly and the ungodly on the final day of judgment.

See Also: → THRONE

SECOND

OT Words

shēnî [שֵׁנִי, 8145]

shēnî is a noun found around 150 times, indicating the ordinal number "second" in about half of these contexts.

The designation "second" is applied to days (cf. Gen. 1:18; Exod. 2:13); months (cf. Gen. 7:11); years (cf. 1 Kgs. 15:25); and specific occasions in time (cf. Lev. 13:58; Isa. 11:11; Jer. 13:3). It is also applied to listings of children (cf. Gen. 30:7) and sacrificial animals (cf. Lev. 5:10; Judg. 6:25).

mishneh [מִשְׁנֶה, 4932]

mishneh is a noun meaning "second," as well as related senses, in about half of the thirty-five occurrences of the term. (→ DOUBLE)

mishneh refers to the "second" item, or person, in a series, or in rank (cf. Gen. 41:43; 1 Sam. 8:2; 2 Sam. 3:3; 2 Kgs. 23:4; Neh. 11:9). It also refers to the "copy" of the law, noted in Deut. 15:18; 17:18; Josh. 8:32.

terēn [תְּרֵין, 8648 (Aramaic)]

terēn is an Aramaic noun occurring twelve times, with the primary meaning "twelve." However, it is translated "second" in Ezra 4:24, referring to the second year of King Darius' reign.

NT Words

deuteros [δεύτερος, *1208*]

deuteros is the dynamic equivalent of ***shēnî*** (see above), the numerical adjective "second." It is found in nearly fifty contexts.

The number "second" is indicated in a variety of contexts. There are references to time, or occasion, in Matt. 26:42. More commonly, ***deuteros*** indicates "second" in a group, or series — the second of the Ten Commandments (Matt. 22:39; Mark 12:31); the "second" death (Rev. 2:11; 20:6, 14; 21:8); and the "second" seal of judgment (Rev. 6:3). Heb. 8:7 speaks of the new covenant as the "second" covenant. See also Heb. 9:3, 7.

SECRET, SECRETLY

OT Words

sôd [סוֹד, 5475]

sôd is a noun meaning "assembly" or "council" in the majority of its nearly twenty occurrences. However, when it is the "council" of Yahweh, it is indicative of God's plans being formed and revealed in secret. Only those privileged to be called into God's presence will gain knowledge of Yahweh's secret counsel (e.g., the prophets). In this regard, Amos 3:7 explicitly refers to these divine secrets. (➞ COUNCIL)

Elsewhere, **sôd** refers to the "secrets" of human beings (cf. Prov. 11:13; 20:19; 25:9).

sēter [סֵתֶר, 5643]

sēter is a noun derived from **sātar** (see below), with the underlying sense of "shelter," "hiding place," or "secret place." It is also used adverbially with the sense of "secretly," "in secret."

The adverbial sense is found, for example, in Deut. 13:6; 2 Sam. 12:12; Ps. 139:15; Prov. 9:17; Jer. 38:16. Isa. 45:19; 48:16 declare that God's word is not spoken in secret.

sēter refers to the "secret place" or "hiding place" of human beings (1 Sam. 19:2). It also refers metaphorically to the "shelter" or "secret place" of God (Pss. 31:20; 61:4; 91:1). God himself is declared to be a "refuge," or "hiding place," in Pss. 32:7; 119:114.

sātar [סָתַר, 5641]

sātar is a verb found in around eighty contexts with the primary sense of "hide," indicating the underlying sense of secret concealment. (➞ HIDE) In several places, however, **sātar** is explicitly translated "secret." The participial noun of the term refers to the "secret things" of Yahweh that belong to him alone (Deut. 29:29). "Secret" faults are indicated in Ps. 19:12. "Secret" love is indicated in Prov. 27:5.

mistār [מִסְתָּר, 4565]

mistār is a noun derived from **sātar** (see above) and occurs ten times with the underlying sense of "secret place" or "hiding place." It is also used adverbially.

The meaning "hiding place" is indicated in Ps. 10:8; Isa. 45:3; Jer. 13:17; 23:24; 49:10. **mistār** also means "ambush" in Lam. 3:10; Pss. 17:12; 64:4.

The adverbial sense of "secretly," "in secret" is found in Ps. 10:9; Hab. 3:14.

'ālam [עָלַם, 5956]

'ālam is a verb occurring around thirty times with the primary meaning "to hide." (➞ HIDE) It is also used adjectivally to refer to "secret" sins (Ps. 90:8), and to "secret" things in the heart of human beings, whether good or bad (Eccl. 12:14).

ta'alummāh [תַּעֲלֻמָּה, 8587]

ta'alummāh is a noun derived from **'ālam** (see above) meaning "secret," indicating "that which is hidden." It is found only three times. Job 11:6 refers to "secrets" of wisdom, and Ps. 44:21 speaks of "secrets" of the heart. See also Job 28:11.

ḥeresh [חֶרֶשׁ, 2791]

ḥeresh is an adverbial form found only in Josh. 2:1, with reference to Joshua sending out spies "in secret" to search out the land of Canaan.

ḥāphā' [חָפָא, 2644]

ḥāphā' is a rare verb found only in 2 Kgs. 17:9 in relation to Israel "acting in secret," as they engage in idolatrous worship.

NT Words

kryptos [κρυπτός, *2927*]

kryptos is an adjective occurring about twenty times, also used adverbially, meaning "secret," "in secret," and indicating "that which is hidden."

Practicing piety "in secret" will earn the favor of God who sees "in secret" (cf. Matt. 6:4, 6, 18). See also John 7:4. Nothing can remain hidden (i.e., secret) from God (Matt. 10:26; Mark 4:22; Luke 8:17; 12:2).

kryptos is used nominally in Rom. 2:16; 1 Cor. 4:5; 14:25 to refer to the "secrets" of human beings, to be judged by God.

Jesus Christ denies having said anything "in secret," with a view to deceive (cf. John 18:20).

kryptō [κρύπτω, *2928*]

kryptō is a verb found in sixteen contexts with the dominant sense "to hide." However, in John 19:38, **kryptō** is used adverbially to refer to the "secret" discipleship of Joseph of Arimathea. (➞ HIDE)

apokryphos [ἀπόκρυφος, *614*]

apokryphos is an adjective found in only three contexts, meaning "secret" (i.e., "kept hidden"). It is used negatively in Mark 4:22; Luke 8:17, indicating that nothing can be kept secret or hidden from the scrutiny of God. See also Col. 2:3.

kryphē [κρυφῇ, *2931*]

kryphē is an adverb found only in Eph. 5:12 with reference to shameful things done "in secret."

lathra [λάθρα, *2977*]

lathra is an adverb found in four places, meaning "secretly" in the sense of "quietly," or "discreetly" (cf. Matt. 1:19; 2:7; John 11:28; Acts 16:37).

See Also: → MYSTERY

SECT

NT Words

hairesis [αἵρεσις, *139*]

hairesis is a noun found in nine contexts meaning "sect," in the sense of a religious or political party or faction. It also has the connotation of "heresy" or "false teaching."

The meaning "sect" in the sense of "party" is found in a number of contexts. It is evident in the general sense of a "faction" in 1 Cor. 11:19; Gal. 5:20. ***hairesis*** refers to the Sadducean "party" (Acts 5:17); the Pharisaic "party" (Acts 15:5; 26:5); the "sect" of the Nazarenes (Acts 24:5); and the "sect" of the Christians (Acts 28:22).

In Acts 24:14; 2 Pet. 2:1, ***hairesis*** is translated "heresy" or "false teaching," referring in the latter text to the false prophets that threatened the spiritual well-being of the first-century church.

SECURE → SAFE

SEDITION → TRAITOR

SEE

OT Words

rā'āh [רָאָה, **7200**]

rā'āh is a common verb, occurring over 1,300 times and meaning "to see" in the majority of these contexts. In addition, ***rā'āh*** can have the sense of "look" — the two meanings are closely related. The action of "seeing" and "looking," with associated nuances, is predicated of both God and human beings.

Where Yahweh is the subject of ***rā'āh***, a number of contexts are in view. With the sense of "observe," or "focus attention on," God is said to have seen his creation, declaring it to be good (cf. Gen. 1:4ff.; Job 28:24). Similarly, Gen. 6:12 declares that God "looked" on the earth, noting the wickedness of humankind (Gen. 6:5). In Gen. 9:16, Yahweh is said to "see" or "look at" the rainbow and remember his covenant promises. Neh. 9:9 records God "seeing" or "viewing" the suffering of his people, and other texts likewise indicate God looking at his people's suffering with a view to alleviating it (cf. Gen. 29:32; Exod. 2:5; Deut. 26:7).

With the sense of "inspect," or "examine," God is said to "see" the ways of human beings (Gen. 11:5; Job 31:4; Ps. 53:2; Isa. 57:2; Jer. 12:3). In Exod. 5:21, he looks on them with a view to punishment.

God also exhorts human beings to "see" and give attention to God and his ways (cf. Exod. 31:2; Deut. 1:8; Ps. 34:8).

Where human beings are involved in "seeing" and "looking," similar nuances are observed. With the sense of "witness," or "observe," human beings are said to "view" or "see" the glory of God (e.g., Ps. 97:6; Isa. 35:2); a vision of God (e.g., Judg. 13:22; 1 Kgs. 22:19; Isa. 6:1ff.; Ezek. 1:1ff.; Amos 9:1); and the redemptive acts of God (e.g., Deut. 29:2ff.; Ps. 98:3; Isa. 52:10). Humankind is said to have seen the judgment of God on his people (Jer. 44:3; Lam. 3:1); the righteousness of God's people (Isa. 62:2); and the futility of life (Eccl. 4:7). Isa. 42:18 declares that people see after being given the gift of sight.

The meaning "see" in the sense of "realize," or "gain mental perception of" is indicated, for example, in Gen. 3:6, where Eve "saw" that the fruit of the forbidden tree was good for eating (cf. also Exod. 32:1; Num. 20:29; Deut. 28:10; Eccl. 3:22). Ezek. 12:2 affirms that the sin of God's people blinds them so they cannot "see" the wrong they are doing.

The sense of "see" or "look" is also indicated in contexts where "examination," "investigation," or "searching" is undertaken. Such "looking" is stated absolutely, as in Gen. 8:13; Josh. 5:13; Neh. 4:14; Ezek. 8:7. In particular, Moses "examines" the burning bush in Exod. 3:2. Priests are required by law to "look for" the presence of disease which might disqualify a person for worship in the tabernacle (cf. Lev. 13:3ff.; 14:3, 37ff.). The occult practice of "examining" the liver is indicated in Ezek. 21:21. The task of "seeing" (i.e., "searching out") the land of Canaan is noted in Num. 32:9; Deut. 3:25.

In other contexts, ***rā'āh*** is translated "look" in the sense of "gaze at" — for example, in Num. 21:8, where the Israelites are urged to "look at" the bronze serpent in order to gain healing (cf. also. Gen. 13:4; 18:16; 1 Sam. 6:19). The meaning "look," with a view to action, is illustrated in Exod. 2:11. The exclamation "Look!" as a demand for attention is found in Exod. 10:10; 2 Kgs. 6:32.

Inanimate objects are declared to be "visible" (lit., "seen"), including the rainbow in Gen. 9:14. See also Gen. 8:5; Ps. 18:15.

rā'āh is also used metaphorically. For example, Job 9:25 declares that "one's days 'see' no good"; and the waters are said to "see" God in Ps. 77:16. The experience of "seeing" death is noted in Ps. 89:48. The shame of God's people "will be seen," as indicated in Jer. 13:26.

nābat [נָבַט, 5027]

nābat is a verb found in nearly eighty contexts, meaning "to look," "look upon," "regard," in the majority of these instances. The explicit meaning "to see" is found in only a handful of these texts — although, as noted in the entry for ***rā'āh***, above, the senses of "see" and "look" are very similar. As with ***rā'āh***, above, the action of "looking" is predicated of both God and humankind.

With the underlying sense of "examine," God is said "to look upon" the ends of the earth, and thereby see everything (cf. Job 28:24; Ps. 33:13; Isa. 18:4). In Ps. 10:14, the examining gaze of Yahweh detects suffering in human beings, and alleviates it (Ps. 102:19). See also Isa. 63:15.

The expression "look down on," in relation to God's activity, is found in Pss. 13:3; 80:14; Lam. 1:1; 2:20; 5:1. In these contexts, the underlying sense of ***nābat*** is that of "to have regard for," "consider," and speaks of God's concern for his people.

In the human sphere, ***nābat*** refers to people "looking (or gazing) at" — for example, Abraham looking at the stars (Gen. 15:5); Moses afraid to look at God (Exod. 3:6); the people looking at the bronze serpent for healing (cf. Num. 21:9). The sense of "look back" is indicated in Gen. 19:17, 21 — an action forbidden to Lot and his wife as they fled from the destruction of Sodom and Gomorrah, yet one that the woman committed and consequently lost her life.

The meaning "look" in the sense of "take notice of" is indicated in 1 Sam. 16:7; Isa. 51:1, 2. Isa. 22:11 records that the people of God did not "look to" God — they took no notice of him.

The specific sense of "see" is noted with respect to God (Ps. 94:9), who is declared to be perfectly capable of "seeing" all in his world. In Ps. 92:11 the psalmist declares that he has seen the downfall of his enemies.

shāqaph [שָׁקַף, 8259]

shāqaph is a verb that occurs around twenty times and means "look," "look down," "look out" throughout its usage, again predicated of both God and human beings.

shāqaph indicates the action of "looking out" a window in Gen. 26:8; Judg. 5:28; 2 Sam. 6:16; 2 Kgs. 9:30; Prov. 7:6. The action of "looking down" is noted in 2 Sam. 24:20.

In an evident theophanic context, the three divine visitors to Abraham "look toward" Sodom in Gen. 18:16.

Yahweh is said "to look down upon" the Egyptian army in Exod. 14:24 with a view to their destruction. Deut. 26:15 contains a plea for God "to look down from" heaven and bless his people. See also Pss. 14:2; 53:2; Lam. 3:50.

In inanimate contexts, mountains are said "to look down upon," or "overlook," the wasteland (cf. Num. 21:20; 23:28). Ps. 85:11 declares that righteousness "looks down from" the sky.

shāgaḥ [שָׁגַח, 7688]

shāgaḥ is a rare verb found only three times, meaning "look at," or "gaze at." Ps. 33:14 refers to Yahweh "looking at" the peoples of the world. The action of people "gazing" is indicated in Song 2:9; Isa. 14:16.

ḥāzāh [חָזָה, 2372]

ḥāzāh is a verb found approximately fifty times, meaning "see" or "behold" in the majority of these contexts, and referring to the action of both God and human beings.

ḥāzāh frequently refers to "seeing" or "beholding" God in vision or theophany. Moses and the seventy elders of Israel are said to behold God on Mt. Sinai (Exod. 24:11); and the psalmist sees God in the temple sanctuary (Ps. 63:2). Only genuine prophets have the privilege of "seeing" God and receiving revelation from him — for example, Balaam (cf. Num. 24:4, 16); Ezekiel (Ezek. 12:27); Isaiah (Isa. 1:1; 2:1; 13:1). See also Amos 1:1; Mic. 1:1; Hab. 1:1. In contrast, false prophets only "see vain things" (cf. Lam. 2:14; Ezek. 13:6ff.; Zech. 10:2). Pss. 11:7; 17:15 declare that the righteous shall see the face of God. Conversely, people will fail to see God because of their sin (cf. Isa. 26:11).

When God is declared to "see," the usage is metaphorical or, more accurately, anthropomorphic. God "sees" the children of human beings (Ps. 11:4) and the righteous (Ps. 17:2).

shûr [שׁוּר, 7789]

shûr is a verb found in sixteen places, meaning "see," "behold," "look" in the majority of these contexts.

General references to "seeing" or "beholding" are found in Job 24:15; 35:5; Num. 23:9. Balaam's prophecy in Num. 24:14 contains his anticipated vision (or sighting) of the coming Messianic King. Skepticism about the human ability to see God is noted in Job 34:29 (cf. also Job 33:14; 35:14). Job 7:8 denotes God "seeing" (or "beholding") human beings.

NT Words

horaō [ὁράω, *3708*];
eidon, oida [εἶδον, οἶδα, *1492*]

horaō is a verb found in nearly 700 places meaning "see" in the majority of these contexts, with a variety of nuances. The terms ***eidon*** and ***oida*** are past tense forms of this verb. These forms also express the meaning "know," which is closely related to "seeing," in the context of mental perception. (➠ KNOW)

References to "seeing" in the physical realm of visual perception include those in Mark 1:10; Luke 9:36; John 1:39; Acts 6:15; 1 Cor. 2:9; Col. 2:1. In particular, John 6:36 refers to people seeing or watching Christ perform miraculous signs.

In John 14:9 Christ declares that "to see" him is equivalent to "seeing" the Father — clearly implying spiritual perception. Seeing, or beholding, the glory of God or a vision from God is indicated, for example, in Luke 1:22; Acts 7:55; Rev. 20:11ff. See also Rev. 4:4; 18:1ff.; 7:1ff. Other contexts declare that human beings cannot "see" God in his essential being (cf. John 1:18; 5:37; 6:46; 1 John 4:20; 1 Tim. 6:16). Luke 2:30 refers to Simeon "seeing" the salvation of God when he was introduced to the infant Jesus and blessed him. John declares that he saw a vision of the "new heavens and the new earth" in Rev. 21:1, 2. See also Matt. 3:16; 16:28.

horaō means "see" in a number of other senses — for example, "take heed" (cf. Matt. 8:4; Acts 22:6; 1 Thess. 5:15); "bear witness to," or "recognize," in the context of affirming Jesus Christ as the son of God (cf. John 1:34; 4:45; 19:35); "realize," or "perceive" (cf. John 6:23; Acts 8:23; Jas. 2:24; Gal. 2:7). In particular, Christ "sees" into the heart of human beings (Luke 9:47), and then "perceives" faith in their hearts (Matt. 9:2; Mark 2:5). ***horaō*** also refers to not "seeing" (i.e., experiencing) death (cf. Luke 2:26; Heb. 11:5,) or "seeing" corruption (Acts 2:27ff.). Luke 9:27; John 3:3 refer to "seeing" the kingdom of God.

theōreō [θεωρέω, *2334*]

theōreō is a verb occurring about sixty times meaning "see," "look," or "behold" in most of these contexts.

The sense of "looking at, or on," as a spectator, is indicated in Matt. 27:55; Mark 12:41. In particular, Christ declares that he saw Satan fall like lightning from heaven (cf. Luke 10:18).

The nuance of "inspect" or "examine" is evident in Matt. 28:1 in relation to the tomb of Jesus.

Other senses of ***theōreō*** include that of "perceive," "realize" (John 4:19; Acts 17:22); "experience" (John 8:51, explicitly denying that any believer will ever "see" eternal death); and "consider," or "assess" (Heb. 7:4).

The plain sense of "seeing" as visual perception is indicated in Mark 3:11; Luke 24:37; John 17:24; Acts 7:56; 10:11.

blepō [βλέπω, *991*]

blepō is a fairly common verb occurring about 130 times. It means "see," "look," along with a variety of associated nuances, predicated of both God and human beings.

Matt. 5:28; 14:30 refer to people "looking on, or at" in the sense of "observe," or "watch." Matt. 18:10 speaks of "observing" the face of God. Acts 8:6 refers to "witnessing" apostolic miracles. See also Acts 2:33. The action of "looking back" is noted in Luke 9:62.

Matt. 12:22; John 9:25 refer to "seeing" after being healed from blindness. Ordinary visual perception is noted in Mark 13:2. The nuance of "impact," or "examine," is evident in Rev. 5:4.

In a number of contexts, ***blepō*** expresses the idea of "seeing" as "understanding," or "realizing," especially in relation to spiritual truth (cf. Matt. 13:13ff.; Mark 8:18; Luke 8:10; John 9:39; Acts 28:26; Rom. 11:10; Heb. 2:9; 2 Cor. 7:8).

The meaning "see," with the sense of "take heed," "take care," is evident in Matt. 24:4; Mark 4:24; 1 Cor. 3:10; Eph. 5:15.

Where God is concerned, ***blepō*** indicates the divine action of "seeing" in the sense of "observing" or "taking note" (cf. Matt. 6:4ff.; 7:3).

anablepō [ἀναβλέπω, *308*]

anablepō is a variant form of ***blepō***, above, meaning "look up," "receive one's sight," to see again after healing from blindness. The term is found in approximately twenty-five contexts.

References to the blind "receiving their sight" and seeing again are found, for example, in Matt. 11:5; Mark 10:51; Luke 7:22; John 9:11ff.; Acts 9:12ff.

The action of "looking, or glancing up" in general is indicated in Mark 8:24; Luke 21:1. Matt. 4:19; Mark 6:41; Luke 9:16 describe "raising one's glance" to heaven.

periblepō [περιβλέπω, *4017*]

periblepō, another variant form of ***blepō***, is a verb found in seven contexts with the literal meaning "to look around" (cf. Mark 3:5, 34; 5:32; 9:8; 10:23; 11:11; Luke 6:10).

emblepō [ἐμβλέπω, *1689*]

The verb ***emblepō***, also related to ***blepō***, is found twelve times in all and means "look, or gaze upon."

Matt. 6:26 contains Jesus' exhortation to "consider," or focus attention on, the birds of the air and note how God cares for them.

Christ is said to "look intently" at those to whom he was ministering (cf. Mark 10:21, 27; Luke 20:17; 22:61; John 1:42). See also Mark 8:25; John 1:36. Acts 1:11 refers to the disciples "looking up" towards heaven, in the wake of Jesus' departure from the earth.

Acts 22:11 refers to Paul's temporary blindness in the aftermath of his dramatic conversion.

atenizō [ἀτενίζω, *816*]

atenizō is a verb found in fourteen contexts with the underlying sense of "to look intently at," or "gaze, or stare at," "fix one's eyes on" (cf. Luke 4:20; Acts 1:10; 6:15; 13:9; 23:1; 2 Cor. 3:7). In particular, 2 Cor. 3:13 speaks of God's people being denied the opportunity to "see" the fading glory on the face of Moses after his descent from Sinai.

parakyptō [παρακύπτω, *3879*]

parakyptō is a verb that occurs five times. It means "look into" in two of these contexts, both of them metaphorical. Jas. 1:25 refers to "looking into" the law of liberty. 1 Pet. 1:12 refers to angels longing "to look into" the fulfillment of God's redemptive purposes revealed to the prophets of old.

skopeō [σκοπέω, *4648*]

skopeō is a verb found eight times, meaning "look" in the sense of "take note of" in Rom. 16:17; Phil. 3:17. In 1 Cor. 4:18, ***skopeō*** is translated "fix one's eyes on" in relation to spiritual realities that are not discerned by normal human means.

aphoraō [ἀφοράω, *872*]

aphoraō is a rare verb found only twice, meaning "see" in the sense of "consider," "assess," or "determine" how things will turn out (Phil. 2:23). In Heb. 12:2 it indicates "looking" to Jesus, or focusing attention upon him, as the one who brings our salvation to fulfillment.

myōpazō [μυωπάζω, *3467*]

myōpazō is a rare verb found only in 2 Pet. 1:9. It describes the condition of "being short-sighted," or seeing dimly, in a spiritual sense — unable to grasp the implications of being granted new life and godliness.

See Also: → LIGHT → TURN

SEED

OT Words

zera' [זֶרַע, 2233]

zera' is a common noun found about 230 times with the primary meaning "seed" in most of these contexts, with a number of associated nuances.

The meaning "seed," referring to grain for sowing, is indicated in Gen. 1:11ff.; 47:19ff.; Lev. 11:37ff.; Ps. 5:10; Ezek. 17:5; Hag. 2:19. Exod. 16:31 refers to "seed" as "fruit," or "vegetation."

More commonly, ***zera'*** means "seed" with reference to "children," "posterity," or "offspring" (cf. Lev. 18:21; 20:2ff.; Deut. 28:59; Ps. 37:28; Isa. 1:4). Elsewhere, "seed" refers to a "lineage," "home," or "nation" (2 Chr. 22:10; Ezra 9:2; Neh. 9:2; Ps. 22:23; Dan. 9:1). Isa. 53:10 refers to the "seed" of the messianic Suffering Servant.

Of special significance is the reference in Gen. 3:15 to the conflict between the "seed" of the serpent and that of the woman, Eve — a prophecy of the utter destruction of the evil one at the hands of the messianic "seed" of the woman. ***zera'*** also refers to the "seed" of Abraham — an incalculable number of descendants promised by God to the patriarch Abraham under terms of the covenant (cf. Gen. 9:9; 12:17; 15:5ff.; 17:7ff.; 28:13ff.; Deut. 1:8; Josh. 24:3; Ps. 105:6); and to the "seed" of David (cf. 1 Chr. 17:11; Ps. 18:50; Jer. 33:22). In each case, the "seed" of promise finds its redemptive-historical fulfillment in the person of Christ, the final "seed" of promise (below).

Gen. 7:3 refers to the "seed" or "offspring" of animals; and Lev. 15:6ff. uses the term "seed" to refer to expressing semen.

kil'ayim **[כִּלְאַיִם, 3610]**

kil'ayim is a rare noun found only twice, meaning "mixed seed." It refers in Lev. 19:19 to the mingling of grain, the offspring of cattle as a result of crossbreeding, and to differing types of woven cloth. Deut. 22:9 refers to "mixed seeds" for sowing or planting.

perudôth **[פְּרֻדוֹת, 6507]**

perudôth is a term found only in Joel 1:17 with reference to "planted seed."

NT Words

sperma [σπέρμα, *4690*]

sperma is the dynamic equivalent for the Hebrew term ***zera'*** (see above), occurring around forty times with the underlying sense of "seed," as well as associated nuances in various contexts.

Seed for planting is indicated, for example, in Matt. 13:24ff.; Mark 4:31; 2 Cor. 9:10 (cf. also 1 Cor. 15:38).

More commonly, ***sperma*** refers to "seed" as "progeny," or "children." General references include those in Matt. 22:24ff.; Mark 12:19ff.

As with the corresponding Hebrew term, ***sperma*** refers to the "posterity" granted by God to Abraham under the promises of the old covenant (cf. Luke 1:55; John 8:33; Rom. 4:13ff.; 9:7ff.; 11:1; Heb. 11:11, 18). Similar mention is made of David's "seed" in John 7:42; Rom. 1:3; 2 Tim. 2:8. ***sperma*** likewise refers to the "nation" of Israel in Gal. 3:29; Heb. 2:16. In a redemptive-historical sense, ***sperma*** indicates that Jesus Christ is the one "seed" of Abraham — the culmination of all of God's redemptive purposes.

speirō [σπείρω, *4687*]

speirō is a verb occurring about fifty times with the principal meaning "to sow seed."

The literal sense of "sowing seed" is indicated in Matt. 6:26; 13:3ff.; Mark 4:3ff.; Luke 8:5. The expression "one reaps what one sows" is found in Matt. 25:24; Luke 12:24; 1 Cor. 15:37; Gal. 6:7, 8.

speirō is used metaphorically to indicate "sowing the seed" of God's word in the hearts of human beings (cf. Matt. 13:19ff.; Mark 4:14ff.; John 4:36ff.; 1 Cor. 9:11). Further symbolic usage is indicated in 1 Cor. 15:42ff., where Paul refers to the human body as "being sown," "perishable," or constituted by God to break down and decompose after physical death. Finally, 1 Pet. 3:18 declares that those who "sow" in peace reap a harvest of righteousness.

sinapi [σίναπι, *4615*]

sinapi is a noun found in five contexts, referring in each case to a "mustard seed" (cf. Matt. 13:31; 17:20; Mark 4:31; Luke 13:19; 17:6).

sporos [σπόρος, *4703*]

sporos is a noun occurring five times, referring literally to "seed (for sowing)" in Mark 4:26, 27; Luke 8:5; 2 Cor. 9:10. In Luke 8:11, ***sporos*** refers to "the word of God."

spora [σπορά, *4701*]

spora is a noun found only in 1 Pet. 2:3 with the metaphorical meaning "seed" in the sense of "physical and finite human existence."

Additional Notes

The most significant aspect of the vocabulary for "seed" throughout the Old and New Testaments is its metaphorical reference to a "lineage," or "posterity," that is promised, initiated, and brought to fulfillment by God himself. "Seed" refers specifically to the innumerable descendants promised to Abraham by Yahweh in relation to blessings guaranteed to him under the terms of the covenant.

Abraham's promised "seed" comes to fulfillment first of all in the nations of Israel. It then finds particular expression in the person of King David and his descendants, the most important of all being the Messiah himself, whom the New Testament clearly identifies as Jesus Christ.

SEEK

OT Words

bāqash **[בָּקַשׁ, 1245]**

bāqash is a verb occurring 225 times meaning "seek," or "search (for)," in most of these occurrences, predicated of both human beings and God.

Human beings "search" for people (cf. Gen. 37:15; Judg. 4:22; 1 Sam. 10:21; 28:7); for animals (1 Sam. 9:3); for places (Gen. 43:30; Ruth 3:1); for peace (Ps. 34:14); and for virtue and wisdom (Prov. 11:27; 14:6; Eccl. 7:25). See also Eccl. 3:6; Isa. 41:7; Prov. 17:19.

The meaning "seek" in the sense of "attempt" is indicated in several places with reference to an intention to kill (cf. Exod. 2:15; 4:24; 1 Sam. 19:2; 1 Kgs. 11:40;

Esth. 3:6; Jer. 38:16). Num. 16:10 refers to the attempt to gain the office of priesthood.

Various texts indicate the intention to seek the Lord, with various aims in view — to worship him (cf. Exod. 33:7; Deut. 4:29; Zech. 8:21); to know him (cf. Ezra 8:22; Ps. 40:16); or to gain an answer to prayer (cf. 2 Sam. 12:16; Ezra 8:23).

Yahweh is said to "seek out" a man after his own heart (1 Sam. 13:14) and his lost people (Ezek. 34:16).

dārash [דָּרַשׁ, 1875]

dārash is a verb found in around 160 places meaning "inquire," or "seek." The latter sense is found in about half of these contexts. (→ ASK)

Human beings "seek" or "search" for animals (cf. Lev. 10:16); peace and prosperity (cf. Deut. 2:3; Jer. 29:7); wisdom (cf. Eccl. 1:3); and pagan gods (cf. 2 Chr. 25:9). ***dārash*** also means "seek" in the sense of "attempting" to take life, or kill (cf. Ps. 38:12).

The intention of "seeking" the Lord is expressed in general terms in Deut. 4:29; 1 Chr. 28:9; Ezra 4:2; Ps. 19:10; Jer. 29:13. In negative contexts, ***dārash*** also refers to the rebellious people of God failing to "seek after" God in Ps. 10:4; Isa. 9:13; 31:1; Jer. 10:21. Exhortations and commands to seek the Lord are found in 1 Chr. 16:11; 2 Chr. 14:4ff.; Isa. 55:6; Hos. 10:12; Amos 5:4ff. "Seeking" the law of the Lord is indicated in Ezra 7:10; Ps. 119:45; Isa. 34:16.

dārash does not often refer to the actions of God. However, 1 Chr. 28:9 refers to God "searching" the hearts of human beings. And in Ezek. 34:11, God "searches for" his sheep (i.e., his people) in order to restore and heal them.

bāqar [בָּקַר, 1239]

bāqar is a verb found seven times and translated "seek out" only in Ezek. 34:11, where it is predicated of Yahweh, who promises to "search" or "seek out" his sheep (i.e., his people), mistreated by corrupt and cruel leaders.

shāḥar [שָׁחַר, 7836]

shāḥar is a verb occurring thirteen times meaning "seek," or "look for," in most of these contexts.

In Job 7:21, the term refers to God "looking for" his servants.

Human beings "seek after God" in Job 8:5; Pss. 63:1; 78:34; Prov. 1:28; 8:17; Isa. 26:9; Hos. 5:15. See also Prov. 7:15; 11:27.

NT Words

zēteō [ζητέω, *2212*]

zēteō is a dynamic equivalent for the Hebrew terms discussed above. It is found in approximately 120 contexts meaning "seek," or "search for," in the great majority of these places.

zēteō refers to people "searching for" wisdom (1 Cor. 1:22); spiritual blessing (Matt. 7:7; Luke 11:19); rest (Matt. 12:43); peace (1 Pet. 3:11); a sign (Mark 8:11); and death (Rev. 9:6). People are also said to "seek after" the kingdom of God (Matt. 6:33; Luke 12:31; 13:24). See also Matt. 2:13; Mark 16:6; Luke 13:6; 1 Cor. 7:27.

The meaning "seek" in the sense of "attempt" is indicated in contexts where there is an intention to destroy or kill (cf. Matt. 2:20; 21:31). In particular, such an intent is recorded in connection with the campaign of the Jewish authorities to have Jesus Christ killed (cf. Matt. 21:46; Mark 11:18; Luke 19:47; John 5:16; 7:1, 19ff.; 8:37ff.). Elsewhere, ***zēteō*** refers to the "attempt" to obtain eternal life or glory (Rom. 2:7; Col. 3:1). See also Luke 17:33. It also refers to people touching Jesus in order to obtain a cure for disease (cf. Luke 6:19).

Christ, as the Son of Man, "seeks" to do the will of God (John 5:44); and "seeks out" those who are spiritually lost in order to save them (cf. Luke 19:10). God is said to seek those who will worship him in John 4:23.

epizēteō [ἐπιζητέω, *1934*]

epizēteō is a variant form of ***zēteō***, above, occurring fourteen times and meaning "seek after," or "search for," in most of these contexts.

People are described as "seeking after" material needs (Matt. 6:32; Luke 12:30); a sign or miracle (Matt. 12:39; 16:4; Mark 8:12; Luke 11:29); and salvation (Rom. 11:7). Heb. 11:14 speaks of the Old Testament saints "looking for" a homeland. Believers are then described as "searching for" an eternal city (Heb. 13:14). See also Acts 12:19.

ekzēteō [ἐκζητέω, *1567*]

ekzēteō is another variant form of ***zēteō*** (see above), found eight times and meaning "seek after" in about half of these contexts.

The intention of "seeking after the Lord" is indicated in Acts 15:17; Heb. 11:6. Rom. 3:11 acknowledges that none seek after the Lord. Heb. 12:17 refers to Esau's abortive attempt to seek a blessing after forfeiting his birthright to Jacob. 1 Pet. 1:10 refers to those "searching for" the fulfillment of God's redemptive purposes for his people.

anazēteō [ἀναζητέω, *327*]

anazēteō is a rare verb found in only two places. Luke 2:44 refers to Jesus' parents "searching for" him among their friends and relatives. In Acts 11:25, Barnabas "looks for" Saul in Tarsus.

SEER

OT Words

rō'eh **[רֹאֶה, 7203]**

rō'eh is a participial noun derived from ***rā'āh*** (→ SEE), occurring twelve times and meaning "seer" (i.e., prophet), referring to one who beholds visions from God and communicates them to the people.

References to Samuel as a "seer" predominate in the usage of ***rō'eh*** (cf. 1 Sam. 9:9ff.; 1 Chr. 9:22; 26:28; 29:29. Hanani is also referred to as a "seer" in 2 Chr. 16:7ff.

ḥōzeh **[חֹזֶה, 2374]**

ḥōzeh is a participial noun derived from ***ḥāzāh*** (→ SEE) and meaning "seer" in most of its twenty-two occurrences.

General references to "seer" include those in 2 Kgs. 17:13; 2 Chr. 33:18ff.; Isa. 29:10; Mic. 3:7. ***ḥōzeh*** refers to God as a "seer" (cf. 2 Sam. 24:11; 1 Chr. 21:9; 29:29); to Heman (cf. 1 Chr. 25:5); to Iddo (cf. 2 Chr. 9:29; 12:15); to Hanani (cf. 2 Chr. 19:2); to Asaph (cf. 2 Chr. 29:30); to Jeduthun (cf. 2 Chr. 35:15); and to Amos (cf. Amos 7:12).

SEIZE

OT Words

'āḥaz **[אָחַז, 270]**

'āḥaz is a verb occurring about seventy times meaning "take hold of," "grasp," "seize." The meaning "seize" is closely related to the first two meanings. (→ HOLD [])

ḥāzaq **[חָזַק, 2388]**

ḥāzaq is a verb occurring around three hundred times with the primary sense of "be strong," or "hold." It also means "seize," or "lay hold of." (→ HOLD [VERB] → STRENGTH)

tāphas **[תָּפַשׂ, 8610]**

tāphas is a verb found in sixty-five contexts with various senses including "take," "catch," "hold," or "seize."

The meaning "seize" in the sense of "catch," or "take hold of," refers to grabbing hold of clothing (Gen. 39:12; 1 Kgs. 11:30); apprehending someone with physical force (Deut. 21:19; 22:28; 1 Kgs. 13:4; 18:40; Ps. 71:11); or seizing someone through ambush (2 Kgs. 7:12). ***tāphas*** also refers to capturing a city (Josh. 8:8; 2 Kgs. 16:9; Jer. 40:10; 50:46).

NT Words

synarpazō [συναρπάζω, *4884*]

synarpazō is a verb found in only four places, meaning "seize by force," or "catch," in each case. Three times, ***synarpazō*** refers to seizing people (cf. Luke 8:29; Acts 6:12; 19:29); and once it refers to a ship being "caught" in a storm (cf. Acts 27:15).

syllambanō [συλλαμβάνω, *4815*]

syllambanō is a verb found in sixteen contexts with the general meaning "take" in the senses of "seize," "capture," in most of these places. (→ CONCEIVE)

The meaning "seize" in the sense of "capture," or "take by force," is indicated in Matt. 26:55; Mark 14:48; Luke 22:54; John 18:24; Acts 1:16, with reference to the capture of Jesus the night before his crucifixion. See also Acts 23:27; 26:21.

epilambanō [ἐπιλαμβάνω, *1949*]

epilambanō is a variant form of ***syllambanō***, above, occurring twenty times with the general meaning "take" in various senses, including "lead," "guide," "seize" (i.e., take hold of). (→ TAKE)

The meaning "seize" in the sense of "capture," "take (violent) hold of" someone, is indicated in Luke 23:26; Acts 16:19; 17:19; 18:17; 21:30.

krateō [κρατέω, *2902*]

krateō is a verb synonymous with ***synarpazō*** and ***syllambanō***, above. It occurs about fifty times with the general meanings "take," "hold," in a number of contexts. ***krateō*** also means "seize" or "capture" in approximately half of these contexts (cf. Matt. 14:3; 22:6; 26:48ff.; Mark 3:21; 14:1, 4ff.; Acts 24:6). (→ HOLD)

See Also: → TAKE

SELL

OT Words

mākar **[מָכַר, 4376]**

mākar is a verb found in approximately eighty contexts, meaning "sell" in a number of different contexts.

General references to the activity of "selling" include those in 1 Kgs. 21:20ff.; Isa. 24:2; Ezek. 7:12ff.

mākar frequently refers to selling people as slaves (cf. Gen. 37:27ff.; Exod. 21:7ff.; Deut. 15:12; 28:68; 2 Kgs. 17:17; Pss. 44:12; 105:17; Jer. 34:14; Joel 3:6ff.; Amos 2:6; Zech. 11:5). In particular, Israel is "sold" into slavery by Yahweh as a punishment for their rebellion against him (cf. Deut. 32:30; Judg. 2:14; 3:8; 4:3; 10:7; 1 Sam. 12:9; Isa. 50:1).

mākar also refers to selling property (Gen. 47:20ff.; Lev. 25:14ff.), as well as cattle (Exod. 21:35; Lev. 27:27ff.), and merchandise in general (2 Kgs. 4:7; Neh. 10:31; 13:16ff.; Prov. 31:24).

There is also a metaphorical prohibition against "selling" truth in Prov. 23:23.

shābar [שָׁבַר, 7666]

shābar is a verb occurring about twenty times with the primary sense of "buying" food. However, in several places it refers to "selling" food (cf. Gen. 41:56; 42:6; Deut. 2:28; Prov. 11:26; Amos 8:5ff.). (→ BUY)

NT Words

pōleō [πωλέω, *4453*]

pōleō is a verb that occurs around twenty times and means "sell." It refers to birds and animals (Matt. 10:29; Luke 12:6; John 2:14ff.); one's possessions (Matt. 13:44; 19:21; Luke 18:22); merchandise (Matt. 21:21; Mark 11:15; Luke 19:45; Rev. 13:17); food (1 Cor. 10:25); clothing (Luke 22:36); and property (Acts 4:34ff.; 5:1).

porphyropōlis [πορφυρόπωλις, *4211*]

porphyropōlis is a rare noun found only in Acts 16:14 with reference to Lydia, a "seller of purple cloth."

SEND

OT Words

shālaḥ [שָׁלַח, 7971]

shālaḥ is a common verb occurring nearly 850 times with the underlying sense of "send," as well as a variety of associated nuances. The act of "sending" is predicated of both God and human beings.

Where Yahweh is involved, ***shālaḥ*** means "send away," in the sense of "expel," in relation to Adam and Eve in the garden of Eden (cf. Gen. 3:23); and in relation to Israel, whom he is said "to divorce" (Jer. 3:8).

With the sense of "send forth," or "send on the way," God is said to send rain on the earth (cf. Job 5:10); food to his creatures (cf. Ps. 78:25); and blessing to his people, involving their salvation (cf. Pss. 20:2; 43:3; Isa. 19:20).

In the context of a specific task, or mission, Yahweh is also said to send his Spirit as an agent of creation (Ps. 104:30); and to send prophets to his people to convey his redemptive purposes (cf. Judg. 6:8; 2 Sam. 12:1; Isa. 6:8; Jer. 1:7; Ezek. 2:3ff.; Hag. 1:12; Zech. 2:9; Mal. 3:1). Of special significance is God's determination to send his Messianic Servant to usher in the climax of the divine kingdom and plan of salvation (cf. Isa. 61:1ff.). See also 1 Sam. 15:1; Ps. 110:2. People are also declared to have been sent by God for specific purposes, such as Moses, the deliverer of his people from Egypt (cf. Exod. 3:12ff.; 7:16; Num. 16:25; Josh. 24:5; Ps. 105:26). See also Gen. 24:7; Exod. 23:20.

In negative contexts, judgment is "sent" by God as a result of rebellion against him, directed against enemy nations (cf. Ps. 18:14; Jer. 25:15ff.; Amos 1:4ff.). Specifically, Yahweh sent plague judgments against Egypt (cf. Exod. 8:21; 9:14; Ps. 78:45); as well as covenant curses against his people (cf. Lev. 26:22; Deut. 28:20; Isa. 10:16; Jer. 9:16; Ezek. 5:17; Hos. 8:14). See also Exod. 23:27; 33:2.

In the human sphere, ***shālaḥ*** likewise expresses the sense of "send forth," "send on the way," in regard to people (cf. Gen:18:16); and animals (cf. Gen. 8:7ff.). In particular, Lev. 16:21 refers to the Israelite priests "sending out" the scapegoat into the wilderness as part of the sacrifice for sin on the Day of Atonement. The action of "divorcing" (i.e., sending away, or dismissing) one's wife is indicated in Deut. 24:1ff.

Gen. 32:3; Num. 20:14; 2 Sam. 11:1ff. refer to "sending" people on a mission or a specific task. In particular, tribal representatives from Israel are "sent out" to search the land of Canaan (cf. Num. 13:16; Deut. 1:22; Josh. 1:16; 7:2, 22).

shelaḥ [שְׁלַח, 7972 (Aramaic)]

shelaḥ is the Aramaic equivalent of ***shālaḥ*** (see above), occurring thirteen times and meaning "send," "send out," "send for."

Ezra 4:11ff.; 5:6ff., 17; 6:13 refer to sending or dispatching letters, as correspondence. Ezra the priest is sent on a mission, when Artaxerxes commissions him to return to his people to teach them the law of God (cf. Ezra 7:14). The meaning "send for," in the sense of a "summons," is indicated in Dan. 3:12.

Yahweh is said to send an angel to protect his servants in Dan. 3:28; 6:22. And in Dan. 5:24 he sends a message of judgment to Belshazzar, last ruler of Babylon.

NT Words

apostellō [ἀποστέλλω, *649*]

apostellō is the dynamic equivalent of ***shālaḥ*** (see above), found in approximately 130 contexts. It means "send," with a variety of nuances and in a variety of contexts.

apostellō refers to "sending" people in the sense of assigning someone a mission or task (cf. Matt. 14:35; Mark 12:2ff.; Luke 14:17; Acts 10:8). In particular, it refers to Herod's royal decree to slaughter all male infants two years old and younger (cf. Matt. 2:16).

Jesus Christ also sends people — for example, he sends his disciples on an evangelistic mission (Matt. 10:5, 16; Mark 6:7; Luke 9:2; 10:1ff.); and to preach in general (cf. Mark 3:14). His angels are sent to uphold the authority of his kingdom and deliver his people from destruction (cf. Matt. 13:14; 24:31). In Luke 24:49, Jesus promises to send the Holy Spirit in accordance with the plan of the Father.

apostellō also refers to God sending Jesus Christ to live among humankind (cf. Matt. 10:40; Mark 9:37; Luke 4:18; John 3:17; 6:29; 17:3ff., 18ff.; 1 John 4:9ff.); and to God sending his prophets to his people (Matt. 11:10; 23:34ff.; Mark 1:2; Luke 7:27; John 1:6; Rev. 22:6). In particular, Acts 7:34ff. indicates that God sent Moses to deliver his people from captivity in Egypt. God also sends angels to comfort and protect believers (cf. Heb. 1:14), and to communicate his plan to his people — as in Luke 1:19, where Gabriel announces to Zechariah that his wife Elizabeth will bear a son, who would become John the Baptist, the forerunner and herald of Jesus Christ.

exapostellō [ἐξαποστέλλω, *1821*]

exapostellō is a variant form of ***apostellō***, above. It occurs thirteen times and means "send away," "send out." It refers to people (Luke 1:53; 20:10ff.; Acts 7:12; 9:30; 11:22; 12:11; 17:14; 22:21); and to God "sending forth" his son, Jesus Christ into the world (Gal. 4:4). Gal. 4:6 affirms that God has sent his Spirit into our hearts.

synapostellō [συναποστέλλω, *4882*]

synapostellō is a rare verb, found only in 2 Cor. 12:18 and meaning "to send with."

pempō [πέμπω, *3992*]

pempō is a synonym for ***apostellō*** (see above), meaning "send" in most of its nearly eighty occurrences in a variety of contexts.

pempō refers to sending someone on an errand or mission (Matt. 14:10; Acts 10:5, 32ff.; Phil. 2:19ff.); to sending a message (Matt. 11:2; Acts 19:31; 23:30); to sending letters to the seven churches of Asia (Rev. 1:11); and to Jesus "sending" his disciples into the world (John 20:21).

In the sense of "expel," or "dismiss," Jesus "sends" a host of evil spirits into a herd of pigs (cf. Mark 5:12).

pempō also refers to God "sending" in a number of contexts. For example, God sends prophets to his people (cf. Luke 4:26) and sends his Son, Jesus Christ to earth to redeem his people (cf. John 1:33; 5:23ff.; 6:38ff.; 12:44ff.; 13:16ff.; Rom. 8:3. God also promises to send his Spirit after Jesus leaves the earth (cf. John 14:26; 15:26; 16:7). And in 2 Thess. 2:11, God is said to send judgment on unbelievers.

metapempō [μεταπέμπω, *3343*]

metapempō is a variant form of ***pempō***, above, found eight times and meaning "send for" or "call for someone" (cf. Acts 10:5, 22, 29; 11:13; 24:24, 26; 25:3).

anapempō [ἀναπέμπω, *375*]

anapempō, another variant form of ***pempō***, is found in five places and means "send," "send again," "send back." It refers to people in each case (cf. Luke 23:7ff.; Phlm. 12).

sympempō [συμπέμπω, *4842*]

sympempō is a rare variant of ***pempō*** (see above), found only twice only in 2 Cor. 8:18, 22. It means "send together with."

ekballō [ἐκβάλλω, *1544*]

ekballō is a verb found in around eighty contexts with the dominant meaning "cast out." (→ CAST) In several contexts, however, ***ekballō*** means "send out," "send away." The sense of "sending people out" on a mission is noted in Matt. 9:38; Luke 10:2; Jas. 2:25. The sense of "send away" or "dismiss" is indicated in Mark 1:43; Acts 13:50.

apolyō [ἀπολύω, *630*]

apolyō is a verb occurring approximately ninety times. It means "release," "put away," as well as associated senses, in most of these contexts. (→ RELEASE) One of these related senses is "send away," referring to people being dismissed (cf. Matt. 14:15ff.; Mark 6:45; 8:3; Luke 9:12). Mark 6:36 speaks of people being sent away to buy food. In Luke 8:38, Jesus "expels" demons from those previously enslaved by the evil spirits.

brechō [βρέχω, *1026*]

brechō is a verb found in seven contexts with the primary meanings "to rain," or "wash." In Matt. 5:45 it refers to God "sending rain."

Additional Notes

The vocabulary of "sending" throughout both Old and New Testaments, in theologically significant contexts, highlights the divine initiative in providing specially chosen servants in order to bring about the fulfillment of Yahweh's redemptive purposes.

In the Old Testament, God sends prophets to his people as the primary vehicle of divine revelation. The prophets receive the word and/or visions of God and pass the message on to the people. Included in their message is the promise of the coming Messiah — both a prophetic and regal figure — who will inaugurate the climactic fulfillment of God's kingdom on earth.

In the New Testament, the motif of "sending" finds its most significant expression in Christ, as the one whom the Father has sent to be the ultimate redeemer of his people. Christ in turn sends his apostles out into the world to propagate the gospel of the kingdom. And, finally, it is the Spirit of God who is "sent out" into the hearts of all God's people to empower and equip them for gospel ministry.

See Also: ➞ CAST

SENTENCE

OT Words

***pitgām* [פִּתְגָם, 6599]**

pitgām is a rare noun found only twice. In Eccl. 8:11 it refers to a judicial "sentence." Esth. 1:20 refers to a royal "decree."

***mishpāt* [מִשְׁפָּט, 4941]**

mishpāt is a very significant term in the Old Testament, referring mostly to the motifs of "justice" and "judgment." (➞ JUDGMENT) In a number of contexts these meanings convey the idea of a judicial "sentence," especially in the context of divine justice or judgment.

NT Words

krinō [κρίνω, *2919*]

krinō is a verb with the predominant sense of "judge," found over one hundred times. It also has the sense of "pass judicial sentence" on. (➞ JUDGE)

epikrinō [ἐπικρίνω, *1948*]

epikrinō is a rare variant form of ***krinō*** (see above), found only in Luke 23:24 and meaning "to give, or pass judicial sentence," in the context of the trial of Christ under the control of the Roman procurator, Pontius Pilate.

apokrima [ἀπόκριμα, *610*]

apokrima is a rare noun derived from ***krinō*** (see above), meaning "sentence" in relation to a metaphorical "sentence of death," found only in 2 Cor. 1:9.

SEPARATE

OT Words

***pārad* [פָּרַד, 6504]**

pārad is a verb found in approximately twenty-five places meaning "separate," or "divide," along with several related nuances.

The meaning "separate" in the sense of "part," or "divide in two," is expressed in relation to rivers (Gen. 2:10); animals (Gen. 30:40); and nations (Gen. 25:23; Deut. 32:8). The sense of "spread out" is indicated in relation to nations (Gen. 10:5, 32; Esth. 3:8); and to a group of people (Neh. 4:19). The action of "separating" in the sense of "leave," or "part company with," is noted with respect to groups of people in Gen. 13:9ff.; Judg. 4:11.

"Separating" as a consequence of death is indicated in Ruth 1:7 (cf. also 2 Sam. 1:23). ***pārad*** also refers to the "parting" of friends as a consequence of rumors (cf. Prov. 16:28; 17:9).

***nāzar* [נָזַר, 5144]**

nāzar is a verb found nine times, meaning "to separate, or dedicate oneself" to Yahweh in the context of making a vow such as the solemn Nazirite oath, described in detail in Num. 6:2ff . See also Zech. 7:3. The meaning "separate (oneself)" is also found in Lev. 15:31; 22:2; in relation to the Israelites' obligation to "keep away from" any situation that will lead to ceremonial impurity.

nāzar is also used negatively to refer to the Israelite practice of "separating (i.e., dedicating) themselves" to the idolatrous system of Baal worship (cf. Ezek. 14:7; Hos. 9:10).

***bādal* [בָּדַל, 914]**

bādal is a verb synonymous with ***pārad*** (see above), with the primary meanings "separate" or "divide" in the majority of its nearly forty occurrences.

The meaning "separate" in the sense of "divide" is indicated in Gen. 1:4, where God is said to separate light from darkness; and night from day (Gen. 1:14, 18). Gen. 1:6ff. describes the separation of the waters from the firmament.

In the context of worship, Exod. 26:33 alludes to the curtain "separating" the holy place and the most holy place.

bādal also means "separate" in the sense of "remove oneself, or someone, away from." Isa. 59:2 affirms that sin separates God from his people. "Separation from" (i.e., removal of) a godless lifestyle is indicated in Ezra 6:21; 10:11. People are "banned" from the congregation of Israel for disobedience (cf. Ezra 10:8). In Num. 16:21, God commands Moses and Aaron to "move away" from the congregation of the Israelites so that the people may be destroyed (cf. also Deut. 29:21).

With the sense of "being set apart for a specific purpose," Israel is declared to "be separate from the world" (cf. 1 Kgs. 8:53; Neh. 9:2). Similarly, Levites are "set apart" from the rest of the Israelite tribes (cf. Num. 8:14; Deut. 10:8). Levitical cities are likewise to "be set apart" from other towns in Israel (cf. Deut. 19:2, 7). Moses and Aaron are "set apart" as spiritual leaders (1 Chr. 23:13).

nēzer [נֵזֶר, 5145]

nēzer is a noun occurring twenty-five times, meaning "crown" and "separation." (→ CROWN) ***nēzer*** refers to the period of "separation" or "dedication" required of the person wanting to take a Nazirite vow (cf. Num. 6:4ff.).

NT Words

aphorizō [ἀφορίζω, *873*]

aphorizō is a verb found in ten contexts, meaning "separate," or "divide."

"Separating" the righteous from the wicked, dividing them into two groups, is referred to in Matt. 13:49; 25:32.

The idea of "setting apart" for gospel ministry is indicated in the usage of ***aphorizō***, meaning "separate" (cf. Acts 13:2; Rom. 1:1).

aphorizō also means "to separate," in the sense "withdraw from the company of" wicked people (cf. 2 Cor. 6:17); and also from fellowship with Gentiles (cf. Gal. 2:12).

chōrizō [χωρίζω, *5563*]

chōrizō is a verb occurring thirteen times. It is synonymous with ***aphorizō***, above, and means "separate" or "divide" in various contexts.

There are clear injunctions laid down in Matt. 19:6; Mark 10:9; 1 Cor. 7:10ff. for married couples not to separate, indicating that "divorce" is in view. The meaning "separate," in the sense of "part company," is indicated in Phlm. 15.

Rom. 8:35, 39 indicate that nothing can "separate" the believer from the love of Christ.

Christ, our great high priest, is declared to be "separate" (i.e., removed) from sinners in Heb. 7:26.

apodiorizō [ἀποδιορίζω, *592*]

apodiorizō is a rare verb found only in Jude 19 meaning "separate," or "cause division."

See Also: → UNCLEAN

SERAPHIM

sārāph [שָׂרָף, 8314]

sārāph is a noun found seven times, meaning "serpent" in five of these contexts. (→ BURN)

In Isa. 6:2, 6, ***sārāph*** refers to the "fiery angelic being" (i.e., seraphim) in the vision accompanying Isaiah's call to ministry.

SERPENT

OT Words

nāḥāsh [נָחָשׁ, 5175]

nāḥāsh is a noun found about thirty times, consistently translated "serpent," or "snake."

Literal references to the reptile are found, for example, in Gen. 49:17; Exod. 4:3; 7:15; Ps. 58:4; Eccl. 10:8; Amos 5:19. Serpents are sent as instruments of divine punishment against the Israelites (cf. Num. 21:6ff.; Deut. 8:15). See also Jer. 8:17; Amos 9:3. Num. 21:9; 2 Kgs. 18:4 refer to the brass serpent raised on a pole in the wilderness as a means of healing afforded by Yahweh to the Israelites afflicted by snake bites. Serpent's food is indicated in Isa. 65:25.

Gen. 3:1ff. records the activity of the serpent in the garden of Eden, controlled by the person of Satan.

Metaphorical references to "serpents" are found in Prov. 23:32; Jer. 46:22. Ps. 140:3 notes the cruel speech of people who have tongues "like a serpent."

tannîn [תַּנִּין, 8577]

tannîn is a noun found in around thirty places with the broader sense of a large voracious animal, translated "(sea) monster," "jackal," or "serpent." The explicit sense of "serpent" is found in Exod. 7:9ff. with literal reference to snakes.

zāḥal **[זָחַל, 2119]**

zāḥal is a rare noun referring to "vipers" in Deut. 32:24.

NT Words

ophis [ὄφις, *3789*]

ophis is a noun found fourteen times, meaning "serpent."

Literal references to these reptiles are found in Matt. 7:10ff.; Mark 16:18; Luke 10:19; 11:11; 1 Cor. 10:9. See also John 3:14 with reference to the bronze serpent of Num. 21:8. 2 Cor. 11:3; Rev. 12:9ff.; 20:2 refer to the serpent in the garden of Eden, the embodiment of satanic deceit, who beguiled Eve.

Matt. 23:33 refers metaphorically to "serpents" in relation to the hypocritical cunning and self-righteousness of the Pharisees. Rev. 9:19 refers to "serpents" as visionary creatures from hell, unleashed on godless humanity.

SERVANT

OT Words

'ebed **[עֶבֶד, 5650]**

'ebed is a common noun occurring around eight hundred times with the meaning "servant," or "slave," in most of these contexts.

Literal references to a "servant" or "slave," indicating a person bonded to his or her master, include those in Gen. 9:25ff.; Exod. 7:10; 8:3ff.; 1 Sam. 8:15ff.; 2 Kgs. 6:11ff. In related contexts, regulations governing the treatment and care of slaves in Israel are noted in Exod. 21:2ff.; 25:39ff.; Deut. 5:14ff.; 23:15; Jer. 34:9ff.

In more theologically significant contexts, ***'ebed*** refers to the "servant" of Yahweh in a variety of circumstances. Individuals are described as "servants" of Yahweh, such as Moses (cf. Exod. 4:10; Num. 12:7ff.; Josh. 8:31ff.); Joshua (cf. Judg. 2:8); Nehemiah (cf. Neh. 1:6ff.); and, significantly, Cyrus the Persian is referred to as a "servant" in Isa. 45:1. See also 1 Kgs. 8:23; Neh. 1:11; Ps. 19:13. The prophets are described as "servants" of Yahweh (2 Kgs. 17:13; Ezra 9:11; Jer. 7:25; Ezek. 38:17; Dan. 9:6; Amos 3:7; Zech. 1:6); as is David (2 Sam. 7:5ff.; 1 Kgs. 3:6); and also Solomon (1 Kgs. 3:7ff.).

A number of significant theological contexts mention Israel as the corporate servant of Yahweh (cf. Isa. 41:8ff.; 42:19; 44:1ff.; 49:3). ***'ebed*** also refers to the individual Messianic Servant who is declared to be the agent for the implementation of Yahweh's climactic plan of redemption (cf. Isa. 42:1; 49:5ff.; 52:13; 53:11). It is sometimes difficult to determine whether references to this "servant" are corporate or individual.

'abad **[עֲבַד, 5649** (Aramaic)**]**

'abad is an Aramaic noun occurring seven times with reference to the "servant" of human beings (Ezra 4:11; Dan. 2:4ff.); and the servant of Yahweh (Ezra 5:11; Dan. 3:2ff.; 6:20).

na'ar **[נַעַר, 5288]**

na'ar is a common noun occurring around 240 times with the primary meanings "young man," "child" in the majority of these contexts. (→ CHILD) ***na'ar*** also means "servant," referring exclusively to household service (e.g., Num. 22:22; Judg. 19:3ff.; Ruth 2:5ff.; 1 Sam. 9:3ff.; 2 Kgs. 4:12; Job 1:15ff.; Isa. 37:6).

shiphḥāh **[שִׁפְחָה, 8198]**

shiphḥāh is noun occurring about sixty times with the primary meanings "(female) servant," "maidservant," "maid" (cf. Gen. 16:1ff.; 33:1ff.; Exod. 11:5; 2 Kgs. 5:26; Jer. 34:9ff.; Joel 2:29).

Occasionally, ***shiphḥāh*** indicates a woman's deference to another man she regards as above her in rank or importance, "your handmaid" (cf. 2 Kgs. 4:2, 16; Ruth 2:13).

sākîr **[שָׂכִיר, 7916]**

sākîr is a noun found seventeen times, meaning "hired servant" in most of these instances (cf. Exod. 12:45; Lev. 19:13; 25:40ff.; Deut. 15:18; Job 7:1ff.; Isa. 16:14; Jer. 46:21; Mal. 3:5).

NT Words

doulos [δοῦλος, *1401*]

doulos is a noun found about 125 times meaning "servant," or "slave," in all of these contexts, both literal and metaphorical.

Literal references to "servant" include those in Matt. 8:9; 13:27ff.; Luke 7:2ff.; Eph. 6:5; Col. 3:11; 1 Tim. 6:1; Rev. 13:16.

References to the "servant(s)" of God are found in Luke 2:29; Acts 2:18; 4:29; Jas. 1:1; 1 Pet. 2:16; Rev. 10:7; 11:18.

The following passages refer to the "servant" of Jesus Christ (e.g., Rom. 1:1; 1 Cor. 7:22; Gal. 1:10; Eph. 6:6; 2 Tim. 2:24; 2 Pet. 1:1; Rev. 1:1; 2:20).

doulos is used metaphorically to indicate the condition of being a "slave" to sin (John 8:34; Rom. 6:16); and a "slave" of corruption (2 Pet. 2:19).

douloō [δουλόω, *1402*]

douloō is a verb that is translated "to bring into slavery or bondage," "to become, make a servant" in each of the eight contexts in which it is found.

The meaning "to be under bondage (i.e., obligation)" is indicated in 1 Cor. 7:15.

Acts 7:6 refers to Israel being "brought into slavery" in Egypt. In 1 Cor. 9:19, Paul speaks of "making himself a slave or servant" to all human beings. Rom. 6:18 refers to one "becoming a slave" of righteousness; 2 Pet. 2:19 to becoming a "slave" to passion. See also Gal. 4:3; Titus 2:3. Rom. 6:22 refers to "becoming servants" of God.

pais [παῖς, *3816*]

pais is a noun with the primary meanings "servant," "child," in around twenty-five occurrences. (→ CHILD)

The meaning "servant," in the literal sense of "a person bonded as a slave," is indicated in Matt. 8:6ff.; 12:18; 14:2; Luke 7:7; 12:45; 15:26.

The designation "servant" is applied to Israel (Luke 1:54); and to David (Luke 1:69; Acts 4:25).

diakonos [διάκονος, *1249*]

diakonos is a noun found in thirty contexts meaning "servant," or "minister," and also "deacon." The usage is varied.

The general sense of "servant" as "one who serves or ministers" is indicated in Matt. 20:26; 23:11; Mark 9:35; 10:43. Household slaves are mentioned in Matt. 22:13; John 2:5, 9.

diakonos refers to servants as "deacons" (1 Tim. 3:8, 12); as "deaconesses" (Rom. 16:1, 27); and as "servants" of the church (cf. Col. 1:25; 1 Tim. 4:6).

The meaning "servant" of Christ is indicated in John 12:26; 1 Cor. 3:5; 2 Cor. 11:23; Eph. 6:21; Col. 1:7; and "servant" of God in Rom. 13:4; 2 Cor. 6:4; 1 Thess. 3:2. Christ himself is described as a "servant" to the circumcised in Rom. 15:8. In stark contrast, ***diakonos*** refers to "servants" of Satan in 2 Cor. 11:15.

diakonos refers also to "ministers" of the new covenant (2 Cor. 3:6); and to "ministers" of the gospel (Eph. 3:7; Col. 1:23).

syndoulos [σύνδουλος, *4889*]

syndoulos is a noun that is consistently translated "fellow-servant" in each of the ten contexts in which it is found. Literal references are indicated in Matt. 18:28ff.; 24:49; Col. 1:7. References are made to one's "fellow-servant" in the Lord in Col. 4:7; Rev. 6:11; 19:10; 22:9.

therapōn [θεράπων, *2324*]

therapōn is a rare term found only in Heb. 3:5 with reference to Moses as a faithful "servant" in God's house.

misthōtos [μισθωτός, *3411*]; *misthios* [μίσθιος, *3407*]

Both of these terms are translated "hired servant." ***misthōtos*** is found four times (Mark 1:20; John 10:12ff.). ***misthios*** occurs only in Luke 15:17, 19.

hypēretēs [ὑπηρέτης, *5257*]

hypēretēs occurs about twenty times with the principal meanings "guard," "officer" in most of these contexts. (→ OFFICER) However, ***hypēretēs*** twice refers to the "servants" of Christ (John 18:36; 1 Cor. 4:1).

oiketēs [οἰκέτης, *3610*]

oiketēs is a noun found five times meaning "servant" in the sense of a "bonded slave" (cf. Luke 16:13; Acts 10:7; Rom. 14:4; Phlm. 25; 1 Pet. 2:18).

Additional Notes

The most significant feature of the vocabulary for "servant" or "slave" throughout the Scriptures is the aspect of such a person being bound to his master by a strict legal and commercial obligation. This obligation was literal in the cultural sphere of the ancient world. Then the idea of a binding obligation is transferred to the spiritual realm when the Old Testament speaks of the messianic "Servant of Yahweh," who is solemnly and personally committed to the redemptive purposes of God, whose mission the "Servant" must undertake.

This motif is carried over indirectly yet substantially to the New Testament, where Christ's unswerving commitment to the will of his Father demonstrates an unambiguous fulfillment of the role of the "Suffering Servant" of Yahweh. Christ is bound to this commitment to God just as surely as a slave is bound to his master, and he fulfills his task with whole-hearted devotion, notwithstanding the enormous cost and pain of such a commitment.

See Also: ➡ SERVE

SERVE, SERVICE

OT Words

***'ābad* [עָבַד, 5647]**

'ābad is a common verb occurring around three hundred times, meaning "to serve" in the majority of these contexts, with a variety of nuances.

The meaning "to serve" (i.e., as a slave) is indicated in general contexts in Gen. 14:4; 1 Sam. 11:1; 17:9; 1 Kgs. 4:21; Jer. 25:11; 27:6ff. In particular, Israel's enslavement in Egypt is indicated in Gen. 15:13; Exod. 1:13. Working as a household servant is noted in Exod. 21:2ff.; 25:39ff.; Deut. 15:12.

The notion of "serving" God in the sense of worshiping him in obedient submission to all his ways is evident in Gen. 27:29; Exod. 3:12; 10:7ff.; Deut. 10:12; Josh. 24:15ff.; 1 Sam. 12:14; Jer. 30:9. The command to serve God is recorded in Deut. 6:13; Josh. 22:5; Pss. 2:11; 100:2; and a refusal to serve him is found in Isa. 60:12. Related to the practice of serving God is "performing service" in the tabernacle (cf. Num. 3:7ff.; 4:24ff.; 8:11ff.; Josh. 22:27).

In contrast, ***'ābad*** is also found in the frequent prohibitions against "serving" (i.e., worshiping) idols (cf. Exod. 20:15; 23:24; Deut. 5:9; 7:16; Josh. 23:7; Jer. 25:6). Israel's rebellion against Yahweh is most often expressed by their idolatrous "serving" of other gods (cf. Deut. 17:3; Josh. 24:2; Judg. 2:11ff.; 3:6ff.; 1 Sam. 8:8; 1 Kgs. 9:6; Pss. 97:7; 106:36; Jer. 5:19; 16:11ff.; 44:3).

***'abôdāh* [עֲבוֹדָה, 5656]**

'abôdāh is a noun derived from ***'ābad*** (see above). It occurs around 140 times and means "service," or "work," in most of these contexts, both human and divine.

"Service," in the general sense of obligation to another, is indicated in Gen. 29:27; Ps. 104:23.

'abôdāh is also translated "work" in the sense of "slavery" (Exod. 1:14; 2:23; 6:6ff.); and "oppressive labor" (1 Kgs. 12:4; Isa. 14:3). The meaning "labor" in a positive sense of working for Yahweh is indicated in Neh. 3:5.

'abôdāh also frequently refers to "service" in the context of ritual worship associated with the tabernacle and temple (cf. Exod. 35:21; 36:1ff.; Num. 3:7ff.; 4:19ff.; Josh. 22:27; 1 Chr. 9:13ff.; 23:24ff.). Ezek. 44:14 speaks of the same "service," but in the context of the prophet's visionary temple; and Ezra 8:20 refers to such "service" in the reconstructed postexilic temple.

***'abîdāh* [עֲבִידָה, 5673** (Aramaic)]

'abîdāh is an Aramaic noun, equivalent to ***'abôdāh*** (see above), meaning "service," "work," or "business affairs." It is found in six places.

The "work" of rebuilding the temple in Jerusalem is indicated in Ezra 4:24; 5:8; 6:7. Ezra 6:18 speaks of the "service" of Yahweh in the sense of "ritual or ceremonial worship." The sense of "business affairs" is evident in Dan. 2:49; 3:12 in relation to Babylon.

***shārat* [שָׁרַת, 8334]**

The verb ***shārat*** is synonymous with ***'ābad*** (see above), and is found approximately one hundred times meaning "to serve," or "minister."

The general sense of "serving" (i.e., working for) someone is evident in Gen. 39:4; Esth. 1:10. Similarly, the meaning "servant," in the sense of one's personal attendant, is indicated in Exod. 24:13; Josh. 1:1; 2 Sam. 13:17; 2 Kgs. 6:15.

shārat usually occurs in the context of the tabernacle and temple, where it refers to the priests and Levites "serving" (cf. Exod. 28:35, 43; 29:30; Num. 1:50; 3:6; Deut. 10:8; 1 Kgs. 8:11; 2 Chr. 5:14; Ezek. 40:46; 44:11ff.).

***pelaḥ* [פְּלַח, 6399** (Aramaic)]

pelaḥ is an Aramaic verb found ten times, meaning "to serve" (as a priest) in the temple (cf. Ezra 7:24). ***pelaḥ*** also refers to serving one's God (i.e., Yahweh) or one's gods (cf. Dan. 3:12ff.; 6:16, 20; 7:14, 27).

***polḥan* [פָּלְחָן, 6402** (Aramaic)]

polḥan is an Aramaic noun derived from the verb ***pelaḥ*** (see above). It is found only in Ezra 7:19, where it refers to the vessels used for the "service" (i.e., worship ritual) of the house of Yahweh.

NT Words

latreuō [λατρεύω, *3000*]

latreuō is a verb found about twenty times, meaning "serve" in the primary sense of "worship, or officiate in a ritual ceremony."

latreuō refers to "serving" or worshiping God in general terms in Matt. 4:10; Luke 1:74; Acts 26:7; Rom. 1:9; Phil. 3:3; 2 Tim. 1:3; Heb. 9:14; 12:28. The contrasting activity of "serving" idols is indicated in Acts 7:42; Rom. 1:25.

In particular, ***latreuō*** refers to "serving" at the temple, indicating the process of conducting and guiding worship there (cf. Acts 7:42; Rom. 1:25).

latreia [λατρεία, *2999*]

latreia is a noun derived from ***latreuō*** (see above). It occurs five times, only in ceremonial contexts, and means "service," or "worship" (cf. John 16:2; Rom. 9:4; Heb. 9:1, 6). Rom. 12:1 contains a metaphorical ceremonial reference, as Paul exhorts his readers to present themselves as living sacrifices to God as an expression of reasonable "worship."

douleuō [δουλεύω, *1398*]

douleuō is a verb found in twenty-five contexts meaning "serve," "do service," "be a slave."

The general sense of "serve" in relation to "being in bond service to a master" is noted in Matt. 6:24; Luke 16:13; John 8:33; Acts 7:7; 1 Tim. 6:2. See also Luke 15:29. Metaphorically, the state of "being in bondage" to sin is evident in Rom. 6:6; Titus 3:3. See also Gal. 4:8, 9.

"Serving" God in a general sense is indicated in Matt. 6:24; Luke 16:13; Acts 20:19; Rom. 7:6, 25; 12:11; Eph. 6:7. Similarly, Rom. 14:18; Col. 3:24 refer to "serving" in gospel ministry.

diakoneō [διακονέω, *1247*]

diakoneō is a verb occurring about forty times with the primary meaning "to minister" or "serve" in most of these contexts.

"Serving" in the general sense of offering hospitality or particular service and help is recorded in Matt. 4:11; 8:15; Mark 1:13; Luke 8:3; John 12:2; 2 Tim. 1:18; Heb. 6:18. Matt. 20:28; Mark 10:45 speak of the purpose of Christ — not to be served, but to serve. Acts 6:2 refers to "serving" tables in the early Christian community.

John 12:26 refers to "serving" Christ; and 1 Tim. 3:10ff. refers to the "service" of deacons.

diakonia [διακονία, *1248*]

diakonia is the noun derived from ***diakoneō*** (see above), found in approximately thirty-five contexts and meaning "ministry," or "service," "serving."

"Serving" as the exercise of hospitality is noted in Luke 10:40; Rom. 12:7.

diakonia means "ministry" in numerous contexts, referring to ministry in general (1 Cor. 12:5; 2 Cor. 9:13; Rev. 2:19); ministry of the word (Acts 6:4); apostolic ministry (Acts 1:17, 25); gospel ministry (Acts 12:25; 2 Cor. 4:1; 2 Cor. 5:18; Eph. 4:12; 1 Tim. 1:2); and the ministry of the Spirit (2 Cor. 3:8ff.). See also 2 Cor. 3:8, 9 which contrast the ministry of life in the Sprit with the "ministry of death."

hypēreteō [ὑπηρετέω, *5256*]

hypēreteō is a verb found in only three places, meaning "to serve" or "minister." David is said to "serve" the purpose of God in Acts 13:36; and the noble action of "ministering to one's needs" is described in Acts 20:34; 24:23.

leitourgia [λειτουργία, *3009*]

leitourgia is a noun found six times, meaning "service," "ministry."

Service in association with temple worship is indicated in Luke 1:23; Heb. 9:21. "Ministry" in general is cited in Phil. 2:30. The "ministry" of generous giving is indicated in 2 Cor. 9:12.

Metaphorical reference to one's "service," or sacrifice for the gospel, is found in Phil. 2:17. The more excellent "ministry" of Christ through the new covenant is described in Heb. 8:6.

SET

OT Words

nātan [נָתַן, 5414]

nātan is a common verb with the predominant meaning "give" in about half of the nearly 2,000 contexts in which it is found. It also has a number of related senses and other meanings. These include "put" and "set," with the underlying sense of "place," and this is predicated of both God and human beings in a wide variety of contexts.

God is said, for example, to set created phenomena in their place (cf. Gen. 1:17; 9:13; Ps. 8:1); and to set (i.e., appoint) a watchman over Israel (cf. Ezek. 33:2ff.), and a king on the throne (1 Kgs. 5:5).

In particular, where human beings are the object of his action, God is said to put blessing on his people (cf. Deut. 11:29), and curses on his enemies (cf. Deut. 30:7). He also puts fear in human hearts (Ezek. 30:13), as well as gladness (cf. Ps. 4:7). Deut. 18:18; Jer. 1:9 affirm that God puts words in the mouths of his prophets. See also Neh. 2:12; 7:5.

In relation to the temple and the Israelite people, Yahweh is said to "set" his sanctuary in the midst of his people (Ezek. 37:26); and to "put" his name in the Jerusalem temple (1 Kgs. 11:36). See also 1 Kgs. 6:19. He is also said to "set" the law before his people (Deut. 4:8; 2 Chr. 7:19; Jer. 9:13; Dan. 9:10).

In the context of the divine renewal of the people of God, Isa. 42:1 affirms that Yahweh will put his Spirit on his Servant, and that he will put the law of God in their hearts (Jer. 31:33). Similarly, Ezek. 11:19; 36:26ff.; 37:14 declare that God will put a new spirit in the hearts of his people.

In terms of judgment, Lev. 17:10; Ezek. 15:7 refer to God "setting" his face against those who oppose him. Jer. 27:8, 14 declare that Yahweh will put a yoke on the neck of his enemies.

nātan describes the action of human beings "setting" in a number of contexts — for example, setting, or placing objects in position (Exod. 28:27, 30; 2 Chr. 4:7ff.; Esth. 6:8; Lev. 1:7; 2:15; Deut. 28:48); and "placing" items in readiness for worship in the tabernacle and temple (Exod. 28:27; Lev. 1:7; 2:15; 4:25ff.; 8:7ff.; Num. 4:7ff.; 1 Kgs. 7:39, 51). In contrast, Lev. 26:1 warns against "setting up" idols for worship, and 1 Kgs. 12:29 records an instance of that culpable action.

People are set or placed in positions of authority in Gen. 41:41. Gen. 39:20 refers to Potiphar putting Joseph in prison.

The expression "to set one's heart" conveys strong determination. It is found in 1 Chr. 22:19 with reference to serving the Lord; and in Ezek. 28:2ff. in relation to opposing Yahweh (i.e., "set one's heart against God"). See also Exod. 19:8.

sûm [שׂוּם, 7760]

sûm is another common verb, occurring around six hundred times with the primary meanings "put," "make," "set," "place," as well as additional nuances. It indicates both human and divine agency.

sûm is found in a wide variety of contexts referring to God's actions. For example, God is said "to put a mark" on Cain (Gen. 4:15); he places a man in Eden (Gen. 2:8); he "sets" a sign among his people (Isa. 66:19; Amos 7:8); he puts words in the mouths of his prophets (Isa. 51:16); and he promises to "set" (i.e., establish) justice on the earth through the Servant of Yahweh (Isa. 42:4). His purpose is to set a king over his people in Deut. 17:14; 1 Sam. 12:13. He is also said to set people in positions of authority (Job 5:11).

Yahweh is also said to "set" his laws and ordinances before his people through Moses (Exod. 21:1; Deut. 4:44). He sets his eyes on his people in judgment (Amos 9:4); and "sets his face" against those who oppose him (cf. Lev. 20:5; Jer. 21:10; 44:11). In regard to worship, Yahweh expresses his clear intention to set, or put, his name in the place of his choice — the site of the tabernacle and, later, the temple in Jerusalem (cf. Deut. 14:24; 12:5, 21; 1 Kgs. 9:3; 11:36; 2 Kgs. 21:4). Ezek. 5:5 declares that Yahweh has "set" Jerusalem at the center of the nations.

sûm also refers to human action in various contexts. For example, Judg. 12:3; Job 13:14 speak of putting one's life in one's hands. The act of putting words into someone's mouth is noted in 2 Sam. 14:3. Exod. 1:11 refers to taskmasters being "set (or placed) in authority" over the people of Israel in Egypt. "Setting an ambush" is noted in Judg. 20:29. Song 8:6 speaks of "setting" one's beloved spouse as a seal on one's heart. In 1 Kgs. 8:21, a place for the ark of the covenant is "set" in the Jerusalem temple. The determination to "set" one's heart on God and his word is indicated in Deut. 32:46. Similarly, the intent of achieving a specific purpose is expressed in the phrase "to set one's face on (or toward)" (cf. Gen. 31:21; 2 Kgs. 12:17; Isa. 50:7; Jer. 44:12). In particular, this expression is used of the prophets, who "set their face" against people in order to bring God's judgment on them (cf. Ezek. 13:17; 20:46; 38:2).

sûm also means "to set up" in the sense of "erect," and it refers to a monument (Gen. 28:18); the tabernacle (Exod. 40:18ff.); and idols for worship (Judg. 18:31; 2 Kgs. 21:7; Jer. 11:13; 32:34).

yāṣag [יָצַג, 3322]

yāṣag is a verb synonymous with ***nātan*** and ***sûm***, above. It occurs sixteen times and means "set," "place" in most of these contexts.

The action of setting, or placing, physical objects in position is indicated in Gen. 30:28; Judg. 6:37; 1 Sam. 5:2; 2 Sam. 6:17; 1 Chr. 16:1. The three latter texts refer specifically to the ark of the covenant. Judg. 7:5 refers to setting people aside. See also Gen. 43:9.

shît [שִׁית, 7896]

The verb ***shît*** is also synonymous with the above terms. The term occurs around ninety times in a variety of contexts, with the primary meanings "set," "put," "lay."

shît has the general sense of "put" or "place" in specific locations with regard to animals (Gen. 30:40); people (2 Sam. 19:28); and a crown on one's head (Ps.

21:3). See also Gen. 48:14. ***shît*** also refers to putting on jewelry in Exod. 33:4.

In other contexts, ***shît*** refers to "setting" or placing people in positions of civil authority (cf. Gen. 41:33). Gen. 3:15 records the promise that God "will put" enmity among the future peoples of the world, between the progeny of the serpent (i.e., Satan) and that of the woman (i.e., between godly and ungodly humanity). The expression "set one's face," conveying the idea of determined effort, is found in Num. 24:1.

shît is also predicted of God, who is said to "set his mind" on human beings (Job 7:17). Ps. 8:6 declares that God "has put" all things under the feet of human beings; and Ps. 9:20 affirms that he has put fear into the hearts of human beings. Ps. 132:11 indicates that God has placed one of David's descendants on the throne. The boundaries of the land of Canaan are declared to have been "set" (i.e., fixed) by God (Exod. 23:31).

'ārak [עָרַךְ, 6186]

'ārak is a verb occurring about eighty times with the primary meaning "to arrange, or set in order."

The general sense of "arrange" or "set in order" is indicated in Josh. 2:6; Judg. 20:20ff.; 1 Sam. 4:2; 2 Sam. 10:8ff.; 1 Chr. 19:9ff.; Jer. 6:23; Joel 2:5. In particular, ***'ārak*** refers to "arranging" the furniture in the tabernacle (cf. Exod. 40:4; Lev. 24:4ff.), and to "setting" the wood for the altar fire (Lev. 1:7ff.; 1 Kgs. 18:23). Several texts refer to "setting up" tables for a banquet (cf. Pss. 23:5; 78:19; Prov. 9:2; Isa. 21:5; 65:11; Ezek. 23:41).

nāsa' [נָסַע, 5265]

nāsa' is a verb found in approximately 150 contexts, meaning "to set out, or depart on a journey" in the majority of these contexts. (→ JOURNEY)

'āmad [עָמַד, 5975]

'āmad is a common verb found approximately 520 times with the dominant sense of "to stand," as well as associated nuances, in the large majority of these contexts.

In several places, ***'āmad*** means "to present" with the underlying sense of "set before (someone)." For example, Joseph is "set" (i.e., presented) before Pharaoh in Gen. 47:7. A jealous husband "sets," or presents, his wife suspected of adultery before the Lord for trial (Num. 5:30). See also Num. 8:13.

Elsewhere, ***'āmad*** means "set, or place in position," as in Judg. 16:25 with regard to Samson being placed between the pillars of the Philistine temple. Isa. 21:6 refers to "setting up" a watchman for the people of Israel. ***'āmad*** refers to "setting up" or "erecting" the temple (Ezra 2:68), and the various gates in the reconstructed temple in Jerusalem (Neh. 3:1ff.).

'āmad also refers to the action of God, who is said "to set people on their feet" with a view to restoring and/or refreshing them (cf. Ps. 31:8; Ezek. 3:4; Dan. 8:18).

nāṣab [נָצַב, 5324]

nāṣab is a verb found in seventy-five places, meaning "to stand" in about half of these contexts. In addition, ***nāṣab*** means "set up" in the sense of "position," or "erect" memorial pillars for a grave (Gen. 35:20; 1 Kgs. 16:34); and idols (2 Kgs. 17:10). Jer. 5:26 refers to "setting" a trap, or snare. See also Jer. 31:21; Lam. 3:12.

rûm [רוּם, 7311]

rûm is a verb found in approximately two hundred places with the primary meanings "lift up," "exalt," as well as associated nuances. However, in a few places ***rûm*** also means "erect," "set up" — referring to a memorial stone (Gen. 31:45), and the temple of the Lord (Ezra 9:9). See also Ps. 27:5.

yānaḥ [יָנַח, 3240]

yānaḥ is found seventy-five times, meaning "leave," "depart," "rest" throughout the majority of its usage. In several places, however, it means "to set down" (i.e., lay down or place), referring exclusively to objects (cf. Deut. 26:4; Judg. 6:18; Zech. 5:11). In particular, 1 Sam. 6:18 refers to placing the ark of the covenant on the rock at Beth Shemesh, after its return from Philistine territory.

gābal [גָּבַל, 1379]

gābal is a verb found five times, meaning "to border" or "set boundaries." The latter sense is explicit in Exod. 19:12, 23.

shākan [שָׁכַן, 7931]

shākan is a verb found around 130 times with the primary meaning "to dwell," frequently referring to Yahweh living among his people in the tabernacle. In Josh. 18:1, however, ***shākan*** refers to the Israelite congregation "setting up" the tabernacle at Shiloh.

qāhāh [קָהָה, 6949]

The verb ***qāhāh*** occurs in four places and means "to set (one's teeth) on edge" in three of these contexts (cf. Jer. 31:29, 30; Ezek. 18:2).

nûaḥ [נוּחַ, 5117]

nûaḥ is a verb found in over 140 contexts, meaning "to rest" in most of these. However, in Ezek. 37:1; 40:1, ***nûaḥ*** refers to Yahweh "setting (Ezekiel) down" in a valley.

NT Words

tithēmi [τίθημι, *5087*]

tithēmi is a verb found in around 100 places, meaning "set," "put," "place," "lay" in the majority of its usage in a variety of contexts.

The general sense of "put" or "set," in relation to placing objects in a certain place, is illustrated in Matt. 5:15; Mark 4:21; Luke 8:16; John 13:4; Acts 4:37. In particular, Luke 23:53; John 19:42; Acts 13:29 refer to "placing" the body of Christ in a tomb; and John 11:34 refers similarly to the body of Lazarus. Rom. 14:13 warns against putting a stumbling block in the way of a fellow believer.

tithēmi also refers to God "putting" or "setting" in a number of places. For example, he promises to put his Spirit on his anointed Servant (i.e., the Messiah) in Matt. 12:18. "Laying" or "setting" a stone in Zion to make human beings stumble is a reference to God placing his Son, Jesus Christ, among human beings (cf. Rom. 9:33; 1 Pet. 2:6ff.). "Setting" (i.e., appointing) various kinds of leaders in the church is indicated in 1 Cor. 12:28; 1 Tim. 1:12; 2 Tim. 1:11, referring to their particular gifts for service. The "appointing" of Christ as the heir of all things is noted in Heb. 1:2. 1 Cor. 15:25 declares that God will "place" all of his enemies under his feet. See also Rev. 10:2; 11:9.

paratithēmi [παρατίθημι, *3908*]

paratithēmi is a variant form of ***tithēmi***, above, occurring around twenty times and meaning "to set before" in about half of these contexts.

Christ is said to "set" parables before the people (Matt. 13:24ff.). In Luke 23:46, he "places" (i.e., commends) his spirit into the hands of his Father.

paratithēmi also refers to "setting" food before people (cf. Mark 6:41; 8:6ff.; Luke 9:16; Acts 16:34; 1 Cor. 10:27).

perititēmi [περιτίθημι, *4060*]

Another variant of ***tithēmi***, above, ***peritithēmi*** is found six times meaning "set (or put) around" in relation to various objects.

Matt. 21:33; Mark 12:1 refer to "setting" a hedge around a vineyard. Roman soldiers place a crown of thorns on the head of Christ (Mark 15:17), and put a robe around him (Matt. 27:28). Matt. 27:48; Mark 15:36; John 19:29 refer to placing a sponge filled with vinegar on a reed for Christ on the cross.

histēmi [ἵστημι, *2476*]

histēmi is a common verb found in nearly 160 contexts with the dominant meaning "to stand." Occasionally, however, it means "set" or "place."

Christ is "set" (or placed) on the pinnacle of the temple by Satan in Matt. 4:5; Luke 4:9. Sheep and goats are placed, metaphorically, at the right and left hand of God — referring to the righteous and the wicked, respectively (Matt. 25:33).

More generally, ***histēmi*** refers to "setting up" false witnesses in Acts 6:13. Other references include those in Matt. 18:2; Mark 9:36; Luke 9:47; John 8:3; Acts 4:7.

keimai [κεῖμαι, *2749*]

keimai is a verb found nearly thirty times, usually with a passive sense — "to be laid," "be set up," "be appointed."

Matt. 5:14 refers to city being set on a hill. Clothes are "laid aside" in Luke 24:12. Luke 2:34 affirms that Christ "is appointed" for the rise and fall of many in Israel. Phil. 2:17 declares that Paul "is set" for the defense of the gospel.

prokeimai [πρόκειμαι, *4295*]

prokeimai is a variant form of ***keimai***, above, found five times with the sense of "to be set," "placed before," "be set forth" in all but one of these contexts.

Hope is "set before" the believer in Heb. 6:18. The race of life is also "set before" believers in Heb. 12:1. Joy is "set before" Christ in Heb. 12:2. In Jude 7, Sodom and Gomorrah are "set forth" as an example of divine punishment.

dynō [δύνω, *1416*]

dynō is a rare verb found only twice, referring to the "setting" sun in Mark 1:32; Luke 4:40.

epibibazō [ἐπιβιβάζω, *1913*]

epibibazō is a verb found five times meaning "to set (or place) upon." It refers exclusively to helping people to mount and ride horses or donkeys (cf. Luke 10:34; 19:35; Acts 23:24).

phroneō [φρονέω, *5426*]

phroneō is a verb occurring around forty times with the primary meaning "think," in various senses.

The phrase "set one's mind on" in Col. 3:2 refers to the desired focus of the believer's heart on preparing himself for eternal life in the hereafter.

See Also: → APPOINT → DIVORCE → ESTABLISH

SEVEN

OT Words

sheba' [שֶׁבַע, 7651]

This noun is found in approximately 350 contexts, indicating the cardinal numeral "seven" in most instances. ***sheba'*** also indicates the ordinal sense of "seventh," as well as compound numerals involving this number.

Mundane usage of this number includes references to age in years (cf. Gen. 5:7, 25ff.; Exod. 6:16); length of time in days (cf. Gen. 7:4ff.); and years (cf. 2 Sam. 2:11). Quantities involving the number "seven" are indicated, for example, with reference to numbers of children (Exod. 2:16; Ezra 2:5ff.; Neh. 7:14ff.); to money, or silver (Exod. 38:25); and to animals marked for sacrifice (Lev. 23:18; Num. 29:2ff.).

"Seven" is used metaphorically in Zech. 3:9, with reference to the "seven eyes (or facets)" of the high priestly stone or diadem, symbolizing Yahweh's all-knowing gaze. See also Zech. 4:2.

Significant periods of time relating to the number "seven" include the seven-day duration of sacred festivals such as Passover (cf. Exod. 12:15ff.; Num. 28:17ff.; Deut. 16:3ff.); Tabernacles (cf. Lev. 23:34ff.); and Weeks (or Harvest) (cf. Deut. 16:13ff.). This duration also applies to the period of priestly ordination (Exod. 29:35) and ceremonial defilement (Lev. 13:4ff.; 15:19ff.; Num. 12:14, 15; 19:11ff.). Lev. 25:8 refers to the period leading up to Jubilee (i.e., the fiftieth year) as "seven Sabbaths of years" (i.e., forty-nine years). Slaves in Israel must also be released every seven years (cf. Deut. 15:1, 9; Jer. 34:14).

shebî'î [שְׁבִיעִי, 7637]

shebî'î is the adjectival form derived from ***sheba'*** (see above), expressing the ordinal sense of "seventh." The term occurs in around 100 contexts.

Significant references to "the seventh" day include God's rest from creative activity (Gen. 2:2, 3; Exod. 20:11; 31:17); the "seventh" day of the festival weeks (Exod. 12:15ff.); and the destruction of Jericho on the "seventh" day (cf. Josh. 6:4, 15, 16).

Most significant are the references to this day as the "Sabbath," referring to the compulsory day of rest under Mosaic law (cf. Exod. 16:20ff.; 20:10, 11; 23:12; 31:15; Lev. 23:3, 8; Deut. 5:14). The institution of the "Sabbath" year is designed to guarantee rest for agricultural land (cf. Exod. 23:11; Lev. 25:4). Lev. 23:24ff.; Neh. 8:2 refer to the "seventh" month, that includes the Day of Atonement ceremony on the tenth day.

Mundane usage of ***shebî'î*** is found in Gen. 8:4; Lev. 13:5ff.; 2 Kgs. 11:4.

shib'îm [שִׁבְעִים, 7657]

The noun ***shib'îm*** occurs around ninety times and means "seventy."

Mundane use of the number is found in Gen. 4:24; 5:12; Exod. 24:1; Num. 7:25ff.; 2 Kgs. 10:7; 2 Chr. 29:32; Ps. 90:10.

In more theologically significant contexts, ***shib'îm*** refers to the "seventy" years of exile, designated by Yahweh for his disobedient people (Jer. 25:11ff.; 29:10; Dan. 9:2; Zech. 1:12; 7:5).

shābûa' [שָׁבוּעַ, 7620]

shābûa' is a noun occurring around twenty times. It is difficult to provide an exact English equivalent, although the term most closely approximates the concept of "a period of seven days or years." It is used literally in mundane contexts as well as in significant symbolic contexts.

Literal "periods of seven days" (or multiples thereof) are noted in Gen. 29:27ff.; Lev. 12:5; Ezek. 45:21; Dan. 10:2, 3. Such a period is also indicated in relation to the Feast of Weeks (or Harvest) in Exod. 34:22; Deut. 16:9ff.; 2 Chr. 8:13; Jer. 5:24.

A very significant symbolic use of ***shābûa'*** in Dan. 9:24ff. refers to a prophetic period of "seventy weeks (of years)" designated by Yahweh as the period from the time of Daniel until the consummation of his plan of redemption through the person of the Messiah.

NT Words

hepta [ἑπτά, *2033*]

hepta is the only term in the New Testament for the cardinal number seven, occurring around ninety times.

Literal, mundane usage includes that in Matt. 12:45; Mark 8:5ff.; Luke 11:26; Acts 6:3; Rev. 1:4, 11.

Significant figurative uses of the number "seven" include Jesus' expression "seventy times seven," referring symbolically to the unlimited capacity of one's forgiving attitude to those who wrong us (cf. Matt. 18:22).

The remaining symbolic uses of "seven" are found exclusively in the book of Revelation. Rev. 1:12ff. refers to the seven golden lampstands that represent the seven churches of Asia. In the same context, reference to the "seven stars" in Rev. 1:16, 20; 2:1; 3:1 is equated with the angels of the seven churches of Asia. Cycles of judgment also revolve around the number seven — ***hepta*** refers to seven seals (Rev. 5:1, 5); seven trumpets (Rev. 8:2); seven bowls (Rev. 16:1; 17:1; 21:9); and "seven angels" of judgment (Rev. 15:1, 6ff.). See also Rev. 10:3, 4; 11:13; 12:3; 13:1; 17:3.

hebdomos [ἕβδομος, *1442*]

hebdomos is an adjectival form designating the ordinal number "seventh," occurring nine times.

It is used literally in John 1:14 and symbolically in Rev. 21:20.

In significant contexts, ***hebdomos*** refers to the "seventh" day (Heb. 4:4); the "seventh" seal of judgment (Rev. 8:1); and the "seventh" angel of judgment (Rev. 10:7; 11:15; 16:17).

hebdomēkontakis [ἑβδομηκοντάκις, *1441*]

This is an adverbial form, indicating the numeral "seventy" in Christ's expression "seventy times seven," which refers symbolically to the limitless number of times he expected his followers to forgive those who had wronged them (cf. Matt. 18:22).

hebdomēkonta [ἑβδομήκοντα, *1440*]

hebdomēkonta is a noun occurring five times, referring to the number "seventy" (cf. Luke 10:1, 17; Acts 23:23). See also Acts 7:14; 27:37.

SEVER → DIVIDE

SHADOW

OT Words

ṣēl [צֵל, 6738]

ṣēl is a noun found in around fifty places meaning "shade," "shadow." It is used both literally and figuratively with several associated nuances.

The meaning "shade" in the sense of "shelter" is indicated in Gen. 19:8; Judg. 9:15; Isa. 25:4; 30:2ff.; Ezek. 31:6.

Literal "shadows" are indicated in relation to a man (2 Kgs. 20:9ff.; Song 2:3; Isa. 38:8); and a mountain (Judg. 9:36). Other mundane references to "shadow" include those in 1 Chr. 29:15; Song 2:17; 4:6; Job 7:2; Jer. 6:4; Hos. 4:13; Jonah 4:5, 6.

In metaphorical contexts, ***ṣēl*** means "shadow" with reference to the transitory nature of life (cf. Job 8:9; Pss. 102:11; 144:4; Eccl. 6:12; 8:13). In Pss. 17:8; 36:7; 57:1; 63:7; Hos. 14:7, the "shadow" of God's wings refers to the protection offered by the presence of God through the golden wings of the sculpted cherubim on the cover of the ark of the covenant. In several places, the "shadow" of God itself is referred to, anthropomorphically speaking (Ps. 91:1; Lam. 4:20; Isa. 49:2; 51:16).

ṣalmāwet [צַלְמָוֶת, 6757]

ṣalmāwet is a noun occurring eighteen times with the consistent meaning "shadow of death," or "deep darkness," all referring metaphorically to the fear of death or the depth of despair.

References to the "deep darkness" of despondency and gloom include those in Job 3:5; 10:21ff.; 28:3; Pss. 44:19; 107:10; Jer. 13:16. Divine deliverance from such darkness is indicated in Pss. 9:2; 107:14; Jer. 2:6. In Job 38:17, this motif is used as an analogy with the terrifying prospect of dying.

Divine protection from the fear of the "shadow of death" is indicated in Ps. 23:4.

telal [טְלַל, 2927 (Aramaic)]

telal is an Aramaic noun found only in Dan. 4:12 with reference to the "shade" of a tree.

NT Words

skia [σκιά, *4639*]

skia is a dynamic equivalent for ***ṣēl*** (see above), meaning "shadow" or "shade" in all seven occurrences.

The literal "shade" or shelter of a tree is indicated in Mark 4:32, and the shadow of a man in Acts 5:15.

Metaphorical reference to the "shadow" of sin and death from which people have been delivered is noted in Matt. 4:16; Luke 1:79. Elsewhere, the "shadows" of old covenant realities anticipate the coming of Christ, who fulfills those realities (cf. Col. 2:17). Examples of the "shadow" phenomenon are found in relation to the tabernacle (Heb. 8:5), and to the law (Heb. 10:1).

aposkiasma [ἀποσκίασμα, *644*]

aposkiasma is a rare noun found only in Jas. 1:17, referring metaphorically to a "shadow" as evidence of change in a person. This is then deemed impossible for God, who never changes.

kataskiazō [κατασκιάζω, *2683*]

kataskiazō is a verb found only in Heb. 9:5, referring to the wings of the golden cherubim "overshadowing" the ark of the covenant.

SHAKE

OT Words

rā'ash [**רָעַשׁ, 7493**]

rā'ash is a verb found thirty times with the dominant meaning "shake," or "tremble."

Most commonly, ***rā'ash*** indicates the shaking or quaking of the earth (e.g., Judg. 5:4; 2 Sam. 22:8; Ps. 18:7; Isa. 14:16; 24:18; Jer. 4:24).

A figurative "shaking" of the earth is recorded in several contexts, indicating the impact of God's wrath or judgment on the nations (cf. Jer. 10:10; Ezek. 26:15; Joel 2:10; 3:16; Nah. 1:5; Hag. 2:6ff., 21). See also Amos 9:1.

nā'ar [**נָעַר, 5287**]

nā'ar is a verb found eleven times and meaning "shake," "shake out" in most of these contexts.

Shaking oneself in a physical sense is indicated in Judg. 16:20; Isa. 52:2 (cf. also Neh. 5:13).

God is said to "shake (people) out" as a judgment against them by removing them from their homes and also from the earth (cf. Neh. 5:13; Job 38:13). See also Isa. 33:9, 15.

gā'ash [**גָּעַשׁ, 1607**]

This verb means "shake" or "quake" in two places. 2 Sam. 22:8; Ps. 18:7 refer to the quaking of the earth in the face of divine judgment.

NT Words

saleuō [σαλεύω, *4531*]

saleuō is a verb meaning "shake" in a variety of contexts. It is found fifteen times.

Literal "shaking" involves the effect of the wind (Matt. 11:7; Luke 7:24); rising floodwaters (Luke 6:48); an earthquake (Acts 16:26); and the Holy Spirit (Acts 4:31). See also Heb. 12:26; Luke 6:38.

In metaphorical contexts, ***saleuō*** refers to the powers of heaven "being shaken" by the impact of the Day of the Lord (cf. Matt. 24:49; Mark 13:25; Luke 21:26). In Acts 2:25, ***saleuō*** is used negatively — David's confidence in God is said "not to be shaken," for he was protected by God from destruction.

ektinassō [ἐκτινάσσω, *1621*]

ektinassō is a verb found four times meaning "shake off," "shake out." Matt. 10:14; Mark 6:11; Acts 13:51 refer to "shaking (the dust) off" one's feet as a sign of contempt for those who refuse to extend hospitality to the servants of Christ. Acts 18:6 refers to the similar action of "shaking out" one's clothing as a sign of rejection of those Jewish citizens who refuse to respond to the message of the gospel of Christ.

seiō [σείω, *4579*]

seiō is a verb found in five contexts meaning "shake," "quake" in all but one place.

seiō refers to an earthquake (Matt. 27:51); to overturning nations (Heb. 12:26); to the emotion of fear (Matt. 28:4); and to the effect of strong wind (Rev. 6:13).

apotinassō [ἀποτινάσσω, *660*]

apotinassō is a rare verb found only twice, meaning "shake off" in both instances. Luke 9:5 refers to "shaking (the dust) off (one's feet)" (see also ***ektinassō***, above). In Acts 28:5, ***apotinassō*** refers to Paul "shaking off" a viper from his arms.

See Also: → TREMBLE

SHAME

OT Words

bôsh [**בּוֹשׁ, 954**]

bôsh is a verb found in approximately one hundred places meaning "to shame," "to be ashamed," "put to shame."

The sense of "be ashamed" in general contexts is indicated in 2 Kgs. 2:17; 8:11; Ezra 8:22; 9:6. In particular, being ashamed of one's sin is noted in Isa. 1:29; Jer. 22:22; Mic. 3:7; Zeph. 3:11. The negative sense of "not ashamed" is evident in Gen. 2:25; Ps. 127:5; Isa. 49:23; 50:7. The meaning "shameless" indicates a hardened conscience in Jer. 6:15; 8:12; and is to be distinguished from the sense of "not being ashamed" for legitimate reasons.

The meaning "put to shame" is frequently predicated of God in relation to both his people as well as his enemies. Such an action of Yahweh toward his enemies is indicated in Pss. 44:7; 53:5; Isa. 41:11; 44:11; 45:16; Jer. 15:9; 51:47; Ezek. 16:52; Hos. 4:19. A plea to God to have one's enemies "confounded" (i.e., put to shame) is recorded in Pss. 35:4, 26; 40:14; Jer. 17:18. Conversely, a plea to God "not to be put to shame" by one's enemies is indicated in Pss. 25:2, 20; 31:1, 17; 119:31. God promises in Joel 2:26ff. never again to "put to shame" his people after their punishment in exile. See also Prov. 12:4; 14:35.

bōshet [בֹּשֶׁת, 1322]

bōshet is a noun derived from ***bôsh*** (see above), meaning "shame," with the underlying sense of "disgrace," in most of its thirty occurrences.

"Shame" in the general moral sense of "disgrace" is indicated in 1 Sam. 20:30; 2 Chr. 32:21; Ezra 9:7; Ps. 40:15; Isa. 30:5; Jer. 3:25.

bōshet is also used in the expression "to put to shame," involving divine judgment on the enemies of God's people (Pss. 109:29; 132:18). In addition, the expression "to know no shame" is noted in Zeph. 3:5, referring to the hardened consciences of the wicked.

bûshāh [בּוּשָׁה, 955]

bûshāh is a passive participial form of ***bôsh*** (see above) with nominal force, occurring four times and meaning "shame" — an emotional response to the presence of sin in one's life. God is said to cover his people with shame in Ps. 89:5. The faces of the people of Jerusalem are covered with shame in Ezek. 7:16, as are those of Edom in Obad. 10. Shame is said to cover the enemies of God's people in Mic. 7:10.

bōshnāh [בָּשְׁנָה, 1317]

bōshnāh is a rare noun derived from ***bôsh*** (see above). It is found only in Hos. 10:6, referring to the "shame" of Israel's sinfulness.

kālam [כָּלַם, 3637]

kālam is a verb synonymous with ***bôsh*** (see above), meaning "put to shame," "be ashamed," in most of its forty occurrences.

The general sense of "being ashamed" (i.e., in disgrace) is illustrated in Num. 12:14; 2 Sam. 10:5; 19:3; Ezek. 16:54ff. Failure to be ashamed through hardness of heart is indicated in Jer. 3:3; 6:15; 8:12. The meaning "put to shame" is also noted in 1 Sam. 20:34; Prov. 28:7. The sense of being "shamed" (i.e., conscience-stricken) by neglecting God's law is predicated of Levites and priests in 2 Chr. 30:15; Ezra 9:6.

The psalmists pleads that God would put his enemies "to shame" (Pss. 35:4; 40:14), and God promises that he will do so (Isa. 41:11), including his enemies among his own people (Jer. 22:22). But the psalmists also pleads that Yahweh not "put to shame" those who belong to him (Pss. 69:6; 74:21), and God promises not to put Israel to shame in an absolute sense (Isa. 45:17; 54:4).

kelimmāh [כְּלִמָּה, 3639]

kelimmāh is a noun derived from ***kālam*** (see above), occurring about thirty times and meaning "shame," "disgrace" throughout.

"Shame," in the general sense of "disgrace," or "dishonor," is indicated in Ps. 4:2; Isa. 45:16; 50:6; Jer. 20:11; Ezek. 32:24ff. ***kelimmāh*** also means "shame" in the sense of "humiliation" with respect to Israel, who foolishly puts her trust in Egypt (Isa. 30:3).

There are invocations against the enemies of God, that they might suffer shame (Ps. 35:26); against the foes of the psalmist (Pss. 71:13; 109:29); and against Judah for her idolatry (Ezek. 16:52ff.).

"Shame" at the realization of one's sin is noted in Pss. 44:15; 69:19; Jer. 3:25; 51:51. Ezek. 36:6ff. also records the "shame," or reproach, of the nations brought against Israel.

ḥāphēr [חָפֵר, 2659]

ḥāphēr is a verb found seventeen times, synonymous with the above terms. It has the primary sense of "be ashamed," as well as associated nuances.

The general sense of "shame" is indicated in Job 6:20; Prov. 13:5; Ps. 34:5. In particular, the action of "bringing shame" (or reproach) on someone is indicated in Prov. 19:26.

There are invocations against one's enemies, for them "to be put to shame" in Pss. 35:26; 40:14; 70:2.

God promises not to "put (his people) to shame" in an absolute sense, but will ultimately deliver them (cf. Isa. 54:4). However, the people's "disgrace" on account of their sin will be real (cf. Jer. 15:9; 50:12; Mic. 3:7).

Metaphorically, the sun is said "to be confounded (or embarrassed)," symbolizing the extinguishing of the sun's light at the coming of the Day of the Lord (cf. Isa. 24:23; also Isa. 33:9).

qālôn [קָלוֹן, 7036]

The noun ***qālôn*** is synonymous with ***kelimmāh*** (see above). It occurs seventeen times and also means "shame," "disgrace," "dishonor" in the majority of these contexts.

General references to "shame," or "disgrace," include those in Job 10:15; Prov. 3:35; Isa. 22:18; Jer. 46:12.

"Shame" as a judgment of God is levied against Judah, who is likened to a prostitute in her "adulterous" relationship with other gods (viz. idolatry), and whose nakedness, indicated metaphorically by the term "shame," will be exposed by God (cf. Jer. 13:26; Hab. 2:16). Hos. 4:7ff. similarly refers to Israel's shame as a consequence of her "harlotry," as does Nah. 3:5 in relation to Nineveh.

yābēsh **[יָבֵשׁ, 3001]**

yābēsh is a fairly common verb, occurring around eighty times, with the primary sense of "dry (up)," "wither." In several contexts, however, ***yābēsh*** means "to shame," "be ashamed."

2 Sam. 19:5 refers to "being covered with shame." The meaning "be ashamed" is found in Isa. 30:5; Jer. 2:26; 8:9; Joel 1:11. Jer. 6:15; 8:12 refer to being "unashamed" as a result of a hardened conscience. References to "putting to shame" include those in Jer. 46:24; 48:1, 20; 50:2; 51:17. The sense of "acting shamefully" through idol worship is found in Hos. 2:5 in relation to the people of Israel.

NT Words

aischynē [αἰσχύνη, *152*]

aischynē is a noun found six times, meaning "shame," "disgrace," "dishonor."

It is used in a general sense in Luke 14:9. ***aischynē*** refers to the "disgrace" arising from the practice of idolatry (Phil. 3:19); to the shame of "crucifixion" (Heb. 12:2); and to a dissolute lifestyle (Jude 13).

Metaphorically, ***aischynē*** refers to the "shame" of one's spiritual nakedness, or bankruptcy (cf. Rev. 3:18).

aischron [αἰσχρόν, *149*]

aischron is a noun synonymous with ***aischynē***, above, found in three places with the general sense of "shame," "disgrace" (1 Cor. 11:6; Eph. 5:12). 1 Cor. 14:35 indicates that it is shameful for a woman to speak in church.

kataischynō [καταισχύνω, *2617*]

kataischynō is a dynamic equivalent for the Hebrew verbs discussed in the OT entry above. It occurs thirteen times, meaning "to put to shame," "dishonor," "be ashamed" in most of these contexts, with various nuances.

The meaning "be ashamed" refers to Jesus' opponents in Luke 13:17. To actively shame or humiliate is the meaning indicated in 1 Cor. 11:22.

With the underlying sense of "dishonor," God is said to shame the wise (1 Cor. 1:27). A man praying with his head covered "dishonors" his head (1 Cor. 11:4). Conversely, a woman praying with her head uncovered "dishonors" herself (1 Cor. 11:5).

Those who persecute followers of Christ are said "to be put to shame" (1 Pet. 3:16). Those who do trust in Christ, however, will not be put to shame (cf. Rom. 9:33; 10:11; 1 Pet. 2:6). See also 2 Cor. 7:14.

entrepō [ἐντρέπω, *1788*]

entrepō is a verb found nine times, and in over half of these contexts it means "to fear" or "reverence." In the remaining places, however, it means to "be ashamed" (cf. 1 Cor. 4:14; 2 Thess. 3:14; Titus 2:8).

entropē [ἐντροπή, *1791*]

entropē is a rare noun derived from ***entrepō*** (see above), meaning "shame" or "disgrace" and found only in 1 Cor. 6:5; 15:34.

atimia [ἀτιμία, *819*]

atimia is a noun occurring seven times with the primary sense of "dishonor," or "shame." It is also occasionally used adjectivally.

The meaning "shameful" is found in 1 Cor. 11:14 with the sense of "degrading." Rom. 1:26 refers to "shameful" and vile passions. The sense of "shame" as a reproach is indicated in 2 Cor. 11:21.

Metaphorically speaking, ***atimia*** means "dishonor" in Rom. 9:21 in relation to "worthless" vessels (cf. also 2 Tim. 2:20). In 1 Cor. 15:43, the human body is said "to be sown in 'dishonor'" (cf. also 2 Cor. 6:8).

atimoō [ἀτιμόω, *821*]

atimoō is a verb found only in Mark 12:4, meaning "to treat shamefully."

atimazō [ἀτιμάζω, *818*]

atimazō is a verb found six times, meaning "to treat shamefully," or "dishonor," as well as associated senses.

The sense of "treat shamefully" (i.e., with contempt) is found in Luke 20:11; Rom. 1:24; Jas. 2:6.

atimazō refers to "dishonoring" Christ (John 8:49) and God (Rom. 2:23), as a consequence of breaking the law.

The meaning "to suffer shame" is indicated in Acts 5:41 in relation to the persecution of Christ's disciples.

hybrizō [ὑβρίζω, *5195*]

hybrizō is a term synonymous with ***atimazō*** (see above). It occurs five times and means "to treat shamefully, or with contempt" (cf. Matt. 22:6; Luke 18:32; Acts 14:5; 1 Thess. 2:2). In Luke 11:45, it means "reproach."

See Also: → NAKED → REPROACH

SHARE

OT Words

ḥēleq [חֵלֶק, **2506**]

ḥēleq is a noun found in approximately seventy places referring primarily to a "share," or "portion," in the sense of "that which is allotted," in a variety of contexts.

In a mundane sense, ***ḥēleq*** refers to sharing food (Gen. 14:24; Num. 31:36; Deut. 18:8), and territory (2 Kgs. 9:10).

The meaning "share" in the sense of "an inherited portion" of land or goods is evident in general contexts in Gen. 37:14; Deut. 10:9; Josh. 15:13. In relation to the land of Canaan as both owned by God and the gift of God, this particular sense of ***ḥēleq*** is indicated in Num. 18:20; Josh. 18:5, 6; Jer. 51:19; Ezek. 45:7ff.; Zech. 2:12. In contrast, the Levites are declared "to have no share" in the land portions of Canaan. Rather, they were supported by the people and were given cities to live in (cf. Deut. 14:27ff.; Josh. 14:4; 18:7). See also 2 Sam. 20:1; Neh. 2:20. Lev. 6:17 refers to the allotted "portion" or "share" of one's offerings to Yahweh.

In metaphorical contexts, ***ḥēleq*** refers, for example, to the people of Yahweh as "his share (or portion)" (Deut. 32:9). In several places, God himself is said to be the "portion" of the believer (cf. Pss. 16:5; 73:26; 119:57; 142:5; Lam. 3:24).

ḥōq [חֹק, **2706**]

ḥōq is a fairly common noun, occurring around 130 times with the primary sense of "statute," or "ordinance," in most of these contexts. However, ***ḥōq*** refers several times to a "portion" or "share" in the sense of a "fixed allowance" (cf. Gen. 47:22 [twice]), and "set tasks" (Prov. 31:15). (→ LAW)

ḥelqāh [חֶלְקָה, **2513**]

ḥelqāh is a noun found in around thirty contexts meaning "portion" or "part" in the sense of a "share" or "that which is set aside." This latter nuance is found only in Deut. 33:21; Job 24:18 with general reference to land portions; and in Jer. 12:10 referring to that which belongs to Yahweh.

mānāh [מָנָה, **4490**]

mānāh is a noun synonymous with the entries above. It occurs fourteen times with the sense of "share," or "portion," in most of these.

General, mundane usage is indicated in 1 Sam. 1:4; Neh. 8:10ff.

The allotted "share" or portion of food for the Levites, as well as their designated "cities," are mentioned in Exod. 29:26; Lev. 7:33; 8:29; 2 Chr. 31:19. Yahweh himself is designated as the allotted "portion" of his people in Ps. 16:5.

menāt [מְנָת, **4521**]

menāt is a synonym for ***mānāh*** (see above) and is found in seven contexts, meaning "share" in the sense of an "allotted portion." It is mentioned in connection with the Levites and priests (2 Chr. 31:4; Neh. 12:44ff.; 13:10); and the king (2 Chr. 31:3). See also Pss. 11:6; 63:10.

NT Words

klēros [κλῆρος, *2819*]

klēros is a noun occurring thirteen times, meaning "lot," "inheritance," in most of these contexts. In several places, however, ***klēros*** has the nuance of "allotted share." It refers, for example, to the traitor Judas Iscariot, who originally "shared" in the ministry of the twelve apostles (cf. Acts 1:17), and also to Matthias, who succeeded him as the result of a ballot (cf. Acts 1:25ff.). Acts 8:21 denies Simon Magus a "share" or "part" in the apostolic ministry, on account of his greed in imagining that he could purchase the gift of the Holy Spirit with money.

metechō [μετέχω, *3348*]

metechō is a verb found eight times, meaning "to become a partaker of," "have a share in."

It refers, for example, to one's right "to share" in material blessings as a remuneration for ministry (cf. 1 Cor. 9:10ff.). 1 Cor. 10:17ff. refers to "sharing" or "partaking" of one bread. Christ is said "to share" our human nature in Heb. 2:14.

metochos [μέτοχος, *3353*]

metochos is an adjective occurring six times meaning "sharing in," "partaker of." It is also used nominally to mean "partner."

metochos refers to believers "sharing" in a heavenly call (Heb. 3:1) and "sharing" in godly discipline (Heb. 12:8). Heb. 3:14 speaks of those who "share" in

Christ; and Heb. 6:4 mentions those who "share" in the Holy Spirit.

symmetochos [συμμέτοχος, *4830*]

symmetochos is a synonym for ***metochos*** (see above). It is twice used as a noun meaning "partaker," or "one who shares in." Eph. 3:6 refers to those who share in the promise of salvation through Jesus Christ. Eph. 5:7 warns against "sharing" in fellowship with the ungodly.

koinōneō [κοινωνέω, *2841*]

koinōneō is a verb found in eight contexts with the underlying sense of "come into communion, or fellowship with," or "become a sharer in."

koinōneō refers to sharing in the spiritual blessings of the Gentiles (Rom. 15:27); sharing in material blessings (Gal. 6:6); and sharing in the sufferings of Christ (1 Pet. 4:13). 1 Tim. 5:22 warns against sharing, or participating in, someone else's sins. See also 2 John 11.

koinōnos [κοινωνός, *2844*]

koinōnos is a noun derived from ***koinōneō***, occurring ten times and meaning "one who shares in" — a partner, or companion.

Partners in ministry are indicated in 2 Cor. 8:23; Phlm. 17. "Sharers" (i.e., companions) in suffering for the gospel are noted in 2 Cor. 1:7; Heb. 10:33. "Those who share" in eternal glory are indicated in 1 Pet. 5:1. See also 2 Pet. 1:4; 1 Cor. 10:18, 20. A mundane usage is found in Luke 5:10 with reference to "partners" in commerce.

synkoinōnos [συγκοινωνός, *4791*]

This term is derived from ***koinōnos*** with the same meaning — "one who shares with," or a "partaker of."

synkoinōnos occurs in a significant metaphorical context in Rom. 11:17, which speaks of Gentile believers who were grafted on to the "olive tree," symbolizing the "elect people" of Israel. They were subsequently designated literally as "partakers of" the spiritual richness of that tree, focusing on Christ. In related contexts, see also 1 Cor. 9:10; Phil. 1:7, which speak of "sharing" in gospel ministry.

synkoinōneō [συγκοινωνέω, *4790*]

synkoinōneō is a variant form of ***koinōneō***, above, occurring three times and meaning "to have fellowship with, or in," "to have a share, or part in."

Eph. 5:11 warns against having a share, or part, in the works of darkness. See also Rev. 18:4 in this regard. And in Phil. 4:14 Paul speaks of "sharing" in his trouble.

symmerizō [συμμερίζω, *4829*]

This is a rare verb found only in 1 Cor. 9:13 with reference to "those who share in" the sacrificial offerings presented at the temple altar.

meris [μερίς, *3310*]

meris is a noun found five times, meaning "part," "portion," or "share." It refers to a participation in the ministry of the kingdom (cf. Acts 8:21), and to the inheritance of the saints (cf. Col. 1:12). See also 2 Cor. 6:15, where Paul asks what a believer "shares" or "has in common" with an unbeliever.

synkakopatheō [συγκακοπαθέω, *4777*]

This verb is found only in 2 Tim. 1:8, meaning "to share in suffering" for the gospel.

metalambanō [μεταλαμβάνω, *3335*]

metalambanō is a verb occurring six times, meaning "to partake of food," "to be a partner." In two of these contexts, the term indicates the sense of "to have (first) share" of the crops (cf. 2 Tim. 2:6), and "to share in" the holiness of God (cf. Heb. 2:10).

SHARP

OT Words

ṣōr [**צֹר, 6864**]

ṣōr is a noun occurring only twice, meaning "sharp stone" or "flint" (Exod. 4:25; Ezek. 3:9).

ḥaddûd [**חַדּוּד, 2303**]

ḥaddûd is an adjective, found only in Job 41:30 with the sense of "sharp," or "pointed."

shānan [**שָׁנַן, 8150**]

shānan is a verb occurring nine times, meaning "sharpen" or "whet" in most of these contexts.

The sharpening of weapons is indicated in Deut. 32:41. Adjectival usage is found in Pss. 45:5; 120:4; Prov. 25:18; Isa. 5:28, with reference to "sharp" weapons.

shānan is used metaphorically in Pss. 64:3; 140:3, indicating the sense of "sharpening" one's tongue.

lāṭash [**לָטַשׁ, 3913**]

lāṭash is a verb synonymous with ***shānan*** (see above). It occurs five times and means "to sharpen" in most of them.

lātash refers to sharpening weapons (Ps. 7:12), and tools (1 Sam. 13:20). There is also an adjectival use of "sharp" in Ps. 52:2.

Job 16:9 refers metaphorically to "sharpening" one's eye.

ḥad [חַד, 2299]

ḥad is an adjectival form occurring four times, meaning "harp." It refers to swords (Ps. 57:4; Prov. 5:4; Isa. 49:2), and to a knife (Ezek. 5:1).

ḥādad [חָדַד, 2300]

ḥādad is a verb found in six places, all with reference to the action of "sharpening." It is used in a general sense in Prov. 17:7 and refers specifically to weapons in Ezek. 21:9ff.

ḥārûṣ [חָרוּץ, 2742]

ḥārûṣ is a passive participial form used adjectivally to refer to a "sharp pointed" object such as a threshing sledge (Isa. 28:27; 41:15; Job 41:30).

NT Words

oxys [ὀξύς, *3691*]

oxys is an adjective with the primary meaning "sharp." It occurs only in the book of Revelation and refers to a sword (Rev. 1:16; 2:12; 19:15) and a sickle (Rev. 2:14ff.).

tomos [τομός, *5114*]

tomos is an adjective found only in Heb. 4:12, used metaphorically to describe the word of God as "sharper" than any two-edged sword.

apotomōs [ἀποτόμως, *664*]

apotomōs is a noun found in only two places, meaning "sharpness" in the sense of "severity," referring to a disposition or mood (cf. 2 Cor. 13:10; Titus 1:13).

SHEAF

OT Words

'alummāh [אֲלֻמָּה, 485]

'alummāh is a noun occurring five times. It means "sheaf" (of grain) in Gen. 37:7 (four times) and refers symbolically to the people of Israel in Ps. 126:6.

'ōmer [עֹמֶר, 6016]

'ōmer is a noun found in fourteen contexts signifying "omer" (a dry measure of grain) in about half of these. In the remaining contexts it refers to a "sheaf" in general agricultural contexts (e.g., Deut. 24:19; Ruth 2:7, 15; Job 24:10); and in reference to the firstfruits of harvest (Lev. 23:10ff.).

'āmîr [עָמִיר, 5995]

'āmîr is a noun found four times, indicating the "sheaf" of harvest (Jer. 9:22; Amos 2:13; Mic. 4:12; Zech. 12:6).

SHEAR

OT Words

gāzaz [גָּזַז, 1494]

gāzaz is a verb occurring fifteen times. It means "to shear" (sheep) or "sheep shearer" (the nominal sense) in most of these contexts (cf. Gen. 31:19; 38:12ff.; Deut. 15:19; 1 Sam. 25:2ff.; 13:23ff.; Isa. 53:7).

NT Words

keirō [κείρω, *2751*]

keirō is the Greek dynamic equivalent for the Hebrew term ***gāzaz*** (see above), found in four contexts. There is one reference to "sheep shearing" (Acts 8:32), with the remaining references signifying the "shaving" of one's head (cf. Acts 18:18; 1 Cor. 11:6).

SHED

OT Words

shāphak [שָׁפַךְ, 8210]

shāphak is a verb found over one hundred times with the primary meaning "pour" or "pour out." In the remaining usage of the term, however, ***shāphak*** means "to shed." (→ POUR)

shāphak usually means "to shed" in the context of murder, or shedding the blood of human beings (e.g., Gen. 9:6; Deut. 19:10; 21:7; 1 Sam. 25:31; 2 Kgs. 21:16; Prov. 1:16; Isa. 59:7; Lam. 4:13; Ezek. 16:38; Joel 3:19).

There is an especially significant use of the term ***shāphak*** in 1 Chr. 28:3, where King David is described as a man who has "shed blood." This is not an indictment of David, however, but rather a recognition that this aspect of his military career was in full accord with God's plan. David was chosen by Yahweh to be the ruler to rid Israel of her enemies, both within and without the land of Canaan.

shāphak refers once to shedding animal blood in a ritual context (Lev. 17:4).

NT Words

ekcheō [ἐκχέω, *1632*]

ekcheō is a verb found in nearly thirty contexts, meaning "to pour" in about half of these occurrences. In the remaining use of ***ekcheō***, the meaning "shed" is indicated. (→ POUR)

Matt. 23:35; Luke 11:50; Acts 22:20; Rom. 3:15; Rev. 16:6 refer to "shedding" the blood of human beings, in the sense of murder. Matt. 26:28; Mark 14:24; Luke 22:20 refer to "shedding" the blood of Christ for the remission of sins. Mundane references to "spilling" (or shedding) liquids are found in Mark 2:22; Luke 5:37.

ekcheō is used metaphorically in Rom. 5:5 with reference to the love of God being "shed abroad" in our hearts.

haimatekchysia [αἱματεκχυσία, *130*]

haimatekchysia is a noun found only in Heb. 9:22, referring to "the shedding" of blood, without which (in the ritual sense) there is no remission of sins.

Additional Notes

In the limited vocabulary for "shed," the Old Testament Hebrew term ***shāphak*** frequently means "to shed" in relation to blood, in the profoundly negative context of committing murder.

However, by way of stark contrast, the New Testament Greek dynamic equivalent term ***ekcheō*** has primary reference to the shedding of the blood of Christ, which has a profound irony that is supremely positive. The sense here is that through the judicial execution of Christ, which was in human terms little different than murder, the will of God for the salvation of his people worldwide was fully accomplished through the stark vehicle of a violent bloodletting.

See Also: → POUR

SHEEP

OT Words

ṣō'n [צֹאן, **6629**]

ṣō'n is a noun found in nearly 300 places meaning "flock," signifying various kinds of small herd animals in about half of these contexts. (→ FLOCK) In the remaining usage, ***ṣō'n*** specifically refers to "sheep." ***ṣō'n*** has both a literal and a symbolic significance.

Literal, mundane references to "sheep" include those in Gen. 4:2; Exod. 9:3; Num. 31:28ff.; 1 Sam. 14:32; 1 Kgs. 1:9; Job 1:3, 16; Ps. 44:11; Isa. 7:21. References to the "Sheep Gate" in Jerusalem are found in Neh. 3:1, 32; 5:18.

Metaphorical use of ***ṣō'n*** centers on the representation of the people of Yahweh as his "sheep" (cf. Pss. 79:13; 95:7; 100:3; Isa. 53:6; Jer. 23:1; 50:6; Ezek. 34:11ff.).

seh [שֶׂה, **7716**]

seh is a noun occurring about fifty times meaning "sheep," "cattle," "lamb." (→ LAMB) Specific references to "sheep" account for nearly half of the usage of ***seh***.

Literal "sheep" are referred to in Exod. 22:1ff.; Deut. 14:4; Judg. 6:14; 1 Sam. 14:34. Sheep are indicated in the context of ritual sacrifice (Lev. 27:26; Deut. 17:1). ***seh*** is also used metaphorically to refer to the people of Israel as "sheep" (Jer. 50:17).

keseb [כֶּשֶׂב, **3775**]

keseb is a variant noun of ***kebes*** (see below). It is found in thirteen places and refers primarily to "sheep."

Mundane usage is found in Gen. 30:32ff.; and the ritual use and sacrifice of "sheep" is recorded in Lev. 1:10; 22:17, 27; Num. 18:17; Deut. 14:4.

rāḥēl [רָחֵל, **7353**]

rāḥēl is a noun occurring four times, referring to a "ewe" in most of these places. In Isa. 53:7, however, this term means "sheep" in relation to the sacrificial nature of the death of the messianic Suffering Servant.

nōqēd [נֹקֵד, **5349**]

nōqēd is a rare noun occurring twice, meaning "sheep breeder" (2 Kgs. 3:4; Amos 1:1).

NT Words

probaton [πρόβατον, *4263*]

probaton is a noun occurring forty times with the primary meaning "sheep," though it may also indicate any kind of small herd animal or cattle.

Mundane usage of the term is found in Matt. 12:11ff.; Luke 15:4ff. Ritual references to "sheep" are indicated in John 2:14ff.

General metaphorical references to "sheep" include those in Matt. 7:15; 10:16; Mark 6:34; Rom. 8:36; 1 Pet. 2:15. There are specific metaphorical references to the "house of Israel" as "sheep" in a number of contexts. ***probaton*** alludes, for example, to Israel as God's "sheep," the object of his affection (cf. Matt. 26:31; John 10:2ff.; Heb. 13:20); and to Israel as "lost sheep" (Matt. 10:6; 15:24). The redeemed people from among the nations are referred to as "sheep" on the Day of Judgment (Matt. 25:32ff.). God's people under one's pastoral care are also described as "sheep" in John 21:16ff. The designation "sheep" in the context of ritual sacrifice also refers to Christ (Acts 8:32).

probatikos [προβατικός, *4262*]

probatikos is an adjectival form derived from ***probaton*** (see above). It is found only in John 5:2, referring to the "Sheep Gate" in Jerusalem.

Additional Notes

Significant metaphorical references to "sheep" are found throughout the Scriptures. Throughout the Old Testament, the people of Israel are described as "sheep," both positively and negatively.

In positive contexts, such "sheep" are precious to Yahweh and are in need of nurture and care. In negative contexts, they are described as being neglected and cruelly mistreated by "godless shepherds" (i.e., the corrupt civil and spiritual leaders of the nation). Yahweh, on the other hand, is the loving, caring shepherd who is fulfilled ultimately in the New Testament in the person of Christ. He also is portrayed as "the good shepherd" (cf. John 10) who lays down his life for "the sheep," or his own people — those who belong to him by faith.

See Also: → LAMB → SHEAR

SHEKEL

OT Words

sheqel **[שֶׁקֶל, 8255]**

sheqel is the chief or standard unit of weight or measure in the Old Testament. It occurs around ninety times.

General references to this measure by weight include those in Exod. 30:13; 1 Sam. 17:7; Ezek. 4:10. Other references to the "shekel" in relation to money, or silver, include those in Gen. 23:15; Lev. 5:15; Josh. 7:21; 2 Sam. 24:24; 1 Chr. 21:25; Neh. 5:15; Amos 8:5.

There are also numerous references to the "shekel of the sanctuary," a standard measure (cf. Exod. 30:24; 38:24ff.; Num. 3:47; 7:13, 25ff.).

In addition, monetary value in shekels is deemed equivalent to the dedication of particular individuals to service for Yahweh (cf. Lev. 27:4ff.).

beqa' **[בֶּקַע, 1235]**

beqa' is a noun found only twice, meaning "half shekel" (cf. Gen. 24:22; Exod. 38:26).

SHELTER → REFUGE

SHEPHERD

OT Words

rā'āh **[רָעָה, 7462]**

rā'āh is a common verb found around 170 times with the primary meanings "to feed" or "pasture" in relation to tending animal herds. The related sense of "to shepherd" is found in nearly half of these contexts. ***rā'āh*** is often used nominally to refer to "shepherds." General references to "shepherds" include those in Gen. 46:34; Amos 3:12.

The remaining usage of ***rā'āh*** is metaphorical. ***rā'āh*** refers to the leaders of the Israelites as "shepherds" (1 Kgs. 22:17; Ezek. 34:5ff., 23; 37:24; Zech. 11:16; 13:7). See also Jer. 51:23. Cyrus, King of Persia, is also designated as a "shepherd" of Yahweh in Isa. 44:28. Yahweh is described as the "shepherd" of Israel in Pss. 23:1; 80:1; Isa. 40:11; Jer. 31:10.

NT Words

poimēn [ποιμήν, *4166*]

poimēn is a noun occurring eighteen times meaning "shepherd," "pastor." It is a dynamic equivalent for the Hebrew term ***rā'āh*** (see above).

Literal references to shepherds include those in Matt. 25:32; Luke 2:8, 15ff.; John 10:2.

The remaining uses of ***poimēn*** are all metaphorical. Matt. 9:36; Mark 6:34 refer to spiritual leaders as "shepherds." Eph. 4:11 refers to "pastors" of a congregation. Christ is depicted as "the good shepherd" in John 10:11ff.; Heb. 13:20; 1 Pet. 2:25.

archipoimēn [ἀρχιποίμην, *750*]

archipoimēn is a variant of ***poimēn*** (see above) found only in 1 Pet. 5:4, referring to Christ as the "chief shepherd."

SHIELD

OT Words

māgēn **[מָגֵן, 4043]**

māgēn is a noun occurring sixty times, meaning "shield" in most of these contexts, both literal and figurative.

Literal references to "shields" as a defensive weapon of war are found in Judg. 5:8; 2 Sam. 1:21; 1 Kgs. 10:17; Neh. 4:16; Ps. 47:9; Isa. 22:6; Ezek. 38:4ff.

Metaphorical use of ***māgēn*** focuses on Yahweh as the "shield" of his people (cf. Gen. 15:1; Deut. 33:29;

2 Sam. 22:3; Pss. 3:3; 18:2; 28:7; 59:11; 115:9ff.; 119:114; Prov. 30:5). 2 Sam. 22:36; Ps. 18:35 refer to Yahweh as "the shield" of salvation.

ṣinnāh [צִנָּה, 6793]

ṣinnāh is a noun synonymous with ***māgēn***, above, occurring around twenty times and meaning "shield" in the majority of these contexts.

Literal references to "shields" as a defensive weapon of war are found in 1 Sam. 17:7, 41; 1 Chr. 12:8; 2 Chr. 11:12; Ps. 35:2; Ezek. 26:8; 38:4.

ṣinnāh is used metaphorically to refer to God as "the shield" of his people, or the one who protects them (Ps. 91:4).

shelet [שֶׁלֶט, 7982]

shelet is a noun found seven times, referring to "shields" in literal contexts (cf. 2 Sam. 8:7; 2 Kgs. 11:10; 1 Chr. 18:7; 2 Chr. 23:7; Song 4:4; Jer. 51:11; Ezek. 27:11).

NT Words

thyreos [θυρεός, *2375*]

thyreos is a term found only in Eph. 6:16, referring metaphorically to a "shield" of faith.

SHINE

OT Words

'ôr [אוֹר, 215]

'ôr is a noun occurring around forty times with the meanings "to be, give light," "shine," in most contexts. In a number of places, the meaning of these two senses overlap. (→ LIGHT)

The literal sense of "shine" (i.e., be bright) is indicated in Ps. 139:12; Prov. 4:18. ***'ôr*** is also used adjectivally in Job 41:32 with the sense of "shining."

More commonly, ***'ôr*** is used metaphorically. Ezek. 43:2 mentions the land "radiating" the glory of God. In several places, the face of Yahweh "shines" upon his people (cf. Num. 6:25; Pss. 31:16; 67:1; 80:3, 7, 19; 119:135; Eccl. 8:1; Dan. 9:17).

yāpha' [יָפַע, 3313]

yāpha' is a verb found in eight places meaning "shine," or "shine forth," principally with reference to God. He is said "to shine forth" in general terms in Ps. 94:1. God "shines forth" from Sinai (Deut. 33:2); from Zion (Ps. 50:2); and from the holy of holies (Ps. 80:1).

The natural phenomenon of "shining" is indicated in Job 37:15 with reference to lightning.

nāgah [נָגַהּ, 5050]

nāgah occurs six times, meaning "to shine" in most of these.

Isa. 13:10 mentions the moon failing to shine. Light is said "to shine" on humankind's ways (Job 22:28), as does the light of salvation on the people of God (Isa. 9:2).

nōgah [נֹגַהּ, 5051]

nōgah is a noun found in nineteen places with the dominant sense of "brightness," including the nuance of "shining."

nōgah refers to the natural phenomenon of the "brightness" of light (Prov. 4:18); of stars (Joel 2:10; 3:15); of the sun (Isa. 60:19); and of a flame (Isa. 4:5).

The "brightness" of divine theophany is indicated in Ezek. 1:4, 13, 27ff.; 10:4. In Amos 5:20, such brightness is predicated of the Day of the Lord. The "brightness" of God is described in 2 Sam. 22:13; Ps. 18:12; Isa. 60:3; Hab. 3:4. A metaphorical brightness is mentioned in relation to Jerusalem in Isa. 62:1.

qāran [קָרַן, 7160]

qāran is a verb found in only four places, meaning "to shine" in connection with the radiant face of Moses after spending time with Yahweh on Mt. Sinai (cf. Exod. 34:29ff.).

zāraḥ [זָרַח, 2224]

zāraḥ is a verb with the dominant sense of "rise," "rise up" in most of its eighteen occurrences. However, in 2 Kgs. 3:22 ***zāraḥ*** refers to the "shining" of the sun.

NT Words

lampō [λάμπω, *2989*]

lampō is a verb found nine times meaning "shine," "give light."

lampō refers to light "shining" (Matt. 5:15); to the metaphorical "light" of one's life (Matt. 5:16); to the "shining" of Moses' face (Matt. 17:2); to the "light" of God's glory in one's heart (2 Cor. 4:6); and to angelic light (Acts 12:7).

eklampō [ἐκλάμπω, *1584*]

eklampō is a variant form of ***lampō***, above, found only in Matt. 13:43 and referring to the righteous who "shine" like the sun.

perilampō [περιλάμπω, *4034*]

Another variant of ***lampō*** (see above), ***perilampō*** is found only twice, expressing the sense of "shine around about" in relation to divine glory (cf. Luke 2:9; Acts 26:13).

phainō [φαίνω, *5316*]

phainō is a verb occurring about thirty times, meaning "appear," "shine" in most of these contexts. (→ APPEAR)

The phenomenon of "shining" is evident in natural contexts referring to lightning (cf. Matt. 24:27); light (cf. John 1:5; 2 Pet. 1:19; Rev. 8:12); the sun (cf. Rev. 1:16); and the moon (cf. Rev. 21:23).

phainō indicates the metaphorical sense of "shining light" in relation to John the Baptist (John 5:35), and believers (Phil. 2:15). The "light" of new life in Christ is indicated in 1 John 2:8.

periastraptō [περιαστράπτω, *4015*]

periastraptō is a verb found three times, identical in meaning to ***perilampō*** (see above). It refers to the glory of God in Acts 9:3; 12:6.

SHIP → BOAT

SHIPWRECK

NT WORDS

nauageō [ναυαγέω, *3489*]

nauageō is a verb found only twice, meaning "to suffer shipwreck," "make shipwreck," in 2 Cor. 11:25; 1 Tim. 1:19.

SHOE → SANDAL

SHOOT (NOUN) → BRANCH

SHOOT (VERB)

OT WORDS

yārāh [יָרָה, **3384**]

yārāh is a verb found about eighty times, meaning "teach," or "shoot," as well as associated nuances. The usage is spread fairly evenly between these two senses. (→ TEACH)

The sense of "shoot" is restricted to the bow and arrow (cf. Exod. 19:13; 1 Sam. 20:36ff.; 2 Sam. 11:20ff.; Pss. 11:2; 64:4ff.; Isa. 37:33).

NT WORDS

proballō [προβάλλω, *4261*]

proballō is a verb meaning "to shoot forth" in relation to plants in Luke 21:30.

SHORE

OT WORDS

sāphāh [שָׂפָה, **8193**]

sāphāh is a noun found in around 180 contexts with a variety of meanings such as "lip," "bank," "brim," "edge," and several other associated meanings. One of these is "shore," or "seashore" (cf. Gen. 22:17; Exod. 14:30; Josh. 11:4; 1 Sam. 13:5; 1 Kgs. 4:29; 9:26).

ḥôph [חוֹף, **2348**]

ḥôph is a synonym for ***sāphāh***, above, found in seven places meaning "(sea)shore" or "coast" (cf. Gen. 49:13; Deut. 1:7; Josh. 9:1; Judg. 5:17; Jer. 47:7; Ezek. 25:16).

NT WORDS

aigialos [αἰγιαλός, *123*]

aigialos is a noun found six times with reference to "shore," "seashore" (cf. Matt. 13:2, 48; John 21:4; Acts 21:5; 27:39, 40).

cheilos [χεῖλος, *5491*]

cheilos is a term meaning "lip" in most of its six occurrences. In Heb. 11:12, ***cheilos*** refers to the "seashore."

SHORT, SHORTEN

OT WORDS

qāṣar [קָצַר, **7114**]

qāṣar is a verb occurring around fifty times, meaning "to reap" and "shorten." The former sense is more common. (→ REAP)

qāṣar means "to shorten" in relation to the hand of God (cf. Num. 11:23; Isa. 50:2; 59:1). The shortening of the days of one's life or youth is noted in Pss. 89:45; 102:23. The days of the wicked are said to be shortened in Prov. 10:27. See also Isa. 28:20.

NT WORDS

hystereō [ὑστερέω, *5302*]

hystereō is a verb with the primary sense of "lack," "fail," "want." Rom. 3:23 describes the state of all humankind, who "have fallen short" of God's standard.

koloboō [κολοβόω, *2856*]

koloboō is a verb found four times with reference to the phenomenon of "shortening" the days of tribulation prior to the return of Christ for the sake of the elect (cf. Matt. 24:22; Mark 13:20).

SHOULDER

OT Words

shekem [שְׁכֶם, 7926]

shekem is a noun occurring about twenty times with primary reference to a person's "shoulder" in the majority of these contexts (e.g., Gen. 9:23; 21:14; Exod. 12:34; Josh. 4:5; 1 Sam. 9:2; Ps. 81:6; Isa. 9:4ff.; 22:22). In one instance, ***shekem*** refers to one's "back" (cf. 1 Sam. 10:9).

zerôa' [זְרוֹעַ, 2220]

zerôa' is a noun found in approximately ninety places, referring primarily to "arms" in both a literal and metaphorical sense. However, in a couple of contexts, ***zerôa'*** refers to the "shoulder" of a ram in the context of sacrifice and worship (cf. Num. 6:19; Deut. 18:3).

kātēph [כָּתֵף, 3802]

kātēph is a noun indicating the rather indefinite sense of "side" in a variety of contexts, in about half of the seventy or so occurrences of the term. The meaning "shoulder" is predominant in the remaining occurrences, as well as one or two related senses.

Reference to "shoulder pieces" of a garment is made in Exod. 28:7ff.; 39:4ff. in relation to the priestly ephod.

The "shoulders" of animals are indicated in Isa. 30:6; Ezek. 24:4. More commonly, the term refers to this part of the human anatomy (cf. Num. 7:9, Judg. 16:3; 1 Sam. 17:6; 1 Chr. 15:15; Isa. 46:7; Ezek. 12:6ff.; 29:18).

kātēph refers metaphorically to the "shoulder" of Philistia with reference to the mountain slopes of that country (Isa. 11:14). The term also refers to an attitude of arrogance in Zech. 7:11 — "turning a stubborn shoulder."

kātēph is also used anthropomorphically of Yahweh, referring to his "shoulders" as a place of security and rest for his people (cf. Deut. 33:12).

NT Words

ōmos [ὦμος, *5606*]

ōmos is a noun referring to the "shoulders" of human beings. It is found only in Matt. 23:4; Luke 15:5.

See Also: → THIGH

SHOUT

OT Words

terû'āh [תְּרוּעָה, 8643]

terû'āh is a noun with a variety of meanings focusing on the sense of "an alarm raised," or "acclamation given," in several different contexts. These include "blowing" trumpets and "shouting." The term is found in around forty contexts.

The meaning "shout," or "shouting," is evident in a number of places. The shouting of the Israelite people results in the destruction of Jericho in Josh. 6:5, 20. The "shout" of alarm in battle is indicated in Jer. 20:16; Ezek. 21:22; Amos 1:14; Zeph. 1:16; 2:2. Pss. 33:3; 89:15 record the shouts of joy in worship. There are also shouts of joy heard at the completion of the postexilic temple in Ezra 3:11ff.; and similar cries on the occasion of the return of the ark of the covenant to Jerusalem in 2 Sam. 6:15; 1 Chr. 15:28. See also 1 Sam. 4:5ff.; 2 Chr. 15:14.

The "shout" of God is also indicated metaphorically in Ps. 47:5 in the context of worship.

rûa' [רוּעַ, 7321]

rûa' is a verb occurring fifty times with the primary meaning "to shout" in the contexts of "sounding, or raising an alarm" or "giving an acclamation."

"Shouting" is commonly indicated in relation to the people of Israel. They shout, for example, to bring about the destruction of Jericho in Josh. 6:5ff. There is shouting for joy at the anticipation of a divine victory over the Philistines (1 Sam. 4:5); at the completion of the reconstructed postexilic temple (Ezra 3:11ff.); and again at the coronation of King Saul (1 Sam. 10:24). The Israelites shout in battle to unsettle the enemy in 1 Sam. 17:20ff. They also shout in praise of God in Pss. 47:1; 66:1; Zech. 9:10 (cf. also Isa. 16:10). The shouting of people in general as an expression of anger and hostility towards others is indicated in Judg. 15:4.

rûa' also refers to creation, which is described as "shouting for joy" (Ps. 65:13; Isa. 44:23).

rēa' [רֵעַ, 7452]

rēa' is a rare participial noun meaning "shouting" in relation to the people of Israel (Exod. 32:17).

teshu'āh [תְּשֻׁאָה, 8663]

teshu'āh is a noun expressing the general sense of "noise" in the four contexts in which it is found. In Zech. 4:7 it refers to the "shouts" of the people of Israel in praise to God for the completion of the postexilic temple.

***rānan* [רָנַן, 7442]**

rānan is a verb with the predominant meanings "sing," "cry aloud," as well as "shout," in most of its fifty or so occurrences. (➠ SING)

Lev. 9:24 records the Israelite people "shouting" in fear before God. Shouting for joy is evident in Job 38:7; Pss. 5:11; 32:11; 132:9; Isa. 12:6. Ps. 78:6 refers to "shouting" in a state of intoxication.

***ṣāwaḥ* [צָוַח, 6681]**

ṣāwaḥ is a rare verb found only in Isa. 42:11 with reference to people "shouting" for joy.

***hêdād* [הֵידָד, 1959]**

hêdād is a noun meaning "shout" in most of its seven occurrences.

hêdād refers to the shout of battle (Isa. 16:9); of victory (Jer. 51:14); of joy for the harvest (Isa. 16:10; Jer. 48:33). Metaphorical reference to Yahweh "shouting" (or roaring) in judgment against the wickedness of human beings is found in Jer. 25:30.

NT Words

epiphōneō [ἐπιφωνέω, *2019*]

epiphōneō is a verb found three times, meaning "cry," "shout out," in each case. The angry shout of a crowd demanding punishment for Jesus Christ at his trial is indicated in Luke 23:21; and also in Acts 22:24 in relation to Paul. See also Acts 12:22.

keleusma [κέλευσμα, *2752*]

keleusma is a rare noun found only in 1 Thess. 4:16, referring to the "shout" of the archangel announcing the return of the Lord on the final day of judgment.

See Also: ➠ CRY

SHOW

OT Words

***rā'āh* [רָאָה, 7200]**

rā'āh is a common verb occurring around 1,300 times with the primary meanings "see," "look," with a wide variety of nuances. Among these nuances is the causative sense of "show," or "manifest" (i.e., cause to be seen), also with a number of associated nuances. Usage is spread fairly evenly between these two senses.

rā'āh is commonly predicated of God with this meaning. With the underlying sense of "reveal," Yahweh is said to show the descendants of Abraham the land of Canaan (Gen. 12:1; Josh. 6:5; Deut. 34:1); to show the way through the wilderness (Deut. 1:33); to show his purposes (2 Kgs. 8:10; Jer. 24:1; Ezek. 11:25; Amos 7:1ff.); to show his divine power (Exod. 9:16); to show the pattern of the tabernacle to Moses (Exod. 25:9, 40); to show the plan of the renewed visionary temple to Ezekiel (Ezek. 40:4); and also to show his glory (Exod. 33:18; Deut. 5:24).

In addition, ***rā'āh*** indicates the sense of "extend to," when it is said that Yahweh shows his mercy (Ps. 85:7); and his salvation (Pss. 50:23; 91:16). In both cases, his people are the objects of his actions. The sense of "demonstrate" is evident in Ps. 78:11, referring to God showing his miraculous power.

Where human beings are concerned, the meaning "show one self to" is noted in 1 Kgs. 18:1 with the sense of "present oneself to." See also Esth. 4:8; Lev. 13:19. The general meaning "show" in the sense of "reveal" is illustrated in Esth. 1:11; Isa. 39:4.

***'āsāh* [עָשָׂה, 6213]**

'āsāh is one of the most common verbs in the Old Testament, with the primary meanings "to do," "make," with a variety of associated meanings — one of which is "to show" or "manifest."

Where human beings are concerned, ***'āsāh*** refers to showing (or demonstrating) kindness (Gen. 20:13; Josh. 2:12; 1 Sam. 20:14; 2 Sam. 9:1), and mercy (Judg. 1:24; Zech. 7:9).

Similarly, God is said to "show" his mercy (2 Chr. 1:8); to show (i.e., extend) salvation to his people (Exod. 14:13); and to "reveal" a sign (Judg. 16:17).

***yāda'* [יָדַע, 3045]**

yāda' is a common verb found in around 1,000 places with the predominant sense of "know," with a variety of related meanings. The sense of "to show" is included here with the underlying connotation of "cause to know."

"Showing" the people of Yahweh the way to live through the law of God is the sense evident in Exod. 18:20; 1 Sam. 10:8; Isa. 40:14. Then there are pleas for God to "show" his people the way to live in Exod. 33:13; Ps. 25:4, 14. Specifically, Ezek. 20:11 indicates that Yahweh shows (i.e., makes known) his laws to his people. The related sense of God "bringing to light" or "revealing" those who are faithful to him is evident in Num. 16:5; Gen. 41:39.

In 1 Sam. 16:3, such a "showing" or "revealing" is predicated of human beings.

NT Words

deiknymi [δείκνυμι, *1166*]

deiknymi is a verb found about thirty times, meaning "show" with a number of associated nuances.

The meaning "show" in the sense of "manifest," or "reveal," is indicated in Matt. 4:8; Mark 14:15; Luke 4:5; John 20:20; Acts 7:3; Rev. 21:10; 22:1ff. In particular, in John 14:8ff. there is a plea for God to "show himself" to his disciples. Heb. 8:5 refers to God showing the pattern of the tabernacle to Moses.

The sense of "to present oneself (before another)" is noted in Matt. 8:4; Mark 1:44; Luke 5:14.

The action of "showing" in the sense of "disclose," or "explain," is noted in Matt. 16:21; Acts 10:28; Jas. 2:18; Rev. 1:1; 4:1; 17:1.

Divine power is indicated in John 2:18; 5:20; 10:32, where God "shows" signs or works of redemption.

epideiknymi [ἐπιδείκνυμι, *1925*]

epideiknymi is a variant of ***deiknymi***, above, meaning "to show" in each of its nine occurrences.

epideiknymi refers to "showing" a sign from heaven ((Matt. 16:1) and "showing" the truth of the Scriptures (Acts 18:28), both in the sense of "demonstrate."

The sense of "disclose," "reveal," or "point out" is indicated in Matt. 22:19; 24:1; Luke 24:40; Acts 9:39.

The sense of "present oneself" is evident in Luke 17:14.

hypodeiknymi [ὑποδείκνυμι, *5263*]

Another variant of ***deiknymi*** (see above), this term occurs seven times and means "to warn," "show."
(→ WARN)

In Acts 9:16, it means "show" in the sense of "reveal," or "explain." In Acts 20:35, the translation is "show" in the sense of "teach."

anadeiknymi [ἀναδείκνυμι, *322*]

This variant of ***deiknymi*** (see above) is found only twice. In Acts 1:24 it is translated "show" in the sense of "disclose," or "reveal."

endeiknymi [ἐνδείκνυμι, *1731*]

This variant of ***deiknymi*** means "show," "show forth" in most of its twelve occurrences.

The sense of "point out," or "prove," is illustrated in Rom. 2:15; 2 Cor. 8:24. The nuance of "demonstrate" is indicated in Titus 2:10; 3:2; Heb. 6:10ff. with reference to people.

God is said to "show" or "demonstrate" his divine power in relation to the hardening of Pharaoh's heart (Rom. 9:17); his wrath against wickedness (Rom. 9:22); and the riches of his grace (Eph. 2:7).

Christ is said to "show forth" or "display" his patience in the hearts of his people in order to sustain them for eternal life (cf. 2 Tim. 1:16).

phaneroō [φανερόω, *5319*]

phaneroō is a verb occurring around sixty times meaning "to (make, be) manifest," "show," with a number of nuances.

General references to "show" in the sense of "present oneself," "demonstrate," or "prove," are found in John 7:4; 2 Cor. 3:3.

God is said to "manifest" or "reveal" his works in the lives of human beings (John 9:3); and to manifest his general revelation to humankind (Rom. 1:9).

Christ is said to "show" or "manifest" himself as the "chief shepherd" (1 Pet. 5:4); to show his glory to human beings (cf. John 2:11); to show his name (cf. John 17:6); and his life (cf. 2 Cor. 4:10ff.). John 21:1 describes the risen Christ "showing" himself to his disciples. 1 John 3:8 declares that Christ "is revealed" to destroy the work of the devil.

paristēmi [παρίστημι, *3936*]

paristēmi is a verb occurring around forty times with the predominant meaning "stand by," along with a number of related senses. One of these associated nuances is that of "to show" in the sense of "present oneself," as noted in Acts 1:3, where the resurrected Christ is said to "have presented himself" alive to his disciples. Also, in 2 Tim. 2:15, Paul gives an exhortation to Timothy "to present himself" to God as a competent teacher of the holy Scriptures.

emphanizō [ἐμφανίζω, *1718*]

emphanizō is a verb occurring ten times, with the varying senses of "inform," "make known," "manifest," "show."

John 14:21 speaks of Christ's promise to "show" or "reveal" himself' to the one who keeps his commandments. In the next verse (i.e., John 14:22), Christ is said "to reveal" himself to his disciples.

See Also: → GRACE → MERCY

SHRINE → TABERNACLE → TEMPLE

SHUT

OT Words

sāgar **[סָגַר, 5462]**

The verb ***sāgar*** means "shut," "shut up," explicitly indicated in over half of the ninety or so occurrences of the term. (→ DELIVER)

The literal sense of "shut in" is evident in Gen. 7:16; 1 Sam. 23:7; Ezek. 3:24 in relation to being "locked in." Isa. 24:22 refers to the state of being "shut" (i.e., confined) in prison. The sense of "hem in" or "surround" is indicated in Exod. 14:3; Job 12:11.

Gen. 19:6; Josh. 2:5; Judg. 3:23; 2 Kgs. 4:4ff.; Neh. 6:10; Jer. 13:9; Ezek. 44:1ff. refer to shutting a door, or gate. In particular, Isa. 60:11 contains the divine promise that the gates of Jerusalem will never be shut.

In several contexts, ***sāgar*** refers to being placed in isolation or quarantine as a consequence of contracting an infectious skin disease.

sāgar also indicates the "shutting" or "closing" of the female womb in 1 Sam. 1:5ff.; Job 3:10.

segar **[סְגַר, 5463 (Aramaic)]**

segar is the Aramaic equivalent of ***sāgar*** (see above). It is found only in Dan. 6:22, with reference to God "shutting" the mouths of the lions and thus sparing Daniel's life.

'āṣar **[עָצַר, 6113]**

'āṣar is a verb found approximately fifty times with a number of meanings, including "shut (up)," "restrain," "halt" (plus related senses). (→ RESTRAIN)

Literal references to being "shut up" or "confined" in prison are found in 1 Kgs. 21:21; 2 Kgs. 9:8; Jer. 33:1.

Jer. 20:9 records the prophet Jeremiah's anguish at "the fire shut up in his bones," referring to a burning compulsion to speak the word of God.

When predicated of God, ***'āṣar*** sometimes refers to him "shutting" or "closing" the wombs of women who fall under divine judgment (cf. Gen. 20:18; Isa. 66:9). In a number of places, Yahweh is said "to shut the heavens" in order to withhold rain from the earth, again as an expression of his judgment (cf. Deut. 11:17; 1 Kgs. 8:35; 2 Chr. 6:26).

qāphaṣ **[קָפַץ, 7092]**

qāphaṣ is a verb meaning "shut" or "close" in most of its seven occurrences. ***qāphaṣ*** refers primarily to "shutting" one's mouth, metaphorically alluding to injustice "shutting her mouth" in Job 5:16 (cf. also Ps. 107:42). Ps. 77:9 makes a hypothetical allusion to Yahweh "closing up" his compassion. Isa. 52:15 refers to kings "shutting their mouths" in astonishment in the face of the deeds of Yahweh's Suffering Servant.

kālā' **[כָּלָא, 3607]**

This term is synonymous with ***'āṣar*** (see above). ***kālā'*** occurs eighteen times, meaning "shut (up)," "restrain," "withhold." (→ RESTRAIN)

The sense of "shut up" or "locked up" is indicated in relation to animals (1 Sam. 6:10); and to people in prison (Jer. 32:2ff.).

kālā' is used metaphorically in Ps. 88:8 to refer to one being "shut in" or "trapped" by one's enemies.

tûaḥ **[טוּחַ, 2902]**

tûaḥ is a verb found in twelve contexts meaning to "plaster," or "daub (with whitewash). The term is translated "shut" only in Isa. 44:18, where it refers metaphorically to Yahweh "plastering" the eyes of apostate idol worshipers in Israel, so that they cannot see (or know) anything of God's truth.

gûph **[גּוּף, 1479]**

gûph is a rare verb found only in Neh. 7:3 with reference to shutting the gates of Jerusalem.

shā'a' **[שָׁעַע, 8173]**

shā'a' is a verb with the predominant meanings "to delight," "fondle." In one context, however, ***shā'a'*** refers to the judgment of God on the people of Israel in "shutting (out)" a knowledge of his word (Isa. 6:10). (→ DELIGHT)

'āṣam **[עָצַם, 6105]**

This verb occurs twenty times with the primary meaning "to be mighty," or "strong." In two places, however, ***'āṣam*** means "shut" with reference to "closing one's eyes." In Isa. 29:10 the action constitutes a divine judgment; and Isa. 33:15 mentions the righteous man "shutting his eyes" against evil.

NT Words

kleiō **[κλείω, *2808*]**

kleiō is a verb meaning "shut," "shut up" in most of its nineteen occurrences.

Literal references to shutting a door are found in Matt. 6:6; 25:10; Luke 11:7; John 20:19ff.; Acts 5:23; 21:30.

The remaining uses of ***kleiō*** are metaphorical. Matt. 23:13 refers to "shutting" the kingdom of God in people's faces. Rev. 3:7ff. refers to "closing the entrance" to the kingdom of heaven by royal, messianic authority. Rev. 20:3 refers to Satan's "confinement" in the bottomless abyss. Rev. 21:25 affirms that the gates of the heavenly Jerusalem will never be shut. See also Luke 4:25; Rev. 11:6.

apokleiō [ἀποκλείω, *608*]

apokleiō is a variant form of ***kleiō***, above, found only in Luke 13:25 with reference to "shutting" the door.

katakleiō [κατακλείω, *2623*]

Another variant of ***kleiō*** (see above), this term is found only twice. In Luke 3:20; Acts 26:10 ***katakleiō*** means being "shut up" or "confined" in prison.

SICK, SICKNESS

OT Words

ḥālāh [חָלָה, 2470]

ḥālāh is a verb found in seventy-five contexts meaning "be sick (or ill)," as well as related nuances.

Literal references to being sick include those in 2 Sam. 13:2ff.; Ps. 35:13; Ezek. 34:4; Hos. 7:5.

ḥālāh is used metaphorically in Prov. 13:12 with reference to "the heart being sick," or being cast down or depressed. Song 2:5 records the emotion of being "sick with love," or overwhelmed.

maḥalāh [מַחֲלָה, 4245]

maḥalāh is a noun derived from ***ḥālāh*** (see above). It is found in six places and means "sickness" or "disease" (cf. Exod. 15:26; 23:25; 1 Kgs. 8:37; 2 Chr. 6:28; 21:15; Prov. 18:14).

ḥolî [חֳלִי, 2483]

ḥolî is a noun synonymous with ***maḥalāh*** (see above), meaning "disease," "sickness" in most of its twenty-four occurrences (e.g., Deut. 7:15; 28:59ff.; 1 Kgs. 17:17; Ps. 41:3; Eccl. 5:17; Isa. 1:5; 38:9).

taḥalû'îm [תַּחֲלוּאִים, 8463]

taḥalû'îm is a noun synonymous with ***maḥalāh*** and ***ḥolî***, above, meaning "sickness," "illness" in most of its five occurrences (cf. Deut. 29:22; 2 Chr. 21:19; Ps. 103:3; Jer. 14:18.)

'ānash [אָנַשׁ, 605]

'ānash is a verb with the primary sense of "to be incurable" for most of its nine occurrences. In 2 Sam. 12:15, however, it means "to fall sick" in relation to the son born to Bathsheba.

NT Words

kakōs [κακῶς, *2560*]

kakōs is an adverbial form used both adjectivally and verbally meaning "be sick, ill" or "diseased" in most of the sixteen contexts in which it is found (cf. Matt. 4:24; 14:35; Mark 1:32ff.; 2:17; Luke 5:31; 7:2).

astheneō [ἀσθενέω, *770*]

astheneō is a verb found thirty-five times with the sense of "to be sick" or "be weak (i.e., from disease, illness)" in most contexts (cf. Matt. 10:8; Mark 6:56; Luke 4:40; John 5:3ff.; Acts 9:37; Rom. 14:2; Jas. 5:14). (➠ WEAK)

asthenēs [ἀσθενής, *772*]

asthenēs is an adjective derived from ***astheneō*** (see above), found in twenty-five places and meaning "sick" or "weak" (i.e., from disease). See Matt. 25:43ff.; Mark 14:38; Luke 10:9; Acts 4:9; 5:15ff.; 1 Cor. 11:30. (➠ WEAK)

astheneia [ἀσθένεια, *769*]

astheneia is a noun derived from ***astheneō*** (see above). It is translated "illness," "disease," or "sickness" throughout the twenty or so occurrences (cf. Matt. 8:17; Luke 5:15; 8:2; 13:11, 12; John 11:4; Acts 28:9; Rom. 8:26; 2 Cor. 12:5ff.; Gal. 4:13; 1 Tim. 5:13; Heb. 4:15). (➠ WEAK)

pyressō [πυρέσσω, *4445*]

pyressō is a verb found only twice, meaning "to be sick with fever" (cf. Matt. 8:14; Mark 1:30).

arrōstos [ἄρρωστος, *732*]

arrōstos is an adjective meaning "sick," "ill" in all five occurrences (cf. Matt. 14:14; Mark 6:5, 13; 16:18; 1 Cor. 11:30).

kamnō [κάμνω, *2577*]

kamnō is a rare verb found in only three places, indicating the sense of "grow weary," "to be sick." The latter sense is found only in Jas. 5:15. (➠ WEARY)

nosos [νόσος, *3554*]

nosos is synonymous with ***astheneia*** (see above) meaning "sickness," "disease" throughout all twelve occurrences of the term (cf. Matt. 4:23ff.; 10:1; Mark 1:34; Luke 4:40; Acts 9:12).

See Also: → POOR → WEAK

SIDE

OT Words

ṣad [צַד, 6654]

ṣad is a noun with the general sense of "side" in various contexts throughout its usage. It occurs thirty times.

The physical "side" of a constructed object is indicated in various places, with reference to Noah's ark (Gen. 6:16); to the tabernacle (Exod. 26:13); to the ark of the covenant (Deut. 31:26); and to the candlestick of the tabernacle (Exod. 25:32).

The general directional phrase "to the side of" is indicated in 1 Sam. 20:20. Ezek. 4:4ff. refers to the action of "lying on one's side." References to being "by someone's side" are found in 1 Sam. 20:25; 2 Sam. 2:16; Ps. 91:7. The physical "side" of a mountain or hill is noted in 1 Sam. 23:26; 2 Sam. 13:34.

Metaphorically speaking, **ṣad** is used in the expression "to be a thorn in one's side" (i.e., to irritate or annoy) as noted in Num. 33:55; Josh. 23:13; Judg. 2:3.

ṣēlā' [צֵלָע, 6763]

ṣēlā' is a noun occurring around forty times with the primary sense of "side," usually referring to the "side" of the human body as well as a "side room" in relation to the tabernacle.

Gen. 2:21, 22 refer to God taking a "rib" from man in order to fashion a "woman." However, the term **ṣēlā'** here may simply refer to the man's "side," from which God took an undesignated part. The precise translation of **ṣēlā'** in this context is ambiguous.

More commonly, **ṣēlā'** refers to physical location, in relation to the "side" of the tabernacle (Exod. 26:26ff.; 36:25ff.); the "side" of the bronze altar of the tabernacle (Exod. 27:7; 38:7); the "side" of the ark of the covenant (Exod. 25:12ff.; 37:3ff.). 2 Sam. 16:13 refers to a "hillside."

1 Kgs. 6:5ff.; Ezek. 41:5ff. refer to the "side rooms" of the temple.

pē'āh [פֵּאָה, 6285]

pē'āh is a noun found approximately sixty times meaning "side," "corner."

The meaning "side" is refers to the four directions of the compass in several contexts. Examples of the north, south, east, and west side, respectively, are found in relation to the tabernacle (cf. Exod. 26:20; 26:18; 27:13; 27:12); Levitical cities (cf. Num. 35:5 — all four directions are mentioned in this single text); and the borders of Canaan (cf. Josh. 15:5; Num. 34:3; Josh. 18:20; Ezek. 47:20). The latter reference in Ezek. 47:20 alludes to the visionary "idealized" land of Canaan. See also Ezek. 45:7; 48:1ff.

kātēph [כָּתֵף, 3802]

kātēph is a noun occurring around seventy times with the primary meanings "side," "shoulder," distributed fairly evenly throughout the usage of the term. (→ SHOULDER)

kātēph refers to the "side" of the tabernacle entrance (Exod. 27:14ff.; 38:14ff.); and the temple (1 Kgs. 6:8; 7:39; Ezek. 40:40ff.; 47:1ff.). The term also refers to the "side" of the ephod garment (Exod. 28:27; 39:20). **kātēph** (like **pē'āh**, above) also refers to "side" in terms of compass direction in the context of the geographic features of Canaanite cities (cf. Josh. 15:8ff.; 18:12ff.).

'ēber [עֵבֶר, 5676]

'ēber is a noun meaning "side" in about half of the ninety or so contexts in which it is found.

In a number of places, the meaning "side" has merely a general directional sense such as "on this (or that) side" (i.e., beyond) (e.g., Num. 21:13; Deut. 1:1; 4:46ff.; Josh. 22:4ff.; 1 Kgs. 4:24; Isa. 9:1).

'ēber also signifies "side" in relation to the flat surface of the two stones inscribed with the Ten Commandments by the hand of God (cf. Exod. 32:15).

yārēk [יָרֵךְ, 3409]

yārēk is a term found around thirty times with the predominant sense of "thigh" (of the human body). It can also mean "side," again in relation to a human body (cf. Exod. 32:27).

yārēk also refers to compass direction in relation to the tabernacle. References to the north, south, and west "side" are illustrated respectively in Exod. 40:22; 40:24; 26:22. See also 1 Kgs. 6:16.

qîr [קִיר, 7023]

qîr is a noun occurring around seventy times with primary reference to a "wall." (→ WALL) However, in several places it indicates the physical "side" of a structure (e.g., the altar of incense in the tabernacle (Exod. 30:3; 37:26) and the bronze altar of sacrifice (Lev. 1:15; 5:9).

reba' **[רֶבַע, 7253]**

reba' is a rare noun, referring to the four "sides" of the cherubim creatures as seen by the prophet Ezekiel in his vision of the heavenly throne room in Ezek. 1:8.

shetar **[שְׂטַר, 7859** (Aramaic)**]**

shetar is a rare Aramaic noun found only in Dan. 7:5 with reference to the raised "side" of the visionary "bear" representing the dual kingdom of Medo-Persia.

NT Words

dexios [δεξιός, *1188*]

dexios is an adjective found in approximately fifty contexts with the dominant sense of "right" (as opposed to "left"). In two places, however, it refers to the "right side." In Mark 16:5 it refers to the tomb of Christ, and in Luke 1:11 to the altar in the temple.

pleura [πλευρά, *4125*]

pleura is a noun found in five places meaning "right side" (i.e., of the body), referring to Christ's crucifixion wound (John 19:34; 20:20ff.); and to Peter (Acts 12:7).

SIEGE, BESIEGE

OT Words

ṣûr **[צוּר, 6696]**

ṣûr is a verb signifying "lay siege," "besiege," as well as related nuances, throughout the majority of its nearly forty occurrences.

Most commonly, ***ṣûr*** relates to the military tactic of laying siege to cities under attack (cf. Deut. 20:12, 19; 2 Sam. 11:1; 1 Kgs. 15:27; Isa. 21:2). In particular, Jerusalem is often designated as a target for siege, constituting a divine punishment for her rebellion against Yahweh (cf. Jer. 21:4; 32:2; Ezek. 4:3; Dan. 1:1). See also Isa. 29:3.

Occasionally, people are depicted as the object of a siege (cf. 1 Sam. 23:8 [King David]; 2 Sam. 20:15; 2 Kgs. 16:5).

In Judg. 9:31, ***ṣûr*** means "to fortify" in relation to cities.

māṣôr **[מָצוֹר, 4692]**

māṣôr is a noun derived from ***ṣûr*** (see above), meaning "siege," and related terms, throughout its twenty-five occurrences.

Military siege is in view in Deut. 20:19ff.; 28:53; 2 Kgs. 24:10; Ps. 31:21; Neh. 3:14; and Jerusalem is again singled out in Jer. 19:9; 52:5; Ezek. 4:3ff.; 5:2, suffering this fate for her lawless rejection of Yahweh. See also Mic. 5:1; Zech. 12:2 in this regard. ***māṣôr*** also refers to "siege works" in 2 Chr. 8:5; 11:5; Ps. 60:9.

māṣôr is also used in certain contexts to refer to a city's "defense" (i.e., a protection against a siege) (cf. 2 Chr. 8:5; 11:5; Ps. 60:9).

ṣārar **[צָרַר, 6887]**

ṣārar is a verb occurring around sixty times and, although it is semantically related to ***ṣûr*** and ***māṣôr***, ***ṣārar*** has a broader range of meanings. The dominant sense of this term is "to besiege." It is used in military contexts in Deut. 28:52; 1 Kgs. 8:37; 2 Chr. 6:28, all related to enacting the divine covenant curse.

SIEVE, SIFT

OT Words

nûa' **[נוּעַ, 5128]**

nûa' is a verb occurring around forty times with a variety of meanings grouped around the action of "shaking." One of these meanings is "to sift," and it is used metaphorically only twice. Amos 9:9 refers to Yahweh "sifting" Israel (i.e., as one shakes with a sieve). See also Nah. 3:12.

nûph **[נוּף, 5130]**

nûph is a verb with the primary sense of "wave," or "shake," as well as related meanings. It is found in around forty contexts. In Isa. 30:28, ***nûph*** indicates Yahweh's judgment against the nations, "sifting" them as in a sieve of destruction.

nāphāh **[נָפָה, 5299]**

nāphāh is a noun derived from ***nûph*** (see above) with the underlying sense of "lifting." It is translated "sieve" in Isa. 30:28, referring metaphorically to Yahweh's "sieve of destruction" against the nations.

kebārāh **[כְּבָרָה, 3531]**

kebārāh is a noun found only in Amos 9:9, referring to a "sieve" as a winnowing instrument.

NT Words

siniazō [σινιάζω, *4617*]

siniazō is a verb found only in Luke 22:31, referring to Peter being "sifted" like wheat, signifying a severe trial of his faith.

SIGH → GROAN

SIGHT → VISION

SIGN

OT Words

'ôt **[אוֹת, 226]**

'ôt is a significant term in the Old Testament occurring around eighty times with primary reference to a "sign," or "miracle." The term's field of meaning ranges from a visible or distinguishing mark to a manifestation of divine revelation, usually but not always accompanied by a miraculous omen.

The "signs" of sun and moon, indicated in Gen. 1:14, refer to the natural phenomena of the created order. In Num. 2:2; Ps. 74:4, ***'ôt*** refers literally to an "ensign" or "standard." In Josh. 2:12, ***'ôt*** refers to a "sign" as a token or pledge exchanged between two parties. Gen. 4:15 records God placing a "sign," or "mark," on Cain's forehead — a physical imprint that identified him as being under a divine curse.

More commonly, ***'ôt*** refers to a "sign" emanating from God himself. It is used, for example, to indicate a symbol of the divine covenant, such as the rainbow (Gen. 9:12ff.). The "sign" of circumcision in Gen. 17:11 functions as a mutual response from God and man: God will note his special people by this mark on the male body; and man will recognize his solemn obligation to carry it out.

Elsewhere, ***'ôt*** indicates a "sign" that constitutes a divine revelation, though without an accompanying miracle. For example, in Exod. 3:12 God expresses his intention to bring Moses back to Horeb to worship him there The Sabbath day is also given to the people of God as a "sign" of "rest," initiated first of all by God and subsequently required of them to observe (cf. Exod. 31:13ff.; Ezek. 20:12, 20). See also Exod. 13:9ff.; Deut. 6:8; Num. 16:38; 1 Sam. 2:34; Isa. 20:3; 38:22 for further examples.

'ôt also indicates a "sign" as a revelation from God together with a miraculous omen or phenomenon. For example, the plague judgments on the land of Egypt preceding the liberation of Israel from slavery in that land are "signs" from Yahweh (cf. Exod. 7:3; 8:23; 10:1ff.; Num. 14:22; Deut. 7:19; 11:31; Josh. 24:17; Neh. 9:10; Pss. 78:43; 135:9; Jer. 32:20ff.). Related to the phenomenon of the plague judgments is the "sign" of the blood on the door frames of Israelite homes in Egypt, required by Yahweh of his people if they were to escape the terrible visitation of the angel of death (cf. Exod. 12:13). Such a "sign" constitutes the heart of the "Passover" sacrifice, and it is one of the central motifs of redemption in the Old Testament. There is also the remarkable "sign" of the Emmanuel child, the anticipation of the coming Messiah in Isa. 7:11, 14 — one who will be born of a virgin. The miraculous crossing of the Jordan River in Josh. 4:6 is also memorialized through the "sign" of the stone pillar erected at the site of the crossing. See also Judg. 6:17; Ezek. 4:3.

'āt **[אָת, 852** (Aramaic)**]**

'āt is a rare Aramaic noun corresponding to the Hebrew ***'ôt*** (see above). It is found only three times, all with reference to the miraculous "signs" Yahweh has performed on behalf of his people (cf. Dan. 4:2, 3; 6:27).

môphēt **[מוֹפֵת, 4159]**

môphēt is a noun synonymous with ***'ôt*** (see above), meaning "sign" in the sense of "wonder" or "miracle" in almost all of its thirty-five occurrences.

It refers to the plague judgments on Egypt as "signs," or "wonders" (cf. Exod. 4:21; 7:3, 9; 11:9ff.; Deut. 6:22; 7:19; 34:11; Neh. 9:10; Ps. 78:43; Jer. 32:20). ***môphēt*** is also used in the context of the Emmanuel "sign" associated with the birth of Maher-Shalah-Hash-Baz and Shear-Jashub, sons of the prophet Isaiah (cf. Isa. 8:18).

môphēt also refers to "signs" or "wonders" as miraculous omens from God (cf. Deut. 13:1ff.; 28:46; 1 Kgs. 13:3ff.; Ps. 105:5). Apocalyptic "signs" of cosmic degeneration on the great Day of the Lord judgment are indicated in Joel 2:30.

An example of a non-miraculous "omen" or "sign" from God is the death of the prophet Ezekiel's wife (Ezek. 24:24), which indicated the certainty of an impending disaster for the people of Judah.

ṣîyûn **[צִיּוּן, 6725]**

ṣîyûn is a rare noun, referring to a "sign" or "guidepost" in Ezek. 39:15.

resham **[רְשַׁם, 7560** (Aramaic)**]**

resham is an Aramaic verb meaning "to sign" a royal decree (cf. Dan. 6:8ff.).

NT Words

sēmeion **[σημεῖον, *4592*]**

sēmeion is a dynamic equivalent for the Hebrew ***'ôt***, with similar significance in the New Testament. It is found in approximately eighty contexts with the primary senses of "sign" or "miracle," again ranging in meaning from a "distinguishing mark" to a significant "divine revelation" usually, though not always, accompanied by a miraculous omen.

The general sense of "sign" as a confirming gesture is illustrated in Matt. 26:48 with reference to Judas' kiss of betrayal identifying Jesus Christ to the Jewish authorities. The meaning "sign" as a "mark" or "signature" is indicated in 2 Thess. 3:17.

The meaning "sign" in the general sense of a confirmation of divine authority is indicated in 1 Cor. 1:22; 14:22. Such signs were demanded of Jesus by the Jewish population (John 2:18; 6:30); by the Pharisees (Matt. 12:38ff.; 16:1ff.; Mark 8:11; Luke 11:16, 29ff.); and were expected by King Herod (Luke 23:8). Highly significant in this regard are the "signs" or miraculous deeds performed by Jesus as indicators of his divine person and authority — although these could only be truly understood through the eyes of faith (cf. John 2:11, 23; 3:2; 4:48, 54; 6:2, 14, 26, 30; 7:31; 11:47; Acts 2:22). John 12:37, in contrast, records a "sign" of unbelief in spite of Jesus' miracles. The early apostles were also granted power to perform miracles, testifying to the divine authority they had received through the Spirit of God (cf. Acts 2:43; 4:16ff.; 5:12, 6:8; Rom. 5:19; 2 Cor. 2:12).

One of the great miraculous "signs" of the New Testament is the birth of Jesus Christ, clearly portrayed as a fulfillment of Old Testament prophecy (cf. Luke 2:12, 34).

References to Yahweh's miraculous "signs" in Egypt are found in Acts 7:36 (cf. also Heb. 2:4). Circumcision, as the "sign" or "seal" of the old covenant, is noted in Rom. 4:11. In contrast, the reality of satanic power and authority is indicated with reference to demonic "signs" or "miracles" in 2 Thess. 2:9; Rev. 16:14; 19:20.

Jesus' disciples ask him for "signs" of the approaching end of the world (Matt. 24:3, 24, 30; Mark 13:4, 22; 16:17ff.; Luke 21:7ff.). ***sēmeion*** also refers to "signs" as symbolic apocalyptic references to the coming final judgment of God against the wicked, and at the same time the vindication and fulfillment of his redemptive purposes in Christ. These are all found in the book of Revelation (cf. Rev. 12:1, 3; 13:13, 14; 15:1).

enneuō [ἐννεύω, *1770*]

enneuō is a rare verb found only in Luke 1:62 with reference to people "making signs," or "gesturing" with face and hands in order to communicate.

dynamis [δύναμις, *1411*]

dynamis is a fairly common noun with the primary sense of "power," "strength" in the majority of its 120 occurrences. (→ POWER) In a few places, however, ***dynamis*** is translated "mighty works" as well as "miracle," or "sign." In essence, these two meanings are synonymous.

References to "mighty works" or "signs" performed by Christ include those in Matt. 11:20ff.; 13:54ff.; Mark 6:2ff.; Luke 19:37; Acts 2:22 (cf. also Matt. 7:22).

References to "miracles" performed by the apostles are found in Acts 8:13; 19:11; 2 Cor. 9:12. This gift is also said to be given to some in the church (cf. 1 Cor. 12:10, 28ff.; Heb. 2:4; Gal. 3:5).

Additional Notes

The vocabulary for "sign" and the related senses of "wonders," "miracles" are particularly significant throughout the Bible. "Sign" terminology focuses on divine revelation, which is frequently accompanied by a miraculous or supernatural intervention on the part of God.

In the Old Testament, particular emphasis is placed on the plague judgments of Yahweh against Egypt that includes the Passover deliverance. A clear case may be made for the Passover rescue constituting the paradigm "sign" of divine redemption in the old covenant.

The New Testament vocabulary centers on the miracles performed by Jesus that reveal his divine person, origin, and authority. Yet only those enlightened by the Spirit of God are able to fully appreciate the significance of Jesus' miraculous "signs."

The consistent motif evident throughout the usage of such vocabulary is that of the revelation of God's redemptive plan for humankind. It is a plan that involves the destruction of all who oppose Yahweh, including sometimes the people of God themselves. In a positive sense, such "sign" revelation demonstrates God's clear intention to accomplish the salvation of his chosen people.

See Also: → STANDARD

SILENCE, SILENT

OT WORDS

dāmam [דָּמַם, 1826]

dāmam is a verb found thirty times meaning "be silent (or still)," as well as the nominal sense of "silence" in about half of these contexts. There are, in addition, several related nuances.

The meaning "be silent" in the sense of "hold one's peace" is indicated in Lev. 10:3. The silence of the wicked is noted in 1 Sam. 2:9; Ps. 31:17. The psalmist cannot be silent, as he is compelled to worship (Ps. 30:12). The meaning "to keep silent" is evident in Job 29:21; 31:34; Lam. 2:10; 3:28; Amos 5:13.

demāmāh **[דְּמָמָה, 1827]**

demāmāh is a rare noun, derived from ***dāmam*** (see above), meaning "silence" in Job 4:16.

dûmîyāh **[דּוּמִיָּה, 1747]**

dûmîyāh is a rare noun found four times with the adjectival sense of "silent" in Pss. 22:2; 39:2.

dûmāh **[דּוּמָה, 1745]**

dûmāh is a rare noun referring metaphorically to the "silence" of death in Pss. 94:17; 115:17.

domî **[דֳּמִי, 1824]**

domî is a rare noun expressing the sense of "silence" in Ps. 83:1 in the psalmist's plea for God "not to keep silence."

ḥārash **[חָרַשׁ, 2790]**

ḥārash is a verb with the primary sense of "keep silent," "keep one's peace," as well as several associated meanings, in about half of the usage of the term (about seventy occurrences). (→ PLOW)

ḥārash refers to human beings who "keep silent" or "hold one's peace" in Gen. 24:21; Num. 30:4ff.; 1 Sam. 10:27; 2 Sam. 13:20; Neh. 5:8; Job 11:3; 13:5ff.; Ps. 32:3; Isa. 36:21.

The meaning "to be silent" is indicated in Job 6:24; Pss. 28:1; 35:22.

God is said to "keep silent" at the wicked in Ps. 50:2. See also Hab. 1:13. Pss. 83:1; 109:1 plead for God not to keep silent.

ḥāsāh **[חָסָה, 2013]**

ḥāsāh is a verb found on eight occasions with the meaning "to keep silent," "hold one's tongue."

The injunction "to keep silent," or "hold one's tongue," is found in Judg. 3:19; Neh. 8:11; Amos 6:10; Hab. 2:20; Zeph. 1:7; Zech. 2:13.

The meaning "to silence" is evident in Num. 13:30. See also Amos 8:3.

ḥāshāh **[חָשָׁה, 2814]**

ḥāshāh is a verb synonymous with ***ḥāsāh*** (see above). ***ḥāshāh*** occurs sixteen times with the sense of "keep silent," "hold one's peace" throughout most of its usage (cf. 1 Kgs. 22:3; Ps. 39:2; Eccl. 3:7; Isa. 42:14; 64:12).

NT Words

siōpaō **[σιωπάω, *4623*]**

siōpaō is a verb found in twelve contexts with the consistent meanings "to keep silent," "hold one's peace" (cf. Matt. 20:31; 26:63; Mark 3:4; 9:34; 10:48; 14:61; Luke 18:39; 19:40; Acts 18:9). Luke 1:20 expresses the sense of "be silent" in the context of being struck dumb, unable to speak.

hēsychazō **[ἡσυχάζω, *2270*]**

hēsychazō is a term synonymous with ***siōpaō*** (see above), found in five places and meaning "hold one's peace," "keep quiet, or silent" (e.g., Luke 14:4; Acts 11:18).

hēsychia **[ἡσυχία, *2271*]**

hēsychia is a noun derived from ***hēsychazō*** (see above), found in four contexts and meaning "silence" in Acts 22:2; 1 Tim. 2:11, 12.

sigaō **[σιγάω, *4601*]**

Another synonym for ***siōpaō*** (see above), ***sigaō*** occurs nine times meaning "keep silence," "hold one's peace" (cf. Luke 9:36; 20:26; Acts 12:17; 15:12ff.; 1 Cor. 14:28ff.).

sigē **[σιγή, *4602*]**

sigē is a rare noun meaning "silence" in Acts 21:40; Rev. 8:1.

phimoō **[φιμόω, *5392*]**

phimoō is a verb found eleven times meaning "(put to) silence," "hold one's peace," "muzzle" (i.e., animals).

The meaning "(put to) silence" is found in contexts where the aim is to prevent someone from speaking (cf. Matt. 22:34; 1 Pet. 2:15). See also Luke 4:35. Mark 1:25 records the command of Christ to the demon to be silent, or quiet, just prior to his being cast out from the man he had previously "possessed."

The Mosaic command forbidding the "muzzling" of an ox is found in 1 Cor. 9:9; 1 Tim. 5:8.

SILVER

OT Words

keseph **[כֶּסֶף, 3701]**

keseph is a common noun occurring in around 400 places meaning "silver," or "money."

The general sense of "money" is evident in Gen. 17:12ff.; 43:12ff.; Lev. 25:37ff.; Eccl. 7:12; Jer. 32:25; Mic. 3:11.

The meaning "silver" is indicated in variety of contexts. It is described as a precious metal, in connection with gold and/or other possessions (e.g., Gen. 13:2; Exod. 3:2; Deut. 2:6; 1 Kgs. 10:21ff. Esth. 1:6; Song 1:11; Isa. 2:7). It is also a unit of currency, as "pieces, or shekels of silver" (cf. Gen. 20:16; Exod. 21:32; Lev. 22:3ff.; Deut. 22:19; 1 Sam. 9:8; Hos. 3:2; Zech. 11:12ff.). Silver is a metal used for manufacturing of idols (cf. Exod. 20:23; Ps. 15:4; Isa. 30:22; Jer. 10:4). It is also utilized in making ritual items for use in the tabernacle and temple (cf. Exod. 26:19ff.; 27:10ff.; Num. 7:13ff.; 1 Kgs. 15:15ff.). Silver trumpets are noted in Num. 10:2. Ceremonial offerings of silver are indicated in Exod. 35:24; Ezra 8:25ff. Silver, as part of the monetary wealth of the tabernacle and temple treasuries, is so described in Josh. 6:19; 1 Kgs. 7:51.

keseph is also used metaphorically in a number of places. The words of God, or his law, are occasionally described as being "like silver" or "more valuable than silver" (cf. Pss. 12:6; 119:72). Wisdom is similarly evaluated in Prov. 2:4; 3:14; 8:19. The phenomenon of "being tested, or refined like silver" is illustrated in Ps. 66:10; Isa. 48:10; Ezek. 22:20ff.; Zech. 13:9; Mal. 3:3.

kesaph [כְּסַף, **3702** (Aramaic)]

kesaph is the Aramaic equivalent of ***keseph***, found thirteen times and meaning "silver," "money."

kesaph refers to vessels of silver belonging to the temple of Jerusalem (Ezra 5:14; 6:5); to silver for the temple treasury (Ezra 7:15ff.); and to the metal in the symbolic statue of King Nebuchadnezzar's dream (Dan. 2:32, 35, 45). The sole reference to "money" is found in Ezra 7:17.

NT Words

argyros [ἄργυρος, *696*]

argyros is a noun occurring five times, all with reference to "silver."

"Silver" as money is indicated in Matt. 10:9; Rev. 18:12. As a valuable metal, it is noted in 1 Cor. 3:12; Jas. 5:3. Acts 17:29 refers to silver as a component of an idol statue.

argyrion [ἀργύριον, *694*]

argyrion is a synonym for ***argyros*** (see above), occurring twenty times. References to "money" are found in Matt. 25:18, 27; 28:12ff.; Mark 14:11; Luke 9:3; 22:5; Acts 7:16; 8:20. "Pieces of silver" are noted in Matt. 26:15; 27:3ff.; Acts 19:19. General references to silver are found in Acts 3:6; 20:33; 1 Pet. 1:18.

argyrous [ἀργυροῦς, *693*]

argyrous is an adjectival form derived from ***argyros*** (see above), meaning "made of silver." It refers to idols in Acts 19:24; Rev. 9:20; and to silver containers in 2 Tim. 2:20.

argyrokopos [ἀργυροκόπος, *695*]

argyrokopos is found only in Acts 19:24, where it refers to a "silversmith"

SIN, SINNER

OT Words

ḥaṭṭā't [חַטָּאת, **2403**]

ḥaṭṭā't is a noun found in around 300 contexts with the two dominant meanings "sin," "sin offering." "Sin" indicates the failure to measure up to the ethical, moral, and ritual standard laid down by God in his revealed law.

General references to "sin" against God include those in Gen. 4:7; Exod. 32:30ff.; Lev. 26:21ff.; 2 Kgs. 15:18ff.; Isa. 3:9; Ezek. 3:20. ***ḥaṭṭā't*** refers to the sins of divination (1 Sam. 15:23); idolatry (1 Kgs. 12:30); and the "sins of the fathers" (1 Kgs. 15:3).

Specific confession for sin is indicated in Ps. 38:18; Dan. 9:20. Prayers for forgiveness of sin are recorded in Exod. 10:17; Pss. 25:18; 51:2; 79:9. God is asked not to forgive the sins of one's enemies (cf. Jer. 18:23). In Jer. 31:34, God promises that he will not remember the "sins of his people" — a promise associated with the anticipation of the new covenant age.

Yahweh graciously forgives sin (Ps. 85:2; Dan. 9:24; Zech. 3:1) and also punishes those who commit sin (Jer. 14:10; Hos. 8:13).

References to ***ḥaṭṭā't*** with the sense of "sin offering" are found in Exod. 29:14; Lev. 4:3ff.; 5:6ff.; 6:17ff.; Num. 5:6ff.; 7:16ff.; Ezra 8:35; Ezek. 43:19ff.

ḥāṭā' [חָטָא, **2398**]

ḥāṭā' is the most common verb meaning "to sin" in the Old Testament, occurring nearly 240 times. ***ḥāṭā'*** has other meanings as well, the most notable of which is "to cleanse." (→ CLEAN)

The predominant context of ***ḥāṭā'*** is that of "sinning" against God (cf. Gen. 20:6; Exod. 32:33; Lev. 5:7ff.; Num. 6:11; 2 Sam. 12:13; 2 Kgs. 21:16ff.; Pss.

41:4; 106:6; Eccl. 7:20; Jer. 3:25). There is an exhortation not to sin found in Ps. 4:4.

On occasion, references are made to "sinning" against people (cf. Gen. 42:22; 1 Sam. 24:11; 1 Kgs. 8:31).

ḥēt' [חֵטְא, **2399**]

ḥēt' is a noun derived from ***ḥāṭā'*** (see above). It is found in about thirty places with the primary sense of "sin," usually against God (cf. Lev. 19:17, 20; Deut. 15:9; 2 Kgs. 10:29; Ps. 51:5; Ezek. 23:49; Dan. 9:16). The psalmist pleads for God to do away with sin in Ps. 51:5.

ḥaṭā'āh [חֲטָאָה, **2401**]

ḥaṭā'āh is a noun found in eight contexts. It is related to ***ḥēt'*** (see above), meaning "sin," "sin offering."

General references to "sin" include those in Gen. 20:9; Exod. 32:21, 30ff.; 2 Kgs. 17:21; Pss. 32:1; 109:7. Ps. 40:6 refers to a "sin offering."

ḥattā' [חַטָּא, **2400**]

ḥattā' is a noun occurring eighteen times, meaning "sinner" throughout (i.e., against God) (cf. Gen. 13:13; Num. 16:38; 1 Sam. 5:8; Pss. 1:1, 5; 25:8; 51:13; Prov. 1:10; Isa. 1:28; Amos 9:10).

NT Words

hamartia [ἁμαρτία, *266*]

hamartia is the dynamic Greek equivalent for the Hebrew ***ḥattā't***, as well as associated senses (see above). This term is found in approximately 170 places with the sense of "sin" throughout, primarily with reference to failing to meet God's revealed moral, ethical, and ritual standards.

The meaning "sin" in the general sense of "violating God's law" is indicated in Matt. 1:21; Mark 1:5; John 8:2ff.; 1 Tim. 5:24; Heb. 10:3ff.; Jas. 2:9. The power of sin and its impact, leading to death, is expressed in Rom. 3:9; 5:12ff., 20ff.; 7:5; Gal. 3:22; Eph. 2:1; Heb. 10:3ff. The importance of the law in fully eradicating sin is described in Heb. 10:4ff. The so-called "man of sin" (i.e., the antichrist) is described in 2 Thess. 2:3.

Mark 1:4; Luke 3:3 refer to John the Baptist's baptism for the forgiveness of sins. Heb. 8:12; 10:17 contain God's promise to remember the sins of his people no more. John 16:8 refers to the role of the Holy Spirit in convicting people of sin.

hamartia also refers to Jesus' claim to forgive sin (cf. Matt. 9:2ff.; Mark 2:5, 9ff.; Luke 5:20ff.; 7:47ff.). The perfection of Christ's nature, being "without sin," is indicated in Heb. 4:15; 1 Pet. 2:22. His eradication of the deadly power of sin is recorded frequently in the New Testament (e.g., Matt. 26:28; Acts 2:38; 10:43; 22:16; Rom. 4:7ff.; 6:6ff.; 8:2ff.; Gal. 1:4; Heb. 1:3; 9:26ff.; 1 Pet. 3:18; 1 John 1:7ff.; Rev. 1:5).

hamartanō [ἁμαρτάνω, *264*]

hamartanō is the principal verb in the New Testament meaning "to sin." It occurs around fifty times and functions as a dynamic equivalent for the Hebrew ***ḥāṭā'*** (see above). It has the same underlying sense of missing the mark that God has established as a standard for his people to follow.

The general sense of human beings "sinning" against God is predominant (cf. Matt. 27:4; Luke 15:18ff.; John 8:11; Rom. 2:12; 3:23; Rom. 5:12ff.; Heb. 3:17). Angels are said to sin against God (2 Pet. 2:4); as does Satan (1 John 3:18). Eph. 4:26 records an exhortation "not to sin."

Sinning against another person is noted in Matt. 18:21; Luke 17:4; 1 Cor. 8:12; as is sinning against one's own body in 1 Cor. 6:18.

1 John 3:9 refers to the destruction of sin in the life of the believer.

hamartōlos [ἁμαρτωλός, *268*]

hamartōlos is a noun derived from ***hamartanō*** (see above) meaning "sinner" throughout its fifty occurrences (cf. Matt. 9:10ff.; Mark 2:15ff.; Luke 5:30ff.; John 9:16, 24ff.; Rom. 3:7; Gal. 2:15ff.; 1 Tim. 1:9; Heb. 12:3; 1 Pet. 4:1ff.).

hamartēma [ἁμάρτημα, *265*]

hamartēma is a synonym for ***hamartia*** (see above), translated "sin" in all four occurrences (cf. Mark 3:28; 4:12; Rom. 3:25; 1 Cor. 6:18).

anamartētos [ἀναμάρτητος, *361*]

anamartētos is an adjective found only in John 8:7, meaning "without sin."

skandalizō [σκανδαλίζω, *4624*]

skandalizō is a verb found in thirty-five contexts with the primary meaning "to offend," "cause offense." In certain contexts, the underlying sense is that of "causing someone to sin" (e.g., Matt. 5:29ff.; 18:6ff.; Mark 9:42ff.; Rom. 14:21; 1 Cor. 8:13).

Additional Notes

The vocabulary used in both Testaments to indicate the phenomenon of "sin," as well as related senses such as "trespass," "iniquity," "transgression," is consistent in its emphasis on humankind's failure to live up to God's revealed standard of righteousness.

The Old Testament makes it clear that sin inevitably brings down the wrath of God, resulting in punishment that is most often linked to material and physical loss or trauma associated with the life of God's people in the land of Canaan. Such chastisement may be summed up as the enactment of covenant curse.

The only remedy for alleviating the terrible consequences of sin under the old covenant lay in the presentation of the sin offering — and it was only effective if the presenter came to the sacrifice with a pure heart. It is clear that the old covenant sacrificial system did not provide a true remedy for Israel's persistent and consistent sinfulness.

New Testament references to "sin" likewise make it clear that failure to deal with sin will result in consequences that are more terrifying than even the physical suffering experienced by the old covenant people of God and the godless Gentile nations. The eternal consequences of unforgiven sin are clearly spelled out in the New Testament revelation.

What is also very clearly indicated is that the atoning sacrifice of Jesus Christ at Calvary is the only effective, divinely ordained means of destroying the dreadful effects of sin on humankind. It paves the way for a full and perfect deliverance from the principle of sin and its terrible impact on humankind. Such a deliverance could only have been anticipated under the old covenant, though it must be emphasized that all godly old covenant believers who truly exercised repentance and saving trust in God came to share in full salvation through the operation of genuine faith in their lives — notwithstanding the inherent weakness in the sacrificial sin offering of the Mosaic covenant.

See Also: ➞ GUILT ➞ INIQUITY ➞ TRANSGRESS ➞ TRESPASS

SING, SONG

OT Words

shîr [שִׁיר, 7891, 7892]

shîr is the most common verb in the Old Testament meaning "to sing." It also has the nominal sense of "singer" throughout most of its ninety or so occurrences. The usage of ***shîr*** focuses almost exclusively on singing praise to Yahweh.

Singing to the Lord as an act of praise for his redemptive deeds is indicated in Exod. 15:1; Judg. 5:1; Isa. 26:1; Jer. 20:13. Singing to the Lord in the specific contexts of worship is recorded in 1 Chr. 16:9; Pss. 13:6; 59:16; 68:4; 96:1ff. Levitical "singers" are also indicated by the nominal use of ***shîr*** (cf. 1 Kgs. 10:12; 1 Chr. 6:33; Ezra 2:41; Neh. 11:22ff.; 12:28ff.; Ezek. 40:44).

shîr also means "song" in approximately ninety places.

Mundane references to "song(s)" include those in Gen. 31:27; 1 Kgs. 4:32; Eccl. 7:5; Isa. 24:9.

Songs rendered to Yahweh, praising him for his saving acts of deliverance on behalf of his people, are noted in Exod. 15:1; 2 Sam. 22:1; Isa. 42:10. Songs sung in the context of worship are noted in 1 Chr. 6:31; 2 Chr. 29:27; Pss. 18:1; 67:1; 126:1; Amos 5:23; 8:10.

Deut. 31:19ff. contains the text of a song referred to as the "Song of Moses" — a witness against the people of Israel, to be learned by them as a reminder of their rebellion against Yahweh.

shîr is also found in the title of the canonical love poem "Song of Songs" (cf. Song 1:1).

rānan [רָנַן, 7442]

rānan is a verb found in around fifty contexts meaning "sing," "rejoice," "shout," "cry out." The meaning "sing" is found in about half of these contexts.

rānan frequently means "sing" in reference to expressing joy to the Lord (cf. Pss. 59:16; 145:7; Isa. 24:14; Jer. 31:12; Zech. 2:10). Such "singing" is predicated metaphorically of the trees of the forest (1 Chr. 16:33; Ps. 96:12); of the heavens (Isa. 44:23; 49:13); and the stars (Job 38:7). Rejoicing in song at Yahweh's deliverance of his people is noted in Pss. 51:14; 95:1. See also Pss. 5:11; 81:1; Prov. 29:6; Isa. 42:11; 54:1.

rinnāh [רִנָּה, 7440]

rinnāh is a noun derived from ***rānan*** (see above). It occurs around thirty times and means "cry," "singing," as well as related nuances. The specific sense of "singing" is found in about one-third of these contexts.

Isa. 14:7 refers generally to singing. Singing in praise of God is recorded in Pss. 105:43; 126:2; and Isa. 35:10; 48:20; 54:1; 55:12 refer to singing for joy at the salvation of the Lord.

In Zeph. 3:17 Yahweh is said "to sing," rejoicing over his people.

renānāh [רְנָנָה, 7445]

renānāh is another noun derived from ***rānan*** (see above). It occurs four times with the primary sense of a "ringing cry" or "shout for joy." In Ps. 100:2 it refers to joyful "singing" in praise of Yahweh.

zāmar **[זָמַר, 2167]**

zāmar is a verb found forty-five times with the primary senses of "praise," "sing."

General references to singing praise to Yahweh include those in 1 Chr. 16:9; Pss. 18:49; 27:6; 59:17; 71:22ff.; Isa. 12:5. In particular, singing praise for his victory over the enemies of Israel is noted in Judg. 5:3; 2 Sam. 22:50.

zammār **[זַמָּר, 2171 (Aramaic)]**

zammār is a rare Aramaic noun referring to Levitical "singers" in Ezra 7:24.

zāmîr **[זָמִיר, 2158]**

zāmîr is a noun occurring six times, meaning "song," "singing" in Job 35:10; Pss. 95:2; 119:54; Song 2:12; Isa. 24:16.

zimrāt **[זִמְרָת, 2176]**

zimrāt is a noun found in three places. It refers to a "song" of praise to God in Exod. 15:2. In Ps. 118:14; Isa. 12:2, Yahweh himself is described as a "song" in celebration of the salvation granted to his people.

negînāh **[נְגִינָה, 5058]**

negînāh is a noun found fourteen times with primary reference to "stringed instruments." However, in a few places it means "song."

The following contexts suggest that these songs are intended to taunt or mock (cf. Job 30:9; Ps. 69:12; Lam. 3:14; 5:14). Isa. 38:20 refers to songs of worship.

NT Words

hymneō [ὑμνέω, *5214*]

hymneō is a verb occurring four times, meaning "sing a hymn," "sing praise" to God (cf. Matt. 26:30; Mark 14:26; Acts 16:25; Heb. 2:12).

psallō [ψάλλω, *5567*]

psallō is a verb found in five contexts, meaning "sing" in relation to psalm-singing or making music in the context of praising God (cf. Rom. 15:9; 1 Cor. 14:15 [twice]; Jas. 5:13; Eph. 5:19).

adō [ᾄδω, *103*]

adō is a verb meaning "sing" in relation to praising God in Eph. 5:19; Col. 3:16; Rev. 5:9; 14:3; 15:3.

ōdē [ᾠδή, *5603*]

ōdē is a noun derived from ***adō*** (see above) meaning "song" in the same five contexts (i.e., Eph. 5:19; Col. 3:16; Rev. 5:9; 14:3; 15:3).

SINK

OT Words

tāba' **[טָבַע, 2883]**

tāba' is a verb meaning "to sink," "sink down into," in most of its ten occurrences. It is usually used in a metaphorical sense.

The Egyptian army is declared to have sunk (i.e., drowned) in the sea in Exod. 15:4.

A stone is said "to sink into" the forehead of the Philistine giant Goliath in 1 Sam. 17:47. Ps. 69:2; Jer. 38:22 describe "sinking into" the mire of distress due to overwhelming circumstances. Jer. 38:6 contains a literal reference to Jeremiah sinking into the mud at the bottom of the well in which he was incarcerated.

Ps. 9:15 alludes to the enemies of Israel "sinking down" into the pit of destruction.

shāqa' **[שָׁקַע, 8257]**

shāqa' is a verb found six times with the underlying sense of "sink down," or "subside." It is explicitly translated "sink" in a metaphorical context in relation to Babylon's destruction at the hand of God (cf. Jer. 51:64).

ṣālal **[צָלַל, 6749]**

ṣālal is a rare verb found only in Exod. 15:10, referring to the Egyptian army "sinking" like lead in the Re(e)d Sea.

NT Words

katapontizō [καταποντίζω, *2670*]

katapontizō is a verb occurring only twice, meaning "sink," or "drown" (cf. Matt. 14:30; 18:6).

bythizō [βυθίζω, *1036*]

bythizō is a rare verb referring to ships "beginning to sink" (Luke 5:7).

SISTER

OT Words

'āḥôt **[אָחוֹת, 269]**

'āḥôt is a standard term in the Old Testament for "sister," occurring around one hundred times with several metaphorical nuances throughout its usage, in addition to the literal sense of "sister."

References to one's "sister" (i.e., sibling) include those in Gen. 4:22; 12:13, 19; 30:1; Exod. 2:4ff.; 1 Kgs. 11:19ff.; 1 Chr. 3:19; Ezek. 22:11. Legislation forbidding someone to take his sister as a wife (implying a sexual relationship) is recorded in Lev. 18:9ff. See also Deut. 27:22; 2 Sam. 13:1.

The meaning "sister" is a term of affection for a new bride in Song 4:9ff.; 5:1ff. ***'āḥôt*** also refers to Judah as Israel's "sister" (Jer. 3:7ff.); and to Samaria and Sodom as the idolatrous "sisters" of Judah (Ezek. 16:4ff.).

dôdāh **[דּוֹדָה, 1733]**

dôdāh is a rare noun occurring three times with reference to one's "aunt" (i.e., one's father's sister) (cf. Exod. 6:20; Lev. 18:14; 20:20).

yebemet **[יְבֶמֶת, 2994]**

yebemet is a noun occurring five times, meaning "sister-in-law" in Deut. 25:7ff.; Ruth 1:15.

NT Words

adelphē [ἀδελφή, *79*]

adelphē is the dynamic equivalent for ***'āḥôt*** (see above), occurring around twenty-five times and meaning "sister" both in the literal sense of one's siblings and also as a term of endearment.

Literal references to "sisters" include those in Matt. 13:56; Mark 10:29ff.; John 11:1ff.; Acts 23:16; Rom. 16:15. Other contexts indicate the sense of "sister" as a platonic term of endearment for a woman, reflecting her status as part of the family of believers (cf. Matt. 12:50; Mark 3:35; Rom. 16:1; 1 Cor. 7:15; Jas. 2:15; 2 John 13).

SIT

OT Words

yāshab **[יָשַׁב, 3427]**

yāshab is a common verb occurring around 1,200 times with the dominant sense of "dwell," "live," "inhabit" with a variety of related senses. One of these is "to sit," evident in around 170 contexts. (→ DWELL)

General unspecified references to sitting down include those in Num. 32:6; Ruth 4:1; 2 Kgs. 7:3ff.; Jer. 36:15; Lev. 15:4ff.

yāshab refers to sitting down to eat (Gen. 27:19; Jer. 16:8; Ezek. 44:3); to "sitting in the gate of the city" as a judge or other civic leader in order to carry out a judicial or civil function (2 Sam. 19:8; Ps. 69:12; Prov. 31:23); to sitting (i.e., keeping company) with the wicked (Pss. 1:1; 26:5 [in the negative]); and to "sitting in darkness," indicating a state of unenlightened ignorance in relation to spiritual truth (Ps. 107:10; Isa. 42:7; Mic. 7:8). "Sitting in the dust" involves a posture of mourning and anguish (cf. Isa. 47:1; Lam. 2:10).

"Sitting on the throne" is predicated of kings in Exod. 11:5; Deut. 17:8; 1 Kgs. 1:13ff.; 8:20ff.; 2 Kgs. 15:12; Jer. 13:13. In 2 Chr. 6:16; Jer. 33:17; Zech. 6:13, God's covenant promise to David indicates that he will never fail to have a descendant "to sit on the throne." Ps. 110:1 contains the invitation of Yahweh to the messianic ruler to "sit at my right hand." Isa. 16:5 refers to the Messianic King sitting on God's throne. The satanic "son of the dawn" makes a blasphemous attempt to usurp the seat of God's throne (Isa. 14:13), as does the demonic spirit of the king of Tyre in Ezek. 28:2

yāshab is also predicated of God, who is said "to sit in judgment" on the nations (Joel 3:12; Ps. 2:4). He is also said "to sit" as a refiner of his people in Mal. 3:3. Pss. 47:8; 99:1 speak of God sitting on his throne.

yetib **[יְתִב, 3488** (Aramaic)**]**

yetib is an Aramaic verb occurring five times meaning "sit in judgment," referring to Yahweh presiding as judge in the heavenly court (cf. Dan. 7:10, 26).

NT Words

kathēmai [κάθημαι, *2521*]

kathēmai is a verb found nearly ninety times with the underlying meaning "sit," as well as associated nuances.

The mundane sense of "sitting down" is evident in Matt. 4:16; Mark 2:6; Luke 5:27; John 6:3; Acts 2:2; 8:28.

The risen Christ sits on (i.e., rides) a horse (Rev. 19:11, 21) as the apocalyptic "rider on the white horse." Jesus rides on a donkey in fulfillment of Old Testament prophecy (John 12:15; cf. Zech. 9:9).

Other metaphorical uses of ***kathēmai*** include those in Matt. 4:16; Luke 1:79, referring to people "sitting in darkness" (i.e., spiritual blindness). The "great harlot" Babylon is described in Rev. 17:9 as "seated" on seven mountains. See also Rev. 17:3, 15. The "Son of Man" is described as sitting on the clouds of heaven in Rev. 14:14ff.

The privileged position of "sitting at the right hand of God" is referred to in Matt. 22:44; 26:64; Mark 12:36; Luke 20:42; 22:69; Acts 2:34; Heb. 1:13. God is portrayed as sitting on his throne in Matt. 23:22; Mark 14:62; Rev. 4:2ff.; 5:1, 13; 6:16; 7:10, 15; 19:4; 20:11; 21:5.

synkathēmai [συγκάθημαι, *4775*]

synkathēmai is a variant form of ***kathēmai***, above, meaning "sit together with" in Mark 14:54; Acts 26:30.

kathizō [καθίζω, *2523*]

kathizō is a verb synonymous with ***kathēmai*** (see above), occurring around fifty times and meaning "sit," "sit down" in most contexts.

Mundane references to sitting down include those in Matt. 5:1; Luke 4:20; Acts 13:14; 1 Cor. 10:7.

kathizō refers to "sitting on thrones" in various contexts — in relation to an earthly ruler (Acts 12:21); to the saints in glory (Luke 22:30; Rev. 20:4); and to the Son of Man upon his throne (Matt. 19:28). The privileged position of sitting at the right hand of the Son of Man in glory is noted in Matt. 20:21ff.; 25:31; Mark 10:37ff. ***kathizō*** also refers to Christ sitting on his throne at the right hand of God (Mark 16:19; Heb. 1:3; 10:12, Rev. 3:21).

synkathizō [συγκαθίζω, *4776*]

synkathizō is a variant form of ***kathizō***, above. It is found only twice and means "sit (down) together with" in a literal sense in Luke 22:55. Eph. 2:6 mentions the believer's spiritual status of "sitting with Christ" in the heavenly places.

anakathizō [ἀνακαθίζω, *339*]

anakathizō is another variant of ***kathizō***, above. It means "sit up" and is found only twice, in Luke 7:15; Acts 9:40.

parakathizō [παρακαθίζω, *3869*]

parakathizō is a rare variant of ***kathizō*** found only in Luke 10:9 with the sense of "sit down at, or beside."

anakeimai [ἀνάκειμαι, *345*]

anakeimai is a verb occurring fourteen times. It means "sit down" in the context of sharing a meal or banquet in the majority of these contexts (cf. Matt. 9:10; 26:7, 20; Mark 14:18; 16:18; Luke 7:37; 22:27; John 6:11; 13:28).

katakeimai [κατάκειμαι, *2621*]

katakeimai is a variant of ***anakeimai***, above. It is found in eleven places and means "lie (down)" in most of these. In four contexts, however, ***katakeimai*** indicates the sense of "sit down" (i.e., at a table for a meal) (cf. Mark 2:15; 14:3; Luke 5:29; 1 Cor. 8:10).

synanakeimai [συνανάκειμαι, *4873*]

Another variant of ***anakeimai***, above, ***synanakeimai*** is a verb found in nine places referring to being seated at a meal (cf. Matt. 9:10; 14:9; Mark 2:15; Luke 14:10, 15; John 12:2).

anaklinō [ἀνακλίνω, *347*]

anaklinō is a verb synonymous with the entries above, meaning "sit down" in the context of feasting in seven places (cf. Matt. 8:11; Mark 6:39; Luke 7:36; 9:15; 12:37; 13:29). See also Matt. 14:19.

kataklinō [κατακλίνω, *2625*]

kataklinō is a verb found in only three places, meaning "sit down" (i.e., to eat) (cf. Luke 9:14; 14:8; 24:30).

anapiptō [ἀναπίπτω, *377*]

anapiptō is another verb synonymous with the preceding entries. It is found in ten places and means "sit down" in the context of taking a meal (cf. Matt. 15:35; Mark 6:40; Luke 11:37; 14:10; 17:7; 22:14; John 6:10; 13:12).

kathezomai [καθέζομαι, *2516*]

kathezomai is a verb with the sense of "sit down" (i.e., take one's seat), found in six places (cf. Matt. 26:55; Luke 2:46; John 4:6; 11:20; 20:12; Acts 6:15).

SKILL, SKILLFUL → WISDOM

SKIN

OT Words

'ôr [עוֹר, **5785**]

'ôr is a noun occurring around one hundred times meaning "skin," "hide."

Animal skins for clothing are indicated in Gen. 3:21; 27:16. General references to "skin" include those in Exod. 25:5; 35:7; Lev. 4:11; Num. 4:6ff.; Jer. 13:23. Ezek. 37:6 refers to bodies being covered with new skin in the context of Ezekiel's vision of the resurrection of the people of Israel. The skin of Moses' face is said to glow after his audience with Yahweh on Mt. Sinai (cf. Exod. 34:29ff.). Skin disease is described in Lev. 13:2ff. Job 2:4 refers to a human being's physical person through the metaphor of "skin."

geled [גֶּלֶד, **1539**]

geled is a rare noun with reference to human "skin," found only in Job 16:15.

SKULL

OT Words

gulgōlet [גֻּלְגֹּלֶת, **1538**]

gulgōlet is a noun occurring twelve times with reference to a human skull. See Judg. 9:53; 2 Kgs. 9:35.

NT Words

kranion [κρανίον, *2898*]

kranion is the dynamic equivalent of the Aramaic term "Golgotha," referring to the hill near Jerusalem designated as the site of Christ's crucifixion, translated "the place of the skull" (cf. Matt. 27:33; Mark 15:22; Luke 23:33; John 19:17).

SKY → HEAVEN

SLAIN → WOUND

SLANDER

OT Words

dibbāh [דִּבָּה, **1681**]

dibbāh is a noun found in nine contexts meaning "slander" in the sense of a malicious report about someone or something (cf. Gen. 37:2; Num. 13:32; Ps. 31:13; Prov. 10:18; Jer. 20:10; Ezek. 36:3).

rāgal [רָגַל, **7270**]

rāgal is a verb found in twenty-five contexts with the primary sense of "spy," "spy out." In 2 Sam. 19:27; Ps. 15:3, however, this term is translated "slander" in the sense of speaking maliciously about someone.

dōphî [דֹּפִי, **1848**]

dōphî is a rare noun found only in Ps. 50:20 with reference to "slandering" one's own brother.

lāshan [לָשַׁן, **3960**]

lāshan is a verb found three times meaning "to slander," to use one's tongue to speak evil of someone (cf. Ps. 101:5; Prov. 30:10).

rākîl [רָכִיל, **7400**]

rākîl is a noun occurring six times denoting a "slanderer," or one who spreads malicious gossip (cf. Lev. 19:16; Prov. 11:13; Jer. 6:28).

NT Words

blasphēmeō [βλασφημέω, *987*]

blasphēmeō is a verb with the predominant sense of "blaspheme" (i.e., against God) in nearly all of its forty or so occurrences. In addition, ***blasphēmeō*** means "speak evil" or "slander" (cf. Matt. 27:39; Mark 15:29; Acts 13:45; Rom. 3:8; Titus 3:2; 2 Pet. 2:2; Jude 8ff.).

diabolos [διάβολος, *1228*]

diabolos is a common term for "devil" found in about forty contexts. ***diabolos*** is also occasionally translated as "slanderer," "accuser," in relation to people (cf. 2 Tim. 3:3; Titus 2:3).

SLAVE → SERVANT

SLAUGHTER, SLAY

OT Words

ḥārēb [חָרֵב, **2717**]

ḥārēb is a verb found forty times with the primary meaning "dry up," "make desolate," "lay waste." The latter meaning has the underlying sense of "destroy," or "eradicate," where "slaughter" is implied. ***ḥārēb*** is explicitly translated "slay" in a couple of contexts (cf. Jer. 50:21, 27; 2 Kgs. 3:23). Isa. 60:12 speaks of "laying waste" to the nations.

qetal [קְטַל, **6992** (Aramaic)]

qetal is an Aramaic verb found in seven places meaning "slay," or "kill" (cf. Dan. 2:13, 14; 3:22; 5:19, 30; 7:11).

makkāh [מַכָּה, **4347**]

makkāh is a noun occurring around fifty times meaning "blow," "wound," "plague," "slaughter." The latter sense is evident in about one-third of the total usage and relates exclusively to the slaughter of battle (cf. Josh. 10:10, 20; Judg. 11:33; 15:8; 1 Sam. 4:10; 6:19; 1 Kgs. 20:21; Isa. 10:26).

maggēphāh [מַגֵּפָה, **4046**]

maggēphāh is a noun synonymous with ***makkāh***, above, occurring around thirty times and meaning "blow," "plague," "slaughter." The sense of "slaughter" relates to the context of a military defeat and is found in 1 Sam. 4:17; 2 Sam. 17:9; 18:7.

tebaḥ [טֶבַח, **2874**]

tebaḥ is a noun meaning "slaughter" in most of its twelve occurrences.

The slaughter of beasts for sacrifice is indicated in Prov. 7:22; Jer. 50:27. Isa. 34:2ff.; Jer. 48:15 speak of the slaughter of the nations. The slaughter of the messianic Suffering Servant is described in Isa. 53:7. Isa. 65:12; Ezek. 21:10, 15 refer to "slaughter" as an expression of divine judgment.

tibḥāh [טִבְחָה, **2878**]

tibḥāh is a noun found in three places meaning "slaughter," used metaphorically in relation to people as "sheep for slaughter" (cf. Ps. 44:22; Jer. 12:3).

matbēaḥ [מַטְבֵּחַ, **4293**]

matbēaḥ is a term found only in Isa. 14:21 with reference to a "slaughtering place" prepared for the Babylonians.

hereg [הֶרֶג, **2027**]

hereg is a noun occurring five times meaning "slaughter" in relation to people (cf. Esth. 9:5; Prov. 24:11; Isa. 27:7; 30:25; Ezek. 26:15).

harēgāh [הֲרֵגָה, **2028**]

harēgāh is a noun synonymous with ***hereg***, above, found five times and meaning "slaughter" in Jer. 7:23; 12:3; 19:6; Zech. 11:4, 7.

qetel [קֶטֶל, **6993**]

qetel is found in Obad. 9 and refers to the "slaughter" of people.

NT Words

sphagē [σφαγή, *4967*]

sphagē is a noun occurring three times with reference to "slaughter" in relation to Jesus Christ's crucifixion (Acts 8:32), and the persecuted saints (Rom. 8:36). See also Jas. 5:5.

phonos [φόνος, *5408*]

This term occurs ten times with predominant literal references to "murder" (Matt. 15:19; Mark 7:21; Luke 23:19; Acts 9:1; Rom. 1:29; Rev. 9:21).

kopē [κοπή, *2871*]

kopē is a rare noun found only in Heb. 7:1 with reference to the "slaughter" of battle.

See Also: → KILL → SACRIFICE

SLEEP

OT Words

shākab [שָׁכַב, **7901**]

shākab is a verb found over two hundred times with the principal meanings "lie (down)," "sleep." The latter sense is found in about fifty of these contexts. (→ LIE)

The literal sense of "sleep" occurs in Gen. 28:11; Deut. 24:12ff.; 1 Sam. 26:7; Job 7:21; Prov. 6:10. Metaphorical references to the "sleep" of death are found in 2 Sam. 7:12; 1 Kgs. 1:21; 2:10; 11:21; 2 Kgs. 10:35; 2 Chr. 9:31.

shēnāh [שֵׁנָה, **8142**]

shēnāh is a noun found over twenty times with the consistent meaning "sleep" throughout (cf. Gen. 28:16; Judg. 16:14; Esth. 6:1; Ps. 76:5; Prov. 4:16; Eccl. 8:16; Dan. 2:1; Zech. 4:1). Jer. 51:39, 57 refer metaphorically to the "sleep" of death.

yāshēn [יָשֵׁן, **3462** (Verb), **3463** (Adjective)]

yāshēn as a verb occurs around twenty times, meaning "to sleep" in most contexts (e.g., Gen. 2:21; Judg. 16:19; Ps. 4:8). Eccl. 5:12; Jer. 51:39 speak of the metaphorical "sleep" of death. See also Dan. 12:11.

The form ***yāshēn*** is also used adjectivally with the sense of "sleeping," "asleep" (cf. 1 Sam. 26:7; 1 Kgs. 3:20; Song 5:2; 7:9).

tardēmāh [תַּרְדֵּמָה, **8639**]

tardēmāh is a noun occurring seven times meaning "deep sleep" or "trance" (cf. Gen. 2:21; 15:12; Job 4:13; Prov. 19:15; Isa. 29:10).

rādam [רָדַם, **7290**]

rādam is a verb occurring seven times meaning "to be (fast) asleep," "fall asleep" (cf. Judg. 4:21; Prov. 10:5; Dan. 8:18; 10:9; Jonah 1:5, 6).

See Also: → ASLEEP

SLOTHFUL → IDLE

SMALL → LITTLE

SMELL

OT Words

rêaḥ **[רֵיחַ, 7381]**

rêaḥ is a noun found in around sixty contexts meaning "smell," or "aroma," in most of these.

The "aroma" of sacrifice that is pleasing to God is indicated in Gen. 8:21; Exod. 29:18; Lev. 1:9ff.; 2:2ff.; 6:15ff.; Num. 28:6ff.; 29:2ff. The sacrifices of idol worshipers are also "fragrant" incense (i.e., a pleasing aroma) to idols (cf. Ezek. 6:13; 16:19; 20:28).

General references to a "fragrant aroma" in relation to perfume are indicated in Song 1:3; 2:12; 4:10. See also Gen. 27:27.

rûaḥ **[רוּחַ, 7306]**

rûaḥ is a verb occurring eleven times, meaning "to smell" in the most of these occurrences.

rûaḥ is predicated of Yahweh when he is said to smell a sacrifice in Gen. 8:21; Lev. 26:31. On the other hand, idols are declared to be incapable of smelling a sacrifice (cf. Deut. 4:28; Ps. 115:6). See also Gen. 27:27; Job 39:25.

NT Words

euōdia [εὐωδία, *2175*]

euōdia is a rare noun found in three places, referring metaphorically to a "sweet smell," or "fragrant aroma." 2 Cor. 2:15 refers to believers as a "sweet aroma" of Christ to God. Eph. 5:2 declares that Christ gave himself as a "fragrant offering" to God. Gifts from the Philippian church are described as a "fragrant offering" to God (Phil. 4:18).

osphrēsis [ὄσφρησις, *3750*]

osphrēsis is a rare noun indicating a "sense of smell," found only in 1 Cor. 12:17.

SMITE → STRIKE

SMOKE

OT Words

'āshān **[עָשָׁן, 6227]**

'āshān is a noun occurring twenty-five times meaning "smoke" throughout, primarily in metaphorical contexts.

Smoke is one of the observable phenomena associated with the divine theophany on Mt. Sinai (cf. Exod. 19:18); as it is in the vision of Isaiah's prophetic call (Isa. 4:5; 6:4). Other theophanic manifestations involving smoke include a smoking fire pot (Gen. 15:17); and smoke pouring from Yahweh's nostrils in anger (2 Sam. 22:9).

The heavens are said to vanish like smoke (Isa. 51:6); as do the enemies of God's people (cf. Isa. 9:18; Pss. 37:20; 68:2). See also Job 41:20; Ps. 102:3; Song 3:6; Isa. 14:31.

Literal references to the smoke of a burning city are found in Josh. 8:20ff.; Judg. 20:38ff.

'āshēn **[עָשֵׁן, 6226]**

'āshēn is an adjectival form meaning "smoking" found only twice. Exod. 20:10 refers to Mt. Sinai as "smoking." Isa. 7:4 speaks of the kings Rezin and Rekah as "smoking firebrands."

'āshan **[עָשַׁן, 6225]**

'āshan is a verb related to ***'āshān*** and ***'āshēn***, above, meaning "to smoke," "fume." It occurs six times.

Mt. Sinai is said "to smoke" in Exod. 19:18 in association with divine theophany. See also Pss. 104:32; 144:5.

Yahweh is said "to smoke" in divine anger in Deut. 29:20; Ps. 74:1.

qîṭôr **[קִיטוֹר, 7008]**

qîṭôr is a noun meaning "smoke" in all but one of the four occurrences of the term. The smoke of burning cities is indicated in Gen. 19:28 (twice); and Ps. 119:83 refers generally to smoke.

NT Words

kapnos [καπνός, *2586*]

The noun ***kapnos*** means "smoke" and is found thirteen times.

Acts 2:19 contains a general reference to "smoke."

Elsewhere, ***kapnos*** is found exclusively in the book of Revelation, referring to the smoke of incense in the temple (Rev. 8:4); smoke from the bottomless pit of destruction (Rev. 9:2ff.); smoke pouring from the mouth of demonic creatures (Rev. 9:17ff.); smoke issuing from the fiery destruction of the demonic "beasts" and the "Babylonian whore" (Rev. 14:11; 18:9, 18; 19:3); and smoke filling the temple in connection with a divine theophany (Rev. 15:8).

SNARE → TRAP

SOBER → TEMPERANCE

SOJOURN, SOJOURNER

OT Words

gûr **[גּוּר, 1481]**

gûr is a verb occurring nearly one hundred times with the primary meaning "sojourn" (i.e., dwell as a stranger in a foreign land) in the majority of these contexts.

General references to "sojourning" include those in Exod. 3:22; Deut. 26:5; Judg. 17:7ff.; Jer. 42:15ff.

The "sojourning" of the patriarchs in Canaan is indicated in Gen. 12:10; 26:3; 35:27; Exod. 6:4; Ps. 105:23.

Legislation concerning the treatment of sojourners is detailed in Lev. 17:8ff.; 19:33ff.; Num. 15:14ff.; Ezra 1:4.

māgûr **[מָגוּר, 4033]**

māgûr is a rare noun found only in Gen. 17:8 referring to Abraham as a "sojourner" in Canaan.

tôshāb **[תּוֹשָׁב, 8453]**

tôshāb is a noun found in fourteen places meaning "sojourner," "stranger," "foreigner."

It refers to Abraham (Gen. 23:4) and to the Israelites in Canaan (Lev. 25:23; Ps. 39:12). Legislation concerning the "sojourner" is found in Exod. 12:45; Lev. 22:10; 25:6, 40ff.; Num. 35:15.

NT Words

paroikos **[πάροικος, *3941*]**

paroikos is a noun occurring four times meaning "stranger," "foreigner," or "sojourner." It refers to the Israelites in Egypt (Acts 7:6, 29); and to believers on earth (Eph. 2:19; 1 Pet. 2:11).

paroikia **[παροικία, *3940*]**

paroikia is a rare noun with the sense of "sojourner," or "stranger," found only in Acts 13:17 with reference to Israelites in Egypt.

Additional Notes

The vocabulary for "sojourner" and related meanings has both a literal and metaphorical sense throughout both Old and New Testaments.

The term ***gûr*** refers literally to "strangers" living in a country not their own. Significantly, this term frequently refers to Abraham and his posterity in their occupation of the land of Canaan. The Israelites were required to adhere to humane legislation concerning the treatment of "aliens," "strangers," or "sojourners" who would come to share in their land. Israel was to treat "sojourners" dwelling alongside them in a compassionate way, just as Yahweh had shown them compassion while they were "sojourners" in Egypt.

In the New Testament, the usage of the terms ***paroikos*** and ***paroikia***, though infrequent, is significant. The phenomenon of "sojourning" in the New Testament focuses on the believer's temporary "sojourn" on earth as a passing, finite preparation for eternity in the consummated kingdom of heaven. Just as the Israelites "sojourned" in Egypt, awaiting their release from captivity and progress toward the promised land of rest, so the new covenant believer "sojourns" here on earth, awaiting his transfer to the eternal reality of fellowship with God and Christ in heavenly glory.

See Also: → ALIEN

SOLDIER

NT Words

stratiōtēs **[στρατιώτης, *4757*]**

stratiōtēs is a noun occurring thirty times, meaning "soldier" throughout.

stratiōtēs frequently refers to the "(common) soldier" (e.g., Matt. 8:9; Mark 15:16; Luke 7:8; John 19:2, 23ff.; Acts 10:7; 12:4ff.; 21:32).

A metaphorical reference to a "soldier" as a devout follower of Christ is found in 2 Tim. 2:3.

See Also: → ARMY

SON

OT Words

bēn **[בֵּן, 1121]**

bēn is a common noun found in nearly 5,000 contexts, meaning "son," "children" in most of these. The former sense occurs in more than half of the usage of ***bēn***.

The literal, mundane sense of "son" as a male child is illustrated in Gen. 4:17; 17:19; 21:2ff.; Exod. 21:9; Lev. 12:6; Deut. 1:31; 1 Kgs. 21:22; Ps. 50:20. A highly significant reference to "son" is recorded in Isa. 7:14; 9:16 in relation to the promised "son" born to the virgin. In the immediate context, this sign given to King Ahaz of Judah concerns the birth of Maher-Shalal-Hash-Baz, who anticipates in a redemptive-historical sense the birth of the promised Messiah to Mary, the mother of the Christ child.

The term ***bēn*** is also commonly used in genealogical listings, referring not only to "son" in the sense of an immediate male offspring, but also in the sense of a "descendant of" (i.e., grandson, or more distant generation) (e.g., Num. 1:5ff.; 1 Sam. 1:1ff.; 1 Chr. 1:43ff.; 4:34ff.; 7:16ff.; 9:4ff.; Neh. 3:2ff.).

The expression "my son" is often used in metaphorical contexts. For example, Yahweh refers to the people of Israel held captive in Egypt as "my son" (in a corporate sense) in Exod. 4:22ff. See also Hos. 11:1. God also uses this expression in 2 Sam. 7:14ff.; 1 Chr. 17:13; Jer. 33:21, referring to the descendant of David as "my son," indicating at one level Solomon, and at another level the anticipated messianic offspring. Ps. 2:7 contains the phrase "my son" in relation to Yahweh's declaration of a filial relationship with the child he "has begotten."

The book of Proverbs frequently uses the expression "my son." In this context, a father is exhorting his son to be wise, which underlies the familial usage of this section (cf. Prov. 1:8ff.; 2:1; 3:1; 4:10; 5:1; 6:1ff.; 19:27; 24:13). This expression also indicates a form of polite endearment or greeting to a servant, messenger, or young man (cf. 1 Sam. 4:16; 26:17; Eccl. 12:12).

Another expression worthy of note involving the use of ***bēn*** is "son of man." At one level it is an oblique way of referring to a "human being." For example, Num. 23:19 declares that Yahweh is definitely not like a "son of man," who is prone to falsehood and other frailties. See also Ps. 8:4. The prophet Ezekiel is also commonly referred to as a "son of man" (e.g., Ezek. 2:1ff.; 3:1ff.; 8:5ff.; 21:2ff.; 33:10ff.). In a theologically significant sense, the expression "Son of Man" is applied to the coming Messianic King in Dan. 7:13.

A unique use of ***bēn*** is found in Dan. 3:25 with reference to the divine-like figure described as a "son of the gods," seen to be closely involved with the miraculous rescue of David's three friends from the blazing furnace.

NT Words

huios [υἱός, *5207*]

huios is the Greek dynamic equivalent for ***bēn*** (see above), occurring nearly four hundred times. It means "son," "child(ren)" throughout its usage, and is used both literally and metaphorically.

huios refers generally to "son" in the literal sense of a male child (e.g., Matt. 7:9; Luke 1:31; John 4:46ff.; Rom. 9:9; Gal. 4:22; Heb. 11:24). ***huios*** also refers to Jesus, the "son" of Mary and Joseph (Matt. 1:21ff.; Mark 6:3; Luke 1:13; John 1:45). Matt. 1:1 uses the word "son" in a genealogical context. The "sons" of Levi are referred to in Heb. 7:5.

Believers are often spoken of as "children," or "sons," of God (cf. Matt. 5:9; Rom. 8:14; Gal. 4:6). 1 Thess. 5:5 refers to believers as "children of light." Matt. 13:48 speaks of "children, or sons of the kingdom." The expression "sons of Abraham" is found in Gal. 3:7. Conversely, unbelievers are referred to as "sons of disobedience" in Eph. 5:6; Col. 3:6. The antichrist figure is described in 2 Thess. 2:3 as "the son of perdition."

Elsewhere, the term "Son" refers to Christ. The phrase "Son of God" is commonly used in reference to Christ (e.g., Matt. 4:3ff.; 16:16; Mark 3:11; Luke 1:35; 15:11ff.; John 10:36; Acts 8:37; Rom. 1:4; 2 Cor. 1:19; Gal. 2:20; Eph. 4:13; Heb. 4:14ff.; 1 John 5:10ff.; Rev. 2:18). In addition, Christ is often referred to simply as "the Son" (cf. Matt. 11:27; Mark 1:1; John 1:18; 5:22ff.; 1 Cor. 15:28; Heb. 1:8; 1 John 2:22ff.). John 3:16 refers to Christ as "the only-begotten Son." Luke 1:32 describes him as the "Son of the most high." The title "Son of Man" is self-consciously taken by Christ as an expression of his fulfillment of the messianic "Son of Man" figure of Dan. 7 (cf. Matt. 8:20; 20:28; Mark 2:10; Luke 5:25; John 1:51; Acts 7:56; Rev. 1:13; 14:14). Christ is also described as the embodiment of the messianic "Son of David" (cf. Matt. 9:27; 12:23; 22:42ff.; Luke 18:38ff.).

God himself refers to Jesus Christ as "my (beloved) Son" in a number of places (cf. Matt. 3:17; Mark 1:11; 9:7; Luke 3:22; 2 Pet. 1:17; Acts 13:33). In Heb. 1:5; 5:5, this designation is expanded with the words ". . . whom I have begotten."

SON-IN-LAW

OT Words

ḥātān **[חָתָן, 2860]**

ḥātān is a noun found nineteen times meaning "bridegroom" and "son-in-law." (→ HUSBAND)

About half of these occurrences contain literal references to "sons-in-law," in the contexts of familial relationships (cf. Gen. 19:12ff.; Judg. 15:6; 19:5; 1 Sam. 18:18; 22:14; 2 Kgs. 8:27; Neh. 6:18; 13:24).

ḥātan **[חָתַן, 2859]**

ḥātan is a verb found about thirty times meaning "join in marriage," as well as the primary nominal senses of "father-in-law" and "son-in-law." The latter sense is found on only five occasions, in 1 Sam. 18:21ff.

SONG → SING

SOOTHSAYING, SORCERER, SORCERY
→ MAGIC

SORROW, SORROWFUL

OT Words

'eṣeb [עֶצֶב, 6089]; 'ōṣeb [עֹצֶב, 6090]

The noun ***'eṣeb*** is found seven times, meaning "sorrow" in the sense of "emotional hurt or pain" (Gen. 3:16; Prov. 10:22).

The synonymous term ***'ōṣeb*** is found in 1 Chr. 4:9; Isa. 14:3.

'iṣṣābôn [עִצָּבוֹן, 6093]

'iṣṣābôn is a variant form of ***'eṣeb***, above. It is found in three places meaning "sorrow" (Gen. 3:16, 17), and "toil" (Gen. 5:29), suggesting that hard labor produces sorrow and frustration.

'aṣṣebet [עַצֶּבֶת, 6094]

'aṣṣebet is a noun related to ***'eṣeb***, above, occurring four times and meaning "sorrow," "pain" (both physical and mental) (cf. Job 9:28; Ps. 16:4; Prov. 10:10; 15:13).

yāgôn [יָגוֹן, 3015]

yāgôn is a noun found in fourteen contexts meaning "sorrow," or grief, anguish (Gen. 42:38; Pss. 13:2; 107:39; Jer. 8:18; 20:18; Ezek. 23:33). Isa. 51:11; Jer. 31:13 contain the promise that the sorrow of God's people will be turned to joy.

ḥîl [חִיל, 2427]

ḥîl is a noun occurring seven times meaning "sorrow" in the sense of "pangs of anguish, torment." The term suggests writhing in anguish, frequently associated with childbirth (cf. Ps. 48:6; Jer. 6:24; 22:23; 50:43; Mic. 4:9). See also Exod. 15:14; Job 6:10.

ka'as [כַּעַס, 3708]

ka'as is a noun that occurs about fifty times, and in half of these places it has the principal sense of "sorrow," "sadness," "grief" (cf. 1 Sam. 1:16; Job 6:2; Ps. 6:7; Prov. 17:25; Eccl. 1:18; 11:10).

mak'ôb [מַכְאוֹב, 4341]

mak'ôb is a term found in sixteen places with the dominant senses of "sorrow," "suffering," indicating both mental and physical anguish.

"Sorrow" in the sense of physical suffering as well as mental anguish is indicated in Exod. 3:7 in relation to the Israelites in Egypt. Such torment is predicated of the Messiah, the "man of sorrows," in Isa. 53:3, 4. See also Pss. 32:10; 69:26.

The "sorrow" of mental and emotional sadness is indicated in Ps. 38:17; Eccl. 1:18; 2:23; Jer. 45:3. Lam. 1:12 refers to the "sorrow" brought about in the wake of divine judgment on the nation of Judah. The "sorrow" of repentance is indicated in 2 Chr. 6:29.

In a couple of places, "sorrow" indicates physical pain and anguish (cf. Job 33:19; Isa. 51:8).

ke'ēb [כְּאֵב, 3511]

ke'ēb is a term found in six places meaning "sorrow," "grief," and "pain." Mental and physical anguish is indicated in Job 2:3; 16:6; while emotional distress is noted in Ps. 39:2; Isa. 17:11; 65:14; Jer. 15:18.

tûgāh [תּוּגָה, 8424]

tûgāh is a noun occurring four times and meaning "grief," "sorrow" in Ps. 119:28; Prov. 10:1; 14:13; 17:21.

NT Words

lypē [λύπη, *3077*]

lypē is a noun found sixteen times meaning "sorrow," "grief" in the majority of these contexts (cf. Luke 22:45; John 16:6, 20, 22; Rom. 9:2; 2 Cor. 2:3). 2 Cor. 7:10 speaks of "sorrow" leading to repentance. In John 16:21, ***lypē*** is translated "pain" in relation to childbirth.

lypeō [λυπέω, *3076*]

lypeō is a verb found around twenty times with a variety of meanings such as "to cause grief," "sorrow," "make sorrowful," "affect with sadness," "be sorry."

lypeō means to "be sorry" (Matt. 14:9; 18:31); "be sorrowful, very sad"(Matt. 19:22; 26:22; Mark 10:22; John 16:20); "cause grief, anguish" (2 Cor. 2:2ff.; 7:8ff.). Eph. 4:30 contains the admonition not "to grieve" the Holy Spirit. See also 1 Thess. 4:13.

perilypos [περίλυπος, *4036*]

perilypos is an adjective found in five contexts meaning "very sad," "sorrowful" in Matt. 26:38; Mark 6:26; 14:34; Luke 18:23, 24.

penthos [πένθος, *3997*]

penthos is a noun meaning "sorrow," "mourning" in Jas. 4:9; Rev. 18:7, 8; 21:4.

odynē [ὀδύνη, *3601*]

odynē is a rare noun found only in Rom. 9:2; 1 Tim. 6:10, meaning "profound sorrow, grief."

odynaō [ὀδυνάω, *3600*]

odynaō is a verb found four times, meaning "to cause sorrow, torment," "be in anguish," in Luke 2:48; 16:24, 25; Acts 20:38.

See Also: ➙ DISTRESS ➙ MOURN

SORRY ➙ REPENT

SOUL

OT Words

nephesh [נֶפֶשׁ, **5315**]

nephesh is a common noun occurring over 750 times with a wide variety of meanings and contexts. It is virtually untranslatable by any one English word. In relation to people, the underlying essence of ***nephesh*** may be described as that quality which lends to human beings their distinctive individuality as creatures made in the image of God. ***nephesh*** is most commonly translated by terms such as "soul," "life," "person," "heart," "mind," though these senses do not exhaust the usage of the term.

The word "soul" denotes "a person's being," or his or her distinctive essence as a person created in God's image. In Hebrew usage, this term is not to be understood merely as the spiritual "part" of a human being in opposition to "physical bodies," for ***nephesh*** may indeed refer to the human physiological constitution. ***nephesh*** does refer to the "heart" and "mind" as the seat of human emotions and intellect. (➙ LIFE ➙ PERSON)

nephesh also refers to animals as "living creatures," distinctive in that they receive the breath of life from the Creator, although they are without the unique personal qualities that distinguish human beings from the animal kingdom.

The meaning "soul," with reference to "person," or "individual," is found in Gen. 12:5; 46:18ff.; Exod. 12:15; Lev. 7:18ff.; Josh. 10:28ff.; Jer. 52:30; Ezek. 13:18ff. Occasionally, the expressions "my soul," "your soul," "his soul" simply indicate pronominal usage such as "I," "you," "him" (cf. Gen. 27:4; Exod. 30:16; Num. 30:5ff.).

nephesh also refers to "the life of the individual" (cf. Gen. 12:13; Exod. 4:19; 2 Sam. 1:9; Ps. 23:3; Prov. 1:18; Jer. 34:20ff.; Amos 2:14). In Pss. 6:4; 17:13; 22:20, the psalmist pleads with God to save his "soul" (i.e., life). Lev. 24:18; Deut. 12:23 also refer to the "life" of the creature.

The "soul" as the "heart," the center of significant emotional attachment or awareness, is indicated in a variety of contexts. General references to this phenomenon include those in Gen. 34:3; Exod. 23:9; 1 Sam. 18:1ff.; Ps. 6:3. Loving God with all one's "soul" (i.e., one's entire being) is indicated in Deut. 4:29; 6:5; 10:12; 11:13; 13:3; 30:6ff. Pouring out one's "soul" in anguish is noted in 1 Sam. 1:15; Ps. 119:167. Giving praise to God "with all one's soul (i.e., heart)" is indicated in Ps. 146:1. See also Isa. 42:1; Mic. 6:7. Returning to God in repentance with all one's soul is evident in 1 Kgs. 8:48. Other references include those in Song 1:7; 3:1ff.; Ezek. 25:6.

The term ***nephesh*** refers to animals as "living creatures" in Gen. 21:24; 2:19; 9:10ff.; Lev. 11:46.

nephesh also refers to a "corpse," or "dead body," in Num. 5:2; 6:6; 9:6ff.; Hag. 2:13.

NT Words

psychē [ψυχή, *5590*]

psychē is an approximate dynamic equivalent for the Hebrew term ***nephesh*** (see above), occurring around sixty times. ***psychē***, however, has a narrower semantic field than its Hebrew equivalent, and it is translated primarily as "soul," "life" in the large majority of these contexts.

This Greek term indicates, as does the Hebrew, that the "soul" is not to be distinguished from the "body" in an absolute sense, for the Scriptures teach that humans are whole, integral beings. There is, however, evidence clearly suggesting that there is a duality within a person's created constitution — humans have a physical body that will perish and decay as well as a "spirit" or "soul" that is immortal and subject to divine judgment for good or ill at the end of time.

This perspective is not as fully developed in the Old Testament as it is in the New. However, as with ***nephesh*** (at least by implication, if not explicitly), ***psychē*** indicates a human being's "soul" as a way of describing his or her unique essence as a being with an inner emotional, rational, and spiritual essence that sets him or her apart from other created (i.e., animal) life forms.

psychē refers to "souls" in the sense of persons, individuals in a number of places (cf. Acts 2:41ff.; Rom. 2:9; 13:1; 1 Pet. 3:20; Rev. 18:13.

More commonly, ***psychē*** also refers to the "soul" of a person, referring to his or her "life"—the animating life force, sustaining earthly existence. The "lives" of people are referred to this way in Matt. 2:20; 16:25ff.; Mark 3:4; Luke 6:9; 12:20ff.; Acts 20:10; Rom. 16:4. In particular, John 13:37ff.; 15:13 speak of the greatest of virtues as laying down one's life for others. Such nobility is, of course, attributed to the person of Christ, who gave up his "life" for the salvation of his people (cf. Matt. 20:28; Mark 10:45; John 10:11; 1 John 3:16).

psychē also indicates the "soul" as that unique, immortal essence of all human beings, equated in many ways to a person's "spirit," which has an eternal destiny. One's "soul" is seen as being clothed with a physical body that will decay after physical death (cf. Matt. 10:28; Acts 2:27; 13:17; Jas. 1:21; 5:20; 1 Pet. 1:9; 2:25; Rev. 6:9; 20:4).

Related to the above sense is the meaning "soul" (in relation to people), indicating the inner spiritual, psychological, and emotional center of one's being. This is occasionally identified as the "heart," or "mind." The usage of ***psychē*** with this shade of meaning does not imply an eternal destiny, but rather an inner quality of life on earth.

Such a perspective is illustrated in the following contexts, where ***psychē*** refers to promised rest for one's "soul" (Matt. 11:29); and to people's "soul" as "heart," or "mind" (Acts 14:2; 15:24; Eph. 6:6; Phil. 1:27, 2 Pet. 2:8). Elsewhere, ***psychē*** refers to one's "soul" in relation to one's "entire being," in an undifferentiated sense — for example, in contexts advocating loving God with all one's "heart" (i.e., all one's soul or being) (cf. Matt. 22:37; Mark 12:30ff.; Luke 10:27). See also Luke 1:46; 12:19. In 1 Thess. 5:23 there is a rare reference to one's "soul," as distinct from "body" and "spirit." The context here, however, would probably suggest an emphasis on the profound relationship between the human physical and spiritual constitution within the phenomenon of the "whole person," rather than indicating human beings merely as a composite of three separate parts. A similar reference is also made in Heb. 4:12; 6:19.

References to the entire emotional being of Christ (i.e., his "soul") are found in Matt. 26:38; John 12:27 in relation to his mental and spiritual anguish prior to his crucifixion, in the garden of Gethsemane.

In a slightly different setting, the expression "my soul" is also predicated of God, metaphorically referring to "himself" (e.g., Matt. 12:18; Heb. 10:38).

Elsewhere, ***psychē*** means "living being" in relation to the first man, Adam (1 Cor. 15:45). In Rev. 16:3, ***psychē*** means "living thing" in relation to marine life.

SOUND

OT Words

qôl **[קוֹל, 6963]**

qôl is a noun occurring over five hundred times with the primary meanings "voice," "sound," "noise" in the majority of these contexts. (→ VOICE) In some places it is difficult to determine whether ***qôl*** indicates "sound," or "voice." ***qôl*** refers literally to the "sound" of a "bell" (Exod. 28:35), and of a trumpet (Josh. 6:5; 2 Sam. 6:15; Jer. 4:19; Ezek. 33:4); as well as to other "sounds" (Lev. 26:36; 2 Kgs. 6:23; Ps. 77:17; Jer. 8:19; Ezek. 33:4).

rûa' **[רוּעַ, 7321]**

rûa' is a verb occurring around fifty times meaning "sound an alarm" in Num. 10:7ff.; 2 Chr. 13:12; Joel 2:1. (→ SHOUT)

shāma' **[שָׁמַע, 8085]**

shāma' is a common verb found in nearly 1,150 contexts with the primary meanings "to hear" or "obey." In a few places, however, ***shāma'*** refers to "sounding a cymbal" (cf. 1 Chr. 15:19; 16:5). See also 1 Chr. 16:42.

tēqa' **[תֵּקַע, 8629]**

tēqa' is a noun found only in Ps. 150:3, referring to the "sound" of a trumpet.

qāl **[קָל, 7032 (Aramaic)]**

qāl is the Aramaic equivalent of ***qôl*** (see above). It occurs twelve times and means "sound," "voice." In Dan. 3:5ff., ***qāl*** refers to the "sound" of the horn (musical instrument).

NT Words

phōnē **[φωνή, *5456*]**

phōnē is a noun found in approximately 140 places with the dominant sense of "voice." In a few contexts, however, it is translated "sound." ***phōnē*** refers to a trumpet sound (Matt. 24:31); to the sound of a trumpet likened to a "voice" (Rev. 1:10; 4:1); to the "sound" of the wind (John 3:8); and to the "sound" of the Holy Spirit coming upon the disciples of Christ, likened to a rushing wind (Acts 2:6). See also Rev. 1:15; 9:9.

salpizō [σαλπίζω, *4537*]

salpizō is a verb occurring twelve times, referring to "sounding a trumpet" in Matt. 6:2; 1 Cor. 15:52. In Rev. 8:6ff.; 9:1, 13; 11:15, trumpets are "sounded" by angels in a cycle of judgment against the wickedness of humankind.

hygiainō [ὑγιαίνω, *5198*]

hygiainō is a verb found in twelve contexts with the sense of "to be well, in good health" (i.e., sound). The term is also used adjectivally to refer to that which is trustworthy or accurate.

The expression "safe and sound" (i.e., in good health) is indicated in Luke 15:27; as is the meaning "to be well" in Luke 5:31; 7:10.

Elsewhere, "sound doctrine," that which is in accordance with the principles of revealed Scripture as given through God and Christ, is indicated in 1 Tim. 1:10; 2 Tim. 4:3; Titus 1:9, 13. Similarly, the "sound words" of Christ and the apostles are noted in 1 Tim. 6:3; 2 Tim. 1:13.

ēchos [ἦχος, *2279*]

ēchos is a rare noun, occurring three times with reference to "sound" or "noise" in Acts 2:2 (rushing wind); Heb. 12:19 (a trumpet).

bolizō [βολίζω, *1001*]

bolizō is a verb, a nautical term, found twice with the exclusive sense of "to sound," "take a sounding," to ascertain water depth beneath a ship (cf. Acts 27:28).

SOW, SOWER

OT Words

zāra' [זָרַע, **2232**]

zāra' is a verb found nearly sixty times with the primary sense of "sow" (i.e., plant seed) in most of these contexts. It is used both literally and metaphorically.

"Sowing" in the sense of scattering seed for planting is indicated in general contexts in Gen. 26:12; Exod. 23:10, 16; Lev. 25:3ff.; Deut. 21:4; Judg. 6:3; Ps. 107:37; Isa. 28:4; Jer. 35:7; Hag. 1:6. In particular, Lev. 19:19 contains a prohibition against sowing a field with mixed seed. Jer. 2:2 refers to the wilderness as a land "not sown."

zāra' is also used metaphorically. Judg. 9:45 refers, for example, to the destruction of a city through the expression "to sow with salt." "Sowing trouble" is noted in Job 4:8 in relation to living an evil lifestyle. Ps. 126:5 alludes to the pain of "sowing in tears" (i.e., suffering calamity). To "sow righteousness" indicates living a godly life in Prov. 22:8; Hos. 10:12. See also Jer. 31:27; Hos. 2:23; 8:7.

zērûa' [זֵרוּעַ, **2221**]

zērûa' is a rare noun derived from ***zāra'*** (see above). It is found only twice, with reference to "that which is sown" (i.e., seed) in Lev. 11:37; Isa. 61:11.

mizra' [מִזְרָע, **4218**]

mizra' is a noun synonymous with ***zērûa'***, above, found only in Isa. 19:7 and referring to "that which is sown."

NT Words

speirō [σπείρω, *4687*]

speirō is a verb occurring some fifty times as a dynamic equivalent to ***zāra'*** (see above), meaning "to sow," as well as the nominal sense of "sower." The use of the term is likewise both literal and metaphorical.

Literal references to "sowing" (i.e., scattering) seed for planting include those in Matt. 6:26; 13:3ff.; Mark 4:3ff., 31; Luke 8:5; John 4:36. References to the "sower" are made in the parable of the sower in Matt. 13:3ff.; Mark 4:3ff.; Luke 8:5.

Metaphorically speaking, ***speirō*** refers to "sowing" the word of God in the hearts of humankind (cf. Matt. 13:19ff.; Mark 4:14ff.). Similarly, 1 Cor. 9:11 refers to "sowing" truth in the lives of believers. The contrast between the earthly and heavenly body of the believer is described with reference to that which is "sown" perishable, but raised imperishable (cf. 1 Cor. 15:37ff.).

sporos [σπόρος, *4703*]

sporos is a noun occurring five times, usually translated as "seed." It is used literally in connection with seed for sowing or planting in Mark 4:26ff.; Luke 8:5. Luke 8:11 refers to the word of God as "seed." See also 2 Cor. 9:10.

SPARE

OT Words

ḥāsak [חָשַׂךְ, **2820**]

ḥāsak is a verb found around thirty times meaning "spare," "keep back," "withhold," as well as several related nuances.

ḥāsak means "to spare" in the sense of "keep back from doing evil" in 1 Sam. 25:39. In 2 Kgs. 5:20ff.; the meaning "spare" has the sense of "to treat with leniency." Disciplinary action is the context of Prov. 13:24, which declares that "sparing" (i.e., withholding) the rod of discipline will spoil the child.

ḥāsak is also predicated of God in Ps. 78:50, where it is affirmed that God "did not spare" the Egyptians from death during the period of the ten plague judgments against that nation.

NT Words

perisseuō [περισσεύω, *4052*]

perisseuō is a verb found in about forty contexts with the underlying meaning "to have an abundance of." In Luke 15:17, ***perisseuō*** expresses the idea of having enough (food) to spare.

pheidomai [φείδομαι, *5339*]

pheidomai is a verb found twelve times with the primary meaning "spare," with the underlying sense of "keeping from harm, or emotional hurt" (cf. 1 Cor. 7:28; 2 Cor. 1:23).

The term is also used negatively to indicate a desire not to preserve from harm. For example, Acts 20:29 refers to cruel leaders of God's people who will abuse (i.e., "not spare") the flock. Rom. 8:32 affirms that God refused to spare his own Son from death in order to fully accomplish his plan of salvation for humankind. See also 2 Pet. 2:4, 5.

See Also: → COMPASSION → FORGIVE

SPEAK → SAY

SPEECH

OT Words

'imrāh [אִמְרָה, **565**]

'imrāh is a term denoting "word(s)," "speech" throughout its nearly forty occurrences. References to "speech" in the sense of a "sustained utterance," i.e., not merely expressing individual words, are found in Gen. 4:23; Deut. 32:2; Ps. 17:6; Isa. 28:23; 29:4; 32:9.

dābār [דָּבָר, **1697**]

dābār is a common noun denoting the primary sense of "word," as well as numerous related meanings, throughout its nearly 1,500 occurrences. One of these related meanings is "speech."

A reference to "speech" in the sense of "human language" is found in Gen. 11:1. A formal judicial "charge" (lit., "speech") is indicated in Deut. 22:17. See also Jer. 31:23.

sāphāh [שָׂפָה, **8193**]

sāphāh is a noun with a variety of meanings including "lip," "language," and "edge," "speech," along with a number of associated nuances. (→ LANGUAGE)

The meanings "speech" and "(human) language" overlap in Gen. 11:1, 7.

The faculty of human "speech" is noted in a general sense in Job 12:20; Prov. 17:7.

peh [פֶּה, **6310**]

peh is a common noun, occurring nearly five hundred times with the predominant meaning "mouth," as well as the derived sense of "commandment," "word." Exod. 4:10 contains a puzzling reference to Moses' aversion to speaking when he protests to Yahweh in response to the command to go to Pharaoh and demand release for the Israelites. Moses claims: "I am slow of speech and tongue," probably indicating some kind of speech impediment.

yehûdît [יְהוּדִית, **3066**]

yehûdît is a term specifically denoting the "language" (or speech) of the Jewish people (cf. 2 Kgs. 18:26ff.; 2 Chr. 32:18; Neh. 13:24; Isa. 36:11ff.). See also Neh. 13:24.

millāh [מִלָּה, **4405**]

millāh is a noun meaning "word," "speech," throughout its nearly forty occurrences. The former sense is dominant, though there is a degree of overlap between the two. References to human "speech" or "speaking" are found in Job 13:17; 21:2; 24:25; 33:1.

'ōmer [אֹמֶר, **562**]

'ōmer is a rare noun denoting "(human) speech" in Ps. 19:2ff.

'ēmer [אֵמֶר, **561**]

'ēmer is a more common variant of ***'ōmer***, above, meaning "word," "speech" throughout its nearly fifty occurrences. The meaning "word(s)" is dominant. Job 6:26; 32:14 refer to the "speech" of human beings.

NT Words

lalia [λαλιά, *2981*]

lalia is a noun occurring four times denoting the faculty of "speech" (Matt. 26:73; Mark 14:7). References to "speech" in the sense of discourse are found in John 4:42; 8:43.

mogilalos [μογιλάλος, *3424*]

mogilalos is a rare adjectival form denoting a "speech impediment" in Mark 7:32.

logos [λόγος, *3056*]

logos is a common noun found 331 times with the predominant meanings "word," "saying." ***logos*** also denotes "speech" in the sense of a "discourse" in Acts 20:7; 1 Cor. 2:1ff.; 4:19; Col. 4:6; Titus 2:8.

The faculty of "speech" is indicated in 2 Cor. 10:10; 11:6.

SPEND

OT Words

kālāh [כָּלָה, 3615]

kālāh is a verb occurring around two hundred times with a variety of senses including "finish," "complete," "use up," as well as a large number of associated nuances. In a number of places it means "spend."

The sense of "use up," or "consume," is indicated with reference to "spending" arrows in battle (Deut. 32:23); food and water (Gen. 21:15; Jer. 37:21); and one's strength (Isa. 49:4).

Spending time is indicated in Job 21:13; 36:11; Ps. 90:9 in relation to one's days, and in Ps. 31:10 with reference to one's life.

shāqal [שָׁקַל, 8254]

shāqal is a verb occurring about twenty times with the primary meaning "to weigh." In Isa. 55:2, however, it refers to spending money.

NT Words

chronotribeō [χρονοτριβέω, *5551*]

chronotribeō is a rare verb found only in Acts 20:16 with reference to "spending" time.

dapanaō [δαπανάω, *1159*]

dapanaō is a verb found in five contexts, meaning "to spend." Mark 5:26; 15:14 refer to people spending all that they have, exhausting their monetary resources. Acts 21:24 refers to "paying one's expenses." See also 2 Cor. 12:15; Jas. 4:3.

prosdapanaō [προσδαπανάω, *4325*]

prosdapanaō is found only in Luke 10:35, meaning "to spend more money."

ekdapanaō [ἐκδαπανάω, *1550*]

ekdapanaō is a verb found only in 2 Cor. 12:15 with reference to "spending oneself wholly" (i.e., to sacrificially give oneself to the welfare of others).

SPICE

OT Words

bōsem [בֹּשֶׂם, 1314]

bōsem is the most common term for "spice(s)" in the Old Testament. It is found around twenty-five times.

Spices are used in the context of ritual worship as one of the components of the oil of anointing (cf. Exod. 25:6; 30:23; 35:8, 28; 2 Kgs. 20:13; 1 Chr. 9:29ff.; Isa. 39:2).

Spices are designated as commercial merchandise in 1 Kgs. 10:2, 10; 2 Chr. 9:1, 24; Ezek. 27:22. Spices are used in the preparation of a perfumed concoction used in the ritual preparation of corpses prior to burial (cf. 2 Chr. 16:14). Spices are also routinely used in the manufacture of perfumes (cf. Esth. 2:12; Song 4:10ff.; 5:13; 6:2; 8:14).

reqaḥ [רֶקַח, 7544]

reqaḥ is found only in Song 8:2 with reference to "spiced" wine.

nekō't [נְכֹאת, 5219]

nekō't is a noun found only twice, with reference to "spices" as merchandise (cf. Gen. 37:25; 43:11).

sam [סַם, 5561]

sam is a noun occurring seventeen times meaning "sweet spice," "fragrant incense," for use in worship at the incense altar (cf. Exod. 25:6; 37:29; 40:27; Lev. 4:7; 2 Chr. 2:4; 13:11).

NT Words

arōma [ἄρωμα, *759*]

arōma is a noun found four times, meaning "spice," "perfume," used in the preparation of a funeral blend for "anointing" corpses in connection with the burial ritual. In the New Testament, this usage focuses exclusively on the body of Christ. The Gospels refer to the group of women who had prepared this perfumed blend of spices, intending to anoint the body of Christ recently laid in the tomb. This action was never performed, since Christ had by then risen from the grave (cf. Mark 16:5; Luke 23:56; 24:1; John 19:40).

SPIRIT

OT Words

rûaḥ [רוּחַ, 7307]

rûaḥ is a common noun, found nearly four hundred times with the predominant sense of "spirit" in relation to both God and human beings. There is also occasional overlap with the sense of "breath." ***rûaḥ*** also means "wind." (➠ WIND)

General references to the Spirit of God include those in Gen. 41:38; Exod. 21:3; Ezek. 1:12ff. The Spirit of God is declared to be at work alongside God in the original creation of the world. Significantly, the Spirit of God is also given as an empowerment for service, an "anointing" as a means of assigning divine authority to a specific function. Such an experience is predicated of the Israelite elders (Num. 11:17ff.); and of prophets, including Balaam (Num. 24:2); Saul (1 Sam. 10:6, 10); and Ezekiel (Ezek. 2:2; 3:12ff.; 11:1, 5; 37:1). David is also "anointed" with the Spirit of God in 1 Sam. 16:13, setting him apart as the eventual successor to Saul, who was declared a failure and had the Spirit of God taken from him, thus losing his authority as ruler of Israel.

References to the Spirit of the Lord (i.e., Yahweh) are also common and constitute simply a variant expression for the Spirit of God.

General references to the Spirit of the Lord include those in Gen. 6:3; Pss. 32:2; 51:11; Isa. 11:2; 40:13; Zech. 4:6. The Spirit of Yahweh is designated as the empowering divine presence that gave the "judges" in Israel their unique power and authority (cf. Judg. 3:10; 6:34; 11:29; 13:25; 14:6, 19; 15:14). The Spirit of Yahweh is poured out on the Messianic Servant of the Lord in Isa. 42:1; 59:21 (on the people of Israel as "corporate Servant"); 61:1. The same outpouring of the Spirit of the Lord is indicated in Ezek. 11:19; 36:26ff.; Joel 2:28ff., anticipating the anointing of the Holy Spirit in the new covenant age.

rûaḥ is also used in reference to "life" in the phrase "breath of life," indicating "life" as the animating spirit of physical existence. This "breath of life" is predicated of animals (Gen. 6:17; Eccl. 3:19), and of people (Job 17:1). In Job 32:8; Ezek. 37:5ff., the phrase "spirit of man" is equated with the "breath of life."

rûaḥ also refers to the "spirit" of human beings, indicating the "mind," or "heart," the center of emotional and rational constitution (cf. Gen. 41:8; Exod. 35:21; Deut. 2:30; 1 Kgs. 21:5; Ezra 1:1; Ps. 51:1; Prov. 16:18; Eccl. 3:21). In this connection, ***rûaḥ*** is explicitly translated "mind" in Ezek. 11:5; 20:32. Other references to the human "spirit" include those in Exod. 28:3; Deut. 34:9; Isa. 29:10; Hos. 4:12.

In contrast, ***rûaḥ*** also refers to an "evil spirit" in 1 Sam. 16:14ff.; 1 Kgs. 22:2ff.

neshāmāh [נְשָׁמָה, 5397]

neshāmāh is a noun occurring around twenty-five times with the primary meaning "breath," applied to both God and human beings. This overlaps with the meaning "spirit," referring to the "breath" or "spirit" that imparts life to the creature.

God breathes the "breath" of life into human beings at creation in Gen. 2:7. Elsewhere, the phenomenon of the divine breath is noted in Gen. 7:22; Job 33:4; Isa. 42:5. Other general references to the "breath of life" include those in Deut. 20:16; Josh. 10:40; 11:11; 1 Kgs. 17:17. In Job 27:3, the "breath of life" is equated with the "Spirit" of God.

NT Words

pneuma [πνεῦμα, *4151*]

pneuma is the dynamic equivalent for the Hebrew term ***rûaḥ*** (see above), found in over 140 contexts. Its root meaning is "spirit," which refers to "the Spirit of God," or "the Holy Spirit," and "the Spirit of Christ," as well as the human spirit — all in a wide variety of contexts.

References to the Holy Spirit are numerous. He is designated as the supernatural agent of conception in the birth of Christ, with Mary as mother of the child (cf. Matt. 1:18ff.; Luke 1:35ff.). Luke 4:1 describes Jesus Christ as being full of the Holy Spirit.

In relation to the people of God, or true followers of Christ, believers are said to be baptized with the Holy Spirit (Matt. 3:11; Mark 1:8; Luke 3:16). The Holy Spirit is given to the new covenant people of God in fulfillment of Old Testament prophecy (cf. Joel 2:28; John 20:23; Acts 1:8; 2:4, 17, 18, 33, 38; 4:31; 8:15ff.; 10:44). The Spirit is also given to believers as a seal, a guarantee of salvation (2 Cor. 1:22; Eph. 1:13). He illuminates divine truth in the believer (cf. 1 Cor. 2:10ff.; Eph. 3:5); gives divine guidance (cf. Acts 8:29; 13:2); and is the source of godly "fruit" or virtues (cf. Gal. 5:22ff.). The Spirit comes upon and indwells the believer as noted in Luke 1:15, 67; Acts 6:3ff.; Rom. 5:5; 8:2ff.; 1 Cor. 3:16; Gal. 3:2ff. The believer is described as the temple of the Holy Spirit in 1 Cor. 6:19ff.; Eph. 2:22. The Holy Spirit is also designated as the agent of regeneration or new birth (John 3:5ff.; 6:63); and as the agent of sanctification (Rom. 15:16; Gal. 5:16ff.).

The Holy Spirit is linked with the triune Godhead in Matt. 28:19; Rom. 1:4. He is also designated as the source of divine revelation through the prophets in 2 Pet. 1:21.

References to the Spirit of God are less common, though the identity with the Holy Spirit is clearly established. He is declared to be the giver of spiritual gifts in 1 Cor. 12:4ff. References to placing the Spirit of God on the Messianic Servant are found in Matt. 12:18; Luke 4:18 — an experience which Christ self-consciously claims as his own. God's unique nature is designated as that of a spirit in John 4:24; 2 Cor. 3:17ff.

pneuma also refers to the "spirit" of human beings. It designates aspects of character, such as those who are "poor in spirit" (cf. Matt. 5:3). The term also indicates the human "spirit" as the heart of the human emotional rational faculty (cf. Matt. 26:41, Luke 1:47; 1 Cor. 5:3ff.; Eph. 4:23; 1 Pet. 3:4). This is also predicated of Christ (Mark 2:8; Luke 2:40; John 11:33).

pneuma also means "life" referring to people (Matt. 27:50; 1 Cor. 5:5); and to the "life" of Christ, which he voluntarily surrendered (lit., "gave up his spirit") to God on the cross (cf. Luke 23:46; John 19:30).

The Spirit of Christ is equated with the Holy Spirit in Phil. 1:19; 1 Pet. 1:11.

pneuma also refers to the "spirit" of human beings in conjunction with their bodies and souls (Heb. 4:12). (➡ SOUL)

Evil spirits, or demons, are also denoted by ***pneuma*** (cf. Matt. 8:16; 12:43; Mark 1:23ff.; Luke 4:36; Acts 8:7; Eph. 2:2; Rev. 16:14). Angels are described as "ministering spirits" in Heb. 1:14.

pneumatikos [πνευματικός, *4152*]

pneumatikos is an adjective derived from ***pneuma*** (see above) meaning "spiritual," referring to both the human and divine spirit.

In the sense of "being derived from God," ***pneumatikos*** is applied to gifts for God's people (Rom. 1:11; 1 Cor. 12:1; 14:1); truth (1 Cor. 2:3); law (Rom. 7:14); songs (Eph. 5:19; Col. 3:16); and understanding (Col. 1:9).

In relation to the non-material world, the designation "spiritual" is applied to blessings (cf. Rom. 15:27; Eph. 1:3); food (cf. 1 Cor. 10:3); the post-resurrection bodies of believers (cf. 1 Cor. 15:44); and sacrifices (cf. 1 Pet. 2:5).

A "spiritual person" is a child of God (cf. 1 Cor. 2:15; 3:1; 14:37; Gal. 6:1); and Christ is the "spiritual Rock" (1 Cor. 10:4).

pneumatikos also refers to "spiritual forces of evil," as in the demonic spirit realm in Eph. 6:12.

pneumatikōs [πνευματικῶς, *4153*]

pneumatikōs is an adverbial form found in only two places. In 1 Cor. 2:14 it refers to those truths "spiritually" discerned only by the spiritual person through Christ. See also Rev. 11:8.

SPLENDOR

OT Words

gā'ôn [**גָּאוֹן, 1347**]

gā'ôn is a noun occurring around fifty times meaning "pride," "majesty" in the majority of occurrences. However, in Isa. 14:11, ***gā'ôn*** means "splendor," referring to the arrogant pride of Babylon.

NT Words

phantasia [φαντασία, *5325*]

phantasia is a rare noun found only in Acts 25:23 indicating the "splendor" of King Agrippa.

SPOIL

OT Words

shālāl [**שָׁלָל, 7998**]

shālāl is a noun occurring seventy times, meaning "spoil," "plunder," or "booty" in relation to the aftermath of a military victory (e.g., Gen. 49:27; Josh. 7:21; 1 Sam. 15:19ff.; Ps. 68:12; Isa. 53:12; Jer. 39:18; Ezek. 7:21; Zech. 2:9).

shālal [**שָׁלַל, 7997**]

shālal is a verb found sixteen times meaning "take spoil," "plunder" in about half of these contexts. The action applies both to Israel and her enemies (e.g., Ps. 76:5; Isa. 10:16; Jer. 50:10; Ezek. 26:12; 9:10; Hab. 2:8; Zech. 2:8).

gāzal [**גָּזַל, 1497**]

gāzal is a verb found thirty times with the primary meanings "to rob" or "seize." In a number of these contexts the sense is that of "to plunder" or "spoil" in the sense of seizing property (cf. Lev. 6:4; Deut. 28:29; Job 20:19; Ps. 35:10).

baz [**בַּז, 957**]

baz is a synonym for ***shālal***, above, occurring about twenty-five times and meaning "spoil," "plunder," or "prey." References to the "spoil" of war include those in Num. 31:32; Jer. 15:13; Ezek. 23:46; 26:5.

In Isa. 8:3, this term forms part of the name given to the son born to Isaiah's wife, "the prophetess." His name is "Maher-Shalal-Hash-Baz," meaning "quick to the plunder, swift to the spoil"; and the child constitutes the initial fulfillment of the Emmanuel sign for King Ahaz of Judah.

bāzaz [**בָּזַז, 962**]

bāzaz is a verb occurring about forty times meaning "to plunder," "despoil" (e.g., Gen. 34:27ff.; Deut. 2:35; 2 Chr. 25:13; Ps. 109:11; Jer. 20:5; Ezek. 26:13; Amos 3:11).

bizzāh [**בִּזָּה, 961**]

bizzāh is a noun meaning "plunder," "spoil" (2 Chr. 14:14; Neh. 4:4; Dan. 11:24, 33).

shāsāh [**שָׁסָה, 8154**]

shāsāh is a verb found twelve times meaning "to spoil," "plunder," as well as the nominal sense of "plunderer" (cf. Judg. 2:14ff.; 1 Sam. 14:48; 2 Kgs. 17:20; Isa. 10:13; Jer. 30:16).

meshissāh [**מְשִׁסָּה, 4933**]

meshissāh is a noun derived from ***shāsāh*** (see above). It is found in six places meaning "spoil," "plunder" (cf. 2 Kgs. 21:14; Isa. 42:22, 24; Jer. 30:16; Hab. 2:7; Zeph. 1:13).

shādad [**שָׁדַד, 7703**]

shādad is a verb found in approximately sixty contexts with the predominant sense of "to spoil" in the sense of "destroy" or "ruin." The term is also used nominally.

References to places being "soiled," "devastated," or "laid waste" include those in Isa. 23:1, 14; 33:1; Jer. 4:20; 9:19; 48:1; 51:50; Joel 1:10.

The nominal sense of "plunderer," or "spoiler," is found in Isa. 21:2; Jer. 12:12; Obad. 5.

malqôaḥ [**מַלְקוֹחַ, 4455**]

malqôaḥ is a noun found eight times meaning "spoil," "booty" in Num. 31:11ff.

NT Words

diarpazō [διαρπάζω, *1283*]

diarpazō is a verb found twice, referring to "plundering," or "spoiling" one's property (Matt. 12:29; Mark 3:27).

harpagē [ἁρπαγή, *724*]

harpagē is a noun found three times meaning "to extort." In Heb. 10:34 it refers to "spoiling" or "plundering" one's goods.

SPREAD

OT Words

pāras [**פָּרַשׂ, 6566**]

pāras is a verb occurring around seventy times with the underlying meaning "to spread," as well as a number of related senses.

pāras has the sense of "spread out" with reference to the wings of cherubim (Exod. 37:9; 1 Kgs. 6:27; 8:7) and the wings of eagles (Deut. 32:11). See also Jer. 48:40; 49:22.

The action of "spreading" a garment over someone signifies a marriage proposal (Ruth 3:9; Ezek. 16:8). Exod. 40:19 describes the tent being spread over the tabernacle. See also Deut. 22:17; Judg. 8:25.

Isa. 19:8 refers to "spreading" fishing nets on the water. ***pāras*** is also used metaphorically in reference to people "spreading a net" in the sense of "setting a trap."

God is also said to "have spread a cloud" over his people to hide them from the pursuing Egyptian army (cf. Ps. 105:39).

pāsāh [**פָּשָׂה, 6581**]

pāsāh is a verb found around twenty times meaning "to spread" throughout.

pāsāh refers to spreading skin disease (Lev. 13:5ff.); and to the spread of mildew in clothing (Lev. 13:51ff.), and in houses (Lev. 14:39ff.).

mishtôaḥ [**מִשְׁטוֹחַ, 4894**]

mishtôaḥ is a noun occurring four times with reference to "a place for spreading (fishing) nets" (cf. Ezek. 26:5, 14 [twice]; 47:10).

parshēz [**פַּרְשֵׁז, 6576**]

parshēz is found only once, with reference to God "spreading" clouds over the face of the moon.

NT Words

strōnnymi [στρώννυμι, *4766*];
hypostrōnnymi [ὑποστρώννυμι, *5291*]

strōnnymi is a verb found in eight places, meaning "spread out" in Matt. 21:8; Mark 11:8, in relation to people spreading their garments on the road to welcome

Christ into Jerusalem as the coming Messianic King. ***hypostrōnnymi*** has the same meaning in Luke 19:36.

diaphēmizō [διαφημίζω, *1310*]

diaphēmizō is a verb occurring three times with the primary sense of "spread abroad." It refers to spreading fame (Matt. 9:31); and news, or a report (Matt. 28:15; Mark 1:45).

dianemō [διανέμω, *1268*]

dianemō is a verb synonymous with ***diaphēmizō***, above. It occurs only once, in Acts 4:17, in relation to "spreading" the message of the Christian gospel.

See Also: → SCATTER

SPRING

OT Words

môṣā' [**מוֹצָא, 4161**]

môṣā' is a participial noun (derived from ***yāsā'*** "to go out," etc.) denoting in general terms "that which issues, goes out," referring to "springs (of water)" in 2 Kgs. 2:21; Isa. 41:18; 58:11.

ṣāmaḥ [**צָמַח, 6779**]

ṣāmaḥ is a verb found about thirty times, meaning "grow," "sprout," "spring up." (→ GROW)

The meanings "sprout," "spring (up)" are predominantly metaphorical in the usage of ***ṣāmaḥ***. Job 5:6 refers to trouble "springing from" the ground. In contexts of spiritual renewal, faithfulness and righteousness are said to "spring from" the earth in Ps. 85:11; Isa. 45:8; 61:11. God declares that he will fashion "new things" that will "spring forth" in the age of new covenant renewal, speaking of the climax of his redemptive purposes in the coming of the Messiah (cf. Isa. 42:9; 43:19). See also Isa. 58:8.

Literal references to grass "sprouting or springing up" from the ground are found in Job 38:27; Isa. 44:4.

pāraḥ [**פָּרַח, 6524**]

pāraḥ is a verb found over thirty times with the literal sense of "bud," "blossom," as well as "break out," "spread," "flourish" in most of its occurrences. However, in two places ***pāraḥ*** refers metaphorically to wickedness and punishment "springing up" on the earth, manifesting divine retribution (cf. Ps. 92:7; Hos. 10:14).

māqôr [**מָקוֹר, 4726**]

māqôr is a noun found in eighteen places with reference to a "fountain," or "spring," in both literal and figurative contexts for the majority of its usage. The metaphorical sense is predominant.

Reference is made to a woman's monthly period flow as her "fountain of blood" in Lev. 12:7; 20:18. The "wellspring" or "fountain" of one's life is said to be found in God (Ps. 36:9). Similarly, the mouth of the righteous one is designated as the "fountain of life" (Prov. 10:11). See also Prov. 13:14; 16:22; 18:4.

Yahweh is described as Israel's "spring (or fountain) of living waters," denoting her divine source of cleansing and protection (Jer. 2:13; 17:13; Zech. 13:1). Jer. 9:1 refers to one's "fountain, spring of tears." See also Jer. 51:36; Hos. 13:15.

shāḥîs [**שָׁחִיס, 7823**]

shāḥîs is a rare noun found only in 2 Kgs. 19:29; Isa. 37:30 denoting grain that "sprouts" by itself in the year after harvest, without replanting.

gullāh [**גֻּלָּה, 1543**]

gullāh is a noun found fourteen times denoting "springs (of water)" for half of this usage (Josh. 15:19; Judg. 1:15). (→ BOWL)

nēbek [**נֵבֶךְ, 5033**]

nēbek is a rare noun found only in Job 38:16 denoting the subterranean "springs" of the sea.

mabbûa' [**מַבּוּעַ, 4002**]

mabbûa' is a noun found only three times, denoting "springs (of water)" in Isa. 35:7; 49:10. See also Eccl. 12:6.

NT Words

blastanō [βλαστάνω, *985*]

blastanō is a verb found in four places indicating the "sprouting" or "springing up" of vegetation in Matt. 13:26; Mark 4:27. Heb. 9:4 refers to the "budding" of Aaron's staff. See also Jas. 5:18.

phyō [φύω, *5453*]

phyō is a verb found in only three places. In Luke 8:6ff. it refers to vegetation "sprouting" or "springing up." The term is used metaphorically in Heb. 12:15, warning believers against allowing the root of bitterness to "spring up" within them.

See Also: → FOUNTAIN → LEAP

SPRINKLE

OT Words

zāraq [זָרַק, 2236]

zāraq is a verb indicating the action of "sprinkling" for most of its usage. It is found in thirty-five contexts.

The sprinkling of ashes is designated as the catalyst for the plague of boils on the Egyptians (cf. Exod. 9:8ff.). See also Job 2:12.

Far more common is the action of sprinkling blood on the altar of sacrifice as part of the ritual for a variety of offerings (cf. Exod. 29:16, 20; Lev. 1:5, 11; 3:8ff.; 9:18; Num. 18:17; 2 Kgs. 16:13ff.; 2 Chr. 30:16). In Exod. 24:6, 8, the sprinkling of blood is associated with the ceremony of covenant ratification.

In another ritual context, the sprinkling of water for ritual cleansing is indicated in Num. 19:13, 20. Similarly, in Ezek. 36:25 the sprinkling of clean water on the hearts of God's people symbolizes the promise of full forgiveness of sin in the new covenant age.

nāzāh [נָזָה, 5137]

nāzāh is a verb occurring around twenty-five times. It is synonymous with ***zāraq*** (see above) and means "sprinkle."

The sprinkling of blood is indicated in a variety of ritual contexts. It is sprinkled on Aaron the high priest, along with other members of the priesthood, as part of their ordination ritual (Exod. 29:21; Lev. 8:30). Blood is also sprinkled before the Lord in front of the holy of holies (Lev. 4:6, 17). Such sprinkling is also performed in relation to the altar of sacrifice (cf. Lev. 5:9; 8:11); and the ark of the covenant during the Day of Atonement ritual (Lev. 16:14ff.). See also Lev. 6:27; 14:7, 16, 27, 51; Isa. 63:3.

Num. 8:7; 19:18ff. refer to sprinkling water for ritual purification.

nāzāh also refers to "spattering" blood on a wall on the occasion of the grisly death of Queen Jezebel in 2 Kgs. 9:33.

NT Words

rhantizō [ῥαντίζω, *4472*]

rhantizō is a verb meaning to "sprinkle" in all four occurrences of the term.

In relation to the sprinkling of blood, ***rhantizō*** refers to the sin offering (Heb. 9:13); to the covenant ratification ceremony (Heb. 9:19); and to hearts "sprinkled clean" from an evil conscience (Heb. 10:22). See also Heb. 9:21.

rhantismos [ῥαντισμός, *4473*]

rhantismos is a noun derived from ***rhantizō*** (see above), found only twice. Heb. 12:24; 1 Pet. 2:5 refer to the "sprinkled" blood of Christ that has eradicated sin once and for all.

Additional Notes

There is a consistency in usage between the Old and New Testament vocabulary for "sprinkling." The sprinkling of blood and water in old covenant ritual sacrifice was an indispensable component of worship that allowed God's people to continue in fellowship with him without penal sanction. However, it is also evident that the old covenant was not designed to fully eliminate the impact of sin on the people of God.

In the New Testament, the significance of "sprinkling" Jesus' blood, referring to his death by crucifixion, is fully realized. The shed blood of Christ guarantees that the penalty of sin has been paid for in full. Such a "sprinkling" in the eyes of God is thus deemed a full satisfaction of his wrath; and forgiveness is freely available for all who repent of their sin and put their trust in Jesus Christ as the one who died for their sins.

SPY → SEARCH

STAFF

OT Words

maqqēl [מַקֵּל, 4731]

maqqēl is a noun denoting a "rod" or "staff" in most of its eighteen occurrences.

Gen. 30:38ff.; Jer. 1:11 refer to "rods" (i.e., branches). Gen. 32:10; Exod. 12:11; 1 Sam. 17:40 refer to a "staff" in the sense of a "walking stick."

General references to a "staff," or "stick," are found in Num. 22:27; 1 Sam. 17:43. In Hos. 4:12, "stick" is associated with idolatry.

Metaphorically, ***maqqēl*** refers to a royal scepter in Jer. 48:17. Two shepherds' crooks, symbolizing the nations of Israel and Judah, are mentioned in Zech. 11:7ff.

matteh [מַטֶּה, 4294]

matteh is a common noun found in nearly 250 contexts with the primary sense of "tribe" in the majority of these occurrences. (→ TRIBE) However, other meanings include "staff," or "rod." Isa. 28:27 refers to a "stick"; and Gen. 38:18 speaks of a "walking stick."

Metaphorically, ***matteh*** also indicates the "staff" of divine anger (viz. Assyria) as an instrument of punishment in Isa. 10:5, 24; 30:32. The "staff" (identified with the wicked) is designated the object of God's anger in Isa. 14:5. The "staff" is identified as a symbol of royal authority in Jer. 48:17. See also Ezek. 29:6.

mish'enet [מִשְׁעֶנֶת, 4938]

mish'enet is a noun denoting a "staff" or "stick" throughout its twelve occurrences.

Exod. 21:19; 2 Kgs. 4:29ff.; Zech. 8:4 refer to a "staff" as a walking stick. ***mish'enet*** refers metaphorically to Yahweh's personal property in Ps. 23:4.

The "staff" as a symbol of high civil office or authority is linked with the "scepter" in Num. 21:28. Egypt is occasionally described as a "broken reed of a staff," denoting her weakness and unreliability in 2 Kgs. 18:21; Isa. 36:6; Ezek. 29:6.

See Also: → SCEPTER

STAIR, STAIRS → STEP

STAND

OT Words

qûm [קוּם, 6965]

qûm is a common verb occurring over six hundred times with a variety of meanings, including "to stand." (→ ARISE)

The meaning "stand," with the underlying sense of "remain in force," is applied to the valuation of property (Lev. 27:14ff.) and vows (Num. 30:4ff.). In relation to God, Isa. 40:8; Jer. 44:28ff. affirm that his word "stands forever"; as do his plan and purposes (Isa. 14:24; 46:10) Negatively speaking, opposition to God will never "stand" (Isa. 8:10).

Pss. 1:5; 24:3 speak of "standing before" God in judgment. The futility of idol worship is affirmed in Isa. 27:9, which declares that no idols will "remain standing." In contrast, the Redeemer himself is said "to stand" in Job 19:25, indicating that he will be an all-conquering figure.

The phenomenon of "standing against" the enemy in battle is described in Josh. 7:12ff.; Ps. 89:43.

nāṣab [נָצַב, 5324]

nāṣab is a verb occurring in seventy-five places meaning "stand," "set," in a variety of contexts and nuances.

General references to people "standing by, or alongside" someone are found in Gen. 18:2; Exod. 7:15; Isa. 22:7.

God himself is portrayed as standing beside a wall in a prophetic vision in Amos 9:1. In the vision of the patriarch Jacob in Gen. 28:17, God is described as "standing above" the ladder leading up to heaven. In another visionary context the angel of the Lord is said "to stand in the way" of Balaam's donkey, blocking its path (cf. Num. 22:23ff.).

An allegorical use of ***nāṣab*** is evident in Prov. 8:2, where Lady Wisdom is said "to take her stand" along the way in order to address the people passing by. In Isa. 3:13 Yahweh is said "to take his stand" against his people in order to judge them.

yāṣab [יָצַב, 3320]

yāṣab is a verb synonymous with ***nāṣab***, above, meaning "stand," along with associated nuances.

General references to "standing" in the mundane sense of taking up a position or location are found in Exod. 2:14; Num. 23:3; 1 Sam. 10:23.

The action of standing, or presenting oneself before another, is evident in Exod. 9:13; Prov. 22:29. In particular, the practice of standing before God is noted in Josh. 24:1; Judg. 20:2; Job 1:6; 2:1; Zech. 6:5. Ps. 5:5 declares that the wicked will be unable to stand before God.

yāṣab describes the attitude of "standing firm," without hesitation or fear (Exod. 14:13; 1 Sam. 12:16; Jer. 46:14), and "standing against," or opposing, someone (Deut. 7:24; 9:2). In particular, Deut. 11:25; Josh. 1:5 record the claim that none will be able to stand against the people of Israel.

'āmad [עָמַד, 5975]

'āmad is one of the most common verbs meaning "stand." It occurs about 520 times, in a variety of contexts with a number of associated senses.

Mundane references to the position of "standing" include those in Gen. 18:8; Josh. 3:17; Ps. 106:30; Isa. 36:2. Moses stands on holy ground in Exod. 3:5, as does Joshua in Josh. 5:15. See also Num. 22:24ff.; Josh. 5:13 in relation to the angel of the Lord "standing."

The position of "standing before the Lord" is commonly noted in the ritual context of praise and worship of Yahweh (cf. Gen. 19:27; Lev. 9:5; Jer. 15:1; 35:19). This is particularly the case with priests and Levites (cf. Deut. 18:5, 7; Ezek. 44:11), who are portrayed as ministering to the people as well. This position is also depicted in the context of facing divine judgment (cf. 1 Sam. 6:20; Nah. 1:6; Mal. 3:2). Significantly, genuine prophets are portrayed as "standing" in the council of Yahweh in order to receive divine revelation. In Zech. 3:1ff., the high priest Joshua is described "standing before" the angel of the Lord, facing the prospect of judgment, but he is subsequently forgiven and renewed by an act of divine mercy.

God himself is said "to take his stand," or to exercise judgment against his people, in Isa. 3:13. See also Exod. 17:6.

'āmad also indicates the enduring qualities of the plans of God which "stand (i.e., endure) forever" (cf. Ps. 33:11). This is also true of God's righteousness (cf. Pss. 111:3; 112:3); and praise for God, (cf. Ps. 111:10).

The expression "stand in the way" means "sharing the lifestyle of." Ps. 1:1 affirms blessing for the person who does not stand in the way of sinners.

The attitude of "standing against," or opposing, someone is indicated in Eccl. 4:12; Dan. 10:13.

The participial form of this verb refers to the people of God standing in his presence, reading from the book of the law. In Dan. 8:17, 18; 10:11, Daniel is found "standing" before God in order to receive a prophetic word. See also Dan. 11:1.

NT Words

histēmi [ἵστημι, *2476*]

histēmi is the most common New Testament term meaning "to stand," and constitutes a dynamic equivalent for the Hebrew ***'āmad*** (see above). ***histēmi*** occurs in nearly 160 places in a variety of contexts with a number of nuances.

Mundane references to "standing" include those in Matt. 2:6; Mark 1:5; Luke 7:38; John 1:26; Acts 1:11. See also Luke 1:11; Acts 7:33; Rev. 12:4.

The meaning "stand" in the sense of "endure," "last," is indicated negatively in Matt. 12:25; Mark 3:24ff.; Luke 11:18, where it is declared that a divided kingdom can never stand.

The process of "standing trial" is noted in Acts 26:6; and Rev. 6:17 speaks of standing before the judgment of God. Rev. 7:9ff. depicts the heavenly host of saints standing before the throne of God in worship.

With reference to the person of Christ, Acts 7:55ff. refers to him standing at the right hand of God (cf. also Rev. 14:1). He is also said to stand at the door of the believer's heart in Rev. 3:20.

The believer is exhorted to "stand" in the grace of God (i.e., live day by day in dependence on him) in Rom. 5:2; 1 Pet. 5:12. Similarly, 1 Cor. 15:1 speaks of "standing" in the gospel. The believer is exhorted to "stand fast" in his faith (Rom. 11:20; 2 Cor. 1:24), and also to "stand against" (i.e., oppose) the trickery of the devil (cf. Eph. 6:11ff.).

In relation to the person of God, his foundation (i.e., his purposes in salvation) is said to stand firm (2 Tim. 2:19).

paristēmi [παρίστημι, *3936*]

paristēmi is a variant form of ***histēmi***, above, occurring around forty-five times and meaning "stand," "stand by" in about one-third of these contexts.

Literal references to "standing by, or near" include those in Mark 14:47; Luke 19:24; John 18:22; Acts 1:10. Luke 1:19 refers to Gabriel "standing" in the presence of God. See also 2 Tim. 4:17.

ephistēmi [ἐφίστημι, *2186*]

ephistēmi is a verb occurring around twenty times, meaning "come (upon)," and "stand," "stand over." Luke 4:39 refers to "standing over" someone; and Luke 24:4; Acts 10:17; 22:13, 20; 23:11 refer to "standing by, or alongside."

synistēmi [συνίστημι, *4921*]

synistēmi is a verb meaning "to commend" in most of its sixteen occurrences. However, in Luke 9:32 it means "to stand alongside with."

periistēmi [περιΐστημι, *4026*]

periistēmi is a verb occurring four times, meaning "stand," "stand around" (cf. John 11:42; Acts 25:7).

stēkō [στήκω, *4739*]

stēkō is a verb found eight times meaning "stand fast," "stand by" throughout.

The position of "standing" in prayer is noted in Mark 11:25.

The metaphorical sense of "stand" is found in Rom. 14:4 in relation to sustaining or maintaining one's office with integrity. In addition, 1 Cor. 16:13; Gal. 5:1; 2 Thess. 2:15; Phil. 4:1 encourage "standing firm" in one's faith. Phil. 1:27 encourages "standing firm" in the unity of the Spirit.

See Also: → ARISE

STANDARD

OT Words

degel [**דֶּגֶל, 1714**]

degel is a noun occurring fourteen times denoting a "standard" or "banner" (i.e., "flag," "ensign") that lends an identity or common characteristic to those who gather under it.

The term is used in connection with the Israelite people in general in Num. 1:52; and with the Israelite tribes in particular (cf. Num. 2:2ff.; 10:14ff.).

nēs **[נֵס, 5251]**

nēs is a noun meaning "standard," "banner" in most of its twenty occurrences. Its usage is largely metaphorical.

Ps. 60:4 refers to a "banner" set by God for those who fear him, as a rallying point. God also sets up a "standard" as a rallying point for the nations. However, the contexts here are all negative, for these "standards" are erected as a precursor to their punishment, a warning of doom (cf. Isa. 5:26; 13:2; 18:3; Jer. 4:6, 21; 50:2; 51:12).

In contrast, ***nēs*** also designates the messianic "root of Jesse" as a "banner" for the exiled people of Yahweh, along with those of the nations who will flock to worship him in the redeemed kingdom of Israel (cf. Isa. 11:10, 12; 49:22; 62:10).

NT Words

kanōn [κανών, *2583*]

kanōn is a noun denoting a "rule" in the sense of a "standard," "principle," or "law" explicitly set by God (cf. 2 Cor. 10:13; Gal. 6:16; Phil. 3:16).

STAR

OT Words

kôkāb **[כּוֹכָב, 3556]**

kôkāb is a noun with the consistent meaning "star" in both a literal and metaphorical sense. The term is found in around forty contexts.

Literal references to "stars" as celestial bodies created by God include those in Gen. 1:16; Exod. 32:13; Deut. 28:62; Ps. 8:3; Eccl. 12:2; Jer. 31:35.

kôkāb is used metaphorically in Num. 24:17 to refer to a "star" coming out of Jacob — a future Messianic King descended from the people of Israel. Amos 5:26 refers to a "star god," indicating a pagan idol.

NT Words

astēr [ἀστήρ, *792*]

astēr is a noun meaning "star" in each of its nearly twenty-five occurrences and constitutes a dynamic equivalent for the Hebrew term ***kôkāb*** (see above).

Literal references to stars as heavenly bodies include those in Matt. 24:29; Mark 13:25; 1 Cor. 15:41. In the book of Revelation, all such references occur in a visionary context (cf. Rev. 6:13; 8:10ff.; 9:1; 12:1, 4). One reference to a star is especially significant. In Matt. 2:2ff., the star from the east is sighted over Bethlehem "announcing" the birth of the Christ child.

In metaphorical contexts, Jude 24 refers to false prophets, among other things, as "wandering stars." The "seven stars" held in the hand of the heavenly Christ symbolize the angels of the seven churches of Asia (cf. Rev. 1:16, 20; 2:1; 3:1). Rev. 2:28; 22:16 refer to Christ as "the morning star."

astron [ἄστρον, *798*]

astron is a variant form of ***astēr*** (see above), found in four places meaning "star."

Luke 21:25; Acts 27:20; Heb. 11:12 refer to stars as heavenly bodies. Acts 7:43 mentions a "star god" in reference to a pagan idol.

phōsphoros [φωσφόρος, *5459*]

phōsphoros is a rare noun found only in 2 Pet. 1:19 with reference to "the morning star," symbolizing the person of Christ.

Additional Notes

The "star" has a distinctive connection with the theme of the promised Messiah, as one who will emerge onto the world stage like a rising star. There is a strong redemptive-historical link between the prophecy of Num. 24:17 and Matt. 2:2ff., with the dominant symbols of a messianic "star." The powerful symbolism of the "star imagery" in the book of Revelation also supports the conclusion that it is Jesus Christ who constitutes the complete fulfillment of the messianic "star" phenomenon, bringing to light the full revelation of that motif — in his birth, life, death, resurrection, and ascension.

STEAL

OT Words

gānab **[גָּנַב, 1589]**

gānab is a verb meaning "steal," "rob" throughout its approximately forty occurrences.

It refers literally to stealing food (cf. Prov. 6:30); livestock (cf. Gen. 30:33; Exod. 22:1); money (cf. Gen. 44:8; Exod. 22:7); personal goods (cf. Gen. 31:19ff.; Josh. 7:11). See also 2 Sam. 21:2. The eighth commandment of the Decalogue, "do not steal," is recorded in Exod. 20:5; Deut. 5:19. See also Lev. 19:11; Jer. 7:9; Hos. 4:2; Zech. 5:3. "Stealing away" persons, or kidnapping, is a criminal practice alluded to in Gen. 40:15; Exod. 21:16; Deut. 24:7; 2 Kgs. 11:2.

Metaphorically, ***gānab*** refers to "stealing someone's heart" (i.e., capturing a person's loyalty and affection) in 2 Sam. 15:6, in connection with Absalom's popularity with the people of Israel. False prophets are said "to steal" the words of Yahweh in Jer. 23:30.

gāzal **[גָּזַל, 1497]**

gāzal is a verb occurring thirty times and meaning "rob," or "steal," usually associated with violent seizure in a number of contexts. (→ SPOIL)

gāzal refers to "stealing" in the sense of "seize," "take away by violent means," in association with property and money (cf. Gen. 21:25; Deut. 28:31; Judg. 9:25; Job 24:2; Mic. 2:2).

Sanctions against theft are recorded in Lev. 19:13; Prov. 22:22. Other general references to robbing or stealing include those in Lev. 6:4; Prov. 28:24; Jer. 22:3; Ezek. 18:7ff.; 22:29.

gezēlāh **[גְּזֵלָה, 1500]**

gezēlāh is a noun derived from ***gāzal*** (see above) denoting "that which is taken by robbery" (i.e., "stolen property") in four places (cf. Lev. 6:4; Ezek. 18:7, 12; 33:15).

NT WORDS

kleptō [κλέπτω, *2813*]

kleptō is a verb meaning "to steal," "rob" in each of the thirteen occurrences of the term (cf. Matt. 6:19ff.; 27:64; 28:13; John 10:10; Rom. 2:21; Eph. 4:28). The commandment "do not steal" is noted in Matt. 9:18; Mark 10:19; Luke 18:20; Rom. 13:9.

sylaō [συλάω, *4813*]

sylaō is a verb found only in 2 Cor. 11:9, referring metaphorically to Paul "robbing" churches by accepting monetary support from them. This statement is tinged with sarcasm.

STEP

OT WORDS

ma'alāh **[מַעֲלָה, 4609]**

ma'alāh is a noun meaning "step(s)," "stairs" in a number of contexts. The term occurs around fifty times.

Literal references to "steps" include those of the tabernacle altar (cf. Exod. 20:26; Ezek. 40:6, 22ff.). See also 2 Kgs. 9:13; Neh. 3:15; 12:37. The "steps" associated with Solomon's throne are noted in 1 Kgs. 10:19ff.; 2 Chr. 9:18.

ma'alāh also refers to "steps" (i.e., paces) cast by a shadow in 2 Kgs. 20:9ff.; Isa. 38:8.

ṣa'ad **[צַעַד, 6806]**

ṣa'ad is a noun synonymous with ***ma'alāh***, above, found fourteen times and meaning "step," "pace," or "stride."

The term is used literally in 2 Sam. 6:13; 22:37.

More commonly, ***ṣa'ad*** refers to "steps" in the symbolic sense of "one's daily life" — for example, in Job 14:16; Ps. 18:36; Prov. 5:5.

'ashur **[אַשֻּׁר, 838]**

'ashur is a noun occurring nine times, denoting "steps" in the general sense of "ways," or "goings," in relation to one's lifestyle in most cases (cf. Job 23:11; Ps. 17:5; Prov. 14:15).

This meaning is also predicated of God, of whom it is said that his steps (i.e., his ways, plans) never falter (cf. Ps. 37:31).

pesa' **[פֶּשַׂע, 6587]**

pesa' is a rare noun, found only in 1 Sam. 20:3, used metaphorically when David claims that there is but "one step" between him and death.

miṣ'ād **[מִצְעָד, 4703]**

miṣ'ād is synonymous with ***'ashur***, above, found three times and meaning "steps" in the sense of "life direction" (cf. Ps. 37:23; Prov. 20:24). See also Dan. 11:42.

'āqēb **[עָקֵב, 6119]**

'āqēb is a noun denoting "steps," "footsteps" in about half of the thirteen occurrences of the term (cf. Pss. 56:6; 77:19; 89:5; Song 1:8).

NT WORDS

ichnos [ἴχνος, *2487*]

ichnos denotes the phenomenon of "steps" in the context of "walking in the steps of . . ." or following or imitating one's example (cf. Rom. 4:12; 2 Cor. 12:18; 1 Pet. 2:21).

STEWARD

NT WORDS

oikonomos [οἰκονόμος, *3623*]

oikonomos is a noun denoting "one who oversees or manages household or civic affairs." This is usually, though not always, the function of a slave. The term is used both literally and metaphorically, and is found in ten contexts.

The literal sense of "manager" or "steward" is found in Luke 12:42; 16:1ff. In Rom. 16:23, the likely translation of ***oikonomos*** is "director of public works."

Metaphorical reference to "stewards" is found in 1 Cor. 4:1ff., where ***oikonomos*** designates the apostles as "custodians" of the gospel message, which is the full account of the mysteries of God's revelation.

Elsewhere, the metaphor of "steward" or "trustee" relates to the role of the old covenant law in the life of God's people, prior to the coming of Christ (cf. Gal. 4:2). Titus 1:7 speaks of the bishop as a "steward of God," and 1 Pet. 4:10 alludes to the "stewards" of God's gifts.

oikonomeō [οἰκονομέω, *3621*]

oikonomeō is a rare verb, found only in Luke 16:2 in relation to "holding the office of a steward."

oikonomia [οἰκονομία, *3622*]

oikonomia is a noun derived from ***oikonomeō***, above, and found in seven places.

The term denotes "the office of a steward" in a literal sense in Luke 16:2ff. In addition, it refers to "the divine plan," involving the outworking of God's purposes in salvation and the spread of the message of redemption (cf. 1 Cor. 9:17; Eph. 1:10; 3:2; Col. 1:25).

epitropos [ἐπίτροπος, *2012*]

epitropos is a noun occurring three times, synonymous with ***oikonomos*** (see above), in relation to a "steward" or "manager" of a household (cf. Matt. 20:8; Luke 8:3).

It is also used metaphorically to denote a "guardian" or "tutor" in relation to the function of the old covenant law for the people of God prior to the coming of Christ (cf. Gal. 4:2).

STICK → WOOD

STIFF-NECKED → STUBBORN

STIR, STIR UP

OT Words

'ûr [עוּר, **5782**]

'ûr is a verb occurring around eighty times. It means "lift up," "arouse," "wake up," and "stir (up)" in a variety of contexts.

The action of "stirring up" is predicated of God in the context of "provoking" or "inciting" a person's spirit, in order to prepare that person or people for a particular course of action in line with his purposes (cf. 1 Chr. 5:26; 2 Chr. 21:16; Isa. 13:14). In particular, Ezra 1:1 records God's action in "stirring up" the heart of Cyrus, the Persian king, to release the people of Yahweh and have them return to their homes in Judah in order to rebuild the temple. In Hag. 1:14, God "stirs" or "moves" the postexilic community, by his Spirit, to complete the work of rebuilding the temple. In Ps. 78:38, the psalmist affirms that God "did not stir up" his own wrath against his people on every occasion. In Prov. 10:12, hatred is said "to stir up" strife. There is in the Song of Songs a repeated exhortation for love not to be "aroused" (i.e., "stirred up") until the appropriate times (cf. Song 2:7; 3:5; 4:16; 5:2; 8:4ff.).

sût [סוּת, **5496**]

sût is a verb with the general sense of "persuading," "enticing," "provoking" someone into a particular course of action, or attitude. The related meaning "stir up" is evident in 1 Sam. 26:9, where God "provokes" or "stirs up" anger; in 1 Kgs. 21:25, where Jezebel "incites" Ahab to wickedness; and in 1 Chr. 21:1, where Satan incites or stirs David up to take an illegitimate census.

gārāh [גָּרָה, **1624**]

gārāh is a verb with the underlying sense of "cause strife," "stir up trouble" (cf. 2 Kgs. 14:10; 2 Chr. 25:19; Prov. 15:18; 28:25; 29:22).

NT Words

synkineō [συγκινέω, *4787*]

synkineō is a rare verb found only in Acts 6:12, with reference to "stirring up commotion," "causing a disturbance."

epegeirō [ἐπεγείρω, *1892*]

epegeirō is a rare verb, synonymous with ***synkineō***, above, meaning "to stir up strife," "cause a civil disturbance" in Acts 14:2.

saleuō [σαλεύω, *4531*]

saleuō is a verb with the primary sense of "shake," occurring fifteen times. In Acts 17:13, however, it refers to "stirring up" or "inciting" a crowd to uproar.

anaseiō [ἀνασείω, *383*]

anaseiō is a verb found on only two occasions. It means "to stir up," "excite" a crowd (cf. Mark 15:11; Luke 23:5).

erethizō [ἐρεθίζω, *2042*]

erethizō is a verb meaning "stir up" or "provoke" in only two contexts.

In 2 Cor. 9:2, the connotation is a positive one. Paul refers to the Corinthian congregation having "provoked" others to good works in generous giving. Col. 3:21 contains the admonition to fathers not to "provoke" (or stir up) their children to wrath.

STONE

OT Words

'eben [**אֶבֶן, 68** (**69** Aramaic)]

'eben is the standard term in the Old Testament for "stone," "rock," including a variety of associated nuances.

Literal references to "stone(s)" include those in Gen. 11:3; Exod. 7:19; Deut. 29:17; 1 Kgs. 5:17ff.; 7:9. Precious stones are noted in Gen. 2:12; Exod. 25:7; Ezek. 10:9; Zech. 3:9. Stones are indicated both as weapons (cf. 1 Sam. 17:50); as well as instruments of execution (cf. Lev. 24:23; Deut. 13:10; Josh. 10:1). Hailstones are noted in Isa. 30:30; Ezek. 13:11, 13; 38:22 — all in relation to divine judgment.

"Pillars of stones" are erected as markers for a site of special significance, usually associated with a theophany, or miraculous divine intervention. In Deut. 27:2ff.; Josh. 4:3ff., they commemorate a divine miracle. Gen. 35:14 refers to a theophany. And in Josh. 24:27, the stone pillar commemorates the location of the Israelite people's ratification of their covenant promise to Yahweh.

The Ten Commandments are inscribed on tablets of stone (cf. Exod. 24:12; 31:18; 34:1ff.; Deut. 4:13; 5:22; 9:9ff.).

'eben also refers metaphorically to Yahweh as "the Rock of Israel" in Gen. 49:24, indicating his unique dependability and security. In relation to this phenomenon, there are also several references to the rejected "stone" becoming the chief cornerstone, constituting a significant messianic prophecy (cf. Ps. 118:22; Isa. 28:16; Hag. 2:5; Zech. 4:7). Isa. 8:14 refers to the messianic ruler of Israel as a "stumbling stone" for the people of Yahweh — for those who refuse to accept his authority and his identity. Ezek. 11:19; 36:26 describe the wonderful anticipated blessing of the new covenant, with reference to the people's "heart of stone" being replaced with a "heart of flesh," signifying a full transformation of attitude — from rebellion to love and faithfulness.

The Aramaic term for "stone" is identical in form and is found in Ezra 5:8; 6:4 with reference to the stones used to reconstruct the Jerusalem temple In Dan. 2:34ff., this Aramaic term refers to the "stone" of Nebuchadnezzar's dream that destroyed the statue representing the kingdoms of the world. The origins of this "stone" are described as beyond the realm of human knowledge and skill (i.e., "not made with human hands") — a stone signifying the all-conquering kingdom of God that expands to fill the whole earth. See also Dan. 5:4, 23; 6:2.

sāqal [**סָקַל, 5619**]

sāqal is a verb found in around twenty contexts with primary reference to executing people by "stoning" (cf. Exod. 8:26; 21:28ff.; Deut. 13:10; 22:21ff.; Josh. 7:25; 1 Kgs. 21:10ff.).

gāzît [**גָּזִית, 1496**]

gāzît is a noun occurring eleven times denoting "hewn, or dressed stone" utilized in the construction of Solomon's temple (cf. 1 Kgs. 5:17; 6:36), as well as his palace (cf. 1 Kgs. 7:9ff.). See also Ezek. 40:42; Isa. 9:10; Amos 5:11.

rāgam [**רָגַם, 7275**]

rāgam is a verb synonymous with ***sāqal*** (see above) indicating "stoning to death" — a common form of execution in the ancient world. It occurs sixteen times (cf. Lev. 20:21; 24:14ff.; Num. 14:10; Deut. 21:21; Josh. 7:25; Ezek. 23:47).

ṣōr [**צֹר, 6864**]

ṣōr is a noun denoting a "sharp stone," or "flint" (cf. Exod. 4:25; Ezek. 3:9).

NT Words

lithos [λίθος, *3037*]

lithos is a noun meaning "stone" throughout its sixty occurrences. It is a dynamic equivalent for the Hebrew term ***'eben*** (see above). ***lithos*** is used both literally and metaphorically. Literal references to "stones" include those in Matt. 3:9; 27:60ff.; Mark 13:2; 2 Cor. 3:7. Precious stones are indicated in 1 Cor. 3:12; Rev. 4:3; 21:11.

As ***'eben*** is used metaphorically to refer to Yahweh, so ***lithos*** is used symbolically to refer to Christ. Following upon the Old Testament usage, there are several references to the "stone" rejected by the builders becoming the chief cornerstone (cf. Matt. 21:42; Mark

12:10; Luke 20:17; 1 Pet. 2:4ff. — an identification self-consciously adopted by Christ). Christ is also identified with the "stumbling stone," upon which those who refuse to accept him as the Messiah will "stumble" (cf. Rom. 9:32, 33; 1 Pet. 2:8).

In 1 Pet. 2:5, believers are described metaphorically as "living stones" forming part of Christ's body.

lithazō [λιθάζω, *3034*]

This verb occurs eight times, meaning "to stone," "pelt with stones" — either to wound or to kill. John 10:31ff.; 11:8 record the unsuccessful attempt to have Jesus stoned. See also Acts 5:26; 4:19; 2 Cor. 11:25; Heb. 11:37.

lithoboleō [λιθοβολέω, *3036*]

lithoboleō is a verb synonymous with ***lithazō***, above, meaning "to kill by stoning" in Matt. 21:35; Luke 13:34; John 8:5; Acts 7:58ff.; Heb. 12:20. See also Mark 12:4.

lithinos [λίθινος, *3035*]

lithinos is an adjective meaning "made of stone" in John 2:6; 2 Cor. 3:3; Rev. 9:20.

akrogōniaios [ἀκρογωνιαῖος, *204*]

akrogōniaios is an adjective meaning "chief corner (stone)" in reference to Christ. It occurs only in Eph. 2:20; 1 Pet. 2:6.

psēphos [ψῆφος, *5586*]

psēphos is a noun denoting a "small smooth stone" (or pebble), referring metaphorically to the "stone" in Rev. 2:17 (twice) on which the new name of Christ will be written.

petrōdēs [πετρώδης, *4075*]

petrōdēs is an adjective referring to "stony" ground in Matt. 13:5, 20; Mark 4:5, 16.

See Also: → ROCK

STORE → TREASURE

STORM

OT Words

sûphāh [**סוּפָה, 5492**]

sûphāh is a noun occurring sixteen times denoting a "storm," or "whirlwind." The former sense implies both wind and rain (cf. Job 21:18; Isa. 29:6; Ezek. 38:9).

sā'āh [**סָעָה, 5584**]

sā'āh is a term found only in Ps. 55:8 with reference to "windstorm."

zerem [**זֶרֶם, 2230**]

zerem is a noun found in nine contexts denoting a "(rain)storm" or "thunderstorm" in most of these places (cf. Isa. 4:6; 25:4; 28:2; 30:30; 32:2).

NT Words

lailaps [λαῖλαψ, *2978*]

lailaps is a term found only three times, meaning "windstorm" in Mark 4:27; Luke 8:23; 2 Pet. 2:17.

See Also: → WHIRLWIND

STRAIGHT

OT Words

tāqan [**תָּקַן, 8626**]

tāqan is a verb found three times, meaning "make straight" (i.e., put right, set in order) in Eccl. 1:15; 7:13. See also Eccl. 12:9.

NT Words

euthys [εὐθύς, *2117*]

euthys is an adjective found in sixteen places, meaning "straight" in the sense of "free from obstacle" in Matt. 3:3; Mark 1:3; Luke 3:4, 5, referring to the preparation of a straight path for the coming Messiah. The sense of "right" or "morally upright" is indicated in Acts 8:21; 13:10; 2 Pet. 2:15.

euthynō [εὐθύνω, *2116*]

euthynō is an adverbial form translated verbally as "to make straight" (i.e., remove obstacles, level out) in John 1:23, citing the prophecy of the coming Messiah in Isa. 40:1ff.

orthos [ὀρθός, *3717*]

orthos is an adjective found twice, meaning "straight" in the sense of "(standing) physically upright" (Acts 14:10), and "morally upright" (Heb. 12:13).

See Also: → RIGHTEOUS

STRAIGHTWAY → SUDDEN

STRANGE, STRANGER → ALIEN → SOJOURN

STREAM → RIVER

STRENGTH, STRENGTHEN, STRONG

OT Words

kōaḥ [כֹּחַ, 3581]

kōaḥ is a noun denoting the qualities of "strength," "power," "might" in most of the approximately 130 uses of the term, with a degree of overlap in all of these senses.

General references to human strength, indicating energy and vitality as well as physical strength, include those in Gen. 31:6; Lev. 26:20; Job 6:11ff.; Prov. 20:29. Loss of "strength" or "power" is noted in Isa. 49:4 in relation to the Messianic Servant of Yahweh (be it temporary), and also in general terms in Pss. 22:15; 31:10; 71:9. The impotence of human might, apart from God, is indicated in Deut. 8:17; 1 Sam. 2:9; Zech. 4:6.

The strength or might of a nation is noted in Dan. 8:6ff., 22ff. Power or strength as derived from Yahweh is indicated in relation to the judges (Judg. 6:14; 16:5ff.); to the prophet Micah (Mic. 3:8); and it is also given to renew or sustain the weak (Isa. 40:29ff.). The strength of beasts is alluded to in Prov. 14:4.

The quality of "power" or "might" attributed to God refers frequently to his miraculous intervention in human affairs to demonstrate his divine authority and right to rule. Yahweh's power in delivering or sustaining his people is indicated particularly in relation to the exodus from Egypt and the plague judgments on that nation (cf. Exod. 9:16; 32:11; Num. 14:17; Deut. 9:29; 2 Kgs. 17:36; Neh. 1:10). Power over the enemies of Yahweh is demonstrated elsewhere in Exod. 15:6; Deut. 4:30. Recognition of Yahweh's innate power and strength is recorded in 1 Chr. 29:12; Job 37:23; Pss. 29:4; 111:6; 147:5; Isa. 40:26; Nah. 1:3.

Divine power in creation is noted in Jer. 10:12; 27:5; 51:15.

gibbôr [גִּבּוֹר, 1368]

gibbôr primarily denotes a "mighty warrior," "valiant man" in the context of military skill and prowess.

gibbôr refers generally to "mighty men," including the heroes of old (Gen. 6:4; 10:8ff.); Israelite warriors (Josh. 1:14; 1 Sam. 9:1; 2 Sam. 1:18ff.; 1 Kgs. 1:8ff.; 1 Chr. 11:10ff.; 12:1ff.; Song 3:7); Israelite judges (Judg. 6:12; 11:1); "mighty warriors" of the Canaanite cities (Josh. 10:2; Judg. 5:13) and of Babylon (Jer. 51:56); and also Goliath the Philistine (1 Sam. 17:51). See also Ezek. 32:27; 39:20.

Other general references to the "strong man" in non-specific contexts include those in Pss. 19:5; 33:15; Prov. 16:32; Isa. 3:2; Jer. 9:23; Joel 2:7.

gibbôr is used adjectivally in relation to Yahweh, describing him as "mighty God" in Neh. 9:32; Ps. 24:8; Jer. 32:18. In Isa. 9:6, this title is given prophetically to the Messianic King.

Angels are described as "mighty ones" in Ps. 103:20.

ḥāzaq [חָזַק, 2388]

ḥāzaq is a common verb with the underlying senses "to strengthen," "be strong," "prevail," as well as a number of related nuances. The term is found in nearly 300 places, with the above meanings found in about one-third of these contexts.

ḥāzaq means "to prevail" in the sense of "be severe," "have a strong hold on," in relation to famine (Gen. 47:20), and in relation to a military victory (1 Sam. 17:50).

The sense of "strengthen oneself" is indicated in Gen. 48:2 with reference to food; and also in 2 Sam. 3:6 in a political context.

The meaning "be strong," in the sense of resolute dependence upon God, is indicated in Deut. 11:8; 31:6ff.; Josh. 1:7ff.; 1 Kgs. 2:2; Isa. 35:4; Hag. 2:4. This meaning is also indicated in relation to effective military power and strength in 2 Sam. 10:11; 1 Kgs. 20:25; Dan. 11:5ff. See also 2 Sam. 13:14; Ezra 9:12.

God is said "to give strength" to the nations (Judg. 3:12; Ezek. 30:24); and to his people (Judg. 7:11; 16:28; Dan. 10:18; Hos. 7:15).

ḥāzāq [חָזָק, 2389]

ḥāzāq is an adjectival form derived from ***ḥāzaq***, above, meaning "strong," "mighty."

The term is used to describe Yahweh as having a "mighty hand," or "strong arm," in contexts where divine power is expressed — usually through miraculous intervention. The most significant of these contexts is Yahweh forcing Egypt to release the people of Israel (cf. Exod. 3:19; 6:1; 13:9; 32:11; Deut. 4:34; 6:21; Dan. 9:15). See also Deut. 3:24; Josh. 4:24; Ps. 136:12; Isa. 28:2, Jer. 21:5; Ezek. 20:33.ff.

Exod. 10:9; 1 Kgs. 19:11 refer to a "mighty wind."

People are described as "strong" in a physical, military sense in Num. 13:18; Josh. 14:11.

'ōz [עֹז, 5797]

'ōz is a noun denoting the qualities of "strength," "power" in the majority of its ninety occurrences.

The power of Yahweh is indicated in the expression "the Lord is (my, our) strength" — an affirmation of security in God to watch over his people (cf. Exod. 15:2; Pss. 28:7ff.; 46:1; Isa. 12:2; Jer. 16:19). Divine strength in effecting deliverance for his people is noted in Exod. 15:13; Ps. 74:13. See also 1 Chr. 16:11; Job 12:16; Pss. 21:1; 96:7.

The strength of human beings, or physical and military prowess, is indicated in general contexts in Lev. 26:19; 2 Sam. 6:14. God gives strength to his Messianic King (1 Sam. 2:10), and to his people (Pss. 29:11; 89:16).

'ōz is also used adjectivally, referring to a "strong tower" or "fortress" in Judg. 9:51. God himself is described as a "strong tower" in Ps. 61:3; Prov. 18:10. A "strong" city is indicated in Prov. 10:15; Isa. 26:1. Prov. 14:26 speaks of a "strong" confidence in God.

gebûrāh [גְּבוּרָה, 1369]

gebûrāh is a noun which occurs around sixty times and means "strength," "might," "power."

The "might," or "power" of God in his redemptive action is indicated in general contexts in Deut. 3:24; Pss. 71:16; 145:4; Isa. 33:13. Praise to God for his "power" or "might" is indicated in 1 Chr. 29:11; Pss. 21:13; 89:13; Jer. 10:6.

The physical or military might of human beings is indicated in Judg. 8:21; Eccl. 9:16; Isa. 36:5. See also 1 Kgs. 15:23; 2 Kgs. 13:8. Mic. 3:8 notes that Yahweh himself gives strength to the servant. The strength of beasts is indicated in Job 39:19.

Metaphorically, strength (i.e., of character) is attributed to Lady Wisdom in Prov. 8:14.

'āṣûm [עָצוּם, 6099]

'āṣûm is an adjective found in thirty contexts meaning "strong," "mighty" throughout.

The quality of being "strong," in the sense of "secure," "thriving" (i.e., blessed by God) is attributed to the nation of Israel as descended from Abraham in Gen. 18:18.

Foreign nations are "strong" in the sense of military might (Exod. 1:9; Deut. 4:38; 9:1; Josh. 23:9; Isa. 8:7; Joel 1:6; Mic. 4:3, 7; Zech. 8:22); as is Israel (Num. 14:12); people blessed by God (Isa. 53:12); and an army (Dan. 11:25). See also Ps. 135:10.

'az [עַז, 5794]

'az is an adjective synonymous with ***'āṣûm***, above, found in twenty contexts meaning "strong," "mighty."

Natural elements are described this way in Exod. 14:21 in relation to wind; and in Isa. 43:16 with reference to waters.

People are described as "strong" in a physical, military sense in Prov. 30:25; Isa. 25:3; Amos 5:9; Num. 13:28; 21:24; 2 Sam. 22:17; Ps. 18:17.

The lion is also designated as "strong" in Judg. 14:11ff.

mā'ôz [מָעוֹז, 4581]

mā'ôz is a noun denoting "strength" in the majority of the forty or so contexts in which it is found. The principal connotation of this term is its association with a "strong place," "refuge," or "fortress" — a place of physical security.

General references to a "stronghold" or "fortress" are found in Isa. 23:14; Dan. 11:7ff.

God is described as a "strong refuge" or "fortress" (2 Sam. 22:33; Pss. 31:2ff.; 37:39; Prov. 10:29; Jer. 16:19; Nah. 1:7); and as one's "strength" (Neh. 8:10; Ps. 27:1; Isa. 25:4).

The "strength" of the nations is alluded to in Isa. 30:3; Ezek. 30:15.

yād [יָד, 3027]

yād is a common noun with the primary meaning "hand" in most of its nearly 1,600 occurrences. In several places, however, ***yād*** expresses the sense of "power."

The "power" or "strength" of people in a military sense is indicated in Deut. 32:36; Josh. 8:20; 2 Kgs. 19:26; Isa. 37:27; Dan. 12:7.

yād refers to the "power" of Satan (Job 1:12); of the sword (Job 5:20); of the grave (Ps. 49:15; Hos. 13:14); of the tongue (Prov. 18:21); and of fire (Isa. 47:14).

ḥōzeq [חֹזֶק, 2392]

ḥōzeq is a noun denoting "strength," "power" in the five contexts. The power of Yahweh in delivering Israel from Egypt is indicated in Exod. 13:3, 14, 16. The power of human beings noted in Amos 6:13; Hag. 2:22.

'āmaṣ [אָמַץ, 553]

'āmaṣ is a verb meaning "to be strong," "strengthen" in the majority of its approximately forty occurrences. (→ COURAGE)

General references to people being strong include those in Gen. 25:23; 2 Sam. 22:18; Pss. 18:17; 142:6; Prov. 24:5.

The meaning "to strengthen" is evident in relation to the servants of Yahweh — for example, Joshua

(Deut. 3:28); and Israel as God's servant (Isa. 41:10). See also Job 16:5; Ps. 89:21. The temple is said to be "strengthened" in 2 Chr. 24:13, in the context of undergoing repairs and renovations.

'āzaz [עָזַז, **5810**]

'āzaz is a verb meaning "strengthen," "prevail," "be strong" in the majority of its twelve occurrences.

The meaning "prevail over (i.e., prove stronger than)" is indicated in Judg. 3:10; 6:2 in relation to a military conquest. See also Ps. 9:19. Divine strength is indicated in Pss. 68:28; 89:13.

'ammîṣ [אַמִּיץ, **533**]

'ammîṣ is an adjective meaning "strong," "mighty" in most of its six occurrences.

The king of Assyria is designated as a "mighty one" in Isa. 28:2. God is also described as "mighty" in Job 9:4, 19; Isa. 40:26. See also 2 Sam. 15:12.

'ôn [אוֹן, **202**]

'ôn is a term found twelve times with the underlying sense of physical might or strength. Reference to human might is found, for example, in Deut. 21:17; Isa. 40:29. Divine strength is indicated in Isa. 40:26. See also Job 20:10.

gābar [גָּבַר, **1396**]

gābar is a verb meaning to "prevail," "be, grow strong" in most of its twenty-three occurrences.

The meaning "prevail" (i.e., become, grow strong) is indicated in relation to "floodwaters" in Gen. 7:18ff.; and in the context of gaining a military advantage in Exod. 17:11; 2 Sam. 11:23. See also 1 Chr. 5:2; Jer. 9:3. God is said to prevail over his enemies in Isa. 42:13.

2 Sam. 1:23 speaks of people being strong, and Job 36:9 alludes to people growing in strength. In Zech. 10:6, God is said to strengthen the house of Judah.

NT Words

ischys [ἰσχύς, *2479*]

ischys is a term denoting "strength," "power," "might" throughout the eleven contexts in which it is found.

Mark 12:30ff.; Luke 10:27 record the command to love God with all one's "strength" (i.e., with one's whole being). 1 Pet. 4:11 affirms that God supplies strength to his people. See also 2 Pet. 2:11.

The "might," or "power," of God is indicated in Eph. 1:19; 6:10; 2 Thess. 1:9; Rev. 7:12. The "strength" of the Lamb, referring to the heavenly Christ, is indicated in Rev. 5:12.

ischyros [ἰσχυρός, *2478*]

ischyros is an adjective derived from ***ischys*** (see above) meaning "strong," "mighty" throughout nearly all thirty occurrences.

Jesus Christ is designated as "mighty" (Matt. 3:11; Mark 1:7; Luke 3:16); as is God (Rev. 18:8). 1 Cor. 1:25 declares that the weakness of God is stronger than human strength, in a context that is clearly hyperbolic.

People are described as "strong" in Matt. 12:29; Luke 11:21ff.; Rev. 19:18. ***ischyros*** describes strength of character in 1 John 2:14; 1 Cor. 4:10. Other general uses of ***ischyros*** include those in 1 Cor. 1:27; 2 Cor. 10:10; Heb. 5:7.

kratos [κράτος, *2904*]

kratos is a noun synonymous with ***ischys***, above, denoting "strength," "force," "power."

References to the "strength," or "power," of God include those in Luke 1:51; Eph. 6:10; Col. 1:11; 1 Tim. 6:16; 1 Pet. 5:11; Jude 25; Rev. 1:6; 5:13.

kratos indicates the "power" of death in Heb. 2:14; and 1 Pet. 4:11 refers to the "dominion" of Christ.

The word of God is described as growing in "force" in Acts 19:20.

stereoō [στερεόω, *4732*]

stereoō is a verb found three times meaning "be made strong" in Acts 3:7, 16, with reference to healing a crippled man. In Acts 16:5, it refers to churches strengthened in their faith.

dynamis [δύναμις, *1411*]

dynamis is the most common term in the New Testament denoting the qualities of "power," "might," "strength" in 120 contexts.

dynamis refers to the "power" of God (Matt. 6:13; 22:29; Mark 12:24; 1 Cor. 1:18; Eph. 1:19; Rev. 11:17); and to the power of the Son of Man coming in glory (Matt. 24:30; Mark 13:26; Luke 21:27).

References to the "mighty deeds" (i.e., the miracles) of Christ include those in Matt. 11:20ff.; Mark 6:5; Luke 10:13; Acts 2:22; 10:38. Similarly, "mighty works" performed by Jesus' followers are noted in Matt. 7:12; 13:54ff.; 14:2; Acts 19:11. Rev. 1:16; 5:12 refer to the power of the heavenly Christ.

The power of the Holy Spirit is indicated in Luke 4:14; Acts 1:8; Rom. 15:13; as is the "powers of the heavens" in Matt. 24:29; Mark 13:25; Luke 21:26. Angelic power is noted in 2 Pet. 2:11. Luke 9:1 speaks of power over demons.

Rom. 8:38 indicates demonic powers, and 2 Thess. 2:9 refers to the power of Satan. Sin's power is described in 1 Cor. 15:56.

The resurrection body is said to be "raised in power" in 1 Cor. 15:43. The power of the resurrection is noted in Phil. 3:10; and the power of the gospel in 1 Thess. 1:5.

The power of John the Baptist is metaphorically designated as the "power of Elijah" in Luke 1:17.

dynatos [δυνατός, *1415*]

dynatos is an adjective derived from ***dynamis*** (see above), meaning "powerful," "mighty," "strong." The term is found thirty-five times.

dynatos describes God as "mighty" (Luke 1:49), and also Moses (Acts 7:22; see also Acts 18:24). Jesus Christ is designated a "mighty prophet" in Luke 24:19.

People are described as being "strong" in character in Rom. 15:11; 2 Cor. 12:10; 13:9.

dynatos expresses the nominal sense of "power" with reference to divine power in Rom. 9:22; 2 Cor. 10:4.

dynateō [δυνατέω, *1414*]

dynateō is a rare verb found only in 2 Cor. 13:3 with reference to the presence of Christ's Spirit "being powerful" among the Corinthian congregation.

See Also: → ABILITY → ARM → AUTHORITY → ROCK

STRETCH, STRETCH OUT

OT Words

shālaḥ [שָׁלַח, **7971**]

shālaḥ is a common verb occurring around 850 times with the underlying meaning "send," as well as a wide variety of related senses. One of these nuances is "to stretch," or "stretch out."

This action is predicated of God in Exod. 3:20; 9:15, where he is said to stretch out his hand in judgment against those who oppose the divine will. 2 Sam. 24:16 refers to an angel doing the same thing in relation to Jerusalem.

Job 30:24 refers to human beings stretching out their hands in a gesture of despair. In Gen. 48:14, this action indicates the administering of a blessing.

nāṭāh [נָטָה, **5186**]

nāṭāh is a verb with the primary sense of "stretch (out)" in a variety of contexts.

God is said to "stretch out his hand" in judgment against his people for their rebellion against him (cf. Isa. 5:25; Jer. 6:12; 15:6; Ezek. 6:14; Zeph. 1:4). The same action indicates God rescuing his people from captivity in Egypt (Deut. 9:29; 2 Kgs. 17:36 [cf. also 1 Kgs. 8:42]). Judgment against the enemies of God is indicated by this action in Ezek. 25:13ff.; Isa. 14:16. The heavens are said to be stretched out by God in Isa. 45:12.

Yahweh commands Moses to stretch his hand out to effect the plague judgments against Egypt (cf. Exod. 7:19; 8:16; 10:12, 21); and to divide the Re(e)d Sea (Exod. 14:16).

Job 11:13 refers to human beings stretching their hands out to God as an expression of devotion.

1 Chr. 21:16 describes the outstretched arm of an angel extended in judgment against Jerusalem.

gāhar [גָּהַר, **1457**]

gāhar is a verb found three times, referring to Elisha "stretching himself out" on the body of a young boy who had died of a fever, and who was subsequently restored to life through this symbolic action (cf. 2 Kgs. 4:34, 35).

NT Words

ekteinō [ἐκτείνω, *1614*]

ekteinō is a verb found sixteen times meaning "stretch out," or "stretch forth," in most of these contexts.

ekteinō refers to Jesus Christ "stretching out" his hand to touch people as a means of effecting a miraculous cure for their affliction (cf. Matt. 8:3; Mark 1:41; Luke 5:13). See also Acts 4:30. It is also used as a gesture of identification in Matt. 12:49. See also Mark 14:31; Acts 26:1.

In one instance, Jesus asks a man to stretch out his own, withered hand — which is subsequently cured (cf. Matt. 12:13; Mark 3:5; Luke 6:10).

STRIFE

OT Words

merîbāh [מְרִיבָה, **4808**]

merîbāh is a noun denoting "strife," or "contention," between people. It is found in seven contexts (cf. Gen. 13:8; Num. 27:14). See also Ps. 95:8; 106:32; Ezek. 47:19; 48:28.

mādôn [**מָדוֹן, 4066**]

mādôn is synonymous with ***merîbāh*** (see above), also denoting "strife," "contention," "discord." It occurs eighteen times (cf. Prov. 6:14; 17:14; 26:20; Jer. 15:10; Hab. 1:3).

maṣṣāh [**מַצָּה, 4683**]

maṣṣāh is another synonym for ***merîbāh*** and ***mādôn***, above, denoting "contention," "strife" in Prov. 13:10; 17:19; Isa. 58:4.

NT Words

eris [ἔρις, *2054*]

eris denotes "strife," "contention," or "quarreling" in the majority of its nine occurrences (cf. Rom. 1:29; 13:13; 1 Cor. 1:11; 2 Cor. 12:20; Phil. 1:15; 1 Tim. 6:4).

eritheia [ἐριθεία, *2052*]

eritheia is a synonym for ***eris*** (see above), found in seven contexts mostly meaning "strife," "dissension," "discord" (cf. Rom. 2:8; 2 Cor. 12:20; Gal. 5:10; Phil. 1:16). The sense of "selfish ambition" is indicated in Phil. 2:3; Jas. 3:14, 16, emphasizing that such an attitude causes disunity and discord among believers.

philoneikia [φιλονεικία, *5379*]

philoneikia is found only in Luke 22:24 with reference to a "dispute" or "quarrel."

logomachia [λογομαχία, *3055*]

logomachia is a term found only in 1 Tim. 6:4 with reference to "controversy" in the context of "quarreling over words."

machē [μάχη, *3163*]

machē is a noun found in four places denoting "quarrels," or "fights" (cf. 2 Cor. 7:5; 2 Tim. 2:23; Titus 3:9; Jas. 4:1).

See Also: → JUDGE → STRIVE

STRIKE

OT Words

nākāh [**נָכָה, 5221**]

nākāh is a verb found in 500 contexts with the primary sense of "strike," or "afflict," as well as related nuances. (→ KILL)

"Striking" is an action predicated of God in the context of judgment and punishment for sin. Yahweh is said to "strike" the earth (Gen. 8:21; Mal. 4:6). He strikes the people of Israel with a plague (Num. 11:33) and promises to "afflict" them with madness when they rebel against him (cf. Deut. 28:28). Divine "affliction" is also viewed as a disciplinary measure in Isa. 1:5; 5:25. Similarly, Yahweh is said to "strike," or "afflict," his enemies in Exod. 3:20; 1 Sam. 5:9. In particular, Yahweh fatally "strikes" the firstborn son of Pharaoh as a component of the final judgment on the nation of Egypt (cf. Exod. 12:12, 29; Num. 3:13; Ps. 78:51). Metaphorically speaking, God is exhorted to "strike" his enemies on the face (Ps. 3:7).

nākāh refers to human beings "striking" as in combat in Gen. 14:5ff. Moses "strikes" the water of the Nile River to initiate a plague judgment on Egypt in Exod. 7:20 (cf. also Exod. 8:16ff.; 9:15ff., 25). He also strikes a rock in Exod. 17:6 to provide a miraculous supply of water for the Israelite people in the wilderness.

nākāh also means "beat" (i.e., administer a beating) in the context of a physical fight (cf. Exod. 5:14; 21:15ff.), or as a judicial sentence (cf. Deut. 5:7). Striking someone on the cheek suggests an insult in Job 16:10.

The phenomenon of being "conscience-stricken" is also indicated in 1 Sam. 24:5; 2 Sam. 24:10.

nāgaph [**נָגַף, 5062**]

nāgaph is a verb synonymous with ***nākāh*** (see above), found approximately fifty times. It means "strike," "injure" in a number of different contexts.

God is said to "strike" or "afflict" the nation of Egypt with plagues (cf. Exod. 8:2; 12:23, 27; Josh. 24:5); and also to punish his own people the same way in Exod. 32:35. See also 2 Sam. 12:15.

In the human sphere, Exod. 21:22 records the instance of people "striking" or "hurting" each other. In a metaphorical context, Ps. 91:12 refers to striking one's foot against a stone.

Exod. 21:35 refers to animals "injuring" other creatures.

hālam [**הָלַם, 1986**]

hālam is a verb found nine times, meaning "strike" in several contexts. It refers to a fatal wounding in Judg. 5:26, and to "beating" in a physical sense in Prov. 23:35. See also Isa. 41:7.

sāphaq [**סָפַק, 5606**]

sāphaq is a verb meaning "strike," "clap," "slap" in most of its ten occurrences.

God is said to "strike" (i.e., punish) people for their sin in Job 34:26; Ezek. 21:12.

People "clap" their hands together in Num. 24:10; Job 27:23, Lam. 2:15. In Jer. 31:19, "slapping" one's thigh constitutes an expression of anguish.

***meḥā'* [מְחָא, 4223]**

meḥā' is an Aramaic verb occurring four times. It means "strike" in Dan. 2:34, 35 in relation to the stone "striking" the feet of the statue in Nebuchadnezzar's dream.

NT Words

***typtō* [τύπτω, *5180*]**

typtō is a verb meaning "strike," "beat," "wound" throughout its usage (fourteen times).

The action of "beating" one's servants is noted in Matt. 24:49; Luke 12:45. "Striking" someone on the face is indicated in Luke 6:29; 22:64; Acts 23:2ff. See also Matt. 27:30; Mark 15:19.

"Striking or beating one's breast" is a sign of repentance in Luke 18:13; 23:48.

***patassō* [πατάσσω, *3960*]**

patassō means "to strike" in several different contexts. The verb occurs ten times.

It is used metaphorically in the expression "to strike the shepherd" with reference to Christ's imminent death (Matt. 26:31; Mark 14:27; Luke 22:50).

General references to people "striking" include the use of a sword in Matt. 26:51; Luke 22:49. See also Acts 7:24; 12:7.

God is said to strike (or afflict) the earth with plagues in the visionary context of Rev. 11:6. See also Rev. 19:15. An angel of God is said to "strike" King Herod with a fatal illness in Acts 12:23.

***derō* [δέρω, *1194*]**

derō is a verb meaning to "beat," "give a beating" (i.e., a physical assault). The term is found in fifteen contexts (cf. Matt. 21:35; Mark 12:3ff.; Luke 12:47ff.; Acts 5:40; 22:19).

derō also refers to the accusers of Christ at his trial "striking" him on the face (John 18:23). See also 2 Cor. 11:20; 1 Cor. 9:26.

***paiō* [παίω, *3817*]**

paiō is a verb found in five places and meaning "strike," "sting."

Mark 14:47; John 18:10 refer to striking someone with a sword. ***paiō*** refers to "striking" Christ on the face in Luke 22:64; Matt. 26:68, in the context of his humiliating treatment at his trial. The "strike," or "sting," of a scorpion is mentioned in Rev. 9:5.

***rhapizō* [ῥαπίζω, *4474*]**

rhapizō is a verb meaning "to slap" (with the hand) in reference to striking the face (Matt. 5:39; 26:6, 7).

***rhapisma* [ῥάπισμα, *4475*]**

rhapisma is a term denoting a "blow or slap on the face," given with the hand (cf. Mark 14:65; John 18:22; 19:3).

STRIVE

OT Words

***rîb* [רִיב, 7378]**

rîb is a verb occurring around seventy times with the basic meaning "to engage in a dispute." It is translated "strive," "contend," "quarrel," as well as the significant extended sense of "to conduct a lawsuit," or "make a formal legal complaint." This latter extended sense is evident in the context of Yahweh's response to Israel's violation of her covenant oath. It also refers to legal disputes among people. There are also several significant related nuances.

The basic meaning "to strive, contend with," in the context of general quarreling or disputing is evident, for example, in Gen. 26:20ff.; Exod. 17:2; 21:18; Judg. 8:1; Neh. 13:11. ***rîb*** also refers to "making a legal complaint" (cf. Prov. 23:11; 25:8ff.; Isa. 1:17). See also Prov. 3:30.

Arguing or disputing with God is indicated in Job 9:3; 33:13; 40:2; Isa. 45:9; Jer. 12:1 (cf. also Job 10:21; 23:6; Ps. 103:9).

Ps. 35:1 contains a plea for God to "contend against" the enemies of the psalmist. The psalmist pleads with God to "defend the cause" of God's people against their enemies in Pss. 43:1; 74:22; 119:154. In a number of places, Yahweh is said "to take up the cause" of his people, defending and protecting them (cf. Isa. 51:22; Jer. 50:34; 51:36; Lam. 3:58; Mic. 7:9).

In a significant theological sense, Yahweh is said "to bring charges against," or "take up a legal indictment against" his people for violating their covenant oath of allegiance in relation to the demand for exclusive loyalty towards him (cf. Isa. 3:13; Jer. 2:9; Mic. 6:1).

nāṣāh **[נָצָה, 5327]**

nāṣāh is a verb found eleven times, meaning "struggle" or "fight" in a physical encounter in most contexts (cf. Exod. 2:13; 21:22; Lev. 24:10; Deut. 25:11). In Num. 26:9, ***nāṣāh*** means "argue," or "dispute."

yārîb **[יָרִיב, 3401]**

yārîb is a verb meaning "strive," "contend," or "quarrel" (cf. Ps. 35:1; Jer. 49:25).

gārāh **[גָּרָה, 1624]**

gārāh is a verb meaning "contend," or "struggle," in some of the fourteen places in which it occurs. Deut. 2:9, 24 refer to a military "struggle." The action of "struggling, or striving" against Yahweh is indicated in Jer. 50:24. See also Prov. 28:4.

'āsaq **[עָשַׂק, 6229]**

'āsaq is a rare verb found only in Gen. 26:20 with reference to "quarreling" between herdsmen.

NT Words

machomai [μάχομαι, *3164*]

machomai is a verb found four times meaning "fight," primarily in the sense of "arguing," or "quarreling" (cf. John 6:52; Acts 7:26; 2 Tim. 2:24; Jas. 4:2).

diamachomai [διαμάχομαι, *1264*]

diamachomai is a rare verb found only in Acts 23:9 meaning "to argue, dispute" vigorously.

agōnizomai [ἀγωνίζομαι, *75*]

agōnizomai is a verb found seven times, meaning "strive" in the sense of "put in a great effort to obtain a result" in the majority of these contexts.

The attitude of "striving" in order to gain salvation is indicated in Luke 13:24; 1 Tim. 6:12; 2 Tim. 4:7. See also John 18:36.

Col. 1:29 refers to the "struggle" to present people mature in Christ.

spoudazō [σπουδάζω, *4704*]

spoudazō is a verb meaning "to strive" in the sense of "make every effort." It is synonymous with ***agōnizomai*** (see above) and occurs eleven times.

Eph. 4:3 refers to "striving to maintain the unity of the Spirit." 2 Tim. 2:15 advocates making the effort to be an accurate and faithful teacher of God's word.

2 Pet. 1:10 refers to striving to make one's calling and election sure, and Heb. 4:11 refers to the struggle to enter into one's eternal rest.

Other general references include those in 1 Thess. 2:17; 2 Tim. 4:9; Titus 3:12; 2 Pet. 1:12; 3:14.

See Also: ➞ FIGHT

STRONG, STRONGHOLD ➞ STRENGTH

STUBBLE ➞ CHAFF

STUBBORN

OT Words

sārar **[סָרַר, 5637]**

sārar is a verb found in seventeen contexts meaning "to be stubborn, or rebellious."

The attitude of being stubborn in the sense of refusing to heed instruction or advice is evident in Deut. 21:18ff.; Neh. 9:29; Prov. 7:11.

References to those who "rebel against" God are found in Pss. 66:7; 68:6, 18; 78:8; Isa. 1:23; 30:1; Jer. 5:23; Hos. 4:16, Zech. 7:11.

qāsheh **[קָשֶׁה, 7186]**

qāsheh is an adjective meaning "stubborn," or "obstinate," in several of the forty or so contexts in which the term occurs. (➞ HARD)

The stubborn attitude of the Israelite people towards Yahweh is noted in Exod. 32:9; 33:3ff.; Deut. 9:6, 13; 31:27; Judg. 2:19; Isa. 48:4; Ezek. 2:4.

qeshî **[קְשִׁי, 7190]**

qeshî is a noun found only in Deut. 9:27, referring to Israel's "stubbornness" towards God.

NT Words

sklērotrachēlos [σκληροτράχηλος, *4644*]

sklērotrachēlos is a rare adjectival form found only in Acts 7:51, denoting people who are "stubborn," "stiff-necked," or "obstinate" — an accusation directed at the Jewish religious leaders by Stephen, the first Christian martyr.

STUMBLE

OT Words

nāgaph **[נָגַף, 5062]**

nāgaph is a verb occurring around fifty times with the primary sense of "strike." However, in Prov. 3:23; Jer. 13:16, it refers to feet stumbling. (➞ STRIKE)

pûq **[פּוּק, 6328]**

pûq is a rare verb found in Isa. 28:7 meaning "stumble" in reference to priests and prophets giving incoherent judgments as a consequence of alcohol abuse.

shāmat **[שָׁמַט, 8058]**

shāmat is a verb found eight times, and in 2 Kgs. 9:33 it refers to oxen "stumbling."

negeph **[נֶגֶף, 5063]**

negeph is a noun derived from ***nāgaph***, above, with the primary meaning "plague." However, in Isa. 8:14 it refers to a "stone of stumbling" — a metaphorical reference to the Messiah, who will bring about the downfall of those who refuse to accept him as such.

NT Words

proskoptō [προσκόπτω, *4350*]

proskoptō is a verb expressing the sense of "stumble" in the majority of its eight occurrences.

A literal reference to stumbling is found in John 11:9ff.

In metaphorical contexts, ***proskoptō*** is translated "stumble" in relation to "falling" (in a spiritual sense) or failing to exercise faith. These consequences are evident in Rom. 9:32; 1 Pet. 2:8, with reference to those who "stumble over" the "stumbling stone," which is Christ. In Rom. 14:21, ***proskoptō*** indicates the action of causing someone "to commit sin" (i.e., stumble).

ptaiō [πταίω, *4417*]

ptaiō is a verb found in six places meaning "stumble." In Rom. 11:11 it refers to the possibility — denied by Paul — of Israel "having lost all hope" of future salvation.

See Also: → FALL → STUMBLING BLOCK

STUMBLING BLOCK

OT Words

mikshôl **[מִכְשׁוֹל, 4383]**

mikshôl is a noun used metaphorically, denoting a "stumbling block" that indicates an impediment to righteous action. Or, negatively, it can be an occasion promoting transgression or ill treatment.

Reference is made to a "stumbling block" for blind people in Lev. 19:14. The term is translated "offense" (i.e., cause for sorrow, or anguish) in 1 Sam. 25:31.

mikshôl also refers to the "rock of offense," denoting the Messiah in Isa. 8:14 — a stumbling block to those who refuse to believe in him.

Other general references to this phenomenon include those in Ps. 119:165; Isa. 57:14; Jer. 6:21; Ezek. 3:20; 7:19; 14:3ff.; 44:12.

NT Words

proskomma [πρόσκομμα, *4348*]

proskomma is a noun occurring six times, a dynamic equivalent to the Hebrew ***mikshôl*** (see above). The term denotes a "stumbling block" with reference to an obstacle that causes people to sin if they are not wary of it.

1 Pet. 2:8; Rom. 9:32, 33 refer to Christ "the stumbling stone" (citing Isa. 8:14) who, if rejected by unbelievers, will bring about their spiritual ruin.

The meaning "stumbling block" in the sense of causing people to sin is evident in Rom. 14:13, 20; 1 Cor. 8:9. These contexts warn against placing such an obstacle in the way of another believer.

skandalon [σκάνδαλον, *4625*]

skandalon is a noun synonymous with ***proskomma*** (see above), denoting a "stumbling block," "offense" or "temptation to sin." The term is found in fifteen contexts.

The meaning "stumbling block" is indicated in Matt. 13:41; 16:23; Rom. 11:9; 1 Cor. 1:23. In particular, Gal. 5:11 refers to the "stumbling block" of the cross. References to Christ as the "rock of offense" are found in Rom. 9:33; 1 Pet. 2:8.

The sense of "temptation to sin" is evident in Matt. 18:7; Luke 17:1; Rom. 14:13; 1 John 2:10.

SUBDUE → SUBJECT

SUBJECT, SUBJECTION

OT Words

kābash **[כָּבַשׁ, 3533]**

kābash is a verb meaning "subdue," "bring into subjection," as well as associated senses. The term is found in fifteen contexts.

In Gen. 1:28, God calls upon human beings "to subdue" the earth in the sense of "make subservient," "dominate," or "bring under control."

Elsewhere, the meaning "subdue" indicates the sense of "bring into subjection," such as the Israelites "subduing" the land of Canaan (cf. Num. 32:22, 29; Josh. 18:1), and David subduing foreign nations (2 Sam. 8:11; 1 Chr. 22:18).

kābash also expresses the idea of "subject to slavery," "bring into bondage," evident in 2 Chr. 28:10; Neh. 5:5; Jer. 34:11, 16.

kāna' [כָּנַע, 3665]

kāna' is a verb found nearly thirty-five times with the primary sense of "to be humble," "be humbled." This term, however, also means "subdue" in the sense of "bring into subjection." There is some overlap in meaning with that of "to humble," or "humiliate."

God is said to "subdue" the enemies of Israel in the sense of "bringing about their defeat" in a military context (cf. Deut. 9:3; Judg. 3:30; 11:33; 1 Sam. 7:13; 2 Sam. 8:1; Ps. 106:42). In particular, in 1 Chr. 17:10 Yahweh promises David that he will "subdue" all his enemies. Elsewhere, Yahweh is said to "subdue" Judah in the sense of "subjecting her to humiliation" because of King Ahaz's covenant faithlessness toward him (cf. 2 Chr. 28:19). See also Job 40:12.

kāna' also refers to Israel being "subdued" (i.e., defeated) in the civil war with Judah.

rādad [רָדַד, 7286]

rādad is a verb occurring four times, meaning "subdue" in relation to "bringing nations into subjection" in Ps. 144:2; Isa. 45:1. In both cases, Yahweh initiates the action.

NT Words

hypotassō [ὑποτάσσω, *5293*]

hypotassō is a verb occurring about forty times with the senses of "subject to," "submit to," "bring into subjection," as well as related nuances.

The meaning "submit," "be subject to" has the underlying sense of "to obey," "be obedient" in a variety of contexts. Jesus willingly submits to his parents' directions in Luke 2:51. There are exhortations to submit to governing authorities in Rom. 13:1; Titus 3:1; 1 Pet. 2:13. Women are to "submit" to their husbands (cf. 1 Cor. 14:24; Eph. 5:22; Col. 3:18; Titus 2:5; 1 Pet. 3:1, 5). Slaves are enjoined to "submit" to their masters (Titus 2:9; 1 Pet. 2:18). Demons are said to "be subject to" (i.e., under the control of) the apostles during their evangelistic mission (Luke 10:17ff.). The unregenerate human mind does not submit itself to the law of God (cf. Rom. 8:7).

Several texts affirm that God "has subjected" all things under his rule (cf. 1 Cor. 15:27ff.; Eph. 1:22; Phil. 3:21; Heb. 2:8). 1 Pet. 3:22 affirms that all things "are subject" to Christ. The church's "submission" to her Lord is noted in Eph. 5:24. Creation is said "to be subjected" to futility by the will of God in Rom. 8:20.

Other general references to the attitude or stance of "submission," "subjection" include those in 1 Cor. 14:32; Eph. 5:21; Heb. 12:9; Jas. 4:7; 1 Pet. 5:5.

enochos [ἔνοχος, *1777*]

enochos is an adjective meaning "in danger of," "liable to" in most of its ten occurrences. However, in Heb. 2:15, ***enochos*** indicates the state of "being held in slavery" (i.e., subject to bondage) through the fear of death.

doulagōgeō [δουλαγωγέω, *1396*]

doulagōgeō is a rare verb found only in 1 Cor. 9:27 with reference to "subduing" the body (i.e., bringing it under control).

hypotagē [ὑποταγή, *5292*]

hypotagē is a noun denoting "subjection" in the sense of "submission," "obedience." It occurs four times, signifying obedience to the gospel (2 Cor. 9:13) and children obeying their parents (1 Tim. 3:4). See also Gal. 2:5; 1 Tim. 2:11.

SUBMIT → SUBJECT

SUBSTANCE → POSSESS

SUCCEED, SUCCESS

OT Words

ṣālēaḥ [צָלֵחַ, 6743]

ṣālēaḥ is a verb with the dominant sense of "succeed," "prosper" in a variety of contexts. It occurs sixty-five times.

The meaning "succeed," "be prosperous" in a material, economic sense is indicated in Gen. 24:21; Jer. 12:1. The success of Joseph in Egypt in Gen. 39:2ff. refers to the improvement, or advancement, in his position or status. Success as a blessing from God is indicated in 1 Chr. 29:23; 2 Chr. 26:5; Isa. 48:15. In particular, the messianic Suffering Servant is said to prosper in Isa. 53:10. To succeed in the sense of accomplishing a task is indicated in the context of military success in 1 Kgs. 22:12; and in building the temple in 1 Chr. 22:11ff. On the other hand, no such success is possible for those who are opposed to God (cf. 2 Chr. 13:12; 24:20; Prov. 28:13; Jer. 22:30). The "little horn" of Dan. 8:12, 24, 25 enjoys a limited success perpetrating his wickedness. The word of God is guaranteed to prosper in Isa. 55:11. Success in conquering Canaan is noted in Josh. 1:8. ***ṣālēaḥ*** also conveys the meaning "to grant success," as noted in Gen. 24:40ff. Prayers for success to be granted are found in Neh. 1:11; Ps. 118:25. Neh. 2:20 indicates faith that God will grant success.

ṣālēaḥ also refers to a tree "thriving" in its growth (Ezek. 17:9, 10).

sākal [שָׂכַל, 7919]

sākal is a verb occurring around sixty times with the dominant sense of "be wise," "understand." In several instances, however, the term also means "prosper," "succeed."

The idea of "prospering," in the sense of enjoying the blessings of the old covenant in the land of Canaan, is indicated in Deut. 19:9; Josh. 1:7. Solomon's success as a godly king is recorded in 1 Kgs. 2:3.

The "messianic branch" (i.e., king) is said to prosper (Jer. 23:5); as is King David (1 Sam. 18:14ff.).

Jer. 10:21; 20:11 deny prosperity or success to those who fail to uphold God's law.

kāshēr [כָּשֵׁר, 3787]

kāshēr is a rare verb meaning "succeed" in Eccl. 11:6 in a non-specific context.

ṣelaḥ [צְלַח, 6744 (Aramaic)]

ṣelaḥ is an Aramaic verb, found in four places, with the sense of "prosper," "succeed," "have success." Ezra 5:8 refers to the people "succeeding," or making progress, in their efforts to rebuild the temple. Ezra 6:14 refers to the postexilic community prospering under the ministries of Haggai and Zechariah. Dan. 6:28 mentions the political and personal prosperity of Daniel.

SUCKLE → NURSE

SUDDEN, SUDDENLY

OT WORDS

pit'ôm [פִּתְאוֹם, 6597]

pit'ôm is an adverbial form occurring twenty-five times with the sense of "suddenly." It is also used adjectivally.

Where human beings are concerned it is used, for example, in the contexts of action (cf. Num. 6:9; Job 9:23); of the onset of terror (cf. Prov. 3:25); of an unexpected attack (cf. Ps. 64:4); of calamity (cf. Prov. 6:15; Isa. 47:11). See also Job 5:3; 9:23; Eccl. 9:12.

God is also said to act suddenly in regard to speaking (cf. Num. 12:4); attacking (cf. Ps. 64:7); and judging his people (cf. Jer. 15:8).

peta' [פֶּתַע, 6621]

peta' is an adjective denoting the sense of "sudden" in Num. 6:9; Prov. 6:15; 29:1; Hab. 2:7.

NT WORDS

exaiphnēs [ἐξαίφνης, *1810*]

exaiphnēs is used adverbially in five contexts denoting the sense of "suddenly" (cf. Mark 13:36; Luke 2:13; 9:39; Acts 9:3; 22:6).

SUFFER

NT WORDS

paschō [πάσχω, *3958*]

paschō is a verb found in around forty places meaning "to suffer," referring to enduring both physical and emotional trauma.

paschō frequently refers to the "suffering" borne by Christ. Christ's suffering on the cross is anticipated in Matt. 16:21; 17:12; Mark 8:31; 9:12; Luke 9:22; 17:25; 22:15. Reflection on his ordeal after the event but prior to his ascension is found in Luke 24:26. The prophetic prediction of his suffering is recorded in Luke 24:46; Acts 3:18. Mention of his "passion" as a matter of history is noted in Acts 1:3; Heb. 2:18; 5:8; 9:26; 13:12; 1 Pet. 2:21. Paul's determination to demonstrate to his fellow countrymen that the Old Testament prophets had actually predicted the suffering of Christ and his subsequent resurrection is indicated in Acts 17:3.

Elsewhere, human suffering is noted in relation to psychological torment (Matt. 27:19); to illness (Mark 5:26); to the agony of persecution (Luke 13:2; Phil. 1:29; 1 Thess. 2:14; 1 Pet. 2:19ff.; 3:17; 4:1; Rev. 2:10); and to suffering in general (1 Cor. 12:26).

adikeō [ἀδικέω, *91*]

adikeō is a verb found nearly thirty times with the predominant sense of "hurt," "do wrong." However, Acts 7:24 refers to Moses having seen one of his Israelite countrymen "suffering wrong" at the hands of an Egyptian overseer.

zēmioō [ζημιόω, *2210*]

zēmioō is a verb found six times meaning "to lose" and also "to suffer loss." The latter sense is indicated in

1 Cor. 3:15, referring to the prospective loss of reward experienced by the believer on the final day of judgment. In Phil. 2:8, Paul declares that he "has suffered the loss" of all things for the sake of Christ.

Additional Notes

The Old and New Testament vocabulary for "suffer" has the dual senses of "permit" or "allow," as well as that of "bearing affliction or pain," both physical and emotional. (→ AFFLICT → PERMIT)

SUN, SUNRISE

OT Words

shemesh **[שֶׁמֶשׁ, 8121]**

shemesh is a noun denoting "the sun" as a created heavenly body in most of the 130 or so contexts in which it is found. ***shemesh*** also conveys the meaning "sunrise." The term is used both literally and metaphorically.

General references to the sun include those in Gen. 15:12ff.; Exod. 16:21; Ps. 74:16; Eccl. 1:3ff.; Jonah 4:8. In particular, Josh 10:12ff. describes the miraculous halting of the sun's progress in the sky for one whole day. It is also designated as an object of worship in Deut. 4:19; 17:3; Ezek. 8:16 — all of which depict episodes of idolatry. Num. 21:11; Josh. 1:15; Isa. 45:6 describe the sunrise.

There are several references to the darkening of the sun as one component of the anticipated cataclysmic dissolution of the universe in the last days (cf. Isa. 13:10; Ezek. 32:7; Joel 2:10, 31; 3:15; Amos 8:9).

In metaphorical contexts, God is described as a "sun," the source of light (cf. Ps. 84:11). The phrase "sun of righteousness" is employed as a divine title in Mal. 4:2. The enigmatic phrase "under the sun" in the book of Ecclesiastes is a common expression that alludes to the entire range of human experience, largely negative in its assessment (cf. Eccl. 1:4; 2:11, 17ff.; 3:16; 4:1ff.; 5:13ff.; 6:1ff.; 7:11; 8:9ff.; 9:3ff.; 10:5). The overall impression is that life is wholly futile, apart from divinely revealed principles for living contained in the law of God.

ḥeres **[חֶרֶס, 2775]**

ḥeres is a rare noun, denoting the sun in Judg. 14:18; Job 9:7.

ḥammāh **[חַמָּה, 2535]**

ḥammāh is a noun synonymous with ***shemesh*** and ***ḥeres.*** It is found in six contexts, with reference to the sun in Job 30:28; Song 6:10; Isa. 24:23; 30:26.

'ôr **[אוֹר, 216]**

'ôr is the common term for "light" in the Old Testament. However, ***'ôr*** refers to the sun in Job 31:26.

mizrāḥ **[מִזְרָח, 4217]**

mizrāḥ is a term with primary reference to the "east," and by extension it refers to the "sunrise" in several places (cf. Num. 21:11; 34:15; Josh. 1:15; 12:1; 19:27).

NT Words

hēlios **[ἥλιος, *2246*]**

hēlios is a noun occurring thirty times, meaning "sun" throughout most of this usage. Literal references to the sun include those in Matt. 5:45; Mark 1:32; Luke 4:40; Acts 13:11; 1 Cor. 15:41; Eph. 4:26; Rev. 7:16; 21:23.

Repeating the Old Testament apocalyptic theme of cosmic disintegration, the darkening of the sun is noted in Matt. 24:29; Mark 13:24; Luke 23:45 (cf. also Luke 21:25); Acts 2:20; Rev. 6:12.

hēlios is also utilized in metaphorical contexts. The righteous are said "to shine like the sun" (Matt. 13:43); as is the face of Christ on the occasion of his transfiguration (Matt. 17:2), and in heaven (Rev. 1:16; 10:1). The woman in Rev. 12:1, most likely at one level a symbolic depiction of Mary the mother of Christ, is described in John's vision as being "clothed with the sun."

Additional Notes

Significant in the usage of "sun" imagery throughout both Old and New Testaments are the references to the darkening of the sun as the sign of impending cosmic dissolution. The Old Testament references are cast in the contexts of apocalyptic-style prophecy in relation to the final Day of the Lord judgment. And in the New Testament, Jesus refers to this same phenomenon as one of the distinctive features that will herald the end of the universe prior to the final judgment.

SUPPER → FEAST

SUPPLICATION

OT Words

teḥinnāh **[תְּחִנָּה, 8467]**

teḥinnāh is a noun denoting the primary sense of "supplication," or "plea." It refers to an "earnest request," mainly in the context of prayer directed to Yahweh. The term occurs around twenty-five times.

This attitude is reflected in Solomon's prayer of dedication for the temple in 1 Kgs. 8:28ff.; 9:3; 1 Chr. 6:19ff. See also Pss. 6:9; 55:1; 119:170; Jer. 36:7; 42:2; Dan. 9:20.

There is also reference to a "plea" directed to King Zedekiah in Jer. 37:20; 38:26.

ḥānan **[חָנַן, 2603]**

ḥānan is a verb with the primary meanings "show mercy, favor, or grace," "be merciful, gracious" in most of its approximately eighty occurrences. In several places, however, ***ḥānan*** means "to make supplication," "plead," "make earnest request" of God in prayer (cf. 1 Kgs. 8:33, 47, 59; 9:3; 2 Chr. 6:24, 37; Job 8:5; Pss. 30:8; 142:1; Hos. 12:4). Such pleading is also directed to human beings (cf. 2 Kgs. 1:13; Esth. 4:8; 8:3).

taḥanûn **[תַּחֲנוּן, 8469]**

taḥanûn is a noun derived from ***ḥānan*** (see above) denoting a "supplication," "plea," or "request" made primarily to God in prayer (cf. 2 Chr. 6:21; Job 41:3; Pss. 28:2, 6; 31:22; 140:6; Jer. 3:21; Dan. 9:3, 17ff.). Such "requests" are also made of human beings in Prov. 18:23.

NT Words

deēsis **[δέησις, *1162*]**

deēsis is a noun meaning "prayer," or "supplication," in most of its nineteen occurrences (cf. Acts 1:14; Eph. 6:18; Phil. 4:6; 1 Tim. 2:1; 5:5). (→ PRAYER)

hiketēria **[ἱκετηρία, *2428*]**

hiketēria is a rare noun found only in Heb. 5:7 with reference to "supplication," or "earnest prayer" offered by Christ to God during his time on earth.

SUPPOSE → THINK

SURE → SAFE → TRUST

SURETY → GUARANTEE

SURROUND

OT Words

sābab **[סָבַב, 5437]**

This verb is found approximately 170 times in the Old Testament with various meanings, including "surround" or "encircle," "go (or come) around," and "turn" (with various nuances of meaning). (→ TURN)

sābab means "surround" about fifty times in the Old Testament. It is used both literally and metaphorically. One of the most striking literal uses of the word is found in the accounts of the conquest of Canaan by the Israelite tribes under the leadership of Joshua. In particular, the destruction of the city of Jericho takes place after the Israelites surround the city, march around it seven times, and then shout, bringing the walls down and destroying the city (cf. Josh. 6:3ff.). A contrasting perspective is given in Josh. 7:9 when, after the defeat inflicted on the Israelites by the citizens of Ai, Joshua expresses the fear that the Canaanites themselves would now surround the Israelites and engulf them.

Other references to ***sābab*** with this literal sense of "surround" are found in Gen. 19:4; Judg. 19:22; 1 Kgs. 5:3; 2 Sam. 18:15; 2 Kgs. 6:15; 2 Chr. 4:3.

sābab is also used in a metaphorical sense to indicate people being "surrounded," or "engulfed," "overwhelmed" by a set of traumatic circumstances. This is evident in the experience of Jonah, for example, when he is thrown overboard into the sea, only to be swallowed by a great fish (cf. Jonah 2:3, 5). David expresses this same sense of overwhelming anxiety and grief in 2 Sam. 22:6. The psalmist also voices his cry of distress at being surrounded by many sorrows and trials (cf. Pss. 17:11; 18:5; 22:12, 16; 88:17; 109:3; 118:10ff.); as does Job (cf. Job 16:13). Israel's sins are described as surrounding her in Hos. 7:2; and even God affirms Israel's wickedness by noting that his people have surrounded him with their lies (cf. Hos. 11:12).

The metaphorical use of ***sābab*** in this sense, however, is not always negative. The psalmist rejoices in the hope, for instance, that God will surround him with songs (cf. Ps. 32:7); and mercy (cf. Ps. 32:10). The prophet Jeremiah records the prophecy that one day a "woman will surround a man." In the context of Jer. 31:22, this promise is revealed as part of the wonderful renewal of God's people, anticipated in the coming age of new covenant blessing, where the marriage between a man and a woman will be characterized by a genuine intimacy of love and compassion.

sābab also means "go (or come) around" in various contexts — a derivative meaning from the primary sense of "surround." It is used this way, for example, to describe the prophetic "circuit" of Samuel, the last of Israel's major judges and a great prophetic figure in Old Testament history. The idea behind this reference in 1 Sam. 7:16 is that Samuel "went around from town to town" teaching and ministering to the people of Israel as he went. This idea of "going around" from one location to another in a literal sense is also found in Eccl. 2:20; 12:5; Ezek. 42:19; Ps. 48:12; Isa. 23:16; Song 3:3; 5:7. The term is also applied in this sense to the course of the rivers mentioned in Gen. 2:11, 13, which watered the garden of Eden.

'āphaph **[אָפַף, 661]**

This term is used five times in the Old Testament with the metaphorical meaning "engulf," or "surround." The orientation is wholly negative, indicating death or trauma in each case (cf. 2 Sam. 22:5; Pss. 18:4; 40:12; 116:3; Jonah 2:5).

nāqaph **[נָקַף, 5362]**

nāqaph is a synonym for ***sābab***, occurring about fifteen times and meaning "surround" and "engulf." The former sense is found in a predominantly literal context (cf. 2 Kgs. 11:8; 2 Chr. 23:7; Josh. 6:3, 11; Ps. 48:12; 2 Kgs. 6:14). The meaning "engulf," however, is largely metaphorical (cf. Job 19:6; Pss. 17:9; 22:16; 88:17; Lam. 3:5).

kātar **[כָּתַר, 3803]**

Another synonym for ***sābab*** and ***nāqaph***, above, ***kātar*** occurs four times. It has the literal meaning "surround" in Judg. 20:43, and the metaphorical sense of "engulf" in Pss. 22:12; 142:7; Hab. 1:4.

NT Words

kykloō [κυκλόω, *2944*]

kykloō is a verb found five times meaning "surround," "encircle."

Luke 21:20 refers to the future "surrounding" of Jerusalem predicted by Christ. Heb. 11:30 refers to the Israelites of old "encircling" Jericho. John 10:24; Acts 14:20 refer to "surrounding" people in general.

perikykloō [περικυκλόω, *4033*]

perikykloō is a rare variant of ***kykloō***, above, found only in Luke 19:43 and referring to the enemies of God's people "surrounding" or "encircling" them.

perikeimai [περίκειμαι, *4029*]

perikeimai is a verb referring metaphorically in Heb. 12:1 to God's people "being surrounded" by a host of faithful witnesses from the old covenant era.

(→ HANG)

SWALLOW

OT Words

bāla' **[בָּלַע, 1104]**

bāla' is a verb found in fifty places with primary reference to "swallowing" in the metaphorical sense of "engulf," or "devour."

General references to such a phenomenon include those in Gen. 41:7, 24; Exod. 7:12; 2 Sam. 17:16; Ps. 69:15; Prov. 1:12. In particular, the earth is described as opening up and "swallowing" people alive as a method of divine capital punishment (cf. Num. 16:30ff.; 26:10; Deut. 11:6; Ps. 106:17). See also Exod. 15:12. Jonah 1:17 refers to a whale swallowing the prophet Jonah alive.

Elsewhere, the use of ***bāla'*** is metaphorical. The fate of being swallowed by the wrath of God is indicated in Ps. 21:9. See also Ps. 124:3. References to being "swallowed up" in the sense of being "destroyed" are found in 2 Sam. 20:19ff.; Job 37:20. The "swallowing up" of death is noted in Isa. 25:8. An unusual expression in Job 7:19, "to swallow saliva," refers to "the passing of a fleeting moment."

NT Words

katapinō [καταπίνω, *2666*]

katapinō is a verb found in seven contexts meaning "swallow," "drink," "devour" in predominantly metaphorical contexts.

The expression "swallow a camel" indicates the act of ignoring very obvious faults or flaws in one's behavior (cf. Matt. 23:24). Rev. 12:16 speaks of the earth swallowing up a river. 1 Cor. 15:54 refers to death being swallowed up in the victory of Christ over sin. Similarly, mortal life is swallowed up to eternal life in 2 Cor. 5:4. The state of being swallowed up (or overwhelmed) by emotion is indicated in 2 Cor. 2:7. Heb. 11:29 speaks of being swallowed up by water, or drowned.

SWEAR

OT Words

shāba' **[שָׁבַע, 7650]**

shāba' is a verb found nearly two hundred times with the primary meanings "swear," or "take an oath" in the large majority of contexts, as well as some related nuances.

The action of swearing by God, indicating the utterance of a solemn oath, is noted in Gen. 21:23ff.; 1 Sam. 28:10; Pss. 63:11; 119:106; 132:2; Jer. 12:16. This term also indicates the sense of "making someone swear an oath" (cf. Gen. 24:37; Josh. 2:17ff.; Judg. 15:12;

1 Sam. 14:28; Neh. 13:25). Lev. 6:3ff.; Jer. 5:2; 7:9; Zech. 5:4 refer to swearing falsely. Num. 30:2; Judg. 21:7 refer to making a vow to the Lord; and Isa. 19:18 refers specifically to swearing allegiance to Yahweh.

There are a number of contexts in which God is said to swear, or utter, an oath. He is said to swear by himself in Gen. 22:16; Ps. 110:4; Isa. 14:24; 45:23; Jer. 44:26. He also makes a solemn oath for the purposes of punishing sin in Deut. 1:35; 1 Sam. 3:14; Ps. 95:11; Isa. 62:8; Jer. 22:5; Amos 4:2; 6:8.

In relation to the destiny of his people, Yahweh swears to give the land of Canaan to the descendants of Abraham under the terms of the covenant promise (cf. Gen. 24:7; 26:3; Exod. 13:5, 11; Num. 32:11; Deut. 26:15; Josh. 1:6; Judg. 2:1; Jer. 32:22). He also swears a covenant promise to David to grant him a perpetual royal lineage (cf. Ps. 89:3). Yahweh is said to "enter into a solemn marriage vow" with his people in Ezek. 16:8.

nāsā' [נָשָׂא, 5375]

nāsā' is a common verb found in over 650 contexts with the primary sense of "lift (up)," "take," "bear." However, in Num. 14:30; Exod. 6:8; Neh. 9:15, the term refers to God's solemn covenant oath in which he "swore" to give the land of Canaan to the descendants of Abraham.

'ālāh [אָלָה, 422 (Verb), 423 (Noun)]

'ālāh as a verb is found in four contexts meaning "utter a curse," "swear an oath." The former sense is indicated in Judg. 17:2. General references to swearing an oath include those in 1 Kgs. 8:31; 2 Chr. 6:22; Hos. 4:2; 10:4.

The noun ***'ālāh*** is identical with its verbal form. It is found in around forty contexts, meaning "curse," "oath."

General references to an "oath" are found in Gen. 24:41; Lev. 5:1; 1 Kgs. 8:31. Num. 5:21ff. refers to an oath that contained a built-in curse.

The oath associated with ratifying the divine covenant is indicated in Deut. 29:12ff.; Ezek. 16:59. More particularly, several contexts speak of the curse sanctions of the covenant (cf. Deut. 29:20ff.; 30:7; Isa. 24:6; Jer. 23:10; Dan. 9:11; Zech. 5:3).

NT Words

omnyō [ὀμνύω, *3660*]

omnyō is a verb found in thirty contexts with the consistent meaning "to swear."

Matt. 5:34ff.; Jas. 5:16 command human beings not to swear (cf. Matt. 23:16ff.). "Invoking a curse" is noted in Matt. 26:74; Mark 14:71. The action of swearing an oath is indicated in Mark 6:23; Heb. 6:16.

With reference to "divine oaths," God is said to grant his people the land of Canaan under the terms of his covenant "promise" (cf. Luke 1:73; Acts 7:17; Heb. 6:13). Acts 2:30 mentions the Davidic covenant oath. See also Heb. 7:21; Rev. 10:6.

omnyō is also used in the context of God bringing a solemn curse against his people by denying them rest in Canaan (cf. Heb. 3:11, 18; 4:3).

Additional Notes

"Swearing" in the Old Testament refers significantly to the covenant oaths made by God and entered into by the people. These refer either to the enjoyment of blessings in the land of Canaan for faithfulness to God, or to enduring disastrous consequences (i.e., curses), including loss of land, for rebellion against God.

In the New Testament, this blessing/curse motif in relation to the oaths of the covenant continues. God has faithfully kept his covenant "vows" and brought them to fulfillment in Christ, who embodies the "rest" to which the old covenant promises pointed. The curse of the covenant is still in force, however, for those who reject Christ.

SWIFT

OT Words

qal [קַל, 7031]

qal is an adjective occurring thirteen times meaning "swift" in most of these contexts. The term is also used adverbially.

In literal contexts, ***qal*** refers to people who are "fleet-footed" (i.e., swift of foot) (cf. 2 Sam. 2:18; Amos 2:15). Other general references to "those who are swift" include those in Eccl. 9:11; Isa. 18:2.

qal is used adverbially in Job 24:18; Isa. 5:26; Joel 3:4. Animals are also described as swift in Isa. 30:16; Jer. 2:23; Lam. 4:19.

qālal [קָלַל, 7043]

qālal is a verb meaning "be swifter than . . ." in five contexts. The dominant meaning is that of "curse," evident in the large majority of its approximately eighty occurrences.

The meaning "to be swifter than . . ." is indicated in relation to eagles (2 Sam. 1:23; Jer. 4:13; Lam. 4:19); and leopards (Hab. 1:8).

In relation to time, ***qālal*** expresses a metaphorical sense. One's days are said to "be swifter than a weaver's shuttle" (Job 7:6) and a runner (Job 9:25).

NT Words

oxys [ὀξύς, *3691*]

oxys is an adjective with the primary meaning "sharp." However, in Rom. 3:15 it means "swift," describing how quickly the wicked move to shed blood.

tachys [ταχύς, *5036*]

tachys is an adjective found only in Jas. 1:19, which contains the exhortation to be "swift to hear, and slow to speak."

tachinos [ταχινός, *5031*]

tachinos is a variant form of ***tachys*** (see above) with reference to the "swift" destruction that will come upon false teachers.

See Also: ➠ HASTE

SWINE

OT Words

ḥazîr [חֲזִיר, **2386**]

ḥazîr occurs around seven times, denoting "swine," "boar," "pig." This animal was deemed unclean by Mosaic law and thus its flesh constituted a forbidden food.

General references to "swine" include those in Ps. 80:13; Prov. 11:27. The flesh of pigs is designated as unclean, and thus forbidden as a food source (Lev. 11:7; Deut. 14:8; Isa. 65:4; 66:17). See also Isa. 66:3, where swine are described as an illegitimate, unclean offering.

NT Words

choiros [χοῖρος, *5519*]

choiros is the dynamic equivalent of the Hebrew *ḥazîr* (see above), denoting "swine," "pigs" in all fourteen occurrences (cf. Matt. 7:6; 8:3ff.; Mark 5:11ff.; Luke 8:32ff.; 15:15, 16).

SWORD

OT Words

ḥereb [חֶרֶב, **2719**]

ḥereb is a common noun found in approximately four hundred places, denoting a "sword" in almost every occurrence. It occurs, however, in a variety of contexts and with a variety of nuances.

Gen. 3:24 refers to a "flaming sword" held by an angel, guarding the way to the tree of life in Eden after Adam and Eve's expulsion from the garden paradise.

Literal references to the sword as a weapon are found in Exod. 32:27; Num. 19:16; Judg. 9:54; 1 Sam. 17:39.

Other references to the sword represent the emergence of trouble or conflict in one's environment, whether personal or corporate. For instance, the expression "live by the sword" is noted in Gen. 27:40. Then there is the curse pronounced upon the family of David, in the wake of the Bathsheba-Uriah incident, that "the sword will never depart" from his house (cf. 2 Sam. 12:10). See also Exod. 15:9. The use of the sword symbolizes military conquest in Gen. 31:26; Num. 21:24; Isa. 3:25. Such a meaning is also conveyed by the phrase "put to the sword" (cf. Deut. 13:15; 1 Sam. 15:8; Josh. 10:28ff.).

In particular, the "sword" is often designated as the instrument of divine punishment against his people (cf. Exod. 5:3; Lev. 26:25, 33; Deut. 28:22; Ps. 78:62; Isa. 1:20; Jer. 19:7; Ezek. 21:3ff.; Hos. 11:6; Amos 9:1ff.). A similar result is expressed through the phrase "the sword of the Lord" (cf. Josh. 5:13; Judg. 7:20; Ps. 45:3; Isa. 34:6; Jer. 47:6). The "sword" of divine judgment is also exercised against the enemies of Yahweh and his people (cf. Judg. 4:15ff.; Isa. 34:5ff.; Jer. 44:13ff.; Ezek. 25:13). In contrast, Isa. 2:4; Joel 3:10; Mic. 4:3 describe the future phenomenon of "swords being turned into plowshares" — a prophetic indicator of the future period of everlasting peace in the kingdom of God.

ḥereb refers metaphorically to tongues that are "sharp swords" in Ps. 57:4. An allegorical reference to "Madam Folly" as a sharp "two-edged sword" is found in Prov. 5:14. See also Prov. 25:18; 30:14

NT Words

machaira [μάχαιρα, *3162*]

machaira is a dynamic equivalent for the Hebrew term ***ḥereb*** (see above), found in around thirty places and consistently denoting a "sword" in both literal and metaphorical contexts.

Matt. 26:5ff.; Mark 14:43ff.; Luke 22:36, 52; John 18:10; Acts 12:2 contain literal references to swords as weapons. Heb. 11:37 refers to being slain by the sword, indicating a savage persecution.

The "sword" is held up in a number of places as symbolic of strife, war, or divine judgment (cf. Matt. 10:34; Luke 21:24; Rev. 13:10). Rom. 13:4 alludes to the authority of governments, given by God, to "exercise the sword" as a means of judicial punishment.

Eph. 6:17 refers to the word of God as the "sword of the Spirit." In Heb. 4:12, the word of God is declared to be sharper than any two-edged sword.

rhomphaia [ῥομφαία, *4501*]

rhomphaia is a noun synonymous with ***machaira***, above, denoting a "sword" in all seven occurrences.

rhomphaia is used exclusively in metaphorical and visionary contexts. Luke 2:35 refers to a "sword piercing the soul," indicating the prospect of a terrible calamity.

The remaining uses of ***rhomphaia*** are all found in the context of John's visionary Apocalypse, where the term consistently indicates a "two-edged sword," symbolizing the exercising of divine judgment (cf. Rev. 1:16; 2:12, 16; 6:8; 19:15, 21).

SYNAGOGUE → ASSEMBLE

T

TABERNACLE

OT Words

mishkān [מִשְׁכָּן, 4908]

mishkān is a noun occurring over three hundred times with the primary sense of "tabernacle," "tent," or "dwelling place," with reference to both God and human beings.

mishkān refers primarily to the ritual shrine, the "tabernacle" of Yahweh that he commanded Moses to build in the aftermath of the Sinai covenant revelation. The significance of this tent shrine lay in the fact that it was the "dwelling place" of God among his people, the focal point of their worship (cf. Exod. 25:9; 26:1ff.; 35:11ff.; 36:13ff.; 40:2ff.; Num. 1:50ff.; 9:15ff.; Josh. 22:19; Pss. 74:7; 132:7). The peculiar sanctity of this structure is emphasized in Num. 17:13; 19:13; 1 Chr. 6:32; 16:39. The tabernacle is specifically identified as the location of God's intimate covenant relationship with his people in Ezek. 37:27; Jer. 30:18; Isa. 32:18.

mishkān also refers in literal, mundane contexts to people's "dwelling places" or "homes." Such general references are found in Num. 16:24; 24:5; Job 39:6; Ps. 78:28. Job 18:21 refers to the "dwellings" of the wicked.

'ōhel [אֹהֶל, 168]

'ōhel is a common noun occurring around 350 times with the sense of "tabernacle," "tent," or "dwelling place." It also refers to both the ritual tabernacle of the Israelites as well as to the dwelling places of people. ***'ōhel*** functions as a synonym for ***mishkān***, though its range of meaning is a little broader.

'ōhel most commonly refers to the tabernacle, the dwelling place of Yahweh and the central ritual shrine of Israelite worship. It is most often translated "tent of meeting" (cf. Exod. 26:9ff.; 33:7ff.; 40:2ff.; Lev. 4:4ff.; 8:3ff.; 16:16ff.; Num. 3:7ff.; 8:15ff.; 16:42ff.; Deut. 31:14; Josh. 18:1; 1 Sam. 2:22; 1 Kgs. 8:4; Pss. 27:5; 78:60). A synonymous expression is found in Isa. 16:5, where ***'ōhel*** refers to the "tent (or tabernacle) of David." ***'ōhel*** also refers to a "tent" pitched in Jerusalem for the ark of the covenant, though it does not refer to the tabernacle (cf. 2 Sam. 6:17).

In mundane contexts, ***'ōhel*** refers generally to people's "dwellings," "tents," or "homes" (cf. Gen. 4:20; Exod. 16:16; Num. 11:10; 2 Kgs. 7:7; Jer. 4:20; 35:10). The "tents" of the Israelites are designated as such in Num. 24:5; Deut. 1:27; Josh. 22:4ff.; 1 Sam. 13:2; Ps. 78:51; Hos. 12:9. References to the "tents" of the wicked are found in Num. 16:2ff.; Job 8:22; Ps. 84:10. The "dwellings" of particular individuals are noted in Gen. 9:21; 12:8; 13:5; 18:1ff.; Judg. 4:17ff.; Josh. 7:21ff. A general reference to a "tent," without indicating a dwelling, is found in 2 Sam. 16:22.

NT Words

skēnē [σκηνή, *4633*]

skēnē is a dynamic Greek equivalent for the Hebrew ***mishkān*** (see above). The term is found approximately twenty times meaning "tent" or "tabernacle" in both literal and figurative contexts.

Literal references to the "tabernacle" of the old covenant era are found in Acts 7:44; 15:16; Heb. 8:5; 13:10. Linked to these references in a theological sense are those which refer to the heavenly "tabernacle" as the true spiritual reality to which the earthly structure pointed (cf. Acts 8:2; Heb. 9:2ff.; Rev. 13:6; 15:5).

skēnē is also translated "booth," or "shelter," in Matt. 17:4; Mark 9:5; Luke 9:33, where Peter proposes (quite irrationally) to have three "shelters" erected to "house" Jesus, Moses, and Elijah, and thus prolong indefinitely their visionary appearance to the disciples on the "Mount of Transfiguration."

Luke 16:9 refers to the eternal "dwelling place" of believers. In Heb. 11:9, ***skēnē*** denotes the ordinary sense of "house."

skēnos [σκῆνος, *4636*]

skēnos is a rare variant of ***skēnē*** (see above), found only twice. In 2 Cor. 5:1, 4 it refers metaphorically to the human body as a "tabernacle," a temporary dwelling place and a prelude to the eternal house prepared for the believer in glory.

skēnōma [σκήνωμα, *4638*]

skēnōma is another less common variant of ***skēnē*** (see above). It refers to the "dwelling" of God in Acts 7:46, citing the old covenant tabernacle. In 2 Pet. 1:13, 14, the term refers metaphorically to the body as a "tabernacle," a temporary dwelling for the spirit of the believer, to be released at death to be with Christ.

skēnopēgia [σκηνοπηγία, *4634*]

skēnopēgia occurs only in John 7:2 with reference to the "Feast of Tabernacles," specifically indicating the activity of building "shelters," or "tents." This festival celebrated God's protection and guidance of his people during their period of wandering in the wilderness, when they lived in "tents," characteristic of a nomadic lifestyle.

Additional Notes

The consistent motif in the vocabulary for "tabernacle" in both Old and New Testaments is that of God's dwelling place among his people. In the Old Testament, ***mishkān*** and ***'ōhel*** refer to the portable tent structure that constituted the focal point of Israelite worship from the time of ratification of the law covenant at Mt. Sinai until the construction of the permanent temple in Jerusalem during the reign of Solomon. Old covenant worship was dominated by ceremonial ritual and sacrifice that centered on the tabernacle (and later the temple), since that structure embodied the symbolic (though real) presence of Yahweh among his people.

This phenomenon is also evident in the New Testament, though it undergoes a transformation in the process. ***skēnē*** and its variants indicate that while the old covenant tabernacle was a distinctly physical object centered on ritual worship, the continuing "dwelling place" of God is now focused in the lives and spirits of new covenant believers. The body is viewed as the "tabernacle," merely a temporary shell that will pass away at physical death and allow the human spirit to enter into the heavenly dwelling of God and Christ. This is the spiritual reality to which the old covenant tabernacle pointed.

See Also: → TEMPLE

TABLE

OT Words

shulḥān [**שֻׁלְחָן, 7979**]

shulḥān is a common noun found in around seventy contexts with the primary meaning "table," in both literal and metaphorical contexts.

shulḥān refers in a number of places to the "table of the presence" — the item of furniture in the holy place on which loaves of bread were continually placed as a memorial offering to Yahweh. This table was found in both the tabernacle (e.g., Exod. 25:23ff.; 37:10ff.; Lev. 24:6; Num. 4:7); and the temple (e.g., 1 Kgs. 7:48; 1 Chr. 28:16; 2 Chr. 4:19). Mal. 1:7, 12 refer to this table being profaned by polluted offerings. Isa. 65:11 records the sin of pagan offerings being offered on this table in ritual idolatry. Tables for ritual use are indicated in Ezekiel's visionary temple in Ezek. 40:39ff.; 41:22; 44:16.

In metaphorical contexts, ***shulḥān*** refers to "tables," indicating the offering of hospitality (cf. Job 36:16; Pss. 69:22; 128:3; Prov. 9:3; Isa. 21:5). In Ps. 23:5, God is said "to prepare a table" before the psalmist in the presence of his enemies. This is suggestive of God's intimate fellowship with his people in the wake of the decisive victory of his enemies. A similar, though more dramatic, picture is illustrated in Ezek. 39:20, where Yahweh "sets a table" for a symbolic feast at which his people can "gorge" themselves on their defeated foes.

Mundane references to "tables" are found in Judg. 1:7; 2 Kgs. 4:10. Royal "tables" where meals are taken are indicated in 1 Sam. 20:29, 34; 2 Sam. 9:7ff.; 1 Kgs. 2:7; 10:5; Isa. 21:5.

NT Words

trapeza [τράπεζα, *5132*]

trapeza is a dynamic equivalent for the Hebrew ***shulḥān*** (see above), occurring thirteen times and referring to "tables" in a variety of contexts.

References to "tables" in the context of eating are found in Matt. 15:27; Luke 16:21; 22:21; Acts 6:2; Rom. 11:9. The tables of the moneychangers in the temple are noted in Matt. 21:12; Mark 11:15; John 2:15. Heb. 9:2 refers to the "table of the presence" in the tabernacle.

In metaphorical contexts, ***trapeza*** refers to God setting up a table in his heavenly kingdom, symbolizing his intention to establish an intimate fellowship with his people there (cf. Luke 22:30). 1 Cor. 10:21 refers to the "table of the Lord," indicating the location for the Lord's Supper.

Additional Notes

There is a definite consistency in the metaphorical references to "table(s)" in both Old and New Testaments. Where "tables" are mentioned in the context of fellowship with God and his people, both ***shulḥān*** and ***trapeza*** emphasize the intimacy of that relationship. The motif of hospitality underlies much of the usage of ***shulḥān*** in the Old Testament, which is then transferred to the divine sphere. God "feasts" with his people in the light of victory over his enemies. Such is the underlying dynamic associated with the "table" of the Lord's Supper in the New Testament, indicating Christ's victory over sin and death through his own act of voluntary self-sacrifice.

TAIL

OT Words

***zānāb* [זָנָב, 2180]**

zānāb is a noun found in eleven contexts meaning "tail."

zānāb refers literally to the tails of snakes (Exod. 4:4); foxes (Judg. 15:4); and a behemoth (Job 40:17).

The remaining occurrences are metaphorical. Referring to human beings, Deut. 28:13, 44; Isa. 9:15 indicate the "tail" as the lowest rank of authority, as opposed to the "head." Isa. 7:4 speaks of the "tail" of two kings about to be destroyed by Yahweh. Isa. 9:14 refers to a comprehensive divine judgment against Israel, in which Yahweh will cut off their "head and tail" (cf. also Isa. 19:15).

NT Words

oura [οὐρά, *3769*]

oura is a noun found five times, referring metaphorically to the "tails" of hellish beasts depicted in the book of Revelation — to scorpions (Rev. 9:10); serpents (Rev. 9:19); and a dragon, i.e., Satan (Rev. 12:4).

TAKE

OT Words

***lāqaḥ* [לָקַח, 3947]**

lāqaḥ is a common verb with the primary meaning "to take," along with a variety of nuances. The term occurs around one thousand times and indicates both divine and human agency.

In the context of divine activity, ***lāqaḥ*** expresses the sense of "take hold of" in relation to man (Gen. 2:15) and man's rib (Gen. 2:21), from which he fashioned woman. Exod. 6:7 speaks of Yahweh taking hold of a people for himself. The meaning "take out," or "remove," is indicated in Gen. 2:23 in relation to God taking woman from man, and in Gen. 3:19 with reference to man's creation, or God taking him out of the ground. David prays in Ps. 51:11 that God will not take the Holy Spirit from him. Deut. 4:20 mentions Yahweh delivering (i.e., taking out) his people from Egyptian captivity. See also Ps. 18:16; Hos. 13:11; Ezek. 3:14; Isa. 51:22. The meaning "take" is also evident in 2 Sam. 7:8, where God declares that he "took" David from his task as shepherd to be the ruler of Israel. Ps. 6:9 refers to God taking, or receiving, prayer. Isa. 47:3 declares that Yahweh will take revenge on Babylon.

In the human sphere, the usage of ***lāqaḥ*** is much broader. The meaning "take hold" is used in relation to picking fruit (Gen. 3:6, 22); presenting firstfruits to God (Deut. 26:2); and accosting a woman in a sexual assault (Gen. 34:2). ***lāqaḥ*** refers to taking hold of objects in a general sense (Num. 16:17ff.; Josh. 9:4; Isa. 8:1), as well as people (Exod. 2:9; Num. 20:25; Jer. 38:6). ***lāqaḥ*** refers in ceremonial contexts to "taking hold" of offerings and presenting them to Yahweh (Exod. 28:5; 29:13ff.; 30:16; Lev. 8:26), as well as other items for worship (Lev. 8:10ff.; 1 Sam. 10:1; 16:13), and also animals for sacrificial slaughter (cf. Judg. 6:25; 1 Sam. 7:9; Ezek. 45:18). The Levites are commanded to "take hold" of the book of the law and place it in the ark of the covenant in Deut. 31:26. See also Judg. 18:17ff. in the context of pagan worship.

The general sense of "take" is also indicated in a variety of contexts. Gen. 4:19; Exod. 2:1; Num. 12:7 refer to "taking" (or marrying) a wife. Deut. 7:3 contains a prohibition against any Israelite taking a Canaanite woman as a wife. See also Deut. 24:1ff.; Judg. 14:2ff.; Ezra 2:61; Hos. 1:2, 3 as further illustrations of this usage. "Taking" blood for sacrificial offerings is indicated in Exod. 12:7; 25:2ff.; Lev. 4:25ff. Taking armies into battle is noted in Josh. 8:12; 1 Sam. 24:2. Taking food for consumption is noted in Gen. 6:21.

lāqaḥ also means "take" in reference to plundering goods, as spoils of war (cf. Gen. 14:11; 1 Sam. 14:32; 30:20). Deut. 3:4ff. refers to taking cities in this fashion as part of a military campaign, and particularly in relation to the conquest of Canaan (cf. Deut. 26:14; Josh. 11:16ff.).

The meaning "take away," "remove" is applied to a birthright (Gen. 27:36); to human remains for burial (1 Sam. 31:13; 2 Sam. 4:12; 18:17); and to people in various contexts (cf. Exod. 14:11; 1 Sam. 8:14). See also Ps. 31:13; Jer. 28:3.

Other nuances of ***lāqaḥ*** meaning "take" include "accept," or "receive," applied to Moses "receiving" the tablets of the law covenant from Yahweh (Exod. 34:4); to people "accepted" by God for service (cf. Num. 1:17; 3:41ff.); and to Levites "receiving" the tithe from the people (Num. 18:26). Prov. 4:10; 8:10 speak of the wisdom of "receiving" the word of God gladly. "Taking" bribes is noted in 1 Sam. 8:3; Amos 5:12. "Selecting" or "taking" people for specific service to God and the nation of Israel is indicated in Deut. 1:15; Josh. 3:12. Stealing (i.e., wrongful "taking") constitutes a culpable action under the law (cf. Josh. 7:1, 11ff.). Note, too, in a very real, though metaphorical, sense David's "theft" of Bathsheba from her husband Uriah (2 Sam. 12:4ff.). The sense of "capture" is applied to the ark of the covenant when the Philistines seized it in their victory over

Israel in 1 Sam. 4:11ff.; 5:1ff. In this sense, Job 1:15ff. speaks of people "taken" as prisoners. See also Jer. 20:5. Esth. 2:7 speaks of Esther as a young girl whom her uncle, Mordecai, "took" (i.e., adopted) as his own daughter.

nāsā' [נָשָׂא, 5375]

nāsā' is a common verb with a number of meanings found in over 650 contexts. The sense of "take" occurs in about eighty of these. (→ BEAR [VERB] → FORGIVE)

The meaning "take" applies to Yahweh in several places where he is said "to take away" or "remove" his people from their land as punishment for their sin (cf. Amos 4:2; Hos. 5:14). In Hos. 14:2, there is a plea for God to "take away" the iniquity of his people.

The remaining usage of ***nāsā'*** with the meaning "take," as well as associated nuances, is found within the human sphere. The sense of "take up" or "pick up" in a physical, literal manner is applied to weapons (Gen. 27:3); bodies for burial (2 Sam. 2:32; 1 Kgs. 13:29; 1 Chr. 10:12); and the ark of the covenant (Josh. 3:6; 2 Chr. 5:4). See also Josh. 4:8. Ps. 116:13 speaks metaphorically of "taking up" the cup of the Lord's salvation. Jer. 9:10; Ezek. 19:1; Mic. 2:4 describe "taking up" a lament.

Num. 1:2; 4:2 refer to "taking" (i.e., conducting) a census; and Ruth 1:4; 2 Chr. 11:21 to taking a wife (i.e., marrying). The prohibition against taking the name of the Lord in vain is noted in the third commandment in Exod. 20:7; Deut. 5:11. The sense of "take away" or "remove" is found in Song 5:7; Mic. 2:2.

In Exod. 10:19, the wind is described as "taking (i.e., blowing) away" the plague of locusts against Egypt.

'āḥaz [אָחַז, 270]

'āḥaz is a verb occurring around seventy times with the primary sense of "grasp," "seize," or "take hold of." (→ HOLD)

lākad [לָכַד, 3920]

This verb occurs around 120 times with the primary senses of "take hold," "seize," "capture," "apprehend." (→ APPREHEND)

gāzal [גָּזַל, 1497]

gāzal is a verb occurring around thirty times with the underlying sense of "steal," "plunder" or "take away," "seize by force."

Gen. 31:31; Job 24:9 refer to the crime of kidnapping, or taking people away by force. The unlawful taking of property, stealing, is mentioned in Lev. 6:4; 19:13; Deut. 28:13; Job 24:2. Grabbing a spear from someone's grasp is indicated in 2 Sam. 23:21; 1 Chr. 11:23. "Taking away" or "depriving" the poor of their rights is condemned in Isa. 10:2. Prov. 4:16 refers metaphorically to one's sleep being taken away (lit. "robbed of sleep").

qāmaṣ [קָמַץ, 7061]

qāmaṣ is a verb found in three contexts meaning "take (a handful)." All settings are ceremonial, referring to the priest taking a handful of flour for a grain offering (Lev. 2:2; Num. 5:12), and for a sin offering (Lev. 5:12).

'āṣal [אָצַל, 680]

'āṣal is a verb found in five contexts meaning "lay aside," "withdraw." In Num. 11:7, 25, ***'āṣal*** refers explicitly to God taking his Spirit from Moses and imparting it to the elders appointed to assist the prophet in leading the people. The idea here is transferral of spiritual authority so that both parties share in the divine endowment.

nephaq [נְפַק, 5312 (Aramaic)]

nephaq is an Aramaic verb occurring ten times with the predominant meanings "take out," "remove." Ezra 5:14; 6:5 refer to the sacred items of the Jerusalem temple taken out by Cyrus in order to return them to the Jews. Dan. 5:2ff. refers to those same items originally taken by Nebuchadnezzar from the Jerusalem temple.

nesā' [נְשָׂא, 5376 (Aramaic)]

nesā' is an Aramaic verb found three times, translated "carry" or "take away" in Ezra 5:15, with reference to the sacred items of the Jerusalem temple, about to be returned to their place of origin.

NT Words

lambanō [λαμβάνω, *2983*]

lambanō is a verb occurring around 260 times with the primary senses of "receive" and "take." The latter meaning accounts for a little under half of its usage, including a variety of nuances.

The meaning "take away" or "remove" is indicated in relation to the loss of one's coat in a lawsuit (cf. Matt. 5:40). Pilate issues the command to have Jesus taken away in John 18:31; 19:6. John 19:40 records that Jesus' body was taken away for burial.

The sense of "take up" is evident in relation to the believer taking up his cross in identification with

Christ in his suffering (cf. Matt. 10:38). Acts 1:25 refers to taking up a position for ministry. In John 10:17, Jesus declares that he will take up his life again after laying it down. See also Matt. 16:9, 10.

lambanō refers to Christ "taking upon" himself the form of a man (Phil. 2:7); as well as the sins and infirmities of his people (Matt. 8:17).

Other nuances of ***lambanō*** associated with "taking" include "to accost," "grab hold of" (cf. Matt. 21:39); "take counsel," "seek advice" (cf. Matt. 27:7); "take courage" (cf. Acts 28:15); and "take" a wife (i.e., marry) (cf. Mark 12:19ff.; Luke 20:28ff.).

The general sense of "taking (hold of)" objects is illustrated in Matt. 13:31; 26:52; Mark 14:22ff.; Luke 6:4; John 6:7; 1 Cor. 11:24; Rev. 5:7; 10:9ff.

paralambanō [παραλαμβάνω, *3880*]

paralambanō is a synonym for ***lambanō*** (see above) with the primary meanings "take," "receive." The term occurs fifty times, with the meaning "take" evident in over half of these contexts. (→ RECEIVE)

The meaning "take" in the sense of "lead," or "bring," is applied to the infant Jesus being taken to Egypt by his parents in Matt. 2:13ff. Satan is described taking Jesus to Jerusalem, to the pinnacle of the temple, in order to tempt him (cf. Matt. 4:5ff.). Other such general references include those in Matt. 12:45; Mark 4:36; Luke 9:28; Acts 15:39.

Elsewhere, ***paralambanō*** refers to "taking" a wife (Matt. 1:20); to Jesus being "taken away" to be crucified (John 19:16); and to persons being "taken up" into heaven (Matt. 24:40; Luke 17:34).

analambanō [ἀναλαμβάνω, *353*]

analambanō is a verb meaning "take," "take up" for most of its approximately thirteen occurrences.

The meaning "take up" relates to Christ ascending into heaven after his resurrection (cf. Mark 16:19; Acts 1:2, 11, 22; 1 Tim. 3:16). The visionary sheet laden with unclean food in Peter's vision is "taken up" into heaven in Acts 10:16. In Eph. 6:13, 16 Paul exhorts his readers to "take up" the whole armor of God.

analambanō is also translated "take" in the sense of "get," "fetch" in Acts 23:31; 2 Tim. 4:11.

epilambanō [ἐπιλαμβάνω, *1949*]

This verb, occurring approximately twenty times, means "take hold of" in the majority of cases.

"Taking hold of" people in the sense of "seizing" them is noted in Luke 23:26; Acts 21:30. Mark 8:29; Heb. 8:9 speak of "taking hold of" someone's hand. An attempt to "take hold of" Jesus' words (i.e., to catch him out) is indicated in Luke 20:20. An exhortation to take hold of eternal life is found in 1 Tim. 6:12, 19. See also Luke 9:47; 14:4; Acts 9:27.

symparalambanō [συμπαραλαμβάνω, *4838*]

This verb means "to take (along) with," as a companion, in all four occurrences (cf. Acts 12:25; 15:37ff.; Gal. 2:1).

proslambanō [προσλαμβάνω, *4355*]

proslambanō is a verb occurring fourteen times meaning "take," "take to oneself," "take (someone) aside" in over half of these contexts.

The action of "taking people aside" is indicated in the following contexts: for teaching (cf. Acts 18:26); for rebuke (cf. Matt. 16:22; Mark 8:32); and the general context of Acts 17:5. Acts 27:33ff. refers to taking food to eat.

harpazō [ἁρπάζω, *726*]

harpazō is a verb found in thirteen places meaning "take by force" in various settings.

"Take away" means "snatch away" in relation to Satan stealing the word of God from the hearts and minds of people who had initially received it (cf. Matt. 13:19). John 10:12 describes the action of the wolf snatching sheep away from the flock. John 10:28ff. contains the divine guarantee that no believer will ever "be snatched out" of the hand of Christ.

harpazō also refers to Paul "being caught (or taken) up" to the third heaven in 2 Cor. 12:2ff. Similarly, believers are promised that they will be caught up with the dead in Christ to meet the Lord in the air when he returns (cf. 1 Thess. 4:17; Rev. 12:5).

harpazō also means "to take by force" in the context of violent action (cf. Matt. 11:12; John 6:15; Acts 23:10).

apairō [ἀπαίρω, *522*]

apairō is a verb found only three times, all referring to Jesus Christ as the "bridegroom" who one day "will be taken away" from his disciples (cf. Matt. 9:15; Mark 2:20; Luke 5:35).

aphaireō [ἀφαιρέω, *851*]

aphaireō is a verb meaning "take away" in most of the ten contexts in which it is found.

Luke 1:25 mentions "taking away" or "removing" one's reproach. Luke 16:3 records the "removal" of a person's employment. In Luke 10:42, Mary (the sister of Lazarus) is told that her opportunity for service to Jesus will not be taken away. Rom. 11:27 refers to God taking away the sins of his people. Heb. 10:4 declares that the blood of bulls and goats can never by itself remove sin. See also Rev. 22:19.

kathaireō [καθαιρέω, *2507*]

This verb occurs in nine places, meaning "take down" in about half of these, all referring to the body of Christ being taken down from the cross (cf. Mark 15:36, 46; Luke 23:53; Acts 13:29).

periaireō [περιαιρέω, *4014*]

periaireō is a verb occurring four times, meaning "take away" in each context. This happens to the veil of sin when a person turns to the Lord in faith (cf. 2 Cor. 3:16). Heb. 10:11 declares that sacrifices by themselves can never take away sin. See also Acts 27:20, 40.

parapherō [παραφέρω, *3911*]

parapherō is found only in Mark 14:36; Luke 22:42, referring to Jesus' plea to his Father that his cup of suffering will be taken away.

ekdyō [ἐκδύω, *1562*]

ekdyō is a verb meaning "taking off," or "stripping," of clothes. It occurs in five places, most of which refer to divesting Christ's garments prior to his crucifixion (cf. Matt. 27:28, 31; Mark 15:20; Luke 10:30). In 2 Cor. 5:4 ***ekdyō*** is used adjectivally, referring to the supposed intermediate state of the believer between death and resurrection to life, describing the person as "unclothed."

Additional Notes

The vocabulary for "taking" in the Old Testament is extensive, with a broad semantic field and a wide variety of associated senses. See, therefore, the entries listed below with synonymous or related vocabulary.

See Also: → APPREHEND → ATTEND → BEAR (VERB) → GATHER → HOLD → KILL → OVERTAKE → RECEIVE → REMOVE → SEIZE

TALK

OT Words

sāphāh [**שָׂפָה, 8193**]

sāphāh is a noun occurring around 180 times with a variety of meanings, including the sense of "talk," or "speech." → EDGE → LANGUAGE → LIP → SHORE → SPEECH

NT Words

syllaleō [συλλαλέω, *4814*]

syllaleō is a verb meaning "talk with," "speak with," or "confer." It occurs six times (cf. Matt. 17:3; Mark 9:4; Luke 4:36; 9:30; 22:4; Acts 25:12).

homileō [ὁμιλέω, *3656*]

homileō is synonymous with ***syllaleō*** (see above), meaning "talk with," "discuss" in four places (cf. Luke 24:14, 15; Acts 20:11; 24:26).

synomileō [συνομιλέω, *4926*]

synomileō is a variant form of ***homileō***, above. It is found only in Acts 10:27, meaning "talk with."

mōrologia [μωρολογία, *3473*]

mōrologia is a noun occurring only once, in Eph. 5:4, indicating the sense of "foolish (or silly) talking."

lalia [λαλιά, *2981*]

lalia is a noun occurring in four contexts meaning "speech" (Matt. 26:73; Mark 14:70), and also "words" (John 4:42).

See Also: → SAY → TELL → WORD

TALL

OT Words

rûm [**רוּם, 7311**]

rûm is a verb found in around 200 places with the primary meanings "lift up," "exalt," as well as a number of associated senses. In several contexts, ***rûm*** is used adjectivally to refer to the tall inhabitants of the land of Canaan (cf. Deut. 1:28; 2:10, 21; 9:2).

qômāh [**קוֹמָה, 6967**]

qômāh is a noun with the predominant meaning "height," as well as related nuances, occurring forty-five times. It is used adjectivally to refer to "tall" cedar trees in 2 Kgs. 19:23; Isa. 37:24.

TARES → WEEDS

TARRY → WAIT

TASTE

OT Words

ta'am [**טַעַם, 2940**]

ta'am is a noun meaning "taste" in around half of its thirteen occurrences.

The taste of manna is described in Exod. 16:31; Num. 11:18. Job 6:6 refers to the taste of an egg white. ***ta'am*** refers metaphorically to the nation of Moab, noting that her "taste" has remained unchanged, and that she will still be subject to severe divine punishment (cf. Jer. 48:11).

tā'am [טָעַם, 2938]

tā'am is a verb meaning "to taste" in most of its eleven occurrences.

tā'am refers almost exclusively to tasting food (cf. 1 Sam. 14:24, 29, 43; 2 Sam. 3:35; 19:35; Job 12:11; 34:3).

In Ps. 34:8, ***tā'am*** is used metaphorically in the exhortation to "taste and see that the Lord is good."

ḥēk [חֵךְ, 2441]

ḥēk is a noun meaning "taste," "mouth" throughout its eighteen occurrences. (→ MOUTH)

General references to "taste" are found in Job 6:30; Prov. 24:13; Song 2:3. ***ḥēk*** refers metaphorically in Ps. 119:103 to the words of the law being sweet to the "taste."

NT Words

geuomai [γεύομαι, *1089*]

geuomai is the sole term in the New Testament indicating the experience of "tasting." It occurs fifteen times and is used both literally and metaphorically.

Literal references to "tasting" food and drink are found in Matt. 27:34; Luke 14:24; John 2:9; Acts 23:14. Col. 2:21 refers to the avoidance of "tasting" certain foods.

Elsewhere, ***geuomai*** is used metaphorically, especially in the context of "tasting" (i.e., experiencing) death. Mention is made of those who "will not taste death" before Christ returns to his heavenly glory, after his resurrection (cf. Matt. 16:28; Mark 9:1; Luke 9:27). See also John 8:52. In particular, Jesus Christ is said to have tasted death for every person in Heb. 2:9.

Other contexts refer to people "tasting" the heavenly gift (Heb. 6:4); the word of God (Heb. 9:5); and the kindness of the Lord (1 Pet. 2:3).

TAX, TAXATION

OT Words

'ārak [עָרַךְ, 6186]

'ārak is a verb found in about eighty contexts with the primary meanings "arrange," "set in order," as well as several associated senses — one of which is "to tax," "make an assessment for taxation." This latter sense is found only in 2 Kgs. 23:35. (→ ARRANGE)

nāgas [נָגַשׂ, 5065]

nāgas is a verb with the dominant sense of "to oppress." (→ OPPRESS) In Dan. 11:20 it refers to those who raise "taxes." ***nāgas*** occurs twenty-three times.

TEACH, TEACHER, TEACHING

OT Words

yārāh [יָרָה, 3384]

yārāh is a verb occurring in around eighty contexts with the two predominant meanings "to teach" or "instruct," and "to shoot," both with related nuances. (→ SHOOT)

In several contexts, Yahweh is described as the one who teaches, in the sense of "inform" or "instruct." Moses is depicted as being taught by him (Exod. 4:12, 15). The people are identified as the target of divine instruction (1 Kgs. 8:36; 2 Chr. 6:27; Job 36:22; Isa. 2:3; Mic. 4:2); as are sinners (Ps. 25:8); and godly people (Pss. 25:12; 32:8).

In other places, various individuals and classes of people are cast in the role of teachers for the people of God — for example, Moses (Exod. 24:12); Samuel (1 Sam. 12:23); and judges and priests (Deut. 17:11; 24:8; 33:10; 2 Kgs. 12:2; 17:27; Ezek. 44:23). The father's pivotal role in the nurture and instruction of his children is laid down in Prov. 4:4. See also Judg. 13:8. Isa. 9:15; Mic. 3:11 refer to wicked prophets who teach the people lies. In a significant metaphorical context, the role of Wisdom (personified) as a teacher is described in Prov. 4:11. The idol deity is indicated as a "teacher of lies" in Hab. 2:18. Human beings plead with God to teach them in Job 6:24; Pss. 27:11; 86:11; 119:33.

General references to the process of teaching include those in Exod. 25:34; Job 12:7; Isa. 28:26. Prov. 5:13; Isa. 30:20 refer to teachers.

lāmad [לָמַד, 3925]

lāmad is a verb occurring around ninety times with the primary meanings "learn," "teach" throughout. (→ LEARN)

General references to the activity of teaching are found in several different contexts. The psalmist pleads with God to teach him his ways and laws (cf. Pss. 25:4ff.; 119:64ff., 108, 124; 143:10). The need for the knowledge of Yahweh to be taught by a third party is set to disappear in the promise of Jer. 31:34. Such knowledge will be given to all in the age of the new covenant when the Spirit of God will indwell each believer. This does not mean that the need for teachers will disappear altogether — only that individual believers will not be entirely dependent on others for their awareness of God. David promises to teach sinners the way of the Lord in Ps. 51:13.

Other contexts speak about teaching from a negative perspective. For example, Jer. 9:5 refers to people being taught to lie; and Jer. 9:14 describes the corrupt teaching of godless parents who led their children into Baal worship. Deut. 20:18 refers to the negative impact of the Canaanites teaching the Israelites their corrupt, pagan ways. Job 21:22; Isa. 40:14 refer to the implied futility or impossibility of attempting to teach God.

lāmad also indicates the activity of teaching in the context of the Israelite worship. The role of Moses in this process is noted in Deut. 4:1ff.; 5:31; 6:1; 31:19ff.; as is the role of priests in 2 Chr. 17:7; Ezra 7:10. The direct participation of Yahweh in teaching his people is indicated in Judg. 3:2; 2 Sam. 22:35; Ps. 94:12. The role of parents in teaching their children is cited in Deut. 11:19. General references to the people's instruction under the law include those in 2 Sam. 1:18; Ps. 34:11; Eccl. 12:9.

zāhar [**זָהַר, 2094**]

zāhar is a verb with the predominant meaning "to warn," "admonish," found in all but one of the twenty-two occurrences of the term. (→ WARN) The exception is Exod. 18:20, which refers to Yahweh's command to Moses to teach the people the divinely revealed laws of the covenant.

yāda' [**יָדַע, 3045**]

yāda' is a common verb occurring nearly nine hundred times with the primary sense of "know," as well as a variety of associated nuances. One of these nuances is the meaning "teach." Godly instruction is in view in Ps. 90:12; Prov. 9:9. Judg. 8:16 speaks of teaching the enemies of Yahweh and his people a harsh lesson, through inflicting severe punishment. Teaching people to sing is in view in 2 Chr. 23:13. See also Job 32:7; 37:19.

'ālaph [**אָלַף, 502**]

'ālaph is a verb found in only four places, meaning "teach" in three of these. Job 15:5 refers to iniquity "teaching" one's mouth. ***'ālaph*** refers to the teaching of human beings (Job 33:33), and to divine instruction (Job 35:11).

leqaḥ [**לֶקַח, 3948**]

leqaḥ is a noun found in nine contexts, meaning "teaching," "learning" throughout most of these. "Teaching" refers to that which is taught and derived from God, and may also be translated "doctrine." See Deut. 32:2; Job 11:4; Prov. 4:2; Isa. 29:24. (→ LEARN)

sākal [**שָׂכַל, 7919**]

sākal is a verb occurring in approximately sixty places with several different meanings. The primary meanings are "to understand," "be wise," along with a variety of nuances. One of these nuances is the meaning "to teach." A general reference to the teaching given to the wise person is found in Prov. 21:11. Instruction given by God and his Spirit is noted in Neh. 9:20; Ps. 32:8. 2 Chr. 30:22 refers to the Levites teaching the people of Israel.

NT Words

didaskō [**διδάσκω, *1321***]

didaskō is the most common verb meaning "to teach" in the New Testament. The term occurs around one hundred times.

The teaching ministry of Christ is described throughout the Gospels and Acts (e.g., Matt. 4:23; 5:2; 13:54; Mark 4:1ff.; Luke 13:22; 20:1; John 6:59; 7:28ff.; Acts 1:1). Paul indicates in Gal. 1:12 that he was not taught the gospel message by any human source, but by the risen Christ himself in a revelation.

General references to human teaching are found in Matt. 5:19; 15:9; Acts 15:1; Rev. 2:14, 20. See also 1 Cor. 11:14. Jesus' command to his disciples to teach others the gospel and disciple them is found in Matt. 28:20. The teaching ministry of the apostles is also frequently indicated (e.g., Mark 6:30; Luke 11:1; Acts 4:2; 5:21; 1 Cor. 4:17; Eph. 4:21; Col. 1:28; 2 Thess. 2:15; 1 Tim. 4:11). Mutual edification (i.e., teaching) among believers is indicated in Col. 3:16; Heb. 5:12. Paul's refusal to admit women to the teaching office in the church is recorded in 1 Tim. 2:12.

The ministry of the Holy Spirit in teaching the people of God is noted in Luke 12:12; John 14:26.

katēcheō [**κατηχέω, *2727***]

katēcheō is a verb occurring eight times meaning "instruct," "inform," or "teach." The usage is largely passive. Being instructed in, or taught, the word of God is a process indicated in Luke 1:4; Acts 18:25; Rom. 2:18; Gal. 6:6. General references to "being informed" are found in Acts 21:21ff. The active sense of "teach" or "instruct" is noted in 1 Cor. 14:19.

heterodidaskaleō [ἑτεροδιδασκαλέω, *2085*]

heterodidaskaleō is a verb found only twice. 1 Tim. 1:3; 6:3 refer to those who "teach a different doctrine" to that of the apostolic tradition of the gospel.

didaktikos [διδακτικός, *1317*]

didaktikos is an adjective signifying the quality of being "apt to teach" or "skilled in teaching." It occurs only in 1 Tim. 3:2; 2 Tim. 2:24 as part of a list of prerequisite characteristics for those aspiring to the office of elder.

didaskalos [διδάσκαλος, *1320*]

didaskalos is a noun derived from ***didaskō*** (see above), occurring around sixty times with the primary sense of "teacher," applied most often as a title for Jesus Christ during his earthly ministry.

The title "teacher" is frequently given to Jesus in the gospel narratives (e.g., Matt. 8:19; 22:16, 24, 36; Mark 4:38; 10:17ff.; Luke 3:12; 11:45; 12:13; John 1:38; 3:2).

References to the teachers of the Jewish people include those in Luke 2:46; John 3:10; Acts 13:1. 1 Tim. 2:7; 2 Tim. 1:11 refer to apostolic teachers, appointed by God for the edification of the church. 1 Cor. 12:28ff.; Eph. 4:11 refer to teachers who are gifted by the Spirit of God, again for the benefit of God's people.

General references to teachers include those in Matt. 10:24ff.; Luke 6:40; Rom. 2:20; 2 Tim. 4:3; Heb. 5:12; Jas. 3:1

nomodidaskalos [νομοδιδάσκαλος, *3547*]

nomodidaskalos is a term denoting the specific office of "teacher of the law," found only three times (Luke 5:17; Acts 5:34; 1 Tim. 1:7).

kalodidaskalos [καλοδιδάσκαλος, *2567*]

kalodidaskalos is an adjective found only in Titus 2:3, referring to those who "teach what is good."

pseudodidaskalos [ψευδοδιδάσκαλος, *5572*]

pseudodidaskalos is a term denoting "a false teacher," found only in 2 Pet. 2:1.

rhabbi [ῥαββί, *4461*]

rhabbi is the Greek transliteration of a Hebrew term that denotes a "teacher" of the law of Moses. It is used seventeen times in the New Testament as a courtesy title for Jesus (e.g., Matt. 23:7ff.; Mark 9:5; 14:65; John 1:38, 49; 4:31; 11:8).

Additional Notes

One of the most significant aspects of the vocabulary for "teaching" throughout the Bible is the fact that genuine teachers of God's people are appointed and equipped by God himself. Under the old covenant, the prophets and priests communicated the word(s) of Yahweh and interpreted them according to the divine intention.

In the New Testament, the genuine teachers of God's people are still equipped and appointed by God. The distinctive difference here lies in the fact that the office of teacher is not restricted to any one class of people. The fundamental prerequisite for the new covenant teacher is the indwelling and equipping of the Holy Spirit. The Spirit imparts the teaching gift to those so chosen, who are then recognized by the Christian community as manifesting such a gift.

The problem of false teachers has always been a problem for the community of God's people. Under the old covenant, false teachers were most often located in the ranks of the prophets, and their punishment was always severe. Distorting and misrepresenting the word of God constituted a capital offense. Such a severe response is not articulated against false teachers in the New Testament in explicit detail, although their condemnation is declared as certain.

See Also: → ADMONISH → CHASTISE → CORRECT → DISCIPLE → DOCTRINE → PREACH

TEAR (VERB)

OT Words

qāra' [קָרַע, 7167]

qāra' is a verb found in sixty places meaning "to tear," as well as various extended meanings.

General references to the action of tearing include those in Exod. 28:32; Lev. 13:56; 1 Sam. 15:27.

More commonly, ***qāra'*** refers to people tearing their clothes as a sign of anguish, or mourning (cf. Gen. 37:29ff.; 44:13; Num. 14:6; Judg. 11:35; 1 Sam. 4:12; 2 Sam. 1:2; 2 Kgs. 2:12; Esth. 4:1; Isa. 36:22; Jer. 41:5). In particular, clothing is torn as an expression of repentance (Josh. 7:6; 1 Kgs. 21:27; 2 Kgs. 22:11; Ezra 9:3ff.). See also Jer. 36:24.

qāra' also refers to "tearing down" the altar of the temple in 1 Kgs. 13:3ff. as a sign of God's judgment against his people.

qāra' is also used metaphorically of God in several contexts, meaning "tear away." In 1 Sam. 15:28; 28:17 God is said to have "torn away" the kingdom from Saul, and from Solomon's son Rehoboam in 1 Kgs. 11:11ff.; 14:8; 2 Kgs. 17:2, for their rebellion against him. See also Ezek. 13:20; Hos. 13:8; Joel 2:13. There is also a plea for God to "tear" the heavens and come down to destroy his enemies (cf. Isa. 64:1).

bāqa' [בָּקַע, 1234]

bāqa' is a verb occurring around fifty times with the primary meaning "split," "divide," as well as a number of associated nuances. One of these nuances is "to tear up," "rip open," suggesting violent action in most of the contexts where this meaning is evident.

The meanings "tear apart," "tear up" are evident in the following contexts. 2 Kgs. 2:24 refers to children being torn apart by a savage bear. Pregnant women are threatened with the prospect of being ripped open and slain by violent, cruel men, and they are actually treated that way in 2 Kgs. 8:12; 15:16; Hos. 13:16; Amos 1:13. In Ezek. 29:7, soldiers in battle are said to have their shoulders "torn apart." Hos. 13:8 uses ***bāqa'*** metaphorically, wherein Israel is declared to be "torn apart" by Yahweh in judgment against them. Cities are described as "torn down" in battle in Ezek. 30:16. Wineskins are described as "torn" in Josh. 9:4.

tāraph [טָרַף, 2963]

tāraph is a verb occurring twenty-five times with the primary meanings "tear," "tear in pieces."

Literal references to people being torn to pieces by wild animals are found in Gen. 37:33; 44:28. The action of wild animals capturing and "tearing" their prey is indicated in Ps. 17:12; Ezek. 22:27; Nah. 2:12. ***tāraph*** is also used metaphorically with reference to God "tearing his people to pieces" in judgment (cf. Jer. 5:6; Hos. 5:14; 6:1; Mic. 5:8).

In other metaphorical contexts, ***tāraph*** indicates "tearing" as a sign of dominant strength in Deut. 33:20. In Job 16:9, Job accuses God of "tearing" him in his wrath (cf. also Job 18:4). In Ps. 50:22, the psalmist describes himself as being torn in the context of persecution from his enemies.

terēphāh [טְרֵפָה, 2966]

terēphāh is a noun occurring eight times, referring to wildlife that has been "torn" (i.e., by wild beasts). General references are found in Gen. 31:39; Exod. 22:13; Nah. 2:12. Elsewhere, such flesh is declared to be ceremonially unclean, unfit for human consumption (cf. Exod. 22:31; Lev. 7:24; 17:15; 22:8; Ezek. 4:14; 44:31).

pāraq [פָּרַק, 6561]

pāraq is a verb found in ten places with the primary meaning "break off," or "split." In two contexts, however, it means "to tear." It refers metaphorically in Ps. 7:2 to the psalmist's description of his enemies "tearing (him) apart" like a lion. See also Zech. 11:16.

NT Words

schizō [σχίζω, *4977*]

schizō is a verb found ten times with the predominant meaning "tear" (i.e., divide in two).

Reference is made to the veil of the temple being "torn in two" at the moment of Christ's death on the cross, signifying the climactic end of the old covenant, with unhindered access to the holy of holies opened for all (cf. Matt. 27:51; Mark 15:38; Luke 23:45).

Other general references to "tearing" cloth include those in Luke 5:36; John 19:24.

See Also: → THRESH

TEARS

OT Words

dim'āh [דִּמְעָה, 1832]

dim'āh is a noun that consistently means "tears" in each of its twenty-three occurrences.

General references to tears of sadness include those in Pss. 56:8; 116:8; Isa. 25:3; Jer. 9:18. Tears brought about by suffering and anguish are noted in 2 Kgs. 20:5; Pss. 6:6; 39:12; 80:12; Eccl. 4:1; Isa. 38:5; Lam. 1:2. Ezek. 24:16 refers explicitly to tears of mourning over the loss of a loved one. The prophet Ezekiel is denied this expression of mourning, at Yahweh's command, over the sudden death of his wife, whom God took from him as a sign that the people of Israel will also soon be bereaved of their loved ones.

NT Words

dakryon [δάκρυον, *1144*]

dakryon is a noun occurring ten times with the consistent sense of "tears." General references to "tears" shed in grief include those in Acts 20:19, 31; 2 Cor. 2:4; 2 Tim. 1:4; Rev. 7:17; 21:4. Tears shed as a consequence of a penitent spirit are noted in Heb. 12:17. Christ shed tears during his life on earth as he earnestly prayed to the Father on behalf of his people (e.g., Heb. 5:7).

See Also: ➞ WEEP

TELL

OT Words

nāgad **[נָגַד, 5046]**

nāgad is a verb found in nearly 400 places expressing the primary meanings "tell," "declare," as well as several related nuances including "announce," "explain." (➞ REPORT)

nāgad commonly refers to the process of "telling" in the sense of "informing," or "communicating," information to people (e.g., Gen. 3:11; 37:11; Exod. 13:8; Judg. 4:12; Esth. 4:7; Isa. 36:22).

nāgad also has the nuance of "explain" or "declare," as in Gen. 41:24; 1 Sam. 9:6ff. Moses "declares" the word of God to the Israelites in Deut. 5:5. Judg. 14:12ff. refers to "telling" (i.e., explaining) a riddle. See also Job 31:37.

nāgad is also translated "tell" in the sense of "reveal," or "disclose," in a number of contexts. This meaning is evident in relation to disclosing secret information (cf. Josh. 2:20; Judg. 16:6; 1 Sam. 19:19); revealing the name of the angel of Yahweh (cf. Judg. 13:6ff.); confessing sins (cf. Josh. 7:19; Ps. 38:18); and a revelation from God (cf. 1 Sam. 3:15; Jer. 36:13ff.; Ezek. 43:10). See also 2 Sam. 17:16; Esth. 2:20; Job 42:3.

nāgad also means "tell" in the sense of "proclaim," especially in relation to expressing praise to God for his redemptive deeds on behalf of his people (cf. Pss. 9:11; 22:31; 50:6; 92:2; 145:4; Isa. 42:12; 57:12). Other settings for this usage include the expectation of impending divine judgment (cf. Jer. 5:20; 46:14; Mic. 3:8); the proclamation of the glory of God among the Gentiles (cf. Isa. 66:19); and the testimony of creation that "proclaims" the handiwork of Yahweh (cf. Ps. 19:1).

In several contexts, ***nāgad*** also denotes the divine action of "telling" in the sense of "declare" or "reveal." This is evident in relation to disclosing the law covenant (cf. Deut. 4:13); revealing a vision to the prophet Isaiah (cf. Isa. 21:2); and conveying his redemptive plan to his people (cf. Isa. 40:21; 42:9; Jer. 33:3). See also Dan. 10:21. In an expression of caustic divine sarcasm, and in judgment against pagan deities, Yahweh appeals to the gods to "tell" their plans to human beings (cf. Isa. 41:23).

'āmar **[אָמַר, 559 (560 Aramaic)]**

'āmar is among the most common verbs found in the Old Testament. It is translated "say," or "speak," in the large majority of its more than 5,300 occurrences. However, it also means "tell" in a significant number of instances, with several associated nuances.

Yahweh is sometimes depicted as "telling" the prophets to speak to the people of Israel. These contexts are concerned with issuing a command (cf. 1 Chr. 17:4; Isa. 6:9; Jer. 15:2; 35:13; Ezek. 3:11; 12:23; 17:22). Divine judgment in this regard is evident in Jer. 28:13, in relation to the condemnation of the false prophet Hananiah; and in Jer. 34:2 in regard to the rebellious King Zedekiah of Judah.

'āmar is also translated "tell" in relation to "informing" people. This usage applies to God (Gen. 22:2; 26:2; Ps. 50:12); and to people (Num. 14:14; 2 Sam. 7:5; 1 Kgs. 18:8ff.; 2 Kgs. 20:5; 1 Chr. 18:17; 2 Chr. 34:23; Job 34:34). The Aramaic equivalent is found in Dan. 2:4, 7, 9, 36, where Daniel relates the contents of the dream vision given to Nebuchadnezzar by Yahweh.

'āmar also has the underlying sense of "explain" in relation to the Israelite elders' responsibility to make clear to the people the details of God's remarkable actions of redemptive activity on their behalf (cf. Deut. 32:7).

dābar **[דָּבַר, 1696]**

This common verb, found in approximately 1,150 places, means "tell," "say," and "speak." (➞ SAY)

dābar means "tell" with reference to the process of "informing" or "explaining" (cf. Gen. 20:8; 24:33; 45:27; Judg. 20:3; 1 Kgs. 20:11; 1 Chr. 21:10; 1 Sam. 10:25).

1 Kgs. 22:16 contains an exhortation to "tell the truth"; and Judg. 16:10ff. refers to telling lies. God conveys his words to the prophet Jeremiah in Jer. 19:2.

sāphar **[סָפַר, 5608]**

sāphar is a verb meaning "number," "count" in most of its approximately 160 occurrences. In a little less than half of these, ***sāphar*** means "tell" in a variety of contexts. (➞ NUMBER)

General references to the meaning "tell" in the sense of "inform" include those in Gen. 24:66; Josh. 2:23; 1 Kgs. 13:11; 2 Kgs. 8:5.

sāphar also means "tell" in the sense of "recount," or "relate the contents of," in connection with dreams (cf. Gen. 37:9; 40:8ff.; 41:8ff.; Judg. 7:13; Jer. 23:27). It also refers to "recounting" the redemptive deeds of

God (cf. Exod. 10:2; Pss. 26:7; 48:13 [also Joel 1:3]) and conveying God's word to his people (cf. Exod. 24:3).

sîaḥ **[שִׂיחַ, 7878]**

The verb ***sîaḥ*** occurs twenty times, meaning "meditate," "speak," "talk," and "tell." (→ MEDITATE)

With reference to "telling," ***sîaḥ*** is used in the context of "reciting" the redemptive deeds of Yahweh (Judg. 5:10; 1 Chr. 16:9; Ps. 105:2).

NT Words

legō [λέγω, *3004*]

legō is a common verb occurring over 1,300 times with the dominant senses of "say," "speak." However, the meaning "tell" is evident in a number of places.

legō means "tell" in relation to conveying news and messages in Matt. 10:27; Mark 1:30; Luke 24:10; Phil. 3:18; 2 Thess. 2:5. In Acts 17:21, ***legō*** describes the process of "discussing" novel philosophies in the context of Athenian society.

legō also means "tell" with the underlying sense of "state," "declare." In Matt. 10:27; Mark 8:30, Jesus issues a command to his followers to tell no one that he is the Christ. Then, in Mark 10:32, Jesus "informs" his disciples what will happen to him as he comes to the end of his earthly life. Jesus also frequently declares, "I tell you . . ." (cf. Luke 12:51; 13:3; 18:8; 22:67; John 13:19; 16:7).

legō also means "tell" in the sense of "explain" in Mark 11:33; Luke 20:8, where Jesus refuses to reveal the true source of his authority to the unbelieving Pharisees.

apangellō [ἀπαγγέλλω, *518*]

apangellō is a verb with the primary meanings "tell," "report," as well as several related senses.

In general contexts, ***apangellō*** indicates the sense of "bring news of," or "report" (e.g., Matt. 2:8; 8:33; 28:9ff.; Mark 6:30; Luke 7:18; 8:36; John 4:51; Acts 12:14). A more formal sense of "bring a report" is indicated in Acts 4:23; 5:22; 28:21; 1 Thess. 1:9.

The term also means "tell" with the nuance of "declare," or "explain" (cf. Luke 8:47; Acts 11:13; 1 Cor. 14:25; Heb. 2:12).

anangellō [ἀναγγέλλω, *312*]

anangellō is a synonym for ***apangellō*** (see above), meaning "tell," "declare" in most of its eighteen occurrences.

The idea of "reporting" is noted in Mark 5:14; John 5:15; Acts 16:38; 1 Pet. 1:12. The nuance of "declare" or "affirm" is found in Acts 14:27; 15:4; 20:27; 1 John 1:5. And the sense of "relate," "recount" is evident in Mark 5:19.

laleō [λαλέω, *2980*]

laleō is a synonym for ***legō*** (see above), occurring around three hundred times and likewise translated "speak," "say." The variant sense of "tell" is found in several places.

The sense of "inform" is found in Luke 12:17; Acts 9:6. ***laleō*** also expresses the sense of "proclaim" in relation to the message of the gospel (cf. Acts 11:14); and to the shepherds' account of Jesus' birth (cf. Luke 2:18ff.) Jesus' claim to "proclaim" the truth is noted in John 8:40.

diēgeomai [διηγέομαι, *1334*]

diēgeomai is a verb found in eight places meaning "tell," "declare." The concept of "bringing a report" or "giving an account of" an incident or news is indicated in Mark 5:16; 9:9; Luke 9:10; Acts 9:27; 12:17; Heb. 11:32. ***diēgeomai*** also has the sense of "declare," or "proclaim" (cf. Luke 8:39). See also Acts 8:33.

eklaleō [ἐκλαλέω, *1583*]

eklaleō occurs only in Acts 23:22 (in the negative), meaning "tell" in the sense of "divulge," or "inform."

alētheuō [ἀληθεύω, *226*]

alētheuō is found only in Gal. 4:16; Eph. 4:15 meaning to "tell the truth."

See Also: → REBUKE → WARN

TEMPERANCE, TEMPERATE

NT Words

enkrateia [ἐγκράτεια, *1466*]

enkrateia is a noun found in three contexts indicating the virtue of "temperance," "restraint," or "self-control." It is used in a general sense in Acts 24:25, and it is listed as a fruit of the Spirit in Gal. 5:23; 2 Pet. 1:6.

enkratēs [ἐγκρατής, *1468*]

enkratēs is an adjective found only in Titus 1:8, referring to the personal quality of "self-control," "temperance."

enkrateuomai [ἐγκρατεύομαι, *1467*]

enkrateuomai is a rare verb found only in 1 Cor. 7:9, 25, referring to the exercise of self-control — the former in relation to sexual desire, the latter in regard to the lifestyle of the athlete.

sōphrōn [σώφρων, *4998*]

sōphrōn is an adjective, synonymous with ***enkratēs***, denoting the quality of "self-control" in 1 Tim. 3:2; Titus 1:8; 2:2, 5.

sōphroneō [σωφρονέω, *4993*]

sōphroneō is a verb found seven times, meaning "to be in (one's) right mind" and "to be self-controlled." The latter sense is indicated in Titus 2:6; 1 Pet. 4:7.

nēphō [νήφω, *3525*]

nēphō is another verb synonymous with ***enkrateuomai*** and ***sōphroneō***, above. It likewise indicates "exercising self-control" or "being temperate, or sober." ***nēphō*** occurs seven times (cf. 1 Thess. 5:6ff.; 2 Tim. 4:5; 1 Pet. 1:13; 4:7; 5:8).

nēphalios [νηφάλιος, *3524*]

nēphalios is another adjective synonymous with ***enkratēs*** and ***sōphrōn***, above, likewise signifying the quality of "sobriety," "temperance," "self-control" (cf. 1 Tim. 3:2, 11; Titus 2:2).

TEMPEST → STORM

TEMPLE

OT Words

hêkāl [הֵיכָל, **1964**]

hêkāl is a noun found approximately eighty times with the primary meanings "temple," "palace," referring primarily to the Israelite ritual sanctuary representing Yahweh's dwelling place among his people. As well as referring explicitly to the Jerusalem temple, ***hêkāl*** also indicates the tabernacle at Shiloh in 1 Sam. 1:9; 3:3. (→ TABERNACLE)

General references to the Jerusalem temple include those in 2 Kgs. 18:16; 2 Chr. 26:16; Jer. 7:4; Amos 8:3; Jonah 2:4ff. The temple construction is described in 1 Kgs. 6:3ff.; 7:21; 2 Chr. 3:17; 4:7ff. The temple is designated as belonging to Yahweh in 2 Sam. 22:7; Pss. 5:7; 27:9; 68:29; Jer. 50:8; Mic. 1:2; Mal. 3:1. Ezek. 8:14 records the practice of blatant idolatry in the temple; and Joel 3:5 refers to idol temples. The "heavenly temple" of Yahweh is described in the prophetic vision of Isaiah's calling in Isa. 6:1.

In relation to the postexilic "Second Temple," Ezra 3:6, 10 refer to its rebuilding, as does Hag. 2:15ff. The promise to rebuild it is found in Isa. 44:28; Zech. 6:12ff. Other general references include those in Neh. 6:10, 11.

The visionary temple of Ezekiel as revealed to him by God is specifically noted in Ezek. 41:1ff.; 42:8.

hêkāl means "palace," referring to royal residences, in Ps. 45:8, 15; Prov. 30:28; Isa. 13:22; Nah. 2:6; 1 Kgs. 21:1; 2 Kgs. 20:18; Dan. 1:4.

hêkal [הֵיכַל, **1965** (Aramaic)]

hêkal is the Aramaic equivalent of ***hêkāl*** (see above), again meaning "temple," "palace." The term is found thirteen times. The royal palace of Babylon is described in Ezra 4:14; 5:14; Dan. 4:4, 29. The Jerusalem temple is indicated in Ezra 5:14; 6:5; Dan. 5:2ff.; 6:18.

bayit [בַּיִת, **1004**]

bayit is a common noun occurring around two thousand times with the predominant meaning "house," as well as a wide variety of related senses, indicating various kinds of dwellings and including the designation "household." One of these related meanings is "temple," found in eleven contexts. ***bayit*** refers to the "house of the Lord" explicitly in 2 Kgs. 11:10, 13; 24:13; 2 Chr. 29:16. This sense is also implicitly indicated in 1 Chr. 6:10; 2 Kgs. 11:11; 2 Chr. 23:10; 35:20. The pagan temple of Dagon is likewise mentioned in 1 Chr. 10:10.

miqdāsh [מִקְדָּשׁ, **4720**]

miqdāsh is a noun translated as "sanctuary" (lit., "holy place") throughout its usage (approximately seventy contexts); though it is evidently synonymous with the temple as the dwelling place of the holy God of Israel. ***miqdāsh*** designates the entire structure of the temple and also refers to the inner temple, or holy of holies. However, the former sense is much more common.

General references to the tabernacle as the "sanctuary" include those in Exod. 15:17; 25:8; Lev. 12:4; 21:12; Num. 3:38. Similar references to the temple are noted in 1 Chr. 22:19; 2 Chr. 20:8; Neh. 10:39; Pss. 73:17; 78:69; Isa. 63:18; Jer. 17:12; Lam. 1:10. See also Ps. 74:7. This term also refers to Ezekiel's visionary temple in Ezek. 44:1, 5ff.; 45:3ff.; 47:12; 48:8ff. The pagan sanctuary of foreign peoples is noted in Isa. 16:12.

Lev. 16:33; 21:23; Jer. 51:51; Ezek. 44:16 refer to the inner sanctuary, or holy of holies.

The sanctuary in general terms is said to belong to Yahweh (Isa. 60:13; Lam. 2:7; Ezek. 8:6), and is defiled by sin (Ezek. 5:11; 23:38; 24:21).

miqdāsh also refers metaphorically to Yahweh as "the sanctuary" of his people in Isa. 8:14; Ezek. 11:16.

qōdesh [קֹדֶשׁ, 6944]

qōdesh is a term found in nearly 500 contexts, a synonym for ***miqdāsh*** (see above). It is used both adjectivally and nominally. The former usage is predominant, meaning "holy" in the majority of contexts. As a noun, ***qōdesh*** means "sanctuary" or "temple" in about seventy places. As with ***miqdāsh***, ***qōdesh*** indicates the sanctuary in general terms (the majority usage), as well as the inner sanctuary, or holy of holies.

General references to the tabernacle include those in Exod. 30:13; 36:1ff.; Lev. 5:15; Num. 3:30ff.; 7:9ff.; and Pss. 20:2; 68:24; Lam. 4:1; Dan. 8:13, 14 mention the temple. ***qōdesh*** also indicates Ezekiel's visionary temple in Ezek. 41:21ff.; 45:2.

The inner sanctuary, or holy of holies, is noted in Lev. 4:6; Num. 3:31; Ps. 63:2; Ezek. 41:21ff.; 45:3.

qōdesh is also used metaphorically to designate the nation of Judah as a sanctuary (cf. Ps. 114:2).

NT Words

hieron [ἱερόν, *2411*]

hieron is a noun meaning "temple" throughout its approximately seventy occurrences. It usually refers to the temple at Jerusalem (cf. Matt. 4:5; 21:12ff.; Mark 11:11ff.; Luke 2:27; 19:45ff.; John 2:14, 15; 8:20; Acts 2:46; 5:20ff.; 21:26ff.; 1 Cor. 9:13). It also refers to the temple of Artemis in Ephesus (Acts 19:27).

naos [ναός, *3485*]

naos is a synonym for ***hieron*** (see above), meaning "temple" throughout its forty-five occurrences. ***naos*** refers primarily to the inner sanctuary (i.e., the holy place) of the temple complex. It also denotes the structure as a whole.

References to the inner sanctuary of the Jerusalem temple include those in Matt. 23:16ff.; Mark 14:58; Luke 1:9, 21; John 2:19ff.; 2 Thess. 2:4; Rev. 3:12; 11:1, 2. In particular, Matt. 27:51; Mark 15:38; Luke 23:45 refer to tearing the veil separating the "holy of holies" from the rest of the temple at the time of Christ's crucifixion. ***naos*** refers to the temple as a whole (Matt. 26:61; 27:5), and also to the pagan "shrine" for the Greek goddess Diana (Acts 19:24). See also Acts 17:24.

naos is also used metaphorically in John 2:21 to refer to the "temple" of Jesus' body. Believers are declared to be "temples" of God's Spirit in 1 Cor. 3:16ff.; 6:19; 2 Cor. 6:16; Eph. 2:21. The book of Revelation contains a number of references to the heavenly "temple," which constitutes the consummate reality of the true "inner sanctuary" (cf. Rev. 7:15; 11:19; 14:15ff.; 15:5ff.; 16:1, 17; 21:22).

eidōleion [εἰδωλεῖον, *1493*]

eidōleion is found only in 1 Cor. 8:10, indicating an idol's "temple," or a temple consecrated for idolatrous worship.

Additional Notes

"Temple" vocabulary throughout both Old and New Testaments is consistent, though the motif undergoes a transformation in the transition from the old to the new covenant age.

From an overall biblical perspective, the "temple" (including the tabernacle) is the the dwelling place of God on earth, the central focal point of Israelite worship.

The New Testament shifts the theological dynamic of the temple motif. Whereas temple worship in the Old Testament was focused on a physical structure and relied on external ritual, in the New Testament there emerges a new focus on the worship of God that transcends the ritual infrastructure of worship in the temple. This new focal point is now concentrated much more on the person of God in Christ and the spiritual realities of the temple phenomenon to which the old covenant pointed.

The tearing of the curtain that screened off the most holy place was a highly significant turning point. After the death of Christ, access to God and the blessings of forgiveness and atonement were no longer limited by restricted passage to an inner sanctuary through the mediation of an earthly priesthood once a year. Now, all those who joined themselves to Christ through faith and repentance would have direct and immediate access to the throne room of God, without the need for an earthly mediator.

The phenomenon of "temple worship" in the new covenant era has thus moved from an earthly structure to a spiritual, heavenly one. The crucial central element is the person of Christ, in whose being the phenomenon of "temple" finds full spiritual manifestation. By way of spiritual bonding, all believers are described as "temples" of the Holy Spirit, joined to Christ by faith and trust. New covenant worship is not defined by an external ritual house of worship.

Significantly, John observes in his vision of the heavenly Jerusalem that there is no separate temple structure. Rather, the entire heavenly city constitutes a "temple manifestation," or the heavenly dwelling of God and Christ together with his people, forever. The Old Testament depiction of temple worship anticipated this reality; the coming of Christ in the New brought this vision of God and the community of his people to its consummate fulfillment.

TEMPT, TEMPTATION

OT Words

nāsāh [נָסָה, 5254]

nāsāh is a verb occurring around forty times meaning "test," "prove," "tempt." The latter sense is found explicitly in about one-third of these contexts, although there is some overlap in meaning between all three nuances. (→ PROOF)

nāsāh refers to Yahweh's action in Gen. 22:1 in "tempting" Abraham to offer up his son Isaac as a sacrifice. Such an action was never to be required of Abraham. Rather, Yahweh was putting the patriarch's faith to a severe test. Hence the underlying sense of ***nāsāh*** in this context is "to test the quality or legitimacy of." Israel was similarly "tested" by Yahweh in the wilderness (cf. Exod. 15:25), in relation to their faith in him.

Where human beings instigate "tempting," it is seen as a sinful, culpable action with God as its object. People are said "to put (God) to the test," as a means of challenging his power and/or authority (cf. Exod. 17:2, 7; Num. 14:22; Pss. 78:18, 41, 56; 95:9; 106:14). See also Isa. 7:2.

NT Words

peirazō [πειράζω, *3985*]

peirazō is a verb occurring about forty times, with the primary meanings "tempt," "put to the test" in the sense of ascertaining the validity or integrity of one's faith in God. ***peirazō*** is therefore to be regarded as a dynamic equivalent for ***nāsāh*** (see above). The term is used in a variety of contexts.

Satan is depicted as "tempting" Christ in the wilderness — attempting, without success, to have him betray his trust in God (cf. Matt. 4:13; Mark 1:13; Luke 4:2; Heb. 2:18; 4:15). 1 Cor. 7:5 also describes Satan's active tempting of Christian couples to violate their marriage vows through sexual misconduct. 1 Thess. 3:5 refers to the devil tempting believers in general.

The Pharisees are frequently described as "tempting" Christ during his earthly ministry, deliberately seeking to trap or ensnare him so as to bring an accusation against him (cf. Matt. 16:1; 19:3; 22:18, 35; Mark 8:11; 10:2; 12:15; Luke 11:16; John 8:16).

Warnings against being tempted to sin are given in Gal. 6:1; and the reality of that state is found in Jas. 1:14. Jas. 1:13 affirms that God is never directly the agent of tempting. The Israelites' sin of "tempting" God in the wilderness is noted in 1 Cor. 10:9; Heb. 3:9. In Acts 5:9, the sin of Ananias and Sapphira in lying to the apostles about the sale of property is described as "tempting (i.e., putting to the test) the Spirit of the Lord" — a sin for which they were struck dead.

1 Cor. 10:13 records the promise that God will keep his people from being "tempted" or "tested" beyond their capacity to cope.

peirasmos [πειρασμός, *3986*]

peirasmos is a noun derived from ***peirazō*** (see above), occurring around twenty times with the consistent meaning "temptation," primarily in the context of incitement to sin. The term is also translated "trial." (→ TRIAL)

The prayer that God will not lead his people into temptation is recorded in Matt. 6:13; Luke 11:14. Luke 8:13 mentions those who fall away, having given in to temptation. Matt. 26:41; Mark 14:38; Luke 22:40, 46 contain exhortations to keep away from temptation. See also 1 Tim. 6:9.

Satan fails completely to ensnare Christ in the temptation to act on his own initiative rather than place his trust in God (cf. Luke 4:13). 1 Cor. 10:13 contains the promise that God will always provide a way of escape for the believer from succumbing to various "temptations," or "trials."

ekpeirazō [ἐκπειράζω, *1598*]

ekpeirazō is a verb found only four times, meaning "tempt," or "put to the test." Matt. 4:7; Luke 4:12 refer to Jesus' rebuke of the devil, appealing to the scriptural command that God must not be tempted. That sin is attributed to the Israelite people during their wandering in the wilderness, who did in fact put God to the test (cf. 1 Cor. 10:9).

apeirastos [ἀπείραστος, *551*]

apeirastos is an adjectival form meaning "cannot be tempted," found only in Jas. 1:13 with reference to God.

TENDER

OT Words

rak [רַךְ, 7390]

rak is an adjective occurring sixteen times, referring to choice, "tender" meat (cf. Gen. 18:7); and a "tender" plant (cf. Ezek. 17:2). The term also refers to the "tender" age and inexperience of youth (cf. 1 Chr. 22:5); and also to a "softness" or "tenderness" of character (cf. Deut. 28:54, 56).

rākak [רָכַךְ, 7401]

rākak is a verb found eight times meaning "to be tender," "faint-hearted" throughout most of this usage.

"Faint-heartedness" in the sense of lack of courage is indicated in Deut. 20:3; Isa. 7:4. Such "faint-heartedness" as a perceived judgment from God is indicated in Job 23:16.

Exhortations not to be "faint-hearted" are recorded in Isa. 7:4; Jer. 51:46.

A "tender heart," or one that is responsive to the prompting of the Spirit of God, is described in 2 Kgs. 22:19; 2 Chr. 34:27.

yônēq [יוֹנֵק, 3126]

yônēq is a term found only in Isa. 53:2, indicating a "tender plant."

NT Words

hapalos [ἁπαλός, *527*]

hapalos is an adjective found only in Matt. 24:32; Mark 13:28, referring to a "tender" branch that is ready to bud.

eusplanchnos [εὔσπλαγχνος, *2155*]

eusplanchnos is an adjective meaning "tender-hearted" (cf. Eph. 4:32; 1 Pet. 3:8).

See Also: → MERCY

TENT → TABERNACLE

TERRIBLE, TERROR

OT Words

deḥal [דְּחַל, 1763 (Aramaic)]

deḥal is an Aramaic verb found six times that functions primarily as an adjective. It means "be afraid," "terrified," or "terrifying," "dreadful." Dan. 2:31; 4:5; 7:7, 19 refer to terrifying visions given by God. Dan. 5:19; 6:26 speak of the terror of powerful armies.

môrā' [מוֹרָא, 4172]

môrā' is a noun derived from ***yārē'*** (→ FEAR) meaning "terror," "fear," or "dread." It is found in thirteen contexts, most of which refer to the "terror" of God's judgments upon wicked humankind (cf. Deut. 4:34; 11:25; 26:8; 34:12; Ps. 9:20; Jer. 32:21). ***môrā'*** also refers to the "terror" or "dread" of God himself. See also Gen. 9:2.

ballāhāh [בַּלָּהָה, 1091]

ballāhāh is a noun with the consistent meaning "terror," or "calamity," sometimes brought about by God as a judgment against wicked people.

General references include those in Job 18:11, 14; 24:17; 27:20; 30:15; Ps. 73:19; Isa. 17:14. God-ordained disasters are evident in Ezek. 26:21; 27:36; 28:19.

See Also: → FEAR

TERRIFY

OT Words

bā'at [בָּעַת, 1204]

bā'at is a verb found sixteen times with the predominant meaning "to terrify," "instill fear," commonly predicated of God against human beings (cf. Job 3:5; 7:14; 9:34; 13:11; 21; 15:24; 18:11; 33:7).

NT Words

ptoeō [πτοέω, *4422*]

ptoeō is a rare verb, found only in Luke 21:9; 24:37, meaning "to terrify," "be afraid."

ekphobeō [ἐκφοβέω, *1629*]

ekphobeō is another rare verb meaning to "frighten," or "terrify," found only in 2 Cor. 10:9.

TEST

OT Words

bāḥan [בָּחַן, 974]

bāḥan is a verb meaning "try," "prove," "examine"; all with the sense of "testing," in several different contexts.

bāḥan refers to "testing" for the purpose of determining someone's genuine intention or integrity (Gen. 42:15; Jer. 6:27); and for the purpose of examining someone's word as truth (Gen. 42:16). ***bāḥan*** is also used in relation to "putting God to the test" (cf. Ps. 95:9; Mal. 3:15). See also Job 7:18; 12:11.

In several places, God is said to "test" the heart of someone to see whether that person is genuine in their devotion to the Lord, or to engender such an attitude (cf. 1 Chr. 29:17; Job 23:10; Pss. 7:9; 26:2; Prov. 17:3; Jer. 11:20; 17:20). Yahweh also "tests" his people through a trial, a traumatic experience, to purge them of their lack of devotion to him (cf. Ps. 81:7; Jer. 9:7; Zech. 13:9).

ṣāraph [צָרַף, **6884**]

ṣāraph occurs around thirty times meaning "try," "prove," or "test." In a number of places ***ṣāraph*** indicates "smelting" or "refining." (→ REFINE)

Judg. 7:4 refers to "testing" for the purpose of proving people's integrity or faithfulness to a task. Ps. 105:19 refers to being tested or vindicated by the word of God.

God's action in "testing" his people to gauge their devotion to him is noted in Pss. 17:3; 28:2; cf. also Ps. 66:10.

NT Words

dokimazō [δοκιμάζω, *1381*]

dokimazō is a verb found thirty times meaning "prove," "examine," "test" throughout.

The process of "testing" (i.e., proofing, or assessing) that which is good is described in Rom. 12:2; Phil. 1:10; 1 Thess. 5:2. Such a process is also indicated in relation to one's love for God (cf. 2 Cor. 8:8); and concerning one's suitability for the office of deacon (cf. 1 Tim. 3:10). ***dokimazō*** is also used in this sense in relation to the life work of the believer, which will be "tested" on the day of judgment.

dokimazō also means "test" with the underlying sense of "to scrutinize," or "examine." This is evident in 1 John 4:1 in relation to believers "testing the spirits," to see whether they are of God. It also refers to the Lord's Supper, as believers are exhorted to "examine" themselves prior to taking the sacrament. See also 2 Cor. 13:5; Gal. 6:4.

Heb. 3:9 refers to the sinful action of the Israelites in putting God to the test.

TESTATOR → COVENANT

TESTIFY, TESTIMONY → WITNESS

THANK, THANKS, THANKSGIVING

OT Words

yedā' [יְדָא, **3029** (Aramaic)]

yedā' is an Aramaic verb found only in Dan. 2:23; 6:10 meaning to "give thanks" to God.

tôdāh [תּוֹדָה, **8426**]

tôdāh is a noun derived from ***yādāh*** (→ PRAISE), meaning "thanks," "thanksgiving" throughout most of the approximately thirty occurrences of the term. The contexts are exclusively ritual, denoting giving thanks to Yahweh — for example, in connection with sacrifice (cf. Lev. 7:12ff.; 22:29; 2 Chr. 29:31; Pss. 50:14; 100:1ff.; Jer. 17:26); in relation to building the walls of Jerusalem (cf. Neh. 12:27ff.); and in singing songs of thanksgiving in worship (cf. Pss. 26:7; 69:30; 147:7; Isa. 51:3; Jer. 30:19).

tôdāh also means "confession" in one or two contexts. (→ CONFESS)

NT Words

eucharisteō [εὐχαριστέω, *2168*]

eucharisteō is a verb meaning "give thanks," "be thankful," primarily in the context of giving thanks to God.

Jesus expresses such thankfulness to the Father in Matt. 15:36; Mark 8:6; John 6:11; 11:41. In particular, he does so at the Passover festival (cf. Matt. 26:27; Mark 14:23; Luke 22:17ff.). See also 1 Cor. 11:24.

People give thanks to Christ for healing them in Luke 17:16.

General references to thanks being offered up to God include those in Luke 18:11; Acts 28:15; Rev. 11:17. In Rom. 1:21, unbelievers refuse to give thanks to God. Paul gives thanks to God for the salvation offered in Christ (cf. Rom. 1:8; 7:25; 1 Cor. 1:4; Eph. 5:20; Col. 1:3). See also Acts 27:35; Eph. 1:16; 1 Thess. 1:2; Phlm. 4.

eucharistia [εὐχαριστία, *2169*]

eucharistia is a noun derived from ***eucharisteō*** (see above). It is found in fifteen places and means "thanks," "thanksgiving," "thankfulness" throughout — primarily in relation to God.

Thanksgiving to God in worship is noted in 1 Cor. 14:16; Rev. 4:9; 7:2. Other general contexts for the expression of gratitude include those in 2 Cor. 4:15; Phil. 4:6; Col. 2:7; 1 Tim. 2:1; 4:3ff.

exomologeō [ἐξομολογέω, *1843*]

exomologeō is a verb expressing the primary meaning "confess." However, in two of the eleven occurrences of the term, the meaning indicated is "give thanks" in relation to Jesus' gratitude to God for making his revelation known not to the proud, who called themselves "wise," but to the "little children," or those who showed genuine faith and dependence on God for all their needs (cf. Matt. 11:25; Luke 10:21).

eucharistos [εὐχάριστος, *2170*]

eucharistos is an adjectival form found only in Col. 3:15 meaning "thankful" in relation to the believer's gratitude for his saving relationship with Christ.

anthomologeomai [ἀνθομολογέομαι, *437*]

This is a rare verb found only in Luke 2:38 in the context of "giving thanks" to God.

See Also: → BLESS → CONFESS → GRACE → PRAISE

THIEF → ROB

THIGH

OT Words

yārēk [יָרֵךְ, **3409**]

yārēk is a noun found in thirty contexts meaning "thigh," or "side," in the literal sense of the "upper portion of the leg." It also refers metaphorically to the male genital organ in association with taking a solemn oath or vow.

In metaphorical contexts, ***yārēk*** is euphemistically translated "thigh." Here the one taking the solemn oath would place his hand on the genital area (i.e., "under the thigh") of the one "receiving" the oath or promise (cf. Gen. 24:2, 9; 47:29). ***yārēk*** also indicates a woman's ability to bear children in the reference to her "thigh" in Num. 5:21ff. This ability will be taken from her as a punishment if she is found guilty of adultery upon failing a trial by ordeal.

yārēk refers literally to "thighs," including that portion of an animal's leg taken as food (Ezek. 24:4); and the human thigh (Gen. 32:25; Isa. 47:2; Jer. 31:19), in particular as the location on the body for strapping on a sword for battle (cf. Judg. 3:16, 21; Song 3:8). See also Isa. 45:3.

The action of striking the thigh as a sign of remorse is indicated in Jer. 31:19; Ezek. 21:12.

shôq [שׁוֹק, **7785**]

shôq is a noun found in around twenty contexts with the specific sense of "thigh" for most of the usage, referring to the upper portion of the human leg, as well as to the upper hind leg of an animal. This latter portion is set aside for human consumption in the context of food set aside for the Israelite priesthood.

This portion of the animal designated as food for priests refers generally to the ram's thigh. It is indicated in the context of the consecration or ordination sacrifice for the priests (cf. Exod. 29:22ff.; Lev. 8:25ff.); as well as for the Nazirite consecration rituals (cf. Num. 6:20).

Other general references to the "thigh" of an animal being set aside for food are found in relation to the fellowship offering (cf. Lev. 7:32ff.; 9:21; 10:14ff.). See also Num. 18:18; 1 Sam. 9:24.

General references to the human "thigh" are found in Ps. 147:10; Prov. 26:27; Song 5:15; Isa. 47:2. In Deut. 28:35, the "thigh" is designated as the site of a boil infestation, an element of the curse of the covenant.

The phrase "hip and thigh" occurs in Judg. 15:8, referring to a vicious slaughter.

yarkāh [יַרְכָה, **3410** (Aramaic)]

yarkāh is an Aramaic noun designating "the (bronze) thighs" of the giant statue in the dream given by God to King Nebuchadnezzar of Babylon (cf. Dan. 2:32).

NT Words

mēros [μηρός, *3382*]

mēros is a noun found only in Rev. 19:16, referring to the "thigh" of Christ, the divine warrior, bearing the name "King of Kings and Lord of Lords" as he rides forth to overthrow all the armies of Satan.

THING

OT Words

dābār [דָּבָר, **1697**]

dābār is a common term primarily denoting a "word," but with numerous related nuances, including the vague sense of "thing." It also indicates the negative meaning "nothing" (Gen. 24:50; Deut. 22:26; Dan. 1:20; Ezek. 11:25; Isa. 39:2; Amos 3:7). Often ***dābār*** denotes "thing" in the sense of "matter," "affair," or "business" (cf. Gen. 21:11; Exod. 33:17; Eccl. 1:8; 12:13; Jer. 20:1; Ezra 7:1; 10:4; Esth. 2:23; Ps. 112:5). ***dābār*** in this sense also refers to blessings and curses (Deut. 30:1); ceremonially unclean objects (Lev. 5:2); sacred offerings (Num. 18:7); and "wicked things" (Deut. 23:9).

NT Words

pragma [πρᾶγμα, *4229*]

pragma is a noun found eleven times with the underlying sense of "something accomplished or done," "an established fact." It is translated "thing," "matter" for the most part; and it is thus a partial dynamic equivalent for ***dābār*** (see above).

The sense of a "transaction" is indicated in Matt. 18:19; Acts 5:4. Reference to "things" fulfilled by divine power is found in Luke 1:1. A "legal dispute or matter" is noted in 1 Cor. 6:1 (cf. also 2 Cor. 7:11). The "matter" of sexual purity is indicated in 1 Thess. 4:6. With reference to God's utter truthfulness, ***pragma*** denotes two unchangeable "things" that make it impossible for God to lie (cf. Heb. 6:18). Heb. 10:1 refers to spiritual "realities." See also Heb. 11:1; Jas. 3:16.

agathos [ἀγαθός, *18*]

agathos is an adjectival form denoting "good things" in a number of contexts. A question as to what "good thing" one must do to gain eternal life is put to Christ in Matt. 19:16. "Doing good" is commended in Eph. 6:8. The possession of "every good thing" in Christ is noted in Phlm. 6. See also John 1:46; Gal. 4:18; 2 Tim. 1:14; Heb. 13:9.

The negative sense of "nothing good" is indicated in relation to human nature in Rom. 7:18.

plasma [πλάσμα, *4110*]

plasma is a rare noun found only in Rom. 9:20, denoting "the thing formed by the potter," or a clay pot.

koinos [κοινός, *2839*]

koinos is an adjective found twelve times with the underlying senses of "common," and "unclean." In Heb. 10:29 it refers to the heinous crime of treating the death of Christ, his shed blood, as an "unholy thing," thereby drawing down the wrath of God.

prōtos [πρῶτος, *4413*]

prōtos is a common adjective found over one hundred times with the primary meaning "first." Much rarer is the meaning "former." In Rev. 21:24 ***prōtos*** refers to the "former things" (i.e., the legal conditions of the old covenant) that have passed away in the wake of the redemptive work of Christ.

Additional Notes

The denotation of "thing(s)" in the New Testament is generally vague and non-specific, other than the references above. The primary usage is made up of particles and pronouns.

THINK, THOUGHT

OT Words

ḥāshab [**חָשַׁב, 2803**]

ḥāshab is a verb occurring around 120 times with various meanings, including "count," "reckon," "consider," "plan," as well as related nuances. These are all senses related to the process of rational human thinking. The general meaning "think" is also included in the usage of ***ḥāshab***, although the meanings overlap in a number of instances.

The process of "thinking" in the sense of "considering," "believing" is indicated in Gen. 38:15; 1 Sam. 1:13; 18:25; Job 6:26. God is said to "think of, or about" his people in the sense of "showing concern" in Ps. 40:17. Ps. 119:59 refers to thinking about, or "contemplating," the ways of the Lord. See also Isa. 10:7.

'āmar [**אָמַר, 559**]

'āmar is a common verb found over 5,300 times with the dominant sense of "say," "speak," as well as numerous related senses. One of these is the meaning "think," indicating the process of rational assessment or consideration (cf. Gen. 20:11; Judg. 15:2; 2 Chr. 13:8; Eccl. 8:17).

maḥashābāh [**מַחֲשָׁבָה, 4284**]

maḥashābāh is a noun occuring approximately sixty times, derived from ***ḥāshab*** (see above). It expresses the primary meaning "thought" in around half of its usage. ***maḥashābāh*** also has several related nuances, such as "plan," "plot," "skill."

General references to the "thoughts" of the human heart include those in 1 Chr. 28:9; Job 21:27; Ps. 94:11. ***maḥashābāh*** refers to wicked thoughts (Gen. 6:5; Ps. 56:5; Prov. 15:26; Isa. 55:7), as well as righteous thoughts (Prov. 12:5; 21:5).

Pss. 33:11; 40:5; Mic. 4:12; Isa. 55:8ff. contain metaphorical references to the "thoughts" of God's heart.

shā'ar [**שָׁעַר, 8176**]

shā'ar is a verb found once, in Prov. 23:7, meaning "think" in the sense of "calculate" or "reason."

NT Words

dokeō [δοκέω, *1380*]

dokeō is a verb with the general meaning "to think" throughout most of its nearly sixty occurrences, in a variety of contexts. The underlying sense is that of "making a rational assessment," or "giving consideration to."

General references to such a process are found in Matt. 6:7; 22:17. "Thinking" in the sense of "believing" is indicated in Matt. 17:25; Luke 19:11; John 11:56; Acts 26:9; 1 Cor. 4:9; 8:2; 12:23. Matt. 22:42 refers to thinking about or believing in Jesus Christ.

dokeō also means "think" in the sense of "suppose" (cf. Mark 6:49; Luke 8:18; 10:36; John 11:13; 2 Cor. 12:19; Jas. 4:5).

dialogismos [διαλογισμός, *1261*]

dialogismos is a noun found fourteen times with the general meaning "thoughts," as well as associated nuances (e.g., "doubts," as well as "thinking," i.e., the process of human reasoning itself).

"Thoughts" in general are indicated in Luke 2:35; 1 Cor. 3:20. Evil thoughts in particular are noted in Matt. 15:19; Mark 7:21; Jas. 2:4. "Doubts" (i.e., "questioning thoughts") are mentioned in Luke 5:22; 6:8; 9:47; 24:38. Luke 9:46; Phil. 2:14 refer to "arguments."

Rom. 1:21 contains the theologically significant affirmation that sin has rendered human "thinking" (i.e., our very thought processes) futile in a moral and spiritual sense.

nomizō [νομίζω, *3543*]

nomizō is a verb found in fifteen places meaning "think," or "suppose" (cf. Matt. 5:17; 20:10; Luke 2:44; Acts 7:25; 17:29; 1 Cor. 7:36).

hyponoeō [ὑπονοέω, *5282*]

hyponoeō is a verb found only three times, meaning "think," "suppose" (cf. Acts 13:35; 25:18; 27:27).

phroneō [φρονέω, *5426*]

phroneō is a verb with a number of meanings, including "think," "agree," "to be like-minded," "regard." ***phroneō*** occurs about forty times. The meaning "think" includes a number of related nuances. (→ AGREE)

Acts 28:22 means "think" with the sense of "express a view or opinion." In Rom. 12:3; 1 Cor. 4:6, ***phroneō*** means "think" with the idea of estimating the level of one's own importance. 1 Cor. 13:11 speaks of "thinking," or "reasoning," like a child.

dianoēma [διανόημα, *1270*]; *epinoia* [ἐπίνοια, *1963*]

These two nouns are rare synonyms for ***dialogismos*** (see above), meaning "thoughts." ***dianoēma*** is found only in Luke 11:17, and ***epinoia*** only in Acts 8:22.

enthymeomai [ἐνθυμέομαι, *1760*]

enthymeomai is a verb found three times meaning "think" in the sense of "ponder," "think about," focusing on one's inner thoughts (cf. Matt. 1:20; 9:4; Acts 10:19).

enthymēsis [ἐνθύμησις, *1761*]

This noun is derived from ***enthymeomai*** (see above). It is found in four contexts, meaning "thought" in the sense of the innermost thoughts of one's heart (cf. Matt. 9:4; 12:25; Acts 17:29; Heb. 4:12).

oimai [οἶμαι, *3633*]

oimai is a verb meaning "think" in the sense of "suppose," found only in John 21:25; Phil. 1:16; Jas. 1:7.

See Also: → CARE → COUNT → RECKON → UNDERSTAND → WORTHY

THIRST, THIRSTY

OT Words

ṣāmēʾ [צָמֵא, **6770** (Verb), **6771** (Adjective)]

ṣāmēʾ is a verb meaning "to thirst," "be thirsty."

Literal references to being thirsty include those in Exod. 17:3; Judg. 4:19; 15:18; Ruth 2:9; Isa. 48:11. See also Isa. 65:13. ***ṣāmēʾ*** is also used metaphorically to indicate "thirsting" after God (cf. Pss. 42:2; 63:1).

ṣāmēʾ is also an adjectival form meaning "thirsty" found in Deut. 29:19; 2 Sam. 17:29; Ps. 107:5; Isa. 21:14; 44:3; 55:1.

ṣāmāʾ [צָמָא, **6772**]

ṣāmāʾ is a noun meaning "thirst" throughout its seventeen occurrences (cf. Exod. 17:3; Neh. 9:15ff.; Ps. 104:11; Isa. 5:13; Ezek. 19:13; Amos 8:11ff.).

ṣimʾāh [צִמְאָה, **6773**]

ṣimʾāh is a rare variant of ***ṣāmāʾ*** (see above). It means "thirst" and is found only in Jer. 2:25.

ṣimmāʾôn [צִמָּאוֹן, **6774**]

ṣimmāʾôn is a noun meaning "thirsty ground," in the context of drought. It occurs only in Deut. 8:15; Ps. 107:33; Isa. 35:7.

NT Words

dipsaō [διψάω, *1372*]

dipsaō is a dynamic equivalent for the verb ***ṣāmēʾ*** (see above). It is found in eighteen places and means "to thirst," "be thirsty."

The experience of literally "being thirsty" is noted in Matt. 25:35ff.; John 4:13ff.; 19:28; Rom. 12:20; 1 Cor. 4:11; Rev. 7:16. ***dipsaō*** is also used metaphorically, indicating "thirsting after" true righteousness and godly living (cf. Matt. 5:6). John 6:35 guarantees that those who believe in Christ shall never thirst again — they shall be satisfied forever in every aspect of their being. See also Rev. 21:6; 22:7.

dipsos [δίψος, *1373*]

dipsos is a rare noun, found only in 2 Cor. 11:27 with reference to "thirst."

THORN

OT Words

ḥôaḥ [חוֹחַ, 2336]

ḥôaḥ is a noun occurring eleven times meaning "thorn," "briar," "bramble" in most of these places.

Several texts mention "thorns" in the sense of "briar bush" (cf. Job 31:40; Song 2:2; Isa. 34:13; Hos. 9:6). A general reference to "thorns" is found in Prov. 26:9.

na'aṣûṣ [נַעֲצוּץ, 5285]

na'aṣûṣ indicates a "thorn bush." It is found only twice (Isa. 7:19; 55:13).

qôṣ [קוֹץ, 6975]

qôṣ is a noun synonymous with ***ḥôaḥ*** and ***na'aṣûṣ***, above, meaning "thorn," "thorn bush" in twelve contexts (cf. Gen. 3:18; Exod. 22:6; Judg. 8:7ff.; 2 Sam. 23:6; Ps. 118:12; Isa. 32:13; Jer. 4:3; Ezek. 28:24; Hos. 10:8).

mesûkāh [מְסוּכָה, 4534]

mesûkāh is a rare noun indicating a "thorn hedge" in Mic. 7:4.

NT Words

skolops [σκόλοψ, *4647*]

skolops is a term found only in 2 Cor. 12:7, referring metaphorically to Paul's "thorn in the flesh" — an unidentified source of pain and anguish given to him by God, after an extraordinary vision of heavenly realities.

akantha [ἄκανθα, *173*]

akantha is a noun found in fourteen contexts, meaning "thorns" or "briars" throughout (cf. Matt. 7:16; 13:7ff.; Mark 4:7; Luke 6:44; John 19:2; Heb. 6:8).

akanthinos [ἀκάνθινος, *174*]

akanthinos is found only in Mark 15:17, referring to the "crown of thorns" placed on the head of Christ prior to his crucifixion.

THOUGHT → THINK

THREATEN

NT Words

apeileō [ἀπειλέω, *546*]

apeileō is a verb found only in 1 Pet. 2:23, meaning "threaten" (used here in the negative).

prosapeileō [προσαπειλέω, *4324*]

prosapeileō is a variant of ***apeileō***, above, meaning "threaten further" in Acts 4:21.

apeilē [ἀπειλή, *547*]

apeilē is a noun (derived from ***apeileō***, above) referring to "threats" in three places (Acts 4:29; 9:1; Eph. 6:9).

THRESH

OT Words

dûsh [דּוּשׁ, 1758]

dûsh is a verb meaning "tread," "trample," or "thresh" in most of its fourteen occurrences, with some overlap in meaning.

The literal action of "threshing" or "treading out" grain is indicated in 1 Chr. 21:20; Isa. 28:27ff.

dûsh also refers metaphorically to "threshing" in the sense of "pulverizing." The contexts denote total military conquest (cf. 2 Kgs. 13:7; Amos 1:3). In particular, Isa. 41:5; Mic. 4:13 refer to Yahweh's consummate victory over the enemies of his people.

ḥābat [חָבַט, 2251]

ḥābat is a verb synonymous with ***dûsh***, above, meaning "thresh," "beat out." It is used literally in relation to grain (Judg. 6:11; Ruth 2:17); and metaphorically in relation to Yahweh "beating" his enemies (Isa. 27:12).

dayish [דַּיִשׁ, 1786]

dayish is a rare noun found only in Lev. 26:5, referring to the "threshing (process)."

***môrag* [מוֹרַג, 4173]**

môrag refers to a "threshing instrument." It is found only three times (2 Sam. 24:22; 1 Chr. 21:23; Isa. 41:15).

***ḥārûṣ* [חָרוּץ, 2742]**

ḥārûṣ is a noun found in eighteen places with the primary sense of "threshing instrument" in some of these contexts. The literal understanding of *ḥārûṣ* refers to a "sharp-pointed implement," and it is used literally only in Isa. 28:27.

Metaphorically, *ḥārûṣ* refers to Israel being fashioned into a "threshing sledge" by Yahweh (Isa. 41:15); and to the "trampling" of a nation (Amos 1:3). See also Job 41:30. (→ DILIGENCE → GOLD)

***gōren* [גֹּרֶן, 1637]**

gōren is a noun found in approximately forty places with the primary meaning "threshing floor" (e.g., Gen. 50:10ff.; Judg. 6:37; Ruth 3:2ff.; Jer. 51:33).

***'iddrê* [אִדְּרֵי, 147 (Aramaic)]**

'iddrê is an Aramaic noun found only in Dan. 2:35, indicating a "threshing floor."

THROAT

OT Words

***gārôn* [גָּרוֹן, 1627]**

gārôn means "throat," "neck" in relation to people in eight contexts (cf. Pss. 69:3; 115:7; 149:6; Jer. 2:25). In Ps. 5:9, the wicked are described as those whose "throat is an open grave."

***lōa'* [לֹעַ, 3930]**

lōa' is a rare noun, occurring only in Prov. 23:2 meaning "throat."

NT Words

***pnigō* [πνίγω, *4155*]**

pnigō is a rare verb denoting the action of "seizing by the throat" (cf. Matt. 18:18).

***larynx* [λάρυγξ, *2995*]**

larynx is another rare noun, the dynamic equivalent of *gārôn* (see above). It is found only in Rom. 3:3, where Paul cites the refrain from Ps. 5:9, describing the "throat" of the wicked as an "open grave."

THRONE

OT Words

***kissē'* [כִּסֵּא, 3678]**

kissē' is a noun occurring in around 130 places meaning "throne," indicating "the seat of royal authority and power," applied to both God and human beings.

Concerning royal office, *kissē'* refers to the "thrones" of human beings in various contexts: to thrones generally (Deut. 17:18; Judg. 3:20; 1 Kgs. 22:10; Esth. 1:2; Prov. 16:12; Isa. 14:9; Hag. 2:22); to the "throne" of Egypt (Gen. 41:40; Exod. 11:5; 12:29); of Israel (1 Kgs. 1:13ff.; 2:4ff.; 10:9; 2 Kgs. 15:12); of Babylon (Isa. 14:9; 47:1); and of Nineveh (Jonah 3:6). A metaphorical usage is found in 1 Sam. 2:8.

kissē' also indicates the "throne" as being synonymous with the "kingdom" established by God (cf. Jer. 13:13; 22:2). In this regard, particular mention is made of the "throne of David" in 2 Sam. 3:10; 7:13ff.; 1 Kgs. 2:12; 1 Chr. 17:12ff.; Ps. 132:11, 12. In Ps. 89:4, 14, 29, 36; Isa. 9:7; Zech. 6:13, references to the Davidic "throne" are indicative of the coming messianic ruler.

All instances of *kissē'* referring to the throne of Yahweh point to his heavenly throne — the seat of divine justice, majesty, and power (cf. 2 Chr. 18:18; Pss. 9:7; 11:4; 45:6; Isa. 6:1; 66:1; Lam. 5:19; Ezek. 1:26; 10:1).

kissē' is also used metaphorically in Prov. 9:14 to refer to the high civil office, the "seat" of authority granted to Lady Wisdom.

***korsē'* [כָּרְסֵא, 3764 (Aramaic)]**

korsē' is a rare Aramaic noun meaning "throne." It refers once to Nebuchadnezzar, king of Babylon (Dan. 5:20), and twice to the "heavenly throne" of Yahweh, and those of lesser authority under him (Dan. 7:9).

***kappōret* [כַּפֹּרֶת, 3727]**

kappōret is a noun derived from the verb *kāphar* meaning "to cover," "make atonement" (→ PROPITIATION) — a ritual term describing the means by which the sin of God's people was dealt with under the old covenant. This was obtained through offering a blood sacrifice that "covered" the sins of the offerer. Hidden by the blood, the offense was rendered null and void.

The term *kappōret* has been translated "mercy seat" in the older English versions, which in modern usage is rendered "atonement cover." This refers to the golden cover of the ark of the covenant on which was sculpted two golden cherubim, whose wings covered the lid of the box. For the Israelites, this constituted the very heart of the worship of Yahweh. This "atonement cover" symbolically represented the very "throne" of God, that was "guarded" in the most holy place of the tabernacle/temple, separated from the rest of the sacred building by a thick curtain. Access to this most sacred of spaces could only be gained once a year, on the Day of Atonement, and then only by the high priest, who offered a sacrifice there for the sin of the Israelite nation for that preceding year.

Thus the meaning "throne" for ***kappōret*** is merely an extension of its symbolic force, pointing to the heavenly reality of divine rule as anticipated by the sanctity of this "atonement cover" of the ark of the covenant.

kappōret is found in around thirty places (e.g., Exod. 25:17ff.; 26:34; 37:6ff.; 40:20; Lev. 16:2, 13ff.; Num. 7:89; 1 Chr. 28:11).

NT Words

thronos [θρόνος, *2362*]

thronos, a dynamic equivalent for ***kissē'*** (see above), is translated "throne" throughout its nearly sixty occurrences, most of which are located in the book of Revelation.

General references to human beings on "thrones" are found in Luke 1:52; Col. 1:16. There are also thrones reserved for the saints in glory, as indicated in Luke 22:30; Rev. 11:16; 20:4.

There are several references to the satanic "throne" — in a general context (Rev. 2:13); to the "throne of the dragon" (Rev. 13:2); and to the "throne of the beast" (Rev. 16:10).

In metaphorical contexts, ***thronos*** denotes the "throne of David," designated as the throne of the Messiah in Luke 1:32; Acts 2:30.

Most commonly, ***thronos*** refers to the heavenly "throne of God" (cf. Matt. 5:34; Acts 7:49; Heb. 4:16; Rev. 1:4; 4:2ff.; 5:1ff.; 7:9ff.; 8:3; 12:5; 14:3ff.; 19:4ff.; 22:1ff.). Rev. 20:11 depicts the "great white throne" judgment of God against the wicked.

thronos also denotes the throne of the Son of Man, referring to the royal standing of the risen Christ in heaven (cf. Matt. 19:28; 25:31; Heb. 1:8; 8:1; Rev. 3:21; 5:6).

bēma [βῆμα, *968*]

bēma is a noun occurring thirteen times meaning "throne," "judgment seat."

The "throne" of Herod is noted in Acts 12:21. More commonly, ***bēma*** means "judgment seat" or "tribunal" in connection with the high office of leading Roman officials (cf. Matt. 27:19; John 19:13; Acts 18:12ff.; 25:6ff.).

bēma also denotes the "throne of Christ" in Rom. 14:10; 2 Cor. 5:10.

hilastērion [ἱλαστήριον, *2435*]

hilastērion is a rare noun, occurring only twice. In Rom. 3:25 the term indicates "atonement" for sin. The other occurrence of ***hilastērion*** is found in Acts 9:5, where it denotes the "atonement cover" of the ark of the covenant, or the earthly, symbolic location of God's throne, pointing to the existence of the divine throne in heaven. (→ PROPITIATION)

Additional Notes

"Throne" vocabulary in both Testaments is most significant in relation to the "atonement cover" or "mercy seat" of the ark of the covenant.

The New Testament vocabulary reinforces and confirms the implication drawn from the Old Testament that the golden lid of the covenant box symbolized the heavenly throne of God. It is from this "throne" that God is seen to have both formed and executed his redemptive plans on behalf of his people; and also directed judgment against them and the nations of the world.

Jesus Christ is said to share the status of divine ruler on the heavenly throne, alongside the Father.

THRONG → CROWD

THROW → CAST

THRUST → DRIVE

THUNDER

OT Words

qôl [קוֹל, **6963**]

qôl is a noun found in around 500 places, primarily meaning "voice," "noise," "sound." One of the subsidiary senses of ***qôl*** is "thunder."

Job 28:26 refers generally to thunder as a natural phenomenon. In Exod. 19:16; 20:18, thunder is an element of the divine theophany at Mt. Sinai.

Thunder is also employed by Yahweh as an aspect of his judgment against Egypt (Exod. 9:23ff.); Philistia (1 Sam. 7:10); and his own people (1 Sam. 12:17ff.).

rā'am [רָעַם, 7481]

rā'am is a verb occurring thirteen times with the primary meaning "to thunder," "make the sound of thunder," in both literal and metaphorical contexts. In a number of places, making the sound of thunder constitutes an expression of divine wrath and/or power (cf. Job 40:9; 37:4ff.; Ps. 29:3).

In other places, Yahweh is said metaphorically "to thunder" against his enemies, referring to God moving out in wrath against his foes in order to crush them (cf. 1 Sam. 2:10; 7:10; 2 Sam. 22:14; Ps. 18:13).

ra'am [רַעַם, 7482]

ra'am is a noun occurring six times meaning "thunder," signifying the theophanic sign of Yahweh's power and authority (cf. Job 26:14; Pss. 77:18; 81:7; 104:7). See also Job 39:25.

NT Words

brontē [βροντή, *1027*]

brontē is a noun meaning "thunder" in each of its twelve occurrences.

References to "thunder" as a natural phenomenon are found in the context of divine revelation that includes judgment (cf. Rev. 4:5; 11:19; 14:2; 16:18), all of which refer to thunder emanating from the throne of God in heaven. See also John 12:28; Rev. 6:1; 8:5; 19:6.

In Mark 3:17, ***brontē*** is used metaphorically as a nickname for a volatile personality in relation to two of Jesus' disciples, James and John, who are described here as "sons of thunder." Rev. 10:3ff. refers to "seven thunders," described as elements of divine judgment against a wayward humanity.

TIDINGS
→ TELL

TIE
→ BIND

TILL
→ WORK

TIME

OT Words

yôm [יוֹם, 3117]

yôm is a common noun found in nearly 2,300 contexts with the primary meaning "day." It also has a number of associated senses, one of which is "time," occurring around sixty times with a variety of nuances. (→ DAY)

Time in the general sense of "duration," or passing moments, is noted in Gen. 4:3; 26:8; Job 15:32.

yôm also indicates "time" as a set point, a designated occasion, or hour. For example, the time of harvest is noted in Num. 13:30; Josh. 3:15; Judg. 15:1; 1 Sam. 9:16; Jer. 39:10; Prov. 25:13.

yôm also has the sense of "time" as a "period of time," as in Lev. 25:50; Deut. 20:19; 1 Sam. 7:2; 2 Sam. 7:11. In particular, the expression "time of trouble" is indicated in Pss. 27:5; 41:1; Prov. 25:19. In several contexts, "time" is identical to the concept of "days" (cf. Neh. 9:32; Eccl. 1:10; Ps. 44:1; Isa. 37:26).

'ēt [עֵת, 6256]

'ēt occurs around three hundred times with the dominant sense of "time" throughout almost the entire usage. As with the synonym ***yôm*** (see above), ***'ēt*** refers to "time" in various contexts.

'ēt refers first of all to "a point in time" (e.g., Gen. 21:22; 24:11; Exod. 9:18; Deut. 1:9; 1 Sam. 20:12; Isa. 48:16; Zeph. 3:20). Ezra 10:14 refers to a "time" arranged for a specific purpose. God also appoints "times" for worship (cf. Neh. 10:34; 13:31); for punishment (cf. 2 Sam. 24:15); and to die (cf. Eccl. 7:17).

'ēt also expresses the phenomenon of "time" as "occasion," or "opportunity" (e.g., Exod. 18:22; 2 Sam. 11:1; Neh. 9:28; Esth. 4:14). The psalmist in Ps. 34:1 affirms that he will praise the Lord "at all times." Job 5:26 refers to the "season" for harvest. Jer. 33:15 employs the phrase "at that time" to indicate a significant redemptive-historical occasion containing a promise. A similar phenomenon is observed in the use of the phrase, "the times of the end" (cf. Dan. 8:17; 11:35, 40; 12:1ff.). Eccl. 10:17 contains the expression "in due season," or "at the right time."

'ēt also expresses "time" as a "period," "age," or "era." The term is used this way, for example, in Lev. 15:25, referring to the "time" of a woman's menstruation. Yahweh also designates certain "times" for specific purposes (cf. Eccl. 3:1ff.). Several contexts refer to "time(s) of trouble" that come under the providential plan and care of God, occasionally as a specific divine judgment (cf. Pss. 9:9; 10:1; Isa. 33:2; Jer. 2:28; 10:15; 11:14; 15:11; 50:31; Ezek. 22:3; Dan. 9:23; Joel 3:1). On occasion, ***'ēt*** refers to "times" as equivalent to one's "days," or life span (cf. Ps. 31:15).

pa'am [פַּעַם, 6471]

pa'am is a noun meaning "time" in the sense of "occurrence" in the majority of its nearly one hundred occurrences. It is nearly always designated as a numerical repetition in the context of ceremonial ritual performance.

Frequent mention is made of ceremonial ritual sacrifice, or elements of the ritual, performed "seven times" (cf. Lev. 4:6, 17; 8:11; 16:14ff.). Such a repetition is also enacted at the "ritual destruction" of the city of Jericho in Josh. 6:4, where the people are instructed to circle the city "seven times." Other illustrations of numerical repetition include those in Gen. 27:36 (two times; twice); Exod. 34:23 (three times); Num. 14:22 (ten times). The phrase "many times" in Ps. 106:43 refers to the frequency of God's deliverance of his people. See also Gen. 29:34; Exod. 8:32.

mô'ēd [**מוֹעֵד, 4150**]

mô'ēd is a noun occurring around 220 times with the dominant sense of "meeting" for most of its usage. However, in a number of places ***mô'ēd*** also refers to "times" in the sense of divinely ordained ritual observations, as well as several related nuances.

"Times" of divinely appointed ritual observation under the Mosaic law include the Passover festival (cf. Exod. 13:10; 23:15; 34:18); and the Sabbatical Year for canceling debts (cf. Deut. 31:10)

In addition, ***mô'ēd*** refers to "(set) times" or "appointed times," as indicated in Gen. 17:21; 18:14; Num. 28:2; 1 Sam. 9:24; 13:8, 11; 2 Sam. 24:15. ***mô'ēd*** also refers to "times" as natural phenomena, such as the setting of the sun (cf. Ps. 104:19). See also Jer. 8:7.

mô'ēd also refers to the divinely appointed eschatological "time of the end" (cf. Dan. 11:27ff.; Hab. 2:3).

zemān [**זְמַן, 2166** (Aramaic)]

zemān is an Aramaic noun found in eleven places meaning "set time," "appointed time" (e.g., Ezra 5:3; Dan. 2:16, 21; 3:7ff.; 4:36; 7:12). In particular, Dan. 6:13 mentions Daniel's set times for prayer. Dan. 7:22 refers to the appointed time set by Yahweh for the saints to receive the kingdom of God. See also Dan. 7:25.

'iddān [**עִדָּן, 5732** (Aramaic)]

'iddān is an Aramaic noun occurring thirteen times meaning "time" in the general sense of "duration of moments" (cf. Dan. 2:8; 4:16, 23ff.); as well as "times" in the context of the ceremonial ritual requirements of the Mosaic law (cf. Dan. 2:21).

mōnîm [**מֹנִים, 4489**]

mōnîm is a rare noun found only twice, meaning "times" in the sense of "occasions." In both contexts, the term refers to the recalculation of wages "ten times over" (cf. Gen. 31:7, 41).

NT Words

chronos [χρόνος, *5550*]

chronos is a noun occurring around fifty times meaning "time" throughout most of the usage of the term in the sense of "measured moments of duration," including assessment of time as either long or short.

General references to measured time include those in Acts 1:6, 21; 17:30; 1 Pet. 4:2. ***chronos*** refers to "time" for giving birth (Luke 1:57); a moment of time (Luke 4:5); a "long time" (Matt. 25:19; Luke 8:27; John 14:9; Acts 8:11; 27:9; Heb. 4:7); and "short times" (John 12:35; Rev. 20:3). See also Acts 20:8; 1 Cor. 16:7.

chronos also refers to "times" fixed by God (Acts 1:7; 3:21), including the fulfillment of prophecy and promise (Acts 7:17; Gal. 4:4), and the designation "last times" (Jude 18).

kairos [καιρός, *2540*]

kairos is a noun occurring nearly ninety times with the primary sense of "time" that is somewhat broader than that of ***chronos*** (see above). ***kairos*** indicates "time" not only in the sense of "measured duration of moments," but also in the sense of "epoch," "age," or "era," which manifests purpose or fulfillment to a greater or lesser degree.

The meaning "time" in the sense of an age or era appointed by God in accordance with his redemptive purposes is evident in a number of contexts. General references include those in Acts 1:7; 7:20; Rom. 3:26. The concept of "this time" or "this present age" is evident in Luke 18:30; Rom. 8:18; 1 Cor. 7:29; 2 Cor. 6:2; Eph. 5:16; Heb. 9:9. The "time" of the fulfillment of divine judgment is noted in Mark 13:33; 1 Pet. 4:17; Rev. 1:3; 11:18; 22:10. Matt. 16:3; Luke 12:56 refer to "the signs of the times" as indicators that this world age may be drawing to a close. The "last times" (i.e., prior to final judgment) are noted in 1 Tim. 4:1; 1 Pet. 1:5 (cf. also 2 Tim. 3:1).

The "time" of the fulfillment of God's purpose and plan in relation to his son, Jesus Christ, and his kingdom, is indicated in several places. Matt. 26:18 refers to Jesus' claim that his "time is at hand" (i.e., his death and resurrection are drawing near). See also John 7:6ff. In relation to the coming kingdom of God, Mark 1:15 refers to John the Baptist's words, "The time has come." Luke 21:24 speaks of "the time of the Gentiles" (i.e., the full extent of their salvation). Rom. 5:6; 1 Tim. 2:6 affirm that Christ died "at the right time." Eph. 1:10 mentions "the fullness of time" (i.e., the consummation of all of God's redemptive purposes).

Additional Notes

"Time" in both Old and New Testaments is not to be regarded merely as a "quantitative" phenomenon (i.e., a measurement of duration), but rather as a fully "qualitative" one, partaking of particular characteristics such as purpose, rationale, redemptive-historical significance and, most importantly, implemented by God himself, the Creator of time.

Time in Scripture has a practical significance that is intimately bound up with the reality of God, who is committed to bring about the fulfillment of his saving purposes for humankind. God created the world in space and time. His own intimate personal involvement with the world culminated in the coming of Christ the Messiah at exactly the right time. God's own son has identified with his fellow human beings in his unique way, thereby gaining salvation for his people that will ultimately transcend space and time in the new heaven and earth.

See Also: → HOUR

TIP → END

TITHE

OT Words

ma'asēr **[מַעֲשֵׂר, 4643]**

ma'asēr is a noun occurring about thirty times, meaning "tithe," or "a tenth part" — that portion of one's goods, produce, and earnings required by Yahweh as his "share," prescribed under the terms of the Mosaic law covenant.

The "tithe" is first mentioned in Gen. 14:20, where the patriarch Abraham pays a tithe to Melchizedek, king of Salem, in recognition of the latter's superior spiritual status.

The tithe demanded by Yahweh was an indisputable principle of the law covenant. In practice, it was the Levites who were the actual recipients of the tithes, receiving them from the people. They were either sacrificial and wholly consumed by fire, or sacrificed in part on the altar and in part given to the Levites, who thus received their means of sustenance. These servants of Yahweh received no direct land inheritance from God, but rather obtained their "inheritance" in kind from the people (cf. Num. 18:21ff.; Deut. 26:12; Neh. 10:38).

General references to the tithe include those in Amos 4:4; Mal. 3:8, 10. Agricultural products given as a tithe are noted in Lev. 22:30; Deut. 14:23; 2 Chr. 31:5; Neh. 10:37. The tithing of cattle is mentioned in Lev. 22:32; 2 Chr. 31:6. See also 2 Chr. 31:6, 12.

Tithes were also to be presented to Yahweh at the central sanctuary, a site to be chosen by him alone (cf. Deut. 12:6, 11, 17).

'āsar **[עָשַׂר, 6237]**

'āsar is a verb found seven times, referring to "paying a tithe" (cf. Gen. 28:22; Deut. 14:22; 26:12; 1 Sam. 8:15, 17; Neh. 10:37ff.).

NT Words

apodekatoō [ἀποδεκατόω, *586*]

apodekatoō is a verb found in four places meaning "to give, pay a tithe," all in the context of worship (cf. Matt. 23:23; Luke 11:42; 18:12; Heb. 7:5).

TOIL → WORK

TOKEN → SIGN

TOMB → GRAVE

TOMORROW

OT Words

māḥār **[מָחָר, 4279]**

māḥār is a noun meaning "tomorrow" in most of its nearly fifty occurrences. The contexts are either mundane (cf. Exod. 16:23; 1 Sam. 20:12ff.; Esth. 5:12; Prov. 3:28; Isa. 56:12); or else they indicate the anticipation of divine action, whether it be intervention on behalf of his people, or judgment against his enemies (cf. Exod. 8:10, 23ff.; 10:4; Num. 16:7; Josh. 3:5; 11:6; Judg. 20:28). ***māḥār*** also anticipates the divine revelation at Mt. Sinai (Exod. 19:10).

NT Words

aurion [αὔριον, *839*]

aurion is an adverbial form found in fourteen places with the consistent meaning "tomorrow" (cf. Matt. 6:30ff.; Luke 10:35; Acts 23:15; Jas. 4:13ff.).

TONGUE

OT Words

***lāshôn* [לָשׁוֹן, 3956]**

lāshôn is a noun with the predominant sense of "tongue" throughout most of its nearly 120 occurrences. ***lāshôn*** is used both literally and figuratively.

Literal references to the tongue as the human organ of speech include those in Judg. 17:5; Job 6:30; 33:2; Ps. 39:1. The tongue is influenced by the Holy Spirit, moving the recipient to speak the divine word he has received (cf. 2 Sam. 23:2). The tongue is used variously to praise God (cf. Pss. 51:14; 66:17; 126:2; Isa. 35:6; 45:23) and to rebel against God (cf. Isa. 1:8). The tongues is described as sinful (Pss. 31:20; 10:7; 78:36; Prov. 6:17; 25:23; Mic. 6:12); and righteous (Pss. 37:30; 119:172; Prov. 10:20; 31:26). The tongue of an animal is also indicated in Job 20:16; Ps. 68:23.

lāshôn is also used metaphorically, meaning "tongue" in the sense of "human language." This usage is evident in general contexts such as Gen. 10:5, 20, 31; Deut. 28:49; Esth. 1:22; Ezek. 3:6; Zech. 8:23. In particular, ***lāshôn*** refers also to the alien language of Israel's captors (Isa. 28:11; 66:18; Jer. 5:15). Elsewhere, the expression "slow of tongue" is used in relation to the speech of Moses, possibly alluding to a speech impediment (cf. Exod. 4:10).

***ḥārash* [חָרַשׁ, 2790]; *ḥāsāh* [חָסָה, 2013]**

These two verbs express the meanings "keep silent," "hold one's tongue." (→ SILENCE)

NT Words

***glōssa* [γλῶσσα, *1100*]**

glōssa is the dynamic equivalent of ***lāshôn*** (see above), a noun occurring fifty times with the meaning "tongue" throughout. As with ***lāshôn***, ***glōssa*** expresses this meaning with differing nuances.

Literal references to the tongue as the organ of speech are found in Mark 7:33ff.; Luke 16:24; Jas. 3:5ff.; Rev. 16:10. It is used to praise God in Acts 2:6; Rom. 14:11; Phil. 2:11; and is also capable of sinful use (cf. Rom. 3:13).

Metaphorically, ***glōssa*** also means "human language." The contexts for this usage involve the direct influence of the Spirit of God (cf. Acts 2:4, 11; 10:46; Rev. 5:9; 7:9; 10:11; 13:7; 14:6; 17:15). In Acts 19:6; 1 Cor. 12:10, 28ff.; 13:1, 8; 14:2ff., the use of ***glōssa*** is often thought to indicate non-human discourse, or ecstatic utterance that bears no relation to ordinary human language. However, there would appear to be no compelling reason to reject the straightforward translation of "human language" in these contexts.

In Acts 2:3, ***glōssa*** refers to the appearance of "tongues" of fire, as a consequence of the Holy Spirit coming down upon the apostles on the Day of Pentecost.

***dialektos* [διάλεκτος, *1258*]**

dialektos is a noun with the consistent sense of "human language" evident in the translation "tongue" throughout each of its six occurrences (cf. Acts 1:19; 2:6, 8; 21:40; 26:14).

***heteroglōssos* [ἑτερόγλωσσος, *2084*]**

heteroglōssos is a rare noun found only in 1 Cor. 14:21, referring to "one who speaks a foreign tongue (i.e., language)."

TOOTH, TEETH

OT Words

***shēn* [שֵׁן, 8127 (8128 Aramaic)]**

shēn is a noun found approximately forty times meaning "tooth," "teeth," as well as some related senses, in most of its usage. (→ IVORY)

Literal references to people's teeth include those in Exod. 21:27; Num. 11:33; Prov. 25:19; Song 6:6. Animal teeth are noted in Deut. 32:24; Job 41:14; Joel 1:6. The Aramaic form, ***shēn***, refers metaphorically to the teeth of the visionary beasts of Daniel's vision (Dan. 7:5, 7, 19).

shēn is also found in a number of other figurative contexts. Yahweh is said to "break the teeth of the wicked" in Pss. 3:7; 58:6. The phrase "eye for eye, tooth for tooth" lies at the heat of the so-called lex talionis (law of retaliation), expressed in Exod. 21:24; Lev. 24:20; Deut. 19:21. Job 19:20 refers to a very narrow escape from disaster in the phrase "by the skin of my teeth." Pss. 37:12; 112:10; Lam. 2:16 refer to "gnashing of teeth" as a sign of physical and emotional anguish. The proverb expressing the provoking or irritation of children in the words ". . . setting their teeth on edge" is recorded in Jer. 31:29, 30; Ezek. 18:2.

***maltā'āh* [מַלְתָּעָה, 4459]**

maltā'āh is a rare noun found in Ps. 58:6, referring to the "great (incisor) tooth" of the lion.

***metall'āh* [מְתַלְּעָה, 4973]**

metall'āh is a rare noun related to ***maltā'āh***, above, referring three times to "the (incisor) teeth" of animals and human beings (cf. Job 29:17; Prov. 30:14; Joel 1:6).

pîphîyot **[פִּיפִיּוֹת, 6374]**

pîphîyot is another rare noun, found only twice. In Isa. 41:15, ***pîphîyot*** refers metaphorically to the "teeth" of a threshing sledge. It is also used adjectivally in Ps. 149:6 with reference to a "double edged" sword.

NT Words

odous [ὀδούς, *3599*]

odous is a noun found in twelve places with consistent reference to a "tooth," or "teeth."

The "lex talionis" of the old covenant law is indicated in Matt. 5:38 (see ***shēn***, above). ***odous*** refers to animal teeth in Rev. 9:8.

Most commonly, ***odous*** is found in the expression "gnashing one's teeth," indicating profound physical and mental anguish (cf. Matt. 22:13; 25:30; Mark 9:18; Luke 13:28; Acts 7:54).

TOP

OT Words

rō'sh **[רֹאשׁ, 7218]**

rō'sh is a common noun, occurring nearly six hundred times meaning "head," "chief," "beginning." ***rō'sh*** has several other related senses, one of which is "top," found in a variety of settings and indicating the highest physical point of the object or structure. ***rō'sh*** refers, for example, to the top of the tower of Babel (Gen. 11:4); a ladder (Gen. 28:12); a rock (Judg. 6:26); a throne (1 Kgs. 10:19); and a tree (Isa. 17:6). ***rō'sh*** also commonly refers to the top of a hill or mountain (e.g., Exod. 17:9ff.; 34:2; Num. 14:40; Judg. 9:17; 1 Kgs. 18:42; Ps. 72:16). In particular, the top of Mt. Sinai is noted in Exod. 19:20; 24:17. (→ HEAD)

qodqōd **[קָדְקֹד, 6936]**

qodqōd is a noun found in twelve places with reference to the "top (or crown) of the head" (cf. Gen. 49:26; Deut. 28:35; 2 Sam. 14:25; Pss. 7:16; 68:21; Isa. 3:17; Jer. 48:45).

ṣammeret **[צַמֶּרֶת, 6788]**

ṣammeret is a term referring to a "tree top" or "the highest branch" of a tree in five places (cf. Ezek. 17:3, 22; 31:3, 10, 14).

See Also: → ROOF

TORCH

OT Words

lappîd **[לַפִּיד, 3940]**

lappîd is a term indicating a "torch," or "firebrand," in about fourteen contexts.

Literal references include those in Gen. 15:17; Judg. 7:16ff.; 15:4ff.; Job 41:19.

Elsewhere, ***lappîd*** is used metaphorically. Isa. 62:1 likens salvation to a "burning torch." Ezek. 1:13 refers to visionary "torches" associated with Ezekiel's "chariot throne." The angelic "man dressed in linen" of Dan. 10:6 is described as having "eyes like burning torches." See also Nah. 2:4; Zech. 12:6.

See Also: → LAMP

TORMENT → AFFLICT → ANGUISH → DISTRESS → JUDGMENT → PUNISH → SORROW → TROUBLE

TOUCH

OT Words

nāga' **[נָגַע, 5060]**

nāga' is a verb found in 150 places with a variety of meanings, the most common being "to touch." All other senses indicated by ***nāga'*** are related to this one, directly or indirectly. (→ REACH)

Most commonly, "touch" has the sense of "come into direct physical contact" with someone or something, expressed in a variety of different contexts. General references include those in Gen. 32:25; Judg. 6:21; 2 Sam. 14:10; Job 6:7. Touching the fruit of the tree of the knowledge of good and evil is forbidden in Gen. 3:3. The wings of the sculpted cherubim on the ark of the covenant are said to touch each other in 1 Kgs. 6:27. Angels are described as touching human beings in 1 Kgs. 19:7; Dan. 8:18; 9:21. There are also various warnings against "touching" laid down in the Mosaic law, including unclean objects (cf. Lev. 11:8; 5:2ff.; 7:18ff.; Deut. 14:8; Isa. 52:11); the most sacred ritual objects (cf. Num. 4:15); and Mt. Sinai, during the theophanic presence of Yahweh (cf. Exod. 19:12). See also Exod. 29:37; Lev. 6:18; Hag. 2:12ff.

nāga' also refers to the act of "touching" with the intent of having intimate sexual contact (cf. Gen. 20:6; Ruth. 2:9).

"Touching" with the intention to physically harm or destroy someone is indicated in Josh. 9:19; 1 Chr. 16:22; Ps. 105:15; Jer. 12:14; Zech. 2:8.

Where Yahweh is the subject of ***nāga'***, he is said to touch the heart of humankind (1 Sam. 10:26); the mountains (Pss. 104:32; 144:5); and also the lips of the prophet (Isa. 6:7; Jer. 1:9; Dan. 10:16), as a prelude to divine revelation.

nāshaq [נָשַׁק, **5401**]

nāshaq is a verb found thirty-five times with the predominant meaning "to kiss"; but in Ezek. 3:13 it refers to the wings of the cherubim "touching" one another. The underlying sense may well relate to a metaphorical "kissing" of the wings.

NT Words

haptomai [ἅπτομαι, *680*]

haptomai is the verbal dynamic equivalent of ***nāga'*** (see above), meaning "touch" throughout its usage, in a variety of contexts.

The action of "touching" in the sense of "making direct physical contact with" is found in a general sense in John 20:17. Christ's miraculous "touching," resulting in the healing of others, is recorded in Matt. 8:3, 15; 9:20ff.; Mark 3:10; 5:28ff.; Luke 5:13; 8:44ff. "Touching" with intent to harm is indicated in 1 John 5:18. The exhortation to touch nothing unclean is found in 2 Cor. 6:17 (cf. also Col. 2:21). 1 Cor. 7:1 refers to "touching" in the context of sexual relationships.

See Also: ➞ FEEL ➞ MEET

TOWER

OT Words

migdāl [מִגְדָּל, **4026**]

migdāl is a noun meaning "tower" in fifty places.

migdāl refers literally to the tower of Babel (Gen. 11:4ff.); to fortified towers, or military defenses (Judg. 8:9, 17; 9:46ff.; 2 Kgs. 9:17; Isa. 2:15); and to towers associated with the city gates of Jerusalem (Neh. 3:1ff.; Ps. 48:12; Jer. 31:38; Ezek. 26:4; Zech. 14:10).

Yahweh is described figuratively as a "strong tower" in Ps. 61:3; Prov. 18:10. See also Song 4:4; 8:10; Isa. 5:2 for other metaphorical uses of ***migdāl***.

misgāb [מִשְׂגָּב, **4869**]

misgāb is a noun occurring seventeen times meaning "stronghold," "fortress," "refuge," "high tower." (➞ REFUGE)

miṣpeh [מִצְפֶּה, **4707**]

miṣpeh is a term found only in 2 Chr. 20:24; Isa. 21:8, indicating a "watchtower."

baḥîn [בַּחִין, **971**]

baḥîn is a rare term found only in Isa. 23:13 with reference to a "siege tower."

NT Words

pyrgos [πύργος, *4444*]

pyrgos is a term indicating a "tower" in only four places (cf. Matt. 21:33; Mark 12:1; Luke 13:4; 14:28).

TOWN ➞ CITY ➞ VILLAGE

TRADE

OT Words

sāḥar [סָחַר, **5503**]

sāḥar is a verb found in twenty contexts, meaning to "engage in trade, or business." It is also used nominally to mean "merchant," or "trader" (cf. Gen. 23:16; 1 Kgs. 10:28; Prov. 31:14; Isa. 13:2; Ezek. 38:13).

The verbal force of "trade" is evident in Gen. 34:10, 12; Jer. 14:18; Ezek. 27:12ff.

rākal [רָכַל, **7402**]

rākal is a verb synonymous with ***sāḥar*** (see above) meaning "to trade," "engage in business." ***rākal*** also functions as a noun, denoting a "merchant," "trader" (cf. 1 Kgs. 10:15; Neh. 3:31ff.; Ezek. 17:4; 27:13ff.).

NT Words

ergazomai [ἐργάζομαι, *2038*]

ergazomai is a verb found in forty contexts with the primary meanings "to work," "labor." However, in a few contexts it means "to trade" in the context of business (cf. Matt. 25:16; Rev. 18:17).

diapragmateuomai [διαπραγματεύομαι, *1281*]

This verb is found only in Luke 9:15, referring to "gaining through trading."

emporos [ἔμπορος, *1713*]

emporos is a noun meaning "merchant," "trader" found in five places (cf. Matt. 13:45; Rev. 18:3, 11, 15, 23).

TRADITION

NT Words

paradosis [παράδοσις, *3862*]

paradosis means "tradition" throughout its thirteen occurrences. The underlying literal sense of ***paradosis*** refers to "that which is handed down," indicating the huge repository of Jewish oral interpretation of the Mosaic law that had accumulated over the centuries. Though in theory this "tradition" was of a lesser standing than Scripture itself, in practice it became equally authoritative and binding. The Pharisees frequently criticized Jesus for failing to observe the "tradition" of the elders. He responded by rebuking them for transgressing the law of God for the sake of that tradition (cf. Matt. 15:2ff.; Mark 7:3ff.). See also Col. 2:8; Gal. 1:14.

More positively, "tradition" in the New Testament can also refer to the "tradition" of the gospel handed on by the apostles (1 Cor. 11:2; 2 Thess. 2:15; 3:6).

TRAITOR

OT Words

bāgad **[בָּגַד, 898]**

bāgad is a verb found in around fifty contexts with the primary meaning "to deal deceitfully, or treacherously with." ***bāgad*** also serves as a noun meaning "traitor," "treacherous one."

The act of "dealing treacherously," or "betrayal," is indicated in Exod. 21:8; Judg. 9:23; Job 6:15; Pss. 25:3; 59:5; Jer. 12:6; Mal. 2:14ff. In Hos. 5:7; 6:7, it is Yahweh who is betrayed by his people.

NT Words

prodotēs [προδότης, *4273*]

prodotēs is a rare noun found in only three places meaning "traitor." Luke 6:16 refers to Judas Iscariot, who betrayed Christ to the authorities. Acts 7:52 refers to the traitors who had Christ put to death. See also 2 Tim. 3:4.

TRAMPLE

OT Words

rāmas **[רָמַס, 7429]**

rāmas is a verb meaning "trample," "tread down" throughout its twenty occurrences.

2 Kgs. 7:17ff.; 9:33 refer to trampling people to death. In 2 Kgs. 14:9, trampling is indicated in a metaphorical context.

Other uses of ***rāmas*** in metaphorical contexts include the trampling of the serpent to death (Ps. 91:13), a possible reference to the messianic victory over Satan; the "trampling" of the Israelites as punishment for their sin (Isa. 28:3); and the "trampling" of the ram (Medo-Persia) by the aggressive goat (Greece) in the vision of Dan. 8:7 (cf. also Dan. 8:10). Isa. 63:3 refers to Yahweh "trampling" the nations (i.e., destroying them). See also Ezek. 34:18. Isa. 1:12 speaks of "trampling" the temple courts, indicating a desecration of the sanctuary. Cities are described as being trampled in Isa. 26:6; Ezek. 26:11. Mic. 5:8 speaks of a lion "trampling" on its prey.

In Isa. 41:25; Nah. 3:14, the potter is described as "treading down" the clay, ready for shaping.

NT Words

katapateō [καταπατέω, *2662*]

katapateō is a verb denoting the action of "trampling," "treading down," "treading under foot" in five contexts. In Luke 8:5, the seed of God's word is trampled under foot and fails to take root in the hearts of those who hear it. Heb. 10:29 speaks of people "trampling" the Son of God, indicating their utter rejection of him. Literal references to "trampling" are found in Matt. 5:13; 7:6; Luke 12:1.

See Also: → TREAD

TRANSFIGURE, TRANSFORM

NT Words

metamorphoō [μεταμορφόω, *3339*]

metamorphoō is a verb found in four places meaning "to transform," "transfigure." In Matt. 17:2; Mark 9:2, ***metamorphoō*** describes Christ's transfiguration (i.e., the transformation of his physical appearance) on the mountain, whereby his three disciples are granted a momentary glimpse of his heavenly glory.

metamorphoō also describes the transformation of the believer through the spiritual renewing of his mind (Rom. 12:2); and into the likeness of Christ in glory (2 Cor. 3:18).

TRANSGRESS, TRANSGRESSION, TRESPASS

OT Words

'ābar **[עָבַר, 5674]**

'ābar is a common verb, occurring in more than 500 contexts with the underlying senses of "pass over, by, or through," "cross over." ***'ābar*** is translated in a large variety of ways. One of these meanings is "transgress." The underlying force of this meaning is the violation of Yahweh's revealed laws and precepts, whereby a person "crosses over" from obedience to disobedience. It is closely related to the sense of "trespass." See the entries below for further discussion.

The sin of transgressing the laws of God in a general sense is noted in Num. 14:41; 2 Chr. 24:20; 1 Sam. 15:24; Isa. 24:5; Dan. 9:11. Specific violation of the Mosaic law covenant is indicated in Deut. 17:2; Josh. 7:11ff.; Judg.

2:20; 2 Kgs. 18:12; Jer. 34:18; Hos. 6:7; 8:1. There is also a denial of transgression in Ps. 17:3; Deut. 26:13.

mā'al [מָעַל, 4603]

mā'al is a verb occurring around thirty-five times meaning "transgress," "trespass" throughout. The meaning "trespass" is closely related to that of "transgress," literally indicating an unlawful invasion of a person's property or territory. The extended meaning "trespass" in Scripture involves a violation of God's law, which is virtually the same as an act of transgression. ***mā'al*** also occasionally refers to an act of infidelity towards other people.

The explicit sense of "transgress or trespass against God's law" is indicated in Lev. 5:15; 26:40; Num. 5:6, 12; Josh. 7:1; 22:16ff.; 1 Chr. 2:7; 28:19. The related meaning "rebel against" God is indicated in Deut. 32:51; Ezra 10:2, 10. Similarly, 2 Chr. 29:6; 30:7; Neh. 1:8 refer to "being unfaithful" to God. Num. 5:27 refers to the act of "being unfaithful" to one's husband, or committing adultery.

pāsha' [פָּשַׁע, 6586]

pāsha' is a verb found about forty times, meaning "transgress," "rebel," as well as related nuances. ***pāsha'*** is also used nominally to mean "sinner," "transgressor." (➡ REBEL)

The act of transgressing against God is noted in a number of places (cf. 1 Kgs. 8:50; Ezra 10:13; Isa. 43:27; 66:24; Jer. 2:18; Ezek. 20:38; Hos. 8:1; Amos 4:4).

Those who break God's law, or "transgressors," are noted in Ps. 37:38; Isa. 1:28; 46:8; Hos. 14:1.

'āsham [אָשַׁם, 816]

'āsham is a verb occurring thirty-five times with the primary meanings "to be guilty," "trespass," as well as several related senses. The context of being guilty here lies in the violation of the law covenant, or being guilty before God. (➡ GUILT)

In Num. 5:7 ***'āsham*** means "trespass" in the sense of committing wrong against other people. In 2 Chr. 19:10, ***'āsham*** refers to trespassing against God and thereby incurring guilt.

'ashmāh [אַשְׁמָה, 819]

'ashmāh is a noun derived from ***'āsham*** (see above) with the predominant meaning "trespass," or "sin," in most of its nineteen occurrences. "Trespass" here implies guilt.

"Trespass," or "sin" against God is indicated in Lev. 4:3; 22:16; 1 Chr. 21:3; 2 Chr. 24:18; Ezra 9:6ff.

pesha' [פֶּשַׁע, 6588]

pesha' is a noun derived from ***pāsha'*** (see above). It is found in approximately ninety places with the dominant sense of "transgression," "trespass," "rebellion," "sin," or "offense." These meanings are virtually all interchangeable in the context of the violation of God's law.

pesha' indicates transgression against God. General references to such violation include those in Exod. 23:21; Lev. 16:16ff.; Isa. 24:20; Lam. 1:5; Ezek. 18:22; Amos 1:3ff.; Mic. 1:13ff. Offenses committed against human beings are indicated in Gen. 31:36; 50:17.

Yahweh's intent to punish human beings for their transgression is noted in Ps. 89:32. The reality or promise of forgiveness for transgression is found in Pss. 32:1; 103:12; Isa. 43:25; 53:5. The latter references in Isaiah mention the messianic Suffering Servant, wounded for the "transgression" of his people.

pesha' is also found in contexts where people plead with God. Pleas for the forgiveness of transgression are found in 1 Kgs. 8:50; Job 7:21; Ps. 51:1ff. Pleas for deliverance from transgression are recorded in Pss. 19:13; 39:8. Ps. 5:10 contains a plea for God to punish the transgression of the psalmist's enemies.

NT Words

parabainō [παραβαίνω, *3845*]

parabainō is a verb denoting the act of "transgressing or violating the law," referring to both the traditions of human beings as well as the commandments of God (cf. Matt. 15:2ff.; Acts 1:25; 2 John 9).

parabasis [παράβασις, *3847*]

parabasis is a noun derived from ***parabainō*** (see above), found in seven places and meaning "transgression" or "violation" in relation to the commands of God (cf. Rom. 2:23; 4:15; 5:14; Gal. 3:19; Heb. 2:2; 9:15).

parabatēs [παραβάτης, *3848*]

parabatēs is another noun derived from ***parabainō*** (see above) meaning "lawbreaker," "transgressor," with exclusive reference to the law of God (cf. Rom. 2:25ff.; Gal. 2:18; Jas. 2:9ff.).

anomos [ἄνομος, *459*]

anomos is a noun synonymous with ***parabatēs*** (see above) meaning "transgressor," "lawbreaker" (i.e., against God).

General references to such people include those in Mark 15:28; Acts 2:23; 1 Tim. 1:9. In Luke 22:37,

Christ's identification with "transgressors" in no way implies the existence of wickedness in his person. 2 Thess. 2:8 mentions "the lawless one" (i.e., the antichrist). ***anomos*** also refers to "lawless deeds" in 2 Pet. 2:8.

In a special use of ***anomos*** in 1 Cor. 9:21, the term refers to "those outside the law" (i.e., Gentiles). Paul, in his determination to win these people for Christ, is intent on identifying with them and describes himself as "outside the law." This does not implicate him in any culpable attitude or action toward God.

paraptōma [παράπτωμα, *3900*]

paraptōma is a noun found in around twenty places meaning "trespass," "sin," "offense," as well as related senses. It functions as a dynamic equivalent for ***pesha'*** (see above).

Offenses committed by people against other people are indicated in Matt. 6:14ff.; 18:35, emphasizing the importance of forgiving one another's trespasses.

General references to trespass against God include those in Matt. 6:14ff.; Mark 11:25ff.; and see also 2 Cor. 5:19; Gal. 6:1; Jas. 5:16. Forgiveness offered by God for "trespass" against him is described in Rom. 11:11ff.; and sin or trespass leading to spiritual death, from which we are delivered in Christ, is noted in Eph. 2:1ff.; Col. 2:13.

Christ's atoning death for our "trespasses" is noted in Rom. 4:25. The "trespass" of one man (i.e., Adam) leading to the condemnation of the entire human race is described in Rom. 5:15ff. Forgiveness for humankind's "sins" is guaranteed by the finished redemptive work of Christ on the cross, as explained in Eph. 1:7.

Additional Notes

The vocabulary for "transgression," as well as various related meanings throughout the Scriptures, clearly has several common denominators. First, the universal, collective guilt of the entire human race is brought about by the violation of God's revealed commands. Secondly, divine judgment for such disobedience is inevitable. Equally certain, however, is the promise of God's forgiveness for such sin, offered through divine initiative.

What is distinctive about the New Testament treatment of the motif of "transgression" is the detailed presentation of the person and work of Christ, whose atoning sacrifice on the cross serves to eradicate forever the sin and penalty of transgression against God for all who repent of such sin and put their faith in Christ.

See Also: → GUILT → INIQUITY → SIN → REBEL → WICKED

TRANSLATE → INTERPRET

TRAP

OT Words

môqēsh [מוֹקֵשׁ, **4170**]

môqēsh is a noun occurring around thirty times, meaning "trap," or "snare."

Literal references to animal or bird traps include those in Job 40:24; Amos 3:5.

Metaphorical use of the term denotes a "trap" for people, implying imminent physical danger or disaster (cf. Exod. 10:7; Josh. 23:13; 1 Sam. 18:21; Ps. 140:5); as well as the threat of apostasy, often in the guise of idolatry (cf. Exod. 23:33; 34:12; Deut. 7:16; Judg. 2:3; 8:27; Pss. 69:22; 106:36). The plight of being "trapped" by sin is indicated in Prov. 12:13; 29:6. The expression "snares of death" denotes an overwhelming catastrophe, as in 2 Sam. 22:6; Ps. 18:5; Prov. 13:14.

paḥ [פַּח, **6341**]

paḥ is a noun occurring around thirty times, synonymous with ***môqēsh***. It is used in a literal sense to indicate trapping birds; and in a figurative sense to express physical, moral, or spiritual danger.

Snares for entrapping birds are found in Pss. 91:3; 124:7; Prov. 7:23; Eccl. 9:12; Amos 3:5. In most of these contexts, however, these references allude to snaring birds as a metaphor for physical and/or moral danger.

Metaphorically, ***paḥ*** refers to a "snare" for Israel, implying physical calamity in Josh. 23:13. In several places, "snares" for the wicked are indicated (cf. Job 18:9; Ps. 69:22; Isa. 24:17ff.; Jer. 48:43ff.). Pss. 119:110; 140:5; 142:3; Jer. 18:22 mention "snares" set by the wicked. In Isa. 8:14, Yahweh himself is described as a "snare" for his people as a judgment for their rebellion against him. The "snare" of idolatry entrapping the nation of Israel is indicated in Ps. 69:22.

nāqash [נָקַשׁ, **5367**]

nāqash is a verb found in four places meaning "lay, set a trap or snare" (cf. Deut. 12:30; 1 Sam. 28:9; Pss. 9:16; 38:12).

qôsh [קוֹשׁ, 6983]

qôsh is a rare verb found only in Isa. 29:21, meaning "to set a trap" in the figurative sense of catching someone out by trickery.

malkōdet [מַלְכֹּדֶת, 4434]

malkōdet is a term found only in Job 18:10, indicating a "trap" or "snare."

yāqōsh [יָקֹשׁ, 3369]

yāqōsh is a verb found in six places. It refers to "setting a trap" for animals and birds in Ps. 124:7. Deut. 7:25 denotes the fate of being "snared" by idolatry. Jer. 50:24 says that Yahweh "sets a trap" for evil people. Ps. 141:9; Prov. 6:2; Eccl. 9:12; Isa. 8:15 speak of being ensnared by evil, or by evil people.

yāqûsh [יָקוּשׁ, 3353]

yāqûsh is a participial form of ***yāqōsh*** (see above). It is used as a noun and refers literally to a "trapper" in Ps. 91:3; Prov. 6:5. It refers metaphorically in Jer. 5:26 to "one who sets a trap."

pāḥaḥ [פָּחַח, 6351]

pāḥaḥ is a rare passive verb used in connection with the Israelite people "trapped" in prisons, referring either to a literal or a metaphorical bondage (Isa. 42:22).

meṣûdāh [מְצוּדָה, 4686]

meṣûdāh is a noun occurring around twenty times. It has the primary meaning "fortress," but in Job 19:6 it refers to a "snare" or "net."

NT WORDS

thēra [θήρα, *2339*]

thēra is a rare noun referring to a moral "trap" or "snare" in Rom. 11:9.

brochos [βρόχος, *1029*]

brochos is a synonym for ***thēra*** (see above), found only in 1 Cor. 7:35.

TRAVAIL → AFFLICT → ANGUISH → PAIN → TROUBLE

TRAVEL, TRAVELER

OT WORDS

hēlek [הֵלֶךְ, 1982]

hēlek is a rare noun derived from the verb ***hālak*** ("to walk"), meaning "traveler" in 2 Sam. 12:4.

'ōraḥ [אֹרַח, 734]

'ōraḥ is another rare term for "traveler," found only in Job 31:32.

nāsa' [נָסַע, 5265]

nāsa' is a verb found in approximately 150 places with the primary meaning "to set out," "depart," as well as several related nuances. One of these nuances is "to journey," or "travel," in a variety of contexts. There is also considerable overlap in meaning in the usage of this term.

nāsa' means "travel" in the sense of "migrate from one region to another" in Gen. 11:2, referring to the world community.

"Traveling" in the context of a journey is indicated in relation to the patriarchal community within Canaan in Gen. 12:9; 33:12ff.; 35:5ff. More commonly, the great journey of the exodus from Egypt, in the "traveling" of the people of Israel through the wilderness and towards the land of Canaan, is indicated (Exod. 12:37; 13:20; 17:1; 40:37; Num. 2:9ff.; 9:17ff.; 10:5ff.; 33:3ff.; Deut. 1:7, 40). See also Josh. 3:1ff.; 9:17.

NT WORDS

synekdēmos [συνέκδημος, *4898*]

synekdēmos is a rare noun found only in Acts 19:29; 2 Cor. 8:19, with reference to "fellow travelers."

dierchomai [διέρχομαι, *1330*]

dierchomai is a verb with the primary sense of "pass through," "go through," occurring around fifty times. The meaning "travel through," "travel about" is found in Luke 5:15; 17:11; John 4:4; Acts 8:4; 9:32; 11:22; 19:1; 1 Cor. 10:1; 16:5.

apodēmeō [ἀποδημέω, *589*]

apodēmeō is a rare verb meaning "go, travel into a far country," found only in Matt. 25:14.

TREAD

OT WORDS

dārak [דָּרַךְ, 1869]

dārak is a verb occurring around sixty times with the predominant meaning "tread" in the sense of "walk on."

"Treading" or "walking on" the land of Canaan in fulfillment of the promise made to Abraham is noted in Deut. 1:36; 11:24ff.; Josh. 1:3. In Mic. 5:5ff., ***dārak*** refers to the Assyrian invader treading on the land.

"Treading" the grapes in the winepresses is referred to in Judg. 9:27; Neh. 13:15; Job 24:11; Isa. 16:10; 63:3; Jer. 48:33; Amos 9:13.

See also Ps. 91:13; 1 Sam. 5:5 for other contexts of literal usage.

Metaphorically, ***dārak*** indicates the "treading down" or "trampling" of one's enemy in the context of military defeat in Judg. 20:43. In Lam. 1:15, Yahweh is described as "having trampled" the people of Judah through the destruction of their land at the hands of the Babylonians.

In other figurative contexts, Yahweh is said to "tread" the waves of the sea (cf. Job 9:8; Hab. 3:15); and the heights of the earth (cf. Amos 4:13; Mic. 1:3). This latter divine action refers to an act of judgment against the wicked, including his own people.

NT Words

pateō [πατέω, *3961*]

pateō is a verb meaning "tread," "tread down" in all five occurrences of the term. Luke 10:19 speaks of treading on serpents. Jerusalem is said to be trodden down by the Gentiles in Luke 21:24; Rev. 11:2. The treading of the winepress in Rev. 14:20; 19:15 indicates divine judgment.

aloaō [ἀλοάω, *248*]

aloaō is a rare verb referring to oxen "treading out the corn" in 1 Cor. 9:9; 1 Tim. 5:18.

TREASURE

OT Words

'ôṣār [**אוֹצָר, 214**]

'ôṣār is a noun found in eighty places with the primary meanings "treasure," "treasury," "storehouse," in both a literal and figurative sense.

Literal references to the "treasuries" of kings include those in 2 Kgs. 16:8; 2 Chr. 12:9. Treasure, or wealth in general, is indicated in Prov. 10:2; 21:20; Isa. 2:7; 39:2ff.; Jer. 20:5; Ezek. 28:4.

Particular mention is made of the "treasury" or "storehouse" of the tabernacle or temple in Josh. 6:19, 24; 1 Kgs. 7:51; 15:18; 2 Kgs. 24:13; 1 Chr. 26:20ff.; Ezra 2:69; Neh. 10:38. In Dan. 1:2 ***'ôṣār*** refers to the treasury of the pagan temple.

'ôṣār is also used metaphorically to refer to Yahweh's "storehouse" in relation to the heavens, from which comes rain (cf. Deut. 28:12). See also Job 38:22; Ps. 135:7; Jer. 10:13. Deut. 32:34 also refers to the heavenly "storehouse" in a vague, undefined way, as a source of divine judgment. See also Isa. 33:6, which refers to "the rich store" of salvation, wisdom, and knowledge.

matmôn [**מַטְמוֹן, 4301**]

matmôn is a noun occurring five times, referring to literal "treasure" or "wealth" in Gen. 43:23; Job 3:21; Prov. 2:4; Jer. 41:8. It has also a metaphorical use in Isa. 45:3.

segullāh [**סְגֻלָּה, 5459**]

segullāh indicates a "special possession" or "treasure," describing the Israelites in their unique relationship with Yahweh as belonging to him (cf. Exod. 19:5; Deut. 7:6; 14:2; 26:18; Ps. 135:4; Mal. 3:17). See also Eccl. 2:8.

genaz [**גְּנַז, 1596** (Aramaic)]

genaz is an Aramaic noun referring to the "royal treasury" of the Persian king, Artaxerxes I, in Ezra 7:20.

ḥōsen [**חֹסֶן, 2633**]

ḥōsen is a noun found in two places, referring to literal treasure in Prov. 27:24; Ezek. 22:25.

'āṣar [**אָצַר, 686**]

'āṣar is a noun indicating "treasure," or "precious stones," in 2 Kgs. 20:17; Neh. 13:13; Isa. 23:18; 39:6.

gizbār [**גִּזְבָּר, 1489**]

gizbār is a rare noun, indicating the sense of "treasurer" in Ezra 1:8.

gizbār [**גִּזְבָּר, 1490** (Aramaic)]

gizbār is a rare Aramaic word indicating "treasurers" in Ezra 7:21.

gedābar [**גְּדָבַר, 1411** (Aramaic)]

gedābar is a synonym for ***gizbār***, above, indicating "treasurers" in Dan. 3:2ff.

sāphan [**שָׂפַן, 8226**]

sāphan is a rare noun found only in Deut. 33:19, meaning "treasures" and implying mineral wealth.

'ātûd [**עָתוּד, 6259**]

'ātûd is a term found only in Isa. 10:13 with reference to "treasuries."

NT Words

thēsauros [θησαυρός, *2344*]

thēsauros is a noun found approximately twenty times meaning "treasure" in the sense of "valuables" in Matt. 2:11; 6:19; 13:44; Heb. 11:26. Metaphorical references to the "treasure" of the heart include those in Matt. 12:35; Luke 6:45; 12:34. Heavenly "treasure" is indicated in Matt. 6:20; Mark 10:21; Luke 18:22; 2 Cor. 4:7. Col. 2:3 affirms that all the "treasures" of wisdom and knowledge are hidden in Christ.

thēsaurizō [θησαυρίζω, *2343*]

thēsaurizō is a verb meaning "lay up," "store up" in relation to wealth or riches in several contexts. Matt. 6:19; Luke 12:21; Jas. 5:3 refer to "laying up" earthly riches; and Matt. 6:20 refers to heavenly riches.

gaza [γάζα, *1047*]

gaza is a rare noun found only in Acts 8:27 with reference to "the treasures" of royalty.

korbanas [κορβανᾶς, *2878*]

korbanas refers to the "sacred treasury" of the temple in Matt. 27:6. It also indicates a gift to God, referred to as "corban" in Mark 7:11.

gazophylakion [γαζοφυλάκιον, *1049*]

gazophylakion is a noun referring five times to the "treasury" of the temple (Mark 12:41ff.; Luke 21:1; John 8:20).

Additional Notes

References to "treasure" or "wealth" in the Old Testament are found in both literal and figurative contexts. Of particular significance is the use of the vocabulary to indicate the spiritual "treasure" found in the rightly ordered covenant relationship between Yahweh and his people. The people of Israel were themselves regarded as God's "treasured possession"; and spiritual wealth was bound up with the qualities of wisdom and knowledge, along with redemption, as indispensable benefits of a saving relationship with God.

In the New Testament, spiritual treasure and the full enjoyment of its benefits are wholly dependent on one being committed to a relationship with the Son of God based on faith and repentance. Thus there is evidence to suggest a redemptive-historical development between the motifs of "treasure" revealed in the Old Testament, and the "treasure" found in Christ in the New.

TREE

OT Words

'ēṣ **[עֵץ, 6086]**

'ēṣ is a common noun, found around three hundred times with the dominant meanings "tree," "wood," as well as related nuances. (→ WOOD)

General references to "tree(s)" include those in Gen. 1:11ff.; 2:16ff.; 3:1ff.; Exod. 9:25; Deut. 20:19; Neh. 10:37; Ps. 105:33; Song 4:14. In particular, Gen. 2:9; 3:22, 24 refer to the "tree of life," and Gen. 2:9, 17; 3:11 to "the tree of the knowledge of good and evil." 1 Kgs. 5:10; 9:11 refer to cedar trees for the construction of the Jerusalem temple.

'ēṣ also refers to "trees" as places of idolatrous worship, forbidden to Israel by God, but nonetheless frequented by the people of God on many occasions (cf. Deut. 12:2; 1 Kgs. 14:23; 2 Kgs. 16:4; 17:10; Jer. 2:20; 3:6ff.; Ezek. 6:13). In addition, ***'ēṣ*** indicates "trees" as places of execution on which people were hanged (though in fact the term "tree" is itself metaphorical in these contexts). In Deut. 21:22ff., the mode of execution actually refers to impaling on a stake. Similar actions are recorded in Josh. 8:29; Esth. 2:23.

There are a number of other metaphorical uses of ***'ēṣ***. Peoples or nations are described as "trees" in the parable of Judg. 9:8ff. In Ezek. 31:4ff., the parable of the cedar tree of Lebanon is equated with the king of Assyria. A godly man in Ps. 1:3 is likened to a "tree" planted by the water in order to derive blessing from God. A dry "tree" constitutes a symbol of sterility in Isa. 56:3. The personification of virtue, Lady Wisdom, is described in Prov. 3:8 as a "tree of life" to all those who lay hold of her (cf. also Prov. 15:4).

The "trees" of Ezekiel's vision in Ezek. 47:7, 12 signify collectively and by implication the "tree of life." These "trees" form part of the transformed landscape wrought by the life-giving river flowing from the temple, down through the Jordan River and into the Dead Sea, making it fresh.

berôsh **[בְּרוֹשׁ, 1265]**

berôsh is a noun occurring twenty times with reference to "fir" or "cypress trees," used in several different contexts.

General references to these tree species are found in 2 Kgs. 19:23; Isa. 14:8; 41:19; Ezek. 31:8. They are also noted as part of the renewed vegetation in a transformed land of Israel (cf. Isa. 55:13). These trees are also designated as construction material for the

Jerusalem temple, along with cedar wood (cf. 1 Kgs. 5:10; 9:11; 2 Chr. 2:8; 3:5).

NT Words

dendron [δένδρον, *1186*]

dendron is a term referring to "tree" throughout all twenty-five occurrences.

General references to trees include those in Matt. 13:32; 21:8; Mark 8:24; Luke 13:19. Trees are also mentioned in the book of Revelation, but these are always found in symbolic contexts (cf. Rev. 7:1ff.; 8:7; 9:4).

A number of metaphorical contexts refer to a person as a "tree," whose true moral character is revealed to God, who stands ready to "chop down" any that bear "bad fruit" (cf. Matt. 3:10; 12:33; Luke 3:9; 6:43ff.).

sykomorea [συκομορέα, *4809*]

sykomorea is found only in Luke 19:4, with reference to a "sycamore tree."

xylon [ξύλον, *3586*]

xylon is a noun found in nearly twenty places, meaning "tree" in exclusively metaphorical contexts. The literal sense of ***xylon*** indicates various products made from wood, such as "clubs," "containers."

One figurative sense of ***xylon*** refers to the "tree" as an instrument of execution — a gibbet, or cross. It is used in relation to Christ's death, as one "who hung on a tree" (cf. Acts 5:30; 10:39; 13:29; Gal. 3:13; 1 Pet. 2:24). In addition, the "tree of life" is depicted in the vision of the heavenly city in Rev. 22:3, 14. See also Rev. 2:7.

See Also: → CEDAR → FIG → FIG TREE → OLIVE → PALM TREE

TREMBLE

OT Words

rāgaz [רָגַז, **7264**]

rāgaz is a verb occurring around forty times with the primary sense of "tremble," as well as a number of related meanings, indicating the physiological response of strong negative emotions such as fear and rage. ***rāgaz*** also refers to the "trembling" of the earth as in an earthquake.

The emotional state of trembling with fear is indicated in Exod. 15:14; Deut. 2:25. In particular, trembling before God in fear is indicated in Ps. 99:1; Isa. 32:11; 64:2; Jer. 33:9; Joel 2:1.

Trembling with rage is noted in 2 Kgs. 19:27ff.; Prov. 29:9. In Isa. 37:28ff., the object of such emotion is Yahweh.

1 Sam. 14:15; 2 Sam. 22:8; Job 9:6; Ps. 18:7; Joel 2:10 refer to the trembling, or quaking, of the earth. In Isa. 13:13, the heavens "tremble" by the action of God.

ḥāphaz [חָפַז, **2648**]

ḥāphaz is a rare verb meaning to "tremble with fear" in Deut. 20:3.

pālaṣ [פָּלַץ, **6426**]

pālaṣ is a verb found only in Job 9:6, referring to the "trembling or shaking" of pillars.

ḥārēd [חָרֵד, **2730**]

ḥārēd is a verb expressing the sense of "tremble" in the context of hearing God's word (cf. 1 Sam. 4:13; Ezra 9:4; 10:3; Isa. 66:2, 5).

rûph [רוּף, **7322**]

rûph is a rare verb found only in Job 26:11 with reference to the pillars of heaven trembling.

ḥûl [חוּל, **2342**]

ḥûl is a verb expressing the underlying sense of "writhe in pain." The meaning "tremble" is used in the context of people trembling in awe of God (Ps. 114:7; Jer. 5:22). It also refers metaphorically to mountains (Hab. 3:10).

ḥārad [חָרַד, **2729**]

ḥārad is a verb found in forty contexts with the primary senses of "frighten," "be afraid," or "tremble." There is overlap in meaning here, for ***ḥārad*** is commonly translated "tremble" with the clear implication of fear as the accompanying emotion. This sense is evident in the case of people facing the prospect of a calamity (cf. Gen. 27:33; 42:28; 1 Sam. 13:7; 14:15; 2 Sam. 17:2; Ezek. 26:16ff.). In Isa. 32:11; Ezek. 32:10, fearful trembling is expressed in relation to imminent divine judgment.

Trembling in awe at God's power and authority is clearly indicated in Hos. 11:10ff.; and at Mt. Sinai there is likewise a reference to the terrified people of Israel trembling before Yahweh.

ḥārad also indicates the trembling or quaking of Mt. Sinai (Exod. 19:18), and of the ends of the earth (Isa. 41:5).

rā'ash [**רָעַשׁ, 7493**]

rā'ash is a verb expressing the primary sense of "tremble," or "shake," throughout its thirty occurrences.

Literal references to earthquakes include those in Judg. 5:4; 2 Sam. 22:8; Pss. 46:3; 77:18; Isa. 24:18; Jer. 4:24; 10:10. The "quaking" of mountains is noted in Nah. 1:5; and the "trembling" of the heavens and the earth in Joel 2:10; 3:16. Metaphorical reference to the "trembling" of the earth as a consequence of divine judgment is indicated in Jer. 50:46; 51:29; Ezek. 26:15; 27:28. Similarly the "shaking of the nations" is indicated in the face of divine judgment in Ezek. 31:16. ***rā'ash*** indicates the shaking of buildings in Ezek. 26:10; Amos 9:1.

People are said to "tremble" before God in fear in Ezek. 38:20.

NT WORDS

phrissō [φρίσσω, *5425*]

phrissō is a verb found only in Jas. 2:19 with reference to demons who "tremble with fear" at the thought of God.

tremō [τρέμω, *5141*]

tremō is synonymous with ***phrissō*** (see above). It is found several times meaning "tremble," "be afraid" (cf. Mark 5:33; Luke 8:47).

entromos [ἔντρομος, *1790*]

entromos is an adjective derived from ***tremō*** (see above), indicating the state of "trembling" in fear (Acts 7:32; 16:29; Heb. 12:21).

tromos [τρόμος, *5156*]

tromos is a noun derived from ***tremō*** (see above). It occurs four times and means "trembling," linked explicitly with fear (1 Cor. 2:3; 2 Cor. 7:15; Eph. 6:5; Phil. 2:12).

TRESPASS ➞ TRANSGRESS

TRIAL

OT WORDS

massāh [**מַסָּה, 4531**]

massāh is a noun meaning "testing," "trial." The term is found in five contexts. The "testing" of the Israelites by Yahweh in the wilderness is indicated in all but one of these (cf. Deut. 4:34; 7:19; 29:3; Ps. 95:8).

bāḥan [**בָּחַן, 974**]

bāḥan is a verb found in around thirty places with the primary meaning "try," or "prove." It is used in a participial nominal sense, with the sense of "testing" from God, in Ezek. 21:13.

NT WORDS

dokimē [δοκιμή, *1382*]

dokimē is a noun indicating the primary meanings "proof," "evidence." In 2 Cor. 8:2, however, the term means "trial," referring to an experience of undefined suffering.

dokimion [δοκίμιον, *1383*]

dokimion is a variant form of ***dokimē*** (see above), found only in Jas. 1:3; 1 Pet. 1:7, meaning "trying," "proving," or "trial" in relation to one's faith.

pyrōsis [πύρωσις, *4451*]

pyrōsis is a noun with the underlying sense of "burning," used metaphorically in 1 Pet. 4:12 to refer to a "fiery trial."

peirasmos [πειρασμός, *3986*]

peirasmos is a noun found in around twenty contexts meaning "trial," "testing," "temptation."

Luke 4:13 refers to Jesus' "trial" or "temptation" by Satan in the wilderness. Heb. 3:8 refers to Israel's "trial" in the wilderness. The prayer that God will not lead his people into "trial" or "temptation" is recorded in Matt. 6:13; Luke 11:4 (cf. also Matt. 26:41). General references to times of "trial" or "testing" are found in Luke 8:13; 1 Tim. 6:19. In particular, times of "testing" for followers of Christ are recorded in Luke 22:28ff.; Acts 20:19; 1 Cor. 10:13; 1 Pet. 1:6; 2 Pet. 2:9; Rev. 3:10.

TRIBE

OT WORDS

matteh [**מַטֶּה, 4294**]

matteh is a common noun found in approximately 250 contexts with several meanings, including the dominant meaning of "tribe," as well as "rod," "staff." (➞ STAFF)

The meaning "tribes" relates exclusively to the tribes of Israel (e.g., Exod. 31:2ff.; Lev. 24:11; Num. 1:4ff.; 2:5ff.; 10:15ff.; 13:2ff.; Josh. 7:1; 14:1ff.; 21:5ff.; 1 Kgs. 7:14; 1 Chr. 6:60ff.).

shēbet [**שֵׁבֶט, 7626**]

shēbet is synonymous with ***matteh*** (see above), found in around 200 contexts and also expressing various meanings such as "tribe," "rod," "scepter," "staff." (➞ SCEPTER) Again, the sense of "tribe" is dominant.

The meaning "tribes" relates primarily to the Israelite clans (e.g., Gen. 49:16; Deut. 1:13ff.; Josh. 4:4ff.; 22:7ff.; Judg. 20:10ff.; 21:15ff.; 2 Sam. 7:7; 1 Kgs. 11:31ff.; Isa. 49:6; Jer. 10:16; Ezek. 47:13ff.; Hos. 5:9). Isa. 19:13 refers to the "tribes" of Egypt.

shebat [**שְׁבַט, 7625** (Aramaic)]

shebat is a rare Aramaic noun indicating the "tribes" of Israel in Ezra 6:17.

NT Words

phylē [φυλή, *5443*]

phylē is a noun found in twenty-five contexts meaning "tribe(s)" throughout.

References to the "tribes" of Israel include those in Matt. 19:28; Luke 2:36; 22:36; Acts 13:21; Rom. 11:1; Phil. 3:5; Heb. 7:13ff.; Rev. 5:5; 7:14ff.; 21:12.

More generally, the "tribes" of the earth, referring to the nations at large, are mentioned in Matt. 24:30; Rev. 7:1; 5:9; 7:9; 11:9; 13:7; 14:6.

See Also: ➞ FAMILY

TRIBULATION

NT Words

thlipsis [θλίψις, *2347*]

thlipsis is a noun found in approximately fifty places with the primary senses of "tribulation," or "persecution," and "affliction."

References to "tribulation" that are largely synonymous with persecution of the Christian church include those in Matt. 13:21; 24:2ff.; Acts 11:19; 14:22; Rom. 2:9; 12:12; Rev. 1:9; 2:9ff.; 7:14.

See Also: ➞ AFFLICT ➞ DISTRESS

TRIBUTE

OT Words

mas [**מַס, 4522**]

mas is a noun expressing the idea of "tribute" under the guise of "slave, or forced labor." The term occurs in approximately twenty contexts with this meaning (cf. Gen. 49:15; Deut. 20:11; Josh. 16:10; 17:13; Judg. 1:28ff.; 1 Kgs. 4:6; 5:13ff.; Esth. 10:1).

middāh [**מִדָּה, 4060**]

middāh is a term denoting a "measure" in most of its nearly forty contexts. However, in Neh. 5:4 it refers to "tax."

NT Words

phoros [φόρος, *5411*]

phoros is a term denoting "tribute," or "tax," in Luke 20:22; 23:2; Rom. 13:6, 7.

didrachmon [δίδραχμον, *1323*]

didrachmon denotes a "half-shekel tax," found only in Matt. 17:24 (twice).

kēnsos [κῆνσος, *2778*]

kēnsos is a term referring to "taxes," or a "toll," found only in Matt. 17:25; 22:17, 29; Mark 12:14.

TRIUMPH

OT Words

'ālaṣ [**עָלַץ, 5970**]

'ālaṣ is a verb found only in Ps. 25:2 with the meaning "triumph" in the cry, "Let not my enemies triumph over me." (➞ JOY)

rûa' [**רוּעַ, 7321**]

rûa' is a verb denoting the actions of "cry," "shout," "make a joyful noise," in most of the fifty or so contexts in which it occurs. In several places, however, ***rûa'*** expresses the sense of "triumphing" over one's enemies (cf. Pss. 41:11; 60:8; 108:9).

gā'āh [**גָּאָה, 1342**]

gā'āh is a rare term expressing the action of Yahweh "triumphing" over his enemies in Exod. 15:1, 21.

NT Words

thriambeuō [θριαμβεύω, *2358*]

thriambeuō is a rare verb found only twice. 2 Cor. 2:14 contains the affirmation that God in Christ always "leads (his people) in triumph." Col. 2:15 then declares that Christ "has triumphed" over his enemies on the cross.

See Also: ➞ JOY

TROUBLE

OT Words

'ākar [**עָכַר, 5916**]

'ākar is a verb meaning "trouble," "stir up," "disturb" throughout its fourteen occurrences.

In Gen. 34:30; Judg. 11:35; 1 Sam. 14:29, ***'ākar*** means "bringing trouble (on someone)." In particular, Yahweh "brings trouble" on Israel because of their sin (cf. Josh. 6:18; 7:25; 1 Chr. 2:7).

The sense of "trouble" or "disturb" is indicated in 1 Kgs. 18:17, 18. "To trouble," or "cause distress" is the meaning evident in Prov. 11:29; 15:6, 27.

bāhal **[בָּהַל, 926]**

bāhal is a verb found around forty times with a variety of meanings. The common underlying sense is "to trouble," usually occurring in the passive voice.

The meaning "be troubled, or dismayed" is indicated in a general sense in Gen. 45:2; Judg. 20:41; Job 4:5; Ps. 104:29; Ezek. 26:1.

The heightened sense of to "be in anguish" is noted in Ps. 6:2; Isa. 21:3. Similarly, the state of being very troubled or terrified is indicated in 1 Sam. 28:1; Ps. 48:5; Ezek. 7:27.

The active voice, meaning "to trouble" or "terrify" is noted in 2 Chr. 32:18; Job 22:10; 23:16; Ps. 83:15.

telā'āh **[תְּלָאָה, 8513]**

telā'āh is a noun denoting "trouble" or "hardship." It occurs only four times (cf. Exod. 18:8; Num. 20:14; Neh. 9:32; Lam. 3:5).

rōgez **[רֹגֶז, 7267]**

rōgez is a general term for "trouble," "turmoil," or "strife" in Job 3:17, 26; 14:1.

mehûmāh **[מְהוּמָה, 4103]**

mehûmāh is a noun denoting "trouble," "turmoil." Turmoil, or confusion, instigated by Yahweh as a judgment against both his people and the nations in general, is noted in Deut. 28:20; Isa. 22:5; Ezek. 7:7; Zech. 14:13. See also 1 Sam. 14:20; 2 Chr. 15:5; Prov. 15:16.

behal **[בְּהַל, 927** (Aramaic)**]**

behal is an Aramaic verb meaning "to be troubled" (in thought and mind) in response to divine revelation (cf. Dan. 4:5, 19; 5:6ff.; 7:15, 28).

pā'am **[פָּעַם, 6470]**

pā'am is a Hebrew synonym for the Aramaic ***behal*** (see above), denoting a state of psychological and mental turmoil (Gen. 41:8; Ps. 77:4; Dan. 2:1ff.).

bā'at **[בָּעַת, 1204]**

bā'at is a verb with the predominant meanings "to make afraid," "terrify." It also signifies the act of "tormenting" in regard to the evil spirit sent by God against Saul to "trouble" him in mind and spirit (cf. 1 Sam. 16:4ff.).

NT Words

kopos [κόπος, *2873*]

kopos is a noun denoting the state of "trouble" or "annoyance." It is used primarily, however, with verbal force, translated "to bother, annoy" in Matt. 26:10; Mark 14:6; Luke 11:7; 18:5. (→ WORK)

skyllō [σκύλλω, *4660*]

skyllō is a verb meaning "trouble," "bother," or "annoy" in Mark 5:35; Luke 7:6; 8:49.

parenochleō [παρενοχλέω, *3926*]

parenochleō is a rare verb found only in Acts 15:19, meaning "to trouble," "make difficult."

ektarassō [ἐκταράσσω, *1613*]

ektarassō is another rare verb meaning to "trouble," or "throw into uproar." It is found only in Acts 16:20.

tarassō [ταράσσω, *5015*]

tarassō is a verb found in approximately twenty contexts meaning "trouble," "cause distress," as well as "be troubled, fearful, or anxious."

The mental state of anxiety is predicated of human beings in Matt. 2:3; Mark 6:50; Luke 1:12; John 11:33; 14:1, 27; 1 Pet. 3:14. Such a condition is also noted in relation to Christ's apprehension at his approaching death (cf. John 12:27; 13:21).

tarassō refers to causing trouble in Acts 15:24; 17:8; Gal. 1:7; 5:10. And in John 5:4ff., ***tarassō*** means "troubling," or agitating, stirring up the water of a pool.

parechō [παρέχω, *3930*]

parechō is a verb found in five contexts meaning "to cause trouble," "irritate," or "bother," often used in the negative (cf. Matt. 26:10; Mark 14:6; Luke 11:7; 18:5; Gal. 6:17).

kakopatheō [κακοπαθέω, *2553*]

kakopatheō is a verb meaning to "endure hardship," or "suffer trouble" (cf. 2 Tim. 2:3, 9; 4:5; Jas. 5:13).

enochleō [ἐνοχλέω, *1776*]

enochleō is a rare term, found only in Heb. 12:15, meaning to "cause trouble" in a spiritual sense.

throeō [θροέω, *2360*]

throeō is a verb found in only three places, meaning to be "troubled," "anxious," or "frightened." It is used only in the negative as an exhortation (cf. Matt. 24:6; Mark 13:7; 2 Thess. 2:2).

diatarassō [διαταράσσω, *1298*]

diatarassō is a rare verb found only in Luke 1:29, meaning "to be troubled, disturbed."

tyrbazō [τυρβάζω, *5182*]

tyrbazō is a synonym for ***diatarassō***, above. It is found only in Luke 10:41 and describes the troubled state of mind of Mary, the sister of Lazarus.

See Also: → AFFLICT → DISTRESS → EVIL → TRIBULATION → WORK

TRUE, TRUTH

OT Words

'emet [אֱמֶת, **571**]

'emet is a noun occurring around 130 times. It means "truth," "faithfulness" in the majority of these contexts. There is considerable overlap between these two meanings. ***'emet*** also functions adjectivally and adverbially, meaning "true," "truly."

The adverbial sense of "truly," or "honorably," "with integrity," is indicated in Gen. 24:19. The sense of "surely" or "certainly" is found in Pss. 15:2; 51:6; 145:18; Jer. 28:9.

'emet refers to "truth" as an absolute virtue (Ps. 45:4; Prov. 22:21; Isa. 59:14; Jer. 9:5; Dan. 8:12); to the "truth" of God's word (1 Kgs. 17:24; Dan. 11:2, Ps. 119:43); to "truth" as a characteristic of God's nature (Pss. 25:5; 86:11; Isa. 10:20; 16:5; Jer. 4:2; 10:10); and to the "truth" of God's laws and words (2 Sam. 7:28; Ps. 119:142, 160). See also Gen. 42:16; Prov. 8:7.

The adjectival use of ***'emet***, denoting the sense of "true" (i.e., in accord with truth) is illustrated in Deut. 13:14; 22:20; 1 Kgs. 10:6; Prov. 14:25; Isa. 43:9; Zech. 7:9. The sense of "certain" or "sure" is found in Josh. 2:12; Ps. 132:11; Prov. 11:18. See also 2 Chr. 15:3.

'omnām [אָמְנָם, **551**]

'omnām is an adverb found in nine contexts, meaning "truly" (i.e., certainly) and in the expression "It is true . . ." (cf. Ruth 3:12; 2 Kgs. 19:17; Job 9:2; 12:2; 19:4ff.; 34:12; 36:4; Isa. 37:18).

'emûnāh [אֱמוּנָה, **530**]

'emûnāh is a noun found in around fifty contexts meaning "faithfulness," "truth," as well as related senses. There is a great deal of overlap between these two primary meanings, with the underlying sense of ***'emûnāh*** indicating the virtue of integrity and wholeness or purity of motive or intention.

"Truth," said to belong to Yahweh, is indicated in Ps. 96:13. The "way of truth" is indicated in Ps. 119:30. The virtue of "truth" is linked to justice in Jer. 5:1ff. Prov. 12:17 refers to "speaking the truth."

The adjectival meaning "true," in the sense of "trustworthy," is indicated with respect to God in Ps. 119:86, 138, and to human beings in Prov. 12:22; 28:20; Isa. 59:4.

NT Words

alēthēs [ἀληθής, *227*]

alēthēs is an adjectival form found in twenty-five contexts meaning "true" in a variety of settings.

The quality of being "true" in the sense of being "endowed with integrity, honesty" describes Christ (Matt. 22:6; Mark 12:14; John 7:18); God (John 8:26; Rom. 3:4); and human beings (2 Cor. 6:8).

In a number of places, ***alēthēs*** denotes the quality "true" in the sense of "that which is in accord with truth" (e.g., John 5:31ff.; 8:13ff.; Phil. 4:8; Titus 1:13; 1 John 2:8, 27).

Similarly, the meaning "true" also signifies that which is "genuine" (e.g., 2 Pet. 2:22; 3 John 12), including the grace of God (cf. 1 Pet. 5:12).

alēthinos [ἀληθινός, *228*]

alēthinos is another adjectival form meaning "true" throughout its nearly thirty occurrences, indicating various related nuances.

The designation "true" is applied to "that which is genuine" in a number of places. It refers, for example, to eternal, spiritual wealth (cf. Luke 16:11); to the spiritual light embodied in the person of Christ (cf. John 1:9; 1 John 2:8); to the believer's heart (cf. Heb. 10:22); to the bread of life, indicating the word of God (John 6:32); to the vine representing Christ as the source of eternal life (cf. John 15:1); and to the tabernacle in heaven, anticipated by the earthly dwelling place of God (cf. Heb. 8:2; 9:24). See also Rev. 19:11.

alēthinos also means "true," designating "that which is in accord with truth" (i.e., the absolute virtue of truth). It is applied to the judgments of God (Rev. 19:2); to the word of God (Rev. 3:7; 19:9; 21:5); to God himself (John

7:28; 17:3; 1 Thess. 1:9; 1 John 5:20; Rev. 6:10); and to apostolic testimony (John 19:35).

alētheia [ἀλήθεια, *225*]

alētheia is the primary term for "truth" in the New Testament, occurring about 110 times in a variety of contexts.

Truth as a virtue, describing "that which accords with reality," is noted in general in Matt. 22:16; Mark 5:33; John 8:40ff.; Rom. 1:18, 25; Eph. 4:25; 1 John 1:6. Truth as the characteristic of God's word is indicated in John 17:17ff.; 2 Tim. 2:15; as is the truth of the gospel (Gal. 2:5, 14; Eph. 1:13; 2 Thess. 2:12; 1 Tim. 2:4; Heb. 10:26).

alētheia is also used with the adverbial sense of "truly" in Col. 1:5.

Truth as an element of the divine character, denoting absolute integrity, is embodied in Christ (cf. John 1:14ff.; 5:33; 14:6; 2 Cor. 11:10; Eph. 4:21); designated as a trait of the Holy Spirit (John 14:17; 15:26; 16:13); and is also a characteristic of God (Rom. 3:7; 15:8).

alēthōs [ἀληθῶς, *230*]

alēthōs is an adverb meaning "truly," "surely" in nearly twenty contexts (e.g., Matt. 14:33; Mark 14:70; John 4:42; 17:8; Acts 12:11).

alētheuō [ἀληθεύω, *226*]

alētheuō is a verb meaning to "tell the truth." It occurs only in Gal. 4:16; Eph. 4:15.

gnēsios [γνήσιος, *1103*]

gnēsios is an adjective found in four places meaning "true," or "genuine," in relation to Christian love (2 Cor. 8:8), and to people (Phil. 4:3; 1 Tim. 1:2; Titus 1:4).

TRUMPET

OT Words

shôphār [**שׁוֹפָר, 7782**]

shôphār is a noun occurring around seventy times with the primary meaning "ram's horn," referring consistently to a "trumpet" used to signal the celebration of ceremonial ritual (cf. Pss. 47:5; 81:3; 98:6; 150:3).

Lev. 25:9 refers literally to the "trumpet" fashioned out of a ram's horn. The instrument is used to herald the arrival of the Year of Jubilee. The word translated "Jubilee" is ***yôbēl***, which is also used to indicate a ram's horn trumpet (see below). However, it is this term ***shôphār*** that denotes the instrument used to announce the arrival of this unique Sabbatical Year. The ***shôphār*** was also used in the miraculous destruction of the city of Jericho, where it was sounded by the Israelite people on the seventh day of their march around that city, precipitating the collapse of the city walls (cf. Josh. 6:4ff.).

Other references to the use of the ***shôphār*** include those in Judg. 3:27; 2 Sam. 15:10; 1 Kgs. 1:34ff.; 2 Chr. 15:14; Job 39:24ff.; Jer. 4:5; Ezek. 33:3ff.; Joel 2:1; Amos 3:6.

The ***shôphār*** in particular was heard on the occasion of the revelation of the law covenant given to Moses on Mt. Sinai. It was sounded by Yahweh at that time (cf. Exod. 19:16ff.; 20:18).

yôbēl [**יוֹבֵל, 3104**]

yôbēl is a noun occurring thirty times with the primary meaning "Jubilee" (i.e., the fiftieth year). However, in several places ***yôbēl*** is translated "ram's horn," from which trumpets were fashioned (cf. Exod. 19:13; Josh. 6:4ff.). (See the entry above for discussion of the use of ***shôphār*** in connection with Jubilee.)

ḥaṣōṣerāh [**חֲצֹצְרָה, 2689**]

ḥaṣōṣerāh is found in approximately thirty contexts, denoting a "trumpet" made of hammered silver used for various purposes in the Israelite community.

Num. 10:8 refers to trumpet construction. General references to trumpets include those in 2 Kgs. 11:14; Neh. 12:35ff.; Hos. 5:8. Trumpets are used in worship (1 Chr. 13:8; 2 Chr. 5:12ff.; Ezra 3:10; Ps. 98:6); in battle (Num. 10:9; 2 Chr. 31:12ff.); and in festivals (Num. 10:10). They are designated as sacred instruments in 2 Kgs. 12:13.

ḥāṣar [**חָצַר, 2690**]

ḥāṣar is a verb meaning "to sound the trumpet." The term is found in eleven contexts (cf. 1 Chr. 15:24; 2 Chr. 5:12; 7:6; 13:14). ***ḥāṣar*** is also used nominally, referring to "trumpeters" in 2 Chr. 5:13; 29:28.

tāqôa' [**תָּקוֹעַ, 8619**]

tāqôa' is a rare term denoting a "trumpet," found only in Ezek. 7:14 in the context of preparing for battle.

NT Words

salpinx [σάλπιγξ, *4536*]

salpinx is a noun denoting a "trumpet" throughout its eleven occurrences.

References to the trumpet heralding the return of Jesus Christ are found in Matt. 24:31; 1 Cor. 15:52; 1 Thess. 4:16. The sounding of the trumpet at the Sinai theophany is noted in Heb. 12:19. A trumpet is sounded in heaven in the presence of the risen Christ-King in Rev. 1:10. See also 1 Cor. 14:8.

In metaphorical contexts, ***salpinx*** is found in Rev. 4:1, referring to a voice that sounds like a trumpet. A trumpet heralds a cycle of divine judgment against wicked humanity in Rev. 8:6, 13; 9:14.

salpizō [σαλπίζω, *4537*]

salpizō is a verb meaning "to sound a trumpet," occurring thirteen times.

The sounding of a trumpet announcing the return of Christ is noted in 1 Cor. 15:52. Trumpet blasts indicating the outpouring of divine wrath against humankind are recorded in Rev. 8:6ff.; 9:1, 13; 11:17. See also Rev. 10:7.

salpistēs [σαλπιστής, *4538*]

salpistēs is a rare noun denoting "trumpeters" in Rev. 18:22.

Additional Notes

"Trumpets" throughout both Old and New Testaments signify important aspects of the divine plan of redemption.

In the first instance, the sound of the trumpet is a focal point of the Sinai theophany whereby Yahweh announces his appearance. Thereafter, the trumpet functions as a key instrument in Israelite worship. It is used at the various festivals to celebrate the victory of God over his enemies and the deliverance of his people. It is especially significant in the destruction of Jericho, and as an accompaniment to God's people in battle.

In the New Testament, the sounding of the trumpet is closely identified with the triumphant return of Jesus Christ as the King of kings. Implicit in his return is the statement of his absolute victory over the powers of evil, which he conquered on the cross. In the book of Revelation, the sounding of the trumpet is a prelude to the outpouring of wrath against the mass of unregenerate, wicked humanity.

Thus the phenomenon of the trumpet call may be closely identified with the manifestation of Yahweh among his people, culminating in the person of Christ. It symbolizes both supreme blessing for God's people, and terrible judgment on those outside of that community.

TRUST

OT Words

ḥāsāh [חָסָה, 2620]

ḥāsāh is a verb found thirty-five times with the primary meaning "seek (a) refuge," indicating the underlying sense of "put (one's) trust in."

The action of "taking refuge" in a general sense with respect to God is indicated in 2 Sam. 22:31; Pss. 2:12; 7:1; Prov. 30:5; Isa. 57:3; Zeph. 3:12. More particularly, 2 Sam. 22:3 speaks of David "taking refuge" in God, "the rock." Many "seek refuge" under the wings of Yahweh in the sanctuary (cf. Ruth 2:12; Pss. 36:7; 57:1; 61:4; 91:4). See also Judg. 9:15.

bātaḥ [בָּטַח, 982]

bātaḥ is the principal verb in the Old Testament meaning "to trust," and it is found with that sense in most of its 120 occurrences. The underlying sense of ***bātaḥ*** is to "have confidence in."

General references to "trusting" include those in Judg. 20:36; 2 Kgs. 18:19ff.; Isa. 59:4. ***bātaḥ*** also refers to trusting in military defenses (Deut. 28:52); in one's leaders (Judg. 9:26); in one's friends (Ps. 41:9); and, more commonly, in God (2 Kgs. 18:5; Pss. 4:5; 22:4ff.; 115:8ff.; Prov. 3:5; Isa. 12:2; Jer. 17:7).

Elsewhere, various objects of people's trust are declared to be futile, or vain, such as wealth (cf. Ps. 49:6; Jer. 48:7); weak military allies (cf. Isa. 36:6, 9); idols (cf. Isa. 42:17; Hab. 2:18); lies (cf. Jer. 13:25; 28:15); one's own righteousness (cf. Ezek. 33:13); and humankind in general (cf. Ps. 118:8ff.; Jer. 9:4; 17:5).

mibtāḥ [מִבְטָח, 4009]

mibtāḥ is a noun derived from ***bātaḥ*** (see above) occurring nine times and meaning "trust," "confidence" in most of these contexts.

General references to "confidence," or "trust," include those in Job 8:14; 18:14; 31:24.

Pss. 40:4; 65:5; 71:5; Prov. 14:26; 22:19; Jer. 17:7 refer to God as the sure object of people's "trust."

Futile objects of one's trust include faithless people (cf. Prov. 25:19) and unreliable allies (cf. Jer. 2:37; 48:13; Ezek. 29:16).

reḥaṣ [רְחַץ, 7365 (Aramaic)]

reḥaṣ is a rare Aramaic verb meaning "trust," referring to the saving confidence placed in Yahweh by Shadrach, Meshach, and Abednego in Dan. 3:28.

NT Words

elpizō [ἐλπίζω, *1679*]

elpizō is a verb found around thirty times with the predominant sense of "hope," or "trust," in a variety of contexts. (→ HOPE) There is also a distinct overlap in meaning between these two senses in several contexts.

elpizō refers to placing trust (i.e., putting one's hope in) in Moses (John 5:45); in Christ (Rom. 15:12; 2 Cor. 1:10; Phil. 2:19); in the living God (1 Tim. 4:10; 5:5); and in wealth (1 Tim. 6:17; 1 Pet. 3:5).

elpizō also means "trust," or "hope," in the sense of "earnestly desire" or "wish for" (2 Cor. 5:11; 13:6; 2 John 12).

peithō [πείθω, *3982*]

peithō is a verb indicating the predominant sense of "persuade" in most of its approximately sixty occurrences. (→ PERSUADE) However, in several places ***peithō*** is also translated "to trust."

Matt. 27:43; Gal. 5:10; Phil. 1:14; Heb. 2:13 refer to trusting in the Lord. 2 Cor. 10:7 speaks of being confident in belonging to Christ. Putting trust in one's wealth is noted in Mark 10:24, and in one's armor in Luke 11:22. In Phlm. 12, Paul describes his "confidence" in the obedience of Philemon. Phil. 3:3ff. disdains any confidence being placed in the "flesh" (i.e., human nature).

parathēkē [παραθήκη, *3866*]

parathēkē is a rare noun found in 2 Tim. 1:12 meaning a "deposit," or "trust," signifying a body of teaching concerning the purity of the gospel which has been entrusted to Timothy by Paul and the other apostles.

See Also: → BELIEF → BELIEVE → CONFIDENCE → REFUGE

TRY → PROOF

TUMULT → UPROAR

TURN

OT Words

sûr [**סוּר, 5493**]

sûr is a verb occurring around three hundred times with various meanings including "remove" (i.e., put, or take away) and "depart." (→ DEPART → REMOVE) In a number of contexts, ***sûr*** has the basic meaning "turn," with the related senses of "turn away," "turn aside."

The literal meaning "turn aside," indicating taking a new direction, is noted in Gen. 19:2ff.; Exod. 3:3ff.; Judg. 4:18; 1 Kgs. 22:32; 1 Sam. 6:12.

The meaning "turn aside" is also evident in metaphorical contexts, where it indicates the sense of "rebel against God," or "wandering from the path of obedience" to him. This action is consistently predicated of Israel (cf. Deut. 9:12ff.; 11:16, 28; 17:17; Judg. 2:17; 1 Kgs. 15:5). See also 1 Sam. 12:20ff. ***sûr*** is also used with active force meaning "to turn (someone) away," to redirect one's purpose or attention (Deut. 7:4). The threat referred to here is linked to the potential spiritual danger posed by the depraved Canaanite culture for the people of Israel, in leading them into an idolatrous lifestyle.

The figurative expression "turn neither to the right nor the left" is to be understood as a moral imperative involving meticulous obedience to the law of God in Deut. 5:32; Josh. 1:7; 23:6. ***sûr*** is also used once literally in the context of the journey of the Israelites towards the land of Canaan (Deut. 2:27).

sûr also means "turn away" in the sense of "reject" in Ps. 66:20, employed in the negative to indicate God's decision not to reject the prayer of his people.

pānāh [**פָּנָה, 6437**]

pānāh is a verb found in 135 contexts meaning "turn," or "look," with a variety of nuances.

The literal sense of "turn away," or "look away," is found in Gen. 18:22. The meaning "turn away" can also metaphorically indicate "rebel against." The sin of "turning away" from Yahweh, for example, is indicated in Deut. 29:18; 30:17; Isa. 53:6; Jer. 2:7. See also Jer. 48:39; 49:24.

pānāh also expresses the literal sense of "turn, or look toward" in Josh. 15:7; 1 Kgs. 7:25; 2 Chr. 20:24. God pleads with the nations to "turn" to him in repentance (Isa. 45:22). The psalmist pleads for God to "turn" and look upon him with favor in Pss. 25:16; 69:16; 119:132.

The meaning "turn" also signifies "making a choice about a course of action" in general terms in Gen. 24:49; 1 Kgs. 2:3; Job 5:1; Eccl. 2:12. In particular, dire penalties are prescribed for those who "turn" to idol worship or occult activity (Lev. 19:4; 20:6; Deut. 31:18; Hos. 3:1).

Literal references to "turning around" and proceeding in a new direction are found in Exod. 7:23; Judg.

18:21; 1 Kgs. 17:3. The Israelites are described thus in Num. 14:25; Deut. 1:7; 2:1ff.

pānāh also expresses the literal meaning "return" (i.e., go back) in Josh. 22:4; Jer. 50:16. In Ezek. 36:9, Yahweh promises to return to his people and renew them.

shûb [שׁוּב, 7725]

shûb is a common verb occurring in over 1,000 contexts with the primary meanings "turn," "return," as well as a number of related senses. (→ REPENT)

The sense of "returning" to one's original state is indicated in relation to physical death (i.e., a return to dust) in Gen. 3:19; Job 34:15; Eccl. 3:20; 12:7. See also Eccl. 1:6. The transitive force of "return" or "restore," "bring back," is used in relation to stolen property (Judg. 17:4); and to former cities of Judah, "brought back" from Edomite control (cf. 2 Kgs. 14:22). In Gen. 8:3, the floodwaters are described as "returning," or "receding," so as to reveal dry land once more.

The literal sense of "returning" to an original location is noted in Gen. 8:9; 31:55; Exod. 4:19ff. This meaning is also applied to water (Exod. 14:28) and to a plague (Lev. 14:43). Judg. 11:31; 1 Sam. 18:6 depict a return from battle; and Ezra 2:1; Isa. 10:4ff.; 35:10; 51:11 depict the significant return of the people of Israel to Canaan. See also Josh. 1:15. The law relating to the "return" of property to the original Israelite owner(s) in the Year of Jubilee is described in Lev. 25:13ff.

The action of "turning away" or "turning back" with transitive force is indicated with respect to one's anger (Gen. 27:44; Prov. 15:1); and to the wrath of God (Num. 25:11). ***shûb*** is often employed in the negative, indicating Yahweh's refusal to turn back his anger, which results in inevitable judgment for those who have sinned against him (cf. Isa. 9:12; 10:4; Jer. 4:8; Amos 1:3ff.; 2:1ff.). Similarly, Yahweh is said "to turn against" his people in punishment for their sin in Josh. 24:20; 1 Kgs. 2:32. In contrast, Jer. 32:40 contains the promise of the new covenant, whereby God solemnly declares that he will never again "turn away" from his people to punish them as he had done in the past.

The meaning "turn from" is applied to Yahweh in Josh. 7:26; Pss. 78:38; 85:3; Hos. 14:4, where he is said to "turn from" his anger. And 1 Kgs. 8:35 contains a plea for God to "turn away from" the sin of his people. In other negative contexts, this meaning is applied to those people who "turn from" Yahweh, or who rebel against him (cf. Num. 32:15; Deut. 23:14; Josh. 22:18; Jer. 34:16; Ezek. 33:18).

In a number of places, "returning" to Yahweh indicates repentance (cf. Deut. 1:45; 4:30 1 Sam. 7:3; 1 Kgs. 8:48; Ps. 22:27; Isa. 19:22; Jer. 18:8; Dan. 9:13; Hos. 6:1). (→ REPENT) Yahweh himself is also depicted as "returning" in several contexts. For example, he returns to enable Sarah to conceive a son in Gen. 18:10ff. Then he acts to fulfill his promise to "bring back" (lit., "causes to return") his people to the land of Canaan after their exile (cf. Deut. 30:3; 1 Kgs. 8:34; Ps. 68:22; Isa. 49:6; Jer. 12:15; 23:3; 29:10ff.; Zech. 10:10). There are various pleas for God to "turn toward" his people in compassion and deliver them (cf. Pss. 6:4; 80:14); to "restore" salvation to his people (cf. Pss. 51:12; 80:7; 126:4); and to "restrain" (i.e., turn away) his anger (cf. Dan. 9:16).

nāṭāh [נָטָה, 5186]

nāṭāh is a verb occurring around two hundred times with the two predominant meanings "stretch (out)" and "turn away." (→ STRETCH)

The literal sense of "turn away," or "turn aside," indicating a physical change of direction, is found in Num. 20:21; 22:23ff. There is a metaphorical application of this sense in Prov. 4:27, where the reader is instructed "not to turn aside" from that which is right. Other figurative contexts include 1 Sam. 8:3, which describes the dishonest practice of "turning aside" after bribes. See also Isa. 30:11.

nāṭāh is used with transitive force in 1 Kgs. 11:2ff.; Job 31:7; Isa. 44:20 to indicate the effect of sin in "turning away" one's heart from serving God. The crime of "turning away" the poor and needy is noted in Job 24:4; Isa. 10:2; Amos 2:7; Mal. 3:5.

In Prov. 21:1, God is said to "turn" the hearts of human beings wherever he wills.

sābab [סָבַב, 5437]

sābab is a verb found in approximately 150 contexts with the fundamental sense of "surround," "turn," along with a variety of related senses.

The meaning "turn" in the sense of "facing a particular direction" is applied to a boundary (Num. 34:4); and to the attitude of prayer (2 Kgs. 20:2; Isa. 38:2), where people "turn" their face to pray to God. ***sābab*** also refers to those who "turn (their face) away" from God in an attitude of rejection (cf. 1 Kgs. 21:4; 2 Chr. 29:6). Conversely, Yahweh is said to "turn" his face from his people in judgment against them (Ezek. 7:22).

The physical action of "turning around" to face the opposite way is noted in Judg. 18:23; 1 Sam. 22:17; 1 Kgs. 8:14; 2 Kgs. 9:18ff. See also Eccl. 1:6. Yahweh is said to "turn around" the hearts of human beings to a right relationship with him (1 Kgs. 18:37; Ezra 6:22).

The physical movement of "returning" to one's home is indicated in 2 Sam. 14:24; 1 Chr. 16:43.

sābab refers to God "turning back" weapons of war in Jer. 21:4. In 1 Chr. 10:14, Yahweh is said to "turn over" (i.e., hand over) the kingdom of Saul to his rival, David. See also Jer. 6:12.

hāphak [הָפַךְ, 2015]

hāphak is a verb found in about one hundred places, with the principal meanings "turn," "overturn," "overthrow," as well as associated nuances.

(→ OVERTHROW)

Gen. 3:24 refers to the sword of the cherubim "turning in all directions." Similarly, ***hāphak*** denotes the action of "turning around" to face in a different direction (1 Sam. 25:12; 2 Chr. 9:12). "Turning one's back" to the enemy is noted in Josh. 7:8; Ps. 78:9. 2 Kgs. 21:13 refers metaphorically to God "turning (a dish) upside down." Diseased skin is described as "turning white" in Lev. 13:3ff.

The meaning "turn into," used transitively in the sense of "change into," or "transform," is predicated of Yahweh in a number of places. Yahweh "changes a rod into a snake" (Exod. 7:15); a river to blood (Exod. 7:17ff.; Pss. 78:44; 105:29); and a curse into a blessing (Deut. 23:5; Neh. 13:2). He is also said to transform sorrow into joy (Esth. 9:22 [implied]; Ps. 30:11; Jer. 31:13); and joy into sorrow, as an element of divine judgment (Lam. 5:15; Amos 8:10). See also 1 Sam. 10:6; Ps. 66:6; Amos 5:8.

Yahweh is said to "turn against" his people in judgment in Lam. 3:3; Isa. 63:10.

tôr [תּוֹר, 8447]

tôr is a rare noun meaning "turn" in the sense of each person in a group having an opportunity to engage in a particular activity. Esth. 2:12, 15 mentions each young woman from the harem of King Ahasuerus (i.e., Xerxes) whose "turn" it was to present herself to him for the evening for his personal pleasure.

lāphat [לָפַת, 3943]

lāphat is a rare verb meaning "turn over," as in one's sleep (Ruth 3:8); and "turn aside" in the sense of "venture away from one's route" (Job 6:18).

sûg [סוּג, 5472]

sûg is a verb occurring fourteen times and meaning "turn," "turn back."

The meaning "turn back" is used with transitive force (i.e., "to drive back") in a number of psalms, where the psalmist utters invocations to have his enemies "driven back" and thus "put to shame" for their defeat (cf. Pss. 35:4; 40:14; 70:2; 129:5; Isa. 42:17).

The other sense of "turn back" is that of "go astray," with reference to a person's heart, in their rebellion against God (cf. Ps. 78:57; Zeph. 1:16). See also Ps. 44:18; Isa. 50:5.

NT Words

strephō [στρέφω, *4762*]

strephō is a verb meaning "turn," "turn around" in a variety of contexts.

Matt. 5:39 refers to "turning" (i.e., offering) one's checks to one's tormentors.

The action of "turning toward (someone)" is noted in the context of speaking to others in Luke 7:44; 9:55; 10:23. See also Acts 7:42.

General references to the physical movement of "turning around" are found in Matt. 16:23; Luke 7:9; John 1:38; 20:14ff. This is done in order to attack in Matt. 7:6.

The meaning "turn into" is noted in the context of the miracle of water changing to blood in Rev. 11:6.

strephō is also translated "turn" with reference to a change of heart resulting in a renewed attitude of devotion to God. Such an attitude is an indispensable prerequisite for entry into the kingdom of heaven (cf. Matt. 18:3). In a negative context, Acts 7:39 records the action of "turning one's heart away from God."

apostrephō [ἀποστρέφω, *654*]

apostrephō is a verb with the primary meaning "turn away" in each of its eleven occurrences. Matt. 5:42 records the request not "to turn someone away" by refusing to lend him some money.

In other contexts, the translation "turn away" indicates the act of "rebelling against," "rejecting," or "refusing." In 2 Tim. 1:15, Paul laments that virtually everyone has "deserted" him. Heb. 12:25 warns of the danger of "rejecting" Christ. Titus 1:14 refers to those who "reject" the truth. See also 2 Tim. 4:4.

Where God is the subject of this verb, he is said "to turn" people from their wickedness (Acts 3:26; Rom. 11:26).

epistrephō [ἐπιστρέφω, *1994*]

epistrephō is a verb meaning "turn," "return" in a variety of contexts throughout its usage (approximately forty times).

The physical movement of "turning around" is noted in Matt. 9:22; Mark 5:30; Luke 17:4; Acts 9:40; Rev. 1:12.

Acts 14:15; 1 Thess. 1:9 refer to "turning" from idolatry to worship the living God. Acts 26:18 speaks similarly of those who "turn" from darkness to light. More commonly, the phenomenon of conversion is denoted by the action of "turning" to God in repentance (cf. Acts 3:19; 9:35; 26:20; 2 Cor. 3:16). God himself is said to "turn" (i.e., bring) people to worship him (Luke 1:16ff.).

epistrephō also means "return" (i.e., come back) in general contexts such as Matt. 24:18; Luke 2:20. Matt. 10:13 specifically refers to peace "returning" to the home. Gal. 4:9 contains a warning against "returning" to a life of enslavement under the law. See also 2 Pet. 2:21ff. In contrast, 1 Pet. 2:25 refers to the joy of "returning" to Christ, the chief shepherd of our souls.

hypostrephō [ὑποστρέφω, *5290*]

hypostrephō is a verb found thirty-five times meaning "turn back," "return."

The general sense of "returning" to one's original point of departure is indicated in Mark 14:40; Luke 7:10; 8:37ff.; 24:9, 33; Acts 8:25; Heb. 7:1. The process of "returning home" is noted in Luke 1:56; 8:39; 11:24.

The meaning "turn back" is used in the sense of "reverting" to an original condition. It is found only in Acts 13:34, referring to Christ as one who will never again "return (i.e., revert) to decay" after having risen from the dead.

anakamptō [ἀνακάμπτω, *344*]

anakamptō is a rare verb found in four places meaning "return," or "come back." Three of these occurrences are in the context of a journey (cf. Matt. 2:12; Acts 18:21; Heb. 11:15). The remaining text speaks of peace "returning" to the disciples on their missionary journey (cf. Luke 10:6).

diastrephō [διαστρέφω, *1294*]

diastrephō is a verb found seven times, meaning "to pervert" in most of these contexts. However, in Acts 13:8, it means "turn (away) from," referring to the sorcerer Elymas' attempt to "turn away" the Roman proconsul form the Christian faith. (→ PERVERSE)

metastrephō [μεταστρέφω, *3344*]

metastrephō is a rare verb meaning "turn into," in the sense of "change into," in two contexts. Acts 2:20 speaks of the sun being turned into darkness before the coming of the Day of the Lord. Jas. 4:9 contains the invocation that laughter be turned into mourning.

TURTLEDOVE → DOVE

TYPE

NT WORDS

typos [τύπος, *5179*]

typos is a noun occurring sixteen times with the underlying literal meaning of a "print," in the sense of a mark on the body left by a wound. ***typos*** also exhibits an expanded metaphorical sense of "pattern," "figure," or "example." This term can also have the technical meaning "type."

The meaning "pattern" refers to that of the temple, duly prescribed by God, as noted in Acts 7:44; Heb. 8:5. It is evident that the temple in Jerusalem constitutes a "typological" anticipation of Christ's eternal dwelling place in heaven alongside his Father. Rom. 6:17 also refers to the apostolic "pattern" of teaching, embodied in the gospel.

The specific sense of "type" indicates a symbolic person, place, object, or event from the Old Testament that prefigures or anticipates the person and work of the Messiah, Jesus Christ, in the New Testament. Adam is declared explicitly to be a "type" of Christ in Rom. 5:14. While the term ***typos*** is rare in the New Testament with this specific meaning, the actual phenomenon of "typology" is everywhere present. The frequency of this phenomenon may be appreciated only when the full extent of the old covenant's anticipation of the person of the Messiah is understood.

typos is also translated "example" in 1 Cor. 10:6, 11, referring to Israel's past sins, for which the people of God received due punishment from God. These "examples" serve as a warning for believers living in the present. Paul also calls upon his readers to imitate the "example" of the apostolic lifestyle (cf. Phil. 3:17; 2 Thess. 3:9; 1 Tim. 4:12; 1 Pet. 5:3; Titus 2:7).

U

UNBELIEF, UNBELIEVER, UNBELIEVING

NT Words

apistia [ἀπιστία, *570*]

apistia is a noun with the consistent meaning "unbelief" in each of the twelve contexts in which it occurs. The sense underlying "unbelief" is that of a lack or absence of saving faith and trust in Christ and/or God (cf. Matt. 13:58; 17:20; Mark 6:6; 9:24; 16:14; Rom. 3:3; 4:20; 11:20ff.; 1 Tim. 1:13; Heb. 3:12, 19).

apeitheia [ἀπείθεια, *543*]

apeitheia is translated as both "unbelief" and "disobedience." The two meanings are clearly linked. Logically, the mindset of "unbelief" may be said to pave the way for the action of "disobedience." ***apeitheia*** is found in six places with this ambiguity (cf. Rom. 11:30ff.; Eph. 2:2; 5:6; Col. 3:6; Heb. 4:6, 11).

apistos [ἄπιστος, *571*]

apistos is an adjective meaning "faithless," or "unbelieving," with respect to a lack of saving trust in God or Christ. ***apistos*** is also used nominally to refer to "unbelievers." The term occurs around twenty-five times.

The adjectival sense of "unbelieving" is applied to Jesus' Jewish audience on several occasions (cf. Matt. 17:17; Mark 9:19; Luke 9:41). See also John 20:27; Titus 1:15.

General references to "unbelievers" include those in Luke 12:46; 1 Cor. 6:6; 7:12ff.; 10:27; 14:22ff.; 2 Cor. 4:4; 6:14ff.; 1 Tim. 5:8; Rev. 21:8.

apeitheō [ἀπειθέω, *544*]

As with ***apeitheia***, above, ***apeitheō*** is a verb that conveys the dual, related senses of "disobey" and "refuse, withhold belief" (i.e., not to believe). ***apeitheō*** is found in sixteen contexts.

In John 3:36 ***apeitheō*** has the sense of "reject" in the context of spurning Christ. The same translation is found in Rom. 2:8.

The ambiguity between "disobeying" and "refusing to believe" the gospel, or the word of God, is preserved in Rom. 11:30, 31; Heb. 3:18; 11:31; 1 Pet. 2:7, 8; 3:1.

Other references to unbelieving Jews are found in Acts 14:2; 19:9; Rom. 15:31.

See Also: → DISOBEDIENCE

UNCERTAIN

NT Words

adēlos [ἄδηλος, *82*]; ***adēlotēs*** [ἀδηλότης, *83*]

These two rare terms indicate "that which is uncertain." ***adēlos*** is an adjective referring to the "uncertain" or "indistinct" sound of a bugle (1 Cor. 14:8); and to graves that are "unmarked" (i.e., uncertain in their location) (Luke 11:44). ***adēlotēs*** is a noun used adjectivally in 1 Tim. 6:17 to refer to "uncertain" riches.

UNCHANGEABLE

NT Words

aparabatos [ἀπαράβατος, *531*]

aparabatos is a rare adjectival form found only in Heb. 7:24, referring to the "unchangeable" high priestly ministry of the risen Christ that will remain forever the same.

UNCIRCUMCISED → CIRCUMCISE

UNCLEAN, UNCLEANNESS

OT Words

tum'āh [טֻמְאָה, **2932**]

tum'āh is a noun that indicates both ritual and moral "uncleanness" associated primarily with the provisions of the Mosaic law covenant. The term occurs around forty times.

General references to ritual or ceremonial uncleanness include those in Lev. 7:20ff.; 22:3; Judg. 13:7, 14 (associated with the Nazirite vow). Elsewhere, such impurity is associated with bodily discharges, as in Lev. 5:3, and especially with female menstruation (cf. Lev. 15:3, 25; 18:19; Ezek. 36:17). Impurity also results from contact with a corpse (cf. Num. 19:13); from infectious skin disease (cf. Lev. 14:19; 15:31); from contact with crawling insects (Lev. 22:5); and is associated with corrupt temple worship (2 Chr. 29:16).

Moral impurity or uncleanness from sin in general is indicated in Lev. 16:16ff. It is linked with the nations in general (Ezra 6:21; 9:11); the citizens of Jerusalem (Lam. 1:9; Ezek. 24:11ff.; 36:25ff.); Judah (Ezek. 22:15); and Israel (Ezek. 39:24). Such impurity is also a result of adultery (cf. Num. 5:19; 2 Sam. 11:4). Zech. 13:2

refers to the "spirit of impurity" from which Israel will be cleansed.

'erwāh [עֶרְוָה, 6172]

'erwāh is a noun denoting "nakedness" in most of its approximately fifty occurrences. However, in two places the term means "uncleanness" in the sense of that which is indecent. In Deut. 23:14 the reference is a general one, pointing to an undefined ritual impurity in the Israelite camp; and in Deut. 24:1 ***'erwāh*** refers to an observed "indecency" or "uncleanness" within a man's wife that led to him divorcing her.

niddāh [נִדָּה, 5079]

niddāh is a noun occurring around forty times that primarily indicates a woman's ritual uncleanness as a result of her regular cycle of menstruation. It may be translated in these contexts either as "impurity" (i.e., "uncleanness") or "menstruation." In both cases, it is the menstrual flow of blood that triggers such ceremonial uncleanness (cf. Lev. 12:2ff.; 15:19ff.; 18:19; Lam. 1:17; Ezek. 18:6; 22:10; 36:17).

niddāh also refers to water set aside for the removal of ritual impurity in Num. 19:9, 13, 20ff.; 31:23. Ritual uncleanness in general is indicated in 2 Chr. 29:5; Ezek. 7:20; Zech. 13:1.

niddāh also refers to the ritual and moral "pollution" of the land of Canaan in Ezra 9:11.

NT Words

akathartos [ἀκάθαρτος, *169*]

akathartos is an adjective found in thirty contexts with the consistent meaning "unclean" throughout, in both a ceremonial and a moral sense. The moral connotation is prominent, referring to "unclean" (i.e., demonic) spirits (cf. Matt. 10:1; 12:43; Mark 1:23ff.; 5:2ff.; Luke 4:33ff.; 9:42; Acts 5:16; Rev. 16:13; 18:2). Eph. 5:5 refers to moral impurity.

Ritual uncleanness is also indicated in Acts 10:14, 28; 11:8; 2 Cor. 6:17. In 1 Cor. 7:14, the designation "unclean" is applied to the children of unbelievers.

koinos [κοινός, *2839*]

koinos is an adjective found ten times meaning "unclean," "defiled," usually in a ceremonial sense.

The designation "unclean" refers to unwashed hands (Mark 7:2); to food (Acts 10:14; 11:8); and to men (Acts 10:28). See also Rom. 14:4.

A notable use of ***koinos*** is found in Heb. 10:29, which denounces all those who would treat the blood of Christ as an "unclean" (or profane) thing — referring to all who reject Christ.

akatharsia [ἀκαθαρσία, *167*]

akatharsia is a noun found in ten contexts meaning "uncleanness," "impurity," primarily in a moral sense.

Moral uncleanness is predicated of the Pharisees, who are condemned by Christ during his public ministry (cf. Matt. 23:27). Morally depraved men and women are so described in Rom. 1:24; 6:19; 2 Cor. 12:21.

The general sense of "uncleanness" or "impurity" as a characteristic (or "fruit") of the unbeliever is indicated in Gal. 5:19; Eph. 4:19; 5:3; Col. 3:5. See also 1 Thess. 2:3; 4:7.

See Also: → DEFILE

UNCLOTHED → NAKED

UNCOVER

OT Words

gālāh [גָּלָה, 1540]

gālāh is a verb occurring around two hundred times with the primary senses of "uncover," and "remove," as well as several associated nuances.
(→ APPEAR → CAPTIVE → REVEAL)

'ārāh [עָרָה, 6168]

'ārāh is a verb found in sixteen places with the primary meaning "uncover," indicating the sense of "reveal," "expose," "lay bare" in several different contexts for most of the usage.

In the context of exposing one's body or revealing one's nakedness, the meaning "uncover" is evident in various places. The curious expression "uncover a woman's flow" is found in Lev. 20:18ff., referring metaphorically to having sexual intercourse during the menstrual period. Such an act was forbidden under the law. Lam. 4:21 speaks of "laying oneself bare," or "stripping naked," as a consequence of drunkenness.

In Ps. 137:7, the meaning "lay bare" has the extended sense of "tear down" with reference to laying a building bare to its foundations. The expression "uncover the shield" is found in Isa. 22:6 indicating preparation for battle. Zeph. 2:14 refers to "exposing" cedar beams in connection with the destruction of buildings.

Isa. 3:17 speaks of Yahweh "laying bare" "the secret parts" of the daughters of Zion, or exposing or uncovering their nakedness. See also Hab. 3:13.

ḥāsaph [**חָשַׂף, 2834**]

ḥāsaph is a verb found in eleven contexts meaning "uncover," "lay bare," "strip off" in several different contexts. Its usage is predominantly figurative.

"Uncovering" or "revealing" men's buttocks is noted in Isa. 20:4 as a sign of shame, associated with nakedness in the context of divine judgment.

Where Yahweh is depicted as the one who "uncovers," or "strips bare," the contexts are uniformly metaphorical, denoting his actions in judgment and redemption. Ps. 29:9, for example, depicts the divine voice "stripping bare" the forests. Isa. 47:2 contains the divine command given to the kingdom of Babylon to "bare her legs," depicting that nation as a woman who will be humiliated through exposing her body, the consequence of Yahweh's judgment against her. Yahweh is described as "stripping Esau bare" in Jer. 49:10, indicating the plundering of all his resources. In Jer. 13:26, ***ḥāsaph*** is translated "lift up" with reference to God pulling up the "skirts" of Jerusalem so as to reveal her nakedness. Again, the context here is one of divine judgment, leading to his people's public humiliation. Elsewhere, Isa. 52:10 depicts Yahweh "laying bare" his arm in preparation for enacting his redemptive purposes for the nations. See also Ezek. 4:7. Joel 1:7 alludes to an invading army "stripping" bark off a tree like a plague of locusts.

NT Words

apostegazō [ἀποστεγάζω, *648*]

apostegazō is a rare verb found only in Mark 2:4 with reference to "uncovering" or "removing" a roof.

akatakalyptos [ἀκατακάλυπτος, *177*]

akatakalyptos is an adjective found only in 1 Cor. 11:5, 13, describing a woman's head as "uncovered" or "unveiled."

UNDEFILED

OT Words

tāmîm [**תָּמִים, 8549**]; ***tām*** [**תָּם, 8535**]

The meaning of the adjectival terms ***tām*** and ***tāmîm*** is bound up primarily with the state of moral and ceremonial purity. Hence they may be translated "spotless," "pure," "without blemish," "blameless," or "undefiled." (→ BLEMISH → PERFECT)

NT Words

amiantos [ἀμίαντος, *283*]

amiantos is an adjective found four times meaning "undefiled" in the sense of being "free from any impurity or flaw."

The designation "undefiled" is applied to the high priestly ministry of Christ in Heb. 7:26. Heb 13:4 contains the injunction to keep the marriage bed undefiled. Pure religion is described as undefiled (Jas. 1:27); as is the eternal inheritance of the unbeliever (1 Pet. 1:4).

UNDERSTAND

OT Words

shāma' [**שָׁמַע, 8085**]

shāma' is a common verb occurring around 1,150 times with the primary meaning "hear," "listen to," "obey" in the large majority of these contexts. There are a number of related nuances evident in the usage of this term, one of which is "to understand."

The facility to understand human language is indicated in Gen. 11:7 with reference to Yahweh confusing the language of the early world community at Babel. A similar prospective punishment is handed down against Israel in Deut. 28:49. Other contexts where languages different from one's own are understood include 2 Kgs. 18:26; Isa. 36:11; Gen. 42:23. See also Ezek. 3:6; Jer. 5:15.

shāma' refers to the God-given ability to understand (i.e., interpret) dreams in Gen. 41:15.

sākal [**שָׂכַל, 7919**]

sākal is a verb found in approximately sixty places meaning "to understand," "be wise," "prosper," or "succeed," as well as several associated senses. (→ SUCCEED)

The meaning "to have understanding, or insight" refers to God's word (Ps. 119:99; Jer. 3:15; Dan. 9:13), and to God's character (Isa. 41:20; Jer. 9:24).

sākal is also used in several places meaning "understand" in the sense of "to discern with wisdom." Pss. 14:2; 53:2 speak of "understanding" the ways of God with a view to living wisely before him. Conversely, Isa. 44:18 denounces idol worshipers for their inability to "discern" spiritual truth.

The meaning "give understanding" in the sense of "make clear" is indicated in relation to God communicating the detailed plans of the temple to King David (cf. 1 Chr. 28:19).

In Dan. 9:25, the angel Gabriel instructs Daniel to "understand" the meaning of the vision he has received, indicating the process of "rational comprehension."

bîn **[בִּין, 995]**

bîn is a verb occurring around 170 times with the dominant sense of "understand," focusing primarily on one's capacity "to discern or perceive with the mind." It also has the nominal sense of "understanding." (→ UNDERSTANDING)

The primary sense of "understand," indicating one's ability to discern, comprehend, or reason is illustrated in a number of places. Ps. 73:17 refers to discerning the destiny of the wicked, and Deut. 32:29; Jer. 23:20; Dan. 12:10 to discerning one's own destiny.

Such discernment or comprehension is not merely rational or intellectual, but is rather linked to godly living. Failure to "understand" in this sense leads to an ungodly lifestyle. "Comprehending" the law of God is noted in Neh. 8:7ff.; Ps. 119:27, 95. Discerning between good and evil is advocated in 1 Kgs. 3:9; Ps. 82:5. See also Prov. 2:9. Such "understanding" is also applied to the fear of the Lord (Prov. 2:5); the ways of the Lord (Hos. 14:9); the attributes of God (Ps. 107:43; Isa. 43:10); and one's path in life (Prov. 20:24). Failure to "understand" God and his demands for right living is a culpable action tantamount to rebellion (cf. Isa. 1:3; 6:9; 56:11); as is the failure to "understand" justice (Prov. 28:5; 29:7).

With God, the ability to exercise discernment or understanding is absolute with respect to people and creation, as illustrated in 1 Chr. 28:9; Job 28:23; Ps. 139:2.

bîn also means "understand" in the sense of "realize," or "perceive." Here the element of rational perception is prominent. General references to this process include those in 2 Sam. 12:19; Neh. 13:7; Job 13:1; Prov. 14:8; Isa. 40:21; Dan. 8:17; 9:2. "Perceiving" the call of God is noted in 1 Sam. 3:8. Realizing the error of one's ways is indicated in Job 6:24; Ps. 19:12.

yāda' **[יָדַע, 3045]**

yāda' is a common verb occurring nearly one thousand times, with the dominant sense of "know." In many of these contexts, "knowing" is equated with "understanding." (→ KNOW)

NT Words

syniēmi [συνίημι, *4920*]

syniēmi is a verb with the consistent meaning "understand" throughout its approximately twenty-five occurrences.

The dominant sense is that of rational and spiritual comprehension, or discernment, of the word of God and the gospel. ***syniēmi*** refers to people "being granted insight" into God's word, the truth of the gospel (cf. Matt. 13:23; Luke 24:45; Rom. 15:21). Conversely, people are declared to be incapable of discerning spiritual truth (e.g., Matt. 13:13ff.; Mark 8:21; Luke 2:50; 18:30; Acts 7:25). Such lack of understanding or comprehension is sometimes deemed to be the result of divine judgment (cf. Mark 4:12; Luke 8:10; Acts 28:26ff.); and is also viewed as one of the characteristics of the wicked (cf. Rom. 3:11; 2 Cor. 10:12).

Matt. 15:10; Mark 7:14 contain exhortations to understand the word of God; and Eph. 5:17 refers to understanding the will of God.

General references to "understanding" in the sense of "realize," or "perceive," are found in Matt. 16:12; 17:13.

noeō [νοέω, *3539*]

noeō is a verb occurring fourteen times meaning "to understand" in the sense of "perceive with the mind," "realize."

General references to the activity of rational perception or discernment include those in Matt. 15:17; 16:9ff.; Mark 7:18; 8:17. In particular, Rom. 1:20 indicates the potential capacity for every person to "realize" (i.e., understand) that God is both real and eternally sovereign in his knowledge and power.

noeō is also translated "understand" with the underlying sense of "comprehend the significance of," or "interpret." This use of the term is indicated in Matt. 24:15; Mark 13:14 in relation to the signs of the times. This sense is also evident in Heb. 11:3, where the "understanding" that the world has been created by the word of God is only possible through the exercise of faith.

Divine judgment is said to prevent people from being able to understand or discern spiritual truth (cf. John 12:40). In contrast, Eph. 3:4 affirms the God-given ability of the believer to understand the significance of the person of Christ. (→ KNOW)

dysnoētos [δυσνόητος, *1425*]

dysnoētos is a rare adjective found only in 2 Pet. 3:16, referring to some of the teaching of the apostle Paul, which Peter regards as "hard to understand."

UNDERSTANDING

OT Words

tebûnāh **[תְּבוּנָה, 8394]**

tebûnāh is a noun occurring around forty times with the primary sense of "understanding." There are several nuances attached to this meaning, though the primary denotation is that of "intelligence," "rational ability or skill."

The nuance of "understanding" that indicates "intelligence" or "rational competence" is illustrated in Exod. 31:3; 35:31; 36:1; 1 Kgs. 7:14 in relation to craftsmen working on the tabernacle and temple. In particular, King Solomon enjoyed this facility in abundance as a consequence of God's gift (cf. 1 Kgs. 4:29). Such a quality is also predicated of God in absolute terms (cf. Job 26:12; Ps. 136:5; Prov. 2:6; Jer. 10:12). In particular, Isa. 40:14 implicitly affirms the impossibility of teaching such "understanding" to God. General references to this kind of understanding are found in Job 12:12ff.; Prov. 2:2; 8:1; 19:8; Ezek. 28:4.

tebûnāh also means "understanding" in the sense of "moral discernment." This quality is noted in Ps. 49:3 in relation to godly wisdom; whereas a total lack of such discernment is evident in the mind of the idol worshiper (cf. Isa. 44:19). See also Deut. 32:28. Lack of moral understanding in relation to justice is evident in a cruel tyrant in Prov. 28:16.

bîn [בִּין, 995]

The dominant meaning of ***bîn*** is "understand" (→ UNDERSTAND), but it is also used nominally with the sense of "understanding." The primary emphasis is on the attribute of rational ability or discernment.

Denoting "intelligence" or "rational competence," ***bîn*** indicates "understanding" in relation to Israelite leaders (Deut. 1:13; Ezra 8:16); to the comprehension of the language of Scripture (Neh. 8:2); and to the skill in interpreting dreams and visions as a gift from God (cf. Dan. 1:17). See also Dan. 1:4. General references to such ability include those in Ps. 32:9; Prov. 1:5; Eccl. 9:11; Isa. 29:16; Dan. 8:23.

bîn also denotes "understanding" that is linked to spiritual wisdom in addition to the element of discernment (cf. Prov. 14:33). This understanding is attributed to the Israelite people by other nations (Deut. 4:6). Solomon requests such understanding from God, and it is granted to him (1 Kgs. 3:11ff.). The absence of any spiritual discernment in the rebellious people of God is noted in Jer. 4:22. The psalmist makes a plea to God for such an understanding in Ps. 119:34, 73.

bînāh [בִּינָה, 998]

bînāh is a synonym for ***bîn*** in its nominal usage (see above) and occurs in around forty contexts.

bînāh denotes "understanding" that is linked with wisdom. This is predicated of Israel (Deut. 4:6); of Daniel and his fellow countrymen in exile (Dan. 1:20; 9:22; 10:1) as a gift from God; and of the coming Messiah (Isa. 11:2). Such understanding is associated with a godly lifestyle in Prov. 4:1ff.; 8:14; 9:10. See also Job 28:12.

Understanding that is linked to keen insight or discernment is attributed to the Israelite leaders (1 Chr. 12:32) and to Solomon (1 Chr. 22:12). Prov. 3:5 warns against relying on one's own "insight." See also Job 20:3; Isa. 29:14. This term also denotes "understanding" that is linked to the skill or ability of temple craftsmen (2 Chr. 2:13).

Finally, "understanding" a foreign language is denied to Israel as part of God's judgment against her.

sekel [שֶׂכֶל, 7922]

sekel is a noun derived from ***sākal*** (→ UNDERSTAND). It is found in sixteen contexts with the primary sense of "understanding" throughout. ***sekel***, however, is also translated "wisdom" or "prudence." The underlying denotation of the term is an understanding that is linked with godly living and wisdom, as well as keen insight (cf. 1 Sam. 25:3; 1 Chr. 22:12; 2 Chr. 2:12; Ezra 8:18; Job 17:4; Ps. 111:10; Prov. 12:8).

In addition, ***sekel*** refers in Neh. 8:8 to the "sense," or the "understanding," of the book of the law. In this context it is most likely that the Levites, who were expounding the law to the postexilic community of God's people, were teaching the people the "meaning" of the Scriptures for their lives.

lēbāb [לֵבָב, 3824]; *lēb* [לֵב, 3820]

These two terms are synonymous, both indicating the basic meaning "heart." ***lēbāb*** occurs around five hundred times; ***lēb*** approximately half that number. The underlying sense of "heart" here refers to the seat of the human intellect, will, and emotions. Various translations of these two terms include "inner man," "mind," "will," "soul," "understanding."

lēbāb means "understanding" in Job 12:3 with reference to one's mind. In Job 34:10, 34, the meaning "understanding" suggests the quality of "intelligence" or "insight."

lēb means "understanding," but also with the sense of "moral discernment," or lack thereof (cf. Prov. 6:32; 9:4, 16; 10:13; 24:30; Jer. 5:21).

manda' [מַנְדַּע, 4486 (Aramaic)]

manda' is a rare Aramaic noun meaning "understanding" in the sense of one's "rational faculty" or "reason" (Dan. 4:34, 36).

sokletānû [**שָׂכְלְתָנוּ, 7924** (Aramaic)]

sokletānû is another rare Aramaic noun found only three times in Dan. 5:11ff., meaning "understanding" in the sense of "keen insight," "intelligence."

NT Words

asynetos [ἀσύνετος, *801*]

asynetos is an adjective found in five contexts meaning "foolish," "without understanding."

Matt. 15:16; Mark 7:18 describe people as "foolish," or "stupid." In Rom. 1:21, 31; 10:19, ***asynetos*** refers to people as "foolish" in the sense of "morally inept."

nous [νοῦς, *3563*]

nous is a noun found in around twenty-five places with the predominant meaning "mind." This sense also overlaps with that of "understanding." In Phil. 4:7; Rev. 13:18, ***nous*** is translated this way with reference to one's "rational ability," or "mind," being the faculty from which "understanding" emanates.

phrēn [φρήν, *5424*]

phrēn is a rare noun meaning "understanding" in the sense of one's faculty of reasoning and discernment, or "thinking" (cf. 1 Cor. 14:20).

synetos [συνετός, *4908*]

synetos is an adjectival form found in four places with the meaning "intelligent"in Matt. 11:25; Luke 10:21; Acts 13:7; 1 Cor. 1:19.

Additional Notes

The vocabulary for "understanding" (both verbal and nominal) is considerably varied in both Testaments. Yet the varied terms are connected by the fact that "understanding" involves "rational insight," or "intelligence," as well as "moral discernment," which is linked to an awareness of and commitment to the demands for godly living.

In the Old Testament it is the "understanding" of the laws and statutes of the covenant, expressing itself in wisdom and obedience directed towards God, that constitutes the theologically significant aspect of this terminology. In the New Testament, this understanding culminates in the right perception and realization of the unique person of Christ. Only an understanding that embraces Jesus Christ, and fully accepts his teaching regarding the need for faith and repentance in him as the way to peace with God, is regarded as legitimate and commendable in the eyes of the New Testament writers.

See Also: → KNOW → MIND

UNEQUALLY → YOKE

UNFAITHFUL → UNBELIEF

UNGODLINESS, UNGODLY

NT Words

asebēs [ἀσεβής, *765*]

asebēs is an adjectival form found nine times meaning "ungodly," referring to all who are devoid of any faith commitment or devotion to God. They are consistently singled out for judgment (cf. Rom. 4:5; 5:6; 1 Tim. 1:9; 1 Pet. 4:18; 2 Pet. 2:5; 3:7; Jude 14, 15).

asebeō [ἀσεβέω, *764*]

asebeō is a rare verb found in only two places, meaning "to live ungodly lives," "be ungodly" (cf. 2 Pet. 2:6; Jude 15).

asebeia [ἀσέβεια, *763*]

asebeia is a noun meaning "ungodliness," denoting a lifestyle devoid of any reverence towards God (cf. Rom. 1:18; 11:26; 2 Tim. 2:16; Titus 2:12; Jude 15, 18).

See Also: → WICKED

UNHOLY → DEFILE

UNITE, UNITY

OT Words

yāḥad [**יָחַד, 3161**]

yāḥad is a verb found on three occasions meaning "unite," or "join."

There is an invocation in Gen. 49:6 against "joining" the council of the violent brothers Simeon and Levi, sons of Jacob. In Ps. 86:11 the psalmist pleads that God will give him an "undivided" or "united" heart for worship. Isa. 14:20 affirms that the king of Babylon "will not join" in burial along with the rulers of other nations. The idea here is that the Babylonian ruler will simply have his body thrown on the ground.

yaḥad [**יַחַד, 3162**]

yaḥad is a noun derived from ***yāḥad*** (see above), occurring about 150 times. It primarily refers to "together" in an adverbial sense. In 1 Chr. 12:17, however, ***yaḥad*** expresses King David's invitation to have fellow Israelites "unite" with him, provided they remain loyal.

NT Words

henotēs [ἑνότης, *1775*]

henotēs is a rare noun signifying the "unity" of the Spirit (Eph. 4:3), and the "unity" of the faith (Eph. 4:13). In both contexts, such a unity, embracing the peace and knowledge of God, is affirmed as a goal to which all believers should aspire within the community of God's people.

homophrōn [ὁμόφρων, *3675*]

homophrōn is a rare adjectival form meaning "harmonious," "being of one mind." It is found in 1 Pet. 3:8 as an exhortation: "Live in unity (i.e., be at peace) with one another."

UNJUST → INIQUITY → UNRIGHTEOUS

UNLAWFUL

NT Words

athemitos [ἀθέμιτος, *111*]

athemitos is an adjective denoting that which is "unlawful," or "lawless," in the context of the revealed standards of God's statutes. It occurs only twice. In Acts 10:28, Peter protests to the Lord that it would be "unlawful" for him to associate with a Gentile in any way. 1 Pet. 4:3 refers to the "lawless" idolatry of the Gentiles.

See Also: → INIQUITY → UNRIGHTEOUS → WICKED

UNLEAVENED → YEAST

UNMARRIED

NT Words

agamos [ἄγαμος, *22*]

agamos is an adjective found in four contexts, used nominally to refer to those who are unmarried, both men and women (cf. 1 Chr. 7:8, 11, 32, 34).

UNMERCIFUL

NT Words

aneleēmōn [ἀνελεήμων, *415*]

aneleēmōn is an adjective found only in Rom. 1:31, describing the wicked as "merciless" or "ruthless."

UNPROFITABLE → WORTHLESS

UNQUENCHABLE

NT Words

asbestos [ἄσβεστος, *762*]

asbestos is an adjective occurring four times, referring in each case to the "unquenchable" fire of eternal punishment for the wicked.

UNREASONABLE

NT Words

alogos [ἄλογος, *249*]

alogos is an adjectival form denoting that which is "unreasonable," or "irrational." It occurs only three times. Acts 25:27 speaks of taking an "unreasonable" course of action. 2 Pet. 2:12; Jude 10 liken false teachers to "irrational" beasts.

UNRIGHTEOUS, UNRIGHTEOUSNESS

NT Words

adikos [ἄδικος, *94*]

adikos is an adjective occurring twelve times meaning "unrighteous," "unjust."

General references to the "unjust," or those who have violated the divinely ordained principles of honesty and integrity, include those in Matt. 5:45; Luke 16:10ff.; 18:11; Acts 24:15; 1 Cor. 6:1. Other references to the "wicked," the "unrighteous," who will be denied entry into the kingdom of God and condemned, are found in 1 Cor. 6:9; 2 Pet. 2:9. 1 Pet. 3:18 declares, remarkably, that Christ died for the "unrighteous." Rom. 3:5 denounces as illegitimate any attempt to charge God with "injustice." See also Heb. 6:10.

See Also: → INIQUITY → UNGODLINESS → WICKED

UNSPEAKABLE

NT Words

anekdiēgētos [ἀνεκδιήγητος, *411*]

anekdiēgētos is an adjective found only in 2 Cor. 9:15, describing the indescribable quality of God's gift of salvation.

arrētos [ἄρρητος, *731*]

arrētos is another rare adjectival form, found only in 2 Cor. 12:4, describing Paul's heavenly vision as a phenomenon that is "unspeakable," "incapable of verbal description."

aneklalētos [ἀνεκλάλητος, *412*]

aneklalētos is an adjective referring to the believer's "unspeakable" (i.e., indescribable) joy in knowing Christ (1 Pet. 1:8).

UNSTABLE

NT Words

akatastatos [ἀκατάστατος, *182*]

akatastatos is an adjective found only in Jas. 1:8 denoting the "unstable" nature of the double-minded person, who doubts the goodness of God.

astēriktos [ἀστήρικτος, *793*]

astēriktos is an adjectival form found in 2 Pet. 2:14, 16. It is used nominally to refer to "unstable persons" who are immature and indecisive in their faith, easily led astray.

UNVEIL

NT Words

anakalyptō [ἀνακαλύπτω, *343*]

anakalyptō is a verb meaning "unveil," or "draw back," "uncover" with the use of a veil. It is used figuratively in both contexts in which it occurs.

2 Cor. 3:14 refers in a negative context to the mind and heart of the unbeliever that remains "veiled" (lit., "not unveiled") to the truth of the gospel until the Spirit of God removes the "veil" of unbelief. 2 Cor. 3:18 mentions the blessed state of the believer who is able to contemplate the glory of God with an "unveiled face." This expression refers metaphorically to a saving understanding of gospel truth, after release from spiritual blindness.

UNWISE → FOOL

UNWORTHY, UNWORTHILY

NT Words

anaxiōs [ἀναξίως, *371*]

anaxiōs is an adverb found on two occasions meaning "unworthily" (1 Cor. 11:27, 29). Here it refers to the sin of profaning the body and blood of Christ by eating the bread and drinking the cup of the Lord's Supper "in an unworthy manner," or participating in the sacrament of the Lord's Supper with an impure motive, or unconfessed sin.

anaxios [ἀνάξιος, *370*]

anaxios is a rare adjectival form meaning "unworthy" in the sense of "incompetent" in 1 Cor. 6:2.

UPRIGHT, UPRIGHTNESS

OT Words

nāṣab [**נָצַב, 5324**]

nāṣab is a verb occurring in seventy-five contexts with the primary meanings "stand," "set up," "erect." It is translated "stand upright" in Gen. 37:7 with reference to the sheaves of grain in Joseph's dream.

qômemîyût [**קוֹמְמִיּוּת, 6968**]

qômemîyût is a rare noun used adverbially only in Lev. 26:13, referring to the people of Israel walking erect, or upright.

yishrāh [**יִשְׁרָה, 3483**]

yishrāh is a rare noun found only in 1 Kgs. 3:6, referring to David's "uprightness" of heart before God, or his moral integrity.

nekōḥah [**נְכֹחָה, 5229**]

nekōḥah is an adjective that is also used nominally with the moral sense of "right," "uprightness." It occurs four times.

A general reference to the "land of uprightness" is found in Isa. 26:10. The virtue of "uprightness" is noted in Isa. 59:14.

nekōḥah is also used adjectivally in Isa. 30:10; Amos 3:10, denoting that which is "right," or "morally upright."

Additional Notes

The large bulk of the vocabulary indicating the virtue of "uprightness" is equated with the sense of "righteousness." (→ RIGHTEOUS)

See Also: → BLEMISH → INTEGRITY

UPROAR

NT Words

thorybos [θόρυβος, *2351*]

thorybos is a noun found seven times with the consistent meaning "uproar," in the context of a "riotous crowd" or a threatened riot (cf. Matt. 26:5; 27:24; Mark

14:2; Acts 20:1; 21:34; 24:18). In addition, Mark 5:38 refers to an "uproar" not in the sense of a riot, but an "outburst of wailing" among the crowd at the death of Jairus' daughter.

thorybeō [θορυβέω, *2350*]

thorybeō is a verb occurring only four times. In two of these contexts, it means "making a loud noise" in mourning the dead (cf. Matt. 9:23; Mark 5:39). Then, in Acts 17:5, ***thorybeō*** indicates the act of "starting a riot." In Acts 20:10 it means "being alarmed," expressed as a negative command.

stasis [στάσις, *4714*]

stasis is a noun expressing the general sense of "uproar" in most of its usage (nine times), with several differing nuances.

"Insurrection" or "revolt," in a political sense, usually involves violence of some kind. The term is used in connection with Barabbas, who was spared execution and whose place on the cross was taken by Jesus Christ (cf. Mark 15:7; Luke 23:19, 25).

stasis also indicates a "riot," or "civil disturbance" (cf. Acts 19:40; 23:7ff.). The apostle Paul is falsely accused of stirring up "riots" in Acts 24:5.

Finally, ***stasis*** denotes a "quarrel" or "argument" in Acts 15:2. The setting of this dispute involves the legalistic "Judaizing party" (probably a Pharisaic group) in conflict with the followers of the apostle Paul.

syncheō [συγχέω, *4797*]

syncheō is a verb occurring five times, meaning "to be in confusion," "stir up confusion" with respect to agitating a crowd (cf. Acts 19:32; 21:27, 31).
(→ CONFOUND)

rhoizēdon [ῥοιζηδόν, *4500*]

rhoizēdon is a rare noun found only in 2 Pet. 3:10, referring to the "loud noise" associated with cosmic dissolution at the end of time.

See Also: → ROAR

UPROOT

OT Words

nāsaḥ [נָסַח, 5255]

nāsaḥ is a verb found four times with the senses of "uproot," "tear down." Deut. 28:63; Ps. 52:5; Prov. 2:22 refer to Yahweh "uprooting" his people from the land of Canaan. Prov. 15:25 mentions "tearing down" the house of the proud.

nātash [נָתַשׁ, 5428]

nātash is a verb expressing the primary meaning "uproot" in the context of divine judgment, whereby Yahweh removes his people from the land of Israel.

Yahweh "uproots" his people from the land in Deut. 29:28, as an element of the covenant curse. Ezek. 19:12 uses the term figuratively. More common is the threat of such divine action (cf. 1 Kgs. 14:15; 2 Chr. 7:20; Jer. 12:14ff.; 31:28; 45:1). A number of texts contain the divine promise to never again uproot the people from the land, as part of Yahweh's program of renewal for Israel (cf. Jer. 24:6; 31:40; 42:10; Amos 9:15).

Yahweh promises to uproot Canaanite idol shrines from the land (cf. Mic. 5:14). Jer. 12:17; 18:7 indicate the uprooting of other nations by divine agency. In Jer. 1:10, the prophet is commissioned by God to "uproot" nations as part of the prophetic charter given to him.

shārash [שָׁרַשׁ, 8327]

shārash is a verb found in eight places with the dual contrasting meanings "take root" and "uproot," primarily in a figurative sense.

The sense of "take root" refers to the prosperity of the fool (Job 5:3), and to the prosperity of the wicked (Jer. 12:2). Ps. 80:9 refers metaphorically to Israel as a vine "taking root" in Israel. See also Isa. 27:6. Job 31:8, 12 refer literally to produce being "uprooted."

Yahweh threatens to "remove" (lit., uproot) his people from the land in Ps. 52:5. And he is also said to "uproot" rulers of the nations, destroying their kingdoms (cf. Isa. 40:24).

'āqar [עָקַר, 6131]

'āqar is a verb meaning "uproot." It is found in two places. Eccl. 3:2 refers generally to "uprooting" (i.e., harvesting) crops. Zeph. 2:4 refers to God's action in "uprooting" (i.e., destroying) the Philistine city of Ekron.

NT Words

ekrizoō [ἐκριζόω, *1610*]

ekrizoō is a verb found in four contexts, meaning "uproot."

There are two figurative contexts of divine judgment in which the metaphor of plants being uprooted by God signifies the destruction of the wicked (cf. Matt. 15:13; Jude 12). The remaining two texts refer in a metaphorical sense to "wheat" (i.e., the righteous) being safeguarded against "uprooting" for judgment (cf. Matt. 13:29). Luke 17:6 mentions a sycamore tree "being uprooted" as a sign of genuine faith. The usage here is evidently hyperbolic.

rhizoō [ῥιζόω, *4492*]

rhizoō indicates the phenomenon of "being rooted, or grounded" in the love of Christ (cf. Eph. 3:17), as well as in Christ himself (cf. Col. 2:7).

URGE

OT Words

pāṣar [**פָּצַר, 6484**]

pāṣar is a verb occurring seven times, meaning "urge," or "press," in most of these contexts. The underlying sense is that of directing a person towards a particular course of action with strong persuasion (cf. Gen. 19:3, 9; 33:11; Judg. 19:7; 2 Kgs. 2:17; 5:16).

'ālaṣ [**אָלַץ, 509**]

'ālaṣ is a rare synonym for ***pāṣar*** (see above) meaning "urge," or "press." It is found only in Judg. 16:16.

pāraṣ [**פָּרַץ, 6555**]

pāraṣ is a verb with the predominant underlying sense of "break." The term occurs in nearly fifty contexts. In 1 Sam. 28:23, ***pāraṣ*** is translated "to urge," in the sense of pushing someone to accept a particular course of action.

USE

OT Words

melā'kāh [**מְלָאכָה, 4399**]

melā'kāh is a noun found in approximately 170 places with the dominant sense of "work," or "business." However, in Lev. 7:24, ***melā'kāh*** is translated "use," describing the fat of dead animals, "which may be put to any other use" except as food.

hāyāh [**הָיָה, 1961**]

hāyāh is the standard Hebrew form of the verb "to be, become," along with associated senses. It occurs about seventy-five times. In Num. 10:2, ***hāyāh*** refers to ceremonial silver trumpets used for summoning the Israelites.

'abôdāh [**עֲבוֹדָה, 5656**]

'abôdāh is the common noun for "service," or "work," occurring about 140 times. In 1 Chr. 28:15 ***'abôdāh*** refers to the ritual "use" (or purpose) of the lampstand in the temple.

NT Words

chraomai [χράομαι, *5530*]

chraomai is a verb with the general meanings "use," "make use of," in half of the twelve contexts in which it occurs.

1 Cor. 7:31 speaks of "making use of" the things of the world. Paul decides "not to make use of" his right to receive payment for his ministry (1 Cor. 9:12, 15). In 2 Cor. 3:10, the apostle hopes that he may "not have to make use of" severe disciplinary measures against the Corinthian congregation. 1 Tim. 1:8 refers to "making proper use of" the law. Paul enjoins Timothy "to use (or take)" a little wine for his stomach ailments (cf. 1 Tim. 5:23).

ginomai [γίνομαι, *1096*]

ginomai is a common verb with the primary meanings "to be, become," as well as associated senses, throughout its over one thousand occurrences. In 1 Thess. 2:5, however, ***ginomai*** means "to use" in the context of Paul's denial that he "used" flattery in order to derive financial gain from his ministry.

USURY → INTEREST

UTENSIL

OT Words

kelî [**כְּלִי, 3627**]

kelî is a noun found in about three hundred places with a variety of meanings. In a number of places, ***kelî*** refers to the large number of "accessories" (lit., utensils) associated with the major items of furniture in the tabernacle (e.g., Exod. 25:39; 30:27ff.; 31:8ff.; 35:13ff.; 40:10; Lev. 8:11; Num. 4:10, 14).

See Also: → ARMS → VESSEL

UTTER → SAY → TELL

UTTERMOST → END

V

VAIN, VANITY

OT Words

sheqer [שֶׁקֶר, 8267]

sheqer is a noun found over one hundred times with the principal sense of "lie," "lying" (i.e., untruth, falsehood). (→ LIE) In one or two places, however, ***sheqer*** means "vain." The phrase "in vain" (i.e., for naught, for no purpose) is indicated in 1 Sam. 25:21. In Jer. 3:23, ***sheqer*** denotes the "deception" (i.e., vain delusion) of idol worship.

shāw' [שָׁוְא, 7723]

shāw' is a noun occurring about fifty times with the predominant sense of "vanity," "vain," indicating "emptiness," or "futility," for most of its usage. These meanings often overlap with the sense of "false."

The adverbial expression "in vain" is also evident in the usage of ***shāw'*** (cf. Ps. 127:1; Jer. 2:30; 6:29; 46:11), suggesting the idea of uselessness or wasted effort. In Exod. 20:7, the third commandment of the Decalogue prohibits taking the Lord's name "in vain." The instruction is aimed at preserving reverential regard for the person of God; and thus ***shāw'*** might also be translated "without due reverence."

The sense of "emptiness" or "futility" is indicated in Job 7:3; Ps. 89:47; Hos. 12:11. Human help is perceived as "useless" (Ps. 60:11); and illicit offerings to Yahweh in Isa. 11:3 are declared to be "worthless."

shāw' refers to the "deceitfulness" of human beings (Job 11:11; Ps. 26:4); to "lies" (Ps. 144:8ff.; Prov. 30:8); and to "destruction" (Isa. 30:28).

hebel [הֶבֶל, 1892]

hebel is a noun with a range of meanings such as "idol," "breath," or "mist." It occurs in around seventy places. The underlying sense of the term is that idols are utterly worthless and futile, and that "breath," or "mist," are phenomena that readily disperse and disappear. ***hebel*** is also used adjectivally.

"Idols," regarded as "vain," or "worthless," are indicated in Deut. 32:21; 1 Kgs. 16:13; 2 Kgs. 17:15; Ps. 31:6; Jer. 2:5; 8:19; Jonah 2:8. See also Jer. 10:3.

hebel also denotes "breath" or "mist" in several metaphorical contexts, referring to that which is momentary and insubstantial (cf. Job 7:16; Pss. 89:5; 78:33; Prov. 21:6; 31:30).

The adverbial expression "in vain," indicating fruitless or wasted effort, is found in Job 9:29. In particular, Isa. 49:4 records the momentary despair of the Suffering Servant of Yahweh, who laments that his labor is "in vain." In Job 35:16, the patriarch is accused of uttering "empty" or "futile" speech.

The theme of "vanity," "futility," or "meaningless activity in life" is one of the principal themes of the book of Ecclesiastes, and ***hebel*** is consistently translated this way throughout (cf. Eccl. 1:2, 14; 2:1, 11ff.; 3:19; 4:14ff.; 5:7ff.; 6:2ff.; 7:6, 15; 8:10ff.; 9:9; 11:8ff.; 12:8).

rîq [רִיק, 7385]

rîq is a noun found twelve times meaning "vanity" in the sense of "emptiness" and "futility"; though the use of the term is primarily adverbial and adjectival.

rîq describes the assistance offered by Egypt to Israel as "futile" (Isa. 30:7). The people of Judah are described as "empty" (i.e., devoid of purpose) in Jer. 51:34.

In Isa. 65:23, God promises that women will not bear children "in vain" — that is, the children will grow strong and healthy. In contrast, Lev. 26:16ff. records an element of the covenant curse, whereby the people of God will sow their crops "in vain" and will not harvest any produce. In Isa. 49:4, the labor of the Messianic Servant is said to be "in vain" (i.e., without purpose). See also Pss. 2:1; 73:13; Jer. 51:58; Hab. 2:13.

Elsewhere, Ps. 4:2 refers to "delusions," or attractions that are false. The context is one of idolatrous worship.

rêq [רֵיק, 7386]

rêq is an adjectival form meaning "empty," "vain," "worthless."

rêq refers literally to empty jars (Judg. 7:16; 2 Kgs. 4:3) and empty pits (Gen. 37:24). See also Isa. 29:4. Deut. 32:47 refers figuratively to "empty" (i.e., meaningless) words.

rêq also refers to "worthless" goals and activities (Prov. 12:11; 28:19); "worthless" (i.e., unproductive) heads of grain (Gen. 41:27); and ruffians or scoundrels (i.e., "worthless" men) (Judg. 9:4; 11:3; 2 Sam. 6:20; 2 Chr. 13:7).

hābal [הָבַל, 1891]

hābal is a verb found in five contexts meaning "to become vain" (i.e., false, worthless), in the context of worshiping idols (cf. 2 Kgs. 17:15; Jer. 2:5) and of meaningless talk (Job 27:12). See also Ps. 62:10. Jer. 23:16 speaks of false prophets "making the people of Judah vain" in the sense of "filling them with false hopes."

tōhû [תֹּהוּ, 8414]

tōhû is a noun occurring twenty times with the primary senses of "vanity," or "vain things." Other meanings include "formlessness," "chaos," or "waste."
(→ FORM → WASTE)

tōhû denotes "useless idols" in 1 Sam. 12:21, and describes as "worthless" those who construct idols. The term also refers to the "confusion" brought to the mind of worshipers through the worship of molten images (Isa. 41:29).

tōhû is also used adjectivally to describe nations as "worthless" in the sight of God (Isa. 40:17, 23). Isa. 59:4 speaks of "futile" arguments in the law courts of Israel. In Isa. 49:4, the Messianic Servant laments (be it momentarily) that his strength is spent "for nothing."

NT Words

matēn [μάτην, *3155*]

matēn is an adverb that depicts the hypocritical worship of the Pharisees as being "in vain" (i.e., of no value) (cf. Matt. 15:9; Mark 7:7).

kenos [κενός, *2756*]

kenos is an adjective meaning "vain," "empty." It also has the adverbial sense "in vain." (→ EMPTY)

The designation "vain" or "futile" is applied to speech (Eph. 5:6; Col. 2:8), and to human beings (Jas. 2:20), indicating their foolishness.

kenos is also used adverbially. The nations plotting "in vain" against God are noted in Acts 4:25 (citing Ps. 2:2). Paul affirms in 1 Cor. 15:10 that the grace of God is never offered "in vain," for no purpose (cf. also 1 Cor. 15:10, 58). Gal. 2:2; Phil. 2:16 warn of the danger of running the race of the Christian life "in vain" (i.e., without receiving the prize of eternal life). See also 1 Thess. 2:1; 3:5.

mataioō [ματαιόω, *3154*]

mataioō is a rare verb found only in Rom. 1:21 which declares that unbelievers "have become vain (i.e., futile)" in their thinking.

mataios [μάταιος, *3152*]

mataios is the adjective derived from ***mataioō*** (see above), denoting that which is "vain" or "useless." ***mataios*** refers to idols (Acts 14:15); to human thoughts (1 Cor. 3:20); and to religion without love (Jas. 1:26). See also 1 Cor. 15:17; Titus 3:9; 1 Pet. 1:18.

mataiologia [ματαιολογία, *3150*]

mataiologia is a rare noun occurring only in 1 Tim. 1:6 with reference to "vain" or "worthless" talk.

mataiologos [ματαιολόγος, *3151*]

mataiologos is a noun found only in Titus 1:10 denoting a "vain talker," or one who utters senseless words.

kenōs [κενῶς, *2761*]

kenōs is an adverb meaning "in vain," found only in Jas. 4:5 as a mistaken assessment of the Scriptures being "without reason."

kenoō [κενόω, *2758*]

kenoō is a verb occurring in five places and meaning primarily "to make vain," "render useless, null and void."

Rom. 4:14 declares that faith "is rendered useless" if people are justified by the law. The power of the cross of Christ is also "rendered useless" without the accompanying proclamation of the gospel. See also 1 Cor. 9:15; 2 Cor. 9:3.

A special use of ***kenoō*** is indicated in Phil. 2:7, which speaks of Christ "having emptied himself" (i.e., made himself nothing), so that he might submit to the humiliation of assuming a human form, simultaneously laying aside his heavenly position for a time in order to do so.

eikē [εἰκῆ, *1500*]

eikē is an adverb meaning "in vain," in the sense of "without reason," or "for nothing." It occurs in seven places.

Rom. 13:4 refers to national governments who "do not use the sword in vain" exercising just punishment. 1 Cor. 15:2 declares that people have believed "in vain" if they do not hold firmly to the message of the gospel. See also Gal. 3:4; 4:11; Col. 2:18.

dōrean [δωρεάν, *1432*]

dōrean is an adverb with the dominant sense of "freely" in most of the nine contexts in which it is found. (→ FREE) In Gal. 2:21, the death of Christ is said to be "in vain" (i.e., useless, futile) if justification is to be gained through the law.

VALLEY

OT Words

'ēmeq [עֵמֶק, **6010**]

'ēmeq is a noun occurring around seventy times with the primary meaning "valley" in a geographic and geological sense.

In a number of places, "valleys" are recorded as the location of battles (cf. Josh. 7:24ff.; 13:19ff.; Judg. 1:19; 7:1ff.; 2 Sam. 5:18ff.; 2 Chr. 20:6; Isa. 22:7; Jer. 31:40). In Hos. 1:5, the Valley of Jezreel is noted as a place where Yahweh brings judgment against his people. In Joel 3:2ff.; Mic. 1:4, valleys are designated as locations for Yahweh's judgment against the nations. In contrast, Isa. 65:10 depicts the Valley of Achor as the object of divine transformation — from battlefield to place of idyllic rest.

General references to valleys in non-military contexts include those in Num. 14:25; Job 39:10; 1 Sam. 6:13; Ps. 65:13; Song 2:1; Isa. 17:5.

gay' [גַּיְא, **1516**]

gay' is a noun denoting a "valley" as well as a "gorge," or "ravine." The term is found in sixty contexts.

Deut. 4:46; 1 Sam. 13:18; Neh. 2:13ff. refer generally to "valleys." ***gay'*** refers to valleys as locations for the outpouring of divine judgment against the people of Israel (Ezek. 6:3; 36:6); and against the nations of Egypt (Ezek. 32:5), Edom (Ezek. 35:8), and Magog (Ezek. 39:11ff.). The Valley of Salt is indicated as a location for battle in 2 Chr. 25:11.

gay' also denotes a "gorge," or "ravine" — a valley with steep sides enclosing it (cf. Num. 21:20; Josh. 8:14; 15:8; 18:16; 1 Sam. 17:3). Included in this usage are references to the Valley of Hinnom outside Jerusalem, a place where idolatrous child sacrifice took place during the period of the divided monarchy in Israel (cf. 2 Kgs. 23:10; 2 Chr. 28:3; 33:6; Jer. 7:31ff.; 19:2; 32:35).

In metaphorical contexts ***gay'*** refers, for example, to "the valley of the shadow of death" in Ps. 23:4. In an eschatological context, Zech. 14:4 refers to the creation of a "valley" at the end of time — the result of splitting the Mount of Olives in two. Isa. 40:4 affirms that "every valley will be lifted up" as part of the removal of all obstacles to the Messianic King coming to his people in Jerusalem. See also Isa. 22:1ff.

naḥal [נַחַל, **5158**]

naḥal is a noun found in approximately 140 places. It means "river," or "stream," in the majority of these contexts, as well as "valley." ***naḥal*** often denotes a "river valley." (→ RIVER)

naḥal denotes "valleys" in general in Gen. 26:17; Num. 21:12; Deut. 1:24; Judg. 16:4; Job 21:33; Prov. 30:17; Song 6:11; Isa. 57:5.

naḥal denotes "river valleys" in Num. 24:6; Deut. 21:4; 2 Kgs. 3:16ff.; Ps. 104:10; Joel 3:18.

biq'āh [בִּקְעָה, **1237**]

biq'āh is a term found in twenty contexts denoting a "plain," or "valley." (→ PLAIN) There is a degree of overlap in these meanings as indicated in Josh. 11:8; 2 Chr. 35:22. But the sense of "valley" is evident in Deut. 8:7; 11:11; Josh. 11:17; Ps. 104:8; Isa. 41:8; Ezek. 37:1ff.

kikkār [כִּכָּר, **3603**]

kikkār is a noun with the primary meaning "talent," denoting a weight of currency, usually in precious metals (gold, silver, etc.), in most of its approximately seventy occurrences. However, in several contexts, ***kikkār*** refers to a "valley," or "plain." In particular, Gen. 17:17, 25ff.; Deut. 24:3 refer to the Valley of Jericho; and Gen. 13:10ff.; 1 Kgs. 7:46; Neh. 12:28 refer to the Jordan Valley.

shephēlāh [שְׁפֵלָה, **8219**]

shephēlāh is a noun found in twenty places denoting a "valley," or "lowland(s)," "foothills." ***shephēlāh*** also designates the coastal strip of land west of the mountain range of Israel and the Mediterranean Sea, the Shephelah. This area is characterized by a series of rivers, river valleys, and river plains, all implied in the designation "lowlands," "foothills" (cf. Deut. 1:7; Josh. 9:1; 10:40; Judg. 1:9; 1 Kgs. 10:27; Jer. 17:26; Obad. 19; Zech. 7:7).

'āphîq [אָפִיק, **650**]

'āphîq is a noun occurring around twenty times with the primary sense of "river," "stream" in the majority of contexts. (→ RIVER) In 2 Sam. 22:16; Ps. 18:15, ***'āphîq*** refers to submarine "valleys" of the oceans.

NT Words

pharanx [φάραγξ, *5327*]

pharanx is a noun found only Luke 3:5 meaning "valley," citing the text of Isa. 40:4: ". . . every valley shall be raised up." This New Testament text affirms that the birth of Christ is a direct fulfillment of the Isaianic prophecy anticipating the coming of the Messianic King.

VALUABLE, VALUE

OT Words

yāqār **[יָקָר, 3368]**

yāqār is an adjective occurring about forty times with the primary meaning "precious," or "valuable."

Jewels, or gemstones, are described as "precious," for example, in 2 Sam. 12:30; 1 Kgs. 10:2ff.; Ezek. 27:22; 28:13. The large stones set aside for the construction of the temple are described as "valuable" in 1 Kgs. 5:17; 7:9ff.; 1 Chr. 29:2. In a significant metaphorical context, ***yāqār*** refers to the "precious" cornerstone set by God himself that points to the coming of the Messiah.

The love of God is described as "precious" (Ps. 36:7); as are the people of God (Lam. 4:2). And Lady Wisdom in Prov. 3:15 is declared to be "more valuable" than jewels.

The meaning "rare" is distinctive in 1 Sam. 3:1, referring to the scarcity of God's word on account of the sinful condition of the Israelite people of the day. The fact that God spoke to Samuel demonstrates his privileged position as the recipient of a highly valued word from God.

yāqar **[יָקַר, 3365]**

yāqar is a verb meaning "to be precious, valuable." It is found in eleven places and refers to the thoughts of God (Ps. 139:15); the value of Israel in God's sight (Isa. 43:4); and the lives of people generally in the sight of God (Ps. 72:14; Isa. 13:12).

yāqar also means "to be costly," as expressed in Ps. 49:8 in relation to the ransom for a human life. See also Zech. 11:13.

meker **[מֶכֶר, 4377]**

meker is a rare noun used adjectivally in Prov. 31:10 to refer to a wife who is "more precious" than jewels.

migdānāh **[מִגְדָּנָה, 4030]**

migdānāh is a noun denoting "valuable, precious gifts" in Gen. 24:53; 2 Chr. 21:3; 32:23; Ezra 1:6.

meged **[מֶגֶד, 4022]**

meged is a variant form of ***migdānāh***, above, denoting "valuable, precious gifts" derived from God in the form of the abundant produce of the land of Canaan (cf. Deut. 33:13ff.). The term also indicates "choice" fruit in Song 4:13ff.; 7:13. ***meged*** is found seven times.

nekōt **[נְכֹת, 5238]**

nekō't is a rare noun denoting "treasure" (i.e., precious commodities) in 2 Kgs. 20:13; Isa. 39:2.

ḥemdāh **[חֶמְדָּה, 2532]**

ḥemdāh is a noun found twenty-five times, with the primary sense of "that which is pleasant, or valuable." The term denotes "valuable goods" in 2 Chr. 21:20; 32:27; 36:10; Hos. 13:15; Nah. 2:9.

'ārak **[עָרַךְ, 6186]**

'ārak is a verb found in about eighty contexts with the almost exclusive sense of "arrange," "set in order." However, it also refers to the priest "setting a value" (i.e., a price) for redemption on a man (Lev. 27:8) and on an animal (Lev. 27:12). (→ ARRANGE)

'ērek **[עֵרֶךְ, 6187]**

'ērek is a noun derived from ***'ārak*** (see above), occurring in around thirty contexts with primary reference to the Levitical "valuation" of people and animals for the purposes of setting a price for their redemption under the terms of the law of Moses (cf. Lev. 27:2ff.; Num. 18:16). See also Lev. 5:15ff.

NT Words

diapherō **[διαφέρω, *1308*]**

diapherō is a verb meaning "to be more valuable, of more value," found in five contexts (cf. Matt. 6:26; 10:31; 12:12; Luke 12:7, 24).

timaō **[τιμάω, *5091*]**

timaō is a verb found in around twenty places with the principal meaning "to honor." Twice, however, it means "set a value, or price on" (cf. Matt. 27:29).

timios **[τίμιος, *5093*]**

timios is an adjective derived from ***timaō*** (see above) meaning "precious," "valuable" in most of its fourteen occurrences. It is applied to gemstones (1 Cor. 3:12; Rev. 17:4; 18:12ff.; 21:11, 19); to one's faith (1 Pet. 1:7); to the blood of Christ (1 Pet. 1:19); and to God's promises (2 Pet. 1:4). See also Acts 20:24; Jas. 5:7.

barytimos **[βαρύτιμος, *927*]**

barytimos is a rare adjectival form found only in Matt. 26:7 denoting ointment or perfume that is "very precious (i.e., expensive)."

entimos [ἔντιμος, *1784*]

entimos is another adjective meaning "prized," "precious." Luke 7:2 refers to a valued slave. Christ the "living stone" is deemed "precious" in God's sight in 1 Pet. 2:4ff. See also Luke 14:8.

isotimos [ἰσότιμος, *2472*]

Another rare variant of the above words, ***isotimos*** is found only in 2 Pet. 1:1 and refers to a faith "of equal value."

polytimos [πολύτιμος, *4186*]

Another adjectival variant of the above entries, ***polytimos*** is found in two places. It indicates a pearl "of great value" in Matt. 13:46, and "very expensive" perfume in John 12:3.

polytelēs [πολυτελής, *4185*]

polytelēs is an adjective synonymous with ***polytimos***, above. It is found three times with the general meaning "precious," "valuable" in relation to perfume (cf. Mark 14:3); garments (cf. 1 Tim. 2:9); and to an intangible (yet very real), gentle, and quiet spirit (1 Pet. 3:4).

ōphelimos [ὠφέλιμος, *5624*]

ōphelimos is an adjective denoting that which is "profitable" (i.e., "of value") in varying degrees. It occurs four times, describing good deeds (Titus 3:8) and bodily fitness and godliness (1 Tim. 4:8). 2 Tim. 3:16 declares that all Scripture is "profitable" for teaching.

euchrēstos [εὔχρηστος, *2173*]

euchrēstos is an adjective synonymous with ***ōphelimos***, above, denoting in three places those who are "useful" in Christian ministry (cf. 2 Tim. 2:21; 4:11; Phlm. 11).

See Also: → HONOR

VANISH

OT Words

mālaḥ [**מָלַח, 4414**]

mālaḥ is a verb found in five places meaning "to season or rub with salt" (cf. Exod. 30:35; Lev. 2:13; Ezek. 16:4). However, in Isa. 51:6 it is translated "to vanish," "disappear," with reference to the apocalyptic dissolution of the heavens at the end of time.

NT Words

aphanismos [ἀφανισμός, *854*]

aphanismos is a noun found only in Heb. 8:13, referring to the superseded Mosaic law covenant that will soon "disappear" (lit., that is ready for disappearing, or vanishing).

See Also: → ABOLISH → CORRUPT

VEIL

OT Words

porōket [**פָּרֹכֶת, 6532**]

porōket is a noun meaning "curtain," or "veil." It is found in twenty-five places with primary reference to the "veil" separating the holy of holies from the remainder of the tabernacle structure (cf. Exod. 26:31ff.; 40:3ff.; Lev. 4:6, 17; 16:2, 12ff.; Num. 4:5; 18:7). 2 Chr. 3:14 refers to that same curtain in the temple. In addition, ***porōket*** denotes the curtains located in the general tabernacle structure (Exod. 38:27; 39:24).

ṣā'îph [**צָעִיף, 6809**]

ṣā'îph is a noun denoting a "veil" with reference to an item of women's clothing. It is found in three places (Gen. 24:65; 38:14, 19).

masweh [**מַסְוֶה, 4533**]

masweh is a synonym for ***ṣā'îph*** (see above), denoting a "veil" that is drawn across the face. It is found only three times (Exod. 34:33ff.), in relation to Moses covering his radiant face after his meeting with Yahweh on Mt. Sinai.

NT Words

kalymma [κάλυμμα, *2571*]

kalymma is a dynamic equivalent for the Hebrew term ***masweh*** (see above), denoting a "veil" for covering the face. It is found in four contexts, referring literally in 2 Cor. 3:13 to the veil used by Moses to cover himself after his meeting with God on Mt. Sinai.

kalymma is also used figuratively in that same passage, referring to the "veil" of spiritual blindness that covers the hearts and minds of unbelieving Jews who refuse to believe in the person of Christ. Only when saving faith in the Son of God is granted to them is that "veil" removed (cf. 2 Cor. 3:14ff.).

katapetasma [καταπέτασμα, *2665*]

katapetasma is the dynamic equivalent for the Hebrew ***porōket*** (see above), denoting the two "curtains," or "veils," that separate the holy place from the outer court of the temple, and the holy of holies from the holy place. This term is found in six contexts, each of them highly significant.

Matt. 27:51; Mark 15:38; Luke 23:45 constitute the three synoptic gospel references to the tearing of the veil that separated the most holy place from the remainder of the sanctuary. The occasion of this shearing of the "veil, or curtain" was the death of Christ — a sacrifice that signaled the effective end of the old covenant legislation. The ritual requirements maintained the strict sanctity of the holy of holies, allowing only the high priest to draw back that veil just once a year in order to offer sacrifice for the people of Israel before the ark of the covenant. This inner sanctuary constituted the symbolic (though very real) dwelling place of God on earth. When this curtain was torn in two at the crucifixion of Christ, it signaled the end of restricted access to God. Now all who trust in the redemptive work of the Savior can gain unrestricted access to the very throne room of God in heaven.

Heb. 6:19; 9:3; 10:20 refer to this temple "veil" in contexts that explain the full significance of Christ's sacrificial death and ongoing, eternal high priestly ministry in heaven on behalf of his peoples. In Heb. 9:3 it is clear (by implication) that ***katapetasma*** also refers to the outer curtain separating the priestly holy place from the general areas of temple worship.

VENGEANCE → AVENGE

VENOM

OT Words

rō'sh **[רֹאשׁ, 7219]**

rō'sh is a noun denoting "poison," or "venom." It is found in twelve contexts, most of them figurative.

The "poison" of an embittered spirit that turns away from the living God is noted in the warning of Deut. 29:18. "Poisonous grapes" and "serpents' venom" are cited in Deut. 32:32ff. as a source of immorality and godlessness for the people of Israel (cf. also Hos. 10:4). Similarly, in an indictment of Israelite society, Amos 6:12 records that justice has been turned into "venom."

"Poisonous food" symbolizes persecution from one's enemies in Ps. 69:21. Yahweh is said to give "poisoned water" to his people in judgment against them (Jer. 8:14; 9:15; 23:15). Lam. 3:19 refers to the "venom" of bitterness.

Job 20:16 refers literally to snake venom.

ḥēmāh **[חֵמָה, 2534]**

ḥēmāh is a noun that primarily denotes the emotion of "wrath," "fury," or "anger" in most of its approximately 120 occurrences. (→ ANGER) In several places, however, the sense of "venom" or "poison" is evident, in predominantly figurative contexts.

In Deut. 32:33, ***ḥēmāh*** designates the "venom of serpents" as the metaphorical quality of the wicked lifestyle of the citizens of Sodom and Gomorrah (cf. also Pss. 58:4; 140:3). In Job 6:4, the "poison" of God's "arrows" is perceived (wrongly) by Job as a campaign of terror against him. Job 20:16 affirms that the "venom of serpents" is to be drunk by the wicked as a judgment from God. The one literal reference to snake venom is found in Deut. 32:24.

NT Words

ios **[ἰός, *2447*]**

ios is a noun found three times. In two of these contexts, it refers figuratively to the "venom" of serpents in relation to the wicked (Rom. 3:13). Jas. 3:8 speaks of the "venom" of the untamed human tongue.

VERILY → TRUE

VESSEL

OT Words

kelî **[כְּלִי, 3627]**

kelî is a noun found in about three hundred places with the rather vague meaning "vessel," or "container." In addition to this mundane sense, ***kelî*** also refers to the "vessels" or "utensils" of the tabernacle and temple. ***kelî*** can also mean "jewels," "precious stones," "instruments." (→ INSTRUMENT → JEWEL)

Mundane references to "vessels" or "containers" include those in Lev. 6:28; Deut. 23:24; 2 Kgs. 4:3ff. The potter's "jar," or "vessel," is indicated in Ps. 2:9; Isa. 30:14. In particular, Jer. 18:4; 19:11; 22:28; 48:38 refer to the potter's "jar" as a symbol for the nation of Judah, a "jar" that will be smashed in accordance with God's judgment against his people. Similarly, in Hos. 8:8, Israel is described as a "useless vessel." Additional examples of this usage are found in Josh. 6:19ff.; 1 Kgs. 7:48ff.; Ezra 1:6ff.; Dan. 1:2. In addition, Isa. 18:2 refers to "boats" as "vessels."

nēbel **[נֵבֶל, 5035]**

nēbel is a noun occurring around forty times with reference to "bottles," "jars," or "pitchers" as containers for liquid. It also refers to an ancient stringed musical instrument such as a "lute" or "psaltery." (→ JAR → LUTE)

mā'n [**מָאן, 3984** (Aramaic)]

mā'n is a noun occurring in seven places, referring to the "vessels" or "articles" taken from the Jerusalem temple by Nebuchadnezzar in 587 B.C. These items were all eventually returned to the people of God (cf. Ezra 5:14ff.; 7:19; Dan. 5:2ff., 23).

NT Words

angeion [**ἀγγεῖον**, *30*]

angeion is a rare noun denoting a "flask" for carrying lamp oil (Matt. 25:4), and a "basket" for sorting fish (Matt. 13:48).

skeuos [σκεῦος, *4632*]

skeuos is a noun found in approximately twenty places primarily meaning "goods," "household utensils." The former sense is found in Matt. 12:29; Luke 17:31; 2 Tim. 2:20. See also Rev. 18:12. Household utensils are indicated in Luke 8:16; John 19:29; Rev. 2:27. Heb. 9:21 refers to the "articles" or "utensils" of the Jerusalem temple under the old covenant.

skeuos is also used figuratively in a number of places. Persons chosen by God for a particular task are designated as "vessels" or "instruments" (Acts 9:15; 2 Tim. 2:21), as are those ordained for a particular destiny (Rom. 9:21ff.). The expression "vessels made of clay" in 2 Cor. 4:7 symbolizes the fragility and purely temporal condition of the human body. The term "vessel" is also a symbol for one's wife in 1 Thess. 4:4; 1 Pet. 3:7.

chalkion [χαλκίον, *5473*]

chalkion is a rare noun found only in Mark 7:4 with reference to a "brass pot, or container," a household utensil.

See Also: → UTENSIL

VEX → TROUBLE

VICTORY, VICTORIOUS

OT Words

teshû'āh [**תְּשׁוּעָה, 8668**]

teshû'āh is a noun occurring around thirty times with the predominant meanings "salvation," "deliverance." (→ SALVATION) ***teshû'āh*** also means "victory," "safety," and there is occasionally some overlap between these four meanings (e.g., 1 Sam. 19:5; 2 Kgs. 5:1; Ps. 144:10; Prov. 21:31). In all of these examples, the "victory" gained was achieved by the power of Yahweh.

teshû'āh means "victory" in 2 Sam. 19:2; 23:10, 12, referring to battles won by Yahweh on behalf of his people.

NT Words

nikos [νῖκος, *3534*]

nikos is a noun denoting "victory" in all four occurrences of the term. Establishing "victory" over injustice as part of the charter of the Messianic King is indicated in Matt. 12:20. The remaining contexts speak of the "victory" over death and sin won by Christ through his own death and resurrection (cf. 1 Cor. 15:54ff.).

nikē [νίκη, *3529*]

nikē is a rare variant form of ***nikos*** (see above), denoting the believer's "victory" over the world, won by faith (cf. 1 John 5:4).

See Also: → OVERCOME → SAVE → WIN

VILE → DISHONOR → FOLLY → SHAME

VILLAGE

OT Words

ḥāṣēr [**חָצֵר, 2691**]

ḥāṣēr is a noun with the primary sense of "court," "courtyard," or "enclosure" in most of its nearly two hundred occurrences. (→ COURT) In a number of places, however, the additional meaning "village" is evident. Unwalled villages are indicated in Lev. 25:31. Other general references to villages are found in Josh. 13:23ff.; 19:6ff.; 1 Chr. 4:32ff.; Neh. 12:28ff.

bat [**בַּת, 1323**]

bat is a common noun with the predominant meaning "daughter" in the large majority of its nearly six hundred occurrences. (→ DAUGHTER) However, in several places, ***bat*** also denotes "villages," or "towns" (cf. Num. 21:25, 32; Josh. 15:45ff.; 2 Chr. 28:18).

kōpher [**כֹּפֶר, 3724**]; ***kāphār*** [**כָּפָר, 3723**]

These two terms mean "village." ***kāphār*** is a rare noun found only in 1 Chr. 27:25; Song 7:11. ***kōpher*** is a more common term, though it refers to "unwalled villages" only in 1 Sam. 6:18. (→ BRIBE → RANSOM)

ḥawwāh **[חַוָּה, 2333]**

The noun ***ḥawwāh*** is synonymous with the terms above, denoting "small towns" or "villages" in four contexts (Num. 32:41; Josh. 13:30; 1 Kgs. 4:13; 1 Chr. 2:23).

perāzāh **[פְּרָזָה, 6519]**

perāzāh occurs three times, referring to "unwalled towns, or villages" (cf. Esth. 9:19; Ezek. 38:11; Zech. 2:4).

NT Words

kōmē [κώμη, *2968*]

kōmē is a noun that occurs approximately thirty times and means "village," "town" (e.g., Matt. 9:35; Mark 6:6, 36, 56; 8:23ff.; Luke 9:6ff.; John 7:42; Acts 8:25).

kōmopolis [κωμόπολις, *2969*]

kōmopolis is a rare variant of ***kōmē*** (see above) referring to "towns," or "villages," in Mark 1:38.

VINE, VINEDRESSER

OT Words

gephen **[גֶּפֶן, 1612]**

gephen is a noun with the consistent meaning "vine" throughout its approximately sixty occurrences, primarily in metaphorical contexts.

General literal references to "vines" are found in Gen. 40:9ff.; Deut. 8:8; Ps. 105:33. Judg. 9:12ff. refers to the "vine" as one component of the so-called "parable of the trees" in Judg. 9:7ff. The destruction of the land of Israel, involving the judgment of Yahweh against his people, leads to the devastation of the nation's agricultural produce, including the vines (cf. Isa. 32:12; Jer. 5:17; 8:13; Hos. 2:12; Joel 1:7, 12). God promises to restore the land of Israel, including the productivity of the land, which involves replanting vines (cf. Hag. 2:19; Zech. 8:12).

In metaphorical contexts, the "vine" is depicted, for example, as the source of the worldview of the wicked, of their immorality and idolatry (cf. Deut. 32:32). The people of Israel are designated as a "vine" that was brought by God out of Egypt (cf. Ps. 80:8, 14; Ezek. 17:6ff.; Hos. 10:1). A wife who will bear her husband many children is described as a "vine" in Ps. 128:3. The "wild vine" noted in Jer. 2:21 symbolizes Israel's spiritual demise. Ezek. 15:6 mentions the "worthless vine," referring to Jerusalem under divine judgment. In Song 7:8, the expression "clusters of the vine" symbolically refers to a woman's breasts.

nāzîr **[נָזִיר, 5139]**

nāzîr denotes one who takes a solemn vow of dedication to Yahweh, a Nazirite. ***nāzîr*** is found primarily in Num. 6. In two places, however, ***nāzîr*** denotes an "undressed, or untended vine" (cf. Lev. 25:5, 11).

kōrēm **[כֹּרֵם, 3755]**

kōrēm denotes a "vinedresser," or one who tends vines. It occurs five times (cf. 2 Kgs. 25:12; 2 Chr. 26:10; Isa. 61:5; Jer. 52:16; Joel 1:11).

sōrēq **[שֹׂרֵק, 8321]**

sōrēq is a noun denoting a "choice vine," found in three places (cf. Gen. 49:11; Isa. 5:2; Jer. 2:21).

NT Words

ampelos [ἄμπελος, *288*]

ampelos is a noun denoting a "vine" in all eight occurrences of the term.

A general reference to the "grape vine" is found in Jas. 3:12. Jesus refers to the "fruit of the vine" at the celebration of the Passover with his disciples, indicating that he will not share it with them again until the consummation of the kingdom of God (cf. Matt. 26:29; Mark 14:25; Luke 22:18). In John 15:1ff., Christ testifies that he is "the true vine," the source of eternal life for all who would entrust themselves to him. Rev. 14:19 refers to the harvesting of "the vine of the earth," alluding to gathering the wicked for judgment.

geōrgos [γεωργός, *1092*]

geōrgos is a noun found only in John 15:1 designating God as the "vinedresser," who "tends" his son Jesus Christ, the "true vine."

ampelourgos [ἀμπελουργός, *289*]

ampelourgos is synonymous with ***geōrgos*** (see above). It too is rare, referring to a "vinedresser" only in Luke 13:7.

Additional Notes

The vocabulary for "vine" in Scripture is significant when referring metaphorically to the people of God.

The image of the "fruitful vine," when applied to Israel, depicts these people in an intimate relationship with their God that yields great blessing for them, measured by the enjoyment of material prosperity expressed largely by an abundance of produce. In contrast, the destruction of vines in Israel symbolizes the devastation of the people of God.

In the New Testament, Christ fulfills the prophetic symbolism of the vine. He identifies himself as the "true vine," to which all who devote themselves to him in faith and repentance truly belong. As long as his followers remain committed to him in faith, and thus remain committed to God as well, they will continue to derive ongoing "nourishment" and "life" from the "vine."

Thus the new covenant phenomenon of the vine embraces the Messiah himself and his people. The powerful metaphor of the vine establishes a clear redemptive-historical continuity between the people of Israel in the old covenant and the person of Christ and his followers in the new.

VINEGAR

OT Words

ḥōmeṣ **[חֹמֶץ, 2558]**

ḥōmeṣ denotes "vinegar" in all six occurrences (cf. Num. 6:3; Ruth 2:14; Ps. 69:21; Prov. 10:26; 25:20).

NT Words

oxos [ὄξος, *3690*]

oxos is the dynamic equivalent for the Hebrew ***ḥōmeṣ***, referring to "vinegar" in several different contexts (cf. Matt. 27:34, 48; Mark 15:36; Luke 23:36; John 19:29, 30).

VINEYARD

OT Words

kerem **[כֶּרֶם, 3754]**

kerem is a noun with the consistent meaning "vineyard" throughout most of its approximately ninety occurrences.

Literal references to "vineyards" are found in Gen. 9:4; Exod. 22:5; Lev. 25:3ff.; Judg. 11:33; 21:20; Ps. 107:37; Prov. 31:16; Isa. 1:8. The destruction of Israel's vineyards constitutes an element of divine judgment against her, through the covenant curse (cf. Amos 4:9; 5:11, 17; Zeph. 1:13). Conversely, one sign of renewed life in the land of Israel as a consequence of the divine transformation is replanting vineyards (cf. Isa. 65:21; Jer. 31:5; 32:15; Ezek. 28:26; Hos. 2:15; Amos 9:14). In Isa. 5:3ff.; Jer. 12:10, the vineyard itself is a symbol of Israel. Elsewhere, the "vineyard" is depicted as part of the symbolic "landscape" of a woman's sexual awareness and experience (cf. Song 7:12).

NT Words

ampelōn [ἀμπελών, *290*]

ampelōn is the dynamic equivalent of the Hebrew ***kerem***, denoting a literal "vineyard" in each of its approximately twenty-five occurrences (cf. Matt. 20:1ff.; 21:28ff.; Mark 12:1ff.; Luke 20:9ff.; 1 Cor. 9:7).

VIOLENCE, VIOLENT

OT Words

ḥāmās **[חָמָס, 2555]**

ḥāmās is a noun denoting "violence" in most of its sixty occurrences. The term is also used adjectivally. The related senses of "cruelty" and "injustice" are also evident in the semantic range of ***ḥāmās***. The meanings "cruelty" and "violence" often overlap.

General references to "violence" as a negative feature of human behavior are found in Gen. 6:11ff.; 2 Sam. 22:3, 49; Ps. 7:16; Prov. 10:6; Jonah 3:8; Hab. 1:2ff. Violence is a characteristic of the people of Judah (Ezek. 7:23; 8:17; 45:9; Mic. 6:12; Mal. 2:16). Violence is also characteristic of the "fallen angel" cast out of heaven for rebellion against Yahweh (cf. Ezek. 28:16). Violence committed against Israel by Edom is indicated in Joel 3:19; Obad. 10. Weapons of violence are indicated in Gen. 49:5. Violence is to be removed from the land as part of the promised divine renewal for Israel (cf. Isa. 60:18). Isa. 53:9 affirms the complete absence of violence from the Suffering Servant. Cruelty and violence are linked together in Judg. 9:24; Ps. 27:12. See also Ps. 140:1ff.

ḥāmas **[חָמַס, 2554]**

ḥāmas is a verb found in eight contexts. In three of these contexts it means "do violence to," or "violate." Jer. 22:3 prohibits the violent handling of the alien in Israel. Ezek. 22:26; Zeph. 3:4 speak of "violating" the law of God (lit. "do violence to").

NT Words

bia [βία, *970*]

bia is a noun denoting "violence" or "force" in relation to people in Acts 5:26; 21:35. Acts 27:41 refers to the "force" of the breaking surf.

hormēma [ὅρμημα, *3731*]

hormēma refers to the "violence" of the destruction of Babylon in Rev. 18:21.

See Also: → FORCE

VIPER

OT Words

'eph'eh **[אֶפְעֶה, 660]**

'eph'eh refers to a "viper," or "adder," in Job 20:16; Isa. 30:6; Isa. 59:5.

NT Words

echidna [ἔχιδνα, *2191*]

echidna is a noun denoting a "viper" in five contexts. Acts 28:3 refers literally to a "viper" that attacked Paul on the island of Malta. The remaining usage is figurative, with John the Baptist denouncing the hypocritical spiritual leaders of Israel as a "brood of vipers" in Matt. 3:7; Luke 3:7. Jesus makes a similar denunciation in Matt. 12:34; 23:33.

See Also: → SERPENT

VIRGIN, VIRGINITY

OT Words

betûlāh **[בְּתוּלָה, 1330]**

betûlāh is the primary term denoting a "virgin," found in fifty contexts and referring in literal settings to an unmarried woman who is chaste, not having "known" a man sexually. The term is also used figuratively.

Literal references to virgins are found in Gen. 24:16; Exod. 22:16ff.; Lev. 21:3; Deut. 22:19ff.; Judg. 19:24; 2 Sam. 13:2; Esth. 2:2ff.; Isa. 6:5; Lam. 1:4.

betûlāh refers metaphorically to Jerusalem and its inhabitants as the "virgin daughter of Zion" in 2 Kgs. 19:21; Isa. 37:22. In particular, Jer. 14:17; Lam. 1:15ff.; 2:13 use this title in the context of God punishing his people for their sinfulness. "Virgin Israel" is condemned for rejecting Yahweh (Jer. 18:13; Amos 5:2), and also receives a promise of forgiveness and renewal from God (Jer. 31:4, 13, 21).

The "virgin daughter of Babylon" in Isa. 47:1 is a title of contempt for the idolatrous ruler of this nation, depicted here as a prostitute.

betûlîm **[בְּתוּלִים, 1331]**

betûlîm is the plural form of ***betûlāh*** (see above). It occurs ten times and denotes a woman's "(state of) virginity" in Lev. 21:13; Deut. 22:14ff.; Judg. 11:37ff.; Ezek. 23:3, 8.

NT Words

parthenos [παρθένος, *3933*]

parthenos is the dynamic equivalent of ***betûlāh*** (see above). It refers to women without sexual experience of a man, as well as (rarely) to men who are likewise designated "virgin." ***parthenos*** occurs fourteen times.

Literal references to women as "virgins" include those in Matt. 25:1, 7, 11; Acts 21:9; 1 Cor. 7:25ff. In particular, Matt. 1:23 refers to the Isaianic prophecy of the "virgin," who will give birth to the Messiah. In Luke 1:27, Mary the betrothed bride of Joseph is identified as a "virgin," and is clearly viewed by the New Testament as the one who fulfills the Old Testament prophecy from Isa. 7:14. In 1 Cor. 7:25, Paul refers to "the unmarried" as a collective designation, presumably, for women and men who are chaste.

In 2 Cor. 11:12, Paul refers figuratively to the community of believers as a "pure (i.e., virgin) bride" betrothed to Christ, "her husband." Rev. 14:4 refers to saints in heaven as those who have not defiled themselves with women, who are "pure," or "chaste." This reference is probably symbolic, using "chastity" as a symbol for separation from a pagan world system, and not sexual purity; for clearly this group contains both men and women.

See Also: → MAID

VIRTUE → GOOD → WORTHY

VISIBLE

NT Words

horatos [ὁρατός, *3707*]

horatos is a rare adjectival form denoting that which is "visible" (i.e., open to view) in creation, fashioned through the divine power of God in Christ (cf. Col. 1:16).

VISION

OT Words

ḥāzôn **[חָזוֹן, 2377]**

ḥāzôn is a noun with the fundamental sense of "vision" found in a variety of contexts. The primary denotation of the term is that of a revelation from God. It occurs thirty-five times.

Visions from God are declared to be rare at the time of Samuel's calling as a prophet (cf. 1 Sam. 3:1). General references to visions include those in Ps. 89:15; Prov. 29:18; Ezek. 12:22ff.; Hos. 12:10. Specifically, visions are given to Isaiah (2 Chr. 32:32; Isa. 1:1); Obadiah (Obad. 1); Nahum (Nah. 1:1); Daniel (Dan. 8:1ff.; 9:21, 24); and also to King David on the occasion of the revelation of Yahweh's covenant promises (cf. 1 Chr. 17:15). In addition, Daniel receives a God-given ability to interpret dreams and visions in Dan. 1:17.

False "visions," derived solely from the human imagination, are condemned by God as illegitimate (Jer. 14:14; 23:16). In contexts of divine judgment, Lam. 2:9; Mic. 3:6 affirm that "visions" from God are denied to the sinful people of Israel and Judah.

mar'eh **[מַרְאֶה, 4758]**

mar'eh is a noun meaning "appearance," "sight," "vision" in most of its approximately one hundred occurrences. The meanings "sight," "appearance," and "vision" often overlap. (→ APPEARANCE)

References to "sight" as the faculty of vision include those in Gen. 2:9; Eccl. 6:9. The visual phenomenon, or "sight," of the burning bush as seen by Moses is noted in Exod. 3:3. See also Deut. 28:34, 67.

pānîm **[פָּנִים, 6440]**

pānîm is a common plural noun form found in approximately 2,100 contexts, and is usually translated "face," "presence." It is also used in the prepositional sense of "before" (i.e., in the presence of). However, ***pānîm*** also means "sight" in a number of places.

"Sight" in the sense of "one's range of vision" is indicated in the context of people in Gen. 23:4ff. References to being "out of God's sight" are found in Josh. 23:5; 2 Sam. 7:9. This expression is also evident in 1 Kgs. 9:7; 2 Kgs. 17:18ff.; 23:27 in the context of "being cast away from the presence of God." See also 1 Chr. 22:8; Ezra 9:9.

maḥazeh **[מַחֲזֶה, 4236]**

maḥazeh is a noun denoting a "vision" from God in three of the four uses of the term (cf. Gen. 15:1; Num. 24:4, 16). In Ezek. 13:7 a "false vision" is in view, for which the false prophets are condemned since Yahweh had not spoken to them.

mar'āh **[מַרְאָה, 4759]**

mar'āh is a noun denoting a "vision" as a mode of divine revelation in most of the twelve occurrences of the term (cf. Gen. 46:2; Num. 12:6; 1 Sam. 3:15; Ezek. 1:1; 8:3; 40:2; 43:3).

ḥizzāyôn **[חִזָּיוֹן, 2384]**

ḥizzāyôn also denotes a "vision." It occurs nine times and refers to "visions" (i.e., revelation) from God in 2 Sam. 7:17; Isa. 22:1ff.; Joel 2:28; Zech. 13:4. ***ḥizzāyôn*** also denotes "visions of the night," presumably indicating "dreams" and including "nightmares" (cf. Job 4:13; 7:14; 20:8; 33:15).

ḥāzût **[חָזוּת, 2380]**

ḥāzût is a noun denoting a "vision" from God in Isa. 21:2; 29:11.

rō'eh **[רֹאֶה, 7203]**

rō'eh is a rare noun referring to seeing "visions" in Isa. 28:7.

ḥēzew **[חֵזֵו, 2376 (Aramaic)]**

ḥēzew is an Aramaic term denoting "visions" given by God. It is found in twelve contexts. Such visions were given to Nebuchadnezzar (cf. Dan. 2:28; 4:5ff.); and to Daniel (cf. Dan. 2:19; 7:1ff.).

ḥāzôt **[חָזוֹת, 2378]**

ḥāzôt is a term found only in 2 Chr. 9:29, referring to "visions" of Iddo the seer.

NT Words

horama **[ὅραμα, *3705*]**

horama is a noun denoting a "vision" in the sense of a revelation from God that is both seen and heard. It is found in twelve contexts.

A vision of God or Christ is indicated in Matt. 17:9, with reference to Christ's transfiguration. Acts 7:31 refers to Moses' "vision" of the burning bush. Visions are also granted to Ananias, who sees the risen Christ in Acts 9:10ff. Peter receives a vision from God (Acts 11:5), as does Cornelius (Acts 10:3, 17, 19). See also Acts 12:9; 16:9ff.; 18:9.

horasis **[ὅρασις, *3706*]**

horasis is a variant form of ***horama***, above, found only three times. It denotes supernatural visions of God (Acts 2:17; Rev. 9:17) and an "appearance" of God that resembles the radiance of precious gemstones (Rev. 4:3).

optasia **[ὀπτασία, *3701*]**

optasia is a noun that also denotes "visions" from heaven, found in four contexts (cf. Luke 24:23; Acts 26:19; 2 Cor. 12:1). Luke 1:22 refers to a vision of an angel bearing the news to the priest Zechariah that his wife would bear a son named John, the forerunner of the Messiah.

anablepō [ἀναβλέπω, *308*]

anablepō is a verb indicating the primary sense of "receive (i.e., recover) one's sight" in the majority of its approximately twenty-five occurrences.

The recovery of sight for the blind is largely due to the miracle cures wrought by Christ during his public ministry (cf. Matt. 11:15; Mark 10:51ff.; Luke 7:22; 18:41ff.; John 9:11ff.). In Acts 9:12ff.; 22:13, Ananias performs such a miracle on the newly-converted Saul of Tarsus.

anablepsis [ἀνάβλεψις, *309*]

anablepsis is a noun derived from ***anablepō***, above. It refers to the "recovery of sight" for the blind in Luke 4:18.

theōria [θεωρία, *2335*]

theōria is found only in Luke 23:48, denoting the "spectacle" of Christ on the cross, as seen by the assembled Jerusalem crowd, who watched him die.

eidos [εἶδος, *1491*]

eidos is a noun expressing the sense of "appearance," "form" in most of its five occurrences. Only in 2 Cor. 5:7 does ***eidos*** mean "sight." Here Paul declares that believers "walk by faith, not by sight," affirming that the exercise of one's physical and rational faculties of perception is not adequate for maintaining a vital relationship with God.

Additional Notes

"Visions" from God throughout Scripture constituted the primary vehicle for communicating God's will and purposes for his people and the nations at large. The contexts are both positive and negative. The revelation of God through visions and dreams culminated in the coming of Christ, who is the ultimate embodiment of God's redemptive plan. Once Christ had finished his life's work, there was no longer any need for visionary communication from God to human beings, since the Holy Spirit is now given to all believers as their means of discerning God's will for their lives through the words of Scripture.

VISIT, VISITATION

OT Words

pāqad [פָּקַד, **6485**]

pāqad is a verb occurring over three hundred times with a range of meanings. The primary meanings include "to number," "appoint," "visit," as well as several related senses. (→ APPOINT → NUMBER) The latter meaning, "to visit," is somewhat archaic English, implying the principal idea of God initiating and delivering blessing and punishment to both his own people and to the nations at large. The catalyst for the negative response of divine punishment is, generally speaking, rebellion against God; whereas the incentive for the outpouring of divine blessing lies in the mercy of God and the commitment to his covenant promises.

"Visiting" Israel in a positive sense involves God blessing them in a variety of ways. For example, he brings them out of Egypt (cf. Gen. 50:24ff.); comes to their aid (Exod. 13:19); brings them salvation (cf. Ps. 106:4); breaks a famine and provides food (cf. Ruth 1:6); and promises to bring them out of the Babylonian captivity (cf. Jer. 27:22; 29:10). See also Exod. 3:16; 4:3; Zech. 10:3.

God also "visits" individuals in different ways — for example, by granting sons to Sarah (Gen. 21:1) and Hannah (1 Sam. 2:21), and by examining or testing others (e.g., Job 7:18; Ps. 17:3).

In contrast, Yahweh also "visits" his people with punishment — for example, by threatening to punish them for their sin against him (cf. Exod. 32:34; Ps. 89:32; Jer. 5:9, 29; 9:9; 23:2; Hos. 2:13; 8:13; Amos 3:14); and by allowing their land to be ravaged (cf. Lev. 18:25). The nations are also "visited" by Yahweh in this way. For example, he "punishes" those who plot evil against him (cf. Isa. 24:22; 26:14ff.; 23:17; Jer. 49:8; 50:31; Lam. 4:22).

The rare modern sense of "paying someone a visit" is indicated only in Judg. 15:1.

pequddāh [פְּקֻדָּה, **6486**]

pequddāh is a form derived from ***pāqad*** (see above), a passive participle used as a noun with the primary meaning "visitation," used almost exclusively in the negative sense of "punishment." It also means "oversight," "charge," "office." (→ OFFICE)

The "visitation" against Israel for rejecting Yahweh is expressed as their "time, or day of punishment" in Isa. 10:3; Jer. 8:12; 10:15; 11:23; 23:12; Hos. 9:7; Mic. 7:4. The same is predicated of the nations of Egypt (Jer. 46:21); Moab (Jer. 48:44); and Babylon (Jer. 50:27).

In Job 10:12, divine "visitation" indicates God's care and nurture.

bô' [בּוֹא, **935**]

bô' is one of the most common verbs in the Old Testament (occurring nearly 2,500 times) with the primary meanings "go," "come," with a large number of related senses. One of these is the expression "to come upon," or "happen to," which implies the idea of a divine visitation, in some contexts similar to the usage of ***pāqad*** and ***pequddāh*** (see above).

This meaning is found in the context of the wrath of God being directed towards the people of Israel, resulting in disaster (cf. Lev. 10:6; Josh. 23:15; 2 Chr. 19:10). A similar fate is handed down to the nations (cf. Deut. 32:35; Isa. 47:1; Jer. 2:3; 46:21). The "coming of the covenant curse upon" Israel is indicated in Deut. 4:3; 28:15; 31:17; 2 Kgs. 8:1; Jer. 6:26; Ezek. 7:2ff.; Amos 4:2; Ezra 9:13.

Less frequently, the blessing of God is said "to come upon" his people (cf. Deut. 33:16; Josh. 23:15).

NT Words

episkeptomai [ἐπισκέπτομαι, *1980*]

episkeptomai is a verb meaning "visit" in several different senses. It occurs eleven times and refers to "paying someone a visit" in order to offer care, support, and help for the sick or imprisoned (cf. Matt. 25:36, 43; Acts 15:36; Jas. 1:27); or to ascertain their well-being, as was Moses' intention in "visiting" his own people in Egypt (cf. Acts 7:23). God is also said to "care for" human beings, his own creation (cf. Heb. 2:6).

God is said to "have visited his people" by sending them his son, Jesus Christ, to accomplish their salvation (cf. Luke 1:68; 7:16) as well as the salvation of a people chosen from the Gentiles (cf. Acts 15:14).

episkopē [ἐπισκοπή, *1984*]

episkopē is a noun denoting both "the office of a bishop" and the "visitation," or "coming," of God. The term occurs four times, with the latter meaning evident in two contexts. One of these contexts refers to "the coming" of God to judge the world (cf. 1 Pet. 2:12); the other in Luke 19:44 refers to the more immediate "coming" of God among his people that will result in the destruction of the temple.

historeō [ἱστορέω, *2477*]

historeō is a verb found only in Gal. 1:18 meaning "to pay a visit to" or "see (someone)."

VOCATION ➞ CALL

VOICE

OT Words

qôl [קוֹל, **6963**]

qôl is a common noun with the principal meanings "voice," or "sound," and including other related senses. The term occurs more than five hundred times. It is sometimes difficult to draw a distinction between these two meanings. (➞ SOUND)

qôl refers to the "voice," or "sound," of God (Gen. 3:8ff.; Deut. 4:12; Ps. 104:7); of animals (Job 4:10); and of created phenomena (Ps. 93:3; Ezek. 1:24).

qôl refers to the voice of people in a variety of contexts. Speech in general is indicated in Gen. 3:17. The expression "lift up one's voice" is found in relation to weeping (cf. Gen. 21:16; Ezra 3:12), and shouting (cf. Judg. 9:7; Prov. 8:1ff.). Isa. 40:3ff. records the voice of the prophet announcing God's purposes in redemption. 2 Sam. 22:7 mentions a voice heard by God. Obedience is defined as "listening to (someone's) voice" (cf. Exod. 4:9; 18:24). Deut. 21:18ff. records an instance of disobedience, indicating a refusal to heed one's parents. See also Num. 20:16; Song 2:14.

qôl also refers to the voice of God in a number of places. Obedience towards God is occasionally defined as "hearing his voice" (cf. Gen. 22:18; Deut. 4:30ff.; 28:1ff.; Josh. 24:4ff.). The divine voice is also heard in theophanic revelation (cf. Num. 7:8, 9; Deut. 5:22ff.; Isa. 6:4ff.; Ezek. 1:25, 28). Dan. 9:10ff. refers to people refusing or failing to obey God's voice. See also Ps. 29:4ff.; Eccl. 12:4; Amos 1:2.

NT Words

phōnē [φωνή, *5456*]

phōnē is a noun occurring around 140 times with the primary sense of "voice," accounting for the large majority of its usage. (➞ SOUND)

phōnē refers to the human voice of prophecy in Matt. 2:18; 3:3; Mark 1:3; Luke 3:4; John 1:23. Other references to voices include those in Mark 1:26; Luke 1:42ff.; Acts 2:14; Rev. 18:23.

The voice of God is heard from heaven, as noted in Matt. 3:17; Luke 3:22; John 12:28ff.; 2 Pet. 1:17ff. It is also evident in theophanic visions (cf. Acts 10:13ff.; 11:7ff.); and is heard in heaven itself (Rev. 16:17; 18:4; 21:3). The voice of the Holy Spirit is indicated in Heb. 3:7, 15; 4:7.

The voice of the archangel is heard at the return of Christ (1 Thess. 4:16). The voices of angels in heaven are heard in Rev. 5:2; 10:3ff.; 18:2. See also Rev. 6:10; 19:1, 6. In contrast, the voices of demons cry out in terror at their confrontation with Christ in Luke 4:33. See also Acts 8:7.

The voice of Christ is heard commanding Lazarus to rise from the dead in John 11:43. His "sheep," his followers, also recognize his voice (cf. John 10:3ff.). The voice of the risen Christ in heaven is likewise recorded in Rev. 1:10ff.; 3:20; 4:1; 14:13. He also addresses Saul in the context of his conversion in Acts 9:4ff.; 22:7ff.

See Also: → SOUND

VOMIT

OT Words

qô' [קוֹא, **6958**]

qô' is a verb meaning "to vomit (up)" "disgorge." It occurs eight times.

Literal references to vomiting include those in Prov. 23:8; 25:16; Jonah 2:10. Metaphorical references to "vomiting" include those in Lev. 18:25, 28; 20:22, referring to the land of Canaan "disgorging" its Israelite inhabitants in response to their defiling the land. See also Job 20:15.

qē' [קֵא, **6892**]

qē' is the noun derived from ***qô'*** (see above) and denotes "vomit" in four places (cf. Prov. 26:11; Isa. 19:14; 28:8; Jer. 48:26).

NT Words

emeō [ἐμέω, *1692*]

emeō is a verb found only in Rev. 3:16, referring to Yahweh's threat to "vomit up" the lukewarm congregation of the church at Laodicea.

exerama [ἐξέραμα, *1829*]

exerama is a noun denoting "vomit," found only in 2 Pet. 2:22.

VOW

OT Words

nēder [נֵדֶר, **5088**]

nēder is a noun denoting a "vow," found in sixty places. The contexts for this usage are varied.

Vows to God are found in Gen. 28:20; Judg. 11:30ff.; 1 Sam. 1:11, 21; Ps. 61:5; Eccl. 5:4. Legislation prescribing various kinds of vows is found in Num. 30:2ff. The Nazirite vow, for example, is described in detail in Num. 6:2ff. Vows requiring, or resulting in, an offering are noted in Lev. 7:16; 22:18ff.; Deut. 12:6ff.; Ps. 50:14; Prov. 7:14. Idolatrous vows made to the Babylonian "Queen of Heaven" are indicated in Jer. 44:25.

nādar [נָדַר, **5087**]

nādar is a verb meaning "to vow," "make a vow" throughout its approximately thirty occurrences.

Gen. 28:20; Num. 21:2; Judg. 11:30ff.; Eccl. 5:4; Isa. 19:2 refer to making a vow to God. Elsewhere, ***nādar*** is found in close proximity with ***nēder***, above.

nēzer [נֵזֶר, **5145**]

nēzer is a noun found in eleven contexts, indicating a "vow of separation" as taken by a Nazirite (Num. 6:4ff.).

NT Words

euchē [εὐχή, *2171*]

euchē is a noun denoting a "vow" in two places, referring to a vow of an indeterminate nature undertaken by Paul and several of his companions (cf. Acts 18:18; 21:23).

See Also: → SWEAR

W

WAGES

OT Words

***maskōret* [מַשְׂכֹּרֶת, 4909]**

maskōret is a noun meaning "wages" in three of its four occurrences (cf. Gen. 29:15; 31:7, 41). The references here are to the ordinary payment of remuneration in return for one's labor.

***sākār* [שָׂכָר, 7939]**

sākār is a noun found about thirty times, meaning "wages" in about half of these contexts. (→ REWARD)

Literal references to "wages" as remuneration for work or services rendered include those in Gen. 30:28ff.; 31:8; Deut. 24:15; 1 Kgs. 5:6; Eccl. 4:9; Ezek. 29:15ff.; Zech. 8:10; Mal. 3:5.

***sākar* [שָׂכַר, 7936]**

sākar is a verb meaning "to earn wages," and conversely "to hire," "hire (oneself) out" for services or labor. ***sākar*** occurs around twenty times, and this latter sense predominates.

The meaning "hire," or "hire out," is indicated in various contexts, most of which involve the payment of money, or wages. The pagan seer Balaam is "hired" by Balak, king of Moab, to curse the Israelites (cf. Deut. 23:4; Neh. 13:2). The employment of mercenaries is noted in Judg. 9:4; 2 Sam. 10:6; 2 Kgs. 7:6; 1 Chr. 19:6ff. See also Judg. 18:4; 1 Sam. 2:5; Ezra 4:5; Heb. 6:12ff.; Prov. 26:10; Isa. 46:6. In Gen. 30:16, Leah "purchases" sexual intercourse with her husband Jacob in an attempt to conceive by him. Hag. 1:6 indicates the explicit sense of "earning wages."

***pe'ullāh* [פְּעֻלָּה, 6468]**

pe'ullāh is a noun found in fourteen places with the primary sense of "wages," or "reward," for services rendered.

Lev. 19:13 refers literally to wages. Prov. 10:16 refers metaphorically to the "wages" of the righteous; and Prov. 11:18, in contrast, mentions the "wages" of the wicked.

Elsewhere, ***pe'ullāh*** refers figuratively to a "reward," or "recompense," for example, given by God to his people (Isa. 40:10; 62:11). Isa. 49:4 indicates a reward belonging to the Messianic Servant of Yahweh (i.e., from Yahweh himself). Isa. 61:8 refers to Yahweh "rewarding" his people as part of the promised blessing of the new covenant. See also Ezek. 29:20. (→ WORK)

NT Words

***opsōnion* [ὀψώνιον, *3800*]**

opsōnion is a noun occurring four times denoting "wages," or "financial support." Luke 3:14 refers to a soldier's wages, or allowance. See also 1 Cor. 9:7. 2 Cor. 11:8 refers to "financial support" provided by churches to the apostle Paul. Rom. 6:23 refers metaphorically to death as the "wages of sin."

***misthos* [μισθός, *3408*]**

misthos is a noun denoting a "reward" in most of its thirty occurrences. (→ REWARD) In several places, however, the meaning "wages" is indicated. Literal references include those in Matt. 20:8; Luke 10:7; John 4:36; Rom. 4:4; 1 Cor. 3:8; 1 Tim. 5:18; Jas. 5:4. 2 Pet. 2:15 refers to the "wages of unrighteousness" desired by Balaam, in relation to his greed and deception.

WAIL → MOURN

WAIT

OT Words

***ṣādāh* [צָדָה, 6658]**

ṣādāh is a rare verb meaning "lie in wait" in Exod. 21:13 in the context of those who "hunt" for a manslayer. ***ṣādāh*** is used similarly in 1 Sam. 24:11.

***'ārab* [אָרַב, 693]**

'ārab is a verb meaning to "lie in wait for" (i.e., "to ambush") in most of its nearly forty occurrences.

Deut. 19:11; Judg. 9:25ff.; 21:20; 1 Sam. 22:8ff.; Lam. 3:10 refer literally to this action. In particular, ***'ārab*** indicates setting ambushes — in the context of the military conquest of Canaan (Josh. 8:2ff.); in relation to Israel's enemies in general (cf. 1 Sam. 15:5; 2 Chr. 20:22); and also in connection with the civil war among the Israelite tribes (cf. Judg. 20:29ff.). In Jer. 51:12, Yahweh is said to lie in wait for the wicked.

'ārab is used metaphorically in several places, where the prostitute is said to "lie in wait," enticing the object of her desire (cf. Job 31:9; Prov 7:12; 23:28).

The wicked also seek to hunt down their victim, the psalmist (cf. Ps 10:9; 59:3). See also Prov. 1:11; 12:6; Mic. 7:2.

ma'arāb [מַאֲרָב, 3993]

ma'arāb is a noun derived from ***'ārab*** (see above), denoting an "ambush" in each of the five contexts in which it is found. It refers first of all to the Israelites lying in wait for the Canaanite people (cf. Josh. 8:9). See also Judg. 9:35; 2 Chr. 13:13. ***ma'arāb*** is also used figuratively of the wicked, who conceal themselves in "ambush" against innocent people (cf. Ps. 10:8ff.).

yāḥal [יָחַל, 3176]

yāḥal is a verb occurring about forty times, meaning "wait" in less than half of these contexts. The dominant sense is that of "hope." (→ HOPE)

General references to "waiting" include those in Job 14:14; 29:21; Mic. 5:7. Gen. 8:12; 1 Sam. 10:8; 13:8 refer to "waiting" for a specific period of time. "Waiting" for the Lord is noted in 2 Kgs. 6:33. In particular, Ps. 69:3 speaks of the psalmist waiting on the Lord, yearning for relief from suffering. Mic. 7:7 indicates the same activity in anticipation of gaining deliverance from trial.

qāwāh [קָוָה, 6960]

qāwāh is a verb meaning to "wait, or look for" someone or something with an underlying sense of expectation or anticipation. It occurs around fifty times.

qāwāh means "to wait, or look for" one's salvation from God (Gen. 49:14; Ps. 130:5; Isa. 51:5); the promised blessing of the land of Canaan (Ps. 37:9, 34); justice (Isa. 5:7; 59:11); and peace (Jer. 8:15; 14:19). Lam. 2:16 mentions the enemies of Judah, who "long for" the day of her destruction.

The sense of "waiting for" God, placing hope in him, is noted in relation to deliverance from trials, or oppression by the wicked (cf. Pss. 25:3ff.; 27:14; 40:1; Prov. 20:22). See also Ps. 39:7; Isa. 8:17; 25:9. Waiting on God for the renewal of one's strength is noted in Isa. 40:31.

qāwāh has the sense of "lie in wait" in Ps. 119:95, attributed to the wicked who seek to ambush and destroy the psalmist.

ḥûl [חוּל, 2342]

ḥûl is a verb found in approximately sixty contexts with the underlying sense of "writhe," often associated with pain. In Ps. 37:7, ***ḥûl*** indicates "waiting patiently" for the Lord. (→ PAIN)

ḥākāh [חָכָה, 2442]

ḥākāh is a verb meaning "to wait" in most of its fourteen occurrences. "Waiting" for morning is indicated in 2 Kgs. 7:9. "Waiting for" the Lord in anticipation of deliverance is noted in Ps. 33:20; Isa. 8:17; 30:18; 64:4. In Zeph. 3:8, God commands his people to wait for him to witness against the nations in judgment. Israel refuses to "wait for" divine counsel in Ps. 106:13.

ḥākāh also means "to lie in wait" (i.e., in ambush) in relation to a thief stalking his victims (cf. Hos. 6:9).

NT Words

enedreuō [ἐνεδρεύω, *1748*]; *enedron* [ἔνεδρον, *1749*]

enedreuō is a verb meaning "to lie in wait for," "set a trap, or ambush." It is found only twice. Luke 11:54 refers to the Pharisees "lying in wait" for Jesus, seeking to ensnare him through what he might say. Acts 23:21 refers to a literal ambush set for the apostle Paul.

The derivative noun ***enedron*** is found only in Acts 23:16 with reference to the ambush set for Paul.

prosdechomai [προσδέχομαι, *4327*]

prosdechomai is a verb meaning "look for," "wait for" with expectancy. It is used in fourteen places. It refers to the coming kingdom of God, for example, in Mark 15:43; Luke 23:51. Luke 2:25 refers to the anticipation of the coming Messiah. Similar expectancy is expressed in relation to the redemption of Jerusalem (Luke 2:38); and to the hope of Christ's return in glory (cf. Titus 2:13; Jude 21). See also Luke 12:36; Acts 23:21.

apekdechomai [ἀπεκδέχομαι, *553*]

apekdechomai is synonymous with ***prosdechomai***, above. It is found in five places. Rom. 8:19ff. refers to believers waiting for the consummation of redemption of the sons of God. "Waiting for" the revelation of Jesus Christ in glory at his return is indicated in 1 Cor. 1:7; Phil. 3:20; Heb. 9:28. See also Gal. 5:5.

prosdokaō [προσδοκάω, *4328*]

prosdokaō is another verb meaning "wait, or look for" in a variety of contexts. The term occurs eighteen times.

General references to "waiting for" people to come, or arrive, are found in Luke 1:21; 12:46; Acts 10:24. See also Acts 3:5.

prosdokaō also refers to waiting expectantly for the coming of the Messiah (cf. Matt. 11:3). See also Matt. 24:50. The anticipation of the day of salvation is noted in Luke 7:19ff.; 2 Pet. 3:12ff.

WAKE

OT Words

qûṣ **[קוּץ, 6974]**

qûṣ is a verb found in around twenty contexts with the predominant meaning "wake up," "awake."

The literal sense of "waking" from sleep is indicated in 1 Sam. 26:12; 2 Kgs. 4:31.

The remaining usage of ***qûṣ*** is metaphorical. Yahweh condemns the wicked to a sleep from which they will "not wake" in Jer. 51:39, 57. The psalmist invokes Yahweh to "rouse himself from sleep" and protect his people (Ps. 44:23); and then to punish the nations (Ps. 59:5). See also Ps. 35:23; Hab. 2:19. Isa. 26:19 invokes the dead to "wake up" and celebrate the joy of their renewed life from God. See also Dan. 12:2.

NT Words

grēgoreō [γρηγορέω, *1127*]

grēgoreō is a verb with the predominant meaning "to watch" in the sense of "keep awake," "give close attention to." It is found around twenty times.

Jesus exhorts his disciples in Gethsemane to "watch" and pray with him (cf. Matt. 26:38ff.; Mark 14:34ff.). Elsewhere, Jesus commands his hearers to "watch" for the day of the Lord's return (cf. Matt. 24:42ff.; Mark 13:34ff.; Luke 12:37ff.). See also Acts 20:31.

There are general exhortations to believers to "keep watch," "keep awake," and safeguard their relationship with the Lord (1 Cor. 16:13; 1 Thess. 5:6; 1 Pet. 5:8; Rev. 3:2ff.; 16:15).

See Also: → ARISE

WALK

OT Words

hālak **[הָלַךְ, 1980];** ***yālak*** **[יָלַךְ, 3212]**

hālak is a common verb (along with the variant ***yālak***) with the predominant meanings "go," "walk," accounting for the large majority of its usage (i.e., around 500 of its nearly one thousand occurrences).

"Walking" (including the sense of "going") is indicated in a variety of contexts. ***hālak*** refers to walking through the land of Canaan (Gen. 12:9; 17:1); through the wilderness (Josh. 5:6); and through the Red Sea (Exod. 15:19). See also Gen. 2:14; Lev. 11:27; Esth. 2:11; Isa. 20:2.

More significantly, ***hālak*** means "walk with God" in the sense of "living a godly life" (cf. Gen. 5:22ff.; 6:9; Deut. 28:9; Judg. 2:17; 1 Sam. 2:30; Pss. 1:1; 26:3; Isa. 38:3; Ezek. 18:17). Similarly, 2 Chr. 11:17; 17:3 speak of those who "walk in the ways of David" (i.e., who copy his godly rule).

Other contexts are negative. Failure "to walk with God" invites condemnation from him (cf. Lev. 26:23ff.; 1 Sam. 8:3ff.; Jer. 32:23; Ezek. 5:7; 20:31ff.). "Walking after other gods" (i.e., worshiping them) is noted in Deut. 8:19; Jer. 7:9. "Walking" in sinful ways is evident in 2 Kgs. 13:11; Ps. 82:5; Isa. 65:2; Amos 2:4; and "walking" in darkness in Isa. 9:2; 50:10; Eccl. 2:14.

hālak is also predicated of Yahweh in a number of places, where he promises to "walk" (i.e., dwell) among his people (Lev. 26:12). In Isa. 52:12, he is said "to walk ahead" of his people to lead them back to Canaan after the exile. In Deut. 23:14, Yahweh is said "to move about" the Israelite camp in order to protect his people.

NT Words

peripateō [περιπατέω, *4043*]

This is a verb occurring around one hundred times with the general, literal sense of "walk (about)," "go," "make one's way." As with the corresponding Hebrew term ***hālak***, ***peripateō*** also means "to live," "conduct one's life" (for good or ill).

Literal references to "walking" include those in Matt. 4:18; Mark 1:16; 6:48ff.; Luke 7:22; John 1:36; 10:23; Acts 3:6ff. Mark 12:38; Luke 20:46 refer to the Pharisees "walking about," "parading themselves." ***peripateō*** also refers metaphorically to the devil seeking out his victims (1 Pet. 5:8).

peripateō is more frequently used in the figurative sense of "walk," indicating the conduct of one's lifestyle, orienting it towards a particular goal (cf. 1 Cor. 3:3; Acts 21:21). Examples include the phenomenon of "walking in the light," denoting a godly lifestyle (cf. John 12:35; Eph. 5:8; 1 John 1:7; Rev. 21:24); and "walking in darkness," suggesting a sinful lifestyle (cf. John 8:12; 11:10; 1 John 1:6; 2:11). See also 2 Cor. 4:2. "Walking in accord with the flesh" also indicates a depraved lifestyle (cf. Rom. 8:4; 2 Cor. 10:2; Eph. 2:2; Col. 3:7).

Other references to godly living include "walking in the Spirit" (cf. Gal. 5:16); "walking in newness of life in Christ" (cf. Rom. 6:4); and "walking worthy of the Lord" (cf. Col. 1:10). See also Rom. 13:13; Eph. 2:10; Col. 4:5; 1 Thess. 4:1; 2 John 6. "Walking by faith" is indicated in 2 Cor. 5:7.

stoicheō [στοιχέω, *4748*]

stoicheō is a verb found five times, used exclusively in the figurative sense of "walk," or engaging in a particular way of life.

"Walking (i.e., living) in accordance with the law of God" is indicated in Acts 21:24; living in harmony with the implications of the new creation in Christ is noted in Gal. 6:16 (cf. also Phil. 3:16). Rom. 4:12 exhorts the reader to follow the example of Abraham's faith (lit., "to walk in the footsteps of"). And Gal. 5:25 commends "walking (i.e., living) in the spirit."

dierchomai [διέρχομαι, *1330*]

dierchomai is a verb occurring around fifty times with the general sense of "go," "pass," "walk through," or "travel," used both literally and figuratively.

General references to this activity are found in Luke 4:30; John 4:4; Acts 8:40; 13:6; 19:1. Specific examples of "traveling" are noted in Acts 11:19; 14:24; 15:41. Evil spirits are said "to pass or walk through" arid regions (Matt. 12:43; Luke 11:24); and Israel's "passing through" the Re(e)d Sea is noted in 1 Cor. 10:1.

dierchomai also refers to Christ "passing through" the heavens (cf. Heb. 4:14); and to the unlikely phenomenon of a camel "passing through the eye of a needle" (Matt. 19:24; Mark 10:25).

Mark 4:35; Luke 8:12; 9:6 refer literally to "going, or walking across" a geographic location.

Additional Notes

By far the most significant aspect of the vocabulary for "walking" in both Testaments is the figurative one, referring to conducting one's lifestyle. In the Old Testament, the term ***hālak*** refers to the absolute necessity of "walking with God" if one is to obtain the blessings of the covenant. This involves an uncompromising commitment to keep his law and to live in lifelong devotion to his service. The identical obligation is laid on the believer in the New Testament, where the dynamically equivalent Greek vocabulary denotes the importance of "walking in the Spirit," or "walking with Christ." The unique perspective of the New Testament demonstrates that in order to live in accordance with God's requirements and thereby please him, one must express absolute devotion and obedience to Christ.

WALL

OT Words

ḥômāh [חוֹמָה, 2346]

ḥômāh is a noun denoting a "wall" throughout most of its nearly 130 occurrences, in both a literal and figurative sense. ***ḥômāh*** is also used adjectivally.

Prov. 18:11 refers to a general, non-specified "wall." More commonly, the walls of a city are noted (e.g., Deut. 3:5; 28:52; Josh. 6:5; Isa. 2:15; Jer. 51:58; 2 Sam. 11:20ff.; Ezek. 26:4ff.). In particular, the walls of Jerusalem are mentioned in 1 Kgs. 3:1; 2 Kgs. 14:13; Neh. 1:3; 2:8ff.; 3:8ff.; 4:1ff.; Isa. 62:6; Jer. 1:15. ***ḥômāh*** is also used as an adjective in Lev. 25:29ff., referring to the "walled" cities of Israel.

Song 8:9ff. refers metaphorically to a "wall." Exod. 14:22, 29 refer to a "wall of water." A "wall" of protection for David's soldiers is indicated in 1 Sam. 25:16. Yahweh is depicted as a "wall of fire" around his people in Zech. 2:5. Then, in Amos 7:7, the prophet is shown a visionary "wall," depicting a symbolic divine assessment of the people of God that finds them grossly wanting.

qîr [קִיר, 7023]

qîr is synonymous with ***ḥômāh*** (see above), found in approximately seventy places with the primary sense of a "wall" of a building. ***qîr*** is also translated "side" in a number of places, referring to a "side wall."

qîr denotes the "walls" of Solomon's temple in 1 Kgs. 6:5ff. It also refers to the walls of a house (Lev. 14:37ff.; Ezek. 8:7ff.), and of a city (Num. 35:4; Josh. 2:15). Other general references include those in Num. 22:25; Isa. 25:4; Ezek. 4:3.

qîr also indicates the "side (wall)" of the tabernacle altar (Exod. 30:3; Lev. 1:15; 5:9), and of the altar of incense (Exod. 37:26).

gādēr [גָּדֵר, 1447]

gādēr is a noun denoting a "wall," "hedge," or "fence" throughout its twelve occurrences.

General references to a "wall" structure include those in Num. 22:24; Eccl. 10:8; Mic. 7:11. Ezek. 42:7 denotes the "wall" of the prophet's visionary temple. Isa. 5:5 refers to the "hedge" of a vineyard. Ps. 62:3 speaks of a "fence" in disrepair.

gādēr is also used in a number of figurative contexts. Ezra 9:9 refers to Yahweh as a "wall of protection" for his people. See also Ps. 80:12; Ezek. 13:5. In Hos. 2:6, Yahweh is said to build a "wall" around his people to block their pathway to freedom.

geder [גֶּדֶר, 1444]

geder is a rare variant form of ***gādēr*** (see above), found in only three places. It refers to a wall of stone (Prov. 24:31), and to the wall associated with the visionary temple of Ezekiel (Ezek. 42:10, 12).

shûr [שׁוּר, 7791]

shûr is a noun found in four places, designating a literal wall in each case (cf. Gen. 49:22; Ps. 18:29; 2 Sam. 22:30; Job 24:11).

kōtel [כֹּתֶל, 3796]

kōtel is a rare noun found only in Song 2:9, referring to "the wall" of a house.

ḥayiṣ [חַיִץ, 2434]

ḥayiṣ is another rare term indicating a "wall" in Ezek. 13:10.

ketal [כְּתַל, 3797 (Aramaic)]

ketal is the Aramaic equivalent of ***kōtel*** (see above), found in only two places. Ezra 5:8 refers to "the wall" of the rebuilt postexilic temple; and Dan. 5:5 refers to "the wall" of the royal palace in Babylon.

NT Words

teichos [τεῖχος, *5038*]

teichos is a noun found in nine contexts, denoting a "city wall" throughout. References to a literal structure include those in Acts 9:25; 2 Cor. 11:33; Heb. 11:30. In Rev. 21:12ff., ***teichos*** is used figuratively to refer to "the wall" surrounding the heavenly city of Jerusalem.

mesotoichon [μεσότοιχον, *3320*]

mesotoichon is a rare noun found only in Eph. 2:14, referring to the "dividing wall" of hostility that has hitherto kept Jew and Gentile from worshiping God together. Now, through the person and work of Christ, that "wall" has been broken down.

WANDER → ERR

WANT → DESIRE → NEED

WARFARE

OT Words

milḥāmāh [מִלְחָמָה, 4421]

milḥāmāh indicates the primary meanings of "war," or "battle," throughout its nearly three hundred occurrences.

Literal references to "war," or "warfare," in general terms include those in Gen. 14:2; Exod. 17:16; Num. 31:14ff.; Deut. 20:1ff.; Josh. 11:18ff.; Judg. 3:1ff.; 1 Sam. 14:20ff.; 1 Kgs. 5:3; Eccl. 3:8; Jer. 4:19.

milḥāmāh also denotes "men of war" (i.e., soldiers) (Num. 31:28; Deut. 2:14ff.; Josh. 5:4ff.; 8:1ff.; Isa. 3:2; Ezek. 27:27), as well as "weapons of war" (Deut. 1:41; Judg. 18:11ff.; Ezek. 32:27). The title "man of war" is given to David by God (1 Chr. 28:3).

Isa. 2:4; Hos. 2:18; Mic. 4:3 refer to the abolition of war as a consequence of divine renewal.

milḥāmāh also designates certain characteristics of Yahweh. He is described figuratively as a "man of war" (Exod. 15:3), and "mighty in battle" (Ps. 24:8). In several places he is depicted as one who controls "the battle" (cf. 1 Chr. 5:22; 2 Chr. 20:15; Ps. 46:9; Zech. 14:2), and also as one who trains and prepares his people for war (cf. Ps. 18:34, 39). Num. 21:14 refers to the "book of the wars of the Lord."

milḥāmāh also denotes specific "battles," or "wars," as in Num. 21:33; Deut. 2:32; Josh. 4:13; Judg. 8:13; 1 Sam. 4:1. In particular, civil war between an Israelite tribal coalition and Benjamin is noted (Judg. 20:14ff.), as is war between Israel and Judah (1 Kgs. 14:30; 15:6ff.; 2 Chr. 12:15). The battles between Israel and the Philistines are described in 1 Kgs. 14:30; 15:6ff.

ṣābā' [צָבָא, 6635]

ṣābā' is a noun with the predominant sense of "host" for the majority of its usage (approximately 450 occurrences). This meaning is commonly associated or identified with the phenomenon of "war," or "battle," including the meaning "army" in a number of places. The meanings "war," "warfare," "battle" are found in approximately fifty contexts. (→ ARMY)

General references to "war" or "battle" include those in Num. 31:3ff.; Deut. 24:5; Josh. 22:12; 1 Sam. 28:1. ***ṣābā'*** refers to "men of war," or "soldiers" (Num. 31:21, 32; 1 Chr. 12:8), and to weapons of war (1 Chr. 12:37). God promises to end warfare for his people in Isa. 40:2.

qerāb [קְרָב, 7128 (7129 Aramaic)]

qerāb is a noun denoting "battle," or "war," in seven contexts.

General references to literal conflict are found in 2 Sam. 17:11; Job 28:23; Pss. 68:30; 78:9; 144:1; Zech. 14:3. Eccl. 9:18 refers to weapons of war. Ps. 55:18ff. refers metaphorically to "battle" in the sense of "opposition," or "strife."

The identical Aramaic form of the term is rare, found only in Dan. 7:21 indicating "war" waged against the saints by the demonic "little horn."

NT Words

polemos [πόλεμος, *4171*]

polemos is a noun denoting "battle," "war," or "fight" in eighteen contexts.

General references to "wars" are found in Matt. 24:6; Mark 13:7; Luke 14:31; Jas. 4:1. Heb. 11:34 refers to those who are mighty in "warfare." The process of preparing for "battle" is described in 1 Cor. 14:8.

The book of Revelation makes a number of references to "war." Here ***polemos*** refers to war waged by Satan and his demonic servants against the people of God (Rev. 12:17; 13:7; 16:14; 20:8), including against the Messiah himself (Rev. 19:19); and to war in the heavenly realm between the archangel Michael and the dragon (Rev. 12:7). Rev. 9:7ff.; 11:7 depict demonic beasts arrayed for battle.

strateuomai [στρατεύομαι, *4754*]

This verb occurs in seven contexts with the primary sense of "to make war," "go to war," used in both literal and figurative contexts.

1 Cor. 9:7 describes "going to war" (i.e., serving as a soldier). 2 Cor. 10:3 refers to "waging war" in a literal sense. ***strateuomai*** refers to figuratively waging war against the spiritual forces of evil in 1 Tim. 1:18. Also in figurative contexts, ungodly passions are said to be "at war" in the hearts of believers (Jas. 4:1; 1 Pet. 2:11).

strateuomai is also given nominal force (i.e., in participial form) in Luke 3:14; 2 Tim. 2:4, referring to "soldiers" (i.e., those who go to war).

strateuma [στράτευμα, *4753*]

strateuma is a noun derived from ***strateuomai***, above, meaning "soldier," "man of war," or "army." It is found in eight contexts.

References to army "troops" or "soldiers" are found in Matt. 22:7; Luke 23:11; Acts 23:10, 27. Rev. 9:16 refers to visionary "men of war," and Rev. 19:14, 19 refer to the "armies" of heaven.

polemeō [πολεμέω, *4170*]

polemeō is a verb found seven times denoting the figurative action of "make war" or "fight."

The general sense of "fight" or "quarrel" is found in Jas. 4:2. The heavenly Christ gives a warning to "wage war" against the godless Nicolaitans of Pergamum in Rev. 2:16. The archangel Michael "wages war" against the dragon in Rev. 12:7. Rev. 13:4 notes the futility of human "opposition" against the satanic sea beast. Rev. 17:14 denotes the armies of Satan seeking "to make war" against the Lamb (i.e., the Messiah). And the messianic rider on the white horse "engages in war" against the enemies of God and his people in Rev. 19:11.

See Also: → FIGHT

WARM → HEAT

WARN

OT Words

zāhar [**זָהַר, 2094**]

zāhar is a verb occurring around twenty times meaning "warn" in the majority of this usage. (→ TEACH)

Warning someone of impending danger is indicated in 2 Kgs. 6:10. People are warned not to sin against the Lord in 2 Chr. 19:10; Ps. 19:11. Eccl. 12:12 warns against adding anything to the words of the wise. Part of the prophet Ezekiel's mandate is to take on the role of watchman, "warning" the people of Israel of the danger of rebelling against Yahweh (cf. Ezek. 3:17ff.; 33:3ff.).

yāsar [**יָסַר, 3256**]

yāsar is a verb expressing the dominant senses of "chasten," "chastise," "instruct" throughout most of its approximately forty occurrences. (→ ADMONISH →INSTRUCT)

The meaning "warn," however, is evident in several of these contexts. Ps. 2:10, for example, warns the kings of the earth against the folly of seeking to thwart the purposes of Yahweh. Isa. 8:11 contains God's warning to the prophet not to adopt the lifestyle of the people of Israel, who are under threat of imminent divine judgment. Similarly, God warns Jerusalem in Jer. 6:8 not to rebel against him, lest they be alienated from him and suffer harsh punishment.

nāgad [**נָגַד, 5046**]

The verb ***nāgad*** is a common verb with the primary meaning "tell," as well as a number of associated nuances throughout most of its nearly four hundred occurrences. Occasionally the meaning "tell" clearly implies the act of "warning" (cf. 1 Sam. 19:2ff.; 20:9; 2 Sam. 17:16ff.; 2 Chr. 20:2).

'ûd [**עוּד, 5749**]

This verb is found in around fifty contexts with the primary meaning "witness," or "testify," throughout. In Jer. 6:10, however, ***'ûd*** means "give warning" in the context of Jeremiah's vain hope that the people of Judah will hear his warning and turn from their sin. (→ WITNESS)

NT Words

prolegō [προλέγω, *4302*]

prolegō is a verb occurring three times meaning "warn," "issue a warning."

2 Cor. 13:2 refers to Paul warning the Corinthian congregation about a painful visit from him if they do not change their sinful ways. Gal. 5:21 warns that those who manifest a consistently sinful lifestyle will not inherit the kingdom of God. 1 Thess. 3:4 contains Paul's recollection of the warning he had previously given to this congregation that they would suffer persecution.

noutheteō [νουθετέω, *3560*]

This verb occurs eight times, meaning "warn," "admonish," "instruct." There is some overlap in meaning here, for in certain contexts "warning" and "admonishing" appear to be identical. In Acts 20:31, for example, Paul reports that he "has exhorted" or "admonished" the Ephesian congregation for three years with tears to maintain their faith in Christ. A similar use is evident in 1 Cor. 4:14; Col. 1:28; 1 Thess. 5:12ff.; 2 Thess. 3:15. In other contexts, admonition is linked to instruction (cf. Rom. 15:14; Col. 3:16).

chrēmatizō [χρηματίζω, *5537*]

chrēmatizō is a verb found nine times with the sense of "being warned (by God)" in about half of these contexts. (➡ REVEAL)

In Matt. 2:12, God warns the magi not to return to Herod after seeing the Christ child, but to go home another way. In Matt. 2:22, Joseph is similarly warned in a dream not to return to Judea with Mary and Jesus. Heb. 11:7 speaks of God warning Noah of the impending universal flood. See also Heb. 12:25.

hypodeiknymi [ὑποδέικνυμι, *5263*]

hypodeiknymi is a verb occurring in six contexts meaning "warn," or "show," throughout. (➡ SHOW) People are warned to flee from the coming judgment of God in Matt. 3:7; Luke 3:7. Jesus warns his hearers to fear God, who can cast someone into hell (cf. Luke 12:5).

WASH, WASHING

OT Words

rāḥaṣ [רָחַץ, **7364**]

rāḥaṣ is a verb meaning "wash," "bathe" throughout most of the approximately seventy contexts in which it is found.

rāḥaṣ refers generally to "washing or bathing oneself" in Exod. 2:5; Ruth 3:3; 2 Kgs. 5:10. See also 1 Kgs. 22:38. Gen. 18:4; Judg. 19:21; Song 5:3 refer to "washing one's feet,"and Gen. 43:31 refers to washing one's face.

Elsewhere, ***rāḥaṣ*** refers to "washing" in the context of ceremonial ritual — for example, for ceremonial cleansing of the body (Lev. 14:8; 15:5ff.; Deut. 23:11; Ps. 26:6). Exod. 29:4; 30:19ff.; 40:31ff.; Lev. 8:6; 16:4, 24ff. specifically refer to priests "washing themselves" in preparation for service. The bronze basin in the tabernacle is the primary vessel for ritual "washing" (Exod. 30:18; 40:30). Exod. 29:17; 40:12; Lev. 1:9, 13; 8:21 refer to "washing" animal carcasses prior to sacrifice.

Metaphorical references to "cleansing (lit., washing) oneself" from sin are found in Isa. 1:16; 4:4. See also Ezek. 16:4, 9. Ps. 58:10 mentions "bathing one's feet" in the blood of the wicked, denoting wholesale victory over such people.

kābas [כָּבַס, **3526**]

The verb ***kābas*** is found in approximately fifty places with the primary sense of "wash," in a variety of contexts. But it refers predominantly to "washing clothes" for ritual purification (e.g., Lev. 6:27; 11:25ff.; 14:8ff.; 15:5ff.; Num. 8:7; 19:7ff.). "Washing clothes" in a mundane context is indicated in Exod. 19:10; 2 Sam. 19:24.

shāṭaph [שָׁטַף, **7857**]

shāṭaph is a verb occurring about thirty times, meaning "overflow" in most of these contexts. In several places, however, the sense of "wash" or "rinse" is indicated. (➡ OVERFLOW)

In the context of ritual purification, Lev. 6:28; 15:12 refer to "washing or rinsing" pots in the tabernacle. Lev. 15:11 refers to "washing" hands. In other contexts, ***shāṭaph*** refers to washing human blood off a chariot (1 Kgs. 22:38), and to floodwaters "washing away" soil (Job 14:19).

dûaḥ [דּוּחַ, **1740**]

dûaḥ is a rare verb meaning "wash," or "rinse," in 2 Chr. 4:6; Ezek. 40:38, referring to the ritual washing of sacrificial animals prior to slaughter. In Isa. 4:4, ***dûaḥ*** refers metaphorically to "washing away" the sins of the daughters of Zion.

raḥṣāh [רַחְצָה, **7367**]

raḥṣāh is a rare verb indicating the "washing" of sheep in Song 4:2; 6:6.

NT Words

niptō [νίπτω, *3538*]

niptō denotes the literal action of "washing" in all seventeen occurrences.

niptō refers to "washing" one's face (Matt. 6:17); one's hands (Matt. 15:2, Mark 7:3); and one's feet (John 13:5ff.; 1 Tim. 5:10). In a miraculous cure of blindness performed by Christ, a man is commanded to "wash off" the clay from his eyes (cf. John 9:7ff.).

aponiptō [ἀπονίπτω, *633*]

aponiptō is found only in Matt. 27:24, referring to Pontius Pilate's public washing of his hands in order to declare himself innocent of the blood of Christ, whom he handed over to be crucified.

baptizō [βαπτίζω, *907*]

baptizō is a verb found in approximately ninety contexts with the primary sense of "baptize." However, in Mark 7:14; Luke 11:38, the term refers to the ritual of "hand washing" prior to eating. (→ BAPTIZE)

brechō [βρέχω, *1026*]

brechō is a verb occurring eight times with the primary sense of "rain." (→ RAIN) However, in Luke 7:38, 44, ***brechō*** refers to a persistent woman "washing," or "wetting," the feet of Jesus with her tears.

louō [λούω, *3068*]

louō is a verb found six times meaning "wash," or "bathe," in most of these contexts. Acts 9:37 refers to "washing" a corpse prior to burial; and "bathing" wounds is noted in Acts 16:33. In a metaphorical context, ***louō*** depicts bodies as "washed with pure water" in Heb. 10:22, denoting their symbolic cleansing from sin.

apolouomai [ἀπολούομαι, *628*]

apolouomai is a rare variant of ***louō***, above, referring to "washing away" sin in Acts 22:16; 1 Cor. 6:11.

plynō [πλύνω, *4150*]

plynō is another rare verb denoting the action of "washing" in only two places. Luke 5:2 refers to "washing" fishing nets. In Rev. 7:14, ***plynō*** refers metaphorically to "washing" the robes of the saints in heaven as a means of describing their purification.

baptismos [βαπτισμός, *909*]

baptismos is the noun derived from ***baptizō*** (see above), denoting "washing" in all but one of its four occurrences. Mark 7:4, 8 refer to washing household utensils. Heb. 9:10 refers to ceremonial "washings." (→ BAPTIZE)

loutron [λουτρόν, *3067*]

loutron is a rare noun denoting the metaphorical action of "washing" or "bathing" in two places. Eph. 5:25 mentions "washing" (i.e., "cleansing") the church by the word of God. Titus 3:5 describes conversion as "the washing" of regeneration, through the Holy Spirit.

Additional Notes

Both Testaments use "washing" terminology to describe the phenomenon of cleansing from sin.

In the Old Testament, the process of ritual washing is a precursor for priestly service. Priests were not to appear before Yahweh without the ceremonial purification that involved washing one's body as well as one's clothes. Such a process is a prelude to gaining atonement in the context of sacrifice for sin. Animal carcasses were also washed prior to sacrifice.

In the New Testament, the ritual significance of "washing" is transferred metaphorically to the work of the atonement affected by Christ, whereby the believer is cleansed from his sin. What was figuratively anticipated under the old covenant, through a literal ceremony, is brought to completion in the new as a direct consequence of the substitutionary sacrifice of Christ on the cross.

WASTE

OT Words

ḥārēb [חָרֵב, 2717]

ḥārēb is a verb with the primary meanings "lay waste," "dry up," "destroy," as well as several related senses. (→ DESOLATE → DRY)

shāmēm [שָׁמֵם, 8074]

shāmēm is a verb expressing the senses of "make desolate," "lay waste," "devastate." (→ DESOLATE)

shammāh [שַׁמָּה, 8047]

The noun ***shammāh*** is found in around forty contexts denoting "waste," "desolation," indicating that which is appalling and horrible.

The meaning "desolation" in the sense of "ruin," or "laying waste," occurs in various contexts with the common denominator of Yahweh, the agent of destruction, exercising judgment against the nations of the world. These nations include Assyria (cf. Zeph.

2:15); Egypt (cf. Jer. 46:19); Moab (cf. Jer. 48:9); Edom (cf. Jer. 49:17); and the earth in general (cf. Ps. 46:8; Isa. 5:9; 24:12). Israel is also targeted as an object of ruin or devastation at the hands of God (cf. Hos. 5:9; Mic. 6:16); as is Judah (cf. Jer. 2:15; 25:11; 29:18; Zech. 7:14).

tōhû [תֹּהוּ, 8414]

tōhû is a noun found in twenty places meaning "without form," "vain" for most of its usage. The meaning "waste," or "wilderness," is indicated in Deut. 32:10; Job 12:24; Ps. 107:40; Jer. 4:23.

shā'āh [שָׁאָה, 7582]

shā'āh is a verb found six times meaning "lay waste," "turn into ruin." 2 Kgs. 19:25; Isa. 6:11; 37:26 record the intention of Yahweh to lay waste the cities of Israel.

meshô'āh [מְשׁוֹאָה, 4875]

meshô'āh is a noun derived from ***shā'āh*** (see above), occurring three times. It denotes "desolate" or "waste" land in Job 30:3; 38:27. Zeph. 1:15 links this term to the Day of the Lord, describing it as a day of "ruin" or "devastation."

bātāh [בָּתָה, 1326]

bātāh is a noun found only in Isa. 5:6, describing the land of Israel as "waste" land — a result of God's judgment against it.

bālaq [בָּלַק, 1110]

bālaq is a rare verb found only twice. Isa. 24:1 refers to God's threat to "lay waste" the earth. In Nah. 2:10, Nineveh is described as having been "laid waste," or "turned into ruins."

māqaq [מָקַק, 4743]

māqaq is a verb with the primary meaning "waste away," referring metaphorically to the effect of sin upon the people of God (cf. Lev. 26:39; Ezek. 4:17). The underlying meaning suggests a state of spiritual or moral decay.

NT Words

diaskorpizō [διασκορπίζω, *1287*]

diaskorpizō is a verb with the dominant sense of "scatter," "scatter abroad." However, in two places it refers to "wasting" or squandering one's wealth or property (cf. Luke 15:13; 16:1).

See Also: → DESTROY → SPOIL

WATCH, WATCHMAN

OT Words

ṣāphāh [צָפָה, 6822]

ṣāphāh is a verb found in nearly forty contexts meaning "watch," "keep watch" in a variety of senses such as "look," "look about," "look after." It is also used nominally to refer to a "watchman."

When predicated of God, ***ṣāphāh*** means "watch" in the sense of "look after" in the so-called "Mizpah benediction" of Gen. 31:49. The context denotes the operation of divine care for his people. It also expresses the sense of "keep a close watch on" in relation to Yahweh's oversight of the nations (Ps. 66:7), and to his watch over the wicked and the good (Prov. 15:3).

When predicated of human beings, ***ṣāphāh*** indicates the action of "watching" in the sense of "look out for" in 1 Sam. 4:13; Ps. 37:32; Jer. 48:19; Lam. 4:17; Nah. 2:1. The term is also used nominally in several places, denoting a "watchman," usually in a military context (cf. 1 Sam. 4:14; 2 Sam. 13:34; 18:24ff.). See also Isa. 56:10.

"Watchman" is also used metaphorically, referring to those who convey the warning of God to his people (cf. Ezek. 3:17; 33:2ff.). It also refers to those who herald the return of God's people to Zion (i.e., the land of Canaan) (Isa. 52:8); and to the prophets of Israel (Jer. 6:17; Hos. 9:8; Mic. 7:4).

shāmar [שָׁמַר, 8104]

shāmar is a common verb occurring over 450 times with the dominant sense of "keep," "guard" for most of its usage. The meanings "watch," "observe" overlap with these two senses, although there are also other occurrences of these meanings. (→ GUARD → KEEP)

The meaning "watch" in the sense of "keep watch over" refers to people in 1 Sam. 19:11 and is predicated of God, indicating "keeping track of people's sins," in Job 14:16.

shāmar is also used nominally to refer to a "watchman" in general contexts (Ps. 130:6; Isa. 21:11; Song 3:3; Isa. 62:6; Jer. 51:12).

shāmar expresses the sense of "observe" primarily in the context of "keeping" or "obeying" the commands of God. (→ KEEP) However, ***shāmar*** also occasionally indicates other senses of "observe" (i.e., "to watch"). For example, Jer. 8:7 refers to birds instinctively "observing" their time of migration. Jonah 2:8 refers to the addictive "observing" of pagan deities by idol worshipers.

'ashmōrāh [**אַשְׁמֹרָה, 821**]

'ashmōrāh is a noun found in seven places denoting the "watch" of the night, or set times of the night ranging from evening till dawn (cf. Exod. 14:24; Judg. 7:19; 1 Sam. 11:11; Pss. 63:6; 90:4; 119:148; Lam. 2:19).

shāqad [**שָׁקַד, 8245**]

shāqad is a verb found in twelve contexts meaning "watch" throughout, with several associated nuances.

The action of "watching" in the sense of "guard" is indicated in relation to the valuable utensils of the temple (Ezra 8:29). Job 21:32 speaks of one "keeping watch" over a tomb. Jer. 1:12 indicates that God "keeps watch" over his word in order to fulfill it. He is said to do likewise over his enemies in order to bring about their ruin (Jer. 31:28); and to his people for their rebellion against him (Jer. 44:27).

The meaning "watch" in the sense of "be, lie awake" is indicated in Pss. 102:7; 127:1.

The sense of "wait expectantly for" is found in Prov. 8:34 in relation to wisdom, and also in Isa. 29:20 in regard to evil.

miṣpeh [**מִצְפֶּה, 4707**]

miṣpeh is a noun denoting a "watchtower," found only in 2 Chr. 20:24; Isa. 21:8.

'îr [**עִיר, 5894** (Aramaic)]

'îr is an Aramaic noun found three times meaning "watcher," or "messenger." It refers to a heavenly angelic being who mediates divine revelation to humankind (cf. Dan. 4:13, 17, 23).

nāṣar [**נָצַר, 5341**]

nāṣar is a verb found in sixty places meaning "keep," or "guard," throughout most of its occurrences. However, in several places ***nāṣar*** also has the nominal sense of "watchtower" (cf. 2 Kgs. 17:9; 18:8); and "watchmen" (Jer. 31:6). (→ KEEP)

NT Words

grēgoreō [γρηγορέω, *1127*]

grēgoreō is a verb occurring around twenty times with the primary meaning "watch," as well as a variety of related nuances.

"Watching" in the sense of "be vigilant," or "pay close attention to" is indicated in the context of waiting for the Day of the Lord (cf. Matt. 24:42; 25:13; Mark 13:35); and also in relation to "guarding" one's house (cf. Matt. 24:43; Mark 13:34; Luke 12:39).

Elsewhere, ***grēgoreō*** means "keep watch" in the sense of "be watchful, alert." Christ pleads with his disciples to "keep watch" with him in Gethsemane during his agony there (cf. Matt. 26:38ff.; Mark 14:34ff.). Such an exhortation is also given in relation to maintaining one's faith (cf. Acts 20:31; 1 Cor. 16:13; 1 Thess. 5:6; 1 Pet. 5:8; Rev. 3:2; 16:15). Col. 4:2 contains an injunction to be watchful in prayer.

grēgoreō means "to be, keep awake" in 1 Thess. 5:10.

agrypneō [ἀγρυπνέω, *69*]

agrypneō is a verb meaning "keep watch," "be vigilant, alert." It is found in four places. Mark 13:33; Luke 21:36 exhort believers to be vigilant in waiting for the return of the Lord. Eph. 6:18 enjoins believers "to be alert" in prayer. "Keeping watch" over the people of God in a pastoral context is indicated in Heb. 13:17.

paratēreō [παρατηρέω, *3906*]

paratēreō is a verb found in six places meaning "watch," "closely observe."

The Pharisees watched Jesus to see if he would heal on the Sabbath (Mark 3:2; Luke 6:7). See also Luke 14:1; 20:20. The enemies of Paul are said to "keep a close watch" on the city gates of Damascus in order to waylay him (cf. Acts 9:24). Gal. 4:10 refers to "keeping" or "observing" ritual festivals.

See Also: → GUARD → KEEP → PRISON

WATER

OT Words

mayim [**מַיִם, 4325**]

mayim is a common noun found in approximately six hundred contexts, denoting "water."

The meaning "waters" in the sense of "bodies of water" is indicated in relation to creation (Gen. 1:2ff.; Lev. 11:9ff.; Ps. 18:15), and to the Re(e)d Sea, the location of Israel's miraculous rescue from the Egyptian army at the hand of God (cf. Exod. 14:21ff.; 15:8ff.; Ps. 78:13). Gen. 6:17; 7:6ff.; 8:1ff.; Pss. 104:6; 106:11 refer to "flood waters." A spring, or well, of water is indicated in Gen. 16:7; 26:18; Judg. 1:15.

The "water gate" is a name given to one of the ancient gates of the city of Jerusalem (cf. Neh. 8:1, 3).

Other general references to "water" include those in Gen. 18:4; Exod. 7:15ff.; Num. 20:2ff.; Deut. 8:15; Judg. 4:19; Ps. 23:2; Dan. 1:12. God miraculously provides water for his people in the wilderness (cf. Neh. 9:15ff.;

Pss. 78:16ff.; 105:41). Exod. 40:7; Lev. 1:9ff.; 6:28; 15:6ff.; Num. 5:17ff. designate water for ritual use.

mayim is also used metaphorically in several places. It refers symbolically to places of suffering or trials (cf. 2 Sam. 22:17; Pss. 18:16; 69:1ff.). Elsewhere, water denotes a divine cleansing from sin (cf. Ezek. 36:25); and a consummate renewal of life (cf. Ezek. 47:1ff.; Zech. 14:8). It also symbolizes human wisdom (Prov. 18:4; 20:5); and salvation (Isa. 12:3). In Jer. 2:13; 17:13, God is described as the "fountain of living waters."

shāqāh [שָׁקָה, 8248]

shāqāh is a verb found in around eighty places with the primary meanings "drink," or "water," as well as several related nuances. In some contexts, the meanings "to drink" and "to water" overlap. (→ DRINK)

shāqāh refers to a river watering the earth (Gen. 2:6ff.); to rain sent by God to "water" the earth (Ps. 104:13); to drinking water for animals (Gen. 24:46; 29:2ff.; Exod. 2:16); to watering crops (Deut. 11:10); and to forcing people to drink (Exod. 32:20). Num. 5:24ff. records of legislation in which a woman is required to drink "bitter water" as a ritual test for sexual immorality.

In metaphorical contexts, ***shāqāh*** denotes God "watering" a vineyard that represents his people Israel (cf. Isa. 27:3). In Joel 3:18, a fountain from the temple is said to water the land of Israel and renew it.

mash'āb [מַשְׁאָב, 4857]

mash'āb is a rare noun denoting a "watering place" in Judg. 5:11.

zarzîph [זַרְזִיף, 2222]

zarzîph is a rare verb, referring to showers of rain that "water" the earth in Ps. 72:6.

NT Words

hydōr [ὕδωρ, *5204*]

hydōr is a noun occurring about eighty times with the consistent meaning "water."

hydōr refers generally to "water" (cf. Matt. 8:32; Mark 9:41; Luke 7:44; John 2:7ff.; 1 Pet. 3:20; Rev. 1:15; 16:4ff.). 2 Pet. 3:6 refers to "flood waters," and 2 Pet. 3:5 to created bodies of water.

Water is used for baptism (Matt. 3:11, 16; Mark 1:8ff.; Luke 3:16; John 1:26ff.; Acts 1:5; 8:36ff.; 11:16), and for ceremonial ritual (Heb. 9:19).

hydōr is used symbolically in several very significant texts. In John 3:5, Christ refers to the importance of being "born of water," indicating a cleansing from sin through personal confession. See also Eph. 5:26; Heb. 10:22. In John 4:10ff.; 7:38, Christ identifies himself as the source of "living water," symbolizing the gift of eternal life and peace with God. Rev. 21:6 refers to the "fountain (or river) of the water of life" in heaven (cf. Rev. 21:6; 22:1, 17).

hydria [ὑδρία, *5201*]

hydria is a rare noun denoting "water pots" in John 2:6ff.; 4:28.

hydropoteō [ὑδροποτέω, *5202*]

hydropoteō is a rare verb referring to "drinking" water in 1 Tim. 5:23.

anydros [ἄνυδρος, *504*]

anydros is an adjective denoting the quality of "waterless" or "dry" (cf. Matt. 12:43; Luke 11:24; 2 Pet. 2:17; Jude 12).

Additional Notes

The principal terms for "water" in both Testaments (viz. ***mayim*** and ***hydōr***) refer to "living water," symbolizing a renewal that is eternally refreshing. Both Yahweh and Christ are indicated as the ultimate sources of such "water," denoting an unbroken relationship of spiritual intimacy for those who partake of it (cf. Ezek. 47; John 4; Rev. 22).

See Also: → DRINK

WAVE OFFERING → OFFER

WAVE (NOUN)

OT Words

mishbār [מִשְׁבָּר, 4867]

mishbār is a noun denoting "waves" in all five occurrences, in both a literal and symbolic sense.

Literal references to "waves" of the sea include those in Ps. 93:4; Jonah 2:3. In Pss. 42:7; 88:7, God is said to stir up "waves," symbolizing trials for the believer. Similarly, in 2 Sam. 22:5, "waves of death" indicate overwhelming affliction.

bāmāh [בָּמָה, 1116]

bāmāh is a noun occurring around one hundred times with the almost exclusive sense of "high place."

In Job 9:8, however, ***bāmāh*** refers also to "waves" of the sea. (→ HIGH PLACE)

gal **[גַּל, 1530]**

gal is a noun found thirty-five times and meaning "waves" in about half of these contexts.

gal refers generally to "ocean waves" (cf. Pss. 65:7; 107:25; Isa. 48:18; Jer. 5:22; Ezek. 26:3). In Ps. 42:7, ***gal*** denotes "waves" as trials sent by God; and in Jer. 51:42, 55, "waves" describe the approach of enemy armies.

NT Words

kyma [κῦμα, *2949*]

kyma is a noun occurring five times. It refers to "waves of the sea" in Matt. 8:24; 14:24; Mark 4:37; Acts 27:41. In Jude 13, the use is symbolic, depicting the harm done by false prophets and teachers in the church.

salos [σάλος, *4535*]

salos is a rare noun denoting "waves" of the sea in Luke 21:25.

klydōn [κλύδων, *2830*]

klydōn is a rare term denoting "raging, storm-tossed waves" in Luke 8:24; Jas. 1:6.

WAY

OT Words

derek **[דֶּרֶךְ, 1870]**

derek is a common noun found nearly seven hundred times with the primary meanings "way," "road," "path," as well as a variety of related nuances.

derek means "way" with a variety of nuances. A general reference to "access" or "thoroughfare" is found in Gen. 3:24. More commonly, ***derek*** refers to a "road" or "highway" (Gen. 16:7; Exod. 23:20; Deut. 14:24; Josh. 2:7; Isa. 43:19; Ezek. 16:31); or a "journey" (Gen. 24:21; Exod. 3:18; Deut. 1:2; Josh. 9:11ff.; Prov. 7:19). The expression "on one's way" refers to one's departure on a journey (cf. Gen. 19:2; Judg. 19:27; 1 Sam. 26:25; Jer. 28:11).

More frequently, ***derek*** is used metaphorically. It denotes, for example, "way" in the sense of a spiritual or moral direction (cf. Gen. 24:48; Ezra 8:21), referring to that which is directed, given by God. Isa. 35:8 refers to the "highway" of holiness. Isa. 40:3; Mal. 3:1 anticipate the "way of the Lord," invoking the coming "Messianic King." In other contexts, "the way of God" denotes his perfection, or righteousness (cf. Pss. 5:8; 10:5; Isa. 55:8; Hos. 14:9).

The meaning "way" also commonly denotes a lifestyle consistent with the will and purpose of God. The contexts here are varied. Instructions and exhortations to keep God's "ways" are found in Gen. 18:19; Exod. 18:20; Deut. 5:33; 30:16; Isa. 30:21; Jer. 7:23. Pleas for God to teach human beings his "ways" are found in Pss. 27:11; 86:11; 119:33. God's "ways" are refused (Job 21:4; Isa. 42:4; Mal. 2:9); upheld (Ps. 18:21); and ignored (Jer. 5:4). Exod. 32:8; Deut. 9:12ff.; Ps. 95:10 record the failure to live by God's "ways." Deut. 28:9; Ps. 128:1 affirm the promise of blessings for those who adhere to the "ways" of the Lord.

derek also denotes "way" with reference to human lifestyle, also in a variety of contexts. General references to the "ways" of people include those in Job 31:4; Ps. 91:11. The "way" of wisdom is noted in Prov. 4:11. Ps. 37:5 speaks of committing one's "way" to the Lord. ***derek*** describes the "way" of the righteous (Ps. 1:6; Prov. 2:8, 20), and of the wicked (Pss. 1:1, 6; 35:6; Isa. 55:7; Jer. 12:1; Ezek. 3:18), which includes references to the people of God (cf. Jer. 2:33; 3:21; Hos. 4:9). Jer. 7:5; 26:13 contain exhortations to change one's "ways" (i.e., repent of one's sin).

mesillāh **[מְסִלָּה, 4546]**

mesillāh is a noun occurring thirty times meaning "highway," "road," "path," used both literally and figuratively.

Literal references to a highway or road include those in Num. 20:19; Judg. 20:31ff.; 1 Sam. 6:12; 2 Kgs. 18:17; Isa. 7:3; 36:2.

Metaphorically, ***mesillāh*** denotes a "way" in the sense of "life" or "lifestyle" (Prov. 16:17), and the way of the wicked (Isa. 59:7). The term also denotes a "highway" in Isa. 40:3 as part of the preparation for the coming of the Messiah.

'ōraḥ **[אֹרַח, 734]**

'ōraḥ is a noun found in sixty contexts meaning "way," "path," "road" in most of these occurrences, both literal and metaphorical.

Literal usage of ***'ōraḥ*** is relatively infrequent, denoting a "road," or "path," for example, in Gen. 49:17; Judg. 5:6. A "journey" or "direction" is indicated in Job 16:22.

More frequently, ***'ōraḥ*** is used figuratively, referring to "lifestyle" or "way of life." General references to "lifestyle" include those in Job 19:8; Ps. 119:9; Prov. 3:6; 5:6. ***'ōraḥ*** refers to the "path of righteousness" (Prov. 2:13; 8:20); the "paths of the righteous" (Prov. 2:20; 15:19; Isa. 26:15); the "ways of justice" (Prov. 2:8); and the "way of the wicked" (Job 8:13; Ps. 17:4; Prov. 1:9).

See also Ps. 119:128. The "way of the Lord" is indicated in Pss. 25:10; 44:18; 119:15; Isa. 2:3; Mic. 4:2.

NT Words

hodos [ὁδός, *3598*]

hodos is a noun occurring around one hundred times with the primary meaning "way" in the literal sense of "road," "route," "journey" and the figurative sense of "way of life," "lifestyle." It constitutes a clear dynamic equivalent for the OT entries above.

Literal references to a "road" or "(well-traveled) path" include those in Matt. 21:8; Mark 10:32; Luke 18:35; Acts 8:26. ***hodos*** refers to a "journey" (Matt. 10:10; Mark 6:8; Luke 2:44; 11:6; Acts 1:12); a "path" or "route" (Matt. 2:12; Mark 4:4; Luke 8:5, 12); and "access" to the temple sanctuary (Heb. 9:8; 10:20).

Figurative usage of ***hodos*** is more common. The meaning "path," or "way," for instance, refers to Christ's claim that he is "the way," affirming that the road to eternal life lies exclusively with him (cf. John 14:6). In contrast, Matt. 7:14 indicates that there is a "broad way" to destruction. Acts 16:17 refers to "the way of salvation," indicating access to eternal life and peace with God. Similarly, Luke 1:79; Rom. 3:17 refer to "the way of peace," implying a state of full reconciliation with God. The phrase "way of righteousness" in Matt. 21:32; 2 Pet. 2:21 refers to a righteous lifestyle. General references to people's "ways," both good and bad, are found in 1 Cor. 4:17; 12:31; Jas. 1:8; 2 Pet. 2:15; Jude 11.

The figurative "way of the Lord," as a prepared "route" for the coming of the Messiah, is indicated in Matt. 3:3; 11:10; Mark 1:2ff.; John 1:23 — all quotations derived from Isa. 40:3. Other general references to "the ways of God," denoting his methods of interacting with his people, include those in Rom. 11:33; Heb. 3:10. His own "righteous paths" are noted in Acts 13:10. In particular, "the way of God," as the divinely prescribed conduct for those who wish to follow him, is noted in Matt. 22:16; Mark 12:14; Luke 1:76; Acts 18:25ff.

Acts 9:2; 19:23; 22:4 describe early Christian disciples as "followers of the way."

See Also: ➞ PATH

WEAK, WEAKEN

OT Words

rāphāh [רָפָה, 7503]

rāphāh is a verb found in around fifty places with the underlying senses of "weaken," "be weak," also expressing the idea of "relax," "fail," "be feeble."

Prov. 18:9; Isa. 13:7; Jer. 49:24 refer to being weak or lazy. 2 Chr. 15:7; Zeph. 3:16 record the exhortation not to allow one's hands to grow weak (i.e., to take courage). Hands that weaken, with reference to the cessation of activity or work, are noted in Neh. 6:9; Jer. 6:24; Ezek. 7:17. The expression "weaken the hands," with the idea of "discouragement," is found in Ezra 4:4; Jer. 38:4.

rāpheh [רָפֶה, 7504]

rāpheh is an adjective derived from ***rāphāh*** (see above). It is found in four places meaning "weak," relating to lack of physical strength (Num. 13:18; 2 Sam. 17:2). In Job 4:3; Isa. 35:3, there is the exhortation to strengthen one's "weak hands,"or to take courage.

ḥālāh [חָלָה, 2470]

ḥālāh is a verb found seventy-five times with the predominant meaning "to be sick, ill." (➞ SICK) In several contexts, however, the term expresses the sense of "become weak," as in Judg. 16:7ff., with reference to Samson's admission to Delilah that cutting his hair would result in the loss of his superhuman strength.

rak [רַךְ, 7390]

rak is an adjective with the primary sense of "tender" in a variety of contexts. (➞ TENDER) However, in 2 Sam. 3:39 the term is incorporated in David's admission that he is "weak" (i.e., lacking in power, authority) at this point in time, though he is the anointed king.

dal [דַּל, 1800]

dal is an adjective with the predominant sense of "poor." (➞ POOR) However, in 2 Sam. 3:1, ***dal*** refers to the disgraced house of Saul growing "weaker and weaker."

NT Words

asthenēs [ἀσθενής, *772*]

asthenēs is an adjective with the dual senses of "weak," "sick," often overlapping in meaning. (➞ SICK)

The meaning "weak" has a variety of connotations. General bodily weakness is indicated in Matt. 26:41; Mark 14:38; 2 Cor. 10:10. Women are referred to in 1 Pet. 3:7 as the weaker sex. The designation "weak" refers to a lack of character (1 Cor. 4:10); to one's conscience lacking in conviction (1 Cor. 8:7ff.); to parts of the body lacking in importance (1 Cor. 12:22); and to the law, which is described in Heb. 7:18 as "weak," or lacking in effective power to deal absolutely with sin.

The weakness of people in relation to a spiritual impotence is indicated in Rom. 5:6; 1 Thess. 5:14. The designation "weak" is also applied to everything in the world that has no reputation (cf. 1 Cor. 1:27; 9:22; Gal. 4:9).

asthenēs is also used hyperbolically to indicate that the "weakness" of God is stronger than human strength (cf. 1 Cor. 1:25).

astheneō [ἀσθενέω, *770*]

astheneō is a verb occurring around forty times with the meanings "to be sick, or weak." (→ SICK)

"Being weak in one's faith" is indicated in Rom. 14:1ff. A passive use is indicated in Rom. 8:3, where the law is said to be "weakened" by the sinful nature, or rendered unable to deal effectively with sin. Other references to "being weak" include those in 2 Cor. 11:21ff., where Paul is said to be lacking in personal presence; and in 2 Cor. 12:10, where his weakness denotes a lack of power and strength. In 2 Cor. 13:3, Christ is designated specifically as one who is "not weak."

astheneia [ἀσθένεια, *769*]

astheneia is a noun found in around twenty-five contexts meaning "sickness," "weakness," "disease." (→ SICK)

"Weakness" in the sense of lack of strength or courage is indicated in 1 Cor. 2:3; Heb. 11:34. Bodily weakness is noted in 1 Cor. 15:43, where the expression "sown in weakness" indicates the finite limitations of the human body (cf. also Heb. 4:15; 5:2; 7:28). Such "weakness" describes the physical distress of Christ on the cross (2 Cor. 13:4).

"Weakness" is also linked with illness and powerlessness in 2 Cor. 11:30; 12:5ff.

adynatos [ἀδύνατος, *102*]

adynatos is an adjective found in ten places with the primary meaning "impossible" in the sense of "impotent," "powerless." (→ IMPOSSIBLE) ***adynatos*** also means "weak" in relation to those who are weak in their faith (Rom. 15:1).

WEALTH → RICH

WEAN

OT Words

gāmal [גָּמַל, **1580**]

The verb ***gāmal*** occurs around forty times and is translated "to reward," "recompense," as well as associated nuances. (→ REWARD) ***gāmal*** is also translated "to wean" in relation to children (Gen. 21:8; 1 Sam. 1:22ff.; 1 Kgs. 11:20; Ps. 131:2; Isa. 11:8; 28:9; Hos. 1:8).

WEAPONS → ARMS

WEAR, WEAR OUT

OT Words

nābēl [נָבֵל, **5034**]

nābēl is a verb found in twenty-five contexts with the dominant meanings "fade," "fade away," "wither." In Exod. 18:18, however, ***nābēl*** means "wear out" with reference to Moses' activity in adjudicating legal disputes for the people of Israel. (→ FADE AWAY)

lābash [לָבַשׁ, **3847**]

lābash is a verb occurring over one hundred times with the primary sense of "to clothe," "put on clothing." In several places, the related sense "to wear" (i.e., clothing) is also found (Deut. 22:11; Esth. 6:8; Job 27:17; Isa. 4:1; Zech. 13:4). (→ CLOTHE)

nāsā' [נָשָׂא, **5375**]

nāsā' is a common verb found in over 650 contexts with the dominant sense of "bear," "lift," "carry," as well as a variety of related meanings. (→ BEAR [VERB])

In addition, ***nāsā'*** means "wear" in the context of priests wearing the linen ephod (cf. 1 Sam. 2:28; 14:3; 22:18).

shāḥaq [שָׁחַק, **7833**]

shāḥaq is a verb found in four places meaning "beat," or "pulverize," in most of these. However, in Job 14:19, the term refers to water "wearing away" stones.

bālāh [בָּלָה, **1086**]

bālāh is a verb found in sixteen places with the meanings "grow old" and "wear out" overlapping in most of them.

Specifically, ***bālāh*** indicates "wearing out" clothing (Deut. 8:4; 29:5; Josh. 9:13; Neh. 9:21; Ps. 102:26; Isa. 50:9). In Isa. 51:6, the earth is said "to wear out."

bāleh [בָּלֶה, **1087**]

bāleh is an adjective denoting "old" or "worn out" sacks, clothes, and wineskins in Josh. 9:4, 5.

belô' [בְּלוֹא, **1094**]

belô' is an adjective referring to "worn out" clothes in Jer. 38:11, 12.

NT Words

phoreō [φορέω, *5409*]

phoreō is a verb expressing the dual meanings "wear" and "bear." (➡ BEAR [VERB])

Matt. 11:8; Jas. 2:3 refer to "wearing" clothing, and Christ "wears" the crown of thorns in John 19:5.

perithesis [περίθεσις, *4025*]

perithesis is a rare noun referring to "wearing" jewelry (1 Pet. 3:3).

endidyskō [ἐνδιδύσκω, *1737*]

endidyskō is a rare verb used in the negative in Luke 8:27 with reference to the Gadarene demoniac, who wore no clothes.

See Also: ➡ CLOTHE

WEARY

OT Words

'āyēph [עָיֵף, **5889**]

'āyēph is an adjective found in seventeen places meaning "weary," "exhausted," "faint."

The "weariness," or "exhaustion," of human beings is indicated, for example, in Deut. 25:18; Judg. 8:4ff.; 2 Sam. 17:29; Isa. 5:27; Jer. 31:25. Isa. 46:1 also speaks of the "weariness" of beasts.

yā'ēph [יָעֵף, **3287**]

yā'ēph is an adjective describing that which is "weary," or "faint." It is predicated of human beings in Judg. 8:15; 2 Sam. 16:2; Isa. 40:29; 50:4.

yā'aph [יָעַף, **3286**]

yā'aph is a verb found nine times, meaning "be, grow weary," "be faint."

God is said to "never grow weary" (cf. Isa. 40:28), and the same is said of young people who wait upon the Lord (cf. Isa. 40:31). People are said "to grow weary" in Isa. 40:30; 44:12; Jer. 2:24; Hab. 2:13.

'ûph [עוּף, **5774**]

'ûph is a verb found in approximately thirty places, meaning "to fly," "be weary" in most of them. (➡ FLY) The meaning "be weary" is found in the context of physical exhaustion in Judg. 4:21; 1 Sam. 14:28ff.; 2 Sam. 21:15.

yāga' [יָגַע, **3021**]

yāga' is a verb occurring around twenty-five times with the primary meaning "to work," including the associated senses of "labor," "toil," as well as "to grow weary," "faint." (➡ WORK)

yāga' refers to people "growing weary," in the sense of being "physically exhausted," in 2 Sam. 23:10; Ps. 6:6; Eccl. 10:15; Isa. 40:30; Isa. 57:10; Lam. 5:5.

Isa. 40:28 declares that God "shall not grow weary," nor shall young people who wait upon the Lord (cf. Isa. 40:31).

Elsewhere, ***yāga'*** means "to make weary" in the sense of "alienate," "make angry" in Isa. 43:24; Mal. 2:17, where Israel "wearies" God through their iniquities.

yāgēa' [יָגֵעַ, **3023**]

yāgēa' is an adjective meaning "weary," "exhausted" in Deut. 25:18; 2 Sam. 17:2; Eccl. 1:8.

yāgîa' [יָגִיעַ, **3019**]

yāgîa' is a rare adjective denoting that which is "weary" or "tired" in Job 3:17.

yegiā'h [יְגִעָה, **3024**]

yegiā'h is a rare noun denoting "weariness" in the sense of "physical fatigue" in Eccl. 12:12.

lā'āh [לָאָה, **3811**]

lā'āh is a verb occurring in nineteen places meaning "to grow weary," "tire oneself" in most of these occurrences.

The meaning "to weary" or "tire oneself" in general contexts is found in Gen. 19:11; Isa. 16:2; Ezek. 24:12. In Jer. 6:11; 20:9, the prophet is "tired" or "weary" of keeping the anger of God pent up inside him. The sense of "grow annoyed at" is found in Isa. 47:13. In this sense, God is said to be "weary" of Israel's sacrifices in Isa. 1:14, and also "tired of" tolerating Israel's sin in Jer. 15:6.

The sense of "make weary," "wear someone out" is found in Jer. 12:5. See also Mic. 6:3. In Job 11:7, the patriarch inappropriately accuses God of "wearing him out."

NT Words

hypōpiazō [ὑπωπιάζω, *5299*]

hypōpiazō is a verb meaning "wear out" or "wear down" as a result of verbal harassment in Luke 18:5. In 1 Cor. 9:27, ***hypōpiazō*** refers to the metaphorical "beating" of one's body in the context of self-discipline. There is arguably some overlap in meaning here.

ekkakeō [ἐκκακέω, *1573*]

ekkakeō is a verb found six times meaning "be weary" in the sense of "grow tired," or "lose heart" (i.e., give up all hope of accomplishing one's goal or maintaining one's faith). The term is always used in the negative.

The concept of never "losing heart" or "giving up" is found in Luke 18:1; 2 Cor. 4:1, 16; Eph. 3:13. The virtue of never growing weary in well doing is noted in Gal. 6:9; 2 Thess. 3:13.

kopiaō [κοπιάω, *2872*]

kopiaō is a verb found in thirty contexts with the primary sense of "to toil," or grow weary through hard work.

Undertaking "labor" in general, without necessarily "growing weary," is noted in Eph. 4:28; Phil. 2:16. More commonly, people's "toiling" is expended in physical exertion, as indicated in Matt. 11:28; Luke 5:5; John 4:6; 2 Tim. 2:6. The idea of "toiling" is also evident in the context of the work of ministry (cf. Acts 20:35; Rom. 16:6, 12; 1 Cor. 4:12; Gal. 4:11; Col. 1:29; 1 Thess. 5:12; 1 Tim. 4:10).

kopiaō is also used metaphorically in Matt. 6:28; Luke 12:27, where the plants of the field are declared not to have engaged in wearying labor or toil.

kamnō [κάμνω, *2577*]

kamnō is a verb found three times meaning "grow weary" (Heb. 12:3; Rev. 7:3); and also "be sick" (Jas. 5:15). (→ SICK)

WEDDING → MARRIAGE

WEEDS

NT Words

zizanion [ζιζάνιον, *2215*]

zizanion is a noun found in eight places denoting "weeds" throughout. ***zizanion*** most likely refers to "darnel," a plant that resembles wheat in its early stages of growth (cf. Matt. 13:25ff.).

WEEK, WEEKS

OT Words

shābûa' [שָׁבוּעַ, **7620**]

shābûa' is a noun occurring twenty times with the underlying sense of "a period of seven," referring to "periods of seven days" (i.e., weeks) or "seven years." This latter sense may be reflected in the use of the term in the book of Daniel, though commentators are divided on whether the expression "seventy weeks" is literal or figurative.

The meaning "week," as a literal period of seven days, is indicated in Gen. 29:27ff.; Lev. 12:5; Jer. 5:24; Ezek. 45:21; Dan. 10:2, 3.

The "Feast of Weeks" festival, so called because it takes place seven weeks after the Passover festival, is noted in Exod. 34:22; Num. 28:26; Deut. 16:9ff.; 2 Chr. 8:13.

The expression "seventy weeks" is found in Dan. 9:24ff.; and is literally rendered "seventy periods of seven." Whether or not this is a reference to a literal period of time is disputed.

NT Words

sabbaton [σάββατον, *4521*]

sabbaton is a common term for "Sabbath" in the New Testament, occurring around seventy times. However, in several places ***sabbaton*** means "week," specifically referring to the first day of the week. See also Matt. 28:1; Mark 16:2ff.; Luke 18:12; 24:1; John 20:19; Acts 20:7; 1 Cor. 16:2. (→ SABBATH)

WEEP, WEEPING

OT Words

bākāh [בָּכָה, **1058**]

bākāh is a verb with the primary sense of "weep," including the senses of "wail," "lament." In the 100 or so occurrences of the term, the contexts are occasions for both joy and sadness.

"Weeping" in the context of despair and sadness is indicated at the perceived threat of death (Gen. 21:16); at the pain of separation (Ruth 1:9, 14; 1 Sam. 20:41); and on the occasion of the death of loved ones (e.g., Gen. 23:2; 1 Sam. 30:4; 2 Sam. 18:33), and the passing of a leader (cf. Num. 20:29; Deut. 34:8; 2 Sam. 1:12). Other contexts for this kind of weeping include the invasion of Assyria and Judah c. 701 B.C. (cf. Isa. 33:7); Jeremiah's pain for his people (cf. Jer. 9:1; 13:17); and the destruction of the city of Jerusalem and the land (cf. Neh. 1:4; Ps. 137:1; Jer. 31:15; Lam. 1:2).

"Weeping" in sorrow for sin is noted in Ezra 10:1; Jer. 50:14 (cf. also Neh. 8:9).

"Weeping" is also evident as a consequence of material loss (cf. Gen. 27:38; Judg. 11:37ff.; 2 Sam. 15:23).

"Lamenting" the pain of divine punishment is indicated in Lev. 10:6; Num. 25:6; Deut. 1:45; Judg. 2:4.

"Weeping" on the occasion of idolatrous worship is recorded in Ezek. 8:14.

Other general references to "weeping in sadness" include those in Gen. 42:24; Num. 11:4; Deut. 21:13; Ezra 3:12; Esth. 8:3; Ps. 126:6; Joel 1:5. Exod. 2:6 refers to "crying" babies.

Less commonly, ***bākāh*** denotes "weeping for joy" (cf. Gen. 29:11; 45:14ff.; 33:4; 46:29).

bekî [בְּכִי, 1065]

bekî is a noun found twenty times with the primary sense of "weeping."

General expressions of grief in weeping include those in Gen. 45:2; Judg. 21:2; Ezra 3:13; Ps. 30:5; Mal. 2:13.

bekî refers to "weeping" in the face of trials and tribulation (Ps. 6:8); "mourning" for the dead (Deut. 34:8; 2 Sam. 13:36); "weeping" over the destruction of Jerusalem (cf. Isa. 22:4; Jer. 3:21; 31:15); and "weeping" with sorrow for sin (Jer. 31:9; Joel 2:12).

dim'āh [דִּמְעָה, 1832]

dim'āh is a noun occurring about twenty times, denoting "tears" throughout.

General references to "tears" of sadness include those in Pss. 39:12; 42:3; 80:5; 116:8; Isa. 16:9; Lam. 1:2; Mal. 1:13. In Isa. 25:8, Yahweh promises to wipe away such tears. Ezekiel is forbidden to shed "tears" in mourning over the death of his wife (Ezek. 24:16).

"Tears of anguish" associated with torment are evident in 2 Kgs. 20:5; Ps. 6:6; Eccl. 4:1; Isa. 38:5; Jer. 9:18. In Jer. 9:1; 13:17; 14:17; Lam. 2:11, "tears" are shed for the condemned people of God.

NT Words

klaiō [κλαίω, *2799*]

klaiō is a verb found in approximately forty contexts meaning "weep" in relation to "mourning" and "suffering."

klaiō refers to the outpouring of grief in weeping in a variety of contexts, including the loss of loved ones (cf. Matt. 2:18; 5:38ff.; Luke 7:13; 8:52; John 11:31ff.); bitter remorse for sin (cf. Matt. 26:75; Mark 14:72; Luke 7:38); Christ's compassion for the rebellious city of Jerusalem (cf. Luke 19:41); and the grief of the disciples over the loss of their Master (cf. John 16:20). Other general references to weeping are found in Luke 6:21ff.; 7:32; 23:28.

klauthmos [κλαυθμός, *2805*]

klauthmos is a noun denoting "weeping" or "wailing" in nine places.

Matt. 2:18 refers to "mourning" the loss of loved ones. "Weeping" as a consequence of suffering the judgment of God is recorded in Matt. 13:42; 22:13; 25:30; Luke 13:28. "Weeping" over the parting of friends and fellow believers is noted in Acts 20:37.

WEIGH, WEIGHT

OT Words

mishqāl [מִשְׁקָל, 4948]

mishqāl is a noun occurring around fifty times with the primary meaning "weight." (→ HEAVY)

The phenomenon of "weight" is evident in a variety of contexts. ***mishqāl*** refers, for example, to the weight of utensils for the temple (cf. 1 Chr. 28:14ff.; Ezra 8:30); ornaments or jewelry (cf. Gen. 24:22; Judg. 8:26); precious metals or money (cf. Gen. 43:21; Josh. 7:21; 1 Kgs. 10:14; 1 Chr. 22:14); military armor (cf. 1 Sam. 17:5; 2 Sam. 21:16); a royal crown (2 Sam. 12:30; 1 Chr. 20:2); and the prophet Ezekiel's hair (cf. Ezek. 5:1). In addition, Lev. 19:35 contains the command to administer just and accurate weights in commercial transactions.

shāqal [שָׁקַל, 8254]

shāqal is a verb expressing the dominant sense of "weigh," "weigh out." It also means "to pay" in several contexts. (→ PAY) ***shāqal*** occurs around twenty times.

The literal use of ***shāqal*** indicates "weighing out" precious metal or money for a commercial transaction (Gen. 23:16; Jer. 32:9ff.); "weighing out" wages for the shepherd of Israel (Zech. 11:12); "weighing" Absalom's hair (2 Sam. 14:26); and "weighing" precious metals for presentation to the temple (Ezra 8:25ff.).

shāqal is also used in a figurative use. For example, Job wishes that his anguish could be weighed in Job 6:2; and he also pleads that he "be weighed" in a just balance. ***shāqal*** is also predicated of God, who is said "to weigh" the mountains in his scales (Isa. 40:12).

tākan [תָּכַן, 8505]

tākan is a verb found nearly twenty times with the underlying meaning "weigh," in both a literal and metaphorical sense. The symbolic meaning "weigh" applies to examining or assessing people's actions.

God "weighs" (i.e., examines) humankind's actions (1 Sam. 2:3); heart (Prov. 21:2; 24:12); and spirit (Prov. 16:2).

2 Kgs. 12:11 refers to literally weighing out (i.e., paying) wages.

teqal [**תְּקַל, 8625** (Aramaic)]

teqal is an Aramaic term found only three times. In Dan. 5:25, 27, the nominal form ***teqēl*** is used, and is left in a transliterated form, "tekel," in English. The literal meaning of ***teqēl*** in these two verses is either "that which is weighed," or a "shekel." In Dan. 5:27, the verbal passive sense of "be weighed" refers to the divine examination of the Babylonian ruler Belshazzar, who is found wanting and will be subject to the punishment of Yahweh. This would lead to the takeover of the empire by the Persians and the death of Belshazzar.

'eben [**אֶבֶן, 68**]

'eben is a noun found around 270 times with the primary sense of "stone." (→ STONE) In several places, ***'eben*** also means "weights" in the context of commercial transactions. "Just, or accurate weights" are demanded by God in Lev. 19:36, and are used by him in Prov. 16:11. The crime of using two different weights in business is indicated in Deut. 25:13; Prov. 20:10, 23; Mic. 6:11. God condemns this practice.

—— NT WORDS ——

baros [βάρος, *922*]

baros is a noun found six times with the predominant sense of "burden," but it is translated "weight" in a figurative context in 2 Cor. 4:17. The context here refers to the glorious destiny of the believer in heaven that far "outweighs" all earthly afflictions during this life.

barys [βαρύς, *926*]

barys is an adjective found in six places meaning "weighty" in the sense of "important," "significant," in Matt. 23:23; 2 Cor. 10:10. (→ HEAVY)

WELCOME → RECEIVE

WELL

—— OT WORDS ——

be'ēr [**בְּאֵר, 875**]

be'ēr is a noun occurring around forty times with the dominant sense of "well," or "pit."

A literal "well," a place for drawing water, is indicated in Gen. 16:4; 21:9ff.; 29:2ff.; Exod. 2:15; Num. 21:16ff.; 2 Sam. 17:18ff.

The metaphorical sense of "pit" as a place of divine judgment for the wicked is indicated in Ps. 55:23. "Pit" is also a complex metaphor suggesting the experiences of "death," "silence," or "darkness," all in the context of a significant trial (cf. Ps. 69:15).

In addition, ***be'ēr*** signifies a "well," denoting one's "wife," the only one from whom her husband ought "to drink" (cf. Prov. 5:15). In Song 4:15, this reference to "well" signifies a new bride's sexual availability. In contrast, Prov. 23:27 refers to a prostitute as a "narrow pit."

—— NT WORDS ——

phrear [φρέαρ, *5421*]

phrear is a noun denoting "well," or "pit," in seven places.

A literal reference to "pit" is found in Luke 14:5; and John 4:11ff. indicates a "well" for drinking. ***phrear*** is also used metaphorically in Rev. 9:1ff. meaning "pit," referring to the entrance of the realm of eternal punishment.

See Also: → FOUNTAIN → PIT

WEST

—— OT WORDS ——

yām [**יָם, 3220**]

yām is a common noun occurring nearly four hundred times and meaning "sea," "west." These two senses are linked in that ***yām*** often refers to the Mediterranean Sea, which lies to the west of the land of Canaan. The meaning "sea" is dominant, accounting for the large majority of this usage. (→ SEA)

The meaning "west," in reference to the compass direction, occurs around seventy times (cf. Gen. 12:4; Exod. 27:12; 38:12; Ezek. 44:12; 42:19). The term is also used adjectivally in several places referring, for example, to the west wind (Exod. 10:19) and to the western boundary of the land of Canaan, the Mediterranean Sea (Num. 34:6; Josh. 15:12). See also Ezek. 48:1ff.

ma'arāb [**מַעֲרָב, 4628**]

ma'arāb is a noun with the exclusive sense of "west," "westward," found in fourteen places.

The general direction "west," "westward" is indicated in 1 Chr. 7:28; 12:15; 26:16ff.; Ps. 75:6; Isa. 43:5; Dan. 8:5. The western side of the city of David is noted in 2 Chr. 32:30.

mābô' [**מָבוֹא, 3996**]

mābô' is a noun occurring twenty-five times with the underlying sense of "going down." It refers in a number of these contexts to the "setting of the sun," which naturally is suggestive of a westerly direction. ***mābô'*** also means "entrance," or "entry." (→ ENTER)

The "setting of the sun" is indicated in Deut. 11:30; Josh. 1:4; Ps. 50:1; Mal. 1:11. The adjective "west" is linked with the direction "east," indicating "from everywhere" with reference to God's promise to deliver his people (Zech. 8:7).

NT Words

dysmē [δυσμή, *1424*]

dysmē is a noun referring to the region of the west in a number of different contexts. It is found five times.

The expression "from east to west" indicates origins from all over the world (cf. Matt. 8:11; Luke 13:29). The region of the sunset is noted in Matt. 24:27. A general reference to the west is found in Luke 12:54. The western gates of the heavenly city are indicated in Rev. 21:13.

WHEAT → GRAIN

WHEEL

OT Words

'ôphan [**אוֹפָן, 212**]

'ôphan is a noun denoting a "wheel" in most of its nearly thirty-five occurrences.

General references to wheels include those in Prov. 20:26; Isa. 28:27. ***'ôphan*** refers to chariot wheels (Exod. 14:25; Nah. 3:2); and to the wheels of the brass water carriers in the temple (1 Kgs. 7:30ff.).

Symbolic references to wheels are found in Ezek. 1:15ff.; 3:13; 10:6ff.; 11:22 in relation to the mysterious heavenly chariot-throne vision of Ezekiel.

galgal [**גַּלְגַּל, 1534**]

galgal is a noun meaning "wheel," as well as the associated nuance of things that whirl or roll (e.g., "whirlwind"). It occurs eleven times.

Ezek. 10:2ff. refers to a "wheel" in general, and Isa. 5:28; Jer. 47:3 refer to "chariot wheels." ***galgal*** also denotes, metaphorically, the "wheels" of the heavenly chariot-throne of Ezekiel's vision (Ezek. 10:2ff.).

galgal also denotes a "whirlwind" in Ps. 77:18 — an element of a theophany. The term also refers to grass blown by the wind, perhaps indicating "tumbleweed" (cf. Ps. 83:13; Isa. 17:13).

'ōben [**אֹבֶן, 70**]

'ōben is a rare noun denoting a "potter's wheel" in Jer. 18:3.

WHIP → SCOURGE

WHIRLWIND

OT Words

sa'ar [**סַעַר, 5591**]

sa'ar is a noun meaning "whirlwind," "windstorm," "storm," "tempest." There is a degree of overlap between these meanings. The term is found approximately twenty-five times. (→ STORM)

Literal references to a whirlwind are found in 2 Kgs. 2:11; Ezek. 13:11ff.

sa'ar also metaphorically denotes a "whirlwind" in Job 38:1; 40:6 as a vehicle for the theophany in which God rebukes Job. Isa. 40:24 also refers to a "whirlwind," denoting the means by which pagan rulers are "blown away" by Yahweh. ***sa'ar*** also refers to a "windstorm," again a vehicle of theophanic revelation of the heavenly courtroom to the prophet Ezekiel (Ezek. 1:4).

sûphāh [**סוּפָה, 5492**]

sûphāh is a noun denoting a "storm," "whirlwind," or "windstorm" in sixteen places. These meanings are interchangeable (e.g., Job 21:18; Prov. 1:27; Isa. 17:13; 66:15; Jer. 4:13). Hos. 8:7; Amos 1:14; Nah. 1:3 refer to a "whirlwind," indicating the destructive judgment of Yahweh.

See Also: → WHEEL

WHISPER

OT Words

lāḥash [**לָחַשׁ, 3907**]

lāḥash is a rare verb meaning "to whisper" in Ps. 41:7, citing the psalmist's fear that all who hate him "are whispering" together in a conspiracy against him. See also 2 Sam. 12:19.

NT Words

psithyristēs [ψιθυριστής, *5588*]

psithyristēs is a rare noun, found only in Rom. 1:29 with reference to those who "whisper" (i.e., gossip) about others.

psithyrismos [ψιθυρισμός, *5587*]

psithyrismos is another rare noun found only in 2 Cor. 12:20, referring to "whisperings" or "gossip."

WHITE

OT Words

lābān [לָבָן, 3836]

lābān is an adjectival form referring to the color "white" throughout its nearly thirty occurrences.

Mundane references to the color "white" include those in Gen. 30:35; Exod. 16:31; Eccl. 3:8. Zech. 1:8 refers to the white horses in Zechariah's visions. **lābān** is also used in Lev. 13:3ff. to describe the appearance of diseased skin as "white," or "bright," rendering the sufferer ceremonially unclean.

bûṣ [בּוּץ, 948]

bûṣ is a noun found in seven places with the literal meaning "byssos" — an expensive Egyptian-made fine white linen.

1 Chr. 4:21; Esth. 1:6; Ezek. 27:16 refer generally to "white linen" in mundane contexts. White linen is one component of the curtains in the temple (cf. 2 Chr. 3:14). White linen was also worn by the Levites and priests in the course of their duties (2 Chr. 5:12).

ḥûr [חוּר, 2353]

ḥûr is a rare noun denoting "white cloth or material" in Esth. 1:6; 8:15.

lābēn [לָבֵן, 3835]

lābēn is a verb with the underlying sense of "be, make white," and the extended sense of "purify." It is found in eight contexts.

The metaphorical expression "to be white as snow," referring to the state of purification from sin, is found in Ps. 51:7; Isa. 1:18; Dan. 11:35.

The passive sense of "be made white" refers to dead branches of a tree in Joel 1:7.

ḥiwwār [חִוָּר, 2358 (Aramaic)]

ḥiwwār is a rare adjective found only in Dan. 7:9, referring to the garment of the "Ancient of Days" in Daniel's vision as "white as snow."

ṣāḥaḥ [צָחַח, 6705]

ṣāḥaḥ is a rare verb meaning "to be radiant," giving the appearance of "whiteness," referring in Lam. 4:7 to the beauty of the leaders of Sodom and Gomorrah.

NT Words

leukos [λευκός, *3022*]

leukos is an adjective meaning "white," as a color and also with the sense of a "brilliant radiance."

General references to "white" are found in Matt. 5:36; Mark 9:3. In John 4:35, fields are declared to be "white for harvest," referring to people ready to receive the news of the gospel. **leukos** also refers to the "white throne" of judgment occupied by God (Rev. 20:11); to the "white horse," bearing Christ the King of kings (Rev. 19:11, 14); to another "white horse" symbolizing military conquest (Rev. 6:2); and to the "white cloud" bearing the Son of Man coming into heaven to receive his kingdom (Rev. 14:14). A number of texts refer to the "white linen garments" of the saints in heaven, signifying their purity (cf. Rev. 3:4, 5; 4:4; 6:11; 7:9, 13). See also Rev. 2:17.

Elsewhere, **leukos** means "white" denoting a brilliant, dazzling radiance. It refers, for example, to the appearance of Christ the King in heaven (cf. Rev. 1:14); to the appearance of Christ's garments during his transfiguration (cf. Matt. 17:2; Luke 9:29); and to angelic clothing (Matt. 28:3; Mark 16:5; John 20:12; Acts 1:10).

leukainō [λευκαίνω, *3021*]

leukainō is a rare verb meaning "to make white," "whiten." It refers literally to clothes in Mark 9:3, and metaphorically to the clothes of the saints in heaven, "made white" (i.e., "purified") in the blood of the Lamb (Rev. 7:14).

lampros [λαμπρός, *2986*]

lampros is an adjective occurring nine times with the underlying sense of that which is "bright," or "clean." Occasionally it refers to brightness of appearance in the sense of "dazzling white" (Acts 10:30). It refers to angelic apparel (Rev. 15:6), and to the clothing of the saints in heaven (Rev. 19:8).

koniaō [κονιάω, *2867*]

koniaō is a rare verb referring to the process of "whitewashing," or covering with lime to impart a white color to something dirty. It refers metaphorically to hypocritical leaders of the people who are likened to "whitewashed tombs" (cf. Matt. 23:27; Acts 23:3).

WHOLE, WHOLLY

OT Words

mālē' [מָלֵא, 4390]

mālē' is a common verb occurring around 250 times with the primary meaning "fill," "fulfill." In several places it expresses the related adverbial sense of "wholly," or "fully." (→ FILL)

Israel's failure to "wholly" follow the commands of Yahweh is noted in Num. 32:11. Joshua and Caleb are commended for "wholly" following the Lord (cf. Num. 32:12; Deut. 1:36; Josh. 14:8ff.).

kālîl [כָּלִיל, 3632]

kālîl is used nominally, adjectivally, and adverbially. It occurs fifteen times and means "entire," "perfect," "whole," as well as associated nuances.

The meaning "wholly," "all" (i.e., to the fullest extent) is indicated in Exod. 28:31; 39:22; Num. 4:6; Isa. 2:8. Burnt offerings are said to be "completely consumed" in Lev. 6:22, 23; Deut. 13:16; 33:10; 1 Sam. 7:9. The adjectival sense of "entire," "whole" is found in Judg. 20:4. (→ PERFECT)

NT Words

hygiainō [ὑγιαίνω, *5198*]

hygiainō is a verb meaning "to be sound," "be whole," as well as related senses. It occurs in twelve places.

The meaning "be whole" (i.e., healthy, well) is indicated in Luke 5:31; 7:10; 3 John 2. The term is also used adjectivally in the expression "safe and sound" (cf. Luke 15:27).

hygiainō means "sound," in the sense of "genuine," in relation to the teaching of Christ (cf. 1 Tim. 6:3), and to sound doctrine in general (cf. 1 Tim. 1:10; 2 Tim. 1:13; 4:3; Titus 2:1). Titus 1:13; Titus 2:2 refer to being "sound" in the faith.

hygiēs [ὑγιής, *5199*]

hygiēs is an adjectival form derived from ***hygiainō*** (see above). It is found in fourteen contexts with the primary senses of "whole," "sound," in predominantly literal contexts.

The meaning "whole" in the sense of "restored," "healed" occurs in the context of Christ's healing ministry. Here ***hygiēs*** refers, for example, to the restoration of a man's withered hand (cf. Matt. 12:13; Mark 3:5; Luke 16:10); to healing a man paralyzed from birth (cf. John 5:6; 7:23); and to the eradication of disease in general (cf. Mark 5:34; John 5:4). This sense is also found in the context of the apostolic healing ministry (cf. Acts 4:10).

hygiēs is also translated "wholesome," "pure" in relation to speech (cf. Titus 2:8).

See Also: → ALL → HEAL

WHORE → FORNICATION → HARLOT → PROSTITUTE

WICKED, WICKEDNESS

OT Words

rāshā' [רָשָׁע, 7563]

rāshā' is a noun occurring around 250 times with the predominant sense of "wicked" throughout. ***rāshā'*** also describes those who are "guilty (of sin)."

General references to the "wicked," those guilty of sinning against God, include those in Gen. 18:23ff.; Exod. 23:7; Pss. 1:1ff.; 37:10ff.; Prov. 10:7; Eccl. 8:10ff.; Isa. 53:9; Ezek. 18:20ff.; Mic. 6:10. There is no peace for the wicked (Jer. 5:26). Pss. 55:3; 119:95, 110 refer to the oppression of the wicked. Frequently, the wicked are declared to have been punished, condemned by God (e.g., Pss. 1:5; 9:5, 16; Isa. 11:4; Jer. 30:23; Ezek. 21:29; 33:8ff.; Mal. 4:3).

rāshā' also denotes "those who are guilty," deserving of death (cf. Num. 35:31; 1 Kgs. 8:32) and condemned by due legal process (cf. Deut. 25:1ff.).

rāsha' [רָשַׁע, 7561]

rāsha' is a verb occurring around thirty times meaning "to be wicked," "act wickedly," "declare guilty."

Exod. 22:9; Deut. 25:1; 1 Kgs. 8:32 refer to "declaring or finding someone guilty" in the context of a legal judgment. Job 32:3 also refers to such a judgment.

The sense of "act wickedly" (i.e., do evil) is evident in 1 Kgs. 8:47; 2 Chr. 20:35; Neh. 9:33; Ps. 106:6. ***rāsha'*** is used in the negative to refer to God (i.e., he "cannot do wrong") in Job 34:12 (cf. also 2 Sam. 22:22; Eccl. 7:17).

belîya'al [בְּלִיַּעַל, 1100]

belîya'al is a noun denoting "wickedness" or "lawlessness." It occurs about thirty times and refers primarily to "wicked" or "lawless" people. The term is also used adjectivally.

Deut. 13:13; Judg. 19:22; 1 Sam. 1:16; 2:12; 1 Kgs. 21:10; Nah. 1:15 refer to wicked people. Deut. 15:9 refers to a "wicked" thought; and Ps. 101:3 indicates anything "wicked" or "worthless."

resha' [רֶשַׁע, 7562]

resha' is synonymous with ***rāshā'*** and ***belîya'al***, above. It occurs thirty times and usually denotes "wickedness," "wrong," but it also refers to "wicked men" in a few instances.

Deut. 9:27 refers to the "wickedness" of the people of Israel, and Jer. 14:20 refers to the "wickedness" of the people of Judah. General references to "wickedness" are found in 1 Sam. 24:13; Ps. 5:4; Prov. 8:7; Eccl. 8:16; Ezek. 3:19. God hates wickedness, as affirmed in Ps. 45:7. Job 34:8; Ps. 10:15 refer to "wicked men." In Job 34:10, the charge that God "acts wickedly" is absolutely denied.

rish'āh [רִשְׁעָה, 7564]

rish'āh is a noun found fifteen times denoting "wickedness" or "guilt."

"Wickedness," in the sense of rebellion against Yahweh, is evident in a number of contexts. It is predicated of pagan nations (Deut. 9:4, 5; Mal. 1:4) and of individuals (Prov. 11:5; Ezek. 18:20; 33:12). Zech. 5:8 personifies "wickedness" as a woman. Other general references include those in Prov. 13:6; Isa. 9:18; Ezek. 5:6; 18:27.

rish'āh is also translated "guilt," with reference to an indictable offense under the law (cf. Deut. 25:2; Mal. 3:15).

rā'a' [רָעַע, 7489]

rā'a' is a verb with the predominant sense of "to act wickedly," "be wicked, bad or evil" throughout most of its nearly one hundred occurrences, as well as associated nuances such as "harm" or "punish." (→ BREAK)

References to "acting wickedly" in a morally offensive, vicious way are found in Gen. 19:7; 43:6; Judg. 19:23. Specific references to "evildoers" (i.e., those who act wickedly) are found in Job 34:24; Pss. 22:16; 37:1; Isa. 1:4.

The meaning "to harm" (or "do wrong to") is predicated of people in Gen. 31:7; Exod. 5:23; Num. 20:15; Deut. 26:6; 1 Sam. 26:21.

Isa. 65:25 refers to "doing evil, or wrong" in a nonspecific context. God is wrongly accused of ill-treating his people in Exod. 5:22; Num. 11:11. God "will bring harm" upon his people for their sinfulness (cf. Josh. 24:20; Jer. 25:29; 31:28). References to "doing wrong" in the context of breaking God's law are found in Lev. 5:4; 1 Sam. 12:25; 2 Kgs. 21:11; Prov. 4:16; Jer. 13:23; Mic. 3:4.

rōa' [רֹעַ, 7455]

rōa' is a noun denoting "wickedness," "evil" relating to unethical behavior and violation of divine statutes. It is found in nineteen contexts.

"Wickedness" as a violation of divine law is noted in Deut. 28:20, where Israel is warned of the covenant curses that will inevitably follow upon their "wickedness." Specific divine condemnation for such wickedness is recorded in Isa. 1:16; Jer. 4:4; 21:12; Hos. 9:15. The general wickedness of the human heart is indicated in 1 Sam. 17:28.

rōa' is also used adjectivally to mean "bad" in the sense of "morally corrupt." The context is a metaphorical one, where "bad (or rotten) figs" signify the moral corruption of the people of Judea (cf. Jer. 24:2ff.; 29:17).

mirsha'at [מִרְשַׁעַת, 4849]

mirsha'at is a rare noun found only in 2 Chr. 24:7, with reference to Queen Athaliah as a "wicked woman."

'ānash [אָנַשׁ, 605]

'ānash is a verb with the root meaning "be incurable" in relation to both physical illness and unrelenting sorrow. Jer. 17:9 describes the human heart as being "incurable," or "beyond cure." The underlying sense is that it is "incurably wicked."

zimmāh [זִמָּה, 2154]

zimmāh is a verb that occurs about thirty times. It is used predominantly with nominal force, referring to "wickedness," primarily in the sense of "lewd, or immoral conduct."

"Wickedness" denotes "immorality" in the following contexts with reference to illicit sexual intimacy (cf. Lev. 18:17; 19:29; 20:14; Judg. 20:6; Job 31:11). In addition, the "wickedness" of idolatry committed by the people of God is evident in Jer. 13:27; Ezek. 16:27, 43, 58; 22:9, 11; 23:21ff.; 24:13; Hos. 6:9.

zimmāh also refers to the "wicked schemes" of evil people (Pss. 26:10; 119:150; Isa. 32:7), and to "evil intent" (Prov. 21:27).

'awwāl [עַוָּל, 5767]

'awwāl is a noun found in five places, denoting those who are "wicked," "ungodly," or "unrighteous" (cf. Job 18:21; 27:7; 29:17; 31:3; Zeph. 3:5).

NT Words

anomos [ἄνομος, *459*]

anomos is an adjective occurring ten times with the fundamental sense of "lawless," referring to those who violate the law of God. It may also be rendered "wicked" and is used both nominally and adjectivally.

Acts 2:23; 2 Pet. 2:8 refer generally to that which is "lawless," or "wicked." Nominal references to "the wicked" or "lawless ones" are found in Mark 15:28; Luke 22:37; 1 Cor. 9:21; 1 Tim. 1:9. In particular, 2 Thess. 2:8 refers to "the antichrist" as "the lawless one."

athesmos [ἄθεσμος, *113*]

athesmos is a rare noun found only twice. In 2 Pet. 2:7; 3:17 it refers to "wicked, or lawless people" and to morally depraved, false teachers, respectively.

ponēria [πονηρία, *4189*]

ponēria is a noun denoting "wickedness" with several different nuances in the seven occurrences of the term. A general designation of "depravity" or "iniquity" underlying the sense of "wickedness" is evident in Mark 7:22; Luke 11:39; Rom. 1:29; 1 Cor. 5:8. "Lawlessness" in the context of rebellion against God is indicated in Acts 3:26. Matt. 22:18 refers to "wickedness" in the sense of "malice." "Wickedness" is also predicated of demonic spirits in Eph. 6:12.

See Also: → EVIL → INIQUITY

WIDE → BROAD

WIDOW

OT Words

'almānāh [אַלְמָנָה, **490**]

'almānāh is a noun occurring around fifty times, consistently translated "widow."

Literal references to "widows" in general contexts are found in Gen. 38:11; 1 Sam. 14:5; 1 Kgs. 17:9ff.; Job 24:21. Mosaic legislation concerning the status, protection, and care of such women is recorded in Exod. 22:22; Lev. 21:14; 22:13; Deut. 10:18; 24:17ff.; 26:12ff.; 27:19. In Isa. 1:17; Jer. 22:13 there are exhortations to protect widows; and Pss. 68:5; 146:9; Prov. 15:25 note that widows are guaranteed protection by God. Conversely, the exploitation and mistreatment of widows are indicated in Isa. 10:2; Jer. 7:6; Ezek. 22:7. The status of widowhood is designated occasionally as the consequence of divine judgment (cf. Exod. 22:24; Jer. 18:21).

'almānāh is also used figuratively in Isa. 47:8, referring to the kingdom of Babylon, whose rulers arrogantly deny that they will ever be "widowed." In Lam. 1:1, Jerusalem herself declares that she has become a "widow" in the aftermath of invasion by the Babylonians.

'almenût [אַלְמְנוּת, **491**]

'almenût is the rare plural noun derived from ***'almānāh*** (see above), meaning "widowhood." It is used literally (Gen. 38:14, 19; 2 Sam. 20:3), and also refers figuratively to Jerusalem in Isa. 54:4, denoting the period of her exile.

'almōn [אַלְמֹן, **489**]

'almōn is a rare noun found only in Isa. 47:9, referring to "widowhood" (i.e., loss of land and exile) imposed on the people of Israel as a divine punishment for rebellion against Yahweh.

NT Words

chēra [χήρα, *5503*]

chēra is a noun occurring around thirty times. It means "widow" in both literal and figurative contexts, though the latter use is rare.

General references to "widows" as a social class are found in Matt. 23:14; Mark 12:40ff.; Luke 4:25ff.; Acts 6:1; 1 Cor. 7:8; 1 Tim. 5:3ff.; Jas. 1:27; and individual women in this category are described in Luke 2:37; 18:3ff.; 21:2.

chēra is also used metaphorically to refer to the city of Babylon in Rev. 18:7, indicating that it is stripped of all power and authority.

WIFE

OT Words

'ishshāh [אִשָּׁה, **802**]

'ishshāh is a very common noun occurring nearly eight hundred times with usage fairly evenly divided between the meanings of "woman" and "wife." (→ WOMAN) In a number of contexts, references to "wife" and "woman" are synonymous.

The natural sense of "wife" is found in general contexts such as Gen. 4:19; Exod. 4:20; Josh. 1:14; Judg. 15:1, 6; Ezra 2:61; Ps. 128:3. In particular, Gen. 2:24ff.; 3:20 refer to Eve as the wife of Adam, constituting the first divinely ordained married couple in creation. A wife is designated as her husband's sexual partner in Gen. 4:1, 17; Prov. 5:18. Canaanite women are forbidden to the sons of Israel as wives (Gen. 28:16; Ezra 10:2ff.). However, other foreign women may be taken as wives (Deut. 21:11ff.; 22:13ff.; Ruth 4:5). See also Prov. 19:14; 31:10.

Instructions in the law concerning "wives" are evident in Exod. 21:3ff.; Lev. 18:8ff.; 20:10ff.; Num. 5:12ff.; Deut. 5:21; 24:1ff.; 28:30. The sexual violation of Israelite wives is depicted as a judgment from God for the people's rebellion against him (Isa. 13:16; Zech. 14:2). The process of divorcing one's wife is recorded in Jer. 3:1; 8:10. Wives of Israelite men guilty of idolatry are noted in Jer. 44:9, 15.

In several contexts, ***'ishshāh*** is used figuratively for Israel and Judah's idolatrous rejection of Yahweh — a wife guilty of adultery (Jer. 3:20; 5:8; Ezek. 16:32; Hos. 1:2; 2:2).

'ishshāh also denotes a "wife" in a number of contexts. In Gen. 2:24ff., Eve is created by God as a "wife" for Adam. Other general references to "wives" include those in Gen. 4:17ff.; 11:29ff.; Exod. 6:20ff.; Judg. 4:4; Ruth 4:4ff.; 1 Sam. 25:3ff.; 2 Sam. 11:3ff.; Ezra 2:61; Ps. 109:9; Prov. 5:18; Jer. 8:10; 44:9ff. In particular, the many "foreign wives" of Solomon who led him astray into idolatry are mentioned in 1 Kgs. 1:1ff. See also Ezra 10:1ff. "Wives" who commit adultery are found in Ezek. 16:32; Hos. 1:2; 3:1; Amos 7:17.

Elsewhere, legislation concerning "wives" and the sanctity of marriage is recorded in Exod. 20:17; 21:3ff.; Lev. 18:8ff.; Num. 5:12ff.; Deut. 5:12; 22:14ff.; 24:1ff.; Jer. 3:1; Mal. 2:14.

bā'al **[בָּעַל, 1166]**

bā'al is a verb found on sixteen occasions with the underlying sense of "marry," and sometimes a "husband." In several places, the term refers to a "married woman" (Gen. 20:3; Prov. 30:23). ***bā'al*** is also used metaphorically to refer to the people of God in intimate relationship with Yahweh, as wife to husband (Isa. 54:1; 62:4).

neshîn **[נְשִׁין, 5389** (Aramaic)**]**

neshîn is a rare noun found only in Dan. 6:24 with reference to "wives."

NT Words

gunē **[γυνή,** ***1135*****]**

gunē is a noun found in over 200 contexts, a dynamic equivalent for ***'ishshāh*** with the dual meanings of "woman," "wife." (→ WOMAN) Again, as with the Hebrew term, there is overlap between these two senses.

Literal references to individual women as wives include those in Matt. 1:20; 5:31; Mark 6:18. Other general references to wives are found in Matt. 22:24ff.; Mark 12:20; Luke 20:29; Rom. 7:21; 1 Cor. 5:1. The creation ordinance of marriage in which "a husband is joined to his wife" is referred to in Matt. 19:5; Mark 10:7.

"Levirate marriage" is referred to in Matt. 22:24ff.; Mark 12:9ff.; Luke 20:28ff. This cultural practice advocated the remarriage of a childless widowed woman to the closest eligible male relative of her deceased husband, so that she could have children by him in order to preserve the family line of her first husband (Eph. 5:22; Col. 3:18ff.; 1 Pet. 3:1).

gunē is used metaphorically in Rev. 19:7; 21:9, referring to the church as the "bride," the "wife" of Christ, the Lamb.

Additional Notes

The vocabulary referring to married women as "wives" throughout both the Old and New Testaments in a number of contexts carries significant theological weight when describing the nature of Israel's relationship with her God. The metaphor of Israel bound to Yahweh in an intimate covenantal relationship as "wife" to "husband" is a very powerful one.

For this reason, the Old Testament writers and prophets view Israel's worship of idols as tantamount to "spiritual adultery" — an attitude and act of betrayal akin to a wife betraying her husband through marital infidelity.

The magnitude of God's mercy and compassion towards his sinful people is demonstrated supremely in the New Testament through the powerful transfer of this marriage metaphor from Yahweh and Israel to Christ and the church. The significant difference in the New Testament is that the redemptive work of Christ results in a perfect consummation of the spiritual intimacy between himself and his people, the church. This relationship will never again be destroyed by "marital infidelity" on the part of the people of God. Significantly, the supreme metaphors of Christ as "bridegroom" and people as "bride" are found in the climactic chapters of the book of Revelation.

See Also: → MARRY

WILD

OT Words

sādeh **[שָׂדֶה, 7704]**

sādeh is a common noun occurring around 330 times with the principal meaning "field." (→ FIELD) However, in several places it has the adjectival sense of "wild."

"Wild beasts," literally "beasts of the field," are found in Lev. 26:22; 2 Kgs. 14:9; Job 39:15. 2 Kgs. 4:39 refers to "wild" plants.

NT Words

agrios [ἄγριος, *66*]

agrios is a rare adjective referring to "wild" or "uncultivated" honey in Matt. 3:4; Mark 1:6.

thērion [θηρίον, *2342*]

thērion is a noun with the general sense of "beast" throughout its nearly fifty occurrences. In several places it refers explicitly to "wild beasts" (cf. Mark 1:13; Acts 10:12; 11:6).

agrielaios [ἀγριέλαιος, *65*]

agrielaios is a rare noun denoting a "wild olive tree," used metaphorically to refer to all Gentile believers who have been brought into the kingdom of God, "grafted onto the olive tree" that represents the Israelite nation (cf. Rom. 11:17, 24).

WILDERNESS → DESERT → PLAIN

WILL, WILLING

OT Words

rāṣôn [רָצוֹן, **7522**]

rāṣôn is a noun with a range of meanings including "favor," "delight," "pleasure," and "will," as well as other related nuances. (→ DELIGHT → FAVOR)

rāṣôn denotes the "will" of God in the sense of his "good pleasure" (cf. Pss. 51:18; 103:21; Ezra 10:11). In Pss. 40:8; 143:10 the psalmist affirms his delight to do the will of God.

The meaning "will" in the sense of one's wish or desire is indicated in Neh. 9:24; Esth. 1:8; Dan. 11:16, 36. References to "doing as one wishes, or pleases" are found in Neh. 9:37; Esth. 9:8; Dan. 8:4.

'ābāh [אָבָה, **14**]

'ābāh is a verb occurring around fifty times with the underlying primary meaning "to be willing," "consent." The overwhelming majority of the usage is negative.

General references to "being unwilling" or "refusing" are found in Gen. 24:5ff.; Exod. 10:27; Deut. 2:30; Judg. 11:17; 1 Sam. 26:23; 2 Sam. 13:14ff. In Deut. 13:8 there is a refusal to show mercy. More significantly, refusing to obey God or listen to him is recorded in Lev. 26:21; Deut. 1:26; 1 Sam. 15:9; Ps. 81:11; Isa. 28:12; 42:24; Ezek. 3:7; 20:8.

'ābāh is also predicated of God in a number of places. Deut. 10:10; 2 Kgs. 8:19; 13:23 affirm that Yahweh is unwilling to destroy his people. Yahweh refuses to listen to Balaam in Deut. 23:5. In Deut. 29:20, he is said to refuse to show mercy, and in 2 Kgs. 24:4 he refuses to pardon.

Isa. 1:19 records a conditional statement to the effect that the people's enjoyment of the land is linked to their willingness to be obedient to God.

mā'ēn [מָאֵן, **3985**]

mā'ēn is a verb occurring around forty times with the consistent meaning "to refuse," "be unwilling." (→ REFUSE)

nādab [נָדַב, **5068**]

nādab is a verb found seventeen times with the underlying sense of "to give freely" or "make offerings to God with a willing heart" (cf. Judg. 5:29; 1 Chr. 29:5ff.; Ezra 1:6; 2:68; 3:5). See also Neh. 11:2.

NT Words

thelō [θέλω, *2309*]

thelō is a dynamic equivalent for the Hebrew verb ***'ābāh*** (see above). The underlying sense is that of to "be willing," "desire," "want," or "wish." As with ***'ābāh***, this term is also used in the negative and is therefore translated "be unwilling," "refuse." With ***thelō***, however, positive and negative usage is more evenly distributed.

thelō occurs in a number of places with the general negative sense of "be unwilling," "refuse" (cf. Matt. 1:19; 21:29; Luke 15:28; 18:13; 1 Cor. 12:1; Gal. 1:7; 1 Thess. 2:18). In particular, John 5:40 speaks of a refusal to come to Christ. Heb 10:5ff. affirms that God "does not want" sacrifices and offerings without an accompanying godly motive.

Elsewhere, ***thelō*** is used positively to indicate the desire to see something done, and is translated thus "to want, or wish." Such a desire is predicated of human beings in Matt. 5:40ff.; 12:23; Mark 6:19; Luke 8:20; 9:23ff.; John 5:6; 8:44; Acts 7:28. In particular, Rom. 7:15ff. refers to Paul's dilemma in not doing what he "wants to do" (cf. also Gal. 5:17); and 2 Tim. 3:12 refers to people "wanting" to live a godly life.

thelō is also used in relation to Christ (cf. Matt. 8:2ff.; Mark 3:13; John 21:23). In particular, Christ is said to yield to the "will" and purpose of the Father (Mark 14:36). Luke 4:6 affirms that Christ delivers authority to whomever "he wills"; and John 5:21 declares that he gives life to whomever "he wills." See also John 17:24.

God is said, for example, to "desire" mercy (Matt. 12:7). Rom. 9:18 declares that God has mercy on whomever he "wills." 1 Tim. 2:4 expresses God's general "desire" that all people will be saved. Phil. 2:13 refers to God's "will" (or purpose) in nurturing believers in a life that will please him. See also Acts 18:21; 1 Cor. 4:19; Jas. 4:15.

thelō also refers metaphorically to the wind in John 3:8, where Christ declares that it blows "wherever it wills."

thelēma [θέλημα, *2307*]

thelēma is a noun derived from ***thelō*** (see above), found in around sixty contexts with the primary meaning "will." The term refers primarily to "that which is desired or intended" and is predicated of both human beings and God. ***thelēma*** has primary reference, however, to the will of God.

References to God's "will," "purpose," or "intent" are varied. Matt. 6:10; Luke 11:2; Acts 21:14 plead for God's will to be done. Those who do "the will" of God are noted in Matt. 7:21; Mark 3:35; Eph. 6:6; 1 John 2:17. And Matt. 26:42; Luke 22:42 refer to Christ's submission to "God's will" in Gethsemane. Christ's determination to do his Father's "will" is expressed in John 4:34; 5:30; 6:3ff.; Heb. 10:9. The "will" of God in relation to the plan of salvation is expressed in Eph. 1:5ff. Knowing the "will of God" is indicated in Rom. 2:18; 12:2. Being called to service by "the will of God" is noted in 1 Cor. 1:1; Eph. 1:1; Col. 1:1; 2 Tim. 1:1. See also 1 Thess. 4:3; 1 Pet. 2:15; Rev. 4:11.

Luke 12:47 refers generally to the "will" of humankind in relation to "desire." See also John 1:13. The evil "purpose" of the Jewish religious leaders plotting to do away with Christ is noted in Luke 23:25.

thelēsis [θέλησις, *2308*]

thelēsis is a rare variant of ***thelēma*** (see above), found only in Heb. 2:4 with reference to the "will" of God that determines the distribution of spiritual gifts to his people.

boulomai [βούλομαι, *1014*]

boulomai is a synonym for ***thelō*** (see above). It occurs about thirty times and expresses the underlying meaning "to will" in the sense of "express a purpose, intention, or desire." It is occasionally used in the negative.

The meaning "to be unwilling" is indicated in Matt. 1:19 in relation to human beings. With respect to God, 2 Pet. 3:9 declares that he is "not willing" that any should perish. In this case, the divine attitude is thought to be characterized by a general desire rather than an explicit purpose.

The meaning "to will" in the sense of "choose," "make a choice," is predicated of Christ in Matt. 11:27; Luke 10:22. In 1 Cor. 12:11, God "chooses" to give various gifts to this people.

The meaning "be willing," or "wish," is predicated of people in general terms (Mark 15:15; Acts 17:20; Jas. 4:4), and also of God (Luke 22:42; Heb. 6:17).

boulomai is also translated "to be determined," "intend" with reference to people (Acts 5:28) and God (Jas. 1:18).

boulēma [βούλημα, *1013*]

boulēma is a rare noun meaning "will," or "purpose." The people's "purpose" (or intention) is indicated in Acts 27:43. God's will or purpose is said to be irresistible in Rom. 9:19. (→ PURPOSE)

eudokeō [εὐδοκέω, *2106*]

eudokeō is a verb found around twenty times with the underlying sense of "be pleased with," or "be willing" (i.e., take pleasure in).

The meaning "be pleased with" refers to God's estimation of his son, Jesus Christ (cf. Matt. 3:17; 12:18; 17:5; Mark 1:11; Luke 3:22; 2 Pet. 1:17).

Elsewhere, ***eudokeō*** is translated "to be willing" with the sense of "take pleasure in doing." This attitude is predicated of God in Luke 12:32 in relation to his desire to grant his kingdom to his people; and in 1 Cor. 1:21 in relation to saving people from their sin. Heb. 10:6ff. affirms that God "takes no pleasure" in offerings presented by people who do not have a right spirit of worship. The "desire" to be "at home with the Lord" rather than to remain in the body is expressed in 2 Cor. 5:8. See also 1 Thess. 2:3; 3:1.

eudokia [εὐδοκία, *2107*]

eudokia is a noun derived from ***eudokeō*** (see above). It is found in nine contexts and means "good will," or "good pleasure," as well as "desire."

God's "good pleasure" is indicated in Phil. 2:13; Matt. 11:26. Luke 2:14 refers specifically to God's "good will" toward humankind (cf. also Luke 10:21; Eph. 1:5). This attitude is predicated of people in Phil. 1:15.

The meaning "will" or "desire" is indicated in Rom. 10:1 with regard to Paul's deep longing that people should be saved.

hekōn [ἑκών, *1635*]

hekōn is a rare adjective with the sense of "one's own will." In Rom. 8:20 creation is subjected to futility "not of its own will," but by God himself. ***hekōn*** refers to Paul's own will in 1 Cor. 9:17.

akōn [ἄκων, *210*]

akōn is a rare adjective found only in 1 Cor. 9:7, referring to something done "against one's will."

prothymos [πρόθυμος, *4289*]

prothymos is an adjective found only three times meaning "willing," "ready."

Matt. 26:41; Mark 14:38 refer to a "willing spirit." A "willing desire" to preach the gospel is noted in Rom. 1:15.

WIN

OT Words

yākōl [יָכֹל, **3201**]

yākōl is a verb occurring about 140 times with the primary sense of "be able." In several places, however, ***yākōl*** is translated "to win" in the sense of "prevail," "have victory over," "overcome."

References to people "overcoming" are found in Gen. 30:8; Jer. 20:10; 38:22; Obad. 7. In particular, David's "prevailing" over Goliath is noted in 1 Sam. 17:9. Gen. 32:25ff. contains the account of Jacob wrestling with and "overcoming" his mysterious angelic opponent at the River Jabbok. See also Hos. 12:4. Ps. 129:2; Jer. 1:19; 15:20; 20:11 affirm that enemies "cannot prevail" over the people of God.

bāqa' [בָּקַע, **1234**]

bāqa' is a verb found in around fifty contexts with the primary sense of "divide," "break up," as well as several associated nuances. In 2 Chr. 32:1, ***bāqa'*** is translated "win," or "conquer," in the context of King Sennacherib seeking to conquer Judean cities in the course of his military campaign at the very end of the eighth century B.C.

See Also: → BREAK → DIVIDE → GAIN → OVERCOME → STRENGTH

WIND

OT Words

rûaḥ [רוּחַ, **7307**]

rûaḥ is a common noun in the Old Testament meaning "spirit" (in relation to both God and human beings), "breath," and "wind." (→ SPIRIT)

As a meteorological phenomenon, God sends "wind" to make the floodwaters subside (Gen. 8:1); as part of the plague judgments against the Egyptians (Exod. 10:13, 19); and to divide the waters of the Re(e)d Sea (cf. Exod. 14:21; 15:10; Isa. 11:15). See also 1 Kgs. 19:11; Ps. 78:36; Jonah 1:4; 4:8. Amos 4:13 affirms that the wind is created by God.

As a natural phenomenon in general contexts, "wind" is found in 2 Sam. 22:1; Job 6:26; 37:17; Ps. 1:4; Ezek. 19:12. In particular, Satan generates a "wind" against Job (cf. Job 1:19).

rûaḥ is used metaphorically in several contexts, likening the following things to "wind": vain words (Job 8:2); futile labor (Eccl. 5:16); and idols (Isa. 41:29).

In Ezek. 37:9, the prophet is commanded to prophesy to the ***rûaḥ***, which could be translated "spirit," "breath of life," in this extraordinary prophetic vision of the transformation and renewal of the people of God.

NT Words

anemos [ἄνεμος, *417*]

anemos is a noun occurring around thirty times denoting "wind" throughout.

"Wind," as a natural phenomenon, is noted in Matt. 7:25ff.; 8:26ff.; Mark 4:37ff.; Luke 7:24; 8:23ff.; Acts 27:4ff.; Rev. 6:13; Jude 12.

anemos is also used metaphorically, denoting the "four winds" of the compass (cf. Matt. 24:31; Rev. 7:1).

notos [νότος, *3558*]

notos is a noun found in seven places meaning "south," "south wind." The latter sense is indicated in Luke 12:55; Acts 27:13; 28:13.

pneuma [πνεῦμα, *4151*]

pneuma is a noun occurring over 140 times with the predominant sense of "spirit." In John 3:8, however, ***pneuma*** denotes the "wind" in a general sense.

pnoē [πνοή, *4157*]

pnoē is a rare noun denoting "wind" in Acts 2:2, where it refers to the supernatural phenomenon of a visitation of the Holy Spirit.

anemizō [ἀνεμίζω, *416*]

anemizō is a rare verb found only in Jas. 1:6, referring to "being driven by the wind."

See Also: → BLOW

WINDOW

OT Words

ḥallôn **[חַלּוֹן, 2474]**

ḥallôn is a noun denoting a "window" throughout most of its thirty occurrences.

General references to the "windows" of a house are found in Gen. 26:8; Josh. 2:15ff.; Judg. 5:28; 2 Sam. 6:16; 2 Kgs. 9:30ff.; Prov. 7:6; Song 2:9; Joel 2:9. ***ḥallôn*** refers to the windows of Noah's ark (Gen. 8:6); of Solomon's temple (1 Kgs. 6:4); and of the visionary temple of Ezekiel (Ezek. 40:16ff.; 41:16, 26).

'arubbāh **[אֲרֻבָּה, 699]**

'arubbāh is a noun referring metaphorically to "windows" in most of its nine occurrences.

Gen. 7:11 refers to opening the "windows of heaven," in relation to the torrential rain that flooded the earth. See also Gen. 8:2; Isa. 24:18; Mal. 3:10. 2 Kgs. 7:2, 19 refer to the hypothetical "windows in heaven" through which God could look. Eccl. 12:3 refers to the "eyes" of an old man.

shāqûph **[שָׁקוּף, 8261]**

shāqûph is a rare noun referring only to the "windows" set in the temple structure (cf. 1 Kgs. 6:4; 7:4).

kawwāh **[כַּוָּה, 3551** (Aramaic)**]**

kawwāh is a rare Aramaic noun found only in Dan. 6:10 with reference to the "windows" of a house.

NT Words

thyris [θυρίς, *2376*]

thyris is a rare noun denoting the "windows" of a house in Acts 20:9; 2 Cor. 11:33.

WINE

OT Words

yayin **[יַיִן, 3196]**

yayin is a noun meaning "wine" (i.e., alcoholic beverage) throughout its 140 occurrences.

General references to "wine" for human consumption include those in Gen. 9:21ff.; 19:32ff.; Num. 6:20; Josh. 9:4; Neh. 2:1; Esth. 1:10; Ps. 104:15; Isa. 5:11ff. Wine is forbidden to the Nazirite during the period of the vow (cf. Num. 6:3ff.; Judg. 13:4ff.), and also to the priests during their ritual service (cf. Lev. 10:9). Wine is an element of a ritual offering in Exod. 29:40; Lev. 23:13; Num. 15:5ff.; Deut. 14:26. Prov. 23:20 refers to a "winebibber."

yayin is also used figuratively. "Wine" symbolizes the wrath of God, "poured from a cup" (cf. Ps. 75:8; Jer. 25:15; 51:7). Prov. 4:17 refers to the "wine of violence" (cf. also Prov. 20:1). "Wine" symbolizes sensual pleasure in Song 5:1.

tîrôsh **[תִּירוֹשׁ, 8492]**

tîrôsh is a noun denoting "new wine" throughout its nearly forty occurrences, indicating wine that has been freshly pressed (cf. Gen. 27:28; 2 Kgs. 18:32ff.; Ps. 4:7; Isa. 36:17; Hos. 2:8ff.; Joel 2:19ff.).

sōbe' **[סֹבֶא, 5435]**

sōbe' is a rare noun indicating "choice wine" in Isa. 1:22.

ḥamar **[חֲמַר, 2562** (Aramaic)**]**

ḥamar is an Aramaic noun denoting "wine" in six places (cf. Ezra 6:9; 7:22; Dan. 5:1ff.).

'āsîs **[עָסִיס, 6071]**

'āsîs is a noun denoting "new wine," in the sense of freshly pressed sweet juice, in most of its five occurrences (cf. Isa. 49:26; Joel 1:5; 3:18; Amos 9:13).

NT Words

oinos [οἶνος, *3631*]

oinos is a dynamic equivalent for ***yayin*** (see above). It denotes "wine" throughout its approximately thirty occurrences, in both a literal and figurative sense.

Literal references to "wine" include those in Matt. 9:17; Mark 15:23; Luke 1:15; 5:37ff.; John 2:3ff.; Rom. 14:21; 1 Tim. 5:23; Rev. 6:6; 18:13. Injunctions not to get drunk with wine, or be addicted to it, are found in Eph. 5:18; 1 Tim. 3:8; Titus 2:3.

oinos also denotes "wine" symbolizing the wrath of God in Rev. 14:10; 16:19. In Rev. 14:8; 17:2; 18:3, ***oinos*** denotes the "wine" of Babylonian "adulteries" (i.e., pagan idolatry).

gleukos [γλεῦκος, *1098*]

gleukos is a rare noun found only in Acts 2:13, denoting "new wine."

See Also: → DRINK → DRUNK

WINEPRESS

OT Words

yeqeb **[יֶקֶב, 3342]**

yeqeb is a noun occurring sixteen times. It means "winepress" or "wine vat" throughout, though in some cases the distinction between "vat" and "press" is not clearly drawn.

General references to a "winepress" include those in Num. 18:27ff.; Deut. 15:14; Judg. 7:25; 2 Kgs. 6:27; Isa. 5:2; Jer. 48:33; Zech. 14:10. "Wine vats" are mentioned in Prov. 3:10; Hos. 9:2; Joel 2:24; 3:13.

gat **[גַּת, 1660]**

gat is synonymous with ***yeqeb*** (see above), denoting a "winepress" in all five occurrences (cf. Judg. 6:11; Neh. 13:15; Isa. 63:2; Lam. 1:15; Joel 3:13).

pûrāh **[פּוּרָה, 6333]**

pûrāh is another synonym for ***yeqeb*** and ***gat***, above. The meaning "winepress" is indicated in Isa. 63:3, referring figuratively to the "winepress" of God's wrath. ***pûrāh*** is used literally in Hag. 2:16.

NT Words

lēnos [ληνός, *3025*]

lēnos is a noun denoting a "winepress" in Matt. 21:33. In Rev. 14:19, 20; 19:15, ***lēnos*** refers metaphorically to a "winepress" as the vehicle for the expression of the wrath of God against the wicked.

WINESKIN → JAR

WING

OT Words

kānāph **[כָּנָף, 3671]**

kānāph is a noun with a diverse range of meanings. The majority sense is that of "wing," as well as indirectly related senses such as "corner," "end."
(→ CORNER → END)

Used adjectivally, ***kānāph*** refers to "winged" creatures in general contexts (e.g., Gen. 1:21; Deut. 4:17; Eccl. 10:20).

Exod. 19:4 refers to the "wings of eagles," metaphorically indicating the means of divine deliverance from trouble. See also Ezek. 17:7.

kānāph also denotes the "wings" of cherubim, both on the ark of the covenant (cf. Exod. 25:20; 37:9; 1 Kgs. 6:24ff.; 8:6ff.; 2 Chr. 3:11ff.), and on the heavenly angelic beings themselves (cf. Isa. 6:2; Ezek. 1:6ff.; 10:5ff.; 11:22). ***kānāph*** also refers to the "wings of Yahweh," signifying the security of his divine protection (cf. Ruth 2:12; Pss. 17:8; 36:7; 61:4; 91:4). 2 Sam. 22:11; Ps. 18:10 speak of the "wings of the wind."

Job 39:13 refers generally to birds' wings. Lev. 1:17 mentions the wings of birds in connection with ritual sacrifice. See also Zech. 5:1.

'ēber **[אֵבֶר, 83]**

'ēber is a rare noun found three times meaning "wings" (cf. Ps. 55:6; Isa. 40:31; Ezek. 17:3).

gaph **[גַּף, 1611** (Aramaic)**]**

gaph is an Aramaic noun denoting the "wings" of birds, found only in Dan. 7:4ff.

NT Words

pteryx [πτέρυξ, *4420*]

pteryx is a noun meaning "wings" in several different contexts. It occurs five times, each in a figurative context.

Matt. 23:37; Luke 13:34 refer to the "wings" of a hen, figuratively indicating a protective, nurturing mother. Rev. 4:8; 9:9 refer to the "wings" of demonic creatures that wreak havoc on humankind. In Rev. 12:4, ***pteryx*** denotes the "wings" of an eagle, symbolically indicating the vehicle of divine deliverance.

WINNOW → SCATTER

WINTER

OT Words

ḥōreph **[חֹרֶף, 2779]**

ḥōreph is a noun found seven times. It means "winter" in most of these contexts, referring literally to the season (cf. Gen. 8:22; Ps. 74:17; Jer. 36:22; Amos 3:15; Zech. 14:8).

setāyw **[סְתָיו, 5638]**

setāyw is a rare noun, found only in Song 2:11 and designating "winter" as the rainy season.

NT Words

cheimōn [χειμών, *5494*]

cheimōn is a dynamic equivalent for ***ḥōreph*** (see above) denoting "winter" in most of the six occurrences (cf. Matt. 24:20; Mark 13:18; John 10:22; 2 Tim. 4:21).

paracheimazō [παραχειμάζω, *3914*]

paracheimazō is a verb occurring four times meaning "to pass, spend the winter" (cf. Acts 27:12; 28:11; 1 Cor. 16:6; Titus 3:12). See also Acts 27:12.

WIPE

OT Words

māḥāh **[מָחָה, 4229]**

māḥāh is a verb found in around forty contexts with the underlying sense of "destroy," translated variously as "obliterate," "blot out," "destroy," and "wipe out." There is some overlap between these meanings. (→ DESTROY)

In the context of divine judgment, God determines to "wipe or blot out" humankind by floodwaters (Gen. 6:7; 7:4). Specific nations are threatened with being "wiped out" by God (Exod. 17:14; Deut. 9:14; 25:19). In Exod. 32:32ff., Moses offers to be "blotted out" of the book written by God. See also Deut. 29:20; Neh. 13:14; Ps. 69:28; Jer. 18:23. The psalmist pleads with God to "wipe out" sins (Pss. 51:1, 9; 109:14). See also Isa. 43:25; Ezek. 6:6.

Isa. 25:8 refers to "wiping away" tears. See also Prov. 6:33.

NT Words

ekmassō [ἐκμάσσω, *1591*]

ekmassō is a verb meaning "wipe off, away." It occurs five times, referring to "wiping away" tears in Luke 7:38, 44, and also to "wiping" perfume from the feet of Christ in John 11:2; 12:3ff.

apomassomai [ἀπομάσσομαι, *631*]

apomassomai is a verb found only in Luke 10:11, referring to "wiping off" dust from one's feet.

exaleiphō [ἐξαλείφω, *1813*]

exaleiphō is a verb meaning "blot out" or "wipe away" in each of its five occurrences.

Acts 3:19 refers to God "blotting out" sin. Similarly, ***exaleiphō*** refers to Christ "blotting out" (i.e., canceling, writing off) the legal indictment against his people in Col. 2:14. In Rev. 3:5, Christ promises that he will never blot out from the Lamb's book of life those who persevere in faith until the end.

God is said to "wipe away" tears from the eyes of the saints in heaven in Rev. 7:17; 21:4.

WISDOM, WISE

OT Words

ḥokmāh **[חָכְמָה, 2451]**

ḥokmāh is a significant term found in approximately 150 places with the dominant sense of "wisdom." Wisdom refers to knowledge coupled with an inner quality that embodies a heart and life in conformity with the purposes and character of God. ***ḥokmāh*** has this meaning throughout most of its usage in a variety of contexts. However, in several places it also has the derivative meaning "skill," or "ability," imparted by the Spirit of Yahweh to particular individuals. (→ UNDERSTANDING)

References to "skills" or "abilities" imparted by the Spirit of God are found in Exod. 28:3; 31:3ff.; 35:26ff.; 36:1, 2; 1 Kgs. 7:14; 1 Chr. 28:21 in relation to craftsmen working on the tabernacle and temple.

"Wisdom" in the general sense of unspecified knowledge that is inherently valuable for right living is indicated, for example, in 2 Sam. 20:22; 1 Kgs. 2:6; Job 4:21; 28:18ff.; Prov. 29:3; Eccl. 1:13ff.; 2:3ff.; 9:10ff.

ḥokmāh also denotes "wisdom" as that knowledge of God which leads to living godly lives in conformity with the divine character. Such "wisdom" is characteristic of Israel, for example, designed and given to reveal God's character and person to the world at large (cf. Deut. 4:6). Elsewhere, this "wisdom" of God is given to particular individuals such as Solomon (cf. 1 Kgs. 3:28; 4:29ff.; 5:12; 10:4ff.; 2 Chr. 1:10ff.; 9:3ff.; Eccl. 2:26; 7:10ff.). See also Deut. 34:9; Isa. 11:2. Godly "wisdom" may be passed down from parent to child in the nurturing of the family (cf. Prov. 5:1). It is clear also that genuine wisdom is derived only from God (cf. Ps. 111:10; Prov. 1:7; 9:10). All of these texts affirm that the "fear of the Lord is the beginning of wisdom."

Other general references to "wisdom" include those in Pss. 51:6; 90:12; Prov. 2:6; 4:7; 10:13; 14:6ff.; Dan. 7:4, 17ff.; Isa. 33:6.

"Wisdom" is indicated as a divine attribute in Job 12:13; Prov. 13:19; Jer. 10:12; 51:15. In Prov. 8:1, 11ff., "wisdom" is personified as the ultimate godly woman.

ḥokmāh also denotes "wisdom" that is false, a mere human pretension that will be destroyed (cf. Isa. 29:14; 47:10; Jer. 8:9). Ezek. 28:4ff. refers to the "wisdom" of the king of Tyre, the embodiment of demonic pride.

ḥākām **[חָכָם, 2450]**

ḥākām is an adjective occurring about 140 times, consistently translated "wise" as well as "skillful." It is also used nominally to refer to a "wise person." The term refers to both human and divine wisdom.

The designation "wise" is used in the unspecified sense of a person of noble character (cf. Gen. 41:33; Deut. 1:13ff.; Ps. 107:43; Prov. 1:5ff.; 15:2ff.; 21:20ff.; Eccl. 2:14ff.; 12:9ff.). General references to the vice of being "worldly wise" are found in Job 5:13; Prov. 3:7; Isa. 5:21.

References to "wise ones" in the pagan sense of "practitioners of occult arts" are found in Gen. 41:8; Exod. 7:11; Esth. 1:13; Isa. 3:3; 19:11ff.; Jer. 51:57; Obad. 8. However, 2 Sam. 14:2 mentions a "wise woman" of uncertain origin.

ḥākām also occasionally refers to "skillful" craftspersons (cf. Jer. 9:12; Ezek. 27:8ff.). In particular, "skilled" workers gifted by God are indicated in the context of the tabernacle and temple construction (cf. Exod. 28:3; 31:6; 35:10, 25; 36:1ff.; 1 Chr. 22:15; 2 Chr. 2:7ff.). In contrast, Jer. 4:22 refers to those who are skilled in evil. Isa. 40:20 refers to a craftsperson who build idols, whose "skill" is put to ungodly purposes.

Finally, the "wise" are explicitly declared to be so endowed by God so that they may conform to his ways and purposes — referring to Israel (Deut. 4:6), and to Solomon (1 Kgs. 2:9; 3:12; 5:7).

ḥākam [חָכַם, 2449]

ḥākam is a verb related to ***ḥokmāh*** and ***ḥākām***, above, occurring about thirty times and meaning "to be wise" "act wisely," "teach wisdom."

1 Kgs. 4:31; Job 32:9; Prov. 13:20; Eccl. 7:23 refer generally to "being wise." See also Exod. 1:10. Exhortations to live wisely are found in Prov. 6:6; 8:33; 23:19. In Pss. 19:7; 119:98, the psalmist affirms that the law of God "makes wise" the simple, and Ps. 105:22 refers to teaching wisdom.

ḥakkîm [חַכִּים, 2445 (Aramaic)]

ḥakkîm is an Aramaic noun, occurring only in the plural and referring to "wise men" in Daniel fourteen times. These "wise men" were in fact pagan magicians or astrologers (cf. Dan. 2:12ff.; 24ff., 48; 4:6, 18; 5:7ff.). In addition, Dan. 2:21 refers to "the wise" as recipients of godly wisdom.

NT Words

sophia [σοφία, *4678*]

sophia is a dynamic equivalent for ***ḥokmāh*** (see above), consistently translated "wisdom" throughout its fifty or so occurrences. ***sophia*** denotes both human and divine wisdom with knowledge, intelligence, and understanding.

sophia generally designates "wisdom" as a gift of God, given to specific individuals in order to equip them to live godly lives. Such "wisdom" includes intelligence and deep understanding. ***sophia*** refers to the wisdom of Solomon (Matt. 12:42; Luke 11:31); Joseph (Acts 7:10); and Moses (Acts 7:22). The people of Jesus' day attributed wisdom to him during his earthly ministry, although not all may have accepted that it came from God (cf. Matt. 13:54; Mark 6:2).

Godly wisdom is given to Christ's disciples and followers (Luke 21:15; Acts 6:3, 10; 1 Cor. 2:6; Col. 1:9; Jas. 3:13, 17; 2 Pet. 3:15). In Col. 4:5, believers are exhorted to ask God for wisdom. Godly wisdom is required for intelligent understanding of spiritual realities (cf. Rev. 13:18; 17:9). Such wisdom is also implicitly attributed to Christ in his boyhood years (cf. Luke 2:40, 52).

Wisdom as a divine attribute is indicated in Luke 11:49; Rom. 11:33; 1 Cor. 1:21, 24; Eph. 3:10; Rev. 7:12. Col. 2:3 indicates that "all the treasures of wisdom" are hidden in Christ. And Rev. 5:12 declares that God gives wisdom. Christ is designated as "our wisdom" in 1 Cor. 1:30; Col. 3:16, wrought by God in the lives of his people. In Matt. 11:19; Luke 7:35, "wisdom" is personified as a woman of noble and godly virtue.

Human wisdom is described as "folly" in the eyes of God (1 Cor. 1:17ff.; 2:1ff.; 3:19; Col. 2:23; Jas. 3:15).

sophos [σοφός, *4680*]

sophos is an adjectival form derived from ***sophia*** (see above) meaning "wise," "skilled." It occurs around twenty times, referring to both human beings and God in a variety of contexts. ***sophos*** is also used nominally.

Matt. 11:25; Luke 10:21; Rom. 1:14 refer to "the wise," "wise ones," indicating that such people see themselves as wise by human standards alone. Matt. 23:34 refers to godly "wise people."

The adjectival sense of "wise" is found in Rom. 1:22; 1 Cor. 1:19ff.; 3:18ff., referring to the folly of human wisdom. In contrast, ***sophos*** also refers to those who are "wise" in the godly sense of being spiritually discerning (cf. Rom. 16:19; 1 Cor. 6:5; Eph. 5:15; Jas. 3:13). This attribute is predicated of God in Rom. 16:27.

The meaning "skilled" refers to a "master builder" in 1 Cor. 3:10.

phronimos [φρόνιμος, *5429*]

phronimos is an adjective found in fourteen places meaning "wise" in the sense of "intelligent" or "prudent," careful to maintain one's own interests in a noble sense.

This characteristic is predicated of people, denoting them as "wise" or "intelligent," capable of insight and understanding (cf. Matt. 7:24; 10:16; 25:2ff.; Luke 12:42; 16:8; 1 Cor. 10:15).

phronimos is also used in a negative sense, where "wise" has the connotation of "conceit" (cf. Rom. 11:25; 12:16).

phronimos also refers to "wisdom" in the context of sarcastic condemnation of foolish people (cf. 1 Cor. 4:10; 2 Cor. 11:19).

phronēsis [φρόνησις, *5428*]

phronēsis is a rare noun denoting "(godly) wisdom" in Luke 1:17, and divine "wisdom" in Eph. 1:8.

magos [μάγος, *3097*]

magos is a noun denoting "wise man," or "sorcerer." It is found in six places. Matt. 2:1, 7, 16 refer to the wise men witnessing the birth of Christ. These were people skilled in the knowledge of natural phenomena, most likely astrologers. ***magos*** also refers to a "(pagan) magician," or "sorcerer," in Acts 13:6, 8.

Additional Notes

A consistent strand of meaning is associated with "wisdom" terminology throughout Scripture.

"Wisdom" in the Old Testament is associated with "skill" and "expertise" in a technical sense. It also refers to an intelligent capacity for knowledge, understanding, and discernment. In the large majority of contexts, such wisdom is either explicitly or implicitly designated as a gift from God. Wisdom is a prerequisite for a rightly ordered relationship with God, resulting in a lifestyle that conforms to God's character and purpose. In short, the "wise" person will please God in all that he or she does.

In the New Testament, the general sense of wisdom as intelligence, understanding, and discernment is likewise evident. Yet the transcendent element of wisdom in the spiritual realm comes to supreme expression in Christ, who is depicted as one who is perfect in wisdom, having received it from God his Father.

Thus the believer, who is personally joined to Christ in faith and repentance, in intimate spiritual union with him, will have access to such wisdom. Indeed, under the new covenant, the only way one can become truly "wise" in the sight of God is to commit oneself to the person of Christ in faith and repentance. For true godly wisdom is found only in him. Only in such a relationship is the believer able to live wisely so as to please God.

See Also: → UNDERSTAND → UNDERSTANDING

WISH → DESIRE → PRAY

WITCHCRAFT → DIVINATION → MAGIC

WITHER

OT Words

nābēl [נָבֵל, 5034]

nābēl is a verb meaning "fade, wear away" and "wither," as well as related nuances. These meanings sometimes overlap.

Ps. 1:3; Isa. 1:30; Jer. 8:13 refer to leaves that "wither" and fall off the branch. See also Ps. 37:2. A metaphorical reference to the earth "withering," or fading away, wearing out, is found in Isa. 24:4.

See Also: → DRY

WITHHOLD → RESTRAIN

WITHSTAND → RESIST

WITNESS

OT Words

'ēdāh [עֵדָה, 5713]; *'ēd* [עֵד, 5707]

These two terms indicate the dual senses of "testimony" and "witness" in a variety of contexts throughout their combined usage of around one hundred occurrences.

References to a "witness," as one who bears testimony to a significant event or transaction, are found in a variety of contexts. General references to "witness(es)" include those in Lev. 5:1; Num. 5:13; 35:30; Deut. 17:6ff.; 19:15; Isa. 8:2; 43:9ff.; Jer. 32:10ff. "Witnesses" to a solemn promise in the context of a covenant oath are described in Gen. 21:30; 31:44; Josh. 24:22; Ruth. 4:9ff. Inanimate "witnesses" to an oath ritual, reminding the parties of their sworn obligation under oath, include a "heap of stones" (Gen. 31:48, 52) and the book of the law — a testimony to the Mosaic law covenant between God and Israel (cf. Deut. 31:26). Other examples are found in Josh. 22:27ff.; Isa. 19:20.

The "Song of Moses" in Deut. 31:19ff. is a poetic "testimony" against the people of Israel.

"False witnesses" are mentioned in 1 Kgs. 21:10; Ps. 27:12; Prov. 6:19; 19:28. Warnings against being a "false witness" are found in Exod. 23:1; Deut. 19:15ff. Prohibitions against "false testimony" (i.e., lying) are found in Exod. 20:16; Deut. 5:20.

In several places, God himself is called upon "to witness." In Gen. 31:50; 1 Sam. 12:5, God's name is invoked to "ratify" the solemnity of a promissory oath. Mic. 1:2 refers to Yahweh being called upon to testify against his people. Jer. 29:23; Mal. 3:5 indicate that God witnesses the sin of his people.

'ēdût [עֵדוּת, **5715**]

'ēdût is the plural form of ***'ēdāh*** (see above), which is translated consistently as "testimony" throughout its usage, referring primarily in a "technical" sense to the tablets of the Mosaic law covenant placed in the ark of the covenant. The underlying sense is that these tablets are a summary of the solemn commitment the people of Israel had made to Yahweh. Thus they "bear witness" to the people's obligation to love and obey their God, who has redeemed them from Egypt. In addition, ***'ēdût*** refers to the ark and the tablets of the "testimony."

Exod. 16:34; 25:16ff.; 31:18; 32:15; 34:29; 40:20 refer to the tablets of the law covenant as the "testimony." In 2 Kgs. 11:12, the "testimony" refers to the copy of the covenant law.

'ēdût is found in the expression "the ark of the testimony" (Exod. 26:33ff.; 30:6; 31:7; 39:35; 40:3ff., 21; Lev. 16:13; Num. 4:15; 7:89; 10:11; 17:7; Josh. 4:16). Similarly, the tabernacle of the "testimony" is indicated in Exod. 38:21; Num. 1:50ff.; 9:15; 17:8.

References to "testimonies" (i.e., divine requirements) synonymous with laws and statutes are found in 1 Kgs. 2:3; 2 Kgs. 23:3; Neh. 9:34; Ps. 19:7; 119:31, 88, 99, 129, 144, 157.

'ûd [עוּד, **5749**]

'ûd is a verb occurring around fifty times with the primary sense of "to bear witness," "testify," as well as related nuances.

"Bearing witness" to a solemn oath in the context of a covenant ratification or renewal is indicated in Deut. 4:26; 30:19; 31:28, with metaphorical reference to heaven and earth.

The meaning "testify" in the sense of "solemnly warn" is indicated in Deut. 8:19, where Moses "warns" the people of Israel against committing idolatry. In 1 Sam. 8:9, Samuel addresses the people with a similar purpose.

Elsewhere, ***'ûd*** is translated "to testify" in a legal sense. 1 Kgs. 21:10ff. refers to King Ahab "bearing false testimony" against Naboth. In several places, God "testifies" against Israel for the violation of their covenant oath (cf. 2 Kgs. 17:13ff.; Neh. 9:26ff.; Ps. 50:7). See also Neh. 13:21; Amos 3:13.

Jer. 32:10, 25, 44 refer to "taking witnesses."

'ānāh [עָנָה, **6030**]

'ānāh is a verb occurring over three hundred times with the primary sense of "to answer." However, in several contexts it means "bear witness against" (cf. 1 Sam. 12:3; Isa. 3:9).

NT Words

martyreō [μαρτυρέω, *3140*]

martyreō is a verb found in around eighty places with the dominant meanings "to testify," "bear witness against," as well as related senses.

The meaning "bear witness to," or "testify," is evident in a variety of contexts. Luke 11:48 refers to testifying to the sins of the fathers of Israel; and John 3:11; 21:24; Rev. 22:16 refer to testimony to the deeds of Jesus. See also John 1:7ff.; Rev. 1:2. Elsewhere, Jesus denies "bearing witness to himself" (John 8:13, 14; 15:26). The works of Christ "bear witness to" his divine nature and origin (John 5:36; 10:25). The Scriptures are said to "bear witness to Christ" (John 5:39; Acts 10:43; Rom. 3:21). God the Father is said to "bear witness to" the Son (John 8:18; 1 John 5:10). See also John 18:37.

The meaning "testify" is also used in a general sense in relation to "speaking well of" people (cf. Luke 4:22; Acts 6:3; 10:22; Heb. 11:39); "reporting" an incident (cf. John 4:39); and general "declaration" (John 7:7; Acts 26:22; 1 Cor. 15:15; Heb. 7:17; John 4:14). See also Acts 23:11.

martyreō is also used nominally to refer to the "witness" the disciples must give of Christ and his works (John 15:27).

martyria [μαρτυρία, *3141*]

martyria is a noun derived from ***martyreō*** (see above). It occurs in around forty contexts and means "witness," "testimony" throughout, in a variety of contexts.

The meaning "testimony" in the general sense of a "report" is indicated in John 1:19; Acts 22:18; Titus 1:13. ***martyria*** refers to God's "testimony" concerning his Son (1 John 5:9ff.); to Jesus' "testimony" about himself (John 5:31ff.; 8:13ff.; Rev. 1:2, 9); and to general "testimony" or "witness" concerning the person and work of Christ (John 3:11, 33; 19:35; 21:24; Rev.

6:9; 11:7; 12:11, 17; 20:4). John 1:7 refers to "witness" to Christ as "the light of the world."

The legal sense of "testimony," "evidence" is used in connection with Jesus at his trial (Mark 14:55ff.; Luke 22:71).

martyrion [μαρτύριον, *3142*]

martyrion is a noun synonymous with ***martyria*** (see above), meaning "witness," "testimony" throughout.

martyrion refers to the "testimony" or "witness" of the gospel to all nations (Matt. 24:14); to the "witness" to the life of Christ (1 Cor. 1:6; 2 Thess. 1:10); and to the "testimony" to the perfect ransom provided by Christ to the Father (1 Tim. 2:6). See also Jas. 5:3; Heb. 3:5.

"Testimony" in the sense of "proof," or "evidence," is indicated in relation to ceremonial cleansing (cf. Mark 1:44; Luke 5:14); to divine rejection (Mark 6:11; Luke 9:5); to the resurrection of Christ (Acts 4:33); and to the presence of godly sincerity in one's conscience (cf. 2 Cor. 1:12). Courtroom "testimony" or "evidence" is indicated in Mark 13:9; Luke 21:13.

Acts 7:44; Rev. 15:5 refer to the "tent of testimony" (i.e., the tabernacle containing the ark of the covenant), with the latter text indicating the heavenly sanctuary.

martys [μάρτυς, *3144*]

martys is a noun denoting a "witness" in a legal, historical sense, as one who bears testimony to significant persons and phenomena. The term occurs around thirty times.

martys refers to a "witness" in the legal sense of presenting testimony in a judicial context in Matt. 18:16; 26:25; Mark 14:63; Acts 7:58; 2 Cor. 13:1; 1 Tim. 5:19; Heb. 10:28.

Acts 1:8, 22; 5:32; 10:39ff.; 22:15; 26:16; 1 Pet. 5:1; Rev. 1:5 mention those who are "witnesses" to the life of Christ and, for following generations in particular, to his death and resurrection.

The apostle Paul occasionally invokes God as his "witness" in order to validate his declaration (e.g., Rom. 1:9; 2 Cor. 1:23; Phil. 1:8; 1 Thess. 2:5).

Reference to a "witness" in general contexts as one who makes a claim is found in 1 Thess. 2:10; 1 Tim. 6:2. "False witnesses" are noted in Acts 6:13 in the trial of Stephen, the first recorded Christian martyr. In Rev. 3:14, Christ himself is declared as the "faithful and true witness."

martys is also translated "martyr" in a number of places, referring to those who give their lives for the cause of the gospel (cf. Acts 22:20; Heb. 12:1 [implied]; Rev. 2:13; 17:6). See also Rev. 11:3.

amartyros [ἀμάρτυρος, *267*]

amartyros is a rare adjective found only in Acts 14:17 meaning "without a witness," or "unattested." It is predicated of God, of whom it is said he did not leave himself without a witness.

pseudomartys [ψευδόμαρτυς, *5575*]

pseudomartys is a noun found only in Mat. 26:60; 1 Cor. 15:15 denoting a "false witness."

pseudomartyreō [ψευδομαρτυρέω, *5576*]

pseudomartyreō is a verb occurring six times meaning "to bear false witness." It is found in contexts rehearsing the ninth commandment in relation to "lying" (cf. Matt. 19:18; Mark 10:19; Luke 18:20; Rom. 13:9); and also in connection with presenting "false testimony" in a court of law, against Christ (cf. Mark 14:56ff.).

pseudomartyria [ψευδομαρτυρία, *5577*]

pseudomartyria is a rare noun found twice. In Matt. 15:19 it denotes "false testimony" as a vice, and in Matt. 26:59 it indicates the "false testimony" presented in relation to Christ at his trial.

katamartyreō [καταμαρτυρέω, *2649*]

katamartyreō is a verb found four times meaning "testify against," "bear witness against," referring to those enemies of Christ at his trial who perjured themselves against him (cf. Matt. 26:62; 27:13; Mark 14:60; 15:4).

symmartyreō [συμμαρτυρέω, *4828*]

symmartyreō is a verb found four times, meaning "bear joint witness to" (Rom. 2:15; 8:16; 9:1). See also Rev. 22:18.

diamartyromai [διαμαρτύρομαι, *1263*]

diamartyromai is a verb expressing the sense of "to testify," "(solemnly) affirm." It occurs fifteen times.

The meaning "testify" in the sense of "warn" is found in Luke 16:28; 1 Thess. 4:6. A solemn charge or exhortation is expressed in Acts 2:40; 1 Tim. 5:21; 2 Tim. 2:14; 4:1; Heb. 2:6.

Acts 8:25 refers to "bearing witness to" the words of the Lord. Acts 10:42 "declares" that Jesus Christ will be the judge of all humankind. Acts 20:21ff. contains the solemn declaration that the central element of the gospel constitutes repentance toward God, and faith in Christ. Acts 18:5; 23:11; 28:23 also contain the unambiguous "declaration" that Jesus is the Christ.

WOMAN

OT Words

'ishshāh [אִשָּׁה, 802]

'ishshāh is a common noun occurring around eight hundred times with the meanings "woman," "wife" in most of the contexts in which it is found. There is often overlap in meaning between these two senses. The term also refers to the "female" of the animal species.

General references to "women" are found in Gen. 3:1ff.; Exod. 1:19; 2:2ff.; Judg. 9:49ff.; Ruth 1:1ff.; 1 Sam. 21:4ff.; Esth. 1:9; Eccles. 7:28; Isa. 45:10; Ezek. 8:10. In particular, Gen. 2:22ff. refers to "woman" as the being created by God from man. Women as harlots are depicted in Exod. 16:30; 1 Kgs. 3:16ff.; Prov. 2:16. Concubines (i.e., women of the harem) are described in Esth. 2:11ff. Lam. 5:11 and Isa. 13:16 mention women who were victims of sexual assault.

Legislation concerning the status and treatment of women is recorded in a number of places (e.g., Lev. 12:2; 15:18ff.; 20:1ff.; Num. 16:2; Deut. 17:5; 21:11; 22:14ff.).

In significant theological contexts, ***'ishshāh*** is used metaphorically to refer to the houses of Israel and Judah as promiscuous "women," describing the practice of idolatry in terms of adulterous prostitution (Ezek. 23:2, 10, 44). And Zech. 5:9 describes the iniquity of the people of Judah as two "women" with the wings of a stork. 1 Sam. 28:7ff. mentions a "witch" (i.e., a woman with a familiar spirit).

In one context, ***'ishshāh*** denotes "female" animals (Gen. 7:2).

neqēbāh [נְקֵבָה, 5347]

neqēbāh is a noun occurring around twenty times with the primary meaning "female," referring both to women and animals.

References to the "female," or the woman created by God along with the male, human beings both created in the divine image, are found in Gen. 1:27; 5:2. It refers to a "daughter" (i.e., a female child) in Lev. 12:5ff. ***neqēbāh*** refers to the "female form" of an idol in Deut. 4:16 and to the "female" of the animal species in Gen. 6:19; 7:3ff.; Lev. 3:1, 6; 4:28ff.; 5:6.

General references to "woman" include those in Lev. 15:33; Num. 31:15; Jer. 31:22. In the context of Mosaic legislation, Lev. 24:4ff. contains a monetary valuation of a "woman" for the purposes of a ritual offering to Yahweh. See also Num. 5:3.

yālad [יָלַד, 3205]

yālad is a common verb form with the primary meaning "to beget," "give birth," as well as several related nuances. (→ BEGET) The participial nominal form, ***yālad,*** is translated "woman in the pangs of labor" and is found in Jer. 6:24; 13:21; 22:23; 49:24; 50:43; Mic. 4:10.

NT Words

gunē [γυνή, *1135*]

gunē, a noun occurring over two hundred times, is the dynamic equivalent for the Hebrew term ***'ishshāh*** (see above). It is translated "woman," "wife." ***gunē*** always refers to a woman, either married or unmarried and, as with ***'ishshāh,*** there is overlap between the two senses.

The general meaning "woman" is indicated in a number of contexts (e.g., Matt. 5:28; 9:20ff.; 11:11; Mark 7:25; Luke 7:37ff.; 8:2ff.; Acts 1:14; 8:12; Rev. 14:4. Specific individuals are referred to in John 4:7ff.; 8:3; Acts 16:14. "Woman" is used as a term of address in John 2:4, when Jesus speaks to his mother.

Legislation involving a "married woman" or "wife" is found in Rom. 7:2; 1 Cor. 7:1ff. A woman's role or function in the context of worship is set out in 1 Cor. 11:3ff.; 14:34ff. 1 Tim. 2:9ff. describes the demeanor required of godly women.

gunē is also used metaphorically to denote a "woman" in John's vision, symbolizing Mary, the mother of Christ (cf. Rev. 12:1ff.). See also Rev. 2:20. In addition, Rev. 17:3ff. describes an evil woman — again in a visionary context — depicting the city of Babylon as a "prostitute," the embodiment of idolatrous blasphemy.

gunaikarion [γυναικάριον, *1133*]

gunaikarion is a rare noun found only in 2 Tim. 3:6, as a term of mild disdain, denoting "weak-willed women."

agamos [ἄγαμος, *22*]

agamos is an adjective referring to "unmarried" or "single women" four times in 1 Cor. 7:8ff., 32ff.

thēlys [θῆλυς, *2338*]

thēlys is an adjectival form, used nominally on five occasions to refer to a "woman" or "female." The designation "female" in conjunction with "male" (i.e., human beings created by God, equal in status as divine image-bearers), is found in Matt. 19:4; Mark 10:6.

General references to "women" are found in Rom. 1:26, 27; Gal. 3:28.

gastēr [γαστήρ, *1064*]

gastēr is a noun denoting a woman who is pregnant (1 Thess. 5:3). (→ WOMB)

presbyteros [πρεσβύτερος, *4245*]

presbyteros is an adjective with the predominent nominal sense of "elder." The adjectival meaning "older" is rare and is used only once in the feminine form, referring to "older women" in 1 Tim. 5:2.

presbytis [πρεσβῦτις, *4247*]

presbytis is a rare feminine noun found only in Titus 2:3, denoting "old women."

Additional Notes

Significant usage of both Hebrew and Greek terminology for "woman," especially ***'ishshāh*** and ***gunē*** respectively, is highly metaphorical.

In the Old Testament, the virtue of wisdom is depicted and personified as a "woman" (Lady Wisdom), as are the vices of immorality and idolatry. In the New Testament, symbolic reference to a woman as a "prostitute" ("Babylon," in Rev. 17) reflects the consummation of parallel imagery derived from the Old Testament (Prov. 1–9; Isa. 47).

The depiction of Israel as "the bride of Yahweh" who "cheats" on him by worshiping other gods and thereby committing "spiritual adultery" further underlines the significance of female imagery throughout Scripture.

See Also: → GIRL → MAID

WOMB

OT Words

beten **[בֶּטֶן, 990]**

beten is a noun found seventy times, usually translated "womb," "belly" in both a literal and figurative sense.

References to a woman's "womb," usually referring to a state of pregnancy (i.e., children in the womb), are found in Gen. 25:23ff.; Judg. 13:5ff.; 16:17; Ps. 139:13. Other general references include those in Job 1:21; 31:15ff.; Pss. 22:9; 71:6; Isa. 46:3; Eccl. 5:15. Ps. 139:13; Isa. 44:2, 24; Jer. 1:5 specifically mention children "formed in the womb" by God. In Isa. 49:1, 5, God's servants are called by him "from the womb" (cf. also Hos. 12:3).

The blessing of fertility, involving the promise of many children as "the fruit of the womb," is noted in Deut. 7:13; 28:4, 11; 30:9; Ps. 127:3. In contrast, the curse of barrenness is indicated in withholding pregnancy where "no fruit of the womb" is forthcoming (cf. Gen. 30:2). ***beten*** also refers to miscarriage, stillbirth, and the slaughter of infants (cf. Deut. 28:18; Isa. 13:18; Hos. 9:16).

Literal references to the "belly" of a man are found in Judg. 3:21ff. ***beten*** also refers anthropomorphically to God, who expels the wicked from his "belly" in Job 20:15.

The remaining occurrences of ***beten*** are metaphorical. Num. 5:21ff. refers to a woman's "swollen belly" in relation to a curse of infertility. The designation "belly" is applied to the "innermost parts" of a man, indicating his inner being (Prov. 20:27ff.). See also Hab. 3:16. Jonah 2:2 refers to the "belly of Sheol," indicating the depths of despair in the realm of the grave.

reḥem **[רֶחֶם, 7358]**

reḥem is a synonym for ***beten*** (see above) and is found approximately twenty-five times. ***reḥem*** is translated "womb" throughout its usage.

Reference to a "womb" closed by God, constituting a divine judgment of infertility, is found in Gen. 20:18. Similarly, the curse of a "miscarrying womb" is indicated in Hos. 9:14. There is also a noteworthy use of ***reḥem*** in 1 Sam. 1:5ff., where the closure of Hannah's "womb" is not a divine judgment, but a divine trial to lead her to cast herself upon God, begging for a son, whom she would dedicate to Yahweh for life. This plea leads to the birth of Samuel, following upon the divine "reopening" of her womb. Elsewhere, a "womb" opened by God indicates a blessing of fertility (cf. Gen. 29:31; 30:22). Job 31:15 refers to children "fashioned in the womb" by God.

General references to a woman's "womb" are found in Num. 12:12; Job 3:11; 10:18; Ps. 58:3; Jer. 20:18. The expression "to open the womb" refers to giving birth and is applied to women (Exod. 13:2; Num. 3:12; 8:16), as well as to animals (Exod. 13:12ff.; 34:19). Jer. 1:5 declares that the prophet was called to serve God from "out of the womb" (i.e., before his birth).

reḥem refers metaphorically in Job 38:8 to the depths of the sea as a "womb." See also Ps. 110:3.

***raḥam* [רַחַם, 7356]**

raḥam is a noun found in around forty places with the primary senses of "mercy," "compassion." In several places, however, ***raḥam*** refers to the "womb." The term signifies fertility, abundant "blessings of the womb" (i.e., many children), in Gen. 49:25. See also Isa. 46:3. Prov. 30:16 contains a metaphorical reference to the grave as "the barren womb," signifying emptiness and despair. (→ MERCY)

NT WORDS

***koilia* [κοιλία, *2836*]**

koilia is a dynamic equivalent for ***beten*** and ***reḥem*** (see above). It occurs about twenty times and means "womb," or "belly" (or stomach) in most of the occurrences. ***koilia*** also refers metaphorically to the "heart" as the seat of human emotions.

The "belly" of a great fish (referring to the experience of the prophet Jonah) is indicated in Matt. 12:40. A person's "belly" (or stomach) is noted in Matt. 15:17; Luke 15:16; 1 Cor. 6:13; Phil. 3:19; Rev. 10:9ff.

References to a woman's (or a mother's) womb are found in Matt. 19:12; Luke 1:15, 41ff.; 23:29; John 3:4; Acts 3:2; 14:8; Gal. 1:15.

A person's inner being is depicted as a "heart" in John 7:38.

***gastēr* [γαστήρ, *1064*]**

gastēr is a noun found in nine places denoting the condition of pregnancy, or "being with child," and in Luke 1:31 it specifically refers to Mary's womb, which will carry the messianic child. Elsewhere, ***gastēr*** denotes "bellies" in reference to gluttony (cf. Titus 1:12).

***mētra* [μήτρα, *3388*]**

mētra is a rare noun referring to a woman's "womb" (Rom. 4:19), and to the womb of both women and female animals (Luke 2:23).

WONDER

OT WORDS

***tāmah* [תָּמַהּ, 8539]**

tāmah is a verb with the underlying senses of "to marvel at," "be amazed," "wonder at." It occurs nine times, referring to the reaction of people in Gen. 43:33; Ps. 48:5; Eccl. 5:8; Isa. 13:8; Jer. 4:9; Hab. 1:5. ***tāmah*** is used figuratively in Job 26:11, where the pillars of heaven are said to "marvel" at God's rebuke.

***pālā'* [פָּלָא, 6381]**

pālā' is a verb found about seventy times with the general sense of "do, work wonders, or marvelous things," with several related meanings. Such actions are predicated of God throughout the usage.

General references to divine miracle-working include those in Judg. 13:19; 1 Chr. 16:9ff.; Job 5:9; Pss. 9:1; 105:2ff.; 107:8ff. ***pālā'*** refers to working "wonders" among God's people (Exod. 34:10; Josh. 3:5; Neh. 9:17; Pss. 78:11; 98:1; Joel 2:26), and to working "signs" against Egypt (Exod. 3:20; Judg. 6:13; Ps. 106:7, 22).

pālā' is also used adjectivally, describing the deeds, or works, of God as "wonderful" (2 Chr. 2:9; Job 37:14; Pss. 26:3; 72:18).

***pele'* [פֶּלֶא, 6382]**

pele' is a noun derived from ***pālā'*** (see above) meaning "wonder," "marvel." It is also used adjectivally.

"Wonders" or "signs" performed by God are indicated in Exod. 15:11; Pss. 77:11ff.; 78:12; 88:10ff.; Dan. 12:6. The designation "wonderful" is either a name given to the promised Messianic King, or an adjective describing him as a Counselor (cf. Isa. 9:6).

***pilî'* [פִּלְאִי, 6383]**

pilî' is a rare adjectival form derived from ***pālā'*** (see above) meaning "wonderful" in the sense of "amazing," or "incomprehensible," suggesting a mysterious hiddenness.

In Judg. 13:18, the angel of the Lord indicates that his name is "Wonderful," suggesting that it is beyond the capacity of the human mind to grasp. In Ps. 139:6, the psalmist declares that the knowledge of Yahweh is too "wonderful" for him to grasp.

***temah* [תְּמַהּ, 8540 (Aramaic)]**

temah is an Aramaic noun occurring three times, referring to a "wonder" or "miracle" wrought by God (cf. Dan. 4:2ff.; 6:27).

NT WORDS

***thaumazō* [θαυμάζω, *2296*]**

thaumazō is a verbal dynamic equivalent for ***tāmah*** (see above), found in approximately fifty contexts with the primary sense of "wonder, or marvel at."

Christ is said to "marvel at" people's faith in him (Matt. 8:10; Luke 7:9). Conversely, he is also "astonished" at the unbelief of his countrymen (Mark 6:6; Luke 7:9).

People are commonly said to "marvel at" the miraculous powers of Christ (Matt. 8:27; Mark 5:20; Luke 8:25; 11:14); and they also express wonder at his words (Luke 4:22). People "marvel at" the news of the birth of the Christ child (Luke 2:18), and also at his resurrection (Luke 24:41). ***thaumazō*** is also found in Mark 15:44; Luke 1:63; 2:33; John 4:27; Acts 2:7; Gal. 1:6. Visions of God also produce a reaction of amazement (Acts 7:31; Rev. 13:3; 17:6ff.).

thaumazō also means "to wonder" in the sense of "be surprised" or even "puzzled at" (cf. Luke 1:21).

thaumasios [θαυμάσιος, *2297*]

thaumasios is an adjectival form derived from ***thaumazō*** (see above), meaning "wonderful" in the sense of "amazing," "marvelous." It is found only in Matt. 21:15, referring to the deeds of Christ.

thaumastos [θαυμαστός, *2298*]

thaumastos is an adjectival form synonymous with ***thaumasios***, above. It is found only in Matt. 21:42 in relation to the "wonderful" (i.e., marvelous) work of salvation wrought by God in Christ.

teras [τέρας, *5059*]

teras is a noun, a dynamic equivalent for ***pele'*** (see above). It occurs in sixteen places meaning "wonder," "miracle," "omen," "sign" throughout.

The meaning "wonder" in the sense of a supernatural phenomenon is indicated in Matt. 24:24; Mark 13:22; 2 Thess. 2:9, where false prophets perform such things in order to try and deceive the elect.

Elsewhere, "wonders" are said to be wrought by God as evidence of his power (John 4:48; Acts 7:36). In particular, these are "omens," constituting a prelude to the final day of judgment (cf. Acts 2:19). "Wonders" were also performed by Christ as a vindication of his divine power and authority (cf. Acts 2:22). Such "miracles" are also performed by the apostles and early Christian leaders as a testimony to their God-given, spirit-empowered ministry, as inheritors of Christ's authority (cf. Acts 2:43; 4:30; 5:12; 6:8; 14:3; 15:12; Rom. 15:19; 2 Cor. 12:12; Heb. 2:4).

See Also: → AMAZE → SIGN

WOOD

OT Words

'ēṣ [עֵץ, **6086**]

'ēṣ is a common noun with the principal meanings "wood," "tree," as well as several related senses throughout the more than three hundred occurrences of the term. (→ TREE)

'ēṣ refers to "wood" or "timber" as material for construction (Gen. 6:14; Lev. 14:45; Num. 13:20; Deut. 10:1; Josh. 9:21ff.; Prov. 26:20; Isa. 30:33; Jer. 28:13); for the manufacture of weapons (cf. Num. 35:18); for making musical instruments (cf. 2 Sam. 6:5); for constructing the tabernacle and temple (Exod. 25:5; 26:15; 1 Kgs. 6:10ff.); for building the ark of the covenant (Exod. 25:10; 37:1); and for other items of tabernacle furniture (cf. Exod. 25:13, 23, 28; 27:1; 30:1ff.; 35:33; 37:4ff.; Lev. 15:12). See also Neh. 2:8.

'ēṣ is also used metaphorically, referring to people as "wood" in the context of being prepared for a fiery destruction (Jer. 5:14).

'ēṣ also refers to "sticks" (2 Kgs. 6:6); and in Num. 15:32ff.; 1 Kgs. 17:10 it denotes "sticks" as firewood. In a figurative context, Israel and Judah are described as two "sticks" (i.e., nations) that will be joined together by God.

'ā' [אָע, **636** (Aramaic)]

'ā' is an Aramaic noun occurring five times denoting "wood," or "timber."

Such material is used for constructing the postexilic temple (Ezra 5:8; 6:4); and for constructing idols (Dan. 5:4, 23). See also Ezra 6:11.

NT Words

xylinos [ξύλινος, *3585*]

xylinos is a rare adjective meaning "wooden," or "made of wood." It refers in 2 Tim. 2:20 to wooden utensils, and in Rev. 9:20 to wooden idols.

See Also: → FOREST → TREE

WOOL

OT Words

ṣemer [צֶמֶר, **6785**]

ṣemer is a noun denoting "wool," as well as the adjectival sense of "woolen," throughout its sixteen occurrences.

Deut. 22:11; 2 Kgs. 3:4; Ezek. 27:18; 34:3; 44:17 refer to "wool," as a fiber used for making clothes. Other general references to "wool" include those in Ps. 147:16; Prov. 31:13; Isa. 1:18; 51:8; Hos. 2:5ff.

Lev. 13:47ff. refers to "woolen" garments, and Judg. 6:37 refers to a "woolen fleece."

'amar **[עֲמַר, 6015** (Aramaic)]

'amar is a rare Aramaic noun denoting "wool" in Dan. 7:9.

NT WORDS

erion [ἔριον, *2053*]

erion is a rare noun referring to "wool" in Heb. 9:19; Rev. 1:4.

WORD

OT WORDS

dābār **[דָּבָר, 1697]**

dābār is a common noun found nearly 1,500 times with a variety of meanings. The most prominent of these is "word," found in a number of contexts.

→ ACT → COMMANDMENT → SAYING
→ SPEECH → THING

dābār denotes "words" in relation to human utterance in a number of places. General references include those in Gen. 24:30; 27:34; Job 9:14; Pss. 55:21; 59:12; Isa. 36:21. ***dābār*** refers to words of parental instruction (Prov. 4:20); lying "words" (Exod. 5:9; Prov. 13:5; Jer. 7:8); "words" of the wicked (Prov. 12:6); "words" of the wise (Eccl. 9:17; 12:11); and the authoritative "words" of Moses received from God (Lev. 10:7; Deut. 1:1). ***dābār*** also refers to similar utterances by Samuel (cf. 1 Sam. 3:19; 4:1); Solomon (cf. 1 Kgs. 5:7); Nehemiah (cf. Neh. 1:1); and Joshua (cf. Josh. 1:18). See also Jer. 23:16; Eccl. 1:1; Isa. 1:1.

"Words" spoken by God are commonly attested. These are evident at the giving of the Sinai law covenant to the people of Israel (cf. Exod. 20:1; 24:3ff.; Deut. 4:10; 5:22; 12:28; Prov. 4:4). See also Job 42:7; Ps. 107:20; Isa. 55:11. ***dābār*** refers specifically to the divine "words" of the law covenant (Exod. 34:28; Deut. 27:8, 26; 28:58; 29:1, 9; 31:30; Josh. 8:34; Judg. 2:4; Neh. 8:9); and also to the Davidic covenant promise (cf. 1 Kgs. 8:26). Ps. 119:9, 16ff.; 65ff.; 101ff. refer to "words" given as a guide to righteous living. God also speaks "words" in judgment against the wicked, including God's own people (cf. Isa. 16:13; 24:3; 29:18; Jer. 36:1ff.; Amos 3:1).

"The word of the Lord" constitutes a technical expression for divine revelation. This is revealed to the patriarchs (Gen. 15:1ff.); to Joshua during the conquest (Josh. 8:27); and commonly to the prophets (e.g., 1 Sam. 3:1, 21; 2 Sam. 7:4; 1 Kgs. 13:1ff.; 17:5ff.; 2 Kgs. 20:16; Jer. 1:2ff.; Hos. 1:1ff.; Joel 1:1; Jonah 1:1; Mic. 1:1, Zeph. 1:1; Hag. 1:1ff.; Zech. 1:1ff.; Mal. 1:1). See also 1 Kgs. 6:11; 1 Chr. 22:8. The "word of the Lord" is found in the law of Moses in the context of binding instructions (cf. Num. 3:16; 15:31).

"The word of the Lord" is characterized by moral uprightness (Ps. 33:4). It is the agent of creation (Ps. 33:6); given in judgment against the wicked (Isa. 28:14); rejected by God's people (Jer. 8:9); and denied to God's people because of their sin.

'ēmer **[אֵמֶר, 561]**

'ēmer is a noun found approximately fifty times meaning "words" or "speech" in the majority of these contexts.

Human "speech," or "utterance," is indicated in general terms in Job 6:25; 33:3; Prov. 19:7. The "speech" of human beings is offered to God in worship (Ps. 19:14), and in prayer (Ps. 54:2). The seductive "words" of the adulteress are found in Prov. 2:16. Lying "words" are noted in Isa. 32:7. ***'ēmer*** also refers to "words of knowledge" (Prov. 19:27; 23:12); godly "words of wisdom" (Prov. 1:2); and "words" of instruction from godly parents (Prov. 2:1; 4:10; 5:7; 7:1, 24).

In the context of general revelation, "words" of God are found in Job 6:10; Ps. 138:4; and they are received by the prophet or seer in Num. 24:4, 16.

The "word(s) of the Lord" are given in the law, in the context of a covenant renewal ceremony (cf. Josh. 24:27); they are kept or treasured in human hearts (Job 22:22); and they are uttered in judgment against the wicked in Israel (Hos. 6:5).

millāh **[מִלָּה, 4405** (**4406** Aramaic)]

millāh is a noun denoting "word," or "speech," in most of its nearly forty occurrences.

2 Sam. 23:2 refers to the "word" of the Spirit of the Lord. The "words of God" are given to comfort those in trouble in Job 4:4.

General references to the "words" of humankind are found in Job 6:26; 15:13; 19:23; 32:14ff.; Ps. 139:4. Foolish "words" are indicated in Job 38:2, and wise "words" in Prov. 23:9.

Ps. 19:4 refers metaphorically to the "words of creation," declaring the glory of God.

The Aramaic form of this term is identical to the Hebrew and is translated "word" in Dan. 2:9; 3:28; 4:31; 5:10; 6:14. It is used metaphorically in Dan. 7:11,

25 to denote "words" spoken by the visionary satanic "little horn."

'imrāh [אִמְרָה, 565]

'imrāh is the feminine form of ***'ēmer*** (see above). It denotes "word(s)" or "speech" throughout its approximately forty occurrences.

Human "words" are offered up in prayer to God (Ps. 17:6). Gen. 4:23 refers to boasting "words."

The "word of God" is equated with his law in Deut. 33:9; Ps. 119:67, 103, 158; Isa. 5:24. In Isa. 28:23; 32:9, people are commanded to hear the words of God. Deut. 32:2 refers metaphorically to the "words of God" spoken through creation.

The "word of the Lord" is affirmed as flawless, true, and perfect in 2 Sam. 22:31; Pss. 12:6; 18:30; Prov. 30:5. It is said to be hidden in the human heart (Ps. 119:11) and to hold the promises of God (Ps. 119:41, 50, 58, 76, 133, 154).

peh [פֶּה, 6310]

peh is a common noun occurring around five hundred times and meaning "mouth" in the majority of these contexts. (→ MOUTH) "Word" is one of the additional senses derived from this primary meaning.

The "word" of human beings is noted as a command in Gen. 41:40. See also Deut. 21:5.

The "word of the Lord" is given in accordance with his law (Num. 3:16, 51; 36:5; 1 Kgs. 13:26); rejected by the Israelites (Num. 20:24); and expressed as a command (Num. 22:18; 27:21; Deut. 34:5; Josh. 19:50; 22:9; 1 Chr. 12:23).

NT Words

logos [λόγος, *3056*]

logos is a dynamic equivalent for the Hebrew term ***dābār*** (see above), signifying "word(s)," "saying," "speech" in the majority of its over 300 occurrences.

The "words" of human beings are indicated in the context of preaching (e.g., Matt. 10:4; Acts 2:22, 40ff.; 4:4; 2 Cor. 1:18). See also Luke 3:4; Matt. 8:8; 12:37. In particular, the "word of the kingdom" signifies gospel preaching (Matt. 13:19ff.; Mark 2:2; 4:14ff.; Acts 6:2ff.; 8:4). In Luke 8:11ff., the "word of God" is equated with the "seed" in the parable of the sower.

The "words of Christ" express the content of his public preaching and teaching. General references to these sayings are found in Matt. 7:24ff.; Mark 10:24; Luke 4:32ff.; 9:26; 10:39; John 2:22; 8:31, 37ff.; 1 Tim. 6:3. Christ's "words" effect miraculous healing (Matt. 8:16); bind people to follow him in obedience and faith (John 14:23; Col. 3:16ff.); and are said to be eternally enduring (Matt. 24:35; Mark 13:31; Luke 21:33).

Specific reference to the "word of God" is found in a variety of contexts. It summarizes the obligation of God's people to obey the commandments of the Lord, and to turn to Christ (cf. Mark 7:13; Luke 11:28; John 5:24, 38; 17:6, 14ff.; Gal. 6:6; Jas. 1:22; 1 John 2:5, 14). The "word of God" is equated with the teaching of Christ (Luke 5:1); revealed through the Hebrew Scriptures (cf. John 15:25; Rom. 9:16ff.; 2 Cor. 4:2); and equated with gospel preaching (Acts 8:14; 11:1; 17:11ff.; Eph. 1:13; Col. 1:15. 1 Thess. 1:5ff.; 2 Tim. 2:11; Heb. 4:2, 12; 1 Pet. 1:23; Rev. 6:9; 20:4). In 2 Pet. 3:5, the "word of God" is depicted as the agent of creation.

In particular, the person of Christ, identified as "the Word," is equated with God the divine being (John 1:1, 14; 1 John 1:1; Rev. 19:13).

The "word," or "message," of wisdom and knowledge is indicated in 1 Cor. 12:8. In 2 Cor. 5:19, the "word of reconciliation" is equated with the gospel. In Rev. 1:3; 22:6ff., "words of prophecy" are identified with the book of Revelation. "Words" taught by the Spirit are indicated in 1 Cor. 2:13. See also Luke 1:20.

Metaphorically speaking, the "word of the cross" in 1 Cor. 1:18 points to the message of Christ's crucifixion, his atoning sacrifice.

rhēma [ῥῆμα, *4487*]

rhēma is a synonym for ***logos*** (see above). It occurs seventy times and means "word," "utterance," "saying," "speech."

rhēma refers to "words" spoken by God as part of the divine revelation to humankind (Matt. 4:14; Luke 2:29; 3:2). In Eph. 6:17, the "word of God" is identified with the "sword of the spirit." In Heb. 11:3, God's "word" or "command" is identified as the agent of creation.

rhēma also refers generally to "words" uttered by human beings (Matt. 12:36; 18:16; Acts 6:11ff.); and to "words" uttered in the context of apostolic preaching (cf. Acts 2:14; 10:37, 44; Rom. 10:8; 1 Pet. 1:25).

Elsewhere, ***rhēma*** denotes the "words" of Jesus in the context of his public teaching and preaching ministry (cf. Matt. 26:75; Mark 9:32; 14:72; Luke 18:34; 24:8; John 5:47; 12:47ff.). These words are equated with gospel preaching (Eph. 5:26; Heb. 1:3); and they reflect the very words of God (John 3:34; 8:47; 18:8). See also John 6:68.

rhēma also metaphorically denotes "words" of creation that proclaim the glory of God (Rom. 10:18).

logomacheō [λογομαχέω, *3054*]

logomacheō is a rare verb found only in 2 Tim. 2:14 meaning "to quarrel about words."

angelia [ἀγγελία, *31*]

angelia is a rare noun, found only in 1 John 3:11, indicating the sense of "message" in the context of divinely revealed principles.

Additional Notes

It is clear from an examination of "word" terminology throughout both Testaments that its most significant usage relates to the phenomenon of divine revelation. Initially such revelation is exclusively verbal, coupled with accompanying dreams and vision. However, in the New Testament it is evident that the climactic revelation of "the word of God" comes to fulfillment in Jesus Christ, the incarnation of the divine Word. In the aftermath of Christ's resurrection and ascension, it is the Spirit of God that enables the believer to fully understand and appropriate the written word(s) of Scripture.

WORK, WORKER

OT Words

'āsāh [עָשָׂה, **6213**]

'āsāh is a common verb with a variety of meanings. It occurs over 2,500 times with the primary senses of "do," "make." There are also a number of derivative meanings, one of which is "to work." → EXECUTE → KEEP → MAKE → OFFER → PREPARATION

The meaning "to work" is predicated of human beings in relation to their skill in making crafts of every kind (cf. Exod. 31:5; 35:32; 39:3; 1 Kgs. 7:14). General references to "laboring," or "working" include those in Josh. 9:14; Neh. 4:6; Hag. 2:14; Prov. 31:13; Eccl. 3:9. In particular, the sense of "act wickedly or deceitfully" is indicated in 1 Kgs. 21:25; Ps. 101:7; Prov. 11:18; Isa. 32:6; Ezek. 33:26; Dan. 11:23; as is the sense of "act righteously" in Isa. 64:5.

Where God is concerned, ***'āsāh*** refers to him "performing acts of deliverance" or "rescuing" his people in 1 Sam. 14:6. See also Ps. 119:126.

ma'aseh [מַעֲשֶׂה, **4639**]

ma'aseh is a noun derived from ***'āsāh*** (see above) with the dominant sense of "work," in a number of contexts.

"Work" in the sense of "labor" is predicated of human beings in general contexts (e.g., Gen. 5:29; Exod. 5:4; Judg. 19:16; Ps. 115:4; Prov. 16:3; Eccl. 2:4; 12:14; Hag. 2:17). "Work" on the Sabbath, however, is forbidden (Exod. 23:12). "Labor" in the sense of an "occupation," "trade," or "business" is indicated in Gen. 46:33; Isa. 17:8; Jer. 10:3.

Specialized forms of "labor" or "work" include "engraving" in "stone and metal," as noted in relation to the tabernacle and temple (cf. Exod. 28:11; 1 Kgs. 7:19ff.). ***ma'aseh*** also refers to "fashioning" and "embroidering" (cf. Exod. 26:1; 28:8; 36:8).

ma'aseh denotes "deeds" or "actions" performed by human beings (e.g., Gen. 20:9). In particular, "deeds" commissioned by God are indicated in Num. 16:28. "Actions" blessed by God are noted in Deut. 2:7; Job 1:10. Eccl. 8:4 mentions the "deeds" of the righteous; and "evil deeds" are evident in Ps. 28:4; Eccl. 4:3. See also Jonah 3:10; Ezek. 16:30.

ma'aseh also denotes "works" or "deeds" performed by God, such as inscribing the two tablets of the law covenant (Exod. 32:16). One of Yahweh's "deeds" is conquering the peoples of Canaan and driving them out, so that the Israelites could live in that land (cf. Exod. 34:10). God's "work" in creation is depicted in Pss. 8:3, 6; 19:1; 102:25; Isa. 64:8.

General references to God's mighty deeds and works on behalf of his people are found in Deut. 3:24; 11:3; Josh. 24:31; Judg. 2:7ff.; Ps. 66:3. Praise for his redemptive "works" is evident in Pss. 107:22; 111:2; 139:14.

melā'kāh [מְלָאכָה, **4399**]

melā'kāh is a noun found nearly 170 times with the underlying sense of "work," also indicating "labor" in general, one's "business," or "occupation."

God's "work" of creation is noted in Gen. 2:2ff. Ps. 73:28 also speaks of the "works" or "deeds" of God, indicating his power and might.

The "work" of human beings, referring to their "occupation," "business," or "trade," is indicated in Gen. 39:11; Ps. 107:23; Prov. 18:9; 22:29; 24:27; Jer. 18:3; Dan. 8:27; Jonah 1:8. In particular, human "craftsmanship" (or skilled handiwork, embroidery, sculpture, etc.) is noted in 1 Kgs. 7:14, 22; Ezek. 28:13.

melā'kāh also denotes human "labor" in a general sense in Exod. 20:9. All "work" is forbidden on the Sabbath (cf. Exod. 12:16; 20:10; 31:14ff.; Lev. 23:3; Deut. 5:13ff.; Jer. 17:22). "Labor" expended in the construction of the temple is indicated in 1 Kgs. 7:51. See also 2 Kgs. 12:14ff.; Ezra 3:8ff.; Hag. 1:14. "Work" on the reconstruction of the city wall of Jerusalem is recorded in Neh. 4:11ff.; 5:16; 6:3ff.

"Work" or "service" in the context of Levitical ritual worship is indicated in Exod. 35:21ff.; 36:1ff.; Lev. 23:21ff.; Num. 4:3. See also Neh. 13:10.

'ābad [עָבַד, 5647]

'ābad is a common verb found approximately three hundred times with the primary meaning "to serve." It also has a number of related meanings, including "till" (i.e., to work the ground).

In several places, ***'ābad*** also means "to work," referring to those who labor in business or construction (cf. 2 Chr. 2:18; Eccl. 5:12). The meaning "till" (i.e., the ground) is found in Gen. 2:5, 15; 3:23; 4:2, 12.

'abôdāh [עֲבוֹדָה, 5656]

'abôdāh is also translated "work" in the sense of "manual labor" (Exod. 5:9ff.), and in the context of tabernacle construction (Exod. 39:32). "Work" is forbidden on the Sabbath (cf. Lev. 23:7ff.). Num. 4:30ff. refers to ritual "service" (or "work"). The term also describes the "tilling" (i.e., working) of the soil in 1 Chr. 27:26.

pā'al [פָּעַל, 6466]

pā'al is a verb occurring about sixty times with the primary meaning "to work" throughout most of its usage, as well as several related nuances.

The meaning "work" in the sense of "do," "accomplish" is predicated of God in Num. 23:23; Deut. 32:37; Job 33:29; Ps. 31:19; Isa. 26:12; 43:13; Hab. 1:5. Ps. 74:12 refers to God, who "accomplishes" salvation.

pā'al refers to human beings who "have done" wrong (Job 36:23), as well as to those who "do" right (Ps. 15:2). The term also refers to the blacksmith "working" (i.e., fashioning) his creations over the fire (cf. Isa. 44:12ff.).

The participial form of ***pā'al*** is used nominally to denote "workers (of iniquity)," or "evil ones," in a number of places (cf. Job 31:3; 34:8; Pss. 5:5; 14:4; 28:3; 64:2; 92:7ff.; Isa. 31:2; Hos. 6:8).

pō'al [פֹּעַל, 6467]

pō'al is a participial noun derived from ***pā'al*** (see above), meaning "work," "deed," "action" throughout most of its nearly forty occurrences.

When predicated of God, ***pō'al*** refers generally to his "works," or his omnipotent, just ways (Deut. 32:4; Pss. 64:9; 90:16; 143:5; Hab. 1:5). See also Isa. 5:12; 45:11.

In the human sphere, ***pō'al*** denotes "work" in the sense of "labor" (Ps. 104:23). In Deut. 33:11, the "work" of one's hands is offered up to God. Other general references to "what one has done" are found in Ruth 2:12; Job 34:11; Prov. 24:12. In particular, "evil deeds" are indicated in Job 36:9; Pss. 9:16; 28:4.

pō'al also denotes the "deeds," or "actions," of human beings, including heroic "deeds" (2 Sam. 23:20; 1 Chr. 11:22); "deeds" of violence (Isa. 59:6); and "deeds" that are evaluated by God in the context of judgment (cf. Jer. 25:14; 50:29).

pe'ullāh [פְּעֻלָּה, 6468]

pe'ullāh is a passive participial form of ***pā'al*** (see above) with the nominal senses of "work," "labor," "wages," "reward" in all fourteen occurrences.

References to "wages," or remuneration for labor undertaken, are found in Lev. 19:13; Prov. 11:18. The expression "wages of righteousness" in Prov. 10:16 figuratively denotes blessings from God.

The meaning "reward," in the sense of "recompense," or "judgment" (from God), is indicated in Ps. 109:29; Isa. 61:8. In particular, Isa. 49:4; 62:11 refer to the Messianic Servant's "reward."

General references to "work" or "labor" are found in 2 Chr. 15:7; Jer. 31:16. The "works" or "deeds" of human beings are likewise noted (Ps. 17:4); as are the "deeds" of the Lord (Ps. 28:5).

'āmal [עָמַל, 5998]

'āmal is a verb meaning "to labor," "toil" in the context of hard, manual work in all eleven occurrences (cf. Ps. 127:1; Jonah 4:10). In particular, Eccl. 1:3; 2:11, 19ff.; 5:16; 8:17 denote "work" or "labor" in relation to fruitless or vain "toil" that seemingly has no meaning. An exception is found in Eccl. 5:18, where "work" is spoken of positively.

miqshāh [מִקְשָׁה, 4749]

miqshāh is a noun found ten times denoting ritual objects of gold and silver, and single pieces of "hammered, or beaten work" — all of which are utilized in the service of the tabernacle (cf. Exod. 25:18, 31, 36; 37:7, 17, 22).

yāga' [יָגַע, 3021]

yāga' is a verb found about thirty times with the underlying meanings "to work," "toil" in the sense of "grow, be weary."

In the human sphere, ***yāga'*** is used in the negative sense of "not growing weary" (cf. Josh. 7:3; 24:13; 2 Sam. 23:10; Job 9:29; Ps. 6:6; Prov. 23:4; Eccl. 10:15; Isa. 40:3ff.; Hab. 2:13).

Such a negative use is also found in relation to God, who likewise "never grows weary" in his work (cf. Isa. 40:28). Isa. 49:14 refers to the "Suffering Servant" who, momentarily at least, admits to the perception of "laboring in vain."

yegîa' [יְגִיעַ, 3018]

yegîa' is a noun derived from ***yāga'*** (see above) denoting "work" or "labor" in most of its sixteen occurrences.

References to the "labor" of one's hands are found in Gen. 31:42; Deut. 28:33; Neh. 5:13; Pss. 78:46; 128:2; Isa. 55:2; Jer. 3:24; Hag. 1:11. Elsewhere, "the fruits of labor" (i.e., wealth) are noted in Isa. 45:14; Ezek. 23:29.

'eṣeb [עֶצֶב, 6089]

'eṣeb is a noun occurring seven times meaning "toil," "labor" (cf. Ps. 127:2; Prov. 5:10; 14:23). Gen. 3:16 refers to "painful childbirth," or giving birth in painful toil. See also Ps. 127:2.

yālad [יָלַד, 3205]

yālad is a common verb found in approximately five hundred contexts with the predominant sense of "beget," "give birth." In a number of contexts, ***yālad*** also refers to the difficulty of this experience for women, describing the birth process as "painful labor" (cf. Gen. 35:16ff.; Ps. 48:6; Jer. 6:24; 13:21; 49:24; 50:43; Mic. 4:9ff.). Another general reference to this process is found in Gen. 38:27.

'alîlāh [עֲלִילָה, 5949]

'alîlāh is a noun found about twenty times denoting "works," "actions," or "deeds."

The culpable, wicked "actions" of human beings that will be judged by God are noted in 1 Sam. 2:3; Pss. 14:1; 77:12.

Yahweh's redemptive "deeds," for which he is to be praised, are evident in 1 Chr. 16:8; Pss. 9:11; 103:7; 105:1; Isa. 12:4. ***'alîlāh*** also denotes divine "acts" of judgment against the wicked (cf. Pss. 66:5; 99:8; 141:4; Ezek. 14:22ff.; 20:43ff.; 21:24; 36:17ff.).

NT Words

ergazomai [ἐργάζομαι, *2038*]

ergazomai is a verb found around forty times meaning "work," "labor."

With reference to human beings, the general sense of "engaging in manual labor" is indicated in Matt. 21:28; Luke 13:14; John 6:27; Rom. 4:4ff.; 1 Cor. 4:12; Eph. 4:28; 2 Thess. 3:10ff. Similarly, ***ergazomai*** also refers to conducting business or trade (Matt. 25:16; Rev. 18:17). In addition, Matt. 7:23 refers to "working (or doing) evil."

1 Cor. 16:10; Col. 3:23; 2 John 18; 3 John 5 refer to engaging in the work of gospel ministry.

ergazomai also denotes, in a nominal sense, the godly "deeds" of the believer (John 3:21).

ergazomai also indicates the work of God in the hearts of human beings, illuminating their hearts (cf. John 5:17), and "performing" miraculous deeds (cf. Acts 13:41). Similarly, in John 6:30; 9:4, Christ is said "to perform" a miraculous sign in order to fulfill the purposes of God.

katergazomai [κατεργάζομαι, *2716*]

katergazomai is a verb found in about thirty contexts, a variant of ***ergazomai***, above, and meaning "to work," "produce," "accomplish."

Suffering and testing is said to "produce," or "bring about," endurance (Rom. 5:3; 2 Cor. 4:17; Jas. 1:3). Conversely, sin is said to "bring about" or "produce" coveting that leads to death (Rom. 7:8, 13). See also 2 Cor. 7:10. In contrast, 2 Cor. 7:11 affirms that godly sorrow "produces" a yearning for righteousness. The work of Christ in producing righteousness in the lives of believers is indicated in Rom. 15:18. In Phil. 2:12, the apostle exhorts believers "to work out" their salvation with fear and trembling.

ergasia [ἐργασία, *2039*]

ergasia is a noun denoting "trade," or "business," as well as "profits" gained from such enterprise. Acts 16:16ff. refers to "profitable gain" derived from one's business or work. Acts 19:24ff. refers generally to "business," "work," or "trade."

ergon [ἔργον, *2041*]

ergon is the predominant Greek term for "work(s)," or "deed(s)," in various contexts. It is found nearly two hundred times.

ergon refers generally to human "works" or "deeds" (cf. Matt. 23:5; Eph. 2:9, 10; 2 Tim. 1:9). 1 Cor. 3:13ff. indicates that such "work" is to be judged by God. Jas. 2:20ff. refers to "works" in relation to one's faith. ***ergon*** refers to good "deeds" (Matt. 5:16; Acts 9:36; 2 Cor. 9:8; 1 Tim. 5:10; 2 Tim. 3:17; Heb. 10:24); evil "deeds"

(Luke 11:48; 2 Pet. 2:8; John 3:19ff.; Jude 15; Rev. 16:11); and "deeds" subject to divine judgment (Rom. 2:6; Eph. 5:11; 1 Pet. 1:17; Rev. 2:2ff.; 3:1ff.; 20:12ff.; 22:12).

"Work" in the sense of formal employment is indicated in Mark 13:34; and in the context of gospel ministry in Acts 13:2; 14:26; 1 Cor. 15:58; Eph. 4:12; 1 Thess. 5:13.

ergon is also used figuratively to denote "workmanship," referring to believers as the fruit of Paul's ministry (cf. 1 Cor. 9:1). The term also denotes "the works of the law" in Rom. 3:20, 28; 4:2ff.; 9:11, 32; 11:6; Gal. 2:16; 3:2ff.

In relation to Christ, ***ergon*** indicates his miraculous signs (i.e., his works) (Matt. 11:2; Luke 24:19; John 5:20; 7:3; Heb. 3:9), and his "work" of redemption (Phil. 3:20).

Rom. 14:20 refers generally to the "work" of God in redemption. The "work" of redemption effected in and through the person of Christ, who is sent by God, is indicated in John 4:34; 5:36; 9:3ff.; 10:25ff.; 14:10ff.; 17:4. The divine "work" in the life of the believer that produces genuine righteousness is noted in Phil. 1:6. Heb. 1:10; 4:3 speak of the "work" of God's hands in creation.

ergon also refers to the "works" of the devil (1 John 3:8).

ergatēs [ἐργάτης, *2040*]

ergatēs is a noun denoting "laborer," "workman" throughout its sixteen occurrences.

General references to "laborer" include those in Matt. 9:37ff.; 10:10; 20:1ff.; Luke 10:2ff.; 1 Tim. 5:16; Jas. 5:4. Acts 19:25; 2 Tim. 2:15 specifically mention a "workman" (i.e., a skilled tradesman). The latter reference indicates one skilled in the knowledge of God's word. Conversely, ***ergatēs*** also denotes "workers of evil, iniquity" (Luke 13:27; 2 Cor. 11:13; Phil. 3:2).

energeō [ἐνεργέω, *1754*]

energeō is a verb found in around twenty contexts meaning "to work," "be at work" in a variety of contexts.

With reference to God, ***energeō*** refers to the divine power "at work" in the life of his people (cf. Eph. 3:20; Phil. 2:13; Col. 1:29). See also Matt. 14:2; Mark 6:14; 1 Cor. 12:11. God is also said to "work" miracles (Gal. 3:5), as he "accomplishes" all things according to his will (cf. Eph. 1:11, 20). The word of God is also said to "be at work" in the life of the believer (1 Thess. 2:13).

Sinful passions are said "to be aroused, produced" by the law in the life of the unbeliever (cf. Rom. 7:5). 2 Cor. 4:12 affirms that death is "at work" in the human body, as is the spirit of Satan in unbelievers (cf. Eph. 2:2). Positively, faith is said to "work" in believers through love (cf. Gal. 5:6).

Gal. 2:8 refers to believers "working" (i.e., engaging) in ministry with one another.

energeia [ἐνέργεια, *1753*]

energeia is a noun occurring eight times, denoting the superhuman "working" of either God or Satan. Satan's activity is noted in 2 Thess. 2:9. God's power is evident in the life of the believer, as noted in Eph. 1:19; 3:7; 4:16; Phil. 3:21; Col. 1:29; 2:12.

synergeō [συνεργέω, *4903*]

synergeō is a verb found in five places, meaning "to work together with," and referring to people working together in ministry (cf. Mark 16:20; 1 Cor. 16:16; 2 Cor. 6:1; Jas. 2:22). ***synergeō*** also refers to things "working together" for the gospel in accord with the purposes of God (Rom. 8:28).

synergos [συνεργός, *4904*]

synergos is a noun occurring thirteen times, denoting "fellow workers" in gospel ministry (cf. Rom. 16:3ff.; 1 Cor. 3:9; 2 Cor. 1:24; 8:23; Phil. 2:25; 4:3; Col. 4:11; Phlm. 1, 24; 3 John 8).

poiēma [ποίημα, *4161*]

poiēma is a rare noun referring to believers as the product of God's "workmanship" (Eph. 2:10).

praxis [πρᾶξις, *4234*]

praxis is a noun occurring six times referring to "works," "deeds."

praxis refers to the "works" of human beings, subject to divine judgment (Matt. 16:27; Luke 23:51; Acts 19:18), and to the "works" of the sinful nature (Rom. 8:13; Col. 3:9).

geōrgeō [γεωργέω, *1090*]

geōrgeō is a rare verb designating the action of "working," or "tilling" the ground, found only in Heb. 6:7.

kopos [κόπος, *2873*]

kopos is a noun denoting "work," "labor" in the majority of its nineteen occurrences. (→ TROUBLE)

General references to "work," "labor" are found in John 4:38; 1 Cor. 3:8; 11:23; 2 Thess. 3:8. The "work" of ministry is noted in 1 Cor. 15:58; 2 Cor. 10:15; 1 Thess. 1:3; Heb. 6:10; Rev. 14:13.

See Also: → SERVE → STRENGTH

WORLD

OT Words

tēbēl [תֵּבֵל, 8398]

tēbēl is a noun denoting "world" throughout its nearly forty occurrences, with a variety of connotations.

"World" in the sense of the "created universe" is indicated in 1 Sam. 2:8; Job 18:18; Pss. 18:15; 24:1; 50:12; Prov. 8:31; Jer. 10:12. ***tēbēl*** also refers to the universal population of the earth (Pss. 9:8; 33:8; Lam. 4:12). The "world" in this sense is explicitly declared to be judged by God (Ps. 96:13; Isa. 13:11). See also Isa. 18:3; 26:9.

tēbēl also denotes the "world" as an entity that includes both people and other created phenomena (cf. Isa. 24:4; 27:6; Nah. 1:5).

ḥeled [חֶלֶד, 2465]

ḥeled is a rare noun denoting "world" in the quasi-philosophical sense of "the age (or spirit) of the world" (cf. Ps. 17:14). It also refers to the "world" generally as the "dwelling place" of human beings (cf. Ps. 49:1).

NT Words

kosmos [κόσμος, *2889*]

kosmos is the dynamic equivalent of the Hebrew term ***tēbēl*** (see above), denoting "world" throughout its nearly two hundred occurrences. There are a variety of connotations associated with this term.

The meaning "world," denoting the realm of humankind inhabited by various kingdoms and nations, is indicated in Matt. 4:8; 13:38; 26:13; Mark 14:19; 16:15; Luke 12:30; Rom. 1:8; 5:12; 1 Tim. 1:15. In John 18:36, Christ explicitly declares, however, that his kingdom is not of this "world." The "world" is said to be illuminated by the true light of the gospel of Christ (cf. Matt. 5:14; John 1:9; 8:12; 9:5; 12:46).

In related contexts, ***kosmos*** also denotes the "world" as the universal community of humankind. This "world" is subject to divine judgment and wrath (Matt. 18:7; John 3:19; 12:31; 16:8; Heb. 11:7; 1 John 2:2); and is also alienated from God (John 14:27; 15:18ff.; 16:28, 33; 17:6, 11ff.; 1 Cor. 1:20ff.; 3:19ff.; 5:10; Phil. 2:15; Jas. 1:27; 1 John 2:15ff.; 4:4ff.). Such a "world" is therefore identified as unbelieving and subject to divine condemnation (cf. John 1:10, 29; 8:23; 1 Cor. 11:32; 2 Pet. 1:4; 2:5). John 14:17 affirms that the "world" is incapable of discerning spiritual truth, and it is also declared to be ruled by the devil (cf. John 14:30; 16:11; Eph. 2:2). In positive contexts, the "world" is granted saving grace, and belief in Christ (cf. John 17:21). It is also designated as the object of God's love (cf. John 3:16ff.) and the salvation of Christ (cf. John 4:42; 6:33; 12:47; 2 Cor. 5:19; 1 John 4:14).

kosmos also refers to the "world" in terms of the universe at the point of creation (cf. Matt. 13:35; 24:21; Luke 11:50; John 17:5, 24; Acts 17:24; Rom. 1:20; Eph. 1:14; Heb. 4:3; 9:26; 1 Pet. 1:20; Rev. 13:8, 17).

Gal. 4:3; Col. 2:8, 20 refer to the "world" as identification with the universe in relation to its elemental spirits, an understanding embraced by the pagans. John 12:25 refers to "this world" in the sense of "this life," "this age."

In addition, ***kosmos*** denotes "world" in the figurative sense of the sum total of one's realized ambition for wealth, power, and prestige (cf. Matt. 16:26; Mark 8:36; Luke 9:25). The term is also used hyperbolically, referring to the "world" as a great number of people (cf. John 12:19; 18:20).

aiōn [αἰών, *165*]

aiōn is a noun occurring about 130 times meaning "age" in the sense of "world" in about one-third of these contexts. It can also mean unending, everlasting duration, as in "forever," "ever more." (→ EVER)

The designation "world" in the sense of "age," indicating the temporal duration of the created universe, is found in general contexts (e.g., Matt. 12:32; Eph. 1:21; 1 Tim. 6:17; Heb. 1:2; 11:3). 1 Cor. 2:7 speaks of God's wisdom evident "before the world began." References to "the end of the age" as the time of judgment are found in Matt. 13:39ff.; 24:3; 28:20; 1 Cor. 10:11; Heb. 9:26. This "age" is designated as evil in 2 Cor. 4:4; Eph. 6:12. See also John 9:32; Acts 15:18; Eph. 3:9. General references to "the sons of this world (i.e., age)," implying hostility to God, are found in Luke 16:8; 20:34. See also Luke 16:8; 20:34; 1 Cor. 1:20; 2:6ff.; 3:18; 2 Tim. 4:10.

aiōn also refers to the future age (or world), to come, depicting eternal life with God (cf. Mark 10:30; Luke 18:30; 20:35; Eph. 2:7; Heb. 6:5 [implied]).

oikoumenē [οἰκουμένη, *3625*]

oikoumenē is a noun denoting "world" throughout its fifteen occurrences.

For the most part, ***oikoumenē*** refers to "world" in the sense of the entire inhabited earth. It is depicted as the sphere for the proclamation of the gospel (Matt. 24:14; Rom. 10:18), and also as the sphere for divine judgment at the end of time (Acts 17:31). Other general references to the "world" in this sense are found in Luke 2:1; Acts 11:28; Heb. 1:6; Rev. 3:10; 12:9; 16:14. See also Luke 4:5; Acts 19:27.

oikoumenē is also used hyperbolically, designating the vast majority of the land of Palestine as "the world" (Acts 17:6; 24:5).

oikoumenē also denotes the world to come as the eternal age (cf. Heb. 2:5).

See Also: ➡ EARTH

WORLDLY

NT Words

kosmikos [κοσμικός, *2886*]

kosmikos is a rare adjective denoting the sense of "worldly" in Titus 2:12 with reference to "worldly desires." In Heb. 9:1 it refers to the "earthly" tabernacle.

WORM

OT Words

rimmāh [**רִמָּה, 7415**]

rimmāh is a noun found in seven places meaning "worm," "maggot," as the cause and evidence of "decay," "rottenness."

The term is used both literally (Exod. 16:24; Job 7:5) and figuratively (Job 17:14; 21:26; 25:6; Isa. 14:11).

tôlā' [**תּוֹלָע, 8438**]

tôlā' is a noun occurring around forty times denoting "worm" in a literal sense, as well as the color "scarlet" — a dye derived from the dried body of the female "coccus" worm.

Literal references to "worm" are found in Exod. 16:20; Deut. 28:31; Jonah 4:7.

References to "scarlet" dye used in coloring materials for the tabernacle are found in Exod. 25:4; 26:1; 27:16; 28:5ff.; 35:23ff.; 36:35ff.; 39:1ff. Such material, as an element of ritual offerings, is also mentioned in Lev. 14:4ff.; 49ff.; Num. 4:8; 19:6.

Metaphorical usage of ***tôlā'***, with reference to the "worm," is found in Job 25:6; Ps. 22:6; Isa. 14:11. In Isa. 1:18, human sin is described as "scarlet."

sās [**סָס, 5580**]

sās is a rare noun denoting "worm" in Isa. 51:8.

NT Words

skōlēx [σκώληξ, *4663*]

skōlēx is a rare noun denoting "the worm" that feeds upon dead bodies (cf. Mark 9:44ff.).

skōlēkobrōtos [σκωληκόβρωτος, *4662*]

skōlēkobrōtos is a rare adjective meaning "eaten by worms," referring in Acts 12:23 to the grisly death suffered by King Herod.

WORSHIP

OT Words

shāḥāh [**שָׁחָה, 7812**]

shāḥāh is a verb depicting the actions of "bowing down" and "worshiping" in most of its approximately 170 occurrences. These two actions are often synonymous. (➡ BOW)

shāḥāh refers to the "worship" of Yahweh in a number of contexts. It is offered by the patriarchs (Gen. 22:5; 24:26); the Israelites (Exod. 4:31; 33:10; 2 Chr. 7:3; Neh. 8:6; Job 1:20; Ps. 22:7ff.; Isa. 27:13; Jer. 7:2); Moses (Exod. 24:1; 34:8); and Joshua (Josh. 5:14). Other general references include those in Judg. 7:15; 1 Sam. 15:25ff.; 2 Sam. 12:20; Ps. 66:4; Isa. 49:7; Zeph. 2:11. Worship is also commanded by God in Deut. 26:10; 1 Chr. 16:29; Ps. 99:9.

shāḥāh also denotes the worshiping of idols, which is cited as a culpable practice (Exod. 32:8; Deut. 29:26; 1 Kgs. 11:33; 2 Kgs. 17:6; Ps. 106:19; Isa. 2:8; Jer. 1:16; 13:10). Such "worship" is forbidden under covenant law on penalty of death, which is both explicit and implicit (cf. Exod. 34:14; Deut. 4:9; 8:19; 17:3; Josh. 23:7; Ps. 81:9). 1 Kgs. 9:6 warns against idolatrous worship. 2 Kgs. 19:37 refers to pagans "worshiping their idols."

segid [**סְגִד, 5457** (Aramaic)]

segid is an Aramaic verb found twelve times meaning "worship," "pay homage to." In Dan. 2:46, King Nebuchadnezzar "pays homage to" Daniel. The same king issues a command for all his people to "worship" the golden image he had erected (cf. Dan. 3:5ff.). "Worshiping" gods in general terms is noted in Dan. 3:28.

'ābad [**עָבַד, 5647**]

'ābad is a common verb found about three hundred times with the predominant sense of "serve," but it occasionally indicates the associated meaning "worship." This is evident in 2 Kgs. 10:19ff.; 17:12ff., where idolatrous worship is practiced by rebellious Israelite people and leaders. (→ SERVE)

NT Words

proskyneō [προσκυνέω, *4352*]

The verb ***proskyneō*** is found in sixty-five places, a dynamic equivalent for ***shāḥāh*** (see above). It means "worship" throughout, in various contexts.

Worship offered to God by human beings is indicated in John 4:20ff.; 1 Cor. 14:25; Rev. 4:10; 5:14; 7:11; 11:16; 14:7; 15:4; 19:4, 10. Various people offer worship to the infant Christ in Matt. 2:2ff. See also Heb. 1:6. Christ is also portrayed as the object of worship in Matt. 8:2; 14:33; Mark 5:6; John 9:38. Satan attempts, without success, to entice Christ to worship him in Matt. 4:9; Mark 4:7. Idolatrous worship is undertaken in Rev. 9:20; 13:4ff.; 14:9ff.; 16:2; 19:20; 20:4; 22:9.

There are general commands for all to "worship" God alone in Matt. 4:10; Mark 4:8. Worship, incorporating the action of "bowing or kneeling down" before Christ, is indicated in Matt. 18:26; 20:20; Mark 15:19.

sebomai [σέβομαι, *4576*]

sebomai is a verb found in ten places meaning "to worship." It also has the adjectival sense of "devout."

The act of worshiping God is indicated in Acts 16:4; 18:7, 13; and "vain worship" is noted in Matt. 15:9; Mark 7:7. The idolatrous worship of the created order is noted in Rom. 1:25. See also Acts 19:27.

Believers are described as "devout" or "God-fearing" in Acts 13:50; 17:4, 17.

latreuō [λατρεύω, *3000*]

latreuō is a verb meaning both "worship" and "serve." (→ SERVE)

eusebeō [εὐσεβέω, *2151*]

eusebeō is a rare verb meaning "to worship" in Acts 17:23 in connection with the "unknown god" of the Athenians. 1 Tim. 5:4 refers to "practicing religious observance."

ethelothrēskeia [ἐθελοθρησκείᾳ, *1479*]

ethelothrēskeia is a rare noun found only in Col. 2:23, referring to "arbitrary, self-imposed worship," which is formulated not for the glory of God but for one's own self-glorification. As such, it is condemned by the apostle.

sebasma [σέβασμα, *4574*]

sebasma is a rare noun found only in Acts 17:23; 2 Thess. 2:4, denoting an "object of worship." Idolatry is involved in both instances.

theosebēs [θεοσεβής, *2318*]

theosebēs is a rare adjective denoting anyone "who worships God." It is found only in John 9:31.

proskynētēs [προσκυνητής, *4353*]

proskynētēs is a rare noun denoting a "worshiper" of God in John 4:23.

thrēskeia [θρησκεία, *2356*]

thrēskeia is a noun indicating "religion," "religious worship." It is found in four places.

Pure "religion" is commended in Jas. 1:26, 27; and the "religion" of the Pharisees is noted in Acts 26:5, in relation to Paul's pre-conversion vocation. Col. 2:18 refers to the ritualistic "religious worship" of angels.

WORTHLESS

OT Words

sākan [סָכַן, 5532]

sākan is a rare verb, used in the adjectival sense of "useless," "worthless," or "unprofitable" in Job 15:3, in relation to "speech," or "talk."

NT Words

achreioō [ἀχρειόω, *889*]

achreioō is a verb found only in Rom. 3:12, referring to all people "becoming worthless, or unprofitable."

achreios [ἀχρεῖος, *888*]

achreios is an adjective found in only two places (Matt. 25:30; Luke 17:10), describing servants as "worthless," "useless," "good-for-nothing."

achrēstos [ἄχρηστος, *890*]

achrēstos is a rare adjective found only in Phlm. 11, indicating the former status of Onesimus as "useless," or "worthless" to his master Philemon.

anōphelēs [ἀνωφελής, *512*]

anōphelēs is another rare adjectival form referring to "worthless" or "unprofitable" argument over the law in Titus 3:9. It also describes as "useless" the former statute of priestly law under the old covenant that could never effectively remove sin and guilt in the life of the Israelite people (cf. Heb. 7:18).

WORTHY

OT Words

hālal [הָלַל, **1984**]

hālal is a common verb with the primary meaning "to praise." It occurs 165 times. In two contexts, however, a passive form of the verb is translated adjectivally as "worthy of praise," referring to God (cf. 2 Sam. 22:4; Ps. 18:3).

NT Words

hikanos [ἱκανός, *2425*]

hikanos is an adjective occurring around forty times with the primary senses of "many," "much," "enough." However, the term also means "worthy," although in the New Testament it occurs only in the negative — with the sense of "unworthy" (cf. Matt. 3:11; 8:8; Mark 1:7; Luke 3:16; 7:6).

axios [ἄξιος, *514*]

axios is an adjective found in around forty contexts with the dominant sense of "worthy," with varying nuances.

The meaning "worthy" in the sense of "deserving" is indicated in Rev. 3:4 in relation to a few members of the congregation at Sardis who are deemed "worthy of praise." Deeds "worthy of repentance" are noted in Matt. 3:8; Luke 3:8; Acts 26:20. Matt. 10:10; Luke 10:7; 1 Tim. 5:8 affirm that a laborer is "worthy of his hire." Sin "deserving" death is referred to in Rom. 1:32. See also Matt. 10:13; Luke 7:4; 12:48; 23:15; 1 Tim. 1:15; 4:9. God is deemed "worthy" to receive praise in Rev. 4:11; 5:12. The negative sense of "unworthy," "undeserving," is indicated in Matt. 22:8; Luke 15:19ff. In several places, people are said to be "unworthy" of Christ (cf. Matt. 22:8; Luke 15:19ff.; Acts 13:25; 23:29; Heb. 11:38).

axioō [ἀξιόω, *515*]

axioō is a verb found in five contexts, meaning "to count, or consider worthy." 2 Thess. 1:11 refers to "being counted worthy" of one's calling by God himself. In 1 Tim. 5:17, Paul expresses the desire that elders "be counted worthy" of double honor. Heb. 3:3 affirms that Jesus should be counted worthy of a greater glory than Moses. See also Heb. 10:29.

kataxioō [καταξιόω, *2661*]

The verb ***kataxioō*** is a derivative form of ***axios***, above. It is found in several contexts, meaning "to judge, or count worthy." Luke 20:35 affirms that believers are "counted worthy" to attain eternal life. In Acts 5:41, the apostles are "judged worthy" to suffer persecution for Christ's sake. See also 2 Thess. 1:5.

axiōs [ἀξίως, *516*]

axiōs is an adverbial form meaning "worthy," in the context of leading a life "worthy" of one's calling (cf. Eph. 4:1; Phil. 1:27; Col. 1:10; 1 Thess. 2:12).

enochos [ἔνοχος, *1777*]

enochos is an adjectival form found ten times with the primary sense of "in danger of" as well as "guilty, or deserving of." The latter sense is found in Matt. 26:66; Mark 14:64, where Christ is declared "worthy" of death by the hostile Jerusalem population.

WOUND

OT Words

makkāh [מַכָּה, **4347**]

makkāh is a noun found about fifty times, meaning "wound," "slaughter," "plague." (→ PLAGUE → SLAUGHTER) It also has several related nuances. ***makkāh*** is also used verbally.

References to a "fatal wound" received in a battle are found in 1 Kgs. 22:35; 2 Kgs. 8:29; 9:15; 2 Chr. 22:6. Metaphorical reference to Israel's "wounds," indicating her pitiable sinful state, is made in Jer. 6:7. See also Zech. 13:6. ***makkāh*** also denotes a "wounding" by grief or sorrow caused by sin (cf. Jer. 10:19; 15:18; 30:12; Mic. 1:9; Nah. 3:19). In Jer. 30:17, Yahweh promises to heal such "wounds" suffered by his people.

Yahweh "inflicts wounds" (Ps. 64:7; Isa. 30:26; Jer. 30:14), which constitute divine punishment for sin.

nākāh [נָכָה, **5221**]

nākāh is a common verb expressing the dominant senses of "kill," "strike," "slay." (→ KILL) However, in 2 Kgs. 8:28 ***nākāh*** means "to inflict wounds" in battle.

pāṣa' [פָּצַע, **6481**]

pāṣa' is a rare verb translated "to wound" in each of its three occurrences. Deut. 23:1 refers to "wounding" a man's testicles by crushing them. "Wounding" by striking is indicated in 1 Kgs. 20:31; Song 5:7.

peṣa' [פֶּצַע, **6482**]

peṣa' is a noun denoting a "wound," or "wounding," in eight places (cf. Gen. 4:23; Exod. 21:25; Job 9:17; Prov. 20:30; 23:29; 27:6; Isa. 1:6).

māḥaṣ [מָחַץ, **4272**]

māḥaṣ is a verb found fourteen times meaning "pierce," "strike through." (→ PIERCE) ***māḥaṣ*** is also translated "to wound" in Deut. 32:39; Job 5:18, where the agent is the hand of God.

ḥēṣ [חֵץ, **2671**]

ḥēṣ is a noun primarily denoting an "arrow" in most of its nearly fifty occurrences. However, Job 34:6 refers to an "arrow wound." (→ ARROW)

māzôr [מָזוֹר, **4204**]

māzôr is a rare noun denoting a "wound" in the figurative sense of an "affliction" occasioned by sin, found only in Jer. 30:13; Hos. 5:13.

ḥālāl [חָלָל, **2491**]

ḥālāl is a verb with the primary meaning "to slay." It occurs around ninety times and is used primarily as a participial form referring to "those who are slain" (i.e., mortally wounded), mostly in a military context and usually "by the sword" (cf. Gen. 34:27; Num. 19:16ff.; Deut. 21:1ff.; 2 Sam. 1:19ff.; 1 Chr. 10:1; Isa. 22:2; Jer. 51:47ff.; Ezek. 6:4ff.; 11:6ff.; 32:20ff.).

Elsewhere, ***ḥālāl*** is translated "wounded" in several contexts (cf. Judg. 9:40; 1 Sam. 17:52; Ps. 69:26; Jer. 51:52; Ezek. 26:15; 30:24).

ḥālāh [חָלָה, **2470**]

ḥālāh is a verb occurring about seventy-five times with the primary sense of "be sick," as well as several related nuances. (→ SICK) In 1 Kgs. 22:34; 2 Chr. 18:33, ***ḥālāh*** is also translated "to wound" (in battle).

ḥabbûrāh [חַבּוּרָה, **2250**]

ḥabbûrāh is a noun found in seven places meaning "bruise," "sore," "wound" (cf. Exod. 21:25; Ps. 38:5; Isa. 1:6; 53:5).

'aṣṣebet [עַצֶּבֶת, **6094**]

'aṣṣebet is a noun found five times with the primary sense of "sorrow." In Prov. 10:10, however, it denotes a "wound."

NT Words

plēgē [πληγή, *4127*]

plēgē is a noun occurring around twenty times meaning "wound," "blow," as well as "plague." (→ PLAGUE)

The sense of "wound" as the result of a beating is indicated in Luke 10:30; Acts 16:23; 2 Cor. 6:5.

plēgē also metaphorically denotes a mortal "wound" inflicted on the satanic beast in Rev. 13:3, 12ff.

kephalaioō [κεφαλαιόω, *2775*]

kephalaioō is a rare verb found only in Mark 12:4 meaning "to wound in the head."

traumatizō [τραυματίζω, *5135*]

traumatizō is a verb found twice, meaning "to inflict a wound" (Luke 20:12; Acts 19:16).

trauma [τραῦμα, *5134*]

trauma is a noun denoting a "wound," found only in Luke 10:34.

See Also: → KILL → PIERCE → STRIKE

WRAP

OT Words

lûṭ [לוּט, **3874**]

lûṭ is a verb found three times. It means "to wrap," indicating "wrapping up" a sword (1 Sam. 21:9) and "wrapping" one's face in a cloak (1 Kgs. 19:13). It also refers metaphorically to the veil of spiritual darkness "spreading over" the nations (Isa. 25:7).

NT Words

entylissō [ἐντυλίσσω, *1794*]

entylissō is a rare verb meaning to "wrap up," "roll together." Matt. 27:59; Luke 23:53 refer to "wrapping up" Jesus' body in a shroud. See also John 20:7.

sparganoō [σπαργανόω, *4683*]

sparganoō is a verb found only in Luke 2:7, 12, referring to "wrapping up" the infant Jesus in strips of cloth.

systellō [συστέλλω, *4958*]

systellō is a rare verb referring to "wrapping up" a body in preparation for burial (Acts 5:6).

eneileō [ἐνειλέω, *1750*]

eneileō is a rare synonym for ***entylissō***, above, referring to "wrapping up" the body of Jesus for burial in Mark 15:46.

WRATH

OT Words

***'ebrāh* [עֶבְרָה, 5678]**

'ebrāh is a noun found approximately thirty times denoting "wrath," "anger," "rage," "fury."

The "wrath" or "rage" of human beings is indicated in general terms in Gen. 49:7; Job 40:11; Amos 1:11. The "wrath" of one's enemies is indicated in Ps. 7:6.

The "wrath" of God is generally expressed as judgment against the wicked (cf. Pss. 78:49; 90:9ff.; Hab. 3:8). Such expression of anger includes the people of God as well (cf. Isa. 9:19; 13:9ff.; Lam. 2:2; Ezek. 21:31; Hos. 5:10; 13:11; Zeph. 1:18). Job 21:30; Prov. 11:4; Ezek. 7:19; Zeph. 1:15 specifically mention the "day of wrath."

***rōgez* [רֹגֶז, 7267]**

rōgez is a noun found in seven contexts, usually denoting "trouble." However, the term indicates "rage" in Hab. 3:2, where the prophet pleads with Yahweh to remember mercy in the midst of "wrath."

See Also: → ANGER

WRESTLE

OT Words

***'ābaq* [אָבַק, 79]**

'ābaq is a rare verb found only twice, meaning "wrestle" in the context of a physical struggle, as in Jacob wrestling with an angelic being (Gen. 32:24ff.). (→ FIGHT → STRIVE)

NT Words

***palē* [πάλη, *3823*]**

palē is a rare noun denoting the "wrestling" or "struggle" of the believer against spiritual powers of darkness (cf. Eph. 6:12).

WRETCHED → DISTRESS → MISERABLE → SORROW → TROUBLE

WRITE, WRITING

OT Words

***kātab* [כָּתַב, 3789]**

kātab is a common verb denoting the action of "writing" in a number of different contexts. It is consistently translated "to write" throughout most of its approximately two hundred occurrences.

Divine instruction to "write" is recorded in Jer. 30:2; 36:2ff., 27ff.; Ezek. 37:16. In another context, such an instruction is given in order to commemorate Yahweh's acts of redemption and his judgment against the enemies of his people (cf. Exod. 17:14).

In other contexts, God himself is said to write. The law of the covenant has Yahweh as its author (cf. Exod. 31:18; 32:15; 34:1, 28; Deut. 4:13; 5:22; 6:10). Other references to the "written" law of God are found in Josh. 1:8; 8:31ff.; 1 Kgs. 2:3; 2 Kgs. 23:21; Ezra 3:2ff.; Neh. 10:34ff. In particular, curse sanctions of the law are held (by implication) to be divinely "written" (cf. Deut. 28:58, 61; 29:20ff.; Dan. 9:11).

In metaphorical contexts "the book" containing the names of the redeemed is declared to "be written" by God (cf. Exod. 32:32; Ps. 69:28; Isa. 4:3). Then, the law of God is to be written on the hearts of his people so that they shall worship him with a new level of purity and devotion — a promise of new covenant renewal (cf. Jer. 31:33). Similarly, the virtues of righteousness and wisdom are "written" on the tablets of the heart (cf. Prov. 3:3; 7:3).

Writing as a human activity is commonly attested. Moses records the laws of God in writing, as indicated in Exod. 24:4, 12; Deut. 27:3; 31:9. He also compiles a written record of the wilderness wanderings of the Israelite people (cf. Num. 33:2). Likewise, Joshua records in writing the renewal of Israel's covenant vows in Josh. 24:26. Parents are instructed to "write down" God's law in order to teach their children (cf. Deut. 6:9). Similarly, Deut. 17:14 lays down the requirement that the king of Israel "make a written copy" of the law of Moses.

Other literary activity includes recording national history, as by the Persians (cf. Esth. 2:23) and recording pagan laws and edicts (Esth. 1:19; 3:9; 8:8). The priestly recordings of extrabiblical historical traditions are noted in 2 Sam. 1:18; 1 Kgs. 14:19; 16:14; 2 Kgs. 15:6, 11; 1 Chr. 29:29. Deut. 24:1ff. refers to writing a bill of divorce. ***kātab*** refers to writing letters (2 Sam. 11:14; 1 Kgs. 21:8; 2 Chr. 32:17; Ezra 4:6, 7); an inscription (Exod. 39:30); and curses (Num. 5:23). See also Num. 17:3; Job 13:26; Isa. 30:8.

***ketab* [כְּתַב, 3790 (Aramaic)]**

The Aramaic term ***ketab*** is found six times, referring to "writing" letters in Ezra 4:8; 5:7, 10; Dan. 6:25. Ezra 6:2 refers to the written records of a Median archival document. Dan. 7:1 speaks of Daniel recording his dream in writing.

miktāb **[מִכְתָּב, 4385]**

miktāb is a noun derived from ***kātab***, above. It is found in nine contexts and denotes "writing" in each instance.

The "writing" of God engraved on tablets of stone, the law of the covenant, is indicated in Exod. 32:16; Deut. 10:4. The engraved (i.e., written) inscription on the high priest's sacred diadem is noted in Exod. 39:30. References to a royal proclamation in writing are found in 2 Chr. 36:22; Ezra 1:1. Written correspondence (i.e., a letter) is indicated in 2 Chr. 21:12.

ketāb **[כְּתָב, 3791]**

ketāb is a synonym for ***miktāb*** (see above), denoting an "edict," or "writing," or "document" in various contexts, and with related nuances, throughout its seventeen occurrences.

Written divine instructions (i.e., plans) for the temple are recorded in 1 Chr. 28:19. Royal directions given by King David are indicated in 2 Chr. 35:4. A royal edict of Persia is noted in Esth. 3:14; 4:8; 8:8ff. The written genealogical register of Levitical priests is indicated in Ezra 2:62; Neh. 7:64. See also Ezek. 13:9.

In other general contexts, written correspondence or letters are referred to in 2 Chr. 2:11; Ezra 4:7. The written script of languages is noted in Esth. 1:22. In Dan. 10:21, reference is made literally to "the scripture (or writing) of truth," a possible metaphorical reference to the destiny of individual people.

NT Words

graphō [γράφω, *1125*]

graphō is a verbal dynamic equivalent of ***kātab*** (see above), occurring around two hundred times. It is consistently translated "write" throughout this usage, in a variety of contexts.

General references to writing activity include those in Luke 1:63; 16:6; 23:38; John 8:6ff.; 19:19ff.; Acts 15:23. Letter writing is indicated in Rom. 16:22; 1 Cor. 5:9; 2 Cor. 1:13; Gal. 1:20; Eph. 3:1; 1 Tim. 3:14; 2 Pet. 3:1. Mark 10:4 records the action of writing a certificate of divorce. Luke 1:3 affirms that Luke the physician wrote his gospel for Theophilus. There are several references to Moses, who wrote down the old covenant law of God (cf. Mark 12:19; Luke 20:28; John 5:46). See also 1 John 2:7ff.

The expression "it is written" constitutes virtually a technical formula denoting a canonical source from the Old Testament. The expression varies somewhat in places, but the meaning is consistent (cf. Matt. 4:4ff.; 26:24, 31; Mark 9:12ff.; Luke 2:23; 4:4ff.; 24:44; John 2:7; 12:14ff.; Acts 1:20; Rom. 3:4, 10; 1 Cor. 1:19; 15:45, 54; Gal. 3:10; Heb. 10:7).

A divine command is given "to write" to the seven churches of Asia Minor (cf. Rev. 2:1–3:7). See also Rev. 21:5; 22:18. A scroll is "inscribed" by God in Rev. 5:1. Names of believers "are written" in the Lamb's "book of life," as noted in Rev. 13:8; 17:8; 20:15; 21:27. (In this regard, see also Exod. 32:32; Ps. 69:28; Isa. 4:3.) Similarly, the name of God the Father "is written" on the foreheads of his people in Rev. 14:1. See also Rev. 17:5.

epistellō [ἐπιστέλλω, *1989*]

epistellō is a rare verb meaning "to write," in the context of communicating instructions (cf. Acts 15:20; 21:25; Heb. 13:22).

epigraphō [ἐπιγράφω, *1924*]

epigraphō is a verb found in five places meaning "to write upon," "inscribe" (cf. Mark 15:26; Acts 17:23; Rev. 21:12). There is also a metaphorical reference to God "writing" his law on the hearts and minds of believers (Heb. 10:16).

prographō [προγράφω, *4270*]

prographō is a verb meaning "to write before," in a temporal sense, referring twice to the Hebrew Scriptures in Rom. 15:4, and once to prior correspondence in Eph. 3:3.

engraphō [ἐγγράφω, *1449*]

engraphō is a verb found only in 2 Cor. 3:2, 3, referring to the faithful, true hearts of believers "engraved" with the Spirit of God.

gramma [γράμμα, *1121*]

gramma is a noun found in fifteen contexts denoting various kinds of "writing."

gramma refers to a commercial bill or account (Luke 16:6ff.); an inscription (Luke 23:38); letters or other correspondence (Acts 28:21); and handwriting (Gal. 6:11). The canonical "writings" of Scripture (i.e., the Old Testament) are indicated in John 5:47; Rom. 2:27; 7:6; 2 Cor. 3:6; 2 Tim. 3:15.

pinakidion [πινακίδιον, *4093*]

pinakidion is a rare noun denoting a "writing tablet" in Luke 1:63.

See Also: → SCRIBE

WRONG

NT Words

adikia [ἀδικία, *93*]

adikia is a noun found in twenty-five contexts with the underlying sense of "moral wrong" throughout. It is translated in various ways.

The meaning "iniquity," in the sense of a violation of God's law, is indicated in Luke 13:27; 16:9; Acts 1:18; Rom. 1:18, 29; 2:8; 2 Thess. 2:10ff.; 2 Tim. 2:19; Heb. 8:12; Jas. 3:6; 2 Pet. 2:13ff.; 1 John 1:9; 5:17.

adikia also denotes "injustice" in Luke 16:8; 18:6; Rom. 9:14. It is also used adjectivally, meaning "false" (John 7:18), and "(morally) wrong" (2 Cor. 12:13).

adikeō [ἀδικέω, *91*]

adikeō is a verb found about thirty times meaning "do wrong," "hurt," "suffer wrong," as well as related nuances.

General references to "doing wrong," or "hurting" include those in Matt. 20:13; Acts 7:26; 25:10ff.; 2 Cor. 7:12; Rev. 6:6; 7:2ff.; 9:4; 22:11. The related sense of "treat unjustly" is indicated in 1 Cor. 6:8; Col. 3:25; Phlm. 18. There are also denials of such action in 2 Cor. 7:2; Gal. 4:12. Rev. 2:11 speaks of "being harmed, or hurt" by the "second death." The meaning "injure" (i.e., to physically hurt) is indicated in Rev. 9:10, 19; 11:5. The sense of "suffer wrong" is found in Acts 7:24; 1 Cor. 6:7.

adikōs [ἀδίκως, *95*]

adikōs is an adverb found only in 1 Pet. 2:19 with reference to suffering "wrongfully" or "unjustly."

See Also: → EVIL → GUILT → INIQUITY → OPPRESS → SIN → TRANSGRESSION → UNGODLINESS → WICKED

Y

YEAR

OT Words

shānāh [שָׁנָה, **8141**]

shānāh is a common noun signifying "year" in virtually all of its approximately nine hundred occurrences in various contexts.

References to "year(s)" as a general, non-specific denotation of time are found in Gen. 1:14; Job 3:6; 10:5; Ps. 31:10; Prov. 3:2; 10:27; Eccl. 6:3, 6; Isa. 34:8.

In relation to a person's age, ***shānāh*** designates "years" in genealogical listings (cf. Gen. 5:3ff.; 11:10ff.). It also refers to people's ages in connection with their ritual monetary value (cf. Lev. 27:3ff.). The minimum age of thirty years is required for the commencement of Levitical, priestly service (cf. Num. 4:3, 23ff.); but see also Num. 8:24. Other general references to "years" include those in Gen. 7:6; 17:17ff.; Deut. 34:7; 2 Sam. 2:10; Job 42:16; Ps. 90:10.

Elsewhere, ***shānāh*** denotes "years," alluding to a significant period of time. Gen. 6:3 refers to a 120-year period of time prior to the judgment of the universal flood (cf. also Gen. 8:3). The round figure of 400 years of Israelite slavery in Egypt is indicated in Gen. 15:13; Exod. 12:40ff. Seven years of alternating famine and plenty are referred to in Gen. 41:26ff. The "year" of Jubilee is mentioned in Lev. 25:10ff.; 27:17ff. And Deut. 15:1ff.; Jer. 34:14 refer to the Sabbath "year" of release for slaves. The seventy "years" of the Judean exile in Babylon are noted in Jer. 25:11ff.; 29:10; Zech. 1:12; 7:5. The "forty-year" period of Israelite wandering in the wilderness is frequently alluded to (cf. Exod. 16:35; Num. 14:33ff.; 32:13; Deut. 1:3; 2:7; 8:2ff.; 29:5; Josh. 5:6; Amos 2:10). The "Sabbath year" of rest for harvest fields is indicated in Lev. 25:3ff.

shānāh also commonly denotes the regnal years of Israelite kings (e.g., 2 Sam. 5:4ff.; 1 Kgs. 11:42; 2 Kgs. 12:1; 14:17ff.; 2 Chr. 16:12ff.; Isa. 6:1; Jer. 1:2ff.; 45:1; 52:31) and the regnal years of pagan kings (cf. Ezra 7:7ff.; Neh. 2:1; Esth. 1:3; Dan. 1:1; 8:1; 9:1; 11:1ff.; Hag. 1:1, 15; Zech. 1:1, 7).

shānāh is also used to denote "year" in the context of the specific time or date for the celebration of ritual festivals (cf. Exod. 12:2, 23:14ff.; 34:23ff.; Lev. 16:34; Deut. 16:16). In related contexts, ***shānāh*** also refers to "one year old" animals without blemish, suitable for ritual sacrifice (cf. Exod. 12:5; 29:38; Lev. 23:12ff.; Num. 6:12; 7:15ff.; 28:3ff.; Ezek. 46:13; Mic. 6:6).

shānāh is used metaphorically to denote a "thousand-year" period, designating an indefinite period of time, a fleeting moment to God (cf. Ps. 90:4). The "year of the Lord's favor," indicating the coming period of new covenant blessing, is indicated in Isa. 61:2. The "year of . . . punishment," expressing an outpouring of divine wrath, is noted in Jer. 11:23; 23:12; 48:44.

yôm [יוֹם, **3117**]

yôm is a common noun found nearly 2,300 times with the predominant sense of "day." (→ DAY) However, in a number of places it also denotes "year(s)."

General, non-specific references to "years" as a period of time are found in Exod. 13:10; Num. 9:22; Judg. 11:40; 2 Sam. 14:26. References to old age in the expression "advanced in years" are found in Josh. 13:1; 1 Kgs. 1:1.

The meaning "yearly" (i.e., annually), in relation to the celebration of ritual festivals or sacrifice, is indicated in Judg. 21:19; 1 Sam. 1:3, 21; 2:19.

shenāh [שְׁנָה, **8140** (Aramaic)]

shenāh is the Aramaic equivalent of ***shānāh*** (see above), found in seven places.

Ezra 5:11 contains a general, non-specific reference to "years." Dan. 5:31 refers to a person's age. The regnal years of kings are indicated in Ezra 4:24; 5:13; 6:3, 15; Dan. 7:1.

shālash [שָׁלַשׁ, **8027**]

shālash is a noun found in nine contexts. It is a variant form of the number "three," meaning "three years old" in Gen. 15:9.

NT Words

etos [ἔτος, *2094*]

etos is the dynamic equivalent for ***shānāh*** (see above), occurring nearly fifty times and meaning "year" throughout.

The designation "years" with reference to specific periods of time is indicated in Matt. 9:20; Mark 5:25; Luke 2:36ff.; John 2:20; 2 Cor. 12:2; Gal. 1:18; Heb. 13:21. References to "years" as periods of indefinite duration are found in Luke 12:19; Acts 24:10; Rom. 15:23.

"Years" as significant periods of time are noted in Acts 7:16; Gal. 3:17 in relation to the 400 years of Israel's captivity in Egypt. Acts 7:36ff.; Heb. 3:9, 17 mention Israel's forty-year wandering in the wilderness.

etos also denotes a person's age in terms of "years" in Luke 2:42; 3:23; John 8:57; 1 Tim. 5:9. Regnal years are also indicated in relation to the Roman emperor (Luke 3:1).

The expression "every year" (i.e., annually) is used to describe the celebration of ritual festivals in Luke 2:41.

etos is also used metaphorically in 2 Pet. 3:8 to refer to a "thousand years" as the equivalent of "one day" in the sight of God. Rev. 20:2ff. refers to the "thousand-year" rule of Christ.

eniautos [ἐνιαυτός, *1763*]

eniautos is a noun found in fourteen places meaning "year" throughout.

General references to a "year" as a point in time, or date, are found in John 11:49ff.; 18:13. ***eniautos*** refers to a period of time in Acts 11:26; 18:11; Jas. 4:13; 5:17; Rev. 9:15, and also in the ritual context of the observance of festivals (Gal. 4:10; Heb. 9:7, 25; 10:1ff.).

The phrase "year of the Lord" is a figurative expression, akin to "the Day of the Lord" — a climactic event in the calendar of redemptive history signifying the coming of the Messiah (cf. Luke 4:19).

perysi [πέρυσι, *4070*]

perysi is an adverb signifying "a year ago," found only twice, in 2 Cor. 8:10; 9:2.

dietēs [διετής, *1332*]

dietēs is a rare adjectival form found only in Matt. 2:16, meaning "two years old."

trietia [τριετία, *5148*]

trietia is a rare noun denoting a period of "three years" (cf. Acts 24:27; 28:30).

dietia [διετία, *1333*]

dietia is a noun found only twice, in Acts 24:27; 28:30, denoting a period of "two years."

hekatontaetēs [ἑκατονταετής, *1541*]

hekatontaetēs is a rare adjective signifying "one hundred years old," found only in Rom. 4:19.

YEAST

OT Words

maṣṣāh [מַצָּה, 4682]

maṣṣāh is a noun occurring around fifty times denoting "unleavened bread" (i.e., bread without yeast) throughout.

The most common usage is a ceremonial one. Eating "unleavened bread" is associated with the Israelite survival of the Passover plague in Egypt, leading to the inauguration of an annual festival (cf. Exod. 12:8ff.; 13:6ff.; 23:15). See also 2 Kgs. 23:9. Legislation prescribed for the Festival of Unleavened Bread is recorded in Exod. 34:18; Lev. 23:6; Num. 9:11; Deut. 16:3ff.; 2 Chr. 8:13; Ezra 6:15. "Unleavened bread" is mentioned in general ceremonial contexts in Exod. 29:2; Lev. 2:4ff.; 6:16; 7:12; Num. 6:15ff.; Judg. 6:19ff.

Gen. 19:3; 1 Sam. 28:24 refer to "unleavened bread" in a non-ritual context.

ḥāmēṣ [חָמֵץ, 2556 (Verb), 2557 (Noun)]

ḥāmēṣ is used both verbally, signifying the state of "being leavened" (i.e., baked with yeast), and nominally, denoting "leaven," or "yeast."

The verbal sense is indicated in general household contexts in relation to food (Exod. 12:19ff.), and to bread dough (Exod. 12:34, 39; Deut. 16:3; Hos. 7:4).

The nominal sense of ***ḥāmēṣ*** is indicated with respect to "leavened bread" in Exod. 12:15; 13:3ff. Bread made with yeast is also generally forbidden in ritual offerings, as noted in Exod. 23:18. But Lev. 7:13; 23:17; Amos 4:5 note exceptions to this prohibition. "Leaven," or "yeast," is itself forbidden in sacrificial offerings (Exod. 34:25; Lev. 2:11; 6:17).

se'ōr [שְׂאֹר, 7603]

se'ōr is a synonym for ***ḥāmēṣ*** (see above) denoting "leaven," or "yeast," in five contexts.

General references to "leaven" are found in Exod. 12:15ff. Its prohibition in ritual offerings is indicated in Lev. 2:11; Deut. 16:4.

NT Words

zymē [ζύμη, *2219*]

zymē is a noun denoting "leaven," or "yeast," in both literal and figurative contexts.

Literal references are found in Matt. 13:33; Luke 13:21.

More significantly, ***zymē*** refers to "the leaven of the Pharisees," denoting their hypocrisy, as recorded in Matt. 16:6ff.; Mark 8:15; Luke 12:1. "Leaven" also signifies the invisible effect of sin in the life and heart of the believer (cf. 1 Cor. 5:6ff.; Gal. 5:9).

zymoō [ζυμόω, *2220*]

zymoō is a verb found in four places indicating the action of "leavening," or "mixing with yeast." It refers literally to baking bread in Matt. 13:33; Luke 13:21. Metaphorically, the action of "leavening" designates infecting one's life with evil intent (cf. 1 Cor. 5:6; Gal. 5:9).

YESTERDAY

OT Words

temôl [תְּמוֹל, **8543**]

temôl is an adverb found approximately twenty times with the general underlying meanings "beforehand," "in times past." In several places, however, it also signifies "yesterday" (cf. Exod. 5:14; 1 Sam. 20:27; 2 Sam. 15:20; Job 8:9).

'emesh [אֶמֶשׁ, **570**]

'emesh is an adverb found in five place with the primary sense of "last night." In 2 Kgs. 9:26, however, it denotes "yesterday."

'etmôl [אֶתְמוֹל, **865**]

'etmôl is an adverbial form synonymous with ***temôl***, above, occurring eight times with the primary senses of "recently," "beforehand." In Ps. 90:4, ***'etmôl*** is translated "yesterday."

NT Words

echthes [ἐχθές, *5504*]

echthes is an adverb meaning "yesterday" in all three occurrences of the term. In John 4:52; Acts 7:28, it is used literally. In Heb. 13:8, ***echthes*** refers metaphorically to Christ's unchanging person "yesterday, today, and forever."

YIELD

OT Words

nātan [נָתַן, **5414**]

nātan is a common verb, occurring nearly two thousand times with the predominant meaning "to give" throughout, along with a number of associated senses. One of these is "yield," found in about fifteen contexts.

The meaning "yield" in the sense of "give up," or "hand over," is indicated primarily in relation to the ground "yielding" its produce (cf. Gen. 4:12; Lev. 25:19; Ps. 85:12; Ezek. 34:27). The sense of "provide" is evident in Gen. 49:20. 2 Chr. 30:8 refers to "yielding," or "submitting," to the Lord.

'āsāh [עָשָׂה, **6213**]

'āsāh is another common verb, found more than 2,500 times, primarily signifying "do," "make." ***'āsāh*** has a large number of associated senses, one of which is "yield."

'āsāh refers, for example, to a vine or tree "bearing" or "yielding" its fruit in Gen. 1:12; Jer. 17:18; Isa. 5:10. In Hos. 8:7, the term denotes the "yield" of standing grain in a field.

zāra' [זָרַע, **2232**]

zāra' is a verb found in approximately fifty places with the primary meaning "to sow" in contexts of scattering seed for the cultivation of food. However, in Gen. 1:11, 12 it has the sense of "bearing" or "yielding" fruit.

NT Words

didōmi [δίδωμι, *1325*]

didōmi is a common verb found in more than 400 contexts with the primary meaning "give," along with several related senses. One of these is "yield," or "bear," with reference to the cultivation of grain (Mark 4:7, 8).

apodidōmi [ἀποδίδωμι, *591*]

apodidōmi is a variant of ***didōmi***, above, found in fifty places with the dominant senses of "pay," "give," "render," in a variety of contexts. However, ***apodidōmi*** denotes trees "yielding," or "bearing," fruit in Rev. 22:2. It also refers metaphorically to discipline "yielding" or "producing" the fruit of righteousness in the lives of believers (cf. Heb. 12:11).

YOKE

OT Words

'ōl [עֹל, **5923**]

'ōl is a noun denoting a "yoke" throughout its approximately forty occurrences. It is predominantly figurative.

Literal references to a "yoke," the instrument designed to keep a pair of beasts of burden walking in tandem, are found in Num. 19:2; 1 Sam. 6:7.

In several contexts, "yoke" denotes the enslavement of persons, from which Yahweh releases, or promises to release, them (cf. Gen. 27:40; Lev. 26:13; Isa. 9:4; 10:27;

Jer. 28:2ff.; 30:8; Ezek. 34:27). The term also designates a "yoke" as a punishment enacted by Yahweh against his people (Deut. 28:48). See also Hos. 11:4. The violation or breaking of the "yoke" of devotion toward Yahweh by his people is indicated in Jer. 2:20; 5:5. "Yoke" also refers to an oppressive regime inflicted by a callous ruler onto his own people (1 Kgs. 12:4ff.; 2 Chr. 10:4ff.), and onto a conquered people (Isa. 47:6; Jer. 27:8ff.).

ṣemed **[צֶמֶד, 6776]**

ṣemed is a noun found in fifteen contexts meaning "couple," "pair," "yoke," or "team" throughout most of the usage.

Literal references to a "yoke," or "pair of oxen," are found in 1 Sam. 11:7; 1 Kgs. 19:19ff.; Job 1:3; 42:12; Jer. 51:23.

môṭāh **[מוֹטָה, 4133]**

môṭāh is a noun occurring twelve times denoting the "yoke" applied to beasts of burden as they plow, or more particularly to the "bars" of the yoke (Lev. 26:13).

môṭāh is also used metaphorically, denoting the "yoke" of oppression from which Yahweh delivers his people (cf. Isa. 58:6ff.; Ezek. 30:18; 34:27), and which he also (conversely) places on the necks of his people as a judgment against them (cf. Jer. 27:2; 28:10ff.).

môṭ **[מוֹט, 4132]**

môṭ is a variant form of ***môṭāh***, above. It is found in six places and denotes a "bar" or "pole" in half of these contexts. The term also metaphorically signifies a "yoke" of oppression inflicted by Nineveh against Israel, which Yahweh will shatter, thereby delivering his people (cf. Nah. 1:13).

NT Words

zygos [ζυγός, *2218*]

zygos is a noun signifying a "yoke" in a figurative sense throughout all six occurrences.

zygos denotes a "yoke" in reference to a "burden" placed by Christ on his people — a burden that is easy to bear. This signifies a commitment to serve him with one's whole being (cf. Matt. 11:29ff.). Acts 15:10 refers to an unwarranted "yoke," a burden of legal obligations placed by Jewish believers onto Gentile converts. In Gal. 5:1, the "yoke" referred to is the law, from which Christians have been delivered. In 1 Tim. 6:1, the "yoke" is the bond of slavery.

heterozygeō [ἑτεροζυγέω, *2086*]

heterozygeō is a rare verb found only in 2 Cor. 6:14 as part of an injunction to believers not "to be unequally yoked together" in marriage with unbelievers.

See Also: → CHILD → GIRL

YOUNG

OT Words

na'ar **[נַעַר, 5288]**

na'ar is a noun occurring about 240 times, denoting for the most part a "young man" or "youth," "child," "lad," "servant." There is often overlap in meaning between "young man," "lad," or "servant." (→ CHILD → SERVANT)

Literal references to a "young man" or "youth" (in both the singular and plural) include those in Gen. 21:12ff.; Exod. 24:5; Num. 11:27; Josh. 8:14ff.; Ruth 2:9; 1 Sam. 2:17; 2 Sam. 14:21; Job 29:8; Isa. 40:30; Zech. 2:4.

References to "the young" as a class of people in contrast to "the old" are found in Josh. 6:21; Esth. 3:13; Isa. 20:4; Jer. 51:22; Lam. 2:21.

The adjectival sense of "young" in years, implying childhood, is found in 2 Chr. 13:7; 34:3; Ps. 37:25.

gôzāl **[גּוֹזָל, 1469]**

gôzāl is a noun found on two occasions only, designating the offspring of birds as their "young" (cf. Gen. 15:9; Deut. 32:11).

'ûl **[עוּל, 5763]**

'ûl is a noun occurring five times, denoting "suckling animals," or "those that are young" (Gen. 33:13; 1 Sam. 6:7ff.; Ps. 78:71). In Isa. 40:11, ***'ûl*** refers metaphorically to God's people as his "young."

bēn **[בֵּן, 1121]**

bēn is a common noun, found in over 5,000 contexts. It most commonly designates "son(s)," "child," "children." There are also a number of related senses, one of which is "young," referring exclusively to the offspring of animals and birds.

The "young" of pigeons are indicated wholly in ritual contexts (cf. Lev. 1:14; 5:7ff.; 12:6ff.; 14:22; 15:14, 29; Num. 6:10).

Then, in Lev. 22:28; Num. 8:8, ***bēn*** also denotes the "young" of cattle.

bāqār [בָּקָר, 1241]

bāqār is a noun occurring about two hundred times, usually denoting "cattle." However, in several related contexts, the term signifies a "young bull" (Lev. 4:3, 14; 9:2; 16:3; 23:18; Num. 7:15ff.; 28:19ff.).

'ephrōaḥ [אֶפְרֹחַ, 667]

'ephrōaḥ is a noun occurring three times denoting the "young" of birds in Deut. 22:6; Job 39:30; Ps. 84:3.

bāḥûr [בָּחוּר, 970]

bāḥûr is a noun occurring about fifty times, denoting "young man," "youth" throughout (cf. Deut. 32:25; Judg. 14:10; Ruth 3:10; 1 Sam. 9:2; 2 Chr. 36:17; Ps. 78:63; Eccl. 11:9; Isa. 9:17; 40:30; Jer. 6:11; Lam. 1:15ff.; Ezek. 9:6; Joel 2:28; Zech. 9:17).

'elem [עֶלֶם, 5958]

'elem is a rare noun designating a "young man," or "youth," in 1 Sam. 17:56; 20:22.

qāṭān [קָטָן, 6996]

qāṭān is an adjective occurring in around 100 contexts, primarily signifying that which is "small," or "little." However, it also designates those who are "young," "younger," "youngest" in relation to family members.

References to the "youngest" son are found in Gen. 9:22; 42:13ff.; Judg. 9:5; 1 Sam. 16:11; 17:14. 2 Sam. 9:12 mentions a "young" son.

The comparative form "younger" is applied to a son (Gen. 27:15; 2 Chr. 21:17; 22:1); a daughter (Gen. 29:16ff.; 1 Sam. 14:49); a brother (Gen. 44:2ff.; Judg. 1:13; 3:9); and a sister (Judg. 15:2; Ezek. 16:46, 61).

ṣā'îr [צָעִיר, 6810]

The noun ***ṣā'îr*** is a synonym for ***qāṭān***, above. It occurs about twenty times, denoting one who is "young," "younger," "youngest" in most of these contexts.

"Younger" men in general are noted in Job 30:1. ***ṣā'îr*** refers to a "younger" brother (Gen. 19:31ff.; 25:23); sister (Gen. 29:26); and son (Gen. 48:14). The "youngest" son is noted in Gen. 43:33; Josh. 6:26; 1 Kgs. 16:34. The adjectival sense of "young" is indicated in Job 32:6.

'ōpher [עֹפֶר, 6082]

'ōpher is a noun denoting a "young deer or stag," found only five times (cf. Song 2:9, 17; 4:5; 7:3; 8:14).

NT Words

neaniskos [νεανίσκος, *3495*]

neaniskos is a noun meaning "young man," "youth" throughout its ten occurrences (cf. Matt. 19:20ff.; Mark 14:51; 16:5; Luke 7:14; Acts 5:10; 1 John 2:13ff.). Acts 2:7 refers to "young men" as a class of people distinct from those who are "old."

nossos [νοσσός, *3502*]

nossos is a rare noun denoting "young pigeons" only in Luke 2:24.

neos [νέος, *3501*]

neos is an adjectival form found in approximately twenty places meaning "new," "young," as well as related senses. (→ NEW)

The designation "young" is applied to men (Acts 5:6; 1 Tim. 5:1), and to women (Titus 2:4). The comparative "younger" is predicated of women (1 Tim. 5:2, 11ff.); of a son (Luke 15:12ff.); of men (Titus 2:6); and in general terms (1 Pet. 5:5). The meaning "youngest" is evident in Luke 22:26. See also John 21:18.

neanias [νεανίας, *3494*]

neanias is a noun indicating a "young man" (cf. Acts 7:58; 20:9; 23:17ff.).

elassōn [ἐλάσσων, *1640*]

elassōn is a comparative adjective denoting "less" in three of its four occurrences. In Rom. 9:12, however, ***elassōn*** refers to Esau, the elder brother who will serve Jacob, the "younger."

See Also: → CHILD

YOUTH

OT Words

nā'ûr [נָעוּר, 5271]

nā'ûr is a noun denoting one's "youth" (i.e., early years) in around fifty contexts.

General references to one's "youth" include those in Gen. 8:21; 46:34; Prov. 2:17; 5:18; Isa. 54:6; Lam. 3:27; Joel 1:8; Mal. 2:14ff. Legislation concerning one's youthful years is found in Lev. 22:13; Num. 30:3, 16. The "early years" of specific individuals are noted in 1 Sam. 17:33; 1 Kgs. 8:12; Ps. 25:7; Ezek. 4:14; Zech. 13:5.

nā'ûr is also used metaphorically, referring to Israel's "youth" in connection with the idyllic early period of her covenant relationship with Yahweh in the wilderness (cf. Jer. 2:2; Ezek. 16:60; Hos. 2:15). A number of texts also recall her sins committed during this period (cf. Jer. 3:24ff.; 22:21; 31:19; 32:30; Ezek. 16:22, 43; 23:3ff.). Such a designation is also applied to pagan rulers (Isa. 47:12ff.; Jer. 48:11).

***'ālûmîm* [עֲלוּמִים, 5934]**

'ālûmîm is a noun synonymous with ***nā'ûr***, above, occurring four times and denoting "youth" in the sense of one's early years. ***'ālûmîm*** is used literally in Job 20:11; 33:25; Ps. 89:45. It refers metaphorically in Isa. 54:4 to Israel's early period in her covenant relationship with Yahweh.

***nō'ar* [נֹעַר, 5290]**

nō'ar is a term denoting "youth," or "childhood," in Job 33:25; 36:14; Ps. 88:15; Prov. 29:21.

***yaldût* [יַלְדוּת, 3208]**

yaldût is another synonym for the terms above, referring to one's "youth" or "childhood" in Ps. 110:3; Eccl. 11:9ff.

***beḥûrôt* [בְּחוּרוֹת, 979]**

beḥûrôt is a rare noun referring to one's "youth" in Eccl. 11:9; 12:1.

NT Words

***neotēs* [νεότης, *3503*]**

neotēs is a noun occurring five times, indicating one's "youth" or "early years" in Matt. 19:20; Mark 10:20; Luke 18:21; Acts 26:4; 1 Tim. 4:12.

***neōterikos* [νεωτερικός, *3512*]**

neōterikos is a rare adjective meaning "youthful" in reference to the passions of one's early years (cf. 2 Tim. 2:22).

See Also: → YOUNG

Z

ZEAL

OT Words

qānā' [קָנָא, 7065]

qānā' is a verb found in approximately thirty places with the predominant senses of "to envy," "be jealous." In several places, however, ***qānā'*** also means "zeal" or "passionate enthusiasm" for a cause, although there is occasional overlap in meaning here. (→ JEALOUS)

Saul's "zeal" for Israel and Judah is noted in 2 Sam. 2:12; and "zeal" for God's name and honor is expressed in Num. 25:11ff.; 1 Kgs. 19:10ff.

qin'āh [קִנְאָה, 7068]

qin'āh is a noun derived from ***qānā'*** (see above) denoting "envy," "jealousy" for most of its forty or so occurrences. (→ JEALOUS) However, as with the verbal root form, ***qin'āh*** also expresses the sense of "zeal" (i.e., passionate desire) in a number of places.

qin'āh refers to "zeal" for the Lord (2 Kgs. 10:16; 19:31); and also for the temple of the Lord (Ps. 69:9). The psalmist's "zeal" is noted in Pss. 69:9; 119:39.

The "zeal" of Yahweh himself in accomplishing his redemptive purposes is noted in Isa. 9:7; 37:32; Ezek. 5:13.

NT Words

zēlos [ζῆλος, *2205*]

zēlos is a noun found in seventeen places, primarily denoting "envy," "jealousy." It also means "zeal" in the sense of "passionate enthusiasm."

John 2:17 records the overwhelming "zeal" consuming Christ in relation to the house of God. "Zeal" for God in general terms is indicated in Rom. 10:2; as is "zeal" for godliness in 2 Cor. 7:11; and for good deeds in 2 Cor. 9:2. Phil. 3:6 refers to "zeal" for the law.

zēlōtēs [ζηλωτής, *2207*]

zēlōtēs is an adjective found in five places with the sense of "zealous," or "eager enthusiasm for." This description is applied to God's law in Acts 21:20 (cf. also Gal. 1:14); to God himself in Acts 22:3; and to good deeds in Titus 2:14. See also 1 Cor. 14:12.

zēloō [ζηλόω, *2206*]

zēloō is a verb signifying the attitude of "being jealous" in six of its twelve occurrences. (→ JEALOUS) The remaining usage expresses the sense of "be zealous, or eager."

"Being zealous" to obtain spiritual gifts is indicated in 1 Cor. 12:31; 14:1, 39. The meaning "covet" is indicated in Jas. 4:2. Gal. 4:18; Rev. 3:19 express zeal in a general non-specific sense.

INDEX OF HEBREW WORDS

Strong's Number	Hebrew Article	English Entry
615	*'āsîr* [אָסִיר]	PRISON
616	*'assîr* [אַסִּיר]	PRISON
618	*'āsām* [אָסָם]	BARN
622	*'āsaph* [אָסַף]	GATHER
631	*'āsar* [אָסַר]	BIND
		PRISON
632	*'esār* [אֱסָר]	BIND
		BOND
636	*'ā'* [אָע]	WOOD
639	*'aph* [אַף]	ANGER
		NOSE
650	*'āphîq* [אָפִיק]	RIVER
		VALLEY
652	*'ōphel* [אֹפֶל]	DARK
653	*'aphēlāh* [אֲפֵלָה]	BLACK
		DARK
657	*'ephes* [אֶפֶס]	END
660	*'eph'eh* [אֶפְעֶה]	VIPER
661	*'āphaph* [אָפַף]	SURROUND
665	*'ēpher* [אֵפֶר]	ASHES
667	*'ephrōaḥ* [אֶפְרֹחַ]	YOUNG
676	*'eṣba'* [אֶצְבַּע]	FINGER
677	*'eṣba'* [אֶצְבַּע]	FINGER
680	*'āṣal* [אָצַל]	TAKE
686	*'āṣar* [אָצַר]	TREASURE
693	*'ārab* [אָרַב]	LIE (VERB)
		WAIT
697	*'arbeh* [אַרְבֶּה]	LOCUST
699	*'arubbāh* [אֲרֻבָּה]	WINDOW
702	*'arba', 'arbā'āh* [אַרְבַּע, אַרְבָּעָה]	FOUR
705	*'arbā'îm* [אַרְבָּעִים]	FORTY
717	*'ārāh* [אָרָה]	GATHER
724	*'arukāh* [אֲרֻכָה]	HEAL
727	*'ārôn* [אָרוֹן]	ARK
		BIER
730	*'erez* [אֶרֶז]	CEDAR
731	*'arzāh* [אַרְזָה]	CEDAR
734	*'ōraḥ* [אֹרַח]	PATH
		TRAVEL
		WAY
738	*'aryēh* [אַרְיֵה]	LION

Strong's Number	Hebrew Article	English Entry
748	*'ārak* [אָרַךְ]	LONG
750	*'erek* [אֶרֶךְ]	LONG-SUFFERING
		PATIENCE
752	*'ārōk* [אָרֹךְ]	LONG
753	*'ōrek* [אֹרֶךְ]	LENGTH
		LONG
759	*'armôn* [אַרְמוֹן]	PALACE
772	*'ara'* [אֲרַע]	EARTH
776	*'ereṣ* [אֶרֶץ]	EARTH
779	*'ārar* [אָרַר]	CURSE
781	*'āras* [אָרַשׂ]	BETROTH
782	*'areshet* [אֲרֶשֶׁת]	REQUEST
784	*'ēsh* [אֵשׁ]	FIRE
787	*'ōsh* [אשׁ]	FOUNDATION
801	*'isheh* [אִשֶּׁה]	OFFERING
802	*'ishshāh* [אִשָּׁה]	WIFE
		WOMAN
811	*'eshkôl* [אֶשְׁכּוֹל]	GRAPE
816	*'āsham* [אָשַׁם]	GUILT
		TRANSGRESS
817	*'āshām* [אָשָׁם]	GUILT
		OFFERING
818	*'āshēm* [אָשֵׁם]	GUILT
819	*'ashmāh* [אַשְׁמָה]	OFFERING
		TRANSGRESS
821	*'ashmōrāh* [אַשְׁמֹרָה]	WATCH
830	*'ashpôt* [אַשְׁפּוֹת]	DUNG
833	*'āshar* [אָשַׁר]	BLESS
835	*'ashrê* [אַשְׁרֵי]	BLESS
838	*'ashur* [אַשֻׁר]	STEP
852	*'āt* [אָת]	SIGN
855	*'ēt* [אֵת]	PLOW
860	*'ātôn* [אָתוֹן]	ASS
861	*'attûn* [אַתּוּן]	FURNACE
865	*'etmôl* [אֶתְמוֹל]	YESTERDAY
874	*bā'ar* [בָּאַר]	EXPLAIN
875	*be'ēr* [בְּאֵר]	WELL
898	*bāgad* [בָּגַד]	TRAITOR
899	*beged* [בֶּגֶד]	CLOTHING
905	*lebad* [לְבַד]	ALONE

Strong's Number	Hebrew Article	English Entry
1739	***dāweh*** [דָּוֶה]	FAINT
1740	***dûaḥ*** [דּוּחַ]	WASH
1742	***dawwāy*** [דַּוָּי]	FAINT
1745	***dûmāh*** [דּוּמָה]	SILENCE
1747	***dûmîyāh*** [דּוּמִיָּה]	SILENCE
1755	***dôr*** [דּוֹר]	AGE
1758	***dûsh*** [דּוּשׁ]	THRESH
1763	***deḥal*** [דְּחַל]	FEAR
		TERRIBLE
1773	***deyô*** [דְּיוֹ]	INK
1777	***dîn*** [דִּין]	JUDGE
		PLEA
1779	***dîn*** [דִּין]	JUDGMENT
		PLEA
1781	***dayyān*** [דַּיָּן]	JUDGE
1786	***dayish*** [דַּיִשׁ]	THRESH
1790	***dak*** [דַּךְ]	OPPRESS
1792	***dāka'*** [דָּכָא]	CRUSH
1798	***dekar*** [דְּכַר]	RAM
1800	***dal*** [דַּל]	POOR
		WEAK
1801	***dālag*** [דָּלַג]	LEAP
1802	***dālāh*** [דָּלָה]	DRAW
1808	***dālît*** [דָּלִית]	BRANCH
1809	***dālal*** [דָּלַל]	LOW
1811	***dālaph*** [דָּלַף]	POUR
1817	***delet*** [דֶּלֶת]	DOOR
1818	***dām*** [דָּם]	BLOOD
1819	***dāmāh*** [דָּמָה]	LIKEN
		PLAN
1820	***dāmāh*** [דָּמָה]	PERISH
1824	***domî*** [דֳּמִי]	SILENCE
1826	***dāmam*** [דָּמַם]	QUIET
		SILENCE
1827	***demāmāh*** [דְּמָמָה]	SILENCE
1828	***dōmen*** [דֹּמֶן]	DUNG
1832	***dim'āh*** [דִּמְעָה]	TEARS
		WEEP
1843	***dēa'*** [דֵּעַ]	KNOW
1844	***dē'āh*** [דֵּעָה]	KNOW
1847	***da'at*** [דַּעַת]	KNOW
1848	***dōphî*** [דֹּפִי]	SLANDER
1849	***dāphaq*** [דָּפַק]	BEAT
		KNOCK
1855	***deqaq*** [דְּקַק]	BREAK
1856	***dāqar*** [דָּקַר]	DRIVE
		PIERCE
1869	***dārak*** [דָּרַךְ]	TREAD
1870	***derek*** [דֶּרֶךְ]	JOURNEY
		WAY
1872	***derā'*** [דְּרָע]	ARM
1875	***dārash*** [דָּרַשׁ]	ASK
		REQUIRE
		SEEK
1877	***deshe'*** [דֶּשֶׁא]	GRASS
		HERB
1878	***dāshēn*** [דָּשֵׁן]	ASHES
1880	***deshen*** [דֶּשֶׁן]	ASHES
1881	***dāt*** [דָּת]	DECREE
		LAW
1883	***dete'*** [דְּתֶא]	GRASS
1891	***hābal*** [הָבַל]	VAIN
1892	***hebel*** [הֶבֶל]	IDOL
		VAIN
1897	***hāgāh*** [הָגָה]	MEDITATE
1916	***hadōm*** [הֲדֹם]	FOOT
1918	***hadas*** [הֲדַס]	MYRTLE
1920	***hādaph*** [הָדַף]	DRIVE
1921	***hādar*** [הָדַר]	HONOR
1926	***hādār*** [הָדָר]	GLORY
1927	***hadārāh*** [הֲדָרָה]	BEAUTIFUL
1935	***hôd*** [הוֹד]	GLORY
		MAJESTY
1947	***hôlēlāh*** [הוֹלֵלָה]	MAD
1952	***hôn*** [הוֹן]	RICH
1959	***hêdād*** [הֵידָד]	SHOUT
1961	***hāyāh*** [הָיָה]	USE
1964	***hêkāl*** [הֵיכָל]	TEMPLE
1965	***hêkal*** [הֵיכַל]	TEMPLE
1980	***hālak*** [הָלַךְ]	WALK
1982	***hēlek*** [הֵלֶךְ]	TRAVEL

Strong's Number	Hebrew Article	English Entry
2388	***ḥāzaq*** [חָזַק]	ENCOURAGE
		HARD
		HOLD (VERB)
		RECOVER
		REPAIR
		RESIST
		SEIZE
		STRENGTH
2389	***ḥāzāq*** [חָזָק]	STRENGTH
2392	***ḥōzeq*** [חֹזֶק]	STRENGTH
2397	***ḥāḥ*** [חָח]	HOOK
2398	***ḥāṭā'*** [חָטָא]	CLEAN
		FAULT
		MISS
		PRACTICE
		SIN
2399	***ḥēṭ'*** [חֵטְא]	SIN
2400	***ḥaṭṭā'*** [חַטָּא]	SIN
2401	***ḥaṭā'āh*** [חֲטָאָה]	SIN
2403	***ḥaṭṭā't*** [חַטָּאת]	OFFERING
		SIN
2406	***ḥiṭṭāh*** [חִטָּה]	GRAIN
2416	***ḥay*** [חַי]	BEAST
		LIFE
		RUN
2418	***ḥayā'*** [חֲיָא]	LIFE
2420	***ḥîdāh*** [חִידָה]	ALLEGORY
		QUESTION
2421	***ḥāyāh*** [חָיָה]	LIFE
		PRESERVE
		QUICKEN
		RECOVER
		RESTORATION
		RESURRECTION
		SAVE
2423	***ḥēwā'*** [חֵיוָא]	BEAST
2427	***ḥîl*** [חִיל]	ANGUISH
		PAIN
		SORROW
2428	***ḥayil*** [חַיִל]	ABILITY
		ARMY
		GOODS
		RICH
2434	***ḥayiṣ*** [חַיִץ]	WALL
2436	***ḥêq*** [חֵיק]	BOSOM
2441	***ḥēk*** [חֵךְ]	MOUTH
		ROOF
		TASTE
2442	***ḥākāh*** [חָכָה]	WAIT
2443	***ḥakkāh*** [חַכָּה]	HOOK
2445	***ḥakkîm*** [חַכִּים]	WISDOM
2449	***ḥākam*** [חָכַם]	WISDOM
2450	***ḥākām*** [חָכָם]	WISDOM
2451	***ḥokmāh*** [חָכְמָה]	WISDOM
2461	***ḥālāb*** [חָלָב]	MILK
2465	***ḥeled*** [חֶלֶד]	WORLD
2470	***ḥālāh*** [חָלָה]	PRAY
		SICK
		WEAK
		WOUND
2472	***ḥalôm*** [חֲלוֹם]	DREAM
2474	***ḥallôn*** [חַלּוֹן]	WINDOW
2479	***ḥalḥālāh*** [חַלְחָלָה]	PAIN
2481	***ḥalî*** [חֲלִי]	JEWEL
2483	***ḥolî*** [חֳלִי]	DISEASE
		GRIEF
		SICK
2484	***ḥelyāh*** [חֶלְיָה]	JEWEL
2485	***ḥālîl*** [חָלִיל]	PIPE
2486	***ḥālîlāh*** [חָלִילָה]	FORBID
2487	***ḥalîphāh*** [חֲלִיפָה]	CHANGE
2488	***ḥalîṣāh*** [חֲלִיצָה]	ARMS
2490	***ḥālal*** [חָלַל]	BEGIN
		DEFILE
		PIPE
2491	***ḥālāl*** [חָלָל]	WOUND
2492	***ḥālam*** [חָלַם]	DREAM
2493	***ḥēlem*** [חֵלֶם]	DREAM
2498	***ḥālaph*** [חָלַף]	CHANGE
		PASS
		RENEW
2499	***ḥalaph*** [חֲלַף]	PASS
2502	***ḥālaṣ*** [חָלַץ]	ARMS
		DELIVER
2505	***ḥālaq*** [חָלַק]	DIVIDE
		RECEIVE
2506	***ḥēleq*** [חֵלֶק]	SHARE

Strong's Number	Hebrew Article	English Entry
3117	***yôm*** [יוֹם]	DAY
		TIME
		YEAR
3123	***yônāh*** [יוֹנָה]	DOVE
3126	***yônēq*** [יוֹנֵק]	PLANT
		TENDER
3138	***yôreh*** [יוֹרֶה]	RAIN
3161	***yāḥad*** [יָחַד]	JOIN
		UNITE
3162	***yaḥad*** [יַחַד]	UNITE
3173	***yāḥîd*** [יָחִיד]	CHILD
		ONLY
3176	***yāḥal*** [יָחַל]	HOPE
		WAIT
3179	***yāḥam*** [יָחַם]	CONCEIVE
3187	***yāḥas*** [יָחַשׂ]	GENEALOGY
3190	***yāṭab*** [יָטַב]	GOOD
		PLEASE
3196	***yayin*** [יַיִן]	WINE
3198	***yākaḥ*** [יָכַח]	DISCIPLINE
		REASON
		REBUKE
3201	***yākōl*** [יָכֹל]	ABILITY
		WIN
3205	***yālad*** [יָלַד]	BEGET
		MIDWIFE
		WOMAN
		WORK
3206	***yeled*** [יֶלֶד]	CHILD
3207	***yaldāh*** [יַלְדָּה]	CHILD
		GIRL
3208	***yaldût*** [יַלְדוּת]	YOUTH
3212	***yālak*** [יָלַךְ]	ALLOW
		FOLLOW
		LEAD (VERB)
		WALK
3213	***yālal*** [יָלַל]	HOWL
3220	***yām*** [יָם]	SEA
		WEST
3221	***yam*** [יַם]	SEA
3225	***yāmîn*** [יָמִין]	RIGHT
3231	***yāman*** [יָמַן]	RIGHT
3233	***yemānî*** [יְמָנִי]	RIGHT
3238	***yānāh*** [יָנָה]	DRIVE
		OPPRESS
3240	***yānaḥ*** [יָנַח]	SET
3243	***yānaq*** [יָנַק]	BABE
		NURSE
3244	***yanshôph*** [יַנְשׁוֹף]	OWL
3245	***yāsad*** [יָסַד]	ESTABLISH
		FOUNDATION
3247	***yesôd*** [יְסוֹד]	FOUNDATION
		RESTORATION
3251	***yāsak*** [יָסַךְ]	POUR
3254	***yāsaph*** [יָסַף]	ADD
		INCREASE
3256	***yāsar*** [יָסַר]	ADMONISH
		CORRECT
		DISCIPLINE
		INSTRUCT
		PUNISH
		WARN
3259	***yā’ad*** [יָעַד]	APPOINT
		ASSEMBLE
		MEET
3276	***yā’al*** [יָעַל]	GAIN
3284	***ya’anāh*** [יַעֲנָה]	OWL
3286	***yā’aph*** [יָעַף]	FAINT
		WEARY
3287	***yā’ēph*** [יָעֵף]	WEARY
3289	***yā’aṣ*** [יָעַץ]	COUNSEL
		DETERMINE
		PLAN
3293	***ya’ar*** [יַעַר]	FOREST
3302	***yāphāh*** [יָפָה]	BEAUTIFUL
3303	***yāpheh*** [יָפֶה]	BEAUTIFUL
3308	***yophî*** [יֳפִי]	BEAUTIFUL
3313	***yāpha’*** [יָפַע]	SHINE
3318	***yāṣā’*** [יָצָא]	LEAVE
3320	***yāṣab*** [יָצַב]	PRESENT
		RESIST
		STAND
3322	***yāṣag*** [יָצַג]	PRESENT
		SET
3323	***yiṣhār*** [יִצְהָר]	OIL
3326	***yāṣûa’*** [יָצוּעַ]	BED

Strong's Number	Hebrew Article	English Entry
3820	*lēb* [לֵב]	HEART
		UNDERSTANDING
3824	*lēbāb* [לֵבָב]	HEART
		UNDERSTANDING
3827	*labbāh* [לַבָּה]	FLAME
3828	*lebônāh* [לְבוֹנָה]	FRANKINCENSE
3830	*lebûsh* [לְבוּשׁ]	CLOTHING
3833	*lābî’* [לָבִיא]	LION
3835	*lābēn* [לָבֵן]	WHITE
3836	*lābān* [לָבָן]	WHITE
3842	*lebānāh* [לְבָנָה]	MOON
3847	*lābash* [לָבַשׁ]	CLOTHE
		WEAR
3848	*lebash* [לְבַשׁ]	CLOTHE
3851	*lahab* [לַהַב]	FLAME
3852	*lehābāh* [לֶהָבָה]	FLAME
3856	*lāhah* [לָהַהּ]	MAD
3857	*lāhat* [לָהַט]	BURN
		FIRE
3858	*lahat* [לַהַט]	FLAME
3867	*lāwāh* [לָוָה]	BORROW
		JOIN
		LEND
3868	*lûz* [לוּז]	PERVERSE
3874	*lût* [לוּט]	WRAP
3885	*lûn* [לוּן]	LODGE
		MURMUR
		NIGHT
3887	*lûṣ* [לוּץ]	AMBASSADOR
		INTERPRET
		MOCK
		SCORN
3898	*lāḥam* [לָחַם]	FIGHT
3899	*leḥem* [לֶחֶם]	BREAD
		FOOD
3905	*lāḥaṣ* [לָחַץ]	AFFLICT
		OPPRESS
3906	*laḥaṣ* [לַחַץ]	AFFLICT
		OPPRESS
3907	*lāḥash* [לָחַשׁ]	WHISPER
3910	*lōt* [לֹט]	MYRRH
3913	*lātash* [לָטַשׁ]	SHARP
3915	*laylāh* [לַיְלָה]	NIGHT
3916	*lêlê* [לֵילֵי]	NIGHT
3918	*layish* [לַיִשׁ]	LION
3920	*lākad* [לָכַד]	APPREHEND
		TAKE
3925	*lāmad* [לָמַד]	LEARN
		TEACH
3928	*limmûd* [לִמּוּד]	DISCIPLE
3930	*lōa’* [לֹעַ]	THROAT
3931	*lā’ab* [לָעַב]	MOCK
3932	*lā’ag* [לָעַג]	LAUGH
3933	*la’ag* [לַעַג]	SCORN
3937	*lā’az* [לָעַז]	LANGUAGE
3940	*lappîd* [לַפִּיד]	LIGHTNING
		TORCH
3943	*lāphat* [לָפַת]	TURN
3944	*lāṣôn* [לָצוֹן]	SCORN
3945	*lāṣaṣ* [לָצַץ]	SCORN
3947	*lāqaḥ* [לָקַח]	MARRY
		RECEIVE
		TAKE
3948	*leqaḥ* [לֶקַח]	LEARN
		TEACH
3950	*lāqat* [לָקַט]	GATHER
3956	*lāshôn* [לָשׁוֹן]	FLAME
		LANGUAGE
		TONGUE
3960	*lāshan* [לָשַׁן]	SLANDER
3961	*lishān* [לִשָּׁן]	LANGUAGE
3966	*me’ōd* [מְאֹד]	ABUNDANCE
3967	*mē’āh* [מֵאָה]	HUNDRED
3971	*mûm* [מוּם]	BLEMISH
3972	*me’ûmāh* [מְאוּמָה]	FAULT
3973	*mā’ôs* [מָאוֹס]	REFUSE
3974	*mā’ôr* [מָאוֹר]	LIGHT
3976	*mō’zenayim* [מֹאזְנַיִם]	BALANCE
3978	*ma’akāl* [מַאֲכָל]	FOOD
3979	*ma’akelet* [מַאֲכֶלֶת]	KNIFE
3984	*mā’n* [מָאן]	VESSEL
3985	*mā’ēn* [מָאֵן]	REFUSE
		WILL

Strong's Number	Hebrew Article	English Entry
3988	***mā'as*** [מָאַס]	DESPISE
		REFUSE
		REJECT
3993	***ma'arāb*** [מַאֲרָב]	WAIT
3994	***me'ērāh*** [מְאֵרָה]	CURSE
3996	***mābô'*** [מָבוֹא]	ENTER
		WEST
3999	***mabbûl*** [מַבּוּל]	FLOOD
4002	***mabbûa'*** [מַבּוּעַ]	SPRING
4005	***mibḥār*** [מִבְחָר]	CHOICE
4009	***mibṭāḥ*** [מִבְטָח]	TRUST
4022	***meged*** [מֶגֶד]	VALUABLE
4026	***migdāl*** [מִגְדָּל]	TOWER
4030	***migdānāh*** [מִגְדָּנָה]	VALUABLE
4033	***māgûr*** [מָגוּר]	SOJOURN
4035	***megûrāh*** [מְגוּרָה]	BARN
4037	***magzērāh*** [מַגְזֵרָה]	AX
4043	***māgēn*** [מָגֵן]	ARMS
		GOD
		SHIELD
4045	***mig'eret*** [מִגְעֶרֶת]	REBUKE
4046	***maggēphāh*** [מַגֵּפָה]	PLAGUE
		SLAUGHTER
4050	***megērāh*** [מְגֵרָה]	AX
4055	***mad*** [מַד]	ARMS
		CLOTHING
4057	***midbār*** [מִדְבָּר]	DESERT
4058	***mādad*** [מָדַד]	MEASURE
4060	***middāh*** [מִדָּה]	MEASURE
		TRIBUTE
4064	***madweh*** [מַדְוֶה]	DISEASE
4066	***mādôn*** [מָדוֹן]	STRIFE
4082	***medînāh*** [מְדִינָה]	REGION
4102	***māhah*** [מָהַהּ]	DELAY
4103	***mehûmāh*** [מְהוּמָה]	TROUBLE
4109	***mahalak*** [מַהֲלָךְ]	JOURNEY
4114	***mahpēkāh*** [מַהְפֵּכָה]	OVERTHROW
4116	***māhar*** [מָהַר]	HASTE
4120	***mehērāh*** [מְהֵרָה]	HASTE
4127	***mûg*** [מוּג]	FAINT
		MELT
4129	***môdā'*** [מוֹדַע]	KIN
4132	***môṭ*** [מוֹט]	YOKE
4133	***môṭāh*** [מוֹטָה]	YOKE
4134	***mûk*** [מוּךְ]	POOR
4135	***mûl*** [מוּל]	CIRCUMCISE
4143	***mûsād*** [מוּסָד]	FOUNDATION
4144	***môsād*** [מוֹסָד]	FOUNDATION
4146	***mûsādāh*** [מוּסָדָה]	FOUNDATION
4147	***môsēr*** [מוֹסֵר]	BAND
		BOND
4148	***mûsār*** [מוּסָר]	CORRECT
		DISCIPLINE
		INSTRUCT
4150	***mô'ēd*** [מוֹעֵד]	ASSEMBLE
		FEAST
		TIME
4159	***môphēt*** [מוֹפֵת]	SIGN
4161	***môṣā'*** [מוֹצָא]	SPRING
4170	***môqēsh*** [מוֹקֵשׁ]	TRAP
4171	***mûr*** [מוּר]	CHANGE
		EXCHANGE
4172	***môrā'*** [מוֹרָא]	FEAR
		TERRIBLE
4173	***môrag*** [מוֹרַג]	INSTRUMENT
		THRESH
4175	***môreh*** [מוֹרֶה]	RAIN
4181	***môrāshāh*** [מוֹרָשָׁה]	POSSESS
4184	***mûsh*** [מוּשׁ]	FEEL
4185	***mûsh*** [מוּשׁ]	DEPART
4186	***môshāb*** [מוֹשָׁב]	DWELL
		SEAT
4191	***mût*** [מוּת]	BODY
		DIE
		KILL
4193	***môt*** [מוֹת]	DEATH
4194	***māwet*** [מָוֶת]	DEATH
4196	***mizbēaḥ*** [מִזְבֵּחַ]	ALTAR
4202	***māzôn*** [מָזוֹן]	FOOD
4204	***māzôr*** [מָזוֹר]	WOUND
4217	***mizrāḥ*** [מִזְרָח]	EAST
		RISE
		SUN

Strong's Number	Hebrew Article	English Entry
4218	***mizra'*** [מִזְרַע]	SOW
4219	***mizraq*** [מִזְרָק]	BOWL
4223	***meḥā'*** [מְחָא]	STRIKE
4229	***māḥāh*** [מָחָה]	BLOT OUT
		DESTROY
		WIPE
4231	***māḥôz*** [מָחוֹז]	HAVEN
4234	***māḥôl*** [מָחוֹל]	DANCE
4236	***maḥazeh*** [מַחֲזֶה]	VISION
4242	***meḥîr*** [מְחִיר]	PRICE
4245	***maḥalāh*** [מַחֲלָה]	DISEASE
		SICK
4246	***meḥōlāh*** [מְחֹלָה]	DANCE
4256	***maḥalōqāt*** [מַחֲלֹקֶת]	DIVISION
4268	***maḥseh*** [מַחְסֶה]	REFUGE
4270	***maḥsôr*** [מַחְסוֹר]	NEED
4272	***māḥaṣ*** [מָחַץ]	PIERCE
		WOUND
4278	***meḥqār*** [מֶחְקָר]	DEEP
4279	***māḥār*** [מָחָר]	TOMORROW
4281	***maḥarēshāh*** [מַחֲרֵשָׁה]	PLOW
4284	***maḥashābāh*** [מַחֲשָׁבָה]	PLAN
		THINK
4285	***maḥshāk*** [מַחְשָׁךְ]	DARK
4291	***mātāh*** [מְטָה]	REACH
4293	***matbēaḥ*** [מַטְבֵּחַ]	SLAUGHTER
4294	***matteh*** [מַטֶּה]	STAFF
		TRIBE
4296	***mittāh*** [מִטָּה]	BED
4301	***matmôn*** [מַטְמוֹן]	TREASURE
4302	***mattā'*** [מַטָּע]	PLANT
4303	***māt'am*** [מַטְעַם]	FOOD
4305	***mātar*** [מָטַר]	RAIN
4306	***mātār*** [מָטָר]	RAIN
4307	***mattārāh*** [מַטָּרָה]	GUARD
4325	***mayim*** [מַיִם]	WATER
4327	***mîn*** [מִין]	KIND (NOUN)
4334	***mîshôr*** [מִישׁוֹר]	PLAIN
4339	***mêshār*** [מֵישָׁר]	RIGHTEOUS
4341	***mak'ôb*** [מַכְאוֹב]	PAIN
		SORROW
4347	***makkāh*** [מַכָּה]	BLOW (NOUN)
		PLAGUE
		SLAUGHTER
		WOUND
4349	***mākôn*** [מָכוֹן]	FOUNDATION
		PLACE (NOUN)
4359	***miklal*** [מִכְלָל]	PERFECT
4364	***makmōr*** [מַכְמֹר]	NET
4365	***mikmōret*** [מִכְמֹרֶת]	NET
4373	***miksāh*** [מִכְסָה]	NUMBER
4376	***mākar*** [מָכַר]	SELL
4377	***meker*** [מֶכֶר]	VALUABLE
4383	***mikshôl*** [מִכְשׁוֹל]	STUMBLING BLOCK
4385	***miktāb*** [מִכְתָּב]	WRITE
4390	***mālē'*** [מָלֵא]	ACCOMPLISH
		FILL
		FULFILL
		OVERFLOW
		WHOLE
4392	***mālē'*** [מָלֵא]	FULL
4393	***melō'*** [מְלֹא]	FILL
4397	***mal'āk*** [מַלְאָךְ]	ANGEL
4399	***melā'kāh*** [מְלָאכָה]	USE
		WORK
4405	***millāh*** [מִלָּה]	SPEECH
		WORD
4410	***melûkāh*** [מְלוּכָה]	KINGDOM
		ROYAL
4411	***mālôn*** [מָלוֹן]	INN
		LODGE
4412	***melûnāh*** [מְלוּנָה]	LODGE
4414	***mālaḥ*** [מָלַח]	VANISH
4417	***melaḥ*** [מֶלַח]	SALT
4419	***mallāḥ*** [מַלָּח]	SAILOR
4421	***milḥāmāh*** [מִלְחָמָה]	WARFARE
4422	***mālat*** [מָלַט]	DELIVER
		ESCAPE
		FLEE
4427	***mālak*** [מָלַךְ]	REIGN
4428	***melek*** [מֶלֶךְ]	GOD
		KING

Strong's Number	Hebrew Article	English Entry
5007	***ne'āṣāh*** [נְאָצָה]	BLASPHEME
5009	***ne'āqāh*** [נְאָקָה]	GROAN
5012	***nābā'*** [נָבָא]	PROPHECY
5013	***nebā'*** [נְבָא]	PROPHECY
5016	***nebû'āh*** [נְבוּאָה]	PROPHECY
5017	***nebû'āh*** [נְבוּאָה]	PROPHECY
5023	***nebizbāh*** [נְבִזְבָּה]	REWARD
5027	***nābat*** [נָבַט]	CONSIDER
		SEE
5029	***nebî'*** [נְבִיא]	PROPHECY
5030	***nābî'*** [נָבִיא]	PROPHECY
5031	***nebî'āh*** [נְבִיאָה]	PROPHECY
5033	***nēbek*** [נֵבֶךְ]	SPRING
5034	***nābēl*** [נָבֵל]	FADE AWAY
		WEAR
		WITHER
5035	***nēbel*** [נֵבֶל]	JAR
		LUTE
		VESSEL
5036	***nābāl*** [נָבָל]	FOOL
5038	***nebēlāh*** [נְבֵלָה]	BODY
5039	***nebālāh*** [נְבָלָה]	FOLLY
5042	***nāba'*** [נָבַע]	POUR
5043	***nebrashtāh*** [נֶבְרַשְׁתָּה]	LAMPSTAND
5046	***nāgad*** [נָגַד]	TELL
		WARN
5050	***nāgah*** [נָגַהּ]	SHINE
5051	***nōgah*** [נֹגַהּ]	BRIGHT
		SHINE
5053	***nōgah*** [נֹגַהּ]	MORNING
5057	***nāgîd*** [נָגִיד]	RULE
5058	***negînāh*** [נְגִינָה]	SING
5059	***nāgan*** [נָגַן]	INSTRUMENT
		PLAY
5060	***nāga'*** [נָגַע]	REACH
		TOUCH
5061	***nega'*** [נֶגַע]	PLAGUE
5062	***nāgaph*** [נָגַף]	BEAT
		STRIKE
		STUMBLE
5063	***negeph*** [נֶגֶף]	PLAGUE
		STUMBLE
5064	***nāgar*** [נָגַר]	POUR
5065	***nāgas*** [נָגַשׂ]	OPPRESS
		TAX
5066	***nāgash*** [נָגַשׁ]	ACCESS
		DRAW
		OFFER
		OVERTAKE
5068	***nādab*** [נָדַב]	OFFER
		WILL
5069	***nedab*** [נְדַב]	OFFERING
5071	***nedābāh*** [נְדָבָה]	FREE
		OFFERING
5074	***nādad*** [נָדַד]	FLEE
5079	***niddāh*** [נִדָּה]	UNCLEAN
5080	***nādaḥ*** [נָדַח]	DRIVE
5081	***nādîb*** [נָדִיב]	NOBLE
5083	***nādān*** [נָדָן]	GIFT
5087	***nādar*** [נָדַר]	VOW
5088	***nēder*** [נֵדֶר]	VOW
5090	***nāhag*** [נָהַג]	DRIVE
		LEAD (VERB)
5092	***nehî*** [נְהִי]	MOURN
5094	***nehôr*** [נְהוֹר]	LIGHT
5095	***nāhal*** [נָהַל]	GUIDE
		LEAD (VERB)
5098	***nāham*** [נָהַם]	ROAR
5099	***naham*** [נַהַם]	ROAR
5100	***nehāmāh*** [נְהָמָה]	ROAR
5102	***nāhar*** [נָהַר]	FLOW
5103	***nehar*** [נְהַר]	RIVER
5104	***nāhār*** [נָהָר]	FLOOD
		RIVER
5105	***nehārāh*** [נְהָרָה]	LIGHT
5117	***nûaḥ*** [נוּחַ]	LEAVE
		QUIET
		REST
		SET
5118	***nôaḥ*** [נוֹחַ]	REST
5127	***nûs*** [נוּס]	FLEE
5128	***nûa'*** [נוּעַ]	SIEVE

Strong's Number	Hebrew Article	English Entry
5291	***na'arāh*** [נַעֲרָה]	CHILD
		GIRL
		MAID
5299	***nāphāh*** [נָפָה]	SIEVE
5301	***nāphaḥ*** [נָפַח]	BLOW (VERB)
		BREATH
5303	***nephîlîm*** [נְפִילִים]	NEPHILIM
5306	***nōphek*** [נֹפֶךְ]	EMERALD
5307	***nāphal*** [נָפַל]	CAST
		FAIL
		FALL
		OVERTHROW
		PERISH
		PRESENT
5309	***nēphel*** [נֵפֶל]	BEGET
5310	***nāphaṣ*** [נָפַץ]	BREAK
		DASH
		SCATTER
5312	***nephaq*** [נְפַק]	TAKE
5314	***nāphash*** [נָפַשׁ]	REFRESH
5315	***nephesh*** [נֶפֶשׁ]	BODY
		CREATE
		LIFE
		MIND
		PERSON
		SOUL
5317	***nōphet*** [נֹפֶת]	HONEY
5324	***nāṣab*** [נָצַב]	APPOINT
		OFFICER
		PRESENT
		SET
		STAND
		UPRIGHT
5327	***nāṣāh*** [נָצָה]	STRIVE
5328	***niṣṣāh*** [נִצָּה]	FLOWER
5329	***menaṣṣēaḥ*** [מְנַצֵּחַ]	MUSIC
5333	***neṣîb*** [נְצִיב]	OFFICER
5337	***nāṣal*** [נָצַל]	DEFEND
		DELIVER
		ESCAPE
		RECOVER
5341	***nāṣar*** [נָצַר]	KEEP
		WATCH
5342	***nēṣer*** [נֵצֶר]	BRANCH
5344	***nāqab*** [נָקַב]	BLASPHEME
		PIERCE
5347	***neqēbāh*** [נְקֵבָה]	WOMAN
5349	***nōqēd*** [נֹקֵד]	SHEEP
5352	***nāqāh*** [נָקָה]	INNOCENCE
5355	***nāqî*** [נָקִי]	INNOCENCE
5358	***nāqam*** [נָקַם]	AVENGE
		PUNISH
5359	***nāqām*** [נָקָם]	AVENGE
5360	***neqāmāh*** [נְקָמָה]	AVENGE
5362	***nāqaph*** [נָקַף]	SURROUND
5365	***nāqar*** [נָקַר]	DIG
5367	***nāqash*** [נָקַשׁ]	TRAP
5375	***nāsā'*** [נָשָׂא]	BEAR (VERB)
		FORGIVE
		RECEIVE
		SWEAR
		TAKE
		WEAR
5376	***nesā'*** [נְשָׂא]	TAKE
5377	***nāshā'*** [נָשָׁא]	DECEIT
5378	***nāshā'*** [נָשָׁא]	DEBT
		INTEREST
5380	***nāshab*** [נָשַׁב]	BLOW (VERB)
5381	***nāsag*** [נָשַׂג]	AFFORD
		OBTAIN
		OVERTAKE
5382	***nāshāh*** [נָשָׁה]	FORGET
5383	***nāshāh*** [נָשָׁה]	INTEREST
5386	***neshî*** [נְשִׁי]	DEBT
5387	***nāsî'*** [נָשִׂיא]	RULE
5389	***neshîn*** [נָשִׁין]	WIFE
5391	***nāshak*** [נָשַׁךְ]	BITE
		INTEREST
5392	***neshek*** [נֶשֶׁךְ]	INTEREST
5397	***neshāmāh*** [נְשָׁמָה]	BREATH
		SPIRIT
5398	***nāshaph*** [נָשַׁף]	BLOW (VERB)
5399	***nesheph*** [נֶשֶׁף]	EVENING
5401	***nāshaq*** [נָשַׁק]	KISS
		TOUCH
5402	***nesheq*** [נֶשֶׁק]	ARMS

Strong's Number	Hebrew Article	English Entry
6041	*'ānî* [עָנִי]	AFFLICT
		HUMBLE
		POOR
6049	*'ānan* [עָנַן]	MAGIC
6051	*'ānan* [עָנָן]	CLOUD
6056	*'anaph* [עֲנַף]	BRANCH
6057	*'ānāph* [עָנָף]	BRANCH
6059	*'ānaq* [עָנַק]	NECKLACE
6060	*'anāq* [עֲנָק]	NECKLACE
6071	*'āsîs* [עָסִיס]	WINE
6074	*'ophî* [עֳפִי]	LEAF
6082	*'ōpher* [עֹפֶר]	YOUNG
6083	*'āphār* [עָפָר]	ASHES
		DUST
6086	*'ēṣ* [עֵץ]	TREE
		WOOD
6087	*'āṣab* [עָצַב]	GRIEF
6089	*'eṣeb* [עֶצֶב]	SORROW
		WORK
6090	*'ōṣeb* [עֹצֶב]	SORROW
6091	*'āṣāb* [עָצָב]	IDOL
6093	*'iṣṣābôn* [עִצָּבוֹן]	SORROW
6094	*'aṣṣebet* [עַצֶּבֶת]	SORROW
		WOUND
6098	*'ēṣāh* [עֵצָה]	ADVICE
6099	*'āṣûm* [עָצוּם]	STRENGTH
6104	*'aṣlût* [עַצְלוּת]	IDLE
6105	*'āṣam* [עָצַם]	BONE
		CLOSE (VERB)
		SHUT
6106	*'eṣem* [עֶצֶם]	BONE
6113	*'āṣar* [עָצַר]	CLOSE (VERB)
		RECOVER
		RESTRAIN
		SHUT
6115	*'ōṣer* [עֹצֶר]	OPPRESS
6116	*'aṣārāh* [עֲצָרָה]	ASSEMBLE
6118	*'ēqeb* [עֵקֶב]	REWARD
6119	*'āqēb* [עָקֵב]	HEEL
		STEP
6121	*'āqōb* [עָקֹב]	DECEIT
6123	*'āqad* [עָקַד]	BIND
6125	*'āqāh* [עָקָה]	OPPRESS
6131	*'āqar* [עָקַר]	UPROOT
6135	*'āqār* [עָקָר]	BARREN
6137	*'aqrāb* [עַקְרָב]	SCORPION
6140	*'āqash* [עָקַשׁ]	PERVERSE
6141	*'iqqēsh* [עִקֵּשׁ]	CROOKED
6148	*'ārab* [עָרַב]	GUARANTEE
		MIX
6149	*'ārab* [עָרַב]	PLEASE
6151	*'arab* [עֲרַב]	MIX
6153	*'ereb* [עֶרֶב]	EVENING
6157	*'ārōb* [עָרֹב]	FLY
6158	*'ôreb* [עוֹרֵב]	RAVEN
6160	*'arābāh* [עֲרָבָה]	PLAIN
6162	*'ērābôn* [עֵרָבוֹן]	DEPOSIT
		GUARANTEE
6168	*'ārāh* [עָרָה]	EMPTY
		NAKED
		POUR
		UNCOVER
6172	*'erwāh* [עֶרְוָה]	NAKED
		UNCLEAN
6173	*'arwāh* [עַרְוָה]	DISHONOR
6174	*'ārôm* [עָרוֹם]	NAKED
6175	*'ārûm* [עָרוּם]	PRUDENCE
6181	*'eryāh* [עֶרְיָה]	NAKED
6184	*'ārîṣ* [עָרִיץ]	OPPRESS
6185	*'arîrî* [עֲרִירִי]	CHILD
6186	*'ārak* [עָרַךְ]	ARRANGE
		ORDER
		PREPARATION
		SET
		TAX
		VALUABLE
6187	*'ērek* [עֵרֶךְ]	VALUABLE
6189	*'ārēl* [עָרֵל]	CIRCUMCISE
6190	*'orlāh* [עָרְלָה]	CIRCUMCISE
6191	*'āram* [עָרַם]	PRUDENCE
6195	*'ormāh* [עָרְמָה]	PRUDENCE
6202	*'āraph* [עָרַף]	NECK

Strong's Number	Hebrew Article	English Entry
6381	*pālā'* [פָּלָא]	IMPOSSIBLE
		WONDER
6382	*pele'* [פֶּלֶא]	WONDER
6383	*pilî'* [פִּלְאִי]	WONDER
6385	*pālag* [פָּלַג]	DIVIDE
6388	*peleg* [פֶּלֶג]	RIVER
6392	*peluggāh* [פְּלֻגָּה]	DIVISION
6399	*pelaḥ* [פְּלַח]	SERVE
6400	*pelaḥ* [פֶּלַח]	PIECE
6402	*polḥan* [פָּלְחַן]	SERVE
6403	*pālaṭ* [פָּלַט]	GOD
6412	*pālîṭ, pālēṭ, pālēṭ* [פָּלִיט, פָּלֵיט, פָּלֵט]	ESCAPE
6414	*pālîl* [פָּלִיל]	JUDGE
6415	*pelîlāh* [פְּלִילָה]	JUDGMENT
6417	*pelîlîyāh* [פְּלִילִיָּה]	JUDGMENT
6419	*pālal* [פָּלַל]	INTERCEDE
		PRAY
6426	*pālaṣ* [פָּלַץ]	TREMBLE
6428	*palash* [פָּלַשׁ]	ROLL
6433	*pum* [פֻּם]	MOUTH
6437	*pānāh* [פָּנָה]	PREPARATION
		TURN
6438	*pinnāh* [פִּנָּה]	CORNER
6440	*pānîm* [פָּנִים]	FACE
		OPEN
		PERSON
		PRESENCE
		VISION
6452	*pāsaḥ* [פָּסַח]	PASS
6453	*pesaḥ* [פֶּסַח]	OFFERING
		PASSOVER
6455	*pisseāḥ* [פִּסֵּחַ]	LAME
6459	*pesel* [פֶּסֶל]	IDOL
6460	*pesantērîn* [פְּסַנְתֵּרִין]	LUTE
6466	*pā'al* [פָּעַל]	CREATE
		WORK
6467	*pō'al* [פֹּעַל]	WORK
6468	*pe'ullāh* [פְּעֻלָּה]	WAGES
		WORK
6470	*pā'am* [פָּעַם]	TROUBLE
6471	*pa'am* [פַּעַם]	TIME
6473	*pā'ar* [פָּעַר]	OPEN
6475	*pāṣāh* [פָּצָה]	OPEN
6481	*pāṣa'* [פָּצַע]	WOUND
6482	*peṣa'* [פֶּצַע]	WOUND
6484	*pāṣar* [פָּצַר]	URGE
6485	*pāqad* [פָּקַד]	APPOINT
		MISS
		NUMBER
		OFFICER
		VISIT
6486	*pequddāh* [פְּקֻדָּה]	OFFICE
		VISIT
6490	*piqqûd* [פִּקּוּד]	COMMANDMENT
6491	*pāqaḥ* [פָּקַח]	OPEN
6496	*pāqîd* [פָּקִיד]	OFFICER
6499	*par* [פַּר]	BULL
6504	*pārad* [פָּרַד]	JOINT
		SCATTER
		SEPARATE
6507	*perudôth* [פְּרֻדוֹת]	SEED
6509	*pārāh* [פָּרָה]	FRUIT
6510	*pārāh* [פָּרָה]	COW
6517	*pārûr* [פָּרוּר]	POT
6519	*perāzāh* [פְּרָזָה]	VILLAGE
6523	*parzel* [פַּרְזֶל]	IRON
6524	*pāraḥ* [פָּרַח]	SPRING
6525	*peraḥ* [פֶּרַח]	FLOWER
6529	*perî* [פְּרִי]	FRUIT
		REWARD
6530	*pārîṣ* [פָּרִיץ]	ROB
6532	*porōket* [פָּרֹכֶת]	VEIL
6536	*pāras* [פָּרַס]	DIVIDE
6545	*pera'* [פֶּרַע]	HAIR
6555	*pāraṣ* [פָּרַץ]	URGE
6561	*pāraq* [פָּרַק]	TEAR (VERB)
6565	*pārar* [פָּרַר]	BREAK
6566	*pāras* [פָּרַשׂ]	SCATTER
		SPREAD
6567	*pārash* [פָּרַשׁ]	SCATTER
6573	*parshegen* [פַּרְשֶׁגֶן]	COPY
6576	*parshēz* [פַּרְשֵׁז]	SPREAD

Strong's Number	Hebrew Article	English Entry
7225	*rē'shît* [רֵאשִׁית]	BEGIN
		FIRSTFRUIT
7227	*rab* [רַב]	ABUNDANCE
		GREAT
		MUCH
		MULTITUDE
7230	*rōb* [רֹב]	ABUNDANCE
		CROWD
		GREAT
		MULTITUDE
7231	*rābab* [רָבַב]	GREAT
7235	*rābāh* [רָבָה]	ABUNDANCE
		INCREASE
7238	*rebû* [רְבוּ]	MAJESTY
7242	*rābîd* [רָבִיד]	NECKLACE
7250	*rāba'* [רָבַע]	LIE (VERB)
7253	*reba'* [רֶבַע]	SIDE
7257	*rābaṣ* [רָבַץ]	LIE
7264	*rāgaz* [רָגַז]	ANGER
		QUAKE
		TREMBLE
7266	*regaz* [רְגַז]	ANGER
7267	*rōgez* [רֹגֶז]	TROUBLE
		WRATH
7270	*rāgal* [רָגַל]	SLANDER
7272	*regel* [רֶגֶל]	FOLLOW
		FOOT
7273	*raglî* [רַגְלִי]	FOOT
7275	*rāgam* [רָגַם]	STONE
7279	*rāgan* [רָגַן]	MURMUR
7280	*rāga'* [רָגַע]	REST
7282	*rāgēa'* [רָגֵעַ]	QUIET
7284	*regash* [רְגַשׁ]	ASSEMBLE
7286	*rādad* [רָדַד]	SUBJECT
7287	*rādāh* [רָדָה]	DOMINION
		RULE
7290	*rādam* [רָדַם]	SLEEP
7291	*rādaph* [רָדַף]	FOLLOW
		PERSECUTE
7301	*rāwāh* [רָוָה]	SATISFY
7306	*rûaḥ* [רוּחַ]	SMELL
7307	*rûaḥ* [רוּחַ]	BREATH
		SPIRIT
		WIND
7310	*rewāyāh* [רְוָיָה]	RUN
7311	*rûm* [רוּם]	EXALT
		LIFT
		OFFER
		RISE
		SET
		TALL
7312	*rûm* [רוּם]	HEIGHT
7321	*rûa'* [רוּעַ]	SHOUT
		SOUND
		TRIUMPH
7322	*rûph* [רוּף]	TREMBLE
7323	*rûṣ* [רוּץ]	GUARD
		RUN
7324	*rûq* [רוּק]	DRAW
		EMPTY
		POUR
7326	*rûsh* [רוּשׁ]	POOR
7328	*rāz* [רָז]	MYSTERY
7336	*rāzan* [רָזַן]	RULE
7337	*rāḥab* [רָחַב]	BROAD
		ENLARGE
		ROOM
7341	*rōḥab* [רֹחַב]	BROAD
7342	*rāḥāb* [רָחָב]	BROAD
		PRIDE
7347	*rēḥayim* [רֵחַיִם]	MILL
7350	*rāḥôq* [רָחוֹק]	FAR
7353	*rāḥēl* [רָחֵל]	SHEEP
7355	*rāḥam* [רָחַם]	MERCY
7356	*raḥam* [רַחַם]	MERCY
		WOMB
7358	*reḥem* [רֶחֶם]	WOMB
7359	*rēḥām* [רֵחָם]	MERCY
7364	*rāḥaṣ* [רָחַץ]	WASH
7365	*reḥaṣ* [רְחַץ]	TRUST
7367	*raḥṣāh* [רַחְצָה]	WASH
7368	*rāḥaq* [רָחַק]	FAR
7376	*rātash* [רָטַשׁ]	DASH

Strong’s Number	Hebrew Article	English Entry
7378	***rîb*** [רִיב]	COMPLAINT
		PLEA
		STRIVE
7379	***rîb*** [רִיב]	ANSWER
		CONDEMN
		LAWSUIT
7381	***rêaḥ*** [רֵיחַ]	SMELL
7385	***rîq*** [רִיק]	VAIN
7386	***rêq*** [רֵיק]	EMPTY
		VAIN
7387	***rêqām*** [רֵיקָם]	EMPTY
7390	***rak*** [רַךְ]	TENDER
		WEAK
7392	***rākab*** [רָכַב]	RIDE
7393	***rekeb*** [רֶכֶב]	CHARIOT
		MILL
7399	***rekûsh*** [רְכוּשׁ]	GOODS
7400	***rākîl*** [רָכִיל]	SLANDER
7401	***rākak*** [רָכַךְ]	FAINT
		TENDER
7402	***rākal*** [רָכַל]	TRADE
7405	***rākas*** [רָכַס]	BIND
7411	***rāmāh*** [רָמָה]	CAST
		DECEIT
7415	***rimmāh*** [רִמָּה]	WORM
7423	***remîyāh*** [רְמִיָּה]	DECEIT
		IDLE
7429	***rāmas*** [רָמַס]	TRAMPLE
7440	***rinnāh*** [רִנָּה]	CRY
		JOY
		SING
7442	***rānan*** [רָנַן]	JOY
		REJOICE
		SHOUT
		SING
7445	***renānāh*** [רְנָנָה]	JOY
		SING
7448	***resen*** [רֶסֶן]	BRIDLE
7451	***ra’*** [רַע]	EVIL
		SAD
7452	***rēa’*** [רֵעַ]	SHOUT
7453	***rēa’*** [רֵעַ]	FRIEND
		NEIGHBOR
7455	***rōa’*** [רֹעַ]	EVIL
		SAD
		WICKED
7458	***rā’āb*** [רָעָב]	FAMINE
7462	***rā’āh*** [רָעָה]	FEED
		SHEPHERD
7463	***rē’eh*** [רֵעֶה]	FRIEND
7468	***re’ût*** [רְעוּת]	NEIGHBOR
7471	***re’î*** [רְעִי]	PASTURE
7474	***ra’yāh*** [רַעְיָה]	LOVE
7481	***rā’am*** [רָעַם]	ROAR
		THUNDER
7482	***ra’am*** [רַעַם]	THUNDER
7489	***rā’a’*** [רָעַע]	AFFLICT
		BREAK
		EVIL
		WICKED
7492	***rā’aṣ*** [רָעַץ]	DASH
7493	***rā’ash*** [רָעַשׁ]	QUAKE
		SHAKE
		TREMBLE
7494	***ra’ash*** [רַעַשׁ]	EARTHQUAKE
		QUAKE
7495	***rāphā’*** [רָפָא]	HEAL
		PHYSICIAN
		REPAIR
7503	***rāphāh*** [רָפָה]	FAIL
		IDLE
		WEAK
7504	***rāpheh*** [רָפֶה]	WEAK
7521	***rāṣāh*** [רָצָה]	ENJOY
7522	***rāṣôn*** [רָצוֹן]	DELIGHT IN
		FAVOR
		WILL
7523	***rāṣaḥ*** [רָצַח]	KILL
7531	***riṣpāh*** [רִצְפָּה]	PAVEMENT
7533	***rāṣaṣ*** [רָצַץ]	BRUISE
		OPPRESS
7540	***rāqad*** [רָקַד]	DANCE
7544	***reqaḥ*** [רֶקַח]	SPICE
7547	***riqqûaḥ*** [רִקּוּחַ]	PERFUME
7560	***resham*** [רְשַׁם]	SIGN

INDEX OF GREEK WORDS

Strong's Number	Greek Article	English Entry
322	***anadeiknymi*** [ἀναδείκνυμι]	APPOINT
		SHOW
324	***anadechomai*** [ἀναδέχομαι]	RECEIVE
325	***anadidōmi*** [ἀναδίδωμι]	DELIVER
326	***anazaō*** [ἀναζάω]	LIFE
327	***anazēteō*** [ἀναζητέω]	SEEK
331	***anathema*** [ἀνάθεμα]	CURSE
332	***anathematizō*** [ἀναθεματίζω]	BIND
		CURSE
		OATH
333	***anatheōreō*** [ἀναθεωρέω]	CONSIDER
336	***anairesis*** [ἀναίρεσις]	DEATH
337	***anaireō*** [ἀναιρέω]	KILL
338	***anaitios*** [ἀναίτιος]	BLAME
		INNOCENCE
339	***anakathizō*** [ἀνακαθίζω]	SIT
341	***anakainoō*** [ἀνακαινόω]	RENEW
342	***anakainōsis*** [ἀνακαίνωσις]	RENEW
343	***anakalyptō*** [ἀνακαλύπτω]	UNVEIL
344	***anakamptō*** [ἀνακάμπτω]	RETURN
		TURN
345	***anakeimai*** [ἀνάκειμαι]	GUEST
		SIT
347	***anaklinō*** [ἀνακλίνω]	SIT
349	***anakrazō*** [ἀνακράζω]	CRY
350	***anakrinō*** [ἀνακρίνω]	ASK
		DISCERN
		EXAMINATION
		JUDGE
		QUESTION
351	***anakrisis*** [ἀνάκρισις]	EXAMINATION
353	***analambanō*** [ἀναλαμβάνω]	TAKE
355	***analiskō*** [ἀναλίσκω]	CONSUME
357	***analogizomai*** [ἀναλογίζομαι]	CONSIDER
358	***analos*** [ἄναλος]	SALT
359	***analysis*** [ἀνάλυσις]	DEPART
360	***analyō*** [ἀναλύω]	DEPART
361	***anamartētos*** [ἀναμάρτητος]	SIN
363	***anamimnēskō*** [ἀναμιμνήσκω]	REMEMBER
364	***anamnēsis*** [ἀνάμνησις]	REMEMBER
365	***ananeoō*** [ἀνανεόω]	RENEW
370	***anaxios*** [ἀνάξιος]	UNWORTHY
371	***anaxiōs*** [ἀναξίως]	UNWORTHY
372	***anapausis*** [ἀνάπαυσις]	REST
373	***anapauō*** [ἀναπαύω]	REFRESH
		REST
374	***anapeithō*** [ἀναπείθω]	PERSUADE
375	***anapempō*** [ἀναπέμπω]	SEND
376	***anapēros*** [ἀνάπηρος]	MAIMED
377	***anapiptō*** [ἀναπίπτω]	SIT
378	***anaplēroō*** [ἀναπληρόω]	FILL
		FULFILL
379	***anapologētos*** [ἀναπολόγητος]	EXCUSE
380	***anaptyssō*** [ἀναπτύσσω]	OPEN
383	***anaseiō*** [ἀνασείω]	STIR
385	***anaspaō*** [ἀνασπάω]	DRAW
386	***anastasis*** [ἀνάστασις]	RESURRECTION
388	***anastauroō*** [ἀνασταυρόω]	CROSS
389	***anastenazō*** [ἀναστενάζω]	GROAN
390	***anastrephō*** [ἀναστρέφω]	RETURN
393	***anatellō*** [ἀνατέλλω]	ARISE
395	***anatolē*** [ἀνατολή]	EAST
397	***anatrephō*** [ἀνατρέφω]	BRING
398	***anaphainō*** [ἀναφαίνω]	APPEAR
399	***anapherō*** [ἀναφέρω]	BEAR (VERB)
		OFFER
402	***anachōreō*** [ἀναχωρέω]	LEAVE
403	***anapsyxis*** [ἀνάψυξις]	REFRESH
404	***anapsychō*** [ἀναψύχω]	REFRESH
410	***anenklētos*** [ἀνέγκλητος]	BLAME
		INNOCENCE
411	***anekdiēgētos*** [ἀνεκδιήγητος]	UNSPEAKABLE
412	***aneklalētos*** [ἀνεκλάλητος]	UNSPEAKABLE
413	***anekleiptos*** [ἀνέκλειπτος]	FAIL
415	***aneleēmōn*** [ἀνελεήμων]	UNMERCIFUL
416	***anemizō*** [ἀνεμίζω]	WIND
417	***anemos*** [ἄνεμος]	WIND
418	***anendektos*** [ἀνένδεκτος]	IMPOSSIBLE
420	***anexikakos*** [ἀνεξίκακος]	PATIENCE
422	***anepaischyntos*** [ἀνεπαίσχυντος]	ASHAMED

Strong's Number	Greek Article	English Entry
423	***anepilēmptos*** [ἀνεπίλημπτος]	BLAME
		INNOCENCE
425	***anesis*** [ἄνεσις]	REST
426	***anetazō*** [ἀνετάζω]	EXAMINATION
429	***aneuriskō*** [ἀνευρίσκω]	FIND
430	***anechomai*** [ἀνέχομαι]	BEAR (VERB)
434	***anēmeros*** [ἀνήμερος]	FIERCE
435	***anēr*** [ἀνήρ]	FELLOW
		HUSBAND
		MAN
436	***anthistēmi*** [ἀνθίστημι]	RESIST
437	***anthomologeomai*** [ἀνθομολογέομαι]	THANK
438	***anthos*** [ἄνθος]	FLOWER
439	***anthrakia*** [ἀνθρακιά]	COALS
		FIRE
440	***anthrax*** [ἄνθραξ]	COALS
444	***anthrōpos*** [ἄνθρωπος]	MAN
450	***anistēmi*** [ἀνίστημι]	ARISE
453	***anoētos*** [ἀνόητος]	FOOL
454	***anoia*** [ἄνοια]	FOLLY
		MAD
455	***anoigō*** [ἀνοίγω]	OPEN
456	***anoikodomeō*** [ἀνοικοδομέω]	BUILD
458	***anomia*** [ἀνομία]	INIQUITY
459	***anomos*** [ἄνομος]	TRANSGRESS
		WICKED
460	***anomōs*** [ἀνόμως]	LAW
465	***antallagma*** [ἀντάλλαγμα]	EXCHANGE
469	***antapodosis*** [ἀνταπόδοσις]	REWARD
470	***antapokrinomai*** [ἀνταποκρίνομαι]	ANSWER
476	***antidikos*** [ἀντίδικος]	ADVERSARY
478	***antikathistēmi*** [ἀντικαθίστημι]	RESIST
479	***antikaleō*** [ἀντικαλέω]	INVITE
480	***antikeimai*** [ἀντίκειμαι]	ADVERSARY
482	***antilambanō*** [ἀντιλαμβάνω]	HELP
483	***antilegō*** [ἀντιλέγω]	DENY
485	***antilogia*** [ἀντιλογία]	DISPUTE
487	***antilytron*** [ἀντίλυτρον]	RANSOM
492	***antiparerchomai*** [ἀντιπαρέρχομαι]	PASS
496	***antipiptō*** [ἀντιπίπτω]	RESIST
498	***antitassomai*** [ἀντιτάσσομαι]	RESIST
500	***antichristos*** [ἀντίχριστος]	ANTICHRIST
501	***antleō*** [ἀντλέω]	DRAW
504	***anydros*** [ἄνυδρος]	DRY
		WATER
508	***anagaion*** [ἀνάγαιον]	ROOM
512	***anōphelēs*** [ἀνωφελής]	WORTHLESS
513	***axinē*** [ἀξίνη]	AX
514	***axios*** [ἄξιος]	REWARD
		WORTHY
515	***axioō*** [ἀξιόω]	WORTHY
516	***axiōs*** [ἀξίως]	WORTHY
517	***aoratos*** [ἀόρατος]	INVISIBLE
518	***apangellō*** [ἀπαγγέλλω]	REPORT
		TELL
519	***apanchō*** [ἀπάγχω]	HANG
520	***apagō*** [ἀπάγω]	DEATH
		LEAD (VERB)
522	***apairō*** [ἀπαίρω]	TAKE
523	***apaiteō*** [ἀπαιτέω]	ASK
		REQUIRE
526	***apallotrioō*** [ἀπαλλοτριόω]	ALIEN
527	***hapalos*** [ἁπαλός]	TENDER
528	***apantaō*** [ἀπαντάω]	MEET
529	***apantēsis*** [ἀπάντησις]	MEET
531	***aparabatos*** [ἀπαράβατος]	UNCHANGEABLE
533	***aparneomai*** [ἀπαρνέομαι]	DENY
535	***apartismos*** [ἀπαρτισμός]	COMPLETE
536	***aparchē*** [ἀπαρχή]	FIRSTFRUIT
537	***hapas*** [ἅπας]	ALL
538	***apataō*** [ἀπατάω]	DECEIT
539	***apatē*** [ἀπάτη]	DECEIT
540	***apatōr*** [ἀπάτωρ]	FATHER
543	***apeitheia*** [ἀπείθεια]	UNBELIEF
544	***apeitheō*** [ἀπειθέω]	BELIEF
		OBEDIENCE
		UNBELIEF
545	***apeithēs*** [ἀπειθής]	DISOBEDIENCE
546	***apeileō*** [ἀπειλέω]	THREATEN
547	***apeilē*** [ἀπειλή]	THREATEN

Strong's Number	Greek Article	English Entry
548	***apeimi*** [ἄπειμι]	ABSENCE
550	***apeipomēn*** [ἀπειπόμην]	RENOUNCE
551	***apeirastos*** [ἀπείραστος]	TEMPT
553	***apekdechomai*** [ἀπεκδέχομαι]	WAIT
554	***apekdyomai*** [ἀπεκδύομαι]	PUT
558	***apeleutheros*** [ἀπελεύθερος]	FREE
564	***aperitmētos*** [ἀπερίτμητος]	CIRCUMCISE
565	***aperchomai*** [ἀπέρχομαι]	LEAVE
		PASS
567	***apechomai*** [ἀπέχομαι]	ABSTAIN
568	***apechō*** [ἀπέχω]	RECEIVE
569	***apisteō*** [ἀπιστέω]	BELIEF
570	***apistia*** [ἀπιστία]	UNBELIEF
571	***apistos*** [ἄπιστος]	FAITHFUL
		UNBELIEF
577	***apoballō*** [ἀποβάλλω]	CAST
579	***apoblētos*** [ἀπόβλητος]	REFUSE
580	***apobolē*** [ἀποβολή]	LOSE
581	***apoginomai*** [ἀπογίνομαι]	DIE
584	***apodeiknymi*** [ἀποδείκνυμι]	APPROVE
		PROOF
585	***apodeixis*** [ἀπόδειξις]	DEMONSTRATION
586	***apodekatoō*** [ἀποδεκατόω]	TITHE
587	***apodektos*** [ἀπόδεκτος]	ACCEPT
588	***apodechomai*** [ἀποδέχομαι]	RECEIVE
589	***apodēmeō*** [ἀποδημέω]	COUNTRY
		JOURNEY
		TRAVEL
590	***apodēmos*** [ἀπόδημος]	JOURNEY
591	***apodidōmi*** [ἀποδίδωμι]	PAY
		REWARD
		YIELD
592	***apodiorizō*** [ἀποδιορίζω]	SEPARATE
593	***apodokimazō*** [ἀποδοκιμάζω]	REJECT
594	***apodochē*** [ἀποδοχή]	ACCEPT
596	***apothēkē*** [ἀποθήκη]	BARN
598	***apothlibō*** [ἀποθλίβω]	CRUSH
		PRESS
599	***apothnēskō*** [ἀποθνήσκω]	DIE
600	***apokathistēmi*** [ἀποκαθίστημι]	RESTORATION
601	***apokalyptō*** [ἀποκαλύπτω]	REVEAL
602	***apokalypsis*** [ἀποκάλυψις]	REVEAL
603	***apokaradokia*** [ἀποκαραδοκία]	EXPECT
604	***apokatallassō*** [ἀποκαταλλάσσω]	RECONCILE
606	***apokeimai*** [ἀπόκειμαι]	APPOINT
607	***apokephalizō*** [ἀποκεφαλίζω]	BEHEAD
608	***apokleiō*** [ἀποκλείω]	SHUT
609	***apokoptō*** [ἀποκόπτω]	CUT
610	***apokrima*** [ἀπόκριμα]	SENTENCE
611	***apokrinomai*** [ἀποκρίνομαι]	ANSWER
612	***apokrisis*** [ἀπόκρισις]	ANSWER
613	***apokryptō*** [ἀποκρύπτω]	HIDE
614	***apokryphos*** [ἀπόκρυφος]	HIDE
		SECRET
615	***apokteinō*** [ἀποκτείνω]	KILL
616	***apokyeō*** [ἀποκυέω]	BEGET
617	***apokyliō*** [ἀποκυλίω]	ROLL
618	***apolambanō*** [ἀπολαμβάνω]	RECEIVE
619	***apolausis*** [ἀπόλαυσις]	ENJOY
620	***apoleipō*** [ἀπολείπω]	LEAVE
		REMAIN
622	***apollymi*** [ἀπόλλυμι]	DESTROY
		LOSE
		PERISH
626	***apologeomai*** [ἀπολογέομαι]	ANSWER
		DEFENSE
		EXCUSE
627	***apologia*** [ἀπολογία]	ANSWER
		DEFENSE
628	***apolouomai*** [ἀπολούομαι]	WASH
629	***apolytrōsis*** [ἀπολύτρωσις]	REDEEM
630	***apolyō*** [ἀπολύω]	ALLOW
		DIVORCE
		FORGIVE
		PUT
		RELEASE
		SEND
631	***apomassomai*** [ἀπομάσσομαι]	WIPE
633	***aponiptō*** [ἀπονίπτω]	WASH
634	***apopiptō*** [ἀποπίπτω]	FALL
635	***apoplanaō*** [ἀποπλανάω]	ERR

Strong's Number	Greek Article	English Entry
762	***asbestos*** [ἄσβεστος]	QUENCH UNQUENCHABLE
763	***asebeia*** [ἀσέβεια]	UNGODLINESS
764	***asebeō*** [ἀσεβέω]	UNGODLINESS
765	***asebēs*** [ἀσεβής]	UNGODLINESS
767	***asēmos*** [ἄσημος]	MEAN (ADJECTIVE)
769	***astheneia*** [ἀσθένεια]	DISEASE SICK WEAK
770	***astheneō*** [ἀσθενέω]	SICK WEAK
772	***asthenēs*** [ἀσθενής]	SICK WEAK
776	***asitia*** [ἀσιτία]	ABSTAIN
782	***aspazomai*** [ἀσπάζομαι]	GREET
783	***aspasmos*** [ἀσπασμός]	GREET
792	***astēr*** [ἀστήρ]	STAR
793	***astēriktos*** [ἀστήρικτος]	UNSTABLE
794	***astorgos*** [ἄστοργος]	NATURAL
795	***astocheō*** [ἀστοχέω]	ERR
796	***astrapē*** [ἀστραπή]	LIGHTNING
797	***astraptō*** [ἀστράπτω]	DAZZLING
798	***astron*** [ἄστρον]	STAR
800	***asymphōnos*** [ἀσύμφωνος]	AGREE
801	***asynetos*** [ἀσύνετος]	FOOL UNDERSTANDING
803	***asphaleia*** [ἀσφάλεια]	SAFE
804	***asphalēs*** [ἀσφαλής]	SAFE
806	***asphalōs*** [ἀσφαλῶς]	SAFE
815	***ateknos*** [ἄτεκνος]	CHILD
816	***atenizō*** [ἀτενίζω]	SEE
818	***atimazō*** [ἀτιμάζω]	ASHAMED DISHONOR SHAME
819	***atimia*** [ἀτιμία]	ASHAMED DISHONOR SHAME
820	***atimos*** [ἄτιμος]	DESPISE DISHONOR
821	***atimoō*** [ἀτιμόω]	ASHAMED SHAME
831	***authenteō*** [αὐθεντέω]	AUTHORITY
832	***auleō*** [αὐλέω]	PIPE
833	***aulē*** [αὐλή]	COURT PALACE
834	***aulētēs*** [αὐλητής]	PIPE
835	***aulizomai*** [αὐλίζομαι]	ABIDE LODGE
836	***aulos*** [αὐλός]	PIPE
837	***auxanō*** [αὐξάνω]	GROW INCREASE
839	***aurion*** [αὔριον]	TOMORROW
843	***autokatakritos*** [αὐτοκατάκριτος]	CONDEMN
845	***autoptēs*** [αὐτόπτης]	EYEWITNESS
850	***auchmēros*** [αὐχμηρός]	DARK
851	***aphaireō*** [ἀφαιρέω]	CUT TAKE
853	***aphanizō*** [ἀφανίζω]	CORRUPT PERISH
854	***aphanismos*** [ἀφανισμός]	VANISH
859	***aphesis*** [ἄφεσις]	FORGIVE
860	***haphē*** [ἁφή]	JOINT
861	***aphtharsia*** [ἀφθαρσία]	CORRUPT IMMORTAL
862	***aphthartos*** [ἄφθαρτος]	CORRUPT IMMORTAL
863	***aphiēmi*** [ἀφίημι]	ALLOW FORGIVE LEAVE
866	***aphilargyros*** [ἀφιλάργυρος]	COVET
867	***aphixis*** [ἄφιξις]	DEPART
868	***aphistēmi*** [ἀφίστημι]	FALL LEAVE
870	***aphobōs*** [ἀφόβως]	FEAR
872	***aphoraō*** [ἀφοράω]	SEE
873	***aphorizō*** [ἀφορίζω]	DIVIDE SEPARATE
875	***aphrizō*** [ἀφρίζω]	FOAM
877	***aphrosynē*** [ἀφροσύνη]	FOLLY
878	***aphrōn*** [ἄφρων]	FOOL
879	***aphypnoō*** [ἀφυπνόω]	ASLEEP
880	***aphōnos*** [ἄφωνος]	DUMB

Strong's Number	Greek Article	English Entry
1016	***bous*** [βοῦς]	OX
1017	***brabeion*** [βραβεῖον]	PRIZE
1018	***brabeuō*** [βραβεύω]	RULE
1023	***brachiōn*** [βραχίων]	ARM
1024	***brachys*** [βραχύς]	LITTLE
1025	***brephos*** [βρέφος]	BABE
1026	***brechō*** [βρέχω]	RAIN
		SEND
		WASH
1027	***brontē*** [βροντή]	THUNDER
1028	***brochē*** [βροχή]	RAIN
1029	***brochos*** [βρόχος]	TRAP
1030	***brygmos*** [βρυγμός]	GNASH
1031	***brychō*** [βρύχω]	GNASH
1033	***brōma*** [βρῶμα]	FOOD
1035	***brōsis*** [βρῶσις]	EAT
		FOOD
1036	***bythizō*** [βυθίζω]	SINK
1039	***byssinos*** [βύσσινος]	LINEN
1040	***byssos*** [βύσσος]	LINEN
1041	***bōmos*** [βωμός]	ALTAR
1044	***gangraina*** [γάγγραινα]	GANGRENE
1047	***gaza*** [γάζα]	TREASURE
1049	***gazophylakion*** [γαζοφυλάκιον]	TREASURE
1051	***gala*** [γάλα]	MILK
1060	***gameō*** [γαμέω]	MARRY
1061	***gamiskō, gamizō*** [γαμίσκω, γαμίζω]	MARRY
1062	***gamos*** [γάμος]	MARRIAGE
1064	***gastēr*** [γαστήρ]	WOMAN
		WOMB
1067	***geenna*** [γέεννα]	HELL
1069	***geitōn*** [γείτων]	NEIGHBOR
1070	***gelaō*** [γελάω]	LAUGH
1071	***gelōs*** [γέλως]	LAUGH
1072	***gemizō*** [γεμίζω]	FILL
1073	***gemō*** [γέμω]	FULL
1074	***genea*** [γενεά]	GENERATION
1075	***genealogeō*** [γενεαλογέω]	DESCEND
		GENEALOGY
1076	***genealogia*** [γενεαλογία]	GENEALOGY
1078	***genesis*** [γένεσις]	GENERATION
1080	***gennaō*** [γεννάω]	BEGET
1081	***gennēma*** [γέννημα]	FRUIT
		GENERATION
1083	***genesis*** [γένεσις]	BEGET
1084	***gennētos*** [γεννητός]	BEGET
1085	***genos*** [γένος]	KIND (NOUN)
		OFFSPRING
1088	***gerōn*** [γέρων]	OLD
1089	***geuomai*** [γεύομαι]	EAT
		TASTE
1090	***geōrgeō*** [γεωργέω]	WORK
1091	***geōrgion*** [γεώργιον]	FIELD
1092	***geōrgos*** [γεωργός]	FARM
		VINE
1093	***gē*** [γῆ]	EARTH
1094	***gēras*** [γῆρας]	OLD
1095	***gēraskō*** [γηράσκω]	OLD
1096	***ginomai*** [γίνομαι]	ARISE
		COME
		USE
1097	***ginōskō*** [γινώσκω]	FEEL
		KNOW
1098	***gleukos*** [γλεῦκος]	WINE
1100	***glōssa*** [γλῶσσα]	TONGUE
1101	***glōssokomon*** [γλωσσόκομον]	BAG
1103	***gnēsios*** [γνήσιος]	TRUE
1105	***gnophos*** [γνόφος]	DARK
1106	***gnōmē*** [γνώμη]	ADVICE
		JUDGMENT
1107	***gnōrizō*** [γνωρίζω]	KNOW
1108	***gnōsis*** [γνῶσις]	KNOW
1110	***gnōstos*** [γνωστός]	KNOW
1111	***gongyzō*** [γογγύζω]	MURMUR
1112	***gongysmos*** [γογγυσμός]	MURMUR
1113	***gongystēs*** [γογγυστής]	MURMUR
1119	***gony*** [γόνυ]	KNEE
1120	***gonypeteō*** [γονυπετέω]	BOW (VERB)
		KNEEL

Strong's Number	Greek Article	English Entry
1252	***diakrinō*** [διακρίνω]	DOUBT
		JUDGE
1253	***diakrisis*** [διάκρισις]	DISCERN
		DISPUTE
1256	***dialegomai*** [διαλέγομαι]	REASON
1257	***dialeipō*** [διαλείπω]	CEASE
1258	***dialektos*** [διάλεκτος]	LANGUAGE
		TONGUE
1259	***diallassomai*** [διαλλάσσομαι]	RECONCILE
1260	***dialogizomai*** [διαλογίζομαι]	REASON
1261	***dialogismos*** [διαλογισμός]	IMAGINE
		THINK
1262	***dialyō*** [διαλύω]	SCATTER
1263	***diamartyromai*** [διαμαρτύρομαι]	CHARGE
		WITNESS
1264	***diamachomai*** [διαμάχομαι]	STRIVE
1265	***diamenō*** [διαμένω]	REMAIN
1266	***diamerizō*** [διαμερίζω]	DIVIDE
1267	***diamerismos*** [διαμερισμός]	DIVISION
1268	***dianemō*** [διανέμω]	SPREAD
1270	***dianoēma*** [διανόημα]	THINK
1271	***dianoia*** [διάνοια]	IMAGINE
		MIND
1272	***dianoigō*** [διανοίγω]	OPEN
1273	***dianyktereuō*** [διανυκτερεύω]	NIGHT
1274	***dianyō*** [διανύω]	FINISH
1276	***diaperaō*** [διαπεράω]	PASS
1277	***diapleō*** [διαπλέω]	SAIL
1279	***diaporeuomai*** [διαπορεύομαι]	JOURNEY
1281	***diapragmateuomai*** [διαπραγματεύομαι]	GAIN
		TRADE
1283	***diarpazō*** [διαρπάζω]	SPOIL
1284	***diarrēgnymi*** [διαρρήγνυμι]	BREAK
1287	***diaskorpizō*** [διασκορπίζω]	SCATTER
		WASTE
1289	***diaspeirō*** [διασπείρω]	SCATTER
1290	***diaspora*** [διασπορά]	SCATTER
1291	***diastellomai*** [διαστέλλομαι]	CHARGE
1293	***diastolē*** [διαστολή]	DISTINCTION
1294	***diastrephō*** [διαστρέφω]	PERVERSE
		TURN
1295	***diasōzō*** [διασώζω]	ESCAPE
		HEAL
		SAFE
		SAVE
1297	***diatagma*** [διάταγμα]	COMMANDMENT
1298	***diatarassō*** [διαταράσσω]	TROUBLE
1299	***diatassō*** [διατάσσω]	COMMAND
1301	***diatēreō*** [διατηρέω]	KEEP
1303	***diatithēmi*** [διατίθημι]	COVENANT
1304	***diatribō*** [διατρίβω]	ABIDE
1305	***diatrophē*** [διατροφή]	FOOD
1306	***diaugazō*** [διαυγάζω]	DAWN
1308	***diapherō*** [διαφέρω]	VALUABLE
1309	***diapheugō*** [διαφεύγω]	ESCAPE
1310	***diaphēmizō*** [διαφημίζω]	SPREAD
1311	***diaphtheirō*** [διαφθείρω]	CORRUPT
		DECAY
		DESTROY
1312	***diaphthora*** [διαφθορά]	CORRUPT
1313	***diaphoros*** [διάφορος]	EXCEL
1314	***diaphylassō*** [διαφυλάσσω]	GUARD
		KEEP
1315	***diacheirizomai*** [διαχειρίζομαι]	KILL
1317	***didaktikos*** [διδακτικός]	TEACH
1319	***didaskalia*** [διδασκαλία]	DOCTRINE
1320	***didaskalos*** [διδάσκαλος]	TEACH
1321	***didaskō*** [διδάσκω]	TEACH
1322	***didachē*** [διδαχή]	DOCTRINE
1323	***didrachmon*** [δίδραχμον]	TRIBUTE
1325	***didōmi*** [δίδωμι]	GIVE
		YIELD
1326	***diegeirō*** [διεγείρω]	ARISE
1329	***diermēneuō*** [διερμηνεύω]	EXPOUND
		INTERPRET
1330	***dierchomai*** [διέρχομαι]	PASS
		PIERCE
		TRAVEL
		WALK
1332	***dietēs*** [διετής]	YEAR
1333	***dietia*** [διετία]	YEAR
1334	***diēgeomai*** [διηγέομαι]	TELL

Strong's Number	Greek Article	English Entry
1442	***hebdomos*** [ἕβδομος]	SEVEN
1445	***Hebraios*** [Ἑβραῖος]	HEBREW
1448	***engizō*** [ἐγγίζω]	APPROACH DRAW
1449	***engraphō*** [ἐγγράφω]	WRITE
1450	***engyos*** [ἔγγυος]	GUARANTEE
1453	***egeirō*** [ἐγείρω]	ARISE
1454	***egersis*** [ἔγερσις]	RESURRECTION
1456	***enkainia*** [ἐγκαίνια]	DEDICATE
1457	***enkainizō*** [ἐγκαινίζω]	DEDICATE
1458	***enkaleō*** [ἐγκαλέω]	ACCUSATION CHARGE
1459	***enkataleipō*** [ἐγκαταλείπω]	LEAVE
1462	***enklēma*** [ἔγκλημα]	ACCUSATION CHARGE
1466	***enkrateia*** [ἐγκράτεια]	TEMPERANCE
1467	***enkrateuomai*** [ἐγκρατεύομαι]	TEMPERANCE
1468	***enkratēs*** [ἐγκρατής]	TEMPERANCE
1470	***enkryptō*** [ἐγκρύπτω]	HIDE
1471	***enkyos*** [ἔγκυος]	CHILD
1472	***enchriō*** [ἐγχρίω]	ANOINT
1474	***edaphizō*** [ἐδαφίζω]	GROUND
1475	***edaphos*** [ἔδαφος]	GROUND
1479	***ethelothrēskeia*** [ἐθελοθρησκείᾳ]	WORSHIP
1481	***ethnarchēs*** [ἐθνάρχης]	GOVERNOR
1482	***ethnikos*** [ἐθνικός]	GENTILES
1483	***ethnikōs*** [ἐθνικῶς]	GENTILES
1484	***ethnos*** [ἔθνος]	GENTILES NATION
1491	***eidos*** [εἶδος]	FORM VISION
1492	***oida*** [οἶδα]	KNOW SEE
1493	***eidōleion*** [εἰδωλεῖον]	TEMPLE
1494	***eidōlothyton*** [εἰδωλόθυτον]	IDOL OFFERING SACRIFICE
1495	***eidōlolatria*** [εἰδωλολατρία]	IDOL
1496	***eidōlolatrēs*** [εἰδωλολάτρης]	IDOL
1497	***eidōlon*** [εἴδωλον]	IDOL
1500	***eikē*** [εἰκῇ]	VAIN
1504	***eikōn*** [εἰκών]	IMAGE
1507	***helissō*** [ἑλίσσω]	ROLL
1514	***eirēneuō*** [εἰρηνεύω]	LIFE PEACE
1515	***eirēnē*** [εἰρήνη]	PEACE
1517	***eirēnopoieō*** [εἰρηνοποιέω]	PEACE
1520	***heis*** [εἷς]	ONE
1523	***eisdechomai*** [εἰσδέχομαι]	RECEIVE
1524	***eiseimi*** [εἴσειμι]	ENTER
1525	***eiserchomai*** [εἰσέρχομαι]	ARISE ENTER
1529	***eisodos*** [εἴσοδος]	COMING (NOUN) ENTER
1531	***eisporeuomai*** [εἰσπορεύομαι]	ENTER
1532	***eistrechō*** [εἰστρέχω]	RUN
1533	***eispherō*** [εἰσφέρω]	LEAD (VERB)
1540	***hekaton*** [ἑκατόν]	HUNDRED
1541	***hekatontaetēs*** [ἑκατονταετής]	YEAR
1542	***hekatontaplasiōn*** [ἑκατονταπλασίων]	HUNDRED
1544	***ekballō*** [ἐκβάλλω]	CAST DRIVE SEND
1545	***ekbasis*** [ἔκβασις]	ESCAPE
1550	***ekdapanaō*** [ἐκδαπανάω]	SPEND
1551	***ekdechomai*** [ἐκδέχομαι]	EXPECT
1553	***ekdēmeō*** [ἐκδημέω]	ABSENCE
1556	***ekdikeō*** [ἐκδικέω]	AVENGE
1557	***ekdikēsis*** [ἐκδίκησις]	AVENGE PUNISH
1558	***ekdikos*** [ἔκδικος]	AVENGE
1559	***ekdiōkō*** [ἐκδιώκω]	DRIVE PERSECUTE
1561	***ekdochē*** [ἐκδοχή]	EXPECT
1562	***ekdyō*** [ἐκδύω]	TAKE
1567	***ekzēteō*** [ἐκζητέω]	REQUIRE SEEK
1568	***ekthambeō*** [ἐκθαμβέω]	AMAZE
1569	***ekthambos*** [ἔκθαμβος]	AMAZE
1571	***ekkathairō*** [ἐκκαθαίρω]	CLEAN

Strong's Number	Greek Article	English Entry
1685	***emballō*** [ἐμβάλλω]	CAST
1686	***embaptō*** [ἐμβάπτω]	BAPTISM
1689	***emblepō*** [ἐμβλέπω]	SEE
1690	***embrimaomai*** [ἐμβριμάομαι]	CHARGE
1692	***emeō*** [ἐμέω]	VOMIT
1694	***Emmanouēl*** [Ἐμμανουήλ]	IMMANUEL
1696	***emmenō*** [ἐμμένω]	CONTINUE
1701	***empaigmos*** [ἐμπαιγμός]	MOCK
1702	***empaizō*** [ἐμπαίζω]	MOCK
1703	***empaiktēs*** [ἐμπαίκτης]	MOCK
1705	***empimplēmi*** [ἐμπίμπλημι]	FILL
1706	***empiptō*** [ἐμπίπτω]	FALL
1707	***emplekō*** [ἐμπλέκω]	ENSNARE
1709	***empneō*** [ἐμπνέω]	BREATH
1713	***emporos*** [ἔμπορος]	TRADE
1718	***emphanizō*** [ἐμφανίζω]	APPEAR
		SHOW
1720	***emphysaō*** [ἐμφυσάω]	BREATH
1723	***enankalizomai*** [ἐναγκαλίζομαι]	ARM
1728	***enarchomai*** [ἐνάρχομαι]	BEGIN
1731	***endeiknymi*** [ἐνδείκνυμι]	SHOW
1732	***endeixis*** [ἔνδειξις]	DEMONSTRATION
1737	***endidyskō*** [ἐνδιδύσκω]	CLOTHE
		WEAR
1740	***endoxazō*** [ἐνδοξάζω]	GLORIFY
1741	***endoxos*** [ἔνδοξος]	GLORY
1742	***endyma*** [ἔνδυμα]	CLOTHING
1743	***endynamoō*** [ἐνδυναμόω]	INCREASE
1746	***endyō*** [ἐνδύω]	CLOTHE
1748	***enedreuō*** [ἐνεδρεύω]	LIE
		WAIT
1749	***enedron*** [ἔνεδρον]	WAIT
1750	***eneileō*** [ἐνειλέω]	WRAP
1753	***energeia*** [ἐνέργεια]	WORK
1754	***energeō*** [ἐνεργέω]	WORK
1757	***eneulogeō*** [ἐνευλογέω]	BLESS
1760	***enthymeomai*** [ἐνθυμέομαι]	THINK
1761	***enthymēsis*** [ἐνθύμησις]	THINK
1763	***eniautos*** [ἐνιαυτός]	YEAR
1764	***enistēmi*** [ἐνίστημι]	PRESENT
1770	***enneuō*** [ἐννεύω]	SIGN
1774	***enoikeō*** [ἐνοικέω]	DWELL
1775	***henotēs*** [ἑνότης]	UNITE
1776	***enochleō*** [ἐνοχλέω]	TROUBLE
1777	***enochos*** [ἔνοχος]	DANGER
		GUILT
		SUBJECT
		WORTHY
1778	***entalma*** [ἔνταλμα]	COMMANDMENT
1779	***entaphiazō*** [ἐνταφιάζω]	BURIAL
1780	***entaphiasmos*** [ἐνταφιασμός]	BURIAL
1781	***entellō*** [ἐντέλλω]	COMMAND
1783	***enteuxis*** [ἔντευξις]	INTERCEDE
		PRAY
1784	***entimos*** [ἔντιμος]	VALUABLE
1785	***entolē*** [ἐντολή]	COMMANDMENT
1788	***entrepō*** [ἐντρέπω]	ASHAMED
		SHAME
1790	***entromos*** [ἔντρομος]	FEAR
		TREMBLE
1791	***entropē*** [ἐντροπή]	ASHAMED
		SHAME
1793	***entynchanō*** [ἐντυγχάνω]	INTERCEDE
1794	***entylissō*** [ἐντυλίσσω]	WRAP
1795	***entypoō*** [ἐντυπόω]	ENGRAVE
1797	***enypniazō*** [ἐνυπνιάζω]	DREAM
1798	***enypnion*** [ἐνύπνιον]	DREAM
1799	***enōpion*** [ἐνώπιον]	PRESENCE
1805	***exagorazō*** [ἐξαγοράζω]	REDEEM
1806	***exagō*** [ἐξάγω]	LEAD (VERB)
1807	***exaireō*** [ἐξαιρέω]	DELIVER
1810	***exaiphnēs*** [ἐξαίφνης]	SUDDEN
1811	***exakoloutheō*** [ἐξακολουθέω]	FOLLOW
1813	***exaleiphō*** [ἐξαλείφω]	BLOT OUT
		WIPE
1814	***exallomai*** [ἐξάλλομαι]	LEAP
1815	***exanastasis*** [ἐξανάστασις]	RESURRECTION
1817	***exanistēmi*** [ἐξανίστημι]	ARISE
		RAISE
1818	***exapataō*** [ἐξαπατάω]	DECEIT

Strong's Number	Greek Article	English Entry
1945	***epikeimai*** [ἐπίκειμαι]	CROWD
1948	***epikrinō*** [ἐπικρίνω]	SENTENCE
1949	***epilambanō*** [ἐπιλαμβάνω]	HOLD (VERB)
		SEIZE
		TAKE
1950	***epilanthanomai*** [ἐπιλανθάνομαι]	FORGET
1951	***epilegō*** [ἐπιλέγω]	CHOICE
1954	***epiloipos*** [ἐπίλοιπος]	REMAIN
1955	***epilysis*** [ἐπίλυσις]	INTERPRET
1956	***epilyō*** [ἐπιλύω]	EXPOUND
1959	***epimeleomai*** [ἐπιμελέομαι]	CARE
1960	***epimelōs*** [ἐπιμελῶς]	DILIGENCE
1961	***epimenō*** [ἐπιμένω]	ABIDE
		CONTINUE
1963	***epinoia*** [ἐπίνοια]	THINK
1967	***epiousios*** [ἐπιούσιος]	DAILY
1968	***epipiptō*** [ἐπιπίπτω]	FALL
1969	***epiplēssō*** [ἐπιπλήσσω]	REBUKE
1971	***epipotheō*** [ἐπιποθέω]	LUST
1972	***epipothēsis*** [ἐπιπόθησις]	DESIRE
1977	***epiriptō*** [ἐπιρίπτω]	CAST
1980	***episkeptomai*** [ἐπισκέπτομαι]	VISIT
1981	***episkēnoō*** [ἐπισκηνόω]	REST
1984	***episkopē*** [ἐπισκοπή]	OFFICE
		VISIT
1985	***episkopos*** [ἐπίσκοπος]	BISHOP
1986	***epispaomai*** [ἐπισπάομαι]	CIRCUMCISE
1987	***epistamai*** [ἐπίσταμαι]	KNOW
1988	***epistatēs*** [ἐπιστάτης]	MASTER
1989	***epistellō*** [ἐπιστέλλω]	WRITE
1992	***epistolē*** [ἐπιστολή]	EPISTLE
		LETTER
1994	***epistrephō*** [ἐπιστρέφω]	RETURN
		TURN
1995	***epistrophē*** [ἐπιστροφή]	CONVERT
1996	***episynagō*** [ἐπισυνάγω]	GATHER
1997	***episynagōgē*** [ἐπισυναγωγή]	ASSEMBLE
		GATHER
1998	***episyntrechō*** [ἐπισυντρέχω]	RUN
2000	***episphalēs*** [ἐπισφαλής]	DANGER
2003	***epitagē*** [ἐπιταγή]	AUTHORITY
		COMMANDMENT
2004	***epitassō*** [ἐπιτάσσω]	COMMAND
2005	***epiteleō*** [ἐπιτελέω]	COMPLETE
2007	***epitithēmi*** [ἐπιτίθημι]	ADD
		PUT
2008	***epitimaō*** [ἐπιτιμάω]	REBUKE
2009	***epitimia*** [ἐπιτιμία]	PUNISH
2010	***epitrepō*** [ἐπιτρέπω]	ALLOW
		PERMIT
2012	***epitropos*** [ἐπίτροπος]	GUARDIAN
		STEWARD
2013	***epitynchanō*** [ἐπιτυγχάνω]	OBTAIN
2014	***epiphainō*** [ἐπιφαίνω]	APPEAR
2015	***epiphaneia*** [ἐπιφάνεια]	APPEAR
2017	***epiphauskō*** [ἐπιφαύσκω]	LIGHT
2019	***epiphōneō*** [ἐπιφωνέω]	CRY
		SHOUT
2020	***epiphōskō*** [ἐπιφώσκω]	DAWN
2022	***epicheō*** [ἐπιχέω]	POUR
2023	***epichorēgeō*** [ἐπιχορηγέω]	ADD
2025	***epichriō*** [ἐπιχρίω]	ANOINT
2026	***epoikodomeō*** [ἐποικοδομέω]	BUILD
2027	***epikellō*** [ἐπικέλλω]	RUN
2030	***epoptēs*** [ἐπόπτης]	EYEWITNESS
2032	***epouranios*** [ἐπουράνιος]	HEAVEN
2033	***hepta*** [ἑπτά]	SEVEN
2038	***ergazomai*** [ἐργάζομαι]	TRADE
		WORK
2039	***ergasia*** [ἐργασία]	CRAFT
		WORK
2040	***ergatēs*** [ἐργάτης]	WORK
2041	***ergon*** [ἔργον]	WORK
2042	***erethizō*** [ἐρεθίζω]	STIR
2047	***erēmia*** [ἐρημία]	DESERT
2048	***erēmos*** [ἔρημος]	DESERT
2049	***erēmoō*** [ἐρημόω]	DESOLATE
2050	***erēmōsis*** [ἐρήμωσις]	DESOLATE
2052	***eritheia*** [ἐριθεία]	STRIFE
2053	***erion*** [ἔριον]	WOOL

Strong's Number	Greek Article	English Entry
2476	*histēmi* [ἵστημι]	APPOINT
		ESTABLISH
		PRESENT
		SET
		STAND
2477	*historeō* [ἱστορέω]	VISIT
2478	*ischyros* [ἰσχυρός]	STRENGTH
2479	*ischys* [ἰσχύς]	ABILITY
		STRENGTH
2480	*ischyō* [ἰσχύω]	ABILITY
2485	*ichthydion* [ἰχθύδιον]	FISH
2486	*ichthys* [ἰχθύς]	FISH
2487	*ichnos* [ἴχνος]	STEP
2503	*iōta* [ἰῶτα]	JOT
2507	*kathaireō* [καθαιρέω]	CAST
		TAKE
2511	*katharizō* [καθαρίζω]	CLEAN
2512	*katharismos* [καθαρισμός]	CLEAN
2513	*katharos* [καθαρός]	CLEAN
2514	*katharotēs* [καθαρότης]	CLEAN
2515	*kathedra* [καθέδρα]	SEAT
2516	*kathezomai* [καθέζομαι]	SIT
2518	*katheudō* [καθεύδω]	ASLEEP
2521	*kathēmai* [κάθημαι]	SIT
2522	*kathēmerinos* [καθημερινός]	DAILY
2523	*kathizō* [καθίζω]	SIT
2525	*kathistēmi* [καθίστημι]	APPOINT
		RULE
2528	*kathoplizō* [καθοπλίζω]	ARMS
2537	*kainos* [καινός]	NEW
2538	*kainotēs* [καινότης]	NEW
2540	*kairos* [καιρός]	TIME
2545	*kaiō* [καίω]	BURN
2549	*kakia* [κακία]	EVIL
2551	*kakologeō* [κακολογέω]	CURSE
2552	*kakopatheia* [κακοπάθεια]	AFFLICT
2553	*kakopatheō* [κακοπαθέω]	AFFLICT
		TROUBLE
2554	*kakopoieō* [κακοποιέω]	EVIL
2555	*kakopoios* [κακοποιός]	EVIL
2556	*kakos* [κακός]	EVIL
2558	*kakoucheō* [κακουχέω]	AFFLICT
2559	*kakoō* [κακόω]	AFFLICT
		EVIL
2560	*kakōs* [κακῶς]	EVIL
		SICK
2561	*kakōsis* [κάκωσις]	AFFLICT
2563	*kalamos* [κάλαμος]	PEN
		REED
2564	*kaleō* [καλέω]	CALL
		INVITE
2565	*kallielaios* [καλλιέλαιος]	OLIVE
2567	*kalodidaskalos* [καλοδιδάσκαλος]	TEACH
2570	*kalos* [καλός]	GOOD
2571	*kalymma* [κάλυμμα]	VEIL
2572	*kalyptō* [καλύπτω]	COVER
		HIDE
2573	*kalōs* [καλῶς]	GOOD
2575	*kaminos* [κάμινος]	FURNACE
2576	*kammyō* [καμμύω]	CLOSE (VERB)
2577	*kamnō* [κάμνω]	SICK
		WEARY
2578	*kamptō* [κάμπτω]	BOW (VERB)
2583	*kanōn* [κανών]	STANDARD
2586	*kapnos* [καπνός]	SMOKE
2588	*kardia* [καρδία]	HEART
2590	*karpos* [καρπός]	FRUIT
2592	*karpophoreō* [καρποφορέω]	BEAR (VERB)
		FRUIT
2593	*karpophoros* [καρποφόρος]	FRUIT
2597	*katabainō* [καταβαίνω]	DESCEND
2598	*kataballō* [καταβάλλω]	CAST
2599	*katabareō* [καταβαρέω]	BURDEN
2602	*katabolē* [καταβολή]	CONCEIVE
		FOUNDATION
2605	*katangellō* [καταγγέλλω]	PREACH
2606	*katagelaō* [καταγελάω]	LAUGH
2607	*kataginōskō* [καταγινώσκω]	CONDEMN
2608	*katagnymi* [κατάγνυμι]	BREAK
2609	*katagō* [κατάγω]	BRING

Strong's Number	Greek Article	English Entry
2611	**katadeō** [καταδέω]	BIND
2612	**katadēlos** [κατάδηλος]	EVIDENCE
2613	**katadikazō** [καταδικάζω]	CONDEMN
2614	**katadiōkō** [καταδιώκω]	FOLLOW
2615	**katadouloō** [καταδουλόω]	BONDAGE
2616	**katadynasteuō** [καταδυναστεύω]	OPPRESS
2617	**kataischynō** [καταισχύνω]	ASHAMED SHAME
2618	**katakaiō** [κατακαίω]	BURN
2619	**katakalyptō** [κατακαλύπτω]	COVER
2620	**katakauchaomai** [κατακαυχάομαι]	BOAST
2621	**katakeimai** [κατάκειμαι]	LIE SIT
2622	**kataklaō** [κατακλάω]	BREAK
2623	**katakleiō** [κατακλείω]	SHUT
2625	**kataklinō** [κατακλίνω]	SIT
2627	**kataklysmos** [κατακλυσμός]	FLOOD
2629	**katakoptō** [κατακόπτω]	CUT
2631	**katakrima** [κατάκριμα]	CONDEMN
2632	**katakrinō** [κατακρίνω]	CONDEMN
2633	**katakrisis** [κατάκρισις]	CONDEMN
2634	**katakyrieuō** [κατακυριεύω]	DOMINION
2638	**katalambanō** [καταλαμβάνω]	APPREHEND ATTAIN OBTAIN
2640	**kataleimma** [κατάλειμμα]	REMNANT
2641	**kataleipō** [καταλείπω]	LEAVE
2643	**katallagē** [καταλλαγή]	ATONEMENT
2644	**katallassō** [καταλλάσσω]	RECONCILE
2646	**katalyma** [κατάλυμα]	GUEST INN
2647	**katalyō** [καταλύω]	CAST DESTROY GUEST
2648	**katamanthanō** [καταμανθάνω]	CONSIDER
2649	**katamartyreō** [καταμαρτυρέω]	WITNESS
2652	**katathema** [κατάθεμα]	CURSE
2653	**katathematizō** [καταθεματίζω]	CURSE
2654	**katanaliskō** [καταναλίσκω]	CONSUME
2655	**katanarkaō** [καταναρκάω]	BURDEN
2657	**katanoeō** [κατανοέω]	CONSIDER
2658	**katantaō** [καταντάω]	ARRIVE ATTAIN
2661	**kataxioō** [καταξιόω]	WORTHY
2662	**katapateō** [καταπατέω]	TRAMPLE
2663	**katapausis** [κατάπαυσις]	REST
2664	**katapauō** [καταπαύω]	REST RESTRAIN
2665	**katapetasma** [καταπέτασμα]	VEIL
2666	**katapinō** [καταπίνω]	DROWN SWALLOW
2667	**katapiptō** [καταπίπτω]	FALL
2668	**katapleō** [καταπλέω]	ARRIVE
2669	**kataponeō** [καταπονέω]	OPPRESS
2670	**katapontizō** [καταποντίζω]	DROWN SINK
2671	**katara** [κατάρα]	CURSE
2672	**kataraomai** [καταράομαι]	CURSE
2673	**katargeō** [καταργέω]	ABOLISH DELIVER
2674	**katarithmeō** [καταριθμέω]	NUMBER
2675	**katartizō** [καταρτίζω]	PERFECT PREPARATION RESTORATION
2680	**kataskeuazō** [κατασκευάζω]	BUILD PREPARATION
2681	**kataskēnoō** [κατασκηνόω]	LODGE NEST
2683	**kataskiazō** [κατασκιάζω]	SHADOW
2687	**katastellō** [καταστέλλω]	QUIET
2696	**katasphragizō** [κατασφραγίζω]	SEAL
2701	**katatrechō** [κατατρέχω]	RUN
2703	**katapheugō** [καταφεύγω]	FLEE
2704	**kataphtheirō** [καταφθείρω]	CORRUPT
2705	**kataphileō** [καταφιλέω]	KISS
2706	**kataphroneō** [καταφρονέω]	DESPISE
2708	**katacheō** [καταχέω]	POUR
2712	**kateidōlos** [κατείδωλος]	IDOL
2714	**katenōpion** [κατενώπιον]	PRESENCE
2715	**katexousiazō** [κατεξουσιάζω]	AUTHORITY
2716	**katergazomai** [κατεργάζομαι]	WORK

Strong's Number	Greek Article	English Entry
2718	***katerchomai*** [κατέρχομαι]	DESCEND
2719	***kataesthiō*** [κατεσθίω]	EAT
2720	***kateuthynō*** [κατευθύνω]	GUIDE
2722	***katechō*** [κατέχω]	HOLD (VERB)
		KEEP
2723	***katēgoreō*** [κατηγορέω]	ACCUSATION
2724	***katēgoria*** [κατηγορία]	ACCUSATION
2725	***katēgoros*** [κατήγορος]	ACCUSATION
2727	***katēcheō*** [κατηχέω]	INSTRUCT
		TEACH
2730	***katoikeō*** [κατοικέω]	DWELL
2736	***katō*** [κάτω]	DOWN
2738	***kauma*** [καῦμα]	HEAT
2739	***kaumatizō*** [καυματίζω]	SCORCH
2740	***kausis*** [καῦσις]	BURN
2742	***kausōn*** [καύσων]	HEAT
2743	***kaustēriazō*** [καυστηριάζω]	IRON
2744	***kauchaomai*** [καυχάομαι]	BOAST
		REJOICE
2745	***kauchēma*** [καύχημα]	BOAST
2746	***kauchēsis*** [καύχησις]	BOAST
2749	***keimai*** [κεῖμαι]	LIE
		SET
2751	***keirō*** [κείρω]	SHEAR
2752	***keleusma*** [κέλευσμα]	SHOUT
2753	***keleuō*** [κελεύω]	COMMAND
2756	***kenos*** [κενός]	EMPTY
		VAIN
2758	***kenoō*** [κενόω]	EMPTY
		VAIN
2761	***kenōs*** [κενῶς]	VAIN
2763	***kerameus*** [κεραμεύς]	POTTER
2765	***keramion*** [κεράμιον]	JAR
2767	***kerannymi*** [κεράννυμι]	POUR
2768	***keras*** [κέρας]	HORN
2769	***keration*** [κεράτιον]	HUSKS
2770	***kerdainō*** [κερδαίνω]	GAIN
2771	***kerdos*** [κέρδος]	GAIN
2772	***kerma*** [κέρμα]	MONEY
2773	***kermatistēs*** [κερματιστής]	MONEY
2775	***kephalaioō*** [κεφαλαιόω]	WOUND
2776	***kephalē*** [κεφαλή]	HEAD
2778	***kēnsos*** [κῆνσος]	TRIBUTE
2779	***kēpos*** [κῆπος]	GARDEN
2782	***kērygma*** [κήρυγμα]	PREACH
2783	***kēryx*** [κῆρυξ]	PREACH
2784	***kēryssō*** [κηρύσσω]	PREACH
2787	***kibōtos*** [κιβωτός]	ARK
2788	***kithara*** [κιθάρα]	HARP
		LUTE
2793	***kindyneuō*** [κινδυνεύω]	DANGER
2795	***kineō*** [κινέω]	REMOVE
2798	***klados*** [κλάδος]	BRANCH
2799	***klaiō*** [κλαίω]	WEEP
2800	***klasis*** [κλάσις]	BREAK
2805	***klauthmos*** [κλαυθμός]	MOURN
		WEEP
2806	***klaō*** [κλάω]	BREAK
2807	***kleis*** [κλείς]	KEY
2808	***kleiō*** [κλείω]	SHUT
2812	***kleptēs*** [κλέπτης]	ROB
2813	***kleptō*** [κλέπτω]	STEAL
2814	***klēma*** [κλῆμα]	BRANCH
2816	***klēronomeō*** [κληρονομέω]	INHERIT
2817	***klēronomia*** [κληρονομία]	INHERIT
2818	***klēronomos*** [κληρονόμος]	HEIR
2819	***klēros*** [κλῆρος]	INHERIT
		LOT
		SHARE
2820	***klēroō*** [κληρόω]	INHERIT
2821	***klēsis*** [κλῆσις]	CALL
2822	***klētos*** [κλητός]	CALL
2823	***klibanos*** [κλίβανος]	OVEN
2824	***klima*** [κλίμα]	REGION
2825	***klinē*** [κλίνη]	BED
2827	***klinō*** [κλίνω]	BOW (VERB)
		FLIGHT
2830	***klydōn*** [κλύδων]	RAGE
		WAVE (NOUN)
2833	***knēthw*** [κνήθω]	ITCH

Strong's Number	Greek Article	English Entry
2836	**koilia** [κοιλία]	BELLY
		WOMB
2837	**koimaō** [κοιμάω]	ASLEEP
		DIE
2839	**koinos** [κοινός]	DEFILE
		THING
		UNCLEAN
2840	**koinoō** [κοινόω]	DEFILE
2841	**koinōneō** [κοινωνέω]	FELLOWSHIP
		SHARE
2842	**koinōnia** [κοινωνία]	FELLOWSHIP
2844	**koinōnos** [κοινωνός]	FELLOWSHIP
		SHARE
2845	**koitē** [κοίτη]	BED
2847	**kokkinos** [κόκκινος]	SCARLET
2848	**kokkos** [κόκκος]	GRAIN
2849	**kolazō** [κολάζω]	PUNISH
2851	**kolasis** [κόλασις]	PUNISH
2853	**kollaō** [κολλάω]	JOIN
2854	**kollourion** [κολλούρίον]	EYE SALVE
2856	**koloboō** [κολοβόω]	SHORT
2859	**kolpos** [κόλπος]	BOSOM
2864	**komē** [κόμη]	HAIR
2865	**komizō** [κομίζω]	RECEIVE
2867	**koniaō** [κονιάω]	WHITE
2868	**koniortos** [κονιορτός]	DUST
2869	**kopazō** [κοπάζω]	CEASE
2870	**kopetos** [κοπετός]	MOURN
2871	**kopē** [κοπή]	SLAUGHTER
2872	**kopiaō** [κοπιάω]	WEARY
2873	**kopos** [κόπος]	TROUBLE
		WORK
2874	**koprion** [κόπριον]	DUNG
2875	**koptō** [κόπτω]	CUT
		MOURN
2876	**korax** [κόραξ]	RAVEN
2877	**korasion** [κοράσιον]	GIRL
		MAID
2878	**korbanas** [κορβανᾶς]	TREASURE
2880	**korennymi** [κορέννυμι]	EAT
2886	**kosmikos** [κοσμικός]	WORLDLY
2888	**kosmokratōr** [κοσμοκράτωρ]	RULE
2889	**kosmos** [κόσμος]	WORLD
2892	**koustōdia** [κουστωδία]	GUARD
2894	**kophinos** [κόφινος]	BASKET
2896	**krazō** [κράζω]	CRY
2898	**kranion** [κρανίον]	CALVARY
		SKULL
2899	**kraspedon** [κράσπεδον]	BORDER
2902	**krateō** [κρατέω]	HOLD (VERB)
		SEIZE
2903	**kratistos** [κράτιστος]	EXCEL
		NOBLE
2904	**kratos** [κράτος]	DOMINION
		STRENGTH
2905	**kraugazō** [κραυγάζω]	CRY
2906	**kraugē** [κραυγή]	CRY
2907	**kreas** [κρέας]	FLESH
2910	**kremannymi** [κρεμάννυμι]	HANG
2915	**krithē** [κριθή]	BARLEY
2916	**krithinos** [κρίθινος]	BARLEY
2917	**krima** [κρίμα]	JUDGMENT
2918	**krinon** [κρίνον]	LILY
2919	**krinō** [κρίνω]	CONDEMN
		JUDGE
		SENTENCE
2920	**krisis** [κρίσις]	ACCUSATION
		JUDGMENT
2922	**kritērion** [κριτήριον]	JUDGMENT
2923	**kritēs** [κριτής]	JUDGE
2925	**krouō** [κρούω]	KNOCK
2927	**kryptos** [κρυπτός]	SECRET
2928	**kryptō** [κρύπτω]	HIDE
		SECRET
2929	**krystallizō** [κρυσταλλίζω]	CLEAR
2931	**kryphē** [κρυφῆ]	SECRET
2932	**ktaomai** [κτάομαι]	GET
2933	**ktēma** [κτῆμα]	POSSESS
2934	**ktēnos** [κτῆνος]	BEAST
2936	**ktizō** [κτίζω]	CREATE
2937	**ktisis** [κτίσις]	CREATE

Strong's Number	Greek Article	English Entry
3415	***mnaomai*** [μνάομαι]	REMEMBER
3417	***mneia*** [μνεία]	REMEMBER
3418	***mnēma*** [μνῆμα]	GRAVE
3419	***mnēmeion*** [μνημεῖον]	GRAVE
3420	***mnēmē*** [μνήμη]	REMEMBER
3421	***mnēmoneuō*** [μνημονεύω]	REMEMBER
3422	***mnēmosynon*** [μνημόσυνον]	REMEMBER
3423	***mnēsteuō*** [μνηστεύω]	BETROTH
3424	***mogilalos*** [μογιλάλος]	IMPEDIMENT
		SPEECH
3428	***moichalis*** [μοιχαλίς]	ADULTERER
3429	***moichaō*** [μοιχάω]	ADULTERER
3430	***moicheia*** [μοιχεία]	ADULTERER
3431	***moicheuō*** [μοιχεύω]	ADULTERER
3432	***moichos*** [μοιχός]	ADULTERER
3435	***molynō*** [μολύνω]	DEFILE
3436	***molysmos*** [μολυσμός]	DEFILE
3437	***momphē*** [μομφή]	COMPLAINT
3439	***monogenēs*** [μονογενής]	BEGET
		ONLY
3440	***monon*** [μόνον]	ALONE
3441	***monos*** [μόνος]	ALONE
3442	***monophthalmos*** [μονόφθαλμος]	EYE
3444	***morphē*** [μορφή]	FORM
3445	***morphoō*** [μορφόω]	FORM
3446	***morphōsis*** [μόρφωσις]	FORM
3451	***mousikos*** [μουσικός]	MUSIC
3455	***mykaomai*** [μυκάομαι]	ROAR
3456	***myktērizō*** [μυκτηρίζω]	MOCK
3458	***mylos*** [μύλος]	MILL
3462	***myrizō*** [μυρίζω]	ANOINT
3466	***mystērion*** [μυστήριον]	MYSTERY
3467	***myōpazō*** [μυωπάζω]	SEE
3469	***mōmaomai*** [μωμάομαι]	BLAME
3470	***mōmos*** [μῶμος]	BLEMISH
3471	***mōrainō*** [μωραίνω]	FOOL
3472	***mōria*** [μωρία]	FOOL
3473	***mōrologia*** [μωρολογία]	TALK
3474	***mōros*** [μωρός]	FOOL
3480	***nazōraios*** [ναζωραῖος]	NAZIRITE
3485	***naos*** [ναός]	TEMPLE
3489	***nauageō*** [ναυαγέω]	SHIPWRECK
3490	***nauklēros*** [ναύκληρος]	OWNER
3492	***nautēs*** [ναύτης]	SAILOR
3494	***neanias*** [νεανίας]	YOUNG
3495	***neaniskos*** [νεανίσκος]	YOUNG
3498	***nekros*** [νεκρός]	DEAD
3499	***nekroō*** [νεκρόω]	DEAD
3501	***neos*** [νέος]	NEW
		YOUNG
3502	***nossos*** [νοσσός]	YOUNG
3503	***neotēs*** [νεότης]	YOUTH
3507	***nephelē*** [νεφέλη]	CLOUD
3509	***nephos*** [νέφος]	CLOUD
3512	***neōterikos*** [νεωτερικός]	YOUTH
3515	***nepiazō*** [νηπιάζω]	CHILD
3516	***nēpios*** [νήπιος]	BABE
		CHILD
3519	***nēsion*** [νησίον]	ISLAND
3520	***nēsos*** [νῆσος]	ISLAND
3521	***nēsteia*** [νηστεία]	FAST
3522	***nēsteuō*** [νηστεύω]	FAST
3523	***nēstis*** [νῆστις]	FAST
3524	***nēphalios*** [νηφάλιος]	TEMPERANCE
3525	***nēphō*** [νήφω]	TEMPERANCE
3528	***nikaō*** [νικάω]	OVERCOME
3529	***nikē*** [νίκη]	VICTORY
3534	***nikos*** [νῖκος]	VICTORY
3538	***niptō*** [νίπτω]	WASH
3539	***noeō*** [νοέω]	CONSIDER
		UNDERSTAND
3540	***noēma*** [νόημα]	MIND
3542	***nomē*** [νομή]	PASTURE
3543	***nomizō*** [νομίζω]	THINK
3544	***nomikos*** [νομικός]	LAWYER
3546	***nomisma*** [νόμισμα]	MONEY
3547	***nomodidaskalos*** [νομοδιδάσκαλος]	LAW
		TEACH

Strong's Number	Greek Article	English Entry
3549	***nomotheteō*** [νομοθετέω]	ENACT
		RECEIVE
3550	***nomothetēs*** [νομοθέτης]	LAWGIVER
3551	***nomos*** [νόμος]	LAW
3554	***nosos*** [νόσος]	DISEASE
		SICK
3558	***notos*** [νότος]	WIND
3559	***nouthesia*** [νουθεσία]	ADMONISH
3560	***noutheteō*** [νουθετέω]	WARN
3561	***neomēnia*** [νεομηνία]	MOON
		NEW
3563	***nous*** [νοῦς]	MIND
		UNDERSTANDING
3565	***nymphē*** [νύμφη]	BRIDE
		DAUGHTER
3566	***nymphios*** [νυμφίος]	BRIDE
3571	***nyx*** [νύξ]	NIGHT
3572	***nyssō*** [νύσσω]	PIERCE
3577	***nōtos*** [νῶτος]	BACK
3578	***xenia*** [ξενία]	INN
		LODGE
3579	***xenizō*** [ξενίζω]	LODGE
3580	***xenodocheō*** [ξενοδοχέω]	LODGE
3582	***xestēs*** [ξέστης]	POT
3583	***xērainō*** [ξηραίνω]	DRY
		RIPE
3584	***xēros*** [ξηρός]	DRY
3585	***xylinos*** [ξύλινος]	WOOD
3586	***xylon*** [ξύλον]	TREE
3590	***ogdoos*** [ὄγδοος]	EIGHT
3594	***hodēgeō*** [ὁδηγέω]	LEAD (VERB)
3595	***hodēgos*** [ὁδηγός]	GUIDE
3596	***hodoiporeō*** [ὁδοιπορέω]	JOURNEY
3598	***hodos*** [ὁδός]	JOURNEY
		WAY
3599	***odous*** [ὀδούς]	TOOTH
3600	***odynaō*** [ὀδυνάω]	ANGUISH
		SORROW
3601	***odynē*** [ὀδύνη]	SORROW
3602	***odyrmos*** [ὀδυρμός]	MOURN
3608	***othonion*** [ὀθόνιον]	LINEN
3610	***oiketēs*** [οἰκέτης]	SERVANT
3611	***oikeō*** [οἰκέω]	DWELL
3614	***oikia*** [οἰκία]	HOUSE
3618	***oikodomeō*** [οἰκοδομέω]	BUILD
		EDIFICATION
3619	***oikodomē*** [οἰκοδομή]	BUILD
		EDIFICATION
3621	***oikonomeō*** [οἰκονομέω]	STEWARD
3622	***oikonomia*** [οἰκονομία]	STEWARD
3623	***oikonomos*** [οἰκονόμος]	STEWARD
3624	***oikos*** [οἶκος]	FAMILY
		HOUSE
3625	***oikoumenē*** [οἰκουμένη]	EARTH
		WORLD
3627	***oikteirō*** [οἰκτείρω]	COMPASSION
		MERCY
3628	***oiktirmos*** [οἰκτιρμός]	MERCY
3629	***oiktirmōn*** [οἰκτίρμων]	MERCY
3631	***oinos*** [οἶνος]	WINE
3632	***oinophlygia*** [οἰνοφλυγία]	DRUNK
3633	***oimai*** [οἶμαι]	THINK
3635	***okneō*** [ὀκνέω]	DELAY
3637	***oktaēmeros*** [ὀκταήμερος]	EIGHT
3638	***oktō*** [ὀκτώ]	EIGHT
3639	***olethros*** [ὄλεθρος]	DESTROY
3640	***oligopistos*** [ὀλιγόπιστος]	FAITH
3641	***oligos*** [ὀλίγος]	FEW
		LITTLE
3645	***olothreuō*** [ὀλοθρεύω]	DESTROY
3646	***holokautōma*** [ὁλοκαύτωμα]	OFFERING
3647	***holoklēria*** [ὁλοκληρία]	PERFECT
3649	***ololyzō*** [ὀλολύζω]	HOWL
3650	***holos*** [ὅλος]	ALL
3653	***olynthos*** [ὄλυνθος]	FIG
3656	***homileō*** [ὁμιλέω]	TALK
3659	***omma*** [ὄμμα]	EYE
3660	***omnyō*** [ὀμνύω]	SWEAR
3666	***homoioō*** [ὁμοιόω]	LIKEN
3670	***homologeō*** [ὁμολογέω]	CONFESS
		PROMISE

Strong's Number	Greek Article	English Entry
3806	***pathos*** [πάθος]	LUST
3807	***paidagōgos*** [παιδαγωγός]	INSTRUCT
3808	***paidarion*** [παιδάριον]	CHILD
3809	***paideia*** [παιδεία]	CHASTEN
		INSTRUCT
3810	***paideutēs*** [παιδευτής]	INSTRUCT
3811	***paideuō*** [παιδεύω]	CHASTEN
		INSTRUCT
		LEARN
3813	***paidion*** [παιδίον]	CHILD
		GIRL
3814	***paidiskē*** [παιδίσκη]	GIRL
		MAID
3816	***pais*** [παῖς]	CHILD
		SERVANT
3817	***paiō*** [παίω]	STRIKE
3820	***palaios*** [παλαιός]	OLD
3822	***palaioō*** [παλαιόω]	DECAY
		OLD
3823	***palē*** [πάλη]	WRESTLE
3824	***palingenesia*** [παλιγγενεσία]	REGENERATION
3829	***pandocheion*** [πανδοχεῖον]	INN
3831	***panēgyris*** [πανήγυρις]	ASSEMBLE
3833	***panoplia*** [πανοπλία]	ARMS
3841	***pantokratōr*** [παντοκράτωρ]	ALMIGHTY
3845	***parabainō*** [παραβαίνω]	TRANSGRESS
3847	***parabasis*** [παράβασις]	TRANSGRESS
3848	***parubatēs*** [παραβάτης]	TRANSGRESS
3850	***parabolē*** [παραβολή]	PARABLE
3852	***parangelia*** [παραγγελία]	CHARGE
3853	***parangellō*** [παραγγέλλω]	COMMAND
3854	***paraginomai*** [παραγίνομαι]	ARRIVE
		PRESENT
3855	***paragō*** [παράγω]	PASS
3856	***paradeigmatizō*** [παραδειγματίζω]	ASHAMED
3857	***paradeisos*** [παράδεισος]	PARADISE
3858	***paradechomai*** [παραδέχομαι]	RECEIVE
3859	***diaparatribē*** [διαπαρατριβή]	DISPUTE
3860	***paradidōmi*** [παραδίδωμι]	DELIVER
		GIVE
3862	***paradosis*** [παράδοσις]	TRADITION
3863	***parazēloō*** [παραζηλόω]	JEALOUS
3865	***paratheōreō*** [παραθεωρέω]	NEGLECT
3866	***parathēkē*** [παραθήκη]	TRUST
3867	***paraineō*** [παραινέω]	ADMONISH
		EXHORT
3868	***paraiteomai*** [παραιτέομαι]	AVOID
		EXCUSE
		REFUSE
3869	***parakathizō*** [παρακαθίζω]	SIT
3870	***parakaleō*** [παρακαλέω]	ASK
		COMFORT
		EXHORT
3874	***paraklēsis*** [παράκλησις]	COMFORT
		EXHORT
3875	***paraklētos*** [παράκλητος]	COMFORT
3876	***parakoē*** [παρακοή]	DISOBEDIENCE
3877	***parakoloutheō*** [παρακολουθέω]	FOLLOW
3879	***parakyptō*** [παρακύπτω]	SEE
3880	***paralambanō*** [παραλαμβάνω]	RECEIVE
		TAKE
3881	***paralegomai*** [παραλέγομαι]	SAIL
3884	***paralogizomai*** [παραλογίζομαι]	DECEIT
3885	***paralytikos*** [παραλυτικός]	PARALYZED
3886	***paralyō*** [παραλύω]	PARALYZED
3887	***paramenō*** [παραμένω]	ABIDE
		CONTINUE
3888	***paramytheomai*** [παραμυθέομαι]	COMFORT
3889	***paramythia*** [παραμυθία]	COMFORT
3894	***parapikrasmos*** [παραπικρασμός]	REBEL
3895	***parapiptō*** [παραπίπτω]	FALL
3896	***parapleō*** [παραπλέω]	SAIL
3899	***paraporeuomai*** [παραπορεύομαι]	PASS
3900	***paraptōma*** [παράπτωμα]	TRANSGRESS
3904	***paraskeuē*** [παρασκευή]	PREPARATION
3906	***paratēreō*** [παρατηρέω]	WATCH
3908	***paratithēmi*** [παρατίθημι]	PUT
		SET
3911	***parapherō*** [παραφέρω]	REMOVE
		TAKE
3913	***paraphronia*** [παραφρονία]	MAD
3914	***paracheimazō*** [παραχειμάζω]	WINTER

Strong's Number	Greek Article	English Entry
4046	***peripoieō*** [περιποιέω]	GAIN
4047	***peripoiēsis*** [περιποίησις]	OBTAIN
		POSSESS
4050	***perisseia*** [περισσεία]	ABUNDANCE
4051	***perisseuma*** [περίσσευμα]	ABUNDANCE
4052	***perisseuō*** [περισσεύω]	ABUNDANCE
		EXCEED
		INCREASE
		REMAIN
		SPARE
4053	***perissos*** [περισσός]	ABUNDANCE
		ADVANTAGE
4054	***perissoteron*** [περισσότερον]	ABUNDANCE
4056	***perissoteron*** [περισσότερον]	ABUNDANCE
4057	***perissōs*** [περισσῶς]	ABUNDANCE
4058	***peristera*** [περιστερά]	DOVE
4059	***peritemnō*** [περιτέμνω]	CIRCUMCISE
4060	***peritithēmi*** [περιτίθημι]	PUT
		SET
4061	***peritomē*** [περιτομή]	CIRCUMCISE
4063	***peritrechō*** [περιτρέχω]	RUN
4065	***periphroneō*** [περιφρονέω]	DESPISE
4066	***perichōros*** [περίχωρος]	COUNTRY
		REGION
4070	***perysi*** [πέρυσι]	YEAR
4071	***peteinon*** [πετεινόν]	BIRD
4072	***petomai*** [πέτομαι]	FLY
4073	***petra*** [πέτρα]	ROCK
4075	***petrōdēs*** [πετρώδης]	STONE
4077	***pēgē*** [πηγή]	FOUNTAIN
4078	***pēgnymi*** [πήγνυμι]	PITCH
4081	***pēlos*** [πηλός]	CLAY
4082	***pēra*** [πήρα]	BAG
4084	***piazō*** [πιάζω]	APPREHEND
		CATCH
4085	***piezō*** [πιέζω]	PRESS
4087	***pikrainō*** [πικραίνω]	BITTER
4088	***pikria*** [πικρία]	BITTER
4089	***pikros*** [πικρός]	BITTER
4090	***pikrōs*** [πικρῶς]	BITTER
4093	***pinakidion*** [πινακίδιον]	WRITE
4094	***pinax*** [πίναξ]	PLATE
4095	***pinō*** [πίνω]	DRINK
4098	***piptō*** [πίπτω]	FALL
4100	***pisteuō*** [πιστεύω]	BELIEF
4102	***pistis*** [πίστις]	FAITH
4103	***pistos*** [πιστός]	FAITHFUL
4105	***planaō*** [πλανάω]	DECEIT
		ERR
4106	***planē*** [πλάνη]	DECEIT
		ERROR
4108	***planos*** [πλάνος]	DECEIT
4110	***plasma*** [πλάσμα]	FORM
		THING
4111	***plassō*** [πλάσσω]	FORM
4114	***platos*** [πλάτος]	BROAD
4115	***platynō*** [πλατύνω]	BROAD
4121	***pleonazō*** [πλεονάζω]	ABUNDANCE
		INCREASE
4122	***pleonekteō*** [πλεονεκτέω]	ADVANTAGE
		DEFRAUD
4123	***pleonektēs*** [πλεονέκτης]	COVET
4124	***pleonexia*** [πλεονεξία]	COVET
4125	***pleura*** [πλευρά]	SIDE
4126	***pleō*** [πλέω]	SAIL
4127	***plēgē*** [πληγή]	PLAGUE
		WOUND
4128	***plēthos*** [πλῆθος]	CROWD
4129	***plēthynō*** [πληθύνω]	ABUNDANCE
4130	***plēthō*** [πλήθω]	FILL
		FINISH
4132	***plēmmyra*** [πλήμμυρα]	FLOOD
4134	***plērēs*** [πλήρης]	FULL
4135	***plērophoreō*** [πληροφορέω]	FULFILL
		PERSUADE
4136	***plērophoria*** [πληροφορία]	ASSURANCE
4137	***plēroō*** [πληρόω]	FILL
		FULFILL
		FULL
4138	***plērōma*** [πλήρωμα]	FILL
		FULFILL
4139	***plēsion*** [πλησίον]	NEIGHBOR

Strong's Number	Greek Article	English Entry
4576	***sebomai*** [σέβομαι]	DEVOUT
		WORSHIP
4578	***seismos*** [σεισμός]	EARTHQUAKE
4579	***seiō*** [σείω]	QUAKE
		SHAKE
4582	***selēnē*** [σελήνη]	MOON
4585	***semidalis*** [σεμίδαλις]	FLOUR
4592	***sēmeion*** [σημεῖον]	SIGN
4597	***sēs*** [σής]	MOTH
4598	***sētobrōtos*** [σητόβρωτος]	MOTH
4601	***sigaō*** [σιγάω]	SILENCE
4602	***sigē*** [σιγή]	SILENCE
4603	***sidērous*** [σιδηροῦς]	IRON
4604	***sidēros*** [σίδηρος]	IRON
4608	***sikera*** [σίκερα]	DRINK
4615	***sinapi*** [σίναπι]	MUSTARD
		SEED
4616	***sindōn*** [σινδών]	LINEN
4617	***siniazō*** [σινιάζω]	SIEVE
4623	***siōpaō*** [σιωπάω]	SILENCE
4624	***skandalizō*** [σκανδαλίζω]	OFFENSE
		SIN
4625	***skandalon*** [σκάνδαλον]	STUMBLING BLOCK
4626	***skaptō*** [σκάπτω]	DIG
4627	***skaphē*** [σκάφη]	BOAT
4628	***skelos*** [σκέλος]	LEG
4632	***skeuos*** [σκεῦος]	GOODS
		VESSEL
4633	***skēnē*** [σκηνή]	TABERNACLE
4634	***skēnopēgia*** [σκηνοπηγία]	TABERNACLE
4636	***skēnos*** [σκῆνος]	TABERNACLE
4637	***skēnoō*** [σκηνόω]	DWELL
4638	***skēnōma*** [σκήνωμα]	TABERNACLE
4639	***skia*** [σκιά]	SHADOW
4640	***skirtaō*** [σκιρτάω]	JOY
		LEAP
4642	***sklēros*** [σκληρός]	HARD
4643	***sklērotēs*** [σκληρότης]	HARD
4644	***sklērotrachēlos*** [σκληροτράχηλος]	STUBBORN
4645	***sklērynō*** [σκληρύνω]	HARD

Strong's Number	Greek Article	English Entry
4646	***skolios*** [σκολιός]	CROOKED
4647	***skolops*** [σκόλοψ]	THORN
4648	***skopeō*** [σκοπέω]	SEE
4649	***skopos*** [σκοπός]	MARK
4650	***skorpizō*** [σκορπίζω]	SCATTER
4651	***skorpios*** [σκορπίος]	SCORPION
4652	***skoteinos*** [σκοτεινός]	DARK
4653	***skotia*** [σκοτία]	DARK
4654	***skotizō*** [σκοτίζω]	DARK
4655	***skotos*** [σκότος]	DARK
4659	***skythrōpos*** [σκυθρωπός]	SAD
4660	***skyllō*** [σκύλλω]	TROUBLE
4662	***skōlēkobrōtos*** [σκωληκόβρωτος]	WORM
4663	***skōlēx*** [σκώληξ]	WORM
4664	***smaragdinos*** [σμαράγδινος]	EMERALD
4665	***smaragdos*** [σμάραγδος]	EMERALD
4666	***smyrna*** [σμύρνα]	MYRRH
4669	***smyrnizō*** [σμυρνίζω]	MYRRH
4673	***soros*** [σορός]	BIER
4676	***soudarion*** [σουδάριον]	HANDKERCHIEF
4678	***sophia*** [σοφία]	WISDOM
4680	***sophos*** [σοφός]	WISDOM
4683	***sparganoō*** [σπαργανόω]	WRAP
4685	***spaō*** [σπάω]	DRAW
4686	***speira*** [σπεῖρα]	BAND
4687	***speirō*** [σπείρω]	SEED
		SOW
4689	***spendomai*** [σπένδομαι]	OFFERING
4690	***sperma*** [σπέρμα]	SEED
4692	***speudō*** [σπεύδω]	HASTE
4693	***spēlaion*** [σπήλαιον]	DEN
4695	***spiloō*** [σπιλόω]	DEFILE
4697	***splanchnizomai*** [σπλαγχνίζομαι]	COMPASSION
4700	***spodos*** [σποδός]	ASHES
4701	***spora*** [σπορά]	SEED
4702	***sporimos*** [σπόριμος]	FIELD
4703	***sporos*** [σπόρος]	SEED
		SOW

Strong's Number	Greek Article	English Entry
4704	**spoudazō** [σπουδάζω]	DILIGENCE
		ENDEAVOR
		STRIVE
4705	**spoudaios** [σπουδαῖος]	DILIGENCE
4706	**spoudaioteros** [σπουδαιότερος]	DILIGENCE
4710	**spoudē** [σπουδή]	DILIGENCE
		HASTE
4711	**spyris** [σπυρίς]	BASKET
4712	**stadion** [στάδιον]	RACE
4713	**stamnos** [στάμνος]	POT
4714	**stasis** [στάσις]	UPROAR
4716	**stauros** [σταυρός]	CROSS
4717	**stauroō** [σταυρόω]	CROSS
4718	**staphylē** [σταφυλή]	GRAPE
4719	**stachys** [στάχυς]	EAR OF CORN
4721	**stegē** [στέγη]	ROOF
4722	**stegō** [στέγω]	BEAR (VERB)
4723	**steira** [στεῖρα]	BARREN
4726	**stenagmos** [στεναγμός]	GROAN
4727	**stenazō** [στενάζω]	GROAN
4728	**stenos** [στενός]	NARROW
4730	**stenochōria** [στενοχωρία]	ANGUISH
		DISTRESS
4731	**stereos** [στερεός]	FIRM
4732	**stereoō** [στερεόω]	ESTABLISH
		STRENGTH
4735	**stephanos** [στέφανος]	CROWN
4737	**stephanoō** [στεφανόω]	CROWN
4738	**stēthos** [στῆθος]	BREAST
4739	**stēkō** [στήκω]	STAND
4741	**stērizō** [στηρίζω]	ESTABLISH
4742	**stigma** [στίγμα]	MARK
4745	**stoa** [στοά]	PORCH
4746	**stoibas** [στοιβάς]	BRANCH
4748	**stoicheō** [στοιχέω]	WALK
4749	**stolē** [στολή]	CLOTHING
4750	**stoma** [στόμα]	EDGE
		FACE
		MOUTH
4753	**strateuma** [στράτευμα]	ARMY
		WARFARE
4754	**strateuomai** [στρατεύομαι]	WARFARE
4755	**stratēgos** [στρατηγός]	CAPTAIN
4757	**stratiōtēs** [στρατιώτης]	SOLDIER
4760	**stratopedon** [στρατόπεδον]	ARMY
4762	**strephō** [στρέφω]	TURN
4766	**strōnnymi** [στρώννυμι]	SPREAD
4767	**stygētos** [στυγητός]	HATE
4768	**stygnazō** [στυγνάζω]	SAD
4769	**stylos** [στῦλος]	PILLAR
4773	**syngenēs** [συγγενής]	KIN
4775	**synkathēmai** [συγκάθημαι]	SIT
4776	**synkathizō** [συγκαθίζω]	SIT
4777	**synkakopatheō** [συγκακοπαθέω]	SHARE
4779	**synkaleō** [συγκαλέω]	CALL
4780	**synkalyptō** [συγκαλύπτω]	COVER
4783	**synkatathesis** [συγκατάθεσις]	AGREE
4784	**synkatatithēmi** [συγκατατίθημι]	CONSENT
4786	**synkerannymi** [συγκεράννυμι]	MIX
4787	**synkineō** [συγκινέω]	STIR
4789	**synklēronomos** [συγκληρονόμος]	HEIR
		JOINT
4790	**synkoinōneō** [συγκοινωνέω]	FELLOWSHIP
		SHARE
4791	**synkoinōnos** [συγκοινωνός]	SHARE
4796	**synchairō** [συγχαίρω]	REJOICE
4797	**syncheō** [συγχέω]	CONFOUND
		UPROAR
4799	**synchysis** [σύγχυσις]	CONFOUND
4800	**syzaō** [συζάω]	LIFE
4801	**syzeugnymi** [συζεύγνυμι]	JOIN
4802	**syzēteō** [συζητέω]	DISPUTE
		QUESTION
4804	**syzētētēs** [συζητητής]	DISPUTE
		PHILOSOPHER
4806	**syzōopoieō** [συζωοποιέω]	QUICKEN
4808	**sykē** [συκῆ]	FIG TREE
4809	**sykomorea** [συκομορέα]	TREE
4810	**sykon** [σῦκον]	FIG

Strong's Number	Greek Article	English Entry
5218	***hypakoē*** [ὑπακοή]	OBEDIENCE
5219	***hypakouō*** [ὑπακούω]	OBEDIENCE
5221	***hypantaō*** [ὑπαντάω]	MEET
5222	***hypantēsis*** [ὑπάντησις]	MEET
5223	***hyparxis*** [ὕπαρξις]	GOODS
5224	***hyparchonta*** [ὑπάρχοντα]	GOODS
5227	***hypenantios*** [ὑπεναντίος]	ADVERSARY
5229	***hyperairō*** [ὑπεραίρω]	EXALT
5232	***hyperauxanō*** [ὑπεραυξάνω]	GROW
5235	***hyperballō*** [ὑπερβάλλω]	EXCEL
5236	***hyperbolē*** [ὑπερβολή]	ABUNDANCE
		EXCEL
5237	***hypereidō*** [ὑπερείδω]	OVERLOOK
5240	***hyperekchynnō*** [ὑπερεκχύννω]	RUN
5241	***hyperentynchanō*** [ὑπερεντυγχάνω]	INTERCEDE
5243	***hyperēphania*** [ὑπερηφανία]	PRIDE
5244	***hyperēphanos*** [ὑπερήφανος]	PRIDE
5248	***hyperperisseuō*** [ὑπερπερισσεύω]	ABUNDANCE
5249	***hyperperissōs*** [ὑπερπερισσῶς]	ABUNDANCE
		MEASURE
5250	***hyperpleonazō*** [ὑπερπλεονάζω]	ABUNDANCE
5251	***hyperypsoō*** [ὑπερυψόω]	EXALT
5253	***hyperōon*** [ὑπερῷον]	ROOM
5255	***hypēkoos*** [ὑπήκοος]	OBEDIENCE
5256	***hypēreteō*** [ὑπηρετέω]	SERVE
5257	***hypēretēs*** [ὑπηρέτης]	OFFICER
		SERVANT
5258	***hypnos*** [ὕπνος]	ASLEEP
5261	***hypogrammos*** [ὑπογραμμός]	EXAMPLE
5262	***hypodeigma*** [ὑπόδειγμα]	COPY
		EXAMPLE
5263	***hypodeiknymi*** [ὑποδείκνυμι]	SHOW
		WARN
5264	***hypodechomai*** [ὑποδέχομαι]	RECEIVE
5268	***hypozygion*** [ὑποζύγιον]	ASS
5272	***hypokrisis*** [ὑπόκρισις]	HYPOCRISY
5273	***hypokritēs*** [ὑποκριτής]	HYPOCRISY
5274	***hypolambanō*** [ὑπολαμβάνω]	ANSWER
5278	***hypomenō*** [ὑπομένω]	ABIDE
		ENDURE
5279	***hypomimnēskō*** [ὑπομιμνήσκω]	REMEMBER
5281	***hypomonē*** [ὑπομονή]	PATIENCE
5282	***hyponoeō*** [ὑπονοέω]	THINK
5284	***hypopleō*** [ὑποπλέω]	SAIL
5285	***hypopneō*** [ὑποπνέω]	BLOW (VERB)
5286	***hypopodion*** [ὑποπόδιον]	FOOT
5287	***hypostasis*** [ὑπόστασις]	ASSURANCE
		CONFIDENCE
5290	***hypostrephō*** [ὑποστρέφω]	RETURN
		TURN
5291	***hypostrōnnymi*** [ὑποστρώννυμι]	SPREAD
5292	***hypotagē*** [ὑποταγή]	SUBJECT
5293	***hypotassō*** [ὑποτάσσω]	PUT
		SUBJECT
5295	***hypotrechō*** [ὑποτρέχω]	RUN
5296	***hypotypōsis*** [ὑποτύπωσις]	EXAMPLE
5297	***hypopherō*** [ὑποφέρω]	BEAR (VERB)
5299	***hypōpiazō*** [ὑπωπιάζω]	WEARY
5302	***hystereō*** [ὑστερέω]	SHORT
5308	***hypsēlos*** [ὑψηλός]	HIGH
5310	***hypsistos*** [ὕψιστος]	HIGH
5311	***hypsos*** [ὕψος]	HEIGHT
5312	***hypsoō*** [ὑψόω]	EXALT
5313	***hypsōma*** [ὕψωμα]	HEIGHT
5315	***phagō*** [φάγω]	EAT
5316	***phainō*** [φαίνω]	APPEAR
		SHINE
5318	***phaneros*** [φανερός]	APPEAR
		KNOW
5319	***phaneroō*** [φανερόω]	APPEAR
		SHOW
5325	***phantasia*** [φαντασία]	SPLENDOR
5326	***phantasma*** [φάντασμα]	APPARITION
5327	***pharanx*** [φάραγξ]	VALLEY
5333	***pharmakos*** [φαρμακός]	MAGIC
5336	***phatnē*** [φάτνη]	MANGER
5337	***phaulos*** [φαῦλος]	EVIL
5338	***phengos*** [φέγγος]	LIGHT
5339	***pheidomai*** [φείδομαι]	SPARE

Strong's Number	Greek Article	English Entry
5453	***phyō*** [φύω]	SPRING
5454	***phōleos*** [φωλεός]	HOLE
5455	***phōneō*** [φωνέω]	CALL
		INVITE
5456	***phōnē*** [φωνή]	SOUND
		VOICE
5457	***phōs*** [φῶς]	LIGHT
5458	***phōstēr*** [φωστήρ]	LIGHT
5459	***phōsphoros*** [φωσφόρος]	STAR
5460	***phōteinos*** [φωτεινός]	LIGHT
5461	***phōtizō*** [φωτίζω]	LIGHT
5462	***phōtismos*** [φωτισμός]	LIGHT
5463	***chairō*** [χαίρω]	FAREWELL
		GREET
		JOY
5464	***chalaza*** [χάλαζα]	HAIL
5467	***chalepos*** [χαλεπός]	FIERCE
5468	***chalinagōgeō*** [χαλιναγωγέω]	BRIDLE
5469	***chalinos*** [χαλινός]	BRIDLE
5470	***chalkeos*** [χάλκεος]	BRASS
5473	***chalkion*** [χαλκίον]	BRASS
		VESSEL
5474	***chalkolibanon*** [χαλκολίβανον]	BRASS
5475	***chalkos*** [χαλκός]	BRASS
		MONEY
5476	***chamai*** [χαμαί]	GROUND
5479	***chara*** [χαρά]	JOY
5480	***charagma*** [χάραγμα]	MARK
5481	***charaktēr*** [χαρακτήρ]	IMAGE
5483	***charizomai*** [χαρίζομαι]	FORGIVE
		GIVE
5485	***charis*** [χάρις]	GRACE
5486	***charisma*** [χάρισμα]	GIFT
5487	***charitoō*** [χαριτόω]	FAVOR
5489	***chartēs*** [χάρτης]	PAPER
5490	***chasma*** [χάσμα]	GULF
5491	***cheilos*** [χεῖλος]	LIP
		SHORE
5494	***cheimōn*** [χειμών]	WINTER
5495	***cheir*** [χείρ]	HAND
5496	***cheiragōgeō*** [χειραγωγέω]	LEAD (VERB)
5500	***cheirotoneō*** [χειροτονέω]	APPOINT
5502	***cheroubim*** [χερουβίμ]	CHERUBIM
5503	***chēra*** [χήρα]	WIDOW
5504	***echthes*** [ἐχθές]	YESTERDAY
5506	***chiliarchos*** [χιλίαρχος]	CAPTAIN
5511	***chlamys*** [χλαμύς]	ROBE
5512	***chleuazō*** [χλευάζω]	MOCK
5513	***chliaros*** [χλιαρός]	LUKEWARM
5517	***choikos*** [χοϊκός]	EARTHEN
5518	***choinix*** [χοῖνιξ]	MEASURE
5519	***choiros*** [χοῖρος]	SWINE
5520	***cholaō*** [χολάω]	ANGER
5522	***chous, choos*** [χοῦς, χόος]	DUST
5525	***choros*** [χορός]	DANCE
5526	***chortazō*** [χορτάζω]	FILL
5528	***chortos*** [χόρτος]	GRASS
5530	***chraomai*** [χράομαι]	USE
5532	***chreia*** [χρεία]	NEED
5533	***chreopheiletēs*** [χρεοφειλέτης]	DEBT
5535	***chrēzō*** [χρῄζω]	NEED
5536	***chrēma*** [χρῆμα]	MONEY
		RICH
5537	***chrēmatizō*** [χρηματίζω]	ADMONISH
		REVEAL
		WARN
5538	***chrēmatismos*** [χρηματισμός]	ANSWER
5541	***chrēsteuomai*** [χρηστεύομαι]	KIND
5543	***chrēstos*** [χρηστός]	KIND
5544	***chrēstotēs*** [χρηστότης]	KIND
5545	***chrisma*** [χρίσμα]	ANOINT
5546	***Christianos*** [Χριστιανός]	CHRISTIAN
5547	***Christos*** [Χριστός]	CHRIST
5548	***chriō*** [χρίω]	ANOINT
5549	***chronizō*** [χρονίζω]	DELAY
5550	***chronos*** [χρόνος]	TIME
5551	***chronotribeō*** [χρονοτριβέω]	SPEND
5552	***chryseos*** [χρύσεος]	GOLD
5554	***chrysodaktylios*** [χρυσοδακτύλιος]	RING